2010 89TH ANNUAL EDITION

WRITER'S MARKET®

COMPLETELY REVISED & UPDATED!

WHERE & HOW TO SELL WHAT YOU WRITE

3,500 listings for book publishers, consumer magazines, trade journals, literary agents, and more

OVER 5 MILLION COPIES SOLD

Complaint Procedure

If you feel you have not been treated fairly by a listing in *Writer's Market* or *Writer's Market Deluxe Edition*, we advise you to take the following steps:

- First try to contact the listing. Sometimes one phone call or a letter can quickly clear up the matter.
- Document all your correspondence with the listing. When you write to us with a complaint, provide the details of your submission, the date of your first contact with the listing and the nature of your subsequent correspondence.
- We will enter your letter into our files and attempt to contact the listing.
- The number and severity of complaints will be considered in our decision whether to delete the listing from the next edition.

Publisher & Editorial Director, Writing Communities: Jane Friedman
Managing Editor, Writer's Digest Market Books: Alice Pope

Writer's Market Web site: www.writersmarket.com
Writer's Digest Web site: www.writersdigest.com

Distributed in Canada by Fraser Direct
100 Armstrong Avenue
Georgetown, ON, Canada L7G 5S4
Tel: (905) 877-4411

Distributed in the U.K. and Europe by David & Charles
Brunel House, Newton Abbot, Devon, TQ12 4PU, England
Tel: (Þpl44) 1626 323200, Fax: (Þpl44) 1626 323319
E-mail: postmaster@davidandcharles.co.uk

Distributed in Australia by Capricorn Link
P.O. Box 704, Windsor, NSW 2756 Australia
Tel: (02) 4577-3555

Library of Congress Catalog Number 31-20772
ISSN: 0084-2729
ISBN-13: 978-1-58297-579-5
ISBN-13: 978-1-58297-580-1 (Writer's Market Deluxe Edition)
ISBN-10: 1-58297-579-5
ISBN-10: 1-58297-580-9 (Writer's Market Deluxe Edition)

Cover design by Claudean Wheeler
Production coordinated by Greg Nock
Illustrations © Dominique Bruneton/PaintoAlto

Attention Booksellers: This is an annual directory of F + W Media, Inc.
Return deadline for this edition is December 31, 2010.

fw media

TEAR ALONG PERFORATION

2010 WRITER'S MARKET KEY TO SYMBOLS

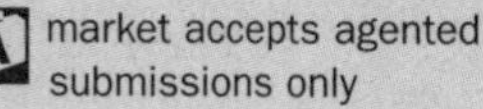

- N market new to this edition
- A market accepts agented submissions only
- market does not accept unsolicited manuscripts
- Canadian market
- market located outside of the U.S. and Canada
- online opportunity
- $ market pays 0-9¢/word or $0-$150/article
- $$ market pays 10-49¢/word or $151-$750/article
- $$$ market pays 50-99¢/word or $751-$1,500/article
- $$$$ market pays $1/word or over $1,500 article
- • comment from the editor of *Writer's Market*
- tips to break in to a specific market

ms, mss manuscript(s)

b&w black & white (photo)

SASE self-addressed, stamped envelope

SAE self-addressed envelope

IRC International Reply Coupon, for use in countries other than your own

(For words and expressions relating specifically to writing and publishing, see the Glossary in the back of this book.)

2010 WRITER'S MARKET KEY TO SYMBOLS

 market new to this edition

 market accepts agented submissions only

 market does not accept unsolicited manuscripts

 Canadian market

market located outside of the U.S. and Canada

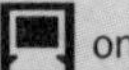 online opportunity

$ market pays 0-9¢/word or $0-$150/article

$ $ market pays 10-49¢/word or $151-$750/article

$ $ $ market pays 50-99¢/word or $751-$1,500/article

$ $ $ $ market pays $1/word or over $1,500 article

• comment from the editor of *Writer's Market*

tips to break in to a specific market

ms, mss manuscript(s)

b&w black & white (photo)

SASE self-addressed, stamped envelope

SAE self-addressed envelope

IRC International Reply Coupon, for use in countries other than your own

(For words and expressions relating specifically to writing and publishing, see the Glossary in the back of this book.)

TEAR ALONG PERFORATION

WritersMarket.com

WHERE & HOW TO SELL WHAT YOU WRITE

- **More Updated Listings –** At WritersMarket.com, you'll find thousands of listings, including the listings that we couldn't fit in the book, as well as listings from our other best selling titles, including *Novel & Short Story Market, Children's Writer's & Illustrator's Market*, and *Guide to Literary Agents*. WritersMarket.com provides the most comprehensive database of verified markets available anywhere.
- **Easy-to-use searchable database –** Looking for a specific magazine or book publisher? Just type in its name. Or widen your prospects with the Advanced Search. You can also search for listings that have been recently updated!
- **Personalized tools –** Store your best-bet markets, and use our popular record-keeping tools to track your submissions. Plus, get new and updated market listings, query reminders, and more – every time you log in!
- **Professional tips & advice –** From pay rate charts to sample query letters, and from how-to articles to Q&A's with literary agents, we have the resources freelance writers need.
- **Industry updates –** Debbie Ridpath Ohi's Market Watch column keeps you up-to-date on the latest publishing industry news, so you'll always be in-the-know.

With subscriptions starting at just $2.29 a month**, WritersMarket.com is the tool you need to take your writing to the next level.

Sign Up Today!

WM10

** $2.29 a month subscription fee based on average monthly cost for bi-annual subscription, billed in one installment of $54.99. Annual subscription rate: $39.99. Monthly subscription rate: $5.99. Prices subject to change.

Contents

BEYOND THE BASICS

LITERARY AGENTS

BOOK PUBLISHERS

CANADIAN BOOK PUBLISHERS

SMALL PRESSES

CONSUMER MAGAZINES

TRADE JOURNALS

NEWSPAPERS

SCREENWRITING

PLAYWRITING

GREETING CARDS

CONTEST & AWARDS

RESOURCES

INDEXES

From the Editor

Successful people—whether freelance writers or professional athletes—have one thing in common: focus. They are able to come through in the clutch on a consistent basis despite the distractions swirling around them. With uncertainty in the economy and as much competition as ever in freelance writing, many writers will likely give up on their dreams of selling articles, books, and screenplays. Let them.

To find success in your own writing, you need to forget the negatives and focus on the positives. Rejection letter? Resubmit with a new angle or move on to other markets on your list. Be persistent and proactive.

As I write this introduction to the 2010 Writer's Market, the economy is about as shaky as it's ever been in my lifetime, but the same principles that brought freelancers success in the "good times" are the same principles that will bring them success now. That starts with focus. Decide what you want to accomplish and then figure out how to make it happen.

If you need some inspiration, check out the Freelance Success Stories article in the Personal Views section of the book. Those three writers had plenty of distractions that could have kept them from success. Instead, they focused on their goals, pushed forward, and made it happen. You can, too.

Until next we meet, keep writing and marketing what you write.

Robert Lee Brewer
Editor, Writer's Market
WritersMarket.com
http://blog.writersdigest.com/poeticasides

P.S. If you currently only use the book, check out www.writersmarket.com, where we make daily updates to a searchable online database of listings and writers can network with each other through a community area.

How to Use *Writer's Market*

Writer's Market is here to help you decide where and how to submit your writing to appropriate markets. Each listing contains information about the editorial focus of the market, how it prefers material to be submitted, payment information, and other helpful tips.

WHAT'S INSIDE?

Since 1921, *Writer's Market* has been giving you the information you need to knowledgeably approach a market. We've continued to develop improvements to help you access that information more efficiently.

Navigational tools. We've designed the pages of *Writer's Market* with you, the user, in mind. Within the pages you will find **readable market listings** and **accessible charts and graphs**. One such chart can be found in the ever-popular **How Much Should I Charge?** on page 58. We've taken all of the updated information in this feature and put it into an easy-to-read and navigate chart, making it convenient for you to find the rates that accompany the freelance jobs you're seeking.

Tabs. You will also find user-friendly tabs for each section of *Writer's Market* so you can quickly find the section you need most. Once inside the Consumer Magazines, Trade Journals and Contests & Awards sections, you'll have subject headings at the top of the page to help guide and speed up your search.

Symbols. There are a variety of symbols that appear before each listing. A complete Key to Symbols & Abbreviations appears on the back inside cover and on a removable bookmark. In Book Publishers, note the which quickly sums up a publisher's interests. In Consumer Magazines, the zeroes in on what areas of that market are particularly open to freelancers—helping you break in. Other symbols let you know whether a listing is new to the book (N), a book publisher accepts only agented writers (A), comparative pay rates for a magazine (**$-$$$$**), and more.

Acquisition names, royalty rates and advances. In the Book Publishers section, we identify acquisition editors with the boldface word **Acquisitions** to help you get your manuscript to the right person. Royalty rates and advances are also highlighted in boldface, as is other important information on the percentage of first-time writers and unagented writers the company publishes, the number of books published, and the number of manuscripts received each year.

Editors, pay rates, and percentage of material written by freelance writers. In the Consumer Magazines and Trade Journals sections, we identify to whom you should send your query or article with the boldface word **Contact**. The amount (percentage) of material accepted from freelance writers, and the pay rates for features, columns and departments, and fillers are also highlighted in boldface to help you quickly identify the information you need to know when considering whether to submit your work.

Query formats. We asked editors how they prefer to receive queries and have indicated in the listings whether they prefer them by mail, e-mail, fax or phone. Be sure to check an editor's individual preference before sending your query.

Articles. Most of the articles are new to this edition. Newer, unpublished writers should be sure to read the articles in **The Basics** section, while more experienced writers should focus on those in the **Beyond the Basics** section. In addition, there is a section devoted to **Personal Views** featuring interviews with and articles by industry professionals and other career-oriented professionals, as well as best-selling authors.

Important Listing Information

1. Listings are based on editorial questionnaires and interviews. They are not advertisements; publishers do not pay for their listings. The markets are not endorsed by *Writer's Market* editors. F + W Media, Inc., Writer's Digest Books, and its employees go to great effort to ascertain the validity of information in this book. However, transactions between users of the information and individuals and/or companies are strictly between those parties.

2. All listings have been verified before publication of this book. If a listing has not changed from last year, then the editor said the market's needs have not changed and the previous listing continues to accurately reflect its policies.

3. *Writer's Market* reserves the right to exclude any listing.

4. When looking for a specific market, check the index. A market may not be listed for one of these reasons:
   - It doesn't solicit freelance material.
   - It doesn't pay for material.
   - It has gone out of business.
   - It has failed to verify or update its listing for this edition.
   - It hasn't answered *Writer's Market* inquiries satisfactorily. (To the best of our ability, and with our readers' help, we try to screen fraudulent listings.)

5. Individual markets that appeared in last year's edition but are not listed in this edition are included in the General Index, with a notation giving the reason for their exclusion.

2010 WRITER'S MARKET KEY TO SYMBOLS

 market new to this edition

market accepts agented submissions only

market does not accept unsolicited manuscripts

Canadian market

market located outside of the U.S. and Canada

online opportunity

$ market pays 0-9¢/word or $0-$150/article

$$ market pays 10-49¢/word or $151-$750/article

$$$ market pays 50-99¢/word or $751-$1,500/article

$$$$ market pays $1/word or over $1,500/article

• comment offering additional market information from the editor of *Writer's Market*

O‒ tips to break into a specific market

ms, mss manuscript(s)

b&w black & white (photo)

SASE self-addressed, stamped envelope

SAE self-addressed envelope

IRC International Reply Coupon, for use in countries other than your own

(For words and expressions relating specifically to writing and publishing, see the Glossary in the back of this book)

Find a handy pull-out bookmark, a quick reference to the icons used in this book, right inside the font cover.

IF *WRITER'S MARKET* IS NEW TO YOU . . .

A quick look at the **Contents** pages will familiarize you with the arrangement of *Writer's Market*. The three largest sections of the book are the market listings of Book Publishers; Consumer Magazines; and Trade Journals. You will also find other sections of market listings for Literary Agents; Newspapers; Screenwriting Markets; Playwriting Markets; Greeting Card Companies; and Contests & Awards.

Narrowing your search

After you've identified the market categories that interest you, you can begin researching specific markets within each section.

Book Publishers are categorized, in the **Book Publishers Subject Index**, according to types of books they are interested in. If, for example, you plan to write a book on a religious topic, simply turn to the Book Publishers Subject Index on page **1079** and look under the Religion subhead in Nonfiction for the names and page numbers of companies that publish such books.

Consumer Magazines and Trade Journals are categorized by subject within their respective sections to make it easier for you to identify markets for your work. If you want to publish an article dealing with retirement, you could look under the Retirement category of Consumer Magazines to find an appropriate market. You would want to keep in mind, however, that magazines in other categories might also be interested in your article. (For example, women's magazines publish such material.)

Interpreting the markets

Once you've identified companies or publications that cover the subjects in which you're interested, you can begin evaluating specific listings to pinpoint the markets most receptive to your work and most beneficial to you.

In evaluating an individual listing, first check the location of the company, the types of material it is interested in seeing, submission requirements, and rights and payment policies. Depending on your personal concerns, any of these items could be a deciding factor as you determine which markets you plan to approach. Many listings also include a reporting time, which lets you know how long it will typically take for the publisher to respond to your initial query or submission. (We suggest that you allow an additional two months for a response, just in case your submission is under further review or the publisher is backlogged.)

Check the Glossary on page **1074** for unfamiliar words. Specific symbols and abbreviations are explained in the Key to Symbols & Abbreviations appearing on the inside cover, as well as on a removable bookmark. The most important abbreviation is SASE—self-addressed, stamped envelope. Always enclose a SASE when you send unsolicited queries, proposals or manuscripts.

A careful reading of the listings will reveal that many editors are very specific about their needs. Your chances of success increase if you follow directions to the letter. Often companies do not accept unsolicited manuscripts and return them unread. If a company does not accept unsolicited manuscripts, it is indicated in the listing with a (⊘) symbol. (Note: You may still be able to query a market that does not accept unsolicited manuscripts.)

Whenever possible, obtain writer's guidelines before submitting material. You can usually obtain guidelines by sending a SASE to the address in the listing. Magazines often post their guidelines on their Web sites, and many book publishers do so as well. Most of the listings indicate how writer's guidelines are made available. You should also familiarize yourself with the company's publications. Many of the listings contain instructions on how to obtain sample copies, catalogs or market lists. The more research you do upfront, the better your chances of acceptance, publication and payment.

Guide to listing features

Below is an example of the market listings you'll find in each section of *Writer's Market*. Note the callouts that identify various format features of the listing.

EASY-TO-USE REFERENCE ICONS

$ $ $ $ PSYCHOLOGY TODAY

Sussex Publishers, Inc., 115 E. 23rd St., 9th Floor, New York NY 10010. (212)260-7210. Fax: (212)260-7445. E-mail: jay@psychologytoday.com. Web site: www.psychologytoday.com. Contact: Jay Dixit, senior editor. Bimonthly magazine. "*Psychology Today* explores every aspect of human behavior, from the cultural trends that shape the way we think and feel to the intricacies of modern neuroscience. We're sort of a hybrid of a science magazine, a health magazine and a self-help magazine. While we're read by many psychologists, therapists and social workers, most of our readers are simply intelligent and curious people interested in the psyche and the self." Estab. 1967. Circ. 331,400. Pays 30 days after publication. Publishes ms an average of 3 months after acceptance. Byline given. Buys first North American serial rights. Editorial lead time 5 months. Accepts queries by mail, e-mail. Responds in 1 month to queries. Sample copy for $3.50. Writer's guidelines online.

Nonfiction "Nearly any subject related to psychology is fair game. We value originality, insight and good reporting; we're not interested in stories or topics that have already been covered ad nauseum by other magazines unless you can provide a fresh new twist and much more depth. We're not interested in simple-minded 'pop psychology.'" No fiction, poetry or first-person essays on "How I Conquered Mental Disorder X." Buys 20-25 mss/year. Query with published clips. Length: 1,500-4,000 words. Pays $1,000-2,500.

Columns/Departments News Editor. News & Trends, 150-300 words. Query with published clips. Pays $150-300.

DIRECT E-MAIL ADDRESSES

SPECIFIC CONTACT NAMES

SPECIFIC PAY RATES

DETAILED SUBMISSIONS GUIDELINES

THE BASICS

Before Your First Sale

Everything in life has to start somewhere and that somewhere is always at the beginning. Stephen King, J.K. Rowling, John Grisham, Nora Roberts—they all had to start at the beginning. It would be great to say becoming a writer is as easy as waving a magic wand over your manuscript and "Poof!'' you're published, but that's not how it happens. While there's no one true "key'' to becoming successful, a long, well-paid writing career *can* happen when you combine four elements:

- Good writing
- Knowledge of writing markets
- Professionalism
- Persistence

Good writing is useless if you don't know which markets will buy your work or how to pitch and sell your writing. If you aren't professional and persistent in your contact with editors, your writing is just that—your writing. But if you are a writer who embraces the above four elements, you have a good chance at becoming a paid, published writer who will reap the benefits of a long and successful career.

As you become more involved with writing, you may read articles or talk to editors and authors with conflicting opinions about the right way to submit your work. The truth is, there are many different routes a writer can follow to get published, but no matter which route you choose, the end is always the same—becoming a published writer.

The following information on submissions has worked for many writers, but it is by no means the be-all-end-all of proper submission guidelines. It's very easy to get wrapped up in the specifics of submitting (Should I put my last name on every page of my manuscript?) and ignore the more important issues (Will this idea on ice fishing in Alaska be appropriate for a regional magazine in Seattle?). Don't allow yourself to become so blinded by submission procedures that you forget common sense. If you use your common sense and develop professional, courteous relations with editors, you will eventually find your own submission style.

DEVELOP YOUR IDEAS, THEN TARGET THE MARKETS

Writers often think of an interesting story, complete the manuscript, and then begin the search for a suitable publisher or magazine. While this approach is common for fiction, poetry and screenwriting, it reduces your chances of success in many nonfiction writing areas. Instead, try choosing categories that interest you and study those sections in *Writer's Market*. Select several listings you consider good prospects for your type of writing. Sometimes the individual listings will even help you generate ideas.

Next, make a list of the potential markets for each idea. Make the initial contact with markets using the method stated in the market listings. If you exhaust your list of possibilities, don't give up. Instead, reevaluate the idea or try another angle. Continue developing ideas and approaching markets. Identify and rank potential markets for an idea and continue the process.

As you submit to the various publications listed in *Writer's Market*, it's important to remember that every magazine is published with a particular audience and slant in mind. Probably the number one complaint we receive from editors is the submissions they receive are completely wrong for their magazines or book line. The first mark of professionalism is to know your market well. Gaining that knowledge starts with *Writer's Market*, but you should also do your own detective work. Search out back issues of the magazines you wish to write for, pick up recent issues at your local newsstand, or visit magazines' Web sites--anything that will help you figure out what subjects specific magazines publish. This research is also helpful in learning what topics have been covered ad nauseum—the topics you should stay away from or approach in a fresh way. Magazines' Web sites are invaluable as most post the current issue of the magazine, as well as back issues, and most offer writer's guidelines.

The same advice is true for submitting to book publishers. Research publisher Web sites for their submission guidelines, recently published titles and their backlist. You can use this information to target your book proposal in a way that fits with a publisher's other titles while not directly competing for sales.

Prepare for rejection and the sometimes lengthy wait. When a submission is returned, check your file folder of potential markets for that idea. Cross off the market that rejected the idea. If the editor has given you suggestions or reasons why the manuscript was not accepted, you might want to incorporate these suggestions when revising your manuscript.

After revising your manuscript mail it to the next market on your list.

Take rejection with a grain of salt

Rejection is a way of life in the publishing world. It's inevitable in a business that deals with such an overwhelming number of applicants for such a limited number of positions. Anyone who has published has lived through many rejections, and writers with thin skin are at a distinct disadvantage. A rejection letter is not a personal attack. It simply indicates your submission is not appropriate for that market. Writers who let rejection dissuade them from pursuing their dream or who react to an editor's "No" with indignation or fury do themselves a disservice. Writers who let rejection stop them do not get published. Resign yourself to facing rejection now. You will live through it, and you'll eventually overcome it.

QUERY AND COVER LETTERS

A query letter is a brief, one-page letter used as a tool to hook an editor and get him interested in your idea. When you send a query letter to a magazine, you are trying to get an editor to buy your idea or article. When you query a book publisher, you are attempting to get an editor interested enough in your idea to request your book proposal or your entire manuscript. (Note: Some book editors prefer to receive book proposals on first contact. Check individual listings for which method editors prefer.)

Here are some basic guidelines to help you create one that's polished and well-organized. For more tips see Query Letter Clinic on page **14**.

- **Limit it to one page, single-spaced**, and address the editor by name (Mr. or Ms. and the surname). *Note*: Do not assume that a person is a Mr. or Ms. unless it is obvious from the name listed. For example, if you are contacting a D.J. Smith, do not assume that D.J. should be preceded by Mr. or Ms. Instead, address the letter to D.J. Smith.
- **Grab the editor's attention with a strong opening.** Some magazine queries, for example, begin with a paragraph meant to approximate the lead of the intended article.
- **Indicate how you intend to develop the article or book.** Give the editor some idea of the work's structure and content.

- **Let the editor know if you have photos** or illustrations available to accompany your magazine article.
- **Mention any expertise or training that qualifies you** to write the article or book. If you've been published before, mention it; if not, don't.
- **End with a direct request to write the article.** Or, if you're pitching a book, ask for the go-ahead to send in a full proposal or the entire manuscript. Give the editor an idea of the expected length and delivery date of your manuscript.

A common question that arises is: If I don't hear from an editor in the reported response time, how do I know when I can safely send the query to another market? Many writers find it helpful to indicate in their queries that if they don't receive a response from the editor (slightly after the listed reporting time), they will assume the editor is not interested. It's best to take this approach, particularly if your topic is timely.

A brief, single-spaced cover letter is helpful when sending a manuscript as it helps personalize the submission. However, if you have previously queried the editor, use the cover letter to politely and briefly remind the editor of that query—when it was sent, what it contained, etc. "Here is the piece on low-fat cooking that I queried you about on December 12. I look forward to hearing from you at your earliest convenience." Do not use the cover letter as a sales pitch.

If you are submitting to a market that accepts unsolicited manuscripts, a cover letter is useful because it personalizes your submission. You can, and should, include information about the manuscript, yourself, your publishing history, and your qualifications.

See Also

In addition to tips on writing queries, The Query Letter Clinic on page 14 offers eight example query letters, some that work and some that don't, as well as editors' comments on why the letters were either successful or failed to garner an assignment or contract.

Querying for fiction

Fiction is sometimes queried, but more often editors prefer receiving material. Many fiction editors won't decide on a submission until they have seen the complete manuscript. When submitting a fiction book idea, most editors prefer to see at least a synopsis and sample

Query Letter Resources

For More Info

The following list of books provide you with more detailed information on writing query letters, cover letters, and book proposals. All titles are published by Writer's Digest Books.

- *Formatting & Submitting Your Manuscript,* 3rd Edition, by Chuck Sambuchino
- *How to Write Attention-Grabbing Query & Cover Letters,* by John Wood
- *How to Write a Book Proposal,* 3rd Edition, by Michael Larsen
- *Writer's Market Companion, 2nd Edition,* by Joe Feiertag and Mary Cupito

chapters (usually the first three). For fiction published in magazines, most editors want to see the complete short story manuscript. If an editor does request a query for fiction, it should include a description of the main theme and story line, including the conflict and resolution. Take a look at individual listings to see what editors prefer to receive.

THE SYNOPSIS

Most fiction books are sold by a complete manuscript, but most editors and agents don't have the time to read a complete manuscript of every wannabe writer. As a result, publishing decision makers use the synopsis and sample chapters to help the screening process of fiction. The synopsis, on its most base level, communicates what the book is about.

The length and depth of a synopsis can change from agent to agent or publisher to publisher. Some will want a synopsis that is 1-2 single-spaced pages; others will want a synopsis that can run up to 25 double-spaced pages. Checking your listings in *Writer's Market*, as well as double-checking with the listing's Web site will help guide you in this respect.

The content should cover all the essential points of the novel from beginning to end and in the correct order. The essential points include main characters, main plot points, and, yes, the ending. Of course, your essential points will vary from the editor who wants a 1-page synopsis to the editor who wants a 25-page synopsis.

NONFICTION BOOK PROPOSALS

Most nonfiction books are sold by a book proposal--a package of materials that details what your book is about, who its intended audience is, and how you intend to write the book. It includes some combination of a cover or query letter, an overview, an outline, author's information sheet, and sample chapters. Editors also want to see information about the audience for your book and about titles that compete with your proposed book.

Submitting a nonfiction book proposal

A proposal package should include the following items:

- **A cover or query letter.** This letter should be a short introduction to the material you include in the proposal.
- **An overview.** This is a brief summary of your book. It should detail your book's subject and give an idea of how that subject will be developed.
- **An outline.** The outline covers your book chapter by chapter and should include all major points covered in each chapter. Some outlines are done in traditional outline form, but most are written in paragraph form.
- **An author's information sheet.** This information should acquaint the editor with your writing background and convince him of your qualifications regarding the subject of your book.
- **Sample chapters.** Many editors like to see sample chapters, especially for a first book. Sample chapters show the editor how you write and develop ideas from your outline.
- **Marketing information.** Facts about how and to whom your book can be successfully marketed are now expected to accompany every book proposal. If you can provide information about the audience for your book and suggest ways the book publisher can reach those people, you will increase your chances of acceptance.
- **Competitive title analysis.** Check the *Subject Guide to Books in Print* for other titles on your topic. Write a one-or two-sentence synopsis of each. Point out how your book differs and improves upon existing topics.

For more information on nonfiction book proposals, read Michael Larsen's *How to Write a Book Proposal* (Writer's Digest Books).

A WORD ABOUT AGENTS

An agent represents a writer's work to publishers, negotiates contracts, follows up to see that contracts are fulfilled, and generally handles a writer's business affairs, leaving the writer free to write. Effective agents are valued for their contacts in the publishing industry, their knowledge about who to approach with certain ideas, their ability to guide an author's career, and their business sense.

While most book publishers listed in *Writer's Market* publish books by unagented writers, some of the larger houses are reluctant to consider submissions that have not reached them through a literary agent. Companies with such a policy are noted by an (🅰) icon at the beginning of the listing, as well as in the submission information within the listing.

Writer's Market includes a list of 85 literary agents who are all members of the Association of Authors' Representatives and who are also actively seeking new and established writers. For a more comprehensive resource on finding and working with an agent, see *2010 Guide to Literary Agents*.

MANUSCRIPT FORMAT

You can increase your chances of publication by following a few standard guidelines regarding the physical format of your manuscript. It should be your goal to make your manuscript readable. Follow these suggestions as you would any other suggestions: Use what works for you and discard what doesn't.

In general, when submitting a manuscript, you should use white, 8½ × 11, 20 lb. paper, and you should also choose a legible, professional looking font (i.e., Times New Roman)—no all-italic or artsy fonts. Your entire manuscript should be double-spaced with a 1½-inch margin on all sides of the page. Once you are ready to print your manuscript, you should print either on a laser printer or an ink-jet printer.

ESTIMATING WORD COUNT

Many computers will provide you with a word count of your manuscript. Your editor will count again after editing the manuscript. Although your computer is counting characters, an editor or production editor is more concerned about the amount of space the text will occupy on a page. Several small headlines or subheads, for instance, will be counted the same by your computer as any other word of text. However, headlines and subheads usually employ a different font size than the body text, so an editor may count them differently to be sure enough space has been estimated for larger type.

For short manuscripts, it's often quickest to count each word on a representative page and multiply by the number of pages. You can get a very rough count by multiplying the number of pages in your manuscript by 250 (the average number of words on a double-spaced typewritten page).

PHOTOGRAPHS AND SLIDES

In some cases, the availability of photographs and slides can be the deciding factor as to whether an editor will accept your submission. This is especially true when querying a publication that relies heavily on photographs, illustrations or artwork to enhance the article (i.e., craft magazines, hobby magazines, etc.). In some instances, the publication may offer additional payment for photographs or illustrations.

Check the individual listings to find out which magazines review photographs and what their submission guidelines are. Most publications prefer you do not send photographs with your submission. However, if photographs or illustrations are available, you should indicate that in your query. As with manuscripts, never send the originals of your photographs or illustrations. Instead, send prints or duplicates of slides and transparencies. Also, more magazines and book publishers are using digital images.

Manuscript Formatting Sample

1. Type your real name (even if you use a pseudonym) and contact information
2. Double-space twice
3. Estimated word count and the rights you are offering
4. Type your title in capital letters, double-space and type "by," double-space again, and type your name (or pseudonym if you're using one)
5. Double-space twice, then indent first paragraph and start text of your manuscript
6. On subsequent pages, type your name, a dash, and the page number in the upper left or right corner

Your name
Your street address
City, State ZIP code
Day and evening phone numbers
E-mail address

50,000 words
World rights

TITLE

by

Your Name

You can increase your chances of publication by following a few standard guidelines regarding the physical format of your article or manuscript. It should be your goal to make your manuscript readable. Use these suggestions as you would any other suggestions: Use what works for you and discard what doesn't.

In general, when submitting a manuscript, you should use white, 8½ x11, 20-lb. bond paper, and you should also choose a legible, professional-looking font (i.e., Times New Roman)—no all-italic or artsy fonts. Your entire manuscript should be double-spaced with a 1½-inch margin on

Your Name - 2

all sides of the page. Once you are ready to print your article or manuscript, you should print either on a laser printer or an ink-jet printer.

Remember, though, articles should either be written after you send a one-page query letter to an editor, and the editor then asks you to write the article. If, however, you are sending an article "on spec" to an editor, you should send both a query letter and the complete article.

Fiction is a little different from nonfiction articles, in that it is only sometimes queried, but more often not. Many fiction editors won't decide on a submission until they have seen the complete manuscript. When submitting a fiction book idea, most editors prefer to see at least a synopsis and sample chapters (usually the first three). For fiction that is pub-

SEND PHOTOCOPIES

If there is one hard-and-fast rule in publishing, it's this: *Never* send the original (or only) copy of your manuscript. Most editors cringe when they find out a writer has sent the only copy of their manuscript. You should always send photocopies of your manuscript.

Some writers choose to send a self-addressed, stamped postcard with a photocopied submission. In their cover letter they suggest if the editor is not interested in their manuscript, it may be tossed out and a reply sent on the postcard. This method is particularly helpful when sending your submissions to international markets.

MAILING SUBMISSIONS

No matter what size manuscript you're mailing, always include a self-addressed, stamped envelope (SASE) with sufficient return postage. The Web site for the U.S. Postal Service (www.usps.com) and the Web site for the Canadian Post (www.canadapost.ca) both have postage calculators if you are unsure of how much postage you'll need to affix.

A book manuscript should be mailed in a sturdy, well-wrapped box. Enclose a self-addressed mailing label and paper clip your return postage to the label. However, be aware that some book publishers do not return unsolicited manuscripts, so make sure you know the practice of the publisher before sending any unsolicited material.

Types of mail service

There are many different mailing service options available to you whether you are sending a query letter or a complete manuscript. You can work with the U.S. Postal Service, United Parcel Service, Federal Express, or any number of private mailing companies. The following are the five most common types of mailing services offered by the U.S. Postal Service.

- **First Class** is a fairly expensive way to mail a manuscript, but many writers prefer it. First-Class mail generally receives better handling and is delivered more quickly than Standard mail.
- **Priority Mail** reaches its destination within two or three days.
- **Standard Mail** rates are available for packages, but be sure to pack your materials carefully because they will be handled roughly. To make sure your package will be returned to you if it is undeliverable, print "Return Postage Guaranteed" under your address.

Mailing Manuscripts

- Fold manuscripts under five pages into thirds, and send in a #10 SASE.
- Mail manuscripts five pages or more unfolded in a 9 x 12 or 10 x 13 SASE.
- For return envelope, fold the envelope in half, address it to yourself, and add a stamp or, if going to Canada or another international destination, International Reply Coupons (available at most post office branches).
- Don't send by Certified Mail–this is a sign of an amateur.

- **Certified Mail** must be signed for when it reaches its destination.
- **Registered Mail** is a high-security method of mailing where the contents are insured. The package is signed in and out of every office it passes through, and a receipt is returned to the sender when the package reaches its destination.

THE BASICS

Query Letter Clinic

Many great writers ask year after year, "Why is it so hard to get published?'' In many cases, these writers have spent years--and possibly thousands of dollars on books and courses--developing their craft. They submit to the appropriate markets, yet rejection is always the end result. The culprit? A weak query letter.

The query letter is often the most important piece of the publishing puzzle. In many cases, it determines whether an editor or agent will even read your manuscript. A good query letter makes a good first impression; a bad query letter earns a swift rejection.

The elements of a query letter

A query letter should sell editors or agents on your idea or convince him to request your finished manuscript. The most effective query letters get into the specifics from the very first line. It's important to remember that the query is a call to action, not a listing of features and benefits.

In addition to selling your idea or manuscript, a query letter can include information on the availability of photographs or artwork. You can include a working title and projected word count. Depending on the piece, you might also mention whether a sidebar might be appropriate and the type of research you plan to conduct. If appropriate, include a tentative deadline and indicate whether the query is being simultaneously submitted.

Biographical information should be included as well, but don't overdo it unless your background actually helps sell the article or proves that you're the only person who could write your proposed piece.

Things to avoid in a query letter

The query letter is not a place to discuss pay rates. This step comes after an editor has agreed to take on your article or book. Besides making an unprofessional impression on an editor, it can also work to your disadvantage in negotiating your fee. If you ask for too much, an editor may not even contact you to see if a lower rate might work. If you ask for too little, you may start an editorial relationship where you are making far less than the normal rate.

You should also avoid rookie mistakes, such as mentioning that your work is copyrighted or including the copyright symbol on your work. While you want to make it clear that you've researched the market, avoid using flattery as a technique for selling your work. It often has the opposite effect of what you intend. In addition, don't hint that you can re-write the piece, as this only leads the editor to think there will be a lot of work involved in shaping up your writing.

Also, never admit several other editors or agents have rejected the query. Always treat your new audience as if they are the first place on your list of submission possibilities.

How to format your query letter

It's OK to break writing rules in a short story or article, but you should follow the rules when it comes to crafting an effective query. Here are guidelines for query writing.

- Use a normal font and typeface, such as Times New Roman and 10- or 12-point type.
- Include your name, address, phone number, e-mail address and Web site, if possible.
- Use a one-inch margin on paper queries.
- Address a specific editor or agent. (Note: The listings in *Writer's Market* provide a contact name for most submissions. It's wise to double-check contact names online or by calling.)
- Limit query letter to one single-spaced page.
- Include self-addressed, stamped envelope or postcard for response with post submissions. Use block paragraph format (no indentations).
- Thank the editor for considering your query.

When and how to follow up

Accidents do happen. Queries may not reach your intended reader. Staff changes or interoffice mail snafus may end up with your query letter thrown away. Or the editor may have set your query off to the side for further consideration and forgotten it. Whatever the case may be, there are some basic guidelines you should use for your follow-up communication.

Most importantly, wait until the reported response time, as indicated in *Writer's Market* or their submission guidelines, has elapsed before contacting an editor or agent. Then, you should send a short and polite e-mail describing the original query sent, the date it was sent, and asking if they received it or made a decision regarding its fate.

The importance of remaining polite and businesslike when following up cannot be stressed enough. Making a bad impression on an editor can often have a ripple effect--as that editor may share his or her bad experience with other editors at the magazine or publishing company.

How the clinic works

As mentioned earlier, the query letter is the most important weapon for getting an assignment or a request for your full manuscript. Published writers know how to craft a well-written, hard-hitting query. What follows are eight queries: four are strong; four are not. Detailed comments show what worked and what did not. As you'll see, there is no cut-and-dried "good" query format; every strong query works on its own merit.

Good Nonfiction Magazine Query

My name is only available on our magazine's Web site and on the masthead. So this writer has done her research.

Here's a story that hasn't been pitched before. I didn't know Morganic was so unique in the market. I'm interested to know more.

The author has access to her interview subject, and she displays knowledge of the magazine by pointing out the correct section in which it would run.

While I probably would've assigned this article based off the idea alone, her past credits do help solidify my decision.

Jimmy Boaz, editor
American Organic Farmer's Digest
8336 Old Dirt Road
Macon, GA 00000

Dear Mr. Boaz,

There are 87 varieties of organic crops grown in the United States, but there's only one farm producing 12 of these—Morganic Corporation.

Located in the heart of Arkansas, this company spent the past decade providing great organic crops at a competitive price helping them grow into the ninth leading organic farming operation in the country. Along the way, they developed the most unique organic offering in North America.

As a seasoned writer with access to Richard Banks, the founder and president of Morganic, I propose writing a profile piece on Banks for your Organic Shakers department. After years of reading this riveting column, I believe the time has come to cover Morganic's rise in the organic farming industry.

The piece would run in the normal 800-1,200 word range with photographs available of Banks and Morganic's operation.

I've been published in *Arkansas Farmer's Deluxe*, *Organic Farming Today* and in several newspapers.

Thank you for your consideration of this article. I hope to hear from you soon.

Sincerely,

Jackie Service
34 Good St.
Little Rock, AR 00000
jackie.service9867@email.com

Bad Nonfiction Magazine Query

This is sexist, and it doesn't address any contact specifically. It shows a complete lack of research on the part of the writer.

An over-the-top, bold claim by a writer who does not impress me with his publishing background.

Insults the magazine, and then reassures me he won't charge too much?

While I do assign material from time-to-time, I prefer writers pitch me on their own ideas after studying the magazine.

I'm sure people aren't going to be knocking down his door anytime soon.

Dear Gentlemen,

I'd like to write the next great article you'll ever publish. My writing credits include exposé pieces I've done for local and community newspapers and for my college English classes. I've been writing for years and years.

Your magazine may not be a big one like *Rolling Stone* or *Sports Illustrated*, but I'm willing to write an interview for you anyway. I know you need material, and I need money (but don't worry I won't charge too much).

Just give me some people to interview, and I'll do the best job you've ever read. It will be amazing, and I can re-write the piece for you if you don't agree. I'm willing to re-write 20 times if needed.

You better hurry up and assign me an article though, because I've sent out letters to lots of other magazines, and I'm sure to be filled up to capacity very soon.

Later gents,

Carl Bighead
76 Bad Query Lane
Big City, NY 00000

Good Fiction Magazine Query

Marcus West
88 Piano Drive
Lexington, KY 00000

August 8, 2008

Jeanette Curic, editor
Wonder Stories
45 Noodle Street
Portland, OR 00000

Dear Ms. Curic,

Please consider the following 1,200-word story, "Turning to the Melon," a quirky coming of age story with a little magical realism thrown in the mix.

After reading *Wonder Stories* for years, I think I've finally written something that would fit with your audience. My previous short story credits include *Stunned Fiction Quarterly* and *Faulty Mindbomb*.

Thank you in advance for considering "Turning to the Melon."

Sincerely,

Marcus West
(123) 456-7890
marcusw87452@email.com

Encl: Manuscript and SASE

Follows the format we established in our guidelines. Being able to follow directions is more important than many writers realize.

Story is in our word count, and the description sounds like the type of story we would consider publishing.

It's flattering to know he reads our magazine. While it won't guarantee publication, it does make me a little more hopeful that the story I'm reading will be a good fit. Also, good to know he's been published before.

I can figure it out, but it's nice to know what other materials were included in the envelope.

This letter is not flashy or gimmicky. It just gives me the basics and puts me in the right frame of mind to read the actual story.

Bad Fiction Magazine Query

To: curic@wonderstories808.com
Subject: A Towering Epic Fantasy

Hello there.

I've written a great fantasy epic novel short story of about 25,000 words that may be included in your magazine if you so desire.

More than 20 years, I've spent chained to my desk in a basement writing out the greatest story of our time. And it can be yours if you so desire to have it.

Just say the word, and I'll ship it over to you. We can talk money and movie rights after your acceptance. I have big plans for this story, and you can be part of that success.

Yours forever (if you so desire),

Harold
(or Harry for friends)

We do not accept e-mail queries or submissions.

This is a little too informal.

First off, what did he write? An epic novel or short story? Second, 25,000 words is way over our 1,500-word max.

I'm lost for words.

Money and movie rights? We pay moderate rates and definitely don't get involved in movies.

I'm sure the writer was just trying to be nice, but this is a little bizarre and kind of a scary stalker ending to the letter. I do not so desire any more contact with "Harry."

Good Nonfiction Book Query

To: corey@bigbookspublishing.com
Subject: Query: Become a Better Parent in 30 Days

Effective subject line. Lets me know exactly what to expect when I open the e-mail.

Dear Mr. Corey,

As a parent of six and a high school teacher for more than a decade, I know first-hand that being a parent is difficult work. Even harder is being a good parent. My proposed title *Taking Care of Yourself and Your Kids: A 30-day Program to Become a Better Parent While Still Living Your Life* would show how to handle real-life situations and still be a good parent.

Good lead. Six kids and teaches high school. I already believe her.

Nice title that would fit well with others that we currently offer.

This book has been years in the making, as it follows the outline I've used successfully in my summer seminars I give on the topic to thousands of parents every year. It really works, because past participants contact me constantly to let me know what a difference my classes have made in their lives.

Her platform as a speaker definitely gets my attention.

In addition to marketing and selling *Taking Care of Yourself and Your Kids* at my summer seminars, I would also be able to sell it through my Web site and promote it through my weekly e-newsletter with over 25,000 subscribers. Of course, it would also make a very nice trade title that I think would sell well in bookstores and possibly retail outlets, such as K-Mart, Wal-Mart and Target.

25,000 e-mail subscribers? She must have a very good voice to gather that many readers.

If you would like to look over my proposal, please just shoot an e-mail back.

Thank you for your consideration.

Sincerely,

Marilyn Parent
8647 Query St.
Norman, OK 00000
mparent8647@email.com
www.marilynsbetterparents.com

I was interested after the first paragraph, but every paragraph after made it impossible to not request her proposal.

Bad Nonfiction Book Query

The subject line is so vague, I almost deleted this e-mail as spam without even opening it.

To: info@bigbookspublishing.com
Subject: a question for you

This almost sounds like a sales pitch for a book. Maybe this is spam after all? The reason we don't publish such a book is easy—we don't do hobby titles.

I really liked this book by Mega Book Publishers called *Build Better Trains in Your Own Backyard*. It was a great book that covered all the basics of model train building. My father and I would read from it together and assemble all the pieces, and it was magical like Christmas all through the year. Why wouldn't you want to publish such a book?

I'm not going to open an attachment from an unknown sender via e-mail, especially of someone who's not the prettiest person. Also, copyrighting your work is the sign of an amateur.

Well, here it is. I've already copyrighted the material for 1999 and can help you promote it if you want to send me on a worldwide book tour. As you can see from my attached digital photo, I'm not the prettiest person, but I am passionate.

1,000 possible buyers is a small market, and I'm not going to pay a writer to do research on a book proposal.

There are at least 1,000 model train builders in the United States alone, and there might be even more than that. I haven't done enough research yet, because I don't know if this is an idea that appeals to you. If you give me maybe $500, I could do that research in a day and get back to you on it.

Anyway, this idea is a good one that brings back lots of memories for me.

Not even a last name? Or contact information? At least, I won't feel guilty for not responding.

Jacob

Good Fiction Book Query

Jeremy Mansfield, editor
Novels R Us Publishing
8787 Big Time Street
New York NY 00000

Dear Mr. Mansfield,

My 62,000-word novel, *Love in April*, is a psychologically complex thriller in the same mold as James Patterson, but with a touch of the supernatural á la Anne Rice.

Supernatural genre bending novels have been money in the bank lately with the emergence of the Anita Blake series and the Highlander series. *Love in April* comes from this same tradition, but like all bestselling fiction makes its own path.

Rebecca Frank is at the top of the modeling world, posing for magazines in exotic locales all over the world and living life to its fullest. Despite all her success, she feels something is missing in her life. Then she runs into Marcus Hunt, a wealthy bachelor with cold blue eyes and an ambiguous past.

Within 24 hours of meeting Marcus, Rebecca's understanding of the world turns upside down, and she finds herself fighting for her life and the love of a man who may not have the ability to return her the favor.

Filled with demons, serial killers, trolls, maniacal clowns and more, this novel will put Rebecca through a gauntlet of trouble and turmoil, leading up to a final climatic realization that may lead to her unraveling.

Love in April should fit in well with your other titles, such as *Bone Dead* and *Carry Me Home*, though it is a unique story. Your Web site mentioned supernatural suspense as a current interest, so I hope this is a good match.

My short fiction has appeared in many mystery magazines, including a prize-winning story in *The Mysterious Oregon Quarterly*. This novel is the first in a series that I'm working on (already half-way through the second).

As stated in your guidelines, I've included the first 30 pages. Thank you for considering *Love in April*.

Sincerely,

Merry Plentiful
54 Willow Road
East Lansing MI 00000
merry865423@email.com

Novel is correct length and has the suspense and supernatural elements we're seeking.

The quick summary sounds like something we would write on the back cover of our paperbacks. That's a good thing, because it identifies the triggers that draw a response out of our readers.

She mentions similar titles we've done and that she's done research on our Web site. She's not afraid to put in a little extra effort.

At the moment, I'm not terribly concerned that this book could become a series, but it is something good to file away in the back of my mind for future use.

Bad Fiction Book Query

Jeremy Mansfield
Novels R Us Publishing
8787 Big Time Street
New York NY 00000

Dear Editor,

My novel has an amazing twist ending that could make it a worldwide phenomenon overnight while you are sleeping. It has spectacular special effects that will probably lead to a multi-million dollar movie deal that will also spawn action figures, lunch boxes, and several other crazy subsidiary rights. I mean, we're talking big-time money here.

While I love to hear enthusiasm from a writer about his or her work, this kind of unchecked excitement is worrisome for an editor.

I'm not going to share the twist until I have a signed contract that authorizes me to a big bank account, because I don't want to have my idea stolen and used to promote whatever new initiative "The Man" has in mind for media nowadays. But let it be known that you will be rewarded handsomely for taking a chance on me.

I need to know the twist to make a decision on whether to accept the manuscript. Plus, I'm troubled by the paranoia and emphasis on making a lot of money.

Did you know that George Lucas once took a chance on an actor named Harrison Ford by casting him as Han Solo in Star Wars? Look at how that's panned out. Ford went on to become a big actor in the Indiana Jones series, *The Fugitive*, *Blade Runner* and more. It's obvious that you taking a risk on me could play out in the same dramatic results.

I'm confused. Does he think he's Harrison Ford?

I realize you've got to make money, and guess what? I want to make money too. So we're on the same page, you and I. We both want to make money, and we'll stop at nothing to do so.

If you want me to start work on this amazing novel with an incredible twist ending, just send a one-page contract agreeing to pay me a lot of money if we hit it big. No other obligations will apply. If it's a bust, I won't sue you for millions.

So that's the twist: He hasn't even written it yet. I can't make a decision without a completed manuscript. There's no way I'm going to offer a contract for a novel that hasn't been written by someone with no experience or idea of how the publishing industry works.

Sincerely,

Kenzel Pain
92 Bad Writer Road
Austin TX 00000

THE BASICS

Freelance Newspaper Writing 101

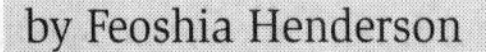

by Feoshia Henderson

Most people have a romantic notion of what it means to be a freelance writer: lounging in your pajamas lingering over coffee and important ideas and words. But if you go for it full-time like I did, the reality is a lot less romantic and a lot of hard, sometimes tedious, work.

After a decade as a newspaper reporter, I finally took the freelance leap. June 19, 2007 became my own personal day of freedom when I left a secure and well-paying job with *The Cincinnati Enquirer* to become a full-time freelance writer and reporter.

And now, I'd like to share with you how I did it, and what I've learned. I've also talked to some other professional freelance writers and newspaper editors, and hope to give you some guidance, a few warnings, and most importantly, hope.

Before I begin, let me start by saying this is really hard to do full-time. It was much more difficult than I thought it would be to establish myself. Also, I have a journalism degree and more than 10 years of writing experience, including about five years working for dailies in a metro area. And I'm no newbie in the freelance world either. I've written on the side for small magazines for about as long as I've been a professional journalist. So, if this is something you want to do full-time realize it might take you a while—meaning several years—to get fully established. It will take an incredible amount of time pitching ideas, selling yourself and facing rejection. Also, you must treat it as a business and not a hobby. That being said, it can be the most rewarding career of your life. You are your own boss and the only limits are what you put on yourself, financially and creatively.

New writing opportunities in newspapers

Newspapers, like so many other businesses, have cut back on staff and other resources. But the boss still expects a steady stream of interesting stories to fill up those column inches. And to compete with the Internet and new media publications, many newspaper companies have started specialty magazines that depend on engaging feature articles.

This has created more opportunities for new and established freelance writers who are looking for welcoming, quality places to publish their work.

If you've never thought about writing for a newspaper, or just want some insight into what editors are looking for, read on. Though editors and newspapers all have different needs, a few themes emerged when they were asked what makes a proposed article—and a writer—stand out.

FEOSHIA HENDERSON is a full-time freelance writer and journalist living in Cincinnati, Ohio. She is a former reporter for the *Cincinnati Enquirer*. Before joining the *Enquirer* staff, she worked for several daily and weekly newspapers in Kentucky. She had been published in *Kentucky Monthly, The Lane Reporter, Catalyst Ohio,* and *The Business Courier of Cincinnati,* among other publications. She also writes for kypost.com.

CityBeat, an alternative urban newsweekly in Cincinnati, Ohio, often looks for writers for their Arts and Entertainment section, especially for music and movie reviews. Travel, Home and Garden and Lifestyle sections are common places where you'll frequently find freelance written articles.

"We tend to look for people who aren't trained writers. We'd rather have someone with expertise in a certain area and passion, and we can help with the writing part," says John Fox, editor and co-publisher of *CityBeat*.

That holds true for more traditional daily newspapers as well. John Bordsen, travel editor for The Charlotte Observer, in North Carolina, says: "Some of the best writers I've used didn't have published clippings. When it comes to background, it's fair game."

Of course, experience does count for something, and it can give you an edge over other writers.

Jacqueline Palfy Klemond is senior editor for specialty publications for the South Dakota Argus Leader in Sioux Falls. She also directs the paper's Lifestyle feature staff. In addition to her newspaper duties, she oversees three magazines (topics include upscale living and pets) that the paper has published for the last three years. For her, experience is key.

"I look for someone who has been published before. Some people are very talented who haven't been published, but it's the first question I ask," Klemond says.

Getting started

If you're new to freelancing and wondering where to start, start by looking at magazines, newspapers or online publications in your area. Write what you know, or what you're interested in. Know of a great local band or painter, does a community group have an interesting outreach project? Those things are fodder for ideas. Generally newspapers aren't going to turn to freelancers for hard news, but for features and travel articles, among other sections. Get in contact with the editor and start pitching some ideas.

Timothy Chambers, an instructor at the University of Hartford, writes op-ed articles for several publications in the U.S. and abroad, including *The Hartford Courant* and *The Korea Times*. He began writing as a way to get his ideas about topical social and cultural issues. He has degrees in philosophy and sticks to the "write what you know" mantra.

"The more experience you have with what you are writing about, the more truthful your writing will be," he says.

Unlike in many cases where you will query an editor to sell and article, Timothy writes his entire op-ed and submits it for approval. He said to keep it to 700 words or less because brevity is a must for newspapers. Timothy submits articles every few months and has been published about a dozen times in the last several years.

Now you might be further along in your freelance writing career and or interested in leaving your current job to pursue freelance full-time. There are several bread-and-butter issues you must examine. Ask yourself these questions: Why do you want to do this? How much monthly income do you need to cover your expenses? Do you have a spouse or partner to help with bills if you're lacking money? Or can you find a part-time job if work is slow? Will you need medical insurance? If you're a parent, will you need childcare during your workday?

And here's a few more: Are you self-motivated? Can you work without a lot of supervision? Can you sell yourself?

After you and your family have examined these issues, if you still decide you want to take the leap. It's time to plan.

Planning to freelance full-time

When I decided to go full-time, one of the first things I did was cut back on expenses and put extra money in my savings account. I saved a few thousand dollars, which was NOT enough. So learn from my mistake, have enough in savings to cover six-to-12 months of living expenses. I can't stress how important this will be in getting started. Chances are it will take you at least this long, if not longer, to get established and find steady work. Also, I paid off most of my non-recurring bills including credit cards and my car. Get financially lean and mean as you can.

Next, I began alerting all of my contacts by e-mail usually, or in person when possible, that I was going to soon make the jump. You might be surprised by who knows somebody, who knows somebody, who's looking for a freelance writer. Family, church members, friends, community groups. Let everyone know.

Put together a portfolio online and on paper. Get a résumé, clips and testimonials from people who you've written for in the past. Also, if you don't have a profile already, set one up on LinkedIn, MySpace or Facebook (or all three!) identifying yourself as a freelance writer. I have gotten several writing jobs (including this one!) by networking online.

Making the move

If possible, ease into full-time freelance writing. In the beginning you'll spend far more time searching for work than you will writing. If it's possible to work at your current job full-time, do it. That's wasn't possible for me, but I wish it had been. Though it's exciting to be your own boss, you could go weeks or maybe months without a substantial paycheck in the beginning. That means one of two things: you have to earn more money elsewhere or spend a lot of time at home broke and creative.

I was lucky in a way, because *The Kentucky Post*, a daily I'd previously worked for went out of business in 2007. The paper needed a freelancer until then. So I worked basically as a daily reporter for about six months. I got a phone call or an e-mail each morning and went out on assignment. It definitely got me through those first six months financially. Otherwise I might have been working a part time job.

Finally, if you want to write articles full time, or just on the side, I'll leave you with this: Don't limit yourself. There are all types of publications that can use the skills of a journalist or newspaper writer. For instance, I write for several business publications and Web sites interviewing business owners, and highlighting local business trends. I also write for an education foundation's magazine where I help explain education policy. There are Web sites, newsletters, magazines, and many types of publications that need good writers. The pay varies by publication so it's really up to you to decide what works best with your budget. Then focus your energy in that area or a couple of areas and go for it. It's best to become an expert in something and write away. Some possible topics include travel, politics, community life, the environment, education or business, transportation, the arts.

As you get more experience under your belt, create your own writing opportunities. I've gone to several small cities in the area and offered to write their newsletters and press releases. They've made for good regular jobs. I've also sent my prior work in education to communications workers at area colleges and universities to let them know I am available to write for them.

"The most important thing I did was self-promotion, and getting my name out there on desks. I also did a lot of cold calling," says Tom Head, a Jackson, Mississippi, writer. He is a nonfiction writer who's also a guide for About.com, an online information network created by The New York Times Company. "That is a wonderful way to find clients and find out what publishers need. A key to my success and being able to sound qualified, sound if that you were made to write on the subject."

That doesn't mean faking qualifications, Head explained, but emphasizing and playing up your strengths on a particular subject.

So, keep your options open, be flexible, be vigilant, and network and you can be a professional newspaper and article writer.

How to Get and Keep a Column

Your whole self-worth can get tied up in publishing a book with the process dragging out for months. Books aren't the only outlet for writers though, what about newspaper columns? They don't pay as well but weekly columns add up. Plus, you can sell an article to multiple papers and send out numerous leads at once.

Topics? Your Passion of course! In minutes I can think of eight columns ideas: gardening, parenting, fun things to do locally, pet health/training, cooking-weekly menus, seasonal-holiday ideas, religious, dining guide.

Here are a few things to keep in mind as you approach newspapers with column ideas:

- Newspapers are struggling. Convince them you'll increase their reader base and gain advertisements. If you're a gardener, garden stores could advertise under your column.
- Get one to sponsor your column—Editor gets a free column.
- Talk to the correct person. With smaller papers, deal with the head editor, larger papers the editor in your area of interest.
- You can't argue with editors but you can diplomatically educate them as to how big a market they're missing. Show how you'll expand their reader base.
- Do I ever run out of topics? No! If you love something there are always new angles, methods and products to test. Keep articles interesting and informative.
- Get readers involved. We did a Kids Outdoor Writing contest. The top four stories were published, the authors taken on a fishing trip and filmed for the TV show "Kid Outdoors."
- Columns open doors. Speaking engagements, seminars, radio interviews and TV shows.
- Keep articles seasonal.
- Usually I select topics. Sometimes I get writing assignments. Never turn one down. Each deal builds momentum.
- First column doesn't pay? You're a writer. Write. It'll sharpen your skills and open doors. An unknown editor read an article and asked me to write some articles for her magazine. I've written five/year ever since.
- Don't grow fainthearted. I get 40 rejects before landing a deal.
- Keep queries brief. Many editors don't reply the first time.
- Photos draw eyes to your article. Some pay extra for photos.
- Enter contests. That's how I got started. Check local newspapers/magazines. I obtained two writing assignments, visited a manufacturer (another article) and $400 in products all while on vacation seeing my mom.
- Newspapers are local. That sets them apart from the Internet. One article won't fit all.
- Most are monthly but I have weekly, bi-monthly and monthly columns.

It's hard to get a column. One you do, it's important to be organized. It can get hectic juggling multiple due dates but don't be late. Be open to criticism and suggestions. Editors are busy, be available but don't wear out your welcome. And be worth more than you're paid.

—Tom Claycomb

THE BASICS

Reasons for Rejection

Six Things That May Be Tripping You Up

by Lisa Abeyta

Not all rejection is the same. While a rejection in our e-mail in box may feel terrible, it's important to determine just what went wrong if we are to turn those rejections into that coveted acceptance letter. *Writer's Market* culled the input of authors, agents and editors to provide you with the tools you need to determine why you're meeting rejection—and what you can do to turn it around.

Is your pitch too vague?

Get specific. Being vague may be a very smart move when you're asked if your friend's outfit makes her look fat. But being anything less than specific in your pitch will inevitably lead to a rejection, no matter how brilliant your idea may be.

"All too often, we see a writer proposing an idea that is not specific or fleshed out enough," says Kate Lawler, Executive Editor of *Ladies Home Journal*.

Powerhouse agent Kristin Nelson, based in Denver, Colorado, agrees. "The biggest trouble is boiling down a 300-page novel, but what we're looking for is that essential plot catalyst that happens in the first 30 pages or so. Many writers have not nailed the pitch blurb."

So how do you nail a pitch? Catch the reader in the first sentence. And the second. And then the third. Start out with a hook, and you're far more likely to hold a reader's attention through the following paragraphs detailing the description of your project, your experience, and why you chose that specific person for a query.

I recently gained the attention of an agent on a pitch for a humor diet book with just such a hook:

> Without quite noticing, I somehow changed from a size four high fashion sales clerk into a frumpy mom in Birkies and stained denim skirts. Instead of chatting with doctor's and lawyer's wives, I started using baby talk and repeating myself—as if the litany of no's I screeched would stop my child from pushing a popcorn seed up his nose while strapped in his car seat behind me. One morning I woke up to see that the lovely young woman was completely gone, replaced by some fat lady in the mirror.

Beyond letting the reader know what the book was about, I tried to craft the words to also give a sense of voice and tone that would be present in the book as well. It was

LISA ABEYTA is a freelance writer and columnist based in Albuquerque, New Mexico, where she lives with her husband and three children. Her work has appeared in a variety of national and local publications.

probably the tenth introductory paragraph I had tried for the query and the third title. When I was finally happy with the product, I pressed send. Five minutes later, I received a request for the full proposal for my nonfiction book—a definite record in my history of querying.

If your introductory sentence is boring, try rearranging and spicing it up.

Be professional: A goofy font is not fun

While the odds may seem to be stacked against writers due to the sheer number of queries and pitches any one editor or agent receives, getting creative can backfire if we're not careful.

Molly Friedrich, one of New York's most respected literary agents whose office receives anywhere from 100 to 150 queries each week, has seen it all. "A letter in italics, pale purple ink, even one that's handwritten ... those are immediately put aside, because they show such a lack of professionalism." She adds that over the years she's received Kleenexes, confetti, and myriad other tchotchke from writers who hope to stand out. They did. Their queries did not.

Kristin Nelson advises that writers should never wing their query letter. "It's almost as important as the complete novel. We've picked a lot of authors from a well-written query letter." Nelson's Denver office, which only accepts e-mail queries, receives around 700 queries each week. Of those, only five or six of those will make it past Nelson's assistant. "If it's really poorly written, we'll assume the sample pages are the same."

To that end, Friedrich also warns against over-hyping yourself. "What happens far too often is when authors try to find comparisons and contrasts, it often comes off as arrogant. Don't go on about who should star in the movie of your book or about your hopes and dreams. Keep it professional with a lively, intelligent and modest query letter."

Oh, and the picture of you with your beloved kitty? Seems that's a no-no, as are photos with your kids, your horse, and the one of you in a field of flowers. Unless you're writing a fitness or beauty book, you have the luxury of being in one of the only forms of media where looks won't help (or hurt) you.

One other thing that will turn off an agent is trying to act like old friends when you are complete strangers. While a friendly tone is always welcome, inappropriate intimacies can close a door. "Here is a query letter that caught my interest," says Friedrich. "It starts out *Dear Ms. Friedrich*. Not Molly. She addresses me professionally, with respect. I like that."

Are you editing out your own unique voice?

Allison Winn Scotch, three-time New York Times Best-selling author and freelance writer, says that she believes the biggest mistake writers make is to lose themselves in their editing. "They write very standard paragraphs, none of their voice comes through," she says. "One of the reasons I was successful is that I wasn't afraid to sort of trust my inner voice. If you write a basic-gray query letter, it is you. If it not fun or playful or intriguing or any three adjectives, why would they want to give a try for this one? People are nervous, want to look professional, perfect, and then they don't let their writing voice come through."

Doris Booth, long-time literary agent, editor and CEO of authorlink.com agrees. "The first element is always your writing. Not just the style of writing but the way you're writing your query. Are you not giving a good sense of conflict or how your characters are different? Agents are too busy. You have to catch us in that first 5, 10, 15 seconds," she says. "Think in terms of television log lines. There are only 10 or 15 seconds to tell us why we should want to watch that movie."

This is such an important point. Figure out what makes you unique in your writing. Let that shine through. No it doesn't mean it is okay to call the agent Dude if that's what you call your friends. But it does mean you should find a way to talk in your unique voice through your letter, not just put words on paper. This is true whether your query is for a 300-word piece in a local publication or a full manuscript to an agent.

Is your concept broad enough for a big audience?

So your query letter pitching your book about the tulip bulbs of Clark County, Ohio, keeps getting rejected by agents on both coasts. You may be one of the few writers who could have a perfectly crafted query letter and still get as much interest as a squash casserole at a cake walk. When your project involves a concept too narrow, you will likely not catch the interest of a national agent. This holds true for nonfiction and fiction alike.

Says Kristin Nelson, "If a book feels too small for me, editors may feel the same way, too."

The same sentiment resounds with Doris Booth. "We're all looking for a fresh idea, something we've not seen before. The first thing we look for is a saleable concept; our gut feeling as to how a manuscript will do in the market."

Ask yourself whether readers everywhere will connect with the concept and characters of your book. Is your idea broad enough to capture the interest of a large cross-section of readers? If not, this may be why your queries are meeting rejection. Find a way to rework your story to appeal to a larger audience, and you may be on your road to acceptance.

Dear Sir or Madam: Mass letters can lead to mass rejection

As tempting as it is with today's quick technology, sending a mass-produced query to editors or agents can put a death knell on a perfectly good idea.

Doris Booth explains what can go wrong. "Every agent has a certain number of contacts specific to certain kinds of work. Let's say I look at a query letter, and I don't know any editors who will be interested in this project. It may be a good query letter, but it won't be one I can represent."

Kristin Nelson adds that her office often receives queries for genres her agency doesn't represent. "Thirty to forty percent of the queries we get are for thrillers, mysteries... titles we don't represent."

Kate Lawler confirms that the same holds true for the magazine industry. "We receive queries proposing an idea that we've published in the last three or four months, people querying and not familiar with the content of the magazine," she says, laughing. "When I was at *Parents Magazine*, I would get queries on teen driving."

Do your research. Just as you do not want to hire an agent who doesn't bother to check which genres a publisher accepts before sending out your book into the publishing world, an agent expects the same of you. Look up an agency to see what types of books are represented. (*Guide to Literary Agents* is a good place to start.) Find the bios of the agents within that agency if possible. And then choose one who has represented and sold something similar to your work. This will not only make it more likely to land an agent, it will also make that agent more likely to be someone who will connect in a strong way to what you have written. You need an agent to be passionate about your work; start by finding an agent in the right genre to make that happen.

Make those changes and get back in the saddle

One of worst mistakes a writer can make is to give up too soon. Almost every writer faces rejections—a lot of them—before they find the right match.

"I think it's only happened once for me," says Kristin Nelson," where we had an author get accepted for representation by us on her very first query. It's very rare that it happens that way."

You also need to look at the feedback, if any, that you are receiving from agents, says Doris Booth. "If one says the concept isn't broad-based enough, another says I don't like the characters, then you can say, 'I need to stick to my guns because that's the opinion only one person'. But if you hear the same thing from two or three, then you need to listen to the feedback you're getting."

One of the pitfalls of mass mailing your query besides failing to refine the letter to a specific person is the chance that you will send a query containing the same flaw to a number of agents who will no longer be interested in your new, revised version. You're best bet is to send it out to only a few at a time so that you can continue to revise your query letter based on the feedback you receive.

Says Allison Winn Scotch, " Trust your instincts, but only to a certain point. Too many times a writer thinks what they've written is really, really good. They don't let it sit long enough to look at it objectively. And they don't bounce their ideas off enough and get feedback."

Each writer has his own limit of rejections before deciding a project is not going to find a home, but it is important to first determine why the project is being rejected and whether you have done everything possible to fix those flaws before abandoning a project. Sure the odds are tough, but somebody is getting accepted. With the right steps, it just may be you.

THE BASICS

Publishing Poetry

A Reality Check

by Nancy Breen

As the former editor of *Poet's Market* (an annual directory, like *Writer's Market*, of magazines, journals, presses, contests and more, but geared to poets), I got a lot of questions about the whole process of writing and submitting poetry. Often similar questions were forwarded to me from *Writer's Market*. Regardless of the source, I tried to treat all such queries with respect and genuine concern for passing along what I hoped was valued information.

There were certain questions, though, that I dreaded receiving—because my answer invariably lead to disillusionment and disappointment as I splashed cold reality into the faces of unsuspecting (and uninformed) poets. Read further if you're curious about these questions, and especially if you're an aspiring poet yourself.

Is there any money in poetry?

It really hurts to tell ambitious writers that their efforts will result in little monetary gain. However, that's the brutal truth about poetry: There's no money in it, at least not for the average hard-working (and even widely published) poet.

Most poetry appears in little magazines and literary journals. These markets are unlikely to pay cash for the poetry they print, offering instead a copy or two of the issue in which the poet's work appears (called a *contributor's copy*). Online literary magazines usually don't pay at all, although many poets see the worldwide exposure of Internet publication as a type of compensation. While there are a few larger literary magazines that do pay, they're quite prestigious and receive thousands of submissions per year while choosing a small percentage for publication. That means intense competition and high rates of rejection. The same is true of the few commercial magazines that publish poetry, such as *The New Yorker* and *The Atlantic Monthly*.

In truth, if you had a poem accepted by every paying magazine and journal, you probably still wouldn't make a decent income.

The situation in poetry book publishing is just as financially grim. Few of the "major" publishers put out many volumes of poetry; and those volumes usually are by our best known, established poets, talented up-and-comers, and major prizewinners. (A few celebrity poetry books may be in the mix; but, obviously, you have to become a celebrity *first* for publishers to take interest in your poetry.)

Most poetry publishers are literary presses, often run through universities and colleges; or they're independent smaller presses. In either case, they don't have large sums of money

NANCY BREEN is the former editor of *Poet's Market* (www.poetsmarket.com). Her chapbooks include: *Rites and Observances* (Finishing Line Press) and *How Time Got Away* (Pudding House Publications). She blogs at www.salmagundiexpress.wordpress.com.

to throw around for advances and royalties.

If you're disappointed, and even depressed by the low financial rewards of poetry publishing, ask yourself: When was the last time you bought a literary magazine or book of poetry? Few readers in America spend their dollars on poetry (and too often that includes the poets themselves).

Can you recommend a publisher for my 300-poem book manuscript?

First, reread the preceding section, especially the paragraphs about book publishers.

Next, if you haven't looked at the poetry shelves of your local bookstore lately, do a little market research. How many 300-poem books do you see? If you find one, is it by a single poet or is it an anthology? If the book is the work of one poet, review the biographical note for the poet's age, publishing history, academic background, awards won and hints about his or her standing in the literary community. If you don't have a similar biography as a poet, don't even think about trying to get such a massive collection of poems published.

Also, if you've never published any of your poems in literary magazines, don't start shopping for a book publisher just yet. The established route poets follow is to publish individual poems in magazines and journals (in print and online) before assembling a collection of any length. By publishing in magazines first, you establish some necessary credentials:

- You demonstrate you're familiar with the world of poetry publishing because you've been an active participant—publishers appreciate that.
- You prove that someone else has read and appreciated your work besides you, your friends and your family.
- You establish a track record of having worked successfully with editors.

There are occasional exceptions to the publish-in-magazines-first approach. The aforementioned celebrity poetry books are one example. And every few years there's a publishing phenomenon like Mattie Stepanek, the young boy with muscular dystrophy who sold millions of copies of his poetry books before his death at 14 in 2004. Such situations are unique unto themselves and represent exceptions, rather than the rule.

Keep in mind, too, that most poets progress from publishing in magazines to assembling a chapbook, rather than book manuscript. What is a chapbook? It's a soft cover publication of about 24-32 pages. Although bookstores don't stock chapbooks (even independent stores don't favor chapbooks because there's no spine showing the title—chapbooks are usually folded and saddle-stapled), chapbooks have become a very popular format. Production values range from simple to extravagant (depending on paper and cover stock), they can be produced and sold economically, and they're easy to offer for sale at readings. No, they don't make money for the poet *or* the press; but as I said earlier, money should never be a primary concern if you're serious about poetry.

Can you recommend an agent who can represent my poetry book?

As I said, there's little money in poetry. Agents work on commission, i.e., a percentage of what the poet is paid. Consequently, 15% of nothing doesn't make poetry attractive to agents.

As always, there may be exceptions. A highly successful poet may have an agent, especially if the poet does other writing that *does* benefit from representation. A beginning poet, though—especially a beginning poet with a manuscript of 300 previously unpublished poems—probably is not going to find an agent. In fact, any poet who comes across an agent who does express interest should be wary. Ask questions, do your homework, don't sign anything until you've thoroughly researched the agent. And *never* pay for representation.

How can I get my self-published book of poetry into bookstores?

Whether your book is truly self-published or printed by a vanity publisher or print-on-demand publisher (known as POD, wherein a publisher stores your book digitally and prints out copies as they're purchased), distribution is going to be a challenge. Bookstores usually work with professional distributors to stock their shelves, an avenue that may be closed to poets who self-publish. Similarly, vanity publishers can't get your books into bookstores without a distributor, no matter what they may claim. POD publishers may rely more on their own online bookstores and author Web sites than working with a distributor.

In most bookstores, a limited amount of shelf space is devoted to poetry. Sometimes independent bookstores (i.e., not owned by national chains) are more open to stocking small press and self-published books; this is especially true if the poet is a local author.

Poets shouldn't focus on bookstores as a sole source of sales. Other methods of selling include offering books through a personal Web site; scheduling readings at coffeehouses, bookstores or even your own church or community center (where you can offer your book for sale to the audience); and sending promotional postcards to potential customers with information about how to order by mail. To learn more, and to brainstorm additional ideas for selling and promotion, try your library for books on self-publishing; or enter "selling self-published books'' or similar phrases into a search engine for a range of information and perspectives on the Web.

And about those anthologies . . .

No reality check for poets would be complete without a mention of those poetry operations that sponsor contests and Web sites, the ones that publish huge anthologies of "winning'' poems. If you choose to participate, that's your decision, but be aware of these points:

- *Everyone* who submits a poem to such contests is "chosen" to appear in an anthology, so there's no quality standard.
- Having a poem published in such an anthology is *not* a legitimate publishing credit (that is, serious publishers don't take such publishing credits seriously).
- If your poem(s) appear in such an anthology, or on an associated public Web site, your work is considered "published" and cannot be submitted to any magazine or contest that does not accept previously published work.

Some poets appreciate the sense of community they find at such Web sites. They simply enjoy seeing their work in print and online, and they don't mind spending huge sums for copies of the anthologies (or for the plaques, coffee mugs and other merchandise that may be available). And that's their prerogative, as long as those poets aren't deceiving themselves about what such publication means. If they use their anthology appearances as selling points to prospective editors and publishers, though, they may find that they and their poetry are not going to be taken seriously.

What are your objectives?

Be realistic about what the world of poetry publishing has to offer and what you hope to achieve. If writing good poetry is more important to you than money, recognition and the other trappings of high stakes publication, then you're on the right path. If, on the other hand, you hope to achieve fame and fortune through your poetry, well—you need a reality check.

PERSONAL VIEWS

Freelance Success Stories

compiled and judged by Robert Lee Brewer

There were more than 120 entries in the 3rd Annual *Writer's Market* Freelance Success Stories Contest. This free contest offers cash prizes to three writers who have not only found freelance success, but who also relate their stories in an enlightening and entertaining way. This year's winners are **Beth Blair**, **Tom Bentley** and **Kristin Bender**.

While these three writers won top honors, the decision was not easy, because the *Writer's Market* readership is filled with successful and great writers. I applaud the efforts of every writer who dares to dream of getting published, but I'm even more impressed with the writers who are bold enough and persistent enough (despite multiple rejections) to make success happen, as opposed to waiting for success to somehow find them. All three of these winners found success by taking chances and delivering quality work on their assignments—and then they took the chance of submitting their success stories, knowing their stories would be competing with other very successful freelancers.

As mentioned in the previous edition of *Writer's Market*, these stories are not presented as the one and only way to get published, or even as the three only ways to get published and find success. These stories are intended to serve as proof that regular people do find success in writing; to inspire new ideas for using unique avenues and opportunities to find success; and to motivate you to create or add your own success stories as a freelance writer.

I hope to read your success story for the 2011 edition of *Writer's Market*. In the meantime, please enjoy the winners of the 2010 contest.

FLYING HIGH FOR FREELANCE SUCCESS

by Beth Blair

Only feet away from me waves are rolling off a turquoise ocean onto a beach so white I can't tell where the waves end and the sand begins. The horizon is dotted with blue and yellow sailboats. On the table next to me sits a maraschino-topped piña colada. How I managed to land here in Providenciales, Turks and Caicos on travel-writing assignment didn't happen overnight. In fact, it began years ago with a vision, passion and plenty of perseverance.

Year after year, for three or four days a week, I boarded a Boeing 737. I was certainly a frequent flier, but not as a passenger. I was the one wearing wings on my chest and a smile on my face as I passed out honey-roasted peanuts and iced beverages. I loved my job. My days were spent meeting interesting people, bonding with cohorts and exploring new destinations.

Every month I anxiously awaited the release of the new monthly inflight magazine. I

ROBERT LEE BREWER is the editor of Writer's Market and Poet's Market. He's a published poet and maintains the Poetic Asides blog at http://blog.writersdigest.com/poeticasides.

took pleasure in flipping through the pages, reading city highlights, restaurant reviews and celebrity profiles. But between you and me, with every issue I envisioned my name on the masthead's contributor list.

I had been dabbling in writing for some time, relaying stories of my childhood or experiences on the plane such as the man who wanted to know what type of bird we had just passed (as we were cruising at 36,000 feet) or the time my fellow flight attendants convinced 137 passengers I was a convict out on parole and that the airline was kindly helping me get back on my feet.

However, "getting published" didn't seem accessible. At the time I thought it was something only "real" writers did. It ends up, if you want something bad enough, anything is possible.

Getting real

I began to read up on freelance writing only to discover I was facing a dilemma. I didn't have any published clips to send to editors with my story ideas. A sleuth by nature, I decided to do a little research and discovered there was at least one way around the clip quandary—send in a completed manuscript. I began searching for appropriate markets that accepted prewritten submissions. After finding several, I went into my computer's saved files and attacked my personal essays with a vengeance. I chopped, diced, flipped, added and deleted words until I felt I had a decent handful of stories. One by one I submitted my narratives, crossing my fingers each time. I certainly had my share of rejections—and I do mean my share and probably a few other writers' worth. Yet, my determination was fierce, forcing me to keep trudging along.

Before I knew it, my handful of hopefuls turned into a handful of clips from publications such as *Chicken Soup for the Bride's Soul* and the *Christian Science Monitor*. I was enjoying getting paid for my writing but I wanted more—I wanted to write articles. Then, it hit me. I could use my flight attendant expertise as part of my query.

I started sending story ideas based on my professional experience—and it worked! In time I had articles published about flying pregnant, flying with children, airports, security, and, well, the list goes on.

Then, a new era began…the person flying pregnant was me. Flying the friendly skies was already quite a challenge since I had a two-hour commute, one-way, at the beginning of each three- or four-day jaunt. My husband and I made a difficult decision: it was time to leave the airline. As sad as it was, I knew this was an opportunity to pursue my dream as a full-time freelance writer while being there for my infant son.

Taking the plunge

Over time I landed a monthly gig writing a monthly newsletter for USATourist.com, a USA travel web site translated into five languages. I was also continuing to grow my writing experience contributing to various publications while gathering a broad collection of clips.

Before long, I had my second child. As my son and daughter grew and with the encouragement of my incredibly supportive husband I was able to get away every so often to attend a press trip or participate in travel writer conferences—something that allowed me to keep my identity as a mother.

Today my published clip collection reminds me of a colorful dessert tray. My print clips cover my favorite topics: weddings, food, spirits, travel, spas and lifestyle while nearly all of my online articles are travel-related. I even started a popular travel blog, TravelingMamas.com, with three of my friends who are also professional travel writers. I've even been flattered by editors tracking me down via my web site to write exciting articles for them while PR people have invited me to explore destinations they represent—indeed, I'm officially living the dream of a travel writer.

Speaking of dreams, I did "return to the skies" via a 1,400-word feature in an inflight magazine. (Yes, that was one fabulous triumph.)

Now, if you'll excuse me. I have an article to outline and a piña colada to review.

CRIME PAYS (but you have to wait 25 years)

by Tom Bentley

When I was in high school, I had no money to buy the records I craved. I fretted about this, but I didn't want to get a job. I realized that some of the local drug and department stores carried most of the records that the music stores did, but that their recordings were tucked away in high aisles cluttered with other goods, far away from registers and the eyes of employees. In a big local drugstore, I bought a record, which was bagged, and then I returned to the record area and put 10 more records in. Terrified, I walked out of the store. Nobody followed.

I was stupid and lucky, but I realized if I were brazen enough, I could do it again. Which I did. And again and again. I systematized my work: Making cheap purchases, I collected bags and legitimate receipts from all the major area stores. I even got a tiny stapler that I carried, to use in those stores that stapled purchases in the shut bag, with the receipt exposed. I'd select my evening store (and bag) and return for plunder. I branched out into clothing, small cassette players and other electronics. I sewed a very broad, very deep pocket into a coat I wore so that I could easily slip things in it. In a mirror, I practiced how to clamp things under my arm under the coat so they couldn't be seen.

I moved on to more overt acts. I carried new briefcases out of stores by their handles, walked out of stores with unrolled sleeping bags, dribbled a new basketball out of a store—I acted as though these were my goods, and that my acts were invisible, which they were. I began selling the goods at school and taking orders. I became a very accomplished shoplifter; I stole things from counters while I talked to the cashiers, just for the thrill.

I continued doing this for a couple of years after high school, until I was caught by a plain-clothes officer in a large grocery store—from which I'd been stealing liquor for a year—with a half-pint of stolen whiskey. Since I was now over 18, I stayed 3 days in jail, because the combined value of four cars (three of my roommates, and one of mine) was determined by the judge to be less than the $500 required for bail. High living it wasn't.

Despite the fact that my first experience running a business was a successful one, I realized that my business principles were compromised. From that point on, I paid for my whiskey (and all those other life incidentals).

Turning things around

Segue about 25 years into the future. Man (that being me) in a fiction-writing class stares numbly at blank page. The assignment was something like, "Take an abstract emotional concept, such as hate, love, pain, guilt, whatever, and construct a lead character who is the deepest embodiment of that abstraction, but bring that character to life."

That gave me all the motivational push of cooked cabbage, but after stewing a bit, a tangential theme bubbled up: present a character who is temperamentally (and declaredly) devoid of the ability to experience a certain emotion. That character: me. Or a certain exaggerated flavor of me, that being the fellow who in his heady shoplifting days would blithely toss off statements like, "I'm not stealing. I'm liberating these goods. All of these stores are just capitalist dogs preying on people."

A more mush-mouthed version of Soggy-Headed Robin Hood probably couldn't be found, but the thought of those silly spoutings put me in mind of a character who thought that if he didn't consciously admit his feelings—in this case, guilt—those feelings didn't exist.

I set to work. I made my protagonist, Douglas, an aloof, hyper-intellectualized, Nietzsche-spewing Catholic high school student, who was an expert shoplifter. He sets up a series of shoplifting "experiments" (escalating in their bravado), which he calmly executes, and then he returns to his home with the goods, where he calculates the value of his thieving and the dearth of his emotional response.

The chink in his armor came in the form of a naïve (and fetching) young classmate who is intrigued by Douglas's odd manner, and who begins a casual flirtation. Douglas decides to incorporate her into his experiment, theorizing that he needed a vulnerable human element to show his true transcendence over guilt. The story had a lot of symbols and a motif critical to its sad end.

When I'd finished the story, I thought it was good enough for presentation in class, though I worried that I'd created a lead character with such exaggerated skills and morbid self-fascination (and, oh dear, based on me) that he would be a kind of straw man, dead on the page. However, it went over fairly well with my classmates, with some caveats.

What next?

I left the story alone for more than a year, until I read about a short story contest at the National Steinbeck Center in Salinas, only a half-hour from my home. I debated whether it was worth paying the application fee to send the story in, because I was flat certain it didn't have a chance of winning, particularly because the judge was John Steinbeck's son, Thomas, also a writer. Though I recognized that they weren't asking that the stories be written in the tang of Steinbeck, those dark voices in my writer's head told me that my themes were too far off base to win.

My shock was tangible when I got the call that I'd won the first-place prize: $1,000 and a luncheon at the Steinbeck Center, with an award presentation from Thomas Steinbeck. I was still in a haze a week later when I went on stage to accept a beautifully engraved glass plaque, a certificate, the check and a warm handshake from Leon Panetta, Bill Clinton's former Chief of Staff and a local resident who had been a last-minute substitute for the ailing Thomas Steinbeck. That was almost 10 years ago, and I still look at that plaque with a flush of pride and happiness.

The prize was a confirmation that I do have the stuff to craft a story, and also an admonition to press forward with my writing, despite all of the night sweats that writers have over the merit of their work. (Not that, of course, pressing forward means those night sweats will go away—just that they can be showered off before you hit the keyboard again.)

In that time since, I've won or been in the top three in a few other short story contests, as well as some nonfiction contests. I was able to finish a novel (yet unpublished) and am slogging, albeit s-l-o-w-l-y, through another. And I don't flinch on the occasions when I'm asked my occupation: my answer is "writer."

It beats shoplifting for a living.

STALKING THE STARS

by Kristin Bender

The road that led me to cover Christina Aguilera's wedding, spy on Brad Pitt and Angelina Jolie in New Orleans, track Jennifer Aniston in Chicago and follow Tom Cruise and Katie Holmes to Rome, Italy was not one I ever expected to travel. After all, I am A Professional Journalist.

I have for 15 years now earned a pretty good living writing for newspapers, magazines and the occasional Web site, but I've always loved the tabloids and gossip mags. I remember flipping through them as a kid, awestruck by stories about two-headed babies, the Loch Ness monster and UFOs that always seem to land in the Midwest.

My love affair endured even after I became a "proper" journalist. I admired tabloids like the *National Enquirer* for scooping the big-shot papers on stories like the O.J. Simpson murder trial and Monica Lewinsky scandal. How did they do it, I wondered?

I would soon find out.

The assignment

The call to join the tabloid-entertainment press came as I was inching through traffic on my way to work in Oakland, where I've been a reporter at the *Oakland Tribune* for the past nine years. A friend who knows an editor at *Life & Style* weekly wanted to know if I was up for a weekend in Napa, ferreting out details on Aguilara's wedding to Jordan Bateman.

"Sure," I replied, concealing the fact I didn't know Jordan Bateman from Justine Bateman. I knew Aguilara was one of those blonde bombshells, but which one exactly?

I should say that I have, over the years, covered visits by dignitaries, ranging from Prince Charles to Bill Clinton. I've ventured into San Francisco Bay Area neighborhoods even the cops are wary of. I've watched surgeons cut into hearts and brains, interviewed UC Berkeley Nobel Laureates and even ridden a bull that was hell-bent on throwing me across the arena.

What I had never done was stalk a movie star or write for a celebrity magazine. Part of me thought the celebrities were too far above me and the magazines that featured them were too far beneath me. But I wanted to give it a shot. Maybe the Loch Ness monster and UFOs do exist. Besides—I was being paid to go to Napa for the weekend.

But first, I had to do some homework.

Learning curve

A few hours of Googling gave me everything I needed to know—and quite a bit I didn't want to know—about Aguilara and her betrothed. I researched the poshest restaurants, hippest nightclubs and swankiest hotels, figuring that's where they'd be. Then I hit paydirt, learning that the happy couple would be staying at the Auberge Du Soleil Inn, where a cottage sets you back $3,500 a night. That would be my first stop.

I was not at all prepared for what I saw. There were reporters and photographers everywhere. Photographers in camouflage, ducking behind bushes, reporters chasing anyone and everyone who might have the smallest shred of information, no matter how inconsequential.

I soon learned that reporting for a celebrity gossip magazine is not like reporting for a newspaper. Oh sure, you have to get people to talk, and most people want to talk. They just don't want to be named. Anonymity isn't the cornerstone of celebrity reporting, it's the entire foundation. People have to know they won't be identified telling you the juicy details or they're not going to tell you the juicy details.

It helps to be friendly but assertive, sincere but not ingratiating. If you can get someone to provide even the slightest details—What kind of champagne did she have delivered to the room? What was he wearing when they left? They did what?—you'll have a good start to the story.

Getting the inside scoop

It's always best to start with a bartender or bell boy, someone like that. They see everything and they're the ones who can, say, get you into the room where Brangelina stayed during a trip to New Orleans.

Ply them for info and you're bound to get something no one else has. I lucked out during the Aguilera wedding when I ran into a couple of restaurant employees—I'd say who, but I promised them I wouldn't—who told me where the couple had eaten dinner the night before. Then I raced off to the Staglin Family Vineyard, where I joined a herd of journalists in waiting 12 hours for Aguilera and Bateman to arrive.

I soon discovered another way that tabloid reporting differs from newspaper reporting. Once you're on a story, you can't leave for anything, with the possible exception of using a bathroom. Duck out for even a minute and that'll be the exact moment your quarry appears. I was glad I had a big bottle of water and a peanut butter sandwich with me.

If following celebrities is a lot like being in the Boy Scouts (be prepared) it's also a lot like being in the Army (hurry up and wait). I once spent hours staking out a Chicago restaurant, hoping for a glimpse of Jennifer Aniston, and finally spotted her in the back room of an Italian eatery playing a drinking game with friends. Score!

It also helps to be resourceful. For example, while standing on a dirt road outside the Napa winery for the Aguilera wedding, I spotted a work crew driving to the wedding site with tables and chairs in their van. I jotted down the name and number on the side of the van and made a call. That call got me to someone else who told me about the winter wonderland theme inside the wedding spot.

Getting lucky

Of course, sometimes you're just lucky. Such was the case for me in Rome when I was sniffing out details about TomKat's wedding. I happened to see the car carrying Tom Cruise hit another car in a dark cobblestone alleyway in the shadow of the hotel where TomKat were staying. I had the story posted online before any of the four zillion other journalists in town that day even knew there'd been an accident.

When I started celebrity reporting more than three years ago, I thought tabloids weren't quite on the same level as "serious" media outlets like newspapers, but now I realize they are and the work is actually harder because you have to fight for every little detail. It's made me a better reporter on all fronts.

I observe more now in my everyday reporting. I listen better and take note of small details I may have ignored before. It's taught me the importance of staying in constant contact with my editors but not being overbearing, calling or e-mailing just to "show" that I am working on a story.

More than three years after that first call came in to cover the Aguilera wedding, I still get an adrenaline rush when I see an e-mail for an assignment from the editor at *Life & Style*. I thought I had something to teach the tabloid-entertainment press but it was they who taught me the most. And oh how the lessons have been fun.

PERSONAL VIEWS

Nonfiction Authors Roundtable

by I.J. Schecter

The list of memorable characters created by fiction authors is long and varied—but in the end, nothing captivates us more than real stories experienced by real people. To render these experiences as compelling literature requires a subtle blend of inspired storytelling and hard-nosed journalism. Here, three expert practitioners of the craft talk about how they approach their work, what they love most about publishing, and how they found nonfiction—or how it found them.

Andrew J. Bacevich is professor of history and international relations at Boston University. A graduate of the US Military Academy, he received his Ph.D. in American diplomatic history from Princeton. He is the author of *The New American Militarism: How Americans Are Seduced by War* and *The Limits of Power: The End of American Exceptionalism*.

Kaylene Johnson is a professional writer and long-time Alaskan who makes her home on a small farm outside Wasilla, Alaska. Her books include *Sarah: How a Hockey Mom Turned the Political Establishment Upside Down*, *Portrait of the Alaska Railroad*, *Trails Across Time: History of an Alaska Mountain Corridor*, and *A Tender Distance*, a memoir of raising sons in Alaska.

Alice Schroeder, a Connecticut transplant from Texas, was an insurance industry analyst and managing director at Morgan Stanley when she met Warren Buffett while doing research on Berkshire Hathaway. The Oracle of Omaha was so impressed with her that he offered her access to his files and to himself. This friendship led to *The Snowball*, described by *Forbes* as "a thoughtful and intimate biography of the globe's wisest investor."

When did you first feel the writing bug? What did you do to feed it, and in what ways did it evolve?

Andrew Bacevich: In high school. Typically, my first efforts were at poetry, for which I showed negligible talent. As a young man, I became enamored with the great American novelists of the '20s and '30s—James T. Farrell was a particular favorite—but I never really tried my hand at fiction. By my mid-twenties, I was dabbling in nonfiction. Only when I got out of the army in my mid-forties did I begin a serious effort to become a writer.

Kaylene Johnson: I've enjoyed writing for as long as I can remember. I loved the way reading transported me to faraway places and how I could feel the longings and laughter of the characters I read about. As a young girl, I loved books and used paper and crayons to make my own picture books. Later, I grew interested in journalism. I worked at a daily newspaper right out of high school and eventually earned an MFA in Writing at Spalding University in Louisville.

I.J. SCHECTER (www.ijschecter.com) is an award-winning writer, interviewer and essayist based in Toronto. His bestselling collection, Slices: Observations from the Wrong Side of the Fairway (John Wiley & Sons), is available in bookstores and online.

Alice Schroeder: I wrote a poem when I was six years old. My father's secretary stole it from his desk and got it published in the newspaper. After that I read obsessively for decades. But I got sidetracked into business and discovered my writing vocation later in life. My analytic skills finally clubbed me over the head with the news that, for 20 years, I had reinvented all my jobs—as a CPA, a regulator, and a Wall Street analyst—as some sort of writing job. By the time I went on leave to write *The Snowball*, writing and editing my Wall Street newsletter had become more important to me than picking stocks.

Once you discovered you wanted to write, did you find that the way you read books changed? Did it go from pleasure to study? Do you read books the same way today as you did when starting out?

Schroeder: Nothing will ever be the same again. Once you understand how writing is created you can't help but bow to writers of every kind and at every level. At the same time, you become a critic. I examine each book like an engineer going over blueprints. I pore over nonfiction, judging the quality of its sourcing, research and argument—delighting in the good and shedding a silent tear at the awful. I read more fiction now; well-written fiction is easier to find and I appreciate the nuances of the art form more than ever—although plot surprises are far rarer. Lastly, I have less patience with those who write for the intelligentsia. I prefer the craftsmanship of a simple piece of writing.

Johnson: I really learned to read as a writer when I attended my undergraduate studies at Vermont College. I had a wonderful mentor who taught his students how to read closely—to analyze and synthesize and absorb language in a way that would inform us as writers. I carried that skill with me to Spalding University, where a rich faculty of esteemed authors helped me to further hone the craft.

Bacevich: The longer I write, the more sensitive I become to the style and approach of other writers—and the less patient I become with mediocrity.

Even though you write about real subjects and events, do you still try to impose structure on your story, or do you prefer to see what direction the research will take you? What's the reason for your preference?

Johnson: The first step for me is to do the research and then see what evolves organically as the storyline. What piques my curiosity? What do I want to learn more about? The answers to those questions help structure how I'll write the piece. For example, I was recently asked to write a short article about the services provided by our local extension service. When I discovered that the extension service was going to offer a Chicken University for new chicken owners wondering how to take care of their poultry, I knew I had to write about *that*. The very notion of such a thing made me laugh.

Schroeder: It is like a science experiment. You start with a working hypothesis, but you let the facts take you toward their conclusion. The little nuances you discover in research are so important that they shape the story. My philosophy is never to get so married to your hypothesis that you aren't willing to abandon it for a better one. Deadlines are a curse of nonfiction—ideally you should be willing to tear the whole thing up the day before it is due and start over, if that makes it a truer, better story.

Bacevich: Almost always. I "see" the book or essay before I begin to write. The final product seldom if ever conforms exactly to that initial vision, but it tends to come close. That process of "seeing" gives me the greatest satisfaction—a combination of discovery and insight.

Put on an editor's hat for a moment. What do you want to see in a manuscript?

Schroeder: Number one, I want to see a story that is really worth telling. Number two, take some risks with the structure. A safe, predictable structure can ruin an otherwise good story. Number three—last but certainly not least—this is nonfiction, so let's limit ourselves to the truth, okay?

Johnson: I'd like to see real thought and polish go into a manuscript. I want it to be the author's best effort. I also want to feel something when I read; I want the author to make me forget the moment and actually participate in the story. And please do the homework. Even a small mistake calls the credibility of the entire work into question.

Bacevich: I'm not a good editor except perhaps of my own work, where I try hard to be critical and demanding.

Give me three pieces of advice for aspiring writers.

Bacevich: Know yourself and your own particular strengths. Persist. Write every day.

Johnson: One: Be committed to the craft of writing—read the great writers and learn from them. Two: Don't be afraid to take assignments for work that you may not love but that will get you published. All writing assignments are an opportunity to hone the craft. Like anything else, writing improves with practice. Plus you'll be building a résumé and a reputation as a professional. Three: Don't forget the particular detail that brings a story to life. For example, in Sarah, the red dress and tiara that Sarah Palin's daughter Piper wore to her mother's inauguration as governor was a detail that made the scene more vivid and human. And a bonus one, but hardly the least important: Don't give up. Study the markets and offer to write to those markets. Be persistent and believe in yourself.

Schroeder: First, do some living so you have some interesting experiences to write about and earn the judgment to edit your material. Second, become an expert. The best nonfiction succeeds because the writer knows more than anyone else about that subject and—secondarily—has learned how to impart that knowledge to others. Third, seek out, listen to and beg for criticism. Since so few people will give you honest feedback, if you find anyone who will admit that your work is crap, buy them a bottle of champagne so they will keep saying it.

Personal Views

What's your ideal writing environment? Does it matter whether you write in the same conditions all the time?

Schroeder: I want to be totally alone but if necessary can write anywhere. When I first met him, my husband, who likes to write in peace and quiet, could not believe it when he saw me writing in airport terminals, in the car (while he was driving—usually) and in my office while it was full of chattering people.

Johnson: Mornings are my best time to write and also, for some reason, later in the evening. Because I'm fresh, mornings are productive times. But the evening is a time when my brain relaxes and if I'm not too tired to write, I can be quite creative. I like to write in a quiet office—or a noisy coffee shop, where I'm forced to tune out the noise.

Bacevich: At home, in my study, in blue jeans, sweatshirt and moccasins, with my aging dog keeping me company.

Have you gotten past the beginning author's frequent experience of his writing seeming brilliant to him one day and abysmal the next? If so, what helped you overcome this syndrome?

Bacevich: I think I have. I no longer view anything I write as brilliant. I know what I can do. The challenge is to consistently hit that standard.

Johnson: I think beginning authors need to get past thinking that everything they write has to be a masterpiece. We all write well and we all have days where nothing seems to work. The important thing is to write—get words on the page, whether they're good or not. Remember, no matter how good the writing is, it can usually be improved, but meanwhile you are slowly but surely adding to the body of your work. So, just write and then worry about going back and making improvements. Whether or not we've created great literature will ultimately be for readers to decide.

Schroeder: This is a beginning author's syndrome?

What's the best part of publishing? What's the most challenging part?

Johnson: One of the best parts of publishing is to see the work you've created in the physical form of an article or book. It's also very gratifying when the people I write about say that I was able to clearly reflect their personality and positions on matters they care about. Even better is getting feedback from readers that understand the intention of the work. The most challenging part is just getting there!

Bacevich: The best part is when the evidence of your labors arrives in the mail: the magazine or journal or that first copy of a new book. The most challenging part is dealing with obtuse editors. I've been blessed—most of the editors I've worked with have been terrific.

Schroeder: The best part is the huge staff of knowledgeable, helpful people who really do know how to get a good book published despite the author's belief that if only she could control it all herself, things would go much better. The most challenging part is the huge staff of knowledgeable, helpful people who try to take control of your book. I drove my editors and production people mad. They probably considered sending an armoured car to my house to take the book away from me. Being a control freak, I battled all the way to the printer, vowing the last word would be mine. And it was.

Name a piece of nonfiction you wish you could have written and/or a nonfiction writer you hold in particularly high esteem.

Schroeder: If I could write like Louis Menand, life would be heaven. Or Karen Armstrong, Jared Diamond. Then there are the most courageous writers like Jarvis Jay Masters and Viktor Frankl. Then John Brooks and J.M. Keynes, deans of the business writers. I also think nonfiction writers should read fiction: Cervantes, Borges, Jane Austen, Cormac McCarthy, Michael Chabon, Jeffrey Eugenides, David Mitchell, Jennifer Egan.

Bacevich: There are so many, I hesitate to provide a list for fearing of leaving some out.

Johnson: E.B. White's powers of observation and ability to craft a sentence will always be an inspiration. I read his work when I need inspiration to elevate my own writing to a higher standard. I enjoy reading memoir. A few titles that stand out are Tobias Wolff's *This Boy's Life*, Frank McCourt's *Angela's Ashes* and Molly Peacock's *Paradise Piece by Piece*.

What's the most unusual research you've done for a story?

Schroeder: Learning all the details of how a slaughterhouse was organized in the 1940s. Would you like to hear about it?

Johnson: Some of my favorite research has been for articles about the Iditarod. This odyssey from Anchorage to Nome is uniquely Alaskan and colorful in so many respects. One of my favorite stories was about Balto, the canine hero of the 1925 diphtheria serum run to Nome. While Balto helped save children in Nome from a diphtheria epidemic, it was children in Cleveland who saved Balto from a subsequent life of squalor.

Bacevich: I suppose it was time spent in Israel doing research for a monograph on Israeli security. There were three of us working as a team. We'd spend the entire day doing interviews and then in the evening return to our beachfront hotel in Tel Aviv. We'd change into swim gear and then head into the sea, where we'd spend an hour or so bobbing in the waves trying to make sense of all we had seen and heard during the day.

How much better are you at handling criticism today than when you started writing?

Schroeder: I love criticism. That probably hasn't changed.

Johnson: It's important to learn and be open to change. I have been part of a writer's group for 17 years and we regularly critique each other's work. The aim of the group is to challenge each other in a spirit of support and respect. All that time in the same group has helped me see the value of good, critical reading.

Bacevich: It always hurts. I remind myself that half the people who criticize don't actually understand what you've written. Their criticism reveals their own ignorance or bias. So you need to blow it off.

What's your favorite moment in the manuscript process?

Schroeder: Getting red-pencilled comments from an editor that I can sink my teeth into.

Johnson: Finding that perfect turn of phrase that encapsulates a feeling or moment or personality.

Bacevich: Two favorites: the Eureka moment of discovery—the insight or inspiration that gets you going; then the moment of completion—when you say: all right, this is done, and it's good.

Three Rapid-Fire Questions

Say I'm about to tackle my first non-fiction project. What advice do you have?

Bacevich: Make sure you choose a topic that you care deeply about. Then ask yourself if others will share that view.

Schroeder: If you spend most of your time addressing your subject and material to make sure the subject is worth writing about, the writing will mostly take care of itself.

Johnson: Think about what you, as a reader, would like to know about the topic and find answers to the questions a reader might ask. Then write it in an engaging way.

What's better, sex or nailing a great sentence?

Schroeder: I think I'll pass on this one...

Johnson: Let me get back to you on that.

Bacevich: As I get older, my appreciation of each increases.

What ingredients make up the ideal writer?

Bacevich: Imagination and doggedness.

Johnson: Curiosity, commitment and continued study of the craft.

Schroeder: You have to wake up in the morning so determined to get the damn book done that you think of entering the kitchen only when you find a Post-it that says Feed the Dog. You have to want criticism so much that you go looking for anybody who will get out a red pencil, mark up your work and make it better. You have to get yourself dirty by rubbing away the sticky parts where your ego has dripped all over the book and gotten stuck between you and your reader. My husband, a voracious reader and an excellent writer, said to me soon after we met that he didn't really understand the old saying that there's nothing to writing, all you do is sit down and open a vein, until he saw me working. You have to slice yourself up. If you don't know what that means, keep writing until you do.

PERSONAL VIEWS

Katie Crouch

No Longer a Girl in a Truck

by Jude Tulli

There was a time when Katie Crouch had abandoned *Girls in Trucks* (Little, Brown, 2008). "It started out as a bunch of short stories and then turned into a novel," Crouch says. "I just kept writing about the same character. It just sort of happened that way." Ultimately, it evolved into "A fairly dark coming of age story about a southern girl."

"It was a long process that started probably in 2001 and the book came from my own experiences just darkened and exaggerated. I wrote the middle chapter in the beginning and just *accordioned* it out," she says, coining a phrase. "I've always written, but then I was writing about an ex-boyfriend that I was really upset about. I would wander around Central Park hoping to run into him. The idea [came to me] of this woman kind of stalking her ex-boyfriend and how dark and desperate that was." Of the character that crystallized, Crouch confides, "She's like my Freudian Id."

Readers of the book often wonder how much the writer has in common with her protagonist. "I did go to Cotillion training school," Crouch says. But that's more or less where the similarities end.

About the development of the manuscript, Crouch says, "I was in an MFA program that was very competitive." Some of the feedback she received there caused her to underestimate the collection's worth. "I abandoned it both because of my own lack of confidence and [some brutal critiquing]. . . My workshop almost killed this book, which would have been too bad because then I wouldn't have been a professional writer."

Like many emerging writers, Crouch "wrote half of another novel that I threw away. I was writing articles for magazines and short stories that never went anywhere. In the middle of this I almost abandoned *Girls in Trucks*."

"It was very painful," she recalls. "I always knew I have this character and I feel like people are going to identify with [the novel]" but she worried that it may have been "too dark, or too disjointed."

"It took a lot of wherewithal," Crouch says. "The fantasy is that you'll just get discovered. You want to be just working on your work alone in a dark room." Yet even laws of physics must leave clues to alert people to their presence. "It's not just about writing in a log cabin. You have to promote yourself both before and after getting published, which is not what you think of when you think of being a writer. You think of Thoreau. By the pond.

Self-promotion

Ultimately Crouch took a cue from her then-boyfriend and offered to intern with an agent in the hopes that she might learn more about the business side of publishing. At least that was her official motive.

JUDE TULLI is a freelance writer from the Sonoran Desert, where he lives with his wife Trish, their six cats and two tanks full of fish.

The subtext: "I wanted to know about how to get an agent," Crouch admits without shame. "That's not something you shout out. We have to be subtle about these things." Diaphanous as such an impetus may be, a little finesse never hurts.

Still, she was honest with herself and the agent, Rob McQuilkin of Lippincott Massie McQuilkin when she met him at a party "We clicked right away. I said I wanted to learn about publishing so I could get my book published. My goal was to eventually give him my work to either represent me or help me find a different agent."

On the face of it the idea makes perfect sense. "It's obvious," Crouch explains, "if they know your face and know you they're going to read more carefully than a letter coming over the transom." Yet it's equally important to leave a positive impression. "It's also good to be helpful," she says. "You want to ingratiate yourself in some way. You don't want to just meet them at a cocktail party and then bug them."

From MFA to agent's intern

The odds are against an agency internship transforming into an agent-client relationship. McQuilkin says that while he would certainly not eschew the stars lining up in such a manner again, Crouch was the first and remains the only intern who has become a client at his agency. "To be perfectly honest," he says, "there is generally no connection between interning in the agency and becoming a client. But I can certainly see how a writer might want to gather insights into all the 'sausage-making' by volunteering his or her services for some length of time at a literary agency."

As an intern, Crouch "read manuscripts and wrote reports on them, which is a great thing to do because you get a sense of what's out there, and what works and what doesn't." Her own method of separating sheep from goats was perhaps no less brutal than any other reader's: "As soon as you see a grammar error that's it. It's done. Not ready. So you learn to be discerning with your own writing." In general, though, Crouch estimates, "I would usually read at least the first third before saying no. A lot of times we'd read the whole thing."

Yet McQuilkin viewed Crouch's undergraduate degree from Brown and her Columbia MFA for fiction as cause for slight "worry that she might be a little overqualified as an intern." To make the most of her experience he made sure that she wasn't "drowning in just basic slush. Her time, I thought, would be best spent reading manuscripts that stood a pretty good chance of being interesting."

It's easy to argue that his approach was right, as her initiation path was not without significant effect upon the lives of other writers. Crouch says, "I found [McQuilkin] a couple of books which he was happy about."

McQuilkin names names: "It was Katie who first read *Pretty Little Dirty* by Amanda Boyden, whom I then took on as a client and set up with Jenny Jackson at Vintage. And Katie contributed some superb edits to *Little Beauties*, the first novel by a poet I'd already been representing, Kim Addonizio. That one went to Simon & Schuster."

Crouch speaks from experience when she says, "Agents *want* something they can sell, it's not like they're there to reject you. Send them the very best thing that you can."

From intern to client

McQuilkin recalls, "It was at least a year or two after Katie had moved on, relocating back to San Francisco, that she asked if I would mind reading a piece she'd written on spec for the *New York Times*. It was just a knock-out." From there, McQuilkin decided, "One thing was for sure: I needed to see those 'short stories' she had been so quiet about."

Crouch sent the manuscript she'd been working on for about four years, though she knew it wasn't finished. "I wouldn't have sent the draft that I gave Rob to an agent blind," she says, "I had a little leeway because he knew me."

McQuilkin was impressed: "When I sat down with the manuscript, I finally realized just how brilliant this Katie Crouch really was." He wasted no time signing his former intern as a client. Then the revisions began.

The year of the red pen

"I would send him a manuscript or print it out and give it to him," Crouch recalls. "It would come back like he shot somebody, there was so much red ink on it. It was pretty ruthless."

McQuilkin concurs, "I am an unreconstructed editor, which is the good or bad luck of any writer I work with, however they choose to see it! With Katie, there were some clear gaps to fill in what was a collection of 'linked stories.'" He sees this as par for the course, "There's always a certain amount of polishing to be done, no matter how sharp a self-editor a writer may be (and Katie, I should say, is *very* sharp)." "We probably went through it seven times," Crouch says. "He was a bit of a slave driver." She would joke, "I hate you, can we just send it out?" As the months went by, it occurred to her that "I'm getting old, I'm not a girl in a truck anymore. I'm a middle-aged woman with no book!"

All told, Crouch recounts, "I rewrote each chapter at least nine times, so I suppose I second guessed everything. The parts of the book I feel most sure about I don't even remember writing. That's when my subconscious took over. I wish that happened every day."

Even without an agent's prompting, Crouch says, "I always over edit everything. Often I find that I've deleted entire sections because I find them 'unnecessary'. Then the story makes no sense so I need to put those sections back in again." She cautions, "It's very easy to over edit. Everything sounds much more interesting with less words! It still needs to make sense, though. And it's important to stick with your voice."

Crouch advocates waiting until one *knows* a work is really ready before submitting it, though she admits there is no empirical formula for identifying the optimal draft of a manuscript. With *Girls in Trucks*, "I could have worked on it till I expired. At some point you have to walk away from it. So I didn't know. I relied on [my agent] to know. And then I relied on my editor to know after that. But I really could have meddled with it forever."

Start the bidding

"Katie's submission went out on a Wednesday," McQuilkin remembers, "and the first response—a very positive one—came in two days later. Judy Clain, [an editor at] Little Brown, got in touch the Monday following, speaking with real excitement and determination about how much she loved the book." With so much buzz abuzz, the book went to auction.

"It was an extremely surreal time," Crouch remembers. "November, 2006. I was working full time in advertising, secretly taking calls from editors in the stairwell. I kept going to meetings about computer brochures and thinking, 'Somewhere in New York, editors are talking about buying my book!' To go from being one of three people who believed in my writing (the others being my agent and my mother) to having major houses bidding on my work was a shock. The entire time I was completely certain it would all fall through."

How did she cope? "I took up smoking (not recommended) and I didn't sleep for a week. Five houses bid on it, but it happened very fast." To her lungs' good fortune, "It was all settled within three days."

McQuilkin's version of the story substitutes nerves for joyful excitement. "Five houses participated in that auction—out of, say, seven or eight that expressed serious interest before that—and we went through five rounds of bidding before finally going to 'best bids.' I should mention that in any auction situation—certainly anything conducted at this agency—the author generally reserves the right to take *every* piece of information into account before [deciding]." Bids can be (and often are) supplemented with "any editorial or publishing vision, as well as marketing plans, that might allow the author to make [an informed decision]."

It was Clain and Little Brown who won the day. McQuilkin wasn't too surprised: "You kind of knew that she and her colleagues were not about to let this one go. And they didn't, when the five-round, five-bidder auction arrived a week later, following a day's worth of meet-and-greets at publishers' offices. It was a lot of fun."

A girl with a book

Crouch was relieved to discover that there wasn't much revision requested from auction to publication. "It was so polished. It was tight; there were almost no mistakes in that manuscript. What I gave Little Brown was very similar to what was published."

McQuilkin is delighted with the reception the book has found. "We are lucky to see Katie's book meeting every hardcover expectation, with a beautiful set-up for next spring's trade paperback release," he says.

What's a writer to do when her hard work finally yields some measure of tangible success? "I've been able to stop working the second jobs for a while and just focus on the writing. It's great, but it's created a bunch of new challenges." Chief among these, time management. "My first few months—I was just a disaster. I would write sporadically and then wander around the city shopping and reading. I did a lot of yoga and was always going out too late."

Joining the Grotto, a writer's co-op in San Francisco, has since helped her to remain focused. "So going to work at an office where a bunch of writers are doing the same thing helps." Her advice born of experience? "Set a routine for yourself. I can't even stress how important [a strict routine] is."

While she occasionally braves straight-from-the-reader reviews on the Internet with varying degrees of angst, Crouch is impervious to critic reviews. "I don't care, because I've been beaten up in my grad program so much." She's happy with her work, and that, to her, is the most important thing. She feels, "This is what I have to say. I worked really hard on it, so if people [don't] like it, or even if they do, it is what it is."

Crouch loves hearing from readers via e-mail and she encourages them to visit her website www.katiecrouch.com and to send any questions or comments. "Of course I want to talk to [my readers]!" she says, "It's hard for me to understand [writers who don't want to correspond with readers]. It's like the best part." For her, writing is about "being able to reach other people and make a tiny little difference in their lives."

Now what?

Crouch's second book is slated for release in 2010, also with Little Brown. *Men and Dogs* is "about a family in the south. A father goes on a fishing trip. And the father doesn't come back. It's a bit of a mystery and it's a story about what happens in the absence of the father."

Crouch finds herself more guarded with this manuscript while it's still in its formative stages. "*Girls in Trucks* almost became for a little while like a make your own pizza. I had so much feedback. [With] this book I'm being protective, and not many people have seen it. In fact I think only three people have seen [*Men and Dogs*]. I feel really good about it. But it's such a different process than the first book." As a result, she's looking forward to seeing how people will respond to it.

What have we learned?

Some of the stories that later became *Girls in Trucks* were published as standalones. "One won the South Carolina fiction prize. Another one was published in the *Washington Review* out of NY University." The theory behind this pursuit is sound: "If one is working on a book of short stories, if you have pieces you can publish then that's a really good idea. It gives you a bit more legitimacy when you send those [query] letters out."

Yet success with a novel is not contingent upon antecedent short story credits. That's a blessing for most writers, as Crouch observes, "It was easier for me to publish a novel than it was for me to get a short story published." For writers capable of crafting in either medium but limited in time and/or energy she suggests, "If one is ambivalent—if you're interested in getting published, [choose] a novel."

Has writing a novel changed her? "I don't think I am the same person at the end of writing a book," Crouch reflects. "I hope not. That's the whole point, isn't it? To come to some realization? I can tell you that I most certainly make the same mistakes as I did before writing *Girls in Trucks*, both on the page and in life. So I am not wiser at all. Just older and more prolific."

Yet her experience has renewed her faith that the promised land of publication she has found after years of hard work and dedication may be attainable for all committed writers. "If you really have a story to tell and a voice that's continuing to reverberate in your head, it will see the light of day."

BEYOND THE BASICS

Minding the Details

Writers who've been successful in getting their work published know that publishing requires two different mind-sets. The first is the actual act of writing the manuscript. The second is the business of writing—the marketing and selling of the manuscript. This shift in perspective is necessary if you want to become a successful career writer. You must keep the business side of the industry in mind as you develop your writing.

Each of the following sections and accompanying sidebars discusses a writing business topic that affects anyone selling a manuscript. Our treatment of the business topics that follow is necessarily limited, so look for short blocks of information and resources throughout this section to help you further research the content.

CONTRACTS AND AGREEMENTS

If you've worked as a freelance writer, you know contracts and agreements vary from publisher to publisher. Some magazine editors work only by verbal agreement, as do many agents; others have elaborate documents you must sign in duplicate and return to the editor before you even begin the assignment. It is essential that you consider all of the elements involved in a contract, whether verbal or written, and know what you stand to gain and lose by agreeing to the contract. Maybe you want to repurpose the article and resell it to a market that is different from the first publication to which you sold it. If that's the case, then you need to know what rights to sell.

In contract negotiations, the writer is usually interested in licensing the work for a particular use, but limiting the publisher's ability to make other uses of the work in the future. It's in the publisher's best interest, however, to secure as many rights as possible, both now and later on. Those are the basic positions of both parties. The contract negotiation involves compromising on questions relating to those basic points—and the amount of compensation to be given the writer for his work. If at any time you are unsure about any part of the contract, it is best to consult a lawyer who specializes in media law and contract negotiation.

A contract is rarely a take-it-or-leave-it proposition. If an editor tells you his company will allow no changes to the contract, you will then have to decide how important the assignment is to you. However, most editors are open to negotiations, so you need to learn how to compromise on points that don't matter to you, and stand your ground on those that do matter.

RIGHTS AND THE WRITER

A creative work can be used in many different ways. As the author of the work, you hold all rights to the work in question. When you agree to have your work published, you are granting a publisher the right to use your work in any number of ways. Whether that right is to publish the manuscript for the first time in a publication, or to publish it as many times and in as many different ways as a publisher wishes, is up to you--it all depends on the agreed-upon terms. As a general rule, the more rights you license away, the less control you have over your work and the money you're paid. You should strive to keep as many rights to your work as you can.

Writers and editors sometimes define rights in a number of different ways. Below you will find a classification of terms as they relate to rights.

- **First Serial Rights**—Rights that the writer offers a newspaper or magazine to publish the manuscript for the first time in any periodical. All other rights remain with the writer. Sometimes the qualifier "North American" is added to these rights to specify a geographical limitation to the license. When content is excerpted from a book scheduled to be published, and it appears in a magazine or newspaper prior to book publication, this is also called first serial rights.
- **One-Time Rights**—Nonexclusive rights (rights that can be licensed to more than one market) purchased by a periodical to publish the work once (also known as simultaneous rights). That is, there is nothing to stop the author from selling the work to other publications at the same time.
- **Second Serial (Reprint) Rights**—Nonexclusive rights given to a newspaper or magazine to publish a manuscript after it has already appeared in another newspaper or magazine.
- **All Rights**—This is exactly what it sounds like. "All rights" means an author is selling every right he has to a work. If you license all rights to your work, you forfeit the right to ever use the work again. If you think you may want to use the article again, you should avoid submitting to such markets or refuse payment and withdraw your material.
- **Electronic Rights**—Rights that cover a broad range of electronic media, from online magazines and databases to CD-ROM magazine anthologies and interactive games. The contract should specify if—and which—electronic rights are included. The presumption is unspecified rights remain with the writer.
- **Subsidiary Rights**—Rights, other than book publication rights, that should be covered in a book contract. These may include various serial rights; movie, TV, audiotape, and other electronic rights; translation rights, etc. The book contract should specify who controls the rights (author or publisher) and what percentage of sales from the licensing of these rights goes to the author.
- **Dramatic, TV, and Motion Picture Rights**—Rights for use of material on the stage, on TV, or in the movies. Often a one-year option to buy such rights is offered (generally for 10 percent of the total price). The party interested in the rights then tries to sell the idea to other people—actors, directors, studios, or TV networks. Some properties are optioned numerous times, but most fail to become full productions. In those cases, the writer can sell the rights again and again.

Sometimes editors don't take the time to specify the rights they are buying. If you sense that an editor is interested in getting stories, but doesn't seem to know what his and the writer's responsibilities are, be wary. In such a case, you'll want to explain what rights you're offering (preferably one-time or first serial rights only) and that you expect additional payment for subsequent use of your work. The Copyright Law that went into

Contracts and Contract Negotiations

For More Info

- **The Authors Guild** (www.authorsguild.org), 31 E. 32nd St., 7th Floor, New York NY 10016. (212)563-5904. Fax: (212)564-5363. E-mail: staff@authorsguild.org.
- **National Writers Union** (www.nwu.org), 113 University Place, 6th Floor, New York NY 10003. (212)254-0279. Fax: (212)254-0673. E-mail: nwu@wu.org.

Filing for Copyright

For More Info

To register your work with the U.S. Copyright Office, you need to complete the following steps.

1. **Fill out an application form** (Form TX), which is available by calling (202)707-9100 or downloading from www.copyright.gov/forms.

2. **Send the application form,** a nonreturnable copy of the work in question, and your application fee to:

   The Library of Congress
   U.S. Copyright Office
   Register of Copyrights
   101 Independence Ave. SE
   Washington DC 20559-6000

effect January 1, 1978, states writers are primarily selling one-time rights to their work unless they—and the publisher—agree otherwise in writing. Book rights are covered fully by contract between the writer and the book publisher.

SELLING SUBSIDIARY RIGHTS

The primary right in book publishing is the right to publish the book itself. All other rights (movie rights, audio rights, book club rights, etc.) are considered secondary, or subsidiary, to the right to print publication. In contract negotiations, authors and their agents traditionally try to avoid granting the publisher subsidiary rights they feel comfortable marketing themselves. Publishers, on the other hand, want to obtain as many of the subsidiary rights as they can.

Larger agencies have experience selling subsidiary rights, and many authors represented by such agents prefer to retain those rights and let their agents do the selling. On the other hand, book publishers have subsidiary rights departments whose sole job is to exploit the subsidiary rights the publisher was able to retain during the contract negotiation.

The marketing of electronic rights can be tricky. With the proliferation of electronic and multimedia formats, publishers, agents, and authors are going to great lengths to make sure contracts specify exactly which electronic rights are being conveyed (or retained). Compensation for these rights is a major source of conflict because many book publishers seek control of them, and many magazines routinely include electronic rights in the purchase of all rights, often with no additional payment.

COPYRIGHT

Copyright law exists to protect creators of original works. It is also designed to encourage the production of creative works by ensuring that artists and writers hold the rights by which they can profit from their hard work.

The moment you finish a piece of writing—or in fact, the second you begin to pen the manuscript--the law recognizes only you can decide how the work is used. Copyright protects your writing, recognizes you (its sole creator) as its owner, and grants you all the rights and benefits that accompany ownership. With very few exceptions, anything you write today will enjoy copyright protection for your lifetime, plus 70 years. Copyright protects "original works of authorship" that are fixed in a tangible form of expression. *Copyright law cannot protect titles, ideas, and facts.*

Some writers are under the mistaken impression that a registered copyright with the U.S. Copyright Office (www.copyright.gov) is necessary to protect their work, and that their work is not protected until they "receive" their copyright paperwork from the government.

This is not true. You don't have to register your work with the U.S. Copyright Office for it to be protected. Registration for your work does, however, offer some additional protection (specifically, the possibility of recovering punitive damages in an infringement suit) as well as legal proof of the date of copyright.

Most magazines are registered with the U.S. Copyright Office as single collective entities themselves; that is, the works that make up the magazine are *not* copyrighted individually in the names of the authors. You'll need to register your article yourself if you wish to have the additional protection of copyright (your name, the year of first publication, and the copyright symbol © appended to any published version of your work. You may use the copyright symbol regardless of whether your work has been registered with the U.S. Copyright Office.

One thing you need to pay particular attention to is work-for-hire arrangements. If you sign a work-for-hire agreement, you are agreeing that your writing will be done as a work for hire, and you will not control the copyright of the completed work—the person or organization who hired you will be the copyright owner. These agreements and transfers of exclusive rights must appear in writing to be legal. In fact, it's a good idea to get every publishing agreement you negotiate in writing before the sale.

FINANCES AND TAXES

You will find that as your writing business expands, so will your need to keep track of writing-related expenses and incomes. Keeping a close eye on these details will prove very helpful when it comes time to report your income to the IRS. It will also help you pay as little tax as possible and keep you aware of the state of your freelance writing as a business. This means you need to set up a detailed tracking and organizing system to log all expenses and income. Without such a system, your writing as a business will eventually fold. If you dislike handling finance-related tasks, you can always hire a professional to oversee these duties for you. However, even if you do hire a professional, you still need to keep all original records. The following tips will help you keep track of the finance-related tasks associated with your freelance business.

- Keep accurate records.
- Separate your writing income and expenses from your personal income and expenses.
- Maintain a separate bank account and credit card for business-related expenses.
- Record every transaction (expenses and earnings) related to your writing.
- Begin keeping records when you make your first writing-related purchase.
- Establish a working, detailed system of tracking expenses and income. Include the date; the source of income (or the vendor of your purchase); a description of what was sold or bought; how the payment was rendered (cash, check, credit card); and the amount of the transaction.
- Keep all check stubs and receipts (cash purchases and credit cards).
- Set up a record-keeping system, such as a file folder system, to store all receipts.

Tax Information

Important

- While we cannot offer you tax advice or interpretations, we can suggest several sources for the most current information.
- Check the IRS Web site (www.irs.gov).
- Call your local IRS office.
- Obtain basic IRS publications by phone or by mail; most are available at libraries and some post offices.

BEYOND THE BASICS

Launching Your Freelance Business

by I.J. Schecter

Starting something from scratch takes guts, faith and a healthy dose of stubborn optimism. Some would argue that deciding to launch a freelance writing practice requires a touch of masochism, too. But let's look at this rationally. First, you aren't starting from scratch; you're starting with talent, knowledge, skill, connections, and, probably, the moral support of a good number of people. Second, starting a writing business is no more or less difficult than starting any other type of business, whether a bakery, real estate brokerage or piano-tuning service. Third, you're peddling an extremely valuable product. Most businesses figure out pretty fast that if they don't know how to communicate, they're going to have a hard time winning customers. And in today's world of short attention spans and stimulus overload, the ability to communicate succinctly and powerfully is more valuable than ever.

PRE-WORK

Before putting your name out there, there are a few things you need to take care of. At the top of the list is getting business cards and letterhead printed. When you do start to tell people about your practice, the last thing you want is to be stuck without a card to hand over. And after you do offer it, hopefully prompting a discussion about your potential client's needs, you'll want to send a follow-up letter immediately—but on your own stationery, not some generic one. From the moment you decide to freelance professionally, you must think of yourself as a brand. Most writers feel hesitant about marketing themselves in any specific way because they don't want to cut off other opportunities. But when you're starting out, establishing a firm brand perception—that is, a clear statement about what you do and why it's valuable—is more important than appearing able do it all. Demonstrate expertise in a few specific areas, and others will inevitably find their way into your lap.

SELLING YOURSELF

Almost all writers share an aversion to self-selling—but it's mostly a function of unfair conditioning. That is, they assume they hate marketing themselves before they even try because other writers have convinced them one can't be a good writer and a good salesman at the same time.

The truth is plenty of good writers are natural salesmen, too, but they feel the superficial selling part undermines the authentic writing part. Take a moment to think about it and you'll realize all businesspeople have to market themselves just like writers do. A restaurateur needs to do more than just open his doors to generate traffic. An investment broker must go beyond merely getting a license if he hopes to succeed. A psychologist wanting to build

I.J. SCHECTER (www.ijschecter.com) is an award-winning writer, interviewer and essayist based in Toronto. His bestselling collection, Slices: Observations from the Wrong Side of the Fairway (John Wiley & Sons), is available in bookstores and online.

a practice ought to take a few steps in addition to simply hanging a shingle. And a writer needs to do more than just write. "This job is about sales as much as it is about writing," says Toronto-based freelancer Ian Harvey. "One of the simple rules guiding my practice is this: Hustle, hustle, hustle."

So how does a writer generate buzz? There are several ways: letters, flyers, brochures, newsletters, blogs, samples, cold calls, and so on. When I launched my practice, the first thing I did (after getting business cards and letterhead printed, of course) was to send out hundreds of introductory letters--to those I knew, to those I didn't know, to people, to businesses . . . to just about everyone whose address I could get. I discriminated little in this initial blitz, though naturally with each letter I dropped into the mailbox I became even more nervous that all the money, time and effort I was expending might lead nowhere.

Then I received a phone call. One of my letters had gone to a high school acquaintance working at a company that manufactured and distributed musical compilations on CD. She had received my letter just as her boss was looking for a writer to help write snappy liner notes. Years later, this company remains one of my biggest corporate clients.

Another of my letters went to an old colleague. He had become the head of an executive degree program at a local university and was preparing to design the program brochure, for which a writer was sorely needed. I won the assignment, which led to another three.

The lesson? You truly never know where work is going to come from. More important, you can't count on finding yourself in the right place at the right time; you have to create the possibility of being there.

GROWING PAINS

There are two parts to selling yourself. First is developing the nerve to do it. Second is developing the right type of skin: rhino. "Rejections are part of the game," says Harvey, "but this is the only game in which rejection doesn't mean no. It means not now, or not for me, or not for me right now. It doesn't mean no forever." While it's fair to spend a little time—very little—getting annoyed or frustrated at rejection, it's best to take that annoyed or frustrated energy and pour it into something productive. Few businesses explode overnight; the ones that end up successful demand lots of grunt work up front, reach a minimum threshold after a few years, and then begin to grow in earnest.

It's imperative you commit to the up-front part. "Most businesses fail because the proprietors underestimate the amount of work required to get the business off the ground and overestimate the revenue in the first year or two," says Paul Lima, a professional writer for over 25 years and author of *The Six-Figure Freelancer*. Adds Vancouver-based freelancer Teresa Murphy, author of more than 1,000 magazine articles, "You need the ability to work 15 hours a day and love it, day in and day out. That means holidays, summer weekends and all-nighters when clients have rush projects. I've worked Boxing Day, New Year's Eve, Easter Sunday until midnight."

Tax Tip

Sure, self-employment doesn't come with medical and dental, but it does offer plenty of opportunities for tax write-offs. Among the expenses you can potentially deduct are car, phone, restaurant meals, postage, magazine purchases, and, if you work from home, a portion of your monthly mortgage (or rent) and utilities. Have a chat with your accountant about this and hold onto your receipts so calculations are easy come tax season. You'll be glad you did.

Answering the Question

Friends familiar with your long-time desire to write may good-naturedly tease you about the risk of giving up your thankless but stable 9-to-5 grind to tackle something so daunting. Former colleagues may wonder aloud about your decision. Busybody aunts will gossip about how no one makes money writing and what a nice doctor or lawyer you would have made.

Change their perception by embracing and celebrating your decision rather than timidly defending it. When people ask, "So what are you doing now?" answer with pride and conviction. Don't say, "I thought I'd give freelancing a go and see how it works out," or "I'm going to try being a freelance writer, though I'm not really sure what that means."

Have your "elevator speech"—a business term for the 30-second spiel that describes what you do—always at the ready. When people ask me what I do, I respond, "I'm a freelance writer and communications consultant." If they want to know more, I tell them my practice is divided evenly between commercial writing, like magazine features, and corporate writing, which entails everything from marketing brochures to ghostwriting business books. Suddenly they're intrigued. They see writing as a real, viable, honest-to-goodness business—not because I've dropped figures but because I've spoken about it in a clear, confident manner.

Let's stop apologizing for being writers. I love being one, and I bet you do, too. Tell anyone who asks.

Of course, if you've decided to take the plunge in the first place, no doubt you've got this much passion and then some, because, like these professionals, you've realized that, despite the challenges of the writing life, nothing in the world makes you feel happier or more fulfilled.

GAINING, AND SUSTAINING, MOMENTUM

Investing the time and energy at the outset will lead to a point of critical mass--that first small group of people interested in your work, the first pebble in your pond. This could include a magazine editor, the president of a company or a friend needing some editing help. To help that first small ripple expand outward, you need to embed two vital behavioral principles.

1. Overdelivery. Whether you're writing an article for your local newspaper, a marketing brochure for a multinational conglomerate or an essay for your best friend's medical school application, do the very best job you can. Your writing is judged every time you put pen to paper or fingers to keys. Force yourself to knock the ball out of the park at every opportunity and you'll develop the kind of reputation that leads to positive word of mouth, constant repeat business and sparkling testimonials.

2. Professionalism. From editors to executives, just about everyone is stretched thin these days—and that's why being known as someone easy to work with can distinguish you from other writers who also deliver solid work. Acting like a professional means a number of things. Dressing a certain way. Acting a certain way. Hitting deadlines. Returning calls and e-mails promptly.

It also means not ever being petty, spiteful or antagonistic. Following the publication of my first short story collection, I lucked into a chance to set up a small table at a prominent outdoor literary festival. Beside me was the editor of an esteemed literary journal--along with her large dog, in a cage a few feet behind us. The dog began barking his head off just as people starting checking out the book tables, and he didn't stop for an hour, scaring off just about anyone who wandered anywhere near me and my book. The woman did nothing. I didn't just want to offer her a few choice words; I wanted to write her a scathing letter several pages long. Friends and family urged me to resist, and, though it was hard, I did. A few years later, when I sent this editor a story for consideration in her journal, she accepted it (though she had no recollection of me from the festival), creating a writing credit that remains one of my most important. The moral? In this business just like any other, people, and circumstances, will irk you--but in almost every case it behooves you to take the high road. Reacting emotionally can only harm you; staying cool can only benefit you.

THE NUMBERS GAME

Writing is dynamic and fluid; it can be endlessly revised, massaged, tweaked, twisted and reversed back over itself. For this reason, it's essential that you get every one of your assignments in writing (no pun intended; OK, slightly intended). Commercial assignments will usually come with a contract; corporate assignments almost never will. To address this, prepare two versions of your own standard agreement. For commercial gigs, this document should include a brief description of the assignment, word count, pay rate, and deadline, along with all the other legal bits you can find by looking up any typical freelance contract.

For corporate assignments, it should include a more detailed description of the project (including each piece of work if there are multiple parts), the agreed timeline, the fee (either an overall flat rate or an hourly rate), and, crucially, a definition of completion. For example, in my standard corporate agreement, I have a clause indicating that, for the agreed-upon fee, I will deliver the described work by the noted deadline and then allow two rounds of requested revisions or suggestions from the client, after which I will start charging extra. This creates clear mutual expectations between the client and me and helps avoid awkward conversations toward the end of the project when the senior partner tries to add an arbitrary comma for the third time.

For corporate work, you'll also have to develop the skill of estimating. It's one thing to name an hourly rate when a potential client first asks; it's another to try to come up with a total number of hours based on his incredibly vague description of the assignment. But come up with one you must--only to be met with, in some cases, a response gently questioning why the work ought to take so long. Here we have a quandary: By and large, people vastly underestimate how long good writing actually takes. I've found the best way to deal with this is to be truthful. I tell my clients up front that writing and communications work tends to take quite a bit longer than non-writers imagine, and that, in fact, most projects end up taking 20 percent more hours than I initially estimate because the client themselves didn't realize going in how much would be involved. As long as I deliver good work, this ceases to be an issue.

How much or how little should you charge for your work? It depends--based on your experience, where you live, and a host of other factors. (See page 57 for a range of rates for different types of writing projects.) Make sure, before you enter any negotiation, that you've decided upon the lowest figure you're willing to accept. Or, as freelancer Colette van Haaren puts it, "You need three things in this business: a good nose to sniff out stories, a thick skin for when rejection hits, and a backbone for when you have to negotiate."

SURE I'M WORKING HARD. IN MY HEAD

Only about half my time is spent actually working on assignments. The other half is spent crafting queries, doing research, maintaining correspondence, or, to be honest, just brainstorming. My favorite part of being a writer is that I can work anywhere, since so much of the work is done between my ears. Often someone will ask me a question, and, when I don't answer, my wife will murmur to him or her, "Oh, he's just working." And she's right.

I also believe, however, that the luxury of being able to do mental work represents an important responsibility. During spells when my plate isn't full with deadlines, I don't rest on my laurels. Instead, I record ideas, I query like crazy, I read other writers, I think about

Where Is Your Stapler?

Many writers and other artists claim that their extreme lack of organization is simply an occupational hazard. Others practically boast about it, claiming it as a distinct imprint of creativity. Whether or not creative types are naturally disinclined toward self-organization, the sooner you decide to get organized and stay organized, the more successful you and your practice will become. Why? Two reasons, one physical, the other mental.

Physically speaking, when your work environment is organized, you spend more time writing and less time trying to locate the calculator or paper clips or this file or that folder. Simple odds dictate that using your time more productively will lead to more work.

The mental aspect is just as important. We all know how aggravating it is having to scramble to find that copy of the current contract for that magazine when we've forgotten what the word count was, or trying desperately to remember where we put the CD with the backup copy of that article after the electrical storm has wiped out our operating system with the deadline looming.

It stands to reason that the less energy you need to put into non-writing activities, the more energy you can direct toward your actual work, improving its overall quality and thereby making you a more desirable commodity. Sure, a little anxiety can be healthy for writing, but it should be anxiety borne of the drive to produce stellar work, not anxiety based on wondering where the stamps got to for the umpteenth time.

Organizing yourself is probably a lot easier than you imagine, and you might even be surprised at how good a little structure makes you feel.

Start small: Buy a box of multicolored file folders, some labels, some CDs or a memory stick, and several upright magazine files. Label one of the magazine files **Contracts**, then place in it different file folders labeled with the subject area for a given contract. For me, these folders include, among others, Bridal, Fitness, Golf, Men's, Gardening, and, of course, Writing and Publishing.

Label another of the magazine files **Current Assignments** and a third **Story Ideas**, and populate them as you did the first. Use consistent colors for specific topics—in other words, gardening always gets a yellow file folder whether it's in the **Story Ideas** or the **Contracts** file. This will make for easy cross-referencing.

And that's just a start. Odds are this small bit of organization will spur you, and soon you'll be creating files for every aspect of your work—character sketches, source notes, dialogue snippets, conferences and retreats, news items.

"Organization is everything," says freelancer Heather Cook, author of *Rookie Reiner: Surviving and Thriving in the Show Pen* (Trafalgar Square Books). "From maintaining accurate records for tax purposes to structuring a weekly plan to include marketing and administrative tasks, it allows me to stay focused and efficient--and that makes my overall work better."

new marketing angles. In short, given the nature of my profession, I have no excuse for down time. "If you don't care about your business, no one else will," says freelancer Sharon Aschaiek. "Use slow times to indirectly generate more work—develop new pitches, follow up with previous editors and clients, explore new marketing avenues. Even use the time to take care of accounting and administrative issues. Just don't let yourself get complacent."

THE BOTTOM LINE

Is freelancing hard work? Sure—damned hard. But it's no harder than any other profession. Like every job, it requires a combination of skill, thoroughness and dependability. The difference is you don't have anyone defining the parameters of the job for you or providing incentives to succeed. The discipline and drive have to come solely from you. Or, in the words of full-time freelancer and book author Lisa Bendall, "All the talent in the world won't help if you aren't willing to put in the time at your desk and actually work. You've got to crack your own whip."

Now get cracking!

BEYOND THE BASICS

How Much Should I Charge?

by Lynn Wasnak

If you're a beginning freelance writer, or don't know many other freelancers, you may wonder how anyone manages to earn enough to eat and pay the rent by writing or performing a mix of writing-related tasks. Yet, smart full-time freelance writers and editors annually gross $35,000 and up—sometimes up into the $150,000-200,000 range. These top-earning freelancers rarely have names known to the general public. (Celebrity writers earn fees far beyond the rates cited in this survey.) But, year after year, they sustain themselves and their families on a freelance income, while maintaining control of their hours and their lives.

Such freelancers take writing and editing seriously—it's their business. Periodically, they sit down and think about the earning potential of their work, and how they can make freelancing more profitable and fun. They know their numbers: what it costs to run their business; what hourly rate they require; how long a job will take. Unless there's a real bonus (a special clip, or a chance to try something new) these writers turn down work that doesn't meet the mark and replace it with a better-paying project.

If you don't know your numbers, take a few minutes to figure them out. Begin by choosing your target annual income—whether it's $25,000 or $100,000. Add in fixed expenses: social security, taxes, and office supplies. Don't forget health insurance and something for your retirement. Once you've determined your annual gross target, divide it by 1,000 billable hours—about 21 hours per week—to determine your target hourly rate.

Remember—this rate is flexible. You can continue doing low-paying work you love as long as you make up for the loss with more lucrative jobs. But you must monitor your rate of earning if you want to reach your goal. If you slip, remind yourself you're in charge. As a freelancer, you can raise prices, chase better-paying jobs, work extra hours, or adjust your spending."

"Sounds great," you may say. "But how do I come up with 1,000 billable hours each year? I'm lucky to find a writing-related job every month or two, and these pay a pittance."

That's where business attitude comes in: network, track your time, join professional organizations, and study the markets. Learn how to query, then query like mad. Take chances by reaching for the next level. Learn to negotiate for a fee you can live on—your plumber does! Then get it in writing.

You'll be surprised how far you can go, and how much you can earn, if you believe in your skills and act on your belief. The rates that follow are a guide to steer you in the right direction.

This report is based on input from sales finalized in 2007 and 2008 only. The data is generated from voluntary surveys completed by members of numerous professional writers' and editors' organizations and specialty groups. We thank these responding groups, listed below, and their members for generously sharing information. If you would like to contribute your input, e-mail lwasnak@fuse.net for a survey.

LYNN WASNAK (www.lynnwasnak.com) was directed to the market for her first paid piece of deathless prose ("Fossils in Your Driveway" published by Journeys in 1968 for $4) by Writer's Market. In the 40 years since, she's made her living as a freelancer and has never looked back.

Advertising, Copywriting & Public Relations	PER HOUR			PER PROJECT			OTHER		
	HIGH	LOW	AVG	HIGH	LOW	AVG	HIGH	LOW	AVG
Advertising copywriting	$125	$40	$77	n/a	n/a	n/a	$2.50/word	38¢/word	$1.59/word
Advertorials	$150	$50	$97	n/a	n/a	n/a	$2.50/word $1,333/page	88¢/word $200/page	$1.43/word $575/page
Book jacket copywriting	$100	$25	$53	$700	$100	$375	$1/word	50¢/word	72¢/word
Campaign development or product launch	$150	$90	$112	$8,750	$1,500	$4,250	n/a	n/a	n/a
Catalog copywriting	$150	$35	$67	n/a	n/a	n/a	$350/item $1,500/page	$25/item $100/page	$84/item $557/page
Copyediting for advertising	$125	$25	$55	n/a	n/a	n/a	n/a	n/a	n/a
Direct-mail copywriting	$125	$55	$89	n/a	n/a	n/a	$4/word $1,200/page	$1/word $200/page	$1.50/word $400/page
E-mail ad copywriting	$125	$55	$78	n/a	n/a	n/a	n/a	n/a	$2/word
Event promotions/publicity	$125	$55	$90	n/a	n/a	n/a	n/a	n/a	$500/day
Fundraising campaign brochure	$110	$69	$91	n/a	n/a	n/a	n/a	n/a	$1/word
Political campaigns, public relations	$150	$43	$91	n/a	n/a	n/a	n/a	n/a	n/a
Press kits	$125	$45	$79	n/a	n/a	n/a	$2/word	50¢/word	$1.30/word
Press/news release	$100	$40	$58	n/a	n/a	n/a	$750/page $2/word	$200/page 40¢/word	$440/page $1.02/word
Public relations for businesses	$150	$40	$77	n/a	n/a	n/a	$500/day	$200/day	$367/day
Public relations for government	$90	$40	$60	n/a	n/a	n/a	n/a	n/a	n/a
Public relations for organizations or nonprofits	$75	$20	$44	n/a	n/a	n/a	n/a	n/a	n/a
Public relations for schools or libraries	$80	$50	$60	n/a	n/a	n/a	n/a	n/a	n/a
Speech writing/editing (general)[1]	$150	$43	$93	$10,000	$2,700	$5,480	$350/min	$100/min	$205/min

1 Per project figures based on 30-minute speech.

	PER HOUR			PER PROJECT			OTHER		
	HIGH	LOW	AVG	HIGH	LOW	AVG	HIGH	LOW	AVG
Speech writing for government officials	$200	$30	$86	n/a	n/a	n/a	$200/min	$110/min	$142/min
Speech writing for political candidates	$150	$60	$92	n/a	n/a	n/a	$200/min	$110/min	$175/min
Audiovisuals & Electronic Communications									
Book summaries (narrative synopsis) for film producers[1]	n/a	n/a	n/a	n/a	n/a	n/a	$1,269/15 min $34/page	$2,114/30 min $15/page	$4,006/60 min $20/page
Business film scripts[2] (training and info)	$150	$50	$100	n/a	$500	n/a	$500/run min	$50/run min	$229/run min
Copyediting audiovisuals	$90	$35	$56	n/a	n/a	n/a	n/a	n/a	$50/page
Corporate product film	$150	$70	$106	n/a	n/a	n/a	$500/run min	$100/run min	$300/run min
Educational/training film scripts	$125	$45	$78	n/a	n/a	n/a	$500/run min	$100/run min	$300/run min
Movie novelization	$100	$35	$68	$15,000	$3,000	$6,750	n/a	n/a	n/a
Radio commercials/PSAs	$85	$30	$56	n/a	n/a	n/a	$850/run min	$120/run min	$504/run min
Radio editorials & essays (no production)	$70	$50	$60	n/a	n/a	n/a	$200/run min	$45/run min	$109/run min
Radio interviews (3 minute interview)	n/a	n/a	n/a	$1,500	$150	$400	n/a	n/a	n/a
Radio stories (over 2 minutes with sound production)	$1,500	$100	$400	n/a	n/a	n/a	n/a	n/a	n/a
Screenwriting (original screenplay)	n/a	n/a	n/a	$106,070	$56,500	$81,285	n/a	n/a	n/a
Script synopsis for agent or film producer	n/a	n/a	n/a	$75	$60	$65	n/a	n/a	n/a
Script synopsis for business	$70	$45	$58	$100	$60	$75	n/a	n/a	n/a

1 Other figures based on length of speech (min=minute).
2 Run min=run minute.

	PER HOUR			PER PROJECT			OTHER		
	HIGH	LOW	AVG	HIGH	LOW	AVG	HIGH	LOW	AVG
Scripts for nontheatrical films for education, business, industry	$125	$55	$80	$5,000	$3,000	$4,083	$500/run min	$100/run min	$300/run min
TV commercials/PSAs[1]	$85	$60	$73	n/a	n/a	n/a	$2,500/ 30 sec spot	$150/ 30 sec spot	$963/ 30 sec spot
TV news story/feature[2]	$100	$70	$90	n/a	n/a	n/a	n/a	n/a	n/a
TV scripts (nontheatrical)	$150	$35	$89	$20,000	$10,000	$15,000	$1,000/day	$550/day	$800/day
TV scripts (teleplay/MOW)[3]	n/a	n/a	n/a	n/a	n/a	n/a	$500/run min	$100/run min	$300/run min
Book Publishing									
Abstracting and abridging	$125	$30	$56	n/a	n/a	n/a	$2/word	$1/word	$1.50/word
Anthology editing	$80	$25	$43	$7,900	$1,200	$3,874	n/a	n/a	n/a
Book proposal consultation	$125	$25	$68	n/a	n/a	n/a	n/a	n/a	n/a
Book proposal writing	$125	$30	$63	$10,000	$3,000	$7,200	n/a	n/a	n/a
Book query critique	$100	$50	$70	$300	$200	$250	n/a	n/a	n/a
Book query writing	n/a	n/a	n/a	$500	$120	$200	n/a	n/a	n/a
Children's book writing (advance against royalties)	n/a	n/a	n/a	n/a	n/a	n/a	$4,400	$450	$1,890
Children's book writing (work for hire)	$75	$50	$63	n/a	n/a	n/a	$5/word	$1/word	$3/word
Content editing (scholarly)	$100	$30	$53	n/a	n/a	n/a	$20/page	$4/page	$6/page
Content editing (textbook)	$100	$25	$48	n/a	n/a	n/a	$9/page	$3/page	$4/page
Content editing (trade)	$100	$29	$49	n/a	n/a	n/a	$40/page	$3.75/page	$7.50/page
Copyediting	$100	$25	$36	n/a	n/a	n/a	$6/page	$1/page	$4/page
Fiction book writing (own)	n/a	n/a	n/a	n/a	n/a	n/a	$40,000	$525	$14,203

1 30 sec spot=30-second spot

2 $1,201 Writers Guild of America minimum/story.

3 TV scripts 30 minutes or less average $6,535/story, $19,603 with teleplay; TV scripts 60 minutes or less average $11,504/story, $28,833 with teleplay.

	PER HOUR			PER PROJECT			OTHER		
	HIGH	LOW	AVG	HIGH	LOW	AVG	HIGH	LOW	AVG
Ghostwriting, as told to[1]	$100	$50	$73	$51,000	$5,500	$20,375	n/a	n/a	n/a
Ghostwriting, no credit	$100	$30	$43	$45,000	$1,500	$18,850	$3/word	$1/word	$1.63/word
Indexing	$40	$22	$30	n/a	n/a	n/a	$6/page	$2.75/page	$4.25/page
Manuscript evaluation and critique	$100	$23	$57	$1,500	$150	$550	n/a	n/a	n/a
Nonfiction book writing (collaborative)	$100	$50	$76	$56,325	$2,000	$17,290	n/a	n/a	n/a
Nonfiction book writing (own) (advance against royalties)	n/a	n/a	n/a	n/a	n/a	n/a	$50,000	$3,000	$11,777
Novel synopsis (general)	$60	$30	$45	$400	$150	$275	$30/page	$10/page	$20/page
Proofreading	$55	$19	$27	n/a	n/a	n/a	$5/page	$2/page	$3.09/page
Research for writers or book publishers	$100	$20	$53	n/a	n/a	n/a	$600/day	$450/day	$525/day
Rewriting	$100	$30	$58	$50,000	$4,000	$14,500	n/a	n/a	n/a
Translation (fiction)[2]	n/a	n/a	n/a	$10,000	$7,000	$8,500	12¢	6¢	9¢
Translation (nonfiction)	n/a	n/a	n/a	n/a	n/a	n/a	15¢	8¢	10¢
Translation (poetry)	n/a	n/a	n/a	n/a	n/a	n/a	$15/page	$0/page	$7.50/page
Business									
Annual reports	$150	$45	$102	$15,000	$1,000	$5,500	n/a	n/a	n/a
Associations and organizations (writing for)	$125	$35	$69	n/a	n/a	n/a	$400/day	$300/day	$350/day
Brochures, fliers, booklets for business	$200	$50	$106	$15,000	$300	$2,777	$2.50/word $800/page	75¢/word $50/page	$1.56/word $387/page
Business & sales letters	$125	$40	$75	n/a	n/a	n/a	$2/word	$1/word	$1.42/page
Business & government research	$100	$35	$69	n/a	n/a	n/a	n/a	n/a	$600/day

1 Per project figures do not include royalty arrangements, which vary from publisher to publisher.
2 Other figures in cents are per target word.

	PER HOUR			PER PROJECT			OTHER		
	HIGH	LOW	AVG	HIGH	LOW	AVG	HIGH	LOW	AVG
Business editing (general)	$125	$35	$63	n/a	n/a	n/a	n/a	n/a	n/a
Business plan	$125	$35	$87	$15,000	$1,000	$6,000	n/a	n/a	$1/word
Business-writing seminars	$200	$60	$103	$8,600	$550	$2,450	n/a	n/a	n/a
Catalogs for businesses	$80	$50	$65	$10,000	$2,000	$5,000	n/a	n/a	n/a
Consultation on communications	$125	$100	$115	n/a	n/a	n/a	$1,200/day	$500/day	$740/day
Copyediting for businesses	$125	$30	$65	n/a	n/a	n/a	$4/page	$2/page	$3/page
Corporate histories	$180	$35	$87	$35,000	$1,000	$12,500	$2/word	$1/word	$1.50/word
Corporate periodicals, editing	$125	$50	$100	n/a	n/a	n/a	$2.50/word	$1/word	$1.83/word
Corporate periodicals, writing	$125	$35	$83	n/a	n/a	n/a	$3/word	$1/word	$1.75/word
Corporate profile	$125	$40	$85	n/a	n/a	$3,000	$2/word	$1/word	$1.50/word
Ghostwriting for business (usually trade magazine articles for business columns)	$125	$50	$98	$3,000	$750	$1,750	$2.50/word n/a	$1.50/word n/a	$2/word $500/day
Government writing	$100	$35	$69	n/a	n/a	n/a	$1.25/word	50¢/word	94¢/word
Grant proposal writing for nonprofits	$125	$30	$69	n/a	n/a	n/a	n/a	n/a	n/a
Newsletters, desktop publishing/production	$130	$30	$67	n/a	n/a	n/a	$750/page	$150/page	$391/page
Newsletters, editing	$125	$25	$88	n/a	n/a	$3,600	$230/page	$150/page	$185/page
Newsletters, writing[1]	$125	$40	$90	$5,000	$800	$2,000	$5/word	$1/word	$2/word
Translation (commercial for government agencies, technical)	n/a	n/a	n/a	n/a	n/a	n/a	$1.40/ target line	$1/ target line	$1.20/ target line
Computer, Scientific & Technical									
Computer-related manual writing	$125	$43	$95	n/a	n/a	n/a	n/a	n/a	n/a

[1] Per project figures based on four-page newsletters.

	PER HOUR			PER PROJECT			OTHER		
	HIGH	LOW	AVG	HIGH	LOW	AVG	HIGH	LOW	AVG
E-mail copywriting	$125	$65	$88	n/a	n/a	$300	$2/word	30¢/word	$1.12/word
Medical and science editing	$125	$20	$56	n/a	n/a	n/a	$4/page	$3/page	$3.50/page
Medical and science proofreading	$125	$35	$61	n/a	n/a	n/a	n/a	n/a	$3/page
Medical and science writing	$250	$35	$93	$5,000	$1,000	$2,875	$2/word	50¢/word	$1.07/word
Online editing	$100	$25	$38	n/a	n/a	n/a	$4/page	$3/page	$3.50/page
Technical editing	$100	$35	$57	n/a	n/a	n/a	n/a	n/a	n/a
Technical writing	$125	$40	$65	n/a	n/a	n/a	n/a	n/a	n/a
Web page design	$150	$35	$76	$4,000	$500	$2,000	n/a	n/a	n/a
Web page editing	$90	$35	$54	n/a	n/a	n/a	n/a	n/a	n/a
Web page writing	$125	$40	$66	n/a	n/a	n/a	$2.62/word	21¢/word	93¢/word
White Papers	$135	$40	$87	$10,000	$2,500	$4,708	n/a	n/a	n/a
Editorial/Design Packages[1]									
Desktop publishing	$125	$35	$67	$6,600	$800	$2,887	$750/page	$100/page	$375/page
Greeting card ideas	n/a	n/a	n/a	n/a	n/a	n/a	$300/card	$50/card	$150/card
Photo brochures[2]	$75	$65	$70	$15,000	$400	$4,913	n/a	n/a	n/a
Photo research	$70	$35	$39	n/a	n/a	n/a	n/a	n/a	n/a
Photography (corporate-commercial)	n/a	n/a	n/a	n/a	$10,000	n/a	$2,500/day	$1,000/day	$2,000/day
Picture editing	$100	$40	$70	n/a	n/a	n/a	$65/picture	$35/picture	$45/picture
Slides/Overheads	$100	$50	$55	$2,500	$500	$1,000	$90/slide	$50/slide	$63/slide
Educational & Literary Services									
Educational consulting and designing business/adult education courses	$100	$45	$66	n/a	n/a	n/a	$2,500/day	$600/day	$900/day

1 For more information about photography rates, see *2009 Photographer's Market*.
2 Per project figures based on 4 pages/8 photos

	PER HOUR			PER PROJECT			OTHER		
	HIGH	LOW	AVG	HIGH	LOW	AVG	HIGH	LOW	AVG
Educational grant and proposal writing	$100	$35	$53	n/a	n/a	n/a	n/a	n/a	n/a
Manuscript evaluation for theses/ dissertations	$90	$25	$47	$1,500	$200	$500	n/a	n/a	n/a
Poetry manuscript critique	$50	$25	$38	n/a	n/a	n/a	n/a	n/a	n/a
Presentations at national conventions (by well-known authors)	$500	$100	$193	n/a	n/a	n/a	$30,000/ event	$1,000/ event	$5,000/ event
Presentations at regional writers' conferences	n/a	n/a	n/a	n/a	n/a	n/a	$1,500/ event	$200/ event	$500/ event
Presentations to local groups, librarians or teachers	$125	$25	$112	n/a	n/a	n/a	$350/event	$50/event	$150/event
Presentations to school classes (5-day visiting artists program)	n/a	n/a	n/a	n/a	n/a	n/a	$3,400	$2,500	$2,750
Readings by poets, fiction writers (highest fees for celebrity writers)	n/a	n/a	n/a	n/a	n/a	n/a	$3,000/event	$50/event	$200/event
Short story manuscript critique	$115	$35	$72	n/a	n/a	n/a	$175/story	$50/story	$115/story
Teaching college course/seminar (includes adult education)	$143	$25	$90	n/a	n/a	n/a	$10,000/course	$1,800 course	$4,110/course
Writers' workshops	$120	$90	$103	n/a	n/a	n/a	$5,000/event	$100/event	$1,459/event
Writing for scholarly journals	$60	$40	$50	n/a	n/a	n/a	$450/article	$100/article	$252/article

Magazines & Trade Journals[1]

	HIGH	LOW	AVG	HIGH	LOW	AVG	HIGH	LOW	AVG
Article manuscript critique	$125	$40	$69	n/a	n/a	n/a	n/a	n/a	n/a
Arts reviewing	n/a	n/a	n/a	$325	$100	$170	$1.20/word	10¢/word	80¢/word
Book reviews	n/a	n/a	n/a	$900	$25	$365	$1.50/word	15¢/word	78¢/word
City magazine, calendar of events column	n/a	n/a	n/a	n/a	n/a	n/a	$200/column $1/word	$75/column 30¢/word	$131/column 75¢/word
Consultation on magazine editorial	$125	$60	$92	n/a	n/a	n/a	n/a	n/a	n/a

1 For specific pay rate information for feature articles, columns/departments, fillers, etc., see individual market listings.

	PER HOUR			PER PROJECT			OTHER		
	HIGH	LOW	AVG	HIGH	LOW	AVG	HIGH	LOW	AVG
Consumer magazine column	n/a	n/a	n/a	n/a	n/a	n/a	$2.50/word $2,500/column	$1/word $75/column	$1.25/word $717/column
Consumer magazine feature articles	n/a	n/a	n/a	$10,000	$100	$3,597	$3.75/word	19¢/word	$1.35/word
Content editing	$100	$30	$49	n/a	n/a	n/a	$5,000/issue	$2,000/issue	$3,167/issue
Copyediting magazines	$60	$20	$39	n/a	n/a	n/a	$10/page	$2.90/page	$6.30/page
Fact checking	$100	$25	$49	n/a	n/a	n/a	n/a	n/a	n/a
Ghostwriting articles (general)	$125	$90	$110	$3,500	$1,100	$2,088	$2.50/word	$1/word	$1.94/word
Magazine research	$100	$25	$50	n/a	n/a	n/a	$500/item	$100/item	$225/item
Proofreading	$60	$17	$34	n/a	n/a	n/a	n/a	n/a	n/a
Reprint fees	n/a	n/a	n/a	$1,000	$20	$350	$1.50/word	10¢/word	59¢/word
Rewriting	$125	$40	$77	n/a	n/a	n/a	n/a	n/a	n/a
Trade journal column	$90	$35	$51	n/a	n/a	n/a	$1/word $600/column	30¢/word $150/column	67¢/word $300/column
Trade journal feature article	$100	$40	$62	$2,000	$350	$991	$3/word	17¢/word	95¢/word
Miscellaneous									
Cartoons (gag, plus illustration)	n/a	n/a	n/a	n/a	n/a	n/a	$575	$15	$100
Comedy writing for nightclub entertainers	n/a	n/a	n/a	n/a	n/a	n/a	$50/joke $500/group	$5/joke $100/group	$38/joke $250/group
Craft projects with instructions	n/a	n/a	n/a	$350	$50	$200	n/a	n/a	65¢/word
Encyclopedia articles	n/a	n/a	n/a	n/a	n/a	n/a	$3,000/article 50¢/word	$50/article 30¢/word	$200/article 40¢/word
Family histories	$80	$30	$65	$25,000	$750	$9,188	n/a	n/a	n/a
Gagwriting for cartoonists	n/a	n/a	n/a	n/a	n/a	n/a	n/a	n/a	$30/gag
Institutional history (church school)	n/a	n/a	n/a	n/a	n/a	n/a	$125/page	$75/page	$100/page
Manuscript typing	n/a	n/a	n/a	n/a	n/a	n/a	$2.50/page	95¢/page	$1.27/page

	PER HOUR			PER PROJECT			OTHER		
	HIGH	LOW	AVG	HIGH	LOW	AVG	HIGH	LOW	AVG
Résumés	n/a	n/a	n/a	$500	$200	$300	n/a	n/a	n/a
Writing contest judging[1]	n/a	n/a	n/a	$250	$0	$55	n/a	n/a	n/a
Newspapers									
Arts reviewing	n/a	n/a	n/a	$200	$15	$93	60¢/word	10¢/word	37¢/word
Book reviews	n/a	n/a	n/a	$350	$25	$150	60¢/word	30¢/word	46¢/word
Column, local	n/a	n/a	n/a	n/a	n/a	n/a	$600/column	$68/column	$171/column
Copyediting	$35	$15	$26	n/a	n/a	n/a	n/a	n/a	n/a
Editing/manuscript evaluation	n/a	n/a	$35	n/a	n/a	n/a	n/a	n/a	n/a
Feature	n/a	n/a	n/a	$1,040	$125	$350	$1.60/word	25¢/word	63¢/word
Obituary copy	n/a	n/a	$20	n/a	n/a	n/a	$225/story	$35/story	$112/story
Proofreading	$25	$15	$19	n/a	n/a	n/a	n/a	n/a	n/a
Reprints	n/a	n/a	n/a	$300	$50	$163	n/a	n/a	n/a
Stringing	n/a	n/a	n/a	n/a	n/a	n/a	$1,000/story	$50/story	$290/story
Syndicated column, self-promoted (rate depends on circulation)	n/a	n/a	n/a	n/a	n/a	n/a	$35/insertion	$4/insertion	$8/insertion

[1] Some pay in gift certificates or books. Judging of finalists may be duty included in workshop speaker's fee.

BEYOND THE BASICS

Build a Platform

Or You'll Miss the Train

by Jeff Yeager

Jeff, you're a wonderful writer!"

Coming from the seasoned New York literary agent, I just wanted those words to hang there, in suspended celebration, while we enjoyed a leisurely lunch at the trendy Manhattan eatery she'd chosen for our meeting. Even though I'm not a dessert fan, I started thinking that maybe I'd stick around after all for some crème brûlée and an espresso or two.

"But the fact is," she continued, "there are lots of wonderful writers—and even lots of truly great writers—who never get a book published." Darn it, so much for basking in the moment. I hadn't even started my salad. Check please!

"The thing that interests me about you, and frankly the reason I agreed to meet with you today, is your platform. I know you're just starting out, but I think publishers will be impressed with the exposure you're already getting and what that means for your platform going forward." I thoughtfully crunched on a crouton from my salad, hoping to suggest that I was contemplating the wisdom of the agent's words. But I'm too honest to be a good bluffer.

"That's fantastic!" I said, enthusiastically spraying the woman I hoped would be my future agent in a shower of soggy crouton crumbs.

"Look," I continued, trying to divert my gaze from what appeared to be an entire crushed baggett clinging to the front of the poor agent's Ann Taylor dress suit. "I really hope you'll agree to represent me, and I want you to know that I always believe in being honest. So I have to confess: I have absolutely no idea what a *platform* is ... although I'm delighted that you think I have such a good one."

WHAT THE HECK IS A PLATFORM?

With that awkward self-confessional a few short years ago, I began my journey—and more importantly my education—into the über competitive, promotion-driven world of book publishing.

Simply put, a platform is a writer's capacity to help promote and market his own work to potential readers. It's a writer's ability to attract a fan base of his own, outside of the promotional efforts of his publisher. It's a writer's ability to get his message out to the world.

Ideally a platform has more than just one plank. For example, it's more than just a strong website or a weekly column in your local newspaper, although either of those planks would be a terrific start. It's a combination of assets, skills, expertise, activities, and professional connections that both strengthen each other and enhance the writer's chances for commercial success.

JEFF YEAGER is the author of *The Ultimate Cheapskate's Road Map to True Riches* (Broadway).

In my case I was lucky enough to inadvertently receive some national television exposure early in my writing career (see 2008 *Writer's Market* Freelance Success Stories), which I then opportunistically parlayed into more press exposure and a growing network of media contacts. By the time I went looking for a literary agent to represent me in a book deal, I'd only had a few articles published and most of those were online. And while the media visibility I'd received prior to that point was not inconsequential, it wasn't nearly enough to carry a book.

But it was a start, and it proved to an agent—and then to a publisher—that I had the wherewithal to build a viable platform; that I was a horse worth betting on. That was two book deals ago, and my platform has since grown to include professional speaking and television reporting gigs, as well as blogging on a number of high traffic websites and authoring articles for a range of national publications.

At first blush my story might seem plucky to the point of being irrelevant to the careers of most writers. After all, how many newbie writers make their media debut on NBC's *Today* show, as I did? But what I've come to appreciate about platform building is this: Even with luck, you need persistence and promotional savvy, and—even without luck—persistence and promotional savvy is probably all you need.

It's also true what they say about making your own luck. Or, as quote-meister H. Jackson Brown, Jr. puts it, "Opportunity dances with those already on the dance floor." The key to building a successful promotional platform is to make sure you're always out there on the dance floor, shakin' what you got.

PRIORITIES AND GETTING STARTED

Given the laundry list of possible tactics for developing a platform (see sidebar), you need to set priorities in order to use your time and resources effectively, while at the same time remaining flexible enough to quickly act on unanticipated opportunities as they come your way. After all, you never know who's going to ask you to dance once you're out there on the floor.

Logically, the first step is to identify the target audience(s) for your writing. The more focused you can be in defining your audience, the more effective you'll be in reaching out to them. For example, if you're writing a book about dieting, you're obviously looking to reach people who would like to lose weight. But can you be even more specific? Maybe your niche is really middle-aged women hoping to lose weight, or parents who want to help their kids lose weight. Or say you write young adult fiction. Does it appeal more to boys or girls, teens or preteens, urban kids or rural kids, or particular YA book discussion groups, etc.?

Now that you know who your audience is, you need to figure out where and how you can best reach them. This is when the brainstorming really starts. What websites or online discussion boards do they frequent? What magazines and other print publications do they read? Are there certain TV or radio shows that appeal to them? Are there any special events they attend, or clubs or associations they join? In short, what are their favorite dance floors?

Identifying publications, media, and other forums through which you can reach your target audience is a never ending process, because they're constantly changing and you're always looking to expand your platform. When you've tapped into one forum, for example a website that caters to middle-aged women hoping to lose weight, always ask the people you meet there what other websites they visit, magazines they read, books the0y've enjoyed, and so on. I call this a *progressive focus group*, relying on everyone I meet in my target audience to educate me further about themselves and where I can find more folks just like them.

IT'S ALL ABOUT CONTENT

Once you've identified your target audience and started building a list of dance floors where they hang out, it's time to introduce yourself, to get to know them, and to make sure they get to know *you*. For most writers, this means providing content; content that helps to establish your reputation, builds name recognition (AKA "brand recognition"), and ideally creates for you a positive notoriety or even celebrity status among members of your target audience.

10 Ways to Build Your Platform

1. Create your own website, keep it current with a blog and other updated content, and make it interactive with forums, contests, surveys, newsletters, a guestbook, etc.
2. Write articles, stories, op-eds, and even letters to the editor for magazines, newsletters, and other print publications read your target audience.
3. Contact other high-traffic websites frequented by your target audience, offer to guest blog or contribute content to them (even for free), link your site to theirs, and participate in their networking forums.
4. Position yourself as *the* go-to source for information regarding your area of expertise by joining related professional organizations, earning certifications, and registering with online and print directories like LinkedIn.com and *Who's Who*, as well as social networking sites like FaceBook and MySpace.
5. Send periodic press releases about yourself, your activities, or some timely aspect of your work/field to targeted print and broadcast media, and offer to sit for an interview—you might be surprised by the response.
6. Hold a publicity event—or dare I say a publicity stunt or gimmick? Challenge your church group to see how much weight they can lose by following the instructions in the diet book you're writing, or hype the mystery novel you're writing by hiding clues around town to the location of the buried treasure—the real treasure might be the media exposure you generate.
7. Give talks, teach classes, offer workshops about your specialty at libraries, schools, churches, and online—but make sure the press knows all about it.
8. Get involved as a volunteer or board member with nonprofit organizations related to your field of interest/expertise; it looks good on your resume and they can be valuable marketing partners for your work.
9. Partner with or co-author a book with a well established, widely recognized expert or celebrity, or try publishing your book through an established franchise like the *Dummies* or *Chicken Soup* serials, where your personal platform is less of a factor.
10. Post your own book trailers and other video content on YouTube, create your own podcasts, or publish your own ezine—even amateurish efforts can catch fire.

If you're a nonfiction writer, you typically provide content from the perspective of being an expert in the field (again, a weight loss expert, for example). If you write fiction, the content you provide is hopefully deemed desirable because of your creative and literary prowess. Who wouldn't want to read the words posted on some obscure website by a future J.K. Rowling?

Content, of course, can take many different forms. It's an article or story you get paid handsomely to write for a national magazine, as well as something you write without compensation for an association newsletter read by your target audience. It's the content of your own website and the guest blogs you write for another high-traffic website frequented by your target audience, and it's also every word you type in a chat room where your audience hangs out, even if it's just passing the time of day. It's the talk you give at the local library about what you do for a living. It's the interview you give on radio or national TV.

The content you provide is the basic building block of your platform, so make sure you have plenty of it and that it reflects the quality and style you want to be associated with. Remember, the most valuable words many authors have ever written are the words they most wish they could take back.

A *VIRTUAL* PLATFORM?

There's no denying that the Internet has had a profound impact on the enterprises of writing and publishing, and also on the ability of an author to develop a platform. Pre-Internet, writers had to rely on traditional print and broadcast media, as well as public appearances and other in-person networking, to gain visibility and establish credibility.

But is it possible to build a promotional platform entirely through online activities—a *virtual platform*, if you will? If you have your own winning website, soft-market yourself through online chat rooms, maybe blog or contribute content to other sites, will that do the trick?

Timothy Ferriss, author of the bestselling book *The 4 Hour Workweek*, attributes much of his success to viral marketing, particularly his efforts to befriend fellow bloggers who then hyped his book. But viral or old school, it all comes back to content. Ferriss said in an interview with Leo Babauta on writetodone.com, "Marketing can get you an initial wave of customers, but you need a good product to go viral ... Focus on making yourself a credible expert vs. pushing a book."

Clearly a strong presence on the Internet can not only be a major plank in an author's platform, but it's also a logical place for many writers to begin building their platforms.

"The barriers (e.g. cost, skill, etc.) for gaining exposure through the Internet are very low," says Kristine Puopolo, Senior Editor with Doubleday Broadway Publishing. "The good news is that almost anyone can publish a blog or create his own website. The bad news is that almost *everyone does* publish a blog and create his own website," she says. Getting noticed on the information superhighway has become increasingly difficult as traffic congestion has increased. "The Internet is a terrific place to create buzz about a book or an author," Puopolo says. "But success is getting that buzz picked up by other media, like TV and print."

So if you were hoping to build your platform solely by sitting at a computer keyboard, Google "try again." Even Ferriss says that his relationships with fellow bloggers were not forged so much over the Internet or even by phone, but by speaking at events they attended and—talk about old school—joining them for some beers afterwards.

COMMON MYTHS ABOUT PLATFORMS

That's not my job, man. Talk to anyone in the publishing business, and the answer is always the same: Gone are the days when authors were just expected to write books and publishers were expected to market them, if those golden days ever existed in the first place. Luke Dempsey knows how it works from both sides of the desk. He's the editor-in-chief of Hudson Street Press, a division of Penguin USA, and he's also author of *A Supremely Bad Idea*, published by Bloomsbury in 2008. "These days book promotion is, at best, a partnership

5 Top-O-Mind Tips

Keep these things in mind as you build your platform, or you'll kick yourself later:

- **Build relationships, not just a Roladex file.** Do you still see yourself in the writing business five years from now? Nurture the relationships you develop with press contacts, readers, and the other folks you encounter in the publishing industry, rather than just milking them for a one-off interview, etc. Keep in touch, do them favors, and treat them as friends so that they'll be glad to help you out again in the future.
- **No publicity is bad publicity...** or at least that's the way the saying goes. And it's true in a great many cases, particularly when you're just starting out and you're relatively unknown. But also remember that it can be hard to shake an unfavorable reputation once the publicity Gods have saddled you with one, so think twice before jumping at publicity for publicity's sake.
- **Mailing lists are golden.** Capturing the names and contact information for everyone you meet—from readers and potential readers to press contacts and booksellers—is key to building your platform. Distribute sign-up lists at your events, collect business cards religiously, and start building a computerized database of your contacts from day one.
- **Remember the "soft" in "soft-marketing."** Particularly when it comes to promoting yourself online, in social networking forums, chat rooms, etc., tread lightly. First get to know the community and contribute content that's not self-promotional before you ever start talking about yourself and your writing. I've never encountered an online forum that doesn't have an eager Spam Master (or ten) to bounce you out if you come on too strong with self-promotion.
- **Recognize your strengths and weaknesses.** It's a truly rare and talented writer who has the skills, resources, and time to develop a robust platform without outside help. Consider hiring a publicist, getting professional "media training," taking a public speaking class, or securing other professional assistance to compliment your strengths and weaknesses.

between an author and a publisher. If an author has a strong platform, it's also more likely that the publisher will get excited about the project and put their backs into it as well."

Only nonfiction authors need a platform. It's true that the publishing industry has historically expected most nonfiction authors to have a strong promotional platform of their own. After all, nonfiction writers are usually considered experts regarding their subject matter, and their expertise should be both in demand and validated by appearing in the media, serving as a source, and writing articles and other content related to their field. But as the book industry has become more competitive, fiction writers are now commonly expected to come to the table with a promotional platform as well.

"It used to be that fiction sold pretty much just as a result of good reviews," Kristine Puopolo says. "But with so many books on the market today and the increased competition for media attention, a fiction author with a compelling personal story, winning personality, or a degree of celebrity definitely has a leg up." Puopolo says that fiction writers can develop their platforms using some of the same techniques as nonfiction writers (e.g. blogs, personal

Creating Effective Press Releases

I often hear from other writers who take one of my workshops or online classes that they do not know how to market their own work. Writing the entire novel was an easier task than approaching stores, newspapers, or online venues about carrying their book. But whether a writer landed a coveted spot with a major publisher, chose to go with a small local press or ventured into the world of print on demand and vanity presses, it often falls on the shoulders of the author to market their own book. A few fortunate authors will gain access to a publicist through their publisher, but many will be completely on their own.

Writing a press release does not have to be a daunting task. In fact, for anyone who has already written a query letter, you are well on your way to mastering a press release. The goal is the same: catch the reader's attention right away, build interest in your project, and motivate the reader to act on your request.

Basic press release format

Beyond the basics of not using all caps (nobody wants to be shouted at, even if you excited) and checking your grammar, start your press release with the following headline: For Immediate Release. The next line should be in bold and should contain the headline of your press release. Follow this with a very brief paragraph summarizing the content below and then with the body of the press release. Finish with a short About the Author paragraph and end with your contact information, including your address, phone number, email and website.

Quality content Is a must

One of the best ways to get your press release past the intern who screens the incessant influx of information is to write your release as a completed article. If your text is compelling, interesting, and complete, you have a much better shot of finding that same text in the Sunday Arts section of the paper. Editors are busy people, and the gift if print-ready text is hard to pass up.

Years ago, when I was working as an artist's representative, I sent press packages to media outlets ahead of each performance in a new city. Editors would often print the press release verbatim, although some would call the artist and conduct an interview. But the press release did its job either way by gaining invaluable publicity before a performance.

Study articles about authors and books. Learn the voice and tone of those articles. Mimic it in your own writing, and you'll be far more likely to generate interest in your project.

Where to send your release

A press release can be a stand alone product or as part of a press package. A package should contain a headshot of yourself and art from your book, both printed and on cd in low and high resolution where possible. The more options you provide, the more likely art will accompany any story published from your press release. It should also include a press copy of the book when possible. You can also attach a sheet with upcoming appearances, other titles, and any other pertinent information.

Press releases can be emailed directly to the appropriate editors or reviewers or uploaded to a variety of online PR distribution sites. And while these sites are great for getting the word out on the web, it is still recommended that you take the time to directly contact the editors who will possibly run your story in print or online. And remember to follow up your press releases with a personal phone call. Nothing will set you apart from the pile of press releases like a friendly follow-up call.

There has been a proliferation of online distribution sites focusing on public relations. Someof these include www/PRWeb.com, www.PRLeap.com, and www.24-7pressrelease.com, and www.epressreleases.com. While many of these sites offer free basic online distribution, there are additional fee-based products for you to consider.

—Lisa Abeyta

appearances, etc.), and also with things like "virtually hosting" book discussion groups online or by phone, joining local and national literary organizations, and participating in other genre specific forums. Fiction or nonfiction, Puopolo says effective platforms grow out of the "authenticity" of the author. "Follow who and what you are. Don't try to be something that you aren't."

Okay, I've built my platform. Now I can get back to writing. As you probably appreciate by now, your platform is not a static set of achievements, but an evolving portfolio of capacities which will hopefully grow and expand along with your writing career. Everything you write, every media appearance you make, every book talk you give, opens a new avenue for extending and strengthening your platform. You need to start building your platform as soon as you start writing—not when you go shopping for a book deal—and the process continues as long as you continue writing. When it comes to your platform as a writer, it's true what they say: "If you're not growing, you're dying."

MORE THAN A MEANS TO AN END

Another common misconception, particularly among new authors, is that platform building is simply a step—perhaps even a necessary evil—in getting your book published.

But here's a bright point to end on: From a business perspective, a robust platform *is* an author's business. In manufacturing terms, it's the sum total of *product lines* that a writer has with which to earn a living. And the payout is that in many cases the non-writing product lines that make up an author's platform may grow to be even more lucrative than writing.

"We're not in the book business. We're in the brand business." That's the prophetic advice Bruce Feiler gave me when I was first starting out. Feiler is a *New York Times* bestselling author of seven books, including *Walking the Bible,* and he has strategically coupled his authorship with television, speaking, and other writing work that has put far more fishes and loaves on his table than writing books alone. In fact Feiler considers the book business to be a "dying industry," which is precisely why he has expanded his product lines.

Stacey Glick, a literary agent with the prestigious firm Dystel and Goderich in New York, wholeheartedly agrees with Feiler. "The thing you need to understand is that most authors can no longer afford to be one dimensional; that is, just authors," she told me. "An author's appeal to a publisher is largely his platform, and his platform in turn benefits from the books he writes. Round and round you go."

And I always value Stacey Glick's advice. After all, she's not only my agent, but she didn't even send me the dry cleaning bill for her Ann Taylor dress suit.

BEYOND THE BASICS

Editor FAQs

by Robert Lee Brewer

The publishing world is filled with so many nooks and crannies that even the most experienced writers have common questions about various topics, such as co-authoring, self-publishing, ghostwriting and more. I know, because writers tend to ask me the same questions whether I'm speaking at a bookstore or a writer's conference, or fielding questions through WritersMarket.com. Here are some of those most frequently asked questions with my most frequently given answers.

What's the trick to getting published?

There really *is* no trick to getting published. There's no tried-and-true gimmick that will build your career for you. Making it as a writer requires a lot of hard work, discipline and perseverance.

The first step is always to work on the craft of writing. You can improve your craft by participating in writer's groups, attending writer's conferences, taking online courses, or going to workshops at local universities. Instructional books on technique (many can be found online at www.WritersDigest.com) can provide exercises, spark ideas, and give advice on plotting, characterization and more.

Once your work is at a publishable level, you should sit down with a pad of paper and outline what your long-term goals are. Then, identify some short-term goals you think will get you there.

It's hard to get somewhere without knowing where you're going, so don't discount this step in the process of becoming a successful writer. Sure, you can change directions if you see a better destination along the way, but it's important that you always have a goal in mind. Your goals will help direct which skills you need to focus on the most and will play an important role in how your writing is crafted.

How does co-authoring work?

In a situation where you wish to co-author a book or article, I suggest defining the roles of each author upfront to avoid ambiguity, hurt feelings, or disputes during the writing process and later on during the submission process. Make sure each author agrees on the goals, responsibilities, rights, compensation and deadlines for the project. Communication throughout the process is key.

When contacting a publisher or agent, it's best to elect one main contact person to avoid confusion. This person should be good at communicating with the publisher or agent and the other co-author or authors.

What about ghostwriting?

Ghostwriting is the process where you take another person's ideas and write an article or book for them, either under their name or "as told to." Authoritative experts with no writing experience use this process, as well as celebrities with stories to tell.

Ghostwriting is not a glamorous job, since you usually don't get credit or recognition, but it does pay the bills for many hard-working and organized writers. As with co-authoring, be sure to get goals, rights, payment, responsibilities, deadlines and other details ironed out before starting any project.

Whether you are looking for a ghostwriter or you wish to become one, the following Web sites can help: www.freelancewriting.com; www.craigslist.org; www.writers-editors.com. On these Web sites, you can look for job openings or post one.

Should I hire an editor or book doctor?

Some writers hire professional editors to strengthen their manuscripts before submitting to publishers or agents. These editors can check for content, flow, do line-by-line edits, offer general critiques, and more (or less—on a case-by-case basis). However, it is often hard to evaluate how good an editor is until you've already invested a good deal of time and money into the process. A much more affordable and possibly more effective solution is to join a writing group in your area or attend a writing workshop that addresses your type of writing. Writer's conferences also offer critiques by professional writers, editors and agents. If these options are not available, then you could try hiring a graduate student from a local college.

You can hunt down possible editors online at the following Web sites: www.writerseditors.com; www.freelancewriting.com; www.absolutewrite.com. Also, check out classified ads in the back of the *Writer's Digest* magazine.

When do I need an agent?

First, you only need an agent if you are writing a book or a screenplay. Second, nonfiction writers need a completed book proposal together before hunting down an agent, and fiction writers need a completed manuscript. Third, agents are most helpful for selling to the larger book publishers, so if you're writing a book that will only appeal to academics or a very small audience, using an agent will not make as much sense.

A good agent will place your work with a publisher; negotiate the best package of subsidiary rights, advance money, and royalty terms possible; help you develop your career as a writer for the short-and long-term; and many also provide guidance in the development of writing projects and promotional opportunities.

For more information on agents, check out *2010 Guide to Literary Agents*, edited by Chuck Sambuchino (Writer's Digest Books). In addition to listing more than 550 agents, this resource is filled with articles explaining how to find and work with an appropriate agent.

Is self-publishing a better option for writers?

Self-publishing is definitely tied up in the whole equation of determining your goals as a writer. Many writers envision publishing a book that will be sold in bookstores, and possibly as a bestseller. If that's your goal, then self-publishing should only be used as a last resort.

Unless you're writing for a very specialized audience or trying to publish a book of poetry, then I suggest trying to get an agent first. If that doesn't work out, try submitting directly to book publishers. If that doesn't work, maybe you need to revise your query letter or manuscript and try again. This is especially true if you keep hearing the same comments and suggestions from agents and editors.

If you've exhausted all these options and you still think you can reach an audience, then self-publishing could be an option for you. However, make sure you research all your self-publishing options to save time, money and headaches. Self-publishing is a very rough road for any writer and often turns into a full-time job with a very low rate of success.

How do I handle a pseudonym?

Many writers working under a pseudonym wonder if they have to deceive their publishers and live a double life. The best policy is to bring your pseudonym up at the beginning of your communication with an agent or editor. In your initial query or cover letter, use your real name, but explain in one sentence somewhere in that letter (and not in the first paragraph) that you write under a pen name. That way payment can be made to your real name, helping you avoid any possible taxation or banking snafus. Also, to avoid confusion, use your pseudonym on the actual manuscript.

Should I copyright my work before submitting?

For all practical and legal purposes, your work is protected by copyright once you put it on paper (or save it electronically). While registering your copyright will add an extra level of protection for your writing against possible manuscript thieves, it is not necessary and can often label you as an amateur. Most cases of plagiarism occur after a work has been published and is under the protection of copyright. Do not write that your work is copyrighted or include a copyright symbol on your manuscript or in your query or cover letter; this will generally get your submission rejected before it is even read.

How do I know a publisher won't steal my work?

As in life, there are no guarantees in publishing. However, it is rare to hear an actual first-person account of an editor or agent stealing someone else's work before it is published. Most people who relay these tall tales of publishing will say "a friend of a friend" had her work stolen by an editor. While there may be a case or two where this has happened, you probably have better odds of winning the lottery than having your work stolen. Whether that's a good or bad thing is open to interpretation.

In addition, *Writer's Market* strives to list only reputable publishers and viable markets within its pages. From including screening questions in our questionnaires to scanning online writer groups and responding to writer complaints, we work to maintain the highest quality directory available to writers trying to get published and paid for their writing. (If you feel you have not been treated fairly by a listing in the book, please follow the Complaint Procedure found on the copyright page of this book—next to the Table of Contents.)

BEYOND THE BASICS

Publishers & Their Imprints

The publishing world is in constant transition. With all the buying, selling, reorganizing, consolidating, and dissolving, it's hard to keep publishers and their imprints straight. To help make sense of these changes, here's a breakdown of major publishers (and their divisions)—who owns whom and which imprints are under each company umbrella. Keep in mind that this information changes frequently. The Web site of each publisher is provided to help you keep an eye on this ever-evolving business.

HACHETTE BOOK GROUP USA

www.hachettebookgroupusa.com

Center Street

FaithWords

Grand Central Publishing
Business Plus
5-Spot
Forever
Springboard Press
Twelve
Vision
Wellness Central

Hachette Book Group Digital Media
Hachette Audio

Little, Brown and Company
Back Bay Books
Bulfinch
Reagan Arthur Books

Little, Brown Books for Young Readers
LB Kids
Poppy

Orbit

Yen Press

HARLEQUIN ENTERPRISES

www.eharlequin.com

Harlequin
Harlequin American Romance
Harlequin Bianca
Harlequin Blaze
Harlequin Deseo
Harlequin Historical
Harlequin Intrigue
Harlequin Jazmin
Harlequin Julia
Harlequin Medical Romance
Harlequin NASCAR
Harlequin NEXT

Harlequin Presents
Harlequin Romance
Harlequin Superromance
Harlequin eBooks
Harlequin Special Releases
Harlequin Nonfiction
Harlequin Historical Undone

HQN Books
HQN eBooks

LUNA
Luna eBooks

MIRA
Mira eBooks

Kimani Press
Kimani Press Arabesque
Kimani Press Kimani Romance
Kimani Press Kimani TRU
Kimani Press New Spirit
Kimani Press Sepia
Kimani Press Special Releases
Kimani Press eBooks

Red Dress Ink
Red Dress eBooks

Silhouette
Silhouette Desire
Silhouette Nocturne
Silhouette Romantic Suspense
Silhouette Special Edition

SPICE
SPICE Books
SPICE Briefs

Steeple Hill
Steeple Hill Café©
Steeple Hill Love Inspired
Steeple Hill Love Inspired Historical
Steeple Hill Love Inspired Suspense
Steeple Hill Women's Fiction

Worldwide Library

Rogue Angel

Worldwide Mystery

HARPERCOLLINS

www.harpercollins.com

HarperMorrow
Amistad
Avon
- Avon A
- Avon Inspire
- Avon Red

Collins
Collins Business
Collins Design
Collins Living
Ecco
Eos
Harper
- Harper Mass Market
- Harper Perennial
- Harper Perennial
- Harper Audio

HarperCollins
- HarperCollins e-Books
- HarperEntertainment
- HarperLuxe
- HarperOne
- HarperStudio

William Morrow
- Morrow Cookbooks

Rayo

HarperCollins Children's Books
Amistad Press
Balzer & Bray
Eos
Collins
Greenwillow Books
Harper Children's Audio
HarperCollins e-books
Harper Festival
HarperTeen
HarperTrophy
Rayo
Katherine Tegen Booler
Tokyo Bop

HarperCollins U.K.
Harper Press
- Blue Door
- Fourth Estate
- The Friday Project
- HarperPress

HarperFiction
- Voyager
- Avon
- HarperCollins Childrens Books

Collins
- Times
- Jane's

HarperCollins Canada
HarperCollinsPublishers
Collins Canada
HarperPerennial Canada
HarperTrophyCanada
Phyllis Bruce Books

HarperCollins Australia

HarperCollins India

HarperCollins New Zealand
- Zondervan
- Zonderkids
- Vida

MACMILLAN US (Holtzbrinck)

http://us.macmillan.com

MacMillan
Farrar, Straus & Giroux
Faber and Faber, Inc
Farrar, Straus
Hill & Wang
North Point Press

First Second

Henry Holt
Henry Holt Books for Young Readers
Holt Paperbacks
Metropolitan
Times

MacMillan Children's
Feiwel & Friends
Farrar, Straus and Giroux Books for Young Readers
Kingfisher
Holt Books for Young Readers
Priddy Books
Roaring Brook Press
Square Fish

Picador

Palgrave MacMillan

Tor/Forge Books
Tor
Forge
Orb
Tor/Seven Seas

St. Martin's Press
Minotaur Press
Thomas Dunne Books
Griffin
St. Martin's Press Paperbacks
Let's Go
Truman Talley Books

Bedford, Freeman & Worth Publishing Group

Bedford/St. Martin's

Hayden-McNeil

W.H. Freeman

Worth Publishers

MacMillan Audio

PENGUIN GROUP (USA), INC.

www.penguingroup.com

Penguin Adult Division
Ace
Alpha
Amy Einhorn Books/Putnam
Avery
Berkley
Dutton
Gotham
HPBooks
Hudson Street Press
Jeremy P. Tarcher
Jove NAL
Penguin
Penguin Press
Perigree
Plume
Portfolio

Riverhead
Sentinel
Viking
Price Stern Sloan

Young Readers Division
Dial
Dutton
Firebird
Frederick Warne
Grosset & Dunlap
Philomel

Puffin Books
Putnam
Razorbill
Speak
Viking

RANDOM HOUSE, INC. (Bertelsmann)

www.randomhouse.com

Crown Publishing Group
Broadway
Crown
Crown Business
Crown Forum
Clarkson Potter
Doubleday Business
Doubleday Religion
Harmony
Potter Craft
Potter Style
Three Rivers Press
Shaye Areheart Books
Waterbrook
Multnomah

Knopf Doubleday Publishing Group
Alfred A. Knopf
Anchor Books
Doubleday
  Doubleday Religion
  Flying Dolphin Press
Broadway
Everyman's Library
Nan A. Talese
Pantheon Books
Schocken Books
Vintage

Monacelli Press

Random House Publishing Group
Ballantine Books
Bantam Dell
Del Rey
Del Rey/Lucas Books
The Dial Press
The Modern Library
One World
Random House Trade Group
Random House Trade Paperbacks
Reader's Circle
Spectra
Spiegel and Grau
Strivers Row Books
Villard Books

Random House Audio Publishing Group
Listening Library
Random House Audio

Random House Children's Books
Kids@Random
Golden Books
Alfred A. Knopf Children's Books
Bantam Beginner Books
Crown Children's Books
David Fickling Books
Delacorte Press
Disney Books for Young Readers
Doubleday Children's Books
Dragonfly
First Time Books
Landmark Books
Laurel-Leaf
Picturebacks
Random House Books for Young Readers
Robin Corey Books
Schwartz and Wade Books
Sesame Workshop
Step into Reading
Stepping Stone Books
Wendy Lamb Books
Yearling

Random House Information Group
Fodor's Travel
Living Language
Prima Games
Princeton Review
RH Puzzles & Games
RH Reference Publishing
Sylvan Learning

Random House International
Arete
McClelland & Stewart Ltd.
Plaza & Janes
RH Australia
RH of Canada Limited
RH Mondadori
RH South America
RH United Kingdom
Transworld UK
Verlagsgruppe RH

SIMON & SCHUSTER

www.simonsays.com

Simon & Schuster Adult Publishing
Atria Books
  Washington Square Press
  Beyond Words
Free Press
Howard Books
Pocket Books
Scribner
Simon & Schuster
Strebor
The Touchstone & Fireside Group

Simon & Schuster Audio
Pimsleur
Simon & Schuster Audioworks
Encore
Sound Ideas
Nightingale Conant

Simon & Schuster Children's Publishing
Aladdin Paperbacks
Atheneum Books for Young Readers
Libros
Para Nin´os
Little Simon®
Little Simon
Inspirations
Margaret K. McElderry Books
Simon & Schuster Books for Young Readers
Simon Pulse
Simon Scribbles
Simon Spotlight®
Simon Spotlight Entertainment

Simon & Schuster International
Simon & Schuster Australia
Simon & Schuster Canada
Simon & Schuster UK

MARKETS

Literary Agents

The literary agencies listed in this section are members of the Association of Authors' Representatives (AAR), which means they do not charge for reading, critiquing, or editing. Some agents in this section may charge clients for office expenses such as photocopying, foreign postage, long-distance phone calls, or express mail services. Make sure you have a clear understanding of what these expenses are before signing any agency agreement.

FOR MORE . . .

The *2010 Guide to Literary Agents* (Writer's Digest Books) offers more than 550 literary agents, as well as information on writers' conferences. It also offers a wealth of information on the author/agent relationship and other related topics.

SUBHEADS

Each listing is broken down into subheads to make locating specific information easier. In the first section, you'll find contact information for each agency. Further information is provided which indicates an agency's size, its willingness to work with a new or previously unpublished writer, and its general areas of interest.

Member Agents Agencies comprised of more than one agent list member agents and their individual specialties to help you determine the most appropriate person for your query letter.

Represents Here agencies specify what nonfiction and fiction subjects they consider.

O- Look for the key icon to quickly learn an agent's areas of specialization or specific strengths.

How to Contact In this section agents specify the type of material they want to receive, how they want to receive it, and how long you should wait for their response.

Terms Provided here are details of an agent's commission, whether a contract is offered, and what additional office expenses you might have to pay if the agent agrees to represent you. Standard commissions range from 10-15 percent for domestic sales, and 15-20 percent for foreign or dramatic sales.

Writers' Conferences Here agents list the conferences they attend.

Tips Agents offer advice and additional instructions for writers looking for representation.

DOMINICK ABEL LITERARY AGENCY, INC.

146 W. 82nd St., #1B, New York NY 10024. (212)877-0710. Fax: (212)595-3133. E-mail: agency@dalainc.com. Member of AAR. Represents 100 clients. Currently handles: nonfiction books adult, novels adult.

How to Contact Query via e-mail.

Terms Agent receives 15% commission on domestic sales. Agent receives 20% commission on foreign sales.

ADAMS LITERARY

7845 Colony Road C4, #215, Charlotte NC 28226. (704)542-1440. Fax: (704)542-1450. E-mail: info@adamsliterary.com. Website: www.adamsliterary.com. **Contact:** Tracey Adams, Josh Adams. Member of AAR. Other memberships include SCBWI.

Member Agents Tracey Adams; Josh Adams.

Represents Adams Literary is a full-service literary agency exclusively representing children's book authors and artists.

How to Contact "Guidelines are posted (and frequently updated) on our Web site."

BRET ADAMS LTD. AGENCY

448 W. 44th St., New York NY 10036. (212)765-5630. E-mail: literary@bretadamsltd.net. **Contact:** Bruce Ostler, Mark Orsini. Member of AAR. Currently handles: movie scripts, TV scripts, stage plays.

Represents movie, TV, feature, TV movie, theatrical stage play. Handles theatre/film and TV projects. No books.

How to Contact Professional recommendation.

ALIVE COMMUNICATIONS, INC.

7680 Goddard St., Suite 200, Colorado Springs CO 80920. (719)260-7080. Fax: (719)260-8223. E-mail: submissions@alivecom.com. Website: www.alivecom.com. Member of AAR. Other memberships include Authors Guild. Represents 100+ clients. 5% of clients are new/unpublished writers. Currently handles: nonfiction books 50%, novels 40%, juvenile books 10%.

Member Agents Rick Christian, president (blockbusters, bestsellers); Lee Hough (popular/commercial nonfiction and fiction, thoughtful spirituality, children's); Beth Jusino (thoughtful/inspirational nonfiction, women's fiction/nonfiction, popular/commercial nonfiction & fiction); Joel Kneedler popular/commercial nonfiction and fiction, thoughtful spirituality, children's).

Represents nonfiction books, novels, short story collections, novellas. **Considers these nonfiction areas:** biography, business, child, how to, memoirs, religion, self help, womens. **Considers these fiction areas:** contemporary, adventure, detective, family, historical, humor, literary, mainstream, mystery, religious, thriller. This agency specializes in fiction, Christian living, how-to and commercial nonfiction. Actively seeking inspirational, literary and mainstream fiction, and work from authors with established track records and platforms. Does not want to receive poetry, scripts or dark themes.

How to Contact Query via e-mail. "Be advised that this agency works primarily with well-established, bestselling, and career authors." Obtains most new clients through recommendations from others.

Terms Agent receives 15% commission on domestic sales. Offers written contract; 2-month notice must be given to terminate contract.

Tips Rewrite and polish until the words on the page shine. Endorsements and great connections may help, provided you can write with power and passion. Network with publishing professionals by making contacts, joining critique groups, and attending writers' conferences in order to make personal connections and to get feedback. Alive Communications, Inc., has established itself as a premiere literary agency. We serve an elite group of authors who are critically acclaimed and commercially successful in both Christian and general markets.

ARCADIA

31 Lake Place N., Danbury CT 06810. E-mail: arcadialit@sbcglobal.net. **Contact:** Victoria Gould Pryor. Member of AAR.

Represents nonfiction books, literary and commercial fiction. **Considers these nonfiction areas:** biography, business, current affairs, health, history, psychology, science, true crime, womens, investigative journalism; culture; classical music; life transforming self-help. "I'm a very hands-on agent, which is necessary in this competitive marketplace. I work with authors on revisions until whatever we present to publishers is as perfect as it can be. I represent talented, dedicated, intelligent and ambitious writers who are looking for a long-term relationship based on professional success and mutual respect." Does not want to receive science fiction/fantasy, horror, humor or children's/YA. "We are only able to read fiction submissions from previously published authors."

How to Contact Query with SASE. This agency accepts e-queries (no attachments).

THE AXELROD AGENCY

55 Main St., P.O. Box 357, Chatham NY 12037. (518)392-2100. Fax: (518)392-2944. E-mail: steve@axelrodagency.com. **Contact:** Steven Axelrod. Member of AAR. Represents 15-20 clients. 1% of clients are new/unpublished writers. Currently handles: nonfiction books 5%, novels 95%.

- Prior to becoming an agent, Mr. Axelrod was a book club editor.

Represents nonfiction books, novels. **Considers these fiction areas:** mystery, romance, womens.
How to Contact Query with SASE. Accepts simultaneous submissions. Responds in 3 weeks to queries. Responds in 6 weeks to mss. Obtains most new clients through recommendations from others.
Terms Agent receives 15% commission on domestic sales. Agent receives 20% commission on foreign sales. No written contract.
Writers Conferences RWA National Conference.

BALKIN AGENCY, INC.

P.O. Box 222, Amherst MA 01004. Phone/Fax: (413)548-9835. E-mail: rick62838@crocker.com. **Contact:** Rick Balkin, president. Member of AAR. Represents 50 clients. 10% of clients are new/unpublished writers. Currently handles: nonfiction books 85%, scholarly books 5%, other 5% reference books .

- Prior to opening his agency, Mr. Balkin served as executive editor with Bobbs-Merrill Company.

Represents nonfiction books, scholarly. **Considers these nonfiction areas:** animals, anthropology, current affairs, health, history, how to, nature, popular culture, science, sociology, translation, biography. This agency specializes in adult nonfiction. Does not want to receive fiction, poetry, screenplays or computer books.
How to Contact Query with SASE. Submit proposal package, outline. Responds in 1 week to queries. Responds in 2 weeks to mss. Obtains most new clients through recommendations from others.
Terms Agent receives 15% commission on domestic sales. Agent receives 20% commission on foreign sales. Offers written contract, binding for 1 year. This agency charges clients for photocopying and express or foreign mail.
Tips "I do not take on books described as bestsellers or potential bestsellers. Any nonfiction work that is either unique, paradigmatic, a contribution, truly witty, or a labor of love is grist for my mill."

MEREDITH BERNSTEIN LITERARY AGENCY

2095 Broadway, Suite 505, New York NY 10023. (212)799-1007. Fax: (212)799-1145. Member of AAR. Represents 85 clients. 20% of clients are new/unpublished writers. Currently handles: nonfiction books 50%, other 50% fiction.

- Prior to opening her agency, Ms. Bernstein served at another agency for 5 years.

Represents nonfiction books, novels. **Considers these fiction areas:** literary, mystery, romance, thriller, young adult. "This agency does not specialize. It is very eclectic."
How to Contact Query with SASE. Accepts simultaneous submissions. Obtains most new clients through recommendations from others, conferences, developing/packaging ideas.
Terms Agent receives 15% commission on domestic sales. Agent receives 20% commission on foreign sales. Charges clients $75 disbursement fee/year.
Writers Conferences Southwest Writers' Conference; Rocky Mountain Fiction Writers' Colorado Gold; Pacific Northwest Writers' Conference; Willamette Writers' Conference; Surrey International Writers' Conference; San Diego State University Writers' Conference.

BLEECKER STREET ASSOCIATES, INC.

532 LaGuardia Place, #617, New York NY 10012. (212)677-4492. Fax: (212)388-0001. E-mail: bleeckerst@hotmail.com. **Contact:** Agnes Birnbaum. Member of AAR. Other memberships include RWA, MWA. Represents 60 clients. 20% of clients are new/unpublished writers. Currently handles: nonfiction books 75%, novels 25%.

- Prior to becoming an agent, Ms. Birnbaum was a senior editor at Simon & Schuster, Dutton/Signet, and other publishing houses.

Represents nonfiction books, novels. **Considers these nonfiction areas:** newage, animals, biography, business, child, computers, cooking, current affairs, ethnic, government, health, history, how to, memoirs, military, money, nature, popular culture, psychology, religion, science, self help, sociology, sports, true crime, womens. **Considers these fiction areas:** ethnic, historical, literary, mystery, romance, thriller, womens. "We're very hands-on and accessible. We try to be truly creative in our submission approaches. We've had especially good luck with first-time authors." Does not want to receive science fiction, westerns, poetry, children's books, academic/scholarly/professional books, plays, scripts, or short stories.
How to Contact Query with SASE. No email, phone, or fax queries. Accepts simultaneous submissions. Responds in 2 weeks to queries. Responds in 1 month to mss. "Obtains most new clients through recommendations from others, solicitations, conferences, plus, I will approach someone with a letter if his/her work impresses me."
Terms Agent receives 15% commission on domestic sales. Agent receives 25% commission on foreign sales. Offers written contract; 1-month notice must be given to terminate contract. Charges for postage, long distance, fax, messengers, photocopies (not to exceed $200).
Tips "Keep query letters short and to the point; include only information pertaining to the book or background as a writer. Try to avoid superlatives in description. Work needs to stand on its own, so how much editing it may have received has no place in a query letter."

BOOKS & SUCH LITERARY AGENCY

52 Mission Circle, Suite 122, PMB 170, Santa Rosa CA 95409. E-mail: representation@booksandsuch.biz. Website: www.booksandsuch.biz. **Contact:** Janet Kobobel Grant, Wendy Lawton, Etta Wilson, Rachel

Zurakowski. Member of AAR. Member of CBA (associate), American Christian Fiction Writers. Represents 150 clients. 5% of clients are new/unpublished writers. Currently handles: nonfiction books 50%, novels 50%.

- Prior to becoming an agent, Ms. Grant was an editor for Zondervan and managing editor for *Focus on the Family*; Ms. Lawton was an author, sculptor and designer of porcelein dolls. Ms. Wilson emphasizes middle grade children's books. Ms. Zurakowski concentrates on material for 20-something or 30-something readers.

Represents nonfiction books, novels, juvenile books. **Considers these nonfiction areas:** child, humor, religion, self help, womens. **Considers these fiction areas:** contemporary, family, historical, mainstream, religious, romance, African American adult. This agency specializes in general and inspirational fiction, romance, and in the Christian booksellers market. Actively seeking well-crafted material that presents Judeo-Christian values, if only subtly.

How to Contact Query via e-mail only, no attachments. Accepts simultaneous submissions. Responds in 1 month to queries. Obtains most new clients through recommendations from others, conferences.

Terms Agent receives 15% commission on domestic sales. Agent receives 20% commission on foreign sales. Offers written contract; 2-month notice must be given to terminate contract. No additional charges.

Writers Conferences Mount Hermon Christian Writers' Conference; Society of Childrens' Writers and Illustrators Conference; Writing for the Soul; American Christian Fiction Writers' Conference; San Francisco Writers' Conference.

Tips "The heart of our agency's motivation is to develop relationships with the authors we serve, to do what we can to shine the light of success on them, and to help be a caretaker of their gifts and time."

GEORGES BORCHARDT, INC.

136 E. 57th St., New York NY 10022. Member of AAR.

Member Agents Anne Borchardt; Georges Borchardt; Valerie Borchardt.

Represents This agency specializes in literary fiction and outstanding nonfiction.

How to Contact *No unsolicited mss.* Obtains most new clients through recommendations from others.

Terms Agent receives 15% commission on domestic sales. Agent receives 20% commission on foreign sales. Offers written contract.

CURTIS BROWN, LTD.

10 Astor Place, New York NY 10003-6935. (212)473-5400. Website: www.curtisbrown.com. Alternate address: Peter Ginsberg, president at CBSF, 1750 Montgomery St., San Francisco CA 94111. (415)954-8566. Member of AAR. Signatory of WGA.

Member Agents Ginger Clark; Katherine Fausset; Holly Frederick; Emilie Jacobson, senior vice president; Elizabeth Hardin; Ginger Knowlton, vice president; Timothy Knowlton, CEO; Laura Blake Peterson; Maureen Walters, senior vice president; Mitchell Waters. San Francisco Office: Nathan Bransford, Peter Ginsberg (President).

Represents nonfiction books, novels, short story collections, juvenile. **Considers these nonfiction areas:** agriculture horticulture, americana, crafts, interior, juvenile, New Age, young, animals, anthropology, art, biography, business, child, computers, cooking, current affairs, education, ethnic, gardening, gay, government, health, history, how to, humor, language, memoirs, military, money, multicultural, music, nature, philosophy, photography, popular culture, psychology, recreation, regional, religion, science, self help, sex, sociology, software, spirituality, sports, film, translation, travel, true crime, womens, creative nonfiction. **Considers these fiction areas:** contemporary, glitz, newage, psychic, adventure, comic, confession, detective, erotica, ethnic, experimental, family, fantasy, feminist, gay, gothic, hi lo, historical, horror, humor, juvenile, literary, mainstream, military, multicultural, multimedia, mystery, occult, picture books, plays, poetry, regional, religious, romance, science, short, spiritual, sports, thriller, translation, western, young, womens.

How to Contact Prefers to read materials exclusively. *No unsolicited mss.* Responds in 3 weeks to queries. Responds in 5 weeks to mss. Obtains most new clients through recommendations from others, solicitations, conferences.

Terms Offers written contract. Charges for some postage (overseas, etc.)

BROWNE & MILLER LITERARY ASSOCIATES

410 S. Michigan Ave., Suite 460, Chicago IL 60605-1465. (312)922-3063. E-mail: mail@browneandmiller.com. **Contact:** Danielle Egan-Miller. Member of AAR. Other memberships include RWA, MWA, Author's Guild. Represents 150 clients. 2%% of clients are new/unpublished writers. Currently handles: nonfiction books 25%, novels 75%.

Represents nonfiction books, novels. **Considers these nonfiction areas:** agriculture horticulture, crafts, animals, anthropology, biography, business, child, cooking, current affairs, ethnic, health, how to, humor, memoirs, money, nature, popular culture, psychology, religion, science, self help, sociology, sports, true crime, womens. **Considers these fiction areas:** glitz, detective, ethnic, family, historical, literary, mainstream, mystery, religious, romance, contemporary, gothic, historical, regency, sports, thriller, paranormal, erotica. We are partial to talented newcomers and experienced authors who are seeking hands-on career management, highly personal representation, and who are interested in being full partners in their books' successes. We are editorially focused and work closely with our authors through the whole publishing process, from proposal to after publication. Actively seeking highly commercial mainstream fiction and nonfiction. Does not represent poetry, short stories, plays, screenplays, articles, or children's books.

How to Contact Query with SASE. *No unsolicited mss.* Prefers to read material exclusively. Put submission in the subject line. Send no attachments. Responds in 6 weeks to queries. Obtains most new clients through referrals, queries by professional/marketable authors.

Terms Agent receives 15% commission on domestic sales. Agent receives 20% commission on foreign sales. Offers written contract, binding for 2 years. Charges clients for photocopying, overseas postage.

Writers Conferences BookExpo America; Frankfurt Book Fair; RWA National Conference; ICRS; London Book Fair; Bouchercon, regional writers conferences.

Tips "If interested in agency representation, be well informed."

MARIA CARVAINIS AGENCY, INC.

1270 Avenue of the Americas, Suite 2320, New York NY 10019. (212)245-6365. Fax: (212)245-7196. E-mail: mca@mariacarvainisagency.com. **Contact:** Maria Carvainis, Donna Bagdasarian. Member of AAR. Signatory of WGA. Other memberships include Authors Guild, Women's Media Group, ABA, MWA, RWA. Represents 75 clients. 10%% of clients are new/unpublished writers. Currently handles: nonfiction books 35%, novels 65%.

- Prior to opening her agency, Ms. Carvainis spent more than 10 years in the publishing industry as a senior editor with Macmillan Publishing, Basic Books, Avon Books, and Crown Publishers. Ms. Carvainis has served as a member of the AAR Board of Directors and AAR Treasurer, as well as serving as chair of the AAR Contracts Committee. She presently serves on the AAR Royalty Committee. Ms. Bagdasarian began her career as an academic at Boston University, then spent 5 years with Addison Wesley Longman as an acquisitions editor before joining the William Morris Agency in 1998. She has represented a breadth of projects, ranging from literary fiction to celebrity memoir.

Member Agents Maria Carvainis, president/literary agent; Donna Bagdasarian, literary agent; June Renschler, literary associate/subsidiary rights manager; Jerome Murphy and Alex Slater, literary assistants.

Represents nonfiction books, novels. **Considers these nonfiction areas:** biography, business, history, memoirs, science, pop science, womens. **Considers these fiction areas:** historical, literary, mainstream, mystery, thriller, young, womens, middle grade. Does not want to receive science fiction or children's picture books.

How to Contact Query with SASE. to queries. Responds in up to 3 months to mss. Obtains most new clients through recommendations from others, conferences, query letters.

Terms Agent receives 15% commission on domestic sales. Agent receives 20% commission on foreign sales. Offers written contract. Charges clients for foreign postage and bulk copying.

Writers Conferences BookExpo America; Frankfurt Book Fair; London Book Fair; Mystery Writers of America; Thrillerfest; Romance Writers of America.

CASTIGLIA LITERARY AGENCY

1155 Camino Del Mar, Suite 510, Del Mar CA 92014. (858)755-8761. Fax: (858)755-7063. Website: home.earthlink.net/~mwgconference/id22.html. Member of AAR. Other memberships include PEN. Represents 50 clients. Currently handles: nonfiction books 55%, novels 45%.

Member Agents Julie Castiglia; Winifred Golden; Sally Van Haitsma; Deborah Ritchken.

Represents nonfiction books, novels. **Considers these nonfiction areas:** animals, anthropology, biography, business, child, cooking, current affairs, ethnic, health, history, language, money, nature, psychology, religion, science, self help, womens. **Considers these fiction areas:** ethnic, literary, mainstream, mystery, womens. Does not want to receive horror, screenplays, poetry or academic nonfiction.

How to Contact Query with SASE. Obtains most new clients through recommendations from others, solicitations, conferences.

Terms Agent receives 15% commission on domestic sales. Agent receives 25% commission on foreign sales. Offers written contract; 6-week notice must be given to terminate contract.

Writers Conferences Santa Barbara Writers' Conference; Southern California Writers' Conference; Surrey International Writers' Conference; San Diego State University Writers' Conference; Willamette Writers' Conference.

Tips "Be professional with submissions. Attend workshops and conferences before you approach an agent."

THE CHOATE AGENCY, LLC

1320 Bolton Road, Pelham NY 10803. E-mail: mickey@thechoateagency.com. Website: www.thechoateagency.com. **Contact:** Mickey Choate. Member of AAR.

Represents nonfiction books, novels. **Considers these nonfiction areas:** history, memoirs, by journalists, military or political figures, biography; cookery/food; journalism; military science; narrative; politics; general science; wine/spirits. **Considers these fiction areas:** historical, mystery, thriller, select literary fiction. Does not want to receive chick lit, cozies or romance.

How to Contact Query with brief synopsis and bio. This agency prefers e-queries, but accepts snail mail queries with SASE.

DON CONGDON ASSOCIATES INC.

156 Fifth Ave., Suite 625, New York NY 10010-7002. (212)645-1229. Fax: (212)727-2688. E-mail: dca@doncongdon.com. **Contact:** Don Congdon, Michael Congdon, Susan Ramer, Cristina Concepcion, Maura Kye-Casella, Katie Kotchman, Katie Grimm. Member of AAR. Represents 100 clients. Currently handles: nonfiction books 60%, other 40% fiction.

Represents nonfiction books, fiction. **Considers these nonfiction areas:** anthropology, biography, child, cooking, current affairs, government, health, history, humor, language, memoirs, military, music, nature, popular culture, psychology, science, film, travel, true crime, womens, creative nonfiction. **Considers these fiction areas:** adventure, detective, literary, mainstream, mystery, short, thriller, womens. Especially interested in narrative nonfiction and literary fiction.

How to Contact Query with SASE or via e-mail (no attachments). Responds in 3 weeks to queries. Responds in 1 month to mss. Obtains most new clients through recommendations from other authors.

Terms Agent receives 15% commission on domestic sales. Agent receives 19% commission on foreign sales. Charges client for extra shipping costs, photocopying, copyright fees, book purchases.

Tips "Writing a query letter with a self-addressed stamped envelope is a must. We cannot guarantee replies to foreign queries via standard mail. No phone calls. We never download attachments to e-mail queries for security reasons, so please copy and paste material into your e-mail."

DH LITERARY, INC.

P.O. Box 805, Nyack NY 10960-0990. E-mail: dhendin@aol.com. **Contact:** David Hendin. Member of AAR. Represents 10 clients. Currently handles: nonfiction books 80%, novels 10%, scholarly books 10%.

- Prior to opening his agency, Mr. Hendin served as president and publisher for Pharos Books/World Almanac, as well as senior VP and COO at sister company United Feature Syndicate.

Represents "We are not accepting new clients. Please do not send queries or submissions."

Terms Agent receives 15% commission on domestic sales. Agent receives 20% commission on foreign sales. Offers written contract, binding for 1 year. Charges for out-of-pocket expenses for overseas postage specifically related to the sale.

THE JONATHAN DOLGER AGENCY

49 E. 96th St., Suite 9B, New York NY 10128. Fax: (212)369-7118. Member of AAR.

Represents nonfiction books, novels. **Considers these nonfiction areas:** biography, history, womens, cultural/social. **Considers these fiction areas:** womens, commercial.

How to Contact Query with SASE. No e-mail queries.

Terms Agent receives 15% commission on domestic sales. Agent receives 25% commission on foreign sales.

Tips "Writers must have been previously published if submitting fiction. We prefer to work with published/established authors, and work with a small number of new/previously unpublished writers."

JANIS A. DONNAUD & ASSOCIATES, INC.

525 Broadway, Second Floor, New York NY 10012. (212)431-2664. Fax: (212)431-2667. E-mail: jdonnaud@aol.com; donnaudassociate@aol.com. **Contact:** Janis A. Donnaud. Member of AAR. Signatory of WGA. Represents 40 clients. 5% of clients are new/unpublished writers. Currently handles: nonfiction books 100%.

- Prior to opening her agency, Ms. Donnaud was vice president and associate publisher of Random House Adult Trade Group.

Represents nonfiction books. **Considers these nonfiction areas:** biography, child, cooking, current affairs, health, humor, psychology, pop, womens, lifestyle. This agency specializes in health, medical, cooking, humor, pop psychology, narrative nonfiction, biography, parenting, and current affairs. We give a lot of service and attention to clients. Does not want to receive "fiction, poetry, mysteries, juvenile books, romances, science fiction, young adult, religious or fantasy."

How to Contact Query with SASE. Submit description of book, 2-3 pages of sample material.Prefers to read materials exclusively. No phone calls. Responds in 1 month to queries. Responds in 1 month to mss. Obtains most new clients through recommendations from others.

Terms Agent receives 15% commission on domestic sales. Agent receives 20% commission on foreign sales. Agent receives 20% commission on film sales. Offers written contract; 1-month notice must be given to terminate contract. Charges clients for messengers, photocopying and purchase of books.

DUNHAM LITERARY, INC.

156 Fifth Ave., Suite 625, New York NY 10010-7002. (212)929-0994. Website: www.dunhamlit.com. **Contact:** Jennie Dunham. Member of AAR. Represents 50 clients. 15% of clients are new/unpublished writers. Currently handles: nonfiction books 25%, novels 25%, juvenile books 50%.

- Prior to opening her agency, Ms. Dunham worked as a literary agent for Russell & Volkening. The Rhoda Weyr Agency is now a division of Dunham Literary, Inc.

Represents nonfiction books, novels, short story collections, juvenile. **Considers these nonfiction areas:** anthropology, biography, ethnic, government, health, history, language, nature, popular culture, psychology, science, womens. **Considers these fiction areas:** ethnic, juvenile, literary, mainstream, picture books, young.

How to Contact Query with SASE. Responds in 1 week to queries. Responds in 2 months to mss. Obtains most new clients through recommendations from others, solicitations.

Terms Agent receives 15% commission on domestic sales. Agent receives 20% commission on foreign sales.

THE LISA EKUS GROUP, LLC

57 North St., Hatfield MA 01038. (413)247-9325. Fax: (413)247-9873. E-mail: LisaEkus@lisaekus.com. Website: www.lisaekus.com. **Contact:** Lisa Ekus-Saffer. Member of AAR.

Represents nonfiction books. **Considers these nonfiction areas:** cooking, occasionally health/well-being and women's issues.

How to Contact Submit a one-page query via e-mail or submit your complete hard copy proposal with title page, proposal contents, concept, bio, marketing, TOC, etc. Include SASE for the return of materials.

Tips "Please do not call. No phone queries."

THE ELAINE P. ENGLISH LITERARY AGENCY

4710 41st St. NW, Suite D, Washington DC 20016. (202)362-5190. Fax: (202)362-5192. E-mail: elaine@elaineenglish.com; kvn.mcadams@yahoo.com. Website: www.elaineenglish.com. **Contact:** Elaine English. Kevin McAdams, Executive V.P., 400 East 11th St., # 7, New York, NY 10009 Member of AAR. Represents 20 clients. 25% of clients are new/unpublished writers. Currently handles: novels 100%.

- Ms. English has been working in publishing for more than 20 years. She is also an attorney specializing in media and publishing law.

Represents novels. **Considers these fiction areas:** historical, multicultural, mystery, romance, single title, historical, contemporary, romantic, suspense, chick lit, erotic, thriller, general women's fiction. The agency is slowly but steadily acquiring in all mentioned areas. Actively seeking women's fiction, including single-title romances. Does not want to receive any science fiction, time travel, children's, or young adult.

How to Contact Prefers e-queries sent to queries@elaineenglish.com. If requested, submit synopsis, first 3 chapters, SASE. Responds in 4-8 weeks to queries; 3 months to requested submissions Obtains most new clients through recommendations from others, conferences, submissions.

Terms Agent receives 15% commission on domestic sales. Agent receives 20% commission on foreign sales. Offers written contract; 30-day notice must be given to terminate contract. Charges only for copying and postage; generally taken from proceeds.

Writers Conferences RWA National Conference; Novelists, Inc.; Malice Domestic; Washington Romance Writers Retreat, among others.

FELICIA ETH LITERARY REPRESENTATION

555 Bryant St., Suite 350, Palo Alto CA 94301-1700. (650)375-1276. Fax: (650)401-8892. E-mail: feliciaeth@aol.com. **Contact:** Felicia Eth. Member of AAR. Represents 25-35 clients. Currently handles: nonfiction books 85%, novels 15% adult.

Represents nonfiction books, novels. **Considers these nonfiction areas:** animals, anthropology, biography, business, child, current affairs, ethnic, government, health, history, nature, popular culture, psychology, science, sociology, true crime, womens. **Considers these fiction areas:** literary, mainstream. This agency specializes in high-quality fiction (preferably mainstream/contemporary) and provocative, intelligent, and thoughtful nonfiction on a wide array of commercial subjects.

How to Contact Query with SASE. Accepts simultaneous submissions. Responds in 3 weeks to queries. Responds in 4-6 weeks to mss.

Terms Agent receives 15% commission on domestic sales. Agent receives 20% commission on foreign sales. Agent receives 20% commission on film sales. Charges clients for photocopying and express mail service.

Writers Conferences "Wide Array - from Squaw Valley to Mills College."

Tips "For nonfiction, established expertise is certainly a plus—as is magazine publication—though not a prerequisite. I am highly dedicated to those projects I represent, but highly selective in what I choose."

MARY EVANS INC.

242 E. Fifth St., New York NY 10003. (212)979-0880. Fax: (212)979-5344. Website: www.maryevansinc.com. Member of AAR.

Member Agents Mary Evans (no unsolicited queries); Devin McIntyre, devin@maryevansinc.com (commericial and literary fiction, narrative nonfiction, pop culture, graphic novels, multicultural, pop science, sports, food).

Represents nonfiction books, novels.

How to Contact Query with SASE. Query with SASE. Query by snail mail. Non-query correspondence can be sent to info(at)maryevansinc.com. Obtains most new clients through recommendations from others, solicitations.

DIANA FINCH LITERARY AGENCY

116 W. 23rd St., Suite 500, New York NY 10011. (646)375-2081. E-mail: diana.finch@verizon.net. **Contact:** Diana Finch. Member of AAR. Represents 40 clients. 20% of clients are new/unpublished writers. Currently handles: nonfiction books 65%, novels 25%, juvenile books 5%, multimedia 5%.

- Prior to opening her agency, Ms. Finch worked at Ellen Levine Literary Agency for 18 years.

Represents nonfiction books, novels, scholarly. **Considers these nonfiction areas:** juvenile, biography, business, child, computers, current affairs, ethnic, government, health, history, how to, humor, memoirs, military, money, music, nature, photography, popular culture, psychology, science, self help, sports, film, translation, true crime, womens. **Considers these fiction areas:** adventure, detective, ethnic, historical, literary, mainstream, thriller, young. Actively seeking narrative nonfiction, popular science, and health topics. "Does not want romance, mysteries, or children's picture books."

How to Contact Query with SASE or via e-mail (no attachments). Accepts simultaneous submissions. Obtains most new clients through recommendations from others.

Terms Agent receives 15% commission on domestic sales. Agent receives 20% commission on foreign sales. Offers written contract. "I charge for photocopying, overseas postage, galleys, and books purchased, and try to recap these costs from earnings received for a client, rather than charging outright."

Tips "Do as much research as you can on agents before you query. Have someone critique your query letter before you send it. It should be only 1 page and describe your book clearly—and why you are writing it—but also demonstrate creativity and a sense of your writing style."

FOX CHASE AGENCY, INC.

701 Lee Road, Suite 102, Chesterbrook Corporate Center, Chesterbrook PA 19087. Member of AAR.

Member Agents A.L. Hart; Jo C. Hart.

Represents nonfiction books, novels.

How to Contact Query with SASE.

JEANNE FREDERICKS LITERARY AGENCY, INC.

221 Benedict Hill Road, New Canaan CT 06840. (203)972-3011. Fax: (203)972-3011. E-mail: jeanne.fredericks@gmail.com. Website: jeannefredericks.com/. **Contact:** Jeanne Fredericks. Member of AAR. Other memberships include Authors Guild. Represents 90 clients. 10% of clients are new/unpublished writers. Currently handles: nonfiction books 100%.

- Prior to opening her agency, Ms. Fredericks was an agent and acting director with the Susan P. Urstadt, Inc. Agency.

Represents nonfiction books. **Considers these nonfiction areas:** animals, autobiography, biography, child guidance, cooking, decorating, finance, foods, gardening, health, history, how-to, interior design, medicine, money, nature, nutrition, parenting, personal improvement, photography, psychology, self-help, sports (not spectator sports), women's issues. This agency specializes in quality adult nonfiction by authorities in their fields. Does not want to receive children's books or fiction.

How to Contact Query first with SASE, then send outline/proposal, 1-2 sample chapters, SASE. Accepts simultaneous submissions. Responds in 3-5 weeks to queries. Responds in 2-4 months to mss. Obtains most new clients through recommendations from others, solicitations, conferences.

Terms Agent receives 15% commission on domestic sales. Agent receives 25% commission on foreign sales with co-agent Offers written contract, binding for 9 months; 2-month notice must be given to terminate contract. Charges client for photocopying of whole proposals and mss, overseas postage, priority mail, express mail services.

Writers Conferences Connecticut Authors and Publishers Association-University Conference; ASJA Writers' Conference; BookExpo America; Garden Writers' Association Annual Symposium; Harvard Medical School CME Course in Publishing.

Tips "Be sure to research competition for your work and be able to justify why there's a need for your book. I enjoy building an author's career, particularly if he/she is professional, hardworking, and courteous. Aside from 17 years of agenting experience, I've had 10 years of editorial experience in adult trade book publishing that enables me to help an author polish a proposal so that it's more appealing to prospective editors. My MBA in marketing also distinguishes me from other agents."

THE FRIEDRICH AGENCY

136 East 57th St., 18th Floor, New York NY 10022. Website: www.friedrichagency.com. **Contact:** Molly Friedrich. Member of AAR. Represents 50+ clients.

- Prior to her current position, Ms. Friedrich was an agent at the Aaron Priest Literary Agency.

Member Agents Molly Friedrich, Founder and Agent (open to queries); Paul Cirone, Foreign Rights Director and Agent(open to queries); Lucy Carson, assistant.

Represents full-length fiction and nonfiction.

How to Contact Query with SASE by mail, or e-mail.

GELFMAN SCHNEIDER LITERARY AGENTS, INC.

250 W. 57th St., Suite 2122, New York NY 10107. (212)245-1993. Fax: (212)245-8678. E-mail: mail@gelfmanschneider.com. **Contact:** Jane Gelfman, Deborah Schneider. Member of AAR. Represents 300+ clients. 10% of clients are new/unpublished writers.

Represents nonfiction books, novels. **Considers these fiction areas:** literary, mainstream, mystery, womens. Does not want to receive romance, science fiction, westerns, or children's books.

How to Contact Query with SASE. Send queries via snail mail only. Responds in 1 month to queries. Responds in 2 months to mss.

Terms Agent receives 15% commission on domestic sales. Agent receives 20% commission on foreign sales. Agent receives 15% commission on film sales. Offers written contract. Charges clients for photocopying and messengers/couriers.

GOODMAN ASSOCIATES

500 West End Ave., New York NY 10024-4317. (212)873-4806. Member of AAR.

Represents Accepting new clients by recommendation only.

REECE HALSEY NORTH/PARIS/NEW YORK

98 Main St., #704, Tiburon CA 94920. Fax: (415)789-9177. E-mail: info@reecehalseynorth.com. Website: www.reecehalseynorth.com. **Contact:** Kimberley Cameron. Member of AAR. 30% of clients are new/unpublished writers. Currently handles: other 50% fiction, 50% nonfiction.

- The Reece Halsey Agency has had an illustrious client list of established writers, including the estate of Aldous Huxley, and has represented Upton Sinclair, William Faulkner, and Henry Miller.

Member Agents Kimberley Cameron, Elizabeth Evans; April Eberhardt, Amy Burkhardt.

Represents nonfiction and fiction. **Considers these nonfiction areas:** biography, current affairs, history, language, popular culture, science, true crime, women's issues, women's studies. **Considers these fiction areas:** contemporary, adventure, detective, ethnic, family, historical, horror, literary, mainstream, mystery, science, thriller, women's fiction. We are looking for a unique and heartfelt voice that conveys a universal truth.

How to Contact Query via e-mail with first 50 pages of novel. Responds in 3-6 weeks to queries. Responds in 1 month to mss. Obtains most new clients through recommendations from others, solicitations.

Terms Agent receives 15% commission on domestic sales. Agent receives 10% commission on film sales. Offers written contract, binding for 1 year.

Writers Conferences Maui Writers Conference; Aspen Summer Words Literary Festival; Willamette Writers Conference, numerous others.

Tips "Please send a polite, well-written query to info@reecehalseynorth.com."

JOHN HAWKINS & ASSOCIATES, INC.

71 W. 23rd St., Suite 1600, New York NY 10010. (212)807-7040. Fax: (212)807-9555. E-mail: jha@jhalit.com. Website: www.jhalit.com. **Contact:** Moses Cardona (moses@jhalit.com). Member of AAR. Represents over 100 clients. 5-10% of clients are new/unpublished writers. Currently handles: nonfiction books 40%, novels 40%, juvenile books 20%.

Member Agents Moses Cardona.

Represents nonfiction books, novels, young adult. **Considers these nonfiction areas:** agriculture horticulture, americana, interior, young, anthropology, art, biography, business, current affairs, education, ethnic, gardening, gay, government, health, history, how to, language, memoirs, money, multicultural, nature, philosophy, popular culture, psychology, recreation, science, self help, sex, sociology, software, film, travel, true crime, music, creative nonfiction. **Considers these fiction areas:** glitz, psychic, adventure, detective, ethnic, experimental, family, feminist, gay, gothic, hi lo, historical, literary, mainstream, military, multicultural, multimedia, mystery, religious, short, sports, thriller, translation, western, young, womens.

How to Contact Submit query, proposal package, outline, SASE. Accepts simultaneous submissions. Responds in 1 month to queries. Obtains most new clients through recommendations from others.

Terms Agent receives 15% commission on domestic sales. Agent receives 20% commission on foreign sales. Charges clients for photocopying.

HOPKINS LITERARY ASSOCIATES

2117 Buffalo Rd., Suite 327, Rochester NY 14624-1507. (585)352-6268. **Contact:** Pam Hopkins. Member of AAR. Other memberships include RWA. Represents 30 clients. 5% of clients are new/unpublished writers. Currently handles: novels 100%.

Represents novels. **Considers these fiction areas:** romance, historical, contemporary, category, womens. This agency specializes in women's fiction, particularly historical, contemporary, and category romance, as well as mainstream work.

How to Contact Submit outline, 3 sample chapters. Accepts simultaneous submissions. Responds in 2 weeks to queries. Responds in 1 month to mss. Obtains most new clients through recommendations from others, solicitations, conferences.

Terms Agent receives 15% commission on domestic sales. Agent receives 20% commission on foreign sales. No written contract.

Writers Conferences RWA National Conference.

INTERNATIONAL CREATIVE MANAGEMENT

825 Eighth Ave., New York NY 10019. (212)556-5600. Website: www.icmtalent.com. **Contact:** Literary Department. Member of AAR. Signatory of WGA.

Member Agents Lisa Bankoff, lbankoff@icmtalent.com (fiction interests include: literary fiction, family saga, historical fiction, offbeat/quirky; nonfiction interests include: history, biography, memoirs, narrative); Patrick Herold, pherold@icmtalent.com; Jennifer Joel, jjoel@icmtalent.com (fiction interests include: literary fiction, commercial fiction, historical fiction, thrillers/suspense; nonfiction interests include: history, sports, art, adventure/true story, pop culture); Esther Newberg; Sloan Harris; Amanda Binky Urban; Heather Schroder;

Kristine Dahl; Andrea Barzvi, abarzvi@icmtalent.com (fiction interests include: chick lit, commercial fiction, women's fiction, thrillers/suspense; nonfiction interests include: sports, celebrity, self-help, dating/relationships, women's issues, pop culture, health and fitness); Tina Dubois Wexler, twexler@icmtalent.com (literary fiction, chick lit, young adult, middle grade, memoir, narrative nonfiction); Kate Lee, klee@icmtalent.com (mystery, commercial fiction, short stories, memoir, dating/relationships, pop culture, humor, journalism).

Represents nonfiction books, novels. "We do not accept unsolicited submissions."

How to Contact Query with SASE. Send queries via snail mail and include an SASE. Target a specific agent. Obtains most new clients through recommendations from others.

Terms Agent receives 15% commission on domestic sales. Agent receives 20% commission on foreign sales.

HARVEY KLINGER, INC.

300 W. 55th St., Suite 11V, New York NY 10019. (212)581-7068. E-mail: queries@harveyklinger.com. Website: www.harveyklinger.com. **Contact:** Harvey Klinger. Member of AAR. Represents 100 clients. 25% of clients are new/unpublished writers. Currently handles: nonfiction books 50%, novels 50%.

Member Agents David Dunton (popular culture, music-related books, literary fiction, young adult, fiction, and memoirs); Sara Crowe (children's and young adult authors, adult fiction and nonfiction, foreign rights sales); Andrea Somberg (literary fiction, commercial fiction, romance, sci-fi/fantasy, mysteries/thrillers, young adult, middle grade, quality narrative nonfiction, popular culture, how-to, self-help, humor, interior design, cookbooks, health/fitness).

Represents nonfiction books, novels. **Considers these nonfiction areas:** biography, cooking, health, psychology, science, self help, spirituality, sports, true crime, womens. **Considers these fiction areas:** glitz, adventure, detective, family, literary, mainstream, mystery, thriller. This agency specializes in big, mainstream, contemporary fiction and nonfiction.

How to Contact Query with SASE. No phone or fax queries. Don't send unsolicited manuscripts or e-mail attachments. Responds in 2 months to queries and mss. Obtains most new clients through recommendations from others.

Terms Agent receives 15% commission on domestic sales. Agent receives 25% commission on foreign sales. Offers written contract. Charges for photocopying mss and overseas postage for mss.

LINDA KONNER LITERARY AGENCY

10 W. 15th St., Suite 1918, New York NY 10011-6829. (212)691-3419. E-mail: ldkonner@cs.com. **Contact:** Linda Konner. Member of AAR. Signatory of WGA. Other memberships include ASJA. Represents 85 clients. 30-35% of clients are new/unpublished writers. Currently handles: nonfiction books 100%.

Represents nonfiction books. **Considers these nonfiction areas:** biography (celebrity only), gay, health, diet/nutrition/fitness, how to, money, personal finance, popular culture, psychology, pop psychology, self help, women's issues; African American and Latino issues; business; parenting; relationships. This agency specializes in health, self-help, and how-to books. Authors/co-authors must be top experts in their field with a substantial media platform.

How to Contact Query with SASE, synopsis, author bio, sufficient return postage. Prefers to read materials exclusively for 2 weeks. Accepts simultaneous submissions. Obtains most new clients through recommendations from others, occasional solicitation among established authors/journalists.

Terms Agent receives 15% commission on domestic sales. Agent receives 25% commission on foreign sales. Offers written contract. Charges one-time fee for domestic expenses; additional expenses may be incurred for foreign sales.

Writers Conferences ASJA Writers Conference, Harvard Medical School's "Publishing Books, Memoirs, and Other Creative Nonfiction" Annual Conference.

MICHAEL LARSEN/ELIZABETH POMADA, LITERARY AGENTS

1029 Jones St., San Francisco CA 94109-5023. (415)673-0939. E-mail: larsenpoma@aol.com. Website: www.larsen-pomada.com. **Contact:** Mike Larsen, Elizabeth Pomada. Member of AAR. Other memberships include Authors Guild, ASJA, PEN, WNBA, California Writers Club, National Speakers Association. Represents 100 clients. 40-45% of clients are new/unpublished writers. Currently handles: nonfiction books 70%, novels 30%.

- Prior to opening their agency, Mr. Larsen and Ms. Pomada were promotion executives for major publishing houses. Mr. Larsen worked for Morrow, Bantam and Pyramid (now part of Berkley); Ms. Pomada worked at Holt, David McKay and The Dial Press. Mr. Larsen is the author of the third editions of *How to Write a Book Proposal* and *How to Get a Literary Agent* as well as the coauthor of *Guerilla Marketing for Writers: 100 Weapons for Selling Your Work*, which will be republished in September 2009.

Member Agents Michael Larsen (nonfiction).

Represents **Considers these nonfiction areas:** anthropology, art, biography, business, current affairs, ethnic, film, foods, gay, government, health, history, humor, memoirs, money, music, nature, , popular culture, psychology, science, sociology, sports, travel, true crime, futurism. **Considers these fiction areas:** contemporary, glitz, adventure, detective, ethnic, experimental, family, fantasy, feminist, gay, historical, humor, literary, mainstream, mystery, religious, romance, contemporary, gothic, historical, chick lit. We have diverse tastes. We look for fresh voices and new ideas. We handle literary, commercial and genre fiction, and the full

range of nonfiction books. Actively seeking commercial, genre and literary fiction. Does not want to receive children's books, plays, short stories, screenplays, pornography, poetry or stories of abuse.
How to Contact Query with SASE. Responds in 8 weeks to pages or submissions.
Terms Agent receives 15% commission on domestic sales. Agent receives 20% (30% for Asia) commission on foreign sales. May charge for printing, postage for multiple submissions, foreign mail, foreign phone calls, galleys, books, legal fees.
Writers Conferences This agency organizes the annual San Francisco Writers' Conference (www.sfwriters.org).
Tips "We love helping writers get the rewards and recognition they deserve. If you can write books that meet the needs of the marketplace and you can promote your books, now is the best time ever to be a writer. We must find new writers to make a living, so we are very eager to hear from new writers whose work will interest large houses, and nonfiction writers who can promote their books. For a list of recent sales, helpful info, and three ways to make yourself irresistible to any publisher, please visit our Web site."

LEVINE GREENBERG LITERARY AGENCY, INC.

307 Seventh Ave., Suite 2407, New York NY 10001. (212)337-0934. Fax: (212)337-0948. Website: www.levinegreenberg.com. Member of AAR. Represents 250 clients. 33%% of clients are new/unpublished writers. Currently handles: nonfiction books 70%, novels 30%.

- Prior to opening his agency, Mr. Levine served as vice president of the Bank Street College of Education.

Member Agents James Levine, Daniel Greenberg, Stephanie Kip Rostan, Lindsay Edgecombe, Danielle Svetcov, Elizabeth Fisher, Victoria Skurnick.
Represents nonfiction books, novels. **Considers these nonfiction areas:** New Age, animals, art, biography, business, child, computers, cooking, gardening, gay, health, money, nature, religion, science, self help, sociology, spirituality, sports, womens. **Considers these fiction areas:** literary, mainstream, mystery, thriller, psychological, womens. This agency specializes in business, psychology, parenting, health/medicine, narrative nonfiction, spirituality, religion, women's issues, and commercial fiction.
How to Contact See Web site for full submission procedure. Obtains most new clients through recommendations from others.
Terms Agent receives 15% commission on domestic sales. Agent receives 20% commission on foreign sales. Offers written contract. Charges clients for out-of-pocket expenses—telephone, fax, postage, photocopying—directly connected to the project.
Writers Conferences ASJA Writers' Conference.
Tips "We focus on editorial development, business representation, and publicity and marketing strategy."

WENDY LIPKIND AGENCY

120 E. 81st St., New York NY 10028. (212)628-9653. Fax: (212)585-1306. E-mail: lipkindag@aol.com. **Contact:** Wendy Lipkind. Member of AAR. Represents 50 clients. Currently handles: nonfiction books 100%.
Represents nonfiction books. **Considers these nonfiction areas:** biography, current affairs, health, history, science, womens, social history; narrative nonfiction. This agency specializes in adult nonfiction.
How to Contact Prefers to read materials exclusively. Accepts e-mail queries only (no attachments). Obtains most new clients through recommendations from others.
Terms Agent receives 15% commission on domestic sales. Agent receives 20% commission on foreign sales. Sometimes offers written contract. Charges clients for foreign postage, messenger service, photocopying, transatlantic calls, faxes.
Tips Send intelligent query letter first. Let me know if you've submitted to other agents.

JULIA LORD LITERARY MANAGEMENT

38 W. Ninth St., #4, New York NY 10011. (212)995-2333. Fax: (212)995-2332. E-mail: julialordliterary@nyc.rr.com. Member of AAR.
Member Agents Julia Lord, owner.
Represents Considers these nonfiction areas: biography, history, humor, nature, science, sports, travel, and adventure, African-American; lifestyle; narrative nonfiction. **Considers these fiction areas:** adventure, historical, literary, mainstream.
How to Contact Query with SASE or via e-mail. Obtains most new clients through recommendations from others, solicitations.

MANUS & ASSOCIATES LITERARY AGENCY, INC.

425 Sherman Ave., Suite 200, Palo Alto CA 94306. (650)470-5151. Fax: (650)470-5159. E-mail: manuslit@manuslit.com. Website: www.manuslit.com. **Contact:** Jillian Manus, Jandy Nelson, Penny Nelson. Member of AAR. Represents 75 clients. 30% of clients are new/unpublished writers. Currently handles: nonfiction books 70%, novels 30%.

- Prior to becoming an agent, Ms. Manus was associate publisher of two national magazines and director of development at Warner Bros. and Universal Studios; she has been a literary agent for 20 years.

Member Agents Jandy Nelson, jandy@manuslit.com (self-help, health, memoirs, narrative nonfiction, women's fiction, literary fiction, multicultural fiction, thrillers); Jillian Manus, jillian@manuslit.com (political, memoirs, self-help, history, sports, women's issues, Latin fiction and nonfiction, thrillers); Penny Nelson, penny@manuslit.com (memoirs, self-help, sports, nonfiction); Dena Fischer (literary fiction, mainstream/commercial fiction, chick lit, women's fiction, historical fiction, ethnic/cultural fiction, narrative nonfiction, parenting, relationships, pop culture, health, sociology, psychology).

Represents nonfiction books, novels. **Considers these nonfiction areas:** biography, business, child, current affairs, ethnic, health, how to, memoirs, money, nature, popular culture, psychology, science, self help, womens, Gen X and Gen Y issues; creative nonfiction. **Considers these fiction areas:** literary, mainstream, multicultural, mystery, thriller, womens, quirky/edgy fiction. "Our agency is unique in the way that we not only sell the material, but we edit, develop concepts, and participate in the marketing effort. We specialize in large, conceptual fiction and nonfiction, and always value a project that can be sold in the TV/feature film market." Actively seeking high-concept thrillers, commercial literary fiction, women's fiction, celebrity biographies, memoirs, multicultural fiction, popular health, women's empowerment and mysteries. No horror, romance, science fiction, fantasy, Western, young adult, children's, poetry, cookbooks or magazine articles.

How to Contact Query with SASE. If requested, submit outline, 2-3 sample chapters. All queries should be sent to the California office. Accepts simultaneous submissions. Responds in 3 months to queries. Responds in 3 months to mss. Obtains most new clients through recommendations from others, solicitations, conferences.

Terms Agent receives 15% commission on domestic sales. Agent receives 20-25% commission on foreign sales. Offers written contract, binding for 2 years; 60-day notice must be given to terminate contract. Charges for photocopying and postage/UPS.

Writers Conferences Maui Writers' Conference; San Diego State University Writers' Conference; Willamette Writers' Conference; BookExpo America; MEGA Book Marketing University.

Tips "Research agents using a variety of sources."

THE DENISE MARCIL LITERARY AGENCY, INC.

156 Fifth Ave., Suite 625, New York NY 10010. (212)337-3402. Fax: (212)727-2688. Website: www.DeniseMarcilAgency.com. **Contact:** Denise Marcil, Anne Marie O'Farrell. Member of AAR.

- Prior to opening her agency, Ms. Marcil served as an editorial assistant with Avon Books and as an assistant editor with Simon & Schuster.

Member Agents Denise Marcil (women's commercial fiction, thrillers, suspense, popular reference, how-to, self-help, health, business, and parenting.

Represents *This agency is currently not taking on new authors.*

Terms Agent receives 15% commission on domestic sales. Agent receives 20% commission on foreign sales. Offers written contract, binding for 2 years. Charges $100/year for postage, photocopying, long-distance calls, etc.

THE EVAN MARSHALL AGENCY

Six Tristam Place, Pine Brook NJ 07058-9445. (973)882-1122. Fax: (973)882-3099. E-mail: evanmarshall@optonline.net. **Contact:** Evan Marshall. Member of AAR. Other memberships include MWA, Sisters in Crime. Currently handles: novels 100%.

Represents novels. **Considers these fiction areas:** adventure, erotica, ethnic, historical, horror, humor, literary, mainstream, mystery, religious, romance, contemporary, gothic, historical, regency, science, western.

How to Contact Query first with SASE; do not enclose material. No e-mail queries. Responds in 1 week to queries. Responds in 3 months to mss. Obtains most new clients through recommendations from others.

Terms Agent receives 15% commission on domestic sales. Agent receives 20% commission on foreign sales. Offers written contract.

MARTIN LITERARY MANAGEMENT

17328 Ventura Blvd., Suite 138, Encino (LA) CA 91316. E-mail: sharlene@martinliterarymanagement.com. Website: www.MartinLiteraryManagement.com. **Contact:** Sharlene Martin. Ginny's address: 2511 West Schaumburg Road, No. 217, Schaumburg, IL 60184 (312) 480-5754 Member of AAR. 75% of clients are new/unpublished writers.

- Prior to becoming an agent, Ms. Martin worked in film/TV production and acquisitions.

Member Agents Sharlene Martin (nonfiction); Ginny Weissman (writers with a developed platform and a book that fits the Mind, Body, Spirit genre, including health, spirituality, religion, diet, exercise, psychology, relationships, and metaphysics).

Represents nonfiction books. **Considers these nonfiction areas:** biography, business, child, current affairs, health, history, how to, humor, memoirs, popular culture, psychology, religion, self help, true crime, womens. This agency has strong ties to film/TV. Actively seeking nonfiction that is highly commercial and that can be adapted to film. "We are being inundated with queries and submissions that are wrongfully being submitted to us, which only results in more frustrated for the writers. Under no circumstances do we accept fiction, screenplays, children's books, or poetry."

How to Contact Query via e-mail with MS Word only. No attachments on queries; place letter in body of e-mail. Accepts simultaneous submissions. Responds in 1 week to queries. Responds in 3-4 weeks to mss. Obtains most new clients through recommendations from others.

Terms Agent receives 15% commission on domestic sales. Agent receives 25% commission on foreign sales.

Offers written contract, binding for 1 year; 1-month notice must be given to terminate contract. Charges author for postage and copying if material is not sent electronically. 99 percent of materials are sent electronically to minimize charges to author for postage and copying.
Tips "Have a strong platform for nonfiction. Please don't call. I welcome e-mail. I'm very responsive when I'm interested in a query and work hard to get my clients materials in the best possible shape before submissions. Do your homework prior to submission and only submit your best efforts. Please review our Web site carefully to make sure we're a good match for your work."

MARGRET MCBRIDE LITERARY AGENCY

7744 Fay Ave., Suite 201, La Jolla CA 92037. (858)454-1550. Fax: (858)454-2156. E-mail: staff@mcbridelit.com. Website: www.mcbrideliterary.com. **Contact:** Michael Daley, submissions manager. Member of AAR. Other memberships include Authors Guild. Represents 55 clients.

- Prior to opening her agency, Ms. McBride worked at Random House, Ballantine Books, and Warner Books.

Represents nonfiction books, novels. **Considers these nonfiction areas:** biography, business, cooking, current affairs, ethnic, government, health, history, how to, money, music, popular culture, psychology, science, self help, sociology, womens, style. **Considers these fiction areas:** adventure, detective, ethnic, historical, humor, literary, mainstream, mystery, thriller, western. This agency specializes in mainstream fiction and nonfiction. Does not want to receive screenplays, romance, poetry, or children's/young adult.
How to Contact Query with synopsis, bio, SASE. No e-mail or fax queries. Accepts simultaneous submissions. Responds in 4-6 weeks to queries. Responds in 6-8 weeks to mss.
Terms Agent receives 15% commission on domestic sales. Agent receives 25% commission on foreign sales. Charges for overnight delivery and photocopying.

THE MCCARTHY AGENCY, LLC

7 Allen St., Rumson NJ 07660. Phone/Fax: (732)741-3065. E-mail: mccarthylit@aol.com. **Contact:** Shawna McCarthy. Member of AAR. Currently handles: nonfiction books 25%, novels 75%.
Member Agents Shawna McCarthy (New Jersey address); Nahvae Frost (Brooklyn address).
Represents nonfiction books, novels. **Considers these nonfiction areas:** biography, history, philosophy, science. **Considers these fiction areas:** fantasy, juvenile, mystery, romance, science, womens.
How to Contact Query via e-mail. Accepts simultaneous submissions.

MENDEL MEDIA GROUP, LLC

115 West 30th St., Suite 800, New York NY 10001. (646)239-9896. Fax: (212)685-4717. E-mail: scott@mendelmedia.com. Website: www.mendelmedia.com. Member of AAR. Represents 40-60 clients.

- Prior to becoming an agent, Mr. Mendel was an academic. "I taught American literature, Yiddish, Jewish studies, and literary theory at the University of Chicago and the University of Illinois at Chicago while working on my PhD in English. I also worked as a freelance technical writer and as the managing editor of a healthcare magazine. In 1998, I began working for the late Jane Jordan Browne, a long-time agent in the book publishing world."

Represents nonfiction books, novels, scholarly, with potential for broad/popular appeal. **Considers these nonfiction areas:** americana, animals, anthropology, art, biography, business, child, cooking, current affairs, education, ethnic, gardening, gay, government, health, history, how to, humor, language, memoirs, military, money, multicultural, music, nature, philosophy, popular culture, psychology, recreation, regional, religion, science, self help, sex, sociology, software, spirituality, sports, true crime, womens, Jewish topics; creative nonfiction. **Considers these fiction areas:** contemporary, glitz, adventure, detective, erotica, ethnic, feminist, gay, historical, humor, juvenile, literary, mainstream, mystery, picture books, religious, romance, sports, thriller, young, Jewish fiction. "I am interested in major works of history, current affairs, biography, business, politics, economics, science, major memoirs, narrative nonfiction, and other sorts of general nonfiction." Actively seeking new, major or definitive work on a subject of broad interest, or a controversial, but authoritative, new book on a subject that affects many people's lives." I also represent more light-hearted nonfiction projects, such as gift or novelty books, when they suit the market particularly well." Does not want "queries about projects written years ago that were unsuccessfully shopped to a long list of trade publishers by either the author or another agent. I am specifically not interested in reading short, category romances (regency, time travel, paranormal, etc.), horror novels, supernatural stories, poetry, original plays, or film scripts."
How to Contact Query with SASE. Do not e-mail or fax queries. For nonfiction, include a complete, fully-edited book proposal with sample chapters. For fiction, include a complete synopsis and no more than 20 pages of sample text. Responds in 2 weeks to queries. Responds in 4-6 weeks to mss. Obtains most new clients through recommendations from others.
Terms Agent receives 15% commission on domestic sales. Agent receives 20% commission on foreign sales. Charges clients for ms duplication, expedited delivery services (when necessary), any overseas shipping, telephone calls/faxes necessary for marketing the author's foreign rights.
Writers Conferences BookExpo America; Frankfurt Book Fair; London Book Fair; RWA National Conference; Modern Language Association Convention; Jerusalem Book Fair.

Tips "While I am not interested in being flattered by a prospective client, it does matter to me that she knows why she is writing to me in the first place. Is one of my clients a colleague of hers? Has she read a book by one of my clients that led her to believe I might be interested in her work? Authors of descriptive nonfiction should have real credentials and expertise in their subject areas, either as academics, journalists, or policy experts, and authors of prescriptive nonfiction should have legitimate expertise and considerable experience communicating their ideas in seminars and workshops, in a successful business, through the media, etc."

MENZA-BARRON AGENCY

511 Avenue of the Americas, #51, New York NY 10011. (212)889-6850. **Contact:** Claudia Menza, Manie Barron. Member of AAR. Represents 100 clients. 50% of clients are new/unpublished writers.

Represents nonfiction books, novels, photographic books, especially interested in African-American material. **Considers these nonfiction areas:** current affairs, education, ethnic, especially African-American, health, history, multicultural, music, photography, psychology, film. This agency specializes editorial assistance and African-American fiction and nonfiction.

How to Contact Query with SASE. Responds in 2-4 weeks to queries. Responds in 2-4 months to mss.

Terms Agent receives 15% commission on domestic sales. Agent receives 20% (if co-agent is used) commission on foreign sales. Agent receives 20% commission on film sales. Offers written contract.

JEAN V. NAGGAR LITERARY AGENCY, INC.

216 E. 75th St., Suite 1E, New York NY 10021. (212)794-1082. E-mail: jvnla@jvnla.com. Website: www.jvnla.com. **Contact:** Jean Naggar. Member of AAR. Other memberships include PEN, Women's Media Group, Women's Forum. Represents 80 clients. 20% of clients are new/unpublished writers. Currently handles: nonfiction books 35%, novels 45%, juvenile books 15%, scholarly books 5%.

- Ms. Naggar has served as president of AAR.

Member Agents Jean Naggar (mainstream fiction, nonfiction); Jennifer Weltz, director (subsidiary rights, children's books); Alice Tasman, senior agent (commercial and literary fiction, thrillers, narrative nonfiction); Jessica Regel, agent (young adult fiction and nonfiction).

Represents nonfiction books, novels. **Considers these nonfiction areas:** juvenile, New Age, biography, child, current affairs, government, health, history, memoirs, psychology, religion, self help, sociology, travel, womens. **Considers these fiction areas:** psychic, adventure, detective, ethnic, family, feminist, historical, literary, mainstream, mystery, thriller. This agency specializes in mainstream fiction and nonfiction and literary fiction with commercial potential.

How to Contact Query via e-mail. Prefers to read materials exclusively. No fax queries. Responds in 1 day to queries. Responds in 2 months to mss. Obtains most new clients through recommendations from others.

Terms Agent receives 15% commission on domestic sales. Agent receives 20% commission on foreign sales. Offers written contract. Charges for overseas mailing, messenger services, book purchases, long-distance telephone, photocopying—all deductible from royalties received.

Writers Conferences Willamette Writers Conference; Pacific Northwest Writers Conference; Bread Loaf Writers Conference; Marymount Manhattan Writers Conference; SEAK Medical & Legal Fiction Writing Conference.

Tips "Use a professional presentation. Because of the avalanche of unsolicited queries that flood the agency every week, we have had to modify our policy. We will now only guarantee to read and respond to queries from writers who come recommended by someone we know. Our areas are general fiction and nonfiction—no children's books by unpublished writers, no multimedia, no screenplays, no formula fiction, and no mysteries by unpublished writers. We recommend patience and fortitude: the courage to be true to your own vision, the fortitude to finish a novel and polish it again and again before sending it out, and the patience to accept rejection gracefully and wait for the stars to align themselves appropriately for success."

SUSAN ANN PROTTER, LITERARY AGENT

320 Central Park West, Suite 12E, New York NY 10025. Website: SusanAnnProtter.com. **Contact:** Susan Protter. Member of AAR. Other memberships include Authors Guild.

- Prior to opening her agency, Ms. Protter was associate director of subsidiary rights at Harper & Row Publishers.

Represents Writers must have a book-length project or ms that is ready to sell. Actively seeking for a limited number of quality new clients writing mysteries, health, science and medical. Nonfiction must be by authors with a platform and be new and original concepts by established professionals. Does not want westerns, romance, children's books, young adult novels, screenplays, plays, poetry, Star Wars, or Star Trek.

How to Contact Query by snail mail are preferable; include SASE.

Terms Charges 15% commission on all sales.

ANN RITTENBERG LITERARY AGENCY, INC.

30 Bond St., New York NY 10012. (212)684-6936. Fax: (212)684-6929. Website: www.rittlit.com. **Contact:** Ann Rittenberg, president and Penn Whaling. Member of AAR. Currently handles: nonfiction books 50%, novels 50%.

Represents nonfiction books, novels. **Considers these nonfiction areas:** biography, history, social/cultural, memoirs, womens. **Considers these fiction areas:** literary. This agent specializes in literary fiction and literary

nonfiction. Does not want to receive Screenplays, genre fiction, Poetry, Self-help.
How to Contact Query with SASE. Submit outline, 3 sample chapters, SASE.Query via snail mail *only*. Accepts simultaneous submissions. Responds in 6 weeks to queries. Responds in 2 months to mss. Obtains most new clients through referrals from established writers and editors.
Terms Agent receives 15% commission on domestic sales. Agent receives 20% commission on foreign sales. Offers written contract. This agency charges clients for photocopying only.

RLR ASSOCIATES, LTD.

Literary Department, 7 W. 51st St., New York NY 10019. (212)541-8641. Fax: (212)262-7084. E-mail: sgould@rlrassociates.net. Website: www.rlrliterary.net. **Contact:** Scott Gould. Member of AAR. Represents 50 clients. 25% of clients are new/unpublished writers. Currently handles: nonfiction books 70%, novels 25%, story collections 5%.
Represents nonfiction books, novels, short story collections, scholarly. **Considers these nonfiction areas:** interior, animals, anthropology, art, biography, business, child, cooking, current affairs, education, ethnic, gay, government, health, history, humor, language, memoirs, money, multicultural, music, nature, photography, popular culture, psychology, religion, science, self help, sociology, sports, translation, travel, true crime, womens. **Considers these fiction areas:** adventure, comic, detective, ethnic, experimental, family, feminist, gay, historical, horror, humor, literary, mainstream, multicultural, mystery, sports, thriller. "We provide a lot of editorial assistance to our clients and have connections." Actively seeking fiction, current affairs, history, art, popular culture, health and business. Does not want to receive screenplays.
How to Contact Query by either e-mail or mail. Accepts simultaneous submissions. Responds in 4-8 weeks to queries. Obtains most new clients through recommendations from others.
Terms Agent receives 15% commission on domestic sales. Agent receives 20% commission on foreign sales. Offers written contract.
Tips "Please check out our Web site for more details on our agency."

B.J. ROBBINS LITERARY AGENCY

5130 Bellaire Ave., North Hollywood CA 91607-2908. (818)760-6602. E-mail: robbinsliterary@aol.com. **Contact:** (Ms.) B.J. Robbins. Member of AAR. Represents 40 clients. 50% of clients are new/unpublished writers. Currently handles: nonfiction books 50%, novels 50%.
Represents nonfiction books, novels. **Considers these nonfiction areas:** biography, current affairs, ethnic, health, how-to, humor, memoirs, music, popular culture, psychology, self help, sociology, sports, film, travel, true crime, womens. **Considers these fiction areas:** detective, ethnic, literary, mainstream, mystery, sports, thriller.
How to Contact Query with SASE. Submit outline/proposal, 3 sample chapters, SASE.Accepts e-mail queries (no attachments). Accepts simultaneous submissions. Responds in 2-6 weeks to queries. Responds in 6-8 weeks to mss. Obtains most new clients through conferences, referrals.
Terms Agent receives 15% commission on domestic sales. Agent receives 20% commission on foreign sales. Offers written contract; 3-month notice must be given to terminate contract. This agency charges clients for postage and photocopying (only after sale of ms).
Writers Conferences Squaw Valley Writers Workshop; San Diego State University Writers' Conference.

THE ROSENBERG GROUP

23 Lincoln Ave., Marblehead MA 01945. (781)990-1341. Fax: (781)990-1344. Website: www.rosenberggroup.com. **Contact:** Barbara Collins Rosenberg. Member of AAR. Other memberships include recognized agent of the RWA. Represents 25 clients. 15% of clients are new/unpublished writers. Currently handles: nonfiction books 30%, novels 30%, scholarly books 10%, other 30% college textbooks.

- Prior to becoming an agent, Ms. Rosenberg was a senior editor for Harcourt.

Represents nonfiction books, novels, textbooks, college textbooks only. **Considers these nonfiction areas:** current affairs, popular culture, psychology, sports, womens, women's health; food/wine/beverages. **Considers these fiction areas:** romance, womens. Ms. Rosenberg is well-versed in the romance market (both category and single title). She is a frequent speaker at romance conferences. Actively seeking romance category or single title in contemporary romantic suspense, and the historical subgenres. Does not want to receive inspirational or spiritual romances.
How to Contact Query with SASE. No e-mail or fax queries; will not respond. Responds in 2 weeks to queries. Responds in 4-6 weeks to mss. Obtains most new clients through recommendations from others, solicitations, conferences.
Terms Agent receives 15% commission on domestic sales. Agent receives 15% commission on foreign sales. Offers written contract; 1-month notice must be given to terminate contract. Charges maximum of $350/year for postage and photocopying.
Writers Conferences RWA National Conference; BookExpo America.

THE SAGALYN AGENCY

4922 Fairmont Ave., Suite 200, Bethesda MD 20814. (301)718-6440. Fax: (301)718-6444. E-mail: query@sagalyn.com. Website: www.sagalyn.com. Member of AAR. Currently handles: nonfiction books 85%, novels 5%, scholarly books 10%.

Member Agents Raphael Sagalyn; Bridget Wagner, Shannon O'Neill.

Represents nonfiction books. **Considers these nonfiction areas:** biography, business, history, memoirs, popular culture, religion, science, journalism. Does not want to receive stage plays, screenplays, poetry, science fiction, fantasy, romance, children's books or young adult books.

How to Contact Please send e-mail queries only (no attachments). Include 1 of these words in the subject line: query, submission, inquiry.

Tips "We receive 1,000-1,200 queries a year, which in turn lead to 2 or 3 new clients. Query via e-mail only. See our Web site for sales information and recent projects."

VICTORIA SANDERS & ASSOCIATES

241 Avenue of the Americas, Suite 11 H, New York NY 10014. (212)633-8811. Fax: (212)633-0525. E-mail: queriesvsa@hotmail.com. Website: www.victoriasanders.com. **Contact:** Victoria Sanders, Diane Dickensheid. Member of AAR. Signatory of WGA. Represents 135 clients. 25% of clients are new/unpublished writers. Currently handles: nonfiction books 30%, novels 70%.

Represents nonfiction books, novels. **Considers these nonfiction areas:** biography, current affairs, ethnic, gay, government, history, humor, language, music, popular culture, psychology, film, translation, womens. **Considers these fiction areas:** contemporary, adventure, ethnic, family, feminist, gay, literary, thriller.

How to Contact Query by e-mail only.

Terms Agent receives 15% commission on domestic sales. Agent receives 20% commission on foreign sales. Offers written contract. Charges for photocopying, messenger, express mail. If in excess of $100, client approval is required.

Tips "Limit query to letter (no calls) and give it your best shot. A good query is going to get a good response."

SUSAN SCHULMAN LITERARY AGENCY

454 West 44th St., New York NY 10036. (212)713-1633. Fax: (212)581-8830. E-mail: queries@schulmanagency.com. Website: www.schulmanagency.com. **Contact:** Susan Schulman. Member of AAR. Signatory of WGA. Other memberships include Dramatists Guild. 10% of clients are new/unpublished writers. Currently handles: nonfiction books 50%, novels 25%, juvenile books 15%, stage plays 10%.

Member Agents Linda Kiss, director of foreign rights; Katherine Stones, theater; Emily Uhry, submissions editor.

Represents Considers these nonfiction areas: anthropology, biography, business, child, cooking, current affairs, education, ethnic, gay, government, health, history, how to, language, memoirs, money, music, nature, popular culture, psychology, religion, self help, sociology, sports, true crime, womens. **Considers these fiction areas:** adventure, detective, feminist, historical, humor, juvenile, literary, mainstream, mystery, picture books, religious, young, womens. "We specialize in books for, by and about women and women's issues including nonfiction self-help books, fiction and theater projects. We also handle the film, television and allied rights for several agencies as well as foreign rights for several publishing houses." Actively seeking new nonfiction. Considers plays. Does not want to receive poetry, television scripts or concepts for television.

How to Contact Query with SASE. Submit outline, synopsis, author bio, 3 sample chapters, SASE. Accepts simultaneous submissions. Responds in 6 weeks to queries. Responds in 6 weeks to mss. Obtains most new clients through recommendations from others, solicitations, conferences.

Terms Agent receives 15% commission on domestic sales. Agent receives 20% commission on foreign sales. Offers written contract; 30-day notice must be given to terminate contract.

Writers Conferences Geneva Writers' Conference (Switzerland); Columbus Writers' Conference; Skidmore Conference of the Independent Women's Writers Group.

Tips "Keep writing!"

THE SEYMOUR AGENCY

475 Miner St., Canton NY 13617. (315)386-1831. E-mail: marysue@twcny.rr.com. Website: www.theseymouragency.com. **Contact:** Mary Sue Seymour. Member of AAR. Signatory of WGA. Other memberships include RWA, Authors Guild. Represents 50 clients. 5% of clients are new/unpublished writers. Currently handles: nonfiction books 50%, other 50% fiction.

- Ms. Seymour is a retired New York State certified teacher.

Represents nonfiction books, novels. **Considers these nonfiction areas:** business, health, how-to, self help, Christian books; cookbooks; any well-written nonfiction that includes a proposal in standard format and 1 sample chapter. **Considers these fiction areas:** religious, Christian books, romance, any type.

How to Contact Query with SASE, synopsis, first 50 pages for romance. Accepts e-mail queries. Accepts simultaneous submissions. Responds in 1 month to queries. Responds in 3 months to mss.

Terms Agent receives 12-15% commission on domestic sales.

WENDY SHERMAN ASSOCIATES, INC.

450 Seventh Ave., Suite 2307, New York NY 10123. (212)279-9027. Fax: (212)279-8863. Website: www.wsherman.com. **Contact:** Wendy Sherman. Member of AAR. Represents 50 clients. 30% of clients are new/

unpublished writers. Currently handles: nonfiction books 50%, novels 50%.

- Prior to opening the agency, Ms. Sherman worked for The Aaron Priest agency and served as vice president, executive director, associate publisher, subsidary rights director, and sales and marketing director in the publishing industry.

Member Agents Wendy Sherman; Michelle Brower.

Represents nonfiction books, novels. **Considers these nonfiction areas:** psychology, narrative; practical. **Considers these fiction areas:** literary, womens, suspense. "We specialize in developing new writers, as well as working with more established writers. My experience as a publisher has proven to be a great asset to my clients."

How to Contact Query with SASE or send outline/proposal, 1 sample chapter. E-mail queries accepted by Ms. Brower only. Considers Accepts simultaneous submissions. Responds in 1 month to queries. Obtains most new clients through recommendations from others.

Terms Agent receives 15% commission on domestic sales. Agent receives 20% commission on foreign sales. Offers written contract.

Tips "The bottom line is: Do your homework. Be as well prepared as possible. Read the books that will help you present yourself and your work with polish. You want your submission to stand out."

ROSALIE SIEGEL, INTERNATIONAL LITERARY AGENCY, INC.

1 Abey Dr., Pennington NJ 08543. (609)737-1007. Fax: (609)737-3708. **Contact:** Rosalie Siegel. Member of AAR. Represents 35 clients. 10% of clients are new/unpublished writers. Currently handles: nonfiction books 45%, novels 45%, other 10% young adult books; short story collections for current clients.

How to Contact Obtains most new clients through referrals from writers and friends.

Terms Agent receives 15% commission on domestic sales. Agent receives 20% commission on foreign sales. Offers written contract; 2-month notice must be given to terminate contract. Charges clients for photocopying.

SPENCERHILL ASSOCIATES

P.O. Box 374, Chatham NY 12037. (518)392-9293. Fax: (518)392-9554. E-mail: ksolem@klsbooks.com; jennifer@klsbooks.com. **Contact:** Karen Solem or Jennifer Schober. Member of AAR. Represents 73 clients. 5% of clients are new/unpublished writers.

- Prior to becoming an agent, Ms. Solem was editor-in-chief at HarperCollins and an associate publisher.

Member Agents Karen Solem; Jennifer Schober.

Represents novels. **Considers these fiction areas:** detective, historical, literary, mainstream, religious, romance, thriller, young. "We handle mostly commercial women's fiction, historical novels, romance (historical, contemporary, paranormal, urban fantasy), thrillers, and mysteries. We also represent Christian fiction." No nonfiction, poetry, science fiction, children's picture books, or scripts.

How to Contact Query jennifer@klsbooks.com with synopsis and first three chapters. E-queries preferred. Responds in 6-8 weeks to queries.

Terms Agent receives 15% commission on domestic sales. Agent receives 20% commission on foreign sales. Offers written contract; 3-month notice must be given to terminate contract.

STEELE-PERKINS LITERARY AGENCY

26 Island Ln., Canandaigua NY 14424. (585)396-9290. Fax: (585)396-3579. E-mail: pattiesp@aol.com. **Contact:** Pattie Steele-Perkins. Member of AAR. Other memberships include RWA. Currently handles: novels 100%.

Represents novels. **Considers these fiction areas:** romance, women's, All genres: category romance, romantic suspense, historical, contemporary, multi-cultural, and inspirational.

How to Contact Submit synopsis and one chapter via e-mail (no attachments) or snail mail. Snail mail submissions require SASE. Accepts simultaneous submissions. Responds in 6 weeks to queries. Obtains most new clients through recommendations from others, queries/solicitations.

Terms Agent receives 15% commission on domestic sales. Offers written contract, binding for 1 year; 1-month notice must be given to terminate contract.

Writers Conferences RWA National Conference; BookExpo America; CBA Convention; Romance Slam Jam.

Tips Be patient. E-mail rather than call. Make sure what you are sending is the best it can be.

STIMOLA LITERARY STUDIO, LLC

306 Chase Court, Edgewater NJ 07020. Phone/Fax: (201)945-9353. E-mail: info@stimolaliterarystudio.com. Website: www.stimolaliterarystudio.com. **Contact:** Rosemary B. Stimola. Member of AAR.

How to Contact Query via e-mail (no unsolicited attachments). Responds in 3 weeks to queries "we wish to pursue further." Responds in 2 months to requested mss. Obtains most new clients through referrals. Unsolicited submissions are still accepted.

Terms Agent receives 15% commission on domestic sales. Agent receives 20% (if subagents are employed) commission on foreign sales.

PATRICIA TEAL LITERARY AGENCY

2036 Vista Del Rosa, Fullerton CA 92831-1336. Phone/Fax: (714)738-8333. **Contact:** Patricia Teal. Member of AAR. Other memberships include RWA, Authors Guild. Represents 20 clients. Currently handles: nonfiction books 10%, other 90% fiction .

Represents nonfiction books, novels. **Considers these nonfiction areas:** animals, biography, child, health, how to, psychology, self help, true crime, womens. **Considers these fiction areas:** glitz, mainstream, mystery, romance (contemporary, historical). This agency specializes in women's fiction, commercial how-to, and self-help nonfiction. Does not want to receive poetry, short stories, articles, science fiction, fantasy, or regency romance.
How to Contact Published authors only may query with SASE. Accepts simultaneous submissions. Responds in 10 days to queries. Responds in 6 weeks to mss. Obtains most new clients through conferences, recommendations from authors and editors.
Terms Agent receives 10-15% commission on domestic sales. Agent receives 20% commission on foreign sales. Offers written contract, binding for 1 year. Charges clients for ms copies.
Writers Conferences RWA Conferences; Asilomar; BookExpo America; Bouchercon; Maui Writers Conference.
Tips "Include SASE with all correspondence. I am taking on published authors only."

S©OTT TREIMEL NY

434 Lafayette St., New York NY 10003. (212)505-8353. Website: ScottTreimelNY.blogspot.com; www.ScottTreimelNY.com. **Contact:** John M. Cusick. Member of AAR. Other memberships include Authors Guild, SCBWI. 10% of clients are new/unpublished writers. Currently handles: other 100% junvenile/teen books.

- Prior to becoming an agent, Mr. Treimel was an assistant to Marilyn E. Marlow at Curtis Brown, a rights agent for Scholastic, a book packager and rights agent for United Feature Syndicate, a freelance editor, a rights consultant for HarperCollins Children's Books, and the founding director of Warner Bros. Worldwide Publishing.

Represents nonfiction books, novels, juvenile, children's, picture books, young adult. This agency specializes in tightly focused segments of the trade and institutional markets. Career clients.
How to Contact Submissions accepted only via Web site.
Terms Agent receives 15% commission on domestic sales. Agent receives 20% commission on foreign sales. Offers verbal or written contract. Charges clients for photocopying, express postage, messengers, and books needed to sell foreign, film and other rights.
Writers Conferences SCBWI NY, NJ, PA, Bologna; The New School; Southwest Writers' Conference; Pikes Peak Writers' Conference.

VERITAS LITERARY AGENCY

601 Van Ness Ave., Opera Plaza, Suite E, San Francisco CA 94102. Website: www.veritasliterary.com. **Contact:** Katherine Boyle. Member of AAR. Other memberships include Author's Guild.
Represents nonfiction books, novels. **Considers these nonfiction areas:** current affairs, government, memoirs, popular culture, womens, narrative nonfiction, art and music biography, natural history, health and wellness, psychology, serious religion (no New Age) and popular science. Does not want to receive romance, sci-fi, poetry or children's books.
How to Contact Query with SASE. This agency prefers a short query letter with no attachments.

RALPH VICINANZA, LTD.

303 W. 18th St., New York NY 10011. (212)924-7090. Fax: (212)691-9644. Member of AAR.
Member Agents Ralph M. Vicinanza; Chris Lotts; Chris Schelling, Matthew Mahoney.
How to Contact This agency takes on new clients by professional recommendation only.
Terms Agent receives 15% commission on domestic sales. Agent receives 20% commission on foreign sales.

WALES LITERARY AGENCY, INC.

P.O. Box 9428, Seattle WA 98109-0428. (206)284-7114. E-mail: waleslit@waleslit.com. Website: www.waleslit.com. **Contact:** Elizabeth Wales, Neal Swain. Member of AAR. Other memberships include Book Publishers' Northwest, Pacific Northwest Booksellers Association, PEN. Represents 65 clients. 10% of clients are new/unpublished writers. Currently handles: nonfiction books 60%, novels 40%.

- Prior to becoming an agent, Ms. Wales worked at Oxford University Press and Viking Penguin.

Member Agents Elizabeth Wales; Neal Swain.
Represents This agency specializes in narrative nonfiction and quality mainstream and literary fiction. Does not handle screenplays, children's literature, genre fiction, or most category nonfiction.
How to Contact Query with cover letter, SASE. No phone or fax queries. Prefers regular mail queries, but accepts 1-page e-mail queries with no attachments. Accepts simultaneous submissions. Responds in 3 weeks to queries. Responds in 6 weeks to mss.
Terms Agent receives 15% commission on domestic sales. Agent receives 20% commission on foreign sales.
Writers Conferences Pacific Northwest Writers Conference; Willamette Writers Conference.
Tips "We are especially interested in work that espouses a progressive cultural or political view, projects a new voice, or simply shares an important, compelling story. We also encourage writers living in the Pacific Northwest, West Coast, Alaska, and Pacific Rim countries, and writers from historically underrepresented groups, such as gay and lesbian writers and writers of color, to submit work (but does not discourage writers outside these areas). Most importantly, whether in fiction or nonfiction, the agency is looking for talented storytellers."

AUDREY R. WOLF LITERARY AGENCY

2510 Virginia Ave. NW, #702N, Washington DC 20037. **Contact:** Audrey Wolf. Member of AAR.
How to Contact Query with SASE.

WOLGEMUTH & ASSOCIATES, INC

8600 Crestgate Circle, Orlando FL 32819. (407)909-9445. Fax: (407)909-9446. E-mail: ewolgemuth@wolgemuthandassociates.com. **Contact:** Erik Wolgemuth. Member of AAR. Represents 60 clients. 10% of clients are new/unpublished writers. Currently handles: nonfiction books 90%, novella 2%, juvenile books 5%, multimedia 3%.

- "We have been in the publishing business since 1976, having been a marketing executive at a number of houses, a publisher, an author, and a founder and owner of a publishing company."

Member Agents Robert D. Wolgemuth; Andrew D. Wolgemuth; Erik S. Wolgemuth.
Represents Material used by Christian families. "We are not considering any new material at this time."
Terms Agent receives 15% commission on domestic sales. Offers written contract, binding for 2-3 years; 30-day notice must be given to terminate contract.

WYLIE-MERRICK LITERARY AGENCY

1138 S. Webster St., Kokomo IN 46902-6357. (765)459-8258. Website: www.wylie-merrick.com. **Contact:** Robert Brown. Member of AAR. RWA Currently handles: nonfiction books 5%, novels 95%.

- Ms. Brown holds a master's degree in language education and is a writing and technology curriculum specialist.

Member Agents Sharene Martin-Browne (juvenile, picture books, young adult); Robert Brown.
Represents "Our clients are all professionals. We specialize only in highly commercial literature. Please note that we no longer represent children's picture books."
How to Contact Correspond via e-mail only. No phone queries, please. Obtains new clients through e-mail queries, conferences, and client/editor/agent recommendations only.
Terms Agent receives 15% commission on domestic sales; 20% commission on foreign or dramatic rights sales. Offers written contract.
Tips "As the publishing industry is not static, please always check our Web site for our most updated needs lists. Also, we maintain an informative blog at www.wyliemerrick.blogspot.com. Both agents, when time permits, can be found on Twitter and Facebook."

SUSAN ZECKENDORF ASSOC., INC.

171 W. 57th St., New York NY 10019. (212)245-2928. **Contact:** Susan Zeckendorf. Member of AAR. Represents 15 clients. 25% of clients are new/unpublished writers. Currently handles: nonfiction books 50%, novels 50%.

- Prior to opening her agency, Ms. Zeckendorf was a counseling psychologist.

Represents nonfiction books, novels. **Considers these nonfiction areas:** biography, health, history, music, psychology, sociology, womens. **Considers these fiction areas:** detective, ethnic, historical, literary, mainstream, mystery, thriller. Actively seeking mysteries, literary fiction, mainstream fiction, thrillers, social history, classical music, and biography. Does not want to receive science fiction, romance, or children's books.
How to Contact Query with SASE. Accepts simultaneous submissions. Responds in 10 days to queries. Responds in 3 weeks to mss.
Terms Agent receives 15% commission on domestic sales. Agent receives 20% commission on foreign sales. Charges for photocopying and messenger services.
Writers Conferences Frontiers in Writing Conference; Oklahoma Festival of Books.
Tips "We are a small agency giving lots of individual attention. We respond quickly to submissions."

MARKETS

Book Publishers

The markets in this year's Book Publishers section offer opportunities in nearly every area of publishing. Large, commercial houses are here as are their smaller counterparts.

The **Book Publishers Subject Index** on page **1079** is the best place to start your search. You'll find it in the back of the book, before the General Index. Subject areas for both fiction and nonfiction are broken out for all of the book publisher listings, including Canadian Publishers and Small Presses.

When you have compiled a list of publishers interested in books in your subject area, read the detailed listings. Pare down your list by cross-referencing two or three subject areas and eliminating the listings only marginally suited to your book. When you have a good list, send for those publishers' catalogs and manuscript guidelines, or check publishers' Web sites, which often contain catalog listings, manuscript preparation guidelines, current contact names, and other information helpful to prospective authors. You want to use this information to make sure your book idea is in line with a publisher's list but is not a duplicate of something already published.

You should also visit bookstores and libraries to see if the publisher's books are well represented. When you find a couple of books the house has published that are similar to yours, write or call the company to find out who edited those books. This extra bit of research could be the key to getting your proposal to precisely the right editor.

Publishers prefer different methods of submission on first contact. Most like to see a one-page query with SASE, especially for nonfiction. Others will accept a brief proposal package that might include an outline and/or a sample chapter. Some publishers will accept submissions from agents only. Each listing in the Book Publishers section includes specific submission methods, if provided by the publisher. Make sure you read each listing carefully to find out exactly what the publisher wants to receive.

When you write your one-page query, give an overview of your book, mention the intended audience, the competition for your book (check local bookstore shelves), and what sets your book apart from the competition. You should also include any previous publishing experience or special training relevant to the subject of your book. For more on queries, read "Query Letter Clinic'' on page 14.

Personalize your query by addressing the editor individually and mentioning what you know about the company from its catalog or books. Never send a form letter as a query. Envelopes addressed to "Editor'' or "Editorial Department'' end up in the dreaded slush pile. Under the heading **Acquisitions**, we list the names of editors who acquire new books for each company, along with the editors' specific areas of expertise. Try your best to send your query to the appropriate editor. Editors move around all the time, so it's in your best interest to look online or call the publishing house to make sure the editor you are addressing your query to is still employed by that publisher.

Author-subsidy publishers not included

Writer's Market is a reference tool to help you sell your writing, and we encourage you to work with publishers that pay a royalty. Subsidy publishing involves paying money to a publishing house to publish a book. The source of the money could be a government, foundation or university grant, or it could be the author of the book. If one of the publishers listed in this book offers you an author-subsidy arrangement (sometimes called "cooperative publishing," "co-publishing," or "joint venture"); or asks you to pay for part or all of the cost of any aspect of publishing (editing services, manuscript critiques, printing, advertising, etc.); or asks you to guarantee the purchase of any number of the books yourself, we would like you to inform us of that company's practices immediately.

INFORMATION AT A GLANCE

There are a number of icons at the beginning of each listing to quickly convey certain information. In the Book Publisher sections, these icons identify new listings (N), Canadian markets (🍁), publishers that accept agented submissions only (A), and publishers who do not accept unsolicited manuscripts (⊘). Different sections of *Writer's Market* include other symbols; check the back inside cover for an explanation of all the symbols used throughout the book.

How much money? What are my odds?

We've also highlighted important information in boldface, the "quick facts" you won't find in any other market guide but should know before you submit your work. These items include: how many manuscripts a publisher buys per year; how many manuscripts from first-time authors; how many manuscripts from unagented writers; the royalty rate a publisher pays; and how large an advance is offered. Standard royalty rates for paperbacks generally range from 7 ½ to 12 ½ percent, and from 10 to 15 percent for hardcovers . Royalty rates for children's books are often lower, generally ranging from 5 to 10 percent; 10 percent for picture books (split between the author and the illustrator).

Publishers, their imprints, and how they are related

In this era of big publishing—and big mergers—the world of publishing has grown even more intertwined. A "family tree" on page 81 lists the imprints and divisions of the largest conglomerate publishers.

Keep in mind that most of the major publishers listed in this family tree do not accept unagented submissions or unsolicited manuscripts. You will find many of these publishers and their imprints listed within the Book Publishers section, and many contain only basic contact information. If you are interested in pursuing any of these publishers, we advise you to see each publisher's Web site for more information.

For a list of publishers according to their subjects of interest, see the Nonfiction and Fiction sections of the Book Publishers Subject Index. Information on book publishers listed in the previous edition of *Writer's Market*, but not included in this edition, can be found in the General Index.

N 23 HOUSE PUBLISHING

405 Moseley St., Jefferson TX 75657. Fax: (214)367-4343. E-mail: editor@23house.com. Website: www.23house.com. **Contact:** Editor. Publishes trade paperback originals and electronic book format. Accepts simultaneous submissions. Book catalog and ms guidelines online.

- "We are looking for regional titles around the U.S., specifically in the folklore and supernatural genre. An idea of the market for the book should be included as part of the proposal."

O┯ "We have produced books in almost every genre."

Nonfiction , haunted locations, interesting history, etc. Submit proposal via e-mail, and we'll go from there.
Recent Title(s) *Natchez: The History and Mystery of the City on the Bluff; Poet of the Pines: The Accumulated Works of Milton Watts; Suzie Wilson takes you from Wilted to Wonderful.*
Tips "Representatives from 23 House attend many writer's conferences every year around the country, and we get the majority of our books from the writers that we meet in person at conferences. Because of that, we take very few mss via email submission. The best way to submit to 23 house is to meet one of our representatives at a conference, give us your best pitch, and we'll go from there."

N ABC-CLIO

130 Cremona Dr., Santa Barbara CA 93117. (805)968-1911. Website: www.abc-clio.com. **Publishes 600 titles/year. 20% of books from first-time authors. 90% from unagented writers.** Accepts simultaneous submissions. Catalog and guidelines available online.
Imprints ABC-CLIO (serves the history profession, history teachers, and students and scholars of history with a complete line of award-winning databases, books, and eBooks, along with social studies reference and curriculum resources for middle and high school libraries and classrooms); Greenwood Press (high-quality, authoritative reference books and general interest topics across the secondary and higher education curriculum); Praeger (widely regarded to scholarly and professional books in the social sciences and humanities, with emphasis in modern history, military studies, psychology, business, current events and social issues, international affairs, politics, visual and performing arts, and literature); Praeger Security International (insightful and timely material on international security, including defense and foreign policy, strategy, regional security, military history, and terrorism); Libraries Unlimited (professional materials for librarians, media specialists, and teachers).

O┯ ABC-CLIO is an award-winning publisher of reference titles, academic and general interest books, electronic resources, and books for librarians and other professionals. Today, ABC-CLIO publishes under 5 well-respected imprints.

Nonfiction Subjects include business, child guidance, education, government, history, humanities, language, music, psychology, religion, social sciences, sociology, sports, womens issues. Query with proposal package, including scope, organization, length of project, whether a complete ms is available or when it will be, CV or rèsumè and SASE.
Recent Title(s) *Encyclopedia of the Arab-Israeli Conflict: A Political, Social and Military History*, by Spencer C. Tucker, ABC-CLIO 2008; *Barack Obama, A Biography*, by Joann F. Price, Greenwood, 2008; *Barack Obama, the New Face of American Politics*, by Martin Dupuis and Keith Boeckelman, Praeger, 2009; *In Peace and War: Interpretations of American Naval History*, by Kenneth J. Hagan and Michael T. McMaster, Praeger Security International, 2008; *Serving Urban Teens*, by Paula Brehm-Heeger, Libraries Unlimited, 2008.
Tips Looking for reference materials and materials for educated general readers. Many of our authors are college professors who have distinguished credentials and who have published research widely in their fields.

⊘ ABDO PUBLISHING CO.

8000 W. 78th St., Suite 310, Edina MN 55439. (800)800-1312. Fax: (952)831-1632. E-mail: info@abdopub.com. Website: www.abdopub.com. **Contact:** Paul Abdo, editor-in-chief. Estab. 1985. Publishes hardcover originals. **Publishes 300 titles/year.**
Imprints ABDO & Daughters; Buddy Books; Checkerboard Library; SandCastle.

- *No unsolicited mss.*

O┯ ABDO publishes nonfiction children's books (pre-kindergarten to 8th grade) for school and public libraries—mainly history, sports, biography, geography, science, and social studies.

Nonfiction Subjects include animals, history, science, sports, geography, social studies. Submit résumé to pabdo@abdopub.com
Recent Title(s) *Lewis and Clark*, by John Hamilton (children's nonfiction); *Tiger Woods*, by Paul Joseph (children's biography).

ABINGDON PRESS

Imprint of The United Methodist Publishing House 201 Eighth Ave. S., P.O. Box 801, Nashville TN 37203. (615)749-6000. Fax: (615)749-6512. Website: www.abingdonpress.com. **Contact:** Robert Ratcliff, senior editor (professional clergy and academic); Judy Newman St. John (children's); Ron Kidd, senior editor (general interest). Estab. 1789. Publishes hardcover and paperback originals; church supplies. **Publishes 120 titles/year. 3,000 queries received/year. 250 mss received/year. 85% from unagented writers. Pays 7 ½- royalty on retail price.** Publishes book 2 years after acceptance of ms. Responds in 2 months to queries. Book catalog available free. Guidelines available online.

Imprints Dimensions for Living; Kingswood Books; Abingdon Press.

- Abingdon Press, America's oldest theological publisher, provides an ecumenical publishing program dedicated to serving the Christian community—clergy, scholars, church leaders, musicians, and general readers—with quality resources in the areas of Bible study, the practice of ministry, theology, devotion, spirituality, inspiration, prayer, music and worship, reference, Christian education, and church supplies.

Nonfiction Subjects include education, religion, theology. Query with outline and samples only.

Recent Title(s) *A History of Preaching*, by Edwards; *Global Bible Commentary*, edited by Patte; *Sanctuary*, by Stevens.

ABI PROFESSIONAL PUBLICATIONS

P.O. Box 149, St. Petersburg FL 33731. (727)556-0950. Fax: (727)556-2560. Website: www.abipropub.com. **Contact:** Art Brown, publisher/editor-in-chief (prosthetics, rehabilitation, dental/medical research). Publishes hardcover and trade paperback originals. **Publishes 6 titles/year. 75-100 queries received/year and 20+ mss received/year. 25% of books from first-time authors. 100% from unagented writers. Pays royalty on revenues generated. Pays small advance.** Publishes book 1+ years after acceptance of ms. Accepts simultaneous submissions. Responds in 6 months to queries.

- No registered, certified, return-receipt submissions accepted.

Nonfiction Subjects include health, medicine. Submit proposal package, outline, representative sample chapters, bio. Submit complete ms. Reviews artwork/photos. Send photocopies.

Recent Title(s) *Managing Polio,* 2nd edition, Lauro Halstead, M.D.

Tips "Audience is allied health professionals, dentists, researchers, patients undergoing physical rehabilitation. We will not review electronic submissions."

HARRY N. ABRAMS, INC.

Subsidiary of La Martiniere Groupe 115 W. 18th St., New York NY 10011. (212)206-7715. Fax: (212)645-8437. E-mail: submissions@abramsbooks.com. Website: www.abramsbooks.com. **Contact:** Managing Editor. Estab. 1949. Publishes hardcover and a few paperback originals. **Publishes 250 titles/year.** Responds in 6 months (if interested) to queries.

Imprints Stewart, Tabori & Chang; Abrams Books for Young Readers; Abrams Gifts & Stationary.

- We publish *only* high-quality illustrated art books, i.e., art, art history, museum exhibition catalogs, written by specialists and scholars in the field.

Nonfiction Subjects include art, architecture, nature, environment, recreation, outdoor. Submit queries, proposals, and mss via mail with SASE. No e-mail submissions. Reviews artwork/photos.

Recent Title(s) *1001 Reasons to Love Horses* , by Sheri Seggerman and Mary Tiegreen ( ); *About NYC*, by Joanne Dugan ( ); *Mother Teresa: A Life of Dedication*, by Raghu Rai ( ).

Tips We are one of the few publishers who publish almost exclusively illustrated books. We consider ourselves the leading publishers of art books and high-quality artwork in the U.S. Once the author has signed a contract to write a book for our firm the author must finish the manuscript to agreed-upon high standards within the schedule agreed upon in the contract.

ABSEY & CO.

23011 Northcrest Dr., Spring TX 77389. (281)257-2340. Fax: (281)251-4676. E-mail: info@absey.biz. Website: www.absey.biz. **Contact:** Edward Wilson, publisher. Publishes hardcover, trade paperback, and mass market paperback originals. **Publishes 6-10 titles/year. 50% of books from first-time authors. 50% from unagented writers. Royalty and advance vary.** Publishes book 1 year after acceptance of ms. Responds in 3 months to queries. Responds in 9 months to manuscripts. Guidelines available online.

- Our goal is to publish original, creative works of literary merit. Currently emphasizing educational, young adult literature. De-emphasizing self-help.

Nonfiction Subjects include education, language, literature, language, literature arts, general nonfiction. Query with SASE.

Fiction Subjects include juvenile, mainstream, contemporary, short story collections. Since we are a small, new press, we are looking for book-length manuscripts with a firm intended audience. Query with SASE.

Recent Title(s) *Adrift*, by Greg Raver-Lampman; *Where I'm From*, by George Ella Lyon (poetry); *Stealing a Million Kisses*, by Jennifer Skaggs.

Tips We work closely and attentively with authors and their work. Does not download mss or accept e-mail submissions.

ACADEMY CHICAGO PUBLISHERS

363 W. Erie St., Suite 7E, Chicago IL 60610-3125. (312)751-7300. Fax: (312)751-7306. E-mail: info@academychicago.com. Website: www.academychicago.com. **Contact:** Anita Miller, editorial director/senior editor. Estab. 1975. Publishes hardcover and some paperback originals and trade paperback reprints. **Publishes**

10 titles/year. Pays 7 -10% royalty on wholesale price. Publishes book 18 months after acceptance of ms. Book catalog available online. Guidelines available online.

O→ We publish quality fiction and nonfiction. Our audience is literate and discriminating. No novelized biography, history, or science fiction.

Nonfiction Subjects include history, travel. Submit proposal package, outline, bio, 3 sample chapters.

Fiction Subjects include historical, mainstream, contemporary, military, war, mystery. We look for quality work, but we do not publish experimental, avant garde novels. Submit proposal package, clips, 3 sample chapters.

Tips At the moment, we are looking for good nonfiction; we certainly want excellent original fiction, but we are swamped. No fax queries, no disks. No electronic submissions. We are always interested in reprinting good out-of-print books.

ACE SCIENCE FICTION AND FANTASY

Imprint of The Berkley Publishing Group, Penguin Group (USA), Inc. 375 Hudson St., New York NY 10014. (212)366-2000. Website: www.penguin.com. **Contact:** Anne Sowards, editor; Jessica Webb, editorial assistant. Estab. 1953. Publishes hardcover, paperback, and trade paperback originals and reprints. **Publishes 75 titles/year. Pays royalty. Pays advance.** Publishes book 1-2 years after acceptance of ms. Responds in 2 months to queries. Responds in 6 months to manuscripts. Guidelines for #10 SASE.

O→ Ace publishes science fiction and fantasy exclusively.

Fiction Subjects include fantasy, science fiction. No other genre accepted. No short stories. Query first with SASE.

Recent Title(s) *Od Magic*, by Patricia A. McKillip; *Accelerando*, by Charles Stross.

ACTA PUBLICATIONS

5559 W. Howard St., Skokie IL 60077. (847)676-2282. Fax: (847)676-2287. E-mail: acta@actapublications.com. Website: www.actapublications.com. **Contact:** Andrew Yankech. Estab. 1958. Publishes trade paperback originals. **Publishes 12 titles/year. 100 queries received/year. 25 mss received/year. 50% of books from first-time authors. 90% from unagented writers. Pays 10-12% royalty on wholesale price.** Publishes book 1 year after acceptance of ms. Responds in 1 month to proposals. Book catalog and ms guidelines available online or with #10 SASE.

O→ "ACTA publishes nonacademic, practical books aimed at the mainline religious market."

Nonfiction Subjects include religion, spirituality. Submit outline, 1 sample chapter. Reviews artwork/photos. Send photocopies.

Recent Title(s) *The Geography of God's Mercy*, by Patrick Hannon (spirituality/stories); *Portraits of Grace*, by James Stephen Behrens (spirituality/photography); *God's Word is Alive*, by Alice Camille (lectionary).

Tips "Don't send a submission unless you have examined our catalog, Web site and several of our books."

ADAMS MEDIA

Division of F+W Media, Inc. 57 Littlefield St., Avon MA 02322. (508)427-7100. Fax: (800)872-5628. E-mail: submissions@adamsmedia.com. Website: www.adamsmedia.com. **Contact:** Paula Munier. Estab. 1980. Publishes hardcover originals, trade paperback originals and reprints. **Publishes more than 250 titles/year. 5,000 queries received/year. 1,500 mss received/year. 40% of books from first-time authors. 40% from unagented writers. Pays standard royalty or makes outright purchase. Pays variable advance.** Publishes book 12-18 months after acceptance of ms. Accepts simultaneous submissions. Responds in 3 months to queries. Guidelines available online.

O→ "Adams Media publishes commercial nonfiction, including self-help, inspiration, women's issues, pop psychology, relationships, business, careers, pets, parenting, New Age, gift books, cookbooks, how-to, reference, and humor. Does not return unsolicited materials. Does not accept electronic submissions."

Recent Title(s) *365 Ways to Live Cheap; WTF?; My Mom Is My Hero; The Maxims of Manhood; Surviving a Layoff*

ADDICUS BOOKS, INC.

P.O. Box 45327, Omaha NE 68145. (402)330-7493. Website: www.addicusbooks.com. **Contact:** Acquisitions Editor. Estab. 1994. **Publishes 10 nonfiction titles/year. 90% of books from first-time authors. 95% from unagented writers. Pays royalty as a percentage of net Pays advance.** Publishes book 9 months after acceptance of ms. Accepts simultaneous submissions. Responds in 1 month to proposals. Guidelines available online.

O→ Addicus Books, Inc. seeks mss with strong national or regional appeal.

Nonfiction Subjects include business, economics, health, medicine, psychology. Query with SASE. Do not send entire ms unless requested. When querying electronically, send only 1-page e-mail, giving an overview of your book and its market. Please do not send attachments unless invited to do so. Additional submission guidelines online.

Recent Title(s) *Understanding Peyronie's Disease*, by Laurence A. Levin, MD.; *The New Fibromyalgia Remedy*, by Daniel Dantini, MD.

Tips We are looking for quick-reference books on health topics. Do some market research to make sure the market is not already flooded with similar books. We're also looking for good true-crime manuscripts, with an interesting story, with twists and turns, behind the crime.

AERONAUTICAL PUBLISHERS

1 Oakglade Circle, Hummelstown PA 17036-9525. (717)566-0468. Fax: (717)566-6423. E-mail: possibilitypress@aol.com. Website: www.aeronauticalpublishers.com. **Contact:** Mike Markowski, publisher. Estab. 1981. Publishes trade paperback originals. **Pays variable royalty.** Responds in 2 months to queries. Guidelines available online.

Imprints American Aeronautical Archives, Aviation Publishers, Aeronautical Publishers.

- Our mission is to help people learn more about aviation and model aviation through the written word.

Nonfiction Subjects include history, aviation, hobbies, recreation, radio control, free flight, indoor models, micro radio control, home-built aircraft, ultralights, and hang gliders. Prefers submission by mail. Include SASE.

Recent Title(s) *Flying Models*, by Don Ross; *Those Magnificent Fast Flying Machines*, by C.B. Hayward.

Tips Our focus is on books of short to medium length that will serve the emerging needs of the hobby. We also want to help youth get started, while enhancing everyone's enjoyment of the hobby. We are looking for authors who are passionate about the hobby, and will champion their book and the messages of their books, supported by efforts at promoting and selling their books.

ALASKA NORTHWEST BOOKS

Graphic Arts Center Publishing P.O. Box 10306, Portland OR 97296-0306. (503)226-2402. Fax: (503)223-1410. Website: www.gacpc.com. **Contact:** Tim Frew, executive editor. Estab. 1959. Publishes hardcover and trade paperback originals and reprints. **Publishes 12 titles/year. 10% of books from first-time authors. 90% from unagented writers. Pays 10-14% royalty on net revenues. Buys mss outright (rarely). Pays advance.** Publishes book an average of 2 years after acceptance of ms. Accepts simultaneous submissions. Responds in 6 months to queries. Book catalog for 9x12 envelope and 6 First-Class stamps. Guidelines available online.

Nonfiction Subjects include nature, environment, recreation, sports, travel, Native American culture, adventure, the arts. Submit outline, sample chapters.

Recent Title(s) *The Winterlake Lodge Cookbook: Culinary Adventures in the Wilderness*; *Portrait of the Alaska Railroad*; *Big-Enough Anna: The Little Sled Dog Who Braved the Arctic*, (children's book).

Tips Book proposals that are professionally written and polished with a clear understanding of the market, receive our most careful consideration. We are looking for originality. We publish a wide range of books for a wide audience. Some of our books are clearly for travelers, others for those interested in outdoor recreation or various regional subjects. If I were a writer trying to market a book today, I would research the competition (existing books) for what I have in mind, and clearly (and concisely) express why my idea is different and better. I would describe the book buyers (and readers)—where they are, how many of them are there, how they can be reached (organizations, publications), why they would want or need my book.

N ALBA HOUSE

2187 Victory Blvd., Staten Island NY 10314-6603. (718)761-0047. Fax: (718)761-0057. E-mail: albabooks@aol.com. Website: www.albahouse.org. **Contact:** Edmund C. Lane, S.S.P., editor. Estab. 1961. Publishes hardcover, trade paperback, and mass market paperback originals. **Publishes 24 titles/year. 300 queries received/year. 150 mss received/year. 20% of books from first-time authors. 100% from unagented writers. Pays 7-10% royalty.** Publishes book 9 months after acceptance of ms. Responds in 1 month to queries. Responds in 1 month to proposals. Responds in 2 months to manuscripts. Book catalog and ms guidelines free.

- Alba House is the North American publishing division of the Society of St. Paul, an International Roman Catholic Missionary Religious Congregation dedicated to spreading the Gospel message.

Nonfiction Manuscripts which contribute, from a Roman Catholic perspective, to the personal, intellectual, and spiritual growth of individuals in the following areas: Scripture, theology and the Church, saints (their lives and teachings), spirituality and prayer, religious life, marriage and family life, liturgy and homily preparation, pastoral concerns, religious education, bereavement, moral and ethical concerns.Subjects include education, philosophy, psychology, religion, spirituality. Reviews artwork/photos. Send photocopies.

Recent Title(s) *Those Mysterious Priests*, by Fulton J. Sheen.

ALGONQUIN BOOKS OF CHAPEL HILL

Workman Publishing P.O. Box 2225, Chapel Hill NC 27515-2225. (919)967-0108. Website: www.algonquin.com. **Contact:** Editorial Department. Publishes hardcover originals. **Publishes 24 titles/year.** Guidelines available online.

- "Algonquin Books publishes quality literary fiction and literary nonfiction."

Nonfiction Query by mail before submitting work. No phone, e-mail or fax queries or submissions. Visit our website for full submission policy to queries.

ALGORA PUBLISHING

222 Riverside Dr., 16th Floor, New York NY 10025-6809. (212)678-0232. Fax: (212)666-3682. E-mail: manuscripts@algora.com. Website: www.algora.com. **Contact:** Martin DeMers, editor (sociology/philosophy/economics); Claudiu A. Secara, publisher (philosophy/international affairs). Publishes hardcover and trade paperback originals and reprints. **Publishes 25 titles/year. 1,500 queries received/year. 800 mss received/year. 20% of books from first-time authors. 85% from unagented writers. Pays $0-1,000 advance.** Publishes book 10-18 months after acceptance of ms. Accepts simultaneous submissions. Responds in 1-2 months to queries. Responds in 1-2 months to proposals. Responds in 2-3 months to manuscripts. Book catalog and ms guidelines online.

- Algora Publishing is an academic-type press, focusing on works by North and South American, European, Asian, and African authors for the educated general reader.

Nonfiction Subjects include anthropology, archeology, creative nonfiction, education, government, politics, history, language, literature, military, war, money, finance, music, dance, nature, environment, philosophy, psychology, religion, science, sociology, translation, womens issues, womens studies, economics. Query by e-mail (preferred) or submit proposal package including outline, 3 sample chapters or complete ms.

Recent Title(s) *Washington Diplomacy*, by John Shaw (international politics); *The Case for the Living Wage*, by Jerold Waltman (political economy); *Electoral Laws and Their Political Consequences*, by Bernard Grofman and Arend Lijphart (political science).

Tips We welcome first-time writers; we help craft an author's raw manuscript into a literary work.

ALLWORTH PRESS

10 E. 23rd St., Suite 510, New York NY 10010-4402. (212)777-8395. Fax: (212)777-8261. E-mail: pub@allworth.com. Website: www.allworth.com. **Contact:** Tad Crawford. Estab. 1989. Publishes hardcover and trade paperback originals. **Publishes 12-18 titles/year. Pays advance.** Responds in 1 month to queries. Responds in 2 months to proposals. Book catalog and ms guidelines free.

- Allworth Press publishes business and self-help information for artists, designers, photographers, authors and film and performing artists, as well as books about business, money and the law for the general public. The press also publishes the best of classic and contemporary writing in art and graphic design. Currently emphasizing photography, graphic & industrial design, performing arts, fine arts and crafts, et al.

Nonfiction Subjects include art, architecture, business, economics, film, cinema, stage, music, dance, photography, film, television, graphic design, performing arts, writing, as well as business and legal guides for the public. Query.

Recent Title(s) *Business & Legal Forms for Authors and Self-Publishers*, by Tad Crawford; *Green Graphic Design*, by Brian Doughtery; *ASMP Professional Business Practices in Photography*, by the American Society of Media Photographers.

Tips We are helping creative people in the arts by giving them practical advice about business and success.

ALPHA WORLD PRESS

530 Oaklawn Avenue, Green Bay WI 54304. (866)855-3720. E-mail: office@alphaworldpress.com. Website: www.alphaworldpress.com. **Contact:** Tracey Vandeveer, owner. Estab. 2006. Publishes trade paperback originals, and mass market paperback originals. **Publishes 12 titles/year. 120 queries received/year. 12 mss received/year. 75%% of books from first-time authors. 100%% from unagented writers. Pays 10-30% royalty on retail price.** Publishes book 3 months after acceptance of ms. Responds in 1 month to queries. Responds in 1 month to proposals. Responds in 2 months to manuscripts. Book catalog available online. Guidelines available free.

Nonfiction Subjects include community, contemporary culture, gay, lesbian, history, social sciences, sports. Submit proposal package, outline. Reviews artwork/photos. Send via e-mail.

Fiction Subjects include adventure, confession, gay, lesbian, historical, horror, humor, juvenile, literary, mainstream, contemporary, mystery, romance, science fiction, short story collections, spiritual, sports, suspense, western, young adult. We publish only lesbian-themed books for the lesbian market. Submit proposal package, 3 sample chapters, clips. Send it via e-mail in pdf or d.

Recent Title(s) *Meditative Rose*, by Lynn Gravbelle; *Made For You*, by Geneva St. James; *Marti Brown and the House of Face*, by Teresa R. Allen.

Tips Our audience is lesbians only.

ALTHOS PUBLISHING

404 Wake Chapel Rd., Fuquay-Varina NC 27526-1936. (919)557-2260. Fax: (919)557-2261. E-mail: info@althos.com. Website: www.althos.com. **Contact:** Michele Chandler. Publishes hardcover and trade paperback originals. **Publishes 50 titles/year. 200 queries received/year. Pays 10% royalty on sales.** Publishes book 1-3 months after acceptance of ms. Responds in 3 months to proposals. Responds in 6 months to manuscripts. Book catalog available online. Guidelines available free.

Althos publishes books that solve problems, reduce cost, or save time.

Nonfiction Query with SASE. Reviews artwork/photos. Send photocopies.

N AMADEUS PRESS

Hal Leonard Publishing Group Hal Leonard Corp., 19 W. 21st St., Suite 201, New York NY 10010. (212)575-9265. Fax: (212)575-9270. Website: www.amadeuspress.com. **Contact:** John Cerullo, Publisher.

"Amadeus Press welcomes submissions pertaining to classical and traditional music and opera. Send proposal including: a letter describing the purpose and audience for your book, along with your background and qualifications; please indicate which word-processing software you use as we ask that final ms be submitted on disk; an outline or table of contents and an estimate of the length of the completed ms in numbers of words or double-spaced pages; a sample chapter or two, printed out (no electronic file transfers, please); sample illustrations as well as an estimate of the total numbers and types (for example, pen-and-ink artwork for line drawings, black-and-white glossy photographic prints, camera-ready music examples) of illustrations planned for your book; your schedule to complete the book. Generally, we ask authors to submit book proposals early in the writing process as this allows us to give editorial advice during the development phase and cuts down the amount of revisions needed later. Due to the large volume of submissions, you may not receive a response from us. If you wish to have the materials you submit returned to you, please so indicate and include return postage."

AMBER COMMUNICATIONS GROUP, INC.

1334 E. Chandler Blvd., Suite 5-D67, Phoenix AZ 85048. Website: www.amberbooks.com. **Contact:** Tony Rose, publisher. Estab. 1998. Publishes trade paperback and mass market paperback originals. Book catalog free or online.

Imprints Amber Books (self-help); Busta Books (celebrity bio); Amber/Wiley (personal finance, beauty); Colossus Books (biographies, famous music personalities); Ambrosia Books (nonfiction, fiction, novels, docudramas).

Amber Communications Group, Inc. is the nation's largest African-American publisher of self-help books and music biographies.

Nonfiction Subjects include beauty, fashion, history, celebrity memoirs, biographies, multicultural, personal finance, relationship advice. Submit proposal or outline with author biography. Please do not e-mail or mail mss unless requested by publisher. Reviews artwork/photos. Send photocopies, not originals.

Fiction Wants African-American topics and interest. Submit proposal or outline.

Recent Title(s) *African American Scholarship Guide for Students & Parents presented by Dante Lee*; *How to Prepare for College*, by Thomas Laveist & William Laveist with a forword by Tom Joyner; *Urban Suicide - the Enemy We Choose Not to See* (Drug Crisis in Black America), by Melvin Blackman; *The African American Writer's Guide to Successful Self Publishing*, by Takesha Powell; *Ready to Die: The Story of Biggie Smalls (Notorious B.I.G.)*, by Jake Brown.

Tips The goal of Amber Communications Group is to expand our catalog comprised of self-help books, and celebrity bio books; and expand our fiction department in print and on software, which pertain to, about, and for the African-American population.

AMERICAN ATHEIST PRESS

P.O. Box 5733, Parsippany NJ 07054-6733. (908)276-7300. Fax: (908)276-7402. E-mail: editor@atheists.org. Website: www.atheists.org. **Contact:** Frank Zindler, editor. Estab. 1963. Publishes trade paperback originals and reprints. Publishes monthly journal, *American Atheist*, for which articles of interest to Atheists are needed. **Publishes 12 titles/year. 40-50% of books from first-time authors. 100% from unagented writers. Pays 5-10% royalty on retail price.** Publishes book within 2 years after acceptance of ms. Accepts simultaneous submissions. Responds in 4 months to queries. Book catalog for 6 ½x9 ½ envelope and First-Class stamps. Guidelines for 9x12 envelope and First-Class stamps.

Imprints Gustav Broukal Press.

We are interested in books that will help atheists gain a deeper understanding of atheism, improve their ability to critique religious propaganda, and assist them in fighting to maintain the `wall of separation between state and church.' Currently emphasizing the politics of religion, science and religion. De-emphasizing Biblical criticism (but still doing some).

Nonfiction Subjects include government, politics, separation of state and church, religion and politics, history, of religion and Atheism, of the effects of religion historically, philosophy, from an Atheist perspective, particularly criticism of religion, religion, Atheism (particularly the lifestyle of Atheism; the history of Atheism; applications of Atheism). Submit outline, sample chapters. Reviews artwork/photos.

Fiction Subjects include humor, satire of religion or of current religious leaders, anything of particular interest to Atheists. We rarely publish any fiction. But we have occasionally released a humorous book. No mainstream. For our press to consider fiction, it would have to tie in with the general focus of our press, which is the promotion of Atheism and free thought. Submit outline, sample chapters.

Recent Title(s) *Living in the Light: Freeing Your Child from the Dark Ages*, by Anne Stone (rearing Atheist children); *The Jesus the Jews Never Knew (Against the Historicity of Jesus)*, by Frank R. Zindler; *Illustrated Stories From the Bible (That They Won't Tell You in Sunday School)*, by Paul Farrell.
Tips We will need more how-to types of material—how to argue with creationists, how to fight for state/church separation, etc. We have an urgent need for literature for young Atheists.

AMERICAN BAR ASSOCIATION PUBLISHING

321 N. Clark St., Chicago IL 60610. (312)988-5000. Fax: (312)988-6030. Website: www.ababooks.org. **Contact:** Kathleen A. Welton, director book publishing. Estab. 1878. Publishes hardcover and trade paperback originals. **Publishes 100 titles/year. 50 queries received/year. 20% of books from first-time authors. 95% from unagented writers.** Publishes book 6 months after acceptance of ms. Accepts simultaneous submissions. Responds in 1 month to queries. Responds in 1 month to proposals. Responds in 3 months to manuscripts. Book catalog and ms guidelines online.

- We are interested in books that help lawyers practice law more effectively, whether it's help in handling clients, structuring a real estate deal, or taking an antitrust case to court.

Nonfiction All areas of legal practice.Subjects include business, economics, computers, electronics, money, finance, software, legal practice. Query with SASE.
Recent Title(s) *McElhaney's Trial Notebook*; *The Creative Lawyer: A Practical Guide to Authentic Satisfaction*, by Michael F. Melcher; *The Curmudgeon's Guide to Practicing Law*, by Mark Herrmann.
Tips ABA books are written for busy, practicing lawyers. The most successful books have a practical, reader-friendly voice. If you can build in features like checklists, exhibits, sample contracts, flow charts, and tables of cases, please do so. The Association also publishes over 60 major national periodicals in a variety of legal areas. Contact Tim Brandhorst, Deputy Director of book publishing, at the above address for guidelines.

N AMERICAN BOOK PUBLISHING

5442 So. 900 East, #146, Salt Lake City Utah 84177. E-mail: info@american-book.com. Website: www.american-book.com. **Contact:** John Rutherford, Acquisitions Dir. (fiction and nonfiction). Trade paperback and electronic originals. **Publishes 70 titles/year. 25% of books from first-time authors. 40% from unagented writers.** Publishes book 9 mos. after acceptance of ms. Accepts simultaneous submissions. Catalog available for 8 x 11 SASE with 8 first-class stamps. Guidelines are free on request and by email.
Imprints American Book Classics, American Book Business Press, American University & Colleges Press, Bedside Books, Millennial Mind Publishing.
Nonfiction Subjects include Americana, anthropology, business, child guidance, communications, community, computers, contemporary culture, cooking, counseling, creative nonfiction, economics, education, electronics, entertainment, environment, ethnic, finance, foods, games, government, history, humanities, language, literary criticism, literature, military, money, multicultural, nature, New Age, nutrition, parenting, philosophy, politics, psychology, real estate, recreation, regional, religion, science, social sciences, software, spirituality, sports, translation, transportation, travel, womens issues. Submit completed ms. Does not review artwork.
Fiction TrueSubjects include adventure, ethnic, experimental, fantasy, feminist, historical, horror, humor, juvenile, mainstream, military, multimedia, mystery, regional, religious, romance, science fiction, short story collections, spiritual, sports, suspense, translation, western, young adult. Submit electronically with email attachments only. Submit completed ms.
Recent Title(s) *Christmas, a Season for Angels*, by Vicki L. Julian; *Finding Eden*, by Annalize Clarke; *Adolescent Sexuality: Too Much Too Soon*, by John E. Perito, M.D.
Tips "We target market readers from most nonfiction and fiction genres, have a large book marketing department and assign a staff member to work with each author to reach their specific target market of readers/buyers. Please request our submission information."

AMERICAN CHEMICAL SOCIETY

Publications/Books Division 1155 16th St. NW, Washington DC 20036. (202)452-2120. Fax: (202)452-8913. E-mail: b_hauserman@acs.org. Website: pubs.acs.org/books/. **Contact:** Bob Hauserman, acquisitions editor. Estab. 1876. Publishes hardcover originals. **Publishes 35 titles/year. Pays royalty.** Accepts simultaneous submissions. Responds in 2 months to proposals. Book catalog available free. Guidelines available online.

- American Chemical Society publishes symposium-based books for chemistry.

Nonfiction Subjects include science.
Recent Title(s) *Infrared Analysis of Peptides and Proteins*, edited by Singh.

AMERICAN CORRECTIONAL ASSOCIATION

206 N. Washington St., Suite 200, Alexandria VA 22314. (703)224-0194. Fax: (703)224-0179. E-mail: aliceh@aca.org. Website: www.aca.org. **Contact:** Alice Heiserman, manager of publications and research. Estab. 1870. Publishes trade paperback originals. **Publishes 18 titles/year. 90% of books from first-time authors. 100% from unagented writers.** Publishes book 1 year after acceptance of ms. Responds in 4 months to queries. Book catalog available free. Guidelines available online.

"American Correctional Association provides practical information on jails, prisons, boot camps, probation, parole, community corrections, juvenile facilities and rehabilitation programs, substance abuse programs, and other areas of corrections."

Nonfiction "We are looking for practical, how-to texts or training materials written for the corrections profession. We are especially interested in books on management, development of first-line supervisors, and security-threat group/management in prisons."Query with SASE. Reviews artwork/photos.

Recent Title(s) *TRY: Treatment Readiness for Youth at Risk*; *Changing Criminal Thinking*; *Becoming a Model Warden*.

Tips "Authors are professionals in the field of corrections. Our audience is made up of corrections professionals and criminal justice students. No books by inmates or former inmates. This publisher advises out-of-town freelance editors, indexers, and proofreaders to refrain from requesting work from them."

AMERICAN COUNSELING ASSOCIATION

5999 Stevenson Ave., Alexandria VA 22304. (703)823-9800. Fax: (703)823-4786. E-mail: cbaker@counseling.org. Website: www.counseling.org. **Contact:** Carolyn C. Baker, director of publications. Estab. 1952. Publishes paperback originals. **Publishes 10-12 titles/year. 1% of books from first-time authors. 90% from unagented writers.** Accepts simultaneous submissions. Responds in 1 month to queries. Guidelines available free.

The American Counseling Association is dedicated to promoting public confidence and trust in the counseling profession. We publish scholarly texts for graduate level students and mental health professionals. We do not publish books for the general public.

Nonfiction Subjects include education, gay, lesbian, health, multicultural, psychology, religion, sociology, spirituality, womens issues. Query with SASE. Submit proposal package, outline, 2 sample chapters, vitae.

Recent Title(s) *The ACA Encyclopedia of Counseling: Youth at Risk, 5th Ed.; Counseling Multiple Heritage Individuals, Couples , and Families; ACA Ethical Standards Casebook, 6th Ed.*, by Barbara Herlihy and Gerald Corey.

Tips Target your market. Your books will not be appropriate for everyone across all disciplines.

AMERICAN FEDERATION OF ASTROLOGERS

6535 S. Rural Rd., Tempe AZ 85283. (480)838-1751. Fax: (480)838-8293. E-mail: afa@msn.com. Website: www.astrologers.com. Estab. 1938. Publishes trade paperback originals and reprints. **Publishes 10-15 titles/year. 10 queries received/year. 20 mss received/year. 50% of books from first-time authors. 100% from unagented writers. Pays 10% royalty.** Publishes book 10 months after acceptance of ms. Accepts simultaneous submissions. Responds in 6 months to manuscripts. Book catalog available free. Guidelines available free.

American Federation of Astrologers publishes astrology books, calendars, charts, and related aids.

Nonfiction Submit complete ms.

Recent Title(s) *The Vertex*, by Donna Henson; *Financial Astrology*, by David Williams; *Forensic Astrology*, by Dave Cambell.

N AMERICAN GIRL PUBLISHING

8400 Fairway Place, Middleton WI 53562. Fax: (608)828-4768. Website: www.americangirl.com. **Contact:** Submissions Editor. Estab. 1986. Publishes hardcover and trade paperback originals. **Publishes 50-60 titles/year. 500 queries received/year. 800 mss received/year. 90% from unagented writers. Pays varying advance.** Accepts simultaneous submissions. Responds in 3 months to queries. Responds in 4 months to manuscripts. Book catalog for #10 SASE. Guidelines for for SASE or on the website.

American Girl publishes fiction and nonfiction for girls 7-12. Not accepting fictional mss at this time. We recommend checking our updated writer's guidelines online for possible changes.

Nonfiction Query with SASE.

Recent Title(s) *Chrissa*, by Mary Casanova; *Mini Mysteries 3*, by Rick Walton.

AMERICAN QUILTER'S SOCIETY

Schroeder Publishing Schroeder Publishing, P.O. Box 3290, Paducah KY 42002-3290. (270)898-7903. Fax: (270)898-1173. E-mail: editor@aqsquilt.com. Website: www.americanquilter.com. **Contact:** Andi Reynolds, executive book editor (primarily how-to and patterns, but other quilting books sometimes published, including quilt-related fiction). Estab. 1984. Publishes trade paperback originals. **Publishes 20-24 titles/year. 20-24,300 queries received/year. Multiple submissions okay. 60% of books from first-time authors. Pays 5% royalty on retail price.** Publishes book 12-18 months. after acceptance of ms. Accepts simultaneous submissions. Responds in 1 week to 2 months to proposals. Proposal guidelines online.

"American Quilter's Society publishes how-to and pattern books for quilters (beginners through intermediate skill level). We are not the publisher for non-quilters writing about quilts."

Nonfiction No queries; proposals only. Note: 1 or 2 completed quilt projects must accompany proposal

Recent Title(s) *Beyond the Block*, by Linda K. Johnson and Jane K. Wells (nonfiction); *Bodacious Appliqué à la Carte*, by Margie Engel; *Hooked on Feathers*, by Sally Terry (fiction); *Heart For a Hero*, by Ed Ditto and Laura D. Patrick.

AMERICAN SOCIETY FOR TRAINING & DEVELOPMENT

1640 King St., Alexandria VA 22313. (800)628-2783. Fax: (703)683-9591. E-mail: mmorrow@astd.org. Website: www.astd.org. **Contact:** Mark Morrow, manager, acquisitions and author relations. Estab. 1944. Publishes trade paperback originals. **Publishes 16-20 titles/year. 50 queries received/year. 25-50 mss received/year. 20% of books from first-time authors. 99% from unagented writers.** Publishes book up to 1 year after acceptance of ms. Accepts simultaneous submissions. Responds in 1 month to queries. Responds in 1 month to proposals. Responds in 1 month to manuscripts. Book catalog and ms guidelines free.

Nonfiction Submit proposal package, outline, 1 sample chapter. Reviews artwork/photos.

Recent Title(s) *Adult Learning Basics*, by William J. Rothwell; *Negotiation Skills Training*, by Lisa J. Downs; *Leaders as Teachers: Unlock the Teaching Potential of Your Company's Best and Brightest*, by Edward Betof (co-published with Berrett Kohler Publishers); and *10 Steps to Successful Coaching*, by Sophie Oberstein.

Tips "Audience includes workplace learning professionals including training professionals and some retail business trade titles. Send a good proposal targeted to our audience."

AMERICAN WATER WORKS ASSOCIATION

6666 W. Quincy Ave., Denver CO 80235. (303)347-6278. Fax: (303)794-7310. E-mail: mkozyra@awwa.org. Website: www.awwa.org/communications/books. **Contact:** Mary Kay Kozyra, Acquisitions Editor. Estab. 1881. Publishes hardcover and trade paperback originals. Responds in 4 months to queries. Book catalog and ms guidelines free.

O┑ "AWWA strives to advance and promote the safety and knowledge of drinking water and related issues to all audiences—from kindergarten through post-doctorate."

Nonfiction Subjects include nature, environment, science, software, drinking water- and wastewater-related topics, operations, treatment, sustainability. Query with SASE. Submit outline, bio, 3 sample chapters. Reviews artwork/photos. Send photocopies.

Recent Title(s) *Climate Change and Water: International Perspectives on Mitigation and Adaptation*, by Joel Smith, Carol Howe, and Jim Henderson, editors.

Tips "See website to download submission instructions."

AMERICA WEST PUBLISHERS

P.O. Box 2208, Carson City NV 89702-2208. (775)885-0700. Fax: (877)726-2632. E-mail: global@nohoax.com. Website: www.nohoax.com. **Contact:** George Green, president. Estab. 1985. Publishes hardcover and trade paperback originals and reprints. **Publishes 20 titles/year. 90% of books from first-time authors. 90% from unagented writers. Pays 10% royalty on wholesale price. Pays $300 average advance.** Publishes book 6 months after acceptance of ms. Accepts simultaneous submissions. Responds in 1 month to queries. Book catalog and ms guidelines free.

Imprints Bridger House Publishers, Inc.

O┑ America West seeks the other side of the picture, political cover-ups, and new health alternatives.

Nonfiction Subjects include business, economics, government, politics, including cover-up, health, medicine, holistic self-help, New Age, UFO-metaphysical. Submit outline, sample chapters. Reviews artwork/photos.

Recent Title(s) *Day of Deception*, by William Thomas.

Tips We currently have materials in all bookstores that have areas of UFOs; also political and economic nonfiction.

AMG PUBLISHERS

6815 Shallowford Rd., Chattanooga TN 37421-1755. (423)894-6060. Fax: (423)894-9511. Website: www.amgpublishers.com. **Contact:** Rick Steele, manager of acquisitions. Publishes hardcover and trade paperback originals, electronic originals, and audio Bible and book originals. **Publishes 25-30 titles/year. 2,500 queries received/year. 500 mss received/year. 25% of books from first-time authors. 25% from unagented writers. Pays 10-14% royalty on net sales.** Publishes book 12-18 months after acceptance of ms. Accepts simultaneous submissions. Responds in 1 month to queries. Responds in 6 months to proposals. Responds in 6 months to manuscripts. Book catalog available online. Guidelines available online.

Imprints Living Ink Books; God and Country.

Nonfiction Subjects include Reference, Bible Study workbooks, Bibles, commentaries. Looking for books that facilitate interaction with Bible, encourage and facilitate spiritual growth. Subjects include Christian living, women's , men's family issues, marriage and divorce issues, devotionals, contemporary issues, biblical reference, applied theology, and apologetics. Prefer queries by e-mail.

Fiction Young Adult (teen and preteen) contemporary and fantasy; historical fiction for adults to expand God and Country imprint. " We are looking for youth/young adult (teen) fantasy that contains spiritual truths. We are also now looking for historical fiction for adults."

Recent Title(s) *Last of the Nephilim* and *The Bones of Makaidos*, by Bryan Davis; Preparing My Hearth for Motherhood, by Ann Stewart; Jeremiah; A Bright Light in a Dark Season; Battlefields and Blessings: Stories of Faith and Courage from World War II.

Tips AMG is open to well-written, niche books that meet immediate needs in the lives of adults and young adults.

AMHERST MEDIA, INC.

175 Rano St., Suite 200, Buffalo NY 14207. (716)874-4450. Fax: (716)874-4508. E-mail: amherstmed@aol.com. Website: www.AmherstMedia.com. **Contact:** Craig Alesse, publisher. Estab. 1974. Publishes trade paperback originals and reprints. **Publishes 30 titles/year. 60% of books from first-time authors. 90% from unagented writers. Pays 6-8% royalty on retail price. Pays advance.** Publishes book 1 year after acceptance of ms. Accepts simultaneous submissions. Responds in 2 months to queries. Book catalog and ms guidelines free.

- Amherst Media publishes how-to photography books.

Nonfiction Subjects include photography. Query with outline, 2 sample chapters, and SASE. Reviews artwork/photos.
Recent Title(s) *Portrait Photographer's Handbook*, by Bill Hurter.
Tips Our audience is made up of beginning to advanced photographers. If I were a writer trying to market a book today, I would fill the need of a specific audience and self-edit in a tight manner.

ANDREWS MCMEEL UNIVERSAL

1130 Walnut St., Kansas City MO 64106-2109. (816)932-6700. Website: www.amuniversal.com. **Contact:** Christine Schillig, vice president/editorial director. Estab. 1973. Publishes hardcover and paperback originals. **Publishes 200 titles/year. Pays royalty on retail price or net receipts. Pays advance.**

- Andrews McMeel publishes general trade books, humor books, miniature gift books, calendars, and stationery products.

Nonfiction Subjects include contemporary culture, general trade, relationships. Agented submissions only.
Recent Title(s) *Things Cooks Love*, by Sur La Table ( ).

APA BOOKS

American Psychological Association 750 First St., NE, Washington DC 20002-4242. (800)374-2721 or (202)336-5792. Fax: (202)336-5502. E-mail: books@apa.org. Website: www.apa.org/books. Publishes hardcover and trade paperback originals. Book catalog available online. Guidelines available online.
Imprints Magination Press (children's books).
Nonfiction Subjects include education, gay, lesbian, multicultural, psychology, science, social sciences, sociology, womens issues, womens studies. Submit cv and prospectus with TOC, intended audience, selling points, and outside competition.
Recent Title(s) *The Dependent Patient: A Practitioner's Guide*, by Robert F. Bornstein, PhD; *A Place to Call Home: After-School Programs for Urban Youth*, by Barton J. Hirsch, PhD; *Law & Mental Health Professionals: Ohio*, by Leon VandeCreek, PhD and Marshall Kapp, JD.
Tips Our press features scholarly books on empirically supported topics for professionals and students in all areas of psychology.

APPALACHIAN MOUNTAIN CLUB BOOKS

5 Joy St., Boston MA 02108. (617)523-0655. Fax: (617)523-0722. E-mail: amcpublications@outdoors.org. Website: www.outdoors.org. **Contact:** Editor-in-Chief. Estab. 1897. Publishes hardcover and trade paperback originals. Accepts simultaneous submissions. Guidelines available online.

- Appalachian Mountain Club publishes hiking guides, paddling guides, nature, conservation, and mountain-subject guides for America's Northeast. We connect recreation to conservation and education.

Nonfiction Subjects include nature, environment, recreation, regional, Northeast outdoor recreation, literary nonfiction, guidebooks. Query with proposal and SASE. Reviews artwork/photos. Send photocopies and transparencies.
Recent Title(s) *AMC's Best Backpacking in New England*; *The Wildest Country: Exploring Thoreau's Maine*; *White Mountain Guide: A Centennial Retrospective*.
Tips Our audience is outdoor recreationists, conservation-minded hikers and canoeists, family outdoor lovers, armchair enthusiasts. Visit our website for proposal submission guidelines and more information.

ARCADE PUBLISHING

116 John St., Suite 2810, New York NY 10038. (212)475-2633. Fax: (212)353-8148. Website: www.arcadepub.com. **Contact:** Jeannette Seaver, publisher/executive editor; Cal Barksdale, executive editor; Casey Ebro, editor; Tessa Aye, assistant editor. Estab. 1988. Publishes hardcover originals, trade paperback reprints. **Publishes 35 titles/year. 5% of books from first-time authors. Pays royalty on retail price.10 author's copies Pays advance.** Publishes book within 18 months after acceptance of ms. Responds in 2 months to queries. Book catalog and ms guidelines for #10 SASE.

- "Arcade prides itself on publishing top-notch literary nonfiction and fiction, with a significant proportion of foreign writers."

Nonfiction Subjects include history, memoirs, nature, environment, travel, popular science, current events. Agented submissions only. Reviews artwork/photos. Send photocopies.
Fiction Subjects include literary, mainstream, contemporary, short story collections, translation. Agented submissions only.
Recent Title(s) *Chaplin: A Life*, by Stephen M. Weissman; *You Want Fries With That?*, by Prioleau Alexander; *What You Should Know About Politics.but Don't*, by Jessamyn Conrad.

ARCADIA PUBLISHING

420 Wando Park Blvd., Mt. Pleasant SC 29464. (843)853-2070. Fax: (843)853-0044. Website: www.arcadiapublishing.com. **Contact:** Editorial Director of correct region of the United States. Estab. 1993. Publishes trade paperback originals. **Publishes 600 titles/year. Pays 8% royalty on retail price.** Publishes book 9 months after acceptance of ms. Accepts simultaneous submissions. Book catalog available online. Guidelines available free.

- Four submissions e-mail addresses are publishingnortheast@arcadiapublishing.com; publishingsouth@arcadiapublishing.com; publishingwest@arcadiapublishing.com; publishingmidwest@arcadiapublishing.com. They are divided by region of the United States.
- Arcadia publishes photographic vintage regional histories. We have more than 3,000 in print in our Images of America series. We have expanded our California program.

Nonfiction Subjects include history, local, regional.
Tips Writers should know that we only publish history titles. The majority of our books are on a city or region, and contain vintage images with limited text.

ARCHEBOOKS PUBLISHING

ArcheBooks Publishing Inc. 9101 W. Sahara Ave., Suite 105-112, Las Vegas NV 89117. (800)358-8101. Fax: (702)987-0256. E-mail: info@archebooks.com. Website: www.archebooks.com. **Contact:** Robert E. Gelinas, publisher. Estab. 2003. Publishes hardcover originals, electronic originals and hardcover reprints. **Publishes 30-40 titles/year. 100+ queries received/year. 50+ mss received/year. 90% of books from first-time authors. Pays royalty on retail price. Minimum of $2,500, subject to negotiation and keeping prior history and corporate policy in mind.** Publishes book 6-9 months after acceptance of ms. Responds in 1 month to queries. Responds in 1 month to proposals. Responds in 1 month to manuscripts. Book catalog available online. Guidelines available online.
Nonfiction Subjects include history, true crime. Agented submissions only. Reviews artwork/photos. Send Digital e-mail attachments.
Fiction Subjects include adventure, fantasy, historical, horror, humor, literary, mainstream, contemporary, military, war, mystery, romance, science fiction, suspense, western, young adult. Writers should be prepared to participate in very aggressive and orchestrated marketing and promotion campaigns, using all the promotional tools and training that we provide, at no charge. We're expanding in all areas. Agented submissions only.
Recent Title(s) *The Don Juan Con*, by Sara Williams; *The Mustard Seed*, by Robert E. Gelinas; *The Planters*, by Bill Rogers.
Tips Learn to write a good book proposal. An article on this topic can be found for free on our website in the Author's Corner section of Writer's Resources.

A-R EDITIONS, INC.

8551 Research Way, Suite 180, Middleton WI 53562. (608)836-9000. Fax: (608)831-8200. Website: www.areditions.com. **Contact:** Pamela Whitcomb, managing editor (Recent Researches Series); James L. Zychowicz, managing editor (Computer Music and Digital Audio Series, adn MLA's Index and Bibliography, Technical Reports, and Basic Manual Series). Estab. 1962. **Publishes 30 titles/year. 40 queries received/year. 30 mss received/year. 75% of books from first-time authors. 100% from unagented writers. Pays royalty or honoraria.** Responds in 1 month to queries. Responds in 3 months to proposals. Responds in 6 months to manuscripts. Book catalog available online. Guidelines available online.

- A-R Editions publishes modern critical editions of music based on current musicological research. Each edition is devoted to works by a single composer or to a single genre of composition. The contents are chosen for their potential interest to scholars and performers, then prepared for publication according to the standards that govern the making of all reliable, historical editions.

Nonfiction Subjects include computers, electronics, music, dance, software, historical music editions. Query with SASE. Submit outline.
Recent Title(s) *New Digital Musical Instruments*, by Eduardo Mirando and Marcelo Wanderley; *Charles Ives: 129 Songs*, edited by H. Wiley Hitchcock.

ARKANSAS RESEARCH, INC.

P.O. Box 303, Conway AR 72033. (501)470-1120. E-mail: desmond@arkansasresearch.com. Website: www.arkansasresearch.com. **Contact:** Desmond Walls Allen, owner. Estab. 1985. Publishes trade paperback originals and reprints. **Publishes 10 titles/year. 10% of books from first-time authors. 100% from unagented writers.**

Pays 5-10% royalty on retail price. Publishes book 6 months after acceptance of ms. Responds in 1 month to queries. Book catalog for $1. Guidelines available free.

O-x Our company opens a world of information to researchers interested in the history of Arkansas.

Nonfiction All Arkansas-related subjects.Subjects include Americana, ethnic, history, hobbies, genealogy, military, war, regional. Query with SASE. Reviews artwork/photos. Send photocopies.

Recent Title(s) *Life & Times From The Clay County Courier Newspaper Published at Corning, Arkansas, 1893-1900.*

ARROW PUBLICATIONS, LLC

9112 Paytley Bridge Lane, Potomac MD 20854-4432. (301)299-9422. Fax: (301)299-9423. E-mail: arrow_info@arrowpub.com. Website: www.arrowpub.com. **Contact:** Tom King, managing editor; Maryan Gibson, acquisition editor. Estab. 1987. Publishes romance fiction in a graphic novel format. **Publishes 50 e-book titles. Paperback version launched in 2009 with 12 English and 12 Spanish titles/year. titles/year. 150 queries received/year. 100 mss received/year. 80% of books from first-time authors. 100% from unagented writers. Makes outright purchase of accepted completed scripts.** Publishes book 4-6 months after acceptance of ms. Responds in 2 month to queries (sent with SASE). Responds in 1 month to scripts sent upon request. Guidelines available online at www.arrowpub.com/writers.htm.

Fiction We are looking for outlines of stories heavy on romance with elements of adventure/intrigue/mystery. We will consider other romance genres such as fantasy, western, inspirational, and historical as long as the romance element is strong. See our e-books section at www.myromancestory.com/ebooks for descriptions of typical titles. Humorous love stories are always appreciated. We need true-to-life romances between consenting adults, with believable conflicts and well-defined characterizations. We publish illustrated romance stories, so we are looking for good dialogue writers. Each story is formatted into a script of 70-75 panels, comprising narrative, dialogue, and art direction. Query with outline first with SASE. Consult submission guidelines at www.arrowpub.com before submitting.

Recent Title(s) *Not the Marrying Kind*, by Cynthia Starr (romance/western); *Good Husband Material*, by Maryan Gibson (romance/contemporary); *Faithfully Yours*, by Alice Gaylord (romance/inspirational); *Love's Redemption*, by Niambi Brown Davis (romance/suspense); *The Beaufort Ghost*, by Nazalie Austin (romance/mystery); *Act of Love*, by Maria Davies (romance/adventure).

Tips Our audience is primarily women 18 and older. View sample stories at www.myromancestory.com and review guidelines online at www.arrowpub.com/writers.htm. Send query with outline only. We do not accept queries or sample chapters for full-length novels in any genre.

ARTE PUBLICO PRESS

University of Houston, 452 Cullen Performance Hall, Houston TX 77204-2004. Fax: (713)743-3080. Website: www.artepublicopress.com. **Contact:** Nicolas Kanellos, editor. Estab. 1979. Publishes hardcover originals, trade paperback originals and reprints. **Publishes 25-30 titles/year. 1,000 queries received/year. 2,000 mss received/year. 50% of books from first-time authors. 80% from unagented writers. Pays 10% royalty on wholesale price.Provides 20 author's copies; 40% discount on subsequent copies. Pays $1,000-3,000 advance.** Publishes book 2 years after acceptance of ms. Accepts simultaneous submissions. Responds in 1 month to queries. Responds in 1 month to proposals. Responds in 4 months to manuscripts. Book catalog available free. Guidelines available online.

Imprints Piñata Books.

O-x We are a showcase for **Hispanic** literary creativity, arts and culture. Our endeavor is to provide a national forum for U.S.-Hispanic literature.

Nonfiction Subjects include ethnic, language, literature, regional, translation, womens issues, womens studies. Query with SASE. Submit outline, 2 sample chapters.

Fiction Subjects include ethnic, literary, mainstream, contemporary, written by U.S.-Hispanic authors. Query with SASE. Submit outline/proposal, clips, 2 sample chapters. Submit complete ms.

Recent Title(s) *Butterflies on Carmen Street/Mariposas en la calle Carmen*, by Monica Brown; *El corrido de Dante*, by Eduardo Gonzalez-Viana; *The Lady from Buenos Aires*, by Diane Gonzales Bertrane.

ASA, AVIATION SUPPLIES & ACADEMICS

7005 132nd Pl. SE, Newcastle WA 98059. (425)235-1500. E-mail: feedback@asa2fly.com. Website: www.asa2fly.com. Book catalog available free.

O-x ASA is an industry leader in the development and sales of aviation supplies, publications, and software for pilots, flight instructors, flight engineers and aviation technicians. All ASA products are developed by a team of researchers, authors and editors.

Nonfiction All subjects must be related to aviation education and training.Subjects include education. Query with outline. Send photocopies.

Recent Title(s) *The Savvy Flight Instructor: Secrets of the Successful CFI*, by Greg Brown.

Tips Two of our specialty series include ASA's *Focus Series*, and ASA *Aviator's Library*. Books in our *Focus Series* concentrate on single-subject areas of aviation knowledge, curriculum and practice. The *Aviator's Library* is comprised of titles of known and/or classic aviation authors or established instructor/authors in the industry, and other aviation specialty titles.

ASCE PRESS

1801 Alexander Bell Dr., Reston VA 20191-4400. (703)295-6275. Fax: (703)295-6278. E-mail: ascepress@asce.org. Website: pubs.asce.org. Estab. 1989. **Publishes 10-15 titles/year. 20% of books from first-time authors. 100% from unagented writers.** Accepts simultaneous submissions. Request ASCE Press book proposal submission guidelines. Guidelines available online.

- ASCE Press publishes technical volumes that are useful to practicing civil engineers and civil engineering students, as well as allied professionals. We publish books by individual authors and editors to advance the civil engineering profession. Currently emphasizing geotechnical, structural engineering, water/environmental, management and engineering history. De-emphasizing highly specialized areas with narrow scope.

Nonfiction We are looking for topics that are useful and instructive to the engineering practitioner.Query with proposal, sample chapters, CV, TOC, and target audience.

Recent Title(s) *Washington Roebling's Father: A Memoir of John A. Roebling*, edited by Donald Sayenga; *Geotechnical Testing, Observation, and Documentation*, by Tim Davis; *Beyond Failure: Forensic Case Studies for Civil Engineers*, by Norbert J. Delatte Jr.

Tips As a traditional publisher of scientific and technical materials, ASCE Press applies rigorous standards to the expertise, scholarship, readability and attractiveness of its books.

ASM PRESS

Book division for the American Society for Microbiology 1752 N. St., NW, Washington DC 20036-2904. (202)737-3600. Fax: (202)942-9342. E-mail: books@asmusa.org. Website: www.asmpress.org. **Contact:** Lindsay Williams (proposal submissions); Gregory Payne, senior editor (all microbiology and related sciences); Eleanor Riemer, consulting editor (food microbiology). Estab. 1899. Publishes hardcover, trade paperback and electronic originals. **Publishes 30 titles/year. 40% of books from first-time authors. 95% from unagented writers. Pays 5-15% royalty on wholesale price. Pays $1,000-10,000 advance.** Publishes book 6-9 months after acceptance of ms. Accepts simultaneous submissions. Responds in 1 month to queries. Responds in 1-2 months to proposals. Responds in 1-4 months to manuscripts. Book catalog available online. Guidelines available online.

Nonfiction Subjects include agriculture, animals, education, health, medicine, history, horticulture, nature, environment, science, microbiology and related sciences. Query with SASE. Submit proposal package, outline, prospectus. Reviews artwork/photos. Send photocopies.

Recent Title(s) *Principles of Virology*, 3rd edition, by Flint, Enquist, Racaniello, Skalba (textbook); *Animalcules*, by Dixon (scientific trade); *Clinical Virology*, 3rd edition, by Richman, Whitley, Hayden (reference manual).

Tips "Credentials are most important."

ASSOCIATION FOR SUPERVISION AND CURRICULUM DEVELOPMENT

1703 N. Beauregard St., Alexandria VA 22311. (703)575-5693. Fax: (703)575-5400. Website: www.ascd.org. **Contact:** Scott Willis, acquisitions director. Estab. 1943. Publishes trade paperback originals. **Publishes 24-30 titles/year. 100 queries received/year. 100 mss received/year. 50% of books from first-time authors. 95% from unagented writers. Pays negotiable royalty on actual monies received.** Publishes book 1 year after acceptance of ms. Accepts simultaneous submissions. Responds in 3 months to proposals. Book catalog and ms guidelines free or online.

- ASCD publishes high-quality professional books for educators.

Nonfiction Subjects include education, for professional educators. Submit full proposal, 2 sample chapters. Reviews artwork/photos. Send photocopies.

Recent Title(s) *Leadership for the Learning: How to Help Students Succeed*, by Carl Glickman; *The Multiple Intelligences of Reading and Writing*, by Thomas Armstrong; *Educating Oppositional and Defiant Children*, by Philip S. Hall, Nancy D. Hall.

ATHENEUM BOOKS FOR YOUNG READERS

Imprint of Simon & Schuster 1230 Avenue of the Americas, New York NY 10020. Website: www.simonsayskids.com. Estab. 1960. Publishes hardcover originals. Accepts simultaneous submissions. Guidelines for #10 SASE.

- Atheneum Books for Young Readers publishes books aimed at children, pre-school through high school.

Nonfiction Subjects include Americana, animals, art, architecture, business, economics, government, politics, health, medicine, history, music, dance, nature, environment, photography, psychology, recreation, religion, science, sociology, sports, travel.

Fiction All in juvenile versions.Subjects include adventure, ethnic, experimental, fantasy, gothic, historical, horror, humor, mainstream, contemporary, mystery, science fiction, sports, suspense, western, Animal. We have few specific needs except for books that are fresh, interesting and well written. Fad topics are dangerous, as are works you haven't polished to the best of your ability. We also don't need safety pamphlets, ABC books, coloring books and board books. In writing picture book texts, avoid the coy and `cutesy,' such as stories about characters with alliterative names. *Query only. No unsolicited mss.*
Recent Title(s) *Billy and the Rebel,* by Deborah Hopkinson, illustrated by Brian Floca; *Imagine a Day,* by Sarah L. Thomson, illustrated by Rob Gonsalves; *Seeds,* written and illustrated by Ken Robbins.

ATLAS VARIETY PUBLISHING

P.O. Box 1117, Palmetto FL 34220. E-mail: acquisitions@atlasvariety.com. Website: www.atlasvariety.com. **Contact:** Elaine Rigoli, co-publisher (nonfiction); Christopher Rigoli, co-publisher (fiction). Estab. 2004. Publishes hardcover and trade paperback originals. **Publishes 4 titles/year. 50% of books from first-time authors. 50% from unagented writers. Pays 6-10% royalty on wholesale price.** Publishes book 12-18 months after acceptance of ms. Responds in 6 months to queries. Responds in 6 months to proposals. Responds in 6 months to manuscripts. Guidelines available online.
Nonfiction Subjects include child guidance, contemporary culture, cooking, foods, nutrition, creative nonfiction, health, medicine, sex, travel, womens issues, womens studies, relationships, pregnancy, weddings. Submit proposal package, outline, an updated resume, 3 sample chapters, SASE. Electronic Query Letters Only! .
Fiction Subjects include fantasy, science fiction. Our fiction department seeks to publish entertaining stories driven by characters readers can relate to. Keep query letters to 1 page, proposal/synopsis to 5 pages, and manuscripts to 50 pages (first 3 chapters). Please visit our Web site to determine which fiction categories we are currently seeking. Submit proposal package, outline, resume, 3 sample chapters, SASE. Electronic Query Letters Only!.
Tips Our readers turn to us to find interesting books that encourage, enrich, and inspire. We're open to new writers who have both a natural talent and a new, interesting voice. Check our website for further information, including guidelines and author resources.

ATRIAD PRESS, LLC

13820 Methuen Green, Dallas TX 75240. (972)671-0002. Fax: (214)367-4343. E-mail: editor@atriadpress.com. Website: www.atriadpress.com. **Contact:** Mitchel Whitington, senior editor. Estab. 2002. Publishes trade paperback originals. Accepts simultaneous submissions. Book catalog available online. Guidelines available online.

- We are currently accepting submissions for three different series: The Haunted Encounters Series (submissions@atriadpress.com); Encuentros Encantados (hector@atriadpress.com); Ghostly Tales from America's Jails (jails@atriadpress.com).

Nonfiction Submit proposal package, outline, bio, 3 sample chapters, via mail or e-mail.
Recent Title(s) *Haunted Encounters: Real-Life Stories of Supernatural Experiences*, (anthology).
Tips The market for ghost stories is huge! It seems to be very broad—and ranges from young to old. Currently, our books are for adults, but we would consider the teen market. Please check your manuscript carefully for errors in spelling and structure.

AVALON BOOKS

Thomas Bouregy & Co., Inc. 160 Madison Ave., 5th Floor, New York NY 10016. (212)598-0222. Fax: (212)979-1862. E-mail: editorial@avalonbooks.com. Website: www.avalonbooks.com. Estab. 1950. Publishes hardcover originals. **Publishes 60 titles/year. Pays 10% royalty. Pays $1,000+ advance.** Publishes book 10-12 months after acceptance of ms. Responds in 1 month to queries. Guidelines available online.
Fiction Subjects include mystery, romance, western. "We publish wholesome contemporary romances, mysteries, historical romances and westerns. Our books are read by adults as well as teenagers, and the characters are all adults. All mysteries are contemporary. We publish contemporary romances (4 every 2 months), historical romances (2 every 2 months), mysteries (2 every 2 months) and traditional westerns (2 every 2 months). Submit first 3 sample chapters, a 2-3 page synopsis and SASE. The manuscripts should be 45,000-70,000 words. Manuscripts that are too long will not be considered. The books should be wholesome fiction, without graphic sex, violence or strong language." Query with SASE.
Recent Title(s) *Everything But a Wedding*, by Holly Jacobs (romance), *His Lordship's Chaperone*, by Shirley Marks (historical romance); *The Puzzle of Piri Reis*, by Kent Conwell (mystery); *The Search for Justice*, by Ron and Judy Culp (western)

AVALON TRAVEL PUBLISHING

Avalon Publishing Group 1700 4th St., Berkeley CA 94710. (510)595-3664. Fax: (510)595-4228. E-mail: acquisitions@avalonpub.com. Website: www.travelmatters.com. Estab. 1973. Publishes trade paperback originals. **Publishes 100 titles/year. 5,000 queries received/year. 25% of books from first-time authors. 95% from unagented writers. Pays up to $17,000 advance.** Publishes book an average of 9 months after acceptance of ms. Accepts simultaneous submissions. Responds in 4 months to queries. Responds in 4 months to proposals. Guidelines available online.

O→ Avalon travel guides feature a combination of practicality and spirit, offering a traveler-to-traveler perspective perfect for planning an afternoon hike, around-the-world journey, or anything in between. ATP publishes 7 major series. Each one has a different emphasis and a different geographic coverage. We're currently expanding our coverage, with a focus on European and Asian destinations. Our main areas of interest are North America, Central America, South America, the Caribbean, and the Pacific. At any given moment, we are seeking to acquire only a handful of specific titles in each of our major series. Check online guidelines for current needs. Follow guidelines closely.

Nonfiction Subjects include regional, travel.

Recent Title(s) *Moon Handbooks Florida Gulf Coast*, by Laura Reiley; *Moon Handbooks Panama*, by William Friar; *Living Abroad in Costa Rica*, by Erin Van Rheenen.

Tips Please note that ATP is only looking for books that fit into current series and is not interested in the following genres: fiction, children's books, and travelogues/travel diaries.

[A] AVON BOOKS

HarperCollins 10 E. 53rd St., New York NY 10022. Website: www.harpercollins.com. **Contact:** Editorial Submissions. Estab. 1941. Publishes trade and mass market paperback originals and reprints. **Royalty negotiable. Pays advance.** Accepts simultaneous submissions. online for Avon romance submissions only. E-mail to: avonromance@harpercollins.com.

Fiction Subjects include romance, contemporary, historical, suspense, and thriller, women's fiction, women's nonfiction. Agented submissions only.

Recent Title(s) *The Secret Diaries of Miss Miranda Cheever*, by Julia Quinn; *Lost & Found*, by Jacqueline Sheehan; *Sanity Savers*, by Dale V. Atkins.

B&H PUBLISHING GROUP

Lifeway Christian Resources 127 Ninth Ave. N., Nashville TN 37234. (615)251-2644. Fax: (615)251-2413. Website: www.bhpublishinggroup.com. **Contact:** Ricky King, associate publisher. Estab. 1934. Publishes hardcover and paperback originals. **Publishes 90-100 titles/year. Pays negotiable royalty** Accepts simultaneous submissions. Responds in 9-12 months to queries. Responds in 9-12 months to manuscripts.

O→ "B&H Publishers publishes books that provide biblical solutions that spiritually transform individuals and cultures. Currently emphasizing inspirational/gift books, general Christian living and books on Christianity and society."

Nonfiction Subjects include religion, spirituality. Query with SASE.

Fiction Subjects include adventure, mystery, religious, general religious, inspirational, religious fantasy, religious mystery/suspense, religious thriller, religious romance, western. "We publish fiction in all the main genres. We want not only a very good story, but also one that sets forth Christian values. Nothing that lacks a positive Christian emphasis (but do not preach, however); nothing that fails to sustain reader interest." Query with SASE.

Recent Title(s) *A Greater Freedom*, by Oliver North; *The Beloved Disciple*, by Beth Moore; *Against All Odds*, by Chuck Norris.

[N] BACKBEAT BOOKS

Hal Leonard Publishing Group 19 W. 21st St., Suite 201, New York NY 10010. (212)575-9265. Fax: (212)575-9270. E-mail: medison@halleonard.com. Website: www.backbeatbooks.com. **Contact:** Mike Edison, Sr. Ed. (rock, jazz, pop culture). hardcover and trade paperback originals; trade paperback reprints. **Publishes 24 titles/year.**

Nonfiction Subjects include music (rock & roll), pop culture. Query by email.

Recent Title(s) *Waiting for the Sun: A Rock and Roll History of Los Angeles*, by Barney Hoskyns (rock history); *A Pure Drop: The Life of Jeff Buckley*, by Jeff Apter (rock bio); *Gruhn's Guide to Vintage Guitars*, by George Gruhn & Walter Carter (musical instruments/guitar).

BAEN PUBLISHING ENTERPRISES

P.O. Box 1403, Riverdale NY 10471-0671. Website: www.baen.com. **Contact:** Toni Weisskopf. Estab. 1983. Publishes hardcover, trade paperback and mass market paperback originals and reprints. Responds in 9-12 months to manuscripts. Book catalog available free. Guidelines available online.

O→ We publish books at the heart of science fiction and fantasy.

Fiction Subjects include fantasy, science fiction. Interested in science fiction novels (based on real science) and fantasy novels that at least strive for originality. Submit synopsis and complete m

Recent Title(s) *The Prometheus Project*, by Steve Shite; *The Course of Empire*, by Eric Flint and K.D. Wentworth; *E. Godz*, by Robert Asprin and Esther Friesner.

Tips See our books before submitting. Send for our writers' guidelines.

BAKER ACADEMIC

Division of Baker Publishing Group 6030 E. Fulton Rd., Ada MI 49301. (616)676-9185. Fax: (616)676-2315. Website: www.bakeracademic.com. Estab. 1939. Publishes hardcover and trade paperback originals. **Publishes 50 titles/year. 10% of books from first-time authors. 85% from unagented writers. Pays advance.** Publishes book 1 year after acceptance of ms. Book catalog for 9 ½x12 ½ SAE with 3 first-class stamps. Guidelines for #10 SASE.

- "Baker Academic publishes religious academic and professional books for students and church leaders. Most of our authors and readers are Christians with academic interests, and our books are purchased from all standard retailers. Does not accept unsolicited queries."

Nonfiction Subjects include anthropology, archeology, education, psychology, religion, womens issues, womens studies, Biblical studies, Christian doctrine, books for pastors and church leaders, contemporary issues.

Recent Title(s) *Apostle Paul*, by Udo Schnelle; *Dictionary for Theological Interpretation of the Bible*, edited by Kevin Vanhoorer, et al.; *The American Evangelical Story*, by Douglas Sweeney.

BAKER BOOKS

Imprint of Baker Publishing Group 6030 E. Fulton Rd., Ada MI 49301. (616)676-9185. Fax: (616)676-9573. Website: www.bakerbooks.com. Estab. 1939. Publishes hardcover and trade paperback originals, and trade paperback reprints. Book catalog for 9 ½x12 ½ envelope and 3 First-Class stamps. Guidelines for #10 SASE.

- "Baker Books publishes popular religious nonfiction reference books and professional books for church leaders. Most of our authors and readers are evangelical Christians, and our books are purchased from Christian bookstores, mail-order retailers, and school bookstores. Does not accept unsolicited queries."

Nonfiction Subjects include child guidance, psychology, religion, womens issues, womens studies, Christian doctrine.

Fiction .

Recent Title(s) *Praying Backwards*, by Bryan Chapell; *The Scandal of the Evangelical Conscience*, by Ronald J. Sider; *The Invisible War*, by Chip Ingram.

BAKER PUBLISHING GROUP

6030 E. Fulton Rd., Ada MI 49301. (616)676-9185. Fax: (616)676-2315. Website: www.bakerpublishinggroup.com.

Imprints Baker Academic; Baker Books; Bethany House; Brazos Press; Chosen; Fleming H. Revell.

- *Does not accept unsolicited queries.*

BALCONY MEDIA, INC.

512 E. Wilson, Suite 213, Glendale CA 91206. (818)956-5313. E-mail: ann@balconypress.com. **Contact:** Ann Gray, publisher. Publishes hardcover and trade paperback originals. **Publishes 6-8 titles/year. 75% of books from first-time authors. 90% from unagented writers. Pays 10% royalty on wholesale price.** Accepts simultaneous submissions. Responds in 1 month to queries. Responds in 1 month to proposals. Responds in 3 months to manuscripts. Book catalog available online.

- We also now publish *Form: pioneering design magazine, bi-monthly to the architecture and design professions.* Editor: Alelxi Drosu, www.formmag.net.

Nonfiction Subjects include art, architecture, ethnic, gardening, history, relative to design, art, architecture, and architecture, regional. Query by e-mail or letter. Submit outline and 2 sample chapters with introduction, if applicable.

Recent Title(s) *Tall Building: Imagining the Skyscraper*, by Scott Johnson; *Water is Key: A Better Future for Africa*, by Gil Garcetti.

Tips Audience consists of architects, designers, and the general public who enjoy those fields. Our books typically cover California subjects, but that is not a restriction. It's always nice when an author has strong ideas about how the book can be effectively marketed. We are not afraid of small niches if a good sales plan can be devised.

BALLANTINE PUBLISHING GROUP

Imprint of Random House, Inc. 1745 Broadway, 18th Floor, New York NY 10019. (212)782-9000. Website: www.randomhouse.com. Estab. 1952. Publishes hardcover, trade paperback, mass market paperback originals. Guidelines available online.

Imprints Ballantine Books, Ballantine Reader's Circle, Del Rey, Del Rey/Lucas Books, Fawcett, Ivy, One World, Wellspring.

- Ballantine Books publishes a wide variety of nonfiction and fiction.

Nonfiction Subjects include animals, child guidance, community, cooking, foods, nutrition, creative nonfiction, education, gay, lesbian, health, medicine, history, language, literature, memoirs, military, war, recreation, religion, sex, spirituality, travel, true crime. Agented submissions only. Reviews artwork/photos. Send

photocopies.

Fiction Subjects include confession, ethnic, fantasy, feminist, gay, lesbian, historical, humor, literary, mainstream, contemporary, womens, military, war, multicultural, mystery, romance, short story collections, spiritual, suspense, translation, general fiction. Agented submissions only.

BANTAM BOOKS FOR YOUNG READERS

Imprint of Random House Children's Books/Random House, Inc. 1745 Broadway, New York NY 10019. (212)782-9000. Website: www.randomhouse.com/kids.

- Not seeking mss at this time.

BANTAM DELACORTE DELL BOOKS FOR YOUNG READERS

Random House Children's Publishing, Random House, Inc. 1745 Broadway, New York NY 10019. (212)782-9000. Fax: (212)782-8234. Website: www.randomhouse.com/kids. Publishes hardcover, trade paperback and mass market paperback series originals, trade paperback reprints. **Publishes approximately 300 titles/year. Pays royalty.**

Imprints Delacorte Press; Doubleday; Laurel Leaf (YA); Yearling (middle grade).

> Bantam Delacorte Dell Books for Young Readers publishes award-winning books by distinguished authors and the most promising new writers. The best way to break in to this market is through its 2 contests, the Delacrote/Yearling Contest and the Delacorte Press Contest for a First Young Adult Novel.

Fiction Subjects include adventure, fantasy, historical, humor, juvenile, mainstream, contemporary, mystery, picture books, suspense, chapter books, middle-grade. *No unsolicited mss or queri*

Recent Title(s) *Forever in Blue: The Fourth Summer of the Sisterhood*, by Ann Brashares; *The Sweet Far Thing*, by Libby Bray; *Hattie Big Sky*, by Kirby Larson.

BARBOUR PUBLISHING, INC.

P.O. Box 719, Uhrichsville OH 44683. E-mail: editors@barbourbooks.com. Website: www.barbourpublishing.com. **Contact:** Paul Muckley, senior editor (nonfiction); Rebecca Germany, senior editor (women's fiction). Estab. 1981. Publishes hardcover, trade paperback and mass market paperback originals and reprints. **Publishes 200 titles/year. 500 queries received/year. 1000 mss received/year. 40% of books from first-time authors. 80% from unagented writers. Pays 0-16% royalty on net price or makes outright purchase of $500-6,000. Pays $500-10,000 advance.** Publishes book 12-24 months after acceptance of ms. Accepts simultaneous submissions. Responds in 1 month to queries. Book catalog online or for 9x12 SAE with 2 first-class stamps. Ms guidelines for #10 SASE or online.

Imprints Heartsong Presents (contact Joanne Simmons, managing editor).

> Barbour Books publishes inspirational/devotional material that is nondenominational and evangelical in nature; Heartsong Presents publishes Christian romance. We're a Christian evangelical publisher.

Nonfiction Subjects include child guidance, cooking, foods, nutrition, money, finance, religion, evangelical Christian, womens issues, womens studies, inspirational/Christian living. Submit outline, 3 sample chapters, SASE. Reviews artwork/photos. Send photocopies.

Fiction Subjects include romance, historical and contemporary, suspense, women's issues. Heartsong romance is 'sweet'—no sex, no bad language. Other genres may be 'grittier'—real-life stories. All must have Christian faith as an underlying basis. Common writer's mistakes are a sketchy proposal, an unbelievable story, and a story that don't fit our guidelines for inspirational romances. Submit clips, 3 sample chapters, SASE.

Recent Title(s) *Power Prayers to Start Your Day*, by Donna K. Maltese (devotional); *The Red Siren*, by M. L. Tyndall (fiction); *School's Out*, by Wanda E. Brunstetter.

Tips Audience is evangelical/Christian conservative, nondenominational, young and old. We're looking for great concepts, not necessarily a big name author or agent. We want to publish books that will consistently sell large numbers, not just `flash in the pan' releases. Send us your ideas!

BAREFOOT BOOKS

2067 Massachusettes Ave., Cambridge MA 02140. Website: www.barefootbooks.com. **Contact:** Submissions Editor. Publishes hardcover and trade paperback originals. **Publishes 30 titles/year. 2,000 queries received/year. 3,000 mss received/year. 35% of books from first-time authors. 60% from unagented writers. Pays 2 ½-5% royalty on retail price. Pays advance.** Publishes book 2 years after acceptance of ms. Accepts simultaneous submissions. Responds in 4 months to queries. Responds in 4 months to proposals. Responds in 4 months to manuscripts. Book catalog for 9x12 SAE stamped with $1.80 postage. Guidelines available online.

> We are a small, independent publishing company that publishes high-quality picture books for children of all ages and specializes in the work of artists andwriters from many cultures. We focus on themes that support independence of spirit, encourage openness to others, and foster a life-long love of learning. Prefers full manuscript.

Fiction Subjects include juvenile. Barefoot Books only publishes children's picture books and anthologies of folktales. We do not publish novels. We encourage authors to send their full manuscript. Always include SASE.
Recent Title(s) *We All Went on Safari: A Counting Journey Through Tanzania*, by Laurie Krebs (early learning picture book); *The Fairie's Gift*, by Tanya Robyn Batt (picture book); *The Lady of Ten Thousand Names: Goddess Stories From Many Cultures*, by Burleigh Mutén (illustrated anthology).
Tips Our audience is made up of children and parents, teachers and students, of many different ages and cultures. Since we are a small publisher, and we definitely publish for a 'niche' market, it is helpful to look at our books and our website before submitting, to see if your book would fit into the type of book we publish.

BARRICADE BOOKS, INC.

185 Bridge Plaza N., Suite 308A, Fort Lee NJ 07024-5900. (201)944-7600. Fax: (201)944-6363. Website: www.barricadebooks.com. **Contact:** Carole Stuart, publisher. Estab. 1991. Publishes hardcover and trade paperback originals, trade paperback reprints. **Publishes 12 titles/year. 200 queries received/year. 100 mss received/year. 80% of books from first-time authors. 50% from unagented writers. Pays 10-12% royalty on retail price for hardcover. Pays advance.** Publishes book 18 months after acceptance of ms. Responds in 1 month to queries.

- "Barricade Books publishes nonfiction, mostly of the controversial type, and books we can promote with authors who can talk about their topics on radio and television and to the press."

Nonfiction Subjects include business, economics, ethnic, gay, lesbian, government, politics, health, medicine, history, nature, environment, psychology, sociology, true crime. Query with SASE. Submit outline, 1-2 sample chapters. Material will not be returned or responded to without SASE. Reviews artwork/photos. Send photocopies.
Recent Title(s) *Mail for Mikey,* by Orson Bean; *Jailing the Johnstown Gang*, by Bruce Mowday.
Tips "Do your homework. Visit bookshops to find publishers who are doing the kinds of books you want to write. Always submit to a person—not just `Editor.' Always enclose a SASE or you may not get a response."

BARRON'S EDUCATIONAL SERIES, INC.

250 Wireless Blvd., Hauppauge NY 11788. (800)645-3476. Fax: (631)434-3723. E-mail: waynebarr@barronseduc.com. Website: www.barronseduc.com. **Contact:** Acquisitions Manager. Estab. 1941. Publishes hardcover, paperback and mass market originals and software. **Publishes 400 titles/year. 2,000 queries received/year. 15% of books from first-time authors. 75% from unagented writers. Pays $3,000-4,000 advance.** Publishes book 18 months after acceptance of ms. Accepts simultaneous submissions. Responds in 3 months to queries. Responds in 8 months to manuscripts. Book catalog available free. Guidelines available online.

- Barron's tends to publish series of books, both for adults and children. No adult fiction. We are always on the lookout for creative nonfiction ideas for children and adults.

Nonfiction Subjects include business, economics, child guidance, education, health, hobbies, language, literature, new age, sports, translation, adult education, foreign language, review books, pet guides, test prep guides. Query with SASE. Submit outline, 2-3 sample chapters. Reviews artwork/photos.
Recent Title(s) *Night at the Museum: Battle of the Smithsonian; Mathopolis: Parting is Such Sweet Sorrow.*
Tips Audience is mostly educated self-learners and students. The writer has the best chance of selling us a book that will fit into one of our series. Children's books have less chance for acceptance because of the glut of submissions. On children's stories, better to send query e-mail without attachments to: Waynebarr@barronseduc.com. SASE must be included for the return of all materials. Please be patient for replies.

BASIC HEALTH PUBLICATIONS, INC.

28812 Top of the World Dr., Laguna Beach CA 92651. (949)715-7327. Fax: (949)715-7328. Website: www.basichealthpub.com. **Contact:** Norman Goldfind, publisher. Estab. 2001. Publishes hard cover trade paperback and mass market paperback originals and reprints. Accepts simultaneous submissions. Book catalog available online. Guidelines for #10 SASE.
Nonfiction Subjects include health, medicine. Submit proposal package, outline, 2-3 sample chapters, introduction.
Recent Title(s) *The Sinatra Solution: Metabolic Cardiology*, by Stephen Sinatra, MD; *Umbilical Cord Stem Cell Therapy: The Gift of Life From Healthy Newborns*, by David Steenblock, MSDD, and Anthony F. Payne, PhD.
Tips "Our audience is over 30, well educated, middle to upper income. We prefer writers with professional credentials (M.D.s, Ph.D.s, N.D.s, etc.), or writers with backgrounds in health and medicine."

BATTELLE PRESS

505 King Ave., Columbus OH 43201. (614)424-6424. E-mail: press@battelle.org. Website: www.battelle.org/bookstore. **Contact:** Joe Sheldrick. Estab. 1980. Publishes hardcover and paperback originals and markets primarily by direct mail. **Publishes 15 titles/year. Pays 10% royalty on wholesale price.** Publishes book 6 months after acceptance of ms. Accepts simultaneous submissions. Responds in 1 month to queries. Book catalog available free. Guidelines available online.

O‑ Battelle Press strives to be a primary source of books and software on science and technology management.

Nonfiction Subjects include science. Query with SASE. Returns submissions with SASE only by writer's request. Reviews artwork/photos. Send photocopies.

Recent Title(s) *Communications Guide*; *Technically Speaking*.

Tips Audience consists of engineers, researchers, scientists and corporate researchers and developers.

BAYLOR UNIVERSITY PRESS

One Bear Place 97363, Waco TX 76798. (254)710-3164. Fax: (254)710-3440. E-mail: carey_newman@baylor.edu. Website: www.baylorpress.com. **Contact:** Carey C. Newman, editor. Publishes hardcover and trade paperback originals. **Publishes 30 titles/year. Pays 10% royalty on wholesale price.** Publishes book 1 year after acceptance of ms. Accepts simultaneous submissions. Responds in 2 months to proposals. Guidelines available online.

O‑ We publish contemporary and historical scholarly works on religion and public life. Currently emphasizing religious studies.

Nonfiction Submit outline, 1-3 sample chapters.

Recent Title(s) *Building Jewish in the Roman East*, by Peter Richardson; *Encyclopedia of Evangelicalism*, by Randall Balmer; *Not Quite American? The Shaping of Arab and Muslim Identity in the United States*, by Yvonne Yazbeck Haddad.

BAYWOOD PUBLISHING CO., INC.

26 Austin Ave., P.O. Box 337, Amityville NY 11701. (631)691-1270. Fax: (631)691-1770. Website: www.baywood.com. **Contact:** Stuart Cohen, managing editor. Estab. 1964. **Publishes 25 titles/year. Pays 7-15% royalty on retail price. Pays advance.** Publishes book within 12 months after acceptance of ms. Book catalog and ms guidelines free or online.

O‑ "Baywood Publishing publishes original and innovative books in the humanities and social sciences, including areas such as health sciences, gerontology, death and bereavement, psychology, technical communications and archaeology."

Nonfiction Subjects include anthropology, archaeology, computers, electronics, education, health, nature, environment, psychology, sociology, womens issues, gerontology. Submit proposal package.

Recent Title(s) *Perspectives on Violence and Violent Death*, edited by Robert G. Stevenson and Gerry R. Cox; *Together with Technology: Writing Review, Enculturation, and Technological Mediation*, by Jason Swarts; *Freedom to Choose: How To Make End-Of-Life Decisions On Your Own Terms*, by George Burnell; *At the Point of Production: Social Analysis of Occupational and Environmental Health*, edited by Charles Levenstein; *Within Reach? Managing Chemical Risks in Small Enterprises*, by David Walters; *Outsourcing Technical Communication: Issues, Policies and Practices*, ed. by Barry L. Thatcher and Carlos Evia.

BEACON HILL PRESS OF KANSAS CITY

Nazarene Publishing House P.O. Box 419527, Kansas City MO 64141. (816)931-1900. Fax: (816)753-4071. **Contact:** Judi Perry, consumer editor. Publishes hardcover and paperback originals. **Publishes 30 titles/year. Pays royalty.** Publishes book 2 years after acceptance of ms. Responds in 3 months to queries.

O‑ "Beacon Hill Press is a Christ-centered publisher that provides authentically Christian resources faithful to God's word and relevant to life."

Nonfiction "Accent on holy living; encouragement in daily Christian life."Query or submit proposal electronically.

Recent Title(s) *Manna*, by Kevin Stirratt; *So Long, Status Quo*, by Susy Flory.

BEACON PRESS

25 Beacon St., Boston MA 02108-2892. (617)742-2110. Fax: (617)723-3097. Website: www.beacon.org. **Contact:** Gayatri Patnaik, senior editor (African-American, Asian-American, Latino, Native American, Jewish, and gay and lesbian studies, anthropology); Joanne Wyckoff, executive editor (child and family issues, environmental concerns); Amy Caldwell, senior editor (poetry, gender studies, gay/lesbian studies, and Cuban studies); Christopher Vyce, assistant editor; Brian Halley, assistant editor. Estab. 1854. Publishes hardcover originals and paperback reprints. **Publishes 60 titles/year. 10% of books from first-time authors. Pays royalty. Pays advance.** Accepts simultaneous submissions. Responds in 3 months to queries.

Imprints Bluestreak Series (innovative literary writing by women of color).

O‑ Beacon Press publishes general interest books that promote the following values: the inherent worth and dignity of every person; justice, equity, and compassion in human relations; acceptance of one another; a free and responsible search for truth and meaning; the goal of world community with peace, liberty, and justice for all; respect for the interdependent web of all existence. Currently emphasizing innovative nonfiction writing by people of all colors. De-emphasizing poetry, children's stories, art books, self-help.

Nonfiction Subjects include anthropology, archeology, child guidance, education, ethnic, gay, lesbian, nature, environment, philosophy, religion, womens issues, womens studies, world affairs. Query with SASE. Submit outline, sample chapters, resume, CV. *Strongly prefers referred submissions, on exclusive.*
Recent Title(s) *Radical Equation*, by Robert Moses and Charles Cobb; *All Souls*, by Michael Patrick McDonald; *Speak to Me*, by Marcie Hershman.
Tips We probably accept only 1 or 2 manuscripts from an unpublished pool of 4,000 submissions/year. No fiction, children's book, or poetry submissions invited. An academic affiliation is helpful.

BEARMANOR MEDIA

P.O. Box 71426, Albany GA 31708. (229)436-4265. Fax: (760)9696. E-mail: books@benohmart.com. Website: www.bearmanormedia.com. Estab. 2001. Publishes trade paperback originals and reprints. **Publishes 25 titles/year. 90% of books from first-time authors. 90% from unagented writers.** Accepts simultaneous submissions. Book catalog for #10 SASE. Guidelines available via e-mail.
Nonfiction , old-time radio, voice actors, old movies, classic television. Query with SASE. Email queries preferred. Submit proposal package, outline, list of credits on the subject.
Recent Title(s) *Son of Harpo Speaks*, by Bill Marx; *Fred MacMurray*, by Charles Tranberg; *John Holmes*, by Jill Nelson.
Tips My readers love the past. Radio, old movies, old television. My own tastes include voice actors and scripts, especially of radio and television no longer available. I prefer books on subjects that haven't previously been covered as full books. It doesn't matter to me if you're a first-time author or have a track record. Just know your subject!

⊘ BEDFORD/ST. MARTIN'S

Division of Holtzbrinck Publishers Boston Office: 75 Arlington St., Boston MA 02116. (617)399-4000. Fax: (617)426-8582., Website: www.bedfordstmartins.com. Estab. 1981. **Publishes 200 titles/year.** Book catalog available online.

- College publisher specializing in English (composition, development, literature, and linguistics); history; communications; business and technical writing; and music.

BEHRMAN HOUSE, INC.

11 Edison Place, Springfield NJ 07081. (973)379-7200. Fax: (973)379-7280. Website: www.behrmanhouse.com. **Contact:** Editorial Committee. Estab. 1921. Accepts simultaneous submissions. Responds in 3 months to queries. Book catalog available free. Guidelines available online.

- "Behrman House publishes quality books and supplementary materials of Jewish content—history, Bible, philosophy, holidays, ethics, Israel, Hebrew—for the classroom and the reading public."

Nonfiction Subjects include ethnic, philosophy, religion. Query with SASE. Submit resume, 2 sample chapters, TOC, target audience. No electronic submissions.
Recent Title(s) *Great Israel Scavenger Hunt*, by Scott Blumenthal (Israel); *Rediscovering the Jewish Holidays*, by Nina Beth Cardin and Gila Gevirtz (Jewish Holidays).

FREDERIC C. BEIL, PUBLISHER, INC.

609 Whitaker St., Savannah GA 31401. (912)233-2446. Fax: (912)233-6456. E-mail: beilbook@beil.com. Website: www.beil.com. **Contact:** Mary Ann Bowman, editor. Estab. 1982. Publishes hardcover originals and reprints. **Publishes 13 titles/year. 3,500 queries received/year. 13 mss received/year. 80% of books from first-time authors. 100% from unagented writers. Pays 7 ½% royalty on retail price.** Publishes book 20 months after acceptance of ms. Accepts simultaneous submissions. Responds in 1 week to queries. Book catalog available free.
Imprints The Sandstone Press; Hypermedia, Inc.

- Frederic C. Beil publishes in the fields of history, literature, and biography.

Nonfiction Subjects include art, architecture, history, language, literature, book arts. Query with SASE. Reviews artwork/photos. Send photocopies.
Fiction Subjects include historical, literary, regional, short story collections, translation, biography. Query with SASE.
Recent Title(s) *Joseph Jefferson: Dean of the American Theatre*, by Arthur Bloom; *Goya, Are You With Me Now?*, by H.E. Francis.
Tips Our objectives are (1) to offer to the reading public carefully selected texts of lasting value; (2) to adhere to high standards in the choice of materials and in bookmaking craftsmanship; (3) to produce books that exemplify good taste in format and design; and (4) to maintain the lowest cost consistent with quality.

BELLWETHER-CROSS PUBLISHING

Imprint of Star Publishing Co., Inc. 940 Emmett Ave., #3, Belmont CA 94002. (650)591-3505. Fax: (650)591-3898. Website: www.starpublishing.com.
Nonfiction Submit cover letter and complete ms with SASE. Reviews artwork/photos. Send photocopies.

Recent Title(s) *Transitional Science*, by H. Sue Way and Gaines B. Jackson; *Daring to Be Different: A Manager's Ascent to Leadership*, by James A. Hatherley.

N BENBELLA BOOKS

6440 N. Central Expy., Suite 503, Dallas TX 75206, United States. Website: www.benbellabooks.com. **Contact:** Glenn Yeffeth, publisher. Hardcover and trade paperback originals. **Publishes 20-25 titles/year.** Publishes book 10 months after acceptance of ms. Accepts simultaneous submissions. Guidelines available online.

Nonfiction Subjects include pop contemporary culture, cooking, foods, nutrition, health, medicine, literary criticism, money, finance, science. Submit proposal package, including: outline, 2 sample chapters (via email).

Recent Title(s) *The China Study*; *You Do Not Talk About Fight Club*.

BENTLEY PUBLISHERS

1734 Massachusetts Ave., Cambridge MA 02138-1804. (617)423-4170. Fax: (617)876-9235. Website: www.bentleypublishers.com. Estab. 1950. Publishes hardcover and trade paperback originals and reprints. Book catalog and ms guidelines for 9x12 SAE with 4 first-class stamps. Proposal guidelines online.

- Bentley Publishers publishes books for automotive enthusiasts. We are interested in books that showcase good research, strong illustrations, and valuable technical information.

Nonfiction Automotive subjects only.Subjects include sports, motor sports. Query with SASE. Submit sample chapters, bio, synopsis, target market. Reviews artwork/photos.

Recent Title(s) *Alex Zanardi: My Sweetest Victory*, by Alex Zanardi and Gianluca Gasparini; *Porsche Boxster Service Manual: 1997-2004*, by Bentley Publishers; *Mercedes-Benz Technical Companion*, by Staff of *The Star* with Mercedes-Benz Club of America.

Tips Our audience is composed of serious, intelligent automobile, sports car, and racing enthusiasts, automotive technicians and high-performance tuners.

BERRETT-KOEHLER PUBLISHERS, INC.

235 Montgomery St., Suite 650, San Francisco CA 94104. (415)288-0260. Fax: (415)362-2512. E-mail: bkpub@bkpub.com. Website: www.bkconnection.com. **Contact:** Jeevan Sivasubramaniam. Publishes hardcover originals, trade paperback originals, mass market paperback originals, hardcover reprints, trade paperback reprints. **Publishes 40 titles/year. 1,300 queries received/year. 800 mss received/year. 20-30% of books from first-time authors. 70% from unagented writers. Pays 10-20% royalty.** Publishes book 10 months after acceptance of ms. Accepts simultaneous submissions. Responds in 1 month to queries. Responds in 1 month to proposals. Responds in 1 month to manuscripts. Book catalog available online. Guidelines available online.

Nonfiction Subjects include business, economics, community, government, politics, New Age, spirituality. Submit proposal package, outline, bio, 1-2 sample chapters. Hard-copy proposals only. Do not e-mail, fax, or phone please. Reviews artwork/photos. Send Send photocopies or originals with SASE.

Recent Title(s) *Alternatives to Globalization*, by Jerry Mander & IFG (current affairs); *Leadership and the New Science*, by Margaret Wheatley (business); *Confessions of an Economic Hit Man*, by John Perkins (*New York Times* bestseller).

Tips Our audience is business lead Use common sense, do your rese

BETHANY HOUSE PUBLISHERS

6030 E. Fulton Rd., Ada MI 49301. (952)829-2500. Fax: (952)996-1304. Website: www.bethanyhouse.com. Estab. 1956. Publishes hardcover and trade paperback originals, mass market paperback reprints. **Publishes 90-100 titles/year. 2% of books from first-time authors. 50% from unagented writers. Pays royalty on net price. Pays advance.** Publishes book 1 year after acceptance of ms. Accepts simultaneous submissions. Responds in 3 months to queries. Book catalog for 9 x 12 envelope and 5 First-Class stamps. Guidelines available online.

- *All unsolicited mss returned unopened.*
- Bethany House Publishers specializes in books that communicate Biblical truth and assist people in both spiritual and practical areas of life. While we do not accept unsolicited queries or proposals via telephone or e-mail, we will consider 1-page queries sent by fax and directed to Adult Nonfiction, Adult Fiction, or Young Adult/Children.

Nonfiction Subjects include child guidance, Biblical disciplines, personal and corporate renewal, emerging generations, devotional, marriage and family, applied theology, inspirational.

Fiction Subjects include historical, young adult, contemporary.

Recent Title(s) *Under God*, by Toby Mae and Michael Tait (nonfiction); *Candle in the Darkness*, by Lynn Austin (fiction); *God Called a Girl*, by Shannon Kubiak Primicerio (YA nonfiction).

Tips Bethany House Publishers' publishing program relates Biblical truth to all areas of life—whether in the framework of a well-told story, of a challenging book for spiritual growth, or of a Bible reference work. We are seeking high quality fiction and nonfiction that will inspire and challenge our audience.

BEYOND WORDS PUBLISHING, INC.

20827 NW Cornell Rd., Suite 500, Hillsboro OR 97124-9808. (503)531-8700. Fax: (503)531-8773. Website: www.beyondword.com. **Contact:** Cynthia Black, editor-in-chief. Estab. 1984. Publishes hardcover and trade paperback originals and paperback reprints. **Publishes 10-15 titles/year.** Accepts simultaneous submissions.

- Does not accept unagented manuscripts. No childrens, young adult, memoir, or fiction.

Tips "*Beyond Words* markets to cultural creatives and women ages 30-60. Titles must have a how-to component, not just personal experience. Study our most recent titles before you submit and check out our website to make sure your book is a good fit for our list."

BLACK ROSE WRITING

7810 Kingsbury Way, San Antonio TX 78240. E-mail: pr@blackrosewriting.com. Website: www.blackrosewriting.com. **Contact:** Reagan Rothe, owner (fiction, autobiography, poetry); Minna Rothe, PR consultant (poetry book, public relations questions and help). Estab. 2006. Publishes hardcover, trade paperback, mass market paperback, and electronic originals. **Publishes 5-10 titles/year. 1,000+ queries received/year. 120 mss received/year. 50% of books from first-time authors. 75% from unagented writers. Pays 10-15% royalty on retail price.** Publishes book 2-4 months after acceptance of ms. Accepts simultaneous submissions. Responds in 3 weeks to queries. Responds in 1 month to proposals. Responds in 1-2 months to manuscripts. Guidelines available online.

- We are open to new submissions until July 1, 2009.

Nonfiction Subjects include animals, art, architecture, child guidance, creative nonfiction, history, military, war, sports. Submit query letter via e-mail or with SASE before sending entire ms. Reviews artwork/photos. Send photocopies.

Fiction Subjects include adventure, fantasy, historical, humor, juvenile, literary, mainstream, contemporary, military, war, mystery, picture books, plays, poetry, poetry in translation, romance, science fiction, short story collections, sports, suspense, western, fable. Send query letter via e-mail

Recent Title(s) *Book of Spells*, by William E. Terry; *Adventures Aboard Rick's Place*, by Terry J. Kotas; Without Redemption, *by Thomas Thorpe;* Dreams and Baseball, by Reagan Rothe.

Tips Black Rose Writing welcomes all writers, but truly focuses on new, talented authors who are seeking their first big recognition and publication. We promise to give you personal feedback on every piece, dedicating ourselves to avoid automated responses or negative outlooks on an individual's subjective work. Please follow our submission guidelines online.

BLACK VELVET SEDUCTIONS PUBLISHING

1350-C W. Southport, Box 249, Indianapolis IN 46217. (888)556-2750. E-mail: lauriesanders@fusemail.com. Website: www.blackvelvetseductions.com. **Contact:** Laurie Sanders, acquisitions editor. Estab. 2005. Publishes trade paperback and electronic originals and reprints. **Publishes about 20 titles/year. 500 queries received/year. 1,000 mss received/year. 90% of books from first-time authors. 100% from unagented writers. Pays 10% royalty for paperbacks; 50% royalty for electronic books.** Publishes book 6-12 months after acceptance of ms. Accepts simultaneous submissions. Responds in 2 months to queries. Responds in 2 months to proposals. Responds in 8-12 months to manuscripts. Catalog free or online. Guidelines online or via e-mail (guidelines@blackvelvetseductions.com).

Imprints Forbidden Experiences (erotic romance of all types); Tender Destinations (sweet romance of all types); Sensous Journeys (sensous romance of all types); Amorous Adventures (romantic suspense).

- We only publish romance novels and romantic short story collections. If the piece is not a romance, we will not accept it. We do not accept mainstream romance or mainstream fiction. We look for well-crafted stories with a high degree of emotional impact.

Fiction Subjects include erotica, erotic romance, historical, romance, multicultural, romance, romance, short story collections romantic stories, suspense, romantic, western, romance. All books must have a strong romance element. Query with SASE. Submit proposal package, clips, 3 sample chapters. Submit complete ms. Prefers e-mail submissions.

Recent Title(s) *Fool Me Once*, by Jessica Joy; *Toy's Story: Acquisition of a Sex Toy*, by Alyssa Aaron.

Tips We publish romance and erotic We look for books written in v

BLEAK HOUSE BOOKS

923 Williamson St., Madison WI 53703. Website: www.bleakhousebooks.com. **Contact:** Submissions. Estab. 1995. **Publishes 15-20 titles/year. 1,000+ queries received/year. 20% of books from first-time authors. 20% from unagented writers. Pays standard royalties. Offers advance.** Publishes book 12-18 months after acceptance of ms. Accepts simultaneous submissions. Responds in 1-2 months to queries. Responds in 2-3 months to manuscripts. Book catalog available online.

Fiction Subjects include literary, mystery. "We are looking for gritty mystery/crime/suspense. Characters should be psychologically complex, flawed, and human. We are rarely interested in cozies and are never interested in animals or inanimate objects that solve mysteries. We want books that are part of a planned series, and we want authors that understand the business of publishing. We are also looking for dark and quirky literary fiction. Tell us a story that hasn't been told before. The most important thing is the quality of writing. Just because your best friends and family loved the book doesn't mean it's going to go over big with everybody else." Query with SASE. *All unsolicited mss returne*

Recent Title(s) *Toros and Torsos*, by Craig McDonald; *Empty Ever After*, by Reed Farrel Coleman; *HogDoggin*, by Anthony Neil Smith; *In the Light of You*, by Nathan Singer.

Tips "Our audience is made up of 2 groups. The first is mystery readers—a group dedicated to quality books that have a satisfying conclusion to the age old questions of 'Whodunit?' The second group reads books to get a different perspective on the human condition, to live through characters they haven't seen or heard from before. These readers aren't afraid of a book that is quirky or disturbed. Do not call us about submission guidelines, your query letter, or anything else that can be answered in this book or others like it. Make sure your book is finished before contacting us."

BLOOMSBURY CHILDREN'S BOOKS

Imprint of Bloomsbury USA 175 Fifth Ave., Suite 300, New York NY 10010. E-mail: bloomsbury.kids@bloomsburyusa.com. Website: www.bloomsburyusa.com. **Publishes 60 titles/year. 25% of books from first-time authors. Pays royalty. Pays advance.** Accepts simultaneous submissions. Responds in 6 months to queries. Responds in 6 months to manuscripts. Book catalog available online. Guidelines available online.

- No phone calls or e-mails.

Fiction Subjects include adventure, fantasy, historical, humor, juvenile, multicultural, mystery, picture books, poetry, science fiction, sports, suspense, young adult, animal, anthology, concept, contemporary, folktales, problem novels. We publish picture books, chapter books, middle grade, and YA novels, and some nonfiction. Query with SASE. Submit clips, first 3 chapters with SASE.

Recent Title(s) *Where Is Coco Going?*, by Sloane Tanen (picture books); *Once Upon a Curse*, by E.D. Baker (middle grade); *Enna Burning*, by Shannon Hale (young adult fantasy).

Tips Do not send originals or only copy. Be sure your work is appropriate for us. Familiarize yourself with our list by going to bookstores or libraries.

⊘ BLUE MOON BOOKS, INC.

Imprint of Avalon Travel 1700 4th St., Berkeley CA 94710. (510)595-3664. Fax: (646)375-2571. Website: www.avalonpub.com. Estab. 1987. Publishes trade paperback and mass market paperback originals. Book catalog available free.

O→ Blue Moon Books is strictly an erotic press; largely fetish-oriented material, B&D, S&M, etc.

Fiction Subjects include erotica.

Recent Title(s) *Amateurs*, by Michael Hemmingson; *Venus in Lace*, by Marcus van Heller; *Confessions of a Left Bank Dominatrix*, by Gala Fur.

BLUEWOOD BOOKS

Imprint of The Siyeh Group, Inc. P.O. Box 689, San Mateo CA 94401. (650)548-0754. **Contact:** Richard Michaels, director. Publishes trade paperback originals. **Publishes 8 titles/year. 20% of books from first-time authors. 100% from unagented writers. Makes work-for-hire assignments—fee depends upon book and writer's expertise. Pays 1/3 fee advance.**

O→ We are looking for qualified writers for nonfiction series—history and biography oriented.

Nonfiction Subjects include Americana, anthropology, archeology, art, architecture, business, economics, government, politics, health, medicine, history, military, war, multicultural, science, sports, womens issues, womens studies. Query with SASE.

Recent Title(s) *True Stories of Baseball's Hall of Famers*, by Russell Roberts (baseball history/biography); *100 Native Americans Who Shaped American History*, by Bonnie Juetner (American history/biography).

Tips Our audience consists of adults and young adults. Our books are written on a newspaper level—clear, concise, well organized, and easy to understand. We encourage potential writers to send us a resume, providing background qualifications and references.

BNA BOOKS

Imprint of The Bureau of National Affairs, Inc. 1801 S. Bell St., Arlington VA 22202. (703)341-5777. Fax: (703)341-1610. Website: www.bnabooks.com. **Contact:** Jim Fattibene, acquisitions manager. Estab. 1929. Publishes hardcover and softcover originals. Accepts simultaneous submissions. Book catalog available online. Guidelines available online.

O→ BNA Books publishes professional reference books written by lawyers, for lawyers.

Nonfiction Submit detailed TOC or outline, cv, intended market, estimated word length.

Recent Title(s) *Pharmaceutical Patent Law*.

Tips Our audience is made up of practicing lawyers and law librarians. We look for authoritative and comprehensive treatises that can be supplemented or revised every year or 2 on legal subjects of interest to those audiences.

BOA EDITIONS, LTD.

250 North Goodman St., Suite 306, Rochester NY 14607. (585)546-3410. Fax: (585)546-3913. E-mail: info@boaeditions.org. Website: www.boaeditions.org. Estab. 1976. Publishes hardcover and trade paperback originals. **Publishes 11-13 titles/year. 1,000 queries received/year. 700 mss received/year. 15% of books from first-time authors. 90% from unagented writers. Negotiates royalties. Pays variable advance.** Publishes book 18 months after acceptance of ms. Accepts simultaneous submissions. Responds in 1 week to queries. Responds in 5 months to manuscripts. Book catalog available online. Guidelines available online.

O━ BOA Editions publishes distinguished collections of poetry, fiction and poetry in translation. Our goal is to publish the finest American contemporary poetry, fiction and poetry in translation.

Fiction Subjects include literary, poetry, poetry in translation, short story collections. "We now publish literary fiction through our American Reader Series. While aesthetic quality is subjective, our fiction will be by authors more concerned with the artfulness of their writing than the twists and turns of plot. Our strongest current interest is in short story collections (and short-short story collections), although we will consider novels. We strongly advise you to read our first published fiction collections."

Recent Title(s) *You & Yours*, by Naomi Shihab Nye; *The Rooster's Wife*, by Russell Edson; *The Heaven-Sent Leaf*, by Katy Lederer.

N BOLD STROKES BOOKS, INC.

P.O. Box 249, City Falls NY 12185. (518)753-6642. Fax: (518)753-6648. E-mail: publisher@boldstrokesbooks.com. Website: www.boldstrokesbooks.com. **Contact:** Len Barot, acq. director (general/genre gay/lesbian fiction). Trade paperback originals and reprints; electronic originals and reprints. **Publishes 60+ titles/year. 300 queries/year; 300 mss/year. 10-20% of books from first-time authors. 99% from unagented writers.** Publishes book 16 months after acceptance of ms. Catalog free on request - PDF. Guidelines online at website.

Imprints BSB Fiction (publishes 30/year), Matinee Books Romances (8/year), Victory Editions Lesbian Fiction (6/year), Liberty Editions Gay Fiction (4/year), Aeros eBooks (12-15/year).

Nonfiction Subjects include gay, lesbian, memoirs, young adult. Submit completed ms with bio, cover letter, and synopsis electronically only. Does not review artwork.

Fiction Subjects include adventure, erotica, fantasy, gay, gothic, historical, horror, lesbian, literary, mainstream, mystery, romance, science fiction, suspense, western, young adult. "Submissions should have a gay, lesbian, transgendered, or bisexual focus and should be positive and life-affirming." Submit completed ms with bio, cover letter, and synopsis—electronically only.

Recent Title(s) *Wall of Silence*, by Gabrielle Goldsby (mystery-2007 Lambda Literary Award winner); *The Lonely Hearts Club*, by Radclyffe (romance-bestseller).

Tips "We are particularly interested in authors who are interested in craft enhancement, technical development, and exploring and expanding traditional genre definitions and boundaries and are looking for a long-term publishing relationship ."

BONUS BOOKS, INC.

1223 Wilshire Blvd., #597, Santa Monica CA 90403. E-mail: submissions@bonusbooks.com. Website: www.bonusbooks.com. **Contact:** Editor. Estab. 1985. Publishes hardcover and trade paperback originals and reprints. Accepts simultaneous submissions. Responds in 6-8 weeks to queries. Book catalog for 9X11 envelope and First-Class stamps. Guidelines for #10 SASE.

O━ Bonus Books publishes quality nonfiction in a variety of categories, including entertainment/pop culture, games/gambling, sports/sports biography, regional (Chicago), broadcasting, fundraising.

Nonfiction Subjects include business, economics, cooking, foods, nutrition, education, health, medicine, hobbies, money, finance, regional, sports, gambling, womens issues, womens studies, pop culture. Query with SASE. Submit outline, bio, 2-3 sample chapters, TOC, SASE. All submissions and queries must include SASE. Reviews artwork/photos. Send .

Recent Title(s) *America's Right Turn*, by David Franke and Richard A. Viguerie; *The On Position*, by Katie Moran; *In the Midst of Wolves*, by Keith Remer.

BOWTIE PRESS

BowTie, Inc. 23172 Plaza Pointe Dr., Suite 230, Laguna Hills CA 92653. E-mail: bowtiepress@bowtieinc.com. Website: www.bowtiepress.com. **Contact:** Acquisitions Editor. Estab. 1995. Publishes hardcover and trade paperback originals. **Publishes 30 titles/year. 250 queries received/year. 50 mss received/year. 20% of books from first-time authors. 90% from unagented writers. Payment varies from author to author** Publishes book 1 year after acceptance of ms. Accepts simultaneous submissions. Responds in 1 month to queries. Responds in 2 months to proposals. Responds in 3 months to manuscripts. Book catalog available online. Guidelines available online.

Imprints Kennel Club Books (Andrew DePrisco); Doral Publishing (Art Stickney); Advanced Vivarium Systems.

Nonfiction Subjects include agriculture, animals, gardening, nature, environment, science, marine subjects, crafts, education. Submit proposal package, outline, sample chapters. Reviews artwork/photos. Send photocopies.

BOYDS MILLS PRESS

815 Church St., Honesdale PA 18431-1895. (570)253-1164. Website: www.boydsmillspress.com. **Contact:** Editorial Department. Estab. 1991. Publishes hardcover originals and trade paperback reprints. **Publishes 50 titles/year. 10,000 mss received/year. 30% of books from first-time authors. 60% from unagented writers. Pays royalty on retail price. Pays variable advance.** Accepts simultaneous submissions. Responds in 3 months to manuscripts. Book catalog available online.

Imprints Wordsong (poetry); Calkins Creek (American history); Front Street

- "Boyds Mills Press publishes a wide range of children's books of literary merit, from preschool through young adult. Currently emphasizing picture books and novels. Time between acceptance and publication depends on acceptance of ms."

Nonfiction Subjects include agriculture, animals, ethnic, history, nature, environment, sports, travel. Query with SASE. Submit proposal package, outline. Reviews artwork/photos.

Fiction Subjects include adventure, ethnic, historical, humor, juvenile, mystery, picture books, young adult, adventure, animal, contemporary, ethnic, historical, humor, mystery, sports. "We look for imaginative stories or concepts with simple, lively language that employs a variety of literary devices, including rhythm, repitition, and when composed properly, rhyme. The stories may entertain or challenge, but the content must be age appropriate for children. For middle and young adult fiction we look for stories told in strong, considered prose driven by well-imagined characters." Query with SASE. Submit outline/synopsis and 3

Recent Title(s) *Red Sled*, by Patricial Thomas (picture book); *Marvels in the Muck*, by Doug Wechsler (nonfiction).

Tips "Our audience is pre-school to young adult. Concentrate first on your writing. Polish it. Then—and only then—select a market. We need books with fresh ideas and characters. We are always interested in multicultural settings."

BRANDEN PUBLISHING CO., INC.

P.O. Box 812094, Wellesley MA 02482. (781)235-3634. Fax: (781)790-1056. Website: www.brandenbooks.com. **Contact:** Adolph Caso, editor. Estab. 1909. Publishes hardcover and trade paperback originals, reprints, and software. **Publishes 15 titles/year. 80% of books from first-time authors. 90% from unagented writers.** Publishes book 10 months after acceptance of ms. Responds in 1 month to queries.

Imprints International Pocket Library and Popular Technology; Four Seas and Brashear; Branden Books.

- "Branden publishes books by or about women, children, military, Italian-American, or African-American themes."

Nonfiction Subjects include Americana, art, architecture, computers, electronics, contemporary culture, education, ethnic, government, politics, health, medicine, history, military, war, music, dance, photography, sociology, software, classics. Paragraph query only with author's vita and SASE. No telephone, e-mail, or fax inquiries. Reviews artwork/photos.

Fiction Subjects include ethnic, histories, integration, historical, literary, military, war, religious, historical-reconstructive, short story collections, translation. Looking for contemporary, fast pace, modern society. Query with SASE. Paragraph query only with auth

Recent Title(s) *Priest to Mafia Don*, by Father Bascio; *Green River Serial Killer*, by Pennie Morehead; *Kaso Verb Conjugation System*, by Adolph Caso ((English, Spanish, Italian)); *Tuskegee Airmen*, 5th edition, by Charles Francis; Tuskegee Airman.

BRENNER MICROCOMPUTING, INC.

Imprint of Brenner Microcomputing, Inc. P.O. Box 721000, San Diego CA 92172. (858)538-0093. Fax: (858)538-0380. E-mail: brenner@brennerbooks.com. Website: www.brennerbooks.com. **Contact:** Jenny Hanson, acquisitions manager (pricing & ranges). Estab. 1982. Publishes trade paperback and electronic originals specializing in pricing and performance time standards. **Publishes 5 titles/year. 1 ms and 6 queries received/year. 5% of books from first-time authors. 98% from unagented writers. Pays 5-15% royalty on wholesale price. Pays $0-1,000 advance.** Publishes book 1 year after acceptance of ms. Accepts simultaneous submissions. Responds in 1 month to queries, proposals, and manuscripts. Book catalog available free. Guidelines for #10 SASE.

BREVET PRESS, INC.

P.O. Box 82, 124 S. Main, Worthington SD 57077-0082. **Contact:** Donald P. Mackintosh, publisher (business); Peter E. Reid, managing editor (technical); A. Melton, editor (Americana); B. Mackintosh, editor (history). Estab. 1972. Publishes hardcover and paperback originals and reprints. **Publishes 15 titles/year. 50% of books from first-time authors. 100% from unagented writers. Pays 5% royalty. Pays $1,000 average advance.** Publishes book 1 year after acceptance of ms. Accepts simultaneous submissions. Responds in 2 months to queries. Book catalog available free.

"Brevet Books seeks nonfiction with market potential and literary excellence."

Nonfiction Subjects include Americana, business, economics, history. Query with SASE. Reviews artwork/photos. Send photocopies.

Tips "Keep sexism out of the manuscripts."

BRISTOL PUBLISHING ENTERPRISES

2714 McCone Ave., Hayward CA 94545. (800)346-4889. Fax: (800)346-7064. Website: bristolcookbooks.com. Estab. 1988. Publishes trade paperback originals. Accepts simultaneous submissions. Book catalog available online.

Imprints Nitty Gritty cookbooks; The Best 50 Recipe Series; Pet Care Series.

Nonfiction Subjects include cooking, foods, nutrition. Send a proposal, or query with possible outline, brief note about author's background, sample of writing, or chapter from ms.

Recent Title(s) *The Best 50 Chocolate Recipes*, by Christie Katona; *No Salt, No Sugar, No Fat*, by Jacqueline Williams and Goldie Silverman (revised edition); *Wraps and Roll-Ups*, by Dona Z. Meilach (revised edition).

Tips Readers of cookbooks are novic Our books educate without int

BROWN BOOKS PUBLISHING GROUP

16200 N. Dallas Pkwy., Suite 170, Dallas TX 75248. (972)381-0009. Fax: (972)248-4336. E-mail: publishing@brownbooks.com. Website: www.brownbooks.com. **Contact:** Janet Harris, senior editor (all genres). Hardcover and trade paperback originals and reprints. **Publishes 150 titles/year. Receives 400 queries/year; 350 mss/year. 85% of books from first-time authors. 100% from unagented writers.** Publishes book 6 months after acceptance of ms. Accepts simultaneous submissions. Catalog not available. Guidelines not available.

Nonfiction Subjects include business, economics, health, medicine, We have covered all subjects. Submit outline, 3 sample chapters, synopsis, and completed ms. Reviews artwork/photos; send electronically.

Fiction "We accept all fiction.""Writers should complete an outline of their story before writing the full ms." Submit synopsis, 3 sample chapters and synopsis. Submit completed ms.

Recent Title(s) *Ebby Halliday: The First Lady of Real Estate*, by Michael Poss (bio); *The Smart Women's Guide to Heart Health*, by Sarah Samaan (health); *Good Christian Bitches*, by Kim Gatlin (gen. fiction/mystery); *Sonnets*, by Robert K. Brown; *Stormy Waters*, by Rosalie Stolinski (poetry).

Tips "Our audience is anyone who reads. Call before submitting."

BUCKNELL UNIVERSITY PRESS

Bucknell University, Lewisburg PA 17837. (570)577-1552. E-mail: clingham@bucknell.edu. Website: www.bucknell.edu/script/upress/. **Contact:** Greg Clingham, director. Estab. 1969. Publishes hardcover originals. **Publishes 35-40 titles/year.** Book catalog available free. Guidelines available online.

In all fields, our criteria are scholarly excellence, critical originality, and interdisciplinary and theoretical expertise and sensitivity.

Nonfiction Subjects include art, architecture, history, language, literature, literary criticism, philosophy, psychology, religion, sociology, English and American literary criticism, literary theory and cultural studies, historiography, art history, modern languages, classics, anthropology, ethnology, cultural and political geography, Hispanic and Latin American studies. Submit proposal package, cv, SASE.

Recent Title(s) *The Selected Essays of Donald Greene*, edited by John Lawrence Abbott; *Brazilian Science Fiction: Cultural Myths and Nationhood in the Land of the Future*, by M. Elizabeth Ginway; *Borges and Translation: The Irreverence of Periphery*, by Sergio Waisman.

BUILDERBOOKS.COM™

National Association of Home Builders 1201 15th St. NW, Washington DC 20005-2800. (800)368-5242. Fax: (202)266-8559. E-mail: publishing@nahb.com. Website: www.builderbooks.com. Publishes books and electronic products for builders, remodelers, developers, sales and marketing professionals, manufacturers, suppliers, and consumers in the residential construction industry. Writers must be experts. **Publishes 10 titles/year. 25% of books from first-time authors. 100% from unagented writers. Pays royalty.** Publishes book 6-12 months after acceptance of ms. Responds in 1-2 months to queries. Book catalog free or on website. Guidelines available via e-mail.

Nonfiction We prefer a detailed outline on a strong residential construction industry topic. Our readers like step-by-step how-to books and electronic products, no history or philosophy of the industry.Query first. E-mail queries accepted. Include electronic and hard copy artwork/photos as part of ms package. Send photocopies.

Recent Title(s) *Trillion Dollar Woman*, by Tara-Nicolle Nelson; *Beyound Warranty: Building Your Referral Business*, by Carol Smith; *Right House, Right Place, Right Time*, by Margaret Wylde.

Tips Audience is primarily home bui Ask for a sample outline.

THE BUREAU FOR AT-RISK YOUTH

2 Skyline Dr., Suite 101, Hawthorne NY 10532. E-mail: submissions@sunburstvm.com. Website: www.

sunburstvm.com. **Contact:** Michelle J. Yannes, editor-in-chief. Estab. 1988. **Publishes 25-50 titles/year. 100% from unagented writers. Payment is on a work-for-hire basis.** Publishes book 1 year after acceptance of ms. Responds in 8 months to queries.

- Publishes materials on youth guidance topics, such as drugs and violence prevention, character education and life skills for young people in grades K-12, and the educators, parents, mental health and juvenile justice professionals who work with them. We accept video/DVD, workbook/activity book, curriculum, or book/booklet series format.

Nonfiction Educational materials for parents, educators and other professionals who work with youth.Subjects include child guidance, education. Query with SASE.

Recent Title(s) *Helping Kids Heal*, by Rebecca Carman.

Tips Publications are sold through direct mail catalogs and Internet. Writers whose expertise is a fit with our customers' interests should send query or proposals since we tailor everything very specifically to meet our audience's needs.

BURFORD BOOKS

32 Morris Ave., Springfield NJ 07081. (973)258-0960. Fax: (973)258-0113. **Contact:** Peter Burford, publisher. Estab. 1997. Publishes hardcover originals, trade paperback originals and reprints. **Publishes 12 titles/year. 300 queries received/year. 200 mss received/year. 30% of books from first-time authors. 60% from unagented writers. Pays royalty on wholesale price.** Publishes book 18 months after acceptance of ms. Accepts simultaneous submissions. Responds in 1 month to queries. Responds in 1 month to proposals. Responds in 2 months to manuscripts. Book catalog and ms guidelines free. See website.

- Burford Books publishes books on all aspects of the outdoors, from backpacking to sports, practical and literary.

Nonfiction Subjects include animals, cooking, foods, nutrition, hobbies, military, war, nature, environment, recreation, sports, travel. Query with SASE. Submit outline. Reviews artwork/photos. Send photocopies.

Recent Title(s) *Saltwater Fishing*, by Jim Freda; *One Hundred Stretches*, by Jim Brown.

BUTTE PUBLICATIONS, INC.

P.O. Box 1328, Hillsboro OR 97123-1328. (503)648-9791. Fax: (503)693-9526. E-mail: service@buttepublications.com. Website: www.buttepublications.com. Estab. 1992. **Publishes several titles/year.** Accepts simultaneous submissions. Responds in 6 or more months to manuscripts. Book catalog and ms guidelines for #10 SASE or online. Guidelines available online.

- Butte Publications, Inc., publishes classroom books related to deafness and language.

Nonfiction Subjects include education, all related to field of deafness and education. Submit proposal package, including author bio, synopsis, market survey, 2-3 sample chapters, SASE and ms (if completed) Reviews artwork/photos. Send photocopies.

Recent Title(s) *Cajun's Song*, by Darlene Toole; *Picture Plus Dictionary*, by Virginia McKinney.

Tips Audience is students, teachers, parents, and professionals in the arena dealing with deafness and hearing loss. We are not seeking autobiographies or novels.

C&T PUBLISHING

1651 Challenge Dr., Concord CA 94520-5206. (925)677-0377. Fax: (925)677-0373. Website: www.ctpub.com. Estab. 1983. Publishes hardcover and trade paperback originals. **Publishes 70 titles/year.** Accepts simultaneous submissions. Responds in 3 months to queries. Book catalog free; proposal guidelines online.

- "C&T publishes well-written, beautifully designed books on quilting and fiber crafts, embroidery, dollmaking, knitting and paper crafts."

Nonfiction Subjects include hobbies, quilting books, occasional quilt picture books, quilt-related crafts, wearable art, needlework, fiber and surface embellishments, other books relating to fabric crafting and paper crafting.

Recent Title(s) *Puzzle Quilts*, by Paula Nadelstern; *Fast Knits Fat Needles*, by Sally Harding.

Tips "In our industry, we find that how-to books have the longest selling life. Quiltmakers, sewing enthusiasts, needle artists, fiber artists and paper crafters are our audience. We like to see new concepts or techniques. Include some great samples, and you'll get our attention quickly. Dynamic design is hard to resist, and if that's your forte, show us what you've done."

CAMBRIDGE EDUCATIONAL

P.O. Box 2053, Princeton NJ 08543. (800)468-4227. Website: www.cambridgeeducational.com. **Contact:** Julian Chiabella, manager of acquisitions. Estab. 1981. Publishes supplemental educational products. **Publishes 30-40 titles/year. 20% of books from first-time authors. 90% from unagented writers. Makes outright purchase of $1,500-4,000. Occasional royalty arrangement.** Publishes book 8 months after acceptance of ms. Accepts simultaneous submissions.

- We are known in the education industry for guidance-related and career search programs. Currently emphasizing social studies and science.

Nonfiction Subjects include child guidance, cooking, foods, nutrition, education, health, medicine, money, finance, science, social sciences, career guidance. Query or submit outline/synopsis and sample chapters. Does not respond unless interested. Reviews artwork/photos.
Recent Title(s) *6 Steps to Getting a Job for People with Disabilities*, by Wayne Forster.
Tips We encourage the submission of high-quality books on timely topics written for young adult audiences at moderate to low readibility levels. Call and request a copy of all our current catalogs, talk to the management about what is timely in the areas you wish to write on, thoroughly research the topic, and write a manuscript that will be read by young adults without being overly technical. Low to moderate readibility yet entertaining, informative and accurate.

⊘ CANDLEWICK PRESS

99 Dover St., Somerville MA 02144. (617)661-3330. Fax: (617)661-0565. Website: www.candlewick.com. **Contact:** Deb Wayshak, executive editor (fiction); Joan Powers, editor-at-large (picture books); Liz Bicknell, editorial director/associate publisher (poetry, picture books, fiction); Mary Lee Donovan, executive editor (picture books, nonfiction/fiction); Hilary Van Dusen, senior editor (nonfiction/fiction); Sarah Ketchersid, senior editor (board, toddler). Estab. 1991. Publishes hardcover and trade paperback originals and reprints. **Publishes 200 titles/year. 5% of books from first-time authors.**

- Candlewick Press publishes high-quality, illustrated children's books for ages infant through young adult. We are a truly child-centered publisher.

Fiction Subjects include juvenile, picture books, young adult. *No unsolicited mss.*
Recent Title(s) *Good Masters! Sweet Ladies! Voices from a Medieval Village*, by Amy Schlitz.
Tips *We no longer accept unsolicited mss.* See our website for further information about us.

CAPITAL BOOKS

22841 Quicksilver Dr., Sterling VA 20166. (703)661-1571. Fax: (703)661-1547. E-mail: kathleen@booksintl.com. Website: www.capital-books.com. **Contact:** Kathleen Hughes, publisher (reference, how-to, lifestyle, regional travel, business). Estab. 1998. Publishes hardcover and trade paperback originals, and trade paperback reprints. **Publishes 20 titles/year. 800 queries received/year. 400 mss received/year. 30% of books from first-time authors. 90% from unagented writers. Pays up to $5,000 advance.** Publishes book 9-12 months after acceptance of ms. Accepts simultaneous submissions. Responds in 6 months to queries. Responds in 6 months to proposals. Responds in 6 months to manuscripts. Book catalog available free. Guidelines available online.
Nonfiction Subjects include child guidance, contemporary culture, cooking, foods, nutrition, health, medicine, money, finance, nature, environment, psychology, regional, travel, business. Submit proposal package, outline, 3 sample chapters, query letter. Reviews artwork/photos. Send photocopies.
Recent Title(s) *Hitting Your Strike: Your Work—Your Way*, by Nan S. Russell; *Tough Questions—Good Answers*, by Thomas F. Calcagni.
Tips Our audience is comprised of enthusiastic readers who look to books for answers and information. Do not send fiction, children's books, or religious titles. Please tell us how you, the author, can help market and sell the book.

⊘ CAPSTONE PRESS

151 Good Counsel Dr., P.O. Box 669, Mankato MN 56002. (507)345-8100. Fax: (507)625-4662. Website: www.capstonepress.com. Publishes hardcover originals. Book catalog available online.
Imprints Edge Books; Blazers Books; Snap Books, Pebble Books; Graphic Library; A+ Books; Pebble Plus; Yellow Umbrella Books; First Facts; Fact Finders; Spanish/Bilingual.

- Capstone Press publishes nonfiction children's books for schools and libraries.

Nonfiction Subjects include Americana, animals, child guidance, cooking, foods, nutrition, health, medicine, history, military, war, multicultural, nature, environment, recreation, science, sports.
Tips Audience is made up of elementary, middle school, and high school students who are just learning how to read, who are experiencing reading difficulties, or who are learning English. Capstone Press does not publish unsolicited mss submitted by authors, nor entertains proposals. Instead, Capstone hires freelance authors to write on nonfiction topics selected by the company. Do not send book proposals. Do not send fiction.

CARDOZA PUBLISHING

5473 S. Eastern Ave., Las Vegas NV 89119. E-mail: submissions@cardozapub.com. Website: www.cardozapub.com. **Contact:** Acquisitions Editor (gaming, gambling, card and casino games, and board games). Estab. 1981. Publishes trade paperback originals and reprints. **Publishes 35-40 titles/year. 20-30 queries received/year. 20-30 mss received/year. 50% of books from first-time authors. 90% from unagented writers. Pays 5-6% royalty on retail price. Pays $1,000-10,000 advance.** Publishes book 7 months after acceptance of ms. Accepts simultaneous submissions. Responds in 2-3 months to manuscripts. Book catalog available online. Guidelines available via e-mail.
Nonfiction Subjects include hobbies, gaming, gambling, backgammon chess, card games. Submit complete ms.

Reviews artwork/photos. Send photocopies.
Recent Title(s) *Super System*, by Doyle Brunson (poker); *Championship Hold 'Em*, by Tom McEvoy and T.J. Cloutier (poker); *Ken Warren Teaches Texas Hold 'Em*, by Ken Warren (poker).
Tips "Audience is professional and recreational gamblers, chess players, card players. We prefer not to deal with agents whenever possible. We publish only titles in a very specific niche market; please do not send us material that will not be relevant to our business."

THE CAREER PRESS, INC.

P.O. Box 687, 3 Tice Rd., Franklin Lakes NJ 07417. (201)848-0310 or (800)227-3371. E-mail: aschwartz@careerpress.com. Website: www.careerpress.com. **Contact:** Michael Pye, director of product development, Adam Schwartz, acquisitions editor. Estab. 1985. Publishes hardcover and paperback originals. Accepts simultaneous submissions. Guidelines available online.
Imprints New Page Books.

- Career Press publishes books for adult readers seeking practical information to improve themselves in careers, business, HR, sales, entrepreneurship, and other related topics, as well as titles on supervision, management and CEOs. New Page Books publishes in the areas of New Age, new science, paranormal, the unexplained, alternative history, spirituality.

Nonfiction Subjects include business, economics, money, finance, recreation, nutrition. Submit outline, bio, table of contents, 2-3 sample chapters, marketing plan, SASE. Or, send complete ms (preferred).
Recent Title(s) *Your Inner CEO*, by Allan Cox; *Play to Your Strengths*, by Andrea Sigetich and Carol Leavitt; *Resumes for the Rest of Us*, by Arnold Boldt.

CAROLRHODA BOOKS, INC.

Imprint of Lerner Publishing Group 241 First Ave. N., Minneapolis MN 55401-1607. Fax: (612)332-7615. Website: www.lernerbooks.com. Estab. 1959. Publishes hardcover originals. Book catalog for 9x12 SAE with $4.50 postage. Guidelines available online.

- Lerner Publishing Group no longer accepts unsolicited submissions in any of our imprints.
- Carolrhoda Books is a children's publisher focused on producing high-quality, socially conscious nonfiction and fiction books with unique and well-developed ideas and angles for young readers that help them learn about and explore the world around them.

Nonfiction Carolrhoda Books seeks creative children's nonfiction.Subjects include ethnic, nature, environment, science.
Fiction Subjects include historical, juvenile, multicultural, picture books, young reader, middle grade and young adult fiction. We continue to add fiction for middle grades and 8-10 picture books per year. Not looking for folktales or anthropomorphic animal stories.
Recent Title(s) *Blackberry Stew*, by Isabell Monk, illustrated by Janice Lee Porter; *A Style All Her Own*, by Laurie Friedman, illustrated by Sharon Watts; *Tooth Fairy's First Night*, by Anne Bowen, illustrated by Jon Berkeley.

CARSON-DELLOSA PUBLISHING CO., INC.

P.O. Box 35665, Greensboro NC 27425-5665. (336)632-0084. Fax: (336)808-3273. Website: www.carsondellosa.com. **Contact:** Julie Killian, Acquisitions. **Publishes 80-90 titles/year. 15-20% of books from first-time authors. 95% from unagented writers. Makes outright purchase.** Accepts simultaneous submissions. Responds in 3 months to proposals. Book catalog available online. Guidelines available free.
Nonfiction We publish supplementary educational materials, such as teacher resource books, workbooks, and activity books.Subjects include education, including Christian education. Submit proposal package, sample chapters or pages, SASE. Reviews artwork/photos. Send photocopies.

CARSTENS PUBLICATIONS, INC.

Hobby Book Division P.O. Box 700, Newton NJ 07860-0700. (973)383-3355. Fax: (973)383-4064. E-mail: carstens@carstens-publications.com. Website: www.carstens-publications.com. **Contact:** Harold H. Carstens, publisher. Estab. 1933. Publishes paperback originals. **Publishes 8 titles/year. 100% from unagented writers. Pays 10% royalty on retail price. Pays advance.** Publishes book 1 year after acceptance of ms. Responds in 2 months to queries. Book catalog for #10 SASE.

- Carstens specializes in books about railroads, model railroads, and airplanes for hobbyists.

Nonfiction Query with SASE. Reviews artwork/photos.
Recent Title(s) *Pennsylvania Railroad Lines East*, by Steve Stewart and Dave Augsburger; *Track Design*, by Bill Schopp.
Tips We need lots of good photos. Material must be in model, hobby, railroad, and transportation field only.

CATHOLIC UNIVERSITY OF AMERICA PRESS

620 Michigan Ave. NE, 240 Leahy Hall, Washington DC 20064. (202)319-5052. Fax: (202)319-4985. E-mail: cua-press@cua.edu. Website: cuapress.cua.edu. **Contact:** James C. Kruggel, acquisitions editor (philosophy,

theology); Dr. David J. McGonagle, director (all other fields). Estab. 1939. **Publishes 30-35 titles/year. 50% of books from first-time authors. 100% from unagented writers. Pays variable royalty on net receipts.** Publishes book 18 months after acceptance of ms. Responds in 5 days to queries. Book catalog on request. Guidelines available online.

- The Catholic University of America Press publishes in the fields of history (ecclesiastical and secular), literature and languages, philosophy, political theory, social studies, and theology. "We have interdisciplinary emphasis on patristics, and medieval studies. We publish works of original scholarship intended for academic libraries, scholars and other professionals and works that offer a synthesis of knowledge of the subject of interest to a general audience or suitable for use in college and university classrooms."

Nonfiction Subjects include government, politics, history, language, literature, philosophy, religion, Church-state relations. Query with outline, sample chapter, cv, and list of previous publications.
Recent Title(s) *Lineages of European Political Thought* by Cary Nederman.
Tips Scholarly monographs and works suitable for adoption as supplementary reading material in courses have the best chance.

CATO INSTITUTE

1000 Massachusetts Ave. NW, Washington DC 20001. (202)842-0200. Website: www.cato.org. **Contact:** Submissions Editor. Estab. 1977. Publishes hardcover originals, trade paperback originals and reprints. **Publishes 12 titles/year. 25% of books from first-time authors. 90% from unagented writers. Makes outright purchase of 1,000-10,000. Pays advance.** Publishes book 9 months after acceptance of ms. Accepts simultaneous submissions. Responds in 3 months to queries. Book catalog available online.

- Cato Institute publishes books on public policy issues from a free-market or libertarian perspective.

Nonfiction Subjects include business, economics, education, government, politics, health, medicine, money, finance, sociology, public policy. Query with SASE.
Recent Title(s) *In Defense of Global Capitalism*, by Johan Norberg; *Voucher Wars*, by Clint Bolick.

CAXTON PRESS

312 Main St., Caldwell ID 83605-3299. (208)459-7421. Fax: (208)459-7450. Website: caxtonpress.com. **Contact:** Wayne Cornell, editor (Western Americana, regional nonfiction). Estab. 1907. Publishes hardcover and trade paperback originals. **Publishes 6-10 titles/year. 50% of books from first-time authors. 60% from unagented writers. Pays royalty. Pays advance.** Publishes book 18 months after acceptance of ms. Accepts simultaneous submissions. Responds in 3 months to queries. Book catalog for 9x12 envelope and First-Class stamps. Guidelines available online.

- "Western Americana nonfiction remains our focus. We define Western Americana as almost any topic that deals with the people or culture of the west, past and present. Currently emphasizing regional issues—primarily Pacific Northwest. De-emphasizing coffee table or photograph-intensive books."

Nonfiction Subjects include Americana, history, regional. Query Reviews artwork/photos.
Recent Title(s) *The Deadliest Indian War in the West*, by Gregory Michel; *Owyhee Canyonlands*, by Mark Lisk; *A Fate Worse Than Death*, by Gregory & Susan Michno.
Tips "Books to us never can or will be primarily articles of merchandise to be produced as cheaply as possible and to be sold like slabs of bacon or packages of cereal over the counter. If there is anything that is really worthwhile in this mad jumble we call the 21st century, it should be books."

CELESTIAL ARTS

Ten Speed Press P.O. Box 7123-S, Berkeley CA 94707. (510)559-1600. Fax: (510)524-1629. Website: www.tenspeed.com. **Contact:** Acquisitions. Estab. 1966. Publishes trade paperback originals and reprints. Accepts simultaneous submissions. Responds in 6-8 weeks to queries. Book catalog available online. Guidelines available online.

- Celestial Arts publishes nonfiction for a forward-thinking, open-minded audience interested in psychology, self-help, spirituality, health and parenting.

Nonfiction Subjects include child guidance, cooking, foods, nutrition, education, health, medicine, New Age, psychology, womens issues, womens studies. Submit proposal package, outline, bio, 1-2 sample chapters, SASE. Reviews artwork/photos. Send photocopies.
Recent Title(s) *Addiction to Love*, by Susan Peabody; *Your Right to Know*, by Andrew Kimbrell; *Girls Speak Out*, by Andrea Johnston.
Tips Audience is fairly well-inform The most completely thought-o

N CENTER FOR THANATOLOGY RESEARCH & EDUCATION, INC.

391 Atlantic Ave., Brooklyn NY 11217. (718)858-3026. E-mail: thanatology@pipeline.com. Website: www.thanatology.org. **Contact:** Director. Estab. 1980. **Publishes 7 titles/year. 10 queries received/year. 3 mss received/year. 15% of books from first-time authors. 100% from unagented writers. Pays 10% royalty on wholesale price.** Publishes book 9 months after acceptance of ms. Responds in 1 month to queries. Responds

in 1 month to proposals. Book catalog and ms guidelines free.

Nonfiction Subjects include education, health, medicine, humanities, psychology, religion, social sciences, sociology, womens issues, womens studies, anthropology. Query with SASE. Reviews artwork/photos. Send photocopies.

Recent Title(s) *Mourning the Living: Coping with the Problems of Substance Abuse*, by F. Selder, Ph.D. (academic/scientific); *Getting the Most Out of Cemetery Visits*, by R. Halporn, M.A. (for educators); *Counting to Zero: Poems on Miscarriage*, by Marion Cohen (poetry on women's grief).

Tips We serve 2 different audiences: One is physicians/social workers/nurses dealing with dying patients and bereaved families. The second relates to all aspects of cemetery lore: recording, preservation, description, art of.

CENTERSTREAM PUBLICATIONS

P.O. Box 17878, Anaheim Hills CA 92817. (714)779-9390. Fax: (714)779-9390. E-mail: centerstrm@aol.com. Website: www.centerstream-usa.com. **Contact:** Ron Middlebrook, Cindy Middlebrook, owners. Estab. 1980. Publishes music hardcover and mass market paperback originals, trade paperback and mass market paperback reprints. **Publishes 12 titles/year. 15 queries received/year. 15 mss received/year. 80% of books from first-time authors. 100% from unagented writers. Pays 10-15% royalty on wholesale price. Pays $300-3,000 advance.** Publishes book 8 months after acceptance of ms. Accepts simultaneous submissions. Responds in 3 months to queries. Book catalog and ms guidelines for #10 SASE.

O→ Centerstream publishes music history and instructional books, all instruments plus DVDs.

Nonfiction Query with SASE.

Recent Title(s) *Guitar Chord Shapes of Charlie Christian*.

CHALICE PRESS

1221 Locust St., Suite 670, St. Louis MO 63103. (314)231-8500. E-mail: submissions@cbp21.com. Website: www.chalicepress.com. **Contact:** Dr. Trent C. Butler, editorial director. Publishes hardcover and trade paperback originals. **Publishes 35 titles/year. 300 queries received/year. 250 mss received/year. 10% of books from first-time authors. 100% from unagented writers.** Publishes book 1 year after acceptance of ms. Accepts simultaneous submissions. Responds in 1 month to queries. Responds in 2 months to proposals. Responds in 3 months to manuscripts. Book catalog available online. Guidelines available online.

Nonfiction Subjects include religion, Christian spirituality. Submit proposal package, outline, 1-2 sample chapters.

Recent Title(s) *Solving the Da Vinci Code Mystery*, by Brandon Gilvin; *Chalice Introduction to the New Testament*, edited by Dennis E. Smith; *Martin Luther King on Creative Living*, by Michael G. Long.

Tips We publish for professors, church ministers, and lay Christian readers.

CHARLESBRIDGE PUBLISHING

85 Main St., Watertown MA 02472. (617)926-0329. Fax: (617)926-5720. Website: www.charlesbridge.com. **Contact:** Submissions Editors. Estab. 1980. Publishes hardcover and trade paperback nonfiction and fiction, children's books for the trade and library markets. **Publishes 30 titles/year. 10-20% of books from first-time authors. 80% from unagented writers. Pays royalty. Pays advance.** Publishes book 2-4 years after acceptance of ms. Guidelines available online.

Imprints Charlesbridge.

O→ "We're always interested in innovative approaches to a difficult genre, the nonfiction picture book."

Nonfiction Subjects include animals, creative nonfiction, history, multicultural, nature, environment, science, social science. *Exclusive submissions only*.

Fiction Strong stories with enduring themes. *Exclusive submissions only*.

Recent Title(s) *The Searcher and Old Tree*, by David McPhail; *Hello, Bumblebee Bat*, by Darrin Lunde; *Wiggle and Waggle*, by Caroline Arnold.

THE CHARLES PRESS, PUBLISHERS

133 North 21st Street, Philadelphia PA 19103. (215)561-2786. Fax: (215)561-0191. E-mail: mailbox@charlespresspub.com. Website: www.charlespresspub.com. **Contact:** Lauren Meltzer, publisher. Estab. 1982. Publishes hardcover and trade paperback originals. Accepts simultaneous submissions. Responds in approximately 1 to 2 months to proposals. Responds in 1 to 2 months to manuscripts. Book catalog available online. Guidelines available online.

O→ Currently emphasizing mental and physical health, psychology, how-to (especially relating to health), comparative religion, aging/eldercare.

Nonfiction Subjects include child guidance, health, medicine, mental health, medicine, physical health, medicine, nursing, psychology, religion, nursing, how-to, aging/eldercare, criminology, true crime. Query or submit proposal package that includes a description of the book, a few representative sample chapters, intended audience, competing titles, author's qualifications/background and SASE. No e-mailed or faxed submissions. Reviews artwork/photos. Send Send photocopies or transparencies.

Recent Title(s) *How Different Religions View Death and Afterlife, Third Edition*, edited by Christopher Johnson, Ph.d. and Marsha McGee, Ph.d.

CHARLES RIVER MEDIA

25 Thomson Place, Boston MA 02210. (617)757-8043. Fax: (617)757-7969. E-mail: crminfo@cengage.com. Website: www.charlesriver.com. **Contact:** Jennifer Blaney. Publishes hardcover and trade paperback originals. **Publishes 60 titles/year. 1,000 queries received/year. 250 mss received/year. 20% of books from first-time authors. 90% from unagented writers. Pays 5-20% royalty on wholesale price. Pays $3,000-20,000 advance.** Publishes book 4 months after acceptance of ms. Accepts simultaneous submissions. Responds in 2 weeks to queries. Book catalog for #10 SASE. Guidelines available online.

O→ Our publishing program concentrates on 6 major areas: Internet, networking, game development, programming, engineering, and graphics. The majority of our titles are considered intermediate, not high-level research monographs, and not for lowest-level general users.

Nonfiction Subjects include computers, electronics. Query with SASE. Submit proposal package, outline, resume, 2 sample chapters. Reviews artwork/photos. Send photocopies and GIF, TIFF, or PDF files.

Recent Title(s) *Game Programming Gems*; *Professional Web Design 2/E*.

Tips We are very receptive to detailed proposals by first-time or nonagented authors. Consult our website for proposal outlines. Manuscripts must be completed within 6 months of contract signing.

CHELSEA GREEN PUBLISHING CO.

P.O. Box 428, White River Junction VT 05001-0428. (802)295-6300. Fax: (802)295-6444. E-mail: submissions@chelseagreen.com. Website: www.chelseagreen.com. **Contact:** Joni Praded, editorial director. Estab. 1984. Publishes hardcover and trade paperback originals and reprints. **Publishes 18-25 titles/year. 600-800 queries received/year. 200-300 mss received/year. 30% of books from first-time authors. 80% from unagented writers. Pays royalty on publisher's net. Pays $2,500-10,000 advance.** Publishes book 18 months after acceptance of ms. Responds in 2 weeks to queries. Responds in 1 month to proposals. Responds in 1 month to manuscripts. Book catalog free or online. Guidelines available online.

O→ For 25 years, Chelsea Green has been the publishing leader for books on the politics and practice of sustainable living. Chelsea Green publishes and distributes books on ethical and sustainable business; food and health; organic gardening and agriculture; green building; nature and the environment; progressive politics and social justice; renewable energy; simple living; and other sustainability topics. Chelsea Green's Sciencewriters series publishes books on cutting-edge topics that advance science and the role it can play in preserving or creating sustainable civilizations and ecosystems.

Nonfiction Subjects include agriculture, alternative lifestyles, ethical & sustainable business, environment, foods, organic gardening, health, green building, progressive politics, science, social justice, simple living, renewable energy; and other sustainability topics. We prefer electronic queries and proposals via email (as a single attachment). If sending via snail mail, submissions will only be returned with SASE. Please review our guidelines carefully before submitting. Reviews artwork/photos.

Fiction We do not publish fiction or children's books.

Recent Title(s) *Obama's Challenge*, by Robert Kutner; *The End of Money and the Future of Civilization*, by Thomas Greco; *The Winter Harvest Handbook*, by Eliot Coleman; *Living Above the Store*, by Martin Melaver; *The Transition Handbook*, by Rob Hopkins; *Wind Energy Basics, 2nd ed.*, by Paul Gipe.

Tips Our readers and our authors are passionate about finding sustainable and viable solutions to contemporary challenges in the fields of energy, food production, economics, and building. It would be helpful for prospective authors to have a look at several of our current books, as well as our website.

CHELSEA HOUSE PUBLISHERS

Infobase Publishing 132 W. 31st St., 17th Floor, New York NY 10001. (800) 322-8755 or (212) 967-8800. Fax: (800)780-7300. E-mail: editorial@factsonfile.com. Website: www.chelseahouse.com. **Contact:** Editorial Assistant. Publishes hardcover originals and reprints. Accepts simultaneous submissions. Book catalog available online. Guidelines for #10 SASE.

O→ We publish curriculum-based nonfiction books for middle school and high school students.

Nonfiction Subjects include Americana, animals, anthropology, archeology, ethnic, gay, lesbian, government, politics, health, medicine, history, hobbies, language, literature, military, war, multicultural, music, dance, nature, environment, recreation, regional, religion, science, sociology, sports, travel, womens issues, womens studies. Query with SASE. Submit proposal package, outline, 2-3 sample chapters, resume. Reviews artwork/photos. Send photocopies.

Recent Title(s) *Point/Counterpoint: Blogging*; *Hepatitis*, (Deadly Disease & Epidemics series); *Natural Resources: Forests*.

Tips Please review our products online or in our bi-annual catalog. Please be sure submissions fit our market of the middle and high school student. Be professional. Send clean, clear submissions that show you read the preferred submission format. Always include SASE.

CHICAGO REVIEW PRESS

814 N. Franklin, Chicago IL 60610-3109. (312)337-0747. Fax: (312)337-5110. E-mail: csherry@chicagoreviewpress.com. Website: www.chicagoreviewpress.com. **Contact:** Cynthia Sherry, associate publisher (general nonfiction, children's); Yuval Taylor, senior editor (African-American and performing arts); Jerome Pohlen, senior editor (educational resources); Susan Bradanini Betz, senior editor (African-American, Latino-American). Estab. 1973. Publishes hardcover and trade paperback originals, and trade paperback reprints. **Publishes 40-50 titles/year. 400 queries received/year. 800 mss received/year. 50% of books from first-time authors. 50% from unagented writers. Pays 7-12 ½% royalty. Pays $3,000-10,000 average advance.** Publishes book 18 months after acceptance of ms. Accepts simultaneous submissions. Responds in 3 months to queries. Book catalog for $3.50. ms guidelines for #10 SASE or online at website.

Imprints Lawrence Hill Books; A Cappella Books (contact Yuval Taylor); Zephyr Press (contact Jerome Pohlen).

- Chicago Review Press publishes intelligent nonfiction on timely subjects for educated readers with special interests.

Nonfiction Subjects include art, architecture, child guidance, creative nonfiction, education, gardening, regional, health, medicine, history, hobbies, memoirs, multicultural, nature, environment, recreation, regional, music. Query with outline, TOC, and 1-2 sample chapters. Reviews artwork/photos.

Recent Title(s) *The Funniest One in the Room: The Lives and Legends of Del Close,* by Kim Howard Johnson.

Tips Along with a table of contents and 1-2 sample chapters, also send a cover letter and a list of credentials with your proposal. Also, provide the following information in your cover letter: audience, market, and competition—who is the book written for and what sets it apart from what's already out there.

CHIVALRY BOOKSHELF

3305 Mayfair Ln., Highland Village TX 75077. (978)418-4774. Fax: (978)418-4774. E-mail: chronique_editor@yahoo.com. Website: www.chivalrybookshelf.com. **Contact:** Brian R. Price, publisher (history, art, philosophy, political science, military, martial arts, fencing). Estab. 1996. Publishes hardcover and trade paperback originals and reprints. **Publishes 12 titles/year. 75 queries received/year. 25 mss received/year. 50% of books from first-time authors. 90% from unagented writers. Pays 5-12% royalty.** Publishes book 6 months after acceptance of ms. Responds in 1 month to queries. Responds in 1 month to proposals. Responds in 2 months to manuscripts. Book catalog available free. Guidelines available online.

Nonfiction Subjects include art, architecture, creative nonfiction, education, government, politics, history, military, war, recreation, sports, martial arts/fencing especially, translation. Query with SASE. Submit proposal package, outline, 1 sample chapter, sample illustrations. Submit complete ms. Reviews artwork/photos.

Recent Title(s) *The Medieval Art of Swordsmanship,* translated and interpreted by Dr. Jeffrey L. Forgeng, co-published with the British Royal Armouries (art history); *Deeds of Arms,* by Dr. Stephen Muhlberger (scholarly/popular translation); *Arte of Defence,* by William E. Wilson (historical fencing).

Tips The bulk of our books are intended for serious amateur scholars and students of history and martial arts. The authors we select tend to have a strong voice, are well read in their chosen field, and submit relatively clean manuscripts.

CHOSEN BOOKS

a division of Baker Publishing Group 3985 Bradwater St., Fairfax VA 22031-3702. (703)764-8250. Fax: (703)764-3995. E-mail: jcampbell@chosenbooks.com. Website: www.chosenbooks.com. **Contact:** Jane Campbell, editorial director. Estab. 1971. Publishes hardcover and trade paperback originals. **Publishes 20 titles/year. 10% of books from first-time authors. 99% from unagented writers. Pays small advance.** Publishes book 12-18 months after acceptance of ms. Accepts simultaneous submissions. Responds in 3 months to queries. Guidelines for #10 SASE.

- We publish well-crafted books that recognize the gifts and ministry of the Holy Spirit, and help the reader live a more empowered and effective life for Jesus Christ.

Nonfiction Submit synopsis, chapter outline, résumé, 2 chapters and SASE or email address. No computer disks or email attachments.

Recent Title(s) *Lord, Help Me Break This Habit: You Can Be Free From Doing the Things You Hate,* by Quin Sherrer and Ruthanne Garlock; *Praying for Israel's Destiny,* by James W. Goll.

Tips We look for solid, practical advice for the growing and maturing Christian from authors with professional or personal experience platforms. No chronicling of life events, please. Narratives have to be theme-driven. State the topic or theme of your book clearly in your query.

CHRISTIAN ED. PUBLISHERS

9260 Trade Place, Suite #100, San Diego CA 92126. (858)578-4700. Fax: (858)578-2431. Website: www.christianedwarehouse.com. **Contact:** Julia Myers, assistant editor. **Publishes 80 titles/year. Makes outright purchase of 3¢/word.** to manuscripts. Book catalog for 9x12 envelope and 4 First-Class stamps. Guidelines for #10 SASE.

O╤ "Christian Ed. Publishers is an independent, nondenominational, evangelical company founded over 50 years ago to produce Christ-centered curriculum materials based on the Word of God for thousands of churches of different denominations throughout the world. Our mission is to introduce children, teens, and adults to a personal faith in Jesus Christ, and to help them grow in their faith and service to the Lord. We publish materials that teach moral and spiritual values while training individuals for a lifetime of Christian service. Currently emphasizing Bible curriculum for preschool-preteen ages."

Nonfiction Subjects include education, Christian, religion. Query with SASE.

Fiction All writing is done on assignment. Query with SASE.

Recent Title(s) *All-Stars for Jesus: Bible Curriculum for Preteens.*

Tips "Read our guidelines carefully before sending us a manuscript. All writing is done on assignment only and must be age appropriate (preschool-6th grade)."

CHRONICLE BOOKS

680 Second St., San Francisco CA 94107. (415)537-4200. Fax: (415)537-4460. Website: www.chroniclebooks.com. **Contact:** Adult Trade Division. Estab. 1966. Publishes hardcover and trade paperback originals. **Publishes 175 titles/year.** Publishes book 18 months after acceptance of ms. Accepts simultaneous submissions. Responds in 3 months to queries. Book catalog for 11X14 envelope and 5 First-Class stamps. Guidelines available online.

Imprints Chronicle Books for Children; GiftWorks (ancillary products, such as stationery, gift books).

O╤ Inspired by the enduring magic and importance of books, our objective is to create and distribute exceptional publishing that is instantly recognizable for its spirit, creativity and value. This objective informs our business relationships and endeavors, be they with customers, authors, suppliers or colleagues.

Nonfiction Subjects include art, architecture, cooking, foods, nutrition, gardening, nature, environment, photography, recreation, regional, design, pop culture, interior design. Query or submit outline/synopsis with artwork and sample chapters

Fiction Submit complete ms.

Recent Title(s) *The Beatles Anthology*, by The Beatles; *Worst-Case Scenario Survival Handbook*, by David Borgenicht and Joshua Piven.

CHRONICLE BOOKS FOR CHILDREN

680 Second St., San Francisco CA 94107. (415)537-4400. Fax: (415)537-4415. Website: www.chroniclekids.com. **Contact:** Children's Division. Publishes hardcover and trade paperback originals. **Publishes 50-60 titles/year. 30,000 queries received/year. 6% of books from first-time authors. 25% from unagented writers. Pays 8% royalty. Pays variable advance.** Publishes book 18-24 months after acceptance of ms. Accepts simultaneous submissions. Responds in 2-4 weeks to queries. Responds in 6 months to manuscripts. Book catalog for 9x12 envelope and 3 First-Class stamps. Guidelines available online.

O╤ Chronicle Books for Children publishes an eclectic mixture of traditional and innovative children's books. Our aim is to publish books that inspire young readers to learn and grow creatively while helping them discover the joy of reading. We're looking for quirky, bold artwork and subject matter. Currently emphasizing picture books. De-emphasizing young adult.

Nonfiction Subjects include animals, art, architecture, multicultural, nature, environment, science. Query with synopsis. Reviews artwork/photos.

Fiction Subjects include mainstream, contemporary, multicultural, young adult, picture books.

Recent Title(s) *The Man Who Went to the Far Side of the Moon*; *Just a Minute*; *Ruby's Wish.*

Tips We are interested in projects that have a unique bent to them—be it in subject matter, writing style, or illustrative technique. As a small list, we are looking for books that will lend our list a distinctive flavor. Primarily we are interested in fiction and nonfiction picture books for children ages up to eight years, and nonfiction books for children ages up to twelve years. We publish board, pop-up, and other novelty formats as well as picture books. We are also interested in early chapter books, middle grade fiction, and young adult projects.

CLARION BOOKS

Houghton Mifflin Co. 215 Park Ave. S., New York NY 10003. Website: www.houghtonmifflinbooks.com. **Contact:** Dinah Stevenson, vice president and publisher; Jennifer B. Greene, senior editor (contemporary fiction, picture books for all ages, nonfiction); Jennifer Wingertzahn, editor (fiction, picture books); Lynne Polvino, editor (fiction, nonfiction, picture books). Estab. 1965. Publishes hardcover originals for children. *Identify multiple submissions.* **Publishes 50 titles/year. Pays 5-10% royalty on retail price. Pays minimum of $4,000 advance.** Publishes book 2 years after acceptance of ms. Responds in 2 months to queries. Guidelines for #10 SASE or online.

O╤ "Clarion Books publishes picture books, nonfiction, and fiction for infants through grade 12. Avoid telling your stories in verse unless you are a professional poet."

Nonfiction Subjects include Americana, history, language, literature, nature, environment, photography, holiday. Query with SASE. Submit proposal package, sample chapters, SASE. Reviews artwork/photos. Send

photocopies.

Fiction Subjects include adventure, historical, humor, suspense, strong character studies, contemporary. "Clarion is highly selective in the areas of historical fiction, fantasy, and science fiction. A novel must be superlatively written in order to find a place on the list. Mss that arrive without an SASE of adequate size will *not* be responded to or returned. Accepts fiction translations." Submit complete ms. No queries, please. Send to only *one* Clarion editor.

Recent Title(s) *The Wednesday Wars*, by Gary D. Schmidt (fiction); *The Wonderful Thing About Hiccups*, by Cece Meng (picture book); *The Real Benedict Arnold*, by Jim Murphy (nonfiction).

Tips "Looks for freshness, enthusiasm—in short, life."

CLEAR LIGHT PUBLISHERS

823 Don Diego, Santa Fe NM 87505-4224. (505)989-9590. E-mail: publish@clearlightbooks.com. **Contact:** Harmon Houghton, publisher. Estab. 1981. Publishes hardcover and trade paperback originals. **Publishes 20-24 titles/year. 100 queries received/year. 10% of books from first-time authors. 50% from unagented writers. Pays 10% royalty on wholesale price. Offers advance, a percent of gross potential.** Publishes book 1 year after acceptance of ms. Accepts simultaneous submissions. Responds in 3 months to queries. Book catalog available free. Guidelines available online.

O→ Clear Light publishes books that accurately depict the positive side of human experience and inspire the spirit.

Nonfiction Subjects include Americana, anthropology, archeology, art, architecture, cooking, foods, nutrition, ethnic, history, nature, environment, philosophy, photography, regional, Southwest. Query with SASE. Reviews artwork/photos. Send photocopies.

Recent Title(s) *American Indian History*, by Robert Venables; *Celebrations Cookbook*, by Myra Baucom; *American Indian Love Stories*, by Herman Grey.

CLEIS PRESS

P.O. Box 14697, San Francisco CA 94114. (415)575-4700. Fax: (415)575-4705. Website: www.cleispress.com. **Contact:** Frederique Delacoste. Estab. 1980. Publishes trade paperback originals and reprints. **Publishes 20 titles/year. 10% of books from first-time authors. 90% from unagented writers. Pays variable royalty on retail price.** Publishes book 2 years after acceptance of ms. Responds in 1 month to queries.

O→ Cleis Press specializes in feminist and gay/lesbian fiction and nonfiction.

Nonfiction Subjects include gay, lesbian, womens issues, womens studies, sexual politics. Query or submit outline and sample chapters

Fiction Subjects include feminist, gay, lesbian, literary. We are looking for high quality fiction by women and men. Submit complete ms. *Writer's Market* recomme

Recent Title(s) *Deconstructing Tyrone*, (nonfiction); *Jia*, (fiction); *Whole Lesbian Sex Book*, (nonfiction).

Tips Be familiar with publishers' catalogs; be absolutely aware of your audience; research potential markets; present fresh new ways of looking at your topic; avoid `PR' language and include publishing history in query letter.

COFFEE HOUSE PRESS

79 13th NE, Suite 110, Minneapolis MN 55413. (612)338-0125. Fax: (612)338-4004. Website: www.coffeehousepress.org. **Contact:** Chris Fischbach, senior editor. Estab. 1984. Publishes hardcover and trade paperback originals. **Publishes 14 titles/year.** Responds in 4-6 weeks to queries. Responds in up to 6 months to manuscripts. Book catalog and ms guidelines online.

Fiction Seeks literary novels, short story collections and poetry. Query first with outline, samp

Recent Title(s) *The Impossibly*, by Laird Hunt; *The California Poem*, by Eleni Sikelianos; *Circle K Cycles*, by Karen Tei Yamashita.

Tips Look for our books at stores and libraries to get a feel for what we like to publish. No phone calls, e-mails, or faxes.

COLLEGE PRESS PUBLISHING CO.

P.O.Box 1132, 223 W. 3rd St., Joplin MO 64801. (800)289-3300. Fax: (417)623-8250. E-mail: books@collegepress.com. Website: www.collegepress.com. **Contact:** Acquisitions Editor. Estab. 1959. Publishes hardcover and trade paperback originals and reprints. Accepts simultaneous submissions. Responds in 3 months to proposals. Responds in 2 months to manuscripts. Book catalog for 9x12 envelope and 5 First-Class stamps. Guidelines available online.

Imprints HeartSpring Publishing (nonacademic Christian, inspirational, devotional and Christian fiction).

O→ College Press is an evangelical Christian publishing house primarily associated with the Christian churches/Church of Christ.

Nonfiction Query with SASE. Submit proposal package, outline, bio, synopsis, TOC, target audience.

Recent Title(s) *Dinner With Skeptics*, by Jeff Vines.

Tips "Our core market is Christian Churches/Churches of Christ and conservative evangelical Christians. Have your material critically reviewed prior to sending it. Make sure that it is non-Calvinistic and that it leans more amillennial (if it is apocalyptic writing)."

CONCORDIA PUBLISHING HOUSE

3558 S. Jefferson Ave., St. Louis MO 63118-3968. (314)268-1187. Fax: (314)268-1329. Website: www.cph.org. **Contact:** Peggy Kuethe, senior editor (children's product, adult devotional, women's resources); Dawn Weinstock, managing production editor (adult nonfiction on Christian spirituality and culture, academic works of interest in Lutheran markets). Estab. 1869. Publishes hardcover and trade paperback originals. **Publishes 30 titles/year.** Guidelines available online.

- "Concordia publishes Protestant, inspirational, theological, family, and juvenile material. All mss must conform to the doctrinal tenets of The Lutheran Church—Missouri Synod. No longer publishes fiction."

Nonfiction Subjects include child guidance, in Christian context, religion, inspirational.
Recent Title(s) *Is God Listening? Making God Part of Your Life*, by Andrew E. Steinmann (Christian living); *I Will Not Be Afraid*, by Michelle Medlock Adams (children's picture).
Tips "Call for information about what we are currently accepting."

CONSORTIUM PUBLISHING

640 Weaver Hill Rd., West Greenwich RI 02817-2261. (401)397-9838. Fax: (401)392-1926. Website: consortiumpublishing.tripod.com/consortiumpub/index.html. **Contact:** John M. Carlevale, chief of publications. Estab. 1990. Publishes trade paperback originals and reprints. **Publishes 12 titles/year. 150 queries received/year. 50 mss received/year. 50% of books from first-time authors. 95% from unagented writers. Pays 10-15% royalty.** Publishes book 3 months after acceptance of ms. Responds in 2 months to queries. Book catalog and ms guidelines for #10 SASE.

- "Consortium publishes books for all levels of the education market."

Nonfiction Subjects include business, economics, child guidance, education, government, politics, health, medicine, history, music, dance, nature, environment, psychology, science, sociology, women's issues, women's studies. Query, or submit proposal package, including TOC, outline, 1 sample chapter, and SASE. Reviews artwork/photos. Send photocopies.
Recent Title(s) *Teaching the Child Under Six, 4th Ed.*, by James L. Hymes, Jr. (education).
Tips "Audience is college and high school students and instructors, elementary school teachers and other trainers."

CONTINUUM INTERNATIONAL PUBLISHING GROUP, LTD.

80 Maiden Lane, Suite 704, New York NY 10038. (212)953-5858. Fax: (212)953-5944. E-mail: info@continuumbooks.com. Website: www.continuumbooks.com. **Contact:** Frank Oveis, VP/senior editor (religious, current affairs). Publishes hardcover originals and paperback textbooks. Book catalog available free. Guidelines available free.

- Continuum publishes textbooks, monographs, and reference works in religious studies, the humanities, arts, and social sciences for students, teachers, and professionals worldwide.

Nonfiction Subjects include anthropology, archeology, business, economics, education, film, cinema, stage, performance, government, politics, history, language, literature, music, dance, popular, philosophy, religion, sociology, linguistics. Submit outline.
Recent Title(s) *Jazz Writings*, by Philip Larkin; *Heavenly Touch*, by Abraham Joshua Heschel; *When the War Came Home*, by Stacy Bannerman.

COPPER CANYON PRESS

P.O. Box 271, Bldg. 313, Port Townsend WA 98368. (360)385-4925. Fax: (360)385-4985. E-mail: poetry@coppercanyonpress.org. Website: www.coppercanyonpress.org. **Contact:** Michael Wiegers, Director/executive editor. Estab. 1972. Publishes trade paperback originals and occasional cloth-bound editions. **Publishes 18 titles/year. 2,000 queries received/year. 1,500 mss received/year. 0% of books from first-time authors. 95% from unagented writers. Pays royalty.** Publishes book 2 years after acceptance of ms. Responds in 4 months to queries. Book catalog available online. Guidelines available online.
Imprints Ausable Press, Chase Twichell (Editor-at-Large, poet)

- The imprint Ausable Press, an independent literary press located in the Adirondack Mountains of northern New York, will join forces with CCR on Jan. 1, 2009. All contracts will be honored. Our offices will be kept open through 2009.
- Copper Canyon Press is dedicated to publishing poetry in a wide range of styles and from a full range of the world's cultures.

Recent Title(s) *Steal Away*, by C.D. Wright; *Twigs & Knucklebones*, by Sarah Lindsay; *The Hands of Day*, by Pablo Neruda.

Tips CCP publishes poetry exclusively and is the largest poetry publisher in the U.S. We will not review queries if guidelines are not followed. We will read queries form poets who have published a book. Please read our query guidelines.

CORNELL UNIVERSITY PRESS

Sage House, 512 E. State St., Ithaca NY 14850. (607)277-2338. Fax: (607)277-2374. Website: www.cornellpress.cornell.edu. Estab. 1869. Publishes hardcover and paperback originals. **Publishes 150 titles/year. Pays royalty. Pays $0-5,000 advance.** Publishes book 1 year after acceptance of ms. Accepts simultaneous submissions. Book catalog available online. Guidelines available online.

Imprints Comstock (contact Heidi Steinmetz Lovette); ILR Press (contact Frances Benson).

- On occasion accepts simultaneous submissions.

O→ "Cornell Press is an academic publisher of nonfiction with particular strengths in anthropology, Asian studies, biological sciences, classics, history, labor and business, literary criticism, politics and international relations, women's studies, Slavic studies, philosophy, urban studies, health care work, regional titles, and security studies. Currently emphasizing sound scholarship that appeals beyond the academic community."

Nonfiction Subjects include agriculture, anthropology, archeology, art, architecture, business, economics, ethnic, government, politics, history, language, literature, military, war, music, dance, philosophy, regional, sociology, translation, womens issues, womens studies, classics, life sciences. Submit resume, cover letter, and prospectus.

Recent Title(s) *Nature of the Rainforest: Costa Rica and Beyond*, by Adrian Forsyth, Foreward by E.O. Wilson, and photography by Michael Fogden and Patricia Fogden; *The Power Problem: How American Military Dominance Makes Us Less Safe, Less Prosperous, and Less Free,* by Christopher A. Preble; *Becoming a Woman in the Age of Letters*, by Dena Goodman.

CORWIN PRESS, INC.

2455 Teller Rd., Thousand Oaks CA 91320. (800)818-7243. Fax: (805)499-2692. E-mail: robb.clouse@corwinpress.com. Website: www.corwinpress.com. **Contact:** Robb Clouse, editorial director; Lizzie Brenkus, acquisitions editor (administration); Cathy Hernandez, acquisitions editor (content, curriculum); Kylee Liegl, acquisitions editor (content, curriculum and exceptional education); Rachel Livsey, senior acquisitions editor (staff development, diversity and research methods); Kathleen McLane, consulting acquisitions editor (exceptional education); Stacy Wagner, associate acquisitions editor (early childhood education and school counseling); Jean Ward, consulting senior acquisitions editor (teaching); Faye Zucker, executive editor (teaching). Estab. 1990. Publishes hardcover and paperback originals. **Publishes 240 titles/year.** Publishes book 7 months after acceptance of ms. Responds in 1-2 months to queries. Guidelines available online.

O→ Corwin Press, Inc., publishes leading-edge, user-friendly publications for education professionals.

Nonfiction Professional-level publications for administrators, teachers, school specialists, policymakers, researchers and others involved with preK-12 education.Subjects include education. Query with SASE.

THE COUNTRYMAN PRESS

P.O. Box 748, Woodstock VT 05091-0748. (802)457-4826. Fax: (802)457-1678. E-mail: countrymanpress@wwnorton.com. Website: www.countrymanpress.com. Estab. 1973. Publishes hardcover originals, trade paperback originals and reprints. **Publishes 60 titles/year. 1,000 queries received/year. 30% of books from first-time authors. 70% from unagented writers. Pays 5-15% royalty on retail price. Pays $1,000-5,000 advance.** Publishes book 18 months after acceptance of ms. Accepts simultaneous submissions. Responds in 2 months to proposals. Book catalog available free. Guidelines available online.

Imprints Backcountry Guides, Berkshire House.

O→ Countryman Press publishes books that encourage physical fitness and appreciation for and understanding of the natural world, self-sufficiency, and adventure.

Nonfiction We publish several series of regional recreation guidebooks—hiking, bicycling, walking, fly-fishing, canoeing, kayaking—and are looking to expand them. We're also looking for books of national interest on travel, gardening, rural living, nature, and fly-fishing.Subjects include cooking, foods, nutrition, gardening, history, nature, environment, recreation, regional, travel, country living. Submit proposal package, outline, bio, 3 sample chapters, market information, SASE. Reviews artwork/photos. Send photocopies.

Recent Title(s) *Eatingwell Comfort Foods Made Easy; San Miguel de Allende: Great Destinations; Old Ghosts of New England; Volunteer Vacations Across America.*

COVENANT COMMUNICATIONS, INC.

920 E. State Rd., American Fork UT 84003. (801)756-9966. Fax: (801)756-1049. E-mail: info@covenant-lds.com. Website: www.covenant-lds.com. **Contact:** Kathryn Jenkins, managing ed. Estab. 1958. **Publishes 80-100 titles/year. 350 queries, 1,200 mss 60% of books from first-time authors. 99% from unagented writers. Pays 6 ½-15% royalty on retail price.** Publishes book 6 months after acceptance of ms. Accepts simultaneous submissions. Responds in 1 month on queries & proposals; 4 months on manuscripts. Guidelines available

online.

- Currently emphasizing inspirational, devotional, historical, biography. Our fiction is also expanding, and we are looking for new approaches to LDS literature and storytelling.

Nonfiction Subjects include history, religion, spirituality. Submit complete ms. Yes. Send photocopies.
Fiction We publish exclusively to the 'Mormon' (The Church of Jesus Christ of Latter-Day Saints) market. Fiction must feature characters who are members of that church, grappling with issues relevant to that religion. Subjects include adventure, historical, mystery, regional, religious, romance, spiritual, suspense. Submit complete ms.
Recent Title(s) *Presidents and Prophets*, by Michael Winder (historical); *Beautiful Zion*, by Al Rounds and Michael Wilcox (historical/gift); *High Country*, by Jennie Hansen (Western); *A Distant Thunder*, by Anita Stansfield (romance)
Tips Our audience is exclusively LDS (Latter-Day Saints, 'Mormon').

COWLEY PUBLICATIONS

Rowman & Littlefield 4501 Forbes Blvd., Suite 200, Lanham MD 20706. Website: www.rowmanlittlefield.com/imprints/cowley.shtml. Estab. 1979. Publishes cloth and paperback originals. **Publishes 5-10 titles/year. 500 queries received/year. 300 mss received/year. 50% of books from first-time authors. 90% from unagented writers. Pays 8-15% royalty on wholesale price. Pays $0-5,000 advance.** Publishes book 12-18 months after acceptance of ms. Accepts simultaneous submissions. Responds in 2 months to queries; 3 months to proposals; 4 months to manuscripts. Book catalog available online. Guidelines available online.

- Purchased by Rowman & Littlefield Publishing Group.

Nonfiction Subjects include religion, spirituality. Query with SASE. Submit proposal package, outline, 1 sample chapter, other materials as specified online.
Recent Title(s) *Conversations With Scripture and With Each Other*," by M. Thomas Shaw, SSJE; *Pilgrims of Christ on the Muslim Road*," by Paul-Gordon Chandler.
Tips "We envision an audience of committed Christians and spiritual seekers of various denominations and faiths. Familiarize yourself with our catalog and our outlook on spiritual and theological formation. Prepare proposals/manuscripts that are of professional caliber and demonstrate an understanding of and commitment to your book's reader."

CQ PRESS

2300 N Street, NW, Suite 800, Washington DC 20037. (202)729-1800. E-mail: ckiino@cqpress.com. Website: www.cqpress.com. **Contact:** Doug Goldenberg-Hart, Shana Wagger (library/reference); Clarisse Kiino (college), Barbara Rogers (staff directories). Estab. 1945. Publishes hardcover and online paperback titles. Accepts simultaneous submissions. Book catalog available free.
Imprints College, Library/Reference, Staff Directories; CQ Electronic Library/CQ Researcher.

- CQ Press seeks to educate the public by publishing authoritative works on American and international politics, policy, and people.

Nonfiction We are interested in American government, public administration, comparative government, and international relations.Subjects include government, politics, history. Submit proposal package, outline. Bio.
Tips Our books present important information on American government and politics, and related issues, with careful attention to accuracy, thoroughness, and readability.

CRAFTSMAN BOOK CO.

6058 Corte Del Cedro, Carlsbad CA 92011. (760)438-7828 or (800)829-8123. Fax: (760)438-0398. Website: www.craftsman-book.com. **Contact:** Laurence D. Jacobs, editorial manager. Estab. 1957. Publishes paperback originals. **Publishes 12 titles/year. 85% of books from first-time authors. 98% from unagented writers. Pays 7 ½-12 ½% royalty on wholesale price or retail price** Publishes book 2 years after acceptance of ms. Accepts simultaneous submissions. Responds in 2 months to queries. Book catalog and ms guidelines free.

- Publishes how-to manuals for professional builders. Currently emphasizing construction software.

Nonfiction All titles are related to construction for professional builders.Query with SASE. Reviews artwork/photos.
Recent Title(s) *Steel-Frame House Construction*, by Tim Waite.
Tips The book should be loaded with step-by-step instructions, illustrations, charts, reference data, forms, samples, cost estimates, rules of thumb, and examples that solve actual problems in the builder's office and in the field. The book must cover the subject completely, become the owner's primary reference on the subject, have a high utility-to-cost ratio, and help the owner make a better living in his chosen field.

CREATIVE HOMEOWNER

24 Park Way, Upper Saddle River NJ 07458. (201)934-7100. Fax: (201)934-8971. E-mail: info@creativehomeowner.com. Website: www.creativehomeowner.com. Estab. 1978. Publishes trade paperback originals. Book catalog available free.

- Creative Homeowner is the one source for the largest selection of quality home-related how-to books, idea books, booklets, and project plans.

Nonfiction Subjects include gardening, crafts/hobbies, home remodeling/building. Query, or submit proposal package, including competitive books (short analysis), outline, and SASE Reviews artwork/photos.

Recent Title(s) *The Painted Home*, by Kerry Skinner; *So Simple Window Style*, by Gail Abbott and Cate Burren; *The Smart Approach to Baby Rooms*, by Joanne Still.

CRICKET BOOKS

Imprint of Carus Publishing 70 E. Lake St., Suite 300, Chicago IL 60601. (603)924-7209. Fax: (603)924-7380. Website: www.cricketmag.com. **Contact:** Submissions Editor. Estab. 1999. Publishes hardcover originals. **Publishes 5 titles/year. Open to first-time authors.** Publishes book 18 months after acceptance of ms.

- *Currently not accepting queries or ms.* Check website for submissions details and updates.

Cricket Books publishes picture books, chapter books, and middle-grade novels.

Fiction Subjects include juvenile, adventure, easy-to-read, fantasy/science fiction fiction, historical, horror, mystery/suspense, problem novels, sports, western, early chapter books and middle-grade fiction.

Recent Title(s) *Dream-of-Jade*, by Lloyd Alexander; *Hercules*, by Geraldine McCaughrean; *Triple-Dare to Be Scared*, by Robert San Souci.

Tips Take a look at the recent titles to see what sort of materials we're interested in, especially for nonfiction. Please note that we aren't doing the sort of strictly educational nonfiction that other publishers specialize in.

CROSS-CULTURAL COMMUNICATIONS

Cross-Cultural Literary Editions, Ltd.; Express Editions; Ostrich Editions 239 Wynsum Ave., Merrick NY 11566-4725. (516)869-5635. Fax: (516)379-1901. E-mail: cccpoetry@aol.com. Website: www.cross-culturalcommunications.com. **Contact:** Stanley H. Barkan, publisher/editor-in-chief (bilingual poetry); Bebe Barkan, Mia Barkan Clarke, art editors (complementary art to poetry editions). Estab. 1971. Publishes hardcover and trade paperback originals. **Publishes 10 titles/year. 200 queries received/year. 50 mss received/year. 25%% of books from first-time authors. 100%% from unagented writers.** Publishes book 12 months after acceptance of ms. Responds in 1 month to proposals. Responds in 2 months to manuscripts. Book catalog (sample flyers) for #10 SASE.

Imprints Expressive Editions (contact Mia Barkan Clarke).

Nonfiction Subjects include language, literature, memoirs, multicultural. Query with SASE. Reviews artwork/photos. Send photocopies.

Fiction Subjects include historical, multicultural, poetry, poetry in translation, translation, Bilingual poetry. We are currently over-committed. Do not query until mid-2009. For bilingual poetry: Submit 3-6 short poems in original language with translation, a brief (3-5 lines) bio of the author and translator(s). Query with SASE.

Recent Title(s) *Memoir from a Swiss Prison*, by Ignazio Silone, translated from the Italian by Stanislao G. Pugliese (memoir); *The Saint-Makers*, by Paul M. Levitt (historical novel); *Skipper Worse*, by Alexander Lange Kielland, translated by Christopher Fauske (historical novel); *The Brush and the Sword: Kasa*, translated by Sung-II Lee (bilingual Korean classical poems in prose).

Tips Best chance: poetry from a translation.

THE CROSSROAD PUBLISHING COMPANY

83 Chestnut Ridge Rd., Chestnut Ridge NY 10977. Fax: (845)517-0181. E-mail: editor@crossroadpublishing.com. Website: www.cpcbooks.com. **Contact:** Attn: Editorial Dept. Estab. 1980. Publishes hardcover and trade paperback originals and reprints. **Publishes 45 titles/year. 1,000 queries received/year. 200 mss received/year. 10% of books from first-time authors. 75% from unagented writers. Pays 6-14% royalty on wholesale price.** Publishes book 14 months after acceptance of ms. Accepts simultaneous submissions. Responds in 6 weeks to queries. Responds in 6 weeks to proposals. Responds in 12 weeks to manuscripts. Book catalog available free. Guidelines available online.

Imprints Crossroad (trade); Herder (classroom/academic).

Nonfiction Subjects include creative nonfiction, ethnic, leadership, philosophy, religion, spirituality, spiritual direction, womens issues, leadership, Catholicism. Query with SASE.

Recent Title(s) *Against the Grain*, by George Weigel; *Secularity and the Gospel*, by Ronald Rolheiser; *The Examen Prayer*, by Timothy Gallagher; *The Bad Catholic's Guide to Good Living*, by John Zmirak and Denise Matychowiak; *What Your Money Means*, by Frank J. Hanna.

Tips Refer to our Web site and catalog for a sense of the range and kinds of books we offer. Follow our application guidelines as posted on our Web site.

CROWN BUSINESS

Random House, Inc. 1745 Broadway, New York NY 10019. (212)572-2275. Fax: (212)572-6192. E-mail: crownbiz@randomhouse.com. Website: www.randomhouse.com/crown. Estab. 1995. Publishes hardcover and trade paperback originals. Accepts simultaneous submissions. Book catalog available online.

- *Agented submissions only.*

Nonfiction Subjects include business, economics, money, finance, management. Query with proposal package including outline, 1-2 sample chapters, market analysis and information on author platform.

Recent Title(s) *The Breakthrough Company*, by Keith R. McFarland; *Know-How*, by Ram Charan; *The Education of an Accidental CEO*, by David Novak.

CSLI PUBLICATIONS

Ventura Hall, Stanford University, Stanford CA 94305-4115. (650)723-1839. Fax: (650)725-2166. E-mail: pubs@csli.stanford.edu. Website: cslipublications.stanford.edu. Publishes hardcover and scholarly paperback originals. Book catalog available free. Guidelines available online.

- *No unsolicited mss.*

O→ CSLI Publications, part of the Center for the Study of Language and Information, specializes in books in the study of language, information, logic, and computation.

Nonfiction Subjects include anthropology, archeology, computers, electronics, language, literature, linguistics, science, logic, cognitive science. Query with SASE or by email.

Recent Title(s) *Handbook of French Semantics*, edited by Francis Corblin and Henriëtte de Swart; *Geometry & Meaning*, by Dominic Widdows.

CUMBERLAND HOUSE PUBLISHING

431 Harding Industrial Dr., Nashville TN 37211. (615)832-1171. Fax: (615)832-0633. Website: www.cumberlandhouse.com. Estab. 1996. Publishes hardcover, trade paperback and mass market originals and reprints. Accepts simultaneous submissions. Responds in 4-6 months to manuscripts. Book catalog for 8x10 envelope and 4 First-Class stamps. Guidelines available online.

Imprints Cumberland House Hearthside; Highland Books; WND Books.

- Accepts mss by US mail only. No electronic or telephone queries will be accepted.

O→ Cumberland House publishes market specific books. We evaluate in terms of how sure we are that we can publish the book successfully and then the quality or uniqueness of a project. No longer seeking to acquire fiction titles.

Nonfiction Subjects include Americana, cooking, foods, nutrition, government, politics, history, military, war, recreation, regional, sports, travel, current affairs, popular culture. Query with SASE. Submit proposal package, outline, 1 sample chapter, synopsis, résumé, SASE. Reviews artwork/photos. Send Send photocopies only; not original copies.

Recent Title(s) *Earl Hamner*, by James E. Person, Jr.; *Atomic Iran*, by Jerome Corsi; *Love Signs*, by Gregory E. Lang.

Tips Audience is adventuresome people who like a fresh approach to things. Writers should tell what their idea is, why it's unique and why somebody would want to buy it—but don't pester us.

[A] BROADWAY BUSINESS

Crown Publishing Group at Random House 1745 Broadway, New York NY 10019. (212)782-9730. Website: www.randomhouse.com. **Contact:** Roger Scholl, editorial dir. Estab. 1989.

- "In addition, I also sign up books in the fields of science, history, and popular culture for the Broadway list."

O→ "We publish original business books in a wide range of areas, from narrative nonfiction to economics, from marketing to leadership, from motivation to books on personal success. See our Spring 2009 titles below."

Nonfiction Agented submissions only.

Recent Title(s) *Ecological Intelligence*, by Daniel Goleman; *Showing Up For Life*, by Bill Gates, Sr.; *Who's Got Your Back*, by Keith Ferrazzi; *The Greatest Man Who Ever Lived*, by Steve Scott; *The Leader's Way*, by The Dalai Lama; Recent Bestsellers: *Sway*, by Ori and Rom Brafman; *Buyology*, by Martin Lindstrom; *Get Motivated*, by Tamara Lowe; *Rubies in the Orchard*, by Lynda Resnick.

DAN RIVER PRESS

Conservatory of American Letters, P.O. Box 298, Thomaston ME 04861-0298. (207)226-7428. E-mail: cal@americanletters.org. Website: www.americanletters.org. **Contact:** Richard S. Danbury, fiction editor. Estab. 1977. Publishes hardcover and paperback originals. **Publishes 6-8 titles/year. Pays 10-15% royalty, 5 author's copies Pays occassional advance.** Publishes book 3-4 months after acceptance of ms. Accepts simultaneous submissions. Responds in 2-3 days to queries. Book catalog for #10 SASE. Guidelines available online.

O→ Small press publisher of fiction and biographies owned by a nonprofit foundation.

Fiction Subjects include space fantasy, sword and sorcery, general, dark fantasy, futuristic, psychological, supernatural, amateur sleuth, police procedural, private eye/hardboiled, general religious, inspirational, religious mystery/suspense, religious thriller, religious romance, contemporary, futuristic/time travel, gothic, historical, romantic suspense, hard science fiction/technological, soft/sociological, amateur sleuth, police procedural, private eye/hardboiled, frontier saga, traditional, outdoors/fishing/hunting/camping/trapping. Accepts anything but porn, sedition, evangelical, and children's literature. Submit publishing history, clips, bio. Cover letter or query should i.

Recent Title(s) *Soft Target: The Air*, by Joel Narlock; *The Mason Dixon project*, by Vincent Grazino.

Tips Spend some time developing a following. Forget the advice that says, 'Your first job is to find a publisher!' That's nonsense. Your first job as a writer is to develop an audience. Do that and a publisher will find you. Forget trying to get good enough; instead, find an audience.

JONATHAN DAVID PUBLISHERS, INC.

68-22 Eliot Ave., Middle Village NY 11379-1194. (718)456-8611. Fax: (718)894-2818. E-mail: submission@jdbooks.com. Website: www.jdbooks.com. **Contact:** David Kolatch, editorial director. Estab. 1948. Publishes hardcover and trade paperback originals and reprints. **Publishes 20-25 titles/year. 50% of books from first-time authors. 90% from unagented writers. Pays royalty, or makes outright purchase.** Publishes book 18 months after acceptance of ms. Responds in 1 month to queries. Responds in 1 month to proposals. Responds in 2 months to manuscripts. Book catalog available online. Guidelines available online.

O→ Jonathan David publishes popular Judaica.

Nonfiction Subjects include cooking, foods, nutrition, creative nonfiction, ethnic, multicultural, religion, sports. Query with SASE. Submit proposal package, outline, resume, 3 sample chapters. Reviews artwork/photos. Send photocopies.

Recent Title(s) *Great Jews in Entertainment*, by Darryl Lyman.

DAW BOOKS, INC.

Distributed by Penguin Group (USA) 375 Hudson St., New York NY 10014-3658. (212)366-2096. Fax: (212)366-2090. Website: www.dawbooks.com. **Contact:** Peter Stampfel, submissions editor. Estab. 1971. Publishes hardcover and paperback originals and reprints. **Publishes 50-60 titles/year. Pays in royalties with an advance negotiable on a book-by-book basis.** Responds in 3 months to manuscripts. Guidelines available online.

- Simultaneous submissions not accepted, unless prior arrangements are made by agent.

O→ DAW Books publishes science fiction and fantasy.

Fiction Subjects include fantasy, science fiction. We are interested in science fiction and fantasy novels. We are also currently seeking modern urban fantasy and paranormals. We like character-driven books with appealing protagonists, engaging plots, and well-constructed worlds. We accept both agented and unagented manuscripts. Submit entire ms, cover letter, SASE.

Recent Title(s) *Foundation*, by Mercedes Lackey (fantasy); *Shadowplay*, by Tad Williams (fantasy); *Regenesis*, by C.J. Cherryh (science fiction).

IVAN R. DEE, PUBLISHER

Imprint of The Rowman & Littlefield Publishing Group 1332 N. Halsted St., Chicago IL 60642-2694. (312)787-6262. Fax: (312)787-6269. E-mail: elephant@ivanrdee.com. Website: www.ivanrdee.com. **Contact:** Ivan R. Dee, president; Stephanie Frerich, managing editor. Estab. 1988. Publishes hardcover originals and trade paperback originals and reprints. **Publishes 50 titles/year. 10% of books from first-time authors. 60% from unagented writers. Pays royalty. Pays advance.** Publishes book 8 months after acceptance of ms. Accepts simultaneous submissions. Responds in 1 month to queries. Responds in 1 month to proposals. Responds in 1 month to manuscripts. Book catalog available free.

Imprints Elephant Paperbacks; New Amsterdam Books; J.S. Sanders Books.

O→ Ivan R. Dee publishes serious nonfiction for general-informed readers.

Nonfiction Subjects include art, architecture, history, language, politics, world affairs, government, contemporary culture, baseball. Submit outline, sample chapters. Reviews artwork/photos.

Recent Title(s) *Notebooks 1951-1959*, by Albert Camus; *But Didn't We Have Fun?*, by Peter Morris; *Safe For Democracy*, by John Prados.

Tips "We publish for an intelligent lay audience and college course adoptions."

DELACORTE BOOKS FOR YOUNG READERS

Imprint of Random House Children's Books/Random House, Inc. 1745 Broadway, New York NY 10019. (212)782-9000. Website: www.randomhouse.com/kids.

- Although not currently accepting unsolicited mss, mss are being sought for 2 contests: Delacorte Dell Yearling Contest for a First Middle-Grade Novel and Delacorte Press Contest for a First Young Adult Novel. Submission guidelines can be found online at www.randomhouse.com/kids/writingcontests.

DEL REY BOOKS

Imprint of Random House Publishing Group 1745 Broadway, 18th Floor, New York NY 10019. (212)782-9000. E-mail: delrey@randomhouse.com. Website: www.randomhouse.com. Estab. 1977. Publishes hardcover, trade paperback, and mass market originals and mass market paperback reprints. **Pays royalty on retail price. Pays competitive advance.**

O→ Del Rey publishes top level fantasy, alternate history, and science fiction.

Fiction Subjects include fantasy, should have the practice of magic as an essential element of the plot, science fiction, well-plotted novels with good characterizations, exotic locales and detailed alien creatures, alternate history. Agented submissions only.

Recent Title(s) *The Salmon of Doubt*, by Douglas Adams; *Weapons of Choice*, by John Birmingham; *The Zenith Angle*, by Bruce Sterling.

Tips Del Rey is a reader's house. Pay particular attention to plotting, strong characters, and dramatic, satisfactory conclusions. It must be/feel believable. That's what the readers like. In terms of mass market, we basically created the field of fantasy bestsellers. Not that it didn't exist before, but we put the mass into mass market.

DIAL BOOKS FOR YOUNG READERS

Imprint of Penguin Group USA 345 Hudson St., New York NY 10014. (212)366-2000. Website: www.penguin.com/youngreaders. **Contact:** Submissions Editor. Estab. 1961. Publishes hardcover originals. **Publishes 50 titles/year. 5,000 queries received/year. 20% of books from first-time authors. Pays royalty. Pays varies advance.** Responds in 4-6 months to queries. Book catalog for 9 X12 envelope and 4 First-Class stamps.

- Dial Books for Young Readers publishes quality picture books for ages 18 months-6 years; lively, believable novels for middle readers and young adults; and occasional nonfiction for middle readers and young adults.

Nonfiction Accepts unsolicited queries.

Fiction Subjects include adventure, fantasy, juvenile, picture books, young adult. Especially looking for lively and well-written novels for middle grade and young adult children involving a convincing plot and believable characters. The subject matter or theme should not already be overworked in previously published books. The approach must not be demeaning to any minority group, nor should the roles of female characters (or others) be stereotyped, though we don't think books should be didactic, or in any way message-y. No topics inappropriate for the juvenile, young adult, and middle grade audiences. No plays. Accepts unsolicited queries an

Recent Title(s) *Little Red Hen*, by Jerry Pinkway; *On the Wings of Horses*, by Richard Peck; *Looking Glass Wars*, by Frank Beddor.

Tips Our readers are anywhere from preschool age to teenage. Picture books must have strong plots, lots of action, unusual premises, or universal themes treated with freshness and originality. Humor works well in these books. A very well-thought-out and intelligently presented book has the best chance of being taken on. Genre isn't as much of a factor as presentation.

DIVERSION PRESS

P.O. Box 150268, Nashville TN 37215. E-mail: diversionpress@yahoo.com. Website: www.diversionpress.com. **Contact:** Attn: Acquisition Editor. Estab. 2008. Publishes hardcover, trade and mass market paperback originals. **Publishes 20-30 titles/year. 75% of books from first-time authors. 95% from unagented writers. Pays -10% royalty on wholesale price.** Publishes book 6-9 months after acceptance of ms. Accepts simultaneous submissions. Responds in 2 weeks to queries. Responds in 1 month to proposals. Guidelines available online.

Nonfiction Subjects include agriculture, Americana, animals, anthropology, archaeology, art, architecture, business, economics, child guidance, community, contemporary culture, cooking, foods, nutrition, education, ethnic, government, politics, health, medicine, history, hobbies, humanities, language, literature, literary criticism, memoirs, military, war, money, finance, multicultural, music, dance, nature, environment, philosophy, psychology, recreation, regional, science, social sciences, sociology, travel, womens issues, womens studies, world affairs. Submit proposal package, outline, bio/c.v. Reviews artwork/photos. Send photocopies.

Fiction Subjects include adventure, fantasy, gothic, historical, horror, humor, literary, mainstream, contemporary, mystery, poetry, science fiction, short story collections, suspense, young adult. We will happily consider any children's or young adult books. If your story has potential to become a series, please address that in your proposal. Fiction short stories and poetry will be considered for our anthology series. See website for details. Submit proposal package, clips, bio/cover letter.

DNA PRESS & NARTEA PUBLISHING

DNA Press P.O. Box 572, Eagleville PA 19408. Fax: (501)694-5495. Website: www.dnapress.com. **Contact:** Xela Schenk, operations manager. Estab. 1998. Publishes hardcover and trade paperback originals. **Publishes 10 titles/year. 500 queries received/year. 400 mss received/year. 90% of books from first-time authors. 100% from unagented writers. Pays 10-15% royalty.** Publishes book 8 months after acceptance of ms. Accepts simultaneous submissions. Responds in 6 weeks to manuscripts. Book catalog and ms guidelines free.

- Book publisher for young adults, children, and adults.

Nonfiction Reviews artwork/photos.

Fiction Subjects include juvenile, science fiction, young adult. All books should be oriented to explaining science even if they do not fall 100% under the category of science fiction. Submit complete ms.

Recent Title(s) *Tax-Free Swaps: Using Section 1031 Like-Kind Exchanges to Preserve Investment Net Worth*, by Bradley T. Borden; *The Secret Diary of Adrian Cat*, by Stuart and Linda MacFarlane.

Tips Quick response, great relationships, high commission/royalty.

TOM DOHERTY ASSOCIATES LLC

175 Fifth Ave., New York NY 10010. Fax: (212)388-0191. E-mail: inquiries@tor.com. Website: www.tor-forge.com. **Contact:** Acquisitions Editor. Estab. 1980. Publishes hardcover trade, paperback, and mass market originals. Book catalog available online. Guidelines available online.

Imprints Forge Books; Orb Books; Tor.

Fiction Subjects include fantasy, horror, mystery, romance, paranormal, science fiction, suspense, western, techno thrillers, American historicals, true crime. Submit synopsis, first 3 chapt

Recent Title(s) *Gardens of the Moon*, by Steven Erikson (fantasy); *Ringworld's Children*, by Larry Nevin (science fiction).

DORAL PUBLISHING, INC.

3 Burroughs, Irvine CA 92618. (800)633-5385. E-mail: doralpub@mindspring.com. Website: www.doralpub.com. **Contact:** Alvin Grossman, publisher; Joe Liddy, marketing manager (purebred dogs). Estab. 1986. Publishes hardcover and trade paperback originals. **Publishes 10 titles/year. 30 queries received/year. 15 mss received/year. 85% from unagented writers. Pays 10% royalty on wholesale price.** Publishes book 6 months after acceptance of ms. Responds in 2 months to queries. Book catalog available free. Guidelines for #10 SASE.

O→ Doral Publishing publishes only books about dogs and dog-related topics, mostly geared for pure-bred dog owners and showing. Currently emphasizing breed books.

Nonfiction Subjects include animals, health, medicine. Query with SASE. Submit outline, 2 sample chapters. Reviews artwork/photos. Send photocopies.

Fiction Subjects include juvenile. Subjects must center around dogs. Either the main character should be a dog or a dog should play an integral role. Query with SASE.

Recent Title(s) *The Bernese Mountain Dog*; *How Wiliy Got His Wings*.

Tips We are currently expanding and are looking for new topics and fresh ideas while staying true to our niche. While we will steadfastly maintain that market—we are always looking for excellent breed books—we also want to explore more `mainstream' topics.

DORCHESTER PUBLISHING CO., INC.

200 Madison Ave., Suite 2000, New York NY 10016. (212)725-8811. Fax: (212)532-1054. Website: www.dorchesterpub.com. **Pays advance.** Guidelines available online.

Imprints Love Spell (romance); Leisure Books (romance, westerns, horror, thrillers); Making It (chick lit).

- No submissions via e-mail or fax.

DOUBLEDAY BOOKS FOR YOUNG READERS

Imprint of Random House Children's Books/Random House, Inc. 1745 Broadway, New York NY 10019. (212)782-9000. Website: www.randomhouse.com/kids.

- Trade picture book list, from preschool to age 8. Not accepting any unsolicited book mss at this time.

DOUBLEDAY BROADWAY PUBLISHING GROUP

Imprint of Random House, Inc. 1745 Broadway, New York NY 10019. (212)782-9000. Fax: (212)782-9700. Website: www.randomhouse.com. Estab. 1897. Publishes hardcover originals. **thousands of queries received/year. thousands of mss received/year. Pays royalty on retail price. Pays advance.**

Imprints Broadway Books; Broadway Business; Doubleday; Doubleday Image; Doubleday Religious Publishing; Main Street Books; Nan A. Talese.

- *Does not accept any unagented submissions.* No exceptions.

O→ Doubleday publishes high-quality fiction and nonfiction.

Nonfiction Subjects include Americana, anthropology, archeology, business, economics, computers, electronics, education, ethnic, government, politics, health, medicine, history, language, literature, money, finance, nature, environment, philosophy, religion, science, sociology, software, sports, translation, womens issues, womens studies. Agented submissions only.

Fiction Subjects include adventure, confession, ethnic, experimental, feminist, gay, lesbian, historical, humor, literary, mainstream, contemporary, religious, short story collections. Agented submissions only.

DOUBLEDAY/IMAGE

Doubleday Broadway Publishing Group, Random House, Inc. 1745 Broadway, New York NY 10019. (212)782-9000. Fax: (212)302-7985. Website: www.randomhouse.com. **Contact:** Trace Murphy, executive editor. Estab. 1956. Publishes hardcover, trade and mass market paperback originals and reprints. **Publishes 12 titles/year. 500 queries received/year. 300 mss received/year. 10% of books from first-time authors. Pays royalty on retail price. Pays varied advance.** Publishes book 18 months after acceptance of ms.

O→ Image Books has grown from a classic Catholic list to include a variety of current and future classics, maintaining a high standard of quality as the finest in religious paperbacks. Also publishes Doubleday paperbacks/hardcovers for general religion, spirituality, including works based in Buddhism, Islam,

Judaism.
Nonfiction Subjects include philosophy, religion, womens issues, womens studies. Agented submissions only.
Recent Title(s) *Papal Sin*, by Garry Wills; *Soul Survivor*, by Philip Yancey; *The Lamb's Supper*, by Scott Hahn.

DOUBLEDAY RELIGIOUS PUBLISHING

Imprint of Doubleday Broadway Publishing Group, Division of Random House, Inc. 1745 Broadway, New York NY 10019. (212)782-9000. Website: www.randomhouse.com. Estab. 1897. Publishes hardcover and trade paperback originals and reprints. Accepts simultaneous submissions.
Imprints Image Books; Galilee; New Jerusalem Bible; Three Leaves Press.
Nonfiction Agented submissions only.

DOVER PUBLICATIONS, INC.

31 E. 2nd St., Mineola NY 11501. (516)294-7000. Fax: (516)873-1401. Website: www.doverpublications.com. **Contact:** John Grafton (math/science reprints). Estab. 1941. Publishes trade paperback originals and reprints. **Publishes 660 titles/year. Makes outright purchase.** Accepts simultaneous submissions. Book catalog available online.
Nonfiction Subjects include agriculture, Americana, animals, anthropology, archeology, art, architecture, cooking, foods, nutrition, health, medicine, history, hobbies, language, literature, music, dance, nature, environment, philosophy, photography, religion, science, sports, translation, travel. Query with SASE. Reviews artwork/photos.
Recent Title(s) *The Waning of the Middle Ages*, by John Huizenga.

DOWN EAST BOOKS

Imprint of Down East Enterprise, Inc. P.O. Box 679, Camden ME 04843-0679. Fax: (207)594-7215. Website: www.downeast.com. **Contact:** Michael Steere, Editor. Estab. 1967. Publishes hardcover and trade paperback originals, trade paperback reprints. **Publishes 24-30 titles/year. 50% of books from first-time authors. 90% from unagented writers. Pays $500 average advance.** Publishes book 1 year after acceptance of ms. Accepts simultaneous submissions. Responds in 3 months to queries. Send SASE for ms guidlines. Send 9 x 12 SASE for guidelines, plus recent catalog.

- Down East Books publishes books that capture and illuminate the unique beauty and character of New England's history, culture, and wild places.

Nonfiction Subjects include Americana, history, nature, environment, recreation, regional, sports. Query with SASE. Do not send CD, DVD, or disk. Reviews artwork/photos.
Fiction Subjects include juvenile, mainstream, contemporary, regional. We publish 2-4 juvenile titles/year (fiction and nonfiction), and 0-1 adult fiction titles/year. Query with SASE.
Recent Title(s) *The Winter Visitors*, by Karel Hayes; *At Home By the Sea*, by Brian Vanden Brink and Bruce Snider; *A Healing Touch*, Richard Russo, Editor.

DUQUESNE UNIVERSITY PRESS

600 Forbes Ave., Pittsburgh PA 15282. (412)396-6610. Fax: (412)396-5984. Website: www.dupress.duq.edu. **Contact:** Susan Wadsworth-Booth, director. Estab. 1927. Publishes hardcover and trade paperback originals. **Publishes 8-12 titles/year. 400 queries received/year. 65 mss received/year. 30% of books from first-time authors. 95% from unagented writers. Pays royalty on net price. Pays (some) advance.** Publishes book 1 year after acceptance of ms. Responds in 1 month to proposals. Responds in 3 months to manuscripts. Book catalog and ms guidelines for #10 SASE. Guidelines available online.

- "Duquesne publishes scholarly monographs in the fields of literary studies (medieval & Renaissance), continental philosophy, ethics, religious studies and existential psychology."

Nonfiction Subjects include language, literature, philosophy, continental, psychology, existential, religion. For scholarly books, query or submit outline, 1 sample chapter, and SASE.
Recent Title(s) *Emmanuel Levinas: His Life and Legacy*, by Salomon Malka; *Psychotherapy as a Human Science*, by Daniel Burston and Roger Frie; *Renaissance Ecology*, by Ken Hiltner.

DUTTON ADULT TRADE

Imprint of Penguin Group (USA), Inc. 375 Hudson St., New York NY 10014. (212)366-2000. Website: us.penguingroup.com. Estab. 1852. Publishes hardcover originals. **Pays royalty. Pays negotiable advance.** Accepts simultaneous submissions. Book catalog for #10 SASE.

- "*Dutton* publishes hardcover, original, mainstream, and contemporary fiction and nonfiction in the areas of memoir, self-help, politics, psychology, and science for a general readership."

Nonfiction Agented submissions only. *No unsolicited mss.*
Fiction Subjects include adventure, historical, literary, mainstream, contemporary, mystery, short story collections, suspense. Agented submissions only. *No unsolicited mss.*

Tips Write the complete manuscript and submit it to an agent or agents. They will know exactly which editor will be interested in a project.

DUTTON CHILDREN'S BOOKS

Imprint of Penguin Group (USA), Inc. 375 Hudson St., New York NY 10014. Website: www.penguin.com. **Contact:** Acquisitions Editor. Estab. 1852. Publishes hardcover originals as well as novelty formats. **Publishes 100 titles/year. 15% of books from first-time authors. Pays royalty on retail price. Pays advance.**

- Dutton Children's Books publishes high-quality fiction and nonfiction for readers ranging from preschoolers to young adults on a variety of subjects. Currently emphasizing middle-grade and young adult novels that offer a fresh perspective. De-emphasizing photographic nonfiction and picture books that teach a lesson.

Nonfiction Subjects include animals, history, US, nature, environment, science. Query with SASE.
Fiction Dutton Children's Books has a diverse, general interest list that includes picture books; easy-to-read books; and fiction for all ages, from first chapter books to young adult readers. Query with SASE.
Recent Title(s) *The Best Pet of All*, by David LaRochelle (picture book); *The Schwa Was Here*, by Neal Shusterman (novel); *Looking for Alaska*, by John Green (young adult novel).

EAKIN PRESS

P.O. Drawer 90159, Austin TX 78709-0159. (512)288-1771. Fax: (512)288-1813. Website: www.eakinpress.com. **Contact:** Virginia Messer, publisher. Estab. 1978. Publishes hardcover and paperback originals and reprints. Accepts simultaneous submissions. Responds in up to 1 year to queries. Book catalog for $1.25. Guidelines available online.

- No electronic submissions.
- Eakin specializes in Texana and Western Americana for adults and juveniles. Currently emphasizing women's studies.

Nonfiction Subjects include Americana, Western, business, economics, cooking, foods, nutrition, ethnic, history, military, war, regional, sports, African American studies. Submit sample chapters, bio, synopsis, publishing credits, SASE.
Fiction Subjects include historical, juvenile. Juvenile fiction for grades K-12, preferably relating to Texas and the Southwest or contemporary. Query or submit outline/synops
Recent Title(s) *Sam Houston Slept Here*, by Bill O'Neal; *Grape Man of Texas*, by Sherrie S. McLeRoy and Roy E. Renfro, Jr., PhD; *Playbills and Popcorn*, by Michael A. Jenkins.

EASTERN WASHINGTON UNIVERSITY PRESS

534 E. Spokane Falls Blvd., Suite 203, Spokane WA 99202. (509)368-6574. Fax: (509)368-6596. E-mail: ewupress@ewu.edu. Website: ewupress.ewu.edu. **Contact:** Christopher Howell, senior editor (poetry, fiction); Ivar Nelson, director (nonfiction); Pamela Holway, managing editor. Estab. 1977. Publishes hardcover and trade paperback originals and reprints. **Publishes 16 titles/year. 300 queries received/year. 15% of books from first-time authors. 10% royalty on monies received** Publishes book 2-4 years after acceptance of ms. Accepts simultaneous submissions. Responds promptly to queries and within 2-3 months to proposals. Book catalog and submission guidelines available online.

- Publishes innovative works that possess freshness in language and theme. It supports and extends the intellectual, educational and public role of the University. Sponsors literary festivals and prizes. Sponsors Blue Lynx Prize For Poetry, Spokane Prize For Short Fiction, and Annual Getlit! Literary Festival. Specializes in works that address the history, culture, literature, and public policy of the Inland Northwest and Northern Rocky Mountain regions of the U.S.

Nonfiction Subjects include anthropology, archaeology, history, language, literature, nature, environment, translation, folklore.
Fiction Accepts novels, story collections and entries for the short fiction contest.Subjects include literary, poetry, regional, short fiction. Query before sending complete ms
Tips Submit complete ms in hard copy—no digital ms submissions. May query by e-mail.

ECLIPSE PRESS

The Blood-Horse, Inc. 3101 Beaumont Centre Circle, Lexington KY 40513. Website: www.eclipsepress.com. **Contact:** Jacqueline Duke, editor (equine). Estab. 1916. Publishes hardcover and trade paperback originals. **Publishes 12-15 titles/year. 100 queries received/year. 50 mss received/year. 20% of books from first-time authors. 40% from unagented writers. Pays $3,000-12,000 advance.** Publishes book 18 months after acceptance of ms. Accepts simultaneous submissions. Responds in 2-3 months to queries. Responds in 2-3 months to proposals. Responds in 2-3 months to manuscripts. Book catalog available free.
Nonfiction Subjects include sports, equine, equestrian. Query with SASE. Submit outline, sample chapters. Reviews artwork/photos.
Tips "Our audience is sports, horse, and racing enthusiasts."

EDUCATOR'S INTERNATIONAL PRESS, INC.

18 Colleen Rd., Troy NY 12180. (518)271-9886. Fax: (518)266-9422. E-mail: bill@edint.com. Website: www.edint.com. **Contact:** William Clockel, publisher. Estab. 1996. Publishes hardcover and trade paperback originals and reprints. Accepts simultaneous submissions. Book catalog and ms guidelines free.

- Educator's International publishes books in all aspects of education, broadly conceived, from pre-kindergarten to postgraduate. We specialize in texts, professional books, videos and other materials for students, faculty, practitioners and researchers. We also publish a full list of books in the areas of women's studies, and social and behavioral sciences.

Nonfiction Subjects include education, language, literature, philosophy, psychology, software, womens studies. Submit TOC, outline, 2-3 chapters, resume with SASE. Reviews artwork/photos.

Recent Title(s) *Journal of Curriculum and Pedagogy*; *Democratic Responses in an Era of Standardization*, (Relationship and the Arts in Teacher Education).

Tips Audience is professors, students, researchers, individuals, libraries.

EDUCATORS PUBLISHING SERVICE

P.O. Box 9031, Cambridge MA 02139-9031. (617)547-6706. Fax: (617)547-3805. Website: www.epsbooks.com. **Contact:** Charles H. Heinle, vice president, Publishing Group. Estab. 1952. **Publishes 26 titles/year. 200 queries received/year. 200 mss received/year. 50% of books from first-time authors. 90% from unagented writers. Pays 5-10% royalty on retail price.** Publishes book 8 months (minimum) after acceptance of ms. Accepts simultaneous submissions. Responds in 1 month to queries. Responds in 3 months to proposals. Responds in 3 months to manuscripts. Book catalog and ms guidelines online.

- EPS accepts queries from educators writing for a school market, authoring materials (primarily K-8) in the reading and language areas. We are interested in materials following pedagogical restraints (such as decodable texts and leveled readers) that we can incorporate into ongoing or future projects, or that form a complete program in themselves.

Nonfiction Subjects include education, reading comprehension, phonics vocabulary development and writing, supplementary texts and workbooks (reading and language arts). Query with SASE.

Recent Title(s) *Words Are Wonderful, Book 3*, by Dorothy Grant Hennings; *Ten Essential Vocabulary Strategies*, by Lee Mountain; *Write About Me*, by Elsie Wilmerding.

Tips Student (K-8) audiences.

EDUPRESS, INC.

W5527 State Road 106, P.O. Box 800, Fort Atkinson WI 53538-0800. (920)563-9571. E-mail: edupress@highsmith.com. Website: www.edupressinc.com. Estab. 1979. Publishes trade paperback originals. Book catalog and ms guidelines free.

- Edupress, Inc., publishes supplemental resources for classroom curriculum. Currently emphasizing more science, math, language arts emphasis than in the past.

Nonfiction Subjects include education, resources for pre-school through middle school.

Tips Audience is classroom teachers and homeschool parents.

EERDMANS BOOKS FOR YOUNG READERS

William B. Eerdmans Publishing Co. 2140 Oak Industrial Dr. NE, Grand Rapids MI 49505. (616)459-4591. Fax: (616)459-6540. Website: www.eerdmans.com/youngreaders. **Contact:** Shannon White, Acquisitions Editor. Board books, picture books, middle reader fiction, young adult fiction, nonfiction, illustrated storybooks. **Publishes 12-17; 10-15 are picture books and 2-4 are fiction for middle grade or young adult. titles/year. 6,000 mss received/year. Pays 5-7% royalty on retail price.** Publishes book Publishes middle reader and YA books in 1 year; publishes picture books in 2-3 years. after acceptance of ms. "We do not accept or reply to queries or submissions via e-mail or fax to queries. Responds in 3-4 months for exclusive submissions sent to Eerdmans Books for Young Readers, cleaerly marked no answer to manuscripts.". Do not call or e-mail to inquire about the status of your manuscript.

- "We are seeking books that encourage independent thinking, problem-solving, creativity, acceptance, kindness. Books that encourage moral values without being didactic or preachy."

Nonfiction Reviews artwork/photos. Send Send color photocopies rather than original art.

Fiction Subjects include juvenile, picture books, young adult, middle reader or young adult. Send exclusive manuscript submissions (marked so on outside of envelope) to acquisitions editor.

Recent Title(s) *A River of Words*, by Jen Bryant, illustrated by Melissa Sweet (2009) Caldecott Honor Book); *Garmann's Summer*, by Stian Hole (2009 Batchelder Honor Book); *Ethan, Suspended*, by Pamela Ehrenberg (novel); *Attack of the Turtle*, by Drew Carlson (novel).

Tips "A submission stands out when it's obvious that someone put time into it—the publisher's name and address is spelled correctly, the package is neat, and all of our submission requirements have been followed precisely. We look for short, concise cover letters that explain why the manuscript fits with our list, and/or how the manuscript fills an important need in the world of children's literature. Send EXCLUSIVE manuscript submissions to acquisitions editor. We regret that due to the volume of material we receive, we cannot comment on manuscripts we are unable to accept."

WILLIAM B. EERDMANS PUBLISHING CO.

2140 Oak Industrial Dr. NE, Grand Rapids MI 49505. (616)459-4591. Fax: (616)459-6540. Website: www.eerdmans.com. **Contact:** Jon Pott, editor-in-chief. Estab. 1911. Publishes hardcover and paperback originals and reprints. Accepts simultaneous submissions. Responds in 4 weeks to queries, possibly longer for mss. Please include e-mail and/or SASE. Book catalog and ms guidelines free.

Imprints Eerdmans Books for Young Readers.

- Will not respond to or accept mss, proposals, or queries sent by e-mail or fax.

O→ "The majority of our adult publications are religious and most of these are academic or semi-academic in character (as opposed to inspirational or celebrity books), though we also publish general trade books on the Christian life. Our nonreligious titles, most of them in regional history or on social issues, aim, similarly, at an educated audience."

Nonfiction Subjects include history, religious, language, literature, philosophy, of religion, psychology, regional, history, religion, sociology, translation, Biblical studies. Query with TOC, 2-3 sample chapters, and SASE for return of ms. Reviews artwork/photos.

Fiction Subjects include religious, children's, general, fantasy. Query with SASE.

Recent Title(s) *Tell it Slant*, by Eugene Peterson; *Rowan's Rule*, by Rupert Shortt; and *A River of Words*, by Jen Bryant, illustrated by Melissa Sweet (illustrator).

ELEPHANT BOOKS

65 Macedonia Rd., Alexander NC 28701. (828)252-9515. Fax: (828)255-8719. E-mail: pat@abooks.com. Website: abooks.com. **Contact:** Editor. Publishes trade paperback originals and reprints. Book catalog available online. Guidelines available online.

- No e-mail or phone submissions.

Nonfiction Subjects include cooking, foods, nutrition, history, military, war, Civil War. Query, or submit outline with 3 sample chapters and proposal package, including potential marketing plans with SASE. Reviews artwork/photos. Send photocopies.

ELLORA'S CAVE PUBLISHING, INC.

1056 Home Ave., Akron OH 44310. E-mail: service@ellorascave.com. Website: www.ellorascave.com. **Contact:** Raelene Gorlinsky, managing editor. Estab. 2000. Publishes electronic originals and reprints. **Pays 37.5% royalty on gross (cover price).** Accepts simultaneous submissions. Responds in 2 months to queries. Responds in 2 months to proposals. Responds in 2-3 months to manuscripts. Book catalog available online. Guidelines available online.

Fiction Subjects include erotica, fantasy, gay, lesbian, gothic, historical, horror, mainstream, contemporary, multicultural, mystery, romance, science fiction, suspense, western. All must be under genre romance. All must have erotic content or author be willing to add sex during editing. Submit proposal package, clips, 3 sample chapters. Send via e-mail in doc or r.

Recent Title(s) *Caught!*, by Lorie O'Clare; *Eden's Curse*, by Elisa Adams; *Immaculate*, by Kate Hill.

Tips Our audience is romance readers who want to read more sex, more detailed sex. They come to us, because we offer not erotica, but Romantica™. Sex with romance, plot, emotion. Remember Ellora's Cave is a Romantica™ site. We publish romance books with an erotic nature. More sex is the motto, but there has to be a storyline—a logical plot and a happy ending.

EMPIRE PUBLISHING SERVICE

P.O. Box 1344, Studio City CA 91614-0344. **Contact:** Joseph Witt. Estab. 1960. Publishes hardcover reprints and trade paperback originals and reprints. **Publishes 40 titles/year. 500 queries received/year. 85 mss received/year. 50% of books from first-time authors. 95% from unagented writers. Pays 6-10% royalty on retail price. Pays variable advance.** Publishes book up to 2 years after acceptance of ms. Responds in 1 month to queries. Responds in 2 months to proposals. Responds in up to 1 year to manuscripts. Book catalog for #10 SASE. Guidelines for $1 or #10 SASE.

Imprints Gaslight Publications; Gaslight Books; Empire Publications; Empire Books; Empire Music.

O→ Submit only Sherlock Holmes, performing arts and health.

Nonfiction Subjects include health, medicine, humor, music, dance, Sherlock Holmes. Query with SASE. Reviews artwork/photos. Send photocopies.

Fiction Subjects include historical, pre-18th century, mystery, Sherlock Holmes. Query with SASE.

Recent Title(s) *Sherlock Holmes and the Adventure of the Clothesline*, by Carolyn Wells; *The Magic of Food*, by James Cohen; *Music, Music* by Nancy Walters.

Ⓐ Ⓩ ENCOUNTER BOOKS

900 Broadway, Suite 400, New York NY 10003-1239. (212)871-6310. Fax: (212)871-6311. E-mail: read@

encounterbooks.com. Website: www.encounterbooks.com. **Contact:** Acquisitions. Hardcover originals and trade paperback reprints. Accepts simultaneous submissions. Book catalog free or online. Guidelines available online.

- *Accepts agented material only. No unsolicited mss/queries.* Reading period is March 1-November 1.

O→ Encounter Books publishes serious nonfiction—books that can alter our society, challenge our morality, stimulate our imaginations—in the areas of history, politics, religion, biography, education, public policy, current affairs, and social sciences.

Nonfiction Subjects include child guidance, education, ethnic, government, politics, health, medicine, history, language, literature, memoirs, military, war, multicultural, philosophy, psychology, religion, science, sociology, womens issues, womens studies, gender studies. Submit proposal package, including outline and 1 sample chapter, SASE. Do not send via e-mail.

Recent Title(s) *Black Rednecks and White Liberals*, by Thomas Sowell; *The Prince of the City*, by Fred Siegel.

ENSLOW PUBLISHERS, INC.

40 Industrial Rd., Box 398, Berkeley Heights NJ 07922. (973)771-9400. Website: www.enslow.com. **Contact:** Brian D. Enslow, editor. Estab. 1977. Publishes hardcover originals. 10% require freelance illustration. **Publishes 250 titles/year. Pays royalty on net price with advance or flat fee. Pays advance.** Publishes book 1 year after acceptance of ms. Responds in 1 month to queries. Guidelines for #10 SASE.

O→ "Enslow publishes hardcover nonfiction series books for young adults and school-age children."

Nonfiction Subjects include health, medicine, history, recreation, Sports, science, sociology.

Recent Title(s) *TV News: Can It Be Trusted?*, by Ray Spangenburg and Kit Moser; *Resisters and Rescuers—Standing Up Against the Holocaust*, by Linda Jacobs Attman.

Tips "We love to receive resumes from experienced writers with good research skills who can think like young people."

ENTREPRENEUR PRESS

2445 McCabe Way, Suite 400, Irvine CA 92614. (949)261-2325. Fax: (949)261-7729. Website: www.entrepreneurpress.com. **Contact:** Jere L. Calmes, publisher; Courtney Thurman, acquisitions editor, Leanne Harvey, director of marketing. Publishes quality hardcover and trade paperbacks. **Publishes 60+ titles/year. 1,200 queries received/year. 600 mss received/year. 40% of books from first-time authors. 60% from unagented writers. Pays competitive net royalty.** Accepts simultaneous submissions. Guidelines available online.

O→ Proposal should include: cover letter, preface, marketing plan, analysis of competition and comparative titles, author bio, TOC, 2 sample chapters. Go to website for more details.

Nonfiction Subjects include business, economics, start-up, small business management, marketing, finance, real estate, careers, personal finance, accounting, motivation, leadership, legal advise, business travel, and management. Query with SASE. Submit proposal package, outline, bio, 2 sample chapters, preface or executive summary, competitive analysis and differentiation. Reviews artwork/photos. Send transparencies and all other applicable information.

Recent Title(s) *Masters of Sales*, by Ivan R. Misner and Don Morgan; *Official Get Rich Guide to Information Marketing*, by Dan Kennedy, Robert Skrob and Bill Glazer; *Startup Guide to Guerrilla Marketing*, by Jay Conrad Levinson and Jeannie Levinson.

Tips We are currently seeking proposals covering sales, small business, startup, real estate, online businesses, marketing, etc.

EOS

Imprint of HarperCollins General Books Group 10 E. 53rd St., New York NY 10022. (212)207-7000. Website: www.eosbooks.com. Estab. 1998. Publishes hardcover originals, trade and mass market paperback originals, and reprints. **Pays royalty on retail price. Pays variable advance.** Guidelines for #10 SASE.

O→ Eos publishes quality science fiction/fantasy with broad appeal.

Fiction Subjects include fantasy, science fiction. Agented submissions only. *All unsolicited mss returne*

Recent Title(s) *Black Juice*, by Margo Lanagan; *Exile's Return*, by Raymond E. Feist; *The Hidden Queen*, by Alma Alexander.

Tips The official HarperCollins submissions policy has changed, and we can no longer accept unsolicited submissions. To submit your science fiction or fantasy novel to Eos, please query first. We strongly urge you to query via e-mail. Your query should be brief—no more than a 2-page description of your book. Do not send chapters or full synopsis at this time. You will receive a response—either a decline or a request for more material—in approximately 1-2 months.

EPICENTER PRESS, INC.

P.O. Box 82368, Kenmore WA 98028. Fax: (425)481-8253. E-mail: info@epicenterpress.com. Website: www.epicenterpress.com. **Contact:** Lael Morgan, 420 Ferry Rd., Saco, ME 04072. Estab. 1987. Publishes hardcover and trade paperback originals. **Publishes 4-8 titles/year. 200 queries received/year. 100 mss received/year.**

75% of books from first-time authors. 90% from unagented writers. Publishes book 12-24 months after acceptance of ms. Responds in 3 months to queries. Book catalog and ms guidelines on website.

- We are a regional press founded in Alaska whose interests include but are not limited to the arts, history, environment, and diverse cultures and lifestyles of the North Pacific and high latitudes.

Nonfiction Our focus is Alaska and the Pacific Northwest. We do not encourage nonfiction titles from outside this region.Subjects include animals, ethnic, history, nature, environment, recreation, regional, womens issues. Submit outline and 3 sample chapters. Reviews artwork/photos. Send photocopies. We are not interested in any content that does not relate in some way to Alaska

EVAN-MOOR EDUCATIONAL PUBLISHERS

18 Lower Ragsdale Dr., Monterey CA 93940-5746. (800)976-1915. Fax: (800)777-4332. Website: www.evan-moor.com. **Contact:** Acquisitions Editor. Estab. 1979. Publishes teaching materials. **Publishes 40-60 titles/year.** Accepts simultaneous submissions. Responds in 3 months to queries. Book catalog and ms guidelines free or on website.

- Our books are teaching ideas, lesson plans, and blackline reproducibles for grades pre-K through 6th in all curriculum areas except music and bilingual. Currently emphasizing writing/language arts, practice materials for home use. De-emphasizing thematic materials. We do not publish children's literary fiction or literary nonfiction.

Nonfiction Subjects include education, teaching materials, grades pre-K through 6th. Submit proposal package, including outline and 3 sample chapters, résumé, SASE.

Recent Title(s) *Basic Phonics Skills*; *Read and Understand Poetry*; *U.S. Facts & Fun*.

Tips Writers should know how classroom/educational materials differ from trade publications. They should request catalogs and submission guidelines before sending queries or manuscripts. Visiting our website will give writers a clear picture of the type of materials we publish.

F+W MEDIA, INC. (BOOK DIVISION)

(formerly F + W Publications, Inc.) 4700 E. Galbraith Rd., Cincinnati OH 45236. (513)531-2690. Website: www.fwmedia.com. **Contact:** President: Sara Domville, President: David Blansfield; Publisher and Editorial Director, Karen Cooper (Adams Media), Publisher and Editorial Director, Dianne Wheeler (Antiques & Collectibles), Publisher and Editorial Director, Jeff Pozorski (Automotives), Publisher and Editorial Director, Jamie Markle (Art), Publisher and Editorial Director, Stephen Bateman (David & Charles), Publisher and Editorial Director, Gary Lynch (Design), Publisher and Editorial Director, Jim Schlender (Firearms & Knives), Publisher and Editorial Director, Guy LeCharles Gonzalez (Horticulture), Publisher and Editorial Director, Scott Tappa (Numismatics), Publisher and Editorial Director, Brad Rucks (Outdoors), Publisher and Editorial Director, Teri Mollison (Scrapbooking), Publisher and Editorial Director, Dean Listle (Sports, Construction Trade), Publisher and Editorial Director, Steve Shanesy (Woodworking), Publisher and Editorial Director, Jane Friedman (Writer's Digest, HOW Books). Estab. 1913. Publishes trade paperback originals and reprints. **Publishes 400 + titles/year.** Guidelines available online.

Imprints Adams Media (general interest series); David & Charles (crafts, equestrian, railroads, soft crafts); HOW Books (graphic design, illustrated, humor, pop culture); IMPACT Books (fantasy art, manga, creative comics and popular culture); Krause Books (antiques and collectibles, automotive, coins and paper money, comics, crafts, games, firearms, militaria, outdoors and hunting, records and CDs, sports, toys); Memory Makers (scrapbooking); North Light Books (crafts, decorative painting, fine art); Popular Woodworking Books (shop skills, woodworking); Warman's (antiques and collectibles, field guides); Writer's Digest Books (writing and reference).

- Please see individual listings for specific submission information about the company's imprints.
- "In October 2008, F + W Media moved from a divisionally structured company to a Community structure, wherein the Publisher and Editorial Director for each community has full responsibility for the books, magazines, online, events, and educational products associated with their community. F + W Media produces more than 400 new books per year, maintains a backlist of more than 2,500 titles, publishes 39 magazines, owns and operates dozens of informational and subscription-based Web sites, and operates a growing number of successful consumer shows annually."

FACTS ON FILE, INC.

Infobase Publishing 132 W. 31st St., 17th Floor, New York NY 10001. (212)967-8800. Fax: (212)339-0326. E-mail: llikoff@factsonfile.com. Website: www.factsonfile.com. **Contact:** Laurie Likoff, Editorial Director (science, fashion, natural history); Frank Darmstadt (science & technology, nature, reference); Owen Lancer, senior editor (American history, women's studies); James Chambers, trade editor (health, pop culture, true crime, sports); Jeff Soloway, acquisitions editor (language/literature). Estab. 1941. Publishes hardcover originals and reprints. **Publishes 135-150 titles/year. 25% from unagented writers. Pays 10% royalty on retail price. Pays $5,000-10,000 advance.** Accepts simultaneous submissions. Responds in 2 months to queries. Book catalog available free. Guidelines available online.

Imprints Checkmark Books.

O-π Facts on File produces high-quality reference materials on a broad range of subjects for the school library market and the general nonfiction trade.

Nonfiction "We publish serious, informational books for a targeted audience. All our books must have strong library interest, but we also distribute books effectively to the trade. Our library books fit the junior and senior high school curriculum."Subjects include contemporary culture, education, health, medicine, history, language, literature, multicultural, recreation, religion, sports, careers, entertainment, natural history, popular culture. Query or submit outline and sample chapter with SASE. No submissions returned without SASE.

Tips "Our audience is school and public libraries for our more reference-oriented books and libraries, schools and bookstores for our less reference-oriented informational titles."

FAIRLEIGH DICKINSON UNIVERSITY PRESS

285 Madison Ave., M-GH2-01, Madison NJ 07940. (973)443-8564. Fax: (973)443-8364. E-mail: fdupress@fdu.edu. Website: www.fdupress.org. **Contact:** Harry Keyishian, director. Estab. 1967. Publishes hardcover originals and occasional paperbacks. **Publishes 30-40 titles/year. 33% of books from first-time authors. 95% from unagented writers.** Publishes book approximately 1 year after acceptance of ms. Responds in 2 weeks to queries.

- "Contract is arranged through Associated University Presses of Cranbury, New Jersey. We are a selection committee only. Non-author subsidy publishes 2% of books."

O-π Fairleigh Dickinson publishes scholarly books for the academic market, in the humanities and social sciences.

Nonfiction Subjects include agriculture, art, architecture, business, economics, contemporary culture, ethnic, film, cinema, stage, gay, lesbian, government, politics, history, local, literary criticism, multicultural, music, dance, philosophy, psychology, regional, religion, sociology, translation, womens issues, womens studies, world affairs, Civil War, film, Jewish studies, scholarly editions. Query with outline, detailed abstract, and sample chapters (if possible). Reviews artwork/photos. Send Send only copies of illustrations during the evaluation process.

Recent Title(s) *Medieval & Renaissance Drama in England*, edited by S. P. Cerasano; *George Eliot U.S.*, by Monika Mueller; *Ashes*, by Grazia Deledda (translated by Jan Kozma).

Tips "Press books are reviewed regularly in leading academic circles. Each year between 150,000-200,000 brochures are mailed to announce new works. Research must be up-to-date. Poor reviews result when bibliographies and notes don't reflect current research. We follow Chicago Manual of Style (15th edition) in scholarly citation. We welcome collections of unpublished conference papers, if they relate to a strong central theme and have scholarly merit. For further details, consult our online catalog."

FANTAGRAPHICS BOOKS

7563 Lake City Way NE, Seattle WA 98115. (206)524-1967. Fax: (206)524-2104. Website: www.fantagraphics.com. **Contact:** Submissions Editor. Estab. 1976. Publishes original trade paperbacks. Responds in 2-3 months to queries. Book catalog available online. Guidelines available online.

O-π Publishes comics for thinking readers. Does not want mainstream genres of superhero, vigilante, horror, fantasy, or science fiction.

Fiction Subjects include comic books. Fantagraphics is an independent company with a modus operandi different from larger, factory-like corporate comics publishers. If your talents are limited to a specific area of expertise (i.e. inking, writing, etc.), then you will need to develop your own team before submitting a project to us. We want to see an idea that is fully fleshed-out in your mind, at least, if not on paper. Submit a minimum of 5 fully-inked pages of art, a synopsis, SASE, and a brief note stating approximately how many issues you have in mind.

Recent Title(s) *In My Darkest Hour*, by Wilfred Santiago; *When We Were Very Maakies*, by Tony Millionaire.

Tips Take note of the originality and diversity of the themes and approaches to drawing in such Fantagraphics titles as *Love & Rockets* (stories of life in Latin America and Chicano L.A.), *Palestine* (journalistic autobiography in the Middle East), *Eightball* (surrealism mixed with kitsch culture in stories alternately humorous and painfully personal), and *Naughty Bits* (feminist humor and short stories which both attack and commiserate). Try to develop your own, equally individual voice; originality, aesthetic maturity, and graphic storytelling skill are the signs by which Fantagraphics judges whether or not your submission is ripe for publication.

FARRAR, STRAUS & GIROUX BOOKS FOR YOUNG READERS

Farrar Straus Giroux, Inc. 18 West 18th St., New York NY 10011. (212)741-6900. E-mail: childrens.editorial@fsgbooks.com. Website: www.fsgkidsbooks.com. **Contact:** Children's Editorial Department. Estab. 1946. Publishes hardcover originals and trade paperback reprints. **Publishes 75 titles/year. 6,000 queries and mss received/year. 5% of books from first-time authors. 50% from unagented writers. Pays 2-6% royalty on retail price for paperbacks, 3-10% for hardcovers. Pays $3,000-25,000 advance.** Publishes book 18 months after acceptance of ms. Accepts simultaneous submissions. Responds in 2 months to queries. Responds in 3

months to manuscripts. Book catalog for 9 X 12 SAE with $1.95 postage. Guidelines available online.
Imprints Frances Foster Books.

O→ We publish original and well-written material for all ages.

Fiction Subjects include juvenile, picture books, young adult, nonfiction. Do not query picture books; just send manuscript. Do not fax or e-mail queries or manuscripts. Query with SASE.
Recent Title(s) *The Cabinet of Wonders*, by Marie Rutkoski (ages 10 up); *How I Learned Geography*, by Uri Shulevitz (Caldecott Honor Book (ages 4-8).
Tips Audience is full age range, preschool to young adult. Specializes in literary fiction.

FATCAT PRESS

P.O. Box 130281, Ann Arbor MI 48113. E-mail: editorial@fatcatpress.com. Website: www.fatcatpress.com. **Contact:** Ellen Bauerle, publisher/acquiring editor (technology, mysteries, Buddhist studies, travel, science fiction). Estab. 2003. Publishes electronic originals and occasional reprints. **Publishes 20 titles/year. 360 queries received/year. 120 mss received/year. 60% of books from first-time authors. 95% from unagented writers.** Publishes book 3 months after acceptance of ms. Responds in 1 month to queries. Responds in 1 month to proposals. Responds in 1 month to manuscripts. Book catalog available online. Guidelines available online.
Nonfiction Subjects include travel, eastern religion and spirituality, technology and society. Query with SASE. Submit proposal package, outline, 2 sample chapters, current e-mail address.
Fiction Subjects include fantasy, mystery, science fiction. We want top-flight writing, unusual points of view, unusual characters. Query via e-mail, or submit co
Tips Our readers are educated, well read, and technologically competent. Many travel extensively.

FAWCETT

The Ballantine Publishing Group, A Division of Random House, Inc. 1745 Broadway, New York NY 10019. E-mail: bfi@randomhouse.com. Website: www.randomhouse.com. Estab. 1955. Publishes paperback originals and reprints.

O→ Major publisher of mystery mass market and trade paperbacks.

Fiction Subjects include mystery. Agented submissions only. *All unsolicited mss returne*

FREDERICK FELL PUBLISHERS, INC.

2131 Hollywood Blvd., Suite 305, Hollywood FL 33020. (954)925-5242. Fax: (954)925-5244. E-mail: info@fellpub.com. Website: www.fellpub.com. **Contact:** Barbara Newman, senior editor. Publishes hardcover and trade paperback originals. **Publishes 40 titles/year. 4,000 queries received/year. 1,000 mss received/year. 95% of books from first-time authors. 95% from unagented writers. Pays negotiable royalty on retail price. Pays up to $10,000 advance.** Publishes book 1 year after acceptance of ms. Accepts simultaneous submissions. Responds in 1 month to queries. Responds in 3 months to proposals. Guidelines available online.

O→ Fell has just launched 25 titles in the *Know-It-All* series. We will be publishing over 125 titles in all genres. Prove to us that your title is the best in this new exciting nonfiction format.

Nonfiction We are reviewing in all categories. Advise us of the top three competitive titles for your work and the reasons why the public would benefit by having your book published.Subjects include business, economics, child guidance, education, ethnic, film, cinema, stage, health, medicine, hobbies, money, finance, spirituality. Submit proposal package, including outline, 3 sample chapters, author bio, publicity ideas, market analysis. Reviews artwork/photos. Send photocopies.
Recent Title(s) *Secrets of Mind Power*, by Harry Lorayne; *Greatest Salesman in the World*, by Og Mandino (illustrated edition).
Tips We are most interested in well-written, timely nonfiction with strong sales potential. We will not consider topics that appeal to a small, select audience. Learn markets and be prepared to help with sales and promotion. Show us how your book is unique or better than the competition.

THE FEMINIST PRESS AT THE CITY UNIVERSITY OF NEW YORK

365 Fifth Ave., Suite 5406, New York NY 10016. (212)817-7925. Fax: (212)817-1593. E-mail: fhowe@gc.cuny.edu. Website: www.feministpress.org. **Contact:** Florence Howe. Estab. 1970. Publishes hardcover and trade paperback originals and reprints.Publishes no original fiction; exceptions are anthologies and international works. Accepts simultaneous submissions. Book catalog available online. Guidelines available online.

O→ Our primary mission is to publish works of fiction by women which preserve and extend women's literary traditions. We emphasize work by multicultural/international women writers.

Nonfiction Subjects include ethnic, gay, lesbian, government, politics, health, medicine, history, language, literature, memoirs, multicultural, music, dance, sociology, translation, womens issues, womens studies. Send e-mail queries only, limited to 2 words with Submission as the subject line. We regret that submissions are no longer accepted through the mail and unsolicited packages will be discarded.
Fiction Subjects include ethnic, feminist, gay, lesbian, literary, short story collections, translation, nonsexist, women's. The Feminist Press publishes only fiction reprints by classic American women authors and imports

and translations of distinguished international women writers. Rarely publishes original fiction.Needs fiction by U.S. women of color writers from 1920-1970 who have fallen out of print. Query by e-mail only; limit 2
Recent Title(s) *The Stories of Fannie Hurst*, by Fannie Hurst; edited by Susan Koppelman; *Developing Power*, by Arvonne S. Fraser and Irene Tinker; *Bunny Lake Is Missing*, by Evelyn Piper.
Tips We cannot accept telephone inquiries regarding proposed submissions.

N FENCE BOOKS

Science Library 320, Univ. of Albany, 1400 Washington Ave., Albany NY 12222. (518)591-8162. E-mail: fence.fencebooks@gmail.com. Website: www.fenceportal.org. Hardcover originals. Guidelines available online.
Fiction Subjects include poetry.
Recent Title(s) *Unspoiled Air*, by Kaisa Ullsvick Miller (poetry); *The Mandarin*, by Aaron Kunin; *Rogue Hemlocks*, by Carl Martin.
Tips At present Fence Books is a self-selecting publisher; mss come to our attention through our contests and through editors' investigations. We hope to become open to submissions of poetry and fiction mss in the near future.

FERGUSON PUBLISHING CO.

Infobase Publishing 132 W. 31st St., 17th Floor, New York NY 10001. (800)322-8755. E-mail: editorial@factsonfile.com. Website: www.fergpubco.com. **Contact:** Editorial Director. Estab. 1940. Publishes hardcover and trade paperback originals. **Publishes 50 titles/year. Pays by project.** Responds in 6 months to queries. Guidelines available online.

- We are primarily a career education publisher that publishes for schools and libraries. We need writers who have expertise in a particular career or career field (for possible full-length books on a specific career or field).

Nonfiction We publish work specifically for the elementary/junior high/high school/college library reference market. Works are generally encyclopedic in nature. Our current focus is career encyclopedias and young adult career sets and series. We consider manuscripts that cross over into the trade market.Query or submit an outline and 1 sample chapter.
Recent Title(s) *Encyclopedia of Careers and Vocational Guidance*, (Careers in Focus: Retail Sales; Career Opportunities: Writing; Career Coach series).
Tips We like writers who know the market—former or current librarians or teachers or guidance counselors.

FIRE ENGINEERING BOOKS & VIDEOS

Imprint of PennWell Corp. 1421 S. Sheridan Rd., Tulsa OK 74112. (918)831-9410. Fax: (918)831-9555. E-mail: bookproposals@pennwell.com. Website: www.pennwellbooks.com. **Contact:** Jerry Naylis, supervising editor. Publishes hardcover and softcover originals. Responds in 1 month to proposals. Book catalog available free.

- Fire Engineering publishes textbooks relevant to firefighting and training. Currently emphasizing strategy and tactics, reserve training, preparedness for terrorist threats, natural disasters, first response to fires and emergencies.

Nonfiction Submit proposal via e-mail.
Recent Title(s) *Fire Officer's Handbook of Tactics, Third Ed.*, by John Norman; *Emergency Rescue Shoring Techniques*, by John O'Connell.
Tips No human-interest stories; technical training only.

FOCAL PRESS

Imprint of Elsevier (USA), Inc. 30 Corporate Dr., Suite 400, Burlington MA 01803. Fax: (781)221-1615. Website: www.focalpress.com. **Contact:** Amorette Petersen, publishing director; for further editorial contacts, visit the contacts page on the company's Web site. Estab. US, 1981; UK, 1938. Publishes hardcover and paperback originals and reprints. **Publishes 80-120 UK-US titles/year; entire firm publishes over 1,000 titles/year. 25% of books from first-time authors. 90% from unagented writers.** Publishes book 6 months after acceptance of ms. Accepts simultaneous submissions. Responds in 2 months to queries. Book catalog for #10 SASE. Guidelines available online.

- Focal Press provides excellent books for students, advanced amateurs, and working professionals involved in all areas of media technology. Topics of interest include photography (digital and traditional techniques), film/video, audio, broadcasting, and cinematography, through to journalism, radio, television, video, and writing. Currently emphasizing graphics, gaming, animation, and multimedia.

Nonfiction Subjects include film, cinema, stage, photography, film, cinematography, broadcasting, theater and performing arts, audio, sound and media technology. Query preferred, or submit outline and sample chapters. Reviews artwork/photos.
Recent Title(s) *Adobe Photoshop CS2 for Photographers*, by Martin Evening (nonfiction).

N A FOGHORN PUBLISHERS

The Scribes Ink, Inc. P.O. Box 8286, Manchester CT 06040-0286. (860)216-5622. Fax: (860)290-8291. E-mail:

foghornpublisher@aol.com. **Contact:** Dr. Aaron D. Lewis, publisher. Publishes hardcover and trade paperback originals. **Publishes 10-20 titles/year. 200 queries received/year. 1,000 mss received/year. 60% of books from first-time authors. Pays 9-15% royalty on wholesale price.** Publishes book 3 months after acceptance of ms. Accepts simultaneous submissions. Responds in 1 month to queries. Responds in 1 month to proposals. Responds in 1 month to manuscripts. Guidelines available free.

Nonfiction Subjects include audio, history, money, finance, religion, spirituality, health/wellness, natural healing. Query with SASE. Submit complete ms. Agented submissions only.

Fiction Subjects include religious, spiritual. Agented submissions only.

Recent Title(s) *The Laws of Thinking*, by E. Bernard Jordan (spritual/self-help); *What in Hell Is Holding You Back*, by Edward Stephens (Christian living).

FORDHAM UNIVERSITY PRESS

2546 Belmont Ave., University Box L, Bronx NY 10458. (718)817-4795. Fax: (718)817-4785. Website: www.fordhampress.com. **Contact:** Helen Tartar, editorial director. Publishes hardcover and trade paperback originals and reprints. Book catalog and ms guidelines free.

- We are a publisher in humanities, accepting scholarly monographs, collections, occasional reprints and general interest titles for consideration. No fiction.

Nonfiction Subjects include anthropology, archeology, art, architecture, education, film, cinema, stage, government, politics, history, language, literature, military, war, World War II, philosophy, regional, New York, religion, science, sociology, translation, business, Jewish studies, media, music. Submit query letter, CV, SASE.

Recent Title(s) *The Search for Major Plagge*, by Michael Good; *Red Tail Captured, Red Tail Free*, by Alexander Jefferson, with Lewis Carlson.

Tips We have an academic and general audience.

FORTRESS PRESS

P.O. Box 1209, Minneapolis MN 55440-1209. (612)330-3300. E-mail: booksub@augsburgfortress.org. Website: www.fortresspress.com. Publishes hardcover and trade paperback originals. **Pays royalty on retail price.** Accepts simultaneous submissions. Book catalog free (call 1-800-328-4648). Guidelines available online.

- Fortress Press publishes academic books in Biblical studies, theology, Christian ethics, church history, and professional books in pastoral care and counseling.

Nonfiction Subjects include religion, womens issues, womens studies, church history, African-American studies. Query with annotated TOC, brief cv, sample pages, SASE. Please study guidelines before submitting.

Recent Title(s) *God & Power: Counter-Apocalyptic Journeys*, by Catherine Keller; *New Testament Theology: Communion and Community*, by Philip F. Esler; *Radical Wisdom: A Feminist Mystical Theology*, by Beverly J. Lanzetta.

N FORTRESS PRESS

Augsburg Fortress Publishers P.O. Box 1209, Minneapolis MN 55440-1209. Website: www.fortresspress.org. **Contact:** Susan Johnson. **Pays royalty.** Guidelines available online under "contact us".

- "Publishes nonfiction books in bible, theology, and ecclesiology geared toward scholarly research and clasroom adoption in colleges and theological seminaries."

FORT ROSS INC. RUSSIAN-AMERICAN PUBLISHING PROJECTS

26 Arthur Place, Yonkers NY 10701. (914)375-6448. E-mail: vkartsev2000@yahoo.com. **Contact:** Dr. Vladimir P. Kartsev, executive director. Estab. 1992. Publishes paperback originals. **Publishes 10 titles/year. 100 queries received/year. 100 mss received/year. 10% of books from first-time authors. 10% from unagented writers. Pays 6-8% royalty on wholesale price or makes outright purchase of $500-1,500. Pays $500-$1,000; negotiable advance.** Publishes book 12 months after acceptance of ms. Accepts simultaneous submissions. Responds in 1 month to queries. Responds in 1 month to proposals. Responds in 3 months to manuscripts.

- Generally, we publish Russia-related books in English or Russian. Sometimes we publish various fiction and nonfiction books in collaboration with the East European publishers in translation. We are looking mainly for well-established authors.

Fiction Subjects include adventure, fantasy, space fantasy, sword and sorcery, horror, mainstream, contemporary, mystery, amateur sleuth, police procedural, private eye/hardboiled, romance, futuristic/time travel, science fiction, hard science fiction/technological, soft/sociological, suspense. Query with SASE.

Recent Title(s) *Cosack Galloped Far Away*, by Nikolas Feodoroff; *Little Hands: The Theme and Variations*, by Oxana Yablonskaya; *Ageless Memory*, by Lorrain; *The Old Man and the Sea*, by Ernest Hemingway (in Russian).

FORUM PUBLISHING CO.

383 E. Main St., Centerport NY 11721. (631)754-5000. Fax: (631)754-0630. Website: www.forum123.com. **Contact:** Martin Stevens. Estab. 1981. Publishes trade paperback originals. **Publishes 12 titles/year. 200**

queries received/year. 25 mss received/year. 75% of books from first-time authors. 75% from unagented writers. Makes outright purchase of 250-750. Publishes book 4 months after acceptance of ms. Accepts simultaneous submissions. Responds in 1 month to manuscripts. Book catalog available free.

"Forum publishes only business titles."

Nonfiction Subjects include business, economics, money, finance. Submit outline. Reviews artwork/photos. Send photocopies.

Recent Title(s) *Selling Information By Mail*, by Glen Gilcrest; *Secrets of Successful Advertising*.

WALTER FOSTER PUBLISHING, INC.

Suite A, Irvine CA 92618. (800)426-0099. Fax: (949)380-7575. E-mail: info@walterfoster.com. Website: www.walterfoster.com. Estab. 1922. Publishes trade paperback originals.

Walter Foster publishes instructional how-to/craft instruction as well as licensed products.

FOX CHAPEL PUBLISHING

1970 Broad St., East Petersburg PA 17520. (717)560-4703. Fax: (717)560-4702. E-mail: editors@foxchapelpublishing.com. Website: www.foxchapelpublishing.com. **Contact:** Peg Couch, acquisitions editor. Publishes hardcover and trade paperback originals and trade paperback reprints. **Publishes 25-40 titles/year. 50% of books from first-time authors. 100% from unagented writers. Pays royalty or makes outright purchase. Pays variable advance.** Publishes book 6-18 months after acceptance of ms. Accepts simultaneous submissions. Responds in 2 months to queries.

Fox Chapel publishes woodworking, woodcarving, and design titles for professionals and hobbyists.

Nonfiction Submission guidelines on website Reviews artwork/photos. Send photocopies.

Recent Title(s) *Celebrating Birch*; *Pinewood Derby Design Secrets*; *Woodworker's Guide to Veneering and Inlay*.

Tips We're looking for knowledgeable artists, craftspeople and woodworkers, all experts in their fields, to write books of lasting value.

FREE PRESS

Simon & Schuster 1230 Avenue of the Americas, New York NY 10020. (212)698-7000. Fax: (212)632-4989. Website: www.simonsays.com. **Contact:** Bruce Nichols, vice president/senior editor (history/serious nonfiction). Estab. 1947. **Publishes 85 titles/year. 15% of books from first-time authors. 10% from unagented writers. Pays variable royalty. Pays advance.** Publishes book 1 year after acceptance of ms. Responds in 2 months to queries.

The Free Press publishes nonfiction.

Recent Title(s) *Against All Enemies*, by Richard Clarke; *The 8th Habit*, by Stephen R. Covey.

FREE SPIRIT PUBLISHING, INC.

217 Fifth Ave. N., Suite 200, Minneapolis MN 55401-1299. (612)338-2068. Fax: (612)337-5050. E-mail: acquisitions@freespirit.com. Website: www.freespirit.com. **Contact:** Acquisitions Editor. Estab. 1983. Publishes trade paperback originals and reprints. **Publishes 18-24 titles/year. 5% of books from first-time authors. 50% from unagented writers. Pays advance.** Book catalog and ms guidelines online.

We believe passionately in empowering kids to learn to think for themselves and make their own good choices.

Nonfiction Subjects include child guidance, education, pre-K-12, study and social sciences skills, special needs, differentiation but not textbooks or basic skills books like reading, counting, etc., health, medicine, mental/emotional health for/about children, psychology for/about children, sociology for/about children. Query with cover letter stating qualifications, intent, and intended audience and market analysis (how your book stands out from the field), along with outline, 2 sample chapters, rèsumè, SASE. Do not send original copies of work.

Recent Title(s) *Good-Bye Bully Machine*; *Real Friends vs. The Other Kind*; *Making Differentiation a Habit*.

Tips Our books are issue-oriented, jargon-free, and solution-focused. Our audience is children, teens, teachers, parents and youth counselors. We are especially concerned with kids' social and emotional well-being and look for books with ready-to-use strategies for coping with today's issues at home or in school—written in every-day language. We are not looking for academic or religious materials, or books that analyze problem's with the nation's school systems. Instead, we want books that offer practical, positive advice so kids can help themselves and parents and teachers can help kids succeed.

FRONT STREET

Boyds Mills Press, 815 Church St., Honesdale PA 18431. Website: www.frontstreetbooks.com. **Contact:** Acquisitions Editor. Estab. 1994. Publishes hardcover originals and trade paperback reprints. **Publishes 10-15 titles/year. 2,000 queries received/year. 5,000 mss received/year. 30% of books from first-time authors. 60% from unagented writers. Pays royalty on retail price. Pays advance.** Publishes book 1 year after acceptance of ms. Accepts simultaneous submissions. Responds in 3 months. Book catalog available online.

Guidelines available online.

O→ "We are an independent publisher of books for children and young adults."

Fiction Subjects include adventure, historical, humor, juvenile, literary, picture books, young adult, adventure, fantasy/science fiction fiction, historical, mystery/suspense, problem novels, sports. Query with SASE. Submit complete ms, if under 100 pages, with SASE. keeps illustration samples on file. Reviews artwork/photos w/ ms. Send photocopies.

Recent Title(s) *The Bear Maker*, by Andrea Cheng; *Drive*, by Nathan Clement; *The Adventurous Deeds of Deadwood Jones*, by Helen Hemphill.

FUTURE HORIZONS

721 W. Abram St., Arlington TX 76013. (817)277-0727. Fax: (817)277-2270. E-mail: kelly@futurehorizons-autism.com. Website: www.futurehorizons-autism.com. **Contact:** Kelly Gilpin. Publishes hardcover originals, trade paperback originals and reprints. **Publishes 10 titles/year. 250 queries received/year. 125 mss received/year. 75% of books from first-time authors. 95% from unagented writers. Pays 10% royalty. Makes outright purchase.** Publishes book 2 months after acceptance of ms. Accepts simultaneous submissions. Responds in 1 month to queries. Responds in 2 months to proposals. Book catalog available free. Guidelines available online.

Nonfiction Subjects include education, about autism/Asperger's syndrome, autism. Submit proposal package, outline. Reviews artwork/photos. Send photocopies.

Recent Title(s) *Unwritten Rules of Social Relationships*, by Dr. Temple Grandin and Sean Barron; *Ten Things Every Child With Autism Wishes You Knew*, by Ellen Notbohm.

Tips Audience is parents, teachers, Books that sell well, have pr

GAUTHIER PUBLICATIONS, INC.

Frog Legs Ink P.O. Box 806241, Saint Clair Shores MI 48080. Fax: (586)279-1515. E-mail: info@gauthierpublications.com. Website: www.gauthierpublications.com. **Contact:** Elizabeth Gauthier, Creative Director (Children's/Fiction). Hardcover originals and Trade paperback originals. **Publishes 10 titles/year. 50% of books from first-time authors. 50% from unagented writers. Pays 5-10% royalty on retail price.** Guidelines available for #10 SASE, or online at website http://gauthierpublications.com, or by email at: submissions@gauthierpublications.com.

Imprints Frog Legs Ink.

Nonfiction Subjects include creative nonfiction, photography. Query with SASE.

Fiction Subjects include adventure, confession, ethnic, experimental, fantasy, feminist, gothic, historical, horror, humor, juvenile, literary, mainstream, contemporary, military, war, multicultural, multimedia, mystery, plays, poetry, poetry in translation, regional, religious, romance. We are particularly interested in mystery, thriller and Young Adult areas for the upcoming year. We do, however, consider most subjects if they are intriguing and well written. Query with SASE.

Recent Title(s) *Milestones*, Armin (young adult novel); *Out of the Nursery*, by Elizabeth Gauthier (Children's Picture Book).

N GENEALOGICAL PUBLISHING CO., INC.

3600 Clipper Mill Rd., Baltimore MD 21211. (410)837-8271. Fax: (410)752-8492. E-mail: info@genealogical.com. Website: www.genealogical.com. **Contact:** Joe Garonzik, mktg. dir. (history & genealogy). hardcover and trade paperback originals and reprints. **Publishes 100 titles/year. 100 queries/year; 20 mss/year. 10% of books from first-time authors. 99% from unagented writers.** Publishes book 6 months after acceptance of ms. Accepts simultaneous submissions. Catalog free on request. Guidelines not available.

Nonfiction TrueSubjects include Americana, ethnic, history, hobbies. Submit outline, 1 sample chapter. Reviews artwork/photos as part of the mss package.

Recent Title(s) *Genealogist's Address Book (6th ed.)*, by Elizabeth P. Bentley (directory); *Social Networking for Genealogists*, by Drew Smith (how-to).

Tips "Our audience is genealogy hobbyists."

GENESIS PRESS, INC.

P.O. Box 101, Columbus MS 39701. (888)463-4461. Fax: (662)329-9399. E-mail: books@genesis-press.com. Website: www.genesis-press.com. Estab. 1993. Publishes hardcover and trade paperback originals and reprints. Responds in 2 months to queries. Responds in 4 months to manuscripts. Guidelines available online.

Imprints Indigo (romance); Black Coral (fiction); Indigo Love Spectrum (interracial romance); Indigo After Dark (erotica); Obsidian (thriller/myster); Indigo Glitz (love stories for young adults); Indigo Vibe (for stylish audience under 35 years old); Mount Blue (Christian); Inca Books (teens); Sage (self-help/inspirational).

O→ Genesis Press is the largest privately owned African-American publisher in the country, focusing on African American, Hispanic, Asian, and interracial fiction.

Nonfiction Submit outline, 3 sample chapters, SASE.

Fiction Subjects include adventure, erotica, ethnic, multicultural, mystery, romance, science fiction, women's.

Submit clips, 3 sample chapters, SASE.

Recent Title(s) *Falling*, by Natalie Dunbar; *Hearts Awakening*, by Veronica Parker.

Tips Be professional. Always include a cover letter and SASE. Follow the submission guidelines posted on our website or send SASE for a copy.

N GGC, INC./PUBLISHING

5107 13th St. NW, Washington DC 20011. (202)541-9700. Fax: (202)541-9750. Website: www.gogardner.com. **Contact:** Garth Gardner, publisher (computer graphics, animation cartoons); Bonney Ford, editor (GGC, art, animation). Publishes trade paperback reprints. **Publishes 10 titles/year. 50 queries received/year. 25 mss received/year. 80% of books from first-time authors. 70% from unagented writers. Pays 10-15% royalty on wholesale price or makes outright purchase.** Publishes book 3 months after acceptance of ms. Accepts simultaneous submissions. Responds in 1 month to queries. Book catalog available online. Guidelines available online.

- GGC publishes books on the subjects of computer graphics, animation, new media, multimedia, art, cartoons, drawing.

Nonfiction Subjects include art, architecture, education, history, computer graphics. Submit proposal package, 2 sample chapters, resume, cover letter. Reviews artwork/photos. Send photocopies.

Recent Title(s) *Gardner's Guide to Creating 2D Animation in a Small Studio*, by Bill Davis; *Career Diary of a Composer*, by Patrick Smith; *Gardner's Guide to Drawing for Animation*, by David Brain.

A Ø DAVID R. GODINE, PUBLISHER, INC.

9 Hamilton Place, Boston MA 02108. (617)451-9600. Fax: (617)350-0250. E-mail: info@godine.com. Website: www.godine.com. Estab. 1970. Publishes hardcover and trade paperback originals and reprints. **Publishes 35 titles/year. Pays royalty on retail price.** Publishes book 3 years after acceptance of ms. Book catalog for 5X8 envelope and 3 First-Class stamps.

- Our particular strengths are books about the history and design of the written word, literary essays, and the best of world fiction in translation. We also have an unusually strong list of children's books, all of them printed in their entirety with no cuts, deletions, or side-stepping to keep the political watchdogs happy.

Nonfiction Subjects include Americana, art, architecture, gardening, literary criticism, nature, environment, photography, literary criticism, book arts, typography. Query with SASE.

Fiction Subjects include historical, literary, translation, literature, novels. *No unsolicited mss* Query with SASE.

Tips Please visit our website for more information about our books and detailed submission policy. No phone calls, please.

N GOLDEN PEACH PUBLISHING

1223 Wilshire Blvd., #1510, Santa Monica CA 90403-5400. E-mail: info@goldenpeachbooks.com. Website: www.goldenpeachbooks.com. Trade paperback originals. **Publishes 20 titles/year.** Accepts simultaneous submissions.

- We focus on quality Chinese, English and bilingual books to bridge the gap between the Eastern and Western worlds.

Nonfiction Subjects include architecture, art, ethnic, health, history, language, literature, medicine, memoirs, multicultural, young adult. Submit proposal package, including outline, 2 sample chapters. Reviews artwork/photos; send photocopies.

Fiction Subjects include adventure, comic books, ethnic, fantasy, juvenile, multicultural, mystery, picture books, young adult. See our website. Submit proposal package, including: synopsis, 3 sample chapters, and illustration copies, if any.

Recent Title(s) *Spine-Related Diseases*, by Wei Guihang (professional); *Princess Pearl, Book One. The Dragon Arch*, by Teri Tao (YA novel); *The Monkey King and the Book of Death*, adapted by Ted Tao (YA novel); *Lotus Lantern*, by Ted Tao (bilingual reader).

THE GRADUATE GROUP

P.O. Box 370351, West Hartford CT 06137-0351. (860)233-2330. Fax: (860)233-2330. E-mail: graduategroup@hotmail.com. Website: www.graduategroup.com. **Contact:** Mara Whitman, partner; Robert Whitman, vice president. Estab. 1964. Publishes trade paperback originals. **Publishes 50 titles/year. 100 queries received/year. 70 mss received/year. 60% of books from first-time authors. 85% from unagented writers. Pays 20% - royalty on retail price.** Publishes book 3 months after acceptance of ms. Accepts simultaneous submissions. Responds in 1 month to queries. Book catalog available free. Guidelines available online.

- The Graduate Group helps college and graduate students better prepare themselves for rewarding careers and helps people advance in the workplace. Currently emphasizing test preparation, career advancement, and materials for prisoners, law enforcement, books on unique careers.

Nonfiction Subjects include business, economics, education, government, politics, health, medicine, money, finance, law enforcement. Submit complete ms and SASE with sufficient postage

Recent Title(s) *Real Life 101: Winning Secrets You Won't Find in Class*, by Debra Yergen; *Getting In: Applicant's Guide to Graduate School Admissions*, by David Burrell.

Tips Audience is career planning of We are open to all submission

GREAT QUOTATIONS PUBLISHING

8102 Lemont Rd., #300, Woodridge IL 60517. (630)390-3580. **Contact:** Ringo Suek, acquisitions editor (humor, relationships, Christian); Jan Stob, acquisitions editor (children's). Estab. 1991. **Publishes 30 titles/year. 1,500 queries received/year. 1,200 mss received/year. 50% of books from first-time authors. 80% from unagented writers.** Publishes book 6 months after acceptance of ms. Accepts simultaneous submissions. Responds in 6 months with SASE to queries. Book catalog for $2. Guidelines for #10 SASE.

O-ᵣ Great Quotations seeks original material for the following general categories: humor, inspiration, motivation, success, romance, tributes to mom/dad/grandma/grandpa, etc. Currently emphasizing humor, relationships. De-emphasizing poetry, self-help. We publish new books twice a year, in July and in January.

Nonfiction Subjects include business, economics, child guidance, nature, environment, religion, sports, womens issues, womens studies. Submit outline, 2 sample chapters. Reviews artwork/photos. Send photocopies and transparencies.

Recent Title(s) *Stress or Sanity*; *If My Teacher Sleeps at School*.

Tips Our books are physically small and generally a very quick read with short sentences. They are available at gift shops and book shops throughout the country. We are aware that most of our books are bought on impulse and given as gifts. We need strong, clever, descriptive titles; beautiful cover art; and brief, positive, upbeat text. Be prepared to submit final manuscript on computer disk, according to our specifications. (It is not necessary to try to format the typesetting of your manuscript to look like a finished book.)

GREENWOOD PUBLISHING GROUP

Reed-Elsevier (USA) Inc. 88 Post Rd. W., Box 5007, Westport CT 06881-5007. (203)226-3571. Fax: (203)222-6009. E-mail: achiffolo@abc-clio.com. Website: www.greenwood.com. **Contact:** See website for list of contact editors by subject area. **Pays variable royalty on net price.** Accepts simultaneous submissions. Book catalog available online. Guidelines available online.

Imprints Praeger (general nonfiction in the social sciences, business, and humanities for public library patrons); Greenwood Press (reference titles for middle, high school, public, and academic libraries); Praeger Security International (nonfiction dealing with security studies broadly defined).

O-ᵣ The Greenwood Publishing Group consists of 3 distinguished imprints with one unifying purpose: to provide the best possible reference and general interest resources in the humanities and the social and hard sciences.

Nonfiction Subjects include business, economics, child guidance, education, government, politics, history, humanities, language, literature, music, dance, psychology, religion, social sciences, sociology, sports, womens issues, womens studies. Query with proposal package, including scope, organization, length of project, whether a complete ms is available or when it will be, CV or resume and SASE.

Recent Title(s) *Relationship Sabotage*, by William J. Matta; *Global Business Etiquette*, by Jeannette S. Martin and Lillian H. Chaney; *The Sound of Stevie Wonder*, by James E. Perone.

Tips No interest in fiction, drama, poetry—looking for reference materials and materials for educated general readers. Many of our authors are college professors who have distinguished credentialsa and who have published research widely in their fields. Greenwood Publishing maintains an excellent website, providing complete catalog, ms guidelines and editorial contacts.

GROUP PUBLISHING, INC.

1515 Cascade Ave., Loveland CO 80538. (970)669-3836. Fax: (970)679-4370. E-mail: kloesche@grouppublishing.com. Website: www.group.com. **Contact:** Kerri Loesche, contract & copyright administrator. Estab. 1974. Publishes trade paperback originals. **Publishes 40 titles/year. 500 queries received/year. 500 mss received/year. 40% of books from first-time authors. 95% from unagented writers. Pays up to 10% royalty on wholesale price or makes outright purchase or work for hire. Pays up to $1,000 advance.** Publishes book 18 months after acceptance of ms. Accepts simultaneous submissions. Responds in 1 month to queries. Responds in 6 months to proposals. Responds in 6 months to manuscripts. Book catalog for 9x12 envelope and 2 First-Class stamps. Guidelines available online.

O-ᵣ Our mission is to equip churches to help children, youth, and adults grow in their relationship with Jesus.

Nonfiction Subjects include education, religion. Query with SASE. Submit proposal package, outline, 3 sample chapters, cover letter, introduction to book, and sample activities if appropriate.

Recent Title(s) *Outflow*, by Steve Sjogren and Dave Ping; *Quiet Strength Bible Study*, by Tony Dungy and Kari Leuthauser; *Hope Lives*, by Amber Van Schooneveld.

Tips Our audience consists of pastors, Christian education directors, youth leaders, and Sunday school teachers.

N GROVE/ATLANTIC, INC.

841 Broadway, New York NY 10003. (212)614-7850. Fax: (212)614-7886. E-mail: info@groveatlantic.com. **Contact:** Morgan Entrekin, publisher (fiction, history, spsorts, current affairs); Elisabeth Schmitz, exec. editor (literary fiction, memoirs). Publishes hardcover and trade paperback originals, and reprints. **Publishes 100 titles/year. 1,000+ queries received/year. 1,000+ mss received/year. 10%% of books from first-time authors. 0%% from unagented writers. Pays 7 ½-12 ½% royalty. Makes outright purchase of 5-500,000.** Publishes book 9 months after acceptance of ms. Accepts simultaneous submissions. Responds in 1 month to queries. Responds in 2 months to proposals. Responds in 4 months to manuscripts. Book catalog available online.

Imprints Black Cat, Atlantic Monthly Press, Grove Press.

Nonfiction Subjects include art, architecture, business, economics, creative nonfiction, education, government, politics, language, literature, memoirs, military, war, philosophy, psychology, science, social sciences, sports, translation. Agented submissions only.

Fiction Subjects include erotica, horror, literary, science fiction, short story collections, suspense, western. Agented submissions only.

GRYPHON HOUSE, INC.

P.O. Box 207, Beltsville MD 20704. (301)595-9500. Fax: (301)595-0051. Website: www.gryphonhouse.com. **Contact:** Kathy Charner, editor-in-chief. Estab. 1971. Publishes trade paperback originals. **Publishes 12-15 titles/year. Pays royalty on wholesale price.** Responds in 3-6 months to queries. Guidelines available online.

- "Gryphon House publishes books that teachers and parents of young children (birth-age 8) consider essential to their daily lives."

Nonfiction Subjects include child guidance, education, early childhood. Submit outline, 2-3 sample chapters, SASE.

Recent Title(s) *Reading Games*, by Jackie Silberg; *Primary Art*, by Mary Ann Kohl; *Preschool Math*, by Robert Williams, Debra Cunningham and Joy Lubawy.

GRYPHON PUBLICATIONS

P.O. Box 209, Brooklyn NY 11228. **Contact:** Gary Lovisi, owner/publisher. Publishes trade paperback originals and reprints. **Publishes 10 titles/year. 500 queries received/year. 1,000 mss received/year. 20% of books from first-time authors. 90% from unagented writers. Makes outright purchase by contract, price varies. Pays no advance.** Publishes book 1-2 years after acceptance of ms. Responds in 1 month to queries to queries. Book catalog and ms guidelines for #10 SASE.

Imprints Paperback Parade Magazine; Hardboiled Magazine; Gryphon Books; Gryphon Doubles.

- "I publish very genre-oriented work (science fiction, crime, pulps) and nonfiction on these topics, authors and artists. It's best to query with an idea first."

Nonfiction Subjects include hobbies, language, literature, book collecting. Query with SASE. Reviews artwork/photos. Send Send photocopies; slides, transparencies may be necessary later.

Fiction "We want cutting-edge fiction, under 3,000 words with impact." For short stories, query or su

Recent Title(s) *Barsom: Edgar Rice Burroughs & the Martian Myth*, by Richard A. Lysoff; *Sherlock Holmes & the Terror Out of Time*, by Ralph Vaughan; *A Trunk Full of Murder*, by Julius Fast.

Tips "We are very particular about novels and book-length work. A first-timer has a better chance with a short story or article. On anything over 4,000 words do not send manuscript, send only query letter with SASE. Always query **first** with an SASE."

N GULF PUBLISHING COMPANY

2 Greenway Plaza, Suite 1020, Houston TX 77046. (713)529-4301. Fax: (713)520-4433. E-mail: svb@gulfpub.com. Website: www.gulfpub.com. **Contact:** Katie Hammon, assoc. pub.; Rusty Meador, pub. (energy, engineering, petroleum, natural gas, offshore, refining, petrochemical, environmental, chemistry). hardcover originals and reprints; electronic originals and reprints. **Publishes 12-15 titles/year. 3-5 queries and mss received in a year. 30% of books from first-time authors. 80% from unagented writers. $1,000-$1,500** Publishes book 8-9 months after acceptance of ms. Accepts simultaneous submissions. Catalog free on request. Guidelines available by email.

Nonfiction , engineering. Submit outline, 1-2 sample chapters, completed ms. Reviews artwork. Send high res. file formats with hi dpi in black & white.

Recent Title(s) *Gulf Drilling Series: Managed Pressure Drilling*, by Bill Rehm, Jerome Schubert, Arash Haghshenas, Amir Paknejad, Jim Hughes; *Well Productivity*, by Boyun Guo, Kai Sun, Ali Ghalamabor; *Advanced Piping Design*, Rutger Botermans, Peter Smith.

Tips "Our audience would be engineers, engineering students, academia, professors, well managers, construction engineers. We recommend getting contributors to help with the writing process—this provides a more comprehensive overview for technical and scientific books. Work harder on artwork. It's expensive and time-consuming for a publisher to redraw a lot of the figures."

N GUN DIGEST BOOKS

F+W Media 700 East State St., Iola WI 54990. (888)457-2873. E-mail: dan.shideler@fwmedia.com. Website: www.krause.com. **Contact:** Dan Shideler, editor (all aspects of firearms history, scholarship, nonpolitical literature). hardcover, trade paperback, mass market paperback, and electronic originals (all). **Publishes 25 titles/year. 75 30% of books from first-time authors. 80% from unagented writers. $2,800-$5,000** Publishes book 7 months after acceptance of ms. Accepts simultaneous submissions. Catalog online at website http://www.krause.com. Guidelines available by email at: corrina.peterson@fwmedia.com.
Imprints Gun Digest Books, Krause Publications.
Nonfiction True, firearms, hunting-related titles only. Submit proposal package, including outline, 2 sample chapters, and author bio; submit completed manuscript. Review artwork/photos (required); high-res digital only (.jpg.tif)
Recent Title(s) *2009 Standard Catalog of Firearms, 19th Ed.*, by Dan Shideler; The Gun Digest® Book of the AK & SKS, by Patrick Sweeney; *The Gun Digest® Book of Concealed Carry*, by Massad Ayoob. http://www.krausebooks.com/category/firearms_knives.
Tips "Our audience is shooters, collectors, hunters, outdoors enthusiasts. We prefer not to work through agents."

HALF HALT PRESS, INC.

P.O. Box 67, Boonsboro MD 21713. (301)733-7119. Fax: (301)733-7408. E-mail: mail@halfhaltpress.com. Website: www.halfhaltpress.com. **Contact:** Elizabeth Rowland, publisher. Estab. 1986. Publishes 90% hardcover and trade paperback originals and 10% reprints. **Publishes 10 titles/year. 25% of books from first-time authors. 50% from unagented writers. Pays 10-12 ½% royalty on retail price.** Publishes book 1 year after acceptance of ms. Responds in 1 month to queries. Book catalog for 6x9 SAE 2 first-class stamps.

- We publish high-quality nonfiction on equestrian topics, books that help riders and trainers do something better.

Nonfiction Subjects include animals, horses, sports. Query with SASE. Reviews artwork/photos.
Recent Title(s) *Dressage in Harmony*, by Walter Zettl.
Tips Writers have the best chance selling us well-written, unique works that teach serious horse people how to do something better. If I were a writer trying to market a book today, I would offer a straightforward presentation, letting the work speak for itself, without hype or hard sell. Allow the publisher to contact the writer, without frequent calling to check status. They haven't forgotten the writer but may have many different proposals at hand; frequent calls to `touch base,' multiplied by the number of submissions, become an annoyance. As the publisher/author relationship becomes close and is based on working well together, early impressions may be important, even to the point of being a consideration in acceptance for publication.

HAMPTON ROADS PUBLISHING CO., INC.

1125 Stoney Ridge Rd., Charlottesville VA 22902. (434)296-2772. Fax: (434)296-5096. E-mail: submissions@hrpub.com. Website: www.hrpub.com. **Contact:** Frank DeMarco, chief editor (metaphysical/visionary fiction); Robert S. Friedman, president (metaphysical, spiritual, inspirational, self-help); Richard Leviton, senior editor (alternative medicine). Estab. 1989. Publishes hardcover and trade paperback originals. Publishes and distributes hardcover and paperback originals on subjects including metaphysics, health, complementary medicine, visionary fiction, and other related topics. **Publishes 35-40 titles/year. 1,000 queries received/year. 1,500 mss received/year. 50% of books from first-time authors. 70% from unagented writers. Pays royalty. Pays $1,000-50,000 advance.** Publishes book 1 year after acceptance of ms. Accepts simultaneous submissions. Responds in 2-4 months to queries. Responds in 1 month to proposals. Responds in 6-12 months to manuscripts. Guidelines available online.

- Please know that we only publish a handful of books every year, and that we pass on many well written, important works, simply because we cannot publish them all. We review each and every proposal very carefully. However, due to the volume of inquiries, we cannot respond to them all individually. Please give us 30 days to review your proposal. If you do not hear back from us within that time, this means we have decided to pursue other book ideas that we feel fit better within our plan.
- Our reason for being is to impact, uplift, and contribute to positive change in the world. We publish books that will enrich and empower the evolving consciousness of mankind.

Nonfiction Subjects include New Age, spirituality. Query with SASE. Submit synopsis, SASE. Reviews artwork/photos. Send photocopies.
Fiction Subjects include literary, spiritual, Visionary fiction, past-life fiction based on actual memories. Fiction should have 1 or more of the following themes: spiritual, inspirational, metaphysical, i.e., past-life

recall, out-of-body experiences, near-death experience, paranormal. Query with SASE. Submit outline, 2 sample chapters, clips. Submit complete ms.
Recent Title(s) *The Beethoven Factor*, by Paul Pearsall; *The Natural Way to Heal*, by Walter Last; *Phoenix Lights*, by Lynn D. Kitei, M.D.

HANCOCK HOUSE PUBLISHERS

1431 Harrison Ave., Blaine WA 98230-5005. (604)538-1114. Fax: (604)538-2262. E-mail: david@hancockwildlife.org. Website: www.hancockwildlife.org. **Contact:** David Hancock. Estab. 1971. Publishes hardcover and trade paperback originals and reprints. **Publishes 12-20 titles/year. 50% of books from first-time authors. 90% from unagented writers. Pays 10% royalty.** Publishes book up to 1 year after acceptance of ms. Accepts simultaneous submissions. Book catalog available free. Guidelines available online.

O→ Hancock House Publishers is the largest North American publisher of wildlife and Native Indian titles. We also cover Pacific Northwest, fishing, history, Canadiana, biographies. We are seeking agriculture, natural history, animal husbandry, conservation, and popular science titles with a regional (Pacific Northwest), national, or international focus. Currently emphasizing nonfiction wildlife, cryptozoology, guide books, native history, biography, fishing.

Nonfiction Centered around Pacific Northwest, local history, nature guide books, international ornithology, and Native Americans.Subjects include agriculture, animals, ethnic, history, horticulture, nature, environment, regional. Submit proposal package, outline, 3 sample chapters, selling points, SASE. Reviews artwork/photos. Send photocopies.
Recent Title(s) *Stagecoaches Across the American West; Wings Over the Wilderness; Bigfoot Encounters.*

HANSER PUBLICATIONS

6915 Valley Ave., Cincinnati OH 45244. (513)527-8800. Fax: (513)527-8801. Website: www.hanserpublications.com. **Contact:** Development Editor. Estab. 1993. Publishes hardcover and paperback originals, and digital educational and training programs. **Publishes 10-15 titles/year. 100 queries received/year. 10-20 mss received/year. 50% of books from first-time authors. 100% from unagented writers.** Publishes book 10 months after acceptance of ms. Accepts simultaneous submissions. Responds in 2 weeks to queries. Responds in 1 month to proposals. Responds in 1 month to manuscripts. Book catalog available free. Guidelines available online.

O→ "Hanser Publications publishes books and electronic media for the manufacturing (both metalworking and plastics) industries. Publications range from basic training materials to advanced reference books."

Nonfiction "We publish how-to texts, references, and technical books, and computer-based learning materials for the manufacturing industries. Titles include award-winning management books, encyclopedic references, and leading references."Submit outline, sample chapters, resume, preface, and comparison to competing or similar titles.
Recent Title(s) *Engineered Rubber Products*, by J.G. Sommer; *Mixing and Compounding*, 2nd edition, by Kamel.
Tips "E-mail submissions speed up response time."

🄰 ⊘ HARCOURT, INC., TRADE DIVISION

Imprint of Houghton Mifflin Harcourt Book Group 215 Park Ave. S., New York NY 10003. Website: www.harcourtbooks.com. Publishes hardcover and trade paperback originals and trade paperback reprints. **Publishes 120 titles/year. 5% of books from first-time authors. 5% from unagented writers. Pays 6-15% royalty on retail price. Pays $2,000 minimum advance.** Accepts simultaneous submissions. Book catalog for 9 x 12 envelope and First-Class stamps. Guidelines available online.
Nonfiction Agented submissions only.
Fiction Agented submissions only.

⊘ HARCOURT CHILDREN'S BOOKS

Imprint of Houghton Mifflin Harcourt Children's Book Group 215 Park Ave. S., New York NY 10003. Website: www.harcourtbooks.com. Estab. 1919. Publishes hardcover originals and trade paperback reprints.
Fiction Subjects include young adult.
Recent Title(s) *Tails*, by Matthew Van Fleet; *The Leaf Man*, by Lois Ehlert; *Each Little Bird That Sings*, Deborah Wiles.

🄰 ⊘ HARPERCOLLINS CHILDREN'S BOOKS GROUP

Imprint of HarperCollins Children's Books Group 10 East 53rd St.,, New York NY 10022. (212)261-6500. Website: www.harperchildrens.com. **Contact:** Jennifer Deason. Publishes hardcover and paperback originals.
Imprints Amistad; Julie Andrews Collection; Avon; Balzer and Bray; Greenwillow Books; HarperAudio; HarperCollins Children's Books; HarperFestival; HarperTempest; Rayo; Katherine Tegen Books.

O→ *No unsolicited mss and/or unagented mss or queries.* The volume of these submissions is so large that we cannot give them the attention they deserve. Such submissions will not be reviewed or returned.

Nonfiction Agented submissions only.

Fiction Subjects include picture books, young adult, chapter books, middle grade, early readers. Agented submissions only. *No unsolicited mss or queri*

Recent Title(s) *The Graveyard Book,* by Neil Gaiman; *Fancy Nancy,* by Jane O'Connor, *Warriors series,* by Erin Hunter; *How to Talk to Girls,* by Alex Greven; and *Pretty Little Liars,* by Sara Shepard.

HARPERCOLLINS GENERAL BOOKS GROUP

Division of HarperCollins Publishers 10 E. 53 St., New York NY 10022. (212)207-7000. Fax: (212)207-7633. Website: www.harpercollins.com.

Imprints Access; Amistad; Avon; Caedmon; Dark Alley; Ecco; Eos; Fourth Estate; HarperAudio; HarperBusiness; HarperCollins; HarperEntertainment; HarperLargePrint; HarperResource; HarperSanFranciso; HarperTorch; Harper Design International; Perennial; PerfectBound; Quill; Rayo; ReganBooks; William Morrow; William Morrow Cookbooks.

- See website for further details.

HARVARD BUSINESS SCHOOL PRESS

Imprint of Harvard Business School Publishing Corp. 60 Harvard Way, Boston MA 02163. (617)783-7400. Fax: (617)783-7489. E-mail: sgreen@hbsp.harvard.edu. Website: www.hbsp.harvard.edu. **Contact:** Sarah Green, editorial coordinator. Estab. 1984. Publishes hardcover originals and several paperback series. **Publishes 40-50 titles/year. Pays escalating royalty on retail price. Advances vary depending on author and market for the book.** Accepts simultaneous submissions. Responds in 1 month to proposals. Responds in 1 month to manuscripts. Book catalog available online. Guidelines available online.

The Harvard Business School Press publishes books for senior and general managers and business scholars. HBS Press is the source of the most influential ideas and conversations that shape business worldwide.

Nonfiction Submit proposal package, outline, sample chapters.

Recent Title(s) *Blue Ocean Strategy,* by Chan Keni and Renee Manborgue; *Resonant Leadership,* by Richard Boyatzis and Annie McKee; *The Ultimate Question,* by Fred Reichheld.

Tips We do not publish books on real estate, personal finance or business parables.

THE HARVARD COMMON PRESS

535 Albany St., Boston MA 02118-2500. (617)423-5803. Fax: (617)695-9794. Website: www.harvardcommonpress.com. **Contact:** Valerie Cimino, executive editor. Estab. 1976. Publishes hardcover and trade paperback originals and reprints. **Publishes 16 titles/year. 20% of books from first-time authors. 40% from unagented writers. Pays royalty. Pays average $2,500-10,000 advance.** Publishes book 1 year after acceptance of ms. Accepts simultaneous submissions. Responds in 2 months to queries. Book catalog for 9x12 envelope and 3 First-Class stamps. Guidelines for #10 SASE or online.

Imprints Gambit Books.

We want strong, practical books that help people gain control over a particular area of their lives. Currently emphasizing cooking, child care/parenting, health. De-emphasizing general instructional books, travel.

Nonfiction Subjects include child guidance, cooking, foods, nutrition, health, medicine. Submit outline. Reviews artwork/photos.

Recent Title(s) *Icebox Desserts,* by Lauren Chattman; *Pie,* by Ken Haedrich; *Not Your Mother's Slow Cooker Cookbook,* by Beth Hensperger and Julie Kaufmann.

Tips We are demanding about the quality of proposals; in addition to strong writing skills and thorough knowledge of the subject matter, we require a detailed analysis of the competition.

HARVEST HOUSE PUBLISHERS

990 Owen Loop N., Eugene OR 97402. (541)343-0123. Fax: (541)302-0731. Website: www.harvesthousepublishers.com. Estab. 1974. Publishes hardcover, trade paperback, and mass market paperback originals and reprints. **Publishes 160 titles/year. 1,500 queries received/year. 1,000 mss received/year. 1% of books from first-time authors. Pays royalty.**

Nonfiction Subjects include anthropology, archeology, business, economics, child guidance, health, medicine, money, finance, religion, womens issues, womens studies, Bible studies.

Fiction *No unsolicited mss, proposals, or artwork.* Agented submissions only.

Recent Title(s) *Praying Through the Bible,* by Stormie Omartian; *Cassidy,* by Lori Wick; *A Young Woman's Walk with God,* by Elizabeth George.

Tips "For first time/nonpublished authors we suggest building their literary résumé by submitting to magazines, or perhaps accruing book contributions."

HASTINGS HOUSE/DAYTRIPS PUBLISHERS

LINI LLC P.O. Box 908, Winter Park FL 32790-0908. (407)339-3600. Fax: (407)339-5900. E-mail: hastingshousebooks.com. Website: www.hastingshousebooks.com. **Contact:** Earl Steinbicker, senior travel editor (edits Daytrips Series). Publishes trade paperback originals and reprints. **Publishes 20 titles/year. 600 queries received/year. 900 mss received/year. 10% of books from first-time authors. 40% from unagented writers.** Publishes book 6-10 months after acceptance of ms. Responds in 2 months to queries.

O- We are primarily focused on expanding our Daytrips Travel Series (facts/guide) nationally and internationally. Currently de-emphasizing all other subjects.

Nonfiction Subjects include travel. Submit outline. Query.

Recent Title(s) *Daytrips Eastern Australia*, by James Postell; *Daytrips Italy*, by Earl Steinbicker (5th edition); *Daytrips Scotland & Wales*, by Judith Frances Duddle.

THE HAWORTH PRESS, INC.

325 Chestnut St., Suite 800, Philadelphia PA 19106. (607)722-5857. Fax: (607)771-0012. Website: www.haworthpress.com. **Contact:** Acquisitions Editor. Estab. 1973. Publishes hardcover and trade paperback originals. **Publishes 100 titles/year. 500 queries received/year. 250 mss received/year. 60% of books from first-time authors. 98% from unagented writers. Pays 7 ½-15% royalty on wholesale price.** Publishes book 1 year after acceptance of ms. Responds in 2 months to proposals. Guidelines available online.

Imprints Best Business Books; Food Products Press; Harrington Park Press; Alice Street Editions; Southern Tier Editions; International Business Press; Pharmaceutical Products Press; The Haworth Clinical Practice Press; The Haworth Hispanic/Latino Press; The Haworth Herbal Press; The Haworth Hospitality Press; The Haworth Information Press; The Haworth Integrative Healing Press; The Haworth Maltreatment & Trauma Press; The Haworth Medical Press; The Haworth Pastoral Press; The Haworth Social Work Practice Press; The Haworth Reference Press; The Haworth Political Press; The Haworth Judaic Press.

O- The Haworth Press is primarily a scholarly press.

Nonfiction Subjects include agriculture, business, economics, child guidance, cooking, foods, nutrition, gay, lesbian, health, medicine, horticulture, money, finance, psychology, sociology, womens issues, womens studies. Submit proposal package, outline, 1-3 sample chapters, bio. Reviews artwork/photos. Send photocopies.

Recent Title(s) *The Body Bears the Burden: Trauma, Dissociation, and Disease*; *The Mental Health Diagnostic Desk Reference: Visual Guides and More for Learning to Use the Diagnostic and Statistical Manual (DSM-IV-TR), 2nd Ed.*; *Handbook of Psychotropic Herbs: A Scientific Analysis of Herbal Remedies for Psychiatric Conditions*.

HAY HOUSE, INC.

P.O. Box 5100, Carlsbad CA 92018-5100. (760)431-7695. Fax: (760)431-6948. E-mail: pgift@hayhouse.com; afreemon@hayhouse.com. Website: www.hayhouse.com. **Contact:** East-coast acquisitions: Patty Gift, West-coast acquisitions: Alex Freemon. Estab. 1985. Publishes hardcover and trade paperback originals. **Publishes 50 titles/year. Pays standard royalty.** Publishes book 14-16 months after acceptance of ms. Accepts simultaneous submissions. Guidelines available online.

Imprints Hay House Lifestyles; New Beginnings Press; SmileyBooks.

O- We publish books, audios, and videos that help heal the planet.

Nonfiction Subjects include cooking, foods, nutrition, education, health, medicine, money, finance, nature, environment, new age, philosophy, psychology, sociology, womens issues, womens studies, mind/body/spirit. Agented submissions only. No email submissions.

Recent Title(s) *Inspiration*, by Dr. Wayne W. Dyer; *Yes, You Can Be a Successful Income Investor!*, by Ben Stein and Phil Demuth; *Secrets & Mysteries of the World*, by Sylvia Browne.

Tips Our audience is concerned with our planet, the healing properties of love, and general self-help principles. If I were a writer trying to market a book today, I would research the market thoroughly to make sure there weren't already too many books on the subject I was interested in writing about. Then I would make sure I had a unique slant on my idea. Simultaneous submissions from agents must include SASE's. No e-mail submissions.

HEALTH COMMUNICATIONS, INC.

3201 SW 15th St., Deerfield Beach FL 33442. (954)360-0909. Fax: (954)360-0034. Website: www.hcibooks.com. **Contact:** Michele Matrisciani, editorial director; Allison Janse, executive editor; Carol Rosenberg, managing editor; Candace Johnson, assistant editor. Estab. 1976. Publishes hardcover and trade paperback nonfiction only. **Publishes 60 titles/year.** Responds in 3-6 months to queries. Responds in 3-6 months to proposals. Guidelines available online.

O- "We are the Life Issues Publisher. Health Communications, Inc., strives to help people grow and improve their lives, from physical and emotional health to finances and interpersonal relationships."

Nonfiction Subjects include child guidance, health, parenting, psychology, womens issues, womens studies, young adult, Self-help.

Recent Title(s) *Zig-zagging*, by Tom Wilson; *Blue Collar and Proud of It*, by Joe Lamacchi with Bridget

Samburg; *Staging Your Comeback*, by Christopher Hopkins; *Success Principles for Teens*, by Jack Canfield and Kent Healy.

WILLIAM S. HEIN & CO., INC.

1285 Main St., Buffalo NY 14209-1987. (716)882-2600. Fax: (716)883-8100. E-mail: sjarrett@wshein.com. Website: www.wshein.com. **Contact:** Sheila Jarrett, publications manager. Estab. 1961. **Publishes 30 titles/year. 80 queries received/year. 40 mss received/year. 30% of books from first-time authors. 100% from unagented writers. Pays 10-20% royalty on net price** Publishes book 9 months after acceptance of ms. Accepts simultaneous submissions. Responds in 3 months to queries. Book catalog available online. Guidelines: send email for info and mss proposal form.

O→ William S. Hein & Co. publishes reference books for law librarians, legal researchers, and those interested in legal writing. Currently emphasizing legal research, legal writing, and legal education.

Nonfiction Subjects include education, government, politics, womens issues, world affairs, legislative histories.

Recent Title(s) *A Higher Law*, by Jeffrey A. Brauch; *Reflections of a Lawyer's Soul*, edited by Amy Timmer & Nelson P. Miller; *Acing Your First Year of Law School 2nd ed.*, by Shana Connell Noyes & Henry S. Noyes; *Congress and Sports Agents: A Legislative History of the Sports Agent Responsibility and Trust Act (SPARTA)*, by Edmund P. Edmonds & William H. Manz; *California Legal Research Handbook 2nd ed.*, by Larry D. Dershem; *1000 Days to the Bar*, by Dennis J. Tonsing; *Librarian's Copyright Companion*, by James S. Heller.

HEINEMANN

Reed Elsevier (USA) Inc. 361 Hanover St., Portsmouth NH 03801-3912. (603)431-7894. Fax: (603)431-7840. E-mail: proposals@heinemann.com. Website: www.heinemann.com. Estab. 1977. Publishes hardcover and trade paperback originals. **Publishes 80-100 titles/year. 50% of books from first-time authors. 75% from unagented writers. Pays royalty on wholesale price. Pays variable advance.** Responds in 6-8 weeks to proposals. Book catalog available free. Guidelines available online.

Imprints Boynton/Cook Publishers.

O→ Heinemann specializes in professional resources for educators and theater professionals. Our goal is to offer a wide selecton of books that satisfy the needs and interests of educators from kindergarten to college. Currently emphasizing literacy education, social studies, mathematics, science, K-12 education through technology, drama and drama education.

Nonfiction Query with SASE. Submit proposal package, outline, 1-2 sample chapters, TOC.

Recent Title(s) *Word Matters*, by Irene Fountas and Gay-Su Pinnell.

Tips Keep your queries (and manuscripts!) short, study the market, be realistic and prepared to promote your book.

HELLGATE PRESS

P.O. Box 3531, Ashland OR 97520. (541)973-5154. E-mail: harley@hellgatepress.com. Website: www.hellgatepress.com. **Contact:** Harley B. Patrick, editor. Estab. 1996. **Publishes 15-20 titles/year. 85% of books from first-time authors. 95% from unagented writers. Pays royalty.** Publishes book 6-9 months after acceptance of ms. Responds in 2 months to queries.

O→ Hellgate Press specializes in military history, other military topics, and travel adventure.

Nonfiction Subjects include history, memoirs, military, war, travel adventure. Query/proposal only with SASE or by e-mail. *Do not send mss.* Reviews artwork/photos. Send photocopies.

Recent Title(s) *Wheels On Fire*, by Michelle Zaremba; *Hello Darling*, by Stanley Morris; *A Patch of Ground*, by Michael Archer.

HENDRICKSON PUBLISHERS, INC.

140 Summit St., P.O. Box 3473, Peabody MA 01961-3473. Fax: (978)573-8276. E-mail: editorial@hendrickson.com. Website: www.hendrickson.com. **Contact:** Shirley Decker-Lucke, editorial director. Estab. 1983. Publishes trade reprints and scholarly material in the areas of New Testament; Hebrew Bible; religion and culture; patristics; Judaism; and practical, historical, and Biblical theology. **Publishes 35 titles/year. 800 queries received/year. 10% of books from first-time authors. 90% from unagented writers.** Publishes book an average of 1 year after acceptance of ms. Responds in 3-4 months to queries. Book catalog and ms guidelines for #10 SASE.

O→ Hendrickson is an academic publisher of books that give insight into Bible understanding (academically) and encourage spiritual growth (popular trade). Currently emphasizing Biblical helps and reference, ministerial helps, Biblical studies and de-emphasizing fiction and biography.

Nonfiction Subjects include religion. Submit outline, sample chapters, and CV.

HENRY HOLT & CO. BOOKS FOR YOUNG READERS

Imprint of Henry Holt & Co., LLC 175 Fifth Ave., New York NY 10010. (646)307-5087. Website: www.henryholtkids.com. **Contact:** Submissions Editor. Publishes hardcover originals of picture books, chapter books, middle grade and young adult novels. **Publishes 70-80 titles/year. 10% of books from first-time authors. 50% from unagented writers. Pays $3,000 and up advance.** Publishes book 18-36 months after acceptance of ms. Book catalog for 8 ½x11 SASE with $1.75 postage. Guidelines available online.

- Please do not send SASE. No response unless interested in publication.

"Henry Holt Books for Young Readers publishes highly original and cutting-edge fiction and nonfiction for all ages, from the very young to the young adult."

Nonfiction Submit complete ms.

Fiction Subjects include adventure, fantasy, historical, mainstream, contemporary, multicultural, picture books, young adult. Juvenile: adventure, animal, contemporary, fantasy, history, multicultural. Picture books: animal, concept, history, mulitcultural, sports. Young adult: contemporary, fantasy, history, multicultural, nature/environment, problem novels, sports. Submit complete ms.

JOSEPH HENRY PRESS

National Academy Press 500 5th St., NW, Lockbox 285, Washington DC 20055. (202)334-3336. Fax: (202)334-2793. E-mail: tsmith@nas.edu. Website: www.jhpress.org. **Contact:** Terrell Smith, project editor. Publishes hardcover and trade paperback originals. **Publishes 15-20 titles/year. 200 queries received/year. 60 mss received/year. 30% of books from first-time authors. 50% from unagented writers. Pays standard trade book list-price royalties. Pays occasional, varying royalty advance.** Publishes book 1 year after acceptance of ms. Accepts simultaneous submissions. Responds in 1 month to queries.

The Joseph Henry Press seeks manuscripts in general science and technology that will appeal to young scientists and established professionals or to interested lay readers within the overall categories of science, technology and health. We'll be looking at everything from astrophysics to the environment to nutrition.

Nonfiction Subjects include health, medicine, nature, environment, psychology, technology, nutrition, physical sciences. Submit proposal package, bio, TOC, prospectus (via mail or e-mail), SASE.

Recent Title(s) *Prime Obsession: Berhard Riemann and the Greatest Unsolved Problem in Mathematics*, by John Derbyshire; *Einstein Defiant: Genius Versus Genius in the Quantum Revolution*, by Edmund Blair Bolles; *Mendel in the Kitchen: A Scientist's View of Genetically Modified Foods*, by Nina V. Fedoroff and Nancy Marie Brown.

HEYDAY BOOKS

Box 9145, Berkeley CA 94709-9145. Fax: (510)549-1889. E-mail: heyday@heydaybooks.com. Website: www.heydaybooks.com. **Contact:** Gayle Wattawa, acquisitions editor. Estab. 1974. Publishes hardcover originals, trade paperback originals and reprints. **Publishes 12-15 titles/year. 50% of books from first-time authors. 90% from unagented writers. Pays 8% royalty on net price.** Publishes book 10 months after acceptance of ms. Responds in 2 months to queries. Responds in 2 months to manuscripts. Book catalog for 7 x 9 SAE with 3 first-class stamps.

Heyday Books publishes nonfiction books and literary anthologies with a strong California focus. We publish books about Native Americans, natural history, history, literature, and recreation, with a strong California focus.

Nonfiction Books about California only.Subjects include Americana, ethnic, history, nature, environment, recreation, regional, travel. Query with outline and synopsis. Reviews artwork/photos.

Recent Title(s) *Dark God of Eros: A William Everson Reader*, edited by Albert Gelpi; *The High Sierra of California*, by Gary Snyder and Tom Killion; *Under the Fifth Sun: Latino Literature from California*, edited by Rick Heidre.

HIDDENSPRING

997 Macarthur Blvd., Mahwah NJ 07430. (201)825-7300. Fax: (201)825-8345. Website: www.hiddenspringbooks.com. **Contact:** Paul McMahon, managing editor (nonfiction/spirituality). Publishes hardcover and trade paperback originals and reprints. **Publishes 10-12 titles/year. 5% of books from first-time authors. 10% from unagented writers. Royalty varies. Pays variable advance.**

- *Currently not accepting unsolicited submissions.*

"Books should always have a spiritual angle—nonfiction with a spiritual twist."

Nonfiction Subjects include Americana, art, architecture, creative nonfiction, ethnic, history, multicultural, psychology, religion.

Recent Title(s) *Frances of Assisi*, by Adrian House; *Before the Living God*, by Ruth Burrows, OCD; *Becoming Who You Are*, by James Martin, SJ.

HILL AND WANG

Farrar Straus & Giroux, Inc. 19 Union Square W., New York NY 10003. (212)741-6900. Fax: (212)633-9385. E-mail: fsg.editorial@fsgbooks.com. Website: www.fsgbooks.com. **Contact:** Thomas LeBien, publisher; Elisabeth Sifton, editor; June Kim, assistant editor. Estab. 1956. Publishes hardcover and trade paperbacks. **Publishes 12 titles/year. 1,500 queries received/year. 50% of books from first-time authors. 50% from**

unagented writers. Pays 10% royalty on retail price to 5,000 copies sold, 12 ½% to 10,000 copies, 15% thereafter on hardcover; 7 ½% on retail price for paperback Publishes book 1 year after acceptance of ms. Accepts simultaneous submissions. Book catalog available free.

- Hill and Wang publishes serious nonfiction books, primarily in history, science, mathematics and the social sciences. We are not considering new fiction, drama, or poetry.

Nonfiction Subjects include government, politics, history, American. Submit outline, sample chapters. SASE and a letter explaining rationale for book .

HILL STREET PRESS

191 E. Broad St., Suite 216, Athens GA 30601. (706)613-7200. Fax: (706)613-7204. E-mail: editorial@hillstreetpress.com. Website: www.hillstreetpress.com. **Contact:** Acquisitions Editor. Estab. 1998. Publishes hardcover originals, trade paperback originals and reprints. **Publishes 20 titles/year. 300+ queries received/year. 5% of books from first-time authors. 2% from unagented writers. Pays varied royalty on wholesale or list price. 12+ months** Accepts simultaneous submissions. Responds in 3 months to queries and proposals. Do not send mss. Book catalog and ms guidelines available online.

Imprints HSP (southern regional nonfiction), Graphedia (graphic novels), College Trivia, Broad Street (children's), Hot Cross Books (crosswords).

- HSP is a Southern regional press. While we are not a scholarly or academic press, our nonfiction titles must meet the standards of research for an exacting general audience.

Nonfiction Subjects include Americana, cooking, foods, nutrition, creative nonfiction, gardening, gay, lesbian, history, memoirs, nature, environment, recreation, regional, Southern, sports, travel, and sports. Submissions must be made by email only and must include cover letter, overview, marketing proposals, and up to three sample chapters. Do not send hard copies to our office. No unsolicited submissions accepted for Crossword or College Trivia imprints.

Fiction We do not publish fiction.

Recent Title(s) *Cooking With Jack, Paranoid Nation, Stone Age Santa, Secretary to a King, Tim & Sally's Beach Adventure.*

Tips Audience is discerning with an interest in the history, current issues, and food of the American South

HIPPOCRENE BOOKS, INC.

171 Madison Ave., New York NY 10016. (212)685-4371. Fax: (212)779-9338. Website: www.hippocrenebooks.com. **Contact:** Rebecca Cole, editor (food and wine); Robert Martin, editor (foreign language, dictionaries, language guides); Sophie Fels, editor (history, nonfiction). Estab. 1971. Publishes hardcover and trade paperback originals. **Publishes 60-80 titles/year. 10% of books from first-time authors. 95% from unagented writers. Pays 6-10% royalty on retail price. Pays $1,500 advance.** Publishes book 16 months after acceptance of ms. Accepts simultaneous submissions. Responds in 2 months to queries. Book catalog for 9 X12 SAE with 5 first-class stamps. Guidelines for #10 SASE.

- We focus on ethnic-interest and language-related titles, particularly on less frequently published languages and often overlooked cultures. Currently emphasizing concise foreign language dictionaries.

Nonfiction Subjects include cooking, foods, nutrition, ethnic, history, language, literature, military, war, multicultural, travel. Submit proposal package, outline, 2 sample chapters, TOC.

Recent Title(s) *Yoruba Practical Dictionary*; *A History of the Islamic World*; *Secrets of Colombian Cooking*.

Tips Our recent successes in publishing general books considered midlist by larger publishers are making us more of a general trade publisher. We continue to do well with reference books like dictionaries and other language related titles. We ask for proposal, sample chapter, and table of contents. If we are interested, we will reply with a request for more material.

HISTORY PUBLISHING COMPANY, INC.

P.O. Box 700, Palisades NY 10964. Fax: (845)359-8282. E-mail: historypublish@aol.com. Website: www.historypublishingco.com. **Contact:** Leslie Hayes, editorial director. Estab. 2001. Publishes hardcover and trade paperback originals and reprints; also, electronic reprints. **Publishes 20 titles/year. 50% of books from first-time authors. 75% from unagented writers. Pays 7-10% royalty on wholesale price. Does not pay advances to unpublished authors.** Publishes book 1 year after acceptance of ms. Accepts simultaneous submissions. Responds in 1 month to queries. Responds in 1 month to proposals. Responds in 2 months to manuscripts. Guidelines via e-mail.

Nonfiction Subjects include Americana, business, economics, contemporary culture, creative nonfiction, government, politics, history, military, war, social sciences, sociology, world affairs. Query with SASE. Submit proposal package, outline, 3 sample chapters. Submit complete ms. Reviews artwork/photos. Send photocopies.

Recent Title(s) *History Publishing Company: Homeland Insecurity; The Words of War; Hunting the American Terrorist; A Lovely Little War; Legerdemain. Today's Books imprint: How To Survive in an Organization; Career of Gold.*

Tips We focus on an audience interested in the events that shaped the world we live in and the events of today that continue to shape that world. Focus on interesting and serious events that will appeal to the contemporary reader. That reader likes easy-to-read history that flows from one page to the next. If you have a good story, we will help you develop it and guide you to a finish.

HOLIDAY HOUSE, INC.

425 Madison Ave., New York NY 10017. (212)688-0085. Fax: (212)421-6134. **Contact:** Mary Cash, editor-in-chief. Estab. 1935. Publishes hardcover originals and paperback reprints. **Publishes 50 titles/year. 5% of books from first-time authors. 50% from unagented writers. Pays royalty on list price, range varies. agent's royalty.** Publishes book 1-2 years after acceptance of ms. Guidelines for #10 SASE.

O→ Holiday House publishes children's and young adult books for the school and library markets. We have a commitment to publishing first-time authors and illustrators. We specialize in quality hardcovers from picture books to young adult, both fiction and nonfiction, primarily for the school and library market.

Nonfiction Subjects include Americana, history, science, Judaica. Query with SASE. Reviews artwork/photos. Send Send photocopies—no originals.

Fiction Subjects include adventure, historical, humor, literary, mainstream, contemporary, Judaica and holiday, animal stories for young readers. Children's books only. Query with SASE. No phone calls, please.

Tips We need manuscripts with strong stories and writing.

HOLMES & MEIER PUBLISHERS, INC.

P.O. Box 943, Teaneck NJ 07666. Website: www.holmesandmeier.com. **Contact:** Maggie Kennedy, managing editor. Estab. 1969. Publishes hardcover and paperback originals. **Publishes 20 titles/year. Pays royalty.** Publishes book an average of 18 months after acceptance of ms. Responds in 6 months to queries. Book catalog available free.

Imprints Africana Publishing Co.

O→ "We are noted as an academic publishing house and are pleased with our reputation for excellence in the field. However, we are also expanding our list to include books of more general interest."

Nonfiction Subjects include art, architecture, business, economics, ethnic, government, politics, history, literary criticism, regional, translation, women's issues, women's studies. Query first with outline, sample chapters, cv and idea of intended market/audience.

⊘ HENRY HOLT & CO. LLC

Holtzbrinck Publishers 175 Fifth Ave., New York NY 10010. (646)307-5095. Fax: (212)633-0748. Website: www.henryholt.com. Estab. 1866.

Imprints Books for Young Readers; John Macrae Books; Metropolitan Books; Owl Books; Times Books.

- *Does not accept unsolicited queries or mss.*

O→ Holt is a general-interest publisher of quality fiction and nonfiction.

Recent Title(s) *The Many Lives of Marilyn Monroe*, by Sarah Churchwell; *Science Friction: Where the Known Meets the Unknown*, by Michael Shermer; *American Mafia: A History of Its Rise to Power*, by Thomas Reppetto.

A ⊘ HONOR BOOKS

Cook Communications Ministries 4050 Lee Vance View, Colorado Springs CO 80918. (719)536-0100. E-mail: info@honorbooks.com. Website: www.honorbooks.com. Publishes hardcover and trade paperback originals. **Pays royalty on wholesale price, makes outright purchase or assigns work for hire Pays negotiable advance.**

- *Currently closed to book proposals.*

O→ We are a Christian publishing house with a mission to inspire and encourage people to draw near to God and to enjoy His love and grace. We are no longer accepting unsolicited mss from writers. Currently emphasizing humor, personal and spiritual growth, children's books, devotions, personal stories.

Nonfiction Subjects include religion, motivation, devotionals.

Recent Title(s) *Welcome Home*, by Liz Cowen Furman; *Breakfast for the Soul*, by Judy Couchman.

Tips Our books are for busy, achievement-oriented people who are looking for a balance between reaching their goals and knowing that God loves them unconditionally. Our books encourage spiritual growth, joyful living and intimacy with God. Write about what you are for and not what you are against. We look for scripts that are biblically based and which inspire readers.

HOUGHTON MIFFLIN BOOKS FOR CHILDREN

Imprint of Houghton Mifflin Trade & Reference Division 222 Berkeley St., Boston MA 02116. (617)351-5959.

Fax: (617)351-1111. E-mail: children's_books@hmco.com. Website: www.houghtonmifflinbooks.com. **Contact:** Erica Zappy, associate editor; Kate O'Sullivan, senior editor; Anne Rider, executive editor; Margaret Raymo, editorial director. Publishes hardcover originals and trade paperback originals and reprints. **Publishes 100 titles/year. 5,000 queries received/year. 14,000 mss received/year. 10% of books from first-time authors. 60% from unagented writers. Pays 5-10% royalty on retail price. Pays variable advance.** Publishes book 18-24 months after acceptance of ms. Accepts simultaneous submissions. Responds in 4-6 months to queries. Guidelines available online.

Imprints Sandpiper Paperback Books; Graphia.

- Does not respond to or return mss unless interested.

O→ Houghton Mifflin gives shape to ideas that educate, inform, and above all, delight.

Nonfiction Subjects include animals, anthropology, archeology, art, architecture, ethnic, history, language, literature, music, dance, nature, environment, science, sports. Query with SASE. Submit sample chapters, synopsis. Reviews artwork/photos. Send photocopies.

Fiction Subjects include adventure, ethnic, historical, humor, juvenile, early readers, literary, mystery, picture books, suspense, young adult, board books. Submit complete ms.

Recent Title(s) *The Willoughbys*, by Lois Lowry; *Hogwash*, by Arthur Geisert; *Trainstop*, by Barbara Lehman.

Tips Faxed or e-mailed manuscripts and proposals are not considered. Complete submission guidelines available on website.

HOUGHTON MIFFLIN HARCOURT CO.

222 Berkeley St., Boston MA 02116. (617)351-5000. Website: www.hmhbooks.com. **Contact:** Submissions Editor. Estab. 1832. Publishes hardcover originals and trade paperback originals and reprints. Book catalog available online.

Imprints American Heritage Dictionaries; Clarion Books; Great Source Education Group; Houghton Mifflin; Houghton Mifflin Books for Children; Houghton Mifflin Paperbacks; Mariner Books; McDougal Littell; Peterson Field Guides; Riverside Publishing; Sunburst Technology; Taylor's Gardening Guides; Edusoft; Promissor; Walter Lorraine Books; Kingfisher.

O→ "Houghton Mifflin Harcourt gives shape to ideas that educate, inform and delight. In a new era of publishing, our legacy of quality thrives as we combine imagination with technology, bringing you new ways to know."

Nonfiction Subjects include audio, agriculture, animals, anthropology, archaeology, cooking, foods, nutrition, ethnic, gardening, gay, lesbian, health, medicine, history, memoirs, military, war, social sciences. Agented submissions only. Unsolicited mss returned unopened.

Fiction Subjects include literary. We are not a mass market publisher. Study the current list. Agented submissions only.

Recent Title(s) *The Namesake*, by Jhumpa Lahiri; *Indignation*, by Philip Roth.

Tips "Our audience is high end literary."

HOUSE OF COLLECTIBLES

Imprint of Random House, Inc., 1745 Broadway, 15th Floor, New York NY 10019. E-mail: houseofcollectibles@randomhouse.com. Website: www.houseofcollectibles.com. Publishes trade and mass market paperback originals. **Royalty on retail price varies. Pays varied advance.** Book catalog available free.

Imprints Official Price Guide series.

O→ One of the premier publishing companies devoted to books on a wide range of antiques and collectibles, House of Collectibles publishes books for the seasoned expert and the beginning collector alike.

Nonfiction Subjects include art, architecture, fine art, architecture, sports, comic books, American patriotic memorabilia, clocks, character toys, coins, stamps, costume jewelry, knives, books, military, glassware, records, arts and crafts, Native American collectibles, pottery, fleamarkets. Accepts unsolicited proposals.

Recent Title(s) *The Official Price Guide to Records*, by Jerry Osborne; *The One-Minute Coin Expert*, by John Travers.

Tips We have been publishing price guides and other books on antiques and collectibles for over 35 years and plan to meet the needs of collectors, dealers, and appraisers well into the 21st century.

HOW BOOKS

Imprint of F+W Media, Inc. 4700 E. Galbraith Rd., Cincinnati OH 45236. (513)531-2690, ext. 1408. E-mail: megan.patrick@fwpubs.com. Website: www.howdesign.com. **Contact:** Megan Patrick, acquisitions editor. Estab. 1985. Publishes hardcover and trade paperback originals. **Publishes 15 titles/year. 50 queries received/year. 5 mss received/year. 50% of books from first-time authors. 50% from unagented writers. Pays 10% royalty on wholesale price. Pays $2,000-6,000 advance.** Publishes book 18-24 months after acceptance of ms. Accepts simultaneous submissions. Responds in 1 month to queries. Responds in 1 month to proposals. Responds in 3 months to manuscripts. Book catalog available online. Guidelines available online.

Nonfiction Subjects include art, architecture, graphic design, creativity, pop culture. Query with SASE. Submit proposal package, outline, 1 sample chapters, sample art or sample design. Reviews artwork/photos. Send photocopies and PDF's (if submitting electronically).

Recent Title(s) *Milk Eggs Vodka*, by Bill Keaggy (humor/pop culture); *Monster Spotter's Guide to North America*, by Scott Francis (humor); *Color Index 2*, by Jim Krause (graphic design).

Tips Audience comprised of graphic designers. Your art, design, or concept.

HUDSON HILLS PRESS, INC.

3556 Main St., Box 205, Manchester VT 05254. (802)362-6450. Fax: (802)362-6459. E-mail: editorial@hudsonhills.com. Website: www.hudsonhills.com. **Contact:** Acquisitions Editor. Estab. 1978. Publishes hardcover and paperback originals. **Publishes 15+ titles/year. 15% of books from first-time authors. 90% from unagented writers. Pays 4-6% royalty on retail price. Pays $3,500 average advance.** Publishes book 1 year after acceptance of ms. Accepts simultaneous submissions. Responds in 2 months to queries. Book catalog for 6 x 9 SAE with 2 first-class stamps.

O→ Hudson Hills Press publishes books about art and photography, including monographs.

Nonfiction Subjects include art, architecture, photography. Query first, then submit outline and sample chapters. Reviews artwork/photos.

Recent Title(s) *Robert Vickrey: The Magic of Realism, by Philip Eliasoph; Kenneth Snelson: Forces Made Visible, by Eleanor Heartney.*

HUMAN KINETICS PUBLISHERS, INC.

P.O. Box 5076, Champaign IL 61825-5076. (800)747-4457. Fax: (217)351-1549. Website: www.humankinetics.com. **Contact:** Ted Miller, VP special acquisitions. Estab. 1974. Publishes hardcover, ebooks, and paperback text and reference books, trade paperback originals, course software and audiovisual. **Publishes 160 titles/year. Pays 10-15% royalty on net income.** Publishes book up to 18 months after acceptance of ms. Accepts simultaneous submissions. Responds in 2 months to queries. Book catalog available free. Guidelines available online.

Imprints HK.

O→ "*Human Kinetics* publishes books which provide expert knowledge in sport and fitness training and techniques, physical education, sports sciences and sports medicine for coaches, athletes and fitness enthusiasts and professionals in the physical action field."

Nonfiction Subjects include education, health, medicine, psychology, recreation, sports, sciences. Submit outline, sample chapters. Reviews artwork/photos.

HUNTER HOUSE

P.O. Box 2914, Alameda CA 94501. (510)865-5282. Fax: (510)865-4295. E-mail: acquisitions@hunterhouse.com. Website: www.hunterhouse.com. **Contact:** Jeanne Brondino, acquisitions editor; Kiran S. Rana, publisher. Estab. 1978. Publishes trade paperback originals and reprints. **Publishes 18 titles/year. 200-300 queries received/year. 100 mss received/year. 50% of books from first-time authors. 80% from unagented writers. Pays 12% royalty on net receipts Pays $500-3,000 advance.** Publishes book 1-2 years after acceptance of ms. Accepts simultaneous submissions. Responds in 2 months to queries. Responds in 3 months to proposals. Book catalog for 8 ½x11 SAE with 3 first-class stamps. Guidelines available online.

O→ Hunter House publishes health books (especially women's health), self-help health, sexuality and couple relationships, violence prevention and intervention. De-emphasizing reference, self-help psychology.

Nonfiction Subjects include health, medicine, self-help, women's health, fitness, relationships, sexuality, personal growth, and violence prevention. Query with proposal package, including synopsis, TOC, and chapter outline, sample chapter, target audience information, competition, and what distinguishes the book. Reviews artwork/photos. Send Send photocopies, proposals generally not returned, requested mss returned with SASE. Reviews artwork/photos as part of ms package.

Recent Title(s) *The Cortisol Connection*, by Shawn Talbott; *Tantric Sex for Women*, by Christa Schulte; *How to Spot a Dangerous Man*, by Sandra Brown.

Tips Audience is concerned people who are looking to educate themselves and their community about real-life issues that affect them. Please send as much information as possible about who your audience is, how your book addresses their needs, and how you reach that audience in your ongoing work.

HUNTER PUBLISHING, INC.

P.O. Box 746, Walpole MA 02081. Fax: (772)546-8040. Website: www.hunterpublishing.com. **Contact:** Kim Andre, editor; Lissa Dailey. Estab. 1985. **Publishes 100 titles/year. 10% of books from first-time authors. 75% from unagented writers. Pays royalty. Pays negotiable advance.** Publishes book 5 months after acceptance of ms. Accepts simultaneous submissions. Responds in 3 weeks to queries. Responds in 1 month to manuscripts. Book catalog for #10 envelope and 4 First-Class stamps.

Imprints Adventure Guides; Romantic Weekends Guides; Alive Guides.

O→ Hunter Publishing publishes practical guides for travelers going to the Caribbean, US, Europe, South

America, and the far reaches of the globe.

Nonfiction Subjects include regional, travel, travel guides. Query, or submit outline/synopsis and sample chapters. Reviews artwork/photos.

Recent Title(s) *Adventure Guide to Canada's Atlantic Provinces*, by Barbara Radcliffe-Rogers.

Tips Guides should be destination-specific, rather than theme-based alone. Thus, `Travel with Kids' is too broad; `Italy with Kids' is OK. Make sure the guide doesn't duplicate what other guide publishers do.

IBEX PUBLISHERS

P.O. Box 30087, Bethesda MD 20824. (301)718-8188. Fax: (301)907-8707. E-mail: info@ibexpub.com. Website: www.ibexpublishers.com. Estab. 1979. Publishes hardcover and trade paperback originals and reprints. **Publishes 10-12 titles/year. Payment varies.** Accepts simultaneous submissions. Book catalog available free.

Imprints Iranbooks Press.

O→ IBEX publishes books about Iran and the Middle East and about Persian culture and literature.

Nonfiction Subjects include cooking, foods, nutrition, language, literature. Query with SASE, or submit proposal package, including outline and 2 sample chapters.

ICONOGRAFIX, INC.

1830A Hanley Rd., P.O. Box 446, Hudson WI 54016. (715)381-9755. Fax: (715)381-9756. E-mail: dcfrautschi@iconografixinc.com. Website: www.enthusiastbooks.com. **Contact:** Dylan Frautschi, acquisitions manager (transportation). Estab. 1992. Publishes trade paperback originals. **Publishes 24 titles/year. 100 queries received/year. 20 mss received/year. 50% of books from first-time authors. 100% from unagented writers. Pays 8-12% royalty on wholesale price. Pays $1,000-3,000 advance.** Publishes book 1 year after acceptance of ms. Accepts simultaneous submissions. Responds in 1 month to queries. Responds in 3 months to proposals. Responds in 3 months to manuscripts. Book catalog and ms guidelines free.

O→ Iconografix publishes special, historical-interest photographic books for transportation equipment enthusiasts. Currently emphasizing emergency vehicles, buses, trucks, railroads, automobiles, auto racing, construction equipment, snowmobiles.

Nonfiction Interested in photo archives.Subjects include Americana, photos from archives of historic places, objects, people, history, hobbies, military, war, transportation (older photos of specific vehicles). Query with SASE, or submit proposal package, including outline. Reviews artwork/photos. Send photocopies.

Recent Title(s) *Trolley Buses Around the World*, by William A. Luke; *Vintage Snowmobilia*, by Jon D. Bertolinol.

N ILR PRESS

Cornell University Press Sage House, 512 E. State St., Ithaca NY 14850. (607)277-2338. Fax: (607)277-2374. **Contact:** Frances Benson, editorial director (fgb2@cornell.edu). Estab. 1945. Publishes hardcover and trade paperback originals and reprints. **Publishes 10-15 titles/year. Pays royalty.** Responds in 2 months to queries. Book catalog available free.

O→ We are interested in manuscripts with innovative perspectives on current workplace issues that concern both academics and the general public.

Nonfiction Subjects include business, economics, government, politics, history, sociology. Query with SASE. Submit outline, sample chapters, cv.

Recent Title(s) The Changing Face of Medicine: Women Doctors and the Evolution of Health Care in America, by Ann K. Boulis and Jerry A. Jacobs(2008); Transnational Tortillas: Race, Gender, and Shop-Floor Politics in Mexico and the United States, by Carolina Bank Muñoz (2008)Condensed Captalism: Campbell Soup and the Pursuit of Cheap production in the Twentieth Century, by Daniel Sidorick (2009);Counter Culture: The American Coffee Shop Waitress, by Candacy A. Taylor (2009).

Tips Manuscripts must be well documented to pass our editorial evaluation, which includes review by academics in related fields.

IMPACT BOOKS

Imprint of F+W Media, Inc. 4700 E. Galbraith Rd., Cincinnati OH 45236. Fax: (513)531-2686. E-mail: pam.wissman@fwmedia.com. Website: www.impact-books.com. **Contact:** Pamela Wissman, editorial director (art instruction for comics, manga, anime, fantasy, popular culture, graffiti, cartooning, body art). Estab. 2004. Publishes trade paperback originals and reprints. **Publishes 10 titles/year. 50 queries received/year. 10-12 mss received/year. 70% of books from first-time authors. 100% from unagented writers.** Publishes book 11 months after acceptance of ms. Accepts simultaneous submissions. Responds in 4 months to queries. Responds in 4 months to proposals. Responds in 2 months to manuscripts. Book catalog available free. Guidelines available online.

Nonfiction Subjects include art, art instruction, contemporary culture, creative nonfiction, hobbies. Submit proposal package, outline, 1 sample chapter, at least 1 example of sample art. Reviews artwork/photos. Send Digital art, hard copies, or anything that represents the art well, preferably in the form the author plans to submit art if contracted.

Recent Title(s) *The Insider's Guide to Creating Comics and Graphic Novels*, by Andy Schmidt; *GRAFF: the Art and Technique of Graffiti*, by Scape Martinez.

Tips Audience comprised primarily of 12- to 18-year-old beginners along the lines of comic buyers, in general—mostly teenagers—but also appealing to a broader audience of young adults 19-30 who need basic techniques. Art must appeal to teenagers and be submitted in a form that will reproduce well. Authors need to know how to teach beginners step-by-step. A sample step-by-step is important.

INCENTIVE PUBLICATIONS, INC.

2400 Crestmoor Rd., Suite 211, Nashville TN 37215. (615)385-2934. Fax: (615)385-2967. Website: www.incentivepublications.com. **Contact:** Patience Camplair, editor. Estab. 1970. Publishes paperback originals. **Publishes 25-30 titles/year. 25% of books from first-time authors. 100% from unagented writers. Pays royalty, or makes outright purchase.** Publishes book an average of 1 year after acceptance of ms. Responds in 1 month to queries. Guidelines available online.

- Incentive publishes developmentally appropriate teacher/parent resource materials and educational workbooks for children in grades K-12. Currently emphasizing primary material. Also interested in character education, English as a second language programs, early learning, current technology, related materials.

Nonfiction Subjects include education. Query with synopsis and detailed outline.

Recent Title(s) *The Ready to Learn Book Series*, by Imogene Forte (Grades pre K-K); *Drumming to the Beat of a Different Marcher*, by Debbie Silver; *As Reading Programs Come and Go, This Is What You Need to Know*, by Judith Cochran.

INDIANA HISTORICAL SOCIETY PRESS

450 W. Ohio St., Indianapolis IN 46202-3269. (317)233-6073. Fax: (317)233-0857. **Contact:** Submissions Editor. Estab. 1830. Publishes hardcover and paperback originals. **Publishes 10 titles/year.** Responds in 1 month to queries.

Nonfiction Subjects include agriculture, art, architecture, business, economics, ethnic, government, politics, history, military, war, sports, family history, children's books. Query with SASE.

Recent Title(s) *Gus Grissom: The Lost Astronaut*, by Ray E. Boomhower; *Skirting the Issue: Stories of Indiana's Historical Women Artists*, by Judith Vale Newton and Carol Ann Weiss; *Captured! A Boy Trapped in the Civil War*, by Mary Blair Immel.

INFORMATION TODAY, INC.

143 Old Marlton Pike, Medford NJ 08055. (609)654-6266. Fax: (609)654-4309. E-mail: jbryans@infotoday.com. Website: www.infotoday.com. **Contact:** John B. Bryans, editor-in-chief/publisher. Publishes hardcover and trade paperback originals. **Publishes 15-20 titles/year. 200 queries received/year. 30 mss received/year. 30% of books from first-time authors. 90% from unagented writers. Pays 10-15% royalty on wholesale price. Pays $500-2,500 advance.** Publishes book 9 months after acceptance of ms. Accepts simultaneous submissions. Responds in 1 month to queries. Responds in 2 months to proposals. Responds in 3 months to manuscripts. Book catalog free or on website. proposal guidelines free or via e-mail as attachment.

Imprints ITI (academic, scholarly, library science); CyberAge Books (high-end consumer and business technology books—emphasis on Internet/WWW topics including online research).

- We look for highly-focused coverage of cutting-edge technology topics, written by established experts and targeted to a tech-savvy readership. Virtually all our titles focus on how information is accessed, used, shared, and transformed into knowledge that can benefit people, business, and society. Currently emphasizing Internet/online technologies, including their social significance; biography, how-to, technical, reference, scholarly. De-emphasizing fiction.

Nonfiction Subjects include business, economics, computers, electronics, education, science, Internet and cyberculture. Query with SASE. Reviews artwork/photos. Send photocopies.

Recent Title(s) *Consider the Source: A Critical Guide to 100 Prominent News and Information Sites on the Web*, by James F. Broderick and Darren W. Miller; *Social Software in Libraries: Building Collaboration, Communication, and Community Online*, by Meredith G. Farkas; *The Extreme Searcher's Internet Handbook: A Guide for the Serious Searcher*, by Randolph Hock.

Tips Our readers include scholars, academics, indexers, librarians, information professionals (ITI imprint), as well as high-end consumer and business users of Internet/WWW/online technologies, and people interested in the marriage of technology with issues of social significance (i.e., cyberculture).

INNER TRADITIONS

Bear & Co. P.O. Box 388, Rochester VT 05767. (802)767-3174. Fax: (802)767-3726. E-mail: submissions@gotoit.com. Website: www.innertraditions.com. **Contact:** Jon Graham, editor. Estab. 1975. Publishes hardcover and trade paperback originals and reprints. **Publishes 60 titles/year. 5,000 queries received/year. 10% of books from first-time authors. 20% from unagented writers. Pays $1,000 average advance.** Publishes book 1 year after acceptance of ms. Responds in 3 months to queries. Responds in 6 months to manuscripts. Book catalog available free. Guidelines available online.

Imprints Destiny Audio Editions; Destiny Books; Destiny Recordings; Healing Arts Press; Inner Traditions; Inner Traditions En Español; Inner Traditions India; Park Street Press; Bear & Company; Bear Cub; Bindu Books.

- Inner Traditions publishes works representing the spiritual, cultural and mythic traditions of the world and works on alternative medicine and holistic health that combine contemporary thought with the knowledge of the world's great healing traditions. Currently emphasizing secret society research, alternative Christianity, indigenous spirituality, ancient history, alternative health, and advanced yoga.

Nonfiction We are interested in the relationship of the spiritual and transformative aspects of world cultures. Subjects include animals, art, architecture, child guidance, contemporary culture, natural foods, ethnic, fashion, health, medicine, alternative medicine, history, ancient history and mythology, music, dance, nature, environment, New Age, philosophy, esoteric, psychology, religion, world affairs religions, sex, spirituality, womens issues, womens studies, indigenous cultures. Query or submit outline and sample chapters with SASE. Does not return mss without SASE. Reviews artwork/photos.

Recent Title(s) *Books on Fire*, by Lucien Polastron; *Death of Religion and the Birth of Spirit*, by Joseph Chilton Pearce; *The Secret Teachings of Plants*, by Stephen Harrod Buhner.

Tips We are not interested in autobiographical stories of self-transformation. We do accept electronic submissions (via e-mail). We are not currently looking at fiction.

INNOVATIVEKIDS®

18 Ann St., Norwalk CT 06854. (203)836-6400. Fax: (203)852-7117. E-mail: marketing@innovativekids.com. Website: www.innovativekids.com. **Contact:** David Linker, editorial director. Trade and mass market paperback originals. **Publishes 50 titles/year.** Publishes book 12 months after acceptance of ms. Accepts simultaneous submissions. Catalog or guidelines not available.

Nonfiction Subjects include animals, crafts, education, entertainment, games. Submit manuscript via mail. Reviews artwork/photos; other original art.

Recent Title(s) *At the Seashore*, by Ruth Koeppel (children's); *The American Revolution*, by Douglas Rife and Gina Capaldi (children's); *Now I'm Reading! Write it! Draw it!* by Nora Gaydos (children's).

Tips Our audience is children from birth to age 12.

INSTITUTE OF POLICE TECHNOLOGY AND MANAGEMENT

University of North Florida 12000 Alumni Dr., Jacksonville FL 32224-2678. (904)620-4786. Fax: (904)620-2453. E-mail: rhodge@unf.edu. Website: www.iptm.org. **Contact:** Richard C. Hodge, editor. Estab. 1980. Usually publishes trade paperback originals. **Publishes 8 titles/year. 30 queries received/year. 12 mss received/year. 50% of books from first-time authors. 100% from unagented writers. Pays 25% royalty on actual sale price, or makes outright purchase of $300-2,000.** Publishes book 6 months after acceptance of ms. Responds in 3 weeks to queries.

- Our publications are principally for law enforcement. Will consider works in nearly every area of law enforcement.

Nonfiction Reviews artwork/photos.

Tips Manuscripts should not be submitted before the author has contacted IPTM's editor by e-mail or telephone. It is best to make this contact before completing a lengthy work such as a manual.

INTERLINK PUBLISHING GROUP, INC.

46 Crosby St., Northampton MA 01060. (413)582-7054. Fax: (413)582-7057. E-mail: info@interlinkbooks.com. Website: www.interlinkbooks.com. **Contact:** Michel Moushabeck, publisher. Estab. 1987. Publishes hardcover and trade paperback originals. **Publishes 50 titles/year. 30% of books from first-time authors. 50% from unagented writers. Pays 6-8% royalty on retail price. Pays small advance.** Publishes book 18 months after acceptance of ms. Accepts simultaneous submissions. Responds in 3-6 months to queries. Book catalog available free. Guidelines available online.

Imprints Crocodile Books, USA; Interlink Books; Olive Branch Press; Clockroot Books.

- Interlink publishes a general trade list of adult fiction and nonfiction with an emphasis on books that have a wide appeal while also meeting high intellectual and literary standards.

Nonfiction Submit outline and sample chapters.

Fiction Subjects include ethnic, international adult. We are looking for translated works relating to the Middle East, Africa or Latin America. Query with SASE. Submit outline, sample chapters.

Recent Title(s) *B as in Beirut*, by Iman Humaydan Younes; *Debunking 9/11 Debunking*, by David Ray Griffin; *Flawed Landscape*, by Sharif S. Elmusa; *The Novel*, by Nawal el Saadawi.

Tips Any submissions that fit well in our publishing program will receive careful attention. A visit to our website, your local bookstore, or library to look at some of our books before you send in your submission is recommended.

INTERNATIONAL CITY/COUNTY MANAGEMENT ASSOCIATION

777 N. Capitol St. NE, Suite 500, Washington DC 20002. (202)962-4262. Fax: (202)962-3500. Website: www.icma.org. **Contact:** Christine Ulrich, editorial director. Estab. 1914. Publishes hardcover and paperback originals. **Publishes 10-15 titles/year. 50 queries received/year. 20 mss received/year. 20% of books from first-time authors. 100% from unagented writers. Makes negotiable outright purchase. Pays occasional advance.** Publishes book 18 months after acceptance of ms. Responds in 2 months to queries. Book catalog available online. Guidelines available online.

O→ Our mission is to create excellence in local government by developing and fostering professional local government management worldwide.

Nonfiction Subjects include government, politics, local. Query with outline and 1 sample chapter. Reviews artwork/photos. Send photocopies.

Recent Title(s) *Emergency Management*; *Service Contracting*; *A Budgeting Guide for Local Government*.

Tips Our mission is to enhance the quality of local government and to support and assist professional local administrators in the United States and other countries.

INTERNATIONAL FOUNDATION OF EMPLOYEE BENEFIT PLANS

18700 W. Bluemound Rd., Brookfield WI 53045. (262)786-6700. Fax: (262)786-8780. E-mail: bookstore@ifebp.org. Website: www.ifebp.org. **Contact:** Dee Birschel, senior director of publications. Estab. 1954. Publishes trade paperback originals. **Publishes 10 titles/year. 15% of books from first-time authors. 80% from unagented writers. Pays 5-15% royalty on wholesale and retail price.** Publishes book 1 year after acceptance of ms. Responds in 3 months to queries. Book catalog available free. Guidelines available online.

O→ IFEBP publishes general and technical monographs on all aspects of employee benefits—pension plans, health insurance, etc.

Nonfiction Subjects limited to health care, pensions, retirement planning and employee benefits and compensation.Query with outline.

Recent Title(s) *Managing Pharmacy Benefits*, by Randy Vogenberg and Joanne Sica; *Effective Benefit Communication*, by Ann Black.

Tips Be aware of interests of employers and the marketplace in benefits topics, for example, pension plan changes, healthcare cost containment.

INTERNATIONAL MARINE

The McGraw-Hill Companies P.O. Box 220, Camden ME 04843-0220. (207)236-4838. Fax: (207)236-6314. Website: www.internationalmarine.com. **Contact:** Acquisitions Editor. Estab. 1969. Publishes hardcover and paperback originals. **Publishes 50 titles/year. 500-700 mss received/year. 30% of books from first-time authors. 60% from unagented writers. Pays standard royalties based on net price. Pays advance.** Publishes book 1 year after acceptance of ms. Responds in 2 months to queries. Guidelines available online.

Imprints Ragged Mountain Press (sports and outdoor books that take you off the beaten path).

O→ International Marine publishes the best books about boats.

Nonfiction Publishes a wide range of subjects include: sea stories, seamanship, boat maintenance, etc.Query first with outline and 2-3 sample chapters. Reviews artwork/photos.

Recent Title(s) *How to Read a Nautical Chart*, by Nigel Caulder; *By the Grace of the Sea: A Woman's Solo Odyssey Around the World*, by Pat Henry; *Coaching Girls' Lacrosse: A Baffled Parent's Guide*, by Janine Tucker.

Tips Writers should be aware of the need for clarity, accuracy and interest. Many progress too far in the actual writing.

N INTERNATIONAL PRESS

P.O. Box 43502, Somerville MA 02143. (617)623-3855. Fax: (617)623-3101. Website: www.intlpress.com. **Contact:** Lisa Lin, general manager (research math and physics). Estab. 1992. Publishes hardcover originals and reprints. **Publishes 12 titles/year. 200 queries received/year. 500 mss received/year. 10% of books from first-time authors. 100% from unagented writers. Pays 3-10% royalty.** Publishes book 6 months after acceptance of ms. Responds in 5 months to queries. Responds in 5 months to proposals. Responds in 1 year to manuscripts. Book catalog available free. Guidelines available online.

Nonfiction Subjects include science. Submit complete ms. Reviews artwork/photos. Send EPS files.

Recent Title(s) *Collected Works on Ricci Flow*; *Current Developments in Mathematics*; *Surveys in Differential Geometry*.

Tips Audience is PhD mathematicians, researchers and students.

INTERNATIONAL SOCIETY FOR TECHNOLOGY IN EDUCATION (ISTE)

175 W. Broadway, Suite 300, Eugene OR 97401. (541)434-8928. Website: www.iste.org. **Contact:** Scott Harter, acquisitions and development editor. Publishes trade paperback originals. **Publishes 10 titles/year. 100 queries received/year. 40 mss received/year. 75% of books from first-time authors. 95% from unagented writers. Pays 10% royalty on retail price.** Publishes book 6-9 months after acceptance of ms. Accepts simultaneous submissions. Responds in 2 weeks to queries. Responds in 1 month to proposals. Responds in 1 month to

manuscripts. Book catalog and ms guidelines online.

O→ Currently emphasizing books on educational technology standards, curriculum integration, professional development, and assessment. De-emphasizing software how-to books.

Nonfiction Submit proposal package, outline, sample chapters, TOC, vita. Reviews artwork/photos. Send photocopies.

Recent Title(s) *1-to-1 Learning*, by Pamela Livingtson; *Nets.S Resources for Student Assessment*, by Peggy Kelly and John Haber; *Digital-Age Literary for Teachers*, by Susan Brooks-Young.

Tips Our audience is K-12 teachers, teacher educators, technology coordinators, and school and district administrators.

INTERNATIONAL WEALTH SUCCESS

P.O. Box 186, Merrick NY 11570-0186. (516)766-5850. Fax: (516)766-5919. **Contact:** Tyler G. Hicks, editor. Estab. 1967. **Publishes 10 titles/year. 100% of books from first-time authors. 100% from unagented writers. Pays 10% royalty on wholesale or retail price. Offers usual advance of $1,000, but this varies depending on author's reputation and nature of book. Buys all rights.** Publishes book 4 months after acceptance of ms. Responds in 1 month to queries. Book catalog and ms guidelines for 9x12 SAE with 3 first-class stamps.

O→ "Our mission is to publish books, newsletters, and self-study courses aimed at helping beginners and experienced business people start, and succeed in, their own small business in the fields of real estate, import-export, mail order, licensing, venture capital, financial brokerage, etc. The large number of layoffs and downsizings have made our publications of greater importance to people seeking financial independence in their own business, free of layoff threats and snarling bosses."

Nonfiction Subjects include business, economics, financing, business success, venture capital, etc. Query. Reviews artwork/photos.

Recent Title(s) *How to Buy and Flip Real Estate for a Profit*, by Rod L. Griffin.

Tips "With the mass layoffs in large and medium-size companies there is an increasing interest in owning your own business. So we focus on more how-to, hands-on material on owning—and becoming successful in—one's own business of any kind. Our market is the BWB—Beginning Wealth Builder. This person has so little money that financial planning is something they never think of. Instead, they want to know what kind of a business they can get into to make some money without a large investment. Write for this market and you have millions of potential readers. Remember—there are a lot more people without money than with money."

INTERVARSITY PRESS

P.O. Box 1400, Downers Grove IL 60515-1426. Website: www.ivpress.com/submissions. **Contact:** David Zimmerman, assoc. ed. (general); Cindy Bunch, sr. ed. (IVP Connect, Formatio); Joel Scandrett (academic, reference); Gary Deddo, sr. ed. (IVP Academic) or Dan Reid, sr. ed. (reference, academic); Al Hsu, assoc. ed. (IVP Books). Estab. 1947. Publishes hardcover originals, trade paperback and mass market paperback originals. **Publishes 110-130 titles/year. 450 queries received/year. 900 mss received/year. 13% of books from first-time authors. 86% from unagented writers. Pays 14-16% royalty on retail price. Outright purchase is $75-1,500. Pays negotiable advance.** Publishes book 18 months after acceptance of ms. Accepts simultaneous submissions. Responds in 3 months to proposals. Book catalog for 9 x 12 SAE and 5 first-class stamps, or online at website. Guidelines available online.

Imprints IVP Academic ; IVP Connect; IVP Books.

- We think of ourselves as the leading publisher of thoughtful Christian books, and we envision our audience to be similarly thoughtful about their Christian lives—people who really want to think through what it means to be a Christ-follower and to live biblically, and then take some concrete steps toward living more in that direction."

O→ "InterVarsity Press publishes a full line of books from an evangelical Christian perspective targeted to an open-minded audience. We serve those in the university, the church, and the world, by publishing books from an evangelical Christian perspective.

Nonfiction TrueSubjects include business, child guidance, contemporary culture, economics, ethinic, government, history, memoirs, multicultural, philosophy, psychology, religion, science, social sciences, sociology, spirituality, women's issues, women's studies. Query with SASE. Does not review artwork.

Recent Title(s) *Culture-Making*, by Andy Crouch (general book/Christian culture critique); *Justification*, by N. T. Wright (academic book/theology of justification.

Tips "The best way to submit to us is to go to a conference where one of our editors are. Networking is key. We're seeking writers who have good ideas and a presence/platform where they've been testing their ideas out (a church, university, on a prominent blog). We need authors who will bring resources to the table for helping to publicize and sell their books (speaking at seminars and conferences, writing for national magazines or newspapers, etc.)."

INTERWEAVE PRESS

201 E. 4th St., Loveland CO 80537. (970)669-7672. Fax: (970)667-8317. Website: www.interweave.com. **Contact:**

Tricia Waddell, book editorial director. Estab. 1975. Publishes hardcover and trade paperback originals. **Publishes 40-45 titles/year. 60% of books from first-time authors. 90% from unagented writers.** Publishes book 6-18 months after acceptance of ms. Accepts simultaneous submissions. Responds in 2 months to queries. Book catalog available online. Guidelines available free.

O→ Interweave Press publishes instructive titles relating to the fiber arts and beadwork topics.

Nonfiction Subjects limited to fiber arts (spinning, knitting, dyeing, weaving, sewing/stiching, art quilting, mixed media/collage) and jewelrymaking (beadwork, stringing, wireworking, metalsmithing).Submit outline, sample chapters. Accepts simultaneous submissions if informed of non-exclusivity. Reviews artwork/photos.

Recent Title(s) *Simply Modern Jewelry*, by Danielle Fox; *Inspired to Knit*, by Michelle Rose Orne; *49 Sensational Skirts*, by Allison Willoughby.

Tips We are looking for very clear, informally written, technically correct manuscripts, generally of a how-to nature, in our specific fiber and beadwork fields only. Our audience includes a variety of creative self-starters who appreciate inspiration and clear instruction. They are often well educated and skillful in many areas.

THE INVISIBLE COLLEGE PRESS

P.O. Box 209, Woodbridge VA 22194-0209. (703)590-4005. E-mail: submissions@invispress.com. Website: www.invispress.com. **Contact:** Dr. Phillip Reynolds, editor (nonfiction); Paul Mossinger, submissions editor (fiction). Publishes trade paperback originals and reprints. **Publishes 12 titles/year. 120 queries received/year. 30 mss received/year. 75% of books from first-time authors. 75% from unagented writers. Pays 10-25% royalty on wholesale price. Pays $100 advance.** Publishes book 4 months after acceptance of ms. Accepts simultaneous submissions. Responds in 1 month to queries. Responds in 1 month to proposals. Responds in 3 months to manuscripts. Book catalog available online. Guidelines available online.

Nonfiction Subjects include creative nonfiction, government, politics, religion, spirituality, conspiracy. Query with SASE. Submit proposal package, outline, 1 sample chapter.

Fiction Subjects include experimental, fantasy, gothic, horror, literary, mainstream, contemporary, occult, religious, science fiction, spiritual, suspense, conspiracy. We only publish fiction related to conspiracies, UFOs, government cover-ups, and the paranormal. Query with SASE. Submit proposal package, clips, 1 sample chapter.

Recent Title(s) *UFO Politics at the White House*, by Larry Bryant (nonfiction); *City of Pillars*, by Dominic Peloso (fiction); *The Third Day*, by Mark Graham (fiction).

Tips Our audience tends to be fans of conspiracies and UFO mythology. They go to UFO conventions, they research who shot JFK, they believe that they are being followed by Men in Black, they wear aluminum-foil hats to stop the CIA from beaming them thought-control rays. We are only interested in work dealing with established conspiracy/UFO mythology. Rosicrucians, Illuminatti, Men in Black, Area 51, Atlantis, etc. If your book doesn't sound like an episode of the *X-Files*, we probably won't consider it.

IRON GATE PUBLISHING

P.O. Box 999, Niwot CO 80544-0999. (303)530-2551. Fax: (303)530-5273. E-mail: editor@irongate.com. Website: www.irongate.com. **Contact:** Dina C. Carson, publisher (how-to, genealogy). Publishes hardcover and trade paperback originals. **Publishes 6-10 titles/year. 100 queries received/year. 20 mss received/year. 30% of books from first-time authors. 10% from unagented writers. Pays royalty on a case-by-case basis.** Publishes book 1 year after acceptance of ms. Accepts simultaneous submissions. Responds in 2 months to proposals. Book catalog and writer's guidelines free or online.

Imprints Reunion Solutions Press; KinderMed Press.

O→ Our readers are people who are looking for solid, how-to advice on planning reunions or self-publishing a genealogy.

Nonfiction Subjects include hobbies, genealogy, reunions, party planning. Query with SASE, or submit proposal package, including outline, 2 sample chapters, and marketing summary. Reviews artwork/photos. Send photocopies.

Recent Title(s) *The Genealogy and Local History Researcher's Self-Publishing Guide*; *Reunion Solutions: Everything You Need to Know to Plan a Family, Class, Military, Association or Corporate Reunion*.

Tips Please look at the other books we publish and tell us in your query letter why your book would fit into our line of books.

JAIN PUBLISHING CO.

P.O. Box 3523, Fremont CA 94539. (510)659-8272. Fax: (510)659-0501. E-mail: mail@jainpub.com. Website: www.jainpub.com. **Contact:** M. Jain, editor-in-chief. Estab. 1989. Publishes hardcover and paperback originals and reprints. **Publishes 12-15 titles/year. 300 queries received/year. 100% from unagented writers. Pays 5-15% royalty on net sales.** Publishes book 12-24 months after acceptance of ms. Responds in 3 months to manuscripts. Book catalog and ms guidelines online.

O→ Jain Publishing Co. publishes college textbooks and supplements, as well as professional and scholarly references, e-books and e-courses.

Nonfiction Subjects include humanities, social sciences, Asian studies, medical, business, scientific/technical. Submit proposal package, publishing history. Reviews artwork/photos. Send photocopies.

Recent Title(s) *A Student Guide to College Composition*, by William Murdiek.

JEWISH LIGHTS PUBLISHING

LongHill Partners, Inc. P.O. Box 237, Sunset Farm Offices, Rt. 4, Woodstock VT 05091. (802)457-4000. Fax: (802)457-4004. Website: www.jewishlights.com. **Contact:** Acquisitions Editor. Estab. 1990. Publishes hardcover and trade paperback originals, trade paperback reprints. **Publishes 30 titles/year. 30% of books from first-time authors. 99% from unagented writers. Pays royalty on net sales, 10% on first printing, then increases.** Publishes book 1 year after acceptance of ms. Accepts simultaneous submissions. Responds in 3 months to queries. Book catalog and ms guidelines online.

"People of all faiths and backgrounds yearn for books that attract, engage, educate and spiritually inspire. Our principal goal is to stimulate thought and help all people learn about who the Jewish people are, where they come from, and what the future can be made to hold."

Nonfiction Subjects include business, economics, with spiritual slant, finding spiritual meaning in one's work, health, medicine, healing/recovery, wellness, aging, life cycle, history, nature, environment, philosophy, religion, theology, spirituality, and inspiration, womens issues, womens studies. Submit proposal package, including cover letter, TOC, 2 sample chapters and SASE (postage must cover weight of ms). Reviews artwork/photos. Send photocopies.

Tips "We publish books for all faiths and backgrounds that also reflect the Jewish wisdom tradition."

JIST PUBLISHING

7321 Shadeland Station, Suite 200, Indianapolis IN 46256-3923, United States. (317)613-4200. Fax: (317)845-1052. E-mail: spines@jist.com. Website: www.jist.com. **Contact:** Susan Pines, associate publisher (career and education reference and library titles); Lori Cates Hand, product line manager, trade and workbooks (Career, job search, and education trade and workbook titles). Estab. 1981. Hardcover and trade paperback originals. **Publishes 60 titles/year. Receives 40 submissions/year 25% of books from first-time authors. 75% from unagented writers. Pays 8-10% royalty on net receipts. Pays advance: 12 months.** Accepts simultaneous submissions. Responds in 6 months to queries, proposals, and mss. Book catalog available online. Guidelines available online.

Our purpose is to provide quality job search, career development, occupational, character education, and life skills information, products, and services that help people manage and improve their lives and careers—and the lives of others. Publishes practical, self-directed tools and training materials that are used in employment and training education, and business settings. Whether reference books, trade books, assessment tools, workbooks, or videos, JIST products foster self-directed job-search attitudes and behaviors.

Nonfiction Subjects include business, economics/economics, education. Submit proposal package, including outline, 1 sample chapter, and author resume, competitive analysis, marketing ideas. Does not review artwork/photos.

Recent Title(s) *10 Best College Majors for Your Personality; Your Dream Job Game Plan; The High Achiever's Secret Codebook; 150 Best Recession-Proof Jobs; Overcoming Barriers to Employment Success.*

Tips Our audiences are students, job seekers, and career changers of all ages and occupations who want to find good jobs quickly and improve their futures. We sell materials through the trade as well as to institutional markets like schools, colleges, and one-stop career centers.

THE JOHNS HOPKINS UNIVERSITY PRESS

2715 N. Charles St., Baltimore MD 21218. (410)516-6900. Fax: (410)516-6968. E-mail: tcl@press.jhu.edu. Website: www.press.jhu.edu. **Contact:** Trevor Lipscombe, editor-in-chief (physics and mathematics; tcl@press.jhu.edu); Jacqueline C. Wehmueller, executive editor (consumer health and history of medicine; jwehmueller@press.jhu.edu); Henry Y.K. Tom, executive editor (social sciences; htom@press.jhu.edu); Wendy Harris, senior acquisitions editor (clinical medicine, public health, health policy; wharris@press.jhu.edu); Robert J. Brugger, senior acquisitions editor (American history, history of science and technology, regional books; rbrugger@press.jhu.edu); Vincent J. Burke, senior acquisitions editor (biology; vjb@press.jhu.edu); Michael B. Lonegro, acquisitions editor (humanities, classics, and ancient studies; mlonegro@press.jhu.edu); Ashleigh McKown, assistant acquisitions editor (higher education; amckown@press.jhu.edu). Estab. 1878. Publishes hardcover originals and reprints, and trade paperback reprints. **Publishes 140 titles/year. Pays royalty.** Publishes book 12 months after acceptance of ms.

Nonfiction Subjects include government, politics, health, medicine, history, humanities, literary criticism, regional, religion, science. Submit proposal package, outline, 1 sample chapter, curriculum vita. Reviews artwork/photos. Send photocopies.

Recent Title(s) *A Contract With the Earth*, by Newt Gingrich; *Abraham Lincoln: A Life*, by Michael Burlingame; *The Quantum Frontier: The Large Hadron Collider*, by Don Lincoln.

JOSSEY-BASS/PFEIFFER

John Wiley & Sons, Inc. 989 Market St., San Francisco CA 94103. (415)433-1740. Fax: (415)433-0499. Website: www.josseybass.com. **Contact:** Paul Foster, publisher (public health and health administration, education K-12, higher and adult education, trade psychology, conflict resolustion, parenting, relationships, Judaica religion and spirituality). **Publishes 250 titles/year. Pays variable royalties. Pays occasional advance.** Publishes book 1 year after acceptance of ms. Accepts simultaneous submissions. Responds in 2-3 months to queries. Guidelines available online.

Nonfiction Subjects include business, economics, education, health, medicine, money, finance, psychology, religion.

Recent Title(s) *No More Misbehavin'*, by Michele Borba; *Hidden Wholeness*, by Parker Palmer; *Teaching With Fire*, by Sam Intrator.

JOURNEYFORTH

Imprint of BJU Press 1700 Wade Hampton Blvd., Greenville SC 29614. (864)242-5100, ext. 4350. Fax: (864)298-0268. E-mail: jb@bjup.com. Website: www.bjup.com. **Contact:** Nancy Lohr, youth acquisitions editor; Suzette Jordan, adult acquisitions editor. Estab. 1974. Publishes paperback originals and reprints. **Publishes 25 titles/year. 10% of books from first-time authors. 8% from unagented writers. Pays royalty.** Publishes book 12-18 months after acceptance of ms. Does accept simultaneous submissions. Responds in 1 month to queries. Responds in 3 months to manuscripts. Book catalog available free. Guidelines available online.

- Small independent publisher of trustworthy novels and biographies for readers pre-school through high school from a conservative Christian perspective.

Fiction Subjects include adventure, historical, animal, easy-to-read, series, mystery, sports, children's/juvenile, suspense, young adult, western. Our fiction is all based on a moral and Christian worldview. Submit 5 sample chapters, synopsis, SASE.

Tips Study the publisher's guidelines. Make sure your work is suitable or you waste time for you and the publisher.

JOURNEY STONE CREATIONS, LLC

3533 Danbury Rd., Fairfield OH 45014. (513)860-5616. Fax: (513)860-0176. Website: www.jscbooks.com. **Contact:** Patricia Stirnkorb, president. Estab. 2004. Publishes hardcover and trade paperback originals. **Publishes 50-100 titles/year. 40-50 queries received/year. 75-90 mss received/year. Pays 6% royalty on wholesale price. Pays minimal advance.** Publishes book 6-12 months after acceptance of ms. Accepts simultaneous submissions. Responds in 1 month to queries. Responds in 4-6 weeks to proposals. Responds in 1-3 months to manuscripts. Book catalog available online. Guidelines available via e-mail.

- We are a new and growing publisher with great plans for the future. All our products must be moral and conservative material to be considered.

Nonfiction Subjects include animals, seasonal, fun. Query with SASE. Submit 3-5 sample chapters or complete manuscript (if under 5 words). Reviews artwork/photos. Send photocopies and assigns art to own artists.

Fiction Subjects include juvenile, picture books, religious, juvenile, young adult, to early teens only. Query with SASE. Submit proposal package, clips, 3-5 sample chapters. Submit complete ms.

Recent Title(s) *Camp Limestone*, by Paul Kijinski; *Never Ceese*, by Suzanne Dent; *The Cat Who Slept All Day*, by John Coniglio.

Tips Audience is kids ages 2-12. Be thorough and concise when

JUDAICA PRESS

123 Ditmas Ave., Brooklyn NY 11218. (718)972-6200. Fax: (718)972-6204. Website: www.judaicapress.com. **Contact:** Nachum Shapiro, managing editor. Estab. 1963. Publishes hardcover and trade paperback originals and reprints. **Publishes 12 titles/year.** Responds in 3 months to queries. Book catalog in print and online.

- We cater to the Orthodox Jewish market.

Nonfiction Looking for Orthodox Judaica in all genres.Subjects include religion, Bible commentary, prayer, holidays, life cycle. Submit ms with SASE.

Recent Title(s) *Scattered Pieces*, by Allison Cohen; *The Practical Guide to Kashrus*, by Rabbi Shaul Wagschal; *How Mitzvah Giraffe Got His Long, Long Neck*, by David Sokoloff.

JUDSON PRESS

P.O. Box 851, Valley Forge PA 19482-0851. (610)768-2118. Fax: (610)768-2441. E-mail: acquisitions@judsonpress.com. Website: www.judsonpress.com. **Contact:** Rebecca Irwin-Diehl. Estab. 1824. Publishes hardcover and paperback originals. **Publishes 12-15 titles/year. 750 queries received/year. Pays royalty or makes outright purchase.** Publishes book 12 months after acceptance of ms. Accepts simultaneous submissions. Responds in 3-6 months to queries. Book catalog for 9 x 12 SAE with 4 first-class stamps. Guidelines available online.

- Our audience is mostly church members and leaders who seek to have a more fulfilling personal spiritual life and want to serve Christ in their churches and other relationships. We have a large African-American readership. Currently emphasizing small group resources. De-emphasizing biography, poetry.

Nonfiction Adult religious nonfiction of 30,000-80,000 words.Subjects include multicultural, religion. Query with SASE. Submit outline, sample chapters.

Recent Title(s) *Playbook for Christian Manhood: 12 Key Plays for Black Teen Boys*, by James C. Perkins; *Morning Meetings with Jesus: 180 Devotions for teachers*, by Susan O'Carroll Drake; *Christian Educators' Guide to Evaluating and Developing Curriculum*, by Nancy Ferguson.

Tips Writers have the best chance selling us practical books assisting clergy or laypersons in their ministry and personal lives. Our audience consists of Protestant church leaders and members. Be sensitive to our workload and adapt to the market's needs. Books on multicultural issues are very welcome. Also seeking books that heighten awareness and sensitivity to issues related to the poor and to social justice.

N JUDSON PRESS

P.O. Box 851, Valley Forge PA 19482-0851. Website: www.judsonpress.com. **Contact:** Rebecca Irwin-Diehl, editor. Trade paperback originals. **Publishes 12-14 titles/year. 500 queries/year; 300 ms/year. 50% of books from first-time authors. 85% from unagented writers. Pays $300-1,000 advance.** Publishes book 14 months after acceptance of ms. Accepts simultaneous submissions. Catalog and guidelines available online at website. Guidelines free on request.

Nonfiction Subjects include ethnic, history-Baptist, multicultural. Query with SASE; submit proposal package, including: outline, 2 sample chapters, CV, and marketing plan.

Tips Our audience is pastors, church leaders, and Christians committed to transformed discipleship. Keep the content practical. What will the readers be equipped and inspired to do in response? Focus your audience. We are theologically moderate, socially progressive, and intentionally multicultural.

KALMBACH PUBLISHING CO.

21027 Crossroads Circle, P.O. Box 1612, Waukesha WI 53187-1612. (262)796-8776. Fax: (262)798-6468. E-mail: books@kalmbach.com. Website: corporate.kalmbach.com. **Contact:** Mark Thompson, editor-in-chief (hobbies); Pat Lantier, executive editor (jewelry and crafts). Estab. 1934. Publishes paperback originals and reprints. **Publishes 40-50 titles/year. 50% of books from first-time authors. 99% from unagented writers. Pays 7% royalty on net receipts. Pays $2,500 advance.** Publishes book 18 months after acceptance of ms. Responds in 2 months to queries.

Nonfiction "Kalmbach publishes reference materials and how-to publications for hobbyists, jewelry-makers, and crafters."Query with 2-3 page detailed outline, sample chapter with photos, drawings, and how-to text. Reviews artwork/photos.

Recent Title(s) *The Model Railroader's Guide to Coal Railroading*, by Tony Koester; *Polymer Pizzazz: 27 Great Polymer Clay Jewelry Projects*.

Tips "Our how-to books are highly visual in their presentation. Any author who wants to publish with us must be able to furnish good photographs and rough drawings before we'll consider his or her book."

KAR-BEN PUBLISHING

A Divison of Lerner Publishing Group 241 First Avenue No., Minneapolis MN 55401, United States. Fax: 612-332-7615. E-mail: editorial@karben.com. Website: www.karben.com. **Contact:** Joni Sussman, publisher (juvenile Judaica). Estab. 1976. Publishes hardcover, trade paperback and electronic originals; hardcover and trade paperback reprints. **Publishes 12-15 titles/year. 800 mss received/year. 70% of books from first-time authors. 70% from unagented writers. Pays 3-5% royalty on wholesale price. Pays $500-2,500 advance.** Publishes book 24 months after acceptance of ms. Accepts simultaneous submissions. Responds in 2 months to queries, proposals, & manuscripts. Book catalog available online; free on request. Guidelines available online.

- "Kar-Ben Publishing publishes high-quality materials on Jewish themes for young children and families."

Nonfiction Subjects include Jewish content children's books only. Submit completed ms. Does not review artwork. Send website info where illustration samples are available for review.

Fiction Subjects include juvenile; Jewish content only. "We seek picture book mss of about 1,000 words on Jewish-themed topics for children." Submit proposal package, including synopsis, 2 sample chapters, and ms if picture book.

Recent Title(s) *Engineer Ari and the Rosh Hoshanah Ride, Jodie's Hannukkah Dig.*

Tips "Do a literature search to make sure similar title doesn't already exist."

KAYA PRODUCTION

116 Pinehurst Ave. #E51, New York NY 10033. (212)740-3519. E-mail: kaya@kaya.com. Website: www.kaya.com. **Contact:** Sunyoung Lee, editor. Publishes hardcover originals and trade paperback originals and reprints. Accepts simultaneous submissions. Responds in 6 months to manuscripts. Book catalog available free. Guidelines available online.

- We do not accept electronic submissions.
- Kaya is an independent literary press dedicated to the publication of innovative literature from the

Asian diaspora.

Nonfiction Subjects include multicultural. Submit proposal package, outline, sample chapters, previous publications, SASE. Reviews artwork/photos. Send photocopies.

Fiction Kaya publishes Asian, Asian-American and Asian diasporic materials. We are looking for innovative writers with a commitment to quality literature. Submit 2-4 sample chapters, clips, SASE.

Recent Title(s) *Where We Once Belonged*, by Sia Figiel (novel); *The Anchored Angel: Selected Writings*, by Jose Garcia Villa, edited by Gileen Tabios.

Tips Audience is people interested in a high standard of literature and who are interested in breaking down easy approaches to multicultural literature.

KENSINGTON PUBLISHING CORP.

850 Third Ave., 16th Floor, New York NY 10022. (212)407-1500. Fax: (212)935-0699. Website: www.kensingtonbooks.com. **Contact:** John Scognamiglio, editorial director, fiction (historical romance, Regency romance, women's contemporary fiction, gay and lesbian fiction and nonfiction, mysteries, suspense, mainstream fiction); Michaela Hamilton, editor-in-chief, Citadel Press (thrillers, mysteries, mainstream fiction, true crime, current events); Kate Duffy, editorial director, romance and women's fiction (historical romance, Regency romance, Brava erotic romance, women's contemporary fiction); Audrey LaFehr, editorial director (women's fiction, romance, romantic suspense, thrillers, erotica); Selena James, executive editor, Dafina Books (African American fiction and nonfiction, inspirational, young adult, romance); Gary Goldstein, senior editor (westerns, true crime, military, sports, how-to, narrative nonfiction); Richard Ember, editor, Citadel Press (biography, film, sports, New Age, spirituality); Danielle Chiotti, senior editor (Dating and relationships, pop culture, humor, women's issues, careers, memoirs, narrative nonfiction, biography, weddings, general self help, Contemporary women's fiction, romance, young adult); Mike Shohl, editor (pop culture, entertainment, music, male interest, fratire, sports, popular science/popular psychology, humor, martial arts, true crime); Peter Senftleben, assistant editor (mainstream fiction, women's contemporary fiction, gay and lesbian fiction, mysteries, suspense, thrillers, romantic suspense, paranormal romance). Estab. 1975. Publishes hardcover and trade paperback originals, mass market paperback originals and reprints. **Publishes over 500 titles/year. 5,000 queries received/year. 2,000 mss received/year. 10% of books from first-time authors. Pays 6-15% royalty on retail price. Makes outright purchase. Pays $2,000 and up advance.** Publishes book 9-12 months after acceptance of ms. Accepts simultaneous submissions. Responds in 1 month to queries. Responds in 1 month to proposals. Responds in 4 months to manuscripts. Book catalog available online.

Imprints Kensington Books; Brava Books; Citadel Press; Dafina Books; Pinnacle Books; Zebra Books.

- Kensington recently purchased the assets of Carol Publishing Group.
- "Kensington focuses on profitable niches and uses aggressive marketing techniques to support its books."

Nonfiction Subjects include alternative, Americana, animals, business, economics, child guidance, contemporary culture, cooking, foods, nutrition, gay, lesbian, health, medicine, history, hobbies, memoirs, military, war, money, finance, multicultural, nature, environment, philosophy, psychology, recreation, regional, sex, sports, travel, true crime, pop culture. Agented submissions only. *No unsolicited mss.* Reviews artwork/photos. Send photocopies.

Fiction Subjects include ethnic, gay, lesbian, historical, horror, mainstream, multicultural, mystery, occult, romance, contemporary, historical, regency, suspense, western, epic, thrillers, women's. Agented submissions only. *No unsolicited mss.*

Recent Title(s) *Cream Puff Murder*, by Joanne Fluke; *Malice*, by Lisa Jackson; *I Hope They Serve Bear in Hell*, by Tucker Max, *Two Rivers*, by T. Greenwood

Tips "Agented submissions only, except for submissions to romance lines. For those lines, query with SASE or submit proposal package including 3 sample chapters, synopsis."

KENT STATE UNIVERSITY PRESS

P.O. Box 5190, Kent OH 44242-0001. (330)672-7913. Fax: (330)672-3104. Website: www.kentstateuniversitypress.com. **Contact:** Joyce Harrison, acquiring editor. Estab. 1965. Publishes hardcover and paperback originals and some reprints. **Publishes 30-35 titles/year. Non-author subsidy publishes 20% of books. Standard minimum book contract on net sales.** Responds in 4 months to queries. Book catalog available free.

- "Kent State publishes primarily scholarly works and titles of regional interest. Currently emphasizing US history, US literary criticism."

Nonfiction Subjects include anthropology, archeology, art, architecture, history, language, literature, literary criticism, regional, true crime, literary criticism, material culture, textile/fashion studies, US foreign relations. Enclose return postage.

KOENISHA PUBLICATIONS

3196 53rd St., Hamilton MI 49419-9626. Phone/Fax: (269)751-4100. E-mail: koenisha@macatawa.org. Website: www.koenisha.com. **Contact:** Sharolett Koenig, publisher; Earl Leon, acquisition editor. Publishes trade paperback originals. **Publishes 10-12 titles/year. 500 queries received/year. 500 mss received/year. 95% of books from first-time authors. 100% from unagented writers.** Publishes book 1 year after acceptance of ms. Accepts simultaneous submissions. Responds in 2 months to queries. Responds in 3 months to proposals. Responds in 3 months to manuscripts. Book catalog available online. Guidelines available online.

Nonfiction Subjects include gardening, hobbies, memoirs, nature, environment. Query with SASE. Submit complete ms. Reviews artwork/photos. Send photocopies.

Fiction Subjects include humor, mainstream, contemporary, mystery, romance, suspense, young adult. Query with SASE. Submit proposal package, clips, 3 sample chapters.

Recent Title(s) *JimJim Meets Poster Guy*, by Gary Crow and Brock Crow (children's read-along); *Cruisin' For a Bruisin'*, by Gayle Wigglesworth (mystery); *The Bonsai Keeper*, by Sharolett Koenig (nonfiction).

Tips "We're not interested in books written to suit a particular line or house or because it's trendy. Instead write a book from your heart—the inspiration or idea that kept you going through the writing process."

KRAUSE BOOKS

Imprint of F + W Media, Inc. 700 E. State St., Iola WI 54990. (715)445-2214. Fax: (715)445-4087. Website: www.krausebooks.com. **Contact:** Paul Kennedy (antiques and collectibles); Corrina Peterson (firearms/outdoors); Candy Wiza (Simple Living). Publishes hardcover and trade paperback originals. **Publishes 80 titles/year. 300 queries received/year. 40 mss received/year. 25% of books from first-time authors. 95% from unagented writers. Pays advance. Photo budget.** Publishes book 18 months after acceptance of ms. Responds in 3 months to proposals. Responds in 2 months to manuscripts. Book catalog for free or on Web site. Guidelines available free.

"We are the world's largest hobby and collectibles publisher."

Nonfiction Submit proposal package, including outline, table of contents, a sample chapter, and letter explaining your project's unique contributions. Reviews artwork/photos. Accepts digital photography. Send Send sample photos.

Recent Title(s) *Hot Wheels: 40 Years*, by Angelo Van Bogart; *Standard Catalog of Winchester Firearms*, by Joseph Cornell; *Altered Style*, by Stephanie Kimura.

Tips Audience consists of serious hobbyists. "Your work should provide a unique contribution to the special interest."

KREGEL PUBLICATIONS

Kregel, Inc. P.O. Box 2607, Grand Rapids MI 49501. (616)451-4775. Fax: (616)451-9330. Website: www.kregelpublications.com. **Contact:** Dennis R. Hillman, publisher. Estab. 1949. Publishes hardcover and trade paperback originals and reprints. **Publishes 90 titles/year. 20% of books from first-time authors. 35% from unagented writers. Pays royalty on wholesale price. Pays negotiable advance.** Publishes book 12-16 months after acceptance of ms. Guidelines available online.

Imprints Editorial Portavoz (Spanish-language works); Kregel Academic & Professional; Kregel Kidzone.

"Our mission as an evangelical Christian publisher is to provide—with integrity and excellence—trusted, Biblically-based resources that challenge and encourage individuals in their Christian lives. Works in theology and Biblical studies should reflect the historic, orthodox Protestant tradition."

Nonfiction We serve evangelical Christian readers and those in career Christian service.

Fiction Subjects include religious, children's, general, inspirational, mystery/suspense, relationships, young adult. Fiction should be geared toward the evangelical Christian market. Wants books with fast-paced, contemporary storylines presenting a strong Christian message in an engaging, entertaining style.

Recent Title(s) *Clopper, The Christmas Donkey*, by Emily King; *Unveiling Islam*, by Ergun Caner and Emir Caner; *Putting Jesus in His Place*, by Robert Bowman.

Tips "Our audience consists of conservative, evangelical Christians, including pastors and ministry students."

KRIEGER PUBLISHING CO.

P.O. Box 9542, Melbourne FL 32902-9542. (321)724-9542. Fax: (321)951-3671. E-mail: info@krieger-publishing.com. Website: www.krieger-publishing.com. **Contact:** Sharan B. Merriam and Ronald M. Cervero, series editor (adult education); David E. Kyvig, series director (local history); James B. Gardner, series editor (public history). Also publishes in the fields of natural sciences, history and space sciences. Estab. 1969. Publishes hardcover and paperback originals and reprints. **Publishes 30 titles/year. 30% of books from first-time authors. 100% from unagented writers. Pays royalty on net price.** Publishes book 9-18 months after acceptance of ms. Responds in 3 months to queries. Book catalog available free.

Imprints Anvil Series; Orbit Series; Public History; Professional Practices in Adult Education and Lifelong Learning Series.

We are a short-run niche publisher providing accurate and well-documented scientific and technical titles for text and reference use, college level and higher.

Nonfiction Subjects include agriculture, animals, education, adult, history, nature, environment, science, space, herpetology. Query with SASE. Reviews artwork/photos.

Recent Title(s) *Children of Divorce*, by William Bernet & Don Ash; *Classic Irises and the Men and Women Who Created Them*, by Clarence E. Mahan.

WENDY LAMB BOOKS

Imprint of Random House Children's Books/Random House, Inc. 1745 Broadway, New York NY 10019. (212)782-9000. Website: www.randomhouse.com. Estab. 2001. Publishes hardcover originals. **Pays royalty.** Accepts simultaneous submissions. Guidelines for #10 SASE.

- Literary fiction and nonfiction for readers 8-15. Query with SASE.

Fiction Subjects include middle grade and young adult.
Tips "Please note that we do not publish picture books. Please send the first ten pages of your ms (or until the end of the first chapter) along with a cover letter, synopsis, and SASE. Before you submit, please take a look at some of our recent titles to get an idea of what we publish."

LARK BOOKS

67 Broadway, Asheville NC 28801. (828)253-0467. Fax: (828)253-7952. Website: www.larkbooks.com. **Contact:** Nicole McConville, acquisitions. Estab. 1976. Publishes hardcover and trade paperback originals and reprints. **Publishes 150 titles/year. 300 queries received/year. 100 mss received/year. 75% of books from first-time authors. 80% from unagented writers.** Publishes book 1 year after acceptance of ms. Accepts simultaneous submissions. Responds in 3 months to queries. Responds in 3 months to proposals. Responds in 3 months to manuscripts. Book catalog available online. Guidelines available online.

O→ Lark Books publishes high quality, highly illustrated books, primarily in the crafts/leisure markets celebrating the creative spirit. We work closely with bookclubs. Our books are either how-to, `gallery' or combination books.

Nonfiction Subjects include nature, environment, photography. Query with SASE. Submit proposal package, outline, 1-2 sample chapters. Query first. If asked, submit outline and 1 sample chapter, sample projects, TOC, visuals. Reviews artwork/photos. Send photocopies.
Recent Title(s) *Doodle-Stitching*, by Aimee Ray.
Tips Make sure your humor submissions are edgy, up to date, and contain a nonfiction element.

LAUREL-LEAF

Imprint of Random House Children's Books/Random House, Inc. 1745 Broadway, New York NY 10019. (212)782-9000. Website: www.randomhouse.com/teens.

- Quality reprint paperback imprint for young adult paperback books. *Does not accept mss.*

LAWYERS & JUDGES PUBLISHING CO.

P.O. Box 30040, Tucson AZ 85751-0040. (520)323-1500. Fax: (520)323-0055. E-mail: sales@lawyersandjudges.com. Website: www.lawyersandjudges.com. **Contact:** Steve Weintraub, president. Estab. 1963. Publishes professional hardcover and trade paperback originals. **Publishes 20 titles/year. 200 queries received/year. 60 mss received/year. 15% of books from first-time authors. 100% from unagented writers.** Publishes book 5 months after acceptance of ms. Accepts simultaneous submissions. Responds in 1 month to queries. Book catalog available free. Guidelines available free.

O→ Lawyers & Judges is a highly specific publishing company, reaching the legal, accident reconstruction, insurance, and medical fields.

Nonfiction Submit proposal package, outline, sample chapters.
Recent Title(s) *Human Factors in Traffic Safety*; *Forensic Science Today*; *Terrorism Law, 3rd Ed.*

LEE & LOW BOOKS

95 Madison Ave., New York NY 10016. E-mail: general@leeandlow.com. Website: www.leeandlow.com. **Contact:** Louise May, editor-in-chief (multicultural children's fiction/nonfiction). Estab. 1991. Publishes hardcover originals and trade paperback reprints of our own titles. **Publishes 12-14 titles/year. Receives 100 queries/year; 1,200 mss/year. 15-20%% of books from first-time authors. 50% from unagented writers. Pays royalty on wholesale price. Pays advance (range depends on project, whether author or author/illustrator).** Publishes book 24-36 months. after acceptance of ms. Responds in 6 months to mss if interested. Book catalog available online or for 9x12 SASE. Guidelines available online; free on request.

O→ Our goals are to meet a growing need for books that address children of color, and to present literature that all children can identify with. We only consider multicultural children's books. Currently emphasizing material for 5-12 year olds. Sponsors a yearly New Voices Award for first-time picture book authors of color. Contest rules online at website or for SASE.

Nonfiction Subjects include young adult, all topics of interest to young readers. Submit completed ms. Reviews artwork/photos only if writer is also a trained illustrator or photographer. Send photocopies.
Fiction Subjects include poetry, young adult. We publish all topics of interest to young readers. Send complete ms.
Recent Title(s) *Capoeira: Game! Dance! Martial Art!*, by George Ancona (children's photo-essay); *Surfer of the*

Century, by Ellie Crowe (illustrated picture book bio); *Bird*, by Zetta Elliott (realistic fiction, illustrated picture book); *Yum! MmMm! ⊠Quèrico!*, by Pat Mora (children's illus. picture book).

Tips Check our website to see the kinds of books we publish. Do not send mss that don't fit our mission.

LEHIGH UNIVERSITY PRESS

B040 Christmas-Saucon Hall 14 E. Packer Ave., Lehigh University, Bethlehem PA 18015. (610)758-3933. Fax: (610)758-6331. E-mail: inlup@lehigh.edu/ ~ inpress/. Website: www.lehigh.edu/library/lup. **Contact:** Scott Paul Gordon, director. Estab. 1985. Publishes nonfiction hardcover originals. **Publishes 10 titles/year. 90-100 queries received/year. 50-60 mss received/year. 70% of books from first-time authors. 100% from unagented writers. Pays royalty.** Publishes book 18 months after acceptance of ms. Responds in 3 months to queries. Book catalog available free. Guidelines available online.

- Currently emphasizing works on 18th-century studies, history of technology, literary criticism, and topics involving Asian Studies. Three series: Studies in Eighteenth-Century America and the Atlantic World and Missionary Work in Asia, and perspectives on Edgar Allen Poe.

Nonfiction Lehigh University Press is a conduit for nonfiction works of scholarly interest to the academic community.Subjects include Americana, art, architecture, history, language, literature, science. Submit proposal package with cover letter, several sample chapters, current CV and SASE.

Recent Title(s) *Thomas Barclay (1728-1793): Consul in France, Diplomat in Barbary*, by Priscilla H. Roberts and Richard S. Roberts; *Pathway to Hell: A Tragedy of the American Civil War*, by Dennis W. Brandt; *CInema of the Occult: New Age, Satanism, WICCA, and Spiritualism in Film*, by Carrol L. Fry.

LEISURE BOOKS

Imprint of Dorchester Publishing Co. 200 Madison Ave., Suite 2000, New York NY 10016. (212)725-8811. Fax: (212)532-1054. Website: www.dorchesterpub.com. **Contact:** Leah Hultenschmidt, editor; Alicia Condon, editorial director; Don D'Auria, executive editor (westerns, thrillers, horror); Christopher Keeslar, senior editor. Estab. 1970. Publishes mass market paperback originals and reprints. Publishes romances, westerns, horror, chick lit and thrillers only. **Publishes 240 titles/year. 20% of books from first-time authors. 20% from unagented writers. Pays royalty on retail price. Pays negotiable advance.** Publishes book 18 months after acceptance of ms. Responds in 6 months to queries. Book catalog for free by calling (800)481-9191. Guidelines available online.

Imprints Love Spell (romance); Leisure (romance, western, thriller, horror); Making It (chick lit).

- Leisure Books/Love Spell is seeking historical, contemporary, time travel, paranormal romances and romantic suspense.

Fiction Subjects include horror, romance, suspense, western, chick lit. All historical romance should be set pre-1900. Westerns should take place West of the Mississippi River before 1900. No sweet romance, science fiction or cozy mysteries. Query with SASE. Submit clips, first 3 chapters. All manuscripts must be typed.

Recent Title(s) *A Knight's Honor*, by Connie Mason (romance); *The Lake*, by Richard Laymon (horror); *Calendar Girl*, by Naomi Neale (chick lit).

N HAL LEONARD BOOKS

Hal Leonard Publishing Group 19 W. 21st St., Suite 201, New York NY 10010. (212)575-9265. Fax: (212)575-9270. **Contact:** Rusty Cutchin, sr. ed. **Publishes 30 titles/year.**

Nonfiction TrueSubjects include music. Query with SASE.

Recent Title(s) *The Desktop Studio*, by Emile D. Menasche (recording); *The Hofner Guitar: A History*, by Gordon Giltrap & Neville Marten (music instruments); *Tipbook Series*, by Hugo Pinksterboer (music techniques & reference).

LERNER PUBLISHING CO.

241 First Ave. N., Minneapolis MN 55401. (612)332-3344. Fax: (612)332-7615. Website: www.lernerbooks.com. Estab. 1959. Publishes hardcover originals, trade paperback originals and reprints.

Imprints Millbrook Press; Twenty-First-Century Books; Carolrhoda Books; First Avenue Editions (paperback reprints for hard/soft deals only); Lerner Publications; LernerClassroom; Kar-Ben Publishing.

- "As of 2007, due to significant increase in volume, Lerner Publishing Group stopped accepting unsolicited submissions for any imprints. We continue to seek target solicitations at specific reading levels and in specific subject areas. The company will list these targeted solicitations on our website and in national newsletters, such as the SCBWI Bulletin."

Nonfiction Subjects include art, architecture, ethnic, history, nature, environment, science, sports.

Fiction Subjects include young adult, problem novels, sports, adventure, mystery.

Tips "To enhance the marketability of your manuscript, you may wish to consider several options: join a group that will help you learn about children's publishing, such as the SCBWI; form or join a critique group that focuses on constructive critiques; find an agent who can help to place your manuscript with the right publisher; and work with an editorial service to improve the quality of your manuscript before submitting it."

LIBRARIES UNLIMITED, INC.

88 Post Rd. W., Westport CT 06881. (800)225-5800. Fax: (203)222-1502. Website: www.lu.com. **Contact:** Barbara Ittner, acquisitions editor (public library titles); Sharon Coatney (school library titles); Sue Easun (academic library titles). Estab. 1964. Publishes hardcover and paperback originals. **Publishes 100 titles/year. 400 queries received/year. 100 mss received/year. 50% of books from first-time authors. 100% from unagented writers.** Publishes book 9 months after acceptance of ms. Accepts simultaneous submissions. Responds in 1 month to queries. Responds in 2 months to proposals. Responds in 2 months to manuscripts. Book catalog and ms guidelines online.

- Libraries Unlimited publishes resources for libraries, librarians, and educators. We are currently emphasizing readers' advisory guides, academic reference works, readers' theatre, literary and technology resources.

Nonfiction Subjects include agriculture, anthropology, archeology, art, architecture, business, economics, education, ethnic, health, medicine, history, language, literature, music, dance, philosophy, psychology, religion, science, sociology, womens issues, womens studies, technology. Submit proposal package, outline, resume, 1 sample chapter. Reviews artwork/photos. Send photocopies.

Recent Title(s) *Information Literacy: Essential Skills for the Information Age*, by Michael B. Eisenberg, Carrie A. Lowe, and Kathleen L. Spitzer; *Picture This! Using Picture Books for Character Education in the Classroom*, by Claire Gatrell Stephens.

Tips We welcome any ideas that combine professional expertise, writing ability, and innovative thinking. Audience is librarians (school, public, academic, and special) and teachers (K-12).

LIGUORI PUBLICATIONS

One Liguori Dr., Liguori MO 63057. (636)464-2500. Fax: (636)464-8449. Website: www.liguori.org. **Contact:** Daniel Michaels, acquisitions editor. Estab. 1947. Publishes paperback originals and reprints under the Ligouri and Libros Ligouri imprints. **Publishes 20-25 titles/year. Pays royalty. Makes outright purchase. Pays varied advance.** Publishes book 2 years after acceptance of ms. Responds in 2 months to queries. Responds in 2 months to proposals. Responds in 3 months to manuscripts. Guidelines available online.

Imprints Libros Liguori; Liguori Books; Liguori/Triumph; Liguori Lifespan.

- Liguori Publications, faithful to the charism of St. Alphonsus, is an apostolate within the mission of the Denver Province. Its mission, a collaborative effort of Redemptorists and laity, is to spread the gospel of Jesus Christ primarily through the print and electronic media. It shares in the Redemptorist priority of giving special attention to the poor and the most abandoned. Currently emphasizing practical spirituality, prayers and devotions, how-to spirituality.

Nonfiction Mss with Catholic sensibility.Subjects include religion, spirituality. Query with SASE. Submit outline, 1 sample chapter.

LILLENAS PUBLISHING CO.

Imprint of Lillenas Drama Resources P.O. Box 419527, Kansas City MO 64109. (816)931-1900. Fax: (816)412-8390. E-mail: drama@lillenas.com. Website: www.lillenasdrama.com. **Contact:** Kim Messer, product manager (Christian drama). Publishes mass market paperback and electronic originals. **Publishes 50+ titles/year. Pays royalty on wholesale price. Makes outright purchase.**

Nonfiction Subjects include religion, life issues. Query with SASE. Submit complete ms.

LINDEN PUBLISHING, INC.

2006 S. Mary, Fresno CA 93721. (559)233-6633. Fax: (559)233-6933. E-mail: richard@lindenpub.com. Website: www.lindenpub.com. **Contact:** Richard Sorsky, president; Kent Sorsky, vice president. Estab. 1976. Publishes trade paperback originals; hardcover and trade paperback reprints. **Publishes 10-12 titles/year. 30+ queries received/year. 5-15 mss received/year. 40% of books from first-time authors. 50% from unagented writers. Pays 7½ -12% royalty on wholesale price. Pays $500-6,000 advance.** Publishes book 18 months after acceptance of ms. Responds in 1 month to queries and proposals. Book catalog available online. Guidelines available via e-mail.

Nonfiction Subjects include history, regional, hobbies, woodworking, Regional California history. Submit proposal package, outline, 3 sample chapters, bio. Reviews artwork/photos. Send electronic files, if available.

Recent Title(s) *The New Influencers, Secrets of Social Media Marketing; Scientists Greater Than Einstein; Global Warming is Good for Business; Elements of Narrative Nonfiction; Refuse to Regain.*

⊘ LIONHEARTED PUBLISHING, INC.

P.O. Box 618, Zephyr Cove NV 89448-0618. (888-546-6478. E-mail: admin@lionhearted.com. Website: www.lionhearted.com. **Contact:** Historical or Contemporary Romantic Fiction Editor. Estab. 1994. Publishes trade paperback originals and e-books. **Publishes 6 titles/year. 90% from unagented writers. Royalties of 10% maximum on paperbacks; 30% on electronic books Pays $100 advance.** Publishes book 18-24 months after acceptance of ms. Responds in 1 month to queries. Responds in 3 months to manuscripts. Book catalog available online. Guidelines available online.

- Submissions are currently closed due to an overflow of submissions. Check website for updates.

O-ᴛ Multiple award-winning, independent publisher of single title paperbacks and e-books.

Fiction Subjects include romance, contemporary, futuristic/time travel, historical, regency period, romantic suspense; over 65,000 words only, romantic comedies. Unsolicited mss returned unopened.

Recent Title(s) *Invited to the Light*, by Bonnie W. Kaye; *Beneath a Blazing Sun*, by J.A. Clarke; *Before an Autumn Wind*, by Katherine Smith.

Tips If you are not an avid reader of romance, don't attempt to write romance. Please read a few of our single-title releases (they are a bit different) before submitting your romance novel.

LISTEN & LIVE AUDIO

P.O. Box 817, Roseland NJ 07068. E-mail: alisa@listenandlive.com. Website: www.listenandlive.com. **Contact:** Alisa Weberman, publisher. Publishes audiobook and trade paperback originals. **Publishes 26 audiobook titles/year. Makes outright purchase.** Book catalog available online.

O-ᴛ We are looking to publish a self-help book about public speaking.

Nonfiction Subjects include audio, CDs, business, economics, child guidance, contemporary culture, creative nonfiction, history, memoirs, military, war, money, finance, sex, travel. Submit proposal package, outline, 2 sample chapters, résumé.

Recent Title(s) *Zingerman's Guide to Giving Great Service*, by Ari Weinzweig (business audio); *The Jane Austin Book Club*, by Karen Joy Fowler (women's audio); *The Perilous Road*, by William O. Steele (classic children's audio).

LITTLE, BROWN

237 Park Avenue, New York NY 10017. Website: www.hbgusa.com. **Contact:** Editorial Department, Trade Division. Estab. 1837. Publishes adult and juvenile hardcover and paperback originals, and reprints. **Pays royalty. Pays varying advance.**

Imprints Little, Brown and Co. Adult Trade; Bulfinch Press; Back Bay Books; Reagan Arthur Books.

- *No unsolicited submissions. Agented submissions only.*

O-ᴛ "The general editorial philosophy for all divisions continues to be broad and flexible, with high quality and the promise of commercial success as always the first considerations."

Nonfiction Subjects include contemporary culture, cooking, foods, nutrition, history, memoirs, nature, environment, science, sports.

Fiction Subjects include experimental, literary, mainstream, contemporary, mystery, short story collections, suspense, thrillers/espionage, translations.

LITTLE, BROWN AND CO. ADULT TRADE BOOKS

Hachette Book Group USA, 1271 Avenue of the Americas, New York NY 10020. (212)522-8700. Fax: (212)522-2067. Website: www.hachettebookgroupusa.com. Estab. 1837. Publishes hardcover originals and paperback originals and reprints.

- *Does not accept unsolicited mss.*

Recent Title(s) *The Way Out*, by Craig Childs; *The True and Outstanding Adventures of the Hunt Sisters*, by Elisabeth Robinson; *Searching for the Sound*, by Phil Lesh.

LITTLE, BROWN AND CO. BOOKS FOR YOUNG READERS

Hachette Book Group USA 237 Park Ave., New York NY 10017. (212)364-1100. Fax: (212)364-0925. Website: www.lb-kids.com. Estab. 1837. Publishes picture books, board books, chapter books, novelty books, and general nonfiction and novels for middle and young adult readers. **Publishes 100-150 titles/year. Pays royalty on retail price. Pays negotiable advance.** Publishes book 1-2 years after acceptance of ms. Accepts simultaneous submissions. Responds in 1 month to queries. Responds in 2 months to proposals. Responds in 2 months to manuscripts.

Imprints Editorial Director, Poppy (young women's commercial fiction imprint): Cynthia Eagan; Editorial Director, LB Kids (novelty and licensed books imprint): Liza Baker.

O-ᴛ Little, Brown and Co. Children's Publishing publishes all formats including board books, picture books, middle grade fiction, and nonfiction YA titles. We are looking for strong writing and presentation, but no predetermined topics.

Nonfiction Subjects include animals, art, architecture, ethnic, gay, lesbian, history, hobbies, nature, environment, recreation, science, sports. Agented submissions only.

Fiction Picture books, middle grade and young adult.Subjects include adventure, fantasy, feminist, gay, lesbian, historical, humor, mystery, science fiction, suspense, chic k lit, multicultural. We are looking for strong fiction for children of all ages in any area. We always prefer full manuscripts for fiction. Agented submissions only.

Recent Title(s) *The Gulps*, by Rosemary Wells, illustrated by Marc Brown; *Hug Time*, by Patrick McDonnel; *Bye-Bye, Big Bad Bullybug!*, by Ed Emberley.

Tips In order to break into the field, authors and illustrators should research their competition and try to come up with something outstandingly different.

LITTLE SIMON

Imprint of Simon & Schuster Children's Publishing Division, Simon & Schuster 1230 Avenue of the Americas, New York NY 10020. (212)698-1295. Fax: (212)698-2794. Website: www.simonsayskids.com. Publishes novelty and branded books only. **Offers advance and royalties.**

- *Currently not accepting unsolicited mss.*
- Our goal is to provide fresh material in an innovative format for preschool to age 8. Our books are often, if not exclusively, format driven.

Nonfiction We publish very few nonfiction titles.Query with SASE.

Fiction Novelty books include many things that do not fit in the traditional hardcover or paperback format, such as pop-up, board book, scratch and sniff, glow in the dark, lift the flap, etc. Children's/juvenile. No picture books. Large part of the list is holiday-themed.

Recent Title(s) *Mother's Day Ribbons*, by Michelle Knudsen, illustrated by John Wallace; *Dear Zoo*, by Rod Campbell; *My Blankie*, by Patricia Ryan Lampl, illustrated by Valeria Petrone.

LIVINGSTON PRESS

University of West Alabama Station 22, Livingston AL 35470. E-mail: jwt@uwa.edu. Website: www.livingstonpress.uwa.edu. **Contact:** Joe Taylor, director. Estab. 1974. Publishes hardcover and trade paperback originals. **Publishes 10-12 titles/year. 50% of books from first-time authors. 100% from unagented writers. Pays 150 contributor's copies, after sales of 1,500, standard royalty** Publishes book 18 months after acceptance of ms. Accepts simultaneous submissions. Responds in 1 month to queries. Responds in 6 mos. - 1 year to manuscripts. Book catalog for SASE. Guidelines available online.

Imprints Swallow's Tale Press.

- Reads mss in March only.
- Livingston Press, as do all literary presses, looks for authorial excellence in style. Currently emphasizing novels. Other than Tartts Contest, we read in June only.

Fiction Subjects include experimental, literary, short story collections, off-beat or Southern. We are interested in form and, of course, style. Query with SASE.

Recent Title(s) *The Soft Room*, by Karen Heuler; *B. Horror and Other Stories*, by Wendell Mayo.

Tips Our readers are interested in literature, often quirky literature that emphasizes form and style. Please visit our website for current needs.

LLEWELLYN ESPAÑOL

2143 Wooddale Dr., Woodbury MN 55125. Website: www.llewellyn.com. Estab. 1993. Publishes mass market and trade reprints. Accepts simultaneous submissions. Guidelines available online.

- "Publishes Spanish-language books for people of any age interested in material discussing mind, body and spirit."

Nonfiction Subjects include health, medicine, New Age, psychology, sex, spirituality, foods/nutrition; angels; magic. Reviews artwork/photos. Send photocopies.

Recent Title(s) *Miguel: Comunicÿndose con el Arcÿngel para la orientación y protección*; *Las llaves del reino: Jesús y la cábala cristiana*, by Migene Gonzalez-Wippler.

LLEWELLYN PUBLICATIONS

Imprint of Llewellyn Worldwide, Ltd. 2143 Wooddale Dr., Woodbury MN 55125. Website: www.llewellyn.com. **Contact:** Acquisitions Editor. Estab. 1901. Publishes trade and mass market paperback originals. **Publishes 100+ titles/year. 30% of books from first-time authors. 50% from unagented writers. Pays 10% royalty on wholesale or retail price.** Accepts simultaneous submissions. Responds in 3 months to queries. Book catalog for 9 x 12 SAE with 4 first-class stamps.

- "Llewellyn publishes New Age fiction and nonfiction exploring new worlds of mind and spirit. Currently emphasizing astrology, alternative health and healing, tarot. De-emphasizing fiction, channeling."

Nonfiction Subjects include cooking, foods, nutrition, health, medicine, nature, environment, New Age, psychology, womens issues, womens studies. Submit outline, sample chapters. Reviews artwork/photos.

Recent Title(s) *Authentic Spirituality*, by Richard N. Potter; *You Are Psychic*, by Debra Katz.

LOFT PRESS, INC.

P.O. Box 150, Fort Valley VA 22652. (540)933-6210. Website: www.loftpress.com. **Contact:** Ann A. Hunter, editor-in-chief. Publishes hardcover and trade paperback originals and reprints. **Publishes 8-16 titles/year. 800 queries received/year. 250 mss received/year. 75% of books from first-time authors. 100% from unagented writers.** Publishes book 6 months after acceptance of ms. Guidelines available online.

Imprints Punch Press, Eschat Press, Far Muse Press (for all contact Stephen R. Hunter, publisher).

Nonfiction Subjects include Americana, art, architecture, business, economics, computers, electronics, government, politics, history, language, literature, memoirs, philosophy, regional, religion, science. Submit proposal package, outline, 1 sample chapter. Reviews artwork/photos. Send photocopies.
Fiction Subjects include literary, poetry, regional, short story collections. Submit proposal package, 1 sample chapter, clips.
Recent Title(s) Essential Self, Your True Identity, by Joseph Walsh; *Quest for Justice*, by Henry E. Hudson; *Telly the White-Liver Woman*, by Isaac Chin; *Zula Remembers*, by Zula Dietrich.

LONELY PLANET PUBLICATIONS

150 Linden St., Oakland CA 94607-2538. (510)893-8555. Fax: (510)893-8563. E-mail: info@lonelyplanet.com. Website: www.lonelyplanet.com. Estab. 1973. Publishes trade paperback originals. **Work-for-hire: 1/3 on contract, 1/3 on submission, 1/3 on approval Pays advance.** Accepts simultaneous submissions. Responds in 3 months to queries. Book catalog available online. Guidelines available online.

- Lonely Planet publishes travel guides, atlases, travel literature, phrasebooks, condensed pocket guides, diving and snorkeling guides.

Nonfiction We only work with contract writers on book ideas that we originate. We do not accept original proposals. Request our writer's guidelines. Send resume and clips of travel writing.Subjects include travel. Query with SASE.
Recent Title(s) *Europe on a Shoestring, 4th Ed.*, by China Williams; *Morocco, 7th Ed.*, by Mara Vorhees; *Vietnam, 8th Ed.*, by Wendy Yanagihara.

LOUISIANA STATE UNIVERSITY PRESS

3990 W. Lakeshore Dr., Baton Rouge LA 70808. (225)578-6295. Fax: (225)578-6461. Website: www.lsu.edu/lsupress. **Contact:** Exec. Ed.: John Easterly (poetry, fiction, literary studies); Sr. Ed.: Rand Dotson (U.S. History & Southern Studies). Estab. 1935. Publishes hardcover and paperback originals, and reprints. Publishes 8 poetry titles per year and 2 works of original fiction as part of the Yellow Shoe Fiction series. **Publishes 80-90 titles/year. 33% of books from first-time authors. 95% from unagented writers. Pays royalty.** Publishes book 1 year after acceptance of ms. Responds in 1 month to queries. Book catalog and ms guidelines free.

- Publishes in the fall and spring.

Nonfiction Subjects include Americana, animals, anthropology, archeology, art, architecture, ethnic, government, politics, history, language, literature, literary criticism, memoirs, military, war, Civil & WWII, music, dance, Southern, Jazz, nature, environment, philosophy, Political, photography, regional, sociology, womens issues, womens studies, world affairs, geography and environmental studies. Query with SASE. Submit proposal package, outline, sample chapters, cover letter, resume.
Fiction Query with SASE. Submit proposal package, sample chapters, resume, clips, and cover letter.
Recent Title(s) *Frontiersman: Daniel Boone and the Making of America* (history), by Meredith Mason Brown; *Revenge of the Teacher's Pet: A Love Story* (fiction), by Darrin Doyle; *Creatures of a Day* (poetry), by Reginald Gibbons.

LOVE INSPIRED

Imprint of Steeple Hill 233 Broadway, Suite 1001, New York NY 10279. (212)553-4200. Fax: (212)227-8969. Website: www.steeplehill.com. **Contact:** Joan Marlow Golan, executive editor (inspirational fiction); Krista Stroever, senior editor (inspirational fiction); Melissa Endlich, editor (inspirational fiction); Emily Rodmell, assistant editor (inspirational fiction). Estab. 1997. Publishes mass market paperback originals. **Publishes 100-120 titles/year. Pays royalty on retail price. Pays advance.** Responds in 3 months to queries. Responds in 3 months to proposals. Responds in 3 months to manuscripts. Guidelines available online.
Fiction Subjects include religious, romance. The Love Inspired line is a series of contemporary, inspirational romances that feature Christian characters facing the many challenges of life and love in today's world. We only publish inspirational romance between 55,000 and 60,000 words. Query with SASE.
Recent Title(s) *Her Perfect Man*, by Jillian Hart; *A Dry Creek Courtship*, by Janet Tronstad.
Tips Please read our guidelines.

LOVE INSPIRED SUSPENSE

Imprint of Steeple Hill 233 Broadway, Suite 1001, New York NY 10279. (212)553-4200. Fax: (212)227-8969. Website: www.steeplehill.com. **Contact:** Joan Marlow Golan, executive editor (inspirational fiction); Krista Stroever, senior editor (inspirational fiction); Melissa Endlich, editor (inspirational fiction); Emily Rodmell, assistant editor (inspirational fiction). Estab. 1997. Publishes mass market paperback originals. **Publishes 100-120 titles/year. Pays royalty on retail price. Pays advance.** Responds in 3 months to queries. Responds in 3 months to proposals. Responds in 3 months to manuscripts. Guidelines available online.
Fiction Subjects include religious, romance, suspense. This series features edge-of-the-seat, comtemporary romantic suspense tales of intrigue and romance featuring Christian characters facing challenges to their faith and to their lives. We only publish novels between 55,000 and 60,000 words. Query with SASE.
Recent Title(s) *The Guardian's Mission*, by Shirlee McCoy; *Double Cross*, by Terri Reed.

Tips Please read our guidelines.

LOVE SPELL

Imprint of Dorchester Publishing Co., Inc. 200 Madison Ave., Suite 2000, New York NY 10016. (212)725-8811. Fax: (212)532-1054. Website: www.dorchesterpub.com. **Contact:** Leah Hultenschmidt, editor; Christopher Keeslar, senior editor; Alicia Condon, editorial director. Publishes mass market paperback originals. **Publishes 48 titles/year. 1,500-2,000 queries received/year. 150-500 mss received/year. 30% of books from first-time authors. 25-30% from unagented writers. Pays royalty on retail price. Pays variable advance.** Publishes book 1 year after acceptance of ms. Responds in 8 months to manuscripts. Book catalog for free or by calling (800)481-9191. Guidelines available online.

- Love Spell publishes the many sub-genres of romance: time-travel, paranormal, futuristic and romantic suspense. Despite the exotic settings, we are still interested in character-driven plots.

Fiction Subjects include romance, futuristic, time travel, paranormal, romantic suspense, whimsical contemporaries. Books industry-wide are getting shorter; we're interested in 90,000 words. Query with SASE. Submit clips. No material will be returned w.

Recent Title(s) *The Deadliest Denial*, by Colleen Thompson; *Shadow Touch*, by Marjorie M. Liu.

N LOVING HEALING PRESS INC.

5145 Pontiac Trail, Ann Arbor MI 48105-9627. (888)761-6268. E-mail: info@lovinghealing.com. Website: www.lovinghealing.com. **Contact:** Victor R. Volkman, Sr. Editor (psychology, self-help, personal growth, trauma recovery). Hardcover originals and reprints; Trade paperback originals and reprints. **Publishes 20 titles/year. Receives 80 queries/year; 40 mss/year 50% of books from first-time authors. 80% from unagented writers.** Publishes book 8 months after acceptance of ms. Accepts simultaneous submissions. Catalog available online at website. Guidelines online at website http://lovinghealing.com/aboutus.

Nonfiction Subjects include child guidance, health, memoirs, psychology, social work. Submit proposal package, including: outline, 3 sample chapters; submit completed ms. Reviews artwork/photos as part of the ms package; send JPEG files.

Fiction Subjects include multicultural, social change. Submit completed ms.

LOYOLA PRESS

3441 N. Ashland Ave., Chicago IL 60657-1397. (773)281-1818. Fax: (773)281-0152. E-mail: editorial@loyolapress.com. Website: www.loyolapress.org. **Contact:** Joseph Durepos, acquisitions editor. Publishes hardcover and trade paperback. **Publishes 20-30 titles/year. 500 queries received/year. Pays standard royalties. Offers reasonable advance.** Accepts simultaneous submissions. Book catalog available online. Guidelines available online.

Imprints Loyola Classics (new editions of classic Catholic literature).

Nonfiction Subjects include religion, spirituality, inspirational, prayer, Catholic life, parish and adult faith formation resources with a special focus on Ignatian spirituality and Jesuit history. Query with SASE.

Recent Title(s) *My Life With the Saints*, by James Martin, S.J.; *Heroic Leadership*, by Chris Lowney; *The Shoemaker's Gospel*, by Daniel Brent.

Tips We're looking for motivated authors who have a passion for the Catholic tradition, to prayer and spirituality, and to helping readers respond to the existence of God in their lives.

⊘ MACADAM/CAGE PUBLISHING, INC.

155 Sansome St., Suite 550, San Francisco CA 94104. (415)986-7502. Fax: (415)986-7414. Website: www.macadamcage.com. **Contact:** Manuscript Submissions. Estab. 1999. Publishes hardcover and trade paperback originals. **Publishes 25-30 titles/year. 5,000 queries received/year. 1,500 mss received/year. 75% of books from first-time authors. 50% from unagented writers. Pays negotiable royalties. Pays negotiable advance.** Publishes book up to 1 year after acceptance of ms. Accepts simultaneous submissions.

- "We look at agented and unagented mss. with equal vigor."
- "MacAdam/Cage publishes quality works of literary fiction that are carefully crafted and tell a bold story. De-emphasizing romance, poetry, Christian or New Age mss."

Nonfiction Subjects include history, memoirs, science, social sciences.

Fiction Subjects include historical, literary, mainstream, contemporary.

Recent Title(s) *The Time Traveler's Wife*, by Audrey Niffenegger; *The Lost Country*, by William Gay; *The Most They Ever Had*, by Rick Bragg.

Tips "We care about great writing and storytelling. We don't really care about 'hot' trends."

N MANDALEY PRESS

720 Rio Grande Dr., Suite 100, Alpharetta GA 30022. E-mail: msatt@mindspring.com. **Contact:** Mark Satterfield, president (business books with a particular interest in sales training). Estab. 2001. Publishes hardcover, trade paperback, and mass market paperback originals. **Publishes 10 titles/year. 50 queries received/year. 50 mss received/year. 80% of books from first-time authors. 100% from unagented writers. Pays 10-20% royalty**

on wholesale price. Publishes book 6 months after acceptance of ms. Accepts simultaneous submissions. Responds in 1 month to queries. Responds in 2 months to proposals. Responds in 2 months to manuscripts.
Nonfiction Subjects include audio, business, economics. Query with SASE. Reviews artwork/photos.

MARINER BOOKS

Houghton Mifflin Trade Division 222 Berkeley St., 8th Floor,, Boston MA 02116. (617)351-5000. Fax: (617)351-1202. Website: www.hmco.com. Estab. 1997. Publishes trade paperback originals and reprints. **Pays royalty on retail price. Makes outright purchase. Pays variable advance.** Book catalog available free.

- Houghton Mifflin books give shape to ideas that educate, inform and delight. Mariner has an eclectic list that notably embraces fiction.

Nonfiction Subjects include education, government, politics, history, nature, environment, philosophy, science, sociology, political thought. Agented submissions only.
Fiction Subjects include literary, mainstream, contemporary. Agented submissions only.
Recent Title(s) *The End of Oil*, by Paul Roberts (politics/environment); *The Namesake*, by Jhumpa Lahiri (literary fiction); *Bury the Chains*, by Adam Hochschild (history).

MCBOOKS PRESS

ID Booth Building, 520 N. Meadow St., Ithaca NY 14850. (607)272-2114. Fax: (607)273-6068. E-mail: jackie@mcbooks.com. Website: www.mcbooks.com. **Contact:** Jackie Swift, editorial director. Estab. 1979. Publishes trade paperback and hardcover originals and reprints. **Publishes 6 titles/year. Pays 5-10% royalty on retail price. Pays $1,000-5,000 advance.** Accepts simultaneous submissions. Responds in 3 months to queries and proposals. Guidelines available online.

- In the current tough book market, the author's ability to use the internet for self promotion is extremely important. Show that you're savvy with personal web sites, blogs, and social networking; and show you know who your audience is and how to generate word-of-mouth.

Nonfiction Query with SASE. Give us a general outline of your book. Let us know how your book differs from what is currently on the market and what your qualifications are for writing it. Give us an idea how you would go about promoting/marketing your book.
Fiction Subjects include historical, nautical, naval and military historical. We will consider any type of fiction. Submission guidelines available on web site. Send cover letter and first 3 chapters, and well-thought-out marketing plan. Query with SASE.
Recent Title(s) *Night of Flames*, by Douglas W. Jacobson; *Four Kings*, by George Kimball; *Better Than Peanut Butter & Jelly, 2nd Ed.*, by Marty Mattare and Wendy Muldawer.

MARGARET K. MCELDERRY BOOKS

Imprint of Simon & Schuster Children's Publishing Division, Simon & Schuster 1230 Sixth Ave., New York NY 10020. (212)698-7000. Website: www.simonsayskids.com. **Contact:** Acquisitions Editor. Estab. 1971. Publishes quality material for preschoolers to 18-year-olds. Publishes hardcover originals. **Publishes 30 titles/year. 4,000 queries received/year. 15% of books from first-time authors. 50% from unagented writers. Average print order is 5,000-10,000 for a first middle grade or young adult book; 7,500-20,000 for a first picture book. Pays royalty on hardcover retail price: 10% fiction; picture book, 5% author and 5% illustrator. Offers $5,000-8,000 advance for new authors.** Publishes book up to 3 years after acceptance of ms. Guidelines for #10 SASE.

- We are more interested in superior writing and illustration than in a particular `type' of book. Currently emphasizing young picture books and funny middle grade fiction.

Nonfiction Subjects include history, adventure.
Fiction Subjects include adventure, fantasy, historical, mainstream, contemporary, mystery, picture books, young adult, or middle grade, All categories (fiction and nonfiction) for juvenile and young adult. We will consider any category. Results depend on the quality of the imagination, the artwork, and the writing. Send query letter with SASE on
Recent Title(s) *Bear Stays Up for Christmas*, by Karma Wilson, illustrated by Jane Chapman (picture book); *Indigo's Star*, by Hilary McKay (middle-grade fiction); *The Legend of Buddy Bush*, by Shelia P. Moses (teen fiction).
Tips Read! The children's book field is competitive. See what's been done and what's out there before submitting. We look for high quality: an originality of ideas, clarity and felicity of expression, a well-organized plot, and strong character-driven stories.

MCFARLAND & CO., INC., PUBLISHERS

Box 611, Jefferson NC 28640. (336)246-4460. Fax: (336)246-5018. E-mail: info@mcfarlandpub.com. Website: www.mcfarlandpub.com. **Contact:** Steve Wilson, editorial director (automotive, general); David Alff, editor (general); Gary Mitchem, acquisitions editor (general, baseball). Estab. 1979. Publishes hardcover and quality paperback originals; a nontrade publisher. **Publishes 350 titles/year. 50% of books from first-time authors. 95% from unagented writers.** Publishes book 10 months after acceptance of ms. Responds in 1 month to queries. Guidelines available online.

- McFarland publishes serious nonfiction in a variety of fields, including general reference, performing arts, popular culture, sports (particularly baseball); women's studies, librarianship, literature, Civil War, history and international studies. Currently emphasizing medieval history, automotive history. De-emphasizing memoirs.

Nonfiction Subjects include art, architecture, automotive, health, medicine, history, military, war/war, popular contemporary culture, music, dance, recreation, sociology, world affairs, sports (very strong), African-American studies (very strong). Query with SASE. Submit outline, sample chapters. Reviews artwork/photos.
Recent Title(s) *American Cars, 1946-1959*, by J. "Kelly" Flory, Jr.; *Classic Home Video Games, 1972-1984*, by Brett Weiss; *African American Mystery Writers*, by Frankie Y. Bailey.
Tips We want well-organized knowledge of an area in which there is not information coverage at present, plus reliability so we don't feel we have to check absolutely everything. Our market is worldwide and libraries are an important part. McFarland also publishes six journals: the *Journal of Information Ethics*, *North Korean Review*, *Base Ball: A Journal of the Early Game*, *Black Ball: A Negro Leagues Journal*, *Clues: A Journal of Detection*, and *Minerva Journal of Women and War*.

N MC PRESS

125 N. Woodland Trail, Double Oak TX 75077. Fax: (682)831-0701. E-mail: mlee@mcpressonline.com. Website: www.mcpressonline.com. **Contact:** Merrikay Lee, president (computer). Estab. 2001. Publishes trade paperback originals. **Publishes 40 titles/year. 100 queries received/year. 50 mss received/year. 5% of books from first-time authors. 5% from unagented writers. Pays 10-16% royalty on wholesale price.** Publishes book 5 months after acceptance of ms. Accepts simultaneous submissions. Responds in 1 month to queries. Responds in 1 month to proposals. Responds in 1 month to manuscripts. Book catalog and ms guidelines free.
Imprints MC Press, IBM Press.
Nonfiction Subjects include computers, electronics. Submit proposal package, outline, 2 sample chapters, abstract. Reviews artwork/photos. Send photocopies.
Recent Title(s) *Understanding the IBM Web Facing Tool*, by Claus Weiss and Emily Bruner (computer); *Eclipse Step-by-Step*, by Jae Pluta (computer).

N ME & MI PUBLISHING

English-Spanish Foundation 128 South County Farm Rd., Suite E, Wheaton IL 60187. Fax: (630)588-9801. E-mail: m3@memima.com. Website: www.memima.com. **Contact:** Mark Wesley, acquisition editor (pre-K-1). Estab. 2001. Publishes hardcover originals. **Publishes 10 titles/year. 30 queries received/year. 30 mss received/year. 30% of books from first-time authors. 70% from unagented writers. Pays 5% royalty on wholesale price. Makes outright purchase of 1,000-3,000.** Publishes book 1 year after acceptance of ms. Accepts simultaneous submissions. Responds in 1 month to queries. Responds in 3 months to proposals. Responds in 4 months to manuscripts. Book catalog available online. Guidelines available via e-mail.
Nonfiction Subjects include ethnic, language, literature, multicultural. Submit complete ms. Reviews artwork/photos. Send photocopies.
Tips Our audience is pre-K to 2nd grade. Our books are bilingual (Spanish and English).

MEADOWBROOK PRESS

5451 Smetana Dr., Minnetonka MN 55343. (952)930-1100. Fax: (952)930-1940. E-mail: editorial@meadowbrookpress.com. Website: www.meadowbrookpress.com. **Contact:** Submissions Editor. Estab. 1975. Publishes trade paperback originals and reprints. **Publishes 12 titles/year. 1,500 queries received/year. 10% of books from first-time authors. Pays 7 ½ % royalty. Pays small advance.** Publishes book 18 months-2 years after acceptance of ms. Accepts simultaneous submissions. Responds only if interested to queries. Book catalog for #10 SASE. Guidelines available online.

- Meadowbrook is a family-oriented press which specializes in parenting and pregnancy books, children's poetry books.

Nonfiction Subjects include child guidance, cooking, foods, nutrition, pregnancy. Query or submit outline with sample chapters.
Recent Title(s) *Tinkle, Tinkle, Little Tot*, by Bruce Lansky, Robert Pottle and friends (childcare); *The Official Lamaze Guide*, by Judith Lothion and Charlotte DeVries (pregnancy).
Tips Always send for guidelines before submitting material. Always submit nonreturnable copies; we do not respond to queries or submissions unless interested.

MENASHA RIDGE PRESS

P.O. Box 43673, Birmingham AL 35243. (205)322-0439. Website: www.menasharidge.com. **Contact:** Molly Merkle, associate publisher (travel, reference); Russell Helms, senior acquisitions editor. Publishes hardcover and trade paperback originals. **Publishes 20 titles/year. 30% of books from first-time authors. 85% from unagented writers. Pays varying royalty. Pays varying advance.** Publishes book 1 year after acceptance of ms. Accepts simultaneous submissions. Responds in 2 months to queries. Book catalog for 9x12 envelope and

4 First-Class stamps.

O→ Menasha Ridge Press publishes distinctive books in the areas of outdoor sports, travel, and diving. Our authors are among the best in their fields.

Nonfiction Subjects include recreation, outdoor, sports, adventure, travel, outdoors. Submit proposal package, resume, clips. Reviews artwork/photos.

Recent Title(s) *Sex in the Outdoors*, by Buck Tilton.

Tips Audience is 25-60, 14-18 years' education, white collar and professional, $30,000 median income, 75% male, 55% east of the Mississippi River.

N MENC

1806 Robert Fulton Dr., Reston VA 20191-4348. Fax: (703)860-9443. Website: www.menc.org. **Contact:** Frances Ponick, director of publications; Ashley Opp, assistant acquisitions editor. Estab. 1907. Publishes hardcover and trade paperback originals. **Publishes 15 titles/year. 75 queries received/year. 50 mss received/year. 40% of books from first-time authors. 100% from unagented writers. Pays royalty on retail price.** Publishes book 1-2 years after acceptance of ms. Responds in 2 months to queries. Responds in 4 months to proposals. Book catalog available online. Guidelines available online.

Nonfiction Subjects include child guidance, education, multicultural, music, dance, music education. Submit proposal package, outline, 1-3 sample chapters, bio, CV, marketing strategy.

Tips Look online for book proposal guidelines. No telephone calls. We are committed to music education books that will serve as the very best resources for music educators, students and their parents.

MERIWETHER PUBLISHING, LTD.

P.O. Box 7710, Colorado Springs CO 80903. Fax: (719)594-9916. E-mail: editor@meriwether.com. **Contact:** Theodore Zape, assoc.l editor. Estab. 1969. Publishes paperback originals and reprints. **Pays 10% royalty or negotiates purchase.** Accepts simultaneous submissions. Responds in 6 weeks. Book catalog and ms guidelines for $2 postage.

O→ "We are specialists in theater arts books and plays for middle grades, high schools, and colleges. We publish textbooks for drama courses of all types. We also publish for mainline liturgical churches—drama activities for church holidays, youth activities, and fundraising entertainment. These may be plays, musicals, or drama-related books. Query with synopsis or submit complete script."

Nonfiction Query with synopsis or submit complete script. "Contemporary Drama Service is now looking for play or musical adaptations of classic stories by famous authors and playwrights. Also looking for parodies of famous movies or historical and/or fictional characters (i.e., Robin Hood, Rip Van Winkle, Buffalo Bill, Huckleberry Finn). Obtains either amateur or all rights."

Fiction Plays and musical comedies for middle grades through college only.Subjects include mainstream, contemporary, plays, and musicals, religious, children's plays and religious Christmas and Easter plays, suspense, all in playscript format, comedy. Query with SASE.

Recent Title(s) *100 Great Monologs*, by Rebecca Young; *Group Improvisation*, by Peter Gwinn; *112 Acting Games*, by Gavin Levy.

Tips "Contemporary Drama Service is looking for creative books on comedy, monologs, staging amateur theatricals, and Christian youth activities. Our writers are usually highly experienced in theatre as teachers or performers. We welcome books that reflect their experience and special knowledge. Any good comedy writer of monologs and short scenes will find a home with us."

MERRIAM PRESS

133 Elm St., Apt. 3R, Bennington VT 05201-2250. (802)447-0313. E-mail: ray@merriam-press.com. Website: www.merriam-press.com. Estab. 1988. Publishes hardcover and softcover trade paperback originals and reprints. **Publishes 12+ titles/year. 70-90% of books from first-time authors. 100% from unagented writers. Pays 10% royalty on actual selling price.** Publishes book 12 months or less after acceptance of ms. Responds quickly (e-mail preferred) to queries. Book catalog available for $1 or visit website to view all available titles and access writer's guidelines and info.

O→ Merriam Press publishes only military history - particularly World War II history.

Nonfiction Subjects include military, war, World War II. Query with SASE or by e-mail first. Reviews artwork/photos. Send photocopies and on floppy disk/CD.

Recent Title(s) *Water in my Veins: The Pauper Who Helped Save a President*, by Ted Robinson; *I Hear No Bugles*, by Robert W. Mercy; *The Mailman Went UA: A Vietnam Memoir*, by David Mulldune; *Here Rests in Honored Glory: Life Stories of our Country's Medal of Honor Recipients*, by Andrew J. Dekever.

Tips Our books are geared for military historians, collectors, model kit builders, war-gamers, veterans, general enthusiasts. We do not publish any fiction or poetry, only WWII military history, military history and veteran memoirs.

METAL POWDER INDUSTRIES FEDERATION

105 College Rd. E., Princeton NJ 08540. (609)452-7700. Fax: (609)987-8523. E-mail: info@mpif.org. Website:

www.mpif.org. **Contact:** Jim Adams, director of technical services; Peggy Lebedz, assistant publications manager. Estab. 1946. Publishes hardcover originals. **Publishes 10 titles/year. Pays 3-12 ½% royalty on wholesale or retail price. Pays $3,000-5,000 advance.** Responds in 1 month to queries.

- Metal Powder Industries publishes monographs, textbooks, handbooks, design guides, conference proceedings, standards, and general titles in the field of powder metallurgy or particulate materials.

Nonfiction Work must relate to powder metallurgy or particulate materials.

Recent Title(s) *Advances in Powder Metallurgy and Particulate Materials*, (conference proceeding).

MICHIGAN STATE UNIVERSITY PRESS

1405 S. Harrison Rd. Manly Miles Bldg., Suite 25, East Lansing MI 48823-5202. (517)355-9543. Fax: (517)432-2611. E-mail: msupress@msu.edu. Website: www.msupress.msu.edu. **Contact:** Martha Bates, acquisitions editor. Estab. 1947. Publishes hardcover and softcover originals. **Pays variable royalty.** Book catalog and ms guidelines for 9X12 SASE or online.

- Distributes books for: University of Calgary Press, Penumbra Press, National Museum of Science (UK), African Books Collective, University of Alberta Press, University of Manitoba Press.
- Michigan State University publishes scholarly books that further scholarship in their particular field. In addition, they publish nonfiction that addresses, in a more contemporary way, social concerns, such as diversity, civil rights, and the environment. They also publish literary fiction and poetry.

Nonfiction Subjects include Americana, American studies, business, economics, creative nonfiction, ethnic, Afro-American studies, government, politics, history, contemporary civil rights , language, literature, literary criticism, regional, Great Lakes regional, Canadian studies, womens issues, womens studies. Submit proposal/outline and sample chapter. Reviews artwork/photos.

Recent Title(s) *5 Years of the 4th Genre*, edited by Martha A. Bates; *Jewish Life in the Industrial Promised Land, 1855-2005*, by Nora Faires and Nancy Hanflik; *My Father on a Bicycle*, by Patricia Clark.

MICROSOFT PRESS

E-mail: 4bkideas@microsoft.com. Website: www.microsoft.com/learning/books. **Contact:** Editor. **Publishes 60 titles/year. 25% of books from first-time authors. 90% from unagented writers.** Book proposal guidelines available online.

Nonfiction We place a great deal of emphasis on your proposal. A proposal provides us with a basis for evaluating the idea of the book and how fully your book fulfills its purpose.Subjects include software.

MILKWEED EDITIONS

1011 Washington Ave. S., Minneapolis MN 55415. (612)332-3192. E-mail: editor@milkweed.org. Website: www.milkweed.org. **Contact:** Patrick Thomas, assoc. ed. Estab. 1979. Publishes hardcover, trade paperback, and electronic originals; trade paperback and electronic reprints. **Publishes 15-20 titles/year. 25% of books from first-time authors. 75% from unagented writers. Pays 7% royalty on retail price. Pays varied advance from $500-10,000.** Publishes book 18 months. after acceptance of ms. Accepts simultaneous submissions. Responds in 6 months to queries, proposals, and mss. Book catalog available online at website. Guidelines available online at website http://www.milkweed.org/content/blogcategory/.

Nonfiction Subjects include agriculture, animals, archaeology, art, contemporary culture, creative nonfiction, environment, gardening, gay, government, history, humanities, language, literature, multicultural, nature, politics, regional, translation, women's issues, world affairs, literary. Submit complete ms with SASE Does not review artwork.

Fiction Subjects include experimental, short story collections, translation, young adult. Novels for adults and for readers 8-13. High literary quality. For adult readers: literary fiction, nonfiction, poetry, essays. For children (ages 8-13): literary novels. Translations welcome for both audiences. Query with SASE, submit completed ms.

Recent Title(s) *The Wet Collection*, by Joni Tevis (creative nonfiction); *The Future of Nature*, ed. by Barry Lopiz (environmental lit); *The Farther Shore*, by Matthew Eck (literary); *Driftless*, by David Rhodes (literary); *Hallelujah Blackout*, by Alex Lemon (poetry);*The Book of Props,* by Wayne Miller (poetry).

Tips "We are looking for excellent writing with the intent of making a humane impact on society. Send for guidelines. Acquaint yourself with our books in terms of style and quality before submitting. Many factors influence our selection process, so don't get discouraged. Nonfiction is focused on literary writing about the natural world, including living well in urban environments."

MINNESOTA HISTORICAL SOCIETY PRESS

Minnesota Historical Society 345 Kellogg Blvd. W., St. Paul MN 55102-1906. (651)259-3200. Fax: (651)297-1345. Website: www.mhspress.org. **Contact:** Ann Regan, editor-in-chief. Estab. 1852. Publishes hardcover, trade paperback and electronic originals; trade paperback and electronic reprints. **Publishes 30 titles/year. 300 queries received/year. 150 mss received/year. 60% of books from first-time authors. 95% from unagented writers. Royalties are negotiated; 5-10% on wholesale price. Pays $1,000 and up.** Publishes book 16 months after acceptance of ms. Accepts simultaneous submissions. Responds in 1 month to queries, 2 months on proposals, 2-4 months on mss. Book catalog online and available free. Guidelines available online and are free.

Imprints Borealis Books, Minnesota Historical Society Press; Ann Regan, editor-in-chief.

Minnesota Historical Society Press publishes both scholarly and general interest books that contribute to the understanding of the Midwest.

Nonfiction Regional works only.Subjects include scholarly, Americana, anthropology, archaeology, art, architecture, community, cooking, foods, nutrition, creative nonfiction, ethnic, government, politics, history, memoirs, multicultural, nature, environment, photography, regional, womens issues, womens studies, Native American studies. Submit proposal package, outline, 1 sample chapter and other materials listed in our online website in author guidelines: CV, brief description, intended audience, readership, length of ms, schedule. Reviews artwork/photos. Send photocopies.

Recent Title(s) *Opening Goliath: Danger and Discovery in Caving*, by Gary J. Griffith; *Tales of the Road: Highway 61*, by Cathy Wurzer; *Tell Me True: Memoir, History, and Writing a Life*, edited by Patricia Hampl and Elaine Tyler May.

MITCHELL LANE PUBLISHERS, INC.

P.O. Box 196, Hockessin DE 19707. (302)234-9426. Fax: (302)234-4742. **Contact:** Barbara Mitchell, publisher. Estab. 1993. Publishes hardcover and library bound originals. **Publishes 85 titles/year. 100 queries received/year. 5 mss received/year. 0% of books from first-time authors. 90% from unagented writers. Makes outright purchase on work-for-hire basis.** Publishes book 1 year after acceptance of ms. Responds only if interested to queries. Book catalog available free.

"Mitchell Lane publishes quality nonfiction for children and young adults."

Nonfiction Subjects include ethnic, multicultural. Query with SASE. *All unsolicited mss discarded.*

Recent Title(s) *How to Convince Your Parents You Can Care for a Pet Mouse*; *Frogs in Danger*, (What's So Great About Harriet Tubman).

Tips "We hire writers on a `work-for-hire' basis to complete book projects we assign. Send resume and writing samples that do not need to be returned."

MODERN LANGUAGE ASSOCIATION OF AMERICA

26 Broadway, 3rd Floor, New York NY 10004-1789. (646)576-5000. Fax: (646)458-0030. **Contact:** Sonia Kane, assistant director of book publications; James Hatch, associate acquisitions editor; Margit Longbrake, associate acquisitions editor. Estab. 1883. Publishes hardcover and paperback originals. **Publishes 15 titles/year. 100% from unagented writers.** Publishes book 1 year after acceptance of ms. Responds in 2 months to manuscripts. Book catalog available free.

The MLA publishes on current issues in literary and linguistic research and teaching of language and literature at postsecondary level.

Nonfiction Subjects include education, language, literature, translation, with companion volume in foreign language, literature, for classroom use. Query with SASE. Submit outline.

Recent Title(s) *Disciplinary Identities: Rhetorical Paths of English, Speech, and Composition*, by Steven Maillous; *Integrating Literature and Writing Instruction*, edited by Judith H. Anderson and Christine R. Farris.

MONDIAL

203 W. 107th St., Suite 6C, New York NY 10025. (212)851-3252. Fax: (208)361-2863. E-mail: contact@mondialbooks.com. Website: www.mondialbooks.com. **Contact:** Andrew Moore, editor. Estab. 1996. Publishes trade paperback originals and reprints. **Publishes 20 titles/year. 2,000 queries received/year. 500 mss received/year 5%% of books from first-time authors. Pays 10-10% royalty on wholesale price** Publishes book 2 months after acceptance of ms. Accepts simultaneous submissions. Guidelines available online.

Nonfiction Subjects include alternative, ethnic, gay, lesbian, history, language, literature, literary criticism, memoirs, multicultural, philosophy, psychology, sex, sociology, translation. Submit proposal package, outline, 1 sample chapters, Send only electronically by e-mail.

Fiction Subjects include adventure, erotica, ethnic, gay, lesbian, historical, literary, mainstream, contemporary, multicultural, mystery, poetry, romance, short story collections, translation.

Recent Title(s) Concise Encyclopedia of the Original Literature of Esperanto (740-page encyclopedia); Two People, by Donald Windham (novel/gay classics); Terminologie und Terminologieplanung in Esperanto, by Wera Blanke (linguistic); *Winter Ridge. A Love Story*, by Bruce Kellner (mature love story); *Bitterness (An African Novel from Zambia)*, by Malama Katulwende (love story and student revolt in Zambia).

MOODY PUBLISHERS

Moody Bible Institute 820 N. LaSalle Blvd., Chicago IL 60610. (312)329-8047. Fax: (312)329-2019. Website: www.moodypublishers.org. **Contact:** Acquisitions Coordinator. Estab. 1894. Publishes hardcover, trade, and mass market paperback originals. **Publishes 60 titles/year. 1,500 queries received/year. 2,000 mss received/year. 1% of books from first-time authors. 80% from unagented writers. Royalty varies. Pays $1,000-10,000 advance.** Publishes book 9-12 months after acceptance of ms. Responds in 2-3 months to queries. Book catalog for 9x12 envelope and 4 First-Class stamps. Guidelines for SASE and on website.

Imprints Northfield Publishing; Lift Every Voice (African American-interest).

- The mission of Moody Publishers is to educate and edify the Christian and to evangelize the non-Christian by ethically publishing conservative, evangelical Christian literature and other media for all ages around the world; and to help provide resources for Moody Bible Institute in its training of future Christian leaders.

Nonfiction Subjects include child guidance, money, finance, religion, spirituality, womens issues, womens studies. Agented submissions only.

Fiction Subjects include fantasy, historical, mystery, religious, children's religious, inspirational, religious mystery/suspense, science fiction, young adult, adventure, fantasy/science fiction fiction, historical, mystery/suspense, series. Query with 1 chapter and SASE.

Recent Title(s) *The Rats of Hamelin*, by Adam and Keith McCune; *Admission*, by Travis Thrasher; *Dawn of a Thousand Nights*, by Tricia Goyer.

Tips In our fiction list, we're looking for Christian storytellers rather than teachers trying to present a message. Your motivation should be to delight the reader. Using your skills to create beautiful works is glorifying to God.

MOREHOUSE PUBLISHING CO.

4475 Linglestown Rd., Harrisburg PA 17112. Fax: (717)541-8136. E-mail: nfitzgerald@cpg.org. Website: www.morehousepublishing.org. **Contact:** Nancy Fitzgerald, editor. Estab. 1884. Publishes hardcover and paperback originals. **Publishes 35 titles/year. 50% of books from first-time authors. Pays small advance.** Publishes book 18 months after acceptance of ms. Accepts simultaneous submissions. Responds in 2-3 months to queries. Guidelines available online.

- Morehouse Publishing publishes mainline Christian books, primarily Episcopal/Anglican works. Currently emphasizing Christian spiritual direction.

Nonfiction Subjects include religion, Christian, womens issues, womens studies, Christian spirituality, Liturgies, congregational resources, issues around Christian life. Submit outline, resume, 1-2 sample chapters, market analysis.

Recent Title(s) *Welcome to Sunday*, by Christopher Webber; *Knitting Into the Mystery*, by Susan Jorgensen; *A Wing and a Prayer*, by Katharine Jefferts Schori.

N MORGAN JAMES PUBLISHING

Morgan James LLC 1225 Franklin Ave., Suite 325, Garden City NY 11530. (516)620-2528. Website: www.morganjamespublishing.com. **Contact:** Rick Frishman, pub. (general nonfiction, business); David Hancock, founder (entrepreneurial business). hardcover, trade paperback, & electronic originals. **Publishes 163 titles/year. 4,500 queries/year; 3,700 mss/year. 60% of books from first-time authors. 80% from unagented writers.** Publishes book 6 months after acceptance of ms. Accepts simultaneous submissions. Catalog & guidelines free on request.

Nonfiction TrueSubjects include business, career guidance, child guidance, communications, computers, counseling, economics, education, electronics, finance, government, health, history, law, medicine, money, real estate, religion. Submit proposal package, including outline, 3 sample chapters; submit completed ms. Does not review artwork/photos.

Recent Title(s) *How I Made My First Million on the Internet*, by Ewen Chia; *Guerrilla Business Secrets*, by Jay Conrad Levinson.

Tips "Study www.morganjamespublishing.com."

MORGAN REYNOLDS PUBLISHING

620 S. Elm St., Suite 223, Greensboro NC 27406. (336)275-1311. Fax: (336)275-1152. E-mail: editorial@morganreynolds.com. Website: www.morganreynolds.com. **Contact:** Casey Cornelius, editor-in-chief. Estab. 1994. Publishes hardcover originals. **Publishes 35 titles/year. 250-300 queries received/year. 100-150 mss received/year. 50% of books from first-time authors. 100% from unagented writers. Pays advance and 10% royalty.** Publishes book 12-18 months after acceptance of ms. Accepts simultaneous submissions. Responds in 3 months to queries. Book catalog available online. Guidelines available online.

- Morgan Reynolds publishes nonfiction books for young-adult readers. We prefer lively, well-written biographies of interesting, contemporary and historical figures for our biography series. Books for our Great Events Series should be insightful and exciting looks at critical periods. Currently emphasizing great scientists and scientific subjects, world history, and world writers. De-emphasizing sports figures.

Nonfiction We do not always publish the obvious subjects. Don't shy away from less-popular subjects.Subjects include Americana, young adult, business, economics, government, politics, history, language, literature, military, war, money, finance, womens issues, womens studies. Query with SASE.

Recent Title(s) *Best of Times*, by Peggy Cervantes; *Nikola Tesla and the Taming of Electricity*, by Lisa J. Aldrich;

Dark Dreams, by Nancy Whitelaw.

Tips Read our writer's guidelines, look at our books, and visit our website.

MORNINGSIDE HOUSE, INC.

Morningside Bookshop 260 Oak St., Dayton OH 45410. (937)461-6736. Fax: (937)461-4260. E-mail: msbooks@erinet.com. Website: www.morningsidebooks.com. **Contact:** Robert J. Younger, publisher. Publishes hardcover and trade paperback originals. **Publishes 10 titles/year. 30 queries received/year. 10 mss received/year. 20% of books from first-time authors. 80% from unagented writers. Pays 10% royalty on retail price. Pays $1,000-2,000 advance.** Publishes book 15 months after acceptance of ms. Accepts simultaneous submissions. Book catalog for $5 or on website.

Imprints Morningside Press;, Press of Morningside Bookshop.

O━ Morningside publishes books for readers interested in the history of the American Civil War.

Nonfiction Subjects include history, military, war. Reviews artwork/photos. Send photocopies.

Recent Title(s) *The Gettysburg Death Roster*, by Robert Krick and Chris Ferguson.

Tips We are only interested in previously unpublished material.

THE MOUNTAINEERS BOOKS

1001 SW Klickitat Way, Suite 201, Seattle WA 98134-1162. (206)223-6303. Fax: (206)223-6306. E-mail: mbooks@mountaineersbooks.org. Website: www.mountaineersbooks.org. **Contact:** Cassandra Conyers, acquisitions editor. Estab. 1961. Publishes 95% hardcover and trade paperback originals and 5% reprints. **Publishes 40 titles/year. 25% of books from first-time authors. 98% from unagented writers. Pays advance.** Publishes book 1 year after acceptance of ms. Responds in 3 months to queries. Book catalog for 9x12 envelope and $1.33 postage First-Class stamps. Guidelines available online.

- See the Contests and Awards section for information on the Barbara Savage/'Miles From Nowhere' Memorial Award for outstanding adventure narratives offered by Mountaineers Books.

O━ Mountaineers Books specializes in expert, authoritative books dealing with mountaineering, hiking, backpacking, skiing, snowshoeing, etc. These can be either how-to-do-it or where-to-do-it (guidebooks). Currently emphasizing regional conservation and natural history.

Nonfiction Subjects include nature, environment, recreation, regional, sports, non-competitive self-propelled, translation, travel, natural history, conservation. Submit outline, 2 sample chapters, bio.

Recent Title(s) *Best Hikes with Dogs: Western Washington*, by Nelson; *Backpacker: More Everyday Wisdom*, by Berger; *Detectives on Everest*, by Hemmleb and Simonson.

Tips The type of book the writer has the best chance of selling to our firm is an authoritative guidebook (*in our field*) to a specific area not otherwise covered; or a how-to that is better than existing competition (again, *in our field*).

MOUNTAIN PRESS PUBLISHING CO.

P.O. Box 2399, Missoula MT 59806-2399. (406)728-1900 or (800)234-5308. Fax: (406)728-1635. E-mail: info@mtnpress.com. Website: www.mountain-press.com. **Contact:** Beth Parker, editor. Estab. 1948. Publishes hardcover and trade paperback originals. **Publishes 15 titles/year. 50% of books from first-time authors. 90% from unagented writers. Pays 7-12% royalty on wholesale price.** Publishes book 2 years after acceptance of ms. Responds in 3 months to queries. Book catalog available online.

- Expanding children's/juvenile nonfiction titles.

O━ We are expanding our Roadside Geology, Geology Underfoot, and Roadside History series (done on a state-by-state basis). We are interested in well-written regional field guides—plants and flowers—and readable history and natural history.

Nonfiction Subjects include animals, history, Western, nature, environment, regional, science, Earth science. Query with SASE. Submit outline, sample chapters. Reviews artwork/photos.

Recent Title(s) *Falcons of North America*, by Kate Davis; *Forgotten Fights*, by Gregory F. and Susan J. Michno; *Roadside Geology of Connecticut and Rhode Island*, by James W. Skehan.

Tips Find out what kind of books a publisher is interested in and tailor your writing to them; research markets and target your audience. Research other books on the same subjects. Make yours different. Don't present your manuscript to a publisher—sell it. Give the information needed to make a decision on a title. Please learn what we publish before sending your proposal. We are a "niche" publisher.

N MOYER BELL, LTD.

549 Old North Rd., Kingston RI 02881-1220. (401)783-5480. Fax: (401)284-0959. Website: www.moyerbellbooks.com. Estab. 1984. Book catalog available online.

O━ Moyer Bell publishes literature, reference, and art books.

Recent Title(s) *The Red Menace*, by Michael Anania (novel); *In Plain Sight*, by Michael Anania (essay); *Camping With the Prince*, by Thomas Bass (science/nature).

N MVP BOOKS

MBI Publishing and Quayside Publishing Group 400 First Avenue N, Suite 300, Minneapolis MN 55401. (612)344-8160. E-mail: jleventhal@mbipublishing.com. Website: www.mvpbooks.com. **Contact:** Josh Leventhal, pub. hardcover and trade paperback originals. **Publishes 15-20 titles/year. Pays advance.** Publishes book 1 year. after acceptance of ms.

- "We seek authors who are strongly committed to helping us promote and sell their books. Please present as focused an idea as possible in a brief submission. Note your credentials for writing the book. Tell all you know about the market niche, existing competition, and marketing possibilities for proposed book."

O- "We publish books for enthusiasts in a wide variety of sports, recreation, and fitness subjects, including heavily illustrated celebrations, narrative works, and how-to instructional guides."

Nonfiction Subjects include sports (baseball, football, basketball, hockey, surfing, golf, bicycling, martial arts, etc.); outdoor activities (hunting and fishing); health and fitness. Query with SASE. WE consider queries from both first-time and experienced authors as well as agented or unagented projects. Submit outline. Reviews artwork/photos. Send sample digital images or transparencies (duplicates and tearsheets only).

Recent Title(s) *New York Yankees and the Meaning of Life*; *St. Louis Cardinals Past & Present*; *Rebound!: Basketball, Busing, Larry Bird, and the Rebirth of Boston*; *Herb Brooks: The Inside Story of a Hockey Mastermind*; *Minnesota Vikings: The Complete Illustrated History*; *The Surfboard: Art, Style, Stroke.*

NAVAL INSTITUTE PRESS

US Naval Institute 291 Wood Ave., Annapolis MD 21402-5034. (410)268-6110. Fax: (410)295-1084. E-mail: esecunda@usni.org. Website: www.usni.org. **Contact:** Paul Wilderson, executive editor; Tom Cutler, senior acquisitions editor; Eric Mills, acquisitions editor. Estab. 1873. **Publishes 80-90 titles/year. 50% of books from first-time authors. 90% from unagented writers.** Guidelines available online.

O- The Naval Institute Press publishes trade and scholarly nonfiction and some fiction. We are interested in national and international security, naval, military, military jointness, intelligence, and special warfare, both current and historical.

Fiction Submit complete ms. Send SASE with sufficient post

⊘ NAVPRESS, (THE PUBLISHING MINISTRY OF THE NAVIGATORS)

P.O. Box 35001, Colorado Springs CO 80935. Fax: (719)260-7223. E-mail: customerservice@navpress.com. Website: www.navpress.com. Estab. 1975. Publishes hardcover, trade paperback, direct and mass market paperback originals and reprints; books and bible studies. **Pays royalty. Pays low or no advances.** Book catalog available free.

Imprints Piñion Press.

Nonfiction Subjects include child guidance, parenting, sociology, spirituality and contemporary culture, Christian living, marriage. Unsolicited mss returned unopened.

Recent Title(s) *Holiness Day by Day*, by Jerry Bridges; *The Crescent Through the Eyes of the Cross*, by Nabeel Jabbour; *Uncompromised Faith*, by S. Michael Craven.

NEAL-SCHUMAN PUBLISHERS, INC.

100 William St., Suite 2004, New York NY 10038-4512. (212)925-8650. Fax: (212)219-8916. Website: www.neal-schuman.com. **Contact:** Paul Harman, V.P./ director of publishing. Estab. 1976. Publishes trade paperback originals. **Publishes 36 titles/year. 150 queries. 80% of books from first-time authors. 100% from unagented writers. Pays 10-25% royalty on wholesale price. Pays infrequent advance.** Publishes book 4 months after acceptance of ms. Accepts simultaneous submissions. Responds in 1 month to queries, proposals, & mss. Book catalog free. Mss guidelines not available.

O- "Neal-Schuman publishes books about library management, information literary titles, the Internet and information technology. Especially soliciting proposals for undergraduate information studies, knowledge management textbooks."

Nonfiction Subjects include computers, electronics, education, software, Internet guides, library and information science, archival studies, records management. Submit proposal package, outline, 1 sample chapter Reviews artwork. Send photocopies.

Recent Title(s) *The Virtual Reference Handbook*, by Diane K. Kovacs; *Information Literary Collaborations That Work*, by Trudie E. Jacobson and Thomas P. Mackey; *The Complete Copyright Liability Handbook*, by Tomas A. Lipinski.

Tips "Our audience is librarians."

N ⊘ TOMMY NELSON

Imprint of Thomas Nelson, Inc. P.O. Box 141000, Nashville TN 37214-1000. (615)889-9000. Fax: (615)902-2219. Website: www.tommynelson.com. Publishes hardcover and trade paperback originals. **Publishes 50-75 titles/year.** Guidelines available online.

- *Does not accept unsolicited mss.*

O→ Tommy Nelson publishes children's Christian nonfiction and fiction for boys and girls up to age 14. We honor God and serve people through books, videos, software and Bibles for children that improve the lives of our customers.

Nonfiction Subjects include religion, Christian evangelical.

Fiction Subjects include adventure, juvenile, mystery, picture books, religious.

Recent Title(s) *Hermie the Common Caterpillar*, by Max Lucado; *Bible for Me Series*, by Andy Holmes; *Shaoey and Dot*, by Mary Beth and Steven Curtis Chapman.

Tips Know the Christian Booksellers Association market. Check out the Christian bookstores to see what sells and what is needed.

NETIMPRESS PUBLISHING, INC.

3186 Michael's Ct., Green Cove Springs FL 32043. (513)464-2082. E-mail: info@netimpress.com. Website: www.netimpress.com. **Contact:** Rod Trent, owner (technology); Brian Knight, owner (technology). Estab. 2002. Publishes trade paperback and electronic originals. **Publishes 50 titles/year. 150 queries received/year. 50 mss received/year. 50% of books from first-time authors. 80% from unagented writers. Pays 50% royalty on retail price.** Publishes book 4 months after acceptance of ms. Accepts simultaneous submissions. Responds in 1 month to queries. Responds in 1 month to proposals. Responds in 1 month to manuscripts. Book catalog available online. Guidelines available via e-mail.

Imprints Start To Finish Guide, Just the FAQs.

Nonfiction Subjects include computers, electronics, software. Query with SASE. Submit proposal package, outline, 1 sample chapters. Reviews artwork/photos. Send Electronic images.

Recent Title(s) *Start To Finish Guide To SMS Delivery*, by Dana Daugherty (technology); *Start To Finish Guide To SQL Server Performance*, by Brian Kelley (technology); *Just the FAQs for SMS*, by Cliff Hobbs (technology).

Tips Our audience is a group of people heavily involved in technology and technology support for companies for which they are employed. These include consultants and IT. Writers must understand the proposed topic very well. They must also be able to communicate technical expertise into easy-to-understand text.

A ⊘ NEW AMERICAN LIBRARY

Penguin Putnam, Inc. 375 Hudson St., New York NY 10014. (212)366-2000. Fax: (212)366-2889. Website: www.penguinputnam.com. Estab. 1948. Publishes mass market and trade paperback originals and reprints. **Pays negotiable royalty. Pays negotiable advance.** Book catalog for SASE.

Imprints Onyx; ROC; Signet; Signet Classic; NAL trade paperback; Signet Eclipse.

O→ NAL publishes commercial fiction and nonfiction for the popular audience.

Nonfiction Subjects include animals, child guidance, ethnic, health, medicine, military, war, psychology, sports, movie tie-in. Agented submissions only.

Fiction Subjects include erotica, ethnic, fantasy, historical, horror, mainstream, contemporary, mystery, romance, science fiction, suspense, western, chicklit. All kinds of commercial fiction. Query with SASE. Agented submissions only. State type of book and past p

Recent Title(s) *How to Be Famous*, by Alison Bond; *Secret Commandos*, by John Plaster; *Notes From the Underbelly*, by Risa Green.

N NEW DIRECTIONS

New Directions Publishing Corp., 80 Eighth Ave., New York NY 10011. Fax: (212)255-0231. E-mail: editorial@ndbooks.com. Website: www.ndpublishing.com. Estab. 1936. Hardcover and trade paperback originals. **Publishes 30 titles/year.** Responds in 3-4 months to queries. Book catalog available online. Guidelines available online.

- Submit by post office mail.

O→ This is a print publication.

Fiction Subjects include ethnic, experimental, historical, humor, literary, poetry, poetry in translation, regional, short story collections, suspense, translation. Submit clips, cover letter, CV, writing credentials, professional experience or otherwise, 1-3 pages of work.

Recent Title(s) *Nazi Literature in the Americas*, by Roberto Bolano (translated from the Spanish by Chris Andrews); *Senselessness*, by Horacio Castellanos Moya (translated from the Spanish by Katherine Silver); *A Coney Island of the Mind-50th Anniversary Edition*, by Lawrence Ferlinghetti (poetry).

Tips Books serve the academic comm Currently, New Directions foc

N NEW FORUMS PRESS

New Forums New Forums Press, P.O. Box 876, Stillwater OK 74076. (405)372-6158. Fax: (405)377-2237. E-mail: dougdollar@newforums.com; ddollar@newforums.com. Website: www.newforums.com. **Contact:** Doug Dollar, president (interests: higher education, Oklahoma-Regional).

NEW HARBINGER PUBLICATIONS

5674 Shattuck Ave., Oakland CA 94609. (510)652-0215. Fax: (510)652-5472. E-mail: proposals@newharbinger.com. Website: www.newharbinger.com. **Contact:** Catharine Sutker, acquisitions director. Estab. 1973. **Publishes 55 titles/year. 1,000 queries received/year. 300 mss received/year. 60% of books from first-time authors. 75% from unagented writers.** Publishes book 1 year after acceptance of ms. Accepts simultaneous submissions. Responds in 2 weeks to queries. Responds in 1 month to proposals. Responds in 2 months to manuscripts. Book catalog available free. Guidelines available online.

O→ We look for psychology and health self-help books that teach readers how to master essential life skills. Mental health professionals who want simple, clear explanations or important psychological techniques and health issues also read our books. Thus, our books must be simple ane easy to understand but also complete and authoritative. Most of our authors are therapists or other helping professionals.

Nonfiction Subjects include health, medicine, psychology, womens issues, womens studies, psycho spirituality, anger management, anxiety, coping, mindfulness skills. Submit proposal package, outline, 2 sample chapters, competing titles, and a compelling, supported reason why the book is unique.

Recent Title(s) *The Gift of ADHD*, by Lara Honos-Webb, PhD; *Get Out of Your Mind and Into Your Life*, by Steven C. Hayes, PhD; *Five Good Minutes*, by Jeffrey Brantley, MD, and Wendy Millstine.

Tips Audience includes psychotherapists and lay readers wanting step-by-step strategies to solve specific problems. Our definition of a self-help psychology or health book is one that teaches essential life skills. The primary goal is to train the reader so that, after reading the book, he or she can deal more effectively with health and/or psychological challenges.

NEW HOPE PUBLISHERS

Woman's Missionary Union P.O. Box 12065, Birmingham AL 35202-2065. (205)991-4950. Fax: (205)991-4015. E-mail: new_hope@wmu.org. Website: www.newhopepublishers.com. **Contact:** Acquisitions Editor. **Publishes 20-28 titles/year. several hundred queries received/year. 25% of books from first-time authors. small% from unagented writers.** Publishes book 2 years after acceptance of ms. Book catalog for 9x12 envelope and 3 First-Class stamps.

O→ Our vision is to challenge believers to understand and be radically involved in the missions of God. This market does not accept unsolicited mss.

Nonfiction We publish books dealing with all facets of Christian life for women and families, including health, discipleship, missions, ministry, Bible studies, spiritual development, parenting, and marriage. We currently do not accept adult fiction or children's picture books. We are particularly interested in niche categories and books on lifestyle development and change.Subjects include child guidance, from Christian perspective, education, Christian church, health, medicine, Christian, multicultural, religion, spiritual development, Bible study, life situations from Christian perspective, ministry, womens issues, womens studies, Christian, church leadership. Prefers a query and prospectus.

Recent Title(s) *Tough Calls*, by Travis Collins; *Pursuing The Christ*, by Jennifer Kennedy Dean; *City Signals*, by Brad Smith

NEW HORIZON PRESS

P.O. Box 669, Far Hills NJ 07931. (908)604-6311. Fax: (908)604-6330. E-mail: nhp@newhorizonpressbooks.com. Website: www.newhorizonpressbooks.com. **Contact:** Dr. Joan S. Dunphy, publisher (nonfiction, social issues, true crime). Estab. 1983. Publishes hardcover and trade paperback originals. **Publishes 12 titles/year. 90% of books from first-time authors. 50% from unagented writers. Pays standard royalty on net receipts. Pays advance.** Publishes book within 2 years after acceptance of ms. Accepts simultaneous submissions. Book catalog available free. Guidelines available online.

Imprints Small Horizons.

O→ New Horizon publishes adult nonfiction featuring true stories of uncommon heroes, true crime, social issues, and self help.

Nonfiction Subjects include child guidance, creative nonfiction, government, politics, health, medicine, nature, environment, psychology, womens issues, womens studies, true crime. Submit proposal package, outline, resume, bio, 3 sample chapters, photo, marketing information.

Recent Title(s) *Murder in Mayberry*, by Mary and Jack Branson; *Thrill Killers*, by Raymond Pingitore and Paul Lonardo; *Boot Camp for the Broken Hearted*, by Audrey Valeriani.

Tips We are a small publisher, thus it is important that the author/publisher have a good working relationship. The author must be willing to promote his book.

NEWMARKET PRESS

18 E. 48th St., New York NY 10017. (212)832-3575. Fax: (212)832-3629. E-mail: mailbox@newmarketpress.com. Website: www.newmarketpress.com. **Contact:** Editorial Department. Publishes hardcover and trade paperback originals and reprints. **Publishes 15-20 titles/year. Pays royalty. Pays varied advance.** Accepts simultaneous submissions. Ms guidelines for #10 SASE or online.

- Currently emphasizing movie tie-in/companion books, health, psychology, parenting. De-emphasizing fiction.

Nonfiction Subjects include child guidance, cooking, foods, nutrition, health, medicine, history, psychology, business/personal finance. Submit proposal package, complete ms, or 1-3 sample chapters, TOC, marketing info, author credentials, SASE.

Recent Title(s) *Condi*, by Antonia Felix; *Hotel Rwanda: Bringing the True Story of an African Hero to Film*, edited by Terry George; *In Good Company*, by Paul Weitz.

NEW SEEDS BOOKS

Imprint of Shambhala Publications 300 Massachusetts Ave., Boston MA 02115. Fax: (617)236-1563. E-mail: editor@newseeds-books.com. Website: www.newseedsbooks.com. **Contact:** David O'Neal, senior editor. Estab. 2005. Publishes hardcover and trade paperback originals, as well as hardcover and trade paperback reprints. **Publishes 90-100 (Shambhala); 10 (New Seeds Books) titles/year. Pays 7.5-15% royalty on retail price.** Publishes book 1 year after acceptance of ms. Accepts simultaneous submissions. Responds in 3 months to queries. Responds in 3 months to proposals. Responds in 3 months to manuscripts. Guidelines available via e-mail.

Nonfiction Subjects include religion, spirituality, contemplative Christianity. Query with SASE. Submit proposal package, outline, bio, 2 sample chapters. Submit complete ms. Reviews artwork/photos. Send photocopies.

Recent Title(s) *Where God Happens: Discovering Christ in One Another*, by Rowan Williams; *The Unknown Sayings of Jesus*, by Marvin Meyer; *Angelic Mistakes*, by Roger Lipsey.

NEW WIN PUBLISHING

Division of Academic Learning Co., LLC 9682 Telstar Ave., Suite 110, El Monte CA 91731. (626)448-4422. E-mail: info@academiclearningcompany.com. Website: www.newwinpublishing.com. **Contact:** Arthur Chou, acquisitions editor. Publishes hardcover and trade paperback originals and reprints. **Publishes 15 titles/year. 70% of books from first-time authors. 60% from unagented writers. Pays 12-15% royalty on net price.** Publishes book 6 months after acceptance of ms. Accepts simultaneous submissions. Responds in 1 month to queries. Responds in 1 month to proposals. Responds in 1 month to manuscripts. Book catalog available online. Guidelines available via e-mail.

Imprints Winchester Press; WBusiness Books.

Nonfiction Subjects include business, economics, child guidance, cooking, foods, nutrition, health, hobbies. Submit proposal package, outline, 2 sample chapters, cover letter. Submit complete ms. Reviews artwork/photos. Send photocopies.

Recent Title(s) *Million Dollar Cup of Tea*, by Tedde McMillen (business); *From Lifeguard To Sun King*, by Robert Bell (business).

NEW WORLD LIBRARY

14 Pamaron Way, Novato CA 94949. (415)884-2100. Fax: (415)884-2199. Website: www.newworldlibrary.com. **Contact:** Jonathan Wichmann, submissions editor. Estab. 1979. Publishes hardcover and trade paperback originals and reprints. **Publishes 35-40 titles/year. 10% of books from first-time authors. 40% from unagented writers.** Accepts simultaneous submissions. Responds in 3 months to queries. Book catalog available free. Guidelines available online.

Imprints H.J. Kramer.

- Prefers e-mail submissions. No longer accepting unsolicited children's mss.
- "NWL is dedicated to publishing books that inspire and challenge us to improve the quality of our lives and our world."

Nonfiction Submit outline, bio, 2-3 sample chapters, SASE. Reviews artwork/photos. Send photocopies.

Recent Title(s) *Zen Wrapped in Karma Dipped in Chocolate*, by Brad Warner; *Happiness From the Inside Out*, by Robert Mack; *The Secret History of Dreaming*, by Robert Moss.

NEW YORK UNIVERSITY PRESS

838 Broadway, New York NY 10003. (212)998-2575. Fax: (212)995-3833. Website: www.nyupress.org. **Contact:** Eric Zinner (cultural studies, literature, media, history); Jennifer Hammer (Jewish studies, psychology, religion, women's studies); Ilene Kalish (sociology, criminology, politics); Deborah Gershenowitz (law, American history). Estab. 1916. Hardcover and trade paperback originals. **Publishes 100 titles/year. 800-1,000 queries received/year. 30% of books from first-time authors. 90% from unagented writers.** Publishes book 9-11 months after acceptance of ms. Accepts simultaneous submissions. Responds in 1-4 months (peer reviewed) to proposals. Guidelines available online.

- New York University Press embraces ideological diversity. We often publish books on the same issue from different poles to generate dialogue, engender and resist pat categorizations.

Nonfiction Subjects include business, economics, ethnic, gay, lesbian, government, politics, language, literature, military, war, psychology, regional, religion, sociology, womens issues, womens studies, American history, anthropology. Query with SASE. Submit proposal package, outline, 1 sample chapter. Reviews artwork/photos. Send photocopies.

N NOLO

950 Parker St., Berkeley CA 94710. (510)549-1976. Fax: (510)859-0025. E-mail: mantha@nolo.com. Website: www.nolo.com. **Contact:** Editorial Department. Estab. 1971. Publishes trade paperback originals. **Publishes 75 new editions and 15 new titles/year. 20% of books from first-time authors. Pays advance.** Accepts simultaneous submissions. Responds in 3 weeks to queries. Responds in 5 weeks to proposals. Guidelines available online.

- We publish practical, do-it-yourself books, software and various electronic products on financial and legal issues that affect individuals, small business, and nonprofit organizations. We specialize in helping people handle their own legal tasks; i.e., write a will, file a small claims lawsuit, start a small business or nonprofit, or apply for a patent.

Nonfiction Subjects include business, economics, money, finance, legal guides in various topics including employment, small business, intellectual property, parenting and education, finance and investment, landlord/ tenant, real estate, and estate planning. Query with SASE. Submit outline, 1 sample chapter.

Recent Title(s) *Credit Repair*, by Robin Leonard; *The Small Business Start-Up Kit*, by Pevi Pakroo; *Effective Fundraising for Nonprofits*, by Ilona Bray.

NOMAD PRESS

2456 Christian St., White River Junction VT 05001. (802)649-1995. Fax: (802)649-2667. E-mail: info@ nomadpress.net. Website: www.nomadpress.net. **Contact:** Acquisitions Editor. Publishes trade paperback originals. **Publishes 10+ titles/year. 10% of books from first-time authors. 90% from unagented writers. Pays royalty on retail price. Makes outright purchase. Pays negotiable advance.** Publishes book 12 months after acceptance of ms. Responds in 1-2 months to manuscripts. Book catalog available online. Guidelines available online.

- Publishes children's nonfiction.

Nonfiction , children's educational, teacher training/education, writing/journalism.

Recent Title(s) *Great Ancient China Projects*, by Lance Kramer (children's nonfiction); *Discover the Amazon: The World's Largest Rainforest*, by Lauri Berkenkamp (children's nonfiction); *Planet Earth: 25 Environmental Projects You Can Build Yourself*, by Kathleen M. Reilly (children's nonfiction).

NORTHERN ILLINOIS UNIVERSITY PRESS

2280 Bethany Rd., DeKalb IL 60115-2854. (815)753-1826. Fax: (815)753-1845. Website: www.niupress.niu.edu. Estab. 1965. **Publishes 20-22 titles/year. Pays 10-15% royalty on wholesale price. Pays advance.** Book catalog available free.

- NIU Press publishes scholarly work and books of general interest to the informed public. We publish mainly history, politics, anthropology, and other social sciences. We are interested also in studies on the Chicago area and Midwest, and in literature in translation. Currently emphasizing history, the social sciences, and cultural studies.

Nonfiction Publishes mainly history, political science, social sciences, philosophy, literary and cultural studies, and regional studies.Subjects include anthropology, archeology, government, politics, history, language, literature, literary criticism, philosophy, regional, social sciences, translation, cultural studies. Query with SASE. Submit outline, 1-3 sample chapters.

Recent Title(s) *Illinois: A History of the Land and Its People*.

NORTH LIGHT BOOKS

Imprint of F+W Media, Inc. 4700 E. Galbraith Rd., Cincinnati OH 45236. Publishes hardcover and trade paperback how-to books. **Publishes 70-75 titles/year. Pays 10% royalty on net receipts and $4,000 advance.** Accepts simultaneous submissions. Responds in 2 months to queries. Book catalog for 9x12 envelope and 6 First-Class stamps.

- "North Light Books publishes art and craft books, including watercolor, drawing, mixed media and decorative painting, knitting, jewelry making, sewing, and needle arts that emphasize illustrated how-to art instruction. Currently emphasizing drawing including traditional, fantasy art, and Japanese-style comics as well as creativity and inspiration."

Nonfiction Art, how-to.Subjects include hobbies, watercolor, realistic drawing, creativity, decorative painting, comics drawing, paper arts, knitting, collage and other craft instruction books. Query with SASE. Submit outline.

Recent Title(s) *Rethinking Acrylic*, by Pat Brady; *Dreamscapes*, by Stephanie Pui-Mun Law; *Knitted Wire Jewelry*, by Samantha Lopez; *Creative Awareness*, by Sheri Gaynor.

NORTH POINT PRESS

Imprint of Farrar Straus & Giroux, Inc. 19 Union Square W., New York NY 10003. (212)741-6900. E-mail: fsg.editorial@fsgbooks.com. Website: www.fsgbooks.com. Estab. 1980. Publishes hardcover and paperback originals. **Pays standard royalty. Pays varied advance.** Accepts simultaneous submissions. Guidelines for #10 SASE.

- We are a broad-based literary trade publisher—high quality writing only.

Nonfiction Subjects include history, nature, environment, religion, no New Age, travel, cultural criticism, music, cooking/food. Query with SASE. Submit outline, 1-2 sample chapters.

Recent Title(s) *Chocolate: A Bittersweet Saga of Dark and Light*, by Mort Rosenblum; *In Fond Remembrance of Me*, by Howard Norman.

NO STARCH PRESS, INC.

555 De Haro St., Suite 250, San Francisco CA 94107. (415)863-9900. Fax: (415)863-9950. E-mail: info@nostarch.com. Website: www.nostarch.com. **Contact:** William Pollock, publisher. Estab. 1994. Publishes trade paperback originals. **Publishes 20-25 titles/year. 100 queries received/year. 5 mss received/year. 80% of books from first-time authors. 90% from unagented writers. Pays 10-15% royalty on wholesale price. Pays advance.** Publishes book 4 months after acceptance of ms. Accepts simultaneous submissions. Book catalog available free.

Imprints Linux Journal Press.

- No Starch Press, Inc., is an independent publishing company committed to producing easy-to-read and information-packed computer books. Currently emphasizing open source, Web development, computer security issues, programming tools, and robotics. More stuff, less fluff.

Nonfiction Subjects include computers, electronics, hobbies, software, Open Source. Submit outline, bio, 1 sample chapter, market rationale. Reviews artwork/photos. Send photocopies.

Recent Title(s) *Hacking: The Art of Exploitation*, by Jon Erickson; *Art of Assembly Language*, by Randall Hyde; *Hacking the XBox*, by Andrew bunnie Huang.

Tips No fluff—content, content, content or just plain fun. Understand how your book fits into the market. Tell us why someone, anyone, will buy your book. Be enthusiastic.

NURSESBOOKS.ORG

American Nurses Association 8515 Georgia Ave., Suite 400, Silver Spring MD 20901-3492. (301)628-5212. Fax: (301)628-5003. E-mail: eric.wurzbacher@ana.org. Website: www.nursesbooks.org. **Contact:** Rosanne Roe, publisher; Eric Wurzbacher, editor/project manager. Publishes professional paperback originals and reprints. **Publishes 10 titles/year. 50 queries received/year. 8-10 mss received/year. 75% of books from first-time authors. 100% from unagented writers.** Publishes book 4 months after acceptance of ms. Responds in 3 months to proposals. Responds in 3 months to manuscripts. Book catalog available online. Guidelines available free.

- Nursebooks.org publishes books designed to help professional nurses in their work and careers. Through the publishing program, Nursebooks.org provides nurses in all practice settings with publications that address cutting-edge issues and form a basis for debate and exploration of this century's most critical health care trends.

Nonfiction Submit outline, 1 sample chapter, CV, list of 3 reviewers and paragraph on audience and how to reach them. Reviews artwork/photos. Send photocopies.

Recent Title(s) *Nursing and Health Care Ethics: A Legacy and A Vision; Genetics and Ethics in Health Care: New Questions in the Age of Genomic Health; Teaching IOM: Implications of the IOM Reports for Nursing Education.*

OAK KNOLL PRESS

310 Delaware St., New Castle DE 19720. (302)328-7232. Fax: (302)328-7274. E-mail: markpm@oakknoll.com. Website: www.oakknoll.com. **Contact:** Mark Parker Miller, publishing director. Estab. 1976. Publishes hardcover and trade paperback originals and reprints. **Publishes 40 titles/year. 250 queries received/year. 100 mss received/year. 50% of books from first-time authors. 100% from unagented writers.** Publishes book 12 months after acceptance of ms. Accepts simultaneous submissions. Guidelines available online.

- Oak Knoll specializes in books about books and manuals on the book arts—preserving the art and lore of the printed word.

Nonfiction Reviews artwork/photos. Send photocopies.

Recent Title(s) *ABC for Book Collectors, 8th Ed.*, by John Carter and Nicolas Barker; *Early Type Specimens*, by John Lane; *The Great Libraries*, by Konstantinos Staikos.

THE OAKLEA PRESS

6912-B Three Chopt Rd., Richmond VA 23226. (804)281-5872. Fax: (804)281-5686. E-mail: info@oakleapress.com. **Contact:** S.H. Martin, publisher. Publishes hardcover and trade paperback originals. **300 queries received/**

year. 50 mss received/year. 50% of books from first-time authors. 90% from unagented writers. Pays 10-20% royalty on wholesale price. Publishes book 6 months after acceptance of ms. Accepts simultaneous submissions. Responds in 1 month to queries. Responds in 1 month to proposals. Responds in 3 months to manuscripts. Book catalog available online.

Nonfiction Submit proposal package, outline, 1 sample chapter and marketing plan.

Recent Title(s) *The Big Squeeze*, by Patricia E. Moody; *Billion Dollar Turnaround*, by William T. Monahan; *Product Development for the Lean Enterprise*, by Michael Kennedy.

OHIO STATE UNIVERSITY PRESS

1070 Carmack Rd., 180 Pressey Hall, Columbus OH 43210-1002. (614)292-6930. Fax: (614)292-2065. E-mail: ohiostatepress@osu.edu. Website: www.ohiostatepress.org. **Contact:** Malcolm Litchfield, director; Sandy Crooms, acquisitions editor. Estab. 1957. **Publishes 30 titles/year. Pays royalty. Pays advance.** Responds in 3 months to queries. Guidelines available online.

- The Ohio State University Press publishes scholarly nonfiction, and offers short fiction and short poetry prizes. Currently emphasizing history, literary studies, political science, women's health, classics, Victoria studies.

Nonfiction Subjects include business, economics, education, government, politics, history, American, language, literature, literary criticism, multicultural, regional, sociology, womens issues, womens studies, criminology, literary criticism, women's health. Query with SASE.

Recent Title(s) *Saving Lives*, by Albert Goldbarth (poetry); *Ohio: History of People*, by Andrew Cayton (nonfiction).

OHIO UNIVERSITY PRESS

19 Circle Dr., The Ridges, Athens OH 45701. (740)593-1155. Fax: (740)593-4536. Website: www.ohioswallow.com. **Contact:** Gillian Berchowitz, senior editor (American history and popular culture, ecology and history, law and society, International studies, Latin American studies, Southern Asian studies, Polish and Polish-American studies, African studies, Appalachian studies); David Sanders, director (literature, literary criticism, midwest studies, Ohioana). Estab. 1964. Publishes hardcover and trade paperback originals and reprints. **Publishes 45-50 titles/year. 500 queries received/year. 50 mss received/year. 20% of books from first-time authors. 95% from unagented writers.** Publishes book 1 year after acceptance of ms. Responds in 1 month to queries. Responds in 1 month to proposals. Responds in 3 months to manuscripts. Book catalog available free. Guidelines available online.

Imprints Ohio University Research in International Studies (Gillian Berchowitz); Swallow Press (David Sanders).

- Ohio University Press publishes and disseminates the fruits of research and creative endeavor, specifically in the areas of literary studies, regional works, philosophy, contemporary history, and African studies. Its charge to produce books of value in service to the academic community and for the enrichment of the broader culture is in keeping with the university's mission of teaching, research and service to its constituents.

Nonfiction Subjects include Americana, anthropology, archaeology, government, history, language, literature, military, nature, politics, regional, sociology, women's issues, women's studies, African studies. Query with SASE. Reviews artwork/photos. Send photocopies.

Recent Title(s) *Evidence of My Existence*, by Jim Lo Scalzo; *For the Prevention of Cruelty*, by Diane L. Beers; *Blank Verse*, by Robert B. Shaw.

Tips Rather than trying to hook the editor on your work, let the material be compelling enough and well-presented enough to do it for you.

ONE WORLD BOOKS

Ballantine Publishing Group, Inc. 1745 Broadway, 18th Floor, New York NY 10019. (212)782-9000. Fax: (212)572-4949. Website: www.randomhouse.com. Estab. 1991. Publishes hardcover, trade and mass market paperback originals and trade paperback reprints. Accepts simultaneous submissions.

- All One World Books must be specifically written for either an African-American, Asian, Native American, or Hispanic audience. No exceptions.

Nonfiction Subjects include Americana, cooking, foods, nutrition, creative nonfiction, ethnic, government, politics, history, memoirs, multicultural, philosophy, psychology, recreation, travel, womens issues, womens studies, African-American studies. Agented submissions only.

Fiction Subjects include adventure, comic books, confession, erotica, ethnic, historical, humor, literary, mainstream, contemporary, multicultural, mystery, regional, romance, suspense, strong need for commercial women's fiction. Agented submissions only.

Recent Title(s) *A One Woman Man*, by Travis Hunter; *Space Between the Stars*, by Deborah Santana; *Black Titan*, by Carol Jenkins and Elizabeth Gardner Hines.

Tips All books must be written in English.

N OPEN COURT PUBLISHING CO.

70 E. Lake Street, Ste. 300, Chicago IL 60601. Website: www.opencourtbooks.com. Estab. 1887. Publishes hardcover and trade paperback originals. **Publishes 20 titles/year. Pays 5-15% royalty on wholesale price.** Publishes book 2 years after acceptance of ms. Book catalog available online. Guidelines available online.

Nonfiction Subjects include philosophy, Asian thought, religious studies and popular culture. Query with SASE. Submit proposal package, outline, 1 sample chapter, TOC, author's cover letter, intended audience.

Recent Title(s) *Pink Floyd and Philosophy*, edited by George Reisch (philosophy); *The Philosophy of Michael Dummett*, edited by Auxier and Hahn (philosophy).

Tips "Audience consists of philosophers and intelligent general readers."

OPEN ROAD PUBLISHING

P.O. Box 284, Cold Spring Harbor NY 11724. (631)692-7172. E-mail: jopenroad@aol.com. Website: openroadguides.com. Estab. 1993. Publishes trade paperback originals. **Publishes 20-22 titles/year. 200 queries received/year. 75 mss received/year. 30% of books from first-time authors. 98% from unagented writers. Pays 5-6% royalty on retail price. Pays $1,000-3,500 advance.** Publishes book 3 months after acceptance of ms. Accepts simultaneous submissions. Responds in 1 month to queries. Responds in 2 months to proposals. Book catalog online. Ms guidelines sent if proposal is accepted.

Imprints Cold Spring Press

- Open Road publishes travel guides and has expanded into other areas with its new imprint, Cold Spring Press, particularly sports/fitness, topical, biographies, history, fantasy.

Nonfiction Subjects include travel guides and travelogues. Query with SASE.

Recent Title(s) *Tahiti & French Polynesia Guide*, by Jan Prince; *Paris With Kids*, by Valerie Gwinner; *Open Road's Best of Ireland*, by Dan Quillen; *Quest For the Kasbah*, by Richard Bangs.

ORANGE FRAZER PRESS, INC.

P.O. Box 214, 37½ W. Main St., Wilmington OH 45177. (937)382-3196. Fax: (937)383-3159. Website: www.orangefrazer.com. **Contact:** John Baskin, editor (sports/history). Publishes hardcover and trade paperback originals. **Publishes 25 titles/year. 50 queries received/year. 35 mss received/year. 80% of books from first-time authors. 100% from unagented writers. Pays 10% royalty on wholesale price. 50% of our books are author-subsidy published/year if the author can afford it. Pays advance.** Publishes book 10 months after acceptance of ms. Accepts simultaneous submissions. Responds in 6 months to proposals. Book catalog and guidelines available free.

Imprints Marcy Hawley, Publisher

- Orange Frazer Press accepts Ohio-related nonfiction only; corporate histories; town celebrations; anniversary books.

Nonfiction Accepts Ohio nonfiction only.Subjects include audio, anthropology, archaeology, art, architecture, business, economics, cooking, foods, nutrition, education, history, nature, environment, photography, regional, sports, travel. Submit proposal package, outline, 3 sample chapters, and marketing plan. Reviews artwork/photos. Send photocopies.

Recent Title(s) *1968: The Year That Saved Ohio State Football*, by David Hyde (sports); *Catch Every Ball; How to Handle Life's Pitches*, by Johnny Bench (sports).

Tips For our commercial titles we focus mainly on sports and biographies. Our readers are interested in sports or curious about famous persons/personalities.

N OREGON STATE UNIVERSITY PRESS

500 Kerr, Corvallis OR 97331. (541)737-3873. Fax: (541)737-3170. E-mail: mary.braun@oregonstate.edu. Website: oregonstate.edu/dept/press. **Contact:** Mary Elizabeth Braun, acquiring editor. Estab. 1962. Publishes hardcover and paperback originals. **Publishes 12-15 titles/year. 75% of books from first-time authors.** Publishes book 1 year after acceptance of ms. Responds in 3 months to queries. Book catalog for 6x9 SAE with 2 first-class stamps. Guidelines available online.

Nonfiction Publishes scholarly books in history, biography, geography, literature, natural resource management, with strong emphasis on Pacific or Northwestern topics.Subjects include regional, science. Submit outline, sample chapters.

Recent Title(s) *Gathering Moss: A Natural & Cultural History of Mosses*, by Robin Wall Kimmerer; *Oregon's Promise: An Interpretive History*, by David Peterson del Mar; *Living with Earthquakes in the Pacific Northwest*, by Robert S. Yeats.

N O'REILLY MEDIA

1005 Gravenstein Highway N., Sebastopol CA 95472. (707)827-7000. Fax: (707)829-0104. E-mail: proposals@oreilly.com. Website: www.oreilly.com. **Contact:** Acquisitions Editor. Guidelines available online.

- We're always looking for new authors and new book ideas. Our ideal author has real technical competence and a passion for explaining things clearly.

Nonfiction Subjects include computers, electronics. Submit proposal package, outline, publishing history, bio.
Tips It helps if you know that we tend to publish 'high end' books rather than books for dummies, and generally don't want yet another book on a topic that's already well covered.

OUR SUNDAY VISITOR PUBLISHING

200 Noll Plaza, Huntington IN 46750-4303. (260)356-8400. Fax: (260)359-9117. E-mail: booksed@osv.com. Website: www.osv.com. **Contact:** Michael Dubruiel, Kelley Renz, acquisitions editors. Estab. 1912. Publishes paperback and hardbound originals. **Publishes 30-40 titles/year. 10% of books from first-time authors. 90% from unagented writers. Pays variable royalty on net receipts. Pays $1,500 average advance.** Publishes book 1-2 years after acceptance of ms. Responds in 3 months to queries. Book catalog for 9x12 envelope and First-Class stamps. ms guidelines for #10 SASE or online.

- We are a Catholic publishing company seeking to educate and deepen our readers in their faith. Currently emphasizing reference, apologetics, and catechetics. De-emphasizing inspirational.

Nonfiction Catholic viewpoints on family, prayer, and devotional books, and Catholic heritage books.Reviews artwork/photos.
Recent Title(s) *De-Coding DaVinci*, by Amy Welborn.
Tips Solid devotional books that are not first person, or lives of the saints and catechetical books have the best chance of selling to our firm. Make it solidly Catholic, unique, without pious platitudes.

THE OVERLOOK PRESS

141 Wooster St., New York NY 10012. (212)673-2210. Fax: (212)673-2296. Website: www.overlookpress.com. Estab. 1971. Publishes hardcover and trade paperback originals and hardcover reprints. **Publishes 100 titles/year.** Book catalog available free.
Imprints .

- "Overlook Press publishes fiction, children's books, and nonfiction."

Nonfiction Subjects include art, architecture, film, cinema, stage, history, regional, New York State, current events, design, health/fitness, how-to, lifestyle, martial arts. Agented submissions only.
Fiction Subjects include literary, some commercial, foreign literature in translation. Agented submissions only.
Recent Title(s) *Dragon's Eye*, by Andy Oakes; *The Brontes*, by Juliet Barker; *Triomf*, translated from the Afrikaans by Leon de Kock.

THE OVERMOUNTAIN PRESS

P.O. Box 1261, Johnson City TN 37605. (423)926-2691. Fax: (423)232-1252. E-mail: submissions@overmtn.com. Website: www.overmountainpress.com. Estab. 1970. Publishes hardcover and trade paperback originals and reprints. Accepts simultaneous submissions. Responds in 1-4 months to manuscripts. Book catalog available free. Guidelines available online.
Imprints Silver Dagger Mysteries.

- The Overmountain Press publishes primarily Appalachian history. Audience is people interested in history of Tennessee, Virginia, North Carolina, Kentucky, and all aspects of this region—Revolutionary War, Civil War, county histories, historical biographies, etc.

Nonfiction Regional works only.Subjects include Americana, cooking, foods, nutrition, ethnic, history, military, war, nature, environment, photography, regional, womens issues, womens studies, Native American, ghostlore, guidebooks, folklore. Submit proposal package, outline, 3 sample chapters, marketing suggestions. Reviews artwork/photos. Send photocopies.
Fiction Subjects include picture books, must have regional flavor. Submit complete ms.
Tips Please, no phone calls.

RICHARD C. OWEN PUBLISHERS, INC.

P.O. Box 585, Katonah NY 10536. (914)232-3903. Website: www.rcowen.com. **Contact:** Janice Boland, director, children's books. Estab. 1982. Publishes book 2-5 years after acceptance of ms. Accepts simultaneous submissions. Ms guidelines for SASE with 52¢ postage.

- Due to high volume and long production time, we are currently limiting to nonfiction submissions only.

Nonfiction Subjects include art, architecture, history, nature, environment, recreation, science, sports, womens issues, womens studies, music, diverse culture, nature.
Tips We don't respond to queries or e-mails. Please do not fax or e-mail us. Because our books are so brief it is better to send entire manuscript. We publish story books with inherent educational value for young readers—books they can read with enjoyment and success. We believe students become enthusiastic, independent, lifelong learners when supported and guided by skillful teachers using good books. The professional development work we do and the books we publish support these beliefs.

P & R PUBLISHING CO.

P.O. Box 817, Phillipsburg NJ 08865. Fax: (908)454-0859. Website: www.prpbooks.com. Estab. 1930. Publishes hardcover originals and trade paperback originals and reprints. **Publishes 40 titles/year. 300 queries received/year. 100 mss received/year. 5% of books from first-time authors. 95% from unagented writers. Pays 10-14% royalty on wholesale price.** Accepts simultaneous submissions. Responds in 3 months to proposals. Guidelines available online.

Nonfiction Subjects include history, religion, spirituality, translation. Only accepts electronic submission with completion of online Author Guidelines. Hard copy mss will not be returned.

Recent Title(s) *Tying the Knot Tighter: Because Marriage Lasts a Lifetime*, by Martha Peace and John Crotts (marriage); *The Law Is Not of Faith: Essays on Works and Grace in the Mosaic Covenant*, edited by Bryan D. Estelle, J. V. Fesko, and David Van Drunen (theology/doctrine); *Where Is God in All of This? Finding God's Purpose in Our Suffering*, by Deborah Howard (Christian living); *The Betrayal: A Novel on John Calvin*, by Douglas Bond (historical fiction).

Tips Our audience is evangelical Christians and seekers. All of our publications are consistent with Biblical teaching, as summarized in the Westminster Standards.

PACIFIC PRESS PUBLISHING ASSOCIATION

Trade Book Division P.O. Box 5353, Nampa ID 83653-5353. (208)465-2500. Fax: (208)465-2531. E-mail: booksubmissions@pacificpress.com. Website: www.pacificpress.com. **Contact:** Scott Cady, acquisitions editor (children's stories, biography, Christian living, spiritual growth); David Jarnes, book editor (theology, doctrine, inspiration). Estab. 1874. Publishes hardcover and trade paperback originals and reprints. **Publishes 35 titles/year. 35% of books from first-time authors. 100% from unagented writers. Pays 8-16% royalty on wholesale price.** Publishes book up to 24 months after acceptance of ms. Responds in 3 months to queries. Guidelines available online.

- We publish books that fit Seventh-day Adventist beliefs only. All titles are Christian and religious. For guidance, see www.adventist.org/beliefs/index.html. Our books fit into the categories of this retail site: www.adventistbookcenter.com.

Nonfiction Subjects include child guidance, cooking, foods, nutrition, vegetarian only, health, history, nature, environment, philosophy, religion, spirituality, womens issues, family living, Christian lifestyle, Bible study, Christian doctrine, prophecy. Query with SASE or e-mail, or submit 3 sample chapters, cover letter with overview of book. Electronic submissions accepted. Reviews artwork/photos.

Fiction Subjects include religious. Pacific Press rarely publishes fiction, but we're interested in developing a line of Seventh-day Adventist fiction in the future. Only proposals accepted; no full manuscripts.

Recent Title(s) *Grounds for Belief*, by Ed Dickerson (doctrine); *Chosen by Grace*, by Stuart Tyner (doctrine); *Peter: Fisher of Men*, by Noni Beth Gibbs (biblical fiction); *Shepherd Warrior*, by Bradley Booth (children's).

Tips Our primary audience is members of the Seventh-day Adventist denomination. Almost all are written by Seventh-day Adventists. Books that do well for us relate the Biblical message to practical human concerns and focus more on the experiential rather than theoretical aspects of Christianity. We are assigning more titles, using less unsolicited material—although we still publish manuscripts from freelance submissions and proposals.

PALADIN PRESS

7077 Winchester Circle, Boulder CO 80301. (303)443-7250. Fax: (303)442-8741. E-mail: editorial@paladin-press.com. Website: www.paladin-press.com. **Contact:** Jon Ford, editorial director. Estab. 1970. Publishes hardcover originals and paperback originals and reprints. **Publishes 50 titles/year. 50% of books from first-time authors. 95% from unagented writers. Pays advance.** Publishes book 1 year after acceptance of ms. Accepts simultaneous submissions. Responds in 2 months to proposals. Book catalog available free.

Imprints Sycamore Island Books; Flying Machines Press; Outer Limits Press; Romance Book Classics.

- Paladin Press publishes the action library of nonfiction in military science, police science, weapons, combat, personal freedom, self-defense, survival.

Nonfiction Paladin Press primarily publishes original manuscripts on military science, weaponry, self-defense, personal privacy, financial freedom, espionage, police science, action careers, guerrilla warfare, and fieldcraft. Subjects include government, politics, military, war. Query with SASE.

Recent Title(s) *Surviving Workplace Violence: What to Do Before a Violent Incident; What to Do When the Violence Explodes*, by Loren W. Christensen.

Tips We need lucid, instructive material aimed at our market and accompanied by sharp, relevant illustrations and photos. As we are primarily a publisher of 'how-to' books, a manuscript that has step-by-step instructions, written in a clear and concise manner (but not strictly outline form) is desirable. No fiction, first-person accounts, children's, religious, or joke books. We are also interested in serious, professional videos and video ideas (contact Michael Rigg).

PALGRAVE MACMILLAN

St. Martin's Press 175 Fifth Ave., New York NY 10010. (212)982-3900. Fax: (212)777-6359. Website: www.palgrave-usa.com. **Contact:** Airié Stuart (history, business, economics, current events, psychology, biography); Anthony Wahl (political science, current events, Asian studies, international relations); Farideh Koohi-Kamali (literature, anthropology, cultural studies, performing arts, Islamic World & Middle East); Amanda Johnson (education, religion, women's studies/history); Ella Pearce (African studies, Latin American studies); Alessandra Bastagli (American history, American studies, world history); Heather Van Dusen (political science, political economy, political theory). Publishes hardcover and trade paperback originals. Accepts simultaneous submissions. Book catalog and ms guidelines online.

- Palgrave wishes to expand on our already successful academic, trade, and reference programs so that we will remain at the forefront of publishing in the global information economy of the 21st century. We publish high-quality academic works and a distinguished range of reference titles, and we expect to see many of our works available in electronic form. We do not accept fiction or poetry.

Nonfiction Subjects include business, economics, creative nonfiction, education, ethnic, gay, lesbian, government, politics, history, language, literature, military, war, money, finance, multicultural, music, dance, philosophy, regional, religion, sociology, spirituality, translation, womens issues, womens studies, humanities. Query with proposal package including outline, 3-4 sample chapters, prospectus, cv and SASE. Reviews artwork/photos.

Recent Title(s) *Future Jihad*, by Walid Phares; *Billions*, by Tom Doctoroff; *AIDS in Asia*, by Susan Houter.

PANTHEON BOOKS

Imprint of Knopf Publishing Group 1745 Broadway 21-1, New York NY 10019. (212)782-9000. Fax: (212)572-6030. Website: www.pantheonbooks.com. **Contact:** Adult Editorial Department. Estab. 1942. Publishes hardcover and trade paperback originals and trade paperback reprints.

- We only accept mss submitted by an agent. You may still send a 20-50 page sample and a SASE to our slushpile. Allow 2-6 months for a response.
- Pantheon Books publishes both Western and non-Western authors of literary fiction and important nonfiction.

Nonfiction Subjects include government, politics, history, memoirs, science, travel.

Fiction Quality fiction, including graphic novels and fairytales/folklore.

Recent Title(s) *Persepolis*, by Marjane Satrapi; *Your Inner Fish*, by Neil Shubin; *The Careful Use of Compliments*, by Alexander McCall Smith.

PARACLETE PRESS

P.O. Box 1568, Orleans MA 02653. (508)255-4685. Fax: (508)255-5705. Website: www.paracletepress.com. **Contact:** Editorial Review Committee. Estab. 1981. Publishes hardcover and trade paperback originals. **Publishes 40 titles/year. 250 mss received/year.** Publishes book up to 2 years after acceptance of ms. Responds in 2 months to queries. Responds in 2 months to manuscripts. Book catalog for 8 ½x11 SASE. Guidelines for #10 SASE.

- "Does not publish poetry, memoirs, or children's books. "
- Publisher of devotionals, new editions of classics, books on prayer, Christian living, spirituality, fiction, compact discs, and videos.

Nonfiction Subjects include religion. Query with SASE. Submit 2-3 sample chapters, TOC, chapter summaries.

Recent Title(s) *The Jesus Creed*, by Scot McKnight; *Engaging the World With Merton*, by M. Basil Pennington, O.C.S.O; *The Illuminated Heart*, by Frederica Mathewes-Green.

PARAGON HOUSE PUBLISHERS

1925 Oakcrest Ave., Suite 7, St. Paul MN 55113-2619. (651)644-3087. Fax: (651)644-0997. E-mail: paragon@paragonhouse.com. Website: www.paragonhouse.com. **Contact:** Rosemary Yokoi, acquisitions editor. Estab. 1962. Publishes hardcover and trade paperback originals and trade paperback reprints. **Publishes 12-15 titles/year. 1,500 queries received/year. 150 mss received/year. 7% of books from first-time authors. 90% from unagented writers. Pays $500-1,500 advance.** Publishes book 12 months after acceptance of ms. Accepts simultaneous submissions. Guidelines available online.

Imprints *Series*: Paragon Issues in Philosophy, Genocide and Holocaust Studies; Omega Books.

- We publish general-interest titles and textbooks that provide the readers greater understanding of society and the world. Currently emphasizing religion, philosophy, economics, and society.

Nonfiction Subjects include government, politics, multicultural, nature, environment, philosophy, psychology, religion, sociology, womens issues, world affairs. Submit proposal package, outline, 2 sample chapters, market breakdown, SASE.

Recent Title(s) *Too Much Medicine: A Doctor's Prescription for Better and More Affordable Healthcare*, by Dennis Gottfried; *Global Ethics: Seminal Essays*, by Thomas Pogge; *Altruism, Intergroup Apology, Forgiveness,* *and Reconciliation*, by Samuel Oliner.

PARKWAY PUBLISHERS, INC.

Box 3678, Boone NC 28607. (828)265-3993. Fax: (828)265-3993. Website: www.parkwaypublishers.com. **Contact:** Rao Aluri, president. Publishes hardcover and trade paperback originals. **Publishes 10-12 titles/year. 15-20 queries received/year. 20 mss received/year. 75% of books from first-time authors. 100% from unagented writers.** Publishes book 8 months after acceptance of ms.

O→ Parkway publishes books on the local history and culture of western North Carolina. We are located on Blue Ridge Parkway and our primary industry is tourism. We are interested in nonfiction books which present the history and culture of western North Carolina to the tourist market. Will consider fiction if it highlights the region.

Nonfiction Subjects include history, biography, tourism, and natural history. Query with SASE. Submit complete ms.

Recent Title(s) *Shuffletown USA and Orville Hicks: Mountain Stories, Mountain Roots.*

N PAUL DRY BOOKS

1616 Walnut St., Suite 808, Philadelphia PA 19103. (215)231-9939. Fax: (215)231-9942. Website: pauldrybooks.com. Hardcover and trade paperback originals, trade paperback reprints. Book catalog available online. Guidelines available online.

Nonfiction Subjects include agriculture, contemporary culture, history, literary criticism, memoirs, multicultural, philosophy, religion, translation, Popular Mathematics. Submit proposal package.

Fiction Subjects include literary, short story collections, translation, young adult, novels. Submit sample chapters, clips, bio. sample 2-3 pages, 1 or 2-pag.

Recent Title(s) *American Places*, by William Zinsser (treasured historic sites); *One is One*, by Barbara Leonie Picard (fiction); *The 64 Sonnets*, Intro by Edward Hirsch (John Keats).

Tips Our aim is to publish lively books 'to awaken, delight, & educate'—to spark conversation. We publish fiction and nonfiction, & essays covering subjects from Homer to Chekhov, bird watching to jazz music, New York City to shogunate Japan.

PAULINE BOOKS & MEDIA

50 St. Paul's Ave., Jamaica Plain MA 02130. (617)522-8911. Fax: (617)541-9805. E-mail: editorial@pauline.org. Website: www.pauline.org. Estab. 1932. Publishes trade paperback originals and reprints. **Publishes 40 titles/year. 15% of books from first-time authors. 05% from unagented writers. 5-15% royalty on wholesale price** Publishes book 11 months after acceptance of ms. Accepts simultaneous submissions. Responds in3 months to queries, proposals, & mss. Book catalog available online. Guidelines available online & by e-mail.

O→ Submissions are evaluated on adherence to Gospel values, harmony with the Catholic tradition, relevance of topic, and quality of writing.

Nonfiction Subjects include child guidance, religion, spirituality. Submit proposal package, including outline, 1- 2 sample chapters, cover letter, synopsis, intended audience & proposed length. Reviews artwork; send photocopies.

Fiction Subjects include juvenile. Children's fiction only. We are now accepting submissions for easy-to-read and middle-reader chapter fiction. Please see our Writer's Guidelines. Submit proposal package, including synopsis, 2 sample chapters, & cover letter; complete ms.

Recent Title(s) *St. Edith Stein: A Spiritual Portrait*, by Dianne Traflet (bio); *Word of Life: Daily Scripture Companion*, by Celia Sirois (scripture reflections)

Tips We target Catholics and other Christians interested in developing their relationship with God.

PAULIST PRESS

997 Macarthur Blvd., Mahwah NJ 07430. (201)825-7300. Fax: (201)825-8345. E-mail: info@paulistpress.com. Website: www.paulistpress.com. **Contact:** Rev. Lawrence Boadt, CSP, editorial director for general submissions; Jennifer Conlan, children's editor. Estab. 1865. Publishes hardcover and paperback originals and paperback reprints. **Pays royalty on net. Pays advance.** Responds in 6-8 weeks to queries. Book catalog available online. Guidelines available online.

O→ Paulist Press publishes "ecumenical theology, Roman Catholic studies, and books on scripture, liturgy, spirituality, church history, and philosophy, as well as works on faith and culture. Our publishing is oriented toward adult-level nonfiction, although we offer a growing selection of children's stories (about 12/year). We do not publish poetry."

Nonfiction Subjects include philosophy (occasionally), religion. Submit 1-2 page summary with rationale for ms, content description, audience info, projected length. Reviews artwork/photos.

Fiction Subjects include Subjects include picture books, ages 2-5, chapter books (ages 8-12). Must have Christian and Catholic themes. Submit resume, ms, SASE. Accepts unsolicited mss, but m.

Recent Title(s) *Praying with St. Paul using Lectio Divina; A Walk Through the New Testament*, by Margaret Ralph; *Good Night and God Bless: A Guide to Convents and Monastery Accommodations in Europe*, by Trish

Clark; *The Devil Can't Cook Spaghetti*, by Michael Esaney.

PEACE HILL PRESS

Affiliate of W.W. Norton 18021 The Glebe Ln., Charles City VA 23030. E-mail: info@peacehillpress.com. Website: www.peacehillpress.com. **Contact:** Peter Buffington, acquisitions editor. Estab. 2001. Publishes hardcover and trade paperback originals. **Publishes 4-8 titles/year. Pays 6-10% royalty on retail price. Pays $500-1,000 advance.** Publishes book 18 months after acceptance of ms. Accepts simultaneous submissions.

Nonfiction Subjects include education, history, language, literature. Submit proposal package, outline, 1 sample chapters. Reviews artwork/photos. Send photocopies.

Fiction Subjects include historical, juvenile, picture books, young adult.

Recent Title(s) *The Story of the World, Vol. 2, revised ed.*, by Susan Wise Bauer.

PEACHTREE CHILDREN'S BOOKS

Peachtree Publishers, Ltd. 1700 Chattahoochee Ave., Atlanta GA 30318-2112. (404)876-8761. Fax: (404)875-2578. E-mail: hello@peachtree-online.com. Website: www.peachtree-online.com. **Contact:** Helen Harriss, submissions editor. Publishes hardcover and trade paperback originals. **Publishes 30 titles/year. 25% of books from first-time authors. 25% from unagented writers. Pays royalty on retail price.** Publishes book 1 year or more after acceptance of ms. Accepts simultaneous submissions. Responds in 6 months to queries. Responds in 6 months to manuscripts. Book catalog for 6 first-class stamps. Guidelines available online.

Imprints Freestone; Peachtree Jr.

- We publish a broad range of subjects and perspectives, with emphasis on innovative plots and strong writing.

Nonfiction Subjects include animals, child guidance, creative nonfiction, education, ethnic, gardening, health, medicine, history, language, literature, literary criticism, multicultural, music, dance, nature, environment, recreation, regional, science, social sciences, sports, travel. Submit complete ms with SASE, or summary and 3 sample chapters with SASE.

Fiction Subjects include juvenile, picture books, young adult. Looking for very well-written middle grade and young adult novels. Submit complete ms with SASE.

Recent Title(s) *Dad, Jackie and Me*, by Myron Uhlberg (children's picture book); *Yellow Star*, by Carmen Agra Deedy (children's picture book); *Dog Sense*, by Sneed Collard (middle reader).

PEACHTREE PUBLISHERS

1700 Chattahoochee Ave., Atlanta GA 30318-2112. (404)876-8761. Fax: (404)875-2578. E-mail: hello@peachtree-online.com. Website: www.peachtree-online.com. **Contact:** Helen Harriss, submissions editor. Estab. 1978. Publishes hardcover and trade paperback originals. **Publishes 30 titles/year. 25% of books from first-time authors. 75% from unagented writers. Pays royalty.Royalty varies. Pays advance.** Publishes book 1 year or more after acceptance of ms. Accepts simultaneous submissions. Responds in 8 months to queries. Responds in 8 months to manuscripts. Book catalog for 9x12 envelope and 6 First-Class stamps. Guidelines available online.

Imprints Peachtree Children's Books (Peachtree Jr., FreeStone).

- Peachtree Publishers specializes in children's books, middle reader and books, young adult, regional guidebooks, parenting and self-help.

Nonfiction Subjects include health, medicine, recreation. Submit outline, 3 sample chapters. Submit complete ms. Include SASE for response.

Fiction Subjects include juvenile, young adult. Absolutely no adult fiction! We are seeking young adult and juvenile works, including mystery and historical fiction, of high literary merit. Query with SASE. Query, submit outline/synopsis

Recent Title(s) *Martina the Beautiful Cockroach*, by Carmen Agra Deedy; *Gabriel's Horses*, by Alison Hart; *The Monster Who Did my Math*, by Danny Schnitzkin.

PELICAN PUBLISHING CO.

1000 Burmaster St., Gretna LA 70053. Website: www.pelicanpub.com. **Contact:** Nina Kooij, editor-in-chief. Estab. 1926. Publishes hardcover, trade paperback and mass market paperback originals and reprints. **Publishes 85 titles/year. 15% of books from first-time authors. 95% from unagented writers. Pays royalty on actual receipts. Advance considered.** Publishes book 9-18 months after acceptance of ms. Responds in 1 month to queries. Responds in 3 months to manuscripts. Book catalog and ms guidelines for SASE or online.

- We believe ideas have consequences. One of the consequences is that they lead to a best-selling book. We publish books to improve and uplift the reader. Currently emphasizing business and history titles.

Nonfiction Subjects include Americana, especially Southern regional, Ozarks, Texas, Florida, and Southwest, art, architecture, ethnic, government, politics, special interest in conservative viewpoint, history, popular, multicultural, American artforms, but will consider others: jazz, blues, Cajun, R&B, regional, religion, for popular audience mostly, but will consider others, sports, motivational (with business slant). Query with SASE.

Reviews artwork/photos.

Fiction Subjects include historical, juvenile, regional or historical focus. We publish maybe 1 novel a year, usually by an author we already have. Almost all proposals are returned. Query with SASE. Submit outline, clips, 2 sample chapters, SASE.

Recent Title(s) *Cookies to Die for!* , by Bev Shaffer (cookbook).

Tips We do extremely well with cookbooks, popular histories, and business. We will continue to build in these areas. The writer must have a clear sense of the market and knowledge of the competition. A query letter should describe the project briefly, give the author's writing and professional credentials, and promotional ideas.

PENNSYLVANIA HISTORICAL AND MUSEUM COMMISSION

Commonwealth of Pennsylvania Keystone Bldg., 400 North St., Harrisburg PA 17120. (717)787-8099. Fax: (717)787-8312. Website: www.phmc.state.pa.us. **Contact:** Diane B. Reed, chief, publications and sales division. Estab. 1913. Publishes hardcover and paperback originals and reprints. **Publishes 6-8 titles/year. Pays 5-10% royalty on retail price or makes outright purchase.** Publishes book 18-24 months after acceptance of ms. Accepts simultaneous submissions. Responds in 4 months to queries. Prepare ms according to the *Chicago Manual of Style*.

O→ We are a public history agency and have a tradition of publishing scholarly and reference works, as well as more popularly styled books that reach an even broader audience interested in some aspect of Pennsylvania's history and heritage.

Nonfiction All books must be related to Pennsylvania, its history or culture. The Commission considers manuscripts on Pennsylvania, specifically on archaeology, history, art (decorative and fine), politics, and biography.Subjects include anthropology, archeology, art, architecture, government, politics, history, travel, historic. Query with SASE. Submit outline, sample chapters.

Recent Title(s) *Classification Guide for Arrowheads and Spearpoints of Eastern Pennsylvania and the Central Middle Atlantic*, by Jay Custer.

Tips Our audience is diverse—students, specialists, and generalists—all of them interested in 1 or more aspects of Pennsylvania's history and culture. Manuscripts must be well researched and documented (footnotes not necessarily required depending on the nature of the manuscript) and interestingly written. Manuscripts must be factually accurate, but in being so, writers must not sacrifice style.

THE PERMANENT PRESS

4170 Noyac Rd., Sag Harbor NY 11963. (631)725-1101. Fax: (631)725-8215. Website: www.thepermanentpress.com. **Contact:** Judith Shepard, editor. Estab. 1978. Publishes hardcover originals. **Publishes 12 titles/year. 60% of books from first-time authors. 60% from unagented writers. Pays 10-15% royalty on wholesale price. Offers $1,000 advance for Permanent Press books; royalty only on Second Chance Press titles.** Publishes book 18 months after acceptance of ms. Accepts simultaneous submissions. Responds in 6 weeks to queries. Responds in 6 months to manuscripts. Book catalog for $2.50 plus SASE. Guidelines for #10 SASE.

O→ "Permanent Press publishes literary fiction. Second Chance Press devotes itself exclusively to re-publishing fine books that are out of print and deserve continued recognition. We endeavor to publish quality writing—primarily fiction—without regard to authors' reputations or track records. Currently emphasizing literary fiction. No poetry, short story collections."

Nonfiction Subjects include history, memoirs. Query with SASE.

Fiction Subjects include literary, mainstream, contemporary, mystery. "Especially looking for high-line literary fiction, artful, original and arresting. Accepts any fiction category as long as it is a well-written, original full-length novel." Query with SASE and first 2 p

Recent Title(s) *The Disappearance*, by Efrem Sigel; *The History of Now*, by Daniel Klein, *Head Wounds,* by Chris Knopf; *When I was Elena*, by Ellen Hiltebrand.

Tips "Audience is the silent minority—people with good taste. We are interested in the writing more than anything and dislike long outlines. The SASE is vital to keep track of things, as we are receiving ever more submissions. No fax queries will be answered. We aren't looking for genre fiction but a compelling, well-written story. Permanent Press does not employ readers and the number of submissions it receives has grown. If the writer sends a query or manuscript that the press is not interested in, a reply may take 6 weeks. If there is interest, it may take 6-8 months."

PFLAUM PUBLISHING GROUP

N90 W16890 Roosevelt Dr., Menomonee Falls WI 53051-7933. (262)502-4222. Fax: (262)502-4224. E-mail: kcannizzo@pflaum.com. **Contact:** Karen A. Cannizzo, editorial director. **Publishes 20 titles/year. Payment may be outright purchase, royalty, or down payment plus royalty.** Book catalog and ms guidelines free.

O→ Pflaum Publishing Group, a division of Peter Li, Inc., serves the specialized market of religious education, primarily Roman Catholic. We provide high quality, theologically sound, practical, and affordable resources that assist religious educators of and ministers to children from preschool through senior high school.

Nonfiction Query with SASE.
Recent Title(s) *Absolutely Advent*; *Totally Lent*.

PHAIDON PRESS

180 Varick St., Suite 1420, New York NY 10014. (212)652-5400. Fax: (212)652-5410. Website: www.phaidon.com. **Contact:** Editorial Submissions. Publishes hardcover and trade paperback originals and reprints. **Publishes 100 titles/year. 500 mss received/year. 40% of books from first-time authors. 90% from unagented writers. Pays royalty on wholesale price, if appropriate Offers advance, if appropriate.** Publishes book 1 year after acceptance of ms. Accepts simultaneous submissions. Responds in 3 months to proposals. Book catalog available free. Guidelines available online.
Imprints Phaidon.
Nonfiction Subjects include art, architecture, photography, design. Submit proposal package and outline, or submit complete ms. Reviews artwork/photos. Send photocopies.

PHI DELTA KAPPA INTERNATIONAL

408 N. Union St., Bloomington IN 47405-3800. (812)339-1156. Fax: (812)339-0018. E-mail: customerservice@pdkintl.org. Website: www.pdkintl.org. **Contact:** Donovan R. Walling, director of publications. Estab. 1906. Publishes hardcover and trade paperback originals. **Publishes 24-30 titles/year. 100 queries received/year. 50-60 mss received/year. 50% of books from first-time authors. 100% from unagented writers. Pays honorarium of $500-5,000.** Publishes book 9 months after acceptance of ms. Responds in 3 months to proposals. Book catalog and ms guidelines free.

- The experts in cultivating great educators for tomorrow and ensuring high-quality education for today.

O→ We publish books for educators—K-12 and higher education. Our professional books are often used in college courses but are never specifically designed as textbooks.

Nonfiction Subjects include child guidance, education, legal issues. Query with SASE. Submit outline, 1 sample chapter. Reviews artwork/photos.
Recent Title(s) *The Nation's Report Card*, edited by Lyle V. Jones and Ingram Olkin; *Evaluating Principals*, by James E. Green.

⊘ PHILOMEL BOOKS

Imprint of Penguin Group (USA), Inc. 345 Hudson St., New York NY 10014. (212)414-3610. **Contact:** Patricia Lee Gauch, editor-at-large; Michael Green, president/publisher. Estab. 1980. Publishes hardcover originals. **Pays royalty. Pays negotiable advance.** Accepts simultaneous submissions. Book catalog for 9x12 envelope and 4 First-Class stamps. Guidelines for #10 SASE.

O→ We look for beautifully written, engaging manuscripts for children and young adults.

Fiction Subjects include adventure, ethnic, fantasy, historical, juvenile, 5-9 years, literary, picture books, regional, short story collections, translation, western, young adult adult, young adult, 10-18 years. Children's picture books (ages 3-8); middle-grade fiction and illustrated chapter books (ages 7-10); young adult novels (ages 10-15). Looking for story-driven novels with a strong cultural voice but which speak universally. *No unsolicited mss*
Recent Title(s) *Snakehead*, by Anthony Horowitz; *Toy Boat*, by Randall de Seve and Loren Long.

PIA/GATFPRESS

Graphic Arts Technical Foundation 200 Deer Run Rd., Sewickley PA 15143-2600. (412)741-6860. Fax: (412)741-2311. E-mail: awoodall@piagatf.org. Website: www.gain.net. **Contact:** Amy Woodall, director (graphic arts, communication, book publishing, printing). Estab. 1924. Publishes trade paperback originals and hardcover reference texts. **Publishes 20 titles/year. 50% of books from first-time authors. 100% from unagented writers. Pays 5-15% royalty on wholesale price.** Publishes book 18 months after acceptance of ms. Responds in 1 month to queries. Book catalog for 9 X 12 envelope and 2 First-Class stamps. Guidelines for #10 SASE.

O→ PIA/GATF's mission is to serve the graphic communications community as the major resource for technical information and services through research and education. Currrently emphasizing career guides for graphic communications and turnkey training curriculums.

Nonfiction Query with SASE, or submit outline, sample chapters, and SASE. Reviews artwork/photos.
Recent Title(s) *Color and Its Reproduction, 3rd Ed.*, by Gary G. Field; *To Be a Profitable Printer*, by Michael Moffit.
Tips We are publishing titles that are updated more frequently, such as *On-Demand Publishing*. Our scope now includes reference titles geared toward general audiences interested in computers, imaging, and Internet, as well as print publishing.

🅰 ⊘ PICADOR USA

Subsidiary of Holtzbrinck Publishers Holdings LLC 175 Fifth Ave., New York NY 10010. (212)674-5151. Fax: (212)253-9627. Website: www.picadorusa.com. Estab. 1994. Publishes hardcover and trade paperback originals and reprints.

- *No unsolicited mss or queries. Agented submissions only.*

O→ Picador publishes high-quality literary fiction and nonfiction.

Recent Title(s) *Housekeeping*, by Marilynne Robinson; *Life on the Outside*, by Jennifer Gonnerman; *Dry*, by Augusten Burroughs.

PICTON PRESS

Picton Corp. P.O. Box 1347, Rockland ME 04841-1347. (207)596-7766. Fax: (207)596-7767. E-mail: sales@pictonpress.com. Website: www.pictonpress.com. Publishes hardcover and mass market paperback originals and reprints, and CDs. **Publishes 30 titles/year. 30 queries received/year. 15 mss received/year. 50% of books from first-time authors. 100% from unagented writers. Pays 0-10% royalty on wholesale price. Makes outright purchase.** Publishes book 6 months after acceptance of ms. Responds in 2 months to queries. Responds in 2 months to proposals. Responds in 3 months to manuscripts. Book catalog available free.

Imprints Cricketfield Press; New England History Press; Penobscot Press; Picton Press.

O→ Picton Press is one of America's oldest, largest, and most respected publishers of genealogical and historical books specializing in research tools for the 17th, 18th, and 19th centuries.

Nonfiction Subjects include Americana, history, hobbies, genealogy. Query with SASE. Submit outline.

Recent Title(s) *Norden: A Guide to Scandinavian Genealogical Research in a Digital World*, by Art Jura.

THE PILGRIM PRESS

700 Prospect Ave. E., Cleveland OH 44115-1100. (216)736-3755. Fax: (216)736-2207. Website: www.thepilgrimpress.com. **Contact:** Timothy G. Staveteig, publisher. Publishes hardcover and trade paperback originals. **Publishes 25 titles/year. 60% of books from first-time authors. 80% from unagented writers. Pays standard royalties. Pays advance.** Publishes book an average of 18 months after acceptance of ms. Responds in 3 months to queries. Book catalog and ms guidelines online.

Nonfiction Subjects include business, economics, gay, lesbian, government, politics, nature, environment, religion, ethics, social issues with a strong commitment to justice—addressing such topics as public policy, sexuality and gender, human rights and minority liberation—primarily in a Christian context, but not exclusively.

Tips "Writers should send books about contemporary social issues. Our audience is liberal, open-minded, socially aware, feminist, church members and clergy, teachers, and seminary professors."

PINEAPPLE PRESS, INC.

P.O. Box 3889, Sarasota FL 34230. Website: www.pineapplepress.com. **Contact:** June Cussen, exec. editor. Estab. 1982. Publishes hardcover and trade paperback originals. **Publishes 25 titles/year. 1,000 queries received/year. 500 mss received/year. 10% of books from first-time authors. 95% from unagented writers. Pays rare advance.** Publishes book 12 months after acceptance of ms. Accepts simultaneous submissions. Responds in 1 month to queries. Responds in 1 month to proposals. Responds in 3 months to manuscripts. Book catalog for 9x12 SAE with $1.25 postage. Guidelines available online.

O→ We are seeking quality nonfiction on diverse topics for the library and book trade markets.

Nonfiction Subjects include regional, Florida. Submit proposal package, outline, 3 sample chapters, and introduction. Reviews artwork/photos. Send photocopies.

Fiction Subjects include regional, Florida. Submit proposal package, 3 sample chapters, clips.

PIÑATA BOOKS

Imprint of Arte Publico Press University of Houston, 452 Cullen Performance Hall, Houston TX 77204-2004. (713)743-2845. Fax: (713)743-3080. Website: www.artepublicopress.com. **Contact:** Nicolas Kanellos, director. Estab. 1994. Publishes hardcover and trade paperback originals. **Publishes 10-15 titles/year. 40% of books from first-time authors. Pays 10% royalty on wholesale price. Pays $1,000-3,000 advance.** Publishes book 2 years after acceptance of ms. Accepts simultaneous submissions. Responds in 1 month to queries. Responds in 6 months to manuscripts. Book catalog and ms guidelines available via website or with #10 SASE.

O→ Piñata Books is dedicated to the publication of children's and young adult literature focusing on US Hispanic culture by US Hispanic authors.

Nonfiction Piñata Books specializes in publication of children's and young adult literature that authentically portrays themes, characters and customs unique to U.S. Hispanic culture.Subjects include ethnic. Query with SASE. Submit outline, 2 sample chapters, synopsis.

Fiction Subjects include adventure, juvenile, picture books, young adult. Query with SASE. Submit clips, 2 sample chapters, SASE.

Recent Title(s) *Walking Stars*, by Victor Villasenor; *The Bakery Lady*, by Pat Mora.

Tips Include cover letter with submission explaining why your manuscript is unique and important, why we should publish it, who will buy it, etc.

PLANNERS PRESS

Imprint of the American Planning Association 122 S. Michigan Ave., Ste. 1600, Chicago IL 60603. (312)431-9100. Fax: (312)431-9985. E-mail: plannerspress@planning.org. Website: www.planning.org/plannerspress/index.htm. **Contact:** Timothy Mennel, Ph.D. (planning practice, urban issues, land use, transportation). Estab. 1970. Publishes hardcover, electronic, and trade paperback originals; and trade paperback and electronic reprints. **Publishes 12 titles/year. 50 queries received/year. 35 mss received/year. 25% of books from first-time authors. 100% from unagented writers. Pays 10-15% royalty on wholesale price. Pays advance.** Publishes book 15 months after acceptance of ms. Accepts simultaneous submissions. Responds in 1 month to queries. Responds in 2 months to proposals and manuscripts. Book catalog online at website www.planningbooks.com. Guidelines available by e-mail at plannerspress@planning.org.

O→ Our books have a narrow audience of city planners and often focus on the tools of city planning.

Nonfiction Subjects include agriculture, business, economics, community, contemporary culture, economics, environment, finance, government, politics, history, horticulture, law, money, finance, nature, environment, politics, real estate, science, social sciences sciences, sociology, transportation, world affairs. Submit proposal package, including: outline, 1 sample chapter and c.v. Submit completed ms. Reviews artwork/photos. Send photocopies.

Fiction We do not publish fiction

Recent Title(s) *Overlooked America and Smart Growth in a Changing World*; The Editors of *Planning* Magazine; *True Urbanism: Living in and Near the Center*; *The High Cost of Free Parking*, by Donald Shoup; *Making Places Special: The Citizen's Guide to Planning*, by Gene Bunnell.

Tips Our audience is professional planners but also anyone interested in community development, urban affairs, sustainability, and related fields.

PLAYERS PRESS, INC.

P.O. Box 1132, Studio City CA 91614-0132. (818)789-4980. **Contact:** Robert W. Gordon, vice president, editorial. Estab. 1965. Publishes hardcover originals and trade paperback originals and reprints. **Publishes 35-70 titles/year. 15% of books from first-time authors. 80% from unagented writers. Pays royalty on wholesale price. Pays advance.** Publishes book 3 months-2 years after acceptance of ms. Responds in 1 week to queries. Responds in up to 1 year to manuscripts. Book catalog for 9x12 envelope and 7 First-Class stamps. Guidelines for #10 SASE.

O→ Players Press publishes support books for the entertainment industries: theater, film, television, dance and technical. Currently emphasizing plays for all ages, theatre crafts, monologues and short scenes for ages 5-9, 11-15, and musicals.

Nonfiction Subjects include film, cinema, stage, performing arts. Query with SASE. Reviews music as part of ms package.

Fiction Plays: Subject matter includes adventure, confession, ethnic, experimental, fantasy, historical, horror, humor, mainstream, mystery, religious romance, science fiction, suspense, western. Submit complete ms for theatrical plays only. Plays must be previously produced.

Recent Title(s) *Women's Wear of the 1930's*, by Hopper/Countryman; *Rhyme Tyme*, by William-Alan Landes; *Borrowed Plumage*, by David Crawford.

Tips "Plays, entertainment industry texts, theater, film and TV books have the only chances of selling to our firm."

⊘ PLAYHOUSE PUBLISHING

1566 Akron-Peninsula Rd., Akron OH 44313. (330)926-1313. Fax: (330)926-1315. Website: www.playhousepublishing.com. **Contact:** Children's Acquisitions Editor. Publishes novelty board books. **Publishes 10-15 titles/year. Work-for-hire. Makes outright purchase.** Publishes book 18-24 months after acceptance of ms. Accepts simultaneous submissions. Responds in 2 months to proposals. Book catalog available online. Guidelines available online.

Imprints Picture Me Books (board books with photos); Nibble Me Books (board books with edibles).

- Playhouse Publishing will no longer accept unsolicited mss sent for review in the mail. Any items sent in the mail will be destroyed. The company encourages writers to submit query letters/book proposals electronically to webmaster@playhousepublishing.com. All copy must be contained in the body of an e-mail. Attachments will not be opened.

O→ We publish novelty board books and juvenile fiction appropriate for children from birth to first grade. All Picture Me Books titles incorporate the `picture me' photo concept. All Nibble Me Books titles incorporate an edible that completes the illustrations.

Fiction Subjects include juvenile.

Recent Title(s) *Squeaky Clean*, by Merry North; *All Gone*, by Merry North; *Pretend & Play Superhero*, by Cathy Hapka.

N POISONED PEN PRESS

6962 E. 1st Ave., #103, Scottsdale AZ 85251. (480)945-3375. Fax: (480)949-1707. E-mail: editor@poisonedpenpress.com. Website: www.poisonedpenpress.com. Estab. 1996. Publishes hardcover originals, and hardcover and trade paperback reprints. **Publishes 36 titles/year. 1,000 queries received/year. 300 mss received/year. 35% of books from first-time authors. 65% from unagented writers. Pays 9-15% royalty on retail price.** Publishes book 10-12 months after acceptance of ms. Responds in 2-3 months to queries. Responds in 2-3 months to proposals. Responds in 6 months to manuscripts. Book catalog available online. Guidelines available online.

- Our publishing goal is to offer well-written mystery novels of crime and/or detection where the puzzle and its resolution are the main forces that move the story forward.

Fiction Subjects include mystery. Mss should generally be longer than 65,000 words and shorter than 100,000 words. Query with SASE. Submit clips, first 3 pages. We must receive both the syno.

Tips Audience is adult readers of mystery fiction.

POPULAR WOODWORKING BOOKS

Imprint of F+W Media, Inc. 4700 Galbraith Rd., Cincinnati OH 45236. (513)531-2690. Website: fwpublications.com/woodworking.asp. **Contact:** David Thiel, executive editor (david.thiel@fwpubs.com). Publishes trade paperback and hardcover originals and reprints. **Publishes 10-12 titles/year. 30 queries received/year. 10 mss received/year. 40% of books from first-time authors. 95% from unagented writers.** Publishes book 1 year after acceptance of ms. Accepts simultaneous submissions. Responds in 1 month to queries.

- Popular Woodworking Books is one of the largest publishers of woodworking books in the world. From perfecting a furniture design to putting on the final coat of finish, our books provide step-by-step instructions and trusted advice from the pros that make them valuable tools for both beginning and advanced woodworkers. Currently emphasizing woodworking jigs and fixtures, furniture and cabinet projects, smaller finely crafted boxes, all styles of furniture. De-emphasizing woodturning, woodcarving, scroll saw projects.

Nonfiction We publish heavily illustrated how-to woodworking books that show, rather than tell, our readers how to accomplish their woodworking goals.Subjects include hobbies, woodworking/wood crafts. Query with SASE, or electronic query. Proposal package should include an outline and digital photos.

Recent Title(s) *The Complete Cabinet Maker's Reference*, by Jeffrey Piontkowski; *Pleasant Hill Shaker Furniture*, by Kerry Pierce; *Workbenches*, by Christopher Schwarz.

Tips Our books are for beginning to advanced woodworking enthusiasts.

POTOMAC BOOKS, INC.

Attn: KO 22841 Quicksilver Dr., Dulles VA 20166. (703)661-1548. Fax: (703)661-1547. Website: www.potomacbooksinc.com. **Contact:** Editorial Department. Estab. 1984. Publishes hardcover and trade paperback originals and reprints. **Publishes 60 titles/year. 900 queries received/year. 20% of books from first-time authors. 70% from unagented writers. Pays royalty on wholesale price. Pays five figure maximum advance.** Publishes book 1 year after acceptance of ms. Accepts simultaneous submissions. Responds in 2 months to queries. Book catalog available free. Guidelines available online.

Imprints Potomac Sports.

- "Potomac Books specializes in national and international affairs, history (especially military and diplomatic), intelligence, biography, reference, and sports. We are particularly interested in authors who can communicate a sophisticated understanding of their topic to general readers, as well as specialists."

Nonfiction Subjects include government, politics, history, military, war, sports, world affairs, national and international affairs. "Query letter should provide a summary of the project, a description of the author's credentials and an analysis of the work's competition. "We are encouraging prospective authors to submit book proposals via e-mail."

Recent Title(s) *Shattered Sword*, by Jonathan Parshall and Anthony Tully; *Wrigley Field*, by Stuart Shea.

Tips "Our audience consists of general nonfiction readers, as well as students, scholars, policymakers and the military."

PPI (PROFESSIONAL PUBLICATIONS, INC.)

1250 Fifth Ave., Belmont CA 94002-3863. (650)593-9119. Fax: (650)592-4519. E-mail: acquisitions@ppi2pass.com. Website: www.ppi2pass.com. Estab. 1975. Publishes hardcover, paperback, and electronic products, CD-ROMs and DVDs. **Publishes 10 titles/year. 5% of books from first-time authors. 100% from unagented writers.** Publishes book 4-18 months after acceptance of ms. Accepts simultaneous submissions. Responds in 1 month to queries. Book catalog and ms guidelines free.

- PPI publishes professional, reference, and licensing preparation materials. PPI wants submissions from both professionals practicing in the field and from experienced instructors. Currently emphasizing engineering, interior design, architecture, landscape architecture and LEED exam review.

Nonfiction Subjects include architecture, science, landscape architecture, engineering mathematics, engineering, surveying, interior design, greenbuilding, sustainable development, and other professional licensure subjects. Please submit ms and proposal outlining market potential, etc. Proposal template available upon request. Reviews artwork/photos.

Recent Title(s) *Six-Minute Solutions for the Civil PE Exam*, various authors; *LEED NC Sample Exam*.

Tips We specialize in books for those people who want to become licensed and/or accredited professionals: engineers, architects, surveyors, interior designers, LEED APs, etc. Exam Prep Lines General include online and print products such as review manuals, practice problems, and sample exams. Demonstrating your understanding of the market, competition, and marketing ideas will help sell us on your proposal.

N PRACTICE MANAGEMENT INFORMATION CORP. (PMIC)

4727 Wilshire Blvd., #300, Los Angeles CA 90010. (323)954-0224. Fax: (323)954-0253. Website: www.medicalbookstore.com. **Contact:** Arthur Gordon, managing editor. Estab. 1986. Publishes hardcover originals. **Publishes 21 titles/year. 100 queries received/year. 50 mss received/year. 10% of books from first-time authors. 90% from unagented writers. Pays $1,000-5,000 advance.** Publishes book 18 months after acceptance of ms. Responds in 6 months to queries.

Imprints PMIC; Health Information Press (HIP).

- PMIC helps healthcare workers understand the business of medicine by publishing books for doctors, medical office and hospital staff, medical managers, insurance coding/billing personnel. HIP seeks to simplify health care for consumers.

Nonfiction Subjects include business, economics, health, medicine, science. Submit proposal package, outline, resume, 3-5 sample chapters, letter stating who is the intended audience and the need/market for such a book.

Recent Title(s) *ICD-9-CM Coding Made Easy*, by James Davis; *Medicare Rules & Regulations*, by Maxine Lewis; *Medical Practice Forms*, by Keith Borglum.

N Ø PRAEGER PUBLISHERS

The Greenwood Publishing Group, Inc. 88 Post Road W., Westport CT 06881. (203)226-3571. Fax: (203)226-6009. **Contact:** Heather Stainer (history, military); Debbie Carvalko (psychology); Suzanne Staszak-Silva (sociology); Nicholas Philipson (business); Eric Levy (cultural studies, media); Hilary Claggett (politics/journalism); Elizabeth Polenza (psychology). Estab. 1949. Publishes hardcover originals. **Publishes 250 titles/year. 5% of books from first-time authors. 90% from unagented writers. Pays rare advance.** Publishes book an average of 12 months. after acceptance of ms. Accepts simultaneous submissions. Responds in 1 month to queries. Book catalog and ms guidelines online.

- Praeger publishes scholarly trade and advanced texts in the the social and behavioral sciences and communications, international relations, and military studies.

Nonfiction Subjects include business, economics, government, politics, history, psychology, sociology, womens issues, womens studies.

Recent Title(s) *An American Paradox: Censorship in a Nation of Free Speech*, Patrick Garry; *Pharmacracy: Medicine and Politics in America*, edited by Thomas Szasz.

PRESTWICK HOUSE, INC.

P.O. Box 658, Clayton DE 19938. Website: www.prestwickhouse.com. Estab. 1980.

Nonfiction Submit proposal package, outline, resume, 1 sample chapter, TOC.

Tips "We market our books primarily for middle and high school English teachers. Submissions should address a direct need of grades 7-12 language arts teachers. Current and former English teachers are encouraged to submit materials developed and used by them successfully in the classroom."

Ø PRICE STERN SLOAN, INC.

Penguin Group (USA) 345 Hudson, New York NY 10014. (212)414-3610. Fax: (212)414-3396. Website: www.us.penguingroup.com. Estab. 1963. **Publishes 75 titles/year. Makes outright purchase. Pays advance.** Book catalog for 9x12 SAE with 5 first-class stamps; ms guidelines for #10 SASE.

Imprints Mad Libs; Mad Libs Jr.; Mr. Men & Little Miss; Serendipity; Wee Sing.

- Price Stern Sloan publishes quirky mass market novelty series for children as well as licensed tie-in books.

Fiction Quirky, funny picture books, novelty books and quirky full color series.

Recent Title(s) *123 Look at Me!*, by Roberta Intrater.

Tips Price Stern Sloan has a unique, humorous, off-the-wall feel.

N PRINCETON ARCHITECTURAL PRESS

37 E. 7th St., New York NY 10003. (212)995-9620. Fax: (212)995-9454. E-mail: submissions@papress.com. Website: www.papress.com. **Contact:** Editorial Submissions. Publishes hardcover and trade paperback originals. **Publishes 50 titles/year. 300 queries received/year. 150 mss received/year. 65% of books from**

first-time authors. 95% from unagented writers. Pays royalty on wholesale price. Publishes book 1 year after acceptance of ms. Accepts simultaneous submissions. Responds in 2 months to queries. Responds in 2 months to proposals. Responds in 2 months to manuscripts. Book catalog available online. Guidelines available online.

Nonfiction Subjects include art, architecture. Submit proposal package, outline, 1 sample chapters, table of contents, sample of art, and survey of competitive titles. Reviews artwork/photos. Send not originals.

Recent Title(s) *45 RPM: A Visual History of the Seven-Inch Record*, edited by Spencer Drate (pictorial collection of record covers); *Inside Design Now: The National Design Triennial*, edited by Donald Albrecht, et. al. (museum catalog of new design work); *Rural Studio*, by Andrea Oppenheimer Dean and Timothy Hursley (monograph on design/build studio).

Tips Princeton Architecture Press publishes fine books on architecture, design, photography, landscape, and visual culture. Our books are acclaimed for their strong and unique editorial vision, unrivaled design sensibility, and high production values at affordable prices.

PRINTING INDUSTRIES OF AMERICA

200 Deer Run Rd., Sewickley PA 15143-2600, United States. (412)741-6860. Fax: (412)741-2311. E-mail: awoodall@printing.org. Website: www.printing.org. **Contact:** Amy Woodall, director (areas of interest: Printing, Graphic Arts, communication). Trade paperback originals and hardcover reference texts. **Publishes 20 titles/year. Receives 20 ms/year, 30 queries 50% of books from first-time authors. 100% from unagented writers.** Publishes book 18 months after acceptance of ms. Accepts simultaneous submissions.

- Formerly PIA/GatfPress

Nonfiction Subjects include business, economics/economics, education, communications, printing & graphic arts. Query with SASE, or submit outline, sample chapters, and SASE. Reviews artwork. Send photocopies.

Recent Title(s) *Color Management Handbook*, by Richard Adams et al. (color handbook); *Printing Estimating, 5th Ed.*, by Philip K. Ruggles (textbook).

PROMETHEUS BOOKS

59 John Glenn Dr., Amherst NY 14228-2119. (800)421-0351. Fax: (716)564-2711. E-mail: editorial@prometheusbooks.com. Website: www.prometheusbooks.com. **Contact:** Steven L. Mitchell, editor-in-chief. Estab. 1969. Publishes hardcover originals, trade paperback originals and reprints. **Publishes 90-100 titles/year. 30% of books from first-time authors. 40% from unagented writers.** Accepts simultaneous submissions. Responds in 2 months to queries. Responds in 3 months to proposals. Responds in 4 months to manuscripts. Book catalog free or online. Guidelines for #10 SASE or online.

Imprints Humanity Books (scholarly and professional monographs in philosophy, social science, sociology, archaeology, black studies, women's studies); PYR (science fiction/fantasy—accepts agented works only by previously published authors—send to the attention of Lou Anders).

O→ "Prometheus Books is a leading independent publisher in philosophy, social science, popular science, and critical thinking. We publish authoritative and thoughtful books by distinguished authors in many categories. Currently emphasizing popular science, health, psychology, social science, current events, business and economics, atheism and critiques of religion."

Nonfiction Subjects include education, government, politics, health, medicine, history, language, literature, New Age, critiquing of, philosophy, psychology, religion, contemporary issues. Submit proposal package including outline, synopsis, potential market, tentative ms length, résumé, and a well-developed query letter with SASE, two or three of author's best chapters. Reviews artwork/photos. Send photocopies.

Recent Title(s) *Evil Genes: Why Rome Fell, Hitler Rose, Enron Failed, and My Sister Stole My Mother's Boyfriend*, by Barbara Oakley; *God: The Failed Hypothesis*, by Victor J. Stenger; *Ad Women: How They Impact What We Need, Want, and Buy*, by Juliann Sivulka; *Will Terrorists Go Nuclear*, by Brian Michael Jenkins; *Cosmic Connection: How Astronomical Events Impact Life On Earth*, by Jeff Kanipe; *The Fabulous Fibonacci Numbers*, by Alfred Posamentier and Ingmar Lehmann; *The Father Factor*, by Stephan B. Poulter; *Distracted*, by Maggie Jackson; *A Question of Murder*, by Cyril H. Wecht and Dawna Kaufmann; *Fifty Reasons People Give For Believing in a God*, by Guy Harrison; *Energy Victory*, by Robert Zubrin; *Disability: The Social, Political, and Ethical Debate*, edited by Robert M. Baird Stuart E. Rosenbaum, and S. Kay Toombs.

Tips "Audience is highly literate with multiple degrees; an audience that is intellectually mature and knows what it wants. They are aware, and we try to provide them with new information on topics of interest to them in mainstream and related areas."

N PROSTAR PUBLICATIONS, INC.

3 Church Circle, #109, Annapolis MD 21401 (800)481-6277. Fax: (800)487-6277. Website: www.prostarpublications.com. **Contact:** Peter Griffes, president (marine-related/how-to/business/technical); Susan Willson, editor (history/memoirs). Estab. 1965. Publishes trade paperback originals. **Publishes 150 titles/year. 120 queries received/year. 25 mss received/year. 50% of books from first-time authors. 100% from unagented writers. Pays 15% royalty on wholesale price. Rarely offers advance.** Publishes book 1 year after acceptance of ms. Accepts simultaneous submissions. Responds in 3 months to queries. Responds in 3 months

to proposals. Book catalog available online.
Imprints Lighthouse Press (Peter Griffes).

O→ Originally, ProStar published only nautical books. Any quality nonfiction book would be of interest.

Nonfiction Subjects include history, memoirs, nature, environment, travel, nautical. Query with SASE. Reviews artwork/photos. Send photocopies.
Recent Title(s) *Age of Cunard*, by Daniel Butler; *They Call Me Kendra*, by Julie Posey; *No More Mondays*, by LaVonne Misner.
Tips We prefer to work directly with the author and seldom work with agents. Please send in a well-written query letter, and we will give your book serious consideration.

PRUETT PUBLISHING

P.O. Box 2140, Boulder CO 80306. (303)449-4919. Fax: (303)443-9019. Website: www.pruettpublishing.com. **Contact:** Jim Pruett, publisher. Estab. 1956. Publishes hardcover and trade paperback originals, trade paperback reprints. **75-80 mss received/year. 90%% of books from first-time authors. 90%% from unagented writers. Pays $1,000-1,500 advance.** Publishes book 12-18 months after acceptance of ms. Accepts simultaneous submissions. Responds in 1 month to queries. Responds in 3 months to proposals. Responds in 3 months to manuscripts.

O→ "We are focused on the mountain West."

Nonfiction Subjects include alternative, Americana, education, history, nature, environment, sports, travel. Query with SASE. Submit outline, 2 sample chapters. Reviews artwork/photos. Send photocopies.
Recent Title(s) *Hikes Around Ft. Collins*, by Melody Edwards ((hiking)); *Telluride Trails*, by Don Scarmuzzi; *OBIT*, by Jim Sheeler ((obituaries)).
Tips We focus on outdoor recreationalists—hikers, fly-fishers, travelers. There has been a movement away from large publisher's mass market books toward small publisher's regional interest books, and in turn distributors and retail outlets are more interested in small publishers. Authors don't need to have a big name to have a good publisher. Look for similar books that you feel are well-produced—consider design, editing, overall quality, and contact those publishers. Get to know several publishers, and find the one that feels right—trust your instincts."

PRUFROCK PRESS, INC.

5926 Balcones Dr., Ste. 220, Austin TX 78731. (512)300-2220. Fax: (512)300-2221. E-mail: info@prufrock.com. Website: www.prufrock.com. **Contact:** Lacy Elwood, Jennifer Robins. Publishes trade paperback originals and reprints. Book catalog and ms guidelines free.

O→ Prufrock Press publishes exciting, innovative and current resources supporting the education of gifted and talented learners.

Nonfiction Subjects include child guidance, education. Submit book prospectus (download form on website).
Recent Title(s) *Ready for Preschool*, by Nancy B. Hertzog; *CSI Expert! Forensic Science for Kids*, by Karen K. Schulz; *School Success for Kids with Asperger's Syndrome*, by Stephan Silverman and Rich Weinfeld.
Tips We are looking for practical, classroom-ready materials that encourage children to creatively learn and think.

Ø PUFFIN BOOKS

Imprint of Penguin Group (USA), Inc. 345 Hudson St., New York NY 10014. (212)366-2000. Website: www.penguinputnam.com. Publishes trade paperback originals and reprints. **Publishes 225 titles/year. Royalty varies. Pays varies advance.** Book catalog for 9x12 SAE with 7 first-class stamps.

O→ Puffin Books publishes high-end trade paperbacks and paperback reprints for preschool children, beginning and middle readers, and young adults.

Nonfiction Subjects include education, for teaching concepts and colors, not academic, history, womens issues, womens studies. *No unsolicited mss.*
Fiction Subjects include picture books, young adult, middle grade, easy-to-read grades 1-3. We do not publish original picture books. *No unsolicited mss.*
Recent Title(s) *The Rules of Survival*, by Nancy Werlin; *Cindy Ella*, by Robin Palmer; *Walk of the Spirits*, by Richie Tankersley Cusick.
Tips Our audience ranges from little children `first books' to young adult (ages 14-16). An original idea has the best luck.

PURDUE UNIVERSITY PRESS

South Campus Courts, Bldg. E, 509 Harrison St., West Lafayette IN 47907-2025. (765)494-2038. E-mail: pupress@purdue.edu. Website: www.thepress.purdue.edu. **Contact:** Acquisitions Editor. Estab. 1960. Publishes hardcover and trade paperback originals and trade paperback reprints. **Publishes 20-25 titles/year.** Book catalog and ms guidelines for 9x12 SASE.
Imprints PuP Books (juvenile reprint series that brings back to publication out-of-print stories illuminating other times in American history)

- We look for books that look at the world as a whole and offer new thoughts and insights into the standard debate. Currently emphasizing technology, human-animal issues, business. De-emphasizing literary studies.

Nonfiction We publish work of quality scholarship and titles with regional (Midwest) flair. Especially interested in innovative contributions to the social sciences and humanities that break new barriers and provide unique views on current topics. Expanding into veterinary medicine, technology, and business topics.Subjects include agriculture, Americana, business,government, politics, health, history, language, literary criticism, philosophy, regional, science, social sciences, sociology. Query before submitting.

Recent Title(s) *Blowing the Whistle on Genocide*, by Rafael Medoff; *New York's Poop Scoop Law*, by Michael Brandow; *What's Buggin' You Now?* by Tom Turpin; *Words at War*, by David B. Sachsman, S. Kittrell Rushing, and Roy Morris Jr.

G.P. PUTNAM'S SONS HARDCOVER

Imprint of Penguin Group (USA), Inc., 375 Hudson, New York NY 10014. (212)366-2000. Fax: (212)366-2664. Website: www.penguinputnam.com. Publishes hardcover originals. **Pays variable royalties on retail price. Pays varies advance.** Accepts simultaneous submissions. Request book catalog through mail order department.

Nonfiction Subjects include animals, business, economics, child guidance, contemporary culture, cooking, foods, nutrition, health, medicine, military, war, nature, environment, religion, science, sports, travel, womens issues, womens studies, celebrity-related topics. Agented submissions only. *No unsolicited mss.*

Fiction Subjects include adventure, literary, mainstream, contemporary, mystery, suspense, women's. Agented submissions only. *No unsolicited mss.*

Recent Title(s) *A Voice for the Dead*, by James Starrs and Katherine Ramsland; *Prince of Fire*, by Daniel Silva.

QUE

Pearson Education 800 E. 96th St., Indianapolis IN 46240. (317)581-3500. E-mail: proposals@quepublishing.com. Website: www.quepublishing.com. Estab. 1981. Publishes hardcover, trade paperback and mass market paperback originals and reprints. **Publishes 100 titles/year. 80% from unagented writers. Pays variable royalty on wholesale price or makes work-for-hire arrangements. Pays varying advance.** Accepts simultaneous submissions. Book catalog and ms guidelines online.

Nonfiction Subjects include computers, electronics, technology, certification. Submit proposal package, resume, TOC, writing sample, competing titles.

Recent Title(s) *MySQL, 3rd Ed.*, by Paul Dubois; *Absolute Beginner's Guide to Project Management*, by Greg Horine; *Teach Yourself to Create Web Pages*, by Preston Gralla and Matt Brown.

QUEST BOOKS

Imprint of Theosophical Publishing House 306 W. Geneva Rd., P.O. Box 270, Wheaton IL 60187. E-mail: submissions@questbooks.net. Website: www.questbooks.net. **Contact:** Richard Smoley, editor. Estab. 1965. Publishes hardcover and trade paperback originals and reprints. **Publishes 12 titles/year. 150 ms; 350 queries received/year. 20% of books from first-time authors. 80% from unagented writers. Pays royalty on retail price. Pays varying advance.** Publishes book 12 months after acceptance of ms. Accepts simultaneous submissions. Responds in 2 months to queries, proposals, & mss. Book catalog available free. Guidelines available online at: www. questbooks.net/aboutquest.cfm#submission.

Imprints Quest Books

- Quest Books is the imprint of the Theosophical Publishing House, the publishing arm of the Theosophical Society in America. Since 1965, Quest books has sold millions of books by leading cultural thinkers on such increasingly popular subjects as transpersonal psychology, comparative religion, deep ecology, spiritual growth, the development of creativity, and alternative health practices.

Nonfiction Subjects include philosophy, psychology, religion, spirituality, New Age, astrology/psychic. Submit proposal package, including outline, 1 sample chapter. Prefer online submissions; no attachments please. Reviews artwork/photos. Writers should send photocopies or transparencies, but note that none will be returned.

Recent Title(s) *Politics and the Occult: The Left, The Right, and the Radically Unseen*, by Gary Lachman (religion & politics); *The Golden Thread: Ageless Wisdom of the Western Mystery Traditions*, by Joscelyn Godwin (religion/spirituality); *War and the Soul: Healing the Nation's Veterans From Post-traumatic Stress Disorder*, by Edward Tick (psychology)

Tips Our audience includes readers interested in spirituality, particularly the world's mystical traditions. Read a few recent Quest titles and submission guidelines before submitting. Know our books and our company goals. Explain how your book or proposal relates to other Quest titles. Quest gives preference to writers with established reputations/successful publications.

QUILL DRIVER BOOKS

1254 Commerce Ave., Sanger CA 93657. (559)876-2170. Fax: (559)876-2180. Website: www.quilldriverbooks.com. **Contact:** Stephen Blake Mettee, publisher. Publishes hardcover and trade paperback originals and reprints. **Publishes 10-12 titles/year. 50% of books from first-time authors. 95% from unagented writers. Pays 4-10% royalty on retail price. Pays $500-5,000 advance.** Publishes book 12 months after acceptance of ms. Accepts simultaneous submissions. Responds in 1 month to queries. Responds in 1 month to proposals. Responds in 3 months to manuscripts. Book catalog and ms guidelines for #10 SASE.

> "We publish a modest number of books per year, each of which, we hope, makes a worthwhile contribution to the human community, and we have a little fun along the way. We are strongly emphasizing our book series: The Best Half of Life series—on subjects which will serve to enhance the lifestyles, life skills, and pleasures of living for those over 50."

Nonfiction Subjects include regional, California, writing, aging. Query with SASE. Submit proposal package. Reviews artwork/photos. Send photocopies.

Recent Title(s) *Live Longer, Live Better*, by Peter H. Gott, MD; *Dr. Ruth's Sex After 50*, by Dr. Ruth K. Westheimer; *Secrets of Social Media Marketing*, by Paul Gillin.

QUITE SPECIFIC MEDIA GROUP, LTD.

7373 Pyramid Place, Hollywood CA 90046. (323)851-5797. Fax: (323)851-5798. E-mail: info@quitespecificmedia.com. Website: www.quitespecificmedia.com. **Contact:** Ralph Pine, editor-in-chief. Estab. 1967. Publishes hardcover originals, trade paperback originals and reprints. **Publishes 12 titles/year. 300 queries received/year. 100 mss received/year. 75% of books from first-time authors. 85% from unagented writers. Pays royalty on wholesale price. Pays varies advance.** Publishes book 18 months after acceptance of ms. Accepts simultaneous submissions. Responds to queries. Book catalog available online. Guidelines available free.

Imprints Costume & Fashion Press; Drama Publishers; By Design Press; Entertainment Pro; Jade Rabbit.

> Quite Specific Media Group is an umbrella company of 5 imprints specializing in costume and fashion, theater and design.

Nonfiction For and about performing arts theory and practice: acting, directing; voice, speech, movement; makeup, masks, wits; costumes, sets, lighting, sound; design and execution; technical theater, stagecraft, equipment; stage management; producing; arts management, all varieties; business and legal aspects; film, radio, television, cable, video; theory, criticism, reference; theater and performance history; costume and fashion.Subjects include fashion, film, cinema, stage, history, literary criticism, translation. Query by e-mail please Reviews artwork/photos.

RANDOM HOUSE AUDIO PUBLISHING GROUP

Subsidiary of Random House, Inc. 1745 Broadway, New York NY 10019. (212)782-9720. Fax: (212)782-9600. Website: www.randomhouse.com.

Imprints Listening Library; Random House Audible; Random House Audio; Random House Audio Assets; Random House Audio Dimensions; Random House Audio Roads; Random House Audio Voices; Random House Price-less.

> Audio publishing for adults and children, offering titles in both abridged and unabridged formats on cassettes, compact discs, and by digital delivery.

Recent Title(s) *Confronting Reality*, by Larry Bossidy and Ram Charan; *To the Last Man*, by Jeff Shaara; *Dragon Rider*, by Cornelia Funke.

RANDOM HOUSE INTERNATIONAL

Division of Random House, Inc. 1745 Broadway, New York NY 10019. (212)572-6106. Fax: (212)572-6045. Website: www.randomhouse.com.

Imprints Arete; McClelland & Stewart Ltd.; Plaza & Janes; Random House Australia; Random House of Canada Ltd.; Random House Mondadori; Random House South Africa; Random House South America; Random House United Kingdom; Transworld UK; Verlagsgruppe Random House.

Recent Title(s) *Saturday*, by Ian McEwan (Random House Australia); *The Family Tree*, by Carole Cadwalladr (Transworld UK); *The Bird Factory*, by David Layton (McClelland & Stewart).

RANDOM HOUSE LARGE PRINT

Division of Random House, Inc. 1745 Broadway, New York NY 10019. (212)782-9720. Fax: (212)782-9600. Website: www.randomhouse.com. Estab. 1990. **Publishes 60 titles/year.**

> Acquires and publishes general interest fiction and nonfiction in large print editions.

RAVENHAWK™ BOOKS

The 6DOF Group 7739 Broadway Blvd., #95, Tucson AZ 85710. E-mail: ravenhawk6dof@yahoo.com. Website: www.ravenhawk.biz. Estab. 1998. Publishes hardcover and paperback originals. **Pays 45-60% royalty.** Publishes book 18 months after acceptance of ms. Responds in weeks to queries. Responds in months to manuscripts. Book catalog available online.

Fiction Subjects include fantasy, space fantasy, sword and sorcery, horror, dark fantasy, futuristic, psychological, supernatural, humor, literary, mainstream, contemporary, mystery, amateur sleuth, cozy, police procedural, private eye/hardboiled, religious, religious mystery/suspense, religious thriller, romance, contemporary, romantic suspense, science fiction, hard science fiction/technological, soft/sociological, short story collections, young adult, adventure, easy-to-read, fantasy/science fiction fiction, horror, mystery/suspense, problem novels, series. Query by invitation only.

RAVEN TREE PRESS

A Division of Delta Publishing Company 1400 Miller Pkwy., McHenry IL 60050. (800)323-8270. Fax: (800)909-9901. E-mail: raven@raventreepress.com. Website: www.raventreepress.com. **Contact:** Check website for most current submission guidelines (children's picture books). Estab. 2000. Publishes hardcover and trade paperback originals. **Publishes 10 titles/year. 1,500 mss received/year. 75% of books from first-time authors. 90% from unagented writers. Pays royalty. Pays variable advance.** Publishes book 2 years after acceptance of ms. Accepts simultaneous submissions. Responds in 2 months to manuscripts. Book catalog available online. Guidelines available online.

Nonfiction Submission guidelines available online. Do not query or send mss without first checking submission guidelines on our website for most current information.

RED HEN PRESS

P.O. Box 3537, Granada Hills CA 91394. (818)831-0649. Fax: (818)831-6659. Website: www.redhen.org. **Contact:** Mark E. Cull, publisher/editor (fiction). Estab. 1993. Publishes trade paperback originals. **Publishes 10 titles/year. 2,000 queries received/year. 500 mss received/year. 10% of books from first-time authors. 90% from unagented writers.** Publishes book 1 year after acceptance of ms. Accepts simultaneous submissions. Responds in 1 month to queries. Responds in 2 months to proposals. Responds in 3 months to manuscripts. Book catalog available free. Guidelines available online.

O-ₜ Red Hen Press is a nonprofit organization specializing in literary fiction and nonfiction. We currently have a backlog and are not accepting unsolicited manuscripts. Currently de-emphasizing poetry.

Nonfiction Subjects include ethnic, gay, lesbian, language, literature, memoirs, womens issues, womens studies, political/social interest. Query with SASE. Reviews artwork/photos. Send photocopies.

Fiction We prefer high-quality literary fiction.Subjects include ethnic, experimental, feminist, gay, lesbian, historical, literary, mainstream, contemporary, poetry, poetry in translation, short story collections. We prefer high-quality literary fiction. Query with SASE.

Recent Title(s) *The Misread City: New Literary Los Angeles*, edited by Dana Gioia and Scott Timberg; *Rebel*, by Tom Hayden.

Tips Audience reads poetry, literary fiction, intelligent nonfiction. If you have an agent, we may be too small since we don't pay advances. Write well. Send queries first. Be willing to help promote your own book.

RED WHEEL/WEISER AND CONARI PRESS

500 Third St., Suite 230, San Francisco CA 94107. (415)978-2665. Fax: (415)359-0142. Website: www.redwheelweiser.com. **Contact:** Pat Bryce, acquisitions editor. Estab. 1956. Publishes hardcover and trade paperback originals and reprints. **Publishes 60-75 titles/year. 2,000 queries received/year. 2,000 mss received/year. 20% of books from first-time authors. 50% from unagented writers. Pays royalty.** Publishes book 1 year after acceptance of ms. Accepts simultaneous submissions. Responds in 3 months to queries. Responds in 3-6 months to proposals. Responds in 3-6 months to manuscripts. Book catalog available free. Guidelines available online.

Imprints Conari Press; Weiser.

Nonfiction Subjects include New Age, spirituality, womens issues, womens studies, parenting. Query with SASE. Submit proposal package, outline, 2 sample chapters, TOC. Reviews artwork/photos. Send photocopies.

Recent Title(s) *Serpent of Light: Beyond 2012*, by Drunvalo Melchizedek; *Attitudes of Gratitude* 10th Anniversary Edition, by MJ Ryan; *The Ledge of Qnetzal, Beyond 2012*, by Jock Whitehouse.

N ROBERT D. REED PUBLISHERS

P.O. Box 1992, Bandon OR 97411, U.S. (541)347-9882. Fax: (541)347-9883. Website: www.rdrpublishers.com. **Contact:** Cleone Lyvonne, ed. Hardcover and trade paperback originals. **Publishes 25-35 titles/year. 500 ms; 2,000 queries 75% of books from first-time authors. 90% from unagented writers.** Publishes book 5 months after acceptance of ms. Accepts simultaneous submissions. Online. By email.

Nonfiction Subjects include alternative lifestyles, business, economics, child guidance, communications, contemporary contemporary culture, counseling, career guidance,education, ethnic, gay, lesbian, nonfiction, health, medicine, history, language, literature, memoirs, military, war, money, finance, multicultural, New Age, philosophy, psychology, sex, social sciences, spirituality, travel, womens issues, womens studies, world affairs. Submit proposal package with outline. Submit completed ms only upon request. Yes.

Fiction Subjects include adventure, fantasy, feminist, historical, humor, literary, military, war, multicultural, mystery, romance, sciencefiction, spiritual, western. We look for high quality work—from authors who will work hard to display their work and travel selling books. Query with SASE or email. Submit proposal package. Submit completed ms by request.

Recent Title(s) *Fearless*, by Steve Chandler (self-help); *Winning Salesmanship*, by Larry Krakow (business); *Avenging Storm*, by Maurice Mayben (novel); *Rendezvous Rock*, by Ricky Bray (novel)

Tips Target trade sales and sales to corporations, organizations and groups. Read over our web site and see what we have done.

REFERENCE SERVICE PRESS

5000 Windplay Dr., Suite 4, El Dorado Hills CA 95762. (916)939-9620. Fax: (916)939-9626. E-mail: info@rspfunding.com. Website: www.rspfunding.com. **Contact:** Stuart Hauser, acquisitions editor. Estab. 1977. Publishes hardcover originals. **Publishes 10-20 titles/year. 100% from unagented writers. Pays 10% royalty. Pays advance.** Publishes book 6 months after acceptance of ms. Accepts simultaneous submissions. Responds in 2 months to queries. Book catalog for #10 SASE.

- Reference Service Press focuses on the development and publication of financial aid resources in any format (print, electronic, e-book, etc.). We are interested in financial aid publications aimed at specific groups (e.g., minorities, women, veterans, the disabled, undergraduates majoring in specific subject areas, specific types of financial aid, etc.).

Nonfiction Specializes in financial aid opportunities for students in or having these characteristics: women, minorities, veterans, the disabled, etc.Subjects include agriculture, art, architecture, business, economics, education, ethnic, health, medicine, history, religion, science, sociology, womens issues, womens studies, disabled. Submit outline, sample chapters.

Recent Title(s) *Financial Aid for Veterans, Military Personnel, and Their Dependents, 2008-2010*; *Directory of Financial Aids for Women, 2007-2009*; *How to Pay for Your Degree in Journalism, 2008-2010.*

Tips Our audience consists of librarians, counselors, researchers, students, re-entry women, scholars, and other fundseekers.

FLEMING H. REVELL PUBLISHING

Division of Baker Book House P.O. Box 6287, Grand Rapids MI 49516. (800)877-2665. Fax: (800)398-3111. Website: www.bakerbooks.com. Estab. 1870. Publishes hardcover, trade paperback and mass market paperback originals. Book catalog and ms guidelines online.

- *No longer accepts unsolicited mss.*
- Revell publishes to the heart (rather than to the head). For 125 years, Revell has been publishing evangelical books for the personal enrichment and spiritual growth of general Christian readers.

Nonfiction Subjects include child guidance, religion, Christian living, marriage.

Fiction Subjects include historical, religious, suspense, contemporary.

Recent Title(s) *Suddenly Unemployed*, by Helen Kooiman Hosier; *The Bride's Handbook*, by Amy J. Tol; *Just Give Me a Little Peace and Quiet*, by Lorilee Craker.

RFF PRESS

Resources for the Future 1616 P St., NW, Washington DC 20036. (202)328-5086. Fax: (202)328-5024. E-mail: rffpress@rff.org. Website: www.rffpress.org. **Contact:** Don Reisman, publisher. Publishes hardcover, trade paperback and electronic originals. **Publishes 15 titles/year. Pays royalty on wholesale price.** Publishes book 6 months after acceptance of ms. Accepts simultaneous submissions. Responds in 1 month to queries. Responds in 1 month to proposals. Responds in 2 months to manuscripts. Book catalog available online. Guidelines available free.

Nonfiction We focus on social science approaches to domestic and international environmental and natural resource issues.Subjects include agriculture, business, economics, government, politics, history, nature, environment, science, urban planning/land-use policy. Submit proposal package, outline. Reviews artwork/photos. Send photocopies.

Recent Title(s) *Perspectives on Sustainable Resources in America*, edited by Roger A. Sedjo; *Taming the Anarchy: Groundwater Governance in South Asia*, by Tushaar Shah; *Liquid City: Megalopolis and the Contemporary Northeast*, by John Rennie Short.

Tips Audience is scholars, policy makers, activists, businesses, government, the general public. Distributed by Johns Hopkins Fulfillment Services.

RIO NUEVO PUBLISHERS

Imprint of Treasure Chest Books P.O. Box 5250, Tucson AZ 85703. Fax: (520)624-5888. E-mail: info@rionuevo.com. Website: www.rionuevo.com. **Contact:** Theresa Kennedy, acquiring editor (adult nonfiction titles about the Southwest). Estab. 1975. Publishes hardcover and trade paperback originals and reprints. **Publishes 12-20 titles/year. 20 queries received/year. 10 mss received/year. 30% of books from first-time authors. 100% from unagented writers. Pays $1,000-4,000 advance.** Publishes book 1 year after acceptance of ms. Accepts simultaneous submissions. Responds in 6 months to queries. Responds in 6 months to proposals. Responds in 6 months to manuscripts. Book catalog available online. Guidelines available via e-mail.

Nonfiction Subjects include animals, cooking, foods, nutrition, gardening, history, nature, environment, regional, religion, spirituality, travel. Query with SASE. Submit proposal package, outline, 2 sample chapters. Reviews artwork/photos. Send photocopies.
Recent Title(s) *Yard Full of Sun: The Story of a Gardener's Obsession That Got a Little Out of Hand*; *The Prickley Pear Cookbook*; *Clouds for Dessert: Sweet Treats From the Wild West*.
Tips We have a general audience of intelligent people interested in the Southwest—nature, history, culture. Many of our books are sold in gift shops throughout the region; we are also distributed nationally by W.W. Norton.

RIVER CITY PUBLISHING

River City Publishing, LLC 1719 Mulberry St., Montgomery AL 36106. (334)265-6753. Fax: (334)265-8880. E-mail: jgilbert@rivercitypublishing.com. Website: www.rivercitypublishing.com. **Contact:** Jim Gilbert, editor. Estab. 1989. Publishes hardcover and trade paperback originals and reprints. **Publishes 8 titles/year. 1,250 queries received/year. 200 mss received/year. 20% of books from first-time authors. 75% from unagented writers. Pays 10% royalty on net revenue. Pays $500-5,000 advance.** Publishes book 1 year after acceptance of ms. Accepts simultaneous submissions. Responds in 3 months to queries. Responds in 4 months to proposals. Responds in 6 months to manuscripts. Guidelines available free.
Imprints Starrhill Press; Elliott & Clark
Nonfiction Subjects include art, architecture, creative nonfiction, government, politics, history, regional, sports, travel. Submit proposal package, outline, 2 sample chapters, author's bio/résumé. Reviews artwork/photos. Send photocopies.
Fiction Subjects include ethnic, historical, literary, multicultural, poetry, regional, southern, short story collections. Submit proposal package, resume, clips, bio, 3 sample chapters.
Recent Title(s) *Murder Creek*, by Joe Formichella (true crime); *The Bear Bryant Funeral Train: Resurrected Edition*, by Brad Vice (short fiction); *Breathing Out the Ghost*, by Kirk Curnutt (fiction).

N A ⊘ RODALE BOOKS

33 E. Minor St., Emmaus PA 18098. (610)967-5171. Fax: (610)967-8961. Website: www.rodale.com. Estab. 1932.

- Rodale Books publishes adult trade titles in categories such health & fitness, cooking, spirituality and pet care.

ROWMAN & LITTLEFIELD PUBLISHING GROUP

4501 Forbes Blvd., Suite 200, Lanham MD 20706. (301)459-3366. Fax: (301)429-5748. Website: www.rowmanlittlefield.com. **Contact:** See website for a detailed list of editors and addresses by subject area. Estab. 1949. Publishes hardcover and trade paperback originals and reprints. **Pays advance.** Guidelines available online.
Imprints Lexington Books; Rowman & Littlefield Publishers; Madison Books; Scarecrow Press; Cooper Square.
Recent Title(s) *Crime, Punishment, and Policing in China*, by Børge Bakken; *The Making of Arab News*, by Noha Mellor; *African Americans in the U.S. Economy*, edited by Cecilia A. Conrad, John Whitehead, Patrick Mason, and James Stewart.

N ROXBURY PUBLISHING CO.

P.O. Box 491044, Los Angeles CA 90049-9044. (310)473-3312. Website: www.roxbury.net. **Contact:** Editor. Estab. 1981. Publishes hardcover and paperback originals and reprints. **Publishes 15-20 titles/year. Pays royalty.** Accepts simultaneous submissions. Responds in 2 months to queries.

- Accepts textbooks (college-level) & supplements only.
- "Roxbury publishes college textbooks in the humanities and social sciences only."

Nonfiction Subjects include humanities, social sciences, sociology, political science. Query with SASE. Submit outline, sample chapters, synopsis. Submit complete ms.

ROYAL FIREWORKS PUBLISHING

1 First Ave., P.O. Box 399, Unionville NY 10988. (845)726-4444. Fax: (845)726-3824. E-mail: mail@rfwp.com. Website: www.rfwp.com. **Contact:** William Neumann, editor (young adult); Dr. T.M. Kemnitz, editor (education). Estab. 1977. Publishes library binding and trade paperback originals, reprints and textbooks. **Publishes 75-140 titles/year. 1,000 queries received/year. 400 mss received/year. 30-50% of books from first-time authors. 98% from unagented writers. Pays 10% royalty on wholesale price.** Publishes book 9 months after acceptance of ms. Responds in 1 month to manuscripts. Book catalog for $3.85. Guidelines for #10 SASE.
Nonfiction Subjects include child guidance, education. Submit complete ms. Reviews artwork/photos. Send photocopies.
Fiction Subjects include young adult. We do novels for children from 8-16. We do a lot of historical fiction,

science fiction, adventure, mystery, sports, etc. We are concerned about the values. Submit complete ms.
Recent Title(s) *Grammar Voyage*, by Michael Thompson; *Double Vision*, by Jerry Chris; *A Few Screws Loose*, by Maryann Easley.
Tips Audience is comprised of gifted children, their parents and teachers, and children (8-18) who read.

RUTGERS UNIVERSITY PRESS

100 Joyce Kilmer Ave., Piscataway NJ 08854-8099. (732)445-7762. Fax: (732)445-7039. Website: rutgerspress.rutgers.edu. **Contact:** Leslie Mitchner, editor-in-chief/associate director (humanities); Adi Hovav, editor (social sciences); Doreen Valentine, editor (science, health & medicine); Beth Kressel, associate editor (Jewish studies). Estab. 1936. Publishes hardcover and trade paperback originals, and reprints. **Publishes 100 titles/year. 1,500 queries received/year. 300 mss received/year. 30% of books from first-time authors. 70% from unagented writers. Pays 7 ½-15% royalty. Pays $1,000-10,000 advance.** Publishes book 1 year after acceptance of ms. Responds in 1 month to proposals. Book catalog online or with SASE. Guidelines available online.

O━ Our Press aims to reach audiences beyond the academic community with accessible scholarly and regional books.

Nonfiction Subjects include art, architecture, art, architecture history, ethnic, film, cinema, stage, gay, lesbian, government, politics, health, medicine, history, multicultural, nature, environment, regional, religion, sociology, womens issues, womens studies, African-American studies. Submit outline, 2-3 sample chapters. Reviews artwork/photos. Send photocopies.
Recent Title(s) *Wrestling with Starbucks: Conscience, Capital, Cappuccino*, by Kim Fellner; *Mama, PhD.: Women Write About Motherhood and Academic Life*, by Elrena Evans and Caroline Grant; *A Shore History of Film*, by Wheeler Winston Dixon and Gwendolyn Audrey Foster.
Tips Both academic and general audiences. Many of our books have potential for undergraduate course use. We are more trade-oriented than most university presses. We are looking for intelligent, well-written, and accessible books. Avoid overly narrow topics.

SAE INTERNATIONAL

400 Commonwealth Dr., Warrendale PA 15096-0001. (724)776-4841. E-mail: writeabook@sae.org. Website: www.sae.org/writeabook. **Contact:** Martha Swiss, intellectual property manager; Kevin Jost, editorial dir.; Erin Moore, product mgr.; Michael Thompson, manager, electronic publishing. Estab. 1905. Publishes hardcover and trade paperback originals, Web and CD-ROM based electronic product. **Publishes 30-40 titles/year. 100 queries received/year. 40 mss received/year. 30-40% of books from first-time authors. 100% from unagented writers. Pays royalty. Pays possible advance.** Publishes book 9-10 months after acceptance of ms. Accepts simultaneous submissions. Responds in 4 months to queries. Book catalog free. Guidelines available online.

O━ Automotive means anything self-propelled. We are a professional society serving engineers, scientists, and researchers in the automobile, aerospace, and off-highway industries.

Nonfiction Query with proposal—see www.sae.org/writeabook for details on submitting a proposal.
Recent Title(s) *Brake Technology Handbook: Analysis Techniques for Racecar Data Acquisition.*
Tips Audience is automotive and aerospace engineers and manager, automotive safety and biomechanics professionals, students, educators, enthusiasts, and historians.

SAFARI PRESS, INC.

15621 Chemical Lane, Bldg. B, Huntington Beach CA 92649-1506. (714)894-9080. Fax: (714)894-4949. E-mail: info@safaripress.com. Website: www.safaripress.com. **Contact:** Jacqueline Neufeld, editor. Estab. 1985. Publishes hardcover originals and reprints, and trade paperback reprints. **Publishes 25-30 titles/year. 70% of books from first-time authors. 80% from unagented writers. Pays 8-15% royalty on wholesale price.** Book catalog for $1. Guidelines available online.

- The editor notes that she receives many mss outside the areas of big-game hunting, wingshooting, and sporting firearms, and these are always rejected.

O━ Safari Press publishes books only on big-game hunting, sporting, firearms, and wingshooting; this includes African, North American, European, Asian, and South American hunting and wingshooting. Does not want books on 'outdoors' topics (hiking, camping, canoeing, etc.).

Nonfiction Query with SASE. Submit outline.
Recent Title(s) *Royal Quest: The Hunting Saga of H.I.H. Prince Abdorreza of Iran;*; *The Best of Holland & Holland: England's Premier Gunmaker;*; *Safari Guide 2007-2008.*

A Ø ST. MARTIN'S PRESS, LLC

Holtzbrinck Publishers 175 Fifth Ave., New York NY 10010. (212)674-5151. Fax: (212)420-9314. Website: www.stmartins.com. Estab. 1952. Publishes hardcover, trade paperback and mass market originals. **Publishes 1,500 titles/year. Pays royalty. Pays advance.** Guidelines available online.
Imprints Minotaur; Thomas Dunne Books; Griffin; Palgrave MacMillan (division); Priddy Books; St. Martin's Press Paperback & Reference Group; St. Martin's Press Trade Division; Truman Talley Books.

O→ General interest publisher of both fiction and nonfiction.

Nonfiction Subjects include business, economics, cooking, foods, nutrition, sports, general nonfiction. Agented submissions only. *No unsolicited mss*

Fiction Subjects include fantasy, historical, horror, literary, mainstream, contemporary, mystery, science fiction, suspense, western, contemporary, general fiction. Agented submissions only. *No unsolicited mss*

SAINT MARY'S PRESS

702 Terrace Heights, Winona MN 55987-1318. (800)533-8095. Fax: (800)344-9225. E-mail: submissions@smp.org. Website: www.smp.org. **Contact:** Submissions Editor. Ms guidelines online or by e-mail.

Nonfiction Subjects include religion, prayers, spirituality. Query with SASE. Submit proposal package, outline, 1 sample chapter, SASE. Brief author biography.

Recent Title(s) *The Catholic Faith Handbook for Youth*; *The Total Faith Initiative*; *Take Ten: Daily Bible Reflections for Teens*.

Tips Request product catalog and/or do research online of Saint Mary Press book lists before submitting proposal.

SALEM PRESS, INC.

Magill's Choice 131 N. El Molino, Suite 350, Pasadena CA 91101. (626)584-0106. Fax: (626)584-1525. Website: www.salempress.com. **Contact:** Dawn P. Dawson. **Publishes 20-22 (50-60 vols.) titles/year. 15 queries received/year. Work-for-hire pays 5-15¢/word.** Responds in 3 months to queries. Responds in 1 month to proposals. Book catalog available online.

Nonfiction Subjects include business, economics, ethnic, government, politics, health, medicine, history, language, literature, military, war, music, dance, nature, environment, philosophy, psychology, science, sociology, womens issues, womens studies. Query with SASE.

SANTA MONICA PRESS LLC

P.O. Box 1076, Santa Monica CA 90406. Website: www.santamonicapress.com. **Contact:** Acquisitions Editor. Estab. 1994. Publishes hardcover and trade paperback originals. **Publishes 15 titles/year. 25% of books from first-time authors. 75% from unagented writers. Pays 4-10% royalty on wholesale price. Pays $500-2,500 advance.** Publishes book 6-18 months after acceptance of ms. Accepts simultaneous submissions. Responds in 1-2 months to proposals. Book catalog for 9x12 SASE with $1.31 postage. Guidelines available online.

O→ "At Santa Monica Press, we're not afraid to cast a wide editorial net. Our eclectic list of lively and modern nonfiction titles includes books in such categories as popular culture, film history, photography, humor, biography, travel, and reference."

Nonfiction Subjects include Americana, architecture, art, contemporary culture, creative nonfiction, education, entertainment, film, games, humanities, language, literature, memoirs, regional, social sciences, sports, travel, Biography, coffee table book, general nonfiction, gift book, humor, illustrated book, reference. Submit proposal package, including outline, 2-3 sample chapters, biography, marketing and publicity plans, analysis of competitive titles, SASE with appropriate postage. Reviews artwork/photos. Send photocopies.

Recent Title(s) *John Van Hamersveld: Post-Future* by John Van Hamersveld; *Roadside Baseball: The Locations of America's Baseball Landmarks* by Chris Epting; *Passings: Death, Dying, and Unexplained Phenomena* by Carole A. Travis-Henikoff; *The Complete History of American Film Criticism* by Jerry Roberts.

Tips "Visit our website before submitting to view our author guidelines and to get a clear idea of the types of books we publish. Carefully analyze your book's competition and tell us what makes your book different—and what makes it better. Also let us know what promotional and marketing opportunities you, as the author, bring to the project."

SARABANDE BOOKS, INC.

2234 Dundee Rd., Suite 200, Louisville KY 40205. (502)458-4028. Fax: (502)458-4065. Website: www.sarabandebooks.org. **Contact:** Sarah Gorham, editor-in-chief. Estab. 1994. Publishes trade paperback originals. **Publishes 10 titles/year. 1,500 queries received/year. 3,000 mss received/year. 35% of books from first-time authors. 75% from unagented writers. Pays royalty.10% on actual income received. Also pays in author's copies. Pays $500-1,000 advance.** Publishes book 18 months after acceptance of ms. Accepts simultaneous submissions. Book catalog available free. contest guidelines for #10 SASE or on website.

O→ "Sarabande Books was founded to publish poetry, short fiction, and creative nonfiction. We look for works of lasting literary value. Please see our titles to get an idea of our taste. Accepts submissions through contests only."

Fiction Subjects include literary, short story collections, novellas, short novels (300 pages maximum, 150 pages minimum).

Recent Title(s) *Portrait of My Mother Who Posed Nude in Wartime*, by Marjorie Sandor; *October*, by Louise Glück.

Tips "Sarabande publishes for a general literary audience. Know your market. Read—and buy—books of literature. Sponsors contests for poetry and fiction."

SAS PUBLISHING

100 SAS Campus Dr., Cary NC 27513-2414. (919)531-0585. Fax: (919)677-4444. Website: support.sas.com/saspress. **Contact:** Julie M. Platt, editor-in-chief. Estab. 1976. Publishes hardcover and trade paperback originals. **Publishes 40 titles/year. 50% of books from first-time authors. 100% from unagented writers. Payment negotiable. Pays negotiable advance.** Responds in 2 weeks to queries. Book catalog and ms guidelines via website or with SASE. Guidelines available online.

O→ SAS publishes books for SAS and JMP software users, both new and experienced.

Nonfiction Subjects include software, statistics. Query with SASE. Submit outline, sample chapters. Reviews artwork/photos.

Recent Title(s) *The Little SAS Book: A Primer, Third Ed.*, by Lora D. Delwiche and Susan J. Slaughter; *SAS for Mixed Models, 2nd Ed.*, by Ramon Littell, George Milliken, Walter Stroup, Russell Wolfinger and Oliver Schenberger.

Tips If I were a writer trying to market a book today, I would concentrate on developing a manuscript that teaches or illustrates a specific concept or application that SAS users will find beneficial in their own environments or can adapt to their own needs.

SASQUATCH BOOKS

119 S. Main, Suite 400, Seattle WA 98104. (206)467-4300. Fax: (206)467-4301. Website: www.sasquatchbooks.com. **Contact:** Gary Luke, editorial director; Terence Maikels, acquisitions editor; Heidi Lenze, acquisitions editor. Estab. 1986. Publishes regional hardcover and trade paperback originals. **Publishes 30 titles/year. 20% of books from first-time authors. 75% from unagented writers. Pays royalty on cover price. Pays wide range advance.** Publishes book 6 months after acceptance of ms. Responds in 3 months to queries. Book catalog for 9x12 envelope and 2 First-Class stamps. Guidelines available online.

O→ Sasquatch Books publishes books for a West Coast regional audience—Alaska to California. Currently emphasizing outdoor recreation, cookbooks, and history.

Nonfiction We are seeking quality nonfiction works about the Pacific Northwest and West Coast regions (including Alaska to California). The literature of place includes how-to and where-to as well as history and narrative nonfiction.Subjects include animals, art, architecture, business, economics, cooking, foods, nutrition, gardening, history, nature, environment, recreation, regional, sports, travel, womens issues, womens studies, outdoors. Query first, then submit outline and sample chapters with SASE.

Recent Title(s) *Out of Left Field*, by Art Thiel; *Book Lust*, by Nancy Pearl; *The Traveling Curmudgeon*, by Jon Winokur.

Tips We sell books through a range of channels in addition to the book trade. Our primary audience consists of active, literate residents of the West Coast.

N SCARECROW PRESS, INC.

Imprint of Rowman & Littlefield Publishing Group 4501 Forbes Blvd., Suite 200, Lanham MD 20706. (301)459-3366. Fax: (301)429-5748. Website: www.scarecrowpress.com. **Contact:** April Snyder, acquisitions editor (information studies, interdisciplinary studies, general reference); Renee Camus, acquisitions editor (music); Stephen Ryan (film and theater); Corinne O. Burton (young adult literature). Estab. 1955. Publishes hardcover originals. **Publishes 165 titles/year. 70% of books from first-time authors. 99% from unagented writers. Pays 8% royalty on net of first 1,000 copies; 10% of net price thereafter.** Publishes book 18 months after acceptance of ms. Responds in 2 months to queries. Catalog and ms guidelines online.

O→ Scarecrow Press publishes several series: Historical Dictionaries (includes countries, religions, international organizations, and area studies); Studies and Documentaries on the History of Popular Entertainment (forthcoming); Society, Culture and Libraries. Emphasis is on any title likely to appeal to libraries. Currently emphasizing jazz, Africana, and educational issues of contemporary interest.

Nonfiction Subjects include film, cinema, stage, language, literature, religion, sports, annotated bibliographies, handbooks and biographical dictionaries in the areas of women's studies and ethnic studies, parapsychology, fine arts and handicrafts, genealogy, sports history, music, movies, stage, library and information science. Query with SASE.

N SCHIFFER PUBLISHING, LTD.

4880 Lower Valley Rd., Atglen PA 19310. (610)593-1777. Fax: (610)593-2002. E-mail: info@schifferbooks.com. Website: www.schifferbooks.com. **Contact:** Tina Skinner. Estab. 1975. **Publishes 10-20 titles/year. Pays royalty on wholesale price.** Responds in 2 weeks to queries. Book catalog available free. Guidelines available online.

Nonfiction Fax or e-mail outline, photos, and book proposal.

Recent Title(s) *Antique Enameled Jewelry*, by Dale Nicholls with Robin Allison; *Mannequins*, by Steven M. Richman; *The Long Campaign*, by John W. Lambert.

Tips We want to publish books for towns or cities with relevant population or active tourism to support book sales. A list of potential town vendors is a helpful start toward selling us on your book idea.

SCHOCKEN BOOKS

Imprint of Knopf Publishing Group, Division of Random House, Inc. 1745 Broadway 21-1, New York NY 10019. (212)572-9000. Fax: (212)572-6030. Website: www.schocken.com. Estab. 1945. Publishes hardcover and trade paperback originals and reprints. **Publishes 9-12 titles/year. Small% of books from first-time authors. small% from unagented writers. Pays varied advance.** Accepts simultaneous submissions.

- Schocken publishes quality Judaica in all areas—fiction, history, biography, current affairs, spirituality and religious practices, popular culture, and cultural studies.

Recent Title(s) *The Wicked Son*, by David Mamet; *Marc Chagall*, by Jonathan Wilson; *The Promise of Politics*, by Hannah Arendt.

SCHOLASTIC LIBRARY PUBLISHING

A division of Scholastic, Inc. 90 Old Sherman Turnpike, Danbury CT 06816. (203)797-3500. Fax: (203)797-3197. Website: www.scholastic.com/librarypublishing. Estab. 1895. Publishes hardcover and trade paperback originals.

Imprints Grolier;, Children's Press; Franklin Watts; Grolier Online.

- *This publisher accepts agented submissions only.*
- Scholastic Library is a leading publisher of reference, educational, and children's books. We provide parents, teachers, and librarians with the tools they need to enlighten children to the pleasure of learning and prepare them for the road ahead.

SCHOLASTIC PRESS

Imprint of Scholastic, Inc. 557 Broadway, New York NY 10012. (212)343-6100. Fax: (212)343-4713. Website: www.scholastic.com. Publishes hardcover originals. **Publishes 30 titles/year. 2,500 queries received/year. 5% of books from first-time authors. Pays royalty on retail price. Pays variable advance.** Publishes book 18-24 months after acceptance of ms. Responds in 3 months to queries. Responds in 6-8 months to manuscripts.

- Scholastic Press publishes fresh, literary picture book fiction and nonfiction; fresh, literary nonseries or nongenre-oriented middle grade and young adult fiction. Currently emphasizing subtly handled treatments of key relationships in children's lives; unusual approaches to commonly dry subjects, such as biography, math, history, or science. De-emphasizing fairy tales (or retellings), board books, genre, or series fiction (mystery, fantasy, etc.).

Nonfiction *Agented submissions and previously published authors only.*

Fiction Subjects include juvenile, picture books, novels. Wants fresh, exciting picture books and novels—inspiring, new talent. *Agented submissions and pre*

SCHOLASTIC PROFESSIONAL PUBLISHING

Imprint of Scholastic, Inc. 524 Broadway, New York NY 10012. Website: www.scholastic.com. **Contact:** Deborah Schecter, editorial director (pre-K-grade 4 teacher resource books and materials); Virginia Dooley, editorial director (grade 4-8 teacher resource books); Lois Bridges, acquisitions editor (theory and practice). Estab. 1989. **Publishes 140+ titles/year. Pays advance.** Responds in 3 months to queries. Book catalog for 9x12 SASE.

- We publish teacher resources to help teachers in their professional growth and to help enrich the curriculum. Currently emphasizing reading and writing, math, standards, testing.

Nonfiction Subjects include education. Query with table of contents, outline, and sample chapter.

Recent Title(s) *Irresistable ABCs*; *Nonfiction in Focus*; *Classroom Management in Photographs*.

Tips Writer should have background working in the classroom with elementary or middle school children, teaching pre-service students, and/or solid background in developing supplementary educational materials for these markets.

SCHROEDER PUBLISHING CO., INC.

P.O. Box 3009, Paducah KY 42002-3009. (270)898-6211. Fax: (270)898-8890. E-mail: editor@collectorbooks.com. Website: www.collectorbooks.com. Estab. 1973. Publishes hardcover and trade paperback orginals. **Publishes 95 titles/year. 150 queries received/year. 100 mss received/year. 60% of books from first-time authors. 100% from unagented writers. Pays 5% royalty on retail price.** Publishes book 6 months after acceptance of ms. Accepts simultaneous submissions. Responds in 1 month to queries. Responds in 1 month to proposals. Responds in 1 month to manuscripts. Book catalog available online. Guidelines available online.

Imprints Collector Books, American Quilter's Society.

Nonfiction Subjects include hobbies, antiques and collectibles. Submit proposal package, outline, 2 sample chapters. Reviews artwork/photos. Send transparencies and prints.

Recent Title(s) *Schroeder's Antiques Price Guide*, by Sharon Huxford (reference); *Vintage Golf Club Collectibles*, by Ronald John (reference); *Collector's Encyclopedia of Depression Glass*, by Gene Florence (reference).

Tips Audience consists of collectors, garage sale and flea market shoppers, antique dealers, E-bay shoppers, and quilters.

SCIENCE & HUMANITIES PRESS

P.O. Box 7151, Chesterfield MO 63006-7151. (636)394-4950. E-mail: publisher@sciencehumanitiespress.com. Website: www.sciencehumanitiespress.com. **Contact:** Dr. Bud Banis, publisher. Publishes trade paperback originals and reprints, and electronic originals and reprints. **Publishes 20-30 titles/year. 1,000 queries received/year. 50 mss received/year. 25% of books from first-time authors. 100% from unagented writers. Pays 8% royalty on retail price.** Publishes book 6-12 after acceptance of ms. Accepts simultaneous submissions. Responds in 2 months to queries. Responds in 2 months to proposals. Responds in 3 months to manuscripts. Book catalog available online. Guidelines available online.

Imprints Science & Humanities Press, BeachHouse Books, MacroPrintBooks (large print editions), Heuristic Books, Early Editions Books.

Nonfiction Subjects include Americana, business, economics, child guidance, computers, electronics, creative nonfiction, education, government, politics, health, medicine, history, hobbies, language, literature, memoirs, military, war, money, finance, philosophy, psychology, recreation, regional, science, sex, sociology, software, spirituality, sports, travel, womens issues, womens studies, math/statistics, management science.

Fiction *Does not accept unsolicited mss.*Subjects include adventure, historical, humor, literary, mainstream, contemporary, military, war, mystery, plays, poetry, regional, romance, short story collections, spiritual, sports, suspense, western, young adult. We prefer books with a theme that gives a market focus. Brief description by e-mail.

Recent Title(s) *To Norma Jeane with Love, Jimmie*, by Jim Dougherty/LC Van Savage (biography); *Growing Up on Route 66*, by Michael Lund (coming of age); *Avoiding Attendants from Hell: A Practical Guide to Finding, Hiring, and Keeping Personal Care Attendants*, by June Price.

Tips Sales are primarily through th Our expertise is electronic p

SCRIBNER

Imprint of Simon & Schuster Adult Publishing Group 1230 Avenue of the Americas, 12th Floor, New York NY 10020. (212)698-7000. Website: www.simonsays.com. **Contact:** Nan Graham (literary fiction, nonfiction); Beth Wareham (fiction); Alexis Gargagliano (literary fiction, nonfiction); Brant Rumble (nonfiction); Colin Harrison (fiction, nonfiction); Samantha Martin (fiction, nonfiction); Whitney Frick (fiction, nonfiction); Kara Watson (fiction, nonfiction); Paul Whitlatch (fiction, nonfiction). Publishes hardcover originals. **Publishes 70-75 titles/year. Thousands queries received/year. 20% of books from first-time authors. 0% from unagented writers. Pays 7 ½-15% royalty. Pays variable advance.** Publishes book 9 months after acceptance of ms. Accepts simultaneous submissions. Responds in 3 months to queries.

Imprints Lisa Drew Books; Scribner Classics (reprints only); Scribner Poetry (by invitation only).

Nonfiction Subjects include education, ethnic, gay, lesbian, health, medicine, history, language, literature, nature, environment, philosophy, psychology, religion, science, criticism. Agented submissions only.

Fiction Subjects include literary, mystery, suspense. Agented submissions only.

Recent Title(s) *Just After Sunset*, by Stephen King; *The Ultramind Solution*, by Mark Hyman; *Nixonland*, by Rick Pearlstein; *Happens Every Day*, by Isabel Gillies.

SEAL PRESS

1700 4th St., Berkeley CA 94710. (510)595-3664. Fax: (510)595-4228. Website: www.sealpress.com. **Contact:** Acquisitions Editor. Estab. 1976. Publishes trade paperback originals. **Publishes 30 titles/year. 1,000 queries received/year. 750 mss received/year. 25% of books from first-time authors. 50% from unagented writers. Pays 7-10% royalty on retail price.Pays variable royalty on retail price. Pays $3,000-10,000 advance. Pays variable advance.** Publishes book 6-12 months after acceptance of ms. Accepts simultaneous submissions. Responds in 2 months to queries. Book catalog and ms guidelines for SASE or online.

Seal Press is an imprint of Avalon Publishing Group, feminist book publisher interested in original, lively, radical, empowering and culturally diverse nonfiction by women addressing contemporary issues from a feminist perspective or speaking positively to the experience of being female. Currently emphasizing women outdoor adventurists, young feminists, political issues for women, health issues, and suriving abuse. De-emphasizing fiction.

Nonfiction Subjects include Americana, child guidance, contemporary culture, creative nonfiction, ethnic, gay, lesbian, memoirs, multicultural, nature, environment, sex, travel, womens issues, womens studies, popular culture, politics, domestic violence, sexual abuse. Query with SASE. Reviews artwork/photos. Send Send photocopies. No original art or photos accepted.

Recent Title(s) *Confessions of a Naughty Mommy*, by Heidi Raykeil; *Invisible Girls*, by Dr. Patti Ferguson; *The Risks of Sunbathing Topless*, by Kate Chynoweth.

Tips Our audience is generally composed of women interested in reading about women's issues addressed from a feminist perspective.

N SEARCH INSTITUTE PRESS

Search Institute 615 First Avenue NE, Minneapolis MN 55413. (612)399-0200. Fax: (612)692-5553. E-mail: acquisitions@search-institute.org. Website: www.search-institute.org. **Contact:** Alison Dotson, ed. trade paperback originals. **Publishes 12-15 titles/year.** Publishes book 12 months after acceptance of ms. Accepts simultaneous submissions. Catalog free on request, online at website. Guidelines online at website.

Nonfiction TrueSubjects include career guidance, child guidance, community, counseling, education, entertainment, games, parenting, public affairs, social sciences, youth leadership, prevention, activities. Query with SASE. Does not review artwork/photos.

Recent Title(s) *Helping Teens Handle Tough Experiences, Great Preschools, Engage Every Parent!, Parenting Preteens With a Purpose.*

Tips "Our audience is educators, youth program leaders, mentors, parents.

SEEDLING PUBLICATIONS, INC.

520 E. Bainbridge St., Elizabethtown PA 17022. (800)233-0759. E-mail: lsalem@jinl.com. Website: www.seedlingpub.com. **Contact:** Josie Stewart, vice president. Estab. 1992. Publishes in an 8-, 12-, or 16-page format for beginning readers. **Publishes 10-20 titles/year. 450 mss received/year. 50% of books from first-time authors. 100% from unagented writers. Makes outright purchase.** Publishes book 1 year after acceptance of ms. Accepts simultaneous submissions. Responds in 9-12 months to queries. Guidelines for #10 SASE.

- Does not accept mss via fax. Does not accept queries at all.
- We are an education niche publisher, producing books for beginning readers. Stories must include language that is natural to young children and story lines that are interesting to 5-7-year-olds and written at their beginning reading level.

Nonfiction Reviews artwork/photos. Send photocopies.

Fiction Subjects include juvenile. Submit complete ms.

Recent Title(s) *Sherman in the Talent Show*, by Betty Erickson; *Moth or Butterfly?*, by Ryan Durney; *The Miller, His Son, and the Donkey*, by Lynn Salem and Josie Stewart.

Tips Follow our guidelines. Do not submit full-length picture books or chapter books. We are an education niche publisher. Our books are for children, ages 5-7, who are just beginning to read independently. We do not accept stories that rhyme or poetry at this time. Try your manuscript with young readers. Listen for text that doesn't flow when the child reads the story. Rewrite until the text sounds natural to beginning readers. Visit our website to be sure your manuscript fits our market.

N SENTIENT PUBLICATIONS

1113 Spruce St., Boulder CO 80302. E-mail: contact@sentientpublications.com. Website: www.sentientpublications.com. **Contact:** Connie Shaw, acq. ed. Estab. 2001. Publishes hardcover and trade paperback originals; trade paperback reprints. **Publishes 12 titles/year. 200 queries received/year. 100 mss received/year. 70%% of books from first-time authors. 50%% from unagented writers. Pays royalty on wholesale price. Pays advance.** Publishes book 6 months after acceptance of ms. Accepts simultaneous submissions. Responds in 1 month to queries. Responds in 2 months to proposals. Responds in 2 months to manuscripts. Book catalog available online.

Nonfiction Subjects include audio, alternative, art, architecture, child guidance, contemporary culture, cooking, foods, nutrition, creative nonfiction, education, gardening, health, medicine, history, language, literature, memoirs, nature, environment, New Age, philosophy, photography, psychology, science, sex, social sciences, sociology, spirituality, travel, womens issues, womens studies. Submit proposal package, See our website. Submit complete ms. Reviews artwork/photos. Send photocopies.

Fiction Subjects include experimental, literary. The quality of the writing is the most important factor. Submit complete ms.

Recent Title(s) *Changing the Course of Autism*, by Bryan Jepson and Jane Johnson ((holistic health)); *If Holden Caulfield Were in My Classroom*, by Bernie Schein ((alternative education)); *God Is an Atheist*, by N. Nosirrah ((novella)).

Tips Our audience would be forward Become familiar with the kind

SEVEN FOOTER PRESS / SEVEN FOOTER KIDS

276 Fifth Ave., Suite 301, New York NY 10001-4556. E-mail: info@sevenfooter.com. Website: www.sevenfooterpress.com. **Contact:** Justin Heimberg, chief creative officer (humor, gift, nonfiction); David Gomberg, president and publisher (children's, illustrated, young adult, sports). Estab. 2004. Publishes hardcover, trade and mass market paperback originals. **Publishes 10-20 titles/year. 200 queries received/year. 50 mss received/year. 50% of books from first-time authors. 50% from unagented writers.** Publishes book 6-12 months after acceptance of ms. Accepts simultaneous submissions. Book catalog available online.

Nonfiction Subjects include creative nonfiction, education, hobbies, regional, sex, sports, travel, college market, games/puzzles, high-concept. Submit proposal package, outline, 2 sample chapters, any visuals or illustrations. Reviews artwork/photos. Send photocopies and scanned artwork or design.

Recent Title(s) *The Hip Grandma's Handbook*, by Linda Oatman-High (humor/reference); *Would You Rather.? For Women*, by Diane Bullock (humor); *Life-Size Zoo*, by Teruyuki Komiya (children's/nature).
Tips The audience for Seven Footer Press titles is Gen X, Gen Y, college, young adults, young professionals, and pop culture fans. The audience for Seven Footer Kids titles is for all children.

SEVEN STORIES PRESS

140 Watts St., New York NY 10013. (212)226-8760. Fax: (212)226-1411. Website: www.sevenstories.com. **Contact:** Daniel Simon; Anna Lui. Estab. 1995. Publishes hardcover and trade paperback originals. **Publishes 40-50 titles/year. 15% of books from first-time authors. 50% from unagented writers. Pays 7-15% royalty on retail price. Pays advance.** Publishes book 1-3 years after acceptance of ms. Accepts simultaneous submissions. Responds in 1 month to queries. Responds in months to manuscripts. Book catalog and ms guidelines free.

- "Seven Stories Press publishes literary fiction and political nonfiction for social justice. Currently emphasizing politics, social justice, biographies, foreign writings."

Nonfiction Query with SASE. "Without SASE enclosed, mss will be disposed, unread."
Fiction Subjects include literary. Query with SASE. "If no SASE enclosed we'll dispose of them unread."
Recent Title(s) *A Man Without a Country*, by Kurt Vonnegut; *Fledgling*, by Octavia E. Butler; *Abolition Democracy*, by Angela Y. Davis.

SHAMBHALA PUBLICATIONS, INC.

300 Massachusetts Ave., Boston MA 02115. (617)424-0030. Fax: (617)236-1563. E-mail: editors@shambhala.com. Website: www.shambhala.com. **Contact:** Eden Steinberg, editor;. Estab. 1969. Publishes hardcover and trade paperback originals and reprints. **Publishes 90-100 titles/year. 2,000 queries received/year. 500-700 mss received/year. 30% of books from first-time authors. 80% from unagented writers. Pays 8% royalty on retail price.** Publishes book 1 year after acceptance of ms. Accepts simultaneous submissions. Responds in 1 month to queries. Responds in 2 months to proposals. Responds in 2 months to manuscripts. Book catalog and ms guidelines free.
Nonfiction Subjects include alternative, art, architecture, creative nonfiction, health, medicine, humanities, language, literature, memoirs, philosophy, religion, spirituality, womens issues, womens studies. Query with SASE. Submit proposal package, outline, resume, 2 sample chapters, synopsis, TOC. Submit complete ms. Reviews artwork/photos.
Fiction Query with SASE. Submit proposal package, outline, resume, clips, 2 sample chapters, TOC. Submit complete ms.

SHEED & WARD BOOK PUBLISHING

Imprint of Rowman & Littlefield Publishing Group 4501 Forbes Blvd., Suite 200, Lanham MD 20706. (301)459-3366. Fax: (301)429-5747. Website: www.sheedandward.com. **Contact:** Sarah Johnson. Publishes hardcover and paperback originals. Book catalog free or on website. Guidelines available online.

- We are looking for books that help our readers, most of whom are college educated, gain access to the riches of the Catholic/Christian tradition. We publish in the areas of history, biography, spirituality, prayer, ethics, ministry, justice, liturgy.

Nonfiction Subjects include religion, spirituality, family life, theology, ethics. Submit proposal package, outline, 2 sample chapters, strong cover letter indicating why the project is unique and compelling. Reviews artwork/photos. Send photocopies.
Recent Title(s) *Becoming Fully Human*, by Joan Chittister, OSB; *Exploring Catholic Literature*, by Mary R. Reichardt.
Tips We prefer that writers get our author guidelines either from our website or via mail before submitting proposals.

SIERRA CLUB BOOKS

85 Second St., San Francisco CA 94105. (415)977-5500. Fax: (415)977-5792. E-mail: books.publishing@sierraclub.org. Website: www.sierraclub.org/books. **Contact:** Danny Moses, editor-in-chief. Estab. 1962. Publishes hardcover and paperback originals and reprints. **Publishes approximately 15 titles/year. 50% from unagented writers. Pays royalty. Pays $5,000-15,000 average advance.** Publishes book 1 year after acceptance of ms. Accepts simultaneous submissions. Responds in 1 month to queries. Responds in 2 months to proposals. Responds in 3 months to manuscripts. Book catalog available online. Guidelines available online.
Imprints Sierra Club Books for Children.

- *Currently not accepting unsolicited mss* or proposals for children's books.
- The Sierra Club was founded to help people to explore, enjoy, and preserve the nation's forests, waters, wildlife, and wilderness. The books program publishes quality trade books about the outdoors and the protection of the natural world.

Nonfiction Subjects include nature, environment. Query with SASE. Reviews artwork/photos. Send photocopies.

Recent Title(s) *Paper or Plastic*, by Daniel Imhoff; *Legacy*, by Nancy Kittle and John Hart; *The Quest for Environmental Justice*, edited by Robert D. Bullard.

SILMAN-JAMES PRESS

3624 Shannon Rd., Los Angeles CA 90027. (323)661-9922. Fax: (323)661-9933. E-mail: silmanjamespress@earthlink.net. Website: www.silmanjamespress.com. Publishes trade paperback originals and reprints. **Pays variable royalty on retail price.** Book catalog available free.

Imprints Siles Press (publishes chess books and other nonfiction subjects).

Nonfiction Pertaining to film, theatre, music, peforming arts.Submit proposal package, outline, 1+ sample chapters. Will accept phone queries. Reviews artwork/photos. Send photocopies.

Recent Title(s) *An Actor Takes a Meeting*, by Stephen Book; *Silman's Complete Endgame Course*, by Jeremy Silman.

Tips Our audience ranges from people with a general interest in film (fans, etc.) to students of film and performing arts to industry professionals. We will accept 'query' phone calls.

⊘ SILVER DAGGER MYSTERIES

The Overmountain Press 325 Walnut St., Johnson City TN 37605. E-mail: contactsd@silverdaggermysteries.com. Website: www.silverdaggermysteries.com. Estab. 1999. Publishes hardcover and trade paperback originals and reprints. Accepts simultaneous submissions. Book catalog and ms guidelines online.

- *Currently closed to submissions.*

O━ Silver Dagger publishes mysteries that take place in the American South. Emphasizing cozies, police procedurals, hard-boiled detectives.

Fiction Subjects include mystery, amateur sleuth, cozy, police procedural, private eye/hardboiled, young adult, mystery. We look for average-length books of 60-80,000 words. *All unsolicited mss returne*

Recent Title(s) *Death by Dissertation*, by Dean James; *Execute the Office*, by Daniel Bailey; *Criminal Appetite*, presented by Jeffrey Marks.

SILVER LAKE PUBLISHING

101 W. Tenth St., Aberdeen WA 98520. (360)532-5758. Fax: (360)532-5728. E-mail: publisher@silverlakepub.com. Website: www.silverlakepub.com. Estab. 1998. Publishes hardcover and trade paperback originals and reprints. **Pays royalty.** Accepts simultaneous submissions. Responds in 6-8 weeks to proposals. Book catalog available free. Guidelines available free.

Nonfiction Subjects include business, economics, money, finance. Submit outline, resume, 2 sample chapters, cover letter, synopsis. Submit via mail only.

Recent Title(s) *Sexual Predators*, by Stephen Dean; *Money and Life*, by Michael Z. Stahl; *Practical Privacy*, by The Silver Lake Editors.

Ⓐ ⊘ SIMON & SCHUSTER, INC.

1230 Avenue of the Americas, New York NY 10020. (212)698-7000. Website: www.simonsays.com. **Pays royalty. Pays advance.** Guidelines available online.

Imprints **Simon & Schuster Adult Publishing Group:** Atria Books (Washington Square Press, Strebor, Beyond Words), The Free Press, Howard Books, Pocket Books (Pocket Star, Star Trek, MTV Books, VH-1 Books, Downtown Press, Karen Hunter Publishing, World Wrestling Entertainment, Paraview Pocket, Juno Books), Scribner (Scribner Classics), Simon & Schuster (Simon & Schuster Classic Editions), Simon Spotlight Entertainment, Threshold Editions, Touchstone-Fireside (Librios en Espanol); **Simon & Schuster Australia:** Audio, Fireside, Kangaroo Press, Martin Books, Pocket Books, Scribner, Simon & Schuster, Touchstone; **Simon & Schuster Children's Publishing:** Aladdin; Atheneum Books for Young Readers (Richard Jackson Books), Libros Para Ninos, Little Simon, Beach Lane Books; Margaret K. McElderry Books, Simon & Schuster Books for Young Readers (Paula Weisman Books), Simon Pulse, Simon Spotlight and Simon Spotlight Entertainment; **Simon & Schuster Audio** (Encore, Nightingale-Conant, Pimsleur Language Programs, Simon & Schuster Audioworks, Simon & Schuster Sound Ideas); **Simon & Schuster Online**; **Simon & Schuster UK:** Fireside, The Free Press, Martin Books, Pocket Books, Scribner, Simon & Schuster, Simon & Schuster Audio, Touchstone, Town House.

- See website for more details.

⊘ SIMON & SCHUSTER BOOKS FOR YOUNG READERS

Imprint of Simon & Schuster Children's Publishing 1230 Avenue of the Americas, New York NY 10020. (212)698-7000. Fax: (212)698-2796. Website: www.simonsayskids.com. Publishes hardcover originals. **Publishes 75 titles/year. Pays variable royalty on retail price.** Publishes book 2-4 years after acceptance of ms. Accepts simultaneous submissions. Responds in 2 months to queries. Responds in 2 months to manuscripts. Guidelines for #10 SASE.

Imprints Paula Wiseman Books.

- *No unsolicited mss.* Queries are accepted via mail.

O→ We publish high-quality fiction and nonfiction for a variety of age groups and a variety of markets. Above all, we strive to publish books that we are passionate about.

Nonfiction Subjects include history, nature, environment, biography. Query with SASE only. *All unsolicited mss returned unopened*

Fiction Subjects include fantasy, historical, humor, juvenile, mystery, picture books, science fiction, young adult, adventure, historical, mystery, contemporary fiction. Query with SASE only. *All u*

Recent Title(s) *Duck for President*, by Doreen Cronin; *Spiderwick*, by Holly Black, illustrated by Tony Di Terlizzi; *Shrimp*, by Rachel Cohn.

SIMON & SCHUSTER CHILDREN'S PUBLISHING

Division of Simon & Schuster, Inc. 1230 Avenue of the Americas, New York NY 10020. (212)698-7000. Website: www.simonsayskids.com. Publishes hardcover and paperback fiction, nonfiction, trade, library, mass market titles, and novelty books for preschool through young adult readers. **Publishes 650 titles/year.**

Imprints Aladdin Paperbacks; Atheneum Books for Young Readers (Richard Jackson Books, Ginee Seo Books); Libros Para Ninos; Little Simon; Margaret K. McElderry Books; Simon & Schuster Books for Young Readers (Paula Wiseman Books); Simon Pulse; Simon Spotlight.

SKINNER HOUSE BOOKS

The Unitarian Universalist Association 25 Beacon St., Boston MA 02108. (617)742-2100 ext. 603. Fax: (617)742-7025. Website: www.uua.org/skinner. **Contact:** Mary Benard, senior editor. Estab. 1975. Publishes trade paperback originals and reprints. **Publishes 10-20 titles/year. 50% of books from first-time authors. 100% from unagented writers.** Publishes book 1 year after acceptance of ms. Responds in 3 months to queries. Book catalog for 6x9 SAE with 3 first-class stamps. Guidelines available online.

O→ We publish titles in Unitarian Universalist faith, liberal religion, history, biography, worship, and issues of social justice. We also publish inspirational titles of poetic prose and meditations. Writers should know that Unitarian Universalism is a liberal religious denomination committed to progressive ideals. Currently emphasizing social justice concerns.

Nonfiction Subjects include gay, lesbian, memoirs, religion, womens issues, womens studies, inspirational, church leadership. Query with SASE. Reviews artwork/photos. Send photocopies.

Recent Title(s) *In Nature's Honor*, by Patricia Montley; *Simply Pray*, by Erik Wikstrom; *Faith Without Certainty*, by Paul Rasor.

Tips From outside our denomination, we are interested in manuscripts that will be of help or interest to liberal churches, Sunday School classes, parents, ministers, and volunteers. Inspirational/spiritual and children's titles must reflect liberal Unitarian Universalist values.

SLACK, INC.

6900 Grove Rd., Thorofare NJ 08086. (856)848-1000. Fax: (856)853-5991. E-mail: jbond@slackinc.com. Website: www.slackbooks.com. **Contact:** John Bond, publisher. Estab. 1960. Publishes hardcover and softcover originals. **Publishes 35 titles/year. 80 queries received/year. 23 mss received/year. 75% of books from first-time authors. 100% from unagented writers. Pays 10% royalty. Pays advance.** Publishes book 8 months after acceptance of ms. Accepts simultaneous submissions. Responds in 1 month to queries. Responds in 1 month to proposals. Responds in 3 months to manuscripts. Book catalog and ms guidelines free. Guidelines available online.

O→ SLACK INC. publishes academic textbooks and professional reference books on various medical topics in an expedient manner.

Nonfiction Subjects include health, medicine, ophthalmology. Submit proposal package, outline, 2 sample chapters, market profile and cv. Reviews artwork/photos. Send photocopies.

Recent Title(s) *Handbook of Ophthalmology*, by Amar Agarural; *Patient Practitionor Interaction*, by Carol Davis.

GIBBS SMITH, PUBLISHER

P.O. Box 667, Layton UT 84041. (801)544-9800. Fax: (801)546-8853. E-mail: info@gibbs-smith.com. Website: www.gibbs-smith.com. **Contact:** Suzanne Taylor, editorial director. Estab. 1969. Publishes hardcover and trade paperback originals. **Publishes 80 titles/year. 3,000-4,000 queries received/year. 50% of books from first-time authors. 75% from unagented writers. Pays 8-14% royalty on gross receipts. Offers advance based on first year saleability projections.** Publishes book 1-2 years after acceptance of ms. Accepts simultaneous submissions. Responds in 1 month to queries. Responds in 10 weeks to proposals. Responds in 10 weeks to manuscripts. Book catalog for 9x12 SAE and $2.13 in postage. Guidelines available online.

O→ We publish books that enrich and inspire humankind. Currently emphasizing interior decorating and design, home reference. De-emphasizing novels and short stories.

Nonfiction Subjects include art, architecture, nature, environment, regional, interior design, cooking, business, western, outdoor/sports/recreation. Query with SASE. Submit outline, several completed chapters, author's cv.

Reviews artwork/photos. Send Send sample illustrations, if applicable.
Fiction Only short works oriented to gift market. Submit synopsis with sample il
Recent Title(s) *Secrets of French Design*, by Betty Lou Phillips (nonfiction); *101 More Things to Do with a Slow Cooker*, by Stephanie Ashcraft and Janet Eyring (cookbook).

SOHO PRESS, INC.

853 Broadway, New York NY 10003. E-mail: soho@sohopress.com. Website: www.sohopress.com. **Contact:** Laura Hruska, editor-in-chief; Katie Herman, editor. Estab. 1986. Publishes hardcover and trade paperback originals; trade paperback reprints. **Publishes 60-70 titles/year. 15-25% of books from first-time authors. 10% from unagented writers. 7.5-15% royalty on retail price (varies under certain circumstances)** Publishes book 18 months after acceptance of ms. Accepts simultaneous submissions. 3 months on queries and mss. Guidelines available online.

- Soho Press publishes primarily fiction, as well as some narrative literary nonfiction and mysteries set abroad. No electronic submissions, only queries by email.

Nonfiction Subjects include creative nonfiction, ethnic, memoirs. Submit 3 sample chapters and a cover letter with a synopsis and author bio; SASE. Send photocopies.
Fiction Subjects include ethnic, historical, humor, literary, mystery, In mysteries, we only publish series with foreign or exotic settings, usually procedurals. Submit 3 sample chapters and cover letter with synopsis, author bio, SASE.
Recent Title(s) *The Elfish Gene*, by Mark Barrowcliffe (memoir); *Chosen Forever*, by Susan Richards (memoir/inspirational); *Year of the Dog*, by Henry Chang (mystery)
Tips Soho Press publishes discerning authors for discriminating readers, finding the strongest possible writers and publishing them. Before submitting, look at our website for an idea of the types of books we publish, and read our submission guidelines.

SOURCEBOOKS, INC.

P.O. Box 4410, Naperville IL 60567. (630)961-3900. Fax: (630)961-2168. Website: www.sourcebooks.com. **Contact:** Todd Stocke, VP/editorial director (nonfiction trade); Deborah Werksman (Sourcebooks Casablanca); Peter Lynch (nonfiction); Daniel Ehrenhaft (Sourcebooks Jabberwocky). Estab. 1987. Publishes hardcover and trade paperback originals. **Publishes 300 titles/year. 30% of books from first-time authors. 25% from unagented writers. Pays royalty on wholesale or list price. Pays advance.** Publishes book 1 year after acceptance of ms. Accepts simultaneous submissions. Responds in 3 months to queries. Book catalog available online. Guidelines available online.
Imprints Sourcebooks Casablanca (romance fiction and love/relationships); Sourcebooks Hysteria (women's humor/gift book); Sourcebooks Landmark (fiction); Sourcebooks MediaFusion (multimedia); Sphinx Publishing (self-help legal); Sourcebooks Jabberwocky (children's).

- "Sourcebooks publishes many forms of fiction and nonfiction titles, including books on parenting, self-help/psychology, business, and health. Focus is on practical, useful information and skills. It also continues to publish in the reference, New Age, history, current affairs, and humor categories. Currently emphasizing gift, women's interest, history, reference, historical fiction, romance genre, and children's."

Nonfiction We seek unique books on traditional subjects and authors who are smart and aggressive.Subjects include biography, gift book, how-to, illustrated book, multimedia, reference, self-help, business, economics, child guidance, history, military, war, money, finance, psychology, science, sports, womens issues, womens studies, contemporary culture. Query with SASE, 2-3 sample chapters (not the first). *No complete mss.* Reviews artwork/photos.
Recent Title(s) *Child's Journey Out of Autism*, by LeAnn Whiffen; *In the Land of Invisible Women*, by Qanta Ahmed.
Tips "Our market is a decidedly trade-oriented bookstore audience. We also have very strong penetration into the gift-store market. Books which cross over between these 2 very different markets do extremely well with us. Our list is a solid mix of unique and general audience titles and series-oriented projects. We are looking for products that break new ground either in their own areas or within the framework of our series of imprints."

SOUTH END PRESS

7 Brookline St., Cambridge MA 02139. (617)547-4002. Fax: (617)547-1333. E-mail: southend@southendpress.org. Website: www.southendpress.org. Estab. 1977. Publishes library and trade paperback originals and reprints. **Publishes 10 titles/year. 400 queries received/year. 100 mss received/year. 30% of books from first-time authors. 95% from unagented writers. Pays 11% royalty on wholesale price. Pays occasionally $500-2,500 advance.** Publishes book 9 months after acceptance of ms. Accepts simultaneous submissions. Responds in up to 3 months to queries. Responds in up to 3 months to proposals. Book catalog available free. Guidelines available online.

- South End Press publishes nonfiction political books with a left/feminist/antiracist perspective.

Nonfiction Subjects include ethnic, gay, lesbian, government, politics, health, medicine, history, nature, environment, environment, philosophy, science, sociology, womens issues, womens studies, economics, world affairs. Query with SASE. Submit 2 sample chapters, intro or conclusion, and annotated TOC. Reviews artwork/photos. Send photocopies.
Recent Title(s) *The Revolution Will Not Be Funded: Beyond the Nonprofit Industrial Complex*, by INCITE! Women of Color Against Violence; *Heat: How to Stop the Planet from Burning*, by George Monbiot.

SOUTHERN ILLINOIS UNIVERSITY PRESS

1915 University Press Dr., SIUC Mail Code 6806, Carbondale IL 62901. (618)453-6626. Fax: (618)453-1221. Website: www.siu.edu/~siupress. **Contact:** Karl Kageff, editor-in-chief (film, regional history, rhetoric); Kristine Priddy, editor (theater, composition); Sylvia Rodrigue, executive editor (Civil War, Reconstruction); Bridget Brown, assistant editor (communication, poetry, popular culture). Estab. 1956. Publishes hardcover and trade paperback originals and reprints. **Publishes 50-60 titles/year. 700 queries received/year. 300 mss received/year. 40% of books from first-time authors. 99% from unagented writers. Pays 5-10% royalty on wholesale price. Rarely offers advance.** Publishes book 1-1 ½ years after acceptance of ms. Responds in 2 months to queries. Book catalog and ms guidelines free.
Imprints Shawnee Books; Shawnee Classics (regional reprint); Crab Orchard Series in Poetry; Theater in the Americas; Studies in Rhetorics and Feminisms; Studies in Writing and Rhetoric; Civil War Campaign in the Heartland.

- Scholarly press specializes in film and theater studies, rhetoric and composition studies, American history, Civil War, regional and nonfiction trade, poetry. No fiction. Currently emphasizing film, theater and American history, especially Civil War.

Recent Title(s) *The Man Who Emptied Death row: Governor George Ryan and the Politics of Crime*, by James L. Merriner; *Marketing to Moviegoers: A Handbook of Strategies and Tactics*, 2nd edition, by Robert Marich; *Lincoln Lessons: Reflections on America's Greatest Leader*, ed. by Frank J. Williams and William D. Pederson; *A Rhetoric of Style*, by Barry Brummett.

N SPECK PRESS

Fulcrum Publishing 4690 Table Mountain Dr., Ste. 100, Golden CO 80403. (303)277-1623. Fax: (303)279-7111. Website: www.speckpress.com. **Contact:** Derek Lawrence, publisher. Estab. 2002. Publishes hardcover, trade paperback, and electronic originals; trade paperback reprints. **Publishes 10 titles/year. 200 queries received/year. 80 mss received/year. 15%% of books from first-time authors. 60%% from unagented writers. Pays royalty on wholesale price.** Publishes book 18 months after acceptance of ms. Accepts simultaneous submissions. Responds in 3 months to queries. Responds in 3 months to proposals. Book catalog available online. Guidelines available online.
Nonfiction Subjects include Americana, architecture, art, contemporary culture, muticultural, music. Query with SASE. Reviews artwork/photos. Send copies, no original artwork.
Recent Title(s) *Roler Derby*, by Catherine Mabe ((popular culture/history)); *Django Reinhardt*, by Michael Dregni ((music/history)).

N SPI BOOKS

99 Spring St., 3rd Floor, New York NY 10012. (212)431-5011. Fax: (212)431-8646. Website: www.spibooks.com. **Contact:** Ian Shapolsky, acquisitions editor (pop culture, how-to, expose, entertainment, Judaica, business, conspiracy, children's). Estab. 1991. Publishes hardcover and trade paperback originals and reprints. **Publishes 20-30 titles/year. 5% of books from first-time authors. 50% from unagented writers. Pays 6-15% royalty on retail price. Pays $1,000-10,000 advance.** Publishes book 3-6 months after acceptance of ms. Accepts simultaneous submissions. Responds in 2 months to queries. Responds in 2 months to proposals. Responds in 2 months to manuscripts. Book catalog available online. Guidelines available free.
Nonfiction Subjects include Americana, animals, business, economics, child guidance, community, contemporary culture, cooking, foods, nutrition, creative nonfiction, education, ethnic, government, politics, health, medicine, history, hobbies, humanities, language, literature, memoirs, military, war, money, finance, multicultural, music, dance, nature, environment, New Age, philosophy, psychology, regional, religion, sex, social sciences, sociology, spirituality, sports, translation, travel, womens issues, womens studies, world affairs, expose. Query with SASE. Submit proposal package, outline, sample chapters. Reviews artwork/photos. Send photocopies.
Recent Title(s) *Don't Be a Slave to What You Crave*, by Dr. Daisy Merey (health); *Princess Diana: The Hidden Evidence*, by King & Beveridge (conspiracy); *Steve Martin: The Magic Years*, by Morris Walker (biography).
Tips Advise us how to reach the market for the legions of interested buyers of your book. Be specific if you can help us target marketing opportunities and promotional possibilities, particularly those that are not obvious. Also, let us know if there are any friends/contacts/connections you can draw upon to assist us in getting the message out about the significance of your book.

SQUARE ONE PUBLISHERS, INC.

115 Herricks Rd., Garden City Park NY 11040. (516)535-2010. Fax: (516)535-2014. Website: www.squareonepublishers.com. **Contact:** Acquisitions Editor. Publishes trade paperback originals. **Publishes 20 titles/year. 500 queries received/year. 100 mss received/year. 95% of books from first-time authors. 95% from unagented writers. Pays 10-15% royalty on wholesale price. Pays variable advance.** Publishes book 10 months after acceptance of ms. Accepts simultaneous submissions. Responds in 1 month to queries. Responds in 1 month to proposals. Responds in 1 month to manuscripts. Book catalog and ms guidelines free or on website. Guidelines available online.

Nonfiction Subjects include business, economics, child guidance, health, medicine, hobbies, money, finance, nature, environment, psychology, religion, spirituality, sports, travel, writers' guides, cooking/foods, gaming/gambling. Query with SASE. Submit proposal package, outline, bio, introduction, synopsis, SASE. Reviews artwork/photos. Send photocopies.

Recent Title(s) *Does Your Baby Have Autism?*, by Osnat Teitelbaum and Philip Teitelbaum, PhD. ((parenting/child development)); *Speaking Scared, Sounding Good*, by Peter Desberg, PhD. ((reference/communication)); *How to Make Real Money Selling Books*, by Brian Jud ((self-help/finance)).

Tips We focus on making our books accessible, accurate, and interesting. They are written for people who are looking for the best place to start, and who don't appreciate the terms 'dummy,' 'idiot,' or 'fool,' on the cover of their books. We look for smartly written, informative books that have a strong point of view, and that are authored by people who know their subjects well.

STACKPOLE BOOKS

5067 Ritter Rd., Mechanicsburg PA 17055. Fax: (717)796-0412. E-mail: jschnell@stackpolebooks.com. Website: www.stackpolebooks.com. **Contact:** Judith Schnell, editorial director (fly fishing, hunting, outdoor sports); Chris Evans, editor (history); Mark Allison, editor (nature); Dave Reisch, editor (military); Kyle Weaver, editor (regional/Pennsylvania). Estab. 1935. Publishes hardcover and paperback originals and reprints. **Publishes 130 titles/year. Pays industry standard advance.** Publishes book 1 year after acceptance of ms. Responds in 1 month to queries.

- Stackpole maintains a growing and vital publishing program by featuring authors who are experts in their fields.

Nonfiction Subjects include history, military, war, nature, environment, recreation, sports, wildlife. Query with SASE. Does not return unsolicited mss. Reviews artwork/photos.

Recent Title(s) *Band of Sisters*; *Fishing Knots*; *True Crime New Jersey*.

Tips Stackpole seeks well-written, authoritative manuscripts for specialized and general trade markets. Proposals should include chapter outline, sample chapter, illustrations, and author's credentials.

STANFORD UNIVERSITY PRESS

1450 Page Mill Rd., Palo Alto CA 94304-1124. (650)723-9434. Fax: (650)725-3457. E-mail: info@www.sup.org. Website: www.sup.org. **Contact:** Muriel Bell (Asian studies, US foreign policy, Asian-American studies); Amanda M. Moran (law, political science, public policy); Martha Cooley (economics, finance, business); Kate Wahl (sociology, anthropology, education, Middle Eastern studies). Estab. 1925. **Pays variable royalty (sometimes none) Pays occasional advance.** Guidelines available online.

- Stanford University Press publishes scholarly books in the humanities and social sciences, along with professional books in business, economics and management science; also high-level textbooks and some books for a more general audience.

Nonfiction Subjects include anthropology, archeology, business, economics, ethnic, studies, gay, lesbian, government, politics, history, humanities, language, literature, literary criticism, and literary theory, nature, environment, philosophy, psychology, religion, science, social sciences, sociology, political science, law, education, history and culture of China, Japan and Latin America, European history, linguistics, geology, medieval and classical studies. Query with prospectus and an outline. Reviews artwork/photos.

Recent Title(s) *Culture and Public Action*; *The Sovereignty Revolution*; *Maps, Myths, and Men*.

Tips The writer's best chance is a work of original scholarship with an argument of some importance.

ST. ANTHONY MESSENGER PRESS

28 W. Liberty St., Cincinnati OH 45202-6498. (513)241-5615. Fax: (513)241-0399. Website: www.americancatholic.org. **Contact:** Lisa Biedenbach, editorial director. Estab. 1970. Publishes trade paperback originals. **Publishes 20-25 titles/year. 300 queries received/year. 50 mss received/year. 5% of books from first-time authors. 99% from unagented writers. Pays $1,000 average advance.** Publishes book 18 months after acceptance of ms. Responds in 2 months to queries, proposals, and mss. Book catalog for 9x12 envelope and 4 First-Class stamps. Guidelines available online.

Imprints Servant Books.

- "St. Anthony Messenger Press/Franciscan Communications seeks to communicate the word that is Jesus Christ in the styles of Saints Francis and Anthony. Through print and electronic media marketed in North America and worldwide, we endeavor to evangelize, inspire, and inform those who search for God and seek a richer Catholic, Christian, human life. Our efforts help support the life, ministry, and charities of the Franciscan Friars of St. John the Baptist Province, who sponsor our work. Currently emphasizing prayer/spirituality."

Nonfiction Query with SASE. Submit outline, Attn: Lisa Biedenbach. Reviews artwork/photos.

Recent Title(s) *Life With Mother Teresa*, by Sebastian Vazhakala, MC; *Franciscan Prayer*, by Ilia Delio, OSF; *Spirituality of Sport*, by Susan Saint Sing.

Tips "Our readers are ordinary `folks in the pews' and those who minister to and educate these folks. Writers need to know the audience and the kind of books we publish. Manuscripts should reflect best and current Catholic theology and doctrine. St. Anthony Messenger Press especially seeks books which will sell in bulk quantities to parishes, teachers, pastoral ministers, etc. They expect to sell at least 5,000 to 7,000 copies of a book."

ST. AUGUSTINE'S PRESS

P.O. Box 2285, South Bend IN 46680-2285. (574)-291-3500. Fax: (574)291-3700. E-mail: bruce@staugustine.net. Website: www.staugustine.net. **Contact:** Bruce Fingerhut, president (philosophy). Publishes hardcover originals and trade paperback originals and reprints. **Publishes 20 titles/year. 350 queries received/year. 100 mss received/year. 2% of books from first-time authors. 95% from unagented writers. Pays 6-15% royalty. Pays $500-5,000 advance.** Publishes book 8 months after acceptance of ms. Accepts simultaneous submissions. Responds in 2-6 months to queries. Responds in 3-8 months to proposals. Responds in 4-8 months to manuscripts. Book catalog available free.

Imprints Carthage Reprints.

- Our market is scholarly in the humanities. We publish in philosophy, religion, cultural history, and history of ideas only.

Nonfiction Subjects include history, of ideas, philosophy, religion. Query with SASE. Reviews artwork/photos. Send photocopies.

Recent Title(s) *The Last Superstition: A Refutation of the New Atheism*, by Edward Feser; *Socrates in the Underworld: On Plato's Gorgias*, by Nalin Ranasinghe; *What Catholics Believe*, by Josef Pieper.

Tips Scholarly and college student audience.

STEEPLE HILL BOOKS

Imprint of Harlequin Enterprises 233 Broadway, Suite 1001, New York NY 10279. (212)553-4200. Fax: (212)227-8969. Website: www.eharlequin.com. **Contact:** Joan Marlow Golan, executive editor; Melissa Endlich, senior editor (inspirational contemp. romance, historical romance, romantic suspense); Tina Colombo, senior editor (inspirational romantic suspense and historical romance); Emily Rodmell, assistant editor. Estab. 1997. Publishes mass market paperback originals and reprints. **Publishes 144 titles/year. Pays royalty on retail price. Pays advance.** 3 months on proposals & mss. Guidelines available online, free on request, for #10 SASE.

Imprints Love Inspired; Love Inspired Suspense; Love Inspired Historical.

- This series of contemporary, inspirational love stories portrays Christian characters facing the many challenges of life, faith, and love in today's world.

Fiction Subjects include historical, mystery, romance, spiritual. Our imprints are inspirational romances that feature Christian characters facing the many challenges of life and love in today's world (and for LIH, in days gone by). We are looking for authors writing from a Christian worldview and conveying their personal faith and ministry values in entertaining fiction that will touch the hearts of believers and seekers everywhere. Query with SASE, submit completed ms.

Recent Title(s) *His Holiday Heart*, by Jillian Hart (love inspired); *Apprentice Father*, by Irene Hannon (contemporary inspirational romance); *Lakeview Protector*, by Shirlee McCoy (love inspired suspense)

Tips Drama, humor, and even a touch of mystery all have a place in Steeple Hill. Subplots are welcome and should further the story's main focus or intertwine in a meaningful way. Secondary characters (children, family, friends, neighbors, fellow church members, etc.) may all contribute to a substantial and satisfying story. These wholesome tales include strong family values and high moral standards. While there is no premarital sex between characters, in the case of romance, a vivid, exciting tone presented with a mature perspective is essential. Although the element of faith must clearly be present, it should be well integrated into the characterizations and plot. The conflict between the main characters should be an emotional one, arising naturally from the well-developed personalities you've created. Suitable stories should also impart an important lesson about the powers of trust and faith.

STEEPLE HILL WOMEN'S FICTION

Imprint of Steeple Hill 233 Broadway, Suite 1001, New York NY 10279. (212)553-4200. Fax: (212)227-8969. Website: www.steeplehill.com. **Contact:** Joan Marlow Golan, executive editor (inspirational fiction); Krista Stroever, senior editor (inspirational fiction); Melissa Endlich, editor (inspirational fiction); Emily Rodmell, assistant editor (inspirational fiction). Estab. 1997. Publishes trade paperback and mass market paperback

originals. **Publishes 100-120 titles/year. Pays royalty on retail price. Pays advance.** Responds in 3 months to queries. Responds in 3 months to proposals. Responds in 3 months to manuscripts. Guidelines available online.
Imprints Steeple Hill Café; Steeple Hill Women's Fiction.
Fiction Subjects include literary, mystery, religious, romance, chick lit. This program is dedicated to publishing inspirational Christian women's fiction that depicts the struggles characters encounter as they learn important lessons about trust and the power of faith. See listing for subgenres. Query with SASE.
Recent Title(s) *Thread of Deceit*, by Catherine Palmer; *The Face*, by Angela Hunt.
Tips Please read our guidelines.

STERLING PUBLISHING

387 Park Ave. S., New York NY 10016. (212)532-7160. Fax: (212)213-2495. Website: www.sterlingpub.com. **Contact:** Category Editor (i.e., Craft Editor or Children's Editor). Estab. 1949. Publishes hardcover and paperback originals and reprints. **Pays royalty. Pays advance.** Guidelines available online.
Imprints Sterling/Chapelle; Lark; Sterling/Tamos; Sterling/Prolific Impressions.

- Sterling publishes highly illustrated, accessible, hands-on, practical books for adults and children.

Nonfiction Publishes nonfiction only.Subjects include alternative, animals, art, architecture, ethnic, gardening, health, medicine, hobbies, New Age, recreation, science, sports, fiber arts, games and puzzles, children's humor, children's science, nature and activities, pets, wine, home decorating, dolls and puppets, ghosts, UFOs, woodworking, crafts, medieval, Celtic subjects, alternative health and healing, new consciousness. Submit outline, publishing history, 1 sample chapter, SASE. Reviews artwork/photos. Send photocopies.
Recent Title(s) *AARP Crash Course in Estate Planning*, by Michael Palermo and Ric Edelman.

STIPES PUBLISHING LLC

P.O. Box 526, Champaign IL 61824-9933. (217)356-8391. Fax: (217)356-5753. E-mail: stipes01@sbcglobal.net. Website: www.stipes.com. **Contact:** Benjamin H. Watts, (engineering, science, business); Robert Watts (agriculture, music, and physical education). Estab. 1925. Publishes hardcover and paperback originals. **Publishes 15-30 titles/year. 50% of books from first-time authors. 95% from unagented writers. Pays 15% maximum royalty on retail price.** Publishes book 4 months after acceptance of ms. Responds in 2 months to queries. Guidelines available online.

- Stipes Publishing is oriented towards the education market and educational books with some emphasis in the trade market.

Nonfiction Subjects include agriculture, business, economics, music, dance, nature, environment, recreation, science. Submit outline, 1 sample chapter.
Recent Title(s) *The AutoCAD 2004 Workbook*, by Philip Age and Ronald Sutliff.

STOEGER PUBLISHING CO.

17603 Indian Head Hwy., Suite 200, Accokeek MD 20607. (301)283-6300. Fax: (301)283-4783. E-mail: submissions@stoegerbooks.com. Website: www.stoegerindustries.com. **Contact:** Jay Langston, publisher. Estab. 1925. Publishes hardback and trade paperback originals. **Publishes 12-15 titles/year. Royalty varies, depending on ms. Pays advance.** Accepts simultaneous submissions. Responds in 2 months to queries. Book catalog available online.

- Stoeger publishes books on hunting, shooting sports, fishing, cooking, nature, and wildlife.

Nonfiction Specializes in reference and how-to books that pertain to hunting, fishing, and appeal to gun enthusiasts.Subjects include cooking, foods, nutrition, sports. Submit outline, sample chapters.
Fiction Specializes in outdoor-related fiction.
Recent Title(s) *Escape in Iraq: The Thomas Hamill Story*; *Gun Trader's Guide, 26th Ed.*; *Hunting Whitetails East & West*.

N STOREY PUBLISHING, LLC

210 MASS MoCA Way, North Adams MA 01247. (413)346-2100. Fax: (413)346-2196. Website: www.storey.com. **Contact:** Deborah Balmuth, editorial director (building, sewing, gift). Estab. 1983. Publishes hardcover and trade paperback originals and reprints. **Publishes 40 titles/year. 600 queries received/year. 150 mss received/year. 25% of books from first-time authors. 60% from unagented writers. Pays royalty. Makes outright purchase. Pays advance.** Publishes book within 2 years after acceptance of ms. Accepts simultaneous submissions. Responds in 1 month to queries. Responds in 3 months to proposals. Responds in 3 months to manuscripts. Book catalog available free. Guidelines available online.

- We publish practical information that encourages personal independence in harmony with the environment.

Nonfiction Subjects include animals, gardening, nature, environment, home, mind/body/spirit, birds, beer and wine, crafts, building, cooking. Reviews artwork/photos.
Recent Title(s) *The Veggie Gardener's Answer Book*, by Barbara W. Ellis; *The Home Creamery*, by Kathy Farrell-Kingsley; *Happy Dog, Happy You*, by Arden Moore.

ST PAULS/ALBA HOUSE

Society of St. Paul 2187 Victory Blvd., Staten Island NY 10314-6603. (718)761-0047. Fax: (718)761-0057. E-mail: edmund_lane@juno.com. Website: www.stpauls.us. **Contact:** Edmund C. Lane, SSP, acquisitions editor. Estab. 1957. Publishes trade paperback and mass market paperback originals and reprints. **Publishes 22 titles/year. 250 queries received/year. 150 mss received/year. 10% of books from first-time authors. 100% from unagented writers. Pays 5-10% royalty.** Publishes book 10 months after acceptance of ms. Responds in 1 month to queries. Responds in 1 month to proposals. Responds in 2 months to manuscripts. Book catalog and ms guidelines free.

Nonfiction Subjects include philosophy, religion, spirituality. Submit complete ms. Reviews artwork/photos. Send photocopies.

Recent Title(s) *Those Mysterious Priests*, by Fulton J. Sheen (spirituality); *Captured Fire*, by S. Joseph Krempa (homiletics).

Tips Our audience is educated Roman Catholic readers interested in matters related to the Church, spirituality, Biblical and theological topics, moral concerns, lives of the saints, etc.

N STRATEGIC BOOK PUBLISHING

AEG Publishing Group 1355 W. Palmetto Pk., Suite 257, Boca Raton FL 33486. Website: www.strategicbookpublishing.com. **Contact:** Robert Williams, V.P. Acquisitions. Estab. 2007. Publishes hardcover, trade paperback, mass market, and electronic originals; reprints. **Publishes 40 titles/year. 4,000 queries received/year. 2,000 mss received/year. 75%% of books from first-time authors. 33%% from unagented writers. Pays 10-20% royalty on wholesale price.** Publishes book 4 months after acceptance of ms. Accepts simultaneous submissions. Responds in 1 month to queries. Responds in 1 month to proposals. Responds in 1 month to manuscripts. Book catalog available online. Guidelines available online.

Imprints AEG Publishing Group

Nonfiction Subjects include agriculture, alternative, Americana, animals, anthropology, archeology, art, architecture, business, economics, child guidance, community, computers, electronics, contemporary culture, cooking, foods, nutrition, creative nonfiction, education, ethnic, fashion, film, cinema, stage, gardening, gay, lesbian, government, politics, health, medicine, history, hobbies, humanities, language, literature, literary criticism, memoirs, military, war, money, finance, multicultural, music, dance, nature, environment, New Age, philosophy, photography, psychology, recreation, regional, religion, science, sex, social sciences, sociology, software, spirituality, sports, translation, travel, true crime, world affairs. Submit complete ms. via e-mail only. Reviews artwork/photos. Send e-mail only.

Recent Title(s) *Understanding Math*, by Don Sutton ((cause)); *The Blow Fish Theory*, by Tricia Dodson ((self-help relationships)).

Tips Nonfiction - 1,000 sales easi Know how you can assist with

STYLUS PUBLISHING, LLC

22883 Quicksilver Dr., Sterling VA 20166. Website: styluspub.com. **Contact:** John von Knorring, publisher. Estab. 1996. Publishes hardcover and trade paperback originals. **Publishes 10-15 titles/year. 50 queries received/year. 6 mss received/year. 50% of books from first-time authors. 100% from unagented writers. Pays 5-10% royalty on wholesale price. Pays advance.** Publishes book 6 months after acceptance of ms. Responds in 1 month to queries. Book catalog available free. Guidelines available online.

- "We publish in higher education (diversity, professional development, distance education, teaching, administration)."

Nonfiction Subjects include education. Query or submit outline, 1 sample chapter with SASE. Reviews artwork/photos. Send photocopies.

Recent Title(s) *Driving Change Through Diversity and Globalization*; *Encountering Faith in the Classroom*.

SUN BOOKS / SUN PUBLISHING

P.O. Box 5588, Santa Fe NM 87502-5588. (505)471-5177. E-mail: info@sunbooks.com. Website: www.sunbooks.com. **Contact:** Skip Whitson, director. Estab. 1973. Publishes trade paperback originals and reprints. **Publishes 10-15 titles/year. 5% of books from first-time authors. 90% from unagented writers. Pays 5% royalty on retail price. Occasionally makes outright purchase.** Publishes book 16 to 18 months after acceptance of ms. Will respond within 2 mos, via e-mail, to queries if interested. Book catalog available online at www.sunbooks.com or www.abooksource.com. Queries via e-mail only, please.

Nonfiction , self-help, leadership, motivational, recovery, inspirational.

Recent Title(s) *Eight Pillars of Prosperity*, by James Allen; *Ambition and Success*, by Orson Swett Marden; *Cheerfulness as a Life Power*, by Orson Swett Marden.

N SUNRISE RIVER PRESS

39966 Grand Ave., North Branch MN 55056. (800)895-4585. Fax: (651)277-1203. E-mail: karinh@sunriseriverpress.com. Website: www.sunriseriverpress.com. **Contact:** Karin Hill. Estab. 1992. **Publishes 30**

titles/year. Pays advance. Accepts simultaneous submissions. Guidelines available online.

- Sunrise River Press is part of a 3-company publishing house that also includes CarTech Books and Specialty Press.

E-mail is preferred method of contact.

Nonfiction Subjects include cooking, foods, nutrition, health, medicine, genetics, immune system maintenance, fitness; also some professional healthcare titles. Check Web site for submission guidelines.

SUPERCOLLEGE

3286 Oak Ct., Belmont CA 94002. Phone/Fax: (650)618-2221. E-mail: supercollege@supercollege.com. Website: www.supercollege.com. Estab. 1998. Publishes trade paperback originals. **Publishes 8-10 titles/year. 50% of books from first-time authors. 70% from unagented writers. Pays royalty on wholesale price or makes outright purchase.** Publishes book 7-9 months after acceptance of ms. Book catalog and writer's guidelines online.

We only publish books on admission, financial aid, scholarships, test preparation, student life, and career preparation for college and graduate students.

Nonfiction Subjects include education, admissions, financial aid, scholarships, test prep, student life, career prep. Submit complete ms. Reviews artwork/photos. Send photocopies.

Recent Title(s) *Our Friendship Rules*, by Peggy Moss and Dee Dee Tardif; *Keep Your Ear on the Ball*, by Genevieve Petrillo.

Tips We want titles that are student and parent friendly, and that are different from other titles in this category. We also seek authors who want to work with a small but dynamic and ambitious publishing company.

SYBEX, INC.

1151 Marina Village Pkwy., Alameda CA 94501. (510)523-8233. Fax: (510)523-2373. E-mail: sybexproposals@wiley.com. Website: www.sybex.com. Estab. 1976. Publishes paperback originals. **Publishes 150 titles/year. Pays standard royalties. Pays competitive advance.** Publishes book 3 months after acceptance of ms. Accepts simultaneous submissions. Responds in 1 month to queries. Book catalog available online. Guidelines available online.

Sybex publishes computer and software titles.

Nonfiction Manuscripts most publishable in the field of PC applications software, hardware, programming languages, operating systems, computer games, Internet/Web certification, and networking.Subjects include computers, electronics, software. Submit outline, 2-3 sample chapters, resume. Reviews artwork/photos. Send Send disk/CD.

Recent Title(s) *Photoshop Elements Solutions*, by Mikkel Haland; *Mastering Windows 2000 Server*, by Mark Minasi; *CCNA: Cisco Certified Network Associate Study Guide*, by Todd Lammle.

Tips Queries/mss may be routed to other editors in the publishing group. Also seeking freelance writers for revising existing works and as contributors in multi-author projects, and freelance editors for editing works in progress.

SYLVAN DELL PUBLISHING

976 Houston Northcutt Blvd., Suite 3, Mt. Pleasant SC 29464. Website: www.sylvandellpublishing.com. **Contact:** Donna German, editor. Estab. 2004. Publishes hardcover, trade paperback, and electronic originals. **Publishes 10 titles/year. < 2,000 mss received/year. 50%% of books from first-time authors. 100%% from unagented writers. Pays 6-8% royalty on wholesale price. Pays small advance.** Publishes book 12-18 months. May hold onto mss of interest for 12 months until acceptance. after acceptance of ms. Accepts simultaneous submissions. Responds in 3 days to queries. Responds in 3 weeks to proposals. Acknowledges receipt of ms submission within 5 days. Book catalog and guidelines available online.

The picture books we publish are usually, but not always, fictional stories that relate to animals, nature, the environment, and science. All books should subtly convey an educational theme through a warm story that is fun to read and that will grab a child's attention. Each book has a 3-5 page *For Creative Minds'* section to reinforce the educational component. This section will have a craft and/or game as well as 'fun facts' to be shared by the parent, teacher, or other adult. Authors do not need to supply this information. Mss. should be < 1,500 words and meet all of the following 4 criteria: Fun to read—mostly fiction with nonfiction facts woven into the story; National or regional in scope; Must tie into early elementary school curriculum; Must be marketable through a niche market such as a zoo, aquarium, or museum gift shop.

Nonfiction Subjects include science, Math. We only accept e-submissions. Reviews artwork/photos. Send 1-2 JPEGS.

Fiction Subjects include picture books, Subjects related to math and science (think *historical fiction*).

Recent Title(s) *Sort It Out!* by Barbara Mariconda; *Ocean Hide and Seek*, by Jennifer Krammer; *Henry the Impatient Heron*, by Donna Love; *One Wolf Howls*, by Scotti Cohn.

Tips We want the children excited about the books. We envision the books being used at home and in the classroom.

SYNERGEBOOKS

11 Spruce Ct., Davenport FL 33837. (863)588-3770. Fax: (863)588-2198. E-mail: synergebooks@aol.com. Website: www.synergebooks.com. **Contact:** Debra Staples, publisher/acquisitions editor. Estab. 1999. Publishes trade paperback and electronic originals. **Publishes 50-70 titles/year. 250 queries received/year. 250 mss received/year. 95% of books from first-time authors. 99.9% from unagented writers. Pays 15-40% royalty; makes outright purchase.** Accepts simultaneous submissions. Book catalog available online at www.synergebooks.com/paperbacks.html. Guidelines available online at www.synergebooks.com/subguide.html.

Nonfiction Subjects include New Age, philosophy, spirituality, travel, young adult. Submit proposal package, 1-3 sample chapters. Reviews artwork/photos. Send jpg via attached mail.

Fiction Subjects include fantasy, historical, horror, humor, mainstream, contemporary, military, war, mystery, poetry, religious, romance, science fiction, short story collections, spiritual, suspense, western, young adult. SynergEbooks published at least 30 new titles a year, and only 1-5 of those are put into print in any given year. SynergEbooks is first and foremost a digital publisher, so most of our marketing budget goes to those formats. Authors are required to direct-sell a minimum of 100 digital copies of a title before it's accepted for print. Submit proposal package, including synopsis, 1-3 sample chapters, and marketing plans.

Recent Title(s) *A Traveler's Highway to Heaven*, by William Bonville (travel); *The Vernal Equinox of Death and Kisses*, by Antonio Hopson (anthology); *New and Easy Poems to Promote Your Health & Safety*, by John Blandly (anthology)

Tips At SynergEbooks, we work with the author to promote their work.

SYRACUSE UNIVERSITY PRESS

621 Skytop Road, Suite 110, Syracuse NY 13244-5290. (315)443-5534. Fax: (315)443-5545. Website: syracuseuniversitypress.syr.edu. **Contact:** Alice R. Pfeiffer, director. Estab. 1943. **Publishes 50 titles/year. 25% of books from first-time authors. 95% from unagented writers.** Publishes book an average of 15 months after acceptance of ms. Book catalog for 9x12 envelope and 3 First-Class stamps. Guidelines available online.

- "Currently emphasizing Middle East studies, Jewish studies, Irish studies, Peace studies, television and popular culture, Native American studies, New York State."

Nonfiction Subjects include regional. Submit query with SASE or online, or submit outline and 2 sample chapters. Reviews artwork/photos.

Recent Title(s) *Besa: Muslims Who Saved Jews in World War II*, by Norman Gershman; *Eminent Persians: The Men and Women Who Made Modern Iran 1941-1979*, by Abbas Milani; *Seven Generations of Iroquois Leadership: The Six Nations Since 1800*, by Lawrence Hauptman; *God and the Editor: My Search for Meaning at the New York Times*, by Robert Phelps.

Tips "We're seeking well-written and well-researched books that will make a significant contribution to the subject areas listed above and will be well-received in the marketplace."

NAN A. TALESE

Imprint of Doubleday 1745 Broadway, New York NY 10019. (212)782-8918. Fax: (212)782-8448. Website: www.nanatalese.com. **Contact:** Nan A. Talese, publisher and editorial director; Ronit Feldman, assistant editor. Publishes hardcover originals. **Publishes 15 titles/year. 400 queries received/year. 400 mss received/year. Pays variable royalty on retail price. Pays varying advance.** *Agented submissions only.*

- Nan A. Talese publishes nonfiction with a powerful guiding narrative and relevance to larger cultural interests, and literary fiction of the highest quality.

Nonfiction Subjects include contemporary culture, history, philosophy, sociology.

Fiction Subjects include literary. Well-written narratives with a compelling story line, good characterization and use of language. We like stories with an edge.

Recent Title(s) *Saturday*, by Ian McEwan; *Albion: The Origins of the English Imagination*, by Peter Ackroyd; *Oryx and Crake*, by Margaret Atwood.

Tips Audience is highly literate people interested in story, information and insight. We want well-written material submitted by agents only. See our website.

JEREMY P. TARCHER, INC.

Imprint of Penguin Group (USA), Inc. 375 Hudson St., New York NY 10014. (212)366-2000. Website: www.penguin.com. **Contact:** Mitch Horowitz, editor-in-chief; Sara Carder, senior editor. Estab. 1972. Publishes hardcover and trade paperback originals and reprints. **Publishes 40-50 titles/year. 1,000 queries received/year. 1,000 mss received/year. 20% of books from first-time authors. 20% from unagented writers. Pays royalty. Pays advance.** Accepts simultaneous submissions.

- Tarcher's vision is to publish ideas and works about human consciousness that are large enough to include all aspects of human experience.

Nonfiction Subjects include health, medicine, nature, environment, philosophy, psychology, religion, Eastern

and Western religions, metaphysics. Query with SASE.
Recent Title(s) *Catching the Big Fish*, by David Lynch; *The Writing Diet*, by Julia Cameron; *Zolz*, by Daniel Pinchbeck.
Tips Our audience seeks personal growth through books. Understand the imprint's focus and categories.

TAYLOR TRADE PUBLISHING

5360 Manhattan Circle, #101, Boulder CO 80303. (303)543-7835. E-mail: rrinehart@rowman.com. Website: www.rlpgtrade.com. **Contact:** Rick Rinehart, editorial director. Publishes hardcover originals, trade paperback originals and reprints. **Publishes 70 titles/year. 15% of books from first-time authors. 65% from unagented writers.** Publishes book 1 year after acceptance of ms. Responds in 2 months to queries.
Nonfiction Subjects include child guidance, cooking, foods, nutrition, gardening, health, medicine, history, Texas/Western, nature, environment, sports, contemporary affairs, music, film, theater, art, nature writing, exploration, women's studies, African-American studies, literary studies. Query with SASE. Submit outline, sample chapters.

TCU PRESS

P.O. Box 298300, TCU, Fort Worth TX 76129. (817)257-7822. Fax: (817)257-5075. **Contact:** Judy Alter, director and Susan Petty, editor. Estab. 1966. Publishes hardcover and trade paper originals, some reprints. **Publishes 9-12 titles/year. 10% of books from first-time authors. 75% from unagented writers.** Publishes book 16-20 months after acceptance of ms. Responds in 3 months to queries.

O→ "TCU publishes scholarly works and regional titles of significance focusing on the history and literature of the American West."

Nonfiction Subjects include Americana, art, architecture, contemporary culture, ethnic, history, language, literature, literary criticism, multicultural, regional, womens issues, womens studies, American studies. Query with SASE. Reviews artwork/photos.
Fiction Subjects include historical, young adult, contemporary.
Recent Title(s) *Echoes of Glory*, by Robert Flynn; *Literary Dallas*, edited by Frances Brannen Vick; *Emily Austin of Texas, 1795-1851*, by Light T. Cummins
Tips "Regional and/or Texana nonfiction has best chance of breaking into our firm. Our list focuses on the history of literature of the American West, although recently we have branched out into literary criticism, women's studies, and Mexican-American studies."

N TEACHERS COLLEGE PRESS

1234 Amsterdam Ave., New York NY 10027. (212)678-3929. Fax: (212)678-4149. Website: www.teacherscollegepress.com. **Contact:** Brian Ellerbeck, executive acquisitions editor. Estab. 1904. Publishes hardcover and paperback originals and reprints. **Publishes 60 titles/year. Pays industry standard royalty. Pays advance.** Publishes book 1 year after acceptance of ms. Responds in 2 months to queries. Book catalog available free. Guidelines available online.

O→ Teachers College Press publishes a wide range of educational titles for all levels of students: early childhood to higher education. Publishing books that respond to, examine, and confront issues pertaining to education, teacher training, and school reform.

Nonfiction Subjects include computers, electronics, education, film, cinema, stage, government, politics, history, philosophy, sociology, womens issues, womens studies. Submit outline, sample chapters.
Recent Title(s) *Cultural Miseducation: In Search of a Democratic Solution*, by Jane Roland Martin.

N TEACHING & LEARNING CO.

1204 Buchanan St., P.O. Box 10, Carthage IL 62321-0010. (217)357-2591. Fax: (217)357-6789. E-mail: customerservice@teachinglearning.com. Website: www.teachinglearning.com. **Contact:** Jill Day, vice president of production. Estab. 1994. **Publishes 60 titles/year. 25 queries received/year. 200 mss received/year. 25% of books from first-time authors. 98% from unagented writers. Pays royalty.** Accepts simultaneous submissions. Responds in 3 months to queries. Responds in 9 months to proposals. Responds in 9 months to manuscripts. Book catalog and ms guidelines free.

O→ Teaching & Learning Co. publishes teacher resources (supplementary activity/idea books) for grades pre K-8. Currently emphasizing more math for all grade levels, more primary science material.

Nonfiction Subjects include art, architecture, education, language, literature, science, teacher resources in language arts, reading, math, science, social studies, arts and crafts, responsibility education. Submit table of contents, introduction, 3 sample chapters with SASE. Reviews artwork/photos. Send photocopies.
Recent Title(s) *Puzzle Paragraphs*, by Christine Boardman Moen; *Four Square Writing Methods (3 books)*, by Evan and Judith Gould; *Social Studies Fast Facts*, by Donna Borst and Mary Ellen Switzer.
Tips Our books are for teachers and parents of pre K-8th grade children.

N TEMPLE UNIVERSITY PRESS

1601 N. Broad St., USB 305, Philadelphia PA 19122-6099. (215)204-8787. Fax: (215)204-4719. E-mail: tempress@

temple.edu. Website: www.temple.edu/tempress/. **Contact:** Alex Holzman, director; Janet Francendese, editor-in-chief; Micah Kleit, executive editor; Mick Gusinde-Duffy, senior acquisitions editor. Estab. 1969. **Publishes 60 titles/year. Pays advance.** Publishes book 10 months after acceptance of ms. Responds in 2 months to queries. Book catalog available free. Guidelines available online.

- Temple University Press has been publishing path-breaking books on Asian-Americans, law, gender issues, film, women's studies and other interesting areas for nearly 40 years.

Nonfiction Subjects include ethnic, government, politics, health, medicine, history, photography, regional, Philadelphia, sociology, labor studies, urban studies, Latin American/Latino, Asian American, African American studies, public policy, women's studies. Query with SASE. Reviews artwork/photos.

Recent Title(s) *From Black Power to Hip Hop*, by Patricia Hill Collins; *The Story Is True*, by Bruce Jackson.

TEN SPEED PRESS

P.O. Box 7123-5, Berkeley CA 94707. (510)559-1600. Fax: (510)524-1052. E-mail: info@tenspeed.com. Website: www.tenspeed.com. Estab. 1971. Publishes trade paperback originals and reprints. **Publishes 120 titles/year. 40% of books from first-time authors. 40% from unagented writers. Pays $2,500 average advance.** Publishes book 1 year after acceptance of ms. Accepts simultaneous submissions. Responds in 3 months to queries. Book catalog for 9x12 envelope and 6 First-Class stamps. Guidelines available online.

Imprints Celestial Arts; Crossing Press; Tricycle Press.

- Ten Speed Press publishes authoritative books for an audience interested in innovative ideas. Currently emphasizing cookbooks, career, business, alternative education, and offbeat general nonfiction gift books.

Nonfiction Subjects include business, economics, child guidance, cooking, foods, nutrition, gardening, health, medicine, money, finance, nature, environment, New Age, mind/body/spirit, recreation, science. Query with SASE. Submit proposal package, sample chapters.

Recent Title(s) *How to Be Happy, Dammit*, by Karen Salmansohn; *The Bread Baker's Apprentice*, by Peter Reinhart.

Tips We like books from people who really know their subject, rather than people who think they've spotted a trend to capitalize on. We like books that will sell for a long time, rather than nine-day wonders. Our audience consists of a well-educated, slightly weird group of people who like food, the outdoors, and take a light, but serious, approach to business and careers. Study the backlist of each publisher you're submitting to and tailor your proposal to what you perceive as their needs. Nothing gets a publisher's attention like someone who knows what he or she is talking about, and nothing falls flat like someone who obviously has no idea who he or she is submitting to.

TEXAS A&M UNIVERSITY PRESS

College Station TX 77843-4354. (979)845-1436. Fax: (979)847-8752. E-mail: d-vance@tamu.edu. Website: www.tamu.edu/upress. **Contact:** Mary Lenn Dixon, editor-in-chief (presidential studies, anthropology, borderlands, western history); Shannon Davies, senior editor (natural history, agriculture). Estab. 1974. **Publishes 60 titles/year. Pays royalty.** Publishes book 1 year after acceptance of ms. Responds in 1 month to queries. Book catalog available free. Guidelines available online.

- Texas A&M University Press publishes a wide range of nonfiction, scholarly trade, and crossover books of regional and national interest, reflecting the interests of the university, the broader scholarly community, and the people of our state and region.

Nonfiction Subjects include agriculture, anthropology, archeology, art, architecture, history, American and Western, language, literature, Texas and western, military, war, nature, environment, regional, Texas and the Southwest, Mexican-US borderlands studies, nautical archaeology, ethnic studies, presidential studies. Nonreturnable queries; e-mail preferred.

Recent Title(s) *Finding Birds on the Great Texas Coastal Birding Trail*, by Ted Lee Eubanks, et al; *The History of Texas Music*, by Gary Hartman.

Tips Proposal requirements are posted on the website.

TILBURY HOUSE, PUBLISHERS

Imprint of Harpswell Press, Inc. 2 Mechanic St., Gardiner ME 04345. (207)582-1899. Fax: (207)582-8227. E-mail: tilbury@tilburyhouse.com. Website: www.tilburyhouse.com. **Contact:** Audrey Maynard, children's book editor. Estab. 1990. Publishes hardcover originals, trade paperback originals. **Publishes 10 titles/year. Pays royalty.** Book catalog available free. Guidelines available online.

Nonfiction Submit complete ms. Reviews artwork/photos. Send photocopies.

Recent Title(s) *Our Friendship Rules*, by Peggy Moss and Dee Dee Tardif; *Keep Your Ear on the Ball*, by Genevieve Petrillo.

TINYHORN

307 4th Ave. S., Minneapolis MN 55415. E-mail: blueghost999@hotmail.com. **Contact:** Marsha Braxton, managing editor. Estab. 2007. Publishes hardcover, trade paperback, and mass market paperback originals

and reprints. **Publishes 100 titles/year. 1,200 queries received/year. 400 mss received/year. 70% of books from first-time authors. 100% from unagented writers.** Publishes book 3-6 months after acceptance of ms. Responds in 2 weeks to queries. Responds in 1 month to manuscripts. Guidelines available online.

Nonfiction Subjects include alternative, animals, anthropology, archeology, art, architecture, business, economics, child guidance, community, computers, electronics, contemporary culture, cooking, foods, nutrition, creative nonfiction, education, ethnic, gardening, gay, lesbian, government, politics, health, medicine, history, hobbies, humanities, language, literature, literary criticism, memoirs, military, war, money, finance, music, dance, nature, environment, New Age, philosophy, psychology, recreation, regional, religion, science, sex, social sciences, sociology, spirituality, sports, travel, womens issues, womens studies, world affairs. Query with SASE. Submit complete ms. Only accept submissions through Web site.

Fiction Subjects include adventure, confession, erotica, ethnic, experimental, fantasy, feminist, gay, lesbian, gothic, historical, horror, humor, juvenile, literary, mainstream, contemporary, military, war, multicultural, multimedia, mystery, occult, plays, regional, religious, romance, science fiction, spiritual, sports, suspense, western, young adult. Submit complete ms. See Web site for submission me

Tips Although we accept unsolicited manuscripts, we have strict standards on the quality of writing we consider, getting a good edit before submitting can do wonders.

THE TOBY PRESS, LTD.

P.O. Box 8531, New Milford CT 06776-8531. Fax: (203)830-8512. Website: www.tobypress.com. **Contact:** Editorial Director (fiction, biography). Publishes hardcover originals and paperbacks. **Publishes 20-25 titles/year. over 2,000 queries received/year. 20% of books from first-time authors. 10% from unagented writers. Pays advance.** Publishes book up to 2 year after acceptance of ms. Accepts simultaneous submissions.

O→ The Toby Press publishes literary fiction.

Fiction Subjects include literary.

Recent Title(s) *Foiglman*, by Aharon Megged; *With*, by Donald Harington.

TODD PUBLICATIONS

P.O. Box 1752, Boca Raton FL 33429. (561)910-0440. E-mail: toddpub@aol.com. Website: www.toddpub.info. **Contact:** Barry Klein, president. Estab. 1973. Publishes reference books and trade paperback originals. **Publishes 10 titles/year. 10% of books from first-time authors. 100% from unagented writers.** Publishes book 3 months after acceptance of ms. Accepts simultaneous submissions. Responds in 1 month to proposals. Book listing available via e-mail.

O→ Todd Publications publishes/distributes reference books and directories of all types.

Nonfiction Subjects include ethnic, health, medicine & fitness. Submit 2 sample chapters.

Recent Title(s) *Aging: Quotations, Poetry, Resources & Bibliography; Wellness & Fitness: Quotations, Hints & Tips, Resources & Bibliography; Mail Order Business Directory*; *Guide to American & International Directories*; *Reference Encyclopedia of the American Indian*.

N TORQUERE PRESS

P.O. Box 2545, Round Rock TX 78680. (512)586-6921. Fax: (866)287-4860. E-mail: submissions@torquerepress.com. Website: www.torquerepress.com. **Contact:** Shawn Clements, submissions editor (homoerotica, suspense, gay/lesbian); Lorna Hivison, senior editor (gay/lesbian romance, historicals). Estab. 2003. Publishes trade paperback originals and electronic originals and reprints. **Publishes 140 titles/year. 500 queries received/year. 200 mss received/year. 25% of books from first-time authors. 100% from unagented writers. Pays 8-40% royalty.Pays $20-40 for anthology stories.** Publishes book 6 months after acceptance of ms. Responds in 1 month to queries. Responds in 1 month to proposals. Responds in 2 months to manuscripts. Book catalog available online. Guidelines available online.

Imprints Top Shelf (Shawn Clements, editor); Single Shots (Shawn Clements, editor); Screwdrivers (M. Rode, editor); High Balls (Alex Draven, editor).

Fiction Subjects include adventure, erotica, gay, lesbian, historical, horror, mainstream, contemporary, multicultural, mystery, occult, romance, science fiction, short story collections, suspense, western. We are a gay and lesbian press focusing on romance and genres of romance. We particularly like paranormal and western romance. Submit proposal package, 3 sample chapters, clips.

Recent Title(s) *Old Town New*, by B.A. Tortuga (contemporary romance); *Broken Road*, by Sean Michael (contemporary romance); *Soul Mates: Bound by Blood*, by Jourdan Lane (paranormal romance).

Tips Our audience is primarily people looking for a familiar romance setting featuring gay or lesbian protagonists. Please read guidelines carefully and familiarize yourself with our lines.

N TOWER PUBLISHING

588 Saco Rd., Standish ME 04084. (207)642-5400. Fax: (207)642-5463. E-mail: info@towerpub.com. Website: www.towerpub.com. **Contact:** Michael Lyons, president. Estab. 1772. Publishes hardcover originals and reprints, trade paperback originals. **Publishes 22 titles/year. 60 queries received/year. 30 mss received/year. 10% of books from first-time authors. 90% from unagented writers.** Publishes book 6 months after

acceptance of ms. Accepts simultaneous submissions. Responds in 1 month to queries. Responds in 2 months to proposals. Responds in 2 months to manuscripts. Book catalog and ms guidelines online.

O┳ Tower Publishing specializes in business and professional directories and legal books.

Nonfiction Subjects include business, economics. Query with SASE. Submit outline.

TRAFALGAR SQUARE BOOKS

P.O. Box 257, N. Pomfret VT 05053-0257. (802)457-1911. Fax: (802)457-1913. E-mail: tsquare@sover.net. Website: www.horseandriderbooks.com. **Contact:** Martha Cook, managing editor. Estab. 1985. Publishes hardcover and trade paperback originals and reprints. **Publishes 10 titles/year. Pays royalty. Pays advance.** Responds in 2 months to queries.

O┳ We publish high quality instructional books for horsemen and horsewomen, always with the horse's welfare in mind.

Nonfiction We publish books for intermediate to advanced riders and horsemen.Subjects include animals, horses. Query with SASE. Submit proposal package, outline, publishing history, 1-2 sample chapters, TOC, and audience for book's subject.

Recent Title(s) *The Rider's Pain-Free Back*, by James Warson; *Clinton Anderson's Down Under Horsemanship*, by Clinton Anderson; *The Ultimate Horse Behavior and Training Book*, by Linda Tellington-Jones.

TRAILS MEDIA GROUP, INC.

923 Williamson St., Madison WI 53703. (608)767-8100. Fax: (608)767-5444. E-mail: mknickelbine@bigearthpublishing.com. Website: www.trailsbooks.com. **Contact:** Mark Knickelbine, managing editor. Publishes hardcover originals, trade paperback originals, and reprints. **Publishes 12 titles/year. Pays royalty. Pays advance.** Responds in 2 months to proposals. Guidelines available online.

Imprints Trails Books; Prairie Oak Press.

- Follow online submission guidelines.

O┳ Trails Media Group publishes exclusively Midwest regional nonfiction. Currently emphasizing travel, sports, recreation, home and garden.

Nonfiction Any work considered must have a strong tie to Wisconsin and/or the Midwest region.Subjects include art, architecture, gardening, history, regional, sports, travel, folklore. Query with SASE. Submit outline, 1 sample chapter.

Recent Title(s) *Before They Were the Packers*, by Dennis J. Gullickson and Carl Hanson; *Great Wisconsin Romantic Weekends*, by Christine des Garennes; *Horsing Around in Wisconsin*, by Anne M. Connor.

Tips We publish works about Wisconsin, Minnesota, Illinois, Iowa, and Indiana.

TRANSNATIONAL PUBLISHERS, INC.

410 Saw Mill River Rd., Ardsley NY 10502. (914)693-5100. Fax: (914)693-4430. E-mail: info@transnationalpubs.com. Website: www.transnationalpubs.com. Estab. 1980. **Publishes 45-50 titles/year. 40-50 queries received/year. 30 mss received/year. 60% of books from first-time authors. 95% from unagented writers. Pays royalty.** Publishes book 6-9 months after acceptance of ms. Accepts simultaneous submissions. Responds in 1 month to queries. Book catalog and ms guidelines free.

O┳ We provide specialized international law publications for the teaching of law and law-related subjects in law school classroom, clinic, and continuing legal education settings. Currently emphasizing any area of international law that is considered a current issue/event.

Nonfiction Subjects include business, economics, government, politics, womens issues, womens studies, international law. Query with SASE. Submit proposal package, sample chapters, TOC, and introduction.

Recent Title(s) *The Jurisprudence on the Rights of the Child*, edited by Cynthia Price Cohen ( ); *The Legislative History of the International Criminal Court*, by M. Cherif Bassiouni ( ); *Humanitarian Intervention*, by Fernando Tesón ( ).

TRAVELERS' TALES

853 Alma St., Palo Alto CA 94301. (650)462-2110. Fax: (650)462-2114. E-mail: submit@travelerstales.com. Website: www.travelerstales.com. **Contact:** James O'Reilly and Larry Habegger, series editors; Sean O'Reilley, editor-at-large (sales/publicity). Publishes inspirational travel books, mostly anthologies and travel advice books. **Publishes 8-10 titles/year. Pays $100 honorarium for anthology pieces.** Accepts simultaneous submissions. Guidelines available online.

Imprints Travelers' Tales Guides; Footsteps; Travelers' Tales Classics.

- Due to the volume of submissions, we do not respond unless the material submitted meets our immediate editorial needs. All stories are read and filed for future use contingent upon meeting editorial guidelines.

Recent Title(s) *The Best Travelers' Tales 2004*; *Hyenas Laughed at Me and Now I Know Why*; *Who's Panties Are Those?*, (women & travel humor book).

Tips We publish personal nonfiction stories and anecdotes—funny, illuminating, adventurous, frightening, or grim. Stories should reflect that unique alchemy that occurs when you enter unfamiliar territory and begin to see the world differently as a result. Stories that have already been published, including book excerpts, are welcome as long as the authors retain the copyright or can obtain permission from the copyright holder to reprint the material. We do not publish fiction.

TRIUMPH BOOKS

542 Dearborn St., Suite 750, Chicago IL 60605. (312)939-3330. Fax: (312)663-3557. Website: www.triumphbooks.com. **Contact:** Tom Bast, editorial director. Estab. 1989. Publishes hardcover originals and trade paperback originals and reprints. Accepts simultaneous submissions. Book catalog available free.

Imprints Triumph Entertainment (pop culture, current events)

Nonfiction Subjects include recreation, sports, health, sports business/motivation. Query with SASE. Reviews artwork/photos. Send photocopies.

Recent Title(s) *It's Only Me: The Ted Williams We Hardly Knew*, by John Underwood; *For the Love of NASCAR*, by Michael Fresina; *Bobby Jones and the Quest for the Grand Slam*, by Catherine Lewis.

TRUMAN STATE UNIVERSITY PRESS

100 E. Normal St., Kirksville MO 63501-4221. (660)785-7336. Fax: (660)785-4480. E-mail: tsup@truman.edu. Website: tsup.truman.edu. **Contact:** Barbara Smith-Mandell (American studies, poetry); Michael Wolfe (early modern studies). **Publishes 13 titles/year.** Guidelines available online.

Recent Title(s) *Haunted Missouri*; *Reformation and Early Modern Europe: A Guide to Research.*

N A ⊘ TWENTY-FIRST CENTURY BOOKS

Imprint of Lerner Publishing Group 241 First Ave. N., Minneapolis MN 55401-1607. (612)332-3344. Fax: (612)332-7615. Website: www.lernerbooks.com. **Contact:** Editorial Department. Publishes hardcover originals.

O→ "We will continue to seek targeted solicitations at specific reading levels and in specific subject areas. The company will list these targeted solicitations on our website and in national newsletters, such as the SCBWI Bulletin."

Nonfiction Subjects include government, politics, health, medicine, history, military, war, nature, environment, science, current events.

Tips "To enhance the marketability of your manuscript, you may wish to consider several options: join a group that will help you learn about children's publishing, such as the SCBWI; form or join a critique group that focuses on constructive critiques; find an agent who can help to place your manuscript with the right publisher; and work with an editorial service to improve the quality of your manuscript before submitting it."

A ⊘ TYNDALE HOUSE PUBLISHERS, INC.

351 Executive Dr., Carol Stream IL 60188. (800)323-9400. Fax: (800)684-0247. Website: www.tyndale.com. **Contact:** Manuscript Review Committee. Estab. 1962. Publishes hardcover and trade paperback originals and mass paperback reprints. **Pays negotiable royalty. Pays negotiable advance.** Accepts simultaneous submissions. Guidelines for 9x12 SAE and $2.40 for postage or visit website.

O→ Tyndale House publishes practical, user-friendly Christian books for the home and family.

Nonfiction Subjects include child guidance, religion, devotional/inspirational.

Fiction Subjects include romance, Christian (children's, general, inspirational, mystery/suspense, thriller, romance). Christian truths must be woven into the story organically. No short story collections. Youth books: character building stories with Christian perspective. Especially interested in ages 10-14. We primarily publish Christian historical romances, with occasional contemporary, suspense, or standalones. Agented submissions only. *No unsolicited mss.*

Recent Title(s) *Danzig Passage*, by Bodie & Brock Thoene; *Croutons for Breakfast*, by Lissa Halls Johnson and Kathy Wierenga; *Stolen Secrets*, by Jerry B. Jenkins and Chris Fabry.

UNITY HOUSE

Unity 1901 N.W. Blue Pkwy., Unity Village MO 64065-0001. (816)524-3550. Fax: (816)347-5518. Website: www.unityonline.org. **Contact:** Sharon Sartin, exec. asst. Estab. 1889. Publishes hardcover, trade paperback, and electronic originals. **Publishes 5-7 titles/year. 50 queries. 5%% of books from first-time authors. 95%% from unagented writers. 10-15% royalty on retail price Pays advance.** Publishes book 5 months after acceptance of ms. Responds in 1 month to queries; 2months to proposals. Free on request & online at website: http://unityonline.org/publications/pdf/productcatalog.pdf. Guidelines available online, by e-mail, & free.

Imprints Unity House

O→ Unity House publishes metaphysical Christian books based on Unity principles, as well as inspirational books on metaphysics and practical spirituality. All manuscripts must reflect a spiritual foundation and express the Unity philosophy, practical Christianity, universal principles, and/or metaphysics.

Nonfiction Writers should be familiar with principles of metaphysical Christianity but not feel bound by them. We are interested in works in the related fields of holistic health, spiritual psychology, and the philosophy of other world religions.Subjects include religion, spirituality, metaphysics, New Thought. Submit proposal package, including: outline, 50 sample chapters. Yes, reviews artwork/photos. Writers should send photocopies.

Recent Title(s) *Sacred Secrets*, edited by Paula Godwin Goppel (anthology); *I of the Storm*, by Gary Simmons

(self-help/spirituality); *That's Just How My Spirit Travels*, by Rosemary Fillmore Rhea.
Tips We target an audience of spiritual seekers.

UNIVERSITY OF ALABAMA PRESS

Box 870380, Tuscaloosa AL 35487. (205)348-5180. Fax: (205)348-9201. Website: www.uapress.ua.edu. **Contact:** Daniel J.J. Ross, director (American history, Southern history and culture, American military history, American religious history, Latin American history, Jewish studies). Estab. 1945. Publishes nonfiction hardcover and paperbound originals, and fiction paperback reprints. **Publishes 70-75 titles/year. 70% of books from first-time authors. 95% from unagented writers. Pays advance.** Responds in 2 weeks to queries. Book catalog available free.
Nonfiction Subjects include anthropology, archeology, community, government, politics, history, language, literature, literary criticism, religion, translation. Query with SASE. Reviews artwork/photos.
Fiction Reprints of works by contemporary, Southern writers. Distributor of Fiction Collective 2 (FC@), avant garde fiction. Query with SASE.
Tips Please direct inquiry to appropriate acquisitions editor. University of Alabama Press responds to an author within 2 weeks upon receiving the ms. If they think it is unsuitable for Alabama's program, they tell the author at once. If the ms warrants it, they begin the peer-review process, which may take 2-4 months to complete. During that process, they keep the author fully informed.

UNIVERSITY OF ALASKA PRESS

P.O. Box 756240, Fairbanks AK 99775-6240. (907)474-5831 or (888)252-6657. Fax: (907)474-5502. E-mail: fypress@uaf.edu. Website: www.uaf.edu/uapress. Estab. 1967. Publishes hardcover originals, trade paperback originals and reprints. **Publishes 10 titles/year.** Publishes book within 2 years after acceptance of ms. Responds in 2 months to queries. Book catalog available free. Guidelines available online.
Imprints Classic Reprints; Oral Biographies; Rasmuson Library Historical Translation Series.

O→ The mission of the University of Alaska Press is to encourage, publish, and disseminate works of scholarship that will enhance the store of knowledge about Alaska and the North Pacific Rim, with a special emphasis on the circumpolar regions.

Nonfiction Subjects include Americana, Alaskana, animals, anthropology, archeology, art, architecture, education, ethnic, government, politics, health, medicine, history, language, literature, military, war, nature, environment, regional, science, translation, womens issues, womens studies. Query with SASE and proposal. Reviews artwork/photos.
Recent Title(s) *Gold Rush Grub*, by Ann Chandonnet; *Geology of Southeast Alaska*, by Harold Stowell; *Into Brown Bear Country*, by Will Troyer.
Tips Writers have the best chance with scholarly nonfiction relating to Alaska, the circumpolar regions and North Pacific Rim. Our audience is made up of scholars, historians, students, libraries, universities, individuals, and the general Alaskan public.

UNIVERSITY OF ARIZONA PRESS

355 S. Euclid Ave., Suite 103, Tucson AZ 85719. (520)621-1441. Fax: (520)621-8899. E-mail: uap@uapress.arizona.edu. Website: www.uapress.arizona.edu. **Contact:** Patti Hartmann, acquiring editor (humanities); Allyson Carter, acquiring editor (social sciences and science). Estab. 1959. Publishes hardcover and paperback originals and reprints. **Royalty terms vary; usual starting point for scholarly monography is after sale of first 1,000 copies. Pays advance.** Responds in 3 months to queries. Book catalog available via website or upon request. Guidelines available online.

O→ University of Arizona is a publisher of scholarly books and books of the Southwest.

Nonfiction Subjects include Americana, anthropology, archeology, ethnic, nature, environment, regional, environmental studies, western, and environmental history. Submit sample chapters, resume, TOC, ms length, audience, comparable books. Reviews artwork/photos.
Recent Title(s) *Elegy for Desire*, by Luis Omar Salinas; *In-Between Places*, by Diane Glancy; *Beyond Desert Walls: Essays from Prison*, by Ken Lamberton.
Tips Perhaps the most common mistake a writer might make is to offer a book manuscript or proposal to a house whose list he or she has not studied carefully. Editors rejoice in receiving material that is clearly targeted to the house's list ('I have approached your firm because my books complement your past publications in .') and presented in a straightforward, businesslike manner.

THE UNIVERSITY OF ARKANSAS PRESS

201 Ozark Ave., Fayetteville AR 72701-1201. (479)575-3246. Fax: (479)575-6044. E-mail: uapress@uark.edu. Website: www.uapress.com. **Contact:** Lawrence J. Malley, director and editor-in-chief. Estab. 1980. Publishes hardcover and trade paperback originals and reprints. **Publishes 30 titles/year. 30% of books from first-time authors. 95% from unagented writers.** Publishes book 1 year after acceptance of ms. Responds in 3 months to proposals. Book catalog and ms guidelines on website or on request.

O→ The University of Arkansas Press publishes series on Ozark studies, the Civil War in the West, poetry and poetics, and sport and society.

Nonfiction Subjects include government, politics, history, Southern, humanities, literary criticism, nature, environment, regional, Arkansas. Query with SASE. Submit outline, sample chapters, resume. cv.

Recent Title(s) *Reading With Oprah*, by Kathleen Rooney; *Looking Back to See*, by Maxine Brown; *Chattahoochee*, by Patrick Phillips.

UNIVERSITY OF CALIFORNIA PRESS

2120 Berkeley Way, Berkeley CA 94720-1012. (510)642-4247. Fax: (510)643-7127. E-mail: askucp@ucpress.edu. Website: www.ucpress.edu. **Contact:** Lynne Withey (public health); Reed Malcolm (religion, politics, Asian studies); Niels Hooper (history); Deborah Kirshman (museum copublications); Sheila Levine (food, regional); Jenny Wapner (natural history, organismal biology); Naomi Schneider (sociology, politics, anthropology, Latin American studies); Blake Edgar (biology, archaeology, viticulture & enology); Stephanie Fay (art); Stan Holwitz (anthropology, public health, Jewish studies); Laura Cerruti (literature, poetry, classics); Mary Francis (music, film); Chuck Crumly (evolution, environment, ecology, biology). Estab. 1893. Publishes hardcover and paperback originals and reprints. **Pays advance.** Response time varies, depending on the subject Enclose return postage to queries. Guidelines available online.

O- University of California Press publishes mostly nonfiction written by scholars.

Nonfiction Subjects include history, nature, environment, translation, art, literature, natural sciences, some high-level popularizations. Submit sample chapters, letter of introduction, cv, TOC.

Fiction Publishes fiction only in translation.

Recent Title(s) *William Dean Howells: A Writer's Life*, by Susan Goodman and Carl Dawson; *A History of Wine in America: From Prohibition to the Present*, by Thomas Pinney; *Biology of Gila Monsters and Beaded Lizards*, by Daniel Beck.

UNIVERSITY OF GEORGIA PRESS

330 Research Dr., Athens GA 30602-4901. (706)369-6130. Fax: (706)369-6131. E-mail: books@ugapress.uga.edu. Website: www.ugapress.org. Estab. 1938. Publishes hardcover originals, trade paperback originals, and reprints. **Publishes 85 titles/year. Pays rare, varying advance.** Publishes book 1 year after acceptance of ms. Responds in 2 months to queries. Book catalog and ms guidelines for #10 SASE or online.

Nonfiction Subjects include government, politics, history, American, nature, environment, regional, environmental studies, literary nonfiction. Query with SASE. Submit bio, 1 sample chapter. Reviews artwork/photos. Send Send if essential to book.

Fiction Short story collections published in Flannery O'Connor Award Competition. Query #1 SASE for guidelines

Recent Title(s) *Equiano, the African: Biography of a Self-Made Man*, by Vincent Carretta; *The Civil Rights Movement in American Memory*, edited by Renee Romano and Leigh Raiford; *Sabbath Creole*, by Juddun Mitcham.

UNIVERSITY OF ILLINOIS PRESS

1325 S. Oak St., Champaign IL 61820-6903. (217)333-0950. Fax: (217)244-8082. E-mail: uipress@uillinois.edu. Website: www.press.uillinois.edu. **Contact:** Willis Regier, director (literature, classics, classical music, sports history); Joan Catapano, associate director and editor-in-chief (women's studies, film, African-American studies); Laurie Matheson (American history, labor history, American music, American studies). Estab. 1918. Publishes hardcover and trade paperback originals and reprints. **Publishes 150 titles/year. 35% of books from first-time authors. 95% from unagented writers. Pays $1,000-1,500 (rarely) advance.** Publishes book 1 year after acceptance of ms. Responds in 1 month to queries. Book catalog for 9x12 envelope and 2 First-Class stamps. Guidelines available online.

O- University of Illinois Press publishes scholarly books and serious nonfiction with a wide range of study interests. Currently emphasizing American history, especially immigration, labor, African-American, and military; American religion, music, women's studies, and film.

Nonfiction Subjects include Americana, animals, cooking, foods, nutrition, government, politics, history, especially American history, language, literature, military, war, music, dance, especially American music, dance, philosophy, regional, sociology, sports, translation, film/cinema/stage. Query with SASE. Submit outline.

Recent Title(s) *Philosophical Writings*, by Simone de Beauvoir (philosophy); *Women for President: Media Bias in Eight Campaigns*, by Erica Falk; *Herndon's Lincoln*, edited by Douglas L. Wilson and Rodney D. Davis.

Tips As a university press, we are required to submit all manuscripts to rigorous scholarly review. Manuscripts need to be clearly original, well written, and based on solid and thorough research. We cannot encourage memoirs or autobiographies.

UNIVERSITY OF IOWA PRESS

100 Kuhl House, Iowa City IA 52242-1000. (319)335-2000. Fax: (319)335-2055. Website: www.uiowapress.org. **Contact:** Holly Carver, director; Joseph Parsons, acquisitions editor. Estab. 1969. Publishes hardcover and paperback originals. **Publishes 35 titles/year. 30% of books from first-time authors. 95% from unagented**

writers. Publishes book 1 year after acceptance of ms. Responds in 6 months to queries. Book catalog available free. Guidelines available online.

O→ "We publish authoritative, original nonfiction that we market mostly by direct mail to groups with special interests in our titles, and by advertising in trade and scholarly publications."

Nonfiction Subjects include anthropology, archeology, creative nonfiction, history, regional, language, literature, nature, environment, American literary studies, medicine and literature. Query with SASE. Submit outline. Reviews artwork/photos.

Fiction Currently publishes the Iowa Short Fiction Award selections. Competition guidelines available.

Recent Title(s) *First We Read, Then We Write: Emerson on the Creative Process*, by Robert D. Richardson.

UNIVERSITY OF MISSOURI PRESS

2910 LeMone Blvd., Columbia MO 65201. (573)882-7641. Fax: (573)884-4498. Website: http://press.umsystems.edu. **Contact:** (Mr.) Clair Willcox. Estab. 1958. Publishes hardcover and paperback originals and paperback reprints. **Publishes 65 titles/year. 40-50% of books from first-time authors. 90% from unagented writers.** Publishes book within 1 year after acceptance of ms. Responds immediately to queries. Responds in 3 months to manuscripts. Book catalog available free. Guidelines available online.

O→ University of Missouri Press publishes primarily scholarly nonfiction in the humanities and social sciences. Currently emphasizing American history, political philosophy, literary criticism, African-American studies, women's studies.

Nonfiction Subjects include history, American, literary criticism, regional, studies of Missouri and the Midwest, social sciences, womens issues, womens studies, political philosophy, African-American studies. Query with SASE. Submit outline, sample chapters.

Recent Title(s) *High-Flying Birds*, by Jerome M. Mileur; *More Than a Farmer's Wife*, Amy Mattson Lauters.

UNIVERSITY OF NEBRASKA PRESS

1111 Lincoln Mall, Lincoln NE 68588-0630. (800)755-1105. Fax: (402)472-6214. E-mail: pressmail@unl.edu. Website: nebraskapress.unl.edu. **Contact:** Ladette Randolph, associate director for development. Publishes hardcover and trade paperback originals and trade paperback reprints. Book catalog available free. Guidelines available online.

Imprints Bison Books (paperback reprints of classic books).

O→ We primarily publish nonfiction books and scholarly journals, along with a few titles per season in contemporary and regional prose and poetry. On occasion, we reprint previously published fiction of established reputation, and we have several programs to publish literary works in translation.

Nonfiction Subjects include agriculture, animals, anthropology, archeology, creative nonfiction, history, memoirs, military, war, multicultural, nature, environment, religion, sports, translation, womens issues, womens studies, Native American studies, American Lives series, experimental fiction by American-Indian writers. Submit book proposal with overview, audience, format, detailed chapter outline, sample chapters, sample bibliography, timetable, CV.

Fiction Series and translation only. Occasionaly reprints fiction of established reputation.

Recent Title(s) *Mad Seasons*, by Karra Porter; *The Broidered Garment* , by Hilda Martinsen Neihardt; *New Perspectives on Native North America*, by Sergei A. Kan and Pauline Turner Strong.

UNIVERSITY OF NEVADA PRESS

Morrill Hall, Mail Stop 0166, Reno NV 89557. (775)784-6573. Fax: (775)784-6200. Website: www.unpress.nevada.edu. **Contact:** Joanne O'Hare, director. Estab. 1961. Publishes hardcover and paperback originals and reprints. **Publishes 25 titles/year.** Guidelines available online.

Nonfiction Subjects include anthropology, archeology, ethnic, studies, history, regional and natural, nature, environment, regional, history and geography, western literature, current affairs, gambling and gaming, Basque studies. Submit proposal. No online submissions. Reviews artwork/photos. Send photocopies.

Fiction Submit proposal package, outline, clips, 2-4 sample chapters.

UNIVERSITY OF NEW MEXICO PRESS

1312 Baschart Rd. SE, Albuquerque NM 87106. (505)277-2346 or (800)249-7737. E-mail: unmpress@unm.edu. Website: www.unmpress.com. **Contact:** Maya Allen-Gallegos, managing editor; W. Clark Whitehorn, editor-in-chief; Lisa S. Pacheco, editor. Estab. 1929. Publishes hardcover originals and trade paperback originals and reprints. **Pays variable royalty. Pays advance.** Book catalog available free. Guidelines available online.

O→ The Press is well known as a publisher in the fields of anthropology, archeology, Latin American studies, photography, architecture and the history and culture of the American West, fiction, some poetry, Chicano/a studies and works by and about American Indians. We focus on American West, Southwest and Latin American regions.

Nonfiction Subjects include Americana, anthropology, archeology, art, architecture, creative nonfiction, ethnic, gardening, gay, lesbian, government, politics, history, language, literature, memoirs, military, war, multicultural, music, dance, nature, environment, photography, regional, religion, science, translation, travel,

womens issues, womens studies, contemporary culture, cinema/stage, true crime, general nonfiction. Query with SASE. Reviews artwork/photos. Send photocopies.
Recent Title(s) *Jemez Spring*, by Rudolfo Anaya; *The Cherokee Nation*, by Robert J. Conley; *Blood of Our Earth*, by Dan C. Jones.

THE UNIVERSITY OF NORTH CAROLINA PRESS

116 S. Boundary St., Chapel Hill NC 27514. (919)966-3561. Fax: (919)966-3829. E-mail: uncpress@unc.edu. Website: www.uncpress.unc.edu. **Contact:** David Perry, editor-in-chief (regional trade, Civil War); Charles Grench, senior editor (American history, European history, law and legal studies, business and economic history, classics, political or social science); Elaine Maisner, senior editor (Latin American studies, religious studies, anthropology, regional trade, folklore); Sian Hunter, senior editor (literary studies, gender studies, American studies, African American studies, social medicine, Appalachian studies, media studies); Mark Simpson-Vos, associate editor (electronic publishing and special projects, American-Indian studies). Publishes hardcover originals, trade paperback originals and reprints. **Publishes 90 titles/year. 500 queries received/ year. 200 mss received/year. 50% of books from first-time authors. 90% from unagented writers. Pays variable royalty on wholesale price. Offers variable advance.** Publishes book 1 year after acceptance of ms. Responds in 3-4 weeks to queries. Responds in 3-4 weeks to proposals. Responds in 2 weeks to manuscripts. Book catalog free or on website. Guidelines available online.

- UNC Press publishes nonfiction books for academic and general audiences. We have a special interest in trade and scholarly titles about our region. We do not, however, publish original fiction, drama, or poetry, memoirs of living persons, or festshriften.

Nonfiction Subjects include Americana, anthropology, archeology, art, architecture, cooking, foods, nutrition, gardening, government, politics, health, medicine, history, language, literature, military, war, multicultural, music, dance, nature, environment, philosophy, photography, regional, religion, translation, womens issues, womens studies, African-American studies, American studies, cultural studies, Latin-American studies, American-Indian studies, media studies, gender studies, social medicine, Appalachian studies. Submit proposal package, outline, CV, cover letter, abstract, and TOC. Reviews artwork/photos. Send photocopies.

UNIVERSITY OF NORTH TEXAS PRESS

1155 Union Circle, #311336, Denton TX 76203-5017. (940)565-2142. E-mail: Ronald.Chrisman@unt.edu; Karen.DeVinney@unt.edu. **Contact:** Ronald Chrisman, director; Karen DeVinney, managing editor. Estab. 1987. Publishes hardcover and trade paperback originals and reprints. **Publishes 14-16 titles/year. 500 queries received/year. 50% of books from first-time authors. 95% from unagented writers.** Publishes book 1-2 years after acceptance of ms. Responds in 1 month to queries. Book catalog for 8 ½x11 SASE. Guidelines available online.

- We are dedicated to producing the highest quality scholarly, academic, and general interest books. We are committed to serving all peoples by publishing stories of their cultures and experiences that have been overlooked. Currently emphasizing military history, Texas history and literature, music, Mexican-American studies.

Nonfiction Subjects include Americana, ethnic, government, politics, history, music, dance, biography, military, war, nature, regional, womens issues/studies. Query with SASE. Reviews artwork/photos. Send photocopies.
Fiction The only fiction we publish is the winner of the Katherine Anne Porter Prize in Short Fiction, an annual, national competition with a $1,000 prize, and publication of the winning manuscript each Fall.
Tips We publish series called War and the Southwest; Texas Folklore Society Publications; the Western Life Series; Practical Guide Series; Al-Filo: Mexican-American studies; North Texas Crime and Criminal Justice; Katherine Anne Porter Prize in Short Fiction; and the North Texas Lives of Musicians Series.

UNIVERSITY OF OKLAHOMA PRESS

2800 Venture Dr., Norman OK 73069. E-mail: cerankin@ou.edu. Website: www.oupress.com. **Contact:** Charles E. Rankin, editor-in-chief. Estab. 1928. Publishes hardcover and paperback originals and reprints. **Publishes 90 titles/year. Pays standard royalty.** Responds promptly to queries. Book catalog for 9x12 SAE with 6 first-class stamps.
Imprints Plains Reprints.

- University of Oklahoma Press publishes books for both scholarly and nonspecialist readers.

Nonfiction Query with SASE. Submit outline, resume, 1-2 sample chapters. Use *Chicago Manual of Style* for ms guidelines. Reviews artwork/photos.
Recent Title(s) *Full Court Quest: The Girls From Fort Shaw Indian School, Basketball Champions of the World*, by Linda Peavy, Ursula Smith (history); *The West of the Imagination, 2nd ed.*, by William H. Goetzmann and William N. Goetzmann (art history); *Plains Apache Ethobotony*, by Julia A. Jordan (Indian studies and natural history).

UNIVERSITY OF PENNSYLVANIA PRESS

3905 Spruce St., Philadelphia PA 19104. (215)898-6261. Fax: (215)898-0404. Website: www.pennpress.org.

Contact: Jerome Singerman, humanities editor; Peter Agree, editor-in-chief and social sciences editor; Jo Joslyn, art and architecture editor; Robert Lockhart, history editor; Bill Finan, politics, international relations.". Estab. 1890. Publishes hardcover and paperback originals, and reprints. **Publishes 100+ titles/year. 20-30% of books from first-time authors. 95% from unagented writers. Royalty determined on book-by-book basis. Pays advance.** Publishes book 10 months after delivery of ms after acceptance of ms. Responds in 3 months to queries. Book catalog available online. Guidelines available online.

Nonfiction "Serious books that serve the scholar and the professional, student and general reader."Subjects include Americana, art, architecture, history, American, art, architecture, literary criticism, sociology, anthropology, literary criticism, cultural studies, ancient studies, medieval studies, urban studies, human rights. Query with SASE. Submit outline, resume. Reviews artwork/photos. Send photocopies.

UNIVERSITY OF SOUTH CAROLINA PRESS

1600 Hampton St., 5th Floor, Columbia SC 29208. (803)777-5243. Fax: (803)777-0160. Website: www.sc.edu/uscpress. **Contact:** Linda Fogle, assistant director for operations (trade books); Jim Denton, acquisitions editor (literature, religious studies, rhetoric, communication, social work); Alexander Moore, acquisitions editor (history, regional studies). Estab. 1944. Publishes hardcover originals, trade paperback originals and reprints. **Publishes 50 titles/year. 500 queries received/year. 150 mss received/year. 30% of books from first-time authors. 95% from unagented writers.** Publishes book 1 year after acceptance of ms. Accepts simultaneous submissions. Responds in 3 months to manuscripts. Book catalog available free. Guidelines available online.

O‑ We focus on scholarly monographs and regional trade books of lasting merit.

Nonfiction Subjects include art, architecture, history, American, Civil War, culinary, maritime, womens, language, literature, regional, religion, rhetoric, communication. Query with SASE, or submit proposal package and outline, and 1 sample chapter and resume with SASE Reviews artwork/photos. Send photocopies.

Recent Title(s) *Mary Black's Family Quilts*, by Laurel Horton; *Sons of Privilege*, by W. Eric Emerson; *Jesus in the Mist: Stories*, by Paul Ruffin.

N UNIVERSITY OF TAMPA PRESS

University of Tampa, 401 W. Kennedy Blvd., Box 19F, Tampa FL 33606-1490. (813)253-6266. Fax: (813)258-7593. E-mail: utpress@ut.edu. Website: utpress.ut.edu/. **Contact:** Donald Morrill, editor (Poetry); Elizabeth Winston, editor (Nonfiction). hardcover originals and reprints; trade paperback originals and reprints. Responds in 3-4 months to queries. Book catalog available online.

Nonfiction Subjects include history, literary criticism, memoirs, military, war, photography, translation. Reviews artwork/photos.

Fiction Subjects include occult, plays, poetry.

Recent Title(s) *The Pinter Review*, ((collected essays)); *Studies in the Fantastic (No. 1)*, edited by S. T. Joshi; *Calenture*, by Kent Shaw ((poems)).

Tips We do not print book-length poetry (except through the annual Tampa Review Prize for Poetry), and rarely publish excerpts. We accept only paper mss. No email or handwritten submissions. Submit between Sept. 1 and Dec. 31.

N THE UNIVERSITY OF TENNESSEE PRESS

110 Conference Center, Knoxville TN 37996. (865)974-3321. Fax: (865)974-3724. Website: www.utpress.org. **Contact:** Scot Danforth, acquisitions editor (scholarly books); Jennifer Siler, director (regional trades, fiction). Estab. 1940. **Publishes 35 titles/year. 35% of books from first-time authors. 99% from unagented writers. Pays negotiable royalty on net receipts.** Book catalog for 12X16 envelope and 2 First-Class stamps. Guidelines available online.

O‑ Our mission is to stimulate scientific and scholarly research in all fields; to channel such studies, either in scholarly or popular form, to a larger number of people; and to extend the regional leadership of the University of Tennessee by stimulating research projects within the South and by nonuniversity authors.

Nonfiction Subjects include Americana, anthropology, archeology, historical, art, architecture, vernacular, history, language, literature, literary criticism, regional, religion, history sociology, anthropology, archeology, biography only, womens issues, womens studies, African-American studies, Appalachian studies, folklore/folklife, material culture. Submit outline, bio, 2 sample chapters. Reviews artwork/photos.

Fiction Query with SASE. Submit clips, bio.

Recent Title(s) *Dictionary of Smoky Mountain English*, by Michael B. Montgomery and Joseph S. Hall.

Tips Our market is in several groups: scholars; educated readers with special interests in given scholarly subjects; and the general educated public interested in Tennessee, Appalachia, and the South. Not all our books appeal to all these groups, of course, but any given book must appeal to at least one of them.

UNIVERSITY OF TEXAS PRESS

P.O. Box 7819, Austin TX 78713-7819. (512)471-4278, ext. 3. Fax: (512)232-7178. E-mail: utpress@uts.cc.utexas.edu. Website: www.utexaspress.com. **Contact:** Theresa May, assistant director/editor-in-chief (social sciences,

Latin American studies); James Burr, sponsoring editor (humanities, classics); William Bishel, sponsoring editor (natural sciences, Texas history); Allison Faust, sponsoring editor (Texana, geography, art, music). Estab. 1952. **Publishes 90 titles/year. 50% of books from first-time authors. 99% from unagented writers. Pays occasional advance.** Publishes book 18-24 months after acceptance of ms. Responds in 3 months to queries. Book catalog available free. Guidelines available online.

- In addition to publishing the results of advanced research for scholars worldwide, UT Press has a special obligation to the people of its state to publish authoritative books on Texas. We do not publish fiction or poetry, except as invited by a series editor, and some Latin American and Middle Eastern literature in translation.

Nonfiction Subjects include anthropology, archeology, art, architecture, ethnic, film, cinema, stage, history, language, literature, literary criticism, nature, environment, regional, science, translation, womens issues, womens studies, natural history, American, Latin American, Native American, Latino, and Middle Eastern studies; classics and the ancient world, film, contemporary regional architecture, geography, ornithology, biology. Query with SASE. Submit outline, 2 sample chapters. Reviews artwork/photos.

Fiction Query with SASE. Submit outline, 2 sample chapters.

Recent Title(s) *The Memory of Bones*, by Houston; *Who Guards the Guardians and How*, by Bruneau; *Women Embracing Islam*, edited by van Nieuwkerk.

Tips It's difficult to make a manuscript over 400 double-spaced pages into a feasible book. Authors should take special care to edit out extraneous material. We look for sharply focused, in-depth treatments of important topics.

N UNIVERSITY OF WASHINGTON PRESS

P.O. Box 50096, Seattle WA 98145-5096. (206)543-4050. Fax: (206)543-3932. E-mail: uwpress@u.washington.edu. Website: www.washington.edu/uwpress/. **Contact:** Marianne Keddington-Lang (Western History, Environmental and Native American Studies). Hardcover originals. **Publishes 70 titles/year.** Book catalog available online.

Nonfiction Subjects include anthropology, archeology, art, architecture, ethnic, Groups in China, history, Western, multicultural, nature, environment, photography, regional, social sciences. Query with SASE. Submit proposal package, outline, sample chapters.

Recent Title(s) *Do Glaciers Listen? Local Knowledge, Colonial Encounters, and Social Imagination*, by Julie Cruikshank; *Making Mountains: New York City and the Catskills*, by David Stradling; *Road to Freedom*, by Julian Cox (Photographs of the Civil Rights Movement 1956-1968).

Tips From the beginning the Press h The Online Guide for authors a

UNIVERSITY PRESS OF COLORADO

5589 Arapahoe, Suite 206C, Boulder CO 80303. (720)406-8849. Fax: (720)406-3443. **Contact:** Darrin Pratt, editor. Estab. 1965. Publishes hardcover and paperback originals. **Publishes 25-30 titles/year. 50% of books from first-time authors. 95% from unagented writers. Pays advance.** Publishes book within 2 years after acceptance of ms. Accepts simultaneous submissions. Responds in 6 months to queries. Book catalog available free.

- "We are a university press that publishes scholarly nonfiction in the disciplines of the American West, Native-American studies, archeology, environmental studies, and regional-interest titles. Currently de-emphasizing fiction, poetry, biography."

Nonfiction Subjects include nature, environment, regional. Query with SASE. Reviews artwork/photos.

Recent Title(s) *A Remarkable Curiosity: Dispatches From a New York City Journalist's 1873 Railroad Trip Across the American West*, by Amos Jay Cummings, compiled and edited by Jerald T. Milanich; *The Geysers of Yellowstone*, 4th edition, by T. Scott Bryan; *Japanese American Resettlement Through the Lens*, by Lane Ryo Hrabayashi with Kenichiro Shimada.

Tips "We have series on mining history and on Mesoamerican worlds."

UNIVERSITY PRESS OF KANSAS

2502 Westbrooke Circle, Lawrence KS 66045-4444. (785)864-4154. Fax: (785)864-4586. E-mail: upress@ku.edu. Website: www.kansaspress.ku.edu. **Contact:** Michael J. Briggs, editor-in-chief (military history, political science, law); Kalyani Fernando, acquisitions editor (western history, American studies, environmental studies, women's studies); Fred M. Woodward, director, (political science, presidency, regional). Estab. 1946. Publishes hardcover originals, trade paperback originals and reprints. **Publishes 55 titles/year. 600 queries received/year. 20% of books from first-time authors. 98% from unagented writers. Pays selective advance.** Publishes book 10 months after acceptance of ms. Responds in 1 month to proposals. Book catalog and ms guidelines free.

- The University Press of Kansas publishes scholarly books that advance knowledge and regional books that contribute to the understanding of Kansas, the Great Plains, and the Midwest.

Nonfiction Subjects include Americana, anthropology, archeology, government, politics, history, military, war, nature, environment, regional, sociology, womens issues, womens studies. Submit outline, sample chapters, cover letter, cv, prospectus. Reviews artwork/photos. Send photocopies.

Recent Title(s) *The Supreme Court*, by Peter Charles Hoffer, William James Hull Hoffer, & N.E.H. Hull; *The Liberals' Moment*, by Bruce Miroff; *Death of the Wehrmacht*, by Robert M. Citino.

UNIVERSITY PRESS OF KENTUCKY

663 S. Limestone St., Lexington KY 40508-4008. (859)257-8434. Fax: (859)323-1873. Website: www.kentuckypress.com. **Contact:** Joyce Harrison, editor-in-chief. Estab. 1943. Publishes hardcover and paperback originals and reprints. **Publishes 60 titles/year. Royalty varies.** Publishes book 1 year after acceptance of ms. Responds in 2 months to queries. Book catalog available free. Guidelines available online.

- We are a scholarly publisher, publishing chiefly for an academic and professional audience, as well as books about Kentucky, the upper South, Appalachia, and the Ohio Valley.

Nonfiction Subjects include history, military, war, history, regional, political science. Query with SASE.

UNIVERSITY PRESS OF MISSISSIPPI

3825 Ridgewood Rd., Jackson MS 39211-6492. (601)432-6205. Fax: (601)432-6217. E-mail: press@ihl.state.ms.us. Website: www.upress.state.ms.us. **Contact:** Craig Gill, editor-in-chief (regional studies, art, folklore). Estab. 1970. Publishes hardcover and paperback originals and reprints. **Publishes 60 titles/year. 20% of books from first-time authors. 90% from unagented writers. Competitive royalties and terms Pays advance.** Publishes book 1 year after acceptance of ms. Responds in 3 months to queries.

- University Press of Mississippi publishes scholarly and trade titles, as well as special series, including: American Made Music; Conversations with Comic Artists; Conversations with Filmmakers; Faulkner and Yoknapatawpha; Literary Conversations; Studies in Popular Culture; Hollywood Legends; Understanding Health and Sickness.

Nonfiction Subjects include Americana, art, architecture, ethnic, minority studies, government, politics, health, medicine, history, language, literature, literary criticism, music, dance, photography, regional, Southern, folklife, literary criticism, popular culture with scholarly emphasis, literary studies. Submit outline, sample chapters, cv.

Recent Title(s) *Anne McCaffrey: A Life With Dragons*, by Robin Roberts; *Roots of a Region: Southern Folk Culture*, by John A. Burrison.

[N] UNLIMITED PUBLISHING LLC

P.O. Box 3007, Bloomington IN 47402. E-mail: info@unlimitedpublishing.com. Website: www.unlimitedpublishing.com. **Contact:** Acquisitions Manager (short nonfiction with a clear audience). **Publishes 25-50 titles/year. Receives 1,000 queries/year; 500 manuscripts/year. 10% of books from first-time authors. 10% from unagented writers.** Publishes book 3 months after acceptance of ms. Catalog online at website http://unlimitedpublishing.com/sitemap.htm.

Imprints Harvardwood Books.

- "We prefer short nonfiction and fiction with a clear audience, and expect authors to be actively involved in publicity. A detailed marketing plan is required with all submissions. Moderate to good computer skills are necessary."

Nonfiction Subjects include agriculture, alternative lifestyles, Americana, animals, anthropology, archaeology, architecture, art, business, career guidance, child guidance, communications, community, computers, contemporary culture, counseling, crafts, creative nonfiction, economics, education, electronics, environment, ethnic, finance, gardening, gay, government, health, history, hobbies, horticulture, humanities, labor, language, law, lesbian, literary criticism, literature, marine subjects, medicine, memoirs, military, money, multicultural, music, nature, parenting, philosophy, politics, psychology, real estate, recreation, regional, religion, science, sex, social sciences, sociology, software, sports, translation, transportation, travel, women's issues, women's studies, world affairs, young adult. Submit proposal package, including: outline and 10-page excerpt in Microsoft Word format, author bio and detailed marketing plan.

Fiction Subjects include adventure, ethnic, experimental, fantasy, feminist, historical, horror, humor, juvenile, literary, mainstream, contemporary, military, war, multicultural, mystery, occult, regional, religious, science fiction fiction, short story collections story collections, spiritual, sports, suspense, translation, war, western, young adult adult. Submit proposal package, including: outline and 10-page excerpt in Microsoft Word format, author bio and detailed marketing plan.

Recent Title(s) *Anything But a Dog! The perfect pet for a girl with congenital CMV (cytomegalovirus)*, by Lisa Saunders (biography-memoir, inspirational, health); *Beijing Journal: A Live, Day-by-Day Account from Backstage at the 2008 Olympics*, by Mark Butler (sports, travel, bio); *The Site*, by Andrew Dawber (adventure, thriller, men's fiction).

Tips "The growth of online bookselling allows authors and publishers to jointly cultivate a tightly targeted grassroots audience in specialty or niche markets before expanding to mainstream book industry channels based on proven public demand."

THE URBAN LAND INSTITUTE

1025 Thomas Jefferson St. NW, Washington DC 20007-5201. (202)624-7000. Fax: (202)624-7140. Website: www.uli.org. **Contact:** Rachelle Levitt, executive vice president/publisher. Estab. 1936. Publishes hardcover and trade paperback originals. **Publishes 15-20 titles/year. 2% of books from first-time authors. 100% from unagented writers. Pays 10% royalty on gross sales.** Publishes book 6 months after acceptance of ms. Book catalog and ms guidelines via website or 9x12 SAE.

"The Urban Land Institute publishes technical books on real estate development and land planning."

Nonfiction Subjects include money, finance, design and development. Query with SASE. Reviews artwork/photos.

Recent Title(s) *Urban Design and the Bottom Line, Getting Real About Urbanism.*

N URJ PRESS

633 Third Ave., New York NY 10017-6778. (212)650-4120. Fax: (212)650-4119. E-mail: press@urj.org. Website: www.urjpress.com. **Contact:** Rabbi Hara Person, editor (subjects related to Judaism). Publishes hardcover and trade paperback originals. **Publishes 22 titles/year. 500 queries received/year. 400 mss received/year. 70% of books from first-time authors. 90% from unagented writers. Pays 3-5% royalty on retail price. Makes outright purchase of 500-2,000. Pays $500-2,000 advance.** Publishes book 9 months after acceptance of ms. Responds in 2 months to queries. Responds in 6 months to proposals. Responds in 6 months to manuscripts. Book catalog and ms guidelines free or on website.

URJ Press publishes books related to Judaism.

Nonfiction Subjects include art, architecture, synagogue, child guidance, Jewish, cooking, foods, nutrition, Jewish, education, Jewish, ethnic, Judaism, government, politics, Israeli/Jewish, history, Jewish, language, literature, Hebrew, military, war, as relates to Judaism, music, dance, nature, environment, philosophy, Jewish, religion, Judaism only, sex, as it relates to Judaism, spirituality, Jewish. Submit proposal package, outline, bio, 1-2 sample chapters.

Fiction Jewish, liberal content. Picture book length only.Subjects include juvenile, children's picture books. Submit complete ms with author

Recent Title(s) *Talmud for Everyday Living: Employer-Employee Relations*, by Hillel Gamoran (nonfiction); *The Gift of Wisdom*, by Steven E. Steinbock (textbook for grades 5-7); *Solomon and the Trees*, by Matt Biers-Ariel (picture book).

Tips Look at some of our books. Have an understanding of the Reform Judaism community. In addition to bookstores, we sell to Jewish congregations and Hebrew day schools.

UTAH STATE UNIVERSITY PRESS

7800 Old Main Hill, Logan UT 84322-7800. (435)797-1362. Fax: (435)797-0313. Website: www.usu.edu/usupress. **Contact:** Michael Spooner, director (composition, poetry); John Alley, editor (history, folklore, fiction. Estab. 1972. Publishes hardcover and trade paperback originals and reprints. **Publishes 18 titles/year. 8% of books from first-time authors.** Publishes book 18 months after acceptance of ms. Responds in 1 month to queries. Book catalog available free. Guidelines available online.

Utah State University Press publishes scholarly works in the academic areas noted below. Currently interested in book-length scholarly mss dealing with folklore studies, composition studies, Native American studies, and history.

Nonfiction Subjects include history, of the West, regional, folklore, the West, Native-American studies, studies in composition and rhetoric. Query with SASE. Reviews artwork/photos. Send photocopies.

Recent Title(s) *The Activist WPA: Changing Stories about Writing and Writers*, by Linda Adler-Kassner; *Literacy, Sexuality, Pedagogy: Theory and Practice for Composition Studies*, by Jonathan Alexander; *Expose of Polygamy: A Lady's Life among the Mormons*, by Fanny Stenhouse (edited by Linda DeSimone).

Tips Utah State University Press also sponsors the annual May Swenson Poetry Award.

VANDERBILT UNIVERSITY PRESS

VU Station B 351813, Nashville TN 37235. (615)322-3585. Fax: (615)343-8823. E-mail: vupress@vanderbilt.edu. Website: www.vanderbiltuniversitypress.com. **Contact:** Michael Ames, director. Publishes hardcover originals and trade paperback originals and reprints. **Publishes 20-25 titles/year. 500 queries received/year. 25% of books from first-time authors. 90% from unagented writers. Pays rare advance.** Publishes book 10 months after acceptance of ms. Accepts simultaneous submissions. Responds in 2 weeks to proposals. Book catalog available free. Guidelines available online.

- Also distributes for and co-publishes with Country Music Foundation.

Vanderbilt University Press publishes books on healthcare, social sciences, education, and regional studies, for both academic and general audiences that are intellectually significant, socially relevant, and of practical importance.

Nonfiction Subjects include Americana, anthropology, archeology, education, ethnic, government, politics, health, medicine, history, language, literature, multicultural, music, dance, nature, environment, philosophy,

womens issues, womens studies. Submit prospectus, sample chapter, cv. Reviews artwork/photos. Send photocopies.
Recent Title(s) *Lost Delta Found*, edited by Robert Gordon and Bruce Nemerov.
Tips Our audience consists of scholars and educated, general readers.

VENTURE PUBLISHING, INC.

1999 Cato Ave., State College PA 16801. (814)234-4561. Fax: (814)234-1651. E-mail: vpublish@venturepublish.com. Website: www.venturepublish.com. Estab. 1978. Publishes hardcover and paperback originals and reprints. **Pays royalty on wholesale price. Pays advance.** Book catalog and ms guidelines for SASE or online.

- Venture Publishing produces quality educational publications, also workbooks for professionals, educators, and students in the fields of recreation, parks, leisure studies, therapeutic recreation and long term care.

Nonfiction Subjects include nature, environment, outdoor recreation management and leadership texts, recreation, sociology, leisure studies, long-term care nursing homes, therapeutic recreation. Submit 1 sample chapter, book proposal, competing titles.
Recent Title(s) *Leisure in Your Life: A New Perspective*, by Geoffrey Godbey; *Leadership in Leisure Services: Making a Difference, 3rd Ed.*, by Debra Jordan; *Leisure for Canadians*, edited by Ron McCarville and Kelly MacKay.

VERSO

20 Jay St., 10th Floor, Brooklyn NY 11201. (718)246-8160. Fax: (718)246-8165. E-mail: versony@versobooks.com. Website: www.versobooks.com. **Contact:** Editorial Department. Estab. 1970. Publishes hardcover and trade paperback originals. **Pays royalty. Pays advance.** Accepts simultaneous submissions. Book catalog available free. Guidelines available online.

- Our books cover economics, politics, cinema studies, and history (among other topics), but all come from a critical, Leftist viewpoint, on the border between trade and academic.

Nonfiction Subjects include business, economics, government, politics, history, philosophy, sociology, womens issues, womens studies. Submit proposal package.
Recent Title(s) *Planet of Slums*, by Mike Davis; *George and Martha*, by Karen Finley; *High Water Everywhere*, by Alexander Cockburn and Jeffry St. Clair.

[A] VILLARD BOOKS

Imprint of Random House Publishing Group 1745 Broadway, New York NY 10019. (212)572-2600. Website: www.atrandom.com. Estab. 1983. Publishes hardcover and trade paperback originals. **Pays negotiable royalty Pays negotiable advance.** Accepts simultaneous submissions.

- Villard Books is the publisher of savvy and sometimes quirky, best-selling hardcovers and trade paperbacks.

Nonfiction , commercial nonfiction. Agented submissions only.
Fiction Commercial fiction Agented submissions only.
Recent Title(s) *Dog Days*, by Jon Katz; *Walking in Circles Before Lying Down*, by Merrill Markoe; *Have You Found Her*, by Janice Erlbaum.

VIVISPHERE PUBLISHING

675 Dutchess Turnpike, Poughkeepsie NY 12603. (845)463-1100, ext. 314. Fax: (845)463-0018. Website: www.vivisphere.com. **Contact:** Lisa Mays. Estab. 1995. Publishes paperback originals and paperback reprints. **Pays royalty.** Publishes book 3-12 months after acceptance of ms. Accepts simultaneous submissions. Responds in 3 months to queries. Book catalog free; ms guidelines free or online.

- "Cookbooks should have a particular slant or appeal to a certain niche. Also publish out-of-print books."

Nonfiction Subjects include history, military, war, New Age, game of bridge. Query with SASE.
Fiction Subjects include feminist, gay, lesbian, historical, horror, literary, mainstream, contemporary, military, war, science fiction, western. Query with SASE.

[N] VOYAGEUR PRESS

400 First Ave.,, Suite 300, Stillwater MN 55401. (651)430-2210. Fax: (651)430-2211. E-mail: mdregni@voyageurpress.com; jleventhal@voyageurpress.com; dprnu@mbipublishing.com; kcornell@voyageurpress.com. **Contact:** Michael Dregni, publisher; Kari Cornell, acquistions editor crafts and cookbooks; Dennis Pernu, senior editor music titles; Josh Leventhal, publisher sports books. Estab. 1972. Publishes hardcover and trade paperback originals. **Publishes 80 titles/year. 1,200 queries received/year. 500 mss received/year. 10% of books from first-time authors. 90% from unagented writers. Pays royalty. Pays advance.** Publishes book 1 year after acceptance of ms. Accepts simultaneous submissions. Responds in 3 months to queries.
Imprints MVP Books

"Voyageur Press (and its sports imprint MVP Books) is internationally known as a leading publisher of quality music, sports, country living, crafts, natural history, and regional books. No children's or poetry books."

Nonfiction Subjects include Americana, cooking, environment, history, hobbies, music, nature, regional, sports, collectibles, country living, knitting and quilting,outdoor recreation. Query with SASE. Submit outline. Send sample digital images or transparencies (duplicates and tearsheets only).

Recent Title(s) *The Snowflake* (popular science and microphotography look at snow crystals); *The Replacements* (oral history of post-punk rock'n'roll band); *The Surfboard* (history of surfboards); *How to Raise Chickens.*

Tips We publish books for an audience interested in regional, natural, and cultural history on a wide variety of subjects. We seek authors strongly committed to helping us promote and sell their books. Please present as focused an idea as possible in a brief submission (1-page cover letter; 2-page outline or proposal). Note your credential for writing the book. Tell all you know about the market niche and marketing possibilities for proposed book.

WALCH PUBLISHING

P.O. Box 658, Portland ME 04104-0658. (207)772-3105. Fax: (207)774-7167. Website: www.walch.com. **Contact:** Susan Blair, editor-in-chief. Estab. 1927. **Publishes 100 titles/year. 10% of books from first-time authors. 95% from unagented writers. Pays 5-8% royalty on flat rate.** Publishes book 6 months after acceptance of ms. Accepts simultaneous submissions. Responds in 2 months to queries. Book catalog for 9x12 envelope and 5 First-Class stamps. Guidelines for #10 SASE.

We focus on English/language arts, math, social studies and science teaching resources for middle school through adult assessment titles.

Nonfiction Formats include teacher resources, reproducibles.Subjects include education, mathematics, middle school, social sciences studies, remedial and special education, government, politics, history, language, literature, science, social sciences, technology. Query with SASE. Reviews artwork/photos.

WALKER AND CO.

Walker Publishing Co. 175 Fifth Ave., 7th Floor, New York NY 10010. (212)727-8300. Fax: (212)727-0984. Website: www.walkeryoungreaders.com. **Contact:** Submissions to Adult Nonfiction Editor limited to agents, published authors, and writers wtih professional credentials in their field of expertise. Children's books to Submissions Editor-Juvenile. Estab. 1959. Publishes hardcover trade originals. Book catalog for 9x12 envelope and 3 First-Class stamps.

Walker publishes general nonfiction on a variety of subjects, as well as children's books.

Nonfiction Subjects include business, economics, health, medicine, history, (science and technology), nature, environment, science, sports, mathematics, self-help. *Adult: agented submissions only*; Juvenile: send synopsis.

Fiction Subjects include juvenile, mystery, adult, picture books. Query with SASE. Send complete ms for picture b

Recent Title(s) *Blood Red Horse*, by K.M. Grant; *The Driving Book*, by Karen Gravelle; *Shelf Life*, by Robert Corbet.

WATERBROOK PRESS

12265 Oracle Blvd., Suite 200, Colorado Springs CO 80921. (719)590-4999. Fax: (719)590-8977. Website: www.waterbrookpress.com. Estab. 1996. Publishes hardcover and trade paperback originals. **Publishes 70 titles/year. 2,000 queries received/year. 15% of books from first-time authors. Pays royalty.** Publishes book 12 months after acceptance of ms. Accepts simultaneous submissions. Responds in 2-3 months to queries. Responds in 2-3 months to proposals. Responds in 2-3 months to manuscripts. Book catalog available online.

Nonfiction Subjects include child guidance, money, finance, religion, spirituality, marriage, Christian living. Agented submissions only.

Fiction Subjects include adventure, historical, literary, mainstream, contemporary, mystery, religious, inspirational, religious mystery/suspense, religious thriller, religious romance, romance, contemporary, historical, science fiction, spiritual, suspense. Agented submissions only.

Recent Title(s) *The Greatest Words Ever Spoken*, by Steven K. Scott; *When the Soul Mends*, by Cindy Woodsmall; *One Month to Live*, by Kerry & Chris Schook.

WATSON-GUPTILL PUBLICATIONS

770 Broadway, New York NY 10003. (646)654-5000. Fax: (646)654-5486. Website: www.watsonguptill.com. **Contact:** The Editors. Publishes hardcover and trade paperback originals and reprints. **150 queries received/year. 50 mss received/year. 50% of books from first-time authors. 75% from unagented writers. Pays royalty on wholesale price.** Publishes book 9 months after acceptance of ms. Responds in 2 months to queries. Responds in 3 months to proposals. Book catalog available free. Guidelines available online.

Imprints Watson-Guptill; Amphoto; Whitney Library of Design; Billboard Books; Back Stage Books.

O→ Watson-Guptill is an arts book publisher.

Nonfiction Subjects include art, architecture, music, dance, photography, lifestyle. Query with SASE. Submit proposal package, outline, 1-2 sample chapters. Reviews artwork/photos. Send photocopies and transparencies.

Recent Title(s) *Manga Mania Shoujo*, by Christopher Hart; *Scared! How to Draw Horror Comic Characters*, by Steve Miller and Bryan Baugh; *Days of Hope and Dreams: An Intimate Portrait of Bruce Springsteen*, by Frank Stefanko.

Tips We are an art book publisher.

WEATHERHILL

Imprint of Shambhala Publications P.O. Box 308, Boston MA 02117. (617)424-0030. Fax: (617)236-1563. E-mail: editors@shambhala.com. Website: www.shambhala.com. Estab. 1962. Publishes hardcover and trade paperback originals and reprints. Accepts simultaneous submissions. Book catalog and ms guidelines free.

O→ Weatherhill publishes exclusively Asia-related nonfiction and Asian fiction and poetry in translation.

Nonfiction Asia-related topics only.Subjects include anthropology, archeology, art, architecture, cooking, foods, nutrition, gardening, history, language, literature, music, dance, nature, environment, photography, regional, religion, sociology, translation, travel, martial arts. Submit outline, resume, 2-3 sample chapters, TOC, SASE. Reviews artwork/photos. Send photocopies.

Fiction We publish only well-known Asian writers in translation. Authors should check funding possibilities from appropriate sources: Japan Foundation, Korea Foundation, etc.

WELCOME ENTERPRISES, INC.

6 W. 18th St., New York NY 10011. (212)989-3200. Fax: (212)989-3205. E-mail: info@welcomebooks.biz. Website: www.welcomebooks.biz. **Contact:** Lena Tabori, publisher/editor; Natasha Tabori Fried, editor; Katrina Fried, editor; Alice Wong, editor. Estab. 1980. **Publishes 10 titles/year.**

Nonfiction Subjects include art, architecture, language, literature, photography. Query with SASE.

Recent Title(s) *The Little Big Book of New York*; *Mom's Almanac.*

N WELLNESS INSTITUTE/SELF-HELP BOOKS, LLC

Selfhelpbooks.com 515 W. North St., Pass Christian MS 39571. Fax: (228)452-0775. Website: www.selfhelpbooks.com. **Contact:** Linda Tell, Ph.D., acquisitions editor. Hardcover originals, trade and mass market paperback originals; electronic originals. **Publishes 10 titles/year. Receives 25 queries/year; 25 mss/year 20% of books from first-time authors. 75% from unagented writers.** Publishes book 6 months from acceptance to publication after acceptance of ms. Catalog available online at website. Guidelines available online at website.

Nonfiction Subjects include health, medicine/medicine, psychology, sex, social sciences, sociology. Submit proposal package with outline. Does not review artwork/photos.

Recent Title(s) *Hazards of Being Male*, by Dr. Herb Goldberg (self-help); *How To Be A Good Parent*, by Dr. Don Fontenelle (self-help)

Tips Our goal is to publish good self-help books and to sell them along with other good self-help books from other publishers through our website, www.selfhelpbooks.com. The vast majority of our authors are Ph.D., MSW, or MD mental health professionals.

N WESLEYAN PUBLISHING HOUSE

P.O. Box 50434, Indianapolis IN 46250. Website: www.wesleyan.org/wph. Hardcover and trade paperback originals. **Publishes 25 titles/year. 150-175 50% of books from first-time authors. 90% from unagented writers.** Publishes book 11 months after acceptance of ms. Accepts simultaneous submissions. Catalog available online at website www.wesleyan.org/wph. Guidelines available online at website www.wesleyan.org/wph/inside/writers_guidelines, and by email.

Nonfiction Subjects include Christianity/religion. Submit proposal package, including outline, 3-5 sample chapters, bio. See writer's guidelines. Does not review artwork.

Fiction Does not publish fiction.

Recent Title(s) *Rethink Your Life*, by Stan Toler (Christian living); *Common Ground*, by Keith Drury (Christian living).

Tips Our books help evangelical Christians learn about the faith or grow in their relationship with God.

WESLEYAN UNIVERSITY PRESS

215 Long Lane, Middletown CT 06459. (860)685-7711. Fax: (860)685-7712. E-mail: stamminen@wesleyan.edu. Website: www.wesleyan.edu/wespress. Estab. 1959. Publishes hardcover originals and paperbacks. Accepts simultaneous submissions. Book catalog available free. Ms guidelines online or with #10 SASE.

O→ Wesleyan University Press is a scholarly press with a focus on poetry, music, dance and cultural studies.

Nonfiction Subjects include music, dance, film/TV & media studies, science fiction studies, dance and poetry. Submit proposal package, outline, sample chapters, cover letter, CV, TOC, anticipated length of ms and date of completion. Reviews artwork/photos. Send photocopies.
Recent Title(s) *Sex and the Slayer*, by Lorna Jarrett; *Door in the Mountain*, by Jean Valentine; *The Begum's Millions*, by Jules Verne.

WESTERNLORE PRESS

P.O. Box 35305, Tucson AZ 85740. (520)297-5491. Fax: (520)297-1722. **Contact:** Lynn R. Bailey, editor. Estab. 1941. **Publishes 6-12 titles/year. Pays standard royalty on retail price.** Responds in 2 months to queries.

O‑ Westernlore publishes Western Americana of a scholarly and semischolarly nature.

Nonfiction Subjects include Americana, anthropology, archaeology, history, regional, historic sights, restoration, ethnohistory pertaining to the American West. Query with SASE.
Recent Title(s) *Too Tough to Die*, by Bailey; *Men & Women of American Mining*, by Bailey & Chaput (2 volumes); *Cochise County Stalwarts, Vol. I & II*, by Bailey & Chaput.

WESTMINSTER JOHN KNOX PRESS

Division of Presbyterian Publishing Corp. 100 Witherspoon St., Louisville KY 40202-1396. Fax: (502)569-5113. Website: www.wjkbooks.com. **Contact:** Gavin Stephens. Publishes hardcover and paperback originals and reprints. **Publishes 100 titles/year. 2,500 queries received/year. 750 mss received/year. 10% of books from first-time authors. Pays royalty on retail price.** Proposal guidelines online.

O‑ All WJK books have a religious/spiritual angle, but are written for various markets—scholarly, professional, and the general reader. Westminster John Knox is affiliated with the Presbyterian Church USA. No phone queries.

Nonfiction Subjects include religion, spirituality. Submit proposal package according to the WJK book proposal guidelines found online.

WHITAKER HOUSE

1030 Hunt Valley Circle, New Kensington PA 15068. E-mail: publisher@whitakerhouse.com. Website: www.whitakerhouse.com. **Contact:** Tom Cox, managing editor. Estab. 1970. hardcover, trade paperback, and mass market originals. **Publishes 50 titles/year. 600 queries received/year. 200 mss received/year. 15% of books from first-time authors. 60% from unagented writers. Pays 5-15% royalty on wholesale price.** Publishes book 3 months after acceptance of ms. Accepts simultaneous submissions. Responds in 3 months to queries. Responds in 3 months to proposals. Responds in 3 months to manuscripts. Book catalog available online. Guidelines available online and by email.
Nonfiction Accepts submissions on any topic as long as they have a Christian perspective.Subjects include religion, Christian. Query with SASE. Does not review artwork/photos.
Fiction All fiction must have a Christian perspective.Subjects include religious, Christian. Query with SASE.
Recent Title(s) *Becoming A Leader*, by Dr. Myles Munroe (Christian living); *Hannah Grace*, by Sharlene MacLaren (romance); *Cursebreaker*, by Nancy Wentz (suspense); *Significant Living*, by Jerry and Shirley Rose.
Tips Audience includes those seeking uplifting and inspirational fiction and nonfiction.

WHITEHORSE PRESS

107 E. Conway Rd., Center Conway NH 03813-4012. (603)356-6556. Fax: (603)356-6590. **Contact:** Dan Kennedy, publisher. Estab. 1988. Publishes trade paperback originals. **Publishes 10-20 titles/year. Pays 10% royalty on wholesale price.** Responds in 1 month to queries.
Nonfiction "We are actively seeking nonfiction books to aid motorcyclists in topics such as motorcycle safety, restoration, repair, and touring. We are especially interested in technical subjects related to motorcycling."Subjects include travel. Query with SASE.
Recent Title(s) *Essential Guide to Motorcycle Maintenance*, by Mark Zimmerman (trade paperback).
Tips "We like to discuss project ideas at an early stage and work with authors to develop those ideas to fit our market."

N WHITE PINE PRESS

P.O. Box 236, Buffalo NY 14201. (716)627-4665. Fax: (716)627-4665. E-mail: wpine@whitepine.org. Website: www.whitepine.org. **Contact:** Dennis Maloney, editor (poetry & translation). Trade paperback originals. **Publishes 10-12 titles/year. 500 queries/yearly 1% of books from first-time authors. 100% from unagented writers.** Publishes book 18 months after acceptance of ms. Accepts simultaneous submissions. Catalog available online at website; for #10 SASE. Guidelines available online at website.
Nonfiction Subjects include language, literature, muticultural, translation, poetry. We do not review artwork/photos
Fiction Subjects include poetry, poetry in translation, translation. We are currently not reading U.S. fiction. We are currently reading unsolicited poetry only as part of our Annual Poetry Contest. The reading period is July

1 - November 30 for fiction and poetry in translation only. For fiction & poetry in translation ONLY—query with SASE; submit proposal package, including synopsis & 2 sample chapters.

N WHITE STONE BOOKS

P.O. Box 2835, Lakeland FL 33806. (918)523-5411. Fax: (918)523-5782. E-mail: info@whitestonebooks.com. Website: www.whitestonebooks.com. **Contact:** Amanda Pilgrim. Estab. 2003. Publishes hardcover, trade paperback, and mass market paperback originals and reprints; also, electronic reprints. **Publishes 25 titles/year. 30% of books from first-time authors.** Publishes book 18 months after acceptance of ms. Accepts simultaneous submissions. Book catalog available free. Guidelines available free.

Nonfiction Subjects include creative nonfiction, education. Submit proposal package, outline, 1 sample chapters, bio. Reviews artwork/photos. Send photocopies.

Fiction Subjects include adventure, historical, humor, juvenile, literary, mainstream, contemporary, military, war, romance, short story collections, western, young adult. We prefer scripts with several connecting layers, with story lines that are compelling and thought provoking. Submit proposal package, 1 sample chapters, clips, bio.

Recent Title(s) *Encounters With Christ*, by Richard Exley; *The Family Blessing*, by Rolf Garborg; *Luke's Passage*, by Max Davis.

N ALBERT WHITMAN & COMPANY

6340 Oakton St., Morton Grove IL 60053. Website: www.albertwhitman.com. **Contact:** Kathleen Tucker, editor-in-chief. Publishes hardcover originals and trade books. **Publishes 30 titles/year. Receives 500 queries/year; 3,000 mss/year. 10% of books from first-time authors. 50% from unagented writers.** Publishes book 18 months after acceptance of ms. Accepts simultaneous submissions. Guidelines available at website.

Nonfiction Subjects include Americana, animals, multicultural. Submit outline and 3 sample chapters. Reviews artwork/photos; send photocopies.

Fiction Subjects include juvenile, picture books, middle-grade novels.

Recent Title(s) *Abe Lincoln Loved Animals*, by Ellen Jackson (picture book); *Polar Bear, Why Is Your World Melting?* by Robert E. Wells (picture book); *The Origami Master*, by Nathaniel Lachenmeyer; *Gus, the Pilgrim Turkey*, by Teresa Bateman (picture book).

Tips Our audience is children ages 3-12. Study our website to get a feeling for the list. We publish trade books that are especially interesting to schools and libraries.

ALBERT WHITMAN & CO.

6340 Oakton St., Morton Grove IL 60053-2723. E-mail: ktucker@awhitmanco.com. Website: www.albertwhitman.com. **Contact:** Kathleen Tucker, editor-in-chief. Estab. 1919. Publishes hardcover originals. **Publishes 30 titles/year. 10% of books from first-time authors. 50% from unagented writers. On retail price: Pays 10% royalty for novels; 5% for picture books. Pays advance.** Publishes book an average of 18 months after acceptance of ms. Accepts simultaneous submissions. Responds in 3 months to queries. Responds in 4 months to proposals and manuscripts. Guidelines online at website.

- Albert Whitman publishes good books for children on a variety of topics: holidays (i.e., Halloween), special needs (such as diabetes), and problems like divorce. The majority of our titles are picture books with less than 1,500 words. De-emphasizing bedtime stories.

Nonfiction Subjects include Americana, animals, muticultural. Submit outline and 3 sample chapters. Reviews artwork/photos; send photocopies.

Fiction Subjects include juvenile, picture books books.

Recent Title(s) *Abe Lincoln Loved Animals*, by Ellen Jackson (picture book); *Polar Bear, Why Is Your World Melting?* by Robert E. Wells (picture book); *The Origami Master*, by Nathaniel Lachenmeyer; *Gus, the Pilgrim Turkey*, by Teresa Bateman (picture book).

Tips We publish trade books that are especially interesting to schools and libraries. We recommend you study our website before submitting your work.

WHITSTON PUBLISHING CO., INC.

P.O. Box 38263, Albany NY 12203. (518)869-9110. Fax: (518)452-2154. Website: www.whitston.com. **Contact:** Paul Laddin. Estab. 1969. Publishes hardcover and trade paperback originals. **Publishes 15-25 titles/year. 500 queries received/year. 20% of books from first-time authors. 100% from unagented writers. Pays royalities after sale of 500 copies** Publishes book 1-2 years after acceptance of ms. Responds in 6 months to queries.

- Whitston focuses on literature, politics, history, business, and the sciences.

Nonfiction We publish nonfiction books in the humanities. We also publish reference bibliographies and indexes.Subjects include art, architecture, business, economics, government, politics, health, medicine, history, language, literature, literary criticism, social sciences. Query with SASE. Reviews artwork/photos.

Recent Title(s) *Mark Twain Among the Scholars*; *Autobiographies by Americans of Color*; *Into the Dragon's Teeth: Warriors' Tales of the Battle of the Bulge*, ( ).

🅽 MICHAEL WIESE PRODUCTIONS

11288 Ventura Blvd., Suite 621, Studio City CA 91604. (818)379-8799 or (206)283-2948. Fax: (818)986-3408. E-mail: kenlee@mwp.com. Website: www.mwp.com. **Contact:** Ken Lee, vice president. Estab. 1981. Publishes trade paperback originals. Accepts simultaneous submissions. Book catalog available online.

- Michael Wiese publishes how-to books for professional film or video makers, film schools and bookstores.

Nonfiction Call before submitting.

Recent Title(s) *Save the Cat! Goes to the Movies*, by Blake Snyder; *The Writer's Journey - 3rd Ed.*, by Chrisopher Vogler; *Writing the TV Drama Series - 2nd Ed.*, by Pamela Douglas.

Tips Audience is professional filmmakers, writers, producers, directors, actors and university film students.

WILDERNESS PRESS

1200 Fifth St., Berkeley CA 94710. (510)558-1666. Fax: (510)558-1696. E-mail: editor@wildernesspress.com. Website: www.wildernesspress.com. **Contact:** Managing Editor. Estab. 1967. Publishes paperback originals. **Publishes 12 titles/year.** Publishes book 8-12 months after acceptance of ms. Responds in 2 months to queries. Book catalog and ms guidelines online.

- Wilderness Press has a long tradition of publishing the highest quality, most accurate hiking and other outdoor activity guidebooks.

Nonfiction Subjects include nature, environment, recreation, trail guides for hikers and backpackers. Download proposal guidelines from website.

Recent Title(s) *Best of California's Missions, Mansions and Museums*; *Stairway Walks in San Francisco*; *Walking Brooklyn*.

🅽 JOHN WILEY & SONS, INC.

111 River St., Hoboken NJ 07030. (201)748-6000. Fax: (201)748-6088. Website: www.wiley.com. **Contact:** Editorial Department. Estab. 1807. Publishes hardcover originals, trade paperback originals and reprints. **Pays competitive rates. Pays advance.** Accepts simultaneous submissions. Book catalog available online. Guidelines available online.

Imprints Jossey-Bass (business/management, leadership, human resource development, education, health, psychology, religion, and public and nonprofit sectors).

- The General Interest group publishes nonfiction books for the consumer market.

Nonfiction Subjects include history, memoirs, psychology, science, popular, African American interest, health/self-improvement, technical, medical. Submit proposal package. Submit complete ms. See website for more details.

Recent Title(s) *Bordeaux and Its Wines, 17th Ed.*, by Charles Cocks; *Penthouse Living*, by Jonathan Bell; *Prevention of Type 2 Diabetes*, edited by Manfred Ganz.

WILLIAM ANDREW, INC.

13 Eaton Ave., Norwich NY 13815. (607)337-5000. Fax: (607)337-5090. E-mail: vhaynes@williamandrew.com. Website: www.williamandrew.com. **Contact:** Valerie Haynes, publications editor. Estab. 1989. Publishes hardcover originals. Accepts simultaneous submissions. Book catalog available online.

Imprints Noyes Publications, Plastics Design Library.

- We are looking for authors who want to write a book or compile data that can be employed by readers in day-to-day activities.

Nonfiction Submit outline with book propsal, SASE Reviews artwork/photos. Send photocopies.

Recent Title(s) *Nanostructured Materials*, by Koch; *Handbook of Molded Part Shrinkage and Warpage*, by Fischer; *Fluoroplastics, Volumes 1 and 2*, by Ebnesajjad.

🅽 🅰 ⊘ WILLIAM MORROW

HarperCollins 10 E. 53rd St., New York NY 10022. (212)207-7000. Fax: (212)207-7145. Website: www.harpercollins.com. **Contact:** Acquisitions Editor. Estab. 1926. **Pays standard royalty on retail price. Pays varying advance.** Book catalog available free.

- William Morrow publishes a wide range of titles that receive much recognition and prestige. A most selective house.

Nonfiction Subjects include art, architecture, cooking, foods, nutrition, history. Agented submissions only.

Fiction Publishes adult ficiton. Morrow accepts only the highest quality submissions in adult fiction. Agented submissions only.

Recent Title(s) *Serpent on the Crown*, by Elizabeth Peters; *The Baker's Apprentice*, by Judith R. Hendricks; *Freakonomics*, by Steven D. Levitt and Stephen J. Dubner.

WILLOW CREEK PRESS

P.O. Box 147, 9931 Highway 70 W., Minocqua WI 54548. (715)358-7010. Fax: (715)358-2807. E-mail: andread@willowcreekpress.com. Website: www.willowcreekpress.com. **Contact:** Andrea Donner, managing editor. Estab.

1986. Publishes hardcover and trade paperback originals and reprints. **Publishes 25 titles/year. 400 queries received/year. 150 mss received/year. 15% of books from first-time authors. 50% from unagented writers. Pays 6-15% royalty on wholesale price. Pays $2,000-5,000 advance.** Publishes book within 18 months after acceptance of ms. Accepts simultaneous submissions. Responds in 2 months to queries. Guidelines available online.

O→ We specialize in nature, outdoor, and sporting topics, including gardening, wildlife, and animal books. Pets, cookbooks, and a few humor books and essays round out our titles. Currently emphasizing pets (mainly dogs and cats), wildlife, outdoor sports (hunting, fishing). De-emphasizing essays, fiction.

Nonfiction Subjects include animals, cooking, foods, nutrition, gardening, nature, environment, recreation, sports, travel, wildlife, pets. Submit outline, 1 sample chapter, SASE. Reviews artwork/photos.

Recent Title(s) *Why Babies Do That*; *Horse Tails & Trails*; *The Little Book of Lap Dogs*.

WILSHIRE BOOK CO.

9731 Variel Ave., Chatsworth CA 91311-4315. (818)700-1522. Fax: (818)700-1527. E-mail: mpowers@mpowers.com. Website: www.mpowers.com. **Contact:** Rights Department. Estab. 1947. Publishes trade paperback originals and reprints. **Publishes 25 titles/year. 1,200 queries received/year. 70% of books from first-time authors. 90% from unagented writers. Pays standard royalty. Pays advance.** Publishes book 6-9 months after acceptance of ms. Accepts simultaneous submissions. Responds in 2 months.

Nonfiction Subjects include psychology, personal success. Submit 3 sample chapters. Submit complete ms. Include outline, author bio, analysis of book's competition and SASE. No e-mail or fax submissions. Reviews artwork/photos. Send photocopies.

Fiction Adult allegories that teach principles of psychological growth or offer guidance in living. Minimum 30,000 words. Submit 3 sample chapters. Submit complete ms. Include outline, author bio, a.

Recent Title(s) *The Dragon Slayer with a Heavy Heart*, by Marcia Powers; *The Secret of Overcoming Verbal Abuse*, by Albert Ellis, PhD, and Marcia Grad Powers; *The Princess Who Believed in Fairy Tales*, by Marcia Grad.

Tips We are vitally interested in all new material we receive. Just as you are hopeful when submitting your manuscript for publication, we are hopeful as we read each one submitted, searching for those we believe could be successful in the marketplace. Writing and publishing must be a team effort. We need you to write what we can sell. We suggest you read the successful books similar to the one you want to write. Analyze them to discover what elements make them winners. Duplicate those elements in your own style, using a creative new approach and fresh material, and you will have written a book we can catapult onto the bestseller list. You are welcome to telephone or e-mail us for immediate feedback on any book concept you may have. To learn more about us and what we publish—and for complete manuscript guidelines—visit our website.

WINDRIVER PUBLISHING, INC.

72 N. WindRiver Rd., Silverton ID 83867-0446. (208)752-1836. Fax: (208)752-1876. E-mail: info@windriverpublishing.com. Website: www.windriverpublishing.com. **Contact:** E. Keith Howick, Jr., president; Gail Howick, vice president/editor-in-chief. Estab. 2003. Publishes hardcover originals and reprints, trade paperback originals, and mass market originals. **Publishes 8 titles/year. 1,000 queries received/year. 300 mss received/year. 95% of books from first-time authors. 90% from unagented writers.** Publishes book 12 months after acceptance of ms. Accepts simultaneous submissions. Responds in 1-2 months to queries. Responds in 4-6 months to proposals. Responds in 4-6 months to manuscripts. Book catalog available online. Guidelines available online.

O→ Authors who wish to submit book proposals for review must do so according to our Submissions Guidelines, which can be found on our website, along with an on-line submission form, which is our preferred submission method. We do not accept submissions of any kind by email.

Nonfiction Subjects include animals, art, architecture, business, economics, computers, electronics, education, gardening, government, politics, health, medicine, history, hobbies, language, literature, nature, environment, New Age, philosophy, religion, science, spirituality, sports, true crime, antiques/collectibles; family/relationships. Follow online instructions for submitting proposal, including synopsis and 3 sample chapters. *Ms submissions by invitation only*. Reviews artwork/photos.

Fiction Subjects include adventure, fantasy, historical, horror, humor, juvenile, literary, military, war, mystery, occult, religious, romance, science fiction, short story collections, spiritual, sports, suspense, western, young adult, drama; espionage; political; psychological; fairy tales/folklore; graphic novels. Follow online instructions.

Recent Title(s) *Stinky Facts of the Mandarin*, by Marion Passey; *Polygamy: The Mormon Enigma*, by E. Keith Howkk.

Tips We do not accept manuscripts containing graphic or gratuitous profanity, sex, or violence. See online instructions for details.

WISCONSIN HISTORICAL SOCIETY PRESS

816 State St., Madison WI 53706. (608)264-6465. Fax: (608)264-6486. E-mail: whspress@wisconsinhistory.org. Website: www.wisconsinhistory.org/whspress/. **Contact:** Kate Thompson, editor. Estab. 1855. Publishes hardcover and trade paperback originals. Trade paperback reprints. **Publishes 12-14 titles/year. 60-75 queries received/year. 20%% of books from first-time authors. 90%% from unagented writers. Pays royalty on wholesale price.** Publishes book 18-24 months after acceptance of ms. to manuscripts. Book catalog available free. Guidelines available online.

Imprints Wisconsin Magazine of History.

Nonfiction Subjects include anthropology, archeology, art, architecture, cooking, foods, nutrition, ethnic, history, (Wisconsin), memoirs, regional, sports, (history). Submit proposal package, form from website. Reviews artwork/photos. Send photocopies.

Tips Our audience reads about Wisc Carefully review the book pro

WISDOM PUBLICATIONS

199 Elm St., Somerville MA 02144. (617)776-7416, ext. 28. Fax: (617)776-7841. E-mail: editors@wisdompubs.org. Website: www.wisdompubs.org. **Contact:** David Kittlestrom, senior editor. Estab. 1976. Publishes hardcover originals and trade paperback originals and reprints. **Publishes 20-25 titles/year. 300 queries received/year. 50% of books from first-time authors. 95% from unagented writers. Pays 4-8% royalty on wholesale price. Pays advance.** Publishes book within 2 years after acceptance of ms. Book catalog and ms guidelines online.

- Wisdom Publications is dedicated to making available authentic Buddhist works for the benefit of all. We publish translations, commentaries, and teachings of past and contemporary Buddhist masters and original works by leading Buddhist scholars. Currently emphasizing popular applied Buddhism, scholarly titles.

Nonfiction Subjects include philosophy, Buddhist or comparative Buddhist/Western, psychology, religion, Buddhism, Tibet. Query with SASE. Reviews artwork/photos. Send photocopies.

Recent Title(s) *Essence of the Heart Sutra*, by The Dalai Lama.

Tips We are basically a publisher of Buddhist books—all schools and traditions of Buddhism. Please see our catalog or our website before you send anything to us to get a sense of what we publish.

WORDWARE PUBLISHING, INC.

1100 Summit Ave., Suite 102, Plano TX 75074. (972)423-0090. Fax: (972)881-9147. E-mail: tmcevoy@wordware.com. Website: www.wordware.com. **Contact:** Acquisitions Editor. Estab. 1983. Publishes trade paperback and mass market paperback originals. **Publishes 20-25 titles/year. 75-100 queries received/year. 30-50 mss received/year. 40% of books from first-time authors. 95% from unagented writers. Royalties/advances negotiated per project.** Publishes book 6 months after acceptance of ms. Accepts simultaneous submissions. Responds in 2 weeks to queries. Book catalog available free. Guidelines available online.

- Wordware publishes computer/electronics books covering a broad range of technologies for professional programmers and developers with special emphasis in game development, animation, and modeling.

Nonfiction Subjects include computers, electronics. Submit proposal package, 2 sample chapters, TOC, target audience summation, competing books.

Recent Title(s) *3DS Max Lighting; Modeling a Character in 3DS Max, 2nd Ed.*; *LightWave 3D 8 Character Animation; Essential LightWave 3D 8; OpenGL Game Development.*

WORKMAN PUBLISHING CO.

225 Varick St., New York NY 10014. Website: www.workman.com. **Contact:** Suzanne Rafer, executive editor (cookbook, child care, parenting, teen interest); Ruth Sullivan, Margot Herrera, Kylie Foxx-McDonald, Jay Schaefer, senior editors. Raquel Jaramillo, senior editor (juvenile); Megan Nicolay, Savannah Ashour (associate editors). Estab. 1967. Publishes hardcover and trade paperback originals, as well as calendars. **Publishes 40 titles/year. thousands of queries received/year. Open to first-time authors. Pays variable royalty on retail price. Pays variable advance.** Publishes book approximately 1 year after acceptance of ms. Accepts simultaneous submissions. Responds in 5 months to queries. Guidelines available online.

Imprints Algonquin, Artisan, Greenwich Workshop Press, Storey, Timber.

- "We are a trade paperback house specializing in a wide range of popular nonfiction. We publish no adult fiction and very little children's fiction. We also publish a full range of full-color wall and Page-A-Day calendars."

Nonfiction Subjects include business, economics, child guidance, cooking, foods, nutrition, gardening, health, medicine, sports, travel. Query with SASE first for guidelines.

Recent Title(s) *Gallop!*, by Rufus Butler Seder; *1,000 Recordings to Hear Before You Die*, by Tom Moon; *I Will Teach You To Be Rich*, by Ramit Sethi.

Tips "No phone calls, please. We do not accept submissions via fax."

N WORLD AUDIENCE

303 Park Ave., New York NY 10010-3657. (646)620-7406. Fax: (646)620-7406. E-mail: info. Website: www.worldaudience.org. **Contact:** M. Stefan Strozier, chief editor (plays, poetry, novel); Kyle Torke, Hareendran Kalliukeel, editor (short stories and novels). Estab. 2004. **Publishes 100 titles/year. 8,000 queries received/year. 4,000 mss received/year. 80% of books from first-time authors. 95% from unagented writers. Pays 15-50% royalty.** Publishes book 3 months after acceptance of ms. Accepts simultaneous submissions. Responds in 1 month to queries. online at www.worldaudience.org, or available for #10 SASE. available at www.worldaudience.org, or by sending an e-mail to info@worldaudience.org.

Imprints Mock Frog Design Press (Australia); Skive Magazine and books.

Nonfiction Subjects include Americana, art, architecture, language, literature, literary criticism, military, war, sex, spirituality, translation, travel, world affairs. Submit proposal package, outline, 3 sample chapters. Reviews artwork/photos. Send .jpg files.

Fiction Subjects include experimental, horror, humor, literary, military, war, plays, poetry, poetry in translation, short story collections, spiritual. We seek excellent writing ability first and foremost. Submit proposal package, 3 sample chapters, clips.

Recent Title(s) *The Audience Book of Theatre Quotes*, by Louis Phillips (quotations); *The Biting Age*, by Ernest Dempsey (satire); *Still in Soil*, by Kyle Torke (poetry).

Tips A world audience reached thro World Audience is a 21st cent

WRITER'S DIGEST BOOKS

Imprint of F+W Media, Inc. 4700 E. Galbraith Rd., Cincinnati OH 45236. E-mail: kelly.nickell@fwmedia.com. Website: www.writersdigest.com/books. **Contact:** Kelly Nickell, executive editor. Estab. 1920. Publishes hardcover originals and trade paperbacks. **Publishes 25 titles/year. 300 queries received/year. 50 mss received/year. 30% from unagented writers. Pays average $4,000 advance.** Publishes book 18 months after acceptance of ms. Accepts simultaneous submissions. Responds in 3 months to queries. Book catalog for 9x12 envelope and 6 First-Class stamps.

- Writer's Digest Books accepts query letters and complete proposals via mail or e-mail at kelly.nickell@fwpubs.com.

O→ Writer's Digest Books is the premiere source for books about writing, publishing instructional and reference books for writers. Typical mss are 80,000 words. E-mail queries strongly preferred; no phone calls please.

Nonfiction Query with SASE. Submit outline, sample chapters, SASE.

Recent Title(s) *The Constant Art of Being a Writer*, by N.M. Kelby; *Write Like the Masters*, by William Cane; *The Daily Writer*, by Fred White; *The Fire in Fiction*, by Donald Maass; *Novel Shortcuts*, by Lauren Whitcomb.

Tips "Most queries we receive are either too broad (how to write fiction) or too niche (how to write erotic horror), and don't reflect a knowledge of our large backlist of 150 titles. We rarely publish new books on journalism, freelancing, magazine article writing or marketing/promotion. We are actively seeking fiction and nonfiction writing technique books with fresh perspectives, interactive and visual writing instruction books, similar to *Pocket Muse*, by Monica Wood; and general reference works that appeal to an audience beyond writers."

⊘ YALE UNIVERSITY PRESS

P.O. Box 209040, New Haven CT 06520. (203)432-0960. Fax: (203)432-0948. Website: www.yale.edu/yup. **Contact:** Jonathan Brent, editorial director (literature, literary studies, theater); Jean E. Thomson Black (science, medicine); Lauren Shapiro (reference books); Keith Condon (education, behavioral/social sciences); Michelle Komie (art, architecture); Patricia Fidler, publisher (art, architecture); Mary Jane Peluso, publisher (languages, ESL); John Kulka (literature, literary studies, philosophy, political science); Michael O'Malley (business, economics, law); Christopher Rogers (history). Estab. 1908. Publishes hardcover and trade paperback originals. Accepts simultaneous submissions. Book catalog and ms guidelines online.

O→ Yale University Press publishes scholarly and general interest books.

Nonfiction Subjects include Americana, anthropology, archeology, art, architecture, business, economics, education, health, medicine, history, language, literature, military, war, music, dance, philosophy, psychology, religion, science, sociology, womens issues, womens studies. Submit sample chapters, cover letter, prospectus, cv, table of contents, SASE. Reviews artwork/photos. Send photocopies.

Recent Title(s) *Methodism: Empire of the Spirit*, by David Hempton; *A Drawing Manual*, by Thomas Eakins; *The Eighties: America in the Age of Reagan*, by John Ehrman.

Tips Audience is scholars, students and general readers.

N YBK PUBLISHERS, INC.

39 Crosby St., New York NY 10013. E-mail: info@ybkpublishers.com. Website: www.ybkpublishers.com. **Contact:** George Ernsberger, editor-in-chief. Estab. 2000. Publishes hardcover and trade paperback originals. **Publishes 12 titles/year. 90%% of books from first-time authors. 100%% from unagented writers. Pays -15% royalty on retail price.** Publishes book 3 months after acceptance of ms. Accepts simultaneous submissions. Responds in 1 month to queries. Responds in 1 month to proposals. Responds in 1 month to manuscripts. Book catalog available online. Guidelines available online.

Nonfiction Reviews artwork/photos.

Tips Our audience wants academic and special interest topics.

YEARLING BOOKS

Imprint of Random House Children's Books/Random House, Inc. 1745 Broadway, New York NY 10019. (212)782-9000. Website: www.randomhouse.com/kids.

- Quality reprint paperback imprint for middle grade paperback books. *Does not accept unsolicited mss.*

ZONDERVAN, A HARPERCOLLINS COMPANY

Division of HarperCollins Publishers 5300 Patterson Ave. SE, Grand Rapids MI 49530-0002. (616)698-6900. Fax: (616)698-3454. E-mail: zpub@zondervan.com. Website: www.zondervan.com. **Contact:** Manuscript Review Editor. Estab. 1931. Publishes hardcover and trade paperback originals and reprints. **Publishes 200 titles/year. 10% of books from first-time authors. 60% from unagented writers. Pays 14% royalty on net amount received on sales of cloth and softcover trade editions; 12% royalty on net amount received on sales of mass market paperbacks. Pays variable advance.** Responds in 2 months to queries. Responds in 3 months to proposals. Responds in 4 months to manuscripts. Guidelines available online.

Imprints Zondervan, Zonderkidz, Youth Specialties, Editorial Vida.

- No longer accepts unsolicited mailed submissions. Instead, submissions may be submitted electronically to (ChristianManuscriptSubmissions.com).
- Our mission is to be the leading Christian communications company meeting the needs of people with resources that glorify Jesus Christ and promote biblical principles.

Nonfiction All religious perspective (evangelical).Subjects include history, humanities, memoirs, religion, Christian living, devotional, bible study resources, preaching, counseling, college and seminary textbooks, discipleship, worship, church renewal for pastors, professionals and lay leaders in ministry, theological, and biblical reference books. Submit TOC, chapter outline, intended audience, curriculum vitae.

Fiction Refer to nonfiction. Inklings-style fiction of high literary quality. Christian relevance in all cases. Will not consider collections of short stories or poetry. Submit TOC, curriculum vitae, chapter outline, intended audience.

Recent Title(s) *The Purpose Driven Life*, by Rick Warren (Christian living); *Ever After*, by Karen Kingsbury (fiction).

ZUMAYA PUBLICATIONS, LLC

3209 S. Interstate 35, #1086, Austin TX 78741. E-mail: acquisitions@zumayapublications.com. Website: www.zumayapublications.com. **Contact:** Elizabeth Burton, executive editor. Estab. 1999. Publishes trade paperback and electronic originals and reprints. **Publishes 20-25 titles/year. 1,000 queries received/year. 100 mss received/year. 75% of books from first-time authors. 98% from unagented writers.** Publishes book 6-24 months after acceptance of ms. Accepts simultaneous submissions. Responds in 6 months to queries. Responds in 6 months to proposals. Responds in 6-9 months to manuscripts. Guidelines available online.

Imprints Zumaya Boundless (GLBT); Zumaya Embraces (romance/women's fiction); Zumaya Enigma (mystery/suspense/thriller); Zumaya Thresholds (YA/middle grade); Zumaya Otherworlds (SF/F/H).

Nonfiction Subjects include creative nonfiction, gay, lesbian, memoirs, New Age, spirituality, true ghost stories. Electronic query only. Reviews artwork/photos. Send digital format.

Fiction Subjects include adventure, fantasy, gay, lesbian, historical, horror, humor, juvenile, literary, mainstream, contemporary, multicultural, mystery, occult, romance, science fiction, short story collections, spiritual, suspense, western, young adult. We are currently oversupplied with speculative fiction and are reviewing submissions in SF, fantasy and paranormal suspense by invitation only. We are much in need of GLBT and YA/middle grade. As with nonfiction, we encourage people to review what we've already published so as to avoid sending us more of the same, at least, insofar as the plot is concerned. In other words, while we're always looking for good specific mysteries, we want original concepts rather than slightly altered versions of what we've already published. Electronic query only.

Recent Title(s) *The Obsidian Seed*, by R. J. Leahy (sf); *Memory's Desire*, by Gale Storm (contemporary romance); *The Emerald City (A Spencer The Adventurer Book)*, by Stephen L. Keeney (middle grade).

Tips We're catering to readers who may have loved last year's best seller but not enough to want to read 10 more just like it. Have something different. If it does not fit standard pigeonholes, that's a plus. On the other hand, it has to have an audience. And if you're not prepared to work with us on promotion and marketing, it would be better to look elsewhere.

MARKETS

Canadian & International Book Publishers

Canadian and international book publishers share the same mission as their U.S. counterparts—publishing timely books on subjects of concern and interest to a targetable audience. Most of the publishers listed in this section, however, differ from U.S. publishers in that their needs tend toward subjects specific to Canada or intended for an international audience. Some are interested in submissions from Canadian writers only. There are many regional publishers that concentrate on region-specific subjects.

U.S. writers hoping to do business with Canadian and international publishers should follow specific paths of research to find out as much about their intended markets as possible. The listings will inform you about what kinds of books the Canadian and international companies publish and tell you whether they are open to receiving submissions from writers in the U.S. To further target your markets and see specific examples of the books these houses are publishing, send for catalogs from publishers, or check their Web sites.

Once you have determined which publishers will accept your work, it is important to understand the differences that exist between U.S. mail and Canadian and international mail. U.S. postage stamps are useless on mailings originating outside of the U.S. When enclosing a SASE for return of your query or manuscript from a Canadian or international publisher, you must include International Reply Coupons (IRCs).

For a list of publishers according to their subjects of interest, see the Nonfiction and Fiction sections of the Book Publishers' Subject Index. Information on book publishers listed in the previous edition of *Writer's Market*, but not included in this edition, can be found in the General Index.

THE ALTHOUSE PRESS

University of Western Ontario, Faculty of Education, 1137 Western Rd., London ON N6G 1G7, Canada. (519)661-2096. Fax: (519)661-3833. E-mail: press@uwo.ca. Website: www.edu.uwo.ca/althousepress. **Contact:** Katherine Butson, editorial assistant. Publishes trade paperback originals and reprints. **Publishes 1-5 titles/year. 60 queries received/year. 19 mss received/year. 50% of books from first-time authors. 100% from unagented writers. Pays 10% royalty. Pays $300 advance.** Publishes book 8-12 months after acceptance of ms. Accepts simultaneous submissions. Responds in 1 month to queries. Responds in 4 months to manuscripts. Book catalog available free. Guidelines available online.

O→ The Althouse Press publishes both scholarly research monographs in education and professional books and materials for educators in elementary schools, secondary schools, and faculties of education. De-emphasizing curricular or instructional materials intended for use by elementary or secondary school students.

Nonfiction Subjects include education, scholarly. Reviews artwork/photos. Send photocopies.

Recent Title(s) *Masculinities and Schooling*, by Blye Frank and Kevin Davison; *Stones in the Sneaker*, by Ellen Singleton and Aniko Varpalotai; *Living Away From Blessings*, by Carina Henriksson.

Tips Audience is practising teachers and graduate education students.

ANNICK PRESS, LTD.

15 Patricia Ave., Toronto ON M2M 1H9, Canada. (416)221-4802. Fax: (416)221-8400. E-mail: annickpress@annickpress.com. Website: www.annickpress.com. **Contact:** Rick Wilks, director; Colleen MacMillan, associate publisher. Publishes picture books, juvenile and YA fiction and nonfiction; specializes in trade books. **Publishes 25 titles/year. 5,000 queries received/year. 3,000 mss received/year. 20% of books from first-time authors. 80-85% from unagented writers.** Publishes book 2 years after acceptance of ms. Book catalog available online. Guidelines available online.

- *Does not accept unsolicited mss.*

O→ Annick Press maintains a commitment to high quality books that entertain and challenge. Our publications share fantasy and stimulate imagination, while encouraging children to trust their judgment and abilities.

Recent Title(s) *The Bite of the Mango*, by Mariatu Kamara with Susan McClelland; *And Ballplayers and Bonesetters: One Hundred Ancient Aztec and Maya Jobs You Might Have Adored or Abhorred*, by Laurie Coulter, illustrated by Martha Newbigging.

ANVIL PRESS

P.O. Box 3008 MPO, Vancouver BC V6B 3X5, Canada. (604)876-8710. Fax: (604)879-2667. E-mail: info@anvilpress.com. Website: www.anvilpress.com. **Contact:** Brian Kaufman. Estab. 1988. Publishes trade paperback originals. **Publishes 8-10 titles/year. 300 queries received/year. 80% of books from first-time authors. 70% from unagented writers. Pays advance.** Publishes book 8 months after acceptance of ms. Accepts simultaneous submissions. Responds in 2 months to queries. Responds in 6 months to manuscripts. Book catalog for 9 x 12 SAE with 2 first-class stamps. Guidelines available online.

- Canadian authors only.

O→ Anvil Press publishes contemporary adult fiction, poetry, and drama, giving voice to up-and-coming Canadian writers, exploring all literary genres, discovering, nurturing, and promoting new Canadian literary talent. Currently emphasizing urban/suburban themed fiction and poetry; de-emphasizing historical novels.

Fiction Subjects include experimental, literary, short story collections. Contemporary, modern literature—no formulaic or genre. Query with SASE.

Recent Title(s) *Stolen*, by Annette LaPointe (fiction); *Confessions of a Small Press Racketeer*, by Stuart Ross (nonfiction); *Bizarre Winery Tragedy*, by Lyle Neff (poetry).

Tips Audience is young, informed, educated, aware, with an opinion, culturally active (films, books, the performing arts). No US authors. Research the appropriate publisher for your work.

ARSENAL PULP PRESS

Suite 200, 341 Water St., Vancouver BC V6B 1B8, Canada. (604)687-4233. Fax: (604)687-4283. E-mail: info@arsenalpulp.com. Website: www.arsenalpulp.com. **Contact:** Brian Lam, publisher. Estab. 1980. Publishes trade paperback originals, and trade paperback reprints. Rarely publishes non-Canadian authors. **Publishes 20 titles/year. 500 queries received/year. 300 mss received/year. 30% of books from first-time authors. 100% from unagented writers.** Publishes book 1 year after acceptance of ms. Accepts simultaneous submissions. Responds in 2 months to queries. Responds in 4 months to proposals. Responds in 4 months to manuscripts. Book catalog for 9x12 SAE with IRCs or online. Guidelines available online.

Imprints Tillacum Library, Advance Editions

Nonfiction Subjects include art, architecture, cooking, foods, nutrition, creative nonfiction, ethnic, Canadian, aboriginal issues, gay, lesbian, history, cultural, language, literature, multicultural, regional, British Columbia, sex, sociology, travel, womens issues, womens studies, film. Submit proposal package, outline, 2-3 sample

chapters. Reviews artwork/photos.
Fiction Subjects include ethnic, general, feminist, gay, lesbian, literary, multicultural, short story collections. Submit proposal package, outline, clips, 2-3 sample chapters.
Recent Title(s) *Fame Us*, by Brian Howell (nonfiction); *La Dolce Vegan*, by Sarah Kramer (nonfiction cookbook); *Soucouyant*, by David Chariandy (fiction).

JONATHAN BALL PUBLISHERS

P.O. Box 33977, Jeppestown 2043, South Africa. (27)(11)622-2900. Fax: (27)(11)601-8183. Website: www.jonathanball.co.za.

Publishes books about South Africa which enlighten and entertain.

Nonfiction Subjects include cooking, foods, nutrition, history, military, war, nature, environment, sports, travel, politics.
Fiction Novels, poetry, drama, classics.
Recent Title(s) *The Mind of South Africa*, by Allister Sparks; *Wrath of the Ancestors*, by AC Jordan; *So Anyway .*, by Helmut Bertelsmann.

BETWEEN THE LINES

720 Bathurst St., Suite 404, Toronto ON M5S 2R4, Canada. (416)535-9914. Fax: (416)535-1484. E-mail: btlbooks@web.ca. Website: www.btlbooks.com. **Contact:** Paul Eprile, editorial coordinator. Publishes trade paperback originals. **Publishes 8 titles/year. 350 queries received/year. 50 mss received/year. 80% of books from first-time authors. 95% from unagented writers. Pays 8% royalty.** Publishes book 1 year after acceptance of ms. Accepts simultaneous submissions. Responds in 2 months to queries. Responds in 2 months to proposals. Responds in 4 months to manuscripts. Book catalog and ms guidelines for 8 ½x 11 SAE and IRCs. Guidelines available online.

We are a small independent house concentrating on politics and public policy issues, social issues, gender issues, international development, education, and the environment. We publish mainly Canadian authors.

Nonfiction Subjects include education, gay, lesbian, government, politics, health, medicine, history, nature, environment, social sciences, sociology, development studies, labor, technology, media, culture. Submit proposal package, outline, resume, 2-3 sample chapters, cover letter, SASE.
Recent Title(s) *Not Paved With Gold*, by Vincenzo Pietropaolo; *Empire's Law*, edited by Amy Bartholomew; *Beyond the Promised Land*, by David F. Noble.

THE BOSTON MILLS PRESS

132 Main St., Erin ON N0B 1T0, Canada. (519)833-2407. Fax: (519)833-2195. E-mail: books@bostonmillspress.com. Website: www.bostonmillspress.com. **Contact:** Noel Hudson, managing editor. Estab. 1974. Publishes hardcover and trade paperback originals. **Publishes 20 titles/year. 40% of books from first-time authors. 95% from unagented writers. Pays 8% royalty on retail price. Pays advance.** Publishes book 6 months-2 years after acceptance of ms. Accepts simultaneous submissions. Responds in 2 months to queries. Book catalog available free.

Boston Mills Press publishes specific market titles of Canadian and American interest including history, transportation, and regional guidebooks. We like very focused books aimed at the North American market.

Nonfiction Subjects include Americana, art, architecture, cooking, foods, nutrition, creative nonfiction, gardening, history, military, war, nature, environment, photography, recreation, regional, sports, travel, Canadiana. Query with SASE. Reviews artwork/photos. Send photocopies.

BRICK BOOKS

Box 20081, 431 Boler Rd., London ON N6K 4G6, Canada. (519)657-8579. E-mail: brick.books@sympatico.ca. Website: www.brickbooks.ca. **Contact:** Don McKay, editor (poetry); Stan Dragland, editor (poetry); Barry Dempster, editor (poetry). Estab. 1975. Publishes trade paperback originals. **Publishes 7 titles/year. 30 queries received/year. 100 mss received/year 30% of books from first-time authors. 100% from unagented writers.** Publishes book 2 years after acceptance of ms. Responds in 3-4 months to queries. Book catalog free or online. Guidelines available online.

- Brick Books has a reading period of January 1-April 30. Mss received outside that period will be returned. No multiple submissions. Pays 10% royalty in book copies only.

Fiction Subjects include poetry.
Recent Title(s) *All Our Wonder Unavenged*, by Don Domanski; *Night Work: The Sawchuk Poems*, by Randall Maggs.
Tips "Writers without previous publications in literary journals or magazines are rarely considered by Brick Books for publication."

BROADVIEW PRESS, INC.

P.O. Box 1243, Peterborough ON K9J 7H5, Canada. (705)743-8990. Fax: (705)743-8353. E-mail: customerservice@broadviewpress.com. Website: www.broadviewpress.com. **Contact:** See Editorial Guidelines online. Estab. 1985. **Publishes over 40 titles/year. 500 queries received/year. 200 mss received/year. 10% of books from first-time authors. 99% from unagented writers. Pays royalty.** Publishes book 12 months after acceptance of ms. Accepts simultaneous submissions. Responds in 1 month to queries. Responds in 2 months to proposals. Responds in 4 months to manuscripts. Book catalog available free. Guidelines available online.

O- We publish in a broad variety of subject areas in the arts and social sciences. We are open to a broad range of political and philosophical viewpoints, from liberal and conservative to libertarian and Marxist, and including a wide range of feminist viewpoints.

Nonfiction Subjects include language, literature, philosophy, religion, politics. Query with SASE. Submit proposal package. Reviews artwork/photos. Send photocopies.

Recent Title(s) *More Precisely*, by Eric Steinhart; *Folk and Fairy Tales*, 4th ed., by Martin Hallet and Barbara Karasek; *Diary of a Nobody*, by George and Weedon Grossmith, ed. by Peter Morton.

Tips Our titles often appeal to a broad readership; we have many books that are as much of interest to the general reader as they are to academics and students.

BROKEN JAW PRESS

Box 596, STN A, Fredericton NB E3B 5A6, Canada. (506)454-5127. Fax: (506)454-5127. E-mail: editors@brokenjaw.com. Website: www.brokenjaw.com. **Contact:** Editorial Board. "Publishes almost exclusively Canadian-authored literary trade paperback originals and reprints". **Publishes 3-6 titles/year. 20% of books from first-time authors. 100% from unagented writers. Pays 10% royalty on retail price. Pays $0-500 advance.** Publishes book 18 months after acceptance of ms. Responds in 1 year to manuscripts. Book catalog for 6x9 SAE with 2 first-class Canadian stamps in Canada or download PDF from website. Guidelines available online.

Imprints Book Rat; Broken Jaw Press; SpareTime Editions; Dead Sea Physh Products; Maritimes Arts Projects Productions.

O- "We publish poetry, fiction, drama and literary nonfiction, including translations and multilingual books."

Nonfiction Subjects include gay, lesbian, history, language, literature, literary criticism, regional, womens issues, womens studies, contemporary culture. Reviews artwork/photos.

Fiction Subjects include literary novels and short story collections stories.

Recent Title(s) *Aquella luz, que estremece/The Light that Makes Us Tremble*, poetry by Nela Rio; Hugh Hazelton, translator; *The York County Jail: A Brief Illustrated History*, George MacBeath and Emelie Hubert.

Tips "Unsolicited manuscripts are not welcome."

CANADIAN LIBRARY ASSOCIATION

328 Frank St., Ottawa ON K2P 0X8, Canada. (613)232-9625. Fax: (613)563-9895. E-mail: publishing@cla.ca. Website: www.cla.ca. Publishes trade paperback originals. **Publishes 1 titles/year. 10 queries received/year. 5 mss received/year. 50% of books from first-time authors. 100% from unagented writers. Pays 10% royalty on wholesale price.** Publishes book 6-12 months after acceptance of ms. Responds in 1 month to queries. Responds in 3 months to proposals. Responds in 3 months to manuscripts. Book catalog and ms guidelines free.

Nonfiction Subjects include history, language, literature, library science. Submit outline. Reviews artwork/photos. Send photocopies.

Tips Our audience is library and information professionals.

CANADIAN PLAINS RESEARCH CENTER

University of Regina, Regina SK S4S 0A2, Canada. (306)585-4795. Fax: (306)585-4699. E-mail: brian.mlazgar@uregina.ca. Website: www.cprc.uregina.ca. **Contact:** Brian Mlazgar, coordinator. Estab. 1973. Publishes scholarly paperback originals and some casebound originals. **Publishes 8-10 titles/year. 35% of books from first-time authors.** Publishes book 2 years after acceptance of ms. Responds in 6 months to queries. Book catalog and ms guidelines free.

O- Canadian Plains Research Center publishes scholarly research on the Canadian plains.

Nonfiction Subjects include business, economics, government, politics, history, nature, environment, regional, sociology. Query with SASE. Submit complete ms. Reviews artwork/photos.

Recent Title(s) *I Could Not Speak My Heart: Education and Social Justice for Gay and Lesbian Youth*, edited by James McNinch and Mary Cronin (19 articles intended for education about the problems faced by gay and lesbian youth).

Tips Pay attention to manuscript preparation and accurate footnoting, according to *Chicago Manual of Style*.

CAPALL BANN PUBLISHING

Auton Farm, Milverton, Somerset, TA4 1NE, United Kingdom. (44)(182)340-1528. Fax: (44)(182)340-1529. E-mail: enquiries@capallbann.co.uk. Website: www.capallbann.co.uk. **Contact:** Julia Day (MBS, healing, animals); Jon Day (MBS, religion). Publishes trade and mass market paperback originals and trade paperback and mass market paperback reprints. **Publishes 46 titles/year. 800 queries received/year. 450 mss received/year. 50% of books from first-time authors. 100% from unagented writers. Pays 10% royalty on net sales.** Publishes book 8 months after acceptance of ms. Accepts simultaneous submissions. Responds in 2-6 weeks to queries. Responds in 2 months to proposals. Responds in 2 months to manuscripts. Book catalog available free. Guidelines available online.

O→ Our mission is to publish books of real value to enhance and improve readers' lives.

Nonfiction Subjects include animals, anthropology, archeology, gardening, health, medicine, music, dance, nature, environment, philosophy, religion, spirituality, womens issues, new age. Submit outline. Reviews artwork/photos. Send photocopies.

Recent Title(s) *The Wizard's Way To Wealth - With Benefit To All and Harm To None*, by Ian Edwards; *The Mystical & Magical World of Faerie*, by Ralph Harvey; *Shamanic Links - A Comprehensive Foundation For Modern Shamanic Practice*, by Adam Bear; *Aphrodisiacs - Aphrodite's Secrets - Sexualilty, Sexual Dysfunction, and a History and A-Z of Aphrodisiacs*, by Linda Louisa Dell.

CARCANET PRESS

Alliance House, 4th Floor, 30 Cross St., Manchester England M2 7AQ, United Kingdom. E-mail: pam@carcanet.co.uk. Website: www.carcanet.co.uk. **Contact:** Michael Schmidt, Editorial & Managing Dir. (poetry, collections, translation, literary criticism, literary history); Judith Willson, Managing Ed. (poetry). Estab. 1969. Hardcover and trade paperback originals.

Imprints Carcanet Poetry.

O→ Carcanet Press is one of Britain's leading poetry publishers. It provides a comprehensive and diverse list of modern and classic poetry in English and in translation.

Fiction Send submissions and book proposals in hard copy only.Submit proposal package, sample chapters, clips, cover letter.

Recent Title(s) *Arioflotga* , by Frank Kuppner (Great Poetic Anthology); *Collected Poems*, by Austin Clarke, ed. by R. Dardis Clarke; *Popeye in Belgrade*, by James Sutherland Smith (21st C, War writings).

Tips For intellectual literary tast To submit to *PN Review*

CHEMTEC PUBLISHING

38 Earswick Dr., Toronto-Scarborough, ON M1E 1C6, Canada. (416)265-2603. Fax: (416)265-1399. E-mail: info@chemtec.org. Website: www.chemtec.org. **Contact:** Anna Wypych, president. Publishes hardcover originals. **Publishes 5 titles/year. 10 queries received/year. 7 mss received/year. 20% of books from first-time authors. Pays 5-15% royalty on retail price.** Publishes book 6 months after acceptance of ms. Accepts simultaneous submissions. Responds in 2 months to queries. Responds in 4 months to manuscripts. Book catalog and ms guidelines free.

O→ Chemtec publishes books on polymer chemistry, physics, and technology. Special emphasis is given to process additives and books which treat subject in comprehensive manner.

Nonfiction Subjects include science, environment. Submit outline, sample chapters.

Recent Title(s) *PVC Degradation and Stabilization*, by George Wypych; *Handbook of Antibloekiny, Release, and Slip Additives*, by George Wypych; *Handbook of Material Weathering, 4th Ed.*, by George Wypych.

Tips Audience is industrial research and universities.

COACH HOUSE BOOKS

401 Huron St. on bpNichol Lane, Toronto ON M5S 2G5, Canada. (416)979-2217. Fax: (416)977-1158. Website: www.chbooks.com. **Contact:** Alana Wilcox, editor. Publishes trade paperback originals by Canadian authors. **Publishes 16 titles/year. 80% of books from first-time authors. 100% from unagented writers. Pays 10% royalty on retail price.** Publishes book 1 year after acceptance of ms. Responds in 6 months to queries. Guidelines available online.

- *All unsolicited mss returned unopened.*

Nonfiction Query with SASE.

Fiction Subjects include experimental, literary, plays. Consult website for submissions policy.

Recent Title(s) *Portable Altamount*, by Brian Joseph Davis (poetry); *Your Secrets Sleep With Me*, by Darren O'Donnell (fiction); *Goodness*, by Michael Redhill (drama).

Tips We are not a general publisher, and publish only Canadian poetry, fiction, artist books and drama. We are interested primarily in innovative or experimental writing.

COTEAU BOOKS

Thunder Creek Publishing Co-operative Ltd. 2517 Victoria Ave., Regina SK S4P 0T2, Canada. (306)777-0170.

Fax: (306)522-5152. E-mail: coteau@coteaubooks.com. Website: www.coteaubooks.com. **Contact:** Geoffrey Ursell, publisher. Estab. 1975. Publishes trade paperback originals and reprints. **Publishes 16 titles/year. 200 queries received/year. 200 mss received/year. 25% of books from first-time authors. 90% from unagented writers. Pays 10% royalty on retail price. 12 months** Responds in 3 months to queries. Responds in 3 months to manuscripts. Book catalog available free. Guidelines available online.

O- Our mission is to publish the finest in Canadian fiction, nonfiction, poetry, drama, and children's literature, with an emphasis on Saskatchewan and prairie writers. De-emphasizing science fiction, picture books.

Nonfiction Subjects include creative nonfiction, ethnic, history, language, literature, memoirs, regional, sports, travel. Submit bio, 3-4 sample chapters, SASE.

Fiction Subjects include ethnic, fantasy, feminist, gay, lesbian, historical, humor, juvenile, literary, mainstream, contemporary, multicultural, multimedia, mystery, plays, poetry, regional, short story collections, spiritual, sports, teen/young adult, novels/short fiction, adult/middle years. *Canadian authors only*. Submit bio, complete ms, SASE.

Recent Title(s) *The Tales of Three Lands Trilogy* (juvenile fantasy series for ages 9 and up); *Mud Girl*, by Alison Acheson (teen fiction); *The Book of Beasts*, by Bernice Friesen (novel); *The Hour of Bad Decisions*, by Russell Wangersky (short stories).

Tips Look at past publications to get an idea of our editorial program. We do not publish romance, horror, or picture books but are interested in juvenile and teen fiction from Canadian authors. Submissions, even queries, must be made in hard copy only. We do not accept simultaneous/multiple submissions.

CRESCENT MOON PUBLISHING

P.O. Box 393, Maidstone Kent ME14 5XU, United Kingdom. (44)(162)272-9593. E-mail: cresmopub@yahoo.co.uk. Website: www.crescentmoon.org.uk. **Contact:** Jeremy Robinson, director (arts, media, cinema, literature); Cassidy Hushes (visual arts). Estab. 1988. Publishes hardcover and trade paperback originals. **Publishes 25 titles/year. 300 queries received/year. 400 mss received/year. 1% of books from first-time authors. 1% from unagented writers. Pays royalty. Pays negotiable advance.** Publishes book 18 months after acceptance of ms. Accepts simultaneous submissions. Responds in 2 months to queries. Responds in 4 months to proposals & mss. Book catalog and ms guidelines free.

Imprints Joe's Press, *Pagan America Magazine*, *Passion Magazine*.

O- "Our mission is to publish the best in contemporary work, in poetry, fiction, and critical studies, and selections from the great writers. Currently emphasizing nonfiction (media, film, music, painting). De-emphasizing children's books."

Nonfiction Subjects include Americana, art, architecture, gardening, government, politics, language, literature, music, dance, philosophy, religion, travel, womens issues, womens studies, cinema, the media, cultural studies. Query with SASE. Submit outline, 2 sample chapters, bio. Reviews artwork/photos. Send photocopies.

Fiction Subjects include erotica, experimental, feminist, gay, lesbian, literary, short story collections, translation. We do not publish much fiction at present but will consider high quality new work. Query with SASE. Submit outline, clips, 2 sample chapters, bio.

Recent Title(s) *J.R.R. Tolkien*, by Jeremy Robinson; *Media Hell: Global Media Warning*, by Oliver Whitehorne; *Colourfield Painting*, by Stuart Morris.

Tips "Our audience is interested in new contemporary writing."

DAYA PUBLISHING HOUSE

1123/74 Deva Ram Park, Tri Nagar Delhi 110035, India. (91)(11)2738-3999. Fax: (91)(11)2326-0116. E-mail: dayabooks.vsnl.com. Website: www.dayabooks.com. Publishes specialist books at the professional level. **Publishes 50 titles/year.**

Nonfiction Subjects include agriculture, animals, anthropology, archeology, art, architecture, business, economics, child guidance, education, history, language, literature, nature, environment, philosophy, religion, science, social sciences, sociology, womens issues, womens studies, engineering, geography, library science, political science, public administration, rural development. Download online questionnaire form and submit it via e-mail or fax.

Recent Title(s) *Advanced Organic Chemistry*, by Akhilesh K. Verma; *Agriculture and Food Security*, by Ram Niwas Sharma; *The Aryan Path of the Buddha*, by K. Manohar Gupta.

DUNDURN PRESS, LTD.

3 Church St., Suite 500, Toronto ON M5E 1M2, Canada. (416)214-5544. Fax: (416)214-5556. E-mail: info@dundurn.com. Website: www.dundurn.com. **Contact:** Barry Jowett (fiction); Tony Hawke (nonfiction). Estab. 1972. Publishes hardcover and trade paperback originals and reprints. **600 queries received/year. 25% of books from first-time authors. 50% from unagented writers.** Publishes book an average of 1 year after acceptance of ms. Accepts simultaneous submissions. Responds in 3 months to queries. Guidelines available online.

Dundurn publishes books by Canadian authors.

Nonfiction Subjects include art, architecture, history, Canadian and military, war, music, dance, drama, regional, art history, theater, serious and popular nonfiction. Submit cover letter, synopsis, cv, sample chapters, SASE/IRC. Submit complete ms.

Fiction Subjects include literary, mystery, young adult. Submit sample chapters, synops

Recent Title(s) *Now You Know Almost Everything*, by Doug Lennox; *Viking Terror*, by Tom Henighan; *The Women of Beaver Hall*, by Evelyn Walters.

DUNEDIN ACADEMIC PRESS LTD

Hudson House, 8 Albany St., Edinburgh EH1 3QB, United Kingdom. (44)(131)473-2397. E-mail: mail@dunedinacademicpress.co.uk. Website: www.dunedinacademicpress.co.uk. **Contact:** Anthony Kinahan, managing director. Estab. 2001. **Publishes 15-20 titles/year. 20% of books from first-time authors. 90% from unagented writers. Pays royalty.** Book catalog available online. Proposal guidelines available online.

Ask for and look over our author proposal guidelines before submitting. Synopses and ideas welcome. Approach first in writing, outlining proposal and identifying the market.

Nonfiction Subjects include education, health policy, vocal music, philosophy, religion, earth science. Look over our author proposal guidelines before submitting. Synopses and ideas welcome. Approach us first in writing, outlining proposal and identifying the market. Reviews artwork/photos.

Recent Title(s) *Mathematical Methods for Earth Scientists*; *Faith Schools in the Twenty-first Century*; *Dementia and Well-being.*

Tips Although located in Scotland, Dunedin's list contains authors and subjects from the wider academic world and DAP's horizons are far broader than our immediate Scottish environment. One of the strengths of Dunedin is that we are able to offer our authors that individual support that comes from dealing with a small independent publisher committed to growth through careful treatment of its authors.

ECW PRESS

2120 Queen St. E., Suite 200, Toronto ON M4E 1E2, Canada. (416)694-3348. Fax: (416)698-9906. E-mail: info@ecwpress.com. Website: www.ecwpress.com. **Contact:** Jack David, president (nonfiction); Michael Holmes, senior editor (fiction, poetry); Jennifer Hale, senior editor (pop culture, entertainment). Estab. 1979. Publishes hardcover and trade paperback originals. **Publishes 50 titles/year. 500 queries received/year. 300 mss received/year. 30% of books from first-time authors. Pays $300-5,000 advance.** Publishes book 18 months after acceptance of ms. Accepts simultaneous submissions. Book catalog available free. Guidelines available online.

Imprints misFit (Michael Holmes, literary editor)

ECW publishes nonfiction about people or subjects that have a substantial fan base. Currently emphasizing books about music, gambling, TV, and sports.

Nonfiction Subjects include business, economics, creative nonfiction, gay, lesbian, government, politics, health, medicine, history, memoirs, money, finance, regional, sex, sports, womens issues, contemporary culture, gambling. Submit proposal package, outline, 4-5 sample chapters, IRC, SASE. Reviews artwork/photos. Send photocopies.

Fiction We publish literary fiction and poetry from Canadian authors exclusively.Subjects include literary, mystery, poetry, short story collections, suspense. Visit company website to view

Recent Title(s) *Too Close to the Falls*, by Catherine Gildiner; *Ghost Rider*, by Neil Peart; *Ashland*, by Gil Adamson (poetry).

Tips Visit our website and read a selection of our books.

EDGE SCIENCE FICTION AND FANTASY PUBLISHING

Box 1714, Calgary AB T2P 2L7, Canada. (403)254-0160. Fax: (403)254-0456. Website: www.edgewebsite.com. Estab. 1996. Publishes hardcover and trade paperback originals. **Publishes 6-8 titles/year. 400 mss received/year. 70% of books from first-time authors. 75% from unagented writers. Pays 10% royalty on wholesale price. Pays negotiable advance.** Publishes book 18 months after acceptance of ms. Responds in 1 month to queries. Responds in 1 month to proposals. Responds in 4-5 months to manuscripts. Guidelines available online.

We want to encourage, produce, and promote thought-provoking and well-written science fiction and fantasy literature.

Fiction Subjects include fantasy, space fantasy, sword and sorcery, science fiction, hard science fiction/technological, soft/sociological. We are looking for all types of fantasy and science fiction, except juvenile/young adult, horror, erotica, religious fiction, short stories, dark/gruesome fantasy, or poetry. Submit outline, 3 sample chapters, clips. Check website or send SAE & IR.

Recent Title(s) *The Black Chalice*, by Marie Jakober; *Eclipse*, by K.A. Bedford; *Stealing Magic*, by Tanya Huff.

Tips Send us your best, polished, completed manuscript. Use proper manuscript format. Take the time before you submit to get a critique from someone who can offer you useful advice. When in doubt, visit our website for helpful resources, FAQs, and other tips.

ÉDITIONS DU NOROÎT

4609 D'Iberville, Bureau 202, Montreal QC H2H 2L9, Canada. (514)727-0005. Fax: (514)723-6660. E-mail: lenoroit@lenoroit.com. Website: www.lenoroit.com. **Contact:** Paul Belanger, director. Publishes trade paperback originals and reprints. **Publishes 20 titles/year. 500 queries received/year. 500 mss received/year. Pays 10% royalty on retail price.** Publishes book 1 year after acceptance of ms. Responds in 4 months to manuscripts.

Editions du Noiroît publishes poetry and essays on poetry.

Recent Title(s) *Origine des Méridiens*, by Paul Bélanger; *Les corps carillonnent*, by Ivan Bielinski; *Piano mélancolique*, by Élise Turcotte.

FERNWOOD PUBLISHING, LTD.

32 Ocenavista Lane, Site 2A, Box 5, Black Pointe NS B0J 1B0, Canada. (902)857-1388. E-mail: errol@fernpub.ca. Website: www.fernwoodpublishing.ca. **Contact:** Errol Sharpe, publisher (social science); Wayne Antony, editor (social science). Publishes trade paperback originals. **Publishes 15-20 titles/year. 80 queries received/year. 30 mss received/year. 40% of books from first-time authors. 100% from unagented writers. Pays 7-10% royalty on wholesale price. Pays advance.** Publishes book 1 year after acceptance of ms. Accepts simultaneous submissions. Responds in 6 weeks to proposals. Guidelines available online.

Fernwood's objective is to publish critical works which challenge existing scholarship.

Nonfiction Subjects include agriculture, anthropology, archeology, business, economics, education, ethnic, gay, lesbian, government, politics, health, medicine, history, language, literature, multicultural, nature, environment, philosophy, regional, sex, sociology, sports, translation, womens issues, womens studies, contemporary culture, world affairs. Submit proposal package, outline, sample chapters. Reviews artwork/photos. Send photocopies.

Recent Title(s) *Challenges and Perils: Social Democracy in Neoliberal Times*, edited by William K. Carroll and R.S. Ratner; *Empire With Imperialism: The Global Dynamics of Neoliberal Capitalism*, by James Petras, Henry Veltmeyer, Luciano Vasapollo and Mauro Casadio; *Cultivating Utopia: Organic Farmers in a Conventional Landscape*, by Kregg Hetherington.

FINDHORN PRESS

305A The Park, Findhorn, Forres Scotland IV36 3TE, United Kingdom. (44)(130)969-0582. Fax: (44)(130)969-0036. Website: www.findhornpress.com. **Contact:** Thierry Bogliolo, publisher. Estab. 1971. Publishes trade paperback originals. **Publishes 20 titles/year. 1,000 queries received/year. 50% of books from first-time authors. 80% from unagented writers. Pays 10-15% royalty on wholesale price.** Publishes book 12 months after acceptance of ms. Responds in 2-3 months to proposals, due to the large number of submissions. Book catalog and ms guidelines online.

Nonfiction Subjects include ealth, nature, spirituality.

Fiction No fiction, short stories, or poetry.

Recent Title(s) *Free Your True Self 2*, by Annie Marquier; *Bodylessons*, by Marian Wolfe Dixon; *The Healing Power of Seashells*, by Daya Sarai Chocron.

FORMAC PUBLISHING CO. LTD.

5502 Atlantic St., Halifax NS B3H 1G4, Canada. (902)421-7022. Fax: (902)425-0166. Website: www.formac.ca. **Contact:** Elizabeth Eve, senior editor (Canadian history and geography). Estab. 1977. Publishes hardcover and trade paperback originals. **Publishes 15-20 titles/year. 200 queries received/year. 150 mss received/year. 20% of books from first-time authors. 75% from unagented writers. Pays 5-10% royalty on wholesale price.** Publishes book 1 year after acceptance of ms. Accepts simultaneous submissions. Responds in 2 months to queries. Responds in 2 months to proposals. Responds in 4 months to manuscripts. Book catalog available free. Guidelines available online.

Nonfiction Subjects include animals, art, architecture, cooking, foods, nutrition, creative nonfiction, government, politics, history, military, war, multicultural, nature, environment, regional, travel, marine subjects, transportation. Submit proposal package, outline, 2 sample chapters, cv or résumé of author(s).

Recent Title(s) *Fastest in the World: The Saga of Canada's Revolutionary Hydrofoils*, by John Boileau (military, transportation, history, illustrated).

Tips For our illustrated books, ou Check out our website and see

GOOSE LANE EDITIONS

500 Beaverbrook Ct., Suite 330, Fredericton, New Brunswick E3B 5X4, Canada. (506)450-4251. Fax: (506)459-4991. Website: www.gooselane.com. **Contact:** Angela Williams, publishing assistant. Estab. 1954. Publishes hardcover and paperback originals and occasional reprints. **Publishes 16-20 titles/year. 20% of books from**

first-time authors. 60% from unagented writers. Pays 8-10% royalty on retail price. Pays $500-3,000, negotiable advance. Responds in 6 months to queries.

- Goose Lane publishes literary fiction and nonfiction from well-read and highly skilled Canadian authors.

Nonfiction Subjects include art, architecture, history, language, literature, nature, environment, regional, womens issues, womens studies. Query with SASE.

Fiction Subjects include literary, novels, short story collections, contemporary. Our needs in fiction never change: Substantial, character-centered literary fiction. Query with SAE with Canadian s

Recent Title(s) *The Nettle Spinner*, by Kathryn Kuitenbrouwer; *Ideas*, edited by Bernie Lucht.

Tips Writers should send us outlines and samples of books that show a very well-read author with highly developed literary skills. Our books are almost all by Canadians living in Canada; we seldom consider submissions from outside Canada. If I were a writer trying to market a book today, I would contact the targeted publisher with a query letter and synopsis, and request manuscript guidelines. Purchase a recent book from the publisher in a relevant area, if possible. Always send an SASE with IRCs or suffient return postage in Canadian stamps for reply to your query and for any material you'd like returned should it not suit our needs.

GUERNICA EDITIONS

Box 117, Station P, Toronto ON M5S 2S6, Canada. (416)658-9888. Fax: (416)657-8885. E-mail: guernicaeditions@cs.com. Website: www.guernicaeditions.com. **Contact:** Antonio D'Alfonso, editor/publisher (poetry, nonfiction, novels). Estab. 1978. Publishes trade paperback originals, reprints, and software. **Publishes 15 titles/year. 750 mss received/year. 20% of books from first-time authors. 99% from unagented writers. Pays 8-10% royalty on retail price, or makes outright purchase of $200-5,000. Pays $200-2,000 advance.** Publishes book 15 months after acceptance of ms. Responds in 1 month to queries. Responds in 6 months to proposals. Responds in 1 year to manuscripts. Book catalog available online.

- Guernica Editions is an independent press dedicated to the bridging of cultures. We do original and translations of fine works. We are seeking essays on authors and translations with less emphasis on poetry.

Nonfiction Subjects include art, architecture, creative nonfiction, ethnic, film, cinema, stage, gay, lesbian, government, politics, history, language, literature, lit-crit, memoirs, multicultural, music, dance, philosophy, psychology, regional, religion, sex, translation, womens issues. Query with SASE. *All unsolicited mss returned unopened.* Reviews artwork/photos. Send photocopies.

Fiction Subjects include erotica, feminist, gay, lesbian, literary, multicultural, plays, poetry, poetry in translation, translation. We wish to open up into the fiction world and focus less on poetry. We specialize in European, especially Italian, translations. Query with SASE. *All unsolicited mss returned unopened.*

Recent Title(s) *At the Copa*, by Marisa Labozzetta; *Intimate Dialogues*, by Hèlène Rioux; *Peace Tower*, by F. G. Paci; *The Trestler House*, by Madeleine Quellette-Michalska.

HARLEQUIN ENTERPRISES, LTD.

225 Duncan Mill Rd., Don Mills ON M3B 3K9, Canada. (416)445-5860. Website: www.eharlequin.com. Estab. 1949. Publishes mass market paperback, trade paperback, and hardcover originals and reprints. **Publishes 1,500 titles/year. Pays royalty. Pays advance.** Publishes book 1-2 years after acceptance of ms. Responds in 6 weeks to queries. Responds in 3 months to manuscripts. Guidelines available online.

Imprints Harlequin Books; Silhouette; MIRA; Luna; HQN Books; Mills & Boon; Steeple Hill Books; Red Dress Ink; Steeple Hill Café.

- Websites: www.eharlequin.com; www.mirabooks.com; www.reddressink.com; www.steeplehill.com; www.luna-books.com.

Fiction Considers all types of serious romance and strong, mainstream, women's fiction. For series, query with SASE. MIRA accepts *agented submissions only*.

Tips "The quickest route to success is to check www.eharlequin.com, the other websites listed above, or write or call for submission guidlines. We acquire first novelists. Before submitting, read as many current titles in the imprint or line of your choice as you can. It's very important to know the genre, what readers are looking for, and the series or imprint most appropriate for your submission."

HARPERCOLLINS CANADA, LTD.

2 Bloor St. E., 20th Floor, Toronto ON M4W 1A8, Canada. (416)975-9334. Fax: (416)975-5223. Website: www.harpercollins.ca. Estab. 1989.

Imprints HarperCollinsPublishers; HarperPerennialCanada (trade paperbacks); HarperTrophyCanada (children's); Phyllis Bruce Books.

- HarperCollins Canada is not accepting unsolicited material at this time.

Recent Title(s) *Hope Diamond*, by Richard Kurin; *Madame Zee*, by Pearl Luke; *Real Life Entertaining*, by Jennifer Rubell.

Canadian & Intl Book Pubs

HELTER SKELTER PUBLISHING

18a Radbourne Rd., London SW12 0DZ, United Kingdom. (44)(208)673-6320. E-mail: sales@helterskelterbooks.com. **Contact:** Graeme Milton, editor. Publishes hardcover and trade paperback originals and trade paperback reprints. **Publishes 10 titles/year. 50 queries received/year. 30 mss received/year. 50% of books from first-time authors. 60% from unagented writers. Pays 8-12½% royalty on retail price.**

Our mission is to publish high quality books about music and cinema subjects of enduring appeal.

Nonfiction Subjects include music. Submit outline, 2 sample chapters. Reviews artwork/photos. Send photocopies.

Recent Title(s) *Natural Born Man: The Life of Jack Johnson; Music in Dreamland: Bill Nelson & Be Bop Deluxe.*

Tips The subject artist should have a career spanning at least five years.

HERITAGE HOUSE PUBLISHING CO., LTD.

#340-1105 Pandora Ave., Victoria BC V8V 3P9, Canada. 250-360-0829. E-mail: editorial@heritagehouse.ca. Website: www.heritagehouse.ca. **Contact:** Rodger Touchie, publisher/president. Publishes trade paperback originals. **Publishes 10-12 titles/year. 200 queries received/year. 60 mss received/year. 50% of books from first-time authors. 90% from unagented writers. Pays 12-15% royalty on net proceeds. Advances are rarely paid.** Publishes book Usually 1 year after acceptance of ms. Responds in 6 months to queries. Book catalog for #10 SASE. Guidelines available online.

Heritage House is primarily a regional publisher of books that celebrate the historical and cultural heritage of Western Canada and, to an extent, the Pacific Northwest; we also publish some titles of national interest and a series of books aimed at young and casual readers, called *Amazing Stories*.

Nonfiction Subjects include regional history, nature, environment, recreation, true crime, first nations, adventure. Query with SASE. Include synopsis, outline, marketing strategy, 2-3 sample chapters, indicate supporting illustrative material available. Reviews artwork/photos. Send photocopies.

Fiction No fiction.

Recent Title(s) *Never Shoot a Stampede Queen: A Rookie Reporter in the Cariboo,* by Mark Leiren-Young; *Country Roads of British Columbia: Exploring the Interior*, by Liz Bryan; *Reena: A Father's Story*, by Manjit Virk; *Robert Service: Under the Spell of the Yukon*, by Enid Mallory; *More Great Dog Stories: Inspirational Tales About Exceptional Dogs*, by Roxanne Willems Snopek.

Tips Our books appeal to residents of and visitors to the northwest quadrant of the continent. We're looking for good stories and good storytellers. We focus on work by Canadian authors.

HIPPOPOTAMUS PRESS

22 Whitewell Rd., Frome, Somerset BA11 4EL, United Kingdom. (44)(173)466-6653. E-mail: rjhippopress@aol.com. **Contact:** R. John, editor; M. Pargitter (poetry); Anna Martin (translation). Estab. 1974. Publishes hardcover and trade paperback originals. **Publishes 6-12 titles/year. 90% of books from first-time authors. 90% from unagented writers. Pays 7 ½-10% royalty on retail price. Pays advance.** Publishes book 10 months after acceptance of ms. Accepts simultaneous submissions. Responds in 1 month to queries. Book catalog available free.

"Hippopotamus Press publishes first, full collections of verse by those well represented in the mainstream poetry magazines of the English-speaking world."

Nonfiction Subjects include language, literature, translation. Query with SASE. Submit complete ms.

Recent Title(s) Touching on Love, by David Clarke; Mystic Bridge, by Edward Lowbury.

Tips We publish books for a literate audience. We have a strong link to the Modernist tradition. Read what we publish.

HOUSE OF ANANSI PRESS

110 Spadina Ave., Suite 801, Toronto ON M5V 2K4, Canada. Fax: (416)363-1017. Website: www.anansi.ca. **Contact:** Lynn Henry, publisher. Estab. 1967. Publishes hardcover and trade paperback originals and paperback reprints. **Publishes 10-15 titles/year. 750 queries received/year. 5% of books from first-time authors. 50% from unagented writers. Pays 8-15% royalty on retail price. Pays $500-2,000 advance.** Publishes book 18 months after acceptance of ms. Accepts simultaneous submissions. Responds in 2 months to queries. Responds in 3 months to proposals. Responds in 4 months to manuscripts. Book catalog available free. Guidelines available online.

Our mission is to publish the best new literary writers in Canada and to continue to grow and adapt along with the Canadian literary community while maintaining Anansi's rich history.

Nonfiction Subjects include anthropology, archeology, gay, lesbian, government, politics, history, language, literature, literary criticism, philosophy, science, sociology, womens issues, womens studies. Query with SASE. Submit outline, 2 sample chapters. Reviews artwork/photos. Send photocopies.

Fiction Subjects include ethnic, general, experimental, feminist, gay, lesbian, literary, short story collections, translation. We publish literary fiction by Canadian authors. Authors must have been published in established

literary magazines and/or journals. We only want to consider sample chapters. Query with SASE. Submit outline, clips, 2 sample chapters.
Recent Title(s) *Alligator*, by Lisa Moore; *Moving Targets*, by Margaret Atwood; *A Short History of Progress*, by Ronald Wright.
Tips Submit often to magazines and journals. Read and buy other writers' work. Know and be a part of your writing community.

INSOMNIAC PRESS

520 Princess Ave., London ON N6B 2B8, Canada. (416)504-6270. E-mail: mike@insomniacpress.com. Website: www.insomniacpress.com. **Contact:** Mike O'Connor, publisher. Estab. 1992. Publishes trade paperback originals and reprints, mass market paperback originals, and electronic originals and reprints. **Publishes 20 titles/year. 250 queries received/year. 1,000 mss received/year. 50% of books from first-time authors. 80% from unagented writers. Pays 10-15% royalty on retail price. Pays $500-1,000 advance.** Publishes book 6 months after acceptance of ms. Accepts simultaneous submissions. Guidelines available online.
Nonfiction Subjects include business, creative nonfiction, gay, lesbian, government, politics, health, medicine, language, literature, money, finance, multicultural, religion, true crime. Query via e-mail, submit proposal package including outline, 2 sample chapters, or submit complete ms. Reviews artwork/photos. Send photocopies.
Fiction Subjects include comic books, ethnic, experimental, gay, lesbian, humor, literary, mainstream, multicultural, mystery, poetry, suspense. We publish a mix of commercial (mysteries) and literary fiction. Query via e-mail, submit proposal.
Recent Title(s) *Dance Hall Road*, by Marion Douglas; *Why Are You So Sad?* by David McFadden; *Stock Market Superstars*, by Bob Thompson.
Tips We envision a mixed readership that appreciates up-and-coming literary fiction and poetry as well as solidly researched and provocative nonfiction. Peruse our website and familiarize yourself with what we've published in the past.

KEY PORTER BOOKS

6 Adelaide St. E, 10th Floor, Toronto ON M5C 1H6, Canada. (416)862-7777. Fax: (416)862-2304. E-mail: info@keyporter.com. Website: www.keyporter.com. **Contact:** Jordan Fenn, publisher. Estab. 1979. Publishes hardcover and trade paperback originals and reprints. **Publishes 100 titles/year. 1,000 queries received/year. Pays royalty.** Responds in 4 months to queries. Responds in 6 months to proposals.
Imprints Key Porter Kids; L&OD.

- No unsolicited mss.

O→ Key Porter specializes in autobiography, biography, children's, cookbook, gift book, how-to, humor, illustrated book, self-help, young adult. Subjects include art, architecture, business, economics, parenting, food, creative nonfiction, gardening, general nonfiction, politics, health, history, humanities, memoirs, military, personal finance, nature, environment, photography, psychology, science, social sciences, sociology, sports, translation, travel, women's issues, world affairs, and literary fiction. Query with SASE. Reviews artwork/photos as part of ms package. Send photocopies only.

KINDRED PRODUCTIONS

1310 Taylor Ave., Winnipeg MB R3M 3Z6, Canada. (204)669-6575. Fax: (204)654-1865. E-mail: kindred@mbconf.ca. Website: www.kindredproductions.com. **Contact:** Mario Buscio, manager. Publishes trade paperback originals and reprints. **Publishes 3 titles/year. 1% of books from first-time authors. 100% from unagented writers.** Publishes book 18 months after acceptance of ms. Accepts simultaneous submissions. Responds in 3 months to queries. Responds in 5 months to manuscripts. Guidelines available online.

O→ Kindred Productions publishes, promotes, and markets print and nonprint resources that will shape our Christian faith and discipleship from a Mennonite Brethren perspective. Currently emphasizing inspirational with cross-over potential. De-emphasizing personal experience, biographical. No children's books or fiction.

Nonfiction Subjects include religion, inspirational. Query with SASE. Submit outline, 2-3 sample chapters.
Recent Title(s) *Being With Jesus*, by Carol Baergen; *Turning the World Upside Down*, by Edmund Janzen; *Out of the Strange Silence*, by Brad Thiessen.
Tips Most of our books are sold to churches, religious bookstores, and schools. We are concentrating on inspirational books. We do not accept children's manuscripts.

N KUNATI INC.

75 First St., Suite 128, Orangeville ON L9W 5B6, Canada. Fax: (905)625-8987. E-mail: info@kunati.com. Website: www.kunati.com. **Contact:** James McKinnon, editor-in-chief (all commercial categories, edgy fiction, literary fiction, memoir, humor); Derek Armstrong, publisher (thrillers, mystery, suspense, non-slasher horror, historical epic, fantasy epic, science fiction, true crime). Estab. 2005. Publishes hardcover originals and trade paperbacks. **Publishes 26 titles/year. 1,200 queries received/year. 450 mss received/year. 80% of books**

from first-time authors. 75% from unagented writers. Pays 10-15% royalty. Publishes book 8 months after acceptance of ms. Accepts simultaneous submissions. Responds in 1 month to queries. Responds in 2-3 months to proposals. Responds in 2 months to manuscripts. You can get a catalog and ms guidelines online, for #10 SASE, or via e-mail.

- Unless you have an absolutely stunning voice, your best opportunity to make us sit up and pay attention is to submit only the most quirky, different, funky, controversial, hiarious, and bizarre material—anything but academic or mainstream. On the other hand, do not bother submitting extremism, quackery, or memoirs without truth. There's a fine line between fun and silly; either entertain to the extreme or present new ideas.

Nonfiction Subjects include creative nonfiction, gardening, health, medicine, memoirs, money, finance, multicultural, nature, environment, New Age, philosophy, psychology, religion, science, sex, social sciences, sociology, spirituality, sports, womens issues, womens studies, world affairs. Query with outline, 3 sample chapters, SASE via mail or e-mail. Reviews artwork/photos. Send photocopies.

Fiction Subjects include adventure, confession, erotica, ethnic, experimental, fantasy, gay, lesbian, gothic, historical, horror, humor, juvenile, literary, mainstream, contemporary, multicultural, mystery, occult, science fiction, sports, suspense, young adult. We don't pay attention to category or genre. If it's edgy, we're interested. Query with short synopsis (tha

Recent Title(s) *Toonamint of Champions*, by Todd Sentell; *Rabid*, by T.K. Kenyon; *Whale Song*, by Cheryl Kaye Tardiff.

Tips Our books cover all audiences Your query letter and synopsis

LES ÉDITIONS DU VERMILLON

305 Saint Patrick St., Ottawa ON K1N 5K4, Canada. (613)241-4032. Fax: (613)241-3109. E-mail: leseditionsduvermillon@rogers.com. Website: www.leseditionsduvermillon.ca. **Contact:** Jacques Flamand, editorial director. Publishes trade paperback originals. **Publishes 15-20 titles/year. Pays 10% royalty.** Publishes book 18 months after acceptance of ms. Responds in 6 months to manuscripts. Book catalog available free.

Fiction Subjects include juvenile, literary, religious, short story collections, young adult.

LEXISNEXIS CANADA, INC.

123 Commerce Valley Dr. E., Suite 700, Markham ON L3T 7W8, Canada. (905)479-2665. Fax: (905)479-2826. E-mail: info@lexisnexis.ca. Website: www.lexisnexis.ca. **Contact:** Product Development Director. **Publishes 100 titles/year. 50% of books from first-time authors. 100% from unagented writers. Pays 5-15% royalty on wholesale price.** Publishes book 4 months after acceptance of ms. Accepts simultaneous submissions. Responds in 1 month to queries. Book catalog available free. Guidelines available online.

- LexisNexis Canada, Inc., publishes professional reference material for the legal, business, and accounting markets under the Butterworths imprint and operates the Quicklaw and LexisNexis online services.

Recent Title(s) *The Canada-U.S. Tax Treaty Text and Commentary*, by Vern Krishna; *The Public Purchasing Law Handbook*, by Robert C. Worthington; *Corporate Law in Quebec*, by Stephan Rousseau.

Tips Audience is legal community, business, medical, accounting professions.

LONE PINE PUBLISHING

10145 81st Ave., Edmonton AB T6E 1W9, Canada. (403)433-9333. Fax: (403)433-9646. Website: www.lonepinepublishing.com. **Contact:** Nancy Foulds, editorial director. Estab. 1980. Publishes trade paperback originals and reprints. **Publishes 30-40 titles/year. 75% of books from first-time authors. 95% from unagented writers. Pays royalty.** Responds in 3 months to queries. Book catalog available free.

Imprints Lone Pine; Home World; Pine Candle; Pine Cone; Ghost House Books.

- Lone Pine publishes natural history and outdoor recreation—including gardening—titles and some popular history and ghost story collections by region. 'The World Outside Your Door' is our motto—helping people appreciate nature and their own special place. Currently emphasizing ghost stories by region and gardening by region.

Nonfiction Subjects include animals, gardening, nature, environment, recreation, regional. Query with SASE. Submit outline, sample chapters. Reviews artwork/photos.

Recent Title(s) *Birds of New York State*, by Bob Budliger and Gregory Kennedy; *Best Garden Plants for Montana*, by Dr. Bob Gough, Cheryl Moore-Gough and Laura Peters; *Ghost Stories of North Carolina*, by Edrick Thay.

Tips Writers have their best chance with recreational or nature guidebooks. Most of our books are strongly regional in nature.

LOON IN BALLOON INC.

133 Weber St. N., Suite #3-513, Waterloo ON N2J 3G9, Canada. E-mail: info@looninballoon.com. Website: www.looninballoon.com. Estab. 2003. Publishes trade paperback originals. **Publishes 5-10 titles/year. 100 mss received/year. 50% of books from first-time authors. 75% from unagented writers. Pays 8-10% royalty on retail price.** Publishes book 6 months after acceptance of ms. Accepts simultaneous submissions. Responds

in 3 months to queries. Responds in 3 months to proposals. Responds in 3 months to manuscripts. Guidelines available online.

Fiction Subjects include adventure, historical, horror, humor, mainstream, contemporary, military, war, mystery, romance, science fiction, suspense, western. Submit proposal package, clips, first 2 chapters.

Recent Title(s) *Murder at Mussel Cove*, by Hugh MacDonald; *Bethesda*, by Adrian White; *The Kremlin in Betrayal*, by Leon Berger.

Tips We publish adult popular fict We are small, but aggressive.

LYNX IMAGES, INC.

P.O. Box 5961, Station A, Toronto ON M5W 1P4, Canada. (416)925-8422. E-mail: submissions@lynximages.com. Website: www.lynximages.com. **Contact:** Russell Floren, president; Andrea Gutsche, director; Barbara Chisholm, producer. Estab. 1988. Publishes hardcover and trade paperback originals. **Publishes 6 titles/year. 100 queries received/year. 50 mss received/year. 80% of books from first-time authors. 80% from unagented writers. Pays 40% advance.** Publishes book 1 year after acceptance of ms. Accepts simultaneous submissions. Responds in 90 days to queries. Guidelines available online.

- Lynx publishes historical tourism, travel, Canadian history, and Great Lakes history. Currently emphasizing travel, history, and nature. De-emphasizing boating, guides.

Nonfiction Subjects include history, nature, environment, travel. Submit proposal, synopsis, bio, market research. Reviews artwork/photos.

Recent Title(s) *Guiding Lights Tragic Shadows: Tales of Great Lakes Lighthouses*, by Ed Butts.

MANOR HOUSE PUBLISHING, INC.

452 Cottingham Crescent, Ancaster ON L9G 3V6, Canada. (905)648-2193. Fax: (905)648-8369. E-mail: mbdavie@manorhouse.biz. Website: www.manor-house.biz. **Contact:** Mike Davie, president (novels, poetry, and nonfiction). Estab. 1998. Publishes hardcover, trade paperback, and mass market paperback originals, and mass market paperback reprints. **Publishes 5-6 titles/year. 30 queries received/year. 20 mss received/year. 90% of books from first-time authors. 90% from unagented writers. Pays 10% royalty on retail price.** Publishes book 12-14 months after acceptance of ms. Accepts simultaneous submissions. Queries and mss to be sent by email only. We will respond in 30 days if interested—if not, there is no response. Do not follow up unless asked to do so. Book catalog available online. Guidelines available via e-mail.

Nonfiction Subjects include alternative, anthropology, business, community, history, sex, social sciences, sociology, spirituality. Query via email. Submit proposal package, outline, bio, 3 sample chapters. Submit complete ms. Reviews artwork/photos. Send photocopies.

Fiction Subjects include adventure, experimental, gothic, historical, horror, humor, juvenile, literary, mystery, occult, poetry, regional, romance, short story collections, young adult. Stories should have Canadian settings and characters should be Canadian, but content should have universal appeal to wide audience. Query via email. Submit proposal package, clips, bio, 3 sample chapters. Submit complete ms.

Recent Title(s) *The Lost Chord*, by Ian Thomas; *Poetry for the Insane: The Full Mental*, by Michael B. Davie; *Poor Little Bitch Girl*, by CJ Sleez.

Tips Our audience includes everyone—the general public/mass audience. Self-edit your work first, make sure it is well written with strong Canadian content.

MAVERICK MUSICALS AND PLAYS

89 Bergann Rd., Maleny QLD 4552, Australia. Phone/Fax: (61)(7)5494-4007. E-mail: helen@mavmuse.com. Website: www.mavmuse.com. **Contact:** The Editor. Estab. 1978. Guidelines available online.

Fiction Subjects include plays. Looking for two-act musicals and one- and two-act plays. See website for more details.

MCCLELLAND & STEWART, LTD.

The Canadian Publishers 75 Sherbourne St., Toronto ON M5A 2P9, Canada. (416)598-1114. Fax: (416)598-7764. E-mail: editorial@mcclelland.com. Website: www.mcclelland.com. Publishes hardcover, trade paperback, and mass market paperback originals and reprints. **Publishes 80 titles/year. 1,500 queries received/year. 10% of books from first-time authors. 30% from unagented writers. Pays 10-15% royalty on retail price (hardcover rates). Pays advance.** Publishes book 1 year after acceptance of ms. Responds in 3 months to proposals.

Imprints McClelland & Stewart; New Canadian Library; Douglas Gibson Books; Emblem Editions (Ellen Seligman, editor).

Nonfiction We publish books primarily by Canadian authors.Subjects include art, architecture, business, economics, gay, lesbian, government, politics, health, medicine, history, language, literature, military, war, music, dance, nature, environment, philosophy, photography, psychology, recreation, religion, science, sociology, sports, translation, travel, womens issues, womens studies, Canadiana. Submit outline. *All unsolicited mss returned unopened.*

Fiction We publish work by established authors, as well as the work of new and developing authors. Query. *All unsolicited mss*

Recent Title(s) *Runaway*, by Alice Munro; *Norman Bray in the Performance of His Life*, by Trevor Cole; *The Mysteries*, by Robert McGill.

MELBOURNE UNIVERSITY PUBLISHING, LTD.

Subsidiary of University of Melbourne 187 Grattan St., Carlton VIC 3053, Australia. (61)(3)934-20300. Fax: (61)(3)9342-0399. E-mail: mup-info@unimelb.edu.au. Website: www.mup.com.au. **Contact:** The Executive Assistant. Estab. 1922. **Publishes 80 titles/year.** Responds to queries in 4 months if interested. Guidelines available online.

Imprints Melbourne University Press; The Miegunyah Press (strong Australian content).

Nonfiction Subjects include art, politics, philosophy, science, social sciences, Aboriginal studies, cultural studies, gender studies, natural history. Submit using MUP Book Proposal Form available online.

Recent Title(s) *TThe Costello Memoirs*, by Peter Costello & Peter Coleman; *Detainee 002*, by Leigh Sales; *First Australians*, by Rachel Perkins; *The Constant Gardener*, by Holly Kerr Forsyth.

MUSSIO VENTURES PUBLISHING LTD.

5811 Beresford St., Burnaby BC V5J1K1, Canada. (604)438-3474. Fax: (604)438-3470. Website: www.backroadmapbooks.com. Estab. 1993. **Publishes 5 titles/year. 5 queries received/year. 2 mss received/year. 25% of books from first-time authors. 0% from unagented writers. Makes outright purchase of 2,000-4,800. Pays $1,000 advance.** Publishes book 12 months after acceptance of ms. Accepts simultaneous submissions. Responds in 1 month to queries. Responds in 1 month to proposals. Responds in 1 month to manuscripts. Book catalog available free.

Nonfiction Subjects include nature, environment, maps and guides. Submit proposal package, outline/proposal, 1 sample chapter. Reviews artwork/photos. Send photocopies and Digital files.

Recent Title(s) *Nova Scotia Backroad Mapbook*, by Linda Akosmitis; *Northern BC Backroad Mapbook*, by Trent Ernst.

Tips Audience includes outdoor recreation enthusiasts and travellers. Provide a proposal including an outline and samples.

NAPOLEON & COMPANY

178 Willowdale Ave., Suite 201, Toronto ON M2N 4Y8, Canada. (416)730-9052. Fax: (416)730-8096. E-mail: napoleon@napoleonandcompany.com. Website: www.napoleonandcompany.com. **Contact:** A. Thompson, editor. Estab. 1990. Publishes hardcover and trade paperback originals and reprints. **Publishes 15 titles/year. 200 queries received/year. 100 mss received/year. 50% of books from first-time authors. 75% from unagented writers.** Publishes book 18 months after acceptance of ms. Accepts simultaneous submissions. Responds in 1 month to queries. Responds in 3 months to proposals. Responds in 6 months to manuscripts. Book catalog and guidelines available online.

- Napoleon is not accepting children's picture books at this time. Rendezvous Crime is not accepting mysteries. Check website for updates. We are accepting general adult fiction only for RendezVous Press and Darkstar Fiction.

O‑‑ Rendezvous publishes adult fiction. Napoleon publishes children's books.

Nonfiction Query with SASE. Submit outline, 1 sample chapter.

Recent Title(s) *Short Candles*, by Rita Donovan; *Too Hot to Handle*, by Mary Jane Maffini; *Treasure at Turtle Lake*, by Peggy Leavey.

Tips Canadian resident authors only.

NATURAL HERITAGE/NATURAL HISTORY, INC.

P.O. Box 95, Station O, Toronto ON M4A 2M8, Canada. (416)694-7907. Fax: (416)690-0819. E-mail: info@naturalheritagebooks.com. Website: www.naturalheritagebooks.com. **Contact:** Barry Penhale, publisher. Publishes trade paperback originals. **Publishes 10-12 titles/year. 50% of books from first-time authors. 85% from unagented writers. Pays 8-10% royalty on retail price.** Publishes book 2-3 years after acceptance of ms. Accepts simultaneous submissions. Responds in 4 months to queries. Responds in 6 months to proposals. Responds in 6 months to manuscripts. Book catalog available free. Guidelines available online.

Imprints Natural Heritage Books.

O‑‑ Currently emphasizing heritage, history, nature.

Nonfiction Subjects include ethnic, history, nature, environment, recreation, regional. Submit outline.

Fiction Query with SASE.

Recent Title(s) *Canoeing a Continent: On the Trail of Alexander Mackenzie*, by Max Finkelstein (nonfiction); *Algonquin Wildlife: Lessons in Survival*, by Norm Quinn (nonfiction); *The Underground Railroad: Next Stop, Toronto!*, by Adrienne Shadd, Afua Cooper, and Karolyn Smardz Frost (young adult nonfiction).

Tips We are a Canadian publisher in the natural heritage and history fields. We publish only Canadian authors or books with significant Canadian content.

NEW AFRICA BOOKS

New Africa Books (Pty) Ltd P.O. Box 46962, Glosderry 7702, South Africa. (27)(21)674-4136. Fax: (27)(21)674-3358. E-mail: info@newafricabooks.co.za. Website: www.newafricabooks.co.za. **Contact:** David Philip, publisher. **Publishes 8-10 titles/year. 40% of books from first-time authors. 80% from unagented writers. Pays royalty.**

Imprints New Africa Education; David Phillip Publishers; Spearhead Press (business, self-improvement, health, natural history, travel, fiction, cookery, and newsworthy books).

Nonfiction Subjects include art, architecture, education, history, memoirs, politics, science, lifestyle.

Fiction Subjects include juvenile, literary.

Recent Title(s) *In the Manure*, by Ronnie Govender; *Soliloquy*, by Stephen Finn; *Soldier Blue*, by Paul Williams.

NEWEST PUBLISHERS LTD.

201, 8540-109 St., Edmonton AB T6G 1E6, Canada. (780)432-9427. Fax: (780)433-3179. Website: www.newestpress.com. **Contact:** Amber Rider, general manager. Estab. 1977. Publishes trade paperback originals. **Publishes 13-16 titles/year. 40% of books from first-time authors. 85% from unagented writers. Pays 10% royalty.** Publishes book 2-3 years after acceptance of ms. Accepts simultaneous submissions. Responds in 6-8 months to queries. Book catalog for 9x12 SASE. Guidelines available online.

O━ NeWest publishes Western Canadian fiction, nonfiction, poetry, and drama.

Nonfiction Subjects include ethnic, government, politics, Western Canada, history, Western Canada, nature, environment, northern, Canadiana. Query.

Fiction Subjects include literary. Our press is interested in Western Canadian writing. Submit complete ms.

Recent Title(s) *Big Rig 2*, by Don McTavish (nonfiction); *The Far Away Home*, by Marci Densiule (short fiction); *Always Someone to Kill the Doves*, by Fred Flahiff (nonfiction).

NEW SOCIETY PUBLISHERS

P.O. Box 189, Gabriola Island BC V0R 1X0, Canada. (250)247-9737. Fax: (250)247-7471. E-mail: info@newsociety.com. Website: www.newsociety.com. **Contact:** Ingrid Witvoet, managing editor/acquisitions. Publishes trade paperback originals and reprints and electronic originals. **Publishes 25 titles/year. 400 queries received/year. 300 mss received/year. 50% of books from first-time authors. 80% from unagented writers. Pays 10-12% royalty on wholesale price. Pays $0-5,000 advance.** Publishes book about 9 months after acceptance of ms. Accepts simultaneous submissions. Responds in 1 month to queries. Responds in 2 months to proposals. Book catalog free or online. Guidelines available online.

Nonfiction Subjects include business, economics, child guidance, creative nonfiction, education, government, politics, memoirs, nature, environment, philosophy, regional, sustainability, open building, peak oil, renewable energy, post carbon prep, sustainable living, gardening & cooking, green building, natural building, ecological design & planning, environment & economy. Query with SASE. Submit proposal package, outline, 2 sample chapters. Reviews artwork/photos. Send photocopies.

Recent Title(s) *Weapons of Mass Instruction: A Schoolteacher's Journey Through the Dark World of Compulsory Schooling*, by John Taylor Gatto (education); *Depletion & Abundance: Life on the New Home Front*, by Sharon Astyk (current affairs); *Reinventing Collapse: The Soviet Experience and American Prospects*, by Dmitry Orlov (current affairs).

Tips Audience is activists, academics. Don't get an agent!

NOVALIS

Bayard Presse Canada 10 Lower Spadina Ave., Suite 400, Toronto ON M5V 2Z2, Canada. (416)363-3303. Fax: (416)363-9409. Website: www.novalis.ca. **Contact:** Kevin Burns, commissioning editor; Michael O'Hearn, publisher; Anne Louise Mahoney, managing editor. Publishes hardcover and trade paperback originals and trade paperback reprints. **Publishes 40 titles/year. 20% of books from first-time authors. Pays 10-15% royalty on wholesale price. Pays $300-2,000 advance.** Publishes book 12-18 months after acceptance of ms. Responds in 2 months to queries. Responds in 1 month to proposals. Responds in 3 months to manuscripts. Book catalog for free or online. Guidelines available free.

O━ Novalis publishes books about faith, religion, and spirituality in their broadest sense. Based in the Catholic tradition, our interest is strongly ecumenical. Regardless of their denominational perspective, our books speak to the heart, mind, and spirit of people seeking to deepen their faith and understanding.

Nonfiction Subjects include child guidance, education, Christian or Catholic, memoirs, multicultural, nature, environment, philosophy, religion, spirituality. Query with SASE.

Recent Title(s) *Restless Churches*, by Reginald W. Bibby; *Drawn to the Mystery of Jesus Through the Gospel of John*, by Jean Vanier; *At the Edge of Our Longing*, by James Conlon.

ONEWORLD PUBLICATIONS

185 Banbury Rd., Oxford OX2 7AR, United Kingdom. (44)(1865)310597. Fax: (44)(1865)310598. E-mail: submissions@oneworld-publications.com. Website: www.oneworld-publications.com. Estab. 1986. Publishes hardcover and trade paperback originals and trade paperback reprints. **Publishes 50 titles/year. 200 queries received/year. 50 mss received/year. 20% of books from first-time authors. 80% from unagented writers. Pays 10% royalty on wholesale price. Pays $1,000-20,000 advance.** Publishes book 15 months after acceptance of ms. Book catalog available online. Guidelines available online.

- We publish accessible but authoritative books, mainly by academics or experts for a general readership and cross-over student market. Authors must be well qualified. Currently emphasizing current affairs, popular science, history, and psychology; de-emphasizing self-help.

Nonfiction Subjects include politics, history, multicultural, philosophy, psychology, religion, science, sociology, womens issues, womens studies. Submit through online proposal form.

Fiction Fiction focusing on well-written literary and commercial fiction from a variety of cultures and periods, many exploring interesting issues and global problems.

Recent Title(s) *Strange Fruit*, by Keenan Malik; *Oilopoly*, by Marshall Goldman; *What's the Point of School*, by Guy Claxton.

Tips We don't require agents—just good proposals with enough hard information.

OOLICHAN BOOKS

P.O. Box 10, Lantzville BC V0R 2H0, Canada. (250)390-4839. Fax: (866)299-0026. E-mail: oolichanbooks@telus.net. Website: www.oolichan.com. **Contact:** Ron Smith, publisher; Hiro Boga, editor; Pat Smith, editor. Estab. 1974. Publishes hardcover and trade paperback originals and reprints. **Publishes 8 titles/year. 2,000 mss received/year. 30% of books from first-time authors. Pays royalty on retail price.** Publishes book 6-12 months after acceptance of ms. Accepts simultaneous submissions. Responds in 1 month to queries. Responds in 1 month to proposals. Responds in 1-3 months to manuscripts. Book catalog available online. Guidelines available online.

- Only publishes Canadian authors.

Nonfiction Subjects include history, regional, community. Submit proposal package, publishing history, bio, cover letter, 3 sample chapters, SASE.

Fiction Subjects include literary. We try to publish at least 2 literary fiction titles each year. We receive many more deserving submissions than we are able to publish, so we publish only outstanding work. We try to balance our list between emerging and established writers, and have published many first-time writers who have gone on to win or be shortlisted for major literary awards, both nationally and internationally. Submit proposal package, publishing history, clips, bio, cover letter, 3 sample chapters, SASE.

Recent Title(s) *Elliot & Me*, by Keith Harrison; *Touching Ecuador*, by W.H. New; *Cartography*, by Rhona McAdam.

Tips Our audience is adult readers who love good books and good literature. Our audience is regional and national, as well as international. Follow our submission guidelines. Check out some of our titles at your local library or bookstore to get an idea of what we publish. Don't send us the only copy of your manuscript. Let us know if your submission is simultaneous, and inform us if it is accepted elsewhere. Above all, keep writing!

ORCA BOOK PUBLISHERS

P.O. Box 5626, Stn. B, Victoria BC V8R 6S4, Canada. Fax: (877)408-1551. E-mail: orca@orcabook.com. Website: www.orcabook.com. **Contact:** Christi Howes, editor (picture books); Sarah Harvey, editor (young readers); Andrew Wooldridge, editor (juvenile and teen fiction); Bob Tyrrell, publisher (YA, teen). Estab. 1984. Publishes hardcover and trade paperback originals, and mass market paperback originals and reprints. **Publishes 30 titles/year. 2,500 queries received/year. 1,000 mss received/year. 20% of books from first-time authors. 75% from unagented writers. Pays 10% royalty.** Publishes book 12-18 months after acceptance of ms. Responds in 1 month to queries. Responds in 2 month to proposals. Responds in 1-2 months to manuscripts. Book catalog for 8½x11 SASE. Guidelines available online.

- Only publishes Canadian authors.

Nonfiction Subjects include multicultural, picture books. Query with SASE.

Fiction Subjects include hi-lo, juvenile (5-9), literary, mainstream, contemporary, young adult (10-18). Ask for guidelines, find out what we publish. Looking for children's fiction. Query with SASE. Submit proposal package, outline, clips, 2-5 sample chapters, SASE.

Recent Title(s) *Sister Wife*, by Shelley Hrdlitschka (teen fiction); *Buttercup's Lovely Day*, by Carolyn Beck (picture book)

Tips Our audience is for students in grades K-12. Know our books, and know the market.

PEARSON EDUCATION: SOUTH AFRICA

P.O. Box 396, Cape Town 8000, South Africa. (27)(21)531-7750. Fax: (27)(21)532-2303. E-mail: info@pearsoned.co.za. Website: www.pearsoned.co.za.

"Publishes education, reference, and lifestyle resources in print and electronic form."
Nonfiction Subjects include business, economics, child guidance, cooking, foods, nutrition, education, health, medicine, religion, science, social sciences, home education, information technology, lifestyle, tourism.
Fiction Subjects include juvenile, romance, novels, true crime.

PEMMICAN PUBLICATIONS, INC.

150 Henry Ave., Winnipeg MB R3B 0J7, Canada. (204)589-6346. Fax: (204)589-2063. Website: www.pemmican.mb.ca. **Contact:** Rihiannen Margarita, managing editor (First Nations, Metis, and Inuit culture and heritage. Estab. 1980. Publishes trade paperback originals and reprints, and electronic reprints. **Publishes 7-10 titles/year. 120 queries received/year. 120 mss received/year. 50% of books from first-time authors. 100% from unagented writers. Pays 10% royalty on retail price** Publishes book 1-2 years after acceptance of ms. Accepts simultaneous submissions. Responds in 1 month to queries. Responds in 1 month to proposals. Responds in 1 year to manuscripts. Book catalog available free. Guidelines available free.
Nonfiction Subjects include alternative, creative nonfiction, education, ethnic, government, politics, history, language, literature, military, war, nature, environment, spirituality. Submit proposal package including outline and 3 sample chapters, or submit complete ms. Reviews artwork/photos. Send photocopies.
Fiction Subjects include adventure, ethnic, fantasy, historical, juvenile, literary, military, war, multicultural, mystery, picture books, short story collections, spiritual, sports, suspense, western, young adult. All manuscripts must be culture and heritage related. Submit proposal package includ
Recent Title(s) *My Children Are My Reward*, by Alex Harpelle (biography); *The Tobanz*, by Edgar Desjarlais (young adult sports); *The Dream Catcher Pool*, by Jane Chartrand (children's fiction).
Tips Audience is anyone who has an interest in Metis, First Nations, and Inuit culture. No agent is necessary.

PENGUIN BOOKS CANADA, LTD.

The Penguin Group 90 Eglinton Ave. E., Suite 700, Toronto ON M4P 2Y3, Canada. (416)925-2249. Fax: (416)925-0068. E-mail: info@penguin.ca. Website: www.penguin.ca. Estab. 1974. **Pays advance.**
Imprints Penguin Canada; Viking Canada; Puffin Canada.
Nonfiction Agented submissions only.
Recent Title(s) *The Great Wall*, by Julia Lovell; *A Whole New Mind*, by Daniel Pink; *The Schwa Was Here*, by Neal Shusterman.

PETER OWEN PUBLISHERS

73 Kenway Road, London SW5 0RE, United Kingdom. (44)(207)373-5628. Fax: (44)(207)373-6760. E-mail: aowen@peterowen.com. Website: www.peterowen.com. **Contact:** Antonia Owen. Publishes hardcover originals and trade paperback originals and reprints. **Publishes 20-30 titles/year. 3,000 queries received/year. 800 mss received/year. 70% from unagented writers. Pays 7 ½-10% royalty. Pays negotiable advance.** Publishes book 1 year after acceptance of ms. Responds in 2 months to queries. Responds in 3 months to proposals. Responds in 3 months to manuscripts. Book catalog for SASE, SAE with IRC or on website.

"We are far more interested in proposals for nonfiction than fiction at the moment. No poetry or short stories."
Nonfiction Subjects include history, literature, memoirs, translation, travel, art, drama, literary, biography. Query with SASE. Submit outline, 1-3 sample chapters. Submit complete ms with return postage or email with attachments including synopsis.
Fiction Subjects include Mainly specialize in literary and translation. "No first novels—Authors should be aware that we publish very little new fiction these days. Will consider excerpts from novels of normal length from established authors if they submit sample chapters and synopses." Query with SASE or by e-mail.
Recent Title(s) *The Life of a Long-Distance Writer: The Biography of Alan Sillitoe* by Richard Bradford; *The Idle Years* by Orhan Kemal.

PLAYLAB PRESS

Metro Arts Bldg., 109 Edward St., Brisbane QLD. 4000, Australia. (61)(7)3220-0841. E-mail: info@playlab.org.au. Website: www.playlab.org.au. **Contact:** The Executive Director. Estab. 1978. **Publishes 1 titles/year.** Responds in 3 months to manuscripts. Guidelines available online.
Nonfiction Subjects include lit-crit.
Fiction Subjects include plays. Submit 2 copies of ms, cover letter.
Recent Title(s) *Not Like Beckett*, by Michael Watts; *Beyond the Neck*, by Tom Holloway; *The Danger Age*, by Kate Mulvany.
Tips Playlab Press is committed to the publication of quality writing for and about theatre and performance, which is of significance to Australia's cultural life. It values socially just and diverse publication outcomes and aims to promote these outcomes in local, national, and international contexts.

PRESSES DE L'UNIVERSITÉ DE MONTREAL

Case postale 6128, Succursale Centre-ville, Montreal QC H3C 3J7, Canada. (514)343-6933. Fax: (514)343-2232. E-mail: pum@umontreal.ca. Website: www.pum.umontreal.ca. **Contact:** Yzabelle Martineau, editor. Publishes hardcover and trade paperback originals. **Publishes 40 titles/year.** Publishes book 6 months after acceptance of ms. Responds in 1 month to queries. Responds in 1 month to proposals. Responds in 3 months to manuscripts. Book catalog and ms guidelines free.

Nonfiction Subjects include education, health, medicine, history, language, literature, philosophy, psychology, sociology, translation. Submit outline, 2 sample chapters.

PRODUCTIVE PUBLICATIONS

P.O. Box 7200 Station A, Toronto ON M5W 1X8, Canada. (416)483-0634. Fax: (416)322-7434. **Contact:** Iain Williamson, owner. Estab. 1985. Publishes trade paperback originals. **Publishes 24 titles/year. 160 queries received/year. 40 mss received/year. 80% of books from first-time authors. 100% from unagented writers. Pays 10% royalty on wholesale price.** Publishes book 6 months after acceptance of ms. Accepts simultaneous submissions. Responds in 1 month to queries. Responds in 1 month to proposals. Responds in 3 months to manuscripts. Book catalog available free.

- Productive Publications publishes books to help readers succeed and to help them meet the challenges of the new information age and global marketplace. Interested in books on business, computer software, the Internet for business purposes, investment, stock market and mutual funds, etc. Currently emphasizing computers, software, small business, business management, entrepreneurship. De-emphasizing jobs, how to get employment.

Nonfiction Subjects include business, economics, small business, economics and management, computers, electronics, money, finance, software, business, economics. Submit outline. Reviews artwork/photos. Send photocopies.

Recent Title(s) *How to Deliver Excellent Customer Service: A Step-by-Step Guide for Every Business*, by Julie Olley; *Start Your Own Successful Home-Based Business Using eBay: Everything You Need to Know to Get Started*, by LEARN2SUCCEED.COM INCORPORATED.

Tips We are looking for books written by knowledgable, experienced experts who can express their ideas clearly and simply.

PURICH PUBLISHING

Box 23032, Market Mall Post Office, Saskatoon SK S7J 5H3, Canada. (306)373-5311. Fax: (306)373-5315. E-mail: purich@sasktel.net. Website: www.purichpublishing.com. **Contact:** Donald Purich, publisher; Karen Bolstad, publisher. Estab. 1992. Publishes trade paperback originals. **Publishes 3-5 titles/year. 20% of books from first-time authors. 100% from unagented writers. Pays 8-12% royalty on retail price.** Publishes book within 4 months of completion of editorial work, after acceptance of ms after acceptance of ms. Accepts simultaneous submissions. Responds in 1 month to queries. Responds in 3 months to manuscripts. Book catalog available free.

- Purich publishes books on law, Aboriginal/Native American issues, and Western Canadian history for the academic and professional trade reference market.

Nonfiction , Aboriginal and social justice issues, Western Canadian history. Query with SASE.

Recent Title(s) *Indigenous Diplomacy and the Rights of Peoples*, by James Sa'ke' j. Youngblood Henderson; *For Future Generations*, by P. Dawn Mills; *Aboriginal Self-Government in Canada* (3rd ed.), edited by Yale D. Belanger; *Moving Toward Justice*, edited by John D. Whyte.

RAINCOAST BOOK DISTRIBUTION, LTD.

9050 Shaughnessy St., Vancouver BC V6P 6E5, Canada. (604)323-7128. Fax: (604)323-2600. E-mail: info@raincoast.com. Website: raincoast.com. Publishes hardcover and trade paperback originals and reprints. **Publishes 60 titles/year. 3,000 queries received/year. 10% of books from first-time authors. 40% from unagented writers. Pays 8-12% royalty on retail price. Pays $1,000-6,000 advance.** Publishes book within 2 years after acceptance of ms. Book catalog for #10 SASE.

Imprints Raincoast Books; Polestar Books (fiction, poetry, literary nonfiction).

Nonfiction Subjects include animals, art, architecture, ethnic, history, nature, environment, photography, recreation, regional, sports, travel. Query with SASE.

Fiction Subjects include literary, short story collections, young adult.

Recent Title(s) *Redress*, by Roy Miki; *Black*, by George Elliott Clarke; *A War Against Truth*, by Paul William Roberts.

REALITY STREET EDITIONS

63 All Saints St., Hastings, E. Sussex TN34-3BN, UK. E-mail: info@realitystreet.co.uk. Website: freespace.virgin.net/reality.street. **Contact:** Ken Edwards, editor/publisher. Estab. 1993. Trade paperback originals. **Publishes 3-4 titles/year.** Book catalog available online.

O→ Reality Street Editions is based in London, publishing new and innovative writing in English and in translation from other languages. Some established writers whose books they have published are Nicole Brossard, Allen Fisher, Barbara Guest, Fanny Howe, Denise Riley, Peter Riley, and Maurice Scully.

Fiction Subjects include ethnic, poetry, poetry in translation, translation, short novels, anthologies.

Recent Title(s) *Rapid Eye Movement*, by Peter Jaeger (dream narrative collaged from multiple sources); *Let Me Tell You*, by Paul Griffiths (a short novel in the Oulipo tradition); *Botsotso*, edited by Allan Kolski Horwitz & Ken Edwards (anthology of contemporary multi-lingual, multi-ethnic poetry from post-apartheid So. Africa).

Tips Our audience likes innovative We're committed to producing

ROCKY MOUNTAIN BOOKS

406-13th Ave. NE, Calgary AB T2E 1C2, Canada. (403)249-9490. Fax: (403)249-2968. E-mail: rmb@heritagehouse.ca. Website: www.rmbooks.com. **Contact:** Fraser Seely, publisher. Publishes trade paperback originals. **Publishes 15 titles/year. 30 queries received/year. 75% of books from first-time authors. 100% from unagented writers. Rarely offers advance.** Publishes book 1 year after acceptance of ms. Accepts simultaneous submissions. Responds in 2 months to queries. Book catalog and ms guidelines free.

O→ Rocky Mountain Books publishes books on outdoor recreation, mountains, and mountaineering in Western Canada.

Nonfiction Subjects include nature, environment, recreation, regional, travel. Query with SASE.

Recent Title(s) *Caves of the Canadian Rockies and Columbia Mountains*, by Jon Rollins; *Exploring Prince George*, by Mike Nash.

RONSDALE PRESS

3350 W. 21st Ave., Vancouver BC V6S 1G7, Canada. (604)738-4688. Fax: (604)731-4548. Website: www.ronsdalepress.com. **Contact:** Ronald B. Hatch, director (fiction, poetry, social commentary); Veronica Hatch, managing director (children's literature). Estab. 1988. Publishes trade paperback originals. **Publishes 10 titles/year. 300 queries received/year. 800 mss received/year. 60% of books from first-time authors. 95% from unagented writers. Pays 10% royalty on retail price.** Publishes book 6 months after acceptance of ms. Accepts simultaneous submissions. Responds in 2 weeks to queries. Responds in 1 month to proposals. Responds in 3 months to manuscripts. Book catalog for #10 SASE. Guidelines available online.

O→ Canadian authors only. Ronsdale publishes fiction, poetry, regional history, biography and autobiography, books of ideas about Canada, as well as young adult historical fiction.

Nonfiction Subjects include history, Canadian, language, literature, nature, environment, regional.

Fiction Subjects include literary, short story collections, novels. *Canadian authors only*. Query with at least the first

Recent Title(s) *Red Goodwin*, by John Wilson (YA historical fiction); *When Eagles Call*, by Susan Dobbie (novel).

Tips Ronsdale Press is a literary publishing house, based in Vancouver, and dedicated to publishing books from across Canada, books that give Canadians new insights into themselves and their country. We aim to publish the best Canadian writers.

SALLY MILNER PUBLISHING, LTD.

734 Woodville Rd., Binda NSW 2583, Australia. (61)(2)4835-6212. Fax: (61)(2)4835-6211. E-mail: info@sallymilner.com.au. Website: www.sallymilner.com.au. **Publishes 12-20 titles/year.**

Imprints Milner Craft Series; Milner Health Series; JB Fairfax Craft; Creative House.

Nonfiction Subjects include crafts, healthy living. Query with SASE.

Recent Title(s) *Ideas For Applique*, by Eileen Campbell, *Freeform Crochet and Beyond*, by Renate Kirkpatrick.

SCRIBE PUBLICATIONS

595 Drummond St., Carlton North VIC 3054, Australia. (61)(3)9349-5955. Fax: (61)(3)9348-2752. E-mail: info@scribepub.com.au. Website: www.scribepub.com.au. Estab. 1976. **Publishes 70 titles/year. 1025% of books from first-time authors. 1020% from unagented writers.** Submission guidelines available on website under Contact Scribe.

Nonfiction Subjects include environment, government, politics, history, memoirs, nature, environment, psychology, current affairs, social issues. Please refer first to our website before contacting us or submitting anything, because we explain there who we will accept proposals from.

Recent Title(s) *Arabian Plights: The Future of the Middle East*, by Peter Rogers; *Atlas of Unknowns: A Novel*, by Tania James; *A Long Time Coming: The 2008 Election and the Victory of Barack Obama*, by Evan Thomas; *The Well-Dressed Ape: A Natural History of Myself*, by Hannah Holmes.

SHEARSMAN PRESS

58 Velwell Rd., Exeter England EX4 4LD, UK. Website: www.shearsman.com. **Contact:** Tony Frazer, editor.

Estab. 1982. Trade paperback originals. **Publishes 45-58 titles/year. Pays 10% royalty on retail price.after 150 copies have sold; authors also receive 10 free copies of their books** Responds in 2-3 months to manuscripts. Book catalog available online. Guidelines available online.

Nonfiction Subjects include memoirs, translation, Essays.

Recent Title(s) *The Look of Goodbye*, by Peter Robinson (poetry collection); *The Council of Heresy-A primer of poetry in a balkanised terrain*, by Andrew Duncan (a study of contemporary poetry); *New and Selected Poems*, by Jennifer Clement.

Tips Book ms submission: most of the ms must have already appeared in the UK or USA magazines of some repute, & it has to fill 70-72 pages of half letter or A5 pages. You must have sufficient return postage. Submissions can also be made by email. It is unlikely that a poet with no track record will be accepted for publication as there is no obvious audience for the work. Try to develop some exposure to the UK& US magazines & try to assemble a ms only later.

SIMON & SCHUSTER UK LTD.

Division of Simon & Schuster, Inc. 222 Gray's Inn Rd., 1st Floor, London WC1X 8HB, UK. (44)(207)316-1900. Fax: (44)(207)316-0332. E-mail: editorial.enquiries@simonandschuster.co.uk. Website: www.simonsays.co.uk. Estab. 1987.

Imprints Simon & Schuster (fiction, memoir, travel, sport, biography, pop culture); Martin Books; Pocket Books; Simon & Schuster Audio; Simon & Schuster Children's.

- Publisher committed to ongoing literary and commercial success across a wide range of imprints. Does not accept unsolicited material.

Recent Title(s) *Child 44*, by Tom Rob Smith; *Fathers & Sons*, by Richard Madeley.

STELLER PRESS LTD.

13, 4335 W. 10th Ave., Vancouver BC V6R 2H6, Canada. (604)222-2955. Fax: (604)222-2965. E-mail: info@stellerpress.com. Website: www.stellerpress.com. **Contact:** Steve Paton (regional interest, outdoors, gardening, history, travel). Publishes trade paperback originals. **75% of books from first-time authors. 100% from unagented writers. Pays royalty on retail price. Pays $500-2,000 advance.**

- Most titles are specific to the Pacific Northwest. Currently emphasizing regional interest, gardening, history, outdoors and travel. De-emphasizing fiction, poetry.

Nonfiction Subjects include gardening, history, nature, environment, regional, travel.

Recent Title(s) *Vancouver Walks*, by Michael Kluckner and John Atkin; *Skytrain Explorer*, by John Atkin.

SUNPENNY PUBISHING

Church Cottage N., Ferry Rd., Carleton St. Peter Norfolk NR1-7BD, UK. E-mail: info@sunpenny.com. Website: www.sunpenny.com. **Contact:** Jo Holloway, ed. Estab. 2007. Publishes hardcover, trade paperback, mass market paperback, and electronic originals. **Publishes 3-5 titles/year. 50%% of books from first-time authors. 90%% from unagented writers. Our contract gives the author 50% of profits, net.** Accepts simultaneous submissions. Responds in 1-2 weeks to queries. Responds in 1-2 months to proposals. Responds in 2-3 months to manuscripts. Book catalog available online. Guidelines available online.

Nonfiction Subjects include animals, child guidance, community, cooking, foods, nutrition, creative nonfiction, ethnic, health, medicine, history, hobbies, memoirs, nature, environment, photography, recreation, regional, religion, spirituality, travel, womens issues, womens studies, Sailing/cruising. Query with SASE. Reviews artwork/photos. Send photocopies and Digital.

Fiction Subjects include adventure, ethnic, historical, humor, literary, mainstream, contemporary, multicultural, mystery, picture books, regional, religious, romance, science fiction, spiritual, sports, suspense, western, young adult, Christian/inspirational. We was books that uplift, carry messages, are thoughtful or experiential. Please read our website—all of the guidelines and information pages—to get to know us.

Recent Title(s) *The Mountains Between*, by Julie McGowan; *Dance of Eagles*, by J.S. Holloway; *Just One More Summer*, by Julie McGowan.

Tips We envision our audience to b We prefer hard copy, but we u

THOMPSON EDUCATIONAL PUBLISHING, INC.

20 Ripley Ave., Toronto ON M6S 3N9, Canada. (416)766-2763. Fax: (416)766-0398. E-mail: publisher@thompsonbooks.com. Website: www.thompsonbooks.com. **Contact:** Keith Thompson, president. **Publishes 10 titles/year. 15 queries received/year. 10 mss received/year. 80% of books from first-time authors. 100% from unagented writers.** Publishes book 1 year after acceptance of ms. Responds in 1 month to queries. Book catalog available free. Guidelines available online.

- Thompson Educational specializes in high-quality educational texts in the social sciences and humanities.

Nonfiction Subjects include business, economics, education, ethnic, government, politics, multicultural, sociology, sports, womens issues, womens studies. Submit outline, resume, 1 sample chapter.

Recent Title(s) *Social Work: A Critical Turn*, edited by Steven Hick, Jan Foot and Richard Pozzuto.

THOMSON CARSWELL

One Corporate Plaza 2075 Kennedy Rd., Toronto ON M1T 3V4, Canada. (416)298-5024. Fax: (416)298-5094. Website: www.carswell.com. **Contact:** Robert Freeman, vice president, legal, accounting and finance, and corporate groups. Publishes hardcover originals. **Publishes 150-200 titles/year. 30-50% of books from first-time authors. Pays 5-15% royalty on wholesale price.** Publishes book 6 months after acceptance of ms. Accepts simultaneous submissions. Responds in 3 months to queries. Book catalog and ms guidelines free.

- Thomson Carswell is Canada's national resource of information and legal interpretations for law, accounting, tax and business professionals.

Nonfiction Submit proposal package, outline, resume.

Tips Audience is Canada and persons interested in Canadian information; professionals in law, tax, accounting fields; business people interested in regulatory material.

TOUCHWOOD EDITIONS

The Heritage Group 340-1105 Pandora Ave., Victoria BC V8V 1L1, Canada. (250)360-0829. Fax: (250)386-0829. E-mail: info@touchwoodeditions.com. Website: www.touchwoodeditions.com. Publishes trade paperback originals and reprints. **Publishes 10-15 titles/year. 40% of books from first-time authors. 90% from unagented writers. Pays 12% royalty on wholesale price.** Publishes book 12-14 months after acceptance of ms. Accepts simultaneous submissions. Responds in 3 months to queries. Book catalog available free.

Nonfiction Subjects include anthropology, archeology, art, architecture, creative nonfiction, government, politics, history, nature, environment, recreation, regional, nautical. Submit TOC, outline, word count, 2-3 sample chapters, synopsis. Reviews artwork/photos. Send photocopies.

Fiction Subjects include historical, mystery. Submit TOC, outline, word count.

Recent Title(s) *Artists in Their Studios*, by Robert Amos; *Sarah's Tea Time*, by Sarah Amos; *The Frog Lake Massacre*, by Bill Gallagher; *Seaweed on the Rocks*, by Stanley Evans; *The Dangerous River*, by R.M. Patterson.

Tips Our area of interest is Western Canada. We would like more creative nonfiction and books about people of note in Canada's history.

TRADEWIND BOOKS

202-1807 Maritime Mews, Granville Island, Vancouver BC V6H 3W7, Canada. (604)662-4405. E-mail: tradewindbooks@mail.lycos.com. Website: www.tradewindbooks.com. **Contact:** Michael Katz, publisher; Carol Frank, art director. Publishes hardcover and trade paperback originals. **Publishes 5 titles/year. 10% of books from first-time authors. 50% from unagented writers. Pays 7% royalty on retail price. Pays variable advance.** Publishes book 3 years after acceptance of ms. Accepts simultaneous submissions. Responds in 2 months to manuscripts. Book catalog and ms guidelines online.

- Tradewind Books publishes juvenile picture books and young adult novels. Requires that submissions include evidence that author has read at least 3 titles published by Tradewind Books.

Fiction Subjects include juvenile, picture books. Send complete ms for picture b

Recent Title(s) *Zig Zag*, by Robert San Souci, illustrated by Stefan Czernecki; *Pacific Seashores*, by Marja Dion Westman, illustrated by George Juharz; *Bamboo*, by Paul Yee, illustrated by Shaoli Wang.

TRENTHAM BOOKS, LTD.

Westview House, 734 London Rd., Stoke on Trent ST4 5NP, United Kingdom. (44)(178)274-5567. E-mail: tb@trentham-books.co.uk. Website: www.trentham-books.co.uk. **Contact:** Gillian Klein, commissioning editor (education, race). Publishes hardcover and trade paperback originals. **Publishes 32 titles/year. 1,000 queries received/year. 600 mss received/year. 60% of books from first-time authors. 70% from unagented writers. Pays 7½% royalty on wholesale price.** Publishes book 4 months after acceptance of ms. Responds in 1 month to queries. Book catalog for #10 SASE. Guidelines available online.

- Our mission is to enhance the work of professionals in education, law, and social work. Currently emphasizing curriculum, professional behavior. De-emphasizing theoretical issues.

Nonfiction Subjects include education, ethnic, multicultural, psychology, womens issues, language/literacy. Query with SASE.

Recent Title(s) *Get Global: A Practical Guide to Integrating the Global Dimension into the Primary Curriculum*, by Tony Pickford, ed.; *Multilingual Europe: Diversity and Learning*, by Charmian Kenner and Tina Hickey, ed.

TURNSTONE PRESS

607-100 Arthur St., Winnipeg MB R3B 1H3, Canada. (204)947-1555. Fax: (204)942-1555. E-mail: info@ravenstonebooks.com. Website: www.ravenstonebooks.com. **Contact:** Todd Besant, managing editor; Sharon Caseburg, acquisitions editor. Estab. 1976. Publishes trade paperback originals, mass market for literary mystery imprint. **Publishes 10-12 titles/year. 800 mss received/year. 25% of books from first-time authors. 75% from unagented writers. Pays 10% royalty on retail price and 10 author's copies. Pays advance.** Publishes book 18 months-2 years after acceptance of ms. Responds in 4 months to queries. Book catalog for #10 SASE. Guidelines available online.

Imprints Ravenstone (literary mystery fiction).

- Turnstone Press is a literary press that publishes Canadian writers with an emphasis on writers from, and writing on, the Canadian West. Currently emphasizing novels, nonfiction travel, adventure travel, poetry. Does not consider formula or mainstream work.

Nonfiction Subjects include travel, adventure travel, cultural/social issues, Canadian literary criticism. Query with SASE, literary cv, and 5-page sample.

Fiction Subjects include literary, regional, Western Canada, short story collections, contemporary, novels. *Canadian authors only*. Query with SASE, literary cv,

Recent Title(s) *Kornukopia*, by David Annandale (action/thriller); *Leaving Wyoming*, by Brent Robillard (novel); *Loving Gertrude Stein*, by Deborah Schnitzer (poetry).

Tips Writers are encouraged to view our list and check if submissions are appropriate. Although we publish new authors, we prefer first-time authors to have publishing credits in literary magazines. We would like to see more adventure travel, as well as eclectic novels. We would like to see `nonformula' writing for the Ravenstone imprint, especially literary thrillers, urban mystery, and noir.

THE UNIVERSITY OF ALBERTA PRESS

Ring House 2, Edmonton AB T6G 2E1, Canada. (780)492-3662. Fax: (780)492-0719. E-mail: pmidgley@mail.library.ualberta.ca. Website: www.uap.ualberta.ca. **Contact:** Peter Midgley. Estab. 1969. Publishes orginals and reprints. **Publishes 18-25 titles/year. Royalties are negotiated.** Publishes book within 2 years (usually) after acceptance of ms. Responds in 3 months to queries. Guidelines available online.

- We do not accept unsolicited novels, short story collections, or poetry. Please see our website for details.

Nonfiction Subjects include history, language, literature, nature, environment, regional, natural history, social policy. Submit cover letter, word count, CV, 1 sample chapter, TOC.

Recent Title(s) *In the News*, by William Carney; *Deep Alberta*, by John Acorn; *Hard Passage*, by Arthur Kroeger.

UNIVERSITY OF CALGARY PRESS

2500 University Dr. NW, Calgary AB T2N 1N4, Canada. (403)220-7578. Fax: (403)282-0085. Website: www.uofcpress.com. **Contact:** John King, senior editor. Publishes hardcover and trade paperback originals and reprints. **Publishes 25 titles/year.** Publishes book 20 months after acceptance of ms. Responds in 1 month to queries. Responds in 2 months to proposals. Responds in 3 months to manuscripts. Book catalog available free. Guidelines available online.

Nonfiction Subjects include art, architecture, philosophy, womens issues, womens studies, world affairs.

Recent Title(s) *Transboundary Policy Changes in the Pacific Border Regions of North America*, edited by James Loucky, Donald K. Alper and J.C. Day.

UNIVERSITY OF OTTAWA PRESS

542 King Edward, Ottawa ON K1N 6N5, Canada. (613)562-5246. Fax: (613)562-5247. E-mail: puo-uop@uottawa.ca. Website: www.uopress.uottawa.ca. **Contact:** Eric Nelson, assistant editor. Estab. 1936. **Publishes 40-50 titles/year. 20% of books from first-time authors. 95% from unagented writers.** Publishes book 12-18 months after acceptance after acceptance of ms. Responds in 1 month to queries. Responds in 6 months to manuscripts. Book catalog and ms guidelines free.

- Publishes books for scholarly and serious nonfiction audiences. This is the only bilingual university press in Canada. Currently emphasizing French in North America, translation studies, philosophy, Canadian studies, criminology, international development, governance.

Nonfiction Subjects include education, government, politics, philosophy, religion, sociology, translation, Canadian literature. Submit outline, sample chapters, CV.

Recent Title(s) *Revolution or Renaissance: Making the Transition From an Economic Age to a Cultural Age*, by D. Paul Schafer; *Histories of Kanatha: Seen and Told*, by Georges Sioui; *Multicultural Dynamics and the Ends of History: Exploring Kant, Hegel and Marx*, by Rèal Fillion.

Tips No unrevised theses! Envision audience of academic specialists and readers of serious nonfiction.

VÉHICULE PRESS

Box 125, Place du Parc Station, Montreal QC H2X 4A3, Canada. (514)844-6073. Fax: (514)844-7543. Website: www.vehiculepress.com. **Contact:** Simon Dardick, president/publisher. Estab. 1973. Publishes trade paperback originals by Canadian authors only. **Publishes 15 titles/year. 20% of books from first-time authors. 95% from unagented writers. Pays 10-15% royalty on retail price. Pays $200-500 advance.** Publishes book 1 year after acceptance of ms. Responds in 4 months to queries. Book catalog for 9 x 12 SAE with IRCs.

Imprints Signal Editions (poetry); Dossier Quebec (history, memoirs); Esplanade Editions (fiction).

- Canadian authors only.

Montreal's Véhicule Press has published the best of Canadian and Quebec literature—fiction, poetry, essays, translations, and social history.

Nonfiction Subjects include government, politics, history, language, literature, memoirs, regional, sociology. Query with SASE. Reviews artwork/photos.

Fiction Contact Andrew Steinmetz.Subjects include feminist, literary, translation, literary novels. Query with SASE.

Recent Title(s) *Mirabel*, by Pierre Nepreu, translated by Judith Cowan; *Seventeen Tomatoes*, by Jasprect Singh; *The Man Who Killed Houdini*, by Don Bell.

WALL & EMERSON, INC.

21 Dale Ave., Suite 533, Toronto ON M4W 1K3, Canada. (416)901-3855. Fax: (416)352-5368. E-mail: wall@wallbooks.com. Website: www.wallbooks.com. **Contact:** Byron E. Wall, president (history of science, mathematics). Estab. 1987. Publishes hardcover originals and reprints. **Publishes 3 titles/year. 10 queries received/year. 8 mss received/year. 50% of books from first-time authors. 100% from unagented writers. Pays 5-12% royalty on wholesale price.** Publishes book 12 months after acceptance of ms. Accepts simultaneous submissions. Responds in 1 month to queries. Responds in 1 month to proposals. Responds in 3 months to manuscripts. Book catalog and ms guidelines free or online.

Currently emphasizing history of science and adult education.

Nonfiction Subjects include education, health, philosophy, science. Submit proposal package, outline, 2 sample chapters.

Recent Title(s) *Delivering Instruction to Adult Learners*, 3rd ed.; *Glimpses of Reality: Episodes in the History of Science*; *The Price of Prosperity: Civilization and the Natural World.*

Tips Our audience consists of college undergraduate students and college libraries. Our ideal writer is a college professor writing a text for a course he or she teaches regularly. If I were a writer trying to market a book today, I would identify the audience for the book and write directly to the audience throughout the book. I would then approach a publisher that publishes books specifically for that audience.

N WEIGL EDUCATIONAL PUBLISHERS, LIMITED

6325 10th St. SE, Calgary AB T2H 2Z9, Canada. (403)233-7747. Fax: (403)233-7769. E-mail: linda@weigl.com. Website: www.weigl.com. **Contact:** Linda Weigl, president/publisher. Publishes hardcover originals and reprints, school library softcover. **Publishes 104 titles/year. 100% from unagented writers. Makes outright purchase.** Responds ASAP to queries. Book catalog available free.

Textbook publisher catering to juvenile and young adult audience (K-12).

Nonfiction Subjects include animals, education, government, politics, history, nature, environment, science. Query with SASE.

Recent Title(s) *Indigenous Peoples*; *Natural Wonders*; *Science Matters*.

WHITECAP BOOKS, LTD.

352 Lynn Ave., North Vancouver BC V7J 2C4, Canada. (640)980-9852. Fax: (604)980-8197. Website: www.whitecap.ca. Publishes hardcover and trade paperback originals. **Publishes 40 titles/year. 500 queries received/year. 1,000 mss received/year. 20% of books from first-time authors. 90% from unagented writers. Pays royalty. Pays negotiated advance.** Publishes book 12 months after acceptance of ms. Accepts simultaneous submissions. Responds in 3 months to proposals.

Whitecap Books publishes a wide range of nonfiction with a Canadian and international focus. Currently emphasizing cooking, wine and spirit, gardening, travel, health and well-being, history, biography, nature and the environment. Also publishes juvenile fiction, young adult fiction, nonfiction, picture books for young children (nature, wildlife and animals).

Nonfiction Subjects include animals, cooking, foods, nutrition, gardening, history, nature, environment, recreation, regional, travel. Submit outline, 1 sample chapter, SASE. Reviews artwork/photos. Send photocopies.

Fiction For children's illustrated fic

Recent Title(s) *Wild Sweets: Chocolate*, by Dominique and Cindy Duby; *Texas: A Visual Journey*, by Claire Philipson; *Saddle Island Series No. 3: Race to the Rescue*, by Sharon Siamon.

Tips We want well-written, well-researched material that presents a fresh approach to a particular topic.

MARKETS

Small Presses

Small press is a relative term. Compared to the dozen or so conglomerates, the rest of the book publishing world may seem to be comprised of small presses. A number of the publishers listed in the Book Publishers section consider themselves small presses and cultivate the image. For our classification, small presses are those that publish, on average, less than 10 books per year.

The publishing opportunities are slightly more limited with the companies listed here than with those in the Book Publishers section. Not only are they publishing fewer books, but small presses are usually not able to market their books as effectively as larger publishers, and their print runs and royalty arrangements are usually smaller.

However, realistic small press publishers don't try to compete with Penguin Group (USA), Inc., or Random House. Most small press publishers get into book publishing for the love of it, not solely for the profit. Of course, every publisher, small or large, wants successful books, but small press publishers often measure success in different ways.

Many writers actually prefer to work with small presses. Since small publishing houses are usually based on the publisher's commitment to the subject matter, and since they work with far fewer authors than the conglomerates, small press authors and their books usually receive more personal attention than the larger publishers can afford to give them. Promotional dollars at the big houses tend to be siphoned toward a few books each season that they have decided are likely to succeed, leaving hundreds of "midlist'' books underpromoted. Since small presses only commit to a very small number of books every year, they are vitally interested in the promotion and distribution of each book.

Just because they publish fewer titles than large publishing houses does not mean small press editors have the time to look at complete manuscripts. In fact, the editors with smaller staffs often have even less time for submissions. The procedure for contacting a small press with your book idea is exactly the same as it is for a larger publisher. Send a one-page query with SASE first. If the press is interested in your proposal, be ready to send an outline or synopsis, and/or a sample chapter or two.For more information on small presses, see *Novel & Short Story Writer's Market* and *Poet's Market* (Writer's Digest Books).

For a list of publishers according to their subjects of interest, see the Nonfiction and Fiction sections of the Book Publishers Subject Index. Information on book publishers listed in the previous edition of *Writer's Market*, but not included in this edition, can be found in the General Index.

ACME PRESS

P.O. Box 1702, Westminster MD 21158-1702. (410)848-7577. E-mail: acmepres@carr.org. **Contact:** (Ms.) E.G. Johnston, managing editor. Estab. 1991. Publishes hardcover and trade paperback originals. **Publishes 1-2 titles/year. Pays 25 author's copies and 50% of profits. Pays small advance.** Publishes book 1 year after acceptance of ms. Accepts simultaneous submissions. Responds in 2 weeks to queries. Responds in 2 months to mss. Book catalog and ms guidelines for #10 SASE.

Fiction Subjects include humor. "We accept submissions on any subject as long as the material is humorous; prefer full-length novels. No cartoons or art (text only). No pornography, poetry, short stories, or children's material." Submit first 3-5 chapters, synopsis

Recent Title(s) *SuperFan*, by Lyn A. Sherwood (funny football novel).

Tips "We are always looking for the great comic novel."

ADAMS-BLAKE PUBLISHING

8041 Sierra St., Fair Oaks CA 95628. (916)962-9296. Website: www.adams-blake.com. **Contact:** Monica Blane, acquisitions editor. Estab. 1992. Publishes trade paperback originals. **Publishes 5 titles/year. 50 queries received/year. 15 mss received/year. 80% of books from first-time authors. 99% from unagented writers. Pays 10% royalty on wholesale price.** Publishes book 9 months after acceptance of ms. Accepts simultaneous submissions. Responds in 3 months on queries, proposals and mss. Catalog not available. Guidelines not available.

> O━ We look for an audience of business and technical readers. We like to look at "oddball" titles that might appeal to people in specific industries, especially financial services (insurance, brokerage, etc.) A big part of our publishing is in the "special markets" or what might be called "premium" or "give away" sales to large companies where we can print for a dollar, sell for three dollars in quantities of many thousands.no returns.

Nonfiction Subjects include business, economics, computers, electronics, counseling, career guidance, labor, money, finance. Query with SASE. Submit proposal package, including outline, 1 sample chapter and marketing information.demographics of readership, pricing, etc. Does not review artwork/photos.

Tips "If you have a book that a large company might buy and give away at sales meetings, send us a query. We like books on sales, especially in specific industries.like 'How to Sell Annuities' or 'How to Sell High-Tech High Tech Equipment.' We look for the title that a company will buy several thousand copies of at a time. We often "personalize" for the company. We look for an audience of business and technical readers. We like to look at 'oddball' titles that might appeal to people in specific industries, especially financial services (insurance, brokerage, etc.) A big part of our publishing is in the 'special markets' or what might be called 'premium' or 'give away' sales to large companies where we can print for a dollar, sell for three dollars in quantities of many thousands.no returns."

ADAMS-HALL PUBLISHING

P.O. Box 491002, Los Angeles CA 90049. (800)888-4452. E-mail: adamshallpublish@aol.com. Website: www.adams-hall.com. **Contact:** Sue Ann Bacon, editorial director. Publishes hardcover and trade paperback originals and reprints. **Publishes 3-4 titles/year. Pays negotiable advance.** Responds in 1 month to queries.

Nonfiction Subjects include money, finance, business. Submit query, title, synopsis, your qualifications, a list of 3 competitive books and how it's widely different from other books. Do not send ms or sample chapters.

Recent Title(s) *Fail Proof Your Business*.

[N] AFFLUENT PUBLISHING CORPORATION

Affluent Publishing 1040 Avenues of the Americas, New York NY 10018. Website: www.affluent-publishing.com. **Contact:** JB Hamilton, editor (mainstream/contemporary). **Publishes 3 titles/year. 50% of books from first-time authors. 50% from unagented writers.** Publishes book 24 months after acceptance of ms. Accepts simultaneous submissions. Guidelines available online at website.

Fiction Subjects include adventure, ethnic, literary, mainstream, mystery, romance, suspense, young adult. Query with SASE

Recent Title(s) *I Apologize*, by Bradley Booth (mainstream/contemporary).

Tips Please follow the submission guidelines posted on our website.

[N] AHSAHTA PRESS

1910 University Dr., MS 1525, Boise ID 83725-1525. (208)426-3134. E-mail: ahsahta@boisestate.edu. **Contact:** Director/Editor-in-Chief: Janet Holmes. Estab. 1974. Publishes trade paperback originals. **Publishes 7 titles/year. 800 mss received/year. 15%% of books from first-time authors. 100%% from unagented writers. Pays 8% royalty on retail price.** Publishes book 6-36 months after acceptance of ms. Accepts simultaneous submissions. We don't accept queries to queries. Responds in 3 months to manuscripts. Book catalog available online.

Recent Title(s) *case sensitive*, by Kate Greenstreet; *Irresponsibility*, by Chris Vitiello; *Zone: Zero*, by Stephanie Strickland.

Tips Ahsahta's motto is that poetry is art, so our readers tend to come to us for the unexpected—poetry that makes them think, reflect, and even do something they haven't done before.

ALONDRA PRESS, LLC

10122 Shadow Wood Dr., #19, Houston TX 77043. E-mail: lark@alondrapress.com. Website: www.alondrapress.com. **Contact:** Kathleen Palmer, chief editor; Penelope Leight, poetry editor. Estab. 2007. Publishes trade paperback originals and reprints. **Publishes 4 titles/year. 75% of books from first-time authors. 75% from unagented writers. Pays $500-1,000 advance.** Publishes book 8 months after acceptance of ms. Accepts simultaneous submissions. Responds in 1 month to queries and proposals. Responds in 3 month to manuscripts. Guidelines available online.

Nonfiction Subjects include anthropology, archaeology, history, philosophy, psychology, translation. Submit complete ms.

Fiction Subjects include literary, poetry. Just send us a few pages, or the entire manuscript, by e-mail only. We will look at it quickly and tell you if it interests us. If it does, we may suggest changes and improvements. If the author is willing to listen to suggestions and make corrections, we will then enter into a negotiation phase for the publication of the book. If the manuscript does not interest us, we will advise the author quickly, and delete it from our e-mail to make room for others.

Recent Title(s) *Nessus the Centaur*, by Henry Hollenbaugh (literary/adventure); *Canyon Chronicles*, by K. Gray Jones (fiction); *Island Journeys*, by Patti M. Marxsen (travel essays).

Tips We will be looking for unusual stories that other firms have not been willing to tackle.

ALPINE PUBLICATIONS

38262 Linman Road, Crawford CO 81415. (970)921-5005. Fax: (970)921-5081. E-mail: alpinepubl@aol.com. Website: alpinepub.com. **Contact:** Ms. B.J. McKinney, publisher. Estab. 1975. Publishes hardcover and trade paperback originals and reprints. **Publishes 6-10 titles/year. 40% of books from first-time authors. 95% from unagented writers. Pays 8-15% royalty on wholesale price. Pays advance.** Publishes book 18 months after acceptance of ms. Accepts simultaneous submissions. Responds in 1-3 weeks to queries. Responds in 1 month to proposals. Responds in 1 month to manuscripts. Book catalog available free. Guidelines available online.

Imprints Blue Ribbon Books.

Nonfiction Subjects include animals. Reviews artwork/photos. Send photocopies.

Fiction No fiction, children's books

Recent Title(s) *Agility Start to Finish*, by Diane Bauman; *Successful Show Dog Handling*, by Peter Green and Mario Migliorini; *Dictionary of Veterinary Terms*, by Jennifer Coates; *Dog Driver*, by Miki and Julie Collins.

Tips Our audience is pet owners, breeders, exhibitors, veterinarians, animal trainers, animal care specialists, and judges. Our books are in-depth and most are heavily illustrated. Look up some of our titles before you submit. See what is unique about our books. Write your proposal to suit our guidelines.

AMBASSADOR BOOKS, INC.

91 Prescott St., Worcester MA 01605. (508)756-2893. Fax: (508)757-7055. Website: www.ambassadorbooks.com. **Contact:** Mr. Chris Driscoll, acquisitions editor. Publishes hardcover and trade paperback originals. **Publishes 9 titles/year. 2,000 queries received/year. 100 mss received/year. 50% of books from first-time authors. 90% from unagented writers. Pays 8-10% royalty on retail price.** Publishes book 1 year after acceptance of ms. Accepts simultaneous submissions. Responds in 3-4 months to queries. Book catalog free or online.

O━ We are a Christian publishing company looking for books of intellectual and/or spiritual excellence.

Nonfiction Books with a spiritual theme.Subjects include creative nonfiction, regional, religion, spirituality, sports, Catholic and Christian books. Query with SASE. Submit complete ms. Reviews artwork/photos. Send photocopies.

Fiction Books with a spiritual/religious theme.Subjects include juvenile, literary, picture books, religious, spiritual, sports, young adult, women's. Query with SASE. Submit complete ms.

Recent Title(s) *A Child's Bedtime Companion*, by Sandy Henry, illustrated by Vera Pavlova; *Praying for a Miracle*, by Gilda D'Agostrio.

AMBER BOOKS PUBLISHING

Amber Communications Group, Inc. 1334 E. Chandler Blvd., Suite 5-D67, Phoenix AZ 85048. Website: www.amberbooks.com. **Contact:** Tony Rose, publisher. Publishes trade paperback and mass market paperback originals. Catalog free or online.

Nonfiction Subjects include beauty, career guidance, fashion, personal finance, muticultural, relationship advice. Reviews artwork/photos as part of ms package. Send photocopies.

Fiction , historic docu-dramas. Wants African-American topics and interests. Submit proposal or outline with author bio. Please do not email or mail mss unless requested by publisher.

Recent Title(s) *African American Scholarship Guide for Students and Parents*, by Dante Lee; *Beautiful Black Hair - Real Solutions for Real Problems*, by Shamboosie; *Is Modeling for You? The Handbook and Guide for the Young Aspiring Black Model*, by Yvonne Rose & Tony Rose; *Prince in the Studio (1975-1995) Vol. I*, by Jake Brown.
Tips "The goal of Amber Books is to expand our catalog, and to expand our fiction department in print and on software."

AMERICAN CATHOLIC PRESS

16565 S. State St., South Holland IL 60473. (312)331-5845. Fax: (708)331-5484. E-mail: acp@acpress.org. Website: www.acpress.org. **Contact:** Rev. Michael Gilligan, PhD, editorial director. Estab. 1967. Publishes hardcover originals and hardcover and paperback reprints. **Publishes 4 titles/year. Makes outright purchase of 25-100.** Guidelines available online.
Nonfiction Subjects include education, music, dance, religion, spirituality.
Tips Most of our sales are by direct mail, although we do work through retail outlets.

AMIGADGET PUBLISHING CO.

P.O. Box 1696, Lexington SC 29071. (803)779-3196. E-mail: amigadget@fotoartista.com. Website: www.fotoartista.com/amigadget. **Contact:** Jay Gross, editor-in-chief. Publishes trade paperback originals. **Publishes 1 titles/year.**
Nonfiction Query via e-mail only. *All unsolicited mss returned unopened.*
Recent Title(s) *The Coffee Experience*, by J. Gross (travel).
Tips We are not currently seeking new paper publishing projects.

THE AMWELL PRESS

P.O. Box 5385, Clinton NJ 08809-0385. (908)638-9033. Fax: (908)638-4728. **Contact:** James Rikhoff, president. Estab. 1976. Publishes hardcover originals. **Publishes 4 titles/year.** Publishes book 18 months after acceptance of ms. Responds in 2 months to queries.

The Amwell Press publishes hunting and fishing nonfiction, but not how-to books on these subjects.

Nonfiction Query with SASE.
Recent Title(s) *Handy to Home*, by Tom Hennessey; *Beyond Hill Country*, by Rikhoff and Sullivan; *A Quail Hunter's Odyssey*, by Dr. Joseph Greenfield.

ANACUS PRESS AND ECOPRESS

Imprint of Finney Co. 8075 215th St. W, Lakeville MN 55044. (952)469-6699. Fax: (952)469-1968. E-mail: feedback@finneyco.com. Website: www.ecopress.com. **Contact:** Alan Krysan, president (bicycling guides, travel). Publishes trade paperback originals. **Publishes variable number of titles/year. Pays 10% royalty on wholesale price.** Responds in 10-12 weeks to queries. Book catalog available online.
Nonfiction Subjects include recreation, regional, travel, travel guides, travelogue, environmental, eco-friendly. Query with SASE.
Recent Title(s) *Fly and Spin Fishing for River Smallmouths*, by Bruce Ingram (travel guide); *The James River Guide*, by Bruce Ingram; *The New River Guide*, by Bruce Ingram.
Tips Audience is cyclists and armchair adventurers.

ANCHORAGE PRESS PLAYS, INC.

617 Baxter Ave., Louisville KY 40204-1105. Phone/Fax: (502)583-2288. E-mail: applays@bellsouth.net. Website: www.applays.com. **Contact:** Marilee H. Miller, publisher. Estab. 1935. Publishes solicited hardcover and trade paperback originals. **Publishes up to 10 titles/year. 50% of books from first-time authors. 80% from unagented writers. Pays 10-15% royalty. Playwrights also receive 50-75% royalties.** Publishes book 1-2 years after acceptance of ms. Accepts simultaneous submissions. Responds in 1 year to manuscripts. Book catalog available online. Review current guidelines online before submission.

We are an international agency for plays for young people. First in the field since 1935. We are primarily a publisher of theatrical plays with limited textbooks.

Nonfiction Subjects include education, theater, child drama, plays. Query. Reviews artwork/photos.
Recent Title(s) *Leaving Hannibal*, by Mary Barile; *Legend of the Poinsettia*, by Roxanne Schroeder-Arce; *TYA: Essays on the Theatre for Young Audiences;* by Moses Goldberg.

ANHINGA PRESS

P.O. Box 10595, Tallahassee FL 32302. (850)422-1408. Fax: (850)442-6323. E-mail: info@anhinga.org. Website: www.anhinga.org. **Contact:** Rick Campbell, editor. Publishes hardcover and trade paperback originals. **Publishes 5 titles/year. Pays 10% royalty on retail price. Offers Anhinga Prize of $2,000.** Accepts simultaneous submissions. Responds in 3 months to queries. Responds in 3 months to proposals. Responds in 3 months to manuscripts. Book catalog for #10 SASE or online. Guidelines available online.

O→ Publishes only full-length collections of poetry (60-80 pages). No individual poems or chapbooks.

Recent Title(s) *Blood Almanac*, by Sandy Langhorn; *Morning of the Red Admirals*, by Robert Dana; *Dubious Angels*, by Keith Ratzlaff.

ARCHIMEDES PRESS, INC.

6 Berkley Rd., Glenville NY 12302. (518)265-3269. Fax: (518)384-1313. E-mail: archimedespress@verizon.net. Website: www.archimedespress.com. **Contact:** Richard DiMaggio, chief editor. Estab. 2002. Publishes broad-based hardcover, trade paperback, and mass market paperback originals. **Publishes 3-6 titles/year. Pays 5-15% royalty.** Publishes book 6 months after acceptance of ms. Responds in 2 months to queries.

O→ Looking for quality nonfiction, business, self-improvement. Also desire funny, up-beat titles.

Nonfiction Subjects include alternative, business, economics, child guidance, community, cooking, foods, nutrition, creative nonfiction, education, government, politics, history, humanities, language, literature, money, finance, photography, sex, social sciences, travel. Query with SASE. Submit sample chapters, marketing plan, SASE. Submit complete ms. Reviews artwork/photos. Send photocopies.

Recent Title(s) *Real Estate Professionals Liability Review*; *Financial Empowerment Infomercials*.

Tips Our audience is the consumer, plain and simple. That means everyone. We are a small press and try hard to avoid the limitations of the industry. While agented submissions are preferred, they are not necessary with professional submissions. We want fresh, creative ideas and will accept unsolicited manuscripts. These, however, will not be returned without a SASE. E-mails are OK. No phone calls, please.

ARIEL STARR PRODUCTIONS, LTD.

P.O. Box 17, Demarest NJ 07627. E-mail: arielstarrprod@aol.com. **Contact:** Attn: Acquisitions Editor. Trade and mass market paperback originals; electronic originals. **Publishes 5 titles/year. Receives 40 queries/year, 4 mss/year. 80% of books from first-time authors. 80% from unagented writers.** Publishes book 12 months after acceptance of ms. Accepts simultaneous submissions. Catalog not available. Guidelines available by email.

Nonfiction Subjects include environment, nature, New Age, religion, spirituality. Query with SASE. Reviews artwork/photos; send photocopies.

Fiction Subjects include adventure, fantasy, poetry, religious, science fiction, spiritual. Query with SASE and one-page proposal.

Recent Title(s) *Focused or Dead*, by George E. Soroka (self-help); *The Dark Chronicles Series*, by Cynthia Soroka (dark fantasy); *Cowboys and Memories*, by Rose Blanchard (poetry).

Tips We want books that stimulate the brain and inspire the mind. Be honest and decent in your queries.

ARJUNA LIBRARY PRESS

Imprint of *Journal of Regional Criticism* 1025 Garner St., D, Space 18, Colorado Springs CO 80905-1774. **Contact:** Count Joseph A. Uphoff, Jr. Publishes CD ROM originals in jpg, asf format. **Publishes 3-6 titles/year. 10 queries received/year. 50 mss received/year. 10% of books from first-time authors. 90% from unagented writers.** Publishes book 6 months after acceptance of ms. Accepts simultaneous submissions. Book catalog available online. Guidelines for #10 SASE.

O→ "*The Journal of Regional Criticism* has now advanced into the Mail Art syntagma within the context of Indefinite Surrealism in the fashion of Indefinite Design for exhibition, reading, website display, artistamps, and criticism by theoretical writing. For demonstration, a dadaist statement has been published at http://hometown.aol.com/druphoff/myhomepage/newsletter.html. The Mail Art system has been evolving to implement the use of blog sites in addition to the production of catalogues and CD-Roms. the Journal of Regional Criticism is now represented on Open Fluxus, FaceBook, and Your Hub (the Colorado Springs Gazette). Older sites include Art Majeur, Flickr, and eSnips. The material value is in signature editions and artistic containers such as rare wood boxes. In commercial terms, the Surrealist Design, like House Mail, offers something of substantial, uncompromising value as a Free Expression, but in addition reserves a supplemental quantity or quality to be purchased or industrialized under a license."

Nonfiction Subjects include anthropology, archeology, art, architecture, creative nonfiction, philosophy, photography, science, surrealism. Submit complete ms. Reviews artwork/photos. Send photocopies, transparencies, artcards or CD ROM: jpg, asf files.

Fiction Subjects include adventure, experimental, fantasy, historical, horror, literary, occult, poetry, poetry in translation, science fiction, translation, surrealism. "The focus being surrealism, the composition should embody principles of the theory in a spirit of experimental inquiry." Submit complete ms.

Recent Title(s) *The Creative Personality*, by Professor S. Giora Shoham; *Thoughtful Fragments*, by Ryan Jackson; *A Cigarette Burn on the Moon*, by Aliya Mehdi.

🄽 ASHLAND POETRY PRESS

401 College Avenue, Ashland OH 44805. (419)289-5110. Fax: (419)289-5255. E-mail: app@ashland.edu. Website: www.ashland.edu/aupoetry. **Contact:** Sarah Wells, managing editor; Deborah Fleming, editor. Estab. 1969. Publishes trade paperback originals. **Publishes 2-3 titles/year. 360 mss received/year. 50%% of books from first-time authors. 100%% from unagented writers. Makes outright purchase of 500-1,000.** Publishes book 10 months after acceptance of ms. Accepts simultaneous submissions. Responds in 1 month to queries. Responds in 6 months to manuscripts. Book catalog available online. Guidelines available online.
Tips We rarely publish a title submitted off the transom outside of our Snyder Prize competition.

ASIAN HUMANITIES PRESS

Jain Publishing Co. P.O. Box 3523, Fremont CA 94539. (510)659-8272. Fax: (510)659-0501. E-mail: mail@jainpub.com. Website: www.jainpub.com. **Contact:** M. Jain, editor-in-chief. Estab. 1989. Publishes hardcover and trade paperback originals and reprints. **Publishes 6 titles/year. 100% from unagented writers.** Publishes book 12-24 months after acceptance of ms. Responds in 3 months to manuscripts. Book catalog available online. Guidelines available online.

- Asian Humanities Press publishes in the areas of humanities and social sciences pertaining to Asia, commonly categorized as Asian Studies. Currently emphasizing undergraduate-level textbooks.

Nonfiction Subjects include language, literature, philosophy, psychology, religion, spirituality, Asian classics, social sciences, art/culture. Submit proposal package, vita, list of prior publications. Reviews artwork/photos. Send photocopies.
Recent Title(s) *A Handbook for Analyzing Chinese Characters*, by Zhifang Ren.

⊘ ASPICOMM MEDIA

Aspicomm Books P.O. Box 1212, Baldwin NY 11510. (516)642-5976. Fax: (516)489-8916. E-mail: rdlagler@aspicomm.com. Website: www.aspicomm.com. **Contact:** Valerie Daniel. Publishes mass market paperback originals. **25 queries received/year. 5 mss received/year. 90% of books from first-time authors. 50% from unagented writers.** Publishes book 6-8 months after acceptance of ms. Responds in 2-3 months to queries. Guidelines available online.
Fiction Subjects include mainstream, contemporary. Query with SASE. Unsolicited mss returned unopened.
Recent Title(s) *Mountain High, Valley Low*, by Renee Flagler; *Miss Guided*, by Renee Flagler; *In Her Mind*, by Renee Flagler.

ASTRAGAL PRESS

Finney Company 8075 215th St. West, Lakeville MN 55044. (866)543-3045. Fax: (952)669-1968. E-mail: feedback@finneyco.com. Website: www.astragalpress.com. Estab. 1983. Publishes trade paperback originals and reprints. Accepts simultaneous submissions. Book catalog and ms guidelines free.

- Our primary audience includes those interested in antique tool collecting, metalworking, carriage building, early sciences and early trades, and railroading.

Nonfiction Query with SASE. Submit sample chapters, TOC, book overview, illustration descriptions. Submit complete ms.
Recent Title(s) *American Milling Machine Builders: 1820-1920*, by Kenneth Cope (Vol. 2); *The Carriage Trimmer's Manual*, by William N. Fitzgerald; *Vintage Woodworking Machinery (Vol. 2)*, by Dana M. Batory.
Tips We sell to niche markets. We are happy to work with knowledgeable amateur authors in developing titles.

A.T. PUBLISHING

23 Lily Lake Rd., Highland NY 12528. (845)691-2021. **Contact:** Anthony Prizzia, publisher (education); John Prizzia, publisher. Estab. 2001. Publishes trade paperback originals. **Publishes 1-3 titles/year. 5-10 queries received/year. 5-10 mss received/year. 100% of books from first-time authors. 100% from unagented writers. Pays 15-25% royalty on retail price. Makes outright purchase of 500-2,500. Pays $500-1,000 advance.** Accepts simultaneous submissions. Responds in 1 month to queries. Responds in 2 months to proposals. Responds in 4 months to manuscripts.
Nonfiction Subjects include cooking, foods, nutrition, education, recreation, science, sports. Query with SASE. Submit complete ms. Reviews artwork/photos. Send photocopies.
Recent Title(s) *The Portion Principle*, by Kaitlin Louie; *The Waiter and Waitress's Guide to a Bigger Income*, by Anthony Thomas; *Why is the Teacher's Butt so Big?* by Debra Craig.
Tips "Audience is people interested in a variety of topics, general. Submit typed manuscript for consideration, including a SASE for return of manuscript."

🄽 AUSABLE PRESS

Copper Canyon Press **Contact:** Chase Twichell, editor/poet (poetry). Estab. 1999.

- This press is closing to join with Copper Canyon Press as an imprint. The office will stay open through 2009.

Tips Our mission is to publish poe We believe that independent p

N AUTUMN HOUSE PRESS

87½ Westwood St., Pittsburgh PA 15211. (412)381-261. E-mail: msimms@autumnhouse.org. Website: www.autumnhouse.org. **Contact:** Michael Simms, editor-in-chief (poetry). Hardcover, trade paperback, and electronic originals. **Publishes 8 titles/year. 1,000 mss/year 10% of books from first-time authors. 100% from unagented writers. Pays $0-2,500 advance.** Publishes book 9 months after acceptance of ms. Accepts simultaneous submissions. Catalog free on request. Guidelines online at website; free on request; or for #10 SASE.

Fiction Subjects include literary. We consider all fiction mss except comic books. Submit only through our annual contest. See guidelines online. Submit completed ms.

Recent Title(s) *Drift and Swerve*, by Samuel Ligon; *New World Order*, by Derek Green; *She Heads into the Wilderness*, by Anne Marie Macari; *The Son of the Horse*, by Samuel Hazo; *Where a Woman*, by Lori Wilson.

Tips The competition to publish with Autumn House is very tough. Submit only your best work.

AVANYU PUBLISHING, INC.

P.O. Box 27134, Albuquerque NM 87125. (505)341-1280. Fax: (505)341-1281. Website: www.avanyu-publishing.com. **Contact:** J. Brent Ricks, president. Estab. 1984. Publishes hardcover and trade paperback originals and reprints. **Publishes 4 titles/year. 30% of books from first-time authors. 90% from unagented writers. Pays 8% maximum royalty on wholesale price. Pays advance.** Publishes book 1 year after acceptance of ms. Responds in 2 months to queries. Book catalog for #10 SASE.

- Avanyu publishes highly-illustrated, history-oriented books on American Indians and adventures in the Southwest.

Nonfiction Subjects include Americana, Southwest, anthropology, archeology, art, architecture, ethnic, history, multicultural, photography, regional, sociology, spirituality. Query with SASE. Reviews artwork/photos.

Recent Title(s) *Kachinas Spirit Beings of the Hopi*; *Mesa Verde Ancient Architecture*; *Hopi Snake Ceremonies*.

Tips Our audience consists of libraries, art collectors, and history students. We publish subjects dealing with modern and historic American Indian matters of all kinds.

BALL PUBLISHING

335 N. River St., Batavia IL 60510-0009. (630)208-9080. Fax: (630)208-9350. E-mail: info@ballpublishing.com; rblanchette@ballpublishing.com. Website: www.ballpublishing.com. **Contact:** Rick Blanchette, editorial director. Publishes hardcover and trade paperback originals. **Publishes 4-6 titles/year.** Accepts simultaneous submissions. Book catalog for 8 ½x11 envelope and 3 First-Class stamps.

- We publish for the book trade and the horticulture trade. Books on both home gardening/landscaping and commercial production are considered.

Nonfiction Subjects include agriculture, gardening, floriculture. Query with SASE. Submit proposal package, outline, 2 sample chapters. Reviews artwork/photos. Send photocopies.

Recent Title(s) *Great Flowering Landscape Shrubs*, by Vincent A. Simeone; *Kids' Container Gardening*, by Cindy Krezel; *Biocontrol in Protected Culture*, by Kevin M. Heinz et al.

Tips We are expanding our book line to home gardeners, while still publishing for green industry professionals. Gardening books should be well thought out and unique in the market. Actively looking for photo books on specific genera and families of flowers and trees.

BANCROFT PRESS

P.O. Box 65360, Baltimore MD 21209-9945. (410)358-0658. Fax: (410)764-1967. E-mail: bruceb@bancroftpress.com. Website: www.bancroftpress.com. **Contact:** Bruce Bortz, editor and publisher (health, investments, politics, history, humor, literary novels, mystery/thrillers, young adult). Publishes hardcover and trade paperback originals. **Publishes 6 titles/year. Pays 6-8% royalty.Pays various royalties on retail price. Pays $750 advance.** Publishes book up to 3 years after acceptance of ms. Accepts simultaneous submissions. Responds in 6-12 months to queries. Responds in 6-12 months to proposals. Responds in 6-12 months to manuscripts. Guidelines available online.

- Bancroft Press is a general trade publisher. We are currently moving into soley publishing young adult fiction and nonfiction as well as adult fiction for young adults (single titles and series). Please, nothing that would be too graphic for anyone under 17 years old.

Nonfiction Our No. 1 priority is publishing books appropriate for young adults, ages 10-18. All quality books on any subject that fit that category will be considered.Subjects include business, economics, government, politics, health, medicine, money, finance, regional, sports, womens issues, womens studies, popular culture. Submit proposal package, outline, 2 sample chapters, competition/market survey.

Fiction Our No. 1 priority is publishing books appropriate for young adults, ages 10-18. All quality books on any subject that fit that category will be considered.Subjects include ethnic, general, feminist, gay, lesbian, historical, humor, literary, mainstream, contemporary, military, war, mystery, amateur sleuth, cozy,

police procedural, private eye/hardboiled, regional, science fiction, hard science fiction/technological, soft/sociological, translation, frontier sage, traditional, young adult, historical, problem novels, series, thrillers.
Recent Title(s) *Like We Care*, by Tom Matthews; *The Case Against My Brother*, by Libby Sternberg; *Mia the Melodramatic*, by Eileen Boggess.

BANTER PRESS

561 Hudson St., Suite 57, New York NY 10014. (718)864-5080. Fax: (718)965-3603. E-mail: info@banterpress.com. Website: www.banterpress.com. **Contact:** David McClintock, president. Estab. 2002. Publishes trade paperback and electronic originals and reprints. **Publishes 1-3 titles/year. 50 queries received/year. 10 mss received/year. 80% of books from first-time authors. 90% from unagented writers. Pays 15% royalty on wholesale price, negotiable.** Publishes book 6-18 months after acceptance of ms. Accepts simultaneous submissions. Responds in 4-12 weeks to queries. Book catalog available online. Guidelines available online.
Imprints Banter Business; Banter Health; Banter Living; Banter Tech.
Nonfiction Subjects include audio, health, written for patients, entrepeneurship, consumer protection, consulting, public speaking, publishing, communication-oriented and teamwork-oriented topics in business, healthcare, computer science, and balanced living. Submit proposal package, outline, maximum sample chapters, bio, analysis of competing books, author's plan for promoting the book. Reviews artwork/photos. Send photocopies; never send originals.
Tips Our readers are curious, technologically savvy professionals who need inspiring, up-to-date business and health information. Please don't mail us manuscripts! E-mail them as Word documents, PDFs, or as plain text files (.txt). Best yet, paste text into a giant e-mail.

BARNEGAT LIGHT PRESS

Pine Barrens Press 3959 Rt. 563, Chatsworth NJ 08019-0607. (609)894-4415. Fax: (609)894-2350. **Contact:** R. Marilyn Schmidt, publisher. Publishes trade paperback originals. **Publishes 4 titles/year. 50 queries received/year. 30 mss received/year. 100% from unagented writers. Makes outright purchase.** Publishes book 6 months after acceptance of ms. Responds in 1 month to queries. Book catalog online.
Imprints Pine Barrens Press.

- "We are a regional publisher emphasizing the mid-Atlantic region. Areas concerned are mid-Atlantic gardening, cooking, and travel."

Nonfiction Subjects include agriculture, cooking, foods, nutrition, gardening, regional, travel. Query with SASE. Reviews artwork/photos. Send photocopies.
Recent Title(s) *Towns Lost But Not Forgotten*, by R. Marilyn Schmidt; *Folk Foods of the Pine Barrens*, by R. Marilyn Schmidt.

BARNWOOD PRESS

4604 47th Ave. S, Seattle WA 98118. E-mail: barnwood@earthlink.net. Website: www.barnwoodpress.org. **Contact:** Tom Koontz, editor. Estab. 1975. Publishes original trade paperbacks. **Publishes 2 titles/year. 25% of books from first-time authors. 100% from unagented writers. Pays 10% of run** Responds in 1 month to queries.

BEAR STAR PRESS

185 Hollow Oak Dr., Cohasset CA 95973. (530)891-0360. Website: www.bearstarpress.com. **Contact:** Beth Spencer, publisher/editor. Estab. 1996. Publishes trade paperback originals. **Publishes 1-3 titles/year. Pays $1,000, and 25 copies to winner of annual Dorothy Brunsman contest.** Publishes book 9 months after acceptance of ms. Accepts simultaneous submissions. Responds in 2 weeks to queries. Guidelines available online.

- "Bear Star is committed to publishing the best poetry it can attract. Each year it sponsors a contest open to poets from Western and Pacific states. From time to time we add to our list other poets from our target area whose work we admire."

Recent Title(s) *Keel Bone*, by Maya Khosla; *The Soup of Something Missing*, by Rick Bursky; *Death of a Mexican and Other Poems*, by Manuel Paul Lopez.
Tips "Send your best work, consider its arrangement. A 'wow' poem early keeps me reading."

BEEMAN JORGENSEN, INC.

7510 Allisonville Rd., Indianapolis IN 46250. (317)841-7677. Fax: (317)849-2001. **Contact:** Brett Johnson, president (automotive/auto racing). Publishes hardcover and trade paperback originals and hardcover reprints. **Publishes 4 titles/year. 10 queries received/year. 50% of books from first-time authors. 100% from unagented writers. Pays 15-30% royalty on wholesale price. Pays up to $1,000 advance.** Publishes book 8 months after acceptance of ms. Responds in 1 month to queries. Responds in 2 months to proposals. Book catalog available free.
Nonfiction Publishes books on automobiles and auto racing.Subjects include sports, auto racing. Query with

SASE. Submit proposal package, outline, 1 sample chapter.

Recent Title(s) *Drag Racing Basics*, by Cindy Crawford (illustrated book); *Road America*, by Tom Schultz (illustrated book); *Porshe 356, Guide to D-I-Y Restoration*, by Jim Kellogg (illustrated book).

Tips Audience is automotive enthusiasts, specific marque owners/enthusiasts, auto racing fans, and participants.

BENDALL BOOKS

145 Tyee Dr., PMB 361, Point Roberts WA 98281. (250)743-2946. Fax: (250)743-2910. E-mail: admin@bendallbooks.com. Website: www.islandnet.com/bendallbooks. **Contact:** Mary Moore, publisher. Publishes trade paperback originals. **Publishes 1 titles/year. 30 queries received/year. 5 mss received/year. 50% of books from first-time authors. 100% from unagented writers. Pays 5-15% royalty on wholesale price.** Publishes book 1 year after acceptance of ms. Accepts simultaneous submissions. Book catalog available free. Guidelines available online.

Nonfiction Subjects include education. Query with SASE.

Recent Title(s) *Daily Meaning*, edited by Allan Neilsen; *Fiction Workshop Companion*, by Jon Volkmer.

BETTERWAY BOOKS

Imprint of F+W Media, Inc. 4700 E. Galbraith Rd., Cincinnati OH 45236. (513)531-2690, ext. 1408. E-mail: jane.friedman@fwpubs.com. Website: www.fwpublications.com. Publishes trade paperback originals. **Publishes 2-4 titles/year. 12 queries received/year. 6 mss received/year. 25% of books from first-time authors. 25% from unagented writers. Pays 8-15% royalty on wholesale price. Pays $3,000-7,000 advance.** Publishes book 18 months after acceptance of ms. Accepts simultaneous submissions. Responds in 1 month to queries. Responds in 1 month to proposals. Responds in 3 months to manuscripts.

Nonfiction Subjects include sports, especially basketball, baseball, tennis, and golf. Query with SASE. Submit proposal package, outline, 1 sample chapters. Reviews artwork/photos. Send photocopies and PDFs (if submitting electronically).

Recent Title(s) *Basketball Drills, Plays, and Strategies*, by Ed Dreyer, et al.; *Coaching Youth Basketball*, by John McCarthy.

Tips Audience comprised of student Make sure your proposal detai

BICK PUBLISHING HOUSE

307 Neck Rd., Madison CT 06443. (203)245-0073. Fax: (203)245-5990. E-mail: bickpubhse@aol.com. Website: www.bickpubhouse.com. **Contact:** Dale Carlson, president (psychology); Hannah Carlson (special needs, disabilities); Irene Ruth (wildlife). Estab. 1994. Publishes trade paperback originals. **Publishes 4 titles/year. 100 queries received/year. 100 mss received/year. 55% of books from first-time authors. 55% from unagented writers. Pays $500-1,000 advance.** Publishes book 12 months after acceptance of ms. Responds in 1 month to queries. Responds in 2 months to proposals. Responds in 3 months to manuscripts. Book catalog available free. Guidelines for #10 SASE.

- Bick Publishing House publishes step-by-step, easy-to-read professional information for the general adult public about physical, psychological, and emotional disabilities or special needs. Currently emphasizing science, psychology for teens.

Nonfiction Subjects include health, medicine, disability/special needs, psychology, young adult or teen science, psychology, wildlife rehabilitation. Query with SASE. Submit proposal package, outline, resume, 3 sample chapters.

Recent Title(s) *Are You Human, or What? Teen Evolutionary Psychology 2008*, by Dale Carlson; *The Courage to Lead Support Groups: Mental Illnesses and Addictions*, by Hannah Carlson; *In and Out of Your Mind Teen Science*, by Dale Carlson; *Who Said What, Philosophy Quotes for Teens: What Are You Doing With Your Life?*, by J. Krishnamurti.

BIRCH BROOK PRESS

P.O. Box 81, Delhi NY 13753. Fax: (607)764-7453. E-mail: birchbrook@copper.net. Website: www.birchbrookpress.info. **Contact:** Editor/publisher: Tom Tolnay; Associate Ed.: Barbara dela Cuesta. Estab. 1982. Publishes trade paperback originals; also, letter press editions are printed in our own shop. **Publishes 4 titles/year. 200+ queries received/year. 200+ mss received/year. 95% from unagented writers. Pays royalty.** Publishes book 6-18 months after acceptance of ms. Accepts simultaneous submissions. Responds in 3-6 months to manuscripts. Book catalog available online.

Imprints Birch Brook Press; Birch Brook Impressions.

Nonfiction , (rare) nonfiction of cultural interest, including stage, film, music, opera, including outdoors.

Fiction Publishes fiction mostly for anthologies with a theme established in-house.Subjects include mainstream, contemporary, poetry, poetry in translation, short fiction (occasionally), sports (outdoors/flyfishing/baseball). Query with SASE.

Recent Title(s) *Human/Nature*, by Lance Lee; *The Alchemy of Words*, by Edward Francisco; *Sea-Crossing of St.*

Small Presses

Brendan, by Matthew Brennan; *Where Things Are When You Lose Them*, by Tom Smith.
Tips Our audience is college educated.

BKMK PRESS

University of Missouri-Kansas City 5101 Rockhill Rd., Kansas City MO 64110-2499. (816)235-2558. Fax: (816)235-2611. E-mail: bkmk@umkc.edu. Website: www.umkc.edu/bkmk. **Contact:** Ben Furnish, managing editor. Estab. 1971. Publishes trade paperback originals. Accepts simultaneous submissions. Responds in 4-6 months to queries. Guidelines available online.

O‑‑ BkMk Press publishes fine literature. Reading period January-June.

Nonfiction Creative nonfiction essays.Submit 25-5 pp. sample and SASE.
Fiction Subjects include literary, short story collections. Query with SASE.
Recent Title(s) *Cleaning a Rainbow*, by Gary Gildner; *Love Letters from a Fat Man*, by Naomi Benarons; *Dream Lives of Butterflies*, by Jaimee Wriston Colbert.
Tips We skew toward readers of literature, particularly contemporary writing. Because of our limited number of titles published per year, we discourage apprentice writers or `scattershot' submissions.

BLACK DOME PRESS CORP.

1011 Route 296, Hensonville NY 12439. (518)734-6357. Fax: (518)734-5802. E-mail: blackdomep@aol.com. Website: www.blackdomepress.com. Estab. 1990. Publishes cloth and trade paperback originals and reprints. Accepts simultaneous submissions. Book catalog available online.
Nonfiction Subjects include history, nature, environment, photography, regional, New York state, Native Americans, grand hotels, geneology, colonial life, quilting, architecture, railroads. Submit proposal package, outline, bio.
Recent Title(s) *American Wilderness*, by Barbara Babcock; *Berkshire & Taconic Trails*, by Edward G. Henry.
Tips Our audience is comprised of New York state residents, tourists, and visitors.

BLACK HERON PRESS

P.O. Box 13396, Mill Creek WA 98082-1396. Website: www.blackheronpress.com. **Contact:** Jerry Gold, publisher. Estab. 1984. Publishes hardcover and trade paperback originals, trade paperback reprints. **Publishes 4 titles/year. 1,500 queries/year 50% of books from first-time authors. 90% from unagented writers. 8% royalty on retail price** Publishes book 24 months after acceptance of ms. Accepts simultaneous submissions. Responds in 6 months on queries and mss. Catalog available online and for 6" x 9" SAE with 3 first-class stamps. For #10 SASE.

O‑‑ Black Heron Press publishes primarily literary fiction.

Nonfiction Subjects include military, war. Submit proposal package, include cover letter & first 40-50 pages of your completed novel. We do not review artwork.
Fiction Subjects include confession, erotica, literary (regardless of genre), military, war, sci-fi, young adult, We publish some science fiction—not fantasy, not Dungeons & Dragons—that makes or implies a social statement. All of our fiction is character driven. Submit proposal package, including cover letter & first 40-50 pages pages of your completed novel.
Recent Title(s) *Anna Begins*, by Jennifer Davenport (YA); *Mantids*, by Ron Dakron (sci-fi/humor); *A Grey Moon Over China*, by Thomas A. Day.
Tips Our Readers love good fiction—they are scattered among all social classes, ethnic groups, & zip code areas. If you can't read our books, at least check out our titles on our website.

BLISS PUBLISHING CO.

P.O. Box 369, Hudson MA 01749. (978)567-9800. Website: www.blisspublishing.com. **Contact:** Stephen H. Clouter, president. Publishes hardcover and trade paperback originals. **Publishes 2-4 titles/year. Pays 10-15% royalty on wholesale price.** Responds in 2 months to queries.
Nonfiction Subjects include government, politics, history, music, dance, nature, environment, recreation, regional. Submit proposal package, outline, resume, 3 sample chapters. SASE.
Recent Title(s) *The Concord, Sudbury and Assabet Rivers, A Guide to Canoeing, Wildlife & History*, by Ron McAdow, illustrated by Gordon Morrison; *Cape Cod Recreation Map & Guide*, by Michael Tougias.

N BLOOMING TREE PRESS

P.O. Box 140934, Austin TX 78714. (512)921-8846. Fax: (512)873-7710. E-mail: bloomingtree@gmail.com. Website: www.bloomingtreepress.com. **Contact:** Bradford Hees: Editorial Director (adult books, graphic novels); Madeline Smoot: Editorial Director (children's books, young adult). Estab. 2000. Publishes hardcover, trade paperback, and mass market paperback originals. **Publishes 8-15 titles/year. 10,000 queries received/year. 1,200 mss received/year. 80%% of books from first-time authors. 90%% from unagented writers. Pays 8-12% royalty on wholesale price.** Publishes book 24 months after acceptance of ms. Accepts simultaneous submissions. Responds in 3 months to queries. Responds in 6 months to proposals. Responds in 6 months to

manuscripts. Book catalog available online. Guidelines available online.
Fiction Subjects include adventure, comic books, fantasy, historical, humor, juvenile, literary, mystery, picture books, romance, science fiction, short story collections, spiritual, young adult. We like to print a wide variety of genres. Agented submissions only. Unsolicited mss returned unopened.
Recent Title(s) *Patrick the Somnambulist*, by Sarah Ackerly ((picture book)); *Dragon Wishes*, by Stacy Nyikos ((mid-grade fiction)).
Tips Our audience is children thro Know your audience and write

N BLUEBRIDGE

Imprint of United Tribes Media, Inc. 240 W. 35th St., Suite 500, New York NY 10001. (212)244-4166. Fax: (212)279-0927. E-mail: janguerth@aol.com. Website: www.bluebridgebooks.com. **Contact:** Jan-Erik Guerth, publisher (general nonfiction). Estab. 2004. Publishes hardcover and trade paperback originals. **Publishes 6-8 titles/year. 1,000 queries received/year. 5% of books from first-time authors. Pays variable royalty on wholesale price. Pays variable advance.** Publishes book 12-24 months after acceptance of ms. Accepts simultaneous submissions. Responds in 1 month to queries. Responds in 1 month to proposals. Book catalog for #10 SASE.
Nonfiction Subjects include Americana, anthropology, archaeology, art, architecture, business, economics, child guidance, contemporary culture, creative nonfiction, ethnic, gardening, gay, lesbian, government, politics, health, medicine, history, humanities, language, literature, literary criticism, multicultural, music, dance, nature, environment, philosophy, psychology, religion, science, social sciences, sociology, spirituality, travel, womens issues, world affairs. Query with SASE or preferably by e-mail.
Recent Title(s) *Revolutionary Spirits*, by Gary Kowalski; *The Gift of Years*, by Joan Chittister; *Horse*, by J. Edward Chamberlin; *The Door of No Return*, by William St. Clair.
Tips We target a broad general audience.

BLUE POPPY PRESS

Imprint of Blue Poppy Enterprises, Inc. 5441 Western Ave., #2, Boulder CO 80301-2733. (303)447-8372. Fax: (303)245-8362. E-mail: info@bluepoppy.com. Website: www.bluepoppy.com. **Contact:** Bob Flaws, editor-in-chief. Estab. 1981. Publishes hardcover and trade paperback originals. **Publishes 3-4 titles/year. 50 queries received/year. 5-10 mss received/year. 30-40% of books from first-time authors. 100% from unagented writers. Pays 8-12% royalty.** Publishes book 1 year after acceptance of ms. Responds in 1 month to queries. Book catalog available free. Guidelines available online.

- Blue Poppy Press is dedicated to expanding and improving the English language literature on acupuncture and Asian medicine for both professional practitioners and lay readers.

Nonfiction Subjects include ethnic, health, medicine. Query with SASE. Submit outline, 1 sample chapter.
Recent Title(s) *Integrated Pharmacology: Combining Modern Pharmacology with Chinese Medicine*, by Dr. Greg Sperber with Bob Flaws; *Principles of Chinese Medical Andrology: An Integrated Approach to Male Reproductive & Urological Health*, by Bob Damone; *Chinese Medicine & Healthy Weight Management: An Evidence-based Integrated Approach*, by Juliette Aiyana.
Tips Audience is practicing acupuncturists, interested in alternatives in healthcare, preventive medicine, Chinese philosophy, and medicine.

A BOOK PEDDLERS

2828 Hedberg Drive, Minnetonka MN 55305. (952)544-1154. Fax: (952)544-1153. E-mail: vlansky@bookpeddlers.com. Website: www.bookpeddlers.com. **Contact:** Vicki Lansky, publisher/editor. Publishes hardcover and trade paperback originals. **Publishes several titles/year. 50 queries received/year. 10 mss received/year. 0% of books from first-time authors. 0% from unagented writers. Pays 10% royalty on wholesale price. Pays advance.** Publishes book 1 year after acceptance of ms. Accepts simultaneous submissions. Responds in 1 week to queries. Book catalog for #10 SASE. Guidelines available online.
Nonfiction Query with SASE.
Recent Title(s) *Coming Clean*, by Schar War (dirty little secrets from a professional housecleaner).
Tips See submission guidelines on website.

BREAKAWAY BOOKS

P.O. Box 24, Halcottsville NY 12438. (212)898-0408. E-mail: information@breakawaybooks.com. Website: www.breakawaybooks.com. **Contact:** Garth Battista, publisher. Estab. 1994. Publishes hardcover and trade paperback originals. **Publishes 8-10 titles/year. 400 queries received/year. 100 mss received/year. 35% of books from first-time authors. 75% from unagented writers. Pays advance.** Publishes book 9 months after acceptance of ms. Accepts simultaneous submissions. Responds in 1 month to queries. Responds in 1 month to proposals. Responds in 2 months to manuscripts. Book catalog and ms guidelines free and online.

- Breakaway Books is a sports literature specialty publisher—only fiction and narrative nonfiction. No how-tos.

Nonfiction Subjects include sports, narrative only, not how-to. Query with SASE or by e-mail.
Fiction Subjects include short story collections, sports stories, translation. Query with SASE. Submit complete ms.
Recent Title(s) *God on the Starting Line*, by Marc Bloom; *The Art of Bicycling*, edited by Justin Belmont; *American Miler*, by Dr. Paul Kiell.
Tips Audience is intelligent, passi We're starting a new children

BREWERS PUBLICATIONS

Imprint of Brewers Association 736 Pearl St., Boulder CO 80302. (303)447-0816. Fax: (303)447-2825. E-mail: kristi@brewersassociation.org. Website: beertown.org. **Contact:** Kristi Switzer, publisher. Estab. 1986. Publishes hardcover and trade paperback originals. **Publishes 2 titles/year. 50% of books from first-time authors. 100% from unagented writers. Pays small advance.** Publishes book 9 months after acceptance of ms. Accepts simultaneous submissions. Responds in 3 months to relevant queries Only those submissions relevant to our needs will receive a response to queries. Guidelines available online.

O-- Brewers Publications is the largest publisher of books on beer-related subjects.

Nonfiction Query first with proposal and sample chapter
Recent Title(s) *Best of American Beer & Food*, by Lucy Saunders; *Great Beers of Belgium*, by Michael Jackson.

BRIGHT MOUNTAIN BOOKS, INC.

206 Riva Ridge Dr., Fairview NC 28730. (828)628-1768. Fax: (828)628-1755. E-mail: booksbmb@charter.net. **Contact:** Cynthia F. Bright, editor. Publishes trade paperback originals and reprints. **Publishes 3 titles/year. 50% of books from first-time authors. 100% from unagented writers. Pays royalty.** Responds in 1 month to queries. Responds in 3 months to manuscripts.
Imprints Historical Images, Ridgetop Books.
Nonfiction Subjects include history, regional. Query with SASE.
Recent Title(s) *Asheville: Mountain Majesty*, by Lou Harshaw; *John Henry Moss*, by Bob Terrell; *The Carolina Mountains*, by Margaret W. Marley.

BRIGHTON PUBLICATIONS, INC.

P.O. Box 120706, St. Paul MN 55112-0706. (800)536-2665. Fax: (651)636-2220. E-mail: sharon@partybooks.com. Website: www.partybooks.com. **Contact:** Sharon E. Dlugosch, editor. Estab. 1977. Publishes trade paperback originals. **100 queries received/year. 100 mss received/year. 50% of books from first-time authors. 100% from unagented writers. Pays 10% royalty on wholesale price.** Accepts simultaneous submissions. Responds in 3 months to queries. Book catalog and ms guidelines for #10 SASE.

O-- Brighton Publications publishes books on celebration or seasonal how-to parties and anything that will help to give a better party such as activities, games, favors, and themes. Currently emphasizing games for meetings, annual parties, picnics, etc., celebration themes, and party/special event planning.

Nonfiction Query with SASE. Submit outline, 2 sample chapters.
Recent Title(s) *Installation Ceremonies for Every Group: 26 Memorable Ways to Install New Officers*, by Pat Hines; *Meeting Room Games: Getting Things Done in Committees*, by Nan Booth.

N BRONZE MAN BOOKS

Bronze Man Books, Millikin Univ., 1184 W. Main, Decatur IL 62522, U.S. (217)424-6264. Website: www.bronzemanbooks.com. **Contact:** Dr. Randy Brooks, editorial board (Area of interest: children's books, fiction, poetry, nonfiction); Edwin Walker, editorial board (art, exhibits, graphic design). Hardcover, trade paperback, & mass market paperback originals. **Publishes 3-4 titles/year. Receives 45 queries; 25 mss. 80% of books from first-time authors. 100% from unagented writers.** Publishes book 6 months after acceptance of ms. Catalog free on request. Guidelines not available.
Nonfiction We do not publish author subsidy books.Subjects include art, architecture, children's, graphic design, exhibits. Query with SASE; submit proposal package, including outline and 3 sample chapters. Reviews artwork/photos. Send photocopies.
Fiction Subjects include art, exhibits, graphic design, general. Submit completed ms.
Recent Title(s) *Robert Marshall Root: Something More Than Praise*, by Edwin Walker (68 pages, nonfiction); *Ants in the Band Room*, by Laura Podeschi (children's trade paperback with audio CD); *Commas & Ampersands*, by Steve Moore (short dramas chapbook); *Millikin University Haiku Anthology* (poetry); *Simple Universal*, by Jeffrey Allen (chapbook, 32 pages); *Mathematics of Fire*, by Josh Wild (chapbook, 24 pages, hand sewn).
Tips The art books are intended for serious collectors and scholars of contemporary art, especially of artists from the Midwestern U.S. These books are published in conjunction with art exhibitions at Millikin University or the Decatur Area Arts Council. The children's books have our broadest audience, and the literary chapbooks are intended for readers of contemporary fiction, drama, and poetry.

BROOKS BOOKS

3720 N. Woodridge Dr., Decatur IL 62526. E-mail: brooksbooks@sbcglobal.net. Website: www.brooksbookshaiku.com. **Contact:** Randy Brooks, editor (haiku poetry, tanka poetry). Publishes hardcover, trade paperback, & electronic originals. **Publishes 2-3 titles/year. 100 queries received/year. 25 mss received/year. 10% of books from first-time authors. 100% from unagented writers. Outright purchase based on wholesale value of 10% of a press run.** Publishes book 6-12 months after acceptance of ms. Responds in 2 months to queries. Responds in 3 months to proposals. Responds in 3 months to manuscripts. Book catalog free on request or online at website. Guidelines free on request, for #10 SASE.

Imprints Brooks Books

O-→ Brooks Books, formerly High/Coo Press, publishes English-language haiku books, chapbooks, magazines, and bibliographies.

Recent Title(s) *HAIKU: the Art of the Short poem, by Tazuo Yamaguchi; Sky In my Teacup: haiku & photographs, by Anne LB Davidson, online edition. See website; Lull Before Dark: Haiku, by Caroline Gourlay; To Hear the Rain: Selected Haiku*, by Peggy Lyles.

Tips The best haiku capture human perception—moments of being alive conveyed through sensory images. They do not explain nor describe nor provide philosophical or political commentary. Haiku are gifts of the here and now, deliberately incomplete so that the reader can enter into the haiku moment to open the gift and experience the feelings and insights of that moment for his or her self. Our readership includes the haiku community, readers of contemporary poetry, teachers and students of Japanese literature and contemporary Japanese poetics.

N BULL PUBLISHING CO.

P.O. Box 1377, Boulder CO 80306. (800)676-2855. Fax: (303)545-6354. Website: www.bullpub.com. **Contact:** James Bull, publisher (self-care, nutrition, women's health, weight control); Lansing Hays, publisher (self-help, psychology). Estab. 1974. Publishes hardcover and trade paperback originals. **Publishes 6-8 titles/year. Pays 10-16% royalty on wholesale price (net to publisher).** Publishes book 6 months after acceptance of ms. Book catalog available free.

O-→ Bull Publishing publishes health and nutrition books for the public with an emphasis on self-care, nutrition, women's health, weight control and psychology.

Nonfiction Subjects include cooking, foods, nutrition, education, health, medicine, womens issues, womens studies. Submit outline, sample chapters. Reviews artwork/photos.

Recent Title(s) *Child of Mine, 3rd Ed.*, by Ellyn Satter; *Hormonal Balance*, by Scott Isaacs.

CADENCE JAZZ BOOKS

Cadence Building, Redwood NY 13679. (315)287-2852. Fax: (315)287-2860. E-mail: cjb@cadencebuilding.com. Website: www.cadencebuilding.com. **Contact:** Bob Rusch, Larry Raye. Estab. 1992. Publishes trade paperback and mass market paperback originals. **Publishes 2 titles/year. 90% of books from first-time authors. 100% from unagented writers. Pays royalty or makes outright purchase. Pays advance.** Publishes book 6-12 months after acceptance of ms. Responds in 1 month to queries.

O-→ Cadence publishes jazz histories and discographies.

Nonfiction Subjects include music, dance, jazz music biographies, discographies and reference works. Submit outline, sample chapters, SASE. Reviews artwork/photos. Send photocopies.

Recent Title(s) *The Earthly Recordings of Sun Ra*, by Robert L. Campbell (discography).

CAMINO BOOKS, INC.

P.O. Box 59026, Philadelphia PA 19102. (215)413-1917. Fax: (215)413-3255. Website: www.caminobooks.com. **Contact:** E. Jutkowitz, publisher. Estab. 1987. Publishes hardcover and trade paperback originals. **Publishes 8 titles/year. 20% of books from first-time authors. Pays $2,000 average advance.** Publishes book 12 months after acceptance of ms. Responds in 2 weeks to queries. Guidelines available online.

O-→ Camino Books, Inc., publishes nonfiction of regional interest to the Mid-Atlantic states.

Nonfiction Subjects include agriculture, Americana, art, architecture, child guidance, cooking, foods, nutrition, ethnic, gardening, government, politics, history, regional, travel. Query with SASE. Submit outline, sample chapters.

Tips The books must be of interest to readers in the Middle Atlantic states, or they should have a clearly defined niche, such as cookbooks.

N CARNEGIE MELLON UNIVERSITY PRESS

5032 Forbes Ave., Pittsburgh PA 15289-1021. (412)268-2861. Fax: (412)268-8706. Website: www.cmu.edu/universitypress/. **Contact:** Cynthia Lamb, editor (nonfiction). Estab. 1972. Hardcover and trade paperback originals. **Publishes 6 titles/year.** Book catalog available online. Guidelines available online.

Nonfiction Subjects include art, architecture, computers, electronics, education, (Higher), history, literary criticism, memoirs, music, dance, science, sociology, translation. Query with SASE.

Fiction Subjects include literary, mainstream, contemporary, poetry, poetry in translation, short story collections, Drama, epistolary novel.
Recent Title(s) *Talking Steel Towns*, by Ellie Wymard (nonfiction); *Getting to Know the Weather*, by Pamela Painter (fiction); *Warhol-o-rama*, by Peter Oresick (poetry).
Tips Please send SASE for judge's decison on our 'first book' contest. Our strength lies in literary publishing with the following series: Contemporary Poetry; Classic Contemporaries (reissuing significant early books by contemporary poets and writers of short fiction); Transation; Short Fiction; Poets in Prose (Titles have included memoir in the form of poets writing about their writing lives, poetry criticism & the epistolary novel).

CAROUSEL PRESS

P.O. Box 6038, Berkeley CA 94706-0038. (510)527-5849. Website: www.carouselpress.com. **Contact:** Carole T. Meyers, editor/publisher. Estab. 1976. Publishes trade paperback originals and reprints. **Publishes 1-2 titles/year. Pays 10-15% royalty on wholesale price. Pays $1,000 advance.** Responds in 1 month to queries.
Nonfiction Subjects include travel, travel-related. Query with SASE.
Recent Title(s) *Weekend Adventures in San Francisco & Northern California.*

N CAVE HOLLOW PRESS

P.O. Drawer J, Warrensburg MO 64093. E-mail: nagel@cavehollowpress.com. Website: www.cavehollowpress.com. **Contact:** R.M. Kinder and Georgia R. Nagel, editors. Estab. 2001. Publishes trade paperback originals. **Publishes 1 titles/year. 70 queries received/year. 6 mss received/year. 80% of books from first-time authors. 100% from unagented writers. Pays 7-12% royalty on wholesale price. Pays negotiable amount in advance.** Publishes book 1 year after acceptance of ms. Accepts simultaneous submissions. Responds in 1-2 months to queries. Responds in 1-2 months to proposals. Responds in 3-6 months to manuscripts. Book catalog for #10 SASE. Guidelines available free.
Fiction Subjects include mainstream, contemporary. Our Web site is updated frequently to reflect the current type of fiction Cave Hollow Press is seeking. Query with SASE.
Recent Title(s) *The Feedsack Dress*, by Carolyn Mulford (young adult); *A Horse Named Kat*, by Lucy Lauer (middle reader); *Triskaideka: Murder, Mystery, Magic, Madness and Mayhem II*, by various writers (anthology).
Tips Our audience varies based on the type of book we are publishing. We specialize in Missouri and Midwest regional fiction. We are interested in talented writers from Missouri and the surrounding Midwest. Check our submission guidelines on the Web site for what type of fiction we are interested in currently.

CHURCH GROWTH INSTITUTE

P.O. Box 7, Elkton MD 21922-0007. (434)525-0022. Fax: (434)525-0608. E-mail: cgimail@churchgrowth.org. Website: www.churchgrowth.org. **Contact:** Cindy Spear, administrator/resource development director. Estab. 1978. Publishes electronic books (pdf), 3-ring-bound manuals, mixed media resource packets. **Publishes 3 titles/year. Pays 6% royalty on retail price.** Publishes book 1 year after acceptance of ms. Accepts simultaneous submissions. Responds in 3 months to queries. Book catalog for 9x12 envelope and 4 First-Class stamps. ms guidelines given after query and outline is received.

- Our mission is to provide practical resources to help pastors, churches, and individuals reach their potential for Christ; to promote spiritual and numerical growth in churches, thereby leading Christians to maturity and lost people to Christ; and to equip pastors so they can equip their church members to do the work of the ministry.

Nonfiction Material should originate from a conservative Christian view and cover topics that will help churches grow, through leadership training, self-evaluation, and new or unique ministries, or enhancing existing ministries. Self-discovery inventories regarding spiritual growth, relationship improvement, etc., are hot items.Subjects include education, religion, church-growth related, ministry, how-to manuals, spiritual growth, relationship-building, evangelism. Query, or submit outline and brief explanation of what the packet will accomplish in the local church and whether it is leadership or lay oriented. Queries accepted by mail or e-mail. No phone queries. Reviews artwork/photos. Send Send photos or images on CD (in TIFF, EPS, or PDF format).
Recent Title(s) *Fruits of the Spirit Assessment*; *Serving God Where You Fit Best*; *How to Develop and Use the Gift of Exhortation.*
Tips We are not accepting textbooks, and are publishing few new printed materials this year—most are online or downloads. Concentrate on how-to manuals and ministry evaluation and diagnostic tools and spiritual or relationship-oriented 'inventories' for individual Christians.

CLARITY PRESS, INC.

3277 Roswell Rd. NE, #469, Atlanta GA 30305. (877)613-1495. Fax: (404)231-3899 and (877)613-7868. E-mail: claritypress@usa.net. Website: www.claritypress.com. **Contact:** Diana G. Collier, editorial director (contemporary social justice issues). Estab. 1984. Publishes hardcover and trade paperback originals. **Publishes**

4 titles/year. Accepts simultaneous submissions. Responds in 1 month to queries.

Nonfiction Publishes books on contemporary issues in US, Middle East and Africa.Subjects include ethnic, world affairs, human rights/socioeconomic and minority issues. Query by email only with synopsis, TOC, résumé, publishing history.

Recent Title(s) *The Power of Israel in the United States*, by James Petras; *Biowarfare and Terrorism*, by Francis A. Boyle.

Tips Check our titles on the Web site.

CLOVER PARK PRESS

P.O. Box 5067, Santa Monica CA 90409-5067. (310)452-7657. E-mail: cloverparkpress@verizon.net. Website: www.cloverparkpress.com. **Contact:** Martha Grant, acquisitions editor. Estab. 1991. Publishes hardcover and trade paperback originals. **Publishes 1-3 titles/year. 800 queries received/year. 500 mss received/year. 90% of books from first-time authors. 80% from unagented writers. Pays royalty. Makes outright purchase. Pays modest advance.** Publishes book less than 12 months. after acceptance of ms. Accepts simultaneous submissions. Responds in 2-4 months to queries, proposals, and to manuscripts. Book catalog available online. Guidelines for #10 SASE.

Nonfiction Subjects include creative nonfiction, multicultural, nature, environment, regional, science, travel, womens issues, womens studies, world affairs. Query with SASE. Submit proposal package, outline, bio, 30-50 pages (including the first chapter), SASE.

Recent Title(s) *Last Moon Dancing: A Memoir of Love and Real Life in Africa*, by Monique Maria Schmidt.

Tips Our audience is primarily women, high school, and college students, readers with curiosity about the world. Initial contact by e-mail or query letter. We welcome good writing. Have patience, we will respond.

CORNELL MARITIME PRESS, INC.

P.O. Box 456, Centreville MD 21617-0456. (410)758-1075. Fax: (410)758-6849. Website: www.cmptp.com. **Contact:** Jonna Jones, managing editor. Estab. 1938. Publishes hardcover originals and quality paperbacks. **Publishes 7-9 titles/year. 80% of books from first-time authors. 99% from unagented writers.** Publishes book 1 year after acceptance of ms. Responds in 2 months to queries.

Imprints *Tidewater* Publishers (regional history, outdoor sports, and wildlife of the Chesapeake Bay and the Delmarva Peninsula).

O→ Cornell Maritime Press publishes books for the merchant marine and a few recreational boating books for professional mariners and yachtsmen. Cornell also publishes a line of leathercraft books.

Nonfiction Look online for current acquisition needs and submission guidelines.

Recent Title(s) *Osprey Adventure*, by Jennifer Keats Curtis; *Beetle Boddiker*, by Priscilla Cummings.

N COSIMO BOOKS

COSIMO, INC. 191 7th Ave., Suite 2F, New York NY 10011-1818, United States. Fax: (212)989-3662. E-mail: info@cosimobooks.com. Website: www.cosimobooks.com. **Contact:** Alexander M. Dolce, CEO. Hardcover & trade paperback originals & reprints; electronic originals; hardcover & trade paperback reprints. **Publishes 5-7 titles/year. 20-25 queries/year; mss by request only 75% of books from first-time authors. 100% from unagented writers. NA** Publishes book 4-6 months after acceptance of ms. Online; free on request. Online; free on request.

Imprints Cosimo Classics, Cosimo Books, Cosimo Reports, Paraview Press

Nonfiction Subjects include alternative, community, contemporary culture, government, politics, health, medicine, history, humanities, memoirs, money, finance, nature, environment, New Age, philosophy, psychology, science, social sciences, sociology, spirituality, womens issues, womens studies, world affairs affairs, environment. Queries by email only. Yes. Send digital images only.

Recent Title(s) *Plunder: Investigating Our Economic Calamity and the Subprime Scandal*, by Danny Schechter

COTTONWOOD PRESS, INC.

109-B Cameron Dr., Fort Collins CO 80525. (800)864-4297. Fax: (970)204-0761. E-mail: cottonwood@cottonwoodpress.com. Website: www.cottonwoodpress.com. **Contact:** Cheryl Thurston, editor. Estab. 1986. Publishes trade paperback originals. **Publishes 2-8 titles/year. 50 queries received/year. 40 mss received/year. 50% of books from first-time authors. 100% from unagented writers.** Publishes book 1 year after acceptance of ms. Accepts simultaneous submissions. Responds in 1 month to queries. Responds in 1 month to proposals. Responds in 3 months to manuscripts. Book catalog for 10x12 envelope and 2 First-Class stamps. Guidelines available online.

O→ Cottonwood Press publishes creative and practical materials for English and language arts teachers, grades 5-12. We believe English should be everyone's favorite subject.

Nonfiction Subjects include education, language, literature. Query with SASE. Submit outline, 1-3 sample chapters.

Recent Title(s) *Phunny Stuph—Proofreading Exercises With a Sense of Humor*, by M.S. Samston; *Twisting Arms—Teaching Students to Write to Persuade*, by Dawn DiPrince; *Rock & Rap in Middle School*, by Sheree Sevilla and Suzanne Stansbury.

Tips We publish only supplemental textbooks for English/language arts teachers, grades 5-12, with an emphasis upon middle school and junior high materials. Don't assume we publish educational materials for all subject areas. We do not. Never submit anything to us before looking at our catalog. We have a very narrow focus and a distinctive style. Writers who don't understand that are wasting their time. On the plus side, we are eager to work with new authors who show a sense of humor and a familiarity with young adolescents.

COUNCIL ON SOCIAL WORK EDUCATION

1725 Duke St., Suite 500, Alexandria VA 22314-3457. (703)683-8080. Fax: (703)683-8099. E-mail: publications@cswe.org. Website: www.cswe.org. **Contact:** Mia Moreno-Hines, publications coordinator. Estab. 1952. Publishes trade paperback originals. **Publishes 4 titles/year. 12 queries received/year. 8 mss received/year. 25% of books from first-time authors. 100% from unagented writers. Pays sliding royalty scale, starting at 10%** Publishes book 1 year after acceptance of ms. Responds in 2 months to queries. Responds in 3 months to proposals. Responds in 3 months to manuscripts. Book catalog and ms guidelines free via website or with SASE.

- O— Council on Social Work Education produces books and resources for social work educators, students and practitioners.

Nonfiction Subjects include education, sociology, social work. Query with proposal package, including cv, outline, 2 sample chapters and SASE. Reviews artwork/photos. Send photocopies.

Recent Title(s) *Group Work Education in the Field*, by Julianne Wayne and Carol S. Cohen; *Ethics Education in Social Work*, by Frederic G. Reamer.

Tips Audience is Social work educators and students and others in the helping professions. Check areas of publication interest on website.

COUNTRY MUSIC FOUNDATION PRESS

222 Fifth Ave. S., Nashville TN 37203. (615)416-2001. Fax: (615)255-2245. Website: www.countrymusichalloffame.com. **Contact:** Jay Orr, senior museum editor; LeAnn Bennett, director of special projects; Michael Gray, associate editor. Publishes hardcover originals and trade paperback originals and reprints. **Publishes 2-4 titles/year. 12 queries received/year. Pays 10% royalty on wholesale price. Pays $1,000-5,000 advance.** Publishes book 1 year after acceptance of ms. Accepts simultaneous submissions. Responds in 2 months to queries. Responds in 3 months to proposals. Responds in 4 months to manuscripts. Book catalog available online. Guidelines available free.

- Also co-publish and hire writers (work-for-hire) for anthologies or for mass-market trade publications where CMF is authored.
- O— "We publish historical, biographical and reference books about country music, many in a joint imprint with Vanderbilt University Press. We require strict factual accuracy and strive to engage an educated general audience. Currently emphasizes histories, biographies, and memoirs with a strong narrative and accessible to an educated general audience. De-emphasizing heavily academic studies."

Nonfiction All must emphasize country music.Subjects include Americana, history, memoirs, music, dance, photography, regional. Query with SASE or submit proposal package, including outline, 1 sample chapter and introduction. Reviews artwork/photos. Send photocopies.

Recent Title(s) *Will the Circle be Unbroken: Country Music in America*, edited by Paul Kingsbury and Alanna Nash; *A Shot in the Dark: Making Records in Nashville 1945-1955*, by Martin Hawkins.

Tips "Our audience is a balance between educated country music fans and scholars. Submit queries or proposals only if you are very knowledgeable about your subject. Our books are in-depth studies written by experts or by music insiders. We aren't especially receptive to inexperienced beginners."

CYCLE PUBLISHING

Van der Plas Publications 1282 Seventh Ave., San Francisco CA 94122. (415)665-8214. Fax: (415)753-8572. Website: www.cyclepublishing.com. **Contact:** Rob van der Plas, publisher/editor. Estab. 1997. Publishes hardcover and trade paperback originals. **Publishes 4 titles/year.** Accepts simultaneous submissions. Book catalog and ms guidelines for #10 SASE.

Nonfiction Subjects include recreation, sports, manufactured homes. Submit complete ms. Reviews artwork/photos.

Recent Title(s) *Mountain Bike Maintenance*; *Buying a Manufactured Home*.

Tips Writers have a good chance selling us books with better and more illustrations and a systematic treatment of the subject. First check what is on the market and ask yourself whether you are writing something that is not yet available and wanted.

Small Presses

CYCLOTOUR GUIDE BOOKS

P.O. Box 10585, Rochester NY 10585-0585. (585)244-6157. Website: www.cyclotour.com. Trade paperback originals. **Publishes 2 titles/year. Receives 25 queries/year and 2 mss/year. 50% of books from first-time authors. 100% from unagented writers.** Publishes book 24 months after acceptance of ms. Accepts simultaneous submissions. Book catalog and ms guidelines online.

Nonfiction Subjects include sports (bicycle only), travel (bicycle tourism). No narrative accounts of their bicycle tour without distance indicators. Query with SASE. Reviews artwork/photos as part of ms package. Send photocopies.

Recent Title(s) *'Round Lake Superior: A Bicyclist's Tour Guide*, Botzman (travel).

Tips Bicyclists. Folks with a dream of bicycle touring. "Check your grammar & spelling. Write logically."

DANA PRESS

900 15th St. NW, Washington DC 20005. (202)408-8800. Fax: (202)408-5599. Website: www.dana.org/books/press. **Contact:** Jane Nevins, editor-in-chief; Dan Gordon, editor. Publishes hardcover and trade paperback originals. **Publishes 4 titles/year. 50% of books from first-time authors. 90% from unagented writers. Pays 7-10% royalty on list price. Pays $10,000-35,000 advance.** Publishes book 1 year after acceptance of ms. Accepts simultaneous submissions. Responds in 2 weeks to queries. Responds in 1 month to proposals. Responds in 2 months to manuscripts. Book catalog and ms guidelines online.

Nonfiction Subjects include health, medicine, memoirs, psychology, science. Reviews artwork/photos. Send photocopies.

Recent Title(s) *A Well-Tempered Mind: Using Music to Help Children Listen and Learn*, by Peter Perret and Janet Fox; *Neuroscience and the Law: Brain, Mind and the Scales of Justice*, edited by Brent Garland; *Back From the Brink: How Crises Spur Doctors to New Discoveries About the Brain*, by Edward J. Sylvester.

Tips The science must be solid, the perspective interesting. Coherent proposals are key. What is new or different about the book? Who is the reader?

DANIEL & DANIEL PUBLISHERS, INC.

P.O. Box 2790, McKinleyville CA 95519. (707)839-3495. Fax: (707)839-3242. E-mail: dandd@danielpublishing.com. Website: www.danielpublishing.com. **Contact:** John Daniel, publisher. Estab. 1980. Publishes hardcover originals and trade paperback originals. Publishes poetry, fiction and nonfiction. **Publishes 4 or fewer titles/year. 50% of books from first-time authors. 90% from unagented writers. Pays 10% royalty on wholesale price. Pays $0-500 advance.** Publishes book 12 months after acceptance of ms. Accepts simultaneous submissions. Responds in 1 month to queries. Responds in 1 month to proposals. Responds in 2 months to manuscripts. Book catalog available online. Guidelines available online.

Imprints John Daniel & Company; Fithian Press (belle lettres: fiction, poetry, memoir, essay); Perseverance Press (literary mysteries).

Nonfiction Subjects include creative nonfiction, memoirs. Query with SASE. Submit proposal package, outline, 5 pages.

Fiction Subjects include literary, short story collections. Query with SASE. Submit proposal package, clips, 5 pages.

Recent Title(s) *Wolf Tones*, by Irving Weinman (novel); *Devora in Exile*, by Barbara Cherne (stories)

Tips Audience includes literate, intelligent general readers. We are very small and very cautious, and we publish fewer books each year, so any submission to us is a long shot. But we welcome your submissions, by mail or e-mail only, please. We don't want submissions by phone, fax or disk.

DANTE UNIVERSITY OF AMERICA PRESS, INC.

P.O. Box 812158, Wellesley MA 02482. Fax: (781)790-1056. E-mail: danteu@danteuniversity.org. Website: www.danteuniversity.org/dpress.html. **Contact:** Josephine Tanner, president. Estab. 1975. Publishes hardcover and trade paperback originals and reprints. **Publishes 5 titles/year. 50% of books from first-time authors. 50% from unagented writers. Pays royalty. Pays negotiable advance.** Publishes book 10 months after acceptance of ms. Responds in 2 months to queries.

> O━ The Dante University Press exists to bring quality, educational books pertaining to our Italian heritage as well as the historical and political studies of America. Profits from the sale of these publications benefit the Foundation, bringing Dante University closer to a reality.

Nonfiction Subjects include history, Italian-American, humanities, translation, from Italian and Latin, general scholarly nonfiction, Renaissance thought and letter, Italian language and linguistics, Italian-American culture, bilingual education. Query with SASE. Reviews artwork/photos.

Fiction Translations from Italian and Latin. Query with SASE.

Recent Title(s) *Italian Poetry*, by Gayle Ridinger; *Marconi My Beloved*, by Maria/Elettra Marconi; *Romeo and Juliet*, by Adolph Caso.

MAY DAVENPORT, PUBLISHERS

26313 Purissima Rd., Los Altos Hills CA 94022. (650)947-1275. Fax: (650)947-1373. E-mail: mdbooks@earthlink.net. Website: www.maydavenportpublishers.com. **Contact:** May Davenport, editor/publisher. Estab. 1976. Publishes hardcover and paperback originals. **Publishes 4 titles/year. 95% of books from first-time authors. 100% from unagented writers. Pays 15% royalty on retail price (if book sells). Pays no advance.** Publishes book 12 months after acceptance of ms. Responds in 1 month to queries. Book catalog and ms guidelines for #10 SASE.

Imprints md Books (nonfiction and fiction).

- May Davenport publishes literature for teenagers (before they graduate from high schools) as supplementary literary material in English courses nationwide. Looking particularly for authors able to write for the teen Internet generation who don't like to read in-depth. Currently emphasizing more upper-level subjects for teens.

Nonfiction Subjects include Americana, language, literature, humorous memoirs for children/young adults. Query with SASE.

Fiction Subjects include humor, literary. We want to focus on novels junior and senior high school teachers can read aloud, share with their reluctant readers in their classrooms. Query with SASE.

Recent Title(s) *Summer of Suspense, a teenage girl's unexpected adventure*, by Frances Drummond Waines (mystery); *Surviving Sarah, the Sequel: Brown Bug and China Doll*, by Dinah Leigh (nonfiction).

Tips Just write your fictional novel humorously. If you can't write that way, create youthful characters so teachers, as well as 15-18-year-old high school readers, will laugh at your descriptive passages and contemporary dialogue. Avoid 1-sentence paragraphs. The audience we want to reach is today's high-tech teens who are talented with digital cameras hooked up to computers. Show them what you can do 'in print' for them and their equipment.

DAWN PUBLICATIONS

12402 Bitney Springs Rd., Nevada City CA 95959. (530)274-7775. Fax: (530)274-7778. Website: www.dawnpub.com. **Contact:** Glenn Hovemann, editor. Estab. 1979. Publishes hardcover and trade paperback originals. **Publishes 6 titles/year. 550 queries received/year. 2,500 mss received/year. 15% of books from first-time authors. 90% from unagented writers. Pays advance.** Publishes book 1 to 2 years after acceptance of ms. Accepts simultaneous submissions. Responds in 2 months to queries. Book catalog available online. Guidelines available online.

- Dawn now accepts mss submissions by e-mail; follow instructions posted on Web site. Submissions by mail still OK.
- Dawn Publications is dedicated to inspiring in children a sense of appreciation for all life on earth. Dawn looks for nature awareness and appreciation titles that promote a relationship with the natural world and specific habitats, usually through inspiring treatment and nonfiction.

Nonfiction Subjects include animals, nature, environment. Query with SASE.

Recent Title(s) *The Web at Dragonfly Pond*, by Brian Fox Ellis; *City Beats*, by S. Kelly Rammell; *If You Were My Baby*, by Fran Hodgkins.

Tips Publishes mostly creative nonfiction with lightness and inspiration.

DBS PRODUCTIONS

P.O. Box 1894, Charlottesville VA 22903. (800)745-1581. Fax: (434)293-5502. E-mail: robert@dbs-sar.com. Website: www.dbs-sar.com. **Contact:** Bob Adams, publisher. Estab. 1989. Publishes hardcover and trade paperback originals. **Publishes 4 titles/year. 10 queries received/year. 10% of books from first-time authors. 100% from unagented writers. Pays 5-20% royalty on retail price.** Publishes book 1 year after acceptance of ms. Responds in 2 weeks to queries. Book catalog on request or on website. Guidelines for #10 SASE.

- dbS Productions produces search and rescue and outdoor first-aid related materials and courses. It offers a selection of publications, videotapes, management kits and tools, and instructional modules.

Nonfiction Subjects include health, medicine. Submit proposal package, outline, 2 sample chapters. Reviews artwork/photos. Send photocopies.

Recent Title(s) *Urban Search*, by C. Young and J. Wehbring.

DEMONTREVILLE PRESS, INC.

P.O. Box 835, Lake Elmo MN 55042-0835. E-mail: publisher@demontrevillepress.com. Website: www.demontrevillepress.com. **Contact:** Kevin Clemens, publisher (automotive fiction and nonfiction). Estab. 2006. Publishes trade paperback originals and reprints. **Publishes 4 titles/year. 150 queries received/year. 100 mss received/year. 90% of books from first-time authors. 90% from unagented writers. Pays 20% royalty on retail price.** Publishes book 18 months after acceptance of ms. Accepts simultaneous submissions. Responds in 3 months to queries. Responds in 4 months to proposals. Responds in 6 months to manuscripts. Book catalog available online. Guidelines available online.

Nonfiction Subjects include creative nonfiction, history, automotive, environment, global climate change. Submit proposal package, outline, 3 sample chapters, bio. Reviews artwork/photos. Send Do not send photos until requested.
Fiction Subjects include current events, environment, adventure, mystery, sports, young adult, automotive, motorcycle. We want novel length automotive or motorcycle historicals and/or adventures. Submit proposal package, 3 sample chapters, clips, bio.
Tips Environmental, energy and transportation nonfiction works are now being accepted. Automotive and motorcycle enthusiasts, adventurers, and history buffs make up our audience.

DISKOTECH, INC.

7930 State Line, Suite 210, Prairie Village KS 66208. (913)432-8606. Fax: (913)432-8606. **Contact:** Jane Locke, submissions editor. Estab. 1989. Publishes multimedia nonfiction and fiction for PC's and the Internet. **Publishes 2 titles/year. Pays 10-15% royalty on wholesale price.** Responds in 2 months to queries.
Nonfiction Authors must supply the multimedia, such as video, music, and animation in html format.Query with SASE.
Fiction Authors must supply the multimedia, such as video, music, and animation and the work in html format.Considers all fiction genres. Query with SASE.
Recent Title(s) *L'Autobiographique* 2009, by Holly Franking, PhD (a new form of literary criticism and so is its Talmudic form); *The Martensville Nightmare CVN®*, Karen Smith (1st multimedia true crime story on CD-Rom, coming soon as a TV movie); *Negative Space CVN®*, Holly Franking (computerized video novel on CD-ROM); *Celebrity lnk CVN®*, (Hypermedia Internet Tabloid).

DOWN THE SHORE PUBLISHING

Box 100, West Creek NJ 08092. Fax: (609)597-0422. E-mail: info@down-the-shore.com. Website: www.down-the-shore.com. Publishes hardcover and trade paperback originals and reprints. **Publishes 6-10 titles/year. Pays royalty on wholesale or retail price, or makes outright purchase.** Accepts simultaneous submissions. Responds in 3 months to queries. Book catalog for 8 x 10 SAE with 2 first-class stamps or on website. Guidelines available online.

- Bear in mind that our market is regional—New Jersey, the Jersey Shore, the mid-Atlantic, and seashore and coastal subjects.

Nonfiction Subjects include Americana, art, architecture, history, nature, environment, regional. Query with SASE. Submit proposal package, 1-2 sample chapters, synopsis. Reviews artwork/photos. Send photocopies.
Fiction Subjects include regional. Query with SASE. Submit proposal package, clips, 1-2 sample chapters.
Recent Title(s) *Four Seasons at the Shore*; *The Oyster Singer*, by Larry Savadove.
Tips Carefully consider whether your proposal is a good fit for our established market.

N DRAM TREE BOOKS

Whittler's Bench Press P.O. Box 7183, Wilmington NC 28406. Website: www.dramtreebooks.com. **Contact:** Jack E. Fryar, Jr., publisher (nonfiction/fiction). Estab. 2000. Publishes trade paperback originals and reprints. **Publishes 8-12 titles/year. 90% of books from first-time authors. 100% from unagented writers. Pays 10-15% royalty on retail price. Pays $250-500 advance.** Publishes book 1 year after acceptance of ms. Responds in 2 months to queries. Responds in 2 months to proposals. Responds in 4 months to manuscripts. Book catalog for #10 SASE. Guidelines available via e-mail.
Imprints Whittler's Bench Press.
Nonfiction Subjects include Americana, art, architecture, creative nonfiction, education, history, hobbies, military, war, regional, travel. Query with SASE. Submit proposal package, outline, 3 sample chapters, bio. Reviews artwork/photos. Send photocopies and JPEGs on CD-ROM.
Recent Title(s) *Rebel Gibraltar: Fort Fisher and Wilmington, CSA*, by James L. Walker, Jr. (Civil War/history); *Wilmington: Lost but Not Forgotten*, by Beverly Tetterton (preservation/architecture); *A History Lover's Guide to Wilmington & the Lower Cape Fear*, by Jack E. Fryar, Jr. (travel).
Tips Our readers are native North Carolinians, recent transplants to the state or tourists visiting our state. We also enjoy a healthy audience among former residents of the Tar Heel State that now reside elsewhere. All of our books have a central theme: North Carolina history (particularly that of the Cape Fear region and North Carolina coast). Don't give us dry names and dates. Tell us a story! Just make sure it's a true one.

EAGLE'S VIEW PUBLISHING

6756 North Fork Rd., Liberty UT 84310. (801)745-0905. Fax: (801)745-0903. Website: www.eaglesviewpub.com. **Contact:** Denise Knight, editor-in-chief. Estab. 1982. Publishes trade paperback originals. **Publishes 2-4 titles/year. 40 queries received/year. 20 mss received/year. 90% of books from first-time authors. 100% from unagented writers. Pays 8-10% royalty on net selling price.** Publishes book 12 months or more after acceptance of ms. Accepts simultaneous submissions. Responds in 1 year to proposals. Book catalog and ms guidelines for $4.00.

O-ᵣ Eagle's View primarily publishes how-to craft books with a subject related to historical or contemporary Native American/Mountain Man/frontier crafts/bead crafts. Currently emphasizing bead-related craft books. De-emphasizing history except for historical Indian crafts.

Nonfiction Subjects include anthropology, archaeology, Native American crafts, ethnic, Native American, history, American frontier historical patterns and books, hobbies, crafts, especially beadwork. Submit outline, 1-2 sample chapters. Reviews artwork/photos. Send photocopies and sample illustrations.

Recent Title(s) *Treasury of Beaded Jewelry*, by Mary Ellen Harte; *Beads and Beadwork of the American Indian*, by William C. Orchard; *Hemp Masters: Getting Knotty*, by Max Lunger.

Tips We will not be publishing any new beaded earrings books for the foreseeable future. We are interested in other craft projects using seed beads, especially books that feature a variety of items, not just different designs for 1 item.

N EARTH-LOVE PUBLISHING HOUSE LTD.

3440 Youngfield St., Suite 353, Wheat Ridge CO 80033. (303)233-9660. Fax: (303)233-9354. **Contact:** Laodeciae Augustine, director. Publishes trade paperback originals. **Publishes 1-2 titles/year. Pays 6-10% royalty on wholesale price.** Responds in 1 month to queries. Responds in 1 month to proposals. Responds in 3 months to manuscripts.

Nonfiction Query with SASE.

Recent Title(s) *Love Is in the Earth—Kaleidoscope Pictorial Supplement Z*, by Melody (mineral reference); *Loves Is in the Earth—Crystal Tarot for the Millennium*, by Melody; *Love Is in the Earth—Reality Checque*, by Melody.

EASTLAND PRESS

P.O. Box 99749, Seattle WA 98139. (206)217-0204. Fax: (206)217-0205. E-mail: info@eastlandpress.com. Website: www.eastlandpress.com. **Contact:** John O'Connor, managing editor. Estab. 1981. Publishes hardcover and trade paperback originals. **Publishes 4-6 titles/year. 25 queries received/year. 30% of books from first-time authors. 90% from unagented writers. Pays 12-15% royalty on receipts.** Publishes book 12 to 24 months after acceptance of ms. Accepts simultaneous submissions. Responds in 1 month to queries. Book catalog available free.

O-ᵣ Eastland Press is interested in textbooks for practitioners of alternative medical therapies, primarily Chinese and physical therapies, and related bodywork.

Nonfiction Subjects include health, medicine. Submit outline and 2-3 sample chapters. Reviews artwork/photos. Send photocopies.

Recent Title(s) *Anatomy of Breathing*, by Blandine Calais-Germain; *The Fasciae: Anatomy, Dysfunction & Treatment*, by Serge Paoletti; *Chinese Herbal Medicine*, by Dan Bensky.

ELDER SIGNS PRESS, INC.

P.O. Box 389, Lake Orion MI 48361-0389. E-mail: editor@eldersignspress.com. Website: www.eldersignspress.com. **Contact:** William Jones, editor. Publishes hardcover and trade paperback originals, along with trade paperback reprints. **Publishes 8+ titles/year. 100+ queries received/year. 60+ mss received/year. 10% of books from first-time authors. 90% from unagented writers. Pays 5-15% royalty on wholesale or net price, or makes outright purchase of $500-$2,000. Pays advance.** Publishes book 6-8 months after acceptance of ms. Responds in 1 month to queries. Responds in 3 months to proposals. Responds in 6 months to manuscripts. Book catalog available online. Writer's guidelines online or via e-mail.

Imprints Dimension; ESP.

Fiction Subjects include adventure, comic, gothic, horror, mystery, science fiction, short story collections, suspense, dark fiction, supernatural, thriller. Strong characters that are round, with developed personality that motivate them, are important to the story. Intriguing plots and the unexpected are also essential. Exploration of the human condition and the unknown are works that make ideal candidates for publication. Submit proposal package, clips, 3 sample chapters.

Recent Title(s) *Twice Dead Things*, by A.A. Attanasio; *Hardboiled Cthulhu*, by various authors; *Hive*, by Tim Curran.

Tips Use the genre as a metaphor instead of a prop or plot device.

N ELKHORN PUBLISHING INC.

P.O. Box 818, Elkhorn NE 68130. (402)315-9600. E-mail: molly@elkhornpublishing.com. Website: www.elkhornpublishing.com. **Contact:** Molly Harper, acquisitions editor. Estab. 2006. **Publishes 3-5 titles/year. 90% of books from first-time authors. 80% from unagented writers. Pays 10-12% royalty. Pays $7,000-20,000 advance.** Publishes book 10 months after acceptance of ms. Accepts simultaneous submissions. Responds in 2 months to queries. Responds in 3 months to proposals. Responds in 3 months to manuscripts. Guidelines available free.

Nonfiction Subjects include Americana, anthropology, archeology, business, economics, community, contemporary culture, government, politics, history, American, memoirs, money, finance, social sciences, sports, particularly baseball. Query with SASE. Reviews artwork/photos.
Fiction Subjects include adventure, historical, mainstream, contemporary, mystery, romance, sports, suspense. No science fiction or fantasy. We want realistic or believable stories. Query with SASE.
Recent Title(s) *Dark Secrets*, by J. Anderson Cross (historical fiction).
Tips Make your pitch brief and to the point. Why will your book sell? What is your audience? Be realistic.

ELYSIAN EDITIONS

Imprint of Princeton Book Co., Publishers 614 Route 130, Hightstown NJ 08520. (609)426-0602. Fax: (609)426-1344. E-mail: elysian@aosi.com. Website: www.dancehorizons.com/elysian.html. **Contact:** Charles Woodford (fitness, yoga, travel, memoir, true adventure). Publishes hardcover and trade paperback originals and reprints. **Publishes 1-3 titles/year. 100 queries received/year. 30 mss received/year. 25% of books from first-time authors. 50% from unagented writers. Pays royalty on retail price. Pays negotiable advance.** Publishes book 9-12 months after acceptance of ms. Accepts simultaneous submissions. Responds in 3 weeks to queries. Responds in 3 weeks to proposals. Responds in 1 month to manuscripts. Book catalog free or on website. Guidelines available free.
Nonfiction Subjects include memoirs, travel, true adventure, fitness, yoga. Submit proposal package, outline, 3 sample chapters. Reviews artwork/photos. Send photocopies.
Recent Title(s) *Paris Discovered: Explorations in the City of Light*; *Inner Focus, Outer Strength: Imagery and Exercise for Health, Strength, and Beauty*.

ENC PRESS

P.O. Box 833, Hoboken NJ 07030. E-mail: publisher@encpress.com. Website: www.encpress.com. **Contact:** Olga Gardner Galvin, publisher. Estab. 2003. Publishes trade paperback originals. **Publishes 2-4 titles/year. 90% of books from first-time authors. 100% from unagented writers. Pays 50% royalty on retail price.** Publishes book 12 months after acceptance of ms. Responds in 6-8 weeks to queries. Responds in 4-6 months to manuscripts. Book catalog available online. Guidelines available online.
Fiction Subjects include humor, mainstream, contemporary, translation, geopolitics, political satire, utopias/dystopias, social satire, picaresque novel. Query through e-mail.
Recent Title(s) *Mean Martin Manning*, by Scott Stein (social satire); *$everance*, by Richard Kaempfer (social satire); *Monkey See*, by Walt Maguire (social satire).
Tips Please submit queries only after reading submissions guidelines.

ERIE CANAL PRODUCTIONS

4 Farmdale St., Clinton NY 13323. E-mail: eriecanal@juno.com. Website: www.eriecanalproductions.com. **Contact:** Scott Fiesthumel, president. Estab. 2001. Publishes trade paperback originals. **Publishes 1-2 titles/year. 50% of books from first-time authors. 100% from unagented writers. Pays negotiable royalty on net profits.** Responds in 1 month to queries. Book catalog available free.
Nonfiction Subjects include Americana, history, sports. Query with SASE. *All unsolicited mss returned unopened.*
Recent Title(s) *The Legend of Wild Bill Setley*, by Tony Kissel; *S. Fiesthumel*, (biography); *Diamond Dynasty*, by Billy Mills; *The Bank With the Gold Dome*, by Scott Fiesthumel.
Tips We publish nonfiction books that look at historical places, events, and people along the traditional route of the Erie Canal through New York State.

EXCALIBUR PUBLICATIONS

P.O. Box 89667, Tucson AZ 85752-9667. (520)575-9057. E-mail: excalibureditor@earthlink.net. **Contact:** Alan M. Petrillo, editor. Estab. 1990. Publishes trade paperback originals. **Publishes 4 titles/year. Pays royalty** Responds in 1 month to queries. Responds in 1 month to manuscripts.

- Excalibur Publications publishes nonfiction historical and military works from all time periods. We do not publish fiction.

Nonfiction Subjects include history, military, war, military, war, strategy and tactics, as well as the history of battles, firearms, arms, and armour, historical personalities. Query with synopsis, first chapter, SASE. Include notes on photos, illustrations, and maps.
Recent Title(s) *Present Sabers: A History of the U.S. Horse Cavalry*, by Allan Heninger; *Japanese Rifles of World War II*, by Duncan O. McCollum; *Famous Faces of World War II*, by Robert Van Osdol.
Tips New writers are welcome, especially those who have a fresh approach to a subject. In addition to a synopsis or proposal, we also like to see a brief bio that indicates any related experience you have, as well as information on particular marketing strategies for your work.

EXECUTIVE EXCELLENCE PUBLISHING

1806 North 1120 West, Provo UT 84604. (801)375-4060. Fax: (801)377-5960. E-mail: editorial@eep.com. Website: www.eep.com. **Contact:** Ken Shelton, editor in chief. Estab. 1984. Publishes hardcover and trade paperback originals and trade paperback reprints. **Publishes 4 titles/year. 300 queries received/year. 150 mss received/year. 35% of books from first-time authors. 95% from unagented writers. Pays 15% on cash received and 50% of subsidary right proceeds.** Publishes book 6-9 months after acceptance of ms. Accepts simultaneous submissions. Responds in 1 month to queries. Responds in 1 month to proposals. Responds in 1 month to manuscripts. Book catalog free or on website.

- Executive Excellence publishes business and self-help titles. We help you—the busy person, executive or entrepreneur—to find a wiser, better way to live your life and lead your organization. Currently emphasizing business innovations for general management and leadership (from the personal perspective). De-emphasizing technical or scholarly textbooks on operational processes and financial management or workbooks.

Nonfiction Subjects include business, economics, leadership/management. Submit proposal package, including outline, 1-2 sample chapters and author bio, company information.

Recent Title(s) *Responsibility 911: With Great Liberty Comes Great Responsibility*, by Daniel Bolz and Ken Shelton, editors; *It's About Excellence: Building Ethically Healthy Organizations*, by David W. Gill; *The 5 Most Important Questions You Must Ask Before You Write Any Ad*, by Edward A. Earle.

Tips Executive Excellence Publishing is an established publishing house with a strong niche in the marketplace. Our magazines, *Leadership Excellence*, *Sales and Service Excellence* and *Personal Excellence*, are distributed monthly in countries across the world. Our authors are on the cutting edge in their fields of leadership, self-help and business and organizational development. We are always looking for strong new talent with something to say, and a burning desire to say it. We expect authors to invest in their work. We do not offer all-expense paid ego trips.

FAIRVIEW PRESS

2450 Riverside Ave., Minneapolis MN 55454. (612)672-4774. Fax: (612)672-4980. E-mail: press@fairview.org. Website: www.fairviewpress.org. **Contact:** Steve Deger, acquisitions and marketing. Estab. 1988. Publishes hardcover and trade paperback originals and reprints. **Publishes 8-12 titles/year. 3,000 queries received/year. 1,500 mss received/year. 40% of books from first-time authors. 65% from unagented writers. Advance and royalties negotiable.** Publishes book 1 year after acceptance of ms. Accepts simultaneous submissions. Responds in 6 months to proposals. Book catalog available free. Guidelines available online.

- Fairview Press publishes books and related materials that educate individuals and families about their physical, emotional, and spiritual health and motivate them to make positive changes in themselves and their communities.

Nonfiction Submit proposal package, outline, bio, 2 sample chapters, marketing ideas, SASE. Reviews artwork/photos. Send photocopies.

Tips Audience is general reader.

FATHER'S PRESS

2424 SE 6th St., Lee's Summit MO 64063. Website: www.fatherspress.com. **Contact:** Mike Smitley, owner (fiction, nonfiction). Estab. 2006. Publishes hardcover, trade paperback, and mass market paperback originals and reprints. **Publishes 6-10 titles/year. Pays 10-15% royalty on wholesale price.** Publishes book 6 months after acceptance of ms. Responds in 1 month to queries and proposals. Responds in 3 months to manuscripts. Guidelines available online.

Nonfiction Subjects include animals, cooking, foods, nutrition, creative nonfiction, history, military, war, nature, regional, religion, travel, womens issues, world affairs. Query with SASE. Unsolicited mss returned unopened. Call or e-mail first Reviews artwork/photos. Send photocopies.

Fiction Subjects include adventure, historical, juvenile, literary, mainstream, contemporary, military, war, mystery, regional, religious, suspense, western, young adult adult. Query with SASE. Unsolicited mss returned unopened. Call or e-mail first.

Recent Title(s) *The Christian and the Struggle With Truth*, by Charles Scheele (Christian); *Six Years' Worth*, by Daniel Lance Wright (fiction); *Spending God's Money*, by Mary Kinney Branson (Christian); *Faith vs. Science*, by Dr. Jerome Goddard (Christian Science); *Disturbing Questions*, by Ron Bourque (social history); *Pressing Matters*, by Larry Tobin (fiction); *All That You Can't Leave Behind*, by Ryan Murphy (Christian); *America Unraveling*, by Dr. L. Scott Smith (social history).

FIELDSTONE ALLIANCE, INC.

60 Plato Blvd. E., Suite 150, St. Paul MN 55107. (651)556-4500. E-mail: vhyman@fieldstonealliance.org. Website: www.fieldstonealliance.org. **Contact:** Vincent Hyman, director. Publishes professional trade paperback originals. **Publishes 6 titles/year. 30 queries received/year. 15 mss received/year. 75% of books from first-**

time authors. 100% from unagented writers. Pays advance. Publishes book 18 months after acceptance of ms. Accepts simultaneous submissions. Responds in 6 weeks to queries. Responds in 6 weeks to proposals. Responds in 3 months to manuscripts. Book catalog and ms guidelines online.

O→ Fieldstone Alliance emphasizes community development, nonprofit organization management, and books for foundations and grant makers. Actively seeking authors and editorial outside vendors of color.

Nonfiction Submit 3 sample chapters, complete topical outline, and full proposal based on online guidelines. Phone query OK before submitting proposal with detailed chapter outline, SASE, statement of the goals of the book, statement of unique selling points, identification of audience, author qualification, competing publications, marketing potential.

Recent Title(s) *The Accidental Techie*; *A Funder's Guide to Evaluation*; *Benchmarking for Nonprofits*.

Tips Writers must be practitioners with a passion for their work in nonprofit management or community building and experience presenting their techniques at conferences. Writers receive preference if they can demonstrate the capacity to help sell their books via trainings, a large established e-mail or client list, or other direct connections with customers, who are largely nonprofit leaders, managers and consultants. We seek practical, not academic books. Our books identify professional challenges faced by our audiences and offer practical, step-by-step solutions. Never send us a manuscript without first checking our online guidelines. Queries showing evidence that the author has not reviewed our guidelines will be ignored.

FILTER PRESS, LLC

P.O. Box 95, Palmer Lake CO 80133-0095. (719)481-2420. Fax: (719)481-2420. E-mail: info@filterpressbooks.com. Website: www.filterpressbooks.com. **Contact:** Doris Baker, president. Estab. 1957. Publishes trade paperback originals and reprints. **Publishes 4-6 titles/year. Pays 10-12% royalty on wholesale price.** Publishes book 1 year after acceptance of ms.

O→ Filter Press specializes in nonfiction of the West.

Nonfiction Subjects include Americana, anthropology, archeology, ethnic, history, regional, crafts and crafts people of the Southwest. Query with outline and SASE. Reviews artwork/photos.

Recent Title(s) *Prunes and Rupe*, by Lydia Griffin.

FINNEY COMPANY, INC.

8075 215th St. W, Lakeville MN 55044. (952)469-6699. Fax: (952)469-1968. E-mail: feedback@finneyco.com. Website: www.finneyco.com. **Contact:** Alan E. Krysan, president. Publishes trade paperback originals. **Publishes 2 titles/year. Pays 10% royalty on wholesale price. Pays advance.** Publishes book 1 year after acceptance of ms. Responds in 10-12 weeks to queries.

Nonfiction Subjects include business, economics, education, career exploration/development. Query with SASE. Reviews artwork/photos.

Recent Title(s) *Planning My Career*, by Capozziello; *On the Job*, edited by Laurie Diethelm, et. al.

N FLASHLIGHT PRESS

527 Empire Blvd., Brooklyn NY 11225. E-mail: editor@flashlightpress.com. Website: www.flashlightpress.com. **Contact:** Shari Dash Greenspan, editor. Estab. 2004. Publishes hardcover and trade paperback originals. **Publishes 2 titles/year. 1,200 queries received/year. 120 mss received/year. 40% of books from first-time authors. 90% from unagented writers. Pays 8-10% royalty on wholesale price.** Publishes book 36 months after acceptance of ms. Accepts simultaneous submissions. Responds in 1 month to queries. Responds in 3 months to manuscripts. Book catalog available online. Guidelines available online.

Fiction Subjects include picture books. We only publish fiction—2 picture books a year, so we're extremely selective. Looking for gems.

Recent Title(s) *I Need my Monster*, by Amanda Noll and Howard McWilliam; *I'm Really Not Tired*, by Lori Sunshine and Jeffrey Ebbeler; *Grandfather's Wrinkles*, by Kathryn England and Richard McFarland; *Grandpa for Sale*, by Dotti Enderle, Vicki Sansum and T. Kyle Gentry.

Tips Our audience is 4-8 years old . Follow our online submissions guide.

FLORICANTO PRESS

Inter American Development 650 Castro St., Suite 120-331, Mountain View CA 94041-2055. (415)552-1879. Fax: (702)995-1410. E-mail: editor@floricantopress.com. Website: www.floricantopress.com. Estab. 1982. Publishes hardcover and trade paperback originals and reprints. Book catalog for #10 SASE. Guidelines available online.

O→ Floricanto Press is dedicated to promoting Latino thought and culture.

Nonfiction Subjects include anthropology, archeology, cooking, foods, nutrition, ethnic, Hispanic, health, medicine, history, language, literature, psychology, womens issues, womens studies. Submit ms with word count, author bio, SASE.

Recent Title(s) *Between Borders: Essays on Chicana/Mexicana History*, by Adelaida del Castillo; *Bring me more Stories: Tales of the Sephardim*, by Sally Benforado; *Borrowing Time: A Latino Sexual Odyssey*, by Carlos T.

Mock, M.D.
Tips Audience is general public interested in Hispanic culture. We need authors that are willing to promote their work heavily.

FLORIDA ACADEMIC PRESS

P.O. Box 540, Gainesville FL 32602. (352)332-5104. Fax: (352)331-6003. E-mail: fapress@gmail.com. Website: www.floridaacademicpress.com. Estab. 1997. Hardcover and trade paperback originals. **Publishes 4-8 titles/year. 2,000 queries received/year. 1,200 mss received/year. 90% of books from first-time authors. 100% from unagented writers. 5-8% royalty on retail price and higher on sales of 2,500+ copies a year.** Publishes book 3 months after acceptance of ms. Responds in 2 months on mss if rejected; 3-4 months if sent for external review. Catalog available online. Guidelines available by email at: fapress@gmail.com.
Nonfiction SASE returns.Subjects include government/politics, philosophy, psychology, social sciences, world affairs. Submit completed ms only and c.v. Query letters or works in progress of little interest—submit only final ms. Reviews artwork/photos. Send photocopies.
Fiction Subjects include historical, literary, mystery. Submit completed ms.
Recent Title(s) *Lucette Desvigness*, by Jerry Curtis (Bio-literary criticism of France's greatest living authoress); *Out of Eden*, by L. F. Baggett (The inter-war period in the Deep South); *Sweet Prince: The Passion of Hamlet*, by Doug Brode.
Tips Match our needs—do not send blindly. Books we accept for publication must be submitted in camera-ready format. The Press covers all publication/promotional expenditures.

N FLYING PEN PRESS

5941 E. Jewell Ave., Denver CO 80222. (303)375-0499. Fax: (303)375-0499. E-mail: publisher@flyingpenpress.com. Website: www.flyingpenpress.com. **Contact:** David A. Rozansky, publisher. Trade paperback and electronic originals. **Publishes 9/2008 titles/year. 60-80 queries/year; 30-40 mss/year. 55% of books from first-time authors. 88% from unagented writers. No advances.** Publishes book 6 months after acceptance of ms. Accepts simultaneous submissions. Catalog free on request; available online at website http://www.flyingpenpress.com/catalog. Guidelines free on request and available online.
Nonfiction Subjects include alternative lifestyles, Americana, animals, anthropology, archaeology, business, career guidance, child guidance, communications, community, computers, contemporary culture, counseling, creative nonfiction, economics, electronics, entertainment, environment, ethnic, finance, games, government, health, history, hobbies, humanities, labor, language, literature, medicine, memoirs, military, money, muticultural, nature, parenting, philosophy, politics, public affairs, recreation, regional (CO, S.W. U.S., Nat'l Parks, Rocky Mountains), science, social sciences, sociology, software, translation, transportation, travel, war, world affairs, aviation, aerospace, game books, travel guides, puzzle books. Submit completed ms by email only. Reviews artwork/photos. Send JPG, TIF, or PDF files.
Fiction Subjects include adventure, comic books, contemporary, ethnic, experimental, fantasy, gothic, historical, horror, humor, literary, mainstream, military, multicultural, mystery, regional, romance, science fiction, short story collections, sports, suspense, translation, western. While we are focused on nonfiction for 2009, we still support our fiction endeavors. We generally look for books that will be commercially viable in the general market, and thus genre titles have the best chance. Submit completed ms by email only.
Recent Title(s) *The Game Day Poker Almanac Official Rules of Poker*, by Kelli Mix (poker rulebook); *Looking Glass*, by James R. Strickland (cyberpunk science fiction); *She Murdered Me With Science*, by David Boop (sci-fi hard boiled detective fusion); Feral World Series (*Migration of the Kamishi, Trials of the Warmland)*, by Gaddy Bergmann (post-apocalyptic lit); *Seventh Daughter*, by Ronnie Seagren (action, adventure).
Tips Don't be shy about approaching us. Our philosophy is to give authors as much respect as we possibly can, and that includes being open and honest with them. We want to see writers wo write professionally and promote themselves accordingly. Understand the book trade and how books are marketed. Authors don't need an agent or writing credits, but there is no excuse for approaching a publisher with a poorly written ms.

FOOTPRINT PRESS, INC.

303 Pine Glen Ct., Englewood FL 34223. Phone/Fax: (941)474-8316. E-mail: info@footprintpress.com. Website: www.footprintpress.com. **Contact:** Sue Freeman, publisher (New York state recreation). Estab. 1997. Publishes trade paperback originals. **Publishes 1 title/year titles/year. 50% of books from first-time authors. 100% from unagented writers. Pays 10% royalty on wholesale price.** Accepts simultaneous submissions. Responds in 1 month to queries. Responds in 1 month to proposals. Responds in 2 months to manuscripts. Book catalog and ms guidelines for #10 SASE or online: www.footprintpress.com.

O→ Footprint Press publishes books pertaining to outdoor recreation in New York state.

Nonfiction Subjects include recreation, regional, sports. Query with SASE.
Recent Title(s) *Cobblestone Quest*, by Rich and Sue Freeman.

FOREIGN POLICY ASSOCIATION

470 Park Ave. S., New York NY 10016. (212)481-8100. Fax: (212)481-9275. E-mail: info@fpa.org. Website: www.fpa.org. Publishes 2 periodicals, an annual eight episode PBS Television series with DVD and an occasional hardcover and trade paperback original. Accepts simultaneous submissions. Book catalog available free.

Imprints Headline Series (quarterly); Great Decisions (annual).

O→ The Foreign Policy Association, a nonpartisan, not-for-profit educational organization founded in 1918, is a catalyst for developing awareness, understanding of and informed opinion on US foreign policy and global issues. Through its balanced, nonpartisan publications, FPA seeks to encourage individuals in schools, communities and the workplace to participate in the foreign policy process.

Nonfiction Subjects include government, politics, history, foreign policy.

Recent Title(s) *Great Decisions 2005*; *Europe: A Year of Living Dangerously*, by Ronald Tiersky, with Alex Tiersky.

Tips Audience is students and people with an interest, but not necessarily any expertise, in foreign policy and international relations.

FORWARD MOVEMENT

300 W. 4th St., Cincinnati OH 45202-2666. (513)721-6659. Fax: (513)721-0729. Website: www.forwardmovement.org. Estab. 1934. Book catalog and ms guidelines free.

O→ Forward Movement was established `to help reinvigorate the life of the church.' Many titles focus on the life of prayer, where our relationship with God is centered, death, marriage, baptism, recovery, joy, the Episcopal Church and more. Currently emphasizing prayer/spirituality.

Nonfiction We are an agency of the Episcopal Church.Subjects include religion. Query with SASE.

Fiction Subjects include juvenile.

Recent Title(s) *De-Cluttering as a Spiritual Activity*, by Donna Schaper; *A Letter Never Sent*, by Alanson B. Houghton.

Tips Audience is primarily Episcopalians and other Christians.

FRIENDS UNITED PRESS

101 Quaker Hill, Richmond IN 47374. (765)962-7573. Fax: (765)966-1293. Website: www.fum.org/shop. **Contact:** Katie Terrell, editor/manager. Estab. 1969. **Publishes 3 titles/year. 100 queries received/year. 80 mss received/year. 50% of books from first-time authors. 99% from unagented writers. Pays 7 ½% royalty on wholesale price.** Publishes book 1 year after acceptance of ms. Accepts simultaneous submissions. Responds in 6 months to queries. Book catalog and ms guidelines free.

O→ "Friends United Press publishes books that reflect Quaker religious practices and testimonies, and energize and equip Friends and others through the power of the Holy Spirit to gather people into fellowships where Jesus Christ is loved, known, and obeyed `as Teacher and Lord.'"

Nonfiction Subjects include history, religion, theology. Submit proposal package. Reviews artwork/photos. Send photocopies.

Recent Title(s) *Enduring Hope: the Impact of the Ramallah Friends Schools*, by Patricia Edwards-Konic; *A Brief Memoir of Elizabeth Fry*, edited by David Goff.

Tips "Quaker titles only."

FRONT ROW EXPERIENCE

540 Discovery Bay Blvd., Discovery Bay CA 94505. (925)634-5710. Fax: (925)634-5710. E-mail: service@frontrowexperience.com. Website: www.frontrowexperience.com. **Contact:** Frank Alexander, editor. Estab. 1974. Publishes trade paperback originals and reprints. **Publishes 1-2 titles/year.** Accepts simultaneous submissions. Responds in 1 month to queries.

Imprints Kokono.

O→ Front Row publishes books on movement education and coordination activities for pre-K to 6th grade.

Nonfiction Query.

Recent Title(s) *Perceptual-Motor Lesson Plans, Level 2*.

Tips Be on target—find out what we want, and only submit queries.

⊘ GAY SUNSHINE PRESS AND LEYLAND PUBLICATIONS

P.O. Box 410690, San Francisco CA 94141-0690. Website: www.leylandpublications.com. **Contact:** Winston Leyland, ed. Estab. 1970. Publishes hardcover originals, trade paperback originals and reprints. **Publishes 2-3 titles/year. Pays royalty, or makes outright purchase.** Responds in 6 weeks to queries. Responds in 2 months to manuscripts. Book catalog for $1.

O→ "Gay history, sex, politics, and culture are the focus of the quality books published by Gay Sunshine Press. Leyland Publications publishes books on popular aspects of gay sexuality and culture.

Nonfiction "We're interested in innovative literary nonfiction which deals with gay lifestyles."Query with SASE.

All unsolicited mss returned unopened.

Fiction Interested in innovative well-written novels on gay themes; also short story collections.Subjects include erotica, experimental, historical, literary, mystery, science fiction, translation, All gay male material only. "We have a high literary standard for fiction. We desire fiction on gay themes of high literary quality and prefer writers who have already had work published in books or literary magazines. We also publish erotica—short stories and novels." Query with SASE. *All unsolicited mss returned.*

Recent Title(s) *Out of the Closet Into Our Hearts: Celebration of Our Gay/Lesbian Family Members.*

GEM GUIDES BOOK CO.

315 Cloverleaf Dr., Suite F, Baldwin Park CA 91706-6510. (626)855-1611. Fax: (626)855-1610. E-mail: gembooks@aol.com. Website: www.gemguidesbooks.com. **Contact:** Kathy Mayerski, editor. Estab. 1965. **Publishes 6-8 titles/year. 60% of books from first-time authors. 100% from unagented writers. Pays 6-10% royalty on retail price.** Publishes book 1 year after acceptance of ms. Accepts simultaneous submissions. Responds in 5 months to queries.

Imprints Gembooks.

O→ Gem Guides prefers nonfiction books for the hobbyist in rocks and minerals; lapidary and jewelry-making; crystals and crystal healing; travel and recreation guide books for the West and Southwest; and other regional local interest. Currently emphasizing how-to, field guides, West/Southwest regional interest. De-emphasizing stories, history, poetry.

Nonfiction Subjects include history, Western, hobbies, rockhounding, prospecting, lapidary, jewelry craft, nature, recreation, regional, Western US, science, earth, travel. Query with outline/synopsis and sample chapters with SASE. Reviews artwork/photos.

Recent Title(s) *Fee Mining and Mineral Adventures in the Eastern U.S.*, by James Martin Monaco and Jeannette Hathaway Monaco; *Baby's Day Out in Southern California: Fun Places to Go With Babies and Toddlers*, by JoBea Holt; *The Rockhound's Handbook*, by James R. Mitchell; *Crystal & Gemstone Divination*, by Gail Butler.

Tips We have a general audience of people interested in recreational activities. Publishers plan and have specific book lines in which they specialize. Learn about the publisher and submit materials compatible with that publisher's product line.

⊘ GIFTED EDUCATION PRESS

10201 Yuma Court, Manassas VA 20109. (703)369-5017. E-mail: mfisher345@comcast.net. Website: www.giftedpress.com. **Contact:** Maurice Fisher, publisher. Estab. 1981. Publishes trade paperback originals. **Publishes 5 titles/year. 20 queries received/year. 10 mss received/year. 90% of books from first-time authors. 100% from unagented writers. Pays 10% royalty on retail price.** Publishes book 4 months after acceptance of ms. Accepts simultaneous submissions. Responds in 1 month to queries. Responds in 1 month to proposals. Responds in 1 month to manuscripts. Book catalog available online. Guidelines available online.

O→ Searching for rigorous texts on teaching science, math and humanities to gifted students.

Nonfiction Subjects include child guidance, computers, electronics, education, history, humanities, philosophy, science, teaching, math, biology, Shakespeare, chemistry, physics, creativity. Query with SASE. *All unsolicited mss returned unopened.* Reviews artwork/photos.

Recent Title(s) *Snibbles*, by Judy Micheletti; *Laboratory Physics Experiments for the Gifted*, by Raja Almukahhal; *Why Don't Birds Get Lost?*, by Franklin H. Bronson.

Tips Audience includes teachers, parents, gift program supervisors, professors. "Be knowledgeable about your subject. Write clearly and don't use educational jargon."

GIVAL PRESS

Gival Press, LLC P.O. Box 3812, Arlington VA 22203. (703)351-0079. E-mail: givalpress@yahoo.com. Website: www.givalpress.com. **Contact:** Robert L. Giron, editor-in-chief (Area of interest: literary). Estab. 1998. Publishes trade paperback, electronic originals, and reprints. **Publishes 5-6 titles/year. over 200 queries received/year. 60 mss received/year. 50%% of books from first-time authors. 70%% from unagented writers. Royalties (% varies)** Publishes book 12 months after acceptance of ms. Accepts simultaneous submissions. Responds in 1 month to queries, 3 months to proposals & mss. Book catalog available online, free on request/for #10 SASE. Guidelines available online, by email, free on request/for #10 SASE.

Imprints Gival Press.

Nonfiction Subjects include creative nonfiction, gay, lesbian, literary criticism, memoirs, multicultural, translation, womens issues/studies, scholarly. Always query first via email; provide plan/ms content, bio, and supportive material. Reviews artwork/photos; query first.

Fiction Subjects include gay, lesbian, literary, multicultural, poetry, translation. Always query first via email; provide description, author's bio, and supportive material.

Recent Title(s) *Twelve Rivers of the Body*, by Elizabeth Oness (literary); *A Tomb on the Periphery*, by John Domini (crime/literary fiction); *Honey*, by Richard Carr (poetry).

Tips "Our audience is those who read literary works with depth to the work. Visit our website—there is much to be read/learned from the numerous pages."

N GLB PUBLISHERS

1028 Howard St., #503, San Francisco CA 94103. (415)621-8307. Website: www.glbpubs.com. Hardcover, trade paperback, and electronic originals; trade paperback and electronic reprints. **Publishes 4-5 titles/year. Receives 50 queries/year; 40 mss/year 20% of books from first-time authors. 90% from unagented writers.** Publishes book 2-3 months after acceptance of ms. Catalog and guidelines free on request and online at website.

Imprints GLB

Nonfiction Subjects include alternative lifestyles, child guidance, contemporary culture, creative nonfiction, entertainment, ethnic, gay, government, health, history, humanities, lesbian, medicine, memoirs, muticultural, New Age, photography, politics, social sciences, travel, women's issues. Reviews artwork/photos. Send originals or scanned files.

Fiction Subjects include adventure, erotica, fantasy, feminist, gay, gothic, historical, humor, literary, multicultural, mystery, plays, poetry, romance, science fiction, short story collections, suspense, western, young adult. Must be gay, lesbian, bisexual, or transgender subjects Submit completed ms.

Recent Title(s) *Crossing Borders*, by Will Carr; *Man In Shadow*, by Russell Thomas; *Basic Butch* Collection of Short Stories, by R. P. Andrews; *Homo Erectus*, by Edward Proffitt.

Tips Our audience consists of "adults of all ages."

GOLDEN WEST BOOKS

P.O. Box 80250, San Marino CA 91118. (626)458-8148. Fax: (626)458-8148. E-mail: trainbook@earthlink.net. Website: www.goldenwestbooks.com. **Contact:** Donald Duke, publisher. Publishes hardcover originals. **Publishes 3-4 titles/year. 8-10 queries received/year. 5 mss received/year. 75% of books from first-time authors. 100% from unagented writers. Pays 8-10% royalty on wholesale price. Pays no advance.** Publishes book 3 months after acceptance of ms. Responds in 3 months to queries. Book catalog and ms guidelines free.

O→ Golden West Books specializes in railroad history.

Nonfiction Subjects include Americana, history. Query with SASE. Reviews artwork/photos.

Recent Title(s) *The Ulster & Delaware Railroad Through the Catskills*, by Gerald M. Best; *The Streamline Era*, by Robert C. Reed; *Electric Railways Around San Francisco Bay*, by Donald Duke.

GOLLEHON PRESS, INC.

6157 28th St. SE, Grand Rapids MI 49546. (616)949-3515. Fax: (616)949-8674. E-mail: john@gollehonbooks.com. Website: www.gollehonbooks.com. **Contact:** Lori Adams, editor. Publishes hardcover, trade paperback, and mass market paperback originals. **Publishes 6-8 titles/year. 100 queries received/year. 30 mss received/year. 85% of books from first-time authors. 90% from unagented writers. Pays 7% royalty on retail price. Pays $500-1,000 advance.** Publishes book usually 6 months after acceptance of ms. Accepts simultaneous submissions. Responds in 1 month (if interested) to proposals. Responds in 2 months to manuscripts. Book catalog and ms guidelines online.

O→ Currently emphasizing theology (life of Christ), political, current events, pets (dogs only, rescue/heroic), self-help, and gardening. *No unsolicited mss*; brief proposals only with first 5 pages of Chapter 1. Writer must have strong credentials to author work.

Nonfiction Submit brief proposal package only with bio and first 5 pages of Chapter 1. We do not return materials unless we specifically request the full manuscript. Reviews artwork/photos. Send Writer must be sure he/she owns all rights to photos, artwork, illustrations, etc., submitted for consideration (all submissions must be free of any third-party claims). Never send original photos or art.

Tips Mail brief book proposal, bio, and a few sample pages only. We will request a full manuscript if interested. We cannot respond to all queries. Full manuscript will be returned if we requested it, and if writer provides SASE. We do not return proposals. Simultaneous submissions are encouraged.

GRAND CANYON ASSOCIATION

P.O. Box 399, 4 Tonto St., Grand Canyon AZ 86023. (928)638-7021. Fax: (928)638-2484. E-mail: tberger@grandcanyon.org. Website: www.grandcanyon.org. **Contact:** Todd R. Berger, director of publishing (Grand Canyon-related geology, natural history, outdoor activities, human history, photography, ecology, etc., posters, postcards and other non-book products). Estab. 1932. Publishes hardcover originals and reprints, and trade paperback originals and reprints. **Publishes 6 titles/year. 100 queries received/year. 70% of books from first-time authors. 99% from unagented writers. Pays royalty on wholesale price. Makes outright purchase.** Publishes book 1 month-2 years after acceptance of ms. Accepts simultaneous submissions. Responds in 2 months to queries. Responds in 2 months to proposals. Responds in 2 months to manuscripts. Book catalog available online. Ms guidelines available by e-mail.

Nonfiction Subjects include animals, anthropology, archaeology, art, architecture, creative nonfiction, history, nature, environment, photography, recreation, regional, science, sports, travel, geology. Query with SASE. Submit proposal package, outline, 3-4 sample chapters, list of publication credits, and samples of previous work. Submit complete ms. Reviews artwork/photos. Send transparencies, color or b&w prints, or digital samples of images.
Recent Title(s) *Grand Canyon: Views Beyond the Beauty* (nature/photography); *Ancient Landscapes of the Colorado Plateau* (nature); *The Adventures of Salt and Soap at Grand Canyon* (children's).
Tips Do not send any proposals that are not directly related to the Grand Canyon or do not have educational value about the Grand Canyon.

GRANITE PUBLISHING, LLC

P.O. Box 1429, Columbus NC 28722. (828)894-8444. Fax: (828)894-8454. E-mail: eileen@souledout.org. Website: www.granitepublishing.us/index.html. **Contact:** Brian Crissey. Publishes trade paperback originals and reprints. **Publishes 4 titles/year. 50 queries received/year. 150 mss received/year. 70% of books from first-time authors. 90% from unagented writers. Pays 7 ½-10% royalty.** Publishes book 16 months after acceptance of ms. Accepts simultaneous submissions. Responds in 6 months to manuscripts.
Imprints Wild Flower Press; Swan-Raven & Co.; Agents of Change.

- Granite Publishing strives to preserve the Earth by publishing books that develop new wisdom about our emerging planetary citizenship, bringing information from the outerworlds to our world. Currently emphasizing indigenous ideas, planetary healing.

Nonfiction Subjects include New Age, planetary paradigm shift. Submit proposal. Reviews artwork/photos. Send photocopies.
Recent Title(s) *Reconciliation*, by Ida Kannenberg; *Raechel's Eyes Volume I & II*, by Helen Littrell and Jean Bilodeaux.

GREAT POTENTIAL PRESS

P.O. Box 5057, Scottsdale AZ 85261. (602)954-4200. Fax: (602)954-0185. E-mail: info@giftedbooks.com. Website: www.giftedbooks.com. **Contact:** Janet Gore, editor, or James T. Webb, Ph.D., president. Estab. 1986. Publishes trade paperback originals. **Publishes 6-10 titles/year. 75 queries received/year. 20-30 mss received/year. 50% of books from first-time authors. 100% from unagented writers. Pays 10% royalty on retail price.** Publishes book 6-12 months after acceptance of ms. Accepts simultaneous submissions. Responds in 2 months to queries. Responds in 3 months to proposals. Responds in 4 months to manuscripts. Book catalog free or on website. Guidelines available online.

- Specializes in non-fiction books that address academic, social and emotional issues of gifted and talented children and adults.

Nonfiction Subjects include child guidance, education, multicultural, psychology, translation, travel, womens issues, gifted/talented children and adults. Submit proposal package, including preface or introduction, TOC, chapter outline, 2-3 sample chapters and an explanation of how work differs from similar published books.
Recent Title(s) *Inspiring Middle School Minds: Gifted, Creative, & Challenging*, by Judy Willis, M.D., M.Ed., *Living with Intensity*, edited by Susan Daniels, Ph.D. and Michael Piechowski, Ph.D., *Boosting Your Baby's Brain Power*, by Holly Engel-Smothers and Susan Heim, and *Academic Advocacy for Gifted Children: A Parent's Complete Guide*, by Barbara Gilman, M.S.
Tips Manuscripts should be clear, cogent, and well-written and should pertain to gifted, talented, and creative persons and/or issues.

GREENE BARK PRESS

P.O. Box 1108, Bridgeport CT 06601. (610)434-2802. Fax: (610)434-2803. Website: www.greenebarkpress.com. **Contact:** Thomas J. Greene, publisher; Tara Maroney, associate publisher. Estab. 1991. Publishes hardcover originals. **Publishes 1-5 titles/year. 100 queries received/year. 6,000 mss received/year. 60% of books from first-time authors. 100% from unagented writers. Pays 10-15% royalty on wholesale price.** Publishes book 1 year after acceptance of ms. Accepts simultaneous submissions. Responds in 2 months to queries. Responds in 6 months to manuscripts. Guidelines for SASE.

- Greene Bark Press only publishes books for children and young adults, mainly picture and read-to books. All of our titles appeal to the imagination and encourage children to read and explore the world through books. We only publish children's fiction—all subjects—but in reading picture book format appealing to ages 3-9 or all ages.

Fiction Subjects include juvenile. Submit complete ms. No queries or ms by e-mail.
Recent Title(s) *The Magical Trunk*, by Gigi Tegge; *Hey! There's a Goblin Under My Throne!*, by Rhett Ransom Pennell; *Edith Ellen Eddy*, by Julee-Ann Granger.
Tips Audience is children who read to themselves and others. Mothers, fathers, grandparents, godparents who read to their respective children, grandchildren. Include SASE, be prepared to wait, do not inquire by telephone.

ALEXANDER HAMILTON INSTITUTE

70 Hilltop Rd., Ramsey NJ 07446-1119. (201)825-3377. Fax: (201)825-8696. Website: www.ahipubs.com. **Contact:** Brian L.P. Zevnik, editor-in-chief; Gloria Ju, editor. Estab. 1909. Publishes 3-ring binder and paperback originals. **Publishes 5-10 titles/year. 50 queries received/year. 10 mss received/year. 25% of books from first-time authors. 95% from unagented writers. Pays 5-8% royalty on retail price. Makes outright purchase of 3,500-7,000. Pays $3,500-7,000 advance.** Publishes book 10 months after acceptance of ms. Accepts simultaneous submissions. Responds in 1 month to queries. Responds in 2 months to manuscripts.

O→ Alexander Hamilton Institute publishes management books for upper-level managers and executives. Currently emphasizing legal issues for HR/personnel.

Nonfiction The main audience is US personnel executives and high-level management.

Recent Title(s) *Employer's Guide to Record-Keeping Requirements*.

Tips We sell exclusively by direct mail or through electronic means to managers and executives. A writer must know his/her field and be able to communicate legal and practical systems and programs.

N HARBOR HOUSE

111 10th St., Augusta GA 30901. (706)738-0354. Fax: (706)823-5999. E-mail: harberhouse@harborhousebooks.com. Website: www.harborhousebooks.com. **Contact:** E. Randall Floyd, publisher/owner. Estab. 1997. Publishes hardcover and trade paperback originals. **Publishes 8-10 titles/year. 200 queries received/year. 100 mss received/year. 90%% of books from first-time authors. 95%% from unagented writers. Pays 7-10% royalty on retail price.** Publishes book 24 months after acceptance of ms. Accepts simultaneous submissions. Responds in 3-6 months to queries. Responds in 3-6 months to proposals. Responds in 6-9 months to manuscripts. Guidelines available online.

Nonfiction Subjects include business, economics, community, contemporary culture, creative nonfiction, government, politics, history, memoirs, military, war, money, finance, nature, environment, philosophy, regional, religion, social sciences, sociology, spirituality, sports, world affairs, the unexplained. Submit proposal package, outline, 3 sample chapters, bio, marketing plan, SASE. Reviews artwork/photos. Send photocopies.

Fiction Subjects include adventure, fantasy, horror, humor, literary, mainstream, contemporary, military, war, mystery, regional, suspense, Thrillers. Submit proposal package, 3 sample chapters, clips, bio, marketing plan, SASE.

Recent Title(s) *A Few Flowers for my Soul*, by Robbie Williams ((relationship book)); *In the Realm of Miracles & Visions*, by E. Randall Floyd ((explanatory)); *Jacob's Daughter*, by Naomi Williams ((contemporary fiction)).

Tips General adult readership. We would like paper submissio

HARTMAN PUBLISHING, INC.

8529 Indian School NE, Albuquerque NM 87112. (505)291-1274. Fax: (505)291-1284. E-mail: susan@hartmanonline.com. Website: www.hartmanonline.com. **Contact:** Susan Alvare, Managing Editor (healthcare education). Publishes trade paperback originals. **Publishes 5-10 titles/year. 50 queries received/year. 25 mss received/year. 50% of books from first-time authors. 100% from unagented writers. Pays 6-12% royalty on wholesale or retail price, or makes outright purchase of $200-600.** Publishes book 4-12 months after acceptance of ms. Accepts simultaneous submissions. Responds in 2 months to proposals. Responds in 3 months to manuscripts. Book catalog available free. Guidelines available online.

Imprints Care Spring (Mark Hartman, publisher).

O→ We publish educational books for employees of nursing homes, home health agencies, hospitals, and providers of eldercare.

Nonfiction Subjects include health, medicine. Submit proposals via e-mail.

HATALA GEROPRODUCTS

P.O. Box 42, Greentop MO 63546. E-mail: editor@geroproducts.com. Website: www.geroproducts.com. **Contact:** Mark Hatala, Ph.D., president (psychology, travel, relationships). Estab. 2002. Publishes hardcover and trade paperback originals. **Publishes 3-4 titles/year. 120 queries received/year. 50 mss received/year. 30% of books from first-time authors. 80% from unagented writers. Pays 5-7½% royalty on retail price. Pays $250-500 advance.** Publishes book 18 months after acceptance of ms. Accepts simultaneous submissions. Responds in 1 month to queries. Responds in 2 months to proposals and manuscripts. Guidelines available online.

Nonfiction Subjects include health, medicine, psychology, sex, travel, seniors, advice. Query with SASE. Submit proposal package, outline, 3 sample chapters, SASE.

Recent Title(s) *Seniorsex*, by Daniel Laury, M.D. (senior relationships); *Mom No More*, by Mignon Matthews (grief); *The Healthy Seniors Cookbook*, by Marilyn McFarlane.

Tips Audience is men and women (but particularly women) over age 60. Books need to be pertinent to the lives of older Americans. No memoirs or poetry.

HAWK PUBLISHING GROUP

7107 S. Yale Ave., #345, Tulsa OK 74136. (918)492-3677. Fax: (918)492-2120. Website: www.hawkpub.com. Estab. 1999. Publishes hardcover and trade paperback originals. **Publishes 6-8 titles/year. 25% of books from first-time authors. 50% from unagented writers. Pays royalty.** Publishes book 1-2 years after acceptance of ms. Accepts simultaneous submissions. Guidelines available online.

- Please visit our website and read the submission guidelines before sending anything to us. The best way to learn what might interest us is to visit the website, read the information there, look at the books, and perhaps even read a few of them.

Fiction Looking for good books of all kinds. Not interested in juvenile, poetry, or short story collections. Submissions will not be return

HEALTH PRESS NA INC.

P.O. Box 37470, Albuquerque NM 87176. (505)888-1394. Fax: (505)888-1521. E-mail: goodbooks@healthpress.com. Website: www.healthpress.com. **Contact:** K. Frazer, editor. Estab. 1988. Publishes hardcover and trade paperback originals. **Publishes 8 titles/year. 90% of books from first-time authors. 90% from unagented writers. Pays standard royalty on wholesale price** Publishes book 1 year after acceptance of ms. Accepts simultaneous submissions. Responds in 3 months to proposals. Book catalog available free. Guidelines available online.

- Health Press publishes books by healthcare professionals on cutting-edge patient education topics.

Nonfiction Subjects include education, health, medicine. Submit proposal package, outline, resume, 3 complete sample chapters. Reviews artwork/photos. Send photocopies.

Recent Title(s) *Keeping a Secret: A Story About Juvenile Rheumatoid Arthritis*; *Peanut Butter Jam: A Story About Peanut Allergy*; *Health and Nutrition Secrets.*

HEALTH PROFESSIONS PRESS

P.O. Box 10624, Baltimore MD 21285-0624. (410)337-9585. Fax: (410)337-8539. E-mail: mmagnus@healthpropress.com. Website: www.healthpropress.com. **Contact:** Mary Magnus, director of publications (aging, long-term care, health administration). Publishes hardcover and trade paperback originals. **Publishes 6-8 titles/year. 70 queries received/year. 12 mss received/year. 50% of books from first-time authors. 100% from unagented writers. Pays 8-18% royalty on wholesale price.** Publishes book 10 months after acceptance of ms. Accepts simultaneous submissions. Responds in 1 month to queries. Responds in 3 months to proposals. Responds in 4 months to manuscripts. Book catalog free or online. Guidelines available online.

- We are a specialty publisher. Our primary audiences are professionals, students, and educated consumers interested in topics related to aging and eldercare.

Nonfiction Subjects include health, medicine, psychology. Query with SASE. Submit proposal package, outline, resume, 1-2 sample chapters, cover letter.

Recent Title(s) *Caring for People With Challenging Behaviors*; *Movement With Meaning*; *Promoting Family Involvement in Long-Term Care Settings.*

HENDRICK-LONG PUBLISHING CO., INC.

10635 Tower Oaks D., Houston TX 77070. (832)912-7323. Fax: (832)912-7353. E-mail: hendrick-long@worldnet.att.net. Website: hendricklongpublishing.com. **Contact:** Vilma Long. Estab. 1969. Publishes hardcover and trade paperback originals and hardcover reprints. **Publishes 4 titles/year. 90% from unagented writers. Pays royalty on selling price Pays advance.** Publishes book 18 months after acceptance of ms. Responds in 3 months to queries. Book catalog for 8½x11 or 9x12 SASE with 4 first-class stamps. Guidelines available online.

- Hendrick-Long publishes historical fiction and nonfiction about Texas and the Southwest for children and young adults.

Nonfiction Subjects include history, regional. Query, or submit outline and 2 sample chapters. Reviews artwork/photos. Send photocopies.

Fiction Subjects include juvenile, young adult. Query with SASE. Submit outline, clips, 2 sample chapters.

Recent Title(s) *Plays & Poems From Texas History* (paperback); *Frederic Remington, Artist of the West, A Picture Biography* (paperback); *Native Americans of Texas*, (paperback, teacher's guide and workbook editions).

HENSLEY PUBLISHING

6116 E. 32nd St., Tulsa OK 74135-5494. (918)664-8520. E-mail: editorial@hensleypublishing.com. Website: www.hensleypublishing.com. **Contact:** Acquisitions Department. Publishes trade paperback originals. **Publishes 5 titles/year. 200 queries received/year. 50% of books from first-time authors. 50% from unagented writers.** Publishes book 18 months after acceptance of ms. Responds in 2 months to queries. Guidelines available online.

- Hensley Publishing publishes Bible studies that offer the reader a wide range of topics. Currently emphasizing 192-page (8½x11) workbook studies and Bible studies of varying sizes and lengths, both

workbook and non-workbook style.
Nonfiction Subjects include child guidance, money, finance, religion, womens issues, marriage/family, various Bible study topics such as topical, general, issue oriented. Query with synopsis and sample chapters.
Recent Title(s) *So You're a Christian! Now What?*, by Catherine Painter; *Walking With God*, by Mindy Ferguson.
Tips Submit something that crosses denominational lines directed toward the large Christian market, not small specialized groups. We serve an interdenominational market—all Christian persuasions. Our goal is to get readers back into studying the Bible instead of studying about the Bible.

HIGH PLAINS PRESS

P.O. Box 123, 403 Cassa Rd., Glendo WY 82213. (307)735-4370. Website: www.highplainspress.com. **Contact:** Nancy Curtis, sr. editor (history of U.S. West); Judy Plazyk, editor (other nonfiction). Estab. 1984. Publishes hardcover and trade paperback originals. **Publishes 4 titles/year. 200 queries received/year. 100 mss received/year. 50% of books from first-time authors. 100% from unagented writers. Pays 10% royalty on wholesale price. Pays < $1,000 advance.** Publishes book 24 months after acceptance of ms. Accepts simultaneous submissions. Responds in 2 months to queries. Responds in 6 months to proposals. Book catalog available online. Guidelines available online.
Nonfiction Subjects include agriculture, animals, creative nonfiction, history, memoirs, nature, environment, regional, Old West. Query with SASE. Submit proposal package, outline, 3 sample chapters. Reviews artwork/photos. Send photocopies.
Fiction Subjects include poetry, western. We publish one volume of poetry a year in our Poetry of the American West series. Almost no fiction. Query with SASE.
Recent Title(s) *Tom Horn: Blood on the Moon*, by Chip Carlson (true crime); *Staking Her Claim: Women Homesteading the West*, by Marcia Meredith Hensley (history); *Small Talk*, by Mary Lou Sanelli (poetry).
Tips "Our audience comprises general readers interested in Intermountain West."

HIGH TIDE PRESS

3650 W. 183rd St., Homewood IL 60430-1809. (708)206-2054. E-mail: managing.editor@hightidepress.com. Website: www.hightidepress.com. **Contact:** Monica Regan, managing editor. Estab. 1995. Publishes hardcover and trade paperback originals. **Publishes 2-3 titles/year. 20 queries received/year. 3 mss received/year. 50% of books from first-time authors. 100% from unagented writers. Royalty. Percentages vary.** Publishes book Publishes book up to 12 months after acceptance. after acceptance of ms. Accepts simultaneous submissions. Responds in 1-3 months to queries, 1-3 months to proposals. Book catalog available online. Guidelines available online at website http://www.hightidepress.com/main/submissions.php.

O‑‑ High Tide Press is a leading provider of resources for disability and nonprofit professionals - publications and training materials on intellectual/developmental disabilities, behavioral health, and nonprofit management.

Nonfiction Subjects include business, economics/economics, education, health, medicine/medicine, how-to, human services, nonprofit management, psychology, reference, All of these topics as they relate to developmental, learning and intellectual disabilities, behavioral health, and human services management. Query via e-mail.
Recent Title(s) *Creating a Meaningful Day: An Innovative Curriculum for People with Significant Intellectual Disabilities*, by Linda Cofield-Van Dyke (professional manual); *Intellectual Disabilities at Your Fingertips: A Health Care Resource*, by Dr. Carl V. Tyler, MD (professional manual).
Tips Our readers are leaders and managers, mostly in the field of human services, and especially those who serve persons with intellectual disabilities or behavioral health needs.

N LAWRENCE HILL BOOKS

Chicago Review Press 814 N. Franklin St., 2nd Floor, Chicago IL 60610. (312)337-0747. Fax: (312)337-5110. **Contact:** Susan Bradanini Betz, senior editor. Publishes hardcover originals and trade paperback originals and reprints. **Publishes 3-10 titles/year. 20 queries received/year. 10 mss received/year. 40% of books from first-time authors. 50% from unagented writers. Pays 7 ½-12 ½% royalty on retail price. Pays $3,000-10,000 advance.** Publishes book 1 year after acceptance of ms. Accepts simultaneous submissions. Responds in 1 month to queries. Responds in 2 months to proposals. Responds in 2 months to manuscripts. Book catalog available free.
Nonfiction Subjects include ethnic, government, politics, history, multicultural. Submit proposal package, outline, 2 sample chapters.
Recent Title(s) *The Thunder of Angels*, by Donnie Williams with Wayne Greenhaw.

HIS WORK CHRISTIAN PUBLISHING

P.O. Box 5732, Ketchikan AK 99901. (206)274-8474. Fax: (614)388-0664 eFax. E-mail: hiswork@hisworkpub.com. Website: www.hisworkpub.com. **Contact:** Angela J. Perez, acquisitions editor. Estab. 2005. Publishes trade paperback and electronic originals and reprints; also, hardcover originals. **Publishes 3-5 titles/year. 100% from unagented writers. Pays 10-20% royalty on wholesale price.** Publishes book 12-24 months after acceptance of ms. Accepts simultaneous submissions. Responds in 1-3 months to queries. Responds in 1-2 months to requested manuscripts. Book catalog available online. Guidelines available online and updated regularly. Please check these before submitting to see what we are looking for.

Nonfiction Subjects include child guidance, cooking, foods, nutrition, creative nonfiction, gardening, health, medicine, history, hobbies, language, literature, memoirs, money, finance, music, dance, photography, recreation, religion, sports. Submit query/proposal package, 3 sample chapters, clips. Reviews artwork/photos. Send photocopies.

Fiction Subjects include humor, juvenile, mystery, picture books, poetry, religious, short story collections, sports, suspense, young adult. Submit query/proposal package, 3 sample chapters, clips.

Tips Audience is children and adults who are looking for the entertainment and relaxation you can only get from jumping into a good book. Submit only your best work to us. Submit only in the genres we are interested in publishing. Do not submit work that is not suitable for a Christian audience.

HOBAR PUBLICATIONS

A division of Finney Co. 8075 215th St. W, Lakeville MN 55044. (952)469-6699. Fax: (952)469-1968. E-mail: feedback@finney-hobar.com. Website: www.finney-hobar.com. **Contact:** Alan E. Krysan, president. Publishes trade paperback originals. **Publishes 4-6 titles/year. 30 queries received/year. 10 mss received/year. 35% of books from first-time authors. 100% from unagented writers. Pays 10% royalty on wholesale price. Pays advance.** Publishes book 1 year after acceptance of ms. Accepts simultaneous submissions. Responds in 10-12 weeks to queries.

O→ Hobar publishes career and technical educational materials.

Nonfiction Subjects include agriculture, animals, business, economics, education, gardening, nature, environment, science, building trades. Query with SASE. Reviews artwork/photos.

Recent Title(s) *Saga of the Grain*, by Ervin Oelke; *E.M. Young*, by Dr. Hiram Drache; *National Safety Tractor and Machinery*.

HOHM PRESS

P.O. Box 31, Prescott AZ 86302. (800)381-2700. Fax: (928)717-1779. Website: www.hohmpress.com. **Contact:** Regina Sara Ryan, managing editor. Estab. 1975. Publishes hardcover and trade paperback originals. **Publishes 6-8 titles/year. 50% of books from first-time authors. Pays 10% royalty on net sales.** Publishes book 18 months after acceptance of ms. Accepts simultaneous submissions. Responds in 3 months to queries.

O→ "*Hohm Press* publishes a range of titles in the areas of transpersonal psychology and spirituality, herbistry, alternative health methods, and nutrition. Not interested in personal health survival stories."

Nonfiction Subjects include health, medicine, natural/alternative health, medicine, philosophy, religion, Hindu, Buddhist, Sufi, or translations of classic texts in major religious traditions, yoga. Query with SASE. No e-mail inquiries, please.

N HOLLIS PUBLISHING CO.

Division of Puritan Press, Inc. 95 Runnells Bridge Rd., Hollis NH 03049. (603)889-4500. Fax: (603)889-6551. E-mail: books@hollispublishing.com. Website: www.hollispublishing.com. **Contact:** Frederick Lyford, editor. Publishes hardcover and trade paperback originals. **Publishes 5 titles/year. 25 queries received/year. 15 mss received/year. 50% of books from first-time authors. 100% from unagented writers. Pays 5-10% royalty on retail price.** Publishes book 6 months after acceptance of ms. Responds in 1 month to queries. Responds in 2 months to manuscripts. Book catalog available free. Guidelines for #10 SASE.

O→ Hollis publishes books on social policy, government, politics, and current and recent events intended for use by professors and their students, college and university libraries, and the general reader. Currently emphasizing works about education, the Internet, government, history-in-the-making, social values and politics.

Nonfiction Subjects include Americana, anthropology, archeology, education, ethnic, government, politics, health, medicine, history, memoirs, nature, environment, regional, sociology, travel. Query with SASE. Submit outline, 2 sample chapters.

Recent Title(s) *Basic Lymphoedema Management: Treatment and Prevention of Problems Associated With Lymphatic Filariasis*, by Gerusa Dreyer, MD, et. al.

N HOST PUBLICATIONS

277 Broadway, Suite 210, New York NY 10007. (212)905-2365. Fax: (212)905-2369. E-mail: tracey@hostpublications.com. Website: www.hostpublications.com. **Contact:** Joe W. Bratcher III and Elzbieta Szoka, co-editors. Estab. 1987. Hardcover and trade paperback originals. Book catalog available online.

O→ Genres are Anthologies, Drama, Novels, Poetry, & Short Stories.

Nonfiction Subjects include memoirs.
Fiction Subjects include ethnic, historical, literary, multicultural, poetry, short story collections.
Recent Title(s) *Homenagem a Alexandrino Severino*, edited by Margo Milleret & Marshall C. Eakin; *The Young Man from Savoy*, by C-F Ramuz (a novel from Switzerland); *Cage*, by Astrid Cabral (poetry from Brazil).
Tips In addition to its catalog of HOST is a press dedicated to

HOWELLS HOUSE

P.O. Box 9546, Washington DC 20016-9546. (202)333-2182. **Contact:** W.D. Howells, publisher. Estab. 1988. Publishes hardcover and trade paperback originals and reprints. **Publishes 0-2 titles/year. 2,000 queries received/year. 300 mss received/year. 95% of books from first-time authors. 95% from unagented writers. Pays 15% net royalty or makes outright purchase. May offer advance.** Publishes book 16 months after acceptance of ms. Accepts simultaneous submissions. Responds in 2 months to proposals.
Imprints The Compass Press; Whalesback Books.

Our interests are institutions and institutional change.

Nonfiction Subjects include Americana, anthropology, archaeology, architecture, art, education, government, history, politics, science, sociology, translation. Query
Fiction Subjects include historical, literary, mainstream, contemporary. Query

N I.C.E. PUBLISHING COMPANY

P.O. Box 749, Telluride CO 81435. (970)209-8092. E-mail: submissions@icepublishing.us. **Contact:** Grit Salewski, acquisitions ed. Estab. 2006. Publishes hardcover, trade paperback, and electronic originals. **Publishes 2-5 titles/year. 20 queries received/year. 5 mss received/year. 50%% of books from first-time authors. 100%% from unagented writers. Pays 10-80% royalty on retail price. Makes outright purchase of 1,000-10,000.** Publishes book 4 months after acceptance of ms. Accepts simultaneous submissions. Responds in 1 month to queries. Responds in 1 month to proposals. Responds in 1 month to manuscripts. Book catalog available online. Guidelines available online.
Nonfiction Subjects include business, economics, community, contemporary culture, cooking, foods, nutrition, creative nonfiction, education, government, politics, history, hobbies, humanities, memoirs, military, war, nature, environment, philosophy, psychology, recreation, religion, science, social sciences, sociology, spirituality, sports, translation, travel, world affairs, Self-defense, firearms, martial arts. Submit proposal package, outline, 2 sample chapters. Submit complete ms. Reviews artwork/photos. Send photocopies.
Fiction Subjects include adventure, historical, military, war, mystery, short story collections, suspense. Query with SASE. Submit proposal package, 3 sample chapters, clips. Submit complete ms.
Recent Title(s) *COMBAT FOCUS SHOOTING*, by R. Pincus ((how-to)); *Warrior Psalms*, by T. Forman ((inspirational)).
Tips Our audience is an educated o Be sure that your premise is

ICS PUBLICATIONS

Institute of Carmelite Studies 2131 Lincoln Rd. NE, Washington DC 20002. (202)832-8489. Fax: (202)832-8967. Website: www.icspublications.org. **Contact:** John Sullivan, OCD. Publishes hardcover and trade paperback originals and reprints. **Publishes 3 titles/year. 10-20 queries received/year. 10 mss received/year. 10% of books from first-time authors. 90-100% from unagented writers. Pays 2-6% royalty on retail price or makes outright purchase. Pays $500 advance.** Publishes book 3 years after acceptance of ms. Responds in 6 months to proposals. Book catalog for 7X10 envelope and 2 First-Class stamps.

Our audience consists of those interested in the Carmelite tradition and in developing their life of prayer and spirituality.

Nonfiction We are looking for significant works on Carmelite history, spirituality, and main figures (Saints Teresa, John of the Cross, Therese of Lisieux, etc.).
Recent Title(s) *The Letters of St. Teresa, vol. 2.*

IDYLL ARBOR, INC.

39129 264th Ave. SE, Enumclaw WA 98022. (360)825-7797. Fax: (360)825-5670. E-mail: editors@idyllarbor.com. Website: www.idyllarbor.com. **Contact:** Tom Blaschko. Estab. 1984. Publishes hardcover and trade paperback originals, and trade paperback reprints. **Publishes 6 titles/year. 50% of books from first-time authors. 100% from unagented writers. Pays 8-15% royalty on wholesale price or retail price.** Publishes book 1 year after acceptance of ms. Accepts simultaneous submissions. Responds in 1 month to queries. Responds in 2 months to proposals. Responds in 6 months to manuscripts. Book catalog and ms guidelines free.
Imprints Issues Press; Pine Winds Press.

Idyll Arbor publishes practical information on the current state and art of healthcare practice. Currently emphasizing therapies (recreational, aquatic, occupational, music, horticultural), and activity directors in long-term care facilities. Issues Press looks at problems in society from video games to returning veterans and their problems reintegrating into the civilian world.

Nonfiction Subjects include health, medicine, for therapists, activity directors, psychology, recreation as therapy, horticulture (used in long-term care activities or health care therapy). Query preferred with outline and 1 sample chapter. Reviews artwork/photos. Send photocopies.
Recent Title(s) *Faces of Combat, PTSD and TBI*, by Eric Newhouse; *Video Games and Your Kids: How Parents Stay in Control*, by Hilarie Cash and Kim McDaniel.
Tips The books must be useful for the health practitioner who meets face to face with patients or the books must be useful for teaching undergraduate and graduate level classes. We are especially looking for therapists with a solid clinical background to write on their area of expertise.

ILLUMINATION ARTS

P.O. Box 1865, Bellevue WA 98009. (425)644-7185. Fax: (425)644-9274. E-mail: liteinfo@illumin.com. Website: www.illumin.com. **Contact:** Ruth Thompson, editorial director (ms submissions). Publishes hardcover originals. **Publishes 1-4 titles/year. Pays royalty on wholesale price. Offers advance for artists.** Reponds in 2 months to queries. Responds in no answer to manuscripts. Book catalog available online. Guidelines available online.

O- Illumination Arts publishes inspirational/spiritual (not religious) children's picture books.

Nonfiction Submit complete ms with SASE Reviews artwork/photos. Send photocopies.
Fiction Subjects include picture books, children's. Prefer under 1,000 words; 1,500 words max. No electronic submissions.
Recent Title(s) *Am I a Color Too?*, by Heidi Cole and Nancy Vogl ; *Mrs. Murphy's Marvelous Mansion*, by Emma Perry Roberts .
Tips A smart writer researches publishing companies thoroughly before submitting and then follows submission guidelines closely.

N IMAGES AND ADJECTIVES PUBLISHING, LLC

P.O. Box 6445, Broomfield CO 80021. E-mail: margaret@imagesandadjectives.com. Website: www.imagesandadjectives.com. **Contact:** Margaret Emerson, president; Cristina Willard, vice-president. Estab. 2008. Publishes trade paperback originals. **Publishes 4 titles/year. 1,200 queries received/year. 50 mss received/year. 50% of books from first-time authors. 0% from unagented writers. Pays 7-10% royalty on wholesale price.** Publishes book 8 months after acceptance of ms. Accepts simultaneous submissions. Responds in 1 month to queries. Responds in 2 months to manuscripts.
Nonfiction Subjects include community, (environmental issues), nature, environment. Submit proposal package, outline, 1 sample chapters. Unsolicited mss returned unopened.
Fiction Subjects include adventure, (see other), juvenile, (see other), nature or environmental issues as strong, primary theme. We want fiction that has a strong pro-environmental theme, or is related to ecopsychology. Please see our website for details. Submit proposal package, 1 sample chapters, clips. Unsolicited mss returned unopened.
Tips Our audience is interested in We welcome first-time authors

IMAGES SI, INC.

Imprint of Images Publishing 109 Woods of Arden Rd., Staten Island NY 10312. (718)966-3694. Fax: (718)966-3695. Website: www.imagesco.com/publishing/index.html. **Contact:** Kimberly Meter. Estab. 1990. Publishes 2 audio books/year. Publishes 6-24 months after acceptance. Accepts simultaneous submissions. Responds in 2-6 months to queries. Responds in 2-6 months to manuscripts. Publisher's catalog and writer's guidelines online.

O- "We are currently looking for hard science fiction short stories only for our line of audio books."

Fiction Needs hard science fiction for audiocassettes and CDs. Query with SASE.
Recent Title(s) *Kirlian Photography*, by John Iovine; *Centauri III*, by George L. Griggs.

N IMMEDIUM

P.O. Box 31846, San Francisco CA 94131. E-mail: pr@immedium.com. Website: www.immedium.com. **Contact:** Amy Ma, acquisitions editor. Estab. 2005. Publishes hardcover and trade paperback originals. **Publishes 4 titles/year. 50 queries received/year. 25 mss received/year. 50%% of books from first-time authors. 90%% from unagented writers. Pays 5% royalty on wholesale price.** Publishes book 24 months after acceptance of ms. Accepts simultaneous submissions. Responds in 1 month to queries. Responds in 2 months to proposals. Responds in 3 months to manuscripts. Book catalog for 9 X 12 envelope and 5 First-Class stamps. Guidelines available online.

O- *Immedium* focuses on publishing children's picture books, Asian American topics, and contemporary arts and culture.

Nonfiction Subjects include art, architecture, multicultural. Query with SASE. Submit proposal package, outline, 2 sample chapters. Submit complete ms. Reviews artwork/photos. Send photocopies.
Fiction Subjects include comic books, picture books. Submit complete ms.

Recent Title(s) *Desert to Dream: A Decade of Burning Man Photography*, by Barbara Traub ((photography)); *The Woollyhoodwinks vs. the Dark Patch*, by Asa Sanchez and Phil Dumensil ((children's picture book)); *The Octonauts & the Frown Fish*, by Meomi ((children's picture book)).

Tips Our audience is children, par Please visit our site and rev

IMPACT PUBLISHERS, INC.

P.O. Box 6016, Atascadero CA 93423-6016. (805)466-5917. E-mail: info@impactpublishers.com. Website: www.impactpublishers.com. **Contact:** Freeman Porter, acquisitions editor. Estab. 1970. Publishes trade paperback originals. **Publishes 6-10 titles/year. 250 queries received/year. 250 mss received/year. 20% of books from first-time authors. 60% from unagented writers. Pays advance.** Publishes book 12-18 months after acceptance of ms. Accepts simultaneous submissions. Responds in 5 months to proposals. Book catalog available free. Guidelines available online.

Imprints Little Imp Books; Rebuilding Books; Practical Therapist series.

- Our purpose is to make the best human services expertise available to the widest possible audience: children, teens, parents, couples, individuals seeking self-help and personal growth, and human service professionals. Currently emphasizing books on divorce recovery for The Rebuilding Books Series. De-emphasizing children's books.

Nonfiction All our books are written by psychologist and other qualified human service professionals and are in the fields of mental health, personal growth, relationships, aging, families, children, and professional psychology.Subjects include child guidance, health, medicine, psychology, professional, caregiving/eldercare. Submit proposal package, including short resume or vita, book description, audience description, outline, 1-3 sample chapters, and SASE.

Recent Title(s) *Moved by the Spirit*, by Jeffrey Kottler and John Carlson; *Your Child's Divorce*, by Marsha Temlock.

Tips Don't call to see if we have received your submission. Include a self-addressed, stamped postcard if you want to know if your manuscript arrived safely. We prefer a nonacademic, readable style. We publish only popular and professional psychology and self-help materials written in `everyday language' by professionals with advanced degrees and significant experience in the human services. Our theme is 'psychology you can use, from professionals you can trust.'

INTERCULTURAL PRESS, INC.

20 Park Plaza, Suite 115A, Boston MA 02110. E-mail: info@interculturalpress.com. Website: www.interculturalpress.com. **Contact:** Judy Carl-Hendrick, managing editor. Estab. 1980. Publishes hardcover and paperback originals. **Publishes 8-12 titles/year. 50% of books from first-time authors. 95% from unagented writers. Pays royalty. Offers small advance occasionally.** Publishes book within 18 months after acceptance of ms. Accepts simultaneous submissions. Responds in 1 month to queries. Book catalog available free. Guidelines available online.

- Intercultural Press publishes materials related to intercultural relations, including the practical concerns of living and working in foreign countries, the impact of cultural differences on personal and professional relationships, and the challenges of interacting with people from unfamiliar cultures, whether at home or abroad. Currently emphasizing international business.

Nonfiction We want books with an international or domestic intercultural or multicultural focus, including those on business operations (how to be effective in intercultural business activities), education (textbooks for teaching intercultural subjects, for instance), and training (for Americans abroad or foreign nationals coming to the United States).Subjects include world affairs, business, education, diversity and multicultural, relocation and cultural adaptation, culture learning, training materials, country-specific guides. Submit proposals, outline, résumé, cv, and potential market information.

Recent Title(s) *The Cultural Imperative: Global Trends in the 21st Century*, by Richard D. Lewis; *Exploring Culture: Excercises, Stories and Synthetic Cultures*, by Gert Jan Hofstede, Paul B. Pedersen and Geert Hofstede.

N INTERNATIONAL PUBLISHERS CO., INC.

239 W. 23 St., New York NY 10011. (212)366-9816. Fax: (212)366-9820. E-mail: service@intpubnyc.com. Website: www.intpubnyc.com. **Contact:** Betty Smith, president. Estab. 1924. Publishes hardcover originals, trade paperback originals and reprints. **Publishes 5-6 titles/year. 50-100 mss received/year. 10% of books from first-time authors. Pays 5-7 ½% royalty on paperbacks; 10% royalty on cloth.** Publishes book 6 months after acceptance of ms. Accepts simultaneous submissions. Responds in 1 month to queries; 6 months to manuscripts. Book catalog online at website. Guidelines online at website.

- International Publishers Co., Inc. emphasizes books based on Marxist science.

Nonfiction Subjects include art, architecture, economics, government, politics, history, philosophy. Query, or submit outline, sample chapters, and SASE. Reviews artwork/photos.

Recent Title(s) *John Brown—The Cost of Freedom*, by Louis A DeCaro, Jr.; *Red Roots, Green Shoots—Marxist Environmentalism*, by Virginia Brodine; *Marxist Ethics—A Short Exposition by Willis Truitt.*

Tips No fiction or poetry.

ITALICA PRESS

595 Main St., Suite 605, New York NY 10044-0047. (212)935-4230. Fax: (212)838-7812. E-mail: inquiries@italicapress.com. Website: www.italicapress.com. **Contact:** Ronald G. Musto and Eileen Gardiner, publishers. Estab. 1985. Publishes trade paperback originals. **Publishes 6 titles/year. 600 queries received/year. 60 mss received/year. 5% of books from first-time authors. 100% from unagented writers. Pays 7-15% royalty on wholesale price.author's copies** Publishes book 1 year after acceptance of ms. Accepts simultaneous submissions. Responds in 1 month to queries. Responds in 4 months to manuscripts. Book catalog available online. Guidelines available online.

- Italica Press publishes English translations of modern Italian fiction and medieval and Renaissance nonfiction.

Nonfiction Subjects include translation. Query with SASE. Reviews artwork/photos. Send photocopies.
Fiction Query with SASE.
Tips We are interested in considering a wide variety of medieval and Renaissance topics (not historical fiction), and for modern works we are only interested in translations from Italian fiction by well-known Italian authors.

ALICE JAMES BOOKS

238 Main St., Farmington ME 04938. (207)778-7071. Fax: (207)778-7071. E-mail: ajb@umf.maine.edu. Website: www.alicejamesbooks.org. Estab. 1973. Publishes trade paperback originals. **Publishes 6 titles/year. 1,000 mss received/year. 50% of books from first-time authors. 100% from unagented writers. Pays through competition awards.** Publishes book 1 to 1 & ½ years after acceptance of ms. Accepts simultaneous submissions. Responds promptly to queries. Responds in 4 months to manuscripts. Book catalog for free or on website. Guidelines for #10 SASE or on website.

- "Alice James Books is a nonprofit cooperative poetry press. The founders' objectives were to give women access to publishing and to involve authors in the publishing process. The cooperative selects mss for publication through both regional and national competitions."

Recent Title(s) *Here, Bullet*, by Brian Turner; *Gloryland*, by Anne Marie Macari; *Goest*, by Cole Swensen.
Tips "Send SASE for contest guidelines or check website. Do not send work without consulting current guidelines."

JAMESON BOOKS, INC.

722 Columbus St., P.O. Box 738, Ottawa IL 61350. (815)434-7905. Fax: (815)434-7907. **Contact:** Jameson G. Campaigne, publisher/editor. Estab. 1986. Publishes hardcover originals. **Publishes 6 titles/year. 500 queries received/year. 300 mss received/year. 33% of books from first-time authors. 33% from unagented writers. Pays 6-15% royalty on retail price. Pays $1,000-25,000 advance.** Publishes book 1 year after acceptance of ms. Accepts simultaneous submissions. Responds in 6 months to queries.

- Jameson Books publishes conservative politics and economics, Chicago area history, and biographies.

Nonfiction Subjects include business, economics, government, politics, history, regional, Chicago area. Query with SASE. Submit 1 sample chapter. Submissions not returned without SASE.
Fiction Interested in pre-cowboy mountain men in American west, before 1820 in east frontier fiction. Query with SASE. Submit outline, clips, 1 sample chapter.
Recent Title(s) *Politics as a Noble Calling*, by F. Clifton White (memoirs); *Capitalism*, by George Reisman; *The Citizen's Guide to Fighting Government*, by Steve Symms and Larry Grupp.

KAEDEN BOOKS

P.O. Box 16190, Rocky River OH 44116. Website: www.kaeden.com. **Contact:** Lisa Stenger, editor. Estab. 1986. Publishes paperback originals. **Publishes 12-20 titles/year. 1,000 mss received/year. 30%% of books from first-time authors. 95%% from unagented writers. Pays royalty. Makes outright purchase. Pays flat fee or royalty by individual arrangement with author depending on book.** Publishes book 6-9 months after acceptance of ms. Accepts simultaneous submissions. Responds in 12 months to manuscripts. Book catalog available online. Guidelines available online.

- "Children's book publisher for education K-2 market: reading stories, fiction/nonfiction, chapter books, science, and social studies materials."

Nonfiction Subjects include animals, creative nonfiction, science, social sciences. Submit complete ms. Reviews artwork/photos. Send photocopies.
Fiction Grades K-3 only.Subjects include adventure, fantasy, historical, humor, mystery, short story collections, sports, suspense. Send a disposable copy of ms a
Recent Title(s) *Sammy Gets A Bath*, by Karen Evans ((early reader)); *Carla's Talent Show*, by Kimberly Beikly ((early reader)); *Adventures of Sophie Bean Red Flyer*, by Kathryn Yeuchak ((early chapter book)).

Tips "Our audience ranges from Kindergarten-2nd grade school children. We are an educational publisher."

KAMEHAMEHA PUBLISHING

Kamehameha Schools 567 S. King St., Suite 118, Honolulu HI 96813. (808)534-8205. E-mail: kspress@ksbe.edu. Website: www.kamehamehapublishing.org. **Contact:** Acquisitions Editor. Publishes hardcover and trade paperback originals and reprints. **Publishes 5-15 titles/year. 10-25% of books from first-time authors. 100% from unagented writers. Makes outright purchase or royalty agreement.** Publishes book up to 2 years after acceptance of ms. Responds in 3 months to queries. Book catalog online or request print copy.

Imprints Kamehameha Schools Press; Kamehameha Schools; Kamehameha Schools Bishop Estate; Pauhi Readers.

- Only writers with substantial and documented expertise in Hawaiian history, Hawaiian culture, Hawaiian language, and/or Hawaiian studies should consider submitting to Kamehameha Schools Press. We prefer to work with writers available to physically meet at our Honolulu offices.

Nonfiction Subjects include education, Hawaiian, history, Hawaiian, regional, Hawaii, translation, Hawaiian. Query with SASE. Reviews artwork/photos. Send photocopies.

N KELSEY STREET PRESS

50 Northgate Ave., Berkeley CA 94708. (510)845-2260. Fax: (510)548-9185. E-mail: amber@kelseyst.com. Website: www.kelseyst.com. Estab. 1974. Hardcover and Trade paperback originals and electronic originals.

- A Berkeley, California press publishing collaborations between women poets and artists. Many of the press's collaborations focus on a central theme or conceit, like the sprawl & spectacle of New York in *Arcade* by Erica Hunt & Alison Saar.

Fiction Subjects include experimental, gay, lesbian, horror, multicultural, mystery, poetry, Prose, Women of Color.

Recent Title(s) *Newcomer Can't Swim*, by Renee Gladman; *Concordance*, poems by Mei-mei Berssenbrugge; drawings by Kiki Smith; *The Addison Street Anthology: Berkeley's Poetry Walk*, ed. by Robert Hass & Jessica Fisher.

Tips You are welcome to submit an email query in 2009.

DENIS KITCHEN PUBLISHING CO., LLC

P.O. Box 2250, Amherst MA 01004-2250. (413)259-1627. Fax: (413)259-1812. E-mail: denis@kitchenandhansen.com. Website: www.deniskitchen.com. **Contact:** Denis Kitchen, publisher (graphic novels, classic comic strips, postcard books, boxed trading cards, graphics, pop culture, alternative culture). Publishes hardcover and trade paperback originals and reprints. **Publishes 4 titles/year. 15% of books from first-time authors. 50% from unagented writers. Pays 6-10% royalty on retail price.Occasionally makes deals based on percentage of wholesale if idea and/or bulk of work is done in-house. Pays $1-5,000 advance.** Publishes book 9-12 months after acceptance of ms. Responds in 4-6 weeks to queries. Responds in 4-6 weeks to proposals. Responds in 4-6 weeks to manuscripts.

- This publisher strongly discourages e-mail submissions.

Nonfiction Query with SASE. Submit proposal package, outline, illustrative matter. Submit complete ms. Reviews artwork/photos. Send photocopies and transparencies.

Fiction Subjects include adventure, erotica, historical, horror, humor, literary, mystery, occult, science fiction, only if in graphic novel form. We do not want pure fiction. We seek cartoonists or writer/illustrator teams who can tell compelling stories with a combination of words and pictures. Query with SASE. Submit sample illustrations/comic pages. Submit complete ms.

Recent Title(s) *Mr. Natural Postcard Book*, by R. Crumb; *The Grasshopper and the Ant*, by Harvey Kurtzman; *Jazz Greats*, by R. Crumb.

Tips Our audience is readers who embrace the graphic novel revolution, who appreciate historical comic strips and books, and those who follow popular and alternative culture. Readers who supported Kitchen Sink Press for 3 decades will find that Denis Kitchen Publishing continues the tradition and precedents established by KSP. We like to discover new talent. The artist who has a day job but a great idea is encouraged to contact us. The pop culture historian who has a new take on an important figure is likewise encouraged. We have few preconceived notions about manuscripts or ideas, though we are decidedly selective. Historically, we have published many first-time authors and artists, some of whom developed into award-winning creators with substantial followings. Artists or illustrators who do not have confidence in their writing should send us self-promotional postcards (our favorite way of spotting new talent).

KITSUNE BOOKS

P.O. Box 1154, Crawfordville FL 32326-1154. E-mail: contact@kitsunebooks.com. Website: www.kitsunebooks.com. **Contact:** Lynn Holschuh, Assistant Editor. Estab. 2006. Publishes trade paperback originals and reprints. **Publishes 4-5 titles/year. 600+ queries received/year. 70 mss received/year. 30% of books from first-time authors. 50% from unagented writers. Pays 6-10% royalty on retail price. Pays $300-500 advance.**

Publishes book 12-18 months after acceptance of ms. Accepts simultaneous submissions. Responds in 2-4 weeks to queries. Responds in 1-3 months to proposals. Responds in 6-9 months to manuscripts. Book catalog available online. Guidelines available online.

Nonfiction Subjects include memoirs, New Age, spirituality, literary commentary, yoga/fitness. Query via e-mail - no hardcopy submissions unless requested. Reviews artwork/photos.

Fiction Subjects include literary, mainstream, contemporary, dark fantasy, short story collections story collections, poetry, speculative, noir, magical realism. We are looking for carefully written fiction that's slightly off the beaten path—interesting novels that don't fit easily into any one category. Graceful command of the language is a plus; technical command of grammar/language mechanics a must. Our latest short story collection is in the Raymond Carver tradition. Looking for authors with a unique voice and style. Query via e-mail. No hardcopy, no previously published material.

Recent Title(s) *Jesus Swept*, by James Protzman (novel); *Living by the Dead*, by Ellen Ashdown (memoir); *You Can't Get There from Here and Other Stories*, by Leonard Nash (literary fiction - 2007 Silver Medal Winner, Florida Book Awards); *The Moving Waters*, by Mary Jane Ryals (poetry collection - 2008-2010 Florida Big Bend Poet Laureate).

Tips Our readership is eclectic, with a taste for the unusual, the artistic and the unexpected. Kitsune Books caters to lovers of literature, poetry, and well-designed and researched nonfiction. We prefer to deal with mss electronically rather than receiving printouts (saves trees). Please read our category guidelines carefully. Although we do accept some genre fiction, please look carefully at what we don't accept before you submit. Interesting novels that don't fit easily into any one category are considered. No self-published material.

N KOMENAR PUBLISHING

1756 Lacassie Ave., Suite 202, Walnut Creek CA 94596-7002. (510)444-2261. Fax: (510)834-2141. Website: www.komenarpublishing.com. **Contact:** Charlotte Cook, president (fiction: mainstream, literary, mystery, historical, science fiction). Estab. 2005. Publishes hardcover originals. **Publishes 2-4 titles/year. 2,000+ mss received/year. 100% of books from first-time authors. Pays royalty.Pays 20% royalties after the first 7,500 books have sold.** Publishes book 1 year after acceptance of ms. Accepts simultaneous submissions. Responds in 1-3 months to manuscripts. Book catalog available online. Guidelines available online.

Fiction Subjects include adventure, ethnic, experimental, historical, humor, literary, mainstream, contemporary, multicultural, mystery, suspense. KOMENAR Publishing believes a novel should be a compelling read. Readers are entitled to stories with strong forward momentum, engaging and dynamic characters, and evocative settings. The story must begin in the first chapter. Submit proposal package, bio, cover letter, first 1 pages of ms. See Web site for additional de.

Recent Title(s) *Outside Child*, by Alice Wilson-Fried (mystery); *Heroes Arise*, by Laurel Anne Hill (literary parable); *My Half of the Sky*, by Jana McBurney-Lin (literary mainstream).

Tips Our audience is comprised of habitual readers. Any experimental craft choices should be applied to the story, not to font, margins or punctuation. Chapters of our books are online. Read a couple. Charlotte Cook is likely to call promising authors. It's a good idea to have some familiarity with our books.

H.J. KRAMER, INC.

In a joint venture with New World Library P.O. Box 1082, Tiburon CA 94920. (415)435-5367. Fax: (415)435-5364. E-mail: hjkramer@jps.net. **Contact:** Jan Phillips. Estab. 1984. Publishes hardcover and trade paperback originals. **Publishes 5-7 titles/year. 1,000 queries received/year. 500 mss received/year. 20% of books from first-time authors. Advance varies.** Publishes book 18 months after acceptance of ms. Book catalog available free.

Imprints Starseed Press Children's Illustrated Books.

Nonfiction Subjects include health, medicine, holistic, spirituality, metaphysical.

Fiction Subjects include juvenile, picture books with themes of self-esteem, nonviolence, and spirituality. Prospective authors please note: Kramer's list is selective and is normally fully slated several seasons in advance.

Recent Title(s) *Saying What's Real*, by Dr. Susan Campbell (nonfiction); *A Goose Named Gilligan*, by Jerry M. Hay (nonfiction for children); *Just for Today*, by Jan Phillips (fiction).

Tips Our books are for people who are interested in personal growth and consciousness-raising. We are not interested in personal stories unless they have universal appeal. We do not accept e-mail submissions of mss although queries will be answered.

LADYBUGPRESS

NewVoices, Inc. 16964 Columbia River Dr., Sonora CA 95370-9111. (209)694-8340. E-mail: georgia@ladybugbooks.com. Website: www.ladybugbooks.com. **Contact:** Georgia Jones, editor-in-chief (new authors). Trade paperback and electronic originals. **Publishes 4-6 titles/year. 30 queries/year; 10 mss/year 90% of books from first-time authors. 100% from unagented writers.** Publishes book 2 months after acceptance of ms. Accepts simultaneous submissions. Catalog and guidelines available online.

Imprints LadybugPress, NewVoices, Ladybug Productions, Partners in Publishing
Nonfiction Subjects include alternative lifestyles, contemporary culture, creative nonfiction, dance, music, social sciences, womens issues, world affairs. Query with SASE; we prefer email submissions. We review artwork/photos; send electronic files.
Fiction Subjects include contemporary, feminist, historical, literary, mainstream, poetry. Our tastes are eclectic. Submit proposal package, including synopsis; we prefer electronic submissions, georgia@ladbugbooks.com.
Recent Title(s) *You Are God*, by Judy Johnston and Michael Love (philosophy); *Lives in Process (audio version)*, by Dottie Moore (spiritual); *Kanai's Journal*, by Kanai Callow (memoir); *Fireflies in Baldwin*, by Lane Willey (suspense); *Isabelle's Appetite*, by Georgia Jones (general fiction); *Feeling We Don't Reveal*, by Elizabeth Castillo (poetry).
Tips We have a lot of information on our website, and have several related sites that give an overview of who we are and what we like to see. Take advantage of this and it will help you make good decisions about submissions.

LAKE CLAREMONT PRESS

P.O. Box 711, Chicago IL 60690. (312)226-8400. Fax: (312)226-8420. E-mail: sharon@lakeclaremont.com. Website: www.lakeclaremont.com. **Contact:** Sharon Woodhouse, publisher. Estab. 1994. Publishes trade paperback originals. **Publishes 6-10 titles/year. 500 queries received/year. 100 mss received/year. 50% of books from first-time authors. 100% from unagented writers. Pays 10-15% royalty on net sales. Pays $500-1,000 advance.** Publishes book 6-12 months after acceptance of ms. Accepts simultaneous submissions. Responds in 1 month to queries. Responds in 2 months to proposals. Responds in 2-6 months to manuscripts. Book catalog available online.

- We specialize in nonfiction books on the Chicago area and its history, particularly by authors with a passion or organizations with a mission.

Nonfiction Subjects include Americana, ethnic, history, nature, environment, regional, regional, travel, womens issues, film/cinema/stage (regional). Query with SASE, or submit proposal package, including outline and 2 sample chapters, or submit complete ms (e-mail queries and proposals preferred).
Recent Title(s) *Today's Chicago Blues*, by Karen Hanson; *Chicago TV Horror Movie Shows: From Shock Theatre to Svengoolie*, by Ted Okuda and Mark Yurkiw.
Tips Please include a market analysis in proposals (who would buy this book and where) and an analysis of similar books available for different regions. Please know what else is out there.

LANGMARC PUBLISHING

P.O. Box 90488, Austin TX 78709-0488. (512)394-0989. Fax: (512)394-0829. E-mail: langmarc@booksails.com. Website: www.langmarc.com. **Contact:** Lois Qualben, president (inspirational). Publishes trade paperback originals. **Publishes 3-5 titles/year. 150 queries received/year. 80 mss received/year. 60% of books from first-time authors. 80% from unagented writers. Pays 10-14% royalty on wholesale price.** Publishes book 18 months after acceptance of ms. Accepts simultaneous submissions. Responds in 3 months to queries. Book catalog available free. Guidelines available online.
Imprints North Sea Press; Harbor Lights Series.
Nonfiction Subjects include child guidance, education. Query with SASE. Reviews artwork/photos. Send photocopies.
Recent Title(s) *Hairball Diaries: The Courage to Speak Up; On the Wings of the Wind: A Journey to Faith; Don't Call Me Shy.*

LARSON PUBLICATIONS

4936 Rt. 414, Burdett NY 14818-9729. (607)546-9342. Fax: (607)546-9344. Website: www.larsonpublications.org. **Contact:** Paul Cash, director. Estab. 1982. Publishes hardcover and trade paperback originals. **Publishes 4-5 titles/year. 5% of books from first-time authors. Pays variable royalty. Seldom offers advance.** Publishes book 1-2 years after acceptance of ms. Accepts simultaneous submissions. Responds in 4-6 months to queries. Visit website for book catalog.
Nonfiction Subjects include philosophy, psychology, religion, spirituality. Query with SASE and outline.
Recent Title(s) *Astronoesis*, by Anthony Damiani.
Tips We look for original studies of comparative spiritual philosophy or personal fruits of independent (transsectarian viewpoint) spiritual research/practice.

LEUCROTA PRESS

P.O. Box 647, Poway CA 92074. (619)534-8169. Fax: (858)592-7684. E-mail: submissions@leucrotapress.com. Website: www.leucrotapress.com. **Contact:** David Peak, acquisitions editor. Estab. 2007. Publishes hardcover, trade paperback and electronic originals. **Publishes 6-10 titles/year. 400 queries received/year. 450-600 mss received/year. 80% of books from first-time authors. 90% from unagented writers. Pays up to $2,000 advance.** Publishes book 9-12 months after acceptance of ms. Accepts simultaneous submissions. Responds in

1 month to queries. Responds in 2 months to proposals. Responds in 3 months to manuscripts. Book catalog available online. Guidelines available online.

Fiction Subjects include fantasy, horror, science fiction, graphic novels, Also publishes a yearly short story anthology. Characterization should be your number one goal. We are looking for character-driven plots, unique settings, established worlds and histories, believable dialogue and new twists on old scenarios. Wow us with something different, something far out of the ordinary. Submit proposal package, three sample chapters, publishing history, cover letter and SASE. Do not submit complete ms unless requested.

Recent Title(s) *Demons of the Past*, by Erin Durante (science fiction); *Low Man*, by T. J. Vargo (horror); *The Kult*, by Shaun Jeffrey (horror); *Blood Sin*, by Toni V. Sweeney (science fiction); *One If By Heaven Two If By Hell*, by Rick Maydak (fantasy).

Tips Visit our Web site to get a feel for our editors, our needs, and overall style and attitude. We have a blog, so post your questions and get feedback from an editor.

LIGHTHOUSE POINT PRESS

100 First Ave., Suite 525, Pittsburgh PA 15222-1517. (412)323-9320. Fax: (412)323-9334. E-mail: info@yearick-millea.com. **Contact:** Ralph W. Yearick, publisher (business/career/general nonfiction). Estab. 1993. Publishes hardcover and trade paperback originals and trade paperback reprints. **Publishes 1-2 titles/year. Pays 5-10% royalty on retail price.** Responds in 6 months to queries.

- O→ Lighthouse Point Press specializes in business/career nonfiction titles, and books that help readers improve their quality of life.

Nonfiction Subjects include business, economics. Submit proposal package, outline, 1-2 sample chapters. Complete manuscripts preferred.

Recent Title(s) *The Heart and Craft of Lifestory Writing: How to Transform Memories into Meaningful Stories*, by Sharon M. Lippincott (writing/reference); *On Track to Quality*, by Dr. James K. Todd (business).

Tips When submitting a manuscript or proposal, please tell us what you see as the target market/audience for the book. Also, be very specific about what you are willing to do to promote the book.

⊘ LOST HORSE PRESS

105 Lost Horse Lane, Sandpoint ID 83864. (208)255-4410. Fax: (208)255-1560. E-mail: losthorsepress@mindspring.com. Website: www.losthorsepress.org. **Contact:** Christine Holbert, editor. Estab. 1998. Publishes hardcover and paperback originals. **Publishes 4 titles/year.** Publishes book 1-2 years after acceptance of ms.

- *Does not accept unsolicited mss. However, we welcome submissions for The Idaho Prize for Poetry, a national competition offering $1000 prize money plus publication for a book-length manuscript. Please check the submission guidelines for The Idaho Prize for Poetry online.*

Fiction Subjects include literary, poetry, regional, Pacific Northwest, short story collections, translation.

Recent Title(s) *Composing Voices*, by Robert Pack (poetry); *Thistle*, by Melissa Kwasny; *A Change of Maps*, by Carolyne Wright.

N LUCKY PRESS, LLC

Lucky Press, LLC, P.O. Box 754, Athens OH 45701-0754. Website: www.luckypress.com. **Contact:** Janice Phelps Williams, editor-in-chief. trade paperback originals. **Publishes 4 titles/year. 24 queries/year; 10 mss/year. 95% of books from first-time authors. 100% from unagented writers. 0-$500** Publishes book 6 months after acceptance of ms. Accepts simultaneous submissions. Catalog available online at website. Guidelines are online at website.

- "We offer personal attention, hope, and encouragement to writers we publish. In return, we ask authors to know their competition, understand what we can provide, and be committed to marketing their book."
- O→ "Lucky Press is a small, independent publisher and a good option for hard-working, talented writers. Our books are sold primarily through Amazon and authors must be comfortable maintaining a blog, and creating social networks to promote their book."

Nonfiction Subjects include animals, crafts, creative nonfiction, health, medicine, regional (OH), spirituality. Submit proposal package, including outline, 2 sample chapters, author bio, 1-page synopsis, list of comparative/competitive titles. Does not review artwork.

Fiction TrueSubjects include historical, literary, mainstream/contemporary, mystery, poetry, regional Ohio or Appalachia, romance, short story collections, young adult. "We'll consider any well-written ms. We are looking for literary fiction, particularly by Ohio authors. Mss should be 30,000-95,000 words; but query with only the first 3 chapters." Submit synopsis, 3 sample chapters, author bio.

Recent Title(s) *For the Love of Greys: The Complete Guide to a Healthy and Happy African Grey*, by Bobbi Brinker (nonfiction/pets); *I Didn't Order This Pink Ribbon*, by Alice Krumm (nonficton/cancer); *The Life and Times of Mister*, by JRM (YA fiction/cats); *Turner's Defense*, by Chris Davey (historical fiction); *The Killing of Strangers*, by Jerry Holt (fiction: Ohio).

Tips "The author is the biggest key to success in our book sales and our best-selling books are by authors with a strong web presence."

THE MAGNI GROUP, INC.

7106 Wellington Point Rd., McKinney TX 75070. (972)540-2050. Fax: (972)540-1057. E-mail: info@magnico.com. Website: www.magnico.com. **Contact:** Evan Reynolds, president. Publishes hardcover originals and trade paperback reprints. **Publishes 5-10 titles/year. 20 queries received/year. 10-20 mss received/year. 50% of books from first-time authors. 80% from unagented writers. Pays royalty on wholesale price. Makes outright purchase. Pays advance.** Publishes book 6 months after acceptance of ms. Responds in 2 months to queries. Book catalog and ms guidelines online.

Imprints Magni Publishing.

Nonfiction Subjects include cooking, foods, nutrition, health, medicine, money, finance, sex, Weight Loss. Submit complete ms. Reviews artwork/photos. Send photocopies.

Recent Title(s) *Natural Remedies From Around the World*; *Natural Cures for Your Dog & Cat*.

MAGNUS PRESS

P.O. Box 2666, Carlsbad CA 92018. (760)806-3743. Fax: (760)806-3689. E-mail: magnuspres@aol.com. Website: www.magnuspress.com. **Contact:** Warren Angel, editorial director. Estab. 1997. Publishes trade paperback originals and reprints. **Publishes 1-3 titles/year. 200 queries received/year. 220 mss received/year. 44% of books from first-time authors. 89% from unagented writers. Pays 6-15% royalty on retail price.** Publishes book 12 months after acceptance of ms. Accepts simultaneous submissions. Responds in 1 month to queries. Responds in 1 month to proposals. Responds in 1 month to manuscripts. Book catalog and ms guidelines for #10 SASE.

Imprints Canticle Books.

Nonfiction Subjects include religion, from a Christian perspective. Submit proposal package, outline, sample chapters, bio.

Recent Title(s) *God's Love in the End Times* (biblical studies); *Adventures of an Alaskan Preacher* (inspirational); *Sports Stories and the Bible*, by Stan Nix (inspirational).

Tips Magnus Press's audience is mainly Christian lay persons, but also includes anyone interested in spirituality and/or Biblical studies and the church. Study our listings and catalog; learn to write effectively for an average reader; read any one of our published books.

N MAIN STREET RAG PUBLISHING COMPANY

P.O. Box 690100, Charlotte NC 28227-7001. (704)573-2516. E-mail: www.mainstreetrag.com. Website: www.mainstreetrag.com. **Contact:** Publisher/Managing Editor: M. Scott Douglas. Estab. 1996. Responds in 3-6 weeks to queries.

Imprints Pure Heart Press (We will publish anything the author or editor is willing to finance.)

- There are 4 ways to get a book of poetry published:1) self-publish using our imprint;2) Enter one of our contests;3) Be invited;4) Be recommended.

Nonfiction Subjects include art, architecture, (we prefer eclectic art, architecture.), creative nonfiction, photography, interview, reviews, essays. Query with SASE. Reviews artwork/photos.

Fiction Subjects include literary, poetry, cartoons, short fiction. We will have 3 new themes starting Jan. 2009: The Commute; Food; Coming Home. (Do not submit until then.) See Current themes online. Address to Short Fiction Anthology for consideration for our anthology. Query with SASE. Submit 2 short stories (6,-

Recent Title(s) *Spinning Words into Gold*, by Maureen Ryan Griffin (A Hands on Guide to the Craft of Writing); *Charlotte's Holy Wars: Religion in a New South City*, by Frye Gaillard; *Bathe in it or sleep*, by Kim Friedman (poetry).

Tips You can request a free electronic newsletter which is a reference for writes, readers and publishers by providing limited information and directing them to links and emails. Current features include: Call for Submissions; Contests; and New Releases. (No email submissions unless overseas, reviews, images, subscribers to *The Mainstreet Rag*. In all cases, query prior to submitting for instructions.

MAISONNEUVE PRESS

P.O. Box 426, College Park MD 20741. (301)277-7505. Fax: (301)277-2467. E-mail: editors@maisonneuvepress.com. Website: www.maisonneuvepress.com. **Contact:** Robert Merrill, editor (politics, literature, philosophy, intellectual history); Dennis Crow, editor (architecture, urban studies, sociology). Publishes hardcover and trade paperback originals. **Publishes 6 titles/year. 5% of books from first-time authors. 100% from unagented writers. Pays 5% royalty on cover price.** Publishes book 1 year after acceptance of ms. Accepts simultaneous submissions. Responds in 1 month to queries. Responds in 1 month to proposals. Responds in 1 month to manuscripts. Book catalog available free. Send letter for guidelines, individual response.

- "Maisonneuve provides solid, first-hand information for serious adult readers: academics and political activists. We do not publish poetry, fiction, or autobiography."

Nonfiction Subjects include education, government, politics, history, language, literature, military, war, philosophy, psychology, sociology, translation, womens issues, womens studies, intellectual history, literary

Small Presses

criticism, social theory, economics, essay collections. Query with SASE. Submit complete ms. Reviews artwork/photos.
Recent Title(s) *The Perpetual Consequences of Fear and Violence: Rethinking the Future*, by Chris Mase; *Iraq and the International Oil System: Why America Went to War in the Gulf*, by Stephen Pelletiere; *Principles of Socialism: Manifesto of 19th Century Democracy*, by Victor Considerant (translation of French original); *Endearing Freedom or Enduring War: The Prospects and Costs of the New American Century*, edited by Carl Mirra.

MANAGEMENT ADVISORY PUBLICATIONS

P.O. Box 81151, Wellesley Hills MA 02481-0001. (781)345-3895. Fax: (781)235-5445. Website: www.masp.com. **Contact:** Jay Kuong, editor (corporate governance, compliance, security, audit, IT, business continuity). Mass market paperback originals. **Publishes 2-10 titles/year. 25 queries/year; 10 mss/year. 5% of books from first-time authors.** Publishes book 3-6 months after acceptance of ms. Catalog not available. Guidelines not available.
Nonfiction Subjects include business, computers, economics, electronics. Submit proposal package.
Recent Title(s) *Achieve a Green Enterprise and a Greene IT Infrastructure.*
Tips Our audience is primarily business and IT professionals and University and Company libraries.

MARINE TECHNIQUES PUBLISHING

126 Western Ave., Suite 266, Augusta ME 04330-7249. (207)622-7984. Fax: (207)621-0821. E-mail: info@marinetechpublishing.com. Website: www.marinetechpublishing.com. **Contact:** James L. Pelletier, president/owner(commercial maritime); Maritime Associates Globally (commercial maritime). Estab. 1983. Trade paperback originals and reprints. **Publishes 2-5 titles/year. 100+ queries received/year. 40+ mss received/year. 50% of books from first-time authors. 75% from unagented writers. Pays 25-55% royalty on wholesale or retail price. Makes outright purchase.** Publishes book 6-12 months after acceptance of ms. Accepts simultaneous submissions. Responds in 2 months to queries, 2 months to proposals, and 2 months to manuscripts. Book catalog available online, by email, and for #10 SASE for $5. Guidelines available by email, and for #10 SASE for $5.

O‑ Publishes only books related to the commercial marine/maritime industry.

Nonfiction Subjects include maritime education, marine subjects, counseling, career guidance, maritime labor, marine engineering, global water transportation, marine subjects, water transportation. Submit proposal package, including all sample chapters; submit completed ms. Reviews artwork/photos as part of the ms package; send photocopies.
Fiction Subjects include adventure, military, war, maritime. Must be commercial maritime/marine related. Submit proposal package, including all sample chapters. Submit complete ms.
Recent Title(s) *Tugging On A Heartstring: The Sequel*, by E.V. Lambert (bio); *An Officer.Not a Gentleman*, by L.J. Lester (bio); *Mariner's Employment Guide*, by J.L. Pelletier (commercial marine employment reference)
Tips Audience consists of commercial marine/maritime firms, persons employed in all aspects of the marine/maritime commercial water-transportation-related industries and recreational fresh and salt water fields, persons interested in seeking employment in the commercial marine industry; firms seeking to sell their products and services to vessel owners, operators, and managers; shipyards, vessel repair yards, recreational and yacht boat building and national and international ports and terminals involved with the commercial marine industry globally worldwide, etc.

MARLOR PRESS, INC.

4304 Brigadoon Dr., St. Paul MN 55126. (651)484-4600. E-mail: marlin.marlor@minn.net. **Contact:** Marlin Bree, publisher. Estab. 1981. Publishes trade paperback originals. **Publishes 2 titles/year. 100 queries received/year. 25 mss received/year. 100% of books from first-time authors. Pays 8-10% royalty on wholesale price.** Publishes book 1 year after acceptance of ms. Responds in 3-6 weeks to queries.

O‑ Currently emphasizing general interest nonfiction children's books and nonfiction boating books.

Nonfiction Subjects include travel, boating. Query first; submit outline with sample chapters only when requested. Do not send full ms. Reviews artwork/photos.
Recent Title(s) *Notable New York*, by Stephen W. Plumb; *The Dangerous Book For Boaters*, by Marlin Bree.

MAUPIN HOUSE PUBLISHING, INC.

2416 NW 71 Place, Gainesville FL 32653. (800)524-0634. Fax: (352)373-5546. E-mail: info@maupinhouse.com. Website: www.maupinhouse.com. **Contact:** Julia Graddy, publisher. Publishes trade paperback originals and reprints. **Publishes 7 titles/year. Pays 10% royalty on retail price.** Responds in 1-2 weeks to queries.

O‑ Maupin House publishes professional resource books for language arts teachers K-12.

Nonfiction Subjects include education, language, literature, writing workshop. Query with SASE or via e-mail.
Recent Title(s) *That's a Great Answer!*; *Flip for Comprehension.*

[N] MAYHAVEN PUBLISHING

P.O. Box 557, Mahomet IL 61853. (217)586-4493. Fax: (217)586-630. E-mail: mayhavenpublishing@mchsi.com. Website: www.mayhavenpublishing.com/pages/about/mayhave%20html. **Contact:** Doris Replogle Wenzel.

Imprints Wild Rose.

- "Mayhaven publishes books and audio books for adults and children by established and first-time authors. From 1997 to 2007 we also offered Mayhaven's Awards for Fiction. We are temporarily suspending the awards, but all other publishing will continue."

Tips "We publish both fiction and nonfiction books and audio books."

MEDICAL GROUP MANAGEMENT ASSOCIATION

104 Inverness Terrace E., Englewood CO 80112. (303)799-1111. Fax: (303)397-1823. E-mail: maust@mgma.com. Website: www.mgma.com. **Contact:** Marilee Aust, publisher (finance, risk and information management, governance, and organizational dynamics); Craig Wiberg, Sr. Knowledge manager (human resources, business and clinical operations, professional ethics/responsibility). Estab. 1926. Publishes professional and scholarly hardcover, paperback, and electronic originals, and trade paperback reprints. **Publishes 6 titles/year. 18 queries received/year. 6 mss received/year. 30% of books from first-time authors. 100% from unagented writers. Pays 8-17% royalty on net sales (twice a year). Pays $2,000-5,000 advance.** Publishes book 6 months after acceptance of ms. Accepts simultaneous submissions. Responds in less than 3 weeks to queries. Responds in 2 months to proposals. Responds in 2 months to manuscripts. Book catalog available online. Writer's guidelines online or via e-mail.

Nonfiction Subjects include audio, business, economics, education, health. Submit proposal package, outline, 3 sample chapters. Submit complete ms. Reviews artwork/photos. Send photocopies.

Recent Title(s) *Data Sanity*, by Davis Balestracchi; *Electronic Health Records*, by Margret Amatakul and Steve Lazarus.

Tips Audience includes medical practice managers and executives. Our books are geared at the business side of medicine.

[N] MEDICAL PHYSICS PUBLISHING

4513 Vernon Blvd., Madison WI 53705. (608)262-4021. Fax: (608)265-2121. Website: www.medicalphysics.org. **Contact:** Betsey Phelps, managing editor. Estab. 1985. Publishes hardcover and paperback originals and reprints. **Publishes 5-6 titles/year. 10-20 queries received/year. 100% from unagented writers. Pays 10% royalty on wholesale price.** Publishes book 1 year after acceptance of ms. Accepts simultaneous submissions. Responds in 6 months to manuscripts. Book catalog available via website or upon request.

- We are a nonprofit, membership organization publishing affordable books in medical physics and related fields. Currently emphasizing biomedical engineering. De-emphasizing books for the general public.

Nonfiction Subjects include health, medicine, symposium proceedings in the fields of medical physics and radiology. Submit complete ms. Reviews artwork/photos. Send Send disposable copies.

Recent Title(s) *A Practical Guide to Intensity-Modulated Radiation Therapy*, by members of the staff of Memorial Sloan-Kettering Cancer Center; *Physics of the Body*, by John R. Cameron, James G. Skofronick and Roderick M. Grant.

MEMORY MAKERS BOOKS

Imprint of F + W Media, Inc. 4700 E. Galbraith Rd., Cincinnati OH 45236. Website: www.memorymakersmagazine.com. **Contact:** Christine Doyle, editorial director. Estab. 1998. Publishes trade paperback originals. **Publishes 3 titles/year. 70% of books from first-time authors. 95% from unagented writers. Pays royalty or flat fee. Pays advance.** Publishes book 12-15 months after acceptance of ms. Accepts simultaneous submissions. Responds in 2 months to queries.

- "Memory Makers Books exclusively publishes titles for the consumer scrapbooking industry in the form of fresh and innovative scrapbooking books. Authors who submit proposal packages must be outstanding scrapbook artists, as well as apt photographers and writers. Authors must possess a well-rounded knowledge of the industry in order to present their special book idea in a concise and complete proposal package to ensure proper evaluation."

Nonfiction Submit a proposal package that includes 40-word synopsis of the book; detailed outline (front and back matter, chapters, sidebars) for a 128-page book; no less than 10 pieces of sample art (jpgs) that illustrate the subject/techniques to be covered in the book; a brief biography and published clips."Subjects include crafts/scrapbooking.

Recent Title(s) *Scrapbook Page Maps*, by Becky Fleck; *Making the Most of Your Scrapbook Supplies*, by Memory Makers Masters; *Scrap Simple*, by Hillary Heidelberg.

Tips "Our readers are savvy scrapbook and paper artists—from beginning to advanced—who are on the lookout for cutting-edge scrapbooking techniques with photo illustration that they can re-create in their own albums with their own photos and journaling. Study our books to see how we present material, then pitch us something fresh, innovative and unlike anything other consumer scrapbooking publishers are producing."

MEYERBOOKS, PUBLISHER

P.O. Box 427, Glenwood IL 60425-0427. (708)757-4950. **Contact:** David Meyer, publisher. Estab. 1976. Publishes hardcover and trade paperback originals and reprints. **Publishes 2 titles/year. Pays 10-15% royalty on wholesale or retail price.** Responds in 3 months to queries.

Imprints David Meyer Magic Books; Waltham Street Press.

- We are currently publishing books on stage magic history. We only consider subjects which have never been presented in book form before. We are not currently considering books on health, herbs, cookery, or general Americana.

Nonfiction Query with SASE.

Recent Title(s) *Inclined Toward Magic: Encounters With Books, Collectors and Conjurors' Lives*, by David Meyer; *Houdini and the Indescribable Phenomenon*, by Robert Lund.

MID-LIST PRESS

4324 12th Ave S., Minneapolis MN 55407-3218. (612)822-3733. Fax: (612)823-8387. Website: www.midlist.org. Estab. 1989. Publishes hardcover and trade paperback originals. **Publishes 3 titles/year.** Publishes book 12-18 months after acceptance of ms. Accepts simultaneous submissions. Guidelines available online.

- "Mid-List Press publishes books of high literary merit and fresh artistic vision by new and emerging writers."

Fiction See guidelines.

Recent Title(s) *Impetuous Sleeper*, by Donald Morrill (essays); *The Writer's Brush: Paintings, Drawings, and Sculpture by Writers*, by Donald Friedman (literature/art); *Pink Harvest: Tales of Happenstance*, by Toni Mirosevich (creative nonfiction); *Handwork*, by Mary Logue (poetry); *To Taste the Water: Poems*, by Norman Minnick (poetry).

Tips "Mid-List Press is an independent press. Mid-List Press publishes fiction, poetry, and creative nonfiction."

MILKWEEDS FOR YOUNG READERS

Milkweed Editions 1011 Washington Ave. S., Suite 300, Minneapolis MN 55415. (612)332-3192. Fax: (612)215-2550. Website: www.milkweed.org. **Contact:** The editors. Estab. 1984. Publishes hardcover and trade paperback originals. **Publishes 3-4 titles/year. 25% of books from first-time authors. 50% from unagented writers. Pays 7% royalty on retail price. Pays variable advance.** Publishes book 1 year after acceptance of ms. Accepts simultaneous submissions. Responds in 6 months to queries. Book catalog for $1.50. Guidelines for #10 SASE or on the website.

- "We are looking first of all for high quality literary writing. We publish books with the intention of making a humane impact on society."

Fiction Subjects include adventure, fantasy, historical, humor, mainstream, contemporary, animal, environmental. Query with SASE.

Recent Title(s) *Perfect*, by Natasha Friend; *The Lot*, by Jutta Richter.

MISSOURI HISTORICAL SOCIETY PRESS

The Missouri Historical Society P.O. Box 11940, St. Louis MO 63112-0040. (314)746-4558 or (314)746-4556. Fax: (314)746-4548. E-mail: vwmonks@mohistory.org. Website: www.mohistory.org. **Contact:** Victoria Monks, publications manager. Publishes hardcover originals and reprints and trade paperback originals and reprints. **Publishes 2-4 titles/year. 30 queries received/year. 20 mss received/year. 10% of books from first-time authors. 80% from unagented writers. Pays 5-10% royalty.** Responds in 1 month to queries. Responds in 1 month to proposals. Responds in 2 months to manuscripts.

Nonfiction Subjects include art, architecture, history, language, literature, multicultural, regional, sports, womens issues, womens studies, popular culture, photography, children's nonfiction. Query with SASE and request author-proposal form.

Recent Title(s) *Lewis and Clark: Across the Divide*, by Carolyn Gilman (regional history); *The Enemy Among Us: POWs in Missouri During World War II*, by David Fiedler (regional history); *A Song of Faith and Hope*, by Frankie Muse Freeman (memoir/African-American history).

Tips We're looking for new perspectives, even if the topics are familiar. You'll get our attention with nontraditional voices and views.

MOMENTUM BOOKS, LLC

117 W. Third St., Royal Oak MI 48067. (800)758-1870. Fax: (248)691-4531. E-mail: info@momentumbooks.com. Website: www.momentumbooks.com. **Contact:** Franklin Foxx, editor. Estab. 1987. **Publishes 6 titles/year. 100 queries received/year. 30 mss received/year. 95% of books from first-time authors. 100% from unagented**

writers. **Pays 10-15% royalty.** Guidelines available online.

Momentum Books publishes Midwest regional nonfiction.

Nonfiction Subjects include history, sports, travel, automotive, current events, biography, entertainment. Submit proposal package, outline, 3 sample chapters, marketing outline.

Recent Title(s) *Turning White*, by Lee Thomas; *Sirens of Chrome*, by Margery Krevsky; *Eight Dogs Named Jack*, by Joe Borri; *Michigan's Columbus*, by Steve Lehto.

MONTANA HISTORICAL SOCIETY PRESS

225 N. Roberts St., Helene MT 59620-1201. (406)444-4741. E-mail: cwhitehorn@state.mt.us. Website: www.montanahistoricalsociety.org. **Contact:** Clark Whitehorn. Estab. 1956. Publishes hardcover originals, trade paperback originals and trade paperback reprints. **Publishes 4 titles/year. 24 queries received/year. 16 mss received/year. 50% of books from first-time authors. 100% from unagented writers. Pays 5-10% royalty on wholesale price.** Publishes book 1 year after acceptance of ms. Responds in 1 month to queries. Responds in 2 months to proposals. Responds in 4 months to manuscripts. Book catalog available online. Guidelines available online.

Nonfiction Subjects include anthropology, archeology, history, military, war, nature, environment, regional, travel. Query with SASE.

Recent Title(s) *Hope in Hard Times*, by Mary Murphy (photo and interpretive essays about Depression-era photographers); *Tenderfoot in Montana*, by Francis Thomson (historical account of the Vigilante era in Montana).

Tips Audience includes history buffs; people with an interest in Yellowstone National Park.

MOUNTAINLAND PUBLISHING, INC.

P.O. Box 150891, Ogden UT 84415. E-mail: editor@mountainlandpublishing.com. **Contact:** Michael Combe, managing editor (fiction & nonfiction). Mass market paperback and electronic originals. **Publishes 6-10 titles/year. 50% of books from first-time authors. 100% from unagented writers.** Publishes book 3 months after acceptance of ms. Accepts simultaneous submissions. Catalog available online at website. Guidelines available online at website.

Nonfiction Subjects include Americana, creative nonfiction, education, history, humanities, literary criticism, memoirs, military, philosophy, regional, religion, science, spirituality, war, world affairs. Query with SASE. Submit proposal package, including outline, 3 sample chapters. Reviews artwork/photos. Send photocopies.

Fiction Subjects include adventure, contemporary, fantasy, historical, horror, humor, juvenile, literary, mainstream, military, multicultural, mystery, regional, religious, romance, science fiction, short story collections, spiritual, sports, suspense, war, western, young adult. Query with SASE. Submit synopsis, 1 sample chapter.

Recent Title(s) *Tales of Two-Bit Street*.

MOUNT OLIVE COLLEGE PRESS

Mount Olive College, 634 Henderson St., Mount Olive NC 28365. (919)658-2502. **Contact:** Dr. Pepper Worthington, director (nonfiction, fiction, poetry, children's stories). Estab. 1990. Publishes trade paperback originals. **Publishes 3 titles/year. 2,500 queries received/year. 75% of books from first-time authors.**

Nonfiction Subjects include creative nonfiction, history, humanities, language, literature, literary criticism, memoirs, philosophy, psychology, religion, sociology, travel, womens issues, womens studies. Submit sample chapters, 3 sample chapters. Reviews artwork/photos. Send photocopies.

Fiction Subjects include literary, poetry, religious, short story collections, spiritual. Submit 3 sample chapters.

MSI PRESS

1760 Airline Hwy., F-203, Hollister CA 95023. Website: www.msipress.com. **Contact:** Betty Leaver, managing ed. (foreign language, humanities, humor, spirituality). Trade paperback originals. **Publishes 8-12 titles/year. 10% of books from first-time authors. 100% from unagented writers.** Publishes book 6 months after acceptance of ms. Accepts simultaneous submissions. Catalog available online at website. Guidelines available at e-mail address: info@msipress.com.

Nonfiction Subjects include education, health, medicine, humanities, language, literature, medicine, psychology, spirituality. Submit proposal package, including: outline, 1 sample chapter, and professional resume. Reviews artwork/photos; send computer disk.

Fiction We have no current plans to publish any more fiction.

Recent Title(s) *Blest Atheist*, by Elizabeth Mahlou (spirituality); *What Works: Helping Students Achieve Near-Native Foreign Language Proficiency*, by CDLC Staff (Scholarly); *The Rise and Fall of Muslim Civil Society*, by Omar Imady (scholarly/political science); *Mommy Poisoned Our House Guest*, by Shenan Leaver (humor); *Road to Damascus*, by Elaine Rippey Imady (memoir); *Thoughts Without a Title*, by Geri Henderson (general interest/collection of fiction & poetry).

Tips We are interested in helping to develop new writers who have good literacy skills but have limited or no publishing experience. We also have the capacity to work with authors with limited English skills whose first language is Arabic, Russian, Spanish, French, German, or Czech.

NAR ASSOCIATES

P.O. Box 233, Barryville NY 12719. (845)557-8713. Website: www.aodceus.com. **Contact:** Nick Roes, Acq. Ed. Estab. 1977. Publishes trade paperback originals. **Publishes 6 titles/year. 10 queries received/year. 10 mss received/year. 80% of books from first-time authors. 100% from unagented writers. Makes outright purchase of $500.** Publishes book 1 month after acceptance of ms. Accepts simultaneous submissions. Responds in 1 month to queries. Responds in 1 month to proposals. Responds in 1 month to manuscripts. Book catalog available online. Guidelines available via e-mail.

Nonfiction Subjects include education, psychology, counseling techniques, professional ethics. Query with SASE. Reviews artwork/photos. Send photocopies.

Recent Title(s) *Cognitive Behavioral Therapy*, by Sara Pascoe, PhD. (home study course); *Teaching Self Advocacy*, by Edward Guild (home study course).

Tips "Our audience consists of addiction counselors, social workers, and other counseling professionals. Use same format as existing coursework currently in publication."

NATUREGRAPH PUBLISHERS, INC.

P.O. Box 1047, Happy Camp CA 96039. Fax: (530)493-5240. E-mail: nature@sisqtel.net. Website: www.naturegraph.com. **Contact:** Barbara Brown, owner. Estab. 1946. Publishes trade paperback originals. **Publishes 2 titles/year. 300 queries received/year. 12 mss received/year. 80% of books from first-time authors. 0% from unagented writers.** Publishes book 24 months after acceptance of ms. Accepts simultaneous submissions. Responds in 1 month to queries. Responds in 2 months to manuscripts. Book catalog for #10 SASE.

Nonfiction Subjects include anthropology, archaeology, multicultural, nature, environment, science, natural history: biology, geology, ecology, astronomy, crafts.

Recent Title(s) *Modoc: The Tribe That Wouldn't Die; Birds in Nest Boxes: How to Help, Study and Enjoy Birds; Enjoying the Native American-Style Flute; The Winds Erase Your Footprints*.

Tips Please—always send a stamped reply envelope. Publishers get hundreds of manuscripts yearly, not just yours.

THE NAUTICAL & AVIATION PUBLISHING CO.

2055 Middleburg Lane, Mt. Pleasant SC 29464. (843)856-0561. Fax: (843)856-3164. **Contact:** Melissa A. Pluta, acquisitions editor. Estab. 1979. Publishes hardcover originals and reprints. **Publishes 5-10 titles/year. 200 queries received/year. Rarely offers advance.** Accepts simultaneous submissions. Responds in 3 weeks to queries. Book catalog available free.

O→ The Nautical & Aviation Publishing Co. publishes naval and military history, fiction, and reference.

Nonfiction Subjects include military, war, American, naval history. Query with SASE. Submit 3 sample chapters, synopsis. Reviews artwork/photos.

Fiction Subjects include historical, military, war, Revolutionary War, War of 1812, Civil War, WW I and II, Persian Gulf, and Marine Corps history. Looks for novels with a strong military history orientation. Submit complete ms with cover

Recent Title(s) *The Civil War in the Carolinas*, by Dan L. Morrill; *Fix Bayonets!*, by John W. Thomason.

Tips We are primarily a nonfiction publisher, but we will review historical fiction of military interest with strong literary merit.

NEW ENGLAND CARTOGRAPHICS, INC.

P.O. Box 9369, North Amherst MA 01059. (413)549-4124. Fax: (413)549-3621. E-mail: geolopes@crocker.com. Website: www.necartographics.com. **Contact:** Chris Ryan, editor; Valerie Vaughan. Publishes trade paperback originals and reprints. **Publishes 3 titles/year. Pays 5-10% royalty on retail price.** Accepts simultaneous submissions. Responds in 2 weeks to queries.

Nonfiction Subjects include nature, environment, recreation, regional, sports. Query with SASE. Submit sample chapters. Reviews artwork/photos. Send photocopies.

Recent Title(s) *Waterfalls of Massachussetts*, by Joseph Bushee, Jr.; *Hiking the SuAsCo Watershed*, by Jill Phelps-Kern; *Birding Western Massachussetts*, by Robert Tougias.

N NEW ISSUES POETRY & PROSE

Western Michigan Univ., 1903 W. Michigan Ave., Kalamazoo MI 49008-5463, United States. (269)387-8185. Fax: (269)387-2562. E-mail: new-issues@wmich.edu. Website: www.wmich.edu/newissues. **Contact:** Managing Editor. Hardcover and trade paperback originals. **Publishes 8 titles/year. 50% of books from first-time authors. 95% from unagented writers.** Publishes book 18 months after acceptance of ms. Accepts simultaneous submissions. Online & free on request. Online, by email, free on request for #10 SASE.

Fiction Subjects include literary, poetry, poetry in translation. All unsolicited mss returned unopened.
Recent Title(s) *The Truth*, by Geoff Rips; *One Tribe*, by M. Evelinn Galang; *Tall If*, by Mark Irwin; *Please*, by Jericho Brown

NEW VICTORIA PUBLISHERS INC.

P.O. Box 13173, Chicago IL 60613. Website: www.newvictoria.com. **Contact:** Patricia Feuerhaken. Trade paperback and hardcover originals. Catalog free on request; for #10 SASE; or online at website. Guidelines free on request; for #10 SASE; or online.
Nonfiction Subjects include alternative, biography, lesbian, history, language, poetry, fiction, literature, memoirs, multicultural, music/dance, mystery, nature, environment, New Age, erotica, translation, womens issues/studies, world affairs, contemporary culture. Query with SASE. Reviews artwork/photos; send photocopies.
Fiction Subjects include adventure, comic books, erotica, fantasy, feminist, gay, ethnic,lesbian, historical, humor, literary, multicultural, mystery, science fiction, spiritual, translation. "We are looking for well-crafted fiction in all genres featuring out lesbian protagonists with a strong sense of self-awareness. Our writers' guidelines are available on our website." Query with SASE.
Recent Title(s) *Queer Japan, by* Barbara Summerhawk, C. McMahill, D. McDonald; *Mommy Deadest*, by Jean Marcy; *Callahoo & Other Lesbian Love Tales*, by LaShonda K. Barnett; *Do Drums Beat There*, by Doe Tabor.
Tips "New writers need to pay attention to structuring your novel and determining the basic conflict."

⊘ NEW VOICES PUBLISHING

Division of KidsTerrain, Inc. P.O. Box 560, Wilmington MA 01887. (978)658-2131. Fax: (978)988-8833. E-mail: rschiano@kidsterrain.com. Website: www.kidsterrain.com. **Contact:** Rita Schiano, executive editor (children's books). Estab. 2000. Publishes hardcover and trade paperback originals. **Publishes 5 titles/year. 95% of books from first-time authors. 95% from unagented writers. Pays 10-15% royalty on wholesale price.** Publishes book 1 year after acceptance of ms. Responds in 1 month to queries. Responds in 3 months to proposals. Responds in 3 months to manuscripts. Book catalog available online. Guidelines available online.

O→ The audience for this company is children ages 4-9, and is not accepting unsolicited mss at this time.
Nonfiction Subjects include child guidance.
Fiction Subjects include juvenile. Query with SASE.
Recent Title(s) *Reaching Home*, by Ron Breazeale.
Tips Know, specifically, what your story/book is about.

NEXT DECADE, INC.

39 Old Farmstead Rd., Chester NJ 07930. (908)879-6625. Fax: (908)879-2920. E-mail: barbara@nextdecade.com. Website: www.nextdecade.com. **Contact:** Barbara Kimmel, president (reference); Carol Rose, editor. Publishes trade paperback originals. **Publishes 2-4 titles/year. Pays 8-15% royalty on wholesale price.** Responds in 1 month to queries. Book catalog available online. Guidelines available online.
Nonfiction Subjects include health, medicine, womens, money, finance, multicultural, senior/retirement issues, real estate.
Recent Title(s) *Retire in Style*, by Warren Bland, PhD; *The Hysterectomy Hoax*, by Stanley West, MD.
Tips We publish books that simplify complex subjects. We are a small, award-winning press that successfully publishes a handful of books each year.

NODIN PRESS

530 N. Third St., Suite 120, Minneapolis MN 55401. (612)333-6300. Fax: (612)333-6303. E-mail: nstill4402@aol.com. **Contact:** Norton Stillman, publisher. Publishes hardcover and trade paperback originals. **Publishes 5 titles/year. 20 queries received/year. 20 mss received/year. 75% of books from first-time authors. 100% from unagented writers. Pays 7 ½% royalty.** Publishes book 6 months after acceptance of ms. Accepts simultaneous submissions. Responds in 6 months to queries. Book catalog and ms guidelines free.

O→ Nodin Press publishes Minnesota regional titles: nonfiction, memoir, sports, poetry.
Nonfiction Subjects include history, ethnic, regional, sports, travel. Query with SASE.
Recent Title(s) *The Great Dan Patch and the Remarkable Mr. Savage*, by Tim Brady; *Tending the Earth, Mending the Spirit*, by Connie Guldman and Richard Mahler; *Kodiak Kings*, by Jason Wood.

NORTH CAROLINA OFFICE OF ARCHIVES AND HISTORY

Historical Publications Section, 4622 Mail Service Center, Raleigh NC 27699-4622. (919)733-7442. Fax: (919)733-1439. E-mail: donna.kelly@ncmail.net. Website: www.ncpublications.com. **Contact:** Donna E. Kelly, administrator (North Carolina and southern history). Publishes hardcover and trade paperback originals. **Publishes 4 titles/year. 20 queries received/year. 25 mss received/year. 5% of books from first-time authors. 100% from unagented writers. Makes one-time payment upon delivery of completed ms.** Publishes book 2 years after acceptance of ms. Accepts simultaneous submissions. Responds in 1 week to queries. Responds in

1 week to proposals. Responds in 2 months to manuscripts. Guidelines for $3.

- We publish *only* titles that relate to North Carolina. The North Carolina Office of Archives and History also publishes the *North Carolina Historical Review*, a scholarly journal of history.

Nonfiction Subjects include history, related to North Carolina, military, war, related to North Carolina, regional, North Carolina and Southern history. Query with SASE. Reviews artwork/photos. Send photocopies.

Recent Title(s) *African Americans in North Carolina*, edited by Alan D. Watson; *A Johnny-Reb Band From Salem*, by Harry H. Hall; *The Old North State Fact Book*, edited by C. Daniel Crews and Lisa D. Bayley.

Tips Audience is public school and college teachers and students, librarians, historians, genealogists, North Carolina citizens, tourists.

NOVA PRESS

11659 Mayfield Ave., Suite 1, Los Angeles CA 90049. (310)207-4078. Fax: (310)571-0908. E-mail: novapress@aol.com. Website: www.novapress.net. **Contact:** Jeff Kolby, president. Estab. 1993. Publishes trade paperback originals. **Publishes 4 titles/year.** Publishes book 6 months after acceptance of ms. Book catalog available free.

- Nova Press publishes only test prep books for college entrance exams (SAT, GRE, GMAT, LSAT, etc.), and closely related reference books, such as college guides and vocabulary books.

Nonfiction Subjects include education, software.

Recent Title(s) *The MCAT Chemistry Book*, by Ajikumar Aryangat.

OAK TREE PRESS

140 E. Palmer, Taylorville IL 62568. (217)824-6500. Fax: (217)824-6500. E-mail: oaktreepub@aol.com. Website: www.oaktreebooks.com. **Contact:** Acquisitions Ed. trade paperback and hardcover books. **No.** Publishes book 6-9 mos. (contract says 18 mos. after signing on) after acceptance of ms. Catalog and guidelines available online.

- "I am always on the lookout for good mysteries, ones that engage fast. I definitely want to add to our Timeless Love list. I am also looking at a lot of nonfiction, especially the in the "how-to" category. We are one of a few publishers who will consider memoirs, especially memoirs of folks who are not famous, and this is because I enjoy reading them myself. In addition, plans are in progress to launch a political/current affairs imprint, and I am actively looking for titles to build this list. Then, of course, there is always that "special something" book that you can't quite describe, but you know it when you see it. "
- "Oak Tree Press is an independent publisher that celebrates writers, and is dedicated to the many great unknowns who are just waiting for the opportunity to break into print. We're looking for mainstream, genre fiction, narrative nonfiction, how-to. Sponsors 3 contests annually: Dark Oak Mystery, Timeless Love Romance and CopTales for true crime and other stories of law enforcement professionals."

Nonfiction True

Fiction True

Tips Perhaps my most extreme pet peeve is receiving queries on projects which we've clearly advertised we don't want: science fiction, fantasy, epic tomes, bigoted diatribes and so on. Second to that is a practice I call "over taping," or the use of yards and yards of tape, or worse yet, the filament tape so that it takes forever to open the package. Finding story pitches on my voice mail is also annoying."

OBERLIN COLLEGE PRESS

50 N. Professor St., Oberlin College, Oberlin OH 44074. (440)775-8408. Fax: (440)775-8124. E-mail: oc.press@oberlin.edu. Website: www.oberlin.edu/ocpress. **Contact:** Linda Slocum, man. ed. Estab. 1969. Publishes hardcover and trade paperback originals. **Publishes 2-3 titles/year. Pays 7½-10% royalty.** Responds promptly to queries. Responds in 1 & ½ months to manuscripts.

Imprints *FIELD: Contemporary Poetry & Poetics*, a magazine published twice annually, FIELD Translation Series, FIELD Poetry Series, FIELD Editions.

- "Even though mss. are considered for the Field Press Series only by invitation, the way we decide what book to publish is through our FIELD Poetry Prize."

Recent Title(s) *Meaning a Cloud*, by John Marshall; *The Extremities*, by Timothy Kelly; *High Lonesome: On the Poetry of Charles Wright*, (poetry).

Tips "Even though mss. are considered for the Field Press Series only by invitation, one can be considered by entering the annual Field Poetry Prize competition."

ONSTAGE PUBLISHING

190 Lime Quarry Road, Suite 106J, Madison AL 35758. (256)308-2300. Website: www.onstagepublishing.com. **Contact:** Dianne Hamilton, senior editor/publisher. Estab. 1999. Publishes mass market paperback originals. **Publishes 3-5 titles/year. 300 queries received/year. 500 mss received/year. 80% of books from first-time authors. 95% from unagented writers. Pays royalty on wholesale price. Pays variable advance.** Publishes book 1-2 years after acceptance of ms. Accepts simultaneous submissions. Responds in 4-6 months to queries.

Responds in 4-6 months to proposals. Responds in 4-6 months to manuscripts. Book catalog available online. Guidelines for #10 SASE or online at website.

Fiction Children's fiction only—Chapter books, middle grades or YA. We're looking for fiction for children ages 8-18. Will accept e-mail queries at: www.onstage123@Knology.net. No picture books or poetry. No short stories.

Recent Title(s) *Flying Boats & Spies*, by Jaime Dodson; *Finder's Magic*, by C.M. Fleming.

Tips "Our audience is third grade to young adult. Study our Web site and get a sense of the kind of books we publish, so that you know whether your manuscript is likely to be right for us."

OOLIGAN PRESS

P.O. Box 751, Portland OR 97207-0751. (503)725-9410. E-mail: ooligan@pdx.edu. Website: www.ooliganpress.pdx.edu. **Contact:** Acquisitions Committee. Estab. 2001. Publishes trade paperback, and electronic originals and reprints. **Publishes 4-6 titles/year. 250-500 queries received/year. 100 mss received/year. 90% of books from first-time authors. 90% from unagented writers. Pays negotiable% royalty on retail price.** Book catalog available online. Guidelines available online.

Nonfiction Subjects include agriculture, alternative, anthropology, archeology, art, architecture, community, contemporary culture, cooking, foods, nutrition, creative nonfiction, education, ethnic, film, cinema, stage, gay, lesbian, government, politics, history, humanities, language, literature, literary criticism, memoirs, multicultural, music, dance, nature, environment, philosophy, regional, religion, social sciences, sociology, spirituality, translation, travel, womens issues, womens studies, world affairs. Query with SASE. Submit proposal package, outline, 4 sample chapters, projected page count, audience, marketing ideas and a list of similar titles. Reviews artwork/photos.

Fiction Subjects include adventure, ethnic, experimental, fantasy, feminist, gay, lesbian, historical, horror, humor, literary, mainstream, contemporary, multicultural, mystery, plays, poetry, poetry in translation, regional, science fiction, short story collections, spiritual, suspense, translation, and middle grade. Query with SASE by traditional

Recent Title(s) *Fort Clatsop: Rebuilding an Icon*, by the Daily Astorian ((nonfiction)); *You Have Time for This*, edited by Mark Budman & Tom Hazuka ((flash fiction)); *Good Friday*, by Tony Wolk ((fiction/alternative history)).

Tips For children's books, our audience will be middle grades and young adult, with marketing to general trade, libraries, and schools. Good marketing ideas increase the chances of a manuscript succeeding.

⊘ ORCHISES PRESS

P.O. Box 320533, Alexandria VA 22320-4533. (703)683-1243. E-mail: lathbury@gmu.edu. Website: mason.gmu.edu/~lathbur. **Contact:** Roger Lathbury, editor-in-chief. Estab. 1983. Publishes hardcover and trade paperback originals and reprints. **Publishes 2-3 titles/year. 1% of books from first-time authors. 95% from unagented writers. Pays 36% of receipts after Orchises has recouped its costs.** Publishes book 1 year after acceptance of ms. Accepts simultaneous submissions. Responds in 3 months to queries. Book catalog for #10 SASE. Guidelines available online.

- *Orchises Press no longer reads unsolicited mss.*

O→ Orchises Press is a general literary publisher specializing in poetry with selected reprints and textbooks. No new fiction or children's books.

Nonfiction Query with SASE. Reviews artwork/photos. Send photocopies.

Recent Title(s) *Library*, by Stephen Akey (nonfiction); *Deniability*, by George Witte (poetry).

N OTTN PUBLISHING

16 Risler St., Stockton NJ 08559. (609)397-4005. Fax: (609)397-4007. E-mail: inquiries@ottnpublishing.com. Website: www.ottnpublishing.com. Hardcover and trade paperback originals. **Publishes 5-10 titles/year. 50 queries received/year 50% of books from first-time authors. 100% from unagented writers.** Publishes book 9 months after acceptance of ms. Accepts simultaneous submissions. Catalog online at website. Guidelines online at website http://www.ottnpublishing.com/contact.htm.

Nonfiction Subjects include government, history, military, politics, war. Query with SASE.

Recent Title(s) *Barack Obama: The Politics of Hope*, by William Michael Davis; *Nathanael Greene: The General Who Saved the Revolution*, by Gregg Mierka; *Sacagawea: Shoshone Explorer*, by Mike Crosby.

Tips Most of our books are published for the school library market, although we do publish some books for an adult audience.

OZARK MOUNTAIN PUBLISHING, INC.

P.O. Box 754, Huntsville AR 72740-0754, U.S. (479)738-2348. Fax: (479)738-2448. E-mail: info@ozarkmt.com. Website: www.ozarkmt.com. **Contact:** Julie Degan, office mgr. (Areas of interest: New age/metaphysics/spiritual). Estab. 1991. Publishes trade paperback originals. **Publishes 8-10 titles/year. 50-75 queries; 150-200 mss 50% of books from first-time authors. 95% from unagented writers. Pays 10-15% royalty on retail**

or wholesale price. Pays $250-500 advance. Publishes book 6-9 months after acceptance of ms. Accepts simultaneous submissions. Responds in 6 months to queries, 7 months on mss. Book catalog free on request. Guidelines available online at website http://www.ozarkmt.com/submissions.htm.

Nonfiction Subjects include new age/metaphysical/body-mind-spirit, philosophy, spirituality. Query with SASE. Submit4-5 sample chapters.

Recent Title(s) *The Convoluted Universe-Book 3*, by Dolores Cannon (metaphysics); *Power of the Magdalene*, by Stuart Wilson & Joann Prentis (spiritual); *Elder Gods of Antiquity*, by M. Don Schorn (ancient history)

Tips We envision our audience to be open minded, spiritually expanding. Please do not call to check on submissions. Do not submit electronically. Send hard copy only.

PAPYRUS/LETTERBOX OF LONDON, USA

Yes You Can 10501 Broom Hill Dr., Suite H, Las Vegas NV 89134-7339. **Contact:** Geoffrey Hutchison-Cleeves, editor-in-chief. Estab. 1946. Publishes hardcover and trade paperback originals. **Publishes 3 titles/year. 80 mss received/year. 1%% of books from first-time authors. 1%% from unagented writers. Pays -10% royalty on wholesale price.** Publishes book 12 months after acceptance of ms. Accepts simultaneous submissions. Responds in 1 month to queries, proposals, and mss. Book catalog for #10 SASE.

Imprints Yes You Can

Nonfiction Subjects include audio, animals, art, architecture, creative nonfiction, music, dance, womens issues, womens studies, Senior singles. Query with SASE. Submit outline. Reviews artwork/photos. Send photocopies.

Fiction Subjects include mainstream, contemporary, plays, and musicals. We are overstocked right now. Query with SASE.

Recent Title(s) *Yes You Can Control Female Incontinence; Out in the Cold*, by Sydney Dawson (adventures in Alaska); *Horse Sense*, by Lynn Burdick; *Mayonnaise*, by Lynn Burdick.

Tips "We publish for educated adults."

PARADISE CAY PUBLICATIONS

P.O. Box 29, Arcata CA 95518-0029. (707)822-7038. Fax: (707)822-9163. E-mail: paracay@humboldt1.com. Website: www.paracay.com. **Contact:** Matt Morehouse, publisher. Publishes hardcover and trade paperback originals and reprints. **Publishes 5 titles/year. 360-480 queries received/year. 240-360 mss received/year. 10% of books from first-time authors. 100% from unagented writers. Pays 10-15% royalty on wholesale price. Makes outright purchase of 1,000-10,000. Pays $0-2,000 advance.** Publishes book 4 months after acceptance of ms. Responds in 1 month to queries. Responds in 1 month to proposals. Responds in 2 months to manuscripts. Book catalog and ms guidelines free on request or online.

Imprints Pardey Books.

Nonfiction Must have strong nautical theme.Subjects include cooking, foods, nutrition, recreation, sports, travel. Query with SASE. Submit proposal package, 2-3 sample chapters . Call first. Reviews artwork/photos. Send photocopies.

Fiction Subjects include adventure, nautical, sailing. All fiction must have a nautical theme. Query with SASE. Submit proposal package, clips, 2-3 sample chapters.

Recent Title(s) *American Practical Navigator*, by Nathaniel Bowditch; *Voyage Toward Vengeance*, (fiction); *Rescue at the Top of the World*.

Tips Audience is recreational sailo Call Matt Morehouse (publisher

PARALLAX PRESS

P.O. Box 7355, Berkeley CA 94707. (510)525-0101, ext. 113. Fax: (510)525-7129. E-mail: rachel@parallax.org. Website: www.parallax.org. **Contact:** Rachel Neumann, senior editor. Estab. 1985. Publishes hardcover and trade paperback originals. **Publishes 5-8 titles/year.** Responds in 6-8 weeks to queries. Book catalog for 1 envelope and 3 First-Class stamps. Ms guidelines for #10 SASE or online.

O→ We focus primarily on engaged Buddhism.

Nonfiction Subjects include multicultural, religion, Buddhism, spirituality. Query with SASE. Submit 1 sample chapter, 1-page proposal. Reviews artwork/photos. Send photocopies.

Recent Title(s) *The World We have*, by Thich Nhat Hanh and Alan Weisman; *World As Lover, World As Self*, by Joanna Macy.

N PEARL EDITIONS

Pearl 3030 E. Second St., Long Beach CA 90803. Website: www.pearlmag.com/pearled.html. **Contact:** Joan Jobe Smith; Marilyn Johnson; Barbara Hauk, co-editors. Estab. 1989. Trade paperback originals (poetry only).

O→ Pearl Poetry Prize ($1,000 plus book publication); Annual Pearl Short Story Contest.

Recent Title(s) *See How We Almost Fly*, by Alison Luterman; *Through the Glorieta Pass*, by Lavonne J. Adams; *Denmark, Kangaroo, Orange*, by Kevin Griffith.

Tips "Our books are not for poetry-lovers only, but also for general readers who are discovering that contemporary poetry can be as readable, dramatic, and entertaining as a good novel or memoir."

PERSPECTIVES PRESS, INC.

P.O. Box 90318, Indianapolis IN 46290-0318. (317)872-3055. E-mail: info@perspectivespress.com. Website: www.perspectivespress.com. **Contact:** Pat Johnston, publisher. Estab. 1982. Publishes hardcover and trade paperback originals. **Publishes 1-4 titles/year. 200 queries received/year. 95% of books from first-time authors. 95% from unagented writers.** Publishes book 1 year after acceptance of ms. Responds in 1 month to queries. Book catalog for #10 SAE and 2 first-class stamps or on website. Guidelines available online.

Our purpose is to promote understanding of infertility issues and alternatives, adoption and closely-related child welfare issues, and to educate and sensitize those personally experiencing these life situations, professionals who work with such clients, and the public at large.

Nonfiction Subjects include child guidance, health, medicine, psychology, sociology. Query with SASE.

Recent Title(s) *Adoption Is a Family Affair*, by Patricia Irwin Johnston; *Having Your Baby Through Egg Donation*, by Ellen Sarasohn Glazer and Evelina Weidman Sterling; *Borya and the Burps*, by Joan MacNamara.

Tips For adults, we are seeking infertility and adoption decision-making materials, books dealing with adoptive or foster parenting issues, books to use with children, books to share with others to help explain infertility, adoption, foster care, third party reproductive assistance, special programming or training manuals, etc. For children, we will consider adoption or foster care-related fiction manuscripts that are appropriate for preschoolers and early elementary school children. We do not consider YA. Nonfiction manuscripts are considered for all ages. No autobiography, memoir or adult fiction. While we would consider a manuscript from a writer who was not personally or professionally involved in these issues, we would be more inclined to accept a manuscript submitted by an infertile person, an adoptee, a birthparent, an adoptive parent, or a professional working with any of these.

PHILOSOPHY DOCUMENTATION CENTER

P.O. Box 7147, Charlottesville VA 22906-7147. (434)220-3300. Fax: (434)220-3301. E-mail: order@pdcnet.org. Website: www.pdcnet.org. **Contact:** Dr. George Leaman, director. Estab. 1966. **Publishes 4 titles/year. 4-6 queries received/year. 4-6 mss received/year. 50% of books from first-time authors. Pays 2 ½-10% royalty. Pays advance.** Publishes book 1 year after acceptance of ms. Responds in 2 months to queries. Book catalog available free.

The Philosophy Documentation Center works in cooperation with publishers, database producers, software developers, journal editors, authors, librarians, and philosophers to create an electronic clearinghouse for philosophical publishing.

Nonfiction Subjects include philosophy, software. Query with SASE. Submit outline.

Recent Title(s) *Proceedings of the World Congress of Philosophy*; *2002-2003 Directory of American Philosophers*.

PICCADILLY BOOKS, LTD.

P.O. Box 25203, Colorado Springs CO 80936-5203. (719)550-9887. Website: www.piccadillybooks.com. **Contact:** Submissions Department. Estab. 1985. Publishes hardcover originals and trade paperback originals and reprints. **Publishes 5-8 titles/year. 70% of books from first-time authors. 95% from unagented writers. Pays 6-10% royalty on retail price.** Publishes book 1 year after acceptance of ms. Accepts simultaneous submissions. Responds only if interested, unless accompanied by a SASE to queries.

"Picadilly publishes nonfiction, diet, nutrition, and health-related books with a focus on alternative and natural medicine."

Nonfiction Subjects include cooking, foods, nutrition, health, medicine, performing arts. Submit outline and sample chapters.

Recent Title(s) *Cocnut Water for Health and Healing*, by Bruce Fife, ND.

Tips "We publish nonfiction, general interest, self-help books currently emphasizing alternative health."

PLANNING/COMMUNICATIONS

7215 Oak Ave., River Forest IL 60305-1935. (708)366-5200. Fax: (708)366-5280. E-mail: dl@planningcommunications.com. Website: jobfindersonline.com. **Contact:** Daniel Lauber, president. Estab. 1979. Publishes hardcover, trade, and mass market paperback originals, trade paperback reprints. **Publishes 3-6 titles/year. 30 queries received/year. 20 mss received/year. 50% of books from first-time authors. 100% from unagented writers.** Publishes book 1 year after acceptance of ms. Accepts simultaneous submissions. Responds in 4 months to queries. Book catalog for $2 or free on website. Guidelines available online.

Planning/Communications publishes books on careers, improving your life, dream fulfillment, ending discrimination, sociology, urban planning, and politics.

Nonfiction Subjects include business, economics, careers, education, government, politics, money, finance, sociology, ending discrimination. Submit outline, 3 sample chapters, SASE. Reviews artwork/photos. Send

photocopies.
Recent Title(s) *Education Job Finder: Where the Jobs are in Primary, Secondary, and Higher Education*, by Daniel Lauber, Diana Lauber, and Deborah Verlench; *Dream It Do It: Inspiring Stories of Dreams Come True*, by Sharon Cook and Graciela Sholander; *How to Get a Job in Europe*, by Cheryl Matherly and Robert Sanborn.
Tips Our editorial mission is to publish books that can make a difference in people's lives—books of substance, not glitz.

N ⊘ PLATYPUS MEDIA, LLC

627 A St. NE, Washington DC 20002. (202)546-1674. Fax: (202)546-2356. E-mail: info@platypusmedia.com. Website: www.platypusmedia.com. **Contact:** Tracey Kilby, editorial assistant (children's—early childhood and science, birth, lactation). Estab. 2000. Publishes hardcover and trade paperback originals. **Publishes 3-4 titles/year. 100 queries received/year. 250 mss received/year. 5% of books from first-time authors. 100% from unagented writers. Pays royalty on wholesale price. Makes outright purchase.** Publishes book 9 months after acceptance of ms. Accepts simultaneous submissions. Responds in 2-4 months to queries. Responds in 2-4 months to proposals. Responds in 2-4 months to manuscripts. Book catalog available free. Guidelines available online.

O-▪ All content should focus on family closeness and child development.

Nonfiction Subjects include child guidance, education, health, medicine, womens issues, womens studies, breastfeeding, childbirth, children's science books. Query with SASE. *All unsolicited mss returned unopened.* Reviews artwork/photos. Send photocopies.
Fiction Subjects include juvenile. Query with SASE. *All unsolicited mss returne*
Recent Title(s) *One Minute Mysteries*, by Eric Yoder and Natalie Yoder; *Look What I See! Where Can I Be? Visiting China*, by Dia L. Michels; *I Was Born to Be a Brother*, by Zaydek G. Michels-Gualtieri.
Tips Audience includes parents, children, teachers, and parenting professionals. We publish just a handful of books each year and most are generated in-house.

PLEXUS PUBLISHING, INC.

143 Old Marlton Pike, Medford NJ 08055-8750. (609)654-6500. Fax: (609)654-4309. E-mail: jbryans@plexuspublishing.com. Website: www.plexuspublishing.com. **Contact:** John B. Bryans, editor-in-chief/publisher. Estab. 1977. Publishes hardcover and paperback originals. **Publishes 4-5 titles/year. 70% of books from first-time authors. 90% from unagented writers. Pays $500-1,000 advance.** Accepts simultaneous submissions. Responds in 3 months to proposals. Book catalog and book proposal guidelines for 10x13 SAE with 4 first-class stamps.

O-▪ Plexus publishes regional-interest (southern New Jersey and the greater Philadelphia area) fiction and nonfiction including mysteries, field guides, nature, travel and history. Also a limited number of titles in health/medicine, biology, ecology, botany, astronomy.

Nonfiction Query with SASE.
Fiction Mysteries and literary novels with a strong regional (southern New Jersey) angle. Query with SASE.
Recent Title(s) *The Philadelphian*, by Richard Powell; *Boardwalk Empire*, by Nelson Johnson.

N POCOL PRESS

6023 Pocol Dr., Clifton VA 20124-1333. (703)830-5862. E-mail: chrisandtom@erols.com. Website: www.pocolpress.com. **Contact:** J. Thomas Hetrick, editor. Estab. 1999. Publishes trade paperback originals. **Publishes 6 titles/year. 90 queries received/year. 20 mss received/year. 90% of books from first-time authors. 100% from unagented writers. Pays 10-12% royalty on wholesale price.** Publishes book less than 12 months after acceptance of ms. Responds in 1 month to queries. Responds in 2 months to manuscripts. Book catalog available online. Guidelines available online.
Fiction Subjects include historical, horror, literary, mainstream, contemporary, military, war, mystery, short story collections, thematic, spiritual, sports, western, Baseball fiction. We specialize in thematic short fiction collections by a single author and baseball fiction. Expert storytellers welcome. Query with SASE.
Recent Title(s) *A Whole New Ballgame: The 1969 Washington Senators*, by Stephen Walker (baseball/biography); *Episode*, by Robert Garner McBrearty (short stories); *From the Quickening*, by Thomas Sheehan (short stories).
Tips Our audience is aged 18 and over.

POLYCHROME PUBLISHING CORP.

4509 N. Francisco, Chicago IL 60625. (773)478-4455. Fax: (773)478-0786. Website: www.polychromebooks.com. Estab. 1990. Publishes hardcover originals and reprints. **Publishes 4 titles/year. 3,000 queries received/year. 7,500-8,000 mss received/year. 50% of books from first-time authors. 100% from unagented writers. Pays royalty Pays advance.** Publishes book 2 years after acceptance of ms. Accepts simultaneous submissions. Responds in 8 months to manuscripts. Book catalog for #10 SASE. Guidelines for #10 SASE or on the website.
Nonfiction Subjects include ethnic. Submit outline, 3 sample chapters. Reviews artwork/photos. Send

photocopies.
Fiction Subjects include ethnic, juvenile, multicultural, particularly Asian-American, picture books, young adult. Submit synopsis and 3 sample c
Recent Title(s) *Striking It Rich: Treasures from Gold Mountain*; *Char Siu Bao Boy*.

POSSIBILITY PRESS

One Oakglade Circle, Hummelstown PA 17036-9525. (717)566-0468. Fax: (717)566-6423. E-mail: info@possibilitypress.com. Website: www.possibilitypress.com. **Contact:** Mike Markowski, publisher. Estab. 1981. Publishes trade paperback originals. **Publishes 4-6 titles/year. 90% of books from first-time authors. 100% from unagented writers. Royalties vary.** Responds in 1 month to queries. Guidelines available online.
Imprints Aeronautical Publishers; Possibility Press; Markowski International Publishers.

O→ Our mission is to help the people of the world grow and become the best they can be, through the written and spoken word.

Nonfiction Subjects include psychology, pop psychology, business, success/motivation, inspiration, entrepreneurship, sales marketing, MLM and home-based business topics, and human interest success stories. Prefers submissions to be mailed. Include SASE.
Fiction Parables that teach lessons about life and success.
Recent Title(s) *Just Ask!*, by Bill McGrane; *Blue*, by Tony Scire and Tony Scire, Jr.; *Yes!*, by John Fuhrman.
Tips Our focus is on creating and publishing short- to medium-length bestsellers written by authors who speak and consult. We're looking for kind and compassionate authors who are passionate about making a difference in the world, and will champion their mission to do so, especially by public speaking.

⊘ THE POST-APOLLO PRESS

35 Marie St., Sausalito CA 94965. (415)332-1458. Fax: (415)332-8045. E-mail: postapollo@earthlink.net. Website: www.postapollopress.com. **Contact:** Simone Fattal, publisher. Estab. 1982. Publishes trade paperback originals and reprints. **Publishes 4 titles/year. Pays 5-7% royalty on wholesale price.** Publishes book 1 ½ years after acceptance of ms. Responds in 3 months to queries. Book catalog and ms guidelines for #10 SASE.

- *Not accepting new mss.*

Nonfiction Subjects include art, architecture, language, literature, translation, womens issues, womens studies. Query.
Fiction Subjects include experimental, literary, plays, spiritual, translation. Many of our books are first translations into English. Submit 1 sample chapter, SASE. The Post-Apollo Press is not .
Recent Title(s) *Memnoir*, by Jack Retallack; *Self-Destruction*, by Laura Moriarty; *Mind-God and the Properties of Nitrogen*, by Fouad Gabriel Naffah, translated from the French by Norma Cole.
Tips We are interested in writers with a fresh and original vision. We often publish foreign literature that is already well known in its original country, but new to the American reader.

PRECEPT PRESS

Bonus Books 1223 Wilshire Blvd., #597, Santa Monica CA 90403. E-mail: submissions@bonusbooks.com. Website: www.bonusbooks.com. **Contact:** Kelley Thornton, acquisitions editor. Estab. 1970. Publishes hardcover and trade paperback originals. **Publishes 3-5 titles/year. 300 queries received/year. 100 mss received/year. 25% of books from first-time authors. 90% from unagented writers. Pays royalty. Pays advance.** Publishes book 1 year after acceptance of ms. Accepts simultaneous submissions. Responds in 3 months to proposals. Guidelines available online.

O→ Precept Press features a wide variety of books for the medical community.

Nonfiction Subjects include health, medicine, clinical medical, oncology texts, science. Query with SASE.
Recent Title(s) *Nutritional Care for High-Risk Newborns*, edited by Groh-Wargo, Thompson & Cox.

THE PRESS AT THE MARYLAND HISTORICAL SOCIETY

201 W. Monument St., Baltimore MD 21201. (410)685-3750. Fax: (410)385-2105. E-mail: press@mdhs.org. Website: www.mdhs.org. **Contact:** Robert I. Cottom, publisher (Maryland-Chesapeake history); Patricia Dockman Anderson, managing editor (Maryland-Chesapeake history). Publishes hardcover and trade paperback originals, and trade paperback reprints. **Publishes 2-4 titles/year. 15-20 queries received/year. 8-10 mss received/year. 50% of books from first-time authors. 100% from unagented writers. Pays 6-10% royalty on retail price.** Publishes book 1-2 years after acceptance of ms. Accepts simultaneous submissions. Responds in 2 months to queries. Responds in 2 months to proposals. Responds in 6 months to manuscripts. Book catalog available online.

O→ The Press at the Maryland Historical Society specializes in Maryland state and Chesapeake regional subjects.

Nonfiction Subjects include anthropology, archeology, art, architecture, history. Query with SASE. Submit proposal package, outline, 1-2 sample chapters.
Recent Title(s) *The Plundering Time*, by Timothy Riordan; *The Great Baltimore Fire*, by Peter B. Petersen; *On*

Africa's Shore: A History of Maryland in Liberia 1834-1857, by Richard L. Hall.
Tips Our audience consists of intelligent readers of Maryland/Chesapeake regional history and biography.

N PRICE WORLD ENTERPRISES, LLC

SportsWorkout.com 1300 W. Belmont Ave., 20g, Chicago IL 60657. Fax: (216)803-0350. Website: www.sportsworkout.com. **Contact:** Robert Price, exec. v.p. Trade and mass market paperback originals. **Publishes 2-5 titles/year titles/year. 35 queries received/year; 20 mss/year 75% of books from first-time authors. 75% from unagented writers.**
Imprints SportsWorkout.com
Nonfiction Subjects include sports, fitness. Submit proposal package, including outline, completed ms; visit our online website for more information (www.sportsworkout.com/publishing). Reviews artwork/photos; send PDF or MS Word docs.
Recent Title(s) *The Ultimate Guide to Weight Training for Fencing; The Ultimate Guide to Weight Training for Skiing; The Ultimate Guide to Weight Training for Bowling.*
Tips The focus of our editorial scope is sports and fitness, with emphasis on instruction for training and performance.

PRINCETON BOOK CO.

614 Route 130, Hightstown NJ 08520. (609)426-0602. Fax: (609)426-1344. E-mail: pbc@dancehorizons.com. Website: www.dancehorizons.com. **Contact:** Charles Woodford, president (dance and adult nonfiction). Publishes hardcover and trade paperback originals and reprints. **Publishes 5-6 titles/year. 50 queries received/year. 100 mss received/year. 80% of books from first-time authors. 100% from unagented writers. Pays negotiable royalty on net receipts.** Publishes book 9-12 months after acceptance of ms. Accepts simultaneous submissions. Responds in 1 week to queries. Responds in 1 week to proposals. Book catalog and ms guidelines free or online.
Imprints Dance Horizons, Elysian Editions.
Nonfiction We publish all sorts of dance-related books including those on fitness and health.Subjects include music, dance. Submit proposal package, outline, 3 sample chapters. Reviews artwork/photos. Send photocopies.
Recent Title(s) *The Nutcracker Backstage*, by Angela Whitehill and William Noble; *The Pointe Book, 2nd Ed.*, by Janice Barringer and Sarah Schlesinger; *Pelvic Power*, by Eric Franklin.

QUICK PUBLISHING, LLC

1610 Long Leaf Circle, St. Louis MO 63146. (314)432-3435. Fax: (314)993-4485. E-mail: quickpublishing@sbcglobal.net. **Contact:** Angie Quick. Publishes trade paperback and hardback originals. **Publishes 1-2 titles/year.** Guidelines available online.

RAVENHAWK BOOKS

The 6DOF Group 7739 E. Broadway Blvd., Tucson AZ 85710. E-mail: ravenhawk6dof@yahoo.com. Website: www.6dofsolutions.com. **Contact:** Carl Lasky, publisher; Shelly Geraci, Exec. ed. (nonfiction/fiction). Estab. 1997. Publishes hardcover, electronic, and trade paperback originals. **Publishes 6-12 titles/year. 1,000 queries received/year. 300 mss received/year. 90%% of books from first-time authors. 80%% from unagented writers. Pays 40-50% royalty on wholesale price.** Publishes book 18 months after acceptance of ms. Accepts simultaneous submissions. Responds in 1 month to queries. Responds in 1 month to proposals. Responds in 3 months to manuscripts. Book catalog available online. Guidelines not available.
Imprints The 6DOF Company
Nonfiction Subjects include Americana, anthropology, astrology, business, community, creative nonfiction, ethnic, government, history, humanities, military, money, multicultural, nature, philosophy, politics, science, sex, social sciences, spirituality, sports, war, womens issues, womens studies, world affairs, young adult. Reviews artwork/photos. Send photocopies.
Fiction Subjects include adventure, confession, erotica, ethnic, experimental, fantasy, gothic, historical, horror, juvenile, literary, mainstream, contemporary, military, war, multicultural, mystery, occult, picture books, romance, spiritual, sports, suspense, western, young adult. Say something unique using powerful language and full-bodied characterizations. We look for dynamic, gripping stories, and fascinating, conflicted characters. Query with SASE.
Tips Our target audience is under 40.

RED ROCK PRESS

459 Columbus Ave., Suite 114, New York NY 10024. Fax: (212)362-6216. E-mail: info@redrockpress.com. Website: www.redrockpress.com. **Contact:** Ilene Barth. Estab. 1998. Publishes hardcover and trade paperback originals. **Publishes 6-8 titles/year. Pays royalty on wholesale price. The amount of the advance offered depends on the project.** Responds in 3-4 months to queries. Book catalog for #10 SASE.

Nonfiction Subjects include creative nonfiction.
Recent Title(s) *I Love You Because.*; *The Christmas Flower Boo.*

REFERENCE PRESS INTERNATIONAL

P.O. Box 4126, Greenwich CT 06831. (203)622-6860. **Contact:** Cheryl Lacoff, senior editor. Publishes hardcover and trade paperback originals. **Publishes 6 titles/year. 50 queries received/year. 20 mss received/year. 75% of books from first-time authors. 90% from unagented writers. Pays royalty. Makes outright purchase. Pays determined by project advance.** Publishes book 6 months after acceptance of ms. Accepts simultaneous submissions. Responds in 3 months to queries.

O→ Reference Press specializes in gift books, instructional, reference, and how-to titles.

Nonfiction Query with SASE. Submit outline, 1-3 sample chapters. Reviews artwork/photos. Send photocopies, not originals.
Recent Title(s) *Who's Who in the Peace Corps*, (alumni directory).

N ROLENTA PRESS

P.O. Box 1365, Springfield NJ 07081-5365. Phone/Fax: (973)564-7252. E-mail: info@rolentapress.com. Website: www.rolentapress.com. Estab. 1994. Publishes trade paperback originals and reprints. **Publishes 5 titles/year. Pays 12-15% royalty on wholesale price.** Publishes book 6 months after acceptance of ms. Accepts simultaneous submissions. Responds in 1 month to queries. Responds in 1 month to proposals. Responds in 2-3 months to manuscripts. Book catalog available online.

O→ Submissions must be video or computer-game related. No stragegy guides or how to break into the business.

Nonfiction Subjects include computers, electronics, software. Query with SASE. Submit proposal package, outline. Reviews artwork/photos. Send photocopies.
Recent Title(s) *Videogames: In the Beginning*, by Ralph H. Baer; *Phoenix: The Fall & Rise of Videogames*, by Leonard Herman.
Tips Audience includes gamers, collectors, and students. Know your subject. It helps to be an authority in the field. We are publishing books by the inventor of videogames and the co-founder of the first videogame magazine.

ROSE PUBLISHING

4733 Torrance Blvd., #259, Torrance CA 90503. (310)353-2100. Fax: (310)353-2116. E-mail: INFO@rose-publishing.com. Website: www.rose-publishing.com. **Contact:** Lynnette Pennings, managing editor. **Publishes 25-30 titles/year. 5% of books from first-time authors. 100% from unagented writers. Makes outright purchase.** Publishes book 18 months after acceptance of ms. Accepts simultaneous submissions. Responds in 3 months to proposals. Responds in 2 months to manuscripts. Book catalog for $1.29 in postage.

O→ We publish Bible reference materials in wall chart, pamphlet, and Powerpoint form, easy-to-understand and appealing to children, teens or adults on Bible study, prayer, basic beliefs, sharing the gospel, creation, apologetics, marriage, family and teens.

Nonfiction Subjects include religion, science, sex, spirituality, Bible studies, Christian history, counseling aids, cults/occult, curriculum, Christian discipleship, stewardship, evangelism/witnessing, Christian living, marriage, prayer, creation, singles issues. Submit proposal package, outline, photocopies of chart contents or poster artwork. Reviews artwork/photos. Send photocopies.
Recent Title(s) *Bible & Christian History Time Lines*; *Questions & Answers on Mormonism*; *Jehovah's Witnesses.*
Tips Audience includes both church (Bible study leaders, Sunday school teachers [all ages], pastors, youth leaders), and home (parents, home schoolers, children, youth, high school, and college). Open to topics that supplement Sunday School curriculum or Bible study, junior high materials, Bible study, reasons to believe, books of the Bible.

SAFER SOCIETY PRESS

P.O. Box 340, Brandon VT 05733. (802)247-3132. Fax: (802)247-4233. Website: www.safersociety.org. **Contact:** Gaen Murphree, editorial director. Estab. 1985. Publishes trade paperback originals. **Publishes 3-4 titles/year. 15-20 queries received/year. 15-20 mss received/year. 90% of books from first-time authors. 100% from unagented writers. Pays 10% royalty on retail price.** Publishes book 1 year after acceptance of ms. Accepts simultaneous submissions. Book catalog available free. Guidelines available online.

O→ Our mission is the prevention and treatment of sexual abuse.

Nonfiction Subjects include psychology, sexual abuse. Query with SASE, submit proposal package, or complete ms Reviews artwork/photos. Send photocopies.
Recent Title(s) *Footprints*, by Krishan G. Hansen, MSW, and Timothy J. Kahn, MSW; *Choices*, by Charlene Steen, PhD, JD.

Tips Audience is persons working in mental health/persons needing self-help books. Pays small fees or low royalties.

SALINA BOOKSHELF

3120 N. Caden Ct., Suite 4, Flagstaff AZ 86004. (928)527-0070. Fax: (928)526-0386. E-mail: tmcconnell@salinabookshelf.com. Website: www.salinabookshelf.com. **Contact:** Tayloe McConnell, editor. Publishes trade paperback originals and reprints. **Publishes 4-5 titles/year. 50% of books from first-time authors. 100% from unagented writers. Pays varying royalty. Pays advance.** Publishes book 1 year after acceptance of ms. Accepts simultaneous submissions. Responds in 3 months to queries.

Nonfiction Subjects include education, ethnic, science. Query with SASE.

Fiction Subjects include juvenile. Submissions should be in English or Navajo. All our books relate to the Navajo language and culture. Query with SASE.

Recent Title(s) *Dine Bizaad Binahoo'ahh: Rediscovering the Navajo Language*, by Evangeline Parsons Yazzie and Margaret Speas.

SALVO PRESS

P.O. Box 7396, Beaverton OR 97007. E-mail: info@salvopress.com. Website: www.salvopress.com. **Contact:** Scott Schmidt, publisher. Estab. 1998. Publishes hardcover and paperback originals and e-books in most formats. **Publishes 3 titles/year. 1200 queries received/year. 50% of books from first-time authors. 80% from unagented writers. Pays 10% royalty.** Publishes book 9 months after acceptance of ms. Responds in 1 month to queries. Responds in 2 months to manuscripts. Book catalog available online. Guidelines available online.

Fiction Subjects include adventure, literary, mystery, amateur sleuth, police procedural, private/hard boiled, science fiction, hard science fiction/technological, suspense, espionage, thriller. Our needs change. Check our website. Query with SASE.

Recent Title(s) *The Cold Edge*, by Trevor Scott; *The Great Planet Robbery*, by Craig DiLouie.

SANDLAPPER PUBLISHING CO., INC.

P.O. Box 730, Orangeburg SC 29116-0730. (803)531-1658. Fax: (803)534-5223. E-mail: agallman1@bellsouth.net. Website: www.sandlapperpublishing.com. **Contact:** Amanda Gallman, managing editor. Estab. 1982. Publishes hardcover and trade paperback originals and reprints. **Publishes 6 titles/year. 80% of books from first-time authors. 95% from unagented writers. Pays 15% maximum royalty on net receipts.** Publishes book 20 months after acceptance of ms. Responds in 3 months to queries. Book catalog and ms guidelines for 9x12 SAE with 4 first-class stamps.

O- We are an independent, regional book publisher specializing in educational nonfiction relating to South Carolina. Emphasizing history and travel.

Nonfiction Subjects include cooking, foods, nutrition, history, humor, regional, culture and cuisine of the Southeast especially South Carolina. Query with SASE. Submit outline, sample chapters. Reviews artwork/photos.

Recent Title(s) *Lowcountry Scenes*, by Jon Wongrey.

Tips Our readers are South Carolinians, visitors to the region's tourist spots, and friends and family that live out-of-state. We are striving to be a leading regional publisher for South Carolina. We will be looking for more history, travel and biography.

N SCARLETTA PRESS

10 S. 5th St., Suite 1105, Minneapolis MN 55402, U.S. (612)455-0252. Website: www.scarlettapress.com. **Publishes 3-6 titles/year. 50% of books from first-time authors. 85% from unagented writers.** Accepts simultaneous submissions. Online.

Nonfiction Subjects include art, architecture, business, economics, career guidance, counseling, history, humanities, language, literature, memoirs, military, war, photography, sociology, translation, world affairs, creative nonfiction. Submit recommendation from industry professional (agent, professor, writer, etc.) and completed ms. Reviews artwork. Email scans (or send CD).

Fiction Subjects include experimental, historical, literary, mainstream, contemporary, multicultural, translation, young adult. All genre fiction should have literary aspirations. Submit recommendation from industry professional (agent, professor, author, etc.) and completed ms.

Recent Title(s) *Tragedy in South Lebanon*, by Cathy Sultan (political science); *The New Writer's Handbook, Vol. 2*, by Philip Martin, ed. (writing how-to); *Greater Trouble in the Lesser Antilles*, by Charles Locks (literary mystery); *Yankee Invasion*, by Ignacio Solares, trans. Timothy Compton (translated historical novel)

Tips Our audience is thoughtful readers looking to expand their horizons. Know your audience, competition, and marketplace. Be prepared to name possible media outlets and contacts you have.

SCRIBLERUS PRESS

548 E. 82nd St., #1B, New York NY 10028. E-mail: editor@scriblerus.net. Website: www.scriblerus.net. **Contact:** Sean Miller, editor. Estab. 2005. Publishes hardcover, trade paperback, and electronic originals. **Publishes 1-5 titles/year. 100 queries received/year. Pays 15-25% royalty on wholesale price.** Publishes book 6 months after acceptance of ms. Accepts simultaneous submissions. Responds in 1 month to queries. Responds in 2 months to manuscripts. Guidelines available online.

- Accepts queries via e-mail only. Snail mail will be refused.

Fiction Subjects include experimental, literary. Submit proposal package, clips, bio, 3 sample chapters.
Recent Title(s) *Riffing on Strings: Creative Writing Inspired by String Theory*.

N SILVERFISH REVIEW PRESS

P.O. Box 3541, Eugene OR 97403. (541)344-5060. E-mail: sfrpress@earthlink.net. Website: www.silverfishreviewpress.com. Estab. 1978. Trade paperback originals. **Publishes 2-3 titles/year. 50% of books from first-time authors. 100% from unagented writers.** Guidelines available online.

"Sponsors the Gerald Cable Book Award. This prize is awarded annually to a book length manuscript of original poetry by an author who has not yet published a full-length collection. There are no restrictions on the kind of poetry or subject matter; translations are not acceptable. Winners will receive one thousand dollars, publication, and twenty-five copies of the book. The winner will be announced in February, 2010. Entries must be postmarked by October 15, 2009. Entries may be submitted by e-mail. See website for instructions."

Recent Title(s) *The Odds of Being*, by Daneen Wardrop (poetry); *Blue to Fill the Empty Heaven*, by Joel Friederich (poetry); *Come the Harvest*, by Paul Hunter (poetry).
Tips "Read recent Silverfish titles."

SLAPERING HOL PRESS

Imprint of The Hudson Valley Writers' Center 300 Riverside Dr., Sleepy Hollow NY 10591. (914)332-5953. Fax: (914)332-4825. E-mail: info@writerscenter.org. Website: www.writerscenter.org. **Contact:** Margo Stever and Suzanne Cleary, co-editors (poetry). Estab. 1990. Publishes chapbooks. **Publishes 1-2 titles/year. 70 queries received/year. 300 mss received/year. 100% of books from first-time authors. 100% from unagented writers.** Publishes book 6 months after acceptance of ms. Accepts simultaneous submissions. Book catalog and competition guidelines for #10 SASE.

Recent Title(s) *A Thirst That's Partly Mine*, by Liz Ahl; *Falling Into Velazquez*, by Mary Kaiser; *A House That Falls*, by Sean Nevin.
Tips Poets should obtain the contest guidelines before submitting.

SOCIETY OF MANUFACTURING ENGINEERS

One SME Dr., Dearborn MI 48128. (313)425-3286. E-mail: publications@sme.org. Website: www.sme.org. **Contact:** Manager. Publishes hardcover and trade paperback originals. **Publishes 6 titles/year. 20 queries received/year. 10 mss received/year. 90% of books from first-time authors. 90% from unagented writers. Pays 10% or more royalty on wholesale or retail price.** Publishes book 8 months after acceptance of ms. Responds in 1 month to queries. Responds in 2 months to proposals. Responds in 1 month to manuscripts. Book catalog and ms guidelines online at www.sme.org/store.

Nonfiction Seeking manuscripts that would assist manufacturing practitioners in increasing their productivity, quality, and/or efficiency.Reviews artwork/photos. Send photocopies.
Recent Title(s) *Hitchhiker's Guide to Lean*; *Factory Man; The Squeeze; Lean 9001*; *Fundamentals of Composites Manufacturing 2nd Edition.*
Tips Audience is manufacturing practitioners and management, individuals wishing to advance their careers in the industry or to enhance productivity, quality, and efficiency within a manufacturing operation.

N SOCRATIC PRESS

P.O. Box 66683, St. Pete Beach FL 33736-6683. (727)367-6177. Publishes hardcover, trade paperback and electronic originals and electronic reprints. **Publishes 2-3 titles/year. Pays 15-50% royalty on retail price.**

Nonfiction Subjects include animals, business, economics, creative nonfiction, government, politics, health, medicine, language, literature, money, finance, nature, environment, philosophy, psychology, science, sex, social sciences, spirituality. Query with SASE. Submit proposal package, outline.
Recent Title(s) *Handbook of the Coming American Revolution*, by Bryant.
Tips "Audience is sceptical, free-thinking, libertarian, inquisitive, uninhibited, curious, iconoclastic."

SOL BOOKS

An imprint of Skywater Publishing Company P.O. Box 24668, Minneapolis MN 55424. E-mail: info@solbooks.com. Website: www.solbooks.com. **Contact:** S. R. Welvaert, prose editor. Estab. 2005. Publishes mass market paperback and electronic originals and reprints. **Publishes 2-4 titles/year. 500 queries received/year. 25% of**

Small Presses

books from first-time authors. 100% from unagented writers. Pays 15% royalty. Pays $250-1,000 advance. Publishes book 1-2 years after acceptance of ms. Accepts simultaneous submissions. Responds in 3 months to queries and proposals. Responds in 3-6 months to manuscripts. Guidelines available online.

Fiction Subjects include adventure, ethnic, experimental, fantasy, gothic, historical, horror, humor, literary, mainstream, contemporary, military, war, multicultural, mystery, poetry, poetry in translation, regional, science fiction, short story collections, sports, suspense, translation, western. We're open to all styles of writing, but what we find more important than scintillating prose is a good story well told, with intriguing characters and a captivating plot. Submit complete ms.

Recent Title(s) *The Prostitutes of Post Office Street*, by Frank Carden (fiction); *Well Deserved*, by Michael Loy Gray (prose); *Gigs*, by John Davis (poetry).

N SOTO PUBLISHING COMPANY

P.O. Box 10, Dade City FL 33526, U.S. Website: www.sotopublishingcompany.com. **Contact:** Pedro Soto, publisher (Areas of interest: All genres, nonfiction, scifi, children's). Hardcover, trade paperback, & electronic originals. **Publishes 3-5 titles/year. 60% of books from first-time authors. 100% from unagented writers. $250-2,500** Publishes book approx. 6-9 months after acceptance of ms. Accepts simultaneous submissions. Online catalog. Guidelines on website and by email at info@sotopublishingcompany.com.

Nonfiction Subjects include alternative, animals, art, architecture, bio, business/economics, child guidance, children's/juvenile, coffee table book, contemporary, cookbook, cooking, foods, nutrition, crafts, creative nonfiction, education, ethnic, gay, lesbian, government, politics, health, medicine, illustrated, history, hobbies, house, home, scholarly, memoirs, military, war, money, finance, multicultural, nature, environment, new age, photography, real estate, recreation, science, sex education,spirituality, sports, translation, travel, womens issues, womens studies, young adult. Query with SASE. For 1st submission, writer should provide a completed, double-spaced, minimum 12pt font size ms, preferably in digital form (hard copy is acceptable). All figures, images, tables.should be submitted as a separate file from ms (text). Partial mss are acceptable. Provide details concerning how you would best go about promoting your work. Reviews artwork. Writers should send photocopies; digital copies preferred.

Fiction Subjects include adventure, ethnic, experimental, fantasy, gay/lesbian, gothic, horror, humor, juvenile, literary, mainstream/contemporary, military/war, multicultural, mystery, occult, picture books, regional, romance, spiritual, sports, suspense, science fiction, short story collections, young adult. See Nonfiction Overview. Query with SASE. Submit completed ms.

Recent Title(s) *Wormy, the Hairy Caterpillar*, and the Rainbow (children's picture book); *Pumps* (children's picture book).

Tips "At Soto Publishing we seek to be a voice for writers of all genres. Our main focus is young adult and children. We seek to provide high quality works that capture and inspire the mind and imaginations of young readers. What makes your story stand out from similar works on the market? What makes it exceptional? Will you be passionate about promoting & marketing your work(s)? If nonfiction, what is your area of expertise? Credentials?"

SOUTHERN METHODIST UNIVERSITY PRESS

P.O. Box 750415, Dallas TX 75275-0415. (214)768-1433. Fax: (214)768-1428. Website: www.tamu.edu/upress/SMU/smugen.html. **Contact:** Kathryn Lang, senior editor. Estab. 1937. Publishes hardcover and trade paperback originals and reprints. **Publishes 8-10 titles/year. 500 queries received/year. 500 mss received/year. 50% of books from first-time authors. 75% from unagented writers. Pays 10% royalty on wholesale price, 10 author's copies. Pays $500 advance.** Publishes book 1 year after acceptance of ms. Accepts simultaneous submissions. Responds in 2 weeks to queries. Responds in 1 month to proposals. Responds in up to 1 year to manuscripts. Book catalog available free. Guidelines available online.

- Southern Methodist University publishes for the general, educated audience in the fields of literary fiction, creative nonfiction, sports, ethics and human values, film and theater, regional studies. Currently emphasizing literary fiction and medical humanities projects. De-emphasizing scholarly, narrowly focused academic studies.

Nonfiction Subjects include creative nonfiction, medical ethics/human values. Query with SASE. Submit outline, bio, 3 sample chapters, TOC. Reviews artwork/photos. Send photocopies.

Fiction Subjects include literary, short story collections, novels. We are willing to look at 'serious' or 'literary' fiction. No mass market, science fiction, formula, thriller, romance. Query with SASE.

Recent Title(s) *The Gateway: Stories*, by T.M. McNally; *Silence Kills: Speaking Out and Saving Lives*, by Lee Gutkind.

ST. BEDE'S PUBLICATIONS

St. Scholastica Priory P.O. Box 545, Petersham MA 01366-0545. (978)724-3213. Fax: (978)724-3216. **Contact:** Acquisitions Editor. Estab. 1977. Publishes hardcover originals, trade paperback originals and reprints. **Publishes 3-4 titles/year. 30-40% of books from first-time authors. 98% from unagented writers. Pays 5-10% royalty**

on wholesale or retail price. Publishes book 2 years after acceptance of ms. Accepts simultaneous submissions. Responds in 2 months to queries. Book catalog and ms guidelines for 9x12 SAE with 2 first-class stamps.

- "St. Bede's Publications is owned and operated by the Roman Catholic nuns of St. Scholastica Priory. The publications are seen as an apostolic outreach. Their mission is to make available to everyone quality books on spiritual subjects such as prayer, scripture, theology, and the lives of holy people."

Nonfiction Subjects include history, philosophy, religion, sex, spirituality, translation, prayer. Query, or submit outline and sample chapters with SASE.
Recent Title(s) *Reading the Gospels with Gregory the Great*, translated by Santha Bhattacharji; *Why Catholic?*, by Father John Pasquini.
Tips "There seems to be a growing interest in monasticism among lay people, and we will be publishing more books in this area. For our theology/philosophy titles our audience is scholars, colleges and universities, seminaries, etc. For our other titles (i.e. prayer, spirituality, lives of saints, etc.) the audience is above-average readers interested in furthering their knowledge in these areas."

STEMMER HOUSE PUBLISHERS

4 White Brook Rd., Gilsum NH 03448. (800)345-6665. Fax: (603)357-2073. E-mail: pbs@pathwaybook.com. Estab. 1975. **Pays advance.** Publishes book 1-2 years after acceptance of ms. Accepts simultaneous submissions. Book catalog for 5 ½x8 ½ envelope and 2 First-Class stamps. Guidelines for #10 SASE.
Imprints The International Design Library®; The NatureEncyclopedia Series.
Nonfiction Subjects include animals, multicultural, nature, environment, arts. Query with SASE.

N ST. JOHANN PRESS

315 Schraalenburgh Rd., Haworth NJ 07641. (201)387-1529. E-mail: d.biesel@att.net. Website: www.stjohannpress.com. hardcover originals, trade paperback originals & reprints. **Publishes 6-8 titles/year. 15/year 50% of books from first-time authors. 95% from unagented writers.** Publishes book 15 months after acceptance of ms. Accepts simultaneous submissions. Catalog online at website. Guidelines free on request.
Nonfiction TrueSubjects include cooking, crafts, foods, history, hobbies, memoirs, military, nutrition, religion, sports (history), war (USMC), Black history in sports. Query with SASE. Reviews artwork/photos as part of the ms package. Send photocopies.
Tips "Our readership is libraries, individuals with special interests, (e.g. sports historians); we also do specialized reference."

STONE BRIDGE PRESS

P.O. Box 8208, Berkeley CA 94707. (510)524-8732. Fax: (510)524-8711. E-mail: sbpedit@stonebridge.com. Website: www.stonebridge.com. **Contact:** Peter Goodman, publisher. Estab. 1989. Publishes hardcover and trade paperback originals. **Publishes 6 titles/year. 100 queries received/year. 75 mss received/year. 15-20% of books from first-time authors. 90% from unagented writers. Pays royalty on wholesale price. Pays variable advance.** Publishes book 2 years after acceptance of ms. Accepts simultaneous submissions. Responds in 4 months to queries. Responds in 6 months to proposals. Responds in 8 months to manuscripts. Book catalog for 2 first-class stamps and SASE. Guidelines available online.
Imprints The Rock Spring Collection of Japanese Literature.

- Stone Bridge Press strives to publish and distribute high-quality informational tools about Japan. Currently emphasizing art/design, spirituality. De-emphasizing business, current affairs, fiction.

Nonfiction Subjects include art, architecture, business, economics, ethnic, language, literature, philosophy, travel, popular culture. Query with SASE. Reviews artwork/photos. Send photocopies.
Fiction Primarily looking at material relating to Japan. Translations only. Query with SASE.
Recent Title(s) *The Yakuza Movie Book*; *Cruising the Anime City*.
Tips Audience is intelligent, worldly readers with an interest in Japan based on personal need or experience. No children's books or commercial fiction. Realize that interest in Japan is a moving target. Please don't submit yesterday's trends or rely on a view of Japan that is outmoded. Stay current!

STONEYDALE PRESS

523 Main St., Stevensville MT 59870. (406)777-2729. Fax: (406)777-2521. Website: www.stoneydale.com. **Contact:** Dale A. Burk, publisher. Estab. 1976. Publishes hardcover and trade paperback originals. **Publishes 6-10 titles/year. 40-50 queries received/year. 6-8 mss received/year. 90% from unagented writers. Pays 12-15% royalty. Pays advance.** Publishes book 12-18 months after acceptance of ms. Responds in 2 months to queries. Book catalog available or see website.

- We seek to publish the best available source books on the Northern Rockies region and Montana in particular, covering such topics as history, historical reminiscence, outdoor recreation with an emphasis on big game hunting.

Nonfiction Subjects include history, regional, sports, historical reminiscences, outdoor recreation with an emphasis on big game hunting. Query with SASE.

Recent Title(s) *Montana Ghost Towns and Gold Camps*, by William Whitfield; *Colter's Run*, by Stephen T. Gough (novel); *Hunting Idaho's Golden Era*, by Fred S. Scott.

STRATA PUBLISHING, INC.

P.O. Box 1303, State College PA 16803. (814)234-8545. Website: www.stratapub.com. **Contact:** Kathleen Domenig, publisher. Publishes hardcover and trade paperback originals. **Publishes 1-3 titles/year. Pays royalty on wholesale price.** Publishes book 1 year after acceptance of ms. Responds in 1 month to queries. Responds in 3-4 months to proposals. Responds in 3 months to manuscripts. Book catalog available online. Guidelines available online.

Nonfiction Query with SASE. Reviews artwork/photos. Send What we need depends on the book.

Recent Title(s) *Readings on Argumentation*, by Angela Aguayo and Timothy Steffensmeier; *Argumentation: Understanding and Shaping Arguments*, by James A. Herrick; *Freedom of Speech in the United States*, by Thomas L. Tedford and Dale A. Herbeck.

Tips "We envision professors and students in college courses on communication and journalism as our audience."

STRIDER NOLAN PUBLISHING, INC.

1990 Heritage Rd., Huntingdon Valley PA 19006. (215)887-3821. Fax: (215)340-3926. E-mail: stridernolanmedia@yahoo.com. Website: www.stridernolanmedia.com. Publishes hardcover, trade paperback. **Publishes 5-10 titles/year. 1,000-2,000 queries received/year. 500-1,000 mss received/year. 50% of books from first-time authors. 50% from unagented writers. Pays royalty on retail price.** Accepts simultaneous submissions. Book catalog available online. Guidelines available online.

O-- No longer accepting queries. Please check website for details.

N STS. JUDE IMPRESS

5537 Waterman Blvd., Suite 2W, St. Louis MO 63112. (314)454-0064. Fax: (314)454-0064. E-mail: stjudes1@mindspring.com. Website: www.stsjudeimpress.org. **Contact:** Lawrence A. Murray, CEO (science, religion). Hardcover, trade paperback, and electronic originals. **Publishes 3-4 titles/year. 15 queries, 4 mss 100% of books from first-time authors. 100% from unagented writers.** Publishes book 9 months after acceptance of ms. Book catalog available online or for #10 SASE. Guidelines not available.

Nonfiction Subjects include anthropology, archaeology, history, photography, religion, science. Query with SASE. Does not review artwork/photos.

Fiction Subjects include adventure, historical, mystery, poetry, science fiction. Query with SASE; submit completed ms on cd.

Recent Title(s) *Science and Religious Essays* (nonfiction); *Arthritis Treatment* (nonfiction); *Everybody Comes to Tangier* (fiction); *Lady or LaMancha* (fiction).

Tips Our audience is well read, well educated. Be clear, clean, and have clever thoughts.

N SUBITO PRESS

Subito Press, Dept. of English, Helems 101, 226 UCB, Boulder CO 80309-0226. E-mail: editors@subitopress.org. Website: www.subitopress.org. Trade paperback originals. Accepts simultaneous submissions.

Imprints Subito Book Contest

Nonfiction See Guidelines online.Subjects include humanities, language, literature, literary criticism, music, dance, philosophy, translation, Interviews.

Fiction Subjects include literary, translation. Submit complete ms. Submit 1 pages, doubled-spac

Recent Title(s) *The Sheep*, by Miltos Sachtouris (poetry); *Floater*, by Keith Buckley (poetry).

Tips We publish innovative fiction/ Submissions are accepted from

SUCCESS PUBLISHING

3419 Dunham Rd., Warsaw NY 14569-9735. **Contact:** Allan H. Smith, president (home-based business); Ginger Smith (business); Dana Herbison (home/craft); Robin Garretson (fiction). Estab. 1982. Publishes mass market paperback originals. **Publishes 6 titles/year. 10 mss received/year. 90% of books from first-time authors. 100% from unagented writers. Pays 7-12% royalty. Pays $500-1,000 advance.** Publishes book 10 months after acceptance of ms. Accepts simultaneous submissions. Responds in 2 months to queries. Book catalog and ms guidelines for #10 SAE with 2 first-class stamps.

O-- "Success publishes guides that focus on the needs of the home entrepreneur to succeed as a viable business. Currently emphasizing starting a new business. De-emphasizing self-help/motivation books. Success Publishing notes that it is looking for ghostwriters."

Nonfiction Subjects include business, economics, child guidance, hobbies, money, finance, craft/home-based business. Query with SASE.

Recent Title(s) *How to Find a Date/Mate*, by Dana Herbison.

Tips "Our audience is made up of housewives, hobbyists, and owners of home-based businesses."

N SWAN ISLE PRESS

P.O. Box 408790, Chicago IL 60640-8790. (773)728-3780. E-mail: info@swanislepress.com. Website: www.swanislepress.com. **Contact:** David Rade, director/editor. Estab. 1999. Publishes hardcover and trade paperback originals. **Publishes 3 titles/year. 1,500 queries received/year. 0% % of books from first-time authors. Pays 7 ½-10% royalty on wholesale price.** Publishes book 12-18 months after acceptance of ms. Responds in 6 months to queries. Responds in 12 months to manuscripts. Book catalog available online. Guidelines available online.

Nonfiction Subjects include art, architecture, creative nonfiction, ethnic, history, humanities, language, literature, literary criticism, memoirs, multicultural, translation. Query with SASE. Submit complete mss only if author receives affirmative response to query. Reviews artwork/photos. Send photocopies.

Fiction Subjects include ethnic, historical, literary, multicultural, poetry, poetry in translation, short story collections, translation. Query with SASE. Submit complete mss. only afte

Recent Title(s) *Midday with Buñel*, by Claudio Isaac ((nonfiction)); *Sebastian's Arrows: Letters and Mementos of Salvador Dalí and Federico Garcia Lora*, Edited, translated with Prologue by Christopher Maurer; *Malambo*, by Lucía Char⊠n Illescas ((fiction)).

SWEDENBORG FOUNDATION PUBLISHERS

320 North Church St., West Chester PA 19380. (610)430-3222. Fax: (610)430-7982. E-mail: editor@swedenborg.com. Website: www.swedenborg.com. **Contact:** Morgan Beard, editor. Estab. 1849. Publishes trade paperback originals and reprints. **Publishes 5 titles/year.** Responds in 1 month to queries. Responds in 3 months to proposals. Responds in 3 months to manuscripts. Book catalog available free. Guidelines available online.

Imprints Chrysalis Books; Swedenborg Foundation Press.

- The Swedenborg Foundation publishes books by and about Emanuel Swedenborg (1688-1772), his ideas, how his ideas have influenced others, and related topics. A Chrysalis book is a spiritually focused book presented with a nonsectarian perspective that appeals to open-minded, well-educated seekers of all traditions. Appropriate topics include—but are not limited to—science, mysticism, spiritual growth and development, wisdom traditions, healing and spirituality, as well as subjects that explore Swedenborgian concepts, such as: near-death experience, angels, Biblical interpretation, mysteries of good and evil, etc. Although Chrysalis Books explore topics of general spirituality, a work must actively engage the thought of Emanuel Swedenborg and show an understanding of his philosophy in order to be accepted for publication.

Nonfiction Subjects include philosophy, psychology, religion, science. Query with SASE. Submit proposal package, outline, sample chapters, synopsis. I personally prefer e-mail. Reviews artwork/photos. Send photocopies.

Recent Title(s) *A Book About Us*, by George Dole; *The Wanderers*, by Naomi Gladish Smith; *Swedenborg, Oetinger, Kant*, by Werner Hanegraaf.

THE SYSTEMSWARE CORPORATION

973 Russell Ave., Suite D, Gaithersburg MD 20879. (301)948-4890. Fax: (301)926-4243. **Contact:** Pat White, editor. Estab. 1987.

Nonfiction Subjects include computers, electronics, software. Query with SASE.

N TECHNICAL ANALYSIS OF STOCKS & COMMODITIES

Technical Analysis, Inc. 4757 California Ave. SW, Seattle WA 98116-4499. (206)938-0570. E-mail: editor@traders.com. Website: www.traders.com. **Contact:** Jayanthi Gopalakrishnan, editor. Estab. 1982. Publishes trade paperback originals and reprints. **Makes outright purchase.** Responds in 6 months to queries.

Nonfiction Query with SASE.

Recent Title(s) *Charting the Stock Market*, by Hutson, Weis, Schroeder (technical analysis).

Tips Only traders and technical analysts really understand the industry. First consideration for publication will be given to material, regardless of topic, that presents the subject in terms that are easily understandable by the novice trader. One of our prime considerations is to instruct, and we must do so in a manner that the lay person can comprehend. This by no means bars material of a complex nature, but the author must first establish the groundwork.

TEXAS WESTERN PRESS

The University of Texas at El Paso, 500 W. University Ave., El Paso TX 79968-0633. (915)747-5688. Fax: (915)747-7515. E-mail: twp@utep.edu. Website: www.utep.edu/twp. **Contact:** Robert L. Stakes, director. Estab. 1952. Publishes hardcover and paperback originals. **Publishes 1 titles/year. Pays standard 10% royalty. Pays advance.** Responds in 2 months to queries. Book catalog available free. Guidelines available online.

Imprints Southwestern Studies.

- Texas Western Press publishes books on the history and cultures of the American Southwest, including the US-Mexico borderlands, West Texas, New Mexico, and northern Mexico. Currently emphasizing developing border issues, economic issues of the border. De-emphasizing coffee table books.

Nonfiction Subjects include education, health, medicine, history, language, literature, nature, environment, regional, science, social sciences. Query with SASE, or submit résumé, 2-3 sample chapters, cover letter, description of ms and special features, list of competing titles.

Recent Title(s) *Jose Cisneros Immigrant Artist*; *Showtime! From Opera Houses to Picture Palaces in El Paso*.

Tips Texas Western Press is interested in books relating to the history of Hispanics in the US. Will experiment with photo-documentary books, and is interested in seeing more contemporary books on border issues. We try to treat our authors professionally, produce handsome, long-lived books and aim for quality, rather than quantity of titles carrying our imprint.

THE MCDONALD & WOODWARD PUBLISHING CO.

431-B E. College St., Granville OH 43023. (740)321-1140. Fax: (740)321-1141. E-mail: mwpubco@mwpubco.com. Website: www.mwpubco.com. **Contact:** Jerry N. McDonald, publisher (area of interest: Archaeology). Estab. 1986. Publishes hardcover and trade paperback originals. **Publishes 5 titles/year. 25 queries received/year. 20 mss received/year. Pays 10% Royalty** Accepts simultaneous submissions. Responds in less than 1 month to queries, proposals & mss. Book catalog available online. Guidelines free on request; by email.

O→ McDonald & Woodward publishes books in natural and cultural history. Currently emphasizing travel, natural and cultural history, and natural resource conservation.

Nonfiction Subjects include animals, anthropology, archaeology, art, architecture, nature, environment, travel. Query with SASE. Reviews artwork/photos. Photos are not required.

Fiction Subjects include historical. Query with SASE.

Recent Title(s) *Yellowstone Wolves: A Chronicle of the Animal, the People, and the Politics*, by Cat Urbigkit (conservation); *Chaining Oregon: Surveying the Public Lands of the Pacific NW. 1851-1855*, by Kay Atwood (historical); *The Teeth of the Lion: The Story of the Beloved and Despised Dandelion*, by Anita Sanchez.

Tips Our books are meant for the curious and educated elements of the general population.

TIDEWATER PUBLISHERS

Cornell Maritime Press, Inc. P.O. Box 456, Centreville MD 21617-0456. (410)758-1075. Fax: (410)758-6849. Website: www.cmptp.com. **Contact:** Jonna Jones, managing editor. Estab. 1938. Publishes hardcover and paperback originals. **Publishes 7-9 titles/year. 41% of books from first-time authors. 99% from unagented writers. Pays 7 ½-15% royalty on retail price.** Publishes book 1 year after acceptance of ms. Responds in 2 months to queries.

O→ Tidewater Publishers issues adult nonfiction and photography works related to the Chesapeake Bay area, Delmarva, or Maryland in general.

Nonfiction Regional subjects only.Subjects include art, architecture, history, regional, sports, boating, outdoor recreation.

Recent Title(s) *Fishing the Chesapeake*, by Lenny Rudow; *Bodine's Chesapeake Bay Country*, by Jennifer Bodine.

Tips Our acquisition needs change frequently. Be sure to check our website under 'Submission Guidelines' for current requirements.

N TO BE READ ALOUD PUBLISHING, INC.

1357 Broadway, Suite 112, New York New York 10018. E-mail: michael@tobereadaloud.org. Website: www.tobereadaloud.org. **Contact:** Michael Powell, president (short stories); Stephen Powell, editor (poetry). Estab. 2006. Publishes trade paperback originals and reprints. **Publishes 4 titles/year. 250 queries received/year. 200 mss received/year. 90% of books from first-time authors. 90% from unagented writers. Makes outright purchase of 100-200.** Publishes book 4 months after acceptance of ms. Accepts simultaneous submissions. Responds in 1 month to queries. Responds in 1 month to proposals. Responds in 1 month to manuscripts. Guidelines available via e-mail.

Nonfiction Subjects include community, contemporary culture, creative nonfiction, education, ethnic, military, war, multicultural, philosophy, sociology. Submit complete ms.

Fiction Subjects include adventure, confession, ethnic, gothic, historical, horror, humor, juvenile, literary, multicultural, mystery, poetry, poetry in translation, science fiction, short story collections, sports, suspense, western. Submit complete ms.

Tips Our audience is high school drama students. Read your selection aloud before submitting.

TOKYO ROSE RECORDS/CHAPULTEPEC PRESS

4222 Chambers, Cincinnati OH 45223. E-mail: chapultepecpress@hotmail.com. Website: www.tokyoroserecords.com. **Contact:** David Garza. Estab. 2001. Publishes trade paperback originals. **Publishes 1-2 titles/year. 50 queries received/year. 10 mss received/year. 50% of books from first-time authors. 100% from unagented writers. Pays 50% of profits and author's copies.** Publishes book 6 months after acceptance of ms. Accepts

simultaneous submissions. Book catalog available online. No submittal guidelines.
Nonfiction Subjects include alternative, art, architecture, contemporary culture, creative nonfiction, ethnic, government, politics, history, humanities, language, literature, literary criticism, memoirs, multicultural, music, dance, nature, environment, philosophy, photography, recreation, regional, translation, world affairs. Submit proposal package, outline, 2-3 sample chapters, artwork samples. Reviews artwork/photos. Send photocopies.
Fiction Subjects include comic books, erotica, ethnic, experimental, humor, literary, multicultural, multimedia, occult, picture books, plays, poetry, poetry in translation, regional, short story collections stories, translation. Submit proposal package, clips, 2-3 sample chapters, artwork samples.
Recent Title(s) *The Compact Duchamp*, by Guy R. Beining; *A Beautiful Woman*, by Roesing Ape; *Teetering on the Brink of Science*, by Shawn Abnoxious.
Tips Tokyo Rose Records/Chapultepec Press specializes in shorter-length publications (100 pages or less). Order sample books by sending $5 payable to David Garza.

TOLLING BELL BOOKS

5555 Oakbrook Parkway, Bldg. 300, Suite 330, Norcross GA 30093. E-mail: info@tollingbellbooks.com. Website: www.tollingbellbooks.com. **Contact:** Lea Thomas, owner (science fiction, mystery, children's). Estab. 2003. Publishes trade paperback originals. **Publishes 2-3 titles/year. 400 queries received/year. 50-100 mss received/year. 50% of books from first-time authors. 90% from unagented writers. Pays royalty. Makes outright purchase.** Publishes book 12-18 months after acceptance of ms. Accepts simultaneous submissions. Responds in 3 months to queries. Responds in 5 months to proposals. Responds in 5 months to manuscripts. Book catalog for $2 (seasonal). Guidelines available online.
Imprints Red Herring Press (mystery); Lil' Bit Books (children's); Andromeda (science fiction)

We specialize in science fiction, mystery, and children's books.

Fiction Subjects include fantasy, juvenile, mystery, picture books, science fiction, young adult. We try to balance our publishing: 1-2 mystery books, 1-2 children's books, and 1 science fiction book. Check our website for what we need and don't need. First query by regular mail.
Recent Title(s) *Obsidian*, (sci-fi); *Runner's High*, (mystery); *Long Lost Teddy*, (children's).
Tips Be sure your work has been proofread (not just spellchecked) for grammar, punctuation, and spelling. It is hard to see the value in a piece of writing if it is full of errors.

TOP PUBLICATIONS, LTD.

3100 Independence Parkway, Suite 311-349, Plano TX 75075. (972)490-9686. Fax: (972)233-0713. E-mail: info@toppub.com. Website: www.toppub.com. **Contact:** Zoila Iglesias, editor. Estab. 1999. Publishes hardcover and paperback originals. **Publishes 4 titles/year. 200 queries received/year. 20 mss received/year. 90% of books from first-time authors. 95% from unagented writers. Pays 15-20% royalty on wholesale price. Pays $250-2,500 advance.** Publishes book 8 months after acceptance of ms. Accepts simultaneous submissions. Acknowledges receipt of queries but only responds if interested in seeing manuscript. Responds in 6 months to manuscripts. Tear sheets available on new titles. Guidelines available online.
Nonfiction We are primarily a fiction publisher and do not solicit submissions of non-fiction works.
Fiction Subjects include adventure, historical, horror, juvenile, mainstream, contemporary, military, war, mystery, regional, romance, science fiction, short story collections, suspense, young adult. It is imperative that our authors realize they will be required to promote their book extensively for it to be a success. Unless they are willing to make this commitment, they shouldn't submit to TOP.
Recent Title(s) *Tarizon: The Liberator*, by William Manchee; *The Curse of Charron*, by H. J. Ralles; *The Exploits of the Second Mrs. Watson*, by Michael Mallory.
Tips Because of the intense competition in this industry, we recommend that our authors write books that appeal to a large mainstream audience to make marketing easier and increase the chances of success. Be patient and don't get your hopes up. We only publish a few titles a year so the odds at getting published at TOP are slim. If we reject your work, don't give it a second thought. It probably doesn't have any reflection on your work. We have to pass on a lot of good material each year simply by the limitations of our time and budget.

TOY BOX PRODUCTIONS

7532 Hickory Hills Court, Whites Creek TN 37189. (615)299-0822. Fax: (615)876-3931. E-mail: toybox@crttoybox.com. Website: www.crttoybox.com. Estab. 1995. Publishes mass market paperback originals. **Publishes 4 titles/year. 100% of books from first-time authors. 100% from unagented writers. Pays 10-15% royalty on wholesale price.** Book catalog available online.

- We are not accepting new submissions at this time.

Nonfiction Subjects include audio, Americana, education, religion. *All unsolicited mss returned unopened.*
Recent Title(s) *The Tuskegee Airmen & Lions, Lions Everywhere*, by Joe Loesch.

TRANSPERSONAL PUBLISHING/AHU PRESS

P.O. Box 7220, Kill Devil Hills NC 27948. E-mail: allenchips@holistictree.com. Website: www.transpersonalpublishing.com. **Contact:** Dr. Allen Chips, managing director (holistic health texts and metaphysics). Estab. 1999. Publishes hardcover, trade originals, and electronic originals; and mass market paperback reprints. **Publishes 3-7 titles/year. 100 queries received/year. 50% of books from first-time authors. 99% from unagented writers. Pays 10% royalty.** Publishes book 9-12 months after acceptance of ms. Accepts simultaneous submissions. Responds in 3 months to proposals. Responds in 3 months to manuscripts. Book catalog and ms guidelines online.

- *Unsolicited mss are discarded.* If asked for a submission, will not return materials.

Nonfiction Reviews artwork/photos. Send photocopies.

Recent Title(s) *Killing Your Cancer Without Killing Yourself, Using Natural Cures*, by Dr. Allen Chips; *After Life From Above, Healings of a Paranormal Nature*, by Anita Billi; *Moving Beyond ADD/ADHD, An Effective, All-Natural Holistic, Mind-Body Approach*, by Kirch and Hart (educational guidebook, 2nd edition).

Tips The best authors are already engaged in regular travel and seminars/workshops, so that book signings are self-initiated. They also demonstrate integrity, honesty, a track record of success, dedication, self-motivation, and a people orientation.

THE TRINITY FOUNDATION

PO Box 68, Unicoi TN 37692. (423)743-0199. Fax: (423)743-2005. E-mail: jrob1517@aol.com. Website: www.trinityfoundation.org. **Contact:** John Robbins. Publishes hardcover and paperback originals and reprints. **Publishes 5 titles/year.** Publishes book 9 months after acceptance of ms. Responds in 1 month to queries. Responds in 1 month to proposals. Responds in 3 months to manuscripts. Book catalog available online.

Nonfiction Only books that conform to the philosophy and theology of the Westminster Confession of Faith. Textbooks subjects include business/economics, education, government/politics, history, philosophy, religion, science.Query with SASE.

TRISTAN PUBLISHING

2355 Louisiana Ave. North, Golden Valley MO 55427. (763)545-1383. Fax: (763)545-1387. Website: www.tristanpublishing.com. **Contact:** Brett Waldman, publisher. Hardcover originals. **Publishes 6-10 titles/year. 1,000 queries and manuscripts/year. 15% of books from first-time authors. 100% from unagented writers.** Publishes book 24 months after acceptance of ms. Accepts simultaneous submissions. Catalog and guidelines free on request. Guidelines available online at website.

Imprints Tristan Publishing; Waldman House Press; Tristan Outdoors.

Nonfiction , inspirational. Query with SASE; submit completed manuscript. Reviews artwork/photos; send photocopies.

Fiction , inspirational, gift books. Query with SASE; submit completed manuscript.

Recent Title(s) *Paw Prints in the Stars*, by Warren Hanson (gift book); *An Imperfect Life*, and *I'm Not Too Busy*, by Jodi Hills (gift books)

Tips "Our audience is adults and children."

TUPELO PRESS

Tupelo Press, P.O.Box 539, Dorset VT 05251. (802)366-8185. Fax: (802)362-1882. E-mail: publisher@tupelopress.org. Website: www.tupelopress.org. Estab. 2001. Guidelines available online.

- We're an independent nonprofit literary press. Also sponsor these upcoming competitions: Dorset Prize: $10,000. Entries must be postmarked between Sept. 1 and Dec. 15, 2008. Guidelines are online; Snowbound Series chapbook Award: $1,000 and 50 copies of chapbook. Closed for 2008.Every July we have Open Submissions. We accept book-length poetry, poetry collections (48 + pages), short story collections, novellas, literary nonfiction/memoirs and up to 80 pages of a novel.

Nonfiction Subjects include memoirs.

Fiction Subjects include poetry, short story collections, Novels. For Novels—submit no more than 100 pages along with a summary of the entire book. If we're interested we'll ask you to send the rest. We accept very few works of prose (1 or 2 per year). Submit complete ms.

Recent Title(s) *After the Gold Rush*, by Lewis Buzbee (fiction); *The Animal gospels*, by Brian Barker (poetry); *Invitation to a Secret Feast*, by Joumana Haddad.

Tips Readers and writers alike have For emerging and established w

TURTLE BOOKS

866 United Nations Plaza, Suite #525, New York NY 10017. (212)644-2020. Fax: (212)223-4387. Website: www.turtlebooks.com. **Contact:** John Whitman, publisher (children's picture books). Publishes hardcover and trade paperback originals. **Publishes 6-8 titles/year. 3,000 mss received/year. 25% of books from first-time authors. 50% from unagented writers. Pays royalty on retail price. Pays advance.** Publishes book 12 months after acceptance of ms. Accepts simultaneous submissions.

Turtle Books publishes only children's picture books (ie, no chapter books, YA or adult).

Nonfiction Subjects include animals, education, history, language, literature, multicultural, nature, environment, regional, any subject suitable for a children's picture book. Submit complete ms. Reviews artwork/photos. Send Send photocopies, no original art.

Fiction Subjects include adventure, ethnic, fantasy, historical, multicultural, regional, sports, western. Subjects suitable for children's picture books. We are looking for good stories which can be illustrated as children's picture books. Submit complete ms. Please do not send queries.

Recent Title(s) *Finding Daddy: A Story of the Great Depression*, by Jo Harper; *The Crab Man*, by Patricia Van West; *Alphabet Fiesta*, by Anne Miranda (children's picture books).

Tips Our preference is for stories rather than concept books. We will consider only children's picture book manuscripts.

THE UNIVERSITY OF AKRON PRESS

Bierce Library 374B, Akron OH 44325-1703. (330)972-5342. Fax: (330)972-8364. E-mail: uapress@uakron.edu. Website: www.uakron.edu/uapress. **Contact:** Mary Biddinger, Series Ed. (Akron Series on Poetry); Prof. Stephen Cutcliffe, Series Ed. (Science, Technology, & Society programs). Estab. 1988. Publishes hardcover and trade paperback originals. **Publishes 8-12 titles/year. 400-500 queries received/year. 100 mss received/year. 40% of books from first-time authors. 100% from unagented writers. Pays 5-10% royalty.** Publishes book 10-12 months after acceptance of ms. Accepts simultaneous submissions. Responds in 2 months to queries. Responds in 2 months to proposals. Responds in 3 months to manuscripts. Book catalog available free. Guidelines available online.

The University of Akron Press strives to be the University's ambassador for scholarship and creative writing at the national and international levels. Currently emphasizing technology and the environment, Ohio history and culture, Ohio politics and poetry. De-emphasizing fiction.

Nonfiction Subjects include business, economics, government, politics, history, humanities, nature, environment, photography, psychology, regional, science, social sciences, environment, technology, political science. Query with SASE. Reviews artwork/photos. Send photocopies.

Recent Title(s) *Chains of Opportunity-The Univ. of Akron & the Emergence of the Polymer Age*, by Mark D. Bowles; *Portraits of Power: Ohio and National Politics, 1964-2004*, by Abe Zaiden, with John C. Green; *The Bride Minaret*, by Heather Derr-Smith.

Tips We have mostly an audience of The scope of the series on Te

N UNIVERSITY OF MAINE PRESS

126A College Ave., Orono ME 04473. (207)866-0573. Fax: (207)866-2084. E-mail: umpress@umit.maine.edu. Website: www.umaine.edu/umpress. **Contact:** Editorial Director. Publishes hardcover and trade paperback originals and reprints. **Publishes 4 titles/year. 50 queries received/year. 25 mss received/year. 50% of books from first-time authors. 90% from unagented writers.** Publishes book 1 year after acceptance of ms.

Nonfiction Subjects include history, regional, science. Query with SASE.

Recent Title(s) *Of Place and Gender*, edited by Marli Weiner; *Woodmen, Horses, and Dynamite*, by C. Max Hilton, FE.

N UNTAPPED TALENT LLC

P.O. Box 396, Hershey PA 17033-0396. (717)707-0720. E-mail: rena.untappedtalent@gmail.com. Website: www.unt2.com. **Contact:** Rena Wilson Fox, (Areas of interest: nonfiction, children's lit, fiction, middle grade). hardcover, trade & mass market paperbacks, & electronic originals. **Publishes 2-10 titles/year. 2,000 queries, 400 mss 80% of books from first-time authors. 80% from unagented writers.** Publishes book 6-12 months, depending on the choice for timing the release. after acceptance of ms. Accepts simultaneous submissions. Catalog and guidelines available online.

As a new publishing company, we only have one title, not enough for a catalog. Please feel free to view the book at our web site.

Nonfiction Subjects include Americana, art, architecture, child guidance, parenting, computers, contemporary culture, cooking, foods, health, medicine, history, memoirs, music, dance, photography, psychology, religion, travel, womens issues/studies, world affairs, young adult. Submit by email: proposal package, outline (if appropriate), 4 sample chapters, & synopsis. Reviews artwork/photos. Send photocopies, computer file.

Fiction Subjects include historical, humor, juvenile, literary, mainstream, contemporary, military, war, multicultural, mystery, regional, religious, romance, suspense, young adult. We have a strong interest in historical fiction. We are looking for books that are current and fully formulated, modern interpretations—even if the story takes place in the past. Submit proposal package with synopsis, 4 sample chapters, and any background information pertinent to the story.

Recent Title(s) *Shunned*, by Arthur L. Ford (fiction).

Tips Follow website instruction, make query brief; if 4 chapters are not many pages, add more; submit to acquisitions editor only.

N UPPER ACCESS, INC.

87 Upper Access Rd., Hinesburg VT 05461. (802)482-2988. Fax: (802)304-1005. E-mail: info@upperaccess.com. Website: www.upperaccess.com. **Contact:** Steve Carlson, Publisher. Estab. 1986. Publishes hardcover and trade paperback originals; hardcover and trade paperback reprints. **Publishes 2-3 titles/year. 200 queries received/ year. 40 mss received/year. 50%% of books from first-time authors. 80%% from unagented writers. Pays 10-20% royalty on wholesale price. $200-500 (Advances are tokens of our good faith; author earnings are from royalties a book sells.)** Publishes book 8 months after acceptance of ms. Accepts simultaneous submissions. Responds in 1 month to queries/manuscripts. Catalog online at website. Guidelines available online.

O-π Publishes nonfiction to improve the quality of life.

Nonfiction Subjects include alternative lifestyles, child guidance, community/public affairs, contemporary culture, cooking, foods, nutrition, creative nonfiction, education, ethnic, gardening, government, politics/ politics, health, medicine, history, humor, humanities, language, literature, multicultural, nature, environment, philosophy, psychology, science, sex, social sciences, sociology, womens issues, womens studies, world affairs affairs, (gay, lesbian/lesbian possible). Query with SASE. "We strongly prefer an initial email describing your proposed title. No attachments please. We will look at paper mail if there is no other way, but email will be reviewed much more quickly and thoroughly." Will request artwork, etc. if and when appropriate. "Discuss this with us in your initial email query."

Fiction "We publish almost no fiction. We have made exceptions, but these are rare. Your may query by email."

Recent Title(s) *About the House with Henri de Marne*, by Henri de Marne (how-to); *Why the Wind Blows: A history of weather and global warming*, by Matthys Levy (environment, science); *Servants of the Fish*, by Myron Arms (environment, history).

Tips "We target intelligent adults willing to challenge the status quo, who are interested in more self-sufficiency with respect for the environment. Most of our books are either unique subjects or unique or different ways of looking at major issues or basic education on subjects that are not well understood by most of the general public. We make a long-term commitment to each book that we publish, trying to find its market as long as possible."

VANDAMERE PRESS

P.O. Box 149, St. Petersburg FL 33731. **Contact:** Jerry Frank, senior acquisitions editor. Estab. 1984. Publishes hardcover and trade paperback originals and reprints. **Publishes 8-15 titles/year. 1,500 queries received/ year and 500 mss received/year. 25% of books from first-time authors. 90% from unagented writers. Pays royalty.on revenues generated. Pays advance.** Publishes book 1 year after acceptance of ms. Accepts simultaneous submissions. Responds in 6 months to queries.

O-π "*Vandamere* publishes high-quality work with solid, well-documented research and minimum author/ political bias."

Nonfiction Subjects include Americana, education, health, medicine, history, military, war, photography, regional, Washington D.C./Mid-Atlantic, disability/healthcare issues. Submit outline, 2-3 sample chapters.

Fiction Subjects include adventure, mystery, suspense. Submit clips, 5-1 sample chapters.

Recent Title(s) *In Honored Glory: Arlington National Cemetery: The Final Post*, by Philip Bigler; *Civil War Fathers: Sons of the Civil War in World War II*, by Tim Pletkovich.

Tips "Authors who can provide endorsements from significant published writers, celebrities, etc., will always be given serious consideration. Clean, easy-to-read, dark copy is essential. Patience in waiting for replies is essential. All unsolicited work is looked at, but at certain times of the year our review schedule will stop. No response without SASE. No electronic submissions or queries!"

VANDERWYK & BURNHAM

P.O. Box 2789, Acton MA 01720. (978)263-7595. Fax: (978)263-0696. Website: www.vandb.com. **Contact:** Meredith Rutter, publisher. Publishes hardcover and trade paperback originals. **Publishes 3-6 titles/year. Pays $500-2,000 advance.** Accepts simultaneous submissions. Responds in 3 months to queries. Guidelines available online.

Nonfiction Subjects include psychology, narrative nonfiction, contemporary issues, aging.

Recent Title(s) *Hidden in Plain Sight: Getting to the Bottom of Puzzling Emotions*; *You're Only Young Twice*; *10 Do-overs to Reawaken Your Spirit*.

N VELÁZQUEZ PRESS

Division of Academic Learning Press 9682 Telstar Ave., Suite 110, El Monte CA 91731. (626)448-3448. E-mail: info@academiclearningcompany.com. Website: www.velazquezpress.com. Publishes hardcover and trade

paperback originals and reprints. **Publishes 5-10 titles/year. Pays 10% royalty on retail price.** Publishes book 6 months after acceptance of ms. Accepts simultaneous submissions. Responds in 2 month to queries. Responds in 2 month to proposals. Responds in 1 month to manuscripts. Book catalog available via e-mail. Guidelines available via e-mail.
Imprints WBusiness Books; ZHealth.
Nonfiction Subjects include education. Submit proposal package, outline, 2 sample chapters, cover letter. Submit complete ms. Reviews artwork/photos. Send photocopies.
Recent Title(s) *Velázquez Spanish and English Dictionary*, (reference/bilingual); *Velázquez World Wide Spanish Dictionary*, (reference/bilingual).

VITESSE PRESS

PMB 367, 45 State St., Montpelier VT 05601-2100. (802)229-4243. Fax: (802)229-6939. E-mail: dick@vitessepress.com. Website: www.vitessepress.com. **Contact:** Richard H. Mansfield, editor. Estab. 1985. Publishes trade paperback originals. **Publishes 2 titles/year.** Responds in 1 month to queries.
Nonfiction Subjects include health, medicine, regional, mountain biking guides, sports.
Recent Title(s) *Cycling Along the Canals of New York*, by Louis Rossi.

VOLCANO PRESS, INC.

P.O. Box 270, Volcano CA 95689-0270. (209)296-7989. Fax: (209)296-4995. E-mail: adam@volcanopress.com. Website: www.volcanopress.com. **Contact:** Ruth Gottstein, editorial consultant; Adam Gottstein, publisher. Estab. 1969. Publishes trade paperback originals. **Publishes 4-6 titles/year. Pays $500-1,000 advance.** Responds in 1 month to queries. Book catalog available free.
Imprints Mother Lode Books

- We believe that the books we are producing today are of even greater value than the gold of yesteryear and that the sybolism of the term `Mother Lode' is still relevant to our work.

Nonfiction Subjects include health, medicine, multicultural, womens issues, womens studies. Query with SASE. No e-mail or fax submissions
Recent Title(s) *Family & Friends Guide to Domestic Violence: How to Listen, Talk & Take Action When Someone You Care About Is Being Abused*, by Elaine Weiss, EdD; *Surviving Domestic Violence: Voices of Women Who Broke Free*, by Elaine Weiss, EdD.
Tips Look at our titles on the Web or in our catalog, and submit materials consistent with what we already publish.

WASHINGTON STATE UNIVERSITY PRESS

P.O. Box 645910, Pullman WA 99164-5910. (800)354-7360. Fax: (509)335-8568. E-mail: wsupress@wsu.edu. Website: www.wsupress.wsu.edu. **Contact:** Glen Lindeman, editor. Estab. 1928. Publishes hardcover originals, trade paperback originals and reprints. **Publishes 4-6 titles/year. 40% of books from first-time authors. 95% from unagented writers. Pays 5% royalty graduated according to sales** Publishes book 18 months after acceptance of ms. Responds in 4 months to queries. Guidelines available online.

- WSU Press publishes books on the history, pre-history, culture, and politics of the West, particularly the Pacific Northwest.

Nonfiction Subjects include cooking, foods, nutrition, (regional), government, politics, history, nature, environment, regional, (cultural studies), essays. Submit outline, sample chapters. Reviews artwork/photos.
Recent Title(s) *Finding Chief Kamiakin: The Life and Legacy of a Northwest Patriot; Crossroads and Connections: Central Washington University Art Alumni Exhibition; Making the Grade: Plucky Schoolmarms of Kittitas Country.*
Tips We have developed our marketing in the direction of regional and local history and have attempted to use this as the base upon which to expand our publishing program. In regional history, the secret is to write a good narrative—a good story—that is substantiated factually. It should be told in an imaginative, clever way. Have visuals (photos, maps, etc.) available to help the reader envision what has happened. Tell the regional history story in a way that ties it to larger, national, and even international events. Weave it into the large pattern of history.

N WAYFINDER PRESS

P.O. Box 217, Ridgway CO 81432-0217. (970)626-5452. **Contact:** Marcus E. Wilson, owner. Estab. 1980. Publishes trade paperback originals. **Publishes 2 titles/year. Pays 8-10% royalty on retail price.** Responds in 1 month to queries.
Nonfiction Subjects include Americana, government, politics, history, nature, environment, photography, recreation, regional, travel. Query with SASE. Submit outline, sample chapters. Reviews artwork/photos.
Recent Title(s) *30 Things to Do in Durango, Colorado; 30 Things to Do in Telluride, Colorado.*
Tips "Writers have the best chance selling us tourist-oriented books. Our audience is the local population and tourists."

WESCOTT COVE PUBLISHING CO.

Subsidiary of NetPV P.O. Box 560989, Rockledge FL 32956. (321)690-2224. Fax: (321)690-0853. E-mail: publisher@wescottcovepublishing.com. Website: www.wescottcovepublishing.com. **Contact:** Will Standley, publisher. Estab. 1968. Publishes trade paperback originals and reprints. **Publishes 4 titles/year.** Accepts simultaneous submissions. Responds in 1 week to queries. Book catalog available free.

O‑‑ We publish the most complete cruising guides, each one an authentic reference for the area covered.

Nonfiction All titles are nautical books; half of them are cruising guides. Mostly we seek out authors knowledgeable in sailing, navigation, cartography and the area we want covered. Then we commission them to write the book.Subjects include history, hobbies, regional, sports, travel, nautical.

WESTERN PSYCHOLOGICAL SERVICES

12031 Wilshire Blvd., Los Angeles CA 90025. (310)478-2061. Fax: (310)478-7838. E-mail: bthomas@wpspublish.com. Website: www.wpspublish.com. **Contact:** Brian Thomas, marketing manager. Estab. 1948. Publishes psychological and educational assessments and some trade paperback originals. **Publishes 2 titles/year. 60 queries received/year. 30 mss received/year. 90% of books from first-time authors. 95% from unagented writers. Pays 5-10% royalty on wholesale price. 12 months** Accepts simultaneous submissions. Responds in 2 months to queries. Book catalog available free. Guidelines available online.

O‑‑ Western Psychological Services publishes psychological and educational assessments that practitioners trust. Our products allow helping professionals to accurately screen, diagnose, and treat people in need. WPS publishes practical books and games used by therapists, counselors, social workers, and others in the helping professionals who work with children and adults.

Nonfiction Subjects include child guidance, psychology, autism, sensory processing disorders. Submit complete ms. Reviews artwork/photos. Send photocopies.

Fiction Children's books dealing with feelings, anger, social skills, autism, family problems, etc. Submit complete ms.

Recent Title(s) *Sensory Integration and the Child*, by A. Jean Ayres, PhD; *To Be Me*, by Rebecca Etlinger.

WESTWINDS PRESS

Imprint of Graphic Arts Center Publishing Company P.O. Box 10306, Portland OR 97296-0306. (503)226-2402. Fax: (503)223-1410. Website: www.gacpc.com. **Contact:** Tim Frew, executive editor. Estab. 1999. Publishes hardcover and trade paperback originals and reprints. **Publishes 5-7 titles/year. 10% of books from first-time authors. 90% from unagented writers. Pays advance.** Publishes book an average of 2 years after acceptance of ms. Accepts simultaneous submissions. Responds in 6 months to queries. Book catalog for 9x12 SAE with 6 first-class stamps. Guidelines available online.

Nonfiction Subjects include history, memoirs, regional, Western regional states—nature, environment, travel, cookbooks, Native American contemporary culture, adventure, outdoor recreation, sports, the arts, and children's books, guidebooks.

Recent Title(s) *Salmon*, (Northwest Homegrown cookbook series); *The Exploding Whale*, (memoir); *Portland Confidential*, (true crime).

Tips Book proposals that are professionally written and polished with a clear understanding of the market receive our most careful consideration. We are looking for originality. We publish a wide range of books for a wide audience. Some of our books are clearly for travelers, others for those interested in outdoor recreation or various regional subjects. If I were a writer trying to market a book today, I would research the competition (existing books) for what I have in mind, and clearly (and concisely) express why my idea is different and better. I would describe the book buyers (and readers)—where they are, how many of them are there, how they can be reached (organizations, publications), why they would want or need my book.

WHITFORD PRESS

Imprint of Schiffer Publishing, Ltd. 4880 Lower Valley Rd., Atglen PA 19310. (610)593-1777. **Contact:** Mary Whitford. Estab. 1975. **Publishes 2-6 titles/year. Pays royalty on wholesale price.** Responds in 2 weeks to queries. Book catalog available free.

Tips We want to publish books for towns or cities with relevant population or active tourism to support book sales. A list of potential town vendors is a helpful start toward selling us on your book idea.

N WHITTLER'S BENCH PRESS

Dram Tree Books P.O. Box 7183, Wilmington NC 28406. E-mail: dramtreebooks@ec.rr.com. Website: www.dramtreebooks.com. **Contact:** Fiction Editor. Estab. 2005. Publishes trade paperback originals and reprints. **Publishes 2-6 titles/year. 90% of books from first-time authors. 100% from unagented writers. Pays 10-15% royalty on retail price. Pays $250-500 advance.** Publishes book 1 year after acceptance of ms. Responds in 2 months to queries. Responds in 2 months to proposals. Responds in 4 months to manuscripts. Guidelines available via e-mail.

Fiction Subjects include adventure, historical, humor, military, war, mystery, regional, suspense. Our main focus is on historical fiction, mysteries and humorous novels—and all of it must have some link to North Carolina. When submitting humorous novels you must make us laugh. Think in terms of books by authors like Michael Malone, T.R. Pearson, Clyde Edgerton, Terry Pratchett, etc. Query with SASE. Submit proposal package, 3 sample chapters, clips.

Tips Our readers are looking for compelling stories that will transport them away from the pressures of the 'real' world for however long they spend with our stories. The North Carolina tie-in is an important part of what will be a Whittler's Bench Press title. Remember they'll be paying good money to be entertained, so give them a story that satisfies. If historical fiction, make sure you get the history right. Finally, always remember: It must have a North Carolina angle of some kind.

WINDWARD PUBLISHING

Imprint of Finney Company 8075 215th St. W., Lakeville MN 55044. (952)469-6699. Fax: (952)469-1968. E-mail: feedback@finney-hobar.com. Website: www.finney-hobar.com. **Contact:** Alan E. Krysan, president. Estab. 1973. Publishes trade paperback originals. **Publishes 6-10 titles/year. 120 queries received/year. 50 mss received/year. 50% of books from first-time authors. 100% from unagented writers. Pays 10% royalty on wholesale price. Pays advance.** Publishes book 6-12 months after acceptance of ms. Accepts simultaneous submissions. Responds in 8-10 weeks to queries.

O→ Windward publishes illustrated natural history, recreation books, and children's books.

Nonfiction Subjects include agriculture, animals, gardening, nature, environment, recreation, science, sports, natural history. Query with SASE. Reviews artwork/photos.

Recent Title(s) *Storm Codes*, by Tracy Nelson Maurer; *My Little Book of Manatees*, by Hope Irvin Marston; *Nightlight*, by Jeannine Anderson.

WOLF DEN BOOKS

5783 S.W. 40th St., #221, Miami FL 33155. (877)667-9737. E-mail: info@wolfdenbooks.com. Website: www.wolfdenbooks.com. **Contact:** Gail Shivel (literary criticism/studies). Estab. 2000. Publishes hardcover, trade paperback and electronic originals and reprints. **Publishes 2 titles/year. 40 queries received/year. 10 mss received/year. 0% of books from first-time authors. 100% from unagented writers. Pays 7½% royalty on retail price. $1,000** Publishes book 12 months. after acceptance of ms. Accepts simultaneous submissions. Responds in 1 month/queries, 2 months/proposals, 4 months/mss. Book catalog available online. Guidelines available via e-mail.

- Do not send postage; mss are not returned.

Nonfiction Subjects include history, humanities, language, literature, literary criticism, philosophy. Query with SASE; submit proposal package, including outline; submit complete ms. Does not review artwork.

Recent Title(s) *Robert Benchley's Wayward Press*, by Robert Benchley (press criticism); *The Columbiad*, by Joel Barlow (American poetry); *Lives of the Most Eminent English Poets*, by Samuel Johnson.

WOODBINE HOUSE

6510 Bells Mill Rd., Bethesda MD 20817. (301)897-3570. Fax: (301)897-5838. E-mail: ngpaul@woodbinehouse.com. Website: www.woodbinehouse.com. **Contact:** Nancy Gray Paul, acquisitions editor. Estab. 1985. Publishes trade paperback originals. **Publishes 10 titles/year. 15% of books from first-time authors. 90% from unagented writers. Pays 10-12% royalty.** Publishes book 18 months after acceptance of ms. Accepts simultaneous submissions. Responds in 3 months to queries. Book catalog for 6x9 SAE with 3 first-class stamps. Guidelines available online.

O→ Woodbine House publishes books for or about individuals with disabilities to help those individuals and their families live fulfilling and satisfying lives in their homes, schools, and communities.

Nonfiction Publishes books for and about children with disabilities.Subjects include specific issues related to a given disability (e.g., communication skills, social sciences skills, feeding issues) and practical guides to issues of concern to parents of children with disabilities (e.g., special education, sibling issues). Submit outline, 3 sample chapters. Reviews artwork/photos.

Fiction Subjects include picture books, children's. Receptive to stories re: developmental and intellectual disabilities, e.g., autism and cerebral palsy. Submit complete ms with SASE.

Recent Title(s) *Self-Help Skills for People With Autism: A Systematic Teaching Approach*, by Stephen R. Anderson, et al.; *Teaching Children With Down Syndrome About Their Bodies, Boundaries, and Sexuality*, by Terri Couwenhoven.

Tips Do not send us a proposal on the basis of this description. Examine our catalog or website and a couple of our books to make sure you are on the right track. Put some thought into how your book could be marketed (aside from in bookstores). Keep cover letters concise and to the point; if it's a subject that interests us, we'll ask to see more.

WORLD LEISURE

P.O. Box 160, Hampstead NH 03841. (617)569-1966. E-mail: leocha@worldleisure.com. Website: www.

worldleisure.com. **Contact:** Charles Leocha, president. Estab. 1977. Publishes trade paperback originals. **Publishes 3-5 titles/year. Pays royalty. Makes outright purchase.** Accepts simultaneous submissions. Responds in 2 months to queries. Book catalog and ms guidelines online.

O─ World Leisure specializes in travel books, activity guidebooks, and self-help titles.

Nonfiction Subjects include recreation, sports, skiing/snowboarding, travel. Submit outline, intro sample chapters, annotated TOC, SASE.

Recent Title(s) *Ski Snowboard America*, by Charles Leocha; *Ski Snowboard Europe*, by Charles Leocha.

N XYZZY PRESS

9105 Concord Hunt Cir., Brentwood TN 37027. (615)585-9836. E-mail: jim@xyzzypress.com. Website: www.xyzzypress.com. **Contact:** Lana Shealy, VP Operations (personal growth/religion). Trade paperback originals. **Publishes 3 titles/year. Receives 30 mss/year; 40 queries/year 70% of books from first-time authors. 100% from unagented writers.** Publishes book 9 months after acceptance of ms. Accepts simultaneous submissions. Catalog and Guidelines available online at website.

Nonfiction Subjects include cooking, foods, nutrition, nature, environment, lifestyle, motivation, food, health, medicine, athletics, personal growth, personal management, personal finances, leisure, entertainment, art, architecture, politics, religion, spirituality, travel. Submit completed ms Reviews artwork/photos

Recent Title(s) *La Bella Vita*, by Helen Ruchti (travelogue and devotional); *New Day Revolution*, by Sam Davidson and Stephen Moseley (environment, sustainability); *The Stories I Keep*, by RoseAne Coleman (inspirational)

Tips Our audiences ranges in age from 20-50. They are urban professionals that want more meaning in their lives—people that are tired of McMansions and more, better, faster.

N YOUR CULTURE GIFTS

P.O. Box 1245, Ellicott City MD 21041, U.S. E-mail: info@yourculturegifts.com. Website: www.yourculturegifts.com. **Contact:** Frank Sauri, Mgr. Trade paperback originals. **Publishes 5 titles/year.** Publishes book 18 months after acceptance of ms. Accepts simultaneous submissions. Catalog and guidelines available online.

O─ Limited to cultural, realistic, historical, creative nonfiction, with language and food components.

Nonfiction Subjects include children's/juvenile, cooking, foods, nutrition, creative nonfiction, history, multicultural, social sciences sciences, young adult. Query with SASE. Reviews artwork/photos. Email samples after request for ms.

Fiction Subjects include ethnic, historical, juvenile, multicultural, young adult. Query with SASE.

Recent Title(s) *Gift of Yucatan: A Short History* (middle grade history) and *Gift of Yucatan: Maria's Rebellion* (middle grade historical fiction), by Trudy Sauri

Tips Our audience is middle grade students, ESL students, unmotivated young adult readers, families. Be committed to a long-term project to share cultural information.

N ZOLAND BOOKS

Steerforth Press 45 Lyme Rd., Suite 208, Hanover NH 03755. Website: www.steerforth.com/zoland/. **Contact:** Editor: Roland Pease (Zoland Poetry annuals). Estab. 1987. Trade paperback originals.

Nonfiction Subjects include translation, travel, (book reviews).

Fiction Subjects include ethnic, experimental, fantasy, historical, horror, humor, literary, military, war, mystery, picture books, plays, poetry, regional, religious, romance, science fiction, short story collections, spiritual, suspense, translation, Folklore.

Recent Title(s) *Phlip Guston's Late Work*, by William Corbett (a memoir); *After Dachau*, by Daniel Quinn (novel); *Big Towns, Big Talk*, by Patricia Smith (poetry).

Tips Zoland Books, which Steerforth Zoland Books publishes contem

Consumer Magazines

Selling your writing to consumer magazines is as much an exercise of your marketing skills as it is of your writing abilities. Editors of consumer magazines are looking not only for good writing, but for good writing which communicates pertinent information to a specific audience—their readers.

Approaching the consumer magazine market

Marketing skills will help you successfully discern a magazine's editorial slant, and write queries and articles that prove your knowledge of the magazine's readership. You can gather clues about a magazine's readership—and establish your credibility with the magazine's editor—in a number of ways:

- **Read** the magazine's listing in *Writer's Market*.
- **Study** a magazine's writer's guidelines.
- **Check** a magazine's Web site.
- **Read** several current issues of the target magazine.
- **Talk** to an editor by phone.

Writers who can correctly and consistently discern a publication's audience and deliver stories that speak to that target readership will win out every time over writers who submit haphazardly.

What editors want

In nonfiction, editors continue to look for short feature articles covering specialized topics. Editors want crisp writing and expertise. If you are not an expert in the area about which you are writing, make yourself one through research. Always query before sending your manuscript. Don't e-mail or fax a query to an editor unless the listing mentions it is acceptable to do so.

Fiction editors prefer to receive complete manuscripts. Writers must keep in mind that marketing fiction is competitive, and editors receive far more material than they can publish. For this reason, they often do not respond to submissions unless they are interested in using the story. More comprehensive information on fiction markets can be found in *Novel & Short Story Writer's Market* (Writer's Digest Books).

Payment

Most magazines listed here have indicated pay rates; some give very specific payment-per-word rates, while others state a range. **(Note: All of the magazines listed in the Consumer Magazines section are paying markets. However, some of the magazines are not identified by payment icons ($-$$$$) because the magazines preferred not to disclose specific payment information.)** Any agreement you come to with a magazine, whether verbal or written, should specify the payment you are to receive and when you are to receive it. Some magazines pay writers only after the piece in question has been published (on publication). Others pay as soon as they have accepted a piece and are sure they are going to use it (on acceptance). In *Writer's Market*, those magazines that pay on acceptance have been highlighted with the phrase **pays on acceptance** set in bold type.

So what is a good pay rate? There are no standards; the principle of supply and demand operates at full throttle in the business of writing and publishing. As long as there are more writers than opportunities for publication, wages for freelancers will never skyrocket. Rates vary widely from one market to the next. Smaller circulation magazines and some departments of the larger magazines will pay a lower rate.

Editors know the listings in *Writer's Market* are read and used by writers with a wide range of experience, from those unpublished writers just starting out, to those with a successful, profitable freelance career. As a result, many magazines publicly report pay rates in the lower end of their actual pay ranges. Experienced writers will be able to successfully negotiate higher pay rates for their material. Newer writers should be encouraged that as their reputation grows (along with their clip file), they will be able to command higher rates. The article "How Much Should I Charge?" on page **61**, gives you an idea of pay ranges for different freelance jobs, including those directly associated with magazines.

INFORMATION AT-A-GLANCE

In the Consumer Magazines section, icons identify comparative payment rates (**$**-**$$$$**); new listings (N); and magazines that do not accept unsolicited manuscripts (⊘). Different sections of *Writer's Market* include other symbols; check the inside back cover for an explanation of all the symbols used throughout the book.

Important information is highlighted in boldface—the "quick facts" you won't find in any other market book, but should know before you submit your work. The word **Contact** identifies the appropriate person to query at each magazine. We also highlight what percentage of the magazine is freelance written; how many manuscripts a magazine buys per year of nonfiction, fiction, poetry, and fillers; and respective pay rates in each category.

Information on publications listed in the previous edition of *Writer's Market*, but not included in this edition, can be found in the General Index.

ANIMAL

$$ FRESHWATER AND MARINE AQUARIUM

Bowtie, Inc., 3 Burroughs, Irvine CA 92618-2804. (949)855-8822. E-mail: emizer@bowtieinc.com. Website: www.fishchannel.com. Clay Jackson. **Contact:** Ethan Mizer, assoc. ed. **95%**. The freshwater and marine aquarium hobby. Our audience tends to be more advanced fish-and coral-keepers as well as planted tank fans. Writers should have aquarium keeping experience themselves. FAMA covers all aspects of fish and coral husbandry. Estab. 1978. Circ. 14,000. Byline given. Pays on publication. Pays $50 kill fee. Publishes ms 6-8 months after acceptance. First North American serial rights purchased. 3 ½ months Accepts queries by mail, e-mail. Accepts simultaneous submissions. 3 weeks on queries, 2 months on mss "If we are interested in a query or ms, we'll e-mail an assignment with guidelines included."

Nonfiction Contact: Ethan Mizer, associate editor. Needs general interest, how-to, interview, new product, personal experience, technical, aquarium-related articles. Every year we do three special issues. Past issues have included aquarium lighting, invertebrates, planted tanks, food, etc. No beginner articles, such as keeping guppies and goldfish. If mid-level to advanced aquarists wouldn't get anything new by reading it, don't send it. Writer should query. 1,500-2,000/words **Pay $300-400; 20¢/word.**

Photos Contact: Ethan Mizer. State availability of photos with submission; send photos. Captions are required. GIF/JPEG files, RAW files, transparencies (35 mm). Digitals must be 300 dpi. If article is on keeping unusual fish, photos should be included. One-time rights.

Columns/Departments All of our columns are assigned and written by established columnists. **$250.**

Tips Check out our website to read about the different topics we cover in our magazine.

$$ AKC GAZETTE

American Kennel Club, Website: www.akc.org/pubs/index.cfm. **85% freelance written**. Monthly magazine. Geared to interests of fanciers of purebred dogs as opposed to commercial interests or pet owners. We require solid expertise from our contributors—we are *not* a pet magazine. Estab. 1889. Circ. 60,000. Byline given. Pays on publication. Offers 10% kill fee. Publishes ms an average of 6 months after acceptance. Buys first North American serial rights, buys electronic rights, buys international rights. Submit seasonal material 6 months in advance. Accepts queries by mail. Responds in 2 months to queries. Guidelines for #10 SASE.

Nonfiction Needs general interest, how-to, humor, interview, photo feature, travel, dog art, training and canine performance sports. No poetry, tributes to individual dogs, or fiction. **Buys 30-40 mss/year.** Length: 1,000-3,000 words. **Pays $300-500.** Pays expenses of writers on assignment.

Photos Photo contest guidelines for #10 SASE. State availability Captions, identification of subjects, model releases required. Reviews color transparencies, prints. Pays $50-200/photo Buys one time rights.

Fiction Annual short fiction contest only. Guidelines for #10 SASE.

Tips Contributors should be involved in the dog fancy or be an expert in the area they write about (veterinary, showing, field trialing, obedience training, dogs in legislation, dog art or history or literature). All submissions are welcome but author must be a credible expert or be able to interview and quote the experts. Veterinary articles must be written by or with veterinarians. Humorous features or personal experiences relative to purebred dogs should have broader applications. For features, know the subject thoroughly and be conversant with jargon peculiar to the sport of dogs.

$$ $$$$ THE AMERICAN QUARTER HORSE JOURNAL

AQHA, 1600 Quarter Horse Dr., Amarillo TX 79104. (806)358-3702. Fax: (806)349-6400. E-mail: jbcampbell@aqha.org. Website: www.aqha.com. **30% freelance written. Prefers to work with published/established writers.** Monthly official publication of the american quarter horse association. covering American Quarter Horses/horse activities/western lifestyle. "Covers the American quarter Horse breed and more than 30 disciplines in which Quarter Horses compete. Business stories, lifestyles stories, how-to stories and others related to the breed and horse activities." Estab. 1948. Circ. 60,000. Byline given. Pays on acceptance. Offers 60% kill fee. Publishes ms an average of 3 months after acceptance. Buys first North American serial rights, buys electronic rights. Editorial lead time 3 months. Submit seasonal material 3 months in advance. Accepts queries by mail, e-mail. Accepts previously published material. Accepts simultaneous submissions. Responds in 1 week to queries. Responds in 1 month to mss. Sample copy free. Guidelines free.

Nonfiction Needs book excerpts, essays, general interest, historical, how-to, fitting, grooming, showing, or anything that relates to owning, showing, or breeding, humor, inspirational, interview, feature-type stories, travel., "Must be about established horses or people who have made a contribution to the business, new prod, opinion, personal exp, photo, technical, equine updates, new surgery procedures, etc.". Annual stallion issue dedicated to the breeding of horses. **Buys 10 mss/year.** Query with published clips. Length: 700-3,000 words. **Pays $250-1,500 for assigned articles. Pays $250-1,500 for unsolicited articles.** Sometimes pays expenses of writers on assignment.

Photos State availability Captions, identification of subjects required. Reviews GIF/JPEG files. Buys all rights.

Columns/Departments Quarter's Worth (Industry news); Horse Health (health items), 750 words. 6 mss/yr.

Query with published clips. **Pays $ $100-$400.**
Tips Writers must have a knowledge of the horse business.

$ $ APPALOOSA JOURNAL

Appaloosa Horse Club, 2720 West Pullman Rd., Moscow ID 83843. (208)882-5578. Fax: (208)882-8150. E-mail: drice@appaloosajournal.com. Website: www.appaloosajournal.com. **40% freelance written**. Monthly magazine covering Appaloosa horses. Estab. 1946. Circ. 25,000. Byline given. Pays on publication. Publishes ms an average of 3 months after acceptance. Buys first North American serial rights, buys electronic rights. Responds in 1 month to queries. Responds in 2 months to mss. Sample copy free. Guidelines available online.

- *Appaloosa Journal* no longer accepts material for columns.

Nonfiction Needs historical, interview, photo feature. **Buys 15-20 mss/year.** Send complete ms. Length: 800-1,800 words. **Pays $200-400.**
Photos Send photos Captions, identification of subjects required. Payment varies
Tips Articles by writers with horse knowledge, news sense, and photography skills are in great demand. If it's a strong article about an Appaloosa, the writer has a pretty good chance of publication. A good understanding of the breed and the industry, breeders, and owners is helpful. Make sure there's some substance and a unique twist.

$ $ AQUARIUM FISH INTERNATIONAL

Fishkeeping—the Art and the Science, Bowtie, Inc., P.O. Box 6050, Mission Viejo CA 92690. Fax: (949)855-3045. E-mail: aquariumfish@bowtieinc.com. Website: www.aquariumfish.com. **Contact:** Patricia Knight, man. ed. **90% freelance written**. Monthly magazine covering fish and other aquatic pets. "Our focus is on beginning and intermediate fish keeping; we also run one advanced saltwater article per issue. Most of our articles concentrate on general fish and aquarium care, but we will also consider other types of articles that may be helpful to those in the fishkeeping hobby. Freshwater and saltwater tanks, and ponds are covered." Estab. 1988. Byline given. Pays on publication. Buys first North American serial rights, buys electronic rights. Accepts queries by mail, e-mail, fax. Responds in 1 month to queries. Responds in 6 months to mss. Guidelines for #10 SASE.
Nonfiction Needs general interest, species profiles, natural history with home care info, new product, press releases only for Product Showcase section, photo feature, caring for fish in aquariums. We do have 1 annual; freelancers should query. No fiction, anthropomorphism, articles on sport fishing, or animals that cannot be kept as pets (i.e., whales, dolphins, manatees, etc.). **Buys 60 mss/year.** Send complete ms. Length: 1,500-2,000 words. **Pays 15¢/word.**
Photos Send for digital image requirements. State availability Identification of subjects required. Reviews 35mm transparencies, 4x5 prints. Offers $15-200/photo. Buys first North American serial rights.
Fillers Needs facts, gags, newsbreaks. variable number Length: 50-200 words.
Tips "Take a look at our guidelines before submitting. Writers are not required to provide photos for submitted articles, but we do encourage it, if possible. It helps if writers are involved in fish keeping themselves. Our writers tend to be experienced fish keepers, detailed researchers, and some scientists."

⊘ 🌐 ARABIAN STUDS & STALLIONS ANNUAL

Vink Publishing, Arabian Studs & Stallions Annual, P.O. Box 8369, Woolloongabba QLD 4102 Australia. (61)(7)3334-8000. Fax: (61)(7)3391-5118. E-mail: sharon@vinkpub.com; montbrae@bigpond.net.au. Website: www.vinkpub.com.au. "Annual magazine covering International Arabian horses and people connected with the Arabian horse from Australia and around the world.".

- Query before submitting.

⊘ 🌐 THE AUSTRALIAN ARABIAN HORSE NEWS

Vink Publishing, P.O. Box 8369, Woolloongabba QLD 4102 Australia. (61)(7)3334-8000. Fax: (61)(7)3391-5118. E-mail: sharon@vinkpub.com. Website: www.arabianhorse.com.au. Quarterly magazine covering Australian Arabian horses.

- Query before submitting.

$ 🌐 BIRDING WORLD

Sea Lawn, Coast Road, Cley next the Sea, Holt Norfolk NR25 7RZ United Kingdom. (44)(126)374-0913. E-mail: steve@birdingworld.co.uk. Website: www.birdingworld.co.uk. Monthly magazine publishing notes about birds and birdwatching. The emphasis is on rarer British and Western Palearctic birds with topical interest. Estab. 1988. No kill fee. Accepts queries by mail, e-mail. Sample copy for £4.50. Guidelines by email.
Nonfiction Pays £2-4/100 words for unsolicited articles.
Photos Reviews digital images, drawings, maps, graphs, paintings. Pays £10-30/color photos; £5-25/b&w photos.

$ $ CAT FANCY

Cat Fancy Query, P.O. Box 6050, Mission Viejo CA 92690. E-mail: query@catfancy.com. Website: www.catfancy.com. **90% freelance written.** Monthly magazine covering all aspects of responsible cat ownership. Estab. 1965. Pays on publication. Buys first North American serial rights. Editorial lead time 6 months. Responds in 3 months to queries. Guidelines available online.

- "*Cat Fancy* does not accept unsolicited mss and only accepts queries from January-May. Queries sent after May will be returned or discarded. Show us how you can contribute something new and unique. No phone queries."

Nonfiction Engaging presentation of expert, up-to-date information. Must be cat oriented. Writing should not be gender specific. Needs how-to, humor, photo feature, travel, behavior, health, lifestyle, cat culture, entertainment. fiction, poetry **Buys 70 mss/year.** Query with published clips. Length: 300-1,000 words. **Pays $50-450.**

Photos "Seeking photos of happy, healthy, well-groomed cats and kittens in indoor settings." Captions, identification of subjects, model releases required. Negotiates payment individually. Buys one time rights.

Tips "Please read recent issues to become acquainted with our style and content."

$ $ THE CHRONICLE OF THE HORSE

P.O. Box 46, Middleburg VA 20118-0046. (540)687-6341. Fax: (540)687-3937. E-mail: staff@chronofhorse.com. Website: www.chronofhorse.com. **80% freelance written.** Weekly magazine covering horses. We cover English riding sports, including horse showing, grand prix jumping competitions, steeplechase racing, foxhunting, dressage, endurance riding, handicapped riding, and combined training. We are the official publication for the national governing bodies of many of the above sports. We feature news, how-to articles on equitation and horse care and interviews with leaders in the various fields. Estab. 1937. Circ. 18,000. Byline given. Pays for features on acceptance; news and other items on publication. Publishes ms an average of 4 months after acceptance. Buys first North American serial rights. Makes work-for-hire assignments. Submit seasonal material 3 months in advance. Accepts queries by mail, e-mail. Responds in 5-6 weeks to queries. Sample copy for $2 and 9x12 SAE. Guidelines available online.

Nonfiction Needs general interest, historical, history of breeds, use of horses in other countries and times, art, etc., how-to, trailer, train, design a course, save money, etc., humor, centered on living with horses or horse people, interview, of nationally known horsemen or the very unusual, technical, horse care, articles on feeding, injuries, care of foals, shoeing, etc. Steeplechase Racing (January); American Horse in Sport and Grand Prix Jumping (February); Horse Show (March); Intercollegiate (April); Kentucky 4-Star Preview (April); Junior and Pony (April); Dressage (June); Horse Care (July); Combined Training (August); Hunt Roster (September); Amateur (November); Stallion (December). No poetry, Q&A interviews, clinic reports, Western riding articles, personal experience or wild horses. **Buys 300 mss/year.** Send complete ms. 6-7 pages **Pays $150-250.**

Photos State availability Identification of subjects required. Reviews e-mailed image, prints or color slides; accepts color for color reproduction. Pays $25-50 Buys one time rights.

Columns/Departments Dressage, Combined Training, Horse Show, Horse Care, Racing over Fences, Young Entry (about young riders, geared for youth), Horses and Humanities, Hunting, Vaulting, Handicapped Riding, Trail Riding, 1,000-1,225 words; News of major competitions (clear assignment with us first), 1,500 words. Query with or without published clips or send complete ms. **Pays $25-200.**

Tips Get our guidelines. Our readers are sophisticated, competitive horsemen. Articles need to go beyond common knowledge. Freelancers often attempt too broad or too basic a subject. We welcome well-written news stories on major events, but clear the assignment with us.

$ COONHOUND BLOODLINES

The Complete Magazine for the Houndsman and Coon Hunter, United Kennel Club, Inc., 100 E. Kilgore Rd., Kalamazoo MI 49002-5584. (269)343-9020. Fax: (269)343-7037. Website: www.ukcdogs.com. **40% freelance written.** Monthly magazine covering all aspects of the 6 Coonhound dog breeds. Writers must retain the 'slang' particular to dog people and to our readers—many of whom are from the South. Estab. 1925. Circ. 16,000. Byline given. Pays on publication. No kill fee. Publishes ms an average of 6 months after acceptance. Buys first North American serial rights. Makes work-for-hire assignments. Editorial lead time 6 months. Submit seasonal material 6 months in advance. Accepts queries by mail, e-mail, fax, phone. Accepts simultaneous submissions. Responds in 6 weeks to queries. Sample copy for $4.50.

Nonfiction Needs general interest, historical, humor, interview, new product, personal experience, photo feature, breed-specific. Six of our 12 issues are each devoted to a specific breed of Coonhound. Treeing Walker (February); English (July); Black & Tan (April); Bluetick (May); Redbone (June); Plott Hound (August), 1,000-3,000 words and photos. **Buys 12-36 mss/year.** Query. Length: 1,000-5,000 words. **Pays variable amount.** Sometimes pays expenses of writers on assignment.

Photos State availability Captions, identification of subjects required. Reviews contact sheets. Negotiates payment individually Buys one time rights.

Fiction Must be about the Coonhound breeds or hunting with hounds. Needs adventure, historical, humorous, mystery. **Buys 3-6 mss/year.** Query. Length: 1,000-3,000 words. **Pay varies.**

Tips Hunting with hounds is a two-century old American tradition and an important part of the American heritage, especially east of the Mississippi. It covers a lifestyle as well as a wonderful segment of the American population, many of whom still live by honest, friendly values.

$ $ DOG FANCY

P.O. Box 6050, Mission Viejo CA 92690-6050. E-mail: barkback@dogfancy.com. Website: www.dogfancy.com. **95% freelance written**. Monthly magazine for men and women of all ages interested in all phases of dog ownership. Estab. 1970. Circ. 250,000. Byline given. Pays on publication. Offers kill fee. Publishes ms an average of 6 months after acceptance. Buys first North American serial rights, buys nonexclusive electronic and other rights. Accepts queries by e-mail. Responds in 2 months to queries. Sample copy for $5.50. Guidelines available online.

- Reading period from January through April.

Nonfiction Needs general interest, how-to, humor, inspirational, interview, photo feature, travel. "No stories written from a dog's point of view." **Buys 80; 10 or fewer from new writers. mss/year.** Query. Length: 800-1,200 words. **Pays 40¢/word**

Photos State availability Reviews transparencies, slides. Offers no additional payment for photos accepted with ms.

Columns/Departments Newshound, Living With Dogs, Sports & Exercise briefs, 500 words. 6 Query by e-mail. **Pays 40¢/word**

Tips "We're looking for the unique experience that enhances the dog/owner relationship. Medical articles are assigned to veterinarians. Note that we write for a lay audience (nontechnical), but we do assume a certain level of intelligence. Read the magazine before making a pitch. Make sure your query is clear, concise, and relevant."

$ DOG SPORTS MAGAZINE

4215 S. Lowell Rd., St. Johns MI 48879. (989)224-7225. Fax: (989)224-6033. Website: www.dogsports.com. **5% freelance written**. Monthly tabloid covering working dogs. Estab. 1979. Circ. 2,000. Byline given. Pays on publication. Publishes ms an average of 1 month after acceptance. Buys first North American serial rights, buys second serial (reprint) rights. Editorial lead time 1 month. Submit seasonal material 1 month in advance. Accepts queries by mail, e-mail. Accepts previously published material. Accepts simultaneous submissions. Sample copy free or online

Nonfiction Needs essays, general interest, how-to, working dogs, humor, interview, technical. **Buys 5 mss/year.** Send complete ms. **Pays $50.**

Photos State availability Captions, identification of subjects required. Reviews prints. Offers no additional payment for photos accepted with ms. Buys all rights.

$ $ EQUESTRIAN MAGAZINE

The Official Magazine of Equestrian Sport Since 1937, United States Equestrian Federation (USEF), 4047 Iron Works Parkway, Lexington KY 40511. (859)225-6934. Fax: (859)231-6662. E-mail: bsosby@usef.org. Website: www.usef.org. **10-30% freelance written**. Magazine published 10 times/year covering the equestrian sport. Estab. 1937. Circ. 77,000. Byline given. Pays on publication. Offers 50% kill fee. Buys first North American serial rights, buys first rights. Editorial lead time 1-5 months. Accepts queries by mail, e-mail, fax, phone. Sample copy and writer's guidelines free.

Nonfiction Needs interview, technical, all equestrian-related. **Buys 20-30 mss/year.** Query with published clips. Length: 500-3,500 words. **Pays $200-500.**

Photos State availability Captions, identification of subjects, model releases required. Reviews contact sheets. Offers $50-200/photo. Buys one time rights.

Columns/Departments Horses of the Past (famous equines); Horse People (famous horsemen/women), both 500-1,000 words. 20-30 Query with published clips. **Pays $100.**

Tips Write via e-mail in first instance with samples, résumé, then mail original clips.

$ EQUINE JOURNAL

103 Roxbury St., Keene NH 03431. (603)357-4271. Fax: (603)357-7851. E-mail: editorial@equinejournal.com. Website: www.equinejournal.com. **90% freelance written**. Monthly tabloid covering horses—all breeds, all disciplines. To educate, entertain, and enable amateurs and professionals alike to stay on top of new developments in the field. Covers horse-related activities from all corners of New England, New York, New Jersey, Pennsylvania, and the Midwest. Estab. 1988. Circ. 26,000. Byline given. Pays on publication. Buys first North American serial rights, buys electronic rights. Editorial lead time 4 months. Accepts queries by mail, e-mail, fax, phone. Responds in 2 months to queries. Guidelines available online.

Nonfiction Needs general interest, how-to, interview. **Buys 100 mss/year.** Send complete ms. Length: 1,500-2,200 words.

Photos Send photos Reviews prints. Pays $10

Columns/Departments Horse Health (health-related topics), 1,200-1,500 words. 12 Query.

EQUUS

656 Quince Orchard Rd., Suite 600, Gaithersburg MD 20878-1409. Fax: (301)990-9015. E-mail: EEQEletters@equinetwork.com. Website: www.equisearch.com. Monthly magazine covering equine behavior. Provides the latest information from the world's top veterinarians, equine researchers, riders, and trainers. Circ. 149,482. No kill fee. Accepts queries by mail. Guidelines available online.

Nonfiction Features on healthcare, behavior, training techniques, veterinary breakthroughs, exercise physiology, etc. Send complete ms. Length: 1,600-3,000 words. **Payment depends on quality, length, and complexity of the story.**

Columns/Departments The Medical Front (research/technology/treatments), 200-400 words; Hands On (everyday horse care), 100-400 words; Roundup (industry news stories), 100-400 words; True Tales (experiences/relationships with horses), 700-2,000 words; Case Report (equine illness/injury), 1,000-2,500 words. Send complete ms. **Payment depends on quality, length, and complexity of the story.**

$ $ FIDO FRIENDLY MAGAZINE

Fido Friendly, Inc., P.O. Box 160, Marsing ID 83639. E-mail: susan@fidofriendly.com. Website: www.fidofriendly.com. **95% freelance written**. Bimonthly magazine covering travel with your dog. "We want articles about all things travel related with your dog". Estab. 2,000. Circ. 44,000. Byline given. Pays on publication. No kill fee. Publishes ms an average of 2 months after acceptance. Buys first North American serial rights, buys electronic rights. Editorial lead time 1-3 months. Submit seasonal material 3 months in advance. Accepts queries by e-mail. Accepts simultaneous submissions. Responds in 2 weeks to queries. Responds in 1 month to mss Sample copy for $7 Guidelines free

Nonfiction Contact: Susan Sims, publisher. Needs essays, general interest, how-to, travel with your dog, humor, inspirational, interview, personal experience, travel. No articles about dog's point of view - dog's voice. **Buys 24 mss/yr. mss/year.** Query with published clips. Length: 600-1,200 words. **Pays 10-20¢ for assigned articles. Pays 10-20¢ for unsolicited articles.**

Photos Contact: Susan Sims. Send photos Captions, identification of subjects, model releases required. Reviews GIF/JPEG files. Offers no additional payment for photos accepted with ms. Buys one time rights.

Columns/Departments Fido Friendly City (City where dogs have lots of options to enjoy restaurants, dog retail stores, dog parks, sports activity.) 6 mss/yr. Query with published clips. **Pays 10-20¢/word**

Fiction Contact: Susan Sims. Needs adventure, (dog). Nothing from dog's point of view. **Buys 0 mss/year.** Query. Length: 600-1,200 words. **Pays $10¢-20¢.**

Tips "Accept copies in lieu of payment. Our readers treat their pets as part of the family. Writing should reflect that."

$ $ FIELD TRIAL MAGAZINE

Androscoggin Publishing, Inc., P.O. Box 298, Milan NH 03588. (603)449-6767. Fax: (603)449-2462. E-mail: birddog@wildblue.net. Website: www.fielddog.com/ftm. **75% freelance written.** Quarterly magazine covering field trials for pointing dogs. "Our readers are knowledgeable sports men and women who want interesting and informative articles about their sport." Estab. 1997. Circ. 6,000. Byline given. Pays on publication. Publishes ms an average of 6 months after acceptance. Buys first North American serial rights. Editorial lead time 3 months. Submit seasonal material 6 months in advance. Accepts queries by mail, e-mail, fax. Accepts simultaneous submissions. Responds in 2 weeks to queries. Responds in 2 months to mss. Sample copy free. Guidelines available online.

Nonfiction Needs book excerpts, essays, general interest, historical, how-to, interview, opinion, personal experience. No hunting articles. **Buys 12-16 mss/year.** Query. Length: 1,000-3,000 words. **Pays $100-300.**

Photos Send photos Captions, identification of subjects required. Offers no additional payment for photos accepted with ms Buys one time rights.

Fiction "Fiction that deals with bird dogs and field trials." **Buys 4 mss/year.** Send complete ms. Length: 1,000-2,500 words. **Pays $100-250.**

Tips "Make sure you have correct and accurate information—we'll work with a writer who has good solid info even if the writing needs work."

$ THE GREYHOUND REVIEW

P.O. Box 543, Abilene KS 67410. (785)263-4660. E-mail: review@ngagreyhounds.com. Website: www.ngagreyhounds.com. **20% freelance written**. Monthly magazine covering greyhound breeding, training, and racing. Estab. 1911. Circ. 3,500. Byline given. Pays on acceptance. No kill fee. Buys first rights. Submit seasonal material 2 months in advance. Responds in 2 weeks to queries. Responds in 1 month to mss. Sample copy for $3. Guidelines free.

Nonfiction "Articles must be targeted at the greyhound industry: from hard news, to special events at racetracks, to the latest medical discoveries." Needs how-to, interview, personal experience. Do not submit gambling systems. **Buys 24 mss/year.** Query. Length: 1,000-10,000 words. **Pays $85-150.**

Reprints Send photocopy. Pays 100% of amount paid for original article.
Photos State availability Identification of subjects required. Reviews digital images. Pays $10-50 photo. Buys one time rights.

$ $ $ HORSE&RIDER

The magazine of western riding, 2000 S. Stemmons Freeway, Ste. 101, Lake Dallas TX 75065. E-mail: horseandrider@equinetwork.com. Website: www.horseandrider.com. **Contact:** Erin Sullivan, Editorial Coordinator. **10% freelance written**. Monthly magazine covering Western horse industry, competition, recreation. "*Horse&Rider*'s mission is to enhance the enjoyment and satisfaction readers derive from horse involvement. We strive to do this by providing the insights, knowledge, and horsemanship skills they need to safely and effectively handle, ride, and appreciate their horses, in and out of the competition arena. We also help them find the time, resources, and energy they need to enjoy their horse to the fullest." Estab. 1961. Circ. 164,000. Byline given. Pays on acceptance. Publishes ms an average of 1 year after acceptance. Buys first North American serial rights. Editorial lead time 2 months. Submit seasonal material 6 months in advance. Accepts queries by mail, e-mail. Responds in 3 months to queries. Responds in 3 months to mss. Sample copy and writer's guidelines online.

- Online magazine carries original content not found in the print edition.

Nonfiction Needs book excerpts, general interest, how-to, horse training, horsemanship, humor, interview, new product, personal experience, photo feature, travel, horse health care, trail riding. **Buys 5-10 mss/year.** Send complete ms. Length: 1,000-3,000 words. **Pays $150-1,000.**
Photos State availability of or send photos Captions, identification of subjects, model releases required. Negotiates payment individually. Buys rights on assignment or stock.
Tips "Writers should have patience, ability to accept critical editing, and extensive knowledge of the Western horse industry and our publication."

$ $ $ THE HORSE

Your Guide To Equine Health Care, P.O. Box 919003, Lexington KY 40591-9003. (859)278-2361. Fax: (859)276-4450. E-mail: kbrown@thehorse.com. Website: www.thehorse.com. **85% freelance written**. Monthly magazine covering equine health, care, management and welfare. *The Horse* is an educational/news magazine geared toward the hands-on horse owner. Estab. 1983. Circ. 55,000. Byline given. Pays on acceptance. Publishes ms an average of 6 months after acceptance. Buys first world and electronic rights Accepts queries by mail, e-mail. Responds in 3 months to queries. Sample copy for $3.95 or online. Guidelines available online.
Nonfiction Needs how-to, technical, topical interviews. No first-person experiences not from professionals; this is a technical magazine to inform horse owners. **Buys 90 mss/year.** Query with published clips. Length: 250-4,000 words. **Pays $60-850.**
Photos Send photos Captions, identification of subjects required. Reviews transparencies. Offers $35-350
Columns/Departments News Front (news on horse health), 100-500 words; Equinomics (economics of horse ownership); Step by Step (feet and leg care); Nutrition; Reproduction; Back to Basics, all 1,500-2,200 words. 50 Query with published clips. **Pays $50-450.**
Tips We publish reliable horse health care and management information from top industry professionals and researchers around the world. Manuscript must be submitted electronically or on disk.

HORSE-CANADA

Horse Publications Group, Box 670, Aurora ON L4G 4J9 Canada. (905)727-0107. Fax: (905)841-1530. E-mail: info@horse-canada.com. Website: www.horse-canada.com. **80% freelance written**. National magazine for horse lovers of all ages. Readers are committed horse owners with many different breeds involved in a variety of disciplines—from beginner riders to industry professionals. *Horsepower* is for horse-crazy kids and is inserted into *Horse Canada* to entertain and educate future equestrians. Circ. 20,000. No kill fee. Buys all rights. Editorial lead time 2 months. Accepts queries by e-mail. Guidelines available online.
Nonfiction Health and management topics, training tips, rural living, and hot industry issues. Query. Length: 750-1,500 words. **Payment varies.**
Photos State availability of or send photos
Columns/Departments The Tail End (humor). **Payment varies.**

$ HORSE CONNECTION

Horse Connection, LLC, 1263 Park St., Suite A, Castle Rock CO 80109. (303)663-1300. Fax: (303)663-1331. Website: www.horseconnection.com. **90% freelance written**. Magazine published 12 times/year covering horse owners and riders. Our readers are horse owners and riders. They specialize in English riding. We primarily focus on show jumping and hunters, dressage, and three-day events, with additional coverage of driving, polo, and endurance. Estab. 1995. Circ. 25,000. Byline given. Pays on publication. No kill fee. Publishes ms an average of 1 month after acceptance. Buys first rights, buys second serial (reprint) rights. Editorial lead time 3 months. Submit seasonal material 3 months in advance. Accepts queries by e-mail. Responds in 1 month to queries. Sample copy for $3.50 or online. Guidelines for #10 SASE or online.

Nonfiction Needs humor, interview, personal experience, event reports. No general interest stories about horses. Nothing negative. No western, racing, or breed specific articles. No my first pony stories. **Buys 30-50 mss/year.** Query with published clips. Length: 500-1,000 words. **Pays $25 for assigned articles. Pays $75 for unsolicited articles.** Sometimes pays expenses of writers on assignment.
Photos State availability Negotiates payment individually Buys one time rights.
Tips Please read the magazine. We are currently focused on the western states and we like stories about English riders from these states.

$ $ HORSE ILLUSTRATED

The Magazine for Hands-On Owners & Riders, BowTie, Inc., P.O. Box 8237, Lexington KY 40533. (859)260-9800. Fax: (859)260-1154. Website: www.horseillustrated.com. **Contact:** Kimberly Abbott. **90% freelance written. Prefers to work with published/established writers but will work with new/unpublished writers.** Monthly magazine covering all aspects of horse ownership. "Our readers are adults, mostly women, between the ages of 18 and 40; stories should be geared to that age group and reflect responsible horse care." Estab. 1976. Circ. 185,000. Byline given. Pays on publication. Publishes ms an average of 8 months after acceptance. Buys one-time rights, requires first North American rights among equine publications. Submit seasonal material 6 months in advance. Accepts queries by mail. Responds in 3 months to queries. Guidelines for #10 SASE and are available online at www.horsechannel.com/horse-magazines/horse-illustrated/submission-guidelines.aspx.
Nonfiction We are looking for authoritative, in-depth features on trends and issues in the horse industry. Such articles must be queried first with a detailed outline of the article and clips. We rarely have a need for fiction. Needs general interest, how-to, horse care, training, veterinary care, inspirational, photo feature. No little girl horse stories, cowboy and Indian stories or anything not *directly* relating to horses. **Buys 20 mss/year.** Query or send complete ms. Length: 1,000-2,000 words. **Pays $200-400.**
Photos Send high-resolution digital images on a CD with thumbnails.
Tips "Freelancers can break in at this publication with feature articles on Western and English training methods; veterinary and general care how-to articles; and horse sports articles. We rarely use personal experience articles. Submit photos with training and how-to articles whenever possible. We have a very good record of developing new freelancers into regular contributors/columnists. We are always looking for fresh talent, but certainly enjoy working with established writers who `know the ropes' as well. We are accepting less unsolicited freelance work—much is now assigned and contracted."

$ I LOVE CATS

I Love Cats Publishing, 1040 First Ave., Suite 323, New York NY 10022. E-mail: ilovecatseditor@sbcglobal.net. Website: www.iluvcats.com. **100% freelance written**. Bimonthly magazine. "*I Love Cats* is a general interest cat magazine for the entire family. It caters to cat lovers of all ages. The stories in the magazine include fiction, nonfiction, how-to, humorous, and columns for the cat lover." Estab. 1989. Circ. 25,000. Byline given. Pays on publication. No kill fee. Publishes ms an average of 2 years after acceptance. Buys all rights. Editorial lead time 6 months. Submit seasonal material 9 months in advance. Accepts queries by mail, e-mail. Responds in 3 months to queries. Sample copy for $5. Guidelines available online.
Nonfiction Needs essays, general interest, how-to, humor, inspirational, interview, new product, opinion, personal experience, photo feature. No poetry. **Buys 50 mss/year.** Send complete ms. Length: 500-1,000 words. **Pays $50-100, or contributor copies or other premiums if requested.** Sometimes pays expenses of writers on assignment.
Photos Please send copies; art will no longer be returned. Send photos Identification of subjects required. Offers no additional payment for photos accepted with ms. Buys all rights.
Fiction Needs adventure, fantasy, historical, humorous, mainstream, mystery, novel concepts, slice-of-life vignettes, suspense. "This is a family magazine. No graphic violence, pornography, or other inappropriate material. *I Love Cats* is strictly 'G-rated.'" **Buys 50 mss/year.** Send complete ms. Length: 500-1,000 words. **Pays $50 and offers contributor copies.**
Fillers Needs anecdotes, facts, short humor. 25 **Pays $25.**
Tips "Please keep stories short and concise. Send complete manuscript with photos, if possible. I buy lots of first-time authors. Nonfiction pieces with color photos are always in short supply. With the exception of the standing columns, the rest of the magazine is open to freelancers. Be witty, humorous, or offer a different approach to writing."

$ $ JUST LABS

A Celebration of the Labrador Retriever, Village Press, 2779 Aero Park Dr., Traverse City MI 49686. Website: www.justlabsmagazine.com. **50% freelance written**. Bimonthly magazine. "*Just Labs* is targeted toward the family Labrador Retriever, and all of our articles help people learn about, live with, train, take care of, and enjoy their dogs. We do not look for articles that pull at the heart strings (those are usually staff-written), but rather we look for articles that teach, inform, and entertain." Estab. 2001. Circ. 20,000. Byline given. Pays on publication. Offers 40% kill fee. Publishes ms an average of 6 months after acceptance. Buys first North

American serial rights. Editorial lead time 6 months. Submit seasonal material 6-8 months in advance. Accepts queries by mail. Responds in 4-6 weeks to queries. Responds in 2 months to mss. Guidelines for #10 SASE.
Nonfiction Needs essays, how-to, (train, health, lifestyle), humor, inspirational, interview, photo feature, technical, travel. We don't want tributes to dogs that have passed on. This is a privilege we reserve for our subscribers. **Buys 30 mss/year mss/year.** Query. Length: 1,000-1,800 words. **Pays $250-400 for assigned articles. Pays $250-400 for unsolicited articles.**
Photos Send photos Captions required. Reviews contact sheets, transparencies, prints, GIF/JPEG files. Offers no additional payment for photos accepted with ms. Buys one time rights.
Tips "Be professional, courteous and understanding of my time. Please be aware that we have been around for several years and have probably published an article on almost every 'dog topic' out there. Those queries providing fresh, unique and interesting angles on common topics will catch our eye."

$ MINIATURE DONKEY TALK

Miniature Donkey Talk, Inc., 1338 Hughes Shop Rd., Westminster MD 21158. (410)875-0118. E-mail: minidonk@qis.net. Website: www.miniaturedonkey.net. **65% freelance written.** Quarterly magazine covering donkeys, with articles on healthcare, promotion, and management of donkeys for owners, breeders, or donkey lovers. Estab. 1987. Circ. 4,925. Byline given. Pays on acceptance. Publishes ms an average of 4 months after acceptance. Buys first rights, buys second serial (reprint) rights. Editorial lead time 2 months. Submit seasonal material 3 months in advance. Accepts queries by mail, e-mail, fax. Accepts previously published material. Responds in 2 weeks to queries. Responds in 1 month to mss. Sample copy for $5. Guidelines free.
Nonfiction We accept breeder profiles—either of yourself or another breeder. We cover nonshow events such as fairs, donkey gatherings, holiday events, etc. We want relevant, informative equine health pieces. We much prefer they deal specifically with donkeys, but will consider articles geared toward horses. If at all possible, substitute the word 'horse' for 'donkey.' We reserve the right to edit, change, delete, or add to health articles. Please be careful with the accuracy of advice or training material, as well as farm management articles and fictional stories on donkeys. Needs book excerpts, humor, interview, personal experience. **Buys 6 mss/year.** Query with published clips. Length: 700-5,000 words. **Pays $25-150.**
Photos State availability Identification of subjects required. Reviews 3x5 prints. Offers no additional payment for photos accepted with ms. Buys one time rights.
Columns/Departments Humor, 2,000 words; Healthcare, 2,000-5,000 words; Management, 2,000 words. 50 Query. **Pays $25-100.**
Tips Simply send your manuscript. If on topic and appropriate, good possibility it will be published. No fiction or poetry.

$ $ MUSHING

P.O. Box 1195, Willow AK 99688. (907)495-2468. E-mail: editor@mushing.com. Website: www.mushing.com. Bimonthly magazine covering "all aspects of the growing sports of dogsledding, skijoring, carting, dog packing, and weight pulling. *Mushing* promotes responsible dog care through feature articles and updates on working animal health care, safety, nutrition, and training." Estab. 1987. Circ. 6,000. Byline given. Pays within 3 months of publication. No kill fee. Publishes ms an average of 4 months after acceptance. Buys first rights, buys second serial (reprint) rights. Submit seasonal material 4 months in advance. Accepts queries by mail, e-mail, fax, phone. Responds in 8 months to queries. Sample copy for $5 ($6 US to Canada). Guidelines available online.
Nonfiction "We consider articles on canine health and nutrition, sled dog behavior and training, musher profiles and interviews, equipment how-to's, trail tips, expedition and race accounts, innovations, sled dog history, current issues, personal experiences, and humor." Needs historical, how-to. Iditarod and Long-Distance Racing (January/February); Ski or Sprint Racing (March/April); Health and Nutrition (May/June); Musher and Dog Profiles, Summer Activities (July/August); Equipment, Fall Training (September/October); Races and Places (November/December). Query with or without published clips. Considers complete ms with SASE. Length: 1,000-2,500 words. **Pays $50-250.** Sometimes pays expenses of writers on assignment.
Photos "We look for good quality color for covers and specials." Send photos Captions, identification of subjects. Reviews digital images only. Pays $20-165/photo Buys one-time and second reprint rights.
Columns/Departments Query with or without published clips or send complete ms.
Fillers Needs anecdotes, facts, newsbreaks, short humor, cartoons, puzzles. Length: 100-250 words. **Pays $20-35.**
Tips "Read our magazine. Know something about dog-driven, dog-powered sports."

$ $ PAINT HORSE JOURNAL

American Paint Horse Association, P.O. Box 961023, Fort Worth TX 76161-0023. (817)834-2742. Website: www.painthorsejournal.com. **10% freelance written. Works with a small number of new/unpublished writers each year.** Monthly magazine for people who raise, breed and show Paint Horses. Estab. 1966. Circ. 20,000. Byline given. Pays on acceptance. Offers negotiable kill fee. Buys first North American serial rights. Submit seasonal material 3 months in advance. Accepts queries by mail, e-mail, fax. Sample copy for $4.50. Guidelines available online.

Nonfiction Needs general interest, personality pieces on well-known owners of Paints, historical, Paint Horses in the past—particular horses and the breed in general, how-to, train and show horses, photo feature, Paint Horses. **Buys 4-5 mss/year.** Query. Length: 1,000-2,000 words. **Pays $100-500.**

Photos Photos must illustrate article and must include registered Paint Horses. Send photos Captions required. Reviews 35mm or larger transparencies, 3x5 or larger color glossy prints, digital images on CD or DVD. Offers no additional payment for photos accepted with accompanying ms.

Tips "Well-written first person articles are welcomed. Submit items that show a definite understanding of the horse business. Be sure you understand precisely what a Paint Horse is as defined by the American Paint Horse Association. Use proper equine terminology. Photos with copy are almost always essential."

N PET NEW ZEALAND

P.O. Box 37 356, Parnell Auckland New Zealand. (64)(9)336-1188. Fax: (64)(9)373-5647. E-mail: enquiries@petmag.co.nz. Website: www.petmag.co.nz. Quarterly magazine covering topics for pet owners and animal lovers. "*Pet New Zealand* promotes public awareness of pet issues, educates through practical advice, features heart-warming stories and pet products, and provides expert advice." No kill fee.

- Query before submitting.

$ $ REPTILES

The World's Leading Reptile Magazine, BowTie, Inc., P.O. Box 6050, Mission Viejo CA 92690. (949)855-8822. E-mail: reptiles@bowtieinc.com. Website: www.reptilesmagazine.com. **20% freelance written**. Monthly magazine covering reptiles and amphibians. *Reptiles* covers "a wide range of topics relating to reptiles and amphibians, including breeding, captive care, field herping, etc." Estab. 1992. Byline given. Pays on publication. Offers 20% kill fee. Publishes ms an average of 6-8 months after acceptance. Buys first North American serial rights, buys electronic rights. Accepts queries by mail, e-mail. Responds in 1 month to queries. Responds in 1-2 months to mss. Sample copy available online. Guidelines available online.

Nonfiction Needs general interest, historical, how-to, interview, personal experience, photo feature, travel. **Buys 10 mss/year.** Query. Length: 1,000-2,000 words. **Pays $250-500.**

Tips "Keep in mind that *Reptiles* has a very knowledgeable readership when it comes to herps. While we accept freelance articles, the bulk of what we publish comes from 'herp people.' Do your research, interview experts, etc., for the best results."

$ ROCKY MOUNTAIN RIDER MAGAZINE

Regional All-Breed Horse Monthly, P.O. Box 995, Hamilton MT 59840. (888)747-1000. E-mail: info@rockymountainrider.com. Website: www.rockymountainrider.com. **90% freelance written.** Monthly magazine for horse owners and enthusiasts. Estab. 1993. Circ. 16,500. Byline given. Pays on publication. No kill fee. Publishes ms an average of 6 months after acceptance. Buys one-time rights. Submit seasonal material 6 months in advance. Accepts simultaneous submissions. Responds in 2 months to queries. Responds in 3 months to mss. Sample copy for $3. Guidelines for #10 SASE.

Nonfiction Needs book excerpts, essays, general interest, historical, humor, interview, personal experience, photo feature, equine medical. **Buys 100 mss/year.** Send complete ms. Length: 500-2,000 words. **Pays $15-100.**

Photos Send photos Captions, identification of subjects required. Reviews 3x5 prints, e-mail digital photos. Pays $5/photo. Buys one time rights.

Poetry Needs light verse, traditional. **Buys 25 poems/year.** Submit maximum 10 poems. Length: 6-36 lines. **Pays $10.**

Fillers Needs anecdotes, facts, gags, short humor. Length: 200-750 words. **Pays $15-30.**

Tips *RMR* is looking for positive, human interest stories that appeal to an audience of horse owners and horse enthusiasts. We accept profiles of unusual people or animals, history, humor, anecdotes, and coverage of regional events. We aren't looking for 'how-to' or training articles, and are not currently looking at any fiction. Our geographical regions of interest is the U.S. West, especially the Rocky Mountain states.

$ $ TROPICAL FISH HOBBYIST MAGAZINE

TFH Publications, Inc., One TFH Plaza, Neptune City NJ 07753. E-mail: AssociateEditor@tfh.com. Website: www.tfhmagazine.com. **90% freelance written**. Monthly magazine covering tropical fish. Estab. 1952. Circ. 35,000. Byline given. Pays on acceptance. No kill fee. Buys all rights. Editorial lead time 3 months. Submit seasonal material 6 months in advance. Accepts queries by e-mail. Responds immediately on electronic queries. Guidelines available online.

Nonfiction We cover any aspect of aquarium science, aquaculture, and the tropical fish hobby. Our readership is diverse—from neophytes to mini reef specialists. We require well-researched, well-written, and factually accurate copy, preferably with photos. **Buys 100-150 mss/year. Pays $100-250.**

Photos State availability Identification of subjects, model releases required. Reviews prints, slides, high-resolution digital images. Negotiates payment individually. Buys multiple nonexclusive rights.

Tips With few exceptions, all communication and submission must be electronic. We want factual, interesting, and relevant articles about the aquarium hobby written by people who are obviously knowledgeable. We publish an enormous variety of article types. Review several past issues to get an idea of the scope.

$ $ USDF CONNECTION

United States Dressage Federation, 4051 Iron Works Parkway, Lexington KY 40511. Website: www.usdf.org. **40% freelance written**. Monthly magazine covering dressage (an equestrian sport). All material must relate to the sport of dressage in the US. Estab. 2000. Circ. 35,000. Byline given. Pays on acceptance. Offers 50% kill fee. Publishes ms an average of 3 months after acceptance. Buys first North American serial rights, buys second serial (reprint) rights. Editorial lead time 3 months. Submit seasonal material 6 months in advance. Accepts queries by mail, e-mail. Accepts previously published material. Responds in 1 month to queries. Responds in 1-2 months to mss. Sample copy for $5. Guidelines available online.

Nonfiction Needs book excerpts, essays, how-to, interview, opinion, personal experience. Does not want general interest equine material or stories that lack a US dressage angle. **Buys 40 mss/year.** Query. Length: 650-3,000 words. **Pays $100-500 for assigned articles. Pays $100-300 for unsolicited articles.** Sometimes pays expenses of writers on assignment.

Photos State availability Captions, identification of subjects required. Reviews prints, GIF/JPEG files. Negotiates payment individually. Buys one time rights.

Columns/Departments Amateur Hour (profiles of adult amateur USDF members), 1,200-1,500 words; Under 21 (profiles of young USDF members), 1,200-1,500 words; Veterinary Connection (dressage-related horse health), 1,500-2,500 words; Mind-Body-Spirit Connection (rider health/fitness, sport psychology), 1,500-2,500 words. 24 Query with published clips. **Pays $150-400.**

Tips Know the organization and the sport. Most successful contributors are active in the horse industry and bring valuable perspectives and insights to their stories and images.

ART & ARCHITECTURE

$ $ AMERICAN ARTIST

29 W. 46th St., 3rd Floor, New York NY 10036. (646)654-5506. E-mail: mail@myamericanartist.com. Website: www.myamericanartist.com. Monthly magazine covering art. "Written to provide information on outstanding representational artists living in the US." Estab. 1937. Circ. 116,526. No kill fee. Editorial lead time 18 weeks. Accepts queries by mail. Responds in 6-8 weeks to queries. Guidelines by email.

Nonfiction Needs essays, exposè, interview, personal experience, technical. Query with published clips and resume Length: 1,500-2,000 words.

$ $ AMERICAN INDIAN ART MAGAZINE

American Indian Art, Inc., 7314 E. Osborn Dr., Scottsdale AZ 85251. (480)994-5445. Fax: (480)945-9533. E-mail: info@aiamagazine.com. Website: www.aiamagazine.com. **97% freelance written. Works with many new/unpublished writers/year.** Quarterly magazine covering Native American art, historic and contemporary, including new research on any aspect of Native American art north of the US-Mexico border. Estab. 1975. Circ. 22,000. Byline given. Pays on publication. No kill fee. Publishes ms an average of 6 months after acceptance. Buys first rights, buys one-time rights. Responds in 6 weeks to queries. Responds in 3 months to mss. Guidelines for #10 SASE or online.

Nonfiction New research on any aspect of Native American art. No previously published work or personal interviews with artists. **Buys 12-18 mss/year.** Query. Length: 6,000-7,000 words. **Pays $150-300.**

Photos An article usually requires 8-15 photographs. Fee schedules and reimbursable expenses are decided upon by the magazine and the author. Buys one time rights.

Tips The magazine is devoted to all aspects of Native American art. Some of our readers are knowledgeable about the field and some know very little. We seek articles that offer something to both groups. Articles reflecting original research are preferred to those summarizing previously published information.

$ $ $ AMERICANSTYLE MAGAZINE

The Rosen Group, 3000 Chestnut Ave., Suite 304, Baltimore MD 21211. (410)889-3093. Fax: (410)243-7089. E-mail: hoped@rosengrp.com. Website: www.americanstyle.com. **80% freelance written**. Bimonthly magazine covering arts, crafts, travel, and interior design. "*AmericanStyle* is a full-color lifestyle publication for people who love art. Our mandate is to nurture collectors with information that will increase their passion for contemporary art and craft and the artists who create it. *AmericanStyle*'s primary audience is contemporary craft collectors and enthusiasts. Readers are college-educated, age 35 +, high-income earners with the financial means to collect art and craft, and to travel to national art and craft events in pursuit of their passions." Estab. 1994. Circ. 60,000. Pays on publication. Publishes ms an average of 9-12 months after acceptance. Buys first North American serial rights. Editorial lead time 9-12 months. Submit seasonal material at least 1 year in

advance. Accepts queries by mail, e-mail. Sample copy for $3. Guidelines available online.
Nonfiction Length: 600-800 words. **Pays $400-800.** Sometimes pays expenses of writers on assignment.
Photos Send photos Captions required. Reviews oversized transparencies, 35mm slides, low resolution e-images. Negotiates payment individually.
Columns/Departments Portfolio (profiles of emerging and established artists); Arts Tour; Arts Walk; Origins; One on One, all appx. 600 words. Query with published clips. **Pays $400-600.**
Tips " This is not a hobby-crafter magazine. Country crafts or home crafting is not our market. We focus on contemporary American craft art, such as ceramics, wood, fiber, glass, metal. Produced by established working artists, most of whom have gallery and/or museum representation."

ARCHITECTURAL DIGEST

The International Magazine of Interior Design, Conde Nast Publications, Inc., 6300 Wilshire Blvd., Los Angeles CA 90048. (323)965-3700. Fax: (323)965-4975. Website: www.architecturaldigest.com. Monthly magazine covering architecture. A global magazine that offers a look at the homes of the rich and famous. Other topics include travel, shopping, automobiles, and technology. Estab. 1920. Circ. 821,992. No kill fee. Accepts queries by mail. Sample copy for $5 on newstands.
Nonfiction Send 3 samples of your work with a brief cover letter. Include a paragraph on who else you've written for and a paragraph on any story ideas you have for *Architectural Digest*. Query with published clips.

$ $ THE ARTIST'S MAGAZINE

F+W Media, Inc., 4700 E. Galbraith Rd., Cincinnati OH 45236. (513)531-2690, ext. 1489. Fax: (513)891-7153. E-mail: tamedit@fwmedia.com. Website: www.artistsmagazine.com. **Contact:** Maureen Bloomfield, Editor-In-Chief. **80% freelance written**. Magazine published 10 times/year covering primarily two-dimensional art for working artists. Ours is a highly visual approach to teaching the serious amateur and professional artists techniques that will help them improve their skills and market their work. The style should be crisp and immediately engaging, written in a voice that speaks directly to artists. Circ. 150,000. Bionote given for feature material. Pays on publication. Offers 8% kill fee. Publishes ms an average of 6 months-1 year after acceptance. Responds in 5 months to queries. Sample copy for $4.99. Guidelines available online.
Nonfiction "The emphasis must be on how the reader can learn some method of improving his artwork; or the marketing of it." No unillustrated articles. **Buys 60 mss/year.** Length: 500-1,200 words. **Pays $300-500 and up.** Sometimes pays expenses of writers on assignment.
Photos Images of artwork must be in the form of 35mm slides, larger transparencies, or high-quality digital files. Full captions must accompany these. Buys all rights.
Tips "Look at several current issues and read the author's guidelines carefully. Remember that our readers are professional artists. Pitch an article; send clips. Do not send a finished article."

$ $ 🌐 ARTLINK

Australia's Leading Contemporary Art Quarterly, Artlink Australia, P.O. Box 8141, Station Arcade, Adelaide SA Australia. (61)(8)8212-8711. Fax: (61)(8)8212-8911. E-mail: info@artlink.com.au. Website: www.artlink.com.au. Quarterly magazine covering contemporary art in Australia. Estab. 1981. Guidelines available online.
Nonfiction Needs general interest. Write or e-mail the editor with your CV and 2-3 examples of previously published writing. **Pays $300/1,000 words.**
Tips Because *Artlink* is a themed magazine which tries to make art relevant across society, we often need to find contributors who have expert knowledge of subjects outside of the art area who can put the work of artists in a broader context.

ARTNEWS

ABC, 48 W. 38th St., New York NY 10018. (212)398-1690. Fax: (212)819-0394. E-mail: info@artnews.com. Website: www.artnews.com. Monthly magazine. *ARTnews* reports on art, personalities, issues, trends and events that shape the international art world. Investigative features focus on art ranging from old masters to contemporary, including painting, sculpture, prints, and photography. Regular columns offer exhibition and book reviews, travel destinations, investment and appreciation advice, design insights, and updates on major art world figures. Estab. 1902. Circ. 84,012. No kill fee. Accepts queries by mail, e-mail, fax, phone.

$ $ ART PAPERS

Atlanta Art Papers, Inc., P.O. Box 5748, Atlanta GA 31107. (404)588-1837. Fax: (404)588-1836. E-mail: editor@artpapers.org. Website: www.artpapers.org. **95% freelance written**. Bimonthly magazine covering contemporary art and artists. *Art Papers*, about regional and national contemporary art and artists, features a variety of perspectives on current art concerns. Each issue presents topical articles, interviews, reviews from across the US, and an extensive and informative artists' classified listings section. Our writers and the artists they cover represent the scope and diversity of the country's art scene. Estab. 1977. Circ. 12,000. Byline given. Pays on publication. No kill fee. Publishes ms an average of 3 months after acceptance. Buys all rights. Editorial lead time 2 months. Submit seasonal material 2 months in advance.

Nonfiction Buys 240 mss/year. **Pays $60-325. unsolicited articles are on spec for unsolicited articles.**
Photos Send photos Identification of subjects required. Reviews color slides, b&w prints. Offers no additional payment for photos accepted with ms.
Columns/Departments Current art concerns and news. 8-10 Query. **Pays $100-175.**

$ ART TIMES

Commentary and Resource for the Fine and Performing Arts, P.O. Box 730, Mount Marion NY 12456-0730. (845)246-6944. Fax: (845)246-6944. E-mail: info@arttimesjournal.com. Website: www.arttimesjournal.com. **10% freelance written**. Monthly tabloid covering the arts (visual, theater, dance, music, literary, etc.). *"Art Times* covers the art fields and is distributed in locations most frequented by those enjoying the arts. Our copies are distributed throughout the lower part of the northeast as well as metropolitan New York area; locations include theaters, galleries, museums, schools, art clubs, cultural centers and the like. Our readers are mostly over 40, affluent, art-conscious and sophisticated. Subscribers are located across US and abroad (Italy, France, Germany, Greece, Russia, etc.)." Estab. 1984. Circ. 28,000. Byline given. Pays on publication. No kill fee. Publishes ms an average of 3 years after acceptance. Buys first North American serial rights, buys first rights. Submit seasonal material 8 months in advance. Accepts simultaneous submissions. Responds in 6 months to queries. Responds in 6 months to mss. Sample copy for sae with 9x12 envelope and 6 First-Class stamps. Writer's guidelines for #10 SASE or online
Fiction Contact: Raymond J. Steiner, fiction editor. "We're looking for short fiction that aspires to be literary." Needs adventure, ethnic, fantasy, historical, humorous, mainstream, science fiction, contemporary. We seek quality literary pieces. Nothing violent, sexist, erotic, juvenile, racist, romantic, political, off-beat, or related to sports or juvenile fiction. **Buys 8-10 mss/year.** Send complete ms. 1,500 words maximum **True**.
Poetry Contact: Raymond J. Steiner, poetry editor. Needs avant-garde, free verse, haiku, light verse, traditional. "We prefer well-crafted 'literary' poems. No excessively sentimental poetry." **Buys 30-35 poems/year.** Submit maximum 6 poems. 20 lines maximum **Offers contributor copies and 1 year's free subscription**.
Tips "Be advised that we are presently on an approximate 3-year lead for short stories, 2-year lead for poetry. We are now receiving 300-400 poems and 40-50 short stories per month. We only publish 2-3 poems and 1 story each issue. Be familiar with *Art Times* and its special audience. *Art Times* has literary leanings with articles written by a staff of scholars knowledgeable in their respective fields. Although an 'arts' publication, we observe no restrictions (other than noted) in accepting fiction/poetry other than a concern for quality writing—subjects can cover anything and not specifically arts."

AUSTRALIAN ART COLLECTOR

Gadfly Media, Level 1, 645 Harris St., Ultimo, Sydney NSW 2007 Australia. (61)(2)9281-7523. Fax: (61)(2)9281-7529. E-mail: susan@gadfly.net.au. Website: www.artcollector.net.au. Quarterly magazine covering Australian art collecting. *Australian Art Collector* is the only Australian publication targeted specifically at people who buy art.
Nonfiction Needs expose, general interest, interview. Query.

$$$$ AZURE DESIGN, ARCHITECTURE AND ART

460 Richmond St. W., Suite 601, Toronto ON M5V 1Y1 Canada. (416)203-9674. Fax: (416)203-9842. E-mail: azure@azureonline.com. Website: www.azuremagazine.com. **75% freelance written**. Magazine covering design and architecture. Estab. 1985. Circ. 20,000. Pays on publication. Offers variable kill fee. Publishes ms an average of 1 month after acceptance. Buys first rights. Editorial lead time up to 45 days. Responds in 6 weeks to queries.
Nonfiction Buys 25-30 mss/year. Length: 350-2,000 words. **Pays $1/word (Canadian).**
Columns/Departments Trailer (essay/photo on something from the built environment); and Forms & Functions (coming exhibitions, happenings in world of design), both 300-350 words. 30 Query. **Pays $1/word (Canadian).**
Tips Try to understand what the magazine is about. Writers must be well versed in the field of architecture and design. It's very unusual to get something from someone I haven't worked quite closely with and gotten a sense of who the writer is. The best way to introduce yourself is by sending clips or writing samples and describing what your background is in the field.

$ BOMB MAGAZINE

New Arts Publications, 80 Hanson Place, Suite 703, Brooklyn NY 11217. (718)636-9100. Fax: (718)636-9200. E-mail: generalinquiries@bombsite.com. Website: www.bombsite.com. Quarterly magazine providing interviews between artists, writers, musicians, directors and actors. Written, edited and produced by industry professionals and funded by those interested in the arts. Publishes work which is unconventional and contains an edge, whether it be in style or subject matter. Estab. 1981. Circ. 36,000. Pays on publication. No kill fee. Publishes ms an average of 3-6 months after acceptance. Buys first rights, buys one-time rights. Editorial lead time 3-4 months. Accepts queries by mail. Responds in 3-5 months to mss. Sample copy for $7, plus $1.59 postage and handling. Guidelines by email.

Fiction Send completed ms with SASE. Needs experimental, novel concepts, contemporary. No genre: romance, science fiction, horror, western. less than 25 pages **Pays $100, and contributor's copies.**
Poetry Send completed ms with SASE. Submit maximum 4-6 poems.
Fillers No more than 25 pages in length
Tips Mss should be typed, double-spaced, proofread and should be final drafts. Purchase a sample issue before submitting work.

$ $ C

international contemporary art, C The Visual Arts Foundation, P.O. Box 5, Station B, Toronto ON M5T 2T2 Canada. (416)539-9495. Fax: (416)539-9903. E-mail: editor@cmagazine.com. Website: www.cmagazine.com. **80% freelance written**. Quarterly magazine covering international contemporary art. *C* provides a vital and vibrant forum for the presentation of contemporary art and the discussion of issues surrounding art in our culture, including feature articles, reviews and reports, as well as original artists' projects. Estab. 1983. Circ. 7,000. Byline given. Pays on publication. Offers kill fee. Offers kill fee Publishes ms an average of 4 months after acceptance. Editorial lead time 3 months. Accepts queries by mail, e-mail, fax. Accepts simultaneous submissions. Responds in 6 weeks to queries. Responds in 4 months to mss. Sample copy for $10 (US). Guidelines for #10 SASE.
Nonfiction Needs essays, general interest, opinion, personal experience. **Buys 50 mss/year.** Length: 1,000-3,000 words. **Pays $150-500 (Canadian), $105-350 (US).**
Photos State availability of or send photos Captions required. Reviews 35mm transparencies or 8x10 prints. Offers no additional payment for photos accepted with ms Buys one-time rights; shared copyright on reprints
Columns/Departments Reviews (review of art exhibitions), 500 words. 30 Query. **Pays $125 (Canadian)**

$ $ DIRECT ART MAGAZINE

Slow Art Productions, 123 Warren St., Hudson NY 12534. E-mail: directartmag@aol.com. Website: www.slowart.com. **75% freelance written**. Semiannual fine art magazine covering alternative, anti-establishment, left-leaning fine art. Estab. 1998. Circ. 10,000. Byline sometimes given. Pays on acceptance. No kill fee. Buys one-time rights, buys electronic rights. Editorial lead time 2 months. Submit seasonal material 3 months in advance. Accepts queries by mail, e-mail. Accepts simultaneous submissions. Responds in 2 weeks to queries. Responds in 1 month to mss. Sample copy for sae with 9x12 envelope and 10 First-Class stamps. Guidelines for #10 SASE.
Nonfiction Needs essays, expose, historical, how-to, humor, inspirational, interview, opinion, personal experience, photo feature, technical. **Buys 4-6 mss/year.** Query with published clips. Length: 1,000-3,000 words. **Pays $100-500.**
Photos State availability of or send photos Reviews 35mm slide transparencies, digital files on CD (TIF format). Negotiates payment individually Buys one time rights.
Columns/Departments Query with published clips. **Pays $100-500.**

EASTERN ART REPORT

EAPGROUP International Media, P.O. Box 13666, London England SW14 8WF United Kingdom. E-mail: info@eapgroup.com. Website: www.eapgroup.com. *EAR* has a worldwide readership—from scholars to connoisseurs—with varying knowledge of or interest in the historical, philosophical, practical, or theoretical aspects of Eastern art. Estab. 1989. No kill fee. Accepts queries by mail, e-mail, fax. Guidelines available online.
Nonfiction International Diary (art-related news, previews, reviews); Art market reports written from an individual perspective; books previews and reviews. Query.
Photos Reviews illustrations, electronic images of at least 300 dpi.

$ ESPACE

SCULPTURE, Le Centre de Diffusion 3D, 4888 rue Saint-Denis, Montreal QC H2J 2L6 Canada. (514)844-9858. Fax: (514)844-3661. E-mail: espace@espace-sculpture.com. Website: www.espace-sculpture.com. **95% freelance written**. Quarterly magazine covering sculpture events. Canada's only sculpture publication, *Espace* represents a critical tool for the understanding of contemporary sculpture. Published 4 times a year, in English and French, *Espace* features interviews, in-depth articles, and special issues related to various aspects of three dimensionality. Foreign contributors guarantee an international perspective and diffusion. Estab. 1987. Circ. 1,400. Byline given. Pays on publication. No kill fee. Publishes ms an average of 3 months after acceptance. Buys all rights. Editorial lead time 5 months. Submit seasonal material 3 months in advance. Accepts queries by mail. Accepts simultaneous submissions. Sample copy free.
Nonfiction Needs essays, expose. **Buys 60 mss/year.** Query. Length: 1,000-1,400 words. **Pays $60/page.**
Photos Send photos Reviews transparencies, prints. Offers no additional payment for photos accepted with ms

LA ARCHITECT

The Magazine of Design in Southern California, Balcony Media, Inc., 512 E. Wilson, Suite 213, Glendale CA

91206. E-mail: Jonathan@formmag.net. Website: www.formmag.net. **80% freelance written**. Bimonthly magazine covering architecture, interiors, landscape, and other design disciplines. *L.A. Architect* is interested in architecture, interiors, product, graphics, and landscape design as well as news about the arts. We encourage designers to keep us informed on projects, techniques, and products that are innovative, new, or nationally newsworthy. We are especially interested in new and renovated projects that illustrate a high degree of design integrity and unique answers to typical problems in the urban cultural and physical environment. Estab. 1999. Circ. 20,000. Byline given. Pays on publication. No kill fee. Publishes ms an average of 3 months after acceptance. Makes work-for-hire assignments. Editorial lead time 4 months. Submit seasonal material 4 months in advance. Accepts queries by mail, e-mail, fax. Responds in 1 month to queries. Responds in 1 month to mss. Sample copy for $5.95. Guidelines available online.

Nonfiction Needs book excerpts, essays, historical, interview, new product. **Buys 20 mss/year.** Length: 500-2,000 words. **Payment negotiable.**

Photos State availability Captions, identification of subjects, model releases required. Offers no additional payment for photos accepted with ms. Buys one time rights.

Columns/Departments .

Tips Our magazine focuses on contemporary and cutting-edge work either happening in Southern California or designed by a Southern California designer. We like to find little-known talent that has not been widely published. We are not like *Architectural Digest* in flavor so avoid highly decorative subjects. Each project, product, or event should be accompanied by a story proposal or brief description and select images. Do not send original art without our written request; we make every effort to return materials we are unable to use, but this is sometimes difficult and we must make advance arrangements for original art.

$ $ THE MAGAZINE ANTIQUES

Brant Publications, 575 Broadway, New York NY 10012. (212)941-2800. Fax: (212)941-2819. E-mail: cdrayton@brantpub.com. Website: www.themagazineantiques.com. **75% freelance written**. Monthly magazine. Articles should present new information in a scholarly format (with footnotes) on the fine and decorative arts, architecture, historic preservation, and landscape architecture. Estab. 1922. Circ. 61,754. Byline given. Pays on publication. No kill fee. Publishes ms an average of 6 months after acceptance. Buys all rights. Editorial lead time 6 months. Submit seasonal material 6 months in advance. Responds in 3 weeks to queries. Responds in 6 months to mss. Sample copy for $10.50 for back issue; $5 for current issue.

Nonfiction Needs historical, scholarly. **Buys 50 mss/year.** Length: 2,850-3,500 words. **Pays $250-500.** Sometimes pays expenses of writers on assignment.

Photos State availability Captions, identification of subjects required. Reviews contact sheets, negatives, transparencies, prints. Buys one time rights.

$ $ $ $ METROPOLIS

The Magazine of Architecture and Design, Bellerophon Publications, 61 W. 23rd St., 4th Floor, New York NY 10010. (212)627-9977. Fax: (212)627-9988. E-mail: edit@metropolismag.com. Website: www.metropolismag.com. **80% freelance written**. Monthly magazine (combined issue July/August) for consumers interested in architecture and design. Estab. 1981. Circ. 45,000. Byline given. Pays 60-90 days after acceptance. No kill fee. Publishes ms an average of 3 months after acceptance. Makes work-for-hire assignments. Submit seasonal material 3 months in advance. Accepts queries by mail, e-mail, fax. Responds in 8 months to queries. Sample copy for $7. Guidelines available online.

Nonfiction Contact: Martin Pedersen, executive editor. Needs essays, design, architecture, urban planning issues and ideas, interview, of multi-disciplinary designers/architects. No profiles on individual architectural practices, information from public relations firms, or fine arts. **Buys 30 mss/year.** Length: 1,500-4,000 words. **Pays $1,500-4,000.**

Photos Captions required. Reviews contact sheets, 35mm or 4 x 5 transparencies, 8 x 10 b&w prints. Payment offered for certain photos. Buys one time rights.

Columns/Departments The Metropolis Observed (architecture, design, and city planning news features), 100-1,200 words, **pays $100-1,200**; Perspective (opinion or personal observation of architecture and design), 1,200 words, **pays $1,200**; Enterprise (the business/development of architecture and design), 1,500 words, **pays $1,500**; In Review (architecture and book review essays), 1,500 words, **pays $1,500**. Direct queries to Belinda Lanks, managing editor. 40 Query with published clips.

Tips *Metropolis* strives to tell the story of design to a lay person with an interest in the built environment, while keeping the professional designer engaged. The magazine examines the various design disciplines (architecture, interior design, product design, graphic design, planning, and preservation) and their social/cultural context. We're looking for the new, the obscure, or the wonderful. Also, be patient and don't expect an immediate answer after submission of query.

$ $ ▣ MIX

IA Declaration of Creative Independence, Parallelogramme Artist-Run Culture and Publishing, Inc., 401

Richmond St. West, Suite 446, Toronto ON M5V 3A8 Canada. (416)506-1012. E-mail: editor@mixmagazine.com. Website: www.mixmagazine.com. **95% freelance written**. Quarterly magazine covering Artist-Run gallery activities. *Mix* represents and investigates contemporary artistic practices and issues, especially in the progressive Canadian artist-run scene. Estab. 1975. Circ. 3,500. Byline given. Pays on publication. Offers 40% kill fee. Publishes ms an average of 6 months after acceptance. Buys first North American serial rights. Editorial lead time 6 months. Submit seasonal material 4 months in advance. Accepts queries by mail, e-mail, fax. Responds in 2 months to queries. Responds in 3 months to mss. Sample copy for $6.95, 8½ × 10¼ SAE and 6 first-class stamps. Guidelines available online.

Nonfiction Needs essays, interview. **Buys 12-20 mss/year.** Query with published clips. Length: 750-3,500 words. **Pays $100-450.**

Reprints Send photocopy of article and information about when and where the article previously appeared.

Photos State availability Captions, identification of subjects required. Buys one time rights.

Columns/Departments Features, 1,000-3,000 words; Art Reviews, 500 words. Query with published clips. **Pays $100-450.**

Tips Read the magazine and other contemporary art magazines. Understand the idea 'artist-run.' We're not interested in 'artsy-phartsy' editorial, but rather pieces that are critical, dynamic, and would be of interest to nonartists too.

$ $ MODERNISM MAGAZINE

199 George St., Lambertville NJ 08530. (609)397-4104. Fax: (609)397-4409. E-mail: andrea@modernismmagazine.com. Website: www.modernismmagazine.com. **Contact:** Andrea Truppin, editor-in-chief. **70% freelance written**. Quarterly magazine covering 20th century design, architecture and decorative arts. "We are interested in design, architecture and decorative arts and the people who created them. Our coverage begins in the 1920s with Art Deco and related movements, and ends with 1980s Post-Modernism, leaving contemporary design to other magazines." Estab. 1998. Circ. 35,000. Byline given. Pays on publication. Offers 25% kill fee. Publishes ms an average of 4 months after acceptance. Buys all rights. We consider the articles to be "work for hire." We don't buy one-time rights. Editorial lead time 6 months. Submit seasonal material 6 months in advance. Accepts queries by mail, e-mail. Accepts previously published material. Accepts simultaneous submissions. Responds in 1 month to queries. Sample copy for $6.95. Guidelines free.

Nonfiction Needs book excerpts, essays, historical, interview, new product, photo feature. No first-person. **Buys 20 mss/year.** Query with published clips. Length: 1,000-2,500 words. **Pays $300-600.**

Reprints Accepts previously published submissions.

Photos State availability of or send photos Captions, identification of subjects required. Reviews contact sheets, transparencies, prints. Negotiates payment individually

Tips "Articles should be well researched, carefully reported, and directed at a popular audience with a special interest in the Modernist movement. Please don't assume readers have prior familiarity with your subject; be sure to tell us the who, what, why, when, and how of whatever you're discussing."

N SOUTHWEST ART

101 Spruce St., Boulder CO 80302. (303)442-0427. Fax: (303)449-0279. E-mail: southwestart@southwestart.com. Website: www.southwestart.com. **60% freelance written**. Monthly magazine directed to art collectors interested in artists, market trends, and art history of the American West. Estab. 1971. Circ. 60,000. Byline given. Pays on acceptance. Publishes ms an average of 1 year after acceptance. Submit seasonal material 8 months in advance. Accepts queries by mail, fax. Responds in 6 months to mss.

Nonfiction Needs book excerpts, interview. No fiction or poetry. **Buys 70 mss/year.** Query with published clips. Length: 1,400-1,600 words.

Photos Photographs, color print-outs, and videotapes will not be considered. Captions, identification of subjects required. Reviews 35mm, 2¼x2¼, 4x5 transparencies. Negotiates rights.

Tips "Research the Southwest art market, send slides or transparencies with queries, and send writing samples demonstrating knowledge of the art world."

$ $ WATERCOLOR

Interweave Press, 29 W. 46th St., 3rd Floor, New York NY 10036. (646)841-0500. E-mail: mail@myamericanartist.com. Website: www.myamericanartist.com. Quarterly magazine devoted to watermedia artists. Circ. 50,000. No kill fee. Editorial lead time 4 months.

Nonfiction Needs essays, interview, personal experience, technical. Query with published clips. Length: 1,500-2,000 words. **Pays $500.**

$ $ WILDLIFE ART

The Art Journal of the Natural World, Pothole Publications, Inc., P.O. Box 219, Ramona CA 92065. Fax: (760)788-9454. E-mail: rmscott-blair@wildlifeartmag.com. Website: www.wildlifeartmag.com. **60% freelance written**. Bimonthly magazine. *Wildlife Art* is the world's foremost magazine of the natural world, featuring wildlife, landscape, and western art. Features living artists as well as wildlife art masters, illustrators, and

conservation organizations. Special emphasis on landscape and plein-air paintings. Audience is collectors, galleries, museums, show promoters worldwide. Estab. 1982. Circ. 30,000. Byline given. Pays on publication. Offers negotiable kill fee. Publishes ms an average of 6 months after acceptance. Buys second serial (reprint) rights. Accepts queries by mail, e-mail. Responds in 6 months to queries. Sample copy for sae with 9x12 envelope and 10 First-Class stamps. Guidelines available online.
Nonfiction Needs general interest, historical, interview. **Buys 40 mss/year.** Query with published clips, include artwork samples. Length: 800-1,500 words. **Pays $150-500.**
Tips Best way to break in is to offer concrete story ideas, new talent, a new unique twist of artistic excellence.

ASSOCIATIONS

$ $ $ $ AAA LIVING

Pace Communications, 1301 Carolina St., Greensboro NC 27401. Fax: (336)383-8272. **70% freelance written.** Published 4 times a year. "AAA Living magazine,published for the Auto Club Group of Dearborn, Michigan, is for members of AAA clubs in 8 Midwest states (IL, N. IN, IA, MI, MN, NE, ND, & WI). Our magazine features lifestyle & travel articles about each state and the region, written by knowledgeable resident writers, as well as coverage of affordable, accessible travel getaways nationally & internationally & information about exclusive AAA products & services." Estab. 1917. Circ. 2.5 million. Byline given. Pays on acceptance. Offers 10% kill fee. Publishes ms an average of 3 months after acceptance. Buys first North American serial rights, buys electronic rights. Editorial lead time 6 months. Submit seasonal material 6 months in advance. Accepts queries by mail, e-mail. Responds in 6 months to mss. Sample copy available online. Guidelines available online.
Nonfiction Needs travel. Query with published clips. Length: 150-1,600 words. **Pays $150-1,800 for assigned articles.** Sometimes pays expenses of writers on assignment.
Photos Send photos Captions, identification of subjects required. Reviews GIF/JPEG files. Negotiates payment individually Buys one time rights.
Tips "Articles should have a strong hook, tell an entertaining story, be unique & should avoid merely listing everything there is to do at a location. Take the readers to places the locals love & visitors would never forget. Color & details are essential. Share a sense of experience that goes beyond 'go here, do this.' Touch the readers' senses. You might find yourself in a quaint downtown surrounded by restored historic buildings, but many towns in the Midwest can claim this. What does that downtown sound like? What's going on in the square behind you? What kinds of smells emanate from nearby restaurants? Your stories should show the readers the destination, not simply tell them about it."

$ $ ACTION

United Spinal Association, 75-20 Astoria Blvd., Jackson Heights NY 11370-1177. (718)803-3782, ext. 279. E-mail: action@unitedspinal.org. Website: www.unitedspinal.org/publications/action. **75% freelance written.** Bimonthly magazine covering living with spinal cord injury. The monthly news magazine of the United Spinal Association is a benefit to members of the organization: people with spinal cord injury or dysfunction, as well as caregivers, parents and some spinal cord injury/dysfunction professionals. All articles should reflect this common interest of the audience. Assume that your audience is better educated in the subject of spinal cord medicine than average, but be careful not to be too technical.Within these seemingly narrow confines, however, a wide variety of subjects are possible. Articles that feature members or programs of United Spinal are preferred, but any article that deals with issues of living with SCI will be considered. Estab. 1946. Circ. 12,000. Byline given. Pays on publication. No kill fee. Publishes ms an average of 2-3 months after acceptance. Buys all rights. Accepts queries by e-mail. Sample copy for sae. Guidelines for sae.
Nonfiction Needs essays, general interest, how-to, humor, interview, new product, personal experience, photo feature, travel, medical research. Does not want articles that treat disabilities as an affliction or cause for pity, or that show the writer does not get that people with disabilities are people like anyone else. **Buys 36 mss/year.** Query. Length: 1,000-1,800 words. **Pays $400.**
Photos Send photos Identification of subjects required. Reviews GIF/JPEG files. Offers no additional payment for photos accepted with ms.
Columns/Departments The Observatory (personal essays on subjects related to disability), 750 words. 60 Query with published clips. **Pays $200.**
Tips It helps (though is not necessary) if you have a disability, or if you can be comfortable with people with disabilities; they are the subjects of most of our articles as well as the bulk of our readership. Our readers are looking for tips on how to live well with mobility impairment. They're concerned with access to jobs, travel, recreation, education, etc. They like to read about how others deal with like situations. They are sophisticated about spinal cord disabilities and don't need to be 'inspired' by the typical stories about people with disabilities that appear in the human interest section of most newspapers.

$ $ $ $ AMERICAN EDUCATOR

American Federation of Teachers, 555 New Jersey Ave. N.W., Washington DC 20001. E-mail: amered@aft.org. Website: www.aft.org/american_educator/index.html. **50% freelance written**. Quarterly magazine covering education, condition of children, and labor issues. *American Educator*, the quaterly magazine of the American Federation of Teachers, reaches over 800,000 public school teachers, higher education faculty, and education researchers and policymakers. The magazine concentrates on significant ideas and practices in education, civics, and the condition of children in America and around the world. Estab. 1977. Circ. 850,000. Byline given. Pays on publication. Offers 50% kill fee. Publishes ms an average of 2-6 months after acceptance. Buys one-time rights, buys electronic rights. Editorial lead time 1 year. Submit seasonal material 6 months in advance. Accepts queries by mail, e-mail, fax. Accepts previously published material. Accepts simultaneous submissions. Responds in 2 months to queries. Responds in 6 months to mss. Sample copy available online. Guidelines available online.

Nonfiction Needs book excerpts, essays, historical, interview, discussions of educational research. No pieces that are not supportive of the public schools. **Buys 8 mss/year.** Query with published clips. Length: 1,000-7,000 words. **Pays $750-3,000 for assigned articles. Pays $300-1,000 for unsolicited articles.** Pays expenses of writers on assignment.

Photos State availability Captions, identification of subjects, model releases required. Reviews contact sheets, negatives, transparencies, 8x10 prints, GIF/JPEG files. Negotiates payment individually. Buys one time rights.

CHRISTIAN MANAGEMENT REPORT

The Latest Leadership and Management Trends and Tools for Members of Christian Management Association, Christian Management Association, P.O. Box 4090, San Clemente CA 92674. (949)487-0900. Fax: (949)487-0927. Website: www.cmaonline.org. **50% freelance written**. Bimonthly magazine covering management and leadership issues for Christian nonprofit organizations and churches. Estab. 1976. Circ. 4,000. Byline given. No kill fee. Publishes ms an average of 4-6 weeks after acceptance. Editorial lead time 3 months. Accepts queries by e-mail, phone. Accepts simultaneous submissions. Responds in 2-4 weeks to queries. Responds in 2-4 weeks to mss. Guidelines by email.

Nonfiction Needs book excerpts, how-to, interview, technical. Query.

$ $ DAC NEWS

Official Publication of the Detroit Athletic Club, Detroit Athletic Club, 241 Madison Ave., Detroit MI 48226. (313)442-1034. Fax: (313)442-1047. E-mail: kenv@thedac.com. **20% freelance written**. Magazine published 10 times/year. *DAC News* is the magazine for Detroit Athletic Club members. It covers club news and events, plus general interest features. Estab. 1916. Circ. 5,000. Byline given. Pays on publication. No kill fee. Publishes ms an average of 3 months after acceptance. Buys one-time rights. Makes work-for-hire assignments. Editorial lead time 3 months. Submit seasonal material 3 months in advance. Accepts queries by mail, phone. Responds in 1 month to queries. Sample copy free.

Nonfiction Needs general interest, historical, photo feature. No politics or social issues—this is an entertainment magazine. We do not acccept unsolicited manuscripts or queries for travel articles. **Buys 2-3 mss/year.** Length: 1,000-2,000 words. **Pays $100-500.** Sometimes pays expenses of writers on assignment.

Photos Illustrations only. State availability Captions, identification of subjects, model releases required. Reviews transparencies, 4x6 prints. Negotiates payment individually. Buys one time rights.

Tips Review our editorial calendar. It tends to repeat from year to year, so a freelancer with a fresh approach to one of these topics will get our attention quickly. It helps if articles have some connection with the DAC, but this is not absolutely necessary. We also welcome articles on Detroit history, Michigan history, or automotive history.

$ $ $ DCM

Data Center Management: Bringing Insight and Ideas to the Data Center Community, AFCOM, 742 E. Chapman Ave., Orange CA 92866. Fax: (714)997-9743. E-mail: afcom@afcom.com. Website: www.afcom.com. **50% freelance written**. Bimonthly magazine covering data center management. *DCM* is the slick, 4-color, bimonthly publication for members of AFCOM, the leading association for data center management. Estab. 1988. Circ. 4,000 worldwide. Byline given. Pays on acceptance for assigned articles and on publication for unsolicited articles. Offers 0-10% kill fee. Publishes ms an average of 3 months after acceptance. Buys all rights. Editorial lead time 6-12 months. Submit seasonal material 6 months in advance. Responds in 1-3 weeks to queries. Responds in 1-3 months to mss. Guidelines available online.

- Prefers queries by e-mail.

Nonfiction Needs how-to, technical, management as it relates to and includes examples of data centers and data center managers. The January/February issue is the annual 'Emerging Technologies' issue. Articles for this issue are visionary and product neutral. No product reviews or general tech articles. **Buys 15+ mss/year.** Query with published clips. 2,000 word maximum **Pays 50¢/word and up, based on writer's expertise.**

Photos We rarely consider freelance photos. State availability Identification of subjects, model releases required.

Reviews TIFF/PDF/GIF/JPEG files. Offers no additional payment for photos accepted with ms. Buys one time rights.
Tips See 'Top 10 Reasons for Rejection' and editorial guidelines online.

$ $ THE ELKS MAGAZINE

The Elks Magazine, 425 W. Diversey Pkwy., Chicago IL 60614-6196. (773)755-4740. E-mail: annai@elks.org. Website: www.elks.org/elksmag. **25% freelance written**. "Magazine covers nonfiction only; published 10 times/year with basic mission of being the voice of the Elks.". All material concerning the news of the Elks is written in-house. Estab. 1922. Circ. 1,037,000. Pays on acceptance. No kill fee. Buys first North American serial rights. Responds in 1 month with a yes/no on ms purchase. Guidelines available online

- Accepts queries by mail, but purchase decision is based on final mss only.

Nonfiction "We're really interested in seeing manuscripts on Americana, history, technology, science, sports, health, or just intriguing topics." No fiction, religion, controversial issues, first-person, fillers, or verse. **Buys 20-30 mss/year.** Send complete ms. Length: 1,500-2,000 words. **Pays 25¢/word.**
Photos "If possible, please advise where photographs may be found. Photographs taken and submitted by the writer are paid for separately at $25 each. Send transparencies, slides. Pays $475 for one-time cover rights."
Columns/Departments "The invited columnists are already selected."
Tips "Please try us first. We'll get back to you soon."

$ $ HUMANITIES

National Endowment for the Humanities, 1100 Pennsylvania Ave. NW, Washington DC 20506. (202)606-8435. Fax: (202)606-8451. E-mail: dskinner@neh.gov. Website: www.neh.gov. **50% freelance written**. Bimonthly magazine covering news in the humanities focused on projects that receive financial support from the agency. Estab. 1980. Circ. 6,000. Byline given. Pays on publication. Publishes ms an average of 2 months after acceptance. Buys all rights. Makes work-for-hire assignments. Editorial lead time 3 months. Submit seasonal material 4 months in advance. Accepts queries by mail, e-mail, fax, phone. Accepts previously published material. Sample copy available online.
Nonfiction Needs book excerpts, historical, interview, photo feature. **Buys 25 mss/year.** Query with published clips. Length: 400-2,500 words. **Pays $300-600.** Sometimes pays expenses of writers on assignment.
Photos Contact: Contact mbiernik@neh.gov. Identification of subjects, model releases required. Offers no additional payment for photos accepted with ms; negotiates payment individually. Buys one time rights.
Columns/Departments In Focus (directors of state humanities councils), 700 words; Breakout (special activities of state humanities councils), 750 words. 12 Query with published clips. **Pays $300.**

$ $ ⊘ KIWANIS

3636 Woodview Trace, Indianapolis IN 46268-3196. (317)875-8755. Fax: (317)879-0204. Website: www.kiwanis.org. **10% freelance written**. Magazine published 6 times/year for business and professional persons and their families. Estab. 1917. Circ. 240,000. Byline given. Pays on acceptance. Offers 40% kill fee. Publishes ms an average of 6 months after acceptance. Buys first rights. Accepts queries by mail, e-mail, fax. Responds in 1 month to queries. Sample copy and writer's guidelines for 9x12 SAE with 5 first class stamps. Guidelines available online.

- No unsolicited mss.

Nonfiction Articles about social and civic betterment, small-business concerns, children, science, education, religion, family, health, recreation, etc. Emphasis on objectivity, intelligent analysis, and thorough research of contemporary issues. Positive tone preferred. Concise, lively writing, absence of clichés, and impartial presentation of controversy required. Articles must include information and quotations from international sources. We have a continuing need for articles that concern helping youth, particularly prenatal through age 5: day care, developmentally appropriate education, early intervention for at-risk children, parent education, safety and health. No fiction, personal essays, profiles, travel pieces, fillers, or verse of any kind. A light or humorous approach is welcomed where the subject is appropriate and all other requirements are observed. **Buys 20 mss/year.** Length: 500-1,200 words. **Pays $300-600.** Sometimes pays expenses of writers on assignment.
Photos We accept photos submitted with manuscripts. Our rate for a manuscript with good photos is higher than for one without. Identification of subjects, model releases required. Buys one time rights.
Tips We will work with any writer who presents a strong feature article idea applicable to our magazine's audience and who will prove he or she knows the craft of writing. First, obtain writer's guidelines and a sample copy. Study for general style and content. When querying, present detailed outline of proposed manuscript's focus and editorial intent. Indicate expert sources to be used, as well as possible Kiwanis sources for quotations and anecdotes. Present a well-researched, smoothly written manuscript that contains a `human quality' with the use of anecdotes, practical examples, quotations, etc.

$ $ THE LION

300 W. 22nd St., Oak Brook IL 60523-8842. E-mail: rkleinfe@lionsclubs.org. Website: www.lionsclubs.org. **35% freelance written. Works with a small number of new/unpublished writers each year.** Monthly magazine

covering service club organization for Lions Club members and their families. Estab. 1918. Circ. 490,000. Byline given. Pays on acceptance. No kill fee. Publishes ms an average of 5 months after acceptance. Buys all rights. Accepts queries by mail, e-mail, fax, phone. Responds in 1 month to queries. Sample copy and writer's guidelines free

Nonfiction Welcomes humor, if sophisticated but clean; no sensationalism. Prefers anecdotes in articles. Needs photo feature, must be of a Lions Club service project, informational (issues of interest to civic-minded individuals). No travel, biography, or personal experiences. **Buys 40 mss/year.** Length: 500-1,500 words. **Pays $100-750.** Sometimes pays expenses of writers on assignment.

Photos Purchased with accompanying ms. Photos should be at least 5x7 glossies; color prints or slides are preferred. We also accept digital photos by e-mail. Be sure photos are clear and as candid as possible. Captions required. Total purchase price for ms includes payment for photos accepted with ms.

Tips Send detailed description of proposed article. Query first and request writer's guidelines and sample copy. Incomplete details on how the Lions involved actually carried out a project and poor quality photos are the most frequent mistakes made by writers in completing an article assignment for us. No gags, fillers, quizzes, or poems are accepted. We are geared increasingly to an international audience. Writers who travel internationally could query for possible assignments, although only locally related expenses could be paid.

$ $ $ THE MEETING PROFESSIONAL MAGAZINE

Meeting Professionals International, 3030 LBJ Freeway, Suite 1700, Dallas TX 75234. E-mail: bpotter@mpiweb.org. Website: www.themeetingprofessional.org. **60% freelance written**. Monthly magazine covering the global meeting idustry. *The Meeting Professional* delivers strategic editorial content on meeting industry trends, opportunities and items of importance in the hope of fostering professional development and career enhancement. The magazine is mailed monthly to 20,000 MPI members and 10,000 qualified nonmember subscribers and meeting industry planners. It is also distributed at major industry shows, such as IT&ME and EIBTM, at MPI conferences, and upon individual request. Circ. 30,000. Byline given. Pays on acceptance. Offers kill fee. Offers a negotiable kill fee. Publishes ms an average of 2-3 months after acceptance. Buys all rights. Editorial lead time 2 months. Submit seasonal material 3 months in advance. Accepts queries by e-mail. Sample copy free. Guidelines by email.

Nonfiction Needs general interest, how-to, interview, travel, industry-related. No duplications from other industry publications. **Buys 60 mss/year.** Query with published clips. Length: 1,000-2,500 words. **Pays 50-75¢/word for assigned articles.**

Tips Understand and have experience within the industry. Writers who are familiar with our magazine and our competitors are better able to get our attention, send better queries, and get assignments.

$ $ PENN LINES

Pennsylvania Rural Electric Association, 212 Locust St., Harrisburg PA 17108-1266. E-mail: peter_fitzgerald@prea.com. Website: www.prea.com/pennlines/plonline.htm. Monthly magazine covering rural life in Pennsylvania. News magazine of Pennsylvania electric cooperatives. Features should be balanced, and they should have a rural focus. Electric cooperative sources (such as consumers) should be used. Estab. 1966. Circ. 140,000. Byline given. Pays on publication. No kill fee. Publishes ms an average of 3 months after acceptance. Buys first rights. Editorial lead time 4 months. Submit seasonal material 4 months in advance. Accepts queries by mail, e-mail. Sample copy available online. Guidelines available online.

Nonfiction Needs general interest, historical, how-to, interview, travel, rural PA only. **Buys 6 mss/year.** Query or send complete ms. Length: 500-2,000 words. **Pays $300-650.**

Photos Captions required. Reviews transparencies, prints, GIF/JPEG files. Negotiates payment individually. Buys one-time rights and right to publish online.

Tips Find topics of statewide interest to rural residents. Detailed information on *Penn Lines'* readers, gleaned from a reader survey, is available online.

THE ROTARIAN

Rotary International, One Rotary Center, 1560 Sherman Ave., Evanston IL 60201. (847)866-3000. Fax: (847)866-8554. Website: www.rotary.org. **40% freelance written**. Monthly magazine for Rotarian business and professional men and women and their families, schools, libraries, hospitals, etc. "Articles should appeal to an international audience and in some way help Rotarians help other people. The organization's rationale is one of hope, encouragement, and belief in the power of individuals talking and working together." Estab. 1911. Circ. 510,000. Byline sometimes given. Pays on acceptance. Offers kill fee. Kill fee negotiable Buys one-time rights, buys all rights. Editorial lead time 4-8 months. Accepts queries by mail, e-mail. Accepts previously published material. Sample copy for $1 (e-mail edbrookc@rotaryintl.org). Guidelines available online.

Nonfiction Needs general interest, humor, inspirational, photo feature, technical, science, travel, lifestyle, sports, business/finance, environmental, health/medicine, social issues. No fiction, religious, or political articles. Query with published clips. Length: 1,500-2,500 words. **Pays negotiable rate.**

Reprints "Send tearsheet, photocopy or typed ms with rights for sale noted and information about when and

where the material previously appeared." Negotiates payment.
Photos State availability Reviews contact sheets, transparencies. Buys one time rights.
Columns/Departments Health; Management; Finance; Travel, all 550-900 words. Query.
Tips "The chief aim of *The Rotarian* is to report Rotary International news. Most of this information comes through Rotary channels and is staff written or edited. The best field for freelance articles is in the general interest category. We prefer queries with a Rotary angle. These stories run the gamut from humor pieces and how-to stories to articles about such significant concerns as business management, technology, world health, and the environment."

SCOTTISH HOME & COUNTRY MAGAZINE

Scottish Women's Rural Institutes, 42 Heriot Row, Edinburgh Scotland EH3 6ES United Kingdom. (44)(131)225-1724. Fax: (44)(131)225-8129. E-mail: swri@swri.demon.co.uk. Website: www.swri.org.uk/magazine.html. Monthly publication that keeps readers in touch with SWRI news and rural events throughout Scotland. No kill fee. Editorial lead time 1 month. Sample copy for £1.35. Guidelines by email.

- SWRI members are not normally paid for submissions.

Nonfiction Crafts, personal histories, social history, health, travel, cookery, general women's interests. Does not want articles on religion or party politics. Send complete ms. Length: 500-1,000 words.

$ $ THE TOASTMASTER

Toastmasters International, P.O. Box 9052, Mission Viejo CA 92690-9052. (949)858-8255. E-mail: submissions@toastmasters.org. Website: www.toastmasters.org. **50% freelance written**. Monthly magazine on public speaking, leadership, and club concerns. "This magazine is sent to members of Toastmasters International, a nonprofit educational association of men and women throughout the world who are interested in developing their communication and leadership skills. Members range from novice to professional speakers and from a wide variety of ethnic and cultural backgrounds, as Toastmasters is an international organization." Estab. 1933. Circ. 235,000 in 11,700 clubs worldwide. Byline given. Pays on acceptance. No kill fee. Publishes ms an average of 1 year after acceptance. Buys first rights, buys second serial (reprint) rights, buys all rights. Submit seasonal material 3-4 months in advance. Accepts queries by mail, e-mail. Accepts previously published material. Accepts simultaneous submissions. Responds in 6-8 weeks to queries. Sample copy for 9 x 12 SASE with 4 first-class stamps. Guidelines available online.

- "Our readers are knowledgeable and experienced public speakers; therefore we accept only authentic, well-researched and well-crafted stories. Show, don't tell! Use sources, quotes from experts and other research to back up your views. The best articles have style, depth, emotional impact and take-away value to the reader. A potential feature article needs an unusual hook, compelling story or unique angle. Profiles of colorful, controversial, historically significant, amusing, unusual or unique people are welcome, but keep in mind that our readers live in 92 different countries, so stay away from profiles of American presidents or sports figures. All submissions must be in English, however. Please query first, or send a draft of your proposed article. We recommend you carefully study several issues of the magazine before submitting a query. We are not responsible for unsolicited articles, artwork or photographs, so please don't send anything you can't afford to lose."

Nonfiction Toastmasters members are requested to view their submissions as contributions to the organization. Sometimes asks for book excerpts and reprints without payment, but original contribution from individuals outside Toastmasters will be paid for at stated rates. Needs how-to, humor, interview, well-known speakers and leaders, communications, leadership, language use. **Buys 50 mss/year.** Please read our guidelines first, then when you are ready, submit through email. Query with published clips by mail or e-mail (preferred). Length: 700-2,000 words. **Compensation for accepted articles depends on whether our submission guidelines are followed, the amount of research involved and the article's general value to us.** Sometimes pays expenses of writers on assignment.
Reprints Send typed ms with rights for sale noted and information about when and where the material previously appeared. Pays 50-70% of amount paid for an original article.
Tips "We are looking primarily for how-to articles on subjects from the broad fields of communications and leadership which can be directly applied by our readers in their self-improvement and club programming efforts. Concrete examples are useful. Avoid sexist or nationalist language. Articles with obvious political or religious slants will not be accepted."

$ TRAIL & TIMBERLINE

The Colorado Mountain Club, 710 10th St., Suite 200, Golden CO 80401. (303)996-2745. Fax: (303)279-9690. E-mail: beckwt@cmc.org. Website: www.cmc.org. **80% freelance written**. Official quarterly publication for the Colorado Mountain Club. Articles in *Trail & Timberline* conform to the mission statement of the Colorado Mountain Club to unite the energy, interest, and knowledge of lovers of the Colorado mountains, to collect and disseminate information, to stimulate public interest, and to encourage preservation of the mountains of Colorado and the Rocky Mountain region. Estab. 1918. Circ. 10,500. Byline given. Pays on publication. No kill

fee. Publishes ms an average of 2 months after acceptance. Buys all rights. Editorial lead time 6 months. Submit seasonal material 6 months in advance. Accepts queries by mail, e-mail. Accepts previously published material. Responds in 1 week to queries. Responds in 1 month to mss. Sample copy for $5. Guidelines available online.
Nonfiction Needs essays, humor, opinion, Switchbacks, personal experience, photo feature, travel, Trip Reports. **Buys 10-15 mss/year.** Send complete ms. Length: 500-2,000 words. **Pays $50.**
Photos Send photos Captions, identification of subjects, model releases required. Reviews contact sheets, 35mm transparencies, 3x5 or larger prints, GIF/JPEG files. Offers no additional payment for photos accepted with ms Buys one time rights.
Poetry Contact: Jared Smith, poetry editor. Needs avant-garde, free verse, traditional. **Buys 6-12 poems/year. Pays $50.**
Tips Writers should be familiar with the purposes and ethos of the Colorado Mountain Club before querying. Writer's guidelines are available and should be consulted—particularly for poetry submissions. All submissions must conform to the mission statement of the Colorado Mountain Club.

$ $ $ VFW MAGAZINE

Veterans of Foreign Wars of the United States, 406 W. 34th St., Suite 523, Kansas City MO 64111. (816)756-3390. Fax: (816)968-1169. E-mail: magazine@vfw.org. Website: www.vfw.org. Tim Dyhouse, managing ed. **Contact:** Rich Kolb, editor-in-chief. **40% freelance written.** Monthly magazine on veterans' affairs, military history, patriotism, defense, and current events. *VFW Magazine* goes to its members worldwide, all having served honorably in the armed forces overseas from World War II through the Iraq and Afghanistan Wars. Estab. 1904. Circ. 1.6 million. Byline given. Pays on acceptance. Offers 50% kill fee. 3-6 months Buys first rights. 6 months Submit seasonal material 6 months in advance. Accepts queries by mail, e-mail, fax. Responds in 2 months to queries. Sample copy for 9x12 SAE with 5 first-class stamps. By e-mail
Nonfiction Contact: Richard Kolb. Veterans' and defense affairs, recognition of veterans and military service, current foreign policy, American armed forces abroad, and international events affecting US national security are in demand. Needs general interest, historical, inspirational. **Buys 25-30 mss/year.** Query with 1-page outline, résumé, and published clips. Length: 1,000-1,500 words. **Pays up to $500-$1,000 max. for assigned articles; $500-$750 max. for unsolicited articles.**
Photos Send photos Reviews contact sheets, negatives, GIF/JPEG files, 5x7 or 8x10 b&w prints. Buys first North American rights.
Tips Absolute accuracy and quotes from relevant individuals are a must. Bibliographies useful if subject required extensive research and/or is open to dispute. Consult *The Associated Press Stylebook* for correct grammar and punctuation. Please enclose a 3-sentence biography describing your military service and your military experience in the field in which you are writing. No phone queries.

VINTAGE SNOWMOBILE MAGAZINE

Vintage Snowmobile Club of America, P.O. Box 130, Grey Eagle MN 56336. (320)285-7066. E-mail: vsca@vsca.com. Website: www.vsca.com. **75% freelance written.** Quarterly magazine covering vintage snowmobiles and collectors. *Vintage Snowmobile Magazine* deals with vintage snowmobiles and is sent to members of the Vintage Snowmobile Club of America. Estab. 1987. Circ. 2,400. Byline sometimes given. Pays on acceptance. No kill fee. Publishes ms an average of 3 months after acceptance. Buys first North American serial rights. Editorial lead time 2 months. Submit seasonal material 3 months in advance. Accepts queries by mail, e-mail, fax, phone.
Nonfiction Needs general interest, historical, humor, photo feature, coverage of shows. Query with published clips. Length: 200-2,000 words.
Photos Send photos Reviews 3x5 prints, GIF/JPEG files. Negotiates payment individually. Buys all rights.
Columns/Departments Featured Sleds Stories, 500 words. Query with published clips.

WALK MAGAZINE

The Ramblers' Association, 2nd Floor, Camelford House, 87-90 Albert Embankment, London England SE1 7TW United Kingdom. (44)(207)339-8500. Fax: (44)(207)339-8501. E-mail: domb@ramblers.org.uk. Website: www.ramblers.org.uk. Quarterly magazine that encourages people to participate in walking, educates people about the countryside, and promotes wider access to—and protection of—the countryside. The magazine is distributed to Ramblers' Association members, organizations, and individuals who want to stay informed on the group's policies. Circ. 140,000. Pays on publication. No kill fee. Editorial lead time 6 weeks. Accepts queries by mail. Sample copy online or for a SASE (A4 and 73 pence). Guidelines by email.

- Book reviews, news stories, and articles on policy issues are normally written in-house.

Nonfiction Feature articles should promote an interest in walking, but should not just profile a location. Articles should describe why a particular walk is special to the writer. It helps if the walk can be accessed by public transportation. Query with synopsis/outline, published clips, SASE. Length: 500-800 words. **Payment is negotiable.**
Photos Send photos Captions required. Reviews 300 dpi digital images. Payment is negotiated.

ASTROLOGY, METAPHYSICAL & NEW AGE

$ $ $ $ BODY & SOUL

Martha Stewart Living Omnimedia, 42 Pleasant St., Watertown MA 02472. (617)926-0200. **60% freelance written**. Magazine published 10 times/year emphasizing personal fulfillment and healthier lifestyles. The audience we reach is primarily female, college-educated, 25-55 years of age, concerned about personal growth, health, earth-friendly living and balance in personal life. Estab. 1974. Circ. 550,000. Byline given. Offers 25% kill fee. Publishes ms an average of 6 months after acceptance. Buys first North American serial rights, buys electronic rights. Editorial lead time 6-8 months. Submit seasonal material 1 year in advance. Accepts queries by mail. Accepts simultaneous submissions. Responds in 2 months to queries. Sample copy for $5 and 9 x 12 SAE.

Nonfiction Needs how-to, inner growth, spiritual, health news, environmental issues, fitness, natural beauty. **Buys 50 mss/year.** Query with published clips. Length: 100-2,500 words. **Pays 75¢-$1.25/word.** Pays expenses of writers on assignment.

Columns/Departments Health, beauty, fitness, home, green living, healthy eating, personal growth, and spirituality, 600-1,300 words. 50 Query with published clips. **Pays 75¢-$1.25/word**

Tips Read the magazine and get a sense of the type of writing run in column. In particular, we are looking for new or interesting approaches to subjects such as mind-body fitness, earth-friendly products, Eastern and herbal medicine, self-help, community, healthy eating, etc. No e-mail or phone queries, please. Begin with a query, résumé and published clips—we will contact you for the manuscript. A query is 1-2 paragraphs—if you need more space than that to present the idea, then you don't have a clear grip on it.

$ $ FATE MAGAZINE

Fate Magazine, Inc., P.O. Box 460, Lakeville MN 55044 U.S. (800)728-2730. Fax: (952)891-6091. E-mail: submissions@fatemag.com. Website: www.fatemag.com. Phyllis Galde, ed.; David Godwin, managing ed. **75% freelance written**. Covering the paranormal, ghosts, ufos, strange science. *Fate* prefers first-person accounts and investigations of the topics we cover. We do not publish fiction or opinion pieces. Estab. 1948. Circ. 15,000. Byline given. Pays after publication. 3-6 months Buys all rights. 3-6 months Accepts queries by mail, e-mail, fax. Accepts simultaneous submissions. Responds in 4-6 months to queries. Online, by e-mail, free Online at website, free

Nonfiction Contact: Andrew Honigman. Personal psychic and mystical experiences, 350-500 words. **Pays $25.** Articles on parapsychology, Fortean phenomena, cryptozoology, spiritual healing, flying saucers, new frontiers of science, and mystical aspects of ancient civilizations, 500-3,000 words. Must include complete authenticating details. Prefers interesting accounts of single events rather than roundups. We very frequently accept manuscripts from new writers; the majority are people's first-person accounts of their own psychic/mystical/spiritual experiences. We do need to have all details, where, when, why, who and what, included for complete documentation. We ask for a notarized statement attesting to truth of the article. Needs general interest, historical, how-to, personal experience, photo feature feature, technical. We do not publish poetry, fiction, editorial/opinion pieces, or book-length mss. **Buys 100 mss/year mss/year.** Query. 500-4,000 words **Pays 10¢/word.** Pays with contributor copies if the writer asks for it.

Photos Contact: Andrew Honigman. Buys slides, prints, or digital photos/illustrations with ms. Send photos with submission. GIF/JPEG files; prints (4 x 6) Pays $10. one-time rights

Columns/Departments Contact: Andrew Honigman. True Mystic Experiences: Short reader-submitted stories of strange experiences; My Proof of Survival: Short, reader-submitted stories of proof of life after death, 300-1,000 words Writer should query. **$25**

Fillers Fillers are especially welcomed and must be be fully authenticated also, and on similar topics. Length: 100-1,000 words. **Pays 10¢/word.**

Tips *Fate* is looking for exciting, first-hand accounts of ufo and paranormal experiences and investigations.

$ NEWWITCH

BBI Media, Inc., P.O. Box 687, Forest Grove OR 97116. (888)724-3966. E-mail: editor@newwitch.com. Website: www.newwitch.com. Quarterly magazine covering paganism, wicca and earth religions. *newWitch* is dedicated to witches, wiccans, neo-pagans, and various other earth-based, pre-Christian, shamanic, and magical practitioners. We hope to reach not only those already involved in what we cover, but the curious and completely new as well. Estab. 2002. Circ. 15,000. Byline given. Pays on publication. Offers 100% kill fee. Buys first world wide periodical and nonexclusive electronic rights. Editorial lead time 3-4 months. Submit seasonal material 6 months in advance. Accepts queries by mail, e-mail, fax, phone. Accepts previously published material. Responds in 1-2 weeks to queries. Responds in 1 month to mss. Sample copy for $6. Guidelines available online.

Nonfiction Particularly interested in how-to spellcrafting and material for solitary pagans and wiccans. Needs book excerpts, essays, historical, how-to, humor, inspirational, interview, new product, opinion, personal experience, photo feature, religious, travel. Send complete ms. Length: 1,000-4,000 words. **Pays 2¢/word**

minimum. Sometimes pays expenses of writers on assignment.
Photos State availability Identification of subjects, model releases required. Reviews GIF/JPEG files. Negotiates payment individually; offers no additional payment for photos accepted with ms. Buys first world wide periodical and nonexclusive electronic rights.
Fiction Needs adventure, erotica, ethnic, fantasy, historical, horror, humorous, mainstream, mystery, novel concepts, religious, romance, suspense. Does not want faction (fictionalized retellings of real events). Avoid gratuitous sex, violence, sentimentality and pagan moralizing. Don't beat our readers with the Rede or the Threefold Law. **Buys 3-4 mss/year.** Send complete ms. Length: 1,000-5,000 words. **Pays 2¢/word minimum.**
Poetry Needs avant-garde, free verse, haiku, light verse, traditional. Submit maximum 3-5 poems. **Pays $15.**
Tips Read the magazine, do your research, write the piece, send it in. That's really the only way to get started as a writer: everything else is window dressing.

$ NEW YORK SPIRIT MAGAZINE

107 Sterling Place, Brooklyn NY 11217. (718)638-3733. Fax: (718)230-3459. E-mail: office@nyspirit.com. Website: www.nyspirit.com. Bimonthly tabloid covering spirituality and personal growth and transformation. We are a magazine that caters to the holistic health community in New York City. Circ. 50,000. Byline given. Pays on acceptance. Publishes ms an average of 3 months after acceptance. Buys first rights. Editorial lead time 1 month. Accepts previously published material. Accepts simultaneous submissions. Responds in 1 month to queries. Sample copy for sae with 8x10 envelope and 10 First-Class stamps. Guidelines available online.
Nonfiction Needs essays, how-to, humor, inspirational, interview, photo feature. **Buys 30 mss/year.** Query. Length: 1,000-3,500 words. **Pays $150 maximum.**
Photos State availability Model releases required.
Columns/Departments Fitness (new ideas in staying fit), 1,500 words. **Pays $150.**
Fiction Needs humorous, mainstream, inspirational. **Buys 5 mss/year.** Query with published clips. Length: 1,000-3,500 words. **Pays $150.**
Tips Be vivid and descriptive. We are very interested in hearing from new writers.

PREDICTION MAGAZINE

IPC Focus Network, Leon House, 233 High St., Croydon CR9 1HZ United Kingdom. E-mail: predictionfeatures@ipcmedia.com. Website: www.predictionmagazine.co.uk. Monthly magazine aimed at women of all ages who are interested in mystical—but practical—solutions to love, family, money, and career issues. Readers are fascinated by life's mysteries and the supernatural, and are looking for upbeat ways to predict their future, understand themselves more, and make their lives happier through positive change. Pays on publication. No kill fee. Editorial lead time 4 months. Accepts queries by mail, e-mail. Respondsi n 6 weeks (if interested). Guidelines available online.
Nonfiction Astrology, divination, psychic phenomena, self-help/personality quizzes, spirituality, ghosts/spirits, angels, crystals, pets, real-life stories. Doesn't accept short stories or poetry. Already has dedicated contributors for horoscopes, tarot, numerology, and dreams. Send complete ms. Length: 800-1,600 words.

$ SHAMAN'S DRUM

A Journal of Experiential Shamanism, Cross-Cultural Shamanism Network, P.O. Box 270, Williams OR 97544. (541)846-1313. Fax: (541)846-1204. **Contact:** Timothy White, editor. **75% freelance written.** Quarterly educational magazine of cross-cultural shamanism. "*Shaman's Drum* seeks contributions directed toward a general but well-informed audience. Our intent is to expand, challenge, and refine our readers' and our understanding of shamanism in practice. Topics include indigenous medicineway practices, contemporary shamanic healing practices, ecstatic spiritual practices, and contemporary shamanic psychotherapies. Our overall focus is cross-cultural, but our editorial approach is culture-specific—we prefer that authors focus on specific ethnic traditions or personal practices about which they have significant firsthand experience. We are looking for examples of not only how shamanism has transformed individual lives but also practical ways it can help ensure survival of life on the planet. We want material that captures the heart and feeling of shamanism and that can inspire people to direct action and participation, and to explore shamanism in greater depth." Estab. 1985. Circ. 6,000. Byline given. Publishes ms an average of 6 months after acceptance. Buys first North American serial rights, buys first rights. Editorial lead time 1 year. Accepts previously published material. Responds in 3 months to queries. Sample copy for $7. Guidelines for #10 SASE.
Nonfiction Needs book excerpts, essays, interview, please query, opinion, personal experience, photo feature. No fiction, poetry, or fillers. **Buys 16 mss/year.** Send complete ms. Length: 5,000-8,000 words. **Pays 5¢/word, depending on how much we have to edit.**
Reprints Send typed manuscript with rights for sale noted and information about when and where the material previously appeared. Pays 50% of amount paid for an original article.
Photos Send photos Identification of subjects required. Reviews contact sheets, transparencies, All size prints. Offers $40-50/photo. Buys one time rights.
Columns/Departments **Contact:** Judy Wells, Earth Circles. Timothy White, Reviews. Earth Circles (news

format, concerned with issues, events, organizations related to shamanism, indigenous peoples, and caretaking Earth); Reviews (in-depth reviews of books about shamanism or closely related subjects such as indigenous lifestyles, ethnobotany, transpersonal healing, and ecstatic spirituality), 500-1,500 words. 8 Query. **Pays 5¢/word.**

Tips "All articles must have a clear relationship to shamanism, but may be on topics which have not traditionally been defined as shamanic. We prefer original material that is based on, or illustrated with, first-hand knowledge and personal experience. Articles should be well documented with descriptive examples and pertinent background information. Photographs and illustrations of high quality are always welcome and can help sell articles."

$ WHOLE LIFE TIMES

1200 S. Hope St., Ste. 300, Los Angeles CA 90015. E-mail: jessica@wholelifetimes.com. Website: www.wholelifetimes.com. Monthly tabloid for cultural creatives. Estab. 1979. Circ. 58,000. Byline given. Pays within 1-2 months after publication. Buys first North American serial rights. Accepts queries by mail, e-mail. Sample copy for $3. Guidelines for #10 SASE.

Nonfiction Healing Arts, Food and Nutrition, Spirituality, New Beginnings, Relationships, Longevity, Arts/Cultures Travel, Vitamins and Supplements, Women's Issues, Sexuality, Science and Metaphysics, Environment/Simple Living. **Buys 60 mss/year.** Send complete ms. **Payment varies.**

Reprints Send typed manuscript with rights for sale noted and information about when and where the material previously appeared. Pays 50% of amount paid for an original article.

Columns/Departments Healing; Parenting; Finance; Food; Personal Growth; Relationships; Humor; Travel; Politics; Sexuality; Spirituality; and Psychology. Length: 750-1,200 words.

Tips Queries should be professionally written and show an awareness of current topics of interest in our subject area. We welcome investigative reporting and are happy to see queries that address topics in a political context. We are especially looking for articles on health and nutrition. No monthly columns sought.

AUTOMOTIVE & MOTORCYCLE

$ $ RIDER MAGAZINE

Ehlert Publishing Group, 2575 Vista Del Mar Dr., Ventura CA 93001. E-mail: editor@ridermagazine.com. Website: www.ridermagazine.com. **60% freelance written**. Monthly magazine covering motorcycling. *Rider* serves the all-brand motorcycle lifestyle/enthusiast with a slant toward travel and touring. Estab. 1974. Circ. 127,000. Byline given. Pays on publication. Offers 25% kill fee. Publishes ms an average of 6-12 months after acceptance. Buys first North American serial rights, buys electronic rights. Editorial lead time 3 months. Submit seasonal material 6 months in advance. Accepts queries by mail. Responds in 2 months to queries. Sample copy for $2.95. Guidelines by email.

Nonfiction Needs general interest, historical, how-to, humor, interview, personal experience, travel. Does not want to see fiction or articles on `How I Began Motorcycling.' **Buys 40-50 mss/year.** Query. Length: 750-1,800 words. **Pays $150-750.**

Photos Send photos Captions required. Reviews contact sheets, transparencies, high quality prints, high resolution (4MP+) digital images. Offers no additional payment for photos accepted with ms. Buys one-time and electronic rights

Columns/Departments Favorite Rides (short trip), 850-1,100 words. 12 Query. **Pays $150-750.**

Tips We rarely accept manuscripts without photos (slides or b&w prints). Query first. Follow guidelines available on request. We are most open to favorite rides, feature stories (must include excellent photography) and material for `Rides, Rallies and Clubs.' Include a map, information on routes, local attractions, restaurants, and scenery in favorite ride submissions.

$ AMERICAN MOTORCYCLIST

American Motorcyclist Association, 13515 Yarmouth Dr., Pickerington OH 43147. Fax: (614)856-1920. Website: www.ama-cycle.org. **10% freelance written**. Monthly magazine for enthusiastic motorcyclists investing considerable time and money in the sport. We emphasize the motorcyclist, not the vehicle. Estab. 1947. Circ. 260,000. Byline given. Pays on publication. No kill fee. Buys first North American serial rights. Editorial lead time 3 months. Submit seasonal material 4 months in advance. Accepts queries by mail, e-mail. Responds in 5 weeks to queries. Responds in 6 weeks to mss. Sample copy for $1.25. Guidelines free.

Nonfiction Needs interview, with interesting personalities in the world of motorcycling, personal experience, travel. **Buys 8 mss/year.** Send complete ms. Length: 1,000-2,500 words. **Pays minimum $8/published column inch.**

Photos Send photos Captions, identification of subjects required. Reviews transparencies, prints. Pays $50/photo minimum. Buys one time rights.

Tips Our major category of freelance stories concerns motorcycling trips to interesting North American destinations. Prefers stories of a timeless nature.

$ $ AUTOMOBILE QUARTERLY

The Connoisseur's Magazine of Motoring Today, Yesterday, and Tomorrow, Automobile Heritage Publishing & Communications LLC, 800 E. 8th St., New Albany IN 47150. Fax: (812)948-2816. E-mail: tpowell@autoquartly.com. Website: www.autoquarterly.com. **Contact:** Tracy Powell, managing editor. **85% freelance written.** Quarterly magazine covering "automotive history, with excellent photography.". Estab. 1962. Circ. 8,000. Byline given. Pays on acceptance. Publishes ms an average of 1 year after acceptance. Buys first international serial rights. Editorial lead time 9 months. Responds in 1 month to queries. Responds in 2 months to mss. Sample copy for $19.95.

Nonfiction Needs historical, photo feature, technical, biographies. **Buys 25 mss/year.** Query. Length: 2,500-5,000 words. **Pays approximately 35¢/word or more.** Sometimes pays expenses of writers on assignment.

Photos State availability Reviews 4 x 5 Buys perpetual rights of published photography per work-for-hire freelance agreement.

Tips "Please query, with clips, via snail mail. No phone calls, please. Study *Automobile Quarterly*'s unique treatment of automotive history first."

$ $ AUTO RESTORER

BowTie, Inc., 3 Burroughs, Irvine CA 92618. (949)855-8822. Fax: (949)855-3045. E-mail: tkade@fancypubs.com. Website: www.autorestorermagazine.com. **85% freelance written**. Monthly magazine covering auto restoration. Our readers own old cars and they work on them. We help our readers by providing as much practical, how-to information as we can about restoration and old cars. Estab. 1989. Pays on publication. Publishes ms an average of 3 months after acceptance. Buys first North American serial rights, buys one-time rights. Submit seasonal material 4 months in advance. Accepts queries by mail, e-mail, fax. Responds in 2 months to queries. Sample copy for $7. Guidelines free.

Nonfiction Needs how-to, auto restoration, new product, photo feature, technical, product evaluation. **Buys 60 mss/year.** Query. Length: 200-2,500 words. **Pays $150/published page, including photos and illustrations.**

Photos Technical drawings that illustrate articles in black ink are welcome. Send photos Reviews contact sheets, transparencies, 5x7 prints. Offers no additional payment for photos accepted with ms.

Tips Query first. Interview the owner of a restored car. Present advice to others on how to do a similar restoration. Seek advice from experts. Go light on history and nonspecific details. Make it something that the magazine regularly uses. Do automotive how-tos.

$ $ $ $ AUTOWEEK

Crain Communications, Inc., 1155 Gratiot Ave., Detroit MI 48207. (313)446-6000. Fax: (313)446-1027. Website: www.autoweek.com. **Contact:** Roger Hart, Managing Editor < person_to_recei > Roger Hart, Managing Editor. **5% freelance written, most by regular contributors**. Biweekly magazine. *AutoWeek* is a biweekly magazine for auto enthusiasts. Estab. 1958. Circ. 300,000. Byline given. Pays on publication. Publishes ms an average of 1 month after acceptance. Buys all rights. Accepts queries by e-mail.

Nonfiction Needs historical, interview. **Buys 5 mss/year.** Query. Length: 100-400 words. **Pays $1/word.**

$ $ BACKROADS

Motorcycles, Travel & Adventure, Backroads, Inc., P.O. Box 317, Branchville NJ 07826. (973)948-4176. Fax: (973)948-0823. E-mail: editor@backroadsusa.com. Website: www.backroadsusa.com. **80% freelance written**. Monthly tabloid covering motorcycle touring. "*Backroads* is a motorcycle tour magazine geared toward getting motorcyclists on the road and traveling. We provide interesting destinations, unique roadside attractions and eateries, plus Rip & Ride Route Sheets. We cater to all brands. If you really ride, you need *Backroads*." Estab. 1995. Circ. 40,000. Byline given. Pays on publication. Buys one-time rights. Editorial lead time 1 month. Submit seasonal material 3 months in advance. Accepts queries by mail, e-mail, fax. Sample copy for $4. Guidelines available online.

Nonfiction Contact: Shira Kamil, editor/publisher. Needs essays, motorcycle/touring, new product, opinion, personal experience, travel. No long diatribes on 'How I got into motorcycles.' Query. Length: 500-2,500 words. **Pays 10¢/word minimum for assigned articles. Pays 5¢/word minimum for unsolicited articles.**

Photos Send photos Offers no additional payment for photos accepted with ms.

Columns/Departments We're Outta Here (weekend destinations), 500-750 words; Great All-American Diner Run (good eateries with great location), 300-800 words; Thoughts from the Road (personal opinion/insights), 250-500 words; Mysterious America (unique and obscure sights), 300-800 words; Big City Getaway (day trips), 500-750 words. 20-24 Query. **Pays $75/article.**

Fillers Needs facts, newsbreaks. Length: 100-250 words.

Tips "We prefer destination-oriented articles in a light, layman's format, with photos (digital images on CD). Stay away from any name-dropping and first-person references."

$ $ $ CANADIAN BIKER MAGAZINE

735 Market St., Victoria BC V8T 2E2 Canada. (250)384-0333. Fax: (250)384-1832. E-mail: edit@canadianbiker.com. Website: www.canadianbiker.com. **65% freelance written**. Magazine covering motorcycling. A family-oriented motorcycle magazine whose purpose is to unite Canadian motorcyclists from coast to coast through the dissemination of information in a non-biased, open forum. The magazine reports on new product, events, touring, racing, vintage and custom motorcycling as well as new industry information. Estab. 1980. Circ. 20,000. Byline given. Publishes ms an average of 1 year after acceptance. Buys first rights. Editorial lead time 3 months. Accepts queries by mail, e-mail, fax, phone. Responds in 6 weeks to queries. Responds in 6 months to mss. Sample copy for $5 or online. Guidelines free.

Nonfiction All nonfiction must include photos and/or illustrations. Needs general interest, historical, how-to, interview, Canadian personalities preferred, new product, technical, travel. **Buys 12 mss/year.** Send complete ms. Length: 500-1,500 words. **Pays $100-200 for assigned articles. Pays $80-150 for unsolicited articles.**

Photos State availability of or send photos Captions, identification of subjects, model releases required. Reviews 4 × 4 transparencies, 3 × 5 prints. Negotiates payment individually. Buys one time rights.

Tips We're looking for more racing features, rider profiles, custom sport bikes, quality touring stories, `extreme' riding articles. Contact editor first before writing anything. Have original ideas, an ability to write from an authoritative point of view, and an ability to supply quality photos to accompany text. Writers should be involved in the motorcycle industry and be intimately familiar with some aspect of the industry which would be of interest to readers. Observations of the industry should be current, timely, and informative.

$ $ $ $ CAR AND DRIVER

Hachette Filipacchi Magazines, Inc., 2002 Hogback Rd., Ann Arbor MI 48105. (734)971-3600. Fax: (734)971-9188. E-mail: editors@caranddriver.com. Website: www.caranddriver.com. Monthly magazine for auto enthusiasts; college-educated, professional, median 24-35 years of age. Estab. 1956. Circ. 1,300,000. Byline given. Pays on acceptance. Offers 25% kill fee. Buys first North American serial rights. Accepts queries by mail, e-mail, fax. Responds in 2 months to queries.

Nonfiction Seek stories about people and trends, including racing. Two recent freelance purchases include news-feature on cities across America banning cruising and feature on how car companies create new car smells. All road tests are staff-written. Unsolicited manuscripts are not accepted. Query letters must be addressed to the Managing Editor. Rates are generous, but few manuscripts are purchased from outside. **Buys 1 mss/year. Pays max $3,000/feature; $750-1,500/short piece.** Pays expenses of writers on assignment.

Photos Color slides and b&w photos sometimes purchased with accompanying ms.

Tips It is best to start off with an interesting query and to stay away from nuts-and-bolts ideas because that will be handled in-house or by an acknowledged expert. Our goal is to be absolutely without flaw in our presentation of automotive facts, but we strive to be every bit as entertaining as we are informative. We do not print this sort of story: `My Dad's Wacky, Lovable Beetle.'

$ $ CAR AUDIO AND ELECTRONICS

Source Interlink, 2400 E. Katella Ave., 11th Floor, Anaheim CA 92806. (714)939-2400. E-mail: featurecar@primedia.com. Website: www.caraudiomag.com. **30% freelance written**. Monthly magazine covering mobile electronics. Circ. 40,000. Byline given. Pays on publication. No kill fee. Publishes ms an average of 5 months after acceptance. Buys first rights, buys electronic rights. Editorial lead time 4 months. Submit seasonal material 5 months in advance. Accepts queries by mail, e-mail. Accepts simultaneous submissions. Responds in 1 week to queries. Responds in 1 month to mss. Sample copy available online. Guidelines available online.

Nonfiction Needs how-to, photo feature, technical. Does not want personal essays, humor, and so on. **Buys 30 mss/year.** Query. Length: 750-1,200 words. **Pays $150-300.**

Photos State availability of or send photos Model releases required. Reviews GIF/JPEG files. Negotiates payment individually.

Columns/Departments Choices (vehicle feature), 400-500 words. 5 Query. **Pays $100-150.**

Tips Most of our freelancers write on assignment. To get in our pool of freelancers, contact us, preferably with published clips. If you are car audio savvy but don't have published clips or don't have published clips that relate to car audio, we may ask you to write a test piece before assigning you a paying article. Another way is to send a query or manuscript on a vehicle you think we'd be interested in featuring. The vehicle should not have run in another magazine, and it should be available for photos.

CAR CRAFT

Primedia Enthusiast Group, 6420 Wilshire Blvd., Los Angeles CA 90048-5515. Website: www.carcraft.com. Monthly magazine. Created to appeal to drag racing and high performance auto owners. Circ. 383,334. No kill fee. Editorial lead time 3 months.

CUSTOM CLASSIC TRUCKS

Source Interlink Media, 774 So. Placentia Ave., Placentia CA 92870. E-mail: john.gilbert@sorc.com. Website:

www.customclassictrucks.com. Monthly magazine. Contains a compilation of technical articles, historical reviews, coverage of top vintage truck events and features dedicated to the fast growing segment of the truck market that includes vintage pickups and sedan deliveries. Circ. 104,376. No kill fee.

$ $ $ FOUR WHEELER MAGAZINE

2400 E. Katella Ave., 11th Floor, Anaheim CA 92806. Website: www.fourwheeler.com. **20% freelance written. Works with a small number of new/unpublished writers each year.** Monthly magazine covering four-wheel-drive vehicles, back-country driving, competition, and travel adventure. Estab. 1963. Circ. 355,466. Pays on publication. No kill fee. Publishes ms an average of 4 months after acceptance. Buys all rights. Submit seasonal material 4 months in advance. Accepts queries by mail.

Nonfiction 4WD competition and travel/adventure articles, technical, how-tos, and vehicle features about unique four-wheel drives. We like the adventure stories that bring four wheeling to life in word and photo: mud-running deserted logging roads, exploring remote, isolated trails or hunting/fishing where the 4x4 is a necessity for success. Query with photos. 1,200-2,000 words; average 4-5 pages when published. **Pays $200-300/feature vehicles; $350-600/travel and adventure; $100-800/technical articles.**

Photos Requires professional quality color slides and b&w prints for every article. Prefers Kodachrome 64 or Fujichrome 50 in 35mm or 2 ¼ formats. Action shots a must for all vehicle features and travel articles. Captions required.

Tips Show us you know how to use a camera as well as the written word. The easiest way for a new writer/photographer to break into our magazine is to read several issues of the magazine, then query with a short vehicle feature that will show his or her potential as a creative writer/photographer.

$ $ ⊘ FRICTION ZONE

Motorcycle Travel and Information, (877)713-9500. E-mail: editor@friction-zone.com. Website: www.friction-zone.com. **60% freelance written.** Monthly magazine covering motorcycles. Estab. 1999. Circ. 26,000. Byline given. Pays on publication. No kill fee. Publishes ms an average of 1 month after acceptance. Buys first North American serial rights. Editorial lead time 6 weeks. Submit seasonal material 2 months in advance. Responds in to queries. Sample copy for $4.50 or on website.

Nonfiction Needs general interest, historical, how-to, humor, inspirational, interview, new product, opinion, photo feature, technical, travel, medical (relating to motorcyclists), book reviews (relating to motorcyclists). Does not accept first-person writing. **Buys 1 mss/year.** Query. Length: 1,000-3,000 words. **Pays 20¢/word.** Sometimes pays expenses of writers on assignment.

Photos Send photos Captions, identification of subjects, model releases required. Reviews negatives, slides. Offers $15/published photo Buys one time rights.

Columns/Departments Health Zone (health issues relating to motorcyclists); Motorcycle Engines 101 (basic motorcycle mechanics); Road Trip (California destination review including hotel, road, restaurant), all 2,000 words. 60 Query. **Pays 20¢/word**

Fiction We want stories concerning motorcycling or motorcyclists. No 'first-person' fiction. Query. Length: 1,000-2,000 words. **Pays 20¢/word.**

Fillers Needs anecdotes, facts, gags, newsbreaks, short humor. Length: 2,000-3,000 words. **Pays 20¢/word**

Tips Query via e-mail with sample writing. Visit our website for more detailed guidelines.

⊘ HOT ROD MAGAZINE

Source Interlink Media, Inc., 6420 Wilshire Bvld., Los Angeles CA 90048-5515. E-mail: inquiries@automotive.com. Website: www.hotrod.com. Monthly magazine covering hot rods. Focuses on 50s and 60s cars outfitted with current drive trains and the nostalgia associated with them. Circ. 700,000. No kill fee. Editorial lead time 3 months.

- Query before submitting.

$ $ IN THE WIND

Paisano Publications, LLC, P.O. Box 3000, Agoura Hills CA 91376-3000. (818)889-8740. Fax: (818)889-1252. E-mail: photos@easyriders.net. Website: www.easyriders.com. **50%% freelance written.** Quarterly magazine. Geared toward the custom (primarily Harley-Davidson) motorcycle rider and enthusiast, *In the Wind* is driven by candid pictorial-action photos of bikes being ridden, and events. Estab. 1978. Circ. 90,000. Byline given. Pays on publication. No kill fee. Publishes ms an average of 9 months after acceptance. Buys all rights. Editorial lead time 6 months. Accepts queries by mail, e-mail. Responds in 2 weeks to queries. Responds in 2 months to mss.

Nonfiction Needs photo feature, event coverage. No long-winded tech articles **Buys 6 mss/year.** Length: 750-1,000 words. **Pays $250-600.** Sometimes pays expenses of writers on assignment.

Photos Send SASE for return. Send photos Identification of subjects, model releases, True required. Reviews transparencies, digital images, b&w, color prints. Buys all rights.

Tips Know the subject. Looking for submissions from people who ride their own bikes.

KEYSTONE MOTORCYCLE PRESS

Blue Moon Publications, P.O. Box 296, Ambridge PA 15003-0296. (724)774-6542. E-mail: kmppress@aol.com. **65% freelance written**. Monthly tabloid covering motorcycling. Our publication is geared toward all motorcyclists & primarily focuses on people & events in the great PA region; hence it is named after the Keystone State. The KMP features product reviews, motorcycle tests, industry news, motorcycling personalities, book reviews, and coverage of major national events. Estab. 1988. Circ. 15,000, plus 2,000 samples and free copies per month. Byline given. Pays on publication. Offers kill fee. varies Publishes ms an average of 2 months after acceptance. Buys first rights. Makes work-for-hire assignments. Editorial lead time 1-2 months. Submit seasonal material 3 months in advance. Accepts queries by mail, e-mail. Responds in 2 weeks to queries. Responds in 1 month to mss. Sample copy free. Guidelines by email.

Nonfiction Needs book excerpts, general interest, historical, how-to, humor, inspirational, interview, new product, (Technical), opinion, (Does not mean letters to the editor), religious, travel, (All must relate to motorcycling). We do not want personal diatribes. Witty, okay; pointless is not. **Buys 8 mss/yr. mss/year.** Query with published clips. Length: 250-1,500 words. Sometimes pays expenses of writers on assignment.

Photos Contact: Marilyn Shields. Send photos Captions, identification of subjects required. Reviews GIF/JPEG files. Negotiates payment individually. negotiable

Columns/Departments Contact: Dan Faingnaert. All Things Considered (Various news clips), 70 words; New Products (Short summaries of new products available), 120 words. 18 mss/yr. Query with published clips. **Pays $$20-$200.**

Fiction Buys 2 mss/yr. mss/year. Query with published clips. Length: 500-2,500 words. **varies-negotiable.**

Poetry Contact: Dan Faingnaert. Needs free verse, haiku, light verse, traditional.

Fillers Contact: Dan Faingnaert. Needs anecdotes, facts, gags, newsbreaks, short humor. 18/yr. variable **variable**

Tips Unique items or news relevant to motorcycling. It is a vast multi-spectrum culture of all types of individuals involved for many different reasons. If one lives in the great PA area, contributing would be very easy. There is much going on in the world of motorcycling now, particularly in light of the current gasoline situation. If one needs some help, try talking to motorcyclists, read a copy of 2 of of *Motorcyclist*, *Cycle World Rider*, or *American Motorcyclist* magazines or surf the WEb for reference materials. If submitting something, do so via email and use the KISS approach: keep it simple, don't embed graphics, photos or illustrations in copy and at least use spell check. Mac users are preferred, but all are welcome.

LATINOS ON WHEELS

On Wheels, Inc., 645 Griswold St., Suite 1209, Detroit MI 48226. (313)237-6883. Fax: (313)237-6886. E-mail: vmenard@onwheelsinc.com. Website: www.onwheelsinc.com/lowmagazine. English-language Quarterly magazine. "Supplement to leading Latino newspapers in the US. Provides Latino car buyers and car enthusiasts with the most relevant automotive trends." Circ. 500,000. No kill fee.

- Query before submitting.

LIVE TO RIDE

News Magazines, Locked Bag 5030, Alexandria NSW 2015 Australia. (61)(02)8062-2612. Fax: (61)(02)8062-2613. E-mail: pugs@livetoride.com.au. Website: www.livetoride.com.au. Monthly magazine covering Harley-Davidsons. "*Live to Ride* is jam-packed full of parties, personalities, bike features, jokes, technical rundown on Harleys, together with motorcycle and product updates." Circ. 24,000.

Nonfiction Needs general interest, interview, new product, technical. Query.

MOTOR TREND

Primedia, 6420 Wilshire Blvd., 7th Floor, Los Angeles CA 90048. Website: www.motortrend.com. **5-10% freelance written. Only works with published/established writers.** Monthly magazine for automotive enthusiasts and general interest consumers. Estab. 1949. Circ. 1,250,000. No kill fee. Publishes ms an average of 3 months after acceptance. Buys all rights. Accepts queries by mail. Responds in 1 month to queries.

Nonfiction Automotive and related subjects that have national appeal. Emphasis on domestic and imported cars, road tests, driving impressions, auto classics, auto, travel, racing, and high-performance features for the enthusiast. Packed with facts. Freelancers should confine queries to photo-illustrated exotic drives and other feature material; road tests and related activity are handled in house. A fact-filled query is suggested for all freelancers.

Photos Buys photos of prototype cars and assorted automotive matter.

NEW ZEALAND 4WD

Adrenalin Publishing Ltd., P.O. Box 65-092, Mairangi Bay Auckland New Zealand. (64)(9)478-4771. Fax: (64)(9)478-4779. E-mail: editor@nz4wd.co.nz. Website: www.nz4wd.co.nz. Magazine published 11 times/year covering topics of interest to 4WD vehicle buyers and drivers, including vehicle selection, accessories/upgrading, 4WD clubs/sports, lifestyle activities associated with 4WD, adventure and track stories, and technical articles. Estab. 1996. No kill fee.

- Query before submitting.

OUTLAW BIKER

Art & Ink Publications, 820 Hamilton St., Charlotte NC 28206-2991. (704)333-3331. Fax: (704)333-3433. E-mail: inked@skinartmag.com. Website: www.outlawbiker.com. **50% freelance written**. Magazine published 4 times/year covering bikers and their lifestyle. All writers must be insiders of biker lifestyle. Features include coverage of biker events, profiles, and humor. Estab. 1983. Circ. 150,000. Byline given. Pays on publication. Publishes ms an average of 3 months after acceptance. Buys first rights. Editorial lead time 3 months. Submit seasonal material 5 months in advance. Accepts queries by mail, e-mail, fax. Accepts previously published material. Accepts simultaneous submissions. Responds in 2 weeks to queries. Responds in 2 months to mss. Sample copy for $5.98. Guidelines for #10 SASE.

Nonfiction Needs historical, humor, new product, personal experience, photo feature, travel. Daytona Special, Sturgis Special (annual bike runs). No first time experiences—our readers already know. **Buys 10-12 mss/year.** Send complete ms. Length: 100-1,000 words.

Photos Send photos Captions, identification of subjects, model releases required. Reviews transparencies, prints. Offers $0-10/photo. Buys one time rights.

Columns/Departments 10-12 Send complete ms.

Fiction Needs adventure, erotica, fantasy, historical, humorous, romance, science fiction, slice-of-life vignettes, suspense. No racism. **Buys 10-12 mss/year.** Send complete ms. Length: 500-2,500 words.

Poetry Needs avant-garde, free verse, haiku, light verse, traditional. **Buys 10-12 poems/year.** Submit maximum 12 poems. Length: 2-1,000 lines.

Fillers Needs anecdotes, facts, gags, newsbreaks, short humor. 10-12 Length: 500-2,000 words.

Tips Writers must be insiders of the biker lifestyle. Manuscripts with accompanying photographs as art are given higher priority.

⊘ POPULAR HOT RODDING

Source Interlink Media, Inc., 774 S. Placentia Ave., Placentia CA 92870. Website: www.popularhotrodding.com. Monthly magazine for the automotive enthusiast; highlights features that emphasize performance, bolt-on accessories, replacement parts, safety, and the sport of drag racing. Circ. 182,000. No kill fee.

- Query before submitting.

$ $ ROAD KING

Parthenon Publishing, 28 White Bridge Rd., Suite 209, Nashville TN 37205. Website: www.roadking.com. **25% freelance written.** Bimonthly magazine covering the trucking industry. Byline given. Pays 3 weeks from acceptance. Offers 30% kill fee. Publishes ms an average of 3 months after acceptance. Buys first North American serial rights, buys all electronic rights. Editorial lead time 3-4 months. Submit seasonal material 4 months in advance. Accepts queries by mail. Accepts simultaneous submissions. Responds in 3-4 weeks to queries. Sample copy for #10 SASE. Guidelines free.

Nonfiction No essays, no humor, no cartoons. **Buys 12 mss/year.** Query with published clips. Length: 100-1,000 words. **Pays $50-500.**

⊘ SPORT COMPACT CAR

Source Interlink Media, Inc., 2400 E. Katella Ave., 11th Floor, Anaheim CA 92806. (714)939-2400. Fax: (714)978-6390. Website: www.sportcompactcarweb.com. Monthly magazine for owners and potential buyers of new compacts who seek inside information regarding performance, personalization, and cosmetic enhancement of the vehicles. Circ. 117,000. No kill fee. Editorial lead time 4 months.

- Query before submitting.

⊘ SPORT RIDER

Source Interlink Media, Inc., 6420 Wilshire Blvd., Los Angeles CA 90048-5515. E-mail: srmail@primedia.com. Website: www.sportrider.com. Bimonthly magazine for enthusiast of sport/street motercycles and emphasizes performance, both in the motorcycle and the rider. Circ. 108,365. No kill fee.

- Query before submitting.

⊘ SUPER CHEVY

Source Interlink Media, Inc., 365 W. Passaic St., Rochelle Park NJ 07662. Website: www.superchevy-web.com. "Monthly magazine covering various forms of motorsports where Cheverolet cars and engines are in competition.". Circ. 198,995. No kill fee.

- "Query before submitting. Ms must be typed on white paper and accompanied by SASE."

Photos Captions, model releases, original material.

$ TRUCKIN' MAGAZINE

World's Leading Truck Publication, Source Interlink Media, Inc., 2400 E. Katella Ave., Suite 700, Anaheim CA 92806. Website: www.truckinweb.com. Monthly magazine. Written for pickup drivers and enthusiasts. Circ. 186,606. No kill fee. Editorial lead time 3 months.

AVIATION

AFRICAN PILOT

Serious About Flying, Published by Wavelengths 10 (Pty) Ltd., 303 Spur Rd., Beaulieu, Kyalami, Midrand Johannesburg South Africa. (27)(11)702-2342. Fax: (27)(11)468-2637. E-mail: editor@africanpilot.co.za. Website: www.africanpilot.co.za. **50% freelance written**. Monthly magazine covering all aspects of general aviation, airline, commercial, and military aviation for consumer value in the sub-continent of Africa. (General aviation hardly exists in the remainder of Africa.) Estab. 2002. Circ. 10,000. Byline given. No kill fee. Editorial lead time 2-3 months. Accepts queries by e-mail. Accepts previously published material. Accepts simultaneous submissions. Sample copy available online. Writer's guidelines online or via e-mail.

Nonfiction Needs general interest, historical, interview, new product, personal experience, photo feature, technical. No articles on aircraft accidents. **Buys up to 60 mss/year.** Send complete ms. Length: 1,200-2,800 words. Sometimes pays expenses of writers on assignment.

Photos Send photos Captions required. Negotiates payment individually. Buys one time rights.

Tips The Web site is update monthly and all articles are fully published online.

$ $ $ $ AIR & SPACE MAGAZINE

Smithsonian Institution, P.O. Box 37012, MRC 951, Washington DC 20013-7012. (202)275-1230. Fax: (202)275-1886. E-mail: editors@si.edu. Website: www.airspacemag.com. **80% freelance written**. Bimonthly magazine covering aviation and aerospace for a nontechnical audience. 'Emphasizes the human rather than the technological, on the ideas behind the events. Features are slanted to a technically curious, but not necessarily technically knowledgeable, audience. We are looking for unique angles to aviation/aerospace stories, history, events, personalities, current and future technologies, that emphasize the human-interest aspect." Estab. 1985. Circ. 225,000. Byline given. Pays on acceptance. Offers kill fee. Buys first North American serial rights. Accepts queries by mail, e-mail, fax. Responds in 3 months to queries. Sample copy for $7. Guidelines available online.

Nonfiction "We are actively seeking stories covering space and general or business aviation." Needs book excerpts, essays, general interest, on aviation/aerospace, historical, humor, photo feature, technical. **Buys 50 mss/year.** Query with published clips. Length: 1,500-3,000 words. **Pays $1,500-3,000.** Pays expenses of writers on assignment.

Photos Refuses unsolicited material. State availability Reviews 35 mm transparencies, digital files.

Columns/Departments Above and Beyond (first person), 1,500-2,000 words; Flights and Fancy (whimsy), approximately 800 words. Soundings (brief items, timely but not breaking news), 500-700 words. 25 Query with published clips. **Pays $150-300.**

Tips "We continue to be interested in stories about space exploration. Also, writing should be clear, accurate, and engaging. It should be free of technical and insider jargon, and generous with explanation and background. The first step every aspiring contributor should take is to study recent issues of the magazine."

$ AUTOPILOT MAGAZINE

The AutoPilot Franchise Systems, 1954 Airport Rd., Suite 250, Atlanta GA 30341. (770)255-1014. Fax: (770)274-2375. Website: www.autopilotmagazine.com. **70% freelance written**. Bimonthly magazine covering aviation. *AutoPilot Magazine* is a lifestyle magazine for the aviation enthusiast. We currently have four editions circulating, including Alabama, Georgia, Florida and the Mid-Atlantic region. This magazine differs from other aviation publications, because its focus is specifically on the pilot. Estab. 2000. Circ. 90,000 for all four editions. Byline given. Pays on acceptance. Buys second serial (reprint) rights. Editorial lead time 2-3 weeks. Accepts queries by mail, e-mail, fax, phone. Sample copy free. Guidelines free.

Nonfiction Needs book excerpts, essays, historical, personal experience, photo feature, travel. Query. Length: 500-900 words. **Pays $100.**

Columns/Departments Airport Spotlight (general aviation airports), 500-800 words; Pilot Profiles, 500-800 words; Notable Aviation Organizations, 900 words; Aviation Museums, 900 words; Aviation Memorials, 600 words. **Pays $100.**

Fillers Needs anecdotes.

Tips Please e-mail with a current resume and 2 writing samples.

$ $ AVIATION HISTORY

Weider History Group, 19300 Promenade Dr., Leesburg VA 20176. E-mail: aviationhistory@weiderhistorygroup.com. Website: www.thehistorynet.com. **95% freelance written**. Bimonthly magazine covering military and civilian aviation from first flight to the jet age. "It aims to make aeronautical history not only factually accurate and complete, but also enjoyable to a varied subscriber and newsstand audience." Estab. 1990. Circ. 50,000. Byline given. Pays on publication. No kill fee. Publishes ms an average of 2 years after acceptance. Buys all rights. Editorial lead time 6 months. Submit seasonal material 1 year in advance. Accepts queries by mail, e-mail, fax. Accepts simultaneous submissions. Responds in 2 months to queries. Responds in 3 months to mss.

Sample copy for $5. Guidelines for #10 SASE or online.
Nonfiction Needs historical, interview, personal experience. **Buys 24 mss/year.** Query. Feature articles should be 3,000-3,500 words, each with a 500-word sidebar where appropriate, author's biography, and book suggestions for further reading **Pays $300.**
Photos State availability of art and photos with submissions, cite sources. We'll order. Identification of subjects required. Reviews contact sheets, negatives, transparencies. Buys one time rights.
Columns/Departments Aviators, Restored, Extremes all 1,500 words or less. Pays $150 and up. Book reviews, 250-500 words, pays minimum $50.
Tips "Choose stories with strong art possibilities. Include a hard copy as well as an IBM- or Macintosh-compatible CD. Write an entertaining, informative, and unusual story that grabs the reader's attention and holds it. All stories must be true. We do not publish fiction or poetry."

$ BALLOON LIFE

9 Madeline Ave., Westport CT 06880. (203)629-1241. E-mail: bill_armstrong@balloonlife.com. Website: www.balloonlife.com. **75% freelance written**. Monthly magazine covering sport of hot air ballooning. Readers participate as pilots, crew, and official observers at events and spectators. Estab. 1986. Circ. 7,000. Byline given. Pays on publication. Offers 50-100% kill fee. Publishes ms an average of 3-4 months after acceptance. Buys first North American serial rights. Submit seasonal material 4 months in advance. Accepts queries by mail, e-mail. Accepts simultaneous submissions. Responds in 2 weeks to queries. Sample copy for 9 x 12 SAE with $2 postage. Guidelines available online.
Nonfiction Needs book excerpts, general interest, how-to, flying hot air balloons, equipment techniques, interview, new product, technical, events/rallies, safety seminars, balloon clubs/organizations, letters to the editor. **Buys 150 mss/year.** Send complete ms. Length: 1,000-1,500 words. **Pays $50-200.**
Photos Send photos Captions, identification of subjects required. Reviews transparencies, prints, high-resolution digital images. Offers $15/inside photos, $50/cover. Buys nonexclusive, all rights.
Columns/Departments Crew Quarters (devoted to some aspect of crewing), 900 words; Preflight (a news and information column), 300-500 words; **pays $50**. Logbook (balloon events that have taken place in last 3-4 months), 300-500 words; **pays $20**. 60 Send complete ms.
Tips This magazine slants toward the technical side of ballooning. We are interested in articles that help to educate and provide safety information. Also stories with manufacturers, important individuals, and/or historic events and technological advances important to ballooning. The magazine attempts to present how-to articles on flying, business opportunities, weather, equipment, etc. Both our feature stories and Logbook sections are where most manuscripts are purchased.

$ $ FLIGHT JOURNAL

The Aviation Adventure—Past, Present and Future, Air Age Publishing, 20 Westport Rd., Wilton CT 06897. Fax: (203)431-3000. E-mail: rogerp@airage.com. Website: www.flightjournal.com/. Bimonthly magazine covering aviation-oriented material, for the most part with a historical overtone, but also with some modern history in the making reporting. Many articles have an 'I was there' or 'from the cockpit' human-interest emphasis. We are not a general aviation magazine. A typical issue will have 2-3 articles on WWII, one odern jet story; it could be hardware and operations with pilot interviews, or a personal story; one historical piece, e.g., early airlines, barnstormers; one semi-technical piece with historical overtones, e.g., low aspect ratio airplanes. No kill fee. Accepts queries by mail, e-mail, fax. Guidelines available.
Nonfiction Needs expose, historical, humor, interview, new product, personal experience, photo feature, technical. We do not want any general aviation articles like 'My Flight to Baja in my 172,' nor detailed recitations of the technical capabilities of an aircraft. Avoid historically accurate, but bland, chronologies of events. Lengthier pieces should be discussed in advance with the editors. Length: 2,500-3,000 words. **Pays $600.**
Photos See submission guidelines. Reviews 5x7 prints. Negotiates payment individually.
Tips Use an unusual slant that makes your story idea unique; unusual pictures for an exciting presentation; fantastic but true accounts; lots of human interest. The designers, builders, pilots and mechanics are what aviation is all about. Send a single page outline of your idea. Provide one or more samples of prior articles, if practical. We like an upbeat style, with humor, where it fits. Use sidebars to divide content of technically dense subjects. If you have a good personal story but aren't a professional-quality writer, we'll help with the writing.

$ $ FLYING ADVENTURES MAGAZINE

Aviation Publishing Corporation, P.O. Box 93613, Pasadena CA 91109-3613. (626)618-4000. E-mail: editor@flyingadventures.com. Website: www.flyingadventures.com. **20% freelance written**. Bimonthly magazine covering lifestyle travel for owners and passengers of private aircraft. "Our articles cover upscale travelers." Estab. 1994. Circ. 135,858. features, no departments Pays on acceptance. No kill fee. Buys all rights. Editorial lead time 2 weeks to 2 months. Accepts queries by e-mail. Accepts previously published material. Accepts simultaneous submissions. immediately. immediately. Sample copy free. Guidelines free.
Nonfiction Needs travel, Lifestyle. Nothing non-relevant, not our style. See magazine. Query with published

clips. Length: 500-1,500 words. **Pays $150-300 for assigned and unsolicited articles.** Sometimes pays expenses of writers on assignment.
Photos Contact: Photographer Director. State availability Captions, identification of subjects, model releases required. Reviews GIF/JPEG files. Negotiates payment individually. Buys all rights.
Columns/Departments Contact: Editor. Numerous Departments, see magazine. 100+ mss/yr. Query with published clips. **Pays $-$150.**
Tips "Send clip that fits our content and style. Must fit our style!"

FLYING MAGAZINE

Hachette Filipacchi Media U.S., Inc., 1633 Broadway, 45th Floor, New York NY 10019. (212)767-4936. Fax: (212)767-4932. E-mail: flyedit@hfmus.com. Website: www.flyingmag.com. Monthly magazine covering aviation. Edited for active pilots through coverage of new product development and application in the general aviation market. Estab. 1927. Circ. 277,875. No kill fee. Editorial lead time 3 months. Accepts queries by mail, e-mail, fax. Sample copy for $4.99.

- *Flying* is almost entirely staff written; use of freelance material is limited.

Nonfiction We are looking for the most unusual and best-written material that suits *Flying*. Most subjects in aviation have already been done so fresher ideas and approaches to stories are particularly valued. We buy 'I Learned About Flying From That' articles, as well as an occasional feature with and without photographs supplied. Send complete ms.
Photos State availability

$ $ ⊘ GENERAL AVIATION NEWS

Flyer Media, Inc., 11120 Gravelly Lake Dr., SW #7, Lakewood WA 98499. (800)426-8538. Fax: (253)471-9911. E-mail: janice@generalaviationnews.com. Website: www.generalaviationnews.com. **20% freelance written. Prefers to work with published/established writers who are pilots.** Monthly magazine covering general aviation across the U.S. Estab. 1949. Circ. 50,000. Byline given. Buys first North American serial rights. Editorial lead time 3-5 months. Accepts queries by e-mail. Accepts simultaneous submissions. Guidelines free.
Nonfiction Needs general interest, how-to, interview, technical, travel. Query. Length: 700-1,000 words. **Pays $75-250.** Sometimes pays expenses of writers on assignment.
Photos Send photos jpeg/eps/tiff files (300 dpi) Payment negotiable.

$ $ PLANE AND PILOT

Werner Publishing Corp., 12121 Wilshire Blvd., 12th Floor, Los Angeles CA 90025-1176. (310)820-1500. Fax: (310)826-5008. E-mail: editor@planeandpilotmag.com. Website: www.planeandpilotmag.com. **80% freelance written**. Monthly magazine covering general aviation. We think a spirited, conversational writing style is most entertaining for our readers. We are read by private and corporate pilots, instructors, students, mechanics and technicians—everyone involved or interested in general aviation. Estab. 1964. Circ. 150,000. Byline given. Pays on publication. Offers kill fee. Publishes ms an average of 4 months after acceptance. Buys all rights. Submit seasonal material 4 months in advance. Accepts previously published material. Responds in 4 months to queries. Sample copy for $5.50. Guidelines available online.
Nonfiction Needs how-to, new product, personal experience, technical, travel, pilot efficiency, pilot reports on aircraft. **Buys 75 mss/year.** Query. Length: 1,200 words. **Pays $200-500.** Pays expenses of writers on assignment.
Reprints Send tearsheet, photocopy or typed ms with rights for sale noted and information about when and where the material previously appeared. Pays 50% of amount paid for original article.
Photos Submit suggested heads, decks and captions for all photos with each story. Submit b&w photos, 8 x 10 prints with glossy finish. Submit color photos in the form of 2 ¼x2 ¼, 4 x 5 or 35mm transparencies in plastic sleeves. Offers $50-300/photo. Buys all rights.
Columns/Departments Readback (any newsworthy items on aircraft and/or people in aviation), 1,200 words; Jobs & Schools (a feature or an interesting school or program in aviation), 900-1,000 words. 30 Send complete ms. **Pays $200-500.**
Tips Pilot proficiency articles are our bread and butter. Manuscripts should be kept under 1,800 words—1,200 words is ideal.

BUSINESS & FINANCE

BUSINESS NATIONAL

$ $ BUSINESS TRAVELER USA

Varquin, 115 W. 30th St., Suite 202, New York NY 10001. (212)725-3500. Fax: (212)725-2646. E-mail: eva@btusonline.com. Website: www.Btusonline.com. **90% freelance written**. Magazine business travel. Estab.

1988. Circ. 150,000. Byline given. No kill fee. Buys all rights. Editorial lead time 2 months. Submit seasonal material 2 months in advance. Accepts queries by mail, e-mail, fax, phone. Accepts simultaneous submissions. Sample copy free.

Nonfiction Needs interview, new product, personal experience, travel. **Buys 100/year mss/year.** Query. Length: 100-1,800 words. **Pays 50¢ a word for assigned articles.**

Columns/Departments Query. **Pays $-50¢ a word.**

$ $ $ $ CORPORATE BOARD MEMBER

Board Member Inc., 475 Park Ave. S., 19th Floor, New York NY 10016. Fax: (212)686-3041. E-mail: cleinster@boardmember.com. Website: www.boardmember.com. **100% freelance written.** Bimonthly magazine covering corporate governance. Our readers are the directors and top executives of publicly-held US corporations. We look for detailed and preferably narrative stories about how individual boards have dealt with the challenges that face them on a daily basis: reforms, shareholder suits, CEO pay, firing and hiring CEOs, setting up new boards, firing useless directors. We're happy to light fires under the feet of boards that are asleep at the switch. We also do service-type pieces, written in the second person, advising directors about new wrinkles in disclosure laws, for example. Estab. 1999. Circ. 60,000. Byline given. Pays on acceptance. Offers 25% kill fee. Publishes ms an average of 3 months after acceptance. Buys all rights. Editorial lead time 4-5 months. Submit seasonal material 4-5 months in advance. Accepts queries by e-mail. Responds in 1 week to queries. Responds in 1 week to mss. Sample copy available online. Guidelines by email.

Nonfiction Best Law Firms in America (July/August); What Directors Think (November/December). Does not want views from 35,000 feet, pontification, opinion, humor, anything devoid of reporting. **Buys 100 mss/year.** Query. Length: 650-2,500 words. **Pays $1,200-5,000.** Pays expenses of writers on assignment.

Tips Don't suggest stories you can't deliver.

$ $ DOLLARS AND SENSE: THE MAGAZINE OF ECONOMIC JUSTICE

Economic Affairs Bureau, 29 Winter St., Boston MA 02108. (617)447-2177. Fax: (617)477-2179. E-mail: dollars@dollarsandsense.org. Website: www.dollarsandsense.org. **10% freelance written.** Bimonthly magazine covering economic, environmental, and social justice. "We explain the workings of the US and international economics, and provide left perspectives on current economic affairs. Our audience is a mix of activists, organizers, academics, unionists, and other socially concerned people." Estab. 1974. Circ. 8,000. Byline given. Pays on publication. No kill fee. Publishes ms an average of 4 months after acceptance. Editorial lead time 3 months. Submit seasonal material 2 months in advance. Accepts queries by mail, e-mail, fax, phone. Sample copy for $5 or on website. Guidelines available online.

Nonfiction Needs exposè, political economics. **Buys 6 mss/year.** Query with published clips. Length: 700-2,500 words. **Pays $0-200.** Sometimes pays expenses of writers on assignment.

Photos State availability Captions, identification of subjects required. Negotiates payment individually. Buys one time rights.

Tips "Be familiar with our magazine and the types of communities interested in reading us. *Dollars and Sense* is a progressive economics magazine that explains in a popular way both the workings of the economy and struggles to change it. Articles may be on the environment, the World Bank, community organizing, urban conflict, inflation, unemployment, union reform, welfare, changes in government regulation—a broad range of topics that have an economic theme. Find samples of our latest issue on our homepage."

$ $ ELLIOTT WAVE INTERNATIONAL PUBLICATIONS

Elliott Wave International, P.O. Box 1618, Gainesville GA 30503. E-mail: customerservice@elliottwave.com. Website: www.elliottwave.com. **10% freelance written.** Our publications are weekly to monthly in print and online formats covering investment markets. An understanding of technical market analysis is indispensible, knowledge of Elliott wave analysis even better. Clear, conversational prose is mandatory. Estab. 1979. Circ. 80,000. Byline sometimes given. Pays on publication. Publishes ms an average of 1 month after acceptance. Buys all rights. Editorial lead time 1 month. Accepts queries by e-mail.

Nonfiction Needs essays, how-to, technical. **Buys 12 mss/year.** Query with published clips. Length: 500-800 words. **Pays $100-200.**

Columns/Departments Pop culture and the stock market, 500-800 words. 12 Query with published clips. **Pays $100-200.**

⊘ FORTUNE

Time, Inc., 1271 Avenue of the Americas, New York NY 10020. (212)522-1212. Fax: (212)522-0810. E-mail: fortunemail_letters@fortunemail.com. Website: www.fortune.com. Biweekly magazine. Edited primarily for high-demographic business people. Specializes in big stories about companies, business personalities, technology, managing, Wall Street, media, marketing, personal finance, politics and policy. Circ. 1,066,000. No kill fee. Editorial lead time 6 weeks.

- Does not accept freelance submissions.

$ $ $ $ HISPANIC BUSINESS

Hispanic Business, Inc., 425 Pine Ave., Santa Barbara CA 93117-3709. (805)964-5539. Fax: (805)964-6139. Website: www.hispanicbusiness.com. **40-50% freelance written.** Monthly magazine covering Hispanic business. For more than 2 decades, *Hispanic Business* magazine has documented the growing affluence and power of the Hispanic community. Our magazine reaches the most educated, affluent Hispanic business and community leaders. Stories should have relevance for the Hispanic business community. Estab. 1979. Circ. 220,000 (rate base); 990,000 (readership base). Byline given. Pays on publication. Offers 50% kill fee. Publishes ms an average of 1 month after acceptance. Buys all rights. Editorial lead time 1-3 months. Submit seasonal material 2 months in advance. Accepts queries by mail. Accepts simultaneous submissions. Responds in 3 weeks to queries. Responds in 1 month to mss. Sample copy free.

Nonfiction Needs interview, travel. **Buys 120 mss/year.** Query résumé and published clips. Length: 650-2,000 words. **Pays $50-1,500.** Sometimes pays expenses of writers on assignment.

Photos State availability Captions required. Reviews GIF/JPEG files. Negotiates payment individually. Buys all rights.

Columns/Departments Tech Pulse (technology); Money Matters (financial), both 800 words. 40 Query with résumé and published clips. **Pays $50-450.**

Tips E-mail or snail mail queries with résumé and published clips are the most effective.

⊘ MONEY

Time, Inc., 1271 Avenue of the Americas, 17th Floor, New York NY 10020. (212)522-1212. Fax: (212)522-0189. E-mail: managing_editor@moneymail.com. Website: money.cnn.com. Monthly magazine covering finance. *Money* magazine offers sophisticated coverage in all aspects of personal finance for individuals, business executives, and personal investors. Estab. 1972. Circ. 1,967,420. No kill fee.

- *Money* magazine does not accept unsolicited manuscripts and almost never uses freelance writers.

$ $ $ MYBUSINESS MAGAZINE

Hammock Publishing, 3322 W. End Ave., Suite 700, Nashville TN 37203. (615)690-3419. E-mail: f. Website: www.mybusinessmag.com. **75% freelance written.** Bimonthly magazine for small businesses. We are a guide to small business success, however that is defined in the new small business economy. We explore the methods and minds behind the trends and celebrate the men and women leading the creation of the new small business economy. Estab. 1999. Circ. 600,000. Byline given. Pays on acceptance. Offers 30% kill fee. Publishes ms an average of 4 months after acceptance. Buys first North American serial rights, buys electronic rights. Editorial lead time 4 months. Submit seasonal material 5 months in advance. Accepts queries by mail. Accepts simultaneous submissions. Responds in 3 weeks to queries. Sample copy free Guidelines available online.

Nonfiction Needs book excerpts, how-to, small business topics, new product. **Buys 8 mss/year.** Query with published clips. Length: 200-1,800 words. **Pays $75-1,000.** Pays expenses of writers on assignment.

Tips *MyBusiness* is sent bimonthly to the 600,000 members of the National Federation of Independent Business. We're here to help small business owners by giving them a range of how-to pieces that evaluate, analyze, and lead to solutions.

$ $ THE NETWORK JOURNAL

Black Professionals and Small Business Magazine, The Network Journal Communication, 39 Broadway, Suite 2120, New York NY 10006. (212)962-3791. Fax: (212)962-3537. E-mail: editors@tnj.com. Website: www.tnj.com. **25% freelance written.** Monthly magazine covering business and career articles. *The Network Journal* caters to black professionals and small-business owners, providing quality coverage on business, financial, technology and career news germane to the black community. Estab. 1993. Circ. 25,000. Byline given. Pays on publication. Buys all rights. Editorial lead time 2 months. Submit seasonal material 3 months in advance. Accepts queries by mail, e-mail, fax, phone. Accepts previously published material. Accepts simultaneous submissions. Sample copy for $1 or online. Writer's guidelines for SASE or online

Nonfiction Needs how-to, interview. Send complete ms. Length: 1,200-1,500 words. **Pays $150-200.** Sometimes pays expenses of writers on assignment.

Photos Send photos Identification of subjects required. Offers $25/photo. Buys one time rights.

Columns/Departments Book reviews, 700-800 words; career management and small business development, 800 words. **Pays $100.**

Tips We are looking for vigorous writing and reporting for our cover stories and feature articles. Pieces should have gripping leads, quotes that actually say something and that come from several sources. Unless it is a column, please do not submit a 1-source story. Always remember that your article must contain a nutgraph—that's usually the third paragraph telling the reader what the story is about and why you are telling it now. Editorializing should be kept to a minimum. If you're writing a column, make sure your opinions are well-supported.

PERDIDO

Leadership with a Conscience, High Tide Press, 3650 W. 183rd St., Homewood IL 60430. (708)206-2054. E-mail: editor@hightidepress.com. Website: www.perdidomagazine.com. Monica Regan, mng. ed. **Contact:** Mary Rundell-Holmes, editor. **60% freelance written**. Quarterly magazine covering leadership and management. We are concerned with what's happening in organizations that are mission-oriented—as opposed to merely profit-oriented. *Perdido* is focused on helping conscientious leaders put innovative ideas into practice. We seek pragmatic articles on management techniques as well as essays on social issues relating to the workplace (not politics or religion). The readership of *Perdido* is comprised mainly of CEOs, executive directors, vice presidents, and program directors of nonprofit and for-profit organizations. We try to make the content of *Perdido* accessible to all decision-makers, whether in the nonprofit or for-profit world, government, or academia. *Perdido* actively pursues diverse opinions and authors from many different fields. Estab. 1994. Circ. 1,300. Byline given. Pays on publication. No kill fee. Publishes ms an average of 3 months after acceptance. Buys first North American serial rights, buys second serial (reprint) rights. 2-3 months Submit seasonal material 2-3 months in advance. Accepts queries by mail, e-mail. Accepts previously published material. Accepts simultaneous submissions. Responds in 2-3 weeks to queries Sample copy online at website Guidelines online at: www.perdidomagazine.com/main/submissions.php

- Especially interesting to *Perdido* readers are new management trends, concepts, practices, philosophies, business leaders and authors. And, the most effective articles are those that back up new ideas with practical applications, and those that use stories or anecdotes to provide the reader with a useful context.

Nonfiction Needs book excerpts, how-to, interview, personal experience (leadership experience only). We do not want anything about new products or specific business, or about any leader in whom you have a personal vested interest. **Buys 4 mss/year mss/year.** Query. Length: 900-2,800 words. **Pays 5-7¢/word for assigned and unsolicited articles. Pays $75 for book reviews. Pays in contributor copies.**

Photos State availability of photos. Send photos with submission. Captions, identification of subjects, model releases required. Reviews 5x7 prints. Negotiates payment individually. Buys one time rights.

Columns/Departments Book Review (new books on management/leadership), 750-900 words; Feature articles, 900-2,800 words. **Pays 5-7¢/word; $75 for book reviews.**

Tips Potential writers for *Perdido* should rely on the magazine's motto—Leadership with a Conscience—as starting point. We're looking for thoughtful reflections on management that help people succeed. While instructive articles are good, we avoid step-by-step recipes. Data and real life examples are very important.

$$$$ PROFIT

Your Guide to Business Success, Rogers Media, 1 Mt. Pleasant Rd., 11th Floor, Toronto ON M4Y 2Y5 Canada. (416)764-1402. Fax: (416)764-1404. Website: www.profitguide.com. **80% freelance written**. Magazine published 6 times/year covering small and medium businesses. We specialize in specific, useful information that helps our readers manage their businesses better. We want Canadian stories only. Estab. 1982. Circ. 110,000. Byline given. Pays on acceptance. Offers variable kill fee. Publishes ms an average of 2 months after acceptance. Buys first North American serial rights, buys electronic rights. Submit seasonal material 6 months in advance. Accepts queries by mail, fax, phone. Responds in 1 month to queries. Responds in 6 weeks to mss. Sample copy for 9x12 SAE with 84¢ postage. Guidelines free.

Nonfiction Needs how-to, business management tips, strategies and Canadian business profiles. **Buys 50 mss/year.** Query with published clips. Length: 800-2,000 words. **Pays $500-2,000.** Pays expenses of writers on assignment.

Columns/Departments Finance (info on raising capital in Canada), 700 words; Marketing (marketing strategies for independent business), 700 words. 80 Query with published clips. **Pays $150-600.**

Tips We're wide open to freelancers with good ideas and some knowledge of business. Read the magazine and understand it before submitting your ideas—which should have a Canadian focus.

SMARTMONEY MAGAZINE

1755 Broadway, 2nd Floor, New York NY 10019. E-mail: editors@smartmoney.com. Website: www.smartmoney.com.

- Query before submitting.

$$ TECHNICAL ANALYSIS OF STOCKS & COMMODITIES

The Traders' Magazine, Technical Analysis, Inc., 4757 California Ave. SW, Seattle WA 98116. (206)938-0570. E-mail: editor@traders.com. Website: www.traders.com. **95% freelance written**. "Magazine covers methods of investing and trading stocks, bonds and commodities (futures), options, mutual funds, and precious metals using technical analysis." Estab. 1982. Circ. 65,000. Byline given. Pays on publication. No kill fee. Publishes ms an average of 6 months after acceptance. Buys all rights. Responds in 3 months to queries. Sample copy for $8. Guidelines available online.

- "Eager to work with new/unpublished writers."

Nonfiction Needs how-to, trade, technical, cartoons, trading and software aids to trading, reviews, utilities, real world trading (actual case studies of trades and their results). No newsletter-type, buy-sell recommendations. The article subject must relate to technical analysis, charting or a numerical technique used to trade securities or futures. Almost universally requires graphics with every article. **Buys 150 mss/year.** Send complete ms. Length: 1,000-4,000 words. **Pays $100-500.**

Reprints Send tearsheet with rights for sale noted and information about when and where the material previously appeared.

Photos Contact: Christine M. Morrison, art director. State availability Captions, identification of subjects, model releases required. Pays $60-350 for b&w or color negatives with prints or positive slides. Buys one time and reprint rights

Columns/Departments Length: 800-1,600 words. 100 Query. **Pays $50-300.**

Fillers Contact: Karen Wasserman, fillers editor. "Must relate to trading stocks, bonds, options, mutual funds, commodities, or precious metals." 20 Length: 500 words. **Pays $20-50.**

Tips "Describe how to use technical analysis, charting, or computer work in day-to-day trading of stocks, bonds, commodities, options, mutual funds, or precious metals. A blow-by-blow account of how a trade was made, including the trader's thought processes, is the very best-received story by our subscribers. One of our primary considerations is to instruct in a manner that the layperson can comprehend. We are not hypercritical of writing style."

BUSINESS REGIONAL

$ $ ALASKA BUSINESS MONTHLY

Alaska Business Publishing, 501 W. Northern Lights Blvd., Suite 100, Anchorage AK 99503-2577. (907)276-4373. Fax: (907)279-2900. E-mail: editor@akbizmag.com. Website: www.akbizmag.com. **Contact:** Debbie Cutler, man. ed. **90% freelance written.** "Our audience is Alaska businessmen and women who rely on us for timely features and up-to-date information about doing business in Alaska." Estab. 1985. Circ. 12,000-14,000. Byline given. Pays on publication. Offers $50 kill fee. Publishes ms an average of 4 months after acceptance. Buys all rights. Editorial lead time 5 months. Submit seasonal material 5 months in advance. Accepts queries by mail, e-mail, fax. Accepts previously published material. Responds in 1 month to queries. Sample copy for 9x12 SAE and 4 first-class stamps. Guidelines free.

Nonfiction Needs general interest, how-to, interview, new product, Alaska, opinion. No fiction, poetry, or anything not pertinent to Alaska. **Buys approximately 130 mss/year.** Send complete ms. Length: 500-2,000 words. **Pays $150-300.** Sometimes pays expenses of writers on assignment.

Photos State availability

Tips "Send a well-written manuscript on a subject of importance to Alaska businesses. We seek informative, entertaining articles on everything from entrepreneurs to heavy industry. We cover all Alaska industry to include mining, tourism, timber, transportation, oil and gas, fisheries, finance, insurance, real estate, communications, medical services, technology, and construction. We also cover Native and environmental issues, and occasionally feature Seattle and other communities in the Pacific Northwest."

$ $ $ $ ALBERTA VENTURE

Venture Publishing Inc., 10259 - 105 St., Edmonton AB T5J 1E3 Canada. (780)990-0839. E-mail: mmccullough@albertaventure.com. Website: www.albertaventure.com. **70% freelance written.** Monthly magazine covering business in Alberta. "Our readers are mostly business owners and managers in Alberta who read the magazine to keep up with trends and run their businesses better." Estab. 1997. Circ. 35,000. Byline given. Pays on publication. Offers 30% kill fee. Publishes ms an average of 2 months after acceptance. Buys first North American serial rights, buys electronic rights. Editorial lead time 3 months. Submit seasonal material 3 months in advance. Accepts queries by e-mail. Responds in 2 weeks to queries. Sample copy available online. Guidelines by email.

Nonfiction Needs how-to, business narrative related to Alberta. Does not want company or product profiles. **Buys 75 mss/year.** Query. Length: 1,000-3,000 words. **Pays $300-2,000 (Canadian).** Pays expenses of writers on assignment.

Photos Contact: Contact Alfredo Zelcer, art director. State availability Identification of subjects required. Reviews GIF/JPEG files. Negotiates payment individually. Buys one time rights.

$ $ ATLANTIC BUSINESS MAGAZINE

Communications Ten, Ltd., P.O. Box 2356, Station C, St. John's NL A1C 6E7 Canada. (709)726-9300. Fax: (709)726-3013. Website: www.atlanticbusinessmagazine.com. **80% freelance written.** Bimonthly magazine covering business in Atlantic Canada. We discuss positive business developments, emphasizing that the 4 Atlantic provinces are a great place to do business. Estab. 1989. Circ. 30,000. Byline given. Pays within 30 days of publication. No kill fee. Publishes ms an average of 2 months after acceptance. Buys one-time rights. Editorial lead time 6 months. Accepts queries by mail, e-mail, fax. Sample copy and writer's guidelines free

Nonfiction Needs expose, general interest, interview, new product. We don't want religious, technical, or

scholarly material. We are not an academic magazine. We are interested only in stories concerning business topics specific to the 4 Canadian provinces of Nova Scotia, New Brunswick, Prince Edward Island, and Newfoundland and Labrador. **Buys 36 mss/year.** Query with published clips. Length: 1,200-2,500 words. **Pays $300-750.** Sometimes pays expenses of writers on assignment.
Photos Send photos Captions, identification of subjects required. Reviews contact sheets, transparencies, prints. Negotiates payment individually Buys one time rights.
Columns/Departments Query with published clips.
Tips Writers should submit their areas of interest as well as samples of their work and, if possible, suggested story ideas.

BCBUSINESS

Canada Wide Magazines & Communications, Ltd., 4180 Lougheed Hwy., 4th Floor, Burnaby BC V5C 6A7 Canada. (604)299-7311. Fax: (604)299-9188. E-mail: mogrady@canadawide.com. Website: www.bcbusinessmagazine.com. **80% freelance written**. Monthly magazine covering significant issues and trends shaping the province's business environment. Stories are lively, topical and extensively researched. Circ. 30,000. Byline given. Pays 2 weeks prior to being published. Offers kill fee. Publishes ms an average of 2 months after acceptance. Buys first rights. Editorial lead time 4 months. Submit seasonal material 4 months in advance. Accepts queries by e-mail. Accepts simultaneous submissions. Responds in 6 weeks to queries. Guidelines free.
Nonfiction Query with published clips. Length: 1,500-2,000 words. Sometimes pays expenses of writers on assignment.
Photos State availability

$ BLUE RIDGE BUSINESS JOURNAL

Landmark, Inc., 302 Second St., 4th Floor, Roanoke VA 24011. (540)777-6460. Fax: (540)777-6471. E-mail: dansmith@bizjournal.com. Website: www.bizjournal.com. **75% freelance written**. Monthly. We take a regional slant on national business trends, products, methods, etc. Interested in localized features and news stories highlighting business activity. Estab. 1989. Circ. 15,000. Byline given. Pays on acceptance. No kill fee. Publishes ms an average of 1 month after acceptance. Buys all rights. Editorial lead time 10 days. Accepts queries by mail, e-mail, fax. Accepts previously published material. Responds immediately. Call the editor for sample copies and/or writer's guidelines. Writers must live in our region.
Nonfiction Health Care and Hospitals; Telecommunications; Building and Construction; Investments; Personal Finance and Retirement Planning; Guide to Architectural; Engineering and Construction Services; and Manufacturing and Industry. No columns or stories that are not pre-approved. **Buys 120-150 mss/year.** Query. Length: 500-2,000 words.
Photos State availability Captions, identification of subjects required. Offers $10/photo. Buys all rights.
Tips Talk to the editor. Offer knowledgeable ideas (if accepted they will be assigned to that writer). We need fast turnaround, accurate reporting, neat dress, non-smokers. More interested in writing samples than educational background.

BUSINESS LONDON

P.O. Box 7400, London ON N5Y 4X3 Canada. (519)472-7601. Fax: (519)473-7859. E-mail: editorial@businesslondon.ca. Website: www.businesslondon.ca. **70% freelance written**. Monthly magazine covering London business. Our audience is primarily small and medium businesses and entrepreneurs. Focus is on success stories and how to better operate your business. Estab. 1987. Circ. 14,000. Byline given. Pays on publication. Offers 50% kill fee. Publishes ms an average of 3 months after acceptance. Buys first rights. Editorial lead time 3 months. Accepts queries by e-mail. Responds in 3 months to mss. Sample copy for #10 SASE. Guidelines free.
Nonfiction Needs how-to, business topics, humor, interview, new product, local only, personal experience, must have a London connection. **Buys 30 mss/year.** Query with published clips. Length: 250-1,500 words.
Photos Send photos Identification of subjects required. Reviews contact sheets, transparencies. Negotiates payment individually. Buys one time rights.
Tips Phone with a great idea. The most valuable things a writer owns are ideas. We'll take a chance on an unknown if the idea is good enough.

BUSINESS NH MAGAZINE

670 N. Commercial St., Suite 110, Manchester NH 03101. (603)626-6354. Fax: (603)626-6359. E-mail: edit@businessnhmagazine.com. Website: www.businessnhmagazine.com. **25% freelance written**. Monthly magazine covering business, politics, and people of New Hampshire. Our audience consists of the owners and top managers of New Hampshire businesses. Estab. 1983. Circ. 15,000. Byline given. Pays on publication. No kill fee. Publishes ms an average of 2 months after acceptance. Accepts queries by e-mail, fax.
Nonfiction Needs how-to, interview. No unsolicited manuscripts; interested in New Hampshire writers only. **Buys 24 mss/year.** Query with published clips and résumé Length: 750-2,500 words. **Payment varies.**
Photos Both b&w and color photos are used. Payment varies. Buys one time rights.

Tips I always want clips and resumes with queries. Freelance stories are almost always assigned. Stories must be local to New Hampshire.

$ $ CINCY MAGAZINE

The Magazine for Business Professionals, Great Lakes Publishing Co., Cincinnati Club Building, 30 Garfield Place, Suite 440, Cincinnati OH 45202. (513)421-2533. Fax: (513)421-2542. E-mail: news@cincymagazine .com. Website: www.cincymagazine.com. **80% freelance written**. Bimonthly magazine Glossy color magazine written for business professionals in Greater Cincinnati, published 10 times annually. *Cincy* is written and designed for the interests of business professionals and executives both at work and away from work, with features, trend stories, news and opinions related to business, along with lifestyle articles on home, dining, shopping, travel, health and more. Estab. 2003. Circ. 15,300. Byline given. Pays on publication. Offers 100% kill fee. Publishes ms an average of 3 months after acceptance. Buys all rights. Editorial lead time 1-3 months. Submit seasonal material 4 months in advance. Accepts queries by mail, e-mail.

Nonfiction Needs general interest, interview. Does not want stock advice. Length: 200-2,000 words. **Pays $75-600.**

Tips Read Cincy online, understand what we want, pitch concisely in e-mail, deliver good writing promptly.

$ $ CORPORATE CONNECTICUT MAGAZINE

The Corporate World at Eye Level, Corporate World LLC, P.O. Box 290726, Wethersfield CT 06129. Fax: (860)257-1924. E-mail: editor@corpct.com. Website: www.corpct.com. **50% freelance written.** Quarterly magazine covering regional reporting, global coverage of corporate/business leaders, entreprenuers. *Corporate Connecticut* is devoted to people who make business happen in the private sector and who create innovative change across public arenas. Centered in the Northeast between New York and Boston, Connecticut is positioned in a coastal corridor with a dense affluent population who are highly mobile, accomplished and educated. Estab. 2001. Byline given. Pays on publication. Offers 25% kill fee. Publishes ms an average of 2-3 months after acceptance. Buys first North American serial rights, buys electronic rights, buys all rights, buys negotiable rights. Editorial lead time 3-6 months. Submit seasonal material 10-12 months in advance. Accepts queries by mail, e-mail. Responds in 2 weeks to queries. Sample copy for #10 SASE.

Nonfiction Interested in pieces on hedge funds, venture capital, high-end travel. Query with published clips. **Pays 35¢/word minimum with varying fees for excellence.**

Photos State availability

Tips Review our online content to get a general feel for the publication. Aim high with content, do research, pitch a unique angle with a global perspective on business and people.

$ CRAIN'S DETROIT BUSINESS

Crain Communications, Inc., 1155 Gratiot, Detroit MI 48207. (313)446-0419. Fax: (313)446-1687. E-mail: achapelle@crain.com. Website: www.crainsdetroit.com. **10% freelance written.** Weekly tabloid covering business in the Detroit metropolitan area—specifically Wayne, Oakland, Macomb, Washtenaw, and Livingston counties. Estab. 1985. Circ. 150,000. Byline given. Pays on publication. No kill fee. Publishes ms an average of 1 month after acceptance. Buys all rights. Accepts queries by mail, e-mail. Sample copy for $1.50. Guidelines available online.

- *Crain's Detroit Business* uses only area writers and local topics.

Nonfiction Needs new product, technical, business. **Buys 20 mss/year.** Query with published clips. 30-40 words/column inch **Pays $10-15/column inch.** Pays expenses of writers on assignment.

Photos State availability

Tips Contact special sections editor in writing with background and, if possible, specific story ideas relating to our type of coverage and coverage area.

$ ✪ IN BUSINESS WINDSOR

Cornerstone Publications, Inc., 1775 Sprucewood Ave., LaSalle ON N9J 1X7 Canada. (519)250-2880. Fax: (519)250-2881. E-mail: gbaxter@inbusinesswindsor.com. Website: www.inbusinesswindsor.com. **70% freelance written**. Monthly magazine covering business. We focus on issues/ideas which are of interest to businesses in and around Windsor and Essex County (Ontario). Most stories deal with business and finance; occasionally we will cover health and sports issues that affect our readers. Estab. 1988. Circ. 10,000. Byline given. Pays on acceptance. No kill fee. Buys first rights. Editorial lead time 3 months. Submit seasonal material 3 months in advance. Accepts queries by mail, e-mail, fax. Responds in 2 weeks to queries. Responds in 1 month to mss. Sample copy for $3.50.

Nonfiction Needs general interest, how-to, interview. **Buys 25 mss/year.** Query with published clips. Length: 800-1,500 words. **Pays $70-150.** Sometimes pays expenses of writers on assignment.

$ $ THE LANE REPORT

Lane Communications Group, 210 E. Main St., 14th Floor, Lexington KY 40507. (859)244-3500. Fax: (859)244-3555. E-mail: aolsen@lanereport.com. Website: www.kybiz.com. **70% freelance written**. Monthly magazine covering statewide business. Estab. 1986. Circ. 15,000. Byline given. Pays on publication. No kill fee. Buys one-time rights. Editorial lead time 6 weeks. Submit seasonal material 3 months in advance. Accepts queries by mail, e-mail, fax. Accepts previously published material. Accepts simultaneous submissions. Responds in 1 month to queries. Sample copy and writer's guidelines free

Nonfiction Needs essays, interview, new product, photo feature. No fiction. **Buys 30-40 mss/year.** Query with published clips. Length: 500-2,000 words. **Pays $150-375.** Sometimes pays expenses of writers on assignment.

Photos State availability Identification of subjects required. Reviews contact sheets, negatives, transparencies, prints, digital images. Negotiates payment individually. Buys one time rights.

Columns/Departments Technology and Business in Kentucky; Advertising; Exploring Kentucky; Perspective; Spotlight on the Arts, all less than 1,000 words.

Tips As Kentucky's only statewide business and economics publication, we look for stories that incorporate perspectives from the Commonwealth's various regions and prominent industries—tying it into the national picture when appropriate. We also look for insightful profiles and interviews of Kentucky's entrepreneurs and business leaders.

$ MERCER BUSINESS MAGAZINE

White Eagle Publishing Company, 2550 Kuser Rd., Trenton State NJ 08691. (609)586-2056. Fax: (609)586-8052. E-mail: maggih@mercerbusiness.com. Website: www.mercerchamber.org. **100% freelance written**. Monthly magazine covering national and local business-related, theme-based topics. *Mercer Business* is a Chamber of Commerce publication, so the slant is pro-business primarily. Also covers nonprofits, education and other related issues. Estab. 1924. Circ. 8,500. Byline given. Pays on publication. Publishes ms an average of 1 month after acceptance. Makes work-for-hire assignments. Editorial lead time 6 weeks. Submit seasonal material 6 weeks in advance. Accepts queries by e-mail. Accepts simultaneous submissions. Responds in 1 week to queries. Sample copy for #10 SASE. Guidelines by email.

Nonfiction Needs humor. Query with published clips. Length: 1,000-1,800 words. **Pays $150 for assigned articles.** Sometimes pays expenses of writers on assignment.

Photos State availability of or send photos Captions, identification of subjects, model releases required. Offers no additional payment for photos accepted with ms.

Fillers Needs gags. 24 Length: 300-500 words.

Tips Query with cover letter preferred after perusal of editorial calendar.

$ $ $ $ ☒ OREGON BUSINESS

MEDIAmerica, Inc., 610 SW Broadway, Suite 200, Portalnd OR 97205. (503)223-0304. Fax: (503)221-6544. E-mail: editor@oregonbusiness.com. Website: www.oregonbusiness.com. **15-25% freelance written**. Monthly magazine covering business in Oregon. Our subscribers inlcude owners of small and medium-sized businesses, government agencies, professional staffs of banks, insurance companies, ad agencies, attorneys and other service providers. We accept *only* stories about Oregon businesses, issues and trends. Estab. 1981. Circ. 50,000. Byline given. Pays on publication. No kill fee. Buys first North American serial rights, buys electronic rights. Editorial lead time 2 months. Accepts queries by mail, e-mail. Sample copy for $4. Guidelines available online.

Nonfiction Features should focus on major trends shaping the state; noteworthy businesses, practices, and leaders; stories with sweeping implications across industry sectors. Query with résumé and 2-3 published clips. Length: 1,200-3,000 words.

Columns/Departments First Person (opinion piece on an issue related to business), 750 words; Around the State (recent news and trends, and how they might shape the future), 100-600 words; Business Tools (practical, how-to suggestions for business managers and owners), 400-600 words; In Character (profile of interesting or quirky member of the business community), 850 words. Query with résumé and 2-3 published clips.

Tips An *Oregon Business* story must meet at least 2 of the following criteria: **Size and location**: The topic must be relevant to Northwest businesses. Featured companies (including franchises) must be based in Oregon or Southwest Washington. **Service**: Our sections (1,200 words) are reserved largely for service pieces focusing on finance, marketing, management or other general business topics. These stories are meant to be instructional, emphasizing problem-solving by example. **Trends**: These are sometimes covered in a section piece, or perhaps a feature story. We aim to be the state's leading business publication so we want to be the first to spot trends that affect Oregon companies. **Exclusivity or strategy**: of an event, whether it's a corporate merger, a dramatic turnaround, a marketing triumph or a PR disaster.

$ $ PRAIRIE BUSINESS

Grand Forks (ND) Herald, Forum Communications Company, 808 Third Ave., #400, Fargo ND 58103. Fax: (701)280-9092. E-mail: rschuster@prairiebizmag.com. Website: www.prairiebizmag.com. **Contact:** Ryan Schuster, submissions editor. **30% freelance written**. Monthly magazine covering business on the Northern Plains (North Dakota, South Dakota, Minnesota). "We attempt to be a resource for business owners/managers, policymakers, educators, and nonprofit administrators, acting as a catalyst for growth in the region by reaching out to an audience of decision makers within the region and also venture capitalists, site selectors, and angel visitors from outside the region." Estab. 2000. Circ. 20,000. Byline given. Pays within 2 weeks of mailing date. No kill fee. Publishes ms an average of 1-2 months after acceptance. Buys all rights. Editorial lead time 2 months. Submit seasonal material 2 months in advance. Accepts queries by e-mail. Accepts previously published material. Accepts simultaneous submissions. Responds in 2 weeks to queries. Sample copy free. Guidelines free.

Nonfiction Needs interview, technical. "Does not want articles that are blatant self-promotion for any interest without providing value for readers." **Buys 36 mss/year.** Query. Length: 800-1,500 words. **Pays 10-15¢/word.**
Photos Send photos Captions, identification of subjects required. Reviews GIF/JPEG files (hi-res). Offers $20-250/photo. Buys one time rights.

PROVIDENCE BUSINESS NEWS

220 W. Exchange St., Suite 210, Providence RI 02903. (401)273-2201, ext. 215. Fax: (401)274-0670. E-mail: murphy@pbn.com. Website: www.pbn.com. Business magazine covering news of importance to the Providence area.

- Query before submitting.

$ ROCHESTER BUSINESS JOURNAL

Rochester Business Journal, Inc., 45 E. Ave., Suite 500, Rochester NY 14604. (585)546-8303. Fax: (585)546-3398. Website: www.rbjdaily.com. **10% freelance written**. Weekly tabloid covering local business. The *Rochester Business Journal* is geared toward corporate executives and owners of small businesses, bringing them leading-edge business coverage and analysis first in the market. Estab. 1984. Circ. 10,000. Byline given. Pays on publication. No kill fee. Publishes ms an average of 1 month after acceptance. Buys first rights, buys second serial (reprint) rights, buys electronic rights. Editorial lead time 6 weeks. Accepts queries by mail, fax. Responds in 1 week to queries. Sample copy for free or by e-mail. Guidelines available online.

Nonfiction Needs how-to, business topics, news features, trend stories with local examples. Do not query about any topics that do not include several local examples—local companies, organizations, universities, etc. **Buys 110 mss/year.** Query with published clips. Length: 1,000-2,000 words. **Pays $150.**
Tips The *Rochester Business Journal* prefers queries from local published writers who can demonstrate the ability to write for a sophisticated audience of business readers. Story ideas should be about business trends illustrated with numerous examples of local companies participating in the change or movement.

$ $ SMARTCEO MAGAZINE

SmartCEO, 2700 Lighthouse Point E., Suite 220A, Baltimore MD 21224. (410)342-9510. Fax: (410)675-5280. Website: www.smartceo.com. **Contact:** Jeanine Gajewski. **25% freelance written**. Monthly magazine covering regional business in the Baltimore, MD and Washington, DC areas. "*SmartCEO* is a regional 'growing company' publication. We are not news; we are a resource full of smart ideas to help educate and inspire decision-makers in the Baltimore and DC areas. Each issue contains features, interviews, case studies, columns and other departments designed to help this region's CEOs face the daily challenges of running a business." Estab. 2001. Circ. 34,000. Byline given. Pays on publication. No kill fee. Publishes ms an average of 2 months after acceptance. Buys all rights. Editorial lead time 5 months. Submit seasonal material 5 months in advance. Accepts queries by e-mail, phone. Responds in 4 weeks to queries. Responds in 2 months to mss. Sample copy available online. Guidelines by email.

Nonfiction Needs essays, interview, Business features or tips. "We do not want pitches on CEOs or companies outside the Baltimore, MD or Washington, DC areas; no product reviews, lifestyle content or book reviews, please." **Buys 20 mss/year. mss/year.** Query. Length: 2,000-5,000 words. **Pays $300-600.** Sometimes pays expenses of writers on assignment.
Photos Contact: Erica Fromherz, art director. State availability Identification of subjects required. Reviews GIF/JPEG files.
Columns/Departments Project to Watch (overview of a local development project in progress and why it is of interest to the business community), 600 words; Q&A and tip-focused coverage of business issues and challenges (each article includes the opinions of 10-20 CEOs), 500-1,000 words. 0-5 mss/year Query.
Tips "When pitching a local CEO, tell us why his/her accomplishments tell an inspiring story with appicable lessons for other CEOs. *SmartCEO* is not news; we are a resource full of smart ideas to help educate and inspire decision-makers in the Baltimore and DC areas. Send your pitch via e-mail and follow up with a phone call."

$ SOMERSET BUSINESS MAGAZINE

White Eagle Printing Company, 2550 Kuser Rd., Trenton State NJ 08691. (609)586-2056. Fax: (609)586-8052. E-mail: maggih@sombusmag.com. Website: www.scbp.org. **100% freelance written**. Monthly magazine covering national and local business-related, theme-based topics. *Somerset Business Magazine* is a Chamber of Commerce publication, so the slant is pro-business primarily. Also covers nonprofits, education and other related issues. Estab. 1924. Circ. 6,500. Pays on publication. Publishes ms an average of 1 month after acceptance. Makes work-for-hire assignments. Editorial lead time 6 weeks. Submit seasonal material 6 weeks in advance. Accepts queries by e-mail. Accepts simultaneous submissions. Responds in 1 week to queries. Sample copy for #10 SASE. Guidelines by email.

Nonfiction Needs humor. Query with published clips. Length: 1,000-1,800 words. **Pays $150 for assigned articles.** Sometimes pays expenses of writers on assignment.

Photos State availability of or send photos Captions, identification of subjects, model releases required. Offers no additional payment for photos accepted with ms.

Tips Query with cover letter preferred after perusal of editorial calendar.

$ $ VERMONT BUSINESS MAGAZINE

2 Church St., Burlington VT 05401. (802)863-8038. Fax: (802)863-8069. E-mail: mcq@vermontbiz.com. Website: www.vermontbiz.com. **80% freelance written.** Monthly tabloid covering business in Vermont. Circ. 8,000. Byline given. Pays on publication. No kill fee. Publishes ms an average of 1 month after acceptance. Buys one-time rights. Responds in 2 months to queries. Sample copy for sae with 11 × 14 envelope and 7 First-Class stamps.

Nonfiction Buys 200 mss/year. Query with published clips. Length: 800-1,800 words. **Pays $100-200.**

Reprints Send tearsheet and information about when and where the material previously appeared.

Photos Send photos Identification of subjects required. Reviews contact sheets. Offers $10-35/photo

Tips Read daily papers and look for business angles for a follow-up article. We look for issue and trend articles rather than company or businessman profiles. Note: Magazine accepts Vermont-specific material only. The articles must be about Vermont.

NATIONAL

⊘ BUSINESSWEEK

McGraw-Hill, Inc., 1221 Avenue of the Americas, 43rd Floor, New York NY 10020-1001. (212)512-2511. Fax: (212)512-4938. Website: www.businessweek.com. Weekly magazine. Circ. 991,000. No kill fee.

- *BusinessWeek* does not accept freelance submissions.

$ $ SFO MAGAZINE

Stocks, Futures and Options, Wasendorf and Associates, 3812 Cedar Heights Dr., Cedar Falls IA 50613. Fax: (319)266-1695. E-mail: editorial@sfomag.com. Website: www.sfomag.com. **90% freelance written.** Monthly magazine covering trading of stocks, futures, options, exchange traded funds and currency pairs. We focus on issues and strategies for the retail individual trader. Our articles are educational and nonpromotional in angle and tone. We try to offer our readers information they can apply immediately to their trading (expository types of articles). Estab. 2000. Circ. 120,000. Byline given. Pays on publication. Offers 20% kill fee. Publishes ms an average of 2 months after acceptance. Buys all rights. Editorial lead time 2.5 months. Accepts queries by e-mail. Accepts simultaneous submissions. Responds in 4 weeks to queries. Sample copy available online. Guidelines by email.

Nonfiction Needs how-to, trading strategies, interview, Inj-depth on financial regulations, laws, etc. See editorial calendar. Each month, we have a 'spotlight' section that takes a look at an issue that may affect the way that an individual retail trader can access or take advantage of the financial markets. These are determined as the year progresses, but general areas of interest would be financial regulation, financial policy, taxes, etc. We do not run book excerpts or material that has been published elsewhere. **Buys 12 mss/year mss/year.** Query with published clips. Length: 600-2,500 words. **Pays $250 min. for assigned articles.** Sometimes pays expenses of writers on assignment.

Tips We look specifically for articles that bring a new idea to our readers for their trading: a new way of using a financial product or ways of 'reading' the markets. We strive to have our articles highly readable by all levels of traders (novice to advanced) and that include a creative angle to grab the reader's attention.

REGIONAL

$ $ THE BUSINESS JOURNAL

Serving San Jose and Silicon Valley, American City Business Journals, Inc., 96 N. Third St., Suite 100, San Jose CA 95112. (408)295-3800. Fax: (408)295-5028. Website: sanjose.bizjournals.com. **2-5% freelance written.** Weekly tabloid covering a wide cross-section of industries. Our stories are written for business people. Our audience is primarily upper-level management. Estab. 1983. Circ. 13,200. Byline given. Pays on publication. Offers $75 kill fee. Buys all rights. Editorial lead time 1 month. Responds in 2 weeks to queries. Sample copy free. Guidelines free.

Nonfiction News/feature articles specifically assigned. **Buys 300 mss/year.** Query. Length: 700-2,500 words. **Pays $175-400.**

Photos State availability Reviews 5 x 7 prints. Offers $25/photo used.

Tips Just call or e-mail (preferable) and say you are interested. We give almost everyone a chance.

CAREER, COLLEGE & ALUMNI

$ $ AFRICAN-AMERICAN CAREER WORLD

Equal Opportunity Publications, Inc., 445 Broad Hollow Rd., Suite 425, Melville NY 11747. (631)421-9421. Fax: (631)421-1352. E-mail: info@eop.com. Website: www.eop.com. **60% freelance written**. Semiannual magazine focused on African-American students and professionals in all disciplines. Estab. 1969. Byline given. Pays on publication. No kill fee. Publishes ms an average of 3 months after acceptance. Buys first North American serial rights. Editorial lead time 3 months. Accepts queries by mail, e-mail, fax, phone. Accepts simultaneous submissions. Sample copy free. Guidelines free.

Nonfiction Needs how-to, get jobs, interview, personal experience. We do not want articles that are too general. Query. Length: 1,500-2,500 words. **Pays $350 for assigned articles.**

Tips Gear articles to our audience.

$ $ AMERICAN CAREERS

Career Communications, Inc., 6701 W. 64th St., Overland Park KS 66202. (800)669-7795. Fax: (913)362-7788. Website: www.carcom.com. **10% freelance written**. Student publication covering careers, career statistics, skills needed to get jobs. *American Careers* provides career, salary, and education information to middle school and high school students. Self-tests help them relate their interests and abilities to future careers. Estab. 1989. Circ. 500,000. Byline given. Pays 1 month after acceptance. No kill fee. Buys all rights. Makes work-for-hire assignments. Accepts queries by mail. Accepts simultaneous submissions. Sample copy for $4. Guidelines for #10 SASE.

Nonfiction Career and education features related to career paths, including arts and communication, business, law, government, finance, construction, technology, health services, human services, manufacturing, engineering, and natural resources and agriculture. No preachy advice to teens or articles that talk down to students. **Buys 5 mss/year.** Query by mail only with published clips Length: 300-1,000 words. **Pays $100-450.**

Photos State availability Captions, identification of subjects, model releases required. Negotiates payment individually. Buys all rights.

Tips Letters of introduction or query letters with samples and resumes are ways we get to know writers. Samples should include how-to articles and career-related articles. Articles written for teenagers also would make good samples. Short feature articles on careers, career-related how-to articles, and self-assessment tools (10-20 point quizzes with scoring information) are primarily what we publish.

$ $ THE BLACK COLLEGIAN

The Career & Self Development Magazine for African-American Students, IMDiversity, Inc., 140 Carondelet St., New Orleans LA 70130. (504)523-0154. Website: www.black-collegian.com. **25% freelance written**. Semiannual magazine for African-American college students and recent graduates with an interest in career and job information, African-American cultural awareness, personalities, history, trends, and current events. Estab. 1970. Circ. 122,000. Byline given. Pays 1 month after publication. Buys one-time rights. Submit seasonal material 2 months in advance. Accepts queries by mail. Responds in 6 months to queries. Sample copy for $5 (includes postage) and 9 x 12 SAE. Guidelines for #10 SASE.

Nonfiction Material on careers, sports, black history, news analysis. Articles on problems and opportunities confronting African-American college students and recent graduates. Needs book excerpts, expose, general interest, historical, how-to, develop employability, inspirational, interview, opinion, personal experience. Query. Length: 900-1,900 words. **Pays $100-500 for assigned articles.**

Photos State availability of or send photos Captions, identification of subjects, model releases required. Reviews 8x10 prints.

Tips Articles are published under primarily 5 broad categories: job hunting information, overviews of career opportunities and industry reports, self-development information, analyses and investigations of conditions and problems that affect African-Americans, and celebrations of African-American success.

BROWN ALUMNI MAGAZINE

Brown University, P.O. Box 1854, 71 George St., Providence RI 02912. (401)863-2873. Fax: (401)863-9599. E-mail: alumni_magazine@brown.edu. Website: www.brownalumnimagazine.com. Bimonthly magazine covering the world of Brown University and its alumni. We are an editorially independent, general interest magazine covering the on-campus world of Brown University and the off-campus world of its alumni. Estab. 1900. Circ. 80,000. Byline given. Pays on acceptance. Publishes ms an average of 3 months after acceptance. Buys North American serial and Web rights. Editorial lead time 3 months. Submit seasonal material 4 months in advance. Accepts queries by mail, e-mail, fax. Responds in several weeks to queries. Sample copy free. Guidelines available online.

Nonfiction Needs book excerpts, essays, expose, general interest, historical, humor, interview, opinion, personal experience, photo feature, travel, profiles. No articles unconnected to Brown or its alumni **Buys 50 mss/year.**

Query with published clips. Length: 150-4,000 words.
Photos State availability Captions, identification of subjects required. Reviews contact sheets, transparencies, prints. Negotiates payment individually Buys one time rights.
Columns/Departments P.O.V. (essays by Brown alumni), 750 words. Send complete ms.
Tips Be imaginative and be specific. A Brown connection is required for all stories in the magazine, but a Brown connection alone does not guarantee our interest. Ask yourself: Why should readers care about your proposed story? Also, we look for depth and objective reporting, not boosterism.

$ $ CIRCLE K MAGAZINE

Kiwanis, 3636 Woodview Trace, Indianapolis IN 46268-3196. Fax: (317)879-0204. E-mail: ckimagazine@kiwanis.org. Website: www.circlek.org. Kasey Jackson. **30% freelance written**. Magazine published once a year. "Our readership consists almost entirely of above-average college students interested in voluntary community service and leadership development. They are politically and socially aware and have a wide range of interests." Circ. 12,000. Byline given. Pays on acceptance. Buys first North American serial rights. Accepts queries by mail, e-mail, fax. Responds in 4 weeks to queries. Sample copy for large SAE with 3 first-class stamps or on website. Guidelines available online.
Nonfiction Articles published in *CKI* are of 2 types—serious and light nonfiction. We are interested in general interest articles on topics concerning college students and their lifestyles, as well as articles dealing with careers, community concerns, and leadership development. No first-person confessions, family histories, or travel pieces. Query. Length: 300-1,500 words. **Pays $100-400.**
Photos Captions required. Purchased with accompanying ms; total price includes both photos and ms.
Tips Query should indicate author's familiarity with the field and sources. Subject treatment must be objective and in-depth, and articles should include illustrative examples and quotes from persons involved in the subject or qualified to speak on it. We are open to working with new writers who present a good article idea and demonstrate that they've done their homework concerning the article subject itself, as well as concerning our magazine's style. We're interested in college-oriented trends, for example: entrepreneur schooling, high-tech classrooms, music, leisure, and health issues.

$ $ CONCORDIA UNIVERSITY MAGAZINE

Advancement and Alumni Relations, Concordia University Magazine, Concordia University, 1455 De Maisonneuve Blvd. W., Montreal QC H3G 1M8 Canada. (514)848-2424, ext. 3826. Fax: (514)848-4510. E-mail: howard.bokser@concordia.ca. Website: magazine.concordia.ca. **60% freelance written**. Quarterly magazine covering matters relating to Concordia University and its alumni. We only cover topics related to research and teaching at Concordia, and student or administrator news, and we profile university alumni. Estab. 1977. Circ. 85,000. Byline given. Pays on acceptance. Offers 50% kill fee. Publishes ms an average of 1 month after acceptance. Buys first rights. Editorial lead time 2 months. Submit seasonal material 2 months in advance. Accepts queries by mail, e-mail. Accepts previously published material. Accepts simultaneous submissions. Responds in 1 month to queries. Responds in 1 month to mss. Sample copy available online. Guidelines free.
Nonfiction Needs book excerpts, general interest, historical, humor, interview, opinion, personal experience, photo feature. **Buys 10 mss/year.** Query with published clips. Length: 1,500-2,000 words. **Pays $350-450.** Sometimes pays expenses of writers on assignment.
Photos State availability Identification of subjects required. Reviews contact sheets, 2x2 transparencies, 4x6 prints, GIF/JPEG files. Negotiates payment individually. Buys one time rights.
Columns/Departments End Piece (opinion or essay), 650 words. 4 Query with published clips. **Pays $275**

$ $ THE EDUCATION HIGHWAY

Diversity Publishing Company, P.O. Box 70158, Nashville TN 37207. (615)299-0075. Fax: (615)299-8090. E-mail: editor@eduhwy.com. Website: www.hbcu247.com. **100% freelance written**. Quarterly website magazine covering historically Black colleges & university life. Estab. 1997. Circ. 500,000. Byline given. within 14 days of publication. No kill fee. Publishes ms an average of 1 month after acceptance. Buys all rights. Editorial lead time 1 month. Accepts queries by e-mail. Accepts simultaneous submissions. Sample copy free. Guidelines available.
Nonfiction Needs essays, expose, general interest, how-to, humor, inspirational, interview, opinion, (does not mean letters to the editor), technical. Black College Sports issue is every Sept. **Buys 24 mss/yr. mss/year.** Query. Length: 450-800 words. **Pays $200 max. for assigned articles. Pays $200 max. for unsolicited articles.** Sometimes pays expenses of writers on assignment.
Tips Contact editor through email.

$ $ EQUAL OPPORTUNITY

The Nation's Only Multi-Ethnic Recruitment Magazine for African-American, Hispanic, Native-American & Asian-American College Grads, Equal Opportunity Publications, Inc., 445 Broad Hollow Rd., Suite 425, Melville NY 11747. (631)421-9421. Fax: (631)421-0359. E-mail: jschneider@eop.com. Website: www.eop.com. **70% freelance written. Prefers to work with published/established writers.** Triannual magazine dedicated to advancing the professional interests of African Americans, Hispanics, Asian Americans, and Native Americans. Our audience is 90% college juniors and seniors; 10% working graduates. An understanding of educational and career problems of minorities is essential. Estab. 1967. Circ. 11,000. Byline given. Pays on publication. Publishes ms an average of 6 months after acceptance. Buys first rights. Editorial lead time 6 months. Submit seasonal material 6 months in advance. Accepts queries by mail, e-mail, fax, phone. Accepts previously published material. Responds in 2 weeks to queries. Responds in 1 month to mss. Sample copy and writer's guidelines for 9x12 SAE with 5 first-class stamps.

- Distributed through college guidance and placement offices.

Nonfiction Needs general interest, specific minority concerns, how-to, job hunting skills, personal finance, better living, coping with discrimination, interview, minority role models, opinion, problems of minorities, personal experience, professional and student study experiences, technical, on career fields offering opportunities for minorites, coverage of minority interests. **Buys 10 mss/year.** Send complete ms. Length: 1,000-2,000 words. **Pays 10¢/word.** Sometimes pays expenses of writers on assignment.
Reprints Send information about when and where the material previously appeared. Pays 10¢/word.
Photos Captions, identification of subjects required. Reviews 35mm color slides and b&w. Buys all rights.
Tips Articles must be geared toward questions and answers faced by minority and women students. We would like to see role-model profiles of professions.

$ $ $ $ HARVARD MAGAZINE

7 Ware St., Cambridge MA 02138-4037. (617)495-5746. Fax: (617)495-0324. Website: www.harvardmagazine.com. **35-50% freelance written**. Bimonthly magazine for Harvard University faculty, alumni, and students. Estab. 1898. Circ. 245,000. Byline given. Pays on publication. No kill fee. Publishes ms an average of 4 months after acceptance. Buys one-time print and website rights. Editorial lead time 1 year. Accepts queries by mail, fax. Responds in 1 month to queries. Responds in 1 month to mss. Sample copy available online.
Nonfiction Needs book excerpts, essays, interview, journalism on Harvard-related intellectual subjects. **Buys 20-30 mss/year.** Query with published clips. Length: 800-10,000 words. **Pays $400-3,000.** Pays expenses of writers on assignment.

$ $ HISPANIC CAREER WORLD

Equal Opportunity Publications, Inc., 445 Broad Hollow Rd., Suite 425, Melville NY 11747. (631)421-9421. Fax: (631)421-1352. E-mail: info@eop.com. Website: www.eop.com. **60% freelance written**. Semiannual magazine aimed at Hispanic students and professionals in all disciplines. Estab. 1969. Byline given. Pays on publication. No kill fee. Publishes ms an average of 3 months after acceptance. Buys first North American serial rights. Editorial lead time 3 months. Accepts queries by mail, e-mail, fax, phone. Accepts simultaneous submissions. Responds in 2 weeks to queries. Responds in 2 months to mss. Sample copy free. Guidelines free.
Nonfiction Needs how-to, find jobs, interview, personal experience. Query. Length: 1,500-2,500 words. **Pays $350 for assigned articles.**
Tips Gear articles to our audience.

$ N NEXT STEP MAGAZINE

Next Step Publishing, Inc., 86 W. Main St., Victor NY 14564. (585)742-1260. Fax: (585)742-1263. E-mail: editor@nextstepmag.com. Website: www.nextstepmag.com. **75% freelance written**. Bimonthly magazine covering LINK Newsletter, Transfer Guide. "Our magazine is a 5-times-a-school-year objective publication for high school juniors & seniors preparing for college. Articles cover college, careers, life & financial aid." Estab. 1995. Circ. distributed in 20,500+ high schools. No kill fee. Publishes ms an average of 6 months after acceptance. Buys all rights. Editorial lead time 6 months. Submit seasonal material 6 months in advance. Accepts queries by e-mail. Sample copy available online. Guidelines by email.
Nonfiction Needs book excerpts, general interest, how-to, interview, personal experience, travel. *Link* is a newsletter published 5 times a year for high school counselors. Articles run 800-1,500 words & should be focused on helping counselors do their jobs better. Past articles have included counseling students with AD/HD, sports scholarships & motivation tactics. **Buys 15 mss/yr. mss/year.** Query. Length: 500-1,000 words. **Pays $75 for assigned articles.**
Columns/Departments Contact: Laura Jeanne Hammond. College Planning (college types, making a decision, admissions); Financial Air (scholarships, financial aid options); SAT/ACT (preparing for the SAT/ACT, study tips), 400-1,000 words; Career Profiles (profile at least 3 professionals in different aspects of a specific industry), 800-1,000 words; Military (careers in the military, different branches, how to join), 400-600 words. 5-10 mss/yr. Query with or without published clips. **Pay varies, averages $75 per article.**
Tips "The best queries are specific, concise & entertaining. Readers should be referred to as 'you', and interviews with expert sources, college faculty, workers in the field or students are required in articles."

$ $ $ $ NOTRE DAME MAGAZINE

University of Notre Dame, 538 Grace Hall, Notre Dame IN 46556-5612. (574)631-5335. Fax: (574)631-6767. E-mail: ndmag@nd.edu. Website: www.nd.edu/~ndmag. **50% freelance written**. Quarterly magazine covering

news of Notre Dame and education and issues affecting contemporary society. "We are a university magazine with a scope as broad as that found at a university, but we place our discussion in a moral, ethical, and spiritual context reflecting our Catholic heritage." Estab. 1972. Circ. 150,000. Byline given. Pays on acceptance. No kill fee. Publishes ms an average of 1 year after acceptance. Buys first rights, buys electronic rights. Accepts queries by mail, e-mail, fax. Responds in 2 months to queries. Sample copy online Guidelines available online.
Nonfiction Needs opinion, personal experience, religious. **Buys 35 mss/year.** Query with published clips. Length: 600-3,000 words. **Pays $250-3,000.** Sometimes pays expenses of writers on assignment.
Photos State availability Identification of subjects, model releases required. Buys one-time and electronic rights.
Columns/Departments CrossCurrents (essays, deal with a wide array of issues—some topical, some personal, some serious, some light). Query with or without published clips or send complete ms.
Tips "The editors are always looking for new writers and fresh ideas. However, the caliber of the magazine and frequency of its publication dictate that the writing meet very high standards. The editors value articles strong in storytelling quality, journalistic technique, and substance. They do not encourage promotional or nostalgia pieces, stories on sports, or essays that are sentimentally religious."

$ $ OREGON QUARTERLY

The Northwest Perspective from the University of Oregon, 130 Chapman Hall, 5228 University of Oregon, Eugene OR 97403-5228. (541)346-5048. Fax: (541)346-5571. E-mail: quarterly@uoregon.edu. Website: www.uoregon.edu/~oq. **50% freelance written**. Quarterly magazine covering people and ideas at the University of Oregon and the Northwest. Estab. 1919. Circ. 100,000. Byline given. Pays on acceptance. Offers 20% kill fee. Publishes ms an average of 3 months after acceptance. Buys first North American serial rights and limited online archiving rights. Accepts queries by mail (preferred), e-mail (very rarely). Accepts previously published material. Responds in 2 months to queries Sample copy for 9 x 12 SAE with 4 first-class stamps Guidelines available online
Nonfiction "Northwest issues and culture from the perspective of UO alumni and faculty." **Buys 30 mss/year.** Query with published clips. Length: 500-3,000 words. **Payment varies—30¢/per cord for departments; features more.** Sometimes pays expenses of writers on assignment.
Reprints Send photocopy and information about when and where the material previously appeared. Pays 50% of amount paid for an original article
Photos State availability Identification of subjects required. Reviews 8x10 prints. Offers $10-25/photo Buys one time rights.
Fiction Publishes novel excerpts by UO professors or grads.
Tips "Query with strong, colorful writing on clear display; clips."

$ $ QUEEN'S ALUMNI REVIEW

Queen's University, 99 University Ave., Kingston ON K7L 3N6 Canada. Fax: (613)533-2060. E-mail: cuthberk@post.queensu.ca. Website: alumnireview.queensu.ca. **25% freelance written**. Quarterly magazine. Estab. 1927. Circ. 106,000. Byline given. Pays on publication. Publishes ms an average of 3 months after acceptance. Buys electronic rights, buys first world serial rights. Editorial lead time 3 months. Submit seasonal material 9 months in advance. Accepts queries by mail, e-mail. Responds in 2 weeks to queries. Responds in 2 weeks to mss. Sample copy and writer's guidelines online.
Nonfiction "We publish feature articles, columns, and articles about alumni, faculty, and staff who are doing unusual or worthwhile things." "Does not want religious or political rants, travel articles, how-to, or general interest pieces that do not refer to or make some reference to our core audience." **Buys 10 mss/year.** Send complete ms. Length: 200-2,500 words. **Pays 50¢/word (Canadian) plus 10% e-rights fee for assigned articles.** Sometimes pays expenses of writers on assignment.
Photos Send photos Identification of subjects required. Reviews transparencies, prints, GIF/JPEG files. Offers $25 minimum or negotiates payment individually.
Columns/Departments Potential freelancers should study our magazine before submitting a query for a column. 10 Query with published clips or send complete ms. **Pays 50¢/word (Canadian)**
Tips "We buy freelance material, but our budget is limited, and so we choose carefully. All articles should have a Queen's angle—one that shows how Queen's alumni, faculty, staff, or friends of the university are involved and engaged in the world. We also look for topical articles that start Queen's specific and go on from there to look at issues of a wide topical interest. The writing should be professional, snappy, informative, and engaging. We always have far more editorial material in hand than we can ever publish. Study our magazine before you submit a query. Our circulation is primarily in Canada, but we also have readers in the US, UK, Hong Kong, Australia, and in more than 100 countries. Our readers are young and old, male and female, well educated, well-travelled, and sophisticated. We look for material that will appeal to a broad constituency."

$ $ RIPON COLLEGE MAGAZINE

P.O. Box 248, 300 Seward St., Ripon WI 54971-0248. (920)748-8322. Fax: (920)748-9262. Website: www.ripon.

edu. **15% freelance written**. Quarterly magazine that contains information relating to Ripon College and is mailed to alumni and friends of the college. Estab. 1851. Circ. 14,000. Byline given. Pays on publication. Publishes ms an average of 3 months after acceptance. Makes work-for-hire assignments. Accepts queries by mail, e-mail, fax, phone. Responds in 2 weeks to queries.

Nonfiction Needs historical, interview. **Buys 4 mss/year.** Send complete ms. Length: 250-1,000 words. **Pays $25-350.**

Photos State availability Captions, model releases required. Reviews contact sheets. Offers additional payment for photos accepted with ms. Buys one time rights.

Tips Story ideas must have a direct connection to Ripon College.

SCHOLASTIC ADMINISTR@TOR MAGAZINE

Scholastic, Inc., 557 Broadway, 5th Floor, New York NY 10012. (212)965-7429. Fax: (212)965-7497. E-mail: lrenwick@scholastic.com. Website: www.scholastic.com/administrator. Magazine published 8 times/year. Focuses on helping today's school administrators and education technology leaders in their efforts to improve the management of schools. Circ. 100,000. No kill fee. Editorial lead time 1 month. Sample copy free.

TRANSFORMATIONS

A Journal of People and Change, Worcester Polytechnic Institute, 100 Institute Rd., Worcester MA 01609-2280. Website: www.wpi.edu/+transformations. **60% freelance written**. Quarterly alumni magazine covering "science and engineering/education/business personalities and related technologies and issues for 34,000 alumni, primarily engineers, scientists, entrepreneurs, managers, media.". Estab. 1897. Circ. 40,000. Byline given. Pays on publication. Publishes ms an average of 6 months after acceptance. Buys one-time rights. Accepts queries by mail, e-mail. Accepts previously published material. Accepts simultaneous submissions. Responds in 1 month to queries. Sample copy available online.

Nonfiction Needs interview, alumni in engineering, science, etc., photo feature, features on people and programs at WPI. Query with published clips. Length: 300-2,000 words. **Pays negotiable rate.** Sometimes pays expenses of writers on assignment.

Photos State availability Captions required. Reviews contact sheets. Pays negotiable rate.

Tips "Submit outline of story, story idea, or published work. Features are most open to freelancers with excellent narrative skills, and an ability to understand and convey complex technologies in an engaging way. Keep in mind that this is an alumni magazine, so most articles focus on the college and its graduates."

$ $ WORKFORCE DIVERSITY FOR ENGINEERING & IT PROFESSIONALS

Equal Opportunity Publications, Inc., 445 Broad Hollow Rd., Suite 425, Melville NY 11747. (631)421-9421. Fax: (631)421-1352. E-mail: info@eop.com. Website: www.eop.com. **60% freelance written**. Quarterly magazine addressing workplace issues affecting technical professional women, members of minority groups, and people with disabilities. Estab. 1969. Byline given. Pays on publication. No kill fee. Publishes ms an average of 3 months after acceptance. Buys first North American serial rights. Editorial lead time 3 months. Accepts queries by mail, e-mail, fax, phone. Accepts simultaneous submissions. Responds in 2 weeks to queries. Responds in 2 months to mss. Sample copy free. Guidelines free.

Nonfiction Needs how-to, find jobs, interview, personal experience. We do not want articles that are too general. Query. Length: 1,500-2,500 words. **Pays $350 for assigned articles.**

Tips Gear articles to our audience.

CHILD CARE & PARENTAL GUIDANCE

$ BAY STATE PARENT MAGAZINE

Holden Landmark, 124 Fay Rd., Framingham MA 01702. (508)405-2454. E-mail: editor@baystateparent.com or spetroni@rcn.com. Website: www.baystateparent.com. **80% freelance written**. Monthly magazine covering parenting. Massachusetts based parenting magazine with a focus on raising a family from birth through middle school. Estab. 1996. Circ. 38,500. Byline given. Pays on publication. Offers 10% kill fee. Publishes ms an average of 2-6 months after acceptance. Buys one-time rights, buys second serial (reprint) rights, buys electronic rights, buys MA exclusive for parenting rights. Editorial lead time 3-4 months. Submit seasonal material 2-6 months in advance. Accepts queries by e-mail. Accepts previously published material. Accepts simultaneous submissions. Responds in 1-4 weeks to queries. Responds in 1 month to mss. Sample copy available online. Guidelines by email.

Nonfiction Needs book excerpts, expose, general interest, how-to, inspirational, interview, new product, photo feature, travel. Arts Guide (annually in Sept.), Adoption issue (Nov.), Think Pink Guide (Oct.), Toy Guide (Dec.), Health & Fitness Guide (Jan.), Finance Guide (Feb.), Mother's Day Guide-May issue, Summer Travel Guide, Winter Travel Guide-Dec. issue, Baby Guide and Pregnancy Guide-Spring issue, Back-to-School Guide (Aug.), all annually. We do not want humor or first-person essays, & non-locally sourced articles outside of MA.

Buys 50-75 mss/yr. mss/year. Query with 2 published and 1 unpublished clip plus resume. Length: 500-1,500 words. **Pays $50-100 for assigned articles. Pays $30-75 for unsolicited articles.** Sometimes pays expenses of writers on assignment.
Photos State availability Captions, identification of subjects, model releases required. Reviews JPEG files (200 dpi min.). Negotiates payment individually. Buys one time rights.
Columns/Departments Adoption Insights (Adoption/Families), Working Mom, Special Needs Parenting, 750-1200 words; Mom's Play Date, 750-1000 words; Family Health, 500-1000 words; Sporting Around (Focus on children & sports), 600-1000 words; Features/news articles (Parenting related), 500-1500 words. 50-100 mss/yr. Query with 1 published & 1 unpublished clip plus resume. **Pays $$60-$100.**
Tips We are VERY VERY local. Interview LOCAL sources from MA.

$ $ CHILDREN'S ADVOCATE

DEFENSOR de los NIÑOS, Action Alliance for Children, 1201 Martin Luther King Jr. Way, Oakland CA 94612. E-mail: aacjean@4children.org. Website: www.4children.org. **60% freelance written**. Bimonthly about issues affecting young children and their families in California. Our readers are low and moderate income parents, child care providers, other children's services providers, and the people who work with those audiences (such as community college teachers) in California. Our articles are brief, engaging, and accessible to people without much education and are published in English, spanish, and Chinese. Our values are equity (ethnic, economic, gender, etc.), the need for greater societal attention and resources to meet the needs of children and families, support and respect for parents and others who care for children, respect for children as active learners, participants, nonviolence, and care for the environment. We have a California focus—we quote parents, child care providers, and 'experts' based in California. Our articles are designed to help people take action for change—in their relationships with children, in their communities, and in public policy advocacy. Estab. 1973. Circ. 22,000. Byline given. Pays on acceptance. Offers 20% kill fee. Publishes ms an average of 1 days after acceptance. Buys first North American serial rights, buys electronic rights. Editorial lead time 2 months. Sample copy free.
Nonfiction Needs general interest, how-to, reports on issues relating to our topics (early care and education, health, education, family support, environmental protection, violence prevention, parenting). none currently planned. We do not print articles on the basis of queries from freelancers. We plan the issues, then contact freelancers we work with to see if they are interested in writing one of the articles we have planned. However, we are interested in hearing from freelancers who feel they may be a good fit with our publication. Check us out at www.4children.org. Must be willing to interview only California sources. If you are interested, please send resume, cover letter, and writing sample. **Buys 30/year mss/year.** Length: 1,525-1,050 words. **Pays $225-450 for assigned articles.** Pays phone bill only.
Photos Contact: Jean Tepperman, editor or Jessine Foss, assistant editor. State availability Reviews prints, GIF/ JPEG.

$ $ N FAMILY

Union County, Morris County, Essex County, Essex County, Central Jersey, Kids Monthly Publications, 1122 Route 22 W., Mountainside NJ 07092. (908)232-2913, ext. 103. Fax: (908)317-9518. E-mail: editor@njfamily.com. Website: www.njfamily.com. **75% freelance written**. Monthly magazine covering parenting and family. Estab. 1991. Circ. 126,000. Byline given. Pays on publication. No kill fee. Publishes ms an average of 2 months after acceptance. Buys first North American serial rights. Editorial lead time 3-6 months. Submit seasonal material 4 months in advance. Accepts queries by e-mail. Accepts previously published material. Accepts simultaneous submissions. Sample copy available online.

- "Our mission is to help New Jersey parents be the best parents they can be. Articles should focus on the facts and what you can do for your child to prevent/promote/help/teach, etc. in any given situation."

Nonfiction Needs book excerpts, new product, personal experience. Raising teens. We do not want self-promotion articles. **Buys 60 mss/year. mss/year.** Send complete ms. Length: 450-1,200 words. **Pays $50-200 for assigned articles. Pays $50-200 for unsolicited articles.** Sometimes pays expenses of writers on assignment.
Columns/Departments Contact: Farn Dupre. School solutions (elementary education in New Jersey), 350-400 words. 12 mss/year. Query with published clips. **Pays $$35-$100.**
Fillers Contact: Lucy Banta, Farn Dupre. Needs facts. 4/year Length: 150-400 words. **Pays $10-$25.**
Tips "Know our audience—parents in New Jersey."

$ HUDSON VALLEY PARENT

The Professional Image, 174 South St., Newburgh NY 12550. E-mail: editor@excitingread.com. Website: www.hvparent.com. **95% freelance written**. Monthly magazine covering parents and families. Estab. 1994. Circ. 80,000. Byline given. Pays on publication. No kill fee. Publishes ms an average of 3 months after acceptance. Buys one-time rights. Editorial lead time 4 months. Submit seasonal material 4 months in advance. Accepts queries by e-mail. Responds in 2-4 weeks to mss. Sample copy free. Guidelines available online.
Nonfiction Needs expose, general interest, humor, interview, personal experience. **Buys 20 mss/yr. mss/year.**

Query. Length: 700-1,200 words. **Pays $70-120 for assigned articles. Pays $25-35 for unsolicited articles.**
Reprints $25-35

$ N ✪ ISLAND PARENT MAGAZINE

The Resource Publication for Vancouver Island Parents, Island Parent Group, 830 Pembroke St., Suite A-10, Victoria BC V8T 1H9 Canada. (250)388-6905. Fax: (250)388-6920. E-mail: editor@islandparent.ca. Website: www.islandparent.ca. **98% freelance written**. Monthly magazine covering parenting. Estab. 1988. Circ. 20,000. Byline given. honorium. No kill fee. Publishes ms an average of 3 months after acceptance. Buys one-time rights, buys electronic rights. Editorial lead time 3 months. Submit seasonal material 3 months in advance. Accepts queries by e-mail. Responds in 4-6 weeks to queries. Sample copy available online. Guidelines available online.

- "Our editorial philosophy is based on the belief that parents need encouragement and useful information. We encourage writers to cover topics of interest to them or that reflect their own experience—we're looking for a variety of perspectives, experiences and beliefs. Our aim is to help readers feel valued, supported and respected. Ideally, we can raise the profile of parenting and help families enjoy each other."

Nonfiction Contact: Sue Fast. Needs book excerpts, essays, general interest, how-to, humor, inspirational, interview, opinion, (does not mean letters to the editor), personal experience, travel. **Buys 80 mss/year. mss/year.** Query. Length: 400-1,800 words. **Pays $35 for assigned articles. Pays $35 for unsolicited articles.**
Photos Send photos Reviews GIF/JPEG files. Offers no additional payment for photos accepted with ms. Buys one time rights.
Fillers Needs anecdotes, facts, gags, newsbreaks, short humor. 10/year Length: 400-650 words. **Pays $$35.**

$ ATLANTA PARENT/ATLANTA BABY

2346 Perimeter Park Dr., Suite 100, Atlanta GA 30341. (770)454-7599. Website: www.atlantaparent.com. **50% freelance written**. Byline given. Pays on publication. Publishes ms an average of 3 months after acceptance. Buys one-time rights. Submit seasonal material 6 months in advance. Accepts queries by mail, e-mail. Accepts previously published material. Responds in 4 months to queries. Sample copy for $3.
Nonfiction Needs general interest, how-to, humor, interview, travel. Private School (January); Camp (February); Birthday Parties (March and September); Maternity and Mothering (May and October); Childcare (July); Back-to-School (August); Teens (September); Holidays (November/December) No religious or philosophical discussions. **Buys 60 mss/year.** Send complete ms. Length: 800-1,500 words. **Pays $5-50.** Sometimes pays expenses of writers on assignment.
Reprints Send tearsheet or photocopy with rights for sale noted and information about when and where the material previously appeared. **Pays $30-50**
Photos State availability of or send photos Reviews 3x5 photos . Offers $10/photo. Buys one time rights.
Tips Articles should be geared to problems or situations of families and parents. Should include down-to-earth tips and be clearly written. No philosophical discussions. We're also looking for well-written humor.

$ $ $ $ BABY TALK

Time, Inc., 530 Fifth Ave., 4th Floor, New York NY 10036. (212)522-4327. Fax: (212)522-8699. E-mail: letters@babytalk.com. Website: www.babytalk.com. Magazine published 10 times/year. *Baby Talk* is written primarily for women who are considering pregnancy or who are expecting a child, and parents of children from birth through 18 months, with the emphasis on pregnancy through first 6 months of life. Estab. 1935. Circ. 2,000,000. Byline given. Accepts queries by mail. Responds in 2 months to queries.
Nonfiction Features cover pregnancy, the basics of baby care, infant/toddler health, growth and development, juvenile equipment and toys, work and day care, marriage and sex—approached from a how-to, service perspective. The message—Here's what you need to know and why—is delivered with smart, crisp style. The tone is confident and reassuring (and, when appropriate, humorous and playful), with the backing of experts. In essence, *Baby Talk* is a training manual of parents facing the day-to-day dilemmas of new parenthood. No phone calls. Query with SASE Length: 1,000-2,000 words. **Pays $500-2,000 depending on length, degree of difficulty, and the writer's experience.**
Columns/Departments Several departments are written by regular contributors. 100-1,250 words. Query with SASE **Pays $100-1,000.**
Tips Please familiarize yourself with the magazine before submitting a query. Take the time to focus your story idea; scattershot queries are a waste of everyone's time. WE do not accept poetry.

BIG APPLE PARENT/QUEENS PARENT/WESTCHESTER PARENT/BROOKLYN PARENT/ROCKLAND PARENT

Davler Media Group, 1040 Avenue of the Americas, New York NY 10018. (212)315-0800. E-mail: hellonwheels@parentsknow.com. Website: www.parentsknow.com. **20% freelance written**. Monthly tabloid covering New York City family life. *BAP* readers live in high-rise Manhattan apartments; it is an educated, upscale audience. Often both parents are working full time in professional occupations. Child-care help tends to be one on one, in the home. Kids attend private schools for the most part. While not quite a suburban approach, some of our

QP and *BK* readers do have backyards (though most live in high-rise apartments). It is a more middle-class audience in Queens and Brooklyn. More kids are in day care centers; majority of kids are in public schools. Our Westchester county edition is for suburban parents. Estab. 1985. Circ. 80,000, *Big Apple*; 70,000, *Queens Parent*; 70,000, *Westchester Parent*; 45,000, *Brooklyn Parent*. Byline given. No longer pays for freelance articles. Offers 50% kill fee. Buys first New York area rights. Submit seasonal material 3 months in advance. Accepts queries by mail, e-mail, fax. Accepts simultaneous submissions. Responds immediately. Sample copy free. Guidelines available online.

Nonfiction Needs book excerpts, expose, general interest, how-to, inspirational, interview, opinion, personal experience, family health, education. We're always looking for news and coverage of controversial issues. Send complete ms. Length: 600-1,000 words.

Reprints Send tearsheet or typed ms with rights for sale noted and information about when and where the material previously appeared.

Columns/Departments Dads; Education; Family Finance. Send complete ms.

Tips We have a very local focus; our aim is to present articles our readers cannot find in national publications. To that end, news stories and human interest pieces must focus on New York and New Yorkers. We are always looking for news and newsy pieces; we keep on top of current events, frequently giving issues that may relate to parenting a local focus so that the idea will work for us as well. We are not currently looking for essays, humor, general child raising, or travel.

$ $ BIRMINGHAM PARENT

Evans Publishing LLC, 115-C Hilltop Business Dr., Pelham AL 35124. (205)739-0090. Fax: (205)739-0073. E-mail: editor@birminghamparent.com. Website: www.birminghamparent.com. **75% freelance written**. Monthly magazine covering family issues, parenting, education, babies to teens, health care, anything involving parents raising children. We are a free, local parenting publication in central Alabama. All of our stories carry some type of local slant. Parenting magazines abound: we are the source for the local market. Estab. 2004. Circ. 40,000. Byline given. Pays within 30 days of publication. Offers 20% kill fee. Publishes ms an average of 3-4 months after acceptance. Buys first North American serial rights, buys second serial (reprint) rights, buys electronic rights. Editorial lead time 3-4 months. Submit seasonal material 4 months in advance. Accepts queries by e-mail. Accepts previously published material. Accepts simultaneous submissions. Responds in 2-3 weeks to queries. Responds in 2-3 months to mss. Sample copy for $3. Guidelines available online.

Nonfiction Needs book excerpts, general interest, how-to, interview, parenting. Does not want first person pieces. Our pieces educate and inform: we don't take stories without sources. **Buys 24 mss/year.** Send complete ms. Length: 350-2,500 words. **Pays $50-350 for assigned articles. Pays $35-200 for unsolicited articles.**

Photos State availability Captions, identification of subjects, model releases required. Reviews GIF/JPEG files. Negotiates payment individually; offers no additional payment for photos accepted with ms. Buys one time rights.

Columns/Departments Parenting Solo (single parenting), 650 words; Baby & Me (dealing with newborns or pregnancy), 650 words; Teens (raising teenagers), 650-1,500 words. 36 Query with published clips or send complete ms. **Pays $35-200.**

Tips We have a local slant. Figure out a way you can present your story so that you can add local slant to it, or suggest to us how to do so. Please no first person opinion pieces—no '10 great gifts for teachers,' for example, without sources. We expect some sources for our informative stories.

$ CHESAPEAKE FAMILY

Jefferson Communications, 929 West St., Suite 307, Annapolis MD 21401. (410)263-1641. Fax: (410)280-0255. E-mail: editor@chesapeakefamily.com. Website: www.chesapeakefamily.com. **80% freelance written**. Monthly magazine covering parenting. *Chesapeake Family* is a free, regional parenting publication serving readers in the Anne Arundel, Calvert, Prince George's, and Queen Anne's counties of Maryland. Our goal is to identify tips, resources, and products that will make our readers' lives easier. We answer the questions they don't have time to ask, doing the research for them so they have the information they need to make better decisions for their families' health, education, and well-being. Articles must have local angle and resources. Estab. 1990. Circ. 40,000. Byline given. Publishes ms an average of 2 months after acceptance. Buys first rights, buys one-time rights, buys second serial (reprint) rights, buys electronic rights. Makes work-for-hire assignments. Editorial lead time 3-6 months. Submit seasonal material 4 months in advance. Accepts queries by mail, e-mail, fax. Accepts previously published material. Accepts simultaneous submissions. Guidelines available online.

Nonfiction Needs how-to, parenting topics: sign your kids up for sports, find out if your child needs braces, etc., interview, local personalities, travel, family-fun destinations. No general, personal essays (however, personal anecdotes leading into a story with general applicability is fine). **Buys 25 mss/year.** Send complete ms. Length: 800-1,200 words. **Pays $75-125. Pays $35-50 for unsolicited articles.**

Photos State availability Model releases required. Reviews prints, GIF/JPEG files. Offers no additional payment for photos accepted with ms, unless original, assigned photo is selected for the cover.

Columns/Departments 25 **Pays $35-50.**

Tips A writer's best chance is to know the issues specific to our local readers. Know how to research the issues well, answer the questions our readers need to know, and give them information they can act on—and present it in a friendly, conversational tone.

$ $ CHICAGO PARENT

141 S. Oak Park Ave., Oak Park IL 60302. (708)386-5555. Fax: (708)524-8360. E-mail: chiparent@chicagoparent.com. Website: www.chicagoparent.com. **60% freelance written**. Monthly tabloid. *Chicago Parent* has a distinctly local approach. We offer information, inspiration, perspective and empathy to Chicago-area parents. Our lively editorial mix has a `we're all in this together' spirit, and articles are thoroughly researched and well written. Estab. 1988. Circ. 125,000 in 3 zones covering the 6-county Chicago metropolitan area. Byline given. Pays on publication. Offers 10-50% kill fee. Publishes ms an average of 2 months after acceptance. Buys first rights, buys electronic rights. Editorial lead time 4 months. Submit seasonal material 4 months in advance. Accepts queries by mail. Responds in 6 weeks to queries. Sample copy for $3.95 and 11 × 17 SAE with $1.65 postage. Guidelines for #10 SASE.

Nonfiction Needs essays, expose, how-to, parent-related, humor, interview, travel, local interest. include Chicago Baby and Healthy Child. No pot-boiler parenting pieces, simultaneous submissions, previously published pieces or non-local writers (from outside the 6-county Chicago metropolitan area). **Buys 40-50 mss/year.** Query with published clips. Length: 200-2,500 words. **Pays $25-300 for assigned articles. Pays $25-100 for unsolicited articles.** Pays expenses of writers on assignment.

Photos State availability Captions, identification of subjects required. Reviews contact sheets, negatives, prints. Offers $0-40/photo; negotiates payment individually. Buys one time rights.

Columns/Departments Healthy Child (kids' health issues), 850 words; Getaway (travel pieces), up to 1,200 words; other columns not open to freelancers. 30 Query with published clips or send complete ms. **Pays $100.**

Tips We don't like pot-boiler parenting topics and don't accept many personal essays unless they are truly compelling.

$ $ COLUMBUS PARENT MAGAZINE

Consumer News Service, 5300 Crosswind Dr., Columbus OH 43216. Fax: (614)461-7527. E-mail: columbusparent@thisweeknews.com. Website: www.columbusparent.com. **50% freelance written**. Monthly magazine covering parenting. A hip, reliable resource for Central Ohio parents who are raising children from birth to 18. Estab. 1988. Circ. 60,000. Byline given. Pays on publication. Offers 10% kill fee. Publishes ms an average of 2 months after acceptance. Buys all rights. Editorial lead time 3 months. Submit seasonal material 5 months in advance. Accepts queries by mail, e-mail, fax. Sample copy available online. Guidelines available online.

Nonfiction Needs general interest, how-to, interview, new product. Does not want personal essays. **Buys 80 mss/year.** Send complete ms. Length: 500-900 words. **Pays 10¢/word.**

Photos State availability Identification of subjects required. Offers no additional payment for photos accepted with ms. Buys one time rights.

Tips Your best bet for breaking in is to be an Ohio resident.

$ CONNECTICUT'S COUNTY KIDS

Journal Register Co., 1175 Post Rd. E., Westport CT 06880-5224. (203)226-8877, ext. 125. Fax: (203)221-7540. E-mail: countykids@ctcentral.com. Website: www.countykids.com. **80-90% freelance written**. Monthly tabloid covering parenting. We publish positive articles (nonfiction) that help parents of today raise children. Estab. 1987. Circ. 30,000. Byline given. Pays on publication. No kill fee. Publishes ms an average of 2 months after acceptance. Buys first North American serial rights, buys first rights, buys one-time rights, buys second serial (reprint) rights. Editorial lead time 6 weeks. Submit seasonal material 2-3 months in advance. Accepts queries by e-mail. Accepts previously published material. Guidelines by email.

Nonfiction Needs essays, general interest, humor, inspirational, new product, opinion, personal experience. Birthday; Maternity; Birthing Services. No fiction. **Buys 24-35 mss/year.** Send complete ms. Length: 600-1,500 words. **Pays $40-100 for assigned articles. Pays $25-40 for unsolicited articles.**

Columns/Departments Mom's View (humorous experiences), 800-1,000 words; Pediatric Health (medical situations), 800 words; Active Family (events shared as a family), 800 words. 15-20 Send complete ms. **Pays $25-40.**

Tips We like to use Connecticut writers when we can, but we do use writers from all over the US. We like all kinds of writing styles.

$ THE FAMILY DIGEST

P.O. Box 40137, Fort Wayne IN 46804. **95% freelance written**. Quarterly magazine. *"The Family Digest* is dedicated to the joy and fulfilment of the Catholic family and its relationship to the Catholic parish. Estab. 1945. Circ. 150,000. Byline given. Pays within 2 months of acceptance. Buys first North American rights. Submit seasonal material 7 months in advance. Accepts previously published material. Responds in 1-2 months to queries. Sample copy and writer's guidelines are available for 6 x 9 SAE with 2 first-class stamps.

Nonfiction Family life, parish life, prayer life, Catholic traditions, spiritual life. Needs how-to, inspirational, lives of the saints., lives of the saints. **Buys 45 unsolicited mss/year.** Send complete ms. Length: 750-1,200 words. **Pays $45-60 for accepted articles.**
Reprints "Send typed manuscript with rights for sale noted and information about when and where the material previously appeared."
Fillers Needs anecdotes, tasteful humor based on personal experience. 12 Length: 25-100 words. **Pays $25.**
Tips "Prospective freelance contributors should be familiar with the publication and the types of articles we accept and publish. We are especially looking for upbeat articles which affirm the simple ways in which the Catholic faith is expressed in daily life. Articles on family and parish life, including seasonal articles, how-to pieces, inspirational, prayer, spiritual life, and Church traditions, will be gladly reviewed for possible acceptance and publication."

$ $ $ $ FAMILYFUN

Disney Publishing, Inc., 47 Pleasant St., Northampton MA 01060. (413)585-0444. Fax: (413)586-5724. E-mail: queries.familyfun@disney.com. Website: www.familyfun.com. Magazine covering activities for families with kids ages 3-12. "*FamilyFun* is about all the great things families can do together. Our writers are either parents or authorities in a covered field." Estab. 1991. Circ. 2,100,000. Byline sometimes given. Pays on acceptance. Offers 25% kill fee. Makes work-for-hire assignments. Editorial lead time 6 months. Submit seasonal material 6 months in advance. Accepts simultaneous submissions. Responds in 3 months to queries. Sample copy for $5. Guidelines available online.
Nonfiction Needs book excerpts, essays, general interest, how-to, crafts, cooking, educational activities, humor, interview, personal experience, photo feature, travel. **Buys dozens of mss/year.** Query with published clips. Length: 850-3,000 words. **Pays $1.25/word.** Pays expenses of writers on assignment.
Photos State availability Identification of subjects, model releases required. Reviews contact sheets, negatives, transparencies. Offers $75-500/photo. Buys all rights.
Columns/Departments "Everyday Fun, Debbie Way, senior editor (simple, quick, practical, inexpensive ideas and projects—outings, crafts, games, nature activities, learning projects, and cooking with children), 200-400 words; query or send ms; **pays per word or $200 for ideas.** Family Getaways, Becky Karush, associate editor (brief, newsy items about family travel, what's new, what's great, and especially, what's a good deal), 100-125 words; send ms; **pays per word or $50 for ideas.** Creative Solutions, Debra Immergut, senior editor (explains fun and inventive ideas that have worked for writer's own family), 1,000 words; query or send ms; **pays $1,250 on acceptance.** Also publishes best letters from writers and readers following column, send to My Great Idea: From Our Readers Editor, 100-150 words, **pays $100 on publication**." 60-80 letters/year; 10-12
Tips "Many of our writers break into *FF* by writing for Everyday Fun or Family Getaways (front-of-the-book departments)."

$ GRAND RAPIDS FAMILY MAGAZINE

Gemini Publications, 549 Ottawa Ave., NW, Suite 201, Grand Rapids MI 49503-1444. (616)459-4545. Fax: (616)459-4800. E-mail: cvalade@geminipub.com. Website: www.grfamily.com. Monthly magazine covering local parenting issues. *Grand Rapids Family* seeks to inform, instruct, amuse, and entertain its readers and their families. Circ. 30,000. Byline given. Pays on publication. Offers $25 kill fee. Buys first North American serial rights, buys simultaneous rights, buys all rights. Makes work-for-hire assignments. Editorial lead time 3 months. Submit seasonal material 4 months in advance. Accepts simultaneous submissions. Responds in 2 months to queries. Responds in 6 months to mss. Guidelines for #10 SASE.
Nonfiction The publication recognizes that parenting is a process that begins before conception/adoption and continues for a lifetime. The issues are diverse and ever changing. *Grand Rapids Family* seeks to identify these issues and give them a local perspective, using local sources and resources. Query. **Pays $25-50.**
Photos State availability Captions, identification of subjects, model releases required. Reviews contact sheets. Offers $25/photo Buys one-time or all rights
Columns/Departments All local: law, finance, humor, opinion, mental health. **Pays $25**

$ N GWINNETT PARENTS MAGAZINE

3651 Peachtree Pkwy., Suite 325, Suwanee GA 30024. (678)935-5116. Fax: (678)935-5115. E-mail: editor@gwinnettparents.com. Website: www.gwinnettparents.com. **Contact:** Terrie Carter, ed. "Our mission is to provide the most comprehensive source of parenting information and local resources for families living in and around Gwinnett County, Georgia." Pays on publication. No kill fee. Publishes ms an average of 1-4 weeks after acceptance. Buys nonexclusive online archival rights rights. Editorial lead time 2 months. Accepts queries by e-mail. Responds in 3-4 weeks to queries. Sample copy by e-mail (paulp@gwinnettparents.com).
Nonfiction Send queries with a brief bio via e-mail with Editorial Submission in the subject line. Length: 500-1,500 words. **Pays $50 for department articles; $75 for features**
Photos Accepts color or b&w high resolution images. No images from the Internet. Identification of subjects, True required.

$ HOME EDUCATION MAGAZINE

P.O. Box 1083, Tonasket WA 98855. (509)486-1351. Website: www.homeedmag.com. **80% freelance written**. Bimonthly magazine covering home-based education. "We feature articles which address the concerns of parents who want to take a direct involvement in the education of their children—concerns such as socialization, how to find curriculums and materials, testing and evaluation, how to tell when your child is ready to begin reading, what to do when homeschooling is difficult, teaching advanced subjects, etc." Estab. 1983. Circ. 32,000. Byline given. Pays on publication. Publishes ms an average of 6 months after acceptance. Buys first North American serial rights, buys first rights, buys one-time rights, buys electronic rights. Submit seasonal material 6 months in advance. Accepts queries by mail. Responds in 2 months to queries. Sample copy for $6.50. Writer's guidelines for #10 SASE, via e-mail, or on Web site.

Nonfiction Needs essays, how-to, related to homeschooling, humor, interview, personal experience, photo feature, technical. **Buys 40-50 mss/year.** Send complete ms. Length: 750-2,500 words. **Pays $50-100.**

Photos Send photos Identification of subjects required. Reviews enlargements, 35mm prints, CD-ROMs. Pays $100/cover; $12/inside photos. Buys one time rights.

Tips "We would like to see how-to articles (that don't preach, just present options); articles on testing, accountability, working with the public schools, socialization, learning disabilities, resources, support groups, legislation, and humor. We need answers to the questions that homeschoolers ask. Please, no teachers telling parents how to teach. Personal experience with homeschooling is the preferred approach."

$ HOMESCHOOLING TODAY

P.O. Box 244, Abingdon VA 24212. (276)628-1686. E-mail: management@homeschooltoday.com. Website: www.homeschooltoday.com. **75% freelance written**. Bimonthly magazine covering homeschooling. "We are a practical magazine for homeschoolers with a broadly Christian perspective." Estab. 1992. Circ. 13,000. Byline given. Pays on publication. Offers 25% kill fee. Publishes ms an average of 1 year after acceptance. Buys first rights. Editorial lead time 6 months. Submit seasonal material 1 year in advance. Accepts simultaneous submissions. Responds in 4 months to mss. Sample copy and writer's guidelines free

Nonfiction Needs book excerpts, how-to, interview, new product. No fiction. **Buys 30 mss/year.** Send complete ms. Length: 500-2,000 words. **Pays 10¢/word.**

Photos State availability Captions, identification of subjects required. Offers no additional payment for photos accepted with ms. Buys one time rights.

$ KIDS LIFE MAGAZINE

Kids Life Publishing of Tuscaloosa, LLC, 1426 22nd Ave., Tuscaloosa AL 35401. Fax: (205)345-1632. E-mail: kidslife@comcast.net. Website: www.kidslifemagazine.com. **50% freelance written**. Bimonthly magazine covering family and child. *Kids Life Magazine* is a one-stop place for families containing everything the Tuscaloosa area offers our children. Estab. 1996. Circ. 30,000. Byline given. Pays on publication. Buys simultaneous rights. Editorial lead time 2 months. Submit seasonal material 4 months in advance. Accepts queries by e-mail. Accepts previously published material. Accepts simultaneous submissions. Sample copy free. Guidelines available online.

Nonfiction We want anything child and family related. Needs personal experience. **Buys 12 mss/year. Pays up to $25.**

Photos Send photos Reviews GIF/JPEG files. Offers no additional payment for photos accepted with ms.

Columns/Departments Reel Life with Jane (movie reviews), 1,000 words; Single Parenting, 750 words; Spiritual, 725 words. 3 **Pays $0-20.**

Fillers Needs facts, gags, short humor. Length: 500 words.

Tips E-mail submissions. We welcome anyone wanting to be published.

$ LIVING

Living for the Whole Family, Shalom Foundation, 1251 Virginia Ave., Harrisonburg VA 22802. E-mail: tgether@aol.com. Website: www.churchoutreach.com. **90% freelance written**. Quarterly tabloid covering family living. Articles focus on giving general encouragement for families of all ages and stages. Estab. 1985. Circ. 250,000. Byline given. Pays on publication. No kill fee. Publishes ms an average of 6-12 months after acceptance. Buys one-time rights, buys electronic rights. Editorial lead time 4-6 months. Submit seasonal material 6 months in advance. Accepts queries by mail, e-mail. Accepts previously published material. Accepts simultaneous submissions. Responds in 2 months to queries. Responds in 2-4 months to mss. Sample copy for sae with 9X12 envelope and 4 First-Class stamps. Guidelines free.

- "Our bias is to use articles 'showing' rather than telling readers how to raise families (stories rather than how-to). We aim for articles that are well written, understandable, challenging (not the same old thing you've read elsewhere); they should stimulate readers to dig a little deeper, but not too deep with academic or technical language; that are interesting and fit our theological perspective (Christian), but are not preachy or overly patriotic. No favorable mentions of smoking, drinking, cursing, etc."

O→ "We want our stories and articles to be very practical and upbeat. Since we go to every home, we do not assume a Christian audience. Writers need to take this into account. Personal experience stories are welcome, but are not the only approach.Our audience? Children, teenagers, singles, married couples, right on through to retired persons. We cover the wide variety of subjects that people face in the home and workplace. (See theme list in our guidelines online.)"

Nonfiction Needs general interest, how-to, humor, inspirational, personal experience. We do not use devotional materials intended for Christian audiences. We seldom use pet stories and receive way too many grief/death/dealing with serious illness stories to use. We encourage stories from non-white writers (excuse the phrase). We publish in March, June, September, and December so holidays that occur in other months are not usually the subject of articles. **Buys 48-52 mss/year.** Query. Length: 500-1,200 words. **Pays $35-60.**

Photos Contact: Dorothy Hartman. State availability. Captions, identification of subjects, model releases required. Reviews 4X6 prints, GIF/JPEG files. Offers $15-25/photo Buys one time rights.

Tips "We prefer 'good news' stories that are uplifting and non-controversial in nature. We want articles that tell stories of people solving problems and dealing with personal issues rather than essays or 'preaching.' If you submit electronically, it is very helpful if you put the specific title of the submission in the subject line and please include your e-mail address in the body of the e-mail or on your manuscript. Also, always please include your address and phone number."

$ METROFAMILY MAGAZINE

Inprint Publishing, 306 S. Bryant C-152, Edmond OK 73034. (405)340-1404. E-mail: editor@metrofamilymagazine.com. Website: www.metrofamilymagazine.com. **60% freelance written**. Monthly tabloid covering parenting. *MetroFamily Magazine* provides local parenting and family fun information for our Central Oklahoma readers. Circ. 30,000. Byline given. Pays on publication. Offers 100% on assignments kill fee. Publishes ms an average of 2-3 months after acceptance. Buys first North American serial rights, buys second serial (reprint) rights, buys simultaneous rights, buys electronic rights. Editorial lead time 2-3 months. Accepts queries by e-mail. Accepts previously published material. Accepts simultaneous submissions. Responds in 3 weeks to queries. Responds in 1 month to mss. Sample copy for sae with 10x13 envelope and 3 First-Class stamps. via e-mail or return with #10 SASE

Nonfiction Needs how-to, parenting issues, education, humor, travel. No poetry, fiction (except for humor column), or anything that doesn't support good, solid family values. Send complete ms. Length: 300-600 words. **Pays $25-50, plus 1 contributor copy.**

Photos State availability Captions, identification of subjects, model releases required. Reviews GIF/JPEG files. Negotiates payment individually. Buys one time rights.

Columns/Departments You've Just Gotta Laugh, humor (600 words). 12 Send complete ms. **Pays $35.**

$ METROKIDS

Resource Publications for Delaware Valley Families, Kidstuff Publications, Inc., 1412-1414 Pine St., Philadelphia PA 19102. (215)291-5560, ext. 102. Fax: (215)291-5563. E-mail: editor@metrokids.com. Website: www.metrokids.com. **25% freelance written**. "Monthly tabloid providing information for parents and kids in Philadelphia and surrounding counties, South Jersey, and Delaware.". Estab. 1990. Circ. 130,000. Byline given. Pays on publication. Buys one-time rights. Submit seasonal material 4 months in advance. Accepts queries by e-mail. Accepts previously published material. Guidelines by email

- Responds only if interested.

Nonfiction Needs general interest, how-to, new product, travel, parenting, health. Educator's Edition—field trips, school enrichment, teacher, professional development (March & September); Camps (December & June); Special Kids—children with special needs (August); Vacations and Theme Parks (May & June); What's Happening—guide to events and activities (January); Kids 'N Care—guide to childcare (July) **Buys 40 mss/year.** Query with published clips. Length: 800-1,500 words. **Pays $50.** Sometimes pays expenses of writers on assignment.

Reprints E-mail summary or complete article and information about when and where the material previously appeared. Pays $35, or $50 if localized after discussion.

Columns/Departments Techno Family (CD-ROM and website reviews); Body Wise (health); Style File (fashion and trends); Woman First (motherhood); Practical Parenting (financial parenting advice); Kids 'N Care (toddlers and daycare); Special Kids (disabilities), all 800-1,000 words. 25. Query. **Pays $25-50.**

Tips "We prefer e-mail queries or submissions. Because they're so numerous, we don't reply unless interested. We are interested in feature articles (on specified topics) or material for our regular departments (with a regional/seasonal base). Articles should cite expert sources and the most up-to-date theories and facts. We are looking for a journalistic style of writing. We are also interested in finding local writers for assignments."

$ $ METRO PARENT MAGAZINE

Metro Parent Publishing Group, 22041 Woodward Ave., Ferndale MI 48220-2520. (248)398-3400. Fax: (248)3399-3970. E-mail: jelliott@metroparent.com. Website: www.metroparent.com. **75% freelance written**. Monthly magazine covering parenting, women's health, education. We are a local magazine on parenting topics and issues of interest to Detroit-area parents. Related issues: *Ann Arbor Parent; African/American Parent; Metro Baby Magazine.* Circ. 85,000. Byline given. Pays on publication. Publishes ms an average of 3 months after acceptance. Buys first rights. Editorial lead time 3 months. Submit seasonal material 3 months in advance. Accepts queries by mail, e-mail. Accepts previously published material. Accepts simultaneous submissions. Responds in 2 weeks to queries. Responds in 3 months to mss. Sample copy for $2.50.

Nonfiction Needs essays, humor, inspirational, personal experience. **Buys 100 mss/year.** Send complete ms. Length: 1,500-2,500 words. **Pays $50-300 for assigned articles.**

Photos State availability Captions required. Offers $100-200/photo or negotiates payment individually. Buys one time rights.

Columns/Departments Women's Health (latest issues of 20-40 year olds), 750-900 words; Solo Parenting (advice for single parents); Family Finance (making sense of money and legal issues); Tweens 'N Teens (handling teen issues), 750-800 words. 50 Send complete ms. **Pays $75-150.**

$ $ PARENT:WISE AUSTIN

Pleticha Publishing Inc., 5501-A Balcones Dr., Suite 102, Austin TX 78731. (512)699-5327. Fax: (512)532-6885. Website: www.parentwiseaustin.com. **25% freelance written.** Monthly magazine covering parenting news, features and issues; mothering issues; maternal feminism; feminism as it pertains to motherhood and work/life balance; serious/thoughtful essays about the parenting experience; humor articles pertaining to the parenting experience. "*Parent:Wise Austin* targets educated, thoughtful readers who want solid information about the parenting experience. We seek to create a warm, nurturing community by providing excellent, well researched articles, thoughtful essays, humor articles, and other articles appealing to parents. Our readers demand in-depth, well written articles; we do not accept, nor will we print, 're-worked' articles on boiler plate topics." Estab. 2004. Circ. 32,000. Byline given. Pays on publication. No kill fee. Publishes ms an average of 2 months after acceptance. Buys first North American serial rights, buys electronic rights. Editorial lead time 6 months. Submit seasonal material 6 months in advance. Accepts queries by e-mail. Responds in 1 week to queries. Responds in 1 month to mss. Sample copy for 41.17 postage. "However, sample copies can be viewed online." Guidelines available online.

Nonfiction Needs essays, humor, opinion, personal experience, travel, hard news, features on parenting issues. Mother's Day issue (May); Father's Day issue (June). "Does not want boiler plate articles or generic articles that have been customized for our market." **Buys 12-20 mss/year.** Query with published clips. Length: 500-2,500 words. **Pays $50-200.** Sometimes pays expenses of writers on assignment.

Photos Contact: Contact Nisa Sharma, art director. State availability Captions, identification of subjects, model releases required. Reviews JPEG files. Offers no additional payment for photos accepted with ms. Buys one-time and electronic rights.

Columns/Departments My Life as a Parent (humor), 500-700 words; Essay (first-person narrative), 500-1,000 words. 24-50 Send complete ms. **Pays $50.**

Poetry Needs avant-garde, free verse, haiku, light verse, traditional. "Does not want poetry that does not pertain to parenting or the parenting experience." **Buys 3-5 poems/year.** Submit maximum 3 poems. Length: 25 lines.

Tips "We are much more likely to accept an Essay or a My Life as a Parent (humor) article than a cover article. Cover articles generally are assigned months in advance to seasoned journalists who know our market; humor and essay articles are accepted without a query and generally publish within a couple of months of acceptance. For cover articles, we prefer detailed queries (e.g., the theme of the article; who you plan to interview; what you hope to 'discover' or how you plan to educate readers) and clips of previous work. Please e-mail queries, clips and questions to the editor. No phone calls."

PARENTGUIDE

PG Media, 419 Park Ave. S., Floor 13, New York NY 10016. (212)213-8840. Fax: (212)447-7734. E-mail: jenna@parentguidenews.com. Website: www.parentguidenews.com. **80% freelance written.** Monthly magazine covering parenting and child-rearing. "We are a tabloid-sized publication catering to the needs and interests of parents who have children under the age of 12 in New York City, New Jersey, Long Island, Westchester and Queens. Our columns and feature articles cover health, education, child-rearing, current events, parenting issues, recreational activities and social events. We also run a complete calendar of local events. We welcome articles from professional authors as well as never-before-published writers." Estab. 1982. Circ. 280,000. Byline given. Does not offer financial compensation. No kill fee. Publishes ms an average of 5 months after acceptance. Buys first rights. Editorial lead time 5 months. Submit seasonal material 6 months in advance. Accepts queries by e-mail. Accepts simultaneous submissions. Sample copy available online. Guidelines free.

Nonfiction Needs how-to, (family-related service pieces), inspirational, interview, personal experience, travel, (education, health, fitness, special needs, parenting).

Fiction Needs confession, humorous, slice-of-life vignettes. Query. Length: 800-1,000 words.

$ $ $ $ PARENTING MAGAZINE (EARLY YEARS AND SCHOOL YEARS EDITIONS)

Bonnier Corporation, 2 Park Ave., New York NY 10016. (212)779-5000. Website: www.parenting.com. Magazine published 10 times/year for mothers of children from birth to 12, and covering both the emotional and practical aspects of parenting. Estab. 1987. Circ. 2,100,000. Byline given. Pays on acceptance. Offers 25% kill fee. Buys a variety of rights, including electronic rights. Guidelines for #10 SASE.

Nonfiction Contact: Articles Editor. Needs book excerpts, personal experience, child development/behavior/health. **Buys 20-30 mss/year.** Query. Length: 1,000-2,500 words. **Pays $1,000-3,000.** Pays expenses of writers on assignment.

Columns/Departments Contact: Query to the specific departmental editor. 50-60 Query. **Pays $50-400.**

Tips "The best guide for writers is the magazine itself. Please familiarize yourself with it before submitting a query."

PARENTS

Meredith Corp., 375 Lexington Ave., 10th Floor, New York NY 10017. (212)499-2000. Fax: (212)499-2077. Website: www.parents.com. Monthly magazine. Estab. 1926. Circ. 1,700,000. Pays on acceptance. Offers 25% kill fee. Submit seasonal material 6-8 months in advance. Accepts queries by mail, e-mail. Responds in 6 weeks to queries. Guidelines available online.

Nonfiction Before you query us, please take a close look at our magazine at the library or newsstand. This will give you a good idea of the different kinds of stories we publish, as well as their tempo and tone. In addition, please take the time to look at the masthead to make sure you are directing your query to the correct department. Query with published clips.

Columns/Departments As They Grow (issues on different stages of development), 1,000 words.

Tips We're a national publication, so we're mainly interested in stories that will appeal to a wide variety of parents. We're always looking for compelling human-interest stories, so you may want to check your local newspaper for ideas. Keep in mind that we can't pursue stories that have appeared in competing national publications.

$ PEDIATRICS FOR PARENTS

Pediatrics for Parents, Inc., 35 Starknaught Heights, Gloucester MA 01930. (215)253-4543. Fax: (973)302-4543. E-mail: richsagall@pedsforparents.com. **50% freelance written**. Monthly newsletter covering children's health. *Pediatrics For Parents* emphasizes an informed, common-sense approach to childhood health care. We stress preventative action, accident prevention, when to call the doctor and when and how to handle a situation at home. We are also looking for articles that describe general, medical and pediatric problems, advances, new treatments, etc. All articles must be medically accurate and useful to parents with children—prenatal to adolescence. Estab. 1981. Circ. 120,000. Byline given. Pays on publication. Publishes ms an average of 4 months after acceptance. Buys first North American serial rights, buys electronic rights. Accepts queries by mail, e-mail, fax. Accepts previously published material. Accepts simultaneous submissions. Responds in 1 month to queries. Sample copy available online. Guidelines available online.

Nonfiction No first person or experience. **Buys 25 mss/year.** Send complete ms. Length: 1,000-1,500 words. **Pays $10-25.**

$ PIKES PEAK PARENT

The Gazette/Freedom Communications, 30 S. Prospect St., Colorado Springs CO 80903. Fax: (719)476-1625. E-mail: parent@gazette.com. Website: www.pikespeakparent.com. **10% freelance written**. Monthly tabloid covering parenting, family and grandparenting. We prefer stories with local angle and local stories. We do not accept unsolicited manuscripts. Estab. 1994. Circ. 35,000. Byline given. Pays on publication. No kill fee. Buys first North American serial rights, buys electronic rights. Editorial lead time 3 months. Submit seasonal material 4 months in advance. Accepts queries by e-mail. Accepts previously published material. Accepts simultaneous submissions. Responds in 1 month to queries. Sample copy available online.

Nonfiction Needs essays, general interest, how-to, medical related to parenting. **Buys 10 mss/year.** Query with published clips. Length: 800-1,000 words. **Pays $20-120.**

Tips Local, local, local—with a fresh slant.

$ $ $ PLUM MAGAZINE

Groundbreak Publishing, 276 Fifth Ave., Suite 302, New York NY 10001. (212)725-9201. Fax: (212)725-9203. E-mail: editor@plummagazine.com. Website: www.plummagazine.com. **90% freelance written**. Annual magazine covering health and lifestyle for pregnant women over age 35. *Plum* is a patient education tool meant to be an adjunct to obstetrics care. It presents information on preconception, prenatal medical care, nutrition, fitness, beauty, fashion, decorating, and travel. It also covers newborn health with articles on baby wellness, nursery necessities, postpartum care, and more. Estab. 2004. Circ. 450,000. Byline sometimes given. Pays on publication. Offers 20% kill fee. Publishes ms an average of 3-6 months after acceptance. Buys all rights. Editorial lead time 6 months. Submit seasonal material 8 months in advance. Accepts queries by e-mail.

Responds in 6 weeks to queries. Sample copy for $7.95. Guidelines by email.
Nonfiction Needs essays, how-to, interview. Query with published clips. Length: 300-3,500 words. **Pays 75¢-$1/word**

$ SACRAMENTO PARENT

Reaching Greater Sacramento & the Sierra Foothills, Family Publishing Inc., 457 Grass Valley Hwy., Suite 5, Auburn CA 95603. (530)888-0573. Fax: (530)888-1536. E-mail: amy@sacramentoparent.com. Website: www.sacramentoparent.com. **50% freelance written**. Monthly magazine covering parenting in the Sacramento region. We look for articles that promote a developmentally appropriate, healthy and peaceful environment for children. Estab. 1992. Circ. 50,000. Byline given. Pays on publication. Offers 10% kill fee. Publishes ms an average of 2 months after acceptance. Buys first North American serial rights, buys electronic rights. Editorial lead time 3 months. Submit seasonal material 4 months in advance. Accepts queries by e-mail. Sample copy free. Guidelines by email.
Nonfiction All articles should be related to parenting. Needs book excerpts, general interest, how-to, humor, interview, opinion, personal experience. **Buys 36 mss/year.** Query. Length: 300-1,000 words. **Pays $30-100.**
Columns/Departments Let's Go! (Sacramento regional family-friendly day trips/excursions/activities), 600 words. **Pays $25-45.**

$ SAN DIEGO FAMILY MAGAZINE

1475 Sixth Ave., 5th Floor, San Diego CA 92101-3200. (619)685-6970. Fax: (619)685-6978. E-mail: Kirsten@sandiegofamily.com. Website: www.sandiegofamily.com. **100% freelance written**. Monthly magazine for parenting and family issues. "*SDFM* is a regional family publication. We focus on providing current, informative and interesting editorial about parenting and family life that educates and entertains." Estab. 1982. Circ. 300,000. Byline given. Pays on publication. No kill fee. Publishes ms an average of 1-6 months after acceptance. Buys first rights, buys second serial (reprint) rights, buys electronic rights. Editorial lead time 4 months. Submit seasonal material 6 months in advance. Accepts queries by mail, e-mail. Accepts previously published material. Accepts simultaneous submissions. Responds in 1 month to queries. Responds in 2 months to mss. Sample copy for $4.50 to P.O. Box 23960, San Diego CA 92193. Guidelines available online.
Nonfiction Needs essays, general interest, how-to, interview, technical, travel, informational articles. Does not want humorous personal essays, opinion pieces, religious or spiritual. **Buys 350-500 mss/year.** Query. Length: 600-1,250 words. **Pays $22-90.**
Reprints Send typed manuscript. with rights for sale ted and information about when and where the material previously appeared. Will respond only if SASE is included.
Fiction "No adult fiction. We only want to see short fiction written for children: 'read aloud' stories, stories for beginning readers (400-500 words)." **Buys 0-12 mss/year.** Send complete ms.
Fillers 0-12 Length: 200-600 words.
Tips "We publish short, informational articles. We give preference to stories about San Diego County personalities/events/etc., and stories that include regional resources for our readers. This is a local publication; don't address a national audience."

$ SCHOLASTIC PARENT & CHILD

Scholastic, Inc., 557 Broadway, New York NY 10012. (212)343-6100. Fax: (212)343-4801. E-mail: parentandchild@scholastic.com. Website: parentandchildonline.com. Bimonthly magazine. Published to keep active parents up-to-date on children's learning and development while in pre-school or child-care enviroment. Circ. 1,224,098. No kill fee. Editorial lead time 10 weeks.

$ $ SOUTH FLORIDA PARENTING

1701 Green Rd., Suite B, Deerfield Beach FL 33441. (954)596-5607. Fax: (954)429-1207. E-mail: krlomer@tribune.com. Website: www.sfparenting.com. **Contact:** Kyara Lomer, ed. **90% freelance written**. Monthly magazine covering parenting, family. "*South Florida Parenting* provides news, information, and a calendar of events for readers in Southeast Florida (Palm Beach, Broward and Miami-Dade counties). The focus is parenting issues, things to do, information about raising children in South Florida." Estab. 1990. Circ. 110,000. Byline given. Pays on publication. No kill fee. Buys one-time rights, buys second serial (reprint) rights. Makes work-for-hire assignments. Editorial lead time 4 months. Submit seasonal material 4 months in advance. Accepts queries by e-mail, fax. Accepts previously published material. Responds in 3 months to queries.

- Preference given to writers based in South Florida.

Nonfiction Needs how-to (parenting issues), interview/profile, family, parenting and children's issues. family fitness, education, spring party guide, fall party guide, kids and the environment, toddler/preschool, preteen Length: 500-1,000 words. **Pays $40-165.**
Reprints Pays $25-50.
Columns/Departments Dad's Perspective, Family Deals, Products for Families, Nutrition, Baby Basics, Travel, Toddler/Preschool, Preteen.

Tips "We want information targeted to the South Florida market. Multicultural and well-sourced is preferred. A unique approach to a universal parenting concern will be considered. Profiles or interviews of courageous parents. Opinion pieces on child rearing should be supported by experts and research should be listed. First-person stories should be fresh and insightful. Only accepts stories in email attachment (nothing that has to be retyped)."

$$ SOUTHWEST FLORIDA PARENT & CHILD

The News-Press, 2442 Dr. Martin Luther King, Jr. Blvd., Fort Myers FL 33901. (239)335-4698. Fax: (239)344-4690. E-mail: pamela@swflparentchild.com. Website: www.gulfcoastmoms.com. **75% freelance written.** Monthly magazine covering parenting. *Southwest Florida Parent & Child* is a regional parenting magazine with an audience of mostly moms but some dads, too. With every article, we strive to give readers information they can use. We aim to be an indispensable resource for our local parents. Estab. 2000. Circ. 25,000. Byline given. Pays on publication. Publishes ms an average of 2-3 months after acceptance. Buys all rights. Editorial lead time 2-3 months. Submit seasonal material 3+ months in advance. Accepts queries by mail, e-mail, fax. Accepts previously published material. Accepts simultaneous submissions.

Nonfiction Needs book excerpts, general interest, how-to, humor, interview, new product, personal experience, photo feature, religious, travel. Does not want personal experience or opinion pieces. **Buys 96-120 mss/year.** Send complete ms. Length: 500-700 words. **Pays $25-200.** Sometimes pays expenses of writers on assignment.

Photos State availability of or send photos Captions, identification of subjects required. Reviews GIF/JPEG files. Negotiates payment individually. Buys all rights.

TIDEWATER PARENT

258 Granby St., Norfolk VA 23510. (757)222-3900. Fax: (757)363-1767. E-mail: jenny.odonnell@portfolioweekly.com. Website: www.tidewaterparent.com. **85% freelance written.** Monthly tabloid targeting families in the Hampton Roads area. All our readers are parents of children ages 0-11. Our readers demand stories that will help them tackle the challenges and demands they face daily as parents. Estab. 1980. Byline given. Pays on publication. Buys first North American serial rights. Editorial lead time 2 months. Submit seasonal material 3 months in advance. Accepts queries by mail, e-mail, fax. Accepts previously published material. Accepts simultaneous submissions. Responds in 1 month to queries. Responds in 4 months to mss. Sample copy free. Guidelines free.

Nonfiction Needs essays, general interest, historical, how-to, humor, interview, personal experience, religious, travel. No poetry or fiction. **Buys 60 mss/year.** Send complete ms. Length: 500-3,000 words.

Photos State availability of or send photos Captions required. Negotiates payment individually. Buys one time rights.

Columns/Departments Music and Video Software (reviews), both 600-800 words; also Where to Go, What to Do, Calendar Spotlight and Voices. 36 Send complete ms.

Tips Articles for *Tidewater Parent* should be informative and relative to parenting. An informal, familiar tone is preferable to a more formal style. Avoid difficult vocabulary and complicated sentence structure. A conversational tone works best. Gain your reader's interest by using real-life situations, people or examples to support what you're saying.

$$$$ TODAY'S PARENT

Rogers Media, Inc., One Mt. Pleasant Rd., 8th Floor, Toronto ON M4Y 2Y5 Canada. Fax: (416)764-2801. E-mail: queries@tpg.rogers.com. Website: www.todaysparent.com. Monthly magazine for parents with children up to the age of 12. Circ. 175,000. No kill fee. Editorial lead time 5 months.

Nonfiction Runs features with a balance between the practical and the philosophical, the light-hearted and the investigative. All articles should be grounded in the reality of Canadian family life. Length: 1,800-2,500 words. **Pays $1,500-2,200.**

Columns/Departments Profile (Canadian who has accomplished something remarkable for the benefit of children), 250 words; **pays $250.** Your Turn (parents share their experiences), 800 words; **pays $200.** Beyond Motherhood (deals with topics not directly related to parenting), 700 words; **pays $800.** Education (tackles straightforward topics and controversial or complex topics), 1,200 words; **pays $1,200-1,500.** Health Behavior (child development and discipline), 1,200 words; **pays $1,200-1,500.** Slice of Life (explores lighter side of parenting), 750 words; **pays $650.**

Tips Because we promote ourselves as a Canadian magazine, we use only Canadian writers.

$$$$ TODAY'S PARENT PREGNANCY & BIRTH

Rogers Media, Inc., One Mt. Pleasant Rd., 8th Floor, Toronto ON M4Y 2Y5 Canada. Website: www.todaysparent.com. **100% freelance written.** Magazine published 3 times/year. *P&B* helps, supports and encourages expectant and new parents with news and features related to pregnancy, birth, human sexuality and parenting. Estab. 1973. Circ. 200,000. Pays on acceptance. Publishes ms an average of 8 months after acceptance. Buys first North American serial rights. Editorial lead time 6 months. Responds in 6 weeks to queries. Guidelines for SASE.

Nonfiction Features about pregnancy, labor and delivery, post partum issues. **Buys 12 mss/year.** Query with published clips. Length: 1,000-2,500 words. **Pays up to $1/word.** Sometimes pays expenses of writers on assignment.
Photos State availability Pay negotiated individually. Rights negotiated individually.
Tips Our writers are professional freelance writers with specific knowledge in the childbirth field. *P&B* is written for a Canadian audience using Canadian research and sources.

$ $ TOLEDO AREA PARENT NEWS

Adams Street Publishing, Co., 1120 Adams St., Toledo OH 43604. (419)244-9859. Fax: (419)244-9871. E-mail: editor@toldeoparent.com. Website: www.toledoparent.com. Monthly tabloid for Northwest Ohio/Southeast Michigan parents. Estab. 1992. Circ. 40,000. Byline given. Pays on publication. No kill fee. Publishes ms an average of 1 month after acceptance. Editorial lead time 3 months. Accepts queries by mail, e-mail, fax. Responds in 1 month to queries. Sample copy for $1.50.
Nonfiction We use only local writers by assignment. We accept queries and opinion pieces only. Send cover letter to be considered for assignments. Needs general interest, interview, opinion. **Buys 10 mss/year.** Length: 1,000-2,500 words. **Pays $75-125.**
Photos State availability Identification of subjects required. Negotiates payment individually. Buys all rights.
Tips We love humorous stories that deal with common parenting issues or features on cutting-edge issues.

TREASURE VALLEY FAMILY MAGAZINE

Family Magazine & Media, Inc., 13191 W. Scotfield St., Boise ID 83713. (208)938-2119. Fax: (208)938-2117. E-mail: magazine@tresurevalleyfamily.com. Website: www.treasurevalleyfamily.com. **90% freelance written**. Monthly magazine covering parenting, education, child development. Geared to parents with children 12 years and younger. Focus on education, interest, activities for children. Positive parenting and healthy families. Estab. 1993. Circ. 20,000. Byline given. Pays on publication. Offers 50% kill fee. Publishes ms an average of 3 months after acceptance. Buys first North American serial rights. Editorial lead time 3 months. Submit seasonal material 3 months in advance. Accepts queries by mail, e-mail. Accepts simultaneous submissions. Responds in 2 months to queries. Sample copy for $2. Guidelines available online.
Nonfiction Family Health and Wellness (January); Early Childhood Education (February); Secondary and Higher Education (March); Summer Camps (April); Youth Sports Guide (May); Family Recreation and Fairs & Festivals (June/July); Back-to-School and extra-curricular Activities (August/September); Teens and College Planning (October); Birthday Party Fun (November); Youth in the Arts and Holiday Traditions (December) Query with published clips. Length: 1,000-1,300 words.
Photos State availability Captions required. Negotiates payment individually Buys one time rights.
Columns/Departments Crafts, travel, finance, parenting. Length: 700-1,000 words. Query with published clips.

$ $ TWINS

The Magazine for Parents of Multiples, 5748 S. College Ave., Unit D, Fort Collins CO 80525-4917. E-mail: twinseditor@twinsmagazine.com. Website: www.twinsmagazine.com. **80% freelance written**. Bimonthly magazine covering parenting multiples. *TWINS* is an international publication that provides informational and educational articles regarding the parenting of twins, triplets, and more. All articles must be multiple specific and have an upbeat, hopeful, and/or positive ending. Estab. 1984. Circ. 55,000. Byline given. Pays on publication. Buys first North American serial rights. Editorial lead time 6 months. Submit seasonal material 8 months in advance. Accepts queries by mail, e-mail, fax. Response time varies. Sample copy for $5 or on website. Guidelines available online.
Nonfiction Interested in seeing twin-specific discipline articles. Needs personal experience, first-person parenting experience, professional experience as it relates to multiples. Nothing on cloning, pregnancy reduction, or fertility issues. **Buys 12 mss/year.** Send complete ms. Length: 650-1,300 words. **Pays $25-250 for assigned articles. Pays $25-100 for unsolicited articles.**
Photos State availability Identification of subjects required. Offers no additional payment for photos accepted with ms.
Columns/Departments Special Miracles (miraculous stories about multiples with a happy ending), 800-850 words. 8-10 Query with or without published clips or send complete ms. **Pays $40-75.**
Tips All department articles must have a happy ending, as well as teach a lesson helpful to parents of multiples.

WHAT'S UP KIDS? FAMILY MAGAZINE

496 Metler Rd., Ridgeville ON L0S 1M0 Canada. E-mail: paul@whatsupkids.com. Website: www.whatsupkids.com. **95% freelance written**. Bimonthly magazine covering topics of interest to young families. Editorial is aimed at parents of kids birth-age 14. Kids Fun Section offers a section just for kids. We're committed to providing top-notch content. Estab. 1995. Circ. 200,000. Byline given. Pays 30 days after publication. Publishes ms an average of 4-6 months after acceptance. Buys first North American serial rights. Editorial lead time 6

months. Submit seasonal material 6 months in advance. Accepts queries by e-mail. Responds in 2 weeks if interested, by e-mail. Writer's guidelines online.

Nonfiction Service articles for families. No religious (one sided), personal experience, ADHD, bullying or anything that's all the talk. **Buys 50 mss/year.** Query with published clips. Length: 300-900 words. **Pays variable amount for assigned articles.** Sometimes pays expenses of writers on assignment.

Columns/Departments Understanding Families; Learning Curves; Family Finances; Baby Steps, all 400-600 words. variable number of Query with published clips. **Payment varies.**

Tips We only accept submissions from Canadian writers. Writers should send cover letter, clips, and query. Please do not call, and include e-mail address on all queries.

COMIC BOOKS

$ THE COMICS JOURNAL

Fantagraphics Books, 7563 Lake City Way NE, Seattle WA 98115. (206)524-1967. Fax: (206)524-2104. E-mail: dean@tcj.com. Website: www.tcj.com. Magazine covering the comics medium from an arts-first perspective on a six-week schedule. "*The Comics Journal* is one of the nation's most respected single-arts magazines, providing its readers with an eclectic mix of industry news, professional interviews, and reviews of current work. Due to its reputation as the American magazine with an interest in comics as an art form, the *Journal* has subscribers worldwide, and in this country serves as an important window into the world of comics for several general arts and news magazines." Byline given. Buys exclusive rights to articles that run in print or online versions for 6 months after initial publication. Rights then revert back to the writer. Accepts queries by mail, e-mail. Guidelines available online.

Nonfiction "We're not the magazine for the discussion of comic 'universes,' character re-boots, and Spider-Man's new costume—beyond, perhaps, the business or cultural implications of such events." Needs essays, interview, opinion, reviews. Send complete ms. Length: 2,000-3,000 words. **Pays 4¢/word, and 1 contributor's copy.**

Columns/Departments On Theory, Art and Craft (2,000-3,000 words); Firing Line (reviews 1,000-5,000 words); Bullets (reviews 400 words or less). Send inquiries, samples **Pays 4¢/word, and 1 contributor's copy.**

Tips "Like most magazines, the best writers guideline is to look at the material within the magazine and give something that approximates that material in terms of approach and sophistication. Anything else is a waste of time."

CONSUMER SERVICE & BUSINESS OPPORTUNITY

CONSUMER REPORTS

Consumers Union of U.S., Inc., 101 Truman Ave., Yonkers NY 10703-1057. (914)378-2000. Fax: (914)378-2904. Website: www.consumerreports.org. **5% freelance written**. Monthly magazine. *Consumer Reports* is the leading product-testing and consumer-service magazine in the US. We buy very little freelance material, mostly from proven writers we have used before for finance and health stories. Estab. 1936. Circ. 14,000,000. No byline given. Pays on acceptance. Offers negotiable kill fee. Publishes ms an average of 2 months after acceptance. Buys all rights. Editorial lead time 4 months. Submit seasonal material 6 months in advance. Accepts queries by mail.

Nonfiction Needs technical, personal finance, personal health. **Buys 12 mss/year.** Query. 1,000 words **Pays variable rate.**

KIPLINGER'S PERSONAL FINANCE

1729 H St. NW, Washington DC 20006. (202)887-6400. Fax: (202)331-1206. Website: www.kiplinger.com. **Contact:** Janet Bodnar, editor. **10% freelance written. Prefers to work with published/established writers**. Monthly magazine for general, adult audience interested in personal finance and consumer information. "*Kiplinger's* is a highly trustworthy source of information on saving and investing, taxes, credit, home ownership, paying for college, retirement planning, automobile buying, and many other personal finance topics." Estab. 1947. Circ. 800,000. Pays on acceptance. No kill fee. Publishes ms an average of 2 months after acceptance. Buys all rights. Responds in 1 month to queries.

Nonfiction "Most material is staff-written, but we accept some freelance. Thorough documentation is required for fact-checking." Query with published clips. Pays expenses of writers on assignment.

Tips "We are looking for a heavy emphasis on personal finance topics. Currently most work is provided by in-house writers."

CONTEMPORARY CULTURE

$ CANADIAN DIMENSION

Dimension Publications, Inc., 91 Albert St., Room 2-E, Winnipeg MB R3B 1G5 Canada. (204)957-1519. Fax: (204)943-4617. E-mail: info@canadiandimension.com. Website: www.canadiandimension.com. **80% freelance written**. Bimonthly magazine covering socialist perspective. We bring a socialist perspective to bear on events across Canada and around the world. Our contributors provide in-depth coverage on popular movements, peace, labour, women, aboriginal justice, environment, third world and eastern Europe. Estab. 1963. Circ. 3,000. Pays on publication. Publishes ms an average of 6 months after acceptance. Accepts previously published material. Accepts simultaneous submissions. Responds in 6 weeks to queries. Sample copy for $2. Guidelines available online.

Nonfiction Needs interview, opinion, reviews. **Buys 8 mss/year.** Length: 500-2,000 words. **Pays $25-100.**

Reprints Send typed manuscript with rights for sale noted and information about when and where the material previously appeared.

$ $ A&U

America's AIDS Magazine, Art & Understanding, Inc., 25 Monroe St., Suite 205, Albany NY 12210-2729. (888)245-4333. Fax: (888)790-1790. E-mail: chaelneedle@mac.com. Website: www.aumag.org. **50% freelance written**. Monthly magazine covering cultural, political, and medical responses to HIV/AIDS. Estab. 1991. Circ. 205,000. Byline given. Pays 3 months after publication. Offers 20% kill fee. Publishes ms an average of 3 months after acceptance. Buys first North American serial rights, buys electronic rights. Editorial lead time 6 months. Accepts queries by mail, e-mail. Accepts simultaneous submissions. Responds in 1 month to queries. Responds in 2 months to mss. Sample copy for $5. Guidelines available online.

Nonfiction Needs AIDS-related book excerpts, essays, general interest, how-to, humor, interview, new product, opinion, personal experience, photo feature, travel, reviews (film, theater, art exhibits, video, music, other media), medical news, artist profiles. **Buys 6 mss/year.** Query with published clips. Length: 800-1,200 words. **Pays $150-300 for assigned articles.**

Photos State availability Captions, identification of subjects, model releases required.

Columns/Departments The Culture of AIDS (reviews of books, music, film), 300 words; Viewpoint (personal opinion), 750 words. 6 Send complete ms. **Pays $50-150.**

Fiction Drama. Send complete ms. Length: less than 1,500 words. **Pays $100.**

Poetry Any length/style (shorter works preferred). **Pays $25.**

Tips "We're looking for more articles on youth and HIV/AIDS; more international coverage; celebrity interviews; more coverage of how the pandemic is affecting historically underrepresented communities."

$ $ $ ADBUSTERS

Adbusters Media Foundation, 1243 W. 7th Ave., Vancouver BC V6H 1B7 Canada. (604)736-9401. Fax: (604)737-6021. E-mail: editor@adbusters.org. Website: www.adbusters.org. **50% freelance written**. Bimonthly magazine. We are an activist journal of the mental environment. Estab. 1989. Circ. 90,000. Byline given. Pays 1 month after publication. Buys first rights. Accepts queries by mail, e-mail, fax. Accepts simultaneous submissions. Guidelines available online.

Nonfiction Needs essays, expose, interview, opinion. **Buys variable mss/year.** Query. Length: 250-3,000 words. **Pays $100/page for unsolicited articles; 50¢/word for solicited articles.**

Fiction Inquire about themes.

Poetry Inquire about themes.

$ $ THE AMERICAN SCHOLAR

Phi Beta Kappa, 1606 New Hampshire Ave. NW, Washington DC 20009. (202)265-3808. Fax: (202)265-0083. E-mail: scholar@pbk.org. **100% freelance written**. Quarterly journal. Our intent is to have articles written by scholars and experts but written in nontechnical language for an intelligent audience. Material covers a wide range in the arts, sciences, current affairs, history, and literature. Estab. 1932. Circ. 30,000. Byline given. Pays on publication. Offers 50% kill fee. Publishes ms an average of 1 year after acceptance. Buys first rights. Editorial lead time 6 months. Submit seasonal material 6 months in advance. Accepts queries by mail, e-mail, fax. Responds in 2 weeks to queries. Responds in 2 months to mss. Sample copy for $9. Guidelines for #10 SASE or via e-mail.

Nonfiction Needs essays, historical, humor. **Buys 40 mss/year.** Query. Length: 3,000-5,000 words. **Pays $500 maximum.**

Poetry Contact: Sandra Costich, poetry editor. We're not considering any unsolicited poetry.

$ BOSTON REVIEW

35 Medford St., Suite 302, Somerville MA 02143. (617)591-0505. Fax: (617)591-0440. E-mail: review@bostonreview.net. Website: www.bostonreview.net. **90% freelance written**. Bimonthly magazine of cultural and political analysis, reviews, fiction, and poetry. "The editors are committed to a society and culture that foster

human diversity and a democracy in which we seek common grounds of principle amidst our many differences. In the hope of advancing these ideals, the *Review* acts as a forum that seeks to enrich the language of public debate." Estab. 1975. Circ. 20,000. Byline given. Publishes ms an average of 4 months after acceptance. Buys first North American serial rights, buys first rights. Accepts simultaneous submissions. Responds in 4 months to queries. Sample copy for $5 or online. Guidelines available online.

Nonfiction "We do not accept unsolicited book reviews. If you would like to be considered for review assignments, please send your resume along with several published clips." **Buys 50 mss/year.** Query with published clips.

Fiction Contact: Junot Diaz, fiction editor. "I'm looking for stories that are emotionally and intellectually substantive and also interesting on the level of language. Things that are shocking, dark, lewd, comic, or even insane are fine so long as the fiction is *controlled* and purposeful in a masterly way. Subtlety, delicacy, and lyricism are attractive too." Needs ethnic, experimental, contemporary, prose poem. No romance, erotica, genre fiction. **Buys 5 mss/year.** Send complete ms. Length: 1,200-5,000 words. **Pays $25-300, and 5 contributor's copies.**

Poetry Contact: Benjamin Paloff and Timothy Donnelly, poetry editors. Reads poetry between September 15 and May 15 each year.

BRIARPATCH MAGAZINE

Briarpatch, Inc., 2138 McIntyre St., Regina SK S4P 2R7 Canada. (306)525-2949. E-mail: editor@briarpatchmagazine.com. Website: www.briarpatchmagazine.com. **90% freelance written.** Magazine published 8 times per year covering social justice, environment, and peace. *Briarpatch* features articles about people who are trying to make the world a better place for everyone who wants social justice. Estab. 1973. Circ. 2,000. Byline given. No kill fee. Buys first rights. Editorial lead time 2 months. Submit seasonal material 2 months in advance. Accepts queries by e-mail. Accepts previously published material. Accepts simultaneous submissions. Responds in 1 week to queries. Responds in 1 month to mss. Sample copy available online. Guidelines available online.

Nonfiction Needs expose, historical, interview, opinion, personal experience, photo feature, political analysis. Women's issue (March); Labor issue (September). **Buys 1-2 mss/year.** Send complete ms. Length: 300-1,200 words.

Photos State availability Reviews 4x6 prints, GIF/JPEG files. Offers no additional payment for photos.

Columns/Departments My Opinion (rant on anything of interest to our readers), 600 words. Send complete ms.

Tips We are looking for hard-hitting exposés, clever things people are doing to oppose oppressive situations, and a bit of humor. We like to think we are a stepping stone for new writers breaking into the paid alternative media scene.

$ $ BROKEN PENCIL

The Magazine of Zine Culture and the Independent Arts, P.O. Box 203, Station P, Toronto ON M5S 2S7 Canada. E-mail: editor@brokenpencil.com. Website: www.brokenpencil.com. **80% freelance written.** Quarterly magazine covering arts and culture. *Broken Pencil* is one of the few magazines in the world devoted exclusively to underground culture and the independent arts. We are a great resource and a lively read! *Broken Pencil* reviews the best zines, books, Web sites, videos and artworks from the underground and reprints the best articles from the alternative press. From the hilarious to the perverse, *Broken Pencil* challenges conformity and demands attention. Estab. 1995. Circ. 5,000. Byline given. Pays on publication. Publishes ms an average of 2-3 months after acceptance. Buys first rights. Accepts queries by mail, e-mail. Guidelines available online.

Nonfiction Needs essays, general interest, historical, humor, interview, opinion, personal experience, photo feature, travel, reviews. Does not want anything about mainstream art and culture. **Buys 8 mss/year.** Query with published clips. Length: 400-2,500 words. **Pays $100-400.** Sometimes pays expenses of writers on assignment.

Photos Send photos Identification of subjects required. Reviews prints, GIF/JPEG files. Negotiates payment individually. Buys one time rights.

Columns/Departments Contact: Contact Erin Kobayashi, books editor; James King, ezines editor; Terence Dick, music editor; Lindsay Gibb, film editor. Books (book reviews and feature articles); Ezines (ezine reviews and feature articles); Music (music reviews and feature articles); Film (film reviews and feature articles), all 200-300 words for reviews and 1,000 words for features. 8 Query with published clips. **Pays $100-400.**

Fiction Contact: Contact Hal Niedzviecki, fiction editor. We're particularly interested in work from emerging writers. Needs adventure, cond novels, confession, erotica, ethnic, experimental, fantasy, historical, horror, humorous, mystery, novel concepts, romance, science fiction, slice-of-life vignettes. **Buys 8 mss/year.** Send complete ms. Length: 500-3,000 words.

Tips Write in to receive a list of upcoming themes and then pitch us stories based around those themes. If you keep your ear to the ground in the alternative and underground arts communities, you will be able to find content appropriate for *Broken Pencil*.

$ $ N BUST MAGAZINE

For Women With Something to Get Off Their Chests, Bust, Inc., 78 5th Ave., 5th Floor, New York NY 10011. E-mail: submissions@bust.com. Website: www.bust.com. **60% freelance written**. Bimonthly magazine covering pop culture for young women. "*Bust* is the groundbreaking, original women's lifestyle magazine & website that is unique in its ability to connect with bright, cutting-edge, influential young women." Estab. 1993. Circ. 100,000. Byline given. Pays on publication. No kill fee. Publishes ms an average of 4 months after acceptance. Buys all rights. Editorial lead time 3-4 months. Submit seasonal material 6 months in advance. Accepts queries by mail, e-mail. Accepts simultaneous submissions. varies. online at www.bust.com/info/submit.html

Nonfiction Needs book excerpts, expose, general interest, historical, how-to, humor, inspirational, interview, new product, personal experience, photo feature, travel. No dates are currently set, but we usually have a fashion issue, a music issue and a *Men We Love* issue periodically. We do not want poetry; no stories not relating to women. **Buys 60 + mss/yr. mss/year.** Query with published clips. Length: 350-3,000 words. **Pays 0-$250 max. for assigned articles. Pays 0-$250 max. for unsolicited articles.** Sometimes pays expenses of writers on assignment.

Photos Contact: Laurie Henzel, Art Director. State availability Identification of subjects, model releases required. Reviews GIF/JPEG files. Negotiates payment individually. Negotiates individually.

Columns/Departments Contact: Emily Rems, Managing Ed. Books (Reviews of books by women) assigned by us, Music (Reviews of music by/about women), Movies (Reviews of movies by/about women), 300 words; One-Handed-Read (Erotic Fiction for Women), 1,200 words. 6 mss/yr. Query with published clips. **Pays $-$100.**

Fiction Contact: Lisa Butterworth, Assoc. Ed. Needs erotica. We only publish erotic fiction. All other content is nonfiction. **Buys 6 mss/yr. mss/year.** Query with published clips. Length: 1,000-1,500 words. **Pays $0-$100.**

Tips "We are always looking for stories that are surprising, and that 'Bust' stereotypes about women."

$ $ COFFEEHOUSE DIGEST

Repton Media LLC, 5348 Vegas Dr., Suite 272, Las Vegas NV 89108-2347. (702)953-1819. Fax: (775)255-1908. E-mail: editor@coffeehousedigest.com. Website: www.coffeehousedigest.com. **50% freelance written**. Bimonthly magazine covering the coffeehouse lifestyle. "We reach an eclectic group of individuals, so our editorial schedule is varied and most certainly not themed. We want cutting edge articles to interest everyone who may walk into a coffee house, but no article longer than it takes to savor a talle latte. Writers may also self-publish their work with byline on our site for consideration as a staff writer in future print issues." Estab. 2006. Circ. 100,000. Offers 50% kill fee. Buys electronic rights. Makes work-for-hire assignments. Accepts queries by e-mail. Accepts simultaneous submissions. Responds in 3 months to queries and 6 months to mss. Sample copy for SAE with 6x9 envelope and 3 First-Class stamps.

Nonfiction Needs expose, general interest, historical, how-to, humor, interview, new product, opinion, technical, travel. Does not want humdrum pieces. **Buys Buys 36/year mss/year.** 1,000 **Pays 10¢/word**

Photos State availability of or send photos Captions, identification of subjects, model releases required. Reviews GIF/JPEG files. Offers no additional payment for photos accepted with ms with one-time rights.

Columns/Departments Percolations (caffeine-induced revelations); The Grind (working world related, whether employee or employer); Blogophile (blogger's insight, best of online communities); Java Junket (not necessarily coffee-related travel); Wired UP (technology); Bon Appetit (anything food or drink related); Spilling the Beans (self-help), all 450 words. Cafe Culture (profiles of coffee houses around the world and happenings); Steaming Reviews (books, music, movies), both 250 words. Barista's Brews (profiles of baristas, tips and how-to's); Extremes (anything to the extreme, example sports); Overdrive (for motorheads, anything with a motor or transportation related); Frothed (opinion), all 450 words. 120 columns. Query. **Pays 10¢/word.**

Tips "Understand the concept of our magazine. We don't just feature stories about coffee, and we are not a trade publication. Come up with some unique storylines for our departments. Accompanying photos or graphics a big plus to get published in our print publication."

$ $ $ COMMENTARY

165 E. 56th St., New York NY 10022. (212)891-1400. Fax: (212)891-6700. Website: www.commentarymagazine.com. Monthly magazine. Estab. 1945. Byline given. Pays on publication. No kill fee. Publishes ms an average of 2 months after acceptance. Buys all rights. Accepts queries by mail.

Nonfiction Needs essays, opinion. **Buys 4 mss/year.** Query. Length: 2,000-8,000 words. **Pays $400-1,200.**

Tips Unsolicited manuscripts must be accompanied by a self-addressed, stamped envelope.

$ $ COMMON GROUND

Common Ground Publishing, 204-4381 Fraser St., Vancouver BC V5V 4G4 Canada. (604)733-2215. Fax: (604)733-4415. E-mail: editor@commonground.ca. Website: www.commonground.ca. **90% freelance written**. Monthly tabloid covering health, environment, spirit, creativity, and wellness. We serve the cultural creative community. Estab. 1982. Circ. 70,000. Byline given. Pays on publication. No kill fee. Publishes ms an average of 1 month after acceptance. Buys one-time rights, buys second serial (reprint) rights. Editorial lead time 2 months. Submit seasonal material 3 months in advance. Accepts queries by e-mail. Accepts simultaneous submissions. Responds in 6 weeks to queries. Responds in 3 months to mss. Sample copy for $5. Guidelines available online.

Nonfiction Topics include health, personal growth, creativity, spirituality, ecology, or short inspiring stories on environment themes. Needs book excerpts, how-to, inspirational, interview, opinion, personal experience, travel, call to action. Send complete ms. Length: 500-2,500 words. **Pays 10¢/word (Canadian).**

Photos State availability Captions, True required. Buys one time rights.

$ $ $ FIRST THINGS

Institute on Religion & Public Life, 156 Fifth Ave., Suite 400, New York NY 10010. (212)627-1985. Fax: (212)627-2184. E-mail: ft@firstthings.com. Website: www.firstthings.com. **70% freelance written**. social and intellectual commentary. "Intellectual journal published 10 times/year containing social and ethical commentary in a broad sense, religious and ethical perspectives on society, culture, law, medicine, church and state, morality and mores." Estab. 1990. Circ. 32,000. Byline given. Pays on publication. Publishes ms an average of 4 months after acceptance. Buys all rights. Editorial lead time 2 months. Submit seasonal material 5 months in advance. Responds in 3 weeks to mss. Sample copy and writer's guidelines for #10 SASE

Nonfiction Needs essays, opinion. **Buys 60 mss/year.** Send complete ms. Length: 1,500-6,000 words. **Pays $400-1,000.** Sometimes pays expenses of writers on assignment.

Poetry Contact: Joseph Bettum, poetry editor. Needs traditional. **Buys 25-30 poems/year.** Length: 4-40 lines. **Pays $50.**

Tips "We prefer complete manuscripts (hard copy, double-spaced) to queries, but will reply if unsure."

$ $ FRANCE TODAY

The Insider's Perspective on French Travel & Culture, 944 Market St., Suite 706, San Francisco CA 94102. (415)981-9088. Fax: (415)981-9177. E-mail: asenges@francetoday.com. Website: www.francetoday.com. **70% freelance written.** Tabloid published 10 times/year covering contemporary France. *France Today* is a feature publication on contemporary France including sociocultural analysis, business, trends, current events, food, wine, and travel. Estab. 1989. Circ. 12,000. Byline given. Pays on publication. Buys first North American serial rights, buys second serial (reprint) rights. Submit seasonal material 4 months in advance. Accepts queries by mail, e-mail, fax. Accepts previously published material. Responds in 3 months to queries. Sample copy for 10x13 SAE with 5 first-class stamps.

Nonfiction Needs essays, expose, general interest, humor, interview, personal experience, travel, historical. Paris, France on the Move, France On a Budget, Summer Travel, France Adventure No travel pieces about well-known tourist attractions. Query with published clips, or articles sent on spec Length: 500-1,500 words. **Pays 10¢/word.**

Reprints Send typed manuscript with rights for sale noted and information about when and where the material previously appeared. Payment varies

Photos Identification of subjects required. Offers $25/photo. Buys one time rights.

THE FUTURIST

Trends, Forecasts, and Ideas About the Future, The World Future, 7910 Woodmont Ave., Suite 450, Bethesda MD 20814. (301)656-8274. Fax: (301)951-0394. E-mail: info@wfs.org. Website: www.wfs.org. **50% freelance written.** Bimonthly magazine covering technological, social, environmental, economic, and public policy trends related to the future. Articles should have something new & significant to say about the future. For example, an article noting that increasing air pollution may damage human health is something everyone has already heard. Writers should remember that the publication focuses on the future, especially the period 5 to 50 years ahead. We cover a wide range of subject areas—virtually everything that will affect our future or will be affected by the changes the future will bring. Past articles have focused on technology, planning, resources, economics, religion, the arts, values, and health. For quality of writing, make points clearly and in a way that holds the reader's interest. A reader should not have to struggle to guess an author's meaning. Use concrete examples and anecdotes to illustrate your points; keep sentences short, mostly under 25 words. Avoid the jargon of a particular profession; when technical terms are necessary, explain them. Estab. 1966. Circ. 16,000. Byline given. We pay only in contributors copies. No kill fee. Publishes ms an average of 4 months after acceptance. Buys all rights. Editorial lead time 2 months. Submit seasonal material 3 months in advance. Accepts queries by mail, e-mail. Accepts previously published material. Accepts simultaneous submissions. Responds in 4 weeks to queries. Guidelines available.

Nonfiction Needs book excerpts, essays, expose, general interest, how-to, interview, photo feature, technical. We don't want articles by authors who aren't experts on what they're writing about, or who can't find expert opinion on the subjects they're covering. Articles we avoid include: (A) overly technical articles that would be of little interest to the general reader; (B) opinion pieces on current government issues; (C) articles by authors with only a casual knowledge of the subject being discussed. *The Futurist* does not publish fiction or poetry. An exception is occasionally made for scenarios presenting fictionalized people in future situations. These scenarios are kept brief. **Buys 7 mss/yr. mss/year.** Send complete ms.

GOOD MAGAZINE

9155 W. Sunset Blvd., West Hollywood CA 90069. (310)691-1030. Fax: (310)691-1033. E-mail: submissions@goodmagazine.com. Website: www.goodmagazine.com. *GOOD* is the integrated media platform for people who want to live well and do good. Estab. 2006.

- Has themed issues.

$ $ KARMA MAGAZINE

2880 Zanker Rd., Suite 203, San Jose CA 95134. E-mail: editorial@karmamagazine.com. Website: www.karmamagazine.com. **75% freelance written**. Quarterly magazine covering nightlife culture. *Karma* is the premier nightlife resource for those who choose to live it up, while remaining on the periphery of cultural insights. It highlights the lifestyles and interests of dedicated nightlife-revelers through comprehensive reviews of clubs, bars, and restaurants around the world. It also includes thought-provoking celebrity profiles and intelligent editorals of art, culture and news accented by quality, stylized photography. *Karma* engages readers with full access to nightlife culture from around the globe, providing a sure grasp on what makes urbanites tick. Estab. 2003. Circ. 50,000. Byline given. Pays on publication. No kill fee. Publishes ms an average of 3 months after acceptance. Buys first North American serial rights, buys first rights, buys one-time rights, buys electronic rights, buys all rights. Editorial lead time 3 months. Submit seasonal material 3 months in advance. Accepts queries by e-mail. Accepts simultaneous submissions. Responds in 1 month to queries. Sample copy available online.

Nonfiction Needs essays, general interest, how-to, interview, new product, opinion, photo feature, technical, travel. No self-congratulatory or self-obsessed personal experiences about the nightclub scene; no story ideas without original angles. Query with published clips. Length: 100-2,500 words. **Pays 25¢/word.** Sometimes pays expenses of writers on assignment.

Photos State availability Captions, identification of subjects required. Reviews contact sheets, prints, GIF/JPEG/PDF files. Negotiates payment individually. Buys one-time rights or all rights.

Columns/Departments Features (celebrity interviews and profiles/news in the club industry), 1,500-2,500 words; Zen (nightlife and pop culture trends—art/music/film/product reviews), 50-500 words; Locus (hot-spot reviews of clubs/bars/restaurants), 500-1,000 words. Each issue, *Karma* also features an off-the-beaten path international destination.

$ THE LIST

The List, Ltd., 14 High St., Edinburgh EH1 1TE Scotland. (44)(131)550-3050. Fax: (44)(131)557-8500. Website: www.list.co.uk. **25% freelance written**. Biweekly magazine covering Glasgow and Edinburgh arts, events, listings, and lifestyle. *The List* is pitched at educated 18-35 year olds. Estab. 1985. Circ. 15,000. Byline given. Pays on publication. Offers 100% kill fee. Publishes ms an average of 2 weeks after acceptance. Buys first rights, buys second serial (reprint) rights. Editorial lead time 1 month. Submit seasonal material 1 month in advance. Accepts queries by mail, e-mail. Accepts simultaneous submissions.

Nonfiction Needs interview, opinion, travel. Query with published clips. 300 words. **Pays £60-80.** Sometimes pays expenses of writers on assignment.

Columns/Departments Reviews, 50-650 words, **pays £16-35**; Book Reviews, 150 words; **pays £14**. Comic Reviews, 100 words; **pays £10**. TV/Video Reviews, 100 words; **pays £10**. Record Reviews, 100 words; **pays £10**. Query with published clips.

$ $ $ $ MOTHER JONES

Foundation for National Progress, 222 Sutter St., Suite 600, San Francisco CA 94108. (415)321-1700. Website: www.motherjones.com. **80% freelance written**. Bimonthly magazine covering politics, investigative reporting, social issues, and pop culture. *Mother Jones* is a `progressive' magazine—but the core of its editorial well is reporting (i.e., fact-based). No slant required. MotherJones.com is an online sister publication. Estab. 1976. Circ. 235,000. Byline given. Pays on publication. Offers 33% kill fee. Publishes ms an average of 4 months after acceptance. Buys first North American serial rights, buys first rights, buys one-time rights, buys electronic rights. Editorial lead time 4 months. Submit seasonal material 6 months in advance. Responds in 2 months to queries. Sample copy for $6 and 9x12 SAE. Guidelines available online.

Nonfiction Needs expose, interview, photo feature, current issues, policy, investigative reporting. **Buys 70-100 mss/year.** Query with published clips. Length: 2,000-5,000 words. **Pays $1/word.** Sometimes pays expenses of writers on assignment.

Columns/Departments Outfront (short, newsy and/or outrageous and/or humorous items), 200-800 words; Profiles of Hellraisers, 500 words. **Pays $1/word.**

Tips We're looking for hard-hitting, investigative reports exposing government cover-ups, corporate malfeasance, scientific myopia, institutional fraud or hypocrisy; thoughtful, provocative articles which challenge the conventional wisdom (on the right or the left) concerning issues of national importance; and timely, people-oriented stories on issues such as the environment, labor, the media, healthcare, consumer protection, and cultural trends. Send a great, short query and establish your credibility as a reporter. Explain what you plan to cover and how you will proceed with the reporting. The query should convey your approach, tone and style, and should answer the following: What are your specific qualifications to write on this topic? What `ins' do you have with your sources? Can you provide full documentation so that your story can be fact-checked?

$ $ NATURALLY

Nude Living and Recreation, Internaturally, Inc., P.O. Box 317, Newfoundland NJ 07435. (973)697-3552. Fax: (973)697-8313. E-mail: naturally@internaturally.com. Website: www.internaturally.com. **80% freelance written**. Quarterly magazine covering nudism and naturism. Write about nudists and naturists. More people stories than travel. Estab. 1980. Circ. 30,000. Byline given. Pays on publication. No kill fee. Publishes ms an average of 3 months after acceptance. Buys first North American serial rights, buys first rights, buys one-time rights, buys second serial (reprint) rights, buys simultaneous rights, buys electronic rights, buys all rights, buys rights. Makes work-for-hire assignments. Editorial lead time 3-6 months. Submit seasonal material 6 months in advance. Accepts queries by mail, phone. Accepts previously published material. Accepts simultaneous submissions. Responds in 2 weeks to queries. Responds in 3 months to mss. Sample copy available online. Guidelines available online.

Nonfiction Needs book excerpts, essays, expose, general interest, historical, how-to, for first-time visitors to nudist park., humor, inspirational, interview, new product, personal experience, photo feature, travel. Free-beach activities, public nude events. We don't want opinion pieces and religious slants. **Buys 50 mss/year mss/year.** Send complete ms. Length: 500-2,000 words. **Pays $80 per page, text or photos min.; $300 max. for assigned articles.**

Photos Send photos Model releases required. $80 per page min.; $200 front cover max. promotional

Columns/Departments Health (nudism/naturism), Travel (nudism/naturism), Celebrities (nudism/naturism). 8 mss/year Send complete ms.

Fiction Needs humorous. Science fiction. **Buys 6-8 mss/year. mss/year.** Send complete ms. Length: 800-2,000 words. **Pays $-$80 per page.**

Poetry Needs avant-garde, free verse, haiku, light verse, traditional. **Buys 3-6/year poems/year.** Submit maximum 3 poems.

Fillers Needs anecdotes, facts, gags, newsbreaks, short humor. 4

Tips Become a nudist/naturist. Appreciate human beings in their natural state.

$ NEW HAVEN ADVOCATE

News & Arts Weekly, New Mass Media, Inc., 900 Chapel St., Suite 1100, New Haven CT 06510. (203)789-0010. Fax: (203)787-1418. E-mail: abromage@newhavenadvocate.com. Website: www.newhavenadvocate.com. **10% freelance written**. Weekly tabloid. Alternative, investigative, cultural reporting with a strong voice. We like to shake things up. Estab. 1975. Circ. 55,000. Byline given. Pays on publication. No kill fee. Buys one-time rights. Buys on speculation. Editorial lead time 1 month. Submit seasonal material 2 months in advance. Accepts simultaneous submissions. Responds in 1 month to queries.

Nonfiction Needs book excerpts, essays, expose, general interest, humor, interview. **Buys 15-20 mss/year.** Query with published clips. Length: 750-2,000 words. **Pays $50-150.** Sometimes pays expenses of writers on assignment.

Photos State availability Captions, identification of subjects, model releases required. Buys one time rights.

Tips Strong local focus; strong literary voice, controversial, easy-reading, contemporary, etc.

THE NEXT AMERICAN CITY

The Next American City, Inc., 1315 Walnut St., Suite 902, Philadelphia PA 19107. E-mail: matt@americancity.org. Website: www.americancity.org. **80% freelance written**. Quarterly magazine covering urban affairs. Estab. 2002. Circ. 3,000. Byline given. No kill fee. Publishes ms an average of 2-3 months after acceptance. Buys all rights. Editorial lead time 3 months. Submit seasonal material 2-3 months in advance. Accepts queries by mail, e-mail. Accepts previously published material. Accepts simultaneous submissions. Responds in 2 weeks to queries. Sample copy available online. Guidelines available online.

Nonfiction Needs book excerpts, essays, expose, historical, humor, interview, personal experience, photo feature, religious, travel. Does not accept pure opinion pieces. Send complete ms. Length: 500-2,800 words.

Photos State availability of or send photos Captions required. Reviews TIFF files. Offers no additional payment for photos accepted with ms. Buys one time rights.

Columns/Departments Architecture; Book Reviews; Planning; Technology; Business; Education; Environment; Labor; Law; Housing & Last Exit. Query with or without published clips or send complete ms.

Tips We encourage authors to make challenging, even controversial points with implications about the future of American metropolitan areas for more specific information on what kinds of articles we accept. Please review our submission guidelines.

THE OLDIE MAGAZINE

Oldie Publications Ltd, 65 Newman St., London England W1T 3EG United Kingdom. (44)(207)436-8801. Fax:

(44)(207)436-8804. E-mail: jeremylewis@theoldie.co.uk. Website: www.theoldie.co.uk. No kill fee. Accepts queries by mail. Responds in 2-3 weeks to mss. Sample copy by email. Guidelines available online.
Nonfiction Send complete ms. Length: 600-1,000 words.
Photos Send photocopies of photographs, cartoons, and illustrations.
Columns/Departments Modern Life (puzzling aspects of today's world); Anorak (owning up to an obsession); The Old Un's Diary (oldun@theoldie.co.uk).
Fiction Buys up to 3 short stories/year. Send complete ms.

$ POETRY CANADA MAGAZINE

Website: www.poetrycanada.com. **90% freelance written**. "Biannual magazine promoting culture and diversity through art, photography, poetry, and articles. Despite its Canadian root, writers from around the world can submit poetry, book reviews, and articles that will help to advance and inspire the reader to learn more about their craft, society, and environment." Estab. 2003. Circ. 500. Byline given. Pays on publication. No kill fee. Publishes ms an average of 3-12 months after acceptance. Buys one-time rights, buys electronic rights. Editorial lead time 3-12 months. Submit seasonal material 6 months in advance. Accepts queries by e-mail. Responds in 3 days to queries. Sample copy and writer's guidelines online.
Nonfiction Needs general interest, historical, how-to, humor, inspirational, photo feature, art feature. **Buys 60-100 mss/year.** Length: 25-800 words. **Pays $5-100 and a contributor copy**
Columns/Departments Book Reviews; Top Ways To; Dead Poets Society; Poets Practice; Interviews. 12-15 **Pays $5-100.**
Poetry All types and styles; no line limit.

$ $ SHEPHERD EXPRESS

Alternative Publications, Inc., 207 E. Buffalo St., Suite 410, Milwaukee WI 53202. (414)276-2222. Fax: (414)276-3312. E-mail: editor@shepherd-express.com. Website: www.shepherd-express.com. **50% freelance written**. Weekly tabloid covering news and arts with a progressive news edge and a hip entertainment perspective. Estab. 1982. Circ. 58,000. Pays 1 month after publication. No kill fee. Publishes ms an average of 1 month after acceptance. Submit seasonal material 2 months in advance. Accepts simultaneous submissions. Sample copy for $3.
Nonfiction Needs book excerpts, essays, expose, opinion. **Buys 200 mss/year.** Send complete ms. Length: 900-2,500 words. **Pays $35-300 for assigned articles. Pays $10-200 for unsolicited articles.** Sometimes pays expenses of writers on assignment.
Photos State availability Captions, identification of subjects, model releases required. Reviews prints. Negotiates payment individually Buys one time rights.
Columns/Departments Opinions (social trends, politics, from progressive slant), 800-1,200 words; Books Reviewed (new books only: Social trends, environment, politics), 600-1,200 words. 10 Send complete ms.
Tips Include solid analysis with point of view in tight but lively writing. Nothing cute. Do not tell us that something is important, tell us why.

$ $ $ THE SUN

The Sun Publishing Co., 107 N. Roberson St., Chapel Hill NC 27516. Fax: (919)932-3101. Website: www.thesunmagazine.org. **90% freelance written**. Monthly magazine. We are open to all kinds of writing, though we favor work of a personal nature. Estab. 1974. Circ. 72,000. Byline given. Pays on publication. Publishes ms an average of 6-12 months after acceptance. Buys first rights, buys one-time rights. Accepts previously published material. Responds in 3-6 months to queries. Responds in 3-6 months to mss. Sample copy for $5. Guidelines available online.
Nonfiction Needs essays, personal experience, spiritual, interview. **Buys 50 mss/year.** Send complete ms. 7,000 words maximum **Pays $300-3,000.**
Reprints Send photocopy and information about when and where the material previously appeared.
Photos Send photos Model releases required. Reviews b&w prints. Offers $100-500/photo Buys one time rights.
Fiction Contact: Sy Safransky, editor. We avoid stereotypical genre pieces like science fiction, romance, western, and horror. Read an issue before submitting. **Buys 20 mss/year.** Send complete ms. 7,000 words maximum **Pays $300-2,000.**
Poetry Needs free verse. Rarely publishes poems that rhyme. **Buys 24 poems/year.** Submit maximum 6 poems. **Pays $100-500.**
Tips Do not send queries except for interviews.

TWENTY 3 MAGAZINE

1086 Corona #24, Denver CO 80218. Website: www.twenty3magazine.com. **70% freelance written**. Bimonthly magazine that explores the dynamic between culture and arts. We want to see new work that is driven with a sense of purpose. Estab. 2005. Circ. 1,000. Byline sometimes given. Does not pay freelance writers at this time. No kill fee. Publishes ms an average of 2 months after acceptance. Buys one-time rights, buys electronic rights for 2 months rights. Submit seasonal material 2 months in advance. Accepts queries by e-mail. Responds in 1 week to queries. Responds in 1 month to mss. Sample copy and writer's guidelines online.

Nonfiction Needs essays, expose, general interest, historical, humor, interview, opinion, personal experience, photo feature, religious, technical, travel. **Buys 30 mss/year.** Query or send complete ms. Length: 300-1,000 words.

Photos State availability of or send photos Reviews GIF/JPEG files. Does not pay for photos. Buys one time rights.

Columns/Departments Hammer & Malice (liberal rant); The Lab (science-related news); America (conservative rant); Jocktails (sports), all 400-800 words. 30

Fiction Contact: Erin Strauss, fiction editor. Needs adventure, ethnic, experimental, fantasy, historical, horror, humorous, mainstream, mystery, science fiction, suspense, western. We do not want to see fiction that runs the same line as a recent television show or movie. Keep the talent as clean as possible, using explitives only when necessary **Buys 18 mss/year.** Send complete ms. Length: 300-2,500 words.

Poetry Contact: Tony Davino, poetry editor. Needs avant-garde, free verse, haiku, light verse, traditional. Does not want poetry about teenage angst. **Buys 60 poems/year.** Submit maximum 3 poems. Length: 4-100 lines.

Fillers Needs gags, newsbreaks, short humor. 20 Length: 10-50 words.

Tips Write well, proofread, and show us—don't tell us—how great you are.

UTNE READER

12 N. 12th St., Ste. 400, Minneapolis MN 55403. (612)338-5040. E-mail: editor@utne.com. Website: www.utne.com. Accepts queries by mail, e-mail. Guidelines available online.

Reprints Send tearsheet or photocopy with rights for sale noted and information about when and where the material previously appeared.

Tips "State the theme(s) clearly, let the narrative flow, and build the story around strong characters and a vivid sense of place. Give us rounded episodes, logically arranged. We do not publish fiction or poetry."

⊘ VANITY FAIR

Conde Nast Publications, Inc., 1166 Avenue of the Americas, 15th Floor, New York NY 10036. (212)790-5100. Fax: (212)790-1822. Website: www.condenet.com. Monthly magazine. *Vanity Fair* is edited for readers with an interest in contemporary society. Circ. 1,131,144. No kill fee.

- Does not buy freelance material or use freelance writers.

DISABILITIES

$ $ ABILITIES

Canada's Lifestyle Magazine for People with Disabilities, Canadian Abilities Foundation, 401-340 College St., Toronto ON M5T 3A9 Canada. (416)923-1885. Fax: (416)923-9829. E-mail: able@abilities.ca. Website: www.abilities.ca. **50% freelance written**. Quarterly magazine covering disability issues. *Abilities* provides information, inspiration, and opportunity to its readers with articles and resources covering health, travel, sports, products, technology, profiles, employment, recreation, and more. Estab. 1987. Circ. 20,000. Byline given. Pays on publication. Offers 50% kill fee. Publishes ms an average of 3 months after acceptance. Buys first rights. Editorial lead time 3 months. Submit seasonal material 4 months in advance. Accepts queries by mail, e-mail, fax. Responds in 3 months to queries. Sample copy free. Writer's guidelines for #10 SASE, online, or by e-mail.

Nonfiction Needs general interest, how-to, humor, inspirational, interview, new product, personal experience, photo feature, travel. Does not want articles that 'preach to the converted'—this means info that people with disabilities likely already know, such as what it's like to have a disability. **Buys 30-40 mss/year.** Query or send complete ms. Length: 500-2,500 words. **Pays $50-400 (Canadian) for assigned articles. Pays $50-350 (Canadian) for unsolicited articles.**

Reprints Sometimes accepts previously published submissions (if stated as such).

Photos State availability

Columns/Departments The Lighter Side (humor), 700 words; Profile, 1,200 words.

Tips " Strongly prefer e-mail queries. When developing story ideas, keep in mind that our readers are in Canada.

$ $ CAREERS & THE DISABLED

Equal Opportunity Publications, 445 Broad Hollow Rd., Suite 425, Melville NY 11747. (631)421-9421. Fax: (631)421-0359. E-mail: jschneider@eop.com. Website: www.eop.com. **60% freelance written.** Magazine published 6 times/year with Fall, Winter, Spring, Summer, and Expo editions; offering role-model profiles and career guidance articles geared toward disabled college students and professionals, and promotes personal and professional growth. Estab. 1967. Circ. 10,000. Byline given. Pays on publication. Publishes ms an average of 6 months after acceptance. Buys first North American serial rights. Editorial lead time 6 months. Submit seasonal material 6 months in advance. Accepts queries by mail, e-mail, fax, phone. Accepts previously published material. Accepts simultaneous submissions. Responds in 3 weeks to queries. Sample copy for 9x12 SAE with 5 first-class stamps. Guidelines free.

Nonfiction Needs essays, general interest, how-to, interview, new product, opinion, personal experience. **Buys 30 mss/year.** Query. Length: 1,000-2,500 words. **Pays 10¢/word.** Sometimes pays expenses of writers on assignment.

Reprints and information about when and where the material previously appeared.

Photos Captions, identification of subjects, model releases required. Reviews transparencies, prints. Buys one time rights.

Tips Be as targeted as possible. Role-model profiles and specific career guidance strategies that offer advice to disabled college students are most needed.

$ $ DIABETES HEALTH

P.O. Box 395, Woodacre CA 94973-0395. (415)488-1141. Fax: (415)488-1922. Website: www.diabetesinterview.com. **40% freelance written**. Monthly tabloid covering diabetes care. *Diabetes Interview* covers the latest in diabetes care, medications, and patient advocacy. Personal accounts are welcome as well as medical-oriented articles by MDs, RNs, and CDEs (certified diabetes educators). Estab. 1991. Circ. 40,000. Byline given. Pays on publication. No kill fee. Publishes ms an average of 2 months after acceptance. Buys all rights. Editorial lead time 2 months. Submit seasonal material 2 months in advance. Accepts queries by mail, e-mail, fax, phone. Sample copy available online. Guidelines free.

Nonfiction Needs essays, how-to, humor, inspirational, interview, new product, opinion, personal experience. **Buys 25 mss/year.** Send complete ms. Length: 500-1,500 words. **Pays 20¢/word.**

Photos State availability of or send photos Negotiates payment individually.

Tips Be actively involved in the diabetes community or have diabetes. However, writers need not have diabetes to write an article, but it must be diabetes-related.

$ $ DIABETES SELF-MANAGEMENT

R.A. Rapaport Publishing, Inc., 150 W. 22nd St., Suite 800, New York NY 10011-2421. (212)989-0200. Fax: (212)989-4786. E-mail: editor@rapaportpublishing.com. Website: www.diabetesselfmanagement.com. **Contact:** Editor. **20% freelance written**. Bimonthly magazine. "We publish how-to health care articles for motivated, intelligent readers who have diabetes and who are actively involved in their own health care management. All articles must have immediate application to their daily living." Estab. 1983. Circ. 380,000. Byline given. Pays on publication. Offers 20% kill fee. Buys all rights. Submit seasonal material 6 months in advance. Accepts queries by mail, e-mail, fax. Responds in 6 weeks to queries. Sample copy for $4 and 9x12 SAE with 6 first-class stamps or online Guidelines for #10 SASE.

Nonfiction Needs how-to, exercise, nutrition, diabetes self-care, product surveys, technical, reviews of products available, foods sold by brand name, pharmacology, travel, considerations and prep for people with diabetes. No personal experiences, personality profiles, exposes, or research breakthroughs. **Buys 10-12 mss/year.** Query with published clips. Length: 2,000-2,500 words. **Pays $400-700 for assigned articles. Pays $200-700 for unsolicited articles.**

Tips "The rule of thumb for any article we publish is that it must be clear, concise, useful, and instructive, and it must have immediate application to the lives of our readers. If your query is accepted, expect heavy editorial supervision."

$ DIALOGUE

Blindskills, Inc., P.O. Box 5181, Salem OR 97304-0181. E-mail: magazine@blindskills.com. Website: www.blindskills.com. **60% freelance written**. Bimonthly journal covering visually impaired people. Estab. 1962. Circ. 1,100. Byline given. Pays on publication. Publishes ms an average of 6 months after acceptance. Buys first rights. Editorial lead time 3 months. Accepts queries by e-mail. One free sample on request. Available in large print, Braille, 4-track audio cassette, and e-mail. Guidelines available online.

Nonfiction Mostly features material written by visually impaired writers. Needs essays, general interest, historical, how-to, life skills methods used by visually impaired people, humor, interview, personal experience, sports, recreation, hobbies. No controversial, explicit sex, religious, or political topics. **Buys 80 mss/year.** Send complete ms. 200-1,000. **Pays $15-35 for assigned articles. Pays $15-25 for unsolicited articles.**

Columns/Departments All material should be relative to blind and visually impaired readers. Living with Low Vision, 1,000 words; Hear's How (dealing with sight loss), 1,000 words. Technology Answer Book, 800 words. 80 Send complete ms. **Pays $10-25.**

HEARING HEALTH

Deafness Research Foundation, P.O. Box 573, Clarksville AR 72830. E-mail: info@drf.org. Website: www.drf.org/hearing_health. Magazine covering issues and concerns pertaining to hearing and hearing loss. Byline given. Pays with contributor copies. Buys nonexclusive print and online rights. Accepts queries by mail, e-mail.

Accepts previously published material. Accepts simultaneous submissions. Guidelines available online.
Nonfiction Topic areas include access, hearing aid technology, cochlear implants, assistive listening devices, telecommunications, success stories, research involving the auditory system, education, coping, tinnitus, balance disorders, disability rights and advocacy. Send complete ms.
Reprints Please do t submit a previously published article unless permission has been obtained in writing that allows the article's use in *Hearing Health*.
Photos State availability Captions required. Reviews high-resolution digital images.
Columns/Departments Features (800-1,500 words); First-person stories (500-1,500 words); Humor (500-750 words); Viewpoints/Op-Ed (350-500 words). Send complete ms.
Poetry Length: lines.

$ KALEIDOSCOPE

Exploring the Experience of Disability Through Literature and the Fine Arts, Kaleidoscope Press, 701 S. Main St., Akron OH 44311-1019. (330)762-9755. Fax: (330)762-0912. E-mail: mshiplett@udsakron.org. Website: www.udsakron.org/kaleidoscope.htm. **Contact:** Mildred Shiplett. **75% freelance written. Eager to work with new/unpublished writers**. Semiannual magazine. "Subscribers include individuals, agencies, and organizations that assist people with disabilities and many university and public libraries. Appreciates work by established writers as well. Especially interested in work by writers with a disability, but features writers both with and without disabilities. Writers without a disability must limit themselves to our focus, while those with a disability may explore any topic (although we prefer original perspectives about experiences with disability)." Estab. 1979. Circ. 1,000. Byline given. Pays on publication. No kill fee. Buys first rights. Rights return to author upon publication. Accepts queries by mail, fax. Accepts previously published material. Accepts simultaneous submissions. Responds in 3 weeks to queries. Responds in 6 months to mss. Sample copy for $6 prepaid. Double-space your work, number the pages, & include name. Guidelines available online.
Nonfiction Articles related to disability. Needs book excerpts, essays, humor, interview, personal experience, book reviews, articles related to disability. **Buys 8-15 mss/year.** 5,000 words maximum **Pays $25-125, plus 2 copies.**
Reprints Send double-spaced typed manuscript with rights for sale noted and information about when and where the material previously appeared. Reprints permitted with credit given to original publication.
Photos Send photos
Fiction Contact: Fiction Editor. Short stories, novel excerpts. Traditional and experimental styles. Works should explore experiences with disability. Use people-first language. Needs Well-developed plots, engaging characters, and realistic dialogue. We lean toward fiction that emphasizes character and emotions rather than action-oriented narratives. No fiction that is stereotypical, patronizing, sentimental, erotic, or maudlin. No romance, religious or dogmatic fiction; no children's literature. 5,000 words maximum **Pays $10-125, and 2 contributor's copies.**
Poetry Do not get caught up in rhyme scheme. High quality with strong imagery and evocative language. Reviews any style. **Buys 12-20 poems/year.** Submit maximum 5 poems.
Tips "Articles and personal experiences should be creative rather than journalistic and with some depth. Writers should use more than just the simple facts and chronology of an experience with disability. Inquire about future themes of upcoming issues. Sample copy very helpful. Works should not use stereotyping, patronizing, or offending language about disability. We seek fresh imagery and thought-provoking language. Please double-space work, number pages & include full name and address."

$ $ PN

Paralyzed Veterans of America, 2111 E. Highland Ave., Suite 180, Phoenix AZ 85016. Fax: (602)224-0507. E-mail: info@pnnews.com. Website: www.pn-magazine.com. Monthly magazine covering news and information for wheelchair users. Writing must pertain to people with disabilities—specifically mobility impairments. Estab. 1946. Circ. 40,000. Byline given. Pays on publication. Publishes ms an average of 2-4 months after acceptance. Buys one-time rights. Editorial lead time 3 months. Submit seasonal material 3 months in advance. Accepts queries by mail, e-mail, fax. Sample copy free. Guidelines free.
Nonfiction Needs how-to, interview, new product, opinion. **Buys 10-12 mss/year.** Send complete ms. Length: 1,200-2,500 words. **Pays $25-250.**

$ $ SPECIALIVING

P.O. Box 1000, Bloomington IL 61702. (309)661-9277. E-mail: gareeb@aol.com. Website: www.specialiving.com. **90% freelance written**. Quarterly online magazine covering the physically disabled/mobility impaired. Estab. 2001. Circ. 12,000. Byline given. Pays on publication. Buys one-time rights. Editorial lead time 3 months. Submit seasonal material 6 months in advance. Accepts queries by mail, e-mail, fax, phone. Accepts simultaneous submissions. Responds in 3 weeks to queries. Sample copy for $3.
Nonfiction Needs how-to, humor, inspirational, interview, new product, personal experience, technical, travel. **Buys 40 mss/year.** Query. Length: 800 words. **Pays 10¢/word.**

Photos State availability Captions, identification of subjects required. Reviews GIF/JPEG files. Offers $10/photo; $50/cover photo. Buys one time rights.
Columns/Departments Shopping Guide; Items. 30 Query.

$ $ SPORTS N SPOKES

Paralyzed Veterans of America, 2111 E. Highland Ave., Suite 180, Phoenix AZ 85016. Fax: (602)224-0507. E-mail: info@pnnews.com. Website: www.sportsnspokes.com. Bimonthly magazine covering wheelchair sports and recreation. Writing must pertain to wheelchair sports and recreation. Estab. 1974. Circ. 25,000. Byline given. Pays on publication. Publishes ms an average of 2-3 months after acceptance. Buys first rights. Editorial lead time 2-3 months. Submit seasonal material 2-3 months in advance. Accepts queries by mail, e-mail, fax. Sample copy free. Guidelines free.
Nonfiction Needs general interest, interview, new product. **Buys 5-6 mss/year.** Send complete ms. Length: 1,200-2,500 words. **Pays $20-250.**

ENTERTAINMENT

$ CINEASTE

America's Leading Magazine on the Art and Politics of the Cinema, Cineaste Publishers, Inc., 243 Fifth Ave., #706, New York NY 10016. (212)366-5720. E-mail: cineaste@cineaste.com. Website: www.cineaste.com. **30% freelance written**. Quarterly magazine covering motion pictures with an emphasis on social and political perspective on cinema. Estab. 1967. Circ. 11,000. Byline given. Pays on publication. Offers 50% kill fee. Publishes ms an average of 4 months after acceptance. Buys first North American serial rights. Editorial lead time 3 months. Submit seasonal material 4 months in advance. Accepts queries by mail, e-mail, fax. Responds in 1 month to queries. Sample copy for $5. Writer's guidelines on website.
Nonfiction Needs book excerpts, essays, expose, historical, humor, interview, opinion. **Buys 20-30 mss/year.** Query with published clips. Length: 2,000-5,000 words. **Pays $30-100.**
Photos State availability Identification of subjects required. Reviews transparencies, 8x10 prints. Offers no additional payment for photos accepted with ms. Buys one time rights.
Columns/Departments Homevideo (topics of general interest or a related group of films); A Second Look (new interpretation of a film classic or a reevaluation of an unjustly neglected release of more recent vintage); Lost and Found (film that may or may not be released or otherwise seen in the US but which is important enough to be brought to the attention of our readers), all 1,000-1,500 words. Query with published clips. **Pays $50 minimum.**
Tips "We dislike academic jargon, obtuse Marxist terminology, film buff trivia, trendy `buzz' phrases, and show biz references. We do not want our writers to speak of how they have `read' or `decoded' a film, but to view, analyze, and interpret. Warning the reader of problems with specific films is more important to us than artificially `puffing' a film because its producers or politics are agreeable. One article format we encourage is an omnibus review of several current films, preferably those not reviewed in a previous issue. Such an article would focus on films that perhaps share a certain political perspective, subject matter, or generic concerns (i.e., films on suburban life, or urban violence, or revisionist Westerns). Like individual film reviews, these articles should incorporate a very brief synopsis of plots for those who haven't seen the films. The main focus, however, should be on the social issues manifested in each film, and how it may reflect something about the current political/social/esthetic climate."

$ DANCE INTERNATIONAL

Scotiabant Dance Centre, Level 6 677 Davie St., Vancouver BC V6B 2G6 Canada. (604)681-1525. Fax: (604)681-7732. E-mail: danceint@direct.ca. Website: www.danceinternational.org. **100% freelance written**. Quarterly magazine covering dance arts. Articles and reviews on current activities in world dance, with occasional historical essays; reviews of dance films, video, and books. Estab. 1973. Circ. 4,500. Byline given. Pays on publication. Offers 50% kill fee. Publishes ms an average of 3 months after acceptance. Buys one-time rights. Editorial lead time 3 months. Submit seasonal material 6 weeks in advance. Accepts queries by mail, e-mail, fax, phone. Responds in 2 weeks to queries. Responds in 1 month to mss. Sample copy for $7. Guidelines for #10 SASE.
Nonfiction Needs book excerpts, essays, historical, interview, personal experience, photo feature. **Buys 100 mss/year.** Query. Length: 1,200-2,200 words. **Pays $40-150.**
Photos Send photos Identification of subjects required. Reviews prints. Offers no additional payment for photos accepted with ms.
Columns/Departments Dance Bookshelf (recent books reviewed), 700-800 words; Regional Reports (events in each region), 1,200 words. 100 Query. **Pays $80.**
Tips Send résumé and samples of recent writings.

$ $ DIRECTED BY

The Cinema Quarterly, Visionary Media, P.O. Box 1722, Glendora CA 91740-1722. Fax: (626)608-0309. E-mail: visionarycinema@yahoo.com. Website: www.directed-by.com. **10% freelance written**. Quarterly magazine covering the craft of directing a motion picture. Our articles are for readers particularly knowledgeable about the art and history of movies from the director's point of view. Our purpose is to communicate our enthusiasm and interest in the craft of cinema. Estab. 1998. Circ. 42,000. Byline given. Pays on publication. Offers 25% kill fee. Publishes ms an average of 3 months after acceptance. Buys all rights. Editorial lead time 3 months. Submit seasonal material 3 months in advance. Accepts queries by mail, e-mail. Accepts simultaneous submissions. Responds in 6 weeks to queries. Sample copy for $5. Writer's guidelines free or by e-mail

Nonfiction Needs interview, photo feature, on-set reports. No gossip, celebrity-oriented material, or movie reviews. **Buys 5 mss/year.** Query. Length: 500-7,500 words. **Pays $50-750.** Sometimes pays expenses of writers on assignment.

Photos State availability Captions, identification of subjects required. Reviews contact sheets. Offers no additional payment for photos accepted with ms Buys all rights.

Columns/Departments Trends (overview/analysis of specific moviemaking movements/genres/subjects), 1,500-2,000 words; Focus (innovative take on the vision of a contemporary director), 1,500-2,000 words; Appreciation (overview of deceased/foreign director), 1,000-1,500 words; Final Cut (spotlight interview with contemporary director), 3,000 words; Perspectives (interviews/articles about film craftspeople who work with a featured director), 1,500-2,000 words. 5 Query. **Pays $50-750.**

Tips We have been inundated with 'shelf-life' article queries and cannot publish even a small fraction of them. As such, we have restricted our interest in freelancers to writers who have direct access to a notable director of a current film which has not been significantly covered in previous issues of magazines; said director must be willing to grant an exclusive peronal interview to *DIRECTED BY*. This is a tough task for a writer, but if you are a serious freelancer and have access to important filmmakers, we are interested in you.

⊘ DISNEY MAGAZINE

Disney Publishing Worldwide, 244 Main St., Northampton MA 01060-3886. (413)585-0444. Fax: (413)587-9335. E-mail: letters.familyfun@disney.com. Website: www.disneymagazine.com. Quarterly magazine. Circ. 480,000. No kill fee.

- Does not buy freelance material or use freelance writers.

EAST END LIGHTS

The Quarterly Magazine for Elton John Fans, 114040 Creditview Rd., P.O. Box 188, Mississauga ON L5C 3Y8 Canada. (416)760-3426. Fax: (905)566-7369. E-mail: eastendlights@sympatico.ca. Website: www.eastendlights.com. **90% freelance written**. Quarterly magazine covering Elton John. In one way or another, a story must relate to Elton John, his activities or associates (past and present). We appeal to discriminating Elton fans. No gushing fanzine material. No current concert reviews. Estab. 1990. Circ. 1,700. Byline given. Pays 3 weeks after publication. Publishes ms an average of 3 months after acceptance. Buys first rights, buys second serial (reprint) rights. Submit seasonal material 6 months in advance. Accepts queries by mail, e-mail, fax. Accepts previously published material. Responds in 2 months to queries. Sample copy for $5.

Nonfiction Needs book excerpts, essays, expose, general interest, historical, humor, interview. **Buys 20 mss/year.** Send complete ms. Length: 400-1,000 words.

Reprints Send tearsheet or photocopy with rights for sale noted and information about when and where the material previously appeared.

Photos State availability Reviews negatives, 5x7 prints, high-resolution digital files. Buys one-time and all rights.

Columns/Departments Clippings (nonwire references to Elton John in other publications), maximum 200 words. 12 Send complete ms.

Tips Approach us with a well-thought-out story idea. We prefer interviews with Elton-related personalities—past or present. Try to land an interview we haven't done. We are particularly interested in music/memorabilia collecting of Elton material.

⊘ ENTERTAINMENT WEEKLY

Time, Inc., 1675 Broadway, 30th Floor, New York NY 10019. (212)522-5600. Fax: (212)522-0074. Website: www.ew.com. Weekly magazine. Written for readers who want the latest reviews, previews and updates of the entertainment world. Circ. 1,600,000. No kill fee. Editorial lead time 4 weeks.

- Does not buy freelance material or use freelance writers.

$ $ FANGORIA

Horror in Entertainment, Starlog Communications, Inc., 1560 Broadway, 9th Floor, Ste. 900, New York NY 10036. Website: www.fangoria.com. **95% freelance written. Works with a small number of new/unpublished writers each year**. Magazine published 10 times/year covering horror films, TV projects, comics, videos, and literature, and those who create them. We provide an assignment sheet (deadlines, info) to writers, thus authorizing queried stories that we're buying. Estab. 1979. Byline given. Pays on publication. Publishes ms an average of 3 months after acceptance. Buys all rights. Submit seasonal material 4 months in advance. Accepts queries by mail. Responds in 6 weeks to queries. Sample copy for $9 and 10x13 SAE with 4 first-class stamps. Guidelines for #10 SASE.

Nonfiction Book excerpts, interview/profile of movie directors, makeup FX artists, screenwriters, producers, actors, noted horror/thriller novelists and others—with genre credits; special FX and special makeup FX how-it-was-dones (on filmmaking only). Occasional think pieces, opinion pieces, reviews, or sub-theme overviews by industry professionals. Avoids most articles on science-fiction films. **Buys 120 mss/year.** Query with published clips. Length: 1,000-3,500 words. **Pays $100-250.** Sometimes pays expenses of writers on assignment.

Photos State availability Captions, identification of subjects required. Reviews transparencies, prints (b&w, color) electronically.

Columns/Departments Monster Invasion (exclusive, early information about new film productions; also mini-interviews with filmmakers and novelists). Query with published clips. **Pays $45-75.**

Tips Other than recommending that you study one or several copies of *Fangoria*, we can only describe it as a horror film magazine consisting primarily of interviews with technicians and filmmakers in the field. Be sure to stress the interview subjects' words—not your own opinions as much. We're very interested in small, independent filmmakers working outside of Hollywood. These people are usually more accessible to writers, and more cooperative. *Fangoria* is also sort of a de facto bible for youngsters interested in movie makeup careers and for young filmmakers. We are devoted only to reel horrors—the fakery of films, the imagery of the horror fiction of a Stephen King or a Clive Barker—we do not want nor would we ever publish articles on real-life horrors, murders, etc. A writer must enjoy horror films and horror fiction to work for us. If the photos in *Fangoria* disgust you, if the sight of (stage) blood repels you, if you feel `superior' to horror (and its fans), you aren't a writer for us and we certainly aren't the market for you. We love giving new writers their first chance to break into print in a national magazine. We are currently looking for Arizona- and Las Vegas-based correspondents, as well as writers stationed in Spain (especially Barcelona), southern US cities, and Eastern Europe.

FILM COMMENT

Film Society of Lincoln Center, 70 Lincoln Center Plaza, New York NY 10023. (212)875-5610. E-mail: editor@filmlinc.com. Website: www.filmlinc.com. **100% freelance written.** Bimonthly magazine covering film criticism and film history. Estab. 1962. Circ. 30,000. Byline given. Pays on publication. Editorial lead time 6 weeks. Accepts queries by mail, e-mail, fax, phone. Accepts simultaneous submissions.

Nonfiction Needs essays, historical, interview, opinion. **Buys 100 mss/year.** Send complete ms. We respond to queries, but rarely assign a writer we don't know. Length: 800-8,000 words.

Photos State availability No additional payment for photos accepted with ms Buys one time rights.

Tips We are more or less impervious to `hooks,' don't worry a whole lot about `who's hot who's not,' or tying in with next fall's surefire big hit. (We think people should write about films they've seen, not films that haven't even been finished.) We appreciate good writing (writing, not journalism) on subjects in which the writer has some personal investment and about which he or she has something noteworthy to say. Demonstrate ability and inclination to write *FC*-worthy articles. We read and consider everything we get, and we do print unknowns and first-timers. Probably the writer with a shorter submission (1,000-2,000 words) has a better chance than with an epic article that would fill half the issue.

$ $ FLICK MAGAZINE

Decipher, Inc., 259 Granby St., Norfolk VA 23510. (757)623-3600. Fax: (757)623-8368. E-mail: julie.matthews@decipher.com. Website: www.flickmagazine.com. **30-40% freelance written.** Mini-magazine distributed in movie theaters that comes out in conjunction with selected movies covering one specific movie per issue. *Flick*'s mission is to match the passion and personality of fans, taking readers inside Hollywood and increasing their connection to the film they are about to view. Estab. 2005. Circ. 2.5 million. Pays on acceptance. No kill fee. Publishes ms an average of 4 months after acceptance. Makes work-for-hire assignments. Editorial lead time 4-5 months. Accepts queries by mail, e-mail.

Nonfiction Needs essays, humor, interview, opinion, personal experience. Query. Length: 500-1,000 words. **Pays $200-500.** Sometimes pays expenses of writers on assignment.

Photos Contact: Art Director (jeff.hellerman@decipher.com).

Columns/Departments Pays $200-500.

Fillers Needs gags, short humor. 5-10 **Pays $200-500.**

Tips Writing for *Flick* is about research, story angles, subject knowledge, and access to movie cast and crew.

⊘ GLOBE

American Media, Inc., 1000 American Media Way, Boca Raton FL 33464. (561)997-7733. Fax: (561)989-1004. E-mail: newstips@globefl.com. Website: www.globemagazine.com. Weekly tabloid. *Globe* is edited for an audience interested in a wide range of human-interest stories, with particular emphasis on celebrities. Circ.

631,705. No kill fee.

- Does not buy freelance material or use freelance writers.

INTERVIEW

Brant Publications, Inc., 575 Broadway, 5th Floor, New York NY 10012. (212)941-2900. Fax: (212)941-2934. E-mail: brantinter@aol.com. Website: www.interviewmagazine.com. Monthly magazine. Explores the inside world of music, film, fashion, art, TV, photography, sports, contemporary life and politics through celebrity interviews. Circ. 200,000. No kill fee. Editorial lead time 2 months.

$ IN TOUCH WEEKLY

Bauer Magazine Limited Partnership, 270 Sylvan Ave., Englewood Cliffs NJ 07632. (201)569-6699. E-mail: contactintouch@intouchweekly.com. Website: www.intouchweekly.com. **10% freelance written**. Weekly magazine covering celebrity news and entertainment. Estab. 2002. Circ. 1,300,000. No byline given. Pays on publication. Buys all rights. Editorial lead time 1 week. Accepts queries by mail, e-mail, phone.

Nonfiction Needs interview, gossip. **Buys 1,300 mss/year.** Query. Length: 100-1,000 words. **Pays $50.**

$ $ MOVIEMAKER MAGAZINE

MovieMaker Publishing Co., 121 Fulton St., Fifth Floor, New York NY 10038. (212)766-4100. Fax: (212)766-4102. E-mail: submissions@moviemaker.com. Website: www.moviemaker.com. **95% freelance written**. Bimonthly magazine covering film, independent cinema, and Hollywood. *MovieMaker*'s editorial is a progressive mix of in-depth interviews and criticism, combined with practical techniques and advice on financing, distribution, and production strategies. Behind-the-scenes discussions with Hollywood's top moviemakers, as well as independents from around the globe, are routinely found in *MovieMaker*'s pages. Estab. 1993. Circ. 55,000. Byline given. Pays within 1 month of publication. Offers kill fee. Offers variable kill fee. Publishes ms an average of 2 months after acceptance. Buys all rights. Editorial lead time 3 months. Submit seasonal material 4 months in advance. Accepts queries by mail, e-mail, fax. Accepts simultaneous submissions. Responds in 2-4 weeks to queries. Responds in 2-4 weeks to mss. Sample copy available online. Guidelines by email.

Nonfiction Needs expose, general interest, historical, how-to, interview, new product, technical. **Buys 20 mss/year.** Query with published clips. Length: 800-3,000 words. **Pays $75-500 for assigned articles.**

Photos State availability Identification of subjects required. Payment varies for photos accepted with ms. Rights purchased negotiable.

Columns/Departments Documentary; Home Cinema (home video/DVD reviews); How They Did It (first-person filmmaking experiences); Festival Beat (film festival reviews); World Cinema (current state of cinema from a particular country). Query with published clips. **Pays $75-300.**

Tips The best way to begin working with *MovieMaker* is to send a list of 'pitches' along with your résumé and clips. As we receive a number of résumés each week, we want to get an early sense of not just your style of writing, but the kinds of subjects that interest you most as they relate to film. E-mail is the preferred method of correspondence, and please allow 1 month before following up on a query or résumé. All queries must be submitted in writing. No phone calls, please.

$ $ $ OK! MAGAZINE

Northern & Shell North America Limited, 475 Fifth Ave., New York NY 10017. E-mail: editor@ok-magazine.com. Website: www.ok-magazine.com. **10% freelance written**. Weekly magazine covering entertainment news. We are a celebrity friendly magazine. We strive not to show celebrities in a negative light. We consider ourselves a cross between *People* and *In Style*. Estab. 2005. Circ. 1,000,000. Byline sometimes given. Pays after publication. Publishes ms an average of 1 month after acceptance. Buys first North American serial rights, buys first rights, buys one-time rights. Editorial lead time 2 weeks. Accepts queries by mail, e-mail, fax.

Nonfiction Needs interview, photo feature. **Buys 50 mss/year.** Query with published clips. Length: 500-2,000 words. **Pays $100-1,000.**

Photos Contact: Contact Maria Collazo, photography director.

⊘ PREMIERE MAGAZINE

Hachette Filipacchi Magazines, 1633 Broadway, 41st Floor, New York NY 10019. (212)767-6000. Fax: (212)767-5450. Website: www.premiere.com. Magazine published 10 times/year.

- Does not buy freelance material or use freelance writers.

$ $ RUE MORGUE

Horror in Culture & Entertainment, Marrs Media, Inc., 2926 Dundas St. W., Toronto ON M6P 1Y8 Canada. E-mail: jovanka@rue-morgue.com. Website: www.rue-morgue.com. **50% freelance written**. Monthly magazine covering horror entertainment. "A knowledge of horror entertainment (films, books, games, toys, etc.)." Estab. 1997. Byline given. Pays on publication. No kill fee. Publishes ms an average of 2-4 months after acceptance. Buys all rights. Editorial lead time 2 months. Submit seasonal material 4 months in advance. Accepts queries by e-mail. Responds in 6 weeks to queries. Responds in 2 months to mss. Guidelines by email.

Nonfiction Needs essays, expose, historical, interview, new product, travel. No fiction. Reviews done by staff writers. **Buys 11/yr mss/year.** Query with published clips or send complete ms. Length: 500-3,500 words. **Pays $95-665.**

Columns/Departments Classic Cut (historical essays on classic horror films, books, games, comic books, music), 500-700 words. 1-2 Query with published clips. **Pays $86**

Tips "The editors are most responsive to special interest articles and analytical essays on cultural/historical topics relating to the horror genre—published examples: Leon Theremin, Soren Kierkegaard, Horror in Fine Art, Murderbilia, The History of the Werewolf."

$ $ $ $ SOUND & VISION

Hachette Filipacchi Media U.S., Inc., 1633 Broadway, New York NY 10019. (212)767-6000. Fax: (212)767-5615. E-mail: soundandvision@hfmus.com. Website: www.soundandvisionmag.com. **Contact:** Mike Mettler, editor-in-chief. **40% freelance written**. Published 8 times/year. "Provides readers with authoritative information on the home entertainment technologies and products that will impact their lives." Estab. 1958. Circ. 400,000. Byline given. Pays on acceptance. Publishes ms an average of 4 months after acceptance. Buys first North American serial rights, buys electronic rights. Accepts queries by mail, e-mail, fax. Sample copy for sae with 9x12 envelope and 11 First-Class stamps.

Nonfiction "Home theater, audio, video and multimedia equipment plus movie, music, and video game reviews, how-to-buy and how-to-use A/V gear, interview/profile." **Buys 25 mss/year.** Query with published clips. Length: 1,500-3,000 words. **Pays $1,000-1,500.**

Tips "Send proposals or outlines, rather than complete articles, along with published clips to establish writing ability. Publisher assumes no responsibility for return or safety of unsolicited art, photos, or manuscripts."

⊘ STAR MAGAZINE

American Media, Inc., 1000 American Media Way, Boca Raton FL 33464-1000. E-mail: letters@starmagazine.com. Website: www.starmagazine.com.

- Query before submitting.

⊘ TV GUIDE

Gemstar-TV Guide Ineternational, Inc., 1211 Avenue of the Americas, 4th Floor, New York NY 10036. (212)852-7500. Fax: (212)852-7470. Website: www.tvguide.com. Weekly magazine. Focuses on all aspects of network, cable, and pay television programming and how it affects and reflects audiences. Circ. 9,097,762. No kill fee.

- Does not buy freelance material or use freelance writers.

⊘ VARIETY

Reed Business Information, 5700 Wilshire Blvd., Suite 120, Los Angeles CA 90036. (323)965-4476. Fax: (323)857-0494. E-mail: news@reedbusiness.com. Website: www.variety.com. Weekly magazine. Circ. 34,000. No kill fee.

- Does not buy freelance material or use freelance writers.

XXL MAGAZINE

Harris Publications, 1115 Broadway, New York NY 10010. Website: www.xxlmag.com. **50% freelance written**. Monthly magazine. *XXL* is hip-hop on a higher level, an upscale urban lifestyle magazine. Estab. 1997. Circ. 350,000. Byline given. Pays on publication. Buys all rights. Editorial lead time 2 months. Submit seasonal material 3 months in advance. Accepts queries by mail.

Nonfiction Needs interview, music, entertainment, luxury materialism. Query with published clips. Length: 200-5,000 words.

Photos State availability Captions, model releases required. Reviews contact sheets, transparencies, prints.

Tips Please send clips, query, and cover letter by mail.

ETHNIC & MINORITY

$ $ $ $ AARP SEGUNDA JUVENTUD

AARP, 601 E St. NW, Washington DC 20049. E-mail: segundajuventud@aarp.org. Website: www.aarpsegundajuventud.org. **75% freelance written**. Bimonthly magazine geared toward 50+ Hispanics. With fresh and relevant editorial content and a mission of inclusiveness and empowerment, *AARP Segunda Juventud* serves more than 800,000 Hispanic AARP members and their families in all 50 states, the District of Columbia, Puerto Rico, and the US Virgin Islands. Estab. 2002. Circ. 800,000. Byline given. Pays on acceptance. Offers 33.33% kill fee. Publishes ms an average of 4 months after acceptance. Buys exclusive first worldwide rights. Editorial lead time 2-12 months. Submit seasonal material 4-12 months in advance. Accepts queries by mail, e-mail. Accepts simultaneous submissions. Responds in 4 months to queries. Responds in 4 months to mss. Sample copy available online.

Nonfiction Must have a Hispanic angle targeting the 50+ audience. Needs general interest, interview, new product, travel, reviews (book, film, music). **Buys 36 mss/year.** Query with published clips. Length: 200-1,500 words. **Pays $1-2/word.** Sometimes pays expenses of writers on assignment.
Photos Send photos Captions, identification of subjects, model releases required. Reviews contact sheets, negatives, transparencies, prints, GIF/JPEG files. Negotiates payment individually.
Columns/Departments Health; Finance; Travel; Celebrity profile; Encore (Hispanic 50+ individuals reinventing themselves). 24 Query with published clips. **Pays $1-2/word.**
Fillers Needs facts. 6 Length: 200-250 words. **Pays $1-2/word.**
Tips Look closely at the last 6 issues to get familiar with the magazine topics. Don't submit queries for topics already covered. Write lively but succinct queries that demonstrate you have done your research into our magazine and our demographic, the 50+ Hispanic.

AFRICAN VOICES

African Voices Communications, Inc., 270 W. 96th St., New York NY 10025. (212)865-2982. Fax: (212)316-3335. E-mail: africanvoices@aol.com. Website: www.africanvoices.com. **85% freelance written**. Quarterly magazine covering art, film, culture. *African Voices* is dedicated to highlighting the art, literature, and history of people of color. Estab. 1992. Circ. 20,000. Byline given. Pays on publication. No kill fee. Publishes ms an average of 3-6 months after acceptance. Buys first North American serial rights. Editorial lead time 3 months. Submit seasonal material 3 months in advance. Accepts queries by mail. Accepts previously published material. Accepts simultaneous submissions. Responds in 3 months to queries. Sample copy for $5 or online. Guidelines available online.
Nonfiction Needs book excerpts, essays, historical, humor, inspirational, interview, photo feature, travel. Query with published clips. Length: 500-2,500 words. **Pays in contributor copies.**
Photos State availability Pays in contributor copies Buys one time rights.
Fiction Contact: Kim Horne, fiction editor. Needs adventure, cond novels, erotica, ethnic, experimental, fantasy, historical, general, horror, humorous, mainstream, mystery, novel concepts, religious, romance, science fiction, serialized, slice-of-life vignettes, suspense, African-American. **Buys 4 mss/year.** Send complete ms. Length: 500-2,500 words. **Pays in contributor copies.**
Poetry Contact: Layding Kaliba, managing editor/poetry editor. Needs avant-garde, free verse, haiku, traditional. **Buys 10 poems/year.** Submit maximum 5 poems. Length: 5-100 lines. **Pays in contributor copies.**

$ $ AFRIQUE NEWSMAGAZINE

Afrique Publishing, Inc., 3525 W. Peterson Ave., Suite 200, Chicago IL 60659. (773)463-7200. Fax: (773)463-7264. E-mail: cli@afriquenewsmagazine.com. Website: www.afriquenewsmagazine.com. **50% freelance written**. Monthly tabloid covering African diaspora. The mission of our publication is to connect and empower people of African descent (Africans, African Americans, West Indians, etc.). Writer must be knowledgeable or willing to learn about these communities. Estab. 1991. Circ. 75,000. Byline given. Pays on publication. Publishes ms an average of 1 month after acceptance. Buys all rights. Editorial lead time 2 months. Submit seasonal material 2 months in advance. Accepts queries by mail, e-mail, fax, phone. Accepts previously published material. Accepts simultaneous submissions. Sample copy available online. Guidelines by email.
Nonfiction Needs book excerpts, essays, expose, general interest, historical, how-to, humor, inspirational, interview, new product, opinion, personal experience, photo feature, religious, technical, travel. **Buys 10 mss/year.** Send complete ms. Length: 200+ words. **Pays 10-30¢/word for assigned articles. Pays 10-20¢/word for unsolicited articles.** Sometimes pays expenses of writers on assignment.
Photos State availability Identification of subjects required. Reviews GIF/JPEG files. Offers no additional payment for photos accepted with ms. Buys all rights.
Columns/Departments West/Central Africa; The Americas; East/Southern Africa; Business, all 500 words. 10 Query. **Pays 10-30¢/word.**
Fiction Needs ethnic, humorous, mainstream. **Buys 10 mss/year.** Query.
Poetry Needs avant-garde, free verse, haiku, light verse, traditional. **Buys 10 poems/year.**
Fillers Needs facts, gags, newsbreaks.

$ AIM MAGAZINE

Aim Publication Association, Milton WA 98354. (253)815-9030. E-mail: editor@aimmagazine.org. Website: aimmagazine.org. **75% freelance written. Works with a small number of new/unpublished writers each year.** Quarterly magazine on social betterment that promotes racial harmony and peace for high school, college, and general audience. Publishes material to purge racism from the human bloodstream through the written word. Estab. 1975. Circ. 10,000. Byline given. Pays on publication. Offers 60% kill fee. Publishes ms an average of 3 months after acceptance. Buys first rights, buys one-time rights. Submit seasonal material 6 months in advance. Accepts queries by mail, e-mail. Accepts simultaneous submissions. Responds in 2 months to queries. Responds in 1 month to mss. Sample copy and writer's guidelines for $4 and 9x12 SAE with $1.70 postage or online

Nonfiction Needs expose, education, general interest, social significance, historical, Black or Indian, how-to, create a more equitable society, interview, one who is making social contributions to community, book reviews, reviews of plays. No religious material. **Buys 16 mss/year.** Send complete ms. Length: 500-800 words. **Pays $25-35.**
Photos Captions, identification of subjects required. Reviews b&w prints.
Fiction Contact: Ruth Apilado, associate editor. Fiction that teaches the brotherhood of man. Needs ethnic, historical, mainstream, suspense. Open. No religious mss. **Buys 20 mss/year.** Send complete ms. Length: 1,000-1,500 words. **Pays $25-35.**
Poetry Needs avant-garde, free verse, light verse. No preachy poetry. **Buys 20 poems/year.** Submit maximum 5 poems. Length: 15-30 lines. **Pays $3-5.**
Fillers Needs anecdotes, newsbreaks, short humor. 30 Length: 50-100 words. **Pays $5.**
Tips Interview anyone of any age who unselfishly is making an unusual contribution to the lives of less fortunate individuals. Include photo and background of person. We look at the nations of the world as part of one family. Short stories and historical pieces about Blacks and Indians are the areas most open to freelancers. Subject matter of submission is of paramount concern for us rather than writing style. Articles and stories showing the similarity in the lives of people with different racial backgrounds are desired.

$ $ AMBASSADOR MAGAZINE

National Italian American Foundation, 1860 19th St. NW, Washington DC 20009. (202)387-0600. Fax: (202)387-0800. E-mail: monica@niaf.org. Website: www.niaf.org. **50% freelance written**. Quarterly magazine for Italian-Americans covering Italian-American history and culture. We publish nonfiction articles on little-known events in Italian-American history and articles on Italian-American culture, traditions, and personalities living and dead. Estab. 1989. Circ. 25,000. Byline given. Pays on approval of final draft. Offers $50 kill fee. Buys second serial (reprint) rights. Editorial lead time 3 months. Accepts queries by mail, e-mail, fax. Accepts previously published material. Accepts simultaneous submissions. Responds in 2 months to queries. Sample copy and writer's guidelines free
Nonfiction Needs historical, interview, photo feature. **Buys 12 mss/year.** Send complete ms. Length: 800-1,500 words. **Pays $250 for photos and article.**
Photos Send photos Captions, identification of subjects required. Reviews contact sheets, prints. Offers no additional payment for photos accepted with ms. Buys one time rights.
Tips Good photos, clear prose, and a good storytelling ability are all prerequisites.

$ $ $ B'NAI B'RITH MAGAZINE

2020 K St. NW, Washington DC 20006. (202)857-2701. E-mail: bbm@bnaibrith.org. Website: bnaibrith.org. **90% freelance written**. Quarterly magazine specializing in social, political, historical, religious, cultural, 'lifestyle,' and service articles relating chiefly to the Jewish communities of North America and Israel. Write for the American Jewish audience, i.e., write about topics from a Jewish perspective, highlighting creativity and innovation in Jewish life. Estab. 1886. Circ. 110,000. Byline given. Pays on publication. Offers 25% kill fee. Publishes ms an average of 6 months after acceptance. Buys first rights. Editorial lead time 3 months. Submit seasonal material 5 months in advance. Accepts queries by mail, e-mail, fax. Accepts simultaneous submissions. Responds in 1 month to queries. Responds in 6 weeks to mss. Sample copy for $2. Writer's guidelines for #10 SASE or by e-mail.
Nonfiction General interest pieces of relevance to the Jewish community of US and abroad. Needs interview, photo feature, religious, travel. No Holocaust memoirs, first-person essays/memoirs, fiction, or poetry. **Buys 14-20 mss/year.** Query with published clips. Length: 1,000-2,500 words. **Pays $300-800 for assigned articles. Pays $300-700 for unsolicited articles.** Sometimes pays expenses of writers on assignment.
Photos Rarely assigned. Buys one time rights.
Columns/Departments Up Front (book, CD reviews, small/short items with Jewish interest), 150-200 words. 3 Query. **Pays $50.**
Tips Know what's going on in the Jewish world. Look at other Jewish publications also. Writers should submit clips with their queries. Read our guidelines carefully and present a good idea expressed well. Proofread your query letter.

$ CELTICLIFE MAGAZINE

Clansman Publishing, Ltd., 1454 Dresden Row, Suite 204, Halifax NS B3J 3T5 Canada. (902)425-5617. Fax: (902)835-0080. E-mail: editorial@celticlife.ca. Website: www.celticlife.ca. **95% freelance written**. Quarterly magazine covering culture of North Americans of Celtic descent. "The magazine chronicles the stories of Celtic people who have settled in North America, with a focus on the stories of those who are not mentioned in history books. We also feature Gaelic language articles, history of Celtic people, traditions, music, and folklore. We profile Celtic musicians and include reviews of Celtic books, music, and videos." Estab. 1987. Circ. 5,000 (per issue). Byline given. Pays 2 months after publication. No kill fee. Publishes ms an average of 2 months after acceptance. Buys all rights with electronic negotiable. rights. Editorial lead time 2 months.

Submit seasonal material 3 months in advance. Accepts queries by mail, e-mail, fax, phone. Accepts previously published material. Responds in 1 week to queries. Responds in 1 month to mss Sample copy available online Guidelines available online

Nonfiction Needs essays, general interest, historical, interview, opinion, personal experience, travel, Gaelic language, Celtic music reviews, profiles of Celtic musicians, Celtic history, traditions, and folklore. No fiction, poetry, historical stories already well publicized. **Buys 100 mss/year.** Query or send complete ms Length: 800-2,500 words. **Pays $50-75 (Canadian). All writers receive a complimentary subscription.**

Photos State availability Captions, identification of subjects, model releases required. Reviews 35mm transparencies, 5x7 prints, JPEG files (200 dpi). We do not pay for photographs.

Columns/Departments Query. **Pays $50-75 (Canadian)**

Tips "The only way to get my attention is to submit a query by e-mail. We are so short staffed that we do not have much time to start a correspondence by regular post."

$ FILIPINAS

A Magazine for All Filipinos, Filipinas Publishing, Inc., GBM Bldg., 1580 Bryant St., Daly City CA 94015. (650)985-2530. Website: www.filipinasmag.com. Monthly magazine focused on Filipino-American affairs. *Filipinas* answers the lack of mainstream media coverage of Filipinos in America. It targets both Filipino immigrants and American-born Filipinos, gives in-depth coverage of political, social, and cultural events in the Philippines and in the Filipino-American community. Features role models, history, travel, food and leisure, issues, and controversies. Estab. 1992. Circ. 40,000. Byline given. Pays on publication. Offers $10 kill fee. Publishes ms an average of 5 months after acceptance. Buys first rights, buys all rights. Editorial lead time 2 months. Submit seasonal material 4 months in advance. Accepts queries by mail, e-mail, fax. Responds in 3 weeks to queries. Responds in 5 months to mss. Writer's guidelines for 9 ½x4 SASE or on website.

- *Unsolicited mss will not be paid.*

Nonfiction Interested in seeing more issue-oriented pieces, unusual topics regarding Filipino-Americans, and stories from the Midwest and other parts of the country other than the coasts. Needs expose, general interest, historical, inspirational, interview, opinion, personal experience, travel. No academic papers. **Buys 80-100 mss/year.** Query with published clips. Length: 800-1,500 words. **Pays $50-75.**

Photos State availability Captions, identification of subjects required. Reviews 2¼x2¼ and 4 x 5 transparencies. Offers $15-25/photo.

Columns/Departments Cultural Currents (Filipino traditions and beliefs), 1,000 words; New Voices (first-person essays by Filipino Americans ages 10-25), 800 words; First Person (open to all Filipinos), 800 words. Query with published clips. **Pays $50-75.**

$ $ GERMAN LIFE

Zeitgeist Publishing, Inc., 1068 National Hwy., LaVale MD 21502. (301)729-6190. Fax: (301)729-1720. E-mail: mslider@germanlife.com. Website: www.germanlife.com. **50% freelance written**. Bimonthly magazine covering German-speaking Europe. *German Life* is for all interested in the diversity of German-speaking culture—past and present—and in the various ways that the US (and North America in general) has been shaped by its German immigrants. The magazine is dedicated to solid reporting on cultural, historical, social, and political events. Estab. 1994. Circ. 40,000. Byline given. Pays on publication. Buys first North American serial rights. Editorial lead time 4 months. Submit seasonal material 6 months in advance. Accepts queries by mail, e-mail. Responds in 2 months to queries. Responds in 3 months to mss. Sample copy for $4.95 and SAE with 4 first-class stamps. Guidelines available online.

Nonfiction Needs general interest, historical, interview, photo feature, travel. Oktoberfest-related (October); Seasonal Relative to Germany, Switzerland, or Austria (December); Travel to German-speaking Europe (April). **Buys 50 mss/year.** Query with published clips. Length: 800-1,500 words. **Pays $200-500 for assigned articles. Pays $200-350 for unsolicited articles.**

Photos State availability Identification of subjects required. Reviews color transparencies, 5x7 color or b&w prints. Offers no additional payment for photos accepted with ms. Buys one time rights.

Columns/Departments German-Americana (regards specific German-American communities, organizations, and/or events past or present), 1,200 words; Profile (portrays prominent Germans, Americans, or German-Americans), 1,000 words; At Home (cuisine, etc. relating to German-speaking Europe), 800 words; Library (reviews of books, videos, CDs, etc.), 300 words. 30 Query with published clips. **Pays $50-150.**

Fillers Needs facts, newsbreaks. Length: 100-300 words. **Pays $50-150.**

Tips The best queries include several informative proposals. Writers should avoid overemphasizing autobiographical experiences/stories.

$ HERITAGE FLORIDA JEWISH NEWS

207 O'Brien Rd., Suite 101, Fern Park FL 32730. (407)834-8787. E-mail: news@orlandoheritage.com. Website: www.heritagefl.com. **20% freelance written**. Weekly tabloid on Jewish subjects of local, national and international scope, except for special issues. Covers news of local, national and international scope of interest

to Jewish readers and not likely to be found in other publications. Estab. 1976. Circ. 3,500. Byline given. Pays on publication. No kill fee. Buys first North American serial rights, buys first rights, buys one-time rights, buys second serial (reprint) rights, buys simultaneous rights. Submit seasonal material 3 months in advance. Accepts queries by e-mail. Accepts previously published material. Responds in 1 month to queries. Sample copy for $1 and 9 x 12 SASE.
Nonfiction Especially needs articles for these annual issues: Rosh Hashanah, Financial, Chanukah, Celebration (wedding and bar mitzvah), Passover, Health and Fitness, House and Home, Back to School, Travel and Savvy Seniors. No fiction, poems, first-person experiences. Needs general interest, interview, opinion, photo feature, religious, travel. **Buys 50 mss/year.** Send query only. Length: 500-1,000 words. **Pays 75¢/column inch.**
Reprints Send typed manuscript with rights for sale noted.
Photos State availability Captions, identification of subjects required. Reviews 8x10 prints. Offers $5/photo. Buys one time rights.

$ HORIZONS - THE JEWISH FAMILY MONTHLY

Targum Press, 22700 W. Eleven Mile Rd., Southfield MI 48034. E-mail: horizons@targum.com. Website: www.targum.com. **100% freelance written**. Monthly magazine covering the Orthodox Jewish family. "We include fiction and nonfiction, memoirs, essays, historical, and informational articles—all of interest to the Orthodox Jew." Estab. 1994. Circ. 7,000. Byline given. Pays 4-6 weeks after publication. No kill fee. Publishes ms an average of 6 months after acceptance. Buys one-time rights. Editorial lead time 6 months. Submit seasonal material 8 months in advance. Accepts queries by mail, e-mail, fax. Responds in 1 week to queries. Responds in 2 months to mss. Writer's guidelines available.
Nonfiction Needs essays, historical, humor, inspirational, interview, opinion, personal experience, photo feature, travel. **Buys 150 mss/year.** Send complete ms. Length: 350-3,000 words. **Pays 8¢/word**
Photos State availability Offers no additional payment for photos accepted with ms. Buys one time rights.
Fiction Contact: Suri Brand, chief ed. Needs historical, humorous, mainstream, slice-of-life vignettes. Nothing not suitable to Orthodox Jewish values. **Buys 10-15 mss/year.** Send complete ms. Length: 300-3,000 words. **Pays $20-100.**
Poetry Needs free verse, haiku, light verse, traditional. **Buys 5-10 poems/year.** Submit maximum 3 poems. Length: 3-20 lines. **Pays $15.**
Fillers Needs anecdotes, short humor. 20. Length: 50-120 words. **Pays $15**
Tips "*Horizons* publishes for the Orthodox Jewish market and therefore only accepts articles that are suitable for our readership. We do not accept submissions dealing with political issues or Jewish legal issues. The tone is light and friendly and we therefore do not accept submissions that are of a scholarly nature. Our writers must be very familiar with our market."

$ INTERNATIONAL EXAMINER

622 S. Washington, Seattle WA 98104. (206)624-3925. Fax: (206)624-3046. E-mail: editor@iexaminer.org. Website: www.iexaminer.org. **75% freelance written**. Biweekly journal of Asian-American news, politics, and arts. We write about Asian-American issues and things of interest to Asian-Americans. We do not want stuff about Asian things (stories on your trip to China, Japanese Tea Ceremony, etc. will be rejected). Yes, we are in English. Estab. 1974. Circ. 12,000. Pays on publication. No kill fee. Publishes ms an average of 1 month after acceptance. Buys one-time rights. Editorial lead time 1 month. Submit seasonal material 2 months in advance. Accepts simultaneous submissions. Guidelines for #10 SASE.
Nonfiction Needs essays, expose, general interest, historical, humor, interview, opinion, personal experience, photo feature. **Buys 100 mss/year.** Query by mail, fax, or e-mail with published clips 750-5,000 words depending on subject **Pays $25-100.** Sometimes pays expenses of writers on assignment.
Reprints Accepts previously published submissions (as long as t published in same area). Send typed ms with rights for sale noted and information about when and where the material previously appeared. Payment negotiable
Photos State availability Captions, identification of subjects required. Reviews contact sheets. Negotiates payment individually Buys one time rights.
Fiction Asian-American authored fiction by or about Asian-Americans. Needs novel concepts. **Buys 1-2 mss/year.** Query.
Tips Write decent, suitable material on a subject of interest to the Asian-American community. All submissions are reviewed; all good ones are contacted. It helps to call and run an idea by the editor before or after sending submissions.

$ $ ITALIAN AMERICA

Official Publication of the Order Sons of Italy in America, 219 E St. NE, Washington DC 20002. (202)547-2900. E-mail: ddesanctis@osia.org. Website: www.osia.org. **20% freelance written**. Quarterly magazine. *Italian America* provides timely information about OSIA, while reporting on individuals, institutions, issues, and events of current or historical significance in the Italian-American community. Estab. 1996. Circ. 65,000. Byline given. Pays on publication. Offers 50% kill fee. Publishes ms an average of 3 months after acceptance. Buys worldwide nonexclusive rights. Editorial lead time 3 months. Accepts queries by mail, e-mail, fax. Accepts simultaneous submissions. Sample copy free. Guidelines available online.

Nonfiction Needs historical, little known historical facts that must relate to Italian Americans, interview, opinion, current events. **Buys 8 mss/year.** Query with published clips. Length: 750-1,000 words. **Pays $50-250.**

Tips We pay particular attention to the quality of graphics that accompany the stories. We are interested in little known facts about historical/cultural Italian America.

$ $ JEWISH ACTION

Union of Orthodox Jewish Congregations of America, 11 Broadway, New York NY 10004. (212)613-8146. Fax: (212)613-0646. E-mail: ja@ou.org. Website: www.ou.org/publications/ja/. **80% freelance written.** Quarterly magazine covering a vibrant approach to Jewish issues, Orthodox lifestyle, and values. Circ. 40,000. Byline given. Pays 2 months after publication. Submit seasonal material 4 months in advance. Responds in 3 months to queries. Sample copy available online. Guidelines for #10 SASE or by e-mail.

- Prefers queries by e-mail. Mail and fax OK.

Nonfiction Current Jewish issues, history, biography, art, inspirational, humor, music, book reviews. We are not looking for Holocaust accounts. We welcome essays about responses to personal or societal challenges. **Buys 30-40 mss/year.** Query with published clips. Length: 1,000-3,000 words. **Pays $100-400 for assigned articles. Pays $75-150 for unsolicited articles.**

Photos Send photos Identification of subjects required.

Columns/Departments Just Between Us (personal opinion on current Jewish life and issues), 1,000 words. 4

Fiction Must have relevance to Orthodox reader. Length: 1,000-2,000 words.

Poetry Buys limited number of poems/year. Pays $25-75.

Tips Remember that your reader is well educated and has a strong commitment to Orthodox Judaism. Articles on the holidays, Israel, and other common topics should offer a fresh insight. Because the magazine is a quarterly, we do not generally publish articles which concern specific timely events.

$ JULUKA

P.O. Box 4675, Palo Verdes Peninsula CA 90274. (866)458-5852. Fax: (310)707-2255. E-mail: info@julukanews.com. Website: www.julukanews.com. Published in the US for those interested in South Africa. Helps South Africans adapt to life in a new country and provides a forum for networking and exchanging ideas, opinions, and resources. No kill fee. Editorial lead time 1 month. Accepts queries by e-mail.

Nonfiction Needs humor, interview, opinion, personal experience, travel, news, book reviews. **Pays 5¢/word** Sometimes pays expenses of writers on assignment.

Photos Send photos

Columns/Departments Travel, 520 words; Art & Culture (artist profiles/gallery events), 200-400 words; Culture Shock (personal stories about life in North American/stories about emigrating), 500 words; Sports 200-400 words; Human Interest (personal experiences), 300-1,000 words; Guest Editorial, 150-350 words; Reader Profiles, 400-800 words; Money Matters (financial news), 150-300 words; News You Can Use (law/insurance/financial planning), 250-350 words.

$ KHABAR

The Community Magazine, Khabar, Inc., 3790 Holcomb Bridge Rd., Suite 101, Norcross GA 30092. (770)451-7666, ext. 115. E-mail: parthiv@khabar.com. Website: www.khabar.com. **50% freelance written.** "Monthly magazine covering the Asian Indian community in and around Georgia.". Content relating to Indian-American and/or immigrant experience. Estab. 1992. Circ. 27,000. Pays on publication. Offers 25% kill fee. Publishes ms an average of 2 months after acceptance. Buys one-time rights, buys second serial (reprint) rights, buys simultaneous rights, buys electronic rights. Editorial lead time 2 months. Submit seasonal material 2 months in advance. Accepts queries by e-mail. Accepts previously published material. Accepts simultaneous submissions. Sample copy free. Guidelines by email.

Nonfiction Needs essays, interview, opinion, personal experience, travel. **Buys 5 mss/year.** Send complete ms. Length: 750-4,000 words. **Pays $100-300 for assigned articles. Pays $75 for unsolicited articles.**

Photos State availability of or send photos Captions, identification of subjects required. Negotiates payment individually.

Columns/Departments Book Review, 1,200 words; Music Review, 800 words; Spotlight (profiles), 1,200-3,000 words. 5 Query with or without published clips or send complete ms. **Pays $75 +.**

Fiction Needs ethnic, Indian American/Asian immigrant. **Buys 5 mss/year.** Query or send complete ms. **Pays $50-100.**

Tips "Ask for our 'editorial guidelines' document by e-mail."

$ $ $ $ LATINA MAGAZINE

Latina Media Ventures, LLC, 1500 Broadway, Suite 700, New York NY 10036. (212)642-0200. E-mail: editor@latina.com. Website: www.latina.com. **40-50% freelance written.** Monthly magazine covering Latina lifestyle.

Latina Magazine is the leading bilingual lifestyle publication for Hispanic women in the US today. Covering the best of Latino fashion, beauty, culture, and food, the magazine also features celebrity profiles and interviews. Estab. 1996. Circ. 250,000. Byline given. Pays on publication. Offers 25% kill fee. Publishes ms an average of 2-3 months after acceptance. Buys first rights, buys second serial (reprint) rights, buys electronic rights. Editorial lead time 3 months. Submit seasonal material 4-5 months in advance. Accepts queries by e-mail. Responds in 1 month to queries. Responds in 1-2 months to mss. Sample copy available online.

- Editors are in charge of their individual sections and pitches should be made directly to them. Do not make pitches directly to the editor-in-chief or the editorial director as they will only be routed to the relevant section editor.

Nonfiction Needs essays, how-to, humor, inspirational, interview, new product, personal experience. The 10 Latinas Who Changed the World (December). We do not feature an extensive amount of celebrity content or entertainment content, and freelancers should be sensitive to this. The magazine does not contain book or album reviews, and we do not write stories covering an artist's new project. We do not attend press junkets and do not cover press conferences. Please note that we are a lifestyle magazine, not an entertainment magazine. **Buys 15-20 mss/year.** Query with published clips. Length: 300-2,200 words. **Pays $1/word.** Pays expenses of writers on assignment.

Photos State availability Identification of subjects required. Reviews contact sheets, transparencies, GIF/JPEG files. Negotiates payment individually. Buys one time rights.

Tips *Latina*'s features cover a wide gamut of topics, including fashion, beauty, wellness, and personal essays. The magazine runs a wide variety of features on news and service topics (from the issues affecting Latina adolescents to stories dealing with anger). If you are going to make a pitch, please keep the following things in mind. All pitches should include statistics or some background reporting that demonstrates why a developing trend is important. Also, give examples of women who can provide a personal perspective. Profiles and essays need to have a strong personal journey angle. We will not cover someone just because they are Hispanic. When pitching stories about a particular person, please let us know the following: timeliness (Is this someone who is somehow tied to breaking news events? Has their story been heard?); the 'wow' factor (Why is this person remarkable? What elements make this story a standout? What sets your subject apart from other women?); target our audience (please note that the magazine targets acculturated, English-dominant Latina women between the ages of 18-39).

$ $ $ MOMENT

The Magazine of Jewish Culture, Politics and Religion, 4115 Wisconsin Ave. NW, Suite 102, Washington DC 20016. (202)364-3300. Fax: (202)364-2636. E-mail: editor@momentmag.com. Website: www.momentmag.com. **90% freelance written**. Bimonthly magazine. *Moment* is an independent Jewish bimonthly general interest magazine that specializes in cultural, political, historical, religious, and lifestyle articles relating chiefly to the North American Jewish community and Israel. Estab. 1975. Circ. 65,000. Byline given. Pays on publication. Publishes ms an average of 6 months after acceptance. Buys first North American serial rights. Editorial lead time 3 months. Submit seasonal material 6 months in advance. Accepts queries by mail, e-mail, fax. Accepts simultaneous submissions. Responds in 1 month to queries. Responds in 3 months to mss. Sample copy for $4.50 and SAE. Guidelines available online.

Nonfiction We look for meaty, colorful, thought-provoking features and essays on Jewish trends and Israel. We occasionally publish book excerpts, memoirs, and profiles. **Buys 25-30 mss/year.** Query with published clips. Length: 2,500-7,000 words. **Pays $200-1,200 for assigned articles. Pays $40-500 for unsolicited articles.**

Photos State availability Identification of subjects required. Negotiates payment individually. Buys one time rights.

Columns/Departments 5765 (snappy pieces about quirky events in Jewish communities, news and ideas to improve Jewish living), 250 words maximum; Olam (first-person pieces, humor, and colorful reportage), 600-1,500 words; Book reviews (fiction and nonfiction) are accepted but generally assigned, 400-800 words. 30 Query with published clips. **Pays $50-250.**

Tips Stories for *Moment* are usually assigned, but unsolicited manuscripts are often selected for publication. Successful features offer readers an in-depth journalistic treatment of an issue, phenomenon, institution, or individual. The more the writer can follow the principle of `show, don't tell,' the better. The majority of the submissions we receive are about The Holocaust and Israel. A writer has a better chance of having an idea accepted if it is not on these subjects.

$ $ NATIVE PEOPLES MAGAZINE

5333 N. 7th St., Suite C-224, Phoenix AZ 85014. (602)265-4855. Fax: (602)265-3113. E-mail: dgibson@nativepeoples.com. Website: www.nativepeoples.com. Bimonthly magazine covering Native Americans. High-quality reproduction with full color throughout. The primary purpose of this magazine is to offer a sensitive portrayal of the arts and lifeways of Native peoples of the Americas. Estab. 1987. Circ. 50,000. Byline given. Pays on publication. Buys one-time rights, buys nonexclusive Web and reprint rights rights. Accepts queries by mail, e-mail, fax. Responds in 2 months to queries. Guidelines available online.

Nonfiction All features by freelancers. Of the departments, Pathways (travel section), History and Viewpoint most open to freelancers. Needs interview, of interesting and leading Natives from all walks of life, with an emphasis on arts, personal experience. **Buys 35 mss/year.** Length: 1,000-2,500 words. **Pays 25¢/word.**
Photos State availability Identification of subjects required. Reviews transparencies, prefers high res digital images and 35mm slides. Inquire for details. Offers $45-150/page rates, $250/cover photos. Buys one-time rights and nonexclusive Web and reprint rights.
Tips We are focused upon authenticity and a positive portrayal of present-day Native American life and cultural practices. Our stories portray role models of Native people, young and old, with a sense of pride in their heritage and culture. Therefore, it is important that the Native American point of view be incorporated in each story.

$ $ RUSSIAN LIFE

RIS Publications, P.O. Box 567, Montpelier VT 05601. Website: www.russianlife.net. **75% freelance written.** Bimonthly magazine covering Russian culture, history, travel, and business. "Our readers are informed Russophiles with an avid interest in all things Russian. But we do not publish personal travel journals or the like." Estab. 1956. Circ. 15,000. Byline given. Pays on publication. Publishes ms an average of 3-6 months after acceptance. Buys first rights. Editorial lead time 2 months. Submit seasonal material 3 months in advance. Accepts queries by mail. Accepts previously published material. Responds in 1 month to queries. Sample copy for sae with 9 x 12 envelope and 6 First-Class stamps. Guidelines available online.
Nonfiction Needs general interest, photo feature, travel. No personal stories, i.e., How I came to love Russia. **Buys 15-20 mss/year.** Query. Length: 1,000-6,000 words. **Pays $100-300.**
Reprints Accepts previously published submissions rarely.
Photos Send photos Captions required. Reviews contact sheets. Negotiates payment individually. Buys one time rights.
Tips "A straightforward query letter with writing sample or manuscript (not returnable) enclosed."

$ $ SCANDINAVIAN REVIEW

The American-Scandinavian Foundation, 58 Park Ave., New York NY 10016. (212)879-9779. E-mail: editor@amscan.org. Website: www.amscan.org. **75% freelance written.** Triannual magazine for contemporary Scandinavia. Audience: Members, embassies, consulates, libraries. Slant: Popular coverage of contemporary affairs in Scandinavia. Estab. 1913. Circ. 4,000. Byline given. Pays on publication. No kill fee. Publishes ms an average of 2 months after acceptance. Buys first North American serial rights, buys second serial (reprint) rights. Editorial lead time 3 months. Submit seasonal material 3 months in advance. Accepts previously published material. Responds in 6 weeks to queries. Sample copy available online. Guidelines free.
Nonfiction Needs general interest, interview, photo feature, travel, must have Scandinavia as topic focus. Scandinavian travel No pornography. **Buys 30 mss/year.** Query with published clips. Length: 1,500-2,000 words. **Pays $300 maximum.**
Photos Captions required. Reviews 3 x 5 transparencies, prints. Pays $25-50/photo; negotiates payment individually. Buys one time rights.

SKIPPING STONES

An Award-Winning Multicultural Magazine, P.O. Box 3939, Eugene OR 97403-0939. (541)342-4956. E-mail: editor@skippingstones.org. Website: www.skippingstones.org. **80% freelance written.** "We promote multicultural awareness, international understanding, nature appreciation, and social responsibility. We suggest authors not make stereotypical generalizations in their articles. We like when authors include their own experiences, or base their articles on their personal immersion experiences in a culture or country." Estab. 1988. Circ. 2,000. Byline given. No kill fee. Publishes ms an average of 4-8 months after acceptance. Buys first North American serial rights, non-exclusive reprint, and electronic rights. Editorial lead time 3-4 months. Submit seasonal material 4 months in advance. Accepts queries by mail, e-mail. Accepts simultaneous submissions. Responds in 2-4 weeks to queries. Responds in 4 months to mss. Sample copy for $6. Writer's guidelines online or for business-sized envelope.
Nonfiction Needs essays, general interest, humor, inspirational, interview, opinion, personal experience, photo feature, travel. No 'preachy' or 'screetchy' articles. **Buys 20-30 mss/year.** Send complete ms. Length: 400-800 words.
Photos Send photos Captions required. Reviews 4X6 prints, low-resolution JPEG files. Offers no additional payment for photos. Buys one time rights.
Fiction Needs adventure, ethnic, historical, humorous, multicultural, international, social issues. **Buys 20 mss/year.** Send complete ms. Length: 300-800 words. **Pays with contributor copies.**
Poetry Only accepts poetry from youth under age 18. **Buys 100-150 poems/year.** Submit maximum 4 poems. Length: 30 lines maximum.
Tips "Be original and innovative. Use multicultural, nature, or cross-cultural themes. Multilingual submissions are welcome."

UPSCALE MAGAZINE

Bronner Brothers, 600 Bronner Brothers Way SW, Atlanta GA 30310. (404)758-7467. E-mail: features@upscalemag.com. Website: www.upscalemagazine.com. Monthly magazine covering topics for upscale African-American/black interests. *Upscale* offers to take the reader to the 'next level' of life's experience. Written for the black reader and consumer, *Upscale* provides information in the realms of business, news, lifestyle, fashion and beauty, and arts and entertainment. Estab. 1989. Circ. 250,000. Byline given. Pays on publication. Offers 25% kill fee. Publishes ms an average of 4 months after acceptance. Buys first North American serial rights. Editorial lead time 3-4 months. Accepts queries by mail. Accepts simultaneous submissions. Responds in 1 month to queries. Sample copy available online. Guidelines available online.

Photos State availability Captions, identification of subjects, model releases required. Negotiates payment individually.

Columns/Departments News & Business (factual, current); Lifestyle (travel, home, wellness, etc.); Beauty & Fashion (tips, trends, upscale fashion, hair); and Arts & Entertainment (artwork, black celebrities, entertainment). 6-10 Query with published clips. **Payment different for each department.**

Tips Make queries informative and exciting. Include entertaining clips. Be familiar with issues affecting black readers. Be able to write about them with ease and intelligence.

$ $ VISTA MAGAZINE

The Magazine for all Hispanics, Hispanic Publishing Corp., 1201 Brickll Ave., Suite 360, Miami FL 33131. (305)416-4644. Fax: (305)416-4344. E-mail: g.godoy@comcast.net. Website: www.vistamagazine.com. **50% freelance written.** Monthly magazine. "Monthly and Sunday supplement-style magazine targeting Hispanic audience. Dual-language, Spanish/English, 50/50%. Stories appear in one language or another, not both. Topics of general interest, but with a Hispanic angle." Estab. 1985. Circ. 1,000,000. Byline given. Pays on publication. Offers 25% kill fee. Publishes ms an average of 2 months after acceptance. Buys all rights. Editorial lead time 2 months. Submit seasonal material 4 months in advance. Accepts queries by mail, e-mail, fax, phone. Sample copy free or online

Nonfiction Needs expose, general interest, historical, how-to, home improvement, inspirational, interview, new product, photo feature, travel. No creative writing, poems, etc. **Buys 40-50 mss/year.** Query with published clips. Length: 500-1,600 words. **Pays $250-450.** Sometimes pays expenses of writers on assignment.

Photos State availability

Columns/Departments In Touch (short profile of someone doing outstanding work in any area, i.e., education, business, health, etc.) **Pays $100.**

Tips "Query by phone is usually best. Articles must be related to Hispanics, be of national interest, timely and, unless assigned by VISTA, should be 850-1,200 words—not longer."

$ WINDSPEAKER

Aboriginal Multi-Media Society of Alberta, 13245-146 St., Edmonton AB T5L 4S8 Canada. (780)455-2700. Fax: (780)455-7639. E-mail: edwind@ammsa.com. Website: www.ammsa.com/windspeaker. **25% freelance written.** Monthly tabloid covering native issues. Focus on events and issues that affect and interest native peoples, national or local. Estab. 1983. Circ. 27,000. Byline given. Pays on publication. Offers kill fee. Publishes ms an average of 1 month after acceptance. Buys first rights. Editorial lead time 1 month. Submit seasonal material 2 months in advance. Accepts queries by mail, e-mail, phone. Accepts simultaneous submissions. Sample copy free. Guidelines available online.

Nonfiction Needs opinion, photo feature, travel, news interview/profile, reviews: books, music, movies. Powwow (June); Travel supplement (May) **Buys 200 mss/year.** Query with published clips and SASE or by phone. Length: 500-800 words. **Pays $3-3.60/published inch.** Sometimes pays expenses of writers on assignment.

Photos Send photos Identification of subjects required. Offers $25-100/photo. Will pay for film and processing. Buys one time rights.

Tips Knowledge of Aboriginal culture and political issues is a great asset.

FOOD & DRINK

BON APPETIT

Conde Nast Publications, Inc., 6300 wilshire Blvd., Los Angeles CA 90048. Website: www.bonappetit.com. **50% freelance written.** Monthly magazine covering fine food, restaurants, and home entertaining. "*Bon Appetit* readers are upscale food enthusiasts and sophisticated travelers. They eat out often and entertain 4-6 times a month." Estab. 1956. Circ. 1,300,000. Byline given. Pays on acceptance. Buys all rights. Submit seasonal material 1 year in advance. Accepts queries by mail. Responds in 6 weeks to queries. Guidelines for #10 SASE.

Nonfiction Needs travel, food-related, food feature, personal essays. No cartoons, quizzes, poetry, historic food

features, or obscure food subjects. **Buys 50 mss/year.** Query with resume and published clips. No phone calls or e-mails. Length: 150-2,000 words. **Pays $100 and up.** Pays expenses of writers on assignment.
Photos Never send photos.
Tips "Writers must have a good knowledge of *Bon Appetit* and the related topics of food, travel, and entertaining (as shown in accompanying clips). A light, lively style is a plus."

$ $ CHILE PEPPER

250 W. 57th St., Suite 728, New York NY 10107. (212)262-2247. E-mail: editor@chilepepper.com. **70% freelance written.** Bimonthly magazine on spicy foods. "The magazine is devoted to spicy foods, and most articles include recipes. We have a very devoted readership who love their food hot!" Estab. 1986. Circ. 85,000. Pays on publication. Buys first rights, buys electronic rights. Submit seasonal material 6 months in advance. Guidelines for #10 SASE.
Nonfiction Needs how-to, cooking and gardening with spicy foods, humor having to do with spicy foods, interview, chefs & business people, travel having to do with spicy foods. **Buys 50 mss/year.** Query by e-mail only. Length: 1,000-3,000 words. **Pays $600 minimum for feature article.**
Reprints Send tearsheet or photocopy and information about when and where the material previously appeared.
Photos State availability. Captions, identification of subjects required. Reviews contact sheets, negatives, transparencies, prints. Offers $25/photo minimum Buys one-time rights.
Tips "We're always interested in queries from *food* writers. Articles about spicy foods with 6-8 recipes are just right. No fillers. No unsolicited manuscripts; queries only. E-mail queries preferred."

CLEAN EATING

Improving your life one meal at a time., Robert Kennedy Publishing, Inc., 5775e McLaughlin Rd., Mississauga ON L5R 3P7 Canada. (905)507-3545/(888)254-0767. E-mail: editorial@cleaneatingmag.com. Website: www.cleaneatingmag.com. Quarterly magazine covering nutrition. *Clean Eating* encourages eating well. Estab. 2007. Circ. 325,000. No kill fee. Buys all rights.
Nonfiction Send with SAE and $5 for return postage.
Tips Editors seek recipes and stories straight from Mother Nature.

$ $ $ DRAFT

Draft Publishing, 4350 E. Camelback Rd., Suite A125, Phoenix AZ 85018. (888)806-4677. E-mail: jessica.daynor@draftmag.com. Website: www.draftmag.com. **60% freelance written.** Bimonthly magazine covering beer and men's lifestyle (including food, travel, sports and leisure). *DRAFT* is a national men's magazine devoted to beer, breweries and the lifestyle and culture that surrounds it. Read by nearly 300,000 men aged 21-45, *DRAFT* offers formal beer reviews, plus coverage of food, travel, sports and leisure. Writers need not have formal beer knowledge (though that's a plus!), but they should be experienced journalists who can appreciate beer and beer culture. Estab. 2006. Circ. 275,000. Byline given. Pays on publication. Offers 20% kill fee. Publishes ms an average of 2 months after acceptance. Buys first rights, buys electronic rights, buys all rights. all rights for 1 year. Editorial lead time 4 months. Submit seasonal material 6 months in advance. Accepts queries by e-mail. Accepts simultaneous submissions. Responds in 3 weeks to queries. Sample copy for $3 (magazine can also be found on most newsstands for $4.99). Guidelines available at www.draftmag.com/submissions.
Nonfiction Needs Accepts features, short front-of-book pieces, how-to's, interviews, travel, food, restaurant and bar pieces, sports and adventure; anything guy-related. The editorial calendar is as follows: November/December: Holiday issue; Jan/Feb: Best of issue; May/June: Food issue; Mar/Apr: Travel issue; July/Aug: All-American issue; Sept/Oct Anniversary issue. Do not want unsolicited mss., beer reviews, brewery profiles. **Buys 80/year. mss/year.** Query with published clips. Length: 250-2,500 words. **50-90¢ for assigned articles.** sometimes (limit agreed upon in advance).
Photos Reviews GIF/JPEG files. Offers no additional payment for photos accepted with ms. varies (either one-time rights or no rights).
Columns/Departments Contact: Chris Staten, associate editor, (chris.staten@draftmag.com) for OnTap and OnTap llife, Jessica Daynor, managing editor, for all other departments. 'On Tap' (short FOB pieces on beer-related subjects, 350 words; 'On Tap Life' (short FOB pieces on NON -beer-related subjects (travel, food, sports, home, leisure), 350 words; 'Trek' (travel pieces [need not relate to beer, but it's a plus]), 950 words; 'Taste' (beer-and food-related incident or unique perspective on beer), 750 words. 50mss/year. Query with published clips. **Pays $50¢-80¢.**
Tips Please see 'What to pitch' and 'what not to pitch' in writer's guidelines.

FOOD & WINE

American Express Publishing Corp., 1120 Avenue of the Americas, 9th Floor, New York NY 10036. (212)382-5600. Fax: (212)764-2177. Website: www.foodandwine.com. Monthly magazine for the reader who enjoys the finer things in life. Editorial focuses on upscale dining, covering resturants, entertaining at home, and travel destinations. Circ. 964,000. No kill fee. Editorial lead time 6 months.

- Does not buy freelance material or use freelance writers.

$ $ $ $ GOURMET

The Magazine of Good Living, Conde Nast Publications, Inc., 4 Times Square, New York NY 10036. (212)286-2860. Website: www.gourmet.com. Monthly magazine for sophisticated readers who have a passion for food and travel. Byline given. Offers 25% kill fee. Accepts queries by mail. Responds in 2 months to queries. Sample copy free.

Nonfiction Looking for articles on reminiscence, single foods, and ethnic cuisines. **Buys 25-30 mss/year.** Query with published clips. Length: 200-3,000 words. Pays expenses of writers on assignment.

$ $ HOME COOKING

DRG, 306 E. Parr Rd., Berne IN 46711-1138. (260)589-4000. Fax: (260)589-8093. E-mail: editor@homecookingmagazine.com. Website: www.homecookingmagazine.com. **35% freelance written**. Bimonthly magazine. Circ. 58,000. Byline given. Pays within 45 days of acceptance. No kill fee. Publishes ms an average of 4 months after acceptance. Buys all rights. Editorial lead time 6 months. Submit seasonal material 6 months in advance. Accepts queries by mail, e-mail. Responds in 1 month to queries. Sample copy for sae with 6x9 envelope and 5 First-Class stamps.

Nonfiction Needs how-to, humor, personal experience, recipes, all in food/cooking area. No health/fitness or travel articles. **Buys 36 mss/year.** Query or send complete ms. 200-350 words, plus 6-10 recipes **Pays $75-200 for assigned articles. Pays $25-200 for unsolicited articles.**

Columns/Departments Pinch of Sage (hints for the home cook), 200-500 words; Kitchen Know-How, 250-1,000 words. 12 Query or send complete ms.

Tips You must request our writer's guidelines and editorial calendar for issue themes. We will gladly e-mail or mail them to you. Please follow our guidelines and schedule for all submissions.

$ $ KASHRUS MAGAZINE

The Bimonthly for the Kosher Consumer and the Trade, The Kashrus Institute, P.O. Box 204, Brooklyn NY 11204. (718)336-8544. E-mail: letters@kashrusmagazine.com. Website: www.kashrusmagazine.com. **25% freelance written. Prefers to work with published/established writers, but will work with new/unpublished writers.** Bimonthly magazine covering the kosher food industry and food production as well as Jewish life in all parts of the world. Estab. 1980. Circ. 10,000. Byline given. Pays on publication. Offers 50% kill fee. Publishes ms an average of 2 months after acceptance. Buys first rights, buys second serial (reprint) rights. Submit seasonal material 2 months in advance. Accepts queries by mail, phone. Accepts previously published material. Accepts simultaneous submissions. Responds in 1 week to queries. Responds in 2 weeks to mss. Sample copy for $2.

Nonfiction Needs general interest, interview, new product, personal experience, photo feature, religious, technical, travel. International Kosher Travel (October); Passover Shopping Guide (March); Domestic Kosher Travel Guide (June). **Buys 8-12 mss/year.** Query with published clips. Length: 1,000-1,500 words. **Pays $100-250 for assigned articles. Pays up to $100 for unsolicited articles.** Sometimes pays expenses of writers on assignment.

Reprints Send tearsheet or photocopy and information about when and where the material previously appeared. Pays 25-50% of amount paid for an original article.

Photos No guidelines; send samples or call. State availability Offers no additional payment for photos accepted with ms. Buys one time rights.

Columns/Departments Book Review (cookbooks, food technology, kosher food), 250-500 words; People In the News (interviews with kosher personalities), 1,000-1,500 words; Regional Kosher Supervision (report on kosher supervision in a city or community), 1,000-1,500 words; Food Technology (new technology or current technology with accompanying pictures), 1,000-1,500 words; Travel (international, national—must include Kosher information and Jewish communities), 1,000-1,500 words; Regional Kosher Cooking, 1,000-1,500 words. 8-12 Query with published clips. **Pays $50-250.**

Tips "*Kashrus Magazine* will do more writing on general food technology, production, and merchandising as well as human interest travelogs and regional writing in 2009 than we have done in the past. Areas most open to freelancers are interviews, food technology, cooking and food preparation, dining, regional reporting, and travel, but we also feature healthy eating and lifestyles, redecorating, catering, and hospitals and health care. We welcome stories on the availability and quality of kosher foods and services in communities across the US and throughout the world. Some of our best stories have been by non-Jewish writers about kosher observance in their region. We also enjoy humorous articles. Just send a query with clips and we'll try to find a storyline that's right for you, or better yet, call us to discuss a storyline."

KRAFT FOOD & FAMILY

Redwood Custom Communications, 37 Front St. E., Toronto ON M5E 1B3 Canada. (416)360-7339. Fax: (416)360-8846. Website: www.kraftkitchens.com. Published 5 times/year. *Kraft Food & Family* is published by Kraft Foods and is directed to Kraft consumers in the United States. The magazine provides simple, realistic food ideas and solutions for time-challenged mothers and working women. No kill fee.

- Does not buy freelance material or use freelance writers.

N SAVEUR MAGAZINE

World Publications, Inc., 15 East 32nd St., 12th Floor, New York NY 10016. (212)219-7400. Website: www.saveur.com. Magazine published 9 times/year. "Saveur seeks out stories from around the globe that weave together culture, tradition, and people through the language of food. On every page the magazine honors a fundamental truth: cooking is one of the most universal - and beautiful - means of human expression. It is written for sophisticated, upscale lovers of food, wine, travel, and adventure." Estab. 1994. Circ. 325,000. No kill fee. Accepts queries by mail, e-mail. Sample copy for $5 at newsstands Guidelines by email

Nonfiction Query with published clips.

Columns/Departments Query with published clips.

Tips "Queries and stories should be detailed and specific, and personal ties to the subject matter are important—let us know why you should be the one to write the story. Familiarize yourself with our departments, and the magazine style as a whole, and pitch your stories accordingly. Also, we rarely assign restaurant-based pieces."

⊘ TASTE OF HOME

Reader's Digest Association, Inc., 5400 S. 60th St., Greendale WI 53129. (414)423-0100. Fax: (414)423-8463. E-mail: editors@tasteofhome.com. Website: www.tasteofhome.com. Bimonthly magazine. *Taste of Home* is dedicated to home cooks, from beginners to the very experienced. Editorial includes recipes and serving suggestions, interviews and ideas from the publication's readers and field editors based around the country, and reviews of new cooking tools and gadgets. Circ. 3.5 million. No kill fee.

- Does not buy freelance material or use freelance writers.

TEA A MAGAZINE

Olde English Tea Company, Inc., 3 Devotion Rd., P.O. Box 348, Scotland CT 06264. (860)456-1145. Fax: (860)456-1023. E-mail: teamag@teamag.com. Website: www.teamag.com. **75% freelance written**. Quarterly magazine covering anything tea related. *Tea A Magazine* is an exciting magazine all about tea, both as a drink and for its cultural significance in art, music, literature, history and society. Estab. 1994. Circ. 9,500. Byline given. Pays on publication. Publishes ms an average of 1 year after acceptance. Buys all rights. Editorial lead time 9 months. Submit seasonal material 6 months in advance. Responds in 6 months to mss. Guidelines by email.

Nonfiction Needs book excerpts, essays, general interest, historical, how-to, humor, interview, personal experience, photo feature, travel. Send complete ms. **Pays negotiable amount.** Sometimes pays expenses of writers on assignment.

Photos Send photos Captions, identification of subjects required. Reviews prints, GIF/JPEG files (300 dpi). Negotiates payment individually. Buys all rights.

Columns/Departments Readers' Stories (personal experience involving tea); Book Reviews (review on tea books). Send complete ms. **Pays negotiable amount.**

Fiction Does not want anything that is not tea related. Send complete ms. **Pays negotiable amount.**

Poetry Needs avant-garde, free verse, haiku, light verse, traditional. Does not want anything that is not tea related.

Tips Please submit full manuscripts with photos and make sure it is tea related.

$$$$ WINE ENTHUSIAST MAGAZINE

Wine Enthusiast Companies, 103 Fairview Park Dr., Elmsford NY 10523. E-mail: tmoriarty@wineenthusiast.net. Website: www.wineenthusiast.com/mag. **40% freelance written**. Monthly magazine covering the lifestyle of wine. Our readers are upscale and educated, but not necessarily super-sophisticated about wine itself. Our informal, irreverent approach appeals to savvy enophiles and newbies alike. Estab. 1988. Circ. 80,000. Byline given. Pays on acceptance. Offers 25% kill fee. Makes work-for-hire assignments. Editorial lead time 4 months. Submit seasonal material 5 months in advance. Accepts queries by e-mail. Responds in 2 weeks to queries. Responds in 2 months to mss.

Nonfiction Needs essays, humor, interview, new product, personal experience. **Buys 5 mss/year. Pays $750-2,500 for assigned articles. Pays $750-2,000 for unsolicited articles.**

Photos Send photos Reviews GIF/JPEG files. Offers $135-400/photo.

$$ WINE PRESS NORTHWEST

P.O. Box 2608, Tri-Cities WA 99302. (509)582-1564. Fax: (509)585-7221. E-mail: edegerman@winepressnw.com. Website: www.winepressnw.com. **Contact:** Eric Degerman, managing editor. **50% freelance written**. Quarterly magazine covering Pacific Northwest wine (Washington, Oregon, British Columbia, Idaho). "We focus narrowly on Pacific Northwest wine. If we write about travel, it's where to go to drink NW wine. If we write about food, it's what goes with NW wine. No beer, no spirits." Estab. 1998. Circ. 12,000. Byline given. Pays on publication. Offers 20% kill fee. Publishes ms an average of 3 months after acceptance. Buys first North

American serial rights, buys electronic rights. Editorial lead time 3 months. Submit seasonal material 3 months in advance. Accepts queries by mail, e-mail, fax. Accepts simultaneous submissions. Responds in 1 month to queries. Sample copy free or online Guidelines free.

Nonfiction Needs general interest, historical, interview, new product, photo feature, travel. No beer, spirits, non-NW (California wine, etc.) **Buys 30 mss/year.** Query with published clips. Length: 1,500-2,500 words. **Pays $300.** Sometimes pays expenses of writers on assignment.

Photos State availability Identification of subjects required. Reviews contact sheets. Negotiates payment individually Buys one time rights.

Tips "Writers must be familiar with *Wine Press Northwest* and should have a passion for the region, its wines, and cuisine."

$ $ $ WINE SPECTATOR

M. Shanken Communications, Inc., 387 Park Ave. S., 8th Floor, New York NY 10016. (212)684-1540. Fax: (212)684-5424. E-mail: winespec@mshanken.com. Website: www.winespectator.com. **20% freelance written. Prefers to work with published/established writers.** Monthly news magazine. Estab. 1976. Circ. 350,000. Byline given. Pays within 30 days of publication. No kill fee. Publishes ms an average of 2 months after acceptance. Buys all rights. Makes work-for-hire assignments. Submit seasonal material 4 months in advance. Accepts queries by mail, fax. Responds in 3 months to queries. Guidelines for #10 SASE.

Nonfiction Needs general interest, news about wine or wine events, interview, of wine, vintners, wineries, opinion, photo feature, travel, dining and other lifestyle pieces. No winery promotional pieces or articles by writers who lack sufficient knowledge to write below just surface data. Query. Length: 100-2,000 words. **Pays $100-1,000.**

Photos Send photos Captions, identification of subjects, model releases required. Pays $75 minimum for color transparencies Buys all rights.

Tips A solid knowledge of wine is a must. Query letters essential, detailing the story idea. New, refreshing ideas which have not been covered before stand a good chance of acceptance. *Wine Spectator* is a consumer-oriented news magazine, but we are interested in some trade stories; brevity is essential.

GAMES & PUZZLES

$ THE BRIDGE BULLETIN

American Contract Bridge League, 2990 Airways Blvd., Memphis TN 38116-3847. (901)332-5586, ext. 1291. Fax: (901)398-7754. E-mail: editor@acbl.org. Website: www.acbl.org. **20% freelance written**. Monthly magazine covering duplicate (tournament) bridge. Estab. 1938. Circ. 155,000. Byline given. Pays on publication. Publishes ms an average of 3 months after acceptance. Buys first rights, buys second serial (reprint) rights. Editorial lead time 2 months. Accepts queries by mail, e-mail. Accepts previously published material. Accepts simultaneous submissions.

Nonfiction Needs book excerpts, essays, how-to, play better bridge, humor, interview, new product, personal experience, photo feature, technical, travel. **Buys 6 mss/year.** Query. Length: 500-2,000 words. **Pays $100/page.**

Photos Color required. State availability Identification of subjects required. Negotiates payment individually Buys all rights.

Tips "Articles must relate to contract bridge in some way. Cartoons on bridge welcome."

$ $ CHESS LIFE

United States Chess Federation, P.O. Box 3967, Crossville TN 38557-3967. (931)787-1234. Fax: (931)787-1200. E-mail: dlucas@uschess.org. Website: www.uschess.org. **15% freelance written. Works with a small number of new/unpublished writers/year.** Monthly magazine. "*Chess Life* is the official publication of the United States Chess Federation, covering news of most major chess events, both here and abroad, with special emphasis on the triumphs and exploits of American players." Estab. 1939. Circ. 85,000. Byline given. No kill fee. Publishes ms an average of 6 months after acceptance. Buys first rights. Submit seasonal material 6 months in advance. Accepts queries by mail, e-mail, fax, phone. Accepts simultaneous submissions. Responds in 3 months to mss. Sample copy and writer's guidelines for 9 × 11 SAE with 5 first-class stamps

Nonfiction All must have some relation to chess. Needs general interest, historical, humor, interview, of a famous chess player or organizer, photo feature, chess centered, technical. No stories about personal experiences with chess. **Buys 30-40 mss/year.** Query with samples if new to publication 3,000 words maximum. **Pays $100/page (800-1,000 words).** Sometimes pays expenses of writers on assignment.

Reprints "Send tearsheet, photocopy or typed ms with rights for sale noted and information about when and where the material previously appeared."

Photos Captions, identification of subjects, model releases required. Reviews b&w contact sheets and prints, and color prints and slides. Pays $25-100 inside; covers negotiable. Buys all or negotiable rights.

Fillers Submit with samples and clips. Buys first or negotiable rights to cartoons and puzzles. **Pays $25 upon acceptance.**
Tips "Articles must be written from an informed point of view. Freelancers in major population areas (except NY and LA) who are interested in short personality profiles and perhaps news reporting have the best opportunities. We're looking for more personality pieces on chess players around the country; not just the stars, but local masters, talented youths, and dedicated volunteers. Freelancers interested in such pieces might let us know of their interest and their range. Could be we know of an interesting story in their territory that needs covering. Examples of published articles include a locally produced chess television program, a meeting of chess set collectors from around the world, chess in our prisons, and chess in the works of several famous writers."

GAMEPRO

IDG Entertainment, 555 12th St., Oakland CA 94607. (510)768-2700. Fax: (510)768-2701. Website: www.gamepro.com. Monthly magazine. *GamePro* is the industry leader among independent multiplatform video gaming magazines. Circ. 517,000. Byline given. No kill fee.

- Contact specific editor. Mostly staff written.

Nonfiction Needs new product. Query.

$ $ POKER AND POOL MAGAZINE

Jester Media, Raleigh NC 27604. E-mail: pokerandpoolmag@aol.com. Website: www.pokerandpoolmagazine.com. **90% freelance written**. Quarterly magazine covering poker and pool. *PPM* is for the player. Informative articles, event calendars, and more. *PPM* is the only magazine of its kind. Estab. 2007. Circ. 25,000. Byline given. Pays on acceptance. Publishes ms an average of 3 months after acceptance. Buys first rights, buys electronic rights. Editorial lead time 2 months. Submit seasonal material 2 months in advance. Accepts queries by mail, e-mail. Responds in 2 weeks to queries. Sample copy available online. Guidelines available online.
Nonfiction Needs book excerpts, essays, expose, general interest, historical, how-to, humor, inspirational, interview, new product, opinion, personal experience, photo feature, technical, travel. Does not want complaints, gripes, bad beat stories, etc. **Buys 50 mss/year.** Query. Length: 100-10,000 words. **Pays $0-200.**
Photos State availability Reviews GIF/JPEG files. Offers $0-50/photo. Buys one time rights.
Fiction Needs adventure, fantasy, historical, horror, humorous, mainstream, mystery, romance, science fiction, slice-of-life vignettes, suspense, western. **Buys 10 mss/year.** Query. Length: 500-10,000 words. **Pays $0-200.**
Poetry Needs avant-garde, free verse, haiku, light verse, traditional. **Buys 10 poems/year.** Submit maximum 5 poems. Length: 3-25 lines.
Fillers Needs anecdotes, facts, gags, newsbreaks, short humor. 50 Length: 10-200 words. **Pays $0-25.**
Tips Know poker or pool. Get your facts right. Don't waste our time if you don't consider yourself a player.

$ $ N POKER PRO MAGAZINE

Poker Pro Media, 4733 W. Atlantic Ave., C-18, Delray Beach FL 33445. E-mail: jwenzel@pokerpromedia.com. Website: www. pokerpromagazine.com. **75% freelance written**. Monthly magazine covering poker, gambling, nightlife. "We want articles about poker and gambling-related articles only; also nightlife in gaming cities and article on gaming destinations." Estab. 2005. Circ. 150,000. Byline given. Pays on publication. No kill fee. Publishes ms an average of 1 month after acceptance. Buys all rights. Editorial lead time 1 ½ months. Submit seasonal material 2 months in advance. Accepts queries by e-mail. Responds in 1 week to queries. Responds in 1 month to mss. Sample copy by email. Guidelines by email.
Nonfiction Needs book excerpts, essays, expose, general interest, historical, how-to, humor, interview, new product, opinion, personal experience, photo feature, travel. **Buys 125 mss/year mss/year.** Query. Length: 800-2,500 words. **Pays $100-$200 for assigned articles. Pays $100-$200 for unsolicited articles.** Sometimes pays expenses of writers on assignment.
Photos State availability Captions, identification of subjects, model releases required. Reviews GIF/JPEG files. Negotiates payment individually. It varies.

WOMAN POKER PLAYER MAGAZINE

915 Chester St., New Westminster BC V3L 4N4 Canada. (604)628-2358. Fax: (516)977-9409. E-mail: editorial@womanpokerplayer.com. Website: www.womanpokerplayer.com. **80% freelance written**. Bimonthly magazine covering poker. *Woman Poker Player* is for the woman who enjoys poker. We are a lifestyle publication that also covers fashion and wellness. Estab. 2005. Circ. 35,000. Byline sometimes given. Pays on publication. No kill fee. Publishes ms an average of 2 months after acceptance. Buys all rights. Editorial lead time 1 month. Submit seasonal material 1 month in advance. Accepts queries by e-mail. Accepts simultaneous submissions. Sample copy free.
Nonfiction Needs book excerpts, humor, interview, poker. Query. Length: 1,100-2,000 words. **Pays variable amount.**
Photos State availability Captions, model releases required. Reviews contact sheets, GIF/JPEG files. Negotiates payment individually. Buys one time rights.
Fiction Needs cond novels, poker. Query. Length: 1,000-2,000 words.

Fillers Needs facts, gags. 6
Tips Send pitch via e-mail stating writing experience.

GAY & LESBIAN INTEREST

$ ECHO MAGAZINE

ACE Publishing, Inc., P.O. Box 16630, Phoenix AZ 85011-6630. (602)266-0550. Fax: (602)266-0773. E-mail: editor@echomag.com. Website: www.echomag.com. **30-40% freelance written**. Biweekly magazine covering gay and lesbian issues. *Echo Magazine* is a newsmagazine for gay, lesbian, bisexual, and transgendered persons in the Phoenix metro area and throughout the state of Arizona. Editorial content needs to be pro-gay, that is, supportive of GLBT equality in all areas of American life. Estab. 1989. Circ. 15,000-18,000. Byline given. Pays on publication. No kill fee. Publishes ms an average of less than 1 month after acceptance. Buys all rights. Editorial lead time 1-2 months. Submit seasonal material 1-2 months in advance. Accepts queries by e-mail. Responds in 2 weeks to queries. Responds in 1 month to mss. Sample copy available online. Guidelines by email.
Nonfiction Needs book excerpts, essays, historical, humor, interview, opinion, personal experience, photo feature, travel. Pride Festival (April); Arts issue (August); Holiday Gift/Decor (December). No articles on topics unrelated to our GLBT readers, or anything that is not pro-gay. **Buys 10-20 mss/year.** Query. Length: 500-2,000 words. **Pays $30-40.**
Photos State availability Captions, identification of subjects, model releases required. Reviews contact sheets, GIF/JPEG files. Negotiates payment individually. Buys all rights.
Columns/Departments Guest Commentary (opinion on GLBT issues), 500-1,000 words; Arts/Entertainment (profiles of GLBT or relevant celebrities, or arts issues), 800-1,500 words. 5-10 Query. **Pays $30-40.**
Tips Know Phoenix (or other areas of Arizona) and its GLBT community. Please don't send nongay-related or nonpro-gay material. Research your topics thoroughly and write professionally. Our print content and online contenty are very similar.

$ $ THE ADVOCATE

Liberation Publications, Inc., 6380 Wilshire Blvd., Suite 1400, Los Angeles CA 90048. (323)852-7200. Fax: (323)852-7272. E-mail: newsroom@advocate.com. Website: www.advocate.com. Biweekly magazine covering national news events with a gay and lesbian perspective on the issues. Estab. 1967. Circ. 120,000. Byline given. Pays on publication. Buys first North American serial rights. Responds in 1 month to queries. Sample copy for $3.95. Guidelines by email.
Nonfiction Here are elements we look for in all articles: *Angling*: An angle is the one editorial tool we have to attract a reader's attention. An *Advocate* editor won't make an assignment unless he or she has worked out a very specific angle with you. Once you've worked out the angle with an editor, don't deviate from it without letting the editor know. Some of the elements we look for in angles are: a news hook; an open question or controversy; a `why' or `how' element or novel twist; national appeal; and tight focus. *Content*: Lesbian and gay news stories in all areas of life: arts, sciences, financial, medical, cyberspace, etc. *Tone*: Tone is the element that makes an emotional connection. Some characteristics we look for: toughness; edginess; fairness and evenhandedness; multiple perspectives. Needs expose, interview, news reporting and investigating. gays on campus, coming out interviews with celebrities, HIV and health Query. Length: 1,200 words. **Pays $550.**
Columns/Departments Arts & Media (news and profiles of well-known gay or lesbians in entertainment) is most open to freelancers, 750 words. Query. **Pays $100-500.**
Tips *The Advocate* is a unique newsmagazine. While we report on gay and lesbian issues and are published by one of the country's oldest and most established gay-owned companies, we also play by the rules of mainstream-not-gay-community-journalism.

$ BENT MAGAZINE

Top Down Productions LLC, E-mail: query@bent-magazine.com. Website: www.bent-magazine.com. **100% freelance written**. Quarterly magazine covering homoerotic romantic literature. "*BENT Magazine* seeks to provide quality romantic fiction and articles of interest to fans of yaoi and slash. All fiction works must focus on a homosexual male main character and/or male/male romance." Estab. 2006. Circ. 40. Byline given. Pays on publication. Publishes ms an average of 1 month after acceptance. Buys first North American serial rights, buys first rights, buys one-time rights, buys second serial (reprint) rights, buys electronic rights. Editorial lead time 4-6 months. Submit seasonal material 4 months in advance. Accepts queries by e-mail. Accepts previously published material. Accepts simultaneous submissions. Responds in 1 week to queries. Responds in 2-4 months to mss. Sample copy available online. Guidelines available online.
Nonfiction Needs book excerpts, essays, general interest, historical, new product, opinion, reviews. Does not want personal experience testimonials. **Buys 36 mss/year.** Send complete ms. Length: 1,000-5,000 words. **Pays $5.**
Columns/Departments Manga Reviews; Book/Movie/Anime Reviews, 1,000 words. 24 Query with or without

published clips or send complete ms. **Pays $5.**
Fiction Needs adventure, erotica, fantasy, historical, horror, humorous, mainstream, mystery, novel concepts, romance, science fiction, serialized, slice-of-life vignettes, suspense, western. Does not want stories that contain heterosexual sex. We are not interested in just-the-sex stories with no development of plot or characters. **Buys 48 mss/year.** Query or send complete ms. Length: 1,000-50,000 words. **Pays $5-30.**
Tips Stories in the sample issue provide a good generalization of what we are looking for. If unsure whether a submission meets the needs of the magazine, please query first with a brief summary/description of the intended work.

$ $ CLOUT MAGAZINE

The Standard for Gays and Lesbians in Southern California, Los Angeles News Group, 300 Oceangate, Suite 150, Long Beach CA 90844. (562)499-1419. Fax: (562)499-1450. E-mail: zamna.avila@presstelegram.com. **99% freelance written**. Bimonthly magazine covering home, travel and entertainment. *Clout* is a new and sophisticated magazine geared toward the more affluent gays and lesbians in the community. Estab. 2008. Circ. 225,000. Byline given. Pays on publication. Offers $50 kill fee. Buys first rights, buys electronic rights. Accepts queries by e-mail.
Nonfiction Needs general interest, historical, how-to, humor, inspirational, interview, opinion, personal experience, photo feature, travel. **Buys 80-100 mss/year.** Query with published clips. Length: 500-2,500 words. **Pays $100-200.**
Photos Send photos Captions, identification of subjects required. Reviews GIF/JPEG files. Offers $125-200/ photo. Buys one time rights.
Columns/Departments She Speaks You Listen (lawyer gives the gay/lesbian perspective on issue); Ask a Hairdresser (advice column for gays and lesbians), both 500 words. Query with published clips. **Pays $125-200.**
Fillers Needs anecdotes, facts, gags, short humor. 8-10 Length: 100-500 words. **Pays $100-150.**
Tips I appreciate people who are local to Southern California, especially Long Beach and have story ideas to contribute. Freelancers must have great work ethics, skillful writing/photo/illustration techniques and flexibility.

$ $ CURVE MAGAZINE

1550 Bryant St., Suite 510, San Francisco CA 94103. E-mail: editor@curvemag.com. Website: www.curvemag.com. **60% freelance written**. Magazine published 10 times/year covering lesbian entertainment, culture, and general interest categories. We want dynamic and provocative articles that deal with issues, ideas, or cultural moments that are of interest or relevance to gay women. Estab. 1990. Circ. 80,000. Byline given. Pays on publication. Offers 25% kill fee. Buys first North American serial rights. Editorial lead time 6 months. Submit seasonal material 6 months in advance. Accepts queries by mail, e-mail, fax. Sample copy for $3.95 with $2 postage. Guidelines available online.
Nonfiction Needs general interest, photo feature, travel, celebrity interview/profile. Sex (February); Travel (March); Fashion + Design (April); Weddings (May); Pride (June); Music (August); School (September); Travel (October); Money/Careers (November); Gift Guide (December). No fiction or poetry. **Buys 100 mss/year.** Query. Length: 200-2,000 words. **Pays 15¢/word.**
Photos Send hi-res photos with submission. Captions, identification of subjects, model releases required. Offers $25-100/photo; negotiates payment individually Buys one time rights.
Tips Feature articles generally fit into 1 of the following categories: Celebrity profiles (lesbian, bisexual, or straight women who are icons for the lesbian community or actively involved in coalition-building with the lesbian community); community segment profiles—i.e., lesbian firefighters, drag kings, sports teams (multiple interviews with a variety of women in different parts of the country representing a diversity of backgrounds); noncelebrity profiles (activities of unknown or low-profile lesbian and bisexual activists/political leaders, athletes, filmmakers, dancers, writers, musicians, etc.); controversial issues (spark a dialogue about issues that divide us as a community, and the ways in which lesbians of different backgrounds fail to understand and support one another). We are not interested in inflammatory articles that incite or enrage readers without offering a channel for action, but we do look for challenging, thought-provoking work. The easiest way to get published in *Curve* is with a front-of-the-book piece for our Curvatures section, topical/fun/newsy pop culture articles that are 100-350 words.

$ THE GAY & LESBIAN REVIEW

Gay & Lesbian Review, Inc., P.O. Box 180300, Boston MA 02118. (617)421-0082. E-mail: HGLR@glreview.com. Website: www.glreview.com. **100% freelance written**. Bimonthly magazine covers gay and lesbian history, culture, and politics. In-depth essays on GLBT history, biography, the arts, political issues, written in clear, lively prose targeted to the 'literate nonspecialist.' Estab. 1994. Circ. 12,000. Byline given. Pays on publication. No kill fee. Buys first rights. Editorial lead time 2 months. Accepts queries by mail, e-mail, phone. Accepts simultaneous submissions. Sample copy free. Guidelines free.

Nonfiction Needs essays, historical, humor, interview, opinion, book reviews. Does not want fiction, memoirs, personal reflections. Query. Length: 1,500-5,000 words. **Pays $100.**
Poetry Needs avant-garde, free verse, traditional. **No payment for poems.**
Tips We prefer that a proposal be e-mailed before a completed draft is sent.

$ $ $ $ GENRE

Genre Publishing, 213 W. 35th St., Suite 402, New York NY 10001. (212)594-8181. Fax: (212)594-8263. E-mail: genre@genremagazine.com. Website: www.genremagazine.com. **60% freelance written**. Monthly magazine. *Genre*, America's best-selling gay men's lifestyle magazine, covers entertainment, fashion, travel, and relationships in a hip, upbeat, upscale voice. Estab. 1991. Circ. 50,000. Byline given. Pays on publication. Offers 25% kill fee. Publishes ms an average of 3 months after acceptance. Buys first North American serial rights, buys electronic rights. Editorial lead time 10 weeks. Submit seasonal material 10 weeks in advance. Accepts queries by mail, e-mail, fax. May only respond if interested. Sample copy for $6.95 ($5 plus $1.95 postage).
Nonfiction Needs essays, expose, general interest, historical, how-to, humor, inspirational, interview, new product, opinion, personal experience, photo feature, religious, travel, relationships, fashion. Not interested in articles on 2 males negotiating a sexual situation or coming out stories. **Buys variable number mss/year.** Query with published clips. Length: 500-1,500 words. **Pays $150-1,600.**
Photos State availability Model releases required. Reviews contact sheets, 3x5 or 5x7 prints. Negotiates payment individually Buys one time rights.
Columns/Departments Body (how to better the body); Mind (how to better the mind); Spirit (how to better the spirit), all 700 words; Reviews (books, movies, music, travel, etc.), 500 words. variable number of Query with published clips or send complete ms. **Pays $200 maximum**
Fiction Needs adventure, experimental, horror, humorous, mainstream, mystery, novel concepts, religious, romance, science fiction, slice-of-life vignettes, suspense. **Buys 10 mss/year.** Send complete ms. Length: 2,000-4,000 words.
Tips Like you, we take our journalistic responsibilities and ethics very seriously, and we subscribe to the highest standards of the profession. We expect our writers to represent original work that is not libelous and does not infringe upon the copyright or violate the right of privacy of any other person, firm or corporation.

$ $ GIRLFRIENDS MAGAZINE

Lesbian Culture, Politics, and Entertainment, H.A.F. Publishing, 3181 Mission St., PMB 30, San Francisco CA 94110. E-mail: staff@girlfriendsmag.com. Website: www.girlfriendsmag.com. Monthly lesbian magazine. *Girlfriends* provides its readers with intelligent, entertaining and visually pleasing coverage of culture, politics, and entertainment—all from an informed and critical lesbian perspective. Estab. 1994. Circ. 75,000. Byline given. Pays on publication. Offers 50% kill fee. Publishes ms an average of 6 months after acceptance. Buys first rights and use for advertising/promoting *Girlfriends*. Editorial lead time 3 months. Submit seasonal material 6 months in advance. Accepts queries by mail, e-mail. Accepts simultaneous submissions. Responds in 3 weeks to queries. Responds in 2 months to mss. Sample copy for $4.95 plus $1.50 postage or online. Guidelines available online.

- *Girlfriends* is not accepting fiction, poetry or fillers.

Nonfiction Needs book excerpts, essays, expose, historical, humor, interview, new product, opinion, personal experience, photo feature, religious, technical, travel, investigative features. Sex, music, bridal, sports and Hollywood issues, breast cancer issue. Special features: Best lesbian restaurants in the US; best places to live. **Buys 20-25 mss/year.** Query with published clips. Length: 1,000-3,500 words. **Pays 15¢/word.**
Reprints Send photocopy or typed ms with rights for sale ted and information about when and where the material previously appeared. Negotiable payment.
Photos Send photos Captions, identification of subjects, model releases required. Reviews contact sheets, 4 × 5 or 2¼ × 2¼ transparencies, prints. Offers $30-50/photo Buys one time rights.
Columns/Departments Book reviews, 900 words; Music reviews, 600 words; Travel, 600 words; Opinion pieces, 1,000 words; Humor, 600 words. Query with published clips. **Pays 15¢/word.**
Tips Be unafraid of controversy—articles should focus on problems and debates raised in lesbian culture, politics, and sexuality. Avoid being `politically correct.' We don't just want to know what's happening in the lesbian world, we want to know how what's happening in the world affects lesbians.

$ $ THE GUIDE

To Gay Travel, Entertainment, Politics, and Sex, Fidelity Publishing, P.O. Box 990593, Boston MA 02199. (617)266-8557. Fax: (617)266-1125. E-mail: letters@guidemag.com. Website: www.guidemag.com. **25% freelance written**. Monthly magazine on the gay and lesbian community. Estab. 1981. Circ. 30,000. Pays on acceptance. Offers negotiable kill fee. Publishes ms an average of 2 months after acceptance. Buys first rights. Submit seasonal material 2 months in advance. Accepts queries by mail, e-mail. Accepts previously published material. Accepts simultaneous submissions. Responds in 3 months to queries. Sample copy for sae with 9x12 envelope and 8 First-Class stamps. Guidelines for #10 SASE.

Nonfiction Needs book excerpts, if yet unpublished, essays, expose, general interest, historical, humor, interview, opinion, personal experience, photo feature, religious. **Buys 24 mss/year.** Send complete ms. Length: 500-5,000 words. **Pays $85-240.**
Reprints Occasionally buys previously published submissions. Pays 100% of amount paid for an original article.
Photos Send photos Captions, identification of subjects, model releases required. Reviews contact sheets. Pays $15/image used Buys one time rights.
Tips Brevity, humor, and militancy appreciated. Writing on sex, political analysis, and humor are particularly appreciated. We purchase very few freelance travel pieces; those that we do buy are usually on less commercial destinations.

$ HX MAGAZINE

Two Queens, Inc., 230 W. 17th St., 8th Floor, New York NY 10011. (212)352-3535. E-mail: info@hx.com. Website: www.hx.com. **25% freelance written**. Weekly magazine covering gay New York City nightlife and entertainment. Estab. 1991. Circ. 39,000. Byline given. Pays on publication. No kill fee. Publishes ms an average of 1 month after acceptance. Buys first North American serial rights, buys second serial (reprint) rights, buys electronic rights. Editorial lead time 2 months. Submit seasonal material 2 months in advance.
Nonfiction Needs general interest, arts and entertainment, celebrity profiles, reviews. **Buys 50 mss/year.** Query with published clips. Length: 500-2,000 words. **Pays $50-150. Pays $25-100 for unsolicited articles.**
Reprints Send tearsheet or photocopy with rights for sale noted and information about when and where the material previously appeared. Pays 50% of amount paid for an original article.
Photos State availability Captions, identification of subjects, model releases required. Reviews contact sheets, negatives, 8x10 prints. Buys one-time, reprint and electronic reprint rights
Columns/Departments 200 Query with published clips. **Pays $25-125.**

$ $ N INSTINCT MAGAZINE

Instinct Publishing, 303 N. Glenoaks Blvd., Suite L-120, Burbank CA 91502. E-mail: editor@instinctmag.com. Website: www.instinctmag.com. **40% freelance written**. Gay men's monthly lifestyle and entertainment magazine. "*Instinct* is a blend of *Cosmo* and *Maxim* for gay men. We're smart, sexy, irreverent, and we always have a sense of humor—a unique style that has made us the #1 gay men's magazine in the US." Estab. 1997. Circ. 115,000. Byline given. Pays on publication. Offers 20% kill fee. Buys all rights. Editorial lead time 2-3 months. Accepts queries by mail, e-mail. Accepts simultaneous submissions. Sample copy available online. Guidelines available online.
Nonfiction Be inventive and specific—an article on 'dating' isn't saying much unless there is a really great hook. Needs expose, general interest, humor, interview, celebrity and non-celebrity, travel, basically anything of interest to gay men will be considered. Does not want first-person accounts or articles. Send complete ms. Length: 850-2,000 words. **Pays $50-300.** Sometimes pays expenses of writers on assignment.
Photos Captions, identification of subjects, model releases required. Negotiates payment individually. Buys all rights.
Columns/Departments Health (gay, off-kilter), 800 words; Fitness (irreverent), 500 words; Movies, Books (edgy, sardonic), 800 words; Music, Video Games (indie, underground), 800 words. **Pays $150-250.**
Tips "While *Instinct* publishes a wide variety of features and columns having to do with gay men's issues, we maintain our signature irreverent, edgy tone throughout. When pitching stories (e-mail is preferred), be as specific as possible, and try to think beyond the normal scope of 'gay relationship' features. An article on 'Dating Tips,' for example, will not be considered, while an article on 'Tips on Dating Two Guys At Once' is more our slant. We rarely accept finished articles. We keep a special eye out for pitches on investigational/expose-type stories geared toward our audience."

MANDATE

225 Broadway, Suite 2801, New York NY 10007-3079. E-mail: mandatemag@aol.com. Website: www.mandatemag.com. Monthly magazine covering gay male erotica & lifestyle. Male photography, freelance erotic fiction, assigned columns & reviews. Estab. 1974. Circ. 100,000. Byline given. Pays on publication. No kill fee. Publishes ms an average of 5 months after acceptance. Buys first North American serial rights. Second Serial (reprint) Rights very rare Editorial lead time 3 months. Accepts queries by mail, e-mail. immediately. Responds in 1 month to mss. Sample copy available online. Guidelines by email.
Nonfiction Nonfiction columns & reviews are staff written or assigned.
Fiction Contact: Managing editor. Needs erotica. No romance, softcore erotica. **Buys 24 (also considers same mss. for *Honcho* & *Torso* magazines. mss/year.** Send complete ms. Length: 2,000-3,500+ words. **Pays $-$150.**

$ $ N MENSBOOK JOURNAL

47 West Communications, LLC, P.O. Box 148, Sturbridge MA 01566. Fax: (508)347-8150. E-mail: editorial@mensbook.com. Website: www.mensbook.com. **Contact:** P.C. Carr, editor/pub. **75% freelance written**.

Quarterly paperback book-serial covering gay men's journal. "We target bright, inquisitive, discerning gay men who share our criticism of the gay culture of pride and want more from gay media. We seek primarily first-person autobiographical pieces—then: biographies, political and social analysis, cartoons, short fiction, commentary, travel, humor." Estab. 2008. Circ. start up. Byline given. Pays on publication. Offers $10 kill fee. Buys first rights. Editorial lead time 4 months. Submit seasonal material 6 months in advance. Accepts queries by e-mail. Responds in 4 weeks to queries. Sample copy sent free by pdf. www.mensbook.com/writersguidelines.htm

Nonfiction Contact: P.C. Carr, publisher. Needs first-person pieces; essays; think-pieces; expose; humor; inspirational profiles of courage and triumph over adversity; interview/profile; religion/philosophy vis-a-vis the gay experience; opinion; travel. "We do not want celebrity profiles/commentary, chatty, campy gossip; sexual conjecture about famous people; film reviews." **Buys Buys 25 mss./yr. mss/year.** Query by e-mail. Length: 1,000-2,500 words. **Pays $20-100 for assigned articles and for unsolicited articles.**

Fiction Contact: Payson Fitch, managing editor. Needs adventure, erotica, fantasy, mystery/suspense, slice-of-life vignettes-of-life vignettes. Nothing poorly written. **Buys 10-12 fiction pieces/yr. mss/year.** Send complete ms. Length: 750-3,000 words.

Poetry Contact: J. K. Small, poetry editor. Needs avant-garde, free verse, haiku, light verse, traditional. **Buys 8/yr. poems/year.**

Tips "Be a tight writer, with a cogent, potent message. Structure your work with well-organized progressive sequencing, edit everything down before you send it over so we know it is the best you can do and we'll work together from there."

$ $ METROSOURCE MAGAZINE

MetroSource Publishing, Inc., 180 Varick St., 5th Floor, New York NY 10014. (212)691-5127. Website: www.metrosource.com. **Contact:** Editor. **75% freelance written**. Magazine published 6 times/year. *MetroSource* is an upscale, glossy, 4-color lifestyle magazine targeted to an urban, professional gay and lesbian readership. Estab. 1990. Circ. 145,000. Byline given. Pays on publication. Publishes ms an average of 2 months after acceptance. Editorial lead time 3 months. Submit seasonal material 4 months in advance. Accepts queries by mail, e-mail, fax, phone. Accepts simultaneous submissions. Sample copy for $5.

Nonfiction Needs expose, interview, opinion, photo feature, travel. **Buys 20 mss/year.** Query with published clips. Length: 1,000-2,500 words. **Pays $100-600.**

Photos State availability Captions, model releases required. Negotiates payment individually

Columns/Departments Book, film, television, and stage reviews; health columns; and personal diary and opinion pieces. Word lengths vary. Query with published clips. **Pays $200**

OUT

Box 1253, Old Chelsea Station, New York NY 10013. (212)242-8100. Fax: (212)242-8338. E-mail: letters@out.com. Website: www.out.com. **70% freelance written**. Monthly national magazine covering gay and lesbian general-interest topics. Our subjects range from current affairs to culture, from fitness to finance. Estab. 1992. Circ. 165,000. Byline given. Pays on publication. Offers 25% kill fee. Publishes ms an average of 3 months after acceptance. Buys first North American serial rights. second serial (reprint) rights for anthologies (additional fee paid) and 30-day reprint rights (additional fee paid if applicable) Editorial lead time 3 months. Submit seasonal material 5 months in advance. Accepts queries by mail. Accepts simultaneous submissions. Responds in 6 weeks to queries. Responds in 2 months to mss.

Nonfiction Needs book excerpts, essays, expose, general interest, historical, humor, interview, new product, opinion, personal experience, photo feature, fashion/lifestyle. **Buys 200 mss/year.** Query with published clips and SASE Length: 50-2,500 words. **Pays variable rate.** Sometimes pays expenses of writers on assignment.

Photos State availability Captions, identification of subjects, model releases required. Reviews contact sheets, transparencies, prints. Negotiates payment individually Buys one time rights.

Tips *Out*'s contributors include editors and writers from the country's top consumer titles: skilled reporters, columnists, and writers with distinctive voices and specific expertise in the fields they cover. But while published clips and relevant experience are a must, the magazine also seeks out fresh, young voices. The best guide to the kind of stories we publish is to review our recent issues. Is there a place for the story you have in mind? Be aware of our long lead time. No phone queries, please.

$ OUTLOOKS

Outlooks Publication Inc., #1B, 1230A 17th Ave. SW, Calgary Alberta T2T 0B8 Canada. (403)228-1157. Fax: (403)228-7735. E-mail: main@outlooks.ca. Website: www.outlooks.ca. **100% freelance written**. Monthly national lifestyle publication for Canada's LGBT community. Estab. 1997. Circ. 31,500. Byline given. Pays on publication. Offers 50% kill fee. Publishes ms an average of 2 months after acceptance. Buys first rights. Editorial lead time 2 months. Submit seasonal material 3 months in advance. Accepts queries by e-mail. Accepts simultaneous submissions. Responds in 2 weeks to queries. Sample copy available online. Guidelines free.

Nonfiction Needs essays, general interest, humor, interview, photo feature feature, travel. Query with published clips. Length: 500-1,500 words. **Pays $100-120.** Sometimes pays expenses of writers on assignment.

Photos State availability Captions required. Reviews contact sheets. Negotiates payment individually. Buys one time rights.
Columns/Departments Book, movie, and music reviews (600-700 words). 120 Query with published clips.
Fiction Needs adventure, erotica, humorous. **Buys 10 mss/year.** Query with published clips. Length: 1,200-1,600 words. **Pays $120-160.**

OUTSMART

Up & Out Communications, 3406 Audubon Place, Houston TX 77006. (713)520-7237. Fax: (713)522-3275. Website: www.outsmartmagazine.com. **50% freelance written**. Monthly magazine concerned with gay, lesbian, bisexual, and transgender issues. *OutSmart* offers vibrant and thoughtful coverage of the stories that appeal most to an educated gay audience. Estab. 1994. Circ. 60,000. Byline given. Pays on publication. No kill fee. Buys one-time rights, buys simultaneous rights. Permission to publish on website. Editorial lead time 3 months. Submit seasonal material 4 months in advance. Accepts queries by mail, e-mail, fax. Responds in 6 weeks to queries. Responds in 2 months to mss. Sample copy and writer's guidelines online
Nonfiction Needs historical, interview, opinion, personal experience, photo feature, travel, health/wellness. **Buys 24 mss/year.** Send complete ms. Length: 450-2,000 words. **Negotiates payment individually.**
Reprints Send photocopy.
Photos State availability Identification of subjects required. Reviews 4x6 prints. Negotiates payment individually Buys one time rights.
Tips *OutSmart* is a mainstream publication that covers culture, politics, personalities, and entertainment as well as local and national news and events. We work to address the diversity of the lesbian, gay, bisexual, and transgender community, fostering understanding among all our readers.

TORSO

225 Broadway, Suite 2801, New York NY 10007-3079. E-mail: torsomag@aol.com. Website: www.torsomag.com. Monthly covering gay male erotica & bodybuilding. Male photography, freelance erotic fiction, assigned columns & reviews. Estab. 1982. Circ. 100,000. Byline given. Pays on publication. No kill fee. Publishes ms an average of 5 months after acceptance. Buys first North American serial rights, buys second serial (reprint) rights, buys electronic rights. Editorial lead time 3 months. Accepts queries by mail, e-mail. immediately. Responds in 1 month to mss. Sample copy available online. Guidelines free.
Nonfiction Nonfiction column & reviews are staff written or assigned. **Pays by agreement. for assigned articles.**
Columns/Departments **Pays for assigned columns/reviews by agreement.**
Fiction Needs erotica. No romance, softcore erotica. **Buys 24 mss/yr. for *Torso*, but same mss. also considered for *Honcho* and *Mandate*. mss/year.** Send complete ms. Length: 2,000-3,500 words.

$ THE WASHINGTON BLADE

Washington Blade, 529 14thSt., NW, Washington DC 20045. (202)797-7000. Fax: (202)797-7040. E-mail: news@washblade.com. Website: www.washblade.com. **20% freelance written**. Nation's oldest and largest weekly newspaper covering the lesbian, gay, bi-sexual and transgender issues. Articles (subjects) should be written from or directed to a gay perspective. Estab. 1969. Circ. 30,000. Byline given. No kill fee. Buys first North American serial rights. Submit seasonal material one month in advance. Accepts queries by mail, e-mail, fax. Responds in within one month to queries.
Nonfiction Most news stories are staff-generated; Writers with news or news feature ideas should inquiere with Joshua Lynsen, news editor. Pay varies.
Reprints Send typed manuscript with rights for sale noted and information about when and where the material previously appeared.
Photos A photo or graphic with feature articles is particularly important. Photos with news stories are appreciated. Send photos by mail or e-mail. Captions required. Pay varies. Photographers on assignment are paid mutually agreed upon fee. Buys all rights.
Columns/Departments Send feature submissions to Joey DiGuglielmo, arts editor. Sent opinion submission to Kevin Naff, editor. Pay varies. No sexually explicit material.
Tips We maintain a highly competent and professional staff of news reporters, and it is difficult to break in here as a freelancer covering news. Include a résumé, good examples of your writing, and know the paper before you send a manuscript for publication. We look for writers who are credible and professional, and for copy that is accurate, fair, timely, and objective in tone. We do not work with writers who play fast and loose with the facts, or who are unprofessional in presentation. Before you send anything, become familiar with our publication. Do not send sexually explicit material.

$ $ XTRA

Toronto's Lesbian & Gay Biweekly, Pink Triangle Press, 491 Church St., Suite 200, Toronto ON M4Y 2C6 Canada. (416)925-6665. Fax: (416)925-6674. E-mail: info@xtra.ca. Website: www.xtra.ca. **80% freelance written**. Biweekly tabloid covering gay, lesbian, bisexual and transgender issues, news, arts and events of interest in

Toronto. *Xtra* is dedicated to lesbian and gay sexual liberation. We publish material that advocates this end, according to the mission statement of the not-for-profit organization Pink Triange Press, which operates the paper. Estab. 1984. Circ. 45,000. Byline given. Pays on publication. No kill fee. Buys first North American serial rights, buys electronic rights. Editorial lead time 1 month. Accepts queries by e-mail. Accepts previously published material. Accepts simultaneous submissions. Responds in 2 weeks to queries. Sample copy available online. Guidelines by email.

Nonfiction Needs book excerpts, essays, interview, opinion, personal experience, travel. US-based stories or profiles of straight people who do not have a direct connection to the LGBT community. Query with published clips. Length: 200-1,600 words. Sometimes pays expenses of writers on assignment. Limit agreed upon in advance

Photos Send photos Captions, identification of subjects, model releases required. Offers $60 minimum Buys Internet rights

Columns/Departments *Xtra* rarely publishes unsolicited columns. 6 Query with published clips.

GENERAL INTEREST

$ $ THE AMERICAN LEGION MAGAZINE

P.O. Box 1055, Indianapolis IN 46206-1055. (317)630-1200. Fax: (317)630-1280. E-mail: magazine@legion.org. Website: www.legion.org. **70% freelance written. Prefers to work with published/established writers, but works with a small number of new/unpublished writers each year.** Monthly magazine. Working through 15,000 community-level posts, the honorably discharged wartime veterans of The American Legion dedicate themselves to God, country and traditional American values. They believe in a strong defense; adequate and compassionate care for veterans and their families; community service; and the wholesome development of our nation's youth. We publish articles that reflect these values. We inform our readers and their families of significant trends and issues affecting our nation, the world and the way we live. Our major features focus on the American flag, national security, foreign affairs, business trends, social issues, health, education, ethics and the arts. We also publish selected general feature articles, articles of special interest to veterans, and question-and-answer interviews with prominent national and world figures. Estab. 1919. Circ. 2,550,000. Byline given. Pays on acceptance. No kill fee. Publishes ms an average of 6 months after acceptance. Buys first North American serial rights. Accepts queries by mail, e-mail, fax. Responds in 2 months to queries. Sample copy for $3.50 and 9 x 12 SAE with 6 first-class stamps. Guidelines for #10 SASE.

Nonfiction Well-reported articles or expert commentaries cover issues/trends in world/national affairs, contemporary problems, general interest, sharply-focused feature subjects. Monthly Q&A with national figures/experts. Needs general interest, interview. No regional topics or promotion of partisan political agendas. No personal experiences or war stories. **Buys 50-60 mss/year.** Query with SASE should explain the subject or issue, article's angle and organization, writer's qualifications, and experts to be interviewed. Length: 300-2,000 words. **Pays 40¢/word and up.**

Photos On assignment.

Tips Queries by new writers should include clips/background/expertise; no longer than 1 ½ pages. Submit suitable material showing you have read several issues. *The American Legion Magazine* considers itself '*the* magazine for a strong America.' Reflect this theme (which includes economy, educational system, moral fiber, social issues, infrastructure, technology and national defense/security). We are a general interest, national magazine, not a strictly military magazine. We are widely read by members of the Washington establishment and other policy makers.

AMERICAN PROFILE

Publishing Group of America, 341 Cool Springs Blvd., 4th Fl., Franklin TN 37067. Website: www.americanprofile.com. **90% freelance written**. Weekly magazine with national and regional editorial celebrating the people, places, and experiences of hometowns across America. The 4-color magazine is distributed through small to medium-size community newspapers. Estab. 2000. Circ. 10,000,000. Byline given. Pays on acceptance. No kill fee. Buys first rights, buys electronic rights, buys 6-month exclusive rights rights. Editorial lead time 6 months. Submit seasonal material 1 year in advance. Accepts queries by mail; include SASE. Responds in 1 month to queries. Responds in 1 month to mss. Guidelines available online.

Nonfiction Needs general interest, how-to, interview. No fiction, nostalgia, poetry, essays. **Buys 250 mss/year.** Query with published clips. Length: 350-1,000 words. Pays expenses of writers on assignment. Must have receipts

Photos State availability Captions, identification of subjects, model releases, True required. Reviews transparencies. Negotiates payment individually. Buys one-time rights, nonexclusive after 6 months.

Columns/Departments Health; Family; Finances; Home; Gardening

Tips "Please visit the website to see our content and writing style."

$$$$ THE ATLANTIC MONTHLY

600 New Hampshire Ave. NW, Washington, DC 20037. (202)266-6000. Website: www.theatlantic.com. Monthly magazine. General magazine for an educated readership with broad cultural and public-affairs interests. Estab. 1857. Circ. 400,000. Byline given. Pays on acceptance. No kill fee. Buys first North American serial rights. Accepts queries by mail. Guidelines available online.

Nonfiction Reportage preferred. Needs book excerpts, essays, general interest, humor, travel. Query with or without published clips or send complete ms to 'Editorial Department' at address above. All unsolicited mss must be accompanied by SASE. Length: 1,000-6,000 words. **Payment varies** Sometimes pays expenses of writers on assignment.

Fiction Contact: C. Michael Curtis, fiction editor. Seeks fiction that is clear, tightly written with strong sense of 'story' and well-defined characters. No longer publishes fiction in the regular magazine. Instead, it will appear in a special newsstand-only fiction issue. Send complete ms. preferred length: 2,000-6,000 words

Poetry Contact: David Barber, poetry editor. **Buys 30-40 poems/year.**

Tips Writers should be aware that this is not a market for beginner's work (nonfiction and fiction), nor is it truly for intermediate work. Study this magazine before sending only your best, most professional work. When making first contact, cover letters are sometimes helpful, particularly if they cite prior publications or involvement in writing programs. Common mistakes: melodrama, inconclusiveness, lack of development, unpersuasive characters and/or dialogue.

$$ AVENTURA MAGAZINE

Discover Magazine, Inc., 18781 Biscayne Blvd., Miami FL 33180. (305)932-2400. E-mail: editorial@aventuramagazine.com. Website: www.aventuramagazine.com. **70% freelance written**. Magazine published 7 times/year covering affluent consumer markets. *AVENTURA Magazine*'s readership identify us as 'the intelligent source to luxury living.' As a horizontally positioned magazine with distribution over 50,000 and readership beyond 125,000, *AVENTURA* is distinguished as the magazine choice for readers pursuing a sophisticated lifestyle and luxury brand. Our typical reader has a household income over $200,000, are well traveled and well-educated. Articles are written for an audience with heightened expectations in all areas of life. Estab. 1998. Circ. 50,000. Byline given. Pays on acceptance. Buys all rights. Editorial lead time 3 months. Submit seasonal material 6 months in advance. Accepts queries by e-mail. Responds in 3 weeks to queries. Sample copy free. Guidelines by email.

Nonfiction Needs expose, interview, travel, luxury living. Does not want to see opinions, essays, religious or how-to pieces. **Buys 1-3 mss/year.** Query. Length: words. **Pays $250+.** Sometimes pays expenses of writers on assignment.

Photos State availability Captions, identification of subjects, model releases required. Reviews GIF/JPEG files. Negotiates payment individually. Buys all rights.

$ ⊘ BIBLIOPHILOS

A Journal of History, Literature, and the Liberal Arts, The Bibliophile Publishing Co., Inc., 200 Security Building, Fairmont WV 26554. (304)366-8107. **65-70% freelance written**. Quarterly literary magazine concentrating on 19th century American and European history and literature. We see ourself as a forum for new and unpublished writers, historians, philosophers, literary critics and reviewers, and those who love animals. Audience is academic-oriented, college graduate, who believes in traditional Aristotelian-Thomistic thought and education, and has a fair streak of the Luddite in him/her. Our ideal reader owns no television, has never sent nor received e-mail, and avoids shopping malls at any cost. He loves books. Estab. 1981. Circ. 400. Byline given. Pays on publication. Publishes ms an average of 1 year after acceptance. Buys first North American serial rights. Editorial lead time 6 months. Submit seasonal material 6 months in advance. Accepts queries by mail. Responds in 2 weeks to queries. Responds in 1 month to mss. Sample copy for $5.25. Guidelines for sae with 9 ½x4 envelope and 2 First-Class stamps.

- Query first only, unaccompanied by any ms.

Nonfiction Needs book excerpts, essays, general interest, historical, humor, interview, opinion, personal experience, photo feature, travel, book review-essay, literary criticism. Upcoming theme issues include an annual all book-review issue, containing 10-15 reviews and review-essays, or poetry about books and reading. Does not want to see anything that Oprah would recommend, or that Erma Bombeck or Ann Landers would think humorous or interesting. No `I found Jesus and it changed my life' material. **Buys 25-30 mss/year.** Query by mail only first, not with any ms included. Length: 1,500-3,000 words. **Pays $5-35.**

Photos State availability Identification of subjects required. Reviews b&w 4x6 prints. Negotiates payment individually. Buys one time rights.

Columns/Departments Features (fiction and nonfiction, short stories), 1,500-3,000 words; Poetry (batches of 5, preferably thematically related), 3-150 lines; Reviews (book reviews or review essays on new books or individual authors, current and past), 1,000-1,500 words; Opinion (man triumphing over technology and technocrats, the facade of modern education, computer fetishism), 1,000-1,500 words. 20 Query by mail only. **Pays $25-40.**

Fiction Contact: Gerald J. Bobango, editor. Needs adventure, ethnic, historical, general, US, Eastern Europe, horror, psychological, supernatural, humorous, mainstream, mystery, police procedural, private eye/hardboiled, courtroom, novel concepts, romance, gothic, historical, regency period, slice-of-life vignettes, suspense, western, frontier saga, traditional, utopian, Orwellian. No `I remember Mama, who was a saint and I miss her terribly'; no gay or lesbian topics; no drug culture material; nothing harping on political correctness; nothing to do with healthy living, HMOs, medical programs, or the welfare state, unless it is against statism in these areas. **Buys 25-30 mss/year.** Length: 1,500-3,000 words. **Pays $25-40.**
Poetry Needs free verse, light verse, traditional. Formal and rhymed verse gets read first.
Tips Query first. Do not send material unsolicited. We shall not respond if you do.

$ $ $ $ DIVERSION

300 W. 57th St., New York NY 10019-5238. (212)969-7500. Fax: (212)969-7563. E-mail: shartford@hearst.com. Website: www.diversion.com. Monthly magazine covering travel and lifestyle, edited for physicians. *Diversion* offers an eclectic mix of interests beyond medicine. Regular features include stories on domestic and foreign travel destinations, food and wine, cars, gardening, photography, books, electronic gear, and the arts. Although *Diversion* doesn't cover health subjects, it does feature profiles of doctors who excel at nonmedical pursuits or who engage in medical volunteer work. Estab. 1973. Circ. 190,000. Byline given. Pays 3 months after acceptance. Offers 25% kill fee. Editorial lead time 6 months. Responds in 1 month to queries. Sample copy for $4.50. Guidelines available
Nonfiction We get so many travel and food queries that we're hard pressed to even read them all. Far better to query us on culture, the arts, sports, technology, etc. Query with proposal, published clips, and author's credentials. Length: 1,800-2,000 words. **Pays 50¢-$1/word.**
Columns/Departments Travel, food & wine, photography, gardening, cars, technology. Length: 1,200 words.

50 SOMETHING

National Seniors, Level 7, 243 Edward St., Brisbane QLD 4000 Australia. (61)(7)3233-9105. E-mail: 50something@nationalseniors.com.au. Website: www.nationalseniors.com.au. Bimonthly magazine covering celebrity profiles, health, the arts, finance, and national and international news, to inform, empower and entertain older Australians. Editorial lead time 2 months.
Nonfiction Needs general interest, interview. Query.

$ $ GRIT

American Life and Traditions, Ogden Publications, 1503 SW 42nd St., Topeka KS 66609. (785)274-4300. Fax: (785)274-4305. E-mail: grit@grit.com. Website: www.grit.com. **90% freelance written. Open to new writers.** Bimonthly magazine. "*Grit* focuses on rural lifestyles, country living and small-scale farming. We are looking for useful, practical information on livestock, gardening, farm equipment, home-and-yard improvement and related topics. We also offer some nostalgia articles in each issue—what it was like living on the farm in the Great Depression, how the family kept the peace during holidays, etc." Estab. 1882. Circ. 117,000. Byline given. Pays on publication. No kill fee. Buys shared rights. Submit seasonal material 6 months in advance. Accepts queries by mail, e-mail. Sample copy and writer's guidelines for $4 and 11X14 SASE with 4 first-class stamps. Guidelines (under Magazine) and sample articles are posted on website.
Nonfiction "The best way to sell work is by reading each issue cover to cover." Query by mail or e-mail. Assignments are made from queries approximately a year in advance. Editorial calendar full for 2009; send queries for 2010 by May 1, 2009. Main features run 1,000-1,200 words. Department features average 800-1,000 words. **Varies: $75 for a short, newsy article for Grit Gazette to $750 or more for long feature articles.**
Photos Professional quality photos or slides accepted with manuscript. We prefer disks or e-mailed low-res digital files to select from. A photo-callout is sent for each issue. Pays $50-$200 per published original photograph.
Fiction We no longer publish fiction.
Tips "Buys shared rights. We work 6 months or more in advance, so no last-minute queries/submissions, please. No unsolicited mss, assignments only."

$ $ $ $ HARPER'S MAGAZINE

666 Broadway, 11th Floor, New York NY 10012. (212)420-5720. Fax: (212)228-5889. Website: www.harpers.org. **90% freelance written**. Monthly magazine for well-educated, socially concerned, widely read men and women who value ideas and good writing. *Harper's Magazine* encourages national discussion on current and significant issues in a format that offers arresting facts and intelligent opinions. By means of its several shorter journalistic forms—Harper's Index, Readings, Forum, and Annotation—as well as with its acclaimed essays, fiction, and reporting, *Harper's* continues the tradition begun with its first issue in 1850: to inform readers across the whole spectrum of political, literary, cultural, and scientific affairs. Estab. 1850. Circ. 230,000. Pays on acceptance. Offers negotiable kill fee. Publishes ms an average of 3 months after acceptance. Rights purchased vary with author and material. Accepts previously published material. Responds in 6 weeks to queries. Sample copy for $5.95.

Nonfiction For writers working with agents or who will query first only, our requirements are: public affairs, literary, international and local reporting, and humor. Publishes 1 major report/issue. Length: 4,000-6,000 words. Publishes 1 major essay/issue. Length: 4,000-6,000 words. These should be construed as topical essays on all manner of subjects (politics, the arts, crime, business, etc.) to which the author can bring the force of passionate and informed statement. Needs humor. No interviews; no profiles. **Buys 2 mss/year.** Query. Length: 4,000-6,000 words.

Reprints Accepted for Readings section. Send typed ms with rights for sale ted and information about when and where the article previously appeared.

Photos Contact: Stacey Clarkson, art director. Occasionally purchased with ms; others by assignment. State availability Pays $50-500.

Fiction Will consider unsolicited fiction. Needs humorous. **Buys 12 mss/year.** Query. Length: 3,000-5,000 words. **Generally pays 50¢-$1/word.**

Tips Some readers expect their magazines to clothe them with opinions in the way that Bloomingdale's dresses them for the opera. The readers of *Harper's Magazine* belong to a different crowd. They strike me as the kind of people who would rather think in their own voices and come to their own conclusions.

$ $ INDUSTRY MAGAZINE

Industry Publications, LLC, 1768 Park Center Dr., Suite 280, Orlando FL 32835. Fax: (407)290-0120. Website: www.industrymagazine.net. **80% freelance written**. Bimonthly magazine covering fashion, entertainment, people, culture. *Industry* combines all the power and swoop of a national, luxury lifestyle, general interest title with the inimitable flair of its regional franchises. Specifically directed at well-educated, affluent, sophisticated residents of its franchise cities, *Industry* offers what typical regional books cannot; content that is at once national and local in scope. Estab. 2002. Circ. 250,000. Byline given. Pays on publication. Offers 33% kill fee. Publishes ms an average of 1 month after acceptance. Buys first rights. Editorial lead time 3 months. Submit seasonal material 5 months in advance. Accepts queries by e-mail, fax. Responds in 1 month to queries. Sample copy by email.

- *Industry Magazine* has editions in Orlando; Tampa Bay; Sarasota; Palm Beach; El Paso; Kansas City; Los Angeles; Staten Island; Phoenix.

Nonfiction Needs general interest, humor, interview, new product, travel, fashion. Does not want stale, PR-type product descriptions. Writers should be witty, but sophisticated and opinionated. **Buys 500 mss/year.** Query with published clips. Length: 450-2,000 words. **Pays $275-600.** Sometimes pays expenses of writers on assignment.

Photos Contact: Contact Kristen Papa, photo editor. Send photos Identification of subjects required. Reviews GIF/JPEG files (300 dpi or higher). Offers no additional payment for photos accepted with ms. Buys one time rights.

Columns/Departments Night Owl (local nightlife for specific regions), 450-600 words; iSpot (places local elite/highrollers are seen), 800 words; Art Scene (local art scene in specific regions), 450-600 words; Restaurant Review (local restaurants in specific regions). 300 Query. **Pays $275-300.**

Tips Pitch ideas based on what you see in the magazine. Do not forget to send clips with your pitch, even if it is not a magazine article. I need to know how well you can write.

$ $ $ $ NATIONAL GEOGRAPHIC MAGAZINE

1145 17th St. NW, Washington DC 20036. (202)857-7000. Fax: (202)492-5767. Website: www.nationalgeographic.com. **60% freelance written. Prefers to work with published/established writers.** Monthly magazine for members of the National Geographic Society. Timely articles written in a compelling, 'eyewitness' style. Arresting photographs that speak to us of the beauty, mystery, and harsh realities of life on earth. Maps of unprecedented detail and accuracy. These are the hallmarks of *National Geographic* magazine. Since 1888, the *Geographic* has been educating readers about the world. Estab. 1888. Circ. 6,800,000.

Nonfiction *National Geographic* publishes general interest, illustrated articles on science, natural history, exploration, cultures and geographical regions. Of the freelance writers assigned, a few are experts in their fields; the remainder are established professionals. Fewer than 1% of unsolicited queries result in assignments. Query (500 words with clips of published articles by mail to Senior Assitant Editor Oliver Payne. Do not send mss. Length: 2,000-8,000 words. Pays expenses of writers on assignment.

Photos Query in care of the Photographic Division.

Tips State the theme(s) clearly, let the narrative flow, and build the story around strong characters and a vivid sense of place. Give us rounded episodes, logically arranged.

$ $ $ NEWSWEEK

251 W. 57th St., New York NY 10019. E-mail: editors@newsweek.com. Website: www.newsweek.com. *Newsweek* is edited to report the week's developments on the newsfront of the world and the nation through news, commentary and analysis. Circ. 3,180,000. No kill fee. Buys non-exclusive world-wide rights.

Columns/Departments Contact: myturn@newsweek.com. Accepts unsolicited mss for My Turn, a column of personal opinion. The 850- 900-word essays for the column must be original, not published elsewhere, and contain verifiable facts. Only responds if interested. **Pays $1,000 on publication.**

$ $ $ THE NEW YORK TIMES MAGAZINE

229 W. 43rd St., New York NY 10036. (212)556-1234. Fax: (212)556-3830. E-mail: magazine@nytimes.com. Website: www.nytimes.com/pages/magazine. *The New York Times Magazine* appears in *The New York Times* on Sunday. The *Arts and Leisure* section appears during the week. The *Op Ed* page appears daily. No kill fee.

- Because of the volume of submissions for the Lives column, the magazine cannot return or respond to unsolicited manuscripts.

Nonfiction *Arts & Leisure*: Wants to encourage imaginativeness in terms of form and approach—stressing ideas, issues, trends, investigations, symbolic reporting and stories delving deeply into the creative achievements and processes of artists and entertainers—and seeks to break away from old-fashioned gushy, fan magazine stuff. Length: 1,500-2,000 words. **Pays $100-350**, depending on length. Address unsolicited articles with SASE to the Arts & Leisure Articles Editor. *Op Ed* page: The Op Ed page is always looking for new material and publishes many people who have never been published before. We want material of universal relevance which people can talk about in a personal way. When writing for the Op Ed page, there is no formula, but the writing itself should have some polish. Don't make the mistake of pontificating on the news. We're not looking for more political columnists. Length: 750 words. **Pays $150.**

$ $ $ THE OLD FARMER'S ALMANAC

Yankee Publishing, Inc., P.O. Box 520, Dublin NH 03444. (603)563-8111. Website: www.Almanac.com. **95% freelance written**. Annual magazine covering weather, gardening, history, oddities, lore. *"The Old Farmer's Almanac* is the oldest continuously published periodical in North America. Since 1792, it has provided useful information for people in all walks of life: tide tables for those who live near the ocean; sunrise tables and planting charts for those who live on the farm or simply enjoy gardening; recipes for those who like to cook; and forecasts for those who don't like the question of weather left up in the air. The words of the *Almanac*'s founder, Robert B. Thomas, guide us still: 'Our main endeavor is to be useful, but with a pleasant degree of humour.'" Estab. 1792. Circ. 3,750,000. Byline given. Pays on acceptance. Offers 25% kill fee. Publishes ms an average of 9 months after acceptance. Buys electronic rights, buys all rights. Editorial lead time 6 months. Submit seasonal material 1 year in advance. Accepts queries by mail. Responds in 3 weeks to queries. Responds in 2 months to mss. Sample copy for $6 at bookstores or online. Guidelines available online.

Nonfiction Needs general interest, historical, how-to, garden, cook, save money, humor, weather, natural remedies, obscure facts, history, popular culture. No personal recollections/accounts, personal/family histories. Query with published clips. Length: 800-2,500 words. **Pays 65¢/word.** Sometimes pays expenses of writers on assignment.

Fillers Needs anecdotes, short humor. 1-2 Length: 100-200 words. **Pays $25.**

Tips *"The Old Farmer's Almanac* is a reference book. Our readers appreciate obscure facts and stories. Read it. Think differently. Read writer's guidelines online."

$ $ $ OPEN SPACES

Open Spaces Publications, Inc., PMB 134, 6327-C SW Capitol Hwy., Portland OR 97239-1937. (503)313-4361. Fax: (503)227-3401. E-mail: info@open-spaces.com. Website: www.open-spaces.com. **95% freelance written**. Quarterly general interest magazine. *Open Spaces* is a forum for informed writing and intelligent thought. Articles are written by experts in various fields. Audience is varied (CEOs and rock climbers, politicos and university presidents, etc.) but is highly educated and loves to read good writing. Estab. 1997. Byline given. Pays on publication. Offers 20% kill fee. Publishes ms an average of 6 months after acceptance. Rights purchased vary with author and material. Editorial lead time 9 months. Accepts queries by mail, fax. Accepts simultaneous submissions. Sample copy for $10. Guidelines available online.

Nonfiction Needs essays, general interest, historical, how-to, if clever, humor, interview, personal experience, travel. **Buys 35 mss/year.** Send complete ms. 1,500-2,500 words; major articles up to 6,000 words. **Pays variable amount.**

Photos State availability Captions, identification of subjects required. Buys one time rights.

Columns/Departments Contact: David Williams, departments editor. Books (substantial topics such as the Booker Prize, The Newbery, etc.); Travel (must reveal insight); Sports (past subjects include rowing, and swing dancing); Unintended Consequences, 1,500-2,500 words. 20-25 Send complete ms. **Payment varies**

Fiction Contact: Ellen Teicher, fiction editor. Quality is far more important than type. Read the magazine. Excellence is the issue—not subject matter. **Buys 8 mss/year.** Length: 2,000-6,000 words. **Payment varies.**

Poetry Contact: Susan Juve-Hu Bucharest, poetry editor. Again, quality is far more important than type.

Fillers Needs anecdotes, short humor, cartoons.

Tips *Open Spaces* reviews all manuscripts submitted in hopes of finding writing of the highest quality. We present a Northwest perspective as well as a national and international one. Best advice is read the magazine.

$ $ $ $ OUTSIDE

Mariah Media, Inc., Outside Plaza, 400 Market St., Santa Fe NM 87501. (505)989-7100. Fax: (505)989-4700. Website: www.outsidemag.com. **60% freelance written**. Monthly magazine covering active lifestyle. Estab. 1977. Circ. 665,000. Byline given. Pays on acceptance. Offers 25% kill fee. Publishes ms an average of 3-6 months after acceptance. Buys first North American serial rights, buys second serial (reprint) rights. Makes work-for-hire assignments. Accepts queries by mail. Guidelines free.

Nonfiction Needs book excerpts, new product, travel. **Buys 300 mss./yr. mss/year.** Query with published clips. Length: 100-5,000 words. **Pays $1.50-2/word for assigned articles. Pays $1-1.50/word for unsolicited articles.** Pays expenses of writers on assignment.

Photos Buys one time rights.

Columns/Departments Pays $$1.50-$2.

$ $ $ $ PARADE

ParadeNet, Inc., 711 Third Ave., New York NY 10017-4014. Website: www.parade.com. **95% freelance written**. Weekly magazine for a general interest audience. Estab. 1941. Circ. 81,000,000. Pays on acceptance. Offers kill fee. Kill fee varies in amount Publishes ms an average of 5 months after acceptance. Buys worldwide exclusive rights for 7 days, plus nonexclusive electronic and other rights in perpetuity. Editorial lead time 1 month. Accepts queries by mail, e-mail, fax. Accepts simultaneous submissions. Sample copy available online. Guidelines available online.

Nonfiction Publishes general interest (on health, trends, social issues or anything of interest to a broad general audience), interview/profile (of news figures, celebrities and people of national significance), and provocative topical pieces of news value. Spot news events are not accepted, as *Parade* has a 2-month lead time. No fiction, fashion, travel, poetry, cartoons, nostalgia, regular columns, personal essays, quizzes, or fillers. Unsolicited queries concerning celebrities, politicians or sports figures are rarely assigned. **Buys 150 mss/year.** Query with published clips. Length: 1,200-1,500 words. **Pays very competitive amount.** Pays expenses of writers on assignment.

Tips If the writer has a specific expertise in the proposed topic, it increases the chances of breaking in. Send a well-researched, well-written 1-page proposal and enclose a SASE. Do not submit completed manuscripts.

⊘ PEOPLE

Time, Inc., 1271 Avenue of the Americas, New York NY 10020. (212)522-1212. Fax: (212)522-1359. E-mail: editor@people.com. Website: www.people.com. Weekly magazine. Designed as a forum for personality journalism through the use of short articles on contemporary news events and people. Circ. 3,617,127. No kill fee. Editorial lead time 3 months.

- Does not buy freelance materials or use freelance writers.

$ THE POLISHING STONE

Refining the Life You Live Into the Life You Love, 20104 87th St. SE, Snohomish WA 98290-7267. E-mail: submissions@polishingstone.com. Website: www.polishingstone.org. **50% freelance written**. Magazine published 5 times/year. *The Polishing Stone* takes an optimistic and realistic look at the environment and quality of life: whole foods, alternative health, earth-friendly and handcrafted products, mindful parenting, relationships, and social and environmental issues. We focus on healthy lifestyles that are close to the earth, sustainable, and in balance. The issues we cover are serious, but we seek a tone of ease because our personal beliefs lean toward hopefulness about possibilities and opportunities for healing. Facts are encouraged as an accurate assessment of a situation, but should not overshadow the offering of solutions and inspiration. In a world where reporting has become synonymous with shock tactics, speaking from the heart is an effective alternative. Estab. 2004. Byline given. Pays on publication. No kill fee. Publishes ms an average of 4 months after acceptance. Buys first North American serial rights. Editorial lead time 4 months. Submit seasonal material 4 months in advance. Accepts queries by mail. Accepts simultaneous submissions. Responds in 1 month to queries. Responds in 2 months to mss. Sample copy available online. Guidelines available online.

Nonfiction Needs book excerpts, essays, general interest, how-to, accepted for the following columns: Whole Foods, From the Ground Up, Everything Herbal, With our Hands and Treading Lightly, humor, inspirational, interview, new product, personal experience. The Polishing Stone is published in February, April, July, September and December. Articles often relate to the season in which they appear. We do not accept travel, religious or technical articles, or any article that focuses on problems without offering solutions. We do not publish reprints. **Buys 75 mss/year.** Query with published clips. Length: 200-1,600 words.

Columns/Departments Whole Foods (preparation of primarily vegetarian foods); From the Ground Up (earth-friendly gardening); Everything Herbal (information about the healing power of herbs); A Balance of Health (practical alternatives for returning to balanced health); Treading Lightly (sustainable products, processes and services); With our Hands (artisans share design for simple hand-made products); Life out Loud (an honest look at how children shape us); Looking Within (spiritual and psychological insights); In Community (the people responsible for healing/changing communities); This Spinning Earth (information and inspiration to heal the earth); In Print & On Screen (reviews of books and movies that explain and encourage). 75 Query with published clips or send complete ms. **Pays $25-100.**

Poetry Needs free verse, haiku, light verse. **Buys 5-10 poems/year.** Submit maximum 4 poems. Length: 5-25 lines.

Fillers Needs anecdotes, facts, short humor. 10-20 Length: 50-175 words. **Pays $10.**

Tips If previously published, send query letter and clips. Otherwise, send a completed ms of no more than 1,600 words. Send both queries and completed mss by mail only. We want to give new writers a chance, especially those who are willing to do the work. For queries, this means providing a clear description of your topic, angle, sources, lead, and reason why the article is a good fit for *The Polishing Stone*. Completed manuscripts should be carefully edited and fact-checked prior to submission. As always, read our magazine as a guide to our content and writing style. Draw on your own experiences and expertise and share from the heart.

PORTLAND MAGAZINE

Maine's City Magazine, 722 Congress St., Portland ME 04102. (207)775-4339. E-mail: portlandmagazine@gmail.com. Website: www.portlandmagazine.com. Monthly city lifestyle magazine—fiction, style, business, real estate, controversy, fashion, cuisine, interviews and art relating to the Maine area. Estab. 1985. Circ. 100,000. Pays on publication. No kill fee. Buys first North American serial rights.

Fiction Contact: Colin Sargent, editor. Send complete ms. 700 words or less

$ $ READER'S DIGEST

The Reader's Digest Association, Inc., Box 100, Pleasantville NY 10572-0100. Website: www.rd.com. Monthly magazine. No kill fee.

Columns/Departments Life; @Work; Off Base, **pays $300**. Laugh; Quotes, **pays $100**. Address your submission to the appropriate humor category.

Tips "Full-length, original articles are usually assigned to regular contributors to the magazine. We do not accept or return unpublished manuscripts. We do, however, accept 1-page queries that clearly detail the article idea—with special emphasis on the arc of the story, your interview access to the main characters, your access to special documents, etc. We look for dramatic narratives, articles about everyday heroes, crime dramas, adventure stories. Do include a separate page of your writing credits. We are not interested in poetry, fiction, or opinion pieces. Please submit article proposals on the website."

$ $ $ $ READER'S DIGEST (CANADA)

1100 Rene Le vesque Blvd. W., Montreal QC H3B 5H5 Canada. E-mail: originals@rd.com. Website: www.readersdigest.ca. **30-50% freelance written**. Monthly magazine of general interest articles and subjects. Estab. 1948. Circ. 1,000,000. Byline given. **Pays on acceptance for original works.** Pays on publication for pickups. Offers $500 (Canadian) kill fee. Buys one-time rights (for reprints), all rights (for original articles). Submit seasonal material 5 months in advance. Accepts queries by mail, e-mail. Accepts previously published material. Guidelines available online.

- Only responds to queries if interested. Prefers Canadian subjects.

Nonfiction We're looking for true stories that depend on emotion and reveal the power of our relationships to help us overcome adversity; also for true first-person accounts of an event that changed a life for the better or led to new insight. No fiction, poetry or articles too specialized, technical or esoteric—read *Reader's Digest* to see what kind of articles we want. Needs general interest, how-to, general interest, humor, jokes, inspirational, personal experience, travel, adventure, crime, health. Query with published clips. Length: 2,000-2,500 words. **Pays $1.50-2.50/word (CDN) depending on story type.** Pays expenses of writers on assignment.

Reprints Query. Payment is negotiable.

Photos State availability

Tips *Reader's Digest* usually finds its freelance writers through other well-known publications in which they have previously been published. There are guidelines available and writers should read *Reader's Digest* to see what kind of stories we look for and how they are written. We do not accept unsolicited manuscripts.

$ REUNIONS MAGAZINE

P.O. Box 11727, Milwaukee WI 53211-0727. (414)263-4567. Fax: (414)263-6331. E-mail: info@reunionsmag.com. Website: www.reunionsmag.com. **85% freelance written**. Quarterly magazine covering reunions—all aspects and types. "*Reunions Magazine* is primarily for people actively planning family, class, military, and other reunions. We want easy, practical ideas about organizing, planning, researching/searching, attending, or promoting reunions." Estab. 1990. Circ. 20,000. Byline given. Pays on publication. Publishes ms an average of 1 year after acceptance. Buys one-time rights. Editorial lead time 6 months. Submit seasonal material 1 year in advance. Accepts queries by mail, e-mail, fax; prefers Word attachments to e-mail. Accepts previously published material. Responds in about 1 year. Sample copy and writer's guidelines for #10 SASE or online.

Nonfiction "We can't get enough about reunion activities, particularly family reunions with multi-generational activities. We would also like more reunion food-related material. Special features: Ethnic/African-American family reunions; food, kids stuff, theme parks, small venues (bed & breakfasts, dormitories, condos); golf, travel and gaming features; themes, cruises, ranch reunions and reunions in various US locations." Needs historical, how-to, humor, interview, new product, personal experience, photo feature, travel, Reunion recipes with reunion anecdote. **Buys 50 mss/year.** Query with published clips. 500-2,500 (prefers work on the short side) **Pays $25-50.**

Reprints Send tearsheet, photocopy or typed ms with rights for sale noted and information about when and where the material previously appeared. Usually pays $10.

Photos Always looking for vertical cover photos screaming: Reunion! Prefers print or e-mail pictures. State availability Captions, identification of subjects, model releases required. Reviews contact sheets, negatives, 35mm transparencies, prints, TIFF/JPEG files (300 dpi or higher) as e-mail attachments. Offers no additional payment for photos accepted with ms.

Fillers Must be reunion-related. Needs anecdotes, facts, short humor. 20-40 Length: 50-250 words. **Pays $5.**

Tips "All copy must be reunion-related with strong, real reunion examples and experiences. Write a lively account of an interesting or unusual reunion, either upcoming or soon after while it's hot. Tell readers why the reunion is special, what went into planning it, and how attendees reacted. Our 'Masterplan' section, about family reunion planning, is a great place for a freelancer to start by telling her/his own reunion story. Send us how-tos or tips about any of the many aspects of reunion organizing or activities. Open your minds to different types of reunions—they're all around!"

$ $ $ $ ROBB REPORT

The Magazine for the Luxury Lifestyle, Curtco Media Labs, 1 Acton Place, Acton MA 01720. (978)264-7500. Fax: (212)264-7501. E-mail: editorial@robbreport.com. Website: www.robbreport.com. **60% freelance written.** Monthly magazine. We are a lifestyle magazine geared toward active, affluent readers. Addresses upscale autos, luxury travel, boating, technology, lifestyles, watches, fashion, sports, investments, collectibles. Estab. 1976. Circ. 111,000. Byline given. Pays on publication. Offers 25% kill fee. Buys first North American serial rights, buys all rights. Submit seasonal material 5 months in advance. Accepts queries by mail, fax. Responds in 2 months to queries. Responds in 1 month to mss. Sample copy for $10.95, plus shipping and handling. Guidelines for #10 SASE.

Nonfiction Needs new product, autos, boats, aircraft, watches, consumer electronics, travel, international and domestic, dining. Home (October); Recreation (March) **Buys 60 mss/year.** Query with published clips. Length: 500-2,000 words. **Pays $1/word.** Sometimes pays expenses of writers on assignment.

Photos State availability Payment depends on article Buys one time rights.

Tips Show zest in your writing, immaculate research, and strong thematic structure, and you can handle most any assignment. We want to put the reader there, whether the article is about test driving a car, fishing for marlin, or touring a luxury home. The best articles will be those that tell compelling stories. Anecdotes should be used liberally, especially for leads, and the fun should show in your writing.

$ $ THE SATURDAY EVENING POST

The Saturday Evening Post Society, 1100 Waterway Blvd., Indianapolis IN 46202. (317)634-1100. Website: www.satevepost.org. **30% freelance written.** Bimonthly general interest, family-oriented magazine focusing on physical fitness, preventive medicine. Ask almost any American if he or she has heard of *The Saturday Evening Post*, and you will find that many have fond recollections of the magazine from their childhood days. Many readers recall sitting with their families on Saturdays awaiting delivery of their *Post* subscription in the mail. *The Saturday Evening Post* has forged a tradition of 'forefront journalism.' *The Saturday Evening Post* continues to stand at the journalistic forefront with its coverage of health, nutrition, and preventive medicine. Estab. 1728. Circ. 350,000. Byline given. Pays on publication. Publishes ms an average of 3 months after acceptance. Buys all rights. Submit seasonal material 4 months in advance. Accepts queries by mail, fax. Accepts simultaneous submissions. Responds in 3 weeks to queries. Responds in 6 weeks to mss.

Nonfiction Needs book excerpts, how-to, gardening, home improvement, humor, interview, medical, health, fitness. No political articles or articles containing sexual innuendo or hypersophistication. **Buys 25 mss/year.** Send complete ms. Length: 2,500-3,000 words. **Pays $25-400.** Sometimes pays expenses of writers on assignment.

Photos State availability Identification of subjects, model releases required. Reviews negatives, transparencies. Offers $50 minimum, negotiable maximum per photo. Buys one-time or all rights.

Columns/Departments Travel (destinations); Post Scripts (well-known humorists); Post People (activities of celebrities). Length 750-1,500. 16 Query with published clips or send complete ms. **Pays $150 minimum, negotiable maximum.**

Fiction Contact: Fiction Editor.

Poetry Needs light verse.

Fillers Contact: Post Scripts Editor. Needs anecdotes, short humor. 200 300 words **Pays $15.**

Tips Areas most open to freelancers are Health, Fitness, Research Breakthroughs, Nutrition, Post Scripts, and Travel. For travel we like text-photo packages, pragmatic tips, side bars, and safe rather than exotic destinations. Query by mail, not phone. Send clips.

$ SENIOR LIVING

Vancouver & Lower Mainland/Vancouver Island, Stratis Publishing Ltd, 153, 1581-H Hillside Ave., Victoria BC V8T 2CI Canada. (250)479-4705. Fax: (250)479-4808. E-mail: office@seniorlivingmag.com. Website: www.seniorlivingmag.com. **100% freelance written**. 12 times per yr. magazine covering active 50+ living. Inspiring editorial profiling 'seniors' (50+) who are active & lead interesting lives. Include articles on health, housing, accessibility, sports, travel, recipes, etc. Estab. 2004. Circ. 41,000. Byline given. quarterly. No kill fee. Publishes an average of 2-3 months after acceptance. Buys all rights. Editorial lead time 3 months. Submit seasonal material 6 months in advance. Accepts queries by e-mail. Accepts previously published material. Accepts simultaneous submissions. Sample copy available online. Guidelines available.

Nonfiction Needs historical, how-to, humor, inspirational, interview, personal experience, travel, active living for 50+. Do not want politics, religion, promotion of business, service or products, humor that demeans 50+ demographic or aging process. **Buys 150 mss/yr. mss/year.** Query. Length: 500-1,200 words. **Pays $35-150 for assigned articles. Pays $35-150 for unsolicited articles.** Sometimes pays expenses of writers on assignment. (limit agreed upon in advance)

Photos Send photos Identification of subjects, model releases required. Reviews GIF/JPEG files. Offers $10-75 per photo. Buys all rights.

Columns/Departments 5-6 mss/yr. Query with published clips. **Pays $$25-$50.**

Tips "Articles need to reflect region in which publication is distributed if about people/profiles/organizations."

$ $ $ $ SMITHSONIAN MAGAZINE

Capital Gallery, Suite 6001, MRC 513, P.O. Box 37012, Washington DC 20013-7012. (202)275-2000. Website: www.smithsonianmag.com. **90% freelance written**. Monthly magazine for associate members of the Smithsonian Institution; 85% with college education. *"Smithsonian Magazine's* mission is to inspire fascination with all the world has to offer by featuring unexpected and entertaining editorial that explores different lifestyles, cultures and peoples, the arts, the wonders of nature and technology, and much more. The highly educated, innovative readers of *Smithsonian* share a unique desire to celebrate life, seeking out the timely as well as timeless, the artistic as well as the academic, and the thought-provoking as well as the humorous." Circ. 2,300,000. Pays on acceptance. Offers 33% kill fee. Publishes ms an average of 6 months after acceptance. Buys first North American serial rights. Editorial lead time 2 months. Submit seasonal material 3 months in advance. Accepts queries by online submission form only. Responds in 3 weeks to queries. Sample copy for $5. Guidelines available online.

Nonfiction Our mandate from the Smithsonian Institution says we are to be interested in the same things which now interest or should interest the institution: Cultural and fine arts, history, natural sciences, hard sciences, etc. **Buys 120-130 feature (up to 5,000 words) and 12 short (500-650 words) mss/year.** Use online submission form. **Pays various rates per feature, $1,500 per short piece.** Pays expenses of writers on assignment.

Photos Purchased with or without ms and on assignment. Illustrations are not the responsibility of authors, but if you do have photographs or illustration materials, please include a selection of them with your submission. In general, 35mm color transparencies or black-and-white prints are perfectly acceptable. Photographs published in the magazine are usually obtained through assignment, stock agencies, or specialized sources. No photo library is maintained and photographs should be submitted only to accompany a specific article proposal. Send photos Captions required. Pays $400/full color page

Columns/Departments Buys 12-15 department articles/year. Length: 1,000-2,000 words. Last Page humor, 550-700 words. Use online submission form. **Pays $1,000-1,500.**

Tips "Send proposals through online submission form only. No e-mail or mail queries, please."

$ SOFA INK QUARTERLY

Sofa Ink, P.O. Box 625, American Fork UT 84003. E-mail: acquisitions@sofaink.com. Website: www.sofaink.com. **95% freelance written**. Quarterly magazine. The magazine is distributed primarily to waiting rooms and lobbies of medical facilities. All of our stories and poetry have positive endings. We like to publish a variety of genres with a focus on good storytelling and word-mastery that does not include swearing, profaning deity, gore, excessive violence or gratuitous sex. Estab. 2005. Circ. 650. Byline given. Pays on acceptance. Publishes ms an average of 3 months after acceptance. Buys first North American serial rights. Submit seasonal material 4 months in advance. Accepts queries by mail, e-mail. Accepts simultaneous submissions. Responds in 1-3 months to queries. Responds in 1-3 months to mss. Sample copy for $6. Guidelines available online.

Nonfiction Needs essays, general interest, historical, humor, inspirational, interview, personal experience. Send complete ms. Length: 7,500 words. **Pays $5, plus 3 contributor copies.**

Photos Identification of subjects, model releases required. Offers no additional payment for photos accepted with ms. Buys one time rights.

Fiction Needs adventure, ethnic, experimental, fantasy, historical, humorous, mainstream, mystery, romance, science fiction, slice-of-life vignettes, suspense, western. Does not want erotic, religious. **Buys 24-30 mss/year.** Send complete ms. Length: 7,500 words. **Pays $5.**

Poetry Needs avant-garde, free verse, haiku, light verse, traditional. **Buys 9-15 poems/year.** Submit maximum 5 poems.
Tips Follow the content guidelines. Electronic submissions should be in a Word attachment rather than in the body of the message.

$ SOMA

SOMA Magazine, Inc., 888 O'Farrell St., Suite 103, San Francisco CA 94109. E-mail: arqt@somamagazine.com. Website: www.somamagazine.com. **5% freelance written**. Monthly magazine covering the arts, music, film, fashion, design, architecture, nightlife, etc. *SOMA* explores the contemporary landscape through insightful writing. Estab. 1986. Circ. 115,000. Byline given. Pays on publication. Offers $30 kill fee. Publishes ms an average of 1-3 months after acceptance. Buys first North American serial rights. Editorial lead time 3 months. Submit seasonal material 3 months in advance. Accepts queries by e-mail. Accepts simultaneous submissions. Responds in 3 months to queries. Sample copy for $3.50. Guidelines free.

$ $ THRIVE NYC

For New York's Boomers and Beyond, Community Media, LLC, 145 6th Ave., 1st Floor, New York NY 10013. (212)229-1890. Fax: (212)229-2790. E-mail: vent@thrivenyc.com. Website: www.nycplus.com. **100% freelance written**. Monthly magazine. We are looking for well-written stories of substance that relate in some way to our 50+ theme. All genres. Estab. 2005. Circ. 50,000. Byline given. Pays on publication. Publishes ms an average of 3-6 months after acceptance. Buys first rights. Editorial lead time 2-3 months. Submit seasonal material 4-5 months in advance. Accepts queries by e-mail. Accepts simultaneous submissions. Responds in 2 months to queries. Responds in 2 months to mss. Sample copy available online. Guidelines by email.
Nonfiction Needs essays, general interest, historical, humor, inspirational, interview, opinion, personal experience. **Buys 110 mss/year.** Query. Length: 900-4,000 words. **Pays $100-300.**
Columns/Departments Memory (personal experience/nostalgia), 800-1,100 words; Mind/Body (50+), 1,000-1,200 words; Food (old and new), 1,000-1,200 words; Work (2nd career/nonretirement), 1,200-1,600 words.
Fiction Needs humorous, mainstream, slice-of-life vignettes.
Tips Go to our website and read as much content as you can.

⊘ TIME

Time Inc. Magazine, Time & Life Bldg., 1271 Avenue of the Americas, New York NY 10020. (212)522-1212. Fax: (212)522-0323. E-mail: letters@time.com. Website: www.time.com. Weekly magazine. *Time* covers the full range of information that is important to people today—breaking news, national and world affairs, business news, societal and lifestyle issues, culture and entertainment news and reviews. Estab. 1923. Circ. 4,150,000. No kill fee.

- *Time* does not accept unsolicited material for publication. The magazine is entirely staff written and produced.

$ $ $ $ TOWN & COUNTRY

The Hearst Corp., 300 W. 57th St., New York NY 10019-3794. Website: www.townandcountrymag.com. **40% freelance written**. Monthly lifestyle magazine. "*Town & Country* is a lifestyle magazine for the affluent market. Features focus on fashion, beauty, travel, interior design, and the arts, as well as individuals' accomplishments and contributions to society.' Estab. 1846. Circ. 488,000. Byline given. Pays on acceptance. Offers 25% kill fee. Buys first North American serial rights, buys electronic rights. Accepts queries by mail. Responds in 2 months to queries.
Nonfiction "We're looking for engaging service articles for a high income, well-educated audience, in numerous categories: travel, personalities, interior design, fashion, beauty, jewelry, health, city news, the arts, philanthropy." Needs general interest, interview, travel. "Rarely publishes work not commissioned by the magazine. Does not publish poetry, short stories, or fiction." **Buys 25 mss/year.** Query by mail only with relevant clips before submitting Column items, 100-300 words; feature stories, 800-2,000 words. **Pays $2/word.**
Tips "We have served the affluent market for over 150 years, and our writers need to be expert in the needs and interests of that market. Most of our freelance writers start by doing short pieces for our front-of-book columns, then progress from there."

$ $ $ YES! MAGAZINE

Positive Futures Network, P.O. Box 10818, Bainbridge Island WA 98110. E-mail: submissions@yesmagazine.org. Website: www.yesmagazine.org. **70% freelance written**. Quarterly magazine covering politics and world affairs; contemporary culture; nature, conservation and ecology. *YES! Magazine* documents how people are creating a more just, sustainable and compassionate world. Each issue includes articles focused on a theme-about solutions to a significant challenge facing our world-and a number of timely, non-theme articles. Our non-theme section provides ongoing coverage of issues like health, climate change, globalization, media reform, faith, democracy, economy and labor, social and racial justice and peace building. To inquire about upcoming themes, send an email to submissions@yesmagazine.org; please be sure to type 'themes' as the subject line. Estab. 1997. Circ. 55,000. Byline given. Pays on publication. Offers kill fee. varies Publishes ms an average of 1-6 months after acceptance. Buys Creative Commons License, see http://www.yesmagazine.org/default.asp?ID=14 rights. Editorial lead time 3-6 months. Submit seasonal material 2-6 months in advance. Accepts queries by mail, e-mail. Sample copy and writer's guidelines online

Nonfiction Please check website for a detailed call for submission before each issue. Needs book excerpts, essays, general interest, how-to, interview, opinion, (does not mean letters to the editor), photo feature. We don't want stories that are negative or too politically partisan. **Buys 60 mss/year. mss/year.** Query with published clips. Length: 100-2,500 words. **Pays $50-1,250 for assigned articles. Pays $50-600 for unsolicited articles.**

Reprints Send photocopy or typed ms with rights for sale noted and information about when and where the material previously appeared.

Photos Buys one time rights.

Columns/Departments Signs of Life (positive news briefs), 100-250 words; Commentary (opinion from thinkers and experts), 500 words; Book and film reviews, 500-800 words. **Pays $$20-$300.**

Tips We're interested in articles that: 'change the story' about what is possible; tell specific success stories of individuals, communities, movements, nations or regions that are addressing society's challenges and problems; offer visions of a better world. We're less interested in articles that: only describe or update a problem (unless there are dramatic new developments, reframings or insights); primarily reinforce a sense of being a victim (and therefore powerless); are written in styles or about topics relevant or accessible only to nararow groups; lack grounding in research or reporting (except for occasional essays); have a partisan or polarizing tone.

HEALTH & FITNESS

HEALTH FREEDOM NEWS

National Health Federation, P.O. Box 688, Monrovia CA 91017. (626)357-2181. Fax: (626)303-0642. E-mail: sct@thenhf.com. Website: www.thenhf.com. Cheri Ties, man. ed. **Contact:** Scott Tips, editor. **50-60%.** Covering health-freedom & alternative health issues. This is a magazine oriented towards consumers and health professionals as the official publication of the world's oldest health-freedom organization. As such, we support the individual's right to buy and consume what he or she freely chooses without unreasonable government interference or restriction. Estab. 1982. Circ. 16,000. Yes Acquires one-time rights, electronic rights (nonexclusive license) 2 months Submit 2 months in advance. Accepts queries by mail, e-mail, fax. Accepts simultaneous submissions. 1-2 weeks on queries; 1-2 months on mss. For $5 By e-mail: ct@thenhf.com

Nonfiction Contact: Scott Tips. Needs essays, expose, general interest, humor, inspirational, interview, personal experience (all from a pro-health-freedom orientation). No product articles. Query. 750-2,000/words **NA**

Photos Contact: Cheri Tips, man. ed. Send photos with submission. Captions, model releases, identification of subjects. Contact sheets, GIF/JPEG files, prints Offers no additional payment for photos accepted with ms. One-time rights.

Columns/Departments Open to suggestions for new columns. Query.

Poetry Contact: Cheri Tips.

$ $ AMERICAN FITNESS

15250 Ventura Blvd., Suite 200, Sherman Oaks CA 91403. Fax: (818)817-0803. E-mail: americanfitness@afaa.com. Website: www.afaa.com. **75% freelance written.** Bimonthly magazine covering exercise and fitness, health, and nutrition. We need timely, in-depth, informative articles on health, fitness, aerobic exercise, sports nutrition, age-specific fitness, and outdoor activity. Absolutely no first-person accounts. Need well-reserched articles for professional readers. Circ. 42,000. Byline given. Pays 30 days after publication. No kill fee. Publishes ms an average of 6 months after acceptance. Submit seasonal material 4 months in advance. Accepts queries by mail, fax. Accepts previously published material. Accepts simultaneous submissions. Responds in 2 months to queries. Sample copy for $4.50 and SAE with 6 first-class stamps.

Nonfiction Needs include health and fitness, including women's issues (pregnancy, family, pre- and post-natal, menopause, and eating disorders); new research findings on exercise techniques and equipment; aerobic exercise; sports nutrition; sports medicine; innovations and trends in aerobic sports; tips on teaching exercise and humorous accounts of fitness motivation; physiology; youth and senior fitness. Needs historical, history of various athletic events, inspirational, sport's leaders motivational pieces, interview, fitness figures, new product, plus equipment review, personal experience, successful fitness story, photo feature, on exercise, fitness, new sport, travel, activity adventures. No articles on unsound nutritional practices, popular trends, or unsafe exercise gimmicks. **Buys 18-25 mss/year.** Send complete ms. Length: 800-1,200 words. **Pays $200 for features, $80 for news.** Sometimes pays expenses of writers on assignment.

Photos Sports, action, fitness, aquatic aerobics competitions, and exercise class. We are especially interested in photos of high-adrenalin sports like rock climbing and mountain biking. Captions, identification of subjects, model releases required. Reviews transparencies, prints. Pays $35 for transparencies Usually buys all rights; other rights purchased depend on use of photo

Columns/Departments Research (latest exercise and fitness findings); Alternative paths (nonmainstream approaches to health, wellness, and fitness); Strength (latest breakthroughs in weight training); Clubscene (profiles and highlights of fitness club industry); Adventure (treks, trails, and global challenges); Food (low-fat/nonfat, high-flavor dishes); Homescene (home-workout alternatives); Clip 'n' Post (concise exercise research to post in health clubs, offices or on refrigerators). Length: 800-1,000 words. Query with published clips or send complete ms. **Pays $100-200.**

Tips Make sure to quote scientific literature or good research studies and several experts with good credentials to validate exercise trend, technique, or issue. Cover a unique aerobics or fitness angle, provide accurate and interesting findings, and write in a lively, intelligent manner. Please, no first-person accouts of 'how I lost weight or discovered running.' *AF* is a good place for first-time authors or regularly published authors who want to sell spin-offs or reprints.

$ $ $ BETTER NUTRITION

Active Interest Media, 300 N. Contintental Blvd., Suite 650, El Segundo CA 90245. (310)356-4100. Fax: (310)356-4110. E-mail: editorial@betternutrition.com. Website: www.betternutrition.com. **57% freelance written.** Monthly magazine covering nutritional news and approaches to optimal health. The new *Better Nutrition* helps people (men, women, families, old and young) integrate nutritious food, the latest and most effective dietary supplements, and exercise/personal care into healthy lifestyles. Estab. 1938. Circ. 460,000. Byline given. Pays on publication. No kill fee. Publishes ms an average of 2 months after acceptance. Buys varies according to article rights. Editorial lead time 3 months. Accepts queries by mail, e-mail. Sample copy free.

Nonfiction Each issue has multiple features, clinical research crystallized into accessible articles on nutrition, health, alternative medicine, disease prevention. **Buys 120-180 mss/year.** Query. Length: 400-1,200 words. **Pays $400-1,000.**

Photos State availability Captions, identification of subjects, model releases required. Reviews 4x5 transparencies, 3x5 prints. Negotiates payment individually Buys one time rights or non-exclusive reprint rights

Tips Be on top of what's newsbreaking in nutrition and supplementation. Interview experts. Fact-check, fact-check, fact-check. Send in a resume (including Social Security/IRS number), a couple of clips, and a list of article possibilities.

$ $ CLIMBING

Primedia Enthusiast Group, Box 420034, Palm Coast FL 32142-0235. (970)963-9449. Fax: (970)963-9442. Website: www.climbing.com. Magazine published 9 times/year covering climbing and mountaineering. Provides features on rock climbing and mountaineering worldwide. Estab. 1970. Circ. 51,000. Pays on publication. No kill fee. Editorial lead time 6 weeks. Accepts queries by e-mail. Sample copy for $4.99. Guidelines available online.

Nonfiction SASE returns Needs interview, interesting climbers, personal experience, climbing adventures, surveys of different areas. Query. Length: 1,500-3,500 words. **Pays 35¢/word.**

Photos State availability Reviews negatives, 35mm transparencies, prints, digital submissions on CD. Pays $25-800

Columns/Departments Query. **Payment varies**

$ $ DELICIOUS LIVING

New Hope Natural Media, 1401 Pearl St., Boulder CO 80302. (303)939-8440. Fax: (303)939-9886. E-mail: deliciousliving@newhope.com. Website: www.deliciouslivingmag.com. **85% freelance written.** Monthly magazine covering natural products, nutrition, alternative medicines, herbal medicines. "*Delicious Living* magazine empowers natural products shoppers to make health-conscious choices in their lives. Our goal is to improve consumers' perception of the value of natural methods in achieving health. To do this, we educate consumers on nutrition, disease prevention, botanical medicines and natural personal care products." Estab. 1985. Circ. 405,000. Byline given. Pays on publication. Offers 20% kill fee. Editorial lead time 6 months. Submit seasonal material 8 months in advance. Accepts simultaneous submissions. Responds in 3 months to queries. Writer's guidelines free.

O━ Does not accept unsolicited manuscripts.

Nonfiction Needs book excerpts, how-to, interview, green living, health nutrition, herbal medicines, alternative medicine, environmental. Query with published clips. Length: 100-1,200 words.

Photos Does not accept submissions

Columns/Departments Fresh Research, How-Tos, Natural-Industry Trends, 75-200/words; Wellness (natural therapies for specific health conditions), 800-1,000/words; Family (issues and topics relevant to raising a natural family), 600-800/words; Beauty (natural personal care). Query with published clips.

Tips "Highlight any previous health/nutrition/medical writing experience. Demonstrate a knowledge of natural medicine, nutrition, or natural products. Health practitioners who demonstrate writing ability are ideal free-lancers."

FIT PREGNANCY

Weider Publications, Inc., 21100 Erwin St., Woodland Hills CA 91367. (818)884-6800. Fax: (818)992-6895. Website: www.fitpregnancy.com. Bimonthly magazine. Circ. 505,000. No kill fee.

- Does not buy freelance material.

$ $ HEALING LIFESTYLES & SPAS

P.O. Box 271207, Louisville CO 80027. (202)441-9557. Fax: (303)926-4099. E-mail: editorial@healinglifestyles.com. Website: www.healinglifestyles.com. **90% freelance written**. *Healing Lifestyles & Spas* is a bimonthly magazine committed to healing, health, and living a well-rounded, more natural life. In each issue we cover retreats, spas, organic living, natural food, herbs, beauty, yoga, alternative medicine, bodywork, spirituality, and features on living a healthy lifestyle. Estab. 1996. Circ. 45,000. Pays on publication. No kill fee. Publishes ms an average of 2-10 months after acceptance. Editorial lead time 6 months. Submit seasonal material 6-9 months in advance. Accepts queries by mail, e-mail. Responds in 6 weeks to queries.

Nonfiction We will consider all in-depth features relating to spas, retreats, lifestyle issues, mind/body well being, yoga, enlightening profiles, and women's health issues. Needs travel, domestic and international. No fiction or poetry. Query. Length: 1,000-2,000 words. **Pays $150-500, depending on length, research, experience, and availability and quality of images.**

Photos If you will be providing your own photography, you must use slide film or provide a Mac-formatted CD with image resolution of at least 300 dpi. Send photos Captions required.

Columns/Departments All Things New & Natural (short pieces outlining new health trends, alternative medicine updates, and other interesting tidbits of information), 50-200 words; Urban Retreats (focuses on a single city and explores its spas and organic living features), 1,200-1,600 words; Health (features on relevant topics ranging from nutrition to health news and updates), 900-1,200 words; Food (nutrition or spa-focused food articles and recipes), 1,000-1,200 words; Ritual (highlights a specific at-home ritual), 500 words; Seasonal Spa (focuses on a seasonal ingredient on the spa menu), 500-700 words; Spa Origins (focuses on particular modalities and healing beliefs from around the world, 1,000-1,200 words; Yoga, 400-800 words; Retreat (highlights a spa or yoga retreat), 500 words; Spa a la carte (explores a new treatment or modality on the spa menu), 600-1,000 words; Insight (focuses on profiles, theme-related articles, and new therapies, healing practices, and newsworthy items), 1,000-2,000 words. Query.

$ $ $ $ HEALTH

Time, Inc., Southern Progress Corp., 2100 Lakeshore Dr., Birmingham AL 35209. (205)445-6000. Fax: (205)445-5123. E-mail: health@timeinc.com. Website: www.health.com. Magazine published 10 times/year covering health, fitness, and nutrition. Our readers are predominantly college-educated women in their 30s, 40s, and 50s. Edited to focus not on illness, but on wellness news, events, ideas, and people. Estab. 1987. Circ. 1,360,000. Byline given. Pays on acceptance. Offers 33% kill fee. Buys first publication and online rights. Accepts queries by mail, fax. Accepts simultaneous submissions. Responds in 2 months to queries. Sample copy for $5 to Back Issues. Guidelines for #10 SASE or via e-mail.

Nonfiction No unsolicited mss. **Buys 25 mss/year.** Query with published clips and SASE. 1,200 words **Pays $1.50-2/word.** Pays expenses of writers on assignment.

Columns/Departments Body, Mind, Fitness, Beauty, Food.

Tips We look for well-articulated ideas with a narrow focus and broad appeal. A query that starts with an unusual local event and hooks it legitimately to some national trend or concern is bound to get our attention. Use quotes, examples and statistics to show why the topic is important and why the approach is workable. We need to see clear evidence of credible research findings pointing to meaningful options for our readers. Stories should offer practical advice and give clear explanations.

$ HOPEKEEPERS

Joyfully Serving the Chronically Ill, Rest Ministries, Inc., P.O. Box 502928, San Diego CA 92150. (888)751-7378. E-mail: rest@restministries.org. Website: www.hopekeepersmagazine.com. **80% freelance written**. Quarterly Christian digital publication for those with chronic illness or pain. "Christian authors are preferred. We are open to health articles as long as they don't promote New Age practices. Prefer sidebars of interesting facts, scripture, etc." Estab. 2004. Circ. 10,000. Byline given. Pays on publication. No kill fee. Publishes ms an average of 3-6 months after acceptance. Buys first rights, buys second serial (reprint) rights, buys electronic rights. Makes work-for-hire assignments. Editorial lead time 4-6 months. Submit seasonal material 6 months in advance. Accepts queries by mail, e-mail. Accepts previously published material. Accepts simultaneous submissions. Responds in 8-12 weeks to queries. Responds in 2 months to mss. Writer's guidelines for #10 SASE or online.

Nonfiction "We are open to any topic with an illness slant and a Christian tone. See guidelines for specific details." Needs book excerpts, essays, how-to, inspirational, interview, new product, opinion, personal experience, religious, technical. "No 'God healed me and can heal you too' articles. Your story cannot be the main content of the piece. The article should be a on a specific topic with your story as an example. We prefer to have other stories as examples, too." Query. Length: 350-1,200 words. **Pays maximum $100.**

Columns/Departments Refreshments (devotional/journal style). 6 Send complete ms. **Pays maximum $50.**
Fillers Needs facts, newsbreaks, short humor. 20 Length: 25-200 words.
Tips "We want fillers that are original, uplifting, and informative, and are interested in how-to articles: how to find contentment, how to know when to change doctors, etc. A large percentage of our publication is open to secular articles with faith-based sidebars."

$ $ IMPACT MAGAZINE

IMPACT Productions, 2007 2nd St. SW, Calgary AB T2S 1S4 Canada. (403)228-0605. E-mail: jay@impactmagazine.ca. Website: www.impactmagazine.ca. **10% freelance written**. Bimonthly magazine covering fitness and sport performance. A leader in the industry, *IMPACT Magazine* is committed to publishing content provided by the best experts in their fields for those who aspire to higher levels of health, fitness, and sport performance. Estab. 1992. Circ. 90,000. Byline given. 30 days after publication. Offers 25% kill fee. Publishes ms an average of 4-6 months after acceptance. Buys first rights, buys electronic rights. Editorial lead time 6 months. Submit seasonal material 6 months in advance. Accepts queries by e-mail. Accepts simultaneous submissions. Responds in 4 weeks to queries. Sample copy available online. Guidelines available online.
Nonfiction Needs general interest, how-to, interview, new product, opinion, technical. **Buys 4 mss/yr. mss/year.** Query. Length: 150-2,000 words. **Pays $0.25/max. for assigned articles. Pays $0.25/max. for unsolicited articles.**
Photos State availability Identification of subjects, model releases required. Reviews contact sheets, GIF/JPEG files (300dpi or greater). Negotiates payment individually. first-time print & all electronic rights

$ $ $ LET'S LIVE MAGAZINE

Basic Media Group, Inc., 11050 Santa Monica Blvd., Ste. 125, Los Angeles CA 90025. (310)445-7500. Fax: (310)445-7583. E-mail: bsalmon@greathealthmag.com. Website: www.letsliveonline.com. **95% freelance written**. Monthly magazine emphasizing health and preventive medicine. We're especially looking for stories that profile a hot, new supplement with growing research to validate its benefits to health and wellness. Estab. 1933. Circ. 1,700,000. Byline given. Pays within 1 month. Publishes ms an average of 4 months after acceptance. Buys all rights. Submit seasonal material 6 months in advance. Accepts queries by mail, e-mail, fax. Responds in 2 months to queries. Responds in 3 months to mss. Sample copy for $5 and 10x13 SAE with 6 first-class stamps or on website. Guidelines for #10 SASE.
Nonfiction Mss must be well-researched, reliably documented and written in a clear, readable style. Needs general interest, effects of vitamins, minerals, herbs and nutrients in improvement of health or afflictions, historical, documentation of experiments or treatments establishing value of nutrients as boon to health, how-to, enhance natural beauty, exercise/bodybuilding, acquire strength and vitality, improve health of adults and/or children and prepare tasty, health meals, interview, benefits of research in establishing prevention as key to good health, background and/or medical history of preventive medicine, MDs or PhDs, in advancement of nutrition, opinion, views of orthomolecular doctors or their patients on balue of health foods toward maintaining good health. No pre-written articles or mainstream medicine pieces such as articles on drugs or surgery. **Buys 2-4 mss/year.** Query with published clips and SASE. Length: 800-1,400 words. **Pays $700-1,200 for features.**
Photos Send photos Captions, model releases required. Reviews transparencies, prints. Pays $50 for 8x10 color prints, 35mm transparencies.
Columns/Departments Natural Medicine Chest Query with published clips and SASE. **Payment varies.**
Tips We want writers with experience in researching nonsurgical medical subjects and interviewing experts with the ability to simplify technical and clinical information for the layman. A captivating lead and structural flow are essential. The most frequent mistakes made by writers are in writing articles that are too technical, in poor style, written for the wrong audience (publication not thoroughly studied), or have unreliable documentation or overzealous faith in the topic reflected by flimsy research and inappropriate tone.

$ $ LIVER HEALTH TODAY

Management and Treatment—A Practical Guide for Patients, Families, and Friends, Quality Publishing, Inc., 523 N. Sam Houston Tollway E., Suite 300, Houston TX 77060. (281)272-2744. Fax: (713)520-1463. E-mail: gdrushel@liverhealthtoday.com. Website: www.liverhealthtoday.org. **70-80% freelance written**. Quarterly magazine covering Hepatitis health news. Estab. 1999. Circ. 25,000. Byline given. Pays on publication. No kill fee. Publishes ms an average of 2 months after acceptance. Buys first North American serial rights, buys electronic rights. Editorial lead time 6 months. Submit seasonal material 4 months in advance. Accepts queries by mail, e-mail. Accepts simultaneous submissions. Responds in 6 weeks to queries. Sample copy and writer's guidelines free.
Nonfiction Needs inspirational, interview, new product, personal experience. We do not want any one-source or no-source articles. **Buys 42-48 mss/year.** Query. Length: 1,500-2,500 words. Sometimes pays expenses of writers on assignment.
Photos Send photos Identification of subjects required. Reviews transparencies, prints, GIF/JPEG files. Offers no additional payment for photos accepted with ms. Rights negotiated, usually purchases one-time rights.

Columns/Departments General news or advice on Hepatitis written by a doctor or healthcare professional, 1,500-2,000 words. 12-18 Query. **Pays $375-500.**

Tips Be specific in your query. Show me that you know the topic you want to write about, and show me that you can write a solid, well-rounded story.

$ $ $ $ MAMM MAGAZINE

Courage, Respect & Survival, MAMM, LLC, 54 W. 22nd St., 4th Floor, New York NY 10010. (646)365-1355. Fax: (646)365-1369. E-mail: editorial@mamm.com. Website: www.mamm.com. **80% freelance written.** Magazine published 10 times/year covering cancer prevention, treatment, and survival for women. *MAMM* gives its readers the essential tools and emotional support they need before, during and after diagnosis of breast, ovarian and other gynecologic cancers. We offer a mix of survivor profiles, conventional and alternative treatment information, investigative features, essays, and cutting-edge news. Estab. 1997. Circ. 100,000. Byline given. Pays within 30 days of publication. Offers 50% kill fee. Publishes ms an average of 3 months after acceptance. Buys exclusive rights up to 3 months after publishing. Submit seasonal material 3-4 months in advance. Accepts simultaneous submissions. Sample copy and writer's guidelines free

Nonfiction Needs book excerpts, essays, expose, how-to, humor, inspirational, interview, opinion, personal experience, photo feature, historic/nostalgic. **Buys 90 mss/year.** Query with published clips. Length: 200-3,000 words. **Pays $100-3,000.** Negotiates coverage of expenses of writers on assignment.

Photos Send photos Identification of subjects required. Reviews contact sheets, negatives. Negotiates payment individually Buys first rights

Columns/Departments Opinion (cultural/political); International Dispatch (experience); Q and A (interview format), all 600 words. 30 Query with published clips. **Pays $400-800.**

$ $ ✪ MAXIMUM FITNESS

For Men, CANUSA Publishing, 5775 McLaughlin Rd., Mississauga ON L5R 3P7 Canada. E-mail: editorial@maxfitmag.com. Website: www.maxfitmag.com. Bimonthly magazine. *American Health & Fitness* is designed to help male fitness enthusiasts (18-39) stay fit, strong, virile, and healthy through sensible diet and exercise. Estab. 2000. Circ. 310,000. Byline given. Pays on acceptance. No kill fee. Publishes ms an average of 6 months after acceptance. Buys all rights. Editorial lead time 4 months. Submit seasonal material 6 months in advance. Accepts queries by mail, e-mail, fax. Responds in 4 months to queries. Responds in 4 months to mss. Sample copy for $5.

Nonfiction Needs how-to, humor, inspirational, fitness stories, interview, new product, personal experience, photo feature, bodybuilding and weight training, health & fitness tips, diet, medical advice, workouts, nutrition. **Buys 80-100 mss/year.** Query or send complete ms. Length: 800-1,500 words. **Pays 25-45¢/word for assigned articles.**

Photos Send photos Captions, identification of subjects required. Reviews 35mm transparencies, 8x10 prints. Offers $35 and up/photo Buys all rights.

Columns/Departments Personal Training; Strength & Conditioning; Fitness; Longevity; Natural Health; Sex. 40 Query or send complete ms.

Fillers Needs anecdotes, facts, gags, newsbreaks, fitness, nutrition, health, short humor. 50-100 Length: 100-200 words.

$ $ $ $ MEN'S HEALTH

Rodale, 33 E. Minor St., Emmaus PA 18098. (610)967-5171. Fax: (610)967-7725. E-mail: online@rodale.com. Website: www.menshealth.com. **50% freelance written.** Magazine published 10 times/year covering men's health and fitness. *Men's Health* is a lifestyle magazine showing men the practical and positive actions that make their lives better, with articles covering fitness, nutrition, relationships, travel, careers, grooming, and health issues. Estab. 1986. Circ. 1,600,000. Pays on acceptance. Offers 25% kill fee. Buys all rights. Accepts queries by mail, fax. Responds in 3 weeks to queries. Guidelines for #10 SASE.

Nonfiction Authoritative information on all aspects of men's physical and emotional health. We rely on writers to seek out the right experts and to either tell a story from a first-person vantage or get good anecdotes. **Buys 30 features/year; 360 short mss/year.** Query with published clips. 1,200-4,000 words for features, 100-300 words for short pieces **Pays $1,000-5,000 for features; $100-500 for short pieces.**

Columns/Departments Length: 750-1,500 words. 80 **Pays $ 750- 2,000.**

Tips We have a wide definition of health. We believe that being successful in every area of your life is being healthy. The magazine focuses on all aspects of health, from stress issues and nutrition, to exercise and sex. It is 50% staff written, 50% from freelancers. The best way to break in is not by covering a particular subject, but by covering it within the magazine's style. There is a very particular tone and voice to the magazine. A writer has to be a good humor writer as well as a good service writer. Prefers mail queries. No phone calls, please.

$ $ $ MUSCLE & FITNESS

Weider Health & Fitness, 21100 Erwin St., Woodland Hills, CA 91367. (818)884-6800. Fax: (818)595-0463. Website: www.muscle-fitness.com. **50% freelance written.** Monthly magazine covering bodybuilding and fitness for healthy, active men and women. It contains a wide range of features and monthly departments devoted to all areas of bodybuilding, health, fitness, sport, injury prevention and treatment, and nutrition. Editorial fulfills 2 functions: information and entertainment. Special attention is devoted to how-to advice and accuracy. Estab. 1950. Circ. 500,000. Pays on publication. No kill fee. Publishes ms an average of 2 months after acceptance. Editorial lead time 5 months. Submit seasonal material 6 months in advance. Accepts queries by mail. Accepts previously published material. Responds in 1 month to queries.

Nonfiction All features and departments are written on assignment. Needs book excerpts, how-to, training, humor, interview, photo feature. **Buys 120 mss/year.** Query with published clips. Length: 800-1,800 words. **Pays $400-1,000.** Pays expenses of writers on assignment.

Reprints Send photocopy with rights for sale noted and information about when and where the material previously appeared. Payment varies.

Photos State availability

Tips Know bodybuilders and bodybuilding. Read our magazine regularly (or at least several issues), come up with new information or a new angle on our subject matter (bodybuilding training, psychology, nutrition, diets, fitness, sports, etc.), then pitch us in terms of providing useful, unique, how-to information for our readers. Send a 1-page query letter (as described in *Writer's Market*) to sell us on your idea and on you as the best writer for that article. Send a sample of your published work.

MUSCLEMAG

MuscleMag International-Building Health, Fitness, Physique, Canusa Products, Inc., 5775 McLaughlin Rd., Mississauga ON L5R-3P7. (905)507-3545. Fax: (905)507-2372. E-mail: editorial@emusclemag.com. Website: www.emusclemag.com. **80% freelance written**. Monthly magazine building health, fitness and physique. Byline given. Pays on acceptance. No kill fee. Publishes ms an average of 6 months after acceptance. Buys all rights. Accepts queries by mail, e-mail. Responds in 4 months to queries. Responds in 4 months to mss. Guidelines available.

Nonfiction Needs how-to, interview, new product, personal experience, photo feature, bodybuilding, strenth training, health, nutrition & fitness. **Pays $80-400 for assigned articles.**

Photos Contact: Jeff Maltby, photo editor. Send photos Captions, identification of subjects required. Reviews 35 mm transparencies, 8x10 prints.

Fillers Needs anecdotes, facts, gags, newsbreaks, fitness, nutrition, health, short humor. 50-100 Length: 100-200 words.

Tips Send in unedited sample articles on training or nutrition to be assessed. Those writers accepted may be added to our roster of freelance writers for future article assignments.

$ $ NATURALLY GOOD MAGAZINE

Naturally Good Magazine, 142 Redwood Dr., Mocksville NC 27028-5434. (336)776-8853. E-mail: editor@naturallygoodmagazine.com. Website: www.naturallygoodmagazine.com. **10% freelance written**. Quarterly magazine covering alternative medicine/health/nutrition. "We are striving for maximum credibility, so writers need to be willing to do lots of research. Our attitude is that God gave us in nature everything we need to live long, healthy lives." Estab. 2008. Byline given. Pays on acceptance. No kill fee. Publishes ms an average of 1 month after acceptance. Buys first rights, buys second serial (reprint) rights, buys electronic rights. Submit seasonal material 2 months in advance. Accepts queries by mail, e-mail. Accepts previously published material. Accepts simultaneous submissions. Responds in 1 week to queries. Responds in 2 weeks to mss Sample copy free by email at sarah@naturallygoodmagazine.com

- "We review all formats."

Nonfiction Contact: Sarah Cain. Needs essays, general interest, inspirational, interview, opinion, personal experience, Alternative health. We do not want anything New Age, Wiccan, or environmental issues. **Buys 20+ mss/yr. mss/year.** Query. Length: 10,000 words. **Pays $20-500 for assigned articles. Pays $10-500 for unsolicited articles.** Sometimes pays expenses of writers on assignment.

Photos Contact: Thomas Corriher, managing editor. State availability Reviews GIF/JPEG. Negotiates payment individually. reprint & electronic

Fillers Contact: Sarah Cain. Needs facts.

Tips "Feel free to contact us. We are very informal. We need articles that are honest, researched, credible, which cite sources of information, and which can withstand scientific criticism."

NATURE & HEALTH

Yaffa Publishing, 17-21 Bellevue St., Surry Hills NSW 2010 Australia. (61)(2)9281-2333. Fax: (61)(2)9281-2750. E-mail: yaffa@yaffa.com.au. Website: www.yaffa.com.au. Bimonthly magazine for people interested in maintaining a naturally healthy lifestyle.

Nonfiction "Nature & Health Magazine is a trusted resource for people who are passionate about their health, and it is the first place they turn to for ideas, information, and advice on complementary medicine and natural therapies. Our articles cover a wide spectrum of relevant topics — self-help and preventive health care, healthy food and cookery, diet and nutrition, anti-aging, herbal medicine, vitamins, drug updates, environmental health issues, exercise, beauty and fitness tips, women's health, relationships, mental and spiritual health, natural pet care, yoga, traditional chinese medicine, ayurveda, psychic healing, eco-travel, sustainability, and personal growth. As a premium quality publication, we require a high standard of contributions. Accuracy, in-depth and 'breaking new ground' are features we look for." Query.

$ $ $ OXYGEN

Serious Fitness for Serious Women, Canusa Products/St. Ives, Inc., 5775 McLaughlin Rd., Mississauga ON L5R 3P7 Canada. (905)507-3545/(888)254-0767. Fax: (905)507-2372. E-mail: editorial@oxygenmag.com. Website: www.oxygenmag.com. **70% freelance written**. Monthly magazine covering women's health and fitness. *Oxygen* encourages various exercise, good nutrition to shape and condition the body. Estab. 1997. Circ. 340,000. Byline given. Pays on acceptance. Offers 25% kill fee. Publishes ms an average of 4 months after acceptance. Buys all rights. Editorial lead time 3 months. Submit seasonal material 6 months in advance. Accepts queries by mail, fax. Responds in 5 weeks to queries. Responds in 2 months to mss. Sample copy for $5.

Nonfiction Needs expose, how-to, training and nutrition, humor, inspirational, interview, new product, personal experience, photo feature. No poorly researched articles that do not genuinely help the readers towards physical fitness, health and physique. **Buys 100 mss/year.** Send complete ms. with SAE and $5 for return postage. Length: 1,400-1,800 words. **Pays $250-1,000.** Sometimes pays expenses of writers on assignment.

Photos State availability of or send photos Identification of subjects required. Reviews contact sheets, 35mm transparencies, prints. Offers $35-500 Buys all rights.

Columns/Departments Nutrition (low-fat recipes), 1,700 words; Weight Training (routines and techniques), 1,800 words; Aerobics (how-tos), 1,700 words. 50 Send complete ms. **Pays $150-500.**

Tips Every editor of every magazine is looking, waiting, hoping and praying for the magic article. The beauty of the writing has to spring from the page; the edge imparted has to excite the reader because of its unbelievable information.

$ $ $ $ POZ

CDM Publishing, LLC, 500 Fifth Ave., Suite 320, New York NY 10110. (212)242-2163. Fax: (212)675-8505. E-mail: editor-in-chief@poz.com. Website: www.poz.com. **25% freelance written**. Monthly national magazine for people impacted by HIV and AIDS. *POZ* is a trusted source of conventional and alternative treatment information, investigative features, survivor profiles, essays and cutting-edge news for people living with AIDS and their caregivers. *POZ* is a lifestyle magazine with both health and cultural content. Estab. 1994. Circ. 125,000. Byline given. Pays 30 days after publication. Offers 25% kill fee. Publishes ms an average of 3 months after acceptance. Buys first rights. Editorial lead time 4 months. Submit seasonal material 4 months in advance. Accepts simultaneous submissions. Sample copy and writer's guidelines free

Nonfiction Needs book excerpts, essays, expose, historical, how-to, humor, inspirational, interview, opinion, personal experience, photo feature. Query with published clips. We take unsolicited mss on speculation only. Length: 200-3,000 words. **Pays $1/word.** Sometimes pays expenses of writers on assignment.

Photos Send photos Identification of subjects required. Reviews contact sheets, negatives. Negotiates payment individually Buys first rights

REPS! MAGAZINE

The Science of Building Muscle, Canusa Products, Inc., 5775 McLaughlin Rd., Mississauga ON L5R-3P7 Canada. (905)507-3545. Fax: (905)507-2372. E-mail: editorial@repsmag.com. Website: www.repsmag.com. Quarterly magazine covering bodybuilding. *Reps! Magazine* brings the best weight-training advice, nutritional news and fat-burning information to help you build the best possible physique. No kill fee. Guidelines available.

Nonfiction Needs how-to, interview, new product, opinion, personal experience, photo feature. Length: 1,000 words. **Pays 25-45¢/word for assigned articles.**

Photos Send photos Captions, identification of subjects required. Reviews 35 mm transparencies, 8x10 prints. Offers $35 and over. Buys all rights.

Columns/Departments 40 mss/yr. Query and/or send complete ms.

Fillers Needs anecdotes, facts, gags, newsbreaks, fitness, nutrition, health, short humor. 50-100/yr. Length: 100-200 words.

$ $ $ $ SHAPE MAGAZINE

Weider Publications, Inc., 21100 Erwin St., Woodland Hills CA 91367. (818)595-0593. Fax: (818)704-7620. Website: www.shapemag.com. **70% freelance written. Prefers to work with published/established writers.** Monthly magazine covering health, fitness, nutrition, and beauty for women ages 18-34. *Shape* reaches women who are committed to healthful, active lifestyles. Our readers are participating in a variety of fitness-related activities, in the gym, at home and outdoors, and they are also proactive about their health and are nutrition conscious. Estab. 1981. Circ. 1,600,000. Pays on acceptance. Offers 33% kill fee. Buys second serial (reprint) rights, buys all rights. Submit seasonal material 8 months in advance. Accepts queries by mail. Responds in 2 months to queries. Sample copy for sae with 9x12 envelope and 4 First-Class stamps. Guidelines available online.

Nonfiction We use some health and fitness articles written by professionals in their specific fields. Needs book excerpts, expose, health, fitness, nutrition related, how-to, get fit, health/fitness, recipes. We rarely publish celebrity question and answer stories, celebrity profiles, or menopausal/hormone replacement therapy stories. **Buys 27 features/year; 36-54 short mss/year.** Query with published clips. 2,500 words/features; 1,000 words/shorter pieces **Pays $1.50/word (on average).**

Tips Review a recent issue of the magazine. Not responsible for unsolicited material. We reserve the right to edit any article.

$ $ $ SPIRITUALITY & HEALTH MAGAZINE

The Soul Body Connection, Spirituality & Health Publishing, Inc., 129½ E. Front St., Traverse City MI 49684. E-mail: editors@spiritualityhealth.com. Website: www.spiritualityhealth.com. **Contact:** Heather Shaw, man. ed. Bimonthly magazine covering research-based spirituality and health. "We look for formally credentialed writers in their fields. We are nondenominational and non-proselytizing. We are not New Age. We appreciate well-written work that offers spiritual seekers from all different traditions help in their unique journeys." Estab. 1998. Circ. 95,000. Byline given. Pays on acceptance. Offers 50% kill fee. Buys electronic rights, buys worldwide rights. Editorial lead time 4 months. Submit seasonal material 6 months in advance. Accepts queries by e-mail. Accepts simultaneous submissions. Responds in 3-4 months to queries. Responds in 2-4 months to mss. Sample copy and writer's guidelines online.

- The most open department is Updates & Observations. Read it to see what we use. (All back issues are on the website.) News must be current with a four-month lead time.

Nonfiction Needs book excerpts, how-to, news shorts. Does not want proselytizing, New Age cures with no scientific basis, "how I recovered from a disease personal essays," psychics, advice columns, profiles of individual healers or practitioners, pieces promoting one way or guru, reviews, poetry or columns. Send complete ms. 300 words for news shorts, otherwise 700 -1,500 words. Sometimes pays expenses of writers on assignment. Limit agreed upon in advance

Tips "Start by pitching really interesting, well-researched news shorts for Updates & Observations. Before you pitch, do a search of our website to see if we've already covered it."

$ $ ⊘ VIBRANT LIFE

A Magazine for Healthful Living, Review and Herald Publishing Association, 55 W. Oak Ridge Dr., Hagerstown MD 21740-7390. (301)393-4019. Fax: (301)393-4055. E-mail: vibrantlife@rhpa.org. Website: www.vibrantlife.com. **80% freelance written. Enjoys working with published/established writers; works with a small number of new/unpublished writers each year.** Bimonthly magazine covering health articles (especially from a prevention angle and with a Christian slant). The average length of time between acceptance of a freelance-written manuscript and publication of the material depends upon the topics: some immediately used; others up to 2 years. Estab. 1885. Circ. 30,000. Byline given. Pays on acceptance. Offers 50% kill fee. Buys first serial, first world serial, or sometimes second serial (reprint) rights. Submit seasonal material 9 months in advance. Accepts queries by mail, e-mail, fax. Accepts previously published material. Responds in 1 month to queries. Sample copy for $1. Guidelines available online.

- Currently closed to submissions.

Nonfiction We seek practical articles promoting better health and a more fulfilled life. We especially like features on breakthroughs in medicine, and most aspects of health. We need articles on how to integrate a person's spiritual life with their health. We'd like more in the areas of exercise, nutrition, water, avoiding addictions of all types, and rest—all done from a wellness perspective. Needs interview, with personalities on health. **Buys 50-60 feature articles/year and 6-12 short mss/year.** Send complete ms. 500-1,500 words for features, 25-250 words for short pieces. **Pays $75-300 for features, $50-75 for short pieces.**

Reprints Send tearsheet and information about when and where the material previously appeared. Pays 50% of amount paid for an original article.

Photos Not interested in b&w photos. Send photos Reviews 35mm transparencies.

Columns/Departments Buys 12-18 department articles/year. Length: 500-650 words. **Pays $75-175.**

Tips *Vibrant Life* is published for baby boomers, particularly young professionals, age 40-55. Articles must be written in an interesting, easy-to-read style. Information must be reliable; no faddism. We are more conservative than other magazines in our field. Request a sample copy, and study the magazine and writer's guidelines.

$ $ $ $ VIM & VIGOR

America's Family Health Magazine, 1010 E. Missouri Ave., Phoenix AZ 85014-2601. (602)395-5850. Fax: (602)395-5853. E-mail: stephaniec@mcmurry.com. **90% freelance written**. Quarterly magazine covering health and healthcare. Estab. 1985. Circ. 800,000. Byline given. Pays on acceptance. Publishes ms an average of 6 months after acceptance. Buys all rights. Sample copy for 9x12 SAE with 8 first-class stamps. Guidelines for #10 SASE.

Nonfiction Absolutely no complete manuscripts will be accepted/returned. All articles are assigned. Send published samples for assignment consideration. Any queries regarding story ideas will be placed on the following year's conference agenda and will be addressed on a topic-by-topic basis. Send published clips and resume by mail or e-mail. Length: 500-1,200 words. **Pays 90¢-$1/word.** Pays expenses of writers on assignment.

Tips Writers must have consumer healthcare experience.

WEBMD THE MAGAZINE

WebMD, E-mail: cparetty@webmd.net. Website: www.webmd.net. www.webmd.net/magazine. **80% freelance written**. Bimonthly magazine covering health, lifestyle health and well-being, some medical. Published by WebMD Health, *WebMD the Magazine* is the print sibling of the website WebMD.com. It aims to broaden our company-wide mandate: 'Better information, better health.' It is a health magazine—with a difference. It is specifically designed and written for people who are about to have what may be the most important conversation of the year with their physician or other medical professional. The magazine's content is therefore developed to be most useful at this critical 'point of care,' to improve and enhance the dialogue between patient and doctor. Our readers are adults (65% women, 35% men) in their 30s, 40s, and 50s (median age is 41) who care about their health, take an active role in their own and their family's wellness, and want the best information possible to make informed healthcare decisions. Estab. 2005. Circ. 1,000,000. Byline given. Pays on acceptance. Offers 30% kill fee. Publishes ms an average of 3 months after acceptance. Buys all rights. Editorial lead time 3-4 months. Submit seasonal material 3-4 months in advance. Accepts queries by e-mail. Accepts previously published material. Sample copy available online.

Tips We only want experienced magazine writers, in the topic areas of consumer health. Writers with experience writing for national women's health magazines preferred. Relevant clips required. Fresh, witty, smart, well-written style, with solid background in health. This is not a publication for writers breaking into the field.

$ $ WHJ/HRHJ

Williamsburg Health Journal/Hampton Roads Health Journal, Rian Enterprises, LLC, 4808 Courthouse St., Suite 204, Williamsburg VA 23188. Fax: (757)645-4473. E-mail: info@thehealthjournals.com. Website: www.williamsburghealth.com. www.hamptonroadshealth.com. **70% freelance written**. Monthly tabloid covering consumer/family health and wellness in the Hampton Roads area. "Articles accepted of local and national interest. Health-savvy, college educated audience of all gender, ages, and backgrounds. " Estab. 2005. Circ. 81,000. Byline given. Pays on publication. Publishes ms an average of 1-2 months after acceptance. Buys first rights, buys second serial (reprint) rights. Editorial lead time 4-6 months. Submit seasonal material 4 months in advance. Accepts queries by mail, e-mail, fax. Accepts previously published material. Accepts simultaneous submissions. Only responds to mss of interest. Sample copy available online. Guidelines available online.

Nonfiction Needs book excerpts, essays, expose, general interest, historical, how-to, humor, inspirational, interview, new product, opinion, personal experience, photo feature, technical, travel. Does not want promotion of products, religious material, anything over 2,000 words. **Buys 100 mss/year.** Query with published clips. Length: 400-1,000 words. **Pays 15¢/word, $50/reprint.** Sometimes pays expenses of writers on assignment.

Tips "Write for the consumer. Remain objective. Entertain. Inform. Surprise us! If you are not a health expert on the topic, consult one. Or two. Or three. Writer's point of view is not sufficient unless submitting a personal essay."

$ $ $ $ YOGA JOURNAL

475 Sasome St., Suite 850, San Francisco CA 94111. (415)591-0555. Fax: (415)591-0733. Website: www.yogajournal.com. **75% freelance written**. Bimonthly magazine covering the practice and philosophy of yoga. Estab. 1975. Circ. 130,000. Byline given. Pays within 90 days of acceptance. Offers kill fee. Offers kill fee on assigned articles. Publishes ms an average of 10 months after acceptance. Buys first North American serial rights. Submit seasonal material 4 months in advance. Accepts queries by mail. Accepts previously published material. Responds in 3 months to queries. Sample copy for $4.99. Guidelines available online.

Nonfiction Yoga is a main concern, but we also highlight other conscious living/New Age personalities and endeavors (nothing too 'woo-woo'). In particular we welcome articles on the following themes: 1) Leaders, spokepersons, and visionaries in the yoga community; 2) The practice of hatha yoga; 3) Applications of yoga to everyday life; 4) Hatha yoga anatomy and kinesiology, and therapeutic yoga; 5) Nutrition and diet, cooking, and natural skin and body care. Needs book excerpts, how-to, yoga, exercise, etc., inspirational, yoga or related, interview, opinion, photo feature, travel, yoga-related. Does not want unsolicited poetry or cartoons. Please avoid New Age jargon and in-house buzz words as much as possible. **Buys 50-60 mss/year.** Query with SASE. Length: 3,000-5,000 words. **Pays $800-2,000.**

Reprints Send tearsheet or photocopy with rights for sale noted and information about when and where the material previously appeared.

Columns/Departments Health (self-care; well-being); Body-Mind (hatha Yoga, other body-mind modalities, meditation, yoga philosophy, Western mysticism); Community (service, profiles, organizations, events), all

1,500-2,000 words. **Pays $400-800.** Living (books, video, arts, music), 800 words. **Pays $200-250.** World of Yoga, Spectrum (brief yoga and healthy living news/events/fillers), 150-600 words. **Pays $50-150.**
Tips Please read our writer's guidelines before submission. Do not e-mail or fax unsolicited manuscripts.

HISTORY

$ N THE TOMBSTONE EPITAPH

National Edition, Tombstone Epitaph, Inc., P.O. BOX, 1880, Tombstone AZ 85638. (520)457-2211. E-mail: info@tombstoneepitaph.com. Website: www.tombstoneepitaph.com. **60% freelance written**. Monthly tabloid covering American west to 1900 (-1935, if there's an Old West connection). "We seek lively, well-written, sourced articles that examine the history and culture of the Old West." Estab. 1880. Byline given. End of calendar year. No kill fee. Publishes ms an average of 3 months after acceptance. Buys first North American serial rights. Editorial lead time 3 months. Submit seasonal material 6 months in advance. Accepts queries by e-mail. Accepts previously published material. Responds in 2 weeks to queries. Responds in 1 month to mss. Sample copy for $3. Guidelines by email.
Nonfiction Needs essays, historical, humor, personal experience, (if historically grounded), travel, Past events as interpreted in film, books, magazines, etc. We do not want poorly sourced stories, contemporary West pieces, fiction, poetry, big 'tell-all' stories. **Buys 25-40 mss/year. mss/year.** Query. Length: 1,000-5,000 words. **Pays $30-50 for assigned articles. Pays $30 max. for unsolicited articles.**
Photos Send photos Captions, identification of subjects required. Reviews GIF/JPEG files. Offers no additional payment for photos accepted with ms. Buys one time rights.
Tips "Writers desiring to break into the Western historical genre are especially encouraged to query. Editor is very willing to work with new talent committed to bright, accurate and polished stories on the history of the Old West. Read a sample copy first, then query."

⊘ AMERICAN HISTORY

Weider History Group, 741 Miller Dr., Suite D-2, Leesburg VA 20175-8994. (703)771-9400. Fax: (703)779-8345. Website: www.historynet.com. **60% freelance written**. Bimonthly magazine of cultural, social, military, and political history published for a general audience. Estab. 1966. Circ. 95,000. Byline given. Pays on acceptance. No kill fee. Buys first rights. Responds in 10 weeks to queries. Sample copy and guidelines for $5 (includes 3rd class postage) or $4 and 9x12 SAE with 4 first-class stamps. Guidelines for #10 SASE.
Nonfiction Features events in the lives of noteworthy historical figures and accounts of important events in American history. Also includes pictorial features on artists, photographers, and graphic subjects. Material is presented on a popular rather than a scholarly level. **Buys 20 mss/year.** Query by mail only with published clips and SASE. 2,000-4,000 words depending on type of article.
Photos Welcomes suggestions for illustrations.
Tips Key prerequisites for publication are thorough research and accurate presentation, precise English usage, and sound organization, a lively style, and a high level of human interest. *Unsolicited manuscripts not considered.* Inappropriate materials include: fiction, book reviews, travelogues, personal/family narratives not of national significance, articles about collectibles/antiques, living artists, local/individual historic buildings/landmarks, and articles of a current editorial nature. Currently seeking articles on significant Civil War subjects. No phone, fax, or e-mail queries, please.

N ⊘ AMERICAN LEGACY

Forbes, Inc., 28 W. 23rd St., 10th Floor, New York NY 10010-5254. (212)367-3100. Fax: (212)367-3151. E-mail: apeterson@americanlegacymag.com. Website: www.americanlegacymagazine.net. Quarterly magazine spotlighting the historical and cultural achievements of African American men and women throughout history. No kill fee. Editorial lead time 6 months.

- Query before submitting.

$ $ AMERICA'S CIVIL WAR

Weider History Group, 741 Miller Dr., Suite D-2, Leesburg VA 20175-8994. (703)771-9400. Fax: (703)779-8345. Website: www.historynet.com. **95% freelance written**. Bimonthly magazine covering popular history and straight historical narrative for both the general reader and the Civil War buff covering strategy, tactics, personalities, arms and equipment. Estab. 1988. Circ. 78,000. Byline given. Pays on publication. No kill fee. Buys all rights. Accepts queries by mail, e-mail, fax. Sample copy for $5. Writer's guidelines for #10 SASE.
Nonfiction Needs historical, book notices, preservation news. **Buys 24 mss/year.** Query. 3,500-4,000 words and a 500-word sidebar. **Pays $300 and up.**
Photos Send photos with submission or cite sources. Captions, identification of subjects required.
Columns/Departments Personality (profiles of Civil War personalities); Men & Material (about weapons used); Commands (about units); Eyewitness to War (historical letters and diary excerpts). Length: 2,000 words. 24

Query. **Pays $150 and up**

Tips All stories must be true. We do not publish fiction or poetry. Write an entertaining, well-researched, informative and unusual story that grabs the reader's attention and holds it. Include suggested readings in a standard format at the end of your piece. Manuscript must be typed, double-spaced on one side of standard white 8 ½x11, 16 to 30 pound paper—no onion skin paper or dot matrix printouts. All submissions are on speculation. Prefer subjects to be on disk (IBM- or Macintosh-compatible floppy disk) as well as a hard copy. Choose stories with strong art possibilities.

$ THE ARTILLERYMAN

Historical Publications, Inc., 234 Monarch Hill Rd., Tunbridge VT 05077. (802)889-3500. Fax: (802)889-5627. E-mail: mail@civilwarnews.com. Website: www.artillerymanmagazine.com. **60% freelance written**. Quarterly magazine covering antique artillery, fortifications, and crew-served weapons 1750-1900 for competition shooters, collectors, and living history reenactors using artillery. Emphasis on Revolutionary War and Civil War but includes everyone interested in pre-1900 artillery and fortifications, preservation, construction of replicas, etc. Estab. 1979. Circ. 1,500. Byline given. Pays on publication. Publishes ms an average of 6 months after acceptance. Buys one-time rights. Accepts queries by mail, e-mail, fax. Accepts previously published material. Accepts simultaneous submissions. Responds in 3 weeks to queries. Sample copy and writer's guidelines for 9x12 SAE with 4 first-class stamps

Nonfiction Interested in artillery only, for sophisticated readers. Not interested in other weapons, battles in general. Needs historical, how-to, reproduce ordnance equipment/sights/implements/tools/accessories, etc., interview, new product, opinion, must be accompanied by detailed background of writer and include references, personal experience, photo feature, technical, must have footnotes, travel, where to find interesting antique cannon. **Buys 24-30 mss/year.** Send complete ms. 300 words minimum **Pays $20-60.**

Reprints Send tearsheet or photocopy and information about when and where the material previously appeared.

Photos Send photos Captions, identification of subjects required. Pays $5 for 5x7 and larger b&w prints

Tips We regularly use freelance contributions for Places-to-Visit, Cannon Safety, The Workshop, and Unit Profiles departments. Also need pieces on unusual cannon or cannon with a known and unique history. To judge whether writing style and/or expertise will suit our needs, writers should ask themselves if they could knowledgeably talk artillery with an expert. Subject matter is of more concern than writer's background.

BRITISH HERITAGE

Weider History Group, 741 Miller Dr., Suite D-2, Leesburg VA 20175-8994. (703)771-9400. Fax: (703)779-8345. E-mail: dana.huntley@weiderhistorygroup.com. Website: www.thehistorynet.com. Bimonthly magazine covering British travel and culture. Stories of British life and history with a sense of place in England, Scotland and Wales. Circ. 77,485. Pays on acceptance. Pays kill fee though never had to. Buys all rights. Editorial lead time 6 months. Accepts queries by e-mail.

Nonfiction Buys 50 mss/year. Query by e-mail. Length: 1,000-2,500 words.

Tips "The first rule still stands: Know thy market."

$ $ $ CIVIL WAR TIMES

Weider History Group, 741 Miller Dr. SE, Suite D-2, Leesburg VA 20175. (703)779-8371. Fax: (703)779-8345. Website: www.historynet.com. **90% freelance written. Works with a small number of new/unpublished writers each year.** Magazine published 6 times/year. *Civil War Times* is the full-spectrum magazine of the Civil War. Specifically, we look for nonpartisan coverage of battles, prominent military and civilian figures, the home front, politics, military technology, common soldier life, prisoners and escapes, period art and photography, the naval war, blockade-running, specific regiments, and much more. Estab. 1962. Circ. 108,000. Pays on acceptance and on publication. Publishes ms an average of 18 months after acceptance. Buys unlimited usage rights. Submit seasonal material 1 year in advance. Responds in 3-6 months to queries. Sample copy for $6. Guidelines for #10 SASE.

Nonfiction Needs interview, photo feature, Civil War historical material. Don't send us a comprehensive article on a well-known major battle. Instead, focus on some part or aspect of such a battle, or some group of soldiers in the battle. Similar advice applies to major historical figures like Lincoln and Lee. Positively no fiction or poetry. **Buys 20 freelance mss/year.** Query with clips and SASE **Pays $75-800.**

Tips We're very open to new submissions. Send query after examining writer's guidelines and several recent issues. Include photocopies of photos that could feasibly accompany the article. Confederate soldiers' diaries and letters are especially welcome.

COMMON PATRIOT

The American Revolutionary War Magazine, Two If By Sea Publishing, LLC, 12995 S. Cleveland Ave., Suite 141 #1776, Fort Myers FL 33907. (239)464-9730. E-mail: editor@commonpatriot.com. Website: www.commonpatriot.com. **100% freelance written**. Quarterly magazine covering the American revolutionary war. Estab. 2005. Byline given. Pays on publication. Publishes ms an average of 4-6 months after acceptance. Buys one-time rights. Submit seasonal material 6 months in advance. Accepts queries by mail, e-mail. Accepts previously published material. Accepts simultaneous submissions. Responds in 1 month to queries. Responds in 2-3 months to mss. Sample copy for $6. Guidelines available online.

Nonfiction Needs book excerpts, general interest, historical, inspirational, interview, personal experience, travel. **Buys 20 mss/year.** Query. Length: 2,500 words. Sometimes pays expenses of writers on assignment.

Photos Send photos Captions, identification of subjects required. Reviews 4x6 prints. Buys one time rights.

Columns/Departments Patriot Profile (biography, history), 500-1,000 words; My Ancestor (genealogy), 500-1,000 words; Am Rev War Today (re-enactments, personal experience, historical), 750-2,000 words; How It Was in Rev War Time (life of being a soldier), 800-1,000 words. 12 Send complete ms.

Tips A well-written article on their 'unknown' common patriot who fought in the American revolutionary war. Check our website for more information.

$ $ GATEWAY

(formerly *Gateway Heritage*), Missouri History Museum, P.O. Box 11940, St. Louis MO 63112-0040. (314)746-4558. Fax: (314)746-4548. E-mail: vwmonks@mohistory.org. Website: www.mohistory.org. **75% freelance written**. Annual magazine covering Missouri history and culture. *Gateway* is a popular cultural history magazine that is primarily a member benefit of the Missouri History Museum. Thus, we have a general audience with an interest in the history and culture of Missouri, and St. Louis in particular. Estab. 1980. Circ. 11,000. Byline given. Pays on publication. Offers $100 kill fee. Publishes ms an average of 6 months to 1 year after acceptance. Buys first North American serial rights. Editorial lead time 6 months. Accepts queries by mail, e-mail, fax. Responds in 1 month to queries. Responds in 2 months to mss. Sample copy for $10. online or send #10 SASE

Nonfiction Needs book excerpts, interview, photo feature, historical, scholarly essays, Missouri biographies, viewpoints on events, first-hand historical accounts, regional architectural history, literary history. No genealogies. **Buys 4-6 mss/year.** Query with writing samples. Length: 4,000-5,000 words. **Pays $300-400 (average).**

Photos State availability

Columns/Departments Origins (essays on the beginnings of organizations, movements, and immigrant communities in St. Louis and Missouri), 1,500-2,500 words; Missouri Biographies (biographical sketches of famous and interesting Missourians), 1,500-2,500 words; Gateway Conversations (interviews); Letters Home (excerpts from letters, diaries, and journals), 1,500-2,500 words. 2-4 **Pays $250-300**

Tips "You'll get our attention with queries reflecting new perspectives on historical and cultural topics."

$ GOOD OLD DAYS

America's Premier Nostalgia Magazine, House of White Birches, 306 E. Parr Rd., Berne IN 46711. Fax: (260)589-8093. E-mail: editor@goodolddaysonline.com. Website: www.goodolddaysonline.com. **75% freelance written**. Monthly magazine of first person nostalgia, 1935-1960. "We look for strong narratives showing life as it was in the middle decades of the 20th century. Our readership is comprised of nostalgia buffs, history enthusiasts, and the people who actually lived and grew up in this era." Byline given. Pays on contract. No kill fee. Publishes ms an average of 8 months after acceptance. Prefers all rights, but will negotiate for First North American serial and one-time rights. Submit seasonal material 10 months in advance. Responds in 2 months to queries. Sample copy for $2. Guidelines available online.

- Queries accepted, but are not necessary.

Nonfiction Regular features: Good Old Days on Wheels (auto, plane, horse-drawn, tram, bicycle, trolley, etc.); Good Old Days In the Kitchen (favorite foods, appliances, ways of cooking, recipes); Home Remedies (herbs and poultices, hometown doctors, harrowing kitchen table operations). Needs historical, humor, personal experience, photo feature, favorite food/recipes, year-round seasonal material, biography, memorable events, fads, fashion, sports, music, literature, entertainment. No fiction accepted. **Buys 350 mss/year.** Query or send complete ms. Length: 500-1,500 words. **Pays $20-100, depending on quality and photos.**

Photos Send original or professionally copied photographs. Do not submit laser-copied prints. Send photos Identification of subjects required.

Tips "Most of our writers are not professionals. We prefer the author's individual voice, warmth, humor, and honesty over technical ability."

$ $ HISTORY MAGAZINE

Moorshead Magazines, 500-505 Consumers Rd., Toronto ON M2J 4V8 Canada. E-mail: magazine@history-magazine.com. Website: www.history-magazine.com. **90% freelance written**. Bimonthly magazine covering social history. A general interest history magazine, focusing on social history up to the outbreak of World War II. Estab. 1999. Byline given. Pays on publication. Publishes ms an average of 6 months after acceptance. Buys electronic rights, buys world serial rights rights. Editorial lead time 6 months. Submit seasonal material 6 months in advance. Accepts queries by mail, e-mail. Responds in 1 month to queries. Responds in 1 month to mss. Sample copy available online. Guidelines available online.

Nonfiction Needs book excerpts, historical. Does not want first-person narratives or revisionist history. **Buys 50**

mss/year. Query. Length: 400-2,500 words. **Pays $50-250.**
Photos State availability Captions required. Reviews GIF/JPEG files. Negotiates payment individually. Buys one time rights.
Tips A love of history helps a lot and a willingness to work with us to present interesting articles on the past to our readers.

$ $ KANSAS JOURNAL OF MILITARY HISTORY

P.O. Box 828, Topeka KS 66601. (785)357-0510. Fax: (785)357-0579. E-mail: karen@ksjournal.com. Website: www.ksjournal.com. **20% freelance written**. Quarterly magazine that celebrates and explores the military history of Kansas and its territories and the Kansans who have served here and abroad, and promotes tourism by showcasing historic sites and landmarks. Estab. 2004. Circ. 4,000. Byline given. Pays on publication. No kill fee. Publishes ms an average of 6 months after acceptance. Buys first North American serial rights. Editorial lead time 6 months. Submit seasonal material 1 year in advance. Accepts queries by mail, e-mail. Accepts previously published material. Accepts simultaneous submissions. Responds in 2 weeks to queries. Responds in 2 months to mss. Sample copy available online. Guidelines available online.
Nonfiction Needs book excerpts, essays, historical, humor, interview, opinion, personal experience, photo feature. Lights, Camera, Kansas: movie stills, posters, etc. relating to film in Kansas. Does not want to receive fiction or poetry. **Buys 10 mss/year.** Query with published clips. Length: 500-1,500 words. **Pays $50-200.**
Photos Send photos Captions, identification of subjects, model releases required. Reviews contact sheets, GIF/JPEG files. Offers no additional payment for photos accepted with ms. Buys one time rights.
Columns/Departments Hand to Hand (opinion, pro/con, historic figures), 800-1,000 words. 5 **Pays $50-200.**
Fillers Needs anecdotes, facts, gags, short humor. 20 Length: 200-300 words. **Pays $25-50.**
Tips We are interested in history that is fun, compelling, and interesting—not academic. The audience is made up of military members, veterans, tourists, and history buffs (novice and knowledgeable).

$ N LIGHTHOUSE DIGEST

Lighthouse Digest, P.O. Box 250, East Machias ME 04630. (207)259-2121. Fax: (207)259-3323. E-mail: timh@lhdigest.com. Website: www.lighthousedigest.com. **Contact:** Tim Harrison, editor. **15% freelance written**. Monthly magazine covering historical, fiction and news events about lighthouses and similar maritime stories. Estab. 1989. Circ. 24,000. Byline given. Pays on publication. No kill fee. Publishes ms an average of 4 months after acceptance. Buys one-time rights, buys electronic rights. Editorial lead time 3 months. Submit seasonal material 3 months in advance. Accepts queries by e-mail. Accepts simultaneous submissions. Responds in 6 weeks to queries. Sample copy free.
Nonfiction Needs expose, general interest, historical, humor, inspirational, personal experience, photo feature, religious, technical, travel. No historical data taken from books. **Buys 30 mss/year.** Send complete ms. 2,500 words maximum **Pays $75.**
Photos Send photos Captions, identification of subjects required. Reviews prints. Offers no additional payment for photos accepted with ms Buys all rights.
Fiction Needs adventure, historical, humorous, mystery, religious, romance, suspense. **Buys 2 mss/year.** Send complete ms. 2,500 words maximum **Pays $75-150.**
Tips "Read our publication and visit the website."

MHQ: THE QUARTERLY JOURNAL OF MILITARY HISTORY

MHQ: The Quarterly Journal of Military History, Weider History Group, 19300 Promenade Dr., Leesburg VA 20176-6500. (703)779-8373. Fax: (703)779-8359. Website: www.historynet.com. **100% freelance written**. Quarterly journal covering military history. *"MHQ* offers readers in-depth articles on the history of warfare from ancient times into the 21st century. Authoritative features and departments cover military strategies, philosophies, campaigns, battles, personalities, weaponry, espionage and perspectives, all written in a lively and readable style. Articles are accompanied by classic works of art, photographs and maps. Readers include serious students of military tactics, strategy, leaders and campaigns, as well as general world history enthusiasts. Many readers are currently in the military or retired officers." Estab. 1988. Circ. 22,000. Byline given. Pays on publication. No kill fee. Buys all rights. Editorial lead time 1 year. Submit seasonal material 1 year in advance. Accepts queries by mail, e-mail, fax. Accepts simultaneous submissions. Sample copy for $23 (hardcover), $13 (softcover); some articles on website. Writer's guidelines for #10 SASE or via e-mail.
Nonfiction Needs historical, personal experience, photo feature. No fiction or stories pertaining to collectibles or reenactments. **Buys 36 mss/year.** Query preferred; also accepts complete ms. Length: 1,500-6,000 words.
Photos Send photos/art with submission. Identification of subjects required. Reviews transparencies, prints. Negotiates payment individually. Buys all rights.
Columns/Departments Artists on War (description of artwork of a military nature); Experience of War (first-person accounts of military incidents); Strategic View (discussion of military theory, strategy); Arms & Men (description of military hardware or unit), all up to 2,500 words. 16 Send complete ms.

Tips "All stories must be true—we publish no fiction. Although we are always looking for variety, some subjects—World War II, the American Civil War, and military biography, for instance—are the focus of so many proposals that we are forced to judge them by relatively rigid criteria. We are always glad to consider articles on these subjects. However, less common topic areas—medieval, Asian, or South American military history, for example—are more likely to attract our attention. The likelihood that articles can be effectively illustrated often determines the ultimate fate of manuscripts. Many otherwise excellent articles have been rejected due to a lack of suitable art or photographs. Regular departments—columns on strategy, tactics, and weaponry—average 1,500 words. While the information we publish is scholarly and substantive, we prefer writing that is light, anecdotal, and above all, engaging, rather than didactic."

MILITARY HISTORY

The Quarterly Juornal of Military History, Weider History Group, 741 Miller Dr.,, Suite D-2, Leesburg VA 20175-8994. (703)771-9400. Fax: (703)779-8345. Website: www.historynet.com. **95% freelance written**. Magazine published 10 times/year covering all military history of the world. We strive to give the general reader accurate, highly readable, often narrative popular history, richly accompanied by period art. Circ. 112,000. Byline given. Pays 30 days after publication. No kill fee. Buys all rights. Submit seasonal material 1 year in advance. Accepts queries by mail, e-mail, fax. Sample copy for $5. Guidelines for #10 SASE.

Nonfiction The best way to break into our magazine is to write an entertaining, informative, and unusual story that grabs the reader's attention and holds it. Needs historical, interview, military figures of commanding interest, personal experience, only occasionally. **Buys 30 mss/year.** Query with published clips. Submit a short, self-explanatory query summarizing the story proposed, its highlights, and/or significance. State also your own expertise, access to sources, or proposed means of developing the pertinent information. 4,000 words with a 500-word sidebar

Columns/Departments Intrigue; Weaponry; Perspectives; Personality; Reviews (books, video, CD-ROMs, software—all relating to military history). Length: 2,000 words. 24 Query with published clips.

Tips We would like journalistically `pure' submissions that adhere to basics, such as full name at first reference, same with rank, and definition of prior or related events, issues cited as context or obscure military `hardware.' Read the magazine, discover our style, and avoid subjects already covered. Pick stories with strong art possibilities (real art and photos), send photocopies, tell us where to order the art. Avoid historical overview; focus upon an event with appropriate and accurate context. Provide bibliography. Tell the story in popular but elegant style. Submissions must be in digital format.

NOSTALGIA MAGAZINE

Enriching Today with the Stories of Yesterday, King's Publishing Group, Inc., P.O. Box 203, Spokane WA 99210. (509)299-4041. E-mail: editor@nostalgiamagazine.net. Website: www.nostalgiamagazine.net. **90% freelance written**. Monthly magazine covering "stories and photos of personal, historical, nostalgic experiences: I remember when. *Nostalgia Magazine* is a journal that gathers photos, personal remembrance stories, diaries, and researched stories of well-known—and more often little-known—people, places, and events, and puts them into 1 monthly volume. We glean the best of the past to share and enrich life now." Byline given. No kill fee. Publishes ms an average of 1 year after acceptance. "Uses simultaneous rights and rights to reprint in our regional editions and affiliated media rights." Editorial lead time 6 months. Submit seasonal material 6 months in advance. Accepts queries by mail, e-mail. Accepts previously published material. Accepts simultaneous submissions. Responds in 6 months to queries. Responds in 6 months to mss. Sample copy for $5. Writer's guidelines available via e-mail or mail

Nonfiction Needs book excerpts, expose, general interest, historical, how-to, humor, inspirational, interview, personal experience, photo feature, religious, travel. Does not want genealogies, current events/news, divisive politics (in historical setting sometimes OK), or glorification of immorality. **Buys 120 mss/year.** Send complete ms. Length: 400-2,000 words.

Photos "Photos are as important as the story. We need 1 candid photo per 400 words of fiction." Send photos Captions, identification of subjects required. Reviews negatives, transparencies, prints, JPEG files. Offers no additional payment for photos accepted with ms. Buys use in all publications and affiliated media only.

Poetry Needs free verse, light verse, traditional. "Does not want avant-garde, contemporary/modern experiences, simple junk." **Buys 3 poems/year.** Submit maximum 1 poems. **Pays in copies.**

Fillers Needs anecdotes, facts, gags, short humor. 50 Length: 50-200 words. **Pays with copies of the magazine.**

Tips Start with an interesting photograph from the past you know, or your own past. Good photos are the key to people reading an interesting story in our magazine. Write the who, what, when, where, why, and how. We need 1 candid photo for every 400 words of text.

$ $ PERSIMMON HILL

National Cowboy & Western Heritage Museum, 1700 NE 63rd St., Oklahoma City OK 73111. (405)478-2250. Fax: (405)478-4714. E-mail: editor@nationalcowboymuseum.org. Website: www.nationalcowboymuseum.org.

Contact: Judy Hilovsky. **70% freelance written. Prefers to work with published/established writers; works with a small number of new/unpublished writers each year.** Quarterly magazine for an audience interested in Western art, Western history, ranching, and rodeo, including historians, artists, ranchers, art galleries, schools, and libraries. Estab. 1970. Circ. 7,500. Byline given. Pays on publication. No kill fee. Publishes ms an average of 18 months after acceptance. Buys first rights. Responds in 3 months to queries. Sample copy for $10.50, including postage. Writer's guidelines for #10 SASE or on website.

Nonfiction Historical and contemporary articles on famous Western figures connected with pioneering the American West, Western art, rodeo, cowboys, etc. (or biographies of such people), stories of Western flora and animal life and environmental subjects. We want thoroughly researched and historically authentic material written in a popular style. May have a humorous approach to subject. No broad, sweeping, superficial pieces; i.e., the California Gold Rush or rehashed pieces on Billy the Kid, etc. **Buys 50-75 mss/year.** Query by mail only with clips. 1,500 words **Pays $150-300.**

Photos Purchased with ms or on assignment. Captions required. Reviews digital images and b&w prints. Pays according to quality and importance for b&w and color photos.

Tips Send us a story that captures the spirit of adventure and indvidualism that typifies the Old West or reveals a facet of the Western lifestyle in comtemporary society. Excellent illustrations for articles are essential! We lean towards scholarly, historical, well-researched articles. We're less focused on Western celebrities than some of the other contemporary Western magazines.

$ $ $ TIMELINE

Ohio Historical Society, 1982 Velma Ave., Columbus OH 43211-2497. (614)297-2360. Fax: (614)297-2367. E-mail: timeline@ohiohistory.org. **90% freelance written. Works with a small number of new/unpublished writers each year.** Quarterly magazine covering history, prehistory, and the natural sciences, directed toward readers in the Midwest. Estab. 1984. Circ. 7,000. Byline given. Pays on acceptance. Offers $75 minimum kill fee. Publishes ms an average of 1 year after acceptance. Buys first North American serial rights, buys all rights. Submit seasonal material 6 months in advance. Accepts queries by mail, e-mail, fax. Responds in 3 weeks to queries. Responds in 6 weeks to mss. Sample copy for $12 and 9x12 SAE. Guidelines for #10 SASE.

Nonfiction Topics include the traditional fields of political, economic, military, and social history; biography; the history of science and technology; archaeology and anthropology; architecture; the fine and decorative arts; and the natural sciences including botany, geology, zoology, ecology, and paleontology. Needs book excerpts, essays, historical, interview, of individuals, photo feature. **Buys 22 mss/year.** Query. 1,500-6,000 words. Also vignettes of 500-1,000 words **Pays $100-800.**

Photos Submissions should include ideas for illustration. Send photos Captions, identification of subjects, model releases required. Reviews contact sheets, transparencies, 8x10 prints. Buys one time rights.

Tips We want crisply written, authoritative narratives for the intelligent lay reader. An Ohio slant may strengthen a submission, but it is not indispensable. Contributors must know enough about their subject to explain it clearly and in an interesting fashion. We use high-quality illustration with all features. If appropriate illustration is unavailable, we can't use the feature. The writer who sends illustration ideas with a manuscript has an advantage, but an often-published illustration won't attract us.

$ TOMBIGBEE COUNTRY MAGAZINE

Old Tyme Tales, History & Humor, Tombigbee Country Magazine, P.O. Box 105, 307 N. James St., Aberdeen MS 39730. (662)369-8551. Website: www.tombigbeecountry.com. **50% freelance written**. Monthly magazine covering nostalgia - history. We fancy ourselves as containing up-beat articles that make our readers feel good about themselves. We attempt to build pride in being an American, from the South and from our particular region along the Tombigbee River (now Tennessee-Tombigbee Waterway) in Mississippi, Alabama and Tennessee. We are an old fashioned, country magazine which takes pride in printing articles by everyday, ordinary people, most of which have never been published before. Estab. 2,000. Circ. 10,000. Byline given. Pays on publication. No kill fee. Publishes ms an average of 1 month after acceptance. Buys all rights. Editorial lead time 2 months. Submit seasonal material 2 months in advance. Accepts queries by mail, e-mail. Accepts previously published material. Accepts simultaneous submissions. Responds in 1 week to queries. Responds in 1 month to mss. Sample copy free. Guidelines free.

- Contributors who submit nonfiction, nostalgia-related articles have the best chance of being published.

Nonfiction Needs book excerpts, essays, general interest, historical, humor, inspirational, personal experience, religious. We are eager for stories on personal experience with celebrities—country musicians, famous southerners. We do not want tributes to family members. **Buys 24+ mss/year.** Query. Length: 800-2,000 words. **Pays $24 for assigned articles. Pays $24 for unsolicited articles.**

Fillers Needs short humor. Length: 25-800 words. **Pays $-0.**

Tips Ask yourself - would this article be of interest to an elder southerner?

$ $ TRACES OF INDIANA AND MIDWESTERN HISTORY

Indiana Historical Society, 450 W. Ohio St., Indianapolis IN 46202-3269. (317)232-1877. Fax: (317)233-0857.

E-mail: rboomhower@indianahistory.org. Website: www.indianahistory.org. **Contact:** Ray E. Boomhower, Senior editor. **80% freelance written.** Quarterly magazine on Indiana history. "Conceived as a vehicle to bring to the public good narrative and analytical history about Indiana in its broader contexts of region and nation, *Traces* explores the lives of artists, writers, performers, soldiers, politicians, entrepreneurs, homemakers, reformers, and naturalists. It has traced the impact of Hoosiers on the nation and the world. In this vein, the editors seek nonfiction articles that are solidly researched, attractively written, and amenable to illustration, and they encourage scholars, journalists, and freelance writers to contribute to the magazine." Estab. 1989. Circ. 8,000. Byline given. No kill fee. Publishes ms an average of 6 months after acceptance. Buys one-time rights. Submit seasonal material 1 year in advance. Responds in 3 months to mss. Guidelines available online.
Nonfiction Book excerpts, historical essays, historical photographic features on topics of biography, literature, folklore, music, visual arts, politics, economics, industry, transportation, and sports. **Buys 20 mss/year.** Send complete ms. Length: 2,000-4,000 words. **Pays $100-500.**
Photos Send photos Captions, identification of subjects, True required. Reviews contact sheets, transparencies, photocopies, prints. Pays reasonable photographic expenses. Buys one time rights.
Tips "Freelancers should be aware of prerequisites for writing history for a broad audience. Should have some awareness of this magazine and other magazines of this type published by Midwestern historical societies. Preference is given to subjects with an Indiana connection and authors who are familiar with *Traces*. Quality of potential illustration is also important."

TRAINS

Kalmbach Publishing Co., P.O. Box 1612, Waukesha WI 53187-1612. (262)796-8776. Fax: (262)796-1142. E-mail: editor@trainsmag.com. Website: www.trainsmag.com. Monthly magazine. "that appeals to consumers interested in learning about the function and history of the railroad industry." Circ. 100,000. No kill fee. Editorial lead time 2 months.

- Query before submitting.

$ $ $ TRUE WEST

True West Publishing, Inc., P.O. Box 8008, Cave Creek AZ 85327. (888)687-1881. Fax: (480)575-1903. E-mail: editor@twmag.com. Website: twmag.com. **70% freelance written. Works with a small number of new/unpublished writers each year.** Magazine published 10 times/year covering Western American history from prehistory 1800 to 1930. "We want reliable research on significant historical topics written in lively prose for an informed general audience. More recent topics may be used if they have a historical angle or retain the Old West flavor of trail dust and saddle leather. True West magazine's features and departments tie the history of the American West (between 1800-1930) to the modern western lifestyle through enticing narrative and intelligent analyses." Estab. 1953. Byline given. Pays on publication. 50% of original fee should the story have run in the publication Buys first North American serial rights and archival rights. Editorial lead time 6 months. Accepts queries by mail, e-mail. Sample copy for $3. Guidelines available online.

- No unsolicited mss.

Nonfiction No fiction, poetry, or unsupported, undocumented tales. **Buys 30 mss/year.** Send query to Meghan Saar at editor@twmag.com Length: 1,000-3,000 words. **Pays $50-800. "Features pay $150-1,000 with a $20 payment for each photo the author provides that is published with the article."**
Photos State availability Captions, identification of subjects, model releases required. Reviews contact sheets, negatives, 4x5 transparencies, 4x5 prints. Offers $20/photo. Buys one time rights.
Columns/Departments Book Reviews, 50-60 words (no unsolicited reviews). Please send in books for review consideration at least 4 months in advance. **Pays $25.**
Fillers Needs anecdotes, facts, gags, newsbreaks, short humor. 30 Length: 50-600 words.
Tips "Read our magazines and follow our guidelines. A freelancer is most likely to break in with us by submitting thoroughly researched, lively prose on relatively obscure topics or by being assigned to write for 1 of our departments. First-person accounts rarely fill our needs. Historical accuracy and strict adherence to the facts are essential. We much prefer material based on primary sources (archives, court records, documents) and should not be based mainly on secondary sources (published books, magazines, and journals). Art is also a huge selling point for us."

VIETNAM

Weider History Group, 741 Miller Dr., Suite D-2, Leesburg VA 20175-8994. (703)771-9400. Fax: (703)779-8345. Website: www.historynet.com. **90% freelance written.** Bimonthly magazine providing in-depth and authoritative accounts of the many complexities that made the war in Vietnam unique, including the people, battles, strategies, perspectives, analysis, and weaponry. Estab. 1988. Circ. 46,000. Byline given. Pays on publication. No kill fee. Buys all rights. Accepts queries by mail, fax. Sample copy for $5. Guidelines for #10 SASE.
Nonfiction Needs historical, military, interview, personal experience. Absolutely no fiction or poetry; we want straight history, as much personal narrative as possible, but not the gung-ho, shoot-'em-up variety, either. **Buys**

24 mss/year. Query. 4,000 words maximum; sidebars 500 words
Photos Send photos with submission or state availability and cite sources. Identification of subjects required.
Columns/Departments Arsenal (about weapons used, all sides); Personality (profiles of the players, all sides); Fighting Forces (various units or types of units: air, sea, rescue); Perspectives. Length: 2,000 words. Query.
Tips Choose stories with strong art possibilities. Send hard copy plus an IBM- or Macintosh-compatible floppy disk. All stories must be true. We do not publish fiction or poetry. All stories should be carefully researched third-person articles or firsthand accounts that give the reader a sense of experiencing historical events.

$ $ WILD WEST

Weider History Group, 741 Miller Dr., SE, Suite D-2, Leesburg VA 20175-8920. (703)771-9400. Fax: (703)779-8345. Website: www.historynet.com. **95% freelance written**. Bimonthly magazine covering the history of the American frontier, from its eastern beginnings to its western terminus. *Wild West* covers the popular (narrative) history of the American West—events, trends, personalities, anything of general interest. Estab. 1988. Circ. 83,500. Byline given. Pays on publication. No kill fee. Publishes ms an average of 2 years after acceptance. Buys all rights. Editorial lead time 10 months. Submit seasonal material 1 year in advance. Accepts queries by mail, e-mail. Accepts simultaneous submissions. Responds in 3 months to queries. Responds in 6 months to mss. Sample copy for $6. Writer's guidelines for #10 SASE or online.
Nonfiction Needs historical, Old West. No excerpts, travel, etc. Articles can be adapted from book. No fiction or poetry—nothing current. **Buys 36 mss/year.** Query. 3,500 words with a 500-word sidebar. **Pays $300.**
Photos State availability Captions, identification of subjects required. Reviews negatives, transparencies. Offers no additional payment for photos accepted with ms. Buys one time rights.
Columns/Departments Gunfighters & Lawmen, 2,000 words; Westerners, 2,000 words; Warriors & Chiefs, 2,000 words; Western Lore, 2,000 words; Guns of the West, 1,500 words; Artists West, 1,500 words; Books Reviews, 250 words. 36 Query. **Pays $150 for departments; book reviews paid by the word, minimum $40.**
Tips Always query the editor with your story idea. Successful queries include a description of sources of information and suggestions for color and b&w photography or artwork. The best way to break into our magazine is to write an entertaining, informative, and unusual story that grabs the reader's attention and holds it. We favor carefully researched, third-person articles that give the reader a sense of experiencing historical events. Include a hard copy as well as an IBM- or Macintosh-compatible floppy disk.

$ $ WORLD WAR II

Weider History Group, 741 Miller Dr., Suite D-2, Leesburg VA 20175-8994. (703)771-9400. Fax: (703)779-8345. Website: www.historynet.com. **95% freelance written. Prefers to work with published/established writers.** Bimonthly magazine covering military operations in World War II—events, personalities, strategy, national policy, etc. Estab. 1986. Circ. 146,000. Byline given. Pays on publication. No kill fee. Buys all rights. Accepts queries by mail, e-mail, fax. Sample copy for $5. Writer's guidelines for #10 SASE.
Nonfiction World War II military history. Submit anniversary-related material 1 year in advance. No fiction. **Buys 24 mss/year.** Query. 4,000 words with a 500-word sidebar. **Pays $300 and up.**
Photos For photos and other art, send photocopies and cite sources. We'll order. State availability Captions, identification of subjects required.
Columns/Departments Undercover (espionage, resistance, sabotage, intelligence gathering, behind the lines, etc.); Personality (WWII personalities of interest); Armament (weapons, their use and development); Commands (unit histories); One Man's War (personal profiles), all 2,000 words. Book reviews, 300-750 words. 30 (plus book reviews) Query. **Pays $150 and up**
Tips List your sources and suggest further readings in standard format at the end of your piece—as a bibliography for our files in case of factual challenge or dispute. All submissions are on speculation. Include a hard copy as well as an IBM- or Macintosh-compatible floppy disk. All stories must be true. We do not publish fiction or poetry. Stories should be carefully researched.

HOBBY & CRAFT

$ N ADORNMENT

The Magazine of Jewelry & Related Arts, Association for the Study of Jewelry & Related Arts, 246 N. Regent St., Port Chester NY 10573. E-mail: ekarlin@usa.net. Website: www.jewelryandrelatedarts.com. www.asjra.net. **50% freelance written.** Quarterly magazine covering jewelry—antique to modern. Fall issue distributed at our annual conference. Estab. 2002. Circ. 1,000+. Byline given. Pays on publication. No kill fee. Publishes ms an average of 3 months after acceptance. Buys first North American serial rights, buys electronic rights. Editorial lead time 3 months. Submit seasonal material 3 months in advance. Accepts queries by mail, e-mail. Accepts previously published material. Responds in 1-2 weeks to queries. Responds in 1 month to mss. Sample copy free. Guidelines free.

- "My readers are collectors, appraisers, antique jewelry dealers, gemologists, jewelry artists, museum curators—anyone with an interest in jewelry."

Nonfiction Needs book excerpts, (reviews), (articles on jewelry), interview, (of jewelry artists), Exhibition reviews—in-depth articles on jewelry subjects. We do not want articles about retail jewelry. We write about ancient, antique, period, and unique and studio jewelers. **Buys 12-15 mss/year mss/year.** Query with published clips. Length: 1,000-3,000 words. **Pays $125 max. for assigned articles. Pays $0 for unsolicited articles.**

Photos We only want photos that accompany articles. We pay $25 for them.

Tips "Know your subject and provide applicable credentials."

$ $ $ $ AMERICAN CRAFT

American Craft Council, 72 Spring St., 6th Floor, New York NY 10012. (212)274-0630. Fax: (212)274-0650. E-mail: awagner@craftcouncil.org. Website: www.americancraftmag.org. **75% freelance written**. Bimonthly magazine covering art/craft/design. Estab. 1943. Circ. 40,000. Byline given. Pays 30 days after acceptance. Offers 25% kill fee. Publishes ms an average of 2 months after acceptance. Buys first North American serial rights, buys electronic rights. Editorial lead time 3 months. Submit seasonal material 3 months in advance. Accepts queries by mail, e-mail. Accepts simultaneous submissions. Responds in 1 month to queries. Responds in 2 months to mss. Sample copy free. Guidelines by email.

Nonfiction Needs essays, general interest, interview, new product, opinion, photo feature, travel. Query with published clips. Length: 1,200-3,000 words. Pays expenses of writers on assignment.

Columns/Departments Critics's Corner (critical essays), 200-2,500 words; Wide World of Craft (travel), 800-1,000 words; Material Culture (material studies), 600-800 words; outskirts (a look at peripheral disciplines), 600-800 words. 10-12 Query with published clips. **Pays $1-1.50/word.**

Tips Keep pitches short and sweet, a paragraph or two at most. Please include visuals with any pitches.

ANCESTRY MAGAZINE

The Generations Network/Ancestry Publishing, 360 West 4800 North, Provo UT 84055. (801)705-7000. E-mail: editor@ancestrymagazine.com. Website: www.ancestrymagazine.com. **60% freelance written**. Bimonthly Magazine covering family history. Byline given. Pays on publication. Publishes ms an average of 3 months after acceptance. Editorial lead time 3 months. Submit seasonal material 6 months in advance. Accepts queries by e-mail. Due to volume of submissions, we report on acceptance only. Guidelines available online.

- Focus on personal history rather than the textbook variety.

Nonfiction Needs essays, historical, humor, interview, opinion, personal experience, photo feature, technical, travel. fiction and poetry

Photos Send photos with submission. State availability Identification of subjects required. Reviews GIF/JPEG files. Offers no additional payment for photos accepted with ms.; negotiates payment individually. Buys all rights.

Columns/Departments Barebones (personal humorous enlightening experience), 450 words; Heirloom (heirloom collection and story), 150 words; Heritage recipe (heritage recipe and story), 150 words; Backstory (photo of ancestor in history and story), 100 words; Breakthrough (problem/solution family history experience story), 75-1,200 words.

Tips Know the audience and the voice we're seeking—we want stories that interest people and motivate them to look for their ancestors.

$ $ ANTIQUE & COLLECTIBLES SHOWCASE

Trajan Publishing Corporation, P.O. Box 1626, Holland Landing ON L9N 1P2 Canada. E-mail: acseditor@rogers.com. Website: www.antiqueandcollectiblesshowcase.ca. **75% freelance written**. Bimonthly magazine covering antiques and contemporary collectibles. Preference is given to Canadian writers, but US writers will be considered if they have a unique angle on a story of interest to Canadian readers. Estab. 2003. Circ. 5,500. Byline given. Pays on publication. Publishes ms an average of 2-3 months after acceptance. Buys first North American serial rights, buys electronic rights. Makes work-for-hire assignments. Editorial lead time 1-3 months. Submit seasonal material 6 months in advance. Accepts queries by mail, e-mail. Responds in 1 month to queries. Sample copy for $5 (Canadian). Guidelines available online.

Nonfiction Needs general interest, how-to, interview, opinion. Does not want poetry, book reports or self-promotion. **Buys 30 mss/year.** Query. Length: 500-1,500 words. **Pays $50-225.**

Photos Send photos Reviews GIF/JPEG files. Offers no additional payment for photos accepted with ms.

Columns/Departments Antiquing in the 21st Century (modern perspective from knowledgeable sources), 750 words; Decorating With Antiques (how to use Great Aunt Gerdie's bookcase), 750 words. 25 Query. **Pays $50-150.**

Tips Antiques are old, but your ideas and your writing shouldn't be. We want to entertain the reader. Form pitches based on the guidelines. Show e-mail subject as Freelance Query.

$ $ ANTIQUES & COLLECTING MAGAZINE

Lightner Publishing, 1006 S. Michigan Ave., Chicago IL 60605. Fax: (312)939-0053. E-mail: editor@acmagazine.com. Website: www.acmagazine.com. **75% freelance written**. Monthly magazine covering antiques and collectibles. Estab. 1931. Circ. 16,000. Byline given. Pays on publication. Publishes ms an average of 6 months after acceptance. Buys first North American serial rights. Editorial lead time 2 months. Submit seasonal material 3 months in advance. Accepts queries by mail, e-mail, fax. Accepts simultaneous submissions. Sample copy free. Guidelines available online.

Nonfiction Needs general interest, historical, interview, personal experience. **Buys 48-60 mss/year.** Send complete ms. Length: 800-1,600 words. **Pays $50-250.**

Photos State availability of or send photos Captions, identification of subjects required. Reviews contact sheets, transparencies, prints, GIF/JPEG files. Offers no additional payment for photos accepted with ms. Buys one time rights.

Fiction Needs historical, humorous, slice-of-life vignettes. **Buys 1-5 mss/year.** Query or send complete ms. **Pays $50-250.**

Fillers Needs anecdotes, facts, short humor.

$ $ ANTIQUE TRADER

F + W Media, Inc., 700 E. State St., Iola WI 54990-0001. (715)445-2214. Fax: (715)445-4087. Website: www.antiquetrader.com. **60% freelance written**. Weekly tabloid covering antiques. We publish quote-heavy stories of timely interest in the antiques field. We cover antiques shows, auctions, and news events. Estab. 1957. Circ. 30,000. Byline given. Pays on publication. Offers 50% kill fee. Publishes ms an average of 1-3 months after acceptance. Buys exclusive rights. Editorial lead time 2 months. Accepts queries by mail, e-mail, fax. Responds in 1 week to queries. Responds in 2 months to mss. Sample copy for cover price, plus postage. Guidelines available online.

Nonfiction Needs book excerpts, general interest, interview, personal experience, show and auction coverage. Does not want the same, dry textbook, historical stories on antiques that appear elsewhere. I want personality and timeliness. **Buys 1,000 + mss/year.** Send complete ms. Length: 750-1,200 words. **Pays $50-200, plus contributor copy.**

Photos State availability Identification of subjects required. Reviews transparencies, prints, GIF/JPEG files. Offers no additional payment for photos accepted with ms. Buys one time rights.

Columns/Departments Dealer Profile (interviews with interesting antiques dealers), 750-1,200 words; Collector Profile (interviews with interesting collectors), 750-1,000 words. 30-60 Query with or without published clips or send complete ms.

$ $ BEAD & BUTTON

Kalmbach Publishing, P.O. Box 1612, Waukesha WI 53187. E-mail: editor@beadandbutton.com. Website: www.beadandbutton.com. **50% freelance written**. *Bead & Button* is a bimonthly magazine devoted to techniques, projects, designs and materials relating to beads, buttons, and accessories. Our readership includes both professional and amateur bead and button makers, hobbyists, and enthusiasts who find satisfaction in making beautiful things. Estab. 1994. Circ. 80,000. Byline given. Pays on acceptance. Offers $75 kill fee. Publishes ms an average of 4 months after acceptance. Buys all rights. Accepts queries by mail, e-mail, fax. Guidelines available online.

Nonfiction Needs historical, on beaded jewelry history, how-to, make beaded jewelry and accessories, humor, inspirational, interview. **Buys 24-30 mss/year.** Send complete ms. Length: 750-3,000 words. **Pays $75-300.**

Photos Send photos Identification of subjects required. Offers no additional payment for photos accepted with ms

Columns/Departments Chic & Easy (fashionable jewelry how-to); Beginner (easy-to-make jewelry how-to); Simply Earrings (fashionable earring how-to); Fun Fashion (trendy jewelry how-to), all 1,000 words. 12 Send complete ms. **Pays $75-150.**

Tips *Bead & Button* magazine primarily publishes how-to articles by the artists who have designed the piece. We publish 2 profiles and 1 historical piece per issue. These would be the only applicable articles for non-artisan writers. Also our humorous and inspirational endpiece might apply.

$ $ BLADE MAGAZINE

The World's #1 Knife Publication, F + W Media, Inc., 700 E. State St., Iola WI 54990-0001. (715)445-2214. Fax: (715)445-4087. E-mail: bladeeditor@fwpubs.com. Website: www.blademag.com. **5% freelance written**. Monthly magazine covering working and using collectible, popular knives. *Blade* prefers in-depth articles focusing on groups of knives, whether military, collectible, high-tech, pocket knives or hunting knives, and how they perform. Estab. 1973. Circ. 39,000. Byline given. Pays on publication. No kill fee. Publishes ms an average of 9 months after acceptance. Buys all rights. Editorial lead time 9 months. Submit seasonal material 9 months in advance. Accepts queries by mail, e-mail, fax. Responds in 3 months to queries. Responds in 6 months to mss. Sample copy for $4.99. Guidelines for sae with 8x11 envelope and 3 First-Class stamps.

Nonfiction Needs general interest, historical, how-to, interview, new product, photo feature, technical. Send complete ms. Length: 700-1,400 words. **Pays $200-300.**

Photos Send photos Captions, identification of subjects required. Reviews transparencies, prints, digital images

(300 dpi at 1200x1200 pixels). Offers no additional payment for photos accepted with ms. Buys all rights.
Fillers Needs anecdotes, facts, newsbreaks. 1-2 Length: 50-200 words. **Pays $25-50.**
Tips We are always willing to read submissions from anyone who has read a few copies and studied the market. The ideal article for us is a piece bringing out the romance, legend, and love of man's oldest tool—the knife. We like articles that place knives in peoples' hands—in life saving situations, adventure modes, etc. (Nothing gory or with the knife as the villain.) People and knives are good copy. We are getting more well-written articles from writers who are reading the publication beforehand. That makes for a harder sell for the quickie writer not willing to do his homework. Go to knife shows and talk to the makers and collectors. Visit knifemakers' shops and knife factories. Read anything and everything you can find on knives and knifemaking.

$ BREW YOUR OWN

The How-to Homebrew Beer Magazine, Battenkill Communications, 5515 Main St., Manchester Center VT 05255. (802)362-3981. Fax: (802)362-2377. E-mail: edit@byo.com. Website: www.byo.com. www.byo.com/about/guidelines. **85% freelance written**. Monthly magazine covering home brewing. Our mission is to provide practical information in an entertaining format. We try to capture the spirit and challenge of brewing while helping our readers brew the best beer they can. Estab. 1995. Circ. 40,000. Byline given. Pays on acceptance. Offers 25% kill fee. Publishes ms an average of 4 months after acceptance. Buys all rights. Editorial lead time 3 months. Submit seasonal material 3 months in advance. Accepts queries by mail, e-mail, fax. Responds in 2 months to queries. Guidelines available online.
Nonfiction Informational pieces on equipment, ingredients, and brewing methods. Needs historical, how-to, home brewing, humor, related to home brewing, interview, of professional brewers who can offer useful tips to home hobbyists, personal experience, trends. **Buys 75 mss/year.** Query with published clips or description of brewing expertise Length: 800-3,000 words. **Pays $50-350, depending on length, complexity of article, and experience of writer.** Sometimes pays expenses of writers on assignment.
Photos State availability Captions required. Reviews contact sheets, transparencies, 5x7 prints, slides, and electronic images. Negotiates payment individually Buys all rights.
Columns/Departments News (humorous, unusual news about homebrewing), 50-250 words; Last Call (humorous stories about homebrewing), 700 words. 12 Query with or without published clips. **Pays $75**
Tips "*Brew Your Own* is for anyone who is interested in brewing beer, from beginners to advanced all-grain brewers. We seek articles that are straightforward and factual, not full of esoteric theories or complex calculations. Our readers tend to be intelligent, upscale, and literate."

$ $ CANADIAN WOODWORKING AND HOME IMPROVEMENT

Develop Your Skills-Tool Your Shop-Build Your Dreams, Sawdust Media, Inc., 51 Maple Ave. N., RR #3, Burford ON N0E 1A0 Canada. (519)449-2444. Fax: (519)449-2445. E-mail: letters@canadianwoodworking.com. Website: www.canadianwoodworking.com. **20% freelance written**. Bimonthly magazine covering woodworking. Estab. 1999. Byline given. Pays on publication. Offers 50% kill fee. Buys all rights. Accepts queries by e-mail. Sample copy available online. Guidelines by email.
Nonfiction Needs how-to, humor, inspirational, new product, personal experience, photo feature, technical. Does not want profile on a woodworker. Query. Length: 500-4,000 words. **Pays $100-600 for assigned articles. Pays $50-400 for unsolicited articles.**
Photos State availability Negotiates payment individually. Buys all rights.

$ $ CERAMICS MONTHLY

600 N. Cleveland Ave., Suite 210, Westerville OH 43082. (614)895-4213. Fax: (614)891-8960. E-mail: editorial@ceramicsmonthly.org. Website: www.ceramicsmonthly.org. **Contact:** Jessica Knapp, assistant editor. **70% freelance written**. Monthly magazine (except July and August) covering the ceramic art and craft field. "Each issue includes articles on potters and ceramics artists from throughout the world, exhibitions, and production processes, as well as critical commentary, book and video reviews, clay and glaze recipes, kiln designs and firing techniques, advice from experts in the field, and ads for available materials and equipment. While principally covering contemporary work, the magazine also looks back at influential artists and events from the past." Estab. 1953. Circ. 39,000. Byline given. Pays on publication. Editorial lead time 3 months. Submit seasonal material 6 months in advance. Accepts queries by mail, e-mail, fax, phone. Responds in 2 months to mss. Guidelines available online.
Nonfiction Needs essays, how-to, interview, opinion, personal experience, technical. **Buys 100 mss/year.** Send complete ms. Length: 500-3,000 words. **Pays 10¢/word.**
Photos Send photos Captions required. Reviews digital images, original slides or 2¼ or 4x5 transparencies.
Columns/Departments Upfront (workshop/exhibition review), 500-1,000 words. 20 Send complete ms.

$ $ CLASSIC TOY TRAINS

Kalmbach Publishing Co., 21027 Crossroads Circle, Waukesha WI 53187. (262)796-8776. Fax: (262)796-1142. E-mail: editor@classictoytrains.com. Website: www.classictoytrains.com. **80% freelance written**. Magazine published 9 times/year covering collectible toy trains (O, S, Standard) like Lionel and American Flyer, etc. For the collector and operator of toy trains, *CTT* offers full-color photos of layouts and collections of toy trains, restoration tips, operating information, new product reviews and information, and insights into the history of toy trains. Estab. 1987. Circ. 50,000. Byline given. Pays on acceptance. Publishes ms an average of 1 year after acceptance. Buys all rights. Editorial lead time 3 months. Submit seasonal material 6 months in advance. Accepts queries by mail, e-mail. Responds in 3 weeks to queries. Responds in 1 month to mss. Sample copy for $5.95, plus postage. Guidelines available online.

Nonfiction Needs general interest, historical, how-to, restore toy trains; design a layout; build accessories; fix broken toy trains, interview, personal experience, photo feature, technical. **Buys 90 mss/year.** Query. Length: 500-5,000 words. **Pays $75-500.** Sometimes pays expenses of writers on assignment.

Photos Send photos Captions required. Reviews 4x5 transparencies, 5x7 prints or 35mm slides preferred. Also accepts hi-res digital photos. Offers no additional payment for photos accepted with ms or $15-75/photo Buys all rights.

Tips It's important to have a thorough understanding of the toy train hobby; most of our freelancers are hobbyists themselves. One-half to two-thirds of *CTT*'s editorial space is devoted to photographs; superior photography is critical.

$ COLLECTORS NEWS

P.O. Box 306, Grundy Center IA 50638. (319)824-6981. Fax: (319)824-3414. E-mail: lkruger@pioneermagazines.com. Website: collectors-news.com. **20% freelance written. Works with a small number of new/unpublished writers each year.** Monthly magazine-size publication on offset, glossy cover, covering antiques, collectibles, and nostalgic memorabilia. Estab. 1959. Circ. 9,000. Byline given. Pays on publication. Publishes ms an average of 1 year after acceptance. Buys first rights. Makes work-for-hire assignments. Submit seasonal material 3 months in advance. Accepts queries by mail, e-mail, fax, phone. Responds in 2 weeks to queries. Responds in 6 weeks to mss. Sample copy for $4 and 9x12 SAE. Guidelines free.

Nonfiction Needs general interest, collectibles, antique to modern, historical, relating to collections or collectors, how-to, display your collection, care for, restore, appraise, locate, add to, etc., interview, covering individual collectors and their hobbies, unique or extensive; celebrity collectors, and limited edition artists, technical, in-depth analysis of a particular antique, collectible, or collecting field, travel, hot antiquing places in the US. 12-month listing of antique and collectible shows, flea markets, and conventions (January includes events January-December; June includes events June-May); Care & Display of Collectibles (September); holidays (October-December) **Buys 36 mss/year.** Query with sample of writing. Length: 800-1,000 words. **Pays $1.10/column inch.**

Photos Articles must be accompanied by photographs for illustration. A selection of 2-8 images is suggested. Articles are eligible for full-color front page consideration when accompanied by high resolution electronic images. Only 1 article is highlighted on the cover/month. Any article providing a color photo selected for front page use receives an additional $25. Captions required. Reviews color or b&w digital images. Payment for photos included in payment for ms. Buys first rights

Tips "Present a professionally written article with quality illustrations—well-researched and documented information."

$ CQ AMATEUR RADIO

The Radio Amateur's Journal, CQ Communications, Inc., 25 Newbridge Rd., Hicksville NY 11801. (516)681-2922. Fax: (516)681-2926. E-mail: cq@cq-amateur-radio.com. Website: www.cq-amateur-radio.com. **Contact:** Gail Sheehan, managing editor or Richard Moseson, editor. **40% freelance written.** Monthly magazine covering amateur (ham) radio. "*CQ* is published for active ham radio operators and is read by radio amateurs in over 100 countries. All articles must deal with amateur radio. Our focus is on operating and on practical projects. A thorough knowledge of amateur radio is required." Estab. 1945. Circ. 60,000. Byline given. Pays on publication. No kill fee. Publishes ms an average of 6 months after acceptance. Buys first North American serial rights. Editorial lead time 4 months. Submit seasonal material 4 months in advance. Accepts queries by mail, e-mail, fax. Responds in 3 weeks to queries. Responds in 3 months to mss. Sample copy free. Guidelines available online.

Nonfiction Needs historical, how-to, interview, personal experience, technical, all related to amateur radio. **Buys 50-60 mss/year.** Query. Length: 2,000-4,000 words. **Pays $40/published page.**

Photos State availability Captions, identification of subjects, model releases required. Reviews contact sheets, 4x6 prints, TIFF or JPEG files with 300 dpi resolution. Offers no additional payment for photos accepted with ms Buys one time rights.

Tips "You must know and understand ham radio and ham radio operators. Most of our writers (95%) are licensed hams. Because our readers span a wide area of interests within amateur radio, don't assume they are already familiar with your topic. Explain. At the same time, don't write down to the readers. They are intelligent, well-educated people who will understand what you're saying when written and explained in plain English."

$ $ CREATING KEEPSAKES

Scrapbook Magazine, Primedia Enthusiast Group, 14850 Pony Express Rd., Bluffdale UT 84065. (801)984-2070. E-mail: marianne.madsen@primedia.com. Website: www.creatingkeepsakes.com. Monthly magazine covering scrapbooks. Written for scrapbook lovers and those with a box of photos high in the closet. Circ. 100,000. No kill fee. Editorial lead time 6 weeks. Accepts queries by mail, e-mail. Guidelines available online.

Nonfiction Accepts articles on a variety of scrapbook and keepsake topics. Query with 2 visuals to illustrate your suggested topic. Length: 800-1,200 words.

Tips Should we opt to pursue the article you've proposed, we will ask you to supply the complete article on disk in WordPerfect, Word or ASCII format. Please supply a paper copy as well. The article should be lively and easy to read, contain solid content, and be broken up with subheads or sidebars as appropriate. We will provide additional guidelines to follow upon acceptance of your query.

$ $ DESIGNS IN MACHINE EMBROIDERY

Great Notions News Corp., 2517 Manana Dr., Dallas TX 75220. (888)739-0555. Fax: (413)723-2027. E-mail: www.designsmagazine@dzgns.com. Website: www.dzgns.com. **75% freelance written**. Bimonthly magazine covering machine embroidery. Projects in *Designs in Machine Embroidery* must feature machine embroidery and teach readers new techniques. Estab. 1998. Circ. 50,000. Byline given. Pays on publication. Publishes ms an average of 2 months after acceptance. Buys all rights. Editorial lead time 4 months. Submit seasonal material 4 months in advance. Accepts queries by mail, e-mail. Responds in 2-3 weeks to queries. Guidelines available online.

Nonfiction Needs how-to, interview, new product, technical. Does not want previously published items. **Buys 60 mss/year.** Query. Length: 250-1,000 words. **Pays $250-500.**

Photos Send photos Captions, identification of subjects, model releases required. Reviews GIF/JPEG files (300 dpi, 4x6 min.). Offers no additional payment for photos accepted with ms.

Tips Projects should be original and fall under one of the following categories: Quilts, Crafts, Clothing, Home Decor. Item or project should be tasteful and mainstream. Since we are an embroidery magazine, the quality of workmanship is critical.

$ $ DOLLS

Jones Publishing, Inc., P.O. Box 5000, Iola WI 54945. (201)497-6444. Fax: (715)445-5000. E-mail: carief@jonespublishing.com. Website: www.dollsmagazine.com. **75% freelance written**. "Magazine published 10 times/year covering dolls, doll artists, and related topics of interest to doll collectors and enthusiasts.". "*Dolls* enhances the joy of collecting by introducing readers to the best new dolls from around the world, along with the artists and designers who create them. It keeps readers up-to-date on shows, sales and special events in the doll world. With beautiful color photography, *Dolls* offers an array of easy-to-read, informative articles that help our collectors select the best buys." Estab. 1982. Circ. 100,000. Byline given. Pays on publication. No kill fee. Buys all rights. Accepts queries by mail, e-mail. Responds in 1 month to queries.

Nonfiction Needs historical, how-to, interview, new product, photo feature. **Buys 55 mss/year.** Send complete ms. Length: 750-1,200 words. **Pays $75-300.**

Photos Send photos Captions, identification of subjects, model releases required. Reviews transparencies. Offers no additional payment for photos accepted with ms. Buys all rights.

Tips "Know the subject matter and artists. Having quality artwork and access to doll artists for interviews are big pluses. We need original ideas of interest to doll lovers."

F+W MEDIA, INC. (MAGAZINE DIVISION)

(formerly F + W Publications, Inc.), 4700 E. Galbraith Rd., Cincinnati OH 45236. (513)531-2690. E-mail: dave.pulvermacher@fwmedia.com. Website: www.fwmedia.com. "Each month, millions of enthusiasts turn to the magazines from F + W for inspiration, instruction, and encouragement. Readers are as varied as our categories, but all are assured of getting the best possible coverage of their favorite hobby." Publishes magazines in the following categories: **antiques and collectibles** (*Antique Trader*); **automotive** (*Military Vehicles, Old Cars Price Guide, Old Cars Weekly*); **coins and paper money** (*Bank Note Reporter, Coins Magazine, Coin Prices, Numismatic News, World Coin News*); **comics** (*Comic Buyers Guide*); **construction** (*Frame Building News, Metal Roofing, Rural Builder*); **fine art** (*Collector's Guide, Pastel Journal, Southwest Art, The Artist's Magazine, Watercolor Artist*); **firearms and knives** (*Blade, Blade Trade, Gun Digest—The Magazine, Gun + Knife Show Calendar*); **genealogy** (*Family Tree Magazine*); **graphic design** (*HOW Magazine, I.D., PRINT*); **horticulture** (*Horticulture*); **militaria** (*Military Trader*); **outdoors and hunting** (*Deer & Deer Hunting, Trapper & Predator Caller, Turkey & Turkey Hunting*); **records and CDs** (*Goldmine*); **scrapbooking** (*Memory Makers Magazine*); **sports** (*Fantasy Sports, Sports Collectors Digest, Tuff Stuff's Sports Collectors Monthly*); **woodworking** (*Popular Woodworking, Woodworking Magazine); **writing** (*Writer's Digest*). No kill fee.

- "Please see individual listings in the Consumer Magazines and Trade Journals sections for specific submission information about each magazine."

$ $ $ FAMILY TREE MAGAZINE

F+W Media, Inc., 4700 E. Galbraith Rd., Cincinnati OH 45236. (513)531-2690. Fax: (513)891-7153. E-mail: ftmedit@fwpubs.com. Website: www.familytreemagazine.com. **75% freelance written**. Bimonthly magazine covering family history, heritage, and genealogy research. *Family Tree Magazine* is a general-interest consumer magazine that helps readers discover, preserve, and celebrate their family's history. We cover genealogy, ethnic heritage, genealogy websites and software, scrapbooking, photography and photo preservation, and other ways that families connect with their past. Estab. 1999. Circ. 70,000. Byline given. Pays on acceptance. Offers 25% kill fee. Publishes ms an average of 6 months after acceptance. Buys first rights, buys electronic rights. Editorial lead time 8 months. Submit seasonal material 8 months in advance. Accepts queries by mail, e-mail. Responds in 1 month to queries. Sample copy for $8 from Web site. Guidelines available online.

Nonfiction Articles are geared to beginner-friendly but must provide in-depth instruction for intermediate and veteran genealogists. We emphasize sidebars, tips, and other reader-friendly 'packaging,' and each article aims to give the reader the resources necessary to take the next step in his or her quest for the past. Needs book excerpts, historical, how-to, genealogy, new product, photography, computer, technical, genealogy software, photography equipment. **Buys 60 mss/year.** Query with published clips. Length: 250-4,500 words. **Pays $25-800.**

Photos State availability Captions required. Reviews color transparencies. Negotiates payment individually. Buys one time rights.

Tips Always query with a specific story idea. Look at sample issues before querying to get a feel for appropriate topics and angles. We see too many broad, general stories on genealogy or records, and personal accounts of `How I found great-aunt Sally' without how-to value.

$ $ FIBERARTS

Contemporary Textile Art and Craft, Interweave Press, 201 E. Fourth St., Loveland CO 80537. (970)613-4679. Fax: (970)669-6117. E-mail: lizg@fiberarts.com. Website: www.fiberarts.com. **85% freelance written**. Magazine published 5 times/year covering textiles as art and craft (contemporary trends in fiber sculpture, weaving, quilting, surface design, stitchery, papermaking, basketry, felting, wearable art, knitting, fashion, crochet, mixed textile techniques, ethnic dying, eccentric tidbits, etc.) for textile artists, craftspeople, collectors, teachers, museum and gallery staffs, and enthusiasts. Estab. 1975. Circ. 27,000. Byline given. Pays on publication. Publishes ms an average of 4 months after acceptance. Buys first rights. Accepts queries by mail. Sample copy for $7.99. Guidelines available online.

Nonfiction "Please be very specific about your proposal. Also, an important consideration in accepting an article is the kind of photos that you can provide as illustration. We like to see photos in advance." Needs essays, interview, artist, opinion, personal experience, photo feature, technical, education, trends, exhibition reviews, textile news, book reviews, ethnic. Query with brief synopsis, SASE, and visuals. No phone queries. Length: 250-2,000 words. **Pays $70-550.**

Photos Color slides, large-format transparencies, or 300 dpi (5-inch-high) TIFF images must accompany every query. "Please include caption information. The names and addresses of those mentioned in the article or to whom the visuals are to be returned are necessary."

Columns/Departments Commentary (thoughtful opinion on a topic of interest to our readers), 400 words; News and Notes; Profiles; The Creative Process; Travel and Traditions; Collecting; Reviews (exhibits and shows; summarize quality, significance, focus and atmosphere, then evaluate selected pieces for aesthetic quality, content and technique. "Because we have an international readership, brief biographical notes or quotes might be pertinent for locally or regionally known artists). (Do not cite works for which visuals are unavailable; you are not eligible to review a show in which you have participated as an artist, organizer, curator or juror.")

Tips "Our writers are usually familiar with textile techniques and textile-art history, but expertise in historical textiles, art, or design can also qualify a new writer. The writer should also be familiar with *Fiberarts* magazine. The professional is essential to the editorial depth of *Fiberarts* and must find timely information in the pages of the magazine, but our editorial philosophy is that the magazine must provide the non-professional textile enthusiast with the inspiration, support, useful information, and direction to keep him or her excited, interested, and committed. Although we address serious issues relating to the fiber arts as well as light, we're looking for an accessible rather than overly scholarly tone."

$ FIBRE FOCUS

Magazine of the Ontario Handweavers and Spinners, 3212 S. Service Rd. W., Oakville ON L6L 6T1 Canada. Website: www.ohs.on.ca. **90% freelance written**. Quarterly magazine covering handweaving, spinning, basketry, beading, and other fibre arts. Our readers are weavers and spinners who also do dyeing, knitting, basketry, feltmaking, papermaking, sheep raising, and craft supply. All articles deal with some aspect of these crafts. Estab. 1957. Circ. 1,000. Byline given. Pays within 30 days after publication. Buys one-time rights. Editorial lead time 6 months. Submit seasonal material 6 months in advance. Accepts previously published material. Responds in 1 month to queries. Sample copy for $8 Canadian. Guidelines available online.

Nonfiction Needs how-to, interview, new product, opinion, personal experience, technical, travel, book reviews.

Buys 40-60 mss/year. Varies **Pays $30 Canadian/published page.**
Photos Send photos Captions, identification of subjects required. Offers additional payment for photos accepted with ms. Buys one time rights.
Tips Visit the OHS website for current information.

$ $ FINE BOOKS & COLLECTIONS

OP Media, LLC, P.O. Box 106, Eureka CA 95502. (707)443-9562. Fax: (707)443-9572. E-mail: scott@finebooksmagazine.com. Website: www.finebooksmagazine.com. **90% freelance written.** Bimonthly magazine covering used and antiquarian bookselling and book collecting. We cover all aspects of selling and collecting out-of-print books. We emphasize good writing, interesting people, and unexpected view points. Estab. 2002. Circ. 5,000. Byline given. Pays on publication. Offers negotiable kill fee. Publishes ms an average of 4 months after acceptance. Buys first North American serial rights, buys second serial (reprint) rights, buys electronic rights. Makes work-for-hire assignments. Editorial lead time 4 months. Submit seasonal material 4 months in advance. Accepts queries by mail, e-mail. Accepts previously published material. Accepts simultaneous submissions. Responds in 1 month to queries. Responds in 2 months to mss. Sample copy for $6.50. Guidelines available online.
Nonfiction Needs book excerpts, essays, expose, general interest, historical, how-to, humor, opinion, personal experience, photo feature, travel. Does not want tales of the gold in my attic vein; stories emphasizing books as an investment. **Buys 40 mss/year.** Query with published clips. Length: 1,000-5,000 words. **Pays $100-400.** Sometimes pays expenses of writers on assignment.
Photos State availability Captions, identification of subjects required. Reviews GIF/JPEG files. Negotiates payment individually. Buys one-time, plus nonexclusive electronic rights
Columns/Departments Digest (news about collectors, booksellers, and bookselling), 350 words; Book Reviews (reviews of books about books, writers, publishers, collecting), 400-800 words.
Tips Tell compelling stories about people and the passion for book collecting. We aim to make academic writing on books accessible to a broad audience and to enliven the writing of aficionados with solid editing and story development.

$ FINESCALE MODELER

Kalmbach Publishing Co., P.O. Box 1612, Waukesha WI 53187. Website: www.finescale.com. **80% freelance written. Eager to work with new/unpublished writers.** "Magazine published 10 times/year devoted to how-to-do-it modeling information for scale model builders who build non-operating aircraft, tanks, boats, automobiles, figures, dioramas, and science fiction and fantasy models.". Circ. 60,000. Byline given. Pays on acceptance. No kill fee. Publishes ms an average of 14 months after acceptance. Buys all rights. Responds in 6 weeks to queries. Responds in 3 months to mss. Sample copy for sae with 9x12 envelope and 3 First-Class stamps.

O→ "Finescale Modeler is especially looking for how-to articles for armor and aircraft modelers.
Nonfiction Needs how-to, build scale models, technical, research information for building models. Query or send complete ms. Length: 750-3,000 words. **Pays $60/published page minimum.**
Photos "Send original high-res digital images, slides, or prints with submission. You can submit digital images at www.contribute.kalmbach.com." Captions, identification of subjects required. Reviews transparencies, color prints. Pays $7.50 minimum for transparencies and $5 minimum for color prints Buys one time rights.
Columns/Departments *FSM* Showcase (photos plus description of model); *FSM* Tips and Techniques (model building hints and tips). 25-50 Send complete ms. **Pays $25-50.**
Tips "A freelancer can best break in first through hints and tips, then through feature articles. Most people who write for *FSM* are modelers first, writers second. This is a specialty magazine for a special, quite expert audience. Essentially, 99% of our writers will come from that audience."

$ $ FINE TOOL JOURNAL

Antique & Collectible Tools, Inc., 27 Fickett Rd., Pownal ME 04069. (207)688-4962. Fax: (207)688-4831. E-mail: ceb@finetoolj.com. Website: www.finetoolj.com. **90% freelance written.** "Quarterly magazine specializing in older or antique hand tools from all traditional trades. Readers are primarily interested in woodworking tools, but some subscribers have interests in such areas as leatherworking, wrenches, kitchen, and machinist tools. Readers range from beginners just getting into the hobby to advanced collectors and organizations.". Estab. 1970. Circ. 2,500. Byline given. Pays on publication. Offers $50 kill fee. Publishes ms an average of 6 months after acceptance. Buys first rights, buys second serial (reprint) rights. Editorial lead time 9 months. Submit seasonal material 6 months in advance. Accepts queries by mail. Accepts previously published material. Responds in 2 months to queries. Responds in 3 months to mss. Sample copy for $5. Guidelines for #10 SASE.
Nonfiction "We're looking for articles about tools from all trades. Interests include collecting, preservation, history, values and price trends, traditional methods and uses, interviews with collectors/users/makers, etc. Most articles published will deal with vintage, pre-1950, hand tools. Also seeking articles on how to use specific tools or how a specific trade was carried out. However, how-to articles must be detailed and not just of general

interest. We do on occasion run articles on modern toolmakers who produce traditional hand tools." Needs general interest, historical, how-to, make, use, fix and tune tools, interview, personal experience, photo feature, technical. **Buys 24 mss/year.** Send complete ms. Length: 400-2,000 words. **Pays $50-200.** Pays expenses of writers on assignment.

Photos Send photos Identification of subjects, model releases required. Reviews 4x5 prints. Negotiates payment individually Buys all rights.

Columns/Departments Stanley Tools (new finds and odd types), 300-400 words; Tips of the Trade (how to use tools), 100-200 words. 12 Send complete ms. **Pays $30-60.**

Tips "The easiest way to get published in the *Journal* is to have personal experience or know someone who can supply the detailed information. We are seeking articles that go deeper than general interest and that knowledge requires experience and/or research. Short of personal experience, find a subject that fits our needs and that interests you. Spend some time learning the ins and outs of the subject and with hard work and a little luck you will earn the right to write about it."

$ $ FINE WOODWORKING

The Taunton Press, P.O. Box 5506, Newtown CT 06470-5506. (800)926-8776. Fax: (203)270-6753. E-mail: fw@taunton.com. Website: www.taunton.com. **Contact:** Betsy Engel. Bimonthly magazine on woodworking in the small shop. "All writers are also skilled woodworkers. It's more important that a contributor be a woodworker than a writer. Our editors (also woodworkers) will provide assistance and travel to shops to shoot all photography needed." Estab. 1975. Circ. 270,000. Byline given. Pays on acceptance. Offers variable kill fee. Buys first rights and rights to republish in other forms and media, as well as use in promo pieces. Submit seasonal material 6 months in advance. Accepts simultaneous submissions. Responds in 1 month to queries. Writer's guidelines free and online

> O→ "We're looking for good articles on almost all aspects of woodworking from the basics of tool use, stock preparation and joinery, to specialized techniques and finishing. We're especially keen on articles about shop-built tools, jigs and fixtures, or any stage of design, construction, finishing and installation of cabinetry and furniture. Whether the subject involves fundamental methods or advanced techniques, we look for high-quality workmanship, thoughtful designs, and safe and proper procedures."

Nonfiction Needs how-to, woodworking. **Buys 120 mss/year.** Send article outline, any helpful drawings or photos, and proposal letter. **Pays $150/magazine page.** Sometimes pays expenses of writers on assignment.

Columns/Departments Fundamentals (basic how-to and concepts for beginning woodworkers); Master Class (advanced techniques); Finish Line (finishing techniques); Question & Answer (woodworking Q&A); Methods of Work (shop tips); Tools & Materials (short reviews of new tools). 400 **Pays $10-150/published page**

Tips "Look for authors guidelines and follow them. Stories about woodworking reported by non-woodworkers are *not* used. Our magazine is essentially reader-written by woodworkers."

$ $ THE HOME SHOP MACHINIST

2779 Aero Park Dr., Traverse City MI 49686. (616)946-3712. Fax: (616)946-3289. E-mail: nknopf@villagepress.com. Website: www.homeshopmachinist.net. **95% freelance written**. Bimonthly magazine covering machining and metalworking for the hobbyist. Circ. 34,000. Byline given. Pays on publication. Publishes ms an average of 2 years after acceptance. Buys first North American serial rights. Responds in 2 months to queries. Sample copy free. Guidelines for 9x12 SASE.

Nonfiction Needs how-to, projects designed to upgrade present shop equipment or hobby model projects that require machining, technical, should pertain to metalworking, machining, drafting, layout, welding or foundry work for the hobbyist. No fiction or people features. **Buys 40 mss/year.** Send complete ms. open—whatever it takes to do a thorough job. **Pays $40/published page, plus $9/published photo.**

Photos Send photos Captions, identification of subjects required. Pays $9-40 for 5x7 b&w prints; $70/page for camera-ready art; $40 for b&w cover photo

Columns/Departments Become familiar with our magazine before submitting. Book Reviews; New Product Reviews; Micro-Machining; Foundry. Length: 600-1,500 words. 25-30 Query. **Pays $40-70.**

Fillers 12-15 Length: 100-300 words. **Pays $30-48.**

Tips The writer should be experienced in the area of metalworking and machining; should be extremely thorough in explanations of methods, processes—always with an eye to safety; and should provide good quality b&w photos and/or clear dimensioned drawings to aid in description. Visuals are of increasing importance to our readers. Carefully planned photos, drawings and charts will carry a submission to our magazine much farther along the path to publication.

$ $ KITPLANES

For Designers, Builders, and Pilots of Experimental Aircraft, A Primedia Publication, Kitplanes, 302 Argonne Ave., Suite B105, Long Beach CA 90803. E-mail: editorial@kitplanes.com. Website: www.kitplanes.com. **50% freelance written. Eager to work with new/unpublished writers.** Monthly magazine covering self-construction of private aircraft for pilots and builders. Estab. 1984. Circ. 72,000. Byline given. Pays on publication. Publishes ms an average of 3 months after acceptance. Buys complete rights, except book rights. Submit seasonal material 6 months in advance. Accepts queries by mail, e-mail. Responds in 4 weeks to queries. Responds in 6 weeks to mss Sample copy for $6 Guidelines available online

Nonfiction "We are looking for articles on specific construction techniques, the use of tools—both hand and power—in aircraft building, the relative merits of various materials, conversions of engines from automobiles for aviation use, and installation of instruments and electronics." Needs general interest, how-to, interview, new product, personal experience, photo feature, technical. No general-interest aviation articles, or My First Solo type of articles. **Buys 80 mss/year.** Query. Length: 500-3,000 words. **Pays $150-500 including story photos.**

Photos State availability of or send photos Captions, identification of subjects required. Pays $300 for cover photos Buys one time rights.

Tips "*Kitplanes* contains very specific information—a writer must be extremely knowledgeable in the field. Major features are entrusted only to known writers. I cannot emphasize enough that articles must be directed at the individual aircraft builder. We need more 'how-to' photo features in all areas of home-built aircraft."

$ $ KNIVES ILLUSTRATED

The Premier Cutlery Magazine, 265 S. Anita Dr., Suite 120, Orange CA 92868. (714)939-9991. Fax: (714)939-9909. E-mail: editorial@knivesillustrated.com. Website: www.knivesillustrated.com. **40-50% freelance written**. Bimonthly magazine covering high-quality factory and custom knives. We publish articles on different types of factory and custom knives, how-to make knives, technical articles, shop tours, articles on knife makers and artists. Must have knowledge about knives and the people who use and make them. We feature the full range of custom and high tech production knives, from miniatures to swords, leaving nothing untouched. We're also known for our outstanding how-to articles and technical features on equipment, materials and knife making supplies. We do not feature knife maker profiles as such, although we do spotlight some makers by featuring a variety of their knives and insight into their background and philosophy. Estab. 1987. Circ. 35,000. Byline given. Pays on publication. No kill fee. Editorial lead time 3 months. Accepts queries by mail, e-mail, fax. Responds in 2 weeks to queries. Sample copy available Guidelines for #10 SASE.

Nonfiction Needs general interest, historical, how-to, interview, new product, photo feature, technical. **Buys 35-40 mss/year.** Query. Length: 400-2,000 words. **Pays $100-500.**

Photos Send photos Captions, identification of subjects, model releases required. Reviews 35mm, 2 ¼ × 2 ¼ , 4x5 transparencies, 5x7 prints, electronic images in TIFF, GIF or JPEG Mac format. Negotiates payment individually

Tips Most of our contributors are involved with knives, either as collectors, makers, engravers, etc. To write about this subject requires knowledge. Writers can do OK if they study some recent issues. If you are interested in submitting work to *Knives Illustrated* magazine, it is suggested you analyze at least 2 or 3 different editions to get a feel for the magazine. It is also recommended that you call or mail in your query to determine if we are interested in the topic you have in mind. While verbal or written approval may be given, all articles are still received on a speculation basis. We cannot approve any article until we have it in hand, whereupon we will make a final decision as to its suitability for our use. Bear in mind we do not suggest you go to the trouble to write an article if there is doubt we can use it promptly.

$ $ THE LEATHER CRAFTERS & SADDLERS JOURNAL

222 Blackburn St., Rhinelander WI 54501-3777. (715)362-5393. Fax: (715)362-5391. E-mail: davidjournal@newnorth.net. **100% freelance written**. Bimonthly magazine. A leather-working publication with how-to, step-by-step instructional articles using patterns for leathercraft, leather art, custom saddle, boot and harness making, etc. A complete resource for leather, tools, machinery, and allied materials, plus leather industry news. Estab. 1990. Circ. 8,000. Byline given. Pays on publication. Publishes ms an average of 4 months after acceptance. Buys first North American serial rights, buys second serial (reprint) rights. Submit seasonal material 6 months in advance. Accepts queries by mail, e-mail, fax, phone. Accepts previously published material. Accepts simultaneous submissions. Responds in 1 month to mss. Sample copy for $6. Guidelines for #10 SASE.

Nonfiction Want only articles that include hands-on, step-by-step, how-to information. **Buys 75 mss/year.** Send complete ms. Length: 500-2,500 words. **Pays $20-250 for assigned articles. Pays $20-150 for unsolicited articles.**

Reprints Send tearsheet or photocopy. Pays 50% of amount paid for an original article.

Photos Send good contrast color print photos and full-size patterns and/or full-size photo-carve patterns with submission. Lack of these reduces payment amount. Captions required.

Columns/Departments Beginners; Intermediate; Artists; Western Design; Saddlemakers; International Design; and Letters (the open exchange of information between all peoples). Length: 500-2,500 words on all.

Tips We want to work with people who understand and know leathercraft and are interested in passing on their knowledge to others. We would prefer to interview people who have achieved a high level in leathercraft skill.

$ LINN'S STAMP NEWS

Amos Press, P.O. Box 29, Sidney OH 45365. (937)498-0801. Fax: (937)498-0886. Website: www.linns.com. **50% freelance written**. Weekly tabloid on the stamp collecting hobby. "All articles must be about philatelic collectibles. Our goal at *Linn's* is to create a weekly publication that is indispensable to stamp collectors." Estab. 1928. Circ. 33,000. Byline given. Pays within 1 month of publication. Publishes ms an average of 3 months after acceptance. Buys first print and electronic rights. Submit seasonal material 2 months in advance. Responds in 6 weeks to queries. Sample copy online. Guidelines available online.

Nonfiction Needs general interest, historical, how-to, interview, technical, club and show news, current issues, auction realization and recent discoveries. "No articles merely giving information on background of stamp subject. Must have philatelic information included." **Buys 50 mss/year.** Send complete ms. 500 words maximum **Pays $40-75.** Sometimes pays expenses of writers on assignment.

Photos Good illustrations a must. Send scans with submission. Captions required. Reviews digital color at twice actual size (300 dpi). Offers no additional payment for photos accepted with ms. Buys all rights.

Tips "Check and double check all facts. Footnotes and bibliographies are not appropriate to newspaper style. Work citation into the text. Even though your subject might be specialized, write understandably. Explain terms. *Linn's* features are aimed at a broad audience of novice and intermediate collectors. Keep this audience in mind. Provide information in such a way to make stamp collecting more interesting to more people."

$ LOST TREASURE, INC.

P.O. Box 451589, Grove OK 74345. (866)469-6224. Fax: (918)786-2192. E-mail: managingeditor@losttreasure.com. Website: www.losttreasure.com. **75% freelance written**. Monthly and annual magazines covering lost treasure. Estab. 1966. Circ. 55,000. Byline given. Pays on publication. Buys all rights. Accepts queries by mail, e-mail, fax. Responds in 1 month to queries. Responds in 2 months to mss. Sample copy for #10 SASE. Guidelines for 10x13 SAE with $1.52 postage or online.

Nonfiction *Lost Treasure* is composed of lost treasure stories, legends, how-to articles, treasure hunting club news, who's who in treasure hunting, tips. Length: 500-1,200 words. *Treasure Cache*, an annual, contains stories about documented treasure caches with a sidebar from the author telling the reader how to search for the cache highlighted in the story. **Buys 225 mss/year.** Query on *Treasure Cache* only. Length: 1,000-2,000 words. **Pays 4¢/word.**

Photos Color or b&w prints, hand-drawn or copied maps, art with source credit with mss will help sell your story.We are always looking for cover photos with or without accompanying ms. Pays $100/published cover photo. Must be vertical. Captions required. Pays $5/published photo

Tips We are only interested in treasures that can be found with metal detectors. Queries welcome but not required. If you write about famous treasures and lost mines, be sure we haven't used your selected topic recently—the story must have a new slant or new information. Source documentation required. How-tos should cover some aspect of treasure hunting and how-to steps should be clearly defined. If you have a *Treasure Cache* story we will, if necessary, help the author with the sidebar telling how to search for the cache in the story. *Lost Treasure* articles should coordinate with theme issues when possible.

$ $ MILITARY TRADER

F + W Media, Inc., 700 E. State St., Iola WI 54990-0001. (715)445-4612. Website: www.militarytrader.com. **50% freelance written**. Magazine covering military collectibles. Dedicated to serving people who collect, preserve, and display military relics. Estab. 1994. Circ. 6,500. Byline given. Pays on publication. No kill fee. Publishes ms an average of 1 month after acceptance. Buys first North American serial rights. Accepts queries by mail, e-mail. Accepts simultaneous submissions. Responds in 1 week to queries. Responds in 1 month to mss. Sample copy for $5.

Nonfiction Needs historical, collection comparisons, artifact identification, reproduction alert. **Buys 40 mss/year.** Send complete ms. Length: 1,300-2,600 words. **Pays $0-200.**

Photos Send photos True required. Reviews contact sheets. Negotiates payment individually. Buys all rights.

Columns/Departments Pays $0-50.

Tips Be knowledgeable on military collectibles and/or military history. Plenty of good photos will make it easier to be published in our publication. Write for the collector: Assume that they already know the basics of historical context. Provide tips on where and how to collect specific items. Articles that teach the reader how to recognize fakes or forgeries are given the highest priority.

$ $ MILITARY VEHICLES

F + W Media, Inc., 700 E. State St., Iola WI 54990-0001. (715)445-4612. Website: www.militaryvehiclesmagazine.com. **50% freelance written**. Bimonthly magazine covering historic military vehicles. Dedicated to serving people who collect, restore, and drive historic military vehicles. Circ. 19,000. Byline given. Pays on publication. No kill fee. Publishes ms an average of 1 month after acceptance. Buys first North American serial rights. Accepts queries by mail, e-mail. Accepts simultaneous submissions. Responds in 1 week to queries. Responds in 1 month to mss. Sample copy for $5.

Nonfiction Needs historical, how-to, technical. **Buys 20 mss/year.** Send complete ms. Length: 1,300-2,600 words. **Pays $0-200.**
Photos True required. Buys all rights.
Columns/Departments Pays $0-75.
Tips Be knowledgeable about military vehicles. This magazine is for a very specialized audience. General automotive journalists will probably not be able to write for this group. The bulk of our content addresses US-manufactured and used vehicles. Plenty of good photos will make it easier to be published in our publication. Write for the collector/restorer: Assume that they already know the basics of historical context. Articles that show how to restore or repair military vehicles are given the highest priority.

$ MODEL CARS MAGAZINE

Golden Bell Press, 2403 Champa St., Denver CO 80205. (303)296-1600. Fax: (303)295-2159. E-mail: gregg@modelcarsmag.com. Website: www.modelcarsmag.com. **25% freelance written**. Magazine published 9 times year covering model cars, trucks, and other automotive models. "*Model Cars Magazine* is the hobby's how-to authority for the automotive modeling hobbiest. We are on the forefront of the hobby, our editorial staff are model car builders, and every single one of our writers have a passion for the hobby that is evident in the articles and stories that we publish. We are the model car magazine written by and for model car builders." Estab. 1999. Circ. 8,500. Byline given. Pays on publication. Publishes ms an average of 2-3 months after acceptance. Buys first North American serial rights. Editorial lead time 2-3 months. Accepts queries by mail, e-mail. Sample copy for $5.50.
Nonfiction We want model car related articles, features and stories. Needs how-to. Length: 600-3,000 words. **Pays $50/page. Pays $25/page for unsolicited articles.** Sometimes pays expenses of writers on assignment.

$ MODEL RAILROADER

Kalmbach Publishing Co., P.O. Box 1612, Waukesha WI 53187. Fax: (262)796-1142. E-mail: mrmag@mrmag.com. Website: www.trains.com. **Contact:** Neil Besougloff, editor. Monthly magazine for hobbyists in scale model railroading. Byline given. Buys exclusive rights. Accepts queries by mail, e-mail, fax. Responds in 2 months to queries.
Nonfiction Wants construction articles on specific model railroad projects (structures, cars, locomotives, scenery, benchwork, etc.). Also photo stories showing model railroads. Query. **Pays base rate of $90/page.**
Photos Buys photos with detailed descriptive captions only. Pays $15 and up, depending on size and use.
Tips "Before you prepare and submit any article, you should write us a short letter of inquiry describing what you want to do. We can then tell you if it fits our needs and save you from working on something we don't want."

$ MONITORING TIMES

Grove Enterprises, Inc., 7546 Hwy. 64 W., Brasstown NC 28902-0098. (828)837-9200. Fax: (828)837-2216. E-mail: editor@monitoringtimes.com. Website: www.monitoringtimes.com. **15% freelance written**. Monthly magazine for radio hobbyists. Estab. 1982. Circ. 15,000. Byline given. Pays on publication. Publishes ms an average of 4 months after acceptance. Buys first North American serial rights, buys second serial (reprint) rights. Submit seasonal material 4 months in advance. Accepts queries by mail, e-mail. Accepts previously published material. Responds in 1 month to queries. Sample copy for 9x12 SAE and 9 first-class stamps Guidelines available online.
Nonfiction Needs general interest, how-to, humor, interview, personal experience, photo feature, technical. **Buys 50 mss/year.** Query. Length: 1,500-3,000 words. **Pays average of $50/published page.**
Reprints Send photocopy and information about when and where the material previously appeared. Pays 50% of amount paid for an original article
Photos Send photos Captions required. Buys one time rights.
Columns/Departments Query managing editor.
Tips Need articles on radio communications systems and shortwave broadcasters. We are accepting more technical projects.

$ NATIONAL COMMUNICATIONS MAGAZINE

Norm Schrein, Inc., P.O. Box 291918, Kettering OH 45429. (937)299-7226. Fax: (937)299-1323. E-mail: norm@bearcat1.com. Website: www.nat-com.org. **100% freelance written**. Bimonthly magazine covering radio as a hobby. Estab. 1990. Circ. 5,000. Byline given. Pays on publication. No kill fee. Publishes ms an average of 2 months after acceptance. Buys all rights. Editorial lead time 2 months. Submit seasonal material 2 months in advance. Accepts queries by phone. Accepts previously published material. Accepts simultaneous submissions. Sample copy for $4.
Nonfiction Needs how-to, interview, new product, personal experience, photo feature, technical. Does not want articles off topic of the publication's audience (radio hobbyists). **Buys 2-3 mss/year.** Query. Length: 300 words. **Pays $75+.**
Photos Send photos Captions, identification of subjects required. Reviews GIF/JPEG files. Offers no additional

payment for photos accepted with ms. Buys all rights.

NEW ZEALAND GENEALOGIST

New Zealand Society of Genealogists, P.O. Box 5523, Moray Place Dunedin New Zealand. (64)(3)467-2036. E-mail: farthing@deepsouth.co.nz. Website: www.genealogy.org.nz. Bimonthly magazine covering articles of interest to NZSG members. No kill fee.

Nonfiction Needs how-to, family reunion notices, information wanted, contact sought, information offered. Query.

Photos Send photos Reviews copies. Do not send originals.

$ NUMISMATIST MAGAZINE

American Numismatic Association, 818 N. Cascade Ave., Colorado Springs CO 80903-3279. (719)632-2646. Fax: (719)634-4085. E-mail: magazine@money.org. Monthly magazine covering numismatics (study of coins, tokens, medals, and paper money). Estab. 1888. Circ. 30,000. Byline given. Pays on publication. No kill fee. Publishes ms an average of 1 year after acceptance. Buys perpetual, but nonexclusive rights. Editorial lead time 2 months. Sample copy free.

Nonfiction Submitted material should present new information and/or constitute a contribution to numismatic education for the experienced collector and beginner alike. Needs book excerpts, essays, historical, opinion, technical. **Buys 45-50 mss/year.** Query or send complete ms 2,500 words maximum **Pays 12¢/word.** Sometimes pays expenses of writers on assignment.

Photos Send photos Captions, identification of subjects required. Negotiates payment individually

Columns/Departments Send complete ms. **Pays $50-150.**

OLD CARS PRICE GUIDE

F + W Media, Inc., 700 E. State St., Iola WI 54990-0001. (715)445-2214. Fax: (715)445-4087. E-mail: oldcarspg@fwpubs.com. Website: www.oldcarspriceguide.net. Bimonthly magazine covering collector vehicle values. Estab. 1978. Circ. 60,000. No kill fee. Sample copy free.

- This publication is not accepting freelance submissions at this time.

$ $ PAPER CRAFTS MAGAZINE

Primedia Magazines, 14850 Pony Express Rd., Bluffdale UT 84065. (800)815-3538. Fax: (801)816-8301. E-mail: editor@papercraftsmag.com. Website: www.papercraftsmag.com. Magazine published 10 times/year designed to help readers make creative and rewarding handmade crafts. The main focus is fresh, craft-related projects our reader can make and display in her home or give as gifts. Estab. 1978. Circ. 300,000. Byline given. Pays on acceptance. Buys all rights. Editorial lead time 6 months. Accepts queries by mail, e-mail. Responds in 1 month to queries. Guidelines for #10 SASE.

Nonfiction Needs how-to. **Buys 300 mss/year.** Query with photo or sketch of how-to project. Do not send the actual project until request. **Pays $100-500.**

Tips We are looking for projects that are fresh, innovative, and in sync with today's trends. We accept projects made with a variety of techniques and media. Projects can fall in several categories, ranging from home decor to gifts, garden accessories to jewelry, and other seasonal craft projects. Submitted projects must be original, never-before-published, copyright-free work that use readily available materials.

$ PIECEWORK MAGAZINE

Interweave Press, Inc., 201 E. 4th St., Loveland CO 80537-5655. (970)669-7672. Fax: (970)667-8317. E-mail: piecework@interweave.com. Website: www.interweave.com. **90% freelance written**. Bimonthly magazine covering needlework history. *PieceWork* celebrates the rich tradition of needlework and the history of the people behind it. Stories and projects on embroidery, cross-stitch, knitting, crocheting, and quilting, along with other textile arts, are featured in each issue. Estab. 1993. Circ. 60,000. Byline given. Pays on publication. Offers 30% kill fee. Buys first North American serial rights. Editorial lead time 6 months. Submit seasonal material 6 months in advance. Accepts queries by mail, e-mail, fax, phone. Responds in 6 months to queries. Sample copy and writer's guidelines free.

Nonfiction Needs book excerpts, historical, how-to, interview, new product. No contemporary needlework articles. **Buys 25-30 mss/year.** Send complete ms. Length: 1,000-5,000 words. **Pays $100/printed page.**

Photos State availability of or send photos Captions, identification of subjects, model releases required. Reviews transparencies, prints. Buys one time rights.

Tips Submit a well-researched article on a historical aspect of needlework complete with information on visuals and suggestion for accompanying project.

$ POPULAR COMMUNICATIONS

CQ Communications, Inc., 25 Newbridge Rd., Hicksville NY 11801. (516)681-2922. Fax: (516)681-2926. E-mail: popularcom@aol.com. Website: www.popular-communications.com. **25% freelance written**. Monthly magazine covering the radio communications hobby. Estab. 1982. Circ. 40,000. Byline given. Pays on publication.

Publishes ms an average of 6 months after acceptance. Buys first North American serial rights. Editorial lead time 3 months. Submit seasonal material 6 months in advance. Accepts queries by mail, e-mail. Responds in 1 month to queries. Responds in 2 months to mss. Sample copy free. Guidelines for #10 SASE.

Nonfiction Needs general interest, how-to, antenna construction, humor, new product, photo feature, technical. **Buys 6-10 mss/year.** Query. Length: 1,800-3,000 words. **Pays $135/printed page.**

Photos State availability Captions, identification of subjects, model releases required. Negotiates payment individually

Tips Either be a radio enthusiast or know one who can help you before sending us an article.

$ $ $ $ POPULAR MECHANICS

Hearst Corp., 300 W. 57th St., New York NY 10019. (212)649-2000. E-mail: popularmechanics@hearst.com. Website: www.popularmechanics.com. **Up to 50% freelance written**. Monthly magazine on technology, science, automotive, home, outdoors. We are a men's service magazine that addresses the diverse interests of today's male, providing him with information to improve the way he lives. We cover stories from do-it-yourself projects to technological advances in aerospace, military, automotive and so on. Estab. 1902. Circ. 1,200,000. Offers 25% kill fee. Publishes ms an average of 6 months after acceptance. Submit seasonal material 6 months in advance.

- **Pays $1/word and up**.

$ $ POPULAR WOODWORKING

F+W Media, Inc., 4700 E. Galbraith Rd., Cincinnati OH 45236. (513)531-2690, ext. 11348. E-mail: megan.fitzpatrick@fwmedia.com. Website: www.popularwoodworking.com. **45% freelance written**. Magazine published 7 times/year. *Popular Woodworking* invites woodworkers of all levels into a community of professionals who share their hard-won shop experience through in-depth projects and technique articles, which help the readers hone their existing skills and develop new ones. Related stories increase the readers' understanding and enjoyment of their craft. Any project submitted must be aesthetically pleasing, of sound construction, and offer a challenge to readers. On the average, we use 4 freelance features per issue. Our primary needs are 'how-to' articles on woodworking. Our secondary need is for articles that will inspire discussion concerning woodworking. Tone of articles should be conversational and informal, as if the writer is speaking directly to the reader. Our readers are the woodworking hobbyist and small woodshop owner. Writers should have an extensive knowledge of woodworking, or be able to communicate information gained from woodworkers. Estab. 1981. Circ. 210,000. Byline given. Pays on acceptance. No kill fee. Publishes ms an average of 10 months after acceptance. Buys all world rights. Submit seasonal material 6 months in advance. Accepts queries by mail, e-mail, fax, phone. Accepts previously published material. Responds in 2 months to queries Sample copy for $5.99 and 9x12 SAE with 6 first-class stamps or online Guidelines available online

Nonfiction Needs how-to (on woodworking projects, with plans), humor (woodworking anecdotes), technical (woodworking techniques). No tool reviews. **Buys 40 mss/year.** Send complete ms. **Pay starts at $200/published page**

Reprints Send photocopy with rights for sale noted and information about when and where the material previously appeared. Pays 25% of amount paid for an original article

Photos Photographic quality affects acceptance. Need high-resolution digital images of step-by-step construction process. Send photos Captions, identification of subjects required.

Columns/Departments Tricks of the Trade (helpful techniques), Out of the Woodwork (thoughts on woodworking as a profession or hobby, can be humorous or serious), 500-600 words. 20 Query.

Tips "Write an `Out of the Woodwork' column for us and then follow up with photos of your projects. Submissions should include materials list, complete diagrams (blueprints not necessary), and discussion of the step-by-step process. We have become more selective on accepting only practical, attractive projects with quality construction for which the authors can supply quality digital photography. We are also looking for more original topics for our other articles."

$ QST

American Radio Relay League, 225 Main St., Newington CT 06111. (860)594-0200. Fax: (860)594-0259. E-mail: qst@arrl.org. Website: www.arrl.org. **90% freelance written**. Monthly magazine covering amateur radio. "*QST* is an ARRL membership journal covering subjects of interest to amateur ('ham') radio operators." Estab. 1915. Circ. 150,000. Byline given. Pays on publication. No kill fee. Publishes ms an average of 6 months after acceptance. Buys all rights. Editorial lead time 6 months. Submit seasonal material 6 months in advance. Accepts queries by mail, e-mail, fax, phone. Responds in 1 week to queries. Responds in 1 month to mss Guidelines available online at: www.arrl.org/qst/aguide

Nonfiction Needs general interest, how-to, technical. Query. Length: 900-3,000 words. **Pays $65-125.** Sometimes pays expenses of writers on assignment.

Photos Send photos Captions, identification of subjects required. Reviews GIF/JPEG files. Offers no additional payment for photos accepted with ms. Buys all rights.

Tips "Submissions must relate to amateur 'ham' radio."

$ $ THE QUILTER

All American Crafts, Inc., 7 Waterloo Rd., Stanhope NJ 07874. (973)347-6900. E-mail: editors@thequiltermag.com. Website: www.thequiltermag.com. **45% freelance written**. Bimonthly magazine on quilting. Estab. 1988. Byline given. Pays on publication. Publishes ms an average of 6 months after acceptance. Submit seasonal material 6 months in advance. Accepts queries by mail, phone. Responds in 2 months to queries. Sample copy for sae with 9x12 envelope and 4 First-Class stamps. Guidelines available online.

Nonfiction Quilts and quilt patterns with instructions, quilt-related projects, interview/profile, photo feature—all quilt related. Query with published clips. Length: 350-1,000 words. **Pays 10-12¢/word.**

Photos Send photos Captions, identification of subjects required. Reviews transparencies, prints. Offers $10-15/photo Buys one-time or all rights

Columns/Departments Feature Teacher (qualified quilt teachers with teaching involved—with slides); Profile (award-winning and interesting quilters). Length: 1,000 words maximum. **Pays 10¢/word, $15/photo**

QUILTER'S NEWSLETTER MAGAZINE

OK Media, 741 Corporate Circle, Suite A, Golden CO 80401. (303)215-5600. Fax: (303)215-5601. Website: www.quiltersnewsletter.com. **Contact:** Jan Magee, Editor-in-Chief. Magazine published 6 times/year covering quilt making. Written for quilt enthusiasts. Estab. 1969. Circ. 185,000. Pays 60 days after publication. No kill fee. Sample copy available online. Guidelines available online.

Nonfiction SASE Returns Needs historical, how-to, design techniques, presentation of a single technique or concept with step-by-step approach, interview, new product, reviews (quilt books and videos). Send complete ms.

Photos Color only, no b&w. Captions required. Reviews 2 x 2, 4 x 5 or larger transparencies, 35mm slides, digital hi-res photos (300 dpi or higher). Negotiates payment individually

Tips "Our decision will be based on the freshness of the material, the interest of the material to our readers, whether we have recently published similar material or already have something similar in our inventory, how well it fits into the balance of the material we have on hand, how much rewriting or editing we think it will require, and the quality of the slides, photos or illustrations you include."

$ $ QUILTER'S WORLD

185 Sweet Rd., Lincoln ME 04457. (207)794-3290. E-mail: sandra_hatch@drgnetwork.com. Website: www.quilters-world.com. **100% freelance written. Works with a small number of new/unpublished writers each year**. Bimonthly magazine covering quilting. "*Quilter's World* is a general quilting publication. We accept articles about special quilters, techniques, coverage of unusual quilts at quilt shows, special interest quilts, human interest articles and patterns. We include 2 articles and 12-15 patterns in every issue. Reader is 30-70 years old, midwestern." Circ. 130,000. Byline given. Pays 45 days after acceptance. No kill fee. Buys all rights. Submit seasonal material 10 months in advance. Accepts queries by mail, e-mail. Responds in 3 months to queries. Guidelines available online.

Nonfiction Needs how-to, interview, new product, photo feature feature, technical, quilters, quilt products. Query or send complete ms **Pays $100-$200 for articles; $50-550 for quilt designs**

Photos State availability Captions required. Reviews Color slides.

Tips "Read several recent issues for style and content."

$ RENAISSANCE MAGAZINE

One Controls Dr., Shelton CT 06484. (800)232-2224. Fax: (800)775-2729. E-mail: editortom@renaissancemagazine.com. Website: www.renaissancemagazine.com. **90% freelance written**. Bimonthly magazine covering the history of the Middle Ages and the Renaissance. Our readers include historians, reenactors, roleplayers, medievalists, and Renaissance Faire enthusiasts. Estab. 1996. Circ. 33,000. Byline given. Pays on publication. Publishes ms an average of 1 year after acceptance. Buys first North American serial rights. Editorial lead time 6 months. Submit seasonal material 4 months in advance. Accepts queries by mail, e-mail, fax, phone. Accepts previously published material. Responds in 3 weeks to queries. Responds in 2 months to mss. Sample copy for $9. Guidelines available online.

- The editor reports an interest in seeing costuming how-to articles; and Renaissance Festival insider articles.

Nonfiction Needs essays, expose, historical, how-to, interview, new product, opinion, photo feature, religious, travel. **Buys 25 mss/year.** Query or send ms Length: 1,000-5,000 words. **Pays 8¢/word.**

Photos State availability Captions, identification of subjects, model releases required. Reviews contact sheets, negatives, transparencies, prints. Pays $7.50/photo. Buys all rights.

Tips Send in all articles in the standard manuscript format with photos/slides or illustrations for suggested use. Writers *must* be open to critique, and all historical articles should also include a recommended reading list. A SASE must be included to receive a response to any submission.

$ $ ROCK & GEM

The Earth's Treasures, Minerals and Jewelry, Miller Magazines, Inc., 290 Maple Court, Suite 232, Ventura CA 93003-7783. (805)644-3824, ext. 29. Fax: (805)644-3875. E-mail: editor@rockngem.com. Website: www.rockngem.com. **99% freelance written.** Monthly magazine covering rockhounding field trips, how-to lapidiary projects, minerals, fossils, gold prospecting, mining, etc. This is not a scientific journal. Its articles appeal to amateurs, beginners, and experts, but its tone is conversational and casual, not stuffy. It's for hobbyists. Estab. 1971. Circ. 55,000. Byline given. Pays on publication. No kill fee. Buys first worldwide serial and electronic reprint rights. Editorial lead time 4 months. Submit seasonal material 6 months in advance. Accepts queries by mail. Guidelines available online.

- Contributor agreement required.

Nonfiction Needs general interest, how-to, personal experience, photo feature, travel. Does not want to see The 25th Anniversary of the Pet Rock, or anything so scientific that it could be a thesis. **Buys 156-200 mss/year.** Send complete ms. Length: 2,000-4,000 words. **Pays $100-250.**

Photos Accepts prints, slides or digital art on disk or CD only (provide thumbnails). Send photos Captions required. Offers no additional payment for photos accepted with ms.

Tips We're looking for more how-to articles and field trips with maps. Read writers guidelines very carefully and follow all instructions in them. Then be patient. Your manuscript may be published within a month or even a year from date of submission.

$ SCALE AUTO

Kalmbach Publishing Co., 21027 Crossroads Circle, P.O. Box 1612, Waukesha WI 53187-1612. (262)796-8776. Fax: (262)796-1383. E-mail: jhaught@kalmbach.com. Website: www.scaleautomag.com. **70% freelance written.** Bimonthly magazine covering model car building. We are looking for model builders, collectors, and enthusiasts who feel their models and/or modeling techniques and experiences would be of interest and benefit to our readership. Estab. 1979. Circ. 35,000. Byline given. Pays on publication. Publishes ms an average of 1 year after acceptance. Buys all rights. Editorial lead time 4 months. Submit seasonal material 4 months in advance. Accepts queries by mail, e-mail, fax, phone. Responds in 3 months to queries. Responds in 3 months to mss. Sample copy and writer's guidelines online.

Nonfiction Needs book excerpts, historical, how-to, build models, do different techniques, interview, personal experience, photo feature, technical. Query or send complete ms Length: 750-3,000 words. **Pays $60/published page.**

Photos When writing how-to articles be sure to take photos during the project. Send photos Captions, identification of subjects, model releases required. Reviews negatives, 35mm color transparencies, color glossy. Negotiates payment individually Buys all rights.

Columns/Departments 50 Query. **Pays $60/page.**

Tips First and foremost, our readers like how-to material: how-to paint, how-to scratchbuild, how-to chop a roof, etc. Basically, our readers want to know how to make their own models better. Therefore, any help or advice you can offer is what modelers want to read. Also, the more photos you send, taken from a variety of views, the better choice we have in putting together an outstanding article layout. Send us more photos than you would ever possibly imagine we could use. This permits us to pick and choose the best of the bunch.

$ SCOTT STAMP MONTHLY

Amos Press Inc., P.O. Box 828, Sidney OH 45365. (937)498-0802. Fax: (937)498-0807. E-mail: ssmeditor@scottonline.com. Website: www.scottonline.com. **70% freelance written.** Monthly magazine covering stamp collecting. Our goal at *Scott Stamp Monthly* is to create a monthly publication that serves every stamp collector, from beginner to advanced with informative and entertaining feature articles covering all aspects of the stamp hobby. Estab. 1868. Circ. 20,000. Byline given. Pays on publication. No kill fee. Publishes ms an average of 6 months after acceptance. Buys first rights, buys electronic rights. Editorial lead time 2 months. Submit seasonal material 6 months in advance. Accepts queries by mail, e-mail, fax, phone. Responds in 6 weeks to queries. Responds in 6 weeks to mss Sample copy for free

Nonfiction Needs general interest, historical, interview, nostalgic, opinion, technical, travel. Does not want non-philatelic articles. **Buys 50 mss/year.** Send complete ms. Length: 2,000 words. **Pays $60+.** Sometimes pays expenses of writers on assignment.

Photos Quality illustrations a must. Send images or photos. Send scans with ms. Captions, identification of subjects required. Reviews digital color at twice actual size (300 dpi). Offers no additional payment for photos accepted with ms. Buys all rights.

Tips "Check and double check all facts. Footnotes and bibliographies are not appropriate to magazine style. Work citation into the text. Even though story subject might be specialized, write understandably. Explain stamp terms. *Scott Stamp Monthly* features are aimed at a broad audience that includes relatively novice collectors. Keep this audience in mind. Provide information in such a way to make stamp collecting more interesting to more people."

$ $ SEW NEWS

Creating for You and Your Home, Primedia Enthusiast Group, 741 Corporate Circle, Suite A, Golden CO 80401. (303)215-5600. Fax: (303)215-5601. E-mail: sewnews@sewnews.com. Website: www.sewnews.com. **70% freelance written. Works with a small number of new/unpublished writers each year.** Monthly magazine covering fashion, gift, and home-dec sewing. Our magazine is for the beginning home sewer to the professional dressmaker. It expresses the fun, creativity, and excitement of sewing. Estab. 1980. Circ. 185,000. Byline given. Pays on publication. No kill fee. Publishes ms an average of 6 months after acceptance. Buys all rights. Submit seasonal material 6 months in advance. Accepts queries by mail, e-mail, fax. Responds in 2 months to mss. Sample copy for $5.99. Guidelines for #10 SAE with 2 first-class stamps or online.

- All stories submitted to *Sew News* must be on disk or by e-mail.

Nonfiction Needs how-to, sewing techniques, interview, interesting personalities in home-sewing field. **Buys 200-240 mss/year.** Query with published clips if available Length: 500-2,000 words. **Pays $25-500.**
Photos Prefers digital images, color photos, or slides. Send photos Identification of subjects required. Payment included in ms price. Buys all rights.
Tips Query first with writing sample and outline of proposed story. Areas most open to freelancers are how-to and sewing techniques; give explicit, step-by-step instructions, plus rough art. We're using more home decorating and soft craft content.

$ SHUTTLE SPINDLE & DYEPOT

Handweavers Guild of America, Inc., 1255 Buford Hwy., Suite 211, Suwanee GA 30024. (678)730-0010. Fax: (678)730-0836. E-mail: hga@weavespindye.org. Website: www.weavespindye.org. **60% freelance written.** Quarterly magazine. Quarterly membership publication of the Handweavers Guild of America, Inc., *Shuttle Spindle & Dyepot* magazine seeks to encourage excellence in contemporary fiber arts and to support the preservation of techniques and traditions in fiber arts. It also provides inspiration for fiber artists of all levels and develops public awareness and appreciation of the fiber arts. *Shuttle Spindle & Dyepot* appeals to a highly educated, creative, and very knowledgeable audience of fiber artists and craftsmen, weavers, spinners, dyers, and basket makers. Estab. 1969. Circ. 30,000. Byline given. Pays on publication. Publishes ms an average of 6 months after acceptance. Buys first North American serial rights, buys second serial (reprint) rights, buys electronic rights. Editorial lead time 8 months. Submit seasonal material 8 months in advance. Accepts queries by mail, e-mail, fax, phone. Sample copy for $8.00 plus shipping. Guidelines available online.
Nonfiction Needs inspirational, interview, new product, personal experience, photo feature, technical, travel. No self-promotional and no articles from those without knowledge of area/art/artists. **Buys 40 mss/year.** Query with published clips. Length: 1,000-2,000 words. **Pays $75-150.**
Photos State availability Captions, identification of subjects, model releases required. Offers no additional payment for photos accepted with ms.
Columns/Departments Books and Videos, News and Information, Calendar and Conference, Travel and Workshop (all fiber/art related).
Tips Become knowledgeable about the fiber arts and artists. The writer should provide an article of importance to the weaving, spinning, dyeing and basket making community. Query by telephone (once familiar with publication) by appointment helps editor and writer.

$ SUNSHINE ARTIST

America's Premier Show & Festival Publication, Palm House Publishing Inc., 4075 L.B. McLeod Rd., Suite E, Orlando FL 32811. (800)597-2573. Fax: (407)228-9862. E-mail: editor@sunshineartist.com. Website: www.sunshineartist.com. Monthly magazine covering art shows in the US. We are the premiere marketing/reference magazine for artists and crafts professionals who earn their living through art shows nationwide. We list more than 2,000 shows monthly, critique many of them, and publish articles on marketing, selling and other issues of concern to professional show circuit artists. Estab. 1972. Circ. 12,000. Byline given. Pays on publication. Publishes ms an average of 3 months after acceptance. Buys first North American serial rights. Responds in 2 months to queries. Sample copy for $5.
Nonfiction We publish articles of interest to artists and crafts professionals who travel the art show circuit. Current topics include marketing, computers, and RV living. No how-to. **Buys 5-10 freelance mss/year.** Send complete ms. Length: 1,000-2,000 words. **Pays $50-150.**
Reprints Send photocopy and information about when and where the material previously appeared.
Photos Send photos Captions, identification of subjects, model releases required. Offers no additional payment for photos accepted with ms.

$ $ TATTOO REVUE

Art & Ink Enterprises, Inc., c/o Art & Ink Enterprises, 820 Hamilton St., Ste. C6, Charlotte NC 28206-2991. (704)333-3331. Fax: (704)333-3433. E-mail: inked@skinartmag.com. Website: www.skinart.com. **25% freelance written.** Interview and profile magazine published 4 times/year covering tattoo artists, their art and lifestyle. All writers must have knowledge of tattoos. Features include interviews with tattoo artists and collectors. Estab.

1990. Circ. 100,000. Byline given. Pays on publication. Publishes ms an average of 3 months after acceptance. Buys one-time rights. Editorial lead time 3 months. Submit seasonal material 5 months in advance. Accepts queries by mail, e-mail, fax. Responds in 2 weeks to queries. Sample copy for $5.98. Guidelines for #10 SASE.
Nonfiction Needs book excerpts, historical, humor, interview, photo feature. Publishes special convention issues—dates and locations provided upon request. No first-time experiences—our readers already know. **Buys 10-30 mss/year.** Send complete ms. Length: 500-2,500 words. **Pays $25-200.**
Photos Send photos Captions, identification of subjects, model releases required. Reviews transparencies, prints. Offers $0-10/photo Buys one time rights.
Columns/Departments 10-30 Query with or without published clips or send complete ms. **Pays $25-50.**
Fillers Needs anecdotes, facts, gags, newsbreaks, short humor. 10-20 Length: 50-2,000 words.
Tips All writers must have knowledge of tattoos! Either giving or receiving.

$ $ TEDDY BEAR REVIEW

Jones Publishing, Inc., N7450 Aanstad Rd., P.O. Box 5000, Iola WI 54945-5000. (715)445-5000. E-mail: editor@teddybearreview.com. Website: www.teddybearreview.com. **65% freelance written. Works with a small number of new/unpublished writers each year.** Bimonthly magazine on teddy bears for collectors, enthusiasts and bearmakers. Estab. 1985. Byline given. Payment upon publication on the last day of the month the issue is mailed. Contact editor for copy of freelance contributor agreement. Submit seasonal material 6 months in advance. Sample copy and writer's guidelines for $2 and 9x12 SAE
Nonfiction Needs historical, how-to, interview. No articles from the bear's point of view. **Buys 30-40 mss/year.** Query with published clips. Length: 900-1,500 words. **Pays $100-350.**
Photos Send photos Captions required. Reviews transparencies, prints. Offers no additional payment for photos accepted with ms Buys one time rights.
Tips We are interested in good, professional writers around the country with a strong knowledge of teddy bears. Historical profile of bear companies, profiles of contemporary artists, and knowledgeable reports on museum collections are of interest.

$ $ THREADS

Taunton Press, 63 S. Main St., P.O. Box 5506, Newtown CT 06470. (203)426-8171. Fax: (203)426-3434. E-mail: th@taunton.com. Website: www.threadsmagazine.com. "Bimonthly magazine covering sewing, garment construction, home decor and embellishments (including quilting and embroidery).". "We're seeking proposals from hands-on authors who first and foremost have a skill. Being an experienced writer is of secondary consideration." Estab. 1985. Circ. 129,000. Byline given. Offers $150 kill fee. Buys one-time rights, buys second serial (reprint) rights. Editorial lead time 4 months. Responds in 1-2 months to queries. Guidelines available online.
Nonfiction We prefer first-person experience. **Pays $150/page.**
Columns/Departments Product reviews; Book reviews; Tips; Closures (stories of a humorous nature). Query. **Pays $150/page**
Tips "Send us a proposal (outline) with photos of your own work (garments, samples, etc.)."

$ $ TOY FARMER

Toy Farmer Publications, 7496 106 Ave. SE, LaMoure ND 58458-9404. (701)883-5206. Fax: (701)883-5209. E-mail: chegvik@toyfarmer.com. Website: www.toyfarmer.com. **70% freelance written.** Monthly magazine covering farm toys. Estab. 1978. Circ. 27,000. Byline given. Pays on publication. Buys first North American serial rights. Editorial lead time 2 months. Submit seasonal material 3 months in advance. Accepts queries by mail, e-mail, fax, phone. Accepts previously published material. Responds in 1 month to queries. Responds in 2 months to mss. Writer's guidelines available upon request.

- Youth involvement is strongly encouraged.

Nonfiction Needs general interest, historical, interview, new product, personal experience, technical, book introductions. **Buys 100 mss/year.** Query with published clips. Length: 800-1,500 words. **Pays 10¢/word.** Sometimes pays expenses of writers on assignment.
Photos Must be 35mm originals or very high resolution digital images. State availability Buys one time rights.

$ $ TOY TRUCKER & CONTRACTOR

Toy Farmer Publications, 7496 106th Ave. SE, LaMoure ND 58458-9404. (701)883-5206. Fax: (701)883-5209. E-mail: chegvik@toyfarmer.com. Website: www.toytrucker.com. **40% freelance written.** Monthly magazine covering collectible toys. We are a magazine on hobby and collectible toy trucks and construction pieces. Estab. 1990. Circ. 6,500. Byline given. Pays on publication. No kill fee. Buys first North American serial rights. Editorial lead time 2 months. Submit seasonal material 3 months in advance. Accepts queries by mail, e-mail, fax, phone. Accepts previously published material. Responds in 1 month to queries. Responds in 2 months to mss. Writer's guidelines available on request.
Nonfiction Needs historical, interview, new product, personal experience, technical. **Buys 35 mss/year.** Query. Length: 800-1,400 words. **Pays 10¢/word.** Sometimes pays expenses of writers on assignment.

Photos Must be 35mm originals or very high resolution digital images. Send photos Captions, identification of subjects, model releases required.
Tips Send sample work that would apply to our magazine. Also, we need more articles on collectors, builders, model kit enthusiasts and small company information. We have regular columns, so a feature should not repeat what our columns do.

$ WESTERN & EASTERN TREASURES

People's Publishing Co., Inc., P.O. Box 219, San Anselmo CA 94979. Website: www.treasurenet.com. **100% freelance written**. Monthly magazine covering hobby/sport of metal detecting/treasure hunting. *"Western & Eastern Treasures* provides concise, yet comprehensive coverage of every aspect of the sport/hobby of metal detecting and treasure hunting with a strong emphasis on current, accurate information; innovative, field-proven advice and instruction; and entertaining, effective presentation." Estab. 1966. Circ. 50,000. Byline given. Pays on publication. No kill fee. Publishes ms an average of 4+ months after acceptance. Buys all rights. Editorial lead time 4 months. Submit seasonal material 3-4 months in advance. Responds in 3 months to mss. Sample copy for sae with 9x12 envelope and 5 First-Class stamps. Guidelines for #10 SASE.
Nonfiction Needs how-to, tips and finds for metal detectorists, interview, only people in metal detecting, personal experience, positive metal detector experiences, technical, only metal detecting hobby-related, helping in local community with metal detecting skills (i.e., helping local police locate evidence at crime scenes—all volunteer basis). *Silver & Gold Annual* (editorial deadline February each year)—looking for articles 1,500+ words, plus photos on the subject of locating silver and/or gold using a metal detector. No fiction, poetry, or puzzles. **Buys 150+ mss/year.** Send complete ms. Length: 1,000-1,500 words. **Pays 3¢/word for articles.**
Photos Send photos Captions, identification of subjects required. Reviews 35mm transparencies, prints, digital scans (minimum 300 dpi). Offers $5 minimum/photo. Buys all rights.

$ $ WOODSHOP NEWS

Soundings Publications, Inc., 10 Bokum Rd., Essex CT 06426-1185. (860)767-8227. Fax: (860)767-1048. E-mail: editorial@woodshopnews.com. Website: www.woodshopnews.com. **20% freelance written.** Monthly tabloid covering woodworking for professionals. Solid business news and features about woodworking companies. Feature stories about interesting professional woodworkers. Some how-to articles. Estab. 1986. Circ. 60,000. Byline given. Pays on publication. Publishes ms an average of 3 months after acceptance. Buys first North American serial rights. Submit seasonal material 4 months in advance. Accepts queries by mail, e-mail, fax. Responds in 1 month to queries. Sample copy available online. Guidelines free.

- *Woodshop News* needs writers in major cities in all regions except the Northeast. Also looking for more editorial opinion pieces.

Nonfiction Needs how-to, query first, interview, new product, opinion, personal experience, photo feature. Key word is newsworthy. No general interest profiles of folksy woodworkers. **Buys 15-25 mss/year.** Send complete ms. Length: 100-1,200 words. **Pays $50-500 for assigned articles. Pays $40-250 for unsolicited articles.** Pays expenses of writers on assignment.
Photos Send photos Captions, identification of subjects required. Reviews contact sheets, prints. Buys one time rights.
Columns/Departments Pro Shop (business advice, marketing, employee relations, taxes, etc., for the professional written by an established professional in the field); Finishing (how-to and techniques, materials, spraybooths, staining; written by experienced finishers), both 1,200-1,500 words. 18 Query. **Pays $200-300.**
Tips The best way to start is a profile of a professional woodworker in your area. Find a unique angle about the person or business and stress this as the theme of your article. Avoid a broad, general-interest theme that would be more appropriate to a daily newspaper. Our readers are professional woodworkers who want more depth and more specifics than would a general readership. If you are profiling a business, we need standard business information such as gross annual earnings/sales, customer base, product line and prices, marketing strategy, etc. Color 35mm or high-res digital photos are a must.

$ $ WOODWORK

A Magazine For All Woodworkers, Ross Periodicals, 42 Digital Dr., #5, Novato CA 94949. (415)382-0580. Fax: (415)382-0587. E-mail: woodwork@rossperiodicals.com. Website: www.woodwork-mag.com. **90% freelance written**. Bimonthly magazine covering woodworking. We are aiming at a broad audience of woodworkers, from the enthusiast to professional. Articles range from intermediate to complex. We cover such subjects as carving, turning, furniture, tools old and new, design, techniques, projects, and more. We also feature profiles of woodworkers, with the emphasis being always on communicating woodworking methods, practices, theories, and techniques. Suggestions for articles are always welcome. Estab. 1986. Circ. 50,000. Byline given. Pays on publication. No kill fee. Buys first North American serial rights, buys second serial (reprint) rights. Accepts queries by mail, e-mail, fax. Sample copy for $5 and 9x12 SAE with 6 first-class stamps. Guidelines for #10 SASE.
Nonfiction All articles must convey a working understanding of the subject matter. Needs how-to, intermediate

to advanced projects, such as furniture, turning, etc., interview, of established woodworkers, photo feature, of interest to woodworkers, technical, tools, techniques. Query. Length: 1,500-2,000 words. **Pays $150-200/published page.**

Photos We accept film (slides or prints) and hi-resolution (300 dpi) digital images. Send photos Captions, identification of subjects required. Pays higher page rate for photos accepted with ms. Buys one time rights.

Columns/Departments Tips and Techniques column, **pays $35-75.** Interview/profiles of established woodworkers (bring out woodworker's philosophy about the craft, opinions about what is happening currently). Good photos of subject's work a must. Section on how-to desirable. Query with published clips.

Tips Our main requirement is that each article must directly concern woodworking. If you are not a woodworker, the interview/profile is your best chance. Good writing is essential, as are good photos. The interview must be entertaining, but informative and pertinent to woodworkers' interests. Include sidebar written by the profile subject.

HOME & GARDEN

ATLANTA HOME IMPROVEMENT

Network Communications, Inc. (NCI), 80 W. Wieuca Rd., Atlanta GA 30342. (404)303-9333. Fax: (404)303-0033. E-mail: editor@homeimprovementmag.com. Website: www.homeimprovementmag.com. **30% freelance written**. Monthly magazine covering home improvement. Estab. 2001. Circ. 40,000. Byline given. Pays on acceptance. No kill fee. Publishes ms an average of 2 months after acceptance. Editorial lead time 3 months. Submit seasonal material 4-5 months in advance. Accepts queries by mail, e-mail. Accepts simultaneous submissions. Responds in 2 weeks to queries. Sample copy free. Guidelines free.

- Our audience is very loca—magazine caters to Atlanta homeowners, so must have an Atlanta slant and include Atlanta home/garden businesses.

Photos State availability of or send photos Identification of subjects required. Reviews GIF/JPEG files. Buys one time rights.

$ $ $ MOUNTAIN HOUSE AND HOME

Planning, Building and Remodeling Your Colorado Home, Colorado Resort Publishing, P.O. Box 8, Vail CO 81658. (970)748-2970. E-mail: knicoletti@coloradoresortpub.com. Website: www.mountainhouseandhome.com. **80% freelance written**. Quarterly magazine covering building, remodeling Colorado homes. We cater to an affluent population of homeowners (including primary, second and third homeowners) who are planning to build or remodel their Colorado home in the mountains or on the western slope. While we feature luxury homes, we also have a slant toward green building. Estab. 2005. Circ. 35,000. Byline given. Pays on publication. No kill fee. Publishes ms an average of 2-3 months after acceptance. Buys all rights. Editorial lead time 12 months. Submit seasonal material 6 months in advance. Accepts queries by e-mail. Responds in 2-4 weeks to queries. Responds in month to mss. Sample copy available online.

Nonfiction Needs interview, new product, Profiles of Colorado homes and features related to them. We do not want do-it-yourself projects. Query with published clips. **Pays $200-650 for assigned articles. We do not buy articles; we only assign articles. for unsolicited articles.**

Photos Send photos Captions required. Reviews GIF/JPEG files. We negotiate payment individually. Buys all rights.

Columns/Departments Your Green Home (tips for environmentally-conscious building, remodeling and living), 300 words. 4 mss/year Query.

Tips Writers should be very familiar with, and preferably live in, the area they are writing about. We set our editorial budget in late spring/early summer for the entire following year, but sometimes we have openings for story ideas; or, more often, we are open to suggestions for featuring a specific, unique home in the area we cover.

$ THE ALMANAC FOR FARMERS & CITY FOLK

Greentree Publishing, Inc., 840 S. Rancho Dr., Suite 4-319, Las Vegas NV 89106. (702)387-6777. Fax: (702)385-1370. Website: www.thealmanac.com. **30-40% freelance written**. Annual almanac of "down-home, folksy material pertaining to farming, gardening, homemaking, animals, etc.". Estab. 1983. Circ. 300,000. Byline given. Pays on publication. No kill fee. Publishes ms an average of 6 months after acceptance. Buys first North American serial rights. Sample copy for $4.99.

- Deadline: March 31.

Nonfiction Needs essays, general interest, historical, how-to, any home or garden project, humor. "No fiction or controversial topics. Please, no first-person pieces!" **Buys 30-40 mss/year.** No queries please. Editorial decisions made from ms only. Send complete ms by mail. Length: 350-1,400 words. **Pays $45/page.**

Poetry Buys 1-6 poems/year. Pays $45 for full pages or $15 for short poems.

Fillers Uses 60/year. Needs anecdotes, facts, short humor, gardening hints. 125 words maximum. **$15 for short**

fillers or page rate for longer fillers

Tips "Typed submissions essential as we scan manuscript. Short, succinct material is preferred. Material should appeal to a wide range of people and should be on the 'folksy' side, preferably with a thread of humor woven in. No first-person pieces (using 'I' or 'my')."

$ $ THE AMERICAN GARDENER

A Publication of the American Horticultural Society, 7931 E. Boulevard Dr., Alexandria VA 22308-1300. (703)768-5700. Fax: (703)768-7533. E-mail: editor@ahs.org. Website: www.ahs.org. **60% freelance written**. Bimonthly magazine covering gardening and horticulture. "This is the official publication of the American Horticultural Society (AHS), a national, nonprofit, membership organization for gardeners, founded in 1922. The AHS mission is 'to open the eyes of all Americans to the vital connection between people and plants, and to inspire all Americans to become responsible caretakers of the earth, to celebrate America's diversity through the art and science of horticulture, and to lead this effort by sharing the society's unique national resources with all Americans.' All articles are also published on members-only website." Estab. 1922. Circ. 36,000. Byline given. Pays on publication. Offers 25% kill fee. Publishes ms an average of 6 months after acceptance. Buys first North American serial rights. Editorial lead time 6 months. Submit seasonal material at least 1 year in advance. Accepts queries by mail. Responds in 3 months to queries. Sample copy for $5. Writer's guidelines by e-mail and online

Nonfiction "Feature-length articles include in-depth profiles of individual plant groups; profiles of prominent American horticulturists and gardeners (living and dead); profiles of unusual public or private gardens; descriptions of historical developments in American gardening; descriptions of innovative landscape design projects (especially relating to use of regionally native plants or naturalistic gardening); and descriptions of important plant breeding and research programs tailored to a lay audience. We run a few how-to articles; these should address relatively complex or unusual topics that most other gardening magazines won't tackle—photography must be provided." **Buys 20 mss/year.** Query with published clips. Length: 1,500-2,500 words. **Pays $300-550, depending on complexity and author's experience.**

Reprints Rarely purchases second rights. Send photocopy of article with information about when and where the material previously appeared. Payment varies.

Photos E-mail or check website for guidelines before submitting. Identification of subjects required. Offers $80-350/photo Buys one-time print rights, plus limited rights to run article on members-only website.

Columns/Departments Natural Connections (explains a natural phenomenon—plant and pollinator relationships, plant and fungus relationships, parasites—that may be observed in nature or in the garden), 750-1,200 words. 5 Query with published clips. **Pays $100-250.**

Tips "The majority of our readers are advanced, passionate amateur gardeners; about 20 percent are horticultural professionals. Most prefer not to use synthetic chemical pesticides. Our articles are intended to bring this knowledgeable group new information, ranging from the latest scientific findings that affect plants, to in-depth profiles of specific plant groups, and the history of gardening and gardens in America."

$ $ ARIZONA HOME & DESIGN

Arizona Business, 1301 N. Central Ave., #1070, Phoenix AZ 85012. (602)277-6045. Fax: (602)650-0827. E-mail: esunna@azbusinessmagazine.com. Website: www.azhomeanddesign.com. **39% freelance written**. Bimonthly magazine covering residential interior design and architecture and products in Arizona. Stories are geared toward an affluent audience living in Arizona who are looking to be inspired by design, rather than learn about how-to projects. Estab. 2000. Circ. 30,000. Byline given. Offers 100% kill fee. Publishes ms an average of 2 months after acceptance. Buys one-time rights. Editorial lead time 3 months. Submit seasonal material 3 months in advance. Accepts queries by mail, e-mail. Accepts simultaneous submissions. Sample copy free. Guidelines free.

Nonfiction Needs general interest, historical, humor, interview, new product, photo feature. Does not want stories without an angle, stories not geared to an affluent reader with a high-end home. Query. Length: 150-2,000 words. **Pays $100-350.**

Photos State availability Identification of subjects required. Reviews negatives, transparencies, prints, GIF/JPEG files. Negotiates payment individually. Buys one time rights.

Columns/Departments Launch (new companies and products); Style Savvy (miscellaneous product showcase); Artery (noteworthy art for the home); Drab2Fab (before and after photos/copy of remodel projects); Inspiration (top 10 picks of home-related products); Social Life (entertaining at home). Home Away from Home department that features second-home properties in and outside of Arizona. Query. **Pays $100-350.**

Tips E-mail managing editor to introduce yourself. Include an organized list of story ideas.

$ $ ATLANTA HOMES AND LIFESTYLES

Network Communications, Inc., 1100 Johnson Ferry Rd., Suite 595, Atlanta GA 30342. (404)252-6670. Fax: (404)252-6673. Website: www.atlantahomesmag.com. **65% freelance written**. Magazine published 12 times/year. *Atlanta Homes and Lifestyles* is designed for the action-oriented, well-educated reader who enjoys his/

her shelter, its design and construction, its environment, and living and entertaining in it. Estab. 1983. Circ. 33,091. Byline given. Pays on publication. Publishes ms an average of 6 months after acceptance. Buys all rights. Accepts queries by mail, fax. Responds in 3 months to queries. Sample copy for $3.95. Guidelines available online.

Nonfiction Needs interview, new product, photo feature, well-designed homes, gardens, local art, remodeling, food, preservation, entertaining. We do not want articles outside respective market area, not written for magazine format, or that are excessively controversial, investigative or that cannot be appropriately illustrated with attractive photography. **Buys 35 mss/year.** Query with published clips. Length: 500-1,200 words. **Pays $100-500.** Sometimes pays expenses of writer on assignment

Photos Most photography is assigned. State availability Captions, identification of subjects, model releases required. Reviews transparencies. Pays $40-50/photo Buys one time rights.

Columns/Departments Pays $50-200.

Tips Query with specific new story ideas rather than previously published material.

$ BACKHOME

Your Hands-On Guide to Sustainable Living, Wordsworth Communications, Inc., P.O. Box 70, Hendersonville NC 28793. (828)696-3838. Fax: (828)696-0700. E-mail: backhome@ioa.com. Website: www.backhomemagazine.com. **80% freelance written**. Bimonthly magazine. *BackHome* encourages readers to take more control over their lives by doing more for themselves: productive organic gardening; building and repairing their homes; utilizing alternative energy systems; raising crops and livestock; building furniture; toys and games and other projects; creative cooking. *BackHome* promotes respect for family activities, community programs, and the environment. Estab. 1990. Circ. 40,000. Byline given. Pays on publication. Offers $25 kill fee at publisher's discretion. Publishes ms an average of 1 year after acceptance. Buys first North American serial rights. Editorial lead time 3 months. Submit seasonal material 6 months in advance. Accepts queries by mail, e-mail, fax, phone. Accepts previously published material. Responds in 6 weeks to queries. Responds in 2 months to mss Sample copy $5 or online Guidelines available online

- The editor reports an interest in seeing more alternative energy experiences, *good* small houses, workshop projects (for handy persons, not experts), and community action others can copy.

Nonfiction Needs how-to, gardening, construction, energy, homebusiness, interview, personal experience, technical, self-sufficiency. No essays or old-timey reminiscences. **Buys 80 mss/year.** Query. Length: 750-5,000 words. **Pays $35 (approximately)/printed page.**

Reprints Send photocopy and information about when and where the material previously appeared. Pays $35/printed page

Photos Send photos Identification of subjects required. Reviews color prints, 35mm slides, JPEG photo attachments of 300 dpi. Offers additional payment for photos published Buys one time rights.

Tips Very specific in relating personal experiences in the areas of gardening, energy, and homebuilding how-to. Third-person approaches to others' experiences are also acceptable but somewhat less desirable. Clear color photo prints, especially those in which people are prominent, help immensely when deciding upon what is accepted.

BATHROOM YEARBOOK

Universal Magazines, Ltd., Unit 5, 6-8 Byfield St., North Ryde NSW 2113 Australia. (61)(2)9887-0367. Fax: (61)9805-0714. E-mail: mgardener@universalmagazines.com.au. Website: www.completehome.com.au. "Annual magazine covering all the latest bathroom products and designs.".

Nonfiction Needs general interest, new product, photo feature. Query.

$ $ $ $ BETTER HOMES AND GARDENS

1716 Locust St., Des Moines IA 50309-3023. (515)284-3044. Fax: (515)284-3763. Website: www.bhg.com. **Contact:** Gayle Butler, Editor-In-Chief. **10-15% freelance written**. Magazine "providing home service information for people who have a serious interest in their homes.". "We read all freelance articles, but much prefer to see a letter of query rather than a finished manuscript." Estab. 1922. Circ. 7,605,000. Pays on acceptance. Buys all rights.

Nonfiction Needs travel, education, gardening, health, cars, home, entertainment. "We do not deal with political subjects or with areas not connected with the home, community, and family. No poetry or fiction." **Pay rates vary**

Tips "Most stories published by this magazine go through a lengthy process of development involving both editor and writer. Some editors will consider only query letters, not unsolicited manuscripts. Direct queries to the department that best suits your storyline."

$ $ BIRDS & BLOOMS

Reiman Publications, 5400 S. 60th St., Greendale WI 53129-1404. (414)423-0100. E-mail: editors@birdsandblooms.com. Website: www.birdsandblooms.com. **15% freelance written**. Bimonthly magazine focusing on the beauty in your own backyard. *Birds & Blooms* is a sharing magazine that lets backyard enthusiasts chat with each other by exchanging personal experiences. This makes *Birds & Blooms* more like a conversation than a magazine, as readers share tips and tricks on producing beautiful blooms and attracting feathered friends to their backyards. Estab. 1995. Circ. 1,900,000. Byline given. Pays on publication. No kill fee. Publishes ms an average of 7 months after acceptance. Buys all rights. Editorial lead time 2 months. Submit seasonal material 4 months in advance. Accepts queries by mail, e-mail. Accepts simultaneous submissions. Responds in 2 months to queries. Responds in 2 months to mss. Sample copy for $2, 9x12 SAE and $1.95 postage. Guidelines for #10 SASE.

Nonfiction Needs essays, how-to, humor, inspirational, personal experience, photo feature, natural crafting and plan items for building backyard accents. No bird rescue or captive bird pieces. **Buys 12-20 mss/year.** Send complete ms. Length: 250-1,000 words. **Pays $100-400.**

Photos Send photos Identification of subjects required. Reviews transparencies, prints. Buys one time rights.

Columns/Departments Backyard Banter (odds, ends and unique things); Bird Tales (backyard bird stories); Local Lookouts (community backyard happenings), all 200 words. 12-20 Send complete ms. **Pays $50-75.**

Fillers Needs anecdotes, facts, gags. 25 Length: 10-250 words. **Pays $10-75.**

Tips Focus on conversational writing—like you're chatting with a neighbor over your fence. Manuscripts full of tips and ideas that people can use in backyards across the country have the best chance of being used. Photos that illustrate these points also increase chances of being used.

BUILD HOME

Universal Magazines, Ltd., Unit 5, 6-8 Byfield St., North Ryde NSW 2113 Australia. (61)(2)9887-0366. Fax: (61)(2)9805-0350. E-mail: kmay@universalmagazines.com.au. Website: www.completehome.com.au. Quarterly magazine featuring kit homes, display homes, split-level homes, manufactured homes and special design projects.

- Query before submitting. Versions of magazine for VIC, NSW and QLD.

$ $ CALIFORNIA HOMES

The Magazine of Architecture, the Arts and Distinctive Design, McFadden-Bray Publishing Corp., P.O. Box 8655, Newport Beach CA 92658. (949)640-1484. Fax: (949)640-1665. E-mail: edit@calhomesmagazine.com. **80% freelance written.** Bimonthly magazine covering California interiors, architecture, some food, travel, history, and current events in the field. Estab. 1997. Circ. 80,000. Byline given. Pays on publication. Offers 50% kill fee. Publishes ms an average of 3 months after acceptance. Buys first North American serial rights. Editorial lead time 3 months. Submit seasonal material 6 months in advance. Accepts queries by mail, e-mail, fax. Responds in 1 month to queries. Responds in 2 months to mss. Sample copy for $7.50. Guidelines for #10 SASE.

Nonfiction Query. Length: 500-1,000 words. **Pays $250-750.** Sometimes pays expenses of writers on assignment.

Photos State availability Captions required. Negotiates payment individually Buys one time rights.

CANADIAN GARDENING MAGAZINE

Transcontinental Media G.P., 25 Sheppard Ave. W., Suite 100, Toronto ON M2N 6S7 Canada. E-mail: editor@canadiangardening.com. Website: www.canadiangardening.com. **Mostly freelance written by assignment.** Magazine published 8 times/year covering Canadian gardening. *Canadian Gardening* is a national magazine aimed at the avid home gardener. Our readers are city gardeners with tiny lots, country gardeners with rolling acreage, indoor gardeners, rooftop gardeners, and enthusiastic beginners and experienced veterans. Estab. 1990. Circ. 152,000. Byline given. Pays on acceptance. Offers 25-50% kill fee. Buys electronic rights. Editorial lead time 4 months. Accepts queries by mail, fax. Accepts simultaneous submissions. Responds in 4 months to queries. Guidelines available online.

Nonfiction Needs how-to, planting and gardening projects, humor, personal experience, technical, plant and garden profiles, practical advice. **Buys 100 mss/year.** Query. Length: 200-1,500 words. **Pays variable amount.** Sometimes pays expenses of writers on assignment.

Photos Send image samples with submission. Reviews color photocopies and PDFs. Negotiates payment individually.

$ $ CANADIAN HOMES & COTTAGES

The In-Home Show, Ltd., 2650 Meadowvale Blvd., Unit 4, Mississauga ON L5N 6M5 Canada. (905)567-1440. Fax: (905)567-1442. E-mail: jnaisby@homesandcottages.com. Website: www.homesandcottages.com. **75% freelance written.** Magazine published 6 times/year covering building and renovating; technically comprehensive articles. Estab. 1987. Circ. 89,500. Byline given. Pays on publication. Offers 10% kill fee. Publishes ms an average of 2 months after acceptance. Buys first North American serial rights. Editorial lead time 3 months. Submit seasonal material 3 months in advance. Accepts queries by mail. Sample copy for SAE. Guidelines for #10 SASE.

Nonfiction Looking for how-to projects and simple home improvement ideas. Needs humor, building and renovation related, new product, technical. **Buys 32 mss/year.** Query. Length: 1,000-2,000 words. **Pays $300-750.** Sometimes pays expenses of writers on assignment.

Photos Send photos Captions, identification of subjects required. Reviews transparencies, prints. Negotiates payment individually Buys one time rights.
Tips Read our magazine before sending in a query. Remember that you are writing to a Canadian audience.

$ $ THE CANADIAN ORGANIC GROWER

1205 Rte 915, New Horton NB E4H 1W1 Canada. E-mail: janet@cog.ca. Website: www.cog.ca/magazine.htm. **100% freelance written**. Quarterly magazine covering organic gardening and farming. "We publish articles that are of interest to organic gardeners, farmers and consumers in Canada. We're always looking for practical how-to articles, as well as farmer profiles. At times, we include news about the organic community, recipes and stories about successful marketing strategies." Estab. 1975. Circ. 4,000. Byline given. Pays on publication. Publishes ms an average of 2-3 months after acceptance. Buys first North American serial rights. Editorial lead time 6 months. Submit seasonal material 6 months in advance. Accepts queries by mail, e-mail. Accepts previously published material. Responds in 3 weeks to queries. Responds in 1 month to mss. Sample copy available online. Guidelines available online.
Nonfiction Needs essays, general interest, how-to, garden, farm, market, process organic food, interview, new product, opinion, technical. Does not want rants. **Buys 25 mss/year.** Query. Length: 500-2,500 words. **Pays $50-250 for assigned articles. Pays $50-200 for unsolicited articles.**
Photos State availability Captions, identification of subjects required. Reviews prints, GIF/JPEG files. Negotiates payment individually. Buys one time rights.

$ CAROLINA HOMES & INTERIORS

MediaServices, Inc., P.O. Box 22617, Charleston SC 29413. (843)881-1481. Fax: (843)849-6717. E-mail: edit@mediaservices1.com. Website: www.carolinahomes.net. **80% freelance written**. 6 issues per year magazine covering coastal Carolina homes and lifestyles. We feature the finest in coastal living. Highlighting builders, designers, communities, vendors and the many recreational alternatives in the Carolinas, coastal Georgia and Florida, *CH&I* is the region's premiere home and lifestyle guide. Estab. 1983. Circ. 65,000. Byline given. Pays 30 days after publication. Offers 50% kill fee. Publishes ms an average of 2 months after acceptance. Buys one-time rights. Editorial lead time 2 months. Submit seasonal material 4 months in advance. Accepts queries by mail, e-mail. Accepts previously published material. Accepts simultaneous submissions. Responds in 2 weeks to queries. Responds in 1-2 months to mss. Sample copy free. Guidelines by email.
Nonfiction Needs general interest, historical, how-to, inspirational, interview, new product, personal experience, technical, travel. **Buys 50 mss/year.** Query with published clips. Length: 300-2,000 words. **Pays 15 cents per word.** Limit agreed upon in advance
Columns/Departments Inner Beauty, 300 words; Outer Beauty, 300 words; Coastal Custom Builders, 430 words; Hot Retirement Towns, 400 words; Things to Do, 500 words; Four!, 500 words; Day Trips, 750 words. 50 Query with published clips. **Pays 15 cents per word**
Tips Be creative. Story ideas should reflect the beauty of the region. All writers are welcome, but local writers are preferred. New writers are encouraged to query.

$ $ $ $ COASTAL LIVING

Southern Progress Corp., 2100 Lakeshore Dr., Birmingham AL 35209. (205)445-6007. Fax: (205)445-8655. E-mail: mamie_walling@timeinc.com. Website: www.coastalliving.com. Bimonthly magazine for those who live or vacation along our nation's coasts. The magazine emphasizes home design and travel, but also covers a wide variety of other lifestyle topics and coastal concerns. Estab. 1997. Circ. 660,000. Pays on acceptance. Offers 25% kill fee. Responds in 2 months to queries. Sample copy available online. Guidelines available online.
Nonfiction The magazine is roughly divided into 5 areas, with regular features, columns and departments for each area. **Currents** offers short, newsy features of 25-200 words written mostly by staff members on new products, seaside events, beach fashions, etc. **Travel** includes outdoor activities, nature experiences, and lodging and dining stories. **Homes** places the accent on casual living, with warm, welcoming houses and rooms designed for living. **Food & Entertainment** is divided into *In the Coastal Kitchen* (recipes and tips) and *Seafood Primer* (basics of buying and preparing seafood). The **Lifestyle** section is a catch all of subjects to help readers live better and more comfortably: *The Good Life* (profiles of people who have moved to the coast), *Coastal Character* (profile of someone connected to a coastal environment), *Collectibles* (treasured items/accessories with a marine connection), *So You Want to Live In.* (profiles of coastal communities), etc. Query with clips and SASE. **Pays $1/word.**
Photos State availability
Tips Query us with ideas that are very specifically targeted to the columns that are currently in the magazine.

$ $ COLORADO HOMES & LIFESTYLES

Wiesner Publishing, LLC, 7009 S. Potomac St., Centennial CO 80112-4029. (303)397-7600. Fax: (303)397-7619. E-mail: mdakotah@coloradohomesmag.com. Website: www.coloradohomesmag.com. **75% freelance written**. Upscale shelter magazine published 9 times/year containing beautiful homes, landscapes, architecture, calendar, antiques, etc. All of Colorado is included. Geared toward home-related and lifestyle areas, personality profiles, etc. Estab. 1981. Circ. 36,000. Byline given. Pays on acceptance. Offers 15% kill fee. Publishes ms an average of 3 months after acceptance. Buys first North American serial rights. Editorial lead time 3 months. Submit seasonal material 1 year in advance. Accepts queries by mail, e-mail. Accepts simultaneous submissions. Responds in 2 months to queries. Sample copy for #10 SASE.

Nonfiction Fine homes and furnishings, regional interior design trends, shopping information, interesting personalities and lifestyles—all with a Colorado slant. No personal essays, religious, humor, technical **Buys 50-75 mss/year.** Query with published clips. Length: 900-1,500 words. **Pays $200-400.** Sometimes pays expenses of writers on assignment. Provide sources with phone numbers

Photos Send photos Identification of subjects, True required. Reviews transparencies, b&w glossy prints, CDs, digital images, slides.

Tips Send query, lead paragraph, clips. Send ideas for story or stories. Include some photos, if applicable. The more interesting and unique the subject, the better. A frequent mistake made by writers is failure to provide material with a style and slant appropriate for the magazine, due to poor understanding of the focus of the magazine.

$ $ CONCRETE HOMES

Publications and Communications, Inc. (PCI), 13581 Pond Springs Rd., Suite 450, Austin TX 78729. Fax: (512)331-3950. E-mail: homes@pcinews.com. Website: concretehomesmagazine.com. **85% freelance written.** Bimonthly magazine covering homes built with concrete. *Concrete Homes* is a publication designed to be informative to consumers, builders, contractors, architects, etc., who are interested in concrete homes. The magazine profiles concrete home projects (they must be complete) and offers how-to and industry news articles. Estab. 1999. Circ. 25,000. Byline given. Pays on publication. Offers 100% kill fee. Publishes ms an average of 2 months after acceptance. Buys all rights. Editorial lead time 2 months. Submit seasonal material 3-4 months in advance. Accepts queries by mail, e-mail. Accepts simultaneous submissions. Responds in 1 month to queries. Responds in 1 month to mss. Sample copy available online. Guidelines available online.

Nonfiction Needs how-to, interview, new product, technical. **Buys 30-40 mss/year.** Query or query with published clips Length: 800-2,000 words. **Pays $200-250.** Sometimes pays expenses of writers on assignment.

Photos State availability Captions required. Reviews 8x10 transparencies, prints, GIF/JPEG files. Offers no additional payment for photos accepted with ms. Buys all rights.

Tips Demonstrate awareness of concrete homes and some knowledge of the construction/building industry.

$ $ $ $ COTTAGE LIFE

Quarto Communications, 54 St. Patrick St., Toronto ON M5T 1V1 Canada. (416)599-2000. Fax: (416)599-4070. E-mail: editorial@cottagelife.com. Website: www.cottagelife.com. **80% freelance written.** Bimonthly magazine. *"Cottage Life* is written and designed for the people who own and spend time at waterfront cottages throughout Canada and bordering US states, with a strong focus on Ontario. The magazine has a strong service slant, combining useful `how-to' journalism with coverage of the people, trends, and issues in cottage country. Regular columns are devoted to boating, fishing, watersports, projects, real estate, cooking, design and decor, nature, personal cottage experience, and environmental, political, and financial issues of concern to cottagers." Estab. 1988. Circ. 70,000. Byline given. Pays on acceptance. Offers 50-100% kill fee. Publishes ms an average of 2 months after acceptance. Buys first North American serial rights. Guidelines available online.

Nonfiction Needs book excerpts, expose, historical, how-to, humor, interview, personal experience, photo feature, technical. **Buys 90 mss/year.** Query with published clips and SAE with Canadian postage or IRCs. Length: 150-3,500 words. **Pays $100-3,000.** Pays expenses of writers on assignment.

Columns/Departments On the Waterfront (front department featuring short news, humor, human interest, and service items), 400 words maximum. **Pays $50-400.** Cooking, Real Estate, Fishing, Nature, Watersports, Decor, Personal Experience, and Issues, all 150-1,200 words. **Pays $100-1,200**. Query with published clips and SAE with Canadian postage or IRCs, or by e-mail.

Tips "If you have not previously written for the magazine, the `On the Waterfront' section is an excellent place to break in."

COUNTRY LIVING

The Hearst Corp., 300 W. 57th St., New York NY 10019. (212)649-3500. Monthly magazine covering home design and interior decorating with an emphasis on country style. A lifestyle magazine for readers who appreciate the warmth and traditions associated with American home and family life. Each monthly issue embraces American country decorating and includes features on furniture, antiques, gardening, home building, real estate, cooking, entertaining and travel. Estab. 1978. Circ. 1,600,000. No kill fee.

Nonfiction Subjects covered include decorating, collecting, cooking, entertaining, gardening/landscaping, home building/remodeling/restoring, travel, and leisure activities. **Buys 20-30 mss/year.** Send complete ms and SASE **Payment varies**

Columns/Departments Query first.

Tips Know the magazine, know the market, and know how to write a good story that will interest *our* readers.

$ $ COUNTRY'S BEST LOG HOMES

F+W Media, Inc., 700 E. State St., Iola WI 54990. E-mail: don.butler@fwpubs.com. Website: www.loghomesnetwork.com. **50% freelance written**. Bimonthly magazine covering milled log homes. *Country's Best Log Homes* focuses solely on milled log homes and related subject matter. It is designed for people who are interested in building a log home and giving them the information they need to finance, design, buy, build, decorate, landscape, and maintain a log home. The feature articles describe individual home owners' experiences in building a log home. Departments discuss the nuts and bolts of log home construction. Estab. 1996. Circ. 120,000. Byline given. Pays on publication. Offers 50% kill fee. Publishes ms an average of 8 months after acceptance. Buys first North American serial rights, buys electronic rights. Editorial lead time 2 months. Accepts queries by e-mail. Responds in 2 months to queries.

- Magazine looking for new freelance writers that would work by assignment only. No unsolicited mss.

Nonfiction Needs historical, deals with historical buildings made of log, such as lodges, Adirondack camps, famous homes, railway stations, etc., how-to, covers anything dealing with building a log home; i.e., how-to select a log home producer, builder contractor, etc., interview, with homeowners, builders, architects, craftspeople of log homes. *No unsolicited mss*; articles by assignment only. **Buys 20 mss/year.** Query with published clips. Length: 800-1,200 words. **Pays $350-450 for assigned articles.**

Photos State availability Captions, identification of subjects, model releases required. Reviews GIF/JPEG files. Negotiates payment individually. Buys one time rights.

Columns/Departments Design (how to design the log home you want); Money (how to find financing for construction; getting the best mortgage rates); Traditions (focus on historic log buildings); Step-by-Step (log home building); all 1,100 words. 30 Query with published clips. **Pays $350-450.**

Tips Send clips that reflect the content of the magazine (architecture, design, decorating, landscaping, building); the clips do not have to be specific to the log home industry.

$ $ $ $ D HOME AND GARDEN MAGAZINE

D Magazine Partners, 4311 Oak Lawn Ave., Dallas TX 75219. (214)939-3636. Fax: (214)748-4153. Website: www.dhomeandgarden.com. **50% freelance written**. Magazine published 7 times/year covering Dallas home and garden. Estab. 1999. Circ. 25,000. Byline given. Pays on acceptance. Offers 25% kill fee. Publishes ms an average of 2-3 months after acceptance. Buys all rights. Editorial lead time 2-3 months. Submit seasonal material 2-3 months in advance. Accepts queries by mail, e-mail, fax, phone. Sample copy available online. Guidelines free.

Nonfiction Green issue (January/February). Does not want anything not specific to Dallas. **Buys 3-5 mss/year.** Query. Length: 800-2,000 words. **Pays $400-1,500.** Sometimes pays expenses of writers on assignment.

Photos Contact: Contact Andrea Tomek, art director. State availability Identification of subjects required. Reviews contact sheets, GIF/JPEG files. Negotiates payment individually. Buys one time rights.

$ $ DREAM HOUSE MAGAZINE

Western Canada's Premier fine home and lifestyle publication, Dream House Publications Inc., 106-873 Beatty St., Vancouver BC V6B 2M6 Canada. (604)681-3463. Fax: (604)681-3494. E-mail: tracey@dreamhousemag.com. Website: www.dreamhousemag.com. **50% freelance written**. Magazine published 8 times/year covering fine homes, luxury lifestyle. *Dream House Magazine* serves its readers the best of the best in fine homes and luxury lifestyles. Estab. 2001. Circ. 28,000. Byline given. Pays within 30 days of publication. Offers 50% kill fee. Publishes ms an average of 1 month after acceptance. Buys first North American serial rights. Editorial lead time 3 months. Submit seasonal material 1 month in advance. Accepts queries by mail, e-mail. Guidelines free.

Nonfiction Needs general interest, historical, humor, interview, new product, photo feature, travel. Does not want memoirs. Query with published clips. Length: 500-800 words. **Pays 25-50¢/word.**

Photos Send photos Reviews TIFF files only (300 dpi at 8x10). Offers no additional payment for photos accepted with ms. Buys one time rights.

Columns/Departments Finance; Real Estate; Insurance, all 500-800 words. Query with published clips.

Tips Read magazine. Study our audience. Be well connected in the luxury marketplace.

$ $ EARLY AMERICAN LIFE

Firelands Media Group LLC, P.O. Box 221228, Shaker Heights OH 44122-0996. E-mail: queries@firelandsmedia.com. Website: www.ealonline.com. **60% freelance written.** Bimonthly magazine for "people who are interested in capturing the warmth and beauty of the 1600-1840 period and using it in their homes and lives today. They are interested in antiques, traditional crafts, architecture, restoration, and collecting.". Estab. 1970. Circ. 90,000. Byline given. Pays on acceptance. No kill fee. Publishes ms an average of 1 year after acceptance. Buys worldwide rights. Accepts queries by mail, e-mail. Responds in 3 months to queries. Sample copy and writer's guidelines for 9x12 SAE with $2.50 postage

Nonfiction "Social history (the story of the people, not epic heroes and battles), travel to historic sites, antiques and reproductions, restoration, architecture, and decorating. We try to entertain as we inform. We're always on the lookout for good pieces on any of our subjects. Would like to see more on how real people did something great to their homes." **Buys 40 mss/year.** Send complete ms. Length: 750-3,000 words. **Pays $350-700, additionally for photos.**

Tips "Our readers are eager for ideas on how to bring early America into their lives. Conceive a new approach to satisfy their related interests in arts, crafts, travel to historic sites, and especially in houses decorated in the Early American style. Write to entertain and inform at the same time. We are visually oriented, so writers are asked to supply images or suggest sources for illustrations."

$ $ $ $ ECOHOME DESIGNS

Your source for sustainable house plans, Hanley Wood, 1 Thomas Cir., #600, Washington DC 20005-5811. (202)729-3525. E-mail: shyoun@hanleywood.com. Website: www.hanleywood.com. **75% freelance written.** Semiannual magazine covering sustainable building, green design, predrawn blueprints. Whether your definition of green building is about the use of sustainable materials or about high performance and energy savings, *Eco-Home Designs* is the perfect place to find the latest editorial about the green building phenomenon as well as predrawn house plans that feature comfortable green designs. Readers will find a wealth of insights about the newest building materials and construction methods, as well as tried-and-true tips on building an energy-efficient custom home. Estab. 2009. Byline given. Pays on acceptance. Offers 50% kill fee. Publishes ms an average of 2 months after acceptance. Makes work-for-hire assignments. Editorial lead time 6 months. Submit seasonal material 3 months in advance. Accepts queries by e-mail. Accepts previously published material. Accepts simultaneous submissions. Responds in 1 week to queries. Responds in 1 month to mss. Guidelines available.

Nonfiction Contact: Simon Hyoun, editor. Needs how-to, choose green building materials; practice green building concepts, new product, photo feature, technical. We do not want personal stories of home building experiences. **Buys 12 mss/yr. mss/year.** Query with published clips. Length: 500-1,000 words. **Pays $.80-$1/ word for assigned articles. Pays $.80-$1/word for unsolicited articles.**

Tips Submissions should demonstrate knowledge of current trends in green building and residential design, as well as the custom home building market.

$ $ $ FINE GARDENING

Taunton Press, 63 S. Main St., P.O. Box 5506, Newtown CT 06470-5506. (203)426-8171. Fax: (203)426-3434. E-mail: fg@taunton.com. Website: www.finegardening.com. Bimonthly magazine. High-value magazine on landscape and ornamental gardening. Articles written by avid gardeners—first person, hands-on gardening experiences. Estab. 1988. Circ. 200,000. Byline given. Pays on acceptance. No kill fee. Publishes ms an average of 6 months after acceptance. Buys all rights. Editorial lead time 1 year. Submit seasonal material 1 year in advance. Accepts queries by mail, e-mail, fax. Guidelines free.

Nonfiction Needs how-to, personal experience, photo feature, book reviews. **Buys 60 mss/year.** Query. Length: 1,000-3,000 words. **Pays $300-1,200.**

Photos Send photos Reviews digital images. Buys serial rights

Columns/Departments Book, video and software reviews (on gardening); Last Word (essays/serious, humorous, fact or fiction). Length: 250-500 words. 30 Query. **Pays $ 50- 200.**

Tips It's most important to have solid first-hand experience as a gardener. Tell us what you've done with your own landscape and plants.

$ $ FINE HOMEBUILDING

The Taunton Press, 63 S. Main St., P.O. Box 5506, Newtown CT 06470-5506. (203)426-8171. Fax: (203)426-3434. E-mail: fh@taunton.com. Website: www.taunton.com. Bimonthly magazine for builders, architects, contractors, owner/builders and others who are seriously involved in building new houses or reviving old ones. Estab. 1981. Circ. 300,000. Byline given. Pays half on acceptance, half on publication. Offers kill fee. Offers on acceptance payment as kill fee. Publishes ms an average of 1 year after acceptance. Buys first rights. Reprint rights Responds in 1 month to queries. Writer's guidelines for SASE and on website.

Nonfiction We're interested in almost all aspects of home building, from laying out foundations to capping cupolas. Query with outline, description, photographs, sketches and SASE. **Pays $150/published page.**

Photos Take lots of work-in-progress photos. Color print film, ASA 400, from either Kodak or Fuji works best. If you prefer to use slide film, use ASA 100. Keep track of the negatives; we will need them for publication. If you're not sure what to use or how to go about it, feel free to call for advice.

Columns/Departments Tools & Materials, Reviews, Questions & Answers, Tips & Techniques, Cross Section, What's the Difference?, Finishing Touches, Great Moments, Breaktime, Drawing Board (design column). Query with outline, description, photographs, sketches and SASE. **Payment varies**

Tips Our chief contributors are home builders, architects and other professionals. We're more interested in your point of view and technical expertise than your prose style. Adopt an easy, conversational style and define any obscure terms for non-specialists. We try to visit all our contributors and rarely publish building projects we haven't seen, or authors we haven't met.

$ GARDEN COMPASS

Streamopolis, 1450 Front St., San Diego CA 92101. (619)239-2202. Fax: (619)239-4621. E-mail: editor@gardencompass.com. Website: www.gardencompass.com. **70% freelance written**. Bimonthly magazine covering gardening. *Garden Compass* is entertaining and offers sound practical advice for West Coast gardeners. Estab. 1992. Circ. 112,000. Byline given. Pays on publication. Offers $50 kill fee. Publishes ms an average of 10 weeks after acceptance. Buys first North American serial rights. Editorial lead time 6 months. Submit seasonal material 6 months in advance. Accepts queries by mail, e-mail. Accepts simultaneous submissions. Responds in 1 month to queries. Sample copy free.

Photos State availability of or send photos Identification of subjects required. Reviews contact sheets, transparencies, GIF/JPEG files. Negotiates payment individually. Buys one time rights.

Columns/Departments Pest Patrol (plant posts/diseases), 400-800 words; e-Gardening (garden info on the Web), 400-800 words; Book Review (gardening books), 400-600 words; Fruit Trees, 800-1,200 words. Query with published clips. **Payment varies.**

Fillers Needs anecdotes, facts, newsbreaks. Length: 30-150 words. **Pays $25**

$ $ $ $ HORTICULTURE

F+W Media, Inc., 4700 E. Galbraith Rd., Cincinnati OH 45236. (513)531-2690. Fax: (513)891-7153. E-mail: meghan.lynch@fwpubs.com. Website: www.hortmag.com. Bimonthly magazine. *Horticulture*, the country's oldest gardening magazine, is designed for active home gardeners. Our goal is to offer a blend of text, photographs and illustrations that will both instruct and inspire readers. Circ. 185,000. Byline given. Offers kill fee. Buys all rights. Submit seasonal material 10 months in advance. Accepts queries by mail, e-mail, fax. Responds in 3 months to queries. Guidelines for SASE or by e-mail.

Nonfiction Articles should be grounded in fact and serve the purpose of helping readers become better gardeners. However, we appreciate good writing and unique voices, and personal experience, anecdote and opinion play a part in our best articles. **Buys 70 mss/year.** Query with published clips, subject background material and SASE. Length: 900-1,200 words. **Pays $600-1,000.**

Columns/Departments Length: 100-800 words. Query with published clips, subject background material and SASE. Include disk where possible. **Pays $50-750.**

Tips We believe every article must offer ideas or illustrate principles that our readers might apply on their own gardens. Our readers want to become better, more creative gardeners.

$ $ $ $ HOUSE BEAUTIFUL

The Hearst Corp., 300 W. 57th St., New York NY 10019. (212)903-5000. Website: www.housebeautiful.com. Monthly magazine. Targeted toward affluent, educated readers ages 30-40. Covers home design and decoration, gardening and entertaining, interior design, architecture and travel. Circ. 865,352. No kill fee. Editorial lead time 3 months.

- Query first.

KITCHENS & BATHROOMS QUARTERLY

Universal Magazines, Ltd., Unit 5, 6-8 Byfield St., North Ryde NSW 2113 Australia. (61)(2)9887-0367. Fax: (61)(2)9887-0350. E-mail: mgardener@universalmagazines.com.au. Website: www.completehome.com.au. "Quarterly magazine for planning, designing, building or renovating your kitchen or bathroom.".

Nonfiction Needs general interest, how-to, new product, photo feature. Query.

KITCHEN YEARBOOK

Universal Magazines, Ltd., Unit 5, 6-8 Byfield St., North Ryde NSW 2113 Australia. (61)(2)9887-0367. Fax: (61)(2)9887-0350. E-mail: mgardener@universalmagazines.com.au. Website: www.completehome.com.au. Annual magazine covering the year's most innovative and inspiring kitchen designs.

Nonfiction Needs general interest, how-to, inspirational, new product, photo feature. Query.

LUXURY KITCHENS & BATHROOMS

Universal Magazines, Ltd., Unit 5, 6-8 Byfield St., North Ryde NSW 2113 Australia. (61)(2)9887-0367. Fax: (61)(2)9887-0350. E-mail: mgardener@universalmagazines.com.au. Website: www.completehome.com.au. Annual magazine covering luxury kitchen and bathroom projects and products.

Nonfiction Needs new product. Query.

$ $ MASTERGARDENER MAGAZINE

Washington State Fruit Commission, 105 S. 18th St., #217, Yakima WA 98901-2177. (509)575-2315. E-mail: jim@mastergardeneronline.com. Website: www.mastergardeneronline.com. **20% freelance written**. Quarterly magazine covering home gardening. Estab. 2007. Circ. 12,000. Byline given. Pays on acceptance. Publishes ms an average of 3 months after acceptance. Buys first rights, buys electronic rights. Accepts queries by mail, e-mail. Accepts simultaneous submissions. Responds in 1 week to queries. Responds in 1 month to mss. Sample copy free. Guidelines free.

Nonfiction "We work with writers to choose topics of mutual interest." **Buys 50 mss/year.** Query. Length: 500-1,500 words. **Pays 40-50¢/word.** Sometimes pays expenses of writers on assignment.

Photos Reviews GIF/JPEG files. Negotiates payment individually. Buys one time rights.

Tips "We appreciate well-written, accurate information. We deal with our writers with honesty and expect the same in return."

$ $ MILWAUKEE HOME & FINE LIVING

Journal Sentinel Specialty Media Division, 4101 W. Burnham St., West Milwaukee WI 53215. (414)647-4748. Fax: (414)647-4745. E-mail: rbundy@journalsentinel.com. Website: www.milwaukee-home.com. **80% freelance written**. Monthly magazine covering homes, gardens, art, furnishings, food, fashion. Estab. 2004. Circ. 17,500. Byline given. Pays on publication. Offers 25% kill fee. Publishes ms an average of 6 months after acceptance. Buys first North American serial rights, electronic rights. Editorial lead time 6 months. Submit seasonal material 1 year in advance. Accepts queries by mail, e-mail. Responds in 6 weeks to queries. Sample copy for sae with 10x13 envelope and 2 First-Class stamps. Guidelines available online.

Nonfiction Needs general interest, historical, interview, nostalgic, photo feature feature, profile. **Buys 80 mss/year.** Query with published clips. Length: 100-1,200 words. **Pays $25-360.** Sometimes pays expenses of writers on assignment.

Columns/Departments Insights (home furnishings, interior design trends, new products); Fine Living (travel, entertaining, food and wine, performing arts); Artisan (local craftspeople); In the Garden (landscaping tips and advice, plant recommendations). **Pays $25-360.**

Tips "Please submit queries on local topics relating to specific homes and gardens, and products that can be obtained in the Milwaukee, Wisconsin, 7-county area. Read the magazine for style and content."

$ $ MOUNTAIN LIVING

Network Communications, Inc., 1777 S. Harrison St., Suite 1200, Denver CO 80210. (303)248-2062. Fax: (303)248-2064. E-mail: irawlings@mountainliving.com. Website: www.mountainliving.com. **50% freelance written**. Magazine published 10 times/year covering architecture, interior design and lifestyle issues for people who live in, visit, or hope to live in the mountains. Estab. 1994. Circ. 48,000. Byline given. Pays on acceptance. Offers 15% kill fee. Publishes ms an average of 4 months after acceptance. Buys one-time magazine rights, plus right to archive piece online. Editorial lead time 6 months. Submit seasonal material 8-12 months in advance. Accepts queries by mail, e-mail. Responds in 6 weeks to queries. Responds in 2 months to mss. Sample copy for $7. Guidelines by email.

Nonfiction Needs photo feature, travel, home features. **Buys 30 mss/year.** Query with published clips. Length: 500-1,000 words. **Pays $250-600.** Sometimes pays expenses of writers on assignment.

Photos Provide photos (slides, transparencies, or on disk, saved as TIFF and at least 300 dpi). State availability All features photography is assigned to photographers who specialize in interior photography. Negotiates payment individually Buys one-time rights plus rights to run photo on Web site.

Columns/Departments ML Recommends; Short Travel Tips; New Product Information; Art; Insider's Guide; Entertaining. Length: 300-800 words. 35 Query with published clips. **Pays $50-500.**

Tips A deep understanding of and respect for the mountain environment is essential. Think out of the box. We love to be surprised. Write a brilliant, short query, and always send clips. Before you query, please read the magazine to get a sense of who we are and what we like.

$ $ $ $ ORGANIC GARDENING

Rodale, 33 E. Minor St., Emmaus PA 18098. (610)967-8363. Fax: (610)967-7722. E-mail: og@rodale.com. Website: www.organicgardening.com. **75% freelance written**. Bimonthly magazine. *Organic Gardening* is for gardeners who enjoy gardening as an integral part of a healthy lifestyle. Editorial shows readers how to grow flowers, edibles, and herbs, as well as information on ecological landscaping. Also covers organic topics including soil building and pest control. Estab. 1942. Circ. 300,000. Byline given. Pays between acceptance and publication. No kill fee. Buys all rights. Accepts queries by mail, fax. Responds in 3 months to queries.

Nonfiction Query with published clips and outline **Pays up to $1/word for experienced writers.**

Tips If you have devised a specific technique that's worked in your garden, have insight into the needs and uses of a particular plant or small group of plants, or have designed whole gardens that integrate well with their environment, and, if you have the capacity to clearly describe what you've learned to other gardeners in a simple but engaging manner, please send us your article ideas. Read a recent issue of the magazine thoroughly before you submit your ideas. If you have an idea that you believe fits with our content, send us a 1-page description of it that will grab our attention in the same manner you intend to entice readers into your article. Be sure to briefly explain why your idea is uniquely suited to our magazine. (We will not publish an article that has already appeared elsewhere. Also, please tell us if you are simultaneously submitting your idea to another magazine.) Tell us about the visual content of your idea—that is, what photographs or illustrations would you suggest be included with your article to get the ideas and information across to readers? If you have photographs, let us know. If you have never been published before, consider whether your idea fits into our Gardener to Gardener department. The shorter, narrowly focused articles in the department and its conversational tone make for a more accessible avenue into the magazine for inexperienced writers.

$ $ ROMANTIC HOMES

Y-Visionary Publishing, 265 Anita Dr., Suite 120, Orange CA 92868. E-mail: editorial@romantichomes.com. Website: www.romantichomesmag.com. **70% freelance written**. Monthly magazine covering home decor. *Romantic Homes* is the magazine for women who want to create a warm, intimate, and casually elegant home—a haven that is both a gathering place for family and friends and a private refuge from the pressures of the outside world. The *Romantic Homes* reader is personally involved in the decor of her home. Features offer unique ideas and how-to advice on decorating, home furnishings, and gardening. Departments focus on floor and wall coverings, paint, textiles, refinishing, architectural elements, artwork, travel, and entertaining. Every article responds to the reader's need to create a beautiful, attainable environment, providing her with the style ideas and resources to achieve her own romantic home. Estab. 1994. Circ. 200,000. Byline given. Pays 30-60 days upon receipt of invoice. No kill fee. Publishes ms an average of 4 months after acceptance. Buys all rights. Editorial lead time 5 months. Submit seasonal material 6 months in advance. Accepts queries by mail, fax. Accepts simultaneous submissions. Responds in 2 weeks to queries. Responds in 2 months to mss. Guidelines for #10 SASE.

Nonfiction Not just for dreaming, *Romantic Homes* combines unique ideas and inspirations with practical how-to advice on decorating, home furnishings, remodeling, and gardening for readers who are actively involved in improving their homes. Every article responds to the reader's need to know how to do it and where to find it. Needs essays, how-to, new product, personal experience, travel. **Buys 150 mss/year.** Query with published clips. Length: 1,000-1,200 words. **Pays $500.**

Photos State availability of or send photos Captions, identification of subjects, model releases required. Reviews transparencies. Buys all rights.

Columns/Departments Departments cover antiques, collectibles, artwork, shopping, travel, refinishing, architectural elements, flower arranging, entertaining, and decorating. Length: 400-600 words. **Pays $250.**

Tips Submit great ideas with photos.

$ $ SAN DIEGO HOME/GARDEN LIFESTYLES

McKinnon Enterprises, Box 719001, San Diego CA 92171-9001. (858)571-1818. Fax: (858)571-6379. E-mail: carlson@sdhg.net; ditler@sdhg.net. **50% freelance written**. Monthly magazine covering homes, gardens, food, intriguing people, real estate, art, culture, and local travel for residents of San Diego city and county. Estab. 1979. Circ. 50,000. Byline given. Pays on publication. No kill fee. Publishes ms an average of 3 months after acceptance. Buys first North American serial rights. Submit seasonal material 3 months in advance. Accepts queries by mail, e-mail, fax, phone. Responds in 3 months to queries. Sample copy for $4.

Nonfiction "Residential architecture and interior design (San Diego-area homes only), remodeling (must be well-designed—little do-it-yourself), residential landscape design, furniture, other features oriented toward upscale readers interested in living the cultured good life in San Diego. Articles must have a local angle." Query with published clips. Length: 700-2,000 words. **Pays $50-375.**

Tips "No out-of-town, out-of-state subject material. Most freelance work is accepted from local writers. Gear stories to the unique quality of San Diego. We try to offer only information unique to San Diego—people, places, shops, resources, etc."

$ $ SEATTLE HOMES & LIFESTYLES

Network Communications, Inc., 1221 E. Pike St., Suite 305, Seattle WA 98122-3930. (206)322-6699. Fax: (206)322-2799. E-mail: gsmith@seattlehomesmag.com. Website: www.seattlehomesmag.com. **60% freelance written**. Magazine published 10 times/year covering home design and lifestyles. *Seattle Homes and Lifestyles* showcases the finest homes and gardens in the Northwest, and the personalities and lifestyles that make this region special. We try to help our readers take full advantage of the resources the region has to offer with in-depth coverage of events, entertaining, shopping, food, and wine. And we write about it with a warm, personal approach that underscores our local perspective. Estab. 1996. Circ. 30,000. Byline given. Pays on acceptance. Offers 25% kill fee. Publishes ms an average of 2 months after acceptance. Buys first rights, buys electronic rights. Editorial lead time 3 months. Submit seasonal material 4 months in advance. Accepts previously published material. Accepts simultaneous submissions. Responds in 4 months to queries.

Nonfiction Needs general interest, how-to, decorating, cooking, interview, photo feature. No essays, travel stories, sports coverage. **Buys 95 mss/year.** Query with published clips via mail. Length: 300-1,500 words. **Pays $150-400.**

Photos State availability Captions, identification of subjects, model releases required. Reviews contact sheets, transparencies, prints. Negotiates payment individually Buys one time rights.

Tips We're always looking for experienced journalists with clips that demonstrate a knack for writing engaging, informative features. We're also looking for writers knowledgeable about architecture and decorating who can communicate a home's flavor and spirit through the written word. Since all stories are assigned by the editor, please do not submit manuscripts. Send a résumé and 3 published samples of your work. Story pitches are not encouraged. Please mail all submissions—do not e-mail or fax. Please don't call—we'll call you if we have an assignment. Writers from the Seattle area only.

$ $ $ SMART HOMEOWNER

Navigator Publishing, P.O. Box 569, Portland ME 04112. (207)772-2466. Fax: (207)772-2879. E-mail: editors@smarthomeownermag.com. Website: www.smarthomeownermag.com. **75% freelance written**. Bimonthly magazine covering smart residential building practices, greenbuilding, energy efficiency, healthy home building and home automation. We tell our readers how to build better homes. Primarily, we focus on 3 areas of residential home building: greenbuilding (eco-friendly building), energy efficiency, and healthy home building. We focus on products and systems homeowners can use to build better homes. We are not a DIY magazine, but rather strive to educate our readers about the options available to them if they are building or remodeling a home. Among the subjects we cover: Energy Star appliances, reclaimed flooring, nontoxic building materials, energy-efficient windows and doors, mold-resistant building materials, efficient heating and cooling systems, and anything else for residential building that is innovative, durable and nontoxic, and that results in a more efficient, healthy, comfortable home. Byline given. Pays half before publication; half on publication. Offers $150 kill fee. Publishes ms an average of 2-4 months after acceptance. Buys first North American serial rights, buys all rights. Makes work-for-hire assignments. Editorial lead time 4 months. Submit seasonal material 4 months in advance. Accepts queries by mail, e-mail, fax. Accepts simultaneous submissions. Responds in 2 weeks to queries. Responds in 1 month to mss. Sample copy available online. Guidelines free.

Nonfiction Needs general interest, interview, new product, technical. Green Issue (May/June); Home Energy Issue (September/October), both annual issues. Does not want DIY articles or anything that's too far out of the mainstream. We are a mainstream greenbuilding magazine. **Buys 45 mss/year.** Query. Length: 800-2,400 words. **Pays $400-1,200.** Sometimes pays expenses of writers on assignment.

Photos State availability Reviews contact sheets, GIF/JPEG files. Negotiates payment individually Buys one time rights.

Columns/Departments Greenbuilding (residential green/eco-friendly residential building); Home Tech (home automation, energy efficient controls), 1,000-1,400 words. 18-25 Query. **Pays $500-700.**

Tips We're particularly interested in what we call 'whole-house' articles, which focus on a single home and the resident homeowners.

SOUTHERN ACCENTS

Southern Progress Corp., 2100 Lakeshore Dr., Birmingham AL 35209. (205)445-6000. Fax: (205)445-6990. Website: www.southernaccents.com. *Southern Accents* celebrates the finest of the South. Estab. 1977. Circ. 370,000. No kill fee. Accepts queries by mail. Responds in 2 months to queries.

Nonfiction Each issue features the finest homes and gardens along with a balance of features that reflect the affluent lifestyles of its readers, including architecture, antiques, entertaining, collecting, and travel. Query by mail with SASE, bio, clips, and photos.

Tips Query us only with specific ideas targeted to our current columns.

$ $ $ ☐ STYLE AT HOME

Transcontinental Media, G.P., 25 Sheppard Ave. W., Suite 100, Toronto ON M2N 6S7 Canada. (416)733-7600. Fax: (416)218-3632. E-mail: letters@styleathome.com. Website: www.styleathome.com. **Contact:** Gail Johnston Habs, editor-in-chief. **85% freelance written**. Magazine published 12 times/year. "The number one magazine choice of Canadian women aged 25 to 54 who have a serious interest in decorating. Provides an authoritative, stylish collection of inspiring and accessible Canadian interiors, decor projects; reports on style design trends." Estab. 1997. Circ. 235,000. Byline given. Pays on acceptance. Offers 50% kill fee. Buys first rights, buys electronic rights. Editorial lead time 4 months. Submit seasonal material 6 months in advance. Accepts queries by e-mail. Responds in 1 month to queries. Responds in 2 weeks to mss. Guidelines by email.

Nonfiction Needs interview, new product. No how-to; these are planned in-house. **Buys 80 mss/year.** Query with published clips; include scouting shots with interior story queries. Length: 300-700 words. **Pays $300-1,000.** Sometimes pays expenses of writers on assignment.

Tips "Break in by familiarizing yourself with the type of interiors we show. Be very up-to-date with the design and home decor market in Canada. Provide a lead to a fabulous home or garden."

$ $ $ SU CASA

At Home in the Southwest, Hacienda Press, 4100 Wolcott Ave. NE, Suite B, Albuquerque NM 87109. (505)344-1783. Fax: (505)345-3295. E-mail: cpoling@sucasamagazine.com. Website: www.sucasamagazine.com. **80% freelance written**. Magazine published 5 times/year covering southwestern homes, building, design, architecture for the reader comtemplating building, remodeling, or decorating a Santa Fe style home. Su Casa is tightly focused on Southwestern home building, architecture and design. In particular, we feature New Mexico homes. We also cover alternative construction, far-out homes and contemporary design. Estab. 1995. Circ. 40,000. Byline given. Pays on acceptance. Offers 50% kill fee. Publishes ms an average of 6 months after acceptance. Buys one-time rights, buys second serial (reprint) rights. Editorial lead time 6-9 months. Submit seasonal material 9 months in advance. Accepts queries by mail, e-mail, fax, phone. Responds in 1 week to queries. Responds in 1 month to mss. Sample copy free. Guidelines free.

- All the departments are assigned long term. We encourage writers to pitch feature story ideas. We don't cover trends or concepts, but rather homes that express them.

Nonfiction Needs book excerpts, essays, interview, personal experience, photo feature. The summer issue covers kitchen and bath topics. Does not want how-to articles, product reviews or features, no trends in southwest homes. **Buys 30 mss/year.** Query with published clips. Length: 1,000-2,500 words. **Pays $250-1,000.** Sometimes pays expenses of writers on assignment. Limit agreed upon in advance

Photos State availability of or send photos Captions, identification of subjects, model releases, True required. Reviews GIF/JPEG files. Offers $25-150/photo. Buys one time rights.

$ $ TEXAS GARDENER

The Magazine for Texas Gardeners, by Texas Gardeners, Suntex Communications, Inc., P.O. Box 9005, Waco TX 76714-9005. (254)848-9393. Fax: (254)848-9779. E-mail: info@texasgardener.com. Website: www.texasgardener.com. **80% freelance written. Works with a small number of new/unpublished writers each year.** Bimonthly magazine covering vegetable and fruit production, ornamentals, and home landscape information for home gardeners in Texas. Estab. 1981. Circ. 20,000. Byline given. Pays on publication. No kill fee. Publishes ms an average of 4 months after acceptance. Buys first North American serial rights, buys all rights. Submit seasonal material 6 months in advance. Accepts queries by mail, e-mail, fax. Responds in 2 months to queries. Sample copy for $4.25 and SAE with 5 first-class stamps. Guidelines for #10 SASE.

Nonfiction We use articles that relate to Texas gardeners. We also like personality profiles on hobby gardeners and professional horticulturists who are doing somehting unique. Needs how-to, humor, interview, photo feature. **Buys 50-60 mss/year.** Query with published clips. Length: 800-2,400 words. **Pays $50-200.**

Photos We prefer superb color and b&w photos; 90% of photos used are color. Send photos Identification of subjects, model releases required. Reviews contact sheets, 2 ¼x2 ¼ or 35mm color transparencies, 8x10 b&w prints. Pays negotiable rates

Columns/Departments Between Neighbors **Pays $25**

Tips First, be a Texan. Then come up with a good idea of interest to home gardeners in this state. Be specific. Stick to feature topics like `How Alley Gardening Became a Texas Tradition.' Leave topics like `How to Control Fire Blight' to the experts. High quality photos could make the difference. We would like to add several writers to our group of regular contributors and would make assignments on a regular basis. Fillers are easy to come up with in-house. We want good writers who can produce accurate and interesting copy. Frequent mistakes made by writers in completing an article assignment for us are that articles are not slanted toward Texas gardening, show inaccurate or too little gardening information, or lack good writing style.

$ $ TEXAS HOME & LIVING

Publications & Communications, Inc., 13581 Pond Springs Rd., Suite 450, Austin TX 78729. (512)381-0576. Fax: (512)331-3950. E-mail: bronas@pcinews.com. Website: www.texasHomeandLiving.com. **75% freelance written**. Bimonthly magazine. "*Texas Home & Living*.the magazine of design, architecture and Texas lifestyle." Estab. 1994. Circ. 50,000. Byline given. Pays on publication. Offers 100% kill fee. Publishes ms an average of 4 months after acceptance. Buys all rights. Editorial lead time 4 months. Submit seasonal material 6 months in advance. Accepts queries by mail, e-mail, fax. Responds in 1 month to queries. Responds in 2 months to mss. Sample copy free. Guidelines available online.

Nonfiction Needs how-to, interview, new product, travel. **Buys 18 mss/year.** Query with published clips. Length: 500-2,000 words. **Pays $200 for assigned articles.** Pays expenses of writers on assignment.

Photos State availability of or send photos Captions required. Reviews negatives, transparencies, prints. Offers no additional payment for photos accepted with ms. Buys all rights.

$ $ $ $ THIS OLD HOUSE MAGAZINE

Time Inc., 135 W. 50th St., 10th Floor, New York NY 10020. (212)522-9465. Fax: (212)522-9435. E-mail: toh_letters@thisoldhouse.com. Website: www.thisoldhouse.com. **40% freelance written**. Magazine published 10 times/year covering home design, renovation, and maintenance. *This Old House* is the ultimate resource for readers whose homes are their passions. The magazine's mission is threefold: to inform with lively service journalism and reporting on innovative new products and materials, to inspire with beautiful examples of fine craftsmanship and elegant architectural design, and to instruct with clear step-by-step projects that will enhance a home or help a homeowner maintain one. The voice of the magazine is not that of a rarefied design maven or a linear Mr. Fix It, but rather that of an eyes-wide-open, in-the-trenches homeowner who's eager for advice, tools, and techniques that'll help him realize his dream of a home. Estab. 1995. Circ. 960,000. Byline

given. Pays on acceptance. Publishes ms an average of 3-6 months after acceptance. Buys all rights. Editorial lead time 3-12 months. Submit seasonal material 1 year in advance. Accepts queries by mail, e-mail.
Nonfiction Needs essays, how-to, new product, technical, must be house-related. **Buys 70 mss/year.** Query with published clips. Length: 250-2,500 words. **Pays $1/word.** Sometimes pays expenses of writers on assignment.
Columns/Departments Around the House (news, new products), 250 words. **Pays $1/word.**

TRADITIONAL HOME

Meredith Corp., 1716 Locust St., Des Moines 50309-3023. (515)284-3762. Fax: (515)284-2083. E-mail: traditionalhome@meredith.com. Website: www.traditionalhome.com. **Contact:** Candace Manroe, Senior Design Editor and Sabine Rothman, Senior Design and Markets Editor. Magazine published 8 times/year. Features articles on building, renovating, and decorating homes in the traditional style. Estab. 1989. Circ. 950,000. No kill fee. Editorial lead time 6 months.

$ $ UNIQUE HOMES

Network Communications, Inc., 327 Wall St., Princeton NJ 08540. (609)688-1110. Fax: (609)688-0201. E-mail: lkim@uniquehomes.com. Website: www.uniquehomes.com. **30% freelance written**. Bimonthly magazine covering luxury real estate for consumers and the high-end real estate industry. Our focus is the luxury real estate market, i.e., the business of buying and selling luxury homes, as well as regional real estate market trends. Byline given. Pays on publication. No kill fee. Publishes ms an average of 3 months after acceptance. Buys all rights. Editorial lead time 4 months. Submit seasonal material 4 months in advance. Accepts queries by mail, e-mail, fax. Responds in 1 month to queries. Responds in 4 months to mss. Sample copy available online.
Nonfiction Looking for high-end luxury real estate profiles on cities and geographical regions. Golf Course Living; Resort Living; Ski Real Estate; Farms, Ranches and Country Estates; Waterfront Homes; International Homes. **Buys 36 mss/year.** Query with published clips and résumé Length: 500-1,500 words. **Pays $150-500.**
Photos State availability Captions required. Reviews transparencies, prints. Offers no additional payment for photos accepted with ms. Buys all rights.
Tips For profiles on specific geographical areas, seeking writers with an in-depth personal knowledge of the luxury real estate trends in those locations. Writers with in-depth knowledge of the high-end residential market (both domestic and abroad) are especially needed.

$ $ VICTORIAN HOMES

Y-Visionary Publishing, LP, 265 S. Anita Dr., Suite 120, Orange CA 92868-3310. (714)939-9991. Fax: (714)939-9909. E-mail: editorial@victorianhomes.com. Website: www.victorianhomesmag.com. **90% freelance written**. Bimonthly magazine covering Victorian home restoration and decoration. *Victorian Homes* is read by Victorian home owners, restorers, house museum management, and others interested in the Victorian revival. Feature articles cover home architecture, interior design, furnishings, and the home's history. Photography is very important to the feature. Estab. 1981. Circ. 100,000. Byline given. Pays on acceptance. Offers $50 kill fee. Publishes ms an average of 1 year after acceptance. Buys first North American serial rights, buys one-time rights. Editorial lead time 4 months. Submit seasonal material 1 year in advance. Accepts queries by mail, e-mail, fax. Accepts simultaneous submissions. Responds in 6 weeks to queries. Responds in 2 months to mss. Sample copy and writer's guidelines for SAE.
Nonfiction Article must deal with structures—no historical articles on Victorian people or lifestyles. Needs how-to, create period style curtains, wall treatments, bathrooms, kitchens, etc., photo feature. **Buys 30-35 mss/year.** Query. Length: 800-1,800 words. **Pays $300-500.** Sometimes pays expenses of writers on assignment.
Photos State availability Captions required. Reviews 2¼x2¼ transparencies. Negotiates payment individually Buys one time rights.

$ $ WATER GARDENING

The Magazine for Pondkeepers, The Water Gardeners, Inc., P.O. Box 607, St. John IN 46373. (219)374-9419. Fax: (219)374-9052. E-mail: wgmag@watergardening.com. Website: www.watergardening.com. **50% freelance written**. Bimonthly magazine. *Water Gardening* is for hobby water gardeners. We prefer articles from a first-person perspective. Estab. 1996. Circ. 25,000. Byline given. Pays on publication. Offers 50% kill fee. Publishes ms an average of 6 months after acceptance. Buys first North American serial rights. Editorial lead time 6 months. Submit seasonal material 6-12 months in advance. Accepts queries by mail, e-mail, fax. Responds in 1 month to queries. Responds in 3 months to mss. Sample copy for $3. Guidelines for #10 SASE.
Nonfiction Needs how-to, construct, maintain, improve ponds, water features, interview, new product, personal experience, photo feature. **Buys 18-20 mss/year.** Query. Length: 600-1,500 words.
Photos State availability Captions, identification of subjects, model releases required. Reviews contact sheets, 3x5 transparencies, 3x5 prints. Negotiates payment individually. Buys one time rights.

WESTERN CANADIAN RESORTS

Vacation Homes and Investment Properties, Source Media Group, 220-5824 2nd St. SW, Calgary AB T2H 0H2

Canada. (403)532-3101. Fax: (403)532-3109. E-mail: laurie.papineau.sourcemediagroup.ca. Website: www.sourcemediagroup.ca. **50% freelance written**. Bimonthly magazine covering recreational investment properties. We cover recreational investment properties & markets, as well as the attached lifestyles—specifically in the areas those properties are in. Estab. 2005. Byline given. Pays on acceptance. Offers 100% kill fee. Buys first rights. Editorial lead time 2 months. Submit seasonal material 2 months in advance. Accepts queries by e-mail. Accepts simultaneous submissions. Responds in 2 weeks to queries. Sample copy free. Guidelines free.
Nonfiction Only on query. **Buys 0 mss/year.** Query. Sometimes pays expenses of writers on assignment.
Photos Contact: Laurie Papineau. State availability Identification of subjects required. Reviews GIF/JPEG files.

HUMOR

$ FUNNY TIMES

A Monthly Humor Review, Funny Times, Inc., P.O. Box 18530, Cleveland Heights OH 44118. (216)371-8600. Fax: (216)371-8696. E-mail: ft@funnytimes.com. Website: www.funnytimes.com. **50% freelance written**. Monthly tabloid for humor. *Funny Times* is a monthly review of America's funniest cartoonists and writers. We are the *Reader's Digest* of modern American humor with a progressive/peace-oriented/environmental/politically activist slant. Estab. 1985. Circ. 70,000. Byline given. Pays on publication. Publishes ms an average of 3 months after acceptance. Buys one-time rights, buys second serial (reprint) rights. Editorial lead time 2 months. Accepts previously published material. Accepts simultaneous submissions. Responds in 3 months to mss. Sample copy for $3 or 9x12 SAE with 3 first-class stamps ($1.14 postage). Guidelines available online.
Nonfiction We only publish humor or interviews with funny people (comedians, comic actors, cartoonists, etc.). Everything we publish is very funny. If your piece isn't extremely funny then don't bother to send it. Don't send us anything that's not outrageously funny. Don't send anything that other people haven't already read and told you they laughed so hard they peed their pants. Needs essays, funny, humor, interview, opinion, humorous, personal experience, absolutely funny. **Buys 60 mss/year.** Send complete ms. Length: 500-700 words. **Pays $60 minimum.**
Columns/Departments Query with published clips.
Fiction Contact: Ray Lesser and Susan Wolpert, editors. Anything funny. **Buys 6 mss/year.** Query with published clips. Length: 500-700 words. **Pays $50-150.**
Fillers Needs short humor. 6 **Pays $20.**
Tips Send us a small packet (1-3 items) of only your very funniest stuff. If this makes us laugh we'll be glad to ask for more. We particularly welcome previously published material that has been well-received elsewhere.

$ $ MAD MAGAZINE

1700 Broadway, New York NY 10019. (212)506-4850. E-mail: submissions@madmagazine.com. Website: www.madmag.com. **100% freelance written**. Monthly magazine always on the lookout for new ways to spoof and to poke fun at hot trends. Estab. 1952. Byline given. Pays on acceptance. Publishes ms an average of 6 months after acceptance. Buys all rights. Submit seasonal material 6 months in advance. Responds in 10 weeks to queries. Sample copy available online. Guidelines available online.
Nonfiction Submit a premise with 3 or 4 examples of how you intend to carry it through, describing the action and visual content. Rough sketches desired but not necessary. One-page gags: 2- to 8-panel cartoon continuities as minimum very funny, maximum hilarious! We're not interested in formats we're already doing or have done to death like 'what they say and what they really mean.' Don't send previously published submissions, riddles, advice columns, TV or movie satires, book manuscripts, top 10 lists, articles about Alfred E. Neuman, poetry, essays, short stories or other text pieces. **Buys 400 mss/year. Pays minimum of $500/page.**
Tips Have fun! Remember to think visually! Surprise us! Freelancers can best break in with satirical nontopical material. Include SASE with each submission. Originality is prized. We like outrageous, silly and/or satirical humor.

INFLIGHT

$ $ $ GO MAGAZINE

INK Publishing, 68 Jay St., Suite 315, Brooklyn NY 11201. (347)294-1220. Fax: (917)591-6247. E-mail: editorial@airtranmagazine.com. Website: www.airtranmagazine.com. **80% freelance written**. Monthly magazine covering travel. "*Go Magazine* is an inflight magazine covering travel, general interest and light business." Estab. 2003. Circ. 100,000. Byline given. net 45 days upon receipt of invoice. Offers 50% kill fee. Publishes ms an average of 3 months after acceptance. Buys first North American serial rights. Editorial lead time 4 months. Submit seasonal material 5 months in advance. Accepts queries by e-mail. Sample copy available online. Guidelines by email.

Nonfiction Needs general interest, interview, photo feature, travel, light business. Does not want first-person travelogues. **Buys 200 mss/year.** Query with published clips. Length: 400-2,000 words. **Pay is negotiable.**
Photos Contact: Shane Luitjens, art director. State availability Reviews GIF/JPEG files. Offers no additional payment for photos accepted with ms. Buys one time rights.
Tips "Review past issues online and study the guidelines to get a true sense of the types of features we are looking for."

$ $ $ HEMISPHERES

Pace Communications for United Airlines, Pace Communications, 1301 Carolina St., Greensboro NC 27401. (336)383-5690. E-mail: Hemiedit@hemispheresmagazine.com. Website: www.hemispheresmagazine.com. **95% freelance written.** Monthly magazine for the educated, sophisticated business and recreational frequent traveler on an airline that spans the globe. *Hemispheres* is an inflight magazine that interprets 'inflight' to be a mode of delivery rather than an editorial genre. As such, Hemispheres' task is to engage, intrigue and entertain its primary readers—an international, culturally diverse group of affluent, educated professionals and executives who frequently travel for business and pleasure on United Airlines. The magazine offers a global perspective and a focus on topics that cross borders as often as the people reading the magazine. That places our emphasis on ideas, concepts, and culture rather than products. We present that perspective in a fresh, artful and sophisticated graphic environment. Estab. 1992. Circ. 500,000. Byline given. Pays on acceptance. Offers 20% kill fee. Publishes ms an average of 4-6 months after acceptance. Buys first worldwide rights. Editorial lead time 8 months. Submit seasonal material 8 months in advance. Accepts queries by mail. Responds in 2 months to queries. Responds in 4 months to mss. Sample copy for $7.50. Guidelines for #10 SASE.
Nonfiction Keeping 'global' in mind, we look for topics that reflect a modern appreciation of the world's cultures and environment. No 'What I did (or am going to do) on a trip.' Needs general interest, humor, personal experience. Query with published clips. Length: 500-3,000 words. **Pays 50¢/word and up.**
Photos Reviews photos only when we request them. State availability Captions, identification of subjects, model releases required. Negotiates payment individually Buys one time rights.
Columns/Departments Making a Difference (Q&A format interview with world leaders, movers, and shakers. A 500-600 word introduction anchors the interview. We want to profile an international mix of men and women representing a variety of topics or issues, but all must truly be making a difference. No puffy celebrity profiles.); 15 Fascinating Facts (a snappy selection of 1- or 2-sentence obscure, intriguing, or travel-service-oriented items that the reader never knew about a city, state, country, or destination.); Executive Secrets (things that top executives know); Case Study (Business strategies of international companies or organizations. No lionizations of CEOs. Strategies should be the emphasis. We want international candidates.); Weekend Breakway (Takes us just outside a major city after a week of business for several activities for a physically active, action-packed weekend. This isn't a sedentary getaway at a property.); Roving Gourmet (Insider's guide to interesting eating in major city, resort area, or region. The slant can be anything from ethnic to expensive; not just best. The 4 featured eateries span a spectrum from hole in the wall, to expense account lunch, and on to big deal dining.); Collecting (occasional 800-word story on collections and collecting that can emphasize travel); Eye on Sports (global look at anything of interest in sports); Vintage Traveler (options for mature, experienced travelers); Savvy Shopper (Insider's tour of best places in the world to shop. Savvy Shopper steps beyond all those stories that just mention the great shopping at a particular destination. A shop-by-shop, gallery-by-gallery tour of the best places in the world.); Science and Technology (Substantive, insightful stories on how technology is changing our lives and the business world. Not just another column on audio components or software. No gift guides!); Aviation Journal (For those fascinated with aviation. Topics range widely.); Terminal Bliss (a great airports guide series); Grape And Grain (wine and spirits with emphasis on education, not one-upmanship); Show Business (films, music, and entertainment); Musings (humor or just curious musings); Quick Quiz (tests to amuse and educate); Travel Trends (brief, practical, invaluable, global, trend-oriented); Book Beat (Tackles topics like the Wodehouse Society, the birth of a book, the competition between local bookshops and national chains. Please, no review proposals.); What the World's Reading (residents explore how current bestsellers tell us what their country is thinking). Length: 1,400 words. Query with published clips. **Pays 50¢/word and up**
Fiction Needs adventure, ethnic, historical, humorous, mainstream, mystery, explorations of those issues common to all people but within the context of a particular culture. **Buys 14 mss/year.** Send complete ms. Length: 1,000-4,000 words. **Pays 50¢/word and up.**
Tips We increasingly require writers of 'destination' pieces or departments to 'live whereof they write.' Increasingly want to hear from US, UK, or other English-speaking/writing journalists (business & travel) who reside outside the US in Europe, South America, Central America, and the Pacific Rim—all areas that United flies. We're not looking for writers who aim at the inflight market. *Hemispheres* broke the fluffy mold of that tired domestic genre. Our monthly readers are a global mix on the cutting edge of the global economy and culture. They don't need to have the world filtered by US writers. We want a Hong Kong restaurant writer to speak for that city's eateries, so we need English-speaking writers around the globe. That's the 'insider' story our readers respect. We use resident writers for departments such as Roving Gourmet, Savvy Shopper, On Location, 3 Perfect Days, and Weekend Breakaway, but authoritative writers can roam in features. Sure we cover the US,

but with a global view: No 'in this country' phraseology. 'Too American' is a frequent complaint for queries. We use UK English spellings in articles that speak from that tradition and we specify costs in local currency first before US dollars. Basically, all of above serves the realization that today, 'global' begins with respect for 'local.' That approach permits a wealth of ways to present culture, travel, and business for a wide readership. We anchor that with a reader-service mission that grounds everything in 'how to do it.'

$ $ HORIZON AIR MAGAZINE

Paradigm Communications Group, 2701 First Ave., Suite 250, Seattle WA 98121. Fax: (206)448-6939. **Contact:** Michele Andrus Dill, Editor. **90% freelance written**. Monthly inflight magazine covering travel, business, and leisure in the Pacific Northwest. *"Horizon Air Magazine* serves a sophisticated audience of business and leisure travelers. Stories must have a Northwest slant." Estab. 1990. Circ. 600,000/month. Byline given. Pays on publication. Offers 33% kill fee. Publishes ms an average of 1 year after acceptance. Buys first North American serial rights, buys electronic rights. Editorial lead time 6 months. Submit seasonal material 5 months in advance. Accepts queries by mail, fax. Sample copy for 10x12 SASE. Guidelines for #10 SASE.

- "Responds only if interested, so include e-mail and phone number but no need to include SASE for queries."

Nonfiction Needs essays, personal, general interest, historical, how-to, humor, interview, personal experience, photo feature, travel, business. Meeting planners' guide, golf, gift guide. No material unrelated to the Pacific Northwest. **Buys approximately 36 mss/year.** Send complete ms. Length: 1,500-3,000 words. **Pays $300-700.** Occasionally

Photos State availability Captions, identification of subjects, model releases required. Reviews transparencies, prints. Negotiates payment individually Buys one time rights.

Columns/Departments Region (Northwest news/profiles), 200-400 words; Air Time (personal essays), 700 words. 15 Query with published clips. **Pays $100 (Region), $250 (Air Time)**

$ $ $ MY MIDWEST

INK Publishing, 68 Jay St., Suite 315, Brooklyn NY 11201. (917)254-4865. Fax: (917)591-6247. E-mail: editorial@mymidwest.com. Website: www.mymidwest.com. **80% freelance written**. Quarterly magazine covering travel. *My Midwest* is an inflight magazine covering travel, general interest and light business. Estab. 2006. Circ. 60,000. Byline given. net 45 upon receipt of invoice. Offers 50% kill fee. Publishes ms an average of 3 months after acceptance. Buys first North American serial rights. Editorial lead time 6 months. Submit seasonal material 7 months in advance. Accepts queries by e-mail. Sample copy available online. Guidelines by email.

Nonfiction Needs general interest, photo feature, travel, light business. Does not want first-person travelogues. **Buys 50 mss/year.** Query with published clips. Length: 700-2,000 words. **Pays $315-900.**

Photos Contact: Shane Luitjens, art director. State availability Reviews GIF/JPEG files. Offers no additional payment for photos accepted with ms. Buys one time rights.

Tips Review past issues online and study the guidelines to get a true sense of the types of features we are looking for.

$ $ $ SIGHTS

INK Publishing, 68 Jay St., Suite 315, Brooklyn NY 11201. (917)254-4865. Fax: (917)591-6247. E-mail: editorial@atasights.com. Website: www.atasights.com. **80% freelance written**. Quarterly magazine covering airline destinations. Estab. 2006. Circ. 55,000. Byline given. net 45 days upon receipt of invoice. Offers 50% kill fee. Publishes ms an average of 3 months after acceptance. Buys first North American serial rights. Editorial lead time 6 months. Submit seasonal material 7 months in advance. Accepts queries by e-mail. Sample copy available online. Guidelines by email.

Nonfiction Needs general interest, photo feature, travel. Does not want travelogues, completed manuscripts. **Buys 50 mss/year.** Query with published clips. Length: 700-2,000 words. **Pays $315-900.**

Photos Contact: Shane Luitjens, art director. State availability Reviews GIF/JPEG files. Offers no additional payment for photos accepted with ms. Buys one time rights.

Tips Review past issues online and study the guidelines to get a true sense of the types of features we are looking for.

$ $ SKYLIGHTS

The Inflight Magazine of Spirit Airlines, Worth International Media Group, Inc., 5979 NW 151 St., Suite 120, Miami Lakes FL 33014. (305)828-0123. Fax: (305)828-0799. Website: www.worthit.com. Bimonthly magazine. Like Spirit Airlines, *Skylights* will be known for its practical and friendly sensibility. This publication is a clean, stylish, user-friendly product. This is not an old-school airline, and *Skylights* is not an old-school inflight. Circ. 5.5 million. Byline sometimes given. Pays on publication. No kill fee. Buys first North American serial rights. Editorial lead time 3-6 months. Submit seasonal material 4 months in advance. Accepts queries by mail. Responds in 4-6 weeks to queries. Writer's guidelines via e-mail at millie@worthit.com.

Nonfiction Needs general interest, humor, interview, new product, travel. No first-person accounts or weighty topics. Stories should be practical and useful, but not something-for-everyone-type articles. **Buys 18 mss/year.**

Query with published clips. Length: 350-1,200 words. **Pays 25-40¢/word.**

Photos State availability Captions, identification of subjects, model releases required. Reviews GIF/JPEG files. Negotiaties payment individually Buys one time rights.

Columns/Departments Events calendar (based on Spirit destinations), 1,200 words; Gizmos (latest and greatest gadgets), 250-word descriptions; Biz (bizz buzz), 650-800 words; Fast Reads (quick finds, books, movies, music, food, wine); Skybuys (hot buys and smart shopping options), 150-word descriptions; Beauty and Health Story (specific aspects of staying well), 800 words. 36 Query with published clips. **25-40¢/word**

Fillers Length: 250-400 words. **25-40¢/word**

$ $ $ $ SPIRIT MAGAZINE

Pace Communications, Inc., Suite 360, 2811 McKinney Ave., Dallas TX 75204. (214)580-8070. Fax: (214)580-2491. E-mail: ideas@spiritmag.com. Website: www.spiritmag.com. Monthly magazine for passengers on Southwest Airlines. Estab. 1992. Circ. 380,000. Byline given. Pays on acceptance. Buys first North American serial rights, buys electronic rights. Responds in 1 month to queries. Guidelines available online.

Nonfiction Seeking lively, accessible, entertaining, relevant, and trendy travel, business, lifestyle, sports, celebrity, food, tech-product stories on newsworthy/noteworthy topics in destinations served by Southwest Airlines; well-researched and reported; multiple source only. Experienced magazine professionals only. **Buys about 40 mss/year.** Query by mail only with published clips. 3,000-6,000 words (features). **Pays $1/word.** Pays expenses of writers on assignment.

Columns/Departments Length: 800-900 words. about 21 Query by mail only with published clips.

Fillers 12 250 words. **variable amount**

Tips *Southwest Airlines Spirit* magazine reaches more than 2.8 million readers every month aboard Southwest Airlines. Our median reader is a college-educated, 32- to 40-year-old traveler with a household income around $90,000. Writers must have proven magazine capabilities, a sense of fun, excellent reporting skills, a smart, hip style, and the ability to provide take-away value to the reader in sidebars, charts, and/or lists.

$ $ SPIRIT OF ALOHA

The Inflight Magazine of Aloha Airlines, Honolulu Publishing Co., Ltd., 707 Richards St., Suite 525, Honolulu HI 96813. (808)524-7400. Fax: (808)531-2306. E-mail: tchapman@honpub.com. Website: www.spiritofaloha.com. **80% freelance written**. Bimonthly magazine covering Hawaii. Estab. 1978. Circ. 100,000. Byline given. Pays on acceptance. Publishes ms an average of 2 months after acceptance. Buys first rights. Editorial lead time 2 months. Submit seasonal material 4 months in advance. Accepts queries by mail, e-mail. Responds in up to 1 month to queries. Guidelines by email.

Nonfiction Should be related to Hawaii. **Buys 40 mss/year.** Query with published clips. Length: 1,500-2,500 words. **Pays $600 and up.**

Photos State availability Captions, identification of subjects, model releases required. Reviews transparencies. Negotiates payment individually Buys one time rights.

$ $ $ STRATOS

Journey Beyond First Class, STRATOS Publishing, 1430 I-85 Parkway, Montgomery AL 36106. E-mail: mnothaft@stratosmag.com. Website: www.stratosmag.com. **90% freelance written**. Magazine published 10 times/year covering luxury lifestyle and travel. Our readers are well-heeled and need exceptional travel experiences that are high end and have an outdoor twist. Estab. 2000. Circ. 65,000. Byline given. Pays on acceptance. Offers 25% kill fee. Publishes ms an average of 3-4 months after acceptance. Buys first North American serial rights. Editorial lead time 3-4 months. Submit seasonal material 6 months in advance. Accepts queries by e-mail. Responds in 1 week to queries.

Nonfiction Needs how-to, interview. Query with published clips. Length: 900-1,500 words. **Pays $600-1,200.** Sometimes pays expenses of writers on assignment.

Photos State availability Identification of subjects required. Reviews GIF/JPEG files. Negotiates payment individually. Buys one time rights.

Tips Pitch to the magazine format and think high end experiences.

$ $ $ $ US AIRWAYS MAGAZINE

Pace Communications, 1301 Carolina St., Greensboro NC 27401. E-mail: edit@usairwaysmag.com. Website: www.usairwaysmag.com. Monthly magazine for travelers on US Airways. We focus on travel, lifestyle and pop culture. Estab. 2006. Circ. 441,000. Byline given. Pays on acceptance. Publishes ms an average of 4 months after acceptance. Buys exclusive worldwide rights for all media for 120 days rights. Editorial lead time 3 months. Accepts queries by mail, e-mail. Responds in 6 weeks to queries. Responds in 1 month to mss. Sample copy for $7.50 or online. Guidelines available online.

Nonfiction Features are highly visual, focusing on some ususual or unique angle of travel, food, business, or other topic approved by a US Airways editor. Needs general interest, personal experience, travel, food, lifestyle, sports. **Buys 200-350 mss/year.** Query with published clips. Length: 100-1,500 words. **Pays $100-1,500.** Sometimes pays expenses of writers on assignment.

Photos State availability Identification of subjects, model releases required. Reviews contact sheets, negatives, transparencies. Negotiates payment individually. Buys one time rights.
Columns/Departments Several columns are authored by a single writer under long-term contract with US Airways Magazine. Departments open to freelance pitches include: All Over the Map; Alter Ego; Straight Talk; Hands On; Shelf Life; In Gear; Get Personal; and Get Away. All of these departments may be viewed on the magazine's Web site.
Tips We look for smart, pithy writing that addresses travel, lifestyle and pop culture. Study the magazine for content, style and tone. Queries for story ideas should be to the point and presented clearly. Any written correspondence should include a SASE.

$ $ $ WASHINGTON FLYER MAGAZINE

1707 L St., NW, Suite 800, Washington DC 20036. (202)331-9393. Fax: (202)331-2043. E-mail: lauren@themagazinegroup.com. Website: www.fly2dc.com. **60% freelance written**. Bimonthly magazine for business and pleasure travelers at Washington National and Washington Dulles International airports INSI. Primarily affluent, well-educated audience that flies frequently in and out of Washington, DC. Estab. 1989. Circ. 182,000. Byline given. Pays on acceptance. Offers 25% kill fee. Buys first North American serial rights. Submit seasonal material 4 months in advance. Accepts queries by mail, e-mail, fax. Responds in 10 weeks to queries. Sample copy for 9x12 SAE with $2 postage. Guidelines available online.
Nonfiction One international destination feature per issue, determined 6 months in advance. One feature per issue on aspect of life in Washington. Needs general interest, interview, travel, business. No personal experiences, poetry, opinion or inspirational. **Buys 20-30 mss/year.** Query with published clips. Length: 800-1,200 words. **Pays $500-900.**
Photos State availability Identification of subjects required. Reviews negatives, almost always color transparencies. Considers additional payment for top-quality photos accepted with ms. Buys one time rights.
Columns/Departments Washington Insider; Travel; Hospitality; Airports and Airlines; Restaurants; Shopping, all 800-1,200 words. Query. **Pays $500-900.**
Tips Know the Washington market and issues relating to frequent business/pleasure travelers as we move toward a global economy. With a bimonthly publication schedule it's important that stories remain viable as possible during the magazine's 2-month 'shelf life.' No telephone calls, please and understand that most assignments are made several months in advance. Queries are best sent via e-mail.

WILD BLUE YONDER

900 South Broadway, Suite 300, Denver CO 80209. (303)296-0039. Fax: (303)296-3410. E-mail: editorial@Gowildblueyonder.com. Website: www.Gowildblueyonder.com. **60% freelance written**. "Prefers queries via e-mail. Don't waste the editor's time. Know the route and the publication before you query." Pays 10 days after publication. Offers $25 kill fee. Sample copy for $5. Guidelines available online.
Fiction Send complete ms.

JUVENILE

$ ADVENTURES

2923 Troost Ave., Kansas City MO 64109. (816)931-1900. Fax: (816)412-8306. E-mail: djbroadbooks@wordaction.com. **25% freelance written**. "Published by Adventures for children ages 6-8. Correlates to the weekly Sunday school lesson." Pays on publication. No kill fee. Publishes ms an average of 1 year after acceptance. Buys all rights. Accepts queries by mail, fax. Responds in 2 months to queries. Sample copy for #10 SASE. Guidelines for #10 SASE.
Columns/Departments Recipes & Crafts, **Pays $15**; Activities, **Pays $15**. Send complete ms.
Fiction "Accepts life application stories that show early elementary children dealing with the issues related to the Bible story, Bible Truth, or lesson goals. Children may interact with friends, family, or other individuals in the stories. Make characters and events realistic. Avoid placing characters in a perfect world or depicting spiritually precocious children." Length: 250 words. **Pays $15.**
Poetry "Short, fun, easy-to-understand, age-appropriate poetry that correlates with the Bible story, Bible Truth, or lesson goals is welcome. We prefer rhythmic, pattern poems, but will accept free verse if reads smoothly out loud." Length: 4-8 lines. **Pays $15.**

$ 🌐 AQUILA MAGAZINE

New Leaf Publishing Ltd, Studio 2, Willowfield Studios, 67a Willowfield Rd., Eastbourne, East Sussex England BN22 8AP United Kingdom. (44)(132)343-1313. Fax: (44)(132)373-1136. E-mail: info@aquila.co.uk. Website: www.aquila.co.uk. Magazine for children 8-12 years old. Circ. 40,000. No kill fee. Sample copy for £5.
Nonfiction Contact the editor to discuss ideas. Features are only likely to be of interest if they are highly original in presentation and content and use specialist/inside knowledge. Query. Length: 600-800 words. **Pays £50-75.**

Fiction Submit either 1 short story or a 2-4 instalments of a story. Each instalment must be satisfying to read in its own right, but also include an ending that tempts the reader to return for the next part. Length: 1,000-1,500 words. **£90/short story; £80/episode for a serial.**

$ $ $ $ BOYS' LIFE

Boy Scouts of America, P.O. Box 152079, Irving TX 75015-2079. (972)580-2366. Fax: (972)580-2079. Website: www.boyslife.org. **Contact:** Michael Goldman, managing editor. **75% freelance written. Prefers to work with published/established writers; works with small number of new/unpublished writers each year.** Monthly magazine covering activities of interest to all boys ages 6-18. Most readers are Boy Scouts or Cub Scouts. *Boys' Life* covers Boy Scout activities and general interest subjects for ages 6-18, Boy Scouts, Cub Scouts and others of that age group. Estab. 1911. Circ. 1,300,000. Pays on acceptance. Publishes ms an average of 1 year after acceptance. Buys one-time rights. Accepts queries by mail. Responds in 2 months to queries. Sample copy for $3.95 and 9x12 SAE. Guidelines for #10 SASE or online.

Nonfiction "Subject matter is broad, everything from professional sports to American history to how to pack a canoe. Look at a current list of the BSA's more than 100 merit badge pamphlets for an idea of the wide range of subjects possible. Uses strong photo features with about 500 words of text. Separate payment or assignment for photos." Needs how-to, photo feature, hobby and craft ideas. **Buys 60 mss/year.** Query with SASE. No phone queries Major articles run 500-1,500 words; preferred length is about 1,000 words, including sidebars and boxes. **Pays $400-1,500.** Pays expenses of writers on assignment.

Columns/Departments "Science, nature, earth, health, sports, space and aviation, cars, computers, entertainment, pets, history, and music are some of the columns for which we use 300-750 words of text. This is a good place to show us what you can do." 100-500 Query Brad Riddell, Associate Editor. **Pays $100-500.**

Fiction Needs adventure, humorous, mystery, young adult, science fiction, western, young adult, sports. **Buys 12-15 mss/year.** Send complete ms. to Paula Murphey, Senior Editor. Length: 1,000-1,500 words. **Pays $750 minimum.**

Tips "We strongly recommend reading at least 12 issues of the magazine before you submit queries. We are a good market for any writer willing to do the necessary homework."

$ BREAD FOR GOD'S CHILDREN

Bread Ministries, Inc., P.O. Box 1017, Arcadia FL 34265. (863)494-6214. Fax: (863)993-0154. E-mail: bread@sunline.net. **10% freelance written**. Published 6-8 times/year. An interdenominational Christian teaching publication published 6-8 times/year written to aid children and youth in leading a Christian life. Estab. 1972. Circ. 10,000. Byline given. Pays on publication. No kill fee. Publishes ms an average of 6 months after acceptance. Buys first rights. Accepts queries by mail. Accepts simultaneous submissions. Responds in 6 months to mss. Three sample copies for 9x12 SAE and 5 first-class stamps. Guidelines for #10 SASE.

Reprints Send tearsheet and information about when and where the material previously appeared.

Columns/Departments Let's Chat (children's Christian values), 500-700 words; Teen Page (youth Christian values), 600-800 words; Idea Page (games, crafts, Bible drills). 5-8 Send complete ms. **Pays $30.**

Fiction We are looking for writers who have a solid knowledge of Biblical principles and are concerned for the youth of today living by those principles. Our stories must be well written, with the story itself getting the message across—no preaching, moralizing, or tag endings. No fantasy, science fiction, or nonChristian themes. **Buys 15-20 mss/year.** Send complete ms. 600-800 words (young children), 900-1,500 words (older children). **Pays $40-50.**

Tips We're looking for more submissions on healing miracles and reconciliation/restoration. Follow usual guidelines for careful writing, editing, and proofreading. We get many manuscripts with misspellings, poor grammar, careless typing. Know your subject—writer should know the Lord to write about the Christian life. Study the publication and our guidelines.

$ CADET QUEST MAGAZINE

P.O. Box 7259, Grand Rapids MI 49510-7259. (616)241-5616. Fax: (616)241-5558. E-mail: submissions@calvinistcadets.org. Website: www.calvinistcadets.org. **Contact:** G. Richard Broene, ed. **40% freelance written. Works with a small number of new/unpublished writers each year.** Magazine published 7 times/year. "*Cadet Quest Magazine* shows boys 9-14 how God is at work in their lives and in the world around them." Estab. 1958. Circ. 9,000. Byline given. Pays on acceptance. No kill fee. Publishes ms an average of 4-11 months after acceptance. Buys first North American serial rights, buys one-time rights, buys second serial (reprint) rights, buys simultaneous rights. Rights purchased vary with author and material. Accepts previously published material. Accepts simultaneous submissions. Responds in 2 months to submissions. Sample copy for 9x12 SASE. Guidelines for #10 SASE.

- Accepts submissions by mail, or by e-mail (must include ms in text of e-mail). Will not open attachments.

Nonfiction Articles about young boys' interests: sports (articles about athletes and developing Christian character through sports; photos appreciated), outdoor activities (camping skills, nature study, survival exercises; practical 'how to do it' approach works best. 'God in nature' themes appreciated), science, crafts, and problems. Emphasis is on a Christian perspective. Needs how-to, humor, inspirational, interview, personal experience, informational. Write for new themes list in February. **Buys 20-25 mss/year.** Send complete ms. Length: 500-1,500 words. **Pays 2-5¢/word.**

Reprints Send typed manuscript with rights for sale noted. Payment varies.

Photos Pays $20-30 for photos purchased with ms

Columns/Departments Project Page (uses simple projects boys 9-14 can do on their own made with easily accessible materials; must provide clear, accurate instructions).

Fiction Considerable fiction is used. Fast-moving stories that appeal to a boy's sense of adventure or sense of humor are welcome. Needs adventure, religious, spiritual, sports, comics. Avoid preachiness. Avoid simplistic answers to complicated problems. Avoid long dialogue and little action. No fantasy, science fiction, fashion, horror or erotica. Send complete ms. Length: 900-1,500 words. **Pays 4-6¢/word, and 1 contributor's copy.**

Tips "Best time to submit stories/articles is early in the year (February-April). Also remember readers are boys ages 9-14. Stories must reflect or add to the theme of the issue and be from a Christian perspective."

$ $ CALLIOPE

Exploring World History, Cobblestone Publishing Co., 30 Grove St., Suite C, Peterborough NH 03458-1454. (603)924-7209. Fax: (603)924-7380. E-mail: cfbakeriii@meganet.net. Website: www.cobblestonepub.com. **50% freelance written**. Magazine published 9 times/year covering world history (East and West) through 1800 AD for 8- 14-year-old kids. Articles must relate to the issue's theme. Lively, original approaches to the subject are the primary concerns of the editors in choosing material. Estab. 1990. Circ. 13,000. Byline given. Pays on publication. No kill fee. Buys all rights. Accepts queries by mail. If interested, responds 5 months before publication date. Sample copy for $5.95, $2 shipping and handling, and 10x13 SASE. Guidelines available online.

Nonfiction Plays, biographies, in-depth nonfiction. Needs essays, general interest, historical, how-to, crafts/woodworking, humor, interview, personal experience, photo feature, technical, travel, recipes. No religious, pornographic, biased, or sophisticated submissions. **Buys 30-40 mss/year.** Query with writing sample, 1-page outline, bibliography, SASE. 700-800/feature articles; 300-600 words/supplemental nonfiction. **Pays 20-25¢/word.**

Photos If you have photographs pertaining to any upcoming theme, please contact the editor by mail or fax, or send them with your query. You may also send images on speculation. Reviews b&w prints, color slides. Pays $15-100/b $25-100/color; cover fees are negotiated. Buys one time rights.

Fiction Needs adventure, historical, biographical, retold legends. **Buys 10 mss/year.** 800 words maximum **Pays 20-25¢/word.**

Fillers Crossword and other word puzzles (no word finds), mazes, and picture puzzles that use the vocabulary of the issue's theme or otherwise relate to the theme. **Pays on an individual basis.**

Tips Authors are urged to use primary resources and up-to-date scholarly resources in their bibliography. In all correspondence, please include your complete address and a telephone number where you can be reached.

$ $ ⊘ CHILDREN'S PLAYMATE MAGAZINE

Children's Better Health Institute, 1100 Waterway Blvd., Indianapolis IN 46202. (317)634-1100. Fax: (317)684-8094. Website: www.childrensplaymatemag.org. **40% freelance written. Eager to work with new/unpublished writers.** Magazine published 8 times/year for children ages 6-8. We are looking for articles, poems, and activities with a health, fitness, or nutrition theme. We try to present our material in a positive light, and we try to incorporate humor and a light approach wherever possible without minimizing the seriousness of what we are saying. Estab. 1929. Circ. 114,907. Byline given. Pays on publication. No kill fee. Buys all rights. Submit seasonal material 8 months in advance. Responds in 3 months to queries. Sample copy for $1.75. Guidelines for SASE or online.

- Closed to submissions until further notice.

Nonfiction We are especially interested in material concerning sports and fitness, including profiles of famous amateur and professional athleters; 'average' atheletes (especially children) who have overcome obstacles to excel in their areas; and new or unusual sports, particularly those in which children can participate. Nonfiction articles dealing with health subjects should be fresh and creative. Avoid encyclopedic or 'preachy' approach. We try to present our health material in a positive manner, incorporate humor and a light approach wherever possible without minimizing the seriousness of the message. Needs interview, famous amateurs and professional athletes, photo feature, recipes (ingredients should be healthful). **Buys 25 mss/year.** Send complete ms. Length: 300-700 words. **Pays up to 17¢/word.**

Photos State availability Captions, model releases required. $15 minimum Buys one time rights.

Fiction Contact: Terry Harshman, editor. Not buying much fiction right now except for rebus stories of 100-300 words and occasional poems. Vocabulary suitable for ages 6-8. Include word count. No adult or adolescent fiction. Send complete ms. Length: 300-700 words. **Pays minimum of 17¢/word and 10 contributor's copies.**

Fillers Recipes, puzzles, dot-to-dots, color-ins, hidden pictures, mazes. Prefers camara-ready activities. Activity guidelines for #10 SASE. 25 **variable amount.**

Tips We would especially like to see more holiday stories, articles, and activities. Please send seasonal material at least 8 months in advance.

$ $ CLUBHOUSE MAGAZINE

Focus on the Family, 8605 Explorer Dr., Colorado Springs CO 80920. (719)531-3400. Website: www.clubhousemagazine.com. **25% freelance written**. Monthly magazine. *Clubhouse* readers are 8-12 year old boys and girls who desire to know more about God and the Bible. Their parents (who typically pay for the membership) want wholesome, educational material with Scriptural or moral insight. The kids want excitement, adventure, action, humor, or mystery. Your job as a writer is to please both the parent and child with each article. Estab. 1987. Circ. 85,000. Byline given. Pays on acceptance. No kill fee. Publishes ms an average of 12-18 months after acceptance. Buys the nonexclusive right to publish in print or electronic form worldwide. Editorial lead time 5 months. Submit seasonal material 9 months in advance. Responds in 2 months to mss. Sample copy for $1.50 with 9x12 SASE. Guidelines for #10 SASE.

Nonfiction Contact: Jesse Florea, editor. Needs essays, how-to, humor, inspirational, interview, personal experience, photo feature, religious. Avoid Bible stories. Avoid informational-only, science, or educational articles. Avoid biographies told encyclopedia or textbook style. **Buys 6 mss/year.** Send complete ms. Length: 800-1,200 words. **Pays $25-450 for assigned articles. Pays 15-25¢/word for unsolicited articles.**

Fiction Contact: Jesse Florea, editor. Needs adventure, humorous, mystery, religious, suspense, holiday. Avoid contemporary, middle-class family settings (existing authors meet this need), poems (rarely printed), stories dealing with boy-girl relationships. **Buys 10 mss/year.** Send complete ms. Length: 400-1,500 words. **Pays $200 and up for first time contributor and 5 contributor's copies; additional copies available.**

Fillers Needs facts, newsbreaks. 2 Length: 40-100 words.

$ $ COBBLESTONE

An Introduction to American History, Cobblestone Publishing, 30 Grove St., Suite C, Peterborough NH 03458. Fax: (603)924-7380. Website: www.cobblestonepub.com. **50**. ages 9-14. "No unsolicited mss. Query first. Prefers to work with published/established writers. Each issue presents a particular theme, making it exciting as well as informative. Half of all subscriptions are for schools. All material must relate to monthly theme." Circ. 15,000. Byline given. Pays on publication. Offers 50% kill fee. Buys all rights. Accepts queries by mail. Accepts simultaneous submissions. Guidelines available on website or for SASE; sample copy for $6.95, $2 shipping/handling, 10x13 SASE

- "It stands apart from other children's magazines by offering a solid look at one subject and stressing strong editorial content, color photographs throughout, and original illustrations."

Nonfiction Needs historical, humor, interview, personal experience, photo feature feature, travel, crafts, recipes, activities. No material that editorializes rather than reports. **Buys 45-50 mss/year mss/year.** Query with writing sample, 1-page outline, bibliography, SASE. 800 words/feature articles; 300-600 words/supplemental nonfiction; up to 700 words maximum/activities **Pays 20-25¢/word.**

Photos Contact: Editor, by mail or fax, or send photos with your query. Captions, identification of subjects Reviews contact sheets, transparencies, prints. $15-100/b&w Buys one time rights.

Fiction Needs adventure, historical, biographical, retold legends. **Buys 5 mss/year.** 800 words maximum **Pays 20-25¢/word.**

Poetry Needs free verse, light verse, traditional. Serious and light verse considered. Must have clear, objective imagery. **Buys 3 poems/year.** 50 lines maximum **Pays on an individual basis.**

Fillers "Crossword and other word puzzles (no word finds), mazes, and picture puzzles that use the vocabulary of the issue's theme or otherwise relate to the theme." **Pays on an individual basis.**

Tips "Review theme lists and past issues to see what we're looking for."

$ $ DIG MAGAZINE

Cobblestone Publishing, 30 Grove St., Suite C, Peterborough NH 03458-1454. (603)924-7209. Fax: (603)924-7380. E-mail: cfbakeriii@meganet.net. Website: www.digonsite.com. **75% freelance written**. Magazine published 9 times/year covering archaeology for kids ages 9-14. Estab. 1999. Circ. 20,000. Byline given. Pays on publication. No kill fee. Publishes ms an average of 1 year after acceptance. Buys all rights. Editorial lead time 1 year. Accepts queries by mail. Responds in several months. Sample copy for $5.95 with 8x11 SASE or $10 without SASE. Guidelines available online.

Nonfiction Needs personal experience, photo feature, travel, archaeological excavation reports. No fiction. Occasional paleontology stories accepted. **Buys 30-40 mss/year.** Query with published clips. Length: 100-1,000 words. **Pays 20-25¢/word.**

Photos State availability Identification of subjects required. Negotiates payment individually Buys one time rights.

Tips Please remember that this is a children's magazine for kids ages 9-14 so the tone is as kid-friendly as possible given the scholarship involved in researching and describing a site or a find.

$ DISCOVERIES

Word Action Publishing Co., 6401 The Paseo, Kansas City MO 64131. (816)333-7000 ext. 2728. Fax: (816)333-4439. E-mail: JJSmith@nazarene.org. **80% freelance written**. Weekly sunday school take-home paper. Our audience is third and fourth graders. We require that the stories relate to the Sunday school lesson for that week. Circ. 18,000. Byline given. Pays on acceptance. No kill fee. Publishes ms an average of 1-2 year after acceptance. Buys multi-use rights. Accepts queries by mail, e-mail, fax. Accepts previously published material. Accepts simultaneous submissions. Responds in 6 weeks to queries. Sample copy for SASE. Guidelines for SASE.

Fiction Submit contemporary, true-to-life portrayals of 8-10 year olds, written for a third- to fourth-grade reading level. Religious themes. Must relate to our theme list. No fantasy, science fiction, abnormally mature or precocious children, personification of animals. Nothing preachy. No unrealistic dialogue. **Buys 25 mss/year.** Send complete ms. Length: words. **Pays $25.**

Fillers Spot cartoons, puzzles (related to the theme), trivia (any miscellaneous area of interest to 8-10 year olds). Length: 50-100 words. **Pays $15 for trivia, puzzles, and cartoons**

Tips Follow our theme list and read the Bible verses that relate to the theme.

$ $ FACES

People, Places and Cultures, Cobblestone Publishing, 30 Grove St., Suite C, Peterborough NH 03458. (603)924-7209. Fax: (603)924-7380. E-mail: facesmag@yahoo.com. Website: www.cobblestonepub.com. **90-100% freelance written**. "Publishes monthly throughout the year, *Faces* covers world culture for ages 9-14. It stands apart from other children's magazines by offering a solid look at one subject and stressing strong editorial content, color photographs throughout, and original illustrations. *Faces* offers an equal balance of feature articles and activities, as well as folktales and legends." Estab. 1984. Circ. 15,000. Byline given. Pays on publication. Offers 50% kill fee. Buys all rights. Accepts queries by mail, e-mail. Accepts simultaneous submissions. Sample copy for $6.95, $2 shipping and handling, 10X13 SASE Guidelines for SASE or on website

Nonfiction "Interviews, personal accounts, in-depth nonfiction highlighting an aspect of the featured culture." Needs historical, humor, interview, personal experience, photo feature, travel, recipes, activities, crafts. **Buys 45-50 mss/year.** Query with writing sample, 1-page outline, bibliography, SASE. 800 words/feature articles; 300-600/supplemental nonfiction; up to 700 words/activities. **Pays 20-25¢/word.**

Photos "Contact the editor by mail or fax, or send photos with your query. You may also send images on speculation." Captions, identification of subjects, model releases required. Reviews contact sheets, transparencies, prints. Pays $15-100/b&w; $25-100/color; cover fees are negotiated. Buys one time rights.

Fiction Needs ethnic, historical, retold legends/folktales, original plays. 800 words maximum. **Pays 20-25¢/word.**

Poetry Serious and light verse considered. Must have clear, objective imagery. 100 lines maximum. **Pays on an individual basis.**

Fillers "Crossword and other word puzzles (no word finds), mazes, and picture puzzles that use the vocabulary of the issue's theme or otherwise relate to the theme." **Pays on an individual basis.**

$ FUN FOR KIDZ

Bluffton News Printing & Publishing, 101 N. Main St., Bluffton OH 45817. Website: www.funforkidzmagazines.com. **60% freelance written**. Bimonthly magazine. We feature children involved in wholesome activities. Byline given. Pays on publication. No kill fee. Publishes ms an average of up to 4 years after acceptance. Buys first rights, buys one-time rights, buys second serial (reprint) rights, buys electronic rights. Accepts queries by mail. Accepts simultaneous submissions. Responds in 4-6 weeks to queries. Responds in 2 months to mss. Sample copy for $6. Writer's guidelines for #10 SASE or online.

Nonfiction Follow our theme list for article needs. We are always looking for creative activities to go with our themes. **Buys about 18 mss/year.** Send complete ms. **Pays 5¢/word for unsolicited articles.**

Photos Send photos Offers $5 maximum/photo Buys one time rights.

Fiction Follow our theme list for fiction needs. No fantasy (magic, wizards, etc.), horror (haunted houses, ghosts, etc.), or Halloween-related stories. **Buys about 10 mss/year.** Send complete ms. Maxiumum 600 words. **Pays 5¢/word.**

Poetry Needs free verse, haiku, light verse, traditional. Poetry must follow our pre-set themes. **Buys about 12 poems/year. Pays $10 minimum.**

Tips Read our guidelines to learn about the kind of material we look for. Always include a SASE when sending in manuscripts for consideration.

$ $ GIRLS' LIFE

Monarch Publishing, 4529 Harford Rd., Baltimore MD 21214. E-mail: mandy@girlslife.com. Website: www.girlslife.com. Bimonthly magazine covering girls ages 9-15. Estab. 1994. Circ. 2,000,000. Byline given. Pays on publication. Publishes ms an average of 3 months after acceptance. Buys all rights. Editorial lead time 4 months. Submit seasonal material 5 months in advance. Accepts queries by mail. Responds in 1 month to

queries. Sample copy for $5 or online Guidelines available online.
Nonfiction Needs book excerpts, essays, general interest, how-to, humor, inspirational, interview, new product, travel, beauty, relationship, sports. Back to School (August/September); Fall, Halloween (October/November); Holidays, Winter (December/January); Valentine's Day, Crushes (February/March); Spring, Mother's Day (April/May); and Summer, Father's Day (June/July) **Buys 40 mss/year.** Query by mail with published clips. Submit complete mss on spec only. Length: 700-2,000 words. **Pays $350/regular column; $500/feature.**
Photos State availability Captions, identification of subjects, model releases required. Reviews contact sheets, negatives, transparencies. Negotiates payment individually
Columns/Departments 20 Query with published clips. **Pays $150-450.**
Tips Send queries with published writing samples and detailed resume. Have new ideas, a voice that speaks to our audience—not *down* to our audience—and supply artwork source.

$ GUIDE

True Stories Pointing to Jesus, Review and Herald Publishing Association, 55 W. Oak Ridge Dr., Hagerstown MD 21740. (301)393-4037. Fax: (301)393-4055. E-mail: guide@rhpa.org. Website: www.guidemagazine.org. **90% freelance written**. Weekly magazine featuring all-true stories showing God's involvement in 10- to 14-year-olds' lives. Estab. 1953. Circ. 32,000. Byline given. Pays on acceptance. No kill fee. Publishes ms an average of 8 months after acceptance. Buys second serial (reprint) rights. first world Editorial lead time 8 months. Submit seasonal material 8 months in advance. Accepts queries by mail, e-mail, fax. Responds in 1 month to queries. Sample copy for 6x9 SAE and 2 first-class stamps Guidelines available online.

- Prefers electronic ms submissions.

Nonfiction Needs religious. No fiction. Nonfiction should set forth a clearly evident spiritual application. **Buys 300 mss/year.** Send complete ms. Length: 500-1,200 words. **Pays $25-140.**
Reprints Send photocopy. Pays 50% of usual rates
Fillers Needs anecdotes, games, puzzles, religious. 75 **Pays $25-50.**
Tips The majority of `misses' are due to the lack of a clearly evident (not `preachy') spiritual application.

$ HIGHLIGHTS FOR CHILDREN

803 Church St., Honesdale PA 18431-1824. (570)253-1080. Fax: (570)251-7847. Website: www.Highlights.com. **Contact:** Christine French Clark, editor-in-chief. **80% freelance written**. Monthly magazine for children up to age 12. "This book of wholesome fun is dedicated to helping children grow in basic skills and knowledge, in creativeness, in ability to think and reason, in sensitivity to others, in high ideals, and worthy ways of living—for children are the world's most important people. We publish stories for beginning and advanced readers. Up to 500 words for beginners (ages 3-7), up to 800 words for advanced (ages 8-12)." Estab. 1946. Pays on acceptance. Buys all rights. Responds in 2 months to queries. Sample copy free. Guidelines on website in "About Us" area.
Nonfiction "We need articles on science, technology, and nature written by persons with strong backgrounds in those fields. Contributions always welcomed from new writers, especially engineers, scientists, historians, teachers, etc., who can make useful, interesting facts accessible to children. Also writers who have lived abroad and can interpret the ways of life, especially of children, in other countries in ways that will foster world brotherhood. Sports material, arts features, biographies, first-person accounts of fieldwork, photo essays, ancient history, high-interest animal articles, world culture, and articles of general interest to children. Direct, original approach, simple style, interesting content, not rewritten from encyclopedias. State background and qualifications for writing factual articles submitted. Include references or sources of information. Articles geared toward our younger readers (3-7) especially welcome, up to 500 words. Also, novel but tested craft ideas with clear directions. Include samples. Projects must require only free or inexpensive, easy-to-obtain materials. Especially desirable if easy enough for early primary grades. Also, fingerplays and action rhymes, easy for young children to grasp and to dramatize. Avoid wordiness. We need creative-thinking puzzles that can be illustrated, optical illusions, brain teasers, games of physical agility, and other `fun' activities of up to 300 words." Accepts queries by mail 800 words maximum **Pays $25 for craft ideas and puzzles; $25 for fingerplays; $150 and up for articles.**
Photos Reviews color 35mm slides, photos, or electronic files.
Fiction "Meaningful stories appealing to both girls and boys, up to age 12. Vivid, full of action. Engaging plot, strong characterization, lively language. Prefers stories in which a child protagonist solves a dilemma through his or her own resources. Seeks stories that the child ages 8-12 will eagerly read, and the child ages 2-7 will like to hear when read aloud (500-800 words). Stories require interesting plots and a number of illustration possiblities. Also need rebuses (picture stories 120 words or under), stories with urban settings, stories for beginning readers (100-500 words), sports and humorous stories, adventures, holiday stories, and mysteries. We also would like to see more material of 1-page length (300 words), both fiction and factual. Needs adventure, fantasy, historical, humorous, animal, contemporary, folktales, multi-cultural, problem-solving, sports. No war, crime or violence. Send complete ms. Length: words. **Pays $150 minimum.**

Tips "We are pleased that many authors of children's literature report that their first published work was in the pages of *Highlights*. It is not our policy to consider fiction on the strength of the reputation of the author. We judge each submission on its own merits. With factual material, however, we do prefer that writers be authorities in their field or people with first-hand experience. In this manner we can avoid the encyclopedic article that merely restates information readily available elsewhere. We don't make assignments. Query with simple letter to establish whether the nonfiction subject is likely to be of interest. A beginning writer should first become familiar with the type of material that *Highlights* publishes. Include special qualifications, if any, of author. Write for the child, not the editor. Write in a voice that children understand and relate to. Speak to today's kids, avoiding didactic, overt messages. Even though our general principles haven't changed over the years, we are contemporary in our approach to issues. Avoid worn themes."

$ $ HUMPTY DUMPTY'S MAGAZINE

Children's Better Health Institute, P.O. Box 567, Indianapolis IN 46206-0567. (317)636-8881. Fax: (317)684-8094. E-mail: plybarger@cbhi.org. Website: www.humptydumptymag.org. **25% freelance written**. Magazine published 8 times/year covering health, nutrition, hygiene, fitness, and safety for children ages 4-6. Our publication is designed to entertain and to educate young readers in healthy lifestyle habits. Fiction, poetry, pencil activities should have an element of good nutrition or fitness. Estab. 1948. Circ. 350,000. Byline given. Pays on publication. Publishes ms an average of 8 months after acceptance. Buys all rights. Editorial lead time 8 months. Submit seasonal material 10 months in advance. Accepts simultaneous submissions. Sample copy for $2.95. Guidelines for SASE or on website.

- All work is on speculation only; queries are not accepted nor are stories assigned.

Nonfiction Material must have a health theme—nutrition, safety, exercise, hygiene. We're looking for articles that encourage readers to develop better health habits without preaching. Very simple factual articles that creatively teach readers about their bodies. We use several puzzles and activities in each issue—dot-to-dot, hidden pictures, and other activities that promote following instructions, developing finger dexterity, and working with numbers and letters. Include word count. **Buys 3-4 mss/year.** Send complete ms. 300 words maximum **Pays 22¢/word.**

Photos Send photos Offers no additonal payment for photos accepted with ms Buys all rights.

Columns/Departments Mix & Fix (no-cook recipes), 100 words. All ingredients must be nutritious—low fat, no sugar, etc.—and tasty. 8 Send complete ms. **Payment varies**

Fiction Contact: Phyllis Lybarger, editor. We use some stories in rhyme and a few easy-to-read stories for the beginning reader. All stories should work well as read-alouds. Currently we need health/sports/fitness stories. We try to present our health material in a positive light, incorporating humor and a light approach wherever possible. Avoid stereotyping. Characters in contemporary stories should be realistic and reflect good, wholesome values. Include word count. No inanimate talking objects, animal stories, or science fiction. **Buys 4-6 mss/year.** Send complete ms. 350 words maximum **Pays 22¢/word for stories, plus 10 contributor's copies.**

Tips We would like to see more holiday stories, articles, and activities. Please send seasonal material at least eight months in advance.

$ $ JACK AND JILL

Children's Better Health Institute, P.O. Box 567, Indianapolis IN 46206-0567. (317)636-8881. Fax: (317)684-8094. E-mail: j.goodman@cbhi.org. Website: www.jackandjillmag.org. **Contact:** Julia Goodman, editor. **50% freelance written**. Bimonthly magazine published 6 times/year for children ages 8-12. "Material will not be returned unless accompanied by SASE with sufficient postage. No queries. May hold material being seriously considered for up to 1 year." Estab. 1938. Circ. 200,000. Byline given. Pays on publication. Publishes ms an average of 8 months after acceptance. Buys all rights. Submit seasonal material 8 months in advance. Responds in 12 weeks to mss. Sample copy for $2.95. Guidelines available online.

Fiction Pays 15¢/word minimum.

Tips "We are constantly looking for new writers who can tell good stories with interesting slants—stories that are not full of out-dated and time-worn expressions. We like to see stories about kids who are smart and capable, but not sarcastic or smug. Problem-solving skills, personal responsibility, and integrity are good topics for us. Obtain current issues of the magazine and study them to determine our present needs and editorial style."

$ $ $ JUNIOR SCHOLASTIC

Scholastic, Inc., 557 Broadway, New York NY 10012-3902. (212)343-6100. Fax: (212)343-6945. E-mail: junior@scholastic.com. Website: www.juniorscholastic.com. Magazine published 18 times/year. Edited for students ages 11-14. Circ. 535,000. No kill fee. Editorial lead time 6 weeks.

MAGIC DRAGON

Association for Encouragement of Children's Creativity, P.O. Box 687, Webster NY 14580. E-mail: magicdragon@rochester.rr.com. Website: www.magicdragonmagazine.com. Quarterly magazine covering children's writing and art. All work is created by children up to age 12 (elementary school grades). We consider stories, poems, and artwork. Estab. 2005. Circ. 3,500. Byline given. Pays 1 contributor copy on publication. No kill fee. Buys

one-time rights. Editorial lead time 3-6 month. Submit seasonal material 6 months in advance. Accepts queries by mail, e-mail. Responds in 2 weeks to queries. Sample copy for $4. Guidelines available online.
Nonfiction Needs essays, humor, inspirational, personal experience. Send complete ms. 250 words maximum.
Photos Include a SASE with all original artwork. If it's a copy, make sure the colors and copy are the same and the lines are clear. Include an explanation of how you created the art (crayon, watercolor, paper sculpture, etc).
Fiction Needs adventure, fantasy, historical, humorous.
Poetry Needs free verse, haiku, light verse, traditional. 30 lines maximum.

$ $ $ $ NATIONAL GEOGRAPHIC KIDS

Dare to Explore, National Geographic Society, 1145 17th St. NW, Washington DC 20036. Website: www.kidsnationalgeographic.com. **70% freelance written**. Magazine published 10 times/year. It's our mission to excite kids about their world. We are the children's magazine that makes learning fun. Estab. 1975. Byline given. Pays on acceptance. Offers 10% kill fee. $100 Publishes ms an average of 6 months after acceptance. Buys all rights. Makes work-for-hire assignments. Editorial lead time 6+ months. Submit seasonal material 6+ months in advance. Accepts queries by mail. Accepts simultaneous submissions. Sample copy for #10 SAE. Guidelines free.
Nonfiction Needs general interest, humor, interview, technical, travel, animals, human interest, science, technology, entertainment, archaeology, pets. "We do not release our editorial calendar. We do not want poetry, sports, fiction, or story ideas that are too young—our audience is between ages 8-14." Query with published clips and resume. Length: 100-1,000 words. **Pays $1/word for assigned articles.** Pays expenses of writers on assignment.
Photos Contact: Jay Sumner, photo director. State availability Captions, identification of subjects, model releases required. Reviews contact sheets, negatives, transparencies, prints. Negotiates payment individually.
Columns/Departments Amazing Animals (animal heroes, stories about animal rescues, interesting/funny animal tales), 100 words; Inside Scoop (fun, kid-friendly news items), 50-70 words. Query with published clips. **Pays $1/word.**
Tips "Submit relevant clips. Writers must have demonstrated experience writing for kids. Read the magazine before submitting. Send query and clips via snail mail—materials will not be returned. No SASE required unless sample copy is requested."

$ NATURE FRIEND

4253 Woodcock Lane, Dayton VA 22821. (540)867-0764. Website: www.dogwoodridgeoutdoors.com. **Contact:** Kevin Shank. **80% freelance written**. Monthly magazine covering nature. "*Nature Friend* includes stories, puzzles, science experiments, nature experiments—all submissions need to honor God as creator." Estab. 1983. Circ. 13,000. Byline given. Pays on publication. No kill fee. Buys first rights, buys one-time rights. Editorial lead time 4 months. Submit seasonal material 6 months in advance. Accepts simultaneous submissions. Responds in 6 months to mss. Sample copy and writer's guidelines for $10 postage paid.
Nonfiction Needs how-to, nature, science experiments, photo feature, articles about interesting/unusual animals. No poetry, evolution, animals depicted in captivity. **Buys 50 mss/year.** Send complete ms. Length: 250-900 words. **Pays 5¢/word.**
Photos Send photos Captions, identification of subjects required. Reviews prints. Offers $20-75/photo Buys one time rights.
Columns/Departments Learning By Doing, 500-900 words. 12 Send complete ms.
Fillers Needs facts, puzzles, short essays on something current in nature. 35 Length: 150-250 words. **5¢/word**
Tips "We want to bring joy and knowledge to children by opening the world of God's creation to them. We endeavor to create a sense of awe about nature's creator and a respect for His creation. I'd like to see more submissions on hands-on things to do with a nature theme (not collecting rocks or leaves—real stuff). Also looking for good stories that are accompanied by good photography."

$ $ NEW MOON

The Magazine for Girls & Their Dreams, New Moon Publishing, Inc., 2 W. First St., #101, Duluth MN 55802. (218)728-5507. Fax: (218)728-0314. E-mail: girl@newmoon.org. Website: www.newmoon.org. **25% freelance written**. Bimonthly magazine covering girls ages 8-14, edited by girls aged 8-14. In general, all material should be pro-girl and feature girls and women as the primary focus. *New Moon* is for every girl who wants her voice heard and her dreams taken seriously. *New Moon* celebrates girls, explores the passage from girl to woman, and builds healthy resistance to gender inequities. The *New Moon* girl is true to herself and *New Moon* helps her as she pursues her unique path in life, moving confidently into the world. Estab. 1992. Circ. 30,000. Byline given. Pays on publication. Publishes ms an average of 6 months after acceptance. Buys all rights. Editorial lead time 6 months. Submit seasonal material 8 months in advance. Accepts queries by mail, e-mail, fax. Accepts simultaneous submissions. Responds in 2 months to mss. Sample copy for $7 or online. Guidelines for SASE or online.

Nonfiction Needs essays, general interest, humor, inspirational, interview, opinion, personal experience, written by girls, photo feature, religious, travel, multicultural/girls from other countries. No fashion, beauty, or dating. **Buys 20 mss/year.** Send complete ms. Length: 600 words. **Pays 6-12¢/word.**
Photos State availability Captions, identification of subjects required. Negotiates payment individually Buys one time rights.
Columns/Departments Women's Work (profile of a woman and her job relating the the theme), 600 words; Herstory (historical woman relating to theme), 600 words. 10 Query. **Pays 6-12¢/word**
Fiction Prefers girl-written material. All girl-centered. Needs adventure, fantasy, historical, humorous, slice-of-life vignettes. **Buys 6 mss/year.** Send complete ms. Length: 1,200-1,400 words. **Pays 6-12¢/word.**
Poetry No poetry by adults.
Tips We'd like to see more girl-written feature articles that relate to a theme. These can be about anything the girl has done personally, or she can write about something she's studied. Please read *New Moon* before submitting to get a sense of our style. Writers and artists who comprehend our goals have the best chance of publication. We love creative articles—both nonfiction and fiction—that are not condescending to our readers. Keep articles to suggested word lengths; avoid stereotypes. Refer to our guidelines and upcoming themes.

$ $ POCKETS

The Upper Room, P.O. Box 340004, Nashville TN 37203-0004. (615)340-7333. Fax: (615)340-7267. E-mail: pockets@upperroom.org. Website: www.pockets.org. **60% freelance written**. Monthly (except February) magazine covering children's and families' spiritual formation. "We are a Christian, inter-denominational publication for children 6-12 years old, focused primarily on the 9-12 age group. Each issue reflects a specific theme." Estab. 1981. Byline given. Pays on acceptance. No kill fee. Publishes ms an average of 1 year after acceptance. Buys first North American serial rights. Submit seasonal material 1 year in advance. Responds in 8 weeks to mss. Each issue reflects a specific theme. Sample copy available with a 9x12 SASE with 4 First-Class stamps attached to envelope. Guidelines on Web site.
Nonfiction "Seek brief biographical sketches, famous or unknown persons, whose lives reflect their Christian commitment and are of particular interest to children. Write in a way that appeals to children. Fictional characters and some elaboration may be included in scripture stories, but the writer must remain faithful to the story." **Buys 10 mss/year.** Length: 400-600 words. **Pays 14¢/word.**
Reprints Accepts one-time previously published submissions. Send ms with rights for sale noted and information about when and where the material previously appeared.
Photos Send 4-6 close-up photos of children actively involved in peacemakers at work activities. Send photos, contact sheets, prints, or digital images. Must be 300 dpi. Pays $25/photo Buys one time rights.
Columns/Departments Poetry and Prayer (related to themes), maximum 24 lines; Family Time, 200-300 words; Peacemakers at Work (profiles of children working for peace, justice, and ecological concerns), 400-600 words. **Pays 14¢/word**. Activities/Games (related to themes). **Pays $25 and up**. Kids Cook (simple recipes children can make alone or with minimal help from an adult). **Pays $25.**
Fiction "Submissions add should contain lots of action, use believable dialogue, be simply written, and be relevant to the problems faced by this age group in every day life. Children need to be able to see themselves in the pages of the magazine. It is important that the tone not be 'preachy' or didactic. Use short sentences and paragraphs. When possible, use concrete words instead of abstractions." Needs adventure, ethnic, historical, general, religious. No violence, science fiction, romance, fantasy, or talking animal stories. **Buys 25-30 mss/year.** Send complete ms. Length: 600-900 words. **Pays 14¢/word, plus 2-5 contributor's copies.**
Poetry Buys 14 poems/year. Length: 4-24 lines. **Pays $2/line, $25 minimum.**
Tips "Theme stories, role models, and retold scripture stories are most open to freelancers. Poetry is also open. It is very helpful if writers read our writers' guidelines and themes on our website."

$ SHINE BRIGHTLY

GEMS Girls' Clubs, P.O. Box 7259, Grand Rapids MI 49510. (616)241-5616. Fax: (616)241-5558. E-mail: christina@gemsgc.org. Website: www.gemsgc.org. **80% freelance written. Works with new and published/established writers.** Monthly magazine. Our purpose is to lead girls into a living relationship with Jesus Christ and to help them see how God is at work in their lives and the world around them. Puzzles, crafts, stories, and articles for girls ages 9-14. Estab. 1971. Circ. 16,000. Byline given. Pays on publication. No kill fee. Publishes ms an average of 1 year after acceptance. Buys first North American serial rights, buys second serial (reprint) rights, buys simultaneous rights. Submit seasonal material 1 year in advance. Accepts previously published material. Accepts simultaneous submissions. Responds in 2 months to queries. Sample copy for 9x12 SAE with 3 first class stamps and $1. Guidelines available online.
Nonfiction We do not want easy solutions or quick character changes from good to bad. No pietistic characters. No 'new girl at school starting over after parents' divorce' stories. Constant mention of God is not necessary if the moral tone of the story is positive. We do not want stories that always have a happy ending. Needs include: biographies and autobiographies of heroes of the faith, informational (write for issue themes), multicultural materials. Needs humor, inspirational, seasonal and holiday, interview, personal experience, avoid the testimony

approach, photo feature, query first, religious, travel, adventure, mystery. **Buys 35 unsolicited mss/year.** Send complete ms. Length: 100-900 words. **Pays 3¢/word, plus 2 copies.**

Reprints Send typed manuscript with rights for sale noted and information about when and where the material previously appeared.

Photos Purchased with or without ms. Appreciate multicultural subjects. Reviews 5x7 or 8x10 clear color glossy prints. Pays $25-50 on publication

Columns/Departments How-to (crafts); puzzles and jokes; quizzes. Length: 200-400 words. Send complete ms. **Pay varies**

Fiction Needs adventure, that girls could experience in their hometowns or places they might realistically visit, ethnic, historical, humorous, mystery, believable only, religious, nothing too preachy, romance, stories that deal with awakening awareness of boys are appreciated, slice-of-life vignettes, suspense, can be serialized. **Buys 20 mss/year.** Send complete ms. Length: 400-900 words. **Pays up to $35.**

Poetry Needs free verse, haiku, light verse, traditional. **Pays $5-15.**

Tips Prefers not to see anything on the adult level, secular material, or violence. Writers frequently oversimplify the articles and often write with a Pollyanna attitude. An author should be able to see his/her writing style as exciting and appealing to girls ages 9-14. The style can be fun, but also teach a truth. Subjects should be current and important to *SHINE brightly* readers. Use our theme update as a guide. We would like to receive material with a multicultural slant.

$ SPARKLE

GEMS Girls' Clubs, P.O. Box 7259, Grand Rapids MI 49510. (616)241-5616. Fax: (616)241-5558. E-mail: sarahv@gemsgc.org. Website: www.gemsgc.org. **80% freelance written.** Magazine published 6 times/year that helps girls in first through third grades grow in a stronger relationship with Jesus Christ. *Sparkle*'s mission is to prepare girls for a life of living out their faith. Our mission is to prepare girls to become world changers. We aspire for girls to passionately shadow Jesus, seeking to live, act and talk so that others are drawn toward the savior. Estab. 2002. Circ. 5,000. Byline given. Pays on publication. Offers $20 kill fee. Buys first North American serial rights, buys first rights, buys one-time rights, buys second serial (reprint) rights, buys simultaneous rights. Editorial lead time 3 months. Submit seasonal material 1 year in advance. Accepts queries by mail. Accepts previously published material. Accepts simultaneous submissions. Responds in 3 weeks to queries. Responds in 3 months to mss. Sample copy for 9x13 SAE, 3 first-class stamps, and $1 for coverage/publication cost. Writer's guidelines for #10 SASE or online.

Nonfiction Needs how-to, crafts/recipes, humor, inspirational, personal experience, photo feature, religious, travel. Constant mention of God is not necessary if the moral tone of the story is positive. **Buys 15 mss/year.** Send complete ms. Length: 100-400 words. **Pays $20/article**

Photos Send photos Identification of subjects required. Reviews at least 5X7 clear color glossy prints, GIF/JPEG files on CD. Offers $25-50/photo. Buys one time rights.

Columns/Departments Crafts; puzzles and jokes; quizzes, all 200-400 words. Send complete ms. **Payment varies.**

Fiction Needs adventure, ethnic, fantasy, humorous, mystery, religious, slice-of-life vignettes. **Buys 10 mss/year.** Send complete ms. Length: 100-400 words. **Pays $20/story.**

Poetry Needs free verse, haiku, light verse, traditional. We do not wish to see anything that is too difficult for a first grader to read. We wish it to remain light. The style can be fun, but also teach a truth. No violence or secular material. **Buys 4 poems/year.** Submit maximum 4 poems.

Fillers Needs facts, short humor. 6 Length: 50-150 words. **Pays $10-15.**

Tips Writers should keep stories simple but not write with a 'Pollyanna' attitude. Authors should see their writing style as exciting and appealing to girls ages 6-9. Subjects should be current and important to *Sparkle* readers. Use our theme as a guide. We would like to receive material with a multicultural slant.

$ $ SPIDER

The Magazine for Children, Cricket Magazine Group, 70 East Lake St., Suite 300, Chicago IL 60601. (312)701-1720. Fax: (312)701-1728. Website: www.cricketmag.com. **85% freelance written.** Monthly reading and activity magazine for children ages 6 to 9. *Spider* introduces children to the highest quality stories, poems, illustrations, articles, and activities. It was created to foster in beginning readers a love of reading and discovery that will last a lifetime. We're looking for writers who respect children's intelligence. Estab. 1994. Circ. 70,000. Byline given. Pays on publication. Accepts previously published material. Accepts simultaneous submissions. Responds in 6 months to mss. Guidelines available online.

Nonfiction Nature, animals, science, foreign culture, history, fine arts and music, humanities topics. Submit complete ms, bibliography, SASE. Length: 300-800 words. **Pays up to 25¢/word.**

Reprints Send photocopy with rights for sale noted and information about when and where the material previously appeared.

Photos For art samples, it is especially helpful to see pieces showing children, animals, action scenes, and several scenes from a narrative showing a character in different situations. Send photocopies/tearsheets. Also

considers photo essays (prefers color, but b&w is also accepted). Captions, identification of subjects, model releases required. Reviews contact sheets, transparencies, 8 × 10 prints.
Fiction Stories should be easy to read. Needs fantasy, humorous, science fiction, folk tales, fairy tales, fables, myths. Length: 300-1,000 words. **Pays up to 25¢/word.**
Poetry Needs free verse, traditional. Submit maximum 5 poems. 20 lines maximum **Pays $3/line maximum.**
Fillers Recipes, crafts, puzzles, games, brainteasers, math and word activities. 1-4 pages **Pays for fillers.**
Tips We'd like to see more of the following: engaging nonfiction, fillers, and 'takeout page' activities; folktales, fairy tales, science fiction, and humorous stories. Most importantly, do not write down to children.

$ STONE SOUP

The Magazine by Young Writers and Artists, Children's Art Foundation, P.O. Box 83, Santa Cruz CA 95063-0083. (831)426-5557. Fax: (831)426-1161. E-mail: editor@stonesoup.com. Website: www.stonesoup.com. **Contact:** Ms. Gerry Mandel, editor. **100% freelance written**. Bimonthly magazine of writing and art by children, including fiction, poetry, book reviews, and art by children through age 13. "Audience is children, teachers, parents, writers, artists. We have a preference for writing and art based on real-life experiences; no formula stories or poems." Estab. 1973. Circ. 20,000. Pays on publication. Publishes ms an average of 4 months after acceptance. Buys all rights. Submit seasonal material 6 months in advance. Sample copy for $5 or online. Guidelines available online.
Nonfiction Needs historical, personal experience, book reviews. **Buys 12 mss/year. Pays $40.**
Fiction Contact: Ms. Gerry Mandel, editor. Needs adventure, ethnic, experimental, fantasy, historical, humorous, mystery, science fiction, slice-of-life vignettes, suspense. We do not like assignments or formula stories of any kind. **Buys 60 mss/year.** Send complete ms. Length: 150-2,500 words. **Pays $40 for stories. Authors also receive 2 copies, a certificate, and discounts on additional copies and on subscriptions.**
Poetry Needs avant-garde, free verse. **Buys 12 poems/year. Pays $40/poem.**
Tips "All writing we publish is by young people ages 13 and under. We do not publish any writing by adults. We can't emphasize enough how important it is to read a couple of issues of the magazine. We have a strong preference for writing on subjects that mean a lot to the author. If you feel strongly about something that happened to you or something you observed, use that feeling as the basis for your story or poem. Stories should have good descriptions, realistic dialogue, and a point to make. In a poem, each word must be chosen carefully. Your poem should present a view of your subject, and a way of using words that are special and all your own."

$ $ ⊘ U.S. KIDS

A Weekly Reader Magazine, Children's Better Health Institute, P.O. Box 567, Indianapolis IN 46206-0567. (317)636-8881. Fax: (317)684-8094. Website: www.cbhi.org/magazines/uskids/index.shtml. **50% freelance written**. Magazine published 8 times/year featuring kids doing extraordinary things, especially activities related to health, sports, the arts, interesting hobbies, the environment, computers, etc. Estab. 1987. Circ. 230,000. Byline given. Pays on publication. Publishes ms an average of 4 months after acceptance. Buys all rights. Editorial lead time 6 months. Submit seasonal material 6 months in advance. Responds in 4 months to mss. Sample copy for $2.95 or online. Guidelines for #10 SASE.

- *U.S. Kids* is being retargeted to a younger audience. Closed to submissions until further notice.

Nonfiction Especially interested in articles with a health/fitness angle. Needs general interest, how-to, interview, science, kids using computers, multicultural. **Buys 16-24 mss/year.** Send complete ms. 400 words maximum **Pays up to 25¢/word.**
Photos State availability Captions, identification of subjects, model releases required. Reviews contact sheets, negatives, transparencies, color photocopies, or prints. Negotiates payment individually Buys one time rights.
Columns/Departments Real Kids (kids doing interesting things); Fit Kids (sports, healthy activities); Computer Zone. Length: 300-400 words. Send complete ms. **Pays up to 25¢/word**
Fiction Buys very little fictional material. **Buys 1-2 mss/year.** Send complete ms. 400 words **Pays up to 25¢/word.**
Poetry Needs light verse, traditional. **Buys 6-8 poems/year.** Submit maximum 6 poems. Length: 8-24 lines. **Pays $25-50.**
Fillers Needs facts, newsbreaks, short humor, puzzles, games, activities. Length: 200-500 words. **Pays 25¢/word**
Tips We are retargeting the magazine for first-, second-, and third-graders, and looking for fun and informative articles on activities and hobbies of interest to younger kids. Special emphasis on fitness, sports, and health. Availability of good photos a plus.

LITERARY & LITTLE

A CAPPELLA ZOO

A cappella Zoo, 100 Harvard Ave. E. #A1, Seattle WA 98102 U.S. Website: www.acappellazoo.com. **Contact:**

Colin Meldrum, editor/publisher. **99%**. Covering experimental and magical realist literary works. "*A cappella Zoo* invites submissions of memorable prose, poetry, drama, and genre-bending works. We are especially excited about magical realism and works that experiment with technique, form, language, and thought." Estab. 2008. Circ. 250. Pays on publication. 4 months First North American serial rights Accepts queries by e-mail at editor@acappellazoo.com. Accepts simultaneous submissions. 2 weeks on queries; 3 months on mss. Guidelines available online

Nonfiction Needs general interest, literary and highly creative. Send complete ms. no minimum words; 7,500 max/words **Pays $5-30 for unsolicited articles.**

Photos Send photos with submission. GIF/JPEG files One-time rights

Fiction Needs Magical realism. **Buys 30 mss/year mss/year.** Send complete ms. no minimum, 7,500 max/ words

Poetry We want *avant-garde* poetry. **Buys 30/year poems/year.** Submit maximum 3 poems.

Tips "We accept only electronic submissions. "

$ $ $ 🄽 DELAWARE BEACH LIFE

Endeavours LLC, Endeavours, LLC, P.O. Box 417, Rehoboth Beach DE 19927. E-mail: info@delawarebeachlife.com. Website: www.delawarebeachlife.com. **Contact:** Terry Plowman, publisher/editor. Covering coastal Delaware. "Delaware Beach Life focuses on coastal Delaware: Fenwick to Lewes. You can go slightly inland as long as there's water and a natural connection to the coast, e.g. Angola or Long neck." Publishes 8 issues/year. Estab. 2002. Circ. 15,000. True Pays on acceptance. 50% kill fee. 4 months Buys first North American serial rights 6 months editorial lead time. Submit seasonal material 12 months in advance. Accepts queries by e-mail. Accepts previously published mss.Reports in 8 weeks/queries; 6 months/mss Sample copy available online at website Guidelines free and by e-mail

- "Delaware Beach Life is the only full-color glossy magazine focused on coastal Delaware's culture and lifestyle. Created by a team of the best freelance writers, the magazines takes a deeper look at the wealth of topics that interest coastal residents. Delaware Beach Life features such top-notch writing and photography that it inspires 95% of its readers to save it as a 'coffee-table' magazine."

Nonfiction Needs book excerpts, essays, general interest, humor, interview, opinion, photo feature feature. Does not want anything not focused on coastal Delaware. Query with published clips. 1,200-3,000/words **Pays $400-1,000 for assigned articles** Does not pay expenses of writers on assignment.

Photos Send photos Photos require captions, identification of subjects. Reviews GIF/JPEG files. Pays $25-100 per photo. Purchases one-time rights.

Columns/Departments Profiles, History, and Opinion (all coastal DE)—1,200/words each. Buys 32 mss/year Query with published clips. **Pays $150-350.**

Fiction Needs adventure, condensed novels, historical, humorous, novel excerpts, Must have coastal theme. Does not want anything not coastal. **Buys Buys 3 mss/year. mss/year.** Query with published clips. 1,000-2,000/words **True.**

Poetry Needs We use avant-garde, free verse, haiku, light verse, and traditional. Does not want anything not coastal. No erotic poetry. **Buys Buys 6 poems/year poems/year.** Submit maximum 3 poem can be submitted at one time. poems. 6-15/lines **Pays $50/max.**

Tips "Review writer's guidelines."

$ $ 🄲 GRAIN LITERARY MAGAZINE

Saskatchewan Writers Guild, P.O. Box 67, Saskatoon SK S7K 3K1 Canada. (306)244-2828. Fax: (306)244-0255. E-mail: grainmag@sasktel.net. Website: www.grainmagazine.ca. **100% freelance written**. Quarterly magazine covering poetry, fiction, creative nonfiction, drama. *Grain* publishes writing of the highest quality, both traditional and innovative in nature. The *Grain* editors' aim: To publish work that challenges readers; to encourage promising new writers; and to produce a well-designed, visually interesting magazine. Estab. 1973. Circ. 1,600. Byline given. Pays on publication. Buys first rights, buys canadian serial rights. Editorial lead time 6 months. Accepts queries by mail. Responds in 1 month to queries. Responds in 4 months to mss. Sample copy for $13 or online. Guidelines for #10 SASE or online.

Nonfiction Interested in creative nonfiction.

Photos Submit 12-20 slides and b&w prints, short statement (200 words), and brief resume. Reviews transparencies, prints. Pays $100 for front cover art, $30/photo.

Fiction Contact: David Carpenter, fiction editor. Literary fiction of all types. Needs experimental, mainstream, contemporary, prose poem. No romance, confession, science fiction, vignettes, mystery. **Buys 40 mss/year.** No more than 30 pages. **Pays $50-225.**

Poetry Needs avant-garde, free verse, haiku, traditional. High quality, imaginative, well-crafted poetry. Submit maximum 8 poems and SASE with postage or IRC's. No sentimental, end-line rhyme, mundane. **Buys 78 poems/year. Pays $40-175.**

Tips Sweat the small stuff. Pay attention to detail, credibility. Make sure you have researched your piece and that the literal and metaphorical support one another.

MAKE

A Chicago literary magazine, P.O. Box 478353, Chicago IL 478353. E-mail: submissions@makemag.com. Website: www.makemag.com. Biannual magazine featuring a series of fiction pieces, poetry, photography, and a nonfiction section, containing interviews, genre reviews, essays, and editorials. chicago is a storyteller's city and *MAKE* is the story's magazine. Editors prefer writers upload their work via an electronic submission system on their site. Circ. 2,000. Byline given. No kill fee.

Nonfiction Needs essays. Send complete ms.

Fiction Needs experimental, mainstream.

Poetry Needs avant-garde, free verse, traditional. Submit maximum 3-5 poems.

Tips This magazine seeks to expand upon the Chicago tradition of informative and innovative writing, while also examining current styles and textures.

5 AM

The Magazine of Contemporary Poetry, Box 205, Spring Church PA 15686. Website: www.5ampoetry.com. Semiannual tabloid covering American poetry; writing from the best small press writers of our time. "Open to most themes." No kill fee. Accepts queries by mail. Responds in 4-6 weeks to mss. Sample copy for $5.

Tips "We read all year. Manuscripts cannot be returned without SASE with sufficient postage."

THE ABSENT WILLOW REVIEW

Tales of Horror, Fantasy & Science Fiction, Absent Willow Publishing, LLC, PO Box 66, Rochester NH 03866. E-mail: editor@absentwillowreview.com and rick@absentwillowreview.com. Website: www.absentwillowreview.com. **100% freelance written**. Monthly webzine covering Horror, Fantasy, and Science Fiction. "We are looking for authors who can show us that they know and understand their craft. That sense of wonder we feel when a story transports us to another time or place is what fuels our passion and keeps us reading. Strong characters are a key to capturing our attention." Estab. 2008. Author to share in proceeds if included in an Anthology. No kill fee. Buys electronic rights, buys Anthology rights. Accepts queries by e-mail. Accepts simultaneous submissions. Online at http://absentwillowreview.com/submissions

Fiction Contact: Rick DeCost. "Stories should fall between 2,000 - 8,000 words in length. Stories above 8,000 words may be considered if deemed exceptional by our editorial staff and must not exceed 10,000 words." Needs fantasy, horror, science fiction. "We do not want to see erotica or excessive gore for the sake of gore. We will not publish stories that may be seen as promoting discrimination against other persons based on gender, age, sexual orientation, religion or race. Violence and profanity are not prohibited but should be used with discretion." Send complete ms. Length: 2,000-8,000 words.

Poetry Contact: Rick DeCost, editor. Needs free verse, light verse, traditional.

Tips "Please visit our website to view our submission guidelines. We are looking for quality works of fiction. The best way to break into our magazine and to be considered for our print anthology is to write a compelling story with memorable characters. If your first submission isn't accepted, keep trying. We love new authors and are always eager to read their work."

N ACORN

A Journal of Contemporary Haiku, Redfox Press, P.O. Box 186, Philadelphia PA 19105. E-mail: acornhaiku@mac.com. **Contact:** Carolyn Hall, editor. Biannual magazine dedicated to publishing the best of contemporary English language haiku, and in particular to showcasing individual poems that reveal the extraordinary moments found in everyday life. Estab. 1998. Publishes ms an average of 1-3 months after acceptance. Reads submissions in January-February and July-August only. Buys first rights, buys one-time rights. Accepts queries by mail, e-mail. Responds in 3 weeks to mss. Guidelines available online.

Poetry Needs haiku. "Decisions made by editor on a rolling basis. Poems judged purely on their own merits, not dependent on other work taken." Sometimes acceptance conditional on minor edits. Often comments on rejected poems. "Does NOT want epigrams, musings, and overt emotion poured into 17 syllables; surreal, science fiction, or political commentary 'ku;' strong puns or raunchy humor. Syllable counting generally not necessary or encouraged." Length: 1-5 lines.

Tips This is primarily a journal for those with a focused interest in haiku, rather than an outlet for the occasional short jottings of longer-form poets. It is a much richer genre than one might surmise from many of the recreational websites that claim to promote 'haiku.'"

$ AFRICAN AMERICAN REVIEW

Saint Louis University, Humanities 317, 3800 Lindell Blvd., St. Louis MO 63108. (314)977-3688. Fax: (314)977-1514. E-mail: keenanam@slu.edu. Website: aar.slu.edu. **65% freelance written**. Quarterly magazine covering African-American literature and culture. Essays on African-American literature, theater, film, art and culture generally; interviews; poetry and fiction by African-American authors; book reviews. Estab. 1967. Circ. 2,000. Byline given. Pays on publication. Publishes ms an average of 1 year after acceptance. Buys first North American serial rights. Editorial lead time 1 year. Responds in 1 month to queries. Responds in 6 months to mss. Sample copy for $12. Guidelines available online.

Nonfiction Needs essays, interview. **Buys 30 mss/year.** Query. Length: 3,500-6,000 words. **Pays $35-80.**
Photos State availability Captions required. Pays $100 for covers.
Fiction Contact: Joycelyn Moody, editor. Needs ethnic, experimental, mainstream. No children's/juvenile/ young adult/teen. **Buys 5 mss/year.** Length: 2,500-5,000 words. **Pays $25-50, 1contributor's copy and 3 offprints.**

$ AGNI

Creative Writing Program, Boston University, 236 Bay State Rd., Boston MA 02215. (617)353-7135. Fax: (617)353-7134. E-mail: agni@bu.edu. Website: www.agnimagazine.org. Biannual magazine. Eclectic literary magazine publishing first-rate poems, essays, translations, and stories. Estab. 1972. Circ. 4,000. Byline given. Pays on publication. Publishes ms an average of 6 months after acceptance. Buys first North American serial rights. Rights to reprint in *AGNI* anthology (with author's consent). Editorial lead time 1 year. Accepts queries by mail. Accepts simultaneous submissions. Responds in 2 weeks to queries. Responds in 4 months to mss. Sample copy for $10 or online. Guidelines available online.

- Reading period September 1-May 31 only. "Online magazine carries original content not found in print edition. All submissions are considered for both."

Fiction Buys stories, prose poems. "No science fiction or romance." **Buys more than 20 mss/year. Pays $10/ page up to $150, 2 contributor's copies, 1-year subscription, and 4 gift copies.**
Poetry Buys more than 120 poems/year poems/year. Submit maximum 5 poems. **Pays $20-150.**
Tips "We're also looking for extraordinary translations from little-translated languages. It is important to look at a copy of *AGNI* before submitting, to see if your work might be compatible. Please write for guidelines or a sample."

$ $ ALASKA QUARTERLY REVIEW

ESB 208, University of Alaska-Anchorage, 3211 Providence Dr., Anchorage AK 99508. (907)786-6916. E-mail: aqr@uaa.alaska.edu. Website: www.uaa.alaska.edu/aqr. **95% freelance written.** Semiannual magazine publishing fiction, poetry, literary nonfiction, and short plays in traditional and experimental styles. "*AQR* publishes fiction, poetry, literary nonfiction and short plays in traditional and experimental styles." Estab. 1982. Circ. 2,700. Byline given. Honorariums on publication when funding permits. Publishes ms an average of 6 months after acceptance. Buys first North American serial rights. Upon request, rights will be transferred back to author after publication. Accepts queries by mail. Responds in 1 month to queries. Responds in 6 months to mss. Sample copy for $6. Guidelines available online.

- *Alaska Quarterly* reports they are always looking for freelance material and new writers.

Nonfiction Literary nonfiction: essays and memoirs. **Buys 0-5 mss/year.** Query. Length: 1,000-20,000 words. **Pays $50-200 subject to funding.**
Fiction Contact: Ronald Spatz, fiction editor. Experimental and traditional literary forms. No romance, children's, or inspirational/religious. Publishes novel excerpts. **Buys 20-26 mss/year.** Also publishes drama: experimental and traditional one-act plays. **Buys 0-2 mss/year.** Needs experimental, contemporary, prose poem. If the works in *Alaska Quarterly Review* have certain characteristics, they are these: freshness, honesty, and a compelling subject. What makes a piece stand out from the multitude of other submissions? The voice of the piece must be strong—idiosyncratic enough to create a unique persona. We look for the demonstration of craft, making the situation palpable and putting it in a form where it becomes emotionally and intellectually complex. One could look through our pages over time and see that many of the pieces published in the *Alaska Quarterly Review* concern everyday life. We're not asking our writers to go outside themselves and their experiences to the absolute exotic to catch our interest. We look for the experiential and revelatory qualities of the work. We will, without hesitation, champion a piece that may be less polished or stylistically sophisticated, if it engages me, surprises me, and resonates for me. The joy in reading such a work is in discovering something true. Moreover, in keeping with our mission to publish new writers, we are looking for voices our readers do not know, voices that may not always be reflected in the dominant culture and that, in all instances, have something important to convey. not exceeding 100 pages **Pays $50-200 subject to funding; pays in contributor's copies and subscriptions when funding is limited.**
Poetry Needs avant-garde, free verse, traditional. No light verse. **Buys 10-30 poems/year.** Submit maximum 10 poems. **Pays $10-50 subject to availability of funds; pays in contributor's copies and subscriptions when funding is limited.**
Tips "All sections are open to freelancers. We rely almost exclusively on unsolicited manuscripts. *AQR* is a nonprofit literary magazine and does not always have funds to pay authors."

ALEHOUSE PRESS

P.O. Box 31655, San Francisco CA 94131. E-mail: query@alehousepress.com. Website: www.alehousepress.com. Annual magazine. In general, unsolicited poetry is considered through the *Alehouse* Happy Hour Poetry Awards. *Alehouse* is happy to consider queries for both essays and book reviews. Our essay topics focus on the current state of poetry, the work of particular poets, plus other appropriate topics of interest. Estab. 2006.

Byline given. No kill fee. Guidelines by email.
Nonfiction Needs essays, Book Reviews. Query.
Poetry Needs avant-garde, free verse, haiku, light verse, traditional. Length: 1-40 lines.

N ALIMENTUM

the lilterature of food, P.O. Box 210028, Nashville TN 37221. E-mail: submissions@alimentumjournal.com. Website: www.alimentumjournal.com. Biannual magazine covering food in literature. "We're seeking fiction, creative nonfiction, and poetry all around the subject of food or drink. We do not read year-round. Check website for reading periods." Byline given. No kill fee. Accepts queries by mail. Accepts simultaneous submissions. Responds in 1-3 months to mss.
Nonfiction Send complete ms.
Fiction Send complete ms.
Poetry Contact: Cortney Davis, poetry editor. Needs avant-garde, free verse, haiku, light verse, traditional. **Buys 5 poems per submission poems/year.**
Tips "No email submissions, only snail mail. Mark outside envelope to the attention of Poetry, Fiction, or Nonfiction Editor."

$ AMERICAN BOOK REVIEW

The Writer's Review, Inc., School of Arts & Sciences, Univ. of Houston-Victoria, 3000 N. Ben Wilson, Victoria TX 77901. (361)570-4848. E-mail: americanbookreview@llstu.edu. Website: www.americanbookreview.org. Bimonthly magazine covering book reviews. We specialize in reviewing books published by independent presses. Estab. 1977. Circ. 15,000. Byline given. Pays on publication. Offers $50 kill fee. Publishes ms an average of 2-4 months after acceptance. Buys one-time rights. Editorial lead time 1 month. Accepts queries by mail, e-mail, fax, phone. Responds in 2 weeks to queries. Responds in 1-2 months to mss. Sample copy for $4. Guidelines available online.
Nonfiction Book reviews. Does not want fiction, poetry, or interviews. Query with published clips. Length: 750-1,250 words. **Pays $50.**
Tips Most of our reviews are assigned, but we occasionally accept unsolicited reviews. Send query and samples of published reviews.

AMERICAN LETTERS AND COMMENTARY

Dept. of English, Univ. of Texas at San Antonio, One UTSA Circle, San Antonio TX 78249. E-mail: amerletters@satx.rr.com. Website: www.amletters.org. Annual magazine covering innovative and challenging poetry, fiction, and nonfiction essays. "Only previously unpublished work is considered. We publish creative nonfiction essays and critical essays with experimental slant/subject matter." No kill fee. Publishes ms an average of 1 year after acceptance. Accepts simultaneous submissions. Guidelines available.
Nonfiction "No resumes, reviews of your work, or lengthy lists of previous publications. Do not send an SASE for response. Submissions will not be returned."
Fiction Needs experimental. 10 pages or less
Poetry Submit maximum 3-5 poems. Length: 10 lines.
Tips "Our reading period is Oct. 1st - Mar. 1st. A brief cover letter is always welcome. Read a recent issue before submitting—75% of submissions are rejected because they don't fit the journal's aesthetic or don't comply with our guidelines. No emailed submissions. We will make contact via email by Sept. 1st for forthcoming issue inclusions. Include an email address in your contact info. All rights are returned to author upon publication."

AMERICAN POETRY REVIEW

American Poetry Review, 1700 Sansom St., Suite 800, Philadelphia PA 19103. (215)496-0439. E-mail: sberg@aprweb.org. Website: www.aprweb.org. Bimonthly pubication covering the very best contemporary poetry and prose from a diverse array of authors. "*American Poetry Review* has helped to make poetry a more public art form without compromising the art of poetry. We publish a broad range of material and bring the diverse international poetry community together." Estab. 1972. Circ. 9,000-12,000. $1,000 prize awarded to 2 poets whose work appeared in *APR* the previous year. No kill fee. Buys first North American serial rights. Accepts queries by mail. Responds in 3 months to mss. Sample copy for $4.25. Online at www.aprweb.org/guidelines.shtml
Nonfiction Needs essays, interview, Review, Translations, Literary Criticism, Social Commentary.
Tips "Do not send mss. by fax or email. Mss. should be typewritten or computer-printed on white 8½ x 11 paper. Prose should be double-spaced. Don't send multiple submissions."

$ $ AMERICAN SHORT FICTION

Badgerdog Literary Publishing, P.O. Box 301209, Austin TX 78703. (512)538-1305. Fax: (512)538-1306. E-mail: editors@americanshortfiction.org. Website: www.americanshortfiction.org. Quarterly magazine publishing new fiction in which transformations of language, narrative, and character occur swiftly, deftly, and unexpectedly. We are drawn to evocative language, unique subject matter, and an overall sense of immediacy. We target

readers who love literary fiction, are drawn to independent publishing, and enjoy short fiction. *ASF* is one of the few journals that focuses solely on fiction. Estab. 1991. Circ. 2,500. Byline given. Pays on publication. Publishes ms an average of 3 months after acceptance. Buys first North American serial rights, buys electronic rights. Accepts simultaneous submissions. Responds in 2 weeks to queries. Responds in 5 months to mss. Guidelines available online.
Fiction Needs experimental, literary, translations. Does not want young adult or genre fiction. However, we are open to publishing mystery or speculative fiction if we feel it has literary value. **Buys 20-25 mss/year.** Send complete ms. Length: 2,000-15,000 words. **Pays $250-500.**

THE AMERICAS

A Quarterly Review of Inter-American Cultural History, 3250-60 Chestnut St., MacAlister 3025, Philadelphia PA 19104. E-mail: americas@drexel.edu. Website: www.drexel.edu/academics/coas/theamericas/. Quarterly magazine One of the principal English-language journals of Latin American history. We publish articles and reviews in history and ethnohistory about all geographical regions of the Americas and their Iberian background. Our review provides a bridge between scholars of all the Americas and on presenting a range of subjects and perspectives. Articles on the cultural, social, religious, and intellectual history of Latin America and the Borderlands are particularly encouraged, as is research which places these themes in a comparative framework with any region of the world. We take a special interest in the history of the Franciscan presence in the Americas. Estab. 1944. No kill fee. Accepts queries by mail, e-mail. Online at www.drexel.edu/academics/coas/theamericas/style.htm.
Nonfiction Needs essays, expose, historical, opinion, religious, Translations. The Inter-American Notes section is an important part of *The Americas*. It includes short reports on archives, research projects, conferences, scholarly competitions and awards, and cultural news. Other featuers include publication of translations of documents that may be of use in classroom teaching. We do not accept unsolicited book reviews.
Tips Wwe prefer MS Word or .rtf file submissions. Mss. should be double-spaced. Use American spelling rather than British. When in doubt, consult The American Heritage Dictionary of the English Language, 3d ed. Use as few capitals as possible. Use endnotes rather than footnotes. Send your electronic ms. as an email attachment. Or, mail two copies.

$ ANCIENT PATHS

Ancient Paths Literary Magazine, P.O. Box 7505, Fairfax Station VA 22039. E-mail: ssburris@cox.net. Website: www.editorskylar.com. **99% freelance written**. Biennial magazine with subtle Christian and universal religious themes. "*Ancient Paths* publishes quality fiction, creative nonfiction and poetry for a literate Christian audience. Religious themes are usually subtle, and the magazine has non-Christian readers as well as some content by non-Christian authors. However, writers should be comfortable appearing in a Christian magazine." Estab. 1998. Circ. 175. Byline given. Pays on publication. No kill fee. Publishes ms an average of 6 months after acceptance. Buys one-time rights. Accepts previously published material. Accepts simultaneous submissions. Responds in 4-5 weeks to queries Sample copy for $10; make checks payable to Skylar Burris.

- *Ancient Paths* is published in January of odd-numbered years. Submission period is March 1-June 1.
- O➛ "Issue 16 will feature two poets (15-20 pages of poetry) and two short story writers (6,000-9,000 words). Featured writers/poets will be paid $50 and one free copy. Query with first three pages of your ms.

Fiction Needs historical, humorous, mainstream, novel concepts, religious, general religious/literary, religious fantasy, religious mystery/suspense, slice-of-life vignettes, literary. No retelling of Bible stories. Literary fiction favored over genre fiction. **Buys 4-10 mss/year.** Send complete ms. Length: 250-2,500 words.
Poetry Needs free verse, traditional. No avant-garde, prose poetry, forced rhyme or poor meter. **Buys 25-60 poems/year.** Submit maximum 5 poems. Length: 4-60 lines. **Pays $2/poem, 1 copy, and discount on additional copies.**
Tips "Make the reader think as well as feel. Do not simply state a moral message; no preaching, nothing didactic. You should have something meaningful to say, but be subtle. Show, don't tell."

$ ANDROIDS2 MAGAZINE

Man's Story 2 Publishing Co., P.O. Box 1082, Roswell GA 30077. E-mail: mansstory2@aol.com. Website: www.mansstory2.com. **80% freelance written**. Online e-zine. *"Man's Story 2 Magazine* strives to recreate the pulp fiction that was published in the magazines of the 1920s through the 1970s with strong emphasis on 3D graphic art." Estab. 2001. Circ. 500. Pays on publication. Publishes ms an average of 3-6 months after acceptance. Buys one-time rights, buys second serial (reprint) rights. Accepts queries by e-mail. Accepts previously published material. Accepts simultaneous submissions. Guidelines available online.

- "Story subjects tend to slant toward the damsel in distress."

Fiction Needs adventure, erotica, fantasy, horror, suspense, pulp fiction. **Buys 30-50 mss/year.** Send complete ms. Length: 1,500-3,500 words. **Pays $25.**

Tips "We suggest interested writers visit our website. Then, read the 1960s style pulp fiction stories posted in our online mini-magazine and/or read one of our magazines, or find an old pulp fiction magazine that was published in the 1960s. If all else fails, e-mail us."

$ ANTIETAM REVIEW

Washington County Arts Council, 14 W. Washington St., Hagerstown MD 21740. (301)791-3132. Fax: (240)420-1754. E-mail: antietamreview@washingtoncountyarts.com (queries only). Website: www.washingtoncountyarts.com. **90% freelance written**. Annual magazine covering fiction, poetry, and b&w photography. Estab. 1982. Circ. 1,000. No kill fee. Buys first North American serial rights. Sample copy for $6.30 (back issue); $8.40 (current issue).

Photos Seeks b&w photos. All subject matter is considered. Contact via mail or e-mail for photo guidelines.

Fiction Needs cond novels, ethnic, experimental, novel concepts, short stories of a literary quality. No religious, romance, erotica, confession, or horror. Maximum 5,000 words **Pays $50-100 and 2 contributor's copies.**

Poetry Needs avant-garde, free verse, traditional. No haiku, religious or rhyme. Submit maximum 3 poems. 30 lines maximum **Pays $25/poemand2contributorcopies.**

Tips We seek high-quality, well-crafted work with significant character development and shift. We look for work that is interesting, involves the reader, and teaches us a new way to view the world. A manuscript stands out because of its energy and flow. Most of our submissions reflect the times (news/current events) more than industry trends. Works should have a compelling voice, originality, and magic. Contributors are encouraged to review past issues.

$ THE ANTIGONISH REVIEW

St. Francis Xavier University, P.O. Box 5000, Antigonish NS B2G 2W5 Canada. (902)867-3962. Fax: (902)867-5563. E-mail: tar@stfx.ca. Website: www.antigonishreview.com. **Contact:** Bonnie McIsaac, office manager. **100% freelance written**. Quarterly magazine. Literary magazine for educated and creative readers. Estab. 1970. Circ. 850. Byline given. Pays on publication. Offers variable kill fee. Publishes ms an average of 8 months after acceptance. Rights retained by author. Editorial lead time 4 months. Submit seasonal material 4 months in advance. Accepts queries by mail, fax. Responds in 1 month to queries. Responds in 6 months to mss. Sample copy for $7 or online Writer's guidelines for #10 SASE or online

Nonfiction Needs essays, interview, book reviews/articles. No academic pieces. **Buys 15-20 mss/year.** Query. Length: 1,500-5,000 words. **Pays $50-150.**

Fiction Literary. No erotica. **Buys 35-40 mss/year.** Send complete ms. Length: 500-5,000 words. **Pays $100 for stories.**

Poetry Buys 100-125 poems/year. Submit maximum 5 poems. **Pays $30/full page.**

Tips "Send for guidelines and/or sample copy. Send ms with cover letter and SASE with submission."

$ ANTIOCH REVIEW

P.O. Box 148, Yellow Springs OH 45387-0148. Website: http://review.antioch.edu. Quarterly magazine for general, literary, and academic audience. Literary and cultural review of contemporary issues, and literature for general readership. Estab. 1941. Circ. 5,000. Byline given. Pays on publication. Publishes ms an average of 10 months after acceptance. Responds in 3-6 months to mss. Sample copy for $7. Guidelines available online.

Nonfiction Contemporary articles in the humanities and social sciences, politics, economics, literature, and all areas of broad intellectual concern. Somewhat scholarly, but never pedantic in style, eschewing all professional jargon. Lively, distinctive prose insisted upon. We *do not* read simultaneous submissions. Length: 2,000-8,000 words. **Pays $15/printed page.**

Fiction Contact: Fiction editor. Quality fiction only, distinctive in style with fresh insights into the human condition. Needs experimental, contemporary. No science fiction, fantasy, or confessions. generally under 8,000 **Pays $15/printed page.**

Poetry No light or inspirational verse. **Pays $15/printed page.**

$ ARC

Canada's National Poetry Magazine, Arc Poetry Society, P.O. Box 81060, Ottawa ON K1P 1B1 Canada. E-mail: arc@arcpoetry.ca. Website: www.arcpoetry.ca. Semiannual magazine featuring poetry, poetry-related articles, and criticism. Our focus is poetry, and Canadian poetry in general, although we do publish writers from elsewhere. We are looking for the best poetry from new and established writers. We often have special issues. Send a SASE for upcoming special issues and contests. Estab. 1978. Circ. 1,500. Byline given. Pays on publication. Publishes ms an average of 6 months after acceptance. Buys one-time rights. Responds in 4 months. Guidelines for #10 SASE.

Nonfiction Needs essays, interview, book reviews. Query first. Length: 500-4,000 words. **Pays $40/printed page (Canadian), and 2 copies.**

Photos Query first. Pays $300 for 10 photos Buys one time rights.

Poetry Needs avant-garde, free verse. E-mail submissions not accepted. **Buys 60 poems/year.** Submit maximum 5 poems. **Pays $40/printed page (Canadian).**

Tips Please include brief biographical note with submission.

ARKANSAS REVIEW

A Journal of Delta Studies, P.O. Box 1890, State University AR 72467. (870)972-3674. Fax: (870)972-3045. E-mail: delta@astate.edu. Website: www.clt.astate.edu/arkreview. **90% freelance written.** Triannual magazine covering the 7-state Mississippi River Delta region. All material, creative and scholarly, published in the *Arkansas Review*, must evoke or respond to the natural and/or cultural experience of the Mississippi River Delta region. Estab. 1998. Circ. 700. Byline given. No kill fee. Buys first North American serial rights. Editorial lead time 4 months. Submit seasonal material 8 months in advance. Accepts queries by mail, fax. Accepts simultaneous submissions. Responds in 2 weeks to queries. Responds in 4 months to mss. Sample copy for $7.50. Guidelines available online.

Nonfiction Needs book excerpts, essays, general interest, historical, interview, personal experience, photo feature. **Buys 2-3 mss/year.** Send complete ms. Length: 500-10,000 words.

Photos Contact: Kim Vickrey, art editor. State availability Reviews contact sheets, GIF/JPEG files. Offers no additional payment for photos accepted with ms. Buys one time rights.

Fiction Needs ethnic, experimental, historical, humorous, mainstream, mystery, novel concepts. **Buys 6-8 mss/year.** Send complete ms. 10,000 words maximum

Poetry Needs avant-garde, free verse, traditional. **Buys 20-24 poems/year.** Submit maximum 6 poems. Length: 1-100 lines.

Tips Submit via mail. E-mails are more likely to be overlooked or lost. Submit a cover letter, but don't try to impress us with credentials or explanations of the submission. Immerse yourself in the literature of the Delta, but provide us with a fresh and original take on its land, its people, its culture. Surprise us. Amuse us. Recognize what makes this region particular as well as universal, and take risks. Help us shape a new Delta literature.

ARSENIC LOBSTER

E-mail: lobster@magere.com. Website: www.arseniclobster.magere.com. (Anthology: annual) (Online: Apr., Aug., Dec.) journal & book covering poetry. Poems should be timeless, rich in imagery and edgy; seeking elegant emotion, articulate experiment. Be compelled to write. No kill fee. Accepts simultaneous submissions. Online at: http://arseniclobster.magere.com/submission.html

Photos Reviews PDF or JPG.

Poetry Contact: Lissa Kiernan, poetry editor. Needs free verse. We do not want political rants or Hallmark poetry. Submit maximum 3-5 poems.

Tips All works must be previously unpublished. Include a lively, short biography. Poetry topics, reviews and criticism, and art/photographs (pdf or jpg attachment only) are also welcome.

$ ARTFUL DODGE

Dept. of English, College of Wooster, Wooster OH 44691. (330)263-2577. Website: www.wooster.edu/artfuldodge. Annual magazine that takes a strong interest in poets who are continually testing what they can get away with successfully in regard to subject, perspective, language, etc., but who also show mastery of the current American poetic techniques—its varied textures and its achievement in the illumination of the particular. There is no theme in this magazine, except literary power. We also have an ongoing interest in translations from Central/Eastern Europe and elsewhere. Estab. 1979. Circ. 1,000. Buys first North American serial rights. Accepts queries by mail. Accepts simultaneous submissions. Responds in 1-6 months to mss. Sample copy for $7. Guidelines for #10 SASE.

Fiction Contact: Marcy Campbell, fiction editor. Needs experimental, prose poem. We judge by literary quality, not by genre. We are especially interested in fine English translations of significant prose writers. Translations should be submitted with original texts. **Pays 2 contributor's copies and honorarium of $5/page, thanks to funding from the Ohio Arts Council.**

Poetry Contact: Philip Brady, poetry editor. We are interested in poems that utilize stylistic persuasions both old and new to good effect. We are not afraid of poems which try to deal with large social, political, historical, and even philosophical questions—especially if the poem emerges from one's own life experience and is not the result of armchair pontificating. We don't want cute, rococo surrealism, someone's warmed-up, left-over notion of an avant-garde that existed 10-100 years ago, or any last bastions of rhymed verse in the civilized world. **Buys 20 poems/year.** Submit maximum 6 poems. **Pays $5/page honorarium and 2 contributor's copies.**

Tips Poets may send books for review consideration; however, there is no guarantee we can review them.

$ ARTS & LETTERS

Journal of Contemporary Culture, Georgia College & State University, Campus Box 89, Milledgeville GA 31061. E-mail: al@gcsu.edu. Website: al.gcsu.edu. Semiannual magazine covering poetry, fiction, creative nonfiction, and commentary on contemporary culture. The journal features the mentors interview series and the world poetry translation series. Also, it is the only journal nationwide to feature authors and artists that represent such an eclectic range of creative work. Estab. 1999. Circ. 1,500. Pays on publication. No kill fee. Publishes ms an average of 6-12 months after acceptance. Rights revert to author after publication. Responds in 2 months to mss. Sample copy for $5, plus $1 for postage. Guidelines available online.

Nonfiction Contact: Karen Salyer McElmurray, creative nonfiction editor. Looking for creative nonfiction.

Fiction Contact: Allen Gee, fiction editor. No genre fiction. **Buys 6 mss/year.** Length: 3,000-7,500 words. **Pays $50 minimum or $10/published page.**

Poetry Contact: Alice Friman, poetry editor.

Tips An obvious, but not gimmicky, attention to fresh usage of language. A solid grasp of the craft of story writing. Fully realized work.

BABEL FRUIT

E-mail: editors@babelfruit.org. Website: www.babelfruit.com. Biannual website covering prose, poetry, and creative nonfiction. "We publish literature of exile, expatriation, repatriation, integration and exploration. We want to read literature under the influence of 'the other.' Travel, look around or reach within. Wherever you see the other." Accepts previously published material.

Nonfiction Needs book excerpts, essays, interview, Translations, Book Reviews, MP3 Recording of Readings (Please send text first.). "Do not send us writing with political intentions. Don't share your recreational drug stories (unless you're very good). We don't accept work that has a primary focus on portraying the other as a victim or oppressor. We are not proponents of the paranormal."

Fiction Needs experimental.

Poetry Submit maximum 3-6 poems.

Tips "If you use an attachment to submit, use: babelfruit.submission.doc and put your name in the subject line. We invite new and established writers."

N THE BALTIMORE REVIEW

A National Journal of Poetry, Fiction, and Creative Nonfiction, P.O. Box 36418, Towson MD 21286. Website: www.baltimorereview.org. **100% freelance written**. Semiannual journal. "The Baltimore Review publishes poetry, fiction, and creative nonfiction from Baltimore and beyond." Estab. 1996. Circ. 1,200. Byline given. Contributor paid in copies. No kill fee. Publishes ms an average of 6 months after acceptance. Buys first North American serial rights. Accepts queries by mail. Accepts simultaneous submissions. Responds in 6 weeks to queries. Responds in 4 months to mss. Sample copy for $10. Guidelines available online.

- "We publish work of high literary quality from established and new writers. No specific preferences regarding theme or style, and all are considered."

Nonfiction Needs essays, interview, personal experience, travel. **Buys 4/year mss/year.** Send complete ms. Length: 1,000-6,000 words. Sometimes pays expenses of writers on assignment. Limit agreed upon in advance.

Photos Send photos Identification of subjects required. Reviews contact sheets. Negotiates payment individually

Fiction Needs ethnic, experimental, novel concepts. No genre fiction. **Buys 25/year mss/year.** Send complete ms. Length: 100-6,000 words.

Poetry Needs avant-garde, free verse, haiku, light verse, traditional. **Buys 25/year poems/year.** Submit maximum 4 poems. 4 pages

Tips "Please read what is being published in other literary journals, including our own. As in any other profession, writers must know what the trends and the major issues are in the field."

N THE BAREFOOT MUSE

A Journal of Formal Metrical Verse, P.O. Box 115, Hainesport NJ 08036. E-mail: editor@barefootmuse.com. Website: www.barefootmuse.com. Semiannual magazine covering formal poetry and metrical verse. "Publishes essays on aspects of formal/metrical poetry, and reviews of books with a noticeable proportion of formal poetry. You may submit your book or chapbook for review. Copies will not be returned. Provides balanced, respectful reviews which shrink neither from praise nor criticism, as tools to inform a prospective buyer/reader. Bios requested along with acceptance notices." Estab. 2005. No kill fee. Accepts queries by mail, e-mail. Accepts previously published material. Accepts simultaneous submissions. Responds in 2 months to mss.

Poetry No free verse; only poems in received forms, or which use meter (rhyme is optional). Submit maximum 3-6 poems.

Tips "Submissions are welcome all year. Editorial deadlines are: May 15th for the June issue, and Nov. 15th for the Dec. issue. Include SASE and email address for reply. I will not open attachments without prior arrangement."

BARRELHOUSE

Website: www.barrelhousemag.com. Biannual magazine featuring fiction, poetry, interviews and essays about music, art and the detritus of popular culture. Byline given. No kill fee. Accepts simultaneous submissions. Responds in 2-3 months to mss.

Nonfiction Needs essays. Send complete ms. **Pays 2 contributor copies.**

Fiction Needs experimental, humorous, mainstream. Send complete ms. **Pays 2 contributor copies.**
Poetry Submit maximum 3-5 poems.
Tips We only take submissions through our fancy pants little online submission center now. Only means only people. do not send with snail mail.

BATEAU PRESS

P.O. Box 2335, Amherst MA 01004. E-mail: submit@bateaupress.org. Website: www.bateaupress.org. www.bateaupress.org. Biannual magazine publishing poetry, flash fiction, short plays, mini reviews, comic strips or graphic narratives, and other illustrations. Byline given. No kill fee. Accepts simultaneous submissions. Responds in 1-4 months to mss.
Nonfiction Send complete ms.
Fiction Send complete ms.
Poetry Needs avant-garde, free verse, haiku, light verse, traditional. Submit maximum 5 poems.
Tips We recommend ordering a copy to better understand our aesthetics. It will save you and us a lot of time and resources.

BELLINGHAM REVIEW

Mail Stop 9053, Western Washington University, Bellingham WA 98225. (360)650-4863. E-mail: bhreview@cc.wwu.edu. Website: www.wwu.edu/bhreview. **100% freelance written.** Annual nonprofit magazine. *Bellingham Review* seeks literature of palpable quality; stories, essays, and poems that nudge the limits of form or execute traditional forms exquisitely. Estab. 1977. Circ. 1,600. Byline given. Pays on publication when funding allows. No kill fee. Publishes ms an average of 6 months after acceptance. Buys first North American serial rights. Editorial lead time 6 months. Accepts simultaneous submissions. Responds in 1-6 months to mss. Sample copy for $7. Guidelines available online.
Nonfiction Contact: Nonfiction Editor. Needs essays, personal experience. Does not want anything nonliterary. **Buys 4-6 mss/year.** Send complete ms. 9,000 words maximum. **Pays as funds allow, plus contributor copies.**
Columns/Departments .
Fiction Contact: Fiction Editor. Literary short fiction. Needs experimental, humorous. Does not want anything nonliterary. **Buys 4-6 mss/year.** Send complete ms. 9,000 words maximum. **Pays as funds allow.**
Poetry Contact: Lori Brack & Matthew Brown. Needs avant-garde, free verse, traditional. Will not use light verse. **Buys 10-30 poems/year.** Submit maximum 3 poems. Indicate approximate word count on prose pieces. **Pays as funds allow.**
Tips Open submission period is from Sept. 15-February 1. Manuscripts arriving between February 2 and September 15 will be returned unread. The *Bellingham Review* holds 3 annual contests: the 49th Parallel Poetry Award, the Annie Dillard Award in Nonfiction, and the Tobias Wolff Award in Fiction. Submissions December 1-March 15, 2009. See the individual listings for these contests under Contests & Awards for full details.

BELOIT POETRY JOURNAL

Beloit Poetry Journal, P.O. Box 151, Farmington ME 04938. (207)778-0020. E-mail: bpj@bpj.org. Website: www.bpj.org. Quarterly magazine covering contemporary poetry. We are open to a wide range of forms and styles in contemporary poetry. We are always watching for new poets, quickened language and poems that offer a new purchase on the political or social landscape. The Chad Walsh Poetry Prize ($3,000) is awarded to the author of the poem or group of poems that are judged to be outstanding during the previous year. Estab. 1950. No kill fee. Responds in 1-16 weeks to queries. Sample copy for $5.
Poetry Length: 5 pages lines. **pays in contributor's copies.**
Tips We seek only unpublished poems or translations of poems not already available in English. We do not accept electronic submissions. We will reply to international submissions by email and read poems submitted from overseas by email. Please buy a sample issue or browse our website archive.

BIG BRIDGE

Big Bridge Press, 2000 Highway 1, Pacifica CA 94044. E-mail: walterblue@bigbridge.org. Website: www.bigbridge.org. Website covering poetry, fiction, nonfiction, essays, journalism and art. *Big Bridge* is a webzine of poetry and everything else. If we like it, we'll publish it. We're interested in poetry, fiction, nonfiction essays, journalism and art (photos, line drawings, performance, installations, siteworks, comix, graphics). No kill fee. Accepts previously published material. Guidelines available.
Nonfiction Needs essays, interview, Reviews.
Photos Contact: Terri Carrion, editor. Reviews negatives, prints, GIF/JPEG files. original work.
Fiction Contact: Vernon Frazer, editor.
Poetry Needs avant-garde, free verse, haiku, light verse, traditional.
Tips Send electronic art and text to: walterblue@bigbridge.org, or mail disks and hard copy (SASE). We are guided by whimsy and passion and urgency. Each issue will feature an online chapbook.

THE BIG UGLY REVIEW

490 Second St., Suite 200, San Francisco CA 94107. E-mail: info@biguglyreview.com. Website: www.biguglyreview.com. **100% freelance written**. Literary magazine published twice a year. *The Big Ugly Review* showcases emerging and established writers, photographers, filmmakers and musicians. Each issue includes fiction (short stories and flash fiction), creative nonfiction, poetry, photo-essays, short films of 5 minutes or less, and original, downloadable songs, all related to that issue's theme. There is also a contest in each issue called And So It Begins. in which writers create a flash fiction story of up to 500 words that begins with a first sentence given on our website. Estab. 2004. Circ. 10,000. Byline given. Publishes ms an average of 1 month after acceptance. Editorial lead time 1-2 months. Accepts queries by mail, e-mail. Accepts previously published material. Accepts simultaneous submissions. Responds in 1 week to queries. Reports 1 month after deadline on mss. Sample copy available online. Guidelines available online.

Nonfiction Needs book excerpts, essays, humor, personal experience, photo feature, creative nonfiction, personal essay, or standalone memoir excerpt inspired by the issue's theme. Please see website for upcoming issue themes. **Buys 15-20 mss/year.** Send complete ms. Length: 3,000 words maximum.

Photos Contact: photo@biguglyreview.com. Send photos Captions required. Reviews GIF/JPEG files. Offers no additional payment for photos accepted with ms.

Fiction Contact: Elizabeth Bernstein, fiction editor. We accept short stories up to 3,000 words on the theme; flash fiction up to 1,000 words on the theme, and submissions to our And So It Begins. contest, in which contributors write a flash fiction story up to 500 words that begins with a sentence we provide on our website. Needs experimental, mainstream, novel concepts, slice-of-life vignettes, literary. Does not want work that is unrelated to the issue's theme. Please check website for theme. **Buys 30-35 mss/year.** Send complete ms.

Poetry Contact: Miriam Pirone, poetry editor. Needs avant-garde, free verse, traditional. **Buys 15-25 poems/year.**

Tips E-mail submissions are preferred over hard copy. Send submissions to the appropriate editor. *The Big Ugly Review* is a nonpaying market at this time. See Web site for complete guidelines.

THE BINNACLE

University of Maine at Machias, 9 O'Brien Ave., Machias ME 04654. E-mail: ummbinnacle@maine.edu. Website: www.umm.maine.edu/binnacle. **100% freelance written**. Semiannual alternative paper format covering general arts. We publish an alternative format journal of literary and visual art. We are restless about the ossification of literature and what to do about it. Estab. 1957. Circ. 300. No kill fee. Publishes ms an average of 3 months after acceptance. Buys one-time rights. Editorial lead time 2-3 months. Submit seasonal material 3 months in advance. Accepts queries by mail, e-mail. Accepts simultaneous submissions. Responds in 1 month to queries. Responds in 3 months to mss. Sample copy for $5. Writer's guidelines online at website or by e-mail.

Nonfiction Needs humor, personal experience. **Buys 1-2 mss/year.** Send complete ms. Length: 100-750 words.

Photos Send photos Reviews prints, GIF/JPEG files. Offers no additional payment for photos accepted with ms. Buys one time rights.

Fiction Needs ethnic, experimental, humorous, mainstream, slice-of-life vignettes. No extreme erotica, fantasy, horror, or religious, but any genre attuned to a general audience can work. **Buys 10-15 mss/year.** Send complete ms. 1,500 words maximum.

Poetry Needs avant-garde, free verse, haiku, light verse, traditional. No greeting card poetry. **Buys 10-15 poems/year.** Submit maximum 5 poems. 100 lines maximum.

Tips We want fiction, poetry, and images that speak to real people, people who have lives, people who have troubles, people who laugh too.

THE BITTER OLEANDER

The Bitter Oleander Press, 4983 Tall Oaks Dr., Fayetteville NY 13066-9776. Fax: (315)637-5056. E-mail: info@bitteroleander.com. Website: www.bitteroleander.com. **100% freelance written**. Semiannual magazine covering poetry and short fiction, and translations of contemporary poetry. "It is the purpose of *The Bitter Oleander* to be highly innovative, freed from the restraints of how language is ruined by repetition." Estab. 1974. Circ. 1,500. Byline given. No kill fee. Publishes ms an average of 1-6 months after acceptance. Buys one-time rights, buys rights revert back to author upon publication rights. Editorial lead time 6 months. Accepts queries by mail, e-mail. Accepts simultaneous submissions. Responds in 1 week to queries. Responds in 1 month to mss. Sample copy for $10. Guidelines available online.

Fiction Needs experimental. Does not want family stories with moralistic plots, and no fantasy that involves hyper-reality of any sort. **Buys 6 mss/year.** Query. Length: 300-2,500 words. **Pays in copies.**

Poetry Needs avant-garde, free verse, haiku. Does not want rhyme and meter. Submit maximum 8 poems. Length: 1-60 lines. **Pays in copies.**

Tips "Study everything the journal has published and get to know the editor's tendencies based on what's written in each issue."

$ BLACK WARRIOR REVIEW

P.O. Box 862936, Tuscaloosa AL 35486-0027. (205)348-4518. Website: www.bwr.ua.edu. **Contact:** Kate Lorenz, ed. **90% freelance written**. Semiannual magazine of fiction, poetry, essays, art, comics and reviews. "We publish contemporary fiction, poetry, reviews, essays, and art for a literary audience. We publish the freshest work we can find." Estab. 1974. Circ. 2,000. Byline given. Pays on publication. Publishes ms an average of 6 months after acceptance. Buys first rights. Accepts simultaneous submissions. Responds in 4 months to mss. Sample copy for $10. Guidelines available online.

Nonfiction Contact: Andy Johnson, nonfiction editor. Needs interview, literary/personal essays. **Buys 5 mss/year.** No queries; send complete ms. **Pays up to $100, copies, and a 1-year subscription.**

Fiction Contact: Christopher Hellwig, ed. Publishes novel excerpts if under contract to be published. One story/chapter per envelope, please. Want work that is conscious of form and well-crafted. We are open to good experimental writing and short-short fiction. No genre fiction please. **Buys 10 mss/year. Pays up to $150, copies, and a 1-year subscription.**

Poetry Contact: Melissa Hull, ed. **Buys 35 poems/year.** Submit maximum 7 poems. **Pays up to $75, copies, and a 1-year subscription.**

Tips "Read *BWR* before submitting. Send us only your best work. Address all submissions to the appropriate genre editor."

BOOK/MARK QUARTERLY REVIEW

P.O. Box 516, Miller Place NY 11764. (631)331-4118. E-mail: cyberpoet@optonline.net. **90% freelance written.** Quarterly newsletter. "*Book/Mark* is dedicated to publishing reviews of books and magazines by small and independent presses. We are eclectic and cover a wide variety of genres and topics, including literary subjects, the arts, popular culture, politics, history, and the sciences." Estab. 1994. Circ. 800. Byline given. No kill fee. Publishes ms an average of 3-6 months after acceptance. Buys first North American serial rights. Editorial lead time 3 months. Submit seasonal material 3-6 months in advance. Accepts queries by mail, e-mail, phone. Accepts previously published material. Accepts simultaneous submissions. Responds in 1 week to queries. Responds in 1 month to mss. Sample copy for $3 and SASE with 1 first-class stamp. Guidelines for #10 SASE.

Nonfiction We only publish book reviews and essays about books. Does not want fiction or poetry. Query. Length: 600-950 words.

Tips "We like reviews that zero in on the virtues and interesting aspects of books. Writers should be empathetic to the topics or close to the genre of each reviewed work."

$ $ BOULEVARD

Opojaz, Inc., 6614 Clayton Rd., PMB 325, Richmond Heights MO 63117. (314)862-2643. Fax: (314)862-2982. **Contact:** Richard Burgin, Editor. **100% freelance written**. Triannual magazine covering fiction, poetry, and essays. "*Boulevard* is a diverse literary magazine presenting original creative work by well-known authors, as well as by writers of exciting promise." Estab. 1985. Circ. 11,000. Byline given. Pays on publication. Offers no kill fee. Publishes ms an average of 9 months after acceptance. Buys first North American serial rights. Accepts queries by mail, phone. Accepts simultaneous submissions. Responds in 2 weeks to queries. Responds in 3 months to mss. Sample copy for $8. Guidelines available online.

O→ "Break in with a touching, intelligent, and original story, poem, or essay."

Nonfiction Needs book excerpts, essays, interview, opinion, photo feature. No pornography, science fiction, children's stories, or westerns. **Buys 10 mss/year.** Send complete ms. 10,000 words maximum. **Pays $20/page, minimum $150.**

Fiction Contact: Richard Burgin, editor. Needs confession, experimental, mainstream, novel excerpts. "We do not want erotica, science fiction, romance, western, or children's stories." **Buys 20 mss/year.** Send complete ms. 8,000 words maximum. **$20/page; minimum $150.**

Poetry Needs avant-garde, free verse, haiku, traditional. "Do not send us light verse." **Buys 80 poems/year.** Submit maximum 5 poems. Length: 200 lines. **$25-250 (sometimes higher).**

Tips "Read the magazine first. The work *Boulevard* publishes is generally recognized as among the finest in the country. We continue to seek more good literary or cultural essays. Send only your best work."

BRAIN, CHILD

The Magazine for Thinking Mothers, March Press, P.O. Box 714, Lexington VA 24450. E-mail: editor@brainchildmag.com. Website: www.brainchildmag.com. **90% freelance written**. Quarterly magazine covering the experience of motherhood. *Brain, Child* reflects modern motherhood—the way it really is. We like to think of *Brain, Child* as a community, for and by mothers who like to think about what raising kids does for (and to) the mind and soul. *Brain, Child* isn't your typical parenting magazine. We couldn't cupcake-decorate our way out of a paper bag. We are more 'literary' than 'how-to,' more *New Yorker* than *Parents*. We shy away from expert advice on childrearing in favor of first-hand reflections by great writers (Jane Smiley, Barbara Ehrenreich, Anne Tyler) on life as a mother. Each quarterly issue is full of essays, features, humor, reviews, fiction, art, cartoons, and our readers' own stories. Our philosophy is pretty simple: Motherhood is worthy of literature. And there are a lot of ways to mother, all of them interesting. We're proud to be publishing articles and essays that are smart, down to earth, sometimes funny, and sometimes poignant. Estab. 2000. Circ. 36,000. Byline given. Pays on publication. No kill fee. Publishes ms an average of 6 months after acceptance. Buys first North American serial rights, buys electronic rights, buys and *Brain, Child* anthology rights. Editorial lead time 3 months. Submit seasonal material 6 months in advance. Accepts queries by mail, e-mail. Accepts simultaneous submissions. Responds in 1 month to queries. Responds in 1-3 months to mss. Sample copy available online. Guidelines available online.

Nonfiction Needs essays, including debate, humor, in-depth features. No how-to articles, advice, or tips. **Buys 40-50 mss/year.** Query with published clips for features and debate essays; send complete ms for essays. Length: 800-5,000 words. **Payment varies.** Sometimes pays expenses of writers on assignment.

Photos State availability Model releases required. Reviews contact sheets, prints, GIF/JPEG files.

Fiction We publish fiction that has a strong motherhood theme. Needs mainstream, literary. No genre fiction. **Buys 4 mss/year.** Send complete ms. Length: 800-5,000 words. **Payment varies.**

$ $ BRICK

Brick, P.O. Box 609, Station P, Toronto ON M5S 2Y4 Canada. Website: www.brickmag.com. **90% freelance written**. Semiannual magazine covering literature and the arts. "We publish literary nonfiction of a very high quality on a range of arts and culture subjects." Estab. 1978. Circ. 4,000. Byline given. Pays on publication. No kill fee. Publishes ms an average of 3 months after acceptance. Buys first world, first serial, one-time English language rights. Editorial lead time 5 months. Responds in 6 months to mss Sample copy for $15, plus $3 shipping Guidelines available online

Nonfiction Needs essays, historical, interview, opinion, travel. No fiction, poetry, personal real-life experience, or book reviews. **Buys 30-40 mss/year.** Send complete ms. Length: 250-2,500 words. **Pays $75-500 (Canadian).**

Photos State availability Reviews transparencies, prints, TIFF/JPEG files. Offers $25-50/photo Buys one time rights.

Tips *"Brick* is interested in polished work by writers who are widely read and in touch with contemporary culture. The magazine is serious, but not fusty. We like to feel the writer's personality in the piece, too."

BRYANT LITERARY REVIEW

Faculty Suite F, Bryant University, 1150 Douglas Pike, Smithfield RI 02917. E-mail: blr@bryant.edu. Website: www.bryant2.bryant.edu/ ~ blr/. Annual magazine covering poetry and fiction up to 5,000 words. Our readers are expected to be sophisticated, educated and familiar with conventions of contemporary literature. Our purpose is cultivation of an active and growing connection between our community and the larger literary culture. Our production values are high and we provide a respected venue for creative writing of every kind from around the world. No kill fee. Guidelines available.

Fiction Contact: Tom Bassett, fiction editor. **Buys 1 short story mss/year.** Length: 5,000 words.

Poetry Contact: Tad Davies, poetry editor. Submit maximum 3-5 poems.

Tips Our reading period is from Sept. 1 - Dec. 31. We only accept hard-copy submissions. Include SASE. We welcome artwork.

BUFFALO CARP

Quad City Arts, 1715 2nd Ave., Rock Island IL 61201. (309)793-1213. Fax: (309)793-1265. E-mail: rcollins@quadcityarts.com. Website: www.quadcityarts.com. **100% freelance written**. Annual magazine. *Buffalo Carp* is an eclectic mix of poetry, fiction, and narrative nonfiction. Our goal is to provide our readers with the best in previously unpublished, contemporary writing. Estab. 1998. Byline given. Pays on publication. Publishes ms an average of 2-4 months after acceptance. Buys first North American serial rights. Editorial lead time 6-8 months. Accepts queries by e-mail. Accepts simultaneous submissions. Responds in 2-4 weeks to queries. Responds in 6-8 months to mss. Sample copy for $5. Guidelines available online.

Nonfiction Needs personal experience, narrative nonfiction (any style). **Buys publishes 1-2 a year mss/year.** Send complete ms. Length: 2,000-3,000 words. **Pays 2 contributor copies.**

Fiction Any style; less interested in genre fiction. Needs adventure, confession, ethnic, experimental, fantasy, humorous, mainstream, mystery, science fiction, slice-of-life vignettes, suspense. Does not want sexually explicit, racist material. **Buys 2-5 mss/year.** Send complete ms. Length: 2,000-3,000 words. **Pays 2 contributor copies.**

Poetry Needs Avant-garde, free verse, light verse, traditional. Any style; no greeting card verse. **Buys 15-25 poems/year.** Submit maximum 5 poems. **Pays 2 contributor copies.**

Tips Send us your best, most interesting work. Worry less about how you would classify the work and more about it being high-quality and stand-out. We are looking to go in new directions with upcoming issues, so send us what you think best represents you and not who your influences are. *Buffalo Carp* is not interested in blending in, and has no interest in homogenized work. Blow us away!

BURNSIDE REVIEW

Website: www.burnsidereview.org. Semiannual magazine. Byline given. No kill fee. Accepts queries by e-mail.

Accepts simultaneous submissions. Responds in 2-4 months to mss. Guidelines available.
Poetry Needs avant-garde, free verse, traditional. Submit maximum 3-5 poems. **Pays contributor copy.**

$ BUTTON

New England's Tiniest Magazine of Poetry, Fiction and Gracious Living, P.O. Box 77, Westminster MA 01473. E-mail: sally@moonsigns.net. Website: www.moonsigns.net. **10% freelance written**. Annual literary magazine. *"Button* is New England's tiniest magazine of poetry, fiction, and gracious living, published once a year. As 'gracious living' is on the cover, we like wit, brevity, cleverly-conceived essay/recipe, poetry that isn't sentimental or song lyrics. I started *Button* so that a century from now, when people read it in landfils or, preferably, libraries, they'll say, 'Gee, what a great time to have lived. I wish I lived back then.' Submit only between April 1 and October 31 please." Estab. 1993. Circ. 1,500. Byline given. Pays on publication. No kill fee. Publishes ms an average of 3-9 months after acceptance. Buys first North American serial rights. Editorial lead time 6 months. Responds in 1 month to queries. Responds in 2 months to mss. Sample copy for $2.50. Guidelines available online.

Nonfiction Needs personal experience, cooking stories. Does not want "the tired, the trite, the sexist, the multiply-folded, the single-spaced, the sentimental, the self-pitying, the swaggering, the infantile (i.e., coruscated whimsy and self-conscious quaint), poems about Why You Can't Be Together and stories about How Complicated Am I. Before you send us anything, sit down and read a poem by Stanley Kunitz or a story by Evelyn Waugh, Louisa May Alcott, or anyone who's visited the poles, and if you still think you've written a damn fine thing, have at it. A word-count on the top of the page is fine—a copyright or 'all rights reserved' reminder makes you look like a beginner." **Buys 1-2 mss/year.** Length: 300-2,000 words. **Pays $10 and up, depending on length of piece.**

Fiction Contact: W.M. Davies, fiction editor. Seeking quality fiction. No genre fiction, science fiction, techno-thriller. "Wants more of anything Herman Melville, Henry James, or Betty MacDonald would like to read." **Buys 1-2 mss/year.** Send complete ms. Length: 300-2,000 words. **Pays honorarium and subscriptions.**

Poetry Needs free verse, traditional. Seeking quality poetry. **Buys 2-4 poems/year.** Submit maximum 3 poems. **Pays $10-25.**

Tips *"Button* writers have been widely published elsewhere, in virtually all the major national magazines. They include, Ralph Lombreglia, Lawrence Millman, They Might Be Giants, Combustible Edison, Sven Birkerts, Stephen McCauley, Amanda Powell, Wayne Wilson, David Barber, Romayne Dawnay, Brendan Galvin, and Diana DerHovanessian. It's $2.50 for a sample, which seems reasonable. Follow the guidelines, make sure you read your work aloud, and don't inflate or deflate your publications and experience. We've published plenty of new folks, but on the merits of the work."

CALYX

A Journal of Art & Literature by Women, Calyx, Inc., P.O. Box B, Corvallis OR 97339. (541)753-9384. Fax: (541)753-0515. E-mail: calyx@proaxis.com. Website: www.calyxpress.org. Biannual journal publishes prose, poetry, art, essays, interviews and critical and book reviews. *"Calyx* exists to publish fine literature and art by women and is committed to publishing the work of all women, including women of color, older women, working class women and other voices that need to be heard. We are committed to discovering and nurturing developing writers." Estab. 1976. Circ. 6,000. No kill fee. Publishes ms an average of 6-12 months after acceptance. Accepts simultaneous submissions. Responds in 4-8 months to mss. Sample copy for $10 plus $4 postage and handling.

- "Annual open submission period is October 1-December 31. Mss received when not open will be returned. Electronic submissions are not accepted. E-mail for guidelines only."

Fiction Length: 5,000 words. **Payment dependent upon grant support. Also receive free issues and 1 volume subscription.**

Tips "Most mss are rejected because the writers are not familiar with *Calyx*—writers should read *Calyx* and be familar with the publication. We look for good writing, imagination and important/interesting subject matter."

$ $ THE CAPILANO REVIEW

2055 Purcell Way, North Vancouver BC V7J 3H5 Canada. E-mail: contact@thecapilanoreview.ca. Website: www.thecapilanoreview.ca. **100% freelance written**. Triannual visual and literary arts magazine that publishes only what the editors consider to be the very best fiction, poetry, drama, or visual art being produced. *TCR* editors are interested in fresh, original work that stimulates and challenges readers. Over the years, the magazine has developed a reputation for pushing beyond the boundaries of traditional art and writing. We are interested in work that is new in concept and in execution. Estab. 1972. Circ. 900. Byline given. Pays on publication. Publishes ms an average of within 1 year after acceptance. Buys first North American serial rights. Accepts queries by mail. Responds in 4 months to mss. Sample copy for $10 (outside of Canada, USD). Guidelines for #10 SASE with IRC or Canadian stamps or online.

Fiction Send complete ms with SASE and Canadian postage or IRCs. Needs experimental, novel concepts,

previously unpublished only, literary. No traditional, conventional fiction. Want to see more innovative, genre-blurring work. **Buys 10-15 mss/year.** 8,000 words **Pays $50-200.**
Poetry Needs avant-garde, free verse. Submit maximum 6-8 poems (with SASE and Canadian postage or IRCs). **Buys 40 poems/year. Pays $50-200.**

CAVE WALL

Cave Wall Press, LLC, P.O. Box 29546, Greensboro NC 29546. E-mail: editor@cavewallpress.com. Website: www.cavewallpress.com. Biannual magazine dedicated to publishing the best in contemporary poetry. Byline given. No kill fee. Buys first North American serial rights. Accepts simultaneous submissions. Responds in 1-5 months to mss.
Poetry Needs avant-garde, free verse, haiku, light verse, traditional. Submit maximum 3-6 poems.
Tips "We encourage you to read an issue of *Cave Wall* before you submit. Find out what kind of poetry we like. Please note that we read blind. Your name should not appear on your poems."

CHA

An Asian Literary Journal, E-mail: editors@asiancha.com. Website: www.asiancha.com. Quarterly website and in the future we'll have a print anthology; covering poetry, short stories, creative nonfiction, drama and reviews from and about Asia. "Strong focus on Asian-themed creative work or work done by Asian writers and artists." Estab. 2007. No kill fee. Accepts previously published material. Accepts simultaneous submissions. Responds in 3 months to mss. by email at: submissions@asiancha.com
Photos Reviews GIF/JPEG files.
Poetry Submit maximum 1-4/year poems.
Tips "Do not send attachments in your email. Include all writing in the body of email. Include a brief biography (100 words). Any submissions received after July 1, 2009 will be considered for Nov. 2009 issue."

$ CHAPMAN

Chapman Publishing, 4 Broughton Place, Edinburgh EH1 3RX Scotland. (44)(131)557-2207. E-mail: chapman-pub@blueyounder.co.uk. Website: www.chapman-pub.co.uk. **100% freelance written**. Magazine published 3 times/year covering poetry, fiction, articles, and reviews. *Chapman*, Scotland's quality literary magazine, is a dynamic force in Scotland, publishing poetry, fiction, criticism, reviews, and articles on theatre, politics, language, and the arts. Our philosophy is to publish new work, from known and unknown writers—mainly Scottish, but also worldwide. Estab. 1970. Circ. 2,000. Pays on publication. No kill fee. Publishes ms an average of 3 months after acceptance. Buys first rights. Accepts queries by mail. Guidelines by email.
Nonfiction Needs essays, expose, general interest, historical, humor, inspirational, interview, personal experience. **Buys 15 mss/year.** Send complete ms. **Pays £10/page (can vary).**
Fiction Needs experimental, historical, humorous, Scottish/ international. No horror or science fiction. Length: 1,000-5,000 words. **Negotiates payment individually.**
Poetry Needs avant-garde, free verse, haiku, light verse, traditional. Submit maximum 10 poems.

THE CHARITON REVIEW

Truman State University Press, The Chariton Review, Truman State Univ., 100 E Normal Ave, Kirksville MO 63501. (800)916-6802. E-mail: tsup@truman.edu. Website: tsup.truman.edu/chariton/index.aspx. Semiannual magazine covering the best in short fiction, poetry, translations, and essays. Estab. 1975. No kill fee. Guidelines available.
Nonfiction Needs essays, Translation.
Tips "All ms. accepted for publication must be supplied in hard copy and electronic copy."

$ THE CHATTAHOOCHEE REVIEW

Georgia Perimeter College, 2101 Womack Rd., Dunwoody GA 30338-4497. (770)274-5147. Website: www.chattahoochee-review.org. Quarterly magazine. We publish a number of Southern writers, but *Chattahoochee Review* is not by design a regional magazine. All themes, forms, and styles are considered as long as they impact the whole person: heart, mind, intuition, and imagination. Estab. 1980. Circ. 1,350. Byline given. Pays on publication. No kill fee. Publishes ms an average of 3 months after acceptance. Buys first rights. Accepts queries by mail. Responds in 2 weeks to queries. Responds in 4 months to mss. Sample copy for $6. Guidelines available online.
Nonfiction We look for distinctive, honest personal essays and creative nonfiction of any kind, including the currently popular memoiristic narrative. We publish interviews with writers of all kinds: literary, academic, journalistic, and popular. We also review selected current offerings in fiction, poetry, and nonfiction, including works on photography and the visual arts. We do not often, if ever, publish technical, critical, theoretical, or scholarly work about literature, although we are interested in essays written for general readers about writers, their careers, and their work. Needs essays, interviews with authors, reviews. **Buys 10 mss/year.** Send complete ms. 5,000 words maximum
Photos State availability Identification of subjects required. Negotiates payment individually. Buys one time

rights.

Fiction Accepts all subject matter except juvenile, science fiction, and romance. **Buys 12 mss/year.** Send complete ms. 6,000 words maximum **Pays $20/page, $250 max and 2 contributor's copies.**

Poetry Needs avant-garde, free verse, haiku, light verse, traditional. **Buys 60 poems/year.** Submit maximum 5 poems. **Pays $50/poem.**

Tips Become familiar with our journal and the type of work we regularly publish.

$ $ CHICKEN SOUP FOR THE SOUL

101 Stories to Open the Heart and Rekindle the Spirit, Chicken Soup for the Soul Enterprises, Inc., P.O, Box 30880, Santa Barbara CA 93130. (805)563-2935. Fax: (805)563-2945. E-mail: webmaster@chickensoupforthesoul.com. Website: www.chickensoup.com. **95% freelance written**. Paperback with 8-12 publications/year featuring inspirational, heartwarming, uplifting short stories. Estab. 1993. Circ. Over 40 titles; 60 million books in print. Byline given. Pays on publication. No kill fee. Publishes ms an average of 8 months after acceptance. Buys one-time rights. Accepts queries by mail, e-mail, fax. Accepts previously published material. Accepts simultaneous submissions. Responds upon consideration. Guidelines available online.

Nonfiction Needs humor, inspirational, personal experience, religious. Traveling sisterhood, Mother-Daughter stories, Christian teen, Christmas stories, stories by and/or about men on love, kindness, parenting, family, Nascar racing, athletes, teachers, fishing, adoption, volunteers. No sermon, essay, eulogy, term paper, journal entry, political, or controversial issues. **Buys 1,000 mss/year.** Send complete ms. Length: 300-1,200 words. **Pays $200.**

Poetry Needs traditional. No controversial poetry. **Buys 50 poems/year.** Submit maximum 5 poems. **Pays $50.**

Fillers Needs anecdotes, facts, gags, short humor. 50 **Pays $200.**

Tips We prefer submissions to be sent via our website. Print submissions should be on 8½x11 paper in 12 point Times New Roman font. Type author's contact information on the first page of story. Stories are to be nonfiction. No anonymous or author unknown submissions are accepted. We do not return submissions.

CIDER PRESS REVIEW

A Journal of Contemporary Poetry, 77 Braddock Lane, Halifax PA 17032. E-mail: ciderpressreview.com. Website: www.ciderpressreview.com. Annual magazine covering the best of new poetry and translations from contemporary writers. No kill fee. Buys first North American serial rights. Guidelines available.

Tips Our reading period is from Apr. 1 - Aug. 31 each year, and full mss. (in conjunction with the CPR Annual Book Award) between Sept. 1 - Nov. 30 each year. Prize is $1,000 and publication for a full length book of poetry and 25 copies.

CIMARRON REVIEW

English Dept., Oklahoma State Univ., 205 Morrell Hall, Stillwater OK 74078. E-mail: cimarronreview@okstate.edu. Website: www.cimarronreview.okstate.edu. Quarterly magazine covering fiction, poetry, essays, and art. "We want strong literary writing. We are partial to fiction in the modern realist tradition and distinctive poetry—lyrical, narrative, etc." Estab. 1967. No kill fee. Buys first North American serial rights. Accepts simultaneous submissions. Responds in 3-6 months to mss. Guidelines available.

Tips "All work must come with SASE. A cover letter is encouraged. No email submissions from authors living in North America. Query first and follow guidelines."

$ THE CINCINNATI REVIEW

P.O. Box 210069, Cincinnati OH 45221-0069. (513)556-3954. E-mail: editors@cincinnatireview.com. Website: www.cincinnatireview.com. **100% freelance written**. Semiannual magazine. A journal devoted to publishing the best new literary fiction and poetry as well as book reviews, essays, and interviews. Estab. 2003. Byline given. Pays on publication. No kill fee. Publishes ms an average of 6 months after acceptance. Buys first North American serial rights, buys electronic rights. Responds in 6 weeks to mss. Sample copy for $7 (back issue) or $9 (current issue), subscription for $15. Considers submissions by mail. No email submissions

- Reads submissions September 1-May 31.

Nonfiction Needs essays, interview, new book fiction and poetry reviews. Query. Length: 1,000-5,000 words. **Pays $25/page.**

Columns/Departments Book Reviews; Fine Art; Literary Fiction; Nonfiction; Poetry. 1,500 words. 10 Query. **Pays $25/page.**

Fiction Contact: Brock Clarke, fiction editor. "Does not want genre fiction." **Buys 13 mss/year.** Query. Length: 125-10,000 words. **Pays $25/page.**

Poetry Contact: Don Bogen, poetry editor. Needs avant-garde, free verse, traditional. **Buys 120 poems/year.** Submit maximum 10 poems. **Pays $30/page.**

N CIPHER JOURNAL

Lucas Klein, New Haven CT E-mail: lklein@cipherjournal.com. Published on a continuing basis. Website covering broad literary translation. "Crack open this often neglected field by melding the invisibility of the translator with the identity of the artist. We also include reviews of translated literature. For a better understanding of our aesthetic, look at our Precedents page. We will post new material as it arrives and will follow no periodical schedule. Please keep posted for changes, updates and new literature." No kill fee. Accepts simultaneous submissions.

Nonfiction Needs essays, translation reviews & non-academic essays.

Tips "We welcome all submissions of works of literary translation and of creative variants along similar themes. This includes poetry, fiction, nonfiction, translation reviews and non-academic essays that are either translations themselves or are in some way relevant to a broader understanding of translation as a concept. We welcome new and original translations."

$ $ CITY SLAB

Urban Tales of the Grotesque, City Slab Publications, 1705 Summit Ave., #314, Seattle WA 98122. (206)226-7430. E-mail: submission@cityslab.com. Website: www.cityslab.com. **90% freelance written**. Quarterly magazine covering horror and horror/crime mix. *City Slab* magazine is hard-edged, adult fiction. Estab. 2002. Byline given. Pays on publication. Publishes ms an average of 3 months after acceptance. Buys first North American serial rights. Accepts queries by mail, e-mail. Responds in 3 weeks to queries. Responds in 2 months to mss. Sample copy for $6. Guidelines available online.

Nonfiction Needs essays, interview, photo feature. **Buys 4 mss/year.** Send complete ms. Length: 2,000-3,000 words. **Pays $50-100, plus contributor copies.**

Photos State availability of or send photos Model releases required. Reviews JPEG files. Offers no additional payment for photos accepted with ms. Buys one time rights.

Fiction *City Slab* wants to publish well thought out, literary-quality horror. Needs erotica, experimental, horror. Does not want to see children/youth in sexually oriented stories. **Buys 24 mss/year.** Send complete ms. 5,000 words maximum **Pays 1-10¢/word**.

Tips Read not only the horror greats—Barker, King, Campbell, Lovecraft, etc.—but also the classics—Dickens, Hemingway, Oates, Steinbeck—to see how a great tale is woven. Recently published fiction by Gerard Hoaurner, Christa Faust, and P.D. Cacek.

CLACKAMAS LITERARY REVIEW

Clackamas Community College, English Dept., Clackamas Community College, 19600 S. Molalla Ave., Oregon City OR 97045. (503)657-6958, ext. 2803. E-mail: clr@clackamas.edu. Website: www.clackamasliteraryreview.org. Semiannual website covering fiction, poetry, and nonfiction of emerging and established writers. No kill fee. Accepts simultaneous submissions. Responds in 4 months to mss. Guidelines available.

Tips Our reading period is open from Sept.-Jan. No electronic submissions. Send poetry and prose separately. SASE for response only; mss. will not be returned. Submissions are limited to 4 poems, 1 short story or 1 essay per submission. Include a current phone number or email address.

CLAY PALM REVIEW

Art and Literary Magazine, OmniPrint, LLC, 8 Huntington St., Suite 307, Shelton CT 06484. (203)929-3292. E-mail: info@claypalmreview.com. Website: www.mbswebcreations.com/claypalm/index.html. Magazine specializing in paint, sculpture, photography, collage as well as poetry, fiction or nonfiction, and essays, interviews or articles on artists, artwork, technique. *Clay Palm Review* was formed from an appreciation of culture, spirituality, the connotative and denotative meaning of words, mannerisms of those around, as well as forms of art and sculpture. CPR is a gallery of word, emotion, communication, silence, desire, passion, earth, ancestors and miracles. CPR urges its audience to absorb the contents, listen to what the pages speak. Let them inspire you to live and keep on living in every sense of the word. No kill fee. Responds in 1-6 months to mss. Guidelines available.

Nonfiction Needs essays, translators, expose, how-to, interview, personal experience, photo feature, technical, travel.

Fiction Contact: Steven Withrow, fiction editor. We do not want rhyme, vulgarity, science fiction, epic poetry, Shakespearean sonnets, 'hallmarkish' material or cliché language. No essays on social or political circumstance; no porn. **Buys Max. 2 short stories (no current line length) mss/year.**

Poetry Submit maximum 5-6 poems.

Tips Consider submitting avant-garde, eccentric and tastefully evocative material. Open to all genres. Include SASE, a brief biography including publication acknowledgments if applicable, a mailing address, email address, phone number (optional) and web address.

$ COLORADO REVIEW

Center for Literary Publishing, Colorado State Univ. - English Dept., 9105 Campus Delivery, Fort Collins CO 80523. (970)491-5449. E-mail: creview@colostate.edu. Website: coloradoreview.colostate.edu. Literary magazine published 3 times/year. Estab. 1956. Circ. 1,100. Byline given. Pays on publication. No kill fee. Publishes ms an average of 6 months after acceptance. Buys first North American serial rights. Rights revert to author upon publication. Editorial lead time 1 year. Responds in 2 months to mss. Sample copy for $10. Guidelines available online.

- Mss are read from September 1 to April 30. Mss received between May 1 and August 30 will be returned unread. Send no more than 1 story at a time.

Nonfiction Buys 6-9 mss/year. Send complete ms. **Pays $5/page.**
Fiction Contact: Stephanie G'Schwind, editor. Short fiction. No genre fiction. Needs ethnic, experimental, mainstream, contemporary. **Buys 15-20 mss/year.** Send complete ms. under 30 ms pages **Pays $5/page.**
Poetry Contact: Don Revell, Sasha Steensen, and Matthew Cooperman , poetry editors. Considers poetry of any style. Send no more than 5 poems at one time. **Buys 60-100 poems/year. Pays $5/page.**

COMBAT

The Literary Expression of Battlefield Touchstones, P.O. Box 3, Circleville WV 26804-0003. E-mail: majordomo@combat.ws. Website: www.combat.ws. **90% freelance written**. Quarterly magazine covering the revelation and exploration of the ramifications of war upon combatants, noncombatants, and their families. Estab. 2003. Byline given. No kill fee. Buys first North American serial rights, buys first rights, buys electronic rights. Editorial lead time 3 months. Submit seasonal material 3 months in advance. Accepts queries by mail, e-mail. Responds in 3 weeks to queries. Responds in 1 month to mss. Sample copy available online. Guidelines available online.
Nonfiction Needs book excerpts, essays, expose, general interest, historical, humor, inspirational, interview, opinion, personal experience, photo feature, religious, technical, travel. Send complete ms. 8,000 words maximum.
Photos Send photos Captions, identification of subjects required. Reviews GIF/JPEG files. Offers no additional payment for photos accepted with ms. Buys one time rights.
Fiction Needs adventure, cond novels, confession, experimental, fantasy, historical, horror, humorous, mystery, novel concepts, religious, science fiction, slice-of-life vignettes, suspense, western. Send complete ms. 8,000 words maximum.
Poetry Needs free verse, haiku, light verse, traditional. Submit maximum 5 poems. 800 words.

COMMON GROUND REVIEW

Publishing Poets Around the World, Western New England College, 40 Prospect St., Unit C1, Westfield MA 01085. E-mail: editors@cgreview.org. Website: http://cgreview.org. Magazine covering poetry from unpublished poets. We want poems with a fresh message, that instill a sense of wonder. This is the official poetry journal of Western New England College. Estab. 1999. No kill fee. Accepts simultaneous submissions. Guidelines available.
Poetry Submit maximum 3 poems. Length: 60 lines.
Tips For poems, use a few good images. Run-on, convoluted imagery may derail the reader. Poems should be condensed and concise, free from words that do not contribute. The subject matter should be worthy of the reader's time and appeal to a wide range of readers. Sometimes the editors may suggest possible revisions.

$ $ CONFRONTATION MAGAZINE

Long Island University's Literary Magazine, Confrontation Press, English Dept., C. W. Post Campus Long Island University, 720 Northern Blvd., Brookville NY 11548-1300. (516)299-2720. Fax: (516)299-2735. E-mail: confrontation@liu.edu. Website: www.liu.edu/confrontation. **75% freelance written**. Semiannual magazine covering all forms and genres of stories, poems, essays, memoirs, and plays. A special section contains book reviews and cultural commentary. We are eclectic in our taste. Excellence of style is our dominant concern. We bring new talent to light. We are open to all submissions, each issue contains original work by famous and lesser-known writers and also contains a thematic supplement that 'confront' a topic; the ensuing confrontation is an attempt to see the many sides of an issue rather than a formed conclusion. Estab. 1968. Circ. 2,000. Byline given. Pays on publication. Offers kill fee. Publishes ms an average of 1 year after acceptance. Buys first North American serial rights, buys first rights, buys one-time rights, buys all rights. Accepts queries by mail, e-mail, phone. Accepts simultaneous submissions. Responds in 3 weeks to queries. Responds in 2 months to mss. Sample copy for $3.

- *Confrontation* does not read mss during June, July, or August and will be returned unread unless commissioned or requested.

Nonfiction Needs essays, personal experience. **Buys 15 mss/year.** Send complete ms. Length: 1,500-5,000 words. **Pays $100-300 for assigned articles. Pays $15-300 for unsolicited articles.**
Photos State availability Offers no additional payment for photos accepted with ms. Buys one time rights.
Fiction We judge on quality, so genre is open. Needs experimental, mainstream, novel concepts, if they are self -contained stories, slice-of-life vignettes, contemporary, prose poem. No 'proselytizing' literature or genre fiction. **Buys 60-75 mss/year.** Send complete ms. 6,000 words **Pays $25-250.**
Poetry Needs avant-garde, free verse, haiku, light verse, traditional. **Buys 60-75 poems/year.** Submit maximum 6 poems. Open **Pays $10-100.**

Tips Most open to fiction and poetry. Prizes are offered for The Sarah Tucker Award for fiction, The H. R. Hays Poetry Award, The Sarah Russo Award (for an essay on the subject of exile), and The John V. Gurry Drama Award.

CONJUNCTIONS

Bard College, 21 East 10th St., New York NY 10003. E-mail: webmaster@conjunctions.com. Website: www.conjunctions.com. Website covering innotive fiction, poetry, drama, criticism, interviews, art and other work by some of the leading literary lights of our time, both established and emerging. We provide a forum for writers & artists whose work challenges acccepted forms and modes of expression, experiments with language and thought, and is fully realized art. Estab. 1988. No kill fee. Accepts queries by mail.

- Unsolicited mss cannot be returned unless accompanied by SASE. Electronic and simultaneous submissions will not be considered.

Nonfiction Needs essays, criticism, Interviews, Art.
Tips Final selection of the material is made based on the literary excellence, originality, and vision of the writing. We have maintained a consistently high editorial and production quality with the intention of attracting a large and varied audience.

$ THE CONNECTICUT POETRY REVIEW

The Connecticut Poetry Review Press, P.O. Box 392, Stonington CT 06378. **60% freelance written**. Annual magazine covering poetry/literature. Estab. 1981. Circ. 500. Byline sometimes given. Pays on acceptance. No kill fee. Buys first rights. Editorial lead time 4 months. Submit seasonal material 4 months in advance. Accepts queries by mail. Responds in 1 month to queries. Responds in 3 months to mss. Sample copy for $5 and #10 SASE. Guidelines for #10 SASE.

Nonfiction Needs book excerpts, essays. **Buys 18 mss/year.**
Fiction Needs experimental.
Poetry Needs avant-garde, free verse, haiku, traditional. No light verse. **Buys 20-30 poems/year.** Submit maximum 4 poems. Length: 3-25 lines. **Pays $5-10.**

N CONNECTICUT REVIEW

Connecticut State University, 39 Woodland St., Hartford CT 06105-2337. **Contact:** Lisa Siedlarz, man. ed. **98% freelance written**. Semiannual magazine. "*Connecticut Review* is a high-quality literary magazine. We take both traditional literary pieces and those on the cutting edge of their genres. We are looking for poetry, fiction, short-shorts, creative essays, and scholarly articles accessible to a general audience. Each issue features an 8-page color fine art section with statements from the painters or photographers featured." Estab. 1967. Circ. 2,000. Byline given. No kill fee. Publishes ms an average of 18 months after acceptance. Buys first rights, buys first electronic rights rights. Accepts queries by mail. Accepts simultaneous submissions. Responds in 6 weeks to queries. Responds in 4 months to mss Sample copy for $12 and 3 first-class stamps Guidelines for #10 SASE

- This market pays in contributor copies only. The submission period is September 1-May 15.

Nonfiction "We are looking for creative and literary essays only. They may be scholarly or personal. They should be both accessible and intellectual." Virtuality (2007); Parable and Culture (2008) Send complete ms. Length: 500-4,000 words.
Photos Send photos Captions, identification of subjects, model releases required. Reviews contact sheets, transparencies, 8 X 10 prints. Offers no additional payment for photos accepted with ms. Buys one-time and electronic rights.
Fiction Needs experimental, literary. "No 'entertainment' fiction, though we don't mind if you entertain us while you plumb for the truth." **Buys 14 mss/year.** Send complete ms. Length: 50-4,000 words.
Poetry Needs avant-garde, free verse, haiku, traditional. No doggerel poetry. **Buys 80 poems/year.** Submit maximum 5 poems.
Tips "We read manuscripts blind—stripping off the cover letter—but the biographical information should be there. Be patient. Our editors are spread over 4 campuses and it takes a while to move the manuscripts around."

CONTE

A journal of narrative writing, E-mail: conte@conteonline.net. Website: www.conteonline.net. Semiannual website covering narrative writing of the highest quality. We publish short stories, chapter-length excerpts from novels and novel mss. and pieces of creative nonfiction. Mention previous publications in your letter and share how you heard about *Conte*. No kill fee. Buys first rights, buys electronic rights. Accepts queries by e-mail.

- We read year-round. We are currently accepting submissions for our winter issue (Nov.-Dec. '08). Deadline and pubilcation date TBD. Query with an excerpt for longer pieces.

Nonfiction Needs travel, Memoirs, engaging journalism. No academic essays.
Fiction Length: 8,000 words.
Poetry Submit maximum 3 poems. Length: 100 lines.

Tips Submit poems in the body of an email to: poetry@conteonline.net, with subject line 'Poetry Submission' followed by the title. We are averse to rhyme schemes and attachments. Submit prose to: prose@conteonline.net, with subject line 'Prose Submission' followed by title. Rich Text (.rtf) attachments are preferred but submissions in the body of an email are acceptable.

$ CONTEMPORARY VERSE 2

The Canadian Journal of Poetry and Critical Writing, Contemporary Verse 2, Inc., 207-100 Arthur St., Winnipeg MB R3B 1H3 Canada. (204)949-1365. Fax: (204)942-5754. E-mail: cv2@mts.net. Website: www.contemporaryverse2.ca. **75% freelance written.** Quarterly magazine covering poetry and critical writing about poetry. *CV2* publishes poetry of demonstrable quality as well as critical writing in the form of interviews, essays, articles, and reviews. With the critical writing we tend to create a discussion of poetry which will interest a broad range of readers, including those who might be skeptical about the value of poetry. Estab. 1975. Circ. 600. Byline given. Pays on publication. Offers 50% kill fee. Buys first North American serial rights, buys second serial (reprint) rights. Editorial lead time 3-6 months. Submit seasonal material 3-6 months in advance. Accepts queries by mail, e-mail, phone. Responds in 2-3 weeks to queries. Responds in 3-8 months to mss. Sample copy for $8. Guidelines available online.

Nonfiction Needs essays, interview, book reviews. No content that is not about poetry. **Buys 10-30 mss/year.** Query. Length: 800-3,000 words. **Pays $40-130 for assigned articles.**

Poetry Needs avant-garde, free verse. No rhyming verse, traditionally inspirational. **Buys 110-120 poems/year.** Submit maximum 6 poems. **Pays $20/poem.**

CRAB CREEK REVIEW

7315 34th Ave. NW, Seattle WA 98117. E-mail: crabcreekreview@gmail.com. Website: www.crabcreekreview.org. Byline given. No kill fee. Buys first North American rights. Accepts queries by mail. Accepts simultaneous submissions. Responds in 3-5 months to mss. Guidelines available online.

- "Nominates for the Pushcart Prize and offers annual Crab Creek Review editors' prize of $100 for the best poem, essay, or short story published in the previous year."

Nonfiction Contact: Jennifer Culkin, nonfiction editor. Submit up to 6,000 words. "No academic or critical essays. "

Fiction Contact: Kerry Banazek, fiction editor. Accepts only the strongest fiction. Prefers shorter work. Needs confession, experimental, humorous, mainstream. Send complete ms. Length: 6,000 words. **Pays in 2 copies.**

Poetry Contact: Lana Ayers, poetry ed. Needs avant-garde, free verse, traditional. Submit maximum 5 poems. **Pays in 2 copies.**

Tips "We currently welcome submissions of poetry, short fiction, and visual art."

$ CRAB ORCHARD REVIEW

A Journal of Creative Works, Southern Illinois University at Carbondale, English Department, Faner Hall, Carbondale IL 62901-4503. (618)453-6833. Fax: (618)453-8224. Website: www.siu.edu/~crborchd. We are a general interest literary journal published twice/year. We strive to be a journal that writers admire and readers enjoy. We publish fiction, poetry, creative nonfiction, fiction translations, interviews and reviews. Estab. 1995. Circ. 2,200. No kill fee. Publishes ms an average of 9-12 months after acceptance. Buys first North American serial rights. Accepts simultaneous submissions. Responds in 3 weeks to queries. Responds in 9 months to mss. Sample copy for $8. Guidelines for #10 SASE.

Fiction Contact: Jon Tribble, managing editor. Needs ethnic, excerpted novel. No science fiction, romance, western, horror, gothic or children's. Wants more novel excerpts that also stand alone as pieces. Length: 1,000-6,500 words. **Pays $100 minimum; $20/page maximum, 2 contributor's copies and a year subscription.**

Tips We publish two issues per volume—one has a theme (we read from May to November for the theme issue), the other doesn't (we read from January through April for the nonthematic issue). Consult our website for information about our upcoming themes.

CRAZYHORSE

College of Charleston, Dept. of English, 66 George St., Charleston SC 29424. (843)953-7740. E-mail: crazyhorse@cofc.edu. Website: crazyhorse.cofc.edu. Semiannual magazine. We like to print a mix of writing regardless of its form, genre, school, or politics. We're especially on the lookout for original writing that doesn't fit the categories and that engages in the work of honest communication. Estab. 2,000. Circ. 1,500. No kill fee. Publishes ms an average of 6-12 months after acceptance. Buys first North American serial rights. Accepts simultaneous submissions. Responds in 1 week to queries. Responds in 3-5 months to mss. Sample copy for $5. Writer's guidelines for SASE or by e-mail.

Fiction Accepts all fiction of fine quality, including short shorts and literary essays. **Buys 12-15 mss/year. Pays 2 contributor's copies and $20 per page.**

Poetry No previously published poems. No fax, e-mail or disk submissions. Cover letter is preferred. Reads submissions year round, but slows down during the summer. **Buys 80 poems/year.** Submit maximum 5 poems. **Pays 2 contributor's copies, plus 1-year subscription (2 issues).**

Tips Write to explore subjects you care about. The subject should be one in which something is at stake. Before sending, ask 'What's reckoned with that's important for other people to read?'

CREAM CITY REVIEW

Dept. of English, Univ. of Wisconsin-Milwaukee, P.O. Box 413, Milwaukee WI 53201. Website: www.creamcityreview.org. Semiannual magazine covering poetry, fiction, and nonfiction by new and established writers. Memorable and energetic fiction, poetry and creative nonfiction. Features reviews of contemporary literature and criticism as well as author interviews and artwork. We are interested in camera-ready art depicting themes appropriate to each issue. No kill fee. Accepts simultaneous submissions. Responds in 2-8 months to mss. Guidelines available.

Nonfiction Contact: nonfiction@creamcityreview.org. Needs essays, (book reviews, 1-10 pp.), interview, personal experience. *CCR* sponsors 3 annual contests judged by established writers for fiction, nonfiction and poetry. The entry fee is $15/story (no longer than 30 pp.) or 3-5 poems. Prize is $1,000 plus publication.

Photos Reviews prints, slides.

Fiction Contact: fiction@creamcityreview.org.

Poetry Contact: poetry@creamcityreview.org. Submit maximum 5 poems.

Tips Please include a few lines about your publication history. CCR seeks to publish a braod range of writings and a broad range of writers with diverse backgrounds. We accept submissions for our annual theme issue from Aug. 1 - Nov. 1, and general submissions from Dec. 1 - Apr. 1. No email submissions, please.

$ CREATIVE NONFICTION

Creative Nonfiction Foundation, 5501 Walnut St., Suite 202, Pittsburgh PA 15232. (412)688-0304. Fax: (412)688-0262. E-mail: information@creativenonfiction.org. Website: www.creativenonfiction.org. **100% freelance written**. Magazine published 3 times/year covering nonfiction—personal essay, memoir, literary journalism. "*Creative Nonfiction* is the voice of the genre. It publishes personal essay, memoir, and literary journalism on a broad range of subjects. Interviews with prominent writers, reviews, and commentary about the genre also appear in its pages." Estab. 1993. Circ. 4,000. Byline given. Pays on publication. No kill fee. Publishes ms an average of 1 year after acceptance. Buys all rights. Editorial lead time 6 months. Accepts simultaneous submissions. Responds in 6 months to mss. Sample copy for $10. Guidelines online.

Nonfiction Needs essays, interview, personal experience, narrative journalism. No poetry, fiction. **Buys 30 mss/year.** Send complete ms. 5,000 words maximum. **Pays $10/page—sometimes more for theme issues.**

Columns/Departments .

Tips "Points to remember when submitting to *Creative Nonfiction:* strong reportage; well-written prose, attentive to language, rich with detail and distinctive voice; an informational quality or 'teaching element'; a compelling, focused, sustained narrative that's well-structured and conveys meaning. Manuscripts will not be accepted via fax or e-mail."

THE DEL SOL REVIEW

The Literary Arts Magazine, Web del Sol, 2020 Pennsylvania Ave., NW, Suite 443, Washington DC 20006. E-mail: editor@webdelsol.com. Website: www.delsolreview.webdelsol.com. Website covering unsolicted poetry, prose poetry, creative nonfiction, short stories, and flash fiction. All forms and styles are considered. The goal of *Del Sol Review* is to publish the best work available. Please note the editors prefer fiction and creative onfiction containing unique and interesting subject matter. Estab. 1998. No kill fee. Buys one-time rights. Accepts queries by e-mail. Guidelines available online.

- Political motives do not compromise, and we do not publish inferior work simply because a 'name' tag comes attached.

Nonfiction Contact: Lorena Knight, managing editor.

Fiction Contact: Lorena Knight, managing editor.

Poetry Contact: Diana Adams.

Tips Submissions will be accepted from Sept. 1, - Dec. 30, 2008. All works should reside in the body of the mail, or attached as an .rtf file. If necessary, italics may be indicated by use of the following characters: [i].[/i].

$ DESCANT

Descant Arts & Letters Foundation, P.O. Box 314, Station P, Toronto ON M5S 2S8 Canada. (416)593-2557. Fax: (416)593-9362. E-mail: info@descant.ca. Website: descant.ca. Quarterly journal. Estab. 1970. Circ. 1,200. Pays on publication. No kill fee. Publishes ms an average of 16 months after acceptance. Editorial lead time 1 year. Accepts queries by mail, e-mail, phone. Sample copy for $8.50 plus postage. Guidelines available online.

- Pays $100 honorarium, plus 1-year's subscription for accepted submissions of any kind.

Nonfiction Needs book excerpts, essays, interview, personal experience, historical.

Photos State availability Reviews contact sheets, prints. Offers no additional payment for photos accepted with ms. Buys one time rights.

Fiction Contact: Karen Mulhallen, editor. Short stories or book excerpts. Maximum length 6,000 words; 3,000 words or less preferred. Needs ethnic, experimental, historical, humorous. No gothic, religious, beat. Send

complete ms. **Pays $100 (Canadian); additional copies $8.**
Poetry Needs free verse, light verse, traditional. Submit maximum 6 poems. **Pays $100.**
Tips Familiarize yourself with our magazine before submitting.

DIAGRAM

Dept. of English, Univ. of Arizona, P.O. Box 210067, Tucson AZ 85721-0067. E-mail: editor@thediagram.com. Website: www.thediagram.com. Website covering poetry, fiction and nonfiction. We sponsor a yearly chapbook competition. "*Diagram* is an electronic journal of text and art, found and created. We're interested in representations, naming, indicating, schematics, labelling and taxonomy of things; in poems that masquerade as stories; in stories that disguise themselves as indices or obituaries." No kill fee. Buys first North American serial rights. Accepts queries by e-mail. Responds in 1 month to mss

- "We sponsor a contest for an unpublished hybrid essay. Hybrids are essays involving fiction, memoir, poetry, art, photography, mathematics—it can take many shapes, marry two or more forms."

Nonfiction Contact: Nicole Walker, nonfiction editor.
Photos Reviews prints, slides, zip disks, magnetic tapes, DCs, punch cards.
Tips "Submit interesting text, images, sound and new media. We value the insides of things, vivisection, urgency, risk, elegance, flamboyance, work that moves us, language that does something new, or does something old - well. We like iteration and reiteration. Ruins and ghosts. Mechanical, moving parts, balloons, and frenzy. We want art and writing that demonstrates/interaction; the processes of things; how functions are accomplished; how things become or expire, move or stand. We'll consider anything. We do not consider email submissions, but encourage electronic submissions via our submissions manager software. Look at the journal and submissions guidelines before submitting."

DMQ REVIEW

The Disquieting Muses Quarterly Review, No public address available, E-mail: editors@dmqreview.com. Website: www.dmqreview.com. Quarterly website covering poetry and artwork. We seek work that represents the diversity of contemporary poetry and demonstrates literary excellence, whether it be lyric, free verse, prose, or experimental form. Estab. 1999. No kill fee. Buys first North American serial rights. Accepts queries by e-mail. Accepts simultaneous submissions. Guidelines available online.
Poetry Needs avant-garde, free verse, traditional. Include a brief bio, 50 words/max. Type Poetry Submission followed by your name in the subject line. Submit maximum 3 poems.
Tips Check our current and past issues and read and follow submission guidelines closely. Important: Copy and include the permission statement with your submission (it's in our guidelines online). For Visual Art submissions: Type 'Art Submission' followed by your name in your email. Send a working URL where we may view samples of your work.

$ DOWNSTATE STORY

1825 Maple Ridge, Peoria IL 61614. (309)688-1409. E-mail: ehopkins@prairienet.org. Website: www.wiu.edu/users/mfgeh/dss. Annual magazine covering short fiction with some connection with Illinois or the Midwest. Estab. 1992. Circ. 500. Pays on acceptance. Publishes ms an average of 1 year after acceptance. Buys first rights. Accepts simultaneous submissions. Responds ASAP. Sample copy for $8. Guidelines available online.
Fiction Contact: Elaine Hopkins, editor. Needs adventure, ethnic, experimental, historical, horror, humorous, mainstream, mystery, romance, science fiction, suspense, western. No porn. **Buys 10 mss/year.** Length: 300-2,000 words. **Pays $50.**
Tips Wants more political fiction. Publishes short shorts and literary essays.

DRUNKEN BOAT

119 Main St., Chester CT 06412. Website: www.drunkenboat.com. covering poetry,prose, photography, video, web art, sound, fiction, nonfiction. "We are soliciting proposals for the design of a special 10th issue dedicated to arts & literature online. The winning designer receives a $2,500 honorarium in return for designing the home page. Open to designers from any discipline, from anywhere in the world. See sample designs online. $25 entry fee." No kill fee. Accepts simultaneous submissions. Responds in 3 months to mss. Guidelines available online.
Nonfiction "We are actively looking to publish more nonfiction. Our aesthetic is very broad. Well-written nonfiction of any length & style from the lyric to the journalistic is welcome. Please submit no more than 2 pieces." Needs book excerpts, essays, interview, personal experience, photo feature, Reviews, translation. **Buys 2 mss/year.** See online submissions manager
Fiction "Please submit one story or piece of longer work. We welcome the well-written in every style, from micro-fiction to hypertext to pieces of novels, original and in translation (with the writer's permission), American & from around the globe."
Poetry Needs avant-garde, traditional. "Submit no more than 3 poems, in a single document. Our aesthetic is very broad. We welcome work ranging from received form to the cutting edge avant-garde, from one line to the multi-page, from collaborations to hybridizations & cut-ups as well as works that use other media in their

composition, originality & in translation (with the writer's permission), American, & from around the globe." Submit maximum 3 poems. Length: 1 lines.
Tips "Submissions should be submitted in Word & rtf format only. (This does not apply to audio, visual & web work.) Accepts chapbooks. See our submissions manager system."

DUBLIN REVIEW

the International Literary Review, Unit 14, Base Enterprise Centri, Ladyswell Rd., Mulhuddart Dublin 15 Ireland. Website: www.dublinquarterly.com. Website covering unique narrative style and technique in literature (plays and novels). Testify to the craetive ingenuity and innovation of Samuel Beckett and James Joyce; assert uninhibited creative imaginations to create a confounding newness—called post-modernism. We accept unpublished short fiction, poetry and essays only. No kill fee. Responds in 3 months to mss.
Nonfiction Needs essays, book reviews.
Fiction We do not want academic conventions. Nothing sexually graphic; no racist and anti-Semitic writings. Our position is that everyone is equal before God. Length: 1,000 words.
Poetry Submit maximum 5 poems.
Tips Submit by email as an attachment (MS Word only). We do not accept submissions by post. Familiarize yourself with our fiction. We want high quality and tasteful submissions. Work must be in English (we like British spellings) and send brief biography in the 3rd person.

ECLECTICA

No public address available, E-mail: editors@eclectica.com. Website: www.eclectica.org. Quarterly website covering finest poetry, fiction, reviews, art, essays and more!. A sterling quality literary magazine on the World Wide Web. Not bound by formula or genre, harnessing technology to further the reading experience and dynamic and interesting in content. Estab. 1996. No kill fee. Buys first North American serial rights, buys one-time, nonexclusive use of electronic rights rights. Accepts simultaneous submissions. Guidelines available.
Nonfiction Contact: Colleen Mondor, review editor; Elizabeth Glixman, interview editor. Needs humor, interview, opinion, travel, satire.
Poetry Contact: Jennifer Finstrom.
Tips Works which cross genres—or create new ones—are encouraged. This includes prose poems, 'heavy' opinion, works combining visual art and writing, electronic multimedia, hypertext/html, and types we have yet to imagine. No length restrictions. We will consider long stories and novel excerpts, and serialization of long pieces. Include short cover letter.

ECOTONE

Creative Writing Dept., Univ. of No. Carolina Wilmington, 601 S. College Rd., Wilmington NC 28403. (910)962-2547. Fax: (910)962-7461. E-mail: info@ecotonejournal.com. Website: www.ecotonejournal.com. Biannual magazine featuring fiction, poetry and nonfiction. "*Ecotone* is a literary journal of place that seeks to publish creative works about the environment and the natural world while avoiding the hushed tones and cliches of much of so-called nature writing. Reading period is Aug. 15 - Apr. 15." Byline given. No kill fee. Accepts simultaneous submissions. Responds in 3-6 months to mss.
Nonfiction Needs personal experience. Send complete ms.
Fiction Needs experimental, mainstream. Send complete ms.
Poetry Needs avant-garde, free verse, haiku, light verse, traditional. Submit maximum 6 poems.
Tips "www.ecotonejournal.com/submissions.html."

$ ELLIPSIS MAGAZINE

Westminster College of Salt Lake City, 1840 S. 1300 E., Salt Lake City UT 84105. (801)832-2321. E-mail: ellipsis@westminstercollege.edu. Website: www.westminstercollege.edu/ellipsis. Annual magazine. *Ellipsis Magazine* needs good literary poetry, fiction, essays, plays and visual art. Estab. 1967. Circ. 2,500. Byline given. Pays on publication. No kill fee. Publishes ms an average of 3 months after acceptance. Buys first North American serial rights. Accepts queries by mail. Accepts simultaneous submissions. Responds in 6 months to mss. Sample copy for $7.50. Guidelines available online.

- Reads submissions August 1 to November 1.

Nonfiction Needs essays.
Fiction Needs good literary fiction and plays. Send complete ms. Length: 6,000 words. **Pays $50 per story and 1 contributor's copy; additional copies $3.50.**
Poetry All accepted poems are eligible for the *Ellipsis* Award which includes a $100 prize. Past judges have included Jorie Graham, Sandra Cisneros, and Stanley Plumly. Submit maximum 3-5 poems. **Pays $10/poem, plus 1 copy.**

$ EPOCH

Cornell University, 251 Goldwin Smith Hall, Cornell University, Ithaca NY 14853. (607)255-3385. Fax: (607)255-6661. **100% freelance written**. Magazine published 3 times/year. "Well-written literary fiction, poetry, personal essays. Newcomers always welcome. Open to mainstream and avant-garde writing." Estab. 1947. Circ. 1,000. Byline given. Pays on publication. Offers 100% kill fee. Publishes ms an average of 6 months after acceptance. Buys first North American serial rights. Editorial lead time 6 months. Submit seasonal material 8 months in advance. Accepts queries by mail. Responds in 2 weeks to queries. Responds in 6 weeks to mss. Sample copy for $5. Guidelines for #10 SASE.

Nonfiction Send complete ms. Needs essays, interview. No inspirational. **Buys 6-8 mss/year.** Send complete ms. Open **Pays $5-10/printed page.**

Photos Send photos Reviews contact sheets, transparencies, any size prints. Negotiates payment individually. Buys one time rights.

Fiction Contact: Joseph Martin, senior editor. Needs ethnic, experimental, mainstream, novel concepts, literary short stories. No genre fiction. Would like to see more Southern fiction (Southern US). **Buys 25-30 mss/year.** Send complete ms. Open. **Pays $5 and up/printed page.**

Poetry Contact: Nancy Vieira Couto. Needs avant-garde, free verse, haiku, light verse, traditional. **Buys 30-75 poems/year.** Submit maximum 7 poems. **Pays $5 up/printed page.**

Tips "Tell your story, speak your poem, straight from the heart. We are attracted to language and to good writing, but we are most interested in what the good writing leads us to, or where."

$ $ EVENT

Douglas College, P.O. Box 2503, New Westminster BC V3L 5B2 Canada. (604)527-5293. Fax: (604)527-5095. Website: event.douglas.bc.ca. **100% freelance written**. Magazine published 3 times/year containing fiction, poetry, creative nonfiction, notes on writing, and reviews. We are eclectic and always open to content that invites involvement. Generally, we like strong narrative. Estab. 1971. Circ. 1,250. Byline given. Pays on publication. Publishes ms an average of 8 months after acceptance. Buys first North American serial rights. Accepts queries by mail, fax. Accepts simultaneous submissions. Responds in 1 month to queries. Responds in 6 months to mss. Sample copy for $5. Guidelines available online.

- *Event* does not read mss in July, August, December, and January. No e-mail submissions. All submissions must include SASE (Canadian postage or IRCs only).

Fiction We look for readability, style, and writing that invites involvement. Submit maximum 2 stories. Needs humorous, contemporary. No technically poor or unoriginal pieces. **Buys 12-15 mss/year.** Send complete ms. 5,000 words maximum **Pays $22/page up to $500.**

Poetry Needs free verse. We tend to appreciate the narrative and sometimes the confessional modes. No light verse. **Buys 30-40 poems/year.** Submit maximum 10 poems. **Pays $25-500.**

Tips Write well and read some past issues of *Event*.

THE EXQUISITE CORPSE

A Journal of Letters and Life, LSU English Dept., P.O. Box 25051, Baton Rouge LA 70803. E-mail: submissions@corpse.org. Website: www.corpse.org. Website covering poetry, letters, fiction, news, drama, mixed genre media. We will read anything—stories, broken language of the heart and loins (poetry, letters, travel reports, news and gossip, mixed genre media with collage, music, sound and web-wide effects. No kill fee. Accepts queries by e-mail. Guidelines available online.

- We prefer works of language genius, provocation, malignant brilliance, practical utopianism, profound terror, sexual delirium, and resolute enmity against commonplace, cliché, and convention.

Nonfiction Needs essays, general interest, travel.

Fiction No more than 15 double-spaced pages for prose. We will occasionally make exceptions for long essays. Submit less than 1,000 words for flash fiction.

Poetry No more than 10 pages for poetry.

Tips We will not accept submissions until May 1, 2009. Would-be contributors should look up previous issues for an idea of how we cause damage and promote health. Only submit by email either in the body or as an attachment with .rtf extension. Name your document after your last name. See our guidelines.

$ FICTION

c/o Department of English, City College, 138th St. & Covenant Ave., New York NY 10031. Website: www.fictioninc.com. Semiannual magazine. "As the name implies, we publish only fiction; we are looking for the best new writing available, leaning toward the unconventional. *Fiction* has traditionally attempted to make accessible the inaccessible, to bring the experimental to a broader audience." Estab. 1972. Circ. 4,000. No kill fee. Publishes ms an average of 1 year after acceptance. Buys first rights. Accepts simultaneous submissions. Responds in 3 months to mss. Sample copy for $7. Guidelines available online.

- Reading period for unsolicited mss is September 15-May 15.

Fiction Needs experimental, humorous, satire, contemporary, literary. translations. No romance, science fiction, etc. **Buys 24-40 mss/year.** Length: 5,000 words. **Pays $114.**

Tips "The guiding principle of *Fiction* has always been to go to terra incognita in the writing of the imagination and to ask that modern fiction set itself serious questions, if often in absurd and comedic voices, interrogating the nature of the real and the fantastic. It represents no particular school of fiction, except the innovative. Its pages have often been a harbor for writers at odds with each other. As a result of its willingness to publish the difficult, experimental, and unusual, while not excluding the well known, *Fiction* has a unique reputation in the US and abroad as a journal of future directions."

$ FIELD: CONTEMPORARY POETRY & POETICS

Oberlin College Press, 50 N. Professor St., Oberlin OH 44074-1091. (440)775-8408. Fax: (440)775-8124. E-mail: oc.press@oberlin.edu. Website: www.oberlin.edu/ocpress. **Contact:** Linda Slocum, man. ed. **60% freelance written.** Biannual magazine of poetry, poetry in translation, and essays on contemporary poetry by poets. Estab. 1969. Circ. 1,500. Byline given. Pays on publication. Buys first rights. Editorial lead time 4 months. Accepts queries by mail, e-mail, fax, phone. Responds in 4-6 weeks to mss. Sample copy for $8. Guidelines available online and for #10 SASE.

- "No electronic submissions yet, but are planning for it. Check website after August 1 for new electronic submission guidelines."

Nonfiction Needs essays, poetry, poetry in translation.
Poetry Contact: Linda Slocum, man. ed. **Buys 120 poems/year.** Submit maximum 5 with sase poems. **Pays $15/page.**
Tips "Submit 3-5 of your best poems with a cover letter and SASE. No simultaneous submissions. Keep trying! Submissions are read year-round."

$ THE FIRST LINE

Blue Cubicle Press, LLC, P.O. Box 250382, Plano TX 75025-0382. E-mail: submission@thefirstline.com. Website: www.thefirstline.com. **95% freelance written.** Quarterly magazine. *The First Line* is a magazine that explores the different directions writers can take when they start from the same place. All stories must be written with the first line provided by the magazine. Estab. 1999. Circ. 1,000. Byline given. Pays on publication. Publishes ms an average of 1 month after acceptance. Buys first North American serial rights, buys electronic rights. Editorial lead time 2 months. Accepts queries by mail, e-mail. Responds in 1 week to queries. Responds in 2 months to mss; responds in 1 month to mss after deadline for that issues closes. Sample copy for $3.50. Guidelines available online.
Nonfiction Needs essays. **Buys 4-8 mss/year.** Query. Length: 600-1,000 words. **Pays $10.**
Fiction Needs adventure, ethnic, experimental, fantasy, historical, horror, humorous, mainstream, mystery, romance, science fiction, suspense, western. No stories that do not start with the issue's first sentence. **Buys 40-60 mss/year.** Send complete ms. Length: 300-3,000 words. **Pays $$20.**

$ FIVE POINTS

A Journal of Literature and Art, Georgia State University, P.O. Box 3999, Atlanta GA 30302-3999. Fax: (404)651-3167. Website: www.webdelsol.com/Five_Points. Triannual. *Five Points* is committed to publishing work that compels the imagination through the use of fresh and convincing language. Estab. 1996. Circ. 2,000. No kill fee. Publishes ms an average of 6 months after acceptance. Buys first North American serial rights. Sample copy for $7.
Fiction Contact: Megan Sexton, executive editor. **Pays $15/page minimum; $250 maximum, free subscription to magazine and 2 contributor's copies; additional copies $4.**

FOLIATE OAK

University of Arkansas-Monticello, Arts & Humanities, 562 University Dr., Monticello AR 71656. (870)460-1247. E-mail: foliateoak@uamont.edu. Website: www.foliateoak.uamont.edu. **100% freelance written.** Monthly magazine covering fiction, creative nonfiction, poetry, and art. We are a general literary magazine for adults. Estab. 1973. Circ. 500. Byline given. No kill fee. Publishes ms an average of 1 month after acceptance. Editorial lead time 1 month. Submit seasonal material 1 month in advance. Accepts queries by e-mail. Accepts simultaneous submissions. Responds in 1 week to queries. Responds in 1 month to mss. Sample copy for #10 SASE. Guidelines available online.
Nonfiction Needs essays, expose, general interest, historical, humor, personal experience. Send complete ms. Length: 200-2,500 words.
Photos Reviews GIF/JPEG files. Offers no additional information for photos accepted with ms.
Fiction Needs adventure, ethnic, experimental, mainstream, slice-of-life vignettes. Does not want horror or confession, or pornographic, racist, or homophobic content. Length: 200-2,500 words.
Poetry Needs avant-garde, free verse, haiku, traditional. Submit maximum 5 poems.

FOURTH GENRE

Explorations in Nonfiction, Michigan State Univ. Press, Dept. of English, 201 Morrill Hall, MSU, East Lansing MI 48824-1036. Website: www.msupress.msw.edu/journals/fg/. Semiannual website covering notable, innovative nonfiction ranging from personal essays and memoirs to literary journalism and personal criticism. "*Fourth Genre* gives writers a showcase for their work and readers a place to find the liveliest and most creative works in the form. Features interviews with prominent nonfiction writers, round table discussions of topical genre issues, mini-essays by selected photographers and visual artists, book reviews." No kill fee.

- Submissions for 2009 Editor's Prize Contest considered beginning Jan. 15, 2009.

Nonfiction Needs essays, reviews and capsule summaries of current books., interview, with prominent nonfiction writers, letters from readers, mini-essays by selected photographs and visual artists.
Tips "Editors invite works that are lyrical, self-interragative, meditative and reflective, as well as expository, analytical, exploratory, or whimsical. The journal encourages a writer-to-reader conversation."

THE FOURTH RIVER

Chatham College, Woodland Rd., Pittsburgh PA 15232. E-mail: fourthriver@chatham.edu. Website: fourthriver.chatham.edu. **100% freelance written**. "Biannual magazine interested in literature that engages and explores the relationship between humans and their environments through writing that is thoughtful, daring, and richly situated at the confluence of place, space, and identity." Estab. 2005. Byline given. Pays with contributor copies only. No kill fee. Buys first North American serial rights. Accepts queries by mail. Accepts simultaneous submissions. Responds in 3 months to mss. Sample copy for $10. Guidelines available online.
Nonfiction Needs book excerpts, essays, expose, general interest, historical, humor, opinion, personal experience, travel. Send complete ms. Maximum 25 pages (double-spaced).
Fiction Needs adventure, cond novels, confession, ethnic, experimental, fantasy, historical, horror, humorous, mainstream, mystery, novel concepts, romance, science fiction, slice-of-life vignettes, suspense, western, literary. Send complete ms. Maximum 25 pages (double-spaced).
Poetry Needs avant-garde, free verse, haiku, light verse, traditional. Submit maximum 3 poems. Maximum 10 pages (double-spaced).

$ FRANK

An International Journal of Contemporary Writing & Art, Association Frank, 32 rue Edouard Vaillant, Montreuil 93100 France. (33)(1)48596658. Fax: (33)(1)4859-6668. E-mail: submissions@readfrank.com. Website: www.readfrank.com; www.frank.ly. **80% freelance written**. Magazine published twice/year covering contemporary writing of all genres. Bilingual. Writing that takes risks and isn't ethnocentric is looked upon favorably. Estab. 1983. Circ. 4,000. Byline given. Pays on publication. Publishes ms an average of 1 year after acceptance. Buys one-time rights. Editorial lead time 6 months. Responds in 1 month to queries. Responds in 2 months to mss. Sample copy for $10. Guidelines available online.
Nonfiction Needs interview, travel. **Buys 2 mss/year.** Query. **Pays $100.**
Photos State availability Negotiates payment individually. Buys one time rights.
Fiction Needs experimental, novel concepts, international. At *Frank*, we publish fiction, poetry, literary and art interviews, and translations. We like work that falls between existing genres and has social or political consciousness. **Buys 8 mss/year.** Send complete ms. Length: 1,000-3,000 words. **Pays $10/printed page.**
Poetry Needs avant-garde. **Buys 20 poems/year.** Submit maximum 10 poems. **Pays $20.**
Tips Suggest what you do or know best. Avoid query form letters—we won't read the manuscript. Looking for excellent literary/cultural interviews with leading American writers or cultural figures. Very receptive to new Foreign Dossiers of writing from a particular country.

FULCRUM: AN ANNUAL OF POETRY AND AESTHETICS

Fulcrum Poetry Press, Inc., 421 Huron Ave., Cambridge MA 02138. Website: www.fulcrumpoetry.com. Annual magazine covering poetry, critical and philosophical essays on poetry, debates and visual art. *Fulcrum* aims to offer an evolving map of what is most important and vibrant in the current poetic process. High quality work and generates a global cross-talk on vital issues among poets, critics, philosophers, artists, psychologists and other humanists. Strives to act as the hub of the global social network that is poetry and thereby to enrich the diversity, flexibility, and aesthetic and communicative capabilities of English. No kill fee. Responds in 1-6 months to mss. Guidelines available.
Nonfiction No book reviews.
Tips We welcome previously unpublished poetry and essays on poetry, poets, poetic form, poetic history, the philosophy of poetry, aesthetics and related subjects. Must be received between June 1 - Aug. 31 with a brief cover letter, SASE, or IRCs. Mss. cannot be returned. No unsolicited visual art. No email submissions. Accepted work will be requested in electronic form.

GARGOYLE MAGAZINE

Paycock Press, 3819 North 13th St., Arlington VA 22201. (703)525-9296. E-mail: gargoyle@gargoylemagazine.com. Annual magazine covering eclectic poetry, fiction, photography, art, essays and interviews. We tend to publish works that are bent or edgy—experimental, magic realism/surrealism. Our next reading period will begin on June 1, 2009. Estab. 1976. No kill fee.

- Electronic submissions preferred.

Nonfiction Needs essays, humor, interview, photo feature.
Fiction Needs experimental, fantasy, horror, Surrealism. Length: 1,000-7,500 words.

$ $$ THE GEORGIA REVIEW

The University of Georgia, University of Georgia, Athens GA 30602-9009. (706)542-3481. Fax: (706)542-0047. E-mail: garev@uga.edu. Website: www.uga.edu/garev. **99% freelance written**. Quarterly journal. Our readers are educated, inquisitive people who read a lot of work in the areas we feature, so they expect only the best in our pages. All work submitted should show evidence that the writer is at least as well-educated and well-read as our readers. Essays should be authoritative but accessible to a range of readers. Estab. 1947. Circ. 4,000. Byline given. Pays on publication. No kill fee. Publishes ms an average of 6 months after acceptance. Buys first North American serial rights. Accepts queries by mail. Responds in 2 weeks to queries. Responds in 2-3 months to mss. Sample copy for $9. Guidelines available online.

- No simultaneous or electronic submissions.

Nonfiction Needs essays. For the most part we are not interested in scholarly articles that are narrow in focus and/or overly burdened with footnotes. The ideal essay for *The Georgia Review* is a provocative, thesis-oriented work that can engage both the intelligent general reader and the specialist. **Buys 12-20 mss/year.** Send complete ms. **Pays $40/published page.**

Photos Send photos Reviews 5x7 prints or larger. Offers no additional payment for photos accepted with ms. Buys one time rights.

Fiction We seek original, excellent writing not bound by type. Ordinarily we do not publish novel excerpts or works translated into English, and we strongly discourage authors from submitting these. **Buys 12-20 mss/year.** Send complete ms. Open **Pays $40/published page.**

Poetry We seek original, excellent poetry. **Buys 60-75 poems/year.** Submit maximum 5 poems. **Pays $3/line.**

Tips Unsolicited manuscripts will not be considered from May 1-August 15 (annually); all such submissions received during that period will be returned unread. Check Web site for submission guidelines.

$ THE GETTYSBURG REVIEW

Gettysburg College, Gettysburg PA 17325. (717)337-6770. Fax: (717)337-6775. Website: www.gettysburgreview.com. Quarterly magazine. "Our concern is quality. Manuscripts submitted here should be extremely well written. Reading period September-May." Estab. 1988. Circ. 3,000. Byline given. Pays on publication. Publishes ms an average of 6 months after acceptance. Buys first North American serial rights. Editorial lead time 1 year. Submit seasonal material 9 months in advance. Accepts queries by mail, fax. Accepts simultaneous submissions. Responds in 1 month to queries. Responds in 3-6 months to mss. Sample copy for $11. Guidelines available online.

Nonfiction Needs essays. **Buys 20 mss/year.** Send complete ms. Length: 3,000-7,000 words. **Pays $30/page.**

Fiction Contact: Mark Drew, assisant editor. High quality, literary. Needs experimental, historical, humorous, mainstream, novel concepts, serialized, contemporary. "We require that fiction be intelligent and esthetically written." **Buys 20 mss/year.** Send complete ms. Length: 2,000-7,000 words. **Pays $30/page.**

Poetry Buys 50 poems/year. Submit maximum 5 poems. **Pays $2.50/line.**

GLASS: A JOURNAL OF POETRY

No public address available, E-mail: glasspoetry@yahoo.com. Website: www.glass-poetry.com. Triannual website covering high quality poetry of all styles, forms and schools. "We are not bound by any specific aesthetic; our mission is to present high quality writing. Easy rhyme and 'light' verse are less likely to inspire us. We want to see poetry that enacts the artistic and creative purity of glass." No kill fee. Buys first North American serial rights. Accepts queries by e-mail. Accepts simultaneous submissions. Responds in 4 months to queries.

- Submissions must follow our guidelines.

Poetry Submit maximum 4 poems.

Tips "Accepts submissions from Sept. - May. We like poems that show a careful understanding of language, sound, passion and creativity and poems that surprise us. Include brief cover letter and biography. Include your email address."

$$ GLIMMER TRAIN STORIES

Glimmer Train Press, Inc., 1211 NW Glisan St., Suite 207, Portland OR 97209. Fax: (503)221-0837. E-mail: eds@glimmertrain.org. Website: www.glimmertrain.org. **90% freelance written**. Quarterly magazine of literary short fiction. "We are interested in literary short stories, particularly by new and lightly published writers." Estab. 1991. Circ. 12,000. Byline given. Pays on acceptance. Publishes ms an average of 18 months after acceptance. Buys first rights. Accepts simultaneous submissions. Responds in 2 months to mss. Sample copy for $12 on Web site. Guidelines available online.

Fiction Buys 40 mss/year. up to 12,000 **Pays $700.**

Tips "Make submissions using their online submission procedure on Web site. Saves paper, time, and allows you to track your submissions. See Glimmer Train's contest listings in contest and awards section."

GREEN MOUNTAINS REVIEW

Johnson State College, 337 College Hill, Johnson VT 05656. E-mail: gmr@jsc.vsc.edu. Semiannual magazine covering poems, stories and creative nonfiction by both well-known authors and promising newcomers. The editors are open to a wide rane of styles and subject matter. No kill fee. Accepts queries by mail. Guidelines available.

Nonfiction Needs essays, book reviews, interview, literary criticism. There may be special issues, as in the past.

Fiction Contact: Leslie Daniels, fiction editor. Length: 1,000-7,500 words.

Poetry Contact: Neil Shepard, poetry editor.

Tips We encourage you to order some of our back issues to acquaint yourself with what has been accepted in the past. Unsolicited mss. are read from Sept. 1 - Mar. 1.

GRIST

The Journal for Writers, English Dept., 301 McClung Tower, Univ. of Tennessee, Knoxville TN 37996. Website: www.gristjournal.com. Annual magazine featuring world class fiction, poetry and creative nonfiction, along with interviews with renowned writers and essayists about craft. *Grist* is distinguished from other journals by a commitment to exploring the nuances of the writer's occupation. Byline given. No kill fee. Accepts simultaneous submissions.

Nonfiction Needs essays, how-to. Send complete ms. **Pays 2 contributor copies.**

Fiction Contact: Brad Tice, fiction editor. Needs experimental, mainstream. Send complete ms. Length: 20,000 words.

Poetry Contact: Josh Robbins, poetry editor. Needs avant-garde, free verse, traditional. Submit maximum 3-7 poems. **Pays 2 contributor copies.**

Tips *Grist* is seeking work from both emerging and established writers, whose work is of high literary quality and value.

$ $ GUD MAGAZINE

Greatest Uncommon Denominator Magazine, Greatest Uncommon Denominator Publishing, P.O. Box 1537, Laconia NH 03247. E-mail: editor@gudmagazine.com. Website: www.gudmagazine.com. **99% freelance written**. Semiannual magazine covering literary content and art. *GUD Magazine* transcends and encompasses the audiences of both genre and literary fiction by featuring fiction, art, poetry, essays and reports, and short drama. Estab. 2006. Byline given. Pays on acceptance. Publishes ms an average of 6 months after acceptance. Buys print and world wide electronic rights from the date of first publication until agreement is terminated in writing, by snail mail, by either party. Editorial lead time 6 months. Submit seasonal material 6 months in advance. Accepts queries by e-mail. Accepts previously published material. Accepts simultaneous submissions. Responds in 6 months to mss. Guidelines available online.

Nonfiction Needs book excerpts, essays, historical, humor, interview, personal experience, photo feature, travel, interesting event. **Buys 2-4 mss/year.** submit complete ms using online form Length: 1-15,000 words. **Pays $450.**

Photos Send photos Model releases required. Reviews GIF/JPEG files. Offers $12 for first rights; $5 for reprints. Buys all rights.

Fiction Needs adventure, cond novels, confession, erotica, ethnic, experimental, fantasy, horror, humorous, novel concepts, science fiction, serialized, suspense. **Buys 40 mss/year.** Length: 1-15,000 words. **Pays $450.**

Poetry Needs avant-garde, free verse, haiku, light verse, traditional. Does not want anything that rhymes 'love' with 'above.' **Buys 12 poems/year.**

Fillers 10 **Pays $5-12.**

Tips We publish work in any genre, plus artwork, factual articles, and interviews. We'll publish something as short as 20 words or as long as 15,000, as long as it grabs us. Be warned: We read a lot. We've seen it all before. We are not easy to impress. Is your work original? Does it have something to say? Read it again. If you genuinely believe it to be so, send it. We do accept simultaneous sumbissions, as well as multiple submissions but read the guidelines first.

$ GULF COAST: A JOURNAL OF LITERATURE AND FINE ARTS

University of Houston, Dept. of English, University of Houston, Houston TX 77204-3013. (713)743-3223. E-mail: editors@gulfcoastmag.org. Website: www.gulfcoastmag.org. "Biannual magazine covering innovative fiction, nonfiction, and poetry for the literary-minded.". Estab. 1986. No kill fee. Accepts queries by mail, phone. Responds in 3-5 months to mss. Guidelines available online.

Nonfiction Contact: Nonfiction editor.

Fiction Contact: Fiction editor. Buys 2-8 ms. a year. **Pays $-$100.**

Poetry Contact: Poetry editor. Submit maximum 1-5 poems.

Tips "Submit only previously unpublished works. Include a cover letter. Stories or essays should be typed, double-spaced, and paginated with your name, address, and phone number on the 1st page, title on subsequent pages. Poems should have your name, address, and phone number on the 1st page of each. Please do not stapled submissions."

GULF STREAM

Creative Writing Program, English Dept., Florida International Univ., 3000 NE 151 St., North Miami FL 33181-3000. E-mail: gulfstreamfiu@yahoo.com. Website: www.gulfstreamlitmag.com. Semiannual covering fiction, oetry, creative nonfiction by emerging and established writers. "Each year we publish 1 open issue and 1 Florida-themed issue." Estab. 1989. No kill fee. Accepts queries by e-mail. Accepts simultaneous submissions.

- Submit online only. "Please read guidelines in full. Submissions that do not conform to our guidelines will be discarded. We read from Sept. 15 - Mar. 15."

Nonfiction Contact: Nick Garnett, nonfiction editor. Needs essays, book reviews, interview, photo feature, black & white.
Photos Reviews black & white prints.
Fiction Length: 1,000-5,000 words.
Poetry Contact: Nick Vagnoni, poetry editor. Submit maximum 5 poems.
Tips "We are currently accepted for the second issue of 'Gulf Stream Online,' a complete online-only analogue of the magazines we have been producing as print journals. Our next print journal has been postponed indefinitely."

THE G.W. REVIEW

The George Washington University, 800 21st St. NW, Marvin Center Box 69, Washington DC 20052. (202)994-7779. E-mail: gwreview@gwu.edu. Website: studentorgs.gwu.edu/gwreview. **100% freelance written**. Annual magazine. "*The G.W. Review* seeks to expose readers to new and emerging writers from both the United States and abroad. New, innovative writing—both in style and subject—is valued above the author's previous publishing history." Estab. 1980. Circ. 1,000. Byline given. No kill fee. Publishes ms an average of 3-6 months after acceptance. Buys first rights. Editorial lead time 3 months. Submit seasonal material 4 months in advance. Accepts queries by mail, e-mail. Accepts simultaneous submissions. Responds in 2 months to queries. Responds in 3-6 months to mss. Sample copy for $4.50. Writer's guidelines online at website or by e-mail.
Nonfiction Needs book excerpts, essays, interview. We do not publish journalism, feature articles, or memoirs not of a literary nature. All nonfiction should be related to arts/culture with an editorial preference for writing/writer-related work. Query. Length: 1,000-3,000 words.
Photos Send photos Reviews GIF/JPEG files. Offers no additional payment for photos accepted with ms. Buys one time rights.
Fiction Needs experimental, mainstream, novel concepts. We do not publish genre fiction (i.e., romance, mystery, crime, etc.). **Buys 6 mss/year.** Send complete ms. Length: 1,000-5,000 words.
Poetry Needs avant-garde, free verse, traditional. **Buys 26 poems/year.** Submit maximum 6 poems.
Tips "We are looking for exciting, risk-taking writing. But don't misconstrue that to mean we only publish experimental work (i.e., cut-up). Your work should be thought-provoking and challenging in its subject matter as well as its style."

N HARVARD REVIEW

Houghton Library of the Harvard College Library, Lamont Library, Harvard University, Cambridge MA 02138. (617)495-9775. Fax: (617)496-3692. E-mail: harvard_review@harvard.edu. Website: www.hcl.harvard.edu/harvardreview/. Semiannual magazine covering poetry, fiction, essays, drama, graphics, and reviews in the spring and fall by an eclectic range of international writers. "We produce a major American literary journal in a wide variety of genres and styles. Previous contributors include Gore Vidal, John Updike, Joyce Carol Oats, Arthur Miller, David Mamet. We also publish the work of emerging and previously unpublished writers." Estab. 1992. No kill fee. Accepts simultaneous submissions. Responds in 6 months to mss.
Nonfiction Needs essays, reviews. If you are interested in reviewing for the *Harvard Review*, write to the editor and enclose 2 or more recent clips. No unsolicited book reviews or genre fiction (romance, horror, detective, etc.).
Photos Contact: Judith Larsen, visual arts editor.
Fiction Contact: Nam Le, fiction editor. Length: 7,000 words.
Poetry Contact: Major Jackson, poetry editor. Submit maximum 5 poems.
Tips "There is no reading period. Include a cover letter citing recent publications or awards and SASE. Mss must be paginated and labeled with author's name on every page. Do not submit more than 2X/yr. We accept email submissions only from overseas. Attach it as a MS Word doc or PDF."

HAWAII REVIEW

University of Hawaii Board of Publications, 1733 Donaghho Rd., Honolulu HI 96822. (808)956-3030. Fax: (808)956-3083. E-mail: hireview@hawaii.edu. Website: www.hawaii-review.org. **100% freelance written**. Semiannual magazine covering fiction, poetry, reviews, and art. Estab. 1973. Circ. 2000. Byline given. Publishes ms an average of 3 months after acceptance. Buys first North American serial rights, buys electronic rights.

Accepts queries by e-mail, fax, phone. Accepts simultaneous submissions. Responds in 3 months to mss. Sample copy for $10. Guidelines available online.

Nonfiction Needs essays, interview. Send complete ms. Length: 0-10,000 words.

Fiction Needs confession, experimental, humorous, novel concepts, short fiction, short stories. "Does not want science fiction/fantasy, erotica, Christian evangelica, horror, cowboy." **Buys 1 mss/year.** Send complete ms.

Poetry Needs avant-garde, free verse, haiku, traditional. Does not want light verse, rhymed poetry, inspirational. **Buys 1 poems/year.** Submit maximum 8 poems.

Tips "Make it new. Offers $500 prize in poetry, nonfiction, and fiction."

$ $ HELIOTROPE

No public address available., E-mail: heliotropeditor@gmail.com. Website: www.heliotropemag.com. Quarterly website covering exceptional fiction articles, poetry, and art. Provides reading pleasure, stories worth telling, and worthwhile observations. We are closed to submissions as the next 2 issues are full. We want to accompany both online and print versions with different art for each issue. Contact Damon: admin@fantasybookspot.com. We have hosted writers like Michael Moorcock, Jeff VanderMeer, Scott Bakker, and more. Estab. 2006. Pays on publication. No kill fee. Buys electronic rights. Accepts queries by e-mail. Responds in 1 month to mss.

Nonfiction Query. Needs interview, opinion. Feature slots will be commissioned. **Pays $90-2,000 for assigned articles.**

Fiction Needs fantasy, horror, mystery, science fiction, If your story is something we can't label, we're interested in that, too. Length: 5,000 words. **Pays $-10 ¢.**

Tips We publish 1 poem per issue. The poem in most cases will be commissioned, thus if interested, please contact: heliotropeditor@gmail.com for consideration. Include cover letter, publishing history/bibliography.

$ HOBART

another literary journal, P.O. Box 1658, Ann Arbor MI 48103. Website: www.hobartpulp.com. Website covering short stories, personal essays, short interviews, comics, roundtable discussions. We tend to like quirky stories like truck driving, mathematics and vagabonding. We like stories with humor (humorous but engaging, literary but not stuffy). We want to get excited about your story and hope you'll send your best work. No kill fee. Accepts queries by e-mail. If our response time is longer than 3 mos., feel free to inquire. Responds in 1-3 months to mss.

- Send submissions to: websubmissions@hobartpulp.com. Query first if you'd like to interview someone for Hobart.

Nonfiction Needs essays, personal., humor, interview, short., Roundtable Discussions. **Pays $50-150.**

Fiction (for print)

Tips The subject line must say 'print submission' and include your name, story title. Attach it as either a Word or .rtf document. For website submissions, we want stories shorter than 2,000 words, though 1,000 is better.

$ THE HOLLINS CRITIC

P.O. Box 9538, Hollins University, Roanoke VA 24020-1538. E-mail: acockrell@hollins.edu. Website: www.hollins.edu/academics/critic. **100% freelance written**. Magazine published 5 times/year. Estab. 1964. Circ. 400. Byline given. Pays on publication. No kill fee. Publishes ms an average of 1 year after acceptance. Buys first North American serial rights. Accepts queries by mail. Accepts simultaneous submissions. Responds in 2 months to mss. Sample copy for $2. Guidelines for #10 SASE.

- No e-mail submissions.

Nonfiction Send complete ms.

Poetry Needs avant-garde, free verse, traditional. We read poetry only from September 1-December 15. **Buys 16-20 poems/year.** Submit maximum 5 poems. **Pays $25.**

Tips We accept unsolicited poetry submissions; all other content is by prearrangement.

HOTEL AMERIKA

Columbia College, English Dept., 600 S. Michigan Ave., Chicago IL 60605. (312)344-8175. E-mail: editors@hotelamerika.net. Website: www.hotelamerika.net. Semiannual magazine. We welcome submissions in all genres of creative writing, generously defined. Estab. 2002. Byline given. No kill fee. Accepts queries by mail. Guidelines available online.

Nonfiction Needs essays, humor, personal experience. Send complete ms.

Fiction Needs confession, experimental, humorous, mainstream. Send complete ms.

Poetry Needs avant-garde, free verse, traditional.

Tips Manuscripts will be considered between Sept. 1 and May 1.

$ THE HUDSON REVIEW

A magazine of literature and the arts, The Hudson Review, Inc., 684 Park Ave., New York NY 10065. Website: www.hudsonreview.com. **100% freelance written**. Quarterly magazine publishing fiction, poetry, essays, book reviews; criticism of literature, art, theatre, dance, film and music; and articles on contemporary cultural developments. Estab. 1948. Circ. 2,000. Byline given. Pays on publication. No kill fee. Publishes ms an average of 6 months after acceptance. Editorial lead time 3 months. Accepts queries by mail. Responds in 2 months to queries. Responds in 3 months to mss. Sample copy for $10. Guidelines for #10 SASE.

Nonfiction Contact: Paula Deitz. Needs essays, general interest, historical, opinion, personal experience, travel. **Buys 4-6 mss/year.** Send complete ms between January 1 and March 31 only 3,500 words maximum **Pays 2½¢/word.**

Fiction Contact: Ronald Koury. Reads between September 1 and November 30 only. **Buys 4 mss/year. Pays 2½¢/word.**

Poetry Contact: Julia Powers, assoc. ed. Reads poems only between April 1 and June 30. **Buys 12-20 poems/year.** Submit maximum 7 poems. **Pays 50¢/line.**

Tips "We do not specialize in publishing any particular 'type' of writing; our sole criterion for accepting unsolicited work is literary quality. The best way for you to get an idea of the range of work we publish is to read a current issue. We do not consider simultaneous submissions. Unsolicited manuscripts submitted outside of specified reading times will be returned unread. Do not send submissions via e-mail."

$ HUNGER MOUNTAIN

The Vermont College Journal of Arts & Letters, Vermont College of Fine Arts, 36 College St., Montpelier VT 05602. Fax: (802)828-8649. E-mail: hungermtn@tui.edu. Website: www.hungermtn.org. **30% freelance written**. Semiannual perfect-bound journal covering high quality fiction, poetry, creative nonfiction, interviews, photography, and artwork reproductions. Accepts high quality work from unknown, emerging, or successful writers and artists. No genre fiction, drama, or academic articles, please. Estab. 2002. Byline given. Pays on publication. No kill fee. Publishes ms an average of 1 year after acceptance. Buys first North American serial rights. Submit seasonal material 6 months in advance. Accepts queries by mail. Responds in 1 month to queries. Responds in 3 months to mss. Sample copy for $10. Writer's guidelines for free, online, or by e-mail

Nonfiction Creative nonfiction only. All book reviews and interviews will be solicited. No informative or instructive articles, please. Prose for young adults is acceptable. Query with published clips. **Pays $5/page (minimum $30).** Sometimes pays expenses of writers on assignment.

Photos Send photos Reviews contact sheets, transparencies, prints, GIF/JPEG files. Slides preferred. Negotiates payment individually. Buys one time rights.

Fiction Needs adventure, ethnic, experimental, novel concepts, high quality short stories and short shorts. No genre fiction, meaning science fiction, fantasy, horror, erotic, etc. Query with published clips. **Pays $25-100.**

Poetry Needs avant-garde, free verse, haiku, traditional. No light verse, humor/quirky/catchy verse, greeting card verse. **Buys 10 poems/year.**

Tips We want high quality work! Submit in duplicate. Manuscripts must be typed, prose double-spaced. Poets submit at least 3 poems. No multiple genre submissions. We need more b&w photography and short shorts. Fresh viewpoints and human interest are very important, as is originality. We are committed to publishing an outstanding journal of arts & letters. Do not send entire novels, manuscripts, or short story collections. Do not send previously published work. See Web site for *Hunger Mountain*-sponsored literary prizes.

$ THE ICONOCLAST

1675 Amazon Rd., Mohegan Lake NY 10547-1804. **90% freelance written**. Quarterly literary magazine. "Aimed for a literate general audience with interests in fine (but accessible) fiction and poetry." Estab. 1992. Circ. 900. Byline given. Pays on publication. No kill fee. Publishes ms an average of 9-12 months after acceptance. Buys first North American serial rights. Editorial lead time 1-2 months. Accepts queries by mail. Responds in 2 weeks to queries. Responds in 1 month to mss. Sample copy for $5. Guidelines for #10 SASE.

Nonfiction Needs essays, humor, reviews, literary/cultural matters. "Does not want anything that would be found in the magazines on the racks of supermarkets or convenience stores." **Buys 6-10 mss/year.** Query. Length: 250-2,500 words. **Pays 1¢/word.**

Photos Line drawings preferred. State availability Reviews 4x6, b&w prints. Negotiates payment individually. Buys one time rights.

Columns/Departments Book reviews (fiction/poetry), 250-500 words. 6 Query. **Pays 1¢/word**

Fiction Contact: Phil Wagner, editor. Buys more fiction and poetry than anything else. Needs adventure, ethnic, experimental, fantasy, humorous, mainstream, novel concepts, science fiction, literary. No character studies, slice-of-life, pieces strong on attitude/weak on plot. **Buys 25 mss/year.** Send complete ms. Length: 250-3,000 words. **Pays 1¢/word.**

Poetry Needs avant-garde, free verse, haiku, light verse, traditional. No religious, greeting card, beginner rhyming. **Buys 75 poems/year.** Submit maximum 4 poems. Length: 2-50 lines. **Pays $2-5.**

Tips "Professional conduct and sincerity help. Know it's the best you can do on a work before sending it out. Skill is the luck of the prepared. Everything counts. We love what we do, and are serious about it—and expect you to share that attitude. Remember: You're writing for paying subscribers. Ask Yourself: Would I pay money to read what I'm sending? We don't reply to submissions without a SASE, nor do we e-mail replies."

$ ILLUMEN

Sam's Dot Publishing, P.O. Box 782, Cedar Rapids IA 52406-0782. E-mail: illumensdp@yahoo.com. Website: www.samsdotpublishing.com/aoife/cover.htm. **Contact:** Karen L. Newman, ed. **100% freelance written.** Semiannual magazine. "*Illumen* publishes speculative poetry and articles about speculative poetry, and reviews of poetry and collections." Estab. 2004. Circ. 40. Byline given. Offers 100% kill fee. Buys first North American serial rights, buys one-time rights, buys second serial (reprint) rights. Editorial lead time 2 months. Submit seasonal material 6 months in advance. Accepts queries by e-mail. Responds in 2 weeks to queries. Responds in 3-4 months to mss. Sample copy for $8. Guidelines available online.

Nonfiction "*Illumen* buys/publishes reviews of poetry and poetry collections, and interviews with poets, writers, and teachers, so long as the interviews are related to the magazine's specialty." **Buys 5-8 mss/year.** Send complete ms. Length: 2,000 words. **Pays $10 for unsolicited articles.**

Poetry Needs avant-garde, free verse, haiku, light verse, traditional. Scifaiku is a difficult sell with us because we also publish a specialty magazine—*Scifaikuest*—for scifaiku and related forms. **Buys 40-50 poems/year.** Submit maximum 5 poems. Length: 200 lines. **Pays 1-2¢/word.**

Tips *Illumen* publishes beginning writers, as well as seasoned veterans. Be sure to read and follow the guidelines before submitting your work. The best advice for beginning writers is to send your best effort, not your first draft.

$ $ IMAGE

3307 Third Ave. W., Seattle WA 98119. (206)281-2988. E-mail: image@imagejournal.org. Website: www.imagejournal.org. **50% freelance written.** Quarterly magazine covering the intersection between art and faith. "*Image* is a unique forum for the best writing and artwork that is informed by—or grapples with—religious faith. We have never been interested in art that merely regurgitates dogma or falls back on easy answers or didacticism. Instead, our focus has been on writing and visual artwork that embody a spiritual struggle, that seek to strike a balance between tradition and a profound openness to the world. Each issue explores this relationship through outstanding fiction, poetry, painting, sculpture, architecture, film, music, interviews, and dance. *Image* also features 4-color reproductions of visual art." Estab. 1989. Circ. 4,500. Byline given. Pays on publication. No kill fee. Publishes ms an average of 8 months after acceptance. Buys first North American serial rights. Accepts queries by mail, e-mail, phone. Responds in 1 month to queries. Responds in 2 months to mss. Sample copy for $16 or online. Guidelines for #10 SASE or online.

Nonfiction Needs essays. No sentimental, preachy, moralistic, or obvious essays. **Buys 10 mss/year.** Send complete ms. Length: 4,000-6,000 words. **Pays $10/page; $150 maximum for all prose articles.**

Fiction "No sentimental, preachy, moralistic, obvious stories, or genre stories (unless they manage to transcend their genre)." **Buys 8 mss/year.** Send complete ms. Length: 4,000-6,000 words. **Pays $10/page; $150 maximum.**

Poetry Buys 24 poems/year. Submit maximum 5 poems. **Pays $2/line; $150 maximum.**

Tips "Read the publication."

$ INDIANA REVIEW

Ballantine Hall 465, Indiana University, Bloomington IN 47405-7103. (812)855-3439. E-mail: inreview@indiana.edu. Website: www.indiana.edu/~inreview. **100% freelance written.** Biannual magazine. *Indiana Review*, a nonprofit organization run by IU graduate students, is a journal of previously unpublished poetry and fiction. Literary interviews and essays are also considered. We publish innovative fiction and poetry. We're interested in energy, originality, and careful attention to craft. While we publish many well-known writers, we also welcome new and emerging poets and fiction writers. Estab. 1976. Circ. 5,000. Byline given. Pays on publication. Publishes ms an average of 3-6 months after acceptance. Buys first North American serial rights. Accepts queries by mail, e-mail. Accepts simultaneous submissions. Responds in 2 or more weeks to queries. Responds in 4 or more months to mss. Sample copy for $9. Guidelines available online.

- Break in with 500-1,000 word book reviews of fiction, poetry, nonfiction, and literary criticism published within the last 2 years.

Nonfiction Needs essays, interview, creative nonfiction, reviews. No coming of age/slice of life pieces. **Buys 5-7 mss/year.** Send complete ms. 9,000 words maximum. **Pays $5/page ($10 minimum), plus 2 contributor's copies.**

Fiction Contact: Danny Nguyen, fiction editor. We look for daring stories which integrate theme, language, character, and form. We like polished writing, humor, and fiction which has consequence beyond the world of its narrator. Needs ethnic, experimental, mainstream, novel concepts, literary, short fictions, translations. No genre fiction. **Buys 14-18 mss/year.** Send complete ms. Length: 250-10,000 words. **Pays $5/page ($10 minimum), plus 2 contributor's copies.**

Poetry Contact: Hannah Faith Notess, poetry editor. We look for poems that are skillful and bold, exhibiting an inventiveness of language with attention to voice and sonics. Experimental, free verse, prose poem, traditional form, lyrical, narrative. **Buys 80 poems/year.** Submit maximum 6 poems. 5 lines minimum **Pays $5/page ($10 minimum), plus 2 contributor's copies.**

Tips We're always looking for nonfiction essays that go beyond merely autobiographical revelation and utilize sophisticated organization and slightly radical narrative strategies. We want essays that are both lyrical and analytical where confession does not mean nostalgia. Read us before you submit. Often reading is slower in summer and holiday months. Only submit work to journals you would proudly subscribe to, then subscribe to a few. Take care to read the latest 2 issues and specifically mention work you identify with and why. Submit work that `stacks up' with the work we've published. Offers annual poetry, fiction, short-short/prose-poem prizes. See website for details.

$ $ INKWELL

Manhattanville College, 2900 Purchase St., Purchase NY 10577. (914)323-7239. Fax: (914)323-3122. E-mail: inkwell@mville.edu. Website: www.inkwelljournal.org. **100% freelance written**. Semiannual magazine covering poetry, fiction, essays, artwork, and photography. Estab. 1995. Byline given. Pays on publication. No kill fee. Publishes ms an average of 4 months after acceptance. Buys first North American serial rights. Editorial lead time 4 months. Accepts simultaneous submissions. Responds in 1 month to queries. Responds in 4-6 months to mss. Sample copy for $6. Guidelines free.

Nonfiction Needs book excerpts, essays, literary essays, memoirs. Does not want children's literature, erotica, pulp adventure, or science fiction. **Buys 3-4 mss/year.** Send complete ms. 5,000 words maximum **Pays $100-350.**

Photos Send photos/artwork with submission. Reviews 5x7 prints, GIF/JPEG files on diskette/cd. Negotiates payment individually. Buys one time rights.

Fiction Needs mainstream, novel concepts, literary. Does not want children's literature, erotica, pulp adventure, or science fiction. **Buys 20 mss/year.** Send complete ms. 5,000 words maximum **Pays $75-150.**

Poetry Needs avant-garde, free verse, traditional. Does not want doggerel, funny poetry, etc. **Buys 40 poems/year.** Submit maximum 5 poems. **Pays $5-10/page.**

Tips "We cannot accept electronic submissions."

INNISFREE POETRY JOURNAL

Cook Communication, No public address available, E-mail: editor@innisfreepoetry.org. Website: www.innisfreepoetry.org. Semiannual online journal publishing contemporary poetry. Our journal continues the series of Closer Looks at the poetry of a leading contemporary poet (Marianne Boruch). Estab. 2005. No kill fee. Buys first North American serial rights. Accepts simultaneous submissions. Guidelines available

Poetry Needs free verse, traditional.

Tips "Welcomes original previously unpublished poems year round. We accept poems only via email from both established and new writers whose work is excellent. We publish well-crafted poems, poems grounded in the specific which speak in fresh language and telling images. And we admire musicality. We welcome those who, like the late Lorenzo Thomas, 'write poems because I can't sing.'"

IN POSSE REVIEW

No public address available, E-mail: submissions@webdelsol.com. Website: www.inpossereview.com. Website covering eclectic fiction, nonfiction, poetry, multi-ethnic anthologies and work in progress/work in print collections. We look for inventive, imaginative, well-crafted work by writers who take risks and are well acquainted with the craft of their genre. Please, no beginners. No kill fee. Accepts queries by e-mail. Guidelines available.

- The theme in Oct. 2008 will be Unconventional Conventions.

Fiction Needs ethnic, Anthologies, mystery, science fiction, suspense, Crime. Length: 1,000-3,500 words.

Tips Query to: In Posse Editor (but please, no submissions). Acceptance of work grants 120 days of electronic rights for *In Posse Review*. Author retains right to publish work in print any time. Work is archived online. Stories should be included in the body of email if possible.

INTERIM

English Dept., University of Nevada, Las Vegas NV 89154-5011. E-mail: claudiakeelan@interim.org. Website: www.interimmag.org. Annual magazine covering creative writing that features poetry, fiction and book reviews. There is no prevailing aesthetic or political philosophy and past contributors include writers as diverse as Martine Bellen, Anselm Berrigan, Brenda Hillman, Anne Porter, and William Carlos Williams. Estab. 1944. No kill fee. Guidelines available.

Tips Open to poetry and short fiction submissions from Sept. 1, 2008 to Apr. 30, 2009.

INTERNATIONAL POETRY REVIEW

Dept. of Romance Languages, Univ. of North Carolina, 2336 MHRA, Greensboro NC 27402-6170. E-mail: smithsom@uncg.edu. Website: www.uncg.edu/rom. **6-10% freelance written**. Semiannual magazine covering poems from contemporary writers in all languages, with facing English translations. Contemporary translation is our primary focus, appearing in bilingual format, along with a limited section, in every issue, of poetry originally written in English. We do not adhere to any one school of translation theory. Estab. 1975. Circ.

< 1,000. No kill fee. Accepts simultaneous submissions. Responds in 3-6 months to mss. Guidelines available.
Poetry Submit maximum 3-5 poems.
Tips "Please indicate clearly if SASE is for nonfiction only. Email submissions accepted only from abroad. Be responsible for securing translation and publication rights as necessary."

$ THE IOWA REVIEW

308 EPB, The University of Iowa, Iowa City IA 52242. Website: iowareview.org. Triannual magazine. Stories, essays, and poems for a general readership interested in contemporary literature. Estab. 1970. Circ. 3,500. Pays on publication. Publishes ms an average of 8-12 months after acceptance. Buys first North American serial rights, buys nonexclusive anthology, classroom, and online serial rights. Responds in 3 months to mss. Sample copy for $9 and online Guidelines available online.

- "This magazine uses the help of colleagues and graduate assistants. Its reading period for unsolicited work is September 1-December 1. From January through April, we read entries to our annual Iowa Awards competition. Check our website for further information."

Fiction "We are open to a range of styles and voices and always hope to be surprised by work we then feel we need." **Pays $25 for the first page and $15 for each additional page, plus 2 contributor's copies and a year-long subscription; additional copies 30% off cover price.**
Tips "We publish essays, reviews, novel excerpts, stories, and poems, and would like for our essays not always to be works of academic criticism. We have no set guidelines as to content or length, but strongly recommend that writers read a sample issue before submitting. **Buys 65-80 unsolicited ms/year**. Submit complete ms with SASE. **Pays $25 for the first page and $15 for each subsequent page of poetry or prose.**"

$ IRREANTUM

A Review of Mormon Literature and Film, The Association for Mormon Letters, P.O. Box 1315, Salt Lake City UT 84110-1315. E-mail: editor@amlpubs.org. Website: www.irreantum.org. Literary journal published 2 times/year. While focused on Mormonism, *Irreantum* is a cultural, humanities-oriented magazine, not a religious magazine. Our guiding principle is that Mormonism is grounded in a sufficiently unusual, cohesive, and extended historical and cultural experience that it has become like a nation, an ethnic culture. We can speak of Mormon literature at least as surely as we can of a Jewish or Southern literature. *Irreantum* publishes stories, one-act dramas, stand-alone novel and drama excerpts, and poetry by, for, or about Mormons (as well as author interviews, essays, and reviews). The journal's audience includes readers of any or no religious faith who are interested in literary exploration of the Mormon culture, mindset, and worldview through Mormon themes and characters either directly or by implication. *Irreantum* is currently the only magazine devoted to Mormon literature. Estab. 1999. Circ. 500. Pays on publication. Publishes ms an average of 3-12 months after acceptance. Buys one-time rights, buys electronic rights. Accepts queries by e-mail. Accepts previously published material. Accepts simultaneous submissions. Responds in 2 weeks to queries. Responds in 2 months to mss. Sample copy for $6. Guidelines by email.

- Also publishes short shorts, literary essays, literary criticism, and poetry.

Fiction Needs adventure, ethnic, Mormon, experimental, fantasy, historical, horror, humorous, mainstream, mystery, religious, romance, science fiction, suspense. **Buys 12 mss/year.** Length: 1,000-5,000 words. **Pays $0-100.**
Tips *Irreantum* is not interested in didactic or polemnical fiction that primarily attempts to prove or disprove Mormon doctrine, history, or corporate policy. We encourage beginning writers to focus on human elements first, with Mormon elements introduced only as natural and organic to the story. Readers can tell if you are honestly trying to explore human experience or if you are writing with a propagandistic agenda either for or against Mormonism. For conservative, orthodox Mormon writers, beware of sentimentalism, simplistic resolutions, and foregone conclusions.

$ 🌐 ISLAND

P.O. Box 210, Sandy Bay Tasmania 7006 Australia. (61)(3)6226-2325. E-mail: island.magazine@utas.edu.au. Website: www.islandmag.com. Quarterly magazine. "*Island* seeks quality fiction, poetry, essays, and articles. A literary magazine with an environmental heart." Circ. 1,500. Buys one-time rights. Accepts queries by mail. Sample copy for $8.95 (Australian). Guidelines available online.
Nonfiction Articles and reviews. **Pays $100 (Australian)/1,000 words**
Fiction Length: up to 2,500 words. **Pays $100 (Australian).**
Poetry Pays $60.

🌐 JACKET

c/-Australian Literary Management, 2-A Booth St., Balmain NSW 2041 Australia. E-mail: p.brown62@gmail.com. Website: jacketmagazine.com. Weekly website covering literature distributed over the internet. Jacket was founded by John Tranter to showcase lively contemporary poetry and prose. Most of the material is original to this magazine, but some is excerpted from or co-produced with hard-to-get books and magazines. I cannot accept unsolicited poetry yet. If you'd like to submit a review, article or interview, send a half-page synopsis with your return email address. Estab. 1997. No kill fee. Buys one-time rights, buys electronic rights. Accepts queries by e-mail. Guidelines available online.

- Jacket's pages are constantly being polished and refined. Make sure you're looking at the latest version of each page by choosing your browser's Reload button to refresh each page you visit.

Nonfiction Needs essays, historical, interview, religious, Book reviews.
Poetry Cannot accept unsolicited poetry.

$ THE JOURNAL

The Ohio State University, 164 W. 17th Ave., Columbus OH 43210. (614)292-4076. Fax: (614)292-7816. E-mail: thejournal@osu.edu. Website: english.osu.edu/research/journals/thejournal/. **100% freelance written.** Semiannual magazine. "We're open to all forms; we tend to favor work that gives evidence of a mature and sophisticated sense of the language." Estab. 1972. Circ. 1,500. Byline given. Pays on publication. Publishes ms an average of 1 year after acceptance. Buys first North American serial rights. Accepts queries by mail. Accepts simultaneous submissions. Responds in 2 weeks to queries. Responds in 2 months to mss. Sample copy for $7 or online. Guidelines available online.
Nonfiction Needs essays, interview. **Buys 2 mss/year.** Query. Length: 2,000-4,000 words. **Pays $20 maximum.**
Columns/Departments Reviews of contemporary poetry, 1,500 words maximum 2 Query. **Pays $20.**
Fiction Needs novel concepts, literary short stories. No romance, science fiction or religious/devotional. Open **Pays $20.**
Poetry Needs avant-garde, free verse, traditional. **Buys 100 poems/year.** Submit maximum 5 poems. **Pays $20.**

THE JOURNAL

once 'of Contemporary Anglo-Scandinavian Poetry', Original Plus, 17 High St., Maryport Cumbria CA15 6BQ UK. 01900 812194. E-mail: smithsssj@aol.com. Website: members.aol.com/smithsssj/index.html. **100% freelance written.** Triannual magazine covering poetry. Estab. 1994. Circ. 150. Byline given. Pays on publication. No kill fee. Publishes ms an average of 6 months after acceptance. Buys all rights. Editorial lead time 6 months. Accepts queries by mail, e-mail. Accepts previously published material. Responds in 4 weeks to queries. Guidelines free.
Tips Send 6 poems; I'll soon let you know if it's not Journal material.

$ KANSAS CITY VOICES

Whispering Prairie Press, P.O. Box 8342, Kansas City KS 66208-0342. E-mail: kcvoices@yahoo.com. Website: kansascityvoices.tripod.com. **100% freelance written.** Annual magazine. *Kansas City Voices* magazine publishes an eclectic mix of fiction, poetry, personal essays, articles and images of artwork. Though we like works that relate to Kansas City and the surrounding area, quality is our primary concern. Estab. 2003. Circ. 1,000. Byline given. Pays on publication. Publishes ms an average of 6 months after acceptance. Buys first North American serial rights. Accepts queries by mail. Accepts simultaneous submissions. Sample copy for $11.45. Guidelines available online.
Nonfiction Needs book excerpts, essays, general interest, historical, how-to, humor, inspirational, interview, personal experience, photo feature, religious, travel. **Buys 10-15 mss/year.** Send complete ms. Length: 800-2,500 words. **Pays $20-100.**
Photos Send photos Offers no additional payment for photos accepted with ms.
Fiction Needs adventure, confession, ethnic, experimental, fantasy, historical, horror, humorous, mainstream, mystery, novel concepts, religious, romance, science fiction, slice-of-life vignettes, suspense, western. Send complete ms. Length: 2,500 words. **Pays $20-100.**
Poetry Needs avant-garde, free verse, light verse, traditional. Does not want haiku. Submit maximum 3 poems. 35 lines maximum **Pays $20-100.**
Tips Familiarize yourself with the magazine, check the Web site and read the guidelines. We have a blind submissions policy, because we want quality work, whether or not it is by writers with long resumes. For fiction, we look for strong stories with active voices. Show, don't tell. Sending us your best work in a proofed, professionally formatted manuscript makes a great first impression.

$ THE KENYON REVIEW

Walton House, 104 College Dr., Gambier OH 43022. (740)427-5208. Fax: (740)427-5417. E-mail: kenyonreview@kenyon.edu. Website: www.kenyonreview.org. **100% freelance written.** Quarterly magazine covering contemporary literature and criticism. An international journal of literature, culture, and the arts dedicated to an inclusive representation of the best in new writing (fiction, poetry, essays, interviews, criticism) from established and emerging writers. Estab. 1939. Circ. 6,000. Byline given. Pays on publication. No kill fee. Publishes ms an average of 1 year after acceptance. Buys first rights. Editorial lead time 1 year. Submit seasonal material 1 year in advance. Responds in 3-4 months to queries. Responds in 4 months to mss. Sample copy $12, includes postage and handling. Please call or e-mail to order. Guidelines available online.

Fiction Contact: Fiction Editor. Needs cond novels, ethnic, experimental, historical, humorous, mainstream, contemporary. 3-15 typeset pages preferred **Pays $30-40/page.**
Tips We no longer accept mailed submissions. Work will only be read if it is submitted through our online program on our Web site. Reading period is September 1-January 31.

$ THE KIT-CAT REVIEW

244 Halstead Ave., Harrison NY 10528. (914)835-4833. E-mail: kitcatreview@gmail.com. **Contact:** Claudia Fletcher, ed. **100% freelance written**. Quarterly magazine. "*The Kit-Cat Review* is named after the 18th Century Kit-Cat Club, whose members included Addison, Steele, Congreve, Vanbrugh, and Garth. It is part of the collections of the Univ. of Wisconsin, Madison, and the State Univ. of New York, Buffalo. Its purpose is to promote/discover excellence and originality." Estab. 1998. Circ. 500. Byline given. Pays on publication. Publishes ms an average of 6-12 months after acceptance. Buys first rights. Accepts queries by mail, phone. Accepts simultaneous submissions. Responds in 1 week to queries. Responds in 2 months to mss. Sample copy for $7 (payable to Claudia Fletcher) Guidelines for SASE.
Nonfiction "Shorter pieces stand a better chance of publication." Needs book excerpts, essays, general interest, historical, humor, interview, personal experience, travel. **Buys 6 mss/year.** Send complete ms with brief bio and SASE 5,000 words maximum **Pays $25-100.**
Fiction Needs ethnic, experimental, novel concepts, slice-of-life vignettes. No stories with O. Henry-type formula endings. Shorter pieces stand a better chance of publication. No science fiction, fantasy, romance, horror, or new age. **Buys 20 mss/year.** Send complete ms. 5,000 words maximum **Pays $25-100 and 2 contributor's copies; additional copies $5.**
Poetry Needs free verse, traditional. No excessively obscure poetry. **Buys 100 poems/year. Pays $20-100.**
Tips "Obtaining a sample copy is strongly suggested. Include a short bio, SASE, and word count for fiction and nonfiction submissions."

LIMP WRIST MAGAZINE

La Vita Poetica Press, P.O. Box 47891, Atlanta GA 30362. E-mail: dustin@limpwristmag.com. Website: www.limpwristmag.com. Website covering poetry and artwork, short fiction, photography and video with a queer sensibility. However, we don't discriminate between hetero vs. homo. We offer a creative writing scholarship ($150) for gay high school seniors. The winner will also win a spot at the 2009 Juniper Summer Writing Institute. We plan to offer a yearly chapbook competition open. No kill fee. Accepts queries by mail, e-mail. Responds in 1-2 months to mss. Guidelines available.

- Submissions must be received by 12/15/2008.

Nonfiction Length: 5,000 words.
Photos For artwork submit up to 3 photos or pieces (all genres accepted) in high resolution. Or submit 1 short film uploaded to a third-party website (MaxVid, YouTube). All artwork should be sent to Montgomery Maxton.
Poetry Submit maximum 5 poems.
Tips Include the statement: 'The work submitted is my own original work and has not been previously published.' Include a brief cover letter email.

LITERARY MAMA

Dept. of English, Pinewood preparatory School, 1114 Orangeburg Rd., Somerville SC 29843. E-mail: lminfo@literarymama.com. Website: www.literarymama.com. Website offering writing about the complexities and many faces of motherhood in a variety of genres. Departments include columns, creative nonfiction, fiction, Literary Reflections, poetry, Profiles & Reviews, and Op Ed. Mothers are interested in reading pieces that are long, complex, ambiguous, deep, raw, irreverent, ironic, body conscious. Circ. 40,000. No kill fee. Accepts queries by e-mail. Accepts simultaneous submissions. No queries. Responds in 3 wks - 3 months to mss. Guidelines available at http://www.literarymama.com/submissions/.
Nonfiction Contact: Kate Haas, Sonya Huber, & Susan Ito. We don't want pieces that read like columns or intellectual reflections on personal experiences; work that would be accepted by the glossy parenting magazines. Length: 500-7,000 words.
Columns/Departments Contact: Alissa McElreath and Delia Scarpitti at lmcolumns@literarymama.com.
Fiction Contact: Suzanne Kamata, Kristina Riggle. E-mail: lmfiction@literarymama.com.
Poetry Contact: Sharon Kraus. E-mail: lmpoetry@literarymama.com. Submit maximum 4 poems.
Tips We seek top-notch creative writing. We also look for quality literary criticism about mother-centric literature and profiles of mother writers. We publish writing with fresh voices, superior craft, vivid imagery. Please send submission (copied into e-mail) to appropriate departmental editors. Include a brief cover letter. We tend to like stark revelation (pathos, humor & joy), clarity, concrete details, strong narrative development; ambiguity, thoughtfulness, delicacy, irreverence, lyricism, sincerity; the elegant. We need the submissions 3 mos. before Oct.: Desiring Motherhood; May: Mother's Day Month; June: Father's Day Month.

$ THE LONDON MAGAZINE

Review of Literature and the Arts, The London Magazine, 32 Addison Grove, London W4 1ER United Kingdom. (44)(208)400-5882. Fax: (44)(208)994-1713. E-mail: editorial@thelondonmagazine.net. Website: www.thelondonmagazine.net. **100% freelance written**. Bimonthly magazine covering literature and the arts. Estab. 1732. Circ. 5,000. Byline given. Pays on publication. Offers kill fee. Kill fee negotiable Publishes ms an average of 4 months after acceptance. Buys first rights. Editorial lead time 3 months. Submit seasonal material 6 months in advance. Accepts queries by mail. Responds in 1 month to queries. Responds in 3 months to mss. Sample copy for £7.50. Guidelines available online.

Nonfiction Needs book excerpts, essays, interview, memoirs. No journalism, reportage, or quasi-marketing. **Buys 16 mss/year.** Send complete ms. 6,000 words maximum. **Pays minimum £20; average £30-50; maximum £150 for a major contribution.**

Fiction Needs adventure, confession, erotica, ethnic, experimental, fantasy, historical, horror, humorous, mainstream, mystery, novel concepts, religious, romance, science fiction, slice-of-life vignettes, suspense. **Buys 32 mss/year.** Send complete ms. 6,000 words maximum. **Pays minimum £20; average £30-50; maximum £150 for a major contribution.**

Poetry Needs avant-garde, free verse, haiku, light verse, traditional. **Buys 60 poems/year.** Submit maximum 6 poems. 1,000 words maximum (negotiable) **Pays minimum £15; maximum rate is negotiable.**

THE LOUISVILLE REVIEW

Spalding University, 8501 S. Fourth St., Louisville KY 40203. (502)585-9911, ext. 2777. Fax: (502)585-7158. E-mail: louisvillereview@spaulding.edu. Website: www.louisvillereview.org. Semiannual magazine covering poetry and fiction, creative nonfiction, and drama; open to almost all themes. We also publish The Children's Corner. Known for excellence nationwide and abroad; fosters the development of new writers. Goal is to import the best writing, to juxtapose the work of established writers with new writers. We seek writing that looks for fresh ways to recreate scenes and feelings. Honest emotion and original imagery are more important to a poem than rhyming and big topics—such as life, moralizing, and other abstractions. No kill fee. Accepts queries by mail. Accepts simultaneous submissions. Sample copy for $4.

- The Review also accepts previously unpublished poetry from students in grades K-12. Must be accompanied by parental permission to publish if accepted.

Poetry Submit maximum 5 poems.

Tips We read year round. See our editorial description.

LULLWATER REVIEW

Emory University, P.O. Box 22036, Atlanta GA 30322. (404)727-6184. E-mail: lullwaterreview@yahoo.com. **80% freelance written**. Semiannual magazine. :*Lullwater Review* seeks submissions that are strong and original. We require no specific genre or subject." Estab. 1990. Circ. 2,000. Byline given. Pays on publication. No kill fee. Publishes ms an average of 1-2 months after acceptance. Buys first North American serial rights. Accepts queries by mail, e-mail, phone. Accepts simultaneous submissions. Responds in 1-3 months to queries. Responds in 3-6 months to mss. Sample copy for $5. Guidelines for #10 SASE.

Nonfiction Needs book excerpts, essays, general interest, historical, humor, inspirational, personal experience, photo feature, travel. **Buys 1-2 mss/year.** Send complete ms. 5,000 words maximum.

Photos Send photos Reviews 8x11 or smaller prints, GIF/JPEG files. Offers no additional payment for photos accepted with ms. Buys first North American serial rights.

Fiction Needs adventure, condensed novels, ethnic, experimental, fantasy, historical, humorous, mainstream, mystery, novel concepts, religious, science fiction, slice-of-life vignettes, suspense, western. No romance or science fiction, please. **Buys 5-7 mss/year.** Send complete ms. 5,000 words maximum. **Pays 3 contributor copies.**

Poetry Needs avant-garde, free verse, light verse, traditional. **Buys 30-40 poems/year.** Submit maximum 6 poems. **Pays 3 contributor copies.**

Tips Be original, honest, and of course, keep trying.

THE LUMBERYARD

Building a New Platform for the Arts, E-mail: info@lumberyardmagazine.com. Website: www.lumberyardmagazine.com. Biannual magazine that's not quite a comic book, not quite a literary magazine. We seek to build a new platform for the arts to speak to the world—to bring literary and visual artistry together, creating a portal for all to enter, experience, and be uplifted in our limited human journey towards understanding. Estab. 2008. No kill fee.

Fiction Send complete ms.

Poetry Needs avant-garde, free verse, traditional. Submit maximum 3 poems.

Tips What do we look for? We like lots of stuff. However, a strong affinity for the concept of design mixed with the literary experience is encouraged, as all work will be placed within the magazine in a spirit of collaboration between visuals and the written word.

LUNA PARK

The Carnival World of Little & Literary Magazines, 313 Elizabeth Ave., Hattiesburg MS 39401. E-mail: lunaparkreview@gmail.com. Website: www.lunaparkreview.com. Quarterly covering fiction, poetry, occasional reviews of literary magazines—any and all forms of literature and art. "Founded on the idea that literary magazines are credible, important and interesting venues for artistic work—at the same time reminiscent of a fine art gallery and a burlesque carnival." Estab. 2008. No kill fee. Guidelines available.

Nonfiction Needs book excerpts, essays, book reviews, interview.

Poetry Contact: Julia Johnson, poetry editor.

Tips "Writers: send your work by email as .doc or .rtf file attachments. We are most interested in intelligent, exciting engagements with the subjects of art and/or publishing. We publish occasionally and quarterly. Feel free to query. Letters to the editor are to be sent by email or to our mailing address. Literary Magazine Publishers: send issue copies to our mailing address. Galleys or final issues are fine."

$ LYRICAL BALLADS MAGAZINE

Classical Publishing, Ltd., E-mail: submissions@lyricalballads.net. Website: www.lyricalballads.net. **75% freelance written.** Monthly newsletter covering literature. "We are looking for either poetry or short fiction. It should be emotional, meaning that its primary aim should be to make the reader feel something—anything at all. Poetry, if not rhyming, should have some standardized form." Estab. 2007. Circ. 1,000. Byline given. Pays on publication. No kill fee. Publishes ms an average of 1-2 months after acceptance. Buys one-time rights. Editorial lead time 2 months. Submit seasonal material 3 months in advance. Accepts queries by e-mail, online submission form. Accepts simultaneous submissions. Responds in 3 months to queries. Responds in 1 month to mss Sample copy available online Guidelines available online

Nonfiction Needs essays. Send complete ms. Length: 300-3,000 words. **Pays $1-10 for assigned articles. Pays $1-10 for unsolicited articles.**

Fiction We accept only literary short fiction and poetry. **Buys 50-60 mss/year. mss/year.** Send complete ms. Length: 500-3,000 words.

Poetry Needs traditional. We do not publish free verse of any kind. **Buys 20-30/year poems/year.** Submit maximum 10 poems. Length: 5-150 lines.

MAD POETS REVIEW

The Mad Poets Society, P.O. Box 1248, Media PA 19063-8248. E-mail: madpoets@comcast.net. Website: www.madpoetsociety.com. Annual covering thought provoking, moving, well-crafted poetry; We encourage beginning poets. We are anxious for work with 'joie de vivre' that startles and inspires. No restrictions on subject, form or style. We have published thousands of poets, including U.S. Poet Laureate Billy Collins as well as other renowned poets. Estab. 1992. Circ. 350. No kill fee. Buys one-time rights. Accepts previously published material. Accepts simultaneous submissions. Responds in 3 months to mss. Sample copy for $13.50.

- We pay writers with contributor copies.

Poetry If you are interested in our annual contest, please review the Contest Guidelines online. 'Mad' does not mean we are looking for crazy, nonsensical ramblings, or poets who are terminally ticked off. Submit maximum 6 poems.

Tips Include SASE, brief cover leter, 3-4 sentence biography. Our reading period runs from Jan. 1 - June 1 only. Poems arriving in the intervening 6 months will be returned unread. You need not be a member to submit work. After submitting, please do not submit again until you have heard from us. We often comment on rejections. The worst case scenario between acceptance and publication is 7-8 mos.

MAGNA

43 Keslake Rd., London England NW6-6DH UK. E-mail: contributions@magmapoetry.com. Website: www.magmapoetry.com. Triannual website covering the best in contemporary poetry and writing about poetry. We look for poems which give a direct sense of what it is to live today—honest about feelings, alert about the world, sometimes funny, always well crafted. We showcase a poet in each issue. A rotating editorship results in different emphasis. A quarter of poems are from poets living abroad, including Ireland, USA, Canada, Australasia. No kill fee. Guidelines available.

- Please submit in the body of an email rather than as an attachment.

Poetry Submit maximum 6 poems.

Tips We welcome unpublished poems and original artwork by post or email. Contribution deadlines for the 3 issues are the end of Feb., mid-July and the end of Oct. Poems are considered for 1 issue only. We write to contributors as soon as a decision is made. Postal contributions must be accompanied by an SAE if posted from the UK or with sufficient international reply coupons if posted abroad. The writer's name must appear on each page or image. Include email address whenever possible.

$ $ MAISONNEUVE

Maisonneuve Magazine Association, 400 de Maisonneuve Blvd. W., Suite 655, Montreal QC H3A 1L4 Canada.

(514)482-5089. Fax: (514)482-6734. E-mail: submissions@maisonneuve.org. Website: www.maisonneuve.org. **90% freelance written**. Quarterly magazine covering eclectic curiousity. What does *Maisonneuve* publish? The sky's the limit—hell, what's in a sky? Poems about nothing? Love 'em. Got a cousin who writes long diatribes against houseflies? How about a really good vignette on the way people walk? Photocopies of your childhood collection of gum-wrappers. Audiofiles of people talking at the Jackson Pollock retrospective. Sonnets to your beloved—they better be good. This is a young magazine, and we're still discovering our limits. You are invited to join in. Estab. 2002. Circ. under 10,000. Byline given. Pays on publication. Offers 25% kill fee. Publishes ms an average of 4-6 months after acceptance. Buys first North American serial rights, buys electronic rights. Editorial lead time 4 months. Submit seasonal material 8 months in advance. Accepts simultaneous submissions. Responds in 2 weeks to queries. Responds in 2 months to mss. Sample copy available online. Guidelines available online.

Nonfiction Needs essays, general interest, historical, humor, interview, personal experience, photo feature. **Buys 20 mss/year.** Query with published clips. Length: 50-5,000 words. **Pays 10¢/word.** Sometimes pays expenses of writers on assignment.

Photos Contact: Contact Jenn McIntyre, art director. State availability Captions, identification of subjects, model releases required. Reviews GIF/JPEG files. Negotiates payment individually. Buys one time rights.

Columns/Departments Open House (witty & whimsical), 800-1,200 words; Profiles + Interviews (character insights), 2,000 words; Studio (spotlight on visual artists/trends), 500 words; Manifesto (passionate calls for change), 800 words. 40-50 Query with published clips. **Pays 10¢/word.**

Fiction Needs adventure, confession, ethnic, experimental, humorous, science fiction, slice-of-life vignettes. **Buys 4 mss/year.** Send complete ms. Length: 1,000-4,000 words. **Pays 10¢/word.**

Poetry Needs avant-garde, free verse, haiku, light verse, traditional. **Buys 16-32 poems/year.** Submit maximum unlimited poems. **Payment varies.**

Fillers Needs anecdotes, facts, short humor. 15 Length: 50-150 words. **Payment varies.**

Tips *Maisonneuve* has been described as a new *New Yorker* for a younger generation, or as *Harper's* meets *Vice*, or as *Vanity Fair* without the vanity—but *Maisonneuve* is its own creature. *Maisonneuve*'s purpose is to keep its readers informed, alert, and entertained, and to dissolve artistic borders between regions, countries, languages and genres. It does this by providing a diverse range of commentary across the arts, sciences, daily and social life. The magazine has a balanced perspective, and 'brings the news' in a wide variety of ways. At its core, *Maisonneuve* asks questions about our lives and provides answers free of cant and cool.

$ THE MALAHAT REVIEW

The University of Victoria, P.O. Box 1700, STN CSC, Victoria BC V8W 2Y2 Canada. (250)721-8524. E-mail: malahat@uvic.ca (for queries only). Website: www.malahatreview.ca. **100% freelance written. Eager to work with new/unpublished writers.** Quarterly magazine covering poetry, fiction, creative non-fiction, and reviews. "We try to achieve a balance of views and styles in each issue. We strive for a mix of the best writing by both established and new writers." Estab. 1967. Circ. 1,500. Byline given. Pays on acceptance. No kill fee. Publishes ms an average of 6 months after acceptance. Buys first world rights. Accepts queries by mail. Responds in 2 weeks to queries. Responds in 3-10 months to mss. Sample copy for $18.45 (US). Guidelines available online.

Nonfiction Query first about review articles, critical essays, interviews, and visual art, which we generally solicit. Include SASE with Canadian postage or IRCs. **Pays $40/magazine page**

Fiction General ficton and poetry. **Buys 12-14 mss/year.** Send complete ms. 8,000 words maximum. **Pays $40/magazine page.**

Poetry Needs avant-garde, free verse, traditional. **Buys 100 poems/year.** 5-10 pages **Pays $40/magazine page.**

Tips "Please do not send more than 1 submission at a time: 4-8 poems or 1 short story (do not mix poetry and fiction in the same submission). See *The Malahat Review*'s Far Horizons for poetry and short fiction, Creative Non-fiction, long poem, and novella contests in the Awards section of our Web site."

$$ MANOA

A Pacific Journal of International Writing, English Dept., University of Hawaii, Honolulu HI 96822. (808)956-3070. Fax: (808)956-3083. E-mail: mjournal-l@hawaii.edu. Website: manoajournal.hawaii.edu. Semiannual magazine. "High quality literary fiction, poetry, essays, personal narrative. In general, each issue is devoted to new work from Pacific and Asian nations. Our audience is international. US writing need not be confined to Pacific settings or subjects. Please see our Web site for more information on what we publish." Estab. 1989. Circ. 2,500 and large online distribution through Project Muse and JSTOR. Byline given. Pays on publication. Buys first North American serial rights, buys non-exclusive, one-time print rights. Editorial lead time 9 months. Accepts simultaneous submissions. Responds in 3 weeks to queries. ; 1 month to poetry mss; 6 months to fiction. Sample copy for $15 (US). Guidelines available online.

Nonfiction No Pacific exotica. Query first. Length: 1,000-5,000 words. **Pays $25/printed page.**

Fiction Query first and/or see Web site. Needs mainstream, contemporary, excerpted novel. No Pacific exotica. **Buys 1-2 in the US (excluding translation) mss/year.** Send complete ms. Length: 1,000-7,500 words. **Pays**

$100-500 normally ($25/printed page).

Poetry No light verse. **Buys 10-20 poems/year.** Submit maximum 5-6 poems. **Pays $25/poem.**

Tips "Not accepting unsolicited manuscripts at this time because of commitments to special projects. See Web site for more information."

MANY MOUNTAINS MOVING

a literary journal of diverse, contemporary voices, 1705 Lombart St., Philadelphia PA 19146. E-mail: jeffreyethan@att.net. Website: www.mmminc.org. Annual covering unpublished poetry, fiction, nonfiction, and art from writers and artists of all walks of life. Open to all forms of poetry, welcoming outstanding, exciting works which reflect the diversity of our many cultures—writing with intelligence, emotion, wit, and craft. Has published Allen Ginsberg, Robert Bly, Isabel Allende, Amiri Baraka, mary Crow, Adrienne Rich. Poetry published in *MMM* has appeared in 'The Best American Poetry' and Pushcart Prize Anthologies. Estab. 1994. contest winnings. No kill fee. Accepts simultaneous submissions. Responds in 3 mos. - 1 year to mss. Guidelines available online.

- Submissions temporary closed due to overwhelming response; check back periodically on website.

Nonfiction Needs essays, Bok Reviews, Translations.

Columns/Departments Many Mountains Moving Poetry & Flash Fiction Contests - Prize: $200 and publication in *MMM* print annual. Finalists also will be considered for publication. Open to all poets and writers whose work is in English. Deadline: Nov. 1, '08. Guidelines and entry fees are online. Poetry Book Contests - Prize: $1,000 and publications in Spring '09. Past deadline.

Fiction Contact: Thaddeus Rutkowski, fiction editor. Length: 1,000-4,000 words.

Poetry Contact: Jeffrey Ethan Lee, Sr. Poetry Editor. Needs avant-garde, free verse, haiku, light verse, traditional.

Tips Invite readers into a truly multicultural exchange.to look through another's eyes at the world, as only literature and art can do, without being too simplistic. Poetry and Flash Fiction Contests' deadline is Nov. 1, 2008. Guidelines and enry fees are online. Prize money from $200, plus publication in our print annual.

MARGIE

The American Journal of Poetry, Intuit House Press, P.O. Box 250, Chesterfield MO 63006-0250. E-mail: margieonl@aol.com. Website: www.margiereview.com. Annual magazine covering superlative poetry without restriction to form, school or subject matter. A distinctive voice is prized. Features the 2008 'Strong Rx Medicine' Best Poem contest (Postmark Deadline: Oct. 31, 2008), online submissions. See Guidelines online. Also, The 2009 Robert E. and Ruth I. Wilson Best Poetry Book Contest (Postmark Deadline: March 14, 2009), postal submissions only. No kill fee. Accepts queries by mail. Accepts simultaneous submissions. Responds in 1-2 months to mss.

Poetry Submit maximum 3-5 poems. **contest awards $1,000.**

Tips Open reading period: June 1st-July 15th. Published in the fall. Open to publishing newer and established poets equally. Subscribers only may submit poetry at any time of the year.

MARGINALIA

CALL Dept., Taylor 115, Gunnison CO 81231. Website: www.western.edu/marginalia. Annual magazine interested in the interplay between the contained text and its surrounding negative space. Byline given. No kill fee. Accepts simultaneous submissions.

Nonfiction Contact: Jane Satterfield, nonfiction editor. Needs essays, creative nonfiction, book reviews. Send complete ms.

Fiction Contact: Alicita Rodriguez, fiction editor. Needs experimental, mainstream. Send complete ms.

Poetry Contact: Joseph Starr and Mark Todd, poetry editors. Needs avant-garde, free verse, traditional. **Buys 3-5 poems/year.**

THE MARLBORO REVIEW

P.O. Box 243, Marlboro VT 05344. E-mail: online at www.marlbororeview.com. Website: www.marlbororeview.com. Semiannual website covering the best in contemporary poetry, fiction, parts-of-novels, long poems, nonfiction, essays. Recent contributors include Stephen Dobyns, Joan Aleshire, Jean Valentine, Robert Hill Long, Carol Frost. Estab. 1996. Pays on publication. No kill fee. Accepts queries by mail. Accepts simultaneous submissions. Guidelines available online.

- Open to short fiction and poetry submissions from Aug. 30, 2008 to May 30, 2009. Include SASE with proper postage, otherwise your work will be discarded unread. Submissions received during the summer break will be returned unread.

Nonfiction Needs essays, Reviews. Criticisms., interview, Translations.

Fiction Contact: Helen Freemont, Margaret Kaufman. Length: 1,000-7,500 words.

Poetry Contact: Ruth Anderson Barnett. No line limits known. Check with publisher.

Tips Check Guideliens for details and restrictions. Open to most themes. We are particularly interested in translation, as well as cultural, scientific, and philosophical issues approached from a writer's sensibility. If you are overseas and must submit electronically, consult with Ellen Dudley before sending any files.

$ THE MASSACHUSETTS REVIEW

South College, University of Massachusetts, Amherst MA 01003-9934. (413)545-2689. Fax: (413)577-0740. E-mail: massrev@external.umass.edu. Website: www.massreview.org. Quarterly magazine. Estab. 1959. Circ. 1,200. Pays on publication. Publishes ms an average of 18 months after acceptance. Buys first North American serial rights. Accepts queries by mail. Accepts simultaneous submissions. Responds in 3 months to mss. Sample copy for $8. Guidelines available online.

- Does not respond to mss without SASE.

Nonfiction Articles on all subjects. No reviews of single books. Send complete ms or query with SASE 6,500 words maximum **Pays $50.**

Fiction Short stories. Wants more prose less than 30 pages. **Buys 10 mss/year.** Send complete ms. 25-30 pages maximum.

Poetry Submit maximum 6 poems. **Pays 50¢/line to $25 maximum.**

Tips "No manuscripts are considered May-September. Electronic submission process on Web site. No fax or e-mail submissions. No simultaneous submissions."

MEMOIR (AND)

Memoir Journal, P.O. Box 1398, Sausalito CA 94966-1398. (415)339-4142. E-mail: admin@memoirjournal.com. Website: www.memoirjournal.com. **100% freelance written**. Semiannual magazine covering memoirs. "*Memoir (and)* publishes memoirs in many forms, from the traditional to the experimental. The editors strive with each issue to include a selection of prose, poetry, graphic memoirs, narrative photography, lies and more from both emerging and established authors." Estab. 2006. (Contributors Notes in each issue) No kill fee. Publishes ms an average of 3 months after acceptance. Buys one-time rights, buys electronic rights, buys rights to publish in future anthologies rights. Accepts queries by mail, e-mail. Accepts simultaneous submissions. Sample copy available online. Guidelines available online.

- We have two reading periods per year, with 4 prizes awarded in each: the *Memoir (and)* Prizes for Prose and Poetry ($500-100 & publication in publication in print and online, plus copies of the journal) and the *Memoir (and)* Prize for Graphic Memoir ($100 & publication in print & online).

Nonfiction Contact: Joan E. Chapman. Needs essays, personal experience, Graphic Memoir. Does not publish themed issues. **Buys 40-80 mss/year mss/year.** Send complete ms. Length: 50-10,000 words. **Pays 0 for assigned or unsolicited articles.**

Photos Send photos Reviews GIF/JPEG files. Offers no additional payment for photos accepted with ms. Buys one time rights.

Poetry Needs avant garde, free verse, haiku, light verse, traditional. **Buys 20-40 poems/year poems/year.** Submit maximum 5 poems.

Tips "The editors particularly invite submissions that push the traditional boundaries of form and content in the exploration of the representation of self. They also just love a well-told memoir."

METAL SCRATCHES

P.O. Box 685, Forest Lake MN 55025. E-mail: metalscratches@metalscratches.com. Website: www.metalscratches.com. **100% freelance written**. "Semiannual publication looking for stories written about the darker side of humanity—fiction with an edge, a metal scratch." Estab. 2003. Circ. 200. Byline given. No kill fee. Publishes ms an average of 6-12 months after acceptance. Buys one-time rights. Accepts queries by mail, e-mail. Accepts simultaneous submissions. Responds in 1 month to mss. Sample copy for $5 (check made out to Kim Mark). Guidelines by email.

Fiction Needs experimental, literary. Does not want horror, science fiction, children's, religion, or poetry. **Buys 12 mss/year.** Send complete ms. 3,500 words maximum

Tips "We are looking for strong character development, and fiction with an edge, a bite. Nothing 'cute' or 'sweet.' Follow our writer's guidelines."

$ MICHIGAN QUARTERLY REVIEW

0576 Rackham Bldg., 915 E. Washington, University of Michigan, Ann Arbor MI 48109-1070. (734)764-9265. E-mail: mqr@umich.edu. Website: www.umich.edu/~mqr. **75% freelance written**. Quarterly magazine. An interdisciplinary journal which publishes mainly essays and reviews, with some high-quality fiction and poetry, for an intellectual, widely read audience. Estab. 1962. Circ. 1,000. Byline given. Pays on publication. No kill fee. Publishes ms an average of 1 year after acceptance. Buys first serial rights. Accepts queries by mail. Responds in 2 months to queries. Responds in 2 months to mss. Sample copy for $4. Guidelines available online.

- "The Laurence Goldstein Award is a $1,000 annual award to the best poem published in the *Michigan Quarterly Review* during the previous year. The Lawrence Foundation Award is a $1,000 annual award to the best short story published in the *Michigan Quarterly Review* during the previous year."

Nonfiction "*MQR* is open to general articles directed at an intellectual audience. Essays ought to have a personal voice and engage a significant subject. Scholarship must be present as a foundation, but we are not interested in specialized essays directed only at professionals in the field. We prefer ruminative essays, written in a fresh style and which reach interesting conclusions. We also like memoirs and interviews with significant historical or cultural resonance." **Buys 35 mss/year.** Query. Length: 2,000-5,000 words. **Pays $10/published page.**

Fiction Contact: Fiction Editor. "No restrictions on subject matter or language. We are very selective. We like stories which are unusual in tone and structure, and innovative in language. No genre fiction written for a market. Would like to see more fiction about social, political, cultural matters, not just centered on a love relationship or dysfunctional family." **Buys 10 mss/year.** Send complete ms. Length: 1,500-7,000 words. **Pays $10/published page.**

Poetry Pays $10/published page.

Tips "Read the journal and assess the range of contents and the level of writing. We have no guidelines to offer or set expectations; every manuscript is judged on its unique qualities. On essays—query with a very thorough description of the argument and a copy of the first page. Watch for announcements of special issues which are usually expanded issues and draw upon a lot of freelance writing. Be aware that this is a university quarterly that publishes a limited amount of fiction and poetry and that it is directed at an educated audience, one that has done a great deal of reading in all types of literature."

THE MIDWEST QUARTERLY

A Journal of Contemporary Thought, 406b Russ Hall, Pittsburg State University, Pittsburg KS 66762. (620)235-4317. Fax: (620)235-4080. E-mail: midwestq@pittstate.edu. Website: www2.pittstate.edu/engl/mwq/mqindex.html. **Contact:** Dr. James B. Schick. Quarterly magazine covering scholarly articles for the academic audience dealing with a broad range of subjects of current interest, and poetry. "We seek discussions of an analytical and speculative nature and well-crafted poems. Poems of interest to us use intense, vivid, concrete and/or surrealistic images to explore the mysterious and surprising interactions of the nature and inner human worlds." Estab. 1959. contest winnings. No kill fee. Accepts queries by mail, e-mail, fax, phone. Guidelines available online.

- "For publication in MQ and eligibility for the annual Emmett Memorial Prize competition, the Editors invite submission of articles on any literary topic, but preferably on Victorian or Modern British Literature, Literary Criticism, or the Teaching of Literature. The winner receives an honorarium and invitation to deliver the annual Emmett Memorial Lecture. Contact Dr. Meats, Chairman, English Dept."

Nonfiction Contact: Tim Bailey, book reviews ed. Needs essays, book of poetry reviews. No heavily documented research studies.

Columns/Departments Book Reviews, Book of Poetry Reviews.

Poetry Contact: Dr. Stephen Meats, poetry ed. Needs avant-garde, traditional.

Tips "The quality and format of book reviews are of special importance to us. Their purpose is to evaluate the significance of new scholarly work: identify its contribution to knowledge and its deficiencies. See Guidelines before submitting."

MISSISSIPPI REVIEW

Univ. of Southern Mississippi, 118 College Dr., #5144, Hattiesburg MS 39406-0001. (601)266-4321. Fax: (601)266-5757. Website: www.mississippireview.com. Semiannual. "Literary publication for those interested in contemporary literature—writers, editors who read to be in touch with current modes." Estab. 1972. Circ. 1,500. No kill fee. Buys first North American serial rights. Sample copy for $10.

- "We do not accept unsolicited manuscripts except under the rules and guidelines of the *Mississippi Review* Prize Competition. See Web site for guidelines."

Fiction Contact: Rie Fortenberry, managing editor. Needs experimental, fantasy, humorous, contemporary, avant-garde and art fiction. No juvenile or genre fiction. 30 pages maximum.

$ $ $ THE MISSOURI REVIEW

357 McReynolds Hall, University of Missouri, Columbia MO 65211. (573)882-4474. Fax: (573)884-4671. E-mail: tmr@missourireview.com. Website: www.missourireview.com. **90% freelance written.** Quarterly magazine. We publish contemporary fiction, poetry, interviews, personal essays, cartoons, special features—such as History as Literature series and Found Text series—for the literary and the general reader interested in a wide range of subjects. Estab. 1978. Circ. 6,500. Byline given. Offers signed contract. Editorial lead time 6 months. Accepts queries by mail. Responds in 2 weeks to queries. Responds in 10 weeks to mss. Sample copy for $8.95 or online Guidelines available online.

Nonfiction Contact: Evelyn Somers, associate editor. Needs book excerpts, essays. No literary criticism. **Buys 10 mss/year.** Send complete ms. **Pays $1,000.**

Fiction Contact: Speer Morgan, editor. Needs ethnic, humorous, mainstream, novel concepts, literary. No genre or flash fiction. **Buys 25 mss/year.** Send complete ms. no preference. **Pays $30/printed page.**

Poetry Contact: Jason Koo, poetry editor. Publishes 3-5 poetry features of 6-12 pages per issue. Please familiarize yourself with the magazine before submitting poetry. **Buys 50 poems/year. Pays $30/printed page.**

Tips Send your best work.

THE MOCHILA REVIEW

Missouri Western State University English, Foreign Languages, & Journalism Dept., Missouri Western State University English, Foreign Languages, & Journalism Dept., 4525 Downs Dr., St. Joseph MO 64507. Website: www.missouriwestern.edu/orgs/mochila/homepage.htm. Annual magazine covering poetry, short stories, creative nonfiction, mixed genre essays, excerpts from longer prose. We are looking for writing that has a respect for the sound of language. We value poems that have to be read aloud so your mouth can feel the shape of the words. Send us writing that conveys a sense of urgency, writing that the writer can't *not* write. We crave fresh and daring work. No kill fee. Accepts queries by mail, e-mail. Accepts simultaneous submissions. Responds in 1 month to mss.

Nonfiction Needs book excerpts, from longer prose, essays, mixed genre.

Fiction Needs novel concepts. Length: 5,000 words.

Tips Send only unpublished work. Mail each genre separately. Word process submissions. If you have not heard back within a month, please feel free to contact us.

$ MODERN HAIKU

An Independent Journal of Haiku and Haiku Studies, P.O. Box 7046, Evanston IL 60204-7046. E-mail: trumbullc@comcast.net. Website: www.modernhaiku.org. **85% freelance written**. Magazine published 3 times/year. *Modern Haiku* publishes high quality material only. Haiku and related genres, articles on haiku, haiku book reviews, and translations comprise its contents. It has an international circulation; subscribers include many university, school, and public libraries." Estab. 1969. Circ. 650. Byline given. Pays on acceptance. No kill fee. Publishes ms an average of 6 months after acceptance. Buys first North American serial rights. Editorial lead time 4 months. Accepts queries by mail, e-mail. Responds in 1 week to queries. Responds in 6-8 weeks to mss. Sample copy for $11 in North America, $13 in Canada, $14 in Mexico, $17 overseas. Guidelines available online.

Nonfiction Needs essays, anything related to haiku. Send complete ms. **Pays $5/page.**

Columns/Departments Haiku & Senryu; Haibun; Essays (on haiku and related genres); Reviews (books of haiku or related genres). 40 essay & review mss/year (most are commissioned). Send complete ms. **Pays $5/page.**

Poetry Needs haiku, senryu, haibun, haiga. Does not want "general poetry, tanka, linked verse forms." **Buys 750 poems/year.** Submit maximum 24 poems. **Pays $1 per haiku.**

Tips "Study the history of haiku, read books about haiku, learn the aesthetics of haiku and methods of composition. Write about your sense perceptions of the suchness of entities; avoid ego-centered interpretations."

MORPHEUS TALES

Morpheus Tales, 116 Muriel St., London N1 9QU— UK. E-mail: morpheustales@blueyonder.co.uk. **100% freelance written**. Quarterly magazine covering horror, science fiction, fantasy. "We publish the best in horror, science fiction and fantasy, both fiction and nonfiction." Estab. 2008. Circ. 1,000. No kill fee. Publishes ms an average of 4 months after acceptance. Buys First British Serial Rights rights. Editorial lead time 3 months. Submit seasonal material 6 months in advance. Accepts queries by e-mail. Responds in 1 week to queries. Responds in 1 month to mss. Sample copy for $7. Guidelines available online.

Nonfiction Needs book excerpts, essays, general interest, how-to, inspirational, interview, new product, opinion, photo feature, Letters to the editor. All material must be based on horror, science fiction or fantasy genre. **Buys 6 mss/year mss/year.** Query. Length: 500-3,000 words. Sometimes pays expenses of writers on assignment.

Fiction Needs experimental, fantasy, horror, mystery, novel concepts, science fiction, serialized, suspense. **Buys 20 mss/year. mss/year.** Send complete ms. Length: 250-300 words.

N+1

The Editors, 68 Jay St., #405, Brooklyn NY 11201. E-mail: queries@nplusonemag.com; fiction@nplusonemag.com. Website: www.nplusonemag.com. seminannual (print); weekly (web-only) magazine covering politics, literature, and culture for our print magazine. N-1 posts new, web-only material, once or twice a week. "The website will be running *n + 1*-type content that because of its timeliness or its genre, cannot appeaer in the print issue. Check the Archive for an indication of the sorts of pieces we run; lengths might range from 500-2,500 words. Articles about global warming and other ecological consequences of contemporary capitalism will be considered first, followed by articles about sports. Book reviews will be read grudgingly, but with something resembling an open mind." No kill fee. Sample copy and guidelines available online.

- "No unsolicited poetry at this time."

Nonfiction "Query with outline of your argument or, better yet, the first 500-1,000 words of your proposed piece. Please attach 2 or 3 samples of your work. If you don't hear back from us within 6 weeks, assume the worst." Needs essays, expose, general interest, interview, opinion, Sports.

Photos Contact: Sabine Rogers.

Fiction Contact: fiction@nplusonemag.com. "In an email, please attach 3 short stories or the ms of a story collection or novels, noting which portions of the submitted work, if any, have been published or accepted for

publication elsewhere."
Tips "Most of the slots available for a given issue will have been filled many months before publication. If you would like to brave the odds, the best submission guidelines are those implied by the magazine itself. Read an issue or 2 through to get a sense of whether your piece might fit into n + 1."

THE NATIONAL POETRY REVIEW

The National Poetry Review Press, C. J. Sage, Editor, The National Poetry Review, P.O. Box 640625, San Jose CA 95164-0625. Website: www.nationalpoetryreview.com. Semiannual magazine covering well-crafted poetry in both formal and free verse. Artwork submissions are also considered for *The National Poetry Review*'s cover. Editor is fond of fresh, formal verse, rich sound, play within form, lyricality, image, metaphor, especially extended metaphor, unique diction and syntax. Contests: *The National Poetry Review* Book Prize Series, The Finch Prize for Poetry. Estab. 2003. No kill fee. Buys first rights. Accepts queries by mail. Accepts simultaneous submissions.

- No unsolicited email submissions. A few editor favorites are S. D. Lishan's 'Eurydice and Loverboy,' John Brehm's 'Songbird,' Kimberly Johnson's 'Sonnet,' Mary Oliver's 'Poppies,' and Margot Schilpp's 'Manifesto.

Poetry No prose poems, simple confessional work, or vulgarity. Submit maximum 3-5 poems. **Payment is 1 copy of the issue in which your work appears and a small honorarium.**
Tips Memorability, innovation, and joie de vivre are important to TNPR. We agree with Frost about delight and wisdom. We believe in the value of rich sound. Send your best, most memorable poems. We tend to prefer I-less poems—poems that do not reference the self—but will consider all excellent, memorable work. Outside the reading period, we only accept submissions from subscribers. Poetry is temporarily closed to submissions. Will be open again from June 1, 2009 to Aug. 31, 2009.

NEON MAGAZINE

A Literary Magazine, UK. E-mail: neonmagazine@ymail.com. Website: www.neonmagazine.co.uk. www.myspace.com/neonlitmag. Quarterly website covering alternative work of any form of poetry and prose, short stories, flash fiction, photographs, artwork and reviews. "Genre work is welcome. Experimentation is encouraged. We like stark poetry and weird prose. We seek work that is beautiful, shocking, intense and memorable. Darker pieces are generally favored over humorous ones. We are not completely averse to more innocent or whimsical creations, but they should be a good fit for the aesthetic of the magazine. We are concerned with themes of isolation, post-modernism, technology, dislocation, apathy, the apocalypse, memory, Kirk Cameron and urban decay." No kill fee. Buys one-time rights. "After publication all rights revert back to you." Accepts queries by e-mail. Reports in 1 month. Query if you have received no reply after 6 weeks. Guidelines available online.

- "We have now finished reading for the print edition of *Neon*. All submissions from now onwards will be considered for the new, online-only edition. Note: *Neon* was previously published as *FourVolts Magazine*."

Nonfiction "Query by email if you would like to have a book, chapbook or magazine reviewed in a future issue. Query with a sample of your work if you would like to write reviews—this is unpaid but you can keep what you review." Needs essays, Reviews. No word limit.
Photos £5 for 1-4 images.
Fiction Needs experimental, horror, humorous, science fiction, suspense. "No nonsensical prose; we are not appreciative of sentimentality." **Buys 8-12 mss/year.** No word limit. **For 1 short story, or 1-2 flash fictions.**
Poetry "No nonsensical poetry; we are not appreciative of sentimentality. Rhyming poetry is discouraged." **Buys 24-30 poems/year.** No word limit.
Tips "Send several poems, one or 2 pieces of prose or several images, pasted in the body of an email. Include the word 'submission' in your subject line. Include a short biographical note (up to 100 words). Read submission guidelines before submitting your work."

NERVE COWBOY

Liquid Paper Press, P.O. Box 4973, Austin TX 78765. Website: www.jwhagins.com/nervecowboy.html. Semiannual. "*Nerve Cowboy* publishes adventurous, comical, disturbing, thought-provoking, accessible poetry and fiction. We like to see work sensitive enough to make the hardest hard-ass cry, funny enough to make the most hopeless brooder laugh and disturbing enough to make us all glad we're not the author of the piece." Estab. 1996. Circ. 350. No kill fee. Publishes ms an average of 6-12 months after acceptance. Buys one-time rights. Accepts previously published material. Responds in 3 weeks to queries. Responds in 3 months to mss. Sample copy for $6. Guidelines available online.
Fiction Contact: Joseph Shields or Jerry Hagins, editors. "No racist, sexist or overly offensive work. Wants more unusual stories with rich description and enough twists and turns that leave the reader thinking." Length: 1,500 words. **Pays 1 contributor's copy.**

$ NEW ENGLAND REVIEW

Middlebury College, Middlebury VT 05753. (802)443-5075. E-mail: nereview@middlebury.edu. Website:

go.middlebury.edu/nereview. Quarterly magazine. Serious literary only. Reads September 1-May 31 (postmarked dates). Estab. 1978. Circ. 2,000. Byline given. Pays on publication. No kill fee. Publishes ms an average of 6 months after acceptance. Buys first North American serial rights, buys first rights, buys second serial (reprint) rights. Accepts simultaneous submissions. Responds in 2 weeks to queries. Responds in 3 months to mss. Sample copy for $8 (add $5 for overseas). Guidelines available online.

- No e-mail submissions.

Nonfiction Serious literary only. Rarely accepts previously published submissions (out of print or previously published abroad only.) **Buys 20-25 mss/year.** Send complete ms. 7,500 words maximum, though exceptions may be made. **Pays $10/page ($20 minimum), and 2 copies.**
Fiction Send 1 story at a time, unless it is very short. Serious literary only, novel excerpts. **Buys 25 mss/year.** Send complete ms. Prose length: 10,000 words maximum, double spaced. Novellas: 30,000 words maximum. **Pays $10/page ($20 minimum), and 2 copies.**
Poetry Buys 75-90 poems/year. Submit maximum 6 poems. **Pays $10/page ($20 minimum), and 2 copies.**
Tips We consider short fiction, including shorts, short-shorts, novellas, and self-contained extracts from novels in both traditional and experimental forms. In nonfiction, we consider a variety of general and literary, but not narrowly scholarly essays; we also publish long and short poems; book reviews; screenplays; graphics; translations; critical reassessments; statements by artists working in various media; interviews; testimonies; and letters from abroad. We are committed to exploration of all forms of contemporary cultural expression in the US and abroad. With few exceptions, we print only work not published previously elsewhere.

$ NEW LETTERS

University of Missouri-Kansas City, University House, 5101 Rockhill Rd., Kansas City MO 64110-2499. (816)235-1168. Fax: (816)235-2611. E-mail: newletters@umkc.edu. Website: www.newletters.org. **100% freelance written**. Quarterly magazine. *New Letters* is intended for the general literary reader. We publish literary fiction, nonfiction, essays, poetry. We also publish art. Estab. 1934. Circ. 5,000. Byline given. Pays on publication. No kill fee. Publishes ms an average of 6 months after acceptance. Buys first North American serial rights. Editorial lead time 6 months. Submit seasonal material 6 months in advance. Accepts queries by mail. Responds in 1 month to queries. Responds in 3 months to mss. Sample copy for $10 or sample articles on website. Guidelines available online.

- Submissions are not read between May 1 and October 1.

Nonfiction Needs essays. No self-help, how-to, or nonliterary work. **Buys 8-10 mss/year.** Send complete ms. 5,000 words maximum. **Pays $40-100.**
Photos Send photos Reviews contact sheets, 2x4 transparencies, prints. Pays $10-40/photo Buys one time rights.
Fiction Contact: Robert Stewart, editor. Needs ethnic, experimental, humorous, mainstream, contemporary. No genre fiction. **Buys 15-20 mss/year.** Send complete ms. 5,000 words maximum. **Pays $30-75.**
Poetry Needs avant-garde, free verse, haiku, traditional. No light verse. **Buys 40-50 poems/year.** Submit maximum 6 poems. Open **Pays $10-25.**
Tips We aren't interested in essays that are footnoted, or essays usually described as scholarly or critical. Our preference is for creative nonfiction or personal essays. We prefer shorter stories and essays to longer ones (an average length is 3,500-4,000 words). We have no rigid preferences as to subject, style, or genre, although commercial efforts tend to put us off. Even so, our only fixed requirement is on good writing.

NEW OHIO REVIEW

English Dept., Ohio Univ., 360 Ellis Hall, Athens OH 45701. E-mail: noreditors@ohio.edu. Website: www.ohiou.edu/nor/. Magazine. Byline given. No kill fee. Accepts queries by mail. Accepts simultaneous submissions. Guidelines available online.
Nonfiction Needs essays, humor. Send complete ms.
Fiction Needs confession, experimental, humorous, mainstream. Send complete ms.
Poetry Needs avant-garde, free verse, haiku, light verse, traditional.
Tips We accept literary submissions in any genre.

$ $ THE NEW QUARTERLY

Canadian Writers & Writing, St. Jerome's University, 290 Westmount Rd. N., Waterloo ON N2L 3G3 Canada. (519)884-8111, ext. 28290. E-mail: editor@tnq.ca. Website: www.tnq.ca. **95% freelance written**. Quarterly book covering Canadian fiction and poetry. Emphasis on emerging writers and genres, but we publish more traditional work as well if the language and narrative structure are fresh. Estab. 1981. Circ. 1,000. Byline given. Pays on publication. No kill fee. Publishes ms an average of 4 months after acceptance. Buys first Canadian rights. Editorial lead time 6 months. Accepts queries by mail. Accepts simultaneous submissions. Responds in 2 weeks to queries. Responds in 4 months to mss. Sample copy for $16.50 (cover price, plus mailing). Guidelines for #10 SASE or online.

- Open to Canadian writers only.

Fiction Contact: Kim Jernigan, Rae Crossman, Mark Spielmacher, Rosalynn Tyo, fiction editors. *Canadian work only*. We are not interested in genre fiction. We are looking for innovative, beautifully crafted, deeply felt literary fiction. **Buys 20-25 mss/year.** Send complete ms. 20 pages maximum **Pays $200/story**.

Poetry Contact: Barbara Carter, Randi Patterson, John Vardon, Erin Noteboom, poetry editors. Needs avant-garde, free verse, traditional. *Canadian work only*. **Buys 40 poems/year.** Submit maximum 5 poems. **Pays $30/poem.**

Tips Reading us is the best way to get our measure. We don't have preconceived ideas about what we're looking for other than that it must be Canadian work (Canadian writers, not necessarily Canadian content). We want something that's fresh, something that will repay a second reading, something in which the language soars and the feeling is complexly rendered.

NEW SOUTH

Campus Box 1894, Georgia State Univ., MSC 8R0322 Unit 8, Atlanta GA 30303-3083. E-mail: www.new_south@langate.gsu.edu. Website: www.review.gsu.edu. Semiannual magazine Dedicated to finding & publishing the best work from artists around the world. After more than 30 years *GSU Review* has become *New South*. Our role as George State University's journal of art & literature has not changed; however, it was time for a revision, a chance for a clearer mission. Byline given. No kill fee. Accepts queries by mail. Accepts simultaneous submissions. Sample copy for $3. Guidelines available online.

Nonfiction Send complete ms. Length: 7,500 words.

Fiction Contact: Peter Fontaine, fiction editor. Send complete ms. Length: 7,500 words.

Poetry Contact: Austin Segrest, poetry editor. **Buys 3 poems/year.**

NEWS POET NEWS

A unique and insightful form of poetry, No public address available, E-mail: contactus@newspoetnews.com. Website: www.newspoetnews.com. Website combining the more thoughtful process of poetry to the communication of news, to create a more insightful form of modern journalism. Our goal is to reestablish the verse news poem as a meaningful verbal expression illuminating and clarifying the ethical and moral questions of our age. To popularize news poems as a vital creative force in revealing the truth behind the often confusing and conflicting events of the 21st century. No kill fee. Buys Affirm that you are the sole author and maintain all rights to the submitted news poem. rights. NPN acquires the right in perpetuity to publish your submitted news poem on this website, without compensation. online at: http://newspoetnews.com/contributors/contributors.htm. Guidelines are subject to change without notice.

Poetry Needs free verse, traditional. Submissions must be in good taste. Do not use ALL CAPS. Submissions cannot be legally defamatory. Length: lines.

Tips Submit each poem in separate email submissions. Include some biographical info. Writers accepted will be notified by email. We reserve the right to discard without notice any submitted news poems that do not follow our guidelines.

$ THE NEW WRITER

P.O. Box 60, Cranbrook Kent TN17 2ZR United Kingdom. (44)(158)021-2626. E-mail: editor@thenewwriter.com. Website: www.thenewwriter.com. Publishes 6 issues per annum. "Contemporary writing magazine which publishes the best in fact, fiction and poetry." Estab. 1996. Circ. 1,500. Pays on publication. No kill fee. Publishes ms an average of 1 year after acceptance. Buys one-time rights. Accepts queries by e-mail, fax. Accepts simultaneous submissions. Responds in 2 months to queries. Responds in 4 months to mss. Sample copy for SASE and A4 SAE with IRCs only. Guidelines for SASE.

Nonfiction "Content should relate to writing." Query. Length: 1,000-2,000 words. **Pays £20-40.**

Fiction *No unsolicited mss.* Accepts fiction from subscribers only. "We will consider most categories apart from stories written for children. No horror, erotic, or cosy fiction." Query with published clips. Length: 2,000-5,000 words. **Pays £10 per story by credit voucher; additional copies for £1.50.**

Poetry Buys 50 poems/year. Submit maximum 3 poems. 40 lines maximum **Pays £3/poem.**

NO MAN'S LAND

Contemporary German-Language Fiction and Poetry in English Translation, P.O. Box 02 13 04, Berlin 10125 Germany. E-mail: isabel@no-man's-land.org. Website: www.no-mans.land.org. Website covering first-ever translations of fiction and poetry by some of the finest young writers working in German today. Our publication plays on the name 'no man's land' while evoking a virtual no man's land of the Berlin Wall, and is now open for exploration. More than just an online literary magazine, it is an information resource and forum for the German- and English-speaking literary communities in Berlin and beyond. No kill fee. Accepts queries by mail, e-mail. Guidelines available online.

Nonfiction Needs book excerpts, Translations. Length: 4,000 words.

Poetry Submit maximum 5 poems.

Tips We are especially interested in work by interesting, important yet under-translated writers. For prose send up to 3 submissions by 1 or different writers: a submission is considered as 1 story or self-contained novel excerpt. For poetry send translations of work by up to 3 poets, each to a max of 5 poems.

NOON: JOURNAL OF THE SHORT POEM

Minami Motomachi 4-49-506, Shinjuku-ku, Tokyo 160-0012 Japan. E-mail: noonpress@mac.com. Website: nc-haiku.blogspot.com/2008/03/noon-journal-of-short-poem.html. Quarterly magazine covering original, unpublished short poems. Philip Rowland asks taht extra time be spent over these short-short poems and sequences so that subtleties of nuance can be teased out. No kill fee.

Poetry Needs haiku. **Pays with contributor copies.**

Tips Please contact Philip Rowland for further details. Selections for 2008 Summer Issue were already made.

$ THE NORTH AMERICAN REVIEW

University of Northern Iowa, 1222 W. 27th St., Cedar Falls IA 50614-0516. (319)273-6455. Fax: (319)273-4326. E-mail: nar@uni.edu. Website: www.webdelsol.com/northamreview/nar/. **90% freelance written.** Bimonthly magazine. "The *NAR* is the oldest literary magazine in America and one of the most respected; though we have no prejudices about the subject matter of material sent to us, our first concern is quality." Estab. 1815. Circ. under 5,000. Byline given. Pays on publication. No kill fee. Publishes ms an average of 1 year after acceptance. Buys first North American serial rights, buys first rights. Accepts queries by mail. Responds in 4 months to mss. Sample copy for $5. Guidelines available online.

- "This is the oldest literary magazine in the country and one of the most prestigious. Also one of the most entertaining—and a tough market for the young writer."

Nonfiction Contact: Ron Sandvik, nonfiction editor. No restrictions; highest quality only. Open **Pays $5/350 words; $20 minimum, $100 maximum.**

Fiction Contact: Grant Tracey, fiction editor. No restrictions; highest quality only. Needs , Wants more well-crafted literary stories that emphasize family concerns. No flat narrative stories where the inferiority of the character is the paramount concern. Open **Pays $5/350 words; $20 minimum, $100 maximum.**

Poetry No restrictions; highest quality only. Open. **Pays $1/line; $20 minimum, $100 maximum.**

Tips "We like stories that start quickly and have a strong narrative arc. Poems that are passionate about subject, language, and image are welcome, whether they are traditional or experimental, whether in formal or free verse (closed or open form). Nonfiction should combine art and fact with the finest writing. We do not accept simultaneous submissions; these will be returned unread. We read poetry, fiction, and nonfiction year-round."

$ NORTH CAROLINA LITERARY REVIEW

A Magazine of North Carolina Literature, Culture, and History, English Dept., East Carolina University, Greenville NC 27858-4353. (252)328-1537. Fax: (252)328-4889. E-mail: bauerm@mail.ecu.edu. Website: www.ecu.edu/nclr. Annual magazine published in summer covering North Carolina writers, literature, culture, history. "Articles should have a North Carolina slant. First consideration is always for quality of work. Although we treat academic and scholarly subjects, we do not wish to see jargon-laden prose; our readers, we hope, are found as often in bookstores and libraries as in academia. We seek to combine the best elements of magazine for serious readers with best of scholarly journal." Estab. 1992. Circ. 750. Byline given. Pays on publication. No kill fee. Publishes ms an average of 1 year after acceptance. Buys first North American serial rights. Rights returned to writer on request. Editorial lead time 6 months. Accepts queries by mail, e-mail. Responds in 1 month to queries. Responds in 6 months to mss. Sample copy for $10-25. Guidelines available online.

Nonfiction North Carolina-related material only. Needs book excerpts, essays, expose, general interest, historical, humor, interview, opinion, personal experience, photo feature, travel, reviews, short narratives, surveys of archives. No jargon-laden academic articles. **Buys 25-35 mss/year.** Query with published clips. Length: 500-5,000 words. **Pays $50-100 honorarium, extra copies, back issues or subscription (negotiable).**

Photos State availability True required. Reviews 5x7 or 8x10 prints; snapshot size or photocopy OK. Pays $25-250. Buys one time rights.

Columns/Departments NC Writers (interviews, biographical/bibliographic essays); Reviews (essay reviews of North Carolina-related fiction, creative nonfiction, or poetry). Query with published clips. **Pays $50-100 honorarium, extra copies, back issues or subscription (negotiable).**

Fiction "Fiction submissions accepted during Doris Betts Prize Competition; see our Submission Guidelines for detail." **Buys 3-4 mss/year.** Query. 5,000 words maximum. **$50-100 honorarium, extra copies, back issues or subscription (negotiable).**

Poetry *North Carolina poets only.* **Buys 5-10 poems/year.** Length: 30-150 lines. **$50-100 honorarium, extra copies, back issues or subscription (negotiable).**

Fillers 2-5 Length: 50-500 words. **$50-100 honorarium, extra copies, back issues or subscription (negotiable)**

Tips "By far the easiest way to break in is with special issue sections. We are especially interested in reports on conferences, readings, meetings that involve North Carolina writers, and personal essays or short narratives with a strong sense of place. See back issues for other departments. Interviews are probably the other easiest place to break in; no discussions of poetics/theory, etc., except in reader-friendly (accessible) language; interviews should be personal, more like conversations, that explore connections between a writer's life and his/her work."

$ NOTRE DAME REVIEW

University of Notre Dame, 840 Flanner Hall, Notre Dame IN 46556. (574)631-6952. Fax: (574)631-4795. E-mail: english.ndreview.1@nd.edu. Website: www.nd.edu/~ndr/review.htm. Semiannual magazine. The *Notre Dame Review* is an indepenent, noncommercial magazine of contemporary American and international fiction, poetry, criticism, and art. We are especially interested in work that takes on big issues by making the invisible seen, that gives voice to the voiceless. In addition to showcasing celebrated authors like Seamus Heaney and Czelaw Milosz, the *Notre Dame Review* introduces readers to authors they may have never encountered before, but who are doing innovative and important work. In conjunction with the *Notre Dame Review*, the online companion to the printed magazine, the *Notre Dame Re-view* engages readers as a community centered in literary rather than commercial concerns, a community we reach out to through critique and commentary as well as aesthetic experience. Estab. 1995. Circ. 2,000. Pays on publication. Publishes ms an average of 6 months after acceptance. Buys first North American serial rights. Accepts simultaneous submissions. Responds in 4 or more months to mss. Sample copy for $6. Guidelines available online.

Fiction Contact: William O'Rourke, fiction editor. We're eclectic. Upcoming theme issues planned. List of upcoming themes or editorial calendar available for SASE. Does not read mss May-August. No genre fiction. **Buys 100 (90 poems, 10 stories) mss/year.** Length: 3,000 words. **Pays $5-25.**

Tips We're looking for high quality work that takes on big issues in a literary way. Please read our back issues before submitting.

NTH POSITION

No public address available, E-mail: val@nthposition.com. Website: www.editred.com/links/submissions/173-nth-position. www.nthposition.com. **5% freelance written**. Website covering all kinds of poetry—from post-modern to mainstream; showcases fresh, urgent voices in poetry and fiction today. Free ezine with politics and opinion, travel writing, fiction and poetry, art reviews and interviews, and some high weirdness. No kill fee. Accepts previously published material. Guidelines available online.

- We can only notify people whose work we accept.

Nonfiction Needs essays, Reviews, opinion, travel.

Photos Art work reviews.

Poetry Contact: Todd Swift. No racisim, nastiness, silkworm farming or diabetes articles. Submit maximum 2-6 poems.

Tips Submit as text in the body of an email, along with a brief bio note (2-3 sentences). If your work is accepted it will be archived into the British Library's permanent collection.

OLD CROW REVIEW

FKB Press, P.O. Box 341, Northampton MA 01060-0341. **90% freelance written**. Semiannual magazine covering poetry, short fiction, interviews. This is a literary journal devoted to including the best new voices in poetry & fiction. Circ. 500-1,000. No byline given. Pays on publication. No kill fee. Editorial lead time 2 months. Accepts queries by mail. Accepts previously published material. Accepts simultaneous submissions. Responds in 2 weeks to queries. Responds in 2 months to mss. Sample copy for $9. Guidelines for #10 SASE.

Nonfiction Contact: Stephen Lindow, editor. Needs interview.

Fiction Needs experimental, novel concepts. **Buys 0 mss/year.**

Poetry Contact: Stephen Lindow, poetry editor. Needs avant-garde, free verse, haiku, light verse, traditional. No greeting card poetry. **Buys 0 poems/year.** Submit maximum 5 poems. Length: 5 lines.

$ ONCE UPON A TIME ONLINE E-ZINE

Once Upon a Time Online, 905 West Franklin St., Monroe NC 28112. E-mail: submissions@onceuponatimeonline.net. Website: www.onceuponatimeonline.net. twice a month website 'zine featuring original, short romantic fiction, as well as author interview and publisher profiles. Estab. 2004. Circ. 200. No kill fee. Buys 1 year exclusive electronic rights rights. Accepts queries by e-mail. Responds in 4-6 weeks to mss. Sample copy free.

Nonfiction Needs interview.

Fiction Pay is based on the author's previous track-record and name recognition. We also compensate with free book cover ads, banners and advertising on various sites in conjunction with our 'zine. Needs erotica, romance, *spicy*, short stories. Length: 3,000-5,000 words. **Pays $$30.**

Tips Please send submissions as an attachment to submissions@onceuponatimeonline.net. Please read our guidelines. If you have a question, don't hesitate to ask. Please send an email to customerservice@onceupnatimeonline.net. Indicate your interest in submitting to our publication, and we'll send you a free back-issue of the 'zine.

ONE LESS MAGAZINE

6 Village Hill Rd., Williamsburg MA 01096. E-mail: onelessartontherange@yahoo.com. Website: www.onelessmag.blogspot.com. Byline given. No kill fee.

Nonfiction Send complete ms.

Fiction Needs experimental, mainstream. Send complete ms.

Poetry Needs avant-garde, free verse, haiku, light verse, traditional. Submit maximum 3-5 poems.

Tips Submit 3-5 pages of poetry, 5-10 pages of prose, or 1-5 pages of artwork.

ORBIS

Quarterly International Literary Journal, 17 Greenhow Ave., West Kirby Wirral CH48 5EL UK. E-mail: carolebaldock@hotmail.com. covering 84 pages of news, reviews, views, letters, features, prose and a lot of poetry, and cover artwork. *Orbis has long been considered one of the top 20 Small Press magazines in the UK. We are interested in social inclusion projects and encouraging access to the Arts, young people, Under 20s and 20somethings. Subjects for discussion: 'day in the life,' technical, topical.* Estab. 1969. No kill fee. Subscribers usually receive an answer re submissions in 3 mos. with the following issue of the magazine.

- Please see Guidelines at: kudoswriting.wordpress.com before submitting.

Nonfiction Contact: Nessa O'Mahony, reviews editor. Needs essays, Reviews, letters, technical, Features. **Writer receives £50.**

Photos Artwork for cover.

Fiction Buys 2/year. mss/year. Length: 500-1,000 words.

Poetry Readers Award - £50 for piece receiving the most votes in each issue. Four winners selected for submissions to Forward Poetry Prize, Single Poem category. Plus £50 split between 4, or more, runners-up. Feature Writer receives £50. NB, work commissioned: 3-4 poems or 1,500 words. **Buys 4 poems/year.**

Tips Enclose SAE with all correspondence. Overseas: 2 IRCs, 3 if work is to be returned. Via email, Overseas only: 2 poems or 1 piece of prose in body. No attachments.

O SWEET FLOWERY ROSES

You submit, we publish, Website: osfrjournal.blogspot.com. **100% freelance written**. Daily magazine covering poetry. You submit, we publish. Wew are devoted to preserving the empowering, cathartic, and basic fun of poetry production and sharing. No hierarchies. No reading fees. We are completist, not elitist. Estab. 2008. Circ. 500+. Byline given. No kill fee. Publishes ms an average of 1-5 days after acceptance. Accepts simultaneous submissions. Guidelines available online.

Poetry Contact: Russell Jaffee, editor-in-chief. Needs avant-garde, free verse, haiku, light verse, traditional.

PACIFIC REVIEW

a west coast arts review annual, San Diego State University Press, San Diego State Univ. Dept of English & Comparative Literature, Arts and Letters 226, San Diego CA 92182-6020. E-mail: pacificreview_sdsu@yahoo.com. Website: www.pacificreview.sdsu.edu/casa1.html. Annual magazine covering fiction, poetry, creative nonfiction, photography, art and cover art. Estab. 1972. No kill fee. Accepts queries by e-mail. Accepts simultaneous submissions. Guidelines available.

Nonfiction Needs essays, Reviews, photo feature, Translations.

Photos Contact: Art Editor. Send images and any style of art via email as attachments. Reviews 300 dpi jpegs or tiff files.

Fiction Contact: Lester O'Connor, fiction & prose editor.

Poetry Contact: Chrissy Rikkers, poetry editor. For translations, include the original poems in the original language you are translating from, and be sure you have acquired the rights from that author. No more than 20 typed pages on 8 ½ x 11 paper.

Tips Enclose SASE for notification. Mss. will not be returned. If you would like to be notified by email please indicate clearly an email address (skip the SASE).

$ PALABRA

A Magazine of Chicano & Latino Literary Art, P.O. Box 86146, Los Angeles CA 90086-0146. E-mail: info@palabralitmag.com. Website: www.palabralitmag.com. Biannual magazine featuring poetry, fiction, short plays, and more. *"PALABRA* is about exploration, risk and ganas—the myriad intersections of thought, language, story and art—*el mas alla of letters*, symbols and spaces into meaning." Byline given. No kill fee. Responds in 3-4 months to mss

Nonfiction Pays $25-35.

Fiction Needs experimental/hybrid, mainstream, novel excerpts, flash fiction, short plays. Does not want genre work (mystery, romance, science fiction, etc.). Send complete ms, unpublished work only. Length: 4,000 words. **Pays $$25-$35.**

Poetry Needs avant garde, free verse, traditional. Submit maximum 5 poems.

PALO ALTO REVIEW

A Journal of Ideas, Palo Alto College, 1400 W. Villaret Blvd., San Antonio TX 78224. (210)486-3249. E-mail: professor78224-par@yahoo.com. Website: www.accd.edu/pac/english/pareview/index.htm. **80% freelance written**. Annual magazine of 80+ pages covering all subjects that can be considered educational—which means almost anything. "We invite original, unpublished writing on a variety of subjects. As a 'journal of ideas,' we look for wide-ranging investigations that have to do with living and learning. Articles, poems, and stories about interesting people, places, and events, are what we are after. Also humor. Our readers want to be stimulated, entertained, and enlightened." Estab. 1992. Circ. 500. Byline given. No kill fee. Publishes ms an average of 3-15 months after acceptance. Buys first North American serial rights. Editorial lead time 3-6 months. Accepts queries by mail. Accepts simultaneous submissions. Responds in 1-2 weeks to queries. Responds in 1-3 months to mss. Sample copy for $5. Guidelines by email.

Nonfiction Needs essays, expose, general interest, historical, how-to, humor, interview, opinion, personal experience, photo feature, travel, book reviews. **Buys 20-25 mss/year.** Send complete ms. 5,000-6,000 words max. **Pays in copies**

Photos State availability Identification of subjects required. Reviews prints, GIF/JPEG files. Offers no additional payment for photos accepted with ms. Buys one time rights.

Fiction Needs adventure, ethnic, historical, humorous, mainstream, mystery, novel concepts, suspense. **Buys 4-6/year mss/year.** Send complete ms. 5,000 words maximum **Pays in copies.**

Poetry Needs avant-garde, free verse, traditional. **Buys 12-16 poems/year.** Submit maximum 5 poems.

Tips "Send for guidelines. Purchase a sample copy. We are willing to work with writers, and we publish many first-time writers. Guidelines inside front cover."

$ $ $ THE PARIS REVIEW

62 White Street, New York NY 10013. (212)343-1333. E-mail: queries@theparisreview.org. Website: www.theparisreview.org. Quarterly magazine. Fiction and poetry of superlative quality, whatever the genre, style or mode. Our contributors include prominent, as well as less well-known and previously unpublished writers. Writers at Work interview series includes important contemporary writers discussing their own work and the craft of writing. Pays on publication. No kill fee. Buys all rights, buys first English-language rights. Accepts queries by mail. Accepts simultaneous submissions. Responds in 4 months to mss. Sample copy for $15 (includes postage). Guidelines available online.

- Address submissions to proper department. Do not make submissions via e-mail.

Fiction Study the publication. Annual Aga Khan Fiction Contest award of $1,000. Send complete ms. no limit **Pays $500-1,000.**

Poetry Contact: Richard Howard, poetry editor. **Pays $35 minimum varies according to length. Awards $1,000 in Bernard F. Conners Poetry Prize contest.**

$ $ PARNASSUS: POETRY IN REVIEW

Poetry in Review Foundation, 205 W. 89th St., #8F, New York NY 10024. (212)362-3492. Fax: (212)875-0148. E-mail: parnew@aol.com. Website: www.parnassuspoetry.com. Annual magazine covering poetry and criticism. "We now publish one double issue a year." Estab. 1972. Circ. 1,800. Byline given. Pays on publication. No kill fee. Publishes ms an average of12-14 months after acceptance. Buys one-time rights. Accepts queries by mail. Responds in 2 months to mss. Sample copy for $15.

Nonfiction Needs essays. **Buys 30 mss/year.** Query with published clips. Length: 1,500-7,500 words. **Pays $200-750.**

Poetry Needs avant garde, free verse, traditional. Accepts most types of poetry. **Buys Buys 3-4 unsolicited poems/year poems/year.**

Tips "Be certain you have read the magazine and are aware of the editor's taste. Blind submissions are a waste of everybody's time. We'd like to see more poems that display intellectual acumen and curiosity about history, science, music, etc., and fewer trivial lyrical poems about the self, or critical prose that's academic and dull. Prose should sing."

PEARL

A Literary Magazine, 3030 E. Second St., Long Beach CA 90803. Website: www.pearlmag.com. Biannual magazine featuring poetry, short fiction, and black and white artwork. We also sponsor the Pearl Poetry Prize, an annual contest for a full length book, as well as the Pearl Short Story Prize. "*Pearl* is an eclectic publication, a place for lively, readable poetry and prose that speaks to real people about real life in direct, living language, profane or sublime." Estab. 1974. Pays with contributor's copy. No kill fee. Publishes ms an average of 6-12 months after acceptance. Accepts queries by mail. Accepts simultaneous submissions. Sample copy for $8. Guidelines available online.

- Submissions are accepted from Jan. - June only. Mss. received between July and Dec. will be returned unread. No email submissions, except from countries outside the U.S. See guidelines.

Photos No photographs. "We only consider camera-ready, black and white spot-art (no shades of gray) that can be reduced without loss of definition or detail. Send clean, high-quality photocopies or original with SASE. Accepted artwork is kept on file and is used as needed."

Fiction "Our annual fiction issue features the winner of our Pearl Short Story Prize contest as well as 'short-shorts,' and some of the longer stories in our contest. Length: 1,200 words. No obscure, experimental fiction. The winner of the Pearl Short Story Prize receives 4250 and 10 copies of the issue the story appears in . A $10 entry fee includes a copy of the magazine; all entries are considered for publication." Nothing sentimental, obscure, predictable, abstract or cliché-ridden poetry or fiction. Length: 1,200 words. **Short Story Prize of $250, 100 copies of the issue the story appears in.**

Poetry "Our poetry issue contains a 12-15 page section featuring the work of a single poet. Entry fee for the Pearl Poetry Prize is $20, which includes a copy of the winning book." No sentimental, obscure, predictable, abstract or cliché-ridden poetry. Submit maximum 3-5 poems. 40 lines max. Send with cover letter and SASE.

Tips "Pays 5 writers with contributor copies. Additional copies may be purchased at a 50% discount."

PEBBLE LAKE REVIEW

15318 Pebble Lake Dr., Houston TX 77095. E-mail: submissions@pebblelakereview.com. Website: www.pebblelakereview.com. **98% freelance written**. Quarterly magazine covering poetry, fiction, creative nonfiction and reviews. *Pebble Lake Review* publishes high quality literary prose and poetry. We strive to publish work by writers whose interest, craft, and usage of words and language reflect in their work. Previous contributors have included Kim Addonizio, Paul Guest, Bob Hicok, Alex Lemon, Timothy Liu, Aimee Nezhukumatathil, Marge Piercy and Eric Shade. We welcome submissions from newer writers if the work exhibits quality. The best indicator of what type of material we accept is to visit our website or order a copy of the publication. Estab. 2003. Circ. 500 (print); 6,000/month (online). Byline given. No kill fee. Publishes ms an average of 3 months after acceptance. Buys one-time rights, buys electronic rights. Editorial lead time 3-6 months. Submit seasonal material 6 months in advance. Accepts queries by mail, e-mail. Accepts simultaneous submissions. Responds in 1 month to queries. Responds in 1-3 months to mss. Sample copy for $10. Guidelines available online.

Nonfiction Needs interview, personal narrative, book reviews. Annual Awards issue, see website for details. Send complete ms. 1,000 maximum for reviews; 3,000 for creative nonfiction

Photos Send photos Identification of subjects required. Reviews GIF/JPEG files. Offers no additional payment for photos accepted with ms. Buys one time rights.

Fiction Needs mainstream, literary. No genre fiction or anything that uses gratuitous violence, language, or sex. Wants more flash/graphic fiction. **Buys 10-12 mss/year.** Send complete ms. 3,000 words maximum

Poetry Needs avant-garde, free verse. No rhyming poetry, greeting-card verse, haiku, light verse, or vampyre (or similar themed) poems. **Buys 75-100 poems/year.** Submit maximum 2-5 poems.

Tips Always be professional, and include a cover letter and SASE for reply. Follow guidelines carefully and study the magazine before submitting. Support independent presses by purchasing a copy or subscription to the publication.

THE PEDESTAL MAGAZINE

6815 Honors Court, Charlotte NC 28210. E-mail: pedmagazine@carolina.rr.com. Website: www.thepedestalmagazine.com. Bimonthly website currently accepting submissions of poetry, fiction, and nonfiction. We are committed to promoting diversity and celebrating the voice of the individual. No kill fee. Buys first rights. All rights reverse back to the author/artist at publication time. We retain the right to publish the piece in any subsequent issue or anthology without additional payment. Accepts queries by e-mail. Accepts simultaneous submissions. Responds in 4-6 weeks to mss. Guidelines available online.

Nonfiction We accept reviews of poetry and short story collections, novels, and nonfiction books. We are currently accepting freelance interviews. Please query prior to submitting the above. Needs essays, Reviews, interview. **Pays 2¢/word. Pays for unsolicited articles.**

Photos Reviews JPEG, GIF files.

Fiction We are receptive to all sorts of high-quality literary fiction. Genre fiction is encouraged as long as it crosses or comments upon its genre and is both character-driven and psychologically acute. We encourage submissions of short fiction, no more than 3 flash fiction pieces at a time. There is no need to query prior to submitting; please submit via the submission form—no email to the editor. Needs experimental, horror, mainstream, mystery, romance, science fiction, Works that don't fit into a specific category. **Buys 10-25 mss/year.** Length: 4,000 words. **Pays $2¢:/word-5¢/word.**

Poetry We are open to a wide variety of poetry, ranging from the highly experimental to the traditionally formal. Submit all poems in 1 form. No need to query before submitting. Submit maximum 6 poems. Length: lines.

Tips If you send us your work, please wait for a response to your first submission before you submit again.

PEMBROKE MAGAZINE

The University of North Carolina at Pembroke and The North Carolina Arts Council, UNCP Box 1510, Pembroke NC 28372-1510. (910)521-6433. E-mail: shelby.stephenson@uncp.edu. Website: www.uncp.edu/pembrokemagazine. Annual magazine covering poetry, fiction, nonfiction, interviews, and visual arts (painting, graphics, sculpture). Prestigious, nationally known *Pembroke Magazine* with international scope has been at the forefront of innovation. Finds overlooked topics and authors. Offers readers a rare opportunity to move through time, across cultures, such as Native American Literature, and into contemporary literature and art. It feeds the desire for understanding. Themes range from immigration, assimilation, exile, alienation, and fragmented identities to romance and metaphysics. We want to tantalize readers to further explorations or, more importantly, self-reflection. Estab. 1969. No kill fee. Responds in 4-7 weeks to mss. Guidelines available online.

Nonfiction Needs essays, interview, photo feature.

Tips Accepts submissions year round though response time will be slower in the summer. Please enclose SASE if you would like your work returned. No electronic submissions.

PILGRIMAGE MAGAZINE

Box 696, Crestone CO 81131. E-mail: info@pilgrimagepress.org. Website: www.pilgrimagepress.org. Biannual magazine Welcoming creative prose and poetry. We favor personal nonfiction on themes of place, spirit, peace and social justice in and beyond the Greater Southwest. Serves an eclectic fellowship of readers, writers, artists, naturalists, contemplatives, activists, seekers, adventurers, and other kindred spirits. Estab. 1976. No kill fee. Guidelines available online.

Nonfiction This year's writing award of $1,000 will be given for the best personal essay that appears in any of the 2008 issues. No entry fee is necessary. See Guidelines for themes of upcoming issues. The winner will be announced on the website by Dec. 20, 2008. Needs essays, historical, humor, personal experience. Maximum of 6,000 words; shorter is better.

Poetry Fit poetry on one page.

Tips Our interests include wildness in all its forms; inward and outward explorations; home ground, the open road, service, witness, peace and justice; symbols, story and myth in contemporary culture; struggle and resilience; insight and transformation; wisdom wherever it is found; and the great mystery of it all. We like good storytellers and a good sense of humor. Must be typed (double-spaced) and submitted along with SASE.

$ 🌐 PLANET-THE WELSH INTERNATIONALIST

P.O. Box 44, Aberystwyth Ceredigion SY23 3ZZ United Kingdom. (44)(197)061-1255. Fax: (44)(197)061-1197. E-mail: planet.enquiries@planetmagazine.org.uk. Website: www.planetmagazine.org.uk. Bimonthly journal. A literary/cultural/political journal centered on Welsh affairs but with a strong interest in minority cultures in Europe and elsewhere. Circ. 1,400. Sample copy for £4. Guidelines available online.

Fiction Would like to see more inventive, imaginative fiction that pays attention to language and experiments with form. No magical realism, horror, science fiction. Length: 1,500-4,000 words. **Pays £50/1,000 words.**

Tips We do not look for fiction which necessarily has a 'Welsh' connection, which some writers assume from our title. We try to publish a broad range of fiction and our main criterion is quality. Try to read copies of any magazine you submit to. Don't write out of the blue to a magazine which might be completely inappropriate for your work. Recognize that you are likely to have a high rejection rate, as magazines tend to favor writers from their own countries.

$ PLEIADES

A Journal of New Writing, Pleiades Press, Department of English, University of Central Missouri, Warrensburg MO 64093. (660)543-4425. Fax: (660)543-8544. E-mail: pleiades@ucmo.edu. Website: www.ucmo.edu/englphil/pleiades. **100% freelance written**. Semiannual journal (5½x8½ perfect bound). "We publish contemporary fiction, poetry, interviews, literary essays, special-interest personal essays, reviews for a general and literary audience from authors from around the world." Estab. 1991. Circ. 3,000. Byline given. Pays on publication. No kill fee. Publishes ms an average of 9 months after acceptance. Buys first North American serial rights, buys second serial (reprint) rights. Occasionally requests rights for TV, radio reading, website. Editorial lead time 9 months. Accepts queries by mail. Accepts simultaneous submissions. Responds in 2 months to queries. Responds in 1-4 months to mss. Sample copy for $5 (back issue); $6 (current issue) Guidelines available online.

- "Also sponsors the Lena-Miles Wever Todd Poetry Series competition, a contest for the best book ms by an American poet. The winner receives $1,000, publication by Pleiades Press, and distribution by Louisiana State University Press. Deadline September 30. Send SASE for guidelines."

Nonfiction Contact: Phone Nguyen, nonfiction ed. "We accept queries for book reviews. Please send queries and clips of previously published reviews to Kevin Prufer. No unsolicited reviews will be accepted." Needs book excerpts, essays, interview, reviews. Nothing pedantic, slick, or shallow. Do not send submissions after May 31. We resume reading nonfiction Sept. 1. **Buys 4-6 mss/year.** Send complete ms. Length: 2,000-4,000 words. **Pays $10.**

Fiction Contact: Matthew Eck and G. B. Crump. We read fiction year-round. Needs ethnic, experimental, humorous, mainstream, novel concepts, magic realism. No science fiction, fantasy, confession, erotica. **Buys 16-20 mss/year.** Send complete ms. Length: 2,000-6,000 words. **Pays $10.**

Poetry Contact: Kevin Prufer and Wayne Miller. Needs avant-garde, free verse, haiku, light verse, traditional. "Nothing didactic, pretentious, or overly sentimental. Do not send poetry after May 31. We resume reading poetry on Sept. 1." **Buys 40-50 poems/year.** Submit maximum 6 poems. **Pays $3/poem, and contributor copies.**
Tips Submit only 1 genre at a time to appropriate editors. Show care for your material and your readers—submit quality work in a professional format. Include cover letter with brief bio and list of publications. Include SASE. Cover art is solicited directly from artists. We accept queries for book reviews. For summer submissions, the Poetry and Nonfiction Editors will no longer accept mss sent between June 1 & August 31. Any sent after May 31 will be held until the end of summer. Please do not send your only copy of anything.

$ $ PLOUGHSHARES

Emerson College, Department M, 120 Boylston St., Boston MA 02116. Website: www.pshares.org. **Contact:** Ladette Randolph, editor. Triquarterly magazine for readers of serious contemporary literature. "Our mission is to present dynamic, contrasting views on what is valid and important in contemporary literature, and to discover and advance significant literary talent. Each issue is guest-edited by a different writer. We no longer structure issues around preconceived themes." Estab. 1971. Circ. 6,000. Pays on publication. Offers 50% kill fee for assigned ms not published. kill fee. Publishes ms an average of 6 months after acceptance. Buys first North American serial rights. Accepts simultaneous submissions. Responds in 5 months to mss. Sample copy for $8.50 (back issue). Guidelines available online.

- "A competitive and highly prestigious market. Rotating and guest editors make cracking the line-up even tougher, since it's difficult to know what is appropriate to send. The reading period is August 1-March 31."

Nonfiction Needs essays, personal and literary; accepted only occasionally. 6,000 words maximum **Pays $25/printed page, $50-250.**
Fiction Needs mainstream, literary. No genre (science fiction, detective, gothic, adventure, etc.), popular formula, or commerical fiction whose purpose is to entertain rather than to illuminate. **Buys 25-35 mss/year.** Length: 300-6,000 words. **Pays $25/printed page, $50-250**.
Poetry Needs avant-garde, free verse, traditional. Open **Pays $25/printed page, $50-250**.
Tips "We no longer structure issues around preconceived themes. If you believe your work is in keeping with our general standards of literary quality and value, submit at any time during our reading period."

PMS

poemmemoirstory, University of Alabama at Birmingham, HB 217, 1530 3rd Ave. South, Birmingham AL 35294-1260. (205)934-5380. Fax: (205)975-5493. E-mail: tmharris@uab.edu. Website: www.pms-journal.org/submissions-guidelines. Annual magazine covering poetry, memoirs and short fiction; contains the best work of the best women writers in the nation. "This is an all women's literary journal. The subject field is wide open." No kill fee. Sample copy for $7.

- Reading period runs from Jan. 1 - Mar. 31. Submissions received at other times of the year will be returned unread.

Nonfiction Needs personal experience. Each issue includes a memoir written by a woman who is not necessary a writer but who has experienced something of historic import. Emily Lyons, the nurse who survived the 1998 New Woman All Women Birgmingham clinic bombing by Eric Rudolph; women who experienced the World Trade Center on 9/11; the Civil Rights Movement in Birmingham, the war in Iraq, and Hurricane Katrina have lent us their stories. Length: 4,300 words.
Fiction Length: 4,300 words.
Poetry Submit maximum 5 poems.
Tips "We seek unpublished original work that we can recycle. Include cover letter, brief bio with SASE. All mss. should be typed on 1-side of 8 X 11 white paper with author's name, address, phone no. and email address on front of each submission."

POETIC MONTHLY MAGAZINE

AG Press/Living the Simple Life, 4133 Hearthside Dr., Wilmington NC 28412. (910)409-5867. E-mail: martin@livingthesimplelife.com. Website: www.poeticmonthly.com. **100% freelance written**. Monthly magazine covering poetry, writing, self-publishing. Follow general theme, relaxed content. Estab. 2006. Byline sometimes given. N/A-Cross Publicity, no pay. No kill fee. Buys Rights Retain with Author rights. Editorial lead time 1 month. Submit seasonal material 1 month in advance. Accepts queries by mail, e-mail, phone. Accepts simultaneous submissions. Responds in 4 weeks to queries. Responds in 1 month to mss. Sample copy available online. Guidelines free.

- Free PDF, POD printing.

Nonfiction Needs book excerpts, essays, general interest, how-to, humor, interview, new product, personal experience, photo feature, General theme. Poetry itself, unknowns submitted to Top 20. Query.
Photos Contact: Martin White. State availability of or send photos Identification of subjects required. Reviews

GIF/JPEG files. Offers no additional payment for photos accepted with ms. Buys one time rights.
Fiction Contact: Martin White. Needs adventure, cond novels, confession, erotica, experimental, fantasy, historical, horror, humorous, mainstream, mystery, novel concepts, romance, serialized, slice-of-life vignettes, suspense. We don't want to to see non-general themes. Query.
Poetry Contact: Martin White. Needs avant-garde, free verse, haiku, light verse, traditional. No cursing words.
Fillers Needs anecdotes, facts, short humor.
Tips Open to guest writers.

$ POETRY

The Poetry Foundation, 444 N. Michigan Ave., Suite 1850, Chicago IL 60611-4034. (312)787-7070. Fax: (312)787-6650. E-mail: editors@poetrymagazine.org. Website: www.poetrymagazine.org. **Contact:** Helen Klaviter. **100% freelance written**. Monthly magazine. Estab. 1912. Circ. 31,000. Byline given. Pays on publication. No kill fee. Publishes ms an average of 9 months after acceptance. Buys first serial rights. Accepts queries by mail. Responds in 1 month to queries and to mss. Sample copy for $3.75 or online at website. Guidelines available online.
Nonfiction Buys 14 mss/year. Query. Length: 1,000-2,000 words. **Pays $150/page.**
Poetry Accepts all styles and subject matter. **Buys 180-250 poems/year.** Submit maximum 4 poems. Open **Pays $10/line ($150 minimum payment).**

POETRY EAST

Dept. of English, DePaul University, 802 W. Belden Ave., Chicago IL 60614. (773)325-7487. Fax: (773)325-7328. E-mail: editor@poetryeast.org. Website: www.poetryeast.org. Semiannual magazine covering poetry, translations, criticism, interviews, and art. An award-winning journal dedicated to publishing poetry that is immediate, accessible, and universal. An independent magazine affiliated with DePaul Univeristy and based in Chicago, IL. No kill fee. Accepts queries by mail. Responds in 4 months to mss.
Nonfiction Needs essays, Literary Criticism, interview.
Photos Art.
Tips *Poetry East* has an open submission policy. Please submit typed mss. and include your name, address, and contact info (phone no. and/or email). Use a #10 envelope. Mss. will not be returned unless accompanied by SASE with sufficient postage.

POETRY INTERNATIONAL

San Diego State University, 5500 Campanile Dr., San Diego CA 92182-6020. (619)594-1522. Fax: (619)594-4998. E-mail: poetryinternational@yahoo.com. Website: www.poetryinternational.sdsu.edu. Annual journal covering new poems from emerging and well-established poets, offering commentary on poetry anthologies, books by individual poets, and poetic criticism, art from around the world. "We intend to continue to publish poetry that makes a difference in people's lives, and startles us anew with the endless capacity of language to awaken our senses and expand our awareness." Estab. 1997. No kill fee Accepts queries by mail. Accepts simultaneous submissions. Responds in 6-8 months to mss. Guidelines available on web site

- Features the Poetry International Prize ($1,000) for best original poem. (Deadline April 15 for 2009.) Submit up to 3 poems with a $10 entry fee.

Nonfiction Needs , Translations, query first for book reviews. Reprints photos.
Fiction Query.
Poetry Features the poetry of a different nation of the world as a special section in each issue. Submit maximum 5 poems.
Tips "Seeks a wide range of styles and subject matter. We read unsolicited mss. only between Sept. 1st and Dec. 31st of each year. Mss. received any other time will be returned unread."

POETRY IRELAND REVIEW

Poetry Ireland, 2 Proud's Lane, Off St. Stephen's Green, Dublin 2 Ireland. 01-4789974. Fax: 01-4780205. E-mail: publications@poetryireland.ie. Website: www.poetryireland.ie. Quarterly literary magazine in book form. Estab. 1978. Circ. 2,000. Pays on publication. No kill fee. Accepts queries by mail, e-mail, fax, phone. Responds in 1 week to queries. Responds in 6 months to mss.
Poetry Needs avant-garde, free verse, haiku, traditional. **Buys 150 poems/year.** Submit maximum 6 poems. **Pays $32/submission.**

POETRY LONDON

London Public Library, Fred Landon Branch, 167 Wortley Rd., London ON Canada. (519)439-6240. E-mail: poetrylondon@yahoo.ca. Website: www.poetrylondon.ca/. Website covering accomplished local poets and emerging poets, and provides national poets a multi-stop Ontario tour. The Oxford Bookshop provides a book sale following each reading. Everyone who enjoys discussing poetry, or learning more about the art form, is welcome to attend the Poetry Workshops. No kill fee. Guidelines available.

Poetry Length: 60 lines.
Tips Sponsoring the Second Annual Poetry London Poetry Writing Contest. $150 in prizes. Invites all London and emerging poets, and Poetry London Workshop participants. One previously unpublished poem per person. Anonymity is preserved. Winners will be notified at least 2 weeks before the April 2009 reading.

POETRY LONDON

81 Lambeth Walk, London England SE11 6DX UK. (207)735-8880. E-mail: mauriceriordan@poetrylondon.co.uk; scottverner@poetrylondon.co.uk. Website: www.poetrylondon.co.uk. covering eclectic international poetry. This is a leading international magazine where new names share pages with acclaimed contemporary poets. No kill fee. Accepts queries by e-mail. Responds in 1-2 months to mss. Guidelines available.
Nonfiction Needs essays, Book Reviews.
Poetry Send submissions of poetry to: Maurice Riordan, 6 Daniels Rd., London SE 15 3LR, UK. Sponsors The Poetry London Competition for prize money (closed for 2008).
Tips Include SASE for our reply.

POETRY MOTEL

Where Poetry Spends a Night On the Road, No public address available, E-mail: reservations@poetrymotel.com. Website: www.poetrymotel.com. Website covering biker poetry. Website under construction. No kill fee.

$ POETRY NEW ZEALAND

34B Methuen Rd., Avondale Auckland New Zealand. E-mail: alstair@ihug.co.nz. Website: www.poetrynz.net. "Each issue has 15-20 pages of poetry from a developing or established poet. The rest of the issue is devoted to a selection of poetry from New Zealand and abroad, plus essays, reviews, and general criticism." Estab. 1951. No kill fee. Accepts queries by mail. Responds in 3 months to mss. Guidelines available online.
Nonfiction Essays (related to poetry), 2,000 words. Submit complete ms, bio, and SASE. **Pays 1 contributor's copy. Overseas subscription for one year: $24 US, libraries: $25 US**
Poetry Accepts any theme/style of poetry. Send complete ms, bio, and SASE. **Pays $30 maximum and 1 copy of the magazine.**

POETRY WALES

Seren, School of English, Bangor University, Gwynedd Wales LL57 2DG UK. E-mail: poetrywales@seren-books.com. Website: poetrywales.co.uk. Quarterly magazine showcasing the best in new poetry, critical features, and reviews from around the world and, of course, from Wales. *Poetry Wales* has a long-standing and international reputation for fine writing and criticism and is committed to bringing the best Welsh writing in English, both past and present, at the same time. One of the UK's most travelled magazines, issues have featured poetry from the USA, Argentina, Japan, Hungary, The Netherlands, Italy, Poland, Slovakia, Galicia, Germany, and Wales. Estab. 1965. No kill fee. Accepts queries by mail. Accepts simultaneous submissions. Guidelines available.
Poetry Contact: Dr. Zoë Skoulding, editor. Needs avant-garde, traditional. *Poetry Wales* emerges from a rich cultural background in which poetry in English exists alongside poetry in Welsh; it therefore welcomes a conversation that sees English-language poetry as part of wider relationships, both within Wales and beyond it. It is open to the possibilities offered by various forms of traditional and experimental, and publishes poetry from a broad range of approaches. Against this background of dynamic contrast it offers a lively and informed critical context for the best new poetry. Submit maximum 6 poems.
Tips We are interested in translation, and in exploring the meaning of local and national identities in a global context. We are at the forefront of some of the most important developments in poetry today.

THE PORTLAND REVIEW

Portland State University, Box 347, Portland OR 97207-0347. (503)7254533. E-mail: theportlandreview@gmail.com. Website: www.portlandreview.org. **Contact:** Chris Cottrell. **98% freelance written**. Triannual magazine covering short fiction, poetry, photography, and art. Estab. 1956. Circ. 1,500. Byline given. No kill fee. Publishes ms an average of 3-6 months after acceptance. Buys first North American serial rights. Accepts simultaneous submissions. Responds in 2-4 months to mss. Sample copy for $9. Guidelines available online. "Automatic rejection of mss not following guidelines."
Photos Black & white only. State availability of or send photos Reviews prints, GIF/JPEG files. Offers no additional payment for photos accepted with ms. Buys one time rights.
Fiction Needs , Flash, vignette, and reviews of small-press publications or emergent authors. No fantasy, detective, or western. **Buys 40 mss/year.** Send complete ms. 5,000 words maximum. **Pays contributor's copies.**
Poetry Needs Avant garde, free verse, haiku, light verse, traditional. **Buys 50 poems/year.** Submit maximum 5 poems.
Tips "View website for current samples and guidelines."

THE PRAGUE REVUE

Bohemia's journal of international literature, No public address available, Europe. E-mail: info@thepraguerevue.com. Magazine covering poems, short stories, essays and plays in all themes and genres. Committed to publishing only the very best writing of the Prague literary scene while establishing an outlet for international writers to publish their work in Central Europe. *Prague* is in the midst of a renaissance of both native and expatriate writing. Estab. 1996. No kill fee. Accepts queries by e-mail. Guidelines available.

Nonfiction Needs essays, photo feature. Query.
Fiction Contact: fiction@thepraguerevue.com. Needs ethnic.
Poetry Contact: poetry@thepraguerevue.com.
Tips Deadline for Issue 9: Oct. 30, 2008. Include a cover letter and brief bio.

$ THE PRAIRIE JOURNAL

Journal of Canadian Literature, Prairie Journal Trust, P.O. Box 61203, Brentwood P.O., Calgary AB T2L 2K6 Canada. E-mail: prairiejournal@yahoo.com. Website: www.geocities.com/prairiejournal. **100% freelance written**. Semiannual magazine publishing quality poetry, short fiction, drama, literary criticism, reviews, bibliography, interviews, profiles, and artwork. "The audience is literary, university, library, scholarly, and creative readers/writers." Estab. 1983. Circ. 600. Byline given. Pays on publication. No kill fee. Publishes ms an average of 4-6 months after acceptance. Buys first North American serial rights, buys electronic rights. In Canada author retains copyright with acknowledgement appreciated. Editorial lead time 4-6 months. Accepts queries by mail, e-mail. Responds in 2 weeks to queries. Responds in 6 months to mss. Sample copy for $5. Guidelines available online.

Nonfiction Needs essays, humor, interview, literary. No inspirational, news, religious, or travel. **Buys 25-40 mss/year.** Query with published clips. Length: 100-3,000 words. **Pays $50-100, plus contributor's copy**
Photos State availability Offers additional payment for photos accepted with ms Rights purchased is negotiable.
Columns/Departments Reviews (books from small presses publishing poetry, short fiction, essays, and criticism), 200-1,000 words. 5 Query with published clips. **Pays $10-50.**
Fiction No genre (romance, horror, western—sagebrush or cowboys), erotic, science fiction, or mystery. **Buys 6 mss/year.** Send complete ms. Length: 100-3,000 words. **Pays $10-75.**
Poetry Needs avant-garde, free verse, haiku. No heroic couplets or greeting card verse. **Buys 25-35 poems/year.** Submit maximum 6-8 poems. Length: 3-50 lines. **Pays $5-50.**
Tips "We publish many, many new writers and are always open to unsolicited submissions because we are 100% freelance. Do not send US stamps, always use IRCs."

PRAIRIE SCHOONER

The University of Nebraska Press, Prairie Schooner, 201 Andrews Hall, University of Nebraska, Lincoln NE 68588-0334. (402)472-0911. E-mail: jengelhardt2@unl.edu. Website: prairieschooner.unl.edu. **100% freelance written**. Quarterly magazine. "We look for the best fiction, poetry, and nonfiction available to publish, and our readers expect to read stories, poems, and essays of extremely high quality. We try to publish a variety of styles, topics, themes, points of view, and writers with a variety of backgrounds in all stages of their careers. We like work that is compelling—intellectually or emotionally—either in form, language, or content." Estab. 1926. Circ. 2,500. Byline given. Pays on publication. Publishes ms an average of 1 year after acceptance. Buys all rights, which are returned to the author upon request after publication. Editorial lead time 6 months. Accepts queries by mail, e-mail. Responds in 1 week to queries. Responds in 3-4 months to mss Sample copy for $6 Guidelines for #10 SASE

- Submissions must be received between September 1 and May 1.

Nonfiction Needs essays, literary/personal, literary or creative nonfiction, memoir, or essays on literature. No scholarly papers that require footnotes. No pieces written only to express a moral lesson or to inspire. There must be depth and literary quality as well. **Buys 6-8 mss/year.** Send complete ms. Length: 250-20,000 words. **Pays 3 copies of the issue in which the writer's work is published**
Fiction "We try to remain open to a variety of styles, themes, and subject matter. We look for high-quality writing, 3-D characters, well-wrought plots, setting, etc. We are open to realistic and/or experimental fiction." Needs ethnic, experimental, mainstream, novel concepts, literary. **Buys 15-25 mss/year.** Send complete ms. **Pays 3 copies of the issue in which the writer's work is published.**
Poetry Needs avant garde, free verse, haiku, light verse, traditional. **Buys 100-120 poems/year.** Submit maximum 7 poems. **Pays 3 copies of the issue in which the writer's work is published.**
Tips "Send us your best, most carefully crafted work and be persistent. Submit again and again. Constantly work on improving your writing. Read widely in literary fiction, nonfiction, and poetry. Read *Prairie Schooner* to know what we publish."

$ PRISM INTERNATIONAL

Department of Creative Writing, Buch E462 Main Mall, University of British Columbia, Vancouver BC V6T

1Z1 Canada. (604)822-2514. Fax: (604)822-3616. E-mail: prism@interchange.ubc.ca. Website: prismmagazine.ca. **100% freelance written. Works with new/unpublished writers.** A quarterly international journal of contemporary writing—fiction, poetry, drama, creative nonfiction and translation. Readership: public and university libraries, individual subscriptions, bookstores—a world-wide audience concerned with the contemporary in literature. Estab. 1959. Circ. 1,200. Pays on publication. No kill fee. Publishes ms an average of 4 months after acceptance. Buys first North American serial rights. Selected authors are paid an additional $10/page for digital rights. Accepts queries by mail. Responds in 4 months to queries. Responds in 3-6 months to mss. Sample copy for $11, more info online. Guidelines available online.

Nonfiction "Creative nonfiction that reads like fiction. Nonfiction pieces should be creative, exploratory, or experimental in tone rather than rhetorical, academic, or journalistic." No reviews, tracts, or scholarly essays. **Pays $20/printed page, and 1-year subscription.**

Fiction For Drama: one-acts/excerpts of no more than 1500 words preferred. Also interested in seeing dramatic monologues. Needs experimental, novel concepts, traditional. "New writing that is contemporary and literary. Short stories and self-contained novel excerpts. Works of translation are eagerly sought and should be accompanied by a copy of the original. Would like to see more translations. No gothic, confession, religious, romance, pornography, or science fiction." **Buys 12-16 mss/year.** Send complete ms. 25 pages maximum **Pays $20/printed page, and 1-year subscription.**

Poetry Needs avant-garde, traditional. **Buys 10 poems/issue.** Submit maximum 6 poems. **Pays $40/printed page, and 1-year subscription.**

Tips "We are looking for new and exciting fiction. Excellence is still our No. 1 criterion. As well as poetry, imaginative nonfiction and fiction, we are especially open to translations of all kinds, very short fiction pieces and drama which work well on the page. Translations must come with a copy of the original language work. We pay an additional $10/printed page to selected authors whose work we place on our online version of *Prism.*"

PUERTO DEL SOL

a journal of new literature, New Mexico State University, English Department, New Mexico State Univ., Box 30001, MSC 3E, Las Cruces NM 88003. E-mail: puerto@nmsu.edu. Website: puertodelsol.org. Semiannual magazine literary fiction, nonfiction and poetry. Estab. 1964. Circ. 1,000. Byline given. We pay in issues. No kill fee. Buys first North American serial rights. Accepts queries by e-mail. Accepts simultaneous submissions. Sample copy online. Guidelines available.

Nonfiction Needs essays, Lyric Essay. **Buys 0 mss/year.** Send complete ms.

Fiction Needs experimental. Send complete ms.

Poetry Needs avant-garde, free verse.

$ $$ QUARTERLY WEST

University of Utah, 255 S. Central Campus Dr., Room 3500, Salt Lake City UT 84112. E-mail: quarterlywest@yahoo.com. Website: www.utah.edu/quarterlywest. Semiannual magazine. We publish fiction, poetry, and nonfiction in long and short formats, and will consider experimental as well as traditional works. Estab. 1976. Circ. 1,900. Pays on publication. Publishes ms an average of 6 months after acceptance. Buys first North American serial rights, buys all rights. Accepts queries by mail. Accepts simultaneous submissions. Responds in 6 months to mss. Sample copy for $7.50 or online Guidelines available online.

Nonfiction Needs essays, interview, personal experience, travel, book reviews. **Buys 6-8 mss/year.** Send complete ms. 10,000 words maximum **Pays $20-100.**

Fiction No preferred lengths; interested in longer, fuller short stories and short shorts. Needs ethnic, experimental, humorous, mainstream, novel concepts, slice-of-life vignettes, short shorts, translations. No detective, science fiction or romance. **Buys 6-10 mss/year.** Send complete ms. **Pays $15-100, and 2 contributor's copies.**

Poetry Needs avant-garde, free verse, traditional. **Buys 40-50 poems/year.** Submit maximum 5 poems. **Pays $15-100.**

Tips We publish a special section of short shorts every issue, and we also sponsor a biennial novella contest. We are open to experimental work—potential contributors should read the magazine! Don't send more than 1 story/submission. Biennial novella competition guidelines available upon request with SASE. We prefer work with interesting language and detail—plot or narrative are less important. We don't do Western themes or religious work.

$$ QUEEN'S QUARTERLY

A Canadian Review, 144 Barrie St., Queen's University, Kingston ON K7L 3N6 Canada. (613)533-2667. Fax: (613)533-6822. E-mail: queens.quarterly@queensu.ca. Website: www.queensu.ca/quarterly. **95% freelance written**. Quarterly magazine covering a wide variety of subjects, including science, humanities, arts and letters, politics, and history for the educated reader. "A general interest intellectual review, featuring articles, book reviews, poetry, and fiction." Estab. 1893. Circ. 3,000. Byline given. Pays on publication. Publishes ms an average of 6-12 months after acceptance. Buys first North American serial rights. Responds in 2-3 months to queries. Sample copy and guidelines available online.

Fiction Contact: Boris Castel, editor. Needs historical, mainstream, novel concepts, short stories, women's. Length: 2,500-3,000 words. **Pays $100-300, 2 contributor's copies and 1-year subscription; additional copies $5.**

Poetry Buys 25 poems/year. Submit maximum 6 poems.

QUICK FICTION

P.O. Box 4445, Salem MA 01970. Website: www.quickfiction.org. Semiannual print and website magazine covering contemporary microfiction stories and narrative prose of 500 words or less for both the print and website journal. This is a New England literary magazine. Open to most themes. Recent issues include Arielle Greenberg, Steve Almond, Stephen Dixon, and James Tates. Estab. 2001. No kill fee. Buys first North American serial rights, buys electronic rights. Actual rights obtained are specific to individual agreement with each author. Accepts previously published material. Accepts simultaneous submissions.

Nonfiction Needs essays, Critical essays, reviews, articles, Oddities.

Fiction Submit a story online in Submission Guidelines. Length: 25-500 words.

Tips Prefers online submissions. Deadline for issue 15 is Feb. 1st. We seek concept pitches for material published exclusively on our website.

N QUIDDITY INTERNATIONAL LITERARY JOURNAL AND PUBLIC-RADIO PROGRAM

Benedictine University at Springfield, 1500 N. 5th St., Springfield IL 62702. Semiannual magazine publishing exemplary poetry and prose from emerging and established writers around the world. "Each work selected is considered for public-radio program feature offered by NPR-member station (WUIS (PRI affiliate)." Byline and contributor note given. Accepts simultaneous submissions.

- "International submissions are encouraged."

Nonfiction Needs Creative nonfiction. Send complete ms. Length: 5,000 word-maximum

Fiction Needs experimental, mainstream, novel excerpts. Send complete ms. Length: 5,000 word-max.

Poetry Needs avant-garde, free verse, traditional. Query first. Submit maximum 5/max. poems.

QWF (QUALITY WOMEN'S FICTION)

AllWriters' Workplace & Workshop, 234 Brook St., Unit 2, Waukesha WI 53188. (262)446-0284. E-mail: qwfsubmissionsusa@yahoo.com. Website: www.allwriters.org. Semiannual magazine published in January and July. Women throughout history have forged a path of strength, creativity and endurance. *QWF* reflects those values and that admiration of women. Estab. 1994. Circ. 1,000. Pays on publication. Buys first North American serial rights. Responds in 3 months to mss. Guidelines available online.

Fiction Reading periods: January issue (September 1-November 30); July issue (March 1-May 31). All fiction genres accepted, as long as the protagonist is a woman, the story evokes emotion, and the story is written by a woman. **Buys 40 mss/year.** Length: up to 5,000 words. **Pays one copy of the magazine.**

Tips Evoke emotion. Present yourself professionally with a clean manuscript and a cover letter.

N RAIN TAXI

Review of Books, Rain Taxi, Inc., P.O. Box 3840, Minneapolis MN 55403-0840. (612)825-1528. Fax: (612)825-1528. E-mail: info@raintaxi.com. Website: www.raintaxi.com. **40% freelance written**. Quarterly magazine covering books. "*Rain Taxi* Review of Books, a nonprofit quarterly, is dedicated to covering literature & the arts, including poetry, graphic novels, cultural critique, & quality fiction in all genres. Winner of an Independent Press Award, *Rain Taxi* is a great vehicle for books & authors that may otherwise get lost in the mainstream media." Estab. 1996. Circ. 18,000. Byline given. Payment in Issues. No kill fee. Publishes ms an average of 2 months after acceptance. Buys first North American serial rights. Editorial lead time 2 months. Submit seasonal material 3 months in advance. Accepts queries by mail, e-mail. Responds in 2 weeks to queries. Responds in 1 month to mss. Sample copy for $5. Guidelines by email.

Nonfiction Contact: Eric Lorberer, editor. Needs essays, interview, Reviews. **Buys 0 mss/year.** Query. Length: 500-2,000 words. **Pays 0 for assigned or unsolicited articles.**

$ THE RAMBLER MAGAZINE

Rambler Publications, LLC, P.O. Box 5070, Chapel Hill NC 27514-5001. (919)545-9789. Fax: (919)545-0921. E-mail: editor@ramblermagazine.com. Website: www.ramblermagazine.com. **85% freelance written.** Bimonthly magazine. *The Rambler Magazine* is interested in fiction, poetry, and nonfiction. Estab. 2003. Circ. 3,000. Byline given. Pays on publication. No kill fee. Publishes ms an average of 6-12 months after acceptance. Buys first rights. Makes work-for-hire assignments. Accepts queries by mail. Accepts previously published material. Responds in 1 month to queries. Responds in 4 months to mss. Sample copy for $7. Guidelines for #10 SASE.

Nonfiction Needs book excerpts, essays, general interest, interview, personal experience, photo feature. **Buys 24 mss/year.** Send complete ms. 8,000 words maximum. **Pays $50, plus 1 contributor copy and one-year subscription.**

Photos State availability Captions, identification of subjects, model releases required. Reviews 4x6 prints, GIF/

JPEG files. Negotiates payment individually. Buys one time rights.
Fiction Needs ethnic, experimental, humorous, mainstream, novel concepts, serialized, short shorts. No genre fiction (science fiction, horror, romance, or children's). **Buys 6-12 mss/year.** Send complete ms. 10,000 words maximum **Pays $50, plus 1 contributor copy and one-year subscription**.
Poetry We are open to all types of poetry. **Buys 12-18 poems/year.** Submit maximum 5 poems. **Pays $25/ poem, plus 2 contributor copies**.
Tips Send us your strongest work. We are interested in writing that knows its objective and achieves it with talent and technique.

RARITAN

A Quarterly Review, 31 Mine St., New Brunswick NJ 08903. (732)932-7887. Fax: (732)932-7855. Quarterly magazine covering literature, history, fiction, and general culture. Estab. 1981. Circ. 3,500. Byline given. Pays on publication. No kill fee. Publishes ms an average of 1 year after acceptance. Buys first North American serial rights. Editorial lead time 5 months. Accepts queries by mail.

- *Raritan* no longer accepts previously published or simultaneous submissions.

Nonfiction Needs book excerpts, essays. **Buys 50 mss/year.** Send 2 copies of complete ms. 15-30 pages

$ RATTAPALLAX

Rattapallax Press, 532 LaGuardia Place, #353, New York NY 10012. (212)560-7459. E-mail: info@rattapallax.com. Website: www.rattapallax.com. **10% freelance written**. Annual magazine covering international fiction and poetry. *Rattapallax* is a literary magazine that focuses on issues dealing with globalization. Estab. 1999. Circ. 3,000. Byline given. Pays on publication. No kill fee. Publishes ms an average of 6 months after acceptance. Buys first North American serial rights, buys South American rights. Editorial lead time 6 months. Submit seasonal material 6 months in advance. Accepts queries by e-mail. Responds in 2 weeks to queries. Responds in 6 months to mss. Sample copy available online. Guidelines available online.
Poetry Needs avant-garde, free verse, traditional. Submit maximum 5 poems. Length: 5-200 lines.

REDACTIONS: POETRY & POETICS

58 So. Main St., 3rd Floor, Brockport NY 14420. E-mail: redactionspoetry@yahoo.com. Website: www.redactions.com. "Every 9 months covering poems, reviews of new books of poems, translations, manifestos, interviews, essays concerning poetry, poetics, poetry movements, or concerning a specific poet or a group of poets; and anything dealing with poetry.". No kill fee. All rights revert back to the author. Accepts queries by e-mail. Accepts simultaneous submissions.
Nonfiction Needs essays, Reviews of new books of poems, interview, Art, Translation.
Reprints "Please mention first publication in *Redactions*."
Poetry "Anything dealing with poetry."
Tips "We only accept submissions by e-mail. We read submissions throughout the year. Email us and attach submission into one Word, Wordpad, Notepad.rtf, or .txt document, or, place in the body of an e-mail. Include brief bio and your snail mail address. Query after 90 days if you haven't heard from us."

RED MOUNTAIN REVIEW

1800 8th Ave. N., Birmingham AL 35203. E-mail: rmrsubmissions@gmail.com. Website: www.redmountainreview.net. Magazine covering poetry, short fiction, nonfiction, chapbooks, interviews, reviews. Features Red Mountain Reading Series and Chapbook Contest ($500 prize plus copies) and trip to a joint reading. Seeks writers who do hard work, who tell the hard truths and who do so expecting little more in return than to be heard. *RMR* gravitates toward work that—for reasons of form, length, subject or project—tends to have a difficult time finding the light of day in mainstream commercial venues. No kill fee. Accepts queries by mail. Accepts simultaneous submissions. Responds in 3 months to queries.
Nonfiction Needs essays, Reviews, interview.
Fiction Length: 1,000-7,500 words.
Poetry Submit maximum 5-7 poems. any length or style
Tips Open to poetry and short fiction submissions from Oct. 1, 2008 to Apr. 30, 2009. Simple goal: to produce fine mags and chapbooks that get noticed, with Birmingham's roots in mind.

RED ROCK REVIEW

College of Southern Nevada, Red Rock Review, Dept. of English J2A, College of Southern Nevada, 3200 E. Cheyenne Ave., North Las Vegas NV 89030. (702)651-4094. E-mail: richard.logsdon@csn.edu. Website: sites.csn.edu/english/redrockreview/. Semiannual magazine covering poetry, fiction and creative nonfiction as well as book reviews. "We are dedicated to the publication of fine contemporary literature." No kill fee. Buys first North American serial rights; All other rights revert to the authors & artists upon publication. rights. Guidelines available online.
Nonfiction Needs essays. No literary criticism. Length: 5,000 words.
Fiction Contact: John Ziebell. Length: 7,500 words.

Poetry Contact: Jean French. Length: 80 lines.
Tips "Open to short fiction and poetry submissions from Sept. 1, 2008 to May 31, 2009. Include SASE, brief bio. No general submissions between June 1st and August 31st. See guidelines online."

RHINO

The Poetry Forum, Inc., P.O. Box 591, Evanston IL 60204. E-mail: rhinobiz@hotmail.com. Website: www.rhinopoetry.org. Annual magazine covering high-quality, diverse poetry, short/shorts and translations by new and established writers. We look for idiosyncratic, lively, passionate, and funny work. We are a proud contributor to the vitality of Illinois' literature. Our diverse group of editors looks for the very best in contemporary writing, and we solicit new work by local, national, and international writers. No kill fee. Buys first North American serial rights. Accepts queries by mail. Accepts simultaneous submissions. Sample copy for $6.

- We also foster a community of writers by presenting readings and workshops both in Evanston and in Normal, IL and awarding cash prizes to poets through two annual programs.

Nonfiction Needs essays, on poetry, humor, Translation.
Photos We are seeking high-quality B&W photos to be released in April 2009. Submissions from Illinois photographers are strongly encouraged. We suggest a body of work that coheres in some way. No slides or electronic files. See back issues for $5.
Fiction Needs humorous, Flash Fiction (.
Poetry Needs avant-garde, free verse, light verse, traditional. *RHINO* occupies a niche somewhere between academia and the emerging Chicago poetry scene—devoted to work that tells stories, provokes thought, and pushes the boundaries in form and feeling—while connecting with the audience. Submit maximum 3-5 poems.
Tips We invite traditional or experimental work reflecting passion, originality, artistic conviction, and a love affair with language. Send typed ms with short cover letter, bio, how you heard about *RHINO*, and/or your past publications. Include #10 SASE and let us know if we should return your poems or just respond. Label each poem with your name, address, phone no., and email address. Send by first class mail.

$ RIVER STYX

Big River Association, 3547 Olive St., Suite 107, St. Louis MO 63103. (314)533-4541. Website: www.riverstyx.org. Triannual magazine. "*River Styx* publishes the highest quality fiction, poetry, interviews, essays, and visual art. We are an internationally distributed multicultural literary magazine. Mss read May-November." Estab. 1975. Byline given. Pays on publication. No kill fee. Publishes ms an average of 1 year after acceptance. Buys first North American serial rights, buys one-time rights. Accepts queries by mail. Accepts simultaneous submissions. Responds in 4 months to mss. Sample copy for $7. Guidelines available online.
Nonfiction Needs essays, interview. **Buys 2-5 mss/year.** Send complete ms. **Pays 2 contributor copies, plus 1 year subscription; pays $8/page if funds are available.**
Photos Send photos Reviews 5x7 or 8x10 b&w and color prints and slides. Pays 2 contributor copies, plus 1-year subscription; $8/page if funds are available Buys one time rights.
Fiction Contact: Richard Newman, editor. Needs ethnic, experimental, mainstream, novel concepts, short stories, literary. No genre fiction, less thinly veiled autobiography. **Buys 6-9 mss/year.** Send complete ms. no more than 23-30 manuscript pages. **Pays 2 contributor copies, plus 1-year subscription; $8/page if funds are available.**
Poetry Needs avant-garde, free verse. No religious. **Buys 40-50 poems/year.** Submit maximum 3-5 poems. **Pays 2 contributor copies, plus a 1-year subscription; $8/page if funds are available.**

R.KV.R.Y.

90 in 90 Press, No known public address, E-mail: victoria.pynchon@gmail.com. Website: www.ninetymeetingsinninetydays.com. Quarterly website covering short stories, poetry and nonfiction of high literary quality every quarter. We prefer stories of character development, psychological penetration, and lyricism, without sentimentality or purple prose. The focus is recovery, not only from alcoholism and drug addiction; also oppression of any kind. Political, ecological, familial, physical. It's a journal of hope and reconciliation with a focus on overcoming obstacles. No kill fee.
Nonfiction Our articles embrace almost every area of adult interest related to recovery as defined here: contemporary affairs, history, fiction, literary criticism, art, music, and the theatre. Material should be presented in a fashion suited to a quarterly that is neither journalistic nor academic. We encourage our academic contributors to free themselves from the constraints imposed by academic journals, letting their knowledge, wisdom and experience rock and roll on these pages.
Photos Art.
Fiction Contact: Rita Williams. Needs historical, Short Stories and Memoirs. **Buys 6 mss/year. mss/year.** Length: 1,500-3,000 (prose) words.
Poetry Contact: Jill Deutsch. Needs traditional. We accept poetry on recovery as it is defined here. Poems should have textured, evocative images, use language with an awareness of how words sound and mean, and

have a definite voice. 1,500-3,000 words for prose
Tips Urges readers to read the links to other literary journals. Tells people who want to submit to read those journals like their lives depend on it. Submit in Word only. See Submission Guidelines online.

ROCKHURST REVIEW

A Fine Arts Journal, Rockhurst College, Kansas City's Jesuit College, 1100 Rockhurst Rd., Kansas City MO 64110-2591. Website: web2.scranton.edu/ajupcal/ru/. Annual magazine covering poetry, essays, fiction, drama and artwork. Each volume features a collection of the finest submissions from the Rockhurst community, compiled by a student-led staff under the direction of Dr. Patricia Cleary Miller. Seeks lively material for Spring, 2009 ed. Estab. 1986. No kill fee. Accepts queries by mail. Guidelines available.
Photos Submit up to 5 b&w or color, glossy photos.
Fiction Fiction/essay: 2,500 words; Drama: 10 pages. Length: 2,500 words.
Poetry Submit maximum 5 poems.
Tips Include brief bio, address, phone no., email address and cover letter to Dr. Patricia Miller. Mail with SASE for Spring notification. Submissions accepted from Sept. 2008 - Jan. 15, 2009. Typed. No return of materials.

$ $ THE SAINT ANN'S REVIEW

A Journal of Contemporary Arts and Letters, Saint Ann's School, 129 Pierrepont St., Brooklyn NY 11201. (718)522-1660. Fax: (718)522-2599. E-mail: sareview@saintannsny.org. Website: www.saintannsreview.com. **100% freelance written**. Semiannual literary magazine. We seek honed work that gives the reader a sense of its necessity. Estab. 2000. Circ. 2,000. Byline given. Pays on publication. No kill fee. Publishes ms an average of 4 months after acceptance. Buys first North American serial rights. Submit seasonal material 4 months in advance. Accepts queries by mail. Responds in 1 month to queries. Responds in 4 months to mss. Sample copy for $8. Guidelines available online.
Nonfiction Needs book excerpts, occasionally, essays, humor, interview, personal experience, photo feature. **Buys 10 mss/year.** Send complete ms. 7,500 words maximum **Pays $40/published page, $250/maximum.**
Photos Send photos Reviews transparencies, prints, GIF/JPEG files, b&w art. Offers $50/photo page or art page, $100 maximum. Buys one time rights.
Columns/Departments Book reviews, 1,500 words. 10 Send complete ms by mail only. **Pays $40/published page, $200 maximum.**
Fiction Needs ethnic, experimental, fantasy, historical, humorous, mainstream, slice-of-life vignettes, translations. **Buys 40 mss/year.** 7,500 words maximum. **Pays $40/published page, $100 maximum.**
Poetry Needs avant-garde, free verse, haiku, light verse, traditional. **Buys 30 poems/year.** Submit maximum 5 poems. **Pays $50/page, $100 maximum.**

SALT HILL

Creative Writing Program, Syracuse University, English Dept., Syracuse University, Syracuse NY 13244. E-mail: salthilljournal@gmail.com. Website: www.salthilljournal.net. **Contact:** Ashley Farmer and Nadxieli Mannello, editors-in-chief. *Salt Hill* is a biannual journal publishing outstanding new poetry, fiction, nonfiction, interviews, and artwork. "Our eclectic taste ranges from traditional to experimental. All we ask is that it's good. Open to most themes." No kill fee. Accepts queries by mail. yesAccepts simultaneous submissions. Guidelines available online
Nonfiction Contact: Mikael Awake, nonfiction editor. Needs essays, Reviews, interview, translation, off-beat travelogues.
Photos Contact: Naxielo Mannello, Art Ed.
Fiction Contact: Kayla Blatchley, Aaron Chambers, Alice Holbrook, fiction editors.
Poetry Contact: Carroll Beauvais, Eric Darby, poetry editors. Needs Needs prose and verse poems. Translations accepted. Submit maximum 3-5 poems/submission poems. No known line limits.
Tips "*Salt Hill* seeks to publish writing that is exciting and necessary, regardless of aesthetic. Rather than trying to fit any subscribed style, send your best work. We recommend reading recent issues or samples on our Web site prior to submitting. Open submissions from Aug. 1-Apr. 1. Enclose SASE for reply. We recycle mss, and encourage you to use a 'Forever' stamp on your SASE. Please send submissions attention to Genre editor."

SANTA CLARA REVIEW

Santa Clara Review, Santa Clara University, P.O. Box 3212, El Camino Real, Santa Clara CA 95053-3212. (408)554-4484. Fax: (408)554-4454. E-mail: info@santaclarareview.com. Website: www.santaclarareview.com. Semiannual magazine covering poetry, fiction, nonfiction, essays, drama/screenplays, photography and art at Santa Clara University. "This is a student-edited literary magazine that draws on SCU students, faculty, staff, as well as writers outside the University. Represents SCU's commitment to the humanities, a tenant of Jesuit education. Accepts only the highest quality material which echoes SCU's dedication to the pursuit of truth, honesty, and social responsibility, within the literary arts. Estab. 1869. No kill fee. Publishes ms an average of 2 months after acceptance. Accepts queries by mail.

- *The Review* is committed to the development of student literary talent, both in editorial and creative

writing skills, and creates a forum for faculty, students and alumni to express their creative energy."
Nonfiction Needs essays, photo feature, Drama/Screenplays.
Fiction Length: 5,000 words or less.
Tips "We are currently accepting submissions for 2009 Fall/Winter issue. If mailing, see guidelines online. All entries must include name, address, phone no., email address, title of work, date of work's completion, dimensions (in inches), medium of the work, cover letter (required for written entries only). No mss. can be returned without SASE. Mss. will be kept at least 4 weeks. SCR is published in Feb. & May. We accept submissions year round."

$ THE SAVAGE KICK LITERARY MAGAZINE

Murder Slim Press, 32c Lichfield Rd., Gt. Yarmouth Norfolk NR31 0EQ United Kingdom. E-mail: moonshine@murderslim.com. Website: www.murderslim.com/savagekick.html. **100% freelance written**. Semiannual magazine. *Savage Kick* primarily deals with viewpoints outside the mainstream.honest emotions told in a raw, simplistic way. It is recommended that you are very familiar with the *SK* style before submitting. We have only accepted 4 new writers in 12 months of the magazine. Ensure you have a distinctive voice and story to tell. Estab. 2005. Circ. 500+. Byline given. Pays on acceptance. Publishes ms an average of up to 2 months after acceptance. Buys all electronic rights for 3 months. Accepts queries by mail, e-mail. Accepts simultaneous submissions. Responds in 7-10 days to queries. Guidelines free.
Nonfiction We only accept articles in relation to the authors featured on our reading list. Needs interview, personal experience. **Buys 10-20 mss/year.** Send complete ms. Length: 500-3,000 words. **Pays $25-35.**
Columns/Departments up to 4 Query. **Pays $25-35.**
Fiction Needs mystery, slice-of-life vignettes, crime. Real-life stories are preferred, unless the work is distinctively extreme within the crime genre. No Poetry of any kind, no mainstream fiction, Oprah-style fiction, Internet/chat language, teen issues, excessive Shakespearean language, surrealism, overworked irony, or genre fiction (horror, fantasy, science fiction, western, erotica, etc.). **Buys 10-25 mss/year.** Send complete ms. Length: 500-6,000 words. **Pays $35.**

$ THE SEATTLE REVIEW

Box 354330, University of Washington, Seattle WA 98195. (206)543-2302. E-mail: seaview@u.washington.edu. Website: www.seattlereview.org. Semiannual magazine. Includes general fiction, poetry, craft essays on writing, and one interview per issue with a Northwest writer. Estab. 1978. Circ. 1,000. Pays on publication. Buys first North American serial rights. Responds in 8 months to mss. Sample copy for $6. Guidelines available online.

- Editors accept submissions only from October 1 through May 31.

Fiction Wants more creative nonfiction. We also publish a series called Writers and their Craft, which deals with aspects of writing fiction (also poetry)—point of view, characterization, etc, rather than literary criticism, each issue. Needs ethnic, experimental, fantasy, historical, horror, humorous, mainstream, mystery, novel concepts, suspense, western, contemporary, feminist, gay, lesbian, literary, psychic/supernatural/occult, regional, translations. Nothing in bad taste (porn, racist, etc.). No genre fiction or science fiction. **Buys 4-10 mss/year.** Send complete ms. Length: 500-10,000 words. **Pays $0-100.**
Tips Beginners do well in our magazine if they send clean, well-written manuscripts. We've published a lot of 'first stories' from all over the country and take pleasure in discovery.

SENECA REVIEW

Hobart and William Smith Colleges, Geneva NY 14456. (315)781-3392. E-mail: senecareview@hws.edu. Website: www.hws.edu/academics/senecareview/index.aspx. Semiannual magazine Seneca Review reads manuscripts of poetry, translations, essays on contemporary poetry, and lyric essays (creative nonfiction that borders on poetry). "The editors have special interest in translations of contemporary poetry from around the world. Publisher of numerous laureates and award-winning poets, we also publish emerging writers and are always open to new, innovative work. Poems from SR are regularly honored by inclusion in The Best American Poetry and Pushcart Prize anthologies. Distributed internationally." No kill fee. Accepts queries by mail. Responds in 3 months to mss. Guidelines available online.
Nonfiction Needs essays, (up to 20 pages), Translation. Past special features have included Irish women's poetry and Irish prison poetry; Iraeli women's poetry; Polish, Catalan, and Albanian poetry; and an issue of essays devoted to Hayden Carruth.
Poetry Submit maximum 3-5 poems.
Tips "One submission per reading period. Mss. received during summer will be returned."

THE SEWANEE REVIEW

University of the South, 735 University Ave., Sewanee TN 37383-1000. (931)598-1246. E-mail: lcouch@sewanee.edu. Website: www.sewanee.edu/sewanee_review. Quarterly magazine. A literary quarterly, publishing original fiction, poetry, essays on literary and related subjects, and book reviews for well-educated readers who appreciate good American and English literature. Estab. 1892. Circ. 2,200. Pays on publication. Buys first North

American serial rights, buys second serial (reprint) rights. Responds in 6-8 weeks to mss. Sample copy for $8.50 ($9.50 outside US). Guidelines available online.

- Does not read mss June 1-August 31.

Fiction Send query letter for essays and reviews. Send complete ms for fiction. No erotica, science fiction, fantasy or excessively violent or profane material. **Buys 10-15 mss/year.** Length: 3,500-7,500 words.
Poetry Send complete ms. Submit maximum 6 poems. Length: 40 lines.

SHEARSMAN

the magazine, Shearsman Books Ltd, Shearsman, 58 Velwell Rd., Exeter England EX4 4LD UK. E-mail: editor@shearsman.com. Website: www.shearsman.com/pages/magazine/home.html. Semiannual website covering contemporary poetry. We are inclined toward the more exploratory end of the current spectrum. Notwithstanding this, however, quality work of a more conservative kind will always be considered seriously, provided that the work is well written. I always look for some rigour in the work, though I will be more forgiving of failure in this regard if the writer is trying to push out the boundaries. Estab. 1981. No kill fee. Accepts queries by mail, e-mail. Guidelines available online.

- I tend to like mixing work from both ends of the spectrum, and firmly believe that good writing can and should cohabit with other forms of good writing, regardless of the aesthetic that drives it.

Poetry No sloppy writing of any kind.
Tips We no longer read through the year. Our reading window for magazines is from 1 Mar.-31 Mar., for the Oct. issue, and from 1 Sept. to 30 Sept. for the April issue. Books may be submitted anytime. See guidelines online. Avoid sending attachments with your emails unless they are in PDF format. Include SASE; no IRCs.

$ SHENANDOAH

The Washington and Lee University Review, Washington and Lee University, Mattingly House, 2 Lee Ave., Lexington VA 24450-2116. (540)458-8765. Fax: (540)458-8461. E-mail: shenandoah@wlu.edu. Website: shenandoah.wlu.edu/faq.html. Triannual magazine. Estab. 1950. Circ. 2,000. Byline given. Pays on publication. No kill fee. Publishes ms an average of 10 months after acceptance. Buys first North American serial rights, buys one-time rights. Responds in 3 months to mss. Sample copy for $12. Guidelines available online.
Nonfiction Needs essays, Book reviews. **Buys 6 mss/year.** Send complete ms. **Pays $25/page ($250 max).**
Fiction Needs mainstream, short stories. No sloppy, hasty, slight fiction. **Buys 15 mss/year.** Send complete ms. **Pays $25/page ($250 max).**
Poetry "No inspirational, confessional poetry." **Buys 70 poems/year.** Submit maximum 5 poems. Open **Pays $2.50/line ($200 max).**

⊘ SHORT STUFF

Bowman Publications, Short Stuff Magazine, Bowman Publications, 301 E. Harmony Rd., Suite 204, Fort Collins CO 80525. (970)232-9066. E-mail: shortstf89@aol.com. **98% freelance written.** Bimonthly magazine. "We are perhaps an enigma in that we publish only clean stories in any genre. We'll tackle any subject, but don't allow obscene language or pornographic description. Our magazine is for grown-ups, not X-rated `adult' fare." Estab. 1989. Circ. 10,400. Byline given. Payment and contract upon publication. Buys first North American serial rights. Editorial lead time 3 months. Submit seasonal material 3 months in advance. Responds in 6 months to mss. Sample copy - send 9x12 SAE with 5 first-class (42¢) stamps. Guidelines for #10 SASE.

- "We are now open to submissions."

Nonfiction Most nonfiction is staff written. Needs humor. We are holiday oriented and each issue reflects the appropriate holidays. **Buys 30 mss/year.** Send complete ms. Include cover letter about the author and synopsis of the story. Length: 500-1,500 words. **Payment varies.**
Photos Send photos Identification of subjects required. Offers no additional payment for photos accepted with ms Buys one time rights.
Fiction Needs adventure, historical, humorous, mainstream, mystery, romance, science fiction, (Seldom), suspense, western. We want to see more humor—not essay format—real stories with humor; 1,000-word mysteries, modern lifestyles. The 1,000-word pieces have the best chance of publication. No erotica; nothing morbid or pornographic. **Buys 144 mss/year.** Send complete ms. Length: 500-1,500 words. **Payment varies.**
Fillers Needs anecdotes, short humor. 200 Length: 20-500 words. **variable amount.**
Tips "Don't send floppy disks or cartridges. We are holiday oriented; mark on outside of envelope if story is for Easter, Mother's Day, etc. We receive 500 manuscripts each month. This is up about 200%. Because of this, I implore writers to send 1 manuscript at a time. I would not use stories from the same author more than once an issue and this means I might keep the others too long. Please don't e-mail your stories! If you have an e-mail address, please include that with cover letter so we can contact you. If no SASE, we destroy the manuscript."

SLICE MAGAZINE

E-mail: submissions@slicemagazine.org. Website: www.slicemagazine.org. Biannual magazine created to provide a forum for dynamic conversations between emerging and established authors. Byline given. No kill fee. Accepts simultaneous submissions. Responds in 2-3 months to mss.

Nonfiction Needs personal experience.
Fiction Needs mainstream, serialized novellas. Send complete ms.

SLIPSTREAM

Dept. W-1, Box 2071, Niagara Falls NY 14301. E-mail: editors@slipstream.org. Website: www.slipstreampress.org/index.html. Annual magazine covering poetry only, black & white photos, drawings and illustrations; A yearly anthology of some of the best poetry and fiction you'll find today in the American small press. "We prefer contemporary urban themes—writing from the grit that is not afraid to bark or bite. We shy away from pastoral, religious, and rhyming verse." Estab. 1980. Chapbook Contest prize is $1,000 plus 50 professionally printed copies of your chapbook. No kill fee. Accepts queries by mail. Accepts previously published material. Accepts simultaneous submissions. Guidelines available online.

- If you're unsure, the editors strongly recommend that you sample a current or back issue of *Slipstream*.

Photos It's better to send scans or photocopies of artwork rather than originals.
Poetry Pastoral, religious, and rhyming verse.
Tips "Reading for general theme issue through 2008—poetry only. Do not submit by email. Include SASE. Send copies of your poems, not originals. See Submission guidelines online."

$ SMITHS KNOLL

Goldings, Golding Lane, Leiston, Suffolk England IP16 4EB UK. Website: www.michael-laskey.co/uk/smiths-knoll.php. Magazine covering contemporary poetry. We are open to new voices. Estab. 1991. Circ. 500. Pays on publication. No kill fee. Publishes ms an average of 2 weeks after acceptance. Accepts queries by mail. Responds in 1 week to mss. Free if you live in the UK. Guidelines available online.

- The name appealed to us because a knoll is a small hill where Smiths, and smiths too, are welcome and belong.

Poetry Submit maximum 4-6 poems.
Tips We're neurotic about proofreading.

SNOW MONKEY

An Eclectic Journal, Ravenna Press, No known public address, E-mail: snowmonkey.editor@comcast.net. Website: www.ravennapress.com/snowmonkey/. Ten times/year website covering original unpublished poems and micro-prose. Seeks writing that's like footprints of the Langur monkeys left at 11,000 feet on Poon Hill, Nepal. Open to most themes. No kill fee. Accepts queries by e-mail. Accepts simultaneous submissions. Responds in 2 months to mss. Guidelines available.
Fiction Up to 10 writers are featured in monthly posting from Sept. through June. Length: 500 words.
Tips Send submissions as text-only in the body of your email. Include your last name in the subject line. We do not currently use bios, but we love to read them.

SOFTBLOW

No public address known, E-mail: editor@softblow.com. Website: www.softblow.com. Monthly website covering poetry online that can claim to have international recognition. We are hosting local writing that could be placed side-by-side with great international works. We hope to better focus the eye back on the poem. We do not exist for a general reading audience, but for unswerving lovers of poetry who also appreciate how far poetry has come over time. We frequently promote to audiences in Singapore, Malaysia, Australia, Hong Kong, the Philippines, Canada, New Zealand, and the States. Estab. 2004. No kill fee. Accepts queries by e-mail. Guidelines available.

- Only 1 or 2 poets will be added at any given time with representative bodies of poems. Featured poets will eventually be put into an Archive Section to make room for new poets. In time, there will be a long section where there will be several poems by a selected poet to span a significant and extensive writing career.

Poetry Prose that defies categorising falls under poetry in my book and is more than welcome at < iSoftblow Submit maximum 4-6 poems.
Tips Paste poems with a short bio in the body of an email. Multiple submissions accepted. No short stories.

$ SOLEADO

Revista de Literatura y Cultura, Dept. of International Language and Culture Studies, IPFW, CM 267, 2101 E. Coliseum Blvd., Fort Wayne IN 46805. (260)481-6630. Fax: (260)481-6985. E-mail: summersj@ipfw.edu. Website: www.soleado.org. **100% freelance written**. Annual magazine covering Spanish-language literary, cultural, and creative writing. Our readers are interested in literature and culture, from creative writing to personal essays and beyond. Spanish is of an ever-growing importance in the US and the world, and our readers and writers are people using that language. *Soleado* is a literary magazine, so academic treatises are not on the list of texts we would be excited to see. The focus of the magazine is on Spanish-language writing, although the national origin of the writer does not matter. The subject matter doesn't have to be Hispanic, either. The one exception to the Spanish-language requirement is that certain texts deal with the difficulties of being bilingual and/or bicultural are welcome to be written in 'Spanglish' when that usage is essential to the text. Please don't send anything written only in English. We publish a very limited selection of work in 'Spanglish'—don't send us anything without having read what we have already published. Estab. 2004. Byline given. Pays on publication. No kill fee. Publishes ms an average of 8 months after acceptance. Buys first North American serial rights, buys first rights, buys one-time rights, buys second serial (reprint) rights, buys simultaneous rights, buys electronic rights, buys anthology rights. Editorial lead time 6 months. Submit seasonal material 1 year in advance. Accepts queries by mail, e-mail. Accepts previously published material. Responds in 1 week to queries. Responds in 3 months to mss. Sample copy and writer's guidelines online.

Nonfiction Needs book excerpts, essays, humor, interview, opinion, personal experience, travel, translations, memoir, creative nonfiction. No how-to, general travel, inspirational, religious or anything written in English. All nonfiction must have a literary or cultural slant. **Buys up to 3 mss/year.** Query. **Pays maximum $50.**

Fiction We are looking for good literary writing in Spanish, from Magical Realism a la García Márquez, to McOndo-esque writing similar to that of Edmundo Paz-Soldán and Alberto Fuguet, to Spanish pulp realism like that of Arturo Pérez-Reverte. Testimonials, experimental works like those of Diamela Eltit, and women's voices like Marcela Serrano and Zoé Valdés are also encouraged. We are not against any particular genre writing, but such stories do have to maintain their hold on the literary, as well as the genre, which is often a difficult task. Needs adventure, ethnic, experimental, fantasy, historical, humorous, mainstream, mystery, novel concepts, science fiction, slice-of-life vignettes, suspense, translations, magical realism. **Buys 2-6 mss/year.** Query or send complete ms. up to 8,000 words **Pays $-50.**

Poetry Needs avant-garde, free verse, light verse, traditional. Avoid poetry that takes us to places we have already seen. The best kind of poetry takes readers somewhere unexpected or via an unexpected path, departing from the familiar just when they thought they had things figured out. **Buys 10-15 poems/year.** Submit maximum 4 poems. 400 words

Fillers Needs short humor. up to 4 1,000 words **Pays $10**

Tips Whether you are or are not a native speaker of Spanish, have someone read over your manuscript for obvious grammatical errors, flow, and continuity of ideas. We are interested in literary translations into Spanish, as well as original writing. Query before sending submission as an e-mail attachment. We publish annually, and the reading period runs from September 1 to March 31 of the following year. Anything that comes between April and August won't get a reply until the new reading period begins.

SONORA REVIEW

University of Arizona's Creative Writing MFA Program, University of Arizona, Dept. of English, Tucson AZ 85721. E-mail: sonora@email.arizona.edu. Website: www.coh.arizona.edu/sonora/. **90% freelance written**. Semiannual magazine. We look for the highest quality poetry, fiction, and nonfiction, with an emphasis on emerging writers. Our magazine has a long-standing tradition of publishing the best new literature and writers. Check out our website for a sample of what we publish and our submission guidelines, or send $6 for a sample back issue. Estab. 1980. Circ. 500. Byline given. No kill fee. Publishes ms an average of 3-4 months after acceptance. Buys first North American serial rights, buys one-time rights, buys electronic rights. Accepts queries by mail. Accepts simultaneous submissions. Responds in 2-5 weeks to queries. Responds in 3 months to mss. Sample copy for $6. Guidelines available online.

Nonfiction Needs book excerpts, essays, interview, personal experience. **Buys 2-4 mss/year.** Send complete ms.

Fiction Needs ethnic, experimental, mainstream, novel concepts. **Buys 6-10 mss/year.** Send complete ms. Length: 1,000-8,000 words. **Pays 2 contributor's copies; additional copies for $4.**

Poetry All poetry welcome. **Buys 20-40 poems/year.** Submit maximum 7 poems.

Tips We have no length requirements, but we usually do not consider poems, stories, or essays that are over 20 pages in length because of space. We publish mostly poems, short stories, and literary nonfiction. We do not read during June or July.

SOUNDINGS EAST

Dept. of English, Salem State College, 352 Lafayette St., Salem MA 01970. (978)542-6000. E-mail: soundingseast@salemstate.edu. Website: www.salemstate.edu/arts/soundings-east.php. Semiannual magazine dedicated to publishing high quality literature covering poetry, fiction and creative nonfiction. Literary journal of Salem State College run by SSC students under the direction of a faculty member. Estab. 1973. Circ. 2,000. No kill fee. Accepts queries by mail.

Tips Reading from Sept. 1 - March 1st.

SOUNDINGS REVIEW

Whidbey Island Writers Association, P.O. Box 1289, Langley WA 98236-1289. (360)331-6714. E-mail: writers@whidbey.com. Website: www.writeonwhidbey.org. **100% freelance written**. Semiannual magazine. We welcome high-quality and accessible poetry, fiction and essays. We are open to all styles and voices, but we are passionate about connecting with readers: a reader should feel a connection on first reading and look forward to reading the material again to find increased depth and understanding. Write for yourself, not other writers, and readers will connect with your characters and their story. Estab. 2008. Circ. 300. Byline given. Pays on publication. No kill fee. Publishes ms an average of 6 months after acceptance. Buys first North American serial rights. one-time anthology rights. Editorial lead time 2 months. Submit seasonal material 6 months in advance. Accepts queries by mail, e-mail. Accepts simultaneous submissions. Responds in 12 weeks to queries. Responds in 3 months to mss. Sample copy for $4.95 WIWA members; $6.50 nonmembers; add $2 for postage to Canada. www.writeonwhidbey.org/publications/soundings.htm.

Nonfiction Needs essays, historical, humor, inspirational, interview, opinion, (does not mean letters to the editor)., personal experience. We do not want political rants or how-to type articles. **Buys 5 mss/year mss/year.** Send complete ms. Length: 3,000 words. **honorarium as budget allows for assigned articles.**

Columns/Departments We sometimes take letters to editor only.

Fiction Needs adventure, ethnic, experimental, fantasy, historical, horror, humorous, mainstream, mystery, novel concepts, religious, romance, science fiction, slice-of-life vignettes, suspense, western. We do not want pornography or extreme violence. **Buys 6 mss/year mss/year.** Send complete ms. Length: 3,000 words. **honrarium as budget allows.**

Poetry Needs avant-garde, free verse, haiku, light verse, traditional. We do not want highly erotic/pornographic or extremely violent poetry; will take experimental only if also accessible. **Buys 30 yearly poems/year.** Submit maximum 6 poems. open, but needs to be very powerful. **honorarium as budget allows.**

SOUTHERN HUMANITIES REVIEW

Auburn University, 9088 Haley Center, Auburn University AL 36849. (334)844-9088. E-mail: shrengl@auburn.edu. Website: www.auburn.edu/english/shr/home.htm. **99% freelance written.** Quarterly perfect-bound journal covering general humanities. *Southern Humanities Review* publishes fiction, poetry, and critical essays on the arts, literature, philosophy, religion, and history for a well-read, scholarly audience. Estab. 1967. Circ. approximately 700. Byline given. No kill fee. We contract for all rights until publication. Then copyright reverts to author. Accepts queries by mail, e-mail. Responds in 1-2 weeks to queries. Sample copy for $5 in U.S.; $7 everywhere else. Guidelines for #10 SASE.

Fiction Buys 4-8 mss/year. Send complete ms. Length: 15,000 words. **Pays 2 contributor copies.**

Poetry Any kind; short poems preferred. **Buys 10-25 poems/year.** Submit maximum 5 poems. **Pays 2 contributor copies.**

$ THE SOUTHERN REVIEW

Louisiana State University, Old President's House, Baton Rouge LA 70803-5001. (225)578-5108. Fax: (225)578-5098. E-mail: southernreview@lsu.edu. Website: www.lsu.edu/tsr. **Contact:** Leslie A. Green, bus. man. **100% freelance written. Works with a moderate number of new/unpublished writers each year; reads unsolicited mss.** Quarterly magazine with emphasis on contemporary literature in the US and abroad. Reading period: September-May. Estab. 1935. Circ. 2,900. Byline given. Pays on publication. No kill fee. Publishes ms an average of 6 months after acceptance. Buys first North American serial rights. Accepts queries by mail. Responds in 2 months to mss. Sample copy for $8. Guidelines available online.

Nonfiction Essays with careful attention to craftsmanship, technique, and seriousness of subject matter. Willing to publish experimental writing if it has a valid artistic purpose. Avoid extremism and sensationalism. Essays should exhibit thoughtful and sometimes severe awareness of the necessity of literary standards in our time. Emphasis on contemporary literature. No footnotes. **Buys 25 mss/year.** Length: 4,000-10,000 words. **Pays $30/page.**

Fiction Contact: Donna Perreault, associate editor. Short stories of lasting literary merit, with emphasis on style and technique; novel excerpts. We emphasize style and substantial content. No mystery, fantasy or religious mss. Length: 4,000-8,000 words. **Pays $30/page.**

Poetry 1-4 pages **Pays $30/page.**

THE SOW'S EAR POETRY REVIEW

The Word Process, P.O. Box 127, Millwood VA 29638-9115. E-mail: rglesman@gmail.com. Website: sows-ear.kitenet.net. **Contact:** Robert Lesman, managing editor. **100% freelance written.** Quarterly magazine. "The Sow's Ear prints fine poetry of all styles and lengths, complemented by black and white art. We also welcome reviews, interviews, and essays related to poetry. We are open to group submissions. Our 'Crossover' section features poetry married to any other art form, including prose, music, and visual media." Estab. 1988. Circ. 700. No byline given. No kill fee. Publishes ms an average of 1-6 months after acceptance. Buys first North American serial rights. Editorial lead time 1-6 months. Submit seasonal material 3 months in advance. Accepts queries by mail, e-mail. Accepts simultaneous submissions. Responds in 2 weeks to queries. Responds in 3 months to mss. Sample copy for $7. Guidelines by email.

Nonfiction Needs essays, related to poetry, interview, of poets, reviews of poetry books. **Buys 6 mss/year.** Query. Length: 1,000-3,000 words.

Photos Model releases required. Reviews prints, GIF/JPEG files. Offers no additional payment for photos accepted with ms. Buys one time rights.

Columns/Departments Review of poetry book published within a year (1,000-3,000 words); Interview with a poet; essay related to poetry. Query.
Poetry Needs avant-garde, free verse, haiku, light verse, traditional. Open to any style or length. **Buys 100/year poems/year.** Submit maximum 5 poems. No limits on line length
Tips "We like work that is carefully crafted, keenly felt, and freshly perceived. We respond to poems with voice, a sense of place, delight in language, and a meaning that unfolds. We look for prose that opens new dimensions to appreciating poetry."

SPOON RIVER POETRY REVIEW

Spoon River Poetry Association, Campus Box 4241, Illinois State University, Normal IL 61790-4241. E-mail: lcqetsi@ilstu.edu. Website: litline.org/spoon/index.html. Semiannual magazine covering contemporary poetry in English from the U.S. and around the world in English translation. Features an Illinois poet (a poet who has an Illinois connection) with an interview and poems. Also publishes reviews of contemporary poetry and poetic theory which address texts and issues in a balanced and intelligent way. Each year there is an Editors' Prize Contest. See contest guidelines online. Prizes of $1,000 and $100. Deadline is Apr. 15th. No kill fee. Guidelines available online.

- *Poet's Market* has named the *SRPR* one of the best reads in the poetry publishing world.

Nonfiction Needs interview.
Columns/Departments Teaching Poetry.
Tips We read submissions from all over the world and nation from Sept. 15-Apr. 15 each year. Include SASE. Mss. postmarked between Apr. 16 & Sept. 14 are returned unread. Reviews of contemporary poetry and poetic theory should address texts and issues in a balanced and intelligent way.

$ STAND MAGAZINE

School of English, University of Leeds, Leeds LS2 9JT United Kingdom. (44)(113)343-4794. E-mail: stand@leeds.ac.uk. Website: www.standmagazine.org. "Quarterly literary magazine. Pays £20 for the first poem or 1,000 words of prose and £5 for each additional piece published in the same issue of the magazine." Estab. 1952. Pays on publication. No kill fee. Accepts queries by mail. Guidelines available online at website.

- "U.S. submissions can be made through the Virginia office (see separate listing)."

$ STORYTELLER

Canada's Short Story Magazine, Tyo Communications, 3687 Twin Falls Place, Ottawa ON K1V 1W6 Canada. E-mail: info@storytellermagazine.com. Website: www.storytellermagazine.com. **99% freelance written.** Quarterly magazine covering fiction. Estab. 1994. Circ. 1,000. Byline given. Pays on publication. No kill fee. Publishes ms an average of 2-3 months after acceptance. Buys first North American serial rights, buys second serial (reprint) rights. Accepts previously published material. Responds in 2-3 months to mss. Sample copy available online. Guidelines available online.
Fiction Needs adventure, confession, ethnic, experimental, fantasy, historical, horror, humorous, mainstream, mystery, romance, science fiction, serialized, slice-of-life vignettes, suspense, western. Does not want religious, erotica, hardcore genre, Americana, stories where nothing happens. **Buys 30-40 mss/year.** Send complete ms. Length: 2,000-6,000 words. **Pays ¼-½¢/word.**
Tips Write the kind of blurb for your story that you'd see on the dust jacket of a novel. If you can't make that blurb sound appealing, we probably don't want to see the story.

THE STORYTELLER

A Writers Magazine, Fossil Creek Publishing, 2441 Washington Rd., Maynard AR 72444. (870)647-2137. Fax: (870)647-2454. E-mail: storyteller1@cox-internet.com. Website: www.thestorytellermagazine.com. **95% freelance written**. Quarterly magazine featuring short stories, essays, nonfiction and poetry. Estab. 1996. Circ. 700. Byline given. Publishes ms an average of 1-12 months after acceptance. Buys first rights. Editorial lead time 6 months. Submit seasonal material 4 months in advance. Accepts queries by mail, e-mail. Accepts previously published material. Accepts simultaneous submissions. Responds in 1 week to queries. Responds in 2 weeks to mss. Sample copy for 4 first-class stamps. Guidelines for #10 SASE.
Nonfiction Needs essays, general interest, historical, how-to, humor, inspirational, opinion, personal experience. Does not want anything graphic, pornographic, or based on Star Trek or Star Wars. Be original with all your work. We don't want 'poor me' articles or stories about how life is hard. We all understand that, but give us something at the end where we can see that things are looking up. **Buys 80 mss/year.** Send complete ms. Length: 1,500 words.
Photos Send photos Identification of subjects required. Reviews 4x6 prints. Offers no additional payment for photos accepted with ms. Buys one time rights.
Fiction Needs adventure, fantasy, historical, horror, humorous, mainstream, mystery, romance, science fiction, slice-of-life vignettes, suspense, western. Does not want anything graphic, religious or bashing—even in fiction. **Buys 180 mss/year.** Send complete ms. Length: 1,500 words.
Poetry Needs avant-garde, free verse, haiku, light verse, traditional. Does not want long rambling. **Buys 220**

poems/year. Submit maximum 3 poems. Length: 40 lines. **$1.00 per poem.**
Fillers Needs anecdotes, facts, short humor. 5-6 Length: 15-50 words.
Tips *The Storyteller* is one of the best places you will find to submit your work, especially new writers. Our best advice, be professional. You have one chance to make a good impression. Don't blow it by being unprofessional.

$ $ THE STRAND MAGAZINE

P.O. Box 1418, Birmingham MI 48012-1418. (248)788-5948. Fax: (248)874-1046. E-mail: strandmag@strandmag.com. Website: www.strandmag.com. Quarterly magazine covering mysteries, short stories, essays, book reviews. After an absence of nearly half a century, the magazine known to millions for bringing Sir Arthur Conan Doyle's ingenious detective, Sherlock Holmes, to the world has once again appeared on the literary scene. First launched in 1891, *The Strand*,included in its pages the works of some of the greatest writers of the 20th century: Agatha Christie, Dorothy Sayers, Margery Allingham, W. Somerset Maugham, Graham Greene, P.G. Wodehouse, H.G. Wells, Aldous Huxley and many others. In 1950, economic difficulties in England caused a drop in circulation which forced the magazine to cease publication. Estab. 1998. Circ. 50,000. Byline given. Pays on acceptance. No kill fee. Publishes ms an average of 4 months after acceptance. Buys first North American serial rights. Accepts queries by e-mail. Responds in 1 month to queries. Guidelines for #10 SASE.
Fiction Contact: A.F. Gulli, editor. Needs horror, humorous, mystery, detective stories, suspense, tales of the unexpected, tales of terror and the supernatural written in the classic tradition of this century's great authors. We are not interested in submissions with any sexual content. Length: 2,000-6,000 words. **Pays $50-175.**
Tips No gratuitous violence, sexual content, or explicit language, please.

STUDIO

A Journal of Christians Writing, 727 Peel St., Albury NSW 2640 Australia. (61)(2)6021-1135. Fax: (61)(2)6021-1135. E-mail: studio00@bigpond.net.au. **Contact:** Paul Grover, man. ed. **80% freelance written**. Quarterly magazine. "*Studio* publishes poetry and prose of literary merit, offers a venue for previously published, new, and aspiring writers, and seeks to create a sense of community among christians who write." Estab. 1980. Circ. 300. Byline given. No kill fee. Publishes ms an average of 6 months after acceptance. Editorial lead time 3 months. Accepts queries by mail, e-mail. Accepts previously published material. Accepts simultaneous submissions. Responds in 1 week to queries and to mss. Sample copy for $10 (AUD). Guidelines by email.
Poetry Needs free verse, haiku, light verse. Submit maximum 2 poems. Length: 10-40 lines. **contributor copy.**

$ $ $ SUBTROPICS

University of Florida, P.O. Box 112075, 4008 Turlington Hall, Gainesville FL 32611-2075. Website: www.english.ufl.edu/subtropics. **100% freelance written**. "Magazine published 3 times/year through the University of Florida's English department. *Subtropics* seeks to publish the best literary fiction, essays, and poetry being written today, both by established and emerging authors. We will consider works of fiction of any length, from short shorts to novellas and self-contained novel excerpts. We give the same latitude to essays. We appreciate work in translation and, from time to time, republish important and compelling stories, essays, and poems that have lapsed out of print by writers no longer living." Estab. 2005. Byline given. Pays on acceptance. Publishes ms an average of 6 months after acceptance. Buys first North American serial rights, buys one-time rights. Responds in 1 month to queries and mss. Guidelines available online
Nonfiction Needs essays, literary nonfiction. No book reviews. **Buys 15 mss/year.** Send complete ms. **Pays $1,000.**
Fiction Literary fiction only, including short-shorts. No genre fiction. **Buys 20 mss/year.** Send complete ms. **Pays $500 for short-shorts; $1,000 for full stories.**
Poetry Buys 50 poems/year. Submit maximum 5 poems. **Pays $100.**
Tips "We publish longer works of fiction, including novellas and excerpts from forthcoming novels. Each issue will include a short-short story of about 250 words on the back cover. We are also interested in publishing works in translation for the magazine's English-speaking audience."

SYCAMORE REVIEW

Purdue University Dept. of English, 500 Oval Dr., West Lafayette IN 47907. E-mail: sycamore@purdue.edu. Website: sycamorereview.com. Semiannual magazine covering poetry, fiction and nonfiction, books reviews and art. Strives to publish the best writing by new and established writers. Looks for well crafted and engaging work, works that illuminate our lives in the collective human search for meaning. We would like to publish more work that takes a reflective look at our national identity and how we are perceived by the world. We look for diversity of voice, pluralistic worldviews, and political and social context. No kill fee. Buys first North American serial rights. Accepts queries by mail.

- *Sycamore Review* is Purdue University's internationally acclaimed literary journal, affiliated with Purdue's College of Liberal Arts and the Dept. of English. Art should present politics in a language that can be felt.

Nonfiction Contact: Jess Mehr. Needs essays, Personal, humor, Literary Memoir, Translation. No outside interviews, previously published work (except translations) or genre pieces (conventional sci fi, romance, horror, etc.) No scholarly articles or journalistic pieces. Please query for book reviews, brief critical essays as well as all art.

Poetry Prose should be typed, double-spaced,with numbered pages and the author's name and the title easily visible on each page. Does not publish creative work by any student currently attending Purdue University. Former students should wait one year before submitting. Submit maximum Submit 4-5 poems in one envelope. Wait until you have received a response to submit again. poems.

Tips We look for originality, brevity, significance, strong dialogue, and vivid detail. We sponsor the Wabash Prize for Poetry ($1,000 award). Deadline: Oct. 17, 2008. All contest submissions will be considered for regular inclusion in the *Sycamore Review*. No email submissions-no exception. Include SASE.

$ TAMPA REVIEW

University of Tampa Press, 401 W. Kennedy Blvd., Tampa FL 33606. (813)253-6266. Fax: (813)258-7593. Website: tampareview.ut.edu. Semiannual magazine published in hardback format. An international literary journal publishing art and literature from Florida and Tampa Bay as well as new work and translations from throughout the world. Estab. 1988. Circ. 500. Byline given. Pays on publication. No kill fee. Publishes ms an average of 10 months after acceptance. Buys first North American serial rights. Editorial lead time 18 months. Accepts queries by mail. Responds in 5 months to mss. Sample copy for $7. Guidelines available online.

Nonfiction Contact: Elizabeth Winston, nonfiction editor. Needs general interest, interview, personal experience, creative nonfiction. No how-to articles, fads, journalistic reprise, etc. **Buys 6 mss/year.** Send complete ms. Length: 250-7,500 words. **Pays $10/printed page.**

Photos State availability Captions, identification of subjects required. Reviews contact sheets, negatives, transparencies, prints, digital files. Offers $10/photo. Buys one time rights.

Fiction Contact: Lisa Birnbaum and Kathleen Ochshorn, fiction editors. Needs ethnic, experimental, fantasy, historical, mainstream, literary. "We are far more interested in quality than in genre. Nothing sentimental as opposed to genuinely moving, nor self-conscious style at the expense of human truth." **Buys 6 mss/year.** Send complete ms. Length: 200-5,000 words. **Pays $10/printed page.**

Poetry Contact: Don Morrill and Martha Serpas, poetry editors. Needs avant-garde, free verse, haiku, light verse, traditional. No greeting card verse, hackneyed, sing-song, rhyme-for-the-sake-of-rhyme. **Buys 45 poems/year.** Submit maximum 10 poems. Length: 2-225 lines.

Tips "Send a clear cover letter stating previous experience or background. Our editorial staff considers submissions between September and December for publication in the following year."

N ⊕ THAT'S LIFE! FAST FICTION

Pacific Magazines, 35-51 Mitchell St., McMahons Point NSW 2060 Australia. E-mail: fictionguidelines@pacificmags.com.au. Quarterly magazine packed with romantic stories, spine-tinglers, humorous reads, tales with a twist and more. Accepts queries by mail (no emails). 8-12 weeks

- "If your story has not been returned after 10 weeks, please send another copy with a letter explaining that it has been sent before."

Fiction "That's Life! Fast Fiction is looking for humorous, positive contemporary stories of 700-2,800 words with a strong plot. If the story has a twist it should arise from the story, rather than from a detail kept from the reader. To check your twist, imagine your story were being made into a film - would the surprise still work?" Needs adventure, horror, humorous, mystery, romance, suspense. 700-2,800/words

Tips "Read several issues of the magazines to get the flavour of the type of fiction we publish. Please avoid straightforward romance ei. boy meets girl and they live happily ever after. Avoid sci-fi and stories narrated by animals or babies. That's Life! is a family magazine. We normally write in chronological order, so keep events in sequence and avoid 'jumping' around time slots, as this can be confusing. Please bear in mind that if your story is themed then it needs to be sent to us about 3 months in advance of the magazine in which it needs to appear."

THE HELIX

Central Connecticut State University's Literary Magazine, Central Connecticut State University, 1615 Stanley St., New Britain CT 06050-4010. (860)832-2740. Fax: (860)832-2784. E-mail: helixmagazine@hotmail.com. Website: clubs.ccsu.edu/helix/. **100% freelance written**. Semiannual magazine covering Creative Writing. *The Helix* magazine is a creative publication funded through the Central connecticut State University's English Department. The magazine has attracted photographers, illustrators, writers, and other artists from across the U.S. and Europe. Magazine editions are distributed to students and published artists. Estab. 1855. Circ. 1,000. Byline sometimes given. Copies. No kill fee. Publishes ms an average of 6 months after acceptance. Buys Writer retains all rights. rights. Editorial lead time 1 & ½ months. Submit seasonal material 1 & ½ months in advance. Accepts queries by e-mail. Accepts previously published material. Accepts simultaneous submissions. Responds in 6 weeks to queries. Responds in 2 months to mss. Sample copy available online. Guidelines available online.

Nonfiction Contact: Michelle Hannon, editor; Dr. Jack Heitner, General Ed. *The Helix* accepts submissions all year round, and prints semi-annually in December and April. The deadline for the December issue is October 20th. Needs book excerpts, essays, expose, general interest, humor, interview, personal experience, photo feature, travel. Pornography. **Buys 50 mss/year mss/year.** Send complete ms. Length: no min.-2,500 words. **Pays 0 for assigned articles. Pays 0 for unsolicited articles.**

Photos Send photos Captions required. Reviews GIF/JPEG files. Artist retains all rights.

Columns/Departments Contact: Michelle Hannon, Dr. Jack Heitner. English Department: Creative writing—fiction, nonfiction, poetry, haiku, etc., 500 words. 50 mss/year Query with published clips or send complete ms. **Pay copies.**

Fiction Contact: Michelle Hannon, editor; Dr. Jack Heitner, general ed. Needs adventure, cond novels, confession, ethnic, experimental, fantasy, historical, horror, humorous, mainstream, mystery, novel concepts, religious, romance, science fiction, serialized, slice-of-life vignettes, suspense, western. Pornography. **Buys 50 mss/year mss/year.** Query with published clips or send complete ms. Length: no min.-2,500 words. **Pays copies.**

Poetry Contact: Michelle Hannon, Dr. Jack Heitner. Needs avant-garde, free verse, haiku, light verse, traditional. **Buys 50 poems/year. poems/year.** Submit maximum The Helix will only publish 3 poems by a single author per issue poems. Length: 350 lines.

Fillers Contact: Michelle Hannon, Dr. Jack Heitner. Needs short humor. Length: 2,500 words.

Tips To be included in *The Helix* magazine, submit work by email to: helixmagazine@hotmail.com before Oct. 20th. Please provide a brief biographical note and contact information. Those authors selected will be contacted in Dec.

$ ⊘ THEMA

Box 8747, Metairie LA 70011-8747. E-mail: thema@cox.net. Website: members.cox.net/thema. **100% freelance written**. Triannual magazine covering a different theme for each issue. Upcoming themes for SASE. *"Thema* is designed to stimulate creative thinking by challenging writers with unusual themes, such as 'The Box Under the Bed' and 'Put It In Your Pocket, Lillian'. Appeals to writers, teachers of creative writing, and general reading audience." Estab. 1988. Circ. 350. Byline given. Pays on acceptance. No kill fee. Publishes ms an average of within 6 months after acceptance. Buys one-time rights. Accepts queries by mail. Accepts previously published material. Accepts simultaneous submissions. Responds in 1 week to queries. Responds in 5 months to mss. Sample copy for $10. Guidelines for #10 SASE.

Reprints "Send typed manuscript with rights for sale noted and information about when and where the material previously appeared." Pays the same amount paid for original

Fiction Contact: Virginia Howard, editor. Needs adventure, ethnic, experimental, fantasy, historical, humorous, mainstream, mystery, novel concepts, religious, science fiction, slice-of-life vignettes, suspense, western, contemporary, sports, prose poem. No erotica. **Buys 30 mss/year.** fewer than 6,000 words preferred **Pays $10-25.**

Poetry Needs avant-garde, free verse, haiku, light verse, traditional. No erotica. **Buys 27 poems/year.** Submit maximum 3 poems. Length: 4-50 lines. **Pays $10**.

Tips "Be familiar with the themes. Don't submit unless you have an upcoming theme in mind. Specify the target theme on the first page of your manuscript or in a cover letter. Put your name on first page of manuscript only. (All submissions are judged in blind review after the deadline for a specified issue.) Most open to fiction and poetry. Don't be hasty when you consider a theme—mull it over and let it ferment in your mind. We appreciate interpretations that are carefully constructed, clever, subtle, and well thought out."

THE MACGUFFIN

Schoolcraft College, 18600 Haggerty Rd., Livonia MI 48152-2696. (734)462-4400, ext. 5327. E-mail: macguffin@schoolcraft.edu. Website: schoolcraft.edu/macguffin. Magazine covering the best new work in contemporary poetry, prose and visual art. Our purpose is to encourage, support and enhance the literary arts in the Schoolcraft College community, the region, the state, and the nation. By fulfilling our role as a national literary journal, we exist to bring national and international prestige to Schoolcraft College. We also sponsor annual literary events and give voice to deserving new writers to share their works with a diverse readership. No kill fee. Buys all rights, buys All rights revert to authors. rights. Accepts queries by mail, e-mail. Responds in 2-4 months to mss. Guidelines available.

Nonfiction Translations are welcome and should be accompanied by a copy of the original text. Translators are responsible for author's permission.

Photos Embedded images are not accessible to the page layout software. EPS or TIFF saved at 300 dpi for photos, and 600 dpi-1,200 dpi for line art. Reviews Original slides, photos, artwork.

Fiction Contact: Elizabeth Kircos. No obvious pornographic material. Length: 5,000 words.

Poetry Needs avant-garde, free verse, light verse, traditional. Prose should be typed and double-spaced. Include word count. One submission per envelope. Poetry should be typed, single-spaced, only one per page. There are no subject biases. Submit maximum 5 poems.

Tips Also sponsors the Poet Hunt Contest. See contest rules online. Do not staple work. Include name, email, address, and the page no. on each page. For email submissions, submit each work in a separate page as a Word doc. attachment. Include SASE, IRCs for reply only. Specify if you want return of your work with sufficient postage.

N THE VIEW FROM HERE/FRONT VIEW SECTION

E-mail: submit.your.words@gmail.com. Website: www.viewfromheremagazine.com. **Contact:** Sydne Nash, editor. "Monthly print/weekly online website covering prose, fiction, and nonfiction essays of personal appeal with a touch of deliberate nonsense combined with editorial comments designed to make you think. We accept only original written work, except by specific invitation. We're a bohemian eclectic online and print zine of great surprise and quality. We don't promote hatred, racism or illegal activities." Authors receive print contributor's copy. No kill fee.
Poetry Submit maximum 3-5 poems.
Tips "Please review our online version, then carefully read and follow our guidelines to submit your work. We accept attachments. Submissions in the body of the email are welcome."

THIN AIR

P.O. Box 6032, Flagstaff AZ 86011. Website: www.thinairmagazine.com. Publishes contemporary voices for a literary-minded audience. Estab. 1995. Circ. 500. Pays with contributor copies. No kill fee. Publishes ms an average of 6-9 months after acceptance. Buys first North American serial rights. Accepts queries by mail, e-mail. Accepts simultaneous submissions. Guidelines available online.
Nonfiction Creative nonfiction. Submit cover letter, bio, and up to 25 pages of your ms.
Photos We accept both b&w and color art and photography. We accept 8x10 photographs of your art. Please do not send slides or negatives.
Fiction Needs cond novels, ethnic, experimental, mainstream. No children's/juvenile, horror, romance, erotica. We would like to see more intelligent comedy.
Poetry Submit maximum 6 poems.

THINK JOURNAL

Reason Publishing LLC, P.O. Box 454, Downingtown PA 19335. E-mail: thinkjournal@yahoo.com. Website: http://web.me.com/christineyurick/think_journal/home_page.html. **100% freelance written**. Quarterly magazine. "*Think Journal* is a quarterly review of poetry, short stories, novel excerpts, and essays. It is for writers who, paraphrasing Aristotle, represent things as they might be/ought to be. The theme of the journal is philosophical, an outlet for poets who live by a certain aesthetic philosophy, one that focuses on form, structure, plot, reason and rationality. Open to different styles and forms of work as long as it has structure and thought behind it." Estab. 2008. Byline given. Publication is payment, along with 1 free contributor's copy. No kill fee. Publishes ms an average of 3-6 months after acceptance. Buys one-time rights. Editorial lead time 3 months. Submit seasonal material 3 months in advance. Accepts queries by mail. Responds in 2-4 weeks to queries. Responds in 1-2 months to mss. Backcopy for cost: $6. Guidelines for sae.
Nonfiction Needs essays, Letter to editor. We do not want ranting, profanity; would only like well thought-out essays that shed light on an intellectual or philosophical topic. Send complete ms. Length: under 2,500 words.
Fiction Needs novel concepts, "Short stories on any topic as long as there is an integration of content and style. We do not want work that doesn't *move*, that doesn't have anything to say. A piece of work that is written beautifully and says nothing will not have a place here." Send complete ms. Length: 2,000-3,000 words.
Poetry Needs free verse, traditional, "The editor is more inclined to publish traditional, formalist work. Free verse poems need to have some underlying structure to be considered. I do not want avant-garde, originality for the sake of originality, words without any connection behind them, work that says and contributes nothing. I am looking for work that makes the reader *think*."
Tips "Submissions are welcome from rational thinkers who believe that words have meaning, and that when you deal with words, you are dealing with the mind. This journal is for those who think. In order to do this, one must first have an 'I.' The basic literary values that will be considered are: content and meaning; words that are logically conceived and arranged; evidence of an active imagination; structure; integration of emotional and intellectual facets. The central criterion for acceptance is merit, which will be judged based on two aspects: content and literary artistry."

THORNY LOCUST

TL Press, P.O. Box 32631, Kansas City MO 64171. (816)501-4178. "*Thorny Locust* is a literary journal produced quarterly in a dusty corner of the publisher's hermitage. We are interested in poetry, fiction, and artwork with some bite (e.g., satire, epigrams, well-structured tirades, black humor, and bleeding heart cynicism.) Absolutely no natural or artificial sweeteners, unless they're the sugar-coating on a strychnine tablet. We are not interested in polemics, gratuitous grotesques, somber surrealism, weeping melancholy, or hate-mongering. To rewrite Jack Conroy, 'We prefer polished vigor to crude banality.'" Estab. 1993. Circ. 200. Pays with contributor copies. No kill fee. Publishes ms an average of 3-4 months after acceptance. Buys one-time rights. Accepts simultaneous submissions.

Photos Black and white line drawings, cartoons, and photographs.

Fiction No restrictions on style; maximum 1,500 words.

Poetry "Formal and casual, conventional and experimental verse are equally welcome. No hard restrictions on length, but we're unlikely to take anything over 2 manuscript pages."

Tips "We publish more poetry than fiction."

$ $ THE THREEPENNY REVIEW

P.O. Box 9131, Berkeley CA 94709. (510)849-4545. Website: www.threepennyreview.com. **100% freelance written. Works with small number of new/unpublished writers each year.** Quarterly tabloid. We are a general interest, national literary magazine with coverage of politics, the visual arts, and the performing arts as well. Estab. 1980. Circ. 9,000. Byline given. Pays on acceptance. Publishes ms an average of 1 year after acceptance. Buys first North American serial rights. Responds in 1 month to queries. Responds in 2 months to mss. Sample copy for $12 or online Guidelines available online.

- Does not read mss from September to December.

Nonfiction Needs essays, expose, historical, personal experience, book, film, theater, dance, music, and art reviews. **Buys 40 mss/year.** Send complete ms. Length: 1,500-4,000 words. **Pays $400.**

Fiction Contact: Wendy Lesser, editor. No fragmentary, sentimental fiction. **Buys 10 mss/year.** Send complete ms. Length: 800-4,000 words. **Pays $400 per poem or Table Talk piece.**

Poetry Needs free verse, traditional. No poems without capital letters or poems without a discernible subject. **Buys 30 poems/year.** Submit maximum 5 poems. **Pays $200.**

Tips Nonfiction (political articles, memoirs, reviews) is most open to freelancers.

TIME OF SINGING

A Magazine of Christian Poetry, P.O. Box 149, Conneaut Lake PA 16316. E-mail: timesing@zoominternet.net. Website: www.timeofsinging.bizland.com. **100% freelance written**. Quarterly booklet. *Time of Singing* publishes 'Christian' poetry in the widest sense, but prefers 'literary type,' not greeting card verse, which has valid but different purposes. Welcome forms, fresh rhyme, well-crafted free verse. Like writers who take chances, who don't feel the need to tie everything up neatly. Estab. 1958. Circ. 250. Byline given. Publishes ms an average of within 1 year after acceptance. Buys first North American serial rights, buys first rights, buys one-time rights, buys second serial (reprint) rights. Editorial lead time 6 months. Submit seasonal material 6 months in advance. Accepts previously published material. Accepts simultaneous submissions. Responds in 3 months to mss. Sample copy for $4/each or 2 for $6. Guidelines for SASE or on Web site.

Poetry Needs free verse, haiku, light verse, traditional. Does not want sermons that rhyme or greeting card type poetry. **Buys 200 poems/year.** Submit maximum 5 poems. Length: 3-60 lines.

Tips Read widely, dead white males and contemporary, 'Christian' and otherwise, and study the craft. Helpful to get honest critique of your work. Cover letter not necessary. Your poems speak for themselves.

$ $ $ TIN HOUSE

McCormack Communications, Box 10500, Portland OR 97210. (503)274-4393. Fax: (503)222-1154. Website: www.tinhouse.com. **Contact:** Win McCormack, Editor-in-Chief; Holly Macarthur, Managing Editor. **90% freelance written**. "We are a general interest literary quarterly. Our watchword is quality. Our audience includes people interested in literature in all its aspects, from the mundane to the exalted." Estab. 1998. Circ. 11,000. Byline given. Pays on publication. No kill fee. Publishes ms an average of 6 months after acceptance. Buys first North American serial rights, buys anthology rights. Editorial lead time 6 months. Submit seasonal material 6 months in advance. Accepts queries by mail. Accepts simultaneous submissions. Responds in 6 weeks to queries. Responds in 3 months to mss. Sample copy for $15. Guidelines available online.

Nonfiction Needs book excerpts, essays, interview, personal experience. Send complete ms. 5,000 words maximum **Pays $50-800 for assigned articles. Pays $50-500 for unsolicited articles.** Sometimes pays expenses of writers on assignment.

Columns/Departments Lost and Found (mini-reviews of forgotten or underappreciated books), up to 500 words; Readable Feasts (fiction or nonfiction literature with recipes), 2,000-3,000 words; Pilgrimage (journey to a personally significant place, especially literary), 2,000-3,000 words. 15-20 Send complete ms. **Pays $50-500.**

Fiction Contact: Rob Spillman, fiction editor. Needs experimental, mainstream, novel concepts, literary. **Buys 15-20 mss/year.** Send complete ms. 5,000 words maximum **Pays $200-800.**

Poetry Contact: Brenda Shaunessy, poetry editor. Needs avant-garde, free verse, traditional. "No prose masquerading as poetry." **Buys 40 poems/year.** Submit maximum 5 poems. **Pays $50-150.**

Tips "Remember to send a SASE with your submission."

TRIQUARTERLY

Northwestern University Press, Northwestern University, 629 Noyes St., Evanston IL 60208-4302. (847)491-7614. Fax: (847)467-2096. E-mail: triquarterly@northwestern.edu. Website: www.triquarterly.org. Triannual magazine covering unsolicited fiction, poetry, and occasionally literary essays and graphic art. We are committed to presenting the finest works of literature and graphic art for discerning readers. By publishing a combination of general issues and occasional special issues such as *for Vladimir Nabokev on his seventieth birthday*, *TriQuarterly* quickly became one of the most widely admired and important literary journals. Estab. 1958. No kill fee. Responds in 3 months to mss. Guidelines available online.

Nonfiction Needs essays, Translation. We do not usually publish philosophical essays.

Tips Work may be submitted without query during our reading period, Oct. 1 to Feb. 28. Mss. submitted between April 1 and Sept. 30 will be returned unreader. All work submitted must be unpublished anywhere. This also applies to translations for which translators must get permission from the author to publish. All mss. should be typed, doubled (poetry may be singled-spaced). Mail to Editors, include SASE.

UPSTREET

Ledgetop Publishing, P.O. Box 105, Richmond MA 01254-0105. (413)441-9702. E-mail: submissions@upstreet-mag.org. Website: www.upstreet-mag.org. **99% freelance written**. Annual magazine covering literary fiction, nonfiction and poetry. Estab. 2005. Circ. 4,000. Byline given. Pays on publication. Publishes ms an average of 6 months after acceptance. Buys first North American serial rights. Editorial lead time 6 months. Accepts queries by e-mail. Accepts simultaneous submissions. Responds in 2 weeks to queries. Responds in 6 months to mss. Sample copy for $12.50. Guidelines by email.

Nonfiction Needs book excerpts, essays, personal experience, literary, personal essay/memoir, lyric essay. Does not want journalism, religious, technical, anything but literary nonfiction. **Buys 8 mss/year.** Send complete ms. Length: 5,000 words.

Fiction Needs experimental, mainstream, novel concepts, quality literary fiction. Does not want run-of-the-mill genre, children's, anything but literary. **Buys 12 mss/year.** Send complete ms. Length: 5,000 words.

Poetry Needs avant-garde, free verse, traditional. Quality is only criterion. **Buys 20 poems/year.** Submit maximum 3 poems.

Tips Get sample copy, submit electronically, and follow guidelines.

U.S. 1 WORKSHEETS

U.S. 1 Poets' Cooperative, U.S. 1 Worksheets, P.O. Box 127, Kingston NJ 08528-0127. E-mail: k-jpalka@comcast.net. Website: www.us1poets.com. Annual journal covering works from U.S. 1 Poets' Cooperative, along with the best works of poetry we receive. "We are looking for well-crafted poetry with a focused point of view. Representative authors: Baron Wormser, Alicia Ostriker, Richard Jones, Bj Ward, Lois Harrod." Estab. 1972. Circ. 500. Accepts simultaneous submissions. Responds in 3-6 months to mss. Guidelines available online.

Fiction "We no longer consider fiction, with the exception of prose poems."

Poetry Submit maximum 5 poems. Submit no more than 7 pages.

Tips "Mss are accepted from April 15-June 30 and are read by rotating editors from the cooperative. Send us something unusual, something we haven't seen before, but make sure it's poetry. Proofread carefully."

$ $ VERBATIM

The Language Quarterly, Word, Inc., P.O. Box 597302, Chicago IL 60659. (800)897-3006. E-mail: editor@verbatimmag.com. Website: www.verbatimmag.com. **75-80% freelance written**. Quarterly magazine covering language and linguistics. *Verbatim* is the only magazine of language and linguistics for the lay person. Estab. 1974. Circ. 1,600. Byline given. Pays on publication. No kill fee. Publishes ms an average of 6-9 months after acceptance. Buys all rights. Editorial lead time 3 months. Submit seasonal material 6 months in advance. Accepts queries by mail, e-mail. Responds in 3 weeks to queries. Responds in 2 months to mss. Sample copy for sae with 9x12 envelope and 6 First-Class stamps. Guidelines available online.

Nonfiction Needs essays, humor, personal experience. Does not want puns or overly cranky prescriptivism. **Buys 24-28 mss/year.** Query. **Pays $25-400 for assigned articles. Pays $25-300 for unsolicited articles.**

Poetry We only publish poems explicitly about language. Poems written in language not enough. **Buys 4-6 poems/year.** Submit maximum 3 poems. Length: 3-75 lines. **Pays $25-50.**

Tips Humorously write about an interesting language, language topic, or jargon. Also, when querying, include 3-4 lines of biographical information about yourself.

VERBSAP

Concise Prose. Enough Said, No public address known., E-mail: editor@verbsap.com. Website covering the best in minimalist prose writing. We accept short stories, flash fiction, creative nonfiction and novel excerpts that stand along. We look for stark, elegant, concise prose. Good: Stories with strong plots and vivid characters; clarity; research; originality; focus; stories that make us weep or laugh; depictions of human frailty or resilience; absurdity. No kill fee. Buys one-time rights, buys Electronic Rights (60 days) rights. All material published online will be archived. Responds in 2 months to mss. Guidelines available online.

Nonfiction Needs interview, Creative. Length: 3,000 words.

Fiction Needs novel concepts, (that stand alone). No fictionalized violence or depictions of drug use; thinly-veiled rewrites of CSI or Law & Order episodes; stories comprised mainly of dialogue or internal monologues;

fables; the torturing of small animals; strong odors; bodily fluids; surprise endings.
Tips We accept submissions during posted reading periods. The next dates will be available shortly. Paste your work in the body of an email. Write 'Submission,' the genre and your name in the subject line. Include your name, email address, and a brief bio. Note that *VerbSap* accepts only original, unpublished work. See Submission guidelines. Query if you haven't heard back in 2 months.

VERSAL

The literary journal of Amsterdam, wordsinhere, Postbus 3865, Amsterdam 1001AR The Netherlands. E-mail: versal@wordsinhere.com. Website: www.wordsinhere.com. Annual website. "We look for the urgent, involved, and unexpected, and are particularly interested in innovative forms and translocal writing." Estab. 2002. Circ. 750. Pays on publication. No kill fee. Publishes ms an average of 3-4 months after acceptance. Buys first rights. Accepts queries by e-mail. Accepts simultaneous submissions. Responds in <1 week to queries. Responds in <2 months to mss. Sample copy available online. Guidelines available.
Nonfiction Query.
Fiction Contact: Robert Glick, editor. Needs experimental, mainstream, novel concepts, Flash fiction, prose poetry. **Buys 10 mss/yr. mss/year. pays in copies.**
Poetry Contact: Megan M. Garr, editor. Needs avant-garde, free verse. **Buys 35/yr. poems/year.** Submit maximum 5 poems. **pays in copies.**
Tips "We ask that all writers interested in submitting work first purchase a copy (available from our website) to get an idea of *Versal*'s personality. All unsolicited submissions must be submitted through our online submission system. The link to this system is live during the submission period, which is Sept. 15-Jan. 15 each year."

$ $ VESTAL REVIEW

A flash fiction magazine, 2609 Dartmouth Dr., Vestal NY 13850. E-mail: submissions@vestalreview.net. Website: www.vestalreview.net. Semi-annual print magazine specializing in flash fiction. We accept only e-mail submissions. Circ. 1,500. Pays on publication. No kill fee. Publishes ms an average of 3-4 months after acceptance. Buys first North American serial rights, buys electronic rights. Accepts queries by e-mail. Accepts simultaneous submissions. Responds in 1 week to queries. Responds in 3 months to mss. Guidelines available online.
Fiction Needs ethnic, horror, mainstream, speculative fiction. Does not read new submissions in January, June, July, and December. All submissions received during these months will be returned unopened. Length: 50-500 words. **Pays 3-10¢/word and 1 contributor's copy; additional copies $10 (plus postage).**
Tips "We like literary fiction, with a plot, that doesn't waste words. Don't send jokes masked as stories."

$ HAYDEN'S FERRY REVIEW

Arizona State University, Box 875002, Arizona State University, Tempe AZ 85287-5002. (480)965-1337. Fax: (480)727-0820. E-mail: hfr@asu.edu. Website: www.haydensferryreview.org. **85% freelance written.** Semiannual magazine. "*Hayden's Ferry Review* publishes the best quality fiction, poetry, and creative nonfiction from new, emerging, and established writers." Estab. 1986. Circ. 1,300. Byline given. Pays on publication. No kill fee. Publishes ms an average of 6 months after acceptance. Buys first North American serial rights. Editorial lead time 5 months. Accepts simultaneous submissions. Responds in 1 week or less to e-mail queries. Responds in 3-4 months to mss. Sample copy for $7.50. Guidelines available online.

- No electronic submissions.

Nonfiction Needs essays, interview, personal experience. **Buys 2 mss/year.** Send complete ms. Open **Pays $25-100.**
Photos Send photos Reviews slides. Offers $25/photo. Buys one time rights.
Fiction Contact: Editors change every 1-2 years. Needs ethnic, experimental, humorous, slice-of-life vignettes, contemporary, prose poem. **Buys 10 mss/year.** Send complete ms. Open **Pays $25-100.**
Poetry Needs avant-garde, free verse, haiku, light verse, traditional. **Buys 60 poems/year.** Submit maximum 6 poems. Open **Pays $25-100.**

$ VIRGINIA QUARTERLY REVIEW

University of Virginia, One West Range, P.O. Box 400223, Charlottesville VA 22904-4223. (434)924-3124. Fax: (434)924-1397. Website: www.vqronline.org. Quarterly magazine. A national journal of literature and thought. A lay, intellectual audience; people who are not out-and-out scholars but who are interested in ideas and literature. Estab. 1925. Circ. 7,000. Byline given. Pays on publication. No kill fee. Publishes ms an average of 4 months after acceptance. Buys first rights. Editorial lead time 6 months. Submit seasonal material 6 months in advance. Responds in 4 months to mss. Sample copy for $14. Guidelines available online.
Nonfiction Needs book excerpts, essays, general interest, historical, reportage, travel. Send complete ms. Length: 2,000-7,000 words. **Pays $.20/word**
Fiction Needs ethnic, mainstream, mystery, novel excerpts, serialized novels. Send complete ms. Length: 3,000-7,000 words. **Pays $100/page maximum.**

Poetry Submit maximum 5 poems. **Pays $5/line.**
Tips "Submissions only accepted online."

$ VIRTUE IN THE ARTS

P.O. Box 11081, Glendale CA 91226. E-mail: info@virtueinthearts.com. Website: www.virtueinthearts.com. **50% freelance written**. Semiannual magazine covering virtues. Each publication features short stories, articles, poetry and artwork relating to a different virtue each time (such as honesty, compassion, trustworthiness, etc.). Estab. 2006. Byline given. Pays on publication. Publishes ms an average of 6 months after acceptance. Buys one-time rights. Editorial lead time 6 months. Submit seasonal material 1 month in advance. Accepts queries by mail, e-mail. Accepts previously published material. Accepts simultaneous submissions. Responds in 6 months to mss. Guidelines by email.
Nonfiction Needs essays. Each issue has a theme. See writer's guidelines for the current theme. Does not want articles that show the virtue in a negative light. **Buys 2 mss/year.** Send complete ms. Length: 100-400 words. **Pays $7.**
Photos Send photos Reviews digital images. Offers $7/photo. Buys one time rights.
Fiction Fiction shedding a positive light on the current theme (a virtue) in an entertaining way. **Buys 2 mss/year.** Send complete ms. Length: 300-1,500 words. **Pays $7.**
Poetry Needs avant-garde, free verse, haiku, light verse, traditional. Poetry needs to reflect the current theme (virtue). Submit maximum 5 poems. Length: 4-32 lines. **Pays $7.**
Tips We're looking for material that promotes virtue. If you promote virtue, you get virtue. Find out the current deadline and the current virtue, then send us your submission.

$ VISIONS-INTERNATIONAL

Black Buzzard Press, 3503 Ferguson Lane, Austin TX 78754. (512)674-3977. **95% freelance written**. Magazine published 2 times/year featuring poetry, essays and reviews. Estab. 1979. Circ. 750. Byline given. Pays on publication. No kill fee. Publishes ms an average of 6 months after acceptance. Buys first North American serial rights. Editorial lead time 1 month. Accepts queries by mail. Responds in 3 weeks to queries. Responds in 2 months to mss. Sample copy for $4.95. Guidelines for #10 SASE.
Nonfiction Needs essays, by assignment after query reviews. Query. 1 page maximum. **Pays $10 and complimentary copies.**
Columns/Departments
Poetry Needs avant-garde, free verse, traditional. "No sentimental, religious, scurrilous, sexist, racist, amateurish, or over 3 pages." **Buys 110 poems/year.** Length: 2-120 lines.
Tips "Know your craft. We are not a magazine for amateurs. We also are interested in translation from modern poets writing in any language into English. No e-mail submissions please."

WASHINGTON SQUARE

Creative Writing Program, New York University, 58 West 10th St., New York NY 10011. E-mail: washingtonsquarereview@gmail.com. Website: www.cwp.fas.nyu.edu/object/cwp.wsr. Semiannual magazine covering fiction and poetry by emerging and established writers. *Washington Square* is a nonprofit, innovative, nationally-distributed literary journal edited and produced by students of the NYU Graduate Creative Writing Program. Also, it sponsors the Washington Square competition which is judged by eminent poets and writers and hosts an annual benefit reading in NYC. *WS* also includes transcriptions of New Salon interviews. A new portfolio provides space for visual artists and photographers. No kill fee. Accepts queries by mail. Accepts simultaneous submissions.

- The magazine now has bold graphic covers and fresh, spare style.

Nonfiction Accepts translations (with renewed focus, presenting readers with international writers in their original languages and English.) Needs interview, Translation.
Fiction 1 short story up to 20 pages.
Poetry Submit maximum 5 poems. 10 pages total
Tips Address submissions to either Fiction/Poetry/Internatonal Editor. We invite you to enter an annual competition in Fiction and Poetry ($500 prize and publication in forthcoming issue). Reading period: August 1 through March 15. Send with SASE for reply and a cover letter with name, address, phone no., email address and title of submission.

$ $ WEBER STUDIES

Voices and Viewpoints of the Contemporary West, Weber State University, 1214 University Circle, Ogden UT 84408-1214. (801)626-6616 or (801)626-6473. E-mail: weberjournal@weber.edu. Website: weberstudies.weber.edu. **70% freelance written**. Magazine and online text archive published 3 times/year covering preservation of and access to wilderness, environmental cooperation, insight derived from living in the West, cultural diversity, changing federal involvement in the region, women and the West, implications of population growth, the contributions of individuals (scholars, artists and community leaders), a sense of place. We seek works that provide insight into the environment and culture (both broadly defined) of the contemporary western US.

We look for good writing that reveals human nature, as well as natural environment. Estab. 1981. Circ. 800-1,000. Byline given. Pays on publication. No kill fee. Publishes ms an average of 6-12 months after acceptance. Buys one-time rights, buys electronic rights. (copyrights revert to authors after publication) Editorial lead time 6 months. Submit seasonal material 6 months in advance. Accepts queries by mail, e-mail, phone. Accepts simultaneous submissions. Responds in 1 month to queries. Responds in 6-9 months to mss. Sample copy for $8. Guidelines for #10 SASE, on website or by e-mail.

Nonfiction Needs essays, historical, interview, opinion, personal experience, photo feature. **Buys 20-25 mss/year.** Send complete ms. Length: 5,000 words. **Pays $150-300, plus 1 contributor copy and 1-year subscription.**

Photos State availability Captions, identification of subjects, model releases required. Reviews 4X6 prints, 4X6 GIF/JPEG files at 300 dpi. Negotiates pay individually. Buys one time rights.

Columns/Departments Send complete ms. **Pays $100-200.**

Fiction Needs adventure, ethnic, historical, humorous, mainstream, novel concepts, religious, slice-of-life vignettes, western. Send complete ms. Length: 5,000 words. **Pays $150-300.**

Poetry Buys 15-20 sets of poems/year. Submit maximum 6 poems. **Pays $100-150.**

$ WEST BRANCH

Bucknell Hall, Bucknell University, Lewisburg PA 17837-2029. (570)577-1853. Fax: (570)577-1885. E-mail: westbranch@bucknell.edu. Website: www.bucknell.edu/westbranch. Semiannual literary magazine. *West Branch* is an aesthetic conversation between the traditional and the innovative in poetry, fiction and nonfiction. It brings writers, new and established, to the rooms where they will be heard, and where they will, no doubt, rearrange the furniture. Byline given. Pays on publication. No kill fee. Buys first North American serial rights. Accepts queries by mail. Sample copy for $3. Guidelines available online.

Nonfiction Needs essays, general interest, literary. **Buys 4-5 mss/year.** Send complete ms. **Pays $20-100 ($10/page).**

Fiction Needs novel concepts, short stories. No genre fiction. **Buys 10-12 mss/year.** Send complete ms. **Pays $20-100 ($10/page).**

Poetry Needs free verse. **Buys 30-40 poems/year.** Submit maximum 6 poems. **Pays $20-100 ($10/page).**

Tips Please send only 1 submission at a time and do not send another work until you have heard about the first. Send no more than 6 poems or 30 pages of prose at once. We accept simultaneous submissions if they are clearly marked as such, and if we are notified immediately upon acceptance elsewhere. Manuscripts must be accompanied by the customary return materials; we cannot respond by e-mail or postcard, except to foreign submissions. All manuscripts should be typed, with the author's name on each page; prose must be double-spaced. We recommend that you acquaint yourself with the magazine before submitting.

$ WEST COAST LINE

A Journal of Contemporary Writing & Criticism, West Coast Review Publishing Society, 2027 E. Annex, 8888 University Dr., Simon Fraser University, Burnaby BC V5A 1S6 Canada. (604)291-4287. Fax: (604)291-4622. E-mail: wcl@sfu.ca. Website: www.sfu.ca/west-coast-line. Triannual magazine of contemporary literature and criticism. Estab. 1990. Circ. 500. Pays on publication. No kill fee. Buys one-time rights. Editorial lead time 4 months. Accepts queries by mail, e-mail. Responds in up to 6 months to queries. Responds in up to 6 months to mss. Sample copy for $10. Guidelines for SASE (US must include IRC).

Nonfiction Needs essays, literary/scholarly/critical, experimental prose. No journalistic articles or articles dealing with nonliterary material. **Buys 8-10 mss/year.** Send complete ms. Length: 1,000-5,000 words. **Pays $8/page, 2 contributor's copies and a 1-year subscription.**

Fiction Needs experimental, novel concepts. **Buys 3-6 mss/year.** Send complete ms. Length: 1,000-7,000 words. **Pays $8/page.**

Poetry Needs avant-garde. No light verse, traditional. **Buys 10-15 poems/year.** Submit maximum maximum 5-6 poems. **Pays $8/page.**

Tips Submissions must be either scholarly or formally innovative. Contributors should be familiar with current literary trends in Canada and the US. Scholars should be aware of current schools of theory. All submissions should be accompanied by a brief cover letter; essays should be formatted according to the MLA guide. The publication is not divided into departments. We accept innovative poetry, fiction, experimental prose, and scholarly essays.

$ WESTERN HUMANITIES REVIEW

University of Utah, English Department, 255 S. Central Campus Dr., Room 3500, Salt Lake City UT 84112-0494. (801)581-6070. Fax: (801)585-5167. E-mail: whr@mail.hum.utah.edu. Website: www.hum.utah.edu/whr. tri-annual magazine for educated readers. Estab. 1947. Circ. 1,000. Pays on publication. No kill fee. Publishes ms an average of 1 year after acceptance. Buys one-time rights. Accepts simultaneous submissions. Sample copy for $10. Guidelines available online.

- Reads mss September 1-May 1. Mss sent outside these dates will be returned unread.

Nonfiction Contact: Barry Weller, editor-in-chief. Authoritative, readable articles on literature, art, philosophy, current events, history, religion, and anything in the humanities. Interdisciplinary articles encouraged. Departments on films and books. **Buys 10-12 unsolicited mss/year.** Send complete ms. **Pays $5/published page.**
Fiction Contact: Karen Brennan and Robin Hemley, fiction editors. Needs experimental, any type. Does not want genre (romance, sci-fi, etc.). **Buys 8-12 mss/year.** Send complete ms. Length: 5,000 words. **Pays $5/ published page (when funds available).**
Poetry Contact: Richard Howard, poetry editor.
Tips Because of changes in our editorial staff, we urge familiarity with recent issues of the magazine. Material will be returned without comment. We do not publish writer's guidelines because we think that the magazine itself conveys an accurate picture of our requirements. Please, no e-mail submissions.

WHISKEY ISLAND MAGAZINE

Dept. of Student Life, Cleveland State University, 2121 Euclid Ave. MC 106, Cleveland OH 44115-2214. E-mail: whiskeyisland@papmail.csuohio.edu. Website: csuohio.edu/poetrycenter. Semiannual magazine covering creative writing, original poetry, fiction, nonfiction, and art submissions year round. This is a nonprofit literary magazine that has been published (in one form or another) by students of Cleveland State University for over 30 years. Also features the Annual Student Creative Writing Contest ($5000-$400-$250). No kill fee. Accepts queries by mail, e-mail. Accepts simultaneous submissions. Responds in 6 months to mss.
Tips See submissions page. Include SASE. Wait at least a year before submitting again.

WILLOW REVIEW

College of Lake County Publications, College of Lake County, 19351 W. Washington St., Grayslake IL 60030-1198. (847)543-2956. E-mail: com426@clcillinois.edu. Website: www.clcillinois.edu/community/willowreview.asp. Magazine covering poems, short fiction, creative nonfiction, reviews of books written by Midwestern writers or published by Midwestern presses. The editors award prizes for best poetry and prose in the issue. Prize awards vary contingent on the current year's budget but normally ranges from $100-400. There is no reading fee or separate application for these prizes. All accepted mss. are eligible. No kill fee. Accepts queries by mail. Guidelines available.
Nonfiction Needs essays, Book Reviews by Midwestern writers or presses. Length: 7,000 words.
Fiction Accepts short fiction.
Tips Include SASE. No email submissions, please.

$ WINDSOR REVIEW

A Journal of the Arts, Dept. of English, University of Windsor, Windsor ON N9B 3P4 Canada. (519)253-3000. Fax: (519)971-3676. E-mail: uwrevu@uwindsor.ca. Website: www.uwindsor.ca. Semiannual magazine. "We try to offer a balance of fiction and poetry distinguished by excellence." Estab. 1965. Circ. 250. Pays on publication. Publishes ms an average of 6 months after acceptance. Buys one-time rights. Accepts queries by e-mail. Responds in 1 month to queries. Responds in 6 weeks to mss. Sample copy for $7 (US). Guidelines available online.
Fiction Contact: Alistair MacLeod, fiction editor. No genre fiction (science fiction, romance), but would consider if writing is good enough. Send complete ms. Length: 1,000-5,000 words. **Pays $25, 1 contributor's copy and a free subscription.**
Poetry Submit maximum 6 poems.
Tips "Good writing, strong characters, and experimental fiction is appreciated."

WORLD LITERATURE TODAY

Literature, Culture, Politics, 630 Parrington Oval, Suite 110, Norman OK 73019-4033. (405)325-4531. E-mail: dsimon@ou.edu or mfjohnson@ou.edu. Website: www.worldliteraturetoday.com. Bimonthly website covering contemporary literature, culture, topics addressing any geographic region or language area. We prefer essays in the tradition of clear and lively discussion intended for a broad audience, with a minimum of scholarly apparatus. We offer a window to world culture for enlightened readers everywhere. To get an idea of the range of our coverage, see recent issues from our home page. Sponsors The Neustadt International Prize for Literature. Estab. 1927. No kill fee. Responds in 6 weeks to mss. Writer's Guidelines and Style Guide on website.
Nonfiction Please inquire about books you would like to review, including author, title, publisher, publication date, price and ISBN. Length: 350-400 words. Reviews of books published the previous year must be received by Sept. 1st of the current year. Needs essays.
Photos Captions required. Reviews 4X6 or 5X7 b&w glossies. prints, GIF/JPEG files (300-600 dpi); PDF or TIF files.
Tips We do not generally accept unsolicited poetry or fiction for publication. In terms of creative writing our general interest, with some exceptions, is in contributions by writers who are born outside the U.S. and with poetry in particular, in poetry translation by writers wo write in languages other than English. Send as fully formatted email attachment.

$ $ THE WRITER'S CHRONICLE

Association of Writers & Writing Programs (AWP), MS 1E3, George Mason University, Fairfax VA 22030-4444. (703)993-4301. Fax: (703)993-4302. E-mail: awp@awpwriter.org. Website: www.awpwriter.org. **90% freelance written**. Published 6 times during the academic year/3 times a semester magazine covering the art and craft of writing. *Writer's Chronicle* strives to: present the best essays on the craft and art of writing poetry, fiction and nonfiction; help overcome the over-specialization of the literary arts by presenting a public forum for the appreciation, debate and analysis of contemporary literature; present the diversity of accomplishments and points of view within contemporary literature; provide serious and committed writers and students of writing the best advice on how to manage their professional lives; provide writers who teach with new pedagogical approaches for their classrooms; provide the members and subscribers with a literary community as a compensation for a devotion to a difficult and lonely art; provide information on publishing opportunities, grants and awards; promote the good works of AWP, its programs and its individual members. Estab. 1967. Circ. 32,000. Byline given. Pays on publication. No kill fee. Buys first North American serial rights. Editorial lead time 3 months. Accepts queries by mail. Accepts simultaneous submissions. Responds in 2 weeks to queries. Sample copy free. Guidelines free.

Nonfiction Needs essays, interview, opinion, (does not mean letters to the editor). No personal essays. **Buys 15-20 mss/year mss/year.** Send complete ms. Length: 2,500-7,000 words. **Pays $11 per 100 words for assigned articles.**

Tips In general, the editors look for articles that demonstrate an excellent working knowledge of literary issues and a generosity of spirit that esteems the arguments of other writers on similar topics. When writing essays on craft, do not use your own work as an example. Keep in mind that 18,000 of our readers are students or just-emerging writers. They must become good readers before they can become good writers, so we expect essays on craft to show exemmplary close readings of a variety of contemporary and older works. Essays must embody erudition, generosity, curiosity and discernment rather than self-involvement. Writers may refer to their own travails and successes if they do so modestly, in small proportion to the other examples. We look for a generosity of spirit-a general love and command of literature as well as an expert, writerly viewpoint.

$ $ THE YALE REVIEW

Yale University, P.O. Box 208243, New Haven CT 06520-8243. (203)432-0499. Fax: (203)432-0510. Website: www.yale.edu/yalereview. **20% freelance written**. Quarterly magazine. Estab. 1911. Circ. 7,000. Pays prior to publication. No kill fee. Publishes ms an average of 6 months after acceptance. Buys one-time rights. Responds in 2 months to queries. Responds in 2 months to mss Sample copy for $9, plus postage Guidelines available online

Nonfiction Authoritative discussions of politics, literature and the arts. No previously published submissions. Send complete ms with cover letter and SASE Length: 3,000-5,000 words. **Pays $400-500.**

Fiction Buys quality fiction. Length: 3,000-5,000 words. **Pays $400-500.**

Poetry Pays $100-250.

$ THE YALOBUSHA REVIEW

The Literary Journal of the University of Mississippi, University of Mississippi Press, P.O. Box 1848, Dept. of English, University MS 38677. (662)915-3175. E-mail: yreditor@yahoo.com. Website: www.olemiss.edu/yalobusha. Annual literary journal seeking quality submissions from around the globe. Reading period is July 15-November 15. Estab. 1995. Circ. 1,000. Buys first North American serial rights. Accepts queries by mail. Accepts simultaneous submissions. Responds in 2-4 months to mss. Sample copy for $5. Guidelines for #10 SASE.

Nonfiction Contact: Nonfiction Editor. Needs essays, general interest, humor, interview, personal experience, travel. Does not want sappy confessional or insights into parenthood. Send complete ms. Length: 500-5,000 words. **Pays honorarium when funding available.**

Fiction Contact: Fiction Editor. Needs experimental, historical, humorous, mainstream, novel concepts, short shorts. **Buys 4-6 mss/year.** Send complete ms. Length: 500-4,000 words. **Pays honorarium when funding available.**

Poetry Needs avant-garde, free verse, light verse, traditional. Submit maximum 3-5 poems.

YEMASSEE

University of South Carolina, Department of English, Columbia SC 29208. (803)777-2085. E-mail: editor@yemasseejournal.org. Website: www.yemasseejournal.org. **90% freelance written**. Semiannual magazine covering fiction, poetry, interviews, creative nonfiction, reviews, one-act plays. *Yemassee* is the University of South Carolina's literary journal. Our readers are interested in high quality fiction, poetry, drama, and creative nonfiction. We have no editorial slant; quality of work is our only concern. Estab. 1993. Circ. 750. Byline given. Publishes ms an average of 4-6 months after acceptance. Buys first North American serial rights, buys electronic rights. Editorial lead time 3 months. Submit seasonal material 2-3 months in advance. Accepts queries by mail, e-mail. Accepts simultaneous submissions. Responds in 2-4 months to queries. Responds in 2-4 months to mss.

Sample copy for $5. Guidelines available online.
Nonfiction Needs book excerpts, essays, expose, general interest, historical, humor, interview, opinion, personal experience, lyric pieces. Does not want inspirational, epiphanic pieces and soapbox diatribes. **Buys 0-1 mss/year.** Send complete ms. Length: 500-5,000 words. **Pays in contributor copies.**
Fiction Contact: Contact: Darien Cavanaugh, co-editor. Needs adventure, experimental, historical, mainstream, novel concepts, romance. **Buys 10 mss/year.** Send complete ms. Length: 250-7,500 words. **Pays in contributor copies.**
Poetry Contact: Contact: Jonathan Maricle, co-editor. Needs avant-garde, free verse, haiku, light verse, traditional. Does not want workshop poems, unpolished drafts, generic/unoriginal themes, bad Hemingway. **Buys 20 poems/year.** Submit maximum 5 poems. Length: 1-120 lines. **Pays in contributor copies.**

$ ZAHIR

A Journal of Speculative Fiction, Zahir Publishing, 315 South Coast Hwy. 101, Suite U8, Encinitas CA 92024. E-mail: stempchin@zahirtales.com. Website: www.zahirtales.com. **100% freelance written.** Triannual magazine covering speculative fiction. We publish literary speculative fiction. Estab. 2003. Byline given. Pays on publication. No kill fee. Publishes ms an average of 2-12 months after acceptance. Buys first rights, buys second serial (reprint) rights. Accepts queries by e-mail. Accepts previously published material. Responds in 1-2 weeks to queries. Responds in 1-3 months to mss. Sample copy for $8 (US), $8.50 (Canada), $12 (international). Writer's guidelines for #10 SASE, by e-mail, or online.
Fiction Needs fantasy, surrealism, magical realism, science fiction, surrealism, magical realism. No children's stories or stories that deal with excessive violence or anything pornographic. **Buys 18-25 mss/year.** Send complete ms. 6,000 words maximum. **Pays $10 and 2 contributor's copies.**
Tips We look for great storytelling and fresh ideas. Let your imagination run wild and capture it in concise, evocative prose.

$ $ $ ZOETROPE: ALL-STORY

Zoetrop: All-Story, The Sentinel Bldg., 916 Kearny St., San Francisco CA 94133. (415)788-7500. Website: www.all-story.com. Quarterly magazine specializing in the best of contemporary short fiction. *Zoetrope: All Story* presents a new generation of classic stories. Estab. 1997. Circ. 20,000. Byline given. No kill fee. Publishes ms an average of 5 months after acceptance. Buys first serial rights. Accepts queries by mail. Responds in 8 months (if SASE included). Sample copy for $8.00. Guidelines available online.

- Does not accept submissions September 1 - December 31.

Fiction Buys 25-35 mss/year. Send complete ms. **Pays $1,000.**

$ ZYZZYVA

The Last Word: West Coast Writers & Artists, P.O. Box 590069, San Francisco CA 94159-0069. (415)752-4393. Fax: (415)752-4391. E-mail: editor@zyzzyva.org. Website: www.zyzzyva.org. **100% freelance written. Works with a small number of new/unpublished writers each year.** Magazine published in March, August, and November. "We feature work by writers currently living on the West Coast or in Alaska and Hawaii only. We are essentially a literary magazine, but of wide-ranging interests and a strong commitment to nonfiction." Estab. 1985. Circ. 2,500. Byline given. Pays on acceptance. No kill fee. Publishes ms an average of 3 months after acceptance. Buys first North American serial and one-time anthology rights. Accepts queries by mail, e-mail. Responds in 1 week to queries. Responds in 1 month to mss. Sample copy for $7 or online. Guidelines available online.
Nonfiction Needs book excerpts, general interest, historical, humor, personal experience. **Buys 50 mss/year.** Query by mail or e-mail. Open **Pays $50.**
Photos Reviews scans only at 300 dpi, 5½.
Fiction Needs ethnic, experimental, humorous, mainstream. **Buys 20 mss/year.** Send complete ms. Length: 100-7,500 words. **Pays $50.**
Poetry Buys 20 poems/year. Submit maximum 5 poems. Length: 3 200 lines. **Pays $50.**
Tips "West Coast writers means those currently living in California, Alaska, Washington, Oregon, or Hawaii."

MEN'S

AMERICAN CURVES

Eye-Candy for Men, Canusa Products, Inc., 5775 McLaughlin Rd., Mississauga ON L5R-3P7 Canada. (905)507-3545/(888)254-0767. E-mail: rico@americancurves.com. Website: www.americancurves.com. 9 times/yr. magazine covering articles on relationships and sex; features female fitness models in sexy attire. Showcasing fitness women; models train with free weights and use cardio equipment to build their sexy bodies and show you how to do the same. With wild stories from our readers and provocative Q&A, *American Curves* has what it takes to fulfill every man's needs, wants and desires. Estab. 2002. Circ. 260,000. Pays on acceptance. No kill fee. Buys all rights. Guidelines available.

Nonfiction Needs expose, interview, personal experience, photo feature. Send submissions with SAE, $5 for return postage. **Pays only with 2 year subscription**

Photos Contact: Jeff Maltby, photo editor.

$ $ $ $ CIGAR AFICIONADO

M. Shanken Communications, Inc., 387 Park Ave. S., 8th Floor, New York NY 10016. (212)684-4224. Fax: (212)684-5424. E-mail: gmott@mshanken.com. Website: www.cigaraficionado.com. **75% freelance written**. Bimonthly magazine for affluent men. Estab. 1992. Circ. 275,000. Byline given. Pays on acceptance. Offers 25% kill fee. Publishes ms an average of 3-6 months after acceptance. Buys all rights. Editorial lead time 6 months. Submit seasonal material 6 months in advance. Accepts queries by e-mail. Responds in 1 month to queries. Responds in 2 months to mss. Sample copy free.

Nonfiction Needs general interest. Query. Length: 1,500-4,000 words. **Pays variable amount.** Pays expenses of writers on assignment.

Photos Contact: Contact Mary Galligun, photo editor.

$ $ $ $ ESQUIRE

Hearst Corp., 300 W. 57th St., 21st. Floor, New York NY 10019. (212)649-4020. E-mail: esquire@hearst.com. Website: www.esquire.com. Monthly magazine covering the ever-changing trends in American culture. Geared toward smart, well-off men. General readership is college educated and sophisticated, between ages 30 and 45. Written mostly by contributing editors on contract. Rarely accepts unsolicited mss. Estab. 1933. Circ. 720,000. Publishes ms an average of 2-6 months after acceptance. Retains first worldwide periodical publication rights for 90 days from cover date. Editorial lead time at least 2 months. Accepts simultaneous submissions. Guidelines for SASE.

Nonfiction Focus is the ever-changing trends in American culture. Topics include current events and politics, social criticism, sports, celebrity profiles, the media, art and music, men's fashion. Queries must be sent by letter. **Buys 4 features and 12 shorter mss/year.** Columns average 1,500 words; features average 5,000 words; short front of book pieces average 200-400 words **Payment varies.**

Photos Uses mostly commissioned photography Payment depends on size and number of photos

Fiction Literary excellence is our only criterion. Needs novel concepts, short stories, memoirs, plays. No pornography, science fiction or 'true romance' stories. Send complete ms.

Tips A writer has the best chance of breaking in at *Esquire* by querying with a specific idea that requires special contacts and expertise. Ideas must be timely and national in scope.

$ GC MAGAZINE

Handel Publishing, P.O. Box 331775, Fort Worth TX 76163. (817)640-1306. Fax: (817)633-9045. E-mail: rosa.gc@sbcglobal.net. **80% freelance written**. Monthly magazine. *GC Magazine* is a general entertainment magazine for men. We include entertainment celebrity interviews (movies, music, books) along with general interest articles for adult males. Estab. 1994. Circ. 53,000. No byline given. Pays on publication. No kill fee. Publishes ms an average of 3 months after acceptance. Buys one-time rights. Editorial lead time 3 months. Submit seasonal material 6 months in advance. Accepts queries by mail, e-mail. Accepts previously published material. Accepts simultaneous submissions. Responds in 3 months to queries. Sample copy for $1.50. Guidelines for #10 SASE.

Nonfiction Needs book excerpts, essays, expose, general interest, historical, how-to, humor, interview, technical, travel, dating tips. **Buys 100 mss/year.** Query. Length: 1,000-2,000 words. **Pays 2¢/word.** Sometimes pays expenses of writers on assignment.

Photos State availability Model releases required. Reviews 3x5 prints, GIF/JPEG files. Offers no additional payment for photos accepted with ms Buys one time rights.

Columns/Departments Actress feature (film actress interviews), 2,500 words; Author feature (book author interviews), 1,500 words; Music feature (singer or band interviews), 1,500 words. 50 Query. **Pays 2¢/word**

Tips Submit material typed and free of errors. Writers should think of magazines like *Maxim* and *Details* when determining article ideas for our magazine. Our primary readership is adult males and we are seeking original and unique articles.

$ $ $ INDY MEN'S MAGAZINE

The Guy's Guide to the Good Life, Table Moose Media, 8500 Keystone Crossing, Suite 100, Indianapolis IN 46240. (317)255-3850. Fax: (317)254-5944. E-mail: lou@indymensmagazine.com. Website: www.indymensmagazine.com. **50% freelance written**. Monthly magazine. Estab. 2002. Circ. 50,000. Byline given. Pays on publication. Offers 10% kill fee. Buys first North American serial rights. Editorial lead time 3 months. Submit seasonal material 1 year in advance. Accepts queries by mail. Accepts simultaneous submissions. Responds in 3 weeks to queries. Responds in 2 months to mss. Sample copy for $5. Guidelines by email.

Nonfiction Needs essays, travel. No generic pieces that could run anywhere. No advocacy pieces. **Buys 50 mss/year.** Query. Length: 100-2,000 words. **Pays $75-500 for assigned articles. Pays $50-400 for unsolicited**

articles. Sometimes pays expenses of writers on assignment.

Photos State availability Identification of subjects required. Reviews contact sheets, transparencies, prints, GIF/JPEG files. Negotiates payment individually. Buys one time rights.

Columns/Departments Balls (opinionated sports pieces), 1,400 words; Dad Files (introspective parenting essays), 1,400 words; Men At Work (Indianapolis men and their jobs), 100-600 words; Trippin' (experiential travel), 1,500 words. 30 Query with published clips. **Pays $75-400.**

Fiction The piece needs to hold our attention from the first paragraph. Needs adventure, fantasy, historical, horror, humorous, mainstream, mystery, science fiction, suspense. **Buys 12 mss/year.** Send complete ms. Length: 1,000-4,000 words. **Pays $50-250.**

Tips We don't believe in wasting our reader's time, whether it's in a 50-word item or a 6,000-word Q&A. Our readers are smart, and they appreciate our sense of humor. Write to entertain and engage.

$$$$ KING

Harris Publications, Inc., 1115 Broadway, 8th Floor, New York NY 10010. (212)467-9675. Fax: (212)807-0216. E-mail: laura@harris-pub.com. Website: www.king-mag.com. **75% freelance written.** Men's lifestyle magazine published 80 times/year. *King* is a general interest men's magazine with a strong editorial voice. Topics include lifestyle, entertainment, news, women, cars, music, fashion, investigative reporting. Estab. 2001. Circ. 270,000. Byline given. Pays on publication. Offers 25% kill fee. Buys all rights. Editorial lead time 2-3 months. Submit seasonal material 4 months in advance. Accepts queries by e-mail. Responds in 1 month to queries. Guidelines free.

Nonfiction Needs essays, expose, general interest. Does not want completed articles. Pitches only. Query with published clips. Length: 2,000-5,000 words. **Pays $1-1.50/word.** Sometimes pays expenses of writers on assignment.

$$$$ SMOKE MAGAZINE

Cigars & Life's Burning Desires, Lockwood Publications, 26 Broadway, Floor 9M, New York NY 10004. (212)391-2060. Fax: (212)827-0945. E-mail: editor@smokemag.com. Website: www.smokemag.com. **50% freelance written.** Quarterly magazine covering cigars and men's lifestyle issues. A large majority of *Smoke's* readers are affluent men, ages 28-50; active, educated and adventurous. Estab. 1995. Circ. 95,000. Byline given. Pays 1 month after publication. Offers 25% kill fee. Publishes ms an average of 3 (average) months after acceptance. Buys first rights. Editorial lead time 2 months. Submit seasonal material 6 months in advance. Accepts queries by mail, e-mail. Accepts simultaneous submissions. Responds in 6 weeks to queries. Responds in 3 months to mss. Sample copy for $4.99.

Nonfiction Needs essays, expose, general interest, historical, how-to, humor, interview, opinion, personal experience, photo feature, technical, travel, true crime. **Buys 8 mss/year.** Query with published clips. Length: 1,500-3,000 words. **Pays $500-1,200.** Sometimes pays expenses of writers on assignment

Photos State availability Identification of subjects required. Reviews 2¼x2¼ transparencies. Negotiates payment individually

Columns/Departments Smoke Undercover (investigative journalism, personal experience); Smoke Screen (TV/film/entertainment issues); Smoke City (cigar-related travel), all 1,500 words. 8 Query with published clips. **Pays $500-1,000.**

Tips Send a short, clear query with clips. Go with your field of expertise: cigars, sports, music, true crime, etc.

$$ UMM (URBAN MALE MAGAZINE)

Canada's Only Lifestyle and Fashion Magazine for Men, UMM Publishing Inc., 300-131 Bank St., Ottawa ON K1P 5N7 Canada. (613)723-6216. Fax: (613)723-1702. E-mail: editor@umm.ca. Website: www.umm.ca. **100% freelance written.** Bimonthly magazine covering men's interests. Our audience is young men, aged 18-24. We focus on Canadian activities, interests, and lifestyle issues. Our magazine is fresh and energetic and we look for original ideas carried out with a spark of intelligence and/or humour (and you'd better spell humour with a `u'). Estab. 1998. Circ. 90,000. Byline given. Pays 1 month after publication. No kill fee. Publishes ms an average of 3 months after acceptance. Buys first North American serial rights. Editorial lead time 3 months. Submit seasonal material 4 months in advance. Accepts queries by e-mail. Accepts simultaneous submissions. Responds in 6 weeks to queries. Responds in 6 weeks to mss.

Nonfiction Needs book excerpts, expose, general interest, historical, how-to, humor, interview, new product, personal experience, travel, adventure, cultural, sports, music. **Buys 80 mss/year.** Query with published clips. Length: 1,200-3,500 words. **Pays $100-400.** Sometimes pays expenses of writers on assignment.

Photos State availability Reviews contact sheets, prints. Negotiates payment individually Buys one time rights.

Fillers Needs anecdotes, facts, short humor. 35 Length: 100-500 words. **Pays $50-150.**

Tips Be familiar with our magazine before querying. We deal with all subjects of interest to young men, especially those with Canadian themes. We are very open-minded. Original ideas and catchy writing are key.

MILITARY

$ $ AIRFORCE

Air Force Association of Canada, P.O Box 2460, Stn D, Ottawa ON K1P 5W6 Canada. (613)232-2303. Fax: (613)232-2156. E-mail: vjohnson@airforce.ca. Website: www.airforce.ca. **5% freelance written**. Quarterly magazine covering Canada's air force heritage. Stories center on Canadian military aviation—past, present and future. Estab. 1977. Circ. 16,000. Byline given. Pays on publication. Publishes ms an average of 6 months after acceptance. Buys all rights. Editorial lead time 3 months. Submit seasonal material 3 months in advance. Accepts queries by mail, e-mail, fax, phone. Accepts previously published material. Accepts simultaneous submissions. Responds in 2 weeks to queries. Responds in 1 month to mss. Sample copy free. Guidelines by email.

Nonfiction Needs historical, interview, personal experience, photo feature. **Buys 2 mss/year.** Query with published clips. Length: 1,500-3,500 words. Sometimes pays expenses of writers on assignment. Limit agreed upon in advance

Photos Send photos Captions, identification of subjects required. Reviews prints, GIF/JPEG files. Buys one time rights.

Fillers Needs anecdotes, facts. About 800 words **Negotiable**

Tips Writers should have a good background in Canadian military history.

$ $ AIR FORCE TIMES

Army Times Publishing Co., 6883 Commercial Dr., Springfield VA 22159. (703)750-8646. Fax: (703)750-8601. E-mail: kmiller@militarytimes.com. Website: www.airforcetimes.com. Weeklies edited separately for Army, Navy, Marine Corps, and Air Force military personnel and their families. They contain career information such as pay raises, promotions, news of legislation affecting the military, housing, base activities and features of interest to military people. Estab. 1940. Byline given. Pays on acceptance. Offers kill fee. Buys first rights. Accepts queries by mail, e-mail, phone. Accepts simultaneous submissions. Responds in 1 month to queries. Sample copy for #10 SASE. Guidelines for #10 SASE.

Nonfiction Features of interest to career military personnel and their families. No advice pieces. **Buys 150-175 mss/year.** Query. Length: 750-2,000 words. **Pays $100-500.**

Columns/Departments Length: 500-900. 75 **Pays $75-125.**

Tips Looking for stories on active duty, reserve and retired military personnel; stories on military matters and localized military issues; stories on successful civilian careers after military service.

$ $ ARMY MAGAZINE

2425 Wilson Blvd., Arlington VA 22201-3385. (703)841-4300. Fax: (703)841-3505. E-mail: armymag@ausa.org. Website: www.ausa.org. **70% freelance written. Prefers to work with published/established writers.** Monthly magazine emphasizing military interests. Estab. 1904. Circ. 90,000. Byline given. Pays on publication. Publishes ms an average of 5 months after acceptance. Buys all rights. Submit seasonal material 3 months in advance. Accepts queries by mail. Sample copy for 9x12 SAE with $1 postage or online Writer's guidelines for 9x12 SAE with $1 postage or online

- *ARMY Magazine* looks for shorter articles.

Nonfiction We would like to see more pieces about little-known episodes involving interesting military personalities. We especially want material lending itself to heavy, contributor-supplied photographic treatment. The first thing a contributor should recognize is that our readership is very savvy militarily. 'Gee-whiz' personal reminiscences get short shrift, unless they hold their own in a company in which long military service, heroism and unusual experiences are commonplace. At the same time, *ARMY* readers like a well-written story with a fresh slant, whether it is about an experience in a foxhole or the fortunes of a corps in battle. Needs historical, military and original, humor, military feature-length articles and anecdotes, interview, photo feature. No rehashed history. No unsolicited book reviews. **Buys 40 mss/year.** Submit complete ms (hard copy and disk) Length: 1,000-1,500 words. **Pays 12-18¢/word.**

Photos Send photos Captions required. Reviews prints, slides, high resolution digital photos. Pays $50-100 for 8x10 b&w glossy prints; $50-350 for 8x10 color glossy prints and 35mm and high resolution digital photos. Buys all rights.

$ $ ARMY TIMES

Army Times Publishing Co., 6883 Commercial Dr., Springfield VA 22159. (703)750-9000. Fax: (703)750-8622. E-mail: aneill@militarytimes.com. Website: www.armytimes.com. Weekly for Army military personnel and their families containing career information such as pay raises, promotions, news of legislation affecting the military, housing, base activities and features of interest to military people. Estab. 1940. Circ. 230,000. Byline given. Pays on acceptance. Offers kill fee. Makes work-for-hire assignments. Accepts queries by mail, e-mail. Accepts simultaneous submissions. Responds in 1 month to queries. Sample copy and writer's guidelines for #10 SASE.

Nonfiction Features of interest to career military personnel and their families: food, relationships, parenting, education, retirement, shelter, health, and fitness, sports, personal appearance, community, recreation, personal finance, entertainment. No advice please. **Buys 150-175 mss/year.** Query. Length: 750-2,000 words. **Pays $100-500.**
Columns/Departments Length: 500-900 words. 75 **Pays $75-125.**
Tips Looking for stories on active duty, reserve and retired military personnel; stories on military matters and localized military issues; stories on successful civilian careers after military service.

$ COMBAT HANDGUNS

Harris Tactical Group, 1115 Broadway, New York NY 10010. (212)807-7100. Fax: (212)807-1479. E-mail: comments@harris-pub.com. Website: www.combathandguns.com. Magazine published 8 times/year covering combat handguns. Written for handgun owners and collectors. Circ. 126,498. No kill fee. Editorial lead time 2 months. Accepts queries by mail, e-mail.
Nonfiction Query.
Photos Send photos Captions required. Reviews GIF/JPEG files.

$ $ MARINE CORPS TIMES

Army Times Publishing Co., 6883 Commercial Dr., Springfield VA 22159. (703)750-9000. Fax: (703)750-8767. E-mail: cmark@militarytimes.com. Website: www.marinecorpstimes.com. Weeklies edited separately for Army, Navy, Marine Corps, and Air Force military personnel and their families. They contain career information such as pay raises, promotions, news of legislation affecting the military, housing, base activities and features of interest to military people. Estab. 1940. Circ. 230,000 (combined). Byline given. Pays on publication. Offers kill fee. Buys first rights. Accepts queries by mail, e-mail, phone. Accepts simultaneous submissions. Responds in 1 month to queries. Sample copy for #10 sase. Guidelines for #10 SASE.
Nonfiction Features of interest to career military personnel and their families, including stories on current military operations and exercises. No advice pieces. **Buys 150-175 mss/year.** Query. Length: 750-2,000 words. **Pays $100-500.**
Columns/Departments Length: 500-900 words. 75 **Pays $75-125.**
Tips Looking for stories on active duty, reserve and retired military personnel; stories on military matters and localized military issues; stories on successful civilian careers after military service.

$ $ $ MILITARY OFFICER

201 N. Washington St., Alexandria VA 22314-2539. (800)234-6622. Fax: (703)838-8179. E-mail: editor@moaa.org. Website: www.moaa.org. **60% freelance written. Prefers to work with published/established writers.** Monthly magazine for officers of the 7 uniformed services and their families. Estab. 1945. Circ. 389,000. Byline given. Pays on acceptance. Publishes ms an average of 1 year after acceptance. Buys first North American serial rights. Accepts queries by e-mail. Responds in 3 months to queries. Sample copy available online. Guidelines available online.
Nonfiction Current military/political affairs, finance, health and wellness, recent military history, travel, military family life-style. Emphasis now on current military and defense issues. "We rarely accept unsolicited manuscripts." **Buys 50 mss/year.** Query with résumé, sample clips Length: 800-2,000 words. **Pays 80¢/word.**
Photos Query with list of stock photo subjects. Original slides and transparencies must be suitable for color separation. Reviews transparencies. Pays $20 for each 8x10 b&w photo (normal halftone) used. Pays $75-250 for inside color; $300 for cover.

$ PARAMETERS

U.S. Army War College Quarterly, U.S. Army War College, 122 Forbes Ave., Carlisle PA 17013-5238. (717)245-4943. E-mail: carl_parameters@conus.army.mil. Website: www.carlisle.army.mil/usawc/parameters. **100% freelance written. Prefers to work with published/established writers or experts in the field.** Readership consists of senior leaders of US defense establishment, both uniformed and civilian, plus members of the media, government, industry and academia. Subjects include national and international security affairs, military strategy, military leadership and management, art and science of warfare, and military history with contemporary relevance. Estab. 1971. Circ. 13,500. Byline given. Pays on publication. No kill fee. Publishes ms an average of 6 months after acceptance. Accepts queries by mail, e-mail, phone. Responds in 6 weeks to queries. Sample copy free or online Guidelines available online.
Nonfiction Prefers articles that deal with current security issues, employ critical analysis, and provide solutions or recommendations. Liveliness and verve, consistent with scholarly integrity, appreciated. Theses, studies, and academic course papers should be adapted to article form prior to submission. Documentation in complete endnotes. Send complete ms. 4,500 words average **Pays $200-300 average.**
Tips Make it short; keep it interesting; get criticism and revise accordingly. Write on a contemporary topic. Tackle a subject only if you are an authority. No fax submissions. Encourage e-mail submissions.

$ $ $ $ SOLDIER OF FORTUNE

The Journal of Professional Adventurers, 5735 Arapahoe Ave., Suite A-5, Boulder CO 80303-1340. (303)449-3750. E-mail: editorsof@aol.com. Website: www.sofmag.com. **50% freelance written**. Monthly magazine covering military, paramilitary, police, combat subjects, and action/adventure. We are an action-oriented magazine; we cover combat hot spots around the world. We also provide timely features on state-of-the-art weapons and equipment; elite military and police units; and historical military operations. Readership is primarily active-duty military, veterans, and law enforcement. Estab. 1975. Circ. 60,000. Byline given. Offers 25% kill fee. Buys first rights. Responds in 3 weeks to queries. Responds in 1 month to mss. Sample copy for $5. Guidelines for #10 SASE.

Nonfiction Needs expose, general interest, historical, how-to, on weapons and their skilled use, humor, interview, new product, personal experience, photo feature, No. 1 on our list, technical, travel, combat reports, military unit reports, and solid Vietnam and Operation Iraqi Freedom articles. No `How I won the war' pieces; no op-ed pieces unless they are fully and factually backgrounded; no knife articles (staff assignments only). All submitted articles should have good art; art will sell us on an article. **Buys 75 mss/year.** Query with or without published clips or send complete ms. Send mss to articles editor; queries to managing editor Length: 2,000-3,000 words. **Pays $150-250/page.**

Reprints Send disk copy, photocopy of article and information about when and where the material previously appeared. Pays 25% of amount paid for an original article

Photos Send photos Captions, identification of subjects required. Reviews contact sheets, transparencies. Pays $500 for cover photo Buys one time rights.

Fillers Contact: Bulletin Board editor. Needs newsbreaks, military/paramilitary related has to be documented. Length: 100-250 words. **Pays $50**

Tips Submit a professionally prepared, complete package. All artwork with cutlines, double-spaced typed manuscript with 5.25 or 3.5 IBM-compatible disk, if available, cover letter including synopsis of article, supporting documentation where applicable, etc. Manuscript must be factual; writers have to do their homework and get all their facts straight. One error means rejection. Vietnam features, if carefully researched and art heavy, will always get a careful look. Combat reports, again, with good art, are No. 1 in our book and stand the best chance of being accepted. Military unit reports from around the world are well received, as are law-enforcement articles (units, police in action). If you write for us, be complete and factual; pros read *Soldier of Fortune*, and are very quick to let us know if we (and the author) err.

MUSIC CONSUMER

$ AMERICAN SONGWRITER MAGAZINE

1303 16th Ave. S., Nashville TN 37212. (615)321-6096. Fax: (615)321-6097. E-mail: info@americansongwriter.com. Website: www.americansongwriter.com. **90% freelance written**. Bimonthly magazine about songwriters and the craft of songwriting for many types of music, including pop, country, rock, metal, jazz, gospel, and r&b. Estab. 1984. Circ. 5,000. Pays on publication. Offers 25% kill fee. Publishes ms an average of 2 months after acceptance. Buys first North American serial rights. Accepts previously published material. Responds in 2 months to queries. Sample copy for $4. Guidelines for #10 SASE or by e-mail.

Nonfiction Needs general interest, interview, new product, technical, home demo studios, movie and TV scores, performance rights organizations. **Buys 20 mss/year.** Query with published clips. Length: 300-1,200 words. **Pays $25-60.**

Reprints Send tearsheet or photocopy and information about when and where the material previously appeared. Pays same amount as paid for an original article

Photos Send photos Identification of subjects required. Reviews 3x5 prints. Offers no additional payment for photos accepeted with ms. Buys one time rights.

Tips *American Songwriter* strives to present articles which can be read a year or 2 after they were written and still be pertinent to the songwriter reading them.

$ $ BLUEGRASS UNLIMITED

Bluegrass Unlimited, Inc., P.O. Box 771, Warrenton VA 20188-0771. (540)349-8181 or (800)BLU-GRAS. Fax: (540)341-0011. E-mail: editor@bluegrassmusic.com. Website: www.bluegrassmusic.com. **10% freelance written. Prefers to work with published/established writers.** Monthly magazine covering bluegrass, acoustic, and old-time country music. Estab. 1966. Circ. 27,000. Byline given. Pays on publication. Offers negotiated kill fee. Publishes ms an average of 4 months after acceptance. Buys first North American serial rights, buys one-time rights, buys second serial (reprint) rights, buys all rights. Submit seasonal material 4 months in advance. Accepts queries by mail, e-mail, fax. Responds in 2 weeks to queries. Responds in 2 months to mss. Sample copy free. Guidelines for #10 SASE.

Nonfiction Needs general interest, historical, how-to, interview, personal experience, photo feature, travel. No

fan-style articles. **Buys 30-40 mss/year.** Query. Open **Pays 10-13¢/word.**
Reprints Send photocopy with rights for sale noted and information about when and where the material previously appeared. Payment is negotiable
Photos State availability of or send photos Identification of subjects required. Reviews 35mm transparencies and 3x5, 5x7 and 8x10 b&w and color prints. Also, reviews/prefers digital 300 dpi or better jpg, tif files, index, contact sheet with digital submissions Pays $50-175 for color; $25-60 for b&w prints; $50-250 for color prints Buys all rights.
Fiction Needs ethnic, humorous. **Buys 3-5 mss/year.** Query. Negotiable **Pays 10-13¢/word.**
Tips We would prefer that articles be informational, based on personal experience or an interview with lots of quotes from subject, profile, humor, etc. We print less than 10% freelance at this time.

$ $ CHAMBER MUSIC

Chamber Music America, 305 Seventh Ave., 5th Floor, New York NY 10001-6008. (212)242-2022. Fax: (212)242-7955. E-mail: egoldensohn@chamber-music.org. Website: www.chamber-music.org. Bimonthly magazine covering chamber music. Estab. 1977. Circ. 13,000. Byline given. Pays on publication. Offers kill fee. Publishes ms an average of 5 months after acceptance. Buys first rights. Editorial lead time 4 months. Accepts queries by mail, phone.
Nonfiction Needs book excerpts, essays, humor, opinion, personal experience, issue-oriented stories of relevance to the chamber music fields written by top music journalists and critics, or music practitioners. No artist profiles, no stories about opera or symphonic work. **Buys 35 mss/year.** Query with published clips. Length: 2,500-3,500 words. **Pays $500 minimum.** Sometimes pays expenses of writers on assignment.
Photos State availability Offers no payment for photos accepted with ms

$ ✠ CHART MAGAZINE

Canada's Music Magazine, Chart Communications, Inc., 41 Britain St., Suite 200, Toronto ON M5A 1R7 Canada. (416)363-3101. Fax: (416)363-3109. E-mail: chart@chartattack.com. Website: www.chartattack.com. **90% freelance written**. Monthly magazine. *Chart Magazine* has a cutting edge attitude toward music and pop culture to fit with youth readership. Estab. 1990. Circ. 40,000 (paid). Byline given. Pays on publication. No kill fee. Publishes ms an average of 3-6 months after acceptance. Buys first North American serial rights, buys electronic rights. Editorial lead time 2 months. Submit seasonal material 3 months in advance. Accepts queries by mail, e-mail, fax, phone. Responds in 4-6 weeks to queries. Responds in 2-3 months to mss. Sample copy for $6 US (via mail order). Guidelines free.
Nonfiction All articles must relate to popular music and/or pop culture. Needs book excerpts, essays, expose, humor, interview, personal experience, photo feature. Nothing that isn't related to popular music and pop culture (i.e., film, books, video games, fashion, etc., that would appeal to a hip youth demographic). Query with published clips and send complete ms. varies. **Payment varies.**
Photos Contact: Steven Balaban, art director. Send photos Negotiates payment individually. Buys all rights.

$ $ GUITAR PLAYER MAGAZINE

New Bay Media, LLC, 1111 Bayhill Dr., Suite 125, San Bruno CA 94403. (650)238-0300. Fax: (650)238-0261. E-mail: mmolenda@musicplayer.com. Website: www.guitarplayer.com. **50% freelance written**. Monthly magazine for persons interested in guitars, guitarists, manufacturers, guitar builders, equipment, careers, etc. Circ. 150,000. Byline given. Pays on acceptance. No kill fee. Publishes ms an average of 3 months after acceptance. Buys first serial and all reprint rights. Accepts queries by e-mail. Responds in 6 weeks to queries. Guidelines for #10 SASE.
Nonfiction Publishes wide variety of articles pertaining to guitars and guitarists: interviews, guitar craftsmen profiles, how-to features—anything amateur and professional guitarists would find fascinating and/or helpful. In interviews with `name' performers, be as technical as possible regarding strings, guitars, techniques, etc. We're not a pop culture magazine, but a magazine for musicians. The essential question: What can the reader take away from a story to become a better player? **Buys 30-40 mss/year.** Query. Open **Pays $250-450.** Sometimes pays expenses of writers on assignment.
Photos Reviews 35 mm color transparencies, b&w glossy prints. Payment varies Buys one time rights.

$ MUSIC FOR THE LOVE OF IT

67 Parkside Dr., Berkeley CA 94705. (510)654-9134. Fax: (510)654-4656. E-mail: tedrust@musicfortheloveofit.com. Website: www.musicfortheloveofit.com. **20% freelance written**. Bimonthly newsletter covering amateur musicianship. A lively, intelligent source of ideas and enthusiasm for a musically literate audience of adult amateur musicians. Estab. 1988. Circ. 600. Byline given. Pays on publication. No kill fee. Publishes ms an average of 2 months after acceptance. Buys one-time rights. Editorial lead time 1 month. Submit seasonal material 1 month in advance. Accepts queries by mail, e-mail, fax, phone. Responds in 1 week to queries. Responds in 1 month to mss. Sample copy for $5. Guidelines available online.
Nonfiction Needs essays, historical, how-to, personal experience, photo feature. No concert reviews, star interviews, CD reviews. **Buys 6 mss/year.** Query. Length: 500-1,500 words. **Pays $50, or gift subscriptions.**

Photos State availability Identification of subjects required. Reviews 4x6 prints or larger. Offers no additional payment for photos accepted with ms Buys one time rights.
Tips We're looking for more good how-to articles on musical styles. Love making music. Know something about it.

$ $ $ SYMPHONY

American Symphony Orchestra League, 33 W. 60th St., Fifth Floor, New York NY 10023. (212)262-5161. Fax: (212)262-5198. E-mail: clare@americanorchestras.org. Website: www.symphony.org. **50% freelance written.** Bimonthly magazine for the orchestra industry and classical music enthusiasts covering classical music, orchestra industry, musicians. Writers should be knowledgeable about classical music and have critical or journalistic/repertorial approach. Circ. 18,000. Byline given. Pays on acceptance. No kill fee. Publishes ms an average of 2 months after acceptance. Buys first rights, buys one-time rights. Editorial lead time 6 months. Submit seasonal material 8 months in advance. Accepts queries by mail, e-mail. Accepts simultaneous submissions. Guidelines available online.
Nonfiction Needs book excerpts, essays, inspirational, interview, opinion, personal experience, rare, photo feature, rare, issue features, trend pieces (by assignment only; pitches welcome). Does not want to see reviews, interviews. **Buys 30 mss/year.** Query with published clips. Length: 1,500-3,500 words. **Pays $500-900.** Sometimes pays expenses of writers on assignment.
Photos Rarely commissions photos or illustrations. State availability of or send photos Captions, identification of subjects required. Reviews contact sheets, negatives, prints, electronic photos (preferred). Offers no additional payment for photos accepted with ms Buys one time rights.
Columns/Departments Repertoire (orchestral music—essays); Comment (personal views and opinions); Currents (electronic media developments); In Print (books); On Record (CD, DVD, video), all 1,000-2,500 words. 12 Query with published clips.
Tips We need writing samples before assigning pieces. We prefer to craft the angle with the writer, rather than adapt an existing piece. Pitches and queries should demonstrate a clear relevance to the American orchestra industry and should be timely.

$ $ $ $ VIBE

215 Lexington Ave., 6th Floor, New York NY 10016. (212)448-7300. Fax: (212)448-7400. Website: www.vibe.com. Monthly magazine covering urban music and culture. *Vibe* chronicles and celebrates urban music and the youth culture that inspires and consumes it. Estab. 1993. Circ. 850,000. Pays on publication. Buys first North American serial rights. Editorial lead time 4 months. Responds in 2 months to queries. Sample copy available on newsstands
Nonfiction Query with published clips, resume and SASE Length: 800-3,000 words. **Pays $1/word.**
Columns/Departments Volume (introductory lifestyle and news-based section), 350-740 words; Revolutions (music reviews), 100-800 words Query with published clips, resume and SASE **Pays $1/word**
Tips A writer's best chance to be published in *Vibe* is through the Volume or Revolutions sections. Keep in mind that *Vibe* is a national magazine, so ideas should have a national scope. People should care as much about the story as people in NYC. Also, *Vibe* has a 4-month lead time. What we work on today will appear in the magazine 4 or more months later. Stories must be timely with respect to this fact.

MYSTERY

$ HARDBOILED

Gryphon Publications, P.O. Box 209, Brooklyn NY 11228. Website: www.gryphonbooks.com. **100% freelance written**. Semiannual book covering crime/mystery fiction and nonfiction. "Hard-hitting crime fiction and private-eye stories—the newest and most cutting-edge work and classic reprints." Estab. 1988. Circ. 1,000. Byline given. Pays on publication. Offers 100% kill fee. Publishes ms an average of 18 months after acceptance. Buys first North American serial rights, buys one-time rights. Editorial lead time 1 year. Submit seasonal material 9 months in advance. Accepts queries by mail, fax. Accepts previously published material. Accepts simultaneous submissions. Responds in 2 weeks to queries. Responds in 1 month to mss. Sample copy for $10. Guidelines for #10 SASE.
Nonfiction Needs book excerpts, essays, expose. **Buys 4-6 mss/year.** Query. Length: 500-3,000 words. **Pays 1 copy.**
Reprints Query first.
Photos State availability
Columns/Departments Occasional review columns/articles on hardboiled writers. 2-4 Query.
Fiction Contact: Gary Lovisi, editor. Needs mystery, private eye, police procedural, noir, hardboiled crime, and private-eye stories, all on the cutting edge. "No pastiches, violence for the sake of violence." **Buys 40 mss/year.** Query or send complete ms. Length: 500-3,000 words. **Pays $5-50.**

Tips "Your best bet for breaking in is short hard crime fiction filled with authenticity and brevity. Try a subscription to *Hardboiled* to get the perfect idea of what we are after."

ALFRED HITCHCOCK'S MYSTERY MAGAZINE

Dell Magazines, 475 Park Ave. S., 11th Floor, New York NY 10016. (212)686-7188. Website: www.themysteryplace.com. **100% freelance written**. Monthly magazine featuring new mystery short stories. Estab. 1956. Circ. 90,000 readers. Byline given. No kill fee. Buys first rights, buys foreign rights. Submit seasonal material 7 months in advance. Responds in 4 months to mss. Sample copy for $6.49 Guidelines for SASE or on website.

Fiction Contact: Linda Landrigan, editor. "Original and well-written mystery and crime fiction. Because this is a mystery magazine, the stories we buy must fall into that genre in some sense or another. We are interested in nearly every kind of mystery: stories of detection of the classic kind, police procedurals, private eye tales, suspense, courtroom dramas, stories of espionage, and so on. We ask only that the story be about crime (or the threat or fear of one). We sometimes accept ghost stories or supernatural tales, but those also should involve a crime." No sensationalism. Send complete ms. Up to 12,000 words **Payment varies.**

Tips "No simultaneous submissions, please. Submissions sent to *Alfred Hitchcock's Mystery Magazine* are not considered for or read by *Ellery Queen's Mystery Magazine*, and vice versa."

$ ELLERY QUEEN'S MYSTERY MAGAZINE

Dell Magazines Fiction Group, 475 Park Ave. S., 11th Floor, New York NY 10016. (212)686-7188. Fax: (212)686-7414. E-mail: elleryqueenmm@dellmagazines.com. Website: www.themysteryplace.com/eqmm. **100% freelance written**. Featuring mystery fiction. "*Ellery Queen's Mystery Magazine* welcomes submissions from both new and established writers. We publish every kind of mystery short story: the psychological suspense tale, the deductive puzzle, the private eye case—the gamut of crime and detection from the realistic (including the policeman's lot and stories of police procedure) to the more imaginative (including 'locked rooms' and 'impossible crimes'). *EQMM* has been in continuous publication since 1941. From the beginning, 3 general criteria have been employed in evaluating submissions: We look for strong writing, an original and exciting plot, and professional craftsmanship. We encourage writers whose work meets these general criteria to read an issue of *EQMM* before making a submission." Estab. 1941. Circ. 120,000. Byline given. Pays on acceptance. No kill fee. Publishes ms an average of 6-12 months after acceptance. Buys first North American serial rights. Accepts simultaneous submissions. Responds in 3 months to mss. Sample copy for $5.50. Guidelines for SASE or online.

Fiction Contact: Janet Hutchings, editor. We always need detective stories. Special consideration given to anything timely and original. Needs mystery. No explicit sex or violence, no gore or horror. Seldom publishes parodies or pastiches. **Buys up to 120 mss/year.** Send complete ms. Most stories 2,500-8,000 words. Accepts longer and shorter submissions—including minute mysteries of 250 words, and novellas of up to 20,000 words from established authors **Pays 5-8¢/word; occasionally higher for established authors.**

Poetry Short mystery verses, limericks. Length: 1 page, double spaced maximum.

Tips "We have a Department of First Stories to encourage writers whose fiction has never before been in print. We publish an average of 10 first stories every year. Mark mss Attn: Dept. of First Stories."

NATURE, CONSERVATION & ECOLOGY

$ $ $ AMERICAN FORESTS

American Forests, P.O. Box 2000, Washington DC 20013. E-mail: mrobbins@amfor.org. Website: www.americanforests.org. **75% freelance written**. Quarterly magazine of trees and forests published by a nonprofit citizens' organization that strives to help people plant and care for trees for ecosystem restoration and healthier communities. Estab. 1895. Circ. 25,000. Byline given. Pays on acceptance. No kill fee. Publishes ms an average of 8 months after acceptance. Buys one-time rights. Submit seasonal material 5 months in advance. Accepts queries by mail, e-mail. Accepts previously published material. Responds in 2 months to queries. Sample copy for $2. Guidelines available online.

Nonfiction All articles should emphasize trees, forests, forestry and related issues. Needs general interest, historical, how-to, humor, inspirational. **Buys 8-12 mss/year.** Query. Length: 1,200-2,000 words. **Pays $250-1,000.**

Reprints Send tearsheet or typed ms with rights for sale noted and information about when and where the material previously appeared. Pays 50% of amount paid for original article

Photos Originals only Send photos Captions required. Reviews 35mm or larger transparencies, glossy color prints. Offers no additional payment for photos accompanying ms. Buys one time rights.

Tips We're looking for more good urban forestry stories, and stories that show cooperation among disparate elements to protect/restore an ecosystem. Query should have honesty and information on photo support. We *do not* accept fiction or poetry at this time.

$ $ APPALACHIAN TRAILWAY NEWS

Appalachian Trail Conservancy, P.O. Box 807, Harpers Ferry WV 25425-0807. (304)535-6331. Fax: (304)535-2667. Website: www.appalachiantrail.org. **40% freelance written**. Bimonthly magazine. Estab. 1925. Circ. 32,000. Byline given. Pays on publication. No kill fee. Buys first North American serial rights, buys second serial (reprint) rights, buys web reprint rights. Responds in 2 months to queries. Sample copy and writer's guidelines online.

- Articles must relate to Appalachian Trail.

Nonfiction Publishes but does not pay for hiking reflections. Needs essays, general interest, historical, how-to, humor, inspirational, interview, photo feature, technical, travel. **Buys 5-10 mss/year.** Query with or without published clips, or send complete ms. Prefers e-mail queries. Length: 250-3,000 words. **Pays $25-300.** Pays expenses of writers on assignment.

Reprints Send photocopy with rights for sale noted and information about when and where the material previously appeared.

Photos State availability Identification of subjects required. Reviews contact sheets, 5x7 prints, slides, digital images. Offers $25-125/photo; $250/cover

Tips Contributors should display a knowledge of or interest in the Appalachian Trail. Those who live in the vicinity of the Trail may opt for an assigned story and should present credentials and subject of interest to the editor.

$ $ $ THE ATLANTIC SALMON JOURNAL

The Atlantic Salmon Federation, P.O. Box 5200, St. Andrews NB E5B 3S8 Canada. Fax: (506)529-4985. Website: www.asf.ca. **50-68% freelance written**. Quarterly magazine covering conservation efforts for the Atlantic salmon, catering to the dedicated angler and conservationist. Circ. 11,000. Byline given. Pays on publication. No kill fee. Publishes ms an average of 6 months after acceptance. Buys first North American serial rights. Buys one-time rights to photos. Submit seasonal material 3 months in advance. Accepts simultaneous submissions. Responds in 2 months to queries. Sample copy for 9x12 SAE with $1 (Canadian), or IRC. Guidelines free.

Nonfiction We are seeking articles that are pertinent to the focus and purpose of our magazine, which is to inform and entertain our membership on all aspects of the Atlantic salmon and its environment, and conservation. Needs expose, historical, how-to, humor, interview, new product, opinion, personal experience, photo feature, technical, travel, conservation. **Buys 15-20 mss/year.** Query with published clips. Length: 2,000 words. **Pays $400-800 for articles with photos.** Sometimes pays expenses of writers on assignment.

Photos State availability Captions, identification of subjects required. Pays $50 minimum; $350-500 for covers; $300 for 2-page spread; $175 for full page photo; $100 for ½-page photo.

Columns/Departments Fit To Be Tied (Conservation issues and salmon research; the design, construction and success of specific flies); interesting characters in the sport and opinion pieces by knowledgeable writers, 900 words; Casting Around (short, informative, entertaining reports, book reviews and quotes from the world of Atlantic salmon angling and conservation). Query. **Pays $50-300.**

Tips Articles must reflect informed and up-to-date knowledge of Atlantic salmon. Writers need not be authorities, but research must be impeccable. Clear, concise writing is essential, and submissions must be typed.

$ $ THE BEAR DELUXE MAGAZINE

Orlo, P.O. Box 10342, Portland OR 97296. (503)242-1047. E-mail: bear@orlo.org. Website: www.orlo.org. **80% freelance written**. Quarterly magazine. *The Bear Deluxe Magazine* is a national independent environmental magazine publishing significant works of reporting, creative nonfiction, literature, visual art and design. Based in the Pacific Northwest, *The Bear Deluxe* reaches across cultural and political divides to engage readers on vital issues effecting the environment. Estab. 1993. Circ. 19,000. Byline given. Pays on publication. Offers 25% kill fee. Publishes ms an average of 6 months after acceptance. Buys first rights, buys one-time rights. Editorial lead time 6 months. Submit seasonal material 9 months in advance. Accepts queries by mail, e-mail. Accepts previously published material. Accepts simultaneous submissions. Responds in 3-6 months to mail queries. Only responds to e-mail queries if interested. Sample copy for $3. Guidelines for #10 SASE or on website.

Nonfiction Needs book excerpts, essays, expose, general interest, interview, new product, opinion, personal experience, photo feature, travel, artist profiles. Publishes 1 theme/2 years **Buys 40 mss/year.** Query with published clips. Length: 250-4,500 words. **Pays $25-400, depending on piece.** Sometimes pays expenses of writers on assignment.

Photos State availability Identification of subjects, model releases required. Reviews contact sheets, transparencies, 8x10 prints. Offers $30/photo Buys one time rights.

Columns/Departments Reviews (almost anything), 300 words; Front of the Book (mix of short news bits, found writing, quirky tidbits), 300-500 words; Portrait of an Artist (artist profiles), 1,200 words; Back of the Book (creative opinion pieces), 650 words. 16 Query with published clips. **Pays $25-400, depending on piece.**

Fiction Stories must have some environmental context, but we view that in a broad sense. Needs adventure, cond novels, historical, horror, humorous, mystery, novel concepts, western. No detective, children's or horror. **Buys 8 mss/year.** Query or send complete ms. Length: 750-4,500 words. **Pays free subscription to the**

magazine, contributor's copies and $25-400, depending on piece; additional copies for postage.

Poetry Needs avant-garde, free verse, haiku, light verse, traditional. **Buys 16-20 poems/year.** Submit maximum 5 poems. 50 lines maximum **Pays $20, subscription, and copies.**

Fillers Needs facts, newsbreaks, short humor. 10 Length: 100-750 words. **$25, subscription, and copies**

Tips Offer to be a stringer for future ideas. Get a copy of the magazine and guidelines, and query us with specific nonfiction ideas and clips. We're looking for original, magazine-style stories, not fluff or PR. Fiction, essay, and poetry writers should know we have an open and blind review policy and should keep sending their best work even if rejected once. Be as specific as possible in queries.

$ $ BIRDER'S WORLD

Kalmbach Publishing Co., P.O. Box 1612, Waukesha WI 53187-1612. Fax: (262)798-6468. E-mail: mail@birdersworld.com. Website: www.birdersworld.com. Bimonthly magazine for birdwatchers who actively look for wild birds in the field. *Birder's World* concentrates on where to find, how to attract, and how to identify wild birds, and on how to understand what they do. Estab. 1987. Circ. 40,000. Byline given. Pays on acceptance. Buys one-time rights. Accepts queries by mail. Guidelines available online.

Nonfiction Needs essays, how-to, attracting birds, interview, personal experience, photo feature, bird photography, travel, birding hotspots in North America and beyond, product reviews/comparisons, bird biology, endangered or threatened birds. No poetry, fiction, or puzzles. **Buys 60 mss/year.** Query with published clips. Length: 500-2,400 words. **Pays $200-450.**

Photos See photo guidelines online. State availability Identification of subjects required. Buys one time rights.

$ BIRD WATCHER'S DIGEST

Pardson Corp., P.O. Box 110, Marietta OH 45750. (740)373-5285. Fax: (740)373-8443. E-mail: editor@birdwatchersdigest.com. Website: www.birdwatchersdigest.com. **60% freelance written. Works with a small number of new/unpublished writers each year.** Bimonthly magazine covering natural history—birds and bird watching. *BWD* is a nontechnical magazine interpreting ornithological material for amateur observers, including the knowledgeable birder, the serious novice and the backyard bird watcher; we strive to provide good reading and good ornithology. Estab. 1978. Circ. 90,000. Byline given. Pays on publication. Publishes ms an average of 2 years after acceptance. Buys one-time rights, buys second serial (reprint) rights. Submit seasonal material 6 months in advance. Accepts previously published material. Responds in 2 months to queries. Sample copy for $3.99 or online. Guidelines available online.

Nonfiction We are especially interested in fresh, lively accounts of closely observed bird behavior and displays and of bird-watching experiences and expeditions. We often need material on backyard subjects such as bird feeding, housing, gardenening on less common species or on unusual or previously unreported behavior of common species. Needs book excerpts, how-to, relating to birds, feeding and attracting, etc., humor, personal experience, travel, limited, we get many. No articles on pet or caged birds; none on raising a baby bird. **Buys 45-60 mss/year.** Send complete ms. Length: 600-3,500 words. **Pays from $100.**

Photos Send photos Reviews transparencies, prints. Pays $75 minimum for transparencies Buys one time rights.

Tips We are aimed at an audience ranging from the backyard bird watcher to the very knowledgeable birder; we include in each issue material that will appeal at various levels. We always strive for a good geographical spread, with material from every section of the country. We leave very technical matters to others, but we want facts and accuracy, depth and quality, directed at the veteran bird watcher and at the enthusiastic novice. We stress the joys and pleasures of bird watching, its environmental contribution, and its value for the individual and society.

$ $ $ CANADIAN WILDLIFE

350 Michael Cowpland Dr., Kanata ON K2M 2W1 Canada. (613)599-9594. Fax: (613)271-9591. E-mail: wild@cwf-fcf.org. **60% freelance written**. Magazine published 6 times/year. Only articles about Canadian subjects by Canadian writers will be considered. covering wildlife conservation. Includes topics pertaining to wildlife, endangered species, conservation, and natural history. Estab. 1995. Circ. 15,000. Byline given. Pays on acceptance. Publishes ms an average of 3 months after acceptance. Buys first North American serial rights, buys All material translated for publication in French-language edition, biosphere rights. Editorial lead time 3 months. Submit seasonal material 4 months in advance. Accepts queries by mail, e-mail. Responds in 6 weeks to queries. Responds in 2 months to mss. Guidelines free.

Nonfiction Needs book excerpts, interview, photo feature, science/nature. No standard travel stories. **Buys 20-25 mss/year.** Query with published clips. Length: 800-2,500 words. **Pays an average of 50 ¢ Cdn per word for assigned articles. Pays $300-1,000 for unsolicited articles.**

Photos Send photos Captions, identification of subjects, model releases required. Reviews transparencies. Negotiates payment individually Buys one time rights.

Tips *Canadian Wildlife* is a benefit of membership in the Canadian Wildlife Federation. Nearly 15,000 people currently receive the magazine. The majority of these men and women are already well versed in topics concerning the environment and natural science; writers, however, should not make assumptions about the extent of a reader's knowledge of topics.

$ $ $ CONSCIOUS CHOICE

The Journal of Ecology & Natural Living, Conscious Enlightenment, LLC, 920 N. Franklin St., Suite 202, Chicago IL 60610-3179. Fax: (312)751-3973. E-mail: editor@consciouschoice.com. Website: www.consciouschoice.com. **95% freelance written**. Monthly tabloid covering the environment, renewable energy, yoga, natural health and medicine, and personal growth and spirituality. Estab. 1988. Circ. 55,000. Byline given. Pays on publication. Offers 50% kill fee. Publishes ms an average of 6 months after acceptance. Buys first North American serial rights, buys electronic rights. Editorial lead time 6 months. Submit seasonal material 6 months in advance. Accepts queries by mail. Accepts simultaneous submissions. Responds in 6 weeks to queries. Responds in 1 month to mss. Sample copy available online. Writer's guidelines free or by e-mail

Nonfiction Needs general interest, to cultural creatives, interview, emphasis on narrative, story telling, environment. **Buys 24 mss/year.** Query with 2-3 published clips. 1,800 words **Pays $150-1,000.** Sometimes pays expenses of writers on assignment.

$ $ EARTH ISLAND JOURNAL

Earth Island Institute, 300 Broadway, Suite 28, San Francisco CA 94133. E-mail: editor@earthisland.org. Website: www.earthisland.org. **80% freelance written**. Quarterly magazine covering the environment/ecology. We are looking for in-depth, vigorously reported stories that reveal the connections between the environment and other contemporary issues. Our audience, though modest, includes many of the leaders of the environmental movement. Article pitches should be geared toward this sophisticated audience. Estab. 1985. Circ. 10,000. Byline given. Pays on publication. Publishes ms an average of 4 months after acceptance. Buys one-time rights, buys electronic rights. Editorial lead time 4 months. Submit seasonal material 4 months in advance. Accepts queries by e-mail. Responds in 4 weeks to queries. Responds in 1 month to mss. Sample copy for $5. Guidelines available online.

Nonfiction Needs book excerpts, essays, expose, general interest, interview, opinion, personal experience, photo feature. We do not want product pitches, services, or company news. **Buys 20/year mss/year.** Query with published clips. Length: 750-4,000 words. **Pays 20¢ a word for unsolicited articles.** Sometimes pays expenses of writers on assignment.

Photos Send photos Reviews contact sheets, GIF/JPEG files. We negotiate payment individually.

Columns/Departments Voices (first person reflection about the environment in a person's life.), 750 words. 4 mss/year Query. **Pays $$50.00.**

Tips Given our audience, we are looking for stories that break new ground when it comes to environmental coverage. We are not going to publish a story 'about recycling.' (I have seriously gotten this pitch.) We MAY, however, be interested in a story about, say, the waste manager in Kansas City, KS who developed an innovative technology for sorting trash, and how his/her scheme is being copied around the world.that is: We are looking for fresh angles on familiar stories, stories that so far have been overlooked by larger publications.

$ $ E THE ENVIRONMENTAL MAGAZINE

Earth Action Network, P.O. Box 5098, Westport CT 06881-5098. (203)854-5559. Fax: (203)866-0602. E-mail: info@emagazine.com. Website: www.emagazine.com. **60% freelance written**. Bimonthly magazine. *E Magazine* was formed for the purpose of acting as a clearinghouse of information, news, and commentary on environmental issues. Estab. 1990. Circ. 50,000. Byline given. Pays on publication. No kill fee. Buys first North American serial rights. Editorial lead time 3 months. Submit seasonal material 6 months in advance. Accepts queries by mail, e-mail, fax. Accepts simultaneous submissions. Sample copy for $5 or online. Guidelines available online.

- The editor reports an interest in seeing more investigative reporting.

Nonfiction On spec or free contributions welcome. Needs expose, environmental, how-to, new product, book review, feature (in-depth articles on key natural environmental issues). **Buys 100 mss/year.** Query with published clips. Length: 100-4,000 words. **Pays 30¢/word.**

Photos State availability Identification of subjects required. Reviews printed samples, e.g., magazine tearsheets, postcards, etc., to be kept on file. Negotiates payment individually Buys one time rights.

Columns/Departments On spec or free contributions welcome. In Brief/Currents (environmental news stories/ trends), 400-1,000 words; Conversations (Q&As with environmental movers and shakers), 2,000 words; Tools for Green Living; Your Health; Eco-Travel; Eco-Home; Eating Right; Green Business; Consumer News (each 700-1,200 words). Query with published clips.

Tips Contact us to obtain writer's guidelines and back issues of our magazine. Tailor your query according to the department/section you feel it would be best suited for. Articles must be lively, well researched, balanced, and relevant to a mainstream, national readership. On spec or free contributions welcome.

$ $ HIGH COUNTRY NEWS

P.O. Box 1090, Paonia CO 81428. (970)527-4898. E-mail: editor@hcn.org. Website: www.hcn.org. **70% freelance**

written. Biweekly nonprofit magazine covering environment, rural communities, and natural resource issues in 11 western states for environmentalists, politicians, companies, college classes, government agencies, grass roots activists, public land managers, etc. Estab. 1970. Circ. 25,000. Byline given. Pays on publication. Kill fee of 1/3 of agreed rate. Publishes ms an average of 2 months after acceptance. Buys all rights. Accepts queries by e-mail. Responds in 2 weeks to queries. Sample copy available online. Guidelines available online at: hcn.org/about/submissions.

Nonfiction "Magazine-style stories with strong storytelling, compelling characters, a clear, jargon-free style, and a dedication to intellectual honesty." **Buys 100 mss/year.** Query. up to 3,000 words **Pay negotiable.** Sometimes pays expenses of writers on assignment.

Photos Send photos Captions, identification of subjects required. Reviews b&w or color prints.

Columns/Departments See guidelines at: hcn.org/about/submissions.

Tips "We use a lot of freelance material. Familiarity with the newsmagazine is a must. Start by writing a query letter. We define 'resources' broadly to include people, culture, and aesthetic values, not just coal, oil, and timber."

$ $ $ MINNESOTA CONSERVATION VOLUNTEER

Minnesota Department of Natural Resources, 500 Lafeyette Rd., St. Paul MN 55155-4046. Website: www.dnr.state.mn.us/magazine. **50% freelance written**. Bimonthly magazine covering Minnesota natural resources, wildlife, natural history, outdoor recreation, and land use. *"Minnesota Conservation Volunteer* is a donor-supported magazine advocating conservation and wise use of Minnesota's natural resources. Material must reflect an appreciation of nature and an ethic of care for the environment. We rely on a variety of sources in our reporting. More than 140,000 Minnesota households, businesses, schools, and other groups subscribe to this conservation magazine." Estab. 1940. Circ. 164,200. Byline given. Pays on acceptance. Offers 30% kill fee. Publishes ms an average of 2 months after acceptance. Buys first North American serial rights, buys Rights to post to website, and archive rights. Editorial lead time 9 months. Submit seasonal material 9 months in advance. Accepts queries by mail, e-mail. Accepts previously published material. Responds in 1 month to queries. Responds in 2 months to mss. Sample copy free or on website Guidelines available online.

Nonfiction Needs book excerpts, essays, expose, general interest, historical, humor, interview, opinion, personal experience, photo feature, travel, Young Naturalist for children. Rarely publishes poetry or uncritical advocacy. **Buys 10 mss/year.** Query with published clips. Length: up to 1,500 words. **Pays 50¢/word for full-length feature articles.** Pays expenses of writers on assignment. up to $300

Photos $100/photo

Columns/Departments Close Encounters (unusual, exciting, or humorous personal wildlife experience in Minnesota), up to 1,500 words; Sense of Place (first- or third-person essay developing character of a Minnesota place), up to 1,500 words; Viewpoint (well-researched and well-reasoned opinion piece), up to 1,500 words; Minnesota Profile (concise description of emblematic state species or geographic feature), 400 words. 10 Query with published clips. **Pays 50¢/word**

Tips "In submitting queries, look beyond topics to *stories:* What is someone doing and why? How does the story end? In submitting a query addressing a particular issue, think of the human impacts and the sources you might consult. Summarize your idea, the story line, and sources in 2 or 3 short paragraphs. While topics must have relevance to Minnesota and give a Minnesota character to the magazine, feel free to round out your research with out-of-state sources."

$ $ $ NATIONAL PARKS

1300 19th St. NW, Suite 300, Washington DC 20036. (202)223-6722. Fax: (202)659-0650. E-mail: npmag@npca.org. Website: www.npca.org/magazine/. **60% freelance written. Prefers to work with published/established writers.** Quarterly magazine for a largely unscientific but highly educated audience interested in preservation of National Park System units, natural areas, and protection of wildlife habitat. Estab. 1919. Circ. 340,000. Pays on acceptance. Offers 33% kill fee. Publishes ms an average of 2 months after acceptance. Responds in 3-4 months to queries. Sample copy for $3 and 9x12 SASE or online. Guidelines available online.

Nonfiction All material must relate to US national parks. Needs expose, on threats, wildlife problems in national parks, descriptive articles about new or proposed national parks and wilderness parks. No poetry, philosophical essays, or first-person narratives. No unsolicited mss. Length: 1,500 words. **Pays $1,300 for 1,500-word features and travel articles.**

Photos Not looking for new photographers. Send photos

Tips Articles should have an original slant or news hook and cover a limited subject, rather than attempt to treat a broad subject superficially. Specific examples, descriptive details, and quotes are always preferable to generalized information. The writer must be able to document factual claims, and statements should be clearly substantiated with evidence within the article. *National Parks* does not publish fiction, poetry, personal essays, or 'My trip to.' stories.

$ $ $ $ NATURAL HISTORY

Natural History, Inc., 36 W. 25th St., 5th Floor, New York NY 10010. E-mail: nhmag@naturalhistorymag.com. Website: www.naturalhistorymag.com. **15% freelance written.** Magazine published 10 times/year for well-educated audience: professional people, scientists, and scholars. Circ. 225,000. Byline given. Pays on acceptance. No kill fee. Publishes ms an average of 3 months after acceptance. Buys first North American serial rights. Becomes an agent for second serial (reprint) rights Submit seasonal material 6 months in advance.

Nonfiction We are seeking new research on mammals, birds, invertebrates, reptiles, ocean life, anthropology, astronomy, preferably written by principal investigators in these fields. Our slant is toward unraveling problems in behavior, ecology, and evolution. **Buys 60 mss/year.** Query by mail or send complete ms Length: 1,500-3,000 words. **Pays $500-2,500.**

Photos Rarely uses 8x10 b&w glossy prints; pays $125/page maximum. Much color is used; pays $300 for inside, and up to $600 for cover. Buys one time rights.

Columns/Departments Journal (reporting from the field); Findings (summary of new or ongoing research); Naturalist At Large; The Living Museum (relates to the American Museum of Natural History); Discovery (natural or cultural history of a specific place).

Tips We expect high standards of writing and research. We do not lobby for causes, environmental, or other. The writer should have a deep knowledge of his subject, then submit original ideas either in query or by manuscript.

$ $ $ NATURE CANADA

85 Alberta St., Suite 900, Ottawa ON K1P 6A4 Canada. (613)562-3447. Fax: (613)562-3371. Website: www.naturecanada.ca. Quarterly magazine covering conservation, natural history and environmental/naturalist community. Editorial content reflects the goals and priorities of Nature Canada as a conservation organization with a focus on our program areas: federally protected areas (national parks, national wildlife areas, etc.), endangered species, and bird conservation through Canada's important bird areas. Nature Canada is written for an audience interested in nature conservation. Nature Canada celebrates, preserves, and protects Canadian nature. We promote the awareness and understanding of the connection between humans and nature and how natural systems support life on Earth. We strive to instill a sense of ownership and belief that these natural systems should be protected. Estab. 1971. Circ. 27,000. Byline given. Pays on publication. Offers $100 kill fee. Publishes ms an average of 3 months after acceptance. Buys all Nature Canada rights (including electronic). Author retains resale rights elsewhere. Editorial lead time 4 months. Submit seasonal material 6 months in advance. Responds in 4 months to mss. Sample copy for $5. Guidelines available online.

Nonfiction Subjects include: Canadian conservation issues; nature education; reconnecting with nature; enviro-friendly lifestyles, products and consumer reports; federal protected areas; endangered species; birds; sustainable development; company and individual profiles; urban nature; how-to; natural history **Buys 12 mss/year.** Query with published clips. Length: 650-2,000 words. **Pays up to 50¢/word (Canadian).**

Photos State availability Identification of subjects required. Offers $50-200/photo (Canadian) Buys one time rights.

Tips Our readers are well-educated and knowledgeable about nature and the environment so contributors should have a good understanding of the subject. We also deal exclusively with Canadian issues and species, except for those relating directly to our international program. E-mail queries preferred. Do not send unsolicited manuscripts. We receive many BC-related queries but need more for the rest of Canada, particularly SK, MB, QC and the Maritimes. Articles must focus on the positive and be supported by science when applicable. We are looking for strong, well-researched writing that is lively, entertaining, enlightening, provocative and, when appropriate, amusing.

$ $ NORTHERN WOODLANDS MAGAZINE

Center for Woodlands Education, Inc., 1776 Center Rd., P.O. Box 471, Corinth VT 05039-0471. (802)439-6292. Fax: (802)439-6296. E-mail: dave@northernwoodlands.org. Website: www.northernwoodlands.org. **40-60% freelance written.** Quarterly magazine covering natural history, conservation, and forest management in the Northeast. "*Northern Woodlands* strives to inspire landowners' sense of stewardship by increasing their awareness of the natural history and the principles of conservation and forestry that are directly related to their land. We also hope to increase the public's awareness of the social, economic, and environmental benefits of a working forest." Estab. 1994. Circ. 12,000. Byline given. Pays 1 month prior to publication. Publishes ms an average of 6 months after acceptance. Buys one-time rights. Editorial lead time 6 months. Submit seasonal material 6 months in advance. Accepts queries by mail, e-mail. Accepts previously published material. Accepts simultaneous submissions. Responds in 1 month to queries. Responds in 1-2 months to mss Sample copy available online Guidelines available online

Nonfiction Contact: Stephen Long, editor. Needs book excerpts, essays, how-to, related to woodland management, interview, related to the Northeastern U.S. No product reviews, first-person travelogues, cute animal stories, opinion, or advocacy pieces. **Buys 15-20 mss/year.** Query with published clips. Length: 500-3,000 words. **Pays 10¢/word.** Sometimes pays expenses of writers on assignment.

Photos State availability Identification of subjects required. Reviews transparencies, prints, high res digital photos. Offers $35-75/photo Buys one time rights.
Columns/Departments Contact: Stephen Long, editor. A Place in Mind (essays on places of personal significance), 600-800 words. **Pays $150**. Knots and Bolts (seasonal natural history items or forest-related news items), 300-600 words. **Pays 10¢/word**. Wood Lit (book reviews), 600 words. **Pays $50**. Field Work (profiles of people who work in the woods, the wood-product industry, or conservation field), 1,500 words. **Pays 10¢/word**. 30 Query with published clips.
Poetry Contact: Jim Schley, poetry editor. Needs free verse, light verse, traditional. **Buys 4 poems/year.** Submit maximum 5 poems. **Pays $25.**
Tips "We will work with subject-matter experts to make their work suitable for our audience."

$ $ OCEAN MAGAZINE

to Celebrate and Protect, P.O. Box 84, Rodanthe NC 27968-0084. (252)256-2296. E-mail: diane@oceanmag.org. Website: www.oceanmag.org. **100% freelance written**. Quarterly magazine covering the ocean, its ecosystem, its creatures, recreation, pollution, energy sources, the love of it. *"OCEAN Magazine* serves to celebrate and protect the greatest, most comprehensive resource for life on earth, our world's ocean. *OCEAN* publishes articles, stories, poems, essays, and photography about the ocean—observations, experiences, scientific and environmental discussions—written with fact and feeling, illustrated with images from nature." Estab. 2003. Circ. 10,000. Byline given. Pays on publication. Publishes ms an average of 2-4 months after acceptance. Buys one-time rights. Editorial lead time 3-6 months. Submit seasonal material 3-6 months in advance. Accepts queries by mail, e-mail (preferable), phone. Accepts previously published material, occasionallyAccepts simultaneous submissions. Responds in 1 day to 4 weeks to queries and mss Sample copy available online Guidelines available online
Nonfiction Needs book excerpts, essays, general interest, historical, inspirational, interview, opinion, personal experience, photo feature, technical, travel, spiritual. Does not want poor writing. **Buys 24-36 mss/year.** Query. Length: 75-5,000 words. **Pays $75-500.**
Photos State availability Identification of subjects, model releases required. Reviews 3x5, 4x6, 5x7, 8x10, 10x12 prints, JPEG files. Negotiates payment individually. Buys one time rights.
Fiction Needs adventure, fantasy, historical, novel concepts, romance, slice-of-life vignettes. **Buys 1-2 mss/year.** Query. Length: 100-2,000 words. **Pays $75-400.**
Poetry Needs avant-garde, free verse, haiku, light verse, traditional. **Buys 12 poems/year.** Submit maximum 6 poems. **Pays $75-150.**
Fillers Needs anecdotes, facts. 4-12 Length: 20-100 words. **Pays $25-50.**
Tips "Submit with a genuine love and concern for the ocean and its creatures."

$ $ $ $ ORION

The Orion Society, 187 Main St., Great Barrington MA 01230. E-mail: orion@orionsociety.org. Website: www.orioonline.org. **90% freelance written**. Bimonthly magazine covering nature and culture. *Orion* is a magazine about the issues of our time: how we live, what we value, what sustains us. *Orion* explores an emerging alternative worldview through essays, literary journalism, short stories, interviews, and reviews, as well as photo essays and portfolios of art. Estab. 1982. Circ. 22,000. Byline given. Pays on publication. No kill fee. Publishes ms an average of 3-12 months after acceptance. Buys first North American serial rights. Editorial lead time 3-9 months. Submit seasonal material 9 months in advance. Accepts queries by mail, e-mail. Accepts simultaneous submissions. Responds in 1-2 months to queries. Responds in 4-6 months to mss. Sample copy available online. Guidelines available online.
Nonfiction Needs essays, expose, historical, humor, personal experience, photo feature, reported feature. No What I learned during my walk in the woods; personal hiking/adventure/travel anecdotes; unsolicited poetry; writing that deals with the natural world in only superficial ways. **Buys 40-50 mss/year.** Send complete ms. Length: 2,000-4,500 words. **Pays $300-2,000.** Pays expenses of writers on assignment.
Photos State availability Reviews contact sheets, prints. Negotiates payment individually. Buys one time rights.
Columns/Departments Point of View (opinion essay by a noted authority), 625 words; Sacred & Mundane (funny, ironic or awe-inspiring ways nature exists within or is created by contemporary culture), 200-600 words; Health & the Environment (emphasizes and explores relationship between human health and a healthy natural world, or forces that threaten both simultaneously), 1,300 words; Reviews (new books, films and recordings related to *Orion's* mission), 250-600 words; Coda (an endpaper), 650 words. 85 Send complete ms. **Pays $25-300.**
Fiction Needs ethnic, historical, humorous, mainstream, slice-of-life vignettes. No manuscripts that don't carry an environmental message or involve the landscape/nature as a major character. Buys up to 1 ms/year. Send complete ms. Length: 1,200-4,000 words. **Pays 10-20¢/word.**
Tips We are most impressed by and most likely to work with writers whose submissions show they know our magazine. If you are proposing a story, your query must: 1. Be detailed in its approach and reflect the care you

will give the story itself; 2. Define where in the magazine you believe the story would be appropriate; 3. Include three tear sheets of previously published work. If you are submitting a manuscript, it must be double-spaced, typed or printed in black ink. Please be sure your name and a page number appear on each page of your submission, and that we have your phone number and SASE.

$ $ $ OUTDOOR AMERICA

Izaak Walton League of America, 707 Conservation Ln., Gaithersburg MD 20878-2983. (301)548-0150. Fax: (301)548-9409. E-mail: oa@iwla.org. Website: www.iwla.org. Quarterly magazine covering national conservation efforts/issues related to and involving members of the Izaak Walton League. A 4-color publication, *Outdoor America* is received by League members, as well as representatives of Congress and the media. Our audience, located predominantly in the midwestern and mid-Atlantic states, enjoys traditional recreational pursuits, such as fishing, hiking, hunting, and boating. All have a keen interest in protecting the future of our natural resources and outdoor recreation heritage. Estab. 1922. Circ. 40,000. Pays on acceptance. Offers 1/3 original rate kill fee. Publishes ms an average of 2 months after acceptance. Buys first North American serial rights. Accepts queries by mail, e-mail. Responds in 2 months to queries. Sample copy for $2.50. Guidelines available online.

Nonfiction Conservation and natural resources issue stories with a direct connection to the work and members of the Izaak Walton League. Features should be 2,000-3,000 words. Essays on outdoor ethics and conservation (1,500-2,000 words). No fiction, poetry, or unsubstantiated opinion pieces. Query or send ms for short columns/news pieces (500 words or less). Features are planned 6-12 months in advance. **Pays $1,000-1,500 for features.**

Photos Send tearsheets or nonreturnable samples. Pays $100-500.

$ $ $ $ SIERRA

85 Second St., 2nd Floor, San Francisco CA 94105. E-mail: sierra.letters@sierraclub.org. Website: www.sierraclub.org. **Works with a small number of new/unpublished writers each year.** Bimonthly magazine emphasizing conservation and environmental politics for people who are well educated, activist, outdoor-oriented, and politically well informed with a dedication to conservation. Estab. 1893. Circ. 695,000. Byline given. Pays on acceptance. Offers negotiable kill fee. Publishes ms an average of 4 months after acceptance. Buys first North American serial rights. Accepts queries by mail, fax. Accepts previously published material. Responds in 2 months to queries. Sample copy for $3 and SASE, or online. Guidelines available online.

- The editor reports an interest in seeing pieces on environmental heroes, thoughtful features on new developments in solving environmental problems, and outdoor adventure stories with a strong environmental element.

Nonfiction Needs expose, well-documented articles on environmental issues of national importance such as energy, wilderness, forests, etc., general interest, well-researched nontechnical pieces on areas of particular environmental concern, interview, photo feature, photo feature essays on threatened or scenic areas, journalistic treatments of semitechnical topic (energy sources, wildlife management, land use, waste management, etc.). No My trip to . or Why we must save wildlife/nature articles; no poetry or general superficial essays on environmentalism; no reporting on purely local environmental issues. **Buys 30-36 mss/year.** Query with published clips. Length: 1,000-3,000 words. **Pays $800-3,000.**

Reprints Send photocopy with rights for sale noted and information about when and where the material previously appeared. Payment negotiable

Photos Send photos Pays maximum $300 for transparencies; more for cover photos Buys one time rights.

Columns/Departments Food for Thought (food's connection to environment); Good Going (adventure journey); Hearth & Home (advice for environmentally sound living); Body Politics (health and the environment); Profiles (biographical look at environmentalists); Hidden Life (exposure of hidden environmental problems in everyday objects); Lay of the Land (national/international concerns), 500-700 words; Mixed Media (essays on environment in the media; book reviews), 200-300 words. **Pays $50-500.**

Tips Queries should include an outline of how the topic would be covered and a mention of the political appropriateness and timeliness of the article. Statements of the writer's qualifications should be included.

$ $ WHISPER IN THE WOODS

Nature Journal, Turning Leaf Productions, LLC, P.O. Box 1014, Traverse City MI 49685-1014. (231)943-0153. E-mail: editor@whisperinthewoods.com. Website: www.whisperinthewoods.com. **100% freelance written.** Quarterly literary art journal covering nature, art and photography. We focus on the appreciation of the beauty of nature. Estab. 2002. Circ. 10,000. Byline sometimes given. Pays on publication. Offers 20% kill fee. Publishes ms an average of 9 months after acceptance. Buys first North American serial rights. Editorial lead time 1 year. Submit seasonal material 1 year in advance. Accepts queries by mail. Accepts previously published material. Accepts simultaneous submissions. Sample copy for $8. Guidelines available online.

Nonfiction Needs essays, inspirational, personal experience, photo feature, travel. Query with published clips. Length: 600-1,500 words. **Pays $20-300.**

Photos State availability Captions required. Reviews contact sheets, GIF/JPEG files. Buys one time rights.
Poetry Contact: Denise Baker, managing editor. Needs avant-garde, free verse, haiku, light verse, traditional. **Buys 4 poems/year.** Submit maximum 5 poems. **Pays $25-40.**
Tips Carefully follow submission guidelines.

$ $ $ $ WILDLIFE CONSERVATION

2300 Southern Blvd., Bronx NY 10460. E-mail: nsimmons@wcs.org. Website: www.wcs.org. Bimonthly magazine for environmentally aware readers. Offers 25% kill fee. Buys first North American serial rights. Accepts simultaneous submissions. Responds in 1 month to queries. Sample copy for $4.95 (plus $1 postage). Writer's guidelines available for SASE or via e-mail.
Nonfiction We want well-reported articles on conservation issues, conservation successes, and straight natural history based on author's research. **Buys 30 mss/year.** Query with published clips. Length: 300-2,000 words. **Pays $1/word for features and department articles, and $150 for short pieces**

PERSONAL COMPUTERS

$ $ $ LAPTOP

Bedford Communications, 1410 Broadway, 21st Floor, New York NY 10018. (212)807-8220. Fax: (212)807-1098. Website: www.laptopmag.com. **60%% freelance written.** Monthly magazine covering mobile computing, such as laptop computers, PDAs, software, and peripherals; industry trends. Publication is geared toward the mobile technology laptop computer buyer, with an emphasis on the small office. Estab. 1991. Byline given. Pays on publication. Offers 20% kill fee. Publishes ms an average of 3 months after acceptance. Buys all rights. Editorial lead time 4 months. Accepts queries by e-mail. Responds in 4 months to queries. Sample copy available online.
Nonfiction Needs how-to, e.g., how-to install a CD-ROM drive, technical, hands-on reviews, features. **Buys 80-100 mss/year.** Length: 300-3,500 words. **Pays $150-1,250.** Sometimes pays expenses of writers on assignment.
Columns/Departments .
Tips Send resume with feature-length clips (technology-related, if possible) to editorial offices. Unsolicited manuscripts are not accepted or returned.

$ $ $ $ MACLIFE

4000 Shoreline Ct., Suite 400, South San Francisco CA 94080. (650)872-1642. Fax: (650)872-1643. E-mail: editor@maclife.com. Website: www.maclife.com. **20% freelance written.** Monthly magazine covering Macintosh computers. "*MacLife* is a magazine for Macintosh computer enthusiasts of all levels. Writers must know, love and own Macintosh computers and/or iPhone, depending on the nature of the query/article." Estab. 1996. Circ. 160,000. Byline given. Pays on publication. No kill fee. Publishes ms an average of 3 months after acceptance. Buys all rights. Editorial lead time 3 months. Submit seasonal material 2 months in advance. Accepts queries by mail, e-mail. Responds in 1 month to queries
Nonfiction "Looking for helpful, entertaining, pop culture-savvy articles and pitches." Needs how-to, new product, technical. No humor, case studies, personal experience, essays. **Buys 10-30 mss/year.** Query. Length: 250-7,500 words. **Pays an average of 35¢/word, depending on the nature & length of assignment.**
Columns/Departments Reviews (always assigned), 300-750 words; How-to's (detailed, step-by-step), 500-2,500 words; features, 1,000-3,500 words. 20 Query with or without published clips. **Pays an average of 35¢/word, depending on the nature & length of assignment.**
Tips "Send us an idea for a short one to two page how-to and/or send us a letter outlining your publishing experience and areas of Mac expertise so we can assign a review to you (reviews editor is Roman Loyola). Your submission should have great practical hands-on benefit to a reader, be fun to read in the author's natural voice, and include lots of screenshot graphics. We require electronic submissions. Impress our reviews editor with well-written reviews of Mac products and then move up to bigger articles from there."

$ $ $ SMART COMPUTING

Sandhills Publishing, 131 W. Grand Dr., Lincoln NE 68521. (800)544-1264. Fax: (402)479-2104. E-mail: editor@smartcomputing.com. Website: www.smartcomputing.com. **45% freelance written.** Monthly magazine. "We focus on plain-English computing articles with an emphasis on tutorials that improve productivity without the purchase of new hardware." Estab. 1990. Circ. 200,000. Byline given. Pays on acceptance. Offers 25% kill fee. Publishes ms an average of 2 months after acceptance. Buys all rights. Editorial lead time 4 months. Submit seasonal material 4 months in advance. Accepts queries by mail, e-mail. Accepts simultaneous submissions. Responds in 1 month to queries. Sample copy for $7.99. Guidelines for #10 SASE.
Nonfiction Needs how-to, new product, technical. No humor, opinion, personal experience. **Buys 250 mss/year.** Query with published clips. Length: 800-3,200 words. **Pays $240-960.** Pays expenses of writers on assignment

up to $75
Photos Send photos Captions required. Offers no additional payment for photos accepted with ms. Buys all rights.
Tips "Focus on practical, how-to computing articles. Our readers are intensely productivity-driven. Carefully review recent issues. We receive many ideas for stories printed in the last 6 months."

WIRED MAGAZINE

Condé Nast Publications, 520 Third St., 3rd Floor, San Francisco CA 94107-1815. (415)276-5000. Fax: (415)276-5150. E-mail: submit@wiredmag.com. Website: www.wired.com/wired. **95% freelance written.** Monthly magazine covering technology and digital culture. We cover the digital revolution and related advances in computers, communications and lifestyles. Estab. 1993. Circ. 500,000. Byline given. Pays on publication. Offers 25% kill fee. Publishes ms an average of 3 months after acceptance. Buys all rights for items less than 1,000 words, first North American serial rights for pieces over 1,000 words. Editorial lead time 3 months. Accepts queries by e-mail. Responds in 3 weeks to queries. Sample copy for $4.95. Guidelines by email.
Nonfiction Needs essays, interview, opinion. No poetry or trade articles. **Buys 85 features, 130 short pieces, 200 reviews, 36 essays, and 50 other mss/year.** Query. Pays expenses of writers on assignment.
Tips Read the magazine. We get too many inappropriate queries. We need quality writers who understand our audience, and who understand how to query.

PHOTOGRAPHY

$ NATURE PHOTOGRAPHER

Nature Photographer Publishing Co., Inc., P.O. Box 220, Lubec ME 04652. (207)733-4201. Fax: (207)733-4202. E-mail: nature_photographer@yahoo.com. Website: www.naturephotographermag.com. Quarterly magazine written by field contributors and editors; write to above address to become a Field Contributor. *Nature Photographer* emphasizes nature photography that uses low-impact and local less-known locations, techniques and ethics. Articles include how-to, travel to world-wide wilderness locations, and how nature photography can be used to benefit the environment and environmental education of the public. Estab. 1990. Circ. 35,000. Pays on publication. Buys one-time rights. Submit seasonal material 8 months in advance. Accepts queries by e-mail. Accepts simultaneous submissions. Responds in 2 months to queries. Sample copy for sae with 9x12 envelope and 6 First-Class stamps. Guidelines by email.
Nonfiction Needs how-to, exposure, creative techniques, techniques to make photography easier, low-impact techniques, macro photography, wildlife, scenics, flowers, photo feature, technical, travel. No articles about photographing in zoos or on game farms. **Buys 56-72 mss/year.** Length: 750-2,500 words. **Pays $75-150.**
Photos Send photos upon request. Do not send with submission. Identification of subjects required. Reviews 35mm and digital images on CD (both scanned and digitally captured images) transparencies. Offers no additional payment for photos accepted with ms. Buys one time rights.
Tips Must have good, solid research and knowledge of subject. Be sure to obtain guidelines before submitting query. If you have not requested guidelines within the last year, request an updated version because *Nature Photographer* is now written by editors and field contributors, and guidelines will outline how you can become a field contributor.

$ $ PC PHOTO

Werner Publishing Corp., 12121 Wilshire Blvd., 12th Floor, Los Angeles CA 90025. (310)820-1500. Fax: (310)826-5008. E-mail: editor@pcphotomag.com. Website: www.pcphotomag.com. **60% freelance written.** Bimonthly magazine covering digital photography. Our magazine is designed to help photographers better use digital technologies to improve their photography. Estab. 1997. Circ. 175,000. Byline given. Pays on publication. No kill fee. Publishes ms an average of 4 months after acceptance. Buys one-time rights. Editorial lead time 6 months. Submit seasonal material 6 months in advance. Accepts queries by mail. Responds in 1 month to queries. Sample copy for #10 SASE or online. Guidelines available online.
Nonfiction Needs how-to, personal experience, photo feature. **Buys 30 mss/year.** Query. 1,200 words **Pays $500 for assigned articles. Pays approximately $400 for unsolicited articles.**
Photos Do not send original transparencies or negatives. Send photos Offers $100-200/photo Buys one time rights.
Tips Since *PCPHOTO* is a photography magazine, we must see photos before any decision can be made on an article, so phone queries are not appropriate. Ultimately, whether we can use a particular piece or not will depend greatly on the photographs and how they fit in with material already in our files. We take a fresh look at the modern photographic world by encouraging photography and the use of new technologies. Editorial is intended to demystify the use of modern equipment by emphasizing practical use of the camera and the computer, highlighting the technique rather than the technical.

$ $ PHOTO TECHNIQUES

Preston Publications, Inc., 6600 W. Touhy Ave., Niles IL 60714. (847)647-2900. Fax: (847)647-1155. E-mail: slewis@prestonpub.com. Website: www.phototechmag.com. **50% freelance written. Prefers to work with experienced photographer-writers; happy to work with excellent photographers whose writing skills are lacking.** Bimonthly publication covering photochemistry, lighting, optics, processing, and printing, Zone System, digital imaging/scanning/printing, special effects, sensitometry, etc. Aimed at serious amateurs. Article conclusions should be able to be duplicated by readers. Estab. 1979. Circ. 20,000. Byline given. Pays within 3 weeks of publication. No kill fee. Publishes ms an average of 6 months after acceptance. Buys one-time rights. Sample copy for $6. Guidelines by email.

Nonfiction Needs how-to, photo feature, technical, product review, special interest articles within the above listed topics. Query or send complete ms Open, but most features run approximately 2,500 words or 3-4 magazine pages **Pays $100-450 for well-researched technical articles.**

Photos Photographers have a much better chance of having their photos published if the photos accompany a written article. Prefers JPEGs scanned at 300 dpi and sent via e-mail or CD-ROM, or prints, slides, and transparencies. Captions, True required. Ms payment includes payment for photos. Buys one time rights.

Tips Study the magazine! Virtually all writers we publish are readers of the magazine. We are now more receptive than ever to articles about photographers, history, aesthetics, and informative backgrounders about specific areas of the photo industry or specific techniques. Successful writers for our magazine are doing what they write about.

$ PICTURE MAGAZINE

319 Lafayette St., No. 135, New York NY 10012. (212)352-2700. Fax: (212)352-2155. E-mail: editorial@picturemagazine.com. Website: www.picturemagazine.com. **100% freelance written**. Bimonthly magazine covering professional photography topics. Estab. 1995. Circ. 16,000. Byline given. Pays on publication. No kill fee. Publishes ms an average of 2 months after acceptance. Buys one-time rights. Editorial lead time 3 months. Submit seasonal material 3 months in advance. Accepts queries by e-mail. Accepts previously published material. Accepts simultaneous submissions. Sample copy free. Guidelines free.

Nonfiction Needs general interest, how-to, interview, new product, photo feature, technical. **Buys 5 mss/year.** Send complete ms. Length: 1,500-2,500 words. **Pays $150.** Pays expenses of writers on assignment.

Photos State availability Captions required. Offers no additional payment for photos accepted with ms. Buys one time rights.

$ $ VIDEOMAKER

Videomaker, Inc., P.O. Box 4591, Chico CA 95927-4591. (530)891-8410. Fax: (530)891-8443. E-mail: editor@videomaker.com. Website: www.videomaker.com. Monthly magazine covering audio and video production, camcorders, editing, computer video, DVDs. Estab. 1985. Circ. 57,814. Byline given. Pays on publication. No kill fee. Publishes ms an average of 4 months after acceptance. Buys electronic rights, buys all rights. Editorial lead time 5 months. Submit seasonal material 5 months in advance. Accepts queries by mail, e-mail. Responds in 3 weeks to queries. Sample copy and writer's guidelines online.

- The magazine's voice is friendly, encouraging; never condescending to the audience.

Nonfiction Needs how-to, technical. Annual Buyer's Guide in October (13th issue of the year) **Buys 34 mss/year.** Query. Length: 800-1,500 words. **Pays $100-300.** Sometimes pays expenses of writers on assignment. Limit agreed upon in advance

Photos Contact: Melissa Hageman, art director. Model releases required. Negotiates payment individually

Fiction Buys 3 mss/year. Query. Length: 400-600 words. **Pays $150-200.**

POLITICS & WORLD AFFAIRS

THE AMERICAN SPECTATOR

1611 N. Kent St., Suite 901, Arlington VA 22209. (703)807-2011. Fax: (703)807-2013. E-mail: editor@spectator.org. Website: www.spectator.org. Monthly magazine. For many years, one ideological viewpoint dominated American print and broadcast journalism. Today, that viewpoint still controls the entertainment and news divisions of the television networks, the mass-circulation news magazines, and the daily newspapers. *American Spectator* has attempted to balance the Left's domination of the media by debunking its perceived wisdom and advancing alternative ideas through spirited writing, insightful essays, humor and, most recently, through well-researched investigative articles that have themselves become news. Estab. 1967. Circ. 50,000. Pays on other. No kill fee. Accepts queries by mail.

Nonfiction Topics include politics, the press, foreign relations, the economy, culture. Stories most suited for publication are timely articles on previously unreported topics with national appeal. Articles should be thoroughly researched with a heavy emphasis on interviewing and reporting, and the facts of the article should be verifiable. We prefer articles in which the facts speak for themselves and shy away from editorial and first

person commentary. No unsolicited poetry, fiction, satire, or crossword puzzles. Query with resume, clips and SASE.
Columns/Departments The Continuing Crisis and Current Wisdom (humor); On the Prowl (Washington insider news). Query with resume, clips and SASE.

ARENA MAGAZINE

P.O. Box 18, North Carlton VIC 3054 Australia. (61)(3)9416-5166. E-mail: magazine@arena.org.au. Website: www.arena.org.au. Bimonthly magazine. "Australia's leading magazine of left political, social and cultural commentary."

- Query before submitting.

Nonfiction Needs essays, letters, political commentary.

$ $ CHURCH & STATE

Americans United for Separation of Church and State, 518 C St. NE, Washington DC 20002. (202)466-3234. Fax: (202)466-3353. E-mail: americansunited@au.org. Website: www.au.org. **10% freelance written**. Monthly magazine emphasizing religious liberty and church/state relations matters. Strongly advocates separation of church and state. Readership is well-educated. Estab. 1947. Circ. 40,000. Pays on acceptance. No kill fee. Publishes ms an average of 2 months after acceptance. Buys all rights. Accepts queries by mail. Accepts simultaneous submissions. Responds in 2 months to queries. Sample copy and writer's guidelines for 9x12 SAE with 3 first-class stamps
Nonfiction Needs expose, general interest, historical, interview. **Buys 11 mss/year.** Query. Length: 800-1,600 words. **Pays $150-300.** Sometimes pays expenses of writers on assignment.
Reprints Send tearsheet, photocopy or typed ms with rights for sale noted and information about when and where the material previously appeared.
Photos Send photos Captions required. Pays negotiable fee for b&w prints Buys one time rights.
Tips We're looking for feature articles on underreported local church-state controversies. We also consider 'viewpoint' essays that offer a unique or personal take on church-state issues. We are not a religious magazine. You need to see our magazine before you try to write for it.

$ COMMONWEAL

A Review of Public Affairs, Religion, Literature and the Arts, Commonweal Foundation, 475 Riverside Dr., Room 405, New York NY 10115. (212)662-4200. Fax: (212)662-4183. E-mail: editors@commonwealmagazine.org. Website: www.commonwealmagazine.org. Biweekly journal of opinion edited by Catholic lay people, dealing with topical issues of the day on public affairs, religion, literature, and the arts. Estab. 1924. Circ. 20,000. Byline given. Pays on publication. No kill fee. Buys all rights. Submit seasonal material 2 months in advance. Responds in 2 months to queries. Sample copy free. Guidelines available online.
Nonfiction Needs essays, general interest, interview, personal experience, religious. **Buys 30 mss/year.** Query with published clips. Length: 2,000-2,500 words. **Pays $75-100.**
Columns/Departments Upfronts (brief, newsy reportorials, giving facts, information and some interpretation behind the headlines of the day), 750-1,000 words; Last Word (usually of a personal nature, on some aspect of the human condition: spiritual, individual, political, or social), 800 words.
Poetry Contact: Rosemary Deen, editor. Needs free verse, traditional. **Buys 20 poems/year. Pays 75¢/line.**
Tips Articles should be written for a general but well-educated audience. While religious articles are always topical, we are less interested in devotional and churchy pieces than in articles which examine the links between `worldly' concerns and religious beliefs.

$ $ THE FREEMAN: IDEAS ON LIBERTY

30 S. Broadway, Irvington-on-Hudson NY 10533. (914)591-7230. Fax: (914)591-8910. E-mail: freeman@fee.org. Website: www.fee.org. **85% freelance written**. Monthly publication for the layman and fairly advanced students of liberty. Estab. 1946. Byline given. Pays on publication. No kill fee. Publishes ms an average of 5 months after acceptance. all rights, including reprint rights. Sample copy for 7 ½x10 ½ SASE with 4 first-class stamps.

- Eager to work with new/unpublished writers.

Nonfiction We want nonfiction clearly analyzing and explaining various aspects of the free market, private property, limited-government philosophy. Though a necessary part of the literature of freedom is the exposure of collectivistic cliches and fallacies, our aim is to emphasize and explain the positive case for individual responsibility and choice in a free-market economy. We avoid name-calling and personality clashes. Ours is an intelligent analysis of the principles underlying a free-market economy. No political strategies or tactics. **Buys 100 mss/year.** Query with SASE. Length: 3,500 words. **Pays 10¢/word.** Sometimes pays expenses of writers on assignment.
Tips It's most rewarding to find freelancers with new insights, fresh points of view. Facts, figures and quotations cited should be fully documented, to their original source, if possible.

$ $ THE NATION

33 Irving Place, New York NY 10003. (212)209-5400. Fax: (212)982-9000. Website: www.thenation.com. **75% freelance written. Works with a small number of new/unpublished writers each year.** "Weekly magazine firmly committed to reporting on the issues of labor, national politics, business, consumer affairs, environmental politics, civil liberties, foreign affairs and the role and future of the Democratic Party.". Estab. 1865. Pays on other. No kill fee. Buys first rights. Accepts queries by mail, e-mail, fax. Sample copy free. Guidelines available online.

Nonfiction "We welcome all articles dealing with the social scene, from an independent perspective. Queries encouraged." **Buys 100 mss/year. Pays $350-500.** Sometimes pays expenses of writers on assignment.

Columns/Departments Editorial, 500-700 words. **Pays $-150.**

Poetry "*The Nation* publishes poetry of outstanding aesthetic quality. Send poems with SASE. See the Contests & Awards section for the Discovery—*The Nation* poetry contest." **Payment negotiable.**

Tips "We are a journal of left/liberal political opinion covering national and international affairs. We are looking both for reporting and for fresh analysis. On the domestic front, we are particularly interested in civil liberties; civil rights; labor, economics, environmental and feminist issues and the role and future of the Democratic Party. Because we have readers all over the country, it's important that stories with a local focus have real national significance. In our foreign affairs coverage we prefer pieces on international political, economic and social developments. As the magazine which published Ralph Nader's first piece (and there is a long list of *Nation* firsts), we are seeking new writers."

⊘ THE NATIONAL VOTER

League of Women Voters, 1730 M St. NW, Suite 1000, Washington DC 20036. (202)429-1965. Fax: (202)429-0854. E-mail: nationalvoter@lwv.org. Website: www.lwv.org. Magazine published 3 times/year. *The National Voter* provides background, perspective and commentary on public policy issues confronting citizens and their leaders at all levels of government. And it empowers people to make a difference in their communities by offering guidance, maturation and models for action. Estab. 1951. Circ. 90,000. Byline given. Pays on publication. No kill fee. Makes work-for-hire assignments. Editorial lead time 2 months. Accepts queries by mail, e-mail. Sample copy free.

- No unsolicited mss.

Photos State availability Captions, identification of subjects required. Offers no additional payment for photos accepted with ms.

$ $ THE PROGRESSIVE

409 E. Main St., Madison WI 53703. (608)257-4626. Fax: (608)257-3373. E-mail: editorial@progressive.org. Website: www.progressive.org. **75% freelance written.** Monthly. Estab. 1909. Byline given. Pays on publication. No kill fee. Publishes ms an average of 6 weeks after acceptance. Accepts queries by mail. Responds in 1 month to queries. Sample copy for 9x12 SAE with 4 first-class stamps or sample articles online. Guidelines available online.

Nonfiction Investigative reporting (exposé of corporate malfeasance and governmental wrongdoing); electoral coverage (a current electoral development that has national implications); social movement pieces (important or interesting event or trend in the labor movement, or the GLBT movement, or in the area of racial justice, disability rights, the environment, women's liberation); foreign policy pieces (a development of huge moral importance where the US role may not be paramount); interviews (a long Q&A with a writer, activist, political figure, or musician who is widely known or doing especially worthwhile work); activism (highlights the work of activists and activist groups; increasingly, we are looking for good photographs of a dynamic or creative action, and we accompany the photos with a caption); book reviews (cover two or three current titles on a major issue of concern). Primarily interested in articles that interpret, from a progressive point of view, domestic and world affairs. Occasional lighter features. *The Progressive* is a *political* publication. General interest is inappropriate. We do not want editorials, satire, historical pieces, philosophical peices or columns. Query. Length: 500-4,000 words. **Pays $500-1,300.**

Poetry Publishes 1 original poem a month. We prefer poems that connect up—in one fashion or another, however obliquely—with political concerns. **Pays $150.**

Tips Sought-after topics include electoral coverage, social movement, foreign policy, activism and book reviews.

$ PROGRESSIVE POPULIST

Journal from America's Heartland, P.O. Box 819, Manchaca TX 78652. (512)828-7245. E-mail: populist@usa.net. Website: www.populist.com. **90% freelance written**. Biweekly tabloid covering politics and economics. We cover issues of interest to workers, small businesses, and family farmers and ranchers. Estab. 1995. Circ. 15,000. Byline given. Pays quarterly. No kill fee. Publishes ms an average of 1 month after acceptance. Buys first North American serial rights, buys second serial (reprint) rights. Editorial lead time 3 weeks. Submit seasonal material 1 month in advance. Accepts queries by mail, e-mail, fax, phone. Accepts previously published material. Accepts simultaneous submissions. Sample copy and writer's guidelines free

Nonfiction We cover politics and economics. We are interested not so much in the dry reporting of campaigns and elections, or the stock markets and GNP, but in how big business is exerting more control over both the government and ordinary people's lives, and what people can do about it. Needs essays, expose, general interest, historical, humor, interview, opinion. We are not much interested in `sound-off' articles about state or national politics, although we accept letters to the editor. We prefer to see more `journalistic' pieces, in which the writer does enough footwork to advance a story beyond the easy realm of opinion. **Buys 400 mss/year.** Query. Length: 600-1,000 words. **Pays $15-50.** Pays writers with contributor copies or other premiums if preferred by writer

Reprints Send photocopy with rights for sale noted and information about when and where the material previously appeared.

Photos State availability Identification of subjects required. Negotiates payment individually Buys one time rights.

Tips We do prefer submissions by e-mail. I find it's easier to work with e-mail and for the writer it probably increases the chances of getting a response.

$ $ $ $ REASON

Free Minds and Free Markets, Reason Foundation, 3415 S. Sepulveda Blvd., Suite 400, Los Angeles CA 90034. (310)391-2245. Fax: (310)390-8986. E-mail: jsanchez@reason.com. Website: www.reason.com. **30% freelance written**. Monthly magazine covering politics, current events, culture, ideas. *Reason* covers politics, culture and ideas from a dynamic libertarian perspective. It features reported works, opinion pieces, and book reviews. Estab. 1968. Circ. 55,000. Byline given. Pays on acceptance. Offers kill fee. Buys first North American serial rights, buys first rights, buys all rights. Editorial lead time 2 months. Submit seasonal material 3 months in advance. Accepts queries by mail, e-mail. Responds in 6 weeks to queries. Responds in 2 months to mss. Sample copy for $4. Guidelines available online.

Nonfiction Needs book excerpts, essays, expose, general interest, humor, interview, opinion. No products, personal experience, how-to, travel. **Buys 50-60 mss/year.** Query with published clips. Length: 850-5,000 words. **Pays $300-2,000.** Sometimes pays expenses of writers on assignment.

Tips We prefer queries of no more than one or two pages with specifically developed ideas about a given topic rather than more general areas of interest. Enclosing a few published clips also helps.

THEORIA

A Journal of Social and Political Theory, Berghahn Books, University of KwaZulu-Natal, P.O. Box 50324, Randjesfontein Johannesburg 1683 South Africa. (27)(11)314-0187. E-mail: deacon@ukzn.ac.za. Website: www.theoria.ukzn.ac.za. **100% freelance written**. "Academic journal published 3 times/year. *Theoria* is an engaged, multidisciplinary peer-reviewed journal of social and political theory. Its purpose is to address—through scholarly debate—the many challenges posed to intellectual life by the major social, political, and economic forces that shape the contemporary world. Thus, it is principally concerned with questions such as how modern systems of power, processes of globalization, and capitalist economic organization bear on matters such as justice, democracy, and truth." Estab. 1947. Circ. 300. Byline sometimes given. No kill fee. Publishes ms an average of 6 months after acceptance. Buys first rights, buys electronic rights. Editorial lead time 3 months. Submit seasonal material 3 months in advance. Accepts queries by mail, e-mail, fax, phone. Responds in 1 week to queries. Responds in 4-5 months to mss. Sample copy for $18. Writer's guidelines online or via e-mail.

Nonfiction Needs book excerpts, essays, expose, general interest, historical, interview, review articles, book reviews, theoretical, philosophical, political, articles. **Buys 1 mss/year.** Send complete ms. Length: 4,000-8,000 words. **Pays 50-200 for assigned articles.** Sometimes pays expenses of writers on assignment.

Photos State availability Identification of subjects required. Reviews GIF/JPEG files. Negotiates payment individually. Buys one time rights.

Columns/Departments Book Reviews, 1,000 words; Review Articles, 5,000 words. 1 Send complete ms.

$ $ WASHINGTON MONTHLY

The Washington Monthly Co., 1319 F St. NW, Suite 810, Washington DC 20004. (202)393-5155. Fax: (202)393-2444. E-mail: editors@washingtonmonthly.com. Website: www.washingtonmonthly.com. **50% freelance written**. Monthly magazine covering politics, policy, media. We are a neo-liberal publication with a long history and specific views—please read our magazine before submitting. Estab. 1969. Circ. 28,000. Byline given. Pays on publication. No kill fee. Publishes ms an average of 2 months after acceptance. Buys all rights. Editorial lead time 2 months. Submit seasonal material 4 months in advance. Accepts queries by mail, e-mail, fax, phone. Responds in 3 weeks to queries. Responds in 2 months to mss. Sample copy for 11 × 17 SAE with 5 first-class stamps or by e-mail. Guidelines available online.

Nonfiction Needs book excerpts, essays, expose, general interest, historical, interview, opinion, personal experience, technical, first-person political. No humor, how-to, or generalized articles. **Buys 20 mss/year.** Send

complete ms. Length: 1,500-5,000 words. **Pays 10¢/word.**
Photos State availability Reviews contact sheets, prints. Negotiates payment individually Buys one time rights.
Columns/Departments 10 Miles Square (about DC); On Political Books, Booknotes (both reviews of current political books), 1,500-3,000 words. 10 Query with published clips or send complete ms. **Pays 10¢/word**
Tips Call our editors to talk about ideas. Always pitch articles showing background research. We're particularly looking for first-hand accounts of working in government. We also like original work showing that the government is or is not doing something important. We have writer's guidelines, but do your research first.

$ $ $ YES! MAGAZINE

Positive Futures Network, P.O. Box 10818, Bainbridge Island WA 98110. E-mail: submissions@yesmagazine.org. Website: www.yesmagazine.org. **70% freelance written.** Quarterly magazine covering politics & world affairs; contemporary culture; nature, conservation, & ecology. *"YES! Magazine* documents how people are creating a more just, sustainable, and compassionate world. Each issue of *YES!* includes a series of articles focused on a theme—about solutions to a significant challenge facing our world—and a number of timely, non-theme articles. Our non-theme section provides ongoing coverage of issues like health, climate change, globalization, media reform, faith, democracy, economy and labor, social and racial justice, and peace building. To inquire about upcoming themes, send an email to submissions@yesmagazine.org; please be sure to type 'themes' as the subject line." Estab. 1997. Circ. 55,000. Byline given. Pays on publication. Offers kill fee. varies Publishes ms an average of 1-6 months after acceptance. Buys Creative Commons License, see http://www.yesmagazine.org/default.asp?ID=14 rights. Editorial lead time 3-6 months. Submit seasonal material 2-6 months in advance. Accepts queries by mail, e-mail. www.yesmagazine.org/default.asp?ID=15
Nonfiction Needs book excerpts, essays, general interest, how-to, interview, opinion, (does not mean letters to the editor), photo feature. "No stories that are negative or too politically partisan stories." **Buys 60 mss/yr. mss/year.** Query with published clips. Length: 100-2,500 words. **Pays $50-1,250 for assigned articles. Pays $50-600 for unsolicited articles.**
Columns/Departments Signs of Life, positive news briefs, 100-250 words; Commentary, opinion from thinkers and experts, 500 words; Book and film reviews, 500-800 words. **Pays $$20-$300.**
Tips "We're interested in articles that: 'Change the story' about what is possible; tell specific success stories of individuals, communities, movements, nations, or regions that are addressing society's challenges and problems; offer visions of a better world.We're less interested in articles that:Only describe or update a problem (unless there are dramatically new developments, reframings, or insights); primarily reinforce a sense of being a victim (and therefore powerless); are written in styles or about topics relevant or accessible only to narrow groups; lack grounding in research or reporting (except for occasional essays)."

PSYCHOLOGY & SELF-IMPROVEMENT

$ $ $ $ GRADPSYCH

American Psychological Association, 750 First St. NE, Washington DC 20009. Fax: (202)336-6103. E-mail: gradpsych@apa.org. Website: www.gradpsych.apags.org/. **50% freelance written. Other Psychology graduate student magazine.** Quarterly magazine We cover issues of interest to psychology graduate students, including career outlook, tips for success in school, profiles of interesting students, and reports on student research. We aim for our articles to be readable, informative and fun. Grad students have enough dry, technical reading to do at school, we don't want to add to it. Estab. 2003. Circ. 60,000. Byline given. Pays on acceptance. Offers $200 kill fee. Publishes ms an average of 4 months after acceptance. Makes work-for-hire assignments. Editorial lead time 3-5 months. Submit seasonal material 4 months in advance. Accepts queries by e-mail. Responds in 2 weeks to queries. Responds in 0 months to mss. Sample copy available online.
Nonfiction Needs general interest, how-to, interview, Jjournalism for grad students. **Buys 25 mss/yr. mss/year.** Query with published clips. Length: 300-2,000 words. **Pays $300-2,000 for assigned articles.** Sometimes pays expenses of writers on assignment.
Photos Contact: Sadie Dingfelder. State availability Identification of subjects, model releases required. Reviews GIF/JPEG files. We negotiate photo payment individually. Buys one time rights.
Tips Check out our Web site and pitch a story on a topic we haven't written on before, or that gives an old topic a new spin. Also, have quality clips.

$ $ $ $ PSYCHOLOGY TODAY

Sussex Publishers, Inc., 115 E. 23rd St., 9th Floor, New York NY 10010. (212)260-7210. Fax: (212)260-7445. E-mail: jay@psychologytoday.com. Website: www.psychologytoday.com. Bimonthly magazine. *Psychology Today* explores every aspect of human behavior, from the cultural trends that shape the way we think and feel to the intricacies of modern neuroscience. We're sort of a hybrid of a science magazine, a health magazine and a self-help magazine. While we're read by many psychologists, therapists and social workers, most of our readers are simply intelligent and curious people interested in the psyche and the self. Estab. 1967. Circ. 331,400. Byline given. 30 days after publication. No kill fee. Publishes ms an average of 3 months after acceptance. Buys first North American serial rights. Editorial lead time 5 months. Accepts queries by mail, e-mail. Responds in 1 month to queries. Sample copy for $3.50. Guidelines available online.

Nonfiction Nearly any subject related to psychology is fair game. We value originality, insight and good reporting; we're not interested in stories or topics that have already been covered *ad nauseum* by other magazines unless you can provide a fresh new twist and much more depth. We're not interested in simple-minded 'pop psychology.' No fiction, poetry or first-person essays on How I Conquered Mental Disorder X. **Buys 20-25 mss/year.** Query with published clips. Length: 1,500-4,000 words. **Pays $1,000-2,500.**

Columns/Departments Contact: News Editor. News & Trends, 150-300 words. Query with published clips. **Pays $150-300.**

$ ROSICRUCIAN DIGEST

Rosicrucian Order, AMORC, 1342 Naglee Ave., San Jose CA 95191-0001. (408)947-3600. Website: www.rosicrucian.org. "Quarterly magazine (international) emphasizing mysticism, science, philosophy, and the arts for educated men and women of all ages seeking alternative answers to life's questions.". Byline given. Pays on acceptance. No kill fee. Publishes ms an average of 6 months after acceptance. Buys first rights, buys second serial (reprint) rights. Accepts queries by mail, phone. Responds in 3 months to queries. Guidelines for #10 SASE.

Nonfiction "How to deal with life—and all it brings us—in a positive and constructive way. Informational articles—new ideas and developments in science, the arts, philosophy, and thought. Historical sketches, biographies, human interest, psychology, philosophical, and inspirational articles. We are always looking for good articles on the contributions of ancient civilizations to today's civilizations, the environment, ecology, inspirational (nonreligious) subjects. Know your subject well and be able to capture the reader's interest in the first paragraph. Be willing to work with the editor to make changes in the manuscript. No religious, astrological, or political material, or articles promoting a particular group or system of thought. Most articles are written by members or donated, but we're always open to freelance submissions. No book-length mss." Query. Length: 1,500-2,000 words. **Pays 6¢/word.**

Reprints Prefers typed ms with rights for sale noted and information about when and where the article previously appeared, but tearsheet or photcopy acceptable. Pays 50% of amount paid for an original article.

Tips "We're looking for more pieces on these subjects: our connection with the past—the important contributions of ancient civilizations to today's world and culture and the relevance of this wisdom to now; how to channel teenage energy/angst into positive, creative, constructive results (preferably written by teachers or others who work with young people—written for frustrated parents); and the vital necessity of raising our environmental consciousness if we are going to survive as a species on this planet."

SCIENCE OF MIND MAGAZINE

2600 W. Magnolia Blvd., Burbank CA 91505. (818)526-7757. E-mail: edit@scienceofmind.com. Website: www.scienceofmind.com. **30% freelance written**. Monthly magazine featuring articles on spirituality, self-help, and inspiration. Our publication centers on oneness of all life and spiritual empowerment through the application of *Science of Mind* principles. Byline given. Pays on acceptance. No kill fee. Publishes ms an average of 5 months after acceptance. Buys first North American serial rights. Submit seasonal material 6 months in advance. Guidelines available online.

Nonfiction Needs book excerpts, essays, inspirational, interview, personal experience, of Science of Mind, spiritual. **Buys 35-45 mss/year.** Length: 750-2,000 words. **Payment varies. Pays in copies for some features written by readers.**

Tips We are interested in how to use spiritual principles in worldly situations or other experiences of a spiritual nature having to do with *Science of Mind* principles.

SHARED VISION

Raven Eagle Partners Co., 873 Beatty St., Suite 301, Vancouver BC V6B 2H6 Canada. (604)733-5062. Fax: (604)731-1050. E-mail: editor@shared-vision.com. Website: www.shared-vision.com. **75% freelance written**. Monthly magazine covering health and wellness, environment, and personal growth. Estab. 1988. Circ. 42,000. Byline given. No kill fee. Editorial lead time 3 months. Submit seasonal material 3 months in advance. Accepts queries by mail, e-mail, fax. Accepts previously published material. Sample copy for $3 Canadian, postage paid. Guidelines available online.

Nonfiction Needs book excerpts, general interest, inspirational, personal experience, travel, health, environment. Query with published clips.

Columns/Departments Footnotes (first-person inspirational). Query with published clips.

Tips Reading the magazine is the optimum method. See Web site for writer's guidelines.

$ SPOTLIGHT ON RECOVERY MAGAZINE

R. Graham Publishing Company, 1454 Rockaway Parkway, #140, Brooklyn NY 11236. (347)831-9373. E-mail:

rgraham_100@msn.com. Website: www.spotlightonrecovery.com. **85% freelance written**. Quarterly magazine covering self-help, recovery, and empowerment. "This is the premiere outreach and resource magazine in New York. Its goal is to be the catalyst for which the human spirit could heal. Everybody knows somebody who has mental illness, substance abuse issues, parenting problems, educational issues, or someone who is homeless, unemployed, physically ill, or the victim of a crime. Many people suffer in silence. *Spotlight on Recovery* will provide a voice to those who suffer in silence and begin the dialogue of recovery." Estab. 2001. Circ. 1,500-2,500. Byline sometimes given. Pays on publication. No kill fee. Publishes ms an average of 2 months after acceptance. Buys second serial (reprint) rights, buys electronic rights. Editorial lead time 1 month. Submit seasonal material 1 month in advance. Accepts queries by mail, e-mail. Accepts simultaneous submissions. Responds in 2 weeks to queries. Responds in 1 month to mss. Sample copy and writer's guidelines free.

Nonfiction Needs book excerpts, interview, opinion, personal experience. **Buys 30-50 mss/year.** Query with published clips. Length: 150-1,500 words. **Pays 5¢/word or $75-80/article.**

Photos State availability Identification of subjects required. Reviews GIF/JPEG files. Pays $5-10/photo. Buys one time rights.

Columns/Departments 4 Query with published clips. **Pays 5¢/word or $75-80/column.**

Fiction Needs ethnic, mainstream, slice-of-life vignettes.

Fillers Needs facts, newsbreaks, short humor. 2 **Pays 5¢/word.**

Tips "Send a query and give a reason why you would choose the subject posted to write about."

REGIONAL

ALABAMA

$ $ ALABAMA HERITAGE

University of Alabama, Box 870342, Tuscaloosa AL 35487-0342. (205)348-7467. Fax: (205)348-7473. Website: www.alabamaheritage.com. **90% freelance written**. *Alabama Heritage* is a nonprofit historical quarterly published by the University of Alabama and the Alabama Department of Archives and History for the intelligent lay reader. We are interested in lively, well-written, and thoroughly researched articles on Alabama/Southern history and culture. Readability and accuracy are essential. Estab. 1986. Byline given. Pays on publication. No kill fee. Buys all rights. Accepts queries by mail, e-mail. Sample copy for $6, plus $2.50 for shipping. Guidelines for #10 SASE or online.

Nonfiction Buys 12-16 feature mss/year and 10-14 short pieces. We do not publish fiction, poetry, articles on current events or living artists, and personal/family reminiscences. Query. Length: 750-4,000 words. **Pays $50-350.**

Photos Identification of subjects required. Reviews contact sheets. Buys one time rights.

Tips Authors need to remember that we regard history as a fascinating subject, not as a dry recounting of dates and facts. Articles that are lively and engaging, in addition to being well researched, will find interested readers among our editors. No term papers, please. All areas are open to freelance writers. Best approach is a written query.

$ $ ALABAMA LIVING

Alabama Rural Electric Assn., P.O. Box 244014, Montgomery AL 36124. (334)215-2732. Fax: (334)215-2733. E-mail: dgates@areapower.com. Website: www.alabamaliving.com. **80% freelance written**. Monthly magazine covering topics of interest to rural and suburban Alabamians. "Our magazine is an editorially balanced, informational and educational service to members of rural electric cooperatives. Our mix regularly includes Alabama history, Alabama features, gardening, outdoor, and consumer pieces." Estab. 1948. Circ. 380,000. Byline given. Pays on acceptance. No kill fee. Editorial lead time 4 months. Submit seasonal material 4 months in advance. Accepts queries by mail, e-mail. Accepts simultaneous submissions. Responds in 1 month to queries. Sample copy free.

Nonfiction Needs historical, rural-oriented, inspirational, Alabama slant, personal experience, Alabama. Gardening (March); Travel (April); Home Improvement (May); Holiday Recipes (December). **Buys 20 mss/year.** Send complete ms. Length: 500-750 words. **Pays $250 minimum for assigned articles. Pays $100 minimum for unsolicited articles.**

Reprints Send typed manuscript with rights for sale noted. Pays $75.

ALASKA

$ $ $ ALASKA

Exploring Life on the Last Frontier, 301 Arctic Slope Ave., Suite 300, Anchorage AK 99518. (907)272-6070. E-mail: tim.woody@alaskamagazine.com. Website: www.alaskamagazine.com. **70% freelance written. Eager**

to work with new/unpublished writers. Magazine published 10 times/year covering topics uniquely Alaskan. Estab. 1935. Circ. 180,000. Byline given. Pays on publication. No kill fee. Publishes ms an average of 6 months after acceptance. Buys first rights, buys one-time rights. Submit seasonal material 1 year in advance. Accepts queries by mail. Responds in 2 months to queries. Responds in 2 months to mss. Sample copy for $3 and 9x12 SAE with 7 first-class stamps. Guidelines available online.

Nonfiction Needs historical, humor, interview, personal experience, photo feature, travel, adventure, outdoor recreation (including hunting, fishing), Alaska destination stories. No fiction or poetry. **Buys 40 mss/year.** Query. Length: 100-2,500 words. **Pays $100-1,250.**

Photos Send photos Captions, identification of subjects required. Reviews 35mm or larger transparencies, slides labeled with your name.

Tips We're looking for top-notch writing—original, well researched, lively. Subjects must be distinctly Alaskan. A story on a mall in Alaska, for example, won't work for us; every state has malls. If you've got a story about a Juneau mall run by someone who is also a bush pilot and part-time trapper, maybe we'd be interested. The point is *Alaska* stories need to be vivid, focused and unique. Alaska is like nowhere else—we need our stories to be the same way.

ARIZONA

$ $ ARIZONA FOOTHILLS MAGAZINE

Media That Deelivers, Inc., 8132 N. 87th Place, Scottsdale AZ 85258. (480)460-5203. Fax: (480)443-1517. E-mail: editorial@azfoothillsmag.com. Website: www.azfoothillsmag.com. **10% freelance written.** Monthly magazine covering Arizona lifesyle. Estab. 1996. Circ. 60,000. Byline given. Pays on publication. No kill fee. Publishes ms an average of 6 months after acceptance. Editorial lead time 6 months. Submit seasonal material at least 4 months in advance. Accepts queries by mail, e-mail. Responds in 1 month to queries. Sample copy for #10 SASE.

Nonfiction Needs general interest, photo feature, travel, fashion, decor, arts, interview. **Buys 10 mss/year.** Query with published clips. Length: 900-2,000 words. **Pays 35-40¢/word for assigned articles.**

Photos Photos may be requested. Captions, identification of subjects, model releases required. Reviews contact sheets, transparencies. Negotiates payment individually Occasionally buys one-time rights.

Columns/Departments Travel, dining, fashion, home decor, design, architecture, wine, shopping, golf, performance & visual arts.

Tips We prefer stories that appeal to our affluent audience written with an upbeat, contemporary approach and reader service in mind.

$ $ $ $ ARIZONA HIGHWAYS

2039 W. Lewis Ave., Phoenix AZ 85009-9988. (602)712-2024. Fax: (602)254-4505. Website: www.arizonahighways.com. **100% freelance written.** Magazine that is state-owned, designed to help attract tourists into and through Arizona. Estab. 1925. Circ. 425,000. Pays on acceptance. No kill fee. Buys first North American serial rights. Accepts queries by mail, e-mail, fax. Responds in 1 month to queries. Responds in 1 month to mss. Guidelines available online.

Nonfiction Feature subjects include narratives and exposition dealing with history, anthropology, nature, wildlife, armchair travel, out of the way places, small towns, Old West history, Indian arts and crafts, travel, etc. Travel articles are experience-based. All must be oriented toward Arizona. We deal with professionals only, so include a list of current credits. **Buys 50 mss/year.** Query with a lead paragraph and brief outline of story Length: 600-1,800 words. **Pays up to $1/word.** Pays expenses of writers on assignment.

Photos Contact: Peter Ensenberger, director of photography. We use transparencies of medium format, 4x5, and 35mm when appropriate to the subject matter, or they display exceptional quality or content. If submitting 35mm, we prefer 100 ISO or slower. Each transparency must be accompanied by information attached to each photograph: where, when, what. No photography will be reviewed by the editors unless the photographer's name appears on each and every transparency. For digital requirements, contact the photography department. Pays $125-600 Buys one time rights.

Columns/Departments Focus on Nature (short feature in first or third person dealing with the unique aspects of a single species of wildlife), 800 words; Along the Way (short essay dealing with life in Arizona, or a personal experience keyed to Arizona), 750 words; Back Road Adventure (personal back-road trips, preferably off the beaten path and outside major metro areas), 1,000 words; Hike of the Month (personal experiences on trails anywhere in Arizona), 500 words. **Pays $50-1,000, depending on department**

Tips Writing must be of professional quality, warm, sincere, in-depth, well peopled, and accurate. Avoid themes that describe first trips to Arizona, the Grand Canyon, the desert, Colorado River running, etc. Emphasis is to be on Arizona adventure and romance as well as flora and fauna, when appropriate, and themes that can be photographed. Double check your manuscript for accuracy. Our typical reader is a 50-something person with the time, the inclination, and the means to travel.

$ $ DESERT LIVING

2525 E. Camelback Rd., Suite 120, Phoenix AZ 85016. (602)667-9798. Fax: (602)508-9454. E-mail: david@desertlivingmag.com. Website: www.desertlivingmag.com. **75% freelance written**. Lifestyle and culture magazine published 8 times/year with an emphasis on modern design, culinary trends, cultural trends, fashion, great thinkers of our time and entertainment. Estab. 1997. Circ. 50,000. Byline given. Pays 1 month after publication. Offers 50% kill fee. Buys first rights, buys electronic rights. Editorial lead time 3 months. Submit seasonal material 3 months in advance. Accepts queries by mail, e-mail, fax. Responds in 3 weeks to queries. Responds in 2 months to mss. Sample copy for e-mail request Guidelines free.

Nonfiction Needs general interest, interview, new product, photo feature, travel, architecture. Query with published clips. Length: 300-1,500 words. **Pays $25-600.**

Photos State availability Identification of subjects, model releases required. Reviews contact sheets, negatives, transparencies, prints. Negotiates payment individually Buys one-time or electronic rights

Columns/Departments See Web site.

$ $ TUCSON LIFESTYLE

Conley Publishing Group, Ltd., Suite 12, 7000 E. Tanque Verde Rd., Tucson AZ 85715-5318. (520)721-2929. Fax: (520)721-8665. E-mail: scott@tucsonlifestyle.com. **Contact:** Scott Barker, executive editor. **90% freelance written. Prefers to work with published/established writers.** Monthly magazine covering Southern Arizona-related events and topics. Estab. 1982. Circ. 32,000. Byline given. Pays on acceptance. No kill fee. Publishes ms an average of 6 months after acceptance. Buys one-time rights, buys second serial (reprint) rights, buys electronic rights. Submit seasonal material 1 year in advance. Accepts queries by mail, e-mail. Responds in 2 months to queries. Responds in 3 months to mss. Sample copy for $3.99, plus $3 postage. Guidelines free.

O→ No fiction, poetry, cartoons, or syndicated columns.

Nonfiction All stories need a Southern Arizona angle. "Avoid obvious tourist attractions and information that most residents of the Southwest are likely to know. No anecdotes masquerading as articles. Not interested in fish-out-of-water, Easterner-visiting-the-Old-West pieces." **Buys 20 mss/year. Pays $50-500.**

Photos Query about photos before submitting anything.

Tips "Read the magazine before submitting anything."

CALIFORNIA

$ $ BRENTWOOD MAGAZINE

PTL Productions, 2118 Wilshire Blvd., #590, Santa Monica CA 90403. (310)390-5209. Fax: (310)390-0261. E-mail: jenny@brentwoodmagazine.com. Website: www.brentwoodmagazine.com. **100% freelance written**. Bimonthly magazine covering entertainment, business, lifestyles, reviews. Wanting in-depth interviews with top entertainers, politicians, and similar individuals. Also travel, sports, adventure. Estab. 1995. Circ. 50,000. Byline given. Pays on publication. Editorial lead time 3 months. Submit seasonal material 3 months in advance. Accepts queries by mail, e-mail, phone. Accepts simultaneous submissions. Sample copy for $5. Writer's guidelines available.

Nonfiction Needs book excerpts, expose, general interest, historical, humor, interview, new product, opinion, personal experience, photo feature, travel. **Buys 80 mss/year.** Query with published clips. Length: 1,000-2,500 words. **Pays 20¢/word.**

Photos State availability Captions, identification of subjects required. Reviews contact sheets, negatives, prints. Offers no additional payment for photos accepted with ms

Columns/Departments Reviews (film/books/theater/museum), 100-500 words; Sports (Southern California angle), 200-600 words. 20 Query with or without published clips or send complete ms. **Pays 15¢/word.**

Tips Los Angeles-based writers preferred for most articles.

$ $ CARLSBAD MAGAZINE

Wheelhouse Media, 2911 State St., Suite J, Carlsbad CA 92008. (760)729-9099. Fax: (760)729-9011. E-mail: carly@carlsbadmagazine.com. Website: www.clickoncarlsbad.com. **80% freelance written**. Bimonthly magazine covering people, places, events, arts in Carlsbad, California. "We are a regional magazine highlighting all things pertaining specifically to Carlsbad. We focus on history, events, people and places that make Carlsbad interesting and unique. Our audience is both Carlsbad residents and visitors or anyone interested in learning more about Carlsbad. We favor a conversational tone that still adheres to standard rules of writing." Estab. 2004. Circ. 35,000. Byline given. Pays on publication. Publishes ms an average of 6 months after acceptance. Buys first North American serial rights. Editorial lead time 4 months. Submit seasonal material 6-12 months in advance. Accepts queries by mail, e-mail. Accepts simultaneous submissions. Responds in 2 months to queries and to mss. Sample copy for $2.31. Guidelines by email.

Nonfiction Needs historical, interview, photo feature, home, garden, arts, events. Does not want self-promoting articles for individuals or businesses, real estate how-to's, advertorials. **Buys 3 mss/year.** Query with published clips. Length: 300-2,700 words. **Pays 20-30¢/word for assigned articles. Pays 20¢/word for unsolicited**

articles. Sometimes pays expenses of writers on assignment.
Photos State availability Reviews GIF/JPEG files. Offers $15-400/photo. Buys one time rights.
Columns/Departments Carlsbad Arts (people, places or things related to cultural arts in Carlsbad); Happenings (events that take place in Carlsbad); Carlsbad Character (unique Carlsbad residents who have contributed to Carlsbad's character); Commerce (Carlsbad business profiles); Surf Scene (subjects pertaining to the beach/surf in Carlsbad), all 500-700 words. Garden (Carlsbad garden feature); Home (Carlsbad home feature), both 700-1,200 words. 60 columns. Query with published clips. **Pays $50 flat fee or 20¢/word.**
Tips "The main thing to remember is that any pitches need to be subjects directly related to Carlsbad. If the subjects focus on surrounding towns, they aren't going to make the cut. We are looking for well-written feature magazine-style articles. E-mail is the preferred method for queries; you will get a response."

$ $ $ $ DIABLO MAGAZINE

The Magazine of the San Francosco East Bay, Diablo Publications, 2520 Camino Diablo, Walnut Creek CA 94597. Fax: (925)943-1045. E-mail: d-mail@maildiablo.com. Website: www.diablomag.com. **50% freelance written**. Monthly magazine covering regional travel, food, homestyle, and profiles in Contra Costa and southern Alameda counties and selected areas of Oakland and Berkeley. Estab. 1979. Circ. 45,000. Byline given. Pays on acceptance. Offers 25% kill fee. Publishes ms an average of 3 months after acceptance. Buys first rights. Editorial lead time 3 months. Submit seasonal material 5 months in advance. Accepts queries by mail, e-mail, fax. Sample copy available online. Guidelines available online.
Nonfiction Needs general interest, interview, new product, photo feature, technical, travel. No restaurant profiles, out of country travel, nonlocal topics. **Buys 60 mss/year.** Query with published clips. Length: 600-3,000 words. **Pays $300-2,000.** Sometimes pays expenses of writers on assignment.
Photos State availability Negotiates payment individually Buys one time rights.
Columns/Departments Education; Parenting; Homestyle; Food; Books; Health; Profiles; Regional Politics. Query with published clips.
Tips We prefer San Francisco Bay area writers who are familiar with the area.

$ LOS ANGELES TIMES MAGAZINE

Los Angeles Times, 202 W. First St., Los Angeles CA 90012. (213)237-7811. Fax: (213)237-7386. Website: www.latimes.com. **50% freelance written**. Monthly magazine of regional general interest. Circ. 1,384,688. Byline given. Payment schedule varies. No kill fee. Publishes ms an average of 2 months after acceptance. Buys first North American serial rights. Submit seasonal material 3 months in advance. Accepts simultaneous submissions. Responds in 2 months to queries. Responds in 2 months to mss. Sample copy and writer's guidelines free
Nonfiction Covers California and the West. Needs essays, reported, general interest, interview, investigative and narrative journalism. Query with published clips. Length: 2,500-4,500 words.
Photos Query first; prefers to assign photos. Captions, identification of subjects, model releases required. Reviews color transparencies, b&w prints. Payment varies. Buys one time rights.
Tips Previous national magazine writing experience preferred.

$ NOB HILL GAZETTE

An Attitude: Not an Address, Nob Hill Gazette, Inc., 5 Third St., San Francisco CA 94103. (415)227-0190. Fax: (415)974-5103. E-mail: nobhillnews@nobhillgazette.com. Website: www.nobhillgazette.com. **95% freelance written**. Monthly magazine covering upscale lifestyles in the Bay Area. *Nob Hill Gazette* is for an upscale readership. Estab. 1978. Circ. 82,000. Byline given. Pays on 15th of month following publication. Offers $50 kill fee. Publishes ms an average of 2-3 months after acceptance. Buys all rights. Editorial lead time 1-2 months. Submit seasonal material 1-2 months in advance. Accepts queries by e-mail. Accepts previously published material. Responds in 2 weeks to queries. Responds in 2 months to mss. Sample copy available online. Guidelines free.
Nonfiction Needs general interest, historical, interview, opinion, photo feature, trends, lifestyles, fashion, health, fitness, entertaining, decor, real estate, charity and philanthropy, culture and the arts. Does not want first person articles, anything commercial (from a business or with a product to sell), profiles of people not active in the community, anything technical, anything on people or events not in the Bay Area. **Buys 75 mss/year.** Query with published clips. Length: 1,200-2,000 words. **Pays $100.** Sometimes pays expenses of writers on assignment.
Photos Contact: Contact Shara Hall, photo coordinator. State availability Captions, identification of subjects required. Reviews GIF/JPEG files. Offers no additional payment for photos accepted with ms. Buys one time rights.
Columns/Departments Contact: Contact Lois Lehrman, publisher. All our columnists are freelancers, but they write for us regularly, so we don't take other submissions.
Tips Before submission, a writer should look at our publication and read the articles to get some idea of our style and range of subjects.

$ $ $ $ OCEAN MAGAZINE

Shoreline Publications, 3334 E. Coast Hwy. #125, Corona del Mar CA 92625. E-mail: editor@oceanmagonline.com. Website: www.oceanmagazine.com. **90% freelance written**. Bimonthly magazine covering beauty, fashion, health, decor. A perfect blend of the hippest trends and freshest ideas, *Ocean* stands apart as the first women's beauty, lifestyle and fashion-forward resource for Southern California. Capturing the essence of one of the most stylish, affluent and globally sought after destinations, *Ocean* appeals to all style-seeking women in search of the inside scoop on West Coast style, shopping, beauty and travel. Estab. 2005. Circ. 45,000. No byline given. Pays on publication. Offers 25% kill fee. Publishes ms an average of 1 month after acceptance. Buys all rights. Editorial lead time 3 months. Submit seasonal material 3 months in advance. Accepts queries by e-mail. Guidelines by email.

Nonfiction Needs general interest, interview, new product. Query with published clips. Length: 800-1,000 words. **Pays 45¢-$1/word.** Sometimes pays expenses of writers on assignment.

Photos Send photos Model releases required. Reviews GIF/JPEG files. Negotiates payment individually. Buys one time rights.

$ $ ORANGE COAST MAGAZINE

The Magazine of Orange County, Orange Coast Kommunications, Inc., 3701 Birch St., Suite 100, Newport Beach CA 92660. (949)862-1133. Fax: (949)862-0133. Website: www.orangecoastmagazine.com. **90% freelance written**. Monthly magazine designed to inform and enlighten the educated, upscale residents of Orange County, California; highly graphic and well researched. Estab. 1974. Circ. 52,000. Byline given. Pays on publication. Offers 20% kill fee. Publishes ms an average of 4 months after acceptance. Buys first North American serial rights. Editorial lead time 5 months. Submit seasonal material 6 months in advance. Accepts queries by mail, e-mail. Accepts simultaneous submissions. Responds in 3 months to queries. Responds in 3 months to mss. Sample copy for #10 SASE and 6 first-class stamps. Guidelines for #10 SASE.

Nonfiction Absolutely no phone queries. Needs general interest, with Orange County focus, inspirational, interview, prominent Orange County citizens, personal experience, celebrity profiles, guides to activities and services. Health, Beauty, and Fitness (January); Dining (March and August); International Travel (April); Home Design (June); Arts (September); Local Travel (October). We do not accept stories that do not have specific Orange County angles. We want profiles on local people, stories on issues going on in our community, informational stories using Orange County-based sources. We cannot emphasize the local angle enough. **Buys up to 65 mss/year.** Query with published clips. Length: 1,000-2,000 words. **Negotiates payment individually.**

Photos State availability Captions, identification of subjects required. Negotiates payment individually. Buys one time rights.

Columns/Departments Short Cuts (stories for the front of the book that focus on Orange County issues, people, and places), 150-250 words. up to 25 Query with published clips. **Negotiates payment individually.**

Tips We're looking for more local personality profiles, analysis of current local issues, local takes on national issues. Most features are assigned to writers we've worked with before. Don't try to sell us `generic' journalism. *Orange Coast* prefers articles with specific and unusual angles focused on Orange County. A lot of freelance writers ignore our Orange County focus. We get far too many generalized manuscripts.

$ $ PALM SPRINGS LIFE

The California Prestige Magazine, Desert Publications, Inc., 303 N. Indian Canyon, Palm Springs CA 92262. (760)325-2333. Fax: (760)325-7008. Website: www.palmspringslife.com. **80% freelance written**. Monthly magazine covering affluent Palm Springs-area desert resort communities. *Palm Springs Life* celebrates the good life. Estab. 1958. Circ. 20,000. Byline given. Pays on publication. Offers negotiable kill fee. Publishes ms an average of 3 months after acceptance. Buys one-time rights (negotiable). Submit seasonal material 6 months in advance. Responds in 4-6 weeks to queries. Sample copy for $3.95. Guidelines available online.

- Increased focus on desert style, home, fashion, art, culture, personalities, celebrities.

Nonfiction Needs book excerpts, essays, interview, feature stories, celebrity, fashion, spa, epicurean. Query with published clips. Length: 500-2,500 words. **Pays $100-500.**

Photos State availability Captions, identification of subjects, model releases required. Reviews contact sheets. Pays $75-350/photo Buys one time rights.

Columns/Departments The Good Life (art, fashion, fine dining, philanthropy, entertainment, luxury living, luxury auto, architecture), 250-750 words. 12 Query with or without published clips. **Pays $200-350.**

$ $ $ SACRAMENTO MAGAZINE

Sacramento Magazines Corp., 706 56th St., Suite 210, Sacramento CA 95819. (916)452-6200. Fax: (916)452-6061. E-mail: krista@sacmag.com. Website: www.sacmag.com. **80% freelance written. Works with a small number of new/unpublished writers each year.** Monthly magazine with a strictly local angle on local issues, human interest and consumer items for readers in the middle to high income brackets. Prefers to work with writers local to Sacramento area. Estab. 1975. Circ. 50,000. Pays on publication. No kill fee. Publishes ms an average of 3 months after acceptance. Generally buys shared North American serial rights and electronic rights.

Accepts queries by mail. Responds in 3 months to queries. Responds in 3 months to mss. Sample copy for $4.50. Guidelines for #10 SASE.

Nonfiction Local isues vital to Sacramento quality of life. No e-mail, fax or phone queries will be answered. **Buys 5 unsolicited feature mss/year.** Query. 1,500-3,000 words, depending on author, subject matter and treatment. **Pays $400 and up.** Sometimes pays expenses of writers on assignment.

Photos Send photos Captions, identification of subjects, True required. Payment varies depending on photographer, subject matter and treatment Buys one time rights.

Columns/Departments Business, home and garden, first person essays, regional travel, gourmet, profile, sports, city arts, health, home and garden, profiles of local people (1,000-1,800 words); UpFront (250-300 words). **Pays $600-800.**

$ $ SACRAMENTO NEWS & REVIEW

Chico Community Publishing, 1015 20th St., Sacramento CA 95814. (916)498-1234. Fax: (916)498-7920. E-mail: melindaw@newsreview.com; kelm@newsreview.com. Website: www.newsreview.com. **Contact:** Melinda Welsh, editor. **25% freelance written.** Alternative news and entertainment weekly magazine. We maintain a high literary standard for submissions; unique or alternative slant. Publication aimed at a young, intellectual audience; submissions should have an edge and strong voice. We have a decided preference for stories with a strong local slant. "Our mission: To publish great newspapers that are successful and enduring. To create a quality work environment that encourages employees to grow professionally while respecting personal welfare. To have a positive impact on our communities and make them better places to live. " Estab. 1989. Circ. 87,000. Byline given. Pays on publication. Offers 10% kill fee. Publishes ms an average of 2 months after acceptance. Buys first rights, buys electronic rights. Editorial lead time 2 months. Submit seasonal material 2 months in advance. Accepts queries by mail, e-mail. Accepts simultaneous submissions. Responds in 1 month to queries. Responds in 2 months to mss. Sample copy for 50¢. Guidelines available online

- Prefers to work with Sacramento-area writers.

Nonfiction Needs essays, expose, general interest, humor, interview, personal experience. Does not want to see travel, product stories, business profile. **Buys 20-30 mss/year.** Query with published clips. Length: 750-5,000 words. **Pays $40-500.** Sometimes pays expenses of writers on assignment.

Photos State availability Identification of subjects required. Reviews 8x10 prints. Negotiates payment individually Buys one time rights.

$ $ SAN DIEGO MAGAZINE

San Diego Magazine Publishing Co., 1450 Front St., San Diego CA 92101. (619)230-9292. Fax: (619)230-0490. E-mail: tblair@sandiegomagazine.com. Website: www.sandiegomag.com. **30% freelance written.** Monthly magazine. We produce informative and entertaining features and investigative reports about politics; community and neighborhood issues; lifestyle; sports; design; dining; arts; and other facets of life in San Diego. Estab. 1948. Circ. 55,000. Byline given. Pays on publication. Offers 25% kill fee. Publishes ms an average of 2 months after acceptance. Buys first North American serial rights, buys second serial (reprint) rights. Editorial lead time 2 months. Submit seasonal material 4 months in advance. Accepts simultaneous submissions.

Nonfiction Needs expose, general interest, historical, how-to, interview, travel, lifestyle. **Buys 12-24 mss/year.** Send complete ms. Length: 1,000-3,000 words. **Pays $250-750.** Sometimes pays expenses of writers on assignment.

Photos State availability Offers no additional payment for photos accepted with ms Buys one time rights.

$ $ $ $ SAN FRANCISCO

243 Vallejo St., San Francisco CA 94111. (415)398-2800. Fax: (415)398-6777. Website: sanfranmag.com. **50% freelance written. Prefers to work with published/established writers.** Monthly city/regional magazine. Estab. 1968. Circ. 180,000. Byline given. Pays on publication. Offers 25% kill fee. Publishes ms an average of 2 months after acceptance. Submit seasonal material 5 months in advance. Responds in 2 months to queries. Responds in 2 months to mss. Sample copy for $3.95.

Nonfiction All stories should relate in some way to the San Francisco Bay Area (travel excepted). Needs expose, interview, travel, arts. Query with published clips. Length: 200-4,000 words. **Pays $100-2,000 and some expenses.**

$ $ $ SAN JOSE

The Magazine for Silicon Valley, Renaissance Publications, Inc., 25 Metro Dr., Suite 550, San Jose CA 95110. (408)975-9300. Fax: (408)975-9900. E-mail: jodi@sanjosemagazine.com. Website: www.sanjosemagazine.com. **10% freelance written.** Monthly magazine. As the lifestyle magazine for those living at center of the technological revolution, we cover the people and places that make Silicon Valley the place to be for the new millennium. All stories must have a local angle, though they should be of national relevance. Estab. 1997. Circ. 60,000. Byline given. Pays on publication. Offers 10% kill fee. Publishes ms an average of 3 months after acceptance. Buys first North American serial rights. pays a flat $25 electronic rights fee. Editorial lead time 18 weeks. Submit seasonal material 6 months in advance. Accepts queries by mail, e-mail, fax. Accepts

simultaneous submissions. Responds in 1 month to queries. Sample copy for $5. Guidelines for #10 SASE.
Nonfiction Needs general interest, interview, photo feature, travel. No technical, trade or articles without a tie-in to Silicon Valley. **Buys 12 mss/year.** Query with published clips. Length: 1,000-2,000 words. **Pays 35¢/word.**
Photos State availability Captions, identification of subjects, model releases required. Offers no additional payment for photos accepted with ms
Columns/Departments Fast Forward (a roundup of trends and personalities and news that has Silicon Valley buzzing; topics include health, history, politics, nonprofits, education, Q&As, business, technology, dining, wine and fashion). 5 Query. **Pays 35¢/word.**
Tips Study our magazine for style and content. Nothing is as exciting as reading a tightly written query and discovering a new writer.

$ SAN LUIS OBISPO COUNTY JOURNAL

654 Osos Street, Suite 10, San Luis Obispo CA 93401. (805)546-0609 or (805)544-8711. Fax: (805)546-8827. E-mail: slojournal@fix.net. **Contact:** Erin Mott. "*The Journal* is strictly local to the Central Coast of California, and the writers are local as well."
Nonfiction Needs general interest. Query.

7X7

Hartle Media, 59 Grant Ave., 4th Floor, San Francisco CA 94108. E-mail: chris@7x7mag.com. Website: www.7x7sf.com. **15% freelance written**. Monthly magazine covering the city of San Francisco. Estab. 2001. Circ. 45,000. Byline given. Pays 60 days following publication. Offers 25% kill fee. Buys first North American serial rights, buys electronic rights, buys nonexclusive reprint rights rights. Editorial lead time 3 months. Submit seasonal material 3-6 months in advance. Accepts queries by mail. Sample copy for $4. Guidelines free.
Nonfiction Although the majority of the magazine is written inhouse, *7x7* accepts freelance queries for both its features section and various departments in the magazine. **Buys 6-10 mss/year.** Query with published clips. **Pays negotiable amount.** Sometimes pays expenses of writers on assignment.
Photos Contact: Contact Stefanie Michejda, photo editor.
Tips Please read the magazine. Stories must appeal to an educated, San Francisco-based audience and, ideally, provide a first-person perspective. Most articles are 500-1,000 words in length.

CANADA/INTERNATIONAL

$ $ ABACO LIFE

Caribe Communications, P.O. Box 37487, Raleigh NC 27627. (919)859-6782. Fax: (919)859-6769. E-mail: jimkerr@mindspring.com. Website: www.abacolife.com. **50% freelance written**. Quarterly magazine covering Abaco, an island group in the Northeast Bahamas. "*Abaco Life* editorial focuses entirely on activities, history, wildlife, resorts, people and other subjects pertaining to the Abacos. Readers include locals, vacationers, second-home owners, and other visitors whose interests range from real estate and resorts to scuba, sailing, fishing, and beaches. The tone is upbeat, adventurous, humorous. No fluff writing for an audience already familiar with the area." Estab. 1979. Circ. 10,000. Byline given. Pays on publication. Offers 40% kill fee. Publishes ms an average of 2 months after acceptance. Buys one-time rights. Editorial lead time 2 months. Submit seasonal material 4 months in advance. Accepts queries by mail, e-mail. Accepts simultaneous submissions. Responds in 2 weeks to queries. Responds in 2 months to mss. Sample copy for $2. Guidelines free.
Nonfiction Needs general interest, historical, how-to, interview, personal experience, photo feature, travel. No general first-time impressions. Articles must be specific, show knowledge and research of the subject and area—`Abaco's Sponge Industry'; `Diving Abaco's Wrecks'; `The Hurricane of '36.' **Buys 8-10 mss/year.** Query or send complete ms Length: 700-2,000 words. **Pays $400-1,000.**
Photos State availability of or send photos Captions, identification of subjects, model releases required. Reviews transparencies, prints. Offers $25-100/photo. Negotiates payment individually. Buys one time rights.
Tips "Travel writers must look deeper than a usual destination piece, and the only real way to do that is spend time in Abaco. Beyond good writing, which is a must, we like submissions on Microsoft Word. We prefer digital photos saved to a disc at 300 dpi minimum JPEG format. Read the magazine to learn its style."

$ $ $ $ ALBERTAVIEWS

AlbertaViews, Ltd., Suite 208-320 23rd Ave. SW, Calgary AB T2S 0J2 Canada. (403)243-5334. Fax: (403)243-8599. E-mail: editor@albertaviews.ab.ca. Website: www.albertaviews.ab.ca. **50% freelance written**. Bimonthly magazine covering Alberta culture: politics, economy, social issues, and art. We are a regional magazine providing thoughtful commentary and background information on issues of concern to Albertans. Most of our writers are Albertans. Estab. 1997. Circ. 30,000. Byline given. Pays on publication. Offers 50% kill fee. Publishes ms an average of 3 months after acceptance. Buys first North American serial rights, buys electronic rights. Editorial lead time 4 months. Submit seasonal material 3 months in advance. Accepts queries by e-mail.

Responds in 6 weeks to queries. Responds in 2 months to mss. Sample copy free. Guidelines available online.

- No phone queries.

Nonfiction Does not want anything not directly related to Alberta Needs essays. **Buys 18 mss/year.** Query with published clips. Length: 3,000-5,000 words. **Pays $1,000-1,500 for assigned articles. Pays $350-750 for unsolicited articles.** Sometimes pays expenses of writers on assignment.

Photos State availability Negotiates payment individually Buys one-time rights, Web rights

Fiction Only fiction by Alberta writers. **Buys 6 mss/year.** Send complete ms. Length: 2,500-4,000 words. **Pays $1,000 maximum.**

$ $ THE ATLANTIC CO-OPERATOR

Promoting Community Ownership, Atlantic Co-operative Publishers, 123 Halifax St., Moncton, New Brunswick E1C 8N5 Canada. Fax: (506)858-6615. E-mail: editor@theatlanticco-operator.coop. Website: www.theatlanticco-operator.coop. **Contact:** Rayanne Brennan, editor-in-chief. **95% freelance written**. Bimonthly tabloid covering co-operatives. "We publish articles of interest to the general public, with a special focus on community ownership and community economic development in Atlantic Canada." Estab. 1933. Byline given. Pays on publication. No kill fee. Publishes ms an average of 2 months after acceptance. Editorial lead time 2 months. Submit seasonal material 2 months in advance. Accepts queries by mail, e-mail, fax. Accepts simultaneous submissions. Responds in 3 weeks to queries.

Nonfiction Needs expose, general interest, historical, interview. No political stories, economical stories, sports. **Buys 90 mss/year.** Query with published clips. Length: 500-2,000 words. **Pays 22¢/word.** Pays expenses of writers on assignment.

Photos State availability Identification of subjects required. Reviews prints, GIF/JPEG files. Offers $25/photo Buys one time rights.

Columns/Departments Health and Lifestyle (anything from recipes to travel), 800 words; International Page (co-operatives in developing countries, good ideas from around the world). 10 Query with published clips.

$ $ $ THE BEAVER

Canada's History Magazine, Canada's National History Society, 56060 Portage Place RPO, Winnipeg MB R3B 0G9 Canada. (204)988-9300. Fax: (204)988-9309. E-mail: editors@historysociety.ca. Website: www.thebeaver.ca. **50% freelance written**. Bimonthly magazine covering Canadian history. Estab. 1920. Circ. 46,000. Byline given. Pays on acceptance. Offers $200 kill fee. Buys first North American serial rights, buys electronic rights. Editorial lead time 4 months. Submit seasonal material 8 months in advance. Accepts queries by e-mail. Accepts simultaneous submissions. Responds in 6 weeks to queries. Responds in 2 months to mss. Sample copy for sae with 9x12 envelope and 2 First-Class stamps. Guidelines available online.

Nonfiction Needs Canadian focus., Subject matter covers the whole range of Canadian history, with emphasis on social history, politics, exploration, discovery and settlement, aboriginal peoples, business & trade, war, culture and sport. Does not want anything unrelated to Canadian history. **Buys 30 mss/year.** Query with published clips, sase. Length: 600-3,500 words. **Pays 50¢/word for major features.** Sometimes pays expenses of writers on assignment.

Photos State availability Identification of subjects, model releases required. Offers no additional payment for photos accepted with ms Buys one time rights.

Columns/Departments Book and other media reviews and Canadian history subjects, 600 words (These are assigned to freelancers with particular areas of expertise, i.e., women's history, labour history, French regime, etc.) 15 columns. **Pays $125**

Tips "*The Beaver* is directed toward a general audience of educated readers, as well as to historians and scholars. We are in the market for lively, well-written, well-researched, and informative articles about Canadian history that focus on all parts of the country and all areas of human activity. Articles are obtained through direct commission and by submission. *The Beaver* publishes articles of various lengths, including long features (from 1,500-3,500 words) that provide an in-depth look at an event, person or era; short, more narrowly focused features (from 600-1,500 words). Longer articles may be considered if their importance warrants publication. Articles should be written in an expository or interpretive style and present the principal themes of Canadian history in an original, interesting and informative way."

$ $ $ CANADIAN GEOGRAPHIC

39 McArthur Ave., Ottawa ON K1L 8L7 Canada. (613)745-4629. Fax: (613)744-0947. Website: www.canadiangeographic.ca. **90% freelance written. Works with a small number of new/unpublished writers each year.** Bimonthly magazine. *Canadian Geographic*'s colorful portraits of our ever-changing population show readers just how important the relationship between the people and the land really is. Estab. 1930. Circ. 240,000. Pays on acceptance. Publishes ms an average of 3 months after acceptance. Buys first Canadian rights. Accepts queries by mail, e-mail, fax. Responds in 1 month to queries. Sample copy for $5.95 (Canadian) and 9x12 SAE or online.

- *Canadian Geographic* reports a need for more articles on earth sciences. Canadian writers only.

Nonfiction Buys authoritative geographical articles, in the broad geographical sense, written for the average person, not for a scientific audience. Predominantly Canadian subjects by Canadian authors. **Buys 30-45 mss/year.** Query. Length: 1,500-3,000 words. **Pays 80¢/word minimum.** Sometimes pays expenses of writers on assignment.
Photos Pays $75-400 for color photos, depending on published size

$ $ COTTAGE

Recreational Living in Western Canada, OP Publishing, Ltd., Suite 500-200, West Esplanade, North Vancouver BC V7M 1A4 Canada. (604)606-4644. Fax: (604)998-3320. E-mail: editor@cottagemagazine.com. Website: www.cottagemagazine.com. **80% freelance written**. "Bimonthly magazine covering do-it-yourself projects, profiles of people and their innovative solutions to building and maintaining their country homes, issues that affect rural individuals and communities, and the R&R aspect of country living.". "Our readers want solid, practical information about living in the country—including alternative energy and sustainable living. The also like to have fun in a wide range of recreational pursuits, from canoeing, fishing, and sailing to water skiing, snowmobiling, and entertaining." Estab. 1992. Circ. 20,000. Byline given. Pays within 1 month of publication. Offers 25% kill fee. Publishes ms an average of 6 months after acceptance. Buys first North American serial rights. Accepts queries by e-mail. Accepts simultaneous submissions. Responds in 1 month to queries.
Nonfiction Buys 18-24 mss/year. Query. Up to 1,500 words. **Pays $100-450 (including visuals).**
Photos Send photos Reviews with negatives prints, slides, digital.
Columns/Departments Utilities (solar and/or wind power), 800 words; Weekend Project (a how-to most homeowners can do themselves), 800 words; Government (new regulations, processes, problems), 800 words; Diversions (advisories, ideas, and how-tos about the fun things that people do), 800 words; InRoads (product reviews), 50-600 words; This Land (personal essays or news-based story with a broader context), 800 words; Last Word or Cabin Life (personal essays and experiences), 800 words; Elements (short articles focusing on a single feature of a cottage), 600 words; Alternatives (applied alternative energy), 600 words. Query. **Pays $75-250.**
Fillers Needs anecdotes, facts, newsbreaks, seasonal tips. 12 Length: 50-200 words. **20¢/word**
Tips "We serve all of Western Canada, so while it's OK to have a main focus on one region, reference should be made to similarities/differences in other provinces. Even technical articles should have some anecdotal content. Some of our best articles come from readers themselves or from writers who can relay that 'personal' feeling. Cottaging is about whimsy and fun as well as maintenance and chores. Images, images, images: We require sharp, quality photos, and the more, the better."

$ DEVON LIFE

Archant Life Ltd, Archant House, Babbage Road, Totnes Devon TQ9 5JA United Kingdom. (44)(180)386-0910. Fax: (44)(180)386-0922. E-mail: devonlife@archant.co.uk. Website: www.devonlife.co.uk. No kill fee. Accepts queries by mail, e-mail. Sample copy available online. Guidelines by email.
Nonfiction 500-750/single-page articles; 1,000-1,200/2-page articles **Pays £60-75/up to 1,200 words; £40-50/up to 750 words**
Photos Send photos Captions required. Reviews transparencies, prints, 300 dpi digital images.

$ $ $ $ HAMILTON MAGAZINE

Town Media, 1074 Cooke Blvd., Burlington ON L7T 4A8 Canada. E-mail: david@townmedia.ca. Website: www.hamiltonmagazine.com. **50% freelance written**. Quarterly magazine devoted to the Greater Hamilton and Golden Horseshoe area. "Mandate: to entertain and inform by spotlighting the best of what our city and region has to offer. We invite readers to take part in a vibrant community by supplying them with authoritative and dynamic coverage of local culture, food, fashion and design. Each story strives to expand your view of the area, every issue an essential resource for exploring, understanding and unlocking the region. Packed with insight, intrigue and suspense, *Hamilton Magazine* delivers the city to your doorstep." Estab. 1978. Byline given. Pays on publication. Offers 50% kill fee. Buys first North American serial rights, buys second serial (reprint) rights. Makes work-for-hire assignments. Editorial lead time 2-3 months. Submit seasonal material 2-3 months in advance. Accepts queries by e-mail. Responds in 1 week to queries and to mss. Sample copy for #10 SASE. Guidelines by email.
Nonfiction Needs book excerpts, essays, expose, historical, how-to, humor, inspirational, interview, personal experience, photo feature, religious, travel. Does not want generic articles that could appear in any mass-market publication. Send complete ms. Length: 800-2,000 words. **Pays $200-1,600 for assigned articles. Pays $100-800 for unsolicited articles.** Sometimes pays expenses of writers on assignment.
Photos Contact: Contact Kate Sharrow, art director. State availability of or send photos Identification of subjects required. Reviews 8x10 prints, JPEG files (8x10 at 300 dpi). Negotiates payment individually. Buys one time rights.
Columns/Departments A&E Art, 1,200-2,000 words; A&E Music, 1,200-2,000 words; A&E Books, 1,200-1,400 words. 12 columns. Send complete ms. **Pays $200-400.**

Tips "Unique local voices are key and a thorough knowledge of the area's history, politics and culture is invaluable."

$ $ MONDAY MAGAZINE

Black Press Ltd., 818 Broughton St., Victoria BC V8W 1E4 Canada. E-mail: editor@mondaymag.com. Website: www.mondaymag.com. **40% freelance written**. Weekly tabloid covering local news. "*Monday Magazine* is Victoria's only alternative newsweekly. For more than 30 years, we have published fresh, informative and alternative perspectives on local events. We prefer lively, concise writing with a sense of humor and insight." Estab. 1975. Circ. 40,000. Byline given. Pays 1-2 months after publication. No kill fee. Publishes ms an average of 1 month after acceptance. Buys first North American serial rights, buys second serial (reprint) rights, buys electronic rights. Makes work-for-hire assignments. Editorial lead time 1-2 months. Submit seasonal material 2 months in advance. Accepts queries by e-mail. Responds in 4-6 weeks to queries. Responds in up to 3 months to mss Guidelines free

Nonfiction Needs expose, general interest, humor, interview, opinion, personal experience, technical, travel. Body, Mind, Spirit (May/October); Student Survival Guide (August). Does not want fiction, poetry, or conspiracy theories. Send complete ms. Length: 300-2,000 words. **Pays 10¢/word**

Photos Send photos Captions, identification of subjects required. Reviews GIF/JPEG files (300 dpi at 4x6). Offers no additional payment for photos accepted with ms. Buys one time rights.

Tips "Local writers tend to have an advantage, as they are familiar with the issues and concerns of interest to a Victoria audience. However, we are interested in perspectives from elsewhere as well, especially on universal topics."

$ $ OUTDOOR CANADA MAGAZINE

25 Sheppard Ave. W., Suite 100, Toronto ON M2N 6S7 Canada. (416)733-7600. Fax: (416)227-8296. E-mail: editorial@outdoorcanada.ca. Website: www.outdoorcanada.ca. **90% freelance written. Works with a small number of new/unpublished writers each year.** "Magazine published 8 times/year emphasizing hunting, fishing, and related pursuits in Canada *only*.". Estab. 1972. Circ. 90,000. Byline given. Pays on publication. No kill fee. Publishes ms an average of 8 months after acceptance. Buys first rights. Submit seasonal material 1 year in advance. Accepts queries by mail, e-mail. Responds in 1 month to queries. Guidelines available online.

Nonfiction Needs how-to, fishing, hunting, outdoor issues, outdoor destinations in Canada. **Buys 35-40 mss/year.** Does not accept unsolicited mss. 2,500 words **Pays $500 and up.**

Reprints Send information about when and where the article previously appeared. Payment varies

Photos Emphasize people in the Canadian outdoors. Captions, model releases required. Pays $100-250 for 35mm transparencies and $400/cover

Fillers 30-40 Length: 100-500 words. **Pays $50 and up**

$ $ $ $ TORONTO LIFE

111 Queen St. E., Suite 320, Toronto ON M5C 1S2 Canada. (416)364-3333. Fax: (416)861-1169. E-mail: editorial@torontolife.com. Website: www.torontolife.com. **95% freelance written. Prefers to work with published/established writers.** Monthly magazine emphasizing local issues and social trends, short humor/satire, and service features for upper income, well-educated and, for the most part, young Torontonians. Circ. 92,039. Byline given. Pays on acceptance. Offers kill fee. Pays 50% kill fee for commissioned articles only. Publishes ms an average of 4 months after acceptance. Buys first North American serial rights. Responds in 3 weeks to queries. Sample copy for $4.95 with SAE and IRCs.

Nonfiction Uses most types of articles. **Buys 17 mss/issue.** Query with published clips and SASE. Length: 1,000-6,000 words. **Pays $500-5,000.**

Columns/Departments We run about 5 columns an issue. They are all freelanced, though most are from regular contributors. They are mostly local in concern and cover politics, business, performing arts, media, design, and food. Length: 2,000 words. Query with published clips and SASE. **Pays $2,000**

Tips Submissions should have strong Toronto orientation.

$ $ THE UKRAINIAN OBSERVER

The Willard Group, 41 Bodgana Khmelnitskoho St., Kiev 01030 Ukraine. (380)(44)502 3005. Fax: (380)(44)501 2342. E-mail: glen.willard@twg.com.ua. Website: www.ukraine-observer.com. **75% freelance written**. Monthly magazine covering Ukrainian news, culture, travel, and history. Our English-language e-zine content is entirely Ukraine-centered. A writer unfamiliar with the country, its politics, or its culture is unlikely to be successful with us. Estab. 2000. Circ. 15,000. Byline given. Pays on publication. Offers 50% kill fee. Publishes ms an average of 2 months after acceptance. Buys all rights. Editorial lead time 1 month. Submit seasonal material 2 months in advance. Accepts queries by mail, e-mail. Responds in 2 weeks to queries. Responds in 1 month to mss. Sample copy free by post to Ukraine addresses only; $3 USD to foreign addresses. Guidelines by email.

Nonfiction Needs general interest, Ukrainian life, history, culture and travel, and significant Ukrainians abroad, historical, Ukrainian history, particular little-known events with significant impact, interview, prominent

Ukrainians or foreign expatriates living in Ukraine, photo feature, current or historical photo feature essays on Ukrainian life, history, culture, and travel, travel, within Ukraine. Does not want poetry, nostalgic family stories, personal experiences or recollections. **Buys 30-40 mss/year.** Send complete ms. Length: 800-1,500 words. **Pays $25-250 for assigned articles. Pays $25-50 for unsolicited articles.** Sometimes pays expenses of writers on assignment.

Photos Send photos Captions, identification of subjects, model releases required. Reviews negatives, GIF/JPEG files. Pays $10/photo. Buys one time rights.

Fiction All fiction should have a Ukrainian setting and/or theme. Needs adventure, ethnic, historical, humorous, mainstream, slice-of-life vignettes. Does not want erotica. **Buys 12 mss/year.** Query or send complete ms. Length: 3,500-4,500 words. **Pays $25-150.**

Tips Obtain, read, and follow our writer's guidelines. We follow Western journalism rules. We are not interested in the writer's opinion—our readers want information to be attributed to experts interviewed for the story. An interesting story that has credible sources and lots of good, direct quotes will be a hit with us. Stories covering political or controversial issues should be balanced and fair.

UP HERE

Explore Canada's Far North, Up Here Publishing, Ltd., P.O. Box 1350, Yellowknife NT X1A 2N9 Canada. (867)766-6710. Fax: (867)873-9876. E-mail: jake@uphere.ca. Website: www.uphere.ca. **50% freelance written**. Magazine published 8 times/year covering general interest about Canada's Far North. We publish features, columns, and shorts about people, wildlife, native cultures, travel, and adventure in Yukon, Northwest Territories, and Nunavut. Be informative, but entertaining. Estab. 1984. Circ. 30,000. Byline given. Pays on publication. Offers 50% kill fee. Buys first North American serial rights. Editorial lead time 6 months. Accepts queries by e-mail. Sample copy for $4.95 (Canadian) and 9x12 SASE.

Nonfiction Needs essays, general interest, how-to, humor, interview, personal experience, photo feature, technical, travel, lifestyle/culture, historical. **Buys 25-30 mss/year.** Query. Length: 1,500-3,000 words. **Fees are negotiable.**

Photos *Please* do not send unsolicited original photos, slides. Send photos Captions, identification of subjects required. Reviews transparencies, prints. Buys one time rights.

Columns/Departments Write for updated guidelines, visit website, or e-mail. 25-30 Query with published clips.

$ $ $ VANCOUVER MAGAZINE

Transcontinental Publications, Inc., Suite 560, 2608 Granville St., Vancouver BC V6H 3V3 Canada. E-mail: mail@vancouvermagazine.com. Website: www.vancouvermagazine.com. **70% freelance written**. Monthly magazine covering the city of Vancouver. Estab. 1967. Circ. 65,000. Byline given. Pays on acceptance. Offers negotiable kill fee. Buys first North American serial rights. Editorial lead time 2 months. Submit seasonal material 6 months in advance. Accepts queries by mail, e-mail, fax, phone. Accepts simultaneous submissions. Responds in 2 weeks to queries. Responds in 1 month to mss. Sample copy for $5. Guidelines for #10 SASE or by e-mail.

Nonfiction We prefer to work with writers from a conceptual stage and have a 6-week lead time. Most stories are under 1,500 words. Please be aware that we don't publish poetry and rarely publish fiction. Needs book excerpts, essays, historical, humor, interview, new product, personal experience, photo feature, travel. **Buys 200 mss/year.** Query. Length: 200-3,000 words. **Pays 50¢/word.** Sometimes pays expenses of writers on assignment.

Photos State availability Captions, identification of subjects, model releases required. Reviews contact sheets, negatives, transparencies, prints, GIF/JPEG files. Negotiates payment individually Buys negotiable rights

Columns/Departments Sport; Media; Business; City Issues, all 1,500 words. Query. **Pays 50¢/word**

Tips Read back issues of the magazine, or visit our website. Almost all of our stories have a strong Vancouver angle. Submit queries by e-mail. Do not send complete stories.

COLORADO

$ SOUTHWEST COLORADO ARTS PERSPECTIVE MAGAZINE

Shared Vision Publishing, P.O. Box 3042, Durango CO 81302. (970)739-3200. E-mail: director@artsperspective.com. Website: www.artsperspective.com. **100% freelance written**. Quarterly tabloid covering art. *"Arts Perspective Magazine* offers a venue for all of the arts. Artists, writers, musicians, dancers, performers and galleries are encourage to showcase their work. A resource for supporters of the arts to share a common thread in the continuum of creative expression." Estab. 2004. Circ. 30,000+. Byline given. Pays on publication. Publishes ms an average of 2 months after acceptance. Buys first North American serial rights, buys first rights, buys one-time rights, buys electronic rights. Editorial lead time 2-5 months. Submit seasonal material 2-5 months in advance. Accepts queries by mail, e-mail, phone. Responds in 2 weeks to queries. Responds in 1 month to mss. Sample copy free. www.artsperspective.com/submissions.php.

Photos Send photos Identification of subjects, model releases required. Reviews GIF/JPEG files. Offers $15-25 per photo. printed online.
Poetry Needs avant-garde, free verse, haiku, light verse, traditional. **Buys 4 yearly poems/year.** Submit maximum 3 poems. Length: 4-45 lines.
Tips "Take me to lunch; sense of humor, please."

$ $ STEAMBOAT MAGAZINE

100 Park Ave., Suite 209, Steamboat Springs CO 80487. (970)871-9413. Fax: (970)871-1922. E-mail: info@steamboatmagazine.com. Website: www.steamboatmagazine.com. **80% freelance written**. Quarterly magazine showcasing the history, people, lifestyles, and interests of Northwest Colorado. Our readers are generally well-educated, well-traveled, upscale, active people visiting our region to ski in winter and recreate in summer. They come from all 50 states and many foreign countries. Writing should be fresh, entertaining, and informative. Estab. 1978. Circ. 20,000. Byline given. Pays 50% on acceptance, 50% on publication. No kill fee. Buys exclusive rights. Submit seasonal material 1 year in advance. Accepts queries by mail, e-mail, fax, phone. Responds in 3 months to queries. Sample copy for $5.95 and SAE with 10 first-class stamps. Guidelines free.
Nonfiction Needs book excerpts, essays, general interest, historical, humor, interview, photo feature, travel. **Buys 10-15 mss/year.** Query with published clips. Length: 150-1,500 words. **Pays $50-300 for assigned articles.** Sometimes pays expenses of writers on assignment.
Photos Prefers to review viewing platforms, JPEGs, and dupes. Will request original transparencies when needed. State availability Captions, identification of subjects required. Pays $50-250/photo Buys one time rights.
Tips Stories must be about Steamboat Springs and the Yampa Valley to be considered. We're looking for new angles on ski/snowboard stories in the winter and activity-related stories, all year round. Please query first with ideas to make sure subjects are fresh and appropriate. We try to make subjects and treatments `timeless' in nature because our magazine is a `keeper' with a multi-year shelf life.

N TELLURIDE MAGAZINE

Big Earth Publishing, Inc., P.O. Box 964, Telluride CO 81435-0964. (970)728-4245. Fax: (970)728-4302. E-mail: duffy@telluridemagazine.com. Website: www.telluridemagazine.com. **Contact:** Mary Duffy, editor-in-chief. 75. Telluride: community, events, recreation, ski resort, surrounding region, San Juan Mountains, history, tourism, mountain living. "*Telluride Magazine* speaks specifically to Telluride and the surrounding mountain environment. Telluride is a resort town supported by the ski industry in winter, festivals in summer, outdoor recreation year round and the unique lifestyle all of that affords. As a National Historic Landmark District with a colorful mining history, it weaves a tale that readers seek out. The local/visitor interaction is key to Telluride's success in making profiles an important part of the content. Telluriders are an environmentally minded and progressive bunch who appreciate efforts toward sustainability and protecting the natural landscape and wilderness that are the region's number one draw." Estab. 1982. Circ. 70,000. True. Pays 60 days from pubication. $50 Buys first rights, first print and electronic rights. 6 months 6 months Accepts queries by e-mail. Responds in 2 weeks on queries; 2 months on mss. Sample copy online at website. Guidelines by email.
Nonfiction Needs historical, humor, nostalgic, personal experience, photo feature, travel, recreation, lifestyle. No articles about places or adventures other than Telluride. **Buys 10/year mss/year.** Query with published clips. 1,000-2,000 **$200-700 for assigned articles; $100-700 for unsolicited articles.** Does not pay expenses.
Photos Send no more than 20 jpeg comps (low-ers) via email or send CD/DVD with submission. Reviews JPEG/TIFF files. Offers $35-300 per photo; negotiates payment individually. Buys one-time rights; includes print and web (electronic).
Columns/Departments Telluride Turns (news and current topics); Mountain Health (health issues related to mountain sports, and living at altitude); Nature Notes (explores the flora, fauna, geology and climate of San Juan Mountains); Green Bytes (sustainable & environmentally sound ideas and products for home building), all 500 words. Buys 40/year Query. **Pays $50-200.**
Fiction "Please contact us; we are very specific about what we will accept." Needs adventure, historical, humorous, slice-of-life vignettes, western, recreation in the mountains. **Buys Buys 2/year mss/year.** Query with published clips. 800-1,200
Poetry Needs any poetry; must reflect mountains or mountain living. **Buys 1/year poems/year.** Submit maximum Submit 6 poems at one time. poems. 3 min. open/max. **Up to $100.**
Fillers anecdotes, facts, short humor. seldom buys fillers. 300-1,000 **Pays up to $500.**

$ $ VAIL-BEAVER CREEK MAGAZINE

Rocky Mountain Media, LLC, P.O. Box 1397, Avon CO 81620. (970)476-6600. Fax: (970)845-0069. E-mail: bergerd@vail.net. Website: www.vailbeavercreekmag.com. **80% freelance written**. Semiannual magazine showcasing the lifestyles and history of the Vail Valley. We are particularly interested in personality profiles, home and design features, the arts, winter and summer recreation/adventure stories, and environmental articles. Estab. 1975. Circ. 30,000. Byline given. Pays on acceptance. Offers 100% kill fee. Publishes ms an average of 6 months after acceptance. Buys one-time rights. Editorial lead time 1 year. Submit seasonal material 1 year in advance. Accepts queries by mail, e-mail. Accepts simultaneous submissions. Responds in 1 month to queries. Responds in 2 months to mss. Sample copy for $5.95 and SAE with 10 first-class stamps. Guidelines free.

Nonfiction Needs essays, general interest, historical, humor, interview, personal experience, photo feature. **Buys 20-25 mss/year.** Query with published clips. Length: 500-3,000 words. **Pays 20-30¢/word.** Sometimes pays expenses of writers on assignment.

Reprints Send typed manuscript with rights for sale noted and information about when and where the material previously appeared.

Photos State availability Captions, identification of subjects, model releases required. Reviews transparencies. Offers $50-250/photo. Buys one time rights.

Tips Be familiar with the Vail Valley and its personality. Approach a story that will be relevant for several years to come. We produce a magazine that is a `keeper.'

CONNECTICUT

$ $ $ 🄽 CONNECTICUT MAGAZINE

Journal Register Co., 35 Nutmeg Dr., Trumbull CT 06611. (203)380-6600. Fax: (203)380-6610. E-mail: dsalm@connecticutmag.com. Website: www.connecticutmag.com. **75% freelance written. Prefers to work with published/established writers who know the state and live/have lived here.** Monthly magazine for an affluent, sophisticated, suburban audience. We want only articles that pertain to living in Connecticut. Estab. 1971. Circ. 93,000. Byline given. Pays on publication. Offers 20% kill fee. Publishes ms an average of 4 months after acceptance. Buys first North American serial rights. Submit seasonal material 4 months in advance. Accepts queries by mail, e-mail, fax. Responds in 6 weeks to queries. Guidelines for #10 SASE.

Nonfiction "Interested in seeing hard-hitting investigative pieces and strong business pieces (not advertorial)." Needs book excerpts, expose, general interest, interview, topics of service to Connecticut readers. Dining/entertainment, northeast/travel, home/garden and Connecticut bride twice/year. Also, business (January) and healthcare once/year. No personal essays. **Buys 50 mss/year.** Query with published clips. 3,000 words maximum. **Pays $600-1,200.** Sometimes pays expenses of writers on assignment.

Photos Send photos Identification of subjects, model releases required. Reviews contact sheets, transparencies. Pays $50 minimum/photo Buys one time rights.

Columns/Departments Business, Health, Politics, Connecticut Calendar, Arts, Dining Out, Gardening, Environment, Education, People, Sports, Media, From the Field (quirky, interesting regional stories with broad appeal). Length: 1,500-2,500 words. 50 Query with published clips. **Pays $400-700.**

Fillers Short pieces about Connecticut trends, curiosities, interesting short subjects, etc. Length: 150-400 words. **Pays $75-150.**

Tips "Make certain your idea has not been covered to death by the local press and can withstand a time lag of a few months. Again, we don't want something that has already received a lot of press."

DELAWARE

$ $ DELAWARE TODAY

3301 Lancaster Pike, Suite 5C, Wilmington DE 19805. (302)656-1809. Fax: (302)656-5843. E-mail: editors@delawaretoday.com. Website: www.delawaretoday.com. **50% freelance written.** Monthly magazine geared toward Delaware people, places and issues. All stories must have Delaware slant. No pitches such as Delawareans will be interested in a national topic. Estab. 1962. Circ. 25,000. Byline given. Pays on publication. Offers 50% kill fee. Publishes ms an average of 4 months after acceptance. all rights for 1 year. Editorial lead time 3 months. Submit seasonal material 6 months in advance. Responds in 2 months to queries. Sample copy for $2.95.

Nonfiction Needs historical, interview, photo feature, lifestyles, issues. Newcomer's Guide to Delaware **Buys 40 mss/year.** Query with published clips. Length: 100-3,000 words. **Pays $50-750.** Sometimes pays expenses of writers on assignment.

Photos State availability Identification of subjects required. Negotiates payment individually. Buys one time rights.

Columns/Departments Business, Health, History, People, all 1,500 words. 24 Query with published clips. **Pays $150-250.**

Fillers Needs anecdotes, newsbreaks, short humor. 10 Length: 100-200 words. **Pays $50-75.**

Tips No story ideas that we would know about, i.e., a profile of the governor. Best bets are profiles of quirky/unique Delawareans that we'd never know about or think of.

DISTRICT OF COLUMBIA

$ $ WASHINGTON CITY PAPER

2390 Champlain St. NW, Washington DC 20009. (202)332-2100. Fax: (202)332-8500. Website: www.washingtoncitypaper.com. **50% freelance written**. Relentlessly local alternative weekly in nation's capital covering city and regional politics, media and arts. No national stories. Estab. 1981. Circ. 93,000. Byline given. Pays on publication. Offers kill fee. Offers 10% kill fee for assigned stories. Publishes ms an average of 6 weeks after acceptance. Buys first rights. Editorial lead time 7-10 days. Responds in 1 month to queries. Guidelines available online.

Nonfiction Our biggest need for freelancers is in the District Line section of the newspaper: short, well-reported and local stories. These range from carefully-drawn profiles to sharp, hooky approaches to reporting on local institutions. We don't want op-ed articles, fiction, poetry, service journalism or play by play accounts of news conferences or events. We also purchase, but more infrequently, longer `cover-length' stories that fit the criteria stated above. Full guide to freelance submissions can be found on website. **Buys 100 mss/year.** District Line: 800-1,500 words; Covers: 2,500-10,000 words **Pays 10-40¢/word.** Sometimes pays expenses of writers on assignment.

Photos Make appointment to show portfolio to art director. Pays minimum of $75.

Columns/Departments Music Writing (eclectic). 100 Query with published clips or send complete ms. **Pays 10-40¢/word.**

Tips Think local. Great ideas are a plus. We are willing to work with anyone who has a strong idea, regardless of vita.

FLORIDA

$ $ $ $ BOCA RATON MAGAZINE

JES Publishing, 6413 Congress Ave., Suite 100, Boca Raton FL 33487. (561)997-8683. Fax: (561)997-8909. Website: www.bocamag.com. **70% freelance written**. Bimonthly lifestyle magazine devoted to the residents of South Florida, featuring fashion, interior design, food, people, places, and issues that shape the affluent South Florida market. Estab. 1981. Circ. 20,000. Byline given. Pays on acceptance. No kill fee. Publishes ms an average of 3 months after acceptance. Buys second serial (reprint) rights. Submit seasonal material 7 months in advance. Accepts simultaneous submissions. Responds in 1 month to queries. Sample copy for $4.95 and 10x13 SAE with 10 first-class stamps. Guidelines for #10 SASE.

Nonfiction Needs general interest, historical, humor, interview, photo feature, travel. Interior Design (September-October); Real Estate (March-April); Best of Boca (July-August). Send complete ms. Length: 800-2,500 words. **Pays $350-1,500.**

Reprints Send tearsheet. Payment varies.

Photos Send photos

Columns/Departments Body & Soul (health, fitness and beauty column, general interest); Hitting Home (family and social interactions); History or Arts (relevant to South Florida), all 1,000 words. Query with published clips or send complete ms. **Pays $350-400.**

Tips We prefer shorter manuscripts, highly localized articles, excellent art/photography.

COASTLINES

Marine Industries Association of Palm Beach County, Inc., P.O. Box 7597, West Palm Beach FL 33405. (561)832-8444. Fax: (561)659-1824. E-mail: alison@marinepbc.org. Website: www.marinepbc.org. biannual magazine. Circ. 25,000+. Byline given. No kill fee. Editorial lead time 3 months. Submit seasonal material 3 months in advance. Guidelines available.

Nonfiction Contact: Alison Pruitt.

Photos Contact: Alison Pruitt, publisher.

$ $ CORAL LIVING

South Florida Life & Leisure, Metropical Media Corp., P.O. Box 140245, Coral Gables FL 33114. (786)552-6464. E-mail: editor@coralliving.com. Website: www.coralliving.com. **80% freelance written**. Quarterly magazine Publish regional stories on life and travel in South Florida. Estab. 2002. Circ. 20,000. Byline given. Pays on publication. Offers %50 kill fee. Publishes ms an average of 4 months after acceptance. Buys first rights, buys one-time rights, buys second serial (reprint) rights, buys simultaneous rights, buys all rights. Makes work-for-hire assignments. Editorial lead time 3-4 months. Submit seasonal material 4 months in advance. Accepts queries by e-mail. Accepts previously published material. Accepts simultaneous submissions. Responds in 2 weeks to queries. Sample copy available online.

Nonfiction Needs book excerpts, essays, general interest, historical, how-to, humor, inspirational, interview, opinion, personal experience, photo feature, travel. We do not want fiction and stories that do not have a regional angle. **Buys 20 mss/year.** Query with published clips. Length: 800-2,500 words. **Pays $150-700 for assigned articles. Pays $150-700 for unsolicited articles.** Sometimes pays expenses of writers on assignment.

Photos State availability of or send photos Identification of subjects, model releases required. Reviews contact

sheets. Negotiates payment individually. Offers no additional payment for photos accepted with ms. Buys one time rights.
Columns/Departments Query with published clips. **Pays $$150-$300.**

$ $ EMERALD COAST MAGAZINE

Rowland Publishing, Inc., 1932 Miccosukee Rd., Tallahassee FL 32308. (850)878-0554. Fax: (850)656-1871. Website: www.emeraldcoastmagazine.com. **50% freelance written**. Bimonthly magazine. Lifestyle publication celebrating life on Florida's Emerald Coast. All content has an Emerald Coast (Northwest Florida) connection. This includes Panama City, Seaside, Sandestin, Destin, Fort Walton Beach, and Pensacola. Estab. 2000. Circ. 18,000. Byline given. Pays on acceptance. No kill fee. Publishes ms an average of 3 months after acceptance. Buys first North American serial rights. Editorial lead time 4 months. Submit seasonal material 6 months in advance. Accepts queries by mail, e-mail. Accepts previously published material. Accepts simultaneous submissions. Responds in 3 months to queries. Responds in 3 months to mss. Sample copy for $4. Guidelines by email.
Nonfiction All must have an Emerald Coast slant. Needs book excerpts, essays, historical, inspirational, interview, new product, personal experience, photo feature. No fiction, poetry, or travel. No general interest—we are Northwest Florida specific. **Buys 10-15 mss/year.** Query with published clips. Length: 1,800-2,000 words. **Pays $100-250.**
Photos Send photos Captions, identification of subjects, model releases required. Reviews prints, GIF/JPEG files. Negotiates payment individually. Buys one time rights.
Tips We're looking for fresh ideas and new slants that are related to Florida's Emerald Coast. Because we work so far in advance, it is difficult to be timely, so be sure to give us ideas that aren't too time specific.

$ $ $ $ FLORIDA INSIDE OUT

404 Washington Ave., Suite 650, Miami Beach FL 33139. (305)532-2544. Website: www.floridainsideout.com. **60% freelance written**. Bimonthly magazine covering architecture and interior design. *Florida Inside Out* is a smart publication for those interested in design, architecture and interiors. It is product-heavy, but also includes many newsy features on the fields we cover. No press releases or pre-packaged features will be published. We accept original material only. Estab. 2004. Circ. 55,000. Byline given. Pays on publication. Offers 20% kill fee. Publishes ms an average of 1-2 months after acceptance. Buys one-time rights. Editorial lead time 2-3 months. Submit seasonal material 3 months in advance. Accepts queries by mail, e-mail, phone. Accepts simultaneous submissions.
Nonfiction Needs book excerpts, essays, general interest, historical, interview, new product, travel. Does not want pre-packaged material. Query with published clips. Length: 150-1,400 words. **Pays $1/word.** Pays expenses of writers on assignment.
Photos Contact: Contact Reynaldo Martin, associate art director. Send photos Identification of subjects required. Reviews GIF/JPEG files. Negotiates payment individually. Buys one time rights.
Columns/Departments Green Matters (landscape, agriculture), 1,000-1,200 words; Fin, Feather, Hoof & Paw (pets and pet-related), 850-1,000 words; History Books (Florida-related history), 850-1,000 words. 18-20 Query. **Pays $1/word.**
Tips Do not approach with anything that has already been published. We assign all of our features, departments, etc. But we do always look for new contributors with fresh ideas.

$ $ FLORIDA MONTHLY MAGAZINE

Florida Media, Inc., 999 Douglas Ave., Suite 3301, Altamonte Springs FL 32714-2063. (407)816-9596. Fax: (407)816-9373. E-mail: exec-editor@floridamagazine.com. Website: www.floridamagazine.com. Monthly lifestyle magazine covering Florida travel, food and dining, heritage, homes and gardens, and all aspects of Florida lifestyle. Full calendar of events each month. Estab. 1981. Circ. 225,235. Byline given. Pays on publication. No kill fee. Publishes ms an average of 5 months after acceptance. Buys first rights. Editorial lead time 3 months. Submit seasonal material 6 months in advance. Accepts queries by mail, e-mail, fax. Responds in 9 months to queries. Sample copy for $5. Guidelines by email.

- Interested in material on areas outside of the larger cities.

Nonfiction Needs historical, interview, travel, general Florida interest, out-of-the-way Florida places, dining, attractions, festivals, shopping, resorts, bed & breakfast reviews, retirement, real estate, business, finance, health, recreation, sports. **Buys 50-60 mss/year.** Query with published clips. Length: 500-2,500 words. **Pays $100-400 for assigned articles. Pays $50-250 for unsolicited articles.**
Photos Send photos Captions required. Reviews 3x5 color prints and slides. Offers $6/photo.
Columns/Departments Golf; Homes & Gardenings; Heritage (all Florida-related); 750 words. 24 Query with published clips. **Pays $75-250.**

$ FT. MYERS MAGAZINE

And Pat, LLC, 15880 Summerlin Rd., Suite 189, Fort Myers FL 33908. E-mail: ftmyers@optonline.net. Website: www.ftmyersmagazine.com. **90% freelance written**. Bimonthly magazine covering regional arts and living for educated, active, successful and creative residents of Lee & Collier Counties, Florida and guests at resorts and hotels in Lee County. "Content: Arts, entertainment, media, travel, sports, health, home, garden, environmental issues." Estab. 2001. Circ. 20,000. Byline given. 30 days after publication. No kill fee. Publishes ms an average of 2-6 months after acceptance. Buys one-time rights, buys second serial (reprint) rights. Editorial lead time 2-4 months. Submit seasonal material 2-4 months in advance. Accepts queries by e-mail. Accepts simultaneous submissions. Responds in 3 months to queries and to mss. Guidelines available online.

Nonfiction Needs essays, general interest, historical, how-to, humor, interview, personal experience, reviews, previews, news, informational. **Buys 10-25 mss/year mss/year.** Send complete ms. Length: 750-1,500 words. **Pays $50-150 or approximately 10¢/word.** Sometimes pays expenses of writers on assignment.

Photos State availability of or send photos Captions, identification of subjects required. Negotiates payment individually; generally offers $25-100/photo or art. Buys one time rights.

Columns/Departments Media: books, music, video, film, theater, Internet, software (news, previews, reviews, interviews, profiles), 750-1,500 words. Lifestyles: art & design, science & technology, house & garden, health & wellness, sports & recreation, travel & leisure, food & drink (news, interviews, previews, reviews, profiles, advice), 750-1,500 words. 60 Query with or without published clips or send complete ms. **Pays $50-150.**

$ $ $ GULFSHORE LIFE

9051 N. Tamiami Trail, Suite 202, Naples FL 34108. (239)449-4111. Fax: (239)594-9986. E-mail: denises@gulfshorelifemag.com. Website: www.gulfshorelifemag.com. **75% freelance written**. Magazine published 10 times/year for southwest Florida, the workings of its natural systems, its history, personalities, culture and lifestyle. Estab. 1970. Circ. 35,000. Byline given. Pays on publication. Publishes ms an average of 4 months after acceptance. Submit seasonal material 8 months in advance. Accepts queries by mail, e-mail, fax. Accepts simultaneous submissions. Sample copy for sae with 9x12 envelope and 10 First-Class stamps.

Nonfiction All articles must be related to southwest Florida. Needs historical, interview, issue/trend. **Buys 100 mss/year.** Query with published clips. Length: 500-3,000 words. **Pays $100-1,000.**

Photos Send photos Identification of subjects, model releases required. Reviews 35mm transparencies, 5x7 prints. Pays $50-100. Buys one time rights.

Tips We buy superbly written stories that illuminate southwest Florida personalities, places and issues. Surprise us!

$ $ JACKSONVILLE

White Publishing Co., 1261 King St., Jacksonville FL 32204. (904)389-3622. Fax: (904)389-3628. Website: www.jacksonvillemag.com. **50% freelance written**. Monthly magazine covering life and business in northeast Florida for upwardly mobile residents of Jacksonville and the Beaches, Orange Park, St. Augustine and Amelia Island, Florida. Estab. 1985. Circ. 25,000. Byline given. Pays on publication. Offers kill fee. Offers 25-33% kill fee to writers on assignment. Buys first North American serial rights, buys second serial (reprint) rights. Editorial lead time 3 months. Submit seasonal material 4 months in advance. Responds in 6 weeks to queries. Responds in 1 month to mss. Sample copy for $5 (includes postage).

Nonfiction All articles *must* have relevance to Jacksonville and Florida's First Coast (Duval, Clay, St. John's, Nassau, Baker counties). Needs book excerpts, expose, general interest, historical, how-to, service articles, humor, interview, personal experience, photo feature, travel, commentary. **Buys 50 mss/year.** Query with published clips. Length: 1,200-3,000 words. **Pays $50-500 for feature length pieces.** Sometimes pays expenses of writers on assignment.

Reprints Send photocopy. Payment varies.

Photos State availability Captions, model releases required. Reviews contact sheets, transparencies. Negotiates payment individually. Buys one time rights.

Columns/Departments Business (trends, success stories, personalities), 1,000-1,200 words; Health (trends, emphasis on people, hopeful outlooks), 1,000-1,200 words; Money (practical personal financial advice using local people, anecdotes and examples), 1,000-1,200 words; Real Estate/Home (service, trends, home photo features), 1,000-1,200 words; Travel (weekends; daytrips; excursions locally and regionally), 1,000-1,200 words; occasional departments and columns covering local history, sports, family issues, etc. 40 **Pays $150-250.**

Tips We are a writer's magazine and demand writing that tells a story with flair.

$ $ PENSACOLA MAGAZINE

Ballinger Publishing, 41 N. Jefferson St., Suite 402, Pensacola FL 32502. E-mail: kelly@ballingerpublishing.com. Website: www.ballingerpublishing.com. **75% freelance written**. Monthly magazine. *Pensacola Magazine*'s articles are written in a casual, conversational tone. We cover a broad range of topics that citizens of Pensacola relate to. Most of our freelance work is assigned, so it is best to send a resume, cover letter and 3 clips to the above e-mail address. Estab. 1987. Circ. 10,000. Byline given. Pays at end of shelf life. Offers 20% kill fee. Buys first rights. Makes work-for-hire assignments. Editorial lead time 1 month. Submit seasonal material 6 months in advance. Accepts queries by e-mail. Accepts previously published material. Accepts simultaneous submissions. Responds in 2 weeks to queries. Sample copy for $1, SASE and 1 First-Class stamp. Guidelines available online.

Nonfiction Wedding (February); Home & Garden (May). Query with published clips. Length: 700-2,100 words. **Pays 10-15¢/word.** Sometimes pays expenses of writers on assignment.

Photos State availability of or send photos Captions, identification of subjects, model releases required. Reviews GIF/JPEG files. Offers $7/photo. Buys one time rights.

Tips We accept submissions for *Pensacola Magazine*, *Northwest Florida's Business Climate*, and *Coming of Age*. Please query by topic via e-mail to shannon@ballingerpublishing.com. If you do not have a specific query topic, please send a resume and three clips via e-mail, and you will be given story assignments if your writing style is appropriate. You do not have to be locally or regionally located to write for us.

$ $ TALLAHASSEE MAGAZINE

Rowland Publishing, Inc., 1932 Miccosukee Rd., Tallahassee FL 32308. E-mail: editorial@rowlandpublishing.com. Website: www.rowlandpublishing.com. **20% freelance written**. Bimonthly magazine covering life in Florida's Capital Region. All content has a Tallahassee, Florida connection. Estab. 1978. Circ. 18,000. Byline given. Pays on acceptance. No kill fee. Publishes ms an average of 2 months after acceptance. Buys first North American serial rights. Editorial lead time 4 months. Submit seasonal material 6 months in advance. Accepts queries by mail, e-mail. Accepts simultaneous submissions. Responds in 3 months to queries. Responds in 3 months to mss. Sample copy for $4. Guidelines by email.

Nonfiction All must have a Tallahassee slant. Needs book excerpts, essays, historical, inspirational, interview, new product, personal experience, photo feature, travel, sports, business, Calendar items. No fiction, poetry, or travel. No general interest—we are Tallahassee, Florida specific. **Buys 15 mss/year.** Query with published clips. Length: 1,000-2,000 words. **Pays $100-250.**

Photos Send photos Captions, identification of subjects, model releases required. Reviews prints, GIF/JPEG files. Negotiates payment individually. Buys one time rights.

Tips We're looking for fresh ideas and new slants that are related to Florida's Capital Region. Because we work so far in advance, it is difficult to be timely, so be sure to give us ideas that aren't too time specific.

$ $ TIMES OF THE ISLANDS

Southwest Florida's Island Coast Magazine, Times of the Islands Inc., P.O. Box 1227, Sanibel FL 33957. (239)472-0205. Fax: (239)395-2125. E-mail: editor@toti.com. Website: www.toti.com. **98% freelance written**. Bimonthly magazine. *Times of the Islands* is a magazine that captures the true essence of island living. It is a high-quality, intriguing publication that captures the beauty, style and spirit of island life; a magazine with vision and substance that appeals not only to residents of Sanibel, Captiva and the barrier islands of Southwest Florida, but to vacationers and mainlanders as wellÃ³anyone who shares a passion for the island mystique and lifestyle. Estab. 1997. Circ. 25,000. Byline given. Pays on publication. No kill fee. Publishes ms an average of 4 months after acceptance. Buys one-time rights, buys electronic rights. Editorial lead time 4 months. Submit seasonal material 4 months in advance. Accepts queries by e-mail. Accepts simultaneous submissions. Responds in 1 week to queries. Responds in 1 month to mss. Sample copy free. Guidelines available online.

Nonfiction Needs general interest, humor, interview, photo feature, travel, cuisine. Query with published clips. Length: 1,000-2,000 words. **Pays $250-400.**

Photos Send photos Captions, identification of subjects required. Reviews contact sheets. Offers $25-50/published photo. Buys one time rights.

Columns/Departments Habitats (homes and living spaces); Arts; Profile (profile of notable person); Coastal Commerce (profile of local business person); Explorer (fun weekend exploration trip); Getaways (traveling trip); Outdoors (outdoor activity); To Your Health (informative health and medical), all 1,000 words. Plus, Making Waves (notable SW Floridians), 300 words. Query with published clips. **Pays $150-250.**

Tips We are looking for exciting, fresh material on subjects that cover anything pertaining to Southwest Florida living.

$ $ N WHERE MAGAZINE

Morris Visitor Publications, 7300 Corporate Center Dr., Suite 303, Miami FL 33126. Fax: (305)892-1005. E-mail: irene.moore@wheremagazine.com. Website: www.wheretraveler.com. **40% freelance written**. Monthly magazine covering Miami tourism. We cover Miami only. We are a tourism guide, so features are only about where to go and what to do in Miami. Writers must be very familiar with Miami. Estab. 1936. Circ. 30,000. Byline for features only, but all writers listed on masthead. Pays on publication. Buys all rights. Editorial lead time 3 months. Submit seasonal material 3 months in advance. Accepts queries by mail, e-mail. Responds in 1 week to queries Sample copy available online Guidelines by email

Nonfiction Needs new product, photo feature, travel, (in Miami). **Buys 0 mss/year.** Query. Length: 1,000 words.

Photos Send photos Captions, identification of subjects, model releases required. Reviews GIF/JPEG files. Negotiates payment individually. Buys all rights.

Columns/Departments Dining; Entertainment; Museums & Attractions; Art Galleries; Shops & Services;

Navigating around Miami, 100 words. Queries for writer clips only per page of 4 blurbs per page.
Tips "We look for a new slant on a 'where to go' or 'what to do' in Miami."

GENERAL REGIONAL

$ $ BLUE RIDGE COUNTRY

Leisure Publishing, 3424 Brambleton Ave., Roanoke VA 24018. (540)989-6138. Fax: (540)989-7603. E-mail: cmodisett@leisurepublishing.com. Website: www.leisurepublishing.com. **90% freelance written**. Bimonthly magazine. "The magazine is designed to celebrate the history, heritage and beauty of the Blue Ridge region. It is aimed at adult, upscale readers who enjoy living or traveling in the mountain regions of Virginia, North Carolina, West Virginia, Maryland, Kentucky, Tennessee, South Carolina, Alabama, and Georgia." Estab. 1988. Circ. 425,000. Byline given. Pays on publication. Offers kill fee. Offers $50 kill fee for commissioned pieces only. Publishes ms an average of 8 months after acceptance. Buys first North American serial rights. Submit seasonal material 6 months in advance. Accepts queries by mail, e-mail, fax; prefer e-mail. Responds in 3-4 months to queries. Responds in 2 months to mss. Sample copy for 9x12 SAE with 6 first-class stamps Guidelines available online.

Nonfiction Looking for more backroads travel, first person outdoor recreation pieces, environmental news, baby boomer era stories, regional history and well-researched regional legend/lore pieces. Needs general interest, historical, personal experience, photo feature, travel. **Buys 25-30 mss/year.** Send complete ms. Length: 200-1,500 words. **Pays $150-250.**

Photos Photos must be shot in region. Outline of region can be found online. Send photos Identification of subjects required. Reviews transparencies. Pays $40-150/photo Buys one time rights.

Columns/Departments Country Roads (shorts on regional news, people, destinations, events, travel, ecology, history, antiques, books); Inns and Getaways (reviews of inns); Mountain Delicacies (cookbooks and recipes); The Hike; On the Mountainside (outdoor recreation pieces). 30-42 Query. **Pays $25-125.**

Fiction Publish occasional previews and book excerpts of regional relevance.

Poetry Publish occasional poetry by regional writers and/or on regional topics in conjunction with photo essays.

Tips "Would like to see more pieces dealing with contemporary history (1940s-70s). Freelancers needed for regional departmental shorts and `macro' issues affecting whole region. Need field reporters from all areas of Blue Ridge region, especially more from Kentucky, Maryland, South Carolina and Alabama. We are also looking for updates on the Blue Ridge Parkway, Appalachian Trail, national forests, ecological issues, preservation movements, affordable travel, and interesting short profiles or regional people."

$ $ $ $ COWBOYS & INDIANS MAGAZINE

The Premier Magazine of the West, USFR Media Group, 6688 N. Central Expressway, Suite 650, Dallas TX 75206. E-mail: queries@cowboysindians.com. Website: www.cowboysindians.com. **60% freelance written**. Magazine published 8 times/year covering people and places of the American West. The Premier Magazine of the West, *Cowboys & Indians* captures the romance, drama, and grandeur of the American frontier—both past and present—like no other publication. Undeniably exclusive, the magazine covers a broad range of lifestyle topics: art, home interiors, travel, fashion, Western film, and Southwestern cuisine. Estab. 1993. Circ. 101,000. Byline given. Pays on publication. Offers 20% kill fee. Publishes ms an average of 2 months after acceptance. Buys first North American serial rights, buys electronic rights. Editorial lead time 4 months. Submit seasonal material 6 months in advance. Accepts queries by mail, e-mail, fax. Sample copy for $5. Guidelines by email.

Nonfiction Needs book excerpts, expose, general interest, historical, interview, photo feature, travel, art. No essays, humor, poetry, or opinion. **Buys 40-50 mss/year.** Query. Length: 500-3,000 words. **Pays $250-5,000 for assigned articles. Pays $250-1,000 for unsolicited articles.**

Photos State availability Captions, identification of subjects required. Reviews contact sheets, 2¼x2¼ transparencies. Negotiates payment individually Buys one time rights.

Columns/Departments Art; Travel; Music; Home Interiors; all 200-1,000 words. 50 Query. **Pays $200-1,500.**

Tips Our readers are educated, intelligent, and well-read Western enthusiasts, many of whom collect Western Americana, read other Western publications, attend shows and have discerning tastes. Therefore, articles should assume a certain level of prior knowledge of Western subjects on the part of the reader. Articles should be readable and interesting to the novice and general interest reader as well. Please keep your style lively, above all things, and fast-moving, with snappy beginnings and endings. Wit and humor are always welcome.

$ $ $ ESTATES WEST MAGAZINE

Media That Deelivers, Inc., 8132 N. 87th Place, Scottsdale AZ 85258. (480)460-5203. Fax: (480)443-1517. E-mail: editorial@estateswest.com; cringer@estateswest.com. Website: www.estateswest.com. **30% freelance written**. Bimonthly magazine affluent living, real estate, architecture, design, and travel throughout the West. Estab. 2000. Circ. 60,000. Byline given. Pays on publication. No kill fee. Publishes ms an average of 6 months after acceptance. Editorial lead time 3-4 months. Submit seasonal material 4 months in advance. Accepts

queries by mail, e-mail. Responds in 1 month to queries. Sample copy and writer's guidelines for #10 SASE.
Nonfiction Needs interview, designers, builders, realtors, architects, new product, travel, decor, real estate. **Buys 10-15 mss/year.** Query with published clips. Length: 900-2,000 words. **Pays 50-60¢/word for assigned articles.**
Photos Send photos with submission per discussion with editor. Photos must be high resolution. Negotiates payment individually. Buys one time rights.

$ $ GUESTLIFE

Monterey Bay/New Mexico/El Paso/Houston/Vancouver, Desert Publications, Inc., 303 N. Indian Canyon Dr., Palm Springs CA 92262. (760)325-2333. Fax: (760)325-7008. Website: www.guestlife.com. **95% freelance written**. Annual prestige hotel room magazine covering history, highlights, and activities of the area named (i.e., *Monterey Bay GuestLife*). *GuestLife* focuses on its respective area and is placed in hotel rooms in that area for the affluent vacationer. Estab. 1979. Byline given. Pays on publication. Offers negotiable kill fee. Publishes ms an average of 9 months after acceptance. Buys electronic rights, buys all rights. Editorial lead time 6 months. Submit seasonal material 8 months in advance. Accepts queries by e-mail. Responds in 1 month to queries. Responds in 1 month to mss. Sample copy for $10.
Nonfiction Needs general interest, regional, historical, photo feature, travel. **Buys 3 mss/year.** Query with published clips. Length: 300-1,500 words. **Pays $100-500.**
Photos State availability Identification of subjects required. Reviews contact sheets. Negotiates payment individually Buys all rights.
Fillers Needs facts. 3 Length: 50-100 words. **Pays $50-100.**

$ $ LAKE

713 State St., La Porte IN 46350. E-mail: info@lakemagazine.com. Website: www.lakemagazine.com. **80% freelance written**. Magazine published 10 times/year covering Lake Michigan, in particular the resort communities of Southeast Michigan and Northwest Indiana. Estab. 2000. Circ. 35,000. Byline given. Pays on acceptance. Offers 15% kill fee. Publishes ms an average of 2 months after acceptance. Buys first North American serial rights. Editorial lead time 2 months. Submit seasonal material 4-5 months in advance. Accepts queries by e-mail. Accepts previously published material. Accepts simultaneous submissions. Sample copy available online.
Nonfiction Needs book excerpts, essays, general interest, historical, humor, interview, new product, personal experience, photo feature, travel. Travel (May and September issues); Kids (June issue). Does not want fiction, poetry. **Buys 100 mss/year.** Send complete ms. Length: 250-2,000 words. **Pays 30-50¢/word.** Sometimes pays expenses of writers on assignment.
Columns/Departments Lake's Grapes (wine), 550 words; Field to Table (regional food); My Lake (well-known Harbor Country residents), 1,000 words; Postcard (profile of Harbor County community), 1,000 words. 40-50 Query with published clips or send complete ms. **Pays 30-50¢/word.**
Tips Pitch shorter stories for our front-of-book section. Send well thought out, in-depth queries explaining what angle you'd use and why it's a good or important story for *Lake* to run.

$ MIDWEST LIVING

Meredith Corp., 1716 Locust St., Des Moines IA 50309-3038. (515)284-3000. Fax: (515)284-3836. Website: www.midwestliving.com. Bimonthly magazine covering Midwestern families. Regional service magazine that celebrates the interest, values, and lifestyles of Midwestern families. Estab. 1987. Circ. 915,000. Pays on acceptance. No kill fee. Buys all rights. Editorial lead time 6 months. Accepts queries by mail, e-mail. Sample copy for $3.95. Guidelines by email.
Nonfiction Needs general interest, good eating, festivals and fairs, historical, interesting slices of Midwestern history, customs, traditions and the people who preserve them, interview, towns, neighborhoods, families,people whose stories exemplify the Midwest spirit an values, travel, Midwestern destinations with emphasis on the fun and affordable. Query.
Photos State availability
Tips As general rule of thumb, we're looking for stories that are useful to the reader with information of ideas they can act on in their own lives. Most important, we want stories that have direct relevance to our Midwest audience.

$ $ MOUNTAIN HOMES/SOUTHERN STYLE

P.O. Box 21535, Roanoke VA 24018. E-mail: mountainhomessouthernstyle.com. Bimonthly magazine celebrating the best of upscale living in the Southern mountains—the homes, the events, the art, the style, the food, and the cities and towns that people today are increasingly seeking out for retirement or as an escape from big city living. "Our territory extends from the Shenandoah Valley of Virginia down into northern Georgia and includes all territory in the mountain regions of Virginia, North Carolina, South Carolina, West Virginia, Tennessee, Maryland and Georgia." Pays on publication. Buys first North American serial rights. Accepts queries by mail. Sample copy for $3 and magazine-sized envelope.

Nonfiction Needs general interest, interview, travel. Query. **Pays $150-300.**
Photos We assign photography according to story needs. Buys one time rights with web and collateral reuse.
Columns/Departments "Destinations (everything there is to tell about a great Southern mountain town, city or locale); Food and Wine (covering Southern vinters, chefs and restaurants); Mountain Style (new trends and sources for unique products); Homes and Gardens (spotlight on homes and gardens—often of those who have chosen to relocate to the mountains), 750-2,000 words." Query. **Pays $100-250.**
Tips "Anything that is well-researched, well-written and tied to the Southern mountains, the second-home and retirement demographic trends, and the area's upscale lifestyle would get strong consideration."

N THE OXFORD AMERICAN

201 Donaghey Ave., Main 107, Conway AR 72035. (501)450-5970. Fax: (501)450-3490. E-mail: oamag@oxfordamericanmag.com. Website: www.oxfordamericanmag.com. **Contact:** Carol Ann Fitzgerald, man. ed. Quarterly literary magazine from the South with a national audience. Circ. 20,000. Pays on publication. Accepts queries by mail. Responds in 2-3 months or sooner to mss. Guidelines available online.

- "*The Oxford American* will consider only unpublished mss that are from and/or about the South. Especially interested in nonfiction from diverse perspectives. Considers excerpts from forthcoming books."

Nonfiction Needs short and long essays (500 to 3,000 words), general interest, how-to, humor, personal experience, travel, reporting, business. Query with SASE or send complete ms.
Photos Uses photos for the cover and throughout issue. Also uses illustration, original art, and comics. Send photos Reviews contact sheets, GIF/JPEG files, slides.
Columns/Departments Odes, Travel, Politics, Business, Writing on Writing, Southerner Abroad, Reports, Literature.
Fiction Stories should be from or about the South. Send complete ms.
Poetry Poems should be from or about the South. Submit maximum 3-5 poems.

SOUTHCOMM PUBLISHING COMPANY, INC.

2600 Abbey Ct., Alpharetta GA 30004. (678)624-1075. Fax: (678)624-1079. E-mail: cwwalker@southcomm.com. Website: www.southcomm.com. "Our magazines primarily are used as marketing and economic development pieces, but they are also used as tourism guides and a source of information for newcomers. As such, our editorial supplies entertaining and informative reading for those visiting the communities for the first time, as well as those who have lived in the area for any period of time. We are looking for writers who are interested in writing dynamic copy about Georgia, Tennessee, South Carolina, North Carolina, Alabama, Virginia, Florida, Pennsylvania, and Texas." Estab. 1985. Byline given. Pays 30 days after acceptance. No kill fee. Publishes ms an average of 1-2 months after acceptance. Buys all rights. Accepts queries by mail, e-mail, fax. Accepts simultaneous submissions. Sample copy and writer's guidelines free.
Nonfiction "Our articles are informative pieces about the communities we're covering. We have 2 types of publications. Our Classic pieces are term paper-style publications, providing a comprehensive overview of all the community has to offer. Our StandOut magazines provide snapshots of community life through articles with a lifestyle publication slant (require interviews and quotes). Classic: Lifestyle; Recreation/Culture; Education; Healthcare; History (community changes over the years); Economic Development; Community/Newcomer Information (important phone numbers and websites). StandOut: Report Card (education stories); Vital Signs (movers an shakers in healthcare); Business Portfolio (what makes the economy work); Claim to Fame (who's who in the community). "We are not looking for article submissions. We will assign stories to writers in which we're interested. Queries should include samples of published works and biographical information." **Buys 50 + mss/year.** Quer or send complete ms. Length: 100-1,000 words. **Pays $25-200.**
Tips "It is not necessary for writers to live in the areas about which they are writing, but it does sometimes help to be familiar with them. We are not looking for writers to submit articles. We solely are interested in contacting writers for articles that we generate with our clients."

SOUTHERN LIVING

Southern Progress Corp., 2100 Lakeshore Dr., Birmingham AL 35209. (205)445-6000. Fax: (205)445-6700. E-mail: sara_askew_jones@timeinc.com. Website: www.southernliving.com. Monthly magazine covering the southern lifestyle. Publication addressing the tastes and interest of contemporary southerners. Estab. 1966. Circ. 2,526,799. No kill fee. Buys all rights. Editorial lead time 3 months. Accepts queries by mail. Sample copy for $4.99 at newsstands. Guidelines by email.
Columns/Departments Southern Journal: Above all, it must be Southern. We need comments on life in this region—written from the standpoint of a person who is intimately familiar with this part of the world. It's personal, almost always involving something that happened to the writer or someone he or she knows very well. We take special note of stories that are contemporary in their point of view. Length: 500-600 words.

$ $ $ $ SUNSET MAGAZINE

Sunset Publishing Corp., 80 Willow Rd., Menlo Park CA 94025-3691. (650)321-3600. Fax: (650)327-7537. Website: www.sunset.com. Monthly magazine covering the lifestyle of the Western states. *Sunset* is a Western lifestyle publication for educated, active consumers. Editorial provides localized information on gardening and travel, food and entertainment, home building and remodeling. Freelance articles should be timely and only about the 13 Western states. Garden section accepts queries by mail. Travel section prefers queries by e-mail. Byline given. Pays on acceptance. No kill fee. Guidelines available online.

Nonfiction Travel items account for the vast majority of *Sunset's* freelance assignments, although we also contract out some short garden items. However *Sunset* is largely staff-written. Needs travel, in the West. **Buys 50-75 mss/year.** Query. Length: 550-750 words. **Pays $1/word.**

Columns/Departments Building & Crafts, Food, Garden, Travel. Travel Guide length: 300-350 words. Direct queries to specific editorial department.

Tips Here are some subjects regularly treated in *Sunset*'s stories and Travel Guide items: Outdoor recreation (i.e., bike tours, bird-watching spots, walking or driving tours of historic districts); indoor adventures (i.e., new museums and displays, hands-on science programs at aquariums or planetariums, specialty shopping); special events (i.e., festivals that celebrate a region's unique social, cultural, or agricultural heritage). Also looking for great weekend getaways, backroad drives, urban adventures and culinary discoveries such as ethnic dining enclaves. Planning and assigning begins a year before publication date.

GEORGIA

$ ATHENS MAGAZINE

The lifestyle magazine of Northeast Georgia, Morris Communications, One Press Place, Athens GA 30603. (706)208-2331. Fax: (706)208-2339. Website: www.athensmagazine.com. **70% freelance written**. Bimonthly + bonus holiday issue magazine. Content focused on Athens, GA community and surrounding area (does not include Atlanta metro). Estab. 1989. Circ. 5,000. Byline given. Pays on publication. Offers 20% kill fee. Publishes ms an average of 6 months after acceptance. Buys first North American serial rights. Editorial lead time 6-9 months. Submit seasonal material 12 months in advance. Accepts queries by mail, e-mail. Responds in 6-8 weeks to queries. Sample copy free. Guidelines available online.

Photos Contact: Katie Davis, art director. State availability Captions, identification of subjects required. Reviews GIF/JPEG files. Negotiates payment individually. Buys one time rights.

Fillers Contact: Margaret Blanchard, editor. Needs anecdotes, facts, short humor. Length: 25-150 words. **Pays $$20-$150.**

Tips I need freelancers who are well-acquainted with Athens area who can write to its unique audience of students, retirees, etc.

$ $ $ ATLANTA LIFE MAGAZINE

2500 Hospital Blvd., Roswell GA 30076. (770)664-6466. Fax: (770)664-6465. E-mail: jsilavent@atlantalifemag.com. Website: www.atlantalifemag.com. **50% freelance written**. Monthly magazine. We are an upscale lifestyle magazine that covers north metro Atlanta. We cover a variety of topics, including sports, fashion, travel, health, finances, home design, etc. Estab. 2006. Byline given. Pays on acceptance. Editorial lead time 2 months. Submit seasonal material 4 months in advance. Accepts queries by e-mail. Sample copy free. Guidelines free.

Nonfiction Needs essays, expose, general interest, historical, how-to, humor, inspirational, interview, new product, personal experience, travel. **Buys 35 mss/year.** Query with published clips. Length: 750-2,000 words. **Pays 25-75¢/word.** Sometimes pays expenses of writers on assignment.

Photos Contact: Contact Natalie Zieky, Creative Director. State availability of or send photos Captions, identification of subjects, model releases required. Reviews GIF/JPEG files. Negotiates payment individually. Buys one time rights.

Columns/Departments Travel; Health/Medical; Sports; Fashion, all 750-1,100 words. Also, Mountain Life and CD/Book Reviews, 750-1,200 words. Query with published clips.

Fillers Needs anecdotes, facts, gags, short humor. 12 Length: 150-350 words.

Tips Submit previously published samples. Have high resolution photo support for your article if possible.

$ $ $ $ ATLANTA MAGAZINE

260 Peachtree St., Suite 300, Atlanta GA 30303. (404)527-5500. Fax: (404)527-5575. Website: www.atlantamagazine.com. The magazine's mission is to engage our community through provacative writing, authoritative reporting, superlative design that illuminates the people, trends, and events that define our city. Circ. 69,000. Byline given. Pays on acceptance. Buys first North American serial rights. Accepts queries by mail. Responds in 3 months to queries. Sample copy available online.

- Almost all content staff written except fiction.

Nonfiction *Atlanta* magazine articulates the special nature of Atlanta and appeals to an audience that wants to understand and celebrate the uniqueness of the city. Needs general interest, interview, travel. **Buys 15-20 mss/year.** Query with published clips. Length: 250-5,000 words. **Pays $200-2,000.**

Fiction Need short stories for annual reading issue (Summer). We prefer all fiction to be by Georgia writers and/or have a Georgia/Southern theme. Length: 1,500-5,000 words.

Tips It's *Atlanta* magazine. If your idea isn't about Atlanta, we're not interested.

$ $ ATLANTA TRIBUNE: THE MAGAZINE

875 Old Roswell Rd, Suite C-100, Roswell GA 30076. (770)587-0501. Fax: (770)642-6501. Website: www.atlantatribune.com. **30% freelance written**. Monthly magazine covering African-American business, careers, technology, wealth-building, politics, and education. The *Atlanta Tribune* is written for Atlanta's black executives, professionals and entrepreneurs with a primary focus of business, careers, technology, wealth-building, politics, and education. Our publication serves as an advisor that offers helpful information and direction to the black entrepreneur. Estab. 1987. Circ. 30,000. Byline given. Pays on publication. Offers 10% kill fee. Buys electronic rights, buys all rights. Editorial lead time 3 months. Submit seasonal material 4 months in advance. Accepts queries by e-mail. Responds in 6 weeks to queries. Sample copy online or mail a request. Guidelines available online.

Nonfiction Our special sections include Black History; Real Estate; Scholarship Roundup. Needs book excerpts, how-to, business, careers, technology, interview, new product, opinion, technical. **Buys 100 mss/year.** Query with published clips. Length: 1,400-2,500 words. **Pays $250-600.** Sometimes pays expenses of writers on assignment.

Photos State availability Identification of subjects, model releases required. Reviews 2¼x2¼ transparencies. Negotiates payment individually. Buys one time rights.

Columns/Departments Business; Careers; Technology; Wealth-Building; Politics and Education; all 400-600 words. 100 Query with published clips. **Pays $100-200.**

Tips Send a well-written, convincing query by e-mail that demonstrates that you have thoroughly read previous issues and reviewed our online writer's guidelines.

$ FLAGPOLE MAGAZINE

P.O. Box 1027, Athens GA 30603. (706)549-9523. Fax: (706)548-8981. E-mail: editor@flagpole.com. Website: www.flagpole.com. **75% freelance written**. Local alternative weekly with a special emphasis on popular (and unpopular) music. Will consider stories on national, international musicians, authors, politicians, etc., even if they don't have a local or regional news peg. However, those stories should be original and irreverent enough to justify inclusion. Of course, local/Southern news/feature stories are best. We like reporting and storytelling more than opinion pieces. Estab. 1987. Circ. 16,000. Byline given. Pays on publication. No kill fee. Publishes ms an average of 1 month after acceptance. Makes work-for-hire assignments. Editorial lead time 2 months. Submit seasonal material 2 months in advance. Responds in 2 weeks to queries. Responds in 1 month to mss. Sample copy online.

Nonfiction Needs book excerpts, essays, expose, interview, new product, personal experience. **Buys 50 mss/year.** Query by e-mail Length: 600-2,000 words.

Reprints Send tearsheet, photocopy or typed ms with rights for sale noted and information about when and where the material previously appeared.

Photos State availability Captions required. Reviews prints. Negotiates payment individually Buys one time rights.

Tips Read our publication online before querying, but don't feel limited by what you see. We can't afford to pay much, so we're open to young/inexperienced writer-journalists looking for clips. Fresh, funny/insightful voices make us happiest, as does reportage over opinion. If you've ever succumbed to the temptation to call a pop record `ethereal' we probably won't bother with your music journalism. No faxed submissions, please.

$ $ GEORGIA BACKROADS

Legacy Communications, Inc., P.O. Box 585, Armuchee GA 30105. E-mail: info@georgiabackroads.com. Website: www.georgiahistory.ws. **70% freelance written**. Quarterly magazine for readers interested in travel, history, and lifestyles in Georgia. Estab. 1984. Circ. 18,861. Byline given. Pays on publication. Offers 25% kill fee. Publishes ms an average of 5 months after acceptance. Buys Usually buys all rights. Rights negotiable. rights. Editorial lead time 3 months. Submit seasonal material 6 months in advance. Accepts queries by mail, e-mail, fax. Sample copy for 9x12 SAE and 8 first-class stamps, or online. Guidelines for #10 SASE.

Nonfiction Needs historical, how-to, survival techniques; mountain living; do-it-yourself home construction and repairs, etc., interview, celebrity, personal experience, anything unique or unusual pertaining to Georgia history, photo feature, any subject of a historic nature which can be photographed in a seasonal context, i.e., old mill with brilliant yellow jonquils in foreground, travel, subjects highlighting travel opportunities in north Georgia. Query with published clips. **Pays $75-350.**

Photos Send photos Captions, identification of subjects, model releases required. Reviews contact sheets, transparencies. Negotiates payment individually. Rights negotiable.

Fiction Needs novel concepts.

Tips Good photography is crucial to acceptance of all articles. Send written queries then *wait* for a response. *No telephone calls, please.* The most useful material involves a first-person experience of an individual who has explored a historic site or scenic locale and *interviewed* a person or persons who were involved with or have first-hand knowledge of a historic site/event. Interviews and quotations are crucial. Articles should be told in writer's own words.

$ $ GEORGIA MAGAZINE

Georgia Electric Membership Corp., P.O. Box 1707, Tucker GA 30085. (770)270-6951. E-mail: aorowski@georgiaemc.com. Website: www.georgiamagazine.org. **50% freelance written**. We are a monthly magazine for and about Georgians, with a friendly, conversational tone and human interest topics. Estab. 1945. Circ. 460,000. Byline given. Pays on publication. No kill fee. Publishes ms an average of 4 months after acceptance. Buys first North American serial rights, buys electronic rights. Editorial lead time 2 months. Submit seasonal material 6 months in advance. Accepts simultaneous submissions. Responds in 1 month to subjects of interest. Sample copy for $2. Guidelines for #10 SASE.

Nonfiction Needs general interest, Georgia-focused, historical, how-to, in the home and garden, humor, inspirational, interview, photo feature, travel. **Buys 24 mss/year.** Query with published clips. 800-1,000 words; 500 words for smaller features and departments. **Pays $150-500.**

Photos State availability Identification of subjects, model releases required. Reviews contact sheets, transparencies, prints. Negotiates payment individually. Buys one time rights.

$ $ KNOW ATLANTA MAGAZINE

New South Publishing, 450 Northride Pkwy., Suite 202, Atlanta GA 30350. (770)650-1102. Fax: (770)650-2848. E-mail: editor1@knowatlanta.com. Website: www.knowatlanta.com. **80% freelance written**. Quarterly magazine covering the Atlanta area. "Our articles offer information on Atlanta that would be useful to newcomers—homes, schools, hospitals, fun things to do, anything that makes their move more comfortable." Estab. 1986. Circ. 192,000. Byline given. Pays on publication. Offers 100% kill fee. Buys first North American serial rights. Editorial lead time 2 months. Submit seasonal material 2 months in advance. Accepts queries by mail, e-mail, fax. Accepts previously published material. Sample copy free.

Nonfiction Needs general interest, how-to, relocate, interview, personal experience, photo feature. No fiction. **Buys 20 mss/year.** Query with clips. Length: 800-1,500 words. **Pays $100-500 for assigned articles. Pays $100-300 for unsolicited articles.** Sometimes pays expenses of writers on assignment.

Photos Send photos with submission, if available. Captions, identification of subjects required. Reviews contact sheets. Negotiates payment individually. Buys one time rights.

$ $ POINTS NORTH MAGAZINE

Serving Atlanta's Stylish Northside, All Points Interactive Media Corp., 568 Peachtree Pkwy., Cumming GA 30041-6820. (770)844-0969. Fax: (770)844-0968. E-mail: julie@ptsnorth.com. Website: www.ptsnorth.com. **85% freelance written**. Monthly magazine covering lifestyle (regional). *Points North* is a first-class lifestyle magazine for affluent residents of suburban communities in north metro Atlanta. Estab. 2000. Circ. 81,000. Byline given. Pays on publication. Offers negotiable (for assigned articles only) kill fee. Publishes ms an average of 1 month after acceptance. Buys electronic rights, buys first serial (in the Southeast with a 6 month moratorium) rights. Editorial lead time 3 months. Submit seasonal material 6 months in advance. Accepts queries by mail, e-mail, fax. Accepts previously published material. Responds in 6-8 weeks to queries. Responds in 6-8 months to mss. Sample copy for $3.

Nonfiction Contact: Managing Editor. Needs general interest, only topics pertaining to Atlanta area, historical, interview, travel. **Buys 50-60 mss/year.** Query with published clips. Length: 1,200-2,500 words. **Pays $250-500.**

Photos We do not accept photos until article acceptance. Do not send photos with query. State availability Captions, identification of subjects, model releases required. Reviews slide transparencies, 4x6 prints, GIF/JPEG files. Offers no additional payment for photos accepted with ms.

Tips The best way for a freelancer, who is interested in being published, is to get a sense of the types of articles we're looking for by reading the magazine.

$ $ SAVANNAH MAGAZINE

Morris Publishing Group, P.O. Box 1088, Savannah GA 31402-1088. Fax: (912)525-0611. E-mail: linda.wittish@savannahnow.com. Website: www.savannahmagazine.com. **95% freelance written**. Bimonthly magazine focusing on homes and entertaining covering coastal lifestyle of Savannah and South Carolina area. "*Savannah Magazine* publishes articles about people, places and events of interest to the residents of the greater Savannah areas, as well as coastal Georgia and the South Carolina low country. We strive to provide our readers with information that is both useful and entertaining—written in a lively, readable style." Estab. 1990. Circ. 14,000. Byline given. Pays on publication. Offers 20% kill fee. Publishes ms an average of 2 months after acceptance. Buys first North American serial rights, buys second serial (reprint) rights. Editorial lead time 2 months. Submit seasonal material 4 months in advance. Accepts queries by mail, e-mail, fax. Accepts simultaneous submissions. Responds in 3 weeks to queries. Responds in 1 month to mss. Sample copy free. Guidelines by email.

Nonfiction Needs general interest, historical, humor, interview, travel. Does not want fiction or poetry. Query with published clips. Length: 750-1,500 words. **Pays $250-450.**

Photos Contact: Contact Michelle Karner, art director. State availability Reviews GIF/JPEG files. Negotiates payment individually. Offers no additional payment for photos accepted with ms. Buys one time rights.

ST. MARYS MAGAZINE

LowCountry Publishing, 711 Mildred St., St. Marys GA 31558. (912)729-1103. Fax: (912)576-3867. E-mail: info@stmarysmagazine.com. Website: www.stmarysmagazine.com. **50% freelance written**. Semiannual magazine covering coastal Georgia. "We want all positive articles." Estab. 2004. Circ. 20,000. Byline given. Pays on acceptance. Offers kill fee. negotiable Publishes ms an average of 2 months after acceptance. Buys first North American serial rights. Editorial lead time 2 months. Submit seasonal material 2 months in advance. Accepts queries by mail, e-mail. Accepts previously published material. Accepts simultaneous submissions. Responds in 2 weeks to queries. Responds in 1 month to mss. Sample copy free. Guidelines free.

Nonfiction Needs general interest, interview, personal experience, travel, history. Query with published clips. Length: 500-2,000 words. **negotiable for assigned articles.** Sometimes pays expenses of writers on assignment.

Photos Send photos Captions, identification of subjects, model releases required. Reviews GIF/JPEG fifles. Negotiates payment individually.

Columns/Departments Grape Expectations (wine review), 500 words; Real people (people of coastal Georgia), 1,000 words. 4 mss/year Query with published clips. **TBD**

Fiction Needs historical, slice-of-life vignettes. **Buys 2 mss/year mss/year.** Query with published clips. Length: 500-2,000 words. **TBD.**

Tips "Review editorial at website."

HAWAII

$ $ $ HONOLULU MAGAZINE

PacificBasin Communications, 1000 Bishop St., Suite 405, Honolulu HI 96813. (808)537-9500. Fax: (808)537-6455. E-mail: kam@pacificbasin.net. Website: www.honolulumagazine.com. **Prefers to work with published/established writers.** Monthly magazine covering general interest topics relating to Hawaii residents. Estab. 1888. Circ. 30,000. Byline given. Pays on publication. No kill fee. Makes work-for-hire assignments. Accepts queries by mail, e-mail. Guidelines available online.

Nonfiction Needs historical, interview, sports, politics, lifestyle trends, all Hawaii-related. "We write for Hawaii residents, so travel articles about Hawaii are not appropriate." Send complete ms. determined when assignments discussed. **Pays $250-1,200.** Sometimes pays expenses of writers on assignment.

Photos Contact: Kristin Lipman, art director. State availability Captions, identification of subjects, model releases required. Pays $50-200/shot.

Columns/Departments Length determined when assignments discussed. Query with published clips or send complete ms. **Pays $100-300.**

IDAHO

$ $ SUN VALLEY MAGAZINE

Valley Publishing, LLC, 12 E. Bullion, Suite B, Hailey ID 83333. (208)788-0770. Fax: (208)788-3881. E-mail: edit@sunvalleymag.com. Website: www.sunvalleymag.com. **95% freelance written**. Quarterly magazine covering the lifestyle of the Sun Valley area. *Sun Valley Magazine* presents the lifestyle of the Sun Valley area and the Wood River Valley, including recreation, culture, profiles, history and the arts. Estab. 1973. Circ. 17,000. Byline given. Pays on publication. No kill fee. Publishes ms an average of 5 months after acceptance. Buys first North American serial rights, buys electronic rights. Editorial lead time 1 year. Submit seasonal material 14 months in advance. Accepts queries by mail. Accepts previously published material. Accepts simultaneous submissions. Responds in 5 weeks to queries. Responds in 2 months to mss. Sample copy for $4.95 and $3 postage. Guidelines for #10 SASE.

Nonfiction All articles are focused specifically on Sun Valley, the Wood River Valley and immediate surrounding areas. Needs historical, interview, photo feature, travel. Sun Valley home design and architecture, Spring; Sun Valley weddings/wedding planner, summer. Query with published clips. **Pays $40-500.** Sometimes pays expenses of writers on assignment.

Reprints Only occasionally purchases reprints.

Photos State availability Identification of subjects, model releases required. Reviews transparencies. Offers $60-275/photo. Buys one-time rights and some electronic rights.

Columns/Departments Conservation issues, winter/summer sports, health & wellness, mountain-related activities and subjects, home (interior design), garden. All columns must have a local slant. Query with published clips. **Pays $40-300.**

Tips Most of our writers are locally based. Also, we rarely take submissions that are not specifically assigned, with the exception of fiction. However, we always appreciate queries.

ILLINOIS

$ $ $ $ CHICAGO MAGAZINE

435 N. Michigan Ave., Suite 1100, Chicago IL 60611. (312)222-8999. E-mail: stritsch@chicagomag.com. Website: www.chicagomag.com. **50% freelance written. Prefers to work with published/established writers.** Monthly magazine for an audience which is 95% from Chicago area; 90% college educated; upper income, overriding interests in the arts, politics, dining, good life in the city and suburbs. Most are in 25-50 age bracket, well-read and articulate. Estab. 1968. Circ. 182,000. Pays on acceptance. No kill fee. Publishes ms an average of 3 months after acceptance. Buys first rights. Submit seasonal material 4 months in advance. Accepts queries by mail, e-mail. Responds in 1 month to queries. For sample copy, send $3 to Circulation Dept. Guidelines for #10 SASE.

Nonfiction On themes relating to the quality of life in Chicago: Past, present, and future. Writers should have a general awareness that the readers will be concerned, influential, longtime Chicagoans. We generally publish material too comprehensive for daily newspapers. Needs expose, humor, personal experience, think pieces, profiles, spot news, historical articles. Does not want anything about events outside the city or profiles on people who no longer live in the city. **Buys 100 mss/year.** Query; indicate specifics, knowledge of city and market, and demonstrable access to sources. Length: 200-6,000 words. **Pays $100-3,000 and up.** Pays expenses of writers on assignment.

Photos Usually assigned separately, not acquired from writers. Reviews 35mm transparencies, color and b&w glossy prints.

Tips Submit detailed queries, be business-like, and avoid clichÃ^ ideas.

$ $ $ $ CHICAGO READER

Chicago's Free Weekly, Chicago Reader, Inc., 11 E. Illinois St., Chicago IL 60611. (312)828-0350. Fax: (312)828-9926. E-mail: mail@chicagoreader.com. Website: www.chicagoreader.com. **50% freelance written**. Weekly Alternative tabloid for Chicago. Estab. 1971. Circ. 120,000. Byline given. Pays on publication. Occasional kill fee. Publishes ms an average of 2 weeks after acceptance. Buys one-time rights. Editorial lead time up to 6 months. Accepts queries by mail, e-mail, fax. Accepts simultaneous submissions. Responds if interested. Sample copy free. Writer's guidelines free or online

Nonfiction Magazine-style features; also book excerpts, essays, humor, interview/profile, opinion, personal experience, photo feature. **Buys 500 mss/year.** Send complete ms. Length: 500-50,000 words. **Pays $100-3,000.** Sometimes pays expenses of writers on assignment.

Reprints Occasionally accepts previously published submissions.

Columns/Departments Local color, 500-2,500 words; arts and entertainment reviews, up to 1,200 words.

Tips Our greatest need is for full-length magazine-style feature stories on Chicago topics. We're *not* looking for: hard news (What the Mayor Said About the Schools Yesterday); commentary and opinion (What I Think About What the Mayor Said About the Schools Yesterday); poetry. We are not particularly interested in stories of national (as opposed to local) scope, or in celebrity for celebrity's sake (€¡ la *Rolling Stone*, *Interview*, etc.). More than half the articles published in the *Reader* each week come from freelancers, and once or twice a month we publish one that's come in `over the transom'—from a writer we've never heard of and may never hear from again. We think that keeping the *Reader* open to the greatest possible number of contributors makes a fresher, less predictable, more interesting paper. We not only publish unsolicited freelance writing, we depend on it. Our last issue in December is dedicated to original fiction.

$ $ CHICAGO SCENE MAGAZINE

233 E. Erie, Suite 603, Chicago IL 60611. Fax: (312)587-7397. E-mail: email@chicago-scene.com. Website: www.chicago-scene.com. **95% freelance written**. Monthly magazine covering dining, nightlife, travel, beauty, entertainment, fitness, style, drinks. *Chicago Scene Magazine* is the premier news and entertainment publication for Chicago's young professional. Estab. 2001. Byline given. Pays on publication. No kill fee. Publishes ms an average of 2 months after acceptance. Buys first North American serial rights. Submit seasonal material 3 months in advance. Accepts queries by e-mail. Sample copy available online. Guidelines free.

Nonfiction Needs how-to, interview, new product, travel. Does not want personal experiences, essays, technical. Query with published clips. Length: 600-2,400 words. **Pays $25-250.**

Columns/Departments Beauty, 840 words; Dining, 1,260-1,680 words; Drinks, 1,260-1,680 words; Fitness, 420-630 words; Travel, 1,260-1,680 words; Nightlife, 1,050-1,680 words; Personal Style, 420 words. Query with published clips. **Pays $25-250.**

$ ILLINOIS ENTERTAINER

657 W. Lake St., Suite A, Chicago IL 60661. (312)922-9333. Fax: (312)922-9341. E-mail: ieeditors@aol.com. Website: www.illinoisentertainer.com. **80% freelance written**. Monthly free magazine covering popular and alternative music, as well as other entertainment: film, media. Estab. 1974. Circ. 55,000. Byline given. Pays on publication. Offers 50% kill fee. Publishes ms an average of 2 months after acceptance. Buys first North American serial rights. Editorial lead time 2 months. Submit seasonal material 2 months in advance. Accepts

queries by mail. Accepts simultaneous submissions. Responds in 2 months to queries. Sample copy for $5.
Nonfiction Needs expose, how-to, humor, interview, new product, reviews. No personal, confessional, inspirational articles. **Buys 75 mss/year.** Query with published clips. Length: 600-2,600 words. **Pays $15-160.** Sometimes pays expenses of writers on assignment.
Reprints Send typed manuscript with rights for sale noted and information about when and where the material previously appeared. Pays 100% of amount paid for an original article.
Photos Send photos Captions, identification of subjects, model releases required. Reviews contact sheets, transparencies, 5x7 prints. Offers $20-200/photo. Buys one time rights.
Columns/Departments Spins (LP reviews), 100-400 words. 200-300 Query with published clips. **Pays $8-25.**
Tips Send clips, rÃˆsumÃˆ, etc. and be patient. Also, sending queries that show you've seen our magazine and have a feel for it greatly increases your publication chances. Don't send unsolicited material. No e-mail solicitations or queries of any kind.

$ $ NORTHWEST QUARTERLY MAGAZINE

Old Northwest Territory, Hughes Media Inc., 728 N. Prospect St., Rockford IL 61101. Fax: (815)316-2301. E-mail: janine@northwestquarterly.com. Website: www.northwestquarterly.com. **80% freelance written.** Quarterly magazine covering regional lifestyle of Northern Illinois and Southern Wisconsin, and also Kane and McHenry counties (Chicago collar counties), highlighting strengths of living and doing business in the area. Estab. 2004. Circ. 21,000. Byline given. Pays on publication. Publishes ms an average of 4-6 months after acceptance. Makes work-for-hire assignments. Editorial lead time 6 months. Submit seasonal material 6 months in advance. Accepts queries by mail, e-mail. Responds in 2 weeks to queries. Responds in 2 months to mss. Sample copy by email. Guidelines by email.
Nonfiction Needs historical, interview, photo feature, regional features. Does not want opinion, fiction, anything unrelated to our geographic region. **Buys 150 mss/year.** Query. Length: 700-2,500 words. **Pays $25-500.** Sometimes pays expenses of writers on assignment.
Photos State availability Captions required. Reviews GIF/JPEG files. Negotiates payment individually. Buys one time rights.
Columns/Departments Health & Fitness, 1,000-2,000 words; Home & Garden, 1,500 words; Destinations & Recreation, 1,000-2,000 words; Environment & Nature, 2,000-3,000 words. 120 Query. **Pays $100-500.**
Fillers Needs short humor. 24 Length: 100-200 words. **Pays $30-50.**
Tips "Any interesting, well-documented feature relating to the 15-county area we cover may be considered. Nature, history, geography, culture and destinations are favorite themes."

$ $ OUTDOOR ILLINOIS

Illinois Department of Natural Resources, One Natural Resources Way, Springfield IL 62702. (217)785-4193. E-mail: dnr.editor@illinois.gov. Website: www.dnr.state.il.us/oi. **25% freelance written.** Monthly magazine covering Illinois cultural and natural resources. *Outdoor Illinois* promotes outdoor activities, Illinois State parks, Illinois natural and cultural resources. Estab. 1973. Circ. 30,000. Byline given. Pays on acceptance. Buys one-time rights. Editorial lead time 4 months. Submit seasonal material 1 year in advance. Accepts queries by mail, e-mail. Responds in 2 weeks to queries. Sample copy free. Guidelines by email.
Nonfiction Needs historical, how-to, humor, interview, photo feature, travel. Does not want first person unless truly has something to say. Query with published clips. Length: 350-1,500 words. **Pays $100-250.**
Photos Contact: Contact Adele Hodde, photography manager. Captions, identification of subjects, model releases required. Reviews contact sheets, GIF/JPEG files. Negotiates payment individually. Buys one time rights.
Tips Write with an Illinois slant to encourage participation in outdoor activities/events.

$ $ WEST SUBURBAN LIVING

C2 Publishing, Inc., 775 Church Rd., Elmhurst IL 60126. (630)834-4994. Fax: (630)834-4996. Website: www.westsuburbanliving.net. **Contact:** Chuck Cozette, Editor. **80% freelance written.** Bimonthly magazine focusing on the western suburbs of Chicago. Estab. 1996. Circ. 25,000. Byline given. Pays on publication. Publishes ms an average of 2-4 months after acceptance. Buys first rights, buys electronic rights. Accepts queries by mail, e-mail, fax. Sample copy available online.
Nonfiction Needs general interest, how-to, travel. "Does not want anything that does not have an angle or tie-in to the area we cover—Chicago's western suburbs." **Buys 15 mss/year. Pays $100-500.** Sometimes pays expenses of writers on assignment.
Photos State availability Model releases required. Offers $50-700/photo; negotiates payment individually.

INDIANA

$ $ EVANSVILLE LIVING

Tucker Publishing Group, 100 NW Second St., Suite 220, Evansville IN 47708. (812)426-2115. Fax: (812)426-2134.

Website: www.evansvilleliving.com. **80-100% freelance written**. Bimonthly magazine covering Evansville, Indiana, and the greater area. *Evansville Living* is the only full-color, glossy, 100+ page city magazine for the Evansville, Indiana, area. Regular departments include: Home Style, Garden Style, Day Tripping, Sporting Life, and Local Flavor (menus). Estab. 2000. Circ. 50,000. Byline given. Pays on acceptance. No kill fee. Publishes ms an average of 3 months after acceptance. Buys all rights. Editorial lead time 6 months. Submit seasonal material 6 months in advance. Accepts queries by mail, e-mail, fax. Accepts previously published material. Sample copy for $5 or online. Guidelines for free or by e-mail.

Nonfiction Needs essays, general interest, historical, photo feature, travel. **Buys 60-80 mss/year.** Query with published clips. Length: 200-2,000 words. **Pays $100-300.** Sometimes pays expenses of writers on assignment.

Photos State availability Captions, identification of subjects required. Reviews contact sheets, negatives, transparencies, prints. Negotiates payment individually Buys all rights.

Columns/Departments Home Style (home); Garden Style (garden); Sporting Life (sports); Local Flavor (menus), all 1,500 words. Query with published clips. **Pays $100-300.**

$ $ $ INDIANAPOLIS MONTHLY

Emmis Publishing Corp., 1 Emmis Plaza, 40 Monument Circle, Suite 100, Indianapolis IN 46204. (317)237-9288. Website: www.indianapolismonthly.com. **30% freelance written. Prefers to work with published/established writers.** "*Indianapolis Monthly* attracts and enlightens its upscale, well-educated readership with bright, lively editorial on subjects ranging from personalities to social issues, fashion to food. Its diverse content and attention to service make it the ultimate source by which the Indianapolis area lives.". Estab. 1977. Circ. 45,000. Byline given. Pays on publication. Offers kill fee. Offers negotiable kill fee. Publishes ms an average of 2 months after acceptance. Buys first North American serial rights, buys one-time rights. Editorial lead time 3 months. Submit seasonal material 3 months in advance. Accepts queries by mail, e-mail. Responds in 6 weeks to queries. Sample copy for $6.10.

- "This magazine is using more first-person essays, but they must have a strong Indianapolis or Indiana tie. It will consider nonfiction book excerpts of material relevant to its readers."

Nonfiction Must have a strong Indianapolis or Indiana angle. Needs book excerpts, by Indiana authors or with strong Indiana ties, essays, expose, general interest, interview, photo feature. No poetry, fiction, or domestic humor; no How Indy Has Changed Since I Left Town, An Outsider's View of the 500, or generic material with no or little tie to Indianapolis/Indiana. **Buys 35 mss/year.** Query by mail with published clips Length: 200-3,000 words. **Pays $50-1,000.**

Photos State availability Captions, identification of subjects, model releases required. Negotiates payment individually. Buys one time rights.

Tips "Our standards are simultaneously broad and narrow: Broad in that we're a general interest magazine spanning a wide spectrum of topics, narrow in that we buy only stories with a heavy emphasis on Indianapolis (and, to a lesser extent, Indiana). Simply inserting an Indy-oriented paragraph into a generic national article won't get it: All stories must pertain primarily to things Hoosier. Once you've cleared that hurdle, however, it's a wide-open field. We've done features on national celebrities—Indianapolis native David Letterman and *Mir* astronaut David Wolf of Indianapolis, to name 2—and we've published 2-paragraph items on such quirky topics as an Indiana gardening supply house that sells insects by mail. Query with clips showing lively writing and solid reporting. No phone queries, please."

$ $ NORTHERN INDIANA LAKES MAGAZINE

1415 W. Coliseum Blvd., Fort Wayne IN 46808. (260)484-0546. Fax: (260)469-0454. E-mail: editor@nilakes.com. Website: www.nilakes.com. **Contact:** Sue Rawlinson, publisher/editor-in-chief. Bimonthly magazine that defines lake living at its best. "*Northern Indiana LAKES Magazine* is the official publication for the good life in northern Indiana. The LAKES country market area is essentially defined as 20 northern Indiana counties: Adams, Allen, DeKalb, Elkhart, Huntington, Jasper, Kosciusko, LaGrange, Lake, LaPorte, Marshall, Newton, Noble, Porter, Pulaski, St. Joseph, Starke, Steuben, Wells and Whitley." Byline given. Pays 2-3 weeks after accepting completed article. Buys one-time rights. Accepts queries by mail. Guidelines by email.

Nonfiction "Our articles take a positive, practical approach to helping readers enjoy and enhance their lifestyle, whether as weekend, seasonal or year-round lake residents. We are not a 'city' magazine that happens to include lake articles; rather, we strive to present articles on issues and subjects unique to the northern Indiana lakes area that cannot be found in any other publication. Our writers help us achieve that goal." Needs general interest, humor, interview, travel. Does not want "personal essays, stories about your vacation, celebrity profiles (with rare exceptions), routine pieces on familiar destinations, completed manuscripts, previously published works." Query with published clips. **Pays 10-50¢/word.**

Tips "Freelance articles are written on assignment, so sending clips and a cover letter explaining your qualifications as a potential writer for *Northern Indiana LAKES* is the best approach. This is not a publication for beginners; please send your best works."

IOWA

$ $ THE IOWAN

Pioneer Communications, Inc., 218 6th Ave., Suite 610, Des Moines IA 50309. Fax: (515)282-0125. E-mail: editor@iowan.com. Website: www.iowan.com. **75% freelance written.** Bimonthly magazine covering the state of Iowa. Our mission statement is: To celebrate the people and communities, the history and traditions, and the culture and events of Iowa that make our readers proud of our state. Estab. 1952. Circ. 25,000. Byline given. Pays on acceptance. Offers $100 kill fee. Publishes ms an average of 3 months after acceptance. Buys first rights. Editorial lead time 8-12 months. Submit seasonal material 6 months in advance. Accepts queries by mail, e-mail. Responds to queries received twice/year. Sample copy for $4.50 + s&h.

Nonfiction Needs book excerpts, essays, general interest, historical, interview, photo feature, travel. **Buys 30 mss/year.** Query with published clips. Length: 1,000-2,000 words. **Pays $250-450.** Sometimes pays expenses of writers on assignment.

Photos Send photos Captions, identification of subjects, model releases required. Reviews contact sheets, GIF/JPEG files (8x10 at 300 dpi min). Negotiates payment individually, according to space rates. Buys one time rights.

Columns/Departments Last Word (essay), 800 words. 6 Query with published clips. **Pays $100.**

Tips Must have submissions in writing, either via e-mail or snail mail. Submitting published clips is preferred.

KANSAS

$ $ KANSAS!

Kansas Department of Commerce, 1000 SW Jackson St., Suite 100, Topeka KS 66612-1354. (785)296-3479. Fax: (785)296-6988. Website: www.kansmag.com. **90% freelance written.** Quarterly magazine emphasizing Kansas travel attractions and events. Estab. 1945. Circ. 38,000. Byline given. Pays on acceptance. No kill fee. Publishes ms an average of 1 year after acceptance. Buys one-time rights. Submit seasonal material 8 months in advance. Accepts queries by mail. Responds in 2 months to queries. Guidelines available online.

Nonfiction Material must be Kansas-oriented and have good potential for color photographs. The focus is on travel with articles about places and events that can be enjoyed by the general public and experimental travel. In other words, events must be open to the public, places also. Query letter should clearly outline story. We are especially interested in Kansas freelancers who can supply their own quality photos. Needs general interest, photo feature, travel. Query by mail. Length: 750-1,250 words. **Pays $200-350.** Pays mileage only for writers on assignment within the State of Kansas.

Photos We are a full-color photo/manuscript publication. Send photos (original transparencies only or CD with images available in high resolution) with query. Captions required. Pays $50-75 (generally included in ms rate) for 35mm or larger format transparencies.

Tips History and nostalgia or essay stories do not fit into our format because they can't be illustrated well with color photos. Submit a query letter describing 1 appropriate idea with outline for possible article and suggestions for photos. Do not send unsolicited manuscripts.

KENTUCKY

$ BACK HOME IN KENTUCKY

Back Home In Kentucky, Inc., P.O. Box 710, Clay City KY 40312-0710. (606)663-1011. Fax: (606)663-1808. E-mail: info@backhomeinky.com. **50% freelance written.** Bimonthly magazine covering Kentucky heritage, people, places, events. We reach Kentuckians and `displaced' Kentuckians living outside the state. Estab. 1977. Circ. 8,000. Byline given. Pays on publication. No kill fee. Publishes ms an average of 4-6 months after acceptance. Buys first North American serial rights. Submit seasonal material 6 months in advance. Responds in 2 months to queries. Sample copy for $3 and 9x12 SAE with $1.23 postage affixed. Guidelines for #10 SASE.

- Interested in profiles of Kentucky people and places, especially historic interest.

Nonfiction Needs historical, Kentucky-related eras or profiles, interview, Kentucky residents or natives, photo feature, Kentucky places and events, travel, unusual/little-known Kentucky places, profiles (Kentucky cooks, gardeners, and craftspersons), memories (Kentucky related). No inspirational or religion. No how-to articles. **Buys 20-25 mss/year.** Send complete ms. Length: 500-2,000 words. **Pays $50-200 for assigned articles. Pays $50-100 for unsolicited articles.**

Photos Looking for digital (high resolution) of Kentucky places of interet. Pays $25-$100 per photo. Photo credits given. For inside photos, send photos with submission. Identification of subjects, model releases required. Reviews transparencies, 4x6 prints. Occasionally offers additional payment for photos accepted with ms. Rights purchased depends on situation.

Columns/Departments Travel, history, profile, and cookbooks (all Kentucky related), 500-2000 words. 10-12 Query with published clips. **Pays $25-50.**

Tips "We work mostly with unpublished or emerging writers who have a feel for Kentucky's people, places, and events. Areas most open are little known places in Kentucky, unusual history, and profiles of interesting Kentuckians, and Kentuckians with unusual hobbies or crafts."

FORT MITCHELL LIVING

Community Publications, Inc., 179 Fairfield Ave., Bellevue KY 41073. (859)291-1412. Fax: (859)291-1417. E-mail: fortmitchell@livingmagazines.com. Website: www.livingmagazines.com. Monthly magazine covering Fort Mitchell community. Estab. 1983. Circ. 4,700. Byline given. Pays on publication. Buys all rights. Editorial lead time 2 months. Submit seasonal material 3 months in advance. Guidelines by email.

Nonfiction Needs book excerpts, essays, expose, general interest, historical, humor, inspirational, interview, new product, personal experience, photo feature, travel. Does not want anything unrelated to Fort Mitchell. Query.

Photos State availability Captions, identification of subjects, model releases required. Reviews contact sheets, negatives, transparencies, prints, GIF/JPEG files. Negotiates payment individually. Buys all rights.

Columns/Departments Financial; Artistic (reviews, etc.); Historic; Food. Query.

Fiction Needs adventure, historical, humorous, mainstream, slice-of-life vignettes of life. Query.

Poetry Needs free verse, light verse, traditional. Please query.

Fillers Please query. Needs anecdotes, short humor.

FORT THOMAS LIVING

Community Publications, Inc., 179 Fairfield Ave., Bellevue KY 41073. (859)291-1412. Fax: (859)291-1417. E-mail: fortthomas@livingmagazines.com. Website: www.livingmagazines.com. **Contact:** Linda Johnson, ed. Monthly magazine covering Fort Thomas community. Estab. 1983. Circ. 4,400. Byline given. Pays on publication. Buys all rights. Editorial lead time 2 months. Submit seasonal material 3 months in advance. Accepts queries by mail, e-mail, fax. Guidelines by email.

Nonfiction Needs book excerpts, essays, expose, general interest, historical, humor, inspirational, interview, new product, personal experience, photo feature, travel. Does not want any material unrelated to Fort Thomas, Kentucky. Query.

Photos State availability Captions, identification of subjects, model releases required. Reviews contact sheets, negatives, transparencies, prints, GIF/JPEG files. Negotiates payment individually. Buys all rights.

Columns/Departments Financial; Artistic (reviews, etc.); Historic; Food. Query.

Fiction Needs adventure, historical, humorous, mainstream, slice-of-life vignettes. Query.

Poetry Needs free verse, light verse, traditional. Please query.

Fillers Please query. Needs anecdotes, short humor.

$ $ KENTUCKY LIVING

Kentucky Association of Electric Co-Ops, P.O. Box 32170, Louisville KY 40232. (502)451-2430. Fax: (502)459-1611. E-mail: e-mail@kentuckyliving.com. Website: www.kentuckyliving.com. **Mostly freelance written. Prefers to work with published/established writers.** Monthly Feature magazine primarily for Kentucky residents. Estab. 1948. Circ. 500,000. Byline given. Pays on acceptance. No kill fee. Publishes ms an average of 12 months after acceptance. Full rights for Kentucky. Submit seasonal material at least 6 months in advance. Accepts previously published material. Accepts simultaneous submissions. Responds in 1 month to queries. Sample copy for sae with 9x12 envelope and 4 First-Class stamps.

Nonfiction Kentucky-related profiles (people, places or events), recreation, travel, leisure, lifestyle articles, book excerpts. Needs , Emphasis on electric industry and ties to Kentucky's electric co-op areas of readership. **Buys 18-24 mss/year.** Send complete ms. **Pays $75-850.** Sometimes pays expenses of writers on assignment.

Photos State availability of or send photos Identification of subjects required. Reviews photo efiles at online link or sent on CD. Payment for photos included in payment for ms.

Tips "The quality of writing and reporting (factual, objective, thorough) is considered in setting payment price. We prefer general interest pieces filled with quotes and anecdotes. Avoid boosterism. Well-researched, well-written feature articles are preferred. All articles must have a strong Kentucky connection."

$ $ KENTUCKY MONTHLY

P.O.Box 559, Frankfort KY 40602. (502)227-0053. Fax: (502)227-5009. E-mail: amanda@kentuckymonthly.com or steve@kentuckymonthly.com. Website: www.kentuckymonthly.com. **75% freelance written**. Monthly magazine. "We publish stories about Kentucky and by Kentuckians, including those who live elsewhere." Estab. 1998. Circ. 40,000. Byline given. Pays within 3 months of publication. No kill fee. Publishes ms an average of 3 months after acceptance. Buys first North American serial rights. Editorial lead time 3 months. Submit seasonal material 4 months in advance. Accepts queries by mail, e-mail, fax. Accepts simultaneous submissions. Responds in 1 month to queries. Responds in 1 month to mss. Sample copy and writer's guidelines online.

Nonfiction Needs book excerpts, general interest, historical, how-to, humor, interview, photo feature, religious, travel, all with a Kentucky angle. **Buys 60 mss/year.** Query. Length: 300-2,000 words. **Pays $25-350 for assigned articles. Pays $20-100 for unsolicited articles.**

Photos State availability Captions required. Reviews negatives. Buys all rights.
Fiction Needs adventure, historical, mainstream, novel concepts, all Kentucky-related stories. **Buys 10 mss/year.** Query with published clips. Length: 1,000-5,000 words. **Pays $50-100.**
Tips "Please read the magazine to get the flavor of what we're publishing each month. We accept articles via e-mail, fax, and mail."

LOUISIANA

$ $ 🄽 PRESERVATION IN PRINT

Preservation Resource Center of New Orleans, 923 Tchoupitoulos St., New Orleans LA 70130. (504)581-7032. Fax: (504)636-3073. E-mail: prc@prcno.org. Website: www.prcno.org. **30% freelance written.** Monthly magazine covering preservation. We want articles about interest in the historic architecture of New Orleans. Estab. 1974. Circ. 10,000. Byline given. Pays on acceptance. No kill fee. Publishes ms an average of 1 month after acceptance. Buys all rights. Editorial lead time 1 month. Submit seasonal material 1-2 months in advance. Accepts queries by mail, e-mail, fax, phone. Accepts simultaneous submissions. Sample copy available online Guidelines free
Nonfiction Needs essays, historical, interview, photo feature, technical. **Buys 30 mss/year mss/year.** Query. Length: 700-1,000 words. **Pays $100-200 for assigned articles.** Sometimes pays expenses of writers on assignment.

MAINE

$ DISCOVER MAINE MAGAZINE

10 Exhcange St., Suite 208, Portland ME 04101. (207)874-7720. Fax: (207)874-7721. E-mail: info@discovermainemagazine.com. **100% freelance written.** Monthly magazine covering Maine history and nostalgia. Sports and hunting/fishing topics are also included. Estab. 1992. Circ. 12,000. Byline given. Pays on publication. No kill fee. Publishes ms an average of 2-3 months after acceptance. Buys one-time rights. Editorial lead time 3 months. Submit seasonal material 3 months in advance. Accepts queries by mail, fax, phone. Accepts previously published material. Accepts simultaneous submissions. Responds in 2 weeks to queries. Responds in 1 month to mss.
Nonfiction Needs historical. Does not want to receive poetry. **Buys 200 mss/year.** Send complete ms. Length: 500-2,000 words. **Pays $20-30**
Photos Send photos Negotiates payment individually. Buys one time rights.
Tips Call first and talk with the publisher.

MARYLAND

$ $ BALTIMORE MAGAZINE

Inner Harbor E. 1000 Lancaster St., Suite 400, Baltimore MD 21202. (410)752-4200. Fax: (410)625-0280. Website: www.baltimoremagazine.net. **50-60% freelance written.** Monthly. Pieces must address an educated, active, affluent reader and must have a very strong Baltimore angle. Estab. 1907. Circ. 70,000. Byline given. Pays within 1 month of publication. Offers kill fee in some cases first rights in all media Submit seasonal material 4 months in advance. Accepts queries by mail, e-mail. Sample copy for $4.45. Guidelines available online.
Nonfiction Needs book excerpts, Baltimore subject or author, essays, expose, general interest, historical, humor, interview, with a Baltimorean, new product, personal experience, photo feature, travel, local and regional to Maryland. Nothing that lacks a strong Baltimore focus or angle. Query by mail with published clips or send complete ms. Length: 1,600-2,500 words. **Pays 30-40¢/word.** Sometimes pays expenses of writers on assignment.
Columns/Departments The shorter pieces are the best places to break into the magazine. Hot Shot, Health, Education, Sports, Parenting, Politics. Length: 1,000-2,500 words. Query with published clips.
Tips Writers who live in the Baltimore area can send rÃˆsumÃˆ and published clips to be considered for first assignment. Must show an understanding of writing that is suitable to an educated magazine reader and show ability to write with authority, describe scenes, help reader experience the subject. Too many writers send us newspaper-style articles. We are seeking: 1) *Human interest features*—strong, even dramatic profiles of Baltimoreans of interest to our readers. 2) *First-person accounts* of experience in Baltimore, or experiences of a Baltimore resident. 3) *Consumer*—according to our editorial needs, and with Baltimore sources. Writers should read/familiarize themselves with style of *Baltimore Magazine* before submitting.

MASSACHUSETTS

BOSTON GLOBE MAGAZINE

P.O. Box 55819, Boston MA 02205-5819. (617)929-2000. Website: www.boston.com/magazine. **75% freelance written.** Weekly magazine. Pays on publication. No kill fee. Publishes ms an average of 2 months after acceptance. Buys non exclusive electronic rights. Editorial lead time 2 months. Submit seasonal material 3 months in advance. Sample copy for sae with 9x12 envelope and 2 First-Class stamps.

Nonfiction Needs book excerpts, first serial rights only, Q&A, narratives, trend pieces, profiles. Especially interested in medicine, education, sports, relationships, parenting, and the arts. No travelogs or poetry. **Buys up to 100 mss/year.** Query; SASE must be included with ms or queries for return. Length: 1,000-4,000 words.

Photos Purchased with accompanying ms or on assignment. Captions required. Reviews contact sheets. Pays standard rates according to size used.

$ $ CAPE COD LIFE

Cape Cod Life, Inc., 270 Communication Way, Building #6, Hyannis MA 02601. (508)775-9800. Fax: (508)775-9801. Website: www.capecodlife.com. **80% freelance written.** Magazine published 7 times/year focusing on area lifestyle, history and culture, people and places, business and industry, and issues and answers for year-round and summer residents of Cape Cod, Nantucket, and Martha's Vineyard as well as nonresidents who spend their leisure time here. Circ. 45,000. Byline given. Pays 90 days after acceptance. Offers 20% kill fee. Buys first North American serial rights. Makes work-for-hire assignments. Submit seasonal material 6 months in advance. Accepts queries by mail. Responds in 3 months to queries. Responds in 3 months to mss. Sample copy for $5. Guidelines for #10 SASE.

Nonfiction Needs book excerpts, general interest, historical, interview, photo feature, travel, outdoors, gardening, nautical, nature, arts, antiques. **Buys 20 mss/year.** Query. Length: 800-1,500 words. **Pays $200-400.**

Photos Photo guidelines for #10 SASE. Captions, identification of subjects required. Pays $25-225 Buys first rights with right to reprint

Tips Freelancers submitting *quality* spec articles with a Cape Cod and Islands angle have a good chance at publication. We like to see a wide selection of writer's clips before giving assignments. We also publish *Cape Cod & Islands Home* covering architecture, landscape design, and interior design with a Cape and Islands focus.

$ $ CAPE COD MAGAZINE

Rabideau Publishing, P.O. Box 208, Yarmouth Port MA 02765. (508)771-6549. Fax: (508)771-3769. E-mail: editor@capecodmagazine.com. Website: www.capecodmagazine.com. **80% freelance written.** Magazine published 9 times/year covering Cape Cod lifestyle. Estab. 1996. Circ. 16,000. Byline given. Pays 30 days after publication. Offers 25% kill fee. Publishes ms an average of 3 months after acceptance. Buys first North American serial rights, buys electronic rights. Editorial lead time 6 months. Submit seasonal material 1 year in advance. Accepts queries by mail, e-mail. Responds in 3 weeks to queries. Responds in 2 months to mss. Sample copy for $5. Guidelines by email.

Nonfiction Needs book excerpts, essays, general interest, historical, humor, interview, personal experience. Does not want cliched pieces, interviews, and puff features. **Buys 3 mss/year.** Send complete ms. Length: 800-2,500 words. **Pays $300-500 for assigned articles. Pays $100-300 for unsolicited articles.** Sometimes pays expenses of writers on assignment.

Photos State availability of or send photos Reviews GIF/JPEG files. Negotiates payment individually. Buys one time rights.

Columns/Departments Last Word (personal observations in typical back page format), 700 words. 4 Query with or without published clips or send complete ms. **Pays $150-300.**

Tips Read good magazines. We strive to offer readers the quality they find in good national magazines, so the more informed they are of what good writing is, the better the chance they'll get published in our magazine. Think of art opportunities. Ideas that do not have good art potential are harder to sell than those that do.

$ $ CHATHAM MAGAZINE

Rabideau Publishing, 396 Main St., Suite 8, Hyannis MA 02601. (508)771-6549. Fax: (508)771-3769. E-mail: editor@capecodmagazine.com. Website: www.chathammag.com. **80% freelance written.** Annual magazine covering Chatham lifestyle. Estab. 2006. Byline given. Pays 30 days after publication. Offers 25% kill fee. Publishes ms an average of 3 months after acceptance. Buys first North American serial rights, buys electronic rights. Editorial lead time 6 months. Submit seasonal material 1 year in advance. Accepts queries by mail, e-mail. Responds in 3 weeks to queries. Responds in 2 months to mss. Sample copy for $5. Guidelines by email.

Nonfiction Needs book excerpts, essays, general interest, historical, humor, interview, personal experience. Send complete ms. Length: 800-2,500 words. **Pays $300-500 for assigned articles. Pays $100-300 for unsolicited articles.** Sometimes pays expenses of writers on assignment.

Photos State availability of or send photos Reviews GIF/JPEG files. Negotiates payment individually. Buys one time rights.

Columns/Departments Hooked (fishing issues), 700 words. 4 Query with or without published clips or send complete ms. **Pays $150-300.**

Tips Read good magazines. We strive to offer readers the quality they find in good national magazines, so the more informed they are of what good writing is, the better the chance they'll get published in our magazine. Think of art opportunities. Ideas that do not have good art potential are harder to sell than those that do.

$ $ WORCESTER MAGAZINE

101 Water St., Worcester MA 01604. (508)749-3166. Fax: (508)749-3165. E-mail: mwarshaw@worcestermag.com. Website: www.worcestermag.com. **10% freelance written**. Weekly tabloid emphasizing the central Massachusetts region, especially the city of Worcester. Estab. 1976. Circ. 40,000. Byline given. Pays on publication. No kill fee. Publishes ms an average of 3 weeks after acceptance. Buys all rights. Submit seasonal material 2 months in advance. Accepts queries by mail, e-mail, fax.

- Does not respond to unsolicited material.

Nonfiction We are interested in any piece with a local angle. Needs essays, expose, area government, corporate, general interest, historical, humor, opinion, local, personal experience, photo feature, religious, interview (local). **Buys less than 75 mss/year.** Length: 500-1,500 words. **Pays 10¢/word.**

MICHIGAN

$ $ $ ANN ARBOR OBSERVER

Ann Arbor Observer Co., 201 E. Catherine, Ann Arbor MI 48104. Fax: (734)769-3375. E-mail: hilton@aaobserver.com. Website: www.arborweb.com. **50% freelance written**. Monthly magazine. We depend heavily on freelancers and we're always glad to talk to new ones. We look for the intelligence and judgment to fully explore complex people and situations, and the ability to convey what makes them interesting. Estab. 1976. Circ. 65,000. Byline given. Pays on publication. No kill fee. Publishes ms an average of 2 months after acceptance. Accepts queries by mail, e-mail, fax, phone. Responds in 3 weeks to queries. Responds in several months to mss. Sample copy for 12½x15 SAE with $3 postage. Guidelines for #10 SASE.

Nonfiction Historical, investigative features, profiles, brief vignettes. Must pertain to Ann Arbor. **Buys 75 mss/year.** Length: 100-5,000 words. **Pays up to $1,000.** Sometimes pays expenses of writers on assignment.

Columns/Departments Up Front (short, interesting tidbits), 150 words. **Pays $100.** Inside Ann Arbor (concise stories), 300-500 words. **Pays $200.** Around Town (unusual, compelling ancedotes), 750-1,500 words. **Pays $150-200.**

Tips If you have an idea for a story, write a 100-200-word description telling us why the story is interesting. We are open most to intelligent, insightful features of up to 5,000 words about interesting aspects of life in Ann Arbor.

$ $ GRAND RAPIDS MAGAZINE

Gemini Publications, 549 Ottawa Ave. NW, Suite 201, Grand Rapids MI 49503-1444. (616)459-4545. Fax: (616)459-4800. E-mail: cvalade@geminipub.com. Website: www.grmag.com. *Grand Rapids* is a general interest life and style magazine designed for those who live in the Grand Rapids metropolitan area or desire to maintain contact with the community. Estab. 1964. Byline given. Pays on publication. No kill fee. Editorial lead time 2 months. Submit seasonal material 2 months in advance. Sample copy for $2 and an SASE with $1.50 postage. Guidelines for #10 SASE.

Nonfiction *Grand Rapids Magazine* is approximately 60 percent service articles—dining guide, calendar, travel, personal finance, humor and reader service sections—and 40 percent topical and issue-oriented editorial that centers on people, politics, problems and trends in the region. In 2003, the editors added a section called 'Design,' which provides a focus on every aspect of the local design community—from Maya Lin's urban park installation and the new 125-acre sculpture park to architecture and the world's Big Three office furniture manufacturers headquartered here. Query. **Pays $25-500.**

HOUR DETROIT

Hour Media, LLC, 117 W. Third St., Royal Oak MI 48067. (248)691-1800. Website: www.hourdetroit.com. **50% freelance written**. Monthly magazine. General interest/lifestyle magazine aimed at a middle- to upper-income readership aged 17-70. Estab. 1996. Circ. 45,000. Byline given. Pays on acceptance. Offers 30% kill fee. Publishes ms an average of 2 months after acceptance. Buys first North American serial rights. Editorial lead time 2 months. Submit seasonal material 1 year in advance. Accepts queries by mail. Sample copy for $6.

Nonfiction Needs expose, general interest, historical, interview, new product, photo feature, technical. **Buys 150 mss/year.** Query with published clips. Length: 300-2,500 words.

Photos State availability

$ $ MICHIGAN HISTORY

Michigan Historical Center, Michigan Dept. of History, Arts & Libraries, 702 W. Kalamazoo, Box 30741, Lansing MI 48909-8241. (800)366-3703. Fax: (517)241-4909. E-mail: editor@michigan.gov. Website: www.michiganhistorymagazine.com. **75% freelance written**. Bimonthly magazine We cover Michigan's history, including a wide range of subtopics, such as aviation, agriculture, African Americans, archaeology, business, disasters, economy, engineering marvels, education, geography, government, war, labor, laws, literature, mritime, music, museums, Native Americans, personal profiles, recreation, politics, religion, sports, science and historic travel ideas. Estab. 1917. Circ. 30,000. Byline given. Pays on publication. Publishes ms an average of 6 months after acceptance. Buys one-time rights, buys electronic rights. Editorial lead time 1 year. Submit seasonal material 1 year in advance. Accepts queries by mail, e-mail, phone. Responds in 3 months to queries. Responds in 6 months to mss. Sample copy free. Guidelines free.

Nonfiction Contact: Christine Schwerin, assistant editor. Needs book excerpts, general interest, historical, interview, personal experience, photo feature. Nothing already published, fictional. **Buys 20-24 mss/year.** Send complete ms. Length: 800-3,500 words. **Pays $100-500.** Sometimes pays expenses of writers on assignment.

Photos Contact: Christine Schwerin, assistant editor. Send photos Identification of subjects, model releases required. Reviews contact sheets, negatives, transparencies, prints, digital photos must be 300 dpi as JPEG or TIFF. Negotiates payment individually. Buys one-time and electronic use rights.

Columns/Departments Columns open to freelancers: Remember the Time (first-person, factual stories, personal experiences that happened in Michigan or to Michiganians-900 words), On This Spot (locations in Michigan where specific, significant historic events have occurred-1,300 words), Back to Basics (simple, basic stories about Michigan's notable personalities, industries or well known events-900 words), History in Your Hometown (accurate, interesting town histories beginning with settlement through modern day, including social, economic, political and religious aspects-1,600 words), The Primary Source (focus on one artifact and its significance to Michigan's history-250 words), Books (send us a review copy of your non-fiction book, must have Michigan or Great Lakes focus). 5 Send complete ms. **Pays $100-400.**

Tips All stories must be well researched, well written, interesting and accurate. Many of our authors are seasoned journalists, graduate students, Ph.D.'s or published book authors. You have a better chance of getting published with us if you skip the query and send us a manuscript. If you do query, be sure to include specific details about your ideas and published clips. Stories about the Upper Peninsula are especially welcome. If your article focuses on history but also has a modern tie-in, your chances of publication are greatly increased. We do not publish any fiction.

$ $ TRAVERSE

Northern Michigan's Magazine, Prism Publications, 148 E. Front St., Traverse City MI 49684. (231)941-8174. Fax: (231)941-8391. Website: www.mynorth.com. **20% freelance written**. Monthly magazine covering northern Michigan life. *Traverse* is a celebration of the life and environment of northern Michigan. Estab. 1981. Circ. 30,000. Byline given. Pays on acceptance. Offers 10% kill fee. Buys first North American serial rights. Editorial lead time 1 year. Submit seasonal material 1 year in advance. Accepts queries by mail, fax, phone. Accepts simultaneous submissions. Responds in 2 months to queries. Sample copy for $3. Guidelines for #10 SASE.

Nonfiction Needs book excerpts, essays, general interest, historical, humor, interview, personal experience, photo feature, travel. No fiction or poetry. **Buys 24 mss/year.** Send complete ms. Length: 1,000-3,200 words. **Pays $150-500.** Sometimes pays expenses of writers on assignment.

Photos State availability Negotiates payment individually. Buys one time rights.

Columns/Departments Up in Michigan Reflection (essays about northern Michigan); Reflection on Home (essays about northern homes), both 700 words. 18 Query with published clips or send complete ms. **Pays $100-200.**

Tips When shaping an article for us, consider first that it must be strongly rooted in our region. The lack of this foundation element is one of the biggest reasons for our rejecting material. If you send us a piece about peaches, even if it does an admirable job of relaying the history of peaches, their medicinal qualities, their nutritional magnificence, and so on, we are likely to reject if it doesn't include local farms as a reference point. We want sidebars and extended captions designed to bring in a reader not enticed by the main subject. We cover the northern portion of the Lower Peninsula and to a lesser degree the Upper Peninsula. General categories of interest include nature and the environment, regional culture, personalities, the arts (visual, performing, literary), crafts, food & dining, homes, history, and outdoor activities (e.g., fishing, golf, skiing, boating, biking, hiking, birding, gardening). We are keenly interested in environmental and land-use issues but seldom use material dealing with such issues as health care, education, social services, criminal justice, and local politics. We use service pieces and a small number of how-to pieces, mostly focused on small projects for the home or yard. Also, we value research. We need articles built with information. Many of the pieces we reject use writing style to fill in for information voids. Style and voice are strongest when used as vehicles for sound research.

MINNESOTA

$ $ LAKE COUNTRY JOURNAL MAGAZINE

Evergreen Press of Brainerd, 201 W. Laurel St., P.O. Box 465, Brainerd MN 56401. (218)828-6424, ext. 14. Fax: (218)825-7816. E-mail: jodi@lakecountryjournal.com. Website: www.lakecountryjournal.com. **Contact:** Jodi Schwen, editor or Tenlee Lund, assistant editor. **90% freelance written**. Bimonthly magazine covering central

Minnesota's lake country. "We target a specific geographical niche in central Minnesota. The writer must be familiar with our area. We promote positive family values, foster a sense of community, increase appreciation for our natural and cultural environments, and provide ideas for enhancing the quality of our lives." Estab. 1996. Circ. 14,500. Byline given. Pays on publication. Offers 25% kill fee. Publishes ms an average of 6 months after acceptance. Buys first North American serial rights, buys second serial (reprint) rights, buys electronic rights. Submit seasonal material 1 year in advance. Accepts queries by mail, e-mail. Responds in 2 months to queries. Responds in 3 months to mss. Sample copy for $6. Guidelines available online.

O- Break in by "submitting department length first—they are not scheduled as far in advance as features. Always in need of original fillers."

Nonfiction Needs essays, general interest, how-to, humor, interview, personal experience, photo feature. "No articles that come from writers who are not familiar with our target geographical location." **Buys 30 mss/year.** Query with or without published clips Length: 1,000-1,500 words. **Pays $100-200.** Sometimes pays expenses of writers on assignment.

Photos State availability Identification of subjects, model releases required. Reviews transparencies. Negotiates payment individually. Buys one time rights.

Columns/Departments Profile-People from Lake Country, 800 words; Essay, 800 words; Health (topics pertinent to central Minnesota living), 500 words. 40 Query with published clips **Pays $50-75.**

Fiction Needs adventure, humorous, mainstream, slice-of-life vignettes, literary, also family fiction appropriate to Lake Country and seasonal fiction. **Buys 6 mss/year.** Length: 1,500 words. **Pays $100-200.**

Poetry Needs free verse. "Never use rhyming verse, avant-garde, experimental, etc." **Buys 6 poems/year.** Submit maximum 4 poems. Length: 8-32 lines. **Pays $25.**

Fillers Needs anecdotes, short humor. 20 Length: 100-300 words. **$25**

Tips "Most of the people who will read your articles live in the north central Minnesota lakes area. All have some significant attachment to the area. We have readers of various ages, backgrounds, and lifestyles. After reading your article, we hope to have a deeper understanding of some aspect of our community, our environment, ourselves, or humanity in general."

$ $ LAKE SUPERIOR MAGAZINE

Lake Superior Port Cities, Inc., P.O. Box 16417, Duluth MN 55816-0417. (218)722-5002. Fax: (218)722-4096. E-mail: edit@lakesuperior.com. Website: www.lakesuperior.com. **40% freelance written. Works with a small number of new/unpublished writers each year. Please include phone number and address with e-mail queries.** Bimonthly magazine covering contemporary and historic people, places and current events around Lake Superior. Estab. 1979. Circ. 20,000. Byline given. Pays on publication. No kill fee. Publishes ms an average of 10 months after acceptance. Buys first North American serial rights, buys second serial (reprint) rights. Submit seasonal material 1 year in advance. Accepts queries by mail, e-mail. Responds in 3 months to queries. Sample copy for $4.95 and 6 first-class stamps. Guidelines available online.

Nonfiction Needs book excerpts, general interest, historical, humor, interview, local, personal experience, photo feature, local, travel, local, city profiles, regional business, some investigative. **Buys 15 mss/year.** Query with published clips. Length: 300-1,800 words. **Pays $60-400.** Sometimes pays expenses of writers on assignment.

Photos Quality photography is our hallmark. Send photos Captions, identification of subjects, model releases required. Reviews contact sheets, 2x2 and larger transparencies, 4x5 prints. Offers $50/image; $150 for covers.

Columns/Departments Current events and things to do (for Events Calendar section), less than 300 words; Around The Circle (media reviews; short pieces on Lake Superior; Great Lakes environmental issues; themes, letters and short pieces on events and highlights of the Lake Superior Region); Essay (nostalgic lake-specific pieces), up to 1,100 words; Profile (single personality profile with photography), up to 900 words. Other headings include Destinations, Wild Superior, Lake Superior Living, Heritage, Recipe Box. 20 Query with published clips. **Pays $60-90.**

Fiction Ethnic, historic, humorous, mainstream, novel excerpts, slice-of-life vignettes, ghost stories. Must be targeted regionally. Wants stories that are Lake Superior related. **Buys 2-3 mss/year.** Query with published clips. Length: 300-2,500 words. **Pays $50-125.**

Tips Well-researched queries are attended to. We actively seek queries from writers in Lake Superior communities. We prefer manuscripts to queries. Provide enough information on why the subject is important to the region and our readers, or why and how something is unique. We want details. The writer must have a thorough knowledge of the subject and how it relates to our region. We prefer a fresh, unused approach to the subject which provides the reader with an emotional involvement. Almost all of our articles feature quality photography, color or black and white. It is a prerequisite of all nonfiction. All submissions should include a *short* biography of author/photographer; mug shot sometimes used. Blanket submissions need not apply.

$ $ $ MPLS. ST. PAUL MAGAZINE

MSP Communications, 220 S. 6th St., Suite 500, Minneapolis MN 55402. (612)339-7571. Fax: (612)339-5806. E-mail: edit@mspmag.com. Website: www.mspmag.com. Monthly magazine. *Mpls. St. Paul Magazine* is a city

magazine serving upscale readers in the Minneapolis-St. Paul metro area. Circ. 80,000. Pays on publication. Buys all rights. Editorial lead time 3 months. Accepts queries by mail, e-mail, fax. Sample copy for $10. Guidelines available online.
Nonfiction Needs book excerpts, essays, general interest, historical, interview, personal experience, photo feature, travel. **Buys 150 mss/year.** Query with published clips. Length: 500-4,000 words. **Pays 50-75¢/word for assigned articles.**

MISSISSIPPI

$ $ MISSISSIPPI MAGAZINE

Downhome Publications, 5 Lakeland Circle, Jackson MS 39216. (601)982-8418. Fax: (601)982-8447. E-mail: editor@mismag.com. Website: www.mississippimagazine.com. **Contact:** Melanie Ward, editor. **90% freelance written**. Bimonthly magazine covering Mississippi—the state and its lifestyles. "We are interested in positive stories reflecting Mississippi's rich traditions and heritage and focusing on the contributions the state and its natives have made to the arts, literature, and culture. In each issue we showcase homes and gardens, in-state travel, food, design, art, and more." Estab. 1982. Circ. 40,000. Byline given. Pays on publication. Offers 25% kill fee. Publishes ms an average of 6 months after acceptance. Buys first North American serial rights. Editorial lead time 6 months. Submit seasonal material 1 year in advance. Accepts queries by mail, fax. Responds in 2 months to queries. Guidelines for #10 SASE or online.
Nonfiction Needs general interest, historical, how-to, home decor, interview, personal experience, travel, in-state. No opinion, political, sports, expose. **Buys 15 mss/year.** Query. Length: 900-1,500 words. **Pays $150-350.**
Photos Send photos with query. Captions, identification of subjects, model releases required. Reviews transparencies, prints, digital images on CD. Negotiates payment individually Buys one time rights.
Columns/Departments Gardening (short informative article on a specific plant or gardening technique), 750-1,000 words; Culture Center (story about an event or person relating to Mississippi's art, music, theatre, or literature), 750-1,000 words; Made in Mississippi (short article about a nationally or internationally known Mississippian or Mississippi company in any field), 600-700 words; On Being Southern (personal essay about life in Mississippi; only ms submissions accepted), 750 words. 6 Query. **Pays $150-225.**

MISSOURI

$ $ 417 MAGAZINE

Southwest Missouri's Life-Improvement Magazine, Whitaker Publishing, 2111 S. Eastgate Ave., Springfield MO 65809. (417)883-7417. Fax: (417)889-7417. E-mail: editor@417mag.com. Website: www.417mag.com. **50% freelance written**. Monthly magazine. *417 Magazine* is a regional title serving southwest Missouri. Our editorial mix includes service journalism and lifestyle content on home, fashion and the arts; as well as narrative and issues pieces. The audience is affluent, educated, mostly female. Estab. 1998. Circ. 20,000. Byline given. Pays on acceptance. Publishes ms an average of 2-3 months after acceptance. Buys first rights, buys second serial (reprint) rights, buys simultaneous rights, buys electronic rights. Editorial lead time 6 months. Accepts queries by e-mail. Responds in 1-2 months to queries. Sample copy by email. Guidelines available online.
Nonfiction Needs essays, expose, general interest, how-to, humor, inspirational, interview, new product, personal experience, photo feature, travel, local book reviews. We are a local magazine, so anything not reflecting our local focus is something we have to pass on. **Buys 175 mss/year.** Query with published clips. Length: 300-3,500 words. **Pays $30-500, sometimes more.** Sometimes pays expenses of writers on assignment.
Tips Read the magazine before contacting us. Send specific ideas with your queries. Submit story ideas of local interest. Send published clips. Be a curious reporter, and ask probing questions.

$ $ KANSAS CITY HOMES & GARDENS

Network Communications, Inc., 4121 W. 83rd St., Suite 110, Prairie Village KS 66208. (913)648-5757. Fax: (913)648-5783. E-mail: adarr@kc-hg.com. Website: kchandg.com. Magazine published 8 times annually. *KCH&G* creates inspirational, credible and compelling content about trends and events in local home and design for affluent homeowners, with beautiful photography, engaging features and expert insight. We help our readers get smarter about where to find and how to buy the best solutions for enhancing their homes. Estab. 1986. Circ. 18,000. Byline given. Pays on publication. No kill fee. Buys one-time rights, buys electronic rights. Editorial lead time 4 months. Submit seasonal material 4 months in advance. Accepts queries by mail, e-mail, fax. Accepts previously published material. Accepts simultaneous submissions. Responds in 1 month to queries. Responds in 1 month to mss. Sample copy for $5.
Nonfiction Buys 8 mss/year. Query with published clips. Length: 600-1,000 words. **Pays $100-350.** Sometimes pays expenses of writers on assignment.
Photos State availability of or send photos Identification of subjects required. Reviews transparencies. Offers no additional payment for photos accepted with ms Buys continual rights.

Tips Focus on local home and garden content for the affluent homeowner.

$ $ MISSOURI LIFE

Missouri Life, Inc., 515 E. Morgan St., Boonville MO 65233. (660)882-9898. Fax: (660)882-9899. E-mail: info@missourilife.com. Website: www.missourilife.com. **85% freelance written**. Bimonthly magazine covering the state of Missouri. *Missouri Life*'s readers are mostly college-educated people with a wide range of travel and lifestyle interests. Our magazine discovers the people, places, and events—both past and present—that make Missouri a great place to live and/or visit. Estab. 1973. Circ. 20,000. Byline given. Pays on publication. Buys all rights, buys nonexclusive rights. Editorial lead time 3 months. Submit seasonal material 6 months in advance. Accepts queries by mail, e-mail, fax. Responds in 2 months to queries. Guidelines available online.

Nonfiction Needs general interest, historical, travel, all Missouri related. Length: 300-2,000 words. **Pays $50-600; 20¢/word.**

Photos State availability in query; buys all rights nonexclusive. Captions, identification of subjects, model releases required. Offers $50-150/photo

Columns/Departments "All Around Missouri (people and places, past and present, written in an almanac style), 300 words; Missouri Artist (features a Missouri artist), 500 words; Made in Missouri (products and businesses native to Missouri), 500 words.

$ RIVER HILLS TRAVELER

Traveler Publishing Co.,, P.O. Box 220, Valley Park MO 63088-0220. (800)874-8423. Fax: (800)874-8423. E-mail: stories@rhtrav.com. Website: www.riverhillstraveler.com. **80% freelance written**. Monthly tabloid covering outdoor sports and nature in the southeast quarter of Missouri, the east and central Ozarks. Topics like those in *Field & Stream* and *National Geographic*. Estab. 1973. Circ. 5,000. Byline given. Pays on publication. No kill fee. Publishes ms an average of 2 months after acceptance. Buys one-time rights. Editorial lead time 2 months. Submit seasonal material 1 year in advance. Accepts queries by e-mail. Accepts simultaneous submissions. Responds in 2 months to queries. Sample copy for SAE or online Guidelines available online.

Nonfiction Needs historical, how-to, humor, opinion, personal experience, photo feature, technical, travel. No stories about other geographic areas. **Buys 80 mss/year.** Query with writing samples. 1,500 word maximum **Pays $15-50.** Sometimes pays expenses of writers on assignment.

Reprints E-mail manuscript with rights for sale noted and information about when and where the material previously appeared.

Photos Send photos Reviews JPEG/TIFF files. Negotiates payment individually. Pays $35 for covers. Buys one time rights.

Tips "We are a `poor man's' *Field & Stream* and *National Geographic*—about the eastern Missouri Ozarks. We prefer stories that relate an adventure that causes a reader to relive an adventure of his own or consider embarking on a similar adventure. Think of an adventure in camping or cooking, not just fishing and hunting. How-to is great, but not simple instructions. We encourage good first-person reporting. We like to get stories as part of an e-mail, not an attached document."

$ RURAL MISSOURI MAGAZINE

Association of Missouri Electric Cooperatives, P.O. Box 1645, Jefferson City MO 65102. E-mail: hberry@ruralmissouri.coop. Website: www.ruralmissouri.coop. **5% freelance written**. Monthly magazine covering rural interests in Missouri; people, places and sights in Missouri. Our audience is comprised of rural electric cooperative members in Missouri. We describe our magazine as 'being devoted to the rural way of life.' Estab. 1948. Circ. 515,000. Byline given. Pays on acceptance. Publishes ms an average of 6 months after acceptance. Buys one-time rights. Editorial lead time 6 months. Submit seasonal material 6 months in advance. Accepts queries by mail, e-mail. Responds in 6-8 weeks to queries. Responds in 6-8 weeks to mss. Sample copy available online. Guidelines available online.

Nonfiction Needs general interest, historical. Does not want personal experiences or nostalgia pieces. Send complete ms. Length: 1,000-1,100 words. **Pays variable amount for each piece.**

Tips We look for tight, well-written history pieces. Remember: History doesn't mean boring. Bring it to life for us—attribute quotes. Make us feel what you're describing to us.

$ $ SPRINGFIELD! MAGAZINE

Springfield Communications, Inc., P.O. Box 4749, Springfield MO 65808-4749. (417)882-4917. **85% freelance written. Eager to work with a small number of new/unpublished writers each year.** This is an extremely local and provincial monthly magazine. No *general* interest articles. Estab. 1979. Circ. 10,000. Byline given. Pays on publication. Publishes ms an average of 3-24 months after acceptance. First serial rights. Submit seasonal material 1 year in advance. Responds in 3 months to queries. Responds in 6 months to mss. Sample copy for $5.30 and 9 ½x12 ½ SAE.

Nonfiction Local interest *only*; no material that could appeal to other magazines elsewhere. Needs book excerpts, Springfield authors only, expose, local topics only, historical, top priority, but must be local history, how-to, humor, interview, needs more on females than males, personal experience, photo feature, travel, 1 page/month. **Buys 150 mss/year.** Query with published clips by mail only or send complete ms with SASE. Length: 500-3,000 words. **Pays $35-250.**

Photos Send photos with query or ms. Needs more photo features of a nostalgic bent. Captions, identification of subjects, model releases required. Reviews contact sheets, 4x6 color, 5x7 b&w glossy prints. Pays $5-$35 for b&w, $10-50 for color. Buys one time rights.

Columns/Departments Length varies, usually 500-2,500 words. 150 Query by mail or send complete ms.

Tips We prefer writers read 8 or 10 copies of our magazine prior to submitting any material for our consideration. The magazine's greatest need is for features which comment on these times in Springfield. We are overstocked with nostalgic pieces right now. We also need profiles about young women and men of distinction.

MONTANA

$ $ MONTANA MAGAZINE

Lee Enterprises, P.O. Box 5630, Helena MT 59604-5630. Fax: (406)443-5480. E-mail: editor@montanamagazine.com. Website: www.montanamagazine.com. **90% freelance written.** Bimonthly magazine. Strictly Montana-oriented magazine that features community profiles, contemporary issues, wildlife and natural history, travel pieces. Estab. 1970. Circ. 40,000. Byline given. No kill fee. Publishes ms an average of 1 year after acceptance. Buys one-time rights. Submit seasonal material 1 year in advance. Accepts simultaneous submissions. Responds in 6 months to queries. Sample copy for $5 or online. Guidelines available online.

- Accepts queries by e-mail. No phone calls.

Nonfiction Query by September for summer material; March for winter material. Needs essays, general interest, interview, photo feature, travel. Special features on summer and winter destination points. No `me and Joe' hiking and hunting tales; no blood-and-guts hunting stories; no poetry; no fiction; no sentimental essays. **Buys 30 mss/year.** Query with samples and SASE Length: 300-3,000 words. **Pays 20¢/word.** Sometimes pays expenses of writers on assignment.

Reprints Send photocopy of article with rights for sale ted and information about when and where the material previously appeared. Pays 50% of amount paid for an original article.

Photos Send photos Captions, identification of subjects, model releases required. Reviews contact sheets, 35mm or larger format transparencies, 5x7 prints. Offers additional payment for photos accepted with ms. Buys one time rights.

Columns/Departments Memories (reminisces of early-day Montana life), 800-1,000 words; Outdoor Recreation, 1,500-2,000 words; Community Festivals, 500 words, plus b&w or color photo; Montana-Specific Humor, 800-1,000 words. Query with samples and SASE

Tips We avoid commonly known topics so Montanans won't ho-hum through more of what they already know. If it's time to revisit a topic, we look for a unique slant.

NEVADA

$ NEVADA HOME MAGAZINE

House and Garden Design, Nevada Home LLC, 780 Smithridge Dr., #200, Reno NV 89502. (775)825-4344. Fax: (775)825-4644. E-mail: lericson@nvhome.biz. Website: www.nvhome.biz. **80% freelance written.** Monthly magazine covering do-it-yourself home improvement, gardening and landscaping specific to the Washoe County, Nevada region. "Stories are all specific to the Reno and Sparks areas. All use local sources as experts. In gardening, the stories must present an understanding of the microclimates here in this area. In home improvement, they must reflect needs and timing based on the local climate and aesthetics." Estab. 2005. Circ. 25,000. Byline given. Pays on publication. No kill fee. Publishes ms an average of 2 months after acceptance. Buys first rights plus usage in all media thereafter, though ownership reverts to writer. Editorial lead time 3 months. Submit seasonal material 4 months in advance. Accepts queries by mail, e-mail. Responds in 3 weeks to queries. Sample copy available online. Guidelines by email.

Nonfiction Needs how-to. Does not want personal experience. **Buys 100 mss/year.** Query. Length: 600-900 words. **Pays $75-125 for assigned articles. Pays $50-100 for unsolicited articles.**

Photos State availability Captions, identification of subjects, model releases required. Reviews GIF/JPEG files. Negotiates payment individually. Buys first rights plus usage in all media thereafter, though ownership reverts to photographer.

Tips "If you have expertise in either home improvement (construction-related work) or gardening, let me know. Depth of related experience counts. Also, all stories are local to the Washoe County, Nevada area. Include your knowledge of, and time spent in, this area."

$ $ NEVADA MAGAZINE

401 N. Carson St., Carson City NV 89701-4291. (775)687-5416. Fax: (775)687-6159. E-mail: editor@nevadamagazine.com. Website: www.nevadamagazine.com. **50% freelance written. Works with a small number of new/unpublished writers each year.** Bimonthly magazine published by the state of Nevada to

promote tourism. Estab. 1936. Circ. 55,000. Byline given. Pays on publication. No kill fee. Publishes ms an average of 6 months after acceptance. Buys first North American serial rights. Submit seasonal material 6 months in advance. Accepts queries by Prefers e-mail. Responds in 1 month to queries.

Nonfiction We use stories and photos on speculation. Nevada topics only. Needs photo feature, travel, lifestyle, dining, recreational. Send detailed query Length: 700-1,000 words. **Pays $50-500.**

Photos Contact: Query art director Tony deRonnebeck (tony@nevadamagazine.com). Reviews digital images. Pays $35-175; cover, $250 Buys one time rights.

Tips Keep in mind the magazine's purpose is to promote Nevada tourism. We look for a light, enthusiastic tone of voice without being too cute.

NEW HAMPSHIRE

$ $ NEW HAMPSHIRE MAGAZINE

McLean Communications, Inc., 150 Dow St., Manchester NH 03101. (603)624-1442. E-mail: editor@nhmagazine.com. Website: www.nhmagazine.com. **50% freelance written**. Monthly magazine devoted to New Hampshire. We want stories written for, by, and about the people of New Hampshire with emphasis on qualities that set us apart from other states. We feature lifestyle, adventure, and home-related stories with a unique local angle. Estab. 1986. Circ. 32,000. Byline given. Pays on publication. Offers 25% kill fee. Buys all rights. Editorial lead time 3 months. Submit seasonal material 3 months in advance. Accepts queries by mail, e-mail, fax. Accepts simultaneous submissions. Responds in 2 months to queries. Responds in 3 months to mss. Guidelines available online.

Nonfiction Needs essays, general interest, historical, photo feature, business. **Buys 30 mss/year.** Query with published clips. Length: 800-2,000 words. **Pays $50-500.** Sometimes pays expenses of writers on assignment.

Photos State availability Captions, identification of subjects, model releases required. Possible additional payment for photos accepted with ms. Rights purchased vary.

Fillers 200-400 words

Tips McLean Communications publishes 1 monthly magazine entitled *New Hampshire Magazine* and a specialty publication called *Destination New Hampshire*. In general, our articles deal with the people of New Hampshire—their lifestyles and interests. We also present localized stories about national and international issues, ideas, and trends. We will only use stories that show our readers how these issues have an impact on their daily lives. We cover a wide range of topics, including healthcare, politics, law, real-life dramas, regional history, medical issues, business, careers, environmental issues, the arts, the outdoors, education, food, recreation, etc. Many of our readers are what we call `The New Traditionalists'—aging Baby Boomers who have embraced solid American values and contemporary New Hampshire lifestyles.

NEW JERSEY

$ $ $ $ NEW JERSEY MONTHLY

The Magazine of the Garden State, New Jersey Monthly, LLC, P.O. Box 920, Morristown NJ 07963-0920. (973)539-8230. Fax: (973)538-2953. Website: www.njmonthly.com. **75-80% freelance written**. Monthly magazine covering just about anything to do with New Jersey, from news, politics, and sports to decorating trends and lifestyle issues. Our readership is well-educated, affluent, and on average our readers have lived in New Jersey 20 years or more. Estab. 1976. Circ. 95,000. Byline given. Pays on completion of fact-checking. Offers 20% kill fee. Publishes ms an average of 3 months after acceptance. Buys first North American serial rights. Editorial lead time 3 months. Submit seasonal material 6 months in advance. Accepts queries by mail, e-mail, fax, phone. Accepts simultaneous submissions. Responds in 2 months to queries.

- This magazine continues to look for strong investigative reporters with novelistic style and solid knowledge of New Jersey issues.

Nonfiction Needs book excerpts, essays, expose, general interest, historical, humor, interview, personal experience, photo feature, travel, within New Jersey, arts, sports, politics. No experience pieces from people who used to live in New Jersey or general pieces that have no New Jersey angle. **Buys 90-100 mss/year.** Query with published magazine clips and SASE. Length: 800-3,000 words. **Pays $750-2,500.** Pays reasonable expenses of writers on assignment with prior approval.

Photos Contact: Donna Panagakos, art director. State availability Identification of subjects, model releases required. Reviews transparencies, prints. Payment negotiated. Buys one time rights.

Columns/Departments Exit Ramp (back page essay usually originating from personal experience but written in a way that tells a broader story of statewide interest), 1,200 words. 12 Query with published clips. **Pays $400.**

Fillers Needs anecdotes, for front-of-book. 12-15 Length: 200-250 words. **$100**

Tips The best approach: Do your homework! Read the past year's issues to get an understanding of our well-written, well-researched articles that tell a tale from a well-established point of view.

$ $ NEW JERSEY SAVVY LIVING

CTB, LLC, 30B Vreeland Rd., Florham Park NJ 07932. (973)966-0997. Fax: (973)966-0210. E-mail: njsavvyliving@ctbintl.com. Website: www.njsavvyliving.com. **90% freelance written**. Bimonthly magazine covering New Jersey residents with affluent lifestyles. *Savvy Living* is a regional magazine for an upscale audience, ages 35-65. We focus on lifestyle topics such as home design, fashion, the arts, travel, personal finance, and health and well being. Estab. 1997. Circ. 50,000. Byline given. Pays on publication. Offers $50 kill fee. Publishes ms an average of 3 months after acceptance. variable rights. Editorial lead time 3 months. Accepts queries by mail. Accepts simultaneous submissions. Response time varies. Sample copy for sae with 9x12 envelope.

Nonfiction Needs interview, people of national and regional importance, photo feature, travel, home/decorating, finance, health, fashion, beauty. No investigative, fiction, personal experience, and non-New Jersey topics (excluding travel). **Buys 50 mss/year.** Query with published clips. Length: 900-2,000 words. **Pays $250-500.**

Photos State availability Captions, identification of subjects, model releases required. Offers no additional payment for photos accepted with ms. Buys one time rights.

Columns/Departments Savvy Shoppers (inside scoop on buying); Dining Out (restaurant review); Home Gourmet (gourmet cooking and entertaining). 25 Query with published clips. **Pays $300.**

Tips Offer ideas of interest to a savvy, upscale New Jersey readership. We love articles that utilize local sources and are well focused and keep our readers informed about trends affecting their lives. We work with experienced and stylish writers. Please provide clips.

$ $ THE SANDPAPER

Newsmagazine of the Jersey Shore, The SandPaper, Inc., 1816 Long Beach Blvd., Surf City NJ 08008-5461. (609)494-5900. Fax: (609)494-1437. E-mail: letters@thesandpaper.net. Weekly tabloid covering subjects of interest to Long Island Beach area residents and visitors. Each issue includes a mix of news, human interest features, opinion columns, and entertainment/calendar listings. Estab. 1976. Circ. 30,000. Byline given. Pays on publication. Offers 100% kill fee. Publishes ms an average of 1 month after acceptance. Buys first rights, buys all rights. Submit seasonal material 3 months in advance. Accepts queries by mail, e-mail, fax, phone. Accepts simultaneous submissions. Responds in 1 month to queries.

Columns/Departments Speakeasy (opinion and slice-of-life, often humorous); Commentary (forum for social science perspectives); both 1,000-1,500 words, preferably with local or Jersey Shore angle. 50 Send complete ms. **Pays $40**

NEW MEXICO

$ $ NEW MEXICO MAGAZINE

Lew Wallace Bldg., 495 Old Santa Fe Trail, Santa Fe NM 87501. (505)827-7447. E-mail: queries@nmmagazine.com. Website: www.nmmagazine.com. **Contact:** Any editor. "Covers areas throughout the state. We want to publish a lively editorial mix, covering both the down-home (like a diner in Tucumcari) and the upscale (a new bistro in world-class Santa Fe). Explore the gamut of the Old West and the New Age.". "Our magazine is about the power of place—in particular more than 120,000 sq. miles of mountains, desert, grasslands, and forest inhabited by a culturally rich mix of individuals. It is an enterprise of the New Mexico Tourism Dept., which strives to make potential visitors aware of our state's multicultural heritage, climate, environment, & uniqueness." Estab. 1923. Circ. 100,000. Pays on acceptance. No kill fee. Publishes ms an average of 2 months after acceptance. Buys first North American serial rights, first publication rights exclusive worldwide. Submit seasonal material 1 year in advance. Accepts queries by mail, e-mail (preferred). Does not accept previously published submissions.Responds to queries if interested. Sample copy for $5. Guidelines for SASE.

- No unsolicited mss. Does not return unsolicited material.

Nonfiction "We look for story ideas about New Mexico experiences, with opinionated storytelling and a first-person point of view when appropriate. Inspire readers to follow in your footsteps. We look for writers—both in New Mexico and elsewhere—who are adept at establishing a theme, then sustaining a story with fresh eyes and true insight. We place a premium on good storytelling, tight composition, and factual accuracy. We expect original work." "Submit your story idea along with a working head and subhead and a paragraph synopsis. Include published clips and a short sum-up about your strengths as a writer. We will consider your proposal as well as your potential to write stories we've conceptualized."

Reprints Rarely publishes reprints but sometimes publishes excerpts from novels and nonfiction books.

Photos "Purchased as portfolio or on assignment. Photographers interested in photo assignments should reference submission guidelines on the contributors' page of our website."

Tips "Does not return unsolicited material."

$ NEW MEXICO WOMAN

New Mexico Woman, Inc., P.O. Box 12955, Albuquerque NM 87195. (505)247-9195. Fax: (505)842-5129. E-mail: heygals@nmwoman.com. Website: www.nmwoman.com. **90% freelance written**. Monthly magazine covering women in business and professional women. Estab. 1983. Circ. 15,000. Pays on publication. Publishes ms an average of 3 months after acceptance. Buys one-time rights. Editorial lead time 2 months. Submit seasonal material 2-3 months in advance. Accepts queries by mail, e-mail, fax. Accepts previously published material. Accepts simultaneous submissions. Guidelines available online.

Nonfiction We are interested primarily in education, opportunities, career options, self improvement, women's health issues, and occasionally articles about home, hobby, travel, lifestyle, or nonprofit programs that serve women in the community. Needs general interest, historical, how-to, humor, inspirational, new product, personal experience. **Buys 5-10 mss/year.** Query. Length: 800-1,600 words. **Pays 5¢/word.**

Photos State availability Captions required. Reviews GIF/JPEG files. Offers no additional payment for photos accepted with ms. Buys one time rights.

Columns/Departments From My Perspective (personal experience); The Inner You (self-improvement); Young Women to Watch (talented young women), all 600 words; and The Seasons of Fitness (fitness advice), 400 words. 12 Query with published clips. **Pays 5¢/word.**

Fillers Needs anecdotes, facts, short humor. Length: 100-150 words. **Pays 5¢/word.**

TRADICION REVISTA

LPD Press, 925 Salamanca N.W., Los Ranchos NM 87107-5647. (505)344-9382. Fax: (505)345-5129. E-mail: LPD_Press@msn.com. Website: www.nmsantos.com. **75% freelance written**. Semiannual magazine covering Southwest history and culture. We publish Southwest art and history, especially the art of New Mexico. Estab. 1995. Circ. 5,000. Byline given. does not pay for articles. No kill fee. Buys Author retains rights. rights. Editorial lead time 6 months. Submit seasonal material 4 months in advance. Accepts queries by e-mail, phone. Accepts simultaneous submissions. Responds in 1 week to queries. Responds in 1 month to mss. Sample copy free.

Nonfiction Needs essays, general interest, historical, interview, photo feature, travel. **Buys 20 (no pay) mss/year. mss/year.** Query. Length: 500-2,000 words.

Photos Send photos Captions required. Reviews GIF/JPEG files. Offers no additional payment for photos accepted with ms. Buys one time rights.

Columns/Departments Query. **no pay.**

NEW YORK

$ $ ADIRONDACK LIFE

P.O. Box 410, Jay NY 12941-0410. (518)946-2191. Fax: (518)946-7461. E-mail: aledit@adirondacklife.com. Website: www.adirondacklife.com. **70% freelance written. Prefers to work with published/established writers.** "Magazine published 8 issues/year, including special Annual Outdoor Guide, emphasizes the Adirondack region and the North Country of New York State in articles covering outdoor activities, history, and natural history directly related to the Adirondacks.". Estab. 1970. Circ. 50,000. Byline given. Pays 30 days after publication. No kill fee. Publishes ms an average of 10 months after acceptance. Buys first North American serial rights, buys Web rights. Submit seasonal material 1 year in advance. Accepts queries by mail, e-mail. Sample copy for $3 and 9x12 SAE. Guidelines available online.

Nonfiction *"Adirondack Life* attempts to capture the unique flavor and ethos of the Adirondack mountains and North Country region through feature articles directly pertaining to the qualities of the area." Outdoors (May); Single-topic Collector's issue (September) **Buys 20-25 unsolicited mss/year.** Query with published clips. Length: 1,000-4,000 words. **Pays 30¢/word.** Sometimes pays expenses of writers on assignment.

Photos "All photos must have been taken in the Adirondacks. Each issue contains a photo feature. Purchased with or without ms on assignment. All photos must be individually identified as to the subject or locale and must bear the photographer's name." Send photos Reviews color transparencies, b&w prints. Pays $150 for full page, b&w, or color; $400 for cover (color only,vertical in format). Credit line given.

Columns/Departments Special Places (unique spots in the Adirondack Park); Watercraft; Barkeater (personal to political essays); Wilderness (environmental issues); Working (careers in the Adirondacks); Home; Yesteryears; Kitchen; Profile; Historic Preservation; Sporting Scene. Length: 1,200-2,400 words. Query with published clips. **Pays 30¢/word.**

Fiction Considers first-serial novel excerpts in its subject matter and region.

Tips "Do not send a personal essay about your meaningful moment in the mountains. We need factual pieces about regional history, sports, culture, and business. We are looking for clear, concise, well-organized manuscripts that are strictly Adirondack in subject. Check back issues to be sure we haven't already covered your topic. Please do not send unsolicited manuscripts via e-mail. Check out our guidelines online."

$ $ BUFFALO SPREE MAGAZINE

David Laurence Publications, Inc., 6215 Sheridan Dr., Buffalo NY 14221. (716)634-0820. Fax: (716)810-0075. E-mail: elicata@buffalospree.com. Website: www.buffalospree.com. **90% freelance written**. City regional magazine published 8 times/year. Estab. 1967. Circ. 25,000. Byline given. Pays on publication. No kill fee. Publishes ms an average of 1 month after acceptance. Buys first North American serial rights. Accepts queries by mail, e-mail, fax. Responds in 6 months to queries. Sample copy for $3.95 and 9x12 SAE with 9 first-class stamps.

Nonfiction Most articles are assigned not unsolicited. Needs interview, travel, issue-oriented features, arts, living, food, regional. Query with rÃ^sumÃ^ and published clips Length: 1,000-2,000 words. **Pays $125-250.**

Tips Send a well-written, compelling query or an interesting topic, and *great* clips. We no longer regularly publish fiction or poetry. Prefers material that is Western New York related.

$ $ $ $ CITY LIMITS

New York's Urban Affairs News Magazine, City Limits Community Information Service, 120 Wall St., 20th Floor, New York NY 10005. (212)479-3344. Fax: (212)344-6457. E-mail: editor@citylimits.org. Website: www.citylimits.org. **50% freelance written**. Monthly magazine covering urban politics and policy. *City Limits* is a 29-year-old nonprofit magazine focusing on issues facing New York City and its neighborhoods, particularly low-income communities. The magazine is strongly committed to investigative journalism, in-depth policy analysis and hard-hitting profiles. Estab. 1976. Circ. 4,000. Byline given. Pays on publication. Offers 50% kill fee. Publishes ms an average of 3 months after acceptance. Buys first North American serial rights, buys second serial (reprint) rights. Editorial lead time 2 months. Accepts queries by mail, e-mail, fax. Accepts simultaneous submissions. Sample copy for $2.95. Guidelines free.

Nonfiction Needs book excerpts, expose, humor, interview, opinion, photo feature. No essays, polemics. **Buys 25 mss/year.** Query with published clips. Length: 400-3,500 words. **Pays $150-2,000 for assigned articles. Pays $100-800 for unsolicited articles.** Pays expenses of writers on assignment.

Photos State availability Reviews contact sheets, negatives, transparencies. Offers $50-100/photo

Columns/Departments Making Change (nonprofit business); Big Idea (policy news); Book Review, all 800 words; Urban Legend (profile); First Hand (Q&A), both 350 words. 15 Query with published clips.

Tips *City Limits'* specialty is covering low-income communities. We want to report untold stories about news affecting neighborhoods at the grassroots. We're looking for stories about housing, health care, criminal justice, child welfare, education, economic development, welfare reform, politics and government.

$ HUDSON VALLEY LIFE

The Professional Image, 174 South St., Newburgh NY 12550. E-mail: editor@excitingread.com. Website: www.hvlifeonline.com. **95% freelance written**. Monthly magazine covering active adults over 45. Estab. 1996. Circ. 15,000. Pays on publication. No kill fee. Publishes ms an average of 3 months after acceptance. Guidelines available.

Nonfiction Needs expose, general interest, humor, interview, personal experience. **Buys 15 mss/yr. mss/year.** Query. Length: 700-1,200 words. **Pays $70-120 for assigned articles. Pays $25-35 for unsolicited articles.**

Reprints $25-35

NEW YORK SPACES

Wainscot Media, 110 Summit Ave., Montvale NJ 07645. (201)571-7003. Fax: (201)782-5319. E-mail: nyspaces@wainscotmedia.com. Website: www.nyspacesmagazine.com. Bimonthly magazine celebrating the best of New York area design. *New York Spaces* is dedicated to helping affluent, acquisitive users enhance their private worldsÃ³making it a remarkable showcase for the design community and advertisers alike. No kill fee.

Nonfiction Needs general interest, how-to. Query.

Photos Submit scouting shots (color prints, copies or low-res .jpg files on CD) for consideration. These images are used solely for the purpose of reviewing and selecting which projects we will publish. We'll be in touch to let you know if your project has been selected. State availability of or send photos Captions, identification of subjects required. Reviews 2 ¼, 4x5, etc. or 35mm slides transparencies, high-resolution digital photos on CD.

$ $ SYRACUSE NEW TIMES

A. Zimmer, Ltd., 1415 W. Genesee St., Syracuse NY 13204. Fax: (315)422-1721. E-mail: editorial@syracusenewtimes.com. Website: www.syracusenewtimes.com. **50% freelance written**. Weekly tabloid covering news, sports, arts, and entertainment. *"Syracuse New Times* is an alternative weekly that is topical, provocative, irreverent, and intensely local." Estab. 1969. Circ. 46,000. Byline given. Pays on publication. No kill fee. Publishes ms an average of 1 month after acceptance. Buys one-time rights. Editorial lead time 3 months. Submit seasonal material 3 months in advance. Accepts simultaneous submissions. Responds in 2 weeks to queries. Responds in 1 month to mss. Sample copy for sae with 9—Š12 envelope and 2 First-Class stamps. Guidelines for #10 SASE.

Nonfiction Needs essays, general interest. **Buys 200 mss/year.** Query by mail with published clips. Length: 250-2,500 words. **Pays $25-200.**

Photos State availability of or send photos Identification of subjects required. Reviews 8x10 prints, color slides. Offers $10-25/photo or negotiates payment individually Buys one time rights.

Tips "Move to Syracuse and query with strong idea."

$ WESTCHESTER ARTSNEWS

Westchester Arts Council, 31 Mamaroneck Ave., White Plains NY 10601. Fax: (914)428-4306. E-mail: jormond@westarts.com. Website: www.westarts.com. **20% freelance written**. Monthly tabloid covering arts and entertainment in Westchester County, New York. We profile artists, arts organizations and write teasers about upcoming exhibitions, concerts, events, theatrical performances, etc. Estab. 1975. Circ. 20,000. Byline given. Pays on publication. Buys all rights. Editorial lead time 1 month. Submit seasonal material 2 months in advance. Accepts queries by mail, e-mail. Sample copy free.

Nonfiction There must be some hook to Westchester County, New York. Query with published clips. Length: 400-500 words. **Pays $75-100.** Pays expenses of writers on assignment.

Tips Please e-mail cover letter, resume, 2 clips. No phone calls please.

NORTH CAROLINA

$ $ AAA CAROLINAS GO MAGAZINE

6600 AAA Dr., Charlotte NC 28212. Fax: (704)569-7815. Website: www.aaacarolinas.com. **Contact:** Tom Crosby, Managing Editor. **20% freelance written**. Member publication for the Carolina affiliate of American Automobile Association covering travel, auto-related issues. "We prefer stories that focus on travel and auto safety in North and South Carolina and surrounding states." Estab. 1922. Circ. 1.1 million. Byline given. Pays on publication. No kill fee. Buys all rights. Editorial lead time 2 months. Accepts queries by mail. Sample copy and writer's guidelines for #10 SASE.

- "The online magazine carries original content not found in the print edition. Contact Brendan Byrnes at btbyrnes@mailaaa.com."

Nonfiction Needs travel, auto safety. Length: 750 words. **Pays $150.**

Photos Send photos Identification of subjects required. Reviews slides. Offers no additional payment for photos accepted with ms. Buys all rights.

Tips "Submit regional stories relating to Carolinas travel."

ALAMANCE MAGAZINE

CCMag Inc., P.O. Box 517, Burlington NC 27216. (336)226-8436. Fax: (336)226-8437. E-mail: alamagkc@bellsouth.net. Website: www.alamancemagazine.com. **90% freelance written**. Monthly magazine. *Alamance Magazine* provides general interest articles for our readers here in Alamance County, North Carolina. Estab. 1986. Circ. 20,000. Byline given. Editorial lead time 3 months. Submit seasonal material 4 months in advance. Accepts queries by mail, e-mail, fax, phone. Accepts simultaneous submissions.

Nonfiction Needs general interest. Query.

$ $ CARY MAGAZINE

SA Cherokee, Westview at Weston, 301 Cascade Pointe Lane, #101, Cary NC 27513. (919)674-6020. Fax: (919)674-6027. E-mail: editor@carymagazine.com. Website: www.carymagazine.com. **40% freelance written.** Bimonthly magazine. "Lifestyle publication for the affluent communities of Cary, Apex, Morrisville, Holly Springs, Fuquay-Varina and RTP. Our editorial objective is to entertain, enlighten and inform our readers with unique and engaging editorial and vivid photography." Estab. 2004. Circ. 23,000. Byline given. Negotiated Buys first North American serial rights. Editorial lead time 3 months. Submit seasonal material 3 months in advance. Accepts queries by mail, e-mail. Responds in 2-4 weeks to queries. Responds in 1 month to mss. Sample copy for $4.95. Guidelines free.

Nonfiction Needs historical, specific to Western Wake County, North Carolina, inspirational, interview, human interest, personal experience. Don't submit articles with no local connection. **Buys 2 mss/year.** Query with published clips. Sometimes pays expenses of writers on assignment.

Photos Freelancers should state the availability of photos with their submission or send the photos with their submission. Identification of subjects required. Reviews GIF/JPEG files. Negotiates payment individually Buys one time rights.

Tips "Prefer experienced feature writers with exceptional interviewing skills who can take a fresh perspective on a topic; writes with a unique flare, but clearly with a good hook to engage the reader and evoke emotion; adheres to AP Style and follows basic journalism conventions; and takes deadlines seriously. E-mail inquiries preferred."

$ $ CHARLOTTE MAGAZINE

Abarta Media, 127 W. Worthington Ave., Suite 208, Charlotte NC 28203. (704)335-7181. Fax: (704)335-3739. E-mail: richard.thurmond@charlottemagazine.com. Website: www.charlottemagazine.com. **75% freelance written**. Monthly magazine covering Charlotte life. This magazine tells its readers things they didn't know about Charlotte, in an interesting, entertaining, and sometimes provocative style. Circ. 40,000. Byline given. Pays within 30 days of acceptance. Offers 25% kill fee. Publishes ms an average of 3 months after acceptance. Buys first North American serial rights. Editorial lead time 3 months. Submit seasonal material 6 months in advance. Accepts queries by mail, e-mail. Accepts simultaneous submissions. Responds in 6 months to mss. Sample copy for 8½—Š11 SAE and $5.

Nonfiction Needs book excerpts, expose, general interest, interview, photo feature, travel. **Buys 35-50 mss/year.** Query with published clips. Length: 200-3,000 words. **Pays 20-40¢/word.** Sometimes pays expenses of writers on assignment.

Photos State availability Identification of subjects required. Negotiates payment individually. Buys one time rights.

Columns/Departments 35-50 **Pays 20-40¢/word**

Tips A story for *Charlotte* magazine could only appear in *Charlotte* magazine. That is, the story and its treatment are particularly germane to this area. Because of this, we rarely work with writers who live outside the Charlotte area.

$ $ FIFTEEN 501

Connecting Life in Durham, Orange and Chatham Counties, Weiss and Hughes Publishing, 189 Wind Chime Ct., Raleigh NC 27615. (919)870-1722. Fax: (919)719-5260. E-mail: dthurber@fifteen501.com. Website: www.fifteen501.com. **50% freelance written.** Quarterly magazine covering lifestyle issues relevant to residents in the US 15/501 corridor of Durham, Orange and Chatham counties. We cover issues important to residents of Durham, Orange and Chatham counties. We're committed to improving our readers' overall quality of life and keeping them informed of the lifestyle amenities there. Estab. 2006. Circ. 30,000. Byline given. within 30 days of publication. Offers 25% kill fee. Publishes ms an average of 2 months after acceptance. Buys all rights. Editorial lead time 2-3 months. Submit seasonal material 6 months in advance. Accepts queries by mail, e-mail. Accepts simultaneous submissions. Responds in 2-4 weeks to queries. Sample copy available online. Guidelines by email.

Nonfiction Needs general interest, historical, how-to, home interiors, landscaping, gardening, technology, inspirational, interview, personal experience, photo feature, technical, travel. Does not want opinion pieces, political or religious topics. Query. Length: 600-1,200 words. **Pays 35¢/word.** Sometimes pays expenses of writers on assignment.

Photos State availability Captions, identification of subjects required. Reviews transparencies, GIF/JPEG files. Offers no additional payment for photos accepted with ms. Rights are negotiable.

Columns/Departments Around Town (local lifestyle topics), 1,000 words; Hometown Stories, 600 words; Travel (around North Carolina), 1,000 words; Home Interiors/Landscaping (varies), 1,000 words; Restaurants (local, fine dining), 600-1,000 words. 20-25 Query. **Pays 35¢/word.**

Tips All queries must be focused on the issues that make Durham, Chapel Hill, Carrboro, Hillsborough and Pittsboro unique and wonderful places to live.

$ $ OUR STATE

Down Home in North Carolina, Mann Media, P.O. Box 4552, Greensboro NC 27404. (336)286-0600. Fax: (336)286-0100. E-mail: editorial@ourstate.com. Website: www.ourstate.com. **95% freelance written.** Monthly magazine covering North Carolina. *Our State* is dedicated to providing editorial about the history, destinations, out-of-the-way places, and culture of North Carolina. Estab. 1933. Circ. 130,000. Byline given. Pays on publication. No kill fee. Publishes ms an average of 6-24 months after acceptance. Buys first North American serial rights. Editorial lead time 4-6 months. Submit seasonal material 4 months in advance. Accepts queries by mail, e-mail, fax. Responds in 6 weeks to queries. Responds in 2 months to mss. Sample copy for $6. Guidelines for #10 SASE.

Nonfiction Needs historical, travel, North Carolina culture, folklore. **Buys 250 mss/year.** Send complete ms. Length: 1,400-1,600 words. **Pays $300-500.**

Photos State availability Reviews 35mm or 4x6 transparencies, digital. Negotiates payment individually. Buys one time rights.

Columns/Departments Tar Heel Memories (remembering something specific about North Carolina), 1,000 words; Tar Heel Profile (profile of interesting North Carolinian), 1,500 words; Tar Heel Literature (review of books by North Carolina writers and about North Carolina), 300 words.

Tips We are developing a style for travel stories that is distinctly *Our State*. That style starts with outstanding photographs, which not only depict an area, but interpret it and thus become an integral part of the presentation. Our stories need not dwell on listings of what can be seen. Concentrate instead on the experience of being there, whether the destination is a hiking trail, a bed and breakfast, a forest, or an urban area. What thoughts and feelings did the experience evoke? We want to know why you went there, what you experienced, and what impressions you came away with. With at least 1 travel story an issue, we run a short sidebar called, 'If You're Going.' It explains how to get to the destination; rates or admission costs if there are any; a schedule of when the attraction is open or list of relevant dates; and an address and phone number for readers to write or call for more information. This sidebar eliminates the need for general-service information in the story.

$ $ WAKE LIVING

Wake County's Premier Lifestyle Publication, Weiss and Hughes Publishing, 189 Wind Chime Ct., Raleigh NC 27615. (919)870-1722. Fax: (919)719-5260. E-mail: dhughes@wakeliving.com. Website: www.wakeliving.com. **50% freelance written**. Quarterly magazine covering lifestyle issues in Wake County, North Carolina. We cover issues important to residents of Wake County. We are committed to improving our readers' overall quality of life and keeping them informed of the lifestyle amenities here. Estab. 2003. Circ. 40,000. Byline given. Pays within 30 days of publication. Offers 25% kill fee. Publishes ms an average of 2 months after acceptance. Buys all rights. Editorial lead time 2-3 months. Submit seasonal material 6 months in advance. Accepts queries by mail, e-mail. Accepts simultaneous submissions. Responds in 2-4 weeks to queries. Sample copy available online. Guidelines available online.

Nonfiction Needs general interest, historical, how-to, home interiors, technology, landscaping, gardening, inspirational, interview, personal experience, photo feature, technical, travel. Does not want opinion pieces, political topics, religious articles. Query. Length: 600-1,200 words. **Pays 35¢/word.** Sometimes pays expenses of writers on assignment.

Photos State availability Captions, identification of subjects required. Reviews transparencies, GIF/JPEG files. Offers no additional payment for photos accepted with ms.

Columns/Departments Around Town (local lifestyle topics); Hometown Stories, 600 words; Travel (around North Carolina); Home Interiors/Landscaping, all 1,000 words. Restaurants (local restaurants, fine dining), 600-1,000 words. 20-25 Query. **Pays 35¢/word.**

Tips Articles must be specifically focused on Wake County/Raleigh metro issues. We like unusual angles about what makes living here unique from other areas.

NORTH DAKOTA

$ $ NORTH DAKOTA LIVING MAGAZINE

North Dakota Association of Rural Electric Cooperatives, 3201 Nygren Dr. NW, P.O. Box 727, Mandan ND 58554-0727. (701)663-6501. Fax: (701)663-3745. E-mail: kbrick@ndarec.com. Website: www.ndarec.com. **20% freelance written**. Monthly magazine covering information of interest to memberships of electric cooperatives and telephone cooperatives. We publish a general interest magazine for North Dakotans. We treat subjects pertaining to living and working in the northern Great Plains. We provide progress reporting on electric cooperatives and telephone cooperatives. Estab. 1954. Circ. 70,000. Byline given. Pays on acceptance. No kill fee. Publishes ms an average of 6 months after acceptance. Buys one-time rights. Makes work-for-hire assignments. Editorial lead time 6 months. Submit seasonal material 6 months in advance. Accepts queries by mail, e-mail. Accepts previously published material. Accepts simultaneous submissions. Sample copy and writer's guidelines not available.

Nonfiction Needs general interest, historical, how-to, humor, interview, new product, travel. **Buys 20 mss/year.** Query with published clips. Length: 1,500-2,000 words. **Pays $100-500 minimum for assigned articles. Pays $300-600 for unsolicited articles.** Sometimes pays expenses of writers on assignment.

Photos State availability Identification of subjects required. Reviews contact sheets. Negotiates payment individually Buys one time rights.

Columns/Departments Energy Use and Financial Planning, both 750 words. 6 Query with published clips. **Pays $100-300.**

Fiction Needs historical, humorous, slice-of-life vignettes, western. **Buys 1 mss/year.** Query with published clips. Length: 1,000-2,500 words. **Pays $100-400.**

Tips Deal with what's real: real data, real people, real experiences, real history, etc.

OHIO

$ $ N AKRON LIFE & LEISURE

The Magazine of Greater Akron, Baker Media Group, 90 S. Maple St., Akron OH 44302. Fax: (330)253-5868. E-mail: klindsey@bakermediagroup.com. Website: www.akronlifeandleisure.com. **10% freelance written**. Monthly magazine Regional magazine covering Summit, Stark, Portage and Medina counties. Estab. 2002. Circ. 15,000. Byline given. Pays on publication. Offers 50% kill fee. Publishes ms an average of 4-6 months after acceptance. Buys all rights. Editorial lead time 2+ months. Submit seasonal material 6 months in advance. Accepts queries by mail, e-mail, fax. Sample copy free. Guidelines free.

Nonfiction Needs essays, general interest, historical, how-to, humor, interview, photo feature, travel. Query with published clips. Length: 300-2,000 words. **Pays $0.10 max/word for assigned and unsolicited articles.**

Photos Contact: Kathy Moorehouse, Creative Director. State availability Captions, identification of subjects, model releases required. Reviews GIF/JPEG files. Negotiates payment individually Buys all rights.

Tips "It's best to submit a detailed query along with samples of previously published works. Include why you think the story is of interest to our readers, and be sure to have a fresh approach."

$ BEND OF THE RIVER MAGAZINE

P.O. Box 859, Maumee OH 43537. (419)893-0022. **98% freelance written. This magazine reports that it is eager to work with all writers. "We buy material that we like whether it is by an experienced writer or not."**. Monthly magazine for readers interested in northwestern Ohio history and nostalgia. Estab. 1972. Circ. 6,500. Byline given. Pays on publication. No kill fee. Publishes ms an average of 1 month after acceptance. Buys one-time rights. Submit seasonal material 2 months in advance. Responds in 1 week to queries. Sample copy for $1.25.

Nonfiction "We are looking for Toledo area articles about famous people and events of Ohio, Michigan and Indiana." Needs historical. **Buys 75 unsolicited mss/year.** Send complete ms. 1,500 words **Pays $50 on average.**

Tips "Our stockpile is low. Send us something!"

$ $ $ CINCINNATI MAGAZINE

Emmis Publishing Corp., 441 Vine St., Suite 200, Cincinnati OH 45202-2039. (513)421-4300. Fax: (513)562-2746. Website: www.cincinnatimagazine.com. Monthly magazine emphasizing Cincinnati living. Circ. 38,000. Byline given. Pays on publication. No kill fee. Buys all periodical rights. Accepts queries by mail, e-mail. Send SASE for writer's guidelines; view content on magazine Web site."

Nonfiction Articles on personalities, business, sports, lifestyle relating to Cincinnati and Northern Kentucky. **Buys 12 mss/year.** Query. Length: 2,500-3,500 words. **Pays $500-1,000.**

Columns/Departments Topics are Cincinnati media, arts and entertainment, people, politics, sports, business, regional. Length: 1,000-1,500 words. 10-15 Query. **Pays $200-400.**

Tips "It's most helpful on us if you query in writing, with clips. All articles have a local focus. No generics, please. Also: No movie, book, theater reviews, poetry, or fiction. For special advertising sections, query special sections editor Marnie Hayutin; for Cincinnati Wedding, query custom publishing editor Steve Smith."

$ $ $ CLEVELAND MAGAZINE

City Magazines, Inc., 1422 Euclid Ave., Suite 730, Cleveland OH 44115. (216)771-2833. Fax: (216)781-6318. E-mail: gleydura@clevelandmagazine.com. Website: www.clevelandmagazine.com. **60% freelance written. Mostly by assignment**. Monthly magazine with a strong Cleveland/Northeast Ohio angle. Estab. 1972. Circ. 50,000. Byline given. Pays on publication. No kill fee. Publishes ms an average of 3 months after acceptance. Buys first rights, buys second serial (reprint) rights, buys electronic rights. Editorial lead time 6 months. Submit seasonal material 8 months in advance. Accepts queries by mail, e-mail, fax. Accepts simultaneous submissions. Responds in 2 months to queries.

Nonfiction Needs general interest, historical, humor, interview, travel, home and garden. Query with published clips. Length: 800-4,000 words. **Pays $250-1,200.**

Columns/Departments My Town (Cleveland first-person stories), 1,100-1,500 words. Query with published clips. **Pays $300**

$ $ $ COLUMBUS MONTHLY

P.O. Box 29913, Columbus OH 43229-7513. (614)888-4567. Fax: (614)848-3838. **40-60% freelance written. Prefers to work with published/established writers.** Monthly magazine emphasizing subjects specifically related to Columbus and Central Ohio. Circ. 35,000. Byline given. Pays on publication. No kill fee. Publishes ms an average of 2 months after acceptance. Buys all rights. Responds in 1 month to queries. Sample copy for $6.50.

Nonfiction "We like query letters that are well written, indicate the author has some familiarity with *Columbus Monthly,* give us enough detail to make a decision and include at least a basic résumé of the writer and clips." **Buys 2-3 unsolicited mss/year.** Query. Length: 250-4,000 words. **Pays $85-900.** Sometimes pays expenses of writers on assignment.

Tips "It makes sense to start small—something for our City Journal section, perhaps. Stories for that section run between 250-500 words."

HYDE PARK LIVING

Community Publications, Inc., 179 Fairfield Ave., Bellevue KY 41073. (859)291-1412. Fax: (859)291-1417. E-mail: hydepark@livingmagazines.com. Website: www.livingmagazines.com. Monthly magazine covering Hyde Park community. Estab. 1983. Circ. 6,800. Byline given. Pays on publication. Buys all rights. Editorial lead time 2 months. Submit seasonal material 3 months in advance. Accepts queries by mail, e-mail, fax. Guidelines by email.

Nonfiction Needs essays, general interest, historical, humor, inspirational, interview, new product, personal experience, photo feature feature, travel. "Does not want anything unrelated to Hyde Park, Ohio." Query.

Photos State availability Captions, identification of subjects, model releases required. Reviews contact sheets, negatives, transparencies, prints, GIF/JPEG files. Negotiates payment individually. Buys all rights.

Columns/Departments Financial; Artistic (reviews, etc.); Historic; Food. Query.

Poetry Needs free verse, light verse, traditional. Please query.
Fillers Please query. Needs anecdotes, short humor.

INDIAN HILL LIVING

Community Publications, Inc., 179 Fairfield Ave., Bellevue KY 41074. (859)291-1412. Fax: (859)291-1417. E-mail: indianhill@livingmagazines.com. Website: www.livingmagazines.com. Monthly magazine covering Indian Hill community. Estab. 1983. Circ. 3,000. Byline given. Pays on publication. Buys all rights. Editorial lead time 2 months. Submit seasonal material 3 months in advance. Accepts queries by mail, e-mail, fax. Guidelines by email.
Nonfiction Needs book excerpts, essays, expose, general interest, historical, humor, inspirational, interview, new product, personal experience, photo feature, travel. Does not want anything unrelated to Indian Hill, Ohio. Query.
Photos State availability Captions, identification of subjects, model releases required. Reviews contact sheets, negatives, transparencies, prints, GIF/JPEG files. Negotiates payment individually. Buys all rights.
Columns/Departments Financial; Artistic (reviews, etc.); Historic; Food. Query.
Fiction Needs adventure, historical, humorous, mainstream, slice-of-life vignettes. Query.
Poetry Needs free verse, light verse, traditional. Please query.
Fillers Please query. Needs anecdotes, short humor.

$ $ $ OHIO MAGAZINE

Great Lakes Publishing Co., 1422 Euclid Ave., Suite 730, Cleveland OH 44115. (216)771-2833. E-mail: editorial@ohiomagazine.com. Website: www.ohiomagazine.com. **50% freelance written**. Monthly magazine emphasizing Ohio-based travel, news and feature material that highlights what's special and unique about the state. Estab. 1978. Circ. 80,000. Byline given. Pays on publication. No kill fee. Publishes ms an average of 6 months after acceptance. Buys first North American serial rights, buys one-time rights, buys second serial (reprint) rights, buys all rights. First serial rights Submit seasonal material 6 months in advance. Accepts queries by mail, e-mail, fax. Responds in 3 months to queries. Responds in 3 months to mss. Sample copy for $3.95 and 9 X 12 SAE or online. Guidelines available online.
Nonfiction Length: 1,000-3,000 words. **Pays $300-1,200.** Sometimes pays expenses of writers on assignment.
Reprints Send tearsheet or photocopy and information about when and where the material previously appeared. Pays 50% of amount paid for an original article
Photos Contact: Rob McGarr, art director. Rate negotiable
Columns/Departments minimum 5 unsolicited **Pays $100-600.**
Tips Freelancers should send all queries in writing (either by mail or e-mail), not by telephone. Successful queries demonstrate an intimate knowledge of the publication. We are looking to increase our circle of writers who can write about the state in an informative and upbeat style. Strong reporting skills are highly valued.

$ $ OVER THE BACK FENCE

Southern Ohio's Own Magazine, Long Point Media, P.O. Box 756, Chillicothe OH 45601. (800)718-5727. Fax: (330)220-3083. E-mail: sarahw@longpointmedia.com. Website: www.backfencemagazine.com. Bimonthly magazine. "We are a regional magazine serving Southern Ohio. *Over The Back Fence* has a wholesome, neighborly style. It appeals to readers from young adults to seniors, showcasing art and travel opportunities in the area." Estab. 1994. Circ. 15,000. Byline given. Pays on publication. No kill fee. Publishes ms an average of 1 year after acceptance. Buys one-time North American serial rights. Makes work-for-hire assignments. Editorial lead time 1 year. Submit seasonal material 1 year in advance. Accepts queries by mail. Accepts simultaneous submissions. Responds in 3 months to queries. Sample copy for $4 or on website. Guidelines available online.
Nonfiction Needs general interest, historical, humor, inspirational, interview, personal experience, photo feature, travel. **Buys 9-12 mss/year.** Send complete ms. Length: 750-1,000 words. **Pays 10¢/word minimum, negotiable depending on experience.**
Reprints Send photocopy of article or short story and typed ms with rights for sale ted, and information about when and where the material previously appeared. Payment negotiable
Photos If sending photos as part of a text/photo package, please request our photo guidelines and submit samples. Captions, identification of subjects, model releases required. $25-100/photo Buys one time rights.
Columns/Departments The Arts, 750-1,000 words; History (relevant to a designated county), 750-1,000 words; 600-850 words; Profiles From Our Past, 300-600 words; Sport & Hobby, 750-1,000 words; Our Neighbors (i.e., people helping others), 750-1,000 words. All must be relevant to Southern Ohio. 24 Query with or without published clips or send complete ms. **Pays 10¢/word minimum, negotiable depending on experience.**
Fiction Needs humorous. **Buys 4 mss/year.** Query with published clips. Length: 600-800 words. **Pays 10¢/word minimum, negotiable depending on experience.**
Tips "Our approach can be equated to a friendly and informative conversation with a neighbor about interesting people, places, and events in Southern Ohio (counties: Adams, Athens, Brown, Clark, Clermont, Clinton, Coshocton, Fayette, Fairfield, Franklin, Gallia, Greene, Guernsey, Highland, Hocking, Holmes, Jackson, Law-

rence, Licking, Madison, Meigs, Miami, Morgan, Muskingum, Noble, Perry, Pickaway, Pike, Ross, Scioto, Vinton, Warren, Washington, and Wayne)."

SYCAMORE LIVING

Community Publications, Inc., 179 Fairfield Ave., Bellevue KY 41073. (859)291-1412. Fax: (859)291-1417. E-mail: sycamore@livingmagazines.com. Website: www.livingmagazines.com. Monthly magazine covering Sycamore community. Estab. 1983. Circ. 6,600. Byline given. Pays on publication. Buys all rights. Editorial lead time 2 months. Submit seasonal material 3 months in advance. Accepts queries by mail, e-mail, fax. Guidelines by email.

Nonfiction Needs book excerpts, essays, expose, general interest, historical, humor, inspirational, interview, new product, personal experience, photo feature, travel. Does not want anything unrelated to Sycamore, Ohio. Query.

Photos State availability Captions, identification of subjects, model releases required. Reviews contact sheets, negatives, transparencies, prints, GIF/JPEG files. Negotiates payment individually. Buys all rights.

Columns/Departments Financial; Artistic (reviews, etc.); Historic; Food. Query.

Fiction Needs adventure, historical, humorous, mainstream, slice-of-life vignettes. Query.

Poetry Needs free verse, light verse, traditional. Please query.

Fillers Please query. Needs anecdotes, short humor.

WYOMING LIVING

Community Publications, Inc., 179 Fairfield Ave., Bellevue KY 41073. (859)291-1412. Fax: (859)291-1417. E-mail: wyoming@livingmagazines.com. Website: www.livingmagazines.com. Monthly magazine covering Wyoming community. Estab. 1983. Circ. 3,400. Byline given. Pays on publication. Buys all rights. Editorial lead time 2 months. Submit seasonal material 3 months in advance. Accepts queries by mail, e-mail, fax. Guidelines by email.

Nonfiction Needs book excerpts, essays, expose, general interest, historical, humor, inspirational, interview, new product, personal experience, photo feature, travel. Does not want anything unrelated to Wyoming, Ohio. Query.

Photos State availability Captions, identification of subjects, model releases required. Reviews contact sheets, negatives, transparencies, prints, GIF/JPEG files. Negotiates payment individually. Buys all rights.

Columns/Departments Financial; Artistic (reviews, etc.); Historic; Food. Query.

Fiction Needs adventure, historical, humorous, mainstream, slice-of-life vignettes. Query.

Poetry Needs free verse, light verse, traditional. Please query.

Fillers Please query. Needs anecdotes, short humor.

OKLAHOMA

$ $ N INTERMISSION

Langdon Publishing, 110 E. 2nd St., Tulsa OK 74103-3212. (918)596-2368. Fax: (918)596-7144. E-mail: nhermann@ci.tulsa.ok.us. Website: www.tulsapac.com. **Contact:** Nancy Hermann. **30% freelance written.** Monthly magazine covering entertainment. "We feature profiles of entertainers appearing at our center, Q&As, stories on the events and entertainers slated for the Tulsa PAC." Byline given. Pays on publication. Offers 50% kill fee. Publishes ms an average of 1 month after acceptance. Buys one-time rights. Editorial lead time 2 months. Submit seasonal material 2 months in advance. Accepts queries by mail, e-mail. Accepts simultaneous submissions. Responds in 2 weeks to queries. Sample copy available online. Guidelines by email.

Nonfiction Needs general interest, interview. Does not want personal experience. **Buys 35 mss/year.** Query with published clips. Length: 600-1,400 words. **Pays $100-200.**

Columns/Departments Q&A (personalities and artists tied into the events at the Tulsa PAC), 1,100 words. 12 Query with published clips. **Pays $100-150.**

Tips "Look ahead at our upcoming events, find an interesting slant on an event. Interview someone who would be of general interest."

$ $ OKLAHOMA TODAY

P.O. Box 1468, Oklahoma City OK 73101. (405)521-2496. Fax: (405)522-4588. E-mail: mccune@oklahomatoday.com. Website: www.oklahomatoday.com. **80% freelance written. Works with approximately 25 new/unpublished writers each year.** Bimonthly magazine covering people, places, and things Oklahoman. We are interested in showing off the best Oklahoma has to offer; we're pretty serious about our travel slant but regularly run history, nature, and personality profiles. Estab. 1956. Circ. 45,000. Byline given. Pays on publication. No kill fee. Publishes ms an average of 6 months after acceptance. Buys first worldwide serial rights. Submit seasonal material 1 year in advance. Accepts queries by mail, e-mail. Responds in 4 months to queries. Sample copy for $3.95 and 9x12 SASE or online. Guidelines available online.

Nonfiction Needs book excerpts, on Oklahoma topics, historical, Oklahoma only, interview, Oklahomans

only, photo feature, in Oklahoma, travel, in Oklahoma. No phone queries. **Buys 20-40 mss/year.** Query with published clips. Length: 250-3,000 words. **Pays $25-750.**
Photos We are especially interested in developing contacts with photographers who live in Oklahoma or have shot here. Send samples. Photo guidelines for SASE. Captions, identification of subjects required. Reviews 4x5, 2¼:x2¼, and 35mm color transparencies, high-quality transparencies, slides, and b&w prints. Pays $50-750 for color Buys one-time rights to use photos for promotional purposes.
Fiction Needs novel concepts, occasionally short fiction.
Tips The best way to become a regular contributor to *Oklahoma Today* is to query us with 1 or more story ideas, each developed to give us an idea of your proposed slant. We're looking for lively, concise, well-researched and reported stories, stories that don't need to be heavily edited and are not newspaper style. We have a 3-person full-time editorial staff, and freelancers who can write and have done their homework get called again and again.

OREGON

$ $ OREGON COAST

4969 Highway 101 N. #2, Florence OR 97439. Website: www.northwestmagazines.com. **65% freelance written**. Bimonthly magazine covering the Oregon Coast. Estab. 1982. Circ. 50,000. Byline given. Pays after publication. Offers 33% (on assigned stories only, not on stories accepted on spec) kill fee. Publishes ms an average of up to 1 year after acceptance. Buys first North American serial rights. Submit seasonal material 6 months in advance. Accepts queries by mail, e-mail. Responds in 3 months to queries. Sample copy for $4.50. Guidelines available on Web site.

- This company also publishes *Northwest Travel*.

Nonfiction "A true regional with general interest, historical/nostalgic, humor, interview/profile, personal experience, photo feature, travel, and nature as pertains to Oregon Coast." **Buys 55 mss/year.** Query with published clips. Length: 500-1,500 words. **Pays $75-350, plus 2 contributor copies.**
Reprints Send tearsheet or photocopy and information about when and where the material previously appeared. Pays an average of 60% of the amount paid for an original article.
Photos Photo submissions with no ms or stand alone or cover photos. Send photos Captions, identification of subjects, True required. Slides or high-resolution digital. Buys one time rights.
Tips "Slant article for readers who do not live at the Oregon Coast. At least 1 historical article is used in each issue. Manuscript/photo packages are preferred over manuscripts with no photos. List photo credits and captions for each photo. Check all facts, proper names, and numbers carefully in photo/manuscript packages. Must pertain to Oregon Coast somehow.

PENNSYLVANIA

$ $ BERKS COUNTY LIVING

201 Washington St., Suite 525, Reading PA 19601. (610)898-1929. Fax: (610)898-1933. E-mail: fscoboria@berkscountyliving.com. Website: www.berkscountyliving.com. **90% freelance written**. Bimonthly magazine covering topics of interest to people living in Berks County, Pennsylvania. Estab. 2000. Circ. 36,000. Byline given. Pays on publication. Offers 25% kill fee. Publishes ms an average of 4 months after acceptance. Buys first North American serial rights. Editorial lead time 3 months. Submit seasonal material 4 months in advance. Accepts queries by mail, e-mail. Accepts previously published material. Accepts simultaneous submissions. Responds in 1 week to queries. Responds in 1 month to mss. Sample copy for sae with 9x12 envelope and 2 First-Class stamps. Guidelines available online.
Nonfiction Articles must be associated with Berks County, Pennsylvania. Needs expose, general interest, historical, how-to, humor, inspirational, interview, new product, photo feature, travel, food, health. **Buys 25 mss/year.** Query. Length: 750-2,000 words. **Pays $150-400.** Sometimes pays expenses of writers on assignment.
Photos State availability Captions, identification of subjects, model releases required. Reviews 35mm or greater transparencies, any size prints. Negotiates payment individually Buys one time rights.

$ $ LEHIGH VALLEY LIVING

The Morning Call, 101 N. 6th St., Allentown PA 18101. (610)820-6773. Fax: (610)820-6663. E-mail: lori.mcferran@mcall.com. Website: www.mcall.com. **100% freelance written**. Monthly magazine covering regional Lehigh Valley lifestyle. "*Lehigh Valley Living* aims to provide information and ideas that reflect real life in our community and will entice and motivate readers to want to learn more. Written and edited for those who are curious about what's new or interesting." Estab. 2005. Circ. 33,000. Byline given. Pays on acceptance. Offers 100% kill fee. Publishes ms an average of 3 months after acceptance. Buys all rights. Editorial lead time 4 months. Accepts queries by mail, e-mail. Accepts simultaneous submissions. Sample copy available online.
Nonfiction Needs general interest, historical, interview, travel, health, entertainment. "We do a bridal focus in

May and October." Does not want anything that does not have a distinct Lehigh Valley focus. **Buys 36-40 mss/year.** Query with published clips. Length: 500-650 words. **Pays $300.**

Photos State availability Identification of subjects, model releases required. Reviews contact sheets, JPEG files. Offers $50/photo. Buys all rights.

Columns/Departments "We're expanding our departments to include topic specialists willing to contribute a column on their area of expertise in exchange for byline. No fee paid."

Tips "Be familiar with the Allentown, Bethlehem, Easton areas. Stories about events and happenings in the region, profiles of people doing unusual or interesting things, and story leads on distinctive homes in the area will get the editor's attention."

$ $ MAIN LINE TODAY

Today Media, Inc., 4699 West Chester Pike, Newtown Square PA 19073. (610)848-6037. Fax: (610)325-5215. Website: www.mainlinetoday.com. **60% freelance written**. Monthly magazine serving Philadelphia's main line and western suburbs. Estab. 1996. Circ. 20,000. Byline given. Pays on publication. Offers 25% kill fee. Publishes ms an average of 3 months after acceptance. Buys first North American serial rights. Editorial lead time 5 months. Submit seasonal material 5 months in advance. Accepts queries by fax. Accepts simultaneous submissions. Responds in 2 weeks to queries. Responds in 1 month to mss. Sample copy free. Guidelines free.

Nonfiction Needs book excerpts, historical, how-to, humor, interview, opinion, photo feature, travel. Health & Wellness Guide (September and March). Query with published clips. Length: 400-3,000 words. **Pays $125-650.** Sometimes pays expenses of writers on assignment.

Photos State availability Identification of subjects, model releases required. Reviews GIF/JPEG files. Negotiates payment individually. Buys one time rights.

Columns/Departments Profile (local personality); Neighborhood (local people/issues); End of the Line (essay/humor); Living Well (health/wellness), all 1,600 words. 50 Query with published clips. **Pays $125-350.**

$ $ MILFORD MAGAZINE

Navigating the Delware River Highlands, Pike Media Partners, P.O. Box 486, 201 W. Harford St., Milford PA 18337. E-mail: editor@milfordmagazine.com. Website: www.milfordmagazine.com. **100% freelance written.** Monthly magazine covering community, culture & nature specific to the Upper Delaware Highlands Regions. We seek to contribute to the best definition of community that is defined not just by demographic charactertistics but by shared values. We value quality of life, diversity,protection of the environemnt, cultivation of the arts, & smart growth. We welcome those new to the area. Mostly, we value integrity & service to those we share this planet with, this continent, & especially those with whom we share the majesty & magnificence of the Delaware River. Estab. 2001. Circ. 20,000. Byline given. Pays on publication. Offers 10% kill fee. Publishes ms an average of 21 months after acceptance. Buys one-time rights. Editorial lead time 2 months. Submit seasonal material 6 months in advance. Accepts queries by mail, e-mail, fax. Accepts previously published material. Accepts simultaneous submissions. Responds in 2 weeks to queries. No mss. please. Sample copy available online. Guidelines for #10 SASE.

- Ours is a free publication.

Nonfiction Needs essays, general interest, historical, how-to, interview, opinion, personal experience, photo feature, travel, Nature. No fiction. No articles unrelated to our geographic area. **Buys 36 mss/yr. mss/year.** Query. Length: 750-2,000 words. **Pays $100-400 for assigned articles. Pays $100-400 for unsolicited articles.**

Photos Contact: James Sheehan, art director. State availability Captions, model releases required. Reviews GIF/JPEG files. Offers no additional payment for photos accepted with ms. Offers $25-175 per photo.

Columns/Departments Look Back (Nostalgia-History related to the area-must include photos(s)), 750 words. 10 mss/yr. Query with or without published clips. **Pay $150**

Tips Be sure you write to our target audience & area. The magazine is a free publication for residents & visitors to the Upper Delaware Highlands Region (NY, NJ & PA).

$ $ PENNSYLVANIA

Pennsylvania Magazine Co., P.O. Box 755, Camp Hill PA 17001-0755. (717)697-4660. E-mail: pamag@aol.com. Website: www.pa-mag.com. **90% freelance written**. Bimonthly magazine covering people, places, events, and history in Pennsylvania. Estab. 1981. Circ. 33,000. Byline given. Pays on acceptance except for articles (by authors unknown to us) sent on speculation. Offers kill fee. 25% kill fee for assigned articles. Publishes ms an average of 9 months after acceptance. Buys first North American serial rights, buys one-time rights. Submit seasonal material 9 months in advance. Accepts queries by mail, e-mail. Responds in 4-6 weeks to queries. Sample copy free. Guidelines for #10 SASE or by e-mail.

Nonfiction Features include general interest, historical, photo feature, vacations and travel, people/family success stories—all dealing with or related to Pennsylvania. Send photocopies of possible illustrations with query or ms. Include SASE. Nothing on Amish topics, hunting, or skiing. **Buys 75-120 mss/year.** Query. Length: 750-2,500 words. **Pays 15¢/word.**

Reprints Send photocopy with rights for sale noted and information about when and where the material previously appeared. Pays 5¢/word

Photos No original slides or transparencies. Photography Essay (highlights annual photo essay contest entries and showcase individual photographers). Captions, True required. Reviews 35mm 2 ¼x2 ¼ color transparencies, 5x7 to 8x10 color prints, digital photos (send printouts and CD). Pays $25-35 for inside photos; $150 for covers Buys one time rights.

Columns/Departments Round Up (short items about people, unusual events, museums, historical topics/ events, family and individually owned consumer-related businesses), 250-1,300 words; Town and Country (items about people or events illustrated with commissioned art), 500 words. Include SASE. Query. **Pays 15¢/ word.**

Tips Our publication depends upon freelance work—send queries.

$ $ PENNSYLVANIA HERITAGE

Pennsylvania Historical and Museum Commission and the Pennsylvania Heritage Society, Commonwealth Keystone Bldg., Plaza Level, 400 North St., Harrisburg PA 17120-0053. (717)787-7522. Fax: (717)787-8312. E-mail: miomalley@state.pa.us. Website: www.paheritage.org. **75% freelance written. Prefers to work with published/established writers.** Quarterly magazine. *Pennsylvania Heritage* introduces readers to Pennsylvania's rich culture and historic legacy; educates and sensitizes them to the value of preserving that heritage; and entertains and involves them in such a way as to ensure that Pennsylvania's past has a future. The magazine is intended for intelligent lay readers. Estab. 1974. Circ. 10,000. Byline given. Pays on publication. Publishes ms an average of 1 year after acceptance. Buys all print and electronic rights for the web. Accepts queries by mail, e-mail. Responds in 10 weeks to queries. Responds in 8 months to mss Sample copy for $5 and 9x12 SAE or online Guidelines for #10 SASE or online

- *Pennsylvania Heritage* is now considering freelance submissions that are shorter in length (2,000-3,000 words); pictorial/photographic essays; biographies of famous (and not-so-famous) Pennsylvanians; and interviews with individuals who have helped shape, make, and preserve the Keystone State's history and heritage.

Nonfiction "Our format requires feature-length articles. Manuscripts with illustrations are especially sought for publication. We are now looking for shorter (2,000 words) manuscripts that are heavily illustrated with publication-quality photographs or artwork. We are eager to work with experienced travel writers for destination pieces on historical sites and museums that make up `The Pennsylvania Trail of History.' Art, science, biographies, industry, business, politics, transportation, military, historic preservation, archaeology, photography, etc." No articles which do not relate to Pennsylvania history or culture. **Buys 20-24 mss/year.** Prefers to see mss with suggested illustrations. Length: 2,000-3,500 words. **Pays $100-500.**

Photos State availability of or send photos Captions, identification of subjects required. $25-200 for transparencies; $5-75 for b&w photos Buys one time rights.

Tips "We are looking for well-written, interesting material that pertains to any aspect of Pennsylvania history or culture. Potential contributors should realize that, although our articles are popularly styled, they are not light, puffy, or breezy; in fact they demand strident documentation and substantiation (sans footnotes). The most frequent mistake made by writers in completing articles for us is making them either too scholarly or too sentimental or nostalgic. We want material which educates, but also entertains. Authors should make history readable and enjoyable. Our goal is to make the Keystone State's history come to life in a meaningful, memorable way."

$ $ PHILADELPHIA STYLE

Philadelphia's Premier Magazine for Lifestyle & Fashion, Philadelphia Style Magazine, LLC, 141 League St., Philadelphia PA 19147. (215)468-6670. Fax: (215)468-6530. E-mail: peter.proko@nichemediallc.com. Website: www.phillystylemag.com. **50% freelance written.** "Bimonthly magazine covering upscale living in the Philadelphia region. Topics include: celebrity interviews, fashion (men's and women's), food, home and design, real estate, dining, beauty, travel, arts and entertainment, and more. Our magazine is a positive look at the best ways to live in the Philadelphia region. Submitted articles should speak to an upscale, educated audience of professionals that live in the Delaware Valley." Estab. 1999. Circ. 60,000. Byline given. Pays on publication. Offers 25% kill fee. Publishes ms an average of 3 months after acceptance. Buys first rights. Editorial lead time 2-4 months. Submit seasonal material 6 months in advance. Accepts queries by mail, e-mail, fax.

Nonfiction Needs general interest, interview, travel, region-specific articles. "We are not looking for articles that do not have a regional spin." **Buys 100+ mss/year.** Send complete ms. Length: 300-2,500 words. **Pays $50-500.**

Columns/Departments Declarations (celebrity interviews and celebrity contributors); Currents (fashion news); Manor (home and design news); Liberties (beauty and travel news); Dish (dining news); Life in the City (fresh, quirky, regional reporting on books, real estate, art, retail, dining, events, and little-known stories/facts about the region), 100-500 words; Vanguard (people on the forefront of Philadelphia's arts, media, fashion, business, and social scene), 500-700 words; In the Neighborhood (reader-friendly reporting on up-and-coming areas of the region including dining, shopping, attractions, and recreation), 2,000-2,500 words. Query with published

clips or send complete ms. **Pays $50-500.**
Tips "Mail queries with clips or manuscripts. Articles should speak to a stylish, educated audience."

$ $ $ $ PITTSBURGH MAGAZINE

WQED Pittsburgh, 4802 Fifth Ave., Pittsburgh PA 15213. (412)622-1360. E-mail: lriley@wged.org. Website: www.pittsburghmag.com. **70% freelance written**. Monthly magazine. *Pittsburgh* presents issues, analyzes problems, and strives to encourage a better understanding of the community. Our region is Western Pennsylvania, Eastern Ohio, Northern West Virginia, and Western Maryland. Estab. 1970. Circ. 75,000. Byline given. Pays on publication. Offers kill fee. Offers kill fee. Publishes ms an average of 2 months after acceptance. Buys first North American serial rights, buys second serial (reprint) rights. Submit seasonal material 6 months in advance. Accepts queries by mail. Responds in 2 months to queries. Sample copy for $2 (old back issues). Writer's guidelines online or via SASE

- The editor reports a need for more hard news and stories targeting readers in their 30s and 40s, especially those with young families. Prefers to work with published/established writers. The monthly magazine is purchased on newsstands and by subscription, and is given to those who contribute $40 or more/year to public TV in western Pennsylvania.

Nonfiction Without exception—whether the topic is business, travel, the arts, or lifestyle—each story is clearly oriented to Pittsburghers of today and to the greater Pittsburgh region of today. Must have greater Pittsburgh angle. No fax, phone, or e-mail queries. No complete mss. Needs expose, lifestyle, sports, informational, service, business, medical, profile. We have minimal interest in historical articles and we do not publish fiction, poetry, advocacy, or personal reminiscence pieces. Query in writing with outline and clips. Length: 1,200-4,000 words. **Pays $300-1,500+.**
Photos Query. Model releases required. Pays prenegotiated expenses of writer on assignment
Columns/Departments The Front (short, front-of-the-book items). Length: 300 words maximum. **Pays $50-150.**
Tips Best bet to break in is through hard news with a region-wide impact or service pieces or profiles with a regional interest. The point is that we want more stories that reflect our region, not just a tiny part. And we *never* consider any story without a strong regional focus. We do not respond to fax and e-mail queries.

$ SUSQUEHANNA LIFE

Central Pennsylvania's Lifestyle Magazine, ELS & Associates, 637 Market St., Lewisburg PA 17837. Fax: (570)524-7796. E-mail: info@susquehannalife.com. Website: www.susquehannalife.com. **80% freelance written**. Quarterly magazine covering Central Pennsylvania lifestyle. Estab. 1993. Circ. 45,000. Byline given. Pays on publication. Offers 50% kill fee. Publishes ms an average of 6-9 months after acceptance. Buys first North American serial rights, buys electronic rights. Editorial lead time 3-6 months. Submit seasonal material 4-6 months in advance. Accepts queries by e-mail. Responds in 4-6 weeks to queries. Responds in 1-3 months to mss. Sample copy for $4.95, plus 5 first-class stamps. Guidelines for #10 SASE.
Nonfiction Needs book excerpts, general interest, historical, how-to, inspirational, related to the region, interview, photo feature, travel. Does not want fiction. **Buys 30-40 mss/year.** Query or send complete ms. Length: 800-1,200 words. **Pays $75-125.** Sometimes pays expenses of writers on assignment.
Photos Send photos Captions, identification of subjects, model releases required. Reviews contact sheets, prints, GIF/JPEG files. Offers $20-25/photo. Buys one time rights.
Poetry Must have a Central PA angle.
Tips When you query, do not address letter to 'Dear Sir'—address the letter to the name of the publisher/editor. Demonstrate your ability to write. You need to be familiar with the type of articles we use and the particular flavor of the region. Only accepts submissions with a Central PA angle.

SOUTH CAROLINA

$ $ HILTON HEAD MONTHLY

P.O. Box 5926, Hilton Head Island SC 29938. Fax: (843)842-5743. E-mail: bkaufman@monthlymag.com. Website: www.hiltonheadmonthly.com. **75% freelance written**. Monthly magazine covering the business, people, and lifestyle of Hilton Head, South Carolina. Our mission is to provide fresh, upbeat reading about the residents, lifestyle and community affairs of Hilton Head Island, an upscale, intensely pro-active resort community on the East Coast. We are not even remotely 'trendy,' but we like to see how national trends/issues play out on a local level. Especially interested in: home design and maintenance, entrepreneurship, health issues, nature, area history, golf/tennis/boating, volunteerism. Circ. 28,000. Byline given. Pays on publication. Offers 50% kill fee. Publishes ms an average of 6 months after acceptance. Buys first North American serial rights. Makes work-for-hire assignments. Editorial lead time 3 months. Submit seasonal material 4 months in advance. Accepts queries by mail, e-mail, fax. Accepts previously published material. Accepts simultaneous submissions. Responds in 1 week to queries. Responds in 4 months to mss. Sample copy for $3.
Nonfiction Needs general interest, historical, history only, how-to, home related, humor, interview, Hilton Head

residents only, opinion, general humor or Hilton Head Island community affairs, personal experience, travel. No exposÃ^ interviews with people who are not Hilton Head residents; profiles of people, events, or businesses in Beaufort, South Carolina; Savannah, Georgia; Charleston; or other surrounding cities, unless it's within a travel piece. **Buys 225-250 mss/year.** Query with published clips.

Photos State availability Reviews contact sheets, prints, slides; any size. Negotiates payment individually Buys one time rights.

Columns/Departments News; Business; Lifestyles (hobbies, health, sports, etc.); Home; Around Town (local events, charities and personalities); People (profiles, weddings, etc.). Query with synopsis. **Pays 15¢/word.**

Tips Give us concise, bullet-style descriptions of what the article covers (in the query letter); choose upbeat, pro-active topics; delight us with your fresh (not trendy) description and word choice.

$ SANDLAPPER

The Magazine of South Carolina, The Sandlapper Society, Inc., P.O. Box 1108, Lexington SC 29071-1108. (803)359-9941. Fax: (803)359-0629. E-mail: aida@sandlapper.org. Website: www.sandlapper.org. **60% freelance written.** Quarterly magazine focusing on the positive aspects of South Carolina. "*Sandlapper* is intended to be read at those times when people want to relax with an attractive, high-quality magazine that entertains and informs them about their state." Estab. 1989. Circ. 18,000 with a readership of 60,000. Byline given. Pays during the dateline period. No kill fee. Publishes ms an average of 1 year after acceptance. Buys first North American serial rights and the right to reprint. Submit seasonal material 6 months in advance. Accepts queries by mail, e-mail, fax. Sample copy available online. Guidelines for #10 SASE.

Nonfiction Feature articles and photo essays about South Carolina's interesting people, places, cuisine, history and culture, things to do. Needs essays, general interest, humor, interview, photo feature. Query with clips and SASE. Length: 500-2,500 words. **Pays $100/published page.** Sometimes pays expenses of writers on assignment.

Photos *Sandlapper* buys b&w prints and art. Photographers should submit working cutlines for each photograph. We accept prints and digital images. Pays $25-75, $100 for cover or centerspread photo

Tips "We're not interested in articles about topical issues, politics, crime, or commercial ventures. Avoid first-person nostalgia and remembrances of places that no longer exist. We look for top-quality literature. Humor is encouraged. Good taste is a standard. Unique angles are critical for acceptance. Dare to be bold, but not too bold."

TENNESSEE

$ $ AT HOME TENNESSEE

Pinpoint Publishing Group, 671 N. Ericson Rd., Suite 200, Cordova TN 38018. (901)684-4155. Fax: (901)684-4156. Website: www.athometn.com. **50% freelance written.** Monthly magazine. Estab. 2002. Circ. 37,000. Byline given. Pays on publication. Offers 50% kill fee. Makes work-for-hire assignments. Editorial lead time 2 months. Submit seasonal material 2-3 months in advance. Accepts queries by e-mail. Responds in 1-2 months to queries. Sample copy for $4.99. Guidelines free.

Nonfiction Needs general interest, how-to, interview, travel, landscaping, arts, design. Does not want opinion. Query with published clips. Length: 400-900 words. **Pays $50-200.**

Photos Contact: Contact Elizabeth Chapman, art director. Send photos Reviews GIF/JPEG files.

$ $ MEMPHIS

Contemporary Media, P.O. Box 1738, Memphis TN 38101. (901)521-9000. Fax: (901)521-0129. Website: www.memphismagazine.com. **30% freelance written. Works with a small number of new/unpublished writers.** Monthly magazine covering Memphis and the local region. Our mission is to provide Memphis with a colorful and informative look at the people, places, lifestyles and businesses that make the Bluff City unique. Estab. 1976. Circ. 24,000. No byline given. Pays on publication. Buys first North American serial rights. Submit seasonal material 3 months in advance. Accepts queries by mail, e-mail, fax.

Nonfiction Virtually all of our material has strong Memphis area connections. Needs essays, general interest, historical, interview, photo feature, travel, Interiors/exteriors, local issues and events. Restaurant Guide and City Guide. **Buys 20 mss/year.** Query with published clips. Length: 500-3,000 words. **Pays 10-30¢/word.** Sometimes pays expenses of writers on assignment.

Photos State availability Reviews contact sheets, transparencies. Buys one time rights.

Fiction One story published annually as part of contest. Open only to those within 150 miles of Memphis. See Web site for details.

$ $ MEMPHIS DOWNTOWNER MAGAZINE

Downtown Productions, Inc., 408 S. Front St., Suite 109, Memphis TN 38103. Fax: (901)525-7128. E-mail: editor@memphisdowntowner.com. Website: www.memphisdowntowner.com. **50% freelance written.** Monthly magazine covering features on positive aspects with a Memphis tie-in, especially to downtown. "We feature people, companies, nonprofits and other issues that the general Memphis public would find interesting, entertaining, and informative. All editorial focuses on the positives Memphis has. No negative commentary or personal judgements. Controversial subjects should be treated fairly and balanced without bias." Estab. 1991. Circ. 30,000. Byline given. Pays on 15th of month in which assignment is published. Offers 25% kill fee. Publishes ms an average of 2-6 months after acceptance. Buys all rights for 90 days, with re-licensing rights thereafter. Editorial lead time 3-6 months. Submit seasonal material 3-6 months in advance. Accepts queries by mail, e-mail. Responds in 2 weeks to queries. Sample copy free. Guidelines by email.

Nonfiction Needs general interest, historical, how-to, humor, interview, personal experience, photo feature. **Buys 40-50 mss/year.** Query with published clips. Length: 600-2,000 words. **Pays scales vary depending on scope of assignment, but typically runs 15¢/word.** Sometimes pays expenses of writers on assignment.

Photos State availability Identification of subjects required. Reviews GIF/JPEG files (300 dpi). Negotiates payment individually.

Columns/Departments So It Goes (G-rated humor), 600-800 words; Discovery 901 (Memphis one-of-a-kinds), 1,000-1,200 words. 6 Query with published clips. **Pays $100-150.**

Fillers Unusual, interesting, or how-to or what to look for appealing to a large, general audience. Needs facts.

Tips "Always pitch an actual story idea. E-mails that simply let us know you're a freelance writer mysteriously disappear from our inboxes. Actually read the magazine before you pitch. Get to know the regular columns and departments. In your pitch, explain where in the magazine you think your story idea would best fit. See Web site for magazine samples and past issues."

TEXAS

$ HILL COUNTRY SUN

T.D. Austin Lane, Inc., 100 Commons Rd., Suite 7, #319, Dripping Springs TX 78620. (512)847-5162. Fax: (512)847-5162. E-mail: melissa@hillcountrysun.com. Website: www.hillcountrysun.com. **75% freelance written.** Monthly tabloid covering traveling in the Central Texas Hill Country. We publish stories of interesting people, places and events in the Central Texas Hill Country. Estab. 1990. Circ. 40,000. Byline given. Pays on acceptance. No kill fee. Publishes ms an average of 2 months after acceptance. Buys one-time rights. Editorial lead time 1 month. Submit seasonal material 2 months in advance. Accepts queries by mail, e-mail. Responds in 1 week to queries. Responds in 1 month to mss. Sample copy free. Guidelines available online.

Nonfiction Needs interview, travel. No first person articles. **Buys 50 mss/year.** Query. Length: 600-800 words. **Pays $50-60.**

Photos State availability of or send photos Identification of subjects required. No additional payment for photos accepted with ms. Buys one time rights.

Tips Writers must be familiar with both the magazine's style and the Texas Hill Country.

$ $ $ HOUSTON PRESS

New Times, Inc., 1621 Milam, Suite 100, Houston TX 77002. (713)280-2400. Fax: (713)280-2444. E-mail: julia.youssefnia@houstonpress.com. Website: www.houstonpress.com. **40% freelance written.** Weekly tabloid covering news and arts stories of interest to a Houston audience. If the same story could run in Seattle, then it's not for us. Estab. 1989. Byline given. Pays on publication. No kill fee. Publishes ms an average of 2 weeks after acceptance. Buys first North American serial rights, buys website rights. Editorial lead time 2 months. Submit seasonal material 3 months in advance. Sample copy for $3.

Nonfiction Needs expose, general interest, interview, arts reviews. Query with published clips. Length: 300-4,500 words. **Pays $10-1,000.** Sometimes pays expenses of writers on assignment.

Photos State availability Identification of subjects required. Negotiates payment individually Buys all rights.

$ $ $ TEXAS HIGHWAYS

The Travel Magazine of Texas, Box 141009, Austin TX 78714-1009. (512)486-5858. Fax: (512)486-5879. Website: www.texashighways.com. **70% freelance written.** Monthly magazine encourages travel within the state and tells the Texas story to readers around the world. Estab. 1974. Circ. 250,000. Pays on acceptance. No kill fee. Publishes ms an average of 1 year after acceptance. Buys first North American serial rights, buys electronic rights. Accepts queries by mail. Responds in 2 months to queries. Guidelines available online.

Nonfiction Subjects should focus on things to do or places to see in Texas. Include historical, cultural, and geographical aspects if appropriate. Text should be meticulously researched. Include anecdotes, historical references, quotations and, where relevant, geologic, botanical, and zoological information. Query with description, published clips, additional background materials (charts, maps, etc.) and SASE. Length: 1,200-1,500 words. **Pays 40-50¢/word.**

Tips We like strong leads that draw in the reader immediately and clear, concise writing. Be specific and avoid superlatives. Avoid overused words. Don't forget the basics—who, what, where, when, why, and how.

$ $ $ $ TEXAS MONTHLY

Emmis Publishing LP, P.O. Box 1569, Austin TX 78767. (512)320-6900. Fax: (512)476-9007. Website: www.texasmonthly.com. **Contact:** Jake Silverstein, editor. **10% freelance written**. Monthly magazine covering Texas. Estab. 1973. Circ. 300,000. Byline given. Pays on acceptance. Publishes ms an average of 1-3 months after acceptance. Buys first North American serial rights, buys first rights, buys one-time rights, buys electronic rights. Editorial lead time 2 months. Submit seasonal material 3 months in advance. Accepts queries by mail, e-mail, fax. Responds in 2 months to queries. Responds in 2 months to mss. Sample copy for $7. Guidelines available online.

Nonfiction Contact: Contact John Broders, associate editor. Needs book excerpts, essays, expose, general interest, interview, personal experience, photo feature, travel. Does not want articles without a Texas connection. **Buys 15 mss/year.** Query. Length: 2,000-5,000 words. **Pays $1/word.** Pays expenses of writers on assignment.

Photos Contact: Contact Leslie Baldwin, photography editor (lbaldwin@texasmonthly.com).

Tips "Stories must appeal to an educated Texas audience. We like solidly researched reporting that uncovers issues of public concern, reveals offbeat and previously unreported topics, or uses a novel approach to familiar topics. Any issue of the magazine would be a helpful guide. We do not use fiction, poetry, or cartoons."

$ $ TEXAS PARKS & WILDLIFE

4200 Smith School Rd, Austin TX 78744. (512)389-8793. Fax: (512)707-1913. E-mail: robert.macias@tpwd.state.tx.us. Website: www.tpwmagazine.com. **80% freelance written**. Monthly magazine featuring articles about "Texas hunting, fishing, birding, outdoor recreation, game and nongame wildlife, state parks, environmental issues. All articles must be about Texas. Estab. 1942. Circ. 150,000. Byline given. Pays on acceptance. Offers kill fee. Kill fee determined by contract, usually $200-250 Publishes ms an average of 4 months after acceptance. Buys first rights. Accepts queries by mail. Responds in 1 month to queries. Responds in 3 months to mss. Sample copy available online. Guidelines available online.

- *Texas Parks & Wildlife* needs more short items for front-of-the-book scout section and wildlife articles written from a natural history perspective (not for hunters)."

Nonfiction Needs general interest, Texas only, how-to, outdoor activities, photo feature, travel, state parks and small towns. **Buys 60 mss/year.** Query with published clips; follow up by e-mail 1 month after submitting query. Length: 500-2,500 words. **Pays 50¢/word.**

Photos Send photos to photo editor Captions, identification of subjects required. Reviews transparencies. Offers $65-500/photo Buys one time rights.

Tips "Queries with a strong seasonal peg are preferred. Our planning progress begins 7 months before the date of publication. That means you have to think ahead. What will Texas outdoor enthusiasts want to read about 7 months from today?"

VERMONT

$ $ VERMONT LIFE MAGAZINE

6 Baldwin St., Montpelier VT 05602-2109. (802)828-3241. Fax: (802)828-3366. E-mail: editors@vtlife.com. Website: www.vermontlife.com. **90% freelance written. Prefers to work with published/established writers.** Quarterly magazine. *Vermont Life* is interested in any article, query, story idea, photograph or photo essay that has to do with Vermont. As the state magazine, we are most favorably impressed with pieces that present positive aspects of life within the state's borders. Estab. 1946. Circ. 75,000. Byline given. Offers kill fee. Publishes ms an average of 9 months after acceptance. Buys first North American serial rights. Submit seasonal material 1 year in advance. Accepts queries by mail, e-mail, fax. Responds in 1 month to queries. Guidelines available online.

Nonfiction Wants articles on today's Vermont, those which portray a typical or, if possible, unique aspect of the state or its people. Style should be literate, clear, and concise. Subtle humor favored. No Vermont clichÃ^s, and please do not send first-person accounts of your vacation trip to Vermont. **Buys 60 mss/year.** Query by letter essential 1,500 words average **Pays 25¢/word.**

Photos Buys photos with mss; buys seasonal photographs alone. Prefers b&w contact sheets to look at first on assigned material. Color submissions must be 4x5 or 35mm transparencies. Gives assignments but only with experienced photographers. Query in writing. Captions, identification of subjects, model releases required. Pays $75-200 inside color; $500 for cover. Buys one time rights.

Tips Writers who read our magazine are given more consideration because they understand that we want authentic articles about Vermont. If a writer has a genuine working knowledge of Vermont, his or her work usually shows it. Vermont is changing and there is much concern here about what this state will be like in years ahead. It is a beautiful, environmentally sound place now and the vast majority of residents want to keep it so. Articles reflecting such concerns in an intelligent, authoritative, non-hysterical way will be given very careful consideration. The growth of tourism makes us interested in intelligent articles about specific places in Vermont, their history and attractions to the traveling public.

VIRGINIA

$ $ ALBEMARLE

Living in Jefferson's Virginia, Carden Jennings Publishing, 375 Greenbrier Dr., Suite 100, Charlottesville VA 22901. (434)817-2000. Fax: (434)817-2020. Website: www.cjp.com. **80% freelance written**. Bimonthly magazine. Lifestyle magazine for central Virginia. Estab. 1987. Circ. 10,000. Byline given. Pays on publication. Offers 30% kill fee. Publishes ms an average of 4 months after acceptance. Buys first North American serial rights. Editorial lead time 6 months. Submit seasonal material 6 months in advance. Accepts queries by mail, fax. Accepts simultaneous submissions. Responds in 1 month to queries. Responds in 2 months to mss. Sample copy for sae with 10x12 envelope and 5 First-Class stamps. Guidelines for #10 SASE.

Nonfiction Needs essays, historical, interview, photo feature, travel. No fiction, poetry or anything without a direct tie to central Virginia. **Buys 30-35 mss/year.** Query with published clips. Length: 900-3,500 words. **Pays $75-225 for assigned articles. Pays $75-175 for unsolicited articles.** Sometimes pays expenses of writers on assignment.

Photos State availability Captions, identification of subjects, model releases required. Reviews transparencies. Negotiates payment individually Buys one time rights.

Columns/Departments Etcetera (personal essay), 900-1,200 words; no food; Leisure (travel, sports), 3,000 words. 20 Query with published clips. **Pays $75-150.**

Tips Be familiar with the central Virginia area and lifestyle. We prefer a regional slant, which should include a focus on someone or something located in the region, or a focus on someone or something from the region making an impact in other parts of the world. Quality writing is a must. Story ideas that lend themselves to multiple sources will give you a leg up on the competition.

$ $ THE ROANOKER

Leisure Publishing Co., 3424 Brambleton Ave., Roanoke VA 24018. (540)989-6138. Fax: (540)989-7603. E-mail: jwood@leisurepublishing.com. Website: www.theroanoker.com. **75% freelance written. Works with a small number of new/unpublished writers each year.** Magazine published 6 times/year. *The Roanoker* is a general interest city magazine for the people of Roanoke, Virginia and the surrounding area. Our readers are primarily upper-income, well-educated professionals between the ages of 35 and 60. Coverage ranges from hard news and consumer information to restaurant reviews and local history. Estab. 1974. Circ. 12,000. Byline given. Pays on publication. No kill fee. Publishes ms an average of 4 months after acceptance. Buys all rights. Makes work-for-hire assignments. Submit seasonal material 4 months in advance. Accepts queries by mail, e-mail, fax. Responds in 2 months to queries. Sample copy for $2 and 9x12 SAE with 5 first-class stamps or online.

Nonfiction We're looking for more photo feature stories based in western Virginia. We place special emphasis on investigative and exposÃˆ articles. Needs expose, historical, how-to, live better in western Virginia, interview, of well-known area personalities, photo feature, travel, Virginia and surrounding states, periodic special sections on fashion, real estate, media, banking, investing. **Buys 30 mss/year.** Send complete ms. 1,400 words maximum **Pays $35-200.**

Photos Send photos Captions, model releases required. Reviews color transparencies, digital submissions. Pays $25-50/published photograph Rights purchased vary

Columns/Departments Skinny (shorts on people, Roanoke-related books, local issues, events, arts and culture).

Tips We're looking for more pieces on contemporary history (1930s-70s). It helps if freelancer lives in the area. The most frequent mistake made by writers in completing an article for us is not having enough Roanoke-area focus: use of area experts, sources, slants, etc.

$ $ VIRGINIA LIVING

Cape Fear Publishing, 109 E. Cary St., Richmond VA 23219. (804)343-7539. Fax: (804)649-0306. E-mail: editor@capefear.com. Website: www.virginialiving.com. **80% freelance written**. Bimonthly magazine covering life and lifestyle in Virginia. We are a large-format (10x13) glossy magazine covering life in Virginia, from food, architecture, and gardening, to issues, profiles, and travel. Estab. 2002. Circ. 70,000. Byline given. Pays on publication. Publishes ms an average of 4-6 months after acceptance. Buys first North American serial rights. Editorial lead time 2-6 months. Submit seasonal material 1 year in advance. Accepts queries by mail. Accepts simultaneous submissions. Responds in 1 month to queries. Responds in 1 month to mss. Sample copy for $5.

Nonfiction Needs book excerpts, essays, expose, general interest, historical, interview, new product, personal experience, photo feature, travel, architecture, design. No fiction, poetry, previously published articles, or stories with a firm grasp of the obvious. **Buys 180 mss/year.** Query with published clips or send complete ms. Length: 300-3,000 words. **Pays 50¢/word.**

Photos Contact: Tyler Darden, art director. Captions, identification of subjects, model releases required. Reviews contact sheets, 6x7 transparencies, 8x10 prints, GIF/JPEG files. Negotiates payment individually. Buys one time rights.

Columns/Departments Beauty; Travel; Books; Events; Sports (all with a unique Virginia slant), all 1,000-1,500 words. 50 Send complete ms. **Pays $120-200.**

Tips I can then sit down with them and read them. In addition, queries should be about fresh subjects in Virginia. Avoid stories about Williamsburg, Chincoteague ponies, Monticello, the Civil War, and other press release-type topics. We prefer to introduce new subjects, faces, and ideas, and get beyond the many clichÃ^s of Virginia. Freelancers would also do well to think about what time of the year they are pitching stories for, as well as art possibilities. We are a large-format magazine close to the size of the old-look magazine, so photography is a key component to our stories.

WASHINGTON

$ $ SEATTLE MAGAZINE

Tiger Oak Publications Inc., 1505 Western Ave., Suite 500, Seattle WA 98101. (206)284-1750. Fax: (206)284-2550. E-mail: rachel.hart@tigeroak.com. Website: www.seattlemagazine.com. Monthly magazine serving the Seattle metropolitan area. Articles should be written with our readers in mind. They are interested in social issues, the arts, politics, homes and gardens, travel and maintaining the region's high quality of life. Estab. 1992. Circ. 45,000. Byline given. Pays on or about 30 days after publication. Offers 25% kill fee. Publishes ms an average of 3 months after acceptance. Buys first rights. Editorial lead time 6 months. Submit seasonal material 6 months in advance. Accepts queries by mail, e-mail, fax. Responds in 2 months to queries. Sample copy for #10 SASE. Guidelines available online.

Nonfiction Needs book excerpts, local, essays, expose, general interest, humor, interview, photo feature, travel, local/regional interest. No longer accepting queries by mail. Query with published clips. Length: 100-2,000 words. **Pays $50 minimum.**

Photos State availability Negotiates payment individually Buys one time rights.

Columns/Departments Scoop, Urban Safari, Voice, Trips, People, Environment, Hot Button, Fitness, Fashion, Eat and Drink Query with published clips. **Pays $225-400.**

Tips The best queries include some idea of a lead and sources of information, plus compelling reasons why the article belongs specifically in *Seattle Magazine*. In addition, queries should demonstrate the writer's familiarity with the magazine. New writers are often assigned front- or back-of-the-book contents, rather than features. However, the editors do not discourage writers from querying for longer articles and are especially interested in receiving trend pieces, in-depth stories with a news hook and cultural criticism with a local angle.

$ $ $ SEATTLE WEEKLY

Village Voice, 1008 Western Ave., Suite 300, Seattle WA 98104. (206)623-0500. Fax: (206)467-4377. Website: seattleweekly.com. **20% freelance written**. Weekly tabloid covering arts, politics, food, business and books with local and regional emphasis. Estab. 1976. Circ. 105,000. Byline given. Pays on publication. Offers variable kill fee. Publishes ms an average of 1 month after acceptance. Buys first North American serial rights. Submit seasonal material 2 months in advance. Responds in 1 month to queries. Sample copy for $3. Guidelines available online.

Nonfiction Needs book excerpts, expose, general interest, historical, Northwest, humor, interview, opinion. **Buys 6-8 mss/year.** Query with cover letter, resume, published clips and SASE Length: 300-4,000 words. **Pays $50-800.** Sometimes pays expenses of writers on assignment.

Reprints Send tearsheet. Payment varies

Tips The *Seattle Weekly* publishes stories on Northwest politics and art, usually written by regional and local writers, for a mostly upscale, urban audience; writing is high-quality magazine style.

WISCONSIN

LABOR PAPER EXTRA!!

Serving Southern Wisconsin, Union-Cooperative Publishing, 3030 39th Ave., Suite 110, Kenosha WI 53144. (262)657-6116. Fax: (262)657-6153. **30% freelance written**. Monthly tabloid covering union/labor news. Estab. 2002. Circ. 12,000. Byline given. Pays on publication. Publishes ms an average of 2 months after acceptance. Buys all rights. Editorial lead time 1 month. Submit seasonal material 1 month in advance. Accepts queries by mail, fax. Accepts simultaneous submissions. Sample copy and writer's guidelines free.

Nonfiction Needs expose, general interest, historical, humor, inspirational. **Buys 4 mss/year.** Query with published clips. Length: 300-1,000 words. Sometimes pays expenses of writers on assignment.

Photos State availability Captions required. Negotiates payment individually.

$ $ MADISON MAGAZINE

Morgan Murphy Media, 7025 Raymond Rd., Madison WI 53719. (608)270-3600. Fax: (608)270-3636. E-mail: bnardi@madisonmagazine.com. Website: www.madisonmagazine.com. **75% freelance written**. Monthly magazine. Estab. 1978. Circ. 18,600. Byline given. Pays on publication. Offers 33% kill fee. Publishes ms an average of 2 months after acceptance. Editorial lead time 3 months. Submit seasonal material 3-4 months in advance. Accepts queries by mail, e-mail. Accepts simultaneous submissions. Responds in 3 weeks to queries. Responds in 3 weeks to mss. Sample copy free. Guidelines available online.

Nonfiction Needs book excerpts, essays, expose, general interest, historical, how-to, humor, inspirational, interview, new product, opinion, personal experience, photo feature, religious, technical, travel.

Photos State availability Reviews contact sheets. Negotiates payment individually. Buys one time rights.

Columns/Departments Your Town (local events) and OverTones (local arts/entertainment), both 300 words; Habitat (local house/garden) and Business (local business), both 800 words. 120 Query with published clips. **Pays variable amount.**

Fillers Needs anecdotes, facts, gags, newsbreaks, short humor. Length: 100 words. **Pays 20-30¢/word.**

Tips Our magazine is local so only articles pertaining to Madison are considered. Specific queries are heavily appreciated. We like fresh, new content taken in a local perspective. Show us what you're like to write for us.

$ $ $ $ MILWAUKEE MAGAZINE

417 E. Chicago St., Milwaukee WI 53202. (414)273-1101. Fax: (414)273-0016. E-mail: milmag@qg.com. Website: www.milwaukeemagazine.com. **40% freelance written**. Monthly magazine. "We publish stories about Milwaukee, of service to Milwaukee-area residents and exploring the area's changing lifestyle, business, arts, politics, and dining." Circ. 40,000. Byline given. Pays on publication. Offers 20% kill fee. Publishes ms an average of 2 months after acceptance. Buys first rights. Submit seasonal material 6 months in advance. Accepts queries by mail, e-mail. Responds in 6 weeks to queries. Sample copy for $4.

Nonfiction Needs essays, expose, general interest, historical, interview, photo feature, travel, food and dining, and other services. "No articles without a strong Milwaukee or Wisconsin angle. Length: 2,500-6,000 words for full-length features; 800 words for 2-page breaker features (short on copy, long on visuals)." **Buys 30-50 mss/year.** Query with published clips. **Pays $800-2,300 for full-length, $250-400 for breaker.** Sometimes pays expenses of writers on assignment.

Columns/Departments Insider (inside information on Milwaukee, exposé, slice-of-life, unconventional angles on current scene), up to 500 words; Mini Reviews for Insider, 125 words. Query with published clips.

Tips "Pitch something for the Insider, or suggest a compelling profile we haven't already done. Submit clips that prove you can do the job. The department most open is Insider. Think short, lively, offbeat, fresh, people-oriented. We are actively seeking freelance writers who can deliver lively, readable copy that helps our readers make the most out of the Milwaukee area. Because we're only human, we'd like writers who can deliver copy on deadline that fits the specifications of our assignment. If you fit this description, we'd love to work with you."

WISCONSIN NATURAL RESOURCES

Wisconsin Department of Natural Resources, P.O. Box 7921, Madison WI 53707-7921. (608)266-1510. Fax: (608)264-6293. E-mail: david.sperling@wi.gov. Website: www.wnrmag.com. **30% freelance written**. Bimonthly magazine covering environment, natural resource management, and outdoor skills. "We cover current issues in Wisconsin aimed to educate and advocate for resource conservation, outdoor recreation, and wise land use." Estab. 1931. Circ. 90,000. Byline given. Publishes ms an average of 8 months after acceptance. Editorial lead time 6 months. Submit seasonal material 1 year in advance. Accepts queries by mail, e-mail. Accepts previously published material. Accepts simultaneous submissions. Responds in 3 weeks to queries. Responds in 6 months to mss. Sample copy free. Guidelines available online.

Nonfiction Needs essays, how-to, photo feature, features on current outdoor issues and environmental issues. Does not want animal rights pieces, poetry or fiction. Query. Length: 1,500-2,700 words.

Photos Also seeks photos of pets at state properties like wildlife areas, campsites, and trails. Send photos Identification of subjects required. Reviews transparencies, JPEG files. Offers no additional payment for photos accepted with ms.

Tips "Provide images that match the copy."

$ $ WISCONSIN TRAILS

P.O. Box 317, Black Earth WI 53515-0317. (608)767-8000. E-mail: hbrown@wistrails.com. Website: wisconsintrails.com. **40% freelance written**. Bimonthly magazine for readers interested in Wisconsin and its contemporary issues, personalities, recreation, history, natural beauty, and arts. Estab. 1960. Circ. 55,000. Byline given. Pays 1 month from publication. No kill fee. Publishes ms an average of 6 months after acceptance. Buys first North American serial rights, buys one-time rights. Submit seasonal material 1 year in advance. Accepts queries by mail, e-mail, fax. Responds in 4 months to queries. Sample copy for $4.95. Guidelines for #10 SASE or online.

Nonfiction Our articles focus on some aspect of Wisconsin life: an interesting town or event, a person or industry, history or the arts, and especially outdoor recreation. No fiction. No articles that are too local for our regional audience, or articles about obvious places to visit in Wisconsin. We need more articles about the new and little-known. **Buys 3 unsolicited mss/year.** Query or send outline Length: 1,000-3,000 words. **Pays 25¢/**

word. Sometimes pays expenses of writers on assignment.

Photos Photographs purchased with or without mss, or on assignment. Color photos usually illustrate an activity, event, region, or striking scenery. Prefer photos with people in scenery. Captions, True required. Reviews 35mm or larger transparencies. Pays $45-175 for inside color; $250 for covers.

Tips When querying, submit well-thought-out ideas about stories specific to people, places, events, arts, outdoor adventures, etc., in Wisconsin. Include published clips with queries. Do some research—many queries we receive are pitching ideas for stories we recently have published. Know the tone, content, and audience of the magazine. Refer to our writer's guidelines, or request them, if necessary.

WYOMING

$ WYOMING RURAL ELECTRIC NEWS (WREN)

P.O. Box 549, Gillette WY 82717. (307)682-7527. Fax: (307)682-7528. E-mail: wren@vcn.com. **20% freelance written**. Monthly magazine for audience of small town residents, vacation-home owners, farmers, and ranchers. Estab. 1954. Circ. 41,000. Byline given. Pays on acceptance. No kill fee. Publishes ms an average of 2 months after acceptance. Buys one-time rights. Submit seasonal material 2 months in advance. Accepts queries by mail, e-mail, fax, phone. Responds in 3 months to queries. Sample copy for $2.50 and 9x12 SASE. Guidelines for #10 SASE.

Nonfiction "We print science, ag, how-to, and human interest but not fiction. Topics of interest in general include: hunting, cooking, gardening, commodities, sugar beets, wheat, oil, coal, hard rock mining, beef cattle, electric technologies such as lawn mowers, car heaters, air cleaners and assorted gadgets, surge protectors, pesticators, etc. Wants science articles with question/answer quiz at end—test your knowledge. Buys electrical appliance articles. Articles welcome that put present and/or future in positive light." No nostalgia, sarcasm, or tongue-in-cheek. **Buys 4-10 mss/year.** Send complete ms. Length: 500-800 words. **Pays up to $140, plus 4 copies.**

Reprints Send tearsheet or photocopy and information about when and where the material previously appeared.

Photos Color only.

Tips "Always looking for fresh, new writers. Submit entire manuscript. Don't submit a regionally set story from some other part of the country. Photos and illustrations (if appropriate) are always welcomed. We want factual articles that are blunt, to the point, accurate."

RELIGIOUS

ALIVE NOW

1908 Grand Ave., P.O. Box 340004, Nashville TN 37203-0004. E-mail: alivenow@upperroom.org. Website: www.alivenow.org. "Bimonthly thematic magazine for a general Christian audience interested in reflection and meditation.". Circ. 40,000. No kill fee. Guidelines available online.

Nonfiction Length: 250-400 words. **Pays $35 and up.**

Fiction Length: 250-400 words. **Pays $35 and up.**

Poetry Needs "Can be avant-garde, free verse — we accept any style.". Length: 10-45 lines.

Tips "We only accept submissions according to our themes."

$ $ AMERICA

106 W. 56th St., New York NY 10019. (212)581-4640. Fax: (212)399-3596. E-mail: articles@americamagazine.org. Website: www.americamagazine.org. Published weekly for adult, educated, largely Roman Catholic audience. Estab. 1909. Byline given. Pays on acceptance. No kill fee. Buys all rights. Responds in 3 weeks to queries. Guidelines available online.

Nonfiction We publish a wide variety of material on religion, politics, economics, ecology, and so forth. We are not a parochial publication, but almost all pieces make some moral or religious point. We are not interested in purely informational pieces or personal narratives which are self-contained and have no larger moral interest. Length: 1,500-2,000 words. **Pays $50-300.**

Poetry Contact: Contact: Rev. James S. Torrens, poetry editor. Only 10-12 poems published a year, thousands turned down. **Buys 10-12 poems/year.** Length: 15-30 lines.

AUSTRALIAN CATHOLICS

Australian Catholics, Ltd., P.O. Box 553, Richmond VIC 3121 Australia. (61)(3)9421-9666. Fax: (61)(3)9421-9600. E-mail: auscaths@jespub.jesuit.org.au. Website: www.australiancatholics.com.au. Magazine published 5 times/year covering the faith and life of Australians. *Australian Catholics* is aimed at all members of the Catholic community, especially young people and the families of students in Catholic schools. Guidelines available online.

Nonfiction Needs religious. Send complete ms. Length: 1,000 words. **Pays negotiable amount.**
Tips We are looking for 'good news' stories.

$ BIBLE ADVOCATE

Bible Advocate, Church of God (Seventh Day), P.O. Box 33677, Denver CO 80233. (303)452-7973. E-mail: bibleadvocate@cog7.org. Website: www.cog7.org/publications/ba/. **25% freelance written**. Religious magazine published 8 times/year. Our purpose is to advocate the Bible and represent the Church of God (Seventh Day) to a Christian audience. Estab. 1863. Circ. 13,500. Byline given. Pays on publication. Offers 50% kill fee. Publishes ms an average of 9 months after acceptance. Buys first rights, buys second serial (reprint) rights, buys electronic rights. Editorial lead time 3 months. Submit seasonal material 6 months in advance. Accepts queries by mail, e-mail; prefers e-mail; attachments ok. Accepts simultaneous submissions. Responds in 2 months to queries. Sample copy for sae with 9x12 envelope and 3 First-Class stamps. Guidelines available online.
Nonfiction Needs inspirational, personal experience, religious, Biblical studies. No articles on Christmas or Easter. **Buys 15-20 mss/year.** Send complete ms and SASE. Length: 1,000-1,200 words. **Pays $25-55.**
Reprints Send typed manuscript with rights for sale noted.
Photos Send photos Identification of subjects required. Reviews prints. Offers payment for photos accepted with ms.
Poetry Needs free verse, traditional. No avant-garde. **Buys 10-12 poems/year.** Submit maximum 5 poems. Length: 5-20 lines. **Pays $20.**
Fillers Needs anecdotes, facts. 5 Length: 50-400 words. **Pays $10-20.**
Tips Be fresh, not preachy! We're trying to reach a younger audience now, so think how you can cover contemporary and biblical topics with this audience in mind. Articles must be in keeping with the doctrinal understanding of the Church of God (Seventh Day). Therefore, the writer should become familiar with what the Church generally accepts as truth as set forth in its doctrinal beliefs. We reserve the right to edit manuscripts to fit our space requirements, doctrinal stands and church terminology. Significant changes are referred to writers for approval. No fax or handwritten submissions, please.

$ $ CATHOLIC DIGEST

P.O. Box 6015, 1 Montauk Ave., Suite 200, New London CT 06320. (800)321-0411. Fax: (860)457-3013. E-mail: cdsubmissions@bayard-inc.com. Website: www.catholicdigest.com. **12% freelance written**. Monthly magazine. Publishes features and advice on topics ranging from health, psychology, humor, adventure, and family, to ethics, spirituality, and Catholics, from modern-day heroes to saints through the ages. Helpful and relevant reading culled from secular and religious periodicals. Estab. 1936. Circ. 275,000. Byline given. Pays on publication. No kill fee. Buys first rights, buys one-time rights, buys second serial (reprint) rights. Editorial lead time 3 months. Submit seasonal material 5 months in advance. Accepts queries by mail, e-mail. Responds in 2 months to mss. Sample copy free
Nonfiction Most articles we use are reprinted. Needs book excerpts, essays, general interest, historical, how-to, humor, inspirational, interview, personal experience, religious, travel. Send complete ms. Length: 750-2,000 words. **Pays $200-400.**
Reprints Send tearsheet or typed ms with rights for sale noted and information about when and where the material previously appeared. Pays $100.
Photos State availability Captions, identification of subjects, model releases required. Reviews contact sheets, transparencies, prints. Negotiates payment individually.
Fillers Contact: Filler Editor. Open Door (statements of true incidents through which people are brought into the Catholic faith, or recover the Catholic faith they had lost), 200-320 words. Also publishes jokes, short anecdotes, and factoids. Finder fees given, depending on length of submission. 200 1 line minimum, 500 words maximum. **Pays $2/per published line (full page width) upon publication.**
Tips Spiritual, self-help, and all wellness is a good bet for us. We would also like to see material with an innovative approach to daily living, articles that show new ways of looking at old ideas, problems. You've got to dig beneath the surface.

$ $ CATHOLIC FORESTER

Catholic Order of Foresters, 355 Shuman Blvd., P.O. Box 3012, Naperville IL 60566-7012. Fax: (630)983-3384. E-mail: magazine@catholicforester.com. Website: www.catholicforester.org. **20% freelance written**. Quarterly magazine for members of the Catholic Order of Foresters, a fraternal insurance benefit society. *Catholic Forester* articles cover varied topics to create a balanced issue for the purpose of informing, educating, and entertaining our readers. Circ. 100,000. Pays on acceptance. Buys first North American serial rights. Editorial lead time 6 months. Submit seasonal material 6 months in advance. Responds in 3 months to mss. Sample copy for sae with 9x12 envelope and 4 First-Class stamps. Guidelines available online.
Nonfiction Needs inspirational, religious, travel, health, parenting, financial, money management, humor. **Buys 12-16 mss/year.** Send complete ms by mail, fax, or e-mail. Rejected material will not be returned without

accompanying SASE Length: 500-1,500 words. **Pays 50¢/word.**
Photos State availability Negotiates payment individually. Buys one time rights.
Fiction Needs humorous, religious. **Buys 12-16 mss/year.** Length: 500-1,500 words. **Pays 50¢/word.**
Poetry Needs light verse, traditional. **Buys 3 poems/year.** 15 lines maximum **Pays 30¢/word.**
Tips Our audience includes a broad age spectrum, ranging from youth to seniors. Nonfiction topics that appeal to our members include health and wellness, money management and budgeting, parenting and family life, interesting travels, insurance, nostalgia, and humor. A good children's story with a positive lesson or message would rate high on our list.

$ $ CELEBRATE LIFE

American Life League, P.O. Box 1350, Stafford VA 22555. (540)659-4171. Fax: (540)659-2586. E-mail: clmag@all.org. Website: www.clmagazine.org. Stephanie Hopping, editor. **Contact:** Jessica Kenney, associate editor. **50% freelance written**. Bimonthly educational magazine covering "pro-life education and human interest.". "We are a religious-based publication specializing in pro-life education through human-interest stories and investigative exposés. Our purpose is to inspire, encourage, motivate, and educate pro-life individuals and activists." Estab. 1979. Circ. 70,000. Byline given. Pays on publication. Buys first, second serial (reprint) rights, or makes work-for-hire assignments. Submit seasonal material 4 months in advance. Accepts queries by mail, e-mail, fax. Accepts previously published material. Accepts simultaneous submissions. Responds in 6 months to mss. Sample copy for sae with 9x12 SAE envelope and 4 First-Class stamps. Guidelines free.
Nonfiction "No fiction, book reviews, poetry, allegory, devotionals." Query with published clips or send complete ms. Length: 400-1,600 words.
Photos Identification of subjects required. Buys one time rights.
Fillers Needs newsbreaks. 5 Length: 75-200 words. **Pays $10.**
Tips "We look for inspiring, educational, or motivational human-interest stories. We are religious based and no exceptions pro-life. All articles must have agreement with the principles expressed in Pope John Paul II's encyclical *Evangelium Vitae*. Our common themes include: abortion, post-abortion healing, sidewalk counseling, adoption, contraception, chastity, euthanasia, eugenics, marriage, opposition to exceptions, organ donation, parenting, political integrity, pro-life/anti-life activities and legislation, pro-life heroes, sanctity of life/personahood, sex education, special needs children/parenting/adoption, and young people in pro-life action."

$ $ $ CHARISMA & CHRISTIAN LIFE

The Magazine About Spirit-Led Living, Strang Communications Co., 600 Rinehart Rd., Lake Mary FL 32746. (407)333-0600. Fax: (407)333-7133. E-mail: charisma@strang.com. Website: www.charismamag.com. **80% freelance written**. Monthly magazine covering items of interest to the Pentecostal or independent charismatic reader. More than half of our readers are Christians who belong to Pentecostal or independent charismatic churches, and numerous others participate in the charismatic renewal in mainline denominations. Estab. 1975. Circ. 250,000. Byline given. Pays on publication. Offers $50 kill fee. Publishes ms an average of 3 months after acceptance. Buys all rights. Editorial lead time 4 months. Submit seasonal material 5 months in advance. Accepts queries by mail, e-mail. Sample copy free. Guidelines by email.
Nonfiction Needs book excerpts, expose, general interest, interview, religious. No fiction, poetry, columns/departments, or sermons. **Buys 40 mss/year.** Query. Length: 2,000-3,000 words. **Pays $1,000 (maximum) for assigned articles.** Pays expenses of writers on assignment.
Photos State availability Model releases required. Reviews contact sheets, 2 ¼x2 ¼ transparencies, 3x5 or larger prints, TIF/JPEG files. Negotiates payment individually. Buys one time rights.
Tips Be especially on the lookout for news stories, trend articles, or interesting personality profiles that relate specifically to the Christian reader.

$ $ THE CHRISTIAN CENTURY

104 S. Michigan Ave., Suite 700, Chicago IL 60603-5901. (312)263-7510. Fax: (312)263-7540. E-mail: main@christiancentury.org. Website: www.christiancentury.org. **90% freelance written. Works with new/unpublished writers.** Biweekly magazine for ecumenically-minded, progressive Protestants, both clergy and lay. Authors must have a critical and analytical perspective on the church and be familiar with contemporary theological discussion. Estab. 1884. Circ. 37,000. Byline given. Pays on publication. No kill fee. Buys all rights. Editorial lead time 1 month. Submit seasonal material 4 months in advance. Accepts queries by mail, e-mail. Responds in 2-4 week to queries. Responds in 2 months to mss. Sample copy for $3.50. Guidelines available online.
Nonfiction We use articles dealing with social problems, ethical dilemmas, political issues, international affairs, and the arts, as well as with theological and ecclesiastical matters. We focus on issues of church and society, and church and culture. Needs essays, humor, interview, opinion, religious. No inspirational. **Buys 150 mss/year.** Send complete ms; query appreciated, but not essential. Length: 1,000-3,000 words. **Pays variable amount for assigned articles. Pays $100-300 for unsolicited articles.**
Photos State availability Reviews any size prints. Buys one time rights.

Poetry Contact: Jill Pelàez Baumgaertner, poetry editor. Needs avant-garde, free verse, haiku, traditional. No sentimental or didactic poetry. **Buys 50 poems/year.** Length: 20 lines. **Pays $50.**
Tips We seek manuscripts that articulate the public meaning of faith, bringing the resources of Christian tradition to bear on such topics as poverty, human rights, economic justice, international relations, national priorities, and popular culture. We are equally interested in articles that probe classical theological themes. We welcome articles that find fresh meaning in old traditions and which adapt or apply religious traditions to new circumstances. Authors should assume that readers are familiar with main themes in Christian history and theology; are not threatened by the historical-critical study of the Bible; and are already engaged in relating faith to social and political issues. Many of our readers are ministers or teachers of religion at the college level.

$ $ CHRISTIAN HOME & SCHOOL

Christian Schools International, 3350 E. Paris Ave. SE, Grand Rapids MI 49512. (616)957-1070, ext. 239. Fax: (616)957-5022. E-mail: abross@csionline.org. **30% freelance written. Works with a small number of new/unpublished writers each year.** Magazine published 4 times/year during the school year covering family life and Christian education. *Christian Home & School* is designed for parents in the United States and Canada who send their children to Christian schools and are concerned about the challenges facing Christian families today. These readers expect a mature, Biblical perspective in the articles, not just a Bible verse tacked onto the end. Estab. 1922. Circ. 67,000. Byline given. Pays on publication. No kill fee. Publishes ms an average of 4 months after acceptance. Buys first North American serial rights. Submit seasonal material 4 months in advance. Accepts queries by mail, e-mail. Responds in 1 month to queries. Sample copy and writer's guidelines for 9x12 SAE with 4 first-class stamps. Writer's guidelines only for #10 SASE or online

- The editor reports an interest in seeing articles on how to experience and express forgiveness in your home, make summer interesting and fun for your kids, help your child make good choices, and raise kids who are opposites, and promote good educational practices in Christian schools.

Nonfiction We publish features on issues that affect the home and school. Needs book excerpts, interview, opinion, personal experience, articles on parenting and school life. **Buys 30 mss/year.** Send complete ms. Length: 1,000-2,000 words. **Pays $175-250.**
Tips Features are the area most open to freelancers. We are publishing articles that deal with contemporary issues that affect parents. Use an informal easy-to-read style rather than a philosophical, academic tone. Try to incorporate vivid imagery and concrete, practical examples from real life. We look for manuscripts with a mature Christian perspective.

$ $ CHRISTIANITY TODAY

465 Gundersen Dr., Carol Stream IL 60188-2498. (630)260-6200. Fax: (630)260-8428. E-mail: cteditor@christianitytoday.com. Website: www.christianitytoday.com. **80% freelance written, but mostly assigned. Works with a small number of new/unpublished writers each year**. Monthly magazine. "*Christianity Today* believes that the vitality of the American church depends on its adhering to and applying the biblical teaching as it meets today's challenges. It attempts to biblically assess people, events, and ideas that shape evangelical life, thought, and mission. It employs analytical reporting, commentary, doctrinal essays, interviews, cultural reviews, and the occasional realistic narrative." Estab. 1956. Circ. 140,000. No kill fee. Publishes ms an average of 6 months after acceptance. Buys first rights. Submit seasonal material at least 8 months in advance. Accepts queries by mail, e-mail, fax. Responds in 3 months to queries. Sample copy and writer's guidelines for 9x12 SAE with 3 first-class stamps.
Nonfiction "Does not buy unsolicited mss." Query required. Length: 1,200-5,200 words. **Pays 25-35¢/word.** Sometimes pays expenses of writers on assignment.
Reprints Rarely accepts previously published submissions. Pays 25% of amount paid for an original article.
Columns/Departments The CT Review (books, the arts, and popular culture). Length: 700-1,500 words. 6 Query only.
Tips "We are developing more of our own manuscripts and requiring a much more professional quality from others. By query only; e-mail preferred."

⊘ CHRISTIAN NEWS NORTHWEST

P.O. Box 974, Newberg OR 97132. Website: www.cnnw.com. No kill fee.

- "*Christian News Northwest* does not need freelance writers."

$ $ CHRYSALIS READER

1745 Gravel Hill Rd., Dillwyn VA 23936. (434)983-3021. E-mail: chrysalis@hovac.com. Website: www.swedenborg.com/chrysalis. **90% freelance written**. Annual magazine Each annual issue focuses on a theme: Lenses (2009), Bridges (2010). "It is very important to send for writer's guidelines and sample copies before submitting. Content of fiction, articles, reviews, poetry, etc., should be directly focused on that issue's theme and directed to the educated, intellectually curious reader." Estab. 1985. Circ. 2,000. Byline given. Pays on publication. Publishes ms an average of 15 months after acceptance. Buys first North American serial rights. Makes work-for-hire assignments. Accepts queries by mail, e-mail. Accepts simultaneous submissions. Responds

in 4 weeks to queries. Responds in 6 months to mss. Sample copy for $10. Guidelines and themes by email.
Nonfiction Needs essays, interview, personal experience. Upcoming special issues include: Lenses, Bridges. "We do not want inspirational or religious articles." Query. Length: 1,500-3,000 words. **Pays $75-100 for assigned articles. Pays $50-150 for unsolicited articles.**
Photos Send suggestions for illustrations with submission. Buys original artwork for cover and inside copy; b&w illustrations related to theme; **pays $25-150.** Captions, identification of subjects required. Offers no additional payment for photos accepted with ms. Buys one time rights.
Fiction Contact: Robert Tucker, fiction editor. Needs adventure, fantasy, historical, science fiction. "No religious works." Query. Length: 1,500-3,000 words.
Poetry Contact: Rob Lawson, series editor. Needs free verse. No religious. **Buys 20 poems/year.** Submit maximum 6 poems. **Pays $25.**

COLUMBIA

1 Columbus Plaza, New Haven CT 06510. (203)752-4398. Fax: (203)752-4109. E-mail: columbia@kofc.org. Website: www.kofc.org/columbia. Monthly magazine for Catholic families. Caters primarily to members of the Knights of Columbus. Estab. 1921. Circ. 1,750,000. Pays on acceptance. No kill fee. Buys first North American serial rights. Accepts queries by mail, e-mail, fax. Sample copy and writer's guidelines free.
Nonfiction Fact articles directed to the Catholic layman and his family dealing with current events, social problems, Catholic apostolic activities, education, ecumenism, rearing a family, literature, science, arts, sports, and leisure. No reprints, poetry, or cartoons. Query with SASE. Length: 750-1,500 words.

$ $ CONSCIENCE

The Newsjournal of Catholic Opinion, Catholics for Choice, 1436 U St. NW, Suite 301, Washington DC 20009-3997. (202)986-6093. E-mail: conscience@catholicsforchoice.org. Website: www.catholicsforchoice.org. **Contact:** Kate Childs Graham. **80% written by nonstaff writers. Publishes 40 freelance submissions yearly; 10% by unpublished writers, 50% by authors who are new to the magazine, 70% by experts.** "Conscience offers in-depth coverage of a range of topics, including contemporary politics, Catholicism, women's rights in society and in religions, US politics, reproductive rights, sexuality and gender, ethics and bioethics, feminist theology, social justice, church and state issues, and the role of religion in formulating public policy." Estab. 1980. Circ. 12,000. Byline given. Pays on publication. No kill fee. Publishes ms an average of 2 months after acceptance. Buys first North American serial rights. Makes work-for-hire assignments. Accepts queries by mail, e-mail. Responds in 4 months to queries. Sample copy free with 9x12 envelope and $1.85 postage. Guidelines for #10 SASE.
Nonfiction "Topics include church-state issues, Catholicism, abortion, contraception, HIV/AIDS, reproductive technologies, sex and sexuality. Informational articles; profiles; interviews; and personal experience and opinion pieces." Needs book excerpts, interview, opinion, personal experience, a small amount, issue analysis. **Buys 4-8 mss/year.** Send complete ms. Length: 1,500-3,500 words. **Pays $200 negotiable.**
Reprints Send typed manuscript with rights for sale noted and information about when and where the material previously appeared. Pays 20-30% of amount paid for an original article.
Columns/Departments Book Reviews, 600-1,200 words. 4-8 **Pays $75.**
Tips "Our readership includes national and international opinion leaders and policymakers, librarians, members of the clergy and the press, and leaders in the fields of theology, ethics, and women's studies. Articles should be written for a diverse and educated audience."

$ $ DECISION

Billy Graham Evangelistic Association, 1 Billy Graham Parkway, Charlotte NC 28201. (704)401-2432. Fax: (704)401-3009. E-mail: submissions@bgea.org. Website: www.decisionmag.org. **5% freelance written. Works each year with small number of new/unpublished writers.** "Magazine published 11 times/year with a mission to extend the ministry of Billy Graham Evangelistic Association; to communicate the Good News of Jesus Christ in such a way that readers will be drawn to make a commitment to Christ; and to encourage, strengthen and equip Christians in evangelism and discipleship.". Estab. 1960. Circ. 400,000. Byline given. Pays on publication. Publishes ms an average of up to 18 months after acceptance. Buys first rights. Assigns work-for-hire mss, articles, projects. Editorial lead time 6 months. Submit seasonal material 6 months in advance. Sample copy for sae with 9x12 envelope and 4 First-Class stamps. Guidelines available online.

- Include telephone number with submission.

Nonfiction Needs personal experience, testimony. **Buys approximately 8 mss/year.** Send complete ms. Length: 400-1,500 words. **Pays $200-400.** Pays expenses of writers on assignment.
Photos State availability Captions, identification of subjects, model releases required. Reviews prints. Buys one time rights.
Columns/Departments Finding Jesus (people who have become Christians through Billy Graham Ministries), 500-600 words. 11 Send complete ms. **Pays $200.**

Tips "Articles should have some connection to the ministry of Billy Graham or Franklin Graham. For example, you may have volunteered in one of these ministries or been touched by them. The article does not need to be entirely about that connection, but it should at least mention the connection. Testimonies and personal experience articles should show how God intervened in your life and how you have been transformed by God. SASE required with submissions."

$ $ DISCIPLESWORLD

A Journal of News, Opinion, and Mission for the Christian Church, DisciplesWorld, Inc., 6325 N. Guilford Ave., Suite 213, Indianapolis IN 46220. (317)375-8846. Fax: (317)375-8849. E-mail: editor@disciplesworld.com. Website: www.disciplesworld.com. **75% freelance written**. Monthly magazine covering faith issues, especially those with a Disciples slant. We are the journal of the Christian Church (Disciples of Christ) in North America. Our denomination numbers roughly 800,000. Disciples are a mainline Protestant group. Our readers are mostly laity, active in their churches, and interested in issues of faithful living, political and church news, ethics, and contemporary social issues. Estab. 2002. Circ. 14,000. Byline given. Pays on publication. No kill fee. Publishes ms an average of 6 months after acceptance. Buys first North American serial rights. Editorial lead time 3 months. Submit seasonal material 3 months in advance. Accepts queries by mail, e-mail. Accepts simultaneous submissions. Responds in 2 weeks to queries. Responds in 2 months to mss. Sample copy for #10 SASE. Guidelines available online.

Nonfiction Needs essays, general interest, inspirational, interview, opinion, personal experience, religious. Does not want preachy or didactic articles. Our style is conversational rather than academic. **Buys 40 mss/year.** Send complete ms. Length: 400-1,500 words. **Pays $100-300 for assigned articles. Pays $25-300 for unsolicited articles.** Sometimes pays expenses of writers on assignment.

Photos Send photos Identification of subjects, model releases required. Negotiates payment individually. Buys one time rights.

Columns/Departments Browsing the Bible (short reflections on the applicability of books of the Bible), 500 words; Speak Out (opinion pieces about issues facing the church), 700 words. 12-15 Send complete ms. **Pays $100.**

Fiction Needs ethnic, mainstream, novel concepts, religious, serialized, slice-of-life vignettes. We're a religious publication, so use common sense! Stories do not have to be overtly 'religious,' but they should be uplifting and positive. **Buys 8-10 mss/year.** Send complete ms. Length: 700-1,500 words. **16¢/word.**

Poetry Needs free verse, light verse, traditional. **Buys 6-10 poems/year.** Submit maximum 3 poems. Length: 30 maximum lines.

Fillers Needs anecdotes, short humor. 20 Length: 25-400 words. **Pays $0-100.**

Tips Send a well-written (and well-proofed!) query explaining what you would like to write about and why you are the person to do it. Write about what you're passionate about. We are especially interested in social justice issues, and we like our writers to take a reasoned and well-argued stand.

$ $ EFCA TODAY

Evangelical Free Church of America, 418 Fourth St., NE, Charlottesville VA 22902. E-mail: dianemc@journeygroup.com. Website: www.efca.org/today. **30% freelance written**. Quarterly magazine. "*EFCA Today*'s purpose is to unify church leaders around the overall mission of the EFCA by bringing its stories and vision to life, and to sharpen those leaders by generating conversations over topics pertinent to faith and life in this 21st century." Estab. 1931. Circ. 44,000. Byline given. Pays on acceptance. Offers 50% kill fee. Publishes ms an average of 3 months after acceptance. Makes work-for-hire assignments. Editorial lead time 5 months. Submit seasonal material 6 months in advance. Accepts queries by mail, e-mail. Rarely accepts previously published material.6 weeks Sample copy for $1 with SAE and 5 first-class stamps Guidelines by email

Nonfiction Needs interview, of EFCA-related subjects, feature articles of EFCA interest, highlighting EFCA subjects. No general-interest inspirational articles. Send complete ms. Length: 200-1,100 words and related/approved expenses for assigned articles. **Pays 23¢/word for first rights, including limited subsidiary rights (free use within an EFCA context).**

Reprints varies.

Columns/Departments On the Radar (significant trends/news of EFCA); Engage (out of the church and into the world); Leader to Leader (what leaders are saying, doing, learning); Catalyst (the passion of EFCA's young leaders; Face to Face (our global family), all between 200 and 600/words. Send complete ms. **Pays 23¢/word and related/approved expenses for assigned articles.**

Tips "One portion of each *EFCA Today* is devoted to a topic designed to stimulate thoughtful dialog and leadership growth, and to highlight how EFCA leaders are already involved in living out that theme. Examples of themes are: new paradigms for 'doing church,' church planting and the 'emerging' church. These articles differ from those in the above sections, in that their primary focus in on the issue rather than the person; the person serves to illustrate the issue. These articles should run between 400 and 800 words. Include contacts for verification of article."

$ $ ENRICHMENT

The General Council of the Assemblies of God, 1445 N. Boonville Ave., Springfield MO 65802. (417)862-2781. Fax: (417)862-0416. E-mail: enrichmentjournal@ag.org. Website: www.enrichmentjournal.ag.org. **15% freelance written.** Quarterly journal covering church leadership and ministry. *Enrichment* offers enriching and encouraging information to equip and empower spirit-filled leaders. Circ. 33,000. Byline given. Pays on publication. No kill fee. Publishes ms an average of 1 year after acceptance. Buys first rights. Editorial lead time 18 months. Submit seasonal material 18 months in advance. Accepts queries by mail, e-mail. Sample copy for $7. Guidelines free.

Nonfiction Needs religious. Send complete ms. Length: 1,000-3,000 words. **Pays up to 15¢/word.**

$ THE EVANGELICAL BAPTIST

Fellowship of Evangelical Baptist Churches in Canada, P.O. Box 457, Guelph ON N1H 6K9 Canada. 519-821-4830. Fax: 519-821-9829. E-mail: eb@fellowship.ca. Website: www.fellowship.ca. **10% freelance written.** Magazine published 4 times/year covering religious, spiritual, Christian living, denominational, and missionary news. We exist to enhance the life and ministry of the church leaders and members in Fellowship Congregations. Estab. 1953. Circ. 3,000. Byline given. Pays on publication. No kill fee. Publishes ms an average of 6 months after acceptance. Buys one-time rights, buys second serial (reprint) rights. Editorial lead time 4 months. Accepts queries by e-mail. Accepts previously published material. Accepts simultaneous submissions. Sample copy available online. Guidelines available online.

Nonfiction Needs religious. No poetry, fiction, puzzles. **Buys 4-6 mss/year.** Send complete ms. Length: 500-900 words. **Pays $50.**

$ EVANGELICAL MISSIONS QUARTERLY

A Professional Journal Serving the Missions Community, Billy Graham Center/Wheaton College, P.O. Box 794, Wheaton IL 60189. (630)752-7158. Fax: (630)752-7155. E-mail: emqjournal@aol.com. Website: www.billygrahamcenter.org/emis. **67% freelance written.** Quarterly magazine covering evangelical missions. This is a professional journal for evangelical missionaries, agency executives, and church members who support global missions ministries. Estab. 1964. Circ. 7,000. Byline given. Pays on publication. Offers negotiable kill fee. Publishes ms an average of 18 months after acceptance. Buys electronic rights, buys all rights. Editorial lead time 1 year. Accepts queries by mail, e-mail, fax, phone. Responds in 2 weeks to queries. Sample copy free Guidelines available online.

Nonfiction Needs essays, interview, opinion, personal experience, religious. No sermons, poetry, straight news. **Buys 24 mss/year.** Query. Length: 800-3,000 words. **Pays $50-100.**

Photos Send photos Identification of subjects required. Offers no additional payment for photos accepted with ms. Buys first rights

Columns/Departments In the Workshop (practical how to's), 800-2,000 words; Perspectives (opinion), 800 words. 8 Query. **Pays $50-100.**

$ $ FAITH & FRIENDS

Inspiration for Living, The Salvation Army, 2 Overlea Blvd., Toronto ON M4H 1P4 Canada. (416)422-6226. Fax: (416)422-6120. E-mail: faithandfriends@can.salvationarmy.org. Website: www.faithandfriends.ca. **25% freelance written.** Monthly magazine covering Christian living and religion. "Our mission statement: to show Jesus Christ at work in the lives of real people, and to provide spiritual resources for those who are new to the Christian faith." Estab. 1996. Circ. 50,000. Byline given. Pays on acceptance. Offers $50 kill fee. Publishes ms an average of 3 months after acceptance. Buys first rights, buys electronic rights. Editorial lead time 3 months. Submit seasonal material 6 months in advance. Accepts queries by mail, e-mail. Accepts previously published material. Responds in 1 week to queries and to mss. Sample copy available online. Guidelines by email.

Nonfiction Needs book excerpts, humor, inspirational, interview, personal experience, photo feature, religious, travel. Does not want sermons, devotionals, or Christian-ese. **Buys 12-24 mss/year.** Query. Length: 500-1,250 words. **Pays $50-200.**

Photos Send photos Captions required. Reviews prints, GIF/JPEG files. Negotiates payment individually. Buys one time rights.

Columns/Departments God in My Life (how life changed by accepting Jesus); Someone Cares (how life changed through someone's intervention), 750 words. 12-18 Query. **Pays $50.**

$ $ FAITH TODAY

To Connect, Equip and Inform Evangelical Christians in Canada, Evangelical Fellowship of Canada, MIP Box 3745, Markham ON L3R 0Y4 Canada. (905)479-5885. Fax: (905)479-4742. Website: www.faithtoday.ca. Bimonthly magazine. "*FT* is the magazine of an association of more than 40 evangelical denominations, but serves evangelicals in all denominations. It focuses on church issues, social issues and personal faith as they are tied to the Canadian context. Writing should explicitly acknowledge that Canadian evangelical context." Estab. 1983. Circ. 18,000. Byline given. Pays on publication. Offers 30-50% kill fee. Publishes ms an average of

4 months after acceptance. Buys first rights. Editorial lead time 4 months. Accepts queries by mail, e-mail, fax. Responds in 6 weeks to queries. Sample copy for SASE in Canadian postage. Guidelines available online.
Nonfiction Needs book excerpts, Canadian authors only, essays, Canadian authors only, interview, Canadian subjects only, opinion, religious, news feature. **Buys 75 mss/year.** Query. Length: 400-2,000 words. **Pays $100-500 Canadian.** Sometimes pays expenses of writers on assignment.
Reprints Send photocopy. Rarely used. Pays 50% of amount paid for an original article.
Photos State availability True required. Reviews contact sheets. Buys one time rights.
Tips "Query should include brief outline and names of the sources you plan to interview in your research. Use Canadian postage on SASE."

$ FORWARD IN CHRIST

The Word from the WELS, WELS, 2929 N. Mayfair Rd., Milwaukee WI 53222-4398. (414)256-3210. Fax: (414)256-3862. E-mail: fic@sab.wels.net. Website: www.wels.net. **5% freelance written**. Monthly magazine covering WELS news, topics, issues. The material usually must be written by or about WELS members. Estab. 1913. Circ. 56,000. Byline given. Pays on publication. No kill fee. Publishes ms an average of 6 months after acceptance. Buys one-time rights. Editorial lead time 3 months. Submit seasonal material 4 months in advance. Accepts queries by mail, e-mail, fax. Responds in 2 months to queries. Sample copy and writer's guidelines free
Nonfiction Needs personal experience, religious. Query. Length: 550-1,200 words. **Pays $75/page, $125/2 pages.** Sometimes pays expenses of writers on assignment.
Photos State availability Captions, identification of subjects, model releases required. Reviews contact sheets. Negotiates payment individually. Buys one-time rights, plus 1 month on Web and in archive
Tips Topics should be of interest to the majority of the members of the synod—the people in the pews. Articles should have a Christian viewpoint, but we don't want sermons. We suggest you carefully read at least 5 or 6 issues with close attention to the length, content, and style of the features.

$$ GROUP MAGAZINE

Group Publishing, Inc., P.O. Box 481, Loveland CO 80539. Fax: (970)292-4373. E-mail: greditor@youthministry.com. Website: www.groupmag.com. **60% freelance written**. Bimonthly magazine covering youth ministry. Writers must be actively involved in youth ministry. Articles we accept are practical, not theoretical, and focused for local church youth workers. Estab. 1974. Circ. 57,000. Byline given. Pays on acceptance. Offers $20 kill fee. Publishes ms an average of 6 months after acceptance. Buys all rights. Submit seasonal material 7 months in advance. Responds in 2 months to queries. Sample copy for $2 and 9 x 12 SAE. Guidelines available online.
Nonfiction Needs how-to, youth ministry issues. No personal testimony, theological or lecture-style articles. **Buys 50-60 mss/year.** Query. Length: 250-2,200 words. **Pays $40-350.** Sometimes pays expenses of writers on assignment.
Tips Submit a youth ministry idea to one of our mini-article sections—we look for tried-and-true ideas youth ministers have used with kids.

HIGHWAY NEWS

Transport For Christ, P.O. Box 117, 1525 River Rd., Marietta PA 17547. (717)426-9977. Fax: (717)426-9980. E-mail: tfcio@transportforchrist.org. Website: www.transportforchrist.org. **Contact:** Inge Koenig. **50% freelance written**. Monthly magazine covering trucking and Christianity. "We publish human interest stories, testimonials, and teachings that have a foundation in Biblical/Christian values. Since truck drivers and their families are our primary readers, we publish works that they will find edifying and helpful." Estab. 1951. Circ. 35,000. Byline given. No kill fee. Publishes ms an average of 1 year after acceptance. Buys We do not buy any rights. rights. Submit seasonal material 1 year in advance. Accepts queries by mail, e-mail, fax. Accepts previously published material. Accepts simultaneous submissions. Responds in 1 month to queries. Responds in 2 months to mss. Sample copy free. Writer's guidelines by e-mail (editor@transportforchrist.org).

- Does not pay writers.

Nonfiction Needs essays, general interest, humor, inspirational, interview, personal experience, photo feature, religious, trucking. No sermons full of personal opinions. **Buys Accepts 20-25 mss/year.** Send complete ms. Length: 600-1,200 words.
Photos Send photos Captions, identification of subjects, model releases required. Reviews prints, GIF/JPEG files. Does not pay for photos. We don't buy anything.
Columns/Departments From the Road (stories by truckers on the road); Devotionals with Trucking theme, both 600 words. Send complete ms.
Fiction Needs humorous, religious, slice-of-life vignettes. No romance or fantasy. We use very little fiction. **Buys Accepts 1 or fewer mss/year.** Send complete ms. Length: 600-1,200 words.
Poetry Needs traditional. Don't send anything unrelated to the trucking industry. **Buys Accepts 2 poems/year.** Submit maximum 10 poems. Length: 4-20 lines. **We don't buy anything.**

Fillers Needs anecdotes, facts, short humor. Length: 20-200 words.
Tips "We are especially interested in human interest stories about truck drivers. Find a trucker doing something unusual or good and write a story about him or her. Be sure to send pictures."

$ HORIZONS

The Magazine for Presbyterian Women, 100 Witherspoon St., Louisville KY 40202-1396. (502)569-5897. Fax: (502)569-8085. Website: www.pcusa.org/horizons/. Bimonthly. "Magazine owned and operated by Presbyterian women offering information and inspiration for Presbyterian women by addressing current issues facing the church and the world." Estab. 1988. Circ. 25,000. Pays on publication. No kill fee. Publishes ms an average of 4 months after acceptance. Buys all rights. Sample copy for $4 and 9x12 SAE. Guidelines for #10 SASE.
Fiction Send complete ms. Length: 800-1,200 words. **Pays $50/600 words and 2 contributor's copies.**

$ $ LIGHT & LIFE MAGAZINE

Free Methodist Church of North America, P.O. Box 535002, Indianapolis IN 46253-5002. (317)244-3660. Fax: (317)248-9055. E-mail: llmauthors@fmcna.org. Website: www.freemethodistchurch.org/Magazine. **Works with a small number of new/unpublished writers each year.** Bimonthly magazine for maturing Christians emphasizing a holiness lifestyle, contemporary issues, and a Christ-centered worldview. Includes pull-out discipleship and evangelism tools and encouragement cards, denominational news. Estab. 1868. Circ. 40,000. Byline given. Pays on acceptance. No kill fee. Buys one-time rights. Sample copy for $4. Guidelines available online.
Nonfiction Query. 1,000-1,500 words (LifeNotes 1,000 words) **Pays 15¢/word.**

$ $ LIGUORIAN

One Liguori Dr., Liguori MO 63057-9999. (636)464-2500. Fax: (636)464-8449. E-mail: liguorianeditor@liguori.org. Website: www.liguorian.org. **Contact:** Fr. Rick Potts, CSSR, Editor-in-Chief. **25% freelance written. Prefers to work with published/established writers.** Magazine published 10 times/year for Catholics. "Our purpose is to lead our readers to a fuller Christian life by helping them better understand the teachings of the gospel and the church and by illustrating how these teachings apply to life and the problems confronting them as members of families, the church, and society." Estab. 1913. Circ. 100,000. Pays on acceptance. Buys first rights. Submit seasonal material 8 months in advance. Accepts queries by mail, e-mail, fax, phone. Responds in 3 months to mss. Sample copy for 9x12 SAE with 3 first-class stamps or online Guidelines for #10 SASE and on website.
Nonfiction Pastoral, practical, and personal approach to the problems and challenges of people today. "No travelogue approach or un-researched ventures into controversial areas. Also, no material found in secular publications—fad subjects that already get enough press, pop psychology, negative or put-down articles." **Buys 30-40 unsolicited mss/year.** Length: 400-2,000 words. **Pays 10-15¢/word and 5 contributor's copies.**
Photos Photographs on assignment only unless submitted with and specific to article.
Fiction Needs religious, senior citizen/retirement. Send complete ms. 1,500-2,000 words preferred **Pays 10-15¢/word and 5 contributor's copies.**

$ $ THE LOOKOUT

For Today's Growing Christian, Standard Publishing, 8805 Governor's Hill Dr., Suite 400, Cincinnati OH 45249. (513)931-4050. Fax: (513)931-0950. E-mail: lookout@standardpub.com. Website: www.lookoutmag.com. **50% freelance written**. Weekly magazine for Christian adults, with emphasis on spiritual growth, family life, and topical issues. Our purpose is to provide Christian adults with practical, Biblical teaching and current information that will help them mature as believers. Estab. 1894. Circ. 75,000. Byline given. Pays on acceptance. Offers 33% kill fee. Publishes ms an average of 1 year after acceptance. Buys first rights. Editorial lead time 9 months. Submit seasonal material 1 year in advance. Accepts simultaneous submissions. Responds in 4-6 weeks to queries. Responds in 10 weeks to mss. Sample copy for $1. Guidelines by email.

- Audience is mainly conservative Christians. Manuscripts only accepted by mail.

Nonfiction Writers need to send for current theme list. We also use inspirational short pieces. Needs inspirational, interview, opinion, personal experience, religious. No fiction or poetry. **Buys 100 mss/year.** Send complete ms. Check guidelines. **Pays 5-12¢/word.**
Photos State availability Identification of subjects required. Offers no additional payment for photos accepted with ms.
Tips *The Lookout* publishes from a theologically conservative, nondenominational, and noncharismatic perspective. It is a member of the Evangelical Press Association. We have readers in every adult age group, but we aim primarily for those aged 30-55. Most readers are married and have elementary to young adult children, but a large number come from other home situations as well. Our emphasis is on the needs of ordinary Christians who want to grow in their faith, rather than on trained theologians or church leaders. As a Christian general-interest magazine, we cover a wide variety of topics—from individual discipleship to family concerns to social involvement. We value well-informed articles that offer lively and clear writing as well as strong application. We often address tough issues and seek to explore fresh ideas or recent developments affecting today's Christians.

$ THE LUTHERAN DIGEST

The Lutheran Digest, Inc., P.O. Box 4250, Hopkins MN 55343. (952)933-2820. Fax: (952)933-5708. E-mail: tldi@lutherandigest.com. Website: www.lutherandigest.com. **95% freelance written**. Quarterly magazine covering Christianity from a Lutheran perspective. "Articles frequently reflect a Lutheran Christian perspective, but are not intended to be sermonettes. Popular stories show how God has intervened in a person's life to help solve a problem." Estab. 1953. Circ. 100,000. Byline given. Pays on acceptance. No kill fee. Publishes ms an average of 6 months after acceptance. Buys first rights, buys second serial (reprint) rights. Editorial lead time 9 months. Submit seasonal material 9 months in advance. Accepts queries by mail. Accepts previously published material. Accepts simultaneous submissions. Responds in 1 month to queries. Responds in 4 months to mss. Sample copy for $3.50. Guidelines available online.

Nonfiction Needs general interest, historical, how-to, personal or spiritual growth, humor, inspirational, personal experience, religious, nature, God's unique creatures. Does not want "to see personal tributes to deceased relatives or friends. They are seldom used unless the subject of the article is well known. We also avoid articles about the moment a person finds Christ as his or her personal savior." **Buys 50-60 mss/year.** Send complete ms. Length: 1,500 words. **Pays $35-50.**

Reprints Accepts previously published submissions. "We prefer this as we are a digest and 70-80% of our articles are reprints."

Photos "We seldom print photos from outside sources." State availability Buys one time rights.

Tips "An article that tugs on the `heart strings' just a little and closes leaving the reader with a sense of hope is a writer's best bet to breaking into *The Lutheran Digest*."

$ LUTHERAN PARTNERS

Augsburg Fortress, Publishers, ELCA (VE), 8765 W. Higgins Rd., Chicago IL 60631-4101. (773)380-2884. Fax: (773)380-2829. E-mail: lutheran.partners@elca.org. Website: www.elca.org/lutheranpartners. **40% freelance written**. Bimonthly magazine covering issues of religious leadership. Lutheran Partners provides a forum for the discussion of issues surrounding gospel-centered ministry which are vital to scripture, theology, leadership, and mission in congregations and other settings of the church. Estab. 1979. Circ. 20,000. Byline given. Pays on publication. No kill fee. Publishes ms an average of 6 months after acceptance. Buys first rights, buys one-time rights, buys second serial (reprint) rights, buys electronic rights. Editorial lead time 6 months. Submit seasonal material 6 months in advance. Accepts queries by mail, e-mail, fax, phone. Accepts previously published material. Accepts simultaneous submissions. Responds in 3 months to queries. Responds in 6 months to mss. Sample copy for $2. Guidelines available online.

- The editor reports an interest in seeing articles on various facets of ministry from the perspectives of ELCA Lutheran ethnic authors (Hispanic, African-American, Asian, Native American, Arab-American), as well as material on youth leadership and ministry, parish education, outreach, and preaching.

Nonfiction Needs historical, how-to, leadership in faith communities, humor, religious cartoon, inspirational, opinion, religious leadership issues, religious, book and DVD reviews (query review editors). No exposès, articles primarily promoting products/services, or anti-religion. **Buys 10-15 mss/year.** Send complete ms. Length: 500-1,500 words. **Pays $25-170.**

Photos State availability Captions, identification of subjects required. Generally offers no additional payment for photos accepted with ms. Buys one time rights.

Columns/Departments Contact: Review Editor. Partners Review (book reviews), 700 words. Query. **Pays in copies**

Fiction Rarely accepts religious fiction. Query.

Poetry Needs free verse, haiku, light verse, traditional. **Buys 3-6 poems/year.** Submit maximum 4 poems. **Pays $50-75.**

Fillers Practical ministry (education, music, youth, social service, administration, worship, etc.) in congregation. 1-3 Length: 500 words. **Pays $25.**

Tips Know congregational life, especially from the perspective of leadership, including both ordained pastor and lay staff. Think current and future leadership needs. It would be good to be familiar with ELCA rostered pastors, lay ministers, and congregations.

$ MENNONITE BRETHREN HERALD

1310 Taylor Ave., Winnipeg MB R3M 3Z6 Canada. (888)669-6575. Fax: (204)654-1865. E-mail: mbherald@mbconf.ca. Website: www.mbherald.com. **25% freelance written**. Monthly family publication read mainly by people of the Mennonite Brethren faith, reaching a wide cross section of professional and occupational groups. Readership includes people from both urban and rural communities. It is intended to inform members of events in the church and the world, serve personal and corporate spiritual needs, serve as a vehicle of communication within the church, serve conference agencies and reflect the history and theology of the Mennonite Brethren Church. Estab. 1962. Circ. 17,000. Byline given. Pays on publication. No kill fee. Publishes ms an average of 6 months after acceptance. Buys one-time rights. Accepts queries by e-mail, fax. Responds in 6 months to queries. Sample copy for $1 and 9x12 SAE with 2 IRCs. Guidelines available online.

• Articles and manuscripts not accepted for publication will be returned if a SASE (Canadian stamps or IRCs) is provided by the writers.

Nonfiction Articles with a Christian family orientation; youth directed, Christian faith and life, and current issues. Wants articles critiquing the values of a secular society, attempting to relate Christian living to the practical situations of daily living; showing how people have related their faith to their vocations. Send complete ms. Length: 250-1,500 words. **Pays $30-40.** Pays expenses of writers on assignment.

Reprints Send tearsheet, photocopy or typed ms with rights for sale noted and information about when and where the material previously appeared. Pays 70% of amount paid for an original article.

Photos Photos purchased with ms.

Columns/Departments Viewpoint (Christian opinion on current topics), 850 words. Crosscurrent (Christian opinion on music, books, art, TV, movies), 350 words.

Poetry 25 lines maximum.

Tips We like simple style, contemporary language and fresh ideas. Writers should take care to avoid religious cliches.

$ $ MESSAGE MAGAZINE

Review and Herald Publishing Association, 55 West Oak Ridge Dr., Hagerstown MD 21740. (301)393-4099. Fax: (301)393-4103. E-mail: wjohnson@rhpa.org. Website: www.messagemagazine.org. **10-20% freelance written.** Bimonthly magazine. "*Message* is the oldest religious journal addressing ethnic issues in the country. Our audience is predominantly Black and Seventh-day Adventist; however, *Message* is an outreach magazine for the churched and un-churched across cultural lines." Estab. 1898. Circ. 110,000. Byline given. Pays on acceptance. No kill fee. Publishes ms an average of 12 months after acceptance. first North American serial rights Editorial lead time 6 months. Submit seasonal material 6 months in advance. Responds in 9 months to queries. Sample copy by email. Guidelines by email.

Nonfiction Needs general interest; how-to (overcome depression, overcome defeat, get closer to God, learn from failure, deal with the economic crises, etc.). **Buys variable number of mss/year.** Send complete ms. Length: 800-1,200 words. **Payment varies. Payment upon acceptance.**

Photos State availability Identification of subjects required. Buys one time rights.

Tips "Please look at the magazine before submitting manuscripts. *Message* publishes a variety of writing styles as long as the writing style is easy to read and flows—please avoid highly technical writing styles."

MESSAGE OF THE OPEN BIBLE

Open Bible Churches, 2020 Bell Ave., Des Moines IA 50315-1096. (515)288-6761. Fax: (515)288-2510. E-mail: andrea@openbible.org. Website: www.openbible.org. **5% freelance written.** *The Message of the Open Bible* is the official bimonthly publication of Open Bible Churches. Its readership consists mostly of people affiliated with Open Bible. Estab. 1932. Circ. 2,700. Byline given. No kill fee. Publishes ms an average of 4-6 months after acceptance. Editorial lead time 6 months. Submit seasonal material 6 months in advance. Accepts queries by mail. Responds in 1 month to queries. Responds in 2 months to mss. Sample copy for sae with 9X12 envelope and 3 First-Class stamps. Writer's guidelines for #10 SASE or by e-mail (message@openbible.org).

• Does not pay for articles.

Nonfiction Needs inspirational, teachings or challenges, interview, personal experience, religious, testimonies, news. No sermons. Send complete ms. Maximum 650 words.

Photos State availability Reviews 5X7 prints, GIF/JPEG files. Doesn't pay for photos.

$ THE MESSENGER OF THE SACRED HEART

Apostleship of Prayer, 661 Greenwood Ave., Toronto ON M4J 4B3 Canada. (416)466-1195. **20% freelance written.** Monthly magazine for Canadian and U.S. Catholics interested in developing a life of prayer and spirituality; stresses the great value of our ordinary actions and lives. Estab. 1891. Circ. 11,000. Byline given. Pays on acceptance. No kill fee. Buys first North American serial rights, buys first rights. Submit seasonal material 5 months in advance. Responds in 1 month to queries. Sample copy for $1 and 7½x10½ SAE. Guidelines for #10 SASE.

Fiction Contact: Rev. F.J. Power, S.J. and Alfred DeManche, editors. Needs religious, stories about people, adventure, heroism, humor, drama. No poetry. **Buys 12 mss/year.** Send complete ms. Length: 750-1,500 words. **Pays 8¢/word, and 3 contributor's copies.**

Tips Develop a story that sustains interest to the end. Do not preach, but use plot and characters to convey the message or theme. Aim to move the heart as well as the mind. Before sending, cut out unnecessary or unrelated words or sentences. If you can, add a light touch or a sense of humor to the story. Your ending should have impact, leaving a moral or faith message for the reader.

$ $ MY DAILY VISITOR

Our Sunday Visitor, Inc., 200 Noll Plaza, Huntington IN 46750. (260)356-8400. Fax: (260)356-8472. E-mail: mdvisitor@osv.com. Website: www.osv.com. **99% freelance written.** Bimonthly magazine of Scripture meditations based on the day's Catholic Mass readings. Circ. 33,000. Byline given. Pays on acceptance. No kill fee. Publishes ms an average of 6 months after acceptance. Buys one-time rights. Accepts queries by mail, e-mail. Responds in 2 months to queries. Sample copy and writer's guidelines for #10 SAE with 3 first-class stamps.

- Sample meditations and guidelines online. Each writer does 1 full month of meditations on assignment basis only.

Nonfiction Needs inspirational, personal experience, religious. **Buys 12 mss/year.** Query with published clips. 130-140 words times the number of days in month. **Pays $500 for 1 month (28-31) of meditations and 5 free copies.**

Tips Previous experience in writing Scripture-based Catholic meditations or essays is helpful.

A NEW HEART

Encouraging Christians in Healthcare, Hospital Christian Fellowship, Inc., P.O. Box 4004, San Clemente CA 92674. (949)496-7655. Fax: (949)496-8465. E-mail: hcfusa@gmail.com. Website: www.hcfusa.com. **50% freelance written**. Quarterly magazine covering articles and true stories that are health-related, with a Christian message, to encourage healthcare workers, patients, and volunteers to meet specific needs. Estab. 1978. Circ. 5,000. Byline given. No kill fee. Publishes ms an average of 4-6 months after acceptance. Buys simultaneous rights. Editorial lead time 6 months. Submit seasonal material 6 months in advance. Accepts queries by mail, e-mail, fax, phone. Accepts previously published material. Accepts simultaneous submissions. Responds in 2 weeks to queries. Sample copy free. Guidelines free.

Nonfiction Needs humor, inspirational, personal experience, religious. No fiction. **Buys 10-20 mss/year.** Query. Length: 500-1,500 words.

Photos State availability of or send photos Captions, identification of subjects required. Offers no additional payment for photos accepted with ms. Buys one time rights.

Columns/Departments Book Review (medical/Christian), 200 words; Events (medical/Christian), 100-200 words; Chaplains (medical/Christian/inspirational), 200-250 words; On the Lighter Side (medical/clean fun), 100-200 words. 4-6 Send complete ms. **Pays in copies.**

Fillers Needs anecdotes, gags, short humor. 4-10 Length: 50-100 words. **Pays in copies.**

$ $ ONE

Catholic Near East Welfare Association, 1011 First Ave., New York NY 10022-4195. (212)826-1480. Fax: (212)826-8979. E-mail: cnewa@cnewa.org. Website: www.cnewa.org. **75% freelance written**. Bimonthly magazine for a Catholic audience with interest in the Near East, particularly its current religious, cultural and political aspects. Estab. 1974. Circ. 100,000. Byline given. Pays on publication. No kill fee. Publishes ms an average of 6 months after acceptance. Buys all rights. Accepts queries by mail, fax. Responds in 1 month to queries. Sample copy and writer's guidelines for 7½x10½ SAE with 2 first-class stamps.

Nonfiction Cultural, devotional, political, historical material on the Near East, with an emphasis on the Eastern Christian churches. Style should be simple, factual, concise. Articles must stem from personal acquaintance with subject matter, or thorough up-to-date research. Length: 1,200-1,800 words. **Pays 20¢/edited word.**

Photos Photographs to accompany manuscript are welcome; they should illustrate the people, places, ceremonies, etc. which are described in the article. We prefer color transparencies but occasionally use b&w. Pay varies depending on use—scale from $50-300.

Tips We are interested in current events in the Near East as they affect the cultural, political and religious lives of the people.

$ $ ON MISSION

North American Mission Board, SBC, 4200 North Point Pkwy., Alpharetta GA 30022-4176. E-mail: onmission@namb.net. Website: www.onmission.com. **25% freelance written**. Quarterly lifestyle magazine that popularizes evangelism, church planting and missions. "*On Mission*'s primary purpose is to tell the story of southern baptist missionaries and to help readers and churches become more intentional about personal evangelism, church planting, and missions. *On Mission* equips Christians for leading people to Christ and encourages churches to reach people through new congregations." Estab. 1998. Circ. 100,000. Byline given. Pays on acceptance. Publishes ms an average of 6 months after acceptance. Buys first rights, buys electronic rights, buys first North American rights. Editorial lead time 9 months. Submit seasonal material 9 months in advance. Accepts queries by mail, e-mail (prefers e-mail). Responds in 6 weeks to queries. Responds in 4 months to mss. Sample copy free or online Guidelines available online.

Nonfiction Needs how-to, humor, personal experience, stories of sharing your faith in Christ with a non-Christian. **Buys 30 mss/year.** Query with published clips. Length: 350-1,200 words. **Pays 25¢/word, more for cover stories.** Pays expenses of writers on assignment.

Photos Most are shot on assignment. Captions, identification of subjects required. Buys all rights.

Columns/Departments 2 Query. **Pays 25¢/word.**

Tips "Readers might be intimidated if those featured appear to be `super Christians' who seem to live on a higher spiritual plane. Try to introduce subjects as three-dimensional, real people. Include anecdotes or examples of their fears and failures, including ways they overcame obstacles. In other words, take the reader inside the heart of the missionary or on mission Christian and reveal the inevitable humanness that makes that person not only believable, but also approachable. We want the reader to feel encouraged to become on mission by identifying with people like them who are featured in the magazine."

$ OPERATION REVEILLE EQUIPPER

Operation Reveille of Mission to Unreached Peoples, P.O. Box 3488, Monument CO 90132-3488. (719)572-5908. E-mail: bside@oprev.org. Website: www.oprev.org. Quarterly newsletter covering Christian cross-cultural ministry. "The newsletter helps service personnel (Evangelical Christians) understand complex religious situations and provides available resources for making a good impression in cross-cultural situations." Estab. 1997. Circ. 1,500. Byline given. Offers 50% kill fee. Buys first rights. Editorial lead time 4 months. Submit seasonal material 4 months in advance. Accepts queries by e-mail. Accepts previously published material. Accepts simultaneous submissions. Responds in 2 weeks to queries. Responds in 1 month to mss. Sample copy available online.

Nonfiction Needs book excerpts, essays, interview, new product, opinion, personal experience, religious. Query. Length: 400-2,500 words. **Pays $50-100 for assigned articles. Pays $25-75 for unsolicited articles.**

Photos State availability Identification of subjects required. Offers $10/photo. Buys one time rights.

Columns/Departments Spiritual Landscape (profiles religious situations in a country or region of conflict), 2,000 words. 3 Query. **Pays $50-100.**

$ $ OUR SUNDAY VISITOR

Our Sunday Visitor, Inc., 200 Noll Plaza, Huntington IN 46750. (260)356-8400. Fax: (260)356-8472. E-mail: jnorton@osv.com. Website: www.osv.com. **70% freelance written. (Mostly assigned).** Weekly tabloid covering world events and culture from a Catholic perspective. Estab. 1912. Circ. 60,000. Byline given. Pays on acceptance. No kill fee. Publishes ms an average of 2-3 weeks after acceptance. Buys first rights. Accepts queries by mail, e-mail.

$ $ $ $ $ OUTREACH MAGAZINE

Outreach, Inc., 2230 Oak Ridge Way, Vista CA 92081-8314. (760)940-0600. Fax: (760)597-2314. E-mail: llowry@outreach.com. Website: www.outreachmagazine.com. **80% freelance written.** Bimonthly magazine covering outreach. *Outreach* is designed to inspire, challenge, and equip churches and church leaders to reach out to their communities with the love of Jesus Christ. Circ. 30,000, plus newsstand. Byline given. Pays on publication. Offers 10% kill fee. Publishes ms an average of 2 months after acceptance. Buys first North American serial rights, buys electronic rights. Editorial lead time 6 months. Submit seasonal material 6 months in advance. Accepts queries by mail, e-mail, fax. Accepts previously published material. Accepts simultaneous submissions. Responds in 2 months to queries. Responds in 8 months to mss. Sample copy free. Guidelines free.

Nonfiction Needs book excerpts, how-to, humor, inspirational, interview, personal experience, photo feature, religious. Vacation Bible School (January); Church Growth—America's Fastest-Growing Churches (Special Issue). Does not want fiction, poetry, non-outreach-related articles. **Buys 30 mss/year.** Query with published clips. Length: 1,200-2,000 words. **Pays $375-600 for assigned articles. Pays $375-500 for unsolicited articles.** Sometimes pays expenses of writers on assignment.

Photos Contact: Christi Osselaer, lead designer. Send photos Identification of subjects required. Reviews GIF/JPEG files. Negotiates payment individually. Buys all rights.

Columns/Departments Contact: Lindy Lowry, editor. Outreach Pulse (short stories about outreach-oriented churches and ministries), 75-250 words; Questions & Perspectives (a first person expert perspective on a question related to outreach), 300-400 words; Soulfires (an as-told-to interview with a person about the stories and people that have fueled their passion for outreach), 900 words; From the Front Line (a profile of a church that is using a transferable idea or concept for outreach), 800 words, plus sidebar; Soujourners (short interviews with everyday people about the stories and people that have informed their worldview and faith perspective), 800 words. 6 mss/year. Query with published clips. **Pays $100-375.**

Fillers Needs facts, gags. 6/year. Length: 25-100 words. **negotiated fee.**

Tips Study our writer's guidelines. Send published clips that showcase tight, bright writing as well as your ability to interview; research; and organize numerous sources into an article; and write a 100-word piece as well as a 1,600-word piece.

$ $ $ $ PAKN TREGER

National Yiddish Book Center, 1021 West St., Amherst MA 01002. E-mail: aatherley@bikher.org. Website: www.yiddishbookcenter.org. **50% freelance written.** Magazine published 2 times/year covering modern and contemporary Yiddish and Jewish culture. Estab. 1980. Circ. 20,000. Byline given. Pays on publication. Publishes ms an average of 3 months after acceptance. Buys one-time rights. Makes work-for-hire assignments. Editorial lead time 4 months. Submit seasonal material 3 months in advance. Accepts queries by mail, e-mail, fax. Accepts simultaneous submissions. Responds in 4 weeks to queries. Responds in 2 months to mss. Sample copy available online. Guidelines by email.

Nonfiction Needs Needs pre-publication book excerpts, essays, humor, interview, travel, graphic novels. Does not want personal memoirs or poetry. **Buys 6-10 mss/year.** Query. Length: 1,200-4,000 words. **Pays $800-2,000 for assigned articles. Pays $350-1,000 for unsolicited articles.** Sometimes pays expenses of writers on assignment.
Photos Contact: Contact Betsey Wolfson, designer. State availability Identification of subjects required. Reviews GIF/JPEG files. Negotiates payment individually. Buys one time rights.
Columns/Departments Let's Learn Yiddish (Yiddish lesson), 1 page Yid/English; Translations (Yiddish-English), 1,200-2,500 words. **Pays $350-1,000.**
Fiction Needs historical, humorous, mystery, novel concepts, serialized, slice-of-life vignettes. **Buys 3 mss/year.** Query. Length: 1,200-6,000 words. **Pays $1,000-2,000.**
Tips Read the magazine and visit our Web site.

$ THE PENTECOSTAL MESSENGER

Messenger Publishing House/Pentecostal Church of God, P.O. Box 850, Joplin MO 64802-0850. (417)624-7050. Fax: (417)624-7102. E-mail: charlotteb@pcg.org. Website: www.pcg.org. Monthly magazine covering Christian, inspirational, religious, leadership news. "Our organization is Pentecostal in nature. Our publication goes out to our ministers and laypeople to educate, inspire and inform them of topics around the world and in our organization that will help them in their daily walk." Estab. 1919. Circ. 5,000. Byline given. Pays on publication. Buys simultaneous rights. Editorial lead time 6 months. Submit themed material 6 months in advance. Accepts queries by mail. Accepts previously published material. Accepts simultaneous submissions. May contact the *Pentecostal Messenger* for a list of monthly themes.
Nonfiction Needs book excerpts, essays, expose, general interest, inspirational, interview, new product, personal experience, religious. **Buys 12-24 mss/year.** Send complete ms. Length: 750-2,000 words. **Pays $15-40.**
Photos Send photos Identification of subjects required. Reviews prints. Offers no additional payment for photos accepted with ms. Buys one time rights.

$ $ ⊘ THE PLAIN TRUTH

Christianity Without the Religion, Plain Truth Ministries, 300 W. Green St., Pasadena CA 91129. Fax: (626)304-8172. E-mail: managing.editor@ptm.org. Website: www.ptm.org. **90% freelance written**. Bimonthly magazine. We seek to reignite the flame of shattered lives by illustrating the joy of a new life in Christ. Estab. 1935. Circ. 70,000. Byline given. Pays on publication. Offers $50 kill fee. Publishes ms an average of 8 months after acceptance. Buys all-language rights for *The Plain Truth* and its affiliated publications. Editorial lead time 6 months. Submit seasonal material 6 months in advance. Accepts queries by mail, e-mail. Accepts simultaneous submissions. Sample copy for sae with 9x12 envelope and 5 First-Class stamps. Guidelines available online.
Nonfiction Needs inspirational, interview, personal experience, religious. **Buys 48-50 mss/year.** Query with published clips and SASE. *No unsolicited mss* Length: 750-2,500 words. **Pays 25¢/word.**
Reprints Send tearsheet or photocopy of article or typed ms with rights for sale ted and information about when and where the article previously appeared with SASE for response. Pays 15¢/word.
Photos State availability Captions required. Reviews transparencies, prints. Negotiates payment individually. Buys one time rights.
Tips Material should offer Biblical solutions to real-life problems. Both first-person and third-person illustrations are encouraged. Articles should take a unique twist on a subject. Material must be insightful and practical for the Christain reader. All articles must be well researched and Biblically accurate without becoming overly scholastic. Use convincing arguments to support your Christian platform. Use vivid word pictures, simple and compelling language, and avoid stuffy academic jargon. Captivating anecdotes are vital.

$ $ POINT

Magazine of Converge Worldwide, Baptist General Conference, 2002 S. Arlington Heights Rd., Arlington Heights IL 60005. Fax: (847)228-5376. E-mail: bputman@baptistgeneral.org. Website: www.bgcworld.org. **5% freelance written**. Nonprofit, religious, evangelical Christian magazine published 6 times/year covering Converge Worldwide. "*Point* is the official magazine of Converge Worldwide (BCG). Almost exclusively uses articles related to Converge, our churches, or by/about Converge people." Circ. 46,000. Byline given. Pays on publication. Offers 50% kill fee. Buys first rights. Editorial lead time 6 months. Submit seasonal material 6 months in advance. Accepts queries by e-mail. Responds in 1 month to queries. Responds in 3 months to mss. Sample copy for #10 SASE. Writer's guidelines, theme list free.
Nonfiction photo, religious Needs , profile, info-graphics, sidebars related to theme. Articles about our people, churches, missions. View online at: www.convergeww.org before sending anything. **Buys 20-30 mss/year.** Query with published clips. Length: 300-1,500 words. **Pays $60-280.** Sometimes pays expenses of writers on assignment.
Photos State availability Captions, identification of subjects, model releases required. Reviews prints, some high-resolution digital. Offers $15-60/photo Buys one time rights.
Columns/Departments Converge Connection (blurbs of news happening in Converge Worldwide), 50-150

words. Send complete ms. **Pays $30.**

Tips "Please study the magazine and the denomination. We will send sample copies to interested freelancers and give further information about our publication needs upon request. Freelancers who are interested in working on assignment are especially welcome."

$ PRAIRIE MESSENGER

Catholic Journal, Benedictine Monks of St. Peter's Abbey, P.O. Box 190, Muenster SK S0K 2Y0 Canada. (306)682-1772. Fax: (306)682-5285. E-mail: pm.canadian@stpeterspress.ca. Website: www.prairiemessenger.ca. **10% freelance written.** Weekly Catholic journal with strong emphasis on social justice, Third World, and ecumenism. Estab. 1904. Circ. 6,900. Byline given. Pays on publication. No kill fee. Publishes ms an average of 4 months after acceptance. Buys first North American serial rights, buys first rights, buys one-time rights, buys second serial (reprint) rights, buys simultaneous rights. Submit seasonal material 3 months in advance. Accepts queries by mail, e-mail, fax, phone. Responds in 2 months to queries. Sample copy for 9x12 SAE with $1 Canadian postage or IRCs. Guidelines available online.

Nonfiction Needs interview, opinion, religious. No articles on abortion. **Buys 15 mss/year.** Send complete ms. Length: 250-600 words. **Pays $55.00.** Sometimes pays expenses of writers on assignment.

Photos Send photos Captions required. Reviews 3x5 prints. Offers $22.50/photo. Buys all rights.

$ $ PRESBYTERIANS TODAY

Presbyterian Church (U.S.A.), 100 Witherspoon St., Louisville KY 40202-1396. (502)569-5637. Fax: (502)569-8632. E-mail: today@pcusa.org. Website: www.pcusa.org/today. **25% freelance written. Prefers to work with published/established writers.** Denominational magazine published 10 times/year covering religion, denominational activities, and public issues for members of the Presbyterian Church (U.S.A.). The magazine's purpose is to increase understanding and appreciation of what the church and its members are doing to live out their Christian faith. Estab. 1867. Circ. 50,000. Byline given. Pays on acceptance. Offers 50% kill fee. Publishes ms an average of 6 months after acceptance. Buys first North American serial rights, buys all rights. Editorial lead time 3 months. Submit seasonal material 3 months in advance. Accepts queries by mail, e-mail, fax, phone. Responds in 2 weeks to queries. Responds in 1 month to mss. Sample copy free Guidelines available online.

Nonfiction Most articles have some direct relevance to a Presbyterian audience; however, *Presbyterians Today* also seeks well-informed articles written for a general audience that help readers deal with the stresses of daily living from a Christian perspective. Needs how-to, everyday Christian living, inspirational, Presbyterian programs, issues, people. **Buys 20 mss/year.** Send complete ms. Length: 1,000-1,800 words. **Pays $300 maximum for assigned articles. Pays $75-300 for unsolicited articles.**

Photos State availability Identification of subjects required. Reviews contact sheets, transparencies, color prints, digital images. Negotiates payment individually. Buys one time rights.

$ $ PRISM MAGAZINE

America's Alternative Evangelical Voice, Evangelicals for Social Action, 6 E. Lancaster Ave., Wynnewood PA 19096. (484)384-2990. E-mail: kristyn@esa-online.org. Website: www.esa-online.org. **50% freelance written.** Bimonthly magazine covering Christianity and social justice. "For holistic, Biblical, socially-concerned, progressive Christians." Estab. 1993. Circ. 2,500. Byline given. Pays on publication. Publishes ms an average of 4-6 months after acceptance. Buys first North American serial rights. Editorial lead time 4 months. Submit seasonal material 4 months in advance. Accepts queries by mail, e-mail. Responds in 1 month to queries. Responds in 3 months to mss. Sample copy for $3. Guidelines free.

- "We're a nonprofit, some writers are pro bono. Occasionally accepts previously published material."

Nonfiction Needs essays on culture/faith, interviews, ministry profiles, reviews, etc. **Buys 10-12/year mss/year.** Send complete ms. Length: 500-3,000 words. **Pays $75 per printed page - about 75¢/word. Pays $25-200 for unsolicited articles.**

Photos Send photos Reviews prints, JPEG files. Pays $25/photo published; $200 if photo used on cover. Buys one time rights.

Tips "We look closely at stories of holistic ministry. It's best to request a sample copy to get to know *PRISM*'s focus/style before submitting—we receive many submissions that are not appropriate."

$ PURPOSE

616 Walnut Ave., Scottdale PA 15683-1999. (724)887-8500. Fax: (724)887-3111. E-mail: horsch@mpn.net. Website: www.mpn.net. **75% freelance written.** Monthly magazine for adults, young and old, general audience with varied interests. Magazine focuses on Christian discipleship—how to be a faithful Christian in the midst of everyday life situations. Uses personal story form to present models and examples to encourage Christians in living a life of faithful discipleship. Estab. 1968. Circ. 8,500. Pays on acceptance. No kill fee. Publishes ms an average of 18 months after acceptance. Buys one-time rights. Submit seasonal material 1 year in advance. Accepts queries by e-mail. Accepts previously published material. Accepts simultaneous submissions. Responds in 3 months to queries. Sample copy and writer's guidelines for 6x9 SAE and $2

Nonfiction Inspirational stories from a Christian perspective. I want upbeat stories that deal with issues faced by believers in family, business, politics, religion, gender, and any other areas—and show how the Christian faith resolves them. *Purpose* conveys truth through quality fiction or true life stories. Our magazine accents Christian discipleship. Christianity affects all of life, and we expect our material to demonstrate this. I would like story-type articles about individuals, groups, and organizations who are intelligently and effectively working at such problems as hunger, poverty, international understanding, peace, justice, etc., because of their faith. Essays, fiction, and how-to-do-it pieces must include a lot of anecdotal, life exposure examples. **Buys 140 mss/year.** E-mail submissions preferred.

Reprints Send tearsheet, photocopy or typed ms with rights for sale noted and information about when and where the material previously appeared.

Photos Photos purchased with ms must be sharp enough for reproduction; requires prints in all cases. Captions required.

Fiction Contact: James E. Horsch, editor. Produce the story with specificity so that it appears to take place somewhere and with real people. Needs historical, related to discipleship theme, humorous, religious. No militaristic/narrow patriotism or racism. Send complete ms. Length: 600 words. **Pays up to 7¢ for stories, and 2 contributor's copies.**

Poetry Needs free verse, light verse, traditional. **Buys 140 poems/year.** Length: 12 lines. **Pays $7.50-20/poem depending on length and quality. Buys one-time rights only.**

Fillers 6¢/word maximum.

QUAKER LIFE

Friends United Meeting, 101 Quaker Hill Dr., Richmond IN 47374. (765)962-7573. Fax: (765)966-1293. E-mail: quakerlife@fum.org. Website: www.fum.org. **Contact:** Katie Terrell. **50% freelance written**. A Christian Quaker magazine published 6 times/year that covers news, inspirational, devotional, peace, equality, and justice issues. Estab. 1960. Circ. 3,000. Byline given. No kill fee. Publishes ms an average of 3-6 months after acceptance. Buys first North American serial rights. Editorial lead time 2-3 months. Submit seasonal material 4-6 months in advance. Accepts queries by mail, e-mail. Accepts simultaneous submissions. Responds in 1 week to queries. Responds in 1-3 months to mss. Sample copy and writer's guidelines free.

Nonfiction Needs book excerpts, general interest, humor, inspirational, interview, personal experience, photo feature, religious, travel, bible study. No poetry or fiction. Query. Length: 400-1,500 words. **Pays 3 contributor's copies**

Photos Reviews b&w or color prints and JPEG files. Occasionally, line drawings and b&w cartoons are used. Send photos Does not pay for photos. Buys one time rights.

Columns/Departments News Brief (newsworthy events among Quakers), 75-200 words; Devotional/ Inspirational (personal insights or spiritual turning points), 750 words; Ideas That Work (ideas from meetings that could be used by others), 750 words; Book/Media Reviews, 75-300 words.

RADIX MAGAZINE

Where Christian Faith Meets Contemporary Culture, Radix Magazine, Inc., P.O. Box 4307, Berkeley CA 94704. (510)548-5329. E-mail: radixmag@aol.com. Website: www.radixmagazine.com. **Contact:** Sharon Gallagher, editor. **10% freelance written**. Quarterly magazine. "*Radix* is for thoughtful Christians who are interested in engaging the world around them." Estab. 1979. Circ. 3,000. Byline given. No kill fee. Publishes ms an average of 6 months after acceptance. interested in first North American serial rights. Editorial lead time 6 months. Submit seasonal material 6 months in advance. Accepts queries by e-mail. Responds in 2 weeks to queries and to mss. Sample copy for $5. Guidelines by email.

- "Needs poetry and book reviews. Email submissions only."

Nonfiction Contact: Sharon Gallagher, editor. Needs essays, religious. Query. Length: 500-2,000 words.

Fiction Needs , book reviews.

Poetry Needs avant-garde, free verse, haiku. "Needs poetry." **Buys 8 poems/year.** Submit maximum 4 poems. Length: 4-20 lines. **Pays 2 contributor copies.**

Tips "We accept very few unsolicited manuscripts. All articles and poems should be based on a Christian world view. Freelancers should have some sense of the magazine's tone and purpose."

RAILROAD EVANGELIST

Railroad Evangelist Association, Inc., P.O. Box 5026, Vancouver WA 98668. (360)699-7208. E-mail: rrjoe@comcast.net. Website: www.railroadevangelist.com. **80% freelance written**. Magazine published 3 times/year covering the railroad industry. "The *Railroad Evangelist*'s purpose and intent is to reach people everywhere with the life-changing gospel of Jesus Christ. The railroad industry is our primary target, along with model railroad and rail fans." Estab. 1938. Circ. 3,000/issue. Byline sometimes given. No kill fee. Editorial lead time 6 weeks. Submit seasonal material 6 weeks in advance. Accepts queries by mail, e-mail. Accepts previously published material. Sample copy for sae with 10x12 envelope and 3 First-Class stamps. Guidelines for #10 SASE.

- All content must be railroad related.

Nonfiction Needs inspirational, interview, personal experience, religious. Query. Length: 300-800 words.
Photos State availability Captions required. Reviews 3x5, 8x10 prints, GIF/JPEG files. Offers no additional payment for photos accepted with ms.
Columns/Departments Right Track (personal testimony), 300-800 words; Ladies Line (personal testimony), 300-500 words; Kids Corner (geared toward children), 50-100 words. Query. **Pays in contributor copies.**
Fiction Needs historical, religious. Query. Length: 300-800 words. **Pays in contributor copies.**
Poetry Needs traditional. Length: 10-100 lines. **Pays in contributor copies.**

$ $ REFORM JUDAISM

Union for Reform Judaism, 633 Third Ave. 7th Floor, New York NY 10017-6778. (212)650-4240. Fax: (212)650-4249. E-mail: rjmagazine@urj.org. Website: www.reformjudaismmag.org. **30% freelance written.** Quarterly magazine of Jewish issues for contemporary Jews. "*Reform Judaism* is the official voice of the Union for Reform Judaism, linking the institutions and affiliates of Reform Judaism with every Reform Jew. *RJ* covers developments within the Movement while interpreting events and Jewish tradition from a Reform perspective." Estab. 1972. Circ. 310,000. Byline given. Pays on publication. Offers kill fee. Offers kill fee for commissioned articles. Publishes ms an average of 3 months after acceptance. Buys first North American serial rights. Submit seasonal material 6 months in advance. Accepts previously published material. Accepts simultaneous submissions. Responds in 2 months to queries and to mss Sample copy for $3.50 Guidelines available online
Nonfiction Needs book excerpts, expose, general interest, historical, inspirational, interview, opinion, personal experience, photo feature, travel. **Buys 30 mss/year.** Submit complete ms with SASE. Cover stories: 2,500-3,500 words; major feature: 1,800-2,500 words; secondary feature: 1,200-1,500 words; department (e.g., Travel): 1,200 words; letters: 200 words maximum; opinion: 525 words maximum. **Pays 30¢/published word.** Sometimes pays expenses of writers on assignment.
Reprints Send tearsheet, photocopy or typed ms with rights for sale and information about when and where the material previously appeared. Usually doesn't publish reprints.
Photos Send photos Identification of subjects required. Reviews 8x10/color or slides, b&w prints, and printouts of electronic images. Payment varies. Buys one time rights.
Fiction Needs humorous, religious, sophisticated, cutting-edge, superb writing. **Buys 4 mss/year.** Send complete ms. Length: 600-2,500 words. **Pays 30¢/published word.**
Tips "We prefer a stamped postcard including the following information/checklist: __Yes, we are interested in publishing; __No, unfortunately the submission doesn't meet our needs; __Maybe, we'd like to hold on to the article for now. Submissions sent this way will receive a faster response."

$ $ RELEVANT

Relevant Media Group, 1220 Alden Rd., Orlando FL 32803. (407)660-1411. Fax: (407)660-8555. E-mail: corene@relevantmediagroup.com. Website: www.relevantmagazine.com. **80% freelance written.** Biweekly magazine covering God, life, and progressive culture. *Relevant* is a lifestyle magazine for Christians in their 20s. Estab. 2002. Circ. 70,000. Byline given. Pays 45 days after publication. Offers 50% kill fee. Publishes ms an average of 6 months after acceptance. Buys first North American serial rights. Editorial lead time 4 months. Submit seasonal material 5 months in advance. Accepts queries by e-mail. Accepts simultaneous submissions. Responds in 6 weeks to queries. Responds in 3 months to mss. Sample copy available online. Guidelines available online.
Nonfiction Needs general interest, how-to, inspirational, interview, new product, personal experience, religious. Don't submit anything that doesn't target ages 18-34. Query with published clips. Length: 1,000-1,500 words. **Pays 10-15¢/word for assigned articles. Pays 10¢/word for unsolicited articles.** Sometimes pays expenses of writers on assignment.
Tips The easiest way to get noticed by our editors is to first submit (donate) stories for online publication.

$ $ THE REPORTER

Women's American ORT, Inc., 75 Maiden Lane, 10th Floor, New York NY 10038. (212)505-7700. Fax: (212)674-3057. E-mail: dasher@waort.org. Website: www.waort.org. **85% freelance written.** Semiannual nonprofit journal published by Jewish women's organization covering Jewish women celebrities, issues of contemporary Jewish culture, Israel, anti-Semitism, women's rights, Jewish travel and the international Jewish community. Estab. 1966. Circ. 50,000. Byline given. Pays on acceptance. No kill fee. Publishes ms an average of 1 year after acceptance. Buys first North American serial rights. Submit seasonal material 6 months in advance. Accepts queries by mail, e-mail. Responds in 3 months to queries. Sample copy for sae with 9x12 envelope and 3 First-Class stamps. Guidelines for #10 SASE.
Nonfiction Cover feature profiles a dynamic Jewish woman making a difference in Judaism, women's issues, education, entertainment, profiles, business, journalism, arts. Needs essays, expose, humor, inspirational, opinion, personal experience, photo feature, religious, travel. Query. 1,800 words maximum **Pays $200 and up.**
Photos Send photos Identification of subjects required.
Columns/Departments Education Horizon; Destination (Jewish sites/travel); Inside Out (Advocacy); Women's

Business; Art Scene (interviews, books, films); Lasting Impression (uplifting/inspirational).
Fiction Length: 800 words. **Pays $150-300.**
Tips Send query only by e-mail or postal mail. Show us a fresh look, not a rehash. Particularly interested in stories of interest to younger readers.

$ REVIEW FOR RELIGIOUS

3601 Lindell Blvd., Room 428, St. Louis MO 63108-3393. (314)633-4610. Fax: (314)633-4611. E-mail: reviewrfr@gmail.com. Website: www.reviewforreligious.org. **100% freelance written**. Quarterly magazine for Roman Catholic priests, brothers, and sisters. Estab. 1942. Byline given. Pays on publication. No kill fee. Publishes ms an average of 9 months after acceptance. Buys first North American serial rights. Rarely buys second serial (reprint) rights. Accepts queries by mail, fax. Responds in 2 months to queries. Guidelines available online.
Nonfiction Not for general audience. Length: 1,500-5,000 words. **Pays $6/page.**
Tips "The writer must know about religious life in the Catholic Church and be familiar with prayer, vows, community life, and ministry."

N SACRED JOURNEY

The Journal of Fellowship in Prayer, Fellowship in Prayer, Inc., 291 Witherspoon St., Princeton NJ 08542. (609)924-6863. Fax: (609)924-6910. E-mail: editorial@sacredjourney.org. Website: www.sacredjourney.org. **70% freelance written**. *Sacred Journey*: The Journal of Fellowship in Prayer is a quarterly multi-faith journal published Winter, Spring, Summer and Autumn. Estab. 1950. Circ. 5,000. No kill fee. Retains one-time rights and then the copyright is returned to the author. Editorial lead time 3 months. Submit seasonal material 4 months in advance. Accepts queries by e-mail (preferably). Accepts previously published material. Accepts simultaneous submissions. Responds within 4 months of receipt. Submission is considered permission for publication. We reserve the right to edit. We will make every effort to contact the author with content revisions Please include or be prepared to provide a bio of 50-words or less and/or a headshot phot to accompany your work, should it be selected for the print journal. Sample copy free. Guidelines available online.

- "We publish articles, poems, and photographs which convey a spiritual orientation to life, promote prayer, meditation, and service to others and present topics that will foster a deeper spirit of unity among humankind. The spiritual insights, practices, and beliefs of women and men from a broad spectrum of religious traditions are welcomed."

Nonfiction "Articles should communicate an inspirational message of universal appeal and may be told through an individual's experience. Articles may be written from a particular religious context; however, the language and message should convey inclusiveness. **Buys 30 mss/year.** Send complete ms. Length: Approx. 750-1,500 words, double-spaced. **"You receive a complimentary one-year subscription to Sacred Journey if you work is selected for publication in the journal or on our website. For publication in the print journal you will also receive 5 copies of the issue in which your work appears."**
Photos "We accept Hi-Res digital photographs and illlustrations for possible publication. Cover photos are typically in color while interior photos are usually in black & white. We favor vertical images, but consider horizontal ones."
Poetry Does not want poetry highly specific to a certain faith tradition. Nothing laden with specific faith terminology, nor a lot of Bibe quotes or other quotes. Submit maximum 5 per submission poems. Limited to 35 lines (occasionally longer).
Tips "We are always seeking original prayers to share the richness of the world's religious traditions."

$$$ SCIENCE & SPIRIT

1319 Eighteenth St., NW, Washington D.C. 20036. Fax: (617)847-5924. E-mail: lwitham@science-spirit.org. Website: www.science-spirit.org. **75% freelance written**. Bimonthly magazine covering science and spirituality. *Science & Spirit* explores the integration of the scientific and spiritual aspects of our culture in a way that is accessible and relevant to everyday living. Examining life's complexities through the lenses of both science and spirituality offers insight neither provides alone. We look for solidly reported pieces relayed in a narrative voice. Circ. 7,500. Byline given. Pays on acceptance. Publishes ms an average of 4 months after acceptance. Makes work-for-hire assignments. Editorial lead time 4-6 months. Submit seasonal material 6 months in advance. Accepts queries by e-mail. Responds in 1 month to queries. Sample copy available online. Guidelines available online.
Nonfiction Needs essays, interview, religious, science, reported pieces. No New Age pieces. In general, we look for solidly reported articles. **Buys 40 mss/year.** Query with published clips. Length: 1,200-2,500 words. **Pays 20-75¢/word for assigned articles. Pays 20-50¢/word for unsolicited articles.** Sometimes pays expenses of writers on assignment.
Tips The best way to improve odds of publication is to really familiarize yourself with the magazine. The most successful submissions are focused pieces that contain unique information about the relationship between science and spirituality. We already know that science, faith, and ethics intersect—we're looking for angles we've never heard before, explored in new and innovative ways.

$ N THE SECRET PLACE

National Ministries, ABC/USA, P.O. Box 851, Valley Forge PA 19482-0851. (610)768-2240. E-mail: thesecretplace@abc-usa.org. **100% freelance written.** Quarterly devotional covering Christian daily devotions. Estab. 1937. Circ. 100,000. Byline given. Pays on acceptance. No kill fee. Buys first rights. Editorial lead time 1 year. Submit seasonal material 9 months in advance. For free sample and guidelines, send 6x9 SASE.

Nonfiction Needs inspirational. **Buys about 400 mss/year.** Send complete ms. Length: 100-200 words. **Pays $20.**

Poetry Needs avant-garde, free verse, light verse, traditional. **Buys 12-15/year poems/year.** Submit maximum 6 poems. Length: 4-30 lines. **Pays $20.**

Tips "Prefers submissions via e-mail."

$ $ $ $ SHAMBHALA SUN

1660 Hollis St., Suite 701, Halifax NS B3J 1V7 Canada. Fax: (902)423-2701. E-mail: magazine@shambhalasun.com. Website: www.shambhalasun.com. **80% freelance written.** Bimonthly magazine covering contemporary life from a Buddhist perspective; Buddhism. We're interested in how a contemplative spiritual practice informs one's view of modern life and experience of it. Estab. 1992. Circ. 75,000. Byline given. Pays on publication. Publishes ms an average of 2-4 months after acceptance. Buys one-time rights, buys electronic rights. Editorial lead time 3 months. Submit seasonal material 6 months in advance. Accepts queries by e-mail, fax. Accepts simultaneous submissions. Responds in 2 weeks to queries. Responds in 1-2 months to mss. Sample copy free. Guidelines free.

Nonfiction Needs book excerpts, essays, how-to, humor, inspirational, interview, opinion, personal experience, photo feature, religious, travel. Does not want unsolicited poetry. **Buys 20 mss/year.** Send complete ms. Length: 800-3,900 words. **Pays $250-2,000 for assigned articles. Pays $100 for unsolicited articles.** Sometimes pays expenses of writers on assignment.

Photos State availability Captions, identification of subjects required. Reviews contact sheets, negatives, transparencies, prints, GIF/JPEG files. Negotiates payment individually. Buys one time rights.

Columns/Departments About a Poem (short essay on a favorite poem), 300 words. 6 Query. **Pays $0-250.**

$ $ SHARING THE VICTORY

Fellowship of Christian Athletes, 8701 Leeds Rd., Kansas City MO 64129. (816)921-0909. Fax: (816)921-8755. E-mail: stv@fca.org. Website: www.fca.org. **50% freelance written. Prefers to work with published/established writers, but works with a growing number of new/unpublished writers each year.** Published 9 times/year. We seek to serve as a ministry tool of the Fellowship of Christian Athletes by informing, inspiring and involving coaches, athletes and all whom they influence, that they may make an impact for Jesus Christ. Estab. 1959. Circ. 80,000. Byline given. Pays on publication. No kill fee. Publishes ms an average of 4 months after acceptance. Buys first rights. Submit seasonal material 6 months in advance. Responds in 3 months to queries. Responds in 3 months to mss. Sample copy for $1 and 9x12 SAE with 3 first-class stamps. Guidelines available online.

Nonfiction Must have FCA connection. Needs inspirational, interview, with name athletes and coaches solid in their faith, personal experience, photo feature. **Buys 5-20 mss/year.** Query. Length: 500-1,000 words.

Photos State availability Reviews contact sheets. Pay based on size of photo. Buys one time rights.

Tips Profiles and interviews of particular interest to coed athlete, primarily high school and college age. Our graphics and editorial content appeal to youth. The area most open to freelancers is profiles on or interviews with well-known athletes or coaches (male, female, minorities) who have been or are involved in some capacity with FCA.

$ SOCIAL JUSTICE REVIEW

3835 Westminster Place, St. Louis MO 63108-3472. (314)371-1653. Fax: (314)371-0889. E-mail: centbur@juno.com. Website: www.socialjusticereview.org. **25% freelance written. Works with a small number of new/unpublished writers each year.** Bimonthly magazine. Estab. 1908. No kill fee. Publishes ms an average of 1 year after acceptance. Buys first North American serial rights. Accepts queries by mail. Sample copy for sae with 9x12 envelope and 3 First-Class stamps.

Nonfiction Query by mail only with SASE. Length: 2,500-3,000 words. **Pays about 2¢/word.**

Reprints Send typed manuscript with rights for sale noted and information about when and where the material previously appeared. Pays about 2¢/word.

Tips Write moderate essays completely compatible with papal teaching and readable to the average person.

$ SPIRITUAL LIFE

2131 Lincoln Rd. NE, Washington DC 20002-1199. (202)832-5505. Fax: (202)832-8967. E-mail: edodonnell@aol.com. Website: www.spiritual-life.org. **80% freelance written. Prefers to work with published/established writers.** Quarterly magazine for largely Christian, well-educated, serious readers. Circ. 12,000. Pays on acceptance. No kill fee. Publishes ms an average of 1 year after acceptance. Buys first North American serial rights. Responds in 2 months to queries. Sample copy and writer's guidelines for 7x10 or larger SAE with 5 first-class stamps.

Nonfiction Serious articles of contemporary spirituality and its pastoral application to everday life. High quality articles about our encounter with God in the present day world. Language of articles should be college level. Technical terminology, if used, should be clearly explained. Material should be presented in a postive manner. Buys inspirational and think pieces. Brief autobiographical information (present occupation, past occupations, books and articles published, etc.) should accompany article. Sentimental articles or those dealing with specific devotional practices not accepted.No fiction or poetry. **Buys 20 mss/year.** Length: 3,000-5,000 words. **Pays $50 minimum, and 2 contributor's copies.**

$ STANDARD

Nazarene International Headquarters, 6401 The Paseo, Kansas City MO 64131. (816)333-7000. Fax: (816)333-4439. Website: www.nazarene.org. **100% freelance written. Works with a small number of new/unpublished writers each year.** Weekly inspirational paper with Christian reading for adults. In *Standard* we want to show Christianity in action, and we prefer to do that through stories that hold the reader's attention. Estab. 1936. Circ. 130,000. Byline given. Pays on acceptance. No kill fee. Publishes ms an average of 14-18 months after acceptance. Buys first or reprint. rights. Submit seasonal material 18 months in advance. Accepts simultaneous submissions. Writer's guidelines and sample copy for SAE with 2 first-class stamps or by e-mail

- Accepts submissions by mail, e-mail. No queries needed.

Fiction Prefers fiction-type stories *showing* Christianity in action. Send complete ms. Length: 600-1,800 words. **Pays 3 ½¢/word for first rights; 2¢/word for reprint rights, and contributor's copies.**

Poetry Needs free verse, haiku, light verse, traditional. Buys poems for Advent and Lent only. **Buys 25 poems/year.** Submit maximum 5 poems. 30 lines **Pays 25¢/line.**

Tips Stories should express Christian principles without being preachy. Setting, plot, and characterization must be realistic.

$ $ ST. ANTHONY MESSENGER

28 W. Liberty St., Cincinnati OH 45202-6498. (513)241-5615. Fax: (513)241-0399. E-mail: stanthony@americancatholic.org. Website: www.americancatholic.org. **55% freelance written.** Monthly general interest magazine for a national readership of Catholic families, most of which have children or grandchildren in grade school, high school, or college. *St. Anthony Messenger* is a Catholic family magazine which aims to help its readers lead more fully human and Christian lives. We publish articles which report on a changing church and world, opinion pieces written from the perspective of Christian faith and values, personality profiles, and fiction which entertains and informs. Estab. 1893. Circ. 305,000. Byline given. Pays on acceptance. No kill fee. Publishes ms an average of 1 year after acceptance. Buys first North American serial rights, buys electronic rights. first worldwide serial rights. Submit seasonal material 6 months in advance. Accepts queries by mail, e-mail, fax. Responds in 3 weeks to queries. Responds in 2 months to mss. Sample copy for 9x12 SAE with 4 first-class stamps. Guidelines available online.

Nonfiction Needs how-to, on psychological and spiritual growth, problems of parenting/better parenting, marriage problems/marriage enrichment, humor, inspirational, interview, opinion, limited use; writer must have special qualifications for topic, personal experience, if pertinent to our purpose, photo feature, informational, social issues. **Buys 35-50 mss/year.** Query with published clips. Length: 1,500-2,500 words. **Pays 20¢/word.** Sometimes pays expenses of writers on assignment.

Fiction Contact: Father Pat McCloskey, O.F.M., editor. Needs mainstream, religious, senior citizen/retirement. We do not want mawkishly sentimental or preachy fiction. Stories are most often rejected for poor plotting and characterization; bad dialogue—listen to how people talk; inadequate motivation. Many stories say nothing, are 'happenings' rather than stories. No fetal journals, no rewritten Bible stories. **Buys 12 mss/year.** Send complete ms. Length: 2,000-3,000 words. **Pays 16¢/word maximum and 2 contributor's copies; $1 charge for extras.**

Poetry Our poetry needs are very limited. Submit maximum 4-5 poems. Up to 20-25 lines; the shorter, the better. **Pays $2/line; $20 minimum.**

Tips The freelancer should consider why his or her proposed article would be appropriate for us, rather than for *Redbook* or *Saturday Review.* We treat human problems of all kinds, but from a religious perspective. Articles should reflect Catholic theology, spirituality, and employ a Catholic terminology and vocabulary. We need more articles on prayer, scripture, Catholic worship. Get authoritative information (not merely library research); we want interviews with experts. Write in popular style; use lots of examples, stories, and personal quotes. Word length is an important consideration.

SUCCESS STORIES

Franklin Publishing Company, 2723 Steamboat Circle, Arlington TX 76006. (817)548-1124. E-mail: ludwigotto@sbcglobal.net. Website: www.franklinpublishing.net. **59% freelance written.** Monthly journal covering positive responses to the problems in life. Estab. 1983. Circ. 1,000. Byline given. Does not pay, but offers 15% discount on issues purchased and 1-year free membership in the International Association of Professionals No kill fee. Publishes ms an average of 1 month after acceptance. Buys one-time rights. Editorial lead time 1 month. Submit seasonal material 3 months in advance. Accepts queries by mail, e-mail. Accepts previously published material. Accepts simultaneous submissions. Responds in 1 week to queries and to mss. Guidelines available online.

Nonfiction Needs book excerpts, essays, general interest, historical, how-to, humor, inspirational, interview, new product, opinion, personal experience, religious, technical, travel. Send complete ms. Length: 750-6,000 words.

Fiction Needs adventure, condensed novels, ethnic, horror, humorous, mainstream, mystery, novel concepts, religious, science fiction, slice-of-life vignettes of life, suspense, western. Send complete ms.

Poetry Needs avantgarde, free verse, haiku, light verse, traditional.

Fillers Needs anecdotes, facts, gags.

N TEACH KIDS!ESSSENTIALS

Child Evangelism Fellowship, Inc., Box 348, Warrenton MO 63383-0348. (636)456-4321. Fax: (636)456-4321. E-mail: yolanda.derstine@cefonline.com. Website: www.cefonline.com. **Contact:** Yolanda Derstine. **90% freelance written**. Monthly newsletter. "Our purpose is to equip Christians to win the world's children to Christ and disciple them. Our readership is Sunday school teachers, Christian education leaders, and children's workers in every phase of Christian ministry to children 4-12 years old." Estab. 1942. Circ. 6,500. Byline given. Publishes ms an average of 1 month after acceptance. All rights reserved. Submit seasonal material 6 months in advance. Accepts queries by e-mail (complete ms.). Responds on acceptance Sample copy and guidelines available online

Nonfiction "Unsolicited articles welcomed from writers with Christian education training or current experience in working with children." Needs "Interested in articles on any aspect of children's ministry.". **Buys 50 mss/year.** Query. Length: 200-300 words. **Pays with subscription.**

Reprints Send photocopy and information about when and where the material previously appeared. Pays by subscription.

$ THESE DAYS

Presbyterian Publishing Corp., 100 Witherspoon St., Louisville KY 40202-1396. (502)569-5102. Fax: (502)569-5113. E-mail: vpatton@presbypub.com. **95% freelance written**. Quarterly magazine covering religious devotionals. *These Days* is published especially for the Cumberland Presbyterian Church, The Presbyterian Church in Canada, The Presbyterian Church (U.S.A.), The United Churches of Canada, and The United Church of Christ as a personal, family, and group devotional guide. Estab. 1970. Circ. 200,000. Byline given. Pays on acceptance. No kill fee. Publishes ms an average of 8 months after acceptance. Buys all rights. Makes work-for-hire assignments. Editorial lead time 8 months. Submit seasonal material 1 year in advance. Accepts queries by mail, e-mail. Responds in 6 months to queries. Responds in 10 months to mss. Sample copy for sae with 6x9 envelope and 3 First-Class stamps. Guidelines for #10 SASE.

Nonfiction Use freelance in all issues. Only devotional material will be accepted. Send for application form and guidelines. Enclose #10 SASE. Publishes very few unsolicited devotionals. **Buys 365 mss/year.** Query. Devotionals, 200 words; These Moments, 475 words; These Times, 750 words **Pays $14.25 for devotions; $30 for These Moments, and $45 for These Times.**

Poetry Buys 2-4 poems/year. Submit maximum 5 poems. Length: 3-20 lines. **Pays $15.**

Tips The best way to be considered is to send a 1-page query that includes your religious affiliation and your religious, writing-related experience, plus a sample devotion in our format and/or published clips of similar material. Read a current issue devotionally to get a feel for the magazine. We would also like to see more minority and Canadian writers.

$ $ THIS ROCK

Catholic Answers, P.O. Box 199000, San Diego CA 92159. (800)291-8000. Website: www.catholic.com. **60% freelance written**. Monthly magazine covering Catholic apologetics and evangelization. Our content explains, defends and promotes Catholic teaching. Estab. 1990. Circ. 24,000. Byline given. Pays on acceptance. Offers variable kill fee. Publishes ms an average of 4 months after acceptance. Buys first rights, buys electronic rights. Accepts queries by e-mail. Responds in 2-4 weeks to queries. Responds in 1-2 months to mss. Sample copy available online. Guidelines by email.

Nonfiction Needs book excerpts, essays, religious, conversion stories. **Buys 50 mss/year.** Send complete ms. Length: 1,500-3,000 words. **Pays $200-350.**

Columns/Departments Damascus Road (stories of conversion to the Catholic Church), 2,000 words. 10 Send complete ms. **Pays $200.**

$ $ TODAY'S CHRISTIAN

Stories of Faith, Hope and God's Love, Christianity Today, 465 Gundersen Dr., Carol Stream IL 60188. (630)260-6200. Fax: (630)480-2004. E-mail: tceditor@todays-christian.com. Website: www.christianitytoday.com/todayschristian. **25% freelance written**. Bimonthly magazine for adult evangelical Christian audience. Estab.

1963. Circ. 75,000. Byline given. Pays on acceptance; on publication for humor pieces. No kill fee. Editorial lead time 5 months. Submit seasonal material 8 months in advance. Accepts queries by mail. Accepts simultaneous submissions. Responds in 1 month to queries. Sample copy for sae with 5—Š8 envelope and 4 First-Class stamps. Guidelines available online.

Nonfiction Needs book excerpts, general interest, historical, humor, inspirational, interview, personal experience, photo feature, religious. **Buys 100-125 mss/year.** Send complete ms. Length: 250-1,500 words. **Pays $125-600 depending on length.** Pays expenses of writers on assignment.

Reprints Send tearsheet, photocopy or typed ms with rights for sale noted and information about when and where the material previously appeared. Pays 35-50% of amount paid for an original article

Photos Send photos Identification of subjects required. Reviews transparencies, prints. Negotiates payment individually. Buys one time rights.

Columns/Departments Contact: Cynthia Thomas, editorial coordinator. Humor Us (adult church humor, kids say and do funny things, and humorous wedding tales), 50-200 words. **Pays $35.**

Fillers Needs anecdotes, short fillers. 10-20 Length: 100-250 words. **Pays $35.**

Tips Most of our articles are reprints or staff written. Freelance competition is keen, so tailor submissions to meet our needs by observing the following: *Today's Christian* audience is truly a general interest one, including men and women, urban professionals and rural homemakers, adults of every age and marital status, and Christians of every church affiliation. We seek to publish a magazine that people from the variety of ethnic groups in North America will find interesting and relevant.

$ $ TODAY'S PENTECOSTAL EVANGEL

The General Council of the Assemblies of God, 1445 N. Boonville, Springfield MO 65802-1894. (417)862-2781. Fax: (417)862-0416. E-mail: tpe@ag.org. Website: www.tpe.ag.org. **5-10% freelance written**. Weekly magazine emphasizing news of the Assemblies of God for members of the Assemblies and other Pentecostal and charismatic Christians. Articles should be inspirational without being preachy. Any devotional writing should take a literal approach to the Bible. A variety of general topics and personal experience accepted with inspirational tie-in. Estab. 1913. Circ. 200,000. Byline given. Pays on acceptance. Offers 100% kill fee. Publishes ms an average of 6 months after acceptance. Buys first North American serial rights, buys one-time rights. Editorial lead time 3 months. Submit seasonal material 6 months in advance. Accepts queries by e-mail. Accepts previously published material. Responds in 2 weeks to queries. Responds in 2 months to mss. Sample copy free. Guidelines available online.

Nonfiction Needs book excerpts, general interest, inspirational, personal experience, religious. Does not want poetry, fiction, self-promotional. **Buys 10-15 mss/year.** Send complete ms. Length: 700-1,200 words. **Pays $25-200.** Pays expenses of writers on assignment.

Tips We publish first-person articles concerning spiritual experiences; that is, answers to prayer for help in a particular situation, of unusual conversions or healings through faith in Christ. All articles submitted to us should be related to religious life. We are Protestant, evangelical, Pentecostal, and any doctrines or practices portrayed should be in harmony with the official position of our denomination (Assemblies of God).

$ TOGETHER

Media For Living, 1251 Virginia Ave., Harrisonburg VA 22802. Website: www.churchoutreach.com. **90% freelance written**. Quarterly tabloid covering religion and inspiration for a nonchurched audience. "*Together* is directed as an outreach publication to those who are not currently involved in a church; therefore, we need general inspirational articles that tell stories of personal change, especially around faith issues. Also, stories that will assist our readers in dealing with the many stresses and trials of everyday life—family, financial, career, community." Estab. 1980. Circ. 20,000. Byline given. Pays on publication. No kill fee. Publishes ms an average of 6-12 months after acceptance. Buys first rights, buys electronic rights. Editorial lead time 6-9 months. Submit seasonal material 6 months in advance. Accepts queries by mail, e-mail. Accepts previously published material. Accepts simultaneous submissions. Responds in 2 months to queries. Responds in 4 months to mss. Sample copy available online. Guidelines available online.

Nonfiction Needs essays, general interest, how-to, humor, inspirational, interview, personal experience, testimony, religious. No pet stories. We have limited room for stories about illness, dying, or grief, but we do use them occasionally. We publish in March, June, September, and December, so holidays that occur in other months are not usually the subject of articles. **Buys 16 mss/year.** Send complete ms. Length: 500-1,200 words. **Pays $35-60.**

Photos State availability. Captions, identification of subjects, model releases required. Reviews 4x6 prints, TIF/JPEG files. Offers $15-25/photo. Buys one time rights.

Tips "We prefer 'good news' stories that are uplifting and noncontroversial in nature. We can use stories of change and growth in religious journey from a Christian slant, including 'salvation' stories. We generally want articles that tell stories of people solving problems and dealing with personal issues rather than essays or 'preaching.' If you submit electronically, it is very helpful if you put the specific title of the submission in the subject line and include your e-mail address in the body of the e-mail or on your manuscript. Also, always include your address and phone number."

TRICYCLE

The Buddhist Review, 92 Vandam St., New York NY 10013. (212)645-1143. Fax: (212)645-1493. E-mail: editorial@tricycle.com. Website: www.tricycle.com. **80% freelance written**. Quarterly magazine covering the impact of Buddhism on Western culture. *Tricycle* readers tend to be well educated and open minded. Estab. 1991. Circ. 60,000. Byline given. Pays on publication. Offers 25% kill fee. Buys one-time rights. Editorial lead time 3 months. Accepts queries by mail, e-mail, fax. Accepts simultaneous submissions. Responds in 3 months to queries & mss Sample copy for $7.95 or online at website Guidelines available online

Nonfiction Needs book excerpts, essays, general interest, historical, humor, inspirational, interview, personal experience, photo feature, religious, travel. **Buys 4-6 mss/year.** Length: 1,000-5,000 words.

Photos State availability Captions, identification of subjects required. Reviews contact sheets. Negotiates payment individually. Buys one-time rights.

Columns/Departments Reviews (film, books, tapes), 600 words; Science and Gen Next, both 700 words. 6-8 Query.

Tips "*Tricycle* is a Buddhist magazine, and we can only consider Buddhist-related submissions."

THE UNITED CHURCH OBSERVER

478 Huron St., Toronto ON M5R 2R3 Canada. (416)960-8500. Fax: (416)960-8477. E-mail: dnwilson@ucobserver.org. Website: www.ucobserver.org. **50% freelance written. Prefers to work with published/established writers.** "Monthly general interest magazine for people associated with The United Church of Canada and non-churchgoers interested in issues of faith, justice, ethics and living.". Deals primarily with events, trends, and policies having religious significance. Most coverage is Canadian, but reports on international or world concerns will be considered. Byline usually given. Pays on publication. No kill fee. Publishes ms an average of 4 months after acceptance. first serial rights and occasionally all rights. Accepts queries by mail, e-mail, fax.

Nonfiction Occasional opinion features only. Longer pieces are usually assigned to known writers. Submissions should be written as news, no more than 1,200 words length, accurate, and well-researched. No poetry. Queries preferred. **Rates depend on subject, author, and work involved.** Pays expenses of writers on assignment as negotiated.

Reprints Send tearsheet or photocopy and information about when and where the material previously appeared. Payment negotiated.

Photos Buys color photographs with mss. Send via e-mail. Payment varies.

Tips "The writer has a better chance of breaking in at our publication with short articles. Include samples of previous magazine writing with query."

$ THE UPPER ROOM

Daily Devotional Guide, P.O. Box 340004, Nashville TN 37203-0004. (615)340-7252. Fax: (615)340-7267. E-mail: theupperroommagazine@upperroom.org. Website: www.upperroom.org. **95% freelance written. Eager to work with new/unpublished writers.** Bimonthly magazine offering a daily inspirational message which includes a Bible reading, text, prayer, `Thought for the Day,' and suggestion for further prayer. Each day's meditation is written by a different person and is usually a personal witness about discovering meaning and power for Christian living through scripture study which illuminates daily life. Circ. 2.2 million (U.S.); 385,000 outside U.S. Byline given. Pays on publication. No kill fee. Publishes ms an average of 1 year after acceptance. Buys first North American serial rights, buys translation rights. Submit seasonal material 14 months in advance. Sample copy and writer's guidelines with a 4x6 SAE and 2 first-class stamps. Guidelines only for #10 SASE or online

- Manuscripts are not returned. If writers include a stamped, self-addressed postcard, we will notify them that their writing has reached us. This does not imply acceptance or interest in purchase. Does not respond unless material is accepted for publication.

Nonfiction Needs inspirational, personal experience, Bible-study insights. Lent and Easter; Advent No poetry, lengthy spiritual journey stories. **Buys 365 unsolicited mss/year.** Send complete ms by mail or e-mail. Length: 300 words. **Pays $25/meditation.**

Tips The best way to break in to our magazine is to send a well-written manuscript that looks at the Christian faith in a fresh way. Standard stories and sermon illustrations are immediately rejected. We very much want to find new writers and welcome good material. We are particularly interested in meditations based on Old Testament characters and stories. Good repeat meditations can lead to work on longer assignments for our other publications, which pay more. A writer who can deal concretely with everyday situations, relate them to the Bible and spiritual truths, and write clear, direct prose should be able to write for *The Upper Room.* We want material that provides for interaction on the part of the reader—meditation suggestions, journaling suggestions, space to reflect and link personal experience with the meditation for the day. Meditations that are personal, authentic, exploratory, and full of sensory detail make good devotional writing.

$ $ U.S. CATHOLIC

Claretian Publications, 205 W. Monroe St., Chicago IL 60606. (312)236-7782. Fax: (312)236-8207. E-mail: editors@uscatholic.org. Website: www.uscatholic.org. **100% freelance written**. Monthly magazine covering Roman Catholic spirituality. *U.S. Catholic* is dedicated to the belief that it makes a difference whether you're Catholic. We invite and help our readers explore the wisdom of their faith tradition and apply their faith to the challenges of the 21st century. Estab. 1935. Circ. 40,000. Byline given. Pays on acceptance. No kill fee. Publishes ms an average of 2-3 months after acceptance. Buys all rights. Editorial lead time 8 months. Submit seasonal material 6 months in advance. Accepts queries by mail, e-mail, fax, phone. Responds in 1 month to queries. Responds in 2 months to mss. Sample copy for large SASE. Guidelines by e-mail or on website.

- Please include SASE with written ms.

Nonfiction Needs essays, inspirational, opinion, personal experience, religious. **Buys 100 mss/year.** Send complete ms. Length: 2,500-3,500 words. **Pays $250-600.** Sometimes pays expenses of writers on assignment.
Photos State availability
Columns/Departments Pays $250-600.
Fiction Contact: Maureen Abood, literary editor. Needs ethnic, mainstream, religious, slice-of-life vignettes. **Buys 4-6 mss/year.** Send complete ms. Length: 2,500-3,000 words. **Pays $300.**
Poetry Contact: Maureen Abood, literary editor. Needs free verse. No light verse. **Buys 12 poems/year.** Submit maximum 5 poems. Length: 50 lines. **Pays $75.**

$ $ THE WAR CRY

The Salvation Army, 615 Slaters Lane, Alexandria VA 22314. (703)684-5500. Fax: (703)684-5539. E-mail: war_cry@usn.salvationarmy.org. **5% freelance written**. Biweekly magazine covering evangelism and Christian growth stories. Estab. 1881. Circ. 250,000. Byline given. Pays on acceptance. No kill fee. Publishes ms an average of 2 months-1 year after acceptance. Buys first rights, buys one-time rights. Editorial lead time 6 weeks. Submit seasonal material 1 year in advance. Responds in 2 months to mss. Sample copy, theme list, and writer's guidelines free for #10 SASE or online
Nonfiction Needs inspirational, interview, personal experience, religious. No missionary stories, confessions. **Buys 25 mss/year.** Send complete ms. **Pays 15-25¢/word for articles; 12¢/word for reprints.**
Photos Identification of subjects required. Offers up to $200/full page or cover; $50/inside. Buys one time rights.
Fillers Needs anecdotes, inspirational. 10-20 Length: 200-500 words. **Pays 15¢/word.**

$ WESLEYAN LIFE

The Wesleyan Publishing House, P.O. Box 50434, Indianapolis IN 46250-0434. (317)774-7909. Fax: (317)774-3924. E-mail: communications@wesleyan.org. Quarterly magazine of The Wesleyan Church. Estab. 1842. Circ. 50,000. Byline given. Pays on publication. No kill fee. Buys first rights or simultaneous rights (prefers first rights). Submit seasonal material 6 months in advance. Accepts simultaneous submissions.
Nonfiction Needs inspirational, religious. No poetry accepted. Send complete ms. Length: 250-400 words. **Pays $25-150.**

$ 🌐 WOMAN ALIVE

Christian Publishing and Outreach, Garcia Estate, Canterbury Road, Worthing West Sussex BN13 1BW United Kingdom. (44)(190)360-4352. Fax: (44)(190)383-0066. E-mail: womanalive@cpo.org.uk. Website: www.womanalive.co.uk. Christian magazine geared specifically toward women. It covers all denominations and seeks to inspire, encourage, and resource women in their faith, helping them to grow in their relationship with God and providing practical help and biblical perspective on the issues impacting their lives. Pays on publication. No kill fee. Accepts queries by mail, e-mail. Sample copy for £1.50, plus postage. Guidelines by email.
Nonfiction Contemporary issues (social/domestic issues affecting the church and women), reports from around the country giving a brief overview of the town and what churches/individuals are doing there, lifestyle, money matters, ethical shopping, work/life balance, homestyle, fashion, creative cookery. Needs how-to, build life skills and discipleship, interview, with Christian women in prominent positions or who are making a difference in their communities/jobs, personal experience, women facing difficult challenges or taking on new challenges, travel, affordable holiday destinations written from a Christian perspective. Submit clips, bio, article summary, ms, SASE. 750-900/1-page article; 1,200-1,300/2-page article; 1,500-1,600/3-page article. **Pays £75/1-page article; £95/2-page article; £125/3-page article.**
Photos Send photos Reviews 300 dpi digital images.

RETIREMENT

$ $ $ $ AARP THE MAGAZINE

AARP, 601 E St. NW, Washington DC 20049. E-mail: member@aarp.org. Website: www.aarp.org. **50% freelance written. Prefers to work with published/established writers.** Bimonthly magazine. *AARP The Magazine* is devoted to the varied needs and active life interests of AARP members, age 50 and over, covering such topics as financial planning, travel, health, careers, retirement, relationships, and social and cultural change. Its editorial content serves the mission of AARP seeking through education, advocacy and service to enhance the quality of life for all by promoting independence, dignity, and purpose. Circ. 21,500,000. Byline given. Pays on acceptance. Offers 25% kill fee. Publishes ms an average of 6 months after acceptance. Buys exclusive first worldwide publication rights. Submit seasonal material 6 months in advance. Accepts queries by mail, e-mail. Responds in 3 months to queries. Sample copy free. Guidelines available online.

Nonfiction Articles can cover finance, health, food, travel, consumerism, general interest topics, and profiles/first-person accounts. Query with published clips. *No unsolicited mss.* Length: Up to 2,000 words. **Pays $1/word.** Sometimes pays expenses of writers on assignment.

Photos Photos purchased with or without accompanying mss. Pays $250 and up for color; $150 and up for b&w.

Tips The most frequent mistake made by writers in completing an article for us is poor follow-through with basic research. The outline is often more interesting than the finished piece. We do not accept unsolicited manuscripts.

$ MATURE YEARS

The United Methodist Publishing House, 201 Eighth Ave. S., Nashville TN 37202-0801. (615)749-6292. Fax: (615)749-6512. E-mail: matureyears@umpublishing.org. **80% freelance written. Prefers to work with published/established writers.** Quarterly magazine designed to help persons in and nearing the retirement years understand and appropriate the resources of the Christian faith in dealing with specific problems and opportunities related to aging. Estab. 1954. Circ. 55,000. Pays on acceptance. No kill fee. Publishes ms an average of 1 year after acceptance. Buys first North American serial rights. Submit seasonal material 14 months in advance. Responds in 2 weeks to queries. Responds in 2 months to mss. Sample copy for $6 and 9x12 SAE. Writer's guidelines for #10 SASE or by e-mail.

Nonfiction Especially important are opportunities for older adults to read about service, adventure, fulfillment, and fun. Needs how-to, hobbies, inspirational, religious, travel, special guidelines, older adult health, finance issues. **Buys 75-80 mss/year.** Send complete ms; e-mail submissions preferred. Length: 900-2,000 words. **Pays $45-125.** Sometimes pays expenses of writers on assignment.

Reprints Send tearsheet, photocopy or typed ms with rights for sale noted and information about when and where the material previously appeared. Pays at same rate as for previously unpublished material.

Photos Send photos Captions, model releases required. Negotiates pay individually. Typically buys one-time rights.

Columns/Departments Health Hints (retirement, health), 900-1,500 words; Going Places (travel, pilgrimage), 1,000-1,500 words; Fragments of Life (personal inspiration), 250-600 words; Modern Revelations (religious/inspirational), 900-1,500 words; Money Matters (personal finance), 1,200-1,800 words; Merry-Go-Round (cartoons, jokes, 4-6 line humorous verse); Puzzle Time (religious puzzles, crosswords). 4 Send complete ms. **Pays $25-45.**

Fiction Contact: Marvin Cropsey, editor. Needs humorous, religious, slice-of-life vignettes, retirement years nostalgia, intergenerational relationships. We don't want anything poking fun at old age, saccharine stories or anything not for older adults. Must show older adults (age 55 plus) in a positive manner. **Buys 4 mss/year.** Send complete ms. Length: 1,000-2,000 words. **Pays $60-125.**

Poetry Needs free verse, haiku, light verse, traditional. **Buys 24 poems/year poems/year.** Submit maximum 6 poems. Length: 3-16 lines. **Pays $5-20.**

$ PLUS

654 Osos St., San Luis Obispo CA 93401. (805)544-8711. Fax: (805)546-8827. E-mail: slojournal@fix.net. Website: slojournal.com. **60% freelance written.** Monthly magazine covering the 25 age group and up but young-at-heart audience. Estab. 1981. Circ. 25,000. Byline given. Pays on publication. No kill fee. Publishes ms an average of 2 months after acceptance. Buys one-time rights. Editorial lead time 2 months. Submit seasonal material 2 months in advance. Accepts queries by mail. Accepts simultaneous submissions. Responds in 2 weeks to queries. Responds in 1 month to mss. Sample copy for 9x12 SAE with $2 postage.

Nonfiction "We favor up-beat articles concerning nostalgia, personality profiles, subtle, not heavy-handed humor, travel, book reviews, entertainment and health related to the California central coast." Needs historical, humor, interview, personal experience, travel, book reviews, entertainment, health. Christmas (December); Travel (October, April) No finance, automotive, heavy humor, poetry, or fiction. **Buys 60-70 mss/year.** Send complete ms. Length: 600-1,400 words. **Pays $50-75.**

Photos Send photos

Tips "Request and read a sample copy before submitting."

RURAL

$ $ BACKWOODS HOME MAGAZINE

P.O. Box 712, Gold Beach OR 97444. (541)247-8900. Fax: (541)247-8600. E-mail: editor@backwoodshome.com. Website: www.backwoodshome.com. **90% freelance written**. Bimonthly magazine covering self-reliance. *Backwoods Home Magazine* is written for people who have a desire to pursue personal independence, self-sufficiency, and their dreams. We offer 'how-to' articles on self-reliance. Estab. 1989. Circ. 38,000. Byline given. Pays on acceptance. Buys first North American serial rights. Editorial lead time 4-6 months. Submit seasonal material 4-6 months in advance. Accepts queries by mail, e-mail. Sample copy for sae with 9x10 envelope and 6 First-Class stamps. Guidelines free.

Nonfiction Needs general interest, how-to, humor, personal experience, technical. **Buys 120 mss/year.** Send complete ms. Length: 500 words. **Pays $30-200.**

Photos Send photos Captions, identification of subjects, model releases required. Offers no additional payment for photos accepted with ms.

$ $ THE COUNTRY CONNECTION

Ontario's Magazine of Choice, Pinecone Publishing, P.O. Box 100, Boulter ON K0L 1G0 Canada. (613)332-3651. Website: www.pinecone.on.ca. **100% freelance written**. Magazine published 4 times/year covering nature, environment, history, heritage, nostalgia, travel and the arts. *The Country Connection* is a magazine for true nature lovers and the rural adventurer. Building on our commitment to heritage, cultural, artistic, and environmental themes, we continually add new topics to illuminate the country experience of people living within nature. Our goal is to chronicle rural life in its many aspects, giving `voice' to the countryside. Estab. 1989. Circ. 4,000. Byline given. Pays on publication. No kill fee. Publishes ms an average of 4 months after acceptance. Buys first rights. Editorial lead time 4 months. Accepts queries by mail, e-mail, phone. Sample copy for $5.64. Guidelines available online.

Nonfiction Needs general interest, historical, humor, opinion, personal experience, travel, lifestyle, leisure, art and culture, vegan recipes. No hunting, fishing, animal husbandry, or pet articles. **Buys 60 mss/year.** Send complete ms. Length: 500-2,000 words. **Pays 10¢/word.**

Photos Send photos Captions required. Reviews transparencies, prints, digital photos on CD. Offers $10-50/ photo Buys one time rights.

Fiction Needs adventure, fantasy, historical, humorous, slice-of-life vignettes, country living. **Buys 10 mss/ year.** Send complete ms. Length: 500-1,500 words. **Pays 10¢/word.**

Tips Canadian content only with a preference for Ontario subject matter. Send manuscript with appropriate support material such as photos, illustrations, maps, etc.

$ $ FARM & RANCH LIVING

Reiman Media Group, 5925 Country Lane, Greendale WI 53129. (414)423-0100. Fax: (414)423-8463. E-mail: editors@farmandranchliving.com. Website: www.farmandranchliving.com. **30% freelance written. Eager to work with new/unpublished writers.** Bimonthly magazine aimed at families that farm or ranch full time. *F&RL* is *not* a `how-to' magazine—it focuses on people rather than products and profits. Estab. 1978. Circ. 400,000. Byline given. Pays on publication. No kill fee. Publishes ms an average of 6 months after acceptance. Buys first rights, buys one-time rights. Submit seasonal material 6 months in advance. Accepts queries by mail, e-mail, fax. Responds in 6 weeks to queries. Sample copy for $2. Guidelines for #10 SASE.

Nonfiction Needs humor, rural only, inspirational, interview, personal experience, farm/ranch related, photo feature, nostalgia, prettiest place in the country (photo/text tour of ranch or farm). No issue-oriented stories (pollution, animal rights, etc.). **Buys 30 mss/year.** Send complete ms. Length: 600-1,200 words. **Pays up to $300 for text/photo package. Payment for Prettiest Place negotiable.**

Reprints Send photocopy with rights for sale noted. Payment negotiable.

Photos Scenic. State availability Pays $75-200 for 35mm color slides. Buys one time rights.

Tips Our readers enjoy stories and features that are upbeat and positive. A freelancer must see *F&RL* to fully appreciate how different it is from other farm publications—ordering a sample is strongly advised (not available on newsstands). Photo features (about interesting farm or ranch families) and personality profiles are most open to freelancers.

$ $ HOBBY FARMS

Rural Living for Pleasure and Profit, Bowtie, Inc., P.O. Box 8237, Lexington KY 40533. Fax: (859)260-9814. E-mail: hobbyfarms@bowtieinc.com. Website: www.hobbyfarms.com. **75% freelance written**. Bimonthly magazine covering small farms and rural lifestyle. *Hobby Farms* is the magazine for rural enthusiasts. Whether you have a small garden or 100 acres, there is something in *Hobby Farms* to educate, enlighten or inspire you. Estab. 2001. Circ. 100,000. Byline given. Pays on publication. Publishes ms an average of 6 months after acceptance. Buys first North American serial rights. Makes work-for-hire assignments. Editorial lead time 3 months. Submit seasonal material 6 months in advance. Accepts queries by mail, e-mail. Responds in 2 months to queries. Responds in 2 months to mss. Guidelines free.

- Writing tone should be conversational, but authoritative.

Nonfiction Needs historical, how-to, farm or livestock management, equipment, etc., interview, personal experience, technical, breed or crop profiles. **Buys 10 mss/year.** Send complete ms. Length: 1,500-2,500 words. Sometimes pays expenses of writers on assignment. Limit agreed upon in advance

Photos State availability of or send photos Identification of subjects, model releases required. Reviews transparencies, GIF/JPEG files. Negotiates payment individually Buys one time rights.

Tips Please state your specific experience with any aspect of farming (livestock, gardening, equipment, marketing, etc).

$ MOTHER EARTH NEWS

Ogden Publications, 1503 SW 42nd St., Topeka KS 66609-1265. (785)274-4300. E-mail: letters@motherearthnews.com. Website: www.motherearthnews.com. **Contact:** Cheryl Long, ed. **Mostly written by staff and team of established freelancers.** Bimonthly magazine emphasizing country living, country skills, natural health and sustainable technologies for both long-time and would-be ruralists. "*Mother Earth News* promotes self-sufficient, financially independent and environmentally aware lifestyles. Many of our feature articles are written by our Contributing Editors, but we also assign articles to freelance writers, particularly those who have experience with our subject matter (both firsthand adn writing experience." Circ. 350,000. Byline given. Pays on publication. No kill fee. Submit seasonal material 5 months in advance. Responds in 6 months to mss. Sample copy for $5. Guidelines for #10 SASE.

Nonfiction Needs how-to, green building, do-it-yourself, organic gardening, whole foods & cooking, natural health, livestock & sustainable farming, renewable energy, 21st century homesteading, nature-environment-community, green transportation. No fiction, please. **Buys 35-50 mss/year.** Query. Please send a short synopsis of the idea, a one-page outline and any relevant digital photos, and samples. If available, please send us copies of one or two published articles, or tell us where to find them online. "Country Lore" length: 100-300/words. "Firsthand Reports" length: 1,500-2,000/words **Pays $25-150.**

Photos "We welcome quality photographs for our two departments."

Columns/Departments Country Lore (helpful how-to tips); 100-300/words; Firsthand Reports (first-person stories about sustainable lifestyles of all sorts), 1,500-2,000/words.

Tips "Read our magazine and take a close look at previous issues to learn more abut the various topics we cover. We assign articles about 6-8 months ahead of publication date, so keep in mind timing and the seasonality of some topics. Our articles provide hands-on, useful information for people who want a more fun, conscientious, sustainable, secure and satisfying lifestyle. Practicality is critical; freelance articles must be informative, well-documented and tightly written in an engaging and energetic voice. For how-to articles, complete, easy-to-understand instructions are essential."

$ RANGE MAGAZINE

The Cowboy Spirit on America's Outback, Purple Coyote Corp., 106 E. Adams St., Suite 201, Carson City NV 89706. (775)884-2200. Fax: (775)884-2213. Website: www.rangemagazine.com. **70% freelance written.** Quarterly magazine. *RANGE* magazine covers ranching and farming and the issues that affect agriculture. Estab. 1991. Pays on publication. Publishes ms an average of 6 months after acceptance. Buys first North American serial rights. Accepts queries by e-mail. Responds in 6-8 weeks to queries. Responds in 3-6 months to mss. Sample copy for $2. Guidelines available online.

Nonfiction Needs book excerpts, humor, interview, personal experience, photo feature. No rodeos or anything by a writer not familiar with *RANGE*. Query. Length: 500-2,000 words. **Pays $50-350.**

Photos Contact: C.J. Hadley, editor/publisher. State availability Captions, identification of subjects required. Reviews 35mm transparencies, 4x6 prints, CDs with contact sheet & captions. Must be high-res digital images. Negotiates payment individually. Buys one time rights.

$ RURAL HERITAGE

PO Box 2067, Cedar Rapids IA 52406-2067. (319)362-3027. E-mail: editor@ruralheritage.com. Website: www.ruralheritage.com. **98% freelance written. Willing to work with a small number of new/unpublished writers.** Bimonthly magazine devoted to the training and care of draft animals. Estab. 1976. Circ. 9,500. Byline given. Pays on publication. No kill fee. Publishes ms an average of 6 months after acceptance. Buys first English language rights. Submit seasonal material 6 months in advance. Accepts queries by mail, e-mail. Responds in 3 months to queries. Sample copy for $8. Guidelines available online.

Nonfiction Needs how-to, farming with draft animals, interview, people using draft animals, photo feature. No articles on *mechanized* farming. **Buys 200 mss/year.** Query or send complete ms. Length: 1,200-1,500 words. **Pays 5¢/word.**

Photos Six covers/year, animals in harness $200. Photo guidelines for #10 SASE or on website. Captions, identification of subjects required. Pays $10. Buys one time rights.

Poetry Needs traditional. **Pays $5-25.**

Tips Thoroughly understand our subject: working draft animals in harness. We'd like more pieces on plans and instructions for constructing various horse-drawn implements and vehicles. Always welcome are: 1.) Detailed descriptions and photos of horse-drawn implements, 2.) Prices and other details of draft animal and implement auctions and sales.

$ $ RURALITE

P.O. Box 558, Forest Grove OR 97116-0558. (503)357-2105. Fax: (503)357-8615. E-mail: curtisc@ruralite.org. Website: www.ruralite.org. **80% freelance written. Works with new, unpublished writers.** Monthly magazine aimed at members of consumer-owned electric utilities throughout 10 western states, including Alaska. Publishes 48 regional editions. Estab. 1954. Circ. 325,000. Byline given. Pays on acceptance. No kill fee. Buys first rights, buys sometimes reprint rights. Accepts queries by mail. Responds in 1 month to queries. Sample copy for 10x13 SAE with 4 first-class stamps; guidelines also online Guidelines available online.

Nonfiction Looking for well-written nonfiction, dealing primarily with human interest topics. Must have strong Northwest perspective and be sensitive to Northwest issues and attitudes. Wide range of topics possible, from energy-related subjects to little-known travel destinations to interesting people living in areas served by consumer-owned electric utilities. Family-related issues, Northwest history (no encyclopedia rewrites), people and events, unusual tidbits that tell the Northwest experience are best chances for a sale. **Buys 50-60 mss/year.** Query. Length: 100-2,000 words. **Pays $50-500.**

Reprints Send typed manuscript with rights for sale noted and information about when and where the material previously appeared.

Photos Illustrated stories are the key to a sale. Stories without art rarely make it. Color prints/negatives, color slides, all formats accepted. No black & white.

Tips Study recent issues. Follow directions when given an assignment. Be able to deliver a complete package (story and photos). We're looking for regular contributors to whom we can assign topics from our story list after they've proven their ability to deliver quality mss.

SCIENCE

$ $ AD ASTRA

The Magazine of the National Space Society, 1155 15th St. NW, Suite 500, Washington DC 20005. (202)429-1600. Fax: (202)463-0659. E-mail: adastra.editor@nss.org. Website: www.nss.org. **90% freelance written.** Quarterly magazine covering the space program. "We publish non-technical, lively articles about all aspects of international space programs, from shuttle missions to planetary probes to plans for the future and commercial space." Estab. 1989. Circ. 38,800. Byline given. Pays on publication. No kill fee. Buys first North American serial rights. Responds when interested. Sample copy for 9x12 SASE.

Nonfiction Needs book excerpts, essays, expose, general interest, interview, opinion, photo feature, technical. No science fiction or UFO stories. Query with published clips. Length: 1,000-2,400 words. **Pays $300-500 for features.**

Photos State availability Identification of subjects required. Reviews color prints, digital, JPEG-IS, GISS. Negotiates pay Buys one time rights.

Tips "We require manuscripts to be in Word or text file formats. Know the field of space technology, programs and policy. Know the players. Look for fresh angles. And, please, know how to write!"

$ $ $ $ AMERICAN ARCHAEOLOGY

The Archaeological Conservancy, 5301 Central Ave. NE, #902, Albuquerque NM 87108-1517. (505)266-9668. Fax: (505)266-0311. E-mail: tacmag@nm.net. Website: www.americanarchaeology.org. **60% freelance written.** Quarterly magazine. "We're a popular archaeology magazine. Our readers are very interested in this science. Our features cover important digs, prominent archaeologists, and most any aspect of the science. We only cover North America." Estab. 1997. Circ. 35,000. Byline given. Pays on acceptance. Offers 20% kill fee. Publishes ms an average of 3 months after acceptance. Buys one-time rights, buys electronic rights. Editorial lead time 3 months. Accepts queries by mail, e-mail, fax. Responds in 3 weeks to queries. Responds in 1 month to mss

Nonfiction No fiction, poetry, humor. **Buys 15 mss/year.** Query with published clips. Length: 1,500-3,000 words. **Pays $1,000-2,000.** Pays expenses of writers on assignment.

Photos State availability Identification of subjects required. Reviews transparencies, prints. Offers $400-600/photo shoot. Negotiates payment individually. Buys one time rights.

Tips "Read the magazine. Features must have a considerable amount of archaeological detail."

$ $ $ $ ARCHAEOLOGY

Archaeological Institute of America, 36-36 33rd St., Long Island NY 11106. (718)472-3050. Fax: (718)472-3051. E-mail: peter@archaeology.org. Website: www.archaeology.org. **50% freelance written.** Magazine. *Archaeology* combines worldwide archaeological findings with photography, specially rendered maps, drawings, and charts.

Articles cover current excavations and recent discoveries, and include personality profiles, technology updates, adventure, travel and studies of ancient cultures. The only magazine of its kind to bring worldwide archaeology to the attention of the general public. Estab. 1948. Circ. 220,000. Byline given. Pays on acceptance. Offers 25% kill fee. Buys world rights. Submit seasonal material 6 months in advance. Accepts queries by mail, e-mail, fax. Accepts simultaneous submissions. Sample copy and writer's guidelines free

Nonfiction Needs essays, general interest. **Buys 6 mss/year.** Query preferred. Length: 1,000-3,000 words. **Pays $2,000 maximum.** Sometimes pays expenses of writers on assignment.

Photos Send photos Identification of subjects, True required. Reviews 4x5 color transparencies, 35mm color slides.

Tips We reach nonspecialist readers interested in art, science, history, and culture. Our reports, regional commentaries, and feature-length articles introduce readers to recent developments in archaeology worldwide.

$ $ ASTRONOMY

Kalmbach Publishing, 21027 Crossroads Circle, P.O. Box 1612, Waukesha WI 53187-1612. (262)796-8776. Fax: (262)798-6468. Website: www.astronomy.com. **Contact:** David J. Eicher, Executive Editor. **50% of articles submitted and written by science writers; includes commissioned and unsolicited.** Monthly magazine covering the science and hobby of astronomy. "Half of our magazine is for hobbyists (who are active observers of the sky); the other half is directed toward armchair astronomers who are intrigued by the science." Estab. 1973. Circ. 122,000. Byline given. Pays on acceptance. No kill fee. Buys first North American serial rights, buys one-time rights, buys all rights. Responds in 1 month to queries. Responds in 3 months to mss. Guidelines for #10 SASE or online.

- "We are governed by what is happening in astronomical research and space exploration. It can be up to a year before we publish a manuscript. Query for electronic submissions."

Nonfiction Needs book excerpts, new product, announcements, photo feature, technical, space, astronomy. **Buys 75 mss/year.** Query. Length: 500-3,000 words. **Pays $100-1,000.**

Photos Send photos Captions, identification of subjects, model releases required. Pays $25/photo

Tips "Submitting to *Astronomy* could be tough. (Take a look at how technical astronomy is.) But if someone is a physics teacher or an amateur astronomer, he or she might want to study the magazine for a year to see the sorts of subjects and approaches we use, and then submit a proposal."

$ $ $ $ BIOSCIENCE

American Institute of Biological Sciences, 1444 Eye St. NW, Suite 200, Washington DC 20005. (202)628-1500. E-mail: features@aibs.org. Website: www.aibs.org. **5% freelance written.** Monthly peer-reviewed scientific journal covering organisms from molecules to the environment. We contract professional science writers to write features on assigned topics, including organismal biology and ecology, but excluding biomedical topics. Estab. 1951. Byline given. Publishes ms an average of 3 months after acceptance. Buys first North American serial rights, buys electronic rights. Editorial lead time 2 months. Accepts queries by e-mail. Responds in 2-3 weeks to queries. Sample copy free. Guidelines free.

Nonfiction Does not want biomedical topics. **Buys 10 mss/year.** Query. Length: 1,500-3,000 words. **Pays $1,500-3,000.** Sometimes pays expenses of writers on assignment.

Tips Queries can cover any area of biology. The story should appeal to a wide scientific audience, yet be accessible to the interested (and somewhat science-literate) layperson. *BioScience* tends to favor research and policy trend stories and avoids personality profiles.

$ $ $ CHEMICAL HERITAGE

Newsmagazine of the Chemical Heritage Foundation, Chemical Heritage Foundation (CHF), 315 Chestnut St., Philadelphia PA 19106-2702. (215)925-2222. E-mail: editor@chemheritage.org. Website: www.chemheritage.org. **40% freelance written.** Quarterly magazine covers history of chemistry and molecular sciences. *Chemical Heritage* reports on the history of the chemical and molecular sciences and industries, on CHF activities, and on other activities of interest to our readers. Estab. 1982. Circ. 25,000. Byline given. Pays on acceptance. Publishes ms an average of 6-12 months after acceptance. Buys all rights. Editorial lead time 4 months. Accepts queries by mail, e-mail, phone. Responds in 1 month to queries. Responds in 1 month to mss. Sample copy free.

Nonfiction We are always particularly interested in celebrating historical anniversaries or discoveries, as well as the history behind timely subjects. Needs book excerpts, essays, historical, interview. No exposes or excessively technical material. Many of our readers are highly educated professionals, but they may not be familiar with, for example, specific chemical processes. **Buys 3-5/year mss/year.** Query. Length: 1,000-3,500 words. **Pays 50¢ to $1/word.**

Photos State availability Captions required. Offers no additional payment for photos accepted with ms. buys one-time print and online rights

Columns/Departments Contact: Content Editor: Christopher Munden (christopherm@chemheritage.org). Book reviews: 200 or 750 words; CHF collections: 300-500 words; policy: 1,000 words; personal remembrances: 750 words; profiles of CHF awardees and oral history subjects: 600-900 words: buys 3-5 mms/year. 10 Query.

Tips CHF operates exhibits at many scientific trade shows and scholarly conferences. Our representatives are always happy to speak to potential authors genuinely interested in the past, present and future of chemistry. We are a good venue for scholars who want to reach a broader audience or for science writers who want to bolster their scholarly credentials.

$ $ COSMOS MAGAZINE

The Science of Everything, Luna Media Pty Ltd., Level 2, 25 Cooper St., Surry Hills, Sydney NSW 2010 Australia. (61)(2)9219-2500. Fax: (61)(2)9281-2360. E-mail: editorial@cosmosmagazine.com. Website: www.cosmosmagazine.com. **90% freelance written**. Monthly magazine covering science. Estab. 2005. Circ. 25,000. Byline given. Pays on acceptance. Offers 50% kill fee. Publishes ms an average of 3 months after acceptance. Buys first rights, buys one-time rights, buys second serial (reprint) rights, buys simultaneous rights. Editorial lead time 2 months. Submit seasonal material 3 months in advance. Accepts queries by e-mail, fax. Accepts previously published material. Accepts simultaneous submissions. Responds in 1 month to queries. Responds in 3 months to mss. Guidelines available online.

Nonfiction Needs book excerpts, essays, expose, historical, humor, interview, opinion, photo feature, travel. **Buys 250 mss/year.** Query with published clips. Length: 700-5,000 words. **Pays 50¢/word for assigned articles. Pays 25¢/word for unsolicited articles.** Sometimes pays expenses of writers on assignment.

Photos State availability Captions, identification of subjects required. Reviews GIF/JPEG files. Pays $15-200/photo; negotiates payment individually. Buys one-time rights and exclusive rights for 3 months.

Columns/Departments Body (medical/health), 700 words; Biosphere (environment/nature), 700 words; First Person (first-person account of an event in science), 800 words; Travelogue (travel to an intriguing/unusual place that involves science), 1,500 words. Query. **Pays $315-450.**

Fiction Needs science fiction. No fantasy—science fiction only. **Buys 12 mss/year.** Length: 2,000-3,500 words. **Pays 25¢/word.**

INTERNATIONAL JOURNAL OF MATHEMATICAL COMBINATORICS

ProQuest Information & Learning, 300 North Zeeb Rd., Ann Arbor MI 48106-1346. (800)521-0600. Website: madis1.iss.ac.cn/IJMC.htm. **100% freelance written**. Quarterly periodical covering mathematics and physics, smarandache multi-space, smarandache geometries. The *International Journal of Mathematical Combinators* deals with smarandache multi-spaces, smarandache geometries, mathematical combinatorics, non-euclidean geometry and topology and their applications to other sciences. Estab. 2007. Byline given. No kill fee. Publishes ms an average of 2 months after acceptance. Buys all rights. Editorial lead time 3 months. Submit seasonal material 1 month in advance. Accepts queries by e-mail. Accepts simultaneous submissions. Responds in 2 months to mss. Guidelines free.

Nonfiction Needs essays, opinion, technical. We have a special volume on smarandache multi-spaces, geometry and mathematical combinatorics. Articles that are not scientifically serious. Send complete ms. no limitation

Photos State availability Reviews GIF/JPEG files. offers no additional payment for photos accepted with ms.

Columns/Departments Mathematics or Physics, no limitation on words.

$ $ $ $ INVENTORS DIGEST

The Magazine For Idea People, Inventors Digest, LLC, 520 Elliot St., Suite 200, Charlotte NC 28211. (704)369-7312. Fax: (704)333-5115. E-mail: info@inventorsdigest.com. Website: www.inventorsdigest.com. **50% freelance written**. Monthly magazine covering inventions, technology, engineering, intellectual property issues. Inventors Digest is committed to educate and inspire entry- and enterprise-level inventors and professional innovators. As the leading print and online publication for the innovation culture, *Inventors Digest* delivers useful, entertaining and cutting-edge information to help its readers succeed. Estab. 1983. Circ. 40,000. Byline given. Pays on publication. Offers 40% kill fee. Publishes ms an average of 2 months after acceptance. Buys all rights. Editorial lead time 2 months. Submit seasonal material 4 months in advance. Accepts queries by mail, e-mail. Responds in 3 weeks to queries. Responds in 1 month to mss. Sample copy available online. Guidelines free.

Nonfiction Needs book excerpts, historical, how-to, secure a patent, find a licensing manufacturer, avoid scams, inspirational, interview, new product, opinion, (does not mean letters to the editor), personal experience, technical. Our editorial calendar is available at our website, http://inventorsdigest.com/images/Inventors%20Digest%20Media%20Kit_R08.pdf. We don't want poetry. No stories that talk about readers-stay away from 'one should do X' construction. Nothing that duplicates what you can read elsewhere. **Buys 4 mss/year. mss/year.** Query. Length: 2,500 words. **Pays $50-TBD for assigned articles. Pays $50-TBD for unsolicited articles.**

Photos Contact: Mike Drummond. State availability Identification of subjects required. Reviews GIF/JPEG files. Negotiates payment individually. Subject to negotiation.

Columns/Departments Contact: Brandon Phillips. Cover (the most important package-puts a key topic in compelling context), 2,000-3,000 words; Radar (news/product snippets), 1,200; Bookshelf (book reviews), 700; Pro Bono (legal issues), 850; Profile (human interest stories on inventors and innovators), BrainChild (celebration of young inventors and innovators), FirstPerson (inventors show how they've overcome hurdles),

1,000; MeetingRoom (learn secrets to success of best inventor groups in the country), 900; TalkBack (Q&A with manufacturers, retailers, etc. in the innovation industry), Five Questions With.(a conversation with some of the brightest and most controversial minds in Technology, manufacturing, academia and other fields), 800. 4 mss/year Query. **Pays $$20.**

Tips We prefer email. If it's a long piece (more than 2,000 words), send a synopsis, captivating us in 300 words. Put 'Article Query' in the subject line. A great story should have conflict or obstacles to overcome. Show us something surprising and why we should care, and put it in context. Sweep, color, scene and strong character anecdotes are important. If there's no conflict-moral, institutional, cultural, obstacles to overcome-there's no story. If you send it in analog form, write to: *Inventors Digest*, Article Query, P.O. Box 36761, Charlotte, NC 28236.

POPULAR SCIENCE

The Future Now, Bonnier Corporation, 2 Park Ave., 9th Floor, New York NY 10016. Website: www.popsci.com. **50% freelance written**. Monthly magazine for the well-educated adult, interested in science, technology, new products. *Popular Science* is devoted to exploring (and explaining) to a nontechnical, but knowledgeable, readership the technical world around us. We cover all of the sciences, engineering, and technology, and above all, products. We are largely a `thing'-oriented publication: things that fly or travel down a turnpike, or go on or under the sea, or cut wood, or reproduce music, or build buildings, or make pictures. We are especially focused on the new, the ingenious, and the useful. Contributors should be as alert to the possibility of selling us pictures and short features as they are to major articles. Freelancers should study the magazine to see what we want and avoid irrelevant submissions. Estab. 1872. Circ. 1,450,000. Byline given. Pays on acceptance. Offers 25% kill fee. Buys first North American serial rights, buys second serial (reprint) rights. Editorial lead time 3 months. Accepts queries by mail, e-mail, fax. Responds in 1 month to queries. Guidelines available online.

Nonfiction We publish stories ranging from hands-on product reviews to investigative feature stories, on everything from black holes to black-budget airplanes. Query.

Tips Probably the easiest way to break in here is by covering a news story in science and technology that we haven't heard about yet. We need people to be acting as scouts for us out there, and we are willing to give the most leeway on these performances. We are interested in good, sharply focused ideas in all areas we cover. We prefer a vivid, journalistic style of writing, with the writer taking the reader along with him, showing the reader what he saw, through words.

SCIENTIA MAGNA

High American Press, 300 N. Zeeb Rd., P.O. Box 1346, Ann Arbor MI 48106-1346. (800)521-0600. E-mail: wpzhang@nwu.edu.cn. Website: www.geocities.com. m_l_perez/scientiamagna.htm. **100% freelance written**. Quarterly magazine covering mathematics. Estab. 2005. Circ. 1,000. Byline given. No kill fee. Publishes ms an average of 6 months after acceptance. Editorial lead time 6 months. Accepts queries by e-mail. Accepts simultaneous submissions. Sample copy free.

Nonfiction Buys 500 mss/year mss/year. Send complete ms.

$ $ $ $ SCIENTIFIC AMERICAN

415 Madison Ave., New York NY 10017. (212)754-0550. Fax: (212)755-1976. E-mail: editors@sciam.com. Website: www.sciam.com. Monthly magazine covering developments and topics of interest in the world of science. Query before submitting. *Scientific American* brings its readers directly to the wellspring of exploration and technological innovation. The magazine specializes in first-hand accounts by the people who actually do the work. Their personal experience provides an authoritative perspective on future growth. Over 100 of our authors have won Nobel Prizes. Complementing those articles are regular departments written by *Scientific American*'s staff of professional journalists, all specialists in their fields. *Scientific American* is the authoritative source of advance information. Authors are the first to report on important breakthroughs, because they're the people who make them. It all goes back to *Scientific American*'s corporate mission: to link those who use knowledge with those who create it. Estab. 1845. Circ. 710,000. No kill fee.

Nonfiction Freelance opportunities mostly in the news scan section; limited opportunity in feature well. **Pays $1/word average.** Pays expenses of writers on assignment.

$ $ SKY & TELESCOPE

The Essential Magazine of Astronomy, New Track Media, 90 Sherman St., Cambridge MA 02140. (617)864-7360. Fax: (617)864-6117. E-mail: editors@skyandtelescope.com. Website: skyandtelescope.com. **15% freelance written**. Monthly magazine covering astronomy. *Sky & Telescope* is the magazine of record for astronomy. We cover amateur activities, research news, equipment, book, and software reviews. Our audience is the amateur astronomer who wants to learn more about the night sky. Estab. 1941. Circ. 110,000. Byline given. Pays on publication. No kill fee. Publishes ms an average of 6 months after acceptance. Buys first rights. Editorial lead time 4 months. Submit seasonal material 1 year in advance. Accepts queries by mail, e-mail, fax. Responds in 3 weeks to queries. Responds in 1 month to mss. Sample copy for $6.99. Guidelines available online.

Nonfiction Needs essays, historical, how-to, opinion, personal experience, photo feature, technical. No poetry,

crosswords, New Age, or alternative cosmologies. **Buys 10 mss/year.** Query. Length: 1,500-2,500 words. **Pays at least 25¢/word.** Sometimes pays expenses of writers on assignment.
Photos Send photos Identification of subjects required. Reviews contact sheets. Negotiates payment individually. Buys one time rights.
Columns/Departments Focal Point (opinion), 700 words; Books & Beyond (reviews), 800 words; The Astronomy Scene (profiles), 1,500 words. 20 Query. **Pays 25¢/word**
Tips We're written exclusively by astronomy professionals, hobbyists, and insiders. Good artwork is key. Keep the text lively and provide captions.

$ $ $ $ ⊘ STARDATE

University of Texas, 1 University Station, A2100, Austin TX 78712. (512)471-5285. Fax: (512)471-5060. Website: stardate.org. **80% freelance written**. Bimonthly magazine covering astronomy. *StarDate* is written for people with an interest in astronomy and what they see in the night sky, but no special astronomy training or background. Estab. 1975. Circ. 10,000. Byline given. Pays on acceptance. Offers 25% kill fee. Publishes ms an average of 4 months after acceptance. Buys first North American serial rights, buys electronic rights. Editorial lead time 6 months. Submit seasonal material 6 months in advance. Accepts queries by mail, e-mail, fax. Responds in 6 weeks to queries. Sample copy and writer's guidelines free

- No unsolicited mss.

Nonfiction Needs general interest, historical, interview, photo feature, technical, travel, research in astronomy. No first-person; first stargazing experiences; paranormal. **Buys 8 mss/year.** Query with published clips. Length: 1,500-3,000 words. **Pays $500-1,500.** Sometimes pays expenses of writers on assignment.
Photos Send photos Identification of subjects required. Reviews transparencies, prints. Negotiates payment individually. Buys one time rights.
Columns/Departments Astro News (short astronomy news item), 250 words. 6 Query with published clips. **Pays $100-200.**
Tips Keep up to date with current astronomy news and space missions. No technical jargon.

$ $ WEATHERWISE

The Magazine About the Weather, Heldref Publications, 1319 18th St. NW, Washington DC 20036. (202)296-6267. Fax: (202)296-5149. E-mail: ww@heldref.org. Website: www.weatherwise.org. **75% freelance written.** Bimonthly magazine covering weather and meteorology. "*Weatherwise* is America's only magazine about the weather. Our readers range from professional weathercasters and scientists to basement-bound hobbyists, but all share a common interest in craving information about weather as it relates to the atmospheric sciences, technology, history, culture, society, art, etc." Estab. 1948. Circ. 11,000. Byline given. Pays on publication. No kill fee. Publishes ms an average of 6 months after acceptance. Buys all rights. Editorial lead time 6-9 months. Submit seasonal material 9 months in advance. Accepts queries by mail, e-mail, fax, phone. Responds in 2 months to queries. Guidelines available online.
Nonfiction Needs book excerpts, essays, general interest, historical, how-to, interview, new product, opinion, personal experience, photo feature, technical, travel. Photo Contest (September/October deadline June 2) No blow-by-blow accounts of the biggest storm to ever hit your backyard. **Buys 15-18 mss/year.** Query with published clips. Length: 2,000-3,000 words. **Pays $200-500 for assigned articles. Pays $0-300 for unsolicited articles.**
Photos Captions, identification of subjects required. Reviews contact sheets, negatives, prints, electronic files. Negotiates payment individually. Buys one time rights.
Columns/Departments Weather Front (news, trends), 300-400 words; Weather Talk (folklore and humor), 650-1,000 words. 12-15 Query with published clips. **Pays $0-200.**
Tips "Don't query us wanting to write about broad types like the Greenhouse Effect, the Ozone Hole, El Ni⊠o, etc. Although these are valid topics, you can bet you won't be able to cover it all in 2,000 words. With these topics and all others, find the story within the story. And whether you're writing about a historical storm or new technology, be sure to focus on the human element—the struggles, triumphs, and other anecdotes of individuals."

SCIENCE FICTION, FANTASY & HORROR

$ $ ANALOG SCIENCE FICTION & FACT

Dell Magazine Fiction Group, 475 Park Ave. S., 11th Floor, New York NY 10016. (212)686-7188. Fax: (212)686-7414. E-mail: analog@dellmagazines.com. Website: www.analogsf.com. **100% freelance written. Eager to work with new/unpublished writers.** Monthly magazine for general future-minded audience. Estab. 1930. Circ. 50,000. Byline given. Pays on acceptance. No kill fee. Publishes ms an average of 10 months after acceptance. Buys first North American serial rights, buys nonexclusive foreign serial rights. Sample copy for $5. Guidelines available online.

Nonfiction Looking for illustrated technical articles dealing with subjects of not only current but future interest, i.e., topics at the present frontiers of research whose likely future developments have implications of wide interest. **Buys 11 mss/year.** Send complete ms. 5,000 words **Pays 6¢/word.**

Fiction Basically, we publish science fiction stories. That is, stories in which some aspect of future science or technology is so integral to the plot that, if that aspect were removed, the story would collapse. The science can be physical, sociological, or psychological. The technology can be anything from electronic engineering to biogenetic engineering. But the stories must be strong and realistic, with believable people doing believable things—no matter how fantastic the background might be. Needs science fiction, hard science/technological, soft/sociological. No fantasy or stories in which the scientific background is implausible or plays no essential role. **Buys 60-100 unsolicited mss/year.** Send complete ms. Length: 2,000-80,000 words. **Pays 4¢/word for novels; 5-6¢/word for novelettes; 6-8¢/word for shorts under 7,500 words; $450-600 for intermediate lengths.**

Tips In query give clear indication of central ideas and themes and general nature of story line—and what is distinctive or unusual about it. We have no hard-and-fast editorial guidelines, because science fiction is such a broad field that I don't want to inhibit a new writer's thinking by imposing 'Thou Shalt Not's.' Besides, a really good story can make an editor swallow his preconceived taboos. I want the best work I can get, regardless of who wrote it—and I need new writers. So I work closely with new writers who show definite promise, but of course it's impossible to do this with every new writer. No occult or fantasy.

$ APEX DIGEST

Apex Science Fiction and Horror Digest/Apex Magazine, Apex Publications, LLC, P.O. Box 24323, Lexington KY 40524. (859)312-3974. E-mail: jason@apexdigest.com. Website: www.apexdigest.com. www.apexbookcompany.com. **Contact:** Mari Adkins, subm. ed. **100% freelance written**. Monthly e-zine publishing dark science fiction. "An elite repository for new and seasoned authors with an other-worldly interest in the unquestioned and slightly bizarre parts of the universe." Estab. 2004. Circ. 10,000 unique visits per month. Byline given. Pays on publication. Offers 30% kill fee. Publishes ms an average of 2 months after acceptance. Buys first World English Language Rights and Non-Exclusive anthology rights. Editorial lead time 2 months. Submit seasonal material 2 months in advance. Accepts queries by e-mail. Responds in 20-30 days to queries and to mss. Sample copy for $6. Guidelines available online.

Fiction Needs , dark science fiction. **Buys 24 mss/year.** Send complete ms. Length: 100-7,500 words. **Pays $20-200.**

Tips "See submissions guidelines at submissions@apexdigest.com."

$ ASIMOV'S SCIENCE FICTION

Dell Magazine Fiction Group, 475 Park Ave. S., 11th Floor, New York NY 10016. (212)686-7188. Fax: (212)686-7414. E-mail: asimovssf@dellmagazines.com. Website: www.asimovs.com. **Contact:** Brian Bieniowski, managing editor. **98% freelance written. Works with a small number of new/unpublished writers each year.** Magazine published 10 times/year, including 2 double issues. "Magazine consists of science fiction and fantasy stories for adults and young adults. Publishes the best short science fiction available." Estab. 1977. Circ. 50,000. Pays on acceptance. No kill fee. Publishes ms an average of 6-12 months after acceptance. Buys first North American serial, nonexclusive foreign serial rights; reprint rights occasionally. Accepts queries by mail. Responds in 2 months to queries. Responds in 3 months to mss. Sample copy for $5. Guidelines for #10 SASE or online.

Fiction "Science fiction primarily. Some fantasy and humor but no sword and sorcery. No explicit sex or violence that isn't integral to the story. It is best to read a great deal of material in the genre to avoid the use of some very old ideas. **Buys 10mss/issue.** Send complete ms and SASE with *all* submissions." Needs fantasy, science fiction, hard science, soft sociological. No horror or psychic/supernatural. Would like to see more hard science fiction. Length: 750-15,000 words. **Pays 5-8¢/word.**

Poetry 40 lines maximum **Pays $1/line.**

Tips "In general, we're looking for `character-oriented' stories, those in which the characters, rather than the science, provide the main focus for the reader's interest. Serious, thoughtful, yet accessible fiction will constitute the majority of our purchases, but there's always room for the humorous as well. Borderline fantasy is fine, but no Sword & Sorcery, please. A good overview would be to consider that all fiction is written to examine or illuminate some aspect of human existence, but that in science fiction the backdrop you work against is the size of the universe. Please do not send us submissions on disk or via e-mail. We've bought some of our best stories from people who have never sold a story before."

$ THE MAGAZINE OF FANTASY & SCIENCE FICTION

Spilogale, Inc., P.O. Box 3447, Hoboken NJ 07030. (201)876-2551. Fax: (201)876-2551. Website: www.fandsf.com. **100% freelance written**. Bimonthly magazine covering science fiction & fantasy. "We have been one of the leading magazines in the realm of fantastic fiction for almost 60 years." Estab. 1949. Circ. 25,000. Byline given. Pays on acceptance. No kill fee. Publishes ms an average of 6-8 months after acceptance. Buys first

North American serial rights. electronic database rights & select foreign right Editorial lead time 6 months. Submit seasonal material 6 months in advance. Responds in 2 months to mss. Sample copy for $6. Guidelines available online.

Columns/Departments Curiosities (Reviews of odd & obscure books), 270 words max. 6 Query. **Pays $-$50.**

Fiction Needs fantasy, horror, science fiction. **Buys 60-80 mss/year.** Send complete ms. Length: 25,000 words. **Pays $$0.06-$0.10.**

Poetry Needs avant-garde, free verse, light verse, traditional. **Buys 1-3 poems/year.** Submit maximum 3 poems.

Tips Read an issue of our magazine before submitting.

$ LEADING EDGE

Science Fiction and Fantasy, 4087 JKB, Provo UT 84602. E-mail: editor@leadingedgemagazine.com. Website: www.leadingedgemagazine.com. **90% freelance written**. Semiannual magazine covering science fiction and fantasy. "*Leading Edge* is a magazine dedicated to new and upcoming talent in the field of science fiction and fantasy." Estab. 1980. Circ. 200. Byline given. Pays on publication. No kill fee. Publishes ms an average of 2-4 months after acceptance. Buys first North American serial rights. Responds in 2-4 months to queries. Sample copy for $5.95. Guidelines available online at website.

- Accepts unsolicited submissions.

Fiction Needs fantasy, science fiction. **Buys 14-16 mss/year mss/year.** Send complete ms by mail. Length: 12,500 words maximum **Pays 1¢/word; $10 minimum.**

Poetry Needs avant-garde, haiku, light verse, traditional. "Publishes 2-4 poems per issue. Poetry should reflect both literary value and popular appeal and should deal with science fiction- or fantasy-related themes." Submit maximum 10 poems. Pays $10 for first 4 pages; $1.50/each subsequent page.

$ THE MAGAZINE OF FANTASY & SCIENCE FICTION

Spilogale, Inc., P.O. Box 3447, Hoboken NJ 07030. E-mail: fandsf@aol.com. Website: www.fsfmag.com. **100% freelance written**. Bimonthly magazine covering fantasy fiction and science fiction. "*The Magazine of Fantasy and Science Fiction* publishes various types of science fiction and fantasy short stories and novellas, making up about 80% of each issue. The balance of each issue is devoted to articles about science fiction, a science column, book and film reviews, cartoons, and competitions." Estab. 1949. Circ. 40,000. Byline given. Pays on acceptance. Publishes ms an average of 9-12 months after acceptance. Buys first North American serial rights, buys foreign serial rights. Submit seasonal material 8 months in advance. Accepts previously published material. Responds in 2 months to queries. Sample copy for $6. Guidelines for SASE, by e-mail or website.

Fiction Contact: Gordon Van Gelder, editor. "Prefers character-oriented stories. We receive a lot of fantasy fiction, but never enough science fiction." Needs adventure, fantasy, space fantasy, sword and sorcery, horror, dark fantasy, futuristic, psychological, supernatural, science fiction, hard science/technological, soft/sociological. No electronic submissions. **Buys 60-90 mss/year.** Send complete ms. Up to 25,000 words. **Pays 5-9¢/word; additional copies $2.10.**

Tips "We need more hard science fiction and humor."

$ MINDFLIGHTS

Double-Edged Publishing Inc., 9618 Misty Brook Cove, Cordova TN 38016. (901)213-3768. E-mail: editor@mindflights.com. Website: www.mindflights.com. **100% freelance written**. Monthly online magazine and quarterly print magazine covering science fiction, fantasy, all genres of speculative fiction and poetry, grounded in a Christian or Christian-friendly worldview. "Paving new roads for Christ-reflected short fiction. Not preachy, but still a reflection of the truth and light. Examples of this are in the writings of C.S. Lewis and Tolkien. We strive to provide quality fiction, poetry and exposition, all in means that respects traditional values and Christian principles. Be uplifting, encouraging with something interesting to our audience—fans of sci-fi and fantasy who are comfortable with an environment committed to a Christian world view." Estab. 2007. Byline given. Pays on acceptance. Publishes ms an average of 2 months after acceptance. Buys first North American serial rights, buys first rights, buys second serial (reprint) rights, buys Non-Exclusive Electronic Rights rights. Editorial lead time 3-4 months. Submit seasonal material 4 months in advance. Responds in 3-4 weeks to mss. Sample copy available online. Guidelines available online at: mindflights.com/guidelines.php.

- No postal submissions accepted. See our portal entry and submission process online.

Nonfiction "We very rarely use nonfiction." Needs expose, general interest, humor, inspirational, interview, opinion, personal experience, religious, Articles on technology, gadgets, science discovery, origins of ancient myths & legends. No preachy, judging, Sunday school items. Do not submit articles unless you are the author. Bashing government leaders less acceptable than rendering opinions of converting books to movies, for example. No works proving or disproving controversial idioms of theology. **Buys 8 mss/year.** Send complete ms. Length: 300-5,000 words. **Pays $5-25.**

Reprints "We will consider reprints but we only accept reprints, and then only if the work is exceptional in both quality and fit."

Fiction Illustrations are compensated with $10 gratuity payment. Needs fantasy, science fiction. Does not want to see any work that does not have a strong speculative element, or that would be offensive to a Christian audience. **Buys 72 mss/year.** Send complete ms. Length: 50-5,000 words. **Pays $5-25.**

Poetry Needs avant-garde, free verse, haiku, light verse, traditional. We accept all forms of poetry, but the work must be speculative in nature. Does not want to see any work that does not have a strong speculative element, or that would be offensive to a Christian audience. **Buys 60 poems/year.** Submit maximum 3 poems. **Pays ½¢ per word,$5/min.-$25/max.**

Tips "Not all works accepted for the online version will also appear in the quarterly print edition. Only a small portion (about a third) of the works accepted for *MindFlights* will appear in our print edition. Most will appear online only. Although our guidelines currently indicate that upon acceptance of a work we will ask for rights for either print, the web, or both, and our contracts clearly indicate which rights we are requesting, we are concerned that authors may be assuming that all works accepted will appear in the print edition. Thank you."

$ NECROLOGY MAGAZINE

Isis International, P.O. Box 510232, Saint Louis MO 63151. E-mail: editor@necrologymag.com. Website: www.necrologymag.com. **100% freelance written**. Quarterly magazine dedicated to horror. We also publish sci-fi and fantasy that contain elements of horror and macabre. Estab. 2006. Circ. 900. Byline sometimes given. Pays on acceptance. Offers 100% kill fee. Publishes ms an average of 9 months after acceptance. Buys first North American serial rights. Editorial lead time 6 months. Submit seasonal material 9 months in advance. Accepts queries by e-mail. Responds in 6 weeks to queries. Responds in 2 months to mss. Sample copy for $4 (print); $1 (ezine). Guidelines available online.

Nonfiction Needs humor, interview. Send complete ms. Length: 1,000-5,000 words. **Pays $50-150 for assigned articles. Pays $10-25 for unsolicited articles.** Sometimes pays expenses of writers on assignment.

Photos Send photos Identification of subjects, model releases required. Reviews GIF/JPEG files. Offers no additional payment for photos accepted with ms; offers $5-25/photo. Buys one time rights.

Columns/Departments 8 Send complete ms. **Pays $10-25.**

Fiction Needs fantasy, horror, science fiction. Does not want to see hack and slash type horror. We'd prefer Lovecraftian style fiction. **Buys 16-20 mss/year.** Send complete ms. Length: 4,000-15,000 words. **Pays $10-25.**

Poetry Needs avant-garde, free verse, haiku, light verse, traditional. **Buys 12-15 poems/year.** Submit maximum 5 poems. Length: 5-100 lines.

Fillers Needs facts, newsbreaks. 8-16 Length: 10-500 words. **Pays $1-25.**

Tips We prefer Lovecraftian style horror and macabre. Do not repeat his works, but expand them into new dark and demented tales. Please view our Web site before submitting work.

$ ON SPEC

P.O. Box 4727, Station South, Edmonton AB T6E 5G6 Canada. (780)413-0215. Fax: (780)413-1538. E-mail: onspec@onspec.ca. Website: www.onspec.ca. **95% freelance written**. Quarterly magazine covering Canadian science fiction, fantasy and horror. "We publish speculative fiction and poetry by new and established writers, with a strong preference for Canadian authored works." Estab. 1989. Circ. 2,000. Byline given. Pays on acceptance. No kill fee. Publishes ms an average of 6-18 months after acceptance. Buys first North American serial rights. Editorial lead time 6 months. Accepts queries by mail. Accepts simultaneous submissions. Responds in 2 weeks to queries. 3 months after deadline to mss. Sample copy for $8. Guidelines for #10 SASE or on website.

- Submission deadlines are February 28, May 31, August 31, and November 30.

Nonfiction Commissioned only.

Fiction Needs fantasy, horror, science fiction, magic realism, ghost stories, fairy stories. No media tie-in or shaggy-alien stories. No condensed or excerpted novels, religious/inspirational stories, fairy tales. **Buys 50 mss/year.** Send complete ms. Length: 1,000-6,000 words. **Pays $50-180 for fiction. Short stories (under 1,000 words): $50 plus 1 contributor's copy.**

Poetry Needs avant-garde, free verse. No rhyming or religious material. **Buys 6 poems/year.** Submit maximum 10 poems. Length: 4-100 lines. **Pays $50 and 1 contributor's copy.**

Tips "We want to see stories with plausible characters, a well-constructed, consistent, and vividly described setting, a strong plot and believable emotions; characters must show us (not tell us) their emotional responses to each other and to the situation and/or challenge they face. Also: don't send us stories written for television. We don't like media tie-ins, so don't watch TV for inspiration! Read, instead! Absolutely no e-mailed or faxed submissions. Strong preference given to submissions by Canadians."

$ PENNY BLOOD

532 LaGuardia Place, Suite 616, New York NY 10012. E-mail: editor@pennyblood.com. Website: www.pennyblood.com. **70% freelance written**. Quarterly magazine covering horror in entertainment. *Penny Blood Magazine* is a survey of horror and cult entertainment. We are looking for horror movie retrospectives and

interviews with genre personalities. Estab. 2004. Circ. 8,000. Byline given. Pays on acceptance. Offers 100% kill fee. Buys all rights. Accepts queries by e-mail. Responds in 2 weeks to queries. Responds in 1 month to mss. Guidelines available online.

Nonfiction Needs essays, interview. **Buys 20-30 mss/year.** Send complete ms. **Pays 3¢/word.**

Tips We accept submissions by e-mail only. We are seeking interviews particularly and our highest pay rates go for these.

$ SCYWEB BEM

Science Fiction & Fantasy Audiozine, Riamac Group, P.O. Box 691298, Charlotte NC 28227. (704)545-8844. E-mail: editor@scywebbem.com. Website: www.scywebbem.com. **100% freelance written**. Quarterly audiozine (CDROM and MP3 download) covering science fiction and fantasy. *SCYWEB BEM* strongly encourages contributors not to alter their writing style to accommodate an audio format, but simply to write the best story possible. They should also go to the 'Submissions' tab on the Web site and click on the link 'a side note about narratives and human psychology.' Estab. 2005. Circ. 3,000. Byline given. Pays on acceptance. Publishes ms an average of 3-6 months after acceptance. Buys first North American serial rights, buys electronic rights, buys first offer on world anthology rights. Editorial lead time 3-6 months. Submit seasonal material 6-9 months in advance. Accepts queries by mail, e-mail. Responds in 1 month to queries. Responds in 2 months to mss. Sample copy for $7.95. Guidelines available online.

Fiction Needs fantasy, science fiction. Does not want graphic sexual content or horror. **Buys 25 mss/year.** Send complete ms. Length: 8,500 words. **Pays $10-50.**

Tips There are a few things that do not translate easily from the written word to the spoken word. Beyond this, writers should do what they've always done: concentrate on telling a good story.

$ TALEBONES

21528 104th St. Court E., Bonney Lake WA 98391. E-mail: info@talebones.com. Website: www.talebones.com. **Contact:** Patrick Swenson, editor. **100% freelance written**. Magazine covering science fiction and dark fantasy. "*Talebones* publishes an eclectic mix of speculative fiction. We want literate stories that entertain readers." Estab. 1995. Circ. 1,000. Byline given. Pays before publication. Offers 100% kill fee. Publishes ms an average of 6 months after acceptance. Buys first North American serial rights, buys electronic rights. Accepts queries by mail, e-mail. Responds in 1 week to queries. Responds in 2 months to mss. Sample copy for $7. Guidelines available online.

Fiction Needs fantasy, horror, science fiction. Does not want "vampire stories, writer stories, or stories about or narrated by young adults or children." **Buys 16 mss/year.** Send complete ms. 6,000 words maximum **Pays 1-2¢/word.**

Poetry Needs avant-garde, free verse, light verse, traditional. **Buys 3-8 poems/year.** Submit maximum 8 poems. **Pays $10 maximum**.

Tips "We publish a wide variety of speculative fiction. Reading a sample copy of *Talebones* will help the writer understand our eclectic tastes. Be professional and humble. We do publish a lot of new writers."

$ TALES OF THE TALISMAN

Hadrosaur Productions, P.O. Box 2194, Mesilla Park NM 88047-2194. E-mail: hadrosaur@zianet.com. Website: www.talesofthetalisman.com. **95% freelance written**. Quarterly magazine covering science fiction and fantasy. "*Tales of the Talisman* is a literary science fiction and fantasy magazine. We publish short stories, poetry, and articles with themes related to science fiction and fantasy. Above all, we are looking for thought-provoking ideas and good writing. Speculative fiction set in the past, present, and future is welcome. Likewise, contemporary or historical fiction is welcome as long as it has a mythic or science fictional element. Our target audience includes adult fans of the science fiction and fantasy genres along with anyone else who enjoys thought-provoking and entertaining writing." Estab. 1995. Circ. 200. Byline given. Pays on acceptance. Offers 100% kill fee. Publishes ms an average of 9 months after acceptance. Buys one-time rights. Editorial lead time 9-12 months. Submit seasonal material 1 year in advance. Accepts queries by mail, e-mail. Accepts previously published material. Responds in 1 week to queries. Responds in 1 month to mss. Sample copy for $8. Guidelines available online.

- Fiction and poetry submissions are limited to reading periods of January 1-February 15 and July 1-August 15.

Nonfiction Needs interview, technical, articles on the craft of writing. "We do not want to see unsolicited articles—please query first if you have an idea that you think would be suitable for *Tales of the Talisman*'s audience. We do not want to see negative or derogatory articles." **Buys 1-3 mss/year.** Query. Length: 1,000-3,000 words. **Pays $10 for assigned articles.**

Fiction Contact: David L. Summers, editor. Needs fantasy, space fantasy, sword and sorcery, horror, science fiction, hard science/technological, soft/sociological. "We do not want to see stories with graphic violence. Do not send 'mainstream' fiction with no science fictional or fantastic elements. Do not send stories with copyrighted characters, unless you're the copyright holder." **Buys 25-30 mss/year.** Send complete ms. Length: 1,000-6,000 words. **Pays $6-10.**

Poetry Needs avant-garde, free verse, haiku, light verse, traditional. "Do not send 'mainstream' poetry with no science fictional or fantastic elements. Do not send poems featuring copyrighted characters, unless you're the copyright holder." **Buys 24-30 poems/year.** Submit maximum 5 poems. Length: 3-50 lines.
Tips "Let your imagination soar to its greatest heights and write down the results. Above all, we are looking for thought-provoking ideas and good writing. Our emphasis is on character-oriented science fiction and fantasy. If we don't believe in the people living the story, we generally won't believe in the story itself. We are open to submissions year-round."

$ VAMPIRES 2 MAGAZINE

Man's Story 2 Publishing Co., P.O. Box 1082, Roswell GA 30077. E-mail: mansstory2@aol.com. Website: www.vampires2.com. **80% freelance written.** "Online E-Zine that s trives to recreate Vampire Romance in the pulp fiction style that was published in the magazines of the 1920s through the 1970s with strong emphasis on 3D graphic art." Estab. 1999. Circ. 500. Pays on publication. No kill fee. Publishes ms an average of 3-6 months after acceptance. Buys one-time rights, buys second serial (reprint) rights. Accepts queries by e-mail only. Accepts previously published material. Accepts simultaneous submissions. Guidelines available online.
Fiction Needs adventure, erotica, fantasy, horror, suspense, pulp fiction involving vampires. **Buys 30-50 mss/year.** Send complete ms. Length: 1,500-3,500 words. **Pays $25.**
Tips "We suggest interested writers visit our website and read our writer's guidelines. Then, read the pulp fiction stories posted in our online mini-magazine and/or read one of our magazines, or find an old pulp fiction magazine that was published in the 1960s. If all else fails, e-mail us."

SEX

$$ EXOTIC MAGAZINE

X Publishing, 314 W. Burnside St., Portland OR 97209. Fax: (503)241-7239. E-mail: exoticunderground2004@yahoo.com. Website: www.xmag.com. Monthly magazine covering adult entertainment, sexuality. *Exotic* is pro-sex, informative, amusing, mature, intelligent. Our readers rent and/or buy adult videos, visit strip clubs and are interested in topics related to the adult entertainment industry and sexuality/culture. Don't talk down to them or fire too far over their heads. Many readers are computer literate and well-traveled. We're also interested in insightful fetish material. We are not a `hard core' publication. Estab. 1993. Circ. 120,000. Byline given. Pays 30 days after publication. No kill fee. Buys first North American serial rights; and online rights; may negotiate second serial (reprint) rights. Accepts queries by fax. Accepts simultaneous submissions. Responds in 2 weeks to queries. Responds in 2 months to mss. Sample copy for sae with 9x12 envelope and 5 First-Class stamps. Guidelines for #10 SASE.
Nonfiction Interested in seeing articles about Viagra, auto racing, gambling, insider porn industry and real sex worker stories. Needs expose, general interest, historical, how-to, humor, interview, travel, News. No men writing as women, articles about being a horny guy, opinion pieces pretending to be fact pieces. **Buys 36 mss/year.** Send complete ms. Length: 1,000-1,800 words. **Pays 10¢/word up to $150.**
Reprints Send typed manuscript with rights for sale noted and information about when and where the material previously appeared. Pays 100% of amount paid for an original article.
Photos Rarely buys photos. Most provided by staff. Model releases required. Reviews prints. Negotiates payment individually.
Fiction We are currently overwhelmed with fiction submissions. Please only send fiction if it's really amazing. Needs erotica, slice-of-life vignettes, must present either erotic element or some vice of modern culture, such as gambling, music, dancing. Send complete ms. Length: 1,000-1,800 words. **Pays 10¢/word up to $150.**
Tips Read adult publications, spend time in the clubs doing more than just tipping and drinking. Look for new insights in adult topics. For the industry to continue to improve, those who cover it must also be educated consumers and affiliates. Please type, spell-check and be realistic about how much time the editor can take `fixing' your manuscript.

$$$$ HUSTLER

HG Inc., 8484 Wilshire Blvd., Suite 900, Beverly Hills CA 90211. Fax: (323)651-2741. E-mail: erampell@lfp.com. Website: www.hustler.com. **60% freelance written.** Magazine published 13 times/year. *Hustler* is the no-nonsense men's magazine, one that is willing to speak frankly about society's sacred cows and expose its hypocrites. The *Hustler* reader expects honest, unflinching looks at hard topicsÃ³sexual, social, political, personality profile, true crime. Estab. 1974. Circ. 750,000. Byline given. Pays as boards ship to printer. Offers 20% kill fee. Publishes ms an average of 3 months after acceptance. Buys all rights. Editorial lead time 4 months. Submit seasonal material 6 months in advance. Accepts queries by mail, e-mail, fax. Responds in 2 weeks to queries. Responds in 1 month to mss. Guidelines for #10 SASE.

- *Hustler* is most interested in well-researched nonfiction reportage focused on sexual practices and subcultures.

Nonfiction Needs book excerpts, expose, general interest, how-to, interview, personal experience, trends. **Buys 30 mss/year.** Query. Length: 3,500-4,000 words. **Pays $1,500.** Sometimes pays expenses of writers on assignment.
Columns/Departments Sex play (some aspect of sex that can be encapsulated in a limited space), 2,500 words. 13 Send complete ms. **Pays $750.**
Fillers Jokes and Graffilthy, bathroom wall humor. **Pays $50-100.**
Tips Don't try and mimic the *Hustler* style. If a writer needs to be molded into our voice, we'll do a better job of it than he or she will. Avoid first- and second-person voice. The ideal manuscript is quote-rich, visual and is narratively driven by events and viewpoints that push one another forward.

$ $ $ $ PENTHOUSE

General Media Communications, 2 Penn Plaza, 11th Floor, New York NY 10121. (212)702-6000. Fax: (212)702-6279. E-mail: pbloch@pmgi.com. Website: www.penthouse.com. Monthly magazine. *Penthouse* is for the sophisticated male. Its editorial scope ranges from outspoken contemporary comment to photography essays of beautiful women. *Penthouse* features interviews with personalities, sociological studies, humor, travel, food and wine, and fashion and grooming for men. Estab. 1969. Circ. 640,000. Byline given. Pays 2 months after acceptance. Offers 25% kill fee. Buys all rights. Editorial lead time 3 months. Accepts simultaneous submissions. Guidelines for #10 SASE.
Nonfiction Needs expose, general interest, to men, interview. **Buys 50 mss/year.** Send complete ms. Length: 4,000-6,000 words. **Pays $3,000.**
Columns/Departments Length: 1,000 words. 25 Query with published clips or send complete ms. **Pays $500.**
Tips Because of our long lead time, writers should think at least 6 months ahead. We take chances. Go against the grain; we like writers who look under rocks and see what hides there.

$ $ $ SWANK

Swank Publications, 210 Route 4 E., Suite 211, Paramus NJ 07652. (201)843-4004. Fax: (201)843-8636. E-mail: editor@swankmag.com. Website: www.swankmag.com. **75% freelance written. Works with new/unpublished writers.** Monthly magazine on sex and sensationalism, lurid. High quality adult erotic entertainment. Audience of men ages 18-38, high school and some college education, medium income, skilled blue-collar professionals, union men, some white-collar. Estab. 1954. Circ. 400,000. Byline given, pseudonym if wanted. Pays on publication. Publishes ms an average of 4 months after acceptance. Buys first North American serial rights. Submit seasonal material 6 months in advance. Accepts queries by mail. Accepts previously published material. Responds in 3 weeks to queries. Responds in 1 month to mss. Sample copy for $6.95. Guidelines for #10 SASE.

- *Swank* reports a need for more nonfiction, non-sex-related articles.

Nonfiction Expose (researched), adventure must be accompanied by color photographs. We buy articles on sex-related topics, which don't need to be accompanied by photos. Interested in unusual lifestyle pieces. How-to, interviews with entertainment, sports and sex industry celebrities. Buys photo pieces on autos, action, adventure. It is strongly recommended that a sample copy is reviewed before submitting material. **Buys 34 mss/year.** Query. **Pays $350-500.** Sometimes pays expenses of writers on assignment.
Reprints Send tearsheet, photocopy or typed ms with rights for sale noted and information about when and where the material previously appeared. Pays 50% of amount paid for an original article.
Photos Contact: Alex Suarez, art director. Articles have a much better chance of being purchased if you have accompanying photos. Model releases required.
Fiction All of the fiction used by *Swank* is erotic in some sense—that is, both theme and content are sexual. New angles are always welcome. We will consider stories that are not strictly sexual in theme (humor, adventure, detective stories, etc.). However, these types of stories are much more likely to be considered if they portray some sexual element, or scene, within their context.
Tips All erotic fiction currently being used by *Swank* must follow certain legal guidelines.

SPORTS

ARCHERY & BOWHUNTING

$ $ BOW & ARROW HUNTING

Action Pursuit Group, 265 S. Anita Dr., Suite 120, Orange CA 92868-3310. (714)939-9991. Fax: (714)939-9909. E-mail: editorial@bowandarrowhunting.com. Website: www.bowandarrowhunting.com. **70% freelance written**. Magazine published 9 times/year covering bowhunting. Dedicated to serve the serious bowhunting enthusiast. Writers must be willing to share their secrets so our readers can become better bowhunters. Estab. 1962. Circ. 90,000. Byline given. Pays on publication. No kill fee. Publishes ms an average of 2 months after acceptance. Buys all rights. Submit seasonal material 6 months in advance. Accepts queries by mail, e-mail. Accepts simultaneous submissions. Responds in 1 month to queries. Responds in 6 weeks to mss. Sample copy and writer's guidelines free

Nonfiction Needs how-to, humor, interview, opinion, personal experience, technical. **Buys 60 mss/year.** Send complete ms. Length: 1,700-3,000 words. **Pays $200-450.**

Photos Send photos Captions required. Reviews contact sheets, 35mm and 2¼x2¼ transparencies, 5x7 prints. Offers no additional payment for photos accepted with ms. Buys one-time or all rights

Fillers Needs facts, newsbreaks. 12 Length: 500 words. **Pays $20-100.**

Tips Inform readers how they can become better at the sport, but don't forget to keep it fun! Sidebars are recommended with every submission.

$ $ BOWHUNTER

The Number One Bowhunting Magazine, InterMedia Outdoors, 6405 Flank Dr., Harrisburg PA 17112. (717)657-9555. Fax: (717)657-9552. E-mail: dwight.schuh@imoutdoors.com. Website: www.bowhunter.com. **50% freelance written.** Bimonthly magazine covering hunting big and small game with bow and arrow. We are a special-interest publication, produced by bowhunters for bowhunters, covering all aspects of the sport. Material included in each issue is designed to entertain and inform readers, making them better bowhunters. Estab. 1971. Circ. 155,000. Byline given. Pays on acceptance. No kill fee. Buys exclusive first, worldwide publication rights. Submit seasonal material 8 months in advance. Accepts queries by mail, e-mail, fax. Responds in 1 month to queries. Responds in 2 months to mss. Sample copy for $2 and 8 ½X11 SAE with appropriate postage. Guidelines for #10 SASE or on website.

Nonfiction We publish a Big Game Special each July but need all material by mid-April. Another annual publication, Whitetail Special, is staff written or by assignment only. Our latest special issue is the Gear Special, which highlights the latest in equipment. We don't want articles that graphically deal with an animal's death. And, please, no articles written from the animal's viewpoint. Needs general interest, how-to, interview, opinion, personal experience, photo feature. **Buys 60 plus mss/year.** Query. Length: 250-2,000 words. **Pays $500 maximum for assigned articles. Pays $100-400 for unsolicited articles.** Sometimes pays expenses of writers on assignment.

Photos Send photos Captions required. Reviews 35mm and 2¼x2¼ transparencies, 5x7 and 8x10 prints, hi-res digital images. Offers $75-250/photo. Buys one time rights.

Fiction Contact: Dwight Schuh, editor. Send complete ms. Length: 500-2,000 words. **Pays $100-350.**

Tips A writer must know bowhunting and be willing to share that knowledge. Writers should anticipate *all* questions a reader might ask, then answer them in the article itself or in an appropriate sidebar. Articles should be written with the reader foremost in mind; we won't be impressed by writers seeking to prove how good they are—either as writers or bowhunters. We care about the reader and don't need writers with 'I' trouble. Features are a good bet because most of our material comes from freelancers. The best advice is: Be yourself. Tell your story the same as if sharing the experience around a campfire. Don't try to write like you think a writer writes.

$ $ BOWHUNTING WORLD

Grand View Media Group, 5959 Baker Rd., Suite 300, Minnetonka MN 55345. (952)405-2280. E-mail: mikes@grandviewmedia.com. Website: www.bowhuntingworld.com. **50% freelance written.** Bimonthly magazine with 3 additional issues for bowhunting and archery enthusiasts who participate in the sport year-round. Estab. 1952. Circ. 95,000. Byline given. Pays on acceptance. No kill fee. Publishes ms an average of 5 months after acceptance. Buys first rights, buys second serial (reprint) rights. Responds in 1 week (e-mail queries). Responds in 6 weeks to mss. Sample copy for $3 and 9x12 SAE with 10 first-class stamps. Guidelines for #10 SASE.

- Accepts queries by mail, but prefers e-mail.

Nonfiction How-to articles with creative slants on knowledgeable selection and use of bowhunting equipment and bowhunting methods. Articles must emphasize knowledgeable use of archery or hunting equipment, and/or specific bowhunting techniques. Contributors must be authorities in the areas of archery and bowhunting. Straight hunting adventure narratives and other types of articles now appear only in special issues. Equipment-oriented aricles must demonstrate wise and insightful selection and use of archery equipment and other gear related to the archery sports. Some product-review, field-test, equipment how-to, and technical pieces will be purchased. We are not interested in articles whose equipment focuses on random mentioning of brands. Technique-oriented aricles most sought are those that briefly cover fundamentals and delve into leading-edge bowhunting or recreational archery methods. **Buys 60 mss/year.** Send complete ms. Length: 1,500-2,500 words. **Pays $350-600.**

Photos We are seeking cover photos that depict specific behavioral traits of the more common big game animals (scraping whitetails, bugling elk, etc.) and well-equipped bowhunters in action. Must include return postage.

Tips Writers are strongly advised to adhere to guidelines and become familiar with our format, as our needs are very specific. Writers are urged to query by e-mail. We prefer detailed outlines of 6 or so article ideas/query. Assignments are made for the next 18 months.

PETERSEN'S BOWHUNTING

Inter Media Partners, 7819 Highland Scenic Rd., Baxter MN 56425. (218)824-2549. Fax: (218)829-2371. Website: www.bowhuntingmag.com. **70% freelance written.** Magazine published 9 times/year covering bowhunting. Very equipment oriented. Our readers are `superenthusiasts,' therefore our writers must have an advanced knowledge of hunting archery. Circ. 175,000. Byline given. Pays on acceptance. No kill fee. Buys all rights. Editorial lead time 6 months. Submit seasonal material 6 months in advance. Accepts queries by mail. Responds in 1 month to queries. Guidelines free.

Nonfiction Emphasis is on how-to instead of personal. Needs how-to, humor, interview, new product, opinion, personal experience, photo feature. **Buys 50 mss/year.** Query. Length: 2,100 words.

Photos Send photos Captions, model releases required. Reviews contact sheets, 35mm transparencies, 5x7 prints, digital. Buys one time rights.

Columns/Departments Departments: True Bowhunting Adventures, 150 words. Query. **Pays $$100.**

BASEBALL

$ FANTASY BASEBALL

F+W Media, Inc., 700 E. State St., Iola WI 54990-0001. (715)445-2214. Fax: (715)445-4087. Website: www.collect.com. Quarterly magazine. Published for fantasy baseball league players. Circ. 130,000. No kill fee. Editorial lead time 6 weeks.

$ JUNIOR BASEBALL

America's Youth Baseball Magazine, 2D Publishing, P.O. Box 9099, Canoga Park CA 91309. (818)710-1234. Fax: (818)710-1877. E-mail: dave@juniorbaseball.com. Website: www.juniorbaseball.com. **25% freelance written.** Bimonthly magazine covering youth baseball. Focused on youth baseball players ages 7-17 (including high school) and their parents/coaches. Edited to various reading levels, depending upon age/skill level of feature. Estab. 1996. Circ. 20,000. Byline given. Pays on publication. No kill fee. Publishes ms an average of 4 months after acceptance. Buys all rights. Editorial lead time 3 months. Submit seasonal material 4 months in advance. Accepts simultaneous submissions. Responds in 2 weeks to queries. Responds in 1 month to mss. Sample copy for $5 and online.

Nonfiction Needs how-to, skills, tips, features, how-to play better baseball, etc., interview, with major league players; only on assignment, personal experience, from coaches' or parents' perspective. No trite first-person articles about your kid. No fiction or poetry. **Buys 8-12 mss/year.** Query. Length: 500-1,000 words. **Pays $50-100.**

Photos Photos can be e-mailed in 300 dpi JPEGs. State availability Captions, identification of subjects required. Reviews 35mm transparencies, 3 x 5 prints. Offers $10-100/photo; negotiates payment individually.

Columns/Departments When I Was a Kid (a current Major League Baseball player profile); Parents Feature (topics of interest to parents of youth ball players); all 1,000-1,500 words. In the Spotlight (news, events, new products), 50-100 words; Hot Prospect (written for the 14 and older competitive player. High school baseball is included, and the focus is on improving the finer points of the game to make the high school team, earn a college scholarship, or attract scouts, written to an adult level), 500-1,000 words. 8-12 **Pays $50-100.**

Tips Must be well-versed in baseball! Having a child who is very involved in the sport, or have extensive hands-on experience in coaching baseball, at the youth, high school or higher level. We can always use accurate, authoritative skills information and good photos to accompany is a big advantage! This magazine is read by experts. No fiction, poems, games, puzzles, etc.

BICYCLING

$ $ $ ADVENTURE CYCLIST

Adventure Cycling Assn., Box 8308, Missoula MT 59807. (406)721-1776, ext. 222. Fax: (406)721-8754. E-mail: magazine@adventurecycling.org. Website: www.adventurecycling.org. **75% freelance written.** Magazine published 9 times/year for Adventure Cycling Association members. Estab. 1975. Circ. 44,000. Byline given. Pays on publication. No kill fee. Buys first rights. Submit seasonal material 9 months in advance. Sample copy and guidelines for 9x12 SAE with 4 first-class stamps. Info available at www.adventurecycling.org/mag.

Nonfiction Needs how-to, humor, interview, photo feature, technical, travel, U.S. or foreign tour accounts. **Buys 20-25 mss/year.** Send complete ms. Length: 800-2,500 words. **Pays $450-1,500.**

Photos People riding bicycles, cultural, detail, architectural, people historic, vertical, horizontal. State availability Identification of subjects, model releases required. Reviews color transparencies.

BICYCLING

Rodale Press, Inc., 400 S. 10th St., Emmaus PA 18098. (610)967-5171. Fax: (610)967-8960. E-mail: bicycling@rodale.com. Website: www.bicycling.com. **50% freelance written**. "*Bicycling* features articles about fitness, training, nutrition, touring, racing, equipment, clothing, maintenance, new technology, industry developments, and other topics of interest to committed bicycle riders. Editorially, we advocate for the sport, industry, and the cycling consumer." Estab. 1961. Circ. 410,000. Byline given. Pays on acceptance. No kill fee. Buys all rights. Submit seasonal material 6 months in advance. Accepts previously published material. Responds in 2 months to queries. Sample copy for $3.50. Guidelines for #10 SASE.

Nonfiction "We are a cycling lifestyle magazine. We seek readable, clear, well-informed pieces that show how cycling is part of our readers' lives. We sometimes run articles that are inspirational, and inspiration might flavor even our most technical pieces. No fiction or poetry." Needs how-to, on all phases of bicycle touring, repair, maintenance, commuting, new products, clothing, riding technique, nutrition for cyclists, conditioning, photo feature, on cycling events, technical, opinions about technology, travel, bicycling must be central here, fitness. **Buys 10 unsolicited mss/year.** Query. **Payment varies** Sometimes pays expenses of writers on assignment.

Reprints Send tearsheet or photocopy and information about when and where the material previously appeared.

Photos State availability of or send photos Captions, model releases required. Pays $15-250/photo.

Tips "Don't send us travel pieces about where you went on summer vacation. Travel/adventure stories have to be about something larger than just visiting someplace on your bike and meeting quirky locals."

$ $ BIKE MAGAZINE

P.O. Box 1028, Dana Point CA 92629. (949)496-5922. Fax: (949)496-7849. E-mail: bikemag@primedia.com. Website: www.bikemag.com. **35% freelance written**. Magazine publishes 8 times/year covering mountain biking. Estab. 1993. Circ. 170,000. Byline given. Pays on publication. Offers 25% kill fee. Publishes ms an average of 2 months after acceptance. Buys first North American serial rights. Editorial lead time 4 months. Submit seasonal material 6 months in advance. Responds in 2 months to queries. Sample copy for $8. Guidelines for #10 SASE.

Nonfiction Writers should submit queries in March (April 1 deadline) for consideration for the following year's editions. All queries received by April 1 will be considered and editors will contact writers about stories they are interested in. Queries should include word count. Needs humor, interview, personal experience, photo feature, travel. **Buys 20 mss/year.** Length: 1,000-2,500 words. **Pays 50¢/word.** Sometimes pays expenses of writers on assignment. $500 maximum

Photos Contact: David Reddick, photo editor. Send photos Captions, identification of subjects required. Reviews color transparencies, b&w prints. Negotiates payment individually. Buys one time rights.

Columns/Departments Splatter (news), 300 words; Urb (details a great ride within 1 hour of a major metropolitan area), 600-700 words. Query year-round for Splatter and Urb. 20 **Pays 50¢/word.**

Tips Remember that we focus on hard core mountain biking, not beginners. We're looking for ideas that deliver the excitement and passion of the sport in ways that aren't common or predictable. Ideas should be vivid, unbiased, irreverent, probing, fun, humorous, funky, quirky, smart, good. Great feature ideas are always welcome, especially features on cultural matters or issues in the sport. However, you're much more likely to get published in *Bike* if you send us great ideas for short articles. In particular we need stories for our Splatter, a front-of-the-book section devoted to news, funny anecdotes, quotes, and odds and ends. These stories range from 50 to 300 words. We also need personality profiles of 600 words or so for our People Who Ride section. Racers are OK but we're more interested in grassroots people with interesting personalities—it doesn't matter if they're Mother Theresas or scumbags, so long as they make mountain biking a little more interesting. Short descriptions of great rides are very welcome for our Urb column; the length should be from 600-700 words.

$ $ CYCLE CALIFORNIA! MAGAZINE

1702-L Meridian Ave., #289, San Jose CA 95125. (408)924-0270. Fax: (408)292-3005. E-mail: tcorral@cyclecalifornia.com. Website: www.cyclecalifornia.com. **75% freelance written**. Magazine published 11 times/year covering Northern California bicycling events, races, people. Issues (topics) covered include bicycle commuting, bicycle politics, touring, racing, nostalgia, history, anything at all to do with riding a bike. Estab. 1995. Circ. 26,000. Byline given. Pays on publication. No kill fee. Publishes ms an average of 3 months after acceptance. Buys first North American serial rights. Editorial lead time 6 weeks. Submit seasonal material 6 weeks in advance. Accepts queries by mail, e-mail. Accepts simultaneous submissions. Responds in 1 month to queries. Sample copy for 10x13 SAE with 3 first-class stamps. Guidelines for #10 SASE.

Nonfiction Needs historical, how-to, interview, opinion, personal experience, technical, travel. Bicycle Tour & Travel (January/February) No articles about any sport that doesn't relate to bicycling, no product reviews. **Buys 36 mss/year.** Query. Length: 500-1,500 words. **Pays 3-10¢/word.**

Photos Send photos Identification of subjects required. Reviews 3 x 5 prints. Negotiates payment individually. Buys one time rights.

Columns/Departments 2-3 Query with published clips. **Pays 3-10¢/word.**

Tips E-mail editor with good ideas. While we don't exclude writers from other parts of the country, articles really should reflect a Northern California slant, or be of general interest to bicyclists. We prefer stories written by people who like and use their bikes.

⊘ CYCLE WORLD

Hachette Filipacchi Media U.S., Inc., 1499 Monrovia Ave., Newport Beach CA 92663. (949)720-5300. Website: www.cycleworld.com. Monthly magazine geared towards motorcycle owners and buyers, accessory buyers, potential buyers and enthusiasts of the overall sport of motorcycling. Circ. 323,690. No kill fee.

- Query before submitting.

$ $ VELONEWS

The Journal of Competitive Cycling, Inside Communications, Inc., 1830 N. 55th St., Boulder CO 80301. (303)440-0601. Fax: (303)444-6788. Website: www.velonews.com. **40% freelance written.** Monthly tabloid covering bicycle racing. Estab. 1972. Circ. 48,000. Byline given. Pays on publication. No kill fee. Publishes ms an average of 1 month after acceptance. Buys one-time worldwide rights. Accepts previously published material. Responds in 3 weeks to queries.

Nonfiction Freelance opportunities include race coverage, reviews (book and videos), health-and-fitness departments. **Buys 80 mss/year.** Query. Length: 300-1,200 words. **Pays $100-400.**

Reprints Send typed manuscript with rights for sale noted and information about when and where the material previously appeared.

Photos State availability Captions, identification of subjects required. Buys one time rights.

BOATING

N ⊘ ⊕ AUSTRALIAN AMATEUR BOATBUILDER

P.O. Box 1254, Burleigh Heights QLD 4220 Australia. (61)(7)5598-2299. Fax: (61)(7)5598-3024. E-mail: info@boatbuilder.com.au. Website: www.boatbuilder.com.au. Quarterly magazine. "*AABB* is an Australian-based specialist publication devoted exclusively to amateur enthusiasts—monohulls, kayaks, multihulls, offshore, off-the-beach, power, racing and cruising." Estab. 1991. Circ. 9,500. No kill fee.

- Query before submitting.

N ⊕ AUSTRALIAN YACHTING

Yaffa Publishing, 17-21 Bellevue St., Surry Hills NSW 2010 Australia. (61)(2)9281-2333. Fax: (61)(2)9281-2750. E-mail: barryhenson@yaffa.com.au. Website: www.yaffa.com.au. **Contact:** Barry Henson, editor. Monthly magazine aimed at the owners and crews of yachts over 20 feet. "*Australian Yachting* covers monohulls, multihulls, inshore and offshore racing, coastal cruising and passage making."

Nonfiction Needs general interest, how-to, interview, new product. Query.

BASS & WALLEYE BOATS

The Magazine of Performance Fishing Boats, Affinity, 20700 Belshaw Ave., Carson CA 90746. (310)537-6322, ext. 118. Fax: (310)537-8735. E-mail: salarid@affinitygroup.com. Website: www.BWBmag.com. **50% freelance written.** *Bass & Walleye Boats* is published 9 times/year for the bass and walleye fisherman/boater. Directed to give priority to the boats, the tech, the how-to, the after-market add-ons and the devices that help anglers enjoy their boating experience. Estab. 1994. Circ. 65,000. Byline given. Pays on acceptance. Offers 25% kill fee. Buys first North American serial rights. Editorial lead time 2 months. Submit seasonal material 3 months in advance. Accepts queries by mail. Sample copy for $3.95 and 9 x 12 SAE with 7 first-class stamps. Guidelines free.

Nonfiction Needs general interest, how-to, interview, photo feature, technical. No fiction. **Buys about 120 mss/year.** Query. Length: 1,000-3,000 words.

Photos State availability Captions, identification of subjects required. Reviews transparencies, 35mm slides. Negotiates payment individually. Buys one time rights.

Tips Write from and for the bass and walleye boaters' perspective.

$ $ $ $ BOAT INTERNATIONAL USA

Boat International Media, 1800 SE 10th Ave., Suite 440, Fort Lauderdale FL 33316. (954)522-2628. Fax: (954)522-2240. E-mail: info@boatinternationalusa.com. Website: www.boatinternational.com. **80% freelance written.** Magazine published 10 times/year covering luxury superyacht industry. Luxury yachting publication aimed at the world's discerning yachting audience. We provide the most exclusive access to superyachts over 100 feet worldwide. Estab. 1995. Circ. 55,000. Byline given. Pays on publication. Offers 50% kill fee. Buys Rights purchased depends on feature. rights. Editorial lead time 2 months. Submit seasonal material 4 months in advance. Accepts queries by e-mail. Responds in 2 months to mss. Sample copy for $3.00. Guidelines free.

Nonfiction anything about boats under 50 feet. Travel/destination pieces that are not superyacht related. **Buys 3/year mss/year.** Query. Length: 500-1,500 words. **Pays $300 minimum, $2,000 maximum for assigned articles.** Sometimes pays expenses of writers on assignment.

Photos Contact: Richard Taranto, art director. State availability Captions required. Reviews contact sheets, GIF/JPESG files. negotiates payment individually Buys one time rights.
Fiction NONE

$ $ $ CHESAPEAKE BAY MAGAZINE

Boating at Its Best, Chesapeake Bay Communications, 1819 Bay Ridge Ave., Annapolis MD 21403. (410)263-2662, ext. 32. Fax: (410)267-6924. E-mail: editor@cbmmag.net. **60% freelance written**. Monthly magazine covering boating and the Chesapeake Bay. Our readers are boaters. Our writers should know boats and boating. Read the magazine before submitting. Estab. 1972. Circ. 46,000. Byline given. Pays within 2 months after acceptance. No kill fee. Publishes ms an average of 1 year after acceptance. Buys first North American serial rights. Editorial lead time 1 year. Submit seasonal material 1 year in advance. Accepts queries by mail, e-mail, fax, phone. Accepts simultaneous submissions. Responds in 2 months to queries. Responds in 3 months to mss. Sample copy for $5.19 prepaid.
Nonfiction Destinations, boating adventures, how-to, marina reviews, history, nature, environment, lifestyles, personal and institutional profiles, boat-type profiles, boatbuilding, boat restoration, boating anecdotes, boating news. **Buys 30 mss/year.** Query with published clips. Length: 300-3,000 words. **Pays $100-1,000.** Pays expenses of writers on assignment.
Photos Captions, identification of subjects required. Offers $75-250/photo, $400/day rate for assignment photography. Buys one time rights.
Tips Send us unedited writing samples (not clips) that show the writer can write, not just string words together. We look for well-organized, lucid, lively, intelligent writing.

$ $ $ $ CRUISING WORLD

The Sailing Co., 55 Hammarland Way, Middletown RI 02842. (401)845-5100. Fax: (401)845-5180. Website: www.cruisingworld.com. **60% freelance written**. Monthly magazine covering sailing, cruising/adventuring, do-it-yourself boat improvements. *Cruising World* is a publication by and for sailboat owners who spend time in home waters as well as voyaging the world. Its readership is extremely loyal, savvy, and driven by independent thinking. Estab. 1974. Circ. 155,000. Byline given. **Pays on acceptance for articles;** on publication for photography. No kill fee. Publishes ms an average of 18 months after acceptance. Buys 6-month, all-world, first time rights (amendable). Editorial lead time 3 months. Submit seasonal material 1 year in advance. Accepts queries by mail. Responds in 2 months to queries. Responds in 4 months to mss. Sample copy free. Guidelines available online.
Nonfiction Needs book excerpts, essays, expose, general interest, historical, how-to, humor, interview, new product, opinion, personal experience, photo feature, technical, travel. No travel articles that have nothing to do with cruising aboard sailboats from 20-50 feet in length. **Buys dozens of mss/year.** Send complete ms. **Pays $50-1,500 for assigned articles. Pays $50-1,000 for unsolicited articles.** Sometimes pays expenses of writers on assignment.
Photos Send high res (minimum 300 DPI) images on CD. Send photos Captions required. Reviews negatives, transparencies, color slides preferred. Payment upon publication. Also buys stand-alone photos. Buys First and One Time Rights.
Columns/Departments Shoreline (sailing news, people, and short features; contact Elaine Lembo), 300 words maximum; Hands-on Sailor (refit, voyaging, seamanship, how-to; contact Mark Pillsbury), 1,000-1,500 words. dozens of Query with or without published clips or send complete ms. **Pays $100-700.**
Tips *Cruising World's* readers know exactly what they want to read, so our best advice to freelancers is to carefully read the magazine and envision which exact section or department would be the appropriate place for proposed submissions.

$ $ GO BOATING MAGAZINE

America's Family Boating Magazine, Duncan McIntosh Co., 17782 Cowan, Suite C, Irvine CA 92614. (949)660-6150. Fax: (949)660-6172. Website: www.goboatingamerica.com. **60% freelance written**. Magazine published 8 times/year covering recreational trailer boats. Typical reader owns a power boat between 14 and 32 feet long and has 3-9 years experience. Boat reports are mostly written by staff while features and most departments are provided by freelancers. We are looking for freelancers who can write well and who have at least a working knowledge of recreational power boating and the industry behind it. Estab. 1997. Circ. 100,000. Pays on publication. No kill fee. Publishes ms an average of 4 months after acceptance. Accepts simultaneous submissions. Responds in 3 months to queries. Sample copy free. Guidelines for #10 SASE.
Nonfiction Needs general interest, how-to, humor, new product, personal experience, travel. **Buys 20-25 mss/year.** Query. Length: 1,400-1,600 words. **Pays $150-450.** Sometimes pays expenses of writers on assignment.
Photos State availability Identification of subjects, model releases required. Reviews transparencies, prints, digital images. Offers $50-250/photo. Buys one time rights.
Fillers Needs anecdotes, facts, newsbreaks. Length: 250-500 words. **Pays $50-100.**

Tips We are looking for solid writers who are familiar with power boating and who can educate, entertain, and enlighten our readers with well-written and researched feature stories.

GOOD OLD BOAT

The Sailing Magazine for the Rest of Us, Partnership for Excellence, Inc., 7340 Niagara Lane N., Maple Grove MN 55311. (763)420-8923. E-mail: karen@goodoldboat.com. Website: www.goodoldboat.com. **Contact:** Karen Larson, ed. **90% freelance written**. Bimonthly magazine covering sailing. "*Good Old Boat* magazine focuses on maintaining, upgrading, and loving cruising sailboats that are 10 years old and older. Readers see themselves as part of a community of sailors who share similar maintenance and replacement concerns which are not generally addressed in the other sailing publications. Our readers do much of the writing about projects they have done on their boats and the joy they receive from sailing them." Estab. 1998. Circ. 30,000. Pays 2 months in advance of publication. No kill fee. Publishes ms an average of 12-18 months after acceptance. Buys first North American serial rights. Editorial lead time 4 months. Submit seasonal material 12-15 months in advance. Accepts queries by mail, e-mail. Accepts simultaneous submissions. Responds in 1-2 weeks to queries. Responds in 2-6 months to mss. Sample copy free. Guidelines available online.

Nonfiction Needs general interest, historical, how-to, interview, personal experience, photo feature, technical. Articles which are written by non-sailors serve no purpose for us. **Buys 150 mss/year.** Query or send complete ms **Payment varies, refer to published rates on website.**

Photos State availability of or send photos. We do not pay additional fees for photos except when they run as covers, center spread photo features, or are specifically requested to support an article.

Tips "Our shorter pieces are the best way to break into our magazine. We publish many Simple Solutions and Quick & Easy pieces. These are how-to tips that have worked for sailors on their boats. In addition, our readers send lists of projects which they've done on their boats and which they could write for publication. We respond to these queries with a thumbs up or down by project. Articles are submitted on speculation, but they have a better chance of being accepted once we have approved of the suggested topic."

$ $ HEARTLAND BOATING

The Waterways Journal, Inc., 319 N. Fourth St., Suite 650, St. Louis MO 63102. (314)241-4310. Fax: (314)241-4207. E-mail: lbraff@heartlandboating.com. Website: www.heartlandboating.com. **90% freelance written**. Magazine published 8 times/year covering recreational boating on the inland waterways of mid-America, from the Great Lakes south to the Gulf of Mexico and over to the east. "Our writers must have experience with, and a great interest in, boating, particularly in the area described above. *Heartland Boating*'s content is both informative and humorous—describing boating life as the heartland boater knows it. We are boaters and enjoy the outdoor, water-oriented way of life. The content reflects the challenge, joy, and excitement of our way of life afloat. We are devoted to both power and sailboating enthusiasts throughout middle America; houseboats are included. The focus is on the freshwater inland rivers and lakes of the heartland, primarily the waters of the Arkansas, Tennessee, Cumberland, Ohio, Missouri, Illinois, and Mississippi rivers, the Tennessee-Tombigbee Waterway, The Gulf Intracoastal Waterway, and the lakes along these waterways." Estab. 1989. Circ. 10,000. Byline given. Pays on publication. No kill fee. Buys first North American serial rights, buys first rights, buys electronic rights. Editorial lead time 3 months. Accepts queries by mail. Accepts previously published material. Responds in 2 months to queries. Sample copy online at website. Choose the Try It For Free! button. Fill out the form, and you will receive 3 free copies. Guidelines for #10 SASE.

- Submission window is May 1-June 15.

Nonfiction Needs how-to, articles about navigation maintenance, upkeep, or making time spent aboard easier and more comfortable, humor, personal experience, technical, Great Loop leg trips, along waterways and on-land stops. Annual houseboat issue in March looks at what is coming out on the houseboat market for the coming year. **Buys 100 mss/year.** Send complete ms. Length: 850-1,500 words. **Pays $40-285.**

Reprints Send tearsheet, photocopy or typed ms and information about when and where the material previously appeared.

Photos Send photos Reviews prints, digital images. Offers no additional payment for photos accepted with ms. Buys one-time print rights and Web rights of photos.

Columns/Departments Books Aboard (assigned book reviews), 400 words. **Buys 8-10 mss/year. Pays $40.** Handy Hints (boat improvement or safety projects), 850 words. **Buys 8 mss/year. Pays $180.** Heartland Haunts (waterside restaurants, bars or B&Bs), 1,000 words. **Buys 16 mss/year. Pays $160.** Query with published clips or send complete ms.

Tips "We plan the next year's schedule starting in May. So submitting material between May 1 and June 15 is the best way to proceed."

$ $ ⊘ HOUSEBOAT MAGAZINE

The Family Magazine for the American Houseboater, Harris Publishing, Inc., 360 B St., Idaho Falls ID 83402. Fax: (208)522-5241. E-mail: blk@houseboatmagazine.com. Website: www.houseboatmagazine.com. **60% freelance written**. "Monthly magazine for houseboaters, who enjoy reading everything that reflects the unique houseboating lifestyle. If it is not a houseboat-specific article, please do not query.". Estab. 1990. Circ. 25,000. Byline given. Pays on acceptance. Offers 25% kill fee. Publishes ms an average of 3 months after acceptance. Buys first North American serial rights, buys electronic rights. Editorial lead time 6 months. Submit seasonal material 6 months in advance. Accepts simultaneous submissions. Responds in 1 month to queries. Sample copy for $5. Guidelines by email.

- No unsolicited mss. Accepts queries by mail and fax, but e-mail strongly preferred.

Nonfiction Needs how-to, interview, new product, personal experience, travel. **Buys 36 mss/year.** Query. Length: 1,500-2,200 words. **Pays $200-500.**

Photos Often required as part of submission package. Color prints discouraged. Digital prints are unacceptable. Seldom purchases photos without ms, but occasionally buys cover photos. Captions, model releases required. Reviews transparencies, high-resolution electronic images. Offers no additional payment for photos accepted with ms Buys one time rights.

Columns/Departments Pays $150-300.

Tips "As a general rule, how-to articles are always in demand. So are stories on unique houseboats or houseboaters. You are less likely to break in with a travel piece that does not revolve around specific people or groups. Personality profile pieces with excellent supporting photography are your best bet."

$ $ LAKELAND BOATING

The Magazine for Great Lakes Boaters, O'Meara-Brown Publications, Inc., 727 S. Dearborn, Suite 812, Chicago IL 60605. (312)276-0610. Fax: (312)276-0619. Website: www.lakelandboating.com. **50% freelance written**. Magazine covering Great Lakes boating. Estab. 1946. Circ. 60,000. Byline given. Pays on publication. No kill fee. Buys first North American serial rights. Accepts queries by e-mail. Responds in 4 months to queries. Sample copy for $5.50 and 9x12 SAE with 6 first-class stamps. Guidelines free.

Nonfiction Needs book excerpts, historical, how-to, interview, personal experience, photo feature, technical, travel, must relate to boating in Great Lakes. No inspirational, religious, exposÃˆ or poetry. **Buys 20-30 mss/year.** Length: 300-1,500 words. **Pays $100-600.**

Photos State availability Captions required. Reviews prefers 35mm transparencies, high-res digital shots. Buys one time rights.

Columns/Departments Bosun's Locker (technical or how-to pieces on boating), 100-1,000 words. 40 Query. **Pays $25-200.**

$ LIVING ABOARD

P.O. Box 91299, Austin TX 78709-1299. (512)892-4446. Fax: (512)892-4448. E-mail: editor@livingaboard.com. Website: www.livingaboard.com. **95% freelance written**. Bimonthly magazine covering living on boats/cruising. Estab. 1973. Circ. 10,000. Byline given. Pays on publication. No kill fee. Publishes ms an average of 3-6 months after acceptance. Buys first North American serial rights, buys first rights, buys one-time rights, buys second serial (reprint) rights. Accepts queries by mail, e-mail, fax. Responds in 1-2 weeks to queries. Responds in 1-2 months to mss. Sample copy available online. Guidelines free.

Nonfiction Needs how-to, buy, furnish, maintain, provision a boat, interview, personal experience, technical, as relates to boats, travel, on the water, Cooking Aboard with Recipes. Send complete ms. **Pays 5¢/word.**

Photos Pays $5/photo; $50/cover photo.

Columns/Departments Cooking Aboard (how to prepare healthy and nutritious meals in the confines of a galley; how to entertain aboard a boat), 1,000-1,500 words; Environmental Notebook (articles pertaining to clean water, fish, waterfowl, water environment), 750-1,000 words. 40 Send complete ms. **Pays 5¢/word**

Tips Articles should have a positive tone and promote the liveaboard lifestyle.

$ NORTHERN BREEZES, SAILING MAGAZINE

Northern Breezes, Inc., 3949 Winnetka Ave. N, Minneapolis MN 55427. Website: www.sailingbreezes.com. **70% freelance written**. Magazine published 8 times/year for the Great Lakes and Midwest sailing community. Focusing on regional cruising, racing, and day sailing. Estab. 1989. Circ. 22,300. Byline given. Pays on publication. No kill fee. Buys first North American serial rights. Editorial lead time 1 months. Submit seasonal material 3 months in advance. Accepts queries by mail, e-mail, fax, phone. Accepts previously published material. Responds in 1 month to queries. Responds in 2 months to mss. Sample copy free. Guidelines available online.

Nonfiction Needs book excerpts, how-to, sailing topics, humor, inspirational, interview, new product, personal experience, photo feature, technical, travel. No boating reviews. **Buys 24 mss/year.** Query with published clips. Length: 300-3,500 words.

Photos Send photos Captions required. Reviews negatives, 35mm slides, 3 x 5 or 4 x 6 prints. "Digital submission preferred." Offers no additional payment for photos accepted with ms. Buys one time rights.

Columns/Departments This Old Boat (sailboat), 500-1,000 words; Surveyor's Notebook, 500-800 words. 8 Query with published clips. **Pays $50-150.**

Tips "Query with a regional connection already in mind."

$ $ $ $ NORTHEAST BOATING MAGAZINE

Northeast Boating at Its Best, Offshore Communications, Inc., 500 Victory Rd., Marina Bay, North Quincy MA 02171. (617)221-1400. Fax: (617)847-1871. E-mail: editors@onortheastboating.net. Website: www.northeastboating.net. **80% freelance written**. Monthly magazine covering power and sailboating on the coast from Maine to New Jersey. Estab. 1976. Circ. 35,000. Byline given. Pays on acceptance. Offers 50% kill fee. Publishes ms an average of 5 months after acceptance. Buys first North American serial rights. Submit seasonal material 6 months in advance. Accepts queries by mail. Accepts simultaneous submissions. Guidelines for #10 SASE.

Nonfiction Articles on boats, boating, New York, New Jersey, and New England coastal places and people, Northeast coastal history. **Buys 90 mss/year.** Send complete ms. Length: 1,200-2,500 words. **Pays $500-1,500 for features, depending on length.**

Photos Identification of subjects required. Reviews 35mm slides and digital images. Pays $150-800. Buys one time rights.

Tips Writers must demonstrate a familiarity with boats and with the Northeast coast. Specifically we are looking for articles on boating destinations, boating events (such as races, rendezvous, and boat parades), on-the-water boating adventures, boating culture, maritime museums, maritime history, boating issues (such as safety and the environment), seamanship, fishing, how-to stories, and essays. Note: Since *Northeast Boating* is a regional magazine, all stories must focus on the area from New Jersey to Maine. We are always open to new people, the best of whom may gradually work their way into regular writing assignments. Important to ask for (and follow) our writer's guidelines if you're not familiar with our magazine.

$ $ PACIFIC YACHTING

Western Canada's Premier Boating Magazine, OP Publishing, Ltd., 200 West Esplanade, Suite 500, Vancouver BC V7M 1A4 Canada. (604)998-3310. Fax: (604)998-3320. E-mail: editor@pacificyachting.com. Website: www.pacificyachting.com. **90% freelance written**. Monthly magazine covering all aspects of recreational boating on British Columbia's coast. "The bulk of our writers and photographers not only come from the local boating community, many of them were long-time *PY* readers before coming aboard as a contributor. The *PY* reader buys the magazine to read about new destinations or changes to old haunts on the British Columbia coast and to learn the latest about boats and gear." Circ. 19,000. Byline given. Pays on publication. No kill fee. Publishes ms an average of 6 months after acceptance. Buys first North American serial rights, buys simultaneous rights. Editorial lead time 4 months. Submit seasonal material 6 months in advance. Accepts queries by mail, e-mail, fax. Sample copy for $6.95, plus postage charged to credit card. Guidelines available online.

Nonfiction Needs historical, British Columbia coast only, how-to, humor, interview, personal experience, technical, boating related, travel, cruising, and destination on the British Columbia coast. "No articles from writers who are obviously not boaters!" Query. Length: 1,500-2,000 words. **Pays $150-500. Pays some expenses of writers on assignment for unsolicited articles.** Pays expenses of writers on assignment.

Photos Send photos Identification of subjects required. Reviews digital photos transparencies, 4 x 6 prints, and slides. Offers no additional payment for photos accepted with ms. Offers $25-400 for photos accepted alone Buys one time rights.

Columns/Departments Currents (current events, trade and people news, boat gatherings, and festivities), 50-250 words. Reflections; Cruising, both 800-1,000 words. Query. **Pay varies.**

Tips "Our reader wants you to balance important navigation details with first-person observations, blending the practical with the romantic. Write tight, write short, write with the reader in mind, write to inform, write to entertain. Be specific, accurate, and historic."

$ $ PONTOON & DECK BOAT

Harris Publishing, Inc., 360 B. St., Idaho Falls ID 83402. (208)524-7000. Fax: (208)522-5241. E-mail: blk@pdbmagazine.com. Website: www.pdbmagazine.com. **15% freelance written**. Magazine published 11 times/year. "We are a boating niche publication geared toward the pontoon and deck boating lifestyle and consumer market. Our audience is comprised of people who utilize these boats for varied family activities and fishing. Our magazine is promotional of the PDB industry and its major players. We seek to give the reader a twofold reason to read our publication: to celebrate the lifestyle, and to do it aboard a first-class craft." Estab. 1995. Circ. 84,000. Byline given. Pays on publication. No kill fee. Buys one-time rights. Editorial lead time 2 months. Submit seasonal material 3 months in advance. Accepts simultaneous submissions. Responds in 6 weeks to queries. Responds in 3 months to mss Sample copy and writer's guidelines free

Nonfiction Needs how-to, personal experience, technical, remodeling, rebuilding. We are saturated with travel pieces; no general boating, humor, fiction, or poetry. **Buys 15 mss/year.** Send complete ms. Length: 600-2,000 words. **Pays $50-300.** Sometimes pays expenses of writers on assignment.

Photos State availability Captions, model releases required. Reviews transparencies. Rights negotiable.

Columns/Departments No Wake Zone (short, fun quips); Better Boater (how-to). 6-12 Query with published clips. **Pays $50-150.**

Tips "Be specific to pontoon and deck boats. Any general boating material goes to the slush pile. The more you can tie together the lifestyle, attitudes, and the PDB industry, the more interest we'll take in what you send us."

$ $ $ POWER & MOTORYACHT

Source Interlink Media, 261 Madison Ave., 6th Floor, New York NY 10016. (212)915-4313. Fax: (212)915-4328. E-mail: diane.byrne@powerandmotoryacht.com. Website: www.powerandmotoryacht.com. **25% freelance written**. Monthly magazine covering powerboats 24 feet and larger with special emphasis on the 35-foot-plus market. Readers have an average of 33 years experience boating, and we give them accurate advice on how to choose, operate, and maintain their boats as well as what electronics and gear will help them pursue their favorite pastime. In addition, since powerboating is truly a lifestyle and not just a hobby for them, *Power & Motoryacht* reports on a host of other topics that affect their enjoyment of the water: chartering, sportfishing, and the environment, among others. Articles must therefore be clear, concise, and authoritative; knowledge of the marine industry is mandatory. Include personal experience and information for marine industry experts where appropriate. Estab. 1985. Circ. 157,000. Byline given. Pays on acceptance. Offers 33% kill fee. Publishes ms an average of 4-6 months after acceptance. Buys all rights. Editorial lead time 4-6 months. Submit seasonal material 4-6 months in advance. Accepts queries by mail, e-mail. Responds in 1 month to queries. Sample copy for 10x12 SASE. Guidelines for #10 SASE or via e-mail.

Nonfiction Needs how-to, interview, personal experience, photo feature, travel. No unsolicited mss or articles about sailboats and/or sailing yachts (including motorsailers or cruise ships). **Buys 20-25 mss/year.** Query with published clips. Length: 800-1,500 words. **Pays $500-1,000 for assigned articles.** Sometimes pays expenses of writers on assignment.

Photos Contact: Aimee Colon, art director. State availability Captions, identification of subjects required. Reviews 8x10 transparencies, GIF/JPEG files (minimum 300 dpi). Offers no additional payment for photos accepted with ms. Buys one-time print and Web rights.

Tips Take a clever or even unique approach to a subject, particularly if the topic is dry/technical. Pitch us on yacht cruises you've taken, particularly if they're in off-the-beaten-path locations.

$ $ POWER BOATING CANADA

1020 Brevik Place, Suites 4 & 5, Mississauga ON L4W 4N7 Canada. (905)624-8218. Fax: (905)624-6764. E-mail: editor@powerboating.com. Website: www.powerboating.com. **70% freelance written**. Bimonthly magazine covering recreational power boating. *Power Boating Canada* offers boating destinations, how-to features, boat tests (usually staff written), lifestyle pieces—with a Canadian slant—and appeal to recreational power boaters across the country. Estab. 1984. Circ. 42,000. Byline given. Pays on publication. No kill fee. Publishes ms an average of 3 months after acceptance. Buys first North American serial rights. Editorial lead time 2 months. Submit seasonal material 3 months in advance. Accepts previously published material. Responds in 1 month to queries. Responds in 2 months to mss. Sample copy free.

Nonfiction Any articles related to the sport of power boating, especially boat tests. Needs historical, how-to, interview, personal experience, travel, boating destinations. No general boating articles or personal anectdotes. **Buys 40-50 mss/year.** Query. Length: 1,200-2,500 words. **Pays $150-300 (Canadian).** Sometimes pays expenses of writers on assignment.

Reprints Send photocopy with rights for sale noted and information about when and where the material previously appeared.

Photos Send photos Captions, identification of subjects required. Reviews contact sheets, negatives, transparencies, prints. Pay varies; no additional payment for photos accepted with ms. Buys one time rights.

$ $ $ SAIL

98 N. Washington St., 2nd Floor, Boston MA 02114. (617)720-8600. Fax: (617)723-0912. E-mail: amy.ullrich@sourceinterlink.com. Website: www.sailmagazine.com. **30% freelance written**. Monthly magazine written and edited for everyone who sails—aboard a coastal or bluewater cruiser, trailerable, one-design or offshore racer, or daysailer. How-to and technical articles concentrate on techniques of sailing and aspects of design and construction, boat systems, and gear; the feature section emphasizes the fun and rewards of sailing in a practical and instructive way. Estab. 1970. Circ. 180,000. Byline given. Pays on acceptance. No kill fee. Publishes ms an average of 1 year after acceptance. Buys first North American and other rights. Accepts queries by mail, e-mail, fax. Responds in 3 months to queries. Guidelines for SASE or online (download).

Nonfiction Needs how-to, personal experience, technical, distance cruising, destinations. Cruising, chartering, commissioning, fitting-out, special race (e.g., America's Cup), Top 10 Boats. **Buys 50 mss/year.** Query. Length: 1,500-3,000 words. **Pays $200-800.** Sometimes pays expenses of writers on assignment.

Photos Prefers transparencies. High-resolution digital photos (300 dpi) are also accepted, as are high-quality color prints (preferably with negatives attached). Captions, identification of subjects, True required. Payment varies, up to $1,000 if photo used on cover.

Columns/Departments Sailing Memories (short essay); Sailing News (cruising, racing, legal, political, environmental); Under Sail (human interest). Query. **Pays $50-400.**

Tips Request an articles' specification sheet. We look for unique ways of viewing sailing. Skim old issues of *Sail* for ideas about the types of articles we publish. Always remember that *Sail* is a sailing magazine. Stay away from gloomy articles detailing all the things that went wrong on your boat. Think constructively and write about how to avoid certain problems. You should focus on a theme or choose some aspect of sailing and discuss a personal attitude or new philosophical approach to the subject. Notice that we have certain issues devoted to special themes—for example, chartering, electronics, commissioning, and the like. Stay away from pieces that chronicle your journey in the day-by-day style of a logbook. These are generally dull and uninteresting. Select specific actions or events (preferably sailing events, not shorebound activities), and build your articles around them. Emphasize the sailing.

$ $ $ SAILING MAGAZINE

125 E. Main St., Port Washington WI 53074-0249. (262)284-3494. Fax: (262)284-7764. E-mail: editorial@sailingmagazine.net. Website: www.sailingmagazine.net. Monthly magazine for the experienced sailor. Estab. 1966. Circ. 45,000. Pays after publication. No kill fee. Buys one-time rights. Accepts queries by mail, e-mail. Responds in 2 months to queries.

Nonfiction Experiences of sailing, cruising, and racing or cruising to interesting locations, whether a small lake near you or islands in the Southern Ocean, with first-hand knowledge and tips for our readers. Top-notch photos with maps, charts, cruising information complete the package. No regatta sports unless there is a story involved. Needs book excerpts, how-to, tech pieces on boats and gear, interview, personal experience, travel, by sail. **Buys 15-20 mss/year.** Length: 750-2,500 words. **Pays $100-800.**

Photos Captions required. Reviews color transparencies. Pays $50-400.

Tips Prefers text in Word on disk for Mac or to e-mail address.

$ $ SAILING WORLD

World Publications, 55 Hammarlund Way, Middletown RI 02842. (401)845-5100. Fax: (401)848-5180. E-mail: editorial@sailingworld.com. Website: www.sailingworld.com. **40% freelance written**. Magazine published 10 times/year covering performance sailing. Estab. 1962. Circ. 60,000. Byline given. Pays on publication. No kill fee. Publishes ms an average of 4 months after acceptance. Buys first North American serial rights. world serial rights Responds in 1 month to queries. Sample copy for $5.

Nonfiction Needs how-to, for racing and performance-oriented sailors, interview, photo feature, Regatta sports and charter. No travelogs. **Buys 5-10 unsolicited mss/year.** Query. Length: 400-1,500 words. **Pays $400 for up to 2,000 words.** Does not pay expenses of writers on assignment unless pre-approved.

Tips Send query with outline and include your experience. Prospective contributors should study recent issues of the magazine to determine appropriate subject matter. The emphasis here is on performance sailing: keep in mind that the *Sailing World* readership is relatively educated about the sport. Unless you are dealing with a totally new aspect of sailing, you can and should discuss ideas on an advanced technical level. `Gee-whiz' impressions from beginning sailors are generally not accepted.

$ $ SEA KAYAKER

Sea Kayaker, Inc., P.O. Box 17029, Seattle WA 98127. (206)789-1326. Fax: (206)781-1141. E-mail: gretchen@seakayakermag.com. Website: www.seakayakermag.com. **95% freelance written**. *Sea Kayaker* is a bimonthly publication with a worldwide readership that covers all aspects of kayak touring. It is well known as an important source of continuing education by the most experienced paddlers. Estab. 1984. Circ. 30,000. Byline given. Pays on publication. Offers 10% kill fee. Publishes ms an average of 6 months after acceptance. Buys first North American serial rights. Editorial lead time 4 months. Submit seasonal material 4 months in advance. Accepts queries by mail, e-mail, fax, phone. Responds in 2 months to queries. Sample copy for $7.30 (US), samples to other countries extra. Guidelines available online.

Nonfiction Needs essays, historical, how-to, on making equipment, humor, new product, personal experience, technical, travel. Unsolicited gear reviews are not accepted. **Buys 50 mss/year.** Send complete ms. Length: 1,500-5,000 words. **Pays 18-20¢/word for assigned articles. Pays 15-17¢/word for unsolicited articles.**

Photos Send photos Captions, identification of subjects required. Reviews transparencies, prints. Offers $15-400. Buys one time rights.

Columns/Departments Technique; Equipment; Do-It-Yourself; Food; Safety; Health; Environment; Book Reviews; all 1,000-2,500 words. 40-45 Query. **Pays 15-20¢/word.**

Tips We consider unsolicited manuscripts that include a SASE, but we give greater priority to brief descriptions (several paragraphs) of proposed articles accompanied by at least 2 samples—published or unpublished—of your writing. Enclose a statement as to why you're qualified to write the piece and indicate whether photographs or illustrations are available to accompany the piece.

SEA MAGAZINE

America's Western Boating Magazine, Duncan McIntosh Co., 17782 Cowan, Suite A, Irvine CA 92614. (949)660-6150, ext. 253. Fax: (949)660-6172. E-mail: lysa@seamag.com. Website: www.goboatingamerica.com. **Contact:**

Lysa Christopher, Managing Editor. Monthly magazine covering West Coast power boating. Estab. 1908. Circ. 50,000. Byline given. Pays on publication. Publishes ms an average of 6 months after acceptance. Buys first North American serial rights. Editorial lead time 3 months. Submit seasonal material 6 months in advance. Accepts simultaneous submissions. Responds in 3 months to queries.

Nonfiction "News you can use is kind of our motto. All articles should aim to help power boat owners make the most of their boating experience." Needs how-to, new product, personal experience, technical, travel. **Buys 36 mss/year.** Send complete ms. Length: 1,000-1,500 words. **Payment varies** Pays expenses of writers on assignment.

Photos State availability of photos. Captions, identification of subjects, model releases required. Reviews transparencies, hi-res digital. Offers $50-250/photo. Buys one time rights.

$ $ SOUTHERN BOATING MAGAZINE

The South's Largest Boating Magazine, Southern Boating & Yachting, Inc., 330 N. Andrews Ave., Ft. Lauderdale FL 33301. (954)522-5515. Fax: (954)522-2260. E-mail: sboating@southernboating.com. Website: southernboating.com. **50% freelance written**. Monthly magazine. Upscale monthly yachting magazine focusing on the Southeast U.S., Bahamas, Caribbean, and Gulf of Mexico. Estab. 1972. Circ. 43,000. Byline given. Pays within 30 days of publication. No kill fee. Publishes ms an average of 2 months after acceptance. Buys one-time rights. Editorial lead time 3 months. Submit seasonal material 3 months in advance. Accepts queries by e-mail. Sample copy for $8.

Nonfiction Needs how-to, boat maintenance, travel, boating related, destination pieces. **Buys 50 mss/year.** Query. Length: 900-1,200 words. **Pays $500-750 with art.**

Photos State availability of or send photos Captions, identification of subjects, model releases required. Reviews transparencies, prints, digital files. Offers $75/photo minimum Buys one time rights.

Columns/Departments Weekend Workshop (how-to/maintenance), 900 words; What's New in Electronics (electronics), 900 words; Engine Room (new developments), 1,000 words. 24 Query first, see media kit for special issue focus. **Pays $600.**

$ $ $ TRAILER BOATS MAGAZINE

Ehlert Publishing Group, Inc., 20700 Belshaw Ave., Carson CA 90746-3510. (310)537-6322. Fax: (310)537-8735. Website: www.trailerboats.com. **50% freelance written**. Monthly magazine covering legally trailerable power boats and related powerboating activities. Estab. 1971. Circ. 100,000. Byline given. Pays on acceptance. No kill fee. Publishes ms an average of 3 months after acceptance. Buys all rights. Editorial lead time 3 months. Submit seasonal material 5 months in advance. Responds in 1 month to queries. Sample copy for 9 x 12 SAE with 7 first-class stamps.

Nonfiction Needs general interest, trailer boating activities, historical, places, events, boats, how-to, repair boats, installation, etc., interview, personal experience, photo feature, technical, travel, boating travel on water or highways, product evaluations. No How I Spent My Summer Vacation stories, or stories not directly connected to trailerable boats and related activities. **Buys 3-4 unsolicited mss/year.** Query. Length: 1,000-2,500 words. **Pays $150-1,000.** Sometimes pays expenses of writers on assignment.

Photos Send photos Captions, identification of subjects, model releases required. Reviews transparencies, 2 ¼x2 ¼ and 35mm slides, and high-resolution digital images (300 dpi). Buys all rights.

Columns/Departments Over the Transom (funny or strange boating photos); Dock Talk (short pieces on boating news, safety, products, profiles of people using boats to do their jobs), all 1,000-1,500 words. 12-13 Query. **Pays $250-500.**

Tips Query should contain short general outline of the intended material; what kind of photos; how the photos illustrate the piece. Write with authority, covering the subject with quotes from experts. Frequent mistakes are not knowing the subject matter or the audience. The writer may have a better chance of breaking in at our publication with short articles and fillers if they are typically hard-to-find articles. We do most major features in-house, but try how-to stories dealing with repairs, installation and towing tips, boat trailer repair. Good color photos will win our hearts every time.

$ WATERFRONT NEWS

Ziegler Publishing Co., Inc., 1515 SW 1st Ave., Ft. Lauderdale FL 33315. (954)524-9450. Fax: (954)524-9464. E-mail: editor@waterfront-news.com. Website: www.waterfront-news.com. **20% freelance written**. Monthly tabloid covering marine and boating topics for the Greater Ft. Lauderdale waterfront community. Estab. 1984. Circ. 20,000. Byline given. Pays on publication. No kill fee. Publishes ms an average of 2 months after acceptance. Buys first rights, buys second serial (reprint) rights, buys simultaneous rights in certain circumstances rights. Submit seasonal material 3 months in advance. Responds in 1 month to queries. Sample copy for sae with 9x12 envelope and 4 First-Class stamps.

Nonfiction Needs interview, of people important in boating, i.e., racers, boat builders, designers, etc. from south Florida, Regional articles on south Florida's waterfront issues; marine communities; travel pieces of interest to boaters, including docking information. Length: 500-1,000 words. **Pays $100-125 for assigned articles.**

Photos Send photos Reviews JPEG/TIFF files.
Tips "No fiction. Keep it under 1,000 words. Photos or illustrations help. Send for a sample copy of *Waterfront News* so you can acquaint yourself with our publication and our unique audience. Although we're not necessarily looking for technical articles, it helps if the writer has sailing or powerboating experience. Writers should be familiar with the region and be specific when dealing with local topics."

$ $ WATERWAY GUIDE

326 First St., Suite 400, Annapolis MD 21403. (443)482-9377. Fax: (443)482-9422. Website: www.waterwayguide.com. **Contact:** Gary Reich, managing editor. **90% freelance written.** Triannual magazine covering intracoastal waterway travel for recreational boats. "Writer must be knowledgeable about navigation and the areas covered by the guide." Estab. 1947. Circ. 30,000. Byline given. Pays on publication. No kill fee. Publishes ms an average of 3 months after acceptance. Buys first North American serial rights, buys electronic rights. Makes work-for-hire assignments. Editorial lead time 4 months. Submit seasonal material 3 months in advance. Accepts queries by mail, phone. Responds in 6 weeks to queries. Responds in 2 months to mss. Sample copy for $39.95 with $3 postage.
Nonfiction Needs essays, historical, how-to, photo feature, technical, travel. **Buys 6 mss/year.** Send complete ms. Length: 250-5,000 words. **Pays $50-500.**
Photos Send photos Captions, identification of subjects required. Reviews transparencies, 3 x 5 prints. Offers $25-50/photo. Buys all rights.
Tips "Must have on-the-water experience and be able to provide new and accurate information on geographic areas covered by *Waterway Guide*."

$ ✪ WAVELENGTH MAGAZINE

Pacific Edge Publishing, 1773 El Verano Dr., Gabriola Island BC V0R 1X6 Canada. (250)247-9093. Fax: (250)247-9083. E-mail: diana@wavelengthmagazine.com. Website: www.wavelengthmagazine.com. **75% freelance written.** Quarterly magazine with a major focus on paddling the Pacific coast. We promote safe paddling, guide paddlers to useful products and services and explore coastal environmental issues. Estab. 1991. Circ. 65,000 print and electronic readers. Byline given. Pays on publication. Publishes ms an average of 4 months after acceptance. Buys first North American serial rights, buys electronic rights. Editorial lead time 4 months. Submit seasonal material 4 months in advance. Accepts queries by mail, e-mail. Sample copy available online. Guidelines available online.
Nonfiction Needs how-to, paddle, travel, humor, new product, personal experience, technical, travel, trips. **Buys 25 mss/year.** Query. Length: 1,000-1,500 words. **Pays $50-75.**
Photos State availability Captions, identification of subjects required. Reviews low res JPEGs. Offers $25-50/photo. Buys first and electronic rights
Tips You must know paddling—although novice paddlers are welcome. A strong environmental or wilderness appreciation component is advisable. We are willing to help refine work with flexible people. E-mail queries preferred. Check out our Editorial Calendar for our upcoming features.

$ $ WOODENBOAT MAGAZINE

The Magazine for Wooden Boat Owners, Builders, and Designers, WoodenBoat Publications, Inc., P.O. Box 78, Brooklin ME 04616. (207)359-4651. Fax: (207)359-8920. Website: www.woodenboat.com. **50% freelance written.** Bimonthly magazine for wooden boat owners, builders, and designers. We are devoted exclusively to the design, building, care, preservation, and use of wooden boats, both commercial and pleasure, old and new, sail and power. We work to convey quality, integrity, and involvement in the creation and care of these craft, to entertain, inform, inspire, and to provide our varied readers with access to individuals who are deeply experienced in the world of wooden boats. Estab. 1974. Circ. 90,000. Byline given. Pays on publication. Offers variable kill fee. Publishes ms an average of 1 year after acceptance. Buys first North American serial rights. Accepts previously published material. Accepts simultaneous submissions. Responds in 2 months to queries. Responds in 2 months to mss. Sample copy for $5.99. Guidelines available online.
Nonfiction Needs technical, repair, restoration, maintenance, use, design, and building wooden boats. No poetry, fiction. **Buys 50 mss/year.** Query with published clips. Length: 1,500-5,000 words. **Pays $300/1,000 words.** Sometimes pays expenses of writers on assignment.
Reprints Send tearsheet or typed ms with rights for sale noted and information about when and where the material previously appeared.
Photos Send photos Identification of subjects required. Reviews negatives. Pays $15-75 b&w, $25-350 color. Buys one time rights.
Columns/Departments Currents pays for information on wooden boat-related events, projects, boatshop activities, etc. Uses same columnists for each issue. Length: 250-1,000 words. Send complete information. **Pays $5-50.**
Tips We appreciate a detailed, articulate query letter, accompanied by photos, that will give us a clear idea of what the author is proposing. We appreciate samples of previously published work. It is important for a

prospective author to become familiar with our magazine. Most work is submitted on speculation. The most common failure is not exploring the subject material in enough depth.

$ $ $ YACHTING

2 Park Ave., 9th Fl., New York NY 10016. Fax: (212)779-5479. E-mail: editor@yachtingmagazine.com. Website: www.yachtingmagazine.com. **30% freelance written**. Monthly magazine. Monthly magazine written and edited for experienced, knowledgeable yachtsmen. Estab. 1907. Circ. 132,000. Byline given. Pays on acceptance. No kill fee. Buys first North American serial rights, buys electronic rights. Editorial lead time 2 months. Submit seasonal material 6 months in advance. Accepts queries by mail, e-mail, fax. Responds in 1 month to queries. Responds in 3 months to mss. Sample copy free. Guidelines available online.

Nonfiction Needs personal experience, technical. **Buys 50 mss/year.** Query with published clips. Length: 750-800 words. **Pays $150-1,500.** Pays expenses of writers on assignment.

Photos Send photos Captions, identification of subjects, model releases required. Reviews transparencies. Negotiates payment individually.

Tips We require considerable expertise in our writing because our audience is experienced and knowledgeable. Vivid descriptions of quaint anchorages and quainter natives are fine, but our readers want to know how the yachtsmen got there, too. They also want to know how their boats work. *Yachting* is edited for experienced, affluent boatowners—power and sail—who don't have the time or the inclination to read sub-standard stories. They love carefully crafted stories about places they've never been or a different spin on places they have, meticulously reported pieces on issues that affect their yachting lives, personal accounts of yachting experiences from which they can learn, engaging profiles of people who share their passion for boats, insightful essays that evoke the history and traditions of the sport and compelling photographs of others enjoying the game as much as they do. They love to know what to buy and how things work. They love to be surprised. They don't mind getting their hands dirty or saving a buck here and there, but they're not interested in learning how to make a masthead light out of a mayonnaise jar. If you love what they love and can communicate like a pro (that means meeting deadlines, writing tight, being obsessively accurate and never misspelling a proper name), we'd love to hear from you.

BOWLING

BOWLING THIS MONTH

P.O. Box 966, San Marcos TX 78667. (512)353-8906. Fax: (512)353-8690. Website: www.bowlingthismonth.com. No kill fee.

- *Bowling This Month* does use freelance articles.

GENERAL INTEREST

$ FIT-4-SPORTS

L.L. Cross Inc, P.O. Box 120327, Clermont FL 34712. (321)438-0838. E-mail: lorettalynn@mac.com. Website: www.fit-4-sports.net. **20% freelance written**. Monthly magazine covering sports, fitness, health and adventure. We write one-on-one interviews with professional athletes, coaches, trainers, as well as content written by doctors, licensed trainers, dietitians, etc. Articles about local athletes as well. Estab. 2003. Circ. 50,000. Byline given. No kill fee. Publishes ms an average of 2-3 months after acceptance. Buys first North American serial rights. Editorial lead time 2-3 months. Submit seasonal material 3-4 months in advance. Accepts queries by mail, e-mail. Accepts simultaneous submissions. Responds in 1-2 weeks to queries. Responds in 2-3 months to mss. Sample copy available online. Guidelines free.

Nonfiction Needs how-to, interview, sports, fitness, health. covering specialty camps, training, interview with professional athletes, trainers, coaches, etc. We do not want generic Q&A, anything thata can be read online, stats, etc. **Buys We purchase maybe 3-4 nonfiction articles; the rest are written for byline purposes. mss/year.** Query. **Pays 25¢ for assigned articles. Pays 25¢ for unsolicited articles.**

Photos State availability Model releases required. Reviews GIF/JPEG files. Buys one time rights.

Columns/Departments Fish Tails (fishing related articles, non-self promotional, etc.), no more than 50 words. 2-3 mss/year Query. **Pays $-$25.**

Tips Read publication on website; articles are written for kids and adults. I don't allow guns, tobacco, alcohol, politicians or lawyers to advertise. Keep it clean and healthy. Be informative, get the story behind the story.

$ $ METROSPORTS

New York, MetroSports Publishing, Inc., 259 W. 30th St., 3rd Floor, New York NY 10001. (212)563-7329. Fax: (212)563-7573. E-mail: melanie@metrosports.com. Website: www.metrosportsny.com. **50% freelance written**. Monthly magazine covering amateur sports and fitness. We focus on participatory sports (not team sports) for an active, young audience that likes to exercise. Estab. 1987. Circ. 100,000. Byline given. Pays on publication. Offers 50% kill fee. Buys first rights, buys electronic rights. Editorial lead time 3 months. Submit seasonal material 6 months in advance. Accepts queries by mail, e-mail, fax. Accepts previously published material. Accepts simultaneous submissions. Responds in 3-4 weeks to queries. Responds in 1-2 months to mss. Sample copy available online. Guidelines by email.

Nonfiction Needs essays, general interest, historical, how-to, train for a triathlon, train for an adventure race, etc., humor, inspirational, interview, new product, opinion, personal experience, technical, travel. Holiday Gift Guide (December). We don't publish anything related to team sports (basketball, baseball, football, etc.), golf, tennis. **Buys 24 mss/year.** Query with published clips. Length: 800-3,000 words. **Pays $100-300.** Sometimes pays expenses of writers on assignment.

Photos State availability Captions, identification of subjects required. Reviews slides transparencies, 3x5 prints, GIF/JPEG files (300 dpi). Negotiates payment individually. Buys one time rights.

Columns/Departments Running (training, nutrition, profiles); Cycling (training, nutrition, profiles), both 800 words. 15 Query with published clips. **Pays $100-250.**

Tips Read the magazine, know what we cover. E-mail queries or mail with published clips. No phone calls, please.

$ OUTDOORS NW

PMB 3311, 10002 Aurora Ave. N. #36, Seattle WA 98133. (206)418-0747. Fax: (206)418-0746. E-mail: info@outdoorsnw.com. Website: www.outdoorsnw.com. **80% freelance written.** Monthly magazine covering outdoor recreation in the Pacific Northwest. "Writers must have a solid knowledge of the sport they are writing about. They must be doers." Estab. 1988. Circ. 40,000. Byline given. Pays on publication. No kill fee. Publishes ms an average of 3 months after acceptance. Buys first rights. Editorial lead time 2 months. Submit seasonal material 4 months in advance. Accepts queries by mail, e-mail, fax. Accepts previously published material. Accepts simultaneous submissions. Sample copy and writer's guidelines for $3.

- Publication changed it's name from Sports Etc.

Nonfiction Needs interview, new product, travel. Query with published clips. Length: 750-1,500 words. **Pays $25-125.** Sometimes pays expenses of writers on assignment.

Photos Send photos Captions, identification of subjects, model releases required. Reviews electronic images only. Buys all rights.

Columns/Departments Faces, Places, Puruits (750 words). 4-6 Query with published clips. **Pays $40-75.**

Tips "*Outdoors NW* is written for the serious Pacific Northwest outdoor recreationalist. The magazine's look, style and editorial content actively engage the reader, delivering insightful perspectives on the sports it has come to be known for—alpine skiing, bicycling, adventure racing, triathlon and multi-sport, hiking, kayaking, marathons, mountain climbing, Nordic skiing, running, and snowboarding. *Outdoors NW* magazine wants vivid writing, telling images, and original perspectives to produce its smart, entertaining monthly."

$ $ ROCKY MOUNTAIN SPORTS MAGAZINE

Rocky Mountain Sports, Inc., P.O. Box 3036,, Boulder CO 80307. (303)477-9770. Fax: (303)477-9747. E-mail: rheaton@rockymountainsports.com. Website: www.rockymountainsports.com. **50% freelance written.** Monthly magazine covering nonteam-related sports in Colorado. "*Rocky* is a magazine for sports-related lifestyles and activities. Our mission is to reflect and inspire the active lifestyle of Rocky Mountain residents." Estab. 1986. Circ. 95,000. Byline given. Pays 60-90 days after publication. Offers 50% kill fee. Publishes ms an average of 1 month after acceptance. Buys first North American serial rights. Editorial lead time 3 months. Submit seasonal material 6 months in advance. Accepts queries by e-mail. Accepts previously published material. Accepts simultaneous submissions. Responds in 1 month to queries. Responds in 2 months to mss. Guidelines by email.

- The editor says she wants to see mountain outdoor sports writing *only. No ball sports, hunting, or fishing.*

Nonfiction Needs general interest, how-to, humor, inspirational, interview, new product, personal experience, travel. Skiing & Snowboarding (November); Nordic/Snowshoeing (December); Marathon (January); Running (March); Adventure Travel (April); Triathlon (May); Paddling and Climbing (June); Road Cycling & Camping (July); Organic (August); Women's Sports & Marathon (September); Health Club (October). Query with published clips. Length: 500-1,500 words. **Pays $50-300.**

Reprints Send photocopy and information about when and where the material previously appeared. Pays 20-25% of amount paid for original article.

Photos State availability Identification of subjects, model releases required. Reviews GIF/JPEG files. Negotiates payment individually. Buys one time rights.

Columns/Departments Starting Lines (short newsy items); Running; Cycling; Climbing; Triathlon; Fitness, Nutrition; Sports Medicine; Off the Beaten Path (sports we don't usually cover). 20 Query. **Pays $25-300.**

Tips Have a Colorado angle to the story, a catchy cover letter, good clips, and demonstrate that you've read and understand our magazine and its readers.

$ SILENT SPORTS

Waupaca Publishing Co., P.O. Box 152, Waupaca WI 54981-9990. (715)258-5546. Fax: (715)258-8162. E-mail: info@silentsports.net. Website: www.silentsports.net. **75% freelance written**. Monthly magazine covering running, cycling, cross-country skiing, canoeing, kayaking, snowshoeing, in-line skating, camping, backpacking, and hiking aimed at people in Wisconsin, Minnesota, northern Illinois, and portions of Michigan and Iowa. Not a coffee table magazine. Our readers are participants from rank amateur weekend athletes to highly competitive racers. Estab. 1984. Circ. 10,000. Byline given. Pays on publication. Offers 20% kill fee. Publishes ms an average of 3 months after acceptance. Buys one-time rights. Submit seasonal material 4 months in advance. Accepts queries by mail, e-mail, fax. Accepts previously published material. Responds in 3 months to queries. Sample copy and writer's guidelines for 10x13 SAE with 7 first-class stamps.

- The editor needs local angles on in-line skating, recreation bicycling, and snowshoeing.

Nonfiction All stories/articles must focus on the Upper Midwest. Needs general interest, how-to, interview, opinion, technical, travel. **Buys 25 mss/year.** Query. 2,500 words maximum. **Pays $15-100.** Sometimes pays expenses of writers on assignment.

Reprints Send typed manuscript with rights for sale noted and information about when and where the material previously appeared. Pays 50% of amount paid for an original article.

Photos State availability Reviews transparencies. Pays $5-15 for b&w story photos; $50-100 for color covers. Buys one time rights.

Tips Where-to-go and personality profiles are areas most open to freelancers. Writers should keep in mind that this is a regional, Midwest-based publication. We want only stories/articles with a focus on our region.

$ $ TWIN CITIES SPORTS

Twin Cities Sports Publishing, Inc., 3009 Holmes Ave. S., Minneapolis MN 55408. (612)825-1034. Fax: (612)825-6452. E-mail: laurie@twincitiessports.com. Website: www.twincitiessports.com. **75% freelance written**. Monthly magazine covering amateur sports and fitness. We focus on participatory sports (not team sports) for an active, young audience that likes to exercise. Estab. 1987. Circ. 40,000. Byline given. Pays on publication. Offers 50% kill fee. Publishes ms an average of 2 months after acceptance. Buys first rights, buys electronic rights. Editorial lead time 3 months. Submit seasonal material 6 months in advance. Accepts queries by mail, e-mail, fax. Accepts previously published material. Accepts simultaneous submissions. Responds in 3-4 weeks to queries. Responds in 1-2 months to mss. Sample copy available online. Guidelines by email.

Nonfiction Needs essays, general interest, historical, how-to, train for a triathlon, set a new 5K P.R., train for an adventure race, humor, inspirational, interview, new product, opinion, personal experience, technical, travel. Holiday Gift Guide (December) We don't publish anything related to team sports (basketball, baseball, football, etc.), golf, tennis. **Buys 24 mss/year.** Query with published clips. Length: 800-3,000 words. **Pays $100-300.** Sometimes pays expenses of writers on assignment.

Photos State availability Captions, identification of subjects required. Reviews slides transparencies, 3x5 prints, GIF/JPEG files (300 dpi). Negotiates payment individually. Buys one time rights.

Columns/Departments Running (training, nutrition, profiles), 800 words; Cycling (training, nutrition, profiles), 800 words; Cool Down (first-person essay), 800-1,000 words. 15 Query with published clips. **Pays $100-250.**

Tips Read the magazine, know what we cover. E-mail queries or mail with published clips. No phone calls, please.

GOLF

$ $ AFRICAN AMERICAN GOLFER'S DIGEST

Nation's leading publication for avid black golfers, 139 Fulton St., Suite 209, New York NY 10038. (212)571-6559. E-mail: debertcook@aol.com. Website: www.africanamericangolfersdigest.com. **100% freelance written**. Quarterly magazine covering golf lifestyle, health, travel destinations and reviews, golf equipment, golfer profiles. Editorial should focus on interests of our market demographic of African Americans with historical, artistic, musical, educational (higher learning), automotive, sports, fashion, entertainment, and other categories of high interest to them. Estab. 2003. Circ. 20,000. Byline given. No kill fee. Publishes ms an average of 3 months after acceptance. Buys all rights. Editorial lead time 3-6 months. Submit seasonal material 3-6 months in advance. Accepts queries by e-mail. Accepts simultaneous submissions. Responds in 3 weeks to queries. Responds in 3 months to mss. Sample copy for $4.99. Guidelines by email.

Nonfiction Needs how-to, interview, new product, personal experience, photo feature, technical, travel, golf-related. **Buys 3 mss/year.** Query. Length: 250-1,500 words. **Pays 25-50¢/word.**

Photos State availability Captions, identification of subjects, model releases required. Reviews GIF/JPEG files (300 dpi or higher at 4x6). Negotiates payment individually. Buys all rights.

Columns/Departments Profiles (celebrities, national leaders, entertainers, corporate leaders, etc., who golf); Travel (destination/golf course reviews); Golf Fashion (jewelry, clothing, accessories). 3 Query. **Pays 25-50¢/word.**

Fillers Needs anecdotes, facts, gags, newsbreaks, short humor. 3 Length: 20-125 words. **Pays 25-50¢/word.**
Tips Emphasize golf and African American appeal.

$ $ ARIZONA, THE STATE OF GOLF

Arizona Golf Association, 7226 N. 16th St., Suite 200, Phoenix AZ 85020. (602)944-3035. Fax: (602)944-3228. Website: www.azgolf.org. **50% freelance written**. Quarterly magazine covering golf in Arizona, the official publication of the Arizona Golf Association. Estab. 1999. Circ. 45,000. Byline given. Pays on acceptance. No kill fee. Buys all rights. Editorial lead time 6 months. Submit seasonal material 3 months in advance. Accepts queries by mail. Accepts previously published material. Accepts simultaneous submissions. Sample copy and writer's guidelines free
Nonfiction Needs book excerpts, essays, historical, how-to, golf, humor, inspirational, interview, new product, opinion, personal experience, photo feature, travel, destinations. **Buys 5-10 mss/year.** Query. Length: 500-2,000 words. **Pays $50-500.** Sometimes pays expenses of writers on assignment.
Photos State availability Captions, identification of subjects required. Reviews contact sheets. Negotiates payment individually. Rights purchased varies.
Columns/Departments Short Strokes (golf news and notes), Improving Your Game (golf tips), Out of Bounds (guest editorial, 800 words). Query.

$ $ $ GOLF CANADA

Official Magazine of the Royal Canadian Golf Association, RCGA/Relevant Communications, Golf House Suite 1, 1333 Dorval Dr., Oakville ON L6M 4X7 Canada. (905)849-9700. Fax: (905)845-7040. Website: www.rcga.org. **80% freelance written**. Magazine published 5 times/year covering Canadian golf. *Golf Canada* is the official magazine of the Royal Canadian Golf Association, published to entertain and enlighten members about RCGA-related activities and to generally support and promote amateur golf in Canada. Estab. 1994. Circ. 159,000. Byline given. Pays on acceptance. Offers 100% kill fee. Buys first translation, electronic rights. Editorial lead time 3 months. Submit seasonal material 6 months in advance. Accepts queries by mail, e-mail, fax, phone. Accepts previously published material. Sample copy free.
Nonfiction Needs historical, interview, new product, opinion, photo feature, travel. No professional golf-related articles **Buys 42 mss/year.** Query with published clips. Length: 750-3,000 words. **Pays 60¢/word, including electronic rights.** Sometimes pays expenses of writers on assignment.
Photos State availability Captions required. Reviews contact sheets, negatives, transparencies, prints. Negotiates payment individually. Buys all rights.
Columns/Departments Guest Column (focus on issues surrounding the Canadian golf community), 700 words. Query. **Pays 60¢/word, including electronic rights**
Tips Keep story ideas focused on Canadian competitive golf.

$ $ $ GOLFING MAGAZINE

Golfer Magazine, Inc., 205 Broad St., Wethersfield CT 06109. (860)563-1633. Fax: (646)607-3001. E-mail: tlanders@golfingmagazine.net. Website: www.golfingmagazineonline.com. **30% freelance written**. Bimonthly magazine covering golf, including travel, products, player profiles and company profiles. Estab. 1999. Circ. 175,000. Byline given. Pays on publication. Offers negotiable kill fee. Buys one-time rights, buys simultaneous rights. Editorial lead time 2 months. Submit seasonal material 2 months in advance. Accepts queries by mail, e-mail. Accepts previously published material. Sample copy free.
Nonfiction All articles must include golf-related tips. Needs book excerpts, new product, photo feature, travel. **Buys 4-5 mss/year.** Query. Length: 700-2,500 words. **Pays $250-1,000 for assigned articles. Pays $100-500 for unsolicited articles.**
Photos State availability Captions required. Reviews GIF/JPEG files. Negotiates payment and rights individually.
Fillers Needs facts, gags. 2-3 **Payment individually determined.**

$ $ GOLF NEWS MAGAZINE

Premier Golf Magazine Since 1984, Golf News Magazine, P.O. Box 1040, Rancho Mirage CA 92270. (760)321-8800. Fax: (760)328-3013. E-mail: golfnews@aol.com. Website: www.golfnewsmag.com. **40% freelance written.** Monthly magazine covering golf. Our publication specializes in the creative treatment of the sport of golf, offering a variety of themes and slants as related to golf. If it's good writing and relates to golf, we're interested. Estab. 1984. Circ. 15,000. Byline given. Pays on acceptance. Publishes ms an average of 3 months after acceptance. Buys first rights. Editorial lead time 2 months. Submit seasonal material 2 months in advance. Accepts queries by mail, e-mail, fax. Accepts previously published material. Accepts simultaneous submissions. Responds in 3 weeks to queries. Responds in 3 weeks to mss. Sample copy for $2 and 9 x 12 SAE with 4 first-class stamps.
Nonfiction We will consider any topic related to golf that is written well with high standards. Needs book excerpts, essays, expose, general interest, historical, humor, inspirational, interview, opinion, personal experience, real estate. **Buys 20 mss/year.** Query with published clips. **Pays $75-350.**

Photos State availability Identification of subjects required. Negotiates payment individually. Buys one time rights.
Columns/Departments Submit ideas. 10 Query with published clips.
Tips Solid, creative, excellent, professional writing. Only good writers need apply. We are a national award-winning magazine looking for the most creative writers we can find.

GOLF TEACHING PROÃ†

United States Golf Teachers Federation, 1295 S.E. Port St. Lucie Blvd., Port St. Lucie FL 34952. (772)335-3216. Fax: (772)335-3822. E-mail: info@usgtf.com. Website: www.golfteachingpro.com. **80% freelance written**. Quarterly magazine covering golf teaching related subjects only. Estab. 1989. Circ. 18,000+. Byline sometimes given. Pays on acceptance. No kill fee. Publishes ms an average of 2-3 months after acceptance. Editorial lead time 2-3 months. Submit seasonal material 2-3 months in advance. Accepts queries by mail, e-mail, fax, phone. Accepts previously published material. Accepts simultaneous submissions. Sample copy available online. Guidelines by email.
Nonfiction Contact: Geoff Bryant. Needs book excerpts, general interest, historical, how-to, golf tips, humor, inspirational, interview, new product, opinion, personal experience, photo feature, technical, all golf teaching related subjects. Query. Sometimes pays expenses of writers on assignment. (limit agreed upon in advance)
Photos Send photos Offers no additional payment for photos accepted with ms.
Columns/Departments Query.
Fiction Query.
Poetry Query.
Fillers Query.

$ $ $ GOLF TIPS

The Game's Most In-Depth Instruction & Equipment Magazine, Werner Publishing Corp., 12121 Wilshire Blvd., Suite 1200, Los Angeles CA 90025. E-mail: editors@golftipsmag.com. Website: www.golftipsmag.com. **95% freelance written**. Magazine published 9 times/year covering golf instruction and equipment. We provide mostly concise, very clear golf instruction pieces for the serious golfer. Estab. 1986. Byline given. Pays on publication. Offers 33% kill fee. Publishes ms an average of 2 months after acceptance. Buys first rights, buys second serial (reprint) rights. Editorial lead time 3 months. Submit seasonal material 4 months in advance. Accepts previously published material. Responds in 1 month to queries. Sample copy free Guidelines available online.
Nonfiction Needs book excerpts, how-to, interview, new product, photo feature, technical, travel, all golf related. Generally golf essays rarely make it. **Buys 125 mss/year.** Send complete ms. Length: 250-2,000 words. **Pays $300-1,000 for assigned articles. Pays $300-800 for unsolicited articles.** Sometimes pays expenses of writers on assignment.
Photos State availability Captions, identification of subjects required. Reviews 2 x 2 transparencies. Negotiates payment individually. Buys all rights.
Columns/Departments Stroke Saver (very clear, concise instruction), 350 words; Lesson Library (book excerpts—usually in a series), 1,000 words; Travel Tips (formatted golf travel), 2,500 words. 40 Query with or without published clips or send complete ms. **Pays $300-850.**
Tips Contact a respected PGA Professional and find out if they're interested in being published. A good writer can turn an interview into a decent instruction piece.

$ $ $ MINNESOTA GOLFER

6550 York Ave. S., Suite 211, Edina MN 55435. (952)927-4643. Fax: (952)927-9642. E-mail: wp@mngolf.org. Website: www.mngolfer.com. **75% freelance written**. Bimonthly magazine covering golf in Minnesota, the official publication of the Minnesota Golf Association. Estab. 1975. Circ. 66,000. Byline given. Pays on acceptance or publication. No kill fee. Buys first rights. Editorial lead time 3 months. Accepts queries by mail, e-mail, fax.
Nonfiction Needs historical, interview, new product, travel, book reviews, instruction, golf course previews. Query with published clips. Length: 400-2,000 words. **Pays $50-750.** Sometimes pays expenses of writers on assignment.
Photos State availability Captions, identification of subjects required. Reviews contact sheets, transparencies, digital images. Negotiates payment individually. Image rights by assignment.
Columns/Departments Punch shots (golf news and notes); Q School (news and information targeted to beginners, junior golfers and women); Great Drives (featuring noteworthy golf holes in Minnesota); Instruction.

$ $ VIRGINIA GOLFER

Touchpoint Publishing, Inc., 600 Founders Bridge Blvd., Midlothian VA 23113. (804)378-2300. Fax: (804)378-2369. Website: www.vsga.org. **65% freelance written**. Bimonthly magazine covering golf in Virginia, the official publication of the Virginia State Golf Association. Estab. 1983. Circ. 45,000. Byline given. Pays on publication. No kill fee. Buys all rights. Editorial lead time 6 months. Submit seasonal material 3 months in advance. Accepts queries by mail, e-mail. Accepts previously published material. Accepts simultaneous submissions. Sample copy and writer's guidelines free

Nonfiction Needs book excerpts, essays, historical, how-to, golf, humor, inspirational, interview, personal experience, photo feature, technical, golf equipment, where to play, golf business. **Buys 30-40 mss/year.** Send complete ms. Length: 500-2,500 words. **Pays $50-200.** Sometimes pays expenses of writers on assignment.

Photos State availability Captions, identification of subjects required. Reviews contact sheets. Negotiates payment individually. Rights purchased varies.

Columns/Departments Chip ins & Three Putts (news notes), Rules Corner (golf rules explanations and discussion), Your Game, Golf Travel (where to play), Great Holes, Q&A, Golf Business (what's happening?), Fashion. Query.

GUNS

$ $ N GUN DIGEST THE MAGAZINE

F + W Media, 700 E. State St., Iola WI 54990. (715)445-2214. Fax: (715)445-4087. E-mail: kevin.michalowski@fwmedia.com. Website: http://www.gundigest.com. **Contact:** Kevin Michalowski, senior editor. **90**. Bimonthly magazine covering firearms. "Gun Digest the Magazine covers all aspects of the firearms community; from collectible guns to tactical gear to reloading and accessories. We also publish gun reviews and tests of new and collectible firearms and news features about firearms legislation. We are 100 percent pro-gun, fully support the NRA and make no bones about our support of Constitutional freedoms." Byline given. Pays on publication. 2 months 3 months 3 months Accepts queries by e-mail. Responds in 3 weeks on queries; 1 month on mss. Free sample copy . Guidelines not available.

Nonfiction "Keep in mind that Writer's Market goes on sale each year in September. List only one-shot issues for which writers will have time to contact you." Needs general interest (firearms related), historical, how-to, interview, new product, nostalgic, profile, technical, All submissions must focus on firearms, accessories or the firearms industry and legislation. Stories that include hunting reference must have as their focus the firearms or ammunition used. The hunting should be secondary. Gun Digest the Magazine also publishes an annual gear guide and 2 issues each year of Tactical Gear Magazine. Tactical Gear is designed for readers interested in self-defense, police and military gear including guns, knives, accessories and fitness. We do not publish "Me and Joe" hunting stories. **Buys 50-75/year mss/year.** Query. 500-3,500 max. **$175-500 for assigned and for unsolicited articles. Does not pay in contributor copies.** Does not pay expenses.

Photos Send photos with submission. Requires captions, identification of subjects. Reviews GIF/JPEG files (and TIF files); 300 DPI submitted on a CD (size) Offers no additional payment for photos accepted with ms. Buys all rights.

Tips "Be an expert in your field. Submit clear copy using the AP stylebook as your guide. Submissions are most easily handled if submitted on a CD. Ms should be saved as an MS Word Doc with photo captions at the bottom of the text. Photo captions and files should have the same names. Do not send mss with photos embedded. Well-researched stories about odd or interesting firearms are always welcomed, should have solid photo support. The Senior Editor will assign gun reviews and tests."

N GUNS AUSTRALIA

Yaffa Publishing, 17-21 Bellevue St., Surry Hills NSW 2010 Australia. (61)(2)9281-2333. Fax: (61)(2)9281-2750. E-mail: yaffa@yaffa.com.au. Website: www.yaffa.com.au. Quarterly magazine delivering comprehensive reviews and the enjoyment of shooting and collecting. "The readers of *Guns Australia* are committed to gun ownership and collecting, target shooting and hunting in Australia."

Nonfiction Needs general interest, how-to, interview, new product. Query.

$ $ MUZZLE BLASTS

National Muzzle Loading Rifle Association, P.O. Box 67, Friendship IN 47021. (812)667-5131. Fax: (812)667-5137. E-mail: mblastdop@seidata.com. Website: www.nmlra.org. **65% freelance written**. Monthly magazine. "Articles must relate to muzzleloading or the muzzleloading era of American history." Estab. 1939. Circ. 20,000. Byline given. Pays on publication. Offers $50 kill fee. Publishes ms an average of 6 months after acceptance. Buys first North American serial rights, buys one-time rights, buys second serial (reprint) rights. Editorial lead time 4 months. Submit seasonal material 6 months in advance. Responds in 1 month to mss. Sample copy and writer's guidelines free

Nonfiction Needs book excerpts, general interest, historical, how-to, humor, interview, new product, personal experience, photo feature, technical, travel. No subjects that do not pertain to muzzleloading. **Buys 80 mss/year.** Query. Length: 2,500 words. **Pays $150 minimum for assigned articles. Pays $50 minimum for unsolicited articles.**

Photos Send photos Captions, model releases required. Reviews 5x7 prints. Negotiates payment individually. Buys one time rights.

Columns/Departments 96 Query. **Pays $50-200.**
Fiction Must pertain to muzzleloading. Needs adventure, historical, humorous. **Buys 6 mss/year.** Query. Length: 2,500 words. **Pays $50-300.**
Fillers Needs facts. **Pays $50.**

HIKING & BACKPACKING

$ $ $ $ BACKPACKER

2520 55th St., Suite 210, Boulder CO 80301. Website: www.backpacker.com. **50% freelance written**. Magazine published 9 times/year covering wilderness travel for backpackers. Estab. 1973. Circ. 295,000. Byline given. Pays on acceptance. No kill fee. Buys one-time rights, buys all rights. Accepts queries by mail, e-mail, fax. Responds in 6 weeks to queries. Guidelines available online.
Nonfiction What we want are features that let us and the readers `feel' the place, and experience your wonderment, excitement, disappointment, or other emotions encountered 'out there.' If we feel like we've been there after reading your story, you've succeeded. Needs essays, expose, historical, how-to, humor, inspirational, interview, new product, personal experience, technical, travel. No step-by-step accounts of what you did on your summer vacation—stories that chronicle every rest stop and gulp of water. Query with published clips. Length: 750-4,000 words. **Pays 60¢-$1/word.**
Photos State availability Payment varies. Buys one time rights.
Columns/Departments Signpost, News From All Over (adventure, environment, wildelife, trails, techniques, organizations, special interests—well-written, entertaining, short, newsy item), 50-500 words; Getaways (great hiking destinations, primarily North America), includes weekend, 250-500 words, weeklong, 250-1000, multi-destination guides, 500-1500 words, and dayhikes, 50-200 words, plus travel news and other items; Fitness (in-the-field health column), 750-1,200 words; Food (food-related aspects of wilderness: nutrition, cooking techniques, recipes, products and gear), 500-750 words; Know How (ranging from beginner to expert focus, written by people with solid expertise, details ways to improve performance, how-to-do-it instructions, information on equipment manufacturers, and places readers can go), 300-1,000 words; Senses (capturing a moment in backcountry through sight, sound, smell, and other senses, paired with an outstanding photo), 150-200 words. 50-75
Tips Our best advice is to read the publication—most freelancers don't know the magazine at all. The best way to break in is with an article for the Weekend Wilderness, Know How, or Signpost Department.

HOCKEY

$ $ MINNESOTA HOCKEY JOURNAL

Official Publication of Minnesota Hockey, Inc., c/o Touchpoint Sports 505, Hwy 169 North, Ste. 465, Minneapolis MN 55441. (763)595-0808. Fax: (763)595-0016. E-mail: greg@touchpointsports.com. Website: www.touchpointsports.com. **50% freelance written**. Journal published 4 times/year. Estab. 2000. Circ. 40,000. Byline given. Pays on publication. No kill fee. Buys all rights. Editorial lead time 6 months. Submit seasonal material 4 months in advance. Accepts previously published material. Accepts simultaneous submissions. Sample copy and writer's guidelines free
Nonfiction Needs essays, general interest, historical, how-to, play hockey, humor, inspirational, interview, new product, opinion, personal experience, photo feature, travel, hockey camps, pro hockey, juniors, college, Olympics, youth, etc. **Buys 3-5 mss/year.** Query. Length: 500-1,500 words. **Pays $100-300.**
Photos State availability Captions, identification of subjects required. Reviews contact sheets. Negotiates payment individually. Rights purchased vary.

$ $ $ USA HOCKEY MAGAZINE

Official Publication of USA Hockey, Touchpoint Sports, 505 Hwy 169 North, Ste 465, Minneapolis MN 55441. (763)595-0808. Fax: (763)595-0016. E-mail: info@touchpointsports.com. Website: www.usahockey.com. **60% freelance written**. Magazine published 10 times/year covering amateur hockey in the US. The world's largest hockey magazine, *USA Hockey Magazine* is the official magazine of USA Hockey, Inc., the national governing body of hockey. Estab. 1980. Circ. 444,000. Byline given. Pays on acceptance or publication. No kill fee. Buys all rights. Editorial lead time 6 months. Submit seasonal material 4 months in advance. Accepts previously published material. Accepts simultaneous submissions. Sample copy and writer's guidelines free
Nonfiction Needs essays, general interest, historical, how-to, play hockey, humor, inspirational, interview, new product, opinion, personal experience, photo feature, travel, hockey camps, pro hockey, juniors, college, NCAA hockey championships, Olympics, youth, etc. **Buys 20-30 mss/year.** Query. Length: 500-5,000 words. **Pays $50-750.** Pays expenses of writers on assignment.
Photos State availability Captions, identification of subjects required. Reviews contact sheets. Negotiates payment individually. Rights purchased varies.
Columns/Departments Short Cuts (news and notes); Coaches' Corner (teaching tips); USA Hockey; Inline

Notebook (news and notes). **Pays $150-250.**
Fiction Needs adventure, humorous, slice-of-life vignettes. **Buys 10-20 mss/year. Pays $150-1,000.**
Fillers Needs anecdotes, facts, gags, newsbreaks, short humor. 20-30 Length: 10-100 words. **Pays $25-250.**
Tips Writers must have a general knowledge and enthusiasm for hockey, including ice, inline, street, and other. The primary audience is youth players in the US.

HORSE RACING

THE AMERICAN QUARTER HORSE RACING JOURNAL

American Quarter Horse Association, P.O. Box 32470, Amarillo TX 79120. (806)376-4811. Website: www.aqha.com/magazines. **10% freelance written**. Monthly magazine promoting American Quarter Horse racing. Articles include training, breeding, nutrition, sports medicine, health, history, etc. Estab. 1988. Circ. 9,000. Pays on acceptance. No kill fee. Publishes ms an average of 3 months after acceptance. Buys first North American serial rights. Submit seasonal material 3 months in advance. Accepts queries by mail. Accepts previously published material. Responds in 1 month to queries. Sample copy and writer's guidelines free
Nonfiction Needs historical, must be on Quarter Horses or people associated with them, how-to, training, opinion, nutrition, health, breeding. Query. Length: 700-1,500 words.
Reprints Send photocopy and information about when and where the material previously appeared.
Photos Send photos Captions, identification of subjects required. Additional payment for photos accepted with ms might be offered.
Tips Query first—you must be familiar with Quarter Horse racing and be knowledgeable of the sport. The *Journal* directs its articles to those who own, train and breed racing Quarter Horses, as well as fans and handicappers. Most open to features covering breeding, raising, training, nutrition and health care utilizing knowledgeable sources with credentials.

$ $ AMERICAN TURF MONTHLY

All Star Sports, Inc., 747 Middle Neck Rd., Suite 103, Great Neck NY 11024. (516)773-4075. Fax: (516)773-2944. E-mail: editor@americanturf.com. Website: www.americanturf.com. **90% freelance written**. Monthly magazine covering Thoroughbred racing, handicapping, and wagering. Squarely focused on Thoroughbred handicapping and wagering. *ATM* is a magazine for horseplayers, not owners, breeders, or 12-year-old girls enthralled with ponies. Estab. 1946. Circ. 28,000. Byline given. Pays on publication. No kill fee. Publishes ms an average of 4 months after acceptance. Makes work-for-hire assignments. Editorial lead time 2 months. Submit seasonal material 2 months in advance. Accepts queries by mail, e-mail. Responds in 1 month to queries. Sample copy and writer's guidelines free
Nonfiction Handicapping and wagering features. Triple Crown/Kentucky Derby (May); Saratoga/Del Mar (August); Breeder's Cup (November) No historical essays, bilious 'guest editorials,' saccharine poetry, fiction. **Buys 50 mss/year.** Query. Length: 800-2,000 words. **Pays $75-300 for assigned articles. Pays $100-500 for unsolicited articles.**
Photos Send photos Identification of subjects required. Reviews 3 x 5 transparencies, prints, 300 dpi TIF images on CD-ROM. Offers $25 interior; $150 for cover. Buys one time rights.
Fillers Needs newsbreaks, short humor. 5 Length: 400 words. **Pays $25.**
Tips Send a good query letter specifically targeted at explaining how this contribution will help our readers to cash a bet at the track!

$ $ HOOF BEATS

United States Trotting Association, 750 Michigan Ave., Columbus OH 43215. Fax: (614)222-6791. E-mail: hoofbeats@ustrotting.com. Website: www.hoofbeatsmagazine.com. **60% freelance written**. Monthly magazine covering harness racing and standardbred horses. Articles and photos must relate to harness racing or standardbreds. We do not accept any topics that do not touch on these 2 subjects. Estab. 1933. Circ. 13,500. Byline given. Pays on publication. Offers 25% kill fee. Publishes ms an average of 2-4 months after acceptance. Buys first North American serial rights, buys second serial (reprint) rights, buys simultaneous rights, buys electronic rights. Makes work-for-hire assignments. Editorial lead time 6 months. Submit seasonal material 6 months in advance. Accepts queries by mail, e-mail, fax. Accepts previously published material. Accepts simultaneous submissions. Responds in 2 weeks to queries. Responds in 1 month to mss. Sample copy available online. Guidelines free.
Nonfiction Needs essays, general interest, historical, how-to, humor, interview, personal experience, photo feature, technical. We do not want any fiction or poetry. **Buys 48-72 mss/year mss/year.** Query. Length: 750-3,000 words. **Pays $100-500. Pays $100-500 for unsolicited articles.**
Photos State availability Identification of subjects required. Reviews contact sheets. We offer $25-100 per photo. Buys one time rights.
Columns/Departments Equine Clinic (standardbreds who overcame major health issues), 900-1,200 words; Bay's Anatomy (veterinary or health issues related to standardbreds), 1,000-1,500 words; Profiles (short profiles

on people or horses in harness racing), 600-1,000 words; Industry Trends (issues impacting standardbreds & harness racing), 1,000-2,000 words. 60 mss/year Query. **Pays $100-500.**

Tips We welcome new writers who know about harness racing or are willing to learn about it. Make sure to read *Hoof Beats* before querying to see our slant & style. We look for informative/promotional stories on harness racing—not exposés on the sport.

HUNTING & FISHING

$ $ ALABAMA GAME & FISH

Game & Fish, 2250 Newmarket Parkway, Suite 110, Marietta GA 30067. (770)953-9222. Fax: (678)279-7512. Website: www.alabamagameandfish.com. See *Game & Fish*. No kill fee.

$ $ AMERICAN ANGLER

735 Broad St., Augusta GA 30904. E-mail: russ.lumpkin@morris.com. Website: www.flyfishingmagazines.com. **95% freelance written**. Bimonthly magazine covering fly fishing. *American Angler* is dedicated to giving fly fishers practical information they can use—wherever they fish, whatever they fish for. Estab. 1976. Circ. 60,000. Byline given. Pays on publication. No kill fee. Publishes ms an average of 6 months after acceptance. Buys first North American serial rights, buys one-time rights. Editorial lead time 3 months. Submit seasonal material 5 months in advance. Accepts queries by mail, fax. Accepts previously published material. Accepts simultaneous submissions. Responds in 6 weeks to queries. Responds in 2 months to mss. Sample copy for $6. Guidelines for #10 SASE.

Nonfiction Needs how-to, most important, personal experience, photo feature, seldom, technical. No promotional flack fo pay back free trips or freebies, no superficial, broad-brush coverage of subjects. **Buys 45-60 mss/year.** Query with published clips. Length: 800-2,200 words. **Pays $200-400.**

Reprints Send information about when and where the material previously appeared. Pay negotiable.

Photos Photographs are important. A fly-tying submission should always include samples of flies to send to our staff photographer, even if photos of the flies are included. Send photos Captions, identification of subjects required. Reviews contact sheets, transparencies. Offers no additional payment for photos accepted with ms. Buys one time rights.

Columns/Departments One-page shorts (problem solvers), 350-750 words. Query with published clips. **Pays $100-300.**

Tips If you are new to this editor, please submit complete queries.

$ $ $ AMERICAN HUNTER

11250 Waples Mill Rd., Fairfax VA 22030-9400. (703)267-1336. Fax: (703)267-3971. E-mail: publications@nrahq.org. Website: www.nra.org. Monthly magazine for hunters who are members of the National Rifle Association (NRA). "*American Hunter* contains articles dealing with various sport hunting and related activities both at home and abroad. With the encouragement of the sport as a prime game management tool, emphasis is on technique, sportsmanship and safety. In each issue hunting equipment and firearms are evaluated, legislative happenings affecting the sport are reported, lore and legend are retold and the business of the Association is recorded in the Official Journal section." Circ. 1,000,000. Byline given. Pays on publication. No kill fee. Buys nonexclusive first North American serial rights with web right. Accepts queries by mail, e-mail. Responds in 6 months to queries. Guidelines for #10 SASE.

Nonfiction Factual material on all phases of hunting: Expository how-to, where-to, and general interest pieces; humor: personal narratives; and semi-technical articles on firearms, wildlife management or hunting. Features fall into five categories: Deer, upland birds, waterfowl, big game and varmints/small game. Pheasants, whitetail tactics, black bear feed areas, mule deer, duck hunters' transport by land and sea, tech topics to be decided; rut strategies, muzzleloader moose and elk, fall turkeys, staying warm, goose talk, long-range muzzleloading Not interested in material on fishing, camping, or firearms knowledge. Query. Length: 1,800-2,000 words. **Pays up to $800.**

Reprints Send typed manuscript with rights for sale noted and information about when and where the material previously appeared.

Photos No additional payment made for photos used with ms; others offered from $125-600

Columns/Departments Hunting Guns, Hunting Loads, destination and adventure, and Public Hunting Grounds. Study back issues for appropriate subject matter and style. Length: 1,200-1,500 words. **Pays $300-450.**

Tips "Although unsolicited manuscripts are accepted, detailed query letters outlining the proposed topic and approach are appreciated and will save both writers and editors a considerable amount of time. If we like your story idea, you will be contacted by mail or phone and given direction on how we'd like the topic covered. NRA Publications accept all manuscripts and photographs for consideration on a speculation basis only. Story angles should be narrow, but coverage must have depth. How-to articles are popular with readers and might range from methods for hunting to techniques on making gear used on successful hunts.

Where-to articles should contain contacts and information needed to arrange a similar hunt. All submissions are judged on three criteria: Story angle (it should be fresh, interesting, and informative); quality of writing (clear and lively—capable of holding the readers' attention throughout); and quality and quantity of accompanying photos (sharpness, reproducability, and connection to text are most important.)"

$ $ ARKANSAS SPORTSMAN

Game & Fish, 2250 Newmarket Parkway, Suite 110, Marietta GA 30067. (770)953-9222. Fax: (678)279-7512. Website: www.arkansassportsmanmag.com. See *Game & Fish*. No kill fee.

BACON BUSTERS

Pig Hunting Guide, Yaffa Publishing, 17-21 Bellevue St., Surry Hills NSW 2010 Australia. (61)(2)9281-2333. Fax: (61)(2)9281-2750. E-mail: editor@baconbusters.com.au. Website: www.yaffa.com.au. **Contact:** Clint Magro, editor. Quarterly magazine covering the hog hunting scene in Australia. "*Bacon Busters* content includes readers' short stories, how-to articles, pig hunting features, technical advice, pig dog profiles and Australia's biggest collection of pig hunting photos. Not to mention the famous Babes & Boars section!" Estab. 1995.

Nonfiction Needs expose, general interest, how-to, interview. Query.

$ $ BASSMASTER MAGAZINE

B.A.S.S. Publications, P.O. Box 10000, Lake Buena Vista FL 32830. (407)566-2277. Fax: (407)566-2072. E-mail: editorial@bassmaster.com. Website: www.bassmaster.com. **80% freelance written**. Magazine published 11 times/year about largemouth, smallmouth, and spotted bass, offering how-to articles for dedicated beginning and advanced bass fishermen, including destinations and new product reviews. Estab. 1968. Circ. 600,000. Byline given. Pays on acceptance. No kill fee. Publishes ms an average of less than 1 year after acceptance. Buys electronic rights. Editorial lead time 2 months. Submit seasonal material 6 months in advance. Accepts queries by mail, e-mail. Responds in 2 months to queries. Sample copy for $2. Guidelines for #10 SASE.

- Needs destination stories (how to fish a certain area) for the Northwest and Northeast.

Nonfiction Needs historical, how-to, patterns, lures, etc., interview, of knowledgeable people in the sport, new product, reels, rods, and bass boats, travel, where to go fish for bass, conservation related to bass fishing. No first-person, personal experience-type articles. **Buys 100 mss/year.** Query. Length: 500-1,500 words. **Pays $100-600.**

Photos Send photos Captions, model releases required. Reviews transparencies. Offers no additional payment for photos accepted with ms, but pays $700 for color cover transparencies. Buys all rights.

Columns/Departments Short Cast/News/Views/Notes/Briefs (upfront regular feature covering news-related events such as new state bass records, unusual bass fishing happenings, conservation, new products, and editorial viewpoints). Length: 250-400 words. **Pays $100-300.**

Tips Editorial direction continues in the short, more direct how-to article. Compact, easy-to-read information is our objective. Shorter articles with good graphics, such as how-to diagrams, step-by-step instruction, etc., will enhance a writer's articles submitted to *Bassmaster Magazine*. The most frequent mistakes made by writers in completing an article for us are poor grammar, poor writing, poor organization, and superficial research. Send in detailed queries outlining specific objectives of article, obtain writer's guidelines. Be as concise as possible.

$ $ THE BIG GAME FISHING JOURNAL

Informational Publications, Inc., 1800 Bay Ave., Point Pleasant NJ 08742. Fax: (732)223-2449. Website: www.biggamefishingjournal.com. **90% freelance written**. Bimonthly magazine covering big game fishing. We require highly instructional articles prepared by qualified writers/fishermen. Estab. 1994. Circ. 45,000. Byline given. Pays on publication. Offers 50% kill fee. Buys first North American serial rights. Editorial lead time 3 months. Submit seasonal material 3 months in advance. Accepts queries by mail, e-mail. Accepts simultaneous submissions. Responds in 2 weeks to queries. Responds in 1 month to mss. Guidelines free.

Nonfiction Needs how-to, interview, technical. **Buys 50-70 mss/year.** Send complete ms. Length: 2,000-3,000 words. **Pays $200-400.** Sometimes pays expenses of writers on assignment.

Photos Send photos Captions required. Reviews transparencies. Offers no additional payment for photos accepted with ms Buys one time rights.

Tips Our format is considerably different than most publications. We prefer to receive articles from qualified anglers on their expertise—if the author is an accomplished writer, all the better. We require highly-instructional articles that teach both novice and expert readers.

$ CALIFORNIA BUCKS

Outdoor News Service, P.O. Box 9007, San Bernardino CA 92427-0007. (909)887-3444. Fax: (909)887-8180. E-mail: cabucks@earthlink.net. Website: www.outdoornewsservice.com. **25% freelance written.**

Quarterly newsletter covering strictly the hunting of deer in CaliforniaÃ³when, where and how. Estab. 2005. Circ. 500. Byline given. Pays on publication. Publishes ms an average of 1-2 months after acceptance. Editorial lead time 3-12 months. Submit seasonal material 3-12 months in advance. Accepts queries by mail, e-mail, fax. Accepts previously published material. Accepts simultaneous submissions. Sample copy by email. Guidelines by email.

Nonfiction Needs expose, historical, how-to, new product, personal experience, technical. Does not want anything that does not deal with deer hunting in California. **Buys 12-18 mss/year.** Query. Length: 200-1,200 words. **Pays $75/printed page.**

Photos State availability Captions, identification of subjects required. Reviews TIFF/JPEG files. Offers no additional payment for photos accepted with ms; pays $25-50/photo separately. Buys one time rights.

Tips We are always looking for individual research pieces on hunters who are successful on taking deer on public lands, especially if the piece detailsÃ³with mapsÃ³where the hunt took place and gives detailed information for our readers.

$ $ CALIFORNIA GAME & FISH

Game & Fish, 2250 Newmarket Parkway, Suite 110, Marietta GA 30067. (770)953-9222. Fax: (678)279-7512. Website: www.californiagameandfish.com. See *Game & Fish* No kill fee.

$ CALIFORNIA HOG HUNTER

A Newsletter Dedicated to Hunting Wild Pigs, Outdoor News Service, P.O. Box 9007, San Bernardino CA 92427-0007. (909)887-3444. Fax: (909)887-8180. E-mail: cahoghunter@earthlink.net. Website: www.outdoornewsservice.com. **25% freelance written**. Quarterly newsletter covering strictly the hunting of wild hogs in CaliforniaÃ³when, where and how. Estab. 1998. Circ. 1,000. Byline given. Pays on publication. Offers kill fee. Publishes ms an average of 1-2 months after acceptance. Editorial lead time 3-12 months. Submit seasonal material 3-12 months in advance. Accepts queries by mail, e-mail, fax. Accepts previously published material. Accepts simultaneous submissions. Responds in 1 month to queries. Sample copy by email. Guidelines by email.

Nonfiction Needs expose, historical, how-to, new product, personal experience, technical. Does not want anything not dealing with hog hunting in California. **Buys 12-18 mss/year.** Query. Length: 200-1,200 words. **Pays $75/printed page.**

Photos State availability Captions, identification of subjects required. Reviews GIF/JPEG files. Offers no additional payment for photos accepted with ms; offers $25-50/photo for those sold separately. Buys one time rights.

Tips We are always looking for individual research pieces on hunters who are successful on taking wild hogs on public lands, especially if the piece details—with maps—where the hunt took place and gives detailed information for our readers.

$ $ DEER & DEER HUNTING

F + W Media, Inc., 700 E. State St., Iola WI 54990-0001. E-mail: dan.schmidt@fwpubs.com. Website: www.deeranddeerhunting.com. **95% freelance written**. Magazine published 10 times/year covering white-tailed deer. "Readers include a cross section of the deer hunting population—individuals who hunt with bow, gun, or camera. The editorial content of the magazine focuses on white-tailed deer biology and behavior, management principle and practices, habitat requirements, natural history of deer, hunting techniques, and hunting ethics. We also publish a wide range of `how-to' articles designed to help hunters locate and get close to deer at all times of the year. The majority of our readership consists of 2-season hunters (bow & gun) and approximately one-third camera hunt." Estab. 1977. Circ. 130,000. Byline given. Pays on acceptance. No kill fee. Publishes ms an average of 18 months after acceptance. Buys all rights. Editorial lead time 6 months. Submit seasonal material 12 months in advance. Accepts queries by mail, e-mail. Responds in 1 month to queries. Responds in 2 months to mss. Sample copy for 9X12 SASE. Guidelines available online.

Nonfiction Needs general interest, historical, how-to, photo feature, technical. No Joe and me articles. **Buys 100 mss/year.** Send complete ms. Length: 1,000-1,700 words. **Pays $150-500 for assigned articles. Pays $150-400 for unsolicited articles.** Sometimes pays expenses of writers on assignment.

Photos Send photos Captions required. Reviews transparencies. Offers $75-250/photo; $600 for cover photos. Buys one time rights.

Columns/Departments Deer Browse (odd occurrences), 500 words. 10 Query. **Pays $50-300.**

Fiction Mood deer hunting pieces. **Buys 9 mss/year.** Send complete ms.

Fillers Needs facts, newsbreaks. 40-50 Length: 100-500 words. **Pays $15-150.**

Tips "Feature articles dealing with deer biology or behavior should be documented by scientific research (the author's or that of others) as opposed to a limited number of personal observations."

$ $ THE DRAKE MAGAZINE

For Those Who Fly-Fish, 1600 Maple St., Fort Collins CO 80521. E-mail: info@drakemag.com. Website:

www.drakemag.com. **70% freelance written**. Biannual magazine for people who love fishing. Byline given. Pays 1 month after publication. No kill fee. Publishes ms an average of 1 year after acceptance. Buys first North American serial rights. Editorial lead time 1 year. Submit seasonal material 1 year in advance. Accepts queries by mail. Responds in 6 months to mss. Guidelines available online.

Nonfiction Needs book excerpts, essays, general interest, historical, humor, interview, opinion, personal experience, photo feature, travel, fishing related. **Buys 8 mss/year.** Query. Length: 250-3,000 words. **Pays 10-20¢/word depending on the amount of work we have to put into the piece.**

Photos State availability Reviews contact sheets, negatives, transparencies. Offers $25-250/photo. Buys one time rights.

$ $ $ FIELD & STREAM

2 Park Ave., New York NY 10016. (212)779-5000. Fax: (212)779-5114. E-mail: fsletters@time4.com. Website: fieldandstream.com. **50% freelance written**. Monthly magazine. Broad-based service magazine for the hunter and fisherman. Editorial content consists of articles of penetrating depth about national hunting, fishing, and related activities. Also humor, personal essays, profiles on outdoor people, conservation, sportsmen's insider secrets, tactics and techniques, and adventures. Estab. 1895. Circ. 1,500,000. Byline given. Pays on acceptance for most articles. No kill fee. Buys first rights. Accepts queries by mail. Responds in 1 month to queries. Guidelines available online.

Nonfiction Length: 1,500 words for features. Payment varies depending on the quality of work, importance of the article. **Pays $800-1,000 and more on a sliding scale for major features.** Query by mail.

Photos Send photos Reviews slides (prefers color). When purchased separately, pays $450 minimum for color. Buys first rights.

Tips Writers are encouraged to submit queries on article ideas. These should be no more than a paragraph or 2, and should include a summary of the idea, including the angle you will hang the story on, and a sense of what makes this piece different from all others on the same or a similar subject. Many queries are turned down because we have no idea what the writer is getting at. Be sure that your letter is absolutely clear. We've found that if you can't sum up the point of the article in a sentence or 2, the article doesn't have a point. Pieces that depend on writing style, such as humor, mood, and nostalgia or essays often can't be queried and may be submitted in manuscript form. The same is true of short tips. All submissions to *Field & Stream* are on an on-spec basis. Before submitting anything, however, we encourage you to *study*, not simply read, the magazine. Many pieces are rejected because they do not fit the tone or style of the magazine, or fail to match the subject of the article with the overall subject matter of *Field & Stream*. Above all, study the magazine before submitting anything.

$ FISHING & HUNTING NEWS

Outdoor Empire Publishing, P.O. Box 3010, Bothell WA 98041. (360)282-4200. Fax: (360)282-4270. E-mail: staff@fhnews.com. Website: www.fhnews.com/. **95% freelance written**. Bimonthly magazine covering fishing and hunting. We focus on upcoming fishing and hunting opportunities in your area—where to go and what to do once you get there. Estab. 1954. Circ. 96,000. Byline given. Pays on publication. No kill fee. Publishes ms an average of 1 month after acceptance. Buys first North American serial rights, buys second serial (reprint) rights, buys electronic rights. Editorial lead time 1 month. Submit seasonal material 2 months in advance. Accepts queries by mail, e-mail. Sample copy and writer's guidelines free

Nonfiction Needs how-to, local fishing and hunting, where-to. **Buys 5,000 mss/year.** Query with published clips. Length: 350-2,000 words. **Pays $25-125 and up.** Seldom pays expenses of writers on assignment.

Photos State availability Captions required. Buys all rights.

Tips *F&H News* is published in 7 local editions across the western U.S., Great Lakes, and mid-Atlantic states. We look for reports of current fishing and hunting opportunity, plus technique- or strategy-related articles that can be used by anglers and hunters in these areas.

$ $ FLORIDA GAME & FISH

Game & Fish, 2250 Newmarket Parkway, Suite 110, Marietta GA 30067. (770)953-9222. Fax: (770)933-9510. Website: www.floridagameandfish.com. See *Game & Fish* No kill fee.

$ $ FLORIDA SPORTSMAN

Wickstrom Communications Division of Primedia Special Interest Publications, 2700 S. Kanner Hwy., Stuart FL 34994. (772)219-7400. Fax: (772)219-6900. E-mail: editor@floridasportsman.com. Website: www.floridasportsman.com. **30% freelance written**. Monthly magazine covering fishing, boating, and related sports—Florida and Caribbean only. *Florida Sportsman* is edited for the boatowner and offshore, coastal, and fresh water fisherman. It provides a how, when, and where approach in its articles, which also includes occasional camping, diving, and hunting stories—plus ecology; in-depth articles and editorials attempting to protect Florida's wilderness, wetlands, and natural beauty. Circ. 115,000. Byline given. Pays on acceptance. No kill fee. Publishes ms an average of 6 months after acceptance. Buys nonexclusive additional rights. Submit seasonal material 6 months in advance. Accepts queries by mail. Responds in 2 months to queries. Responds in 1 month to mss. Sample copy free. Guidelines for #10 SASE.

Nonfiction We use reader service pieces almost entirely—how-to, where-to, etc. One or 2 environmental pieces/issue as well. Writers must be Florida based, or have lengthy experience in Florida outdoors. All articles must have strong Florida emphasis. We do not want to see general how-to-fish-or-boat pieces which might well appear in a national or wide-regional magazine. Needs essays, environment or nature, how-to, fishing, hunting, boating, humor, outdoors angle, personal experience, in fishing, etc., technical, boats, tackle, etc., as particularly suitable for Florida specialities. **Buys 40-60 mss/year.** Query. Length: 1,500-2,500 words. **Pays $475.**

Photos Send photos Reviews 35mm transparencies, 4x5 and larger prints. Offers no additional payment for photos accepted with ms. Pays up to $750 for cover photos. Buys all rights.

Tips Feature articles are most open to freelancers; however there is little chance of acceptance unless contributor is an accomplished and avid outdoorsman *and* a competent writer-photographer with considerable experience in Florida.

$ $ FLW OUTDOORS MAGAZINE

Bass Edition, Walleye Edition, Saltwater Edition, FLW Outdoors, 30 Gamble Lane, Benton KY 42025. E-mail: jsealock@flwoutdoors.com. Website: www.flwoutdoors.com. **40% freelance written.** Magazine published 8 times/year in 3 editions (24 magazines/year) covering fishing for bass, walleye, redfish, kingfish, stripers, etc. *FLW Outdoors Magazine* caters to all anglers from beginning weekend anglers to hardcore professional anglers. Our magazine seeks to educate as well as entertain anglers with cutting-edge techniques and new product innovations being used by America's top fishermen. Estab. 1979. Circ. 100,000+. Byline given. Pays on acceptance. Publishes ms an average of 4 months after acceptance. Buys first rights. Makes work-for-hire assignments. Editorial lead time 5 months. Submit seasonal material 1 year in advance. Accepts queries by mail, e-mail. Sample copy free. Guidelines free.

Nonfiction Needs how-to, new product, photo feature, technical, travel. Does not want me-and-Bubba-went-fishing type stories; stories about author's first trip to catch a certain type of fish; stories in the first person about catching a fish. **Buys 50-75 mss/year.** Query. Length: 2,000-2,500 words. **Pays $400-500.** Sometimes pays expenses of writers on assignment.

Photos State availability Captions required. Reviews contact sheets, GIF/JPEG files. Offers $50-200/photo. Buys one time rights.

Columns/Departments Destinations; Environment; Boat Tech; Tackle Maintenance. 20-30 Query. **Pays $100-300.**

Tips We're looking to be the first place anglers look for the best new products and the hottest fish-catching techniques across the country.

$ FLY FISHERMAN MAGAZINE

6405 Flank Dr., Harrisburg PA 17112. (717)540-6704. Fax: (717)657-9552. Website: www.flyfisherman.com. Published 6 times/year covering fly fishing. Written for anglers who fish primarily with a fly rod and for other anglers who would like to learn more about fly fishing. Circ. 120,358. No kill fee.

$ $ FUR-FISH-GAME

2878 E. Main, Columbus OH 43209-9947. E-mail: ffgcox@ameritech.net. **65% freelance written.** Monthly magazine for outdoorsmen of all ages who are interested in hunting, fishing, trapping, dogs, camping, conservation, and related topics. Estab. 1900. Circ. 111,000. Byline given. Pays on acceptance. No kill fee. Publishes ms an average of 7 months after acceptance. Buys first rights, buys all rights. Responds in 2 months to queries. Sample copy for $1 and 9x12 SAE. Guidelines for #10 SASE.

Nonfiction We are looking for informative, down-to-earth stories about hunting, fishing, trapping, dogs, camping, boating, conservation, and related subjects. Nostalgic articles are also used. Many of our stories are `how-to' and should appeal to small-town and rural readers who are true outdoorsmen. Some recents articles have told how to train a gun dog, catch big-water catfish, outfit a bowhunter, and trap late-season muskrat. We also use personal experience stories and an occasional profile, such as an article about an old-time trapper. `Where-to' stories are used occasionally if they have broad appeal. Query. Length: 500-3,000 words. **Pays $50-250 or more for features depending upon quality, photo support, and importance to magazine.**

Photos Send photos Captions, True required. Reviews transparencies, color 5x7 or 8x10 prints, digital photos on CD only with thumbnail sheet of small images and a numbered caption sheet. Pays $35 for separate freelance photos.

Tips We are always looking for quality how-to articles about fish, game animals, or birds that are popular with everyday outdoorsmen but often overlooked in other publications, such as catfish, bluegill, crappie, squirrel, rabbit, crows, etc. We also use articles on standard seasonal subjects such as deer and pheasant, but like to see a fresh approach or new technique. Instructional trapping articles are useful all year. Articles on gun dogs, ginseng, and do-it-yourself projects are also popular with our readers. An assortment of photos and/or sketches greatly enhances any manuscript, and sidebars, where applicable, can also help. No phone queries, please.

$ $ GAME & FISH

2250 Newmarket Pkwy., Suite 110, Marietta GA 30067. (770)953-9222. Fax: (770)933-9510. E-mail: ken.dunwoody@inoutdoors.com. Website: www.gameandfishmag.com. **90% freelance written.** Publishes 30 different monthly outdoor magazines, each one covering the fishing and hunting opportunities in a particular state or region (see individual titles to contact editors). Estab. 1975. Circ. 570,000. Byline given. Pays 3 months prior to cover date of issue. Offers negotiable kill fee. Publishes ms an average of 7 months after acceptance. Buys first North American serial rights. Submit seasonal material 8 months in advance. Accepts queries by mail, e-mail, fax. Responds in 3 months to queries. Sample copy for $3.50 and 9 x 12 SASE. Guidelines for #10 SASE.

Nonfiction Prefers queries over unsolicited mss. Length: 1,500-2,400 words. **Pays $150-300; additional payment made for electronic rights.**

Photos Captions, identification of subjects required. Reviews transparencies, prints, digital images. Cover photos $250, inside color $75, and b&w $25. Buys one time rights.

Tips Our readers are experienced anglers and hunters, and we try to provide them with useful, specific articles about where, when, and how to enjoy the best hunting and fishing in their state or region. We also cover topics concerning game and fish management. Most articles should be tightly focused and aimed at outdoorsmen in 1 particular state. After familiarizing themselves with our magazine(s), writers should query the appropriate state editor (see individual listings) or send to Ken Dunwoody.

$ $ GEORGIA SPORTSMAN

Game & Fish, 2250 Newmarket Parkway, Suite 110, Marietta GA 30067. (770)953-9222. Fax: (770)933-9510. E-mail: jimmy.jacobs@primedia.com. Website: www.georgiasportsmanmag.com. See *Game & Fish* No kill fee.

$ $ $ N GRAY'S SPORTING JOURNAL

MCC Magazines, LLC, 1 10th St., Suite 380, Augusta GA 30901. E-mail: russ@lumpkin@morris.com. Website: www.grayssportingjournal.com. **75% freelance written**. 7 issues per year magazine High-end hunting and fishing—think *Field & Stream* meets *The New Yorker*. "We expect competent, vividly written prose—fact or fiction—that has high entertainment value for a very sophisticated audience of experienced hunters and anglers. We do not consider previously published material. We do, however, occasionally run prepublication book excerpts. To get a feel for what Gray's publishes, review several back issues. Note that we do not, as a rule, publish 'how-to' articles; this is the province of our regular columnists." Estab. 1975. Circ. 32,000. Byline given. Pays on publication. No kill fee. Publishes ms an average of 12 months after acceptance. Buys first North American serial rights. Editorial lead time 14 months. Submit seasonal material 16 months in advance. Accepts simultaneous submissions. Responds in 3 months to mss. Guidelines available online.

Nonfiction Needs essays, historical, humor, personal experience, photo feature, travel. Gray's publishes three themed issues each year: August is always entirely devoted to upland birdhunting; April to fly fishing; December to sporting travel. All other issues—February, May, September, November—focus on seasonally appropriate themes. Each issue always features a travel piece, from exotic destinations to right around the corner. We publish no how-to of any kind. **Buys 20-30 mss/year. mss/year.** Send complete ms. Length: 1,500-12,000 words. **Pays $600-1,000 for unsolicited articles.**

Photos State availability Reviews contact sheets, GIF/JPEG files. We negotiate payment individually.

Fiction Needs adventure, experimental, historical, humorous, slice-of-life vignettes, All fiction must have some aspect of hunting or fishing at the core. If some aspect of hunting or fishing isn't at the core of the story, it has zero chance of interesting *Gray's*. **Buys 20 mss/year mss/year.** Send complete ms. Length: 1,500-12,000 words. **Pays $600-1,000.**

Poetry Needs avant-garde, haiku, light verse, traditional. **Buys 7/year poems/year.** Submit maximum 3 poems. Length: 10-40 lines.

Tips "Write something different, write something well—fiction or nonfiction—write something that goes to the heart of hunting or fishing more elegantly, more inspirationally, than the 1,500 or so other unsolicited manuscripts we review each year. For best results, submit by e-mail. Mail submissions can take weeks longer to hear back."

$ $ GREAT PLAINS GAME & FISH

Game & Fish, 2250 Newmarket Parkway, Suite 110, Marietta GA 30067. (770)953-9222. Fax: (770)933-9510. Website: www.greatplainsgameandfish.com. See *Game & Fish* No kill fee.

$ $ ILLINOIS GAME & FISH

Game & Fish, 2250 Newmarket Parkway, Suite 110, Marietta GA 30067. (770)953-9222. Fax: (770)933-9510.

Website: www.illinoisgameandfish.com. See *Game & Fish* No kill fee.

$ $ INDIANA GAME & FISH

Game & Fish, 2250 Newmarket Parkway, Suite 110, Marietta GA 30067. (770)953-9222. Fax: (770)933-9510. Website: www.indianagameandfish.com. See *Game & Fish* No kill fee.

$ $ IOWA GAME & FISH

Game & Fish, 2250 Newmarket Parkway, Suite 110, Marietta GA 30067. (770)953-9222. Fax: (770)933-9510. Website: www.iowagameandfish.com. See *Game & Fish* No kill fee.

$ $ KENTUCKY GAME & FISH

Game & Fish, 2250 Newmarket Parkway, Suite 110, Marietta GA 30067. (770)953-9222. Fax: (770)933-9510. Website: www.kentuckygameandfish.com. See *Game & Fish* No kill fee.

$ $ LOUISIANA GAME & FISH

Game & Fish, 2250 Newmarket Parkway, Suite 110, Marietta GA 30067. (770)953-9222. Fax: (770)933-9510. Website: www.lagameandfish.com. See *Game & Fish* No kill fee.

$ $ THE MAINE SPORTSMAN

P.O. Box 910, Yarmouth ME 04096. (207)846-9501. Fax: (207)846-1434. E-mail: harry.vanderweide@verizon.net. Website: www.mainesportsman.com. **80% freelance written**. Monthly tabloid. Eager to work with new/unpublished writers, but because we run over 30 regular columns, it's hard to get into *The Maine Sportsman* as a beginner. Estab. 1972. Circ. 30,000. Byline given. Pays during month of publication. No kill fee. Publishes ms an average of 3 months after acceptance. Buys first rights. Accepts queries by mail, e-mail. Accepts previously published material. Responds in 2 weeks to queries.

Nonfiction We publish only articles about Maine hunting and fishing activities. Any well-written, researched, knowledgeable article about that subject area is likely to be accepted by us. **Buys 25-40 mss/year.** Send complete ms via e-mail Length: 200-2,000 words. **Pays $20-300.** Sometimes pays expenses of writers on assignment.

Reprints Yes, send typed ms via e-mail or query with rights for sale noted. Pays 100% of amount paid for an original article

Photos Send color slides, color prints, or JPGs/TIFFs via e-mail. Pays $5-50 for b&w print.

Tips We publish numerous special sections each year and are eager to buy Maine-oriented articles on snowmobiling, ice fishing, boating, salt water and deer hunting. Send articles or queries.

$ $ MARLIN

P.O. Box 8500, Winter Park FL 32790. (407)628-4802. Fax: (407)628-7061. Website: www.marlinmag.com. **90% freelance written**. Magazine published 8 times/year covering the sport of big game fishing (billfish, tuna, dorado, and wahoo). Our readers are sophisticated, affluent, and serious about their sport—they expect a high-class, well-written magazine that provides information and practical advice. Estab. 1982. Circ. 50,000. Byline given. Pays on acceptance. No kill fee. Publishes ms an average of 3 months after acceptance. Buys first North American serial rights. Submit seasonal material 3 months in advance. Accepts previously published material. Sample copy free with SASE Guidelines available online.

Nonfiction Needs general interest, how-to, bait-rigging, tackle maintenance, etc., new product, personal experience, photo feature, technical, travel. No freshwater fishing stories. No 'Me & Joe went fishing' stories. **Buys 30-50 mss/year.** Query with published clips. Length: 800-3,000 words. **Pays $250-500.**

Reprints Send photocopy and information about when and where the material previously appeared. Pays 50-75% of amount paid for original article.

Photos State availability Reviews original slides. Offers $50-300 for inside use, $1,000 for a cover. Buys one time rights.

Columns/Departments Tournament Reports (reports on winners of major big game fishing tournaments), 200-400 words; Blue Water Currents (news features), 100-400 words. 25 Query. **Pays $75-250.**

Tips Tournament reports are a good way to break in to *Marlin*. Make them short but accurate, and provide photos of fishing action or winners' award shots (*not* dead fish hanging up at the docks). We always need how-tos and news items. Our destination pieces (travel stories) emphasize where and when to fish, but also include information on where to stay. For features: Crisp, high-action stories with emphasis on exotic nature, adventure, personality, etc.—nothing flowery or academic. Technical/how-to: concise and informational—specific details. News: Again, concise with good details—watch for legislation affecting big game fishing, outstanding catches, new clubs and organizations, new trends, and conservation issues.

$ MICHIGAN OUT-OF-DOORS

P.O. Box 30235, Lansing MI 48909. (517)371-1041. Fax: (517)371-1505. Website: www.mucc.org. **75% freelance written**. Monthly magazine emphasizing Michigan outdoor recreation, especially hunting and fishing, conservation, nature, and environmental affairs. Estab. 1947. Circ. 90,000. Byline given. Pays on acceptance. No kill fee. Publishes ms an average of 6 months after acceptance. Buys first North American serial rights. Submit seasonal material 6 months in advance. Accepts queries by mail, phone. Responds in 1 month to queries. Sample copy for $3.50. Guidelines for free or on website.

Nonfiction Stories must have a Michigan slant unless they treat a subject of universal interest to our readers. Needs expose, historical, how-to, interview, opinion, personal experience, photo feature. Archery Deer and Small Game Hunting (October); Firearm Deer Hunting (November); Cross-country Skiing and Early-ice Lake Fishing (December or January); Camping/Hiking (May); Family Fishing (June). No humor or poetry. **Buys 96 mss/year.** Send complete ms. Length: 1,000-2,000 words. **Pays $90 minimum for feature stories.**

Photos Captions required. Offers no additional payment for photos accepted with ms; others $20-175. Buys one time rights.

Tips Top priority is placed on true accounts of personal adventures in the out-of-doors—well-written tales of very unusual incidents encountered while hunting, fishing, camping, hiking, etc.

$ $ MICHIGAN SPORTSMAN

Game & Fish, 2250 Newmarket Parkway, Suite 110, Marietta GA 30067. (770)953-9222. Fax: (770)933-9510. Website: www.michigansportsmanmag.com. See *Game & Fish* No kill fee.

$ $ MID-ATLANTIC GAME & FISH

Game & Fish, 2250 Newmarket Parkway, Suite 110, Marietta GA 30067. (770)953-9222. Fax: (770)933-9510. Website: www.midatlanticgameandfish.com. See *Game & Fish* No kill fee.

$ MIDWEST OUTDOORS

MidWest Outdoors, Ltd., 111 Shore Dr., Burr Ridge IL 60527-5885. (630)887-7722. Fax: (630)887-1958. Website: www.midwestoutdoors.com. **100% freelance written**. Monthly tabloid emphasizing fishing, hunting, camping, and boating. Estab. 1967. Byline given. Pays on publication. No kill fee. Publishes ms an average of 3 months after acceptance. Buys simultaneous rights. Submit seasonal material 2 months in advance. Accepts previously published material. Accepts simultaneous submissions. Responds in 3 weeks to queries. Sample copy for $1 or online. Guidelines for #10 SASE or online.

- "Submissions must be e-mailed to info@midwestoutdoors.com (Microsoft Word format preferred)."

Nonfiction Needs how-to, fishing, hunting, camping in the Midwest, where-to-go (fishing, hunting, camping within 500 miles of Chicago). "We do not want to see any articles on `my first fishing, hunting, or camping experiences,' `cleaning my tackle box,'`tackle tune-up,' 'making fishing fun for kids,' or `catch and release.'" **Buys 1,800 unsolicited mss/year.** Send complete ms. Length: 1,000-1,500 words. **Pays $15-30.**

Photos Captions required. Reviews slides and b&w prints. Offers no additional payment for photos accompanying ms. Buys all rights.

Columns/Departments Fishing; Hunting. Send complete ms. **Pays $30.**

Tips "Break in with a great unknown fishing hole or new technique within 500 miles of Chicago. Where, how, when, and why. Know the type of publication you are sending material to."

$ $ MINNESOTA SPORTSMAN

Game & Fish, 2250 Newmarket Parkway, Suite 110, Marietta GA 30067. (770)953-9222. Fax: (770)933-9510. Website: www.minnesotasportsmanmag.com. See *Game & Fish* No kill fee.

$ $ MISSISSIPPI GAME & FISH

Game & Fish, 2250 Newmarket Parkway, Suite 110, Marietta GA 30067. (770)953-9222. Fax: (770)933-9510. Website: www.mississippigameandfish.com. See *Game & Fish* No kill fee.

$ $ MISSOURI GAME & FISH

Game & Fish, 2250 Newmarket Parkway, Suite 110, Marietta GA 30067. (770)953-9222. Fax: (770)933-9510. Website: www.missourigameandfish.com. See *Game & Fish* No kill fee.

$ $ MUSKY HUNTER MAGAZINE

P.O. Box 340, St. Germain WI 54558. (715)477-2178. Fax: (715)477-8858. **90% freelance written**. Bimonthly magazine on musky fishing. Serves the vertical market of musky fishing enthusiasts. We're interested in how-to, where-to articles. Estab. 1988. Circ. 37,000. Byline given. Pays on publication. No kill fee. Publishes ms an average of 4 months after acceptance. Buys first rights, buys one-time rights. Submit seasonal material 4 months in advance. Responds in 2 months to queries. Sample copy for 9 x 12 SAE with $2.79 postage Guidelines for #10 SASE.

Nonfiction Needs historical, related only to musky fishing, how-to, catch muskies, modify lures, boats, and tackle for musky fishing, personal experience, must be musky fishing experience, technical, fishing equipment, travel, to lakes and areas for musky fishing. **Buys 50 mss/year.** Send complete ms. Length: 1,000-2,500 words. **Pays $100-300 for assigned articles. Pays $50-300 for unsolicited articles.**

Photos Send photos Identification of subjects required. Reviews 35mm transparencies, 3x5 prints, high resolution digital images preferred. Offers no additional payment for photos accepted with ms. Buys one time rights.

$ $ NEW ENGLAND GAME & FISH

Game & Fish, 2250 Newmarket Parkway, Suite 110, Marietta GA 30067. (770)953-9222. Fax: (770)933-9510. Website: www.newenglandgameandfish.com. See *Game & Fish* No kill fee.

$ $ NEW YORK GAME & FISH

Game & Fish, 2250 Newmarket Parkway, Suite 110, Marietta GA 30067. (770)953-9222. Fax: (770)933-9510. Website: www.newyorkgameandfish.com. See *Game & Fish* No kill fee.

$ $ NORTH AMERICAN WHITETAIL

Game & Fish, 2250 Newmarket Pkwy., Suite 110, Marietta GA 30067. (770)953-9222. Fax: (770)933-9510. Website: northamericanwhitetail.com. **70% freelance written**. Magazine published 8 times/year about hunting trophy-class white-tailed deer in North America, primarily the US. We provide the serious hunter with highly sophisticated information about trophy-class whitetails and how, when, and where to hunt them. We are not a general hunting magazine or a magazine for the very occasional deer hunter. Estab. 1982. Circ. 150,000. Byline given. Pays 65 days prior to cover date of issue. Offers negotiable kill fee. Publishes ms an average of 6 months after acceptance. Buys first North American serial rights. Submit seasonal material 10 months in advance. Accepts queries by mail, e-mail, phone. Responds in 3 months to mss. Sample copy for $3.50 and 9x12 SAE with 7 first-class stamps. Guidelines for #10 SASE.

Nonfiction Needs how-to, interview. **Buys 50 mss/year.** Query. Length: 1,000-3,000 words. **Pays $150-400.**

Photos Send photos Captions, identification of subjects required. Reviews 35mm transparencies, color prints, high quality digital images. Offers no additional payment for photos accepted with ms. Buys one time rights.

Columns/Departments Trails and Tails (nostalgic, humorous, or other entertaining styles of deer-hunting material, fictional or nonfictional), 1,200 words. 8 Send complete ms. **Pays $150.**

Tips Our articles are written by persons who are deer hunters first, writers second. Our hard-core hunting audience can see through material produced by nonhunters or those with only marginal deer-hunting expertise. We have a continual need for expert profiles/interviews. Study the magazine to see what type of hunting expert it takes to qualify for our use, and look at how those articles have been directed by the writers. Good photography of the interviewee and his hunting results must accompany such pieces.

$ $ NORTH CAROLINA GAME & FISH

Game & Fish, 2250 Newmarket Parkway, Suite 110, Marietta GA 30067. (770)953-9222. Fax: (770)933-9510. Website: www.ncgameandfish.com. See *Game & Fish* No kill fee.

$ $ OHIO GAME & FISH

Game & Fish, 2250 Newmarket Parkway, Suite 110, Marietta GA 30067. (770)953-9222. Fax: (770)933-9510. Website: www.ohiogameandfish.com. See *Game & Fish* No kill fee.

$ $ OKLAHOMA GAME & FISH

Game & Fish, 2250 Newmarket Parkway, Suite 110, Marietta GA 30067. (770)953-9222. Fax: (770)933-9510. Website: www.oklahomagameandfish.com. See *Game & Fish* No kill fee.

$ $ ONTARIO OUT OF DOORS

Ontario Federation of Anglers and Hunters, P.O. Box 8500, Peterborough ON K9J 0B4 Canada. (705)748-0076. Fax: (705)748-3415. Website: www.ontariooutofdoors.com. **Contact:** John Kerr, editor-in-chief. **80% freelance written**. Magazine published 10 times/year covering the outdoors (hunting, fishing). Estab. 1968. Circ. 93,865. Byline given. Pays on acceptance. Publishes ms an average of 6 months after acceptance. Buys first rights, buys electronic rights. Editorial lead time 1 year. Submit seasonal material 2 months in advance. Accepts queries by mail, e-mail, fax. Responds in 3 months to queries. Writer's guidelines free

Nonfiction Needs interview, opinion, technical, travel, wildlife management. No `Me and Joe' features. **Buys 100 mss/year.** Length: 500-2,500 words. **Pays $950 maximum for assigned articles.**

Fiction Pays $500 maximum.

Tips "It is suggested that writers query prior to submission."

$ THE OUTDOORS MAGAZINE

For the Better Hunter, Angler & Trapper, Elk Publishing, Inc., 531 Main St., Colchester VT 05446. (802)879-2013. Fax: (802)879-2015. E-mail: kyle@elkpublishing.com. Website: www.outdoorsmagazine.net. **80% freelance written**. Monthly magazine covering wildlife conservation. Northeast hunting, fishing, and trapping magazine covering news, tips, destinations, and good old-fashioned stories. Estab. 1996. Circ.

20,000. Byline given. Pays on publication. Offers 10% kill fee. Publishes ms an average of 1 year after acceptance. Buys first North American serial rights. Editorial lead time 1 year. Submit seasonal material 6 months in advance. Accepts queries by mail. Accepts previously published material. Responds in 1 month to queries. Responds in 3 month to mss. Sample copy online or by e-mail Guidelines free.

Nonfiction Needs book excerpts, essays, expose, general interest, historical, how-to, interview, new product, opinion, personal experience, technical. **Buys 200 mss/year.** Query with published clips. Length: 750-2,500 words. **Pays $20-150 for assigned articles.**

Photos State availability Identification of subjects required. Reviews contact sheets. Pays $15-75/photo. Buys one time rights.

Columns/Departments 100 Query with published clips. **Pays $20-60.**

Fillers Needs anecdotes, facts.

Tips *Know* the publication, not just read it, so you understand the audience. Patience and thoroughness will go a long way.

$ $ ⊘ PENNSYLVANIA ANGLER & BOATER

Pennsylvania Fish & Boat Commission, P.O. Box 67000, Harrisburg PA 17106-7000. (717)705-7833. E-mail: ra-pfbcmagazine@state.pa.us. Website: www.fish.state.pa.us. **40% freelance written**. Bimonthly magazine covering fishing, boating, and related conservation topics in Pennsylvania. Circ. 28,000. Byline given. Pays 2 months after acceptance. Publishes ms an average of 8 months after acceptance. Submit seasonal material 8 months in advance. Responds in 1 month to queries. Responds in 2 months to mss. Sample copy for 9x12 SAE with 9 first-class stamps. Guidelines for #10 SASE.

- No unsolicited mss.

Nonfiction Needs how-to, and where-to, technical. No saltwater or hunting material. **Buys 75 mss/year.** Query. Length: 500-2,500 words. **Pays $25-300.**

Photos Send photos Captions, identification of subjects, model releases required. Reviews 35mm and larger transparencies, hi-res digital submissions on CD (preferred). Offers no additional payment for photos accompanying mss. Rights purchased vary.

$ $ PENNSYLVANIA GAME & FISH

Game & Fish, 2250 Newmarket Parkway, Suite 110, Marietta GA 30067. (770)953-9222. Fax: (770)933-9510. Website: www.pagameandfish.com. See *Game & Fish* No kill fee.

$ $ RACK MAGAZINE

Adventures in Trophy Hunting, Buckmasters, Ltd., 10350 U.S. Hwy. 80 E., Montgomery AL 36117. (800)240-3337. Fax: (334)215-3535. E-mail: mhandley@buckmasters.com. Website: www.rackmag.com. **50% freelance written**. monthly, July-December magazine covering big game hunting. "All features are either first- or third-person narratives detailing the successful hunts for world-class, big game animals—mostly white-tailed deer and other North American species." Estab. 1998. Circ. 100,000. Byline given. Pays on publication. No kill fee. Publishes ms an average of 9 months after acceptance. Buys first North American serial rights, buys second serial (reprint) rights. Editorial lead time 9-12 months. Submit seasonal material 9 months in advance. Accepts queries by e-mail. Accepts previously published material. Accepts simultaneous submissions. Responds in 1 month to queries. Responds in 2 months to mss. Sample copy free. Guidelines free.

Nonfiction Needs personal experience. We're interested only in articles chronicling successful hunts. **Buys 40-50 mss/year.** Query. Length: 750-1,500 words. **Pays $175-325 for assigned articles. Pays $175-325 for unsolicited articles.**

Photos Send photos Captions, identification of subjects required. Reviews transparencies, prints, GIF/JPEG files. Buys one time rights.

Tips "Ask for and read the writer's guidelines."

$ $ ROCKY MOUNTAIN GAME & FISH

Game & Fish, 2250 Newmarket Parkway, Suite 110, Marietta GA 30067. (770)935-9222. Fax: (770)933-9510. Website: www.rmgameandfish.com. See *Game & Fish* No kill fee.

$ $ SALT WATER SPORTSMAN MAGAZINE

460 N. Orlando Ave., Suite 200, New York NY 32789. (212)779-5003. Fax: (212)779-5025. E-mail: john.brownlee@bonniecorp.com. Website: www.saltwatersportsman.com. **85% freelance written**. Monthly magazine. *Salt Water Sportsman* is edited for serious marine sport fishermen whose lifestyle includes the pursuit of game fish in US waters and around the world. It provides information on fishing trends, techniques, and destinations, both local and international. Each issue reviews offshore and inshore fishing boats, high-tech electronics, innovative tackle, engines, and other new products. Coverage also focuses on sound fisheries management and conservation. Circ. 170,000. Byline given. Pays on acceptance. Offers kill fee. Publishes ms an average of 5 months after acceptance. Buys first North American serial rights.

Submit seasonal material 8 months in advance. Accepts queries by mail, e-mail, fax. Responds in 1 month to queries. Sample copy for #10 SASE. Guidelines available online.
Nonfiction Readers want solid how-to, where-to information written in an enjoyable, easy-to-read style. Personal anecdotes help the reader identify with the writer. Needs how-to, personal experience, technical, travel, to fishing areas. **Buys 100 mss/year.** Query. Length: 1,200-2,000 words. **Pays $300-750.**
Reprints Send tearsheet. Pays up to 50% of amount paid for original article.
Photos Captions required. Reviews color slides. Pays $1,500 minimum for 35mm, 2 ¼x2 ¼ or 8 x 10 transparencies for cover.
Columns/Departments Sportsman's Tips (short, how-to tips and techniques on salt water fishing, emphasis is on building, repairing, or reconditioning specific items or gear). Send complete ms.
Tips There are a lot of knowledgeable fishermen/budding writers out there who could be valuable to us with a little coaching. Many don't think they can write a story for us, but they'd be surprised. We work with writers. Shorter articles that get to the point which are accompanied by good, sharp photos are hard for us to turn down. Having to delete unnecessary wordage—conversation, clichés, etc.—that writers feel is mandatory is annoying. Often they don't devote enough attention to specific fishing information.

$ $ SHOTGUN SPORTS MAGAZINE

P.O. Box 6810, Auburn CA 95604. (530)889-2220. Fax: (530)889-9106. E-mail: shotgun@shotgunsportsmagazine.com. Website: www.shotgunsportsmagazine.com. **50% freelance written. Welcomes new writers.** Monthly magazine covering all the shotgun sports and shotgun hunting—sporting clays, trap, skeet, hunting, gunsmithing, shotshell patterning, shotsell reloading, mental training for the shotgun sports, shotgun tests, anything shotgun. Pays on publication. No kill fee. Publishes ms an average of 1-6 months after acceptance. Buys all rights. Sample copy and writer's guidelines available by contacting Linda Martin, production coordinator.

- Responds within 3 weeks. Subscription: $32.95 (U.S.); $39.95 (Canada); $70 (foreign).

Nonfiction Current needs: Anything with a 'shotgun' subject. Tests, think pieces, roundups, historical, interviews, etc. No articles promoting a specific club or sponsored hunting trip, etc. Submit complete ms with photos by mail with SASE. Can submit by e-mail. Length: 1,000-5,000 words. **Pays $50-200.**
Reprints Photo
Photos 5x7 or 8x10 b&w or 4-color with appropriate captions. On disk or e-mailed at least 5-inches and 300 dpi (contact Graphics Artist for details). Reviews transparencies (35 mm or larger), b&w, or 4-color. Send photos
Tips Do not fax manuscript. Send good photos. Take a fresh approach. Create a professional, yet friendly article. Send diagrams, maps, and photos of unique details, if needed. For interviews, more interested in 'words of wisdom' than a list of accomplishments. Reloading articles must include source information and backup data. Check your facts and data! If you can't think of a fresh approach, don't bother. If it's not about shotguns or shotgunners, don't send it. Never say, 'You don't need to check my data; I never make mistakes.'

$ $ SOUTH CAROLINA GAME & FISH

Game & Fish, 2250 Newmarket Parkway, Suite 110, Marietta GA 30067. (770)953-9222. Fax: (770)933-9510. Website: www.scgameandfish.com. See *Game & Fish* No kill fee.

$ $ $ $ SPORT FISHING

The Magazine of Saltwater Fishing, World Publications, 460 N. Orlando Ave., Suite 200, Winter Park FL 32789. (407)628-4802. Fax: (407)628-7061. E-mail: doug.olander@worldpub.net. Website: www.sportfishingmag.com. **50% freelance written**. Magazine published 10 times/year covering saltwater anglingÃ³saltwater fish and fisheries. *Sport Fishing*'s readers are middle-aged, affluent, mostly male, who are generally proficient in and very educated to their sport. We are about fishing from boatsÃ³not from surf or jetties. Estab. 1985. Circ. 250,000. Byline given. Pays on acceptance. Offers 25% kill fee. Publishes ms an average of 6-12 months after acceptance. Buys first North American serial rights, buys electronic rights. Editorial lead time 2-12 months. Submit seasonal material 1 year in advance. Accepts queries by e-mail. Responds in 1 week to queries. Responds in 1 month to mss. Sample copy for #10 SASE. Guidelines available online.
Nonfiction Needs general interest, how-to. Query. Length: 2,500-3,000 words. **Pays $500-750 for text only; $1,500+ possible for complete package with photos.**
Photos State availability Reviews GIF/JPEG files. Offers $75-400/photo. Buys one time rights.
Tips Queries please; no over-the-transom submissions. Meet or beat deadlines. Include quality photos when you can. Quote the experts. Balance information with readability. Include sidebars.

$ $ $ SPORTS AFIELD

The Premier Hunting Adventure Magazine, Field Sports Publishing, 15621 Chemical Lane, Huntington Beach CA 92649. (714)894-9080. E-mail: letters@sportsafield.com. Website: www.sportsafield.com. **60%**

freelance written. Magazine published 6 times/year covering big game hunting. "We cater to the upscale hunting market, especially hunters who travel to exotic destinations like Alaska and Africa. We are not a deer hunting magazine, and we do not cover fishing." Estab. 1887. Circ. 50,000. Byline given. Pays 1 month prior to publication. Publishes ms an average of 6 months after acceptance. Buys first North American serial rights, first rights, and electronic rights. Editorial lead time 4 months. Submit seasonal material 5 months in advance. Accepts queries by mail, e-mail. Responds in 2 months to queries and to mss Sample copy for $6.99 Guidelines available online

Nonfiction Needs personal experience, travel. **Buys 6-8 mss/year.** Query. Length: 1,500-2,500 words. **Pays $500-800.**

Photos State availability Captions, model releases required. Reviews 35mm slides transparencies, TIF/JPEG files. Offers no additional payment for photos accepted with ms. Buys first time rights.

Fillers Needs newsbreaks. 30 Length: 200-500 words. **Pays $75-150.**

$ $ TENNESSEE SPORTSMAN

Game & Fish, 2250 Newmarket Parkway, Suite 110, Marietta GA 30067. (770)953-9222. Fax: (770)933-9510. Website: www.tennesseesportsmanmag.com. See *Game & Fish* No kill fee.

$ $ TEXAS SPORTSMAN

Game & Fish, 2250 Newmarket Parkway, Suite 110, Marietta GA 30067. (770)953-9222. Fax: (770)933-9510. Website: www.texassportsmanmag.com. See *Game & Fish* No kill fee.

$ $ TRAPPER & PREDATOR CALLER

F+W Media, Inc., 700 E. State St., Iola WI 54990. (715)445-2214. E-mail: jared.blohm@fwmedia.com. Website: www.trapperpredatorcaller.com. **95% freelance written**. Tabloid published 10 times/year covering trapping and predator calling, fur trade. "Must have mid-level to advanced knowledge, because *T&PC* is heavily how-to focused." Estab. 1975. Circ. 44,000. Byline given. Pays on publication. No kill fee. Publishes ms an average of 6 months after acceptance. Buys one-time rights. Editorial lead time 1 year. Submit seasonal material 1 year in advance. Accepts queries by e-mail.

Nonfiction Needs how-to, interview, personal experience, travel. **Buys 100 mss/year.** Send complete ms. Length: 1,000-2,500 words. **Pays $250 for assigned articles.**

Photos Send photos Reviews negatives, prints. Buys full rights.

$ $ TURKEY CALL

National Wild Turkey Federation, P.O. Box 530, Edgefield SC 29824-0530. (803)637-3106. Fax: (803)637-0034. E-mail: turkeycall@nwtf.net. Website: www.nwtf.org//tv_magazines/turkeycall-magazine.html. **50-60% freelance written**. "Bimonthly educational magazine for members of the National Wild Turkey Federation. Topics covered include hunting, history, restoration, management, biology, and distribution of wild turkey." Estab. 1973. Circ. 180,000. Byline given. Pays on acceptance. No kill fee. Publishes ms an average of 6 months after acceptance. Buys first North American serial rights. Editorial lead time 1 year. Accepts queries by mail, e-mail. Responds in 2 months to queries Sample copy for $3 and 9x12 SAE Guidelines available online

- Submit queries by June 1 of each year.

Nonfiction "Feature articles dealing with the hunting and management of the American wild turkey. Must be accurate information and must appeal to national readership of turkey hunters and wildlife management experts. Queries with suggested sidebars preferred; speculative submissions discouraged." Query (preferred) or send complete ms. Length: 700-2,500 words. **Pays $100 for short fillers; $200-500 for features.**

Photos "We want quality photos submitted with features. Illustrations also acceptable. We are using more and more inside color illustrations. No typical hunter-holding-dead-turkey photos or setups using mounted birds or domestic turkeys. Photos with how-to stories must make the techniques clear (i.e., how to make a turkey call; how to sculpt or carve a bird in wood)." Identification of subjects, model releases required. Reviews transparencies, high resolution digital images. Buys one-time rights.

Fiction Must contribute to the education, enlightenment, or entertainment of readers in some special way.

Tips "The writer should simply keep in mind that the audience is `expert' on wild turkey management, hunting, life history, and restoration/conservation history. He/she must know the subject. We are buying more third person, more fiction, more humor—in an attempt to avoid the `predictability trap' of a single subject magazine."

$ $ VIRGINIA GAME & FISH

Game & Fish, 2250 Newmarket Parkway, Suite 110, Marietta GA 30067. (770)953-9222. Fax: (770)933-9510. Website: www.virginiagameandfish.com. See *Game & Fish* No kill fee.

$ $ WASHINGTON-OREGON GAME & FISH

Game & Fish, 2250 Newmarket Parkway, Suite 110, Marietta GA 30067. (770)953-9222. Fax: (770)933-9510. Website: www.wogameandfish.com. See *Game & Fish* No kill fee.

$ $ WEST VIRGINIA GAME & FISH

Game & Fish, 2250 Newmarket Parkway, Suite 110, Marietta GA 30067. (770)953-9222. Fax: (770)933-9510. Website: www.wvgameandfish.com. See *Game & Fish* No kill fee.

$ $ WISCONSIN OUTDOOR JOURNAL

F+W Media, Inc., 700 E. State St., Iola WI 54990-0001. (715)445-2214. E-mail: jacob.edson@fwpubs.com. Website: www.wisoutdoorjournal.com. **90% freelance written**. Magazine published 8 times/year covering Wisconsin fishing, hunting, and outdoor lifestyles. Estab. 1987. Circ. 25,000. Byline given. Pays on acceptance. No kill fee. Publishes ms an average of 1 year after acceptance. Buys one-time rights. Editorial lead time 1 year. Submit seasonal material 1 year in advance. Accepts queries by e-mail.

Nonfiction Needs book excerpts, expose, how-to, humor, interview, personal experience, travel, within Wisconsin. **Buys 45-50 mss/year.** Query or send complete ms. **Pays $150-225 for assigned articles. Pays $200 for unsolicited articles.**

Photos Send photos Identification of subjects required. Reviews negatives, prints. Offers $25-200/photo. Buys one time rights.

Fiction Needs adventure, historical, nostalgic. No eulogies of a good hunting dog. **Buys 10 mss/year.** Send complete ms. Length: 1,500-2,000 words. **Pays $100-250.**

$ $ WISCONSIN SPORTSMAN

Game & Fish, 2250 Newmarket Parkway, Suite 110, Marietta GA 30067. (770)953-9222. Fax: (770)933-9510. Website: www.wisconsinsportsmanmag.com. See *Game & Fish* No kill fee.

MARTIAL ARTS

AUSTRALASIAN TAEKWONDO

Blitz Publications, P.O. Box 4075, Mulgrave VIC 3170 Australia. (61)(3)9574-8999. Fax: (61)(3)9574-8899. E-mail: taekwondo@blitzmag.com.au. Website: www.sportzblitz.net. Magazine covering the martial art of taekwondo. *"Australasian Taekwondo Magazine* features exclusive interviews, tournament reports, sports medicine, articles on the world's best martial artists, unique styles, personalities, Poomse, black belt patterns, fitness tips, health and street self defense strategies, combat/sports psychology as well as unrivalled coverage of local news, taekwondo events and nutrition."

Nonfiction Needs general interest, how-to, interview, new product. Query.

$ $ BLACK BELT

Black Belt Communications, LLC, 24900 Anza Dr., Unit E, Valencia CA 91355. Fax: (661)257-3028. E-mail: byoung@aimmedia.com. Website: www.blackbeltmag.com. **80% freelance written. Works with a small number of new/unpublished writers each year.** Monthly magazine emphasizing martial arts for both experienced practitioner and layman. Estab. 1961. Circ. 100,000. Pays on publication. No kill fee. Publishes ms an average of 1 year after acceptance. Buys all rights. Accepts queries by mail, e-mail, fax. Accepts simultaneous submissions. Responds in 3 weeks to queries. Guidelines available online.

Nonfiction Needs expose, how-to, interview, new product, personal experience, technical, travel, Informational. We never use personality profiles. **Buys 40-50 mss/year.** Query with outline 1,200 words minimum. **Pays $100-300.**

Photos Very seldom buys photographs without accompanying ms. Captions, model releases required. Total purchase price for ms includes payment for photos.

BLITZ AUSTRALASIAN MARTIAL ARTS MAGAZINE

Blitz Publications, P.O. Box 4075, Mulgrave VIC 3170 Australia. (61)(3)9574-8999. Fax: (61)(3)9574-8899. E-mail: ben@blitzmag.com.au. Website: www.sportzblitz.net. *"Blitz Australasian Martial Arts* monthly magazine features interviews and articles on the world's best martial arts and combat sports personalities, unique styles, technique and fitness tips, health and self-defense strategies, combat psychology, as well as unrivaled coverage of local fight news, events, nutrition and sports supplements.".

Nonfiction Needs general interest, how-to. Query.

$ $ INSIDE KUNG-FU

The Ultimate In Martial Arts Coverage!, CFW Enterprises, 4201 Vanowen Place, Burbank CA 91505. (818)845-2656. Fax: (818)845-7761. E-mail: davecater@cfwenterprises.com. **90% freelance written**. Monthly magazine for those with traditional, modern, athletic, and intellectual tastes. The magazine slants toward little-known martial arts and little-known aspects of established martial arts. Estab. 1973.

Circ. 125,000. Byline given. Pays on publication date on magazine cover. Publishes ms an average of 6 months after acceptance. Buys first North American serial rights. Editorial lead time 6 months. Submit seasonal material 6 months in advance. Accepts simultaneous submissions. Responds in 1 month to queries. Responds in 2 months to mss. Sample copy for $5.95 and 9x12 SAE with 5 first class stamps. Guidelines for #10 SASE.

Nonfiction Articles must be technically or historically accurate. *Inside Kung-Fu* is looking for external type articles (fighting, weapons, multiple hackers). Needs book excerpts, essays, expose, topics relating to martial arts, general interest, historical, how-to, primarily technical materials, inspirational, interview, new product, personal experience, photo feature, technical, travel, cultural/philosophical. No sports coverage, first-person articles, or articles which constitute personal aggrandizement. **Buys 120 mss/year.** Query or send complete ms. 1,500-3,000 words (8-10 pages, typewritten and double-spaced) **Pays $125-175.**

Reprints Send tearsheet or typed ms with rights for sale noted and information about when and where the material previously appeared. No payment

Photos State availability of or send photos Captions, identification of subjects, model releases required. Reviews contact sheets, negatives, 5x7 or 8x10 color prints. No additional payment for photos Buys all rights.

Fiction Fiction must be short (1,000-2,000 words) and relate to the martial arts. We buy very few fiction pieces. Needs adventure, historical, humorous, mystery, novel concepts, suspense. **Buys 2-3 mss/year.**

Tips See what interests the writer. May have a better chance of breaking in at our publication with short articles and fillers since smaller pieces allow us to gauge individual ability, but we're flexible—quality writers get published, period. The most frequent mistakes made by writers in completing an article for us are ignoring photo requirements and model releases (always No. 1—and who knows why? All requirements are spelled out in writer's guidelines).

$ $ N JOURNAL OF ASIAN MARTIAL ARTS

Via Media Publishing Co., 941 Calle Mejia #822, Santa Fe NM 87501. Website: www.goviamedia.com. **90% freelance written**. "Quarterly magazine covering all historical and cultural aspects related to Asian martial arts, offering a mature, well-rounded view of this uniquely fascinating subject. Although the journal treats the subject with academic accuracy (references at end), writing need not lose the reader!". Estab. 1991. Byline given. Pays on publication. No kill fee. Publishes ms an average of 1 year after acceptance. Buys first rights, buys second serial (reprint) rights. Submit seasonal material 6 months in advance. Responds in 1 month to queries. Responds in 2 months to mss. Sample copy for $10. Guidelines for #10 SASE.

Nonfiction All articles should be backed with solid, reliable reference material. Needs essays, expose, historical, how-to, martial art techniques and materials, e.g., weapons, interview, personal experience, photo feature, place or person, religious, technical, travel. No articles overburdened with technical/foreign/scholarly vocabulary, or material slanted as indirect advertising or for personal aggrandizement. **Buys 30 mss/year.** Query with short background and martial arts experience. Length: 2,000-10,000 words. **Pays $150-500.**

Photos State availability Identification of subjects, model releases required. Reviews contact sheets, negatives, transparencies, prints. Offers no additional payment for photos accepted with ms. Buys one-time and reprint rights.

Columns/Departments Location (city, area, specific site, Asian or non-Asian, showing value for martial arts, researchers, history); Media Review (film, book, video, museum for aspects of academic and artistic interest).**Length:** 1,000-2,500 words. 16 Query. **Pays $50-200.**

Fiction Needs adventure, historical, humorous, slice-of-life vignettes, translation. No material that does not focus on martial arts culture. **Buys 1 mss/year.** Query. Length: 1,000-10,000 words. **Pays $50-500, or copies.**

Poetry Needs avant-garde, free verse, haiku, light verse, traditional. No poetry that does not focus on martial arts culture. **Buys 2 poems/year.** Submit maximum 10 poems. **Pays $10-100, or copies.**

Fillers Needs anecdotes, facts, gags, newsbreaks, short humor. 2 Length: 25-500 words. **Pays $1-50, or copies.**

Tips "Always query before sending a manuscript. We are open to varied types of articles; most however require a strong academic grasp of Asian culture. For those not having this background, we suggest trying a museum review, or interview, where authorities can be questioned, quoted, and provide supportive illustrations. We especially desire articles/reports from Asia, with photo illustrations, particularly of a martial art style, so readers can visually understand the unique attributes of that style, its applications, evolution, etc. `Location' and media reports are special areas that writers may consider, especially if they live in a location of martial art significance."

$ KUNG FU TAI CHI

Wisdom for Body and Mind, Pacific Rim Publishing, 40748 Encyclopedia Circle, Fremont CA 94538. (510)656-5100. Fax: (510)656-8844. E-mail: gene@kungfumagazine.com. Website: www.kungfumagazine.

com. **70% freelance written**. Bimonthly magazine covering Chinese martial arts and culture. "*Kung Fu Tai Chi* covers the full range of Kung Fu culture, including healing, philosophy, meditation, yoga, Fengshui, Buddhism, Taoism, history, and the latest events in art and culture, plus insightful features on the martial arts." Circ. 20,000. Byline given. Pays on publication. No kill fee. Buys first North American serial rights, buys electronic rights. Editorial lead time 4 months. Submit seasonal material 4 months in advance. Accepts queries by mail, e-mail, fax, phone. Responds in 2 months to queries. Responds in 3 months to mss. Sample copy for $3.99 or online. Guidelines available online.

Nonfiction Needs general interest, historical, interview, personal experience, religious, technical, travel, cultural perspectives. No poetry or fiction. **Buys 70 mss/year.** Query. Length: 500-2,500 words. **Pays $35-125.**

Photos Send photos Captions, identification of subjects required. Reviews 5x7 prints, GIF/JPEG files. Offers no additional payment for photos accepted with ms Buys one time rights.

Tips "Check out our website and get an idea of past articles."

$ $ T'AI CHI

Leading International Magazine of T'ai Chi Ch'uan, Wayfarer Publications, P.O. Box 39938, Los Angeles CA 90039. (323)665-7773. Fax: (323)665-1627. E-mail: taichi@tai-chi.com. Website: www.tai-chi.com/magazine.htm. **Contact:** Marvin Smalheiser, Editor. **90% freelance written**. Quarterly magazine covering T'ai Chi Ch'uan as a martial art and for health and fitness. "Covers T'ai Chi Ch'uan and other internal martial arts, plus qigong and Chinese health, nutrition, and philosophical disciplines. Readers are practitioners or laymen interested in developing skills and insight for self-defense, health, and self-improvement." Estab. 1977. Circ. 50,000. Byline given. Pays on publication. No kill fee. Publishes ms an average of 3 months after acceptance. Buys first North American serial rights. Editorial lead time 3 months. Submit seasonal material 6 months in advance. Accepts queries by mail, e-mail, fax. Responds in 3 weeks to queries. Responds in 3 months to mss. Sample copy for $3.95. Guidelines available online.

Nonfiction Needs book excerpts, essays, how-to, on T'ai Chi Ch'uan, qigong, and related Chinese disciplines, interview, personal experience. "Do not want articles promoting an individual, system, or school." **Buys 50 mss/year.** Send complete ms. Length: 1,200-4,500 words. **Pays $75-500.**

Photos Send photos Captions, identification of subjects, model releases required. Reviews color transparencies, color or b&w 4x6 or 5x7 prints, digital files suitable for print production. "Offers no additional payment for photos accepted with ms, but overall payment takes into consideration the number and quality of photos." Buys one-time and reprint rights.

Tips "Think and write for practitioners and laymen who want information and insight, and who are trying to work through problems to improve skills and their health. No promotional material."

$ $ N ULTIMATE GRAPPLING

Apprise Media, 2400 E. Katella Ave., Suite 300, Anaheim CA 92806. (714)939-9991. Fax: (714)939-9909. E-mail: doug.jeffrey@apg-media.com. Website: www.ultimategrapplingmag.com. Monthly magazine covering mixed martial arts, grappling. "We are interested in anything and everything about mixed martial arts.lifestyle to events to training to strategy." Estab. 2,000. Byline given. Pays on publication. Offers 20% kill fee. Publishes ms an average of 1-3 months after acceptance. Buys first North American serial rights. Editorial lead time 3 months. Submit seasonal material 3 months in advance. Accepts queries by mail, e-mail. Responds in 2 months to mss. Sample copy free. Guidelines free.

Nonfiction Needs book excerpts, expose, general interest, historical, how-to, inspirational, interview, new product, personal experience, photo feature, technical. **Buys 30 mss/year mss/year.** Query. Length: 500-1,500 words. **Pays $150-500 for assigned articles. Pays $150-500 for unsolicited articles.** Sometimes pays expenses of writers on assignment.

Photos State availability TBD

Columns/Departments Beyond Fighting (lifestyle of fighters); Exercises to bolster MMA game and general fitness. 30 mss/year Query with or without published clips. **Pays $-$125.**

Tips "Know the subject material. Be creative. Be unique. Be accessible and flexible and open to input. Those who can produce on short notice are invaluable."

MISCELLANEOUS SPORTS

$ ACTION PURSUIT GAMES

265 S. Anita Dr., Suite 120, Orange CA 92868. E-mail: editor@actionpursuitgames.com. Website: www.actionpursuitgames.com. **60%% freelance written**. Monthly magazine covering paintball. Estab. 1987. Circ. 85,000. Byline given. Pays on publication. No kill fee. Publishes ms an average of 2 months after acceptance. Buys electronic rights. print rights Editorial lead time 3 months. Submit seasonal material 6 months in advance. Accepts queries by e-mail. Sample copy for sae with 9x12 envelope and 5 First-Class stamps. Guidelines available online.

Nonfiction Needs essays, expose, general interest, historical, how-to, humor, interview, new product, opinion, personal experience, technical, travel, all paintball-related. No sexually oriented material **Buys 100+ mss/year.** Length: 500-1,000 words. **Pays $100.** Sometimes pays expenses of writers on assignment.
Photos Send photos Captions, identification of subjects, model releases required. Reviews transparencies, prints. Negotiates payment individually. Buys all rights, web and print
Columns/Departments Guest Commentary, 400 words; TNT (tournament news), 500-800 words; Young Guns, 300 words; Scenario Game Reporting, 300-500 words. 24 **Pays $100.**
Fiction Needs adventure, historical, must be paintball related. **Buys 1-2 mss/year.** Send complete ms. Length: 500 words. **Pays $100.**
Poetry Needs avant-garde, free verse, haiku, light verse, traditional. **Buys 1-2 poems/year.** Submit maximum 1 poems. Length: 20 lines.
Fillers Needs anecdotes, gags. 2-4 Length: 20-50 words. **Pays $25.**
Tips Good graphic support is critical. Read writer's guidelines at website; read website, www.actionpursuitgames.com, and magazine.

$ $ AMERICAN CHEERLEADER

Macfadden Performing Arts Media LLC, 110 William St., 23rd Floor, New York NY 10038. (646)459-4800. Fax: (646)459-4900. E-mail: mwalker@americancheerleader.com. Website: www.americancheerleader.com. **30% freelance written**. Bimonthly magazine covering high school, college, and competitive cheerleading. We try to keep a young, informative voice for all articles—'for cheerleaders, by cheerleaders.' Estab. 1995. Circ. 200,000. Byline given. Pays on publication. Offers 25% kill fee. Publishes ms an average of 4 months after acceptance. Buys all rights. Editorial lead time 3 months. Submit seasonal material 4 months in advance. Accepts queries by mail, e-mail. Responds in 4 weeks to queries. Responds in 2 months to mss. Sample copy for $2.95. Guidelines free.
Nonfiction Needs how-to, cheering techniques, routines, pep songs, etc., interview, celebrities and media personalities who cheered. Tryouts (April); Camp Basics (June); College (October); Competition (December). No professional cheerleading stories, i.e., no Dallas Cowboy cheerleaders. **Buys 12-16 mss/year.** Query with published clips. Length: 400-1,500 words. **Pays $100-250 for assigned articles. Pays $100 maximum for unsolicited articles.** Sometimes pays expenses of writers on assignment.
Photos State availability Model releases required. Reviews transparencies, 5x7 prints. Offers $50/photo. Rights purchased varies.
Columns/Departments Gameday Beauty (skin care, celeb how-tos), 600 words; Health & Fitness (teen athletes), 1,000 words; Profiles (winning squads), 1,000 words. 12 Query with published clips. **Pays $100-250.**
Tips We invite proposals from freelance writers who are involved in or have been involved in cheerleading—i.e., coaches, sponsors, or cheerleaders. Our writing style is upbeat and `sporty' to catch and hold the attention of our teenaged readers. Articles should be broken down into lots of sidebars, bulleted lists, Q&As, etc.

$ $ $ ATV MAGAZINE/ATV SPORT

Ehlert Publishing, 6420 Sycamore Lane, Maple Grove MN 55369. Fax: (763)383-4499. E-mail: terickson@ehlertpublishing.com. Website: www.atvmagonline.com. www.atvsport.com. **20% freelance written**. Bimonthly magazine covering all-terrain vehicles. Devoted to covering all the things ATV owners enjoy, from hunting to racing, farming to trail riding. Byline given. Pays on magazine shipment to printer. Buys all rights. Editorial lead time 6 months. Accepts queries by mail, e-mail, fax. Responds in 3 weeks to queries. Sample copy and writer's guidelines for #10 SASE
Nonfiction Needs how-to, interview, new product, personal experience, photo feature, technical, travel. **Buys 15-20 mss/year.** Query with published clips. Length: 200-2,000 words. **Pays $100-1,000.** Sometimes pays expenses of writers on assignment.
Photos State availability Captions, identification of subjects required. Negotiates payment individually. Rights purchased vary.
Tips Writers must have experience with ATVs, and should own one or have regular access to at least one ATV.

$ $ BVM

Beach Volleyball Magazine, STN Media Co., 700 Torrance Blvd., Suite C, Redondo Beach CA 90277. (310)792-2226. Fax: (310)792-2231. E-mail: ryan@bvmag.com. Website: www.bvmag.com. **60% freelance written**. Semiannual magazine covering all things, all ages of beach volleyball from an enthusiast slant. Writers must possess a Gen X/Y voice with an understanding of beach culture. Beach volleyball players and/or fans preferred. Writers should at least be familiar with the sport of volleyball and its application in the sand. This includes rules and regulations and leading personalities of the sport. Estab. 2006. Circ. 30,000.

Byline given. Pays on publication. No kill fee. Buys one-time rights. Editorial lead time 2 months. Submit seasonal material 2 months in advance. Accepts queries by e-mail. Accepts simultaneous submissions. Sample copy free. Guidelines free.

Nonfiction Needs general interest, historical, how-to, humor, inspirational, interview, new product, opinion, personal experience, photo feature, travel. Does not want game reporting. *BVM* is a lifestyle magazine looking for lifestyle feature content. Query with published clips. Length: 600-1,200 words. **Pays $150-300.**

Photos Contact: Contact Vince Rios, art director. Send photos Captions, identification of subjects, model releases required. Reviews contact sheets, GIF/JPEG files. Negotiates payment individually. Buys all rights.

Columns/Departments Health & Fitness (training and nutrition tips for all ages); Beach News (current events), both 500 words. 12 Query with published clips. **Pays $150-300.**

Fillers Needs anecdotes, facts, newsbreaks. Length: 50-150 words. **Pays $0-50.**

Tips This is an enthusiast magazine. Writers should be able to exhibit familiarity with and interest in beach volleyball and the surrounding culture. Previous sports writing and/or lifestyle feature experience preferred. Story ideas should have a firm grasp on topics of interest to beach volleyball community. Playing experience a definite plus, as is a demonstrated knowledge of sport history and knowledge, or the ability to quickly come up to speed and take direction.

$ CANADIAN RODEO NEWS

Canadian Rodeo News, Ltd., #223, 2116 27th Ave. NE, Calgary AB T2E 7A6 Canada. (403)250-7292. Fax: (403)250-6926. E-mail: editor@rodeocanada.com. Website: www.rodeocanada.com. **80% freelance written**. Monthly tabloid covering Canada's professional rodeo (CPRA) personalities and livestock. Read by rodeo participants and fans. Estab. 1964. Circ. 4,000. Byline given. Pays on publication. No kill fee. Publishes ms an average of 1 month after acceptance. Buys first rights, buys second serial (reprint) rights. Editorial lead time 1 month. Submit seasonal material 1 month in advance. Accepts queries by mail, e-mail, fax. Accepts simultaneous submissions. Responds in 1 month to queries. Responds in 2 months to mss.

Nonfiction Needs general interest, historical, interview. **Buys 70-80 mss/year.** Query. Length: 400-1,200 words. **Pays $30-60.**

Reprints Send photocopy of article or typed ms with rights for sale noted and information about when and where the material previously appeared. Pays 100% of amount paid for an original article.

Photos Send photos Reviews digital only. Offers $15-25/cover photo. Buys one time rights.

Tips Best to call first with the story idea to inquire if it is suitable for publication. Readers are very knowledgeable of the sport, so writers need to be as well.

$ FANTASY SPORTS

F+W Media, Inc., 700 E. State St., Iola WI 54990-0001. (715)445-2214. Fax: (715)445-4087. Website: fantasysportsmag.com. **10% freelance written**. Quarterly magazine covering fantasy baseball and football. Fantasy advice—how-to win. Estab. 1989. Circ. 100,000. Byline given. Pays on publication. Offers negotiable kill fee. Publishes ms an average of 3 months after acceptance. Makes work-for-hire assignments. Editorial lead time 4 months. Submit seasonal material 4 months in advance. Accepts queries by e-mail. Sample copy free.

Tips Send an e-mail suggestion to ambrosiusg@krause.com.

$ $ FENCERS QUARTERLY MAGAZINE

848 S. Kimbrough, Springfield MO 65806. (417)866-4370. E-mail: editor@fencersquarterly.com. Website: www.fencersquarterly.com. **60% freelance written**. Quarterly magazine covering fencing, fencers, history of sword/fencing/dueling, modern techniques and systems, controversies, personalities of fencing, personal experience. This is a publication for all fencers and those interested in fencing; we favor the grassroots level rather than the highly-promoted elite. Readers will have a grasp of terminology of the sword and refined fencing skills—writers must be familiar with fencing and current changes and controversies. We are happy to air any point of view on any fencing subject, but the material must be well-researched and logically presented. Estab. 1996. Circ. 5,000. Byline given. Pays prior to or at publication. Offers 25% kill fee. Publishes ms an average of 6 months after acceptance. Buys first North American serial rights, buys second serial (reprint) rights, buys electronic rights. Makes work-for-hire assignments. Editorial lead time 3 months. Submit seasonal material 6 months in advance. Accepts queries by mail, e-mail. Accepts simultaneous submissions. Sample copy by request. Guidelines available online.

- Responds in 1 week or less for e-mail; 1 month for snail mail if SASE; no reply if no SASE and material not usable.

Nonfiction All article types acceptable—however, we have seldom used fiction or poetry (though will consider if has special relationship to fencing). How-to should reflect some aspect of fencing or gear.

Personal experience welcome. No articles that lack logical progression of thought, articles that rant, `my weapon is better than your weapon' emotionalism, puff pieces, or public relations stuff. **Buys 100 mss/year.** Send complete ms. Length: 100-4,000 words. **Pays $100-200 (rarely) for assigned articles. Pays $10-60 for unsolicited articles.**

Photos Send photos by mail or as e-mail attachment. Prefers prints, all sizes. Captions, identification of subjects, model releases required. Negotiates payment individually. Buys all rights.

Columns/Departments Cutting-edge news (sword or fencing related), 100 words; Reviews (books/films), 300 words; Fencing Generations (profile), 200-300 words; Tournament Results (veteran events only, please), 200 words. 40 Send complete ms. **Pays $10-20.**

Fiction Will consider all as long as strong fencing/sword slant is major element. No erotica. Query or send complete ms. 1,500 words maximum. **Pays $25-100.**

Poetry Will consider all which have distinct fencing/sword element as central. No erotica. Submit maximum 10 poems. Up to 100 lines. **Pays $10.**

Fillers Needs anecdotes, facts, gags, newsbreaks. 30 100 words maximum. **Pays $5.**

Tips We love new writers! Professionally presented work impresses us. We prefer complete submissions, and e-mail or disk (in rich text format) are our favorites. Ask for our writer's guidelines. Always aim your writing to knowledgeable fencers who are fascinated by this subject, take their fencing seriously, and want to know more about its history, current events, and controversies. Action photos should show proper form—no flailing or tangled-up images, please. We want to know what the 'real' fencer is up to these days, not just what the Olympic contenders are doing. If we don't use your piece, we'll tell you why not.

INTERNATIONAL KICKBOXER

Blitz Publications, P.O. Box 4075, Mulgrave VIC 4075 Australia. (61)(3)9574-8999. Fax: (61)(3)9574-8899. E-mail: ben@blitzmag.com.au. Website: www.sportzblitz.net. Magazine covering the local and international kickboxing scene. "International Kickboxer has followed the growth of kickboxing and Muay Thai is dedicated to bringing the reader the latest news, fitness tips, training techniques, fight strategies, Boxing drills, cardio kick boxing, conditioning exercises, combat tactics, sports nutrition advice and much more. Some of the big names featured include Mark Hunt, Stan 'The Man' Longinidis, Sam Greco, Gurkan Ozkan, Ian Jacobs, Paul 'Hurricane' Briggs, 'John' Wayne Parr and many more. International Kickboxer Magazine covers events like the prestigious K-1 GP, Tarik Solak's K-1 Oceania, as well as Shootboxing and Muay Thai events from the WMC, ISKA, WKA, WKBF and WMTA. "

Nonfiction Needs general interest, how-to. Query.

$ LACROSSE MAGAZINE

US Lacrosse, 113 W. University Pkwy., Baltimore MD 21210. (410)235-6882. Fax: (410)366-6735. E-mail: pkrome@uslacrosse.org. Website: www.uslacrosse.org. **60% freelance written.** *Lacrosse Magazine* is the only national feature publication devoted to the sport of lacrosse. It is a benefit of membership in U.S. Lacrosse, a nonprofit organization devoted to promoting the growth of lacrosse and preserving its history. Estab. 1978. Circ. 235,000. Byline given. Pays on publication. No kill fee. Publishes ms an average of 2 months after acceptance. Buys one-time rights. Editorial lead time 2 months. Submit seasonal material 2 months in advance. Sample copy free. Guidelines free.

Nonfiction Needs book excerpts, general interest, historical, how-to, drills, conditioning, x's and o'x, etc., interview, new product, opinion, personal experience, photo feature, technical. **Buys 30-40 mss/year.** Length: 500-1,750 words. **Payment negotiable.** Sometimes pays expenses of writers on assignment.

Photos State availability Captions, identification of subjects required. Reviews contact sheets, 4x6 prints. Negotiates payment individually. Buys one time rights.

Columns/Departments First Person (personal experience), 1,000 words; Fitness (conditioning/strength/exercise), 500-1,000 words; How-to, 500-1,000 words. 10-15 **Payment negotiable.**

Tips As the national development center of lacrosse, we are particularly interested in stories about the growth of the sport in non-traditional areas of the U.S. and abroad, written for an audience already knowledgeable about the game.

$ $ POINTE MAGAZINE

Ballet At Its Best, MacFadden Performing Arts Media, LLC, 110 William St., 23rd Floor, New York NY 10038. (646)459-4800. Fax: (646)459-4900. E-mail: pointe@lifestylemedia.com. Website: www.pointemagazine.com. Bimonthly magazine covering ballet. *Pointe Magazine* is the only magazine dedicated to ballet. It offers practicalities on ballet careers as well as news and features. Estab. 2000. Circ. 38,000. Byline given. Pays on publication. Buys all rights. Responds in 1 month to queries. Responds in 1 month to mss. Sample copy for sae with 9x12 envelope and 6 First-Class stamps.

Nonfiction Needs historical, how-to, interview, biography, careers, health, news. **Buys 60 mss/year.** Query with published clips. Length: 400-1,500 words. **Pays $125-400.**

Photos Contact: Colin Fowler, photo editor. State availability Captions required. Reviews 214x2¼ or 35 mm transparencies, 8x11 prints. Negotiates payment individually. Buys one time rights.

$ $ POLO PLAYERS' EDITION

Rizzo Management Corp., 3500 Fairlane Farms Rd., Suite 9, Wellington FL 33414-8749. (561)793-9524. Fax: (561)793-9576. E-mail: info@poloplayersedition.com. Website: www.poloplayersedition.com. Monthly magazine on poloÃ³the sport and lifestyle. Our readers are affluent, well educated, well read, and highly sophisticated. Circ. 6,150. Pays on acceptance. Offers kill fee. Kill fee varies. Publishes ms an average of 2 months after acceptance. Buys first North American serial rights. Makes work-for-hire assignments. Submit seasonal material 3 months in advance. Accepts queries by mail, e-mail, fax. Accepts simultaneous submissions. Responds in 3 months to queries. Guidelines for #10 SAE with 2 stamps.

Nonfiction Needs historical, interview, personal experience, photo feature, technical, travel. Annual Art Issue/Gift Buying Guide; Winter Preview/Florida Supplement. **Buys 20 mss/year.** Send complete ms. Length: 800-3,000 words. **Pays $150-400 for assigned articles. Pays $100-300 for unsolicited articles.** Sometimes pays expenses of writers on assignment.

Reprints Send tearsheet or typed ms with rights for sale noted and information about when and where the material previously appeared. Pays 50% of amount paid for an original article.

Photos State availability of or send photos Captions required. Reviews contact sheets, transparencies, prints. Offers $20-150/photo. Buys one time rights.

Columns/Departments Yesteryears (historical pieces), 500 words; Profiles (clubs and players), 800-1,000 words. 15 Query with published clips. **Pays $100-300.**

Tips Query us on a personality or club profile or historic piece or, if you know the game, state availability to cover a tournament. Keep in mind that ours is a sophisticated, well-educated audience.

$ PRORODEO SPORTS NEWS

Professional Rodeo Cowboys Association, 101 ProRodeo Dr., Colorado Springs CO 80919. (719)593-8840. Fax: (719)548-4889. Website: www.prorodeo.com. **10% freelance written**. Biweekly magazine covering professional rodeo. "Our readers are extremely knowledgeable about the sport of rodeo, and anyone who writes for us should have that same in-depth knowledge. Estab. 1952. Circ. 27,000. Byline given. Pays on publication. No kill fee. Publishes ms an average of 1 month after acceptance. Buys first rights, buys one-time rights. Makes work-for-hire assignments. Editorial lead time 2 months. Submit seasonal material 2 months in advance. Responds in 2 weeks to queries Sample copy for #10 SASE Guidelines free

Nonfiction Needs historical, how-to, interview, photo feature, technical. **Pays $50-100.**

Photos State availability Identification of subjects required. Reviews digital images and hard copy portfolios. Offers $15-85/photo. Buys one time rights.

$ RUGBY MAGAZINE

Rugby Press, Ltd., 459 Columbus Ave., #1200, New York NY 10024. (212)787-1160. Fax: (212)787-1161. E-mail: rugbymag@aol.com. Website: www.rugbymag.com. **75% freelance written**. Monthly magazine. *Rugby Magazine* is the journal of record for the sport of rugby in the U.S. Our demographics are among the best in the country. Estab. 1975. Circ. 10,000. Byline given. Pays on publication. No kill fee. Publishes ms an average of 2 months after acceptance. Buys all rights. Editorial lead time 1 month. Submit seasonal material 2 months in advance. Accepts queries by mail, e-mail, fax, phone. Accepts simultaneous submissions. Responds in 2 weeks to queries. Responds in 1 month to mss. Sample copy for $4. Guidelines free.

Nonfiction Needs book excerpts, essays, general interest, historical, how-to, humor, interview, new product, opinion, personal experience, photo feature, technical, travel. **Buys 15 mss/year.** Send complete ms. Length: 600-2,000 words. **Pays $50 minimum.** Pays expenses of writers on assignment.

Reprints Send tearsheet or typed ms with rights for sale noted and information about when and where the material previously appeared. Payment varies.

Photos Send photos Reviews negatives, transparencies, prints. Offers no additional payment for photos accepted with ms. Buys all rights.

Columns/Departments Nutrition (athletic nutrition), 900 words; Referees' Corner, 1,200 words. 2-3 Query with published clips. **Pays $50 maximum.**

Fiction Needs cond novels, humorous, novel concepts, slice-of-life vignettes. **Buys 1-3 mss/year.** Query with published clips. Length: 1,000-2,500 words. **Pays $100.**

Tips Give us a call. Send along your stories or photos; we're happy to take a look. Tournament stories are a good way to get yourself published in *Rugby Magazine*.

$ SKYDIVING

1725 N. Lexington Ave., DeLand FL 32724. (386)736-4793. Fax: (386)736-9786. E-mail: sue@skydivingmagazine.com. Website: skydivingmagazine.com. **25% freelance written**. Monthly tabloid featuring skydiving for sport parachutists, worldwide dealers and equipment manufacturers. *Skydiving* is a news magazine. Its purpose is to deliver timely, useful and interesting information about the equipment, techniques, events, people and places of parachuting. Our scope is national. *Skydiving*'s audience spans the entire spectrum of jumpers, from first-jump students to veterans with thousands of skydives. Some readers are riggers with a keen interest in the technical aspects of parachutes, while others are weekend `fun' jumpers who want information to help them make travel plans and equipment purchases. Circ. 14,200. Byline given. Pays on publication. No kill fee. Publishes ms an average of 3 months after acceptance. Buys one-time rights. Accepts previously published material. Accepts simultaneous submissions. Responds in 1 month to queries. Sample copy for $2. Guidelines available online.

Nonfiction Average issue includes 3 feature articles and 3 columns of technical information. Send us news and information on how-to, where-to, equipment, techniques, events and outstanding personalities who skydive. We want articles written by people who have a solid knowledge of parachuting. No personal experience or human interest articles. Query. Length: 500-1,000 words. **Pays $25-100.** Sometimes pays expenses of writers on assignment.

Photos State availability Captions required. Reviews 5x7 and larger b&w glossy prints. Offers no additional payment for photos accepted with ms.

Fillers Needs newsbreaks. Length: 100-200 words. **$25 minimum.**

Tips The most frequent mistake made by writers in completing articles for us is that the writer isn't knowledgeable about the sport of parachuting. Articles about events are especially time-sensitive so yours must be submitted quickly. We welcome contributions about equipment. Even short, `quick look' articles about new products are appropriate for *Skydiving*. If you know of a drop zone or other place that jumpers would like to visit, write an article describing its features and tell them why you liked it and what they can expect to find if they visit it. Avoid first-person articles.

$ $ TENNIS WEEK

304 Park Ave. South, 8th Fl., New York NY 10010. Website: www.tennisweek.com. **10% freelance written.** Monthly magazine covering tennis. For readers who are either tennis fanatics or involved in the business of tennis. Estab. 1974. Circ. 107,253. Byline given. Pays on publication. No kill fee. Buys all rights. Editorial lead time 1 month. Submit seasonal material 1 month in advance. Responds in 1 month to queries. Sample copy for $4.

Nonfiction Buys 15 mss/year. Query. Length: 1,000-2,000 words. **Pays $300.**

$ $ WINDY CITY SPORTS

Windy City Publishing, 1450 W. Randolph St., Chicago IL 60607. (312)421-1551. Fax: (312)421-1454. E-mail: jeff@windycitysports.com. Website: www.windycitysports.com. **50% freelance written.** Monthly tabloid. Writers should have knowledge of the sport they've been hired to cover. In most cases, these are endurance sports, such as running, cycling, triathlon, or adventure racing. Please read the magazine and visit the website to famliarize yourself with our subject matter and our style. Poorly-tailored queries reflect badly on your journalistic skills. If you query us on a golf story, you will not only suffer the shame of rejection, but your name shall be added to our 'clueless freelancer' list, and we will joke about you at the water cooler. Circ. 110,000. Byline given. Pays on publication. No kill fee. Publishes ms an average of 1 month after acceptance. Buys one-time rights. Editorial lead time 2 months. Accepts queries by e-mail. Sample copy and writer's guidelines online.

Nonfiction Needs essays, general interest, how-to, humor, interview, opinion, personal experience, photo feature, technical. **Buys up to 35 mss/year.** Query with published clips. Length: 700-1,500 words. **Pays $150-300 for assigned articles. Pays $0-300 for unsolicited articles.** Sometimes pays expenses of writers on assignment.

Photos Send photos Captions, identification of subjects required. Reviews prints. Negotiates payment individually Buys one time rights.

Columns/Departments Cool Down (humorous, personal experience), 800-1,000 words; Nutrition (advice and information on diet), 500-800 words; Health/Wellness (advice and information on general health), 500-800 words. Query with published clips. **Pays $50-150.**

Tips You should try to make it fun. We like to see anecdotes, great quotes and vivid descriptions. Quote Chicago area people as often as possible. If that's not possible, try to stick to the Midwest or people with Chicago connections.

MOTOR SPORTS

$ DIRT RIDER

Source Interlink Media, Inc., 6420 Wilshire Blvd., 17th Floor, Los Angeles CA 90048. (323)782-2390. Fax: (323)782-2372. E-mail: drmail@primedia.com. Website: www.dirtrider.com. Monthly magazine devoted to the sport of off-road motorcycle riding that showcases the many ways enthusiast can enjoy dirt bikes. Circ. 201,342. No kill fee.

4-WHEEL & OFF ROAD

Source Interlink Media, 6420 Wilshire Blvd., Los Angeles CA 90048. (323)782-2000. Fax: (323)782-2704. E-mail: 4wheeloffroad@sourceinterlink.com. Website: www.4wheeloffroad.com. Monthly magazine covering off road driving. Intended for the connoisseur of four wheel drive vehicles and their specific applications. Estab. 1977. Circ. 379,284. No kill fee.

Nonfiction Needs how-to, new product, product evaluations, travel, trail destinations, legal issues.

$ THE HOOK MAGAZINE

The Magazine for Antique & Classic Tractor Pullers, Greer Town, Inc., 209 S. Marshall, Box 16, Marshfield MO 65706. (417)468-7000. Fax: (417)859-6075. E-mail: editor@hookmagazine.com. Website: www.hookmagazine.com. **Contact:** Dana Greer Marlin, Owner/Pres. **80% freelance written**. Bimonthly magazine covering tractor pulling. Estab. 1992. Circ. 6,000. Byline given. Pays on publication. No kill fee. Buys one-time rights, buys electronic rights. Editorial lead time 6 months. Submit seasonal material 6 months in advance. Accepts queries by mail, e-mail, fax. Accepts previously published material. Accepts simultaneous submissions. Responds in 3 weeks to queries. Responds in 2 months to mss. Sample copy for 8 ½x11 SAE with 4 first-class stamps or online. Guidelines for #10 SASE.

"Our magazine is easy to break into. Puller profiles are your best bet. Features on individuals and their tractors, how they got into the sport, what they want from competing."

Nonfiction Needs how-to, interview, new product, personal experience, photo feature, technical, event coverage. **Buys 25 mss/year.** Send complete ms. Length: 500-1,500 words. **Pays $70 for technical articles; $35 for others.**

Photos Send photos Captions, identification of subjects, model releases required. Reviews 3x5 prints. Negotiates payment individually. Buys one-time and online rights.

Fillers Needs anecdotes, short humor. 6 Length: 100 words.

Tips "Write 'real'; our readers don't respond well to scholarly tomes. Use your everyday voice in all submissions and your chances will go up radically."

$ $ ROAD RACER X

Filter Publications, 122 Vista del Rio Dr., Morgantown WV 26508. (304)284-0080. Fax: (304)284-0081. E-mail: letters@roadracerx.com. Website: www.roadracerx.com. **25% freelance written**. 8 issues per year magazine covering motorcycle road racing. We cover the sport from a lifestyle/personality perspective. We don't do many technical stories or road tests. Estab. 2003. Circ. 35,000. Byline given. Pays on publication. No kill fee. Publishes ms an average of 2 months after acceptance. Buys one-time rights. Editorial lead time 2 months. Submit seasonal material 1 month in advance. Accepts queries by e-mail. Responds in 1 month to queries. Sample copy for #10 SASE. Guidelines available.

Nonfiction Needs historical, (road racing), interview, (racers). We publish official event programs for several important events, including the Red Bull U.S. Grand Prix & the Miller Motorsports Park World Superbike race. We do not want road tests. **Buys 8 mss/yr. mss/year.** Query. Length: 2,000-3,000 words. **Pays $400-600 for assigned articles. Pays $400-600 for unsolicited articles.** Sometimes pays expenses of writers on assignment. (limit agreed upon in advance)

Photos Contact: Matt Ware. State availability Reviews GIF/JPEG files. Negotiates payment individually. Buys one time rights.

Columns/Departments Contact: Chris Jonnum. 8 mss/yr. Query. **Pays $$25-$100.**

Tips In order for your work to appeal to our readers, you must know the world of motorcycle road racing.

$ $ SAND SPORTS MAGAZINE

Wright Publishing Co., Inc., P.O. Box 2260, Costa Mesa CA 92628. (714)979-2560, ext. 107. Fax: (714)979-3998. Website: www.sandsports.net. **Contact:** Michael Sommer, Managing Editor. **20% freelance written**. Bimonthly magazine covering vehicles for off-road and sand dunes. Estab. 1995. Circ. 35,000. Byline given. Pays on publication. Buys first rights, buys one-time rights. Editorial lead time 3 months. Submit seasonal material 6 months in advance. Accepts queries by mail. Sample copy and writer's guidelines free

Nonfiction Needs how-to, technical-mechanical, photo feature, technical. **Buys 20 mss/year.** Query. 1,500 words minimum **Pays $175/page.** Sometimes pays expenses of writers on assignment.

Photos Send photos Captions, identification of subjects, model releases required. Reviews color slides or high res digital images. Negotiates payment individually. Buys one time rights.

$ $ SPEEDWAY ILLUSTRATED

Performance Media, LLC, 107 Elm St., Salisbury MA 01952. (978)465-9099. Fax: (978)465-9033. E-mail: editorial@speedwayillustrated.com. Website: www.speedwayillustrated.com. **40% freelance written**. Monthly magazine covering stock car racing. Estab. 2000. Circ. 146,000. Byline given. Pays on publication. No kill fee. Buys first rights. Editorial lead time 6 weeks. Accepts queries by mail, e-mail, fax. Responds in 2 weeks to queries. Sample copy free.

Nonfiction Needs interview, opinion, personal experience, photo feature, technical. **Buys 30 mss/year.** Query. **Pays variable rate.**
Photos Send photos Captions, identification of subjects, model releases required. Reviews transparencies, digital. Offers $40-250/photo. Buys all rights.
Tips We seek short, high-interest value pieces that are accompanied by strong photography, in short—knock our socks off.

RUNNING

$ INSIDE TEXAS RUNNING

14201 Memorial Dr., Suite 204, Houston TX 77079. (281)759-0555. Fax: (281)759-7766. E-mail: lance@runningmags.com. Website: www.insidetexasrunning.com. **70% freelance written**. Monthly (except June and August) tabloid covering running and running-related events. Our audience is made up of Texas runners who may also be interested in cross training. Estab. 1977. Circ. 10,000. Byline given. Pays on publication. No kill fee. Publishes ms an average of 2 months after acceptance. Buys one-time, exclusive Texas rights. Submit seasonal material 2 months in advance. Responds in 1 month to mss. Sample copy for $4.95. Guidelines for #10 SASE.
Nonfiction Various topics of interest to runners: Profiles of newsworthy Texas runners of all abilities; unusual events; training interviews. Shoe Review (March); Fall Race Review (September); Marathon Focus (October); Resource Guide (December). **Buys 20 mss/year.** Send complete ms. Length: 500-1,500 words. **Pays $100 maximum for assigned articles. Pays $50 maximum for unsolicited articles.**
Reprints Send tearsheet, photocopy or typed ms with rights for sale noted and information about when and where the material previously appeared.
Photos Send photos Captions required. Offers $25 maximum/photo. Buys one time rights.
Tips Writers should be familiar with the sport and the publication.

$$ NEW YORK RUNNER

New York Road Runners, 9 E. 89th St., New York NY 10128. (212)423-2260. Fax: (212)423-0879. E-mail: webmaster@nyrr.org. Website: www.nyrr.org. Quarterly magazine covering running, walking, nutrition, and fitness. Estab. 1958. Circ. 45,000. Byline given. Pays on acceptance. Buys first North American serial rights. Submit seasonal material 4 months in advance. Accepts queries by mail, e-mail, fax. Responds in 2 months to queries. Sample copy for $3.

- Material should be of interest to members of the New York Road Runners.

Nonfiction Running and marathon articles. Needs interview, of runners. **Buys 15 mss/year.** Query. Length: 750-1,000 words. **Pays $50-350.**
Columns/Departments Running Briefs (anything noteworthy in the running world), 250-500 words. Query.
Tips Be knowledgeable about the sport of running.

$$$$ RUNNER'S WORLD

Rodale, 135 N. 6th St., Emmaus PA 18098. (610)967-8441. Fax: (610)967-8883. E-mail: rwedit@rodale.com. Website: www.runnersworld.com. **5% freelance written**. Monthly magazine on running, mainly long-distance running. The magazine for and about distance running, training, health and fitness, nutrition, motivation, injury prevention, race coverage, personalities of the sport. Estab. 1966. Circ. 500,000. Byline given. Pays on publication. No kill fee. Publishes ms an average of 6 months after acceptance. Buys all rights. Submit seasonal material 6 months in advance. Accepts queries by mail. Responds in 2 months to queries. Guidelines available online.
Nonfiction Needs how-to, train, prevent injuries, interview, personal experience. No my first marathon stories. No poetry. **Buys 5-7 mss/year.** Query. **Pays $1,500-2,000.** Pays expenses of writers on assignment.
Photos State availability Identification of subjects required. Buys one time rights.
Columns/Departments Finish Line (back-of-the-magazine essay, personal experienceÃ³humor). 24 Send complete ms. **Pays $300**
Tips We are always looking for `Adventure Runs' from readers—runs in wild, remote, beautiful, and interesting places. These are rarely race stories but more like backtracking/running adventures. Great color slides are crucial, 2,000 words maximum.

$$ RUNNING TIMES

The Runner's Best Resource, Rodale, Inc., c/o Zephyr Media, P.O. Box 20627, Boulder CO 80308. (203)761-1113. Fax: (203)761-9933. E-mail: editor@runningtimes.com. Website: www.runningtimes.com. **40% freelance written**. Magazine published 10 times/year covering distance running and racing. "*Running Times* is the national magazine for the experienced running participant and fan. Our audience

is knowledgeable about the sport and active in running and racing. All editorial relates specifically to running: improving performance, enhancing enjoyment, or exploring events, places, and people in the sport." Estab. 1977. Circ. 102,000. Byline given. Pays on publication. No kill fee. Publishes ms an average of 3 months after acceptance. Buys first North American serial rights, buys second serial (reprint) rights, buys electronic rights. Editorial lead time 4-6 months. Submit seasonal material 6 months in advance. Accepts queries by mail, e-mail. Responds in 1 month to queries. Responds in 2 months to mss. Sample copy for $8. Guidelines available online.
Nonfiction Needs book excerpts, essays, historical, how-to, training, humor, inspirational, interview, new product, opinion, personal experience, with theme, purpose, evidence of additional research and/ or special expertise, photo feature, news, reports. No basic, beginner how-to, generic fitness/nutrition, or generic first-person accounts. **Buys 35 mss/year.** Query. Length: 1,500-3,000 words. **Pays $200-1,,000 for assigned articles. Pays $150-300 for unsolicited articles.** Sometimes pays expenses of writers on assignment.
Photos State availability Identification of subjects required. Negotiates payment individually. Buys one time rights.
Columns/Departments Training (short topics related to enhancing performance), 1,000 words; Sports-Med (application of medical knowledge to running), 1,000 words; Nutrition (application of nutritional principles to running performance), 1,000 words. 10 Query. **Pays $50-200.**
Fiction Any genre, with running-related theme or characters. Buys 1 ms/year. Send complete ms. Length: 1,500-3,000 words. **Pays $100-500.**
Tips "Thoroughly get to know runners and the running culture, both at the participant level and the professional, elite level."

$ $ TRAIL RUNNER

The Magazine of Running Adventure, Big Stone Publishing, 417 Main St., Unit N, Carbondale CO 81623. (970)704-1442. Fax: (970)963-4965. E-mail: mbenge@bigstonepub.com. Website: www.trailrunnermag.com. **65% freelance written**. Bimonthly magazine covering all aspects of off-road running. The only nationally circulated 4-color glossy magazine dedicated to covering trail running. Estab. 1999. Circ. 20,000. Byline given. Pays on publication. Offers $50 kill fee. Publishes ms an average of 2 months after acceptance. Buys first North American serial rights, buys electronic rights. Editorial lead time 3 months. Submit seasonal material 5 months in advance. Accepts queries by mail, e-mail. Accepts simultaneous submissions. Responds in 3 weeks to queries. Responds in 2 months to mss. Sample copy for $3. Guidelines available online.
Nonfiction Needs essays, expose, general interest, historical, how-to, humor, inspirational, interview, new product, opinion, personal experience, photo feature, technical, travel, racing. No gear reviews, race results. **Buys 30-40 mss/year.** Query with published clips. Length: 800-2,000 words. **Pays 30¢/word.** Sometimes pays expenses of writers on assignment.
Photos Send photos Identification of subjects, model releases required. Reviews 35mm transparencies, prints. Offers $50-250/photo. Buys one time rights.
Columns/Departments Contact: Garett Graubins, senior editor. Training (race training, altitude training, etc.), 800 words; Adventure (off-beat aspects of trail running), 600-800 words; Wanderings (personal essay on any topic related to trail running), 600 words; Urban Escapes (urban trails accessible in and around major US sites), 800 words; Personalities (profile of a trail running personality), 1,000 words. 5-10 Query with published clips. **Pays 30-40¢/word.**
Fiction Needs adventure, fantasy, slice-of-life vignettes. **Buys 1-2 mss/year.** Query with published clips. Length: 1,000-1,500 words. **Pays 25-35¢/word.**
Fillers Needs anecdotes, facts, gags, newsbreaks, short humor. 50-60 Length: 75-400 words. **Pays 25-35¢/word.**
Tips Best way to break in is with interesting and unique trail running news, notes, and nonsense from around the world. Also, check the website for more info.

$ $ TRIATHLETE MAGAZINE

The World's Largest Triathlon Magazine, Triathlon Group of North America, 328 Encinitas Blvd., Suite 100, Encinitas CA 92024. (760)634-4100. Fax: (760)634-4110. E-mail: cam@triathletemag.com. Website: www.triathletemag.com. **50% freelance written**. Monthly magazine. In general, articles should appeal to seasoned triathletes, as well as eager newcomers to the sport. Our audience includes everyone from competitive athletes to people considering their first event. Estab. 1983. Circ. 53,864. Byline given. Pays on publication. No kill fee. Buys second serial (reprint) rights, buys all rights. Editorial lead time 3 months. Submit seasonal material 6 months in advance. Accepts queries by mail, e-mail. Accepts simultaneous submissions. Sample copy for $5.
Nonfiction Needs how-to, interview, new product, photo feature, technical. No first-person pieces about your experience in triathlon or my-first-triathlon stories. **Buys 36 mss/year.** Query with published clips.

Length: 1,000-3,000 words. **Pays $200-600.** Sometimes pays expenses of writers on assignment.
Photos State availability Reviews transparencies. Offers $50-300/photo. Buys first North American rights.
Tips Writers should know the sport and be familiar with the nuances and history. Training-specific articles that focus on new, but scientifically based, methods are good, as are seasonal training pieces.

$ WASHINGTON RUNNING REPORT

Capital Running Company, 13710 Ashby Rd., Rockville MD 20853-2903. (301)871-0005. Fax: (301)871-0006. E-mail: kathy@runwashington.com. Website: www.runwashington.com. **90% freelance written.** Bimonthly tabloid covering running and racing in Washington, DC, metropolitan area, including Baltimore and Richmond metro areas. "*Washington Running Report* is written by runners for runners. Features include runner rankings, training tips and advice, feature articles on races, race results, race calendar, humor, product reviews, and other articles of interest to runners." Estab. 1984. Circ. 35,000. Byline given. Pays on publication. Publishes ms an average of 2-4 months after acceptance. Buys first rights, buys one-time rights, buys second serial (reprint) rights, buys simultaneous rights, buys electronic rights. Makes work-for-hire assignments. Editorial lead time 1 month. Submit seasonal material 3 months in advance. Accepts queries by mail, e-mail, fax, phone. Accepts previously published material. Accepts simultaneous submissions. Responds in 2-3 weeks to queries. Responds in 1-2 months to mss. Sample copy free.
Nonfiction Needs book excerpts, essays, expose, general interest, historical, how-to, humor, inspirational, interview, new product, opinion, personal experience, photo feature, technical, travel. **Buys 10-12 mss/year.** Query. Length: 500-2,800 words. **Pays $75 for assigned articles. Pays $50 for unsolicited articles.**
Photos Send photos Captions, identification of subjects required. Reviews contact sheets, 4x6 prints, GIF/JPEG files. Offers $20-50/photo. Buys all rights.
Columns/Departments Traveling Runner (races in exotic locales), 1,400 words; Training Tips (how to run faster, racing strategy), 750 words; Sports Medicine (new developments in the field), 750 words. 3-4 Query with or without published clips or send complete ms. **Pays $50.**
Fiction Needs adventure, cond novels, experimental, fantasy, historical, humorous, mainstream, mystery, slice-of-life vignettes. **Buys 1-2 mss/year.** Send complete ms. Length: 750-1,500 words. **Pays $50.**
Fillers Needs anecdotes, facts, gags, newsbreaks, short humor. 6 Length: 50-250 words. **Pays $50.**
Tips "Submit timely articles about running and racing in the DC area; original humor pieces; coverage of a large race in our area."

SKIING & SNOW SPORTS

$ AMERICAN SNOWMOBILER

Kalmbach Publishing Co., P.O. Box 1612, Waukesha WI 53187. Website: www.amsnow.com. **Contact:** Mark Savage, ed. **30% freelance written**. Magazine published 6 times seasonally covering snowmobiling. Estab. 1985. Circ. 50,000. Byline given. Pays on acceptance. No kill fee. Publishes an average of 4 months after acceptance. Buys all rights. Editorial lead time 4 months. Submit seasonal material 6 months in advance. Accepts queries by mail, e-mail, fax. Responds in 1 month to queries. Responds in 2 months to mss. Guidelines available online.
Nonfiction "Seeking race coverage for online." Needs general interest, historical, how-to, interview, personal experience, photo feature, travel. **Buys 10 mss/year.** Query with published clips. Length: 500-1,200 words. **Pay varies for assigned articles.Pays $100 minimum for unsolicited articles.**
Photos State availability Captions, identification of subjects, model releases required. Offers no additional payment for photos accepted with ms. Buys all rights.

$ SKATING

United States Figure Skating Association, 20 First St., Colorado Springs CO 80906-3697. (719)635-5200. Fax: (719)635-9548. E-mail: info@usfigureskating.org. Website: www.usfsa.org. Magazine published 10 times/year. *Skating* magazine is the official publication of U.S. Figure Skating, and thus we cover skating at both the championship and grass roots level. Estab. 1923. Circ. 45,000. Byline given. Pays on publication. No kill fee. Publishes ms an average of 3 months after acceptance. Buys first rights. Accepts queries by mail, e-mail, fax.
Nonfiction Needs general interest, historical, how-to, interview, background and interests of skaters, volunteers, or other U.S. Figure Skating members, photo feature, technical and competition reports, figure skating issues and trends, sports medicine. **Buys 10 mss/year.** Query. Length: 500-2,500 words. **Payment varies**
Photos Photos purchased with or without accompanying ms. Query. Pays $10 for 8x10 or 5x7 b&w glossy prints, and $25 for color prints or transparencies.
Columns/Departments Ice Breaker (news briefs); Foreign Competition Reports; Health and Fitness; In Synch (synchronized skating news); Takeoff (up-and-coming athletes), all 500-2,000 words.

Tips We want writing by experienced persons knowledgeable in the technical and artistic aspects of figure skating with a new outlook on the development of the sport. Knowledge and background in technical aspects of figure skating is helpful, but not necessary to the quality of writing expected. We would like to see articles and short features on U.S. Figure Skating volunteers, skaters, and other U.S. Figure Skating members who normally wouldn't get recognized, as opposed to features on championship-level athletes, which are usually assigned to regular contributors. Good quality color photos are a must with submissions. Also would be interested in seeing figure skating 'issues and trends' articles, instead of just profiles. No professional skater material. Synchronized skating and adult skating are the 2 fastest growing aspects of the U.S. Figure Skating. We would like to see more stories dealing with these unique athletes.

$ $ $ $ SKIING

Time 4 Media, Inc., 929 Pearl St., Suite 200, Boulder CO 80302. (303)448-7600. Fax: (303)448-7676. E-mail: editors@time4.com. Website: www.skiingmag.com. Magazine published 7 times/year for skiers who deeply love winter, who live for travel, adventure, instruction, gear, and news. *Skiing* is the user's guide to winter adventure. It is equal parts jaw-dropping inspiration and practical information, action and utility, attitude and advice. It relates the lifestyles of dedicated skiers and captures their spirit of daring and exploration. Dramatic photography transports readers to spine-tingling mountains with breathtaking immediacy. Reading *Skiing* is almost as much fun as being there. Estab. 1948. Circ. 400,000. Byline given. Offers 40% kill fee.

Nonfiction Buys 10-15 feature (1,500-2,000 words) and 12-24 short (100-500 words) mss/year. Query. **Pays $1,000-2,500/feature; $100-500/short piece.**

Columns/Departments Length: 200-1,000 words. 2-3 Query. **Pays $150-1,000.**

Tips Consider less obvious subjects: smaller ski areas, specific local ski cultures, unknown aspects of popular resorts. Be expressive, not merely descriptive. We want readers to feel the adventure in your writing—to tingle with the excitement of skiing steep powder, of meeting intriguing people, of reaching new goals or achieving dramatic new insights. We want readers to have fun, to see the humor in and the lighter side of skiing and their fellow skiers.

$ $ $ ⊘ SKI MAGAZINE

Times Mirror Magazines, 5720 Flatiron Parkway, Boulder CO 80301. E-mail: editor@skimag.com. Website: www.skimag.com. **60% freelance written**. Magazine published 8 times/year. *Ski* is a ski-lifestyle publication written and edited for recreational skiers. Its content is intended to help them ski better (technique), buy better (equipment and skiwear), and introduce them to new experiences, people, and adventures. Estab. 1936. Circ. 430,000. Byline given. Pays on acceptance. Offers 15% kill fee. Publishes ms an average of 3 months after acceptance. Buys first North American serial rights. Submit seasonal material 8 months in advance. Accepts queries by mail, e-mail. Sample copy for sae with 9x12 envelope and 5 First-Class stamps.

- Does not accept unsolicited mss, and assumes no responsibility for their return.

Nonfiction Needs essays, historical, how-to, humor, interview, personal experience. **Buys 5-10 mss/year.** Send complete ms. Length: 1,000-3,500 words. **Pays $500-1,000 for assigned articles. Pays $300-700 for unsolicited articles.** Pays expenses of writers on assignment.

Photos Send photos Captions, identification of subjects, model releases required. Offers $75-300/photo. Buys one time rights.

Fillers Needs facts, short humor. 10 Length: 60-75 words. **Pays $50-75.**

Tips Writers must have an extensive familiarity with the sport and know what concerns, interests, and amuses skiers. Start with short pieces ('hometown hills,' 'dining out,' 'sleeping in'). Columns are most open to freelancers.

$ $ SNOWEST MAGAZINE

Harris Publishing, 360 B St., Idaho Falls ID 83402. (208)524-7000. Fax: (208)522-5241. E-mail: lindstrm@snowest.com. Website: snowest.com. **10-25% freelance written**. Monthly magazine. "*SnoWest* covers the sport of snowmobiling, products, and personalities in the western states. This includes mountain riding, deep powder, and trail riding, as well as destination pieces, tech tips, and new model reviews." Estab. 1972. Circ. 140,000. Byline given. Pays on publication. No kill fee. Publishes ms an average of 2 months after acceptance. Buys first North American serial rights. Editorial lead time 6 months. Submit seasonal material 3 months in advance. Sample copy and writer's guidelines free

Nonfiction Needs how-to, fix a snowmobile, make it high performance, new product, technical, travel. **Buys 3-5 mss/year.** Query with published clips. Length: 500-1,500 words. **Pays $150-300.**

Photos Send photos Captions, identification of subjects required. Negotiates payment individually. Buys one time rights.

$ $ SNOW GOER

Affinity Media, 6420 Sycamore Lane, Maple Grove MN 55369. Fax: (763)383-4499. E-mail: terickson@

affinitygroup.com. Website: www.snowgoer.com. **5% freelance written**. Magazine published 7 times/year covering snowmobiling. "*Snow Goer* is a hard-hitting, tell-it-like-it-is magazine designed for the ultra-active snowmobile enthusiast. It is fun, exciting, innovative, and on the cutting edge of technology and trends." Estab. 1967. Circ. 66,000. Byline given. Pays on publication. No kill fee. Publishes ms an average of 5 months after acceptance. Buys first rights, buys one-time rights. Editorial lead time 5 months. Submit seasonal material 6 months in advance. Accepts queries by mail, e-mail, fax. Accepts simultaneous submissions. Responds in 3 months to queries. Sample copy for sae with 8x10 envelope and 4 First-Class stamps.

Nonfiction Needs general interest, how-to, interview, new product, personal experience, photo feature, technical, travel. **Buys 6 mss/year.** Query. Length: 500-4,000 words. **Pays $50-500.** Sometimes pays expenses of writers on assignment.

Photos State availability Captions, identification of subjects required. Reviews contact sheets, prints. Negotiates payment individually. Buys one-time rights or all rights.

WATER SPORTS

$ DIVER

241 E. 1st St., North Vancouver BC V7L 1B4 Canada. (604)948-9937. Fax: (604)948-9985. E-mail: editor@divermag.com. Website: www.divermag.com. Magazine published 8 times/year emphasizing scuba diving, ocean science, and technology for a well-educated, outdoor-oriented readership. Circ. 7,000. No kill fee. Accepts queries by mail, e-mail.

Nonfiction Well-written and illustrated Canadian and North American regional dive destination articles. Most travel articles are committed up to a year in advance, and there is limited scope for new material. Reading period for unsolicited articles July through August. Length: 500-1,000 words. **Pays $2.50/column inch.**

Photos Captions, identification of subjects required. Reviews 5x7 prints, JPEG/TIFF files (300 dpi), slides, maps, drawings.

$ $ PADDLER MAGAZINE

World's No. 1 Canoeing, Kayaking and Rafting Magazine, Paddlesport Publishing, 12040 98th Ave. NE, Suite 205, Kirkland WA 98034. E-mail: mike@paddlermagazine.com. Website: www.paddlermagazine.com. **70% freelance written**. Bimonthly magazine covering paddle sports. *Paddler* magazine is written by and for those knowledgeable about river running, flatwater canoeing and sea kayaking. Our core audience is the intermediate to advanced paddler, yet we strive to cover the entire range from beginners to experts. Our editorial coverage is divided between whitewater rafting, whitewater kayaking, canoeing and sea kayaking. We strive for balance between the Eastern and Western U.S. paddling scenes and regularly cover international expeditions. We also try to integrate the Canadian paddling community into each publication. Estab. 1991. Circ. 40,000. Byline given. Pays on publication. No kill fee. Publishes ms an average of 6 months after acceptance. Buys first North American serial rights, buys one-time electronic rights rights. Editorial lead time 3 months. Submit seasonal material 6 months in advance. Accepts queries by mail, e-mail. Responds in 6 months to queries. Sample copy for $3 with 8 ½—Š11 SASE. Guidelines available online.

Nonfiction Needs book excerpts, essays, general interest, historical, how-to, humor, inspirational, interview, new product, opinion, personal experience, photo feature, technical, travel, must be paddlesport related. **Buys 75 mss/year.** Query. Length: 100-3,000 words. **Pays 10-25¢/word (more for established writers) for assigned articles. Pays 10-20¢/word for unsolicited articles.** Sometimes pays expenses of writers on assignment.

Photos Submissions should include photos or other art. State availability Reviews contact sheets, negatives, transparencies. Offers $25-200/photo. Buys one time rights.

Columns/Departments Hotline (timely news and exciting developments relating to the paddling community. Stories should be lively and newsworthy), 150-750 words; Paddle People (unique people involved in the sport and industry leaders), 600-800 words; Destinations (informs paddlers of unique places to paddleÃ³we often follow regional themes and cover all paddling disciplines); submissions should include map and photo, 800 words. Marketplace (gear reviews, gadgets and new products, and is about equipment paddlers use, from boats and paddles to collapsible chairs, bivy sacks and other accessories), 250-800 words. Paddle Tales (short, humorous anecdotes), 75-300 words. Skills (a How-to forum for experts to share tricks of the trade, from playboating techniques to cooking in the backcountry), 250-1,000 words. Query. **Pays 20-25¢/word.**

Tips We prefer queries, but will look at manuscripts on speculation. No phone queries please. Be familiar with the magazine and offer us unique, exciting ideas. Most positive responses to queries are on spec, but we will occasionally make assignments.

$ $ ROWING NEWS

The Magazine of Rowing, The Independent Rowing News, Inc., 85 Mechanic St., Suite 440, Lebanon NH 03766. E-mail: editor@rowingnews.com. Website: www.rowingnews.com. **75% freelance written**. Monthly magazine covering rowing (the Olympic sport). We write for a North American readership, serving the rowing community with features, how-to, and dispatches from the rowing world at large. Estab. 1994. Circ. 20,000. Byline given. Pays on publication. No kill fee. Publishes ms an average of 1-2 months after acceptance. Makes work-for-hire assignments. Editorial lead time 1-12 months. Submit seasonal material 1-2 months in advance. Responds in 6 weeks to queries. Sample copy available online. Guidelines free.

Nonfiction Needs essays, how-to, rowing only, interview, new product, personal experience, rowing, travel. Everything must be directedly related to rowing. **Buys 12 mss/year mss/year.** Query with published clips. Length: 1,500-5,000 words. Sometimes pays expenses of writers on assignment.

Photos True required. Reviews JPEG/TIFF. Negotiates payment individually. Buys one time rights.

Tips Make sure you are familiar with the magazine.

SCUBA DIVING

a Division of F + W Media, Inc., 6600 Abercorn St., Suite 208, Savannah GA 31405. (912)351-0855. Fax: (912)351-0735. E-mail: edit@scubadiving.com. Website: www.scubadiving.com. Monthly magazine covering scuba diving. Edited for scuba divers of all skill levels. Estab. 1992. Circ. 175,000. No kill fee. Buys all rights. Editorial lead time 10 weeks. Accepts queries by mail, e-mail, fax, phone. Sample copy for $3.50. Guidelines by email.

Nonfiction No first person essays or puff pieces on dive destinations and operators. Query.

Columns/Departments Currents (lively and engaging stories that are heavy on news and/or how-to information), 500 words or less; North American Travel (great diving/scuba adventures that are close to home and can be done in a long weekend), 750 words, including a getting there and dive conditions sidebar. Query.

$ ⊘ SURFER MAGAZINE

Primedia Enthusiast Group, P.O. Box 1028, Dana Point CA 92629-5028. (949)661-5115. E-mail: chris.mauro@primedia.com. Website: www.surfermag.com. Monthly magazine edited for the avid surfers and those who follow the beach, wave riding scene. Circ. 118,570. No kill fee. Editorial lead time 10 weeks.

- Query before submitting.

$ $ SWIMMING WORLD MAGAZINE

Sports Publications International, P.O. Box 20337, Sedona AZ 86341. (928)284-4005. Fax: (928)284-2477. E-mail: editorial@swimmingworldmagazine.com. Website: www.swimmingworldmagazine.com. **30% freelance written**. Bimonthly magazine about competitive swimming. Readers are fitness-oriented adults from varied social and professional backgrounds who share swimming as part of their lifestyle. Submit 250-word synopsis of your article. Estab. 1960. Circ. 50,000. Byline given. Pays on publication. Buys all rights. Editorial lead time 2 months. Submit seasonal material 3 months in advance. Accepts queries by mail, e-mail, fax. Accepts simultaneous submissions. Responds in 1 month to queries. Guidelines available online.

- Included in this publication are *Swimming Technique*, *Swim Magazine*, and *Junior Swimmer*.

Nonfiction Articles need to be informative as well as interesting. In addition to fitness and health articles, we are interested in exploring fascinating topics dealing with swimming for the adult reader. Needs book excerpts, essays, expose, general interest, historical, how-to, training plans and techniques, humor, inspirational, interview, people associated with fitness and competitive swimming, new product, articles describing new products for fitness and competitive training, personal experience, photo feature, technical, travel, general health. **Buys 30 mss/year.** Query. Length: 250-2,500 words. **Pays $75-400.**

Photos Send photos Captions, identification of subjects, model releases required. Reviews high-resolution digital images. Negotiates payment individually.

$ THE WATER SKIER

USA Water Ski, 1251 Holy Cow Rd., Polk City FL 33868-8200. (863)324-4341. Fax: (863)325-8259. E-mail: satkinson@usawaterski.org. Website: www.usawaterski.org. **10-20% freelance written**. Magazine published 7 times/year. *The Water Skier* is the membership magazine of USA Water Ski, the national governing body for organized water skiing in the United States. The magazine has a controlled circulation and is available only to USA Water Ski's membership, which is made up of 20,000 active competitive water skiers and 10,000 members who are supporting the sport. These supporting members may participate in the sport but they don't compete. The editorial content of the magazine features distinctive and informative writing about the sport of water skiing only. Estab. 1951. Circ. 30,000. Byline given. Offers 30% kill fee. Editorial lead time 4 months. Submit seasonal material 6 months in advance. Responds in 2 weeks to queries. Sample copy for $3.50. Guidelines for #10 SASE.

Nonfiction Needs historical, has to pertain to water skiing, interview, call for assignment, new product, boating and water ski equipment, travel, water ski vacation destinations. **Buys 10-15 mss/year.** Query. Length: 1,500-3,000 words. **Pays $100-150.**
Reprints Send photocopy. Payment negotiable.
Photos State availability Captions, identification of subjects required. Reviews contact sheets. Negotiates payment individually. Buys all rights.
Columns/Departments The Water Skier News (small news items about people and events in the sport), 400-500 words. Other topics include safety, training (3-event, barefoot, disabled, show ski, ski race, kneeboard, and wakeboard); champions on their way; new products. Query. **Pays $50-100.**
Tips Contact the editor through a query letter (please, no phone calls) with an idea. Avoid instruction, these articles are written by professionals. Concentrate on articles about the people of the sport. We are always looking for interesting stories about people in the sport. Also, short news features which will make a reader say to himself, `Hey, I didn't know that.' Keep in mind that the publication is highly specialized about the sport of water skiing.

TEEN & YOUNG ADULT

$ $ BREAKAWAY MAGAZINE

Focus on the Family, 8605 Explorer Dr., Colorado Springs CO 80920. (719)531-3400. Website: www.breakawaymag.com. **25% freelance written**. Monthly magazine covering extreme sports, Christian music artists, and new technology relevant to teen boys. This fast-paced, 4-color publication is designed to creatively teach, entertain, inspire, and challenge the emerging teenager. It also seeks to strengthen a boy's self-esteem, provide role models, guide a healthy awakening to girls, make the Bible relevant, and deepen their love for family, friends, church, and Jesus Christ. Estab. 1990. Circ. 90,000. Byline given. Pays on acceptance. Offers $25 kill fee. Publishes ms an average of 5-12 months after acceptance. Buys first North American serial rights, buys first rights, buys one-time rights, buys electronic rights. Editorial lead time 5 months. Submit seasonal material 8 months in advance. Accepts queries by mail. Responds in 2-3 months to queries. Responds in 2-3 months to mss. Sample copy for $1.50 and 9x12 SASE with 3 first-class stamps. Guidelines for #10 SASE.
Nonfiction Needs inspirational, interview, personal experience. **Buys up to 6 mss/year.** Send complete ms. Length: 700-2,000 words. **Pays 12-15¢/word.**
Columns/Departments Epic Truth (spiritual/Biblical application devotional for teen guys), 800 words; Weird, Wild, WOW! (technology, culture, science), 200-400 words. 2-3 Send complete ms. **Pays 12-15¢/word**
Fiction Needs adventure, humorous, religious, suspense. Avoid Christian jargon, clichÃ^s, preaching, and other dialogue that isn't realistic or that interrupts the flow of the story. **Buys 3-4 mss/year.** Send complete ms. Length: 600-2,000 words. **Pays 15-20¢/word.**
Tips Some of our readers get spiritual nurture at home and at church; many don't. To reach both groups, the articles must be written in ways that are compelling, bright, out of the ordinary. Nearly every adult in a boy's life is an authority figure. We would like you, through the magazine, to be seen as a friend! We also want *Breakaway* to be a magazine any pre-Christian teen could pick up and understand without first learning 'Christianese.' Stories should spiritually challenge, yet be spiritually inviting.

$ $ CICADA MAGAZINE

Cricket Magazine Group, 140 S. Dearborn St., Suite 1450, Chicago IL 60603. (312)701-1720. Fax: (312)701-1728. Website: www.cricketmag.com. **80% freelance written**. Bimonthly literary magazine for ages 14 and up. Publishes original short stories, poems, and first-person essays written for teens and young adults. Estab. 1998. Circ. 17,000. Byline given. Pays on publication. Accepts previously published material. Accepts simultaneous submissions. Responds in 3 months to mss. Guidelines available online.
Nonfiction Looking for first-person experiences that are relevant and interesting to teenagers. Needs essays, personal experience, book reviews. Submit complete ms, SASE. 5,000 words maximum; 300-500 words/book reviews. **Pays up to 25¢/word.**
Reprints Send typed manuscript. Payment varies.
Photos Send photocopies/tearsheets of artwork.
Fiction The main protagonist should be at least 14 and preferably older. Stories should have a genuine teen sensibility and be aimed at readers in high school or college. Needs adventure, fantasy, historical, humorous, mainstream, novel concepts, romance, science fiction, contemporary, realistic, novellas (1/issue). 5,000 words maximum (up to 15,000 words/novellas). **Pays up to 25¢/word.**
Poetry Needs free verse, light verse, traditional. 25 lines maximum. **Pays up to $3/line.**

$ $ $ $ COSMOGIRL!

A Cool New Magazine for Teens, The Hearst Corp., 224 W. 57th St., 3rd Floor, New York NY 10019. (212)649-3852. E-mail: inbox@cosmogirl.com. Website: www.cosmogirl.com. Monthly magazine covering fashion, beauty, photos and profiles of young celebs, advice, health and fitness, dating, relationships and finance. CosmoGIRL! has the voice of a cool older sister. The magazine is conversational, funny, down-to-earth, and honest. We never talk down to our readers, who are 12- to 22-year-old young women. Estab. 1999. Circ. 1,350,000. Byline given. Offers 25% kill fee. Buys all rights. Editorial lead time 3-4 months. Accepts queries by mail. Responds in 2 months to queries. Guidelines by email.

Nonfiction Contact: Look at the masthead of a current issue for the appropriate editor. Looking for features with a news bent that pertains to teenagers' lives; quizzes; relationship stories; dynamic first-person stories. Needs interview, opinion, personal experience. **Pays $1/ word.** Pays expenses of writers on assignment.

Photos Put name, phone # and address on back of all photos. Send photos

$ $ GUIDEPOSTS SWEET 16

1050 Broadway, Suite 6, Chesterton IN 46304. (219)929-4429. Fax: (219)926-3839. E-mail: writers@sweet16mag.com. Website: www.sweet16mag.com. **90% freelance written.** Bimonthly magazine serving as an inspiration for teens. *Sweet 16* is a general interest magazine for teenage girls (ages 11-17). We are an inspirational publication that offers true, first-person stories about real teens. Our watchwords are 'wholesome,' 'current,' 'fun,' and 'inspiring.' We also publish shorter pieces on fashion, beauty, celebrity, boys, embarrassing moments, and advice columns. Estab. 1998. Circ. 145,000. Byline sometimes given. Pays on acceptance. Offers 25% kill fee. Buys all rights. Editorial lead time 6 months. Submit seasonal material 6 months in advance. Accepts queries by mail, e-mail. Accepts simultaneous submissions. Responds in 6 weeks to queries. Responds in 6 weeks to mss. Sample copy for $4.50. Guidelines available online.

Nonfiction Nothing written from an adult point of view. Needs how-to, humor, inspirational, interview, personal experience. **Buys 80 mss/year.** Query. Length: 200-1,500 words. **Pays $300-500 for assigned articles. Pays $100-300 for unsolicited articles.** Pays expenses of writers on assignment.

Photos State availability Identification of subjects required. Negotiates payment individually. Buys one time rights.

Columns/Departments Quiz (teen-related topics/teen language), 500-600 words; Positive Thinker (first-person stories of teen who've overcome something remarkable and kept a positive outlook), 300 words; Mysterious Moments (first-person strange-but-true stories), 250 words; Too Good to be True (profile of a cute wholesome teen guy who has more than looks/has done something very cool/has overcome something extraordinary), 400 words. 40 Query with published clips. **Pays $175-400.**

Tips We are eagerly looking for a number of things: teen profiles, quizzes, DIYs. Most of all, though, we are about TRUE STORIES in the *Guideposts* tradition. Teens in dangerous, inspiring, miraculous situations. These first-person (ghostwritten) true narratives are the backbone of *Sweet 16*—and what sets us apart from other publications.

$ GUMBO MAGAZINE

The National Magazine Written by Teens for Teens, Strive Media Institute, 1818 N. Dr. Martin Luther King Dr., Milwaukee WI 53212. (414)374-3511. Fax: (414)374-3512. E-mail: info@mygumbo.com. Website: www.mygumbo.com. **25% freelance written.** Bimonthly magazine covering teen issues (arts, entertainment, social issues, etc.). All articles must be written by teens (13-19 year-olds) and for teens. Tone is modern, hip, and urban. No adults may write for magazine. Estab. 1998. Circ. 25,000. Byline given. Pays on publication. No kill fee. Publishes ms an average of 6 months after acceptance. Buys one-time rights. Editorial lead time 6 months. Submit seasonal material 6 months in advance. Accepts queries by mail, e-mail, fax. Accepts previously published material. Accepts simultaneous submissions. Responds in 2 weeks to queries. Responds in 2 months to mss. Sample copy free. Guidelines free.

Nonfiction Needs general interest, humor, inspirational, interview, opinion, personal experience, photo feature, technical, book & CD reviews. Does not want unsolicited articles or fiction other than poetry. All news stories require approval from Managing Editor prior to submission. **Buys 50-70 mss/year.** Query. Length: 500-1,000 words. **Pays $25.** Sometimes pays expenses of writers on assignment.

Photos State availability of or send photos Captions, identification of subjects required. Reviews prints, GIF/JPEG files. Offers no additional payment for photos accepted with ms. Buys one time rights.

Poetry Needs avant-garde, free verse, haiku, light verse, traditional. Any poetry is acceptable provided author is 13-19 years of age. Submit maximum 3 poems. Length: 5-50 lines.

Tips Writers need to apply online or mail in an application from an issue of the magazine.

$ $ IGNITE YOUR FAITH

465 Gundersen Dr., Carol Stream IL 60188. (630)260-6200. Fax: (630)480-2004. E-mail: iyf@igniteyourfaith.com. Website: www.igniteyourfaith.com. **35% freelance written.** Bimonthly magazine published 9 times/year for the Christian life as it relates to today's teen. "*Ignite Your Faith* is a magazine for high-school

teenagers. Our editorial slant is not overtly religious. The indirect style is intended to create a safety zone with our readers and to reflect our philosophy that God is interested in all of life. Therefore, we publish `message stories' side by side with general interest, humor, etc. We are also looking for stories that help high school students consider a Christian college education." Estab. 1942. Circ. 100,000. Byline given. Pays on acceptance. Offers 50% kill fee. Publishes ms an average of 5 months after acceptance. Buys first rights, buys one-time rights. Editorial lead time 4 months. Responds in 6 weeks to queries. Sample copy for $3 and 9½x11 SAE with 3 first-class stamps. Guidelines available online.

- No unsolicited mss.

Nonfiction Needs humor, personal experience, photo feature. **Buys 15-20 mss/year.** Query with published clips. Length: 750-1,500 words. **Pays 15-20¢/word minimum.**
Reprints Send tearsheet, photocopy or typed ms with rights for sale noted and information about when and where the material previously appeared. Pays $50.
Fiction Contact: Chris Lutes, editor. **Buys 1-5/year mss/year.** Query. Length: 1,000-1,500 words. **Pays 20-25¢/word, and 2 contributor's copies.**
Tips "The best way to break in to *Ignite Your Faith* is through writing first-person or as-told-to first-person stories. We want stories that capture a teen's everyday `life lesson' experience. A first-person story must be highly descriptive and incorporate fictional technique. While avoiding simplistic religious answers, the story should demonstrate that Christian values or beliefs brought about a change in the young person's life. But query first with theme information telling the way this story would work for our audience."

$ INSIGHT

Because Life Is Full of Decisions, The Review and Herald Publishing Association, 55 W. Oak Ridge Dr., Hagerstown MD 21740. (301)393-4038. E-mail: insight@rhpa.org. Website: www.insightmagazine.org. **80% freelance written.** Weekly magazine covering spiritual life of teenagers. *Insight* publishes true dramatic stories, interviews, and community and mission service features that relate directly to the lives of Christian teenagers, particularly those with a Seventh-day Adventist background. Estab. 1970. Circ. 20,000. Byline given. Pays on publication. No kill fee. Publishes ms an average of 4 months after acceptance. Buys first rights, buys second serial (reprint) rights. Editorial lead time 6 months. Submit seasonal material 6 months in advance. Accepts queries by mail, e-mail, fax. Responds in 1 month to mss. Sample copy for $2 and #10 SASE. Guidelines available online.

- 'Big Deal' appears in *Insight* often, covering a topic of importance to teens. Each feature contains: An opening story involving real teens (can be written in first-person), Scripture Picture (a sidebar that discusses what the Bible says about the topic) and another sidebar (optional) that adds more perspective and help.

Nonfiction Needs how-to, teen relationships and experiences, humor, interview, personal experience, photo feature, religious. **Buys 120 mss/year.** Send complete ms. Length: 500-2,000 words. **Pays $25-150 for assigned articles. Pays $25-125 for unsolicited articles.**
Reprints Send typed manuscript with rights for sale noted and information about when and where the material previously appeared. Pays $50.
Photos State availability Model releases required. Reviews contact sheets, negatives, transparencies, prints. Negotiates payment individually. Buys one time rights.
Columns/Departments Big Deal (topic of importance to teens) 1,200-1,700 words; Interviews (Christian culture figures, especially musicians), 2,000 words; It Happened to Me (first-person teen experiences containing spiritual insights), 1,000 words; On the Edge (dramatic true stories about Christians), 2,000 words; So I Said.(true short stories in the first person of common, everyday events and experiences that taught the writer something), 300-500 words. Send complete ms. **Pays $25-125.**
Tips Skim 2 months of *Insight*. Write about your teen experiences. Use informed, contemporary style and vocabulary. Follow Jesus' life and example.

$ $ LISTEN MAGAZINE

Celebrating Positive Choices, The Health Connection, 55 W. Oak Ridge Dr., Hagerstown MD 21740. (301)393-4010. E-mail: editor@listenmagazine.org. Website: www.listenmagazine.org. **80% freelance written**. Monthly magazine specializing in tobacco, drug, and alcohol prevention, presenting positive alternatives to various tobacco, drug, and alcohol dependencies. *Listen* is used in many high school classes and by professionals: medical personnel, counselors, law enforcement officers, educators, youth workers, etc. *Listen* publishes true stories about giving teens choices about real-life situations and moral issues in a secular way. Circ. 20,000. Byline given. Publishes ms an average of 6 months after acceptance. Pays on acceptance for first rights for use in *Listen*, reprints, and associated material. Accepts queries by mail, e-mail. Accepts previously published material. Accepts simultaneous submissions. Responds in 2 months to queries. Sample copy for $2 and 9x12 SASE. Guidelines available online.
Nonfiction Seeks articles on positive, practical ways in which teens can cope with everyday conflicts and develop self-esteem. Subjects may or may not have a direct connection to drug use. Especially interested

in youth-slanted articles or personality interviews encouraging nonalcoholic and nondrug ways of life and showing positive alternatives. Also interested in good activity articles of interest to teens; sports or hobbies to interest a teen. Teenage point of view is essential. **Pays $150 for Personalities (1,000 words); $125 for hobby/sport/activity (800 words); $100 for factuals (800 words); $80 for true stories and self-help/ social skills articles (800 words); $50 for quizzes (500 words); and 3 contributor's copies (additional copies $2). Buys 30-50 unsolicited mss/year.** Query.

Reprints Send photocopy of article or typed ms with rights for sale ted and information about when and where the material previously appeared. Pays their regular rates.

Photos Color photos preferred, but b&w acceptable. Captions required. Purchased with accompanying ms.

Tips In query, briefly summarize article idea and logic of why you feel it's good. Make sure you've read the magazine to understand our approach. Yearly theme lists available on our Web site.

$ $ LIVE

A Weekly Journal of Practical Christian Living, Gospel Publishing House, 1445 N. Boonville Ave., Springfield MO 65802-1894. (417)862-1447. Fax: (417)862-6059. E-mail: rl-live@gph.org. Website: www.radiantlife.org. **100% freelance written.** Weekly magazine for weekly distribution covering practical Christian living. *LIVE* is a take-home paper distributed weekly in young adult and adult Sunday school classes. We seek to encourage Christians in living for God through fiction and true stories which apply Biblical principles to everyday problems. Estab. 1928. Circ. 50,000. Byline given. Pays on acceptance. No kill fee. Publishes ms an average of 18 months after acceptance. Buys first rights, buys second serial (reprint) rights. Editorial lead time 12 months. Submit seasonal material 18 months in advance. Accepts queries by mail, e-mail. Accepts simultaneous submissions. Responds in 2 weeks to queries. Responds in 6 weeks to mss. Sample copy for #10 SASE. Guidelines for #10 SASE or on website.

Nonfiction Needs inspirational, religious. No preachy articles or stories that refer to religious myths (e.g., Santa Claus, Easter Bunny, etc.) **Buys 50-100 mss/year.** Send complete ms. Length: 400-1,200 words. **Pays 7-10¢/word.**

Reprints Send tearsheet, photocopy or typed ms with rights for sale noted and information about when and where the material previously appeared. Pays 7¢/word.

Photos Send photos Identification of subjects required. Reviews 35mm transparencies and 3 x 4 prints or larger. Offers $35-60/photo. Buys one time rights.

Fiction Contact: Paul W. Smith, editor. Needs religious, inspirational, prose poem. No preachy fiction, fiction about Bible characters, or stories that refer to religious myths (e.g., Santa Claus, Easter Bunny, etc.). No science or Bible fiction. No controversial stories about such subjects as feminism, war or capital punishment. **Buys 20-50 mss/year.** Send complete ms. Length: 800-1,200 words. **Pays 7-10¢/word.**

Poetry Needs free verse, haiku, light verse, traditional. **Buys 15-24 poems/year.** Submit maximum 3 poems. Length: 12-25 lines. **Pays $35-60.**

Fillers Needs anecdotes, short humor. 12-36 Length: 300-600 words. **7-10¢/word.**

Tips Don't moralize or be preachy. Provide human interest articles with Biblical life application. Stories should consist of action, not just thought-life; interaction, not just insight. Heroes and heroines should rise above failures, take risks for God, prove that scriptural principles meet their needs. Conflict and suspense should increase to a climax! Avoid pious conclusions. Characters should be interesting, believable, and re-alistic. Avoid stereotypes. Characters should be active, not just pawns to move the plot along. They should confront conflict and change in believable ways. Describe the character's looks and reveal his personality through his actions to such an extent that the reader feels he has met that person. Readers should care about the character enough to finish the story. Feature racial, ethnic, and regional characters in rural and urban settings.

$ $ THE NEW ERA

50 E. North Temple, Salt Lake City UT 84150. (801)240-2951. Fax: (801)240-2270. E-mail: newera@ldschurch.org. Website: www.newera.lds.org. **Contact:** Richard M. Romney, managing editor. **20% freelance written.** Monthly magazine for young people (ages 12-18) of the Church of Jesus Christ of Latter-day Saints (Mormon), their church leaders and teachers. Estab. 1971. Circ. 230,000. Byline given. Pays on acceptance. No kill fee. Publishes ms an average of 1 year after acceptance. Buys all rights. Submit seasonal material 1 year in advance. Accepts queries by mail, e-mail, fax. Responds in 2 months to queries. Sample copy for $1.50. Guidelines available online.

Nonfiction "Material that shows how the Church of Jesus Christ of Latter-day Saints is relevant in the lives of young people today. Must capture the excitement of being a young Latter-day Saint. Special interest in the experiences of young Mormons in other countries. No general library research or formula pieces without the *New Era* slant and feel." Needs how-to, humor, inspirational, interview, personal experience, informational. Query. Length: 150-1,200 words. **Pays $25-350/article.**

Photos Uses b&w photos and transparencies with manuscripts. Individual photos used for *Photo of the*

Month Payment depends on use, $10-125 per photo.
Columns/Departments What's Up? (news of young Mormons around the world); How I Know; Scripture Lifeline. **Pays $25-125/article.**
Poetry Needs free verse, light verse, traditional, all other forms. Must relate to editorial viewpoint. **Pays $25 and up.**
Tips "The writer must be able to write from a Mormon point of view. We're especially looking for stories about successful family relationships and personal growth. Well-written, personal experiences are always in demand."

$ $ SAFE & STYLISH

TBRA Publishing, LLC, P.O. Box 632426, Nacogdoches TX 75963. Fax: (936)560-4155. E-mail: michael@tobereadaloud.org. Website: www.tobereadaloud.org. **100% freelance written.** Semiannual magazine covering issues related to prom and graduation for high school junior and senior students. Keep the 17-reader in mind. Write about issues related to style, safety or college. What did you wish you knew when you were 17? Estab. 2007. Circ. 40,000. Byline sometimes given. Pays on publication. Offers $25 kill fee. Publishes ms an average of 4 months after acceptance. Makes work-for-hire assignments. Editorial lead time 4-6 months. Submit seasonal material 4-6 months in advance. Accepts queries by mail, e-mail, fax. Responds in 4-6 weeks to queries. Sample copy for #10 SASE. Guidelines by email.
Nonfiction Needs essays, expose, how-to, humor, inspirational, interview, new product, personal experience, photo feature, travel, fashion advice. How to survive as a college freshman; staying safe and having fun on prom night; getting big scholarships for college. **Buys 4-8 mss/year.** Query. Length: 300-1,200 words. **Pays $100-500 for assigned articles. Pays $50-250 for unsolicited articles.** Sometimes pays expenses of writers on assignment.
Photos State availability Reviews GIF/JPEG files. Offers no additional payment for photos accepted with ms. Buys one time rights.
Columns/Departments Mission Accessorize (hair, make-up, shoes), 400 words; Ask Momma Dora (advice column), 200 words. 6-8 Query. **Pays $100-500.**
Fiction Needs adventure, humorous, mystery, romance, suspense. Does not want erotica. **Buys 2 mss/year.** Query. Length: 600-1,000 words. **Pays $100-500.**
Poetry Needs free verse. **Buys 2 poems/year.** Submit maximum 5 poems. Length: 8-40 lines.
Fillers Needs anecdotes, facts, gags, newsbreaks, short humor. 3-5 Length: 30-200 words. **Pays $50-250.**
Tips Any advice a 17 year old doesn't know (and couldn't find in a 5-minute Google search) in the areas of prom, relationships, college and safety.

SCHOLASTIC ACTION

Scholastic, Inc., 557 Broadway, New York NY 10012-3902. (212)343-6100. Fax: (212)343-6945. E-mail: actionmag@scholastic.com. Website: www.scholastic.com. Published 14 times/year. Written for teenagers with profiles of TV and movie celebrities and famous athletes. It also includes true teen nonfiction articles and vocabulary activities. Circ. 200,000. No kill fee. Editorial lead time 2 months.

$ $ $ $ SEVENTEEN

1440 Broadway, 13th Floor, New York NY 10018. (917)934-6500. Fax: (917)934-6574. Website: www.seventeen.com. **20% freelance written.** Monthly magazine. *Seventeen* is a young woman's first fashion and beauty magazine. Tailored for young women in their teens and early twenties, *Seventeen* covers fashion, beauty, health, fitness, food, college, entertainment, fiction, plus crucial personal and global issues. Estab. 1944. Circ. 2,400,000. Byline given. Pays on acceptance. Offers 25% kill fee. Publishes ms an average of 6 months after acceptance. Buys one-time rights. Accepts queries by mail. Responds in 3 months to queries. Writer's guidelines available online
Nonfiction Articles and features of general interest to young women who are concerned with intimate relationships and how to realize their potential in the world; strong emphasis on topicality and service. Send brief outline and query, including typical lead paragraph, summing up basic idea of article, with clips of previously published works. Articles are commissioned after outlines are submitted and approved. Length: 1,200-2,500 words. **Pays $1/word, occasionally more.** Pays expenses of writers on assignment.
Photos Photos usually by assignment only.
Tips Writers have to ask themselves whether or not they feel they can find the right tone for a *Seventeen* article—a tone which is empathetic, yet never patronizing; lively, yet not superficial. Not all writers feel comfortable with, understand, or like teenagers. If you don't like them, *Seventeen* is the wrong market for you. An excellent way to break in to the magazine is by contributing ideas for quizzes or the 'My Story' (personal essay) column.

$ $ TEEN MAGAZINE

Hearst Magazines, 3000 Ocean Park Blvd., Suite 3048, Santa Monica CA 90405. (310)664-2950. Fax: (310)664-2959. Website: www.teenmag.com. Quarterly magazine. for a Jr. high school female audience; median age is 14 years old. *TEEN* teens are upbeat and want to be informed. Estab. 1957. Pays on acceptance. No kill fee. Buys all rights.

- Bylines not guaranteed.

Nonfiction Does not want to see adult-oriented, adult point of view. **Pays $200-600.**
Fiction Does not want to see that which does not apply to our market—i.e., science fiction, history, religious, adult-oriented. **Pays $$200-800-400.**

$ WINNER

Saying No To Drugs and Yes To Life, The Health Connection, 55 W. Oak Ridge Dr., Hagerstown MD 21740. (301)393-4082. Fax: (301)393-4088. E-mail: winner@healthconnection.org. Website: www.winnermagazine.org. **30% freelance written**. Monthly magazine covering positive lifestyle choices for students in grades 4-6. *Winner* is a teaching tool to help students learn the dangers in abusive substances, such as tobacco, alcohol, and other drugs, as well as at-risk behaviors. It also focuses on everyday problems such as dealing with divorce, sibling rivalry, coping with grief, and healthy diet, to mention just a few. Estab. 1956. Circ. 12,000. Byline sometimes given. Pays on acceptance. Offers 50% kill fee. Publishes ms an average of 6-9 months after acceptance. Buys first North American serial rights, buys first rights. Editorial lead time 5 months. Submit seasonal material 6-8 months in advance. Accepts queries by mail, e-mail, fax, phone. Accepts simultaneous submissions. Responds in 4-6 weeks to queries. Responds in 2-3 months to mss. Sample copy for $2 and 9x12 SAE with 2 first-class stamps. Guidelines for SASE, by e-mail, fax or on website.
Nonfiction Needs general interest, humor, drug/alcohol/tobacco activities, personalities, family relationships, friends. No occult, mysteries. I prefer true-to-life stories. Query or send complete ms. Length: 600-650 words. **Pays $50-80.** Sometimes pays expenses of writers on assignment.
Photos State availability of or send photos Model releases required. Reviews GIF/JPEG files. Negotiates payment individually. Buys one time rights.
Columns/Departments Personality (kids making a difference in their community), 600-650 words; Fun & Games (dangers of tobacco, alcohol, and other drugs), 400 words. 9 Query. **Pays $50-80.**
Fiction No suspense or mystery. **Buys 18 mss/year.** Send complete ms. Length: 600-650 words. **Pays $50-80.**

$ $ YOUNG SALVATIONIST

The Salvation Army, P.O. Box 269, Alexandria VA 22313-0269. (703)684-5500. Fax: (703)684-5539. E-mail: ys@usn.salvationarmy.org. **Contact:** Captain Amy Reardon. **10% freelance written**. Monthly magazine for high school and early college youth. Only material with Christian perspective with practical real-life application will be considered. Circ. 48,000. Byline given. Pays on acceptance. No kill fee. Publishes ms an average of 6 months after acceptance. Buys first North American serial rights, buys first rights, buys one-time rights, buys second serial (reprint) rights. Submit seasonal material 6 months in advance. Accepts queries by Accepts complete mss by mail and e-mail. Responds in 2 months to mss. Sample copy for 9 x 12 SAE with 3 first-class stamps or on website. Writer's guidelines and theme list for #10 SASE or on website.

- "Works with a small number of new/unpublished writers each year."

Nonfiction "Articles should deal with issues of relevance to young people today; avoid 'preachiness' or moralizing." Needs how-to, humor, inspirational, interview, personal experience, photo feature, religious. **Buys 10 mss/year.** Send complete ms. Length: 1,000-1,500 words. **Pays 15¢/word for first rights.**
Reprints Send tearsheet, photocopy or typed ms with rights for sale noted and information about when and where the material previously appeared. Pays 10¢/word for reprints.
Fiction Only a small amount is used. Needs adventure, fantasy, humorous, religious, romance, science fiction, (all from a Christian perspective). **Buys few mss/year.** Length: 500-1,200 words. **Pays 15¢/word.**
Tips "Study magazine, familiarize yourself with the unique `Salvationist' perspective of *Young Salvationist*; learn a little about the Salvation Army; media, sports, sex, and dating are strongest appeal."

TRAVEL, CAMPING & TRAILER

$ AAA GOING PLACES

Magazine for Today's Traveler, AAA Auto Club South, 1515 N. Westshore Blvd., Tampa FL 33607. (813)289-5923. Fax: (813)288-7935. **50% freelance written**. Bimonthly magazine on auto tips, cruise travel, tours. Estab. 1982. Circ. 2,500,000. Byline given. Pays on publication. No kill fee. Publishes ms an average of 6 months after acceptance. Buys one-time rights. Submit seasonal material 9 months in advance. Accepts simultaneous submissions. Responds in 2 months to mss. Writer's guidelines for SAE.
Nonfiction Travel stories feature domestic and international destinations with practical information and where to stay, dine, and shop, as well as personal anecdotes and historical background. Needs historical,

how-to, humor, interview, personal experience, photo feature, travel. **Buys 15 mss/year.** Send complete ms. Length: 500-1,200 words. **Pays $50/printed page.**

Photos State availability Captions required. Reviews 2—Š2 transparencies, 300 dpi digital images. Offers no additional payment for photos accepted with ms

Columns/Departments What's Happening (local attractions in Florida, Georgia, or Tennessee).

Tips We prefer lively, upbeat stories that appeal to a well-traveled, sophisticated audience, bearing in mind that AAA is a conservative company.

$ $ RECREATION NEWS

Official Publication of the RecGov.org, 204 Greenwood Rd., Linthicum MD 21090. (410)944-4852. Website: www.recreationnews.com. **Contact:** Marvin Bond, editor. **75% freelance written**. Monthly guide to leisure-time activities for federal and private industry workers covering Mid-Atlantic travel destinations, outdoor recreation, and cultural activities. Estab. 1982. Circ. 115,000. Byline given. Pays on publication. No kill fee. Publishes ms an average of 6 months after acceptance. Buys first rights, buys second serial (reprint) rights. Submit seasonal material 10 months in advance. Accepts queries by mail, e-mail, phone. Accepts previously published material. Accepts simultaneous submissions. Responds in 2 months to queries. See sample copy and writer's guidelines online

Nonfiction Needs Mid-Atlantic travel destinations, outdoor recreation. skiing (December), golf (April), Theme Parks (July) Query with published clips or links. Length: 600-900 words. **Pays $50-300.**

Reprints Send tearsheet or typed ms with rights for sale noted and information about when and where the material previously appeared. Pays $50.

Tips "Our articles are lively and conversational and deal with specific travel destinations in the Mid-Atlantic. We do not buy international or Caribbean stories. Outdoor recreation of all kinds is good, but avoid first-person narrative. Stories need to include info on nearby places of interest, places to eat, and places to stay. Keep contact information in separate box at end of story."

$ $ AAA MIDWEST TRAVELER

AAA Auto Club of Missouri, 12901 N. 40 Dr., St. Louis MO 63141. (314)523-7350 ext. 6301. Fax: (314)523-6982. E-mail: dreinhardt@aaamissouri.com. **Contact:** Deborah Reinhardt, Managing Editor. **80% freelance written**. Bimonthly magazine covering travel and automotive safety. "We provide members with useful information on travel, auto safety and related topics." Estab. 1901. Circ. 500,000. Byline given. Pays on acceptance. Offers $50 kill fee. Buys first North American serial rights, buys second serial (reprint) rights, buys electronic rights. Editorial lead time 1 year. Submit seasonal material 6 months in advance. Accepts queries by mail, e-mail, fax. Accepts simultaneous submissions. Responds in 1 month to queries. Responds in 1 month to mss. Sample copy for sae with 10x13 envelope and 4 First-Class stamps. Guidelines for #10 SASE.

Nonfiction Needs travel. No humor, fiction, poetry or cartoons. **Buys 20-30 mss/year.** Query; query with published clips the first time. Length: 800-1,200 words. **Pays $400.**

Photos State availability Captions required. Reviews transparencies, prints . Offers no additional payment for photos accepted with ms Buys one-time and electronic rights

Tips "Send queries between December and February, as we plan our calendar for the following year. Request a copy. Serious writers ask for media kit to help them target their piece. Send a SASE or download online. Travel destinations and tips are most open to freelancers; all departments and auto-related news handled by staff. We see too many `Here's a recount of our family vacation' manuscripts. Go easy on first-person accounts."

$ $ ARUBA NIGHTS

Nights Publications, Inc., 1751 Richardson St., Suite 5.530, Montreal QC H3K 1G6 Canada. (514)931-1987. Fax: (514)931-6273. E-mail: editor@nightspublications.com. Website: www.nightspublications.com. **Contact:** Jennifer McMorran, ed. **90% freelance written**. Annual magazine covering the Aruban vacation lifestyle experience with an upscale, upbeat touch. Estab. 1988. Circ. 245,000. Byline given for feature articles. Pays on acceptance. No kill fee. Publishes ms an average of 9 months after acceptance. Buys North American and Caribbean serial rights. Editorial lead time 1 month. Accepts queries by mail, e-mail, fax. Responds in 2 weeks to queries. Responds in 1 month to mss. Guidelines by email.

- "Let the reader experience the story; utilize the senses; be descriptive; be specific."

Nonfiction Needs general interest, historical, how-to, relative to Aruba vacationers, humor, inspirational, interview, opinion, personal experience, photo feature, travel, ecotourism, Aruban culture, art, activities, entertainment, topics relative to vacationers in Aruba. No negative pieces. **Buys 5-15 mss/year.** Query with published clips. Email queries preferred. Length: 250-750 words. **Pays $100-300.**

Photos State availability Captions, identification of subjects, model releases required. Reviews transparencies. Pays $50/photo Buys one time rights.

Tips "Be descriptive and entertaining and make sure stories are factually correct. Stories should immerse the reader in a sensory adventure. Focus on specific, individual aspects of the Aruban lifestyle and vacation experience (e.g., art, music, culture, a colorful local character, a personal experience, etc.), rather than generalized overviews. Magazine caters to visitors who are already on Aruba, so ensure your story is of interest to this audience."

$ $ ASU TRAVEL GUIDE

ASU Travel Guide, Inc., 448 Ignacio Blvd. #333, Novato CA 94949. (415)898-9500. Fax: (415)898-9501. E-mail: editor@asutravelguide.com. Website: www.asutravelguide.com. **80% freelance written.** Quarterly guidebook covering international travel features and travel discounts for well-traveled airline employees. Estab. 1970. Circ. 36,000. Byline given. Pays on acceptance. No kill fee. Publishes ms an average of 4 months after acceptance. Buys first North American serial rights, buys first rights, buys second serial (reprint) rights. Submit seasonal material 6 months in advance. Accepts previously published material. Accepts simultaneous submissions. Responds in 1 year to queries. Responds in 1 year to mss. Sample copy for sae with 6x9 envelope and 5 First-Class stamps. Guidelines for #10 SASE.

Nonfiction International travel articles similar to those run in consumer magazines. Not interested in amateur efforts from inexperienced travelers or personal experience articles that don't give useful information to other travelers. Destination pieces only; no Tips on Luggage articles. Unsolicited mss or queries without SASE will not be acknowledged. No telephone queries. Needs travel, international. **Buys 12 mss/year.** Length: 1,800 words. **Pays $200.**

Reprints Send tearsheet and information about when and where the material previously appeared. Pays 100% of amount paid for an original article

Photos Interested in clear, high-contrast photos. Reviews 5x7 and 8x10 b&w or color prints, JPEGs (300 dpi). Payment for photos is included in article price; photos from tourist offices are acceptable.

Tips Query with samples of travel writing and a list of places you've recently visited. We appreciate clean and simple style. Keep verbs in the active tense and involve the reader in what you write. Avoid `cute' writing, coined words, and stale clichés. The most frequent mistakes made by writers in completing an article for us are: 1) Lazy writing—using words to describe a place that could describe any destination such as `there is so much to do in (fill in destination) that whole guidebooks have been written about it'; 2) Including fare and tour package information—our readers make arrangements through their own airline.

$ ✪ BONAIRE NIGHTS

Nights Publications, Inc., 1751 Richardson St., Suite 5.530, Montreal QC H3K 1G6 Canada. (514)931-1987. Fax: (514)931-6273. E-mail: editor@nightspublications.com. **90% freelance written.** Annual magazine covering Bonaire vacation experience. Estab. 1993. Circ. 80,000. Byline given for features. No kill fee. Buys North American and Caribbean serial rights. Editorial lead time 1 month. Accepts queries by mail, e-mail, fax. Responds in 2 weeks to queries. Responds in 1 month to mss. Guidelines by email.

Nonfiction Needs general interest, historical, how-to, humor, interview, opinion, personal experience, photo feature, travel, lifestyle, local culture, art, architecture, activities, scuba diving, snorkeling, ecotourism. **Buys 6-9 mss/year.** E-mail submissions preferred. Mailed mss must include an e-mail address for correspondence. Length: 250-750 words. **Pays $100.**

Photos State availability Captions, identification of subjects, model releases required. Pays $50/published photo.

Tips Focus on the Bonaire lifestyle, what sets it apart from other islands. We want personal experience on specific attractions and culture, not generalized overviews. Be positive and provide an angle that will appeal to vacationers who are already there. Our style is upbeat, friendly, fluid, and descriptive.

$ CAMPERWAYS, MIDWEST RV TRAVELER, FLORIDA RV TRAVELER, NORTHEAST OUTDOORS, SOUTHERN RV

Woodall Publications Corp., 2575 Vista Del Mar Dr., Ventura CA 93001. (888)656-6669. E-mail: info@woodallpub.com. Website: www.woodalls.com. **75%% freelance written.** Monthly tabloids covering RV lifestyle. We're looking for articles of interest to RVers. Lifestyle articles, destinations, technical tips, interesting events and the like make up the bulk of our publications. We also look for region-specific travel and special interest articles. Circ. 30,000. Byline given. Pays on acceptance. Offers 50% kill fee. Buys first North American serial rights. Accepts queries by mail, e-mail. Sample copy free. Guidelines for #10 SASE.

- Accepts queries in June, July, and August for upcoming year.

Nonfiction Needs how-to, personal experience, technical, travel. No Camping From Hell articles. **Buys approximately 500 mss/year.** Length: 500-2,000 words. **Payment varies**

Photos Prefers slides and large (5x7, 300 dpi) digital images. State availability Captions, identification of subjects required. Reviews negatives, 4—Š5 transparencies, 4—Š5 prints. Buys first North American serial rights

Tips Ã®Be an expert in RVing. Make your work readable to a wide variety of readers, from novices to full-timers.Ã®

$ 🅽 CAMPING TODAY

Official Publication of the Family Campers & RVers, 126 Hermitage Rd., Butler PA 16001-8509. (724)283-7401. Website: www.fcrv.org. **Contact:** DeWayne Johnston, ed. **30% freelance written.** Monthly official membership publication of the fcrv. "*Camping Today* is the largest nonprofit family camping and RV organization in the U.s. and Canada. Members are heavily oriented toward RV travel. Concentration is on member activities in chapters. Group is also interested in conservation and wildlife. The majority of members are retired." Estab. 1983. Circ. 10,000. Byline given. Pays on publication. No kill fee. Publishes ms an average of 6 months after acceptance. Buys one-time rights. Submit seasonal material 3 months in advance. Accepts simultaneous submissions. Responds in 2 months to queries and to mss. Sample copy and guidelines for 4 first-class stamps. Guidelines for #10 SASE.

Nonfiction Needs humor, camping or travel related, interview, interesting campers, new product, technical, RVs related, travel, interesting places to visit by RV, camping. **Buys 10-15 mss/year.** Query by mail only or send complete ms with photos. Length: 750-2,000 words. **Pays $50-150.**

Reprints Send typed manuscript with rights for sale noted and information about when and where the material previously appeared. Pays 35-50% of amount paid for original article

Photos Need b&w or sharp color prints. Send photos Captions required.

Tips "Freelance material on RV travel, RV maintenance/safety, and items of general camping interest throughout the United States and Canada will receive special attention. Good photos increase your chances. See website."

$ $ 🌐 CNN TRAVELLER

Highbury House, 47 Brunswick Place, London N1 6EB England. (44)(207)613-6949. E-mail: dan.hayes@ink-publishing.com. Website: www.cnntraveller.com. **50% freelance written.** Bimonthly magazine covering travel. *CNN Traveller* takes readers on a fascinating journey to some of the most intriguing and exotic places in the world. It marries the best in travel journalism and photography with the news values of CNN. The magazines takes an issues-led view of travel, getting behind the headlines with articles that are guaranteed to be intriguing and thought-provoking every issue. Estab. 1998. Circ. 106,500. Byline given. Pays 1 month after publication. Offers 50% kill fee. Publishes ms an average of 3 months after acceptance. Buys all rights. Editorial lead time 2-6 months. Submit seasonal material 4 months in advance. Accepts queries by e-mail, fax. Sample copy available online. Guidelines free.

Nonfiction Needs book excerpts, travel. **Buys 50 mss/year.** Query with published clips. Length: 600-2,000 words. **Pays £120-400 ($225-750) for assigned articles. Pays £100-400 ($190-750) for unsolicited articles.**

Photos State availability Captions required. Reviews GIF/JPEG files. Negotiates payment individually. Buys one time rights.

Columns/Departments 10 Query with published clips. **Pays £100-200 ($190-375).**

$ $ $ COAST TO COAST MAGAZINE

Affinity Group, Inc., 2575 Vista Del Mar Dr., Ventura CA 93001. (805)667-4100. E-mail: vlaw@affinitygroup.com. Website: www.coastresorts.com. **80% freelance written.** Magazine published 6 times/year for members of Coast to Coast Resorts. "*Coast to Coast* focuses on North American travel, outdoor recreation, camping and RV parks, 75,000 Estab. 1983. Byline given. Pays on acceptance. Offers 33% kill fee. Publishes ms an average of 4 months after acceptance. Buys first North American serial rights, prints and electronic. Editorial lead time 5 months. Submit seasonal material 5 months in advance. Accepts queries by mail, e-mail, fax. Accepts previously published material. Accepts simultaneous submissions. Responds in 6-8 weeks to queries. Responds in 1-2 months to mss Sample copy for $4 and 9x12 SASE Guidelines for #10 SASE

Nonfiction Needs book excerpts, essays, general interest, how-to, interview, new product, personal experience, photo feature, technical, travel. No poetry, cartoons. **Buys 70 mss/year.** Send complete ms. Length: 800-2,500 words. **Pays $75-1,200.**

Reprints Send photocopy and information about when and where the material previously appeared. Pays approximately 50% of amount paid for original article

Photos sharp, color-saturated high-res digital images, particularly of North American destinations and RV travel

Columns/Departments Pays $ 150-400.

Tips "Send clips or other writing samples with queries, or story ideas will not be considered."

$ $ 🅲 CURACAO NIGHTS

Nights Publications, Inc., 1751 Richardson St., Suite 5.530, Montreal QC H3K 1G6 Canada. (514)931-1987. Fax: (514)931-6273. E-mail: editor@nightspublications.com. **Contact:** Jennifer McMorran, ed.

90% freelance written. Annual magazine covering the Curacao vacation experience. "We are seeking upbeat, entertaining lifestyle articles; colorful profiles of locals; lively features on culture, activities, nightlife, ecotourism, special events, gambling, how-to features, humor. Our audience is North American vacationers." Estab. 1989. Circ. 165,000. Byline given. No kill fee. Buys North American and Caribbean serial rights. Editorial lead time 1 month. Accepts queries by mail, e-mail, fax. Responds in 2 weeks to queries. Responds in 1 month to mss. Guidelines by email.

Nonfiction Needs general interest, historical, how-to, help a vacationer get the most from their vacation, humor, interview, opinion, personal experience, photo feature, travel, ecotourism, lifestyle, local culture, art, activities, nightlife, topics relative to vacationers in Curacao. No negative pieces, generic copy, or stale rewrites. **Buys 5-10 mss/year.** Query with published clips; e-mail submissions are preferred. Length: 250-750 words. **Pays $100-300.**

Photos State availability Captions, identification of subjects, model releases required. Reviews transparencies. Pays $50/photo Buys one time rights.

Tips "Demonstrate your voice in your query letter. Focus on individual aspects of the island lifestyle and vacation experience (e.g., art, music, culture, a colorful local character, a personal experience, etc.), rather than a generalized overview. Provide an angle that will be entertaining to vacationers who are already on the island. Our style is upbeat, friendly, and fluid."

$ $ FAMILY MOTOR COACHING

Official Publication of the Family Motor Coach Association, 8291 Clough Pike, Cincinnati OH 45244. (513)474-3622. Fax: (513)388-5286. E-mail: magazine@fmca.com. Website: www.fmca.com. **Contact:** Robbin Gould, editor. **80% freelance written. We prefer that writers be experienced RVers.** Monthly magazine emphasizing travel by motorhome, motorhome mechanics, maintenance, and other technical information. "*Family Motor Coaching* magazine is edited for the members and prospective members of the Family Motor Coach Association who own or are about to purchase self-contained, motorized recreational vehicles known as motorhomes. Featured are articles on travel and recreation, association news and activities, plus articles on new products and motorhome maintenance and repair. Approximately 1/3 of editorial content is devoted to travel and entertainment, 1/3 to association news, and 1/3 to new products, industry news, and motorhome maintenance." Estab. 1963. Circ. 140,000. Byline given. Pays on acceptance. Publishes ms an average of 8 months after acceptance. Buys first North American serial rights and electronic rights. Submit seasonal material 4 months in advance. Accepts queries by mail, e-mail, fax. Responds in 3 months to queries. Sample copy for $3.99; $5 if paying by credit card. Guidelines for #10 SASE or request PDF by e-mail.

Nonfiction Needs how-to, do-it-yourself motorhome projects and modifications, humor, interview, new product, technical, motorhome travel (various areas of North America accessible by motorhome), bus conversions, nostalgia. **Buys 50-75 mss/year.** Query with published clips. Length: 1,000-2,000 words. **Pays $100-500, depending on article category.**

Photos State availability Captions, model releases, True required. Offers no additional payment for b&w contact sheets, 35mm 2¼x2¼ color transparencies, or high-resolution electronic images (300 dpi and at least 4x6 in size). Prefers first North American serial and electronic rights to editorial but will consider one-time rights on photos only.

Tips "The greatest number of contributions we receive are travel; therefore, that area is the most competitive. However, it also represents the easiest way to break in to our publication. Articles should be written for those traveling by self-contained motorhome. The destinations must be accessible to motorhome travelers and any peculiar road conditions should be mentioned."

$ GO MAGAZINE

AAA Carolinas, 6600 AAA Dr., Charlotte NC 28212. (704)569-7733. Fax: (704)569-7815. E-mail: trcrosby@aaaqa.com. Website: www.aaacarolinas.com. Bimonthly magazine covering travel, automotive, safety (traffic), and insurance. Consumer-oriented membership publication providing information on things such as car buying, vacations, travel safety problems, etc. Estab. 1928. Circ. 910,000. Pays on publication. No kill fee. Makes work-for-hire assignments. Editorial lead time 3-4 months. Accepts queries by mail, fax. Responds in 6 weeks to queries. Responds in 3 months to mss. Sample copy for sae with 1 envelope and 4 First-Class stamps. Guidelines for #10 SASE.

Nonfiction Needs how-to, fix auto, travel safety, etc., travel, automotive insurance, traffic safety. **Buys 16-18 mss/year.** Query with published clips. Length: 600-900 words. **Pays $150/published story.**

Photos Send photos Offers no additional payment for photos accepted with ms. Buys one time rights.

$ $ HIGHROADS

AAA Arizona, 3144 N. 7th Ave., Phoenix AZ 85013. (602)650-2732. Fax: (602)241-2917. E-mail: highroads@arizona.aaa.com. Website: www.aaa.com. **50% freelance written**. Bimonthly magazine covering Travel/Automotive. Our magazine goes out to our 470,000+ AAA Arizona members on a bimonthly basis. The

mean age of ur audience is around 60 years old. We look for intelligent, engaging writing covering auto and travel-related topics. Byline given. Pays on publication. Offers 30% kill fee. Buys first North American serial rights. Editorial lead time 6 months. Submit seasonal material 6 months in advance. Accepts queries by mail, e-mail, fax. Accepts simultaneous submissions. Sample copy for #10 SASE. Guidelines by email.
Nonfiction Needs travel, Auto-related. Articles unrelated to travel, automotive or Arizona living. **Buys 21 mss/year.** Query with published clips. Length: 500-2,000 words. **Pays $0.35/word for assigned articles. Pays $0.35/word for unsolicited articles.**
Photos Contact: Sherri Rowland, Art Director. Identification of subjects required. Offers $75-500 per photo Buys one time rights.
Columns/Departments Contact: Lindsay DeChacco. Weekender (Weekend destinations near Arizona), Road Trip (Day activities in Arizona), Charming Stays (A charming inn or B&B in Arizona); 500 to 700 words. 10 **Pays $-$0.35.**

$ $ HIGHWAYS

The Official Publication of the Good Sam Club, Affinity Group, Inc., 2575 Vista Del Mar Dr., Ventura CA 93001. (805)667-4100. Fax: (805)667-4454. E-mail: goodsam@goodsamclub.com. Website: www.goodsamclub.com/highways. **30% freelance written**. Monthly magazine covering recreational vehicle lifestyle. All of our readers own some type of RV—a motorhome, trailer, pop-up, tent—so our stories need to include places that you can go with large vehicles, and campgrounds in and around the area where they can spend the night. Estab. 1966. Circ. 975,000. Byline given. Pays on acceptance. Offers 50% kill fee. Publishes ms an average of 6 months after acceptance. Buys first North American serial rights, buys electronic rights. Accepts queries by e-mail. Responds in 2 weeks to queries. Sample copy and writer's guidelines free or online
Nonfiction Needs how-to, repair/replace something on an RV, humor, technical, travel, all RV related. **Buys 15-20 mss/year.** Query. Length: 800-1,100 words.
Photos Do not send or e-mail unless approved by staff.
Columns/Departments On the Road (issue related); RV Insight (for people new to the RV lifestyle); Action Line (consumer help); Tech Topics (tech Q&A); Camp Cuisine (cooking in an RV); Product Previews (new products). No plans on adding new columns/departments.
Tips Know something about RVing. People who drive motorhomes or pull trailers have unique needs that have to be incorporated into our stories. We're looking for well-written, first-person stories that convey the fun of this lifestyle and way to travel.

$ $ INTERNATIONAL LIVING

International Living Publishing, Ltd., Elysium House, Ballytruckle, Waterford Ireland (800)643-2479. Fax: 353-51-304-561. E-mail: editor@internationalliving.com. Website: www.internationalliving.com. **50% freelance written**. Monthly magazine covering retirement, travel, investment, and real estate overseas. We do not want descriptions of how beautiful places are. We want specifics, recommendations, contacts, prices, names, addresses, phone numbers, etc. We want offbeat locations and off-the-beaten-track spots. Estab. 1981. Circ. 500,000. Byline given. Pays on publication. Offers 25-50% kill fee. Publishes ms an average of 3 months after acceptance. Buys all rights. Editorial lead time 2 months. Submit seasonal material 3 months in advance. Accepts queries by mail, e-mail, fax. Accepts simultaneous submissions. Responds in 2 months to mss. Sample copy for #10 SASE. Guidelines available online.
Nonfiction Needs how-to, get a job, buy real estate, get cheap airfares overseas, start a business, etc., interview, entrepreneur or retiree abroad, new product, travel, personal experience, travel, shopping, cruises. We produce special issues each year focusing on Asia, Eastern Europe, and Latin America. No descriptive, run-of-the-mill travel articles. **Buys 100 mss/year.** Send complete ms. Length: 500-2,000 words. **Pays $200-500 for assigned articles. Pays $100-400 for unsolicited articles.**
Photos State availability Identification of subjects required. Reviews contact sheets, negatives, transparencies, prints. Offers $50/photo. Buys all rights.
Fillers Needs facts. 20 Length: 50-250 words. **Pays $25-50.**
Tips Make recommendations in your articles. We want first-hand accounts. Tell us how to do things: how to catch a cab, order a meal, buy a souvenir, buy property, start a business, etc. *International Living*'s philosophy is that the world is full of opportunities to do whatever you want, whenever you want. We will show you how.

$ THE INTERNATIONAL RAILWAY TRAVELER

Hardy Publishing Co., Inc., P.O. Box 3747, San Diego CA 92163. (619)260-1332. Fax: (619)296-4220. E-mail: irteditor@aol.com. Website: www.irtsociety.com. **100% freelance written**. Monthly newsletter covering rail travel. Estab. 1983. Circ. 3,500. Byline given. Pays within 1 month of the publication date. Offers 25% kill fee. Buys first North American serial rights, buys all electronic rights. Editorial lead time 4 months. Submit seasonal material 6 months in advance. Responds in 1 month to queries. Responds in 2 months to mss. Sample copy for $6. Guidelines for #10 SASE or via e-mail.

Nonfiction Needs general interest, how-to, interview, new product, opinion, personal experience, travel, book reviews. **Buys 48-60 mss/year.** Send complete ms. Length: 800-1,200 words. **Pays 3¢/word.**

Photos Include SASE for return of photos. Send photos Captions, identification of subjects required. Reviews contact sheets, negatives, transparencies, 8x10 (preferred) and 5x7 prints, digital photos preferred (minimum 300 dpi). Offers $10 b $20 cover photo. Costs of converting slides and negatives to prints are deducted from payment. Buys first North American serial rights, all electronic rights

Tips We want factual articles concerning world rail travel which would not appear in the mass-market travel magazines. *IRT* readers and editors love stories and photos on off-beat train trips as well as more conventional train trips covered in unconventional ways. With *IRT,* the focus is on the train travel experience, not a blow-by-blow description of the view from the train window. Be sure to include details (prices, passes, schedule info, etc.) for readers who might want to take the trip. E-mail queries, submissions encouraged. Digital photo submissions (at least 300 dpi) are encouraged. Please stay within word-count guidelines.

$ $ $ $ ISLANDS

World Publications, 460 N. Orlando Ave., Suite 200, Winter Park FL 32789. (407)628-4802. E-mail: storyideas@islands.com. Website: www.islands.com. **80% freelance written**. Magazine published 8 times/year. We cover accessible and once-in-a-lifetime islands from many different perspectives: travel, culture, lifestyle. We ask our authors to give us the essence of the island and do it with literary flair. Estab. 1981. Circ. 250,000. Byline given. Pays on publication. Offers 25% kill fee. Publishes ms an average of 8 months after acceptance. Buys all rights. Accepts queries by e-mail. Responds in 2 months to queries. Responds in 6 weeks to mss Sample copy for $6 E-mail us for writer's guidelines

Nonfiction Needs book excerpts, essays, general interest, interview, photo feature, travel, service shorts, island-related material. **Buys 25 feature mss/year.** Send complete ms. Length: 2,000-4,000 words. **Pays $750-2,500.** Sometimes pays expenses of writers on assignment.

Photos "Fine color photography is a special attraction of *Islands*, and we look for superb composition, technical quality, and editorial applicability. Will not accept or be responsible for unsolicited images or artwork."

Columns/Departments Discovers section (island related news), 100-250 words; Taste (island cuisine), 900-1,000 words; Travel Tales (personal essay), 900-1,100 words; Live the Life (island expat Q&A). Query with published clips. **Pays $25-1,000.**

$ $ MEXICO TRAVEL & LIFE

Turistampa LLC, 5850 San Felipe, Suite 500, Houston TX 77057. (713)706-6153. E-mail: jack@mexicotravelandlife.com. Website: www.mexicotravelandlife.com. **70% freelance written**. Quarterly magazine covering travel in Mexico. *Mexico Travel & Life* is a full-color magazine with heavy photo content. It is written to serve the needs and interests of the 20 million visitors to Mexico every year. Estab. 2007. Circ. 100,000. Byline given. Pays on publication. Publishes ms an average of 3 months after acceptance. Buys one-time rights, buys electronic rights. Editorial lead time 3 months. Submit seasonal material 6 months in advance. Accepts queries by e-mail. Accepts previously published material. Accepts simultaneous submissions. Responds in 2 weeks to queries. Responds in 1 month to mss. Guidelines free.

Nonfiction Needs travel. Does not want political or religious. **Buys 24 mss/year.** Query. Length: 1,000-1,200 words. **Pays $300-500.**

Photos Contact: Jenny Lopez, creative director. State availability Captions, identification of subjects, model releases required. Offers no additional payment for photos accepted with ms. Buys one time rights.

Columns/Departments Vistas (single photo with max of 50-100 words); Gusto (food or restaurant article with photo of chef, restaurant interior, entree photo and recipe). 4-8 Query. **Pays $50-300.**

Tips Photography is key to publication. Query and acceptance times are reduced by sending low res photography with manuscript.

$ $ MOTORHOME

Affinity, 2575 Vista Del Mar Dr., Ventura CA 93001. (805)667-4100. Fax: (805)667-4484. Website: www.motorhomemagazine.com. **60% freelance written**. Monthly magazine. "*MotorHome* is a magazine for owners and prospective buyers of motorized recreational vehicles who are active outdoorsmen and wide-ranging travelers. We cover all aspects of the RV lifestyle; editorial material is both technical and nontechnical in nature. Regular features include tests and descriptions of various models of motorhomes, travel adventures, and hobbies pursued in such vehicles, objective analysis of equipment and supplies for such vehicles, and do-it-yourself articles. Guides within the magazine provide listings of manufacturers, rentals, and other sources of equipment and accessories of interest to enthusiasts. Articles must have an RV slant and excellent photography accompanying text." Estab. 1968. Circ. 150,000. Byline given. Pays on acceptance. Offers 30% kill fee. Publishes ms an average of within 1 year after acceptance. Buys first North American serial rights, buys electronic rights. Editorial lead time 4 months. Submit seasonal material 6 months in advance. Accepts queries by mail, fax. Responds in 1 month to queries. Responds in 2 months to mss. Sample copy free. Guidelines for #10 SASE.

Nonfiction Needs general interest, historical, how-to, humor, interview, new product, personal experience, photo feature, technical, travel, celebrity profiles, recreation, lifestyle, legislation, all RV related. No diaries of RV trips or negative RV experiences. **Buys 120 mss/year.** Query with published clips. Length: 250-2,500 words. **Pays $300-600.**

Photos Digital photography accepted. Send photos Captions, identification of subjects, model releases required. Reviews 35mm slides. Offers no additional payment for art accepted with ms. Pays $500 for covers. Buys one time rights.

Columns/Departments Crossroads (offbeat briefs of people, places, and events of interest to travelers), 100-200 words; Keepers (tips, resources). Query with published clips or send complete ms. **Pays $100**

Tips "If a freelancer has an idea for a good article, it's best to send a query and include possible photo locations to illustrate the article. We prefer to assign articles and work with the author in developing a piece suitable to our audience. We are in a specialized field with very enthusiastic readers who appreciate articles by authors who actually enjoy motorhomes. The following areas are most open: Crossroads—brief descriptions of places to see or special events, with 1 photo/slide, 100-200 words; travel—places to go with a motorhome, where to stay, what to see and do, etc.; and how-to—personal projects on author's motorhomes to make travel easier, unique projects, accessories. Also articles on motorhome-owning celebrities, humorous experiences. Be sure to submit appropriate photography with at least 1 good motorhome shot to illustrate travel articles. No phone queries, please."

$ $ 🍁 NORTH AMERICAN INNS MAGAZINE

Harworth Publishing Inc., Box 998, Guelph ON N1H 6N1 Canada. (519)767-6059. Fax: (519)821-0479. E-mail: editor@harworthpublishing.com. Website: www.innsmagazine.com. *North American Inns* is a national publication for travel, dining and pastimes. It focuses on inns, beds & breakfasts, resorts and travel in North America. The magazine is targeted to travelers looking for exquisite getaways. Accepts queries by e-mail. Guidelines by email.

Nonfiction Needs general interest, interview, new product, opinion, personal experience, travel. Query. Length: 300-600 words. **Pays $175-250 (Canadian).**

Fillers Short quips or nominations at 75 words are **$25 each**. All stories submitted have to accompany photos. Please e-mail photos to designer@harworthpublishing.com.

$ $ NORTHWEST TRAVEL

Northwest Regional Magazines, 4969 Hwy. 101 N., Suite 2, Florence OR 97439. (541)997-8401 or (800)348-8401. Fax: (541)902-0400. Website: www.northwestmagazines.com. **60% freelance written**. Bimonthly magazine. "We like energetic writing about popular activities and destinations in the Pacific Northwest. *Northwest Travel* aims to give readers practical ideas on where to go in the region. Magazine covers Oregon, Washington, Idaho, British Columbia, Alaska and western Montana." Estab. 1991. Circ. 50,000. Pays after publication. No kill fee. Publishes ms an average of 8 months after acceptance. Buys first North American serial rights. Submit seasonal material 6 months in advance. Accepts queries by mail, e-mail. Responds in 3 months to queries. Responds in 3 months to mss. Sample copy for $4.50. Guidelines available online.

Nonfiction Needs historical, interview, rarely, photo feature, travel in Northwest region. No "cliché-ridden pieces on places that everyone covers." **Buys 40 mss/year.** Query with or without published clips. Submit copy on CD or via e-mail. Length: 1,000-1,500 words. **Pays $100-500 for feature articles, and contributor copies.**

Reprints Send photocopy and information about when and where the material previously appeared. Pays 50% of amount paid for original article

Photos Provide credit and model release information on cover photos. Digital photos on CD (300 dpi 8 ½x11 ½). State availability Captions, identification of subjects, True required. Reviews transparencies, prefers dupes. Pays $425 for cover; $100 for stand-alone photos; $100 for Back Page. Buys one time rights.

Columns/Departments Worth a Stop (brief items describing places worth a stop), 350-500 words. **Pays $50-100**. Back Page (photo and large caption package on a specific activity, season, or festival with some technical photo info), 80 words and 1 slide. **Pays $100**. 25-30

Tips "Write fresh, lively copy (avoid cliché), and cover exciting travel topics in the region that haven't been covered in other magazines. A story with stunning photos will get serious consideration. The department most open to freelancers is the Worth a Stop department. Take us to fascinating places we may not otherwise discover."

$ PATHFINDERS

Travel Information for People of Color, 6325 Germantown Ave., Philadelphia PA 19144. (215)438-2140. Fax: (215)438-2144. E-mail: editors@pathfinderstravel.com. Website: www.pathfinderstravel.com. **75% freelance written**. Bimonthly magazine covering travel for people of color, primarily African-Americans. We look for lively, original, well-written stories that provide a good sense of place, with useful information and fresh ideas about travel and the travel industry. Our main audience is African-Americans, though we do look for articles relating to other persons of color: Native Americans, Hispanics and Asians. Estab. 1997. Circ. 100,000. Byline given. Pays on publication. Buys first North American serial rights, buys electronic rights. Accepts queries by mail, e-mail. Responds in 1 month to queries. Responds in 2 months to mss. Sample copy at bookstores (Barnes & Noble, Borders) Guidelines available online.

Nonfiction Interested in seeing more Native American stories, places that our readers can visit and rodeos (be sure to tie-in African-American cowboys). Needs essays, historical, how-to, personal experience, photo feature, travel, all vacation travel oriented. No more pitches on Jamaica. We get these all the time. **Buys 16-20 mss/year.** Send complete ms. 1,200-1,400 words for cover stories; 1,000-1,200 words for features. **Pays $200.**

Photos State availability

Columns/Departments Chef's Table, Post Cards from Home; Looking Back; City of the Month, 500-600 words. Send complete ms. **Pays $150.**

Tips We prefer seeing finished articles rather than queries. All articles are submitted on spec. Articles should be saved in either WordPerfect of Microsoft Word, double-spaced and saved as a text-only file. Include a hard copy. E-mail articles are accepted only by request of the editor. No historical articles.

$ $ PILOT GETAWAYS MAGAZINE

Airventure Publishing LLC, P.O. Box 550, Glendale CA 91209-0550. (818)241-1890. Fax: (818)241-1895. E-mail: editor@pilotgetaways.com. Website: www.pilotgetaways.com. **90% freelance written**. Bimonthly magazine covering aviation travel for private pilots. *Pilot Getaways* is a travel magazine for private pilots. Our articles cover destinations that are easily accessible by private aircraft, including details such as airport transportation, convenient hotels, and attractions. Other regular features include Fly-in dining, Flying Tips, and Bush Flying. Estab. 1998. Circ. 20,000. Byline given. Pays on publication. No kill fee. Buys first North American serial rights, buys electronic rights. Editorial lead time 4 months. Submit seasonal material 9 months in advance. Accepts queries by mail, e-mail, fax, phone. Accepts simultaneous submissions. Responds in 2 weeks to queries. Responds in 2 months to mss. Sample copy and writer's guidelines free

Nonfiction Needs travel, specifically travel guide articles. We rarely publish articles about events that have already occurred, such as travel logs about trips the authors have taken or air show reports. **Buys 30 mss/year.** Query. Length: 1,000-3,500 words. **Pays $100-500.**

Photos State availability Captions, identification of subjects required. Reviews contact sheets, negatives, 35mm transparencies, prints, GIF/JPEG/TIFF files. Negotiates payment individually Buys one time rights.

Columns/Departments Weekend Getaways (short fly-in getaways), 2,000 words; Fly-in Dining (reviews of airport restaurants), 1,200 words; Flying Tips (tips and pointers on flying technique), 1,000 words; Bush Flying (getaways to unpaved destinations), 1,500 words. 20 Query. **Pays $100-500.**

Tips *Pilot Getaways* follows a specific format, which is factual and informative. We rarely publish travel logs that chronicle a particular journey. Rather, we prefer travel guides with phone numbers, addresses, prices, etc., so that our readers can plan their own trips. The exact format is described in our writer's guidelines.

$ $ $ PORTHOLE CRUISE MAGAZINE

Panoff Publishing, 4517 NW 31st Ave., Ft. Lauderdale FL 33309-3403. (954)377-7777. Fax: (954)377-7000. E-mail: bpanoff@ppigroup.com. Website: www.porthole.com. **70% freelance written**. Bimonthly magazine covering the cruise industry. *Porthole Cruise Magazine* entices its readers to take a cruise vacation by delivering information that is timely, accurate, colorful, and entertaining. Estab. 1992. Circ. 80,000. Byline given. Pays on publication. Offers 20% kill fee. Publishes ms an average of 6 months after acceptance. Buys first North American serial rights. Editorial lead time 8 months. Submit seasonal material 5 months in advance. Accepts queries by e-mail. Accepts simultaneous submissions.

Nonfiction Needs general interest, cruise related, historical, how-to, pick a cruise, not get seasick, travel tips, humor, interview, crew on board or industry executives, new product, personal experience, photo feature, travel, off-the-beaten-path, adventure, ports, destinations, cruises, onboard fashion, spa articles, duty-free shopping, port shopping, ship reviews. No articles on destinations that can't be reached by ship. **Buys 60 mss/year.** Length: 1,000-1,200 words. **Pays $500-600 for assigned feature articles.**

Photos Contact: Linda Douthat, creative director. State availability Captions, identification of subjects, model releases required. Reviews digital images and original transparencies. Rates available upon request to ldouthat@ppigroup.com Buys one time rights.

$ $ THE SOUTHERN TRAVELER

AAA Auto Club of Missouri, 12901 N. Forty Dr., St. Louis MO 63141. (314)523-7350. Fax: (314)523-6982. Website: www.aaa.com/traveler. **80% freelance written**. Bimonthly magazine. Estab. 1997. Circ. 210,000. Byline given. Pays on acceptance. No kill fee. Buys first North American serial rights, buys second serial (reprint) rights. Accepts simultaneous submissions. Responds in 1 month to queries. Responds in 1 month to mss. Sample copy for sae with 12 ½ X 9 ½ envelope and 3 First-Class stamps. Guidelines available online.

Nonfiction We feature articles on regional and world travel, area history, auto safety, highway and transportation news. **Buys 30 mss/year.** Query. 1,200 words maximum. **Pays $300 maximum.**

Reprints Send typed manuscript with rights for sale noted and information about when and where the material previously appeared. Pays $125-200

Photos State availability Captions required. Reviews transparencies. Offers no additional payment for photos accepted with ms One-time photo reprint rights.

Tips Editorial schedule is set 6-9 months in advance (available online). Some stories available throughout the year, but most are assigned early. Travel destinations and tips are most open to freelancers; auto-related topics handled by staff. Make story bright and quick to read. We see too many `Here's what I did on my vacation' manuscripts. Go easy on first-person accounts.

$ $ $ $ SPA

Healthy Living, Travel & Renewal, World Publications, 415 Jackson St., San Francisco CA 94111. (760)966-6226. Fax: (760)966-6266. Website: www.spamagazine.com. Bimonthly magazine covering health spas: treatments, travel, cuisine, fitness, beauty. Approachable and accessible, authoritative and full of advice, *Spa* is the place to turn for information and tips on nutrition, spa cuisine/recipes, beauty, health, skin care, spa travel, fitness, well-being and renewal. Byline given. Offers 25% kill fee. Buys first North American serial rights, buys all rights. Editorial lead time 3 months. Accepts queries by mail. Sample copy for $6.

Columns/Departments In Touch (spa news, treatments, destinations); Body (nutrition, health & fitness, spa therapies); Rituals (spa at home, beauty, home, books & music, mind/body).

$ $ SPA LIFE

Harworth Publishing, Inc., Box 998, Guelph ON N1H 6N1 Canada. (519)767-6059. Fax: (519)821-0479. E-mail: editor@harworthpublishing.com. *Spa Life* is about more than just spas. With favorite recipes from featured spa destinations, mouth-watering treats are at your fingertips. *Spa Life* is also dedicated to personal and health issues. Estab. 2000. No kill fee. Accepts queries by e-mail. Guidelines by email.

Nonfiction Needs general interest, interview, new product, personal experience, travel. Length: 300-600 words. **Pays $75-200 (Canadian).**

Fillers photos e-mailed to: designer@harworthpublishing.com.

Tips Describe the treatments/food and surroundings. Include all information to make it easy for readers to get more info and make reservations. Make it personal and fun; the reader has to feel they know you and can relate.

$ $ ST. MAARTEN NIGHTS

Nights Publications, Inc., 1751 Richardson St., Suite 5.530, Montreal QC H3K 1G6 Canada. (514)931-1987. Fax: (514)931-6273. E-mail: editor@nightspublications.com. Website: www.nightspublications.com. **Contact:** Jennifer McMorran, ed. **90% freelance written**. Annual magazine covering the St. Maarten/St. Martin vacation experience seeking upbeat, entertaining, lifestyle articles. Our audience is the North American vacationer. Estab. 1981. Circ. 225,000. Byline given. Pays on acceptance. No kill fee. Publishes ms an average of 9 months after acceptance. Buys North American and Caribbean serial rights. Editorial lead time 1 month. Accepts queries by mail, e-mail, fax. Responds in 2 weeks to queries. Responds in 1 month to mss. Guidelines by email.

- "Let the reader experience the story; utilize the senses; be descriptive; be specific."

Nonfiction "Lifestyle with a lively, upscale touch." Needs general interest, historical, how-to, gamble (for example), humor, interview, opinion, personal experience, photo feature, travel, colorful profiles of islanders, sailing, ecological, ecotourism, local culture, art, activities, entertainment, nightlife, special events, topics relative to vacationers in St. Maarten/St. Martin. **Buys 8-10 mss/year.** Query with published clips. Length: 250-750 words. **Pays $100-300.**

Photos State availability Captions, identification of subjects, model releases required. Reviews transparencies. Pays $50/photo Buys one time rights.

Tips "Our style is upbeat, friendly, fluid, and descriptive. Our magazines cater to tourists who are already at the destination, so ensure your story is of interest to this particular audience. We welcome stories that offer fresh angles to familiar tourist-related topics. E-mail queries preferred. All submissions must include an e-mail address for correspondence."

$ $ TIMES OF THE ISLANDS

Sampling the Soul of the Turks and Caicos Islands,, Times Publications, Ltd., P.O. Box 234, Lucille Lightbourne Bldg., #7, Providenciales Turks & Caicos Islands British West Indies. (649)946-4788. Fax: (649)946-4788. E-mail: timespub@tciway.tc. Website: www.timespub.tc. **60% freelance written**. Quarterly magazine covering the Turks & Caicos Islands. "*Times of the Islands* is used by the public and private sector to inform visitors and potential investors/developers about the Islands. It goes beyond a superficial overview of tourist attractions with in-depth articles about natural history, island heritage, local personalities, new development, offshore finance, sporting activities, visitors' experiences, and Caribbean fiction." Estab. 1988. Circ. 10,000. Byline given. Pays on publication. No kill fee. Publishes ms an average of 6 months after acceptance. Buys second serial (reprint) rights. Publication rights for 6 months with respect to other publications distributed in Caribbean. Editorial lead time 4 months. Submit seasonal material at least 4 months in advance. Accepts queries by e-mail. Accepts simultaneous submissions. Responds in 6 weeks to queries. Responds in 2 months to mss. Sample copy for $6. Guidelines available online.

Nonfiction Needs book excerpts, essays, general interest, Caribbean art, culture, cooking, crafts, historical, humor, interview, locals, personal experience, trips to the Islands, photo feature, technical, island businesses, travel, book reviews, nature, ecology, business (offshore finance), watersports. **Buys 20 mss/year.** Query. Length: 500-3,000 words. **Pays $200-600.**

Reprints Send photocopy and information about when and where the material previously appeared. Payment varies

Photos Send photos Identification of subjects required. Reviews digital photos. Pays $15-100/photo

Columns/Departments On Holiday (unique experiences of visitors to Turks & Caicos), 500-1,500 words. 4 Query. **Pays $200**

Fiction Needs adventure, sailing, diving, ethnic, Caribbean, historical, Caribbean, humorous, travel-related, mystery, novel concepts. **Buys 2-3 mss/year.** Query. Length: 1,000-3,000 words. **Pays $250-400.**

Tips "Make sure that the query/article specifically relates to the Turks and Caicos Islands. The theme can be general (ecotourism, for instance), but the manuscript should contain specific and current references to the Islands. We're a high-quality magazine, with a small budget and staff, and are very open-minded to ideas (and manuscripts). Writers who have visited the Islands at least once would probably have a better perspective from which to write."

$ $ TRAILER LIFE

America's No. 1 RV Magazine, Affinity Group, Inc., 2575 Vista Del Mar Dr., Ventura CA 93001. Fax: (805)667-4484. E-mail: info@trailerlife.com. Website: www.trailerlife.com. **40% freelance written**. Monthly magazine. *Trailer Life* magazine is written specifically for active people whose overall lifestyle is based on travel and recreation in their RV. Every issue includes product tests, travel articles, and other features—ranging from lifestyle to vehicle maintenance. Estab. 1941. Circ. 270,000. Byline given. Pays on acceptance. Offers kill fee. Offers 30% kill fee for assigned articles that are not acceptable. Publishes ms an average of 6 months after acceptance. Buys first North American serial rights, buys electronic rights. Editorial lead time 4 months. Submit seasonal material 6 months in advance. Accepts queries by mail. Responds in 2 months to queries. Responds in 2 months to mss. Sample copy free. Guidelines for #10 SASE.

Nonfiction Needs historical, how-to, technical, humor, new product, opinion, personal experience, travel. No vehicle tests, product evaluations or road tests; tech material is strictly assigned. No diaries or trip logs, no non-RV trips; nothing without an RV-hook. **Buys 75 mss/year.** Query. Length: 250-2,500 words. **Pays $125-700.** Sometimes pays expenses of writers on assignment.

Photos Send photos Identification of subjects, model releases required. Reviews transparencies, b&w contact sheets . Offers no additional payment for photos accepted with ms, does pay for supplemental photos Buys one-time and occasionally electronic rights.

Columns/Departments Campground Spotlight (report with 1 photo of campground recommended for RVers), 250 words; Around the Bend (news, trends of interest to RVers), 100 words; Etcetera (useful tips and information affecting RVers), 240 words. 70 Query or send complete ms **Pays $75-250.**

Tips Prerequisite: Must have RV focus. Photos must be magazine quality. These are the two biggest reasons why manuscripts are rejected. Our readers are travel enthusiasts who own all types of RVs (travel trailers, truck campers, van conversions, motorhomes, tent trailers, fifth-wheels) in which they explore North America and beyond, embrace the great outdoors in national, state and private parks. They're very active and very adventurous.

$ N TRANSITIONS ABROAD

P.O. Box 745, Bennington VT 05201. Phone/Fax: (802)442-4827. E-mail: webeditor@transitionsabroad.com. Website: www.transitionsabroad.com. **80-90% freelance written**. Bimonthly magazine resource for low-budget international travel, often with an educational or volunteer/work component. Focus is on enriching, informed, affordable, and responsible travel. Estab. 1977. Circ. 12,000. Byline given. Pays on publication. No kill fee. Buys first rights, buys second serial (reprint) rights. Accepts queries by e-mail. Responds in 1 month to queries and mss Sample copy for $6.45 Guidelines available online

Nonfiction "Lead articles (up to 1,500 words) provide first-hand practical information on independent travel to featured country or region (see topics schedule). Also, how to find educational and specialty travel opportunities, practical information (evaluation of courses, special interest and study tours, economy travel), travel (new learning and cultural travel ideas). Foreign travel only. Few destination (tourist) pieces or first-person narratives. *Transitions Abroad* is a resource magazine for independent, educated, and adventurous travelers, not for armchair travelers or those addicted to packaged tours or cruises. Emphasis on information which must be usable by readers and on interaction with people in host country." **Buys 120 unsolicited mss/year.** Prefer e-mail queries that indicate familiarity with the magazine. Query with credentials and SASE. Include author's bio and e-mail with submissions. Length: 500-1,500 words. **Pays $2/column inch.**

Photos Send photos when submission is accepted. Captions, identification of subjects required. Pays $10-25 for color prints or color slides (prints preferred), $150 for covers. Buys one time rights.

Columns/Departments Worldwide Travel Bargains (destinations, activities, and accommodations for budget travelers—featured in every issue); Tour and Program Notes (new courses or travel programs); Travel Resources (new information and ideas for independent travel); Working Traveler (how to find jobs and what to expect); Activity Vacations (travel opportunities that involve action and learning, usually by direct involvement in host culture); Responsible Travel (information on community-organized tours). Length: 1,000 words maximum. 60 Send complete ms. **Pays $2/column inch**

Fillers Info Exchange (information, preferably first hand—having to do with travel, particularly offbeat educational travel and work or study abroad). 30 750 words maximum. **Pays complimentary 1-year subscription**

Tips "We like nuts and bolts stuff, practical information, especially on how to work, live, and cut costs abroad. Our readers want usable information on planning a travel itinerary. Be specific: names, addresses, current costs. We are very interested in educational and long-stay travel and study abroad for adults and senior citizens. *Overseas Travel Planner* published each year in July provides best information sources on work, study, and independent travel abroad. Each bimonthly issue contains a worldwide directory of educational and specialty travel programs."

$ TRAVEL NATURALLY

Internaturally, Inc., P.O. Box 317, Newfoundland NJ 07435-0317. (973)697-3552. Fax: (973)697-8313. E-mail: naturally@internaturally.com. Website: www.internaturally.com. **90% freelance written.** Quarterly magazine covering wholesome family nude recreation and travel locations. *Travel Naturally* looks at why millions of people believe that removing clothes in public is a good idea, and at places specifically created for that purpose—with good humor, but also in earnest. *Travel Naturally* takes you to places where your personal freedom is the only agenda, and to places where textile-free living is a serious commitment. Estab. 1981. Circ. 35,000. Byline given. Pays on publication. No kill fee. Buys first rights, buys one-time rights. Editorial lead time 4 months. Submit seasonal material 4 months in advance. Accepts queries by mail, e-mail, fax. Accepts simultaneous submissions. Sample copy for $9. Guidelines available online.

Nonfiction Frequent contributors and regular columnists, who develop a following through *Travel Naturally*, are paid from the Frequent Contributors Budget. Payments increase on the basis of frequency of participation. Needs general interest, interview, personal experience, photo feature, travel. **Buys 12 mss/year.** Send complete ms. 2 pages. **Pays $80/published page, including photos.**

Reprints Pays 50% of original rate.

Photos Send photos Reviews contact sheets, negatives, transparencies, prints, high resolution digital images. Buys one time rights.

Fillers Needs anecdotes, facts, gags, newsbreaks, short humor, poems, artwork. **Payment is pro-rated based on length.**

Tips *Travel Naturally* invokes the philosophies of naturism and nudism, but also activities and beliefs in the mainstream that express themselves, barely: spiritual awareness, New Age customs, pagan and religious rites, alternative and fringe lifestyle beliefs, artistic expressions, and many individual nude interests. Our higher purpose is simply to help restore our sense of self. Although the term `nude recreation' may, for some, conjure up visions of sexual frivolities inappropriate for youngsters—because that can also be technically true—these topics are outside the scope of *Travel Naturally* magazine. Here the emphasis is on the many varieties of human beings, of all ages and backgrounds, recreating in their most natural state, at extraordinary places, their reasons for doing so, and the benefits they derive. We incorporate a travel department to advise and book vacations in locations reviewed in travel articles.

$ TRAVEL SMART

Communications House, Inc., P.O. Box 397, Dobbs Ferry NY 10522. E-mail: travelsmartnow@aol.com. Website: travelsmartnewsletter.com. Monthly newsletter covering information on good-value travel. Estab.

1976. Circ. 20,000. Pays on publication. No kill fee. Buys all rights. Accepts queries by mail, e-mail. Responds in 6 weeks to queries. Responds in 6 weeks to mss. Sample copy for sae with 9 X 12 envelope and 3 First-Class stamps. Guidelines for sae with 9 X 12 envelope and 3 First-Class stamps.
Nonfiction Interested primarily in bargains or little-known deals on transportation, lodging, food, unusual destinations that are really good values. No destination stories on major Caribbean islands, London, New York, no travelogs, `my vacation,' poetry, fillers. No photos or illustrations other than maps. Just hard facts. We are not part of `Rosy fingers of dawn.' school. Write for guidelines, then query. Query. Length: 100-1,500 words. **Pays $150 maximum.**
Tips When you travel, check out small hotels offering good prices, good restaurants, and send us brief rundown (with prices, phone numbers, addresses). Information must be current. Include your phone number with submission, because we sometimes make immediate assignments.

$ $ VERGE MAGAZINE

Travel With Purpose, Verge Magazine Inc., P.O. Box 147, Peterborough ON K9J 6Y5 Canada. E-mail: contributing@vergemagazine.org. Website: www.vergemagazine.org. **60% freelance written.** Quarterly magazine Each issue takes you around the world, with people who are doing something different & making a difference doing it. This is the magazine resource for those wanting to volunteer, work, study or adventure overseas. "*Verge* is the magazine for people who travel with purpose. It explores ways to get out & see the world by volunteering, working & studying overseas. Our readers are typically young (17-40 yrs.), or young at heart, active, independent travelers. Editorial content is intended to inform & motivate the reader by profiling unique individuals & experiences that are timely & socially relevant. We look for articles that are issue driven & combine an engaging & well=told story with nuts & bolts how-to information. Wherever possible & applicable, eforsts should be made to provide sources where readers can find out more about the subject, or ways in which readers can become involved in the issue covered." Estab. 2002. Circ. 10,000. Byline given. Pays on publication. No kill fee. Publishes ms an average of 6 months after acceptance. Buys first North American serial rights, buys second serial (reprint) rights, buys electronic rights. Submit seasonal material 8-12 months in advance. Accepts queries by mail, e-mail. Responds in 8 weeks to queries. Responds in 2 months to mss. Sample copy for $6 plus shipping. Guidelines available online.
Nonfiction Contact: Julia Steinecke. Needs how-to, humor, interview, travel, News. "We do not want pure travelogues, predictable tourist experiences, luxury travel, stories highighting a specific company or organisation." **Buys 30-40 mss/yr. mss/year.** Send complete ms. Length: 600-1,000 words. **Pays $60-500 for assigned articles. Pays $60-250 for unsolicited articles.**
Photos Send link to online portfolio to editor@vergemagazine.ca or mail portfolio on CD or DVD to *Verge Magazine*. Captions required. Reviews GIF/JPEG files. Negotiates payment individually.
Columns/Departments Contact: Julia Steinecke. 20-30 mss/yr. Query with published clips. **Pays $$60-$250.**
Tips "Writers should read the guidelines & tell us which dept. their query fits best. should refer to travel undertaken in the past year if possible."

$ WESTERN RV NEWS & RECREATION

Website: www.westernrvnews.com. Monthly magazine for owners of recreational vehicles and those interested in the RV lifestyle. Estab. 1966. Byline given. Buys first rights, buys second serial (reprint) rights. Accepts queries by e-mail. Accepts simultaneous submissions. Guidelines available online.

- All correspondence should come through links on the Web site. Do not send snail mail, call or e-mail directly. Visit the Web pages for submission guidelines and contact forms.

Nonfiction Needs how-to, RV oriented, purchasing considerations, maintenance, humor, RV experiences, new product, with ancillary interest to RV lifestyle, personal experience, varying or unique RV lifestyles, technical, RV systems or hardware, travel. No articles without an RV slant. **Buys 100 mss/year.** Submit complete ms by e-mail only via Web site. Length: 250-1,400 words. **Pays 8¢/word for first rights.**
Photos Prints are accepted with article at a rate of $5/photo used. Digital photos are also accepted through e-mail or on disk (CD, Zip, etc.), but must be at a minimum resolution of 300 dpi at published size (generally, 5x7 inches is adequate). Captions, identification of subjects, model releases required.
Fillers Encourage anecdotes, RV-related tips, and short humor. Length: 50-250 words. **Pays $5-25.**
Tips our editorial mix strives to provide full-color travel features and destinations, useful repair and technical articles, how-to advice, and product reviews. Regular columns written by on-the-road RVers share the back-roads and first-hand experiences of the part-time and full-time RV lifestyle. Our readers say that generations of their families have subscribed to Western RV News & Recreation for many years, and they continue to enjoy Western RV News & Recreation from cover to cover.

$ $ WOODALL'S REGIONALS

2575 Vista Del Mar Dr., Ventura CA 93001. Website: www.woodalls.com. Monthly magazine for RV and

camping enthusiasts. Woodall's Regionals include *CamperWays, Midwest RV Traveler, Northeast Outdoors, Florida RV Traveler*. Byline given. Buys first rights. Accepts queries by mail, e-mail. Responds in 1-2 months to queries. Sample copy free. Guidelines free.
Nonfiction We need interesting and tightly focused feature stories on RV travel and lifestyle, and technical articles that speak to both novices and experienced RVers. **Buys 300 mss/year.** Query with published clips. Length: 1,000-1,400 words. **Pays $180-220/feature; $75-100/department article and short piece.**

WOMENS

ALL YOU MAGAZINE

Time Inc., 135 W. 50th St., 2nd Floor, New York NY 10020. E-mail: feedback@allyou.com. Website: www.allyou.com. No kill fee.

- Query before submitting.

$ $ $ BRIDAL GUIDE

R.F.P., LLC, 330 Seventh Ave., 10th Floor, New York NY 10001. (212)838-7733; (800)472-7744. Fax: (212)308-7165. E-mail: editorial@bridalguide.com. Website: www.bridalguide.com. **20% freelance written**. Bimonthly magazine covering relationships, sexuality, fitness, wedding planning, psychology, finance, travel. Only works with experienced/published writers. Pays on acceptance. No kill fee. Accepts queries by mail. Responds in 3 months to queries. Responds in 3 months to mss. Sample copy for $5 and SAE with 4 first-class stamps. Writer's guidelines available.
Nonfiction Please do not send queries concerning beauty, fashion, or home design stories since we produce them in-house. We do not accept personal wedding essays, fiction, or poetry. Address travel queries to travel editor. All correspondence accompanied by an SASE will be answered. **Buys 100 mss/year.** Query with published clips from national consumer magazines. Length: 1,000-2,000 words. **Pays 50¢/word.**
Photos Photography and illustration submissions should be sent to the art department.
Tips We are looking for service-oriented, well-researched pieces that are journalistically written. Writers we work with use at least 3 top expert sources, such as physicians, book authors, and business people in the appropriate field. Our tone is conversational, yet authoritative. Features are also generally filled with real-life anecdotes. We also do features that are completely real-person based—such as roundtables of bridesmaids discussing their experiences, or grooms-to-be talking about their feelings about getting married. In queries, we are looking for a well-thought-out idea, the specific angle of focus the writer intends to take, and the sources he or she intends to use. Queries should be brief and snappy—and titles should be supplied to give the editor an even better idea of the direction the writer is going in.

$ $ $ $ CHATELAINE

One Mount Pleasant Rd., 8th Floor, Toronto ON M4Y 2Y5 Canada. (416)764-2879. Fax: (416)764-2431. E-mail: storyideas@chatelaine.rogers.com. Website: www.chatelaine.com. Monthly magazine. *Chatelaine* is edited for Canadian women ages 25-49, their changing attitudes and lifestyles. Key editorial ingredients include health, finance, social issues and trends, as well as fashion, beauty, food and home decor. Regular departments include Health pages, Entertainment, Humour, How-to. Byline given. Pays on acceptance. Offers 25-50% kill fee. Buys first rights, buys electronic rights. Accepts queries by mail.
Nonfiction Seeks agenda-setting reports on Canadian national issues and trends as well as pieces on health, careers, personal finance and other facts of Canadian life. **Buys 50 mss/year.** Query with published clips and SASE Length: 1,000-2,500 words. **Pays $1,000-2,500.** Pays expenses of writers on assignment.
Columns/Departments Length: 500-1,000 words. Query with published clips and SASE **Pays $500-750.**

CHRISTIAN WOMAN

Inspired Living, Media Inc./Initiate Media, P.O. Box 163, North Sydney NSW 2059 Australia. (61)(2)8437-3541. Fax: (61)(2)9999-2053. E-mail: jbaxter@mediaincorporated.org. Website: www.christianwoman.com.au. Bimonthly magazine covering issues important to Christian women.

- Australian and New Zealand writers given preference.

Nonfiction Needs inspirational, interview, religious. Query.

$ $ $ $ CONCEIVE MAGAZINE

The Experts on Getting Pregnant, 622 E. Washington St., Suite 440, Orlando FL 32801. (407)447-2456. Fax: (407)770-1760. Website: www.conceiveonline.com. **50% freelance written**. "Bimonthly magazine covering reproductive health, fertility, conception, infertility, adoption.". Estab. 2004. Circ. 200,000+. Byline given. Pays on acceptance. Offers 25% kill fee. Publishes ms an average of 3 months after acceptance. Buys all rights. Editorial lead time 6 months. Submit seasonal material 6 months in advance. Accepts queries by e-mail, online submission form. Guidelines available online.

- E-mail queries should be sent through online contact form.

Nonfiction Needs book excerpts, essays, interview, new product, personal experience. "I am inundated with queries from writers who want to recount their own 'journey to parenthood.' I have plenty of personal stories; I need well-reported, well-written health and lifestyle pieces." Query with published clips. Length: 500-2,000 words. **Pays $250-2,000.** Pays expenses of writers on assignment.

Columns/Departments Adam + Eve (marriage/relationship), 750-1,000 words; Boxers + Briefs (men/fertility), 750 words; Family is Born (success stories), 750-1,500 words; Conceived (early pregnancy), 750-1,500 words. Query with published clips. **Pays $250-1,000.**

Tips "We are the first and only consumer magazine in the pre-pregnancy (fertility and conception) category. We are not a pregnancy or parenting journal, or an infertility magazine."

$$$$ ELLE

Hachette Filipacchi Media U.S., Inc., 1633 Broadway, 44th Floor, New York NY 10019. (212)767-5800. Fax: (212)489-4211. Website: www.elle.com. Monthly magazine. Edited for the modern, sophisticated, affluent, well-traveled woman in her twenties to early thirties. Circ. 1,100,000. No kill fee. Editorial lead time 3 months.

- Query first.

$$$ FAMILY CIRCLE MAGAZINE

Meredith Corporation, 375 Lexington Ave., 9th Floor, New York NY 10017. Website: www.familycircle.com. **80% freelance written**. Magazine published every 3 weeks. We are a national women's service magazine which covers many stages of a woman's life, along with her everyday concerns about social, family, and health issues. Submissions should focus on families with children ages 8-16. Estab. 1932. Circ. 4,200,000. Byline given. Offers 20% kill fee. Buys one-time rights, buys all rights. Editorial lead time 4 months. Submit seasonal material 4 months in advance. Responds in 2 months to queries. Responds in 2 months to mss. For back issues, send $6.95 to P.O. Box 3156, Harlan IA 51537. Guidelines available online.

Nonfiction We look for well-written, well-reported stories told through interesting anecdotes and insightful writing. We want well-researched service journalism on all subjects. Needs essays, opinion, personal experience, women's interest subjects such as family and personal relationships, children, physical and mental health, nutrition and self-improvement. No fiction or poetry. **Buys 200 mss/year.** Submit detailed outline, 2 clips, cover letter describing your publishing history, SASE or IRCs. Length: 1,000-2,500 words. **Pays $1/word.**

Tips Query letters should be concise and to the point. Also, writers should keep close tabs on *Family Circle* and other women's magazines to avoid submitting recently run subject matter.

$$$$ ✪ FLARE MAGAZINE

One Mt. Pleasant Rd., 8th Floor, Toronto ON M4Y 2Y5 Canada. (416)764-2863. Fax: (416)764-2866. E-mail: editors@flare.com. Website: www.flare.com. Monthly magazine for women ages 17-34. Byline given. Offers 50% kill fee. Buys first North American serial rights, buys electronic rights. Accepts queries by e-mail. Response time varies. Sample copy for #10 SASE. Guidelines available online.

Nonfiction Looking for women's fashion, beauty, health, sociological trends and celebrities. **Buys 24 mss/year.** Query. Length: 200-1,200 words. **Pays $1/word.** Pays expenses of writers on assignment.

Tips Study our masthead to determine if your topic is handled by regular contributing staff or a staff member.

GIRLFRIENDZ

The Thinking Woman's Magazine, JNT Communications, LLC, 6 Brookville Dr., Cherry Hill NJ 08003. E-mail: tobi@girlfriendzmag.com. Website: www.girlfriendzmag.com. **80% freelance written**. Quarterly magazine covering Baby Boomer women. "As a publication by and for Baby Boomer women, we are most interested in entertaining, educating and empowering our readers. Our target is smart women born between 1946 and 1964. We like a little humor in our articles, but only if it's appropriate and subtle. And most importantly, all facts must be checked for accuracy. We insist on well-researched and well-documented information." Estab. 2007. Circ. 33,000. Byline given. Headshot and bio included. "As a startup, we are unable to pay our writers." No kill fee. Buys first North American serial rights, buys electronic rights. Editorial lead time 3 months. Submit seasonal material 6 months in advance. Accepts queries by e-mail. Accepts previously published material. Accepts simultaneous submissions. Responds in 2 weeks to queries. Sample copy for $5. Guidelines available online.

Nonfiction Needs book excerpts, expose, historical, how-to, humor, interview, (celebrities only), new product, articles of interest to women born 1946-1964. "We do not want fiction, essays or poetry." **Buys Accepts 20/year mss/year.** Query. Length: 735-1,200 words. Sometimes pays expenses of writers on assignment.

Photos State availability Captions, identification of subjects required. Reviews JPEGs and/or PDFs, 300 dpi. We offer no additional payment for photos accepted with mss. Buys one time rights.

Tips "Please do not call us or fax a query or manuscript. E-mail only. Please query only—no manuscripts. And please, no fiction, essays or poetry. We are interested in nonfiction articles that will make Boomer women think. We also like articles with subjects that our audience can identify with, though we're not looking for Sandwich Generation articles. Also, no articles on pre-schoolers or pregnancy. Our readers have children who are either just starting to exit elementary school, are in middle school, high school or college; are just getting married; are just having children, or already have children. We are also looking for an ethnic mix of writers."

$ $ $ $ GLAMOUR

Conde Nast Publications, Inc., 4 Times Square, 16th floor, New York NY 10036. (212)286-2860. Fax: (212)286-7731. Website: www.glamour.com. Monthly magazine covering subjects ranging from fashion, beauty and health, personal relationships, career, travel, food and entertainment. *Glamour* is edited for the contemporary woman, and informs her of the trends and recommends how she can adapt them to her needs, and motivates her to take action. Estab. 1939. No kill fee.

Nonfiction Needs personal experience, relationships, travel.

$ $ $ $ GOOD HOUSEKEEPING

Hearst Corp., 300 W. 57th St., 28th Floor, New York NY 10019-5288. (212)649-2200. Website: www.goodhousekeeping.com. Monthly magazine. *Good Housekeeping* is edited for the `New Traditionalist.' Articles which focus on food, fitness, beauty, and child care draw upon the resources of the Good Housekeeping Institute. Editorial includes human interest stories, articles that focus on social issues, money management, health news, travel. Circ. 5,000,000. Byline given. Pays on acceptance. Offers 25% kill fee. Buys first North American serial rights. Submit seasonal material 6 months in advance. Responds in 2-3 months to queries. Responds in 2-3 months to mss. For sample copy, call (212)649-2359. Guidelines for #10 SASE.

Nonfiction Consumer, social issues, dramatic narrative, nutrition, work, relationships, psychology, trends. **Buys 4-6 mss/issue mss/year.** Query. Length: 1,500-2,500 words. Pays expenses of writers on assignment.

Photos Contact: Melissa Paterno, art director. Toni Paciello, photo editor. Photos purchased on assignment mostly. State availability Model releases required. Pays $100-350 for b $200-400 for color photos.

Columns/Departments Profiles (inspirational, activist or heroic women), 400-600 words. Query with published clips. **Pays $1/word for items 300-600 words.**

Fiction Contact: Laura Mathews, fiction editor. No longer accepts unagented fiction submissions. Because of heavy volume of fiction submissions, *Good Housekeeping* is not accepting unsolicited submissions at this time. Agented submissions only. 1,500 words (short-shorts); novel according to merit of material; average 5,000 word short stories. **Pays $1,000 minimum.**

Tips Always send a SASE and clips. We prefer to see a query first. Do not send material on subjects already covered in-house by the Good Housekeeping Institute—these include food, beauty, needlework and crafts.

$ $ GRACE ORMONDE WEDDING STYLE

Elegant Publishing, Inc., P.O. Box 89, Barrington RI 02806. Fax: (401)245-5371. E-mail: jessica@weddingstylemagazine.com. Website: www.weddingstylemagazine.com. **90% freelance written.** Semiannual magazine covering weddings catering to the affluent bride. Estab. 1997. Circ. 500,000. Pays on publication. No kill fee. Publishes ms an average of 4 months after acceptance. Buys all rights. Editorial lead time 1 month. Sample copy available online. Guidelines by email.

- Does not accept queries.

Photos State availability Reviews transparencies. Negotiates payment individually

Tips E-mail resume and 5 clips/samples in any area of writing.

$ $ HER SPORTS

Active Sports Lifestyles, Wet Dog Media, 1499 Beach Dr. SE, Suite B, St. Petersburg FL 33701. E-mail: editorial@hersports.com. Website: www.hersports.com. **60% freelance written.** Bimonthly magazine covering women's outdoor, individual sports. *Her Sports* is for active women ages 25-49 who regard sports and being active an important part of their lifestyle. Our readers are beyond 'quick-fix diets' and '5-minute' exercise routines, and are looking for a way to balance being active and healthy with a busy lifestyle. We focus on health, nutrition, and sports, and sports training, travel, and profiles on everyday athletes and professional athletes with unique and motivational stories. Estab. 2004. Circ. 85,000. Byline given. Pays on publication. Offers 50% kill fee. Publishes ms an average of 3 months after acceptance. Buys all rights. Editorial lead time 3 months. Submit seasonal material 6-8 months in advance. Accepts queries by e-mail. Responds in 6-8 weeks to queries. Responds in 1 month to mss. Sample copy for $4.99 and SASE with 5 first-class stamps. Guidelines available online.

Nonfiction Needs personal experience. Please do not send articles pertaining to team sports; we cover only outdoor individual sports. **Buys 6 mss/year.** Query with published clips. Length: 800-1,200 words. **Pays $200-600 for assigned articles.**

Photos Contact: Kristin Mayer, creative director. State availability Captions, identification of subjects required. Reviews GIF/JPEG files. Negotiates payment individually. Buys one time rights.

Columns/Departments Active Updates, Fitness, Health, Fit Foods, 1,200 words; Discoveries (travel articles of interest to active women), 1,500-2,000 words; Weekend Warrior (how-to tips for mastering the sports we cover), 1,000-1,200 words; Her Story (short profile on everyday athletes who are an inspiration to others), 650 words. at least 24 Query.

Tips Persistence pays off but burying the editor with multiple submissions will quickly lose you points. If you're asked to check back in 2 months, do so, but if the editor tells you she's on deadline, simply inquire about a better time to get back in touch.

$ $ HOPE FOR WOMEN

P.O. Box 3241, Muncie IN 47307. (765)284-4673. Fax: (765)284-0919. E-mail: publisher@hopeforwomenmag.org. Website: www.hopeforwomenmag.org. **90% freelance written**. Bimonthly lifestyle magazine that offers faith, love, and virtue for the modern Christian Woman. *Hope for Women* presents refreshing, inspirational articles in an engaging and authentic tone to women from various walks of life. The magazine encourages readers and deals with real-world issues—all while adhering to Christian values and principles. Estab. 2005. Circ. 10,000. Byline given. Pays on publication. Publishes ms an average of 4-6 months after acceptance. Buys first rights, buys electronic rights. Editorial lead time 4-6 months. Accepts queries by mail, e-mail, fax. Guidelines by email.

- Web site is being revamped.

Nonfiction Needs book excerpts, essays, general interest, how-to, humor, inspirational, interview, new product, opinion, personal experience, photo feature, religious, travel. Query. 500 words (minimum) **Pays 10-20¢/word.** Sometimes pays expenses of writers on assignment.

Columns/Departments Relationships (nurturing positive relationships—marriage, dating, divorce, single life), 800-1,200 words; Light (reports on issues such as infidelity, homosexuality, addiction, and domestic violence), 500-800 words; Journey (essays on finding your identity with Christ), 500-800 words; Marketplace (finance/money management), 800-1,200 words); E-Spot (book, music, TV, and film reviews), 500-800 words; Family First (parenting encouragement and instruction), 800-1,500 words; Health/Fitness (nutrition/exercise), 800-1,200 words; The Look (fashion/beauty tips), 500-800 words; Home Essentials (home/garden how-to), 500-800 words. Query. **Pays 10-20¢/word.**

Tips Our readers are a diverse group of women, ages 25-54. They want to read articles about real women dealing with real problems. Because our readers are balancing work and family, they want information that is presented in a no-nonsense fashion that is relevant and readable.

I DO . FOR BRIDES

2400 Lake Park Dr., Suite 440, Smyrna GA 30080. (678)589-8800. E-mail: jgibbs@idoforbrides.com. Website: www.idoforbrides.com. **30% freelance written**. Quarterly magazine covering the bridal industry. The magazine includes tips for wedding preparation, bridal attire, honeymoon and wedding destinations. Publishes 4 regional versions: Alabama, Georgia, Tennessee, and Washington DC/Maryland/Virginia. Estab. 1996. Circ. 160,000. Byline given. No kill fee. Publishes ms an average of 8 months after acceptance. Buys all rights. Editorial lead time 8 months. Submit seasonal material 8 months in advance. Accepts queries by mail, e-mail. Accepts simultaneous submissions.

Nonfiction Needs book excerpts, essays, general interest, historical, how-to, bridal-related, humor, inspirational, interview, new product, opinion, personal experience, photo feature, religious, travel. **Buys 8 mss/year.** Query. Length: 300-1,000 words. **Pays variable rate.**

$ $ $ $ ☒ LADIES' HOME JOURNAL

Meredith Corp., 125 Park Ave., 20th Floor, New York NY 10017-5516. (212)557-6600. Fax: (212)455-1313. E-mail: lhj@mdp.com. Website: www.lhj.com. **50% freelance written**. Monthly magazine focusing on issues of concern to women 30-45. They cover a broader range of news and political issues than many women's magazines. *Ladies' Home Journal* is for active, empowered women who are evolving in new directions. It addresses informational needs with highly focused features and articles on a variety of topics: self, style, family, home, world, health, and food. Estab. 1882. Circ. 4.1 million. Pays on acceptance. Offers 25% kill fee. Publishes ms an average of 4-12 months after acceptance. Buys first North American serial rights. Rights bought vary with submission. Editorial lead time 4 months. Accepts queries by mail, e-mail. Accepts simultaneous submissions. Responds in 3 months to queries. Guidelines available online.

Nonfiction Submissions on the following subjects should be directed to the editor listed for each: investigative reports, news-related features, psychology/relationships/sex, celebrities/entertainment. Send 1-2 page query, SASE, rÃˆsumÃˆ, clips via mail or e-mail (preferred). Length: 2,000-3,000 words. **Pays**

$2,000-4,000. Pays expenses of writers on assignment.
Photos *LHJ* arranges for its own photography almost all the time. State availability Captions, identification of subjects, model releases required. Offers variable payment for photos accepted with ms. Rights bought vary with submission.
Fiction Only short stories and novels submitted by an agent or publisher will be considered. No poetry of any kind. **Buys 12 mss/year.** Send complete ms. 2,000-2,500

$ $ THE LINK & VISITOR

Baptist Women of Ontario and Quebec, 100 - 304 The East Mall, Etobicoke ON M9B 6E2 Canada. (416)622-8600 ext. 305. E-mail: rjames@baptistwomen.com. Website: www.baptistwomen.com. **50% freelance written.** Magazine published 6 times/ year designed to help Baptist women grow their world, faith, relationships, creativity, and mission vision-evangelical, egalitarian, Canadian. Estab. 1878. Circ. 3,500. Byline given. Pays on publication. No kill fee. Publishes ms an average of 6 months after acceptance. Buys one-time rights, buys second serial (reprint) rights, buys simultaneous rights. Makes work-for-hire assignments. Editorial lead time 2 months. Submit seasonal material 4 months in advance. Accepts simultaneous submissions. Sample copy for 9x12 SAE with 2 first-class Canadian stamps. Guidelines available online.
Nonfiction Articles must be Biblically literate. No easy answers, American mindset or U.S. focus, retelling of Bible stories, sermons. Needs inspirational, interview, religious. **Buys 30-35 mss/year.** Send complete ms. Length: 750-2,000 words. **Pays 5-12¢/word (Canadian).** Sometimes pays expenses of writers on assignment.
Photos State availability Captions required. Offers no additional payment for photos accepted with ms. Buys one time rights.
Tips We cannot use unsolicited manuscripts from non-Canadian writers. When submitting by e-mail, please send stories as messages, not as attachments.

$ LONG ISLAND WOMAN

Maraj, Inc., P.O. Box 176, Malverne NY 11565. E-mail: editor@liwomanonline.com. Website: www.liwomanonline.com. **40% freelance written.** Monthly magazine covering issues of importance to women—health, family, finance, arts, entertainment, fitness, travel, home. Estab. 2001. Circ. 40,000. Byline given. Pays within 1 month of publication. Offers 33% kill fee. Publishes ms an average of 3 months after acceptance. Buys one-time rights for print and online use. Editorial lead time 3 months. Submit seasonal material 3 months in advance. Accepts queries by mail, e-mail. Accepts previously published material. Accepts simultaneous submissions. Responds in 8 weeks to queries. Responds in 3 months to mss. Sample copy for $5. Guidelines available online.

- Responds if interested in using reprints that were submitted.

Nonfiction Needs book excerpts, general interest, how-to, humor, interview, new product, travel, reviews. **Buys 25-30 mss/year.** Send complete ms. Length: 500-1,800 words. **Pays $35-150.**
Photos State availability of or send photos Captions, identification of subjects, model releases required. Reviews 5x7 prints.
Columns/Departments Humor; Health Issues; Family Issues; Financial and Business Issues; Book Reviews and Books; Arts and Entertainment; Travel and Leisure; Home and Garden; Fitness.

$ $ $ $ MARIE CLAIRE

The Hearst Publishing Corp., 1790 Broadway, 3rd Floor, New York NY 10019. (212)649-5000. Fax: (212)649-5050. E-mail: joannacoles@hearst.com. Website: www.marieclaire.com. Monthly magazine written for today's younger working woman with a smart service-oriented view. Estab. 1937. Circ. 952,223. No kill fee. Editorial lead time 6 months.

MARIE CLAIRE MAGAZINE

Pacific Magazines, 35-51 Mitchell St., McMahons Point NSW 2060 Australia. (61)(2)9464-3300. Fax: (61)(2)9464-3483. Website: www.pacificmags.com.au. **Contact:** Jackie Frank, ed. Monthly magazine for today's intelligent, thinking woman who likes to be challenged and informed at all levels. Circ. 116,500.

- We have a readership of 522,000.

Nonfiction Needs general interest, how-to, interview, new product, photo feature. Query.

$ $ $ $ MS. MAGAZINE

433 S. Beverly Dr., Beverly Hills CA 90212. (310)556-2515. Fax: (310)556-2514. E-mail: mkort@msmagazine.com. Website: www.msmagazine.com. **70% freelance written.** Quarterly magazine on women's issues and news. Estab. 1972. Circ. 150,000. Byline given. Offers 25% kill fee. Buys all rights. Responds in 3 months to queries. Responds in 3 months to mss. Sample copy for $9. Guidelines available online.
Nonfiction International and national (U.S.) news, the arts, books, popular culture, feminist theory and scholarship, ecofeminism, women's health, political and economic affairs. **Buys 4-5 feature (2,000-3,000**

words) and 4-5 short (500 words) mss/year. Query with published clips. Length: 300-3,500 words. **Pays $1/word, 50¢/word for news stories and book review.**
Columns/Departments 6-10 **Pays $1/word**
Tips Needs international and national women's news, investigative reporting, personal narratives, and prize-winning journalists and feminist thinkers.

$ $ NA'AMAT WOMAN

Magazine of NA'AMAT USA, Na'Amat USA, 350 Fifth Ave., Suite 4700, New York NY 10118-4700. Fax: (212)563-5710. E-mail: judith@naamat.org. Website: www.naamat.org. **80% freelance written**. Quarterly magazine covering Jewish issues/subjects. "We cover issues and topics of interest to the Jewish community in the U.S., Israel, and the rest of the world with emphasis on Jewish women's issues." Estab. 1926. Circ. 13,000. Byline given. Pays on publication. No kill fee. Publishes ms an average of 6 months after acceptance. Buys first North American serial rights, buys second serial (reprint) rights. Makes work-for-hire assignments. Submit seasonal material 6 months in advance. Accepts queries by mail, e-mail. Accepts simultaneous submissions. Responds in 4 weeks to queries. Responds in 3 months to mss Sample copy for $2 Guidelines by email
Nonfiction "Articles must be of particular interest to the Jewish community." Needs book excerpts, essays, historical, interview, personal experience, photo feature, travel, Jewish topics & issues, political & social issues & women's issues. **Buys 16-20 mss/year.** Send complete ms. **Pays 10-20¢/word for assigned and unsolicited articles.** Sometimes pays expenses of writers on assignment.
Photos State availability Reviews GIF/JPEG files. Negotiates payment individually. Buys one time rights.
Fiction Contact: Judith A. Sokoloff, editor. We want serious fiction, with insight, reflection and consciousness. Needs novel excerpts, literary with Jewish content. We do not want fiction that is mostly dialogue. No corny Jewish humor. No Holocaust fiction. **Buys 1-2 mss/year. mss/year.** Query with published clips or send complete ms. Length: 2,000-3,000 words. **Pays 10-20¢/word for assigned articles and for unsolicited articles.**

$ $ $ $ PREGNANCY

A New Look at Motherhood, Future US, Inc., 4000 Shoreline Ct., Suite 400, S. San Francisco CA 94080-1960. (650)872-1642. E-mail: editors@pregnancymagazine.com. Website: www.pregnancymagazine.com. **40% freelance written**. Magazine covering products, wellness, technology fashion, and beauty for pregnant women; and products, health, and child care for babies up to 12 mos. old. "A large part of our audience is first-time moms who seek advice & information about health, relationships, diet, celebrities, fashion, & green living for pregnant women and babies up to 12 mos. old. Our readers are first-time and experienced moms (and dads) who want articles that are relevant to their modern lives. Our goal is to help our readers feel confident and prepared for pregnancy and parenthood by providing the best information for today's parents." Estab. 2000. Circ. 250,000. Offers kill fee. TBD Editorial lead time 5 months. Submit seasonal material 5-6 months in advance. Guidelines available
Nonfiction Buys 60 mss/yr. mss/year. Length: 50-2,000 words.
Tips "Interested freelancers should first read *Pregnancy*'s Writer's Guidelines, which are available for download from the website (click the Contact Us button). When sending pitch ideas, be sure to follow those guidelines carefully."

P31 WOMAN

Bringing God's Peace, Perspective, and Purpose to Today's Busy Woman, Proverbs 31 Ministries, 616-G Matthews-Mint Hill Rd., Charlotte NC 28105. (704)849-2270. E-mail: janet@proverbs31.org. Website: www.proverbs31.org. **50% freelance written**. Monthly magazine covering Christian issues for women. The *P31 Woman* provides Christian wives and mothers with articles that encourage them in their faith and support them in the many roles they have as women. We look for articles that have a Biblical foundation and offer inspiration, yet have a practical application to everyday life. Estab. 1992. Circ. 10,000. Byline given. No kill fee. Publishes ms an average of 6 months after acceptance. No rights purchased. Editorial lead time 5 months. Submit seasonal material 5-6 months in advance. Accepts queries by mail, e-mail. Accepts previously published material. Accepts simultaneous submissions. Responds in 2-4 weeks to queries. Responds in 1-2 months to mss. Sample copy online or $2 for hard copy. Guidelines available online.
Nonfiction Needs humor, inspirational, personal experience, religious. No biographical stories or articles about men's issues. Send complete ms. Length: 200-1,000 words. **Pays in contributor copies.**

RESOURCES FOR FEMINIST RESEARCH

RFR/DRF (Resources for Feminist Research), OISE, University of Toronto, 252 Bloor St. W., Toronto ON M5S 1V6 Canada. E-mail: rfrdrf@oise.utoronto.ca. Website: www.oise.utoronto.ca/rfr. Semiannual academic journal covering feminist research in an interdisciplinary, international perspective. Estab. 1972. Circ. 2,500. Byline given. Publishes ms an average of 1 year after acceptance. Buys all rights. Editorial lead time 1 year. Accepts queries by e-mail. Responds in 2 weeks to queries. Responds in 6-8 months to mss Guidelines free

Nonfiction Needs essays, academic articles and book reviews. Does not want nonacademic articles. Send complete ms. Length: 3,000-5,000 words.

Photos Send photos Identification of subjects required. Reviews prints, GIF/JPEG files. Offers no additional payment for photos accepted with ms. Buys one time rights.

$ $ SKIRT! MAGAZINE

Morris Communications, 7 Radcliffe St., Suite 302, Charleston SC 29403. (843)958-0028. Fax: (843)958-0029. E-mail: editor@skirt.com. Website: www.skirt.com. **50% freelance written**. Monthly magazine covering women's interest. *Skirt!* is all about women—their work, play, families, creativity, style, health, wealth, bodies, and souls. The magazine's attitude is spirited, independent, outspoken, serious, playful, irreverent, sometimes controversial, and always passionate. Estab. 1994. Circ. 285,000. Byline given. Pays on publication. No kill fee. Publishes ms an average of 2 months after acceptance. Buys one-time rights. Editorial lead time 2-3 months. Submit seasonal material 2-3 months in advance. Accepts queries by e-mail. Accepts simultaneous submissions. Responds in 6-8 weeks to queries. Responds in 1-2 months to mss. Sample copy for $5. Guidelines available online.

Nonfiction Needs essays, humor, personal experience. Do not send feature articles. We only accept submissions of completed personal essays. **Buys 100+ mss/year.** Send complete ms. Length: 900-1,200 words. **Pays $150-200.**

Photos We feature a different color photo, painting, or illustration on the cover each month. Each issue also features a b&w photo by a female photographer. Submit artwork via e-mail or mail (include SASE). Reviews Slides, high-resolution digital files. Does not pay for photos or artwork, but the artist's bio is published.

Tips Surprise and charm us. We look for fearless essays that take chances with content and subject. *Skirt!* is not your average women's magazine. We push the envelope and select content that makes our readers think.

$ STRUT

Signature Media, 615 W. Lafayette, Detroi MI 48226. (313)222-2381. E-mail: talktous@strutmag.com. Website: www.strutmag.com. **75% freelance written**. Monthly magazine covering women's issues. *Strut* is designed to surprise, charm and entertain. It celebrates women's opinions and expressions. In addition to expertise shared by women on fashion, dÃˆcor and health experts, *Strut* publishes 3-5 essays each month on topics related to themes. All nonfiction must capture the variety and diversity of women's lives and interests. Preference given to work by metro Detroit writers, but all quality work will be considered. Estab. 2004. Circ. 135,000. Byline given. Pays on publication. No kill fee. Publishes ms an average of 1 month after acceptance. Buys one-time rights. Editorial lead time 3-5 months. Submit seasonal material 3-5 months in advance. Accepts queries by e-mail. Accepts simultaneous submissions. Sample copy free.

Nonfiction Needs book excerpts, essays, new product, personal experience. We do not want diatribes against men. Send complete ms. Length: 700-800 words. **$100 min. TBD for assigned articles.$100 min. TBD for unsolicited articles.** Sometimes pays expenses of writers on assignment.

Photos We are looking for original paintings, illustrations (color or black & white), cartoons and fine art photographs that evoke a sense of place, attitude and fun. Preference given to work by metro Detroit artists, but all quality work considered. We are looking for original, unpublished fine art, representational of a woman or women.

$ $ THAT'S LIFE!

Bauer Publishing, Academic House, 24-28 Oval Rd., London England NW1 7DT United Kingdom. (44)(207)241-8000. Website: www.bauer.co.uk. Weekly publication combining real-life stories with classic women's editorial and a real sense of humour. Aimed at women 20-35 years old. Estab. 1995. Circ. 550,000. No kill fee. Submit seasonal material 3 months in advance. Accepts queries by mail. Responds in 6 weeks to mss. Guidelines by email.

Fiction Stories should have a strong plot and a good twist. A sexy relationships/scene can feature strongly, but isn't essential—the plot twist is much more important. The writing should be chronological and fast moving. A maximum of 4 characters is advisable. Avoid straightforward romance, historical backgrounds, science fiction, and stories told by animals or small children. Graphic murders and sex crimes—especially those involving children—are not acceptable. Send complete ms. 700 words **£400**.

Tips Study the magazine for a few weeks to get an idea of our style and flavor.

$ $ TODAY'S BRIDE

Family Communications, 65 The East Mall, Toronto ON M8Z SW3 Canada. (416)537-2604. Fax: (416)538-1794. E-mail: info@canadianbride.com. Website: www.todaysbride.ca. www.canadianbride.com. **20% freelance written**. Semiannual magazine. Magazine provides information to engaged couples on all aspects of wedding planning, including tips, fashion advice, etc. There are also beauty, home, groom, and honeymoon travel sections. Estab. 1979. Circ. 102,000. Byline given. Pays on acceptance. No kill fee. Buys all rights. Editorial lead time 6 months. Accepts queries by mail, e-mail, fax. Accepts simultaneous submissions. Responds in 2 weeks-1 month.

Nonfiction Needs humor, opinion, personal experience. No travel pieces. Send complete ms. Length: 800-1,400 words. **Pays $250-300.**

Photos Send photos Identification of subjects required. Reviews transparencies, prints. Negotiates payment individually. Rights purchased negotiated on individual basis.

Tips Send us tight writing about topics relevant to all brides and grooms. Stories for grooms, especially those written by/about grooms, are also encouraged.

$ $ TODAY'S CHRISTIAN WOMAN

465 Gundersen Dr., Carol Stream IL 60188-2498. (630)260-6200. Fax: (630)260-0114. E-mail: tcwedit@christianitytoday.com. Website: www.todayschristianwoman.com. **Contact:** Ginger Kolbaba, editor, Cynthia Thomas, editorial coordinator. **50% freelance written.** Bimonthly magazine for Christian women of all ages, single and married, homemakers, and career women. *"Today's Christian Woman* seeks to help women deal with the contemporary issues and hot topics that impact their lives, as well as provide depth, balance, and a Biblical perspective to the relationships they grapple with daily in the following arenas: family, friendship, faith, marriage, single life, self, work, and health." Estab. 1978. Circ. 230,000. Byline given. Pays on acceptance. No kill fee. Publishes ms an average of 6-12 months after acceptance. Buys first rights. Submit seasonal material 9 months in advance. Accepts queries by mail, e-mail, fax. Responds in 2 months to queries. Responds in 2 months to mss. Sample copy for $5. Writer's guidelines for #10 SASE or online

Nonfiction How-to, narrative, inspirational. *Practical* spiritual living articles, 1,200-1,500 words. Humor (light, first-person pieces that include some spiritual distinctive), 1,000 words. Issues (third-person, anecdotal articles that report on scope of trends or hot topics, and provide perspective and practical take away on issues, plus sidebars), 1,500 words. Needs how-to, inspirational. Query. No unsolicited mss. The query should include article summary, purpose, and reader value, author's qualifications, suggested length, date to send, and SASE for reply. **Pays 20-25¢/word.**

Tips "Articles should be practical and contain a distinct evangelical Christian perspective. While *TCW* adheres strictly to this underlying perspective in all its editorial content, articles should refrain from using language that assumes a reader's familiarity with Christian or church-oriented terminology. Bible quotes and references should be used selectively. All Bible quotes should be taken from the New International Version if possible. All articles should be highly anecdotal, personal in tone, and universal in appeal."

$ $ $ $ WISH

St. Joseph Media, 111 Queen St. E., Suite 320, Toronto ON M5C 1S2 Canada. E-mail: jane@wish.ca. Website: www.wish.ca. Pays on acceptance. No kill fee. Guidelines available online.

Nonfiction Fashion, beauty, home decor, food, family, relationships, health & wellness, fitness. Query. **Pays $1/word.**

$ $ WOMAN'S LIFE

A Publication of Woman's Life Insurance Society, 1338 Military St., P.O. Box 5020, Port Huron MI 48061-5020. (800)521-9292. Fax: (810)985-6970. E-mail: wkrabach@womanslife.org. Website: www.womanslife.org. **30% freelance written.** Quarterly magazine published for a primarily female membership to help them care for themselves and their families. Estab. 1892. Circ. 32,000. Byline given. Pays on publication. No kill fee. Publishes ms an average of 1 year after acceptance. Buys one-time rights, buys second serial (reprint) rights, buys simultaneous rights. Submit seasonal material 6 months in advance. Accepts queries by mail, e-mail, fax. Accepts simultaneous submissions. Responds in 1 year to queries and to mss. Sample copy for sae with 9 X 12 envelope and 4 First-Class stamps. Guidelines for #10 SASE.

- "Works only with published/established writers."

Nonfiction "Looking primarily for general interest stories for women aged 25-55 regarding physical, mental, and emotional health and fitness; and financial/fiscal health and fitness. We would like to see more creative financial pieces that are directed at women." **Buys 4-10 mss/year.** Send complete ms. Length: 1,000-2,000 words. **Pays $150-500.**

Reprints Send tearsheet, photocopy or typed ms with rights for sale noted and information about when and where the material previously appeared. Pays 15% of amount paid for an original article

Photos Only interested in photos included with ms. Identification of subjects, model releases required.

$ WOMEN IN BUSINESS

American Business Women's Association (The ABWA Co., Inc.), 9100 Ward Pkwy., P.O. Box 8728, Kansas City MO 64114-0728. (816)361-6621. Fax: (816)361-4991. E-mail: abwa@abwa.org. Website: www.abwa.org. **30% freelance written.** Bimonthly magazine covering issues affecting working women. How-to features for career women on business trends, small-business ownership, self-improvement, and retirement issues. Profiles business women. Estab. 1949. Circ. 45,000. Byline given. Pays on acceptance. No kill fee. Publishes ms an average of 3 months after acceptance. Buys first North American serial rights. Editorial lead time 3 months. Accepts queries by mail, e-mail, fax. Accepts simultaneous submissions. Responds in 3 weeks to queries. Responds in 2 months to mss. Sample copy for sae with 9x12 envelope and 4 First-Class stamps. Guidelines for #10 SASE.

Nonfiction Needs how-to, interview, computer/Internet. No fiction or poetry. **Buys 3% of submitted mss/year.** Query. Length: 500-1,000 words. **Pays $100/500 words.**

Photos State availability Identification of subjects required. Reviews prints. Offers no additional payment for photos accepted with ms Buys all rights.

Columns/Departments Life After Business (concerns of retired business women); It's Your Business (entrepreneurial advice for business owners); Health Spot (health issues that affect women in the work place). Length: 500-750 words. Query. **Pays $100/500 words**

YORKSHIRE WOMEN'S LIFE

P.O. Box 113, Leeds LS8 2WX United Kingdom. E-mail: ywlmagenquiries@btinternet.com. Website: www.yorkshirewomenslife.co.uk. No kill fee. Guidelines by email.

Nonfiction Needs general interest, women's issues, personal experience, author describes some aspect of her life in first person, reviews of theatres/art exhibitions/books. Does not want cooking/recipes, short stories, or poetry. Submit 200-word proposal, published clips, bio, SAE.

Photos "Accepts color copies via post from female visual artists. Include a short CV."

MARKETS

Trade Journals

Many writers who pick up *Writer's Market* for the first time do so with the hope of selling an article to one of the popular, high-profile consumer magazines found on newsstands and in bookstores. Many of those writers are surprised to find an entire world of magazine publishing exists outside the realm of commercial magazines—trade journals. Writers who *have* discovered trade journals have found a market that offers the chance to publish regularly in subject areas they find interesting, editors who are typically more accessible than their commercial counterparts, and pay rates that rival those of the big-name magazines. **(Note: All of the magazines listed in the Trade Journals section are paying markets. However, some of the magazines are not identified by payment rates ($—$$$$) because the magazines preferred not to disclose specific payment information.)**

Trade journal is the general term for any publication focusing on a particular occupation or industry. Other terms used to describe the different types of trade publications are business, technical, and professional journals. They are read by truck drivers, bricklayers, farmers, fishermen, heart surgeons, and just about everyone else working in a trade or profession. Trade periodicals are sharply angled to the specifics of the professions on which they report. They offer business-related news, features, and service articles that will foster their readers' professional development.

Editors at trade journals tell us their audience is made up of knowledgeable and highly interested readers. Writers for trade journals have to either possess knowledge about the field in question or be able to report it accurately from interviews with those who do. Writers who have or can develop a good grasp of a specialized body of knowledge will find trade magazine editors who are eager to hear from them.

An ideal way to begin your foray into trade journals is to write for those that report on your present profession. Whether you've been teaching dance, farming, or working as a paralegal, begin by familiarizing yourself with the magazines that serve your occupation. After you've read enough issues to have a feel for the kinds of pieces the magazines run, approach the editors with your own article ideas. If you don't have experience in a profession but can demonstrate an ability to understand (and write about) the intricacies and issues of a particular trade that interests you, editors will still be willing to hear from you.

Information on trade publications listed in the previous edition of *Writer's Market*, but not included in this edition, can be found in the General Index.

ADVERTISING, MARKETING & PR

ADNEWS

Yaffa Publishing, 17-21 Bellevue St., Surry Hills NSW 2010 Australia. (61)(2)9281-2333. Fax: (61)(2)9281-2750. E-mail: yaffa@yaffa.com.au. Website: www.yaffa.com.au. Biweekly magazine covering advertising, marketing and media industries of Australia.

Nonfiction Needs how-to, interview. Query.

$ $ $ ADVANTAGES MAGAZINE

The Advertising Specialty Institute, 4800 Street Rd., Trevose PA 19053. (215)953-3337. Website: www.advantagesinfo.com. **40% freelance written**. Monthly magazine covering promotional products (branded T-shirts, mugs, pens, etc.). *Advantages* is a 15-issue publication targeted to promotional products salespeople. Its main objective is to be a comprehensive source of sales strategies, information and inspiration through articles, columns, case histories and product showcases. The magazine is presented in a fun and easy-to-read format to keep busy salespeople interested and entertained. The easy-to-use reader response system makes it fast and simple to request product information from suppliers featured in showcases. We want our subscribers to look forward to its arrival and to believe that *Advantages* is the one magazine they can't do without. Estab. 1997. Circ. 40,000. Byline given. Pays on acceptance. Publishes ms an average of 1-2 months after acceptance. Buys all rights. Editorial lead time 1 month. Submit seasonal material 1 month in advance. Accepts queries by e-mail, phone. Accepts simultaneous submissions. Sample copy free. Guidelines free.

Nonfiction Full-length features on market opportunities and selling-related topics. **Buys 40 mss/year.** Query. Length: 2,500-3,500 words. **Pays $500-1,000+.**

Tips Just send me an e-mail, especially if you have any previous experience writing on the promotional products industry and/or sales topics in general.

AUSTRALIAN CREATIVE

Yaffa Publishing, 17-21 Bellevue St., Surry Hills NSW 2010 Australia. (61)(2)9281-2333. Fax: (61)(2)9281-2750. E-mail: yaffa@yaffa.com.au. Website: www.yaffa.com.au. Bimonthly magazine catering to the creative services industry.

Nonfiction Needs general interest, how-to, inspirational, interview, new product, technical. Query.

$ $ $ BRAND PACKAGING

Stagnito Communications, 155 Pfingsten Rd., Suite 205, Deerfield IL 60015. (847)405-4000. Fax: (847)405-4100. E-mail: acevedoj@bnpmedia.com. Website: www.brandpackaging.com. **15% freelance written**. Magazine published 10 times/year covering how packaging can be a marketing tool. We publish strategies and tactics to make products stand out on the shelf. Our market is brand managers who are marketers but need to know something about packaging. Estab. 1997. Circ. 33,000. Byline given. Pays on acceptance. Publishes ms an average of 2 months after acceptance. Makes work-for-hire assignments. Editorial lead time 3 months. Submit seasonal material 3 months in advance. Accepts queries by mail, fax. Sample copy free.

Nonfiction Needs how-to, interview, new product. **Buys 10 mss/year.** Send complete ms. Length: 600-2,400 words. **Pays 40-50¢/word.**

Photos State availability Identification of subjects required. Reviews contact sheets, 35mm transparencies, 4x5 prints. Negotiates payment individually Buys one time rights.

Columns/Departments Emerging Technology (new packaging technology), 600 words. 10 Query. **Pays $150-300.**

Tips Be knowledgeable on marketing techniques and be able to grasp packaging techniques. Be sure you focus on packaging as a marketing tool. Use concrete examples. We are not seeking case histories at this time.

$ DECA DIMENSIONS

1908 Association Dr., Reston VA 20191. (703)860-5000. Fax: (703)860-4013. E-mail: chuck_beatty@deca.org. Website: www.deca.org. **30% freelance written**. Quarterly magazine covering marketing, professional development, business, career training during school year (no issues published May-August). *DECA Dimensions* is the membership magazine for DECA—The Association of Marketing Students—primarily ages 15-19 in all 50 states, the U.S. territories, Germany, and Canada. The magazine is delivered through the classroom. Students are interested in developing professional, leadership, and career skills. Estab. 1947. Circ. 160,000. Byline given. Pays on publication. No kill fee. Buys first rights, buys second serial (reprint) rights. Editorial lead time 3 months. Submit seasonal material 4 months in advance. Accepts queries by mail, e-mail, fax, phone. Accepts simultaneous submissions. Sample copy free.

Nonfiction Interested in seeing trends/forecast information of interest to audience (How do you forecast? Why? What are the trends for the next 5 years in fashion or retail?). Needs essays, general interest, how-to, get jobs, start business, plan for college, etc., interview, business leads, personal experience, working, leadership development. **Buys 10 mss/year.** Send complete ms. Length: 800-1,000 words. **Pays $125 for assigned articles. Pays $100 for unsolicited articles.**

Reprints Send typed manuscript and information about when and where the material previously appeared. Pays 85% of amount paid for an original article

Columns/Departments Professional Development; Leadership, 350-500 words. 6 Send complete ms. **Pays $ 75-100.**

$ $ FPO MAGAZINE

For Publications Only, Auras Custom Publishing, 8435 Georgia Ave., Silver Spring MD 20910. (301)587-4300. Fax: (301)587-6836. E-mail: editor@fpomagazine.com. Website: www.fpomagazine.com. **Contact:** Rob Sugar, editor. **50% freelance written**. Quarterly magazine covering creative and production. "*[FPO] Magazine* is a print and online resource for publication professionals, publishers, editors, designers, and production managers that focuses on the creative side of magazine publishing." Estab. 2007. Circ. 10,000. Byline given. Pays on publication. Offers 25% kill fee. Publishes ms an average of 3-4 months after acceptance. Buys first North American serial rights, buys electronic rights. Editorial lead time 3 months. Accepts queries by mail, e-mail, fax, phone. Accepts previously published material. Accepts simultaneous submissions. Sample copy by email. Guidelines available online.

Nonfiction All articles must relate to magazine design or publishing. Needs essays, historical, how-to, humor, interview, new product, technical. 100 Top Tips (late Fall 2008) **Buys 10-12 mss/year.** Query. **Pays 50¢/word.** Sometimes pays expenses of writers on assignment.

Photos State availability Captions, model releases required. Reviews GIF/JPEG files. Negotiates payment individually.

Columns/Departments Cover Charge; Re: Write; Re: Design; Creative Briefs, all 500 words. 20-25 Query. **Pays 50¢/word.**

Fillers Needs anecdotes, facts, gags, short humor. Length: 100-400 words. **Pays $25-50.**

Tips "Experience working on a magazine helps, along with an understanding of graphic design."

MEDIA INC.

Pacific Northwest Media, Marketing and Creative Services News, P.O. Box 24365, Seattle WA 98124-0365. (206)382-9220. Fax: (206)382-9437. E-mail: mbaumgarten@media-inc.com. Website: www.media-inc.com. **30% freelance written**. Bimonthly magazine covering Northwest US media, advertising, marketing, and creative-service industries. Audience is Northwest ad agencies, marketing professionals, media, and creative-service professionals. Estab. 1987. Circ. 10,000. Byline given. No kill fee. Responds in 1 month to queries. Sample copy for sae with 9x12 envelope and 6 First-Class stamps.

Tips It is best if writers live in the Pacific Northwest and can report on local news and events in Media Inc.'s areas of business coverage.

NETWORKING TIMES

Moving the Heart of Business, Gabriel Media Group, 11418 Kokopeli Place, Chatsworth CA 91311. (818)727-2000. Website: www.networkingtimes.com. **30% freelance written**. Bimonthly magazine covering network marketing and direct sales. *Networking Times* is an advertisement-free educational journal for professional networkers worldwide, available at major bookstores and by subscription. We don't mention any company names, instead filling the pages with practical information that covers two areas: acquisition of skills and building the right mindset to be successful in the world of marketing today. Estab. 2001. Circ. 12,000. Byline given. Pays on publication. Buys all rights. Editorial lead time 3 months. Submit seasonal material 3 months in advance. Accepts queries by e-mail. Sample copy for $9.97. Guidelines by email.

$ $ O'DWYER'S PR REPORT

271 Madison Ave., #600, New York NY 10016. Fax: (212)683-2750. E-mail: jack@odwyerpr.com. Website: www.odwyerpr.com. Monthly magazine providing PR articles. Many of the contributors are PR people publicizing themselves while analyzing something. Byline given. No kill fee. Accepts queries by mail.

Nonfiction We use op-ed pieces and news articles about PR trends. Needs opinion. Query. **Pays $250.**

$ $ $ PROMO MAGAZINE

Insights and Ideas for Building Brands, Penton Media, 244 W. 17th St., New York NY 10011. (212)204-4222. Fax: (203)358-9900. E-mail: larry.jaffee@penton.com. Website: www.promomagazine.com. **5% freelance written**. Monthly magazine covering promotion marketing. *Promo* serves marketers, and stories must be informative, well written, and familiar with the subject matter. Estab. 1987. Circ. 25,000. Byline given. Pays on publication. Offers 25% kill fee. Publishes ms an average of 2 months after acceptance. Buys first North American serial rights. Editorial lead time 3 months. Submit seasonal material 3 months in advance. Responds in 1 month to queries. Sample copy for $5.

Nonfiction Needs expose, general interest, how-to, marketing programs, interview, new product, promotion. No general marketing stories not heavily involved in promotions. Generally does not accept unsolicited mss, query first. **Buys 6-10 mss/year.** Query with published clips. Variable **Pays $1,000 maximum for assigned articles. Pays $500 maximum for unsolicited articles.** Sometimes pays expenses of writers on assignment.

Photos State availability Captions, identification of subjects, model releases required. Reviews contact sheets,

negatives. Negotiates payment individually
Tips Understand that our stories aim to teach marketing professionals about successful promotion strategies. Case studies or new promos have the best chance.

SHOPPER MARKETING

In-Store Marketing Institute, 7400 Skokie Blvd., Skokie IL 60077. (847)675-7400. Fax: (847)675-7494. E-mail: dan_ochwat@instoremarketer.org. Website: www.shoppermarketingmag.com. www.hoytpub.com/poptimes. **80% freelance written**. Monthly tabloid covering advertising and primarily the in-store marketing industry. "We cover how brands market to the shopper at retail, what insights/research did they gather to reach that shopper and how did they activate the program at retail. We write case studies on large branded fixtures, displays, packaging, retail media, and events. We write major category reports, company profiles, trends features, and more. Our readers are marketers and retailers, and a small selection of P-O-P producers (the guys that build the displays)." Circ. 20,000 Estab. 1988. Byline given. Pays on acceptance. Offers no kill fee. Buys all rights. Editorial lead time 2 months. Submit seasonal material 3 months in advance. Accepts queries by e-mail. Accepts simultaneous submissions. Responds in 1 month to queries. Sample copy free. Guidelines free.

$ $ SIGN BUILDER ILLUSTRATED

The How-To Magazine, Simmons-Boardman Publishing Corp., 345 Hudson St., 12th Floor, New York NY 10014. (212)620-7223. E-mail: jwooten@sbpub.com. Website: www.signshop.com. **40% freelance written**. Monthly magazine covering sign and graphic industry. *Sign Builder Illustrated* targets sign professionals where they work: on the shop floor. Our topics cover the broadest spectrum of the sign industry, from design to fabrication, installation, maintenance and repair. Our readers own a similarly wide range of shops, including commercial, vinyl, sign erection and maintenance, electrical and neon, architectural, and awnings. Estab. 1987. Circ. 14,500. Byline given. Pays on acceptance. Offers 10% kill fee. Publishes ms an average of 3 months after acceptance. Buys all rights. Editorial lead time 3 months. Submit seasonal material 4 months in advance. Accepts queries by mail, e-mail, fax, phone. Accepts simultaneous submissions. Responds in 1 month to queries. Sample copy and writer's guidelines free.
Nonfiction Needs historical, how-to, humor, interview, photo feature, technical. **Buys 50-60 mss/year.** Query. Length: 1,000-1,500 words. **Pays $250-550 for assigned articles.**
Photos Send photos Captions, identification of subjects required. Reviews 3x5 prints. Negotiates payment individually Buys all rights.
Tips Be very knowledgeable about a portion of the sign industry you are covering. We want our readers to come away from each article with at least one good idea, one new technique, or one more `trick of the trade.' At the same time, we don't want a purely textbook listing of `do this, do that.' Our readers enjoy *Sign Builder Illustrated* because the publication speaks to them in a clear and lively fashion, from one sign professional to another. We want to engage the reader who has been in the business for some time. While there might be a place for basic instruction in new techniques, our average paid subscriber has been in business over 20 years, employs over seven people, and averages $800,000 in annual sales. These people aren't neophytes content with retread articles they can find anywhere. It's important for our writers to use anecdotes and examples drawn from the daily sign business.

$ $ SIGNCRAFT

The Magazine for Today's Sign Maker, SignCraft Publishing Co., Inc., P.O. Box 60031, Fort Myers FL 33906. (239)939-4644. Fax: (239)939-0607. E-mail: signcraft@signcraft.com. Website: www.signcraft.com. **10% freelance written**. Bimonthly magazine covering the sign industry. "Like any trade magazine, we need material of direct benefit to our readers. We can't afford space for material of marginal interest." Estab. 1980. Circ. 14,000. Byline given. Pays on publication. Offers negotiable kill fee. Publishes ms an average of 6 months after acceptance. Buys first North American serial rights, buys all rights. Accepts queries by mail, e-mail, fax. Responds in 1 month to queries Sample copy and writer's guidelines for $3
Nonfiction "All articles should be directly related to quality commercial signs. If you are familiar with the sign trade, we'd like to hear from you." Needs interview. **Buys 10 mss/year.** Query. Length: 500-2,000 words.

ART, DESIGN & COLLECTIBLES

$ $ AIRBRUSH ACTION MAGAZINE

Action, Inc., 3209 Atlantic Ave., P.O. Box 438, Allenwood NJ 08720. (732)223-7878. Fax: (732)223-2855. E-mail: editor@airbrushaction.com. Website: www.airbrushaction.com. **80% freelance written**. Bimonthly magazine covering the spectrum of airbrush applications: automotive and custom paint applications, illustration, T-shirt airbrushing, fine art, automotive and sign painting, hobby/craft applications, wall murals, fingernails, temporary tattoos, artist profiles, reviews, and more. Estab. 1985. Circ. 35,000. Byline given. Pays 1 month after publication. Publishes ms an average of 6 months after acceptance. Buys all rights. Editorial lead time 6 months. Submit seasonal material 6 months in advance. Accepts queries by mail, e-mail, fax, phone. Accepts simultaneous submissions.

Nonfiction Current primary focus is on automotive, motorcycle, and helmet kustom kulture arts. Needs how-to, humor, inspirational, interview, new product, personal experience, technical. Nothing unrelated to airbrush. Query with published clips. **Pays 15¢/word.** Sometimes pays expenses of writers on assignment.

Photos Digital images preferred. Send photos Captions, identification of subjects, model releases required. Negotiates payment individually. Buys all rights.

Columns/Departments Query with published clips.

Tips Send bio and writing samples. Send well-written technical information pertaining to airbrush art. We publish a lot of artist profiles—they all sound the same. Looking for new pizzazz!

$ $ ANTIQUEWEEK

DMG World Media (USA), P.O. Box 90, Knightstown IN 46148-0090. (800)876-5133, ext. 189. Fax: (800)695-8153. E-mail: connie@antiqueweek.com. Website: www.antiqueweek.com. **80% freelance written**. Weekly tabloid covering antiques and collectibles with 3 editions: Eastern, Central and National, plus monthly *AntiqueWest*. *AntiqueWeek* has a wide range of readership from dealers and auctioneers to collectors, both advanced and novice. Our readers demand accurate information presented in an entertaining style. Estab. 1968. Circ. 50,000. Byline given. Pays on publication. Offers kill fee. Offers 10% kill fee or $25. Buys first rights, buys second serial (reprint) rights. Submit seasonal material 1 month in advance. Accepts queries by mail, e-mail. Sample copy free. Guidelines by email.

Nonfiction Needs historical, how-to, interview, opinion, personal experience, antique show and auction reports, feature articles on particular types of antiques and collectibles. **Buys 400-500 mss/year.** Query. Length: 1,000-2,000 words. **Pays $50-250.**

Reprints Send electronic copy with rights for sale noted and information about when and where the material previously appeared.

Photos All material must be submitted electronically via e-mail or on CD. Send photos Identification of subjects required.

Tips Writers should know their topics thoroughly. Feature articles must be well researched and clearly written. An interview and profile article with a knowledgeable collector might be the break for a first-time contributor. We seek a balanced mix of information on traditional antiques and 20th century collectibles.

$ THE APPRAISERS STANDARD

New England Appraisers Association, 5 Gill Terrace, Ludlow VT 05149-1003. (802)228-7444. Fax: (802)228-7444. E-mail: llt44@ludl.tds.net. Website: www.newenglandappraisers.net. **Contact:** Linda L. Tucker, ed. **50% freelance written. Works with a small number of new/unpublished writers each year**. Quarterly publication covering the appraisals of antiques, art, collectibles, jewelry, coins, stamps, and real estate. "The writer should be knowledgeable on the subject, and the article should be written with appraisers in mind, with prices quoted for objects, good pictures, and descriptions of articles being written about." Estab. 1980. Circ. 1,300. Short bio and byline given. Pays on publication. No kill fee. Publishes ms an average of 1 year after acceptance. Buys first and simultaneous rights. Submit seasonal material 2 months in advance. Accepts queries by mail, e-mail. Accepts simultaneous submissions. Responds in 1 month to queries. Responds in 2 months to mss. Sample copy for 9x12 SAE with 78¢ postage. Guidelines for #10 SASE.

- "I would like writers to focus on particular types of antiques: i.e. types of furniture, glass, artwork, etc., giving information on the history of this type of antique, good photos, recent sale prices, etc."

Nonfiction "All geared toward professional appraisers." Needs interview, personal experience, technical, travel. Send complete ms. Length: 700 words. **Pays $60.**

Reprints "Send typed manuscript with rights for sale noted and information about when and where the material previously appeared."

Photos Send photos Identification of subjects required. Reviews negatives, prints. Offers no additional payment for photos accepted with ms. Buys one time rights.

Tips "Interviewing members of the association for articles, reviewing, shows, and large auctions are all ways for writers who are not in the field to write articles for us. Articles should be geared to provide information which will help the appraisers with ascertaining value, detecting forgeries or reproductions, or simply providing advice on appraising the articles."

ARCHITECTURAL PRODUCT NEWS

Architecture Media, Level 3, 4 Princes St., Port Melbourne VIC 3207 Australia. (61)(3)9646-4760. Fax: (61)(3)9646-4918. E-mail: apn@archmedia.com.au. Website: www.archmedia.com.au. Bimonthly magazine covering the latest building and design products. Circ. 25,000.

- Query before submitting.

ARCHITECTURAL RECORD

McGraw-Hill, 2 Penn Plaza, 9th Floor, New York NY 10121. (212)904-2594. Fax: (212)904-4256. Website: www.architecturalrecord.com. **50% freelance written**. Monthly magazine covering architecture and design. Our readers are architects, designers, and related professionals. Estab. 1891. Circ. 110,000. Byline given. Pays on publication. Offers 25% kill fee. Publishes ms an average of 2 months after acceptance. Buys all rights. Editorial lead time 2 months. Submit seasonal material 2 months in advance. Accepts queries by mail. Responds in 2 weeks to queries. Responds in 2 months to mss. Sample copy and writer's guidelines online.

ARCHITECTURE AUSTRALIA

Architecture Media, Level 3, 4 Princes St., Port Melbourne VIC 3207 Australia. (61)(3)9646-4760. Fax: (61)(3)9646-4918. E-mail: aa@archmedia.com.au. Website: www.archmedia.com.au. Bimonthly magazine covering the architecture industry. Circ. 14,500.

- Query before submitting.

ARCHITECTURE NEW ZEALAND

AGM, Private Bag 99-915, Newmarket Auckland 1031 New Zealand. (64)(9)846-2722. Fax: (64)(9)846-8742. E-mail: johnw@agm.co.nz. Website: www.agm.co.nz. Bimonthly magazine covering issues relating to building design, construction, and management. This is the official magazine of the New Zealand Institute of Architects. It provides national coverage of the best residential, commercial, and institutional architecture, plus constructive criticism and issues of professional practice. No kill fee.

- Query before submitting.

$ $ ART CALENDAR MAGAZINE

The Business Magazine for Visual Artists, 1500 Park Center Dr., Orlando FL 32835. (407)563-7000. Fax: (407)563-7099. E-mail: khall@artcalendar.com. Website: www.artcalendar.com. **75% freelance written**. Monthly magazine. Estab. 1986. Circ. 20,000. Pays on publication. No kill fee. Accepts previously published material. Sample print copy for $5. Guidelines available online.

- We welcome nuts-and-bolts, practical articles of interest to professional visual artists, emerging or professional. Examples: How-to's, first-person stories on how an artist has built his career or an aspect of it, interviews with artists (business/career-building emphasis), web strategies, and pieces on business practices and other topics of use to artists. The tone of our magazine is practical, and uplifting.

Nonfiction Needs essays, the psychology of creativity, how-to, interview, successful artists with a focus on what made them successful, networking articles, marketing topics, technical articles (new equipment, new media, computer software, Internet marketing.), cartoons, art law, including pending legislation that affects artists (copyright law, Internet regulations, etc.). We like nuts-and-bolts information about making a living as an artist. We do not run reviews or art historical pieces, nor do we like writing characterized by 'critic-speak,' philosophical hyperbole, psychological arrogance, politics, or New Age religion. Also, we do not condone a get-rich-quick attitude. Send complete ms. **Pays $250.**

Reprints Send photocopy or typed ms and information about when and where the material previously appeared. Pays $50

Photos Reviews b&w glossy or color prints. Pays $25

Columns/Departments If an artist or freelancer sends us good articles regularly, and based on results we feel that he is able to produce a column at least 3 times per year, we will invite him to be a contributing writer. If a gifted artist-writer can commit to producing an article on a monthly basis, we will offer him a regular column and the title contributing editor. Send complete ms.

Tips " We strongly suggest that you reade a copy of the publication before submitting a proposal. Most queries are rejected because they are too general for our audience."

ARTICHOKE

Architecture Media, Level 3, 4 Princes St., Port Melbourne VIC 3207 Australia. (61)(3)9646-4760. Fax: (61)(3)9646-4918. E-mail: artichoke@archmedia.com.au. Website: www.archmedia.com.au. Quarterly magazine covering interior architecture and Australia's contemporary design. Circ. 7,000.

Nonfiction Needs general interest, how-to, technical. Query.

$ $ ART MATERIALS RETAILER

Fahy-Williams Publishing, P.O. Box 1080, Geneva NY 14456. (315)789-0458. Fax: (315)789-4263. E-mail: tmanzer@fwpi.com. Website: www.artmaterialsretailer.com. **10% freelance written**. Quarterly magazine. Estab. 1998. Byline given. Pays on publication. No kill fee. Buys one-time rights. Editorial lead time 2 months. Submit seasonal material 3 months in advance. Accepts simultaneous submissions. Responds in 3 weeks to queries. Responds in 3 months to mss. Sample copy and writer's guidelines free.

Nonfiction Needs book excerpts, how-to, interview, personal experience. **Buys 2 mss/year.** Send complete ms. Length: 1,500-3,000 words. **Pays $50-250.** Sometimes pays expenses of writers on assignment.

Photos State availability Identification of subjects required. Reviews transparencies. Offers no additional payment for photos accepted with ms. Buys one time rights.

Fillers Needs anecdotes, facts, newsbreaks. 5 Length: 500-1,500 words. **Pays $50-125.**

Tips We like to review manuscripts rather than queries. Artwork (photos, drawings, etc.) is a real plus. We enjoy (our readers enjoy) practical, nuts-and-bolts, news-you-can-use articles.

$ ARTS MANAGEMENT

110 Riverside Dr., Suite 4E, New York NY 10024. (212)579-2039. **1% freelance written**. Magazine published 5 times/year for cultural institutions. Estab. 1962. Circ. 6,000. Byline given. Pays on publication. No kill fee. Buys all rights. Accepts queries by mail. Responds in 2 months to queries. Guidelines for #10 SASE.

- "*Arts Management* is almost completely staff-written and uses very little outside material."

Nonfiction Short articles, 400-900 words, tightly written, expository, explaining how arts administrators solved problems in publicity, fund raising, and general administration; actual case histories emphasizing the how-to. "Also short articles on the economics and sociology of the arts and important trends in the nonprofit cultural field. Must be fact filled, well organized, and without rhetoric." No photographs or pictures. **Pays 2-4¢/word.**

HOUSES

Architecture Media, Level 3, 4 Princes St., Port Melbourne VIC 3207 Australia. (61)(3)9646-4760. Fax: (61)(3)9646-4918. E-mail: houses@archmedia.com.au. Website: www.archmedia.com.au. Bimonthly magazine. *HOUSES* is Australia's multi-award winning residential architecture magazine. Its high quality editorial environment features contemporary projects and interiorsÃ³with outstanding graphic design, informative reviews, excellent photography, detailed floor plans and product lists. Circ. 23,500.

Nonfiction Needs general interest, photo feature. Query.

$ $ $ HOW

Design Ideas at Work, F+W Media, Inc., 4700 E. Galbraith Rd., Cincinnati OH 45236. (513)531-2222. Fax: (513)531-2902. E-mail: editorial@howdesign.com. Website: www.howdesign.com. **75% freelance written.** Bimonthly magazine covering graphic design profession. *HOW: Design Ideas at Work* strives to serve the business, technological and creative needs of graphic-design professionals. The magazine provides a practical mix of essential business information, up-to-date technological tips, the creative whys and hows behind noteworthy projects, and profiles of professionals who are impacting design. The ultimate goal of *HOW* is to help designers, whether they work for a design firm or for an inhouse design department, run successful, creative, profitable studios. Estab. 1985. Circ. 40,000. Byline given. Pays on acceptance. No kill fee. Buys first North American serial rights. Responds in 6 weeks to queries. Sample copy for cover price plus $1.50 (cover price varies per issue). Writer's guidelines and editorial calendar online.

Nonfiction Features cover noteworthy design projects, interviews with leading creative professionals, profiles of established and up-and-coming firms, business and creativity topics for graphic designers. Self-Promotion Annual (September/October); Business Annual (November/December); International Annual of Design (March/April); Creativity/Paper/Stock Photography (May/June); Digital Design Annual (July/August) No how-to articles for beginning artists or fine-art-oriented articles. **Buys 40 mss/year.** Query with published clips and samples of subject's work, artwork or design. Length: 1,500-2,000 words. **Pays $700-900.** Sometimes pays expenses of writers on assignment.

Photos State availability Captions required. Reviews Information updated and verified. Buys one time rights.

Columns/Departments Design Disciplines (focuses on lucrative fields for designers/illustrators); Workspace (takes an inside look at the design of creatives' studios), 1,200-1,500 words. 35 Query with published clips. **Pays $250-400.**

Tips We look for writers who can recognize graphic designers on the cutting-edge of their industry, both creatively and business-wise. Writers must have an eye for detail, and be able to relay *HOW*'s editorial style in an interesting, concise manner—without omitting any details. Showing you've done your homework on a subject—and that you can go beyond asking `those same old questions'—will give you a big advantage.

$ $ INTERIOR LANDSCAPE BUSINESS MAGAZINE

(formerly *Interior Business Magazine*), GIE Media, Inc., 4020 Kinross Lakes Pkwy., Suite 201, Richfield OH 44286. (800)456-0707. Fax: (330)659-0823. E-mail: ccode@gie.net. Website: www.interiorbusinessonline.com. **5-10% freelance written**. Magazine covering interior landscaping. *Interior Business* addresses the concerns of the professional interior landscape contractor. It's devoted to the business management needs of interior landscape professionals. Estab. 2000. Circ. 6,000. Pays on publication. No kill fee. Publishes ms an average of 3 months after acceptance. Editorial lead time 3 months. Submit seasonal material 5 months in advance. Responds in 1 week to queries.

Nonfiction No articles oriented to the consumer or homeowner. **Buys 2 mss/year.** Length: 1,000-2,500 words. **Pays $250-500.**

Tips Know the audience. It's the professional business person, not the consumer.

$ $ THE PASTEL JOURNAL

The Magazine for Pastel Artists, F+W Media, Inc., 4700 E. Galbraith Rd., Cincinnati OH 45236. (513)531-2690. Fax: (513)891-7153. Website: www.pasteljournal.com. **Contact:** Anne Hevener. Bimonthly magazine covering pastel art. "*The Pastel Journal* is the only national magazine devoted to the medium of pastel. Addressing the working professional as well as passionate amateurs, *The Pastel Journal* offers inspiration, information, and instruction to our readers." Estab. 1999. Circ. 22,000. Byline given. Pays on acceptance. Offers 25% kill fee.

Publishes ms an average of 3-6 months after acceptance. Buys all rights. Editorial lead time 6 months. Submit seasonal material 6 months in advance. Accepts queries by mail. Accepts simultaneous submissions. Responds in 4-6 weeks to queries. Writer's guidelines free.

Nonfiction Needs how-to, interview, new product, profile. Does not want articles that aren't art-related. Review magazine before submitting. Query with or without published clips. Length: 500-2,500 words. **Pays $150-750.**

Photos State availability of or send photos Captions required. Reviews transparencies, prints, GIF/JPEG files. Offers no additional payment for photos accepted with ms. Buys all rights.

$ $ $ PRINT

America's Graphic Design Magazine, F+W Media, Inc., 38 E. 29th St., 3rd Floor, New York NY 10016. (212)447-1400. Fax: (212)447-5231. E-mail: info@printmag.com. Website: www.printmag.com. **75% freelance written**. Bimonthly magazine covering graphic design and visual culture. *PRINT*'s articles, written by design specialists and cultural critics, focus on the social, political, and historical context of graphic design, and on the places where consumer culture and popular culture meet. We aim to produce a general interest magazine for professionals with engagingly written text and lavish illustrations. By covering a broad spectrum of topics, both international and local, we try to demonstrate the significance of design in the world at large. Estab. 1940. Circ. 45,000. Byline given. Pays on acceptance. Offers 25% kill fee. Publishes ms an average of 3 months after acceptance. Buys first North American serial rights. Editorial lead time 3 months. Submit seasonal material 3 months in advance. Accepts queries by e-mail. Responds in 2 weeks to queries. Responds in 1 month to mss.

Nonfiction Needs essays, interview, opinion. **Buys 35-40 mss/year.** Query with published clips. Length: 1,000-2,500 words. **Pays $1,250.** Sometimes pays expenses of writers on assignment.

Columns/Departments Query with published clips. **Pays $800.**

Tips Be well versed in issues related to the field of graphic design; don't submit ideas that are too general or geared to nonprofessionals.

$ TEXAS ARCHITECT

Texas Society of Architects, 816 Congress Ave., Suite 970, Austin TX 78701. (512)478-7386. Fax: (512)478-0528. Website: www.texasarchitect.org. **30% freelance written. Mostly written by unpaid members of the professional society**. Bimonthly journal covering architecture and architects of Texas. *Texas Architect* is a highly visually-oriented look at Texas architecture, design, and urban planning. Articles cover varied subtopics within architecture. Readers are mostly architects and related building professionals. Estab. 1951. Circ. 12,000. Byline given. Pays on publication. No kill fee. Publishes ms an average of 3 months after acceptance. Buys one-time rights, buys all rights. Makes work-for-hire assignments. Submit seasonal material 4 months in advance. Accepts queries by mail, e-mail. Responds in 6 weeks to queries. Guidelines available online.

Nonfiction Needs interview, photo feature, technical, book reviews. Query with published clips. Length: 100-2,000 words. **Pays $50-100 for assigned articles.**

Photos Send photos Identification of subjects required. Reviews contact sheets, 35mm or 4x5 transparencies, 4x5 prints. Offers no additional payment for photos accepted with ms. Buys one time rights.

Columns/Departments News (timely reports on architectural issues, projects, and people), 100-500 words. 10 Query with published clips. **Pays $50-100.**

TOY & HOBBY RETAILER

Yaffa Publishing, 17-21 Bellevue St., Surry Hills NSW 2010 Australia. (61)(2)9281-2333. Fax: (61)(2)9281-2750. E-mail: yaffa@yaffa.com.au. Website: www.yaffa.com.au. Magazine published 11 times/year covering Australian toy industry.

Nonfiction Needs general interest, interview, new product. Query.

$ $ WATERCOLOR ARTIST

The No. 1 Magazine for Watercolor Artists, F+W Media, Inc., 4700 E. Galbraith Rd., Cincinnati OH 45236. (513)531-2690. Fax: (513)531-2902. Website: www.watercolorartistmagazine.com. Bimonthly magazine covering water media arts. "*Watercolor Artist* is the definitive source of how-to instruction and creative inspiration for artists working in water-based media." Estab. 1984. Circ. 53,000. Byline given. Pays on acceptance. Offers 10% kill fee. Publishes ms an average of 3-6 months after acceptance. Buys all rights. Editorial lead time 6 months. Submit seasonal material 6 months in advance. Accepts queries by mail. Accepts simultaneous submissions. Responds in 4-6 weeks to queries. Sample copy and writer's guidelines free.

Nonfiction Needs book excerpts, essays, how-to, inspirational, interview, new product, personal experience. "Does not want articles that aren't art-related. Review magazine before submitting." **Buys 36 mss/year.** Send complete ms. Length: 350-2,500 words. **Pays $150-600.**

Photos State availability of or send photos Captions required. Reviews transparencies, prints, slides, GIF/JPEG files. Buys one time rights.

AUTO & TRUCK

AUSTRALASIAN PAINT & PANEL

Yaffa Publishing, 17-21 Bellevue St., Surry Hills NSW 2010 Australia. (61)(2)9281-2333. Fax: (61)(2)9281-2750. E-mail: yaffa@yaffa.com.au. Website: www.yaffa.com.au. Bimonthly magazine for owners, managers, purchasers, and end-users of equipment in every area of motor body repair shops and associated organizations throughout Australia.

- Query before submitting.

AUSTRALIAN AUTOMOTIVE AFTERMARKET MAGAZINE

Australian Automotive Aftermarket Association, P.O. Box 225, Keilor VIC 3036 Australia. (61)(3)9336-3422. E-mail: editor@aaaa.com.au. Website: www.aftermarket.com.au/aftermarket/. Magazine published 7 times/year covering the Australian automotive aftermarket industry. Circ. 10,000.

Nonfiction Needs new product, technical, trade talk, industry news, AAAA trade show and calendar of events. Query.

AUSTRALIAN WORKSHOP MANAGER

AAEN, Ltd., P.O. Box 271, Lutwyche QLD 4030 Australia. (61)(7)3356-6155. Fax: (61)(7)3356-6130. E-mail: office@aaen.com.au. Website: www.aaen.com.au. Bimonthly magazine for professionals in the automotive industry.

- Query before submitting.

$ $ AUTOINC.

Automotive Service Association, P.O. Box 929, Bedford TX 76095. (800)272-7467. Fax: (817)685-0225. E-mail: leonad@asashop.org. Website: www.autoinc.org. **10% freelance written**. Monthly magazine covering independent automotive repair. The mission of *AutoInc.*, ASA's official publication, is to be the informational authority for ASA and industry members nationwide. Its purpose is to enhance the professionalism of these members through management, technical and legislative articles, researched and written with the highest regard for accuracy, quality, and integrity. Estab. 1952. Circ. 14,000. Byline given. Pays on publication. No kill fee. Publishes ms an average of 3 months after acceptance. Buys all rights. Editorial lead time 2 months. Accepts queries by mail, e-mail, fax. Accepts simultaneous submissions. Responds in 6 weeks to queries. Responds in 2 months to mss. Sample copy for $5 or online. Guidelines available online.

Nonfiction Needs how-to, automotive repair, technical. No coverage of staff moves or financial reports. **Buys 6 mss/year.** Query with published clips. Length: 1,200 words. **Pays $300.** Sometimes pays phone expenses of writers on assignment.

Photos State availability of or send photos Captions, identification of subjects, model releases required. Reviews 2—Š3 transparencies, 3—Š5 prints, high resolution digital images. Negotiates payment individually Buys one-time and electronic rights

Tips Learn about the automotive repair industry, specifically the independent shop segment. Understand the high-tech requirements needed to succeed today. We target professional repair shop owners rather than consumers.

AUTOMOTIVE ELECTRICAL & AIR CONDITIONING NEWS

AAEN, Ltd., P.O. Box 271, Lutwyche QLD 4030 Australia. (61)(7)3356-6155. Fax: (61)(7)3356-6130. E-mail: office@aaen.com.au. Website: www.aaen.com.au. Magazine covering industry news. Estab. 1992.

- Query before submitting.

$ $ BUSINESS FLEET

Bobit Publishing, 3520 Challenger St., Torrance CA 90501-1711. (310)533-2400. E-mail: chris.brown@bobit.com. Website: www.businessfleet.com. **10% freelance written**. Bimonthly magazine covering businesses which operate 10-50 company vehicles. While it's a trade publication aimed at a business audience, *Business Fleet* has a lively, conversational style. The best way to get a feel for our `slant' is to read the magazine. Estab. 2000. Circ. 100,000. Byline given. Pays on publication. Offers 25% kill fee. Publishes ms an average of 3 months after acceptance. Buys first rights, buys second serial (reprint) rights, buys electronic rights. Editorial lead time 2 months. Submit seasonal material 2 months in advance. Accepts queries by mail, e-mail, fax. Responds in 3 weeks to queries. Responds in 2 months to mss. Sample copy and writer's guidelines free.

Nonfiction Needs how-to, interview, new product, personal experience, photo feature, technical. **Buys 16 mss/year.** Query with published clips. Length: 500-2,000 words. **Pays $100-400.** Sometimes pays expenses of writers on assignment.

Photos State availability Captions required. Reviews 3x5 prints. Negotiates payment individually Buys one-time, reprint, and electronic rights

Tips Our mission is to educate our target audience on more economical and efficient ways of operating company vehicles, and to inform the audience of the latest vehicles, products, and services available to small commercial companies. Be knowledgeable about automotive and fleet-oriented subjects.

$ $ CASP

Canadian Aftermarket Service Professional, Publications Rousseau et Associes, Inc., 2938 Terrasse Abenaquis, Suite 110, Longueuil QC J4M 2B3 Canada. (450)448-2220. Fax: (450)448-1041. E-mail: sgbrown@xplornet.com. Website: www.autosphere.ca. **30% freelance written**. Magazine published 8 times/year covering the Canadian automotive aftermarket. "*CASP* presents many aspects of the automotive aftermarket: new products, technology, industry image, HR, management." Estab. 2003. Circ. 18,000. Byline given. Pays on publication. Publishes ms an average of 2 months after acceptance. Buys first rights, buys second serial (reprint) rights, buys electronic rights. Editorial lead time 2 months. Submit seasonal material 2 months in advance. Accepts queries by e-mail. Accepts previously published material. Accepts simultaneous submissions. Responds in 2 weeks to queries. Responds in 2 months to mss. Sample copy free. Guidelines by email.
Nonfiction Needs general interest, how-to, inspirational, interview, new product, technical. Does not want opinion pieces. **Buys 6 mss/year.** Query with published clips. Length: 550-610 words. **Pays up to $200 (Canadian).**
Photos Send photos Captions required. Reviews GIF/JPEG files. Offers no additional payment for photos accepted with ms. Buys all rights.
Fillers Needs facts. 2 Length: 550-610 words. **Pays $0-200.**

$ $ FENDERBENDER

DeWitt Publishing, 1043 Grand Ave. #372, St. Paul MN 55105. (651)224-6207. Fax: (651)224-6212. E-mail: editor@fenderbender.com. Website: www.fenderbender.com. **Contact:** Karen Olson, managing editor. **50% freelance written**. Monthly magazine covering automotive collision repair. Estab. 1999. Circ. 58,000. Byline given. Pays on publication. Offers 20% kill fee. Publishes ms an average of 2 months after acceptance. Buys first North American serial rights, buys second serial (reprint) rights, buys electronic rights. Editorial lead time 3 months. Submit seasonal material 6 months in advance. Accepts queries by e-mail. Accepts simultaneous submissions. Responds in 1-2 months to queries. Responds in 2-3 months to mss. Sample copy for sae with 10x13 envelope and 6 First-Class stamps. Guidelines available online.
Nonfiction Needs expose, how-to, inspirational, interview, technical. Does not want personal narratives or any other first-person stories. No poems or creative writing manuscripts. Query with published clips. Length: 1,800-2,500 words. **Pays 25-60¢/word.** Sometimes pays expenses of writers on assignment.
Photos Send photos Captions, identification of subjects, model releases required. Reviews PDF, GIF/JPEG files. Offers no additional payment for photos accepted with ms. Buys one time rights.
Columns/Departments Q&A, 600 words; Shakes, Rattles & Rollovers; Rearview Mirror Query with published clips. **Pays 25-35¢/word.**
Tips "Potential writers need to be knowledgeable about the auto collision repair industry. They should also know standard business practices and be able to explain to shop owners how they can run their businesses better."

$ $ FLEET EXECUTIVE

The Magazine of Vehicle Management, The National Association of Fleet Administrators, Inc., 125 Village Blvd., Suite 200, Princeton NJ 08540. (609)720-0882. Fax: (732)494-6789. E-mail: publications@nafa.org. Website: www.nafa.org. **30% freelance written**. Magazine published 8 times/year covering automotive fleet management. *NAFA Fleet Executive* focuses on car, van, and light-duty truck management in US and Canadian corporations, government agencies, and utilities. Editorial emphasis is on general automotive issues; improving jobs skills, productivity, and professionalism; legislation and regulation; alternative fuels; safety; interviews with prominent industry personalities; technology; association news; public service fleet management; and light-duty truck fleet management. Estab. 1957. Circ. 4,000. No byline given. Pays on publication. No kill fee. Publishes ms an average of 4 months after acceptance. Buys all rights. Editorial lead time 2 months. Accepts queries by mail. Accepts simultaneous submissions. Responds in 1 month to queries. Sample copy available online. Guidelines free.
Nonfiction NAFA hosts its Fleet Management Institute, an educational conference and trade show, which is held in a different city in the US and Canada each year. *Fleet Executive* would consider articles on regional attractions, particularly those that might be of interest to the automotive industry, for use in a conference preview issue of the magazine. The preview issue is published one month prior to the conference. Information about the conference, its host city, and conference dates in a given year may be found on NAFA's website, www.nafa.org, or by calling the association at (732)494-8100. Needs interview, technical. **Buys 24 mss/year.** Query with published clips. Length: 500-3,000 words. **Pays $500 maximum.**
Photos State availability Reviews electronic images.
Tips The sample articles online at www.nafa.org/fleetexecutive should help writers get a feel of the journalistic style we require.

MOTOR AGE

Advanstar Communications, Inc., 24950 Country Club Blvd., Suite 200, North Olmsted OH 44070. Fax: (440)891-2675. Website: www.motorage.com. Monthly magazine. Edited as a technical journal for automotive service dealers and technicians in the U.S. Estab. 1899. Circ. 143,147. No kill fee.

OLD CARS WEEKLY

News & Marketplace, a Division of F + W Media, Inc., 700 E. State St., Iola WI 54990-0001. (715)445-4612. Fax: (715)445-2214. E-mail: angelo.vanbogart@fwpubs.com. Website: www.oldcarsweekly.com. www.thisoldcar.com. **30% freelance written**. Weekly tabloid for anyone restoring, selling or driving an old car. Estab. 1971. Circ. 65,000. Byline given. Pays within 2 months after publication date. No kill fee. Publishes ms an average of 6 months after acceptance. Call circulation department for sample copy. Guidelines for #10 SASE.

Nonfiction Needs how-to, technical, auction prices realized lists. No Grandpa's Car, My First Car or My Car themes from freelance contributors. **Buys 1,600 mss/year.** Send complete ms. Length: 400-1,600 words. **Payment varies.**

Photos Send photos Captions, identification of subjects required. Pays $5/photo. Offers no additional payment for photos accepted with ms

Tips "Seventy-five percent of our material is done by a small group of regular contributors. Many new writers break in here, but we are usually overstocked with material and never seek nostalgic or historical pieces from new authors. Our big need is for well-written items that fit odd pieces in a tabloid page layout. Budding authors should try some short, catchy items that help us fill odd-ball `news holes' with interesting writing. Authors with good skills can work up to longer stories. The best queries are `checklists' where we can quickly mark a `yes' or `no' to article ideas."

$ $ $ OVERDRIVE

The Voice of the American Trucker, Randall-Reilly Publishing Co./Overdrive, Inc., 3200 Rice Mine Rd., Tuscaloosa AL 35406. (205)349-2990. Fax: (205)750-8070. E-mail: mheine@randallpub.com. Website: www.etrucker.com. **5% freelance written**. Monthly magazine for independent truckers. Estab. 1961. Circ. 100,000. Byline given. Pays on publication. Offers 10% kill fee. Publishes ms an average of 2 months after acceptance. Buys all North American rights, including electronic rights. Responds in 2 months to queries. Sample copy for 9x12 SASE.

Nonfiction All must be related to independent trucker interest. Needs essays, expose, how-to, truck maintenance and operation, interview, successful independent truckers, personal experience, photo feature, technical. Send complete ms. Length: 500-2,500 words. **Pays $300-1,500 for assigned articles.**

Photos Photo fees negotiable. Buys all rights.

Tips Talk to independent truckers. Develop a good knowledge of their concerns as small-business owners, truck drivers, and individuals. We prefer articles that quote experts, people in the industry, and truckers, to first-person expositions on a subject. Get straight facts. Look for good material on truck safety, on effects of government regulations, and on rates and business relationships between independent truckers, brokers, carriers, and shippers.

PARTS & PEOPLE

Automotive Counseling & Publishing Co., P.O. Box 18731, Denver CO 80218. Fax: (303)765-4650. E-mail: editor@partsandpeople.com. Website: www.partsandpeople.com. **Contact:** Lance Buchner, publisher. **5% freelance written**. Six monthly magazines covering the automotive industry. Estab. 1985. Circ. 60,000. Byline given. Pays on publication. Offers 10% kill fee. Buys all rights. Editorial lead time 1 month. Submit seasonal material 2 months in advance. Accepts queries by mail, e-mail. Accepts simultaneous submissions. Sample copy for $2.

Nonfiction Needs how-to, new product, photo feature, technical, business features. **Buys 20 mss/year.** Query. Length: 250-1,200 words. **Payment varies** Sometimes pays expenses of writers on assignment.

Photos Send photos Reviews 3x5 prints. Negotiates payment individually Buys all rights.

Columns/Departments 20 Query. **Payment varies.**

Fillers Needs anecdotes, facts. 4-9 Length: 15-100 words. **Variable amount.**

$ ROAD KING MAGAZINE

For the Professional Driver, Parthenon Publishing, 28 White Bridge Rd., Suite 209, Nashville TN 37205. (615)627-2250. Fax: (615)690-3401. Website: www.roadking.com. **80% freelance written**. Bimonthly magazine. *Road King* is published bimonthly for long-haul truckers. It celebrates the lifestyle and work and profiles interesting and/or successful drivers. It also reports on subjects of interest to our audience, including outdoors, vehicles, music, and trade issues. Estab. 1963. Circ. 229,900. Byline given. Pays 3 weeks after acceptance. Offers negotiable kill fee. Publishes ms an average of 4 months after acceptance. Buys first North American serial rights, buys electronic rights. Editorial lead time 4 months. Submit seasonal material 6 months in advance. Accepts queries by mail, e-mail. Responds in 2 months to queries. Sample copy for sae with 9x12 envelope and 5 First-Class stamps. Guidelines available online.

Nonfiction Needs how-to, trucking-related, interview, new product, photo feature, technical, travel. Road Gear (the latest tools, techniques and industry developments to help truckers run a smarter, more efficient trucking business); At Home on the Road (creature comfort products, services, and information for the road life, including what's new, useful, interesting, or fun for cyber-trucking drivers). No fiction, poetry. **Buys 20 mss/year.** Query with published clips. Length: 850-2,000 words. **Payment negotiable** Sometimes pays expenses of writers on assignment.

Photos State availability Identification of subjects, model releases required. Reviews contact sheets. Negotiates payment individually. Buys negotiable rights.

Columns/Departments Lead Driver (profile of outstanding trucker), 250-500 words; Roadrunner (new products, services suited to the business of trucking or to truckers' lifestyles), 100-250 words. 6-10 Query. **Payment negotiable.**

Fillers Needs anecdotes, facts, gags, short humor. Length: 100-250 words. **Pays $50.**

$ $ TIRE NEWS

Publications Rousseau et Associes Inc., 2938 Terrasse Abenaquis, Suite 110, Longueuil QC J4M 2B3 Canada. (450)448-2220. Fax: (450)448-1041. Website: www.publicationsrousseau.com. Bimonthly magazine covering Canadian tire industry. *Tire News* focuses on education/training, industry image, management, new tires, new techniques, marketing, HR, etc. Estab. 2004. Circ. 16,000. Byline given. Pays on publication. Publishes ms an average of 2 months after acceptance. Buys first rights, buys second serial (reprint) rights, buys electronic rights. Editorial lead time 2 months. Submit seasonal material 2 months in advance. Accepts previously published material. Accepts simultaneous submissions. Responds in 2 weeks to queries. Responds in 2 months to mss. Sample copy free. Guidelines by email.

Nonfiction Needs general interest, how-to, inspirational, interview, new product, technical. Does not want opinion pieces. **Buys 5 mss/year.** Query with published clips. Length: 550-610 words. **Pays up to $200 (Canadian).**

Photos Send photos Captions required. Reviews GIF/JPEG files. Offers no additional payment for photos accepted with ms. Buys all rights.

Fillers Needs facts. 2 Length: 550-610 words. **Pays $0-200.**

$ $ TOWING & RECOVERY FOOTNOTES

Reaching more than 100,000 industry professionals monthly, Dominion Enterprises, 150 Granby St., Norfolk VA 23510. (757)351-8633. Fax: (757)233-7047. E-mail: bcandler@traderonline.com. Website: www.trfootnotes.com. **100% freelance written.** Monthly trade newspaper and marketplace for the nation's towing and recovery industry. Estab. 1991. Circ. 28,000. Byline given. within 2-3 weeks of acceptance. No kill fee. Publishes ms an average of 2-3 months after acceptance. Buys first, one-time rights. Editorial lead time 2 months. Submit seasonal material 2 months in advance. Accepts queries by mail, e-mail, phone. Accepts previously published material. Responds in 2 weeks to queries. Responds in 1 month to mss. Sample copy free. Guidelines free.

Nonfiction Needs historical, how-to, humor, interview, new product, opinion, personal experience, photo feature, technical. **Buys 500 mss/year.** Query with published clips. Length: 800-2,000 words. **Pays $200-$600 for assigned articles.**

Photos Send photos Captions, identification of subjects required. Reviews GIF/JPEG files. Negotiates payment individually. Buys one time rights.

Columns/Departments Columns vary from issue to issue; no regular departments available to freelancers; columns are given names appropriate to topic, and often repeat no matter who the author is. 250 Query with published clips. **Pays $$150-$300.**

TRUCK AUSTRALIA

FPC Magazines, 170-180 Bourke Rd., Alexandria NSW 2015 Australia. (61)(2)9353-6666. Fax: (61)(2)9353-6699. E-mail: jgibson@fpc.com.au. Website: www.truckaustralia.com.au. Bimonthly magazine for fleet managers and trucking industry professionals.

Nonfiction Needs general interest, how-to, interview, new product, technical. Query.

WARD'S AUTOWORLD

Primedia Business Magazines and Media, 3000 Town Center, Suite 2750, Southfield MI 48075-1245. (248)357-0800. Fax: (248)357-0810. Website: www.wardsauto.com. Monthly magazine. for personnel involved in the original equipment manufacturing industry. Circ. 101,349. No kill fee. Editorial lead time 1 month.

- Query before submitting.

WARD'S DEALER BUSINESS

Primedia Business Magazines and Media, 3000 Town Center, Suite 2750, Southfield MI 48075-1245. (248)357-0800. Fax: (248)357-0810. Website: www.wardsauto.com. Monthly magazine edited for personnel involved in aftermarket sales. Circ. 30,000. No kill fee. Editorial lead time 1 month.

- Query before submitting.

$ $ WESTERN CANADA HIGHWAY NEWS

Craig Kelman & Associates, 2020 Portage Ave., 3rd Floor, Winnipeg MB R3J 0K4 Canada. (204)985-9785. Fax: (204)985-9795. E-mail: terry@kelman.ca. **Contact:** Terry Ross, managing editor. **30% freelance written.** Quarterly magazine covering trucking. "The official magazine of the Alberta, Saskatchewan, and Manitoba trucking associations." Estab. 1995. Circ. 4,500. Byline given. Pays on publication. No kill fee. Publishes ms an average of 2 months after acceptance. Buys one-time rights. Editorial lead time 3 months. Submit seasonal material 3 months in advance. Accepts simultaneous submissions. Responds in 1 month to queries and mss. Sample copy for 10x13 SAE with 1 IRC Guidelines for #10 SASE.

Nonfiction Needs essays, general interest, how-to, run a trucking business, interview, new product, opinion, personal experience, photo feature, technical, profiles in excellence (bios of trucking or associate firms enjoying success). **Buys 8-10 mss/year.** Query. Length: 500-3,000 words. **Pays 18-25¢/word.** Sometimes pays expenses of writers on assignment.

Photos State availability Identification of subjects required. Reviews 4x6 prints. Buys one time rights.

Columns/Departments Safety (new safety innovation/products), 500 words; Trade Talk (new products), 300 words. Query. **Pays 18-25¢/word.**

Tips "Our publication is fairly time sensitive regarding issues affecting the trucking industry in Western Canada. Current `hot' topics are international trucking, security, driver fatigue, health and safety, emissions control, and national/international highway systems."

AVIATION & SPACE

$ $ AIRCRAFT MAINTENANCE TECHNOLOGY

Cygnus Business Media, 1233 Janesville Ave., Fort Atkinson WI 53538. (920)563-6388. Fax: (920)569-4603. E-mail: joe.escobar@cygnusb2b.com. Website: www.amtonline.com. **10% freelance written.** Magazine published 10 times/year covering aircraft maintenance. *Aircraft Maintenance Technology* provides aircraft maintenance professionals worldwide with a curriculum of technical, professional, and managerial development information that enables them to more efficiently and effectively perform their jobs. Estab. 1989. Circ. 41,500 worldwide. Byline given. Pays on publication. No kill fee. Publishes ms an average of 2 months after acceptance. Buys all rights. Makes work-for-hire assignments. Editorial lead time 3 months. Submit seasonal material 6 months in advance. Accepts queries by mail, e-mail, fax. Accepts simultaneous submissions. Responds in 2 weeks to queries. Responds in 1 month to mss. Sample copy free. Guidelines for #10 SASE or by e-mail.

Nonfiction Needs how-to, technical, safety. Aviation career issue (August) No travel/pilot-oriented pieces. **Buys 10-12 mss/year.** Query with published clips. 600-1,500 words, technical articles 2,000 words **Pays $200.**

Photos State availability Captions, identification of subjects, model releases required. Offers no additional payment for photos accepted with ms Buys one time rights.

Columns/Departments Professionalism, 1,000-1,500 words; Safety Matters, 600-1,000 words; Human Factors, 600-1,000 words. 10-12 Query with published clips. **Pays $200**

Tips This is a technical magazine approved by the FAA and Transport Canada for recurrency training for technicians. Freelancers should have a strong background in aviation, particularly maintenance, to be considered for technical articles. Columns/Departments: Freelancers still should have a strong knowledge of aviation to slant professionalism, safety, and human factors pieces to that audience.

$ $ AIR LINE PILOT

The Magazine of Professional Flight Deck Crews, Air Line Pilots Association, 1625 Massachusetts Ave. NW, Washington DC 20036. E-mail: magazine@alpa.org. Website: www.alpa.org. **2% freelance written. Prefers to work with published/established writers; works with a small number of new/unpublished writers each year.** Magazine published 10 times/year for airline pilots covering commercial aviation industry information—economics, avionics, equipment, systems, safety—that affects a pilot's life in a professional sense. Also includes information about management/labor relations trends, contract negotiations, etc. Estab. 1931. Circ. 90,000. Pays on acceptance. Offers 50% kill fee. Publishes ms an average of 6 months after acceptance. Buys all rights except book rights. Submit seasonal material 6 months in advance. Responds in 2 months to queries. Sample copy for $2. Guidelines available online.

Nonfiction Needs humor, inspirational, photo feature, technical. **Buys 5 mss/year.** Query with or without published clips or send complete ms and SASE. Length: 700-3,000 words. **Pays $100-600 for assigned articles. Pays $50-600 for unsolicited articles.**

Reprints Send photocopy of article or typed ms with rights for sale noted and information about when and where the material previously appeared. Payment varies

Photos Our greatest need is for strikingly original cover photographs featuring ALPA flight deck crew members and their airlines in their operating environment. See list of airlines with ALPA Pilots online. Send photos Identification of subjects required. Reviews contact sheets, 35mm transparencies, 8x10 prints, digital must be 300 dpi at 8x11. Will review low res thumbnail images. Offers $10-35/b&w photo, $30-50 for color used inside and $450 for color used as cover. For cover photography, shoot vertical rather than horizontal. Buys all rights for cover photos, one-time rights for inside color

Tips For our feature section, we seek aviation industry information that affects the life of a professional pilot's career. We also seek material that affects a pilot's life from a job security and work environment standpoint. Any airline pilot featured in an article must be an Air Line Pilot Association member in good standing. Our readers are very experienced and require a high level of technical accuracy in both written material and photographs.

$ $ AIRPORT OPERATIONS

Flight Safety Foundation, Suite 300, 601 Madison St., Alexandria VA 22314-1756. (703)739-6700. Fax: (703)739-6708. Website: www.flightsafety.org. **25% freelance written**. Bimonthly newsletter covering safety aspects of airport operations. *Airport Operations* directs attention to ground operations that involve aircraft and other equipment, airport personnel and services, air traffic control (ATC), and passengers. Estab. 1974. Circ. 2,000. Byline given. Pays on publication. No kill fee. Publishes ms an average of 3 months after acceptance. Buys all rights. Editorial lead time 3 months. Accepts queries by mail, e-mail, fax. Accepts previously published material. Responds in 3 weeks to queries. Sample copy available online. Guidelines available online.

Nonfiction Needs technical. No argumentation, crusading, inspiration, anecdotes, or humor. **Buys 6 mss/year.** Query. Length: 2,500-8,750 words. **Pays $200/printed page, plus 6 copies of publication.**

Photos Send photos Captions, identification of subjects, model releases required. Reviews contact sheets, negatives, 35mm or larger transparencies, 5x7 minimum prints, GIF/JPEG files. Offers $25/photo. Buys all rights.

Tips Study the guidelines carefully. Be concerned above all with accuracy, fairness, and objectivity, but if you have information that you believe meets those standards, do not hesitate to query even if you aren't sure of format or style. If you have the content we need, our editorial staff will work with you to put the material into shape.

$ $ AVIATION INTERNATIONAL NEWS

The Convention News Co., 214 Franklin Ave., Midland Park NJ 07432. (201)444-5075. Fax: (201)444-4647. E-mail: editor@ainonline.com. Website: www.ainonline.com. **30-40% freelance written**. Monthly magazine (with daily onsite issues published at 3 conventions and 2 international air shows each year) and twice-weekly AINalerts via e-mail covering business and commercial aviation with news features, special reports, aircraft evaluations, and surveys on business aviation worldwide, written for business pilots and industry professionals. While the heartbeat of *AIN* is driven by the news it carries, the human touch is not neglected. We pride ourselves on our people stories about the industry's `movers and shakers' and others in aviation who make a difference. Estab. 1972. Circ. 40,000. Byline given. **Pays on acceptance and upon receipt of writer's invoice.** Offers variable kill fee. Publishes ms an average of 2 months after acceptance. Buys first North American serial and second serial (reprint) rights and makes work-for-hire assignments. Editorial lead time 2 months. Submit seasonal material 3 months in advance. Accepts queries by mail, e-mail, fax. Responds in 6 weeks to queries. Responds in 2 months to mss. Sample copy for $10. Writer's guidelines for 9x12 SAE with 3 first-class stamps.

- Do not send mss by e-mail unless requested.

Nonfiction We hire freelancers to work on our staff at 3 aviation conventions and 2 international airshows each year. Must have strong reporting and writing skills and knowledge of aviation. Needs how-to, aviation, interview, new product, opinion, personal experience, photo feature, technical. No puff pieces. Our readers expect serious, real news. We don't pull any punches. *AIN* is not a 'good news' publication: It tells the story, both good and bad. **Buys 150-200 mss/year.** Query with published clips. Length: 200-3,000 words. **Pays 40¢/word to first timers, higher rates to proven *AIN* freelancers.** Pays expenses of writers on assignment.

Photos Send photos Captions required. Reviews contact sheets, transparencies, prints, TIFF files (300 dpi). Negotiates payment individually. Buys one time rights.

Tips Our core freelancers are professional pilots with good writing skills, or good journalists and reporters with an interest in aviation (some with pilot licenses) or technical experts in the aviation industry. The ideal *AIN* writer has an intense interest in and strong knowledge of aviation, a talent for writing news stories, and journalistic cussedness. Hit me with a strong news story relating to business aviation that takes me by surprise—something from your local area or area of expertise. Make it readable, fact-filled, and in the inverted-pyramid style. Double-check facts and names. Interview the right people. Send me good, clear photos and illustrations. Send me well-written, logically ordered copy. Do this for me consistently and we may take you along on our staff to one of the conventions in the U.S. or an airshow in Paris, Singapore, London, or Dubai.

$ $ AVIATION MAINTENANCE

Access Intelligence, 4 Choke Cherry Rd., 2nd Floor, Rockville MD 20850. (301)354-1831. Fax: (301)340-8741. E-mail: jfinnegan@accessintel.com. Website: www.aviationmx.com. **40% freelance written**. Monthly magazine covering aircraft maintenance from small to large aircraft. *Aviation Maintenance* delivers news and information about the aircraft maintenance business for mechanics and management at maintenance shops, airlines, and corporate flight departments. Estab. 1982. Circ. 25,000. Byline given. Pays on acceptance. Offers kill fee. Kill fee varies Publishes ms an average of 2 months after acceptance. Buys all rights. Editorial lead time 3 months. Submit seasonal material 3 months in advance. Accepts queries by mail, e-mail, fax, phone.

Responds in 1 week to queries. Responds in 1 month to mss. Sample copy available online. Guidelines free.
Nonfiction Needs expose, interview, technical. No fiction, technical how-to, or poetry. **Buys 20 mss/year.** Query. Length: 200-500 words. **Pays 50¢/word.** Pays expenses of writers on assignment.
Photos State availability Captions, identification of subjects required. Negotiates payment individually. Buys all rights.
Columns/Departments 12 Query with or without published clips. **Pays $500.**
Tips Writer must be intimately familiar with, or involved in, aviation, either as a pilot or preferably a mechanic or a professional aviation writer. Best place to break in is in the Intelligence News section or the Industry Insights column (see Web site).

$ AVIATION MECHANICS BULLETIN

Flight Safety Foundation, Suite 300, 601 Madison St., Alexandria VA 22314-1756. (703)739-6700. Fax: (703)739-6708. Website: www.flightsafety.org. **25% freelance written**. Bimonthly newsletter covering safety aspects of aviation maintenance (airline and corporate). Estab. 1953. Circ. 2,000. Byline given. Pays on publication. No kill fee. Publishes ms an average of 3 months after acceptance. Buys all rights. Editorial lead time 3 months. Accepts queries by mail, e-mail, fax. Accepts previously published material. Responds in 3 weeks to queries. Sample copy available online. Guidelines available online.
Nonfiction Needs technical. No argumentation, crusading, inspiration, anecdotes, or humor. **Buys 6 mss/year.** Query. Length: 2,000-5,500 words. **Pays $100/printed pocket-sized page, plus 6 copies of publication.**
Photos Send photos Captions, identification of subjects, model releases required. Reviews contact sheets, negatives, 35mm or larger transparencies, 5x7 minimum prints, GIF/JPEG files. Offers $25/photo. Buys all rights.
Tips Study guidelines carefully. Be concerned above all with accuracy, but if you have information that you believe meets those standards, do not hesitate to query even if you aren't sure of format or style. If you have the content we need, our editorial staff will work with you to put the material into shape.

$ $ CABIN CREW SAFETY

Flight Safety Foundation, Suite 300, 601 Madison St., Alexandria VA 22314-1756. (703)739-6700. Fax: (703)739-6708. Website: www.flightsafety.org. **25% freelance written**. Bimonthly newsletter covering safety aspects of aircraft cabins (airline and corporate aviation) for cabin crews and passengers. Estab. 1956. Circ. 2,000. Byline given. Pays on publication. No kill fee. Publishes ms an average of 3 months after acceptance. Buys all rights. Editorial lead time 3 months. Accepts queries by mail, e-mail, fax. Accepts previously published material. Responds in 3 weeks to queries. Sample copy available online. Guidelines available online.
Nonfiction Needs technical. No argumentation, crusading, inspiration, anecdotes, or humor. **Buys 6 mss/year.** Query. Length: 2,500-8,750 words. **Pays $200/printed page, plus 6 copies of publication.**
Photos Send photos Captions, identification of subjects, model releases required. Reviews contact sheets, negatives, 35mm or larger transparencies, 5x7 minimum prints, GIF/JPEG files. Offers $25/photo. Buys all rights.
Tips Study guidelines carefully. Be concerned above all with accuracy, fairness, and objectivity, but if you have information that you believe meets those standards, do not hesitate to query even if you aren't sure of format or style. If you have the content we need, our editorial staff will work with you to put the material into shape.

$ $ FLIGHT SAFETY DIGEST

Flight Safety Foundation, Suite 300, 601 Madison St., Alexandria VA 22314-1756. (703)739-6700. Fax: (703)739-6708. Website: www.flightsafety.org. **25% freelance written**. Monthly magazine covering significant issues in airline and corporate aviation safety. *Flight Safety Digest* offers the page space to explore subjects in greater detail than in other Foundation periodicals. Estab. 1982. Circ. 2,000. Byline given. Pays on publication. No kill fee. Publishes ms an average of 3 months after acceptance. Buys all rights. Editorial lead time 3 months. Accepts queries by mail, e-mail, fax. Accepts previously published material. Responds in 3 weeks to queries. Sample copy available online. Guidelines available online.
Nonfiction Needs technical. No argumentation, crusading, inspiration, anecdotes, or humor. **Buys 6 mss/year.** Query. Length: 4,000-15,000 words. **Pays $200/printed page, plus 6 copies of publication.**
Photos Send photos Captions, identification of subjects, model releases required. Reviews contact sheets, negatives, 35mm or larger transparencies, 5x7 minimum prints, GIF/JPEG files. Offers $25/photo. Buys all rights.
Tips Study guidelines carefully. Be concerned above all with accuracy, fairness, and objectivity, but if you have information that you believe meets those standards, do not hesitate to query even if you aren't sure of format or style. If you have the content we need, our editorial staff will work with you to put the material into shape.

$ $ GROUND SUPPORT WORLDWIDE MAGAZINE

Cygnus Business Media, 1233 Janesville Ave., Fort Atkinson WI 53538. (920)563-1622. Fax: (920)563-1699. E-mail: karen.reinhardt@cygnusb2bpub.com. Website: www.groundsupportworldwide.com. **20% freelance written**. Magazine published 10 times/year. Our readers are those aviation professionals who are involved in ground support—the equipment manufacturers, the suppliers, the ramp operators, ground handlers, airport and airline managers. We cover issues of interest to this community—deicing, ramp safety, equipment technology, pollution, etc. Estab. 1993. Circ. 15,000. Pays on publication. No kill fee. Publishes ms an average of 2 months after acceptance. Buys all rights. Editorial lead time 2 months. Accepts queries by mail, e-mail, fax. Responds in 3 weeks to queries. Responds in 3 months to mss. Sample copy for sae with 9—Š11 envelope and 5 First-Class stamps.

Nonfiction Needs how-to, use or maintain certain equipment, interview, new product, opinion, photo feature, technical aspects of ground support and issues, industry events, meetings, new rules and regulations. **Buys 12-20 mss/year.** Send complete ms. Length: 500-2,000 words. **Pays $100-300.**

Photos Send photos Identification of subjects required. Reviews 35mm prints, electronic preferred, slides. Offers additional payment for photos accepted with ms. Buys all rights.

Tips Write about subjects that relate to ground services. Write in clear and simple terms—personal experience is always welcome. If you have an aviation background or ground support experience, let us know.

$ $ HELICOPTER SAFETY

Flight Safety Foundation, Suite 300, 601 Madison St., Alexandria VA 22314-1756. (703)739-6700. Fax: (703)739-6708. Website: www.flightsafety.org. **50% freelance written**. Bimonthly newsletter covering safety aspects of helicopter operations. *Helicopter Safety* highlights the broad spectrum of real-world helicopter operations. Topics have ranged from design principles and primary training to helicopter utilization in offshore applications and in emergency medical service (EMS). Estab. 1956. Circ. 2,000. Byline given. Pays on publication. No kill fee. Publishes ms an average of 3 months after acceptance. Buys all rights. Editorial lead time 3 months. Accepts queries by mail, e-mail, fax. Accepts previously published material. Responds in 3 weeks to queries. Sample copy available online. Guidelines available online.

Nonfiction Needs technical. No argumentation, crusading, inspiration, anecdotes, or humor. **Buys 6 mss/year.** Query. Length: 2,500-8,750 words. **Pays $200/printed page, plus 6 copies of publication.**

Photos Send photos Captions, identification of subjects, model releases required. Reviews contact sheets, negatives, 35mm or larger transparencies, 5x7 minimum prints. Offers $25/photo. Buys all rights.

Tips Study guidelines carefully. Be concerned above all with accuracy, fairness, and objectivity, but if you have information that you believe meets those standards, do not hesitate to query even if you aren't sure of format or style. If you have the content we need, our editorial staff will work with you to put the material into shape.

$ $ HUMAN FACTORS & AVIATION MEDICINE

Flight Safety Foundation, Suite 300, 601 Madison St., Alexandria VA 22314-1756. (703)739-6700. Fax: (703)739-6708. Website: www.flightsafety.org. **50% freelance written**. Bimonthly newsletter covering medical aspects of aviation, primarily for airline and corporate aviation pilots. *Human Factors & Aviation Medicine* allows specialists, researchers, and physicians to present information critical to the training, performance, and health of aviation professionals. Estab. 1953. Circ. 2,000. Byline given. Pays on publication. No kill fee. Publishes ms an average of 3 months after acceptance. Buys all rights. Editorial lead time 3 months. Accepts queries by mail, e-mail, fax. Accepts previously published material. Responds in 3 weeks to queries. Sample copy available online. Guidelines available online.

Nonfiction Needs technical. No argumentation, crusading, inspiration, anecdotes, or humor. **Buys 6 mss/year.** Query. Length: 2,500-8,750 words. **Pays $200/printed page, plus 6 copies of publication.**

Photos Send photos Captions, identification of subjects, model releases required. Reviews contact sheets, negatives, 35mm or larger transparencies, 5x7 minimum prints, GIF/JPEG files. Offers $25/photo. Buys all rights.

Tips Study guidelines carefully. Be concerned above all with accuracy, fairness, and objectivity, but if you have information that you believe meets those standards, do not hesitate to query even if you aren't sure of format or style. If you have the content we need, our editorial staff will work with you to put the material into shape.

$ $ $ PROFESSIONAL PILOT

Queensmith Communications, 30 S. Quaker Lane, Suite 300, Alexandria VA 22314. (703)370-0606. Fax: (703)370-7082. E-mail: editor@propilotmag.com. Website: www.propilotmag.com. **75% freelance written.** Monthly magazine covering corporate , non combat government, law enforcement and various other types of professional aviation. The typical reader has a sophisticated grasp of piloting/aviation knowledge and is interested in articles that help him/her do the job better or more efficiently. Estab. 1967. Circ. 40,000. Byline given. Pays on publication. Offers kill fee. Kill fee negotiable. Publishes ms an average of 2-3 months after acceptance. Buys all rights. Accepts queries by mail, e-mail, fax.

Nonfiction Typical subjects include new aircraft design, new product reviews (especially avionics), pilot techniques, profiles of fixed base operations, profiles of corporate flight departments and technological advances. All issues have a theme such as regional airline operations, maintenance, avionics, helicopters, etc. **Buys 40 mss/year.** Query. Length: 750-2,500 words. **Pays $200-1,000, depending on length. A fee for the article will be established at the time of assignment.** Sometimes pays expenses of writers on assignment.

Photos Prefers transparencies or high resolution 300 JPEG digital images. Send photos Captions, identification of subjects required. Additional payment for photos negotiable. Buys all rights.

Tips Query first. Freelancer should be a professional pilot or have background in aviation. Authors should indicate relevant aviation experience and pilot credentials (certificates, ratings and hours). We place a greater emphasis on corporate operations and pilot concerns.

BEAUTY & SALON

$ $ BEAUTY STORE BUSINESS

Creative Age Communications, 7628 Densmore Ave., Van Nuys CA 91406-2042. (818)782-7328, ext. 353. Fax: (818)782-7450. E-mail: mbirenbaum@creativeage.com. **50% freelance written**. Monthly magazine covering beauty store business management, news and beauty products. The primary readers of the publication are owners, managers, and buyers at open-to-the-public beauty stores, including general-market and multicultural market-oriented ones with or without salon services. Our secondary readers are those at beauty stores only open to salon industry professionals. We also go to beauty distributors. Estab. 1994. Circ. 15,000. Byline given. Pays on acceptance. Offers kill fee. Offers negotiable kill fee. Publishes ms an average of 3 months after acceptance. Buys all rights. Editorial lead time 3 months. Submit seasonal material 4 months in advance. Accepts queries by mail, e-mail, fax. Responds in 1 week to queries. Responds in 2 weeks, if interested. Sample copy free.

Nonfiction If your business-management article will help a specialty retailer or small business owner, it should be of assistance to our readers. If you're a writer who is/was a hairstylist, nail tech or esthetician, has an interest in professional beauty products or is fluent in Korean, we'd like to talk to you. We're also interested in hearing from illustrators/cartoonists and puzzle writers. Needs how-to, business management, merchandising, e-commerce, retailing, interview, industry leaders/beauty store owners. **Buys 20-30 mss/year.** Query. Length: 1,800-2,200 words. **Pays $250-525 for assigned articles.** Sometimes pays expenses of writers on assignment.

Photos Do not send computer art electronically. State availability Captions, identification of subjects required. Reviews transparencies, computer art (artists work on Macs, request 300 dpi, on CD or Zip disk, saved as JPEG, TIFF, or EPS). Negotiates payment individually. Buys all rights.

🌐 BELLA BEAUTY MAGAZINE

Bella Media, Level 2, 294 New South Head Rd., Double Bay NSW 2028 Australia. (61)(2)9362-1555. Fax: (61)(2)9362-1556. E-mail: acsm@bellamedia.com.au. Website: www.cosmeticsurgerymagazine.com.au/bella_beauty.html. Quarterly magazine containing the latest information on products and services, plus local and international beauty and cosmetic industry news and happenings. Estab. 2005. Circ. 20,000.

Nonfiction Needs general interest, how-to, new product. Query.

$ $ 🍁 COSMETICS

Canada's Business Magazine for the Cosmetics, Fragrance, Toiletry, and Personal Care Industry, Rogers, 1 Mt. Pleasant Rd., 7th Floor, Toronto ON M4Y 2Y5 Canada. (416)764-1680. Fax: (416)764-1704. E-mail: dave.lackie@cosmetics.rogers.com. Website: www.cosmeticsmag.com. **10% freelance written**. Bimonthly magazine. Our main reader segment is the retail trade—department stores, drugstores, salons, estheticians—owners and cosmeticians/beauty advisors; plus manufacturers, distributors, agents, and suppliers to the industry. Estab. 1972. Circ. 13,000. Byline given. Pays on acceptance. Offers 50% kill fee. Publishes ms an average of 3 months after acceptance. Buys all rights. Editorial lead time 4 months. Submit seasonal material 4 months in advance. Accepts queries by mail. Responds in 1 month to queries. Sample copy for $6 (Canadian) and 8% GST.

Nonfiction Needs general interest, interview, photo feature. **Buys 1 mss/year.** Query. Length: 250-1,200 words. **Pays 25¢/word.** Sometimes pays expenses of writers on assignment.

Photos Send photos Captions, identification of subjects, model releases required. Reviews 2½ up to 8x10 transparencies, 4x6 up to 8x10 prints, 35mm slides, e-mail pictures in 300 dpi JPEG format. Offers no additional payment for photos accepted with ms. Buys all rights.

Columns/Departments All articles assigned on a regular basis from correspondents and columnists that we know personally from the industry.

Tips Must have broad knowledge of the Canadian cosmetics, fragrance, and toiletries industry and retail business. 99.9% of freelance articles are assigned by the editor to writers involved with the Canadian cosmetics business.

$ $ DAYSPA

The Premiere Spa Business Source, Creative Age Publications, 7628 Densmore Ave., Van Nuys CA 91406. (818)782-7328. Fax: (818)782-7450. E-mail: dayspa@creativeage.com. Website: www.dayspamagazine.com. **Contact:** Rhonda J. Wilson. **50% freelance written**. Monthly magazine covering the business of day spas, skin care salons, wellness centers. "*Dayspa* includes only well-targeted business articles directed at the owners and managers of high-end, multi-service salons, day spas, resort spas, and destination spas." Estab. 1996. Circ. 31,000. Byline given. Pays on acceptance. No kill fee. Publishes ms an average of 4 months after acceptance. Buys first rights, buys one-time rights. Editorial lead time 4 months. Submit seasonal material 4 months in advance. Accepts queries by mail, e-mail, fax, phone. Responds in 2 months to queries. Sample copy for $5.

Nonfiction Buys 40 mss/year. Query. Length: 1,200-3,000 words. **Pays $150-600.**
Photos Send photos Identification of subjects, model releases required. Negotiates payment individually. Buys one time rights.
Columns/Departments Legal Pad (legal issues affecting salons/spas); Money Matters (financial issues); Management Workshop (spa management issues), all 1,200-1,500 words. 20 Query. **Pays $150-300.**

DERMASCOPE MAGAZINE

The Encyclopedia of Aesthetics & Spa Therapy, Geneva Corp., 2611 N. Belt Line Rd., Suite 1011, Sunnyvale TX 75182. (972)226-2309. Fax: (972)226-2339. E-mail: casey@dermascope.com. Website: www.dermascope.com. Monthly magazine covering aesthetics (skin care) and body and spa therapy. Our magazine is a source of practical advice and continuing education for skin care, body, and spa therapy professionals. Our main readers are salon, day spa, and destination spa owners, managers, or technicians and aesthetics students. Estab. 1976. Circ. 15,000. Byline given. No kill fee. Publishes ms an average of 6 months after acceptance. Editorial lead time 3 months. Submit seasonal material 6 months in advance. Accepts queries by mail, fax. Responds in 1 month to queries. Responds in 6 months to mss. Sample copy available by phone.

- A copyright waiver must be signed guaranteeing article has not been submitted elsewhere. We do not pay for articles.

Nonfiction Interested in seeing nonproduct-specific how-to articles with photographs. Needs book excerpts, general interest, historical, how-to, inspirational, personal experience, photo feature, technical. Query with published clips. Length: 1,500-2,500 words.
Photos State availability Captions, identification of subjects, model releases required. Reviews 4x5 prints. Offers no payment for photos accepted with ms.
Tips Write from the practitioner's point of view. Step-by-step how-to's that show the skin care and body and spa therapist practical methodology are a plus. Would like more business and finance ideas, applicable to the industry.

INSTYLE

The Intermedia Group, Ltd., P.O. Box 55, Glebe NSW 2037 Australia. (61)(2)9660-2113. Fax: (61)(2)9660-4419. E-mail: cameron@intermedia.com.au. Website: www.intermedia.com.au. Bimonthly magazine. *Instyle* is dedicated to educating and entertaining Australia's hairdressing elite with a mix of new product information, salon and company profiles, star hairdresser interviews and trends from the worlds of fashion and celebrity.
Nonfiction Needs interview, new product, trends. Query.

MASSAGE & BODYWORK

Associated Bodywork & Massage Professionals, 25188 Genesee Trail Rd., Suite 200, Golden CO80401 (303)674-8478 or (800)458-2267. Fax: (303)674-0859. E-mail: editor@abmp.com. Website: www.massageandbodywork.com. **85% freelance written**. Bimonthly magazine covering therapeutic massage/bodywork. "A trade publication for the massage therapist, and bodyworker. An all-inclusive publication encompassing everything from traditional Swedish massage to energy work to other complementary therapies (i.e., homeopathy, herbs, aromatherapy, etc.)." Pays on acceptance. No kill fee. Publishes ms an average of 6 months after acceptance. Buys first North American serial rights, buys one-time rights, buys electronic rights. Editorial lead time 6 months. Submit seasonal material 6 months in advance. Accepts queries by e-mail. Responds in 60 days to queries. Guidelines available online.
Nonfiction Needs how-to, technique/modality, interview, opinion, personal experience, technical. No fiction. **Buys 60-75 mss/year.** Query with published clips. Length: 1,000-3,000 words.
Photos Not interested in photo submissions separate from feature queries. State availability Captions, identification of subjects, model releases required. Reviews digital images (300 dpi). Negotiates payment individually. Buys one time rights.
Columns/Departments 20.
Tips "Know your topic. Offer suggestions for art to accompany your submission. *Massage & Bodywork* looks for interesting, tightly focused stories concerning a particular modality or technique of massage, bodywork, and somatic therapies. The editorial staff welcomes the opportunity to review mss which may be relevant to the field of massage and bodywork in addition to more general pieces pertaining to complementary and alternative medicine. This would include the widely varying modalities of massage and bodywork (from Swedish massage to Polarity therapy), specific technical or ancillary therapies, including such topics as biomagnetics, aromatherapy, and facial rejuvenation. Reference lists relating to technical articles should include the author, title, publisher, and publication date of works cited according to Chicago Manual of Style. Word count: 1,500-3,000 words; longer articles negotiable."

$ $ MASSAGE MAGAZINE

Exploring Today's Touch Therapies, 5150 Palm Valley Rd., Suite 103, Ponte Vedra Beach FL 32082. (904)285-9944. E-mail: kmenahan@massagemag.com. Website: www.massagemag.com. **60% freelance written**. Bimonthly magazine covering massage and other touch therapies. Estab. 1985. Circ. 50,000. Byline given. Pays on publication. Publishes ms an average of 4 months-1 year after acceptance. Buys first North American serial rights. Accepts queries by e-mail. Responds in 2 months to queries. Responds in 3 months to mss. Sample copy for $6.95. Guidelines available online.

Nonfiction Needs book excerpts, essays, general interest, how-to, interview, personal experience, photo feature, technical, experiential. Length: 600-2,000 words. **Pays $75-300.**

Reprints Send tearsheet of article and electronic ms with rights for sale noted and information about when and where the material previously appeared. Pays 50-75% of amount paid for an original article

Photos Send photos with submission via e-mail. Identification of subjects, True required. Offers $25-100/photo Buys one time rights.

Columns/Departments Profiles; News and Current Events; Practice Building (business); Technique; Body/Mind. Length: 800-1,200 words. **$75-300 for assigned articles**

Fillers Needs facts, newsbreaks. Length: 100-800 words. **Pays $125 maximum**

Tips Our readers seek practical information on how to help their clients, improve their techniques, and/or make their businesses more successful, as well as feature articles that place massage therapy in a positive or inspiring light. Since most of our readers are professional therapists, we do not publish articles on topics like 'How Massage Can Help You Relax.' Please study a few back issues so you know what types of topics and tone we're looking for.

$ $ NAILPRO, THE MAGAZINE FOR NAIL PROFESSIONALS

Creative Age Publications, 7628 Densmore Ave., Van Nuys CA 91406. (818)782-7328. Fax: (818)782-7450. E-mail: syaggy@creativeage.com. Website: www.nailpro.com. **75% freelance written.** Monthly magazine written for manicurists and nail technicians working in a full-service salon or nails-only salons. "It covers technical and business aspects of working in a salon and operating nailcare services, as well as the nailcare industry in general. Estab. 1989. Circ. 65,000. Byline given. Pays on acceptance. No kill fee. Publishes ms an average of 6 months after acceptance. Buys first North American serial rights. Editorial lead time 3 months. Submit seasonal material 3 months in advance. Accepts queries by mail, e-mail, fax. Accepts simultaneous submissions. Responds in 6 weeks to queries Sample copy for $2 and 8 ½x11 SASE

Nonfiction Needs book excerpts, how-to, humor, inspirational, interview, personal experience, photo feature, technical. No general interest articles or business articles not geared to the nail-care industry. **Buys 50 mss/year.** Query. Length: 1,000-3,000 words. **Pays $150-450.**

Reprints Send typed manuscript with rights for sale noted and information about when and where the material previously appeared. Pays 25-50% of amount paid for an original article.

Photos Send photos Identification of subjects, model releases required. Reviews transparencies, prints. Negotiates payment individually.

Columns/Departments "All Business (articles on building salon business, marketing & advertising, dealing with employees), 1,500-2,000 words; Attitudes (aspects of operating a nail salon and trends in the nail industry), 1,200-2,000 words." 50 Query. **Pays $250-350.**

$ $ ⊘ NAILS

Bobit Business Media, 3520 Challenger St., Torrance CA 90503. (310)533-2400. Fax: (310)533-2507. E-mail: hannah.lee@bobit.com. Website: www.nailsmag.com. **10% freelance written.** Monthly magazine. *NAILS* seeks to educate its readers on new techniques and products, nail anatomy and health, customer relations, working safely with chemicals, salon sanitation, and the business aspects of running a salon. Estab. 1983. Circ. 55,000. Byline given. Pays on acceptance. No kill fee. Buys all rights. Submit seasonal material 4 months in advance. Accepts queries by mail, e-mail, fax. Responds in 3 months to queries. Sample copy and writer's guidelines for #10 SASE.

Nonfiction Needs historical, how-to, inspirational, interview, personal experience, photo feature, technical. No articles on one particular product, company profiles or articles slanted toward a particular company or manufacturer. **Buys 20 mss/year.** Query with published clips. Length: 1,200-3,000 words. **Pays $200-500.** Sometimes pays expenses of writers on assignment.

Photos State availability Captions, identification of subjects, model releases required. Reviews contact sheets, transparencies, prints (any standard size acceptable). Offers $50-200/photo. Buys all rights.

Tips Send clips and query; *do not send unsolicited manscripts.* We would like to see ideas for articles on a unique salon or a business article that focuses on a specific aspect or problem encountered when working in a salon. The Modern Nail Salon section, which profiles nail salons and full-service salons, is most open to freelancers. Focus on an innovative business idea or unique point of view. Articles from experts on specific business issues—insurance, handling difficult employees, cultivating clients—are encouraged.

⊘ 🌐 PROFESSIONAL BEAUTY

The Intermedia Group, Ltd., P.O. Box 55, Glebe NSW 2037 Australia. (61)(2)9660-2113. Fax: (61)(2)9660-4419. E-mail: info@intermedia.com.au. Website: www.intermedia.com.au. Quarterly magazine covering the Australian professional beauty sector. Circ. 10,000.

- Query before submitting.

$ $ PULSE MAGAZINE

The Magazine for the Spa Professional, HOST Communications Inc., 2365 Harrodsburg Rd., Suite A325, Lexington KY 40511. Fax: (859)226-4445. E-mail: pulse@ispastaff.com. Website: www.experienceispa.com/ispa/pulse. **Contact:** Rebekah Sellers, assistant editor. **20% freelance written**. Magazine published 10 times/year covering spa industry. "*Pulse* is the magazine for the spa professional. As the official publication of the International SPA Association, its purpose is to advance the business of the spa professionals by informing them of the latest trends and practices and promoting the wellness aspects of spa. *Pulse* connects people, nurtures their personal and professional growth, and enhances their ability to network and succeed in the spa industry." Estab. 1991. Circ. 5,300. Byline given. Pays on publication. Publishes ms an average of 1 month after acceptance. Buys all rights. Editorial lead time 3 months. Submit seasonal material 4 months in advance. Accepts queries by e-mail. Sample copy for #10 SASE. Guidelines by email.

Nonfiction Needs general interest, how-to, interview, new product. Does not want articles focused on spas that are not members of ISPA, consumer-focused articles (market is the spa industry professional), or features on hot tubs (not *that* spa industry). **Buys 8-10 mss/year.** Query with published clips. Length: 800-2,000 words. **Pays $250-500.** Sometimes pays expenses of writers on assignment.

Photos Contact: Contact Rebekah Sellers, assistant editor. Send photos Captions required. Reviews GIF/JPEG files. Negotiates payment individually. Buys one time rights.

Tips "Understand the nuances of association publishing (different than consumer and B2B). Send published clips, not Word documents. Experience in writing for health and wellness market is helpful. Only feature ISPA member companies in the magazine; visit our Web site to learn more about our industry and to see if your pitch includes member companies before making contact."

$ $ SKIN DEEP

Education for Today's Skin Care Professional, Associated Skin Care Professionals, 25188 Genesee Trail Rd., Suite 200, Golden CO 80401. (800)789-0411. E-mail: nbrunner@ascpskincare.com. Website: www.ascpskincare.com. **Contact:** Nora Brunner, ed. **80% freelance written**. Bimonthly magazine covering technical, educational and business information for estheticians with an emphasis on solo practitioners and spa/salon employees or independent contractors. "Our audience is the U.S. individual skin care practitioner who may work on her own and/or in a spa or salon setting. We keep her up to date on skin care trends and techniques and ways to earn more income doing waxing, facials, peels, microdermabrasion, body wraps and other skin treatments. Our product-neutral stories may include novel spa treatments within the esthetician scope of practice. We do not cover treatments that involve needles or lasers, or invasive treatments like ear candling, colonics or plastic surgery. Successful stories have included how-tos on paraffin facials, aromatherapy body wraps, waxing tips, how to read ingredient labels, how to improve word-of-mouth advertising, and how to choose an online scheduling software package. These are light think pieces; for example, taking time for yourself, getting organized, feng shui, etc. Book excerpts work well. We don't usually pay for lifestyle essays." Estab. 2003. Circ. 7,500 +. Byline given. Pays on acceptance. No kill fee. Publishes ms an average of 4-6 months after acceptance. Buys all rights. Editorial lead time 4-5 months. Submit seasonal material 7 months in advance. Accepts queries by e-mail. Responds in 2 weeks to queries. Sample copy free. Guidelines available.

Nonfiction Needs book excerpts and essays(500-word lifestyle essays), how-to, new product, submit to leslie@abmp.com. We don't run general consumer beauty material and very rarely run a new product that is available through retail outlets. 'New' products means introduced in the last 12 months. We do not run industry personnel announcements or stories on individual spas/salons or getaways. We don't cover hair or nails. **Buys 12 mss/year.** Query. Length: 800-2,300 words. **Pays $75-$300 for assigned articles.**

Columns/Departments Ask the Expert (Practical marketing & technical info, how-to (no pay)), 300-500 words; Lifestyle (See above (no pay)), 500 words. Query.

Tips "Visit the Media Corner at www.ascpskincare.com to learn about what we do. Submit a brief query with an idea to determine if you are on the right track. State specifically what value this has to esthetician and her work/income."

$ $ SKIN INC. MAGAZINE

Spa Business Solutions, Allured Business Media, 336 Gundersen Dr., Suite A, Carol Stream IL 60188. (630)653-2155. Fax: (630)653-2192. E-mail: taschetta-millane@allured.com. Website: www.skininc.com. **Contact:** Melinda Taschetta-Millane, editor. **30% freelance written**. Magazine published 12 times/year. "Manuscripts considered for publication that contain original and new information in the general fields of skin care and makeup, dermatological and esthetician-assisted surgical techniques. The subject may cover the science of skin, the business of skin care and makeup, and plastic surgeons on healthy (i.e., nondiseased) skin." Estab. 1988. Circ. 30,000. Byline given. Pays on publication. No kill fee. Publishes ms an average of 6 months after acceptance. Buys all rights. Editorial lead time 6 months. Submit seasonal material 1 year in advance. Accepts queries by mail, e-mail, fax, phone. Responds in 3 weeks to queries. Responds in 1 month to mss. Sample copy and writer's guidelines free.

Nonfiction Needs general interest, how-to, interview, personal experience, technical. **Buys 6 mss/year.** Query with published clips. Length: 2,000 words. **Pays $100-300 for assigned articles. Pays $50-200 for unsolicited**

articles.
Photos State availability Captions, identification of subjects, model releases required. Reviews 3x5 prints. Offers no additional payment for photos accepted with ms. Buys one time rights.
Columns/Departments Finance (tips and solutions for managing money), 2,000-2,500 words; Personnel (managing personnel), 2,000-2,500 words; Marketing (marketing tips for salon owners), 2,000-2,500 words; Retail (retailing products and services in the salon environment), 2,000-2,500 words. Query with published clips. **Pays $50-200.**
Fillers Needs facts, newsbreaks. 6 Length: 250-500 words. **Pays $50-100.**
Tips "Have an understanding of the professional spa industry."

BEVERAGES & BOTTLING

$ $ BAR & BEVERAGE BUSINESS MAGAZINE

Mercury Publications, Ltd., 1740 Wellington Ave., Winnipeg MB R3H 0E8 Canada. (204)954-2085. Fax: (204)954-2057. E-mail: editorial@mercury.mb.ca. Website: www.barandbeverage.com. **33% freelance written.** Bimonthly magazine providing information on the latest trends, happenings, buying-selling of beverages and product merchandising. Estab. 1998. Circ. 16,077. Byline given. Pays 30-45 days from receipt of invoice. Offers 33% kill fee. Buys all rights. Submit seasonal material 3 months in advance. Accepts simultaneous submissions. Sample copy and writer's guidelines free or by e-mail

- Does not accept queries for specific stories. Assigns stories to Canadian writers.

Nonfiction Needs how-to, making a good drink, training staff, etc., interview. Industry reports, profiles on companies. Query with published clips. Length: 500-9,000 words. **Pays 25-35¢/word.** Sometimes pays expenses of writers on assignment.
Photos State availability Captions required. Reviews negatives, transparencies, 3—Š5 prints, JPEG, EPS or TIFF files. Negotiates payment individually Buys all rights.
Columns/Departments Out There (bar & bev news in various parts of the country), 100-500 words. Query. **Pays $0-100.**

$ BEER, WINE & SPIRITS BEVERAGE RETAILER

The Marketing & Merchandising Magazine for Off-Premise Innovators, Oxford Publishing Co., 307 W. Jackson Ave., Oxford MS 38655-2154. (662)236-5510. Fax: (662)236-5541. E-mail: brenda@oxpub.com. Website: www.beverage-retailer.com. **2-5% freelance written.** Magazine published 6 times a year covering alcohol beverage retail industry (off-premise). Our readership of off-premise beverage alcohol retailers (owners and operators of package liquor stores, wine cellars, beer barns, etc.) appreciates our magazine's total focus on helping them increase their revenue and profits. We particulary emphasize stories on retailers' own ideas and efforts to market their products and their stores' images. Estab. 1997. Circ. 20,000. Byline given. Pays on acceptance. No kill fee. Publishes ms an average of 7 months after acceptance. Buys first North American serial rights. Editorial lead time 6 months. Submit seasonal material 6 months in advance. Accepts queries by mail. Responds in 2 weeks to queries. Responds in 1 month to mss. Sample copy for $5 or online at website.
Nonfiction Needs general interest, how-to, interview, industry commentary. No book reviews; no product stories narrowly focused on one manufacturer's product; no general stories on beverage categories (scotch, tequila, etc.) unless trend-oriented. **Buys 4-6 mss/year.** Send complete ms. Length: 350-800 words. **Pays $100 for assigned articles.** Phone expenses only
Photos State availability of or send photos Captions, identification of subjects, model releases required. Reviews contact sheets, transparencies (all sizes), prints (all sizes). Offers no additional payment for photos accepted with ms on most features. Negotiates payment individually on cover stories and major features. Buys all rights.
Columns/Departments Successful Retailers (What business practice, unique facility feature, or other quality makes this business so successful?), 350-400 words; Marketing & Merchandising (brief stories of innovative efforts by retailers—displays, tastings and other events, celebrity appearances, special sales, etc.) 50-350 words. Query with published clips or send complete ms. **Pays $25-100.**
Tips Rely solely on off-premise beverage alcohol retailers (and, in some cases, leading industry experts) as your sources. Make certain every line of your story focuses on telling the reader how to improve his business' revenue and profits. Keep your story short, and include colorful, intelligent, and concise retailer quotes. Include a few relevant and irresistible statistics. We particularly appreciate trend or analysis stories when we get them early enough to publish them in a timely fashion.

$ $ THE BEVERAGE JOURNAL

Michigan Edition, MI Licensed Beverage Association, P.O. Box 4067, East Lansing MI 48826. (517)374-9611. Fax: (517)374-1165. E-mail: editor@mlba.org. Website: www.mlba.org. **40-50% freelance written.** Monthly magazine covering hospitality industry. A monthly trade magazine devoted to the beer, wine, and spirits industry in Michigan. It is dedicated to serving those who make their living serving the public and the state through the orderly and responsible sale of beverages. Estab. 1983. Circ. 4,200. Pays on publication. No kill fee. Buys one-time rights, buys second serial (reprint) rights. Makes work-for-hire assignments. Editorial lead time 3 months. Submit seasonal material 3 months in advance. Accepts queries by mail, e-mail. Responds in 2 weeks to queries. Responds in 1 month to mss. Sample copy for $5 or online

Nonfiction Needs essays, general interest, historical, how-to, make a drink, human resources, tips, etc, humor, interview, new product, opinion, personal experience, photo feature, technical. **Buys 24 mss/year.** Send complete ms. Length: 1,000 words. **Pays $20-200.**

Columns/Departments Open to essay content ideas. Interviews (legislators, others), 750-1,000 words; personal experience (waitstaff, customer, bartenders), 500 words. 12 Send complete ms. **Pays $25-100.**

Tips We are particularly interested in nonfiction concerning responsible consumption/serving of alcohol. We are looking for product reviews, company profiles, personal experiences, and news articles that would benefit our audience. Our audience is a busy group of business owners and hospitality professionals striving to obtain pertinent information that is not too wordy.

$ $ PATTERSON'S CALIFORNIA BEVERAGE JOURNAL

Interactive Color, Inc., 4910 San Fernando Rd., Glendale CA 91204. (818)291-1125. Fax: (818)547-4607. E-mail: mmay@interactivecolor.com. Website: www.beveragelink.com. **25% freelance written**. Monthly magazine covering the alcohol, beverage, and wine industries. *Patterson's* reports on the latest news in product information, merchandising, company appointments, developments in the wine industry, and consumer trends. Our readers can be informed, up-to-date and confident in their purchasing decisions. Estab. 1962. Circ. 25,000. Byline given. Offers kill fee. Offers negotiable kill fee. Editorial lead time 1 month. Submit seasonal material 1 month in advance. Accepts queries by mail, e-mail, fax. Sample copy and writer's guidelines free.

Nonfiction Needs interview, new product, market reports. No consumer-oriented articles or negative slants on industry as a whole. **Buys 200 mss/year.** Query with published clips. Length: 500-750 words. **Pays $60-200.**

Photos State availability Captions, identification of subjects required. Reviews transparencies. Offers no additional payment for photos accepted with ms. Buys all rights.

Columns/Departments Query with published clips.

$ $ PRACTICAL WINERY & VINEYARD

PWV, Inc., 58 Paul Dr., Suite D, San Rafael CA 94903-2054. (415)479-5819. Fax: (415)492-9325. E-mail: tina@practicalwinery.com. Website: www.practicalwinery.com. **50% freelance written**. Bimonthly magazine covering winemaking, grapegrowing, wine marketing. "*Practical Winery & Vineyard* is a technical trade journal for winemakers and grapegrowers. All articles are fact-checked and peer-reviewed prior to publication to ensure 100% accuracy, readability, and practical useful application for readers. NO consumer-focused wine articles, please." Estab. 1979. Circ. 4,000. Byline given. Pays on publication. No kill fee. Publishes ms an average of 6-9 months after acceptance. Buys first North American serial rights, buys electronic rights. Editorial lead time 6-9 months. Submit seasonal material 9 months in advance. Accepts queries by mail, e-mail, fax. Responds in 1-2 weeks to queries. Responds in 1 month to mss. Guidelines by email.

Nonfiction Contact: Tina L. Vierra, associate publisher. Needs how-to, technical. "Each issue has a specific topic/focus. Please see Editorial Calendar for 2009. We do not want any wine consumer trends, retail info, wine tasting notes, no food, travel, wine lifestyles." **Buys 25 mss/year. mss/year.** Query with published clips. Length: 1,000-3,000 words. **Pays 25-50¢ a word for assigned articles. Pays 25-35¢ a word for unsolicited articles.**

Photos Contact: Tina L. Vierra, associate publisher. State availability Captions required. Reviews GIF/JPEG files. Offers no additional payment for photos accepted with ms.

Tips "Query with CV, tech articles only, must have knowledge of technical aspects of winemaking/grapegrowing."

TEA & COFFEE TRADE JOURNAL

Lockwood Publications, 26 Broadway, Floor 9M, New York NY 10004. (212)391-2060. Fax: (212)827-0945. E-mail: editor@teaandcoffee.net. Website: www.teaandcoffee.net. Monthly magazine covering tea and coffee industry. This is a comprehensive magazine dedicated to providing in-depth articles on all aspects of the tea & coffee industries. *Tea & Coffee Trade Journal* provides the latest informaton on everything from producing countries to retail trends. Estab. 1901. Byline given. Pays on publication. No kill fee. Publishes ms an average of 3 months after acceptance. Buys first North American serial rights. Editorial lead time 2 months. Submit seasonal material 6 months in advance. Accepts queries by mail, e-mail. Accepts simultaneous submissions. Responds in days to queries. Responds in days to mss. Sample copy free. Guidelines free.

$ $ $ VINEYARD & WINERY MANAGEMENT

P.O. Box 2358, Windsor CA 95492-2358. (707)836-6820. Fax: (707)836-6825. Website: www.vwm-online.com. **70% freelance written**. Bimonthly magazine of professional importance to grape growers, winemakers, and winery sales and business people. Estab. 1975. Circ. 6,500. Byline given. Pays on publication. No kill fee. Buys first North American serial rights, buys simultaneous rights. Accepts queries by e-mail. Responds in 3 weeks to queries. Responds in 1 month to mss. Sample copy free. Guidelines for #10 SASE.

Nonfiction Subjects are technical in nature and explore the various methods people in these career paths use to succeed and the equipment and techniques they use successfully. Business articles and management topics are also featured. The audience is national with western dominance. Needs how-to, interview, new product, technical. **Buys 30 mss/year.** Query. Length: 1,800-5,000 words. **Pays $30-1,000.** Sometimes pays expenses of writers on assignment.

Photos State availability Captions, identification of subjects required. Reviews contact sheets, negatives, transparencies, digital photos. Black & white often purchased for $20 each to accompany story material; 35mm and/or 4x5 transparencies for $50 and up; 6/year of vineyard and/or winery scene related to story.

Tips We're looking for long-term relationships with authors who know the business and write well. Electronic submissions required; query for formats.

$ $ WINES & VINES MAGAZINE

The Voice of the Grape and Wine Industry, Wine Communications Group, 1800 Lincoln Ave., San Rafael CA 94901. (415)453-9700. Fax: (415)453-2517. E-mail: edit@winesandvines.com. Website: www.winesandvines.com. **50% freelance written**. Monthly magazine covering the North American winegrape and winemaking industry. "Since 1919 *Wines & Vines Magazine* has been the authoritative voice of the wine and grape industry—from prohibition to phylloxera, we have covered it all. Our paid circulation reaches all 50 states and many foreign countries. Because we are intended for the trade—including growers, winemakers, winery owners, wholesalers, restauranteurs, and serious amateurs—we accept more technical, informative articles. We do not accept wine reviews, wine country tours, or anything of a wine consumer nature." Estab. 1919. Circ. 5,000. Byline given. Pays 30 days after acceptance. No kill fee. Publishes ms an average of 3 months after acceptance. Buys first rights, buys electronic rights. Editorial lead time 2 months. Submit seasonal material 4 months in advance. Accepts queries by e-mail. Responds in 2-3 weeks to queries. Sample copy for $5. Guidelines free.

Nonfiction Needs interview, new product, technical. "No wine reviews, wine country travelogues, 'lifestyle' pieces, or anything aimed at wine consumers. Our readers are professionals in the field." **Buys 60 mss/year.** Query with published clips. Length: 1,000-2,000 words. **Pays flat fee of $500 for assigned articles.**

Photos Prefers JPEG files (JPEG, 300 dpi minimum). Can use high-quality prints. State availability of or send photos Captions, identification of subjects required. Does not pay for photos submitted by author, but will give photo credit.

BOOK & BOOKSTORE

AUSTRALIAN ACADEMIC & RESEARCH LIBRARIES

Australian Academic & Research Libraries, P.O. Box 6335, Kingston ACT 2604 Australia. (61)(2)6215-8222. Fax: (61)(2)6282-2249. E-mail: aarl@alia.org.au. Website: alia.org.au/publishing/aarl. Quarterly magazine covering all aspects of librarianship in university and college libraries, including the technical and further education sector, and in research libraries of all types.

- Query before submitting.

AUSTRALIAN BOOK REVIEW

P.O. Box 2320, Richmond South VIC 3121 Australia. (61)(3)9429-6700. Fax: (61)(3)9429-2288. E-mail: abr@vicnet.net.au. Website: www.vicnet.net.au/~abr. Magazine published 10 times/year covering book reviews.

- Query before submitting.

$ THE BLOOMSBURY REVIEW

A Book Magazine, Dept. WM, Owaissa Communications Co., Inc., P.O. Box 8928, Denver CO 80201. (303)455-3123. Fax: (303)455-7039. E-mail: bloomsb@aol.com. **75% freelance written**. Bimonthly tabloid covering books and book-related matters. We publish book reviews, interviews with writers and poets, literary essays, and original poetry. Our audience consists of educated, literate, nonspecialized readers. Estab. 1980. Circ. 50,000. Byline given. Pays on publication. No kill fee. Publishes ms an average of 4-6 months after acceptance. Buys first rights, buys one-time rights. Accepts queries by mail. Responds in 4 months to queries. Sample copy for $5 and 9x12 SASE. Guidelines for #10 SASE.

Nonfiction Summer issue features reviews, etc., about the American West. We do not publish fiction. Needs essays, interview, book reviews. **Buys 60 mss/year.** Send complete ms. Length: 800-1,500 words. **Pays $10-20. Sometimes pays writers with contributor copies or other premiums if writer agrees.**

Reprints Considered but t encouraged. Send photocopy of article and information about when and where the article previously appeared.

Photos State availability Reviews prints. Offers no additional payment for photos accepted with ms. Buys one time rights.

Columns/Departments Book reviews and essays, 500-1,500 words. 6 Query with published clips or send complete ms. **Pays $10-20.**

Poetry Contact: Ray Gonzalez, poetry editor. Needs avant-garde, free verse, haiku, traditional. **Buys 20 poems/year.** Submit maximum 5 poems. **Pays $5-10.**

Tips We appreciate receiving published clips and/or completed manuscripts. Please—no rough drafts. Book reviews should be of new books (within 6 months of publication).

$ $ FOREWORD MAGAZINE

ForeWord Magazine, Inc., 129 ½ E. Front St., Traverse City MI 49684. (231)933-3699. Fax: (231)933-3899. Website: www.forewordmagazine.com. **95% freelance written.** Bimonthly magazine covering independent and university presses for booksellers and librarians with articles, news, book reviews. Estab. 1998. Circ. 8,000. Byline given. Pays 2 months after publication. No kill fee. Publishes ms an average of 2-3 months after acceptance. Buys all rights. Editorial lead time 3-4 months. Submit seasonal material 5 months in advance. Accepts queries by mail, e-mail. Responds in 1 month to queries. Responds in 1 month to mss. Sample copy for $10 and 8½x11 SASE with $1.50 postage.

Nonfiction Query with published clips. Length: 400-1,500 words. **Pays $25-200 for assigned articles.**

Tips Be knowledgeable about the needs of booksellers and librarians—remember we are an industry trade journal, not a how-to or consumer publication. We review books prior to publication, so book reviews are always assigned—but send us a note telling subjects you wish to review, as well as a resume.

THE HORN BOOK MAGAZINE

The Horn Book, Inc., 56 Roland St., Suite 200, Boston MA 02129. (617)628-0225. Fax: (617)628-0882. Website: www.hbook.com. **75% freelance written. Prefers to work with published/established writers.** Bimonthly magazine covering children's literature for librarians, booksellers, professors, teachers and students of children's literature. Estab. 1924. Circ. 16,000. Byline given. Pays on publication. No kill fee. Publishes ms an average of 4 months after acceptance. Submit seasonal material 6 months in advance. Accepts queries by mail, e-mail, fax. Accepts simultaneous submissions. Responds in 3 months to queries. Sample copy and writer's guidelines online

Nonfiction "Interested in seeing strong, authoritative pieces about children's books and contemporary culture. Writers should be familiar with the magazine and its contents." Needs interview, children's book authors and illustrators, topics of interest to the children's bookworld. **Buys 20 mss/year.** Query or send complete ms. Length: 1,000-2,800 words. **Pays honorarium upon publication**

Tips "Writers have a better chance of breaking into our publication with a query letter on a specific article they want to write."

THE NEW YORK REVIEW OF BOOKS

435 Hudson St., 3rd Floor, New York NY 10014. (212)757-8070. Fax: (212)333-5374. E-mail: editor@nybooks.com. Website: www.nybooks.com. **Contact:** Robert B. Silvers. Biweekly magazine covering books and authors. Circ. 125,000.

Nonfiction Needs interview, reviews. Query.

$ VIDEO LIBRARIAN

8705 Honeycomb Court NW, Seabeck WA 98380. (360)830-9345. Fax: (360)830-9346. E-mail: vidlib@videolibrarian.com. Website: www.videolibrarian.com. **75% freelance written.** Bimonthly magazine covering DVD reviews for librarians. "*Video Librarian* reviews approximately 225 titles in each issue: children's, documentaries, how-to's, movies, TV, music and anime." Estab. 1986. Circ. 2,000. Byline given. Pays on publication. Publishes ms an average of 2 months after acceptance. Buys one-time rights, buys second serial (reprint) rights, buys electronic rights. Makes work-for-hire assignments. Editorial lead time 2 months. Accepts queries by e-mail. Accepts previously published material. Accepts simultaneous submissions. Responds in 1 week to queries. Sample copy for $11.

Nonfiction Buys 500+ mss/year. Query with published clips. Length: 200-300 words. **Pays $10-20/review.**

Tips "We are looking for DVD reviewers with a wide range of interests, good critical eye, and strong writing skills."

BRICK, GLASS & CERAMICS

$ $ GLASS MAGAZINE

For the Architectural Glass Industry, National Glass Association, 8200 Greensboro Dr., Suite 302, McLean VA 22102. (866)342-5642. Fax: (703)442-0630. E-mail: editorialinfo@glass.org. Website: www.glass.org. **10% freelance written. Prefers to work with published/established writers.** Monthly magazine covering the architectural glass industry. Circ. 28,289. Byline given. Pays on acceptance. Offers kill fee. Kill fee varies. Publishes ms an average of 6 months after acceptance. Buys first rights. Accepts queries by mail, e-mail, fax. Responds in 2 months to mss. Sample copy for $5 and 9x12 SAE with 10 first-class stamps.

Nonfiction Needs interview, of various glass businesses; profiles of industry people or glass business owners,

new product, technical, about glazing processes. **Buys 5 mss/year.** Query with published clips. 1,000 words minimum. **Pays $150-300.**
Photos State availability
Tips *Glass Magazine* is doing more inhouse writing; freelance cut by half. Do not send in general glass use stories. Research the industry first, then query.

$ STAINED GLASS

Stained Glass Association of America, 10009 E. 62nd St., Raytown MO 64133. E-mail: quarterly@sgaaonline.com. Website: www.stainedglass.org. **70% freelance written**. Quarterly magazine. Since 1906, *Stained Glass* has been the official voice of the Stained Glass Association of America. As the oldest, most respected stained glass publication in North America, *Stained Glass* preserves the techniques of the past as well as illustrates the trends of the future. This vital information, of significant value to the professional stained glass studio, is also of interest to those for whom stained glass is an avocation or hobby. Estab. 1906. Circ. 8,000. Byline given. Pays on publication. No kill fee. Publishes ms an average of 1 year after acceptance. Buys one-time rights. Editorial lead time 6 months. Submit seasonal material 8 months in advance. Accepts queries by mail, e-mail, fax. Responds in 3 months to queries. Sample copy and writer's guideline free
Nonfiction Strong need for technical and how to create architectural type stained glass. Glass etching, use of etched glass in stained glass compositions, framing. Needs how-to, humor, interview, new product, opinion, photo feature, technical. **Buys 9 mss/year.** Query or send complete ms but must include photos or slides—very heavy on photos. **Pays $125/illustrated article; $75/nonillustrated.**
Reprints Accepts previously published submissions from nstained glass publications only. Send tearsheet of article. Payment negotiable.
Photos Send photos Identification of subjects required. Reviews 4x5 transparencies, send slides with submission. Pays $75 for non-illustrated. Pays $125, plus 3 copies for line art or photography. Buys one time rights.
Columns/Departments Columns must be illustrated. Teknixs (technical, how-to, stained and glass art), word length varies by subject. 4 Query or send complete ms, but must be illustrated.
Tips We need more technical articles. Writers should be extremely well versed in the glass arts. Photographs are extremely important and must be of very high quality. Submissions without photographs or illustrations are seldom considered unless something special and writer states that photos are available. However, prefer to see with submission.

$ $ US GLASS, METAL & GLAZING

Key Communications, Inc., P.O. Box 569, Garrisonville VA 22463. (540)720-5584. Fax: (540)720-5687. E-mail: info@glass.com. Website: www.usglassmag.com. **25% freelance written**. Monthly magazine for companies involved in the flat glass trades. Estab. 1966. Circ. 27,000. Byline given. Pays on publication. No kill fee. Publishes ms an average of 3 months after acceptance. Buys all rights. Editorial lead time 3 months. Submit seasonal material 2 months in advance. Accepts queries by mail, e-mail, fax. Accepts simultaneous submissions. Responds in 1 month to queries. Responds in 2 months to mss. Sample copy and writer's guidelines online.
Nonfiction Buys 12 mss/year. Query with published clips. **Pays $300-600 for assigned articles.** Sometimes pays expenses of writers on assignment.
Photos State availability Captions, identification of subjects required. Reviews contact sheets. Offers no additional payment for photos accepted with ms. Buys first North American rights.

BUILDING INTERIORS

$ $ FABRICS + FURNISHINGS INTERNATIONAL

SIPCO Publications + Events, 1133 Pleasantville Rd., P.O. 161, Briarcliff NY 10510. (914)923-0616. Fax: (914)923-0018. E-mail: rgoldberg@sipco.net. Website: www.sipco.net. **10% freelance written.** Bimonthly magazine covering commercial, hospitality interior design, manufacturing. *F+FI* covers news from vendors who supply hospitality interiors industry. Estab. 1990. Circ. 11,000+. Byline given. Pays on publication. Offers $100 kill fee. Editorial lead time 3 months. Submit seasonal material 3 months in advance. Accepts queries by e-mail. Accepts simultaneous submissions. Sample copy available online.
Nonfiction Needs interview, technical. Does not opinion, consumer pieces. Our readers must learn something from our stories. Query with published clips. Length: 500-1,000 words. **Pays $250-350.**
Photos Send photos Captions, identification of subjects required. Reviews GIF/JPEG files. Offers no additional payment for photos accepted with ms.
Tips Give us a lead on a new project that we haven't heard about. Have pictures of space and ability to interview designer on how they made it work.

FLOOR COVERING NEWS

The publication more retailers prefer, Ro-El Productions, 550 W. Old Country Rd., Suite 204, Hicksville NY 11801. (516)932-7860. Fax: (516)932-7639. E-mail: fcnews@optonline.net. Website: www.floorcoveringnews.

net. **15% freelance written**. Biweekly tabloid covering the floor covering industry for retailers, salespeople, installers, distributors and designers, as well as manufacturers. We are a journalistic-style publication that writes for the flooring industry. While we use industry jargon and have our own nuances, we use the AP and New York Times stylebooks as general guidelines. Estab. 1986. Circ. 16,000. Byline given. Pays on acceptance. Publishes ms an average of 1 month after acceptance. Buys exclusivity rights for within the flooring industry trades, which includes the Internet. Editorial lead time 2 months. Accepts previously published material. Accepts simultaneous submissions. Responds in 2-3 weeks to queries. Sample copy for $4.

Nonfiction Needs book excerpts, expose, historical, interview, new product, photo feature, technical. Does not want puff pieces and commercials. **Buys 30-40 mss/year.** Query. **Pays negotiable amount.** Pays expenses of writers on assignment.

Photos Send photos Captions, identification of subjects, model releases required. Reviews contact sheets, prints, JPEG/TIFF files (300 dpi, 4x4 minimum). Offers no additional payment for photos accepted with ms; negotiates payment individually.

HOME TEXTILES TODAY

The Business and Fashion Newspaper of the Home Textiles Industry, Reed Business Information, 360 Park Ave. S., New York NY 10010. (646)746-7290. Fax: (646)746-7300. E-mail: jnegley@reedbusiness.com. Website: www.hometextilestoday.com. **5% freelance written**. Tabloid published 33 times/year covering home textiles retailers, manufacturers and importers/exporters. Our readers are interested in business trends and statistics about business trends related to their niche in the home furnishings market. Estab. 1979. Circ. 7,700. Byline given. Pays on publication. Offers 30% kill fee. Publishes ms an average of 2 weeks after acceptance. Buys all rights. Editorial lead time 1-2 weeks. Submit seasonal material 3 weeks in advance. Accepts queries by mail, e-mail, fax, phone. Accepts simultaneous submissions. Responds in 2 weeks to queries. Responds in 2 weeks to mss. Sample copy free. Guidelines free.

Tips Information has to be focused on home textiles business—sheets, towels, bedding, curtains, rugs, table linens, kitchen textiles, curtains. Most of our readers are doing volume business at discount chains, mass market retailers, big boxes and department stores.

IE MAGAZINE

IE Publishing, P.O. Box 414179, Craighall Park 2024 South Africa. (27)(11)883-1283. Fax: (27)(11)883-1822. Website: www.iemagazine.co.za. **10% freelance written**. Bimonthly magazine. We are an architecture and interior design-based publication, focusing mainly on new projects in South Africa. We also cover some product and general design news, as well as international trends. Estab. 2001. Circ. 3,500-5,000. Byline given. Pays on publication. No kill fee. Buys all rights. Editorial lead time 2 months. Submit seasonal material 2 months in advance. Accepts queries by e-mail. Accepts previously published material.

Nonfiction Needs new product, technical, architecture, design. Query. Length: 700-1,400 words. **Pays R1.50/word.**

Photos Captions required. Offers no additional payment for photos accepted with ms. Buys all rights.

Columns/Departments Design Divas (successful business women in design industry); International Trends (trade fairs, etc); My Home, My City (local architect's perspective on his/her city). Query.

INTERIOR FITOUT

The Intermedia Group, Ltd., P.O. Box 55, Glebe NSW 2037 Australia. (61)(2)9660-2113. Fax: (61)(2)9660-4419. E-mail: info@intermedia.com.au. Website: www.intermedia.com.au. Bimonthly magazine covering retail and commercial interior design. Estab. 1997.

- Query before submitting.

$ $ KITCHEN & BATH DESIGN NEWS

Cygnus Business Media, 3 Huntington Quadrangle, Suite 301N, Melville NY 11747. Fax: (631)845-7218. E-mail: janice.costa@cygnuspub.com. Website: www.kitchenbathdesign.com. **15% freelance written**. Monthly tabloid for kitchen and bath dealers and design professionals, offering design, business and marketing advice to help our readers be more successful. It is not a consumer publication about design, a book for do-it-yourselfers, or a magazine created to showcase pretty pictures of kitchens and baths. Rather, we cover the professional kitchen and bath design industry in depth, looking at the specific challenges facing these professionals, and how they address these challenges. Estab. 1983. Circ. 51,000. Byline given. Pays on publication. Publishes ms an average of 2-3 months after acceptance. Buys all rights. Editorial lead time 2 months. Accepts queries by mail, e-mail, fax. Responds in 2-4 weeks to queries. Sample copy available online. Guidelines by email.

Nonfiction Needs how-to, interview. Does not want consumer stories; generic business stories; I remodeled my kitchen and it's so beautiful stories. This is a magazine for trade professionals, so stories need to be both slanted for these professionals, as well as sophisticated enough so that people who have been working in the field 30 years can still learn something from them. **Buys 16 mss/year.** Query with published clips. Length: 1,100-3,000 words. **Pays $200-650.** Sometimes pays expenses of writers on assignment.

Photos Send photos Identification of subjects required. Offers no additional payment for photos accepted with ms.

Tips This is a trade magazine for kitchen and bath dealers and designers, so trade experience and knowledge of the industry are essential. We look for writers who already know the unique challenges facing this industry, as well as the major players, acronyms, etc. This is not a market for beginners, and the vast majority of our freelancers are either design professionals, or experienced in the industry.

$ $ QUALIFIED REMODELER

The Business Management Tool for Professional Remodelers, Cygnus Business Media, P.O. Box 803, Fort Atkinson WI 53538. E-mail: chaya.chang@cygnuspub.com. Website: www.qualifiedremodeler.com. **5% freelance written**. Monthly magazine covering residential remodeling. Estab. 1975. Circ. 83,500. Byline given. Pays on acceptance. No kill fee. Publishes ms an average of 1 month after acceptance. Buys all rights. Editorial lead time 3 months. Submit seasonal material 2 months in advance. Accepts queries by mail, e-mail, fax, phone. Sample copy available online.

Nonfiction Needs how-to, business management, new product, photo feature, best practices articles, innovative design. **Buys 12 mss/year.** Query with published clips. Length: 1,200-2,500 words. **Pays $300-600 for assigned articles. Pays $200-400 for unsolicited articles.** Sometimes pays expenses of writers on assignment.

Photos Send photos Reviews negatives, transparencies. Negotiates payment individually. Buys one time rights.

Columns/Departments Query with published clips. **Pays $400**

Tips We focus on business management issues faced by remodeling contractors. For example, sales, marketing, liability, taxes, and just about any matter addressing small business operation.

$ $ $ $ REMODELING

HanleyWood, LLC, One Thomas Circle NW, Suite 600, Washington DC 20005. (202)452-0800. Fax: (202)785-1974. E-mail: ibush@hanleywood.com. Website: www.remodelingmagazine.com. **10% freelance written**. Monthly magazine covering residential and light commercial remodeling. We cover the best new ideas in remodeling design, business, construction and products. Estab. 1985. Circ. 80,000. Byline given. Pays on publication. Offers 5¢/word kill fee. Publishes ms an average of 3 months after acceptance. Buys first North American serial rights. Accepts queries by mail, e-mail, fax. Sample copy free.

Nonfiction Needs interview, new product, technical, small business trends. **Buys 6 mss/year.** Query with published clips. Length: 250-1,000 words. **Pays $1/word.** Sometimes pays expenses of writers on assignment.

Photos State availability Captions, identification of subjects, model releases required. Reviews 4x5 transparencies, slides, 8x10 prints. Offers $25-125/photo. Buys one time rights.

Tips We specialize in service journalism for remodeling contractors. Knowledge of the industry is essential.

$ $ WALLS & CEILINGS

2401 W. Big Beaver Rd., Suite 700, Troy MI 48084. (248)244-6404. Fax: (248)362-5103. E-mail: wyattj@bnpmedia.com. Website: www.wconline.com. **20% freelance written**. Monthly magazine for contractors involved in lathing and plastering, drywall, acoustics, fireproofing, curtain walls, and movable partitions, together with manufacturers, dealers, and architects. Estab. 1938. Circ. 30,000. Byline given. Pays on publication. No kill fee. Publishes ms an average of 6 months after acceptance. Buys all rights. Submit seasonal material 4 months in advance. Accepts queries by mail, e-mail, phone. Accepts simultaneous submissions. Responds in 6 months to queries. Sample copy for 9x12 SAE with $2 postage. Guidelines for #10 SASE.

Nonfiction Needs how-to, drywall and plaster construction and business management, technical. **Buys 20 mss/year.** Query or send complete ms. Length: 1,000-1,500 words. **Pays $50-500.** Sometimes pays expenses of writers on assignment.

Reprints Send tearsheet or photocopy with rights for sale noted and information about when and where the material previously appeared. Pays 50% of the amount paid for an original article.

Photos Send photos Captions, identification of subjects required. Reviews contact sheets, negatives, transparencies, prints. Buys one time rights.

BUSINESS MANAGEMENT

$ $ ASSOCIATION & MEETING DIRECTOR

Canada's Number One Association Management & Meeting Magazine, August Communications, 225-530 Century St., Winnipeg MB R3H 0Y4 Canada. (888)573-1136. Fax: (866)957-0217. E-mail: r.mcilroy@august.ca. Website: www.associationdirector.ca. **70% freelance written**. Bimonthly magazine covering association management and corporate meeting planners. *Association & Meeting Director* is direct mailed to Canadian association executives and corporate meeting professionals. It has the aim of exploring both the Canadian corporate and association marketplace. Estab. 2000. Circ. 15,000. Byline given. Pays 1 month after publication. No kill fee. Publishes ms an average of 2 months after acceptance. Buys all rights. Editorial lead time 3 months. Submit seasonal material 3 months in advance. Accepts queries by mail, e-mail, fax. Responds in 1 week to queries. Sample copy and writer's guidelines free.

Nonfiction Needs how-to, inspirational, interview, new product, technical, travel. **Buys 18 mss/year.** Query with published clips. Length: 700-2,000 words. **Pays 20-40¢/word for assigned articles.**
Photos State availability Identification of subjects required. Reviews GIF/JPEG files. Negotiates payment individually. Buys all rights.
Columns/Departments 12 Query with published clips. **Pays 20-40¢/word**

BEDROOM MAGAZINE

The Marketing Arm Group, Inc., 11826 Shoemaker Court, Charlotte NC 28270. (704)841-8323. Fax: (704)841-0616. E-mail: daler@rtppub.com. Website: www.bedroom-mag.com. Quarterly magazine mailed to more than 18,000 home furnishings retailers, buyers, owners and managers. We only cover one thing: mattresses, beds, top-of-bed, sleep products. We are a narrow, long-standing trade journal. Circ. 20,000.

$ $ $ $ BEDTIMES

The Business Journal for the Sleep Products Industry, International Sleep Products Association, 501 Wythe St., Alexandria VA 22314-1917. (703)683-8371. E-mail: jpalm@sleepproducts.org. Website: www.sleepproducts.org. **20-40% freelance written**. Monthly magazine covering the mattress manufacturing industry. "Our news and features are straightforward—we are not a lobbying vehicle for our association. No special slant." Estab. 1917. Circ. 3,800. Byline given. Pays on acceptance. No kill fee. Publishes ms an average of 3 months after acceptance. Buys first North American serial rights. Editorial lead time 2 months. Accepts queries by e-mail. Accepts simultaneous submissions. Responds in 1 month to queries. Sample copy for $4. Guidelines by email.
Nonfiction No pieces that do not relate to business in general or mattress industry in particular. **Buys 15-25/year mss/year.** Query with published clips. Length: 500-2,500 words. **Pays 50-$1/word for short features; $2,000 for cover story.**
Photos State availability Identification of subjects required. Negotiates payment individually. Buys one time rights.
Tips "Cover topics have included annual industry forecast; e-commerce; flammability and home furnishings; the risks and rewards of marketing overseas; the evolving family business; the shifting workplace environment; and what do consumers really want?"

$ $ $ $ BLACK MBA MAGAZINE

Official Publication of NBMBAA, P&L Publishing Ltd., 9730 S. Western Ave., Suite 320, Evergreen Park IL 60805. (708)422-1506. Fax: (708)422-1507. E-mail: robert@blackmbamagazine.net. Website: www.blackmbamagazine.net. **80% freelance written**. Quarterly magazine covering business career strategy, economic development, and financial management. Estab. 1997. Circ. 45,000. Byline given. Pays after publication. Offers 10-20% or $500 kill fee. Publishes ms an average of 1 month after acceptance. Buys all rights. Editorial lead time 2-3 months. Submit seasonal material 3-4 months in advance. Accepts queries by mail, e-mail, fax.
Photos State availability of or send photos Identification of subjects required. Reviews ZIP disk. Offers no additional payment for photos accepted with ms. Buys one time rights.
Columns/Departments Management Strategies (leadership development), 1,200-1,700 words; Features (business management, entreprenuerial finance); Finance; Technology. Send complete ms. **Pays $500-1,000.**

$ $ $ BUSINESS TRAVEL EXECUTIVE

Managed Travel & Procurement Solutions, 11 Ryerson Ave., Suite 200, Pompton Plains NJ 07405. E-mail: jferring@askbte.com. Website: www.askbte.com. **90% freelance written**. Monthly magazine covering corporate procurement of travel services. "We are not a travel magazine. We publish articles designed to help corporate purchasers of travel negotiate contracts, enforce policy, select automated services, track business travelers and account for their safety and expenditures, understand changes in the various industries associated with travel. Do not submit manuscripts without an assignment. Look at the website for an idea of what we publish." Byline given. Pays on publication. No kill fee. Publishes ms an average of 2 months after acceptance. Buys first North American serial rights. Editorial lead time 0-3 months. Accepts queries by e-mail.
Nonfiction Needs how-to, technical. **Buys 48 mss/year.** Query. Length: 800-2,000 words. **Pays $200-800.**
Columns/Departments Meeting Place (meeting planning and management); Hotel Pulse (hotel negotiations, contracting and compliance); Security Watch (travel safety), all 1,000 words. 24 Query. **Pays $200-400.**

CA MAGAZINE

Canadian Institute of Chartered Accountants, 277 Wellington St. W, Toronto ON M5V 3H2 Canada. (416)977-3222. Fax: (416)204-3409. E-mail: camagazineinfo@cica.ca. Website: www.camagazine.com. **30% freelance written**. Magazine published 10 times/year covering accounting. *CA Magazine* is the leading accounting publication in Canada and the preferred information source for chartered accountants and financial executives. It provides a forum for discussion and debate on professional, financial, and other business issues. Estab. 1911. Circ. 74,834. Byline given. Pays on acceptance. Offers 30% kill fee. Publishes ms an average of 3 months after acceptance. Buys all rights. Editorial lead time 4 months. Accepts queries by e-mail. Responds in 1 month to queries. Sample copy and writer's guidelines online
Nonfiction Needs book excerpts, financial/accounting business. **Buys 30 mss/year.** Query. Length: 2,500-3,500

words. **Pays honorarium for chartered accountants; freelance rate varies.**

⊘ CIO INSIGHT

Ziff-Davis Media, Inc., 28 E. 28th St., New York NY 10016. (212)503-3500. Fax: (212)503-5636. Website: www.cioinsight.com. Monthly magazine covering team management, wireless strategies, investment planning and profits, and Web-hosting security issues. Written for senior-level executives with key interests in strategic information technology, including CIOs, chief technology officers and IS/IT/MIS vice presidents and managers. No kill fee. Accepts queries by e-mail. Accepts previously published material. Guidelines available online.

- No unsolicited mss.

Nonfiction We welcome well-thought out story proposals from experienced journalists and experts in technology and business subjects. If you have a compelling and/or original story idea, you may send us your pitch via e-mail. We are particularly interested in case studies, trend and analysis articles, and ideas for whiteboards. Story pitches should be clear about the focus of the proposed article, why the topic is timely, and the key questions to be answered in the article.

$ $ CONTRACTING PROFITS

Trade Press Publishing, 2100 W. Florist Ave., Milwaukee WI 53209. (414)228-7701. Fax: (414)228-1134. Website: www.cleanlink.com/cp. **40% freelance written**. Magazine published 10 times/year covering building service contracting, business management advice. We are the pocket MBA for this industry—focusing not only on cleaning-specific topics, but also discussing how to run businesses better and increase profits through a variety of management articles. Estab. 1995. Circ. 32,000. Byline given. Pays within 30 days of acceptance. No kill fee. Buys all rights. Editorial lead time 2 months. Submit seasonal material 3 months in advance. Accepts queries by mail, e-mail. Responds in weeks to queries. Sample copy available online. Guidelines free.

Nonfiction Needs expose, how-to, interview, technical. No product-related reviews or testimonials. **Buys 30 mss/year.** Query with published clips. Length: 1,000-1,500 words. **Pays $100-500.** Sometimes pays expenses of writers on assignment.

Columns/Departments Query with published clips.

Tips Read back issues on our website and be able to understand some of those topics prior to calling.

$ $ CONTRACT MANAGEMENT

National Contract Management Association, 8260 Greensboro Dr., Suite 200, McLean VA 22102. (571)382-0082. Fax: (703)448-0939. E-mail: miedema@ncmahq.org. Website: www.ncmahq.org. **10% freelance written**. Monthly magazine covering contract and business management. Most of the articles published in *Contract Management (CM)* are written by members, although one does not have to be an NCMA member to be published in the magazine. Articles should concern some aspect of the contract management profession, whether at the level of a beginner or that of the advanced practitioner. Estab. 1960. Circ. 23,000. Byline given. Pays on publication. No kill fee. Publishes ms an average of 3 months after acceptance. Buys one-time rights. Editorial lead time 10 weeks. Submit seasonal material 3 months in advance. Accepts queries by mail, e-mail, fax, phone. Accepts previously published material. Accepts simultaneous submissions. Responds in 2 weeks to queries. Responds in 1 month to mss. Sample copy and writer's guidelines free

Nonfiction Needs essays, general interest, how-to, humor, inspirational, new product, opinion, technical. No company or CEO profiles—please read a copy of publication before submitting. **Buys 6-10 mss/year.** Query with published clips. Length: 2,500-3,000 words. **Pays $300, association members paid in 3 copies.**

Photos State availability Captions, identification of subjects required. Offers no additional payment for photos accepted with ms Buys one time rights.

Columns/Departments Professional Development (self-improvement in business), 1,000-1,500 words; Back to Basics (basic how-tos and discussions), 1,500-2,000 words. 2 Query with published clips. **Pays $300**

Tips Query and read at least 1 issue. Visit website to better understand our audience.

CONVENTION SOUTH

P.O. Box 2267, Gulf Shores AL 36547. (251)968-5300. Fax: (251)968-4532. E-mail: info@conventionsouth.com. Website: www.conventionsouth.com. **50% freelance written**. Monthly business journal for meeting planners who plan events in the South. Topics relate to the meetings industry—how-to articles, industry news, destination spotlights. Estab. 1983. Circ. 16,000. Byline given. Pays on publication. No kill fee. Publishes ms an average of 2 months after acceptance. Buys first rights, buys second serial (reprint) rights. Editorial lead time 3 months. Submit seasonal material 4 months in advance. Accepts queries by mail, e-mail, fax. Accepts simultaneous submissions. Responds in 2 months to queries. Sample copy free. Guidelines for #10 SASE.

Nonfiction Needs how-to, relative to meeting planning/travel, interview, photo feature, technical, travel. **Buys 50 mss/year.** Query. Length: 750-1,250 words. **Payment negotiable.** Sometimes pays expenses of writers on assignment.

Reprints Send photocopy and information about when and where the material previously appeared. Payment negotiable.

Photos Send photos Captions, identification of subjects required. Reviews 5x7 prints. Offers no additional payment for photos accepted with ms. Buys one time rights.

Columns/Departments How-to (related to meetings), 700 words. 12 Query with published clips. **Payment negotiable.**

Tips Know who our audience is and make sure articles are appropriate for them.

EMPLOYEE ASSISTANCE REPORT

Impact Publications, 1439 Churchill St., Crystal Plaza, Units 302-303, Waupaca WI 54981. (800)350-4422. Fax: (715)258-9048. E-mail: info@impact-publications.com. Website: www.impact-publications.com. **0% freelance written. As opposed to paid freelance writers, most articles in this newsletter are either written by Employee Assistance Report staff or by employee assistance professionals—in exchange for free publicity for their EAP.** Monthly newsletter covering work-life issues of interest to employee assistance professionals (i.e. EAPs). Familiarity with needs and interests of employee assistance professionals. General work-life issues can be useful, but they are definitely not as useful as articles written specifically for this audience. Estab. 1998. Byline given. Writers generally not compensated financially. No kill fee. Publishes ms an average of 3 months after acceptance. Buys all rights. Editorial lead time 3 months. Accepts queries by e-mail, phone. Accepts previously published material. Accepts simultaneous submissions. Guidelines available.

Nonfiction Needs how-to, How-to means how-to resolve a particular issue or topic., interview, new product, Book reviews. Articles that are too long, too general, and/or that insist upon payment. **Buys 0 mss/year.** Query. Length: 1,000-1,300 words.

Photos State availability Offers no additional payment for photos accepted with ms.

Columns/Departments Contact: Mike Jacquart. Legal Lines (legal issues affectingn workplace), Washington Beat (legislative issues affecting the workplace), clinical Perspective (clinical/behavioral health issues affecting workplace), 500 words; On the Job (everyday work-life issues our readers run into), 300 words. 0

Tips Recognize that we work months ahead—contact editor as far in advance as possible, look at a copy of our editorial calendar on our website—it usually is available in early-to-mid fall for the following year. Recognize that we have a very spescific, professional audience and be willing to work with us as far as non-paid compensation arrangements.

$ $ EXECUTIVE UPDATE

Greater Washington Society of Association Executives, Reagan Building & International Trade Center, 1300 Pennsylvania Ave. NW, Washington DC 20004. (202)326-9545. Fax: (202)326-0999. Website: www.executiveupdate.com. **60% freelance written**. Monthly magazine exploring a broad range of association management issues and for introducing and discussing management and leadership philosophies. It is written for individuals at all levels of association management, with emphasis on senior staff and CEOs. Estab. 1979. Circ. 14,000. Byline given. Pays on acceptance. Offers 20% kill fee. Publishes ms an average of 6 months after acceptance. Buys first rights. Editorial lead time 3 months. Submit seasonal material 6 months in advance. Accepts queries by mail, e-mail, fax, phone. Accepts simultaneous submissions. Responds in 1 month to queries. Responds in 2 months to mss. Sample copy free. Guidelines available online.

Nonfiction Needs how-to, humor, interview, opinion, personal experience, travel, management and workplace issues. **Buys 24-36 mss/year.** Query with published clips. Length: 2,000-2,500 words. **Pays $500-700.** Pays expenses of writers on assignment.

Columns/Departments Intelligence (new ways to tackle day-to-day issues), 500-700 words; Off the Cuff (guest column for association executives). Query. **Pays $100-200.**

$ $ EXPANSION MANAGEMENT MAGAZINE

Growth Strategies for Companies On the Move, Penton Media, Inc., 1300 E. 9th St., Cleveland OH 44114. (216)931-9578. Fax: (216)931-9145. **50% freelance written**. Monthly magazine covering economic development. Estab. 1986. Circ. 45,000. Byline given. Pays on acceptance. No kill fee. Publishes ms an average of 1 month after acceptance. Buys all rights. Makes work-for-hire assignments. Editorial lead time 2 months. Sample copy for $7. Guidelines free.

Nonfiction *Expansion Management* presents articles and industry reports examining relocation trends, strategic planning, work force hiring, economic development agencies, and relocation consultants and state, province, and county reviews and profiles to help readers select future expansions and relocation sites. **Buys 120 mss/year.** Query with published clips. Length: 800-1,200 words. **Pays $200-400 for assigned articles.** Sometimes pays expenses of writers on assignment.

Photos Send photos Captions required. Offers no additional payment for photos accepted with ms. Buys one time rights.

Tips Send clips first, then call me.

$ $ $ EXPO

Atwood Publishing, LLC, 7015 College Blvd., Suite 600, Overland Park KS 66211. (913)344-1303. Fax: (913)344-1486. E-mail: dtormohlen@ascendmedia.com. Website: www.expoweb.com. **80% freelance written**. Magazine covering expositions. *EXPO* is the information and education resource for the exposition industry. It is the only magazine dedicated exclusively to the people with direct responsibility for planning, promoting and operating trade and consumer shows. Our readers are show managers and their staff, association executives, independent show producers and industry suppliers. Every issue of *EXPO* contains in-depth, how-to features and departments that focus on the practical aspects of exposition management, including administration, promotion and operations. Byline given. Pays on publication. Offers 50% kill fee. Buys first North American serial rights. Editorial lead time 3 months. Accepts queries by mail, e-mail, fax. Responds in 3 weeks to queries. Sample copy free. Guidelines available online.

Nonfiction Needs how-to, interview. Query with published clips. Length: 600-2,400 words. **Pays 50¢/word.** Pays expenses of writers on assignment.

Photos State availability

Columns/Departments Profile (personality profile), 650 words; Exhibitor Matters (exhibitor issues) and EXPOTech (technology), both 600-1,300 words. 10 Query with published clips.

Tips *EXPO* now offers shorter features and departments, while continuing to offer in-depth reporting. Editorial is more concise, using synopsis, bullets and tidbits whenever possible. Every article needs sidebars, call-outs, graphs, charts, etc., to create entry points for readers. Headlines and leads are more provocative. And writers should elevate the level of shop talk, demonstrating that *EXPO* is the leader in the industry. We plan our editorial calendar about one year in advance, but we are always open to new ideas. Please query before submitting a story to *EXPO*—tell us about your idea and what our readers would learn. Include your qualifications to write about the subject and the sources you plan to contact.

$ $ $ FAMILY BUSINESS MAGAZINE

The Guide for Family Companies, Family Business Publishing Co., Family Business Magazine, 1845 Walnut St., Philadelphia PA 19103. Fax: (215)405-6078. E-mail: bspector@familybusinessmagazine.com. Website: www.familybusinessmagazine.com. **Contact:** Barbara Spector, editor-in-chief. **50% freelance written**. Quarterly magazine covering family-owned companies. "Written expressly for family company owners and advisors. Focuses on business and human dynamic issues unique to family enterprises. Offers practical guidance and tried-and-true solutions for business stakeholders." Estab. 1989. Circ. 6,000. Byline given. Pays on acceptance. Offers 30% kill fee. Publishes ms an average of 9-12 months after acceptance. Buys first rights, buys electronic rights. Editorial lead time 4 months. Submit seasonal material 6 months in advance. Accepts queries by e-mail. Guidelines available online.

Nonfiction Needs how-to, family business related only, interview, personal experience. "No small business articles, articles that aren't specifically related to multi-generational family companies (no general business advice). No success stories—there must be an underlying family or business lesson. **No payment for articles written by family business advisors and other service providers.**" **Buys 24 mss/year.** Query with published clips. E-mail queries preferred. Length: 1,500-2,000 words. **Pays $50-1,400 for articles written by freelance reporters.**

Photos State availability Captions, identification of subjects, model releases required. Offers $50-600 maximum/shoot. Buys first, electronic, reprint rights.

$ $ IN TENTS

The Magazine for the Tent-Rental and Special-Event Industries, Industrial Fabrics Association International, 1801 County Rd. B W., Roseville MN 55113-4061. (651)225-6970. Fax: (651)225-6966. E-mail: intents@ifai.com. Website: www.ifai.com. **50% freelance written**. Bimonthly magazine covering tent-rental and special-event industries. Estab. 1994. Circ. 12,000. Byline given. Pays on acceptance. No kill fee. Publishes ms an average of 2 months after acceptance. Buys all rights. Editorial lead time 3 months. Accepts queries by mail, e-mail, fax. Sample copy and writer's guidelines free.

Nonfiction Needs how-to, interview, new product, photo feature, technical. **Buys 12-18 mss/year.** Query. Length: 800-2,000 words. **Pays $300-500.** Sometimes pays expenses of writers on assignment.

Photos State availability Captions, identification of subjects, model releases required. Reviews contact sheets, negatives, prints, digital images. Negotiates payment individually.

Tips We look for lively, intelligent writing that makes technical subjects come alive.

$ $ MAINEBIZ

Maine's Business News Source, Mainebiz Publications, Inc., 30 Milk St., 3rd Floor, Portland ME 04101. (207)761-8379. Fax: (207)761-0732. E-mail: tsmith@mainebiz.biz. Website: www.mainebiz.biz. **25% freelance written**. Biweekly tabloid covering business in Maine. *Mainebiz* is read by business decision makers across the state. They look to the publication for business news and analysis. Estab. 1994. Circ. 13,000. Byline given. Pays on publication. Offers 10% kill fee. Publishes ms an average of 1 month after acceptance. Buys all rights. Editorial lead time 1 month. Submit seasonal material 2 months in advance. Accepts queries by mail, e-mail. Responds in 3 weeks to queries. Sample copy available online. Guidelines available online.

Nonfiction All pieces are reported and must comply with accepted journalistic standards. We only publish stories about business in Maine. Needs essays, expose, interview, business trends. See website for editorial calendar. **Buys 50+ mss/year.** Query with published clips. Length: 500-2,500 words. **Pays $50-250.** Pays expenses of writers on assignment.

Photos State availability Identification of subjects required. Reviews GIF/JPEG files. Negotiates payment individually. Buys one time rights.

Tips Stories should be well thought out with specific relevance to Maine. Arts and culture-related queries are welcome, as long as there is a business angle. We appreciate unusual angles on business stories and regularly work with new freelancers. Please, no queries unless you have read the paper.

$ $ NATIVE AMERICAN CASINO

Dellas Publications LLC, 1446 Front St., Suite 200, San Diego CA 92101. (619)223-0782. Fax: (619)223-0761. E-mail: mdellas@nacasino.com. Website: www.nacasino.com. **30% freelance written.** Monthly magazine covering the Indian casino industry. *Native American Casino* (NAC) is a monthly, business-to-business magazine dedicated to the growth and prosperity of the Native American businessperson. Our articles aid casino managers in running their various departments, articles also focus on new or expanding Indian casinos, interviews, and topics that people can use to improve any business they wish to pursue. Our readers are the casino managers and tribal leaders/members. Estab. 2000. Circ. 30,000. Byline given. Pays on publication. Publishes ms an average of 2 months after acceptance. Buys all rights. Editorial lead time 2 months. Submit seasonal material 2 months in advance. Accepts queries by e-mail. Accepts simultaneous submissions. Sample copy free. Guidelines by email.

Nonfiction Needs historical, how-to, inspirational, interview, technical, travel. Does not want advertorials, articles degrading or giving any kind of negative impression on Native Americans or the gaming industry, or articles with sexual content or profanity. **Buys 24-36 mss/year.** Query with published clips. Length: 900-2,000 words. **Pays $200-300.**

Photos Contact: Contact Kristina Ushakov, creative director. State availability Captions, identification of subjects, model releases required. Reviews 5x7 prints, GIF/JPEG files (300 dpi). Offers no additional payment for photos accepted with ms. Buys one time rights.

Tips I encourage all freelancers interested to visit our Web site to get familiar with *NAC*. I would also like them to visit www.indiangaming.com to read about the National Indian Gaming Association and become familiar with our industry.

⊘ NORTHEAST EXPORT

A Magazine for New England Companies Engaged in International Trade, Commerce Publishing Company, Inc., P.O. Box 254, Northborough MA 01532. (508)351-2925. Fax: (508)351-2930. E-mail: editor@northeast-export.com. Website: www.northeast-export.com. **30% freelance written.** Bimonthly business-to-business magazine. *Northeast Export* is the only publication directly targeted at New England's international trade community. All stories relate to issues affecting New England companies and feature only New England-based profiles and examples. Estab. 1997. Circ. 13,500. Byline given. Pays on acceptance. Offers 10% kill fee. Buys all rights. Editorial lead time 2 months. Accepts queries by mail, e-mail, fax. Sample copy free.

Nonfiction Needs how-to, interview, travel, industry trends/analysis. **Buys 10-12 mss/year.** Query with published clips and SASE. *No unsolicited mss*. Length: 800-1,200 words. **Payment varies**

Photos State availability of or send photos Captions, identification of subjects, model releases required. Reviews 2 ¼ transparencies, 5x7 prints. Negotiates payment individually. Buys one time rights.

Tips We're looking for writers with availability; the ability to write clearly about tough, sometimes very technical subjects; the fortitude to slog through industry jargon to get the story straight; a knowledge of international trade issues and/or New England transportation infrastructure. We're interested in freelancers with business writing and magazine experience, especially those with contacts in the New England manufacturing, finance, and transportation communities.

$ $ PROGRESSIVE RENTALS

The Voice of the Rental-Purchase Industry, Association of Progressive Rental Organizations, 1504 Robin Hood Trail, Austin TX 78703. (800)204-2776. Fax: (512)794-0097. Website: www.aprovision.org. **50% freelance written.** Bimonthly magazine covering the rent-to-own industry. *Progressive Rentals* is the only publication representing the rent-to-own industry and members of APRO. The magazine covers timely news and features affecting the industry, association activities, and member profiles. Awarded best 4-color magazine by the American Society of Association Executives in 1999. Estab. 1980. Circ. 5,500. Byline given. Pays on acceptance. Offers 25% kill fee. Publishes ms an average of 2 months after acceptance. Buys first North American serial rights. Editorial lead time 2 months. Submit seasonal material 4 months in advance. Accepts queries by mail, e-mail, fax, phone. Accepts simultaneous submissions. Responds in 1 month to queries. Responds in 2 months to mss. Sample copy free.

Nonfiction Needs expose, general interest, how-to, inspirational, interview, technical, industry features. **Buys 12 mss/year.** Query with published clips. Length: 1,200-2,500 words. **Pays $150-700.** Sometimes pays expenses of writers on assignment.

RENTAL MANAGEMENT

American Rental Association, 1900 19th St., Moline IL 61265. (309)764-2475. Fax: (309)764-1533. Website: www.rentalmanagementmag.com. **50% freelance written.** Monthly magazine for the equipment rental industry worldwide (*not* property, real estate, appliances, furniture, or cars), emphasizing management topics in particular but also marketing, merchandising, technology, etc. Estab. 1970. Circ. 18,500. Byline given. Pays on acceptance. No kill fee. Publishes ms an average of 3 months after acceptance. Buys first North American serial rights. Editorial lead time 2 months. Submit seasonal material 3 months in advance. Accepts queries by mail, e-mail, fax.

Nonfiction Buys 25-30 mss/year. Query with published clips. Does not respond to unsolicited work unless being considered for publication. Length: 600-1,500 words. **Payment negotiable.** Sometimes pays expenses of writers on assignment.

Reprints Send tearsheet or typed ms with rights for sale noted and information about when and where the material previously appeared.

Photos Reviews contact sheets, negatives (35mm or 2 ¼), transparencies, prints (any size), digital (300 dpi EPS/TIFF/JPEG on e-mail or CD). State availability Identification of subjects required. Negotiates payment individually. Buys one time rights.

Tips Show me you can write maturely, cogently, and fluently on management matters of direct and compelling interest to the small-business owner or manager in a larger operation; no sloppiness, no unexamined thoughts, no stiffness or affectation—genuine, direct, and worthwhile English. Knowledge of the equipment rental industry is a distinct plus.

$ $ RETAILERS + RESOURCES

CBA Service Corp., P.O. Box 62000, Colorado Springs CO 80962. Fax: (719)272-3510. E-mail: info@cbaonline.org. Website: www.cbaonline.org. **40% freelance written**. Monthly magazine covering the Christian retail industry. "Writers must have knowledge of and direct experience in the Christian retail industry. Subject matter must specifically pertain to the Christian retail audience." Estab. 1968. Byline given. Pays on publication. No kill fee. Publishes ms an average of 3 months after acceptance. Buys all rights. Editorial lead time 3 months. Submit seasonal material 6 months in advance. Accepts queries by e-mail. Responds in 2 months to queries. Sample copy for $9.50 or online

Nonfiction Buys 24 mss/year. Query. Length: 750-1,500 words. **Pays 30¢/word.**

Tips "Only experts on Christian retail industry, completely familiar with retail audience and their needs and considerations, should submit a query. Do not submit articles unless requested."

$ $ RETAIL INFO SYSTEMS NEWS

Where Retail Management Shops for Technology, Edgell Communications, 4 Middlebury Blvd., Randolph NJ 07869. (973)252-0100. Fax: (973)252-9020. Website: www.risnews.com. **65% freelance written**. Monthly magazine. Readers are functional managers/executives in all types of retail and consumer goods firms. They are making major improvements in company operations and in alliances with customers/suppliers. Estab. 1988. Circ. 20,000. Byline sometimes given. Pays on publication. No kill fee. Publishes ms an average of 2 months after acceptance. Buys first North American serial rights, buys second serial (reprint) rights, buys electronic rights, buys all rights. Editorial lead time 3 months. Submit seasonal material 3 months in advance. Accepts queries by mail. Sample copy available online.

Nonfiction Needs essays, expose, how-to, humor, interview, technical. **Buys 80 mss/year.** Query with published clips. Length: 700-1,900 words. **Pays $600-1,200 for assigned articles.** Sometimes pays expenses of writers on assignment.

Photos State availability of or send photos Identification of subjects required. Negotiates payment individually. Buys one-time rights plus reprint, if applicable.

Columns/Departments News/trends (analysis of current events), 150-300 words. 4 Query with published clips. **Pays $100-300.**

Tips Case histories about companies achieving substantial results using advanced management practices and/or advanced technology are best.

$ $ SECURITY DEALER

Cygnus Publishing, 445 Broad Hollow Rd., Melville NY 11747. (631)845-2700. Fax: (631)845-2376. E-mail: susan.brady@secdealer.com. **25% freelance written**. Monthly magazine for electronic alarm dealers, burglary and fire installers, with technical, business, sales and marketing information. Circ. 25,000. Byline sometimes given. Pays 3 weeks after publication. No kill fee. Publishes ms an average of 4 months after acceptance. Buys first North American serial rights. Accepts simultaneous submissions.

Nonfiction Needs how-to, interview, technical. No consumer pieces. Query by mail only. Length: 1,000-3,000 words. **Pays $300 for assigned articles. Pays $100-200 for unsolicited articles.** Sometimes pays expenses of writers on assignment.

Photos State availability Captions, identification of subjects required. Reviews contact sheets, transparencies. Offers $25 additional payment for photos accepted with ms.

Columns/Departments Closed Circuit TV, Access Control (both on application, installation, new products), 500-1,000 words. 25 Query by mail only. **Pays $100-150.**

Tips The areas of our publication most open to freelancers are technical innovations, trends in the alarm industry, and crime patterns as related to the business as well as business finance and management pieces.

SMALL TIMES

Big News in Small Tech, Small Times, Division of Penn Well Corp., c/o Penn Well Corp., 1421 S. Sheridan Rd., Tulka OK 74112. (603)891-9194. Fax: (603)262-1027. E-mail: news@smalltimes.com. Website: www.smalltimes.com. Bimonthly magazine. *Small Times* magazine details technological advances, applications, and investment opportunities to help business leaders stay informed about the rapidly changing business of small tech, from biotech to defense, telecom to transportation. Estab. 2001. Circ. 26,000. No kill fee.

Nonfiction Query.

$ $ ⊘ SMART BUSINESS

Pittsburgh Edition, SBN, Inc., 2186 Frankstown Rd., #313, Pittsburgh PA 15212. (412)371-0451. Fax: (412)371-0452. E-mail: rmarano@sbnonline.com. Website: www.sbnonline.com. Monthly magazine. We provide information and insight designed to help companies grow. Our focus is on CEOs of local companies with 100 or more employees and their successful business strategies, with the ultimate goal of educating their peers. Our target audience is business owners and other top executives. Estab. 1994. Circ. 12,000. No kill fee. Editorial lead time 2 months.

Nonfiction Needs how-to, interview, opinion. No basic profiles about `interesting' companies or stories about companies with no ties to Pittsburgh.

Photos Reviews high resolution digital images.

Tips We have articles localized to the Pittsburgh and surrounding areas. The short description of what we do is tell readers how CEOs do their jobs. Our feature stories focus exclusively on CEOs. Our readers are their peers, and want information and guidance that can help them to better manage their organizations.

$ $ SMART BUSINESS

Smart Business Network, Inc., 835 Sharon Dr., Cleveland OH 44145. (440)250-7000. Fax: (440)250-7001. E-mail: dsklein@sbnonline.com. Website: www.sbnonline.com. **5% freelance written**. Monthly business magazine with an audience made up of business owners and top decision makers. *Smart Business* is one of the fastest growing national chains of regional management journals for corporate executives. Every issue delves into the minds of the most innovative executives in each of our regions to report on how market leaders got to the top and what strategies they use to stay there. Estab. 1989. Byline given. Pays on publication. Offers 50% kill fee. Publishes ms an average of 2 months after acceptance. Buys first North American serial rights, buys second serial (reprint) rights, buys electronic rights. Editorial lead time 3 months. Submit seasonal material 3 months in advance. Accepts queries by mail, e-mail. Responds in 2 weeks to queries. Responds in 1 month to mss. Sample copy available online. Guidelines by email.

- Publishes local editions in Dallas, Houston, St. Louis, Northern California, San Diego, Orange County, Tampa Bay/St. Petersburg, Miami, Philadephia, Cincinnati, Detroit, Los Angeles, Broward/Palm Beach, Cleveland, Akron/Canton, Columbus, Pittsburgh, Atlanta, Chicago, and Indianapolis.

Nonfiction Needs how-to, interview. No breaking news or news features. **Buys 10-12 mss/year.** Query with published clips. Length: 1,150-2,000 words. **Pays $200-500.** Sometimes pays expenses of writers on assignment.

Photos State availability Identification of subjects required. Reviews negatives, prints. Offers no additional payment for photos accepted with ms Buys one-time, reprint, or Web rights

Tips The best way to submit to *Smart Business* is to read us—either online or in print. Remember, our audience is made up of top level business executives and owners.

$ $ STAMATS MEETINGS MEDIA

550 Montgomery St., Suite 750, San Francisco CA 94111. Fax: (415)788-1358. E-mail: tyler.davidson@meetingsmedia.com. Website: www.meetingsmedia.com. **75% freelance written**. Monthly tabloid covering meeting, event, and conference planning. Estab. 1986. Circ. *Meetings East* and *Meetings South* 22,000; *Meetings West* 26,000. Byline given. Pays 1 month after publication. No kill fee. Publishes ms an average of 1 month after acceptance. Buys first North American serial rights, buys electronic rights. Editorial lead time 3 months. Submit seasonal material 3 months in advance. Accepts queries by mail, e-mail, fax. Responds in 3 weeks to queries. Sample copy for sae with 9—Š13 envelope and 5 First-Class stamps.

Nonfiction Needs how-to, travel, as it pertains to meetings and conventions. No first-person fluff. We are a business magazine. **Buys 150 mss/year.** Query with published clips. Length: 1,200-2,000 words. **Pays $500 flat rate/package.**

Photos State availability Identification of subjects required. Offers no additional payment for photos accepted with ms. Buys one time rights.

Tips We're always looking for freelance writers who are local to our destination stories. For Site Inspections, get in touch in late September or early October, when we usually have the following year's editorial calendar available.

$ THE STATE JOURNAL

West V Media Management, LLC, 13 Kanawha Blvd. W., Suite 100, Charleston WV 25302. (304)344-1630. E-mail: dpage@statejournal.com. Website: www.statejournal.com. **30% freelance written**. We are a weekly

journal dedicated to providing stories of interest to the business community in West Virginia. Estab. 1984. Circ. 10,000. Byline given. Pays on publication. No kill fee. Publishes ms an average of 3 weeks after acceptance. Buys first rights. Submit seasonal material 4 months in advance. Accepts queries by mail, e-mail, fax. Sample copy and writer's guidelines for #10 SASE.
Nonfiction Needs general interest, interview, new product, (all business related). **Buys 400 mss/year.** Query. Length: 250-1,500 words. **Pays $50.** Sometimes pays expenses of writers on assignment.
Photos State availability Captions required. Reviews contact sheets. Offers $15/photo. Buys one time rights.
Tips Localize your work—mention West Virginia specifically in the article; or talk to business people in West Virginia.

$ SUPERVISION MAGAZINE

National Research Bureau, 320 Valley St., Burlington IA 52601. (319)752-5415. E-mail: national@willinet.net. Website: www.national-research-bureau.com. **80% freelance written**. Monthly magazine covering management and supervision. *SuperVision Magazine* explains complex issues in a clear and understandable format. Articles written by both experts and scholars provide practical and concise answers to issues facing today's supervisors and managers. Estab. 1939. Circ. 500. Byline given. Pays on acceptance. Publishes ms an average of 1 month after acceptance. Buys all rights. Editorial lead time 1 month. Submit seasonal material 2 months in advance. Accepts queries by e-mail. Sample copy free. Guidelines free.
Nonfiction Needs personal experience. Send complete ms. Length: 1,500-1,800 words. **Pays 4¢/word.**

$ $ SUSTAINABLE INDUSTRIES JOURNAL NW

Sustainable Industries Media, LLC, 3941 SE Hawthorne Blvd., Portland OR 97214. (503)226-7798. Fax: (503)226-7917. E-mail: brian@celilo.net. Website: www.sijournal.com. **20% freelance written**. Monthly magazine covering environmental innovation in business (Northwest focus). We seek high quality, balanced reporting aimed at business readers. More compelling writing than is typical in standard trade journals. Estab. 2003. Circ. 2,500. Byline sometimes given. Pays on publication. No kill fee. Publishes ms an average of 1-3 months after acceptance. Buys all rights. Editorial lead time 1-2 months. Accepts queries by mail, e-mail, fax. Accepts simultaneous submissions.
Nonfiction Needs general interest, how-to, interview, new product, opinion, news briefs. Themes rotate on the following topics: Agriculture & Natural Resources; Green Building; Energy; Government; Manufacturing & Technology; Retail & Service; Transportation & Tourism—though all topics are covered in each issue. No prosaic essays or extra-long pieces. Query with published clips. Length: 500-1,500 words. **Pays $0-500.**
Photos State availability Reviews prints, GIF/JPEG files. Offers no additional payment for photos accepted with ms. Buys all rights.
Columns/Departments Guest columns accepted, but not compensated. Business trade columns on specific industries, 500-1,000 words. Query.

$ $ 🌐 VENECONOMY/VENECONOMÍA

VenEconomía, Edificio Gran Sabana, Piso 1, Avendia Abraham Lincoln No. 174, Blvd. de Sabana Grande, Caracas Venezuela. (58)(212)761-8121. Fax: (58)(212)762-8160. E-mail: mercadeo@veneconomia.com. Website: www.veneconomÃŒa.com; www.veneconomy.com. **70% freelance written**. Monthly business magazine covering business, political and social issues in Venezuela. *VenEconomy*'s subscribers are mostly businesspeople, both Venezuelans and foreigners doing business in Venezuela. Some academics and diplomats also read our magazine. The magazine is published monthly both in English and Spanish—freelancers may query us in either language. Our slant is decidedly pro-business, but not dogmatically conservative. Development, human rights, political and environmental issues are covered from a business-friendly angle. Estab. 1983. Byline given. Pays on publication. Offers 50% kill fee. Publishes ms an average of 1 month after acceptance. Makes work-for-hire assignments. Editorial lead time 1-2 months. Submit seasonal material 1 month in advance. Accepts queries by e-mail. Accepts simultaneous submissions. Responds in 2 weeks to queries. Responds in 4 months to mss. Sample copy by email.
Nonfiction Contact: Francisco Toro, political editor. Needs essays, expose, interview, new product, opinion. No first-person stories or travel articles. **Buys 50 mss/year.** Query. Length: 1,100-3,200 words. **Pays 10-15¢/word for assigned articles.** Sometimes pays expenses of writers on assignment.
Tips A Venezuela tie-in is absolutely indispensable. While most of our readers are businesspeople, *VenEconomy* does not limit itself strictly to business-magazine fare. Our aim is to give our readers a sophisticated understanding of the main issues affecting the country as a whole. Stories about successful Venezuelan companies, or foreign companies doing business successfully with Venezuela are particularly welcome. Stories about the oil-sector, especially as it relates to Venezuela, are useful. Other promising topics for freelancers outside Venezuela include international trade and trade negotiations, US-Venezuela bilateral diplomatic relations, international investors' perceptions of business prospects in Venezuela, and international organizations' assessments of environmental, human rights, or democracy and development issues in Venezuela, etc. Both straight reportage and somewhat more opinionated pieces are acceptable, articles that straddle the borderline between reportage and opinion are best. Before querying, ask yourself: Would this be of interest to me if I was doing business in or with Venezuela?

$ $ $ WORLD TRADE

452 25th St., Hermosa Beach CA 90254. (310)980-5537. E-mail: laras@worldtrademag.com. Website: www.worldtrademag.com. **50% freelance written**. Monthly magazine covering international business. Estab. 1988. Circ. 75,000. Byline given. Pays on publication. No kill fee. Publishes ms an average of 1 month after acceptance. Buys all rights. Editorial lead time 3 months. Accepts queries by mail, fax.

Nonfiction See our editorial calendar online. Needs interview, technical, market reports, finance, logistics. **Buys 40-50 mss/year.** Query with published clips. Length: 450-1,500 words. **Pays 50¢/word.**

Photos State availability Identification of subjects required. Reviews transparencies, prints. Negotiates payment individually. Buys all rights.

Columns/Departments International Business Services, 800 words; Shipping, Supply Chain Management, Logistics, 800 words; Software & Technology, 800 words; Economic Development (US, International), 800 words. 40-50 **Pays 50¢/word.**

Tips We seek writers with expertise in their subject areas, as well as solid researching and writing skills. We want analysts more than reporters. We don't accept unsolicited manuscripts, and we don't want phone calls. Please read *World Trade* before sending a query.

CHURCH ADMINISTRATION & MINISTRY

$ CHRISTIAN COMMUNICATOR

9118 W. Elmwood Dr., #1G, Niles IL 60714-5820. (847)296-3964. Fax: (847)296-0754. E-mail: ljohnson@wordprocommunications.com. **90% freelance written**. Monthly magazine covering Christian writing and speaking. Circ. 4,000. Byline given. Pays on publication. No kill fee. Publishes ms an average of 6-12 months after acceptance. Buys first rights, buys second serial (reprint) rights. Editorial lead time 3 months. Submit seasonal material 9 months in advance. Accepts queries by e-mail. Responds in 4-6 weeks to queries. Responds in 6-8 weeks to mss. Sample copy for SAE and 5 first-class stamps. Writer's guidelines for SASE or by e-mail.

Nonfiction Needs how-to, interview, opinion, book reviews. **Buys 90 mss/year.** Query or send complete ms only by e-mail. Length: 650-1,000 words. **Pays $10.**

Columns/Departments Speaking, 650-1,000 words. 11 Query. **Pays $10.**

Poetry Needs free verse, light verse, traditional. **Buys 22 poems/year.** Submit maximum 3 poems. Length: 4-20 lines. **Pays $5.**

Fillers Needs anecdotes, short humor. 10-30 Length: 75-300 words. **Pays CD.**

Tips "We primarily use 'how to' articles and personality features on experienced writers and editors. However, we're willing to look at any other pieces geared to the writing life."

THE CHRISTIAN LIBRARIAN

Association of Christian Librarians, P.O. Box 4, Cedarville OH 45314. E-mail: info@acl.org. Website: www.acl.org. **80% freelance written**. Magazine published 3 times/year covering Christian librarianship in higher education. *The Christian Librarian* is directed to Christian librarians in institutions of higher learning and publishes articles on Christian interpretation of librarianship, theory and practice of library science, bibliographic essays, reviews, and human-interest articles relating to books and libraries. Estab. 1956. Circ. 800. Byline given. No kill fee. Buys first rights. Editorial lead time 3 months. Accepts queries by e-mail. Responds in 1 month to mss. Sample copy for $5. Guidelines free.

Nonfiction Needs how-to, librarianship, technical, bibliographic essays. No articles on faith outside the realm of librarianship or articles based on specific church denomination. Do not send book reviews that haven't been requested by the Review Editor. Send complete ms. Length: 1,000-5,000 words.

$ THE CLERGY JOURNAL

Personal and Professional Development for Pastors and Church Administrators, Logos Productions, Inc., 6160 Carmen Ave. E., Inver Grove Heights MN 55076-4422. E-mail: editorial@logosstaff.com. Website: www.logosproductions.com. **98% freelance written**. Magazine published 9 times/year covering articles for continuing education and practical help for Christian clergy who are currently serving congregations. The focus of *The Clergy Journal* is personal and professional development for clergy. Each issue focuses on a current topic related to ministers and the church, and also includes preaching illustrations, sermons, and worship aids based on the Revised Common Lectionary. There is an insert in each issue on financial management topics. Most readers are from mainline Protestant traditions, especially Methodist, Presbyterian, Lutheran, and United Church of Christ. Estab. 1924. Circ. 6,000. Byline given. Pays on publication. No kill fee. Publishes ms an average of 9 months after acceptance. Buys first rights. Makes work-for-hire assignments. Editorial lead time 4 months. Submit seasonal material 9 months in advance. Accepts queries by e-mail. Responds in 2 weeks to queries. Responds in 2 months to mss. Sample copy free. Guidelines by email.

Nonfiction We are seeking articles that address current issues of interest to Christian clergy; emphasis on practical help for parish pastors. Needs religious. **Buys 90 mss/year.** Query or send complete ms. Length:

1,200-1,500 words. **Pays $125 for assigned articles.**

Tips Here are my 4 'pet peeves' as an editor: 1. Manuscripts that are over the word count. 2. Manuscripts that do not respect the reader. 3. Manuscripts that are not well organized. 4. Manuscripts that do not have an appropriate 'human touch.'

$ CREATOR MAGAZINE

Bimonthly Magazine of Balanced Music Ministries, P.O. Box 3538, Pismo Beach CA 93448. (707)837-9071. E-mail: creator@creatormagazine.com. Website: www.creatormagazine.com. **35% freelance written.** Bimonthly magazine. Most readers are church music directors and worship leaders. Content focuses on the spectrum of worship styles from praise and worship to traditional to liturgical. All denominations subscribe. Articles on worship, choir rehearsal, handbells, children's/youth choirs, technique, relationships, etc. Estab. 1978. Circ. 6,000. Byline given. Pays on publication. No kill fee. Publishes ms an average of 3 months after acceptance. Buys first rights, buys one-time rights, buys second serial (reprint) rights. Occasionally buys no rights. Editorial lead time 3 months. Submit seasonal material 4 months in advance. Accepts queries by mail. Accepts simultaneous submissions. Sample copy for sae with 9x12 envelope and 5 First-Class stamps. Guidelines free.

Nonfiction Needs essays, how-to, be a better church musician, choir director, rehearsal technician, etc., humor, short personal perspectives, inspirational, interview, call first, new product, call first, opinion, personal experience, photo feature, religious, technical, choral technique. July/August is directed toward adult choir members, rather than directors **Buys 20 mss/year.** Query or send complete ms. Length: 1,000-10,000 words. **Pays $30-75 for assigned articles. Pays $30-60 for unsolicited articles.** Pays expenses of writers on assignment.

Photos State availability of or send photos Captions required. Reviews negatives, 8x10 prints. Offers no additional payment for photos accepted with ms. Buys one time rights.

Columns/Departments Hints & Humor (music ministry short ideas, cute anecdotes, ministry experience), 75-250 words; Inspiration (motivational ministry stories), 200-500 words; Children/Youth (articles about specific choirs), 1,000-5,000 words. 15 Query or send complete ms. **Pays $20-60.**

Tips Request guidelines and stick to them. If theme is relevant and guidelines are followed, we'll probably publish your article.

$ $ GROUP MAGAZINE

Group Publishing, Inc., P.O. Box 481, Loveland CO 80539. E-mail: kloesche@group.com. Website: www.groupmag.com. **50% freelance written**. Bimonthly magazine for Christian youth workers. *Group* is the interdenominational magazine for leaders of Christian youth groups. *Group*'s purpose is to supply ideas, practical help, inspiration, and training for youth leaders. Estab. 1974. Circ. 55,000. Byline sometimes given. Pays on acceptance. No kill fee. Buys all rights. Editorial lead time 4 months. Submit seasonal material 5 months in advance. Accepts queries by mail, e-mail, fax. Responds in 6 weeks to queries. Responds in 2 months to mss. Sample copy for $2, plus 10x12 SAE and 3 first-class stamps Guidelines available online.

Nonfiction Needs inspirational, personal experience, religious. No fiction. **Buys 100 mss/year.** Query. Length: 175-2,000 words. **Pays $150-250.** Sometimes pays expenses of writers on assignment.

Columns/Departments Try This One (short ideas for group use), 300 words; Hands-On-Help (tips for youth leaders), 175 words; Strange But True (profiles remarkable youth ministry experience), 500 words. **Pays $40.**

$ $ THE JOURNAL OF ADVENTIST EDUCATION

General Conference of SDA, 12501 Old Columbia Pike, Silver Spring MD 20904-6600. (301)680-5069. Fax: (301)622-9627. E-mail: rumbleb@gc.adventist.org. Website: http://jae.education.org. **Contact:** Beverly J. Robinson-Rumble, editor. Bimonthly (except skips issue in summer) professional journal covering teachers and administrators in Seventh Day Adventist school systems. Estab. 1939. Circ. 10,500. Byline given. Pays on publication. No kill fee. Publishes ms an average of 1 year after acceptance. Buys first rights. Editorial lead time 1 year. Accepts queries by mail, e-mail, fax, phone. Responds in 6 weeks to queries. Responds in 4 months to mss. Sample copy for sae with 10x12 envelope and 5 First-Class stamps. Guidelines available online.

Nonfiction Theme issues have assigned authors. Needs book excerpts, essays, how-to, education-related , personal experience, photo feature, religious, education. "No brief first-person stories about Sunday Schools." Query. Length: 1,000-1,500 words. **Pays $25-300.**

Reprints Send tearsheet or photocopy and information about when and where the material previously appeared.

Photos Submit glossy prints, high resolution (300 dpi) scans or digital photos in TIFF/JPEG format. No PowerPoint presentations or photos imbedded in Word documents. Include photo of author with submission. State availability of or send photos Captions required. Negotiates payment individually. Buys one time rights.

Tips "Articles may deal with educational theory or practice, although the *Journal* seeks to emphasize the practical. Articles dealing with the creative and effective use of methods to enhance teaching skills or learning in the classroom are especially welcome. Whether theoretical or practical, such essays should demonstrate the skillful integration of Seventh-day Adventist faith/values and learning."

JOURNAL OF CHURCH AND STATE

J.M. Dawson Institute of Church and State Studies, Baylor University, One Bear Place, #97308, Waco TX 76798-7308. (254)710-1510. Fax: (254)710-1571. E-mail: Suzanne_Sellers@baylor.edu. Website: www.baylor.edu/church_state. **70% freelance written.** Quarterly journal covering law, social studies, religion, philosophy, and history. Published quarterly, this publication is read by an interdisciplinary, scholarly audience and covers topics such as law, social studies, religion, philosophy, and history. Its focus is to examine the interaction of religion and government worldwide. Estab. 1959. Circ. 1,600. No kill fee. Publishes ms an average of 3 months after acceptance. Buys all rights. Accepts queries by mail, e-mail. Responds in 1 week to queries. Responds in 3-4 months to mss. Sample copy for $8. Guidelines free.

Nonfiction Needs essays, historical, religious, law. Query or send complete ms.

$ KIDS' MINISTRY IDEAS

Review and Herald Publishing Association, 55 W. Oak Ridge Dr., Hagerstown MD 21740. (301)393-4115. Fax: (301)393-4055. E-mail: kidsmin@rhpa.org. **95% freelance written.** A quarterly resource for children's leaders, those involved in Vacation Bible School and Story Hours, home school teachers, etc. *Kids' Ministry Ideas* provides affirmation, pertinent and informative articles, program ideas, resource suggestions, and answers to questions from a Seventh-day Adventist Christian perspective. Estab. 1991. Circ. 3,000. Byline given. Pays on acceptance. Publishes ms an average of 3 months after acceptance. Buys first North American serial rights, buys electronic rights. Editorial lead time 3 months. Submit seasonal material 6 months in advance. Accepts queries by mail, e-mail, fax. Responds in 3 weeks to queries. Responds in 3 months to mss. Sample copy and writer's guidelines free

Nonfiction Needs inspirational, new product, related to children's ministry, articles fitting the mission of. **Buys 40-60 mss/year.** Send complete ms. Length: 300-1,000 words. **Pays $30-100 for assigned articles. Pays $30-70 for unsolicited articles.**

Photos State availability Captions required. Buys one time rights.

Columns/Departments 20-30 Query. **Pays $30-100.**

Tips Request writer's guidelines and a sample issue.

$ LAUSANNE WORLD PULSE

Evangelism and Missions Information Service/Wheaton College, P.O. Box 794, Wheaton IL 60189. (630)752-7158. Fax: (630)752-7155. E-mail: info@lausanneworldpulse.com. Website: www.worldpulseonline.com. **60% freelance written.** Semimonthly print and online newsletter covering mission news and trends. We provide current information about evangelical Christian missions and churches around the world. Most articles are news-oriented, although we do publish some features and interviews. Estab. 1965. Circ. 3,000. Byline given. Pays on publication. Publishes ms an average of 2 months after acceptance. Buys first rights. Editorial lead time 2 months. Sample copy and writer's guidelines free

- Prefers queries by e-mail.

Nonfiction Needs interview, photo feature, religious, technical. Does not want anything that does not cover the world of evangelical missions. **Buys 50-60 mss/year.** Query with published clips. Length: 300-1,000 words. **Pays $25-100.**

Photos Send photos Reviews contact sheets. Pays $25 for use of all photos accompanying an article.

Tips Have a knowledge of and appreciation for the evangelical missions community, as well as for cross-cultural issues. Writing must be economical, with a judicious use of quotes and examples.

$ $ LEADERSHIP

Real Ministry in a Complex World, Christianity Today International, 465 Gundersen Dr., Carol Stream IL 60188. (630)260-6200. Fax: (630)260-0114. E-mail: ljeditor@leadershipjournal.net. Website: www.leadershipjournal.net. **75% freelance written. Works with a small number of new/unpublished writers each year.** Quarterly magazine. Writers must have a knowledge of and sympathy for the unique expectations placed on pastors and local church leaders. Each article must support points by illustrating from real life experiences in local churches. Estab. 1980. Circ. 57,000. Byline given. Pays on acceptance. Offers 33% kill fee. Publishes ms an average of 6 months after acceptance. Buys first rights, buys electronic rights. Editorial lead time 6 months. Submit seasonal material 6 months in advance. Accepts queries by mail, e-mail, fax. Responds in 3 weeks to queries. Responds in 2 months to mss. Sample copy for $5 or online Guidelines available online.

Nonfiction Needs how-to, humor, interview, personal experience, sermon illustrations. No articles from writers who have never read our journal. **Buys 60 mss/year.** Query. Length: 300-3,000 words. **Pays $35-400.** Sometimes pays expenses of writers on assignment.

Columns/Departments Contact: Eric Reed, managing editor. Toolkit (book/software reviews), 500 words. 8 Query.

Tips Every article in *Leadership* must provide practical help for problems that church leaders face. *Leadership* articles are not essays expounding a topic or editorials arguing a position or homilies explaining Biblical principles. They are how-to articles, based on first-person accounts of real-life experiences in ministry. They allow our readers to see `over the shoulder' of a colleague in ministry who then reflects on those experiences and identifies the lessons learned. As you know, a magazine's slant is a specific personality that readers expect (and it's what they've sent us their subscription money to provide). Our style is that of friendly conversation rather than directive discourse—what I learned about local church ministry rather than what you need to do.

$ MOMENTUM

Official Journal of the National Catholic Educational Association, National Catholic Educational Association, 1077 30th St. NW, Suite 100, Washington DC 20007-3852. (202)337-6232. Fax: (202)333-6706. E-mail: momentum@ncea.org. Website: www.ncea.org. **Contact:** Brian E. Gray, editor. **65% freelance written**. Quarterly educational journal covering educational issues in Catholic schools and parishes. "*Momentum* is a membership journal of the National Catholic Educational Association. The audience is educators and administrators in Catholic schools K-12, and parish programs." Estab. 1970. Circ. 23,000. Byline given. Pays on publication. No kill fee. Publishes ms an average of 3 months after acceptance. Buys first rights. Accepts queries by e-mail. Sample copy for $5 SASE and 8 first-class stamps. Guidelines available online.

Nonfiction Educational trends, issues, research. No articles unrelated to educational and catechesis issues. **Buys 40-60 mss/year.** Query and send complete ms. Length: 1,500 words. **Pays $75 maximum.**

Photos State availability Captions, identification of subjects required. Reviews prints. Offers no additional payment for photos accepted with ms

Columns/Departments From the Field (practical application in classroom); DRE Directions (parish catechesis), both 700 words. 10 Query and send complete ms. **Pays $50.**

$ $ OUTREACH MAGAZINE

Outreach Inc., 2230 Oak Ridge Way, Vista CA 92081-8341. (760)940-0600. Fax: (760)597-2314. E-mail: lwarren@outreach.com. Website: www.outreachmagazine.com. **80% freelance written**. Bimonthly magazine designed to inspire, challenge and equip churches and church leaders to reach out to their communities with the love of Jesus Christ. Circ. 30,000. Byline given. Pays on publication. Offers 10% kill fee. Publishes ms an average of 2 months after acceptance. Buys first North American serial rights, buys electronic rights. Editorial lead time 6 months. Submit seasonal material 6 months in advance. Accepts queries by mail, e-mail, fax. Accepts previously published material. Accepts simultaneous submissions. Responds in 2 months to queries. Responds in 8 months to mss. Sample copy and writer's guidelines free.

Nonfiction Needs book excerpts, how-to, humor, inspirational, interview, personal experience, photo feature, religious. Vacation Bible School (January); America's Fastest Growing Churches (July/August 2005). Does not want fiction, poetry, or non-outreach-related articles. **Buys 30 mss/year.** Query with published clips. Length: 1,200-2,000 words. **Pays $375-600 for assigned articles. Pays $375-400 for unsolicited articles.** Pays some expensesLimit agreed upon in advance.

Photos Contact: Christi Riddell, lead designer. Send photos Identification of subjects required. Reviews GIF/JPEG files. Negotiates payment individually. Buys all rights.

Columns/Departments Outreach Pulse (short stories about outreach-oriented churches and ministries), 75-250 words; Questions & Perspectives (first-person expert perspective on a question related to outreach), 300-400 words; Soulfires (interview piece with a person about the stories and people that have fueled their passion for outreach), 900 words; From the Front Line (profile of a church that is using a transferable idea for outreach), 800 words plus sidebars; Sounourners (short interviews with everyday people about the stories and people that have informed their worldview and faith perspective), 800 words; Frames (short personality profiles); POV (2-page interview with a significant voice in the church). at least 6 Query with published clips. **Pays $100-375.**

Fillers Needs facts, gags. 2 Length: 25-100 words. **Payment is negotiated.**

Tips Study our writer's guidelines. Send published clips that showcase tight, bright writing, as well as your ability to interview, research, organize numerous sources into an article, and write a 100-word piece as well as a 1,600-word piece.

$ $ THE PRIEST

Our Sunday Visitor, Inc., 200 Noll Plaza, Huntington IN 46750-4304. (260)356-8400. Fax: (260)359-9117. E-mail: tpriest@osv.com. Website: www.osv.com. **40% freelance written**. Monthly magazine. We run articles that will aid priests in their day-to-day ministry. Includes items on spirituality, counseling, administration, theology, personalities, the saints, etc. Byline given. Pays on acceptance. No kill fee. Buys first North American serial rights. Editorial lead time 3 months. Submit seasonal material 4 months in advance. Accepts queries by mail, e-mail, fax, phone. Responds in 5 weeks to queries. Responds in 3 months to mss. Sample copy and writer's guidelines free.

Nonfiction Needs essays, historical, humor, inspirational, interview, opinion, personal experience, photo feature, religious. **Buys 96 mss/year.** Send complete ms. Length: 1,500 words. **Pays $200 minimum for assigned articles. Pays $50 minimum for unsolicited articles.**

Photos Send photos Captions, identification of subjects required. Reviews transparencies, prints. Negotiates payment individually. Buys one time rights.

Tips Please do not stray from the magisterium of the Catholic Church.

RESOURCE

Nazarene Publishing House, 6401 The Paseo, Kansas City MO 64131. (816)333-7000, ext. 2343. Fax: (816)363-7092. E-mail: ssmith@nazarene.org. **95% freelance written**. *Resource* is a denominationally-produced quarterly magazine which contains information useful to Sunday School teachers and workers interested in extending their knowledge and skills to their particular aged-group ministry. Estab. 1976. Circ. 30,000. Pays on publication. Offers kill fee. Publishes ms an average of 9-12 months after acceptance. Buys first rights, buys one-time rights, buys second serial (reprint) rights, buys simultaneous rights, buys all rights. Editorial lead time 9 months. Submit seasonal material 9-12 months in advance. Accepts queries by mail, e-mail, fax, phone. Accepts previously published material. Accepts simultaneous submissions. Responds in 2-3 weeks to queries. Sample copy free. Guidelines by email.

Nonfiction Focus on an issue, skill, or concern central to a particular age-group ministry. Topics include: skill development, inspirational/motivational, spiritual formation, roles of a teach, building community and fellowship, evangelism, outreach, organizational tips, etc. **Pays 5¢/word for all rights; 3¢/word for first rights; and 2¢/word for reprint rights**

$ $ REV! MAGAZINE

P.O. Box 481, Loveland CO 80539-0481. (970)669-3836. Fax: (970)292-4373. E-mail: lsparks@group.com. Website: www.revmagazine.com. **25% freelance written**. Bimonthly magazine for pastors. We offer practical solutions to revolutionize and revitalize ministry. Estab. 1997. Circ. 45,000. Byline given. Pays on acceptance. No kill fee. Publishes ms an average of 6 months after acceptance. Makes work-for-hire assignments. Editorial lead time 6 months. Submit seasonal material 8 months in advance. Accepts queries by mail, e-mail. Responds in 2 months to queries. Guidelines available online.

Nonfiction Ministry, leadership, and personal articles with practical application. No devotions, articles for church members, theological pieces. **Buys 18-24 mss/year.** Query or send complete ms. Length: 1,800-2,000 words. **Pays $300-400.**

Columns/Departments Work (preaching, worship, discipleship, outreach, church business & administration, leadership); Life (personal growth, pastor's family); Culture (trends, facts), all 250-3,000 words. 25 Send complete ms. **Pays $100-500.**

Fillers 3 **Pays $50.**

Tips We are looking for creative and practical ideas that pastors and other leaders of churches of all sizes can use.

$ RTJ

The Magazine for Catechist Formation, Twenty-Third Publications, P.O. Box 180, Mystic CT 06355. (800)321-0411. Fax: (860)437-6246. E-mail: aberger@twenty-thirdpublications.com. Website: www.religionteachersjournal.com. Monthly magazine for Catholic catechists and religion teachers. The mission of *RTJ* is to encourage and assist Catholic DREs and catechists in their vocation to proclaim the gospel message and lead others to the joy of following Jesus Christ. *RTJ* provides professional support, theological content, age appropriate methodology and teaching tools. Estab. 1966. Circ. 30,000. Byline given. Pays on acceptance. Publishes ms an average of 3-20 months after acceptance. Buys first rights, buys one-time rights. Editorial lead time 4 months. Submit seasonal material 6 months in advance. Accepts queries by mail, e-mail. Accepts simultaneous submissions. Responds in 1-2 weeks to queries. Responds in 1-2 months to mss. Sample copy for sae with 9x12 envelope and 3 First-Class stamps. Guidelines free.

Nonfiction Needs how-to, inspirational, personal experience, religious, articles on celebrating church seasons, sacraments, on morality, on prayer, on saints. Sacraments; Prayer; Advent/Christmas; Lent/Easter. All should be written by people who have experience in religious education, or a good background in Catholic faith. Does not want fiction, poems, plays, articles written for Catholic school teachers (i.e., math, English, etc.), or articles that are academic rather than catechetical in nature. **Buys 35-40 mss/year.** Send complete ms. Length: 600-1,300 words. **Pays $100-125 for assigned articles. Pays $75-125 for unsolicited articles.**

Columns/Departments Catechist to Catechist (brief articles on crafts, games, etc., for religion lessons); Faith and Fun (full page religious word games, puzzles, mazes, etc., for children). 30 Send complete ms. **Pays $20-125.**

Tips We look for clear, concise articles written from experience. Articles should help readers move from theory/doctrine to concrete application. Unsolicited manuscripts not returned without SASE. No fancy formatting; no handwritten manuscripts. Author should be able to furnish article on disk or via e-mail if possible.

$ TEACHERS INTERACTION

Concordia Publishing House, 3558 S. Jefferson Ave., St. Louis MO 63118-3968. (314)268-1083. Fax: (314)268-1329. E-mail: tom.nummela@cph.org. **5% freelance written**. Quarterly magazine of practical, inspirational, theological articles for volunteer Sunday school teachers. Material must be true to the doctrines of the Lutheran Church—Missouri Synod. Estab. 1960. Circ. 6,000. Byline given. Pays on publication. No kill fee. Publishes ms an average of 1 year after acceptance. Buys all rights. Submit seasonal material 1 year in advance. Accepts

queries by mail, e-mail, fax. Responds in 3 weeks to mss. Sample copy for $5.50. Guidelines for #10 SASE.
Nonfiction Needs how-to, practical help/ideas used successfully in own classroom, inspirational, to the church school worker—must be in accordance with LCMS doctrine, personal experience, of Sunday School teachers. No freelance theological articles. **Buys 6 mss/year.** Send complete ms. Length: 1,200 words. **Pays up to $120.**
Fillers *Teachers Interaction* buys short 'Toolbox' items—activities and ideas planned and used successfully in a church school classroom. 48 200 words maximum. **Pays $20-40.**
Tips Practical or `it happened to me' articles would have the best chance. Also short items—ideas used in classrooms; seasonal and in conjunction with our Sunday school material. Our format emphasizes volunteer Sunday school teachers.

TECHNOLOGIES FOR WORSHIP MAGAZINE

Inspiration Technology Companies, Inc., 3891 Holborn Rd., Queensville ON L0G 1R0 Canada. (905)473-9822. Fax: (905)473-9928. E-mail: inspiration@tfwm.com. Website: www.tfwm.com. **Contact:** Kevin Rogers Cobus, managing editor. **100% freelance written**. Magazine published 10 times/year covering technologies for churches and ministries. "A leading educational resource for advancing technology for churches and ministries." Estab. 1992. Circ. 25,000. No kill fee. Editorial lead time 40 days. Accepts queries by mail, e-mail, fax, phone. Accepts previously published material. Accepts simultaneous submissions. Sample copy free. Guidelines available online.
Nonfiction Needs how-to, inspirational, new product, religious. Does not want any religious article that does not relate to implementing technology into the church. Send complete ms. Length: 250-1,500 words.
Photos Send photos Captions required. Reviews GIF/JPEG/PDF files (high resolution). Offers no additional payment for photos accepted with ms.
Columns/Departments Church Network News (newspaper clippings, etc.); 5 Minutes With.
Tips "Just send relevant industry material. All submissions are considered. No payments are ever made."

$ $ TODAY'S CATHOLIC TEACHER

Peter Li Education Group, 2621 Dryden Rd., Suite 300, Dayton OH 45439. (937)293-1415. Fax: (937)293-1310. E-mail: mnoschang@peterli.com. Website: www.catholicteacher.com. **60% freelance written**. Magazine published 6 times/year during school year covering Catholic education for grades K-12. "We look for topics of interest and practical help to teachers in Catholic elementary schools in all curriculum areas including religion technology, discipline, motivation." Estab. 1972. Circ. 50,000. Byline given. Pays on publication. No kill fee. Publishes ms an average of 2 months after acceptance. Buys first and all rights and makes work-for-hire assignments. Editorial lead time 3 months. Submit seasonal material 6 months in advance. Accepts queries by mail, e-mail, fax. Accepts simultaneous submissions. Responds in 1 month to queries. Responds in 3 months to mss. Sample copy for $3 or on website. Guidelines available online.
Nonfiction Interested in articles detailing ways to incorporate Catholic values into academic subjects other than religion class. Needs essays, how-to, humor, interview, personal experience. No articles pertaining to public education. **Buys 15 mss/year.** Query or send complete ms. Length: 1,500-3,000 words. **Pays $150-300.** Sometimes pays expenses of writers on assignment.
Photos State availability Captions, identification of subjects, model releases required. Reviews transparencies, prints. Offers $20-50/photo. Buys one time rights.
Tips "Although our readership is primarily classroom teachers, *Today's Catholic Teacher* is also read by principals, supervisors, superintendents, boards of education, pastors, and parents. *Today's Catholic Teacher* aims to be for Catholic educators a source of information not available elsewhere. The focus of articles should span the interests of teachers from early childhood through junior high. Articles may be directed to just one age group, yet have wider implications. Preference is given to material directed to teachers in grades 4-8. The desired magazine style is direct, concise, informative, and accurate. Writing should be enjoyable to read, informal rather than scholarly, lively, and free of educational jargon."

$ $ $ WORSHIP LEADER MAGAZINE

26311 Junipero Serra, #130, San Juan Capistrano CA 92675. (949)240-9339. Fax: (949)240-0038. E-mail: editor@wlmag.com. Website: www.worshipleader.com. **80% freelance written**. Bimonthly magazine covering all aspects of Christian worship. *Worship Leader Magazine* exists to challenge, serve, equip, and train those involved in leading the 21st century church in worship. The intended readership is the worship team (all those who plan and lead) of the local church. Estab. 1992. Circ. 50,000. Byline given. Pays on publication. Offers 50% kill fee. Buys first North American serial rights, buys all rights. Editorial lead time 3 months. Submit seasonal material 6 months in advance. Responds in 6 weeks to queries. Responds in 3 months to mss. Sample copy for $5. Guidelines available online.
Nonfiction Needs general interest, how-to, related to purpose/audience, inspirational, interview, opinion. **Buys 15-30 mss/year.** Query with published clips. Length: 1,200-2,000 words. **Pays $200-800 for assigned articles. Pays $200-500 for unsolicited articles.** Sometimes pays expenses of writers on assignment.
Photos State availability Identification of subjects required. Negotiate payment individually. Buys one time rights.

Tips Our goal has been and is to provide the tools and information pastors, worship leaders, and ministers of music, youth, and the arts need to facilitate and enhance worship in their churches. In achieving this goal, we strive to maintain high journalistic standards, Biblical soundness, and theological neutrality. Our intent is to present the philosophical, scholarly insight on worship, as well as the day-to-day, `putting it all together' side of worship, while celebrating our unity and diversity.

$ $ YOUR CHURCH

Helping You With the Business of Ministry, Christianity Today, Inc., 465 Gundersen Dr., Carol Stream IL 60188. (630)260-6200. Fax: (630)260-0451. E-mail: yceditor@yourchurch.net. Website: www.yourchurch.net. **90% freelance written**. Bimonthly magazine covering church administration and products. Articles pertain to the business aspects of ministry pastors are called upon to perform: administration, purchasing, management, technology, building, etc. Estab. 1955. Circ. 85,000 (controlled). Byline given. Pays on acceptance. No kill fee. Publishes ms an average of 3-4 months after acceptance. Buys first rights, buys electronic rights. Editorial lead time 6 weeks. Submit seasonal material 5 months in advance. Accepts queries by mail, e-mail, fax. Accepts previously published material. Responds in 1 month to queries. Responds in 3 months to mss. Sample copy for sae with 9x12 envelope and 4 First-Class stamps. Guidelines free.
Nonfiction Needs how-to, new product, technical. **Buys 50-60 mss/year.** Send complete ms. Length: 1,000-4,000 words. **Pays 15-20¢/word.** Sometimes pays expenses of writers on assignment.
Tips The editorial is generally geared toward brief and helpful articles dealing with some form of church business. Concise, bulleted points from experts in the field are typical for our articles.

$ YOUTH AND CHRISTIAN EDUCATION LEADERSHIP

Pathway Press, 1080 Montgomery Ave., P.O. Box 2250, Cleveland TN 37311. (800)553-8506. Fax: (800)546-7590. E-mail: tammy_hatfield@pathwaypress.org. Website: www.pathwaypress.org. **25% freelance written**. Quarterly magazine covering Christian education. *Youth and Christian Education Leadership* is written for teachers, youth pastors, children's pastors, and other local Christian education workers. Estab. 1976. Circ. 12,000. Pays on publication. No kill fee. Publishes ms an average of 6 months after acceptance. Buys first or one-time rights. Editorial lead time 3 months. Submit seasonal material 6 months in advance. Accepts queries by mail, e-mail. Accepts simultaneous submissions. Responds in 3 months to mss. Sample copy for $1.25 and 9x12 SASE. Writer's guidelines online or by e-mail.
Nonfiction Needs how-to, humor, in-class experience, inspire, interview, motivational, seasonal short skits. **Buys 16 mss/year.** Send complete ms; include SSN. Send SASE for return of ms. Length: 400-1,200 words. **$25-50**
Reprints Send typed, double-spaced ms with rights for sale and information about when and where the material previously appeared. Pays 80% of amount paid for an original article.
Photos State availability Reviews contact sheets, transparencies. Negotiates payment individually. Buys one time rights.
Columns/Departments Sunday School Leadership; Reaching Out (creative evangelism); The Pastor and Christian Education; Preschool; Elementary; Teen; Adult; Drawing Closer; Kids Church, all 500-1,000 words. Send complete ms with SASE. **Pays $25-50.**
Tips "Become familiar with the publication's content and submit appropriate material. We are continually looking for 'fresh ideas' that have proven to be successful."

$ $ YOUTHWORKER JOURNAL

Salem Publishing, 104 Woodmont Blvd., Suite 300, Nashville TN 37205-9759. E-mail: articles@youthworker.com. Website: www.youthworker.com. **100% freelance written**. Bimonthly magazine covering professional youth ministry in the church and parachurch. We exist to help meet the personal and professional needs of career, Christian youth workers in the church and parachurch. Proposals accepted on the posted theme, according to the writer's guidelines on our website. It's not enough to write well—you must know youth ministry. Estab. 1984. Circ. 20,000. Byline given. Pays on publication. No kill fee. Publishes ms an average of 3 months after acceptance. Articles must be first published with us, and we buy unrestricted use for print and electronic media. Editorial lead time 6 months. Submit seasonal material 6 months in advance. Accepts queries by e-mail. Responds in 6 months to queries. Sample copy for $5. Guidelines available online.
Nonfiction Needs essays, new product, youth ministry books only, personal experience, photo feature, religious. Query. Length: 250-3,000 words. **Pays $50-200.** Sometimes pays expenses of writers on assignment.
Photos Send photos Reviews GIF/JPEG files. Negotiates payment individually.

CLOTHING

APPAREL

801 Gervais St., Suite 101, Columbia SC 29201. (803)771-7500. Fax: (803)799-1461. Website: www.apparelmag.com. **25% freelance written**. Monthly magazine for CEO's and top management in apparel and soft goods

businesses including manufacturers and retailers. Circ. 18,000. Byline given. Pays on receipt of article. No kill fee. Buys all rights. Responds in 2 weeks to queries. Sample copy free. Guidelines free.

Columns/Departments R Winning Strategies; International Watch; Best Practices; Retail Strategies; Production Solutions.

Tips Articles should be written in a style appealing to busy top managers and should in some way foster thought or new ideas, or present solutions/alternatives to common industry problems/concerns. CEOs are most interested in quick read pieces that are also informative and substantive. Articles should not be based on opinions but should be developed through interviews with industry manufacturers, retailers, or other experts, etc. Sidebars may be included to expand upon certain aspects within the article. If available, illustrations, graphs/charts, or photographs should accompany the article.

$ $ EMB-EMBROIDERY/MONOGRAM BUSINESS

1145 Sanctuary Parkway, Suite 355, Alpharetta GA 30004. (770)291-5534. Fax: (770)777-8733. E-mail: rlebovitz@impressionsmag.com. Website: www.impressionsmag.com. **30% freelance written.** Monthly magazine covering computerized embroidery and digitizing design. Readable, practical business and/or technical articles that show our readers how to succeed in their profession. Estab. 1994. Circ. 20,000. Byline given. Pays on publication. No kill fee. Publishes ms an average of 3 months after acceptance. Buys all rights. Editorial lead time 3 months. Submit seasonal material 6 months in advance. Accepts queries by mail, e-mail. Accepts simultaneous submissions. Sample copy for $10.

Nonfiction Needs how-to, embroidery, sales, marketing, design, general business info, interview, new product, photo feature, technical, computerized embroidery. **Buys 40 mss/year.** Query. Length: 800-2,000 words. **Pays $200 and up for assigned articles.**

Photos Send photos Reviews transparencies, prints. Negotiates payment individually.

Tips Show us you have specified knowledge, experience, or contacts in the embroidery industry or a related field.

$ $ $ FOOTWEAR PLUS

Symphony Publishing, 8 W. 38th St., New York NY 10018. (646)278-1550. Fax: (646)278-1553. E-mail: nyeditorial@symphonypublishing.com. Website: www.footwearplusmagazine.com. **20% freelance written.** Monthly magazine covering footwear fashion and business. "A business-to-business publication targeted at footwear retailers. Covering all categories of footwear and age ranges with a focus on new trends, brands and consumer buying habits, as well as retailer advice on operating the store more effectively." Estab. 1990. Circ. 18,000. Byline given. Pays on publication. No kill fee. Publishes ms an average of 1-2 months after acceptance. Buys second serial (reprint) rights, buys electronic rights. Editorial lead time 1-2 months. Accepts queries by e-mail. Sample copy for $5.

Nonfiction Needs interview, new product, technical. Does not want pieces unrelated to footwear/fashion industry. **Buys 10-20 mss/year.** Query. Length: 500-2,500 words. **Pays $1,000 maximum.** Sometimes pays expenses of writers on assignment.

$ $ MADE TO MEASURE

Halper Publishing Co., 830 Moseley Rd., Highland Park IL 60035. Fax: (847)780-2902. E-mail: mtm@halper.com. Website: www.madetomeasuremag.com. **50% freelance written.** Semiannual magazine covering uniforms and career apparel. A semi-annual magazine/buyers' reference containing leading sources of supply, equipment, and services of every description related to the Uniform, Career Apparel, and allied trades, throughout the entire US. Estab. 1930. Circ. 25,000. Byline given. Pays on acceptance. No kill fee. Publishes ms an average of 2 months after acceptance. Buys first North American serial rights. Editorial lead time 4 months. Submit seasonal material 4 months in advance. Accepts queries by mail, e-mail. Accepts simultaneous submissions. Responds in 3 weeks to queries. Sample copy available online.

Nonfiction Please only consider sending queries related to companies that wear or make uniforms, career apparel, or identify apparel. Needs interview, new product, personal experience, photo feature, technical. **Buys 6-8 mss/year.** Query with published clips. Length: 1,000-3,000 words. **Pays $300-500.** Sometimes pays expenses of writers on assignment.

Photos State availability Reviews contact sheets, any prints. Negotiates payment individually. Buys one time rights.

Tips We look for features about large and small companies who wear uniforms (restaurants, hotels, industrial, medical, public safety, etc.).

RAGTRADER

Yaffa Publishing, 17-21 Bellevue St., Surry Hills NSW 2010 Australia. (61)(2)9281-2333. Fax: (61)(2)9281-2750. E-mail: yaffa@yaffa.com.au. Website: www.yaffa.com.au. Magazine published 24 times/year covering the latest fashion trends for the fashion retail and international runway industry. *Ragtrader* features all the latest gossip on the local industry along with news, views, directional looks and topical features.

Nonfiction Needs general interest, new product. Query.

$ $ TEXTILE WORLD

Billian Publishing Co., 2100 Powers Ferry Rd., Suite 300, Atlanta GA 30339. (770)955-5656. Fax: (770)952-0669. E-mail: editor@textileworld.com. Website: www.textileworld.com. **5% freelance written.** Bimonthly magazine covering the business of textile, apparel, and fiber industries with considerable technical focus on products and processes. No puff pieces pushing a particular product. Estab. 1868. Byline given. Pays on publication. No kill fee. Buys first North American serial rights.

Nonfiction Needs technical, business. **Buys 10 mss/year.** Query. 500 words minimum. **Pays $200/published page.**

Photos Send photos Captions required. Reviews prints. Offers no additional payment for photos accepted with ms. Buys one time rights.

CONSTRUCTION & CONTRACTING

$ $ ADVANCED MATERIALS & COMPOSITES NEWS PLUS COMPOSITES ENEWS

International Business & Technology Intelligence on High Performance M&P, Composites Worldwide, Inc., 991-C Lomas Santa Fe Dr., MC469, Solana Beach CA 92075-2125. (858)755-1372. E-mail: info@compositesnews.com. Website: www.compositesnews.com. **1% freelance written.** Bimonthly newsletter covering advanced materials and fiber-reinforced polymer composites, plus a weekly electronic version called *Composite eNews*, reaching over 15,000 subscribers and many more pass-along readers. *Advanced Materials & Composites News* covers markets, applications, materials, processes, and organizations for all sectors of the global hi-tech materials world. Audience is management, academics, researchers, government, suppliers, and fabricators. Focus on news about growth opportunities. Estab. 1978. Circ. 15,000+. Byline sometimes given. Pays on publication. No kill fee. Publishes ms an average of 1 month after acceptance. Buys all rights. Editorial lead time 2 weeks. Submit seasonal material 1 month in advance. Accepts queries by e-mail. Responds in 1 week to queries. Responds in 1 month to mss. Sample copy for #10 SASE.

Nonfiction Needs new product, technical, industry information. **Buys 4-6 mss/year.** Query. 300 words. **Pays $200/final printed page.**

Photos State availability Captions, identification of subjects, model releases required. Reviews 4x5 transparencies, prints, 35mm slides, JPEGs (much preferred). Offers no additional payment for photos accepted with ms Buys all rights.

AUSTRALIAN JOURNAL OF CONSTRUCTION, ECONOMICS AND BUILDING

P.O. Box 301, Deakin West ACT 2600 Australia. (61)(2)6282-2222. Fax: (61)(2)6285-2427. E-mail: linda@aiqs.com.au. Website: www.aiqs.com.au. Semiannual magazine covering construction economics and building in Australia. Guidelines available online.

Nonfiction Needs technical. Send complete ms. Length: 5,000 words.

Photos Reviews transparencies, prints.

$ $ AUTOMATED BUILDER

CMN Associates, Inc., 1445 Donlon St., Suite 16, Ventura CA 93003. (805)642-9735. Fax: (805)642-8820. E-mail: info@automatedbuilder.com. Website: www.automatedbuilder.com. **Contact:** Don O. Carlson, editor and publisher. **10% freelance written.** Monthly magazine specializing in management for industrialized (manufactured) housing and volume home builders. "Our material is technical in content and concerned with new technologies or improved methods for in-plant building and components related to building. Online content is uploaded from the monthly print material." Estab. 1964. Circ. 25,000. Byline given. Pays on acceptance. No kill fee. Publishes ms an average of 3 months after acceptance. Buys first North American serial rights. Editorial lead time 2 months. Submit seasonal material 2 months in advance. Accepts queries by mail, e-mail, fax. Responds in 2 weeks to queries. Sample copy free.

Nonfiction Case history articles on successful home building companies which may be 1) production (big volume) home builders; 2) mobile home manufacturers; 3) modular home manufacturers; 4) prefabricated (panelized) home manufacturers; 5) house component manufacturers; or 6) special unit (in-plant commercial building) manufacturers. Also uses interviews, photo features, and technical articles. "No architect or plan `dreams.' Housing projects must be built or under construction." **Buys 6-8 mss/year.** Query. Phone queries OK. Length: 250-500 words. **Pays $350 for stories including photos.**

Photos Wants 4x5, 5x7, or 8x10 glossies or disks. State availability Captions, identification of subjects required. Offers no additional payment for photos accepted with ms.

Tips "Stories often are too long, too loose; we prefer 500-750 words. We prefer a phone query on feature articles. If accepted on query, article usually will not be rejected later."

BCME

FPC Magazines, 170-180 Bourke Rd., Alexandria NSW 2015 Australia. (61)(2)9353-6666. Fax: (61)(2)9353-6699. E-mail: bcme@fpcpower.com.au. Website: www.bcme.com.au. Bimonthly magazine covering building products, services news, and industry views for the key decision makers and experts in the design and building industry. *BCME* provides its readers with in-depth interviews of industry leaders providing insight into industry trends in Australia and overseas. Circ. 17,700.

Nonfiction Needs general interest, how-to, interview, new product. Query.

$ $ BUILDERNEWS MAGAZINE

Pacific NW Sales & Marketing, Inc., 500 W. 8th St., Suite 270, Vancouver WA 98660. (360)906-0793. Fax: (360)906-0794. Website: www.buildernewsmag.com. Articles must address pressing topics for builders in our region with a special emphasis on the business aspects of construction. Estab. 1996. Circ. 35,000. Byline given. Pays on acceptance of revised ms. No kill fee. Publishes ms an average of 1 month after acceptance. Buys first North American serial rights, buys electronic rights. Editorial lead time 2 months. Submit seasonal material 3 months in advance. Accepts queries by mail, e-mail, fax. Responds in 1 week to queries. Responds in 1 month to mss. Sample copy for free or online. Guidelines free.

Nonfiction Needs how-to, interview, new product, technical. No personal bios unless they teach a valuable lesson to those in the building industry. **Buys 400 mss/year.** Query. Length: 500-2,500 words. **Pays $200-500.** Sometimes pays expenses of writers on assignment.

Photos State availability Captions, identification of subjects, model releases required. Offers no additional payment for photos accepted with ms. Buys first North American serial and electronic rights.

Columns/Departments Engineering; Construction; Architecture & Design; Tools & Materials; Heavy Equipment; Business & Economics; Legal Matters; E-build; Building Green, all 750-2,500 words. Query.

Tips Writers should have an understanding of the residential building industry and its terminology and be prepared to provide a resume, writing samples, and story synopsis.

CAM MAGAZINE

Construction Association of Michigan, 43636 S. Woodward Ave., Bloomfield Hills MI 48302. (248)972-1000. Fax: (248)972-1001. Website: www.cam-online.com. **5% freelance written**. Monthly magazine covering all facets of the Michigan construction industry. *CAM Magazine* is devoted to the growth and progress of individuals and companies serving and servicing the industry. It provides a forum on new construction-related technology, products, and services, plus publishes information on industry personnel changes and advancements. Estab. 1980. Circ. 4,300. Byline given. No kill fee. Buys all rights. Editorial lead time 2 months. Submit seasonal material 3 months in advance. Accepts queries by mail, e-mail, fax, phone. Sample copy and editorial subject calendar with query and SASE.

Nonfiction Michigan construction-related only. Query with published clips. Features: 1,000-2,000 words; will also review short pieces.

Photos Digital format preferred. Send photos Offers no payment for photos accepted with ms.

Tips Anyone having current knowledge or expertise on trends and innovations related to commercial construction is welcome to submit articles. Our readers are construction experts.

$ $ CONCRETE CONSTRUCTION

Hanley-Wood, LLC., 426 S. Westgate St., Addison IL 60101. (630)543-0870. Fax: (630)543-3112. E-mail: preband@hanleywood.com. Website: www.worldofconcrete.com. **20% freelance written**. Monthly magazine for concrete contractors, engineers, architects, specifiers, and others who design and build residential, commercial, industrial, and public works, cast-in-place concrete structures. It also covers job stories and new equipment in the industry. Estab. 1956. Circ. 80,000. Byline given. Pays on acceptance. No kill fee. Publishes ms an average of 4 months after acceptance. Editorial lead time 4 months. Submit seasonal material 4 months in advance. Accepts queries by mail, e-mail, fax. Responds in 2 weeks to queries. Responds in 1 month to mss. Sample copy and writer's guidelines free.

Nonfiction Needs how-to, new product, personal experience, photo feature, technical, job stories. **Buys 7-10 mss/year.** Query with published clips. 2,000 words maximum **Pays $250 or more for assigned articles. Pays $200 minimum for unsolicited articles.** Pays expenses of writers on assignment.

Photos Send photos Captions required. Reviews contact sheets, negatives, transparencies, prints. Offers no additional payment for photos accepted with ms. Buys one time rights.

Tips Have a good understanding of the concrete construction industry. How-to stories accepted only from industry experts. Job stories must cover procedures, materials, and equipment used as well as the project's scope.

$ $ $ THE CONCRETE PRODUCER

Hanley-Wood, LLC, 426 S. Westgate St., Addison IL 60101. (630)543-0870. Fax: (630)543-3112. Website: www.theconcreteproducer.com. **25% freelance written**. Monthly magazine covering concrete production. Our audience consists of producers who have succeeded in making concrete the preferred building material through management, operating, quality control, use of the latest technology, or use of superior materials. Estab. 1982. Circ. 18,000. Byline given. Pays on acceptance. No kill fee. Publishes ms an average of 2 months after acceptance. Editorial lead time 4 months. Accepts queries by mail, e-mail, fax, phone. Responds in 1 week to queries. Responds in 2 months to mss. Sample copy for $4. Guidelines free.

Nonfiction Needs how-to, promote concrete, new product, technical. **Buys 10 mss/year.** Send complete ms. Length: 500-2,000 words. **Pays $200-1,000.** Sometimes pays expenses of writers on assignment.
Photos Scan photos at 300 dpi. State availability Captions, identification of subjects required. Reviews transparencies, prints. Offers no additional payment for photos accepted with ms.

$ $ FRAME BUILDING NEWS

The Official Publication of the National Frame Builders Association, A Division of F + W Media, Inc., 700 E. State St., Iola WI 54990-0001. (715)445-4612, ext. 428. Fax: (715)445-4087. E-mail: renee.russell@fwmedia.com. Website: www.framebuildingnews.com. **10% freelance written.** Magazine published 5 times/year covering post-frame building. "*Frame Building News* is the official publication of the National Frame Builders Association, which represents contractors who specialize in post-frame building construction." Estab. 1990. Circ. 20,000. Byline given. Pays on publication. Publishes ms an average of 3 months after acceptance. Buys all rights. Editorial lead time 3 months. Submit seasonal material 3 months in advance. Accepts queries by mail. Accepts simultaneous submissions. Sample copy free.
Nonfiction Needs book excerpts, historical, how-to, interview, new product, opinion, photo feature, technical. No advertorials. **Buys 15 mss/year.** Query with published clips. 750 words minimum. **Pays $100-500 for assigned articles.**
Photos Send photos Captions, identification of subjects required. Reviews GIF/JPEG files. Negotiates payment individually. Buys all rights.
Columns/Departments Money Talk (taxes for business); Tech Talk (computers for builders); Tool Talk (tools); Management Insights (business management), all 1,000 words. 15 Send complete ms. **Pays $0-500.**
Tips "Read our magazine online for a sense of our typical subject matter and audience. Contact by regular mail is best. No advertorials, please."

$ HARD HAT NEWS

Lee Publications, Inc., 6113 State Highway 5, Palatine Bridge NY 13428. (518)673-3237. Fax: (518)673-2381. E-mail: rlindsay@leepub.com. Website: www.hardhat.com. **Contact:** Robert Lindsay. **80% freelance written.** Biweekly tabloid covering heavy construction, equipment, road, and bridge work. "Our readers are contractors and heavy construction workers involved in excavation, highways, bridges, utility construction, and underground construction." Estab. 1980. Circ. 58,000. Byline given. No kill fee. Editorial lead time 2 weeks. Submit seasonal material 2 weeks in advance. Accepts queries by mail, e-mail, fax, phone. Sample copy and writer's guidelines free.
Nonfiction Job stories (a brief overall description of the project, the names and addresses of the companies and contractors involved, and a description of the equipment used, including manufacturers' names and model numbers; quotes from the people in charge, as well as photos, are important, as are the names of the dealers providing the equipment). Needs interview, new product, opinion, photo feature, technical. Send complete ms. Length: 800-2,000 words. **Pays $2.50/inch.** Sometimes pays expenses of writers on assignment.
Photos Send photos Captions, identification of subjects required. Reviews prints, digital preferred. Offers $15/photo.
Columns/Departments Association News; Parts and Repairs; Attachments; Trucks and Trailers; People on the Move.
Tips "Every issue has a focus—see our editorial calender. Special consideration is given to a story that coincides with the focus. A color photo is necessary for the front page. Vertical shots work best. We need more writers in metro NY area. Also, we are expanding our distribution into the Mid-Atlantic states and need writers in Virginia, Tennessee, North Carolina, Michigan, New Jersey and South Carolina."

$ $ HOME ENERGY MAGAZINE

Advancing Home Performance, Home Energy Magazine, 2124 Kittredge St., Suite 95, Berkeley CA 94704. (510)52405405. Fax: (510)486-4673. E-mail: contact@homeenergy.org. Website: www.homeenergy.org. **10% freelance written.** Bimonthly magazine covering green home building and renovation. Estab. 1984. Circ. 5,000. Byline given. Pays on publication. Offers 10% kill fee. Publishes ms an average of 4 months after acceptance. Buys all rights. Editorial lead time 4 months. Accepts queries by e-mail. Responds in 2 weeks to queries. Responds in 2 months to mss. Guidelines by email.

- Our readers are building contractors, energy auditors, and weatherization professionals. They expect technical detail, accuracy, and brevity.

Nonfiction Needs interview, technical. We do not want articles for consumers/general public. **Buys 6 mss/year. mss/year.** Query with published clips. Length: 900-3,500 words. **Pays 20¢/word; $400 max. for assigned articles. Pays 20¢/word; $400 max. for unsolicited articles.**

$ $ $ INTERIOR CONSTRUCTION

The Resource for the Ceilings & Interior Systems Construction Industry, Ceilings & Interior Systems Construction Association, 405 Illinois Ave., Unit 2B, St. Charles IL 60174. (630)584-1919. Fax: (630)584-2003. E-mail: cisca@cisca.org. Website: www.cisca.org. **1-2 features per issue.** Quarterly magazine Acoustics and commercial specialty ceiling construction. Estab. 1950. Circ. 3,000. Byline given. Pays on publication. No kill fee. Publishes

ms an average of 1 ½ months after acceptance. Buys all rights. Editorial lead time 2-3 months. Accepts queries by e-mail. Sample copy by email. Guidelines available.
Nonfiction Needs new product, technical. Query with published clips. Length: 700-1,700 words. **Pays $400 min., $800 max. for assigned articles.**

$ $ KEYSTONE BUILDER MAGAZINE

Pennsylvania Builders Association, 600 N. 12th St., Lemoyne PA 17043. (717)730-4380. Fax: (717)730-4396. E-mail: admin@pabuilders.org. Website: www.pabuilders.org. **10% freelance written**. "Bimonthly trade publication for builders, remodelers, subcontractors, and other affiliates of the home building industry in Pennsylvania." Estab. 1988. Circ. 9,300. Byline given. Pays on publication. No kill fee. Publishes ms an average of 1 year after acceptance. Buys one-time rights. Editorial lead time 3 months. Submit seasonal material 9 months in advance. Accepts queries by mail, e-mail. Accepts simultaneous submissions. Responds in 2 weeks to queries. Responds in 3 months to mss. Sample copy free. Guidelines by email.
Nonfiction Needs general interest, how-to, new product, technical. No personnel or company profiles. **Buys 1-2 mss/year.** Send complete ms. Length: 200-500 words. **Pays $200.**
Photos Send photos Captions, identification of subjects required. Reviews digital images Negotiates payment individually Buys one time rights.

$ $ MC MAGAZINE

The Voice of the Manufactured Concrete Products Industry, National Precast Concrete Association, 10333 N. Meridian St., Suite 272, Indianapolis IN 46290. (317)571-9500. Fax: (317)571-0041. E-mail: rhyink@precast.org. Website: www.precast.org. **75% freelance written**. Bimonthly magazine covering manufactured concrete products. *MC Magazine* is a publication for owners and managers of factory-produced concrete products used in construction. We publish business articles, technical articles, company profiles, safety articles, and project profiles, with the intent of educating our readers in order to increase the quality and use of precast concrete. Estab. 1995. Circ. 8,500. Byline given. Pays on acceptance. No kill fee. Publishes ms an average of 6 months after acceptance. Buys first North American serial rights, buys second serial (reprint) rights, buys all rights. Editorial lead time 3 months. Accepts queries by mail, e-mail, fax. Accepts simultaneous submissions. Responds in 1 month to queries. Responds in 2 months to mss. Sample copy available online. Guidelines available online.
Nonfiction Needs how-to, business, interview, technical, concrete manufacturing. No humor, essays, fiction, or fillers. **Buys 8-14 mss/year.** Query or send complete ms. Length: 1,500-2,500 words. **Pays $250-750.** Sometimes pays expenses of writers on assignment.
Photos State availability Captions required. Offers no additional payment for photos accepted with ms. Buys all rights.
Tips Understand the audience and the purpose of the magazine. Understanding audience interests and needs is important and expressing a willingness to tailor a subject to get the right slant is critical. Our primary freelance needs are about general business or technology topics. Of course, if you are an engineer or a writer specializing in industry, construction, or manufacturing technology, other possibilities may exist. Writing style should be concise, yet lively and entertaining. Avoid clichÃ^s. We require a third-person perspective, and encourage a positive tone and active voice. For stylistic matters, follow the *AP Style Book*.

$ $ METAL ROOFING MAGAZINE

a Division of F + W Media, Inc., 700 E. Iola St., Iola WI 54990-0001. (715)445-4612, ext. 13281. Fax: (715)445-4087. E-mail: jim.austin@fwmedia.com. Website: www.metalroofingmag.com. **10% freelance written**. Bimonthly magazine covering roofing. *Metal Roofing Magazine* offers contractors, designers, suppliers, architects and others in the construction industry a wealth of information on metal roofing—a growing segment of the roofing trade. Estab. 2000. Circ. 26,000. Byline given. Pays on publication. Publishes ms an average of 3 months after acceptance. Buys all rights. Editorial lead time 3 months. Submit seasonal material 3 months in advance. Accepts queries by mail. Accepts simultaneous submissions. Sample copy free.
Nonfiction Needs book excerpts, historical, how-to, interview, new product, opinion, photo feature, technical. No advertorials. **Buys 15 mss/year.** Query with published clips. 750 words minimum. **Pays $100-500 for assigned articles.**
Photos Send photos Captions, identification of subjects required. Reviews GIF/JPEG files. Negotiates payment individually. Buys all rights.
Columns/Departments Gutter Opportunities; Stay Cool; Metal Roofing Details; Spec It. 15 Send complete ms. **Pays $0-500.**
Tips "Read our magazine online for a sense of our typical subject matter and audience. Contact by regular mail is best."

MICHIGAN CONTRACTOR & BUILDER

1917 Savannah Lane, Ypsilanti MI 48198-3674. (734)482-0272. Fax: (734)482-0291. E-mail: akalousdian@reedbusiness.com. **25% freelance written**. Weekly magazine covering the commercial construction industry in Michigan (no home building). *Michigan Contractor & Builder's* audience is contractors, equipment suppliers, engineers, and architects. The magazine reports on construction projects in Michigan. It does not cover homebuilding. Stories should focus on news or innovative techniques or materials in construction. Estab. 1907. Byline given. Pays 1 month after publication. No kill fee. Buys all rights. Accepts queries by mail, e-mail, fax, phone. Sample copy free.

Nonfiction Michigan construction projects. Query with published clips. 1,000 words with 5-7 photos. **Payment is negotiable**

Photos Send photos Captions required. Reviews high resolution digital photos. Offers no additional payment for photos accepted with ms. Buys all rights.

$ $ PERMANENT BUILDINGS & FOUNDATIONS (PBF)

R.W. Nielsen Co., 575 E. Center St., Provo UT 84606. (801)794-1393. Fax: (801)804-6691. E-mail: rnielsen@permanentbuildings.com. Website: www.permanentbuildings.com. **80% freelance written**. Magazine published 8 times/year. *PBF* readers are general contractors who build residential and light commercial concrete buildings. Editorial focus is on new technologies to build solid, energy efficient structures, insulated concrete walls, waterproofing, underpinning, roofing and the business of contracting and construction. No highway, bridge or large industrial construction. Estab. 1989. Circ. 30,000. Byline given. Pays on publication. No kill fee. Buys first North American serial rights. Editorial lead time 1 month. Submit seasonal material 2 months in advance. Accepts queries by mail, e-mail, phone. Responds immediately. Responds in 1 month to mss. Sample copy for 9x12 SASE or online. Writer's guidelines free or online.

Nonfiction Needs how-to, construction methods, management techniques, humor, interview, new product, technical, tool reviews, environment/green building. **Buys 90-100 mss/year.** Query. Length: 500-1,500 words. **Pays 30-60¢/word.**

Photos State availability Captions, identification of subjects required. Reviews digital images (300 dpi). Offers no additional payment for photos accepted with ms. Buys North American rights.

Columns/Departments Marketing Tips, 250-500 words; Q&A (solutions to contractor problems), 200-500 words. Query.

$ $ POB MAGAZINE

BNP Media, 2401 W. Big Beaver Rd., Suite 700, Troy MI 48084. (248)362-3700. E-mail: hohnerl@bnpmedia.com. Website: www.pobonline.com. **5% freelance written.** Monthly magazine covering surveying, mapping and geomatics. Estab. 1975. Circ. 39,000. Byline given. Pays on publication. Publishes ms an average of 3 months after acceptance. Buys first North American serial rights. Editorial lead time 3 months. Accepts queries by e-mail, phone. Sample copy available online. Guidelines available online.

Nonfiction Query. Length: 1,700-2,200 words. **Pays $400.**

Photos State availability Captions, identification of subjects required. Reviews GIF/JPEG files. Offers no additional payment for photos accepted with ms. Buys one time rights.

Tips They must know our profession and industry.

PROFESSIONAL BUILDER

Reed Business Information, 2000 Clearwater Dr., Oak Brook IL 60523. (630)288-8000. Fax: (630)288-8145. E-mail: erin.hallstrom@reedbusiness.com. Website: probuilder.com. Magazine published 14 times/year covering the business of home building. Designed as a resource to help builders run succesful and profitable home building businesses. Circ. 127,277. No kill fee. Editorial lead time 6 months. Accepts queries by mail, e-mail.

$ $ RURAL BUILDER

The Business Management Magazine for Rural Contractors, a Division of F+W Media, Inc., 700 E. State St., Iola WI 54990-0001. (715)445-4612, ext. 13644. Fax: (715)445-4087. E-mail: renee.russell@fwmedia.com. Website: www.ruralbuilder.com. **10% freelance written**. Magazine published 7 times/year covering rural building. *"Builder* serves diversified town and country builders, offering them help managing their businesses through editorial and advertising material about metal, wood, post-frame, and masonry construction." Estab. 1967. Circ. 30,000. Byline given. Pays on publication. Publishes ms an average of 3 months after acceptance. Buys all rights. Editorial lead time 3 months. Submit seasonal material 3 months in advance. Accepts queries by mail. Accepts simultaneous submissions. Sample copy free.

Nonfiction Needs book excerpts, historical, how-to, interview, new product, opinion, photo feature, technical. No advertorials. **Buys 15 mss/year.** Query with published clips. 750 words minimum. **Pays $100-500.**

Photos Send photos Captions, identification of subjects required. Reviews GIF/JPEG files. Negotiates payment individually. Buys all rights.

Columns/Departments Money Talk (taxes for business); Tech Talk (computers for builders); Tool Talk (tools); Management Insights (business management); all 1,000 words. 15 Send complete ms. **Pays $0-500.**

Tips "Read our magazine online for a sense of our typical subject matter and audience. Contact by regular mail is best. No advertorials, please."

$ $ UNDERGROUND CONSTRUCTION

Oildom Publishing Co. of Texas, Inc., P.O. Box 941669, Houston TX 77094-8669. (281)558-6930. Fax: (281)558-

7029. E-mail: rcarpenter@oildom.com. Website: www.oildompublishing.com. **35% freelance written.** Monthly magazine covering underground oil and gas pipeline, water and sewer pipeline, cable construction for contractors and owning companies. Circ. 38,000. No kill fee. Publishes ms an average of 6 months after acceptance. Buys first North American serial rights. Accepts queries by mail, e-mail, fax, phone. Responds in 1 month to mss. Sample copy for sae.

Nonfiction Needs how-to, job stories and industry issues. Query with published clips. Length: 1,000-2,000 words. **Pays $3-500.** Sometimes pays expenses of writers on assignment.

Photos Send photos Captions required. Reviews color prints and slides. Buys one time rights.

DRUGS, HEALTH CARE & MEDICAL PRODUCTS

$ $ $ $ N ACP INTERNIST/ACP HOSPITALIST

American College of Physicians, 191 N. Independence Mall W., Philadelphia PA 19106. (215)351-2400. E-mail: acpinternist@acponline.org. Website: www.acpinternist.org. www.acphospitalist.org. **40% freelance written.** Monthly magazine covering Internal Medicine/Hospital Medicine. "We write for specialists in internal medicine, not a consumer audience. Topics include clinical medicine, practice management, health information technology, Medicare issues." Estab. 1981. Circ. 85,000 (Internist), 24,000 (Hospitalist). Byline given. Offers kill fee. Negotiable Publishes ms an average of 2 months after acceptance. Buys electronic rights. Makes work-for-hire assignments. Editorial lead time 4 months. Submit seasonal material 6 months in advance. Accepts queries by e-mail. Sample copy available online Guidelines free

Nonfiction Needs interview. Query with published clips. Length: 700-2,000 words. **Pays $500-2,000 for assigned articles.** Pays expenses of writers on assignment.

Photos Contact: Ryan Dubosar, senior editor. State availability Reviews TIFF/JPEG files. Negotiates payment individually

AUSTRALIAN AND NEW ZEALAND JOURNAL OF PUBLIC HEALTH

P.O. Box 351, North Melbourne VIC 3051 Australia. (61)(3)9329-3535. Fax: (61)(3)9329-3550. E-mail: anzjph@substitution.com.au. Website: www.phaa.net.au. Bimonthly magazine. Guidelines available online.

Nonfiction Needs general interest, technical. Send complete ms. Length: 500-3,500 words.

Tips Contributors come from almost all of the human, natural and social science disciplines.

AUSTRALIAN HEALTH REVIEW

Australasian Medical Publishing Company, Locked Bag 3030, Strawberry Hills NSW 2012 Australia. (61)(2)9562-6640. Fax: (61)(2)9562-6699. E-mail: ahr@ampco.com.au. Website: www.aushealthcare.com.au. Quarterly magazine for the Australian Healthcare Association. "*AHR* provides information for decision makers in the health care industry and is read by health care professionals, managers, planners and policy makers throughout Australia and the region." Byline given. Buys all rights. Guidelines available online.

Nonfiction Needs opinion, feature articles, research notes, case studies, book reviews, editorials. Send complete ms. Length: 500-5,000 words.

Photos Send photos Offers no additional payment for photos accepted with ms. Buys all rights.

AUSTRALIAN JOURNAL OF PHARMACY

APPCo, Level 5, 8 Thomas St., Chatswood NSW 2057 Australia. (61)(2)8117 9500. Fax: (61)(2)8117 9511. E-mail: matthew.eton@appco.com.au. Website: www.appco.com.au. Monthly magazine covering news, health features, developments in pharmacy practice, new products, pharmacy education, research, legal and financial issues, conferences and special events. Circ. 15,400.

Nonfiction Needs general interest, how-to, interview, new product, technical. Query.

HOSPITAL & AGEDCARE

Yaffa Publishing, 17-21 Bellevue St., Surry Hills NSW 2010 Australia. (61)(2)9281-2333. Fax: (61)(2)9281-2750. E-mail: hospital@yaffa.com.au. Website: www.yaffa.com.au. **Contact:** Karen Burge, editor. Monthly magazine covering independent, incisive news and features targeting healthcare managers, including politics, finance, clinical care, health IT and profession-based issues. "Australia's leading magazine for hospital and care managers." Circ. 8,000. Yes publication 2 months Accepts queries by mail.

Nonfiction Needs general interest, how-to, interview, new product, opinion, photo feature feature. **Buys 10 mss/year.** Query. 1,200-2,000 **Pays 50¢ per commission word, max. for assigned articles.**

Columns/Departments Pays 50¢ per commissioned word.

JUCM

The Journal of Urgent Care Medicine, Braveheart Publishing, 2 Split Rock Rd., Mahwah NJ 07430. (201)529-4014. Fax: (201)529-4007. E-mail: editor@jucm.com. Website: www.jucm.com. **80% freelance written.** Monthly magazine covering clinical and practice management issues relevant to the field of urgent care medicine.

JUCM supports the evolution of urgent care medicine by creating content that addresses both the clinical needs and practice management challenges or urgent care clinicians, managers and owners. Hence, each article must offer practical, concrete ways to improve care offered or management of the business. Estab. 2006. Circ. 13,000. Byline given. Does not pay contributors at present. No kill fee. Publishes ms an average of 6 months after acceptance. Buys simultaneous rights. Editorial lead time 2 months. Submit seasonal material 4 months in advance. Accepts queries by e-mail. Accepts simultaneous submissions. Responds in 1 month to queries. Responds in 1-2 months to mss. Sample copy free. Guidelines free.

Nonfiction Contact: J. Harris Fleming, Jr. Needs essays, how-to, Clinical topics, opinion. We don't want any articles that promote a particular product or company. **Buys 22 mss/year mss/year.** Query. Length: 1,200-3,200 words.

$ $ N LABTALK

LabTalk, P.O. Box 1945, Big Bear Lake CA 92315. (909)866-5590. Fax: (909)866-5577. E-mail: cwalker@framesdata.com. Website: www.framesdata.com. **20% freelance written**. Magazine published 6 times/year for the eye wear industry. "*Sunwear Vision* brings readers current information on all the latest designs and innovations available in the field of fashion and sports sunwear." Estab. 1970. Circ. 30,000. Byline given. Pays 1 month prior to publication. No kill fee. Publishes ms an average of 3 months after acceptance. Buys first North American serial rights. Editorial lead time 3 months. Submit seasonal material 3 months in advance. Accepts simultaneous submissions. Responds in 1 week to queries. Sample copy for sae with 8x10 envelope and 2 First-Class stamps.

Nonfiction Needs how-to, new product. **Buys 10 mss/year.** Query with published clips. Length: 800-1,600 words. **Pays $00-800.**

Photos Send photos Captions, identification of subjects required. Offers no additional payment for photos accepted with ms. Buys one time rights.

Tips "Write for the doctor. How can doctors make more money selling sunwear?"

PHARMACY TODAY

CMPMedica (NZ) Ltd., 3 Shea Terrace, Takapuna Auckland New Zealand. (64)(9)488-4290. Fax: (64)(9)489-6240. E-mail: asvendsen@pharmacy-today.co.nz. Website: www.pharmacy-today.co.nz. Trade journal providing the pharmaceutical industry with news on business, politics, clinical pharmacy, and medicines. No kill fee.

- Query before submitting.

$ $ $ VALIDATION TIMES

Bio Research Compliance Report, Adverse Event Reporting News, Washington Information Source Co., 208 S. King St., Suite 303, Leesburg VA 20175. (703)779-8777. Fax: (703)779-2508. E-mail: publisher@fdainfo.com. Website: www.fdainfo.com. Monthly newsletters covering regulation of pharmaceutical and medical devices. We write to executives who have to keep up on changing FDA policies and regulations, and on what their competitors are doing at the agency. Estab. 1992. Byline given. Pays on publication. No kill fee. Publishes ms an average of 1 month after acceptance. Makes work-for-hire assignments. Editorial lead time 1 month. Submit seasonal material 1 month in advance. Accepts queries by mail. Responds in 1 month to queries. Sample copy and writer's guidelines free.

Nonfiction Needs how-to, technical, regulatory. No lay interest pieces. **Buys 50-100 mss/year.** Query. Length: 600-1,500 words. **Pays $100/half day; $200 full day to cover meetings and same rate for writing.** Sometimes pays expenses of writers on assignment.

Tips If you're covering a conference for non-competing publications, call me with a drug or device regulatory angle.

EDUCATION & COUNSELING

ILLINOIS

CATALYST CHICAGO

Community Renewal Society, 332 S. Michigan Ave., Suite 500, Chicago IL 60604. E-mail: editorial@catalyst-chicago.org. Website: www.catalyst-chicago.org. 5 times/year-print; semi-monthly online magazine Urban education in Chicago. *Catalyst Chicago* provides in-depth, authoritative reporting on urban education & school improvement to a wide-ranging, well-informed audience that includes parents, teachers, district officials, resesearchers, policymakers, legislators & activists. Writing for *Catalyst Chicago* readership requires substantial background knowledge or research, & the ability to make the research & reporting readable for a wide audience. Estab. 1990. Circ. 10,000. Byline given. Pays on publication. Offers 20% kill fee. Publishes ms an average of 1-2 months after acceptance. Buys first rights, buys electronic rights. Editorial lead time 4 months. Accepts queries by mail, e-mail. Times vary on reporting back. Sample copy for sae with $2 envelope. Guidelines free.

Nonfiction Needs interview, opinion, as assigned. Query. varies
Photos Contact: Christine Wachter, Presentation Editor. Identification of subjects, model releases required. Reviews GIF/JPEG files. Negotiates payment individually. Buys one time rights.
Tips Please query first. We do not generally buy over-the-transom articles. Your query should show knowledge of education & state clearly how the proposed article would shed light on some aspect of school improvement in Chicago.

$ ARTS & ACTIVITIES

Publishers' Development Corp., Dept. WM, 12345 World Trade Dr., San Diego CA 92128. (858)605-0242. Fax: (858)605-0247. E-mail: ed@artsandactivities.com. Website: www.artsandactivities.com. **95% freelance written. Eager to work with new/unpublished writers.** Monthly (except July and August) magazine covering art education at levels from preschool through college for educators and therapists engaged in arts and crafts education and training. Estab. 1932. Circ. 20,000. Byline given. Pays on publication. No kill fee. Publishes ms an average of 1 year after acceptance. Buys first North American serial rights. Submit seasonal material 6 months in advance. Accepts queries by mail. Responds in 3 months to queries. Sample copy for sae with 9x12 envelope and 8 First-Class stamps. Guidelines available online.
Nonfiction Needs historical, arts, activities, history, how-to, classroom art experiences, artists' techniques, interview, of artists, opinion, on arts activities curriculum, ideas of how-to do things better, philosophy of art education, personal experience, this ties in with the how-to, we like it to be personal, no recipe style, articles of exceptional art programs. **Buys 80-100 mss/year.** Length: 200-2,000 words. **Pays $35-150.**
Tips Frequently in unsolicited manuscripts, writers obviously have not studied the magazine to see what style of articles we publish. Send for a sample copy to familiarize yourself with our style and needs. The best way to find out if his/her writing style suits our needs is for the author to submit a manuscript on speculation. We prefer an anecdotal style of writing, so that readers will feel as though they are there in the art room as the lesson/project is taking place. Also, good quality photographs of student artwork are important. We are a visual art magazine!

$ THE ATA MAGAZINE

The Alberta Teachers' Association, 11010 142nd St., Edmonton AB T5N 2R1 Canada. (780)447-9400. Fax: (780)455-6481. E-mail: postmaster@teachers.ab.ca. Website: www.teachers.ab.ca. Quarterly magazine covering education. Estab. 1920. Circ. 39,500. Byline given. Pays on publication. No kill fee. Publishes ms an average of 4 months after acceptance. Buys one-time rights. Editorial lead time 2 months. Submit seasonal material 2 months in advance. Accepts queries by mail, e-mail, fax, phone. Accepts simultaneous submissions. Responds in 2 months to queries. Sample copy free. Guidelines available online.
Nonfiction Education-related topics. Query with published clips. Length: 500-1,250 words. **Pays $75 (Canadian).**
Photos Send photos Captions required. Reviews 4x6 prints. Negotiates payment individually. Negotiates rights.

AUSTRALIAN JOURNAL OF ADULT LEARNING

Adult Learning Australia, Inc., Centre for Research in Education, Equity and Work, University of South Australia (Building 64), Mawson Lakes Blvd., Mawson Lakes SA 5095 Australia. (61)(8)8302-6246. Fax: (61)(8)8302-6832. E-mail: roger.harris@unisa.edu.au. Website: www.ala.asn.au. "Academic journal published 3 times/year covering adult learning in Australia and internationally.".
Nonfiction Needs general interest, how-to. Query.

AUSTRALIAN JOURNAL OF EARLY CHILDHOOD

Early Childhood Australia, Inc., P.O. Box 7105, Watson ACT 2602 Australia. (61)(2)6242-1800. Fax: (61)(2)6242-1818. E-mail: publishing@earlychildhood.org.au. Website: www.earlychildhoodaustralia.org.au. **Contact:** Dave Kingwell, publishing and marketing manager. Nonprofit early childhood advocacy organisation, acting in the interests of young children aged from bith to eight years of age, their families and those in the early childhood field. Specialist publisher of early childhood magazines, journals, and booklets. Guidelines available online.
Nonfiction Please read author guidelines, available online, or contact publishing department for submission details. Needs essays. Send complete ms. Length: Magazine articles, 600-1,000 words; research-based papers, 3,000-6,500 words ; submissions for booklets, approximately 5,000 words.

AUSTRALIAN SCREEN EDUCATION

P.O. Box 2040, St. Kilda West VIC 3182 Australia. (61)(3)9525-5302. Fax: (61)(3)9537-2325. E-mail: assistanteditor@atom.org.au. Website: www.metromagazine.com.au. Quarterly magazine written by and for teachers and students in secondary and primary schools, covering all curriculum areas. Guidelines available online.
Nonfiction Needs general interest, interview, reviews, classroom activities. E-mail proposals or complete article. Length: 1,000-3,000 words.

Photos Reviews TIFF/JPEG files.

CATECHIST

Peter Li, Inc., 2621 Dryden Rd., Suite 300, Dayton OH 45439. E-mail: kdotterweich@peterli.com. Website: www.catechist.com. **75% freelance written**. Magazine published 7 times/year covering Catholic education, grades K-6. Our articles target teachers of children in religious education parish programs. Estab. 1961. Circ. 52,000. Byline given. Pays on publication. Publishes ms an average of 8 months after acceptance. Buys first North American serial rights. Editorial lead time 1 year. Submit seasonal material 1 year in advance. Accepts queries by mail, e-mail, fax. Responds in 2 weeks to queries. Responds in 2 months to mss. Sample copy for $3.50. Guidelines available online.

Nonfiction Needs how-to, personal experience, religious. Advent/Christmas (November-December); Sacrament (January). Does not want product profiles. **Buys 15 mss/year.** Query. Length: 500-1,000 words. **Pays negotiable amount.**

Tips Call the editor with specific questions.

$ $ EARLYCHILDHOOD NEWS

Excelligence Learning Corp., 2 Lower Ragsdale, Suite 200, Monterey CA 93940. (831)333-5771. Fax: (831)333-5595. E-mail: batkinson@excelligencemail.com. Website: www.earlychildhoodnews.com. **80% freelance written**. Monthly magazine covering early childhood education. Targets teachers and parents of young children (infants to age 8). Estab. 1988. Circ. 55,000. Byline given. Pays on publication. No kill fee. Publishes ms an average of 2-3 months after acceptance. Buys all rights. Editorial lead time 2-4 months. Submit seasonal material 4 months in advance. Accepts queries by mail, e-mail, fax. Responds in 4-6 weeks to queries. Responds in 2-4 months to mss. Guidelines available online.

Nonfiction Needs essays, general interest, inspirational, interview, research-based. Why Humor is the Best Teacher, Classroom Design (January/February); Promoting Development Through Play (March/April); Sizzling Summer Programs, Summer Reading (May/June); Meeting the Needs of Infants & Toddlers, Safety, Preschool Behavior (August/September); How to Measure Learning, Directors' Choice Awards (October); Crystal Clear Communication with Parents, Music, Teaching Kids with Special Needs (November/December). No personal stories or fiction. **Buys 40-50 mss/year.** Query. Length: 500-1,200 words. **Pays $100-300 for assigned articles. Pays $100-300 for unsolicited articles.**

Poetry Needs light verse, traditional. Poems should have a teacher-directed audience. No poetry not related to children, teachers, or early childhood. **Buys 6 poems/year.** Length: 10-60 lines. **Pays $50-250.**

Tips Knowing about the publication and the types of articles we publish is greatly appreciated. Query letters are preferred over complete manuscripts.

EDUCATION TODAY

Masterprint Ltd., P.O. Box 641, New Plymouth New Zealand. (64)(6)7559500. Fax: (64)(6)7552624. E-mail: melva.orm@cler.net.nz. Website: www.education-today.co.nz. Magazine covering news and issues for educational professionals. No kill fee.

- Query before submitting.

$ THE FORENSIC TEACHER

Wide Open Minds Educational Services, P.O. Box 5263, Wilmington DE 19808. E-mail: admin@theforensicteacher.com. Website: www.theforensicteacher.com. **70% freelance written**. Quarterly magazine covering forensic education. "Our readers are middle, high and post-secondary teachers who are looking for better, easier and more engaging ways to teach forensics as well as law enforcement and scientific forensic experts. Our writers understand this and are writing from a forensic or educational background, or both." Estab. 2006. Circ. 30,000. Byline given. Pays 60 days after publication. No kill fee. Publishes ms an average of 6 months after acceptance. Buys first North American serial rights, buys second serial (reprint) rights, buys all electronic rights. Editorial lead time 6 months. Submit seasonal material 6 months in advance. Accepts queries by mail, e-mail. Accepts simultaneous submissions. Responds in 2 weeks to queries. Responds in 2 months to mss. Sample copy for $5. Guidelines available online.

Nonfiction Needs how-to, personal experience, photo feature, technical, lesson plans. Does not want poetry, fiction or anything unrelated to medicine, law, forensics or teaching. **Buys 18 mss/year.** Send complete ms. Length: 400-2,000 words. **Pays 2¢/word.**

Photos State availability Captions required. Reviews GIF/JPEG files/pdf. Negotiates payment individually. Buys first North American serial rights, second serial reprint rights, all electronic rights

Columns/Departments Needs lesson experiences or ideas, personal or professional experiences with a branch of forensics. "If you've done it in your classroom please share it with us. Also, if you're a professional, please tell our readers how they can duplicate the lesson/demo/experiment in their classrooms. Please share what you know."

Fillers Needs facts, newsbreaks. 15 Length: 50-200 words. **Pays 2¢/word.**

Tips "Your article will benefit forensics teachers and their students. It should inform, entertain and enlighten the teacher and the students. Would you read it if you were a busy forensics teacher?"

$ $ HISPANIC OUTLOOK IN HIGHER EDUCATION

210 Route 4 E., Suite 310, Paramus NJ 07652. (201)587-8800, ext 100. Fax: (201)587-9105. E-mail: sloutlook@aol.com. Website: www.hispanicoutlook.com. **50% freelance written**. Biweekly magazine. We're looking for higher education story articles, with a focus on Hispanics and the advancements made by and for Hispanics in higher education. Circ. 28,000. Byline given. Pays on publication. No kill fee. Publishes ms an average of 2 months after acceptance. Editorial lead time 2 months. Submit seasonal material 3 months in advance. Accepts queries by mail, e-mail, fax. Accepts simultaneous submissions. Sample copy free.

Nonfiction Needs historical, interview, of academic or scholar, opinion, on higher education, personal experience, all regarding higher education only. **Buys 20-25 mss/year.** Query with published clips. Length: 1,800-2,200 words. **Pays $500 minimum for assigned articles.** Pays expenses of writers on assignment.

Photos Send photos Reviews color or b&w prints, digital images must be 300 dpi (call for e-mail photo address). Offers no additional payment for photos accepted with ms.

Tips Articles explore the Hispanic experience in higher education. Special theme issues address sports, law, health, corporations, heritage, women, and a wide range of similar issues; however, articles need not fall under those umbrellas.

INSTRUCTOR MAGAZINE

For Teachers of Grades K-8, Scholastic, Inc., P.O. Box 713, New York NY 10013. E-mail: instructor@scholastic.com. Website: www.scholastic.com/instructor. Magazine 8 times/year geared toward teachers, curriculum coordinators, principals, and supervisors of kindergarten through 8th grade classes. Circ. 200,391. No kill fee. Editorial lead time 4 months. Submit seasonal material 6 months in advance. Accepts queries by mail, e-mail. Sample copy available by calling (866)436-2455. Guidelines available online.

Nonfiction Send complete ms. Length: 800-1,200 words.

Columns/Departments Activities and Tips (for teachers), 250 words; Lesson Units (lesson-planning units on a specific curriculum area or theme), 400-800 words. Send complete ms.

Tips As you write, think: How can I make this article most useful for teachers? Write in your natural voice. We shy away from wordy, academic prose. Let us know what grade/subject you teach and name and location of your school.

MUSIC EDUCATORS JOURNAL

MENC: The National Association for Music Education, 1806 Robert Fulton Dr., Reston VA 20191-4348. E-mail: caroline@menc.org. Website: www.menc.org. **100% freelance written**. Bimonthly magazine covering music education. *MEJ* is a peer-reviewed journal that offers timely articles on teaching approaches and philosophies, current trends, issues in music education, and the latest in products and services. Byline given. Does not pay freelance writers at this time. No kill fee. Publishes ms an average of 6-12 months after acceptance. Buys all rights. Accepts queries by mail, e-mail, fax. Guidelines available online.

Nonfiction Needs essays, how-to, related to teaching music, new product. **Buys 30 mss/year.** Send complete ms. Length: 1,800-3,500 words.

Tips Most of our authors are music teachers or university-level professors of music education. Although a music education degree is not a requirement, very few articles by those outside the field are accepted for publication.

$ $ PTO TODAY

The #1 Resource for Parent Groups, PTO Today, Inc., 100 Stonewall Blvd., Suite 3, Wrentham MA 02093. (800)644-3561. Fax: (508)384-6108. E-mail: editor@ptotoday.com. Website: www.ptotoday.com. **50% freelance written**. Magazine published 6 times during the school year covering the work of school parent-teacher groups. "We celebrate the work of school parent volunteers and provide resources to help them do that work more effectively." Estab. 1999. Circ. 80,000. Byline given. Pays on acceptance. Offers 30% kill fee. Publishes ms an average of 4-6 months after acceptance. Buys first North American serial rights, buys electronic rights, buys all rights. Editorial lead time 4 months. Submit seasonal material 4 months in advance. Accepts queries by e-mail. Guidelines by email.

Nonfiction Needs expose, general interest, how-to, anything related to PTO/PTA, interview, personal experience. **Buys 20 mss/year.** Query. Length: 600-2,000 words. **Pays 20-40¢/word for assigned articles. Pays $50-500 for unsolicited articles.** Sometimes pays expenses of writers on assignment.

Photos State availability Identification of subjects required. Negotiates payment individually Buys one time rights.

Tips "It's difficult for us to find talented writers with strong experience with parent groups. This experience is a big plus. Also, it helps to review our writer's guidelines before querying. All queries must have a strong parent group angle."

$ SCHOOLARTS MAGAZINE

50 Portland St., Worcester MA 01608-9959. Fax: (610)683-8229. Website: www.davis-art.com. **85% freelance written**. Monthly magazine (September-May), serving arts and craft education profession, K-12, higher

education, and museum education programs written by and for art teachers. Estab. 1901. Pays on publication. No kill fee. Publishes ms an average of 3 months after acceptance. Buys all rights. Accepts queries by mail, phone. Responds in 3 months to queries. Guidelines available online.

Nonfiction Articles on art and craft activities in schools. Should include description and photos of activity in progress, as well as examples of finished artwork. Query or send complete ms and SASE. Length: 600-1,400 words. **Pays $30-150.**

Tips We prefer articles on actual art projects or techniques done by students in actual classroom situations. Philosophical and theoretical aspects of art and art education are usually handled by our contributing editors. Our articles are reviewed and accepted on merit and each is tailored to meet our needs. Keep in mind that art teachers want practical tips above all—more hands-on information than academic theory. Write your article with the accompanying photographs in hand. The most frequent mistakes made by writers are bad visual material (photographs, drawings) submitted with articles, a lack of complete descriptions of art processes, and no rationale behind programs or activities. Familiarity with the field of art education is essential. Review recent issues of *SchoolArts*.

TEACHERS & WRITERS MAGAZINE

Teachers & Writers Collaborative, 520 Eighth Ave., Suite 2020, New York NY 10018. (212)691-6590. Fax: (212)675-0171. E-mail: editors@twc.org. Website: www.twc.org/pubs. **75% freelance written**. Quarterly magazine covering how to teach creative writing (kindergarten through university). "*Teachers & Writers* offers readers a rich array of educational and writerly insights." Estab. 1967. Circ. 5,000. Byline given. Pays on publication. No kill fee. Publishes ms an average of 4-6 months after acceptance. Buys one-time rights. Editorial lead time 4 months. Submit seasonal material 4-6 months in advance. Accepts queries by e-mail. Accepts simultaneous submissions. Responds in 4-8 weeks to queries. Responds in 3-6 months to mss. Sample copy for $5 Guidelines by email.

Nonfiction Needs book excerpts, on creative writing education, essays, interview, opinion, personal experience, creative writing exercises.

$ TEACHERS OF VISION

A Publication of Christian Educators Association, 227 N. Magnolia Ave., Suite 2, Anaheim CA 92801. (714)761-1476. Fax: (714)761-1679. E-mail: TOV@ceai.org. Website: www.ceai.org. **70% freelance written**. Magazine published 4 times/year for Christians in public education. "*Teachers of Vision*'s articles inspire, inform, and equip teachers and administrators in the educational arena. Readers look for teacher tips, integrating faith and work, and general interest education articles. Topics include subject matter, religious expression and activity in public schools, and legal rights of Christian educators. Our audience is primarily public school educators. Other readers include teachers in private schools, university professors, school administrators, parents, and school board members." Estab. 1953. Circ. 10,000. Byline given. Pays on publication. No kill fee. Publishes ms an average of 6 months after acceptance. Buys first North American serial rights, buys second serial (reprint) rights, buys electronic rights. Editorial lead time 4 months. Submit seasonal material 4 months in advance. Accepts queries by mail, e-mail, fax. Accepts simultaneous submissions. Responds in 1 month to queries. Responds in 3-4 months to mss. Sample copy for sae with 9x12 envelope and 4 First-Class stamps. Guidelines available online.

Nonfiction Needs how-to, humor, inspirational, interview, opinion, personal experience, religious. Nothing preachy. **Buys 50-60 mss/year.** Query or send complete ms if 2,000 words or less. Length: 600-2,500 words. **Pays $30-40.**

Photos State availability Offers no additional payment for photos accepted with ms. Buys one-time, web and reprint rights by members for educational purposes.

Columns/Departments Query. **Pays $10-40.**

Fillers Send with SASE—must relate to public education.

Tips "We are looking for material on living out one's faith in appropriate, legal ways in the public school setting."

TEACHING MUSIC

MENC: The National Association for Music Education, 1806 Robert Fulton Dr., Reston VA 20191-4348. E-mail: caroline@menc.org. Website: www.menc.org. Bimonthly journal covering music education. *Teaching Music* is a peer-reviewed journal that offers music educators a forum for the exchange of practical ideas that will help them become more effective teachers. Written in an easy-to-read, conversational style, the magazine includes timely information to interest, inform, and inspire music teachers and those who support their work. Byline given. Does not pay writers at this time. No kill fee. Publishes ms an average of 18 months after acceptance. Buys all rights. Editorial lead time 12-18 months. Accepts queries by mail, e-mail, fax, phone. Responds in 1 week to queries. Responds in 3 months to mss. Guidelines available online.

Nonfiction Needs how-to, inspirational, personal experience. **Buys 30 mss/year.** Send complete ms. Length: 1,000-1,500 words.

Photos Pays $10/photo.

$ $ $ $ TEACHING TOLERANCE

The Southern Poverty Law Center, 400 Washington Ave., Montgomery AL 36104. (334)956-8200. Fax: (334)956-8488. Website: www.teachingtolerance.org. **30% freelance written**. Semiannual magazine. *Teaching Tolerance* is dedicated to helping K-12 teachers promote tolerance and understanding between widely diverse groups of students. Includes articles, teaching ideas, and reviews of other resources available to educators. Estab. 1991. Circ. 600,000. Byline given. Pays on acceptance. No kill fee. Buys all rights. Editorial lead time 6 months. Submit seasonal material 6 months in advance. Accepts queries by mail, fax. Sample copy and writer's guidelines free or online

Nonfiction Needs essays, how-to, classroom techniques, personal experience, classroom, photo feature. No jargon, rhetoric or academic analysis. No theoretical discussions on the pros/cons of multicultural education. **Buys 2-4 mss/year.** Submit outlines or complete mss. Length: 1,000-3,000 words. **Pays $500-3,000.** Pays expenses of writers on assignment.

Photos State availability Captions, identification of subjects required. Reviews contact sheets, transparencies. Buys one time rights.

Columns/Departments Essays (personal reflection, how-to, school program), 400-800 words; Idea Exchange (special projects, successful anti-bias activities), 250-500 words; Student Writings (short essays dealing with diversity, tolerance, justice), 300-500 words. 8-12 Query with published clips. **Pays $50 1,000.**

Tips We want lively, simple, concise writing. The writing style should be descriptive and reflective, showing the strength of programs dealing successfully with diversity by employing clear descriptions of real scenes and interactions, and by using quotes from teachers and students. We ask that prospective writers study previous issues of the magazine before making submission. Most open to articles that have a strong classroom focus. We are interested in approaches to teaching tolerance and promoting understanding that really work—approaches we might not have heard of. We want to inform our readers; we also want to inspire and encourage them. We know what's happening nationally; we want to know what's happening in your neighborhood classroom.

$ TECH DIRECTIONS

Prakken Publications, Inc., P.O. Box 8623, Ann Arbor MI 48107-8623. (734)975-2800. Fax: (734)975-2787. E-mail: susanne@techdirections.com. Website: www.techdirections.com. **100% freelance written. Eager to work with new/unpublished writers.** Monthly (except June and July) magazine covering issues, trends, and activities of interest to science, technical, and technology educators at the elementary through post-secondary school levels. Estab. 1934. Circ. 40,000. Byline given. Pays on publication. No kill fee. Publishes ms an average of 1 year after acceptance. Buys all rights. Responds in 1 month to queries. Sample copy for $5. Guidelines available online.

Nonfiction Uses articles pertinent to the various teaching areas in science and technology education (woodwork, electronics, drafting, physics, graphic arts, computer training, etc.). Prefers authors who have direct connection with the field of science and/or technical education. The outlook should be on innovation in educational programs, processes, or projects that directly apply to the technical education area. Main focus: technical career and education. Needs general interest, how-to, personal experience, technical, think pieces. **Buys 50 unsolicited mss/year.** Length: 2,000-3,000 words. **Pays $50-150.**

Photos Send photos Reviews color prints. Payment for photos included in payment for ms. Will accept electronic art as well.

Columns/Departments Direct from Washington (education news from Washington DC); Technology Today (new products under development); Technologies Past (profiles the inventors of last century); Mastering Computers, Technology Concepts (project orientation).

Tips We are most interested in articles written by technology and science educators about their class projects and their ideas about the field. We need more and more technology-related articles, especially written for the community college level.

ELECTRONICS & COMMUNICATION

$ $ THE ACUTA JOURNAL OF TELECOMMUNICATIONS IN HIGHER EDUCATION

ACUTA, 152 W. Zandale Dr., Suite 200, Lexington KY 40503-2486. (859)278-3338. Fax: (859)278-3268. E-mail: pscott@acuta.org. Website: www.acuta.org. **Contact:** Patricia Scott, communications manager. **20% freelance written**. Quarterly professional association journal covering information communications technology (ICT) in higher education. "Our audience includes, primarily, middle to upper management in the IT/telecommunications department on college/university campuses. They are highly skilled, technology-oriented professionals who provide data, voice, and video communications services for residential and academic purposes." Estab. 1997. Circ. 2,200. Byline given. Pays on publication. No kill fee. Publishes ms an average of 6 months after acceptance. Buys first rights. Editorial lead time 6 months. Accepts queries by mail, e-mail, fax, phone. Responds in 1 month to queries. Responds in 2 months to mss. Sample copy for sae with 9x12 envelope and 6 First-Class stamps. Guidelines free.

Nonfiction Each issue has a focus. Available with writer's guidelines. We are only interested in articles described in article types. Needs how-to, ICT, technical, technology, case study, college/university application of technology. **Buys 6-8 mss/year.** Query. Length: 1,200-4,000 words. **Pays 8-10¢/word.** Sometimes pays expenses of writers on assignment.
Photos State availability Captions, model releases required. Reviews prints. Offers no additional payment for photos accepted with ms.
Tips "Our audience expects every article to be relevant to information communications technology on the college/university campus, whether it is related to technology, facilities, or management. Writers must read back issues to understand this focus and the level of technicality we expect."

AUSTRALIAN TELECOM

First Charlton Communications, Level 8, 122 Arthur St., North Sydney NSW 2060 Australia. (61)(2)9955-6299. Fax: (61)(2)9957-1512. E-mail: peter@charlton.com.au. Website: www.charlton.com.au. Bimonthly magazine for people in telecommunications/IT who need to know about the events driving their own companies and their computers.
Nonfiction *Australian Telecom* tracks the news, views and players in the Australian industry. Needs general interest, interview. Query.

AV SPECIALIST

AV Specialist Mena FZ LLC, P.O. Box 502314, Dubai United Arab Emirates. (971)(4)391-4718. E-mail: kevan@avspecialist.tv. Website: www.avspecialist.tv. **15% freelance written**. Bimonthly trade journal covering the film, broadcast, production, and post-production process. Estab. 1989. Pays half of writers on acceptance, half on publication. No kill fee. Buys all rights in the Middle East, Africa, and India. Accepts queries by e-mail. Responds in 1 week to mss. Guidelines available online.
Nonfiction Refer to the online submission guidelines for the 2006 editorial calendar. Submit complete ms as text in the body of an e-mail.

$ $ CABLING BUSINESS MAGAZINE

Cabling Publications, Inc., 12035 Shiloh Rd., Suite 350, Dallas TX 75228. (214)328-1717. Fax: (214)319-6077. E-mail: margaret@cablingbusiness.com. Website: www.cablingbusiness.com. **30% freelance written**. Monthly magazine covering telecommunications, cable manufacturing, volP, wireless, broadband, structured cabling. "Each month, *Cabling Business Magazine* offers readers a broad mix of information relating to premises cabling, including industry news, standards updates, design and installation tutorials, and case studies highlighting successes achieved with the industry's latest technologies. Our editors are experts in the field and can pinpoint the timely material most relevant to the cabling professional. With input and contributions from the top minds in the industry, the editorial staff brings readers real-world information they can use. Online access since 2007." Estab. 1991. Circ. 15,000. Byline given. Pays on publication. No kill fee. Publishes ms an average of 1-2 months after acceptance. Buys second serial (reprint) rights. Editorial lead time 2 months. Submit seasonal material 2 months in advance. Accepts queries by e-mail. Accepts simultaneous submissions. Responds in 1 week to queries and to mss. Sample copy available online. Guidelines by email.
Nonfiction Contact: Margaret Patterson. Needs how-to, interview, new product, opinion, personal experience, technical. No vendor/product specific infomercials. **Buys 6 mss/yr. mss/year.** Query. Length: 1,500-2,500 words. **Pays $400 max. for assigned articles. Pays $400 max. for unsolicited articles.**
Photos Contact: Margaret Patterson. State availability Captions, identification of subjects, model releases required. Reviews GIF/JPEG files. Offers no additional payment for photos accepted with ms. Buys all rights.
Columns/Departments Contact: Margaret Patterson. New Products (latest technology from industry), 350 words; Testing Equipment Q&A (work with specific companies on testing information), Cable Q&A (work with specific companies on cable questions from around the industry), 800 words; Terminology/Calendar, 200 words. Query. **Pays $-$400.**
Tips "Contact Margaret@cablingbusiness.com with a query-list of specific items covered in proposed article and how it relates to our industry-also know what our magazine covers and be sure to check out the editorial calendar on the website."

$ $ DIGITAL OUTPUT

The Only Magazine Dedicated to Capture, Creation, Output and Finishing, The Doyle Group, 5150 Palm Valley Rd., Suite 103, Ponte Vedra Beach FL 32082. (904)285-6020. Fax: (904)285-9944. E-mail: cmason@digitaloutput.net. Website: www.digitaloutput.net. **70% freelance written**. Monthly magazine covering electronic prepress, desktop publishing, and digital imaging, with articles ranging from digital capture and design to electronic prepress and digital printing. *Digital Output* is a national business publication for electronic publishers and digital imagers, providing monthly articles which examine the latest technologies and digital methods and discuss how to profit from them. Our readers include service bureaus, prepress and reprographic houses, designers, commercial printers, wide-format printers, ad agencies, corporate communications, sign shops, and others. Estab. 1994. Circ. 30,000. Byline given. Pays on publication. Offers 10-20% kill fee. Publishes ms an average of 2 months after acceptance. Buys one-time rights including electronic rights for archival posting. Editorial lead time 3 months. Submit seasonal material 3 months in advance. Accepts queries by mail, e-mail. Responds in 3 weeks to queries. Responds in 1 month to mss. Sample copy for $4.50 or online.

Nonfiction Needs how-to, interview, technical, case studies. **Buys 36 mss/year.** Query with published clips or hyperlinks to posted clips. Length: 1,500-4,000 words. **Pays $250-600.**

Photos Send photos

Tips Our readers are graphic arts professionals. The freelance writers we use are deeply immersed in the technology of commercial printing, desktop publishing, digital imaging, color management, PDF workflow, inkjet printing, and similar topics.

$ $ ELECTRONIC SERVICING & TECHNOLOGY

The Professional Magazine for Electronics and Computer Servicing, P.O. Box 12487, Overland Park KS 66282-2487. (913)492-4857. Fax: (913)492-4857. E-mail: cpersedit@aol.com. **80% freelance written**. Monthly magazine for service technicians, field service personnel, and avid servicing enthusiasts, who service audio, video, and computer equipment. Estab. 1950. Circ. 15,000. Byline given. Pays on publication. No kill fee. Publishes ms an average of 4 months after acceptance. Buys one-time rights. Editorial lead time 2 months. Accepts queries by mail, e-mail, fax, phone. Accepts simultaneous submissions. Responds in 1 month to queries. Responds in 2 months to mss. Sample copy free. Guidelines free.

Nonfiction Needs book excerpts, how-to, service consumer electronics, new product, technical. **Buys 40 mss/year.** Query or send complete ms. **Pays $50/page.**

Reprints Send typed manuscript with rights for sale noted and information about when and where the material previously appeared.

Photos Send photos Offers no additional payment for photos accepted with ms. Buys one time rights.

Columns/Departments Business Corner (business tips); Computer Corner (computer servicing tips); Video Corner (understanding/servicing TV and video), all 1,000-2,000 words. 30 Query, or send complete ms. **Pays $100-300.**

Tips Writers should have a strong background in electronics, especially consumer electronics servicing. Understand the information needs of consumer electronics service technicians, and be able to write articles that address specific areas of those needs.

HOME THEATER

Primedia Enthusiast Group, 6420 Wilshire Blvd., Los Angeles CA 90048-5502. (323)782-2000. Fax: (323)782-2080. E-mail: htletters@primedia.com. Website: www.hometheatermag.com. Monthly magazine covering audio, video, high-end components, and movies and music. Covers the home theater lifestyle. Estab. 1995. Circ. 109,422. No kill fee. Accepts queries by e-mail. Sample copy for $4.95.

Nonfiction Query with published clips.

Columns/Departments Query with published clips.

RFID PRODUCT NEWS

The Comprehensive News Source for RFID Users, manufacturers, and Vendors, ST Media Group, 19 Wilson Ave., West Chester PA 19382-4815. (610)296-3001. Fax: (610)296-1553. E-mail: eric.vanosten@stmediagroup.com. Website: www.rfidproductnews.com. **90% freelance written**. Weekly e-newsletter and Web site covering radio frequency identification (RFID). "Try to make articles accessible to any reader, regardless of radio frequency knowledge." Estab. 2004. Circ. 9,000. Byline given. Does not pay, but invites people to write for us to spread radio frequency knowledge. No kill fee. Publishes ms an average of 3 months after acceptance. Editorial lead time varies Accepts queries by e-mail. Accepts simultaneous submissions. Responds in month to mss. Sample copy available online. Guidelines by e-mail.

Nonfiction Needs how-to, new product, opinion, personal experience, photo feature, technical, legal, case studies. Query. Length: 600-1,800 words.

Photos State availability Captions, identification of subjects required. Reviews GIF/JPEG files. negotiable

Columns/Departments News Desk (RFID news); New Products (New RFID products), 300 words; Ask the Expert (expert Q&A); The Legal Side (RFID legal topics), 1,200 words. Query.

$ $ SQL SERVER MAGAZINE

Penton Media, 221 E. 29th St., Loveland CO 80538. (970)663-4700. Fax: (970)667-2321. E-mail: articles@sqlmag.com. Website: www.sqlmag.com. **35% freelance written**. Monthly magazine covering Microsoft SQL Server. *SQL Server Magazine* is the only magazine completely devoted to helping developers and DBAs master new and emerging SQL Server technologies and issues. It provides practical advice and lots of code examples for SQL Server developers and administrators, and includes how-to articles, tips, tricks, and programming techniques offered by SQL Server experts. Estab. 1999. Circ. 20,000. Byline given. Pays on publication. Offers $100 kill fee. Publishes ms an average of 6 months after acceptance. Buys all rights. Editorial lead time 4+ months. Accepts queries by mail, e-mail. Responds in 6 weeks to queries. Responds

in 2-3 months to mss. Sample copy available online. Guidelines available online.
Nonfiction Needs how-to, technical, SQL Server administration and programming. Nothing promoting third-party products or companies. **Buys 25-35 mss/year.** Send complete ms. Length: 1,800-3,000 words. **Pays $200 for feature articles; $500 for Focus articles.**
Columns/Departments Contact: R2R Editor. Send all column/department submissions to r2r@sqlmag.com. Reader to Reader (helpful SQL Server hints and tips from readers), 200-400 words. 6-12 Send complete ms. **Pays $50**
Tips Read back issues and make sure that your proposed article doesn't overlap previous coverage. When proposing articles, state specifically how your article would contain new information compared to previously published information, and what benefit your information would be to *SQL Server Magazine*'s readership.

TECH TRADER MAGAZINE

The Intermedia Group, Ltd., Tech Trader Magazine, Unit 39, 100 Harris St., Pyrmont NSW 2009 Australia. (61)(2)9660-2113. Fax: (61)(2)9660-4419. E-mail: kymberly@intermedia.com.au. Website: www.intermedia.com.au. Monthly magazine covering consumer electronics industry. "Tech Trader Magazine delivers the latest news, opinion, features, product reviews, overseas reports, and new products together in one lively publication." Circ. 9,000.
Nonfiction Needs general interest, new product. Query.

ENERGY & UTILITIES

PIPELINE & GAS JOURNAL

Oildom Publishing, 1160 Dairy Ashford, Suite 610, Houston TX 77079. (281)558-6930. Fax: (281)558-7029. E-mail: rtubb@oildom.com. Website: www.oildompublishing.com. Rita Tubb, man. ed. **Contact:** Jeff Share, editor. **15%**. Covering pipeline operations worldwide. zEdited for personnel engaged in energy pipeline design construction operations, as well as marketing, storage, supply, risk management and regulatory affairs, natural gas transmission and distribution companies. " Estab. 1859. Circ. 26,800. Yes Pays on publication. 2 months All rights purchased. 1 month Accepts queries by e-mail at jshare@oildom.com. 2-3 weeks on queries; 1-2 months on mss Free Online at http://pgjonline.com
Nonfiction Contact: Editor. Needs interview, new product, travel, case studies. Query. 2,000-3,000/words
Columns/Departments Contact: Sr. Ed.: lbullion@oildom.com. What's New: Product type items, 100/words; New Products: Product items, 50-100/words; Business New: Personnel Change, 25-35/words; Company New: 35-50/words

$ $ ALTERNATIVE ENERGY RETAILER

Zackin Publications, Inc., P.O. Box 2180, Waterbury CT 06722. (800)325-6745. Fax: (203)262-4680. E-mail: griffin@aer-online.com. Website: www.aer-online.com. **5% freelance written. Prefers to work with published/established writers.** Monthly magazine on selling home hearth products—chiefly solid fuel and gas-burning appliances. We seek detailed how-to tips for retailers to improve business. Most freelance material purchased is about retailers and how they succeed. Estab. 1980. Circ. 10,000. Pays on publication. No kill fee. Publishes ms an average of 2 months after acceptance. Buys first North American serial rights. Submit seasonal material 4 months in advance. Accepts queries by mail, e-mail, fax, phone. Responds in 2 weeks to queries. Sample copy for sae with 9x12 envelope and 4 First-Class stamps. Guidelines available online.
Nonfiction Needs how-to, improve retail profits and business know-how, interview, of successful retailers in this field. No general business articles not adapted to this industry. **Buys 10 mss/year.** Query. Length: 1,000 words. **Pays $200.**
Photos State availability Identification of subjects required. Reviews color transparencies. Pays $25-125 maximum for 5x7 b&w prints. Buys one time rights.
Tips A freelancer can best break into our publication with features about readers (retailers). Stick to details about what has made this person a success.

AUSTRALASIAN POWER TRANSMISSION & DISTRIBUTION

P.O. Box 1195, Kenmore QLD 4069 Australia. (61)(7)3374-2877. Fax: (61)(7)3374-2899. E-mail: roland@powertrans.com.au. Website: www.powertrans.com.au. Bimonthly magazine for the electricity supply industries of Australia and New Zealand. Estab. 1996. Circ. 8,000.
Nonfiction Needs technical. Query.

$ $ ELECTRICAL APPARATUS

The Magazine of Electromechanical & Electronic Application & Maintenance, Barks Publications, Inc., 400 N. Michigan Ave., Chicago IL 60611-4104. (312)321-9440. Fax: (312)321-1288. "Monthly magazine for persons

working in electrical and electronic maintenance, in industrial plants and service and sales centers, who install and service electric motors, transformers, generators, controls, and related equipment.". Estab. 1967. Circ. 16,000. Byline given. Pays on publication. No kill fee. Publishes ms an average of 1 month after acceptance. Buys all rights unless other arrangements made. Accepts queries by mail, fax. Responds in 1 week to queries. Responds in 2 weeks to mss.
Nonfiction Needs technical. Length: 1,500-2,500 words. **Pays $250-500 for assigned articles.**
Tips "All feature articles are assigned to staff and contributing editors and correspondents. Professionals interested in appointments as contributing editors and correspondents should submit resume and article outlines, including illustration suggestions. Writers should be competent with a camera, which should be described in resume. Technical expertise is absolutely necessary, preferably an E.E. degree, or practical experience. We are also book publishers and some of the material in *EA* is now in book form, bringing the authors royalties. Also publishes an annual directory, subtitled *ElectroMechanical Bench Reference.*"

$ $ ELECTRICAL BUSINESS

CLB Media, Inc., 240 Edward St., Aurora ON L4G 3S9 Canada. (905)727-0077. Fax: (905)727-0017. E-mail: acapkun@clbmedia.ca. Website: www.ebmag.com. **35% freelance written**. Tabloid published 10 times/year covering the Canadian electrical industry. *Electrical Business* targets electrical contractors and electricians. It provides practical information readers can use right away in their work and for running their business and assets. Estab. 1964. Circ. 18,097. Byline given. Pays on acceptance. Offers 50% kill fee. Publishes ms an average of 1-2 months after acceptance. Buys simultaneous rights. Editorial lead time 3 months. Submit seasonal material 6 months in advance. Accepts queries by e-mail, phone. Accepts simultaneous submissions. Responds in 1 month to queries. Responds in 1 month to mss. Sample copy available online. Guidelines free.
Nonfiction Needs how-to, technical. Summer Blockbuster issue (June/July); Special Homebuilders' issue (November/December). **Buys 15 mss/year.** Query. Length: 800-1,200 words. **Pays 40¢/word.** Sometimes pays expenses of writers on assignment.
Photos State availability Captions, identification of subjects, model releases required. Reviews GIF/JPEG files. Negotiates payment individually. Buys simultaneous rights.
Columns/Departments Atlantic Focus (stories from Atlantic Canada); Western Focus (stories from Western Canada, including Manitoba); Trucks for the Trade (articles pertaining to the vehicles used by electrical contractors); Tools for the Trade (articles pertaining to tools used by contractors); all 800 words. 6 Query. **Pays 40¢/word.**
Tips Call me, and we'll talk about what I need, and how you can provide it. Stories must have Canadian content.

$ $ PUBLIC POWER

Dept. WM, 2301 M St. NW, Washington DC 20037-1484. (202)467-2948. Fax: (202)467-2910. E-mail: jlabella@appanet.org. Website: www.appanet.org. **60% freelance written. Prefers to work with published/established writers.** Bimonthly trade journal. Estab. 1942. Byline given. Pays on acceptance. No kill fee. Publishes ms an average of 3 months after acceptance. Accepts queries by mail, e-mail, fax. Responds in 6 months to queries. Sample copy and writer's guidelines free
Nonfiction Features on municipal and other local publicly owned electric utilities. **Pays $600 and up.**
Photos Reviews electronic photos (minimum 300 dpi at reproduction size), transparencies, slides, and prints.
Tips We look for writers who are familiar with energy policy issues.

$ $ $ TEXAS CO-OP POWER

Texas Electric Cooperatives, Inc., 2550 S. IH-35, Austin TX 78704. (512)454-0311. Website: www.texascooppower.com. **50% freelance written**. Monthly magazine covering rural and suburban Texas life, people, and places. *Texas Co-op Power* provides 1 million households and businesses educational and technical information about electric cooperatives in a high-quality and entertaining format to promote the general welfare of cooperatives, their member-owners, and the areas in which they serve. Estab. 1948. Circ. 1 million. Byline given. after any necessary rewrites. No kill fee. Publishes ms an average of 6 months after acceptance. Buys first rights, buys electronic rights. Editorial lead time 4-5 months. Submit seasonal material 6 months in advance. Accepts queries by mail, e-mail, fax. Accepts simultaneous submissions. Responds in 1 month to queries. Responds in 3 months to mss. Sample copy available online. Guidelines for #10 sase.
Nonfiction Needs general interest, historical, interview, photo feature, travel. **Buys 30 mss/year.** Query with published clips. Length: 800-1,200 words. **Pays $400-1,000.** Sometimes pays expenses of writers on assignment.
Photos State availability Identification of subjects, model releases required. Reviews transparencies, prints. Negotiates payment individually. Buys one time rights.
Tips We're looking for Texas-related, rural-based articles, often first-person, always lively and interesting.

ENGINEERING & TECHNOLOGY

$ $ $ CABLING NETWORKING SYSTEMS

12 Concorde Place, Suite 800, North York ON M3C 4J2 Canada. (416)510-6752. Fax: (416)510-5134. E-mail: pbarker@cnsmagazine.com. Website: www.cablingsystems.com. **50% freelance written**. Magazine published 8 times/year covering structured cabling/telecommunications industry. *Cabling Systems* is written for engineers, designers, contractors, and end users who design, specify, purchase, install, test and maintain structured cabling and telecommunications products and systems. Estab. 1998. Circ. 11,000. Byline given. Pays on publication. No kill fee. Publishes ms an average of 1 month after acceptance. Buys all rights. Editorial lead time 3 months. Submit seasonal material 1 month in advance. Accepts queries by mail, e-mail, phone. Accepts simultaneous submissions. Sample copy available online. Guidelines free.

Nonfiction Needs technical, case studies, features. No reprints or previously written articles. All articles are assigned by editor based on query or need of publication. **Buys 12 mss/year.** Query with published clips. Length: 1,500-2,500 words. **Pays 40-50¢/word.** Sometimes pays expenses of writers on assignment.

Photos State availability Captions, identification of subjects required. Reviews contact sheets, prints. Negotiates payment individually.

Columns/Departments Focus on Engineering/Design; Focus on Installation; Focus on Maintenance/Testing, all 1,500 words. 7 Query with published clips. **Pays 40-50¢/word.**

Tips Visit our website to see back issues, and visit links on our website for background.

$ $ $ CANADIAN CONSULTING ENGINEER

Business Information Group, 12 Condorde Place, Suite 800, Toronto ON M3C 4J2 Canada. (416)510-5119. Fax: (416)510-5134. E-mail: bparsons@ccemag.com. Website: www.canadianconsultingengineer.com. **Contact:** Bronwen Parsons, editor. **20%% freelance written**. Bimonthly magazine covering consulting engineering in private practice. Estab. 1958. Circ. 8,900. Byline given depending on length of story Pays on publication. Offers 50% kill fee. Publishes ms an average of 4 months after acceptance. Buys first North American serial rights. Editorial lead time 6 months. Responds in 3 months to mss. Sample copy free.

- Canadian content only. Impartial editorial required.

Nonfiction Needs historical, new product, technical, engineering/construction projects, environmental/construction issues. **Buys 8-10 mss/year.** Length: 300-1,500 words. **Pays $200-1,000 (Canadian).** Sometimes pays expenses of writers on assignment.

Photos State availability Negotiates payment individually. Buys one time rights.

Columns/Departments Export (selling consulting engineering services abroad); Management (managing consulting engineering businesses); On-Line (trends in CAD systems); Employment; Business; Construction and Environmental Law (Canada), all 800 words. 4 Query with published clips. **Pays $250-400.**

THE CHIEF MAGAZINE

First Charlton Communications, Level 8, 122 Arthur St., North Sydney NSW 2060 Australia. (61)(2)9955-6299. Fax: (61)(2)9957-1512. E-mail: pctc@charlton.com.au. Website: www.charlton.com.au. Monthly magazine covering new technology and trends in the IT industry, and profiles of leading Australian CEOs. *The Chief* aims to inform chief executives as to how technology will affect their company, and help them wade through the often confusing jargon which surrounds technology.

Nonfiction Needs interview, new product, technical. Query.

$ $ COMPOSITES MANUFACTURING MAGAZINE

The Official Publication of the American Composites Manufacturers Association, (formerly *Composites Fabrication Magazine*), American Composites Manufacturers Association, 1010 N. Glebe Rd., Suite 450, Arlington VA 22201. (703)525-0511. Fax: (703)525-0743. E-mail: arusnak@acmanet.org. Website: www.cfmagazine.org. Monthly magazine covering any industry that uses reinforced composites: marine, aerospace, infrastructure, automotive, transportation, corrosion, architecture, tub and shower, sports, and recreation. Primarily, we publish educational pieces, the how-to of the shop environment. We also publish marketing, business trends, and economic forecasts relevant to the composites industry. Estab. 1979. Circ. 12,000. Byline given. Pays on acceptance. No kill fee. Publishes ms an average of 2-3 months after acceptance. Buys all rights. Editorial lead time 2 months. Accepts queries by e-mail. Accepts previously published material. Accepts simultaneous submissions. Responds in 1 week to queries. Responds in 1 month to mss. Sample copy free. Guidelines by email.

Nonfiction Needs how-to, composites manufacturing, new product, technical, marketing, related business trends and forecasts. Each January we publish a World Market Report where we cover all niche markets and all geographic areas relevant to the composites industry. Freelance material will be considered strongly for this issue. No need to query company or personal profiles unless there is an extremely unique or novel angle. **Buys 5-10 mss/year.** Query. Length: 1,500-4,000 words. **Pays 20-40¢/word (negotiable).** Sometimes pays expenses of writers on assignment.

Columns/Departments We publish columns on HR, relevant government legislation, industry lessons learned, regulatory affairs, and technology. Average word length for columns is 500 words. We would entertain any new column idea that hits hard on industry matters. Query. **Pays $300-350.**

Tips The best way to break into the magazine is to empathize with the entrepreneurial and technical background of readership, and come up with an exclusive, original, creative story idea. We pride ourselves on not looking or acting like any other trade publication (composites industry or otherwise). Our editor is very open to suggestions, but they must be unique. Don't waste his time with canned articles dressed up to look exclusive. This is the best way to get on the 'immediate rejection list.'

DESIGN NEWS

Reed Business Information, 225 Wyman St., Waltham MA 02451. (781)734-8188. Fax: (781)290-3188. E-mail: kfield@reedbusiness.com. Website: www.designnews.com. Magazine published 18 times/year dedicated to reporting on the latest technology that OEM design engineers can use in their jobs. Circ. 170,000. No kill fee. Editorial lead time 4-6 months.

ECN ELECTRONIC COMPONENT NEWS

Reed Business Information, 100 Enterprise Dr., Suite 600, Box 912, Rockaway NJ 07866. (973)292-7037. Fax: (973)292-0783. E-mail: akalnoskas@reedbusiness.com. Website: www.ecnmag.com. Monthly magazine. Provides design engineers and engineering management in electronics OEM with a monthly update on new products and literature. Circ. 131,052. No kill fee. Editorial lead time 2 months.

EMBEDDED TECHNOLOGY

Tech Briefs Media Group, 1466 Broadway, Ste. 910, New York NY 10036. (212)490-3999. E-mail: bruce@abpi.net. Website: www.techbriefsmediagroup.com. **100% freelance written**. Bimonthly magazine covering embedded, industrial, and COTS computers. *Embedded Technology*'s audience consists of computer and electronics engineers, designers, scientists, technicians, and systems integrators, and since ET is published in conjunction with NASA Tech Briefs, we probably have a few rocket scientists in the mix as well. Articles tend to be highly technical in nature and cover everything from the latest ASICs and FPGAs to single board computers and data transfer protocols. Estab. 2005. Circ. 71,000. Byline given. No monetary payment. No kill fee. Publishes ms an average of 3-6 months after acceptance. Buys all rights. Editorial lead time 3-6 months. Accepts queries by e-mail. Sample copy available online. Guidelines available.

Nonfiction Contact: Bruce A. Bennett. Needs technical. We don't want anything non-technical. Query. Length: 1,200-1,500 words.

Tips Our authors tend to work in the embedded computing industry and have solid academic and professional credentials. They're writing for professional and peer recognition, not monetary reward.

$ $ INTERFACE TECH NEWS

Northern New England's Technology Newspaper, Millyard Communications, Inc., 670 N. Commercial St., Suite 110, Manchester NH 03101. (603)626-6354. Fax: (603)626-6359. E-mail: msaturley@millyardcommunications.com. Website: www.interfacetechnews.com. **85% freelance written**. Monthly newspaper covering people, companies and cutting edge technology in Northern New England. Stories must have a local, northern New England angle. Who are the people shaping tomorrow's tech industry? Why should you care? Estab. 1997. Circ. 11,000. Byline given. Pays on publication. Offers 25% kill fee. Publishes ms an average of 2-3 months after acceptance. Buys first North American serial rights. Editorial lead time 3 months. Submit seasonal material 3 months in advance. Accepts queries by mail, e-mail. Accepts previously published material. Responds in 2 weeks to queries. Sample copy free. Guidelines free.

Nonfiction Needs how-to, interview, new product, opinion, technical, case studies. Does not want stories about companies, people or products not based in northern New England. **Buys 60 mss/year.** Query with published clips. Length: 600-1,500 words. **Pays $150-300.** Sometimes pays expenses of writers on assignment.

Photos Contact: Contact Greg Duval, creative director. Send photos Identification of subjects required. Reviews GIF/JPEG files. Offers $25-50/photo. Buys one time rights.

Columns/Departments Industry Watch (exploring tech advancements in specific industries), 600-800 words; From the Bench (case law, legislation, lobbyist activity), 600-800 words; Tech Download (explanation of bleeding-edge tech), 800 words; Interface Case Study (in-depth look at a problem solved by technology), 800-900 words. 50 Query with published clips. **Pays $200-250.**

Tips We usually start off new writers with a shorter piece, around 600 words. If they work out, we start assigning longer stories. Experience in journalism and a working knowledge of tech required.

LASER FOCUS WORLD MAGAZINE

PennWell, 98 Spit Brook Rd., Nashua NH 03062-2801. (603)891-0123. Fax: (603)891-0574. Website: www.laserfocusworld.com. **1% freelance written**. "Monthly magazine for physicists, scientists, and engineers involved in the research and development, design, manufacturing, and applications of lasers, laser systems, and all other segments of optoelectronic technologies.". Estab. 1968. Circ. 66,000. Byline given unless anonymity requested. No kill fee. Publishes ms an average of 6 months after acceptance. Buys all rights.

Accepts queries by mail, e-mail, fax, phone. Responds in 1 month to queries Sample copy free Guidelines available online

- Check online guidelines for specific contacts.

Nonfiction "Lasers, laser systems, fiberoptics, optics, detectors, sensors, imaging, and other optoelectronic materials, components, instrumentation, and systems. Each article should serve our reader's need by either stimulating ideas, increasing technical competence, or improving design capabilities in the following areas: natural light and radiation sources, artificial light and radiation sources, light modulators, optical materials and components, image detectors, energy detectors, information displays, image processing, information storage and processing, subsystem and system testing, support equipment, and other related areas." No flighty prose, material not written for our readership, or irrelevant material. Query first with a clear statement and outline of why the article would be important to our readers.

Photos Drawings: Rough drawings accepted and finished by staff technical illustrator. Send photos Reviews 4x5 color transparencies, 8x10 b&w glossies.

Tips "The writer has a better chance of breaking in at our publication with short articles because shorter articles are easier to schedule, but they must address more carefully our requirements for technical coverage. Most of our submitted materials come from technical experts in the areas we cover. The most frequent mistake made by writers in completing articles for us is that the articles are too commercial, i.e., emphasize a given product or technology from one company. Also, articles are not the right technical depth, too thin, or too scientific."

$ $ LD+A

Lighting Design & Application, Illuminating Engineering Society of North America, 120 Wall St., 17th Floor, New York NY 10005. (212)248-5000. Fax: (212)248-5017. E-mail: ptarricone@iesna.org. Website: www.iesna.org. **10% freelance written**. Monthly magazine. *LD+A* is geared to professionals in lighting design and the lighting field in architecture, retail, entertainment, etc. Estab. 1971. Circ. 10,000. Byline given. Pays on acceptance. No kill fee. Publishes ms an average of 4 months after acceptance. Buys all rights. Editorial lead time 2 months. Submit seasonal material 4 months in advance. Accepts queries by mail, e-mail, fax, phone. Accepts simultaneous submissions. Responds in 2 weeks to queries. Sample copy free.

Nonfiction Every year we have entertainment, outdoor, retail and arts, and exhibits issues. Needs historical, how-to, opinion, personal experience, photo feature, technical. No articles blatantly promoting a product, company, or individual. **Buys 6-10 mss/year.** Query. Length: 1,500-2,200 words.

Photos Send photos Captions required. Reviews JPEG/TIFF files. Offers no additional payment for photos accepted with ms.

Columns/Departments Essay by Invitation (industry trends), 1,200 words. Query. **Does not pay for columns.**

Tips Most of our features detail the ins and outs of a specific lighting project. From museums to stadiums and highways, *LD+A* gives its readers an in-depth look at how the designer(s) reached their goals.

$ $ MANUFACTURING & TECHNOLOGY EJOURNAL

The Manufacturers Group Inc., P.O. Box 4310, Lexington KY 40544. Fax: (859)223-6709. E-mail: editor@industrysearch.com. Website: www.mfr.tech.com. **40% freelance written**. Weekly website Manufacturing & technology. Editorial targets middle and upper management—Presidents, Plant Managers, Engineering, Purchasing. Editorial includes features on operations and management, new plants, acquisitions, expansions, new products. Estab. 1976 (print). Circ. 10,000 plus weekly (email) 5,000 weekly online. Byline given. 30 days followiong publication. Offers 25% kill fee. Publishes ms an average of 2 weeks after acceptance. Buys first North American serial rights. Editorial lead time 2 weeks. Submit seasonal material 2 weeks in advance. Sample copy available online. Guidelines by email.

Nonfiction Needs new product, opinion, technical, New plants, expansions, acquisitions. Most articles are assignments. We have assigned features on timely issues relating to economics, environmental, manufacturing trends, employment. Open to feature suggestions by outline only. Marketing, opinion. General interest, inspirational, personal, travel, book excerpts. Length: 750-1,200 words. **Pays $0.20/word published.**

Columns/Departments New Plants (Manufacturing, Technology), Acquisitions (Manufacturing, Technology), New Technology, Expansions (Manufacturing, Technology). Query. **Pays $-$0.20/word.**

$ $ $ MINNESOTA TECHNOLOGY

Inside Technology and Manufacturing Business, Minnesota Technology, Inc., 111 Third Ave. S., Minneapolis MN 55401. (612)373-2900. Fax: (612)373-2901. E-mail: editor@mntech.org. Website: mntechnologymag.com. **90% freelance written**. Magazine published 5 times/year. *Minnesota Technology* is read 5 times a year by owners and top management of Minnesota's technology and manufacturing companies. The magazine covers technology trends and issues, global trade, management techniques, and finance. We profile new and growing companies, new products, and the innovators and entrepreneurs of Minnesota's technology sector. Estab. 1991. Circ. 16,000. Byline given. Pays on publication. Offers 10% kill fee. Publishes ms an average of 3 months after acceptance. Buys first North American serial rights for print and Web version of magazine. Editorial lead time 1 month. Submit seasonal material 1 year in advance. Accepts queries by mail, e-mail.

Guidelines available online.

Nonfiction Needs general interest, how-to, interview. **Buys 60 mss/year.** Query with published clips. **Pays $150-1,000.**

Columns/Departments Feature Well (Q&A format, provocative ideas from Minnesota business and industry leaders), 2,000 words; Up Front (mini profiles, anecdotal news items), 250-500 words. Query with published clips.

$ $ MINORITY ENGINEER

An Equal Opportunity Career Publication for Professional and Graduating Minority Engineers, Equal Opportunity Publications, Inc., 445 Broad Hollow Rd., Suite 425, Melville NY 11747. (631)421-9421. Fax: (516)421-0359. E-mail: jschneider@eop.com. Website: www.eop.com. **60% freelance written. Prefers to work with published/established writers.** Triannual magazine covering career guidance for minority engineering students and minority professional engineers. Job information. Estab. 1969. Circ. 15,000. Byline given. Pays on publication. No kill fee. Publishes ms an average of 3 months after acceptance. Buys first North American serial rights. Editorial lead time 3 months. Accepts queries by mail, e-mail, fax, phone. Accepts simultaneous submissions. Responds in 2 weeks to queries. Responds in 2 months to mss. Sample copy and writer's guidelines for 9x12 SAE with 5 first-class stamps Guidelines free.

Nonfiction We're interested in articles dealing with career guidance and job opportunities for minority engineers. Needs book excerpts, general interest, on specific minority engineering concerns, how-to, land a job, keep a job, etc., interview, minority engineer role models, opinion, problems of ethnic minorities, personal experience, student and career experiences, technical, on career fields offering opportunities for minority engineers, articles on job search techniques, role models. No general information. Query. Length: 1,500-2,500 words. **Pays $350 for assigned articles.** Sometimes pays expenses of writers on assignment.

Reprints Send typed manuscript with rights for sale noted and information about when and where the material previously appeared. Pays 100% of amount paid for an original article.

Photos State availability

Tips Articles should focus on career guidance, role model and industry prospects for minority engineers. Prefer articles related to careers, not politically or socially sensitive.

PHOTONICS TECH BRIEFS

Tech Briefs Media Group, 1466 Broadway, Ste. 910, New York NY 10036. (212)490-3999. E-mail: bruce@abpi.net. Website: www.techbriefsmediagroup.com. **100% freelance written**. 8 times a year magazine covering lasers, optics, and photonic systems. "*Photonics Tech Briefs*' audience consists of engineers, designers, scientists, and technicians working in all aspects of the laser, optics, and photonics industries. Since we're published in conjunction with NASA Tech Briefs, we probably have a few honest-to-goodness rocket scientists in the mix as well. Articles tend to be highly technical in nature and cover everything from lasers, fiber optics and infrared technology to biophotonics, photovoltaics, and digital imaging systems." Circ. 102,698. Byline given. No monetary payment. No kill fee. Publishes ms an average of 3-6 months after acceptance. Buys all rights. Editorial lead time 3-6 months. Accepts queries by e-mail. Sample copy available online. Guidelines available.

Nonfiction Contact: Bruce A. Bennett. Needs technical. We don't want anything non-technical. **Buys 0 mss/year.** Query without published clips or send complete ms. Length: 1,200-1,500 words.

Tips "Our authors tend to work in the photonics/optics industry and have solid academic and professional credentials. They're writing for professional and peer recognition, not monetary reward."

PROFESSIONAL SURVEYOR MAGAZINE

Reed Business Geo, Inc., 100 Tuscanny Drive, Frederick MD 21702-5958. (301)682-6101. Fax: (301)682-6105. E-mail: psm@gitcamerica.com. Website: www.profsurv.com. **50% freelance written**. Monthly magazine Surveying. This publication covers all facets of surveying and related activities such as satellite positioning (GPS), laser scanning, remote sensing, photogrammetry and mapping. The audience is mainly surveyors. Estab. 1982. Circ. 40,000. Byline given. Pays on publication. No kill fee. Publishes ms an average of 2 months after acceptance. Buys first North American serial rights, buys second serial (reprint) rights. Editorial lead time 3 months. Accepts queries by e-mail. Responds in 2 weeks to queries. Responds in 1 month to mss. Sample copy available online.

Nonfiction Needs book excerpts, general interest, historical, how-to, humor, interview, new product, opinion, personal experience, technical, case histories. Aerial Mapping Supplement. Length: 1000-2000 words. **Pays $300-500 for assigned articles.** Sometimes pays expenses of writers on assignment.

Photos Contact: JoAnne Howland, art director. Send photos Captions required. Reviews GIF/JPEG files. offers no additional money for photos

Columns/Departments Contact: Shelly Cox, managing editor. Book Review, Aerial Perspective, 3D Scanning, Business Angle (all 1,250 words). 50 Query. **Pays $$200-$400.**

Tips For features, we're always looking for surveying-related case histories or discussions of new technology. We also seek contributors for our columns.

$ $ $ $ RAILWAY TRACK AND STRUCTURES

RT&S, Simmons-Boardman Publishing, 20 S. Clark St., Chicago IL 60603-1838. (312)683-0130. Fax: (312)683-0131. Website: www.rtands.com. **1% freelance written**. Monthly magazine covering railroad civil engineering. *RT&S* is a nuts-and-bolts journal to help railroad civil engineers do their jobs better. Estab. 1904. Circ. 9,500. Byline given. Pays on publication. Offers 90% kill fee. Publishes ms an average of 1 month after acceptance. Buys one-time rights. Editorial lead time 2 months. Submit seasonal material 3 months in advance. Accepts queries by mail, fax, phone. Accepts previously published material. Accepts simultaneous submissions. Responds in 1 month to queries. Responds in 1 month to mss. Sample copy available online.

Nonfiction Needs how-to, new product, technical. Does not want nostalgia or railroadiana. **Buys 1 mss/year.** Query. Length: 900-2,000 words. **Pays $500-1,000.** Sometimes pays expenses of writers on assignment.

Photos State availability Captions, identification of subjects, model releases required. Reviews GIF/JPEG files. Negotiates payment individually. Buys one time rights.

Tips "We prefer writers with a civil engineering background and railroad experience."

UTILITY PRODUCTS MAGAZINE

Pennwell Publishing, 114 Trade Center Dr., Suite A, Birmingham AL 35244. (888)985-9229, ext. 222. E-mail: kellies@pennwell.com. Website: www.utilityproducts.com. **95% freelance written**. Monthly magazine covering electric, TELCO, CATV utilities. "Non-commercial slant. We like to hear about problems the utility industry is facing and what new technologies, tools, etc. are available to solve these problems. Case studies and bylined articles are both accepted. The audience ranges from management to the people out in the field." Estab. 1997. Circ. 45,000. Byline given. non-paid only. No kill fee. Publishes ms an average of 1-5 months after acceptance. Editorial lead time 2 months. Submit seasonal material 3 months in advance. Accepts queries by e-mail, phone. Responds in 1 week to queries. Responds in 1 month to mss. Sample copy free. Guidelines by email.

Nonfiction Needs new product, personal experience, photo feature, technical. Please see our 2009 editorial calendar. No commercial-based articles; advertorial. **Buys 0 mss/year.** Send complete ms. Length: 1,500-2,200 words.

Photos Contact: Kellie Sandrik, managing editor. Send photos Reviews GIF/JPEG files. Offers no additional payment for photos accepted with ms. Buys one time rights.

Tips "Read our magazine and look at our website—know our magazine and market. Query well in advance of the deadline. Query with several story pitches if possible."

$ $ WOMAN ENGINEER

An Equal Opportunity Career Publication for Graduating Women and Experienced Professionals, Equal Opportunity Publications, Inc., 445 Broad Hollow Rd., Suite 425, Melville NY 11747. (631)421-9421. Fax: (631)421-0359. E-mail: info@eop.com. Website: www.eop.com. **60% freelance written. Works with a small number of new/unpublished writers each year.** Triannual magazine aimed at advancing the careers of women engineering students and professional women engineers. Job information. Estab. 1968. Circ. 16,000. Byline given. Pays on publication. No kill fee. Publishes ms an average of 3 months after acceptance. Buys first North American serial rights. Editorial lead time 3 months. Accepts queries by mail, e-mail, fax, phone. Responds in 2 weeks to queries. Responds in 2 months to mss. Sample copy and writer's guidelines free Guidelines free.

Nonfiction Interested in articles dealing with career guidance and job opportunities for women engineers. Looking for manuscripts showing how to land an engineering position and advance professionally. We want features on job-search techniques, engineering disciplines offering career opportunities to women; companies with career advancement opportunities for women; problems facing women engineers and how to cope with such problems; and role-model profiles of successful women engineers, especially in major U.S. corporations. Needs how-to, find jobs, interview, personal experience. Query. Length: 1,500-2,500 words. **Pays $350 for assigned articles.**

Photos Captions, identification of subjects required. Reviews color slides but will accept b&w. Buys all rights.

Tips We are looking for first-person `As I See It, personal perspectives.' Gear it to our audience.

ENTERTAINMENT & THE ARTS

$ $ $ AMERICAN CINEMATOGRAPHER

The International Journal of Film & Digital Production Techniques, American Society of Cinematographers, 1782 N. Orange Dr., Hollywood CA 90028. (323)969-4333. Fax: (323)876-4973. E-mail: stephen@ascmag.com. Website: www.theasc.com. **90% freelance written**. Monthly magazine covering cinematography (motion picture, TV, music video, commercial). *American Cinematographer* is a trade publication devoted to the art and craft of cinematography. Our readers are predominantly film-industry professionals. Estab. 1919. Circ. 45,000. Byline given. Pays on publication. Offers 50% kill fee. Publishes ms an average of 2-3 months after acceptance. Buys all rights. Editorial lead time 2 months. Submit seasonal material 3 months in advance. Accepts queries by mail, e-mail, phone. Responds in 2 weeks to queries. Responds in 2 months to mss. Sample copy and writer's guidelines free.

Nonfiction Contact: Stephen Pizzello, editor. Needs interview, new product, technical. No reviews, opinion pieces. **Buys 20-25 mss/year.** Query with published clips. Length: 1,500-4,000 words. **Pays $600-1,200.** Sometimes pays expenses of writers on assignment.

Tips Familiarity with the technical side of film production and the ability to present that information in an articulate fashion to our audience are crucial.

$ $ AMERICAN THEATRE

Theatre Communications Group, 520 8th Ave., 24th Floor, New York NY 10018. (212)609-5900. E-mail: atminfo@tcg.org. Website: www.tcg.org. **60% freelance written**. Monthly magazine covering theatre. Our focus is American regional nonprofit theatre. Estab. 1982. Circ. 100,000. Byline given. Pays on publication. Editorial lead time 3 months. Submit seasonal material 3 months in advance. Accepts queries by mail, e-mail, fax, phone. Accepts previously published material. Accepts simultaneous submissions. Sample copy available online. Guidelines available online.

Nonfiction Needs book excerpts, essays, expose, general interest, historical, how-to, humor, inspirational, interview, opinion, personal experience, photo feature, travel. Training (January); International (May/June); Season Preview (October). Query with published clips. Length: 200-2,000 words. **Pays $150-200.**

Photos Contact: Contact Kitty Sven, art director. Send photos Captions required. Reviews JPEG files. Negotiates payment individually.

Tips American nonprofit regional theatre. Don't pitch music or film festivals. Must be about theatre.

BACK STAGE EAST

VNU Business Media, 770 Broadway, 4th Floor, New York NY 10003. (646)654-5500. Fax: (646)654-5743. E-mail: editorial@backstage.com. Website: www.backstage.com. Weekly magazine covering performing arts. *Back Stage* was created for actors, singers, dancers, and associated performing arts professionals. Circ. 33,000. No kill fee. Accepts queries by mail. Sample copy for $3.25; $2.95 for New York, New Jersey, Connecticut.

$ $ BOXOFFICE MAGAZINE

Media Enterprises LP, 155 S. El Molino Ave., Suite 100, Pasadena CA 91101. (626)396-0250. Fax: (626)396-0248. E-mail: editorial@boxoffice.com. Website: www.boxoffice.com. **15% freelance written**. Magazine about the motion picture industry for executives and managers working in the film business, including movie theater owners and operators, Hollywood studio personnel and leaders in allied industries. Estab. 1920. Circ. 6,000. Byline given. Pays on publication. No kill fee. Publishes ms an average of 3 months after acceptance. Buys first print and all electronic rights. Submit seasonal material 5 months in advance. Accepts queries by mail, e-mail, fax. Sample copy for $5 in US; $10 outside US.

Nonfiction We are a business news magazine about the motion picture industry in general and the theater industry in particular, and as such publish stories on business trends, developments, problems, and opportunities facing the industry. Almost any story will be considered, including corporate profiles, but we don't want gossip, film or celebrity coverage. Needs book excerpts, essays, interview, new product, personal experience, photo feature, technical, investigative all regarding movie theatre business. Query with published clips. Length: 800-2,500 words. **Pays 10¢/word.**

Photos State availability Captions required. Reviews prints, slides and JPEG files. Pays $10 per published image.

Tips Purchase a sample copy and read it. Then, write a clear, comprehensive outline of the proposed story, and enclose a resume and published clips to the managing editor.

$ $ CAMPUS ACTIVITIES

Cameo Publishing Group, P.O. Box 509, Prosperity SC 29127. (800)728-2950. Fax: (803)712-6703. E-mail: cameopublishing@earthlink.net. Website: www.campusactivitiesmagazine.com; www.cameopublishing.com; www.americanentertainmentmagazine.com. **75% freelance written**. Magazine published 8 times/year covering entertainment on college campuses. *Campus Activities* goes to entertainment buyers on every campus in the U.S. Features stories on artists (national and regional), speakers, and the programs at individual schools. Estab. 1991. Circ. 9,872. Byline given. Pays on publication. Offers kill fee. Offers 15% kill fee if accepted and not run. Publishes ms an average of 2 months after acceptance. Buys first rights, buys second serial (reprint) rights, buys electronic rights. Editorial lead time 2 months. Submit seasonal material 2 months in advance. Accepts queries by mail, e-mail, fax. Accepts simultaneous submissions. Responds in 1 month to queries. Responds in 2 months to mss. Sample copy for $3.50. Guidelines free.

Nonfiction Needs interview, photo feature. Accepts no unsolicited articles. **Buys 40 mss/year.** Query. Length: 1,400-3,000 words. **Pays 13¢/word.** Sometimes pays expenses of writers on assignment.

Photos State availability Identification of subjects required. Reviews contact sheets, negatives, 3x5 transparencies, 8x10 prints, electronic media at 300 dpi or higher. Negotiates payment individually. Buys

one time rights.
Tips Writers who have ideas, proposals, and special project requests should contact the publisher prior to any commitment to work on such a story. The publisher welcomes innovative and creative ideas for stories and works with writers on such proposals which have significant impact on our readers.

$ $ CREATE MAGAZINE

Fueling the Professional Creative Community, Brahn Communications, Inc., 5842 S. Semoran Blvd., Orlando FL 32822. Fax: (407)207-0405. E-mail: contribute@createmagazine.com. Website: www.createmagazine.com. **90% freelance written**. Quarterly magazine covering advertising, design, photography, printing, film & video, audio & music, animation, new media. *Create Magazine* is the largest trade publication serving the creative community. We are looking for experts in our respective industries who have writing experience. We are constantly looking for local writers in the 20 cities where we are published to get the latest scoop on the local creative community. Estab. 2000. Circ. 100,000. Byline given. Pays on publication. No kill fee. Publishes ms an average of 4 months after acceptance. Buys first North American serial rights, buys electronic rights. Editorial lead time 4-12 months. Submit seasonal material 5 months in advance. Accepts queries by e-mail, fax. Accepts simultaneous submissions. Responds in 4-6 weeks to queries. Responds in to mss. Sample copy for $7.95. Guidelines available online.
Nonfiction Needs how-to, use design/photo feature software, inspirational, new product, photo feature, technical. Does not want downtrodden musings and frustrations of particular industries. How poorly certain products perform and stream of consciousness writings are not accepted. Query with published clips. Length: 500-2,500 words. **Pays minimum $300 for assigned articles.**
Photos State availability Captions required. Reviews GIF/JPEG files. Offers no additional payment for photos accepted with ms
Tips Have plenty of contacts in these industries: advertising, new media, photography, film & video, design, printing, audio & music. Be located in one of our 20 markets (Central Florida, South Florida, Southern California, Atlanta, Chicago, New York—see website for all 20).

$ $ DANCE TEACHER

The Practical Magazine of Dance, McFadden Performing Arts Media, 110 William St., 23rd Floor, New York NY 10038. Fax: (646)459-4000. E-mail: jtu@dancemedia.com. Website: www.dance-teacher.com. **60% freelance written**. Monthly magazine. Our readers are professional dance educators, business persons, and related professionals in all forms of dance. Estab. 1979. Circ. 25,000. Byline given. Pays on publication. No kill fee. Publishes ms an average of 3 months after acceptance. Negotiates rights and permission to reprint on request. Submit seasonal material 6 months in advance. Accepts queries by mail, e-mail, fax, phone. Responds in 3 months to mss. Sample copy for sae with 9x12 envelope and 6 First-Class stamps. Guidelines available online.
Nonfiction Needs how-to, teach, health, business, legal. Summer Programs (January); Music & More (May); Costumes and Production Preview (November); College/Training Schools (December). No PR or puff pieces. All articles must be well researched. **Buys 50 mss/year.** Query. Length: 700-2,000 words. **Pays $100-300.**
Photos Send photos Reviews contact sheets, negatives, transparencies, prints. Limited photo budget.
Tips Read several issues—particularly seasonal. Stay within writer's guidelines.

$ $ DRAMATICS MAGAZINE

Educational Theatre Association, 2343 Auburn Ave., Cincinnati OH 45219-2815. (513)421-3900. Fax: (513)421-7077. E-mail: dcorathers@edta.org. Website: www.edta.org. **70% freelance written**. Monthly magazine for theater arts students, teachers, and others interested in theater arts education. *Dramatics* is designed to provide serious, committed young theater students and their teachers with the skills and knowledge they need to make better theater; to be a resource that will help high school juniors and seniors make an informed decision about whether to pursue a career in theater, and about how to do so; and to prepare high school students to be knowledgeable, appreciative audience members for the rest of their lives. Estab. 1929. Circ. 40,000. Byline given. Pays on acceptance. No kill fee. Publishes ms an average of 3 months after acceptance. Buys first North American serial rights. Submit seasonal material 3 months in advance. Accepts queries by mail, e-mail, fax. Accepts previously published material. Accepts simultaneous submissions. Responds in 3 months to queries. Responds in more than 3 months to mss. Sample copy for 9x12 SAE with 5 first-class stamps. Guidelines available online.
Nonfiction Needs how-to, technical theater, directing, acting, etc., humor, inspirational, interview, photo feature, technical. **Buys 30 mss/year.** Send complete ms. Length: 750-3,000 words. **Pays $50-400.** Sometimes pays expenses of writers on assignment.
Reprints Send tearsheet, photocopy or typed ms with rights for sale noted and information about when and where the material previously appeared. Pays up to 75% of amount paid for original.
Photos Query. Purchased with accompanying ms. Reviews high-res JPEG files on CD. Total price for ms usually includes payment for photos.
Fiction Drama (one-act and full-length plays). Prefers unpublished scripts that have been produced at least

once. No plays for children, Christmas plays, or plays written with no attention paid to the conventions of theater. **Buys 5-9 mss/year.** Send complete ms. **Pays $100-400.**

Tips Writers who have some practical experience in theater, especially in technical areas, have a leg-up here, but we'll work with anybody who has a good idea. Some freelancers have become regular contributors, others ignore style suggestions included in our writer's guidelines.

$ $ MAKE-UP ARTIST MAGAZINE

Motion Picture, Television, Theatre, Print, 4018 NE 112th Ave., Suite D-8, Vancouver WA 98682. (360)882-3488. E-mail: news@makeupmag.com. Website: www.makeupmag.com. **90% freelance written**. Bimonthly magazine covering all types of professional make-up artistry. Our audience is a mixture of high-level make-up artists, make-up students, and movie buffs. Writers should be comfortable with technical writing, and should have substantial knowledge of at least one area of makeup, such as effects or fashion. This is an entertainment-industry magazine so writing should have an element of fun and storytelling. Good interview skills required. Estab. 1996. Circ. 12,000. Byline given. Pays within 30 days of publication. No kill fee. Buys all rights. Editorial lead time 6 weeks. Submit seasonal material 2 months in advance. Accepts queries by mail, e-mail, phone. Accepts simultaneous submissions. Sample copy for $7. Guidelines by email.

Nonfiction Needs book excerpts, essays, historical, how-to, humor, inspirational, interview, new product, opinion, personal experience, photo feature, technical, travel. Does not want fluff pieces about consumer beauty products. **Buys 20+ mss/year.** Query with published clips. Length: 500-3,000 words. **Pays 20-50¢/word.** Sometimes pays expenses of writers on assignment.

Photos Contact: Contact Elizabeth Grattan, make-up artist. Send photos Captions, identification of subjects required. Reviews prints, GIF/JPEG files. Negotiates payment individually. Buys all rights.

Columns/Departments Cameo (short yet thorough look at a makeup artist not covered in a feature story), 800 words (15 photos); Lab Tech (how-to advice for effects artists, usually written by a current makeup artist working in a lab), 800 words (3 photos); Backstage (analysis, interview, tips and behind the scenes info on a theatrical production's makeup), 800 words (3 photos). 30 Query with published clips. **Pays $100.**

Tips Read books about professional makeup artistry (see list in FAQ section of our Web site). Read online interviews with makeup artists. Read makeup-oriented mainstream magazines, such as *Allure*. Read *Cinefex* and other film-industry publications. Meet and talk to makeup artists and makeup students.

$ SCREEN MAGAZINE

Screen Enterprises, Inc., 222 W. Ontario St., Suite 500, Chicago IL 60610. (312)640-0800. Fax: (312)640-1928. E-mail: coverage@screenmag.com. Website: www.screenmag.com. **5% freelance written**. Biweekly Chicago-based trade magazine covering advertising and film production in the Midwest and national markets. *Screen* is written for Midwest producers (and other creatives involved) of commercials, AV, features, independent corporate and multimedia. Estab. 1979. Circ. 15,000. Byline given. Pays on publication. No kill fee. Makes work-for-hire assignments. Accepts queries by e-mail. Responds in 3 weeks to queries. Sample copy available online.

Nonfiction Needs interview, new product, technical. No general AV; nothing specific to other markets; no no-brainers or opinion. **Buys 26 mss/year.** Query with published clips. Length: 750-1,500 words. **Pays $50.**

Photos Send photos Captions required. Reviews prints. Offers no additional payment for photos accepted with ms.

Tips Our readers want to know facts and figures. They want to know the news about a company or an individual. We provide exclusive news of this market, in as much depth as space allows without being boring, with lots of specific information and details. We write knowledgably about the market we serve. We recognize the film/video-making process is a difficult one because it 1) is often technical, 2) has implications not immediately discerned.

$ SOUTHERN THEATRE

Southeastern Theatre Conference, P.O. Box 9868, Greensboro NC 27429-0868. (336)292-6041. E-mail: deanna@setc.org. Website: www.setc.org. **Contact:** Deanna Thompson, ed. **100% freelance written**. Quarterly magazine covering all aspects of theater in the Southeast, from innovative theater companies, to important trends, to people making a difference in the region. All stories must be written in a popular magazine style but with subject matter appropriate for theater professionals (not the general public). The audience includes members of the Southeastern Theatre Conference, founded in 1949 and the nation's largest regional theater organization. These members include individuals involved in professional, community, college/university, children's, and secondary school theater. The magazine also is purchased by more than 100 libraries. Estab. 1962. Circ. 4,200. Byline given. Pays on publication. No kill fee. Publishes ms an average of 3 months after acceptance. Buys first North American serial rights, first rights, one-time rights, second serial (reprint) rights, electronic rights. Editorial lead time 3 months. Submit seasonal material 6 months in advance. Accepts queries by mail, e-mail. Responds in 3 months to queries. Responds in 6 months to mss. Sample copy for $10. Guidelines available online.

Nonfiction Looking for stories on design/technology, playwriting, acting, directing—all with a Southeastern connection. Needs general interest, innovative theaters and theater programs, trend stories, interview, people making a difference in Southeastern theater. Playwriting (Fall issue, all stories submitted by January 1) No scholarly articles. **Buys 15-20 mss/year.** Send complete ms. Length: 1,000-3,000 words. **Pays $50 for feature stories.**

Photos State availability of or send photos Captions, identification of subjects, model releases required. Reviews transparencies, prints. Offers no additional payment for photos accepted with ms.

Columns/Departments *Outside the Box* (innovative solutions to problems faced by designers and technicians), *400 Words* (column where the theater professionals can sound off on issues), 400 words; 800-1,000 words; *Words, Words, Words* (reviews of books on theater), 400 words. Query or send complete ms **No payment for columns.**

Tips "Look for a theater or theater person in your area that is doing something different or innovative that would be of interest to others in the profession, then write about that theater or person in a compelling way. We also are looking for well-written trend stories (talk to theaters in your area about trends that are affecting them), and we especially like stories that help our readers do their jobs more effectively. Send an e-mail detailing a well-developed story idea, and ask if we're interested."

VARIETY

Reed Elsevier, 5700 Wilshire Blvd., Suite 120, Los Angeles CA 90069. (323)965-4476. E-mail: specials@reedbusiness.com. Website: www.variety.com. **100% freelance written**. Weekly magazine covering entertainment industry. We require a strong knowledge of how the entertainment industry works beyond what is covered in the consumer press. Estab. 1905. Circ. 63,000. Byline given. Pays on publication. Offers 50% kill fee. Buys all rights. Editorial lead time 2-3 months. Accepts queries by e-mail. Responds in 1 week to queries. Sample copy available online. Guidelines by email.

Nonfiction Needs interview, new product. Does not want opinion pieces. Query.

FARM

AGRICULTURAL EQUIPMENT

$ AG WEEKLY

Lee Agri-Media, P.O. Box 507, Twin Falls ID 83303. Fax: (208)734-9667. E-mail: carol.dumas@lee.net. Website: www.agweekly.com. **25% freelance written**. Biweekly tabloid covering regional farming and ranching with emphasis on Idaho. *Ag Weekly* is an agricultural publication covering production, markets, regulation, politics. Writers need to be familiar with Idaho agricultural commodities. Byline given. Pays on publication. Publishes ms an average of 1 month after acceptance. Buys first rights. Editorial lead time 1 month. Submit seasonal material 1 month in advance. Accepts queries by e-mail. Accepts previously published material. Accepts simultaneous submissions. Responds in 2 weeks to queries. Responds in 1 month to mss. Sample copy available online. Guidelines for #10 sase.

Nonfiction Needs interview, new product, opinion, travel, ag-related. Does not want anything other than local/regional ag-related articles. No cowboy poetry. **Buys 100 mss/year.** Query. Length: 250-700 words. **Pays $30-80.**

Photos State availability Captions required. Reviews GIF/JPEG files. Offers $20-45/photo. Buys one time rights.

$ $ IMPLEMENT & TRACTOR

Farm Journal, 120 West 4th St., Cedar Falls IA 50613. (319)277-3599. Fax: (319)277-3783. E-mail: mfischer@farmjournal.com or cfinck@farmjournal.com. Website: www.implementandtractor.com. **Contact:** Margy Fischer or Charlene Finck. **10% freelance written**. Bimonthly magazine covering the agricultural equipment industry. *"Implement & Tractor* offers equipment reviews and business news for agricultural equipment dealers, ag equipment manufacturers, distributors, and aftermarket suppliers." Estab. 1895. Circ. 5,000. Byline given. Pays on publication. No kill fee. Publishes ms an average of 3-4 months after acceptance. Buys all rights. Editorial lead time 2 months. Accepts queries by mail, e-mail, fax. Responds in 2 months to queries. Sample copy for $6.

CROPS & SOIL MANAGEMENT

$ $ AMERICAN AND WESTERN FRUIT GROWER

Meister Media Worldwide, 37733 Euclid Ave., Willoughby OH 44094. (440)942-2000. E-mail: bdsparks@meistermedia.com. Website: www.fruitgrower.com. **3% freelance written**. Annual magazine covering commercial fruit growing. How-to articles are best. Estab. 1880. Circ. 44,000. Byline given. Pays on publication. No kill fee. Publishes ms an average of 4 months after acceptance. Buys first rights. Editorial lead time 2 months. Submit seasonal material 4 months in advance. Accepts queries by mail, e-mail, fax, phone. Responds in 2 weeks to queries. Responds in 2 months to mss. Sample copy and writer's guidelines free.

Nonfiction Needs how-to, better grow fruit crops. **Buys 6-10 mss/year.** Send complete ms. Length: 800-1,200 words. **Pays $200-250.** Sometimes pays expenses of writers on assignment.

Photos Send photos Reviews prints, slides. Negotiates payment individually. Buys one time rights.

THE AUSTRALIAN & NEW ZEALAND GRAPEGROWER AND WINEMAKER

Ryan Publications, Ltd., P.O. Box 54, Goodwood SA 5034 Australia. (61)(8)8292-0888. Fax: (61)(8)8293-4666. E-mail: editor@grapeandwine.com.au. Website: www.grapeandwine.com.au. Monthly magazine providing vignerons and winemakers with an abundance of practical information to assist them to make premium quality wines for domestic and discerning export markets. Estab. 1963.

Nonfiction Needs general interest, how-to, interview, new product, personal experience, technical. Query.

AUSTRALIAN CANEGROWERS

Canegrowers, Canegrowers Building, 190-194 Edward St., Brisbane QLD 4000 Australia. (61)(7)3864-6444. Fax: (61)(7)3864-6429. E-mail: enquiry@canegrowers.com.au. Website: www.canegrowers.com.au. Magazine published 25 times/year covering Australia's cane growing industry.

Nonfiction Needs general interest, technical. Query.

AUSTRALIAN GRAIN

Greenmount Press, P.O. Box 766, Toowoomba QLD 4350 Australia. (61)(7)4659-3555. Fax: (61)(7)4638-4520. E-mail: grain@greenmountpress.com.au. Website: www.ausgrain.com.au. Bimonthly magazine covering technical and marketing information to the Australian grain industry. Estab. 1990.

Nonfiction Needs general interest, technical. Query.

AUSTRALIAN JOURNAL OF EXPERIMENTAL AGRICULTURE

CSIRO Publishing, P.O. Box 1139, 150 Oxford St., Collingwood VIC 3066 Australia. (61)(3)9662-7500. Fax: (61)(3)9662-7555. E-mail: john.manger@csiro.au. Website: www.publish.csiro.au/journals/ajea. **Contact:** John Manger, pub. dir. Departments: Books, Journals, Multimedia Accepts queries by mail, e-mail. Guidelines available online.

Nonfiction Needs technical, science, environment, Australiana, natural history. Send complete ms.

$ $ COTTON GROWER MAGAZINE

Meister Media Worldwide, 65 Germantown Court, #202, Cordova TN 38018. (901)756-8822. E-mail: frgiles@meistermedia.com. **5% freelance written**. Monthly magazine covering cotton production, cotton markets and related subjects. Readers are mostly cotton producers who seek information on production practices, equipment and products related to cotton. Estab. 1901. Circ. 43,000. Byline given. Pays on acceptance. No kill fee. Publishes ms an average of 2 months after acceptance. Buys first rights. Editorial lead time 2 months. Submit seasonal material 2 months in advance. Accepts queries by mail, e-mail, fax, phone. Accepts simultaneous submissions. Sample copy free.

Nonfiction Needs interview, new product, photo feature, technical. No fiction or humorous pieces. **Buys 5-10 mss/year.** Query with published clips. Length: 500-800 words. **Pays $200-400.** Sometimes pays expenses of writers on assignment.

Photos State availability Captions, identification of subjects required. Reviews transparencies. Offers no additional payment for photos accepted with ms. Buys all rights.

$ THE FRUIT GROWERS NEWS

Great American Publishing, P.O. Box 128, Sparta MI 49345. (616)887-9008. Fax: (616)887-2666. E-mail: editor@fruitgrowersnews.com. Website: www.fruitgrowersnews.com. **15% freelance written**. Monthly tabloid covering agriculture. Our objective is to provide commercial fruit growers of all sizes with information to help them succeed. Estab. 1970. Circ. 15,000. Pays on publication. No kill fee. Publishes ms an average of 2 months after acceptance. Makes work-for-hire assignments. Editorial lead time 1-2 months. Submit seasonal material 3 months in advance. Accepts queries by mail, e-mail, fax. Accepts simultaneous submissions. Responds in 2 weeks to queries. Responds in 1 month to mss. Sample copy free.

Nonfiction Needs general interest, interview, new product. No advertorials, other puff pieces. **Buys 25 mss/year.** Query with published clips and resume. Length: 800-1,200 words. **Pays $100-125.** Sometimes pays expenses of writers on assignment.

Photos Send photos Captions required. Reviews prints. Offers $15/photo. Buys one time rights.

$ $ GOOD FRUIT GROWER

Washington State Fruit Commission, 105 S. 18th St., #217, Yakima WA 98901-2177. (509)575-2315. E-mail: jim.black@goodfruit.com. Website: www.goodfruit.com. **20% freelance written**. Semi-monthly magazine covering tree fruit/grape growing. Estab. 1946. Circ. 11,000. Byline given. Pays on acceptance. Publishes ms an average of 3 months after acceptance. Buys first rights, buys electronic rights. Accepts queries by mail,

e-mail. Accepts simultaneous submissions. Responds in 1 week to queries. Responds in 1 month to mss. Sample copy free. Guidelines free.
Nonfiction "We work with writers to choose topics of mutual interest." **Buys 50 mss/year.** Query. Length: 500-1,500 words. **Pays 40-50¢/word.** Sometimes pays expenses of writers on assignment.
Photos Contact: Jim Black. Reviews GIF/JPEG files. Negotiates payment individually. Buys one time rights.
Tips "We want well-written, accurate information. We deal with our writers honestly and expect the same in return."

$ GRAIN JOURNAL

Country Publications, Inc., 3065 Pershing Ct., Decatur IL 62526. Fax: (217)877-6647. E-mail: ed@grainnet.com. Website: www.grainnet.com. **5% freelance written**. Bimonthly magazine covering grain handling and merchandising. *Grain Journal* serves the North American grain industry, from the smallest country grain elevators and feed mills to major export terminals. Estab. 1972. Circ. 12,000. Byline sometimes given. Pays on publication. No kill fee. Publishes ms an average of 2 months after acceptance. Buys first rights. Editorial lead time 2 months. Submit seasonal material 2 months in advance. Accepts simultaneous submissions. Sample copy free.
Nonfiction Needs how-to, interview, new product, technical. Query. 750 words maximum. **Pays $100.**
Photos Send photos Captions, identification of subjects required. Reviews contact sheets, negatives, transparencies, 3x5 prints, electronic files. Offers $50-100/photo. Buys one time rights.
Tips Call with your idea. We'll let you know if it is suitable for our publication.

NEW ZEALAND COMMERCIAL GROWER

P.O. Box 10-232, Wellington New Zealand. (64)(4)472-3795. Fax: (64)(4)471-2861. E-mail: comgrow@xtra.co.nz. Website: www.thegrower.co.nz. Trade journal published 11 times/year covering information for commercial growers of fresh vegetables, including potatoes, tomatoes, asparagus, and buttercup squash. Circ. 4,500. No kill fee.

- Query before submitting.

$ ONION WORLD

Columbia Publishing, 413-B N. 20th Ave., Yakima WA 98902. (509)248-2452, ext. 105. Fax: (509)248-4056. E-mail: dbrent@columbiapublications.com. Website: www.onionworld.net. **25% freelance written**. Monthly magazine covering the world of onion production and marketing for onion growers and shippers. Estab. 1985. Circ. 5,500. Byline given. Pays on publication. No kill fee. Publishes ms an average of 1 month after acceptance. Buys first North American serial rights. Submit seasonal material 1 month in advance. Accepts queries by mail, e-mail, fax, phone. Accepts simultaneous submissions. Responds in 1 month to queries. Sample copy for sae with 9x12 envelope and 5 First-Class stamps.

- Columbia Publishing also produces *The Tomato Magazine*, *Potato Country* and *Carrot Country*.

Nonfiction Needs general interest, historical, interview. **Buys 30 mss/year.** Query. Length: 1,200-1,250 words. **Pays $5/column inch for assigned articles.**
Reprints Send photocopy and information about when and where the material previously appeared. Pays 50% of amount paid for an original article.
Photos Send photos Captions, identification of subjects required. Offers no additional payment for photos accepted with ms, unless it's a cover shot. Buys all rights.
Tips Writers should be familiar with growing and marketing onions. We use a lot of feature stories on growers, shippers, and others in the onion trade—what they are doing, their problems, solutions, marketing plans, etc.

$ SPUDMAN

Great American Publishing, P.O. Box 128, Sparta MI 49345. Fax: (616)887-2666. Website: www.spudman.com. **15% freelance written**. Monthly magazine covering potato industryÃ³growing, packing, processing, chipping. Estab. 1964. Circ. 10,000. Byline given. Pays on publication. Offers $75 kill fee. Publishes ms an average of 2 months after acceptance. Buys first North American serial rights, buys electronic rights. Editorial lead time 2 months. Submit seasonal material 4 months in advance. Accepts queries by mail, e-mail. Accepts previously published material. Responds in 2-3 weeks to queries. Sample copy for sae with 8 ½x11 envelope and 3 First-Class stamps. Guidelines for #10 sase.

$ THE VEGETABLE GROWERS NEWS

Great American Publishing, P.O. Box 128, Sparta MI 49345. (616)887-9008. Fax: (616)887-2666. E-mail: editor@vegetablegrowersnews.com. Website: www.vegetablegrowersnews.com. **15% freelance written**. Monthly tabloid covering agriculture. Our objective is to provide commercial vegetable growers of all sizes with information to help them succeed. Estab. 1970. Circ. 16,000. Pays on publication. No kill fee. Publishes ms an average of 2 months after acceptance. Makes work-for-hire assignments. Editorial lead time 1-2 months. Submit seasonal material 3 months in advance. Accepts queries by mail, e-mail, fax. Accepts simultaneous submissions. Responds in 2 weeks to queries. Responds in 1 month to mss. Sample copy free.

Nonfiction Needs general interest, interview, new product. No advertorials, other puff pieces. **Buys 25 mss/year.** Query with published clips and resume. Length: 800-1,200 words. **Pays $100-125.** Sometimes pays expenses of writers on assignment.
Photos Send photos Captions required. Reviews prints. Offers $15/photo. Buys one time rights.

DAIRY FARMING

$ $ HOARD'S DAIRYMAN

W.D. Hoard and Sons, Co., P.O. Box 801, Fort Atkinson WI 53538. (920)563-5551. Fax: (920)563-7298. E-mail: hoards@hoards.com. Website: www.hoards.com. Tabloid published 20 times/year covering dairy industry. We publish semi-technical information published for dairy-farm families and their advisors. Estab. 1885. Circ. 100,000. Byline given. Pays on acceptance. No kill fee. Publishes ms an average of 4 months after acceptance. Buys first rights. Editorial lead time 2 months. Submit seasonal material 3 months in advance. Accepts queries by mail, e-mail, fax. Responds in 2 weeks to queries. Responds in 1 month to mss. Sample copy for 12X15 SAE and $3. Guidelines for #10 sase.
Nonfiction Needs how-to, technical. **Buys 60 mss/year.** Query. Length: 800-1,500 words. **Pays $150-350.**
Photos Send photos Reviews 2X2 transparencies. Offers no additional payment for photos accepted with ms.

$ $ WESTERN DAIRYBUSINESS

Dairy Business Communications, Heritage Complex, Suite 218, 4500 S. Laspina, Tulare CA 93274. (559)687-3160. Fax: (559)687-3166. E-mail: rgoble@dairybusiness.com. Website: www.dairybusiness.com. **10% freelance written. Prefers to work with published/established writers.** Monthly magazine dealing with large-herd commercial dairy industry. Rarely publishes information about non-Western producers or dairy groups and events. Estab. 1922. Circ. 11,500. Byline given. Pays on publication. No kill fee. Publishes ms an average of 3 months after acceptance. Buys first North American serial rights. Submit seasonal material 3 months in advance. Accepts queries by e-mail. Responds in 1 month to queries. Sample copy for sae with 9x12 envelope and 4 First-Class stamps.
Nonfiction "Special emphasis on: environmental stewardship, animal welfare, herd health, herd management systems, business management, facilities/equipment, forage/cropping." Needs interview, new product, opinion, industry analysis, industry analysis. No religion, nostalgia, politics, or 'mom and pop' dairies. Query, or e-mail complete ms. Length: 300-1,500 words. **Pays $25-400.**
Reprints "Seldom accepts previously published submissions. Send information about when and where the article previously appeared." Pays 50% of amount paid for an original article.
Photos Photos are a critical part of story packages. Send photos Captions, identification of subjects required. Reviews contact sheets, 35mm or 2 ¼x2 ¼ transparencies. Pays $25 for b $50-100 for color. Buys one time rights.
Tips "Know the market and the industry, be well-versed in large-herd dairy management and business."

$ WESTERN DAIRY FARMER

Bowes Publishers, Ltd., 4504—61 Ave., Leduc AB T9E 3Z1 Canada. (780)980-7488. Fax: (780)986-6397. E-mail: editor-wdf-caf@webcoleduc.com. Website: www.westerndairyfarmer.com. **70% freelance written.** Bimonthly magazine covering the dairy industry. *Western Dairy Farmer* is a trade publication dealing with issues surrounding the dairy industry. The magazine features innovative articles on animal health, industry changes, new methods of dairying, and personal experiences. Sometimes highlights successful farmers. Estab. 1991. Circ. 6,300. Byline given. Pays on publication. No kill fee. Publishes ms an average of 4 months after acceptance. Buys all rights. Editorial lead time 2 months. Submit seasonal material 2 months in advance. Accepts queries by mail, e-mail, fax. Responds in 2 weeks to queries. Responds in 2 months to mss. Sample copy for 9x12 SAE.
Nonfiction All topics/submissions must be related to the dairy industry. Needs general interest, how-to, interview, new product, personal experience, only exceptional stories, technical. Not interested in anything vague, trite, or not dairy related. **Buys 50 mss/year.** Query or send complete ms Length: 900-1,200 words. **Pays $75-150.**
Photos State availability Captions, identification of subjects, model releases required. Reviews GIF/JPEG files. Offers no additional payment for photos accepted with ms. Buys all rights.
Tips Know the industry inside and out. Provide contact names and phone numbers (both for writers and subjects) with submissions. Remember, this is a specialized trade publication, and our readers are well-aquainted with the issues and appreciate new up-to-date information.

LIVESTOCK

$ $ ANGUS BEEF BULLETIN

Angus Productions, Inc., 3201 Frederick Ave., St. Joseph MO 64506. (816)383-5270. Fax: (816)233-6575.

E-mail: shermel@angusjournal.com. Website: www.angusbeefbulletin.com. **45% freelance written**. Tabloid published 5 times/year covering commercial cattle industry. The *Bulletin* is mailed free to commercial cattlemen who have purchased an Angus bull and had the registration transferred to them and to others who sign a request card. Estab. 1985. Circ. 97,000. Byline given. Pays on publication. No kill fee. Publishes ms an average of 3 months after acceptance. Buys first rights, buys electronic rights. Editorial lead time 3 months. Submit seasonal material 3 months in advance. Accepts queries by mail, e-mail. Accepts simultaneous submissions. Responds in 3 weeks to queries. Responds in 3 months to mss. Sample copy for $5. Guidelines for #10 sase.

Nonfiction Needs how-to, cattle production, interview, technical, cattle production. **Buys 10 mss/year.** Query with published clips. Length: 800-2,500 words. **Pays $50-600.** Pays expenses of writers on assignment.

Photos Send photos Identification of subjects required. Reviews 5x7 transparencies, 5x7 glossy prints. Offers $25/photo. Buys all rights.

Tips Read the publication and have a firm grasp of the commercial cattle industry and how the Angus breed fits in that industry.

$ $ $ ANGUS JOURNAL

Angus Productions Inc., 3201 Frederick Ave., St. Joseph MO 64506-2997. (816)383-5270. Fax: (816)233-6575. E-mail: shermel@angusjournal.com. Website: www.angusjournal.com. **40% freelance written**. Monthly magazine covering Angus cattle. The *Angus Journal* is the official magazine of the American Angus Association. Its primary function as such is to report to the membership association activities and information pertinent to raising Angus cattle. Estab. 1919. Circ. 17,000. Byline given. Pays on publication. No kill fee. Publishes ms an average of 3 months after acceptance. Buys first rights, buys electronic rights. Editorial lead time 2 months. Submit seasonal material 3 months in advance. Accepts queries by mail, e-mail, fax. Accepts simultaneous submissions. Responds in 3 weeks to queries. Responds in 2 months to mss. Sample copy for $5. Guidelines for #10 sase.

Nonfiction Needs how-to, cattle production, interview, technical, related to cattle. **Buys 20-30 mss/year.** Query with published clips. Length: 800-3,500 words. **Pays $50-1,000.** Pays expenses of writers on assignment.

Photos Send photos Identification of subjects required. Reviews 5x7 glossy prints. Offers $25-400/photo. Buys all rights.

Tips Read the magazine and have a firm grasp of the cattle industry.

$ $ THE BRAHMAN JOURNAL

17269 FM 1887, Hempstead TX 77445. (979)826-4347. Fax: (979)826-8352. **10% freelance written**. Monthly magazine covering Brahman cattle. Estab. 1971. Circ. 4,000. Byline given. Pays on publication. No kill fee. Publishes ms an average of 2 months after acceptance. Buys first North American serial rights, buys one-time rights, buys second serial (reprint) rights. Makes work-for-hire assignments. Submit seasonal material 3 months in advance. Sample copy for sae with 9x12 envelope and 5 First-Class stamps.

Nonfiction Needs general interest, historical, interview. Pre-Houston, International Sale Catalog (February); Houston Livestock Show Issue (March); Performance, Houston Results (April); Herd Bull Issue (May); Youth Issue (June); All-American Issue (July); International Issue (August); All-American Results (September); Pre-National Show (October); Calendar Issue (November); Directory Issue (December). **Buys 3-4 mss/year.** Query with published clips. Length: 1,200-3,000 words. **Pays $100-250.**

Reprints Send typed manuscript with rights for sale noted. Pays 50% of amount paid for an original article.

Photos Photos needed for article purchase. Send photos Captions required. Reviews 4x5 prints. Offers no additional payment for photos accepted with ms. Buys one time rights.

$ $ THE CATTLEMAN

Texas and Southwestern Cattle Raisers Association, 1301 W. 7th St., Ft. Worth TX 76102-2660. E-mail: lionel@texascattleraisers.org. Website: www.thecattlemanmagazine.com. **25% freelance written**. Monthly magazine covering the Texas/Oklahoma beef cattle industry. We specialize in in-depth, management-type articles related to range and pasture, beef cattle production, animal health, nutrition, and marketing. We want `how-to' articles. Estab. 1914. Circ. 15,400. Byline given. Pays on acceptance. No kill fee. Publishes ms an average of 2 months after acceptance. Buys exclusive and one-time rights, plus rights to post on website in month of publication. Editorial lead time 2 months. Submit seasonal material 6 months in advance. Accepts queries by mail, e-mail. Sample copy free. Guidelines available online.

Nonfiction Needs how-to, interview, new product, personal experience, technical, ag research. Editorial calendar themes include: Horses (January); Range and Pasture (February); Livestock Marketing (July); Hereford and Wildlife (August); Feedlots (September); Bull Buyers (October); Ranch Safety (December). Does not want to see anything not specifically related to beef production in the Southwest. **Buys 20 mss/year.** Query with published clips. Length: 1,500-2,000 words. **Pays $200-350 for assigned articles. Pays $100-350 for unsolicited articles.** Sometimes pays expenses of writers on assignment.

Photos Identification of subjects required. Reviews transparencies, prints, digital files. Offers no additional payment for photos accepted with ms. Buys one time rights.

Tips In our most recent readership survey, subscribers said they were most interested in the following topics in this order: range/pasture, property rights, animal health, water, new innovations, and marketing. *The Cattleman* prefers to work on an assignment basis. However, prospective contributors are urged to write the managing editor of the magazine to inquire of interest on a proposed subject. Occasionally, the editor will return a manuscript to a potential contributor for cutting, polishing, checking, rewriting, or condensing. Be able to demonstrate background/knowledge in this field. Include tearsheets from similar magazines.

$ $ FEED LOT MAGAZINE

Feed Lot Magazine, Inc., P.O. Box 850, Dighton KS 67839. (620)397-2838. Fax: (620)397-2839. E-mail: feedlot@st-tel.net. Website: www.feedlotmagazine.com. **40% freelance written**. Bimonthly magazine. "The editorial information content fits a dual role: large feedlots and their related cow/calf operations, and large 500pl cow/calf, 100pl stocker operations. The information covers all phases of production from breeding, genetics, animal health, nutrition, equipment design, research through finishing fat cattle. *Feed Lot* publishes a mix of new information and timely articles which directly affect the cattle industry." Estab. 1993. Circ. 12,000. Byline given. Pays on publication. Offers 50% kill fee. Publishes ms an average of 2 months after acceptance. Buys all rights. Editorial lead time 2 months. Submit seasonal material 6 months in advance. Accepts queries by mail, e-mail, fax. Responds in 1 month to queries. Sample copy and writer's guidelines for $1.50

Nonfiction Needs interview, new product, cattle-related, photo feature. Send complete ms. Length: 100-400 words. **Pays 20¢/word.**

Reprints Send tearsheet or typed ms with rights for sale noted and information about when and where the material previously appeared. Pays 50% of amount paid for an original article.

Photos State availability of or send photos Captions, model releases required. Reviews contact sheets. Negotiates payment individually. Buys all rights.

Tips "Know what you are writing about—have a good knowledge of the subject."

$ SHEEP! MAGAZINE

Countryside Publications, Ltd., 145 Industrial Dr., Medford WI 54451. (715)785-7979. Fax: (715)785-7414. Website: www.sheepmagazine.com. **35% freelance written. Prefers to work with published/established writers**. Bimonthly magazine. We're looking for clear, concise, useful information for sheep raisers who have a few sheep to a 1,000 ewe flock. Estab. 1980. Circ. 8,000. Byline given. Pays on publication. Offers $30 kill fee. Buys all rights or makes work-for-hire assignments. Submit seasonal material 3 months in advance.

Nonfiction Health and husbandry articles should be written by someone with extensive experience or appropriate credentials (i.e., a veterinarian or animal scientist). Accepts informative articles (on personalities and/or political, legal, or environmental issues affecting the sheep industry); features (on small businesses that promote wool products and stories about local and regional sheep producers' groups and their activities); and first-person narratives. Needs book excerpts, how-to, on innovative lamb and wool marketing and promotion techniques, efficient record-keeping systems, or specific aspects of health and husbandry, interview, on experienced sheep producers who detail the economics and management of their operation, new product, of value to sheep producers; should be written by someone who has used them, technical, on genetics health and nutrition. **Buys 80 mss/year.** Send complete ms. Length: 750-2,500 words. **Pays $45-150.**

Photos Color—vertical compositions of sheep and/or people—for cover. Use only b&w inside magazine. Black & white, 35mm photos or other visuals improve chances of a sale. Identification of subjects required. Buys all rights.

Tips Send us your best ideas and photos! We love good writing!

MANAGEMENT

$ AG JOURNAL

Arkansas Valley Publishing, P.O. Box 500, La Junta CO 81050. (719)384-8121. Fax: (719)384-8157. E-mail: ag-publish@centurytel.net. Website: www.agjournalonline.com. **20% freelance written**. Weekly journal covering agriculture. The *Ag Journal* covers people, issues and events relevant to ag producers in our seven state region (Colorado, Kansas, Oklahoma, Texas, Wyoming, Nebraska, New Mexico). Estab. 1949. Circ. 11,000. Byline given. Pays on publication. No kill fee. Publishes ms an average of 2 weeks after acceptance. Buys first rights, buys one-time rights. Makes work-for-hire assignments. Editorial lead time 1 month. Submit seasonal material 1 month in advance. Accepts queries by e-mail. Accepts previously published material. Responds in 2 weeks to queries. Sample copy and writer's guidelines free.

Nonfiction Needs how-to, interview, new product, opinion, photo feature, technical. Query by e-mail only. **Pays 4¢/word.** Sometimes pays expenses of writers on assignment.

Photos State availability Captions, identification of subjects required. Offers $8/photo. Buys one time rights.

$ $ NEW HOLLAND NEWS AND ACRES MAGAZINE

P.O. Box 1895, New Holland PA 17557-0903. Website: www.newholland.com/na. **Contact:** Gary Martin, ed. **75% freelance written. Works with a small number of new/unpublished writers each year.** Each magazine published 4 times/year covering agriculture and non-farm country living; designed to entertain and inform farm families and rural homeowners and provide ideas for small acreage outdoor projects. Estab. 1960. Byline given. Pays on acceptance. Offers negotiable kill fee. Publishes ms an average of 8 months after acceptance. Buys first North American serial rights. Submit seasonal material 8 months in advance. Accepts queries by mail. Responds in 2 months to queries. Sample copy and writer's guidelines for 9x12 SAE with 2 first-class stamps

- "Break in with features about people and their unique and attractive country living projects, such as outdoor pets (horses, camels, birds), building projects (cabins, barns, restorations), trees, flowers, landscaping, outdoor activities, part-time farms and businesses, and country-related antique collections."

Nonfiction "We need strong photo support for articles of 1,200-1,700 words on farm management, farm human interest and rural lifestyles." **Buys 40 mss/year.** Query. **Pays $700-900.** Pays expenses of writers on assignment.

Photos Professional photos only. Captions, identification of subjects, model releases required. Reviews color photos in any format. Pays $50-300, $500 for cover shot. Buys one time rights.

Tips "We want stories about people who are doing something unique that looks good in photos. Do not write lifeless reports about inanimate subjects."

SMALL FARM TODAY

The How-to Magazine of Alternative and Traditional Crops, Livestock, and Direct Marketing, Missouri Farm Publishing, Inc., Ridge Top Ranch, 3903 W. Ridge Trail Rd., Clark MO 65243-9525. (573)687-3525. E-mail: smallfarm@socket.net. Website: www.smallfarmtoday.com. Bimonthly magazine for small farmers and small-acreage landowners interested in diversification, direct marketing, alternative crops, horses, draft animals, small livestock, exotic and minor breeds, home-based businesses, gardening, vegetable and small fruit crops. Estab. 1984 as *Missouri Farm Magazine*. Circ. 12,000. Byline given. Pays 60 days after publication. No kill fee. Publishes ms an average of 6 months after acceptance. Buys first serial and nonexclusive reprint rights (right to reprint article in an anthology). Submit seasonal material 4 months in advance. Accepts queries by mail, e-mail. Responds in 3 months to queries. Sample copy for $3. Guidelines available online.

Nonfiction Practical and how-to (small farming, gardening, alternative crops/livestock). Poultry (January); Wool & Fiber (March); Aquaculture (July); Equipment (November) Query letters recommended. Length: 1,200-2,600 words.

Reprints Send tearsheet, photocopy or typed ms with rights for sale noted and information about when and where the material previously appeared. Pays 57% of amount paid for an original article.

Photos Send photos Captions required. Offers $6 for inside photos and $10 for cover photos. Pays $4 for negatives or slides. Buys one-time and nonexclusive reprint rights (for anthologies).

Tips No poetry or humor. Your topic must apply to the small farm or acreage. It helps to provide more practical and helpful information without the fluff. We need `how-to' articles (how-to grow, raise, market, build, etc.), as well as articles about small farmers who are experiencing success through diversification, specialty/alternative crops and livestock, and direct marketing.

$ 🌐 SMALLHOLDER MAGAZINE

Newsquest Media Group, Hook House, Hook Road, Wimblington, March Cambs PE15 0QL United Kingdom. Phone/Fax: (44)(135)474-1538. E-mail: liz.wright1@btconnect.com. Website: www.smallholder.co.uk. No kill fee. Accepts queries by e-mail. Sample copy available online. Guidelines by email.

Nonfiction Length: 700-1,400 words. **Pays 4£/word.**

Photos Send photos Reviews 300 dpi digital images. Pays £5-50.

MISCELLANEOUS FARM

$ $ ACRES U.S.A.

The Voice of Eco-Agriculture, P.O. Box 91299, Austin TX 78709-1299. (512)892-4400. Fax: (512)892-4448. E-mail: editor@acresusa.com. Website: www.acresusa.com. "Monthly trade journal written by people who have a sincere interest in the principles of organic and sustainable agriculture." Estab. 1970. Circ. 18,000. Byline given. Pays on publication. No kill fee. Buys first North American serial rights. Editorial lead time 4 months. Submit seasonal material 6 months in advance. Accepts queries by mail, e-mail, fax. Accepts simultaneous submissions. Sample copy and writer's guidelines free.

Nonfiction Needs expose, how-to, personal experience. Seeds (January), Soil Fertility & Testing (March), Cattle & Grazing (May), Poultry (July), Composting/Compost Tea (September), Tillage & Equipment (November). Does not want poetry, fillers, product profiles, or anything with a promotional tone. **Buys about 50 mss/year.** Send complete ms. Length: 1,000-2,500 words. **Pays 10¢/word**

Photos State availability of or send photos Captions, identification of subjects required. Reviews GIF/JPEG/TIF files. Negotiates payment individually. Buys one time rights.

ALBA BIENNIAL REPORT

Alba, P.O. Box 6264, Salinas CA 93912. (831)758-1469. Fax: (831)758-3665. E-mail: brett@albafarmers.org. Website: www.albafarmers.org. Quarterly newsletter covering small-scale farming done by minority farmers in California. Provides a variety of services and resources that aim to increase the success of Latino farmers. Works to help farmers overcome barriers, create opportunities for them to benefit from organic farming techniques and open new markets. No kill fee. Guidelines available.

AUSTRALASIAN FARMERS' & DEALERS' JOURNAL

22 Stradbroke Ave., Brighton VIC 3187 Australia. (61)(3)9592-7167. Fax: (61)(3)9592-7336. E-mail: peterlevy@afdj.com.au. Website: www.afdj.com.au. Quarterly magazine. Accepts queries by mail, e-mail, fax, phone.
Nonfiction Needs general interest. Query.

$ $ BEE CULTURE

P.O. Box 706, Medina OH 44256-0706. Fax: (330)725-5624. E-mail: kim@beeculture.com. Website: www.beeculture.com. **50% freelance written**. natural science of honey bees. "Monthly magazine for beekeepers and those interested in the natural science of honey bees, with environmentally-oriented articles relating to honey bees or pollination." Estab. 1873. Pays on publication. No kill fee. Publishes ms an average of 4 months after acceptance. Buys first North American serial rights. Accepts queries by mail, e-mail, fax, phone. Responds in 1 month to mss. Sample copy for sae with 9x12 envelope and 5 First-Class stamps. Guidelines available online.
Nonfiction "Interested in articles giving new ideas on managing bees. Also looking for articles on honey bee/environment connections or relationships. Also uses success stories about commercial beekeepers." Needs interview, personal experience, photo feature. No how I began beekeeping articles. No highly advanced, technical, and scientific abstracts, or impractical advice. 2,000 words average. **Pays $100-250.**
Reprints Send photocopy and information about when and where the material previously appeared. Pays about the same as for an original article, on negotiation.
Photos B&W or color prints, 5x7 standard, but 3x5 are OK. 35mm slides, mid-format transparencies are excellent. Electronic images accepted and encouraged. Pays $7-10 each, $50 for cover photos.
Tips "Do an interview story on commercial beekeepers who are cooperative enough to furnish accurate, factual information on their operations. Frequent mistakes made by writers in completing articles are that they are too general in nature and lack management knowledge."

$ $ $ PRODUCE BUSINESS

Phoenix Media Network Inc., P.O. Box 810425, Boca Raton FL 33481-0425. (561)994-1118. E-mail: kwhitacre@phoenixmedianet.com. **90% freelance written**. Monthly magazine covering produce and floral marketing. We address the buying end of the produce/floral industry, concentrating on supermarkets, chain restaurants, etc. Estab. 1985. Circ. 16,000. Byline given. Pays 30 days after publication. Offers $50 kill fee. Buys all rights. Editorial lead time 2 months. Accepts queries by e-mail. Sample copy free. Guidelines free.
Nonfiction All articles are assigned to conform to our editorial calendar. Does not want unsolicited articles. **Buys 150 mss/year.** Query with published clips. Length: 1,200-10,000 words. **Pays $240-1,200.** Pays expenses of writers on assignment.

REGIONAL FARM

$ $ AMERICAN AGRICULTURIST

5227 Baltimore Pike, Littlestown PA 17340. (717)359-0150. Fax: (717)359-0250. E-mail: jvogel@farmprogress.com. Website: www.farmprogress.com. **20% freelance written**. Monthly magazine covering "cutting-edge technology and news to help farmers improve their operations.". We publish cutting-edge technology with ready on-farm application. Estab. 1842. Circ. 32,000. Pays on publication. No kill fee. Publishes ms an average of 3 months after acceptance. Buys first rights. Editorial lead time 3 months. Submit seasonal material 3 months in advance. Accepts queries by e-mail, fax, phone. Accepts simultaneous submissions. Responds in 2 weeks to queries. Responds in 1 month to mss. Guidelines for #10 SASE.
Nonfiction Needs how-to, humor, inspirational, interview, new product, personal experience, photo feature feature, technical, "No stories without a strong tie to Mid-Atlantic farming.". **Buys 20 mss/year.** Query. Length: 500-1,000 words. **Pays $150-300.** Sometimes pays expenses of writers on assignment.
Photos Send photos Captions, identification of subjects, model releases required. Reviews transparencies, prints, GIF/JPEG files. Offers $75-200/photo Buys one time rights.
Columns/Departments Contact: Kathleen O'Connor, editorial assistant. Country Air (humor, nostalgia, inspirational), 300-400 words; Family Favorites, 100 words. 36 Send complete ms. **Pays $15-50.**
Poetry Contact: Kathleen O'Connor, editorial assistant. Needs free verse, light verse, traditional. All poetry must have a link to New York farming. **Buys 2 poems/year.** Length: 12-40 lines. **Pays $50.**

$ CENTRAL ALBERTA FARMER

Bowes Publishers, Ltd., 4504—61 Ave., Leduc AB T9E 3Z1 Canada. (780)986-2271. Fax: (780)986-6397. E-mail: editor-wdf-caf@webcoleduc.com. Website: www.albertafarmer.com. **10% freelance written**. Monthly tabloid covering farming issues specific to or affecting farmers in central Alberta, Canada. *Central Alberta Farmer* is an industry magazine-type product that deals with issues in farming. It also highlights value-added efforts in agriculture and features stories on rural lifestyles. Estab. 1993. Circ. 36,000. Byline given. Pays on publication. No kill fee. Publishes ms an average of 3 months after acceptance. Buys all rights. Editorial lead time 3 months. Submit seasonal material 4 months in advance. Accepts queries by mail, e-mail, fax. Accepts simultaneous submissions. Responds in 2 weeks to queries. Responds in 2 months to mss. Sample copy for 9x12 SAE.

Nonfiction All articles must be related to an aspect of farming in the area *Central Alberta Farmer* covers. Freelance articles must be exceptional. Not many are accepted. Needs general interest, how-to, interview, new product, personal experience, technical. Not interested in anything trite or trivial. **Buys 5 mss/year.** Query or send complete ms Length: 1,000-1,500 words. **Pays $20-30.**

Photos State availability Captions, identification of subjects, model releases required. Reviews GIF/JPEG files. Offers no additional payment for photos accepted with ms. Buys all rights.

Tips Know the industry well. Provide names and phone numbers with submissions (both yours and the people in the article). This is a difficult publication to break into because most copy is generated in-house. So, your submission must be far above average.

$ $ FLORIDA GROWER

The Voice of Florida Agriculture for More Than 90 Years, Meister Media Worldwide, 1555 Howell Branch Rd., Suite C-204, Winter Park FL 32789. (407)539-6552. Fax: (407)539-6544. E-mail: rcpadrick@meistermedia.com. Website: www.floridagrower.net. **10% freelance written**. Monthly magazine edited for the Florida farmer with commercial production interest primarily in citrus, vegetables, and other ag endeavors. Our goal is to provide articles which update and inform on such areas as production, ag financing, farm labor relations, technology, safety, education, and regulation. Estab. 1907. Circ. 12,200. Byline given. Pays on publication. No kill fee. Buys all rights. Editorial lead time 2 months. Submit seasonal material 3 months in advance. Accepts queries by mail, e-mail, fax, phone. Responds in 1 month to queries. Sample copy for sae with 9x12 envelope and 5 First-Class stamps. Guidelines free.

Nonfiction Needs interview, photo feature, technical. Query with published clips. Length: 700-1,000 words. **Pays $150-250.**

Photos Send photos

$ THE LAND

Minnesota's Favorite Ag Publication, Free Press Co., P.O. Box 3169, Mankato MN 56002-3169. (507)345-4523. E-mail: editor@thelandonline.com. Website: www.thelandonline.com. **40% freelance written**. Weekly tabloid covering farming in Minnesota. Although we're not tightly focused on any one type of farming, our articles must be of interest to farmers. In other words, will your article topic have an impact on people who live and work in rural areas? Prefers to work with Minnesota writers. Estab. 1976. Circ. 33,000. Byline given. Pays on acceptance. No kill fee. Publishes ms an average of 2 months after acceptance. Buys first North American serial rights. Editorial lead time 2 months. Submit seasonal material 2 months in advance. Accepts queries by mail, e-mail. Responds in 3 weeks to queries. Responds in 2 months to mss. Sample copy free. Guidelines for #10 SASE.

Nonfiction Needs general interest, ag, how-to, crop, livestock production, marketing. **Buys 80 mss/year.** Query. Length: 500-750 words. **Pays $50-70 for assigned articles.**

Photos Send photos Reviews contact sheets. Negotiates payment individually. Buys one time rights.

Columns/Departments Query. **Pays $10-50.**

Tips Be enthused about rural Minnesota life and agriculture and be willing to work with our editors. We try to stress relevance. When sending me a query, convince me the story belongs in a Minnesota farm publication.

$ $ MAINE ORGANIC FARMER & GARDENER

Maine Organic Farmers & Gardeners Association, 662 Slab City Rd., Lincolnville ME 04849. (207)763-3043. E-mail: jenglish@midcoast.com. Website: www.mofga.org. **40% freelance written. Prefers to work with published/established local writers.** Quarterly newspaper. "The *MOF&G* promotes and encourages sustainable agriculture and environmentally sound living. Our primary focus is organic farming, gardening, and forestry, but we also deal with local, national, and international agriculture, food, and environmental issues." Estab. 1976. Circ. 10,000. Byline and bio offered. Pays on publication. No kill fee. Publishes ms an average of 8 months after acceptance. Buys first North American serial rights, buys first rights, buys one-time rights, buys second serial (reprint) rights. Submit seasonal material 1 year in advance. Accepts queries by mail, e-mail. Accepts simultaneous submissions. Responds in 2 months to queries. Sample copy for $2 and SAE with 7 first-class stamps; from MOFGA, P.O. Box 170, Unity ME 04988. Guidelines free.

Nonfiction "Book reviews; how-to based on personal experience, research reports, interviews; profiles of farmers, gardeners, plants; information on renewable energy, recycling, nutrition, health, nontoxic pest control, organic farm management and marketing. We use profiles of New England organic farmers and gardeners and news reports (500-1,000 words) dealing with U.S./international sustainable ag research and development, rural development, recycling projects, environmental and agricultural problems and solutions, organic farms with broad impact, cooperatives and community projects." **Buys 30 mss/year.** Send complete ms. Length: 250-3,000 words. **Pays $25-300.**

Reprints E-mail manuscript with rights for sale noted and information about when and where the material previously appeared. Pays 50% of amount paid for an original article.

Photos State availability of photos with query. Captions, identification of subjects, model releases required. Buys one time rights.

Tips "We are a nonprofit organization. Our publication's primary mission is to inform and educate, but we also want readers to enjoy the articles. Most of our articles are written by our staff or by freelancers who have been associated with the publication for several years."

FINANCE

$ $ $ ADVISOR'S EDGE

Canada's Magazine for the Financial Professional, Rogers Media, Inc., 156 Front St. W., 4th Floor, Toronto ON M5J 2L6 Canada. E-mail: deanne.gage@advisor.rogers.com. Website: www.advisorsedge.ca. Monthly magazine covering the financial industry (financial advisors and investment advisors). *Advisor's Edge* focuses on sales and marketing opportunities for the financial advisor (how they can build their business and improve relationships with clients. Estab. 1998. Circ. 36,000. Byline given. Pays on publication. Offers 25% kill fee. Publishes ms an average of 3 months after acceptance. Buys one-time rights, buys electronic rights. Editorial lead time 3 months. Accepts queries by e-mail. Sample copy available online.

Nonfiction We are looking for articles that help advisors do their jobs better. Needs how-to, interview. No articles that aren't relevant to how a financial advisor does his/her job. **Buys 12 mss/year.** Query with published clips. Length: 1,500-2,000 words. **Pays $900 (Canadian).**

$ $ $ AFP EXCHANGE

Association for Financial Professionals, 4520 E. West Hwy., Suite 750, Bethesda MD 20814. (301)907-2862. E-mail: exchange@afponline.org. Website: www.afponline.org. **20% freelance written.** Monthly magazine covering corporate treasury, corporate finance, B2B payments issues, corporate risk management, accounting and regulatory issues from the perspective of corporations. Welcome interviews with CFOs and senior level practitioners. Best practices and practical information for corporate CFOs and treasurers. Tone is professional, intended to appeal to financial professionals on the job. Estab. 1979. Circ. 25,000. Byline given. Pays on publication. Offers kill fee. Pays negotiable kill fee in advance. Buys all rights. Editorial lead time 2 months. Submit seasonal material 3 months in advance. Accepts queries by e-mail. Responds in 1 week to queries. Responds in 1 month to mss. Guidelines available online.

Nonfiction Contact: Exchange Magazine Editor. Needs book excerpts, how-to, interview, personal experience, technical. PR-type articles pointing to any type of product or solution **Buys 3-4 year mss/year.** Query. Length: 1,100-1,800 words. **Pays 75¢/word minimum, &1.00 maximum for assigned articles.**

Columns/Departments Cash Flow Forecasting (practical tips for treasurers, CFOs); Financial Reporting (insight, practical tips); Risk Management (practical tips for treasurers, CFOs); Corporate Payments (practical tips for treasurers), all 1,000-1,300 words; Professional Development (success stories, career related, about high level financial professionals), 1,100 words. 10 Query. **Pays $75¢/word-$1.00/word.**

Fillers Needs anecdotes. open to consideration Length: 400-700 words. **Pays $75¢-75¢.**

Tips Accepted submissions deal with high-level issues relevant to today's corporate CFO or treasurer, including issues of global trade, global finance, accounting, M&A, risk management, corporate cash management, international regulatory issues, communications issues with corporate boards and shareholders, and especially new issues on the horizon. Preference given to articles by or about corporate practitioners in the finance function of mid-to large-size corporations in the U.S. or abroad. Also purchase articles by accomplished financial writers. Cannot accept content that points to any product, 'solution' or that promotes any vendor. Should not be considered a PR outlet. Authors may be required to sign agreement.

AUSTRALIAN BANKING & FINANCE

First Charlton Communications, Level 8, 122 Arthur St., North Sydney NSW 2060 Australia. (61)(2)9955-6299. Fax: (61)(2)9957-1512. E-mail: pctc@charlton.com.au. Website: www.charlton.com.au. Magazine published 22 times/year covering the dynamic financial services sector. *Australian Banking & Finance*helps senior executives make crucial decisions about the future by keeping them informed of the major issues and trends affecting their industry through unique editorial coverage and a constant stream of professional events supporting the industry's development.

Nonfiction Needs general interest. Query.

THE AUSTRALIAN ECONOMIC REVIEW

Melbourne Institute of Applied Economic and Social Research, The University of Melbourne, Melbourne VIC 3010 Australia. E-mail: aer@melbourneinstitute.com. Website: www.melbourneinstitute.com. Quarterly magazine applying economic analysis to a wide range of macroeconomic and microeconomic topics relevant to both economic and social policy issues. Guidelines available online.

Nonfiction Needs essays. Send complete ms.

BANKING STRATEGIES

Bank Administration Institute (BAI), 1 N. Franklin St., Suite 1000, Chicago IL 60606. E-mail: bankingstrategies@bai.org. Website: www.bai.org/bankingstrategies. **70% freelance written**. Magazine covering banking and financial services. Magazine covers banking from a strategic and managerial perspective for its senior financial executive audience. Each issue includes in-depth trend articles and interviews with influential executives. Offers variable kill fee. Buys all rights. Accepts queries by e-mail. Responds almost immediately.

Nonfiction Needs how-to, articles that help institutions be more effective and competitive in the marketplace, interview, executive interviews. No topic queries, we assign stories to freelancers. I'm looking for qualifications as opposed to topic queries. I need experienced writers/reporters. **Buys 30 mss/year.** E-queries preferred.

Tips Demonstrate ability and financial services expertise. I'm looking for freelancers who can write according to our standards, which are quite high.

$ $ $ CREDIT TODAY

Tomorrow's Tools for Today's Credit Professionals, P.O. Box 720, Roanoke VA 24004. (540)343-7500. E-mail: editor@credittoday.net. Website: www.credittoday.net. **50% freelance written**. Monthly newsletter covering business or trade credit. Make pieces actionable, personable, and a quick read. Estab. 1997. No byline given. Pays on acceptance. Publishes ms an average of 2 months after acceptance. Buys all rights. Editorial lead time 1-2 months. Accepts queries by e-mail. Sample copy free. Guidelines free.

Nonfiction Needs how-to, interview, technical. Does not want puff pieces promoting a particular product or vendor. **Buys 20 mss/year.** Send complete ms. Length: 700-1,800 words. **Pays $200-1,400.**

$ $ EQUITIES MAGAZINE, LLC

2118 Wilshire Blvd. #722, Santa Monica CA 90403. (914)723-6702. Fax: (914)723-0176. E-mail: equitymag@aol.com. Website: www.equitiesmagazine.com. **50% freelance written**. We are a seven-issues-a-year financial magazine covering the fastest-growing public companies in the world. We study the management of companies and act as critics reviewing their performances. We aspire to be 'The Shareholder's Friend.' We want to be a bridge between quality public companies and sophisticated investors. Estab. 1951. Circ. 18,000. Byline given. Pays on publication. No kill fee. Publishes ms an average of 2 months after acceptance. Buys all rights. Accepts queries by mail. Sample copy for sae with 9x12 envelope and 5 First-Class stamps.

Nonfiction We must know the writer first as we are careful about whom we publish. A letter of introduction with resume and clips is the best way to introduce yourself. Financial writing requires specialized knowledge and a feel for people as well, which can be a tough combination to find. Carries guest columns by famous money managers who are not writing for cash payments, but to showcase their ideas and approach. Needs expose, new product, technical. **Buys 30 mss/year.** Query with published clips. Length: 300-1,500 words. **Pays $250-750 for assigned articles, more for very difficult or investigative pieces.** Pays expenses of writers on assignment.

Photos Send color photos with submission. Identification of subjects required. Reviews contact sheets, negatives, transparencies, prints. Offers no additional payment for photos accepted with ms.

Columns/Departments Pays $25-75 for assigned items only.

Tips Give us an idea for a story on a specific publically-owned company, whose stock is traded on NASDAQ, the NYSE, or American Stock Exchange. Anyone who enjoys analyzing a business and telling the story of the people who started it, or run it today, is a potential *Equities* contributor. But to protect our readers and ourselves, we are careful about who writes for us. We do not want writers who are trading the stocks of the companies they profile. Business writing is an exciting area and our stories reflect that. If a writer relies on numbers and percentages to tell his story, rather than the individuals involved, the result will be numbingly dull.

$ $ $ THE FEDERAL CREDIT UNION

National Association of Federal Credit Unions, 3138 N. 10th St., Arlington VA 22201. (703)522-4770. Fax: (703)524-1082. E-mail: tfcu@nafcu.org. Website: www.nafcu.org. **30% freelance written**. Looking for writers with financial, banking, or credit union experience, but will work with inexperienced (unpublished) writers based on writing skill. Published bimonthly, *The Federal Credit Union* is the official publication of the National Association of Federal Credit Unions. The magazine is dedicated to providing credit union management, staff, and volunteers with in-depth information (HR, technology, security, board management, etc.) they can use to fulfill their duties and better serve their members. The editorial focus includes coverage of management issues, operations, and technology as well as volunteer-related issues. Estab. 1967. Circ.

8,000. Byline given. Pays on publication. No kill fee. Publishes ms an average of 3 months after acceptance. Buys first North American serial rights, rights to publish and archive online. Submit seasonal material 5 months in advance. Accepts queries by mail, e-mail, fax. Accepts simultaneous submissions. Responds in 2 months to queries. Sample copy for sae with 10x13 envelope and 5 First-Class stamps. Guidelines for #10 sase.

Nonfiction Needs humor, inspirational, interview. Query with published clips and SASE. Length: 1,200-2,000 words. **Pays $400-1,000.**

Photos Send photos Identification of subjects, model releases required. Reviews 35mm transparencies, 5x7 prints, high-resolution photos. Offers no additional payment for photos accepted with ms. Pays $50-500. Buys all rights.

Tips We would like more articles on how credit unions are using technology to serve their members and more articles on leading-edge technologies they can use in their operations. If you can write on current trends in technology, human resources, or strategic planning, you stand a better chance of being published than if you wrote on other topics.

ILLINOIS BANKER

Illinois Bankers Association, 133 S. Fourth St., Suite 300, Springfield IL 62701. (217)789-9340. Fax: (217)789-5410. Our audience is approximately 3,000 bankers and vendors related to the banking industry. The purpose of the publication is to educate and inform readers on major public policy issues affecting banking today, as well as provide new ideas that can be applied to day-to-day operations and management. Writers may not sell or promote a product or service. Estab. 1891. Circ. 2,800. Byline given. No kill fee. Publishes ms an average of 3 months after acceptance. Buys first North American serial rights. Editorial lead time 2 months. Accepts simultaneous submissions. Responds in 3 months to queries. Sample copy and writer's guidelines free.

Nonfiction It is *IBA* policy that writers do not sell or promote a particular product, service, or organization within the content of an article written for publication. Needs essays, historical, interview, new product, opinion, personal experience. Query. Length: 1,000-1,500 words.

Photos State availability Captions, identification of subjects required. Reviews contact sheets, negatives, transparencies, prints.

Tips Articles published in *Illinois Banker* address current issues of key importance to the banking industry in Illinois. Our intention is to keep readers informed of the latest industry news, developments, and trends, as well as provide necessary technical information. We publish articles on any topic that affects the banking industry, provided the content is in agreement with Association policy and position. Because we are a trade association, most articles need to be reviewed by an advisory committee before publication; therefore, the earlier they are submitted the better. Some recent topics include: agriculture, bank architecture, commercial and consumer credit, marketing, operations/cost control, security, and technology. In addition, articles are also considered on the topics of economic development and business/banking trends in Illinois and the Midwest region.

INVESTMENT NEWS

Crain Communications, 711 Third Ave., 3rd Floor, New York NY 10017. (212)210-0775. Fax: (212)210-0444. E-mail: jpavia@crain.com. Website: www.investmentnews.com. **10% freelance written**. Weekly magazine, newsletter, tabloid covering financial planning and investing. It covers the business of personal finance to keep its audience of planners, brokers and other tax investment professionals informed of the latest news about their industry. Estab. 1997. Circ. 60,000. Byline given. Pays on publication. Offers kill fee. Negotiate kill fee. Publishes ms an average of 1 month after acceptance. Buys all rights. Makes work-for-hire assignments. Editorial lead time 2 weeks. Submit seasonal material 1 month in advance. Sample copy and writer's guidelines free.

Tips Come to us with a specific pitch, preferably based on a news tip. We prefer to be contacted by fax or e-mail.

MORTGAGE BANKING

The Magazine of Real Estate Finance, Mortgage Bankers Association, 1919 Pennsylvania Ave., NW, Washington DC 20006. (202)557-2853. Fax: (202)721-0245. E-mail: jhewitt@mortgagebankers.org. Website: www.mortgagebankingmagazine.com. Monthly magazine covering real estate finance. Timely examinations of major news and trends in the business of mortgage lending for both commercial and residential real estate. Estab. 1939. Circ. 10,000. Byline given. Pays on acceptance. Offers kill fee. Negotiates kill fee. Publishes ms an average of 2 months after acceptance. Buys one-time rights. Makes work-for-hire assignments. Editorial lead time 2 months. Submit seasonal material 3 months in advance. Accepts queries by mail, e-mail, fax. Accepts simultaneous submissions. Responds in 1 month to queries. Responds in 4 months to mss. Sample copy and writer's guidelines free

Nonfiction Needs book excerpts, essays, interview, opinion. Commercial Real Estate Special Supplemental Issue (January); Internet Guide Supplemental Issue (September). **Buys 30 mss/year.** Query. 3,000 words **Writers' fees negotiable.** Sometimes pays expenses of writers on assignment.

Photos State availability Identification of subjects, model releases required. Reviews prints. Negotiates payment individually. Buys one time rights.
Columns/Departments Book reviews (current, relevant material), 300 words; executive essay (industry executive's personal views on relevant topic), 750-1,000 words. 2 Query. **Pay negotiated.**
Tips Trends in technology, current and upcoming legislation that will affect the mortgage industry are good focus.

$ $ $ $ ON WALL STREET

Source Media, One State St. Plaza, 26th Floor, New York NY 10004. (212)803-8783. E-mail: frances.mcmorris@sourcemedia.com. Website: www.onwallstreet.com. **50% freelance written**. Monthly magazine for retail stockbrokers. We help 95,000+ stockbrockers build their business. Estab. 1991. Circ. 95,000. Byline given. Pays on publication. No kill fee. Publishes ms an average of 1-2 months after acceptance. Buys all rights. Editorial lead time 3 months. Submit seasonal material 4 months in advance. Accepts queries by e-mail. Responds in 1-2 months to queries. Responds in 2 month to mss. Sample copy for $10.
Nonfiction Needs how-to, interview. No investment-related articles about hot stocks, nor funds or hot alternative investments. **Buys 30 mss/year.** Query. Length: 1,000-3,000 words. **Pays $1/word.**
Photos State availability Identification of subjects required. Reviews contact sheets. Negotiates payment individually. Buys all rights.
Tips Articles should be written for a professional, not consumer, audience.

$ $ SERVICING MANAGEMENT

The Magazine for Loan Servicing Professionals, Zackin Publications, P.O. Box 2180, Waterbury CT 06722. (800)325-6745. Fax: (203)262-4680. E-mail: bates@sm-online.com. Website: www.sm-online.com. **15% freelance written**. Monthly magazine covering residential mortgage servicing. Estab. 1989. Circ. 20,000. Byline given. Pays on acceptance. No kill fee. Publishes ms an average of 2 months after acceptance. Buys all rights. Accepts queries by mail, e-mail, fax. Responds in 2 weeks to queries. Sample copy free. Guidelines available online.
Nonfiction Needs how-to, interview, new product, technical. **Buys 10 mss/year.** Query. Length: 1,500-2,500 words.
Photos State availability Identification of subjects required. Reviews contact sheets. Offers no additional payment for photos accepted with ms. Buys all rights.
Columns/Departments 5 Query. **Pays $200.**

TRADERS MAGAZINE

1 State St. Plaza, 27th Floor, New York NY 10004. (212)803-8366. Fax: (212)295-1725. E-mail: michael.scotti@sourcemedia.com. Website: www.tradersmagazine.com. **35% freelance written**. Monthly magazine plus 2 specials covering equity trading and technology. Provides comprehensive coverage of how institutional trading is performed on NASDAQ and the New York Stock Exchange. Byline given. Pays on publication. No kill fee. Publishes ms an average of 2 months after acceptance. Buys all rights. Editorial lead time 2 months. Submit seasonal material 3 months in advance. Accepts queries by mail, e-mail, phone. Sample copy free to writers on assignment.
Nonfiction Needs book excerpts, expose, general interest, historical, how-to, humor, interview, new product, opinion, personal experience, religious, technical. Correspondent clearing (every market) and market making survey of broker dealers. No stories that are related to fixed income and other non-equity topics. **Buys 12-20 mss/year.** Send complete ms. Length: 750-2,800 words.
Columns/Departments Special Features (market regulation and human interest), 1600 words; Trading & Technology, 1,600 words; Washington Watch (market regulation), 750 words. Query with published clips.
Fiction Needs ethnic, Irish and Italian American, historical, humorous, mystery, science fiction, slice-of-life vignettes. No erotica. **Buys 1 mss/year.** Query or send complete ms. Length: 2,100-2,800 words.
Tips Boil it all down and don't bore the hell out of readers. Advice from a distinguished scribe which we pass along. Learn to explain equity market making and institutional trading in a simple, direct manner. Don't waffle. Have a trader explain the business to you if necessary. The *Traders Magazine* is highly regarded among Wall Street insiders, trading honchos, and Washington pundits alike.

$ $ $ $ N USAA MAGAZINE

A Member's Guide to Financial Security, USAA, 9800 Fredericksburg Rd., San Antonio TX 78288. Website: www.usaa.com/maglinks. **80% freelance written**. Quarterly magazine covering financial security for USAA members. "Conservative, common-sense approach to personal finance issues. Especially interested in how-to articles and pieces with actionable tips." Estab. 1970. Circ. 4.2 million. Byline given. Pays on acceptance. Offers 25% kill fee. Publishes ms an average of 4 months after acceptance. Buys all rights. Editorial lead time 6 months. Submit seasonal material 6 months in advance. Accepts queries by e-mail. Responds in 6-8 weeks to queries. No mss. accepted. Sample copy available online. Guidelines by email.
Nonfiction Needs general interest, (finance), historical, (military), how-to, (personal finance), interview, (military/financial), personal experience, (finance). No poetry, photos, lifestyle unrelated to military or

personal finance. **Buys 20 mss/year mss/year.** Query with published clips. Length: 750-1,500 words. **Pays $750-1,500 for assigned articles.** Sometimes pays expenses of writers on assignment.

Tips "Story must take a unique or innovative approach to the personal finance topic. Piece must be actionable and useful. (Not philosophical or academic.)"

$ $ $ $ WEALTH MANAGER

33-41 Newark St., 2nd Floor, Hoboken NJ 07030. E-mail: rkoreto@highlinemedia.com. Website: www.wealthmanagermag.com. **90% freelance written**. Magazine published 11 times/year for financial advisors. Stories should provide insight and information for the financial adviser. Put yourself on the adviser's side of the table and cover the issues thoroughly from his/her perspective. The piece should delve beneath the surface. We need specific examples, professional caveats, advice from professionals. Estab. 1999. Circ. 50,000. Byline given. Pays on acceptance. No kill fee. Publishes ms an average of 3 months after acceptance. Buys first North American serial rights. Editorial lead time 4 months. Submit seasonal material 4 months in advance. Accepts queries by e-mail. Responds in 1 month to queries.

Nonfiction Needs book excerpts, interview, technical. Do not submit anything that does not deal with financial planning issues or the financial markets. **Buys 30-40 mss/year.** Query with published clips. Length: 1,500-3,000 words. **Pays $1.50/word for assigned articles.**

Tips *Wealth Manager* is a trade magazine. All pieces should be written from the perspective of a financial adviser who has wealthy clients.

SOUTH CAROLINA

PALMETTO BANKER

The Official Publication of the SC Bankers Association, South Carolina Bankers Association, P.O. Box 1483, Columbia SC 29202. (803)779-0850. Fax: (803)256-8150. Website: www.scbankers.org. **15% freelance written**. Quarterly magazine covering Banking in South Carolina, trends & industry. We focus only on banking trends, regulations, laws, news, economic development of SC, technology and education of bankers. Estab. 1967. Circ. 1,600. Byline given. Doesn't pay for submissions. No kill fee. Publishes ms an average of 6 months after acceptance. Editorial lead time 6 months. Submit seasonal material 3 months in advance. Accepts queries by mail, fax. Accepts previously published material. Accepts simultaneous submissions. Sample copy free.

Nonfiction Needs technical. I don't want anything that does not pertain to banking trends, operations or technology. Anything that smacks of product sales. **Buys 0 mss/year.** Send complete ms. Length: 600-1,500 words. **Pays 0 for assigned articles. Pays 0 for unsolicited articles.**

Photos Send photos Model releases required. Reviews GIF/JPEG files. Offers no additional payment for photos accepted with ms.

Tips Recommendations/referrals from other State banking/national banking associations are helpful.

FISHING

AUSMARINE

Baird Publications, 135 Sturt St., Southbank VIC 3006 Australia. (61)(3)9645-0411. Fax: (61)(3)9645-0475. E-mail: marinfo@baird.com.au. Website: www.baird.com.au. Monthly magazine covering the Australian commercial fishing and government marine industry. "*Ausmarine* offers its readers information and ideas as to how to improve the efficiency and profitability of their business operations through the adoption of new technology and equipment, improved operational techniques and systems, and by simply providing them with the information required to make the right business decisions." Estab. 1978.

Nonfiction Query.

FISHING BOAT WORLD

Baird Publications, 135 Sturt St., Southbank VIC 3006 Australia. (61)(3)9645-0411. Fax: (61)(3)9645-0475. E-mail: marinfo@baird.com.au. Website: www.baird.com.au. Monthly magazine supplies the most accurate and up-to-date information regarding the boats, products, personalities and politics that affect the commercial fishing industry. *Fishing Boat World* offers its readers information and ideas as to how to improve the efficiency and profitability of their business operations through the adoption of new vessels, technology and equipment, improved operational techniques and systems, and by simply providing them with the information required to make the right business decisions. Estab. 1989.

Nonfiction Needs general interest, how-to, new product, technical. Query.

$ $ PACIFIC FISHING

Northwest Publishing Center, 1710 S. Norman St., Seattle WA 98144. (206)709-1840. Fax: (206)324-8939. E-mail: jholland@pfmag.com. Website: www.pfmag.com. **75% freelance written. Works with some new/**

unpublished writers. Monthly magazine for commercial fishermen and others in the commercial fishing industry throughout Alaska, the west coast, and the Pacific. *Pacific Fishing* views the fisherman as a small businessman and covers all aspects of the industry, including harvesting, processing, and marketing. Estab. 1979. Circ. 8,000. Byline given. Pays on publication. No kill fee. Publishes ms an average of 2 months after acceptance. Buys first North American serial and unlimited re-use rights. Accepts queries by mail, e-mail, fax, phone. Variable response time. Sample copy and writer's guidelines for 9x12 SAE with 10 first-class stamps

Nonfiction Articles must be concerned specifically with commercial fishing. We view fishermen as small business operators and professionals who are innovative and success-oriented. To appeal to this reader, *Pacific Fishing offers 4 basic features: technical, how-to articles that give fishermen hands-on tips that will make their operation more efficient and profitable; practical, well-researched business articles discussing the dollars and cents of fishing, processing, and marketing; profiles of a fisherman, processor, or company with emphasis on practical business and technical areas; and in-depth analysis of political, social, fisheries management, and resource issues that have a direct bearing on commercial fishermen.* **Buys 20 mss/year.** Query noting whether photos are available, and enclose samples of previous work and SASE. Varies, one-paragraph news items to 3,000-word features. **Pays 20¢/word for most assignments.** Sometimes pays expenses of writers on assignment.

Photos We need good, high-quality photography, especially color, of commercial fishing. We prefer 35mm color slides or JPEG files of at least 300 dpi. Our rates are $200 for cover; $50-100 for inside color; $25-75 for b $10 for table of contents.

Tips Read the magazine before sending a query. Make your pitch fit the magazine. If you haven't read it, don't waste your time and ours.

FLORIST, NURSERIES & LANDSCAPERS

$ $ DIGGER

Oregon Association of Nurseries, 29751 SW Town Center Loop W., Wilsonville OR 97070. (503)682-5089. Fax: (503)682-5099. E-mail: csivesind@oan.org. Website: www.oan.org. **50% freelance written**. Monthly magazine covering nursery and greenhouse industry. Our readers are mainly nursery and greenhouse operators and owners who propagate nursery stock/crops, so we write with them in mind. Circ. 8,000. Byline given. Pays on receipt of copy. Offers 100% kill fee. Publishes ms an average of 2 months after acceptance. Buys first North American serial rights. Editorial lead time 6 weeks. Submit seasonal material 2 months in advance. Accepts queries by mail, e-mail, fax, phone. Sample copy and writer's guidelines free

Nonfiction Needs general interest, how-to, propagation techniques, other crop-growing tips, interview, personal experience, technical. Farwest Edition (August)—this is a triple-size issue that runs in tandem with our annual trade show (14,500 circulation for this issue). No articles not related or pertinent to nursery and greenhouse industry. **Buys 20-30 mss/year.** Query. Length: 800-2,000 words. **Pays $125-400 for assigned articles. Pays $100-300 for unsolicited articles.** Sometimes pays expenses of writers on assignment.

Photos State availability Captions, identification of subjects required. Reviews high-res digital images sent by e-mail or on CD preferred. Offers $25-150/photo Buys one-time rights, which includes Web posting.

Tips Our best freelancers are familiar with or have experience in the horticultural industry. Some `green' knowledge is a definite advantage.

$ GROWERTALKS

Ball Publishing, 335 N. River St., P.O. Box 9, Batavia IL 60510. (630)208-9080. Fax: (630)208-9350. E-mail: beytes@growertalks.com. Website: www.growertalks.com. **50% freelance written**. Monthly magazine. *GrowerTalks* serves the commercial greenhouse grower. Editorial emphasis is on floricultural crops: bedding plants, potted floral crops, foliage and fresh cut flowers. Our readers are growers, managers, and owners. We're looking for writers who've had experience in the greenhouse industry. Estab. 1937. Circ. 9,500. Byline given. Pays on publication. No kill fee. Publishes ms an average of 3 months after acceptance. Buys first North American serial rights. Editorial lead time 4 months. Submit seasonal material 3 months in advance. Accepts queries by mail, e-mail, fax. Responds in 1 month to queries. Sample copy and writer's guidelines free

Nonfiction Needs how-to, time- or money-saving projects for professional flower/plant growers, interview, ornamental horticulture growers, personal experience, of a grower, technical, about growing process in greenhouse setting. No articles that promote only one product. **Buys 36 mss/year.** Query. Length: 1,200-1,600 words. **Pays $125 minimum for assigned articles. Pays $75 minimum for unsolicited articles.**

Photos State availability Captions, identification of subjects, model releases required. Reviews 2½x2½ slides and 3x5 prints. Negotiates payment individually. Buys one time rights.

Tips Discuss magazine with ornamental horticulture growers to find out what topics that have or haven't appeared in the magazine interest them.

$ $ THE GROWING EDGE

New Moon Publishing, Inc., P.O. Box 1027, Corvallis OR 97339. (541)757-8477. Fax: (541)757-0028. Website: www.growingedge.com. **85% freelance written**. Bimonthly magazine covering indoor and outdoor high-tech gardening techniques and tips. Estab. 1980. Circ. 20,000. Byline given. Pays on publication. No kill fee. Publishes ms an average of 3 months after acceptance. Buys first serial and reprint rights. Submit seasonal material 6 months in advance. Accepts queries by mail, e-mail. Responds in 3 months to queries. Sample copy for $3. Guidelines available online.

Nonfiction Needs how-to, interview, personal experience, must be technical, book reviews, general horticulture and agriculture. Query. Length: 500-3,500 words. **Pays 20¢/word (10¢ for first rights, 5¢ for nonexclusive reprint and nonexclusive electronic rights).**

Reprints Send tearsheet, photocopy or typed ms with rights for sale noted and information about when and where the material previously appeared. Payment negotiable.

Photos Pays $25-175. Pays on publication. Credit line given. Buys first and reprint rights.

Tips Looking for more hydroponics articles and information that will give the reader/gardener/farmer the growing edge in high-tech gardening and farming on topics such as high intensity grow lights, water conservation, drip irrigation, advanced organic fertilizers, new seed varieties, and greenhouse cultivation.

LANDSCAPE AUSTRALIA

Universal Magazines, Ltd., Unit 5, 6-8 Byfield St., North Ryde NSW 2113 Australia. (61)(2)9887-0399. Fax: (61)(2)9805-0714. E-mail: landscape@universalmagazines.com.au. Website: www.universalmagazines.com.au. Quarterly magazine for professionals working in landscape, urban design or land-use planning.

Nonfiction Needs general interest, how-to, photo feature, case studies. Query.

$ $ ORNAMENTAL OUTLOOK

Your Connection To The South's Horticulture Industry, Meister Media Worldwide, 1555 Howell Branch Rd., Suite C204, Winter Park FL 32789. (407)539-6552. Fax: (407)539-6544. E-mail: pprusnak@meistermedia.com. Website: www.ornamentaloutlook.com. **Contact:** Paul Rusnak, managing editor. **20% freelance written**. Monthly magazine. "*Ornamental Outlook* is written for commercial growers of ornamental plants and landscapers in Florida. Our goal is to provide interesting and informative articles on such topics as production, legislation, safety, technology, pest control, water management, and new varieties, as they apply to Southeast growers and landscapers." Estab. 1991. Circ. 11,000. Byline given. Pays on publication. No kill fee. Publishes ms an average of 4 months after acceptance. Buys all rights. Editorial lead time 2 months. Submit seasonal material 3 months in advance. Accepts queries by mail, e-mail, fax, phone. Responds in 3 months to queries. Sample copy for sae with 9x12 envelope and 5 First-Class stamps. Guidelines free.

Nonfiction Needs interview, photo feature, technical. No first-person articles. No word-for-word meeting transcripts or all-quote articles. Query with published clips. Length: 600-1,000 words. **Pays $150-300/article including photos.**

Photos Send photos Captions, identification of subjects required. Reviews contact sheets, transparencies, prints. Buys one time rights.

Tips "I am most impressed by written queries that address specific subjects of interest to our audience, which is the Florida landscaper and grower of commercial horticulture. Our biggest demand is for features, about 700 words, that follow subjects listed on our editorial calendar (which is sent with guidelines). Please do not send articles of national or consumer interest."

$ $ TREE CARE INDUSTRY MAGAZINE

Tree Care Industry Association, 136 Harvey Rd., londonderry NH 03053. (800)733-2622 or (603)314-5380. Fax: (603)314-5386. E-mail: staruk@tcia.org. Website: www.treecareindustry.org. **50% freelance written.** Monthly magazine covering tree care and landscape maintenance. Estab. 1990. Circ. 27,500. Byline given. Pays within 1 month of publication. No kill fee. Publishes manuscripts an average of 3 months after acceptance. Buys all rights. Editorial lead time 10 weeks. Submit seasonal material 3 months in advance. Accepts queries by e-mail. Responds within 2 days to queries. Responds in 2 months to manuscripts. View PDFs online Guidelines free

Nonfiction Needs book excerpts, historical, interview, new product, technical. **Buys Buys 60 manuscripts/year mss/year.** Query with published clips. Length: 900-3,500 words. **Pays negotiable rate.**

Photos Send photos with submission by e-mail or FTP site. Captions, identification of subjects required. Reviews prints. Negotiate payment individually. Buys one-time and Web rights.

Columns/Departments 40 Send complete manuscript. **Pays $100 and up.**

Tips "Preference is given to writers with background and knowledge of the tree care industry; our focus is relatively narrow."

GOVERNMENT & PUBLIC SERVICE

MPC TODAY

Associated Mail and Parcel Centers, 5411 E. State St., Suite 202, Rockford IL 61108. Fax: (815)316-8256. Website: www.ampc.org. Ellen Peters, editor. **Contact:** Jim Kitzmiller, gen. manger. **85**. Mail and Parcel Industry/Retail Shipping Stores. Our readers are the owners and operators of retail shipping and business service stores. These are convenience stores for packing, shipping, and other services including mailbox rental and mail forwarding. The stores are both independent and franchise operated; they are small and generally family or owner operated. The biggest obstacle to success is for the owner to leave the store for training, networking, planning, managing, and sales. Estab. 1984. Circ. 12 months: 2,400; 3 months: 10,000. Yes. publication. 3 months Buys one-time rights. 3 months. Accepts queries by mail, e-mail at articles@ampc.org. Accepts previously published submissions.Accepts simultaneous submissions. Sample copy online at website

Nonfiction Needs essays, how-to, inspirational, interview, new product, technical, Typical topics can be packing, shipping, mailbox rentals, freight shipping, UPS, FedEx, DHL, USPS, bulk mailing, copy service, binding, laminating, retail fill items, packaging supplies, custom boxes, customer service, store profiles, and diversified profit centers. Send complete ms. 500-2,000/words. **Pays $50-150 for assigned articles and for unsolicited articles.** Pays expenses sometimes (limit agreed upon in advance).Does not pay with contributor copies or other premiums rather than cash.

Photos Contact: Jim Kitzmiller, gen. manager. Send photos with submission. Requires identification of subjects. Review GIF/JPEG files Offers no additional payment for photos accepted with ms. Purchases one-time rights.

Columns/Departments Column pays $50-150.

Tips It is important that you be very knowledgeable about the subject of the mail and parcel industry you are covering. Our articles are usually written by store owners or vendors to the industry, but that is not a requirement. Our readers run the gamut of new store owners to 30-year veterans and the articles can be geared to anywhere in between, but must be accurate and engaging. Although best practices of store operations is important, our missions is to help our members become more successful, more profitable, and the articles should support that.

$ $ AMERICAN CITY & COUNTY

Penton Media, 6151 Powers Ferry Rd. NW, Suite 200, Atlanta GA 30339. (770)618-0199. Fax: (770)618-0349. E-mail: lindsay.isaacs@penton.com. Website: www.americancityandcounty.com. **40% freelance written.** Monthly magazine covering local and state government in the United States. *American City & County* is received by more than 82,000 elected and appointed local and state government officials and public and private engineers. Included in the circulation list are administrators, supervisors and department heads of municipal, county, township, state and special district governments. Estab. 1909. Circ. 82,000. Byline given. Pays on publication. Offers 25% kill fee. Publishes ms an average of 2 months after acceptance. Buys all rights. Editorial lead time 3 months. Accepts queries by e-mail. Accepts simultaneous submissions. Sample copy available online. Guidelines by email.

Nonfiction Needs new product, local and state government news analysis. **Buys 36 mss/year.** Query. Length: 600-2,000 words. **Pays $600.** Sometimes pays expenses of writers on assignment.

Photos State availability Captions required. Reviews GIF/JPEG files. Negotiates payment individually. Buys all rights.

Columns/Departments Issues & Trends (local and state government news analysis), 500-700 words. 24 Query. **Pays $150-250.**

Tips We use only third-person articles. We do not tell the reader what to do; we offer the facts and assume the reader will make his or her own informed decision. We cover city and county government and state highway departments. We do not cover state legislatures or the federal government, except as they affect local government.

ATLANTIC FIREFIGHTER

The Voice of the Fire Service in Atlantic Canada, Hilden Publishing, Ltd., P.O. Box 919, Amherst NS B4H 4E1 Canada. E-mail: info@atlanticfirefighter.ca. Website: www.atlanticfirefighter.ca. Monthly magazine. Circ. 7,000. Accepts queries by e-mail. Guidelines available online.

Nonfiction Needs general interest, interview. Send complete ms.

Tips Just e-mail your article as a Word document.

AUSTRALASIAN PARKS AND LEISURE

P.O. Box 210, Bendigo Central VIC 3552 Australia. E-mail: office@park-leisure.com.au. Website: www.parks-leisure.com.au. Quarterly magazine including general professional articles, notes, announcements, photographic features, refereed academic articles and more. *"Australasian Parks and Leisure*'s major function is to provide a professional service to members of the 2 organizations and to provide opportunities for the dissemination of information and ideas in the field of parks and leisure." Guidelines available online.

Nonfiction Needs general interest, how-to, technical. Query. Length: 1,000-1,500 words.

Photos Captions, identification of subjects required. Reviews JPEG files (300 dpi).

Tips "Articles should be written in direct, informative style, avoiding jargon and too much abstract material."

AUSTRALIAN DEFENCE BUSINESS REVIEW

P.O. Box 250, Mawson ACT 2607 Australia. (61)(2)6260-4855. Fax: (61)(2)6260-3977. E-mail: busicom@ozemail.com.au. Website: www.adbr.com.au. Magazine for defence business executives. Estab. 1982.

- Query before submitting.

AUSTRALIAN JOURNAL OF EMERGENCY MANAGEMENT

Mount Macedon Rd., 601 Mount Macedon VIC 3441 Australia. (61)(03)5421-5100. E-mail: ajem@ema.gov.au. Website: www.ema.gov.au. Quarterly magazine. Estab. 1986. Guidelines available online.
Nonfiction Needs how-to, technical. Send complete ms. Length: 3,000 words.
Photos Reviews JPEG/TIFF/EPS (300 dpi).

AUSTRALIAN JOURNAL OF INTERNATIONAL AFFAIRS

Taylor & Francis Group, Dept. of International Relations, Research School of Pacific & Asian Studies, The Australian National University, Canberra ACT 0200 Australia. Website: www.aiia.asn.au. Quarterly magazine covering high quality scholarly research on international political, social, economic and legal issues, especially within the Asia-Pacific region. Guidelines available online.
Nonfiction Needs technical. Send complete ms.

AUSTRALIAN JOURNAL OF PUBLIC ADMINISTRATION

Blackwell Publishing, Political Science Program, RSSS, Australian National University, Canberra ACT 0200 Australia. E-mail: ajpa@anu.edu.au. Website: www.blackwellpublishers.co.uk. Magazine committed to the study and practice of public administration, public management and policy making. Buys all rights. Guidelines available online.
Nonfiction Needs general interest, interview, technical, book reviews. Send complete ms. Length: 300-7,000 words.

AUSTRALIAN SOCIAL WORK

Australian Association of Social Workers, P.O. Box 4956, Kingston ACT 2604 Australia. (61)(2)6273-5024. Fax: (61)(2)6273-5020. E-mail: suew@aasw.asn.au. Website: www.aasw.asn.au. Quarterly magazine addressing contemporary thinking on social work, social welfare and social policy. Guidelines available online.
Nonfiction Needs general interest, how-to, interview, technical. Send complete ms. Length: 5,000 words.
Tips We're especially interested in articles which add to existing knowledge, or open up new or neglected areas in the profession.

BLUE LINE MAGAZINE

Canada's National Law Enforcement Magazine, 12A-4981 Highway 7 East, Suite 254, Markham ON L3R 1N1 Canada. (905)640-3048. Fax: (905)640-7547. E-mail: blueline@blueline.ca. Website: www.blueline.ca. Monthly magazine keeping readers on the leading edge of information, whether it be case law, training issues or technology trends. Estab. 1989. Circ. 12,000.
Nonfiction Needs general interest, how-to, interview, new product. Query.

CANADIAN FIREFIGHTER AND EMS QUARTERLY

105 Donly Dr., Simcoe ON NY3 4N5 Canada. (905)847-9743. E-mail: canfirefight@annexweb.com. Website: www.firefightingincanada.com. Quarterly magazine covering fire fighting in Canada.
Nonfiction Needs general interest, how-to, interview, technical. Query.

$ $ COUNTY

Texas Association of Counties, P.O. Box 2131, Austin TX 78768. (512)478-8753. Fax: (512)477-1324. E-mail: jiml@county.org. Website: www.county.org. **15% freelance written**. Bimonthly magazine covering county and state government in Texas. We provide elected and appointed county officials with insights and information that help them do their jobs and enhances communications among the independent office-holders in the courthouse. Estab. 1988. Circ. 5,500. Byline given. Pays on acceptance. No kill fee. Publishes ms an average of 2 months after acceptance. Makes work-for-hire assignments. Editorial lead time 2 months. Submit seasonal material 4 months in advance. Accepts queries by mail, e-mail, phone. Responds in 2 weeks to queries. Responds in 1 month to mss. Sample copy and writer's guidelines for 8x10 SAE with 3 first-class stamps
Nonfiction Needs historical, photo feature, government innovations. **Buys 5 mss/year.** Query with published clips. Length: 1,000-3,000 words. **Pays $500-700.** Sometimes pays expenses of writers on assignment.
Photos State availability Captions, identification of subjects, model releases required. Negotiates payment individually Buys all rights.
Columns/Departments Safety; Human Resources; Risk Management (all directed toward education of Texas

county officials), maximum length 1,000 words. 2 Query with published clips. **Pays $500**
Tips Identify innovative practices or developing trends that affect Texas county officials, and have the basic journalism skills to write a multi-sourced, informative feature.

EVIDENCE TECHNOLOGY MAGAZINE

P.O. Box 555, Kearney MO 64060. E-mail: kmayo@evidencemagazine.com. Website: www.evidencemagazine.com. "Bimonthly magazine providing news and information relating to the collection, processing and preservation of evidence.". Accepts queries by e-mail. Guidelines available online
Nonfiction Needs general interest, how-to, interview, new product, technical. Query. **Pays 2 contributor copies.**
Photos Reviews JPEG files (300 dpi or larger).
Tips "Opening a dialogue with the editor will give you the opportunity to get guidelines on length, style and deadlines."

FIRE APPARATUS & EMERGENCY EQUIPMENT

234 Monarch Hill Rd., Turnbridge VT 05077. (802)889-9800. Fax: (802)889-9608. E-mail: news@firemagazine.com. Website: www.fireapparatusmagazine.com. Monthly magazine focused on fire trucks, tools and new technology.
Nonfiction Needs general interest, how-to, new product, technical. Query.

$ $ FIRE CHIEF

Primedia Business, 330 N. Wabash, Suite 2300, Chicago IL 60611. (312)840-8410. Fax: (312)595-0295. E-mail: jwilmoth@primediabusiness.com. Website: www.firechief.com. **60% freelance written.** Monthly magazine. *Fire Chief* is the management magazine of the fire service, addressing the administrative, personnel, training, prevention/education, professional development, and operational issues faced by chiefs and other fire officers, whether in paid, volunteer, or combination departments. We're potentially interested in any article that can help them do their jobs better, whether that's as incident commanders, financial managers, supervisors, leaders, trainers, planners, or ambassadors to municipal officials or the public. Estab. 1956. Circ. 53,000. Byline given. Pays on publication. Offers kill fee. Kill fee negotiable. Publishes ms an average of 6 months after acceptance. Buys first rights, buys one-time rights, buys second serial (reprint) rights, buys all rights. Editorial lead time 2 months. Submit seasonal material 4 months in advance. Accepts queries by mail, e-mail, fax. Responds in 1 month to queries. Responds in 2 months to mss. Sample copy and writer's guidelines free or online
Nonfiction If your department has made some changes in its structure, budget, mission, or organizational culture (or really did reinvent itself in a serious way), an account of that process, including the mistakes made and lessons learned, could be a winner. Similarly, if you've observed certain things that fire departments typically could do a lot better and you think you have the solution, let us know. Needs how-to, technical. **Buys 50-60 mss/year.** Query with published clips. Length: 1,500-8,000 words. **Pays $50-400.** Sometimes pays expenses of writers on assignment.
Photos State availability Captions, identification of subjects required. Reviews transparencies, prints. Buys one-time or reprint rights.
Columns/Departments Training Perspectives; EMS Viewpoints; Sound Off; Volunteer Voice; all 1,000-1,800 words.
Tips Writers who are unfamiliar with the fire service are very unlikely to place anything with us. Many pieces that we reject are either too unfocused or too abstract. We want articles that help keep fire chiefs well informed and effective at their jobs.

FIRE ENGINEERING

21-00 Route 208 S., Fair Lawn NJ 07410. (800)962-6484, ext. 5047. E-mail: dianef@pennwell.com. Website: www.fireengineering.com. Monthly magazine covering issues of importance to firefighters. Accepts queries by mail, e-mail. Responds in 2-3 months to mss. Guidelines available online.
Nonfiction Themes: Training/Instructor Development, Engine Company Operations, Technical Rescue, Fire Protection, EMS, Truck Company Operations, Apparatus, Fire Technology, Firefighter Safety and Health, Officer Development, and Leadership and Management. Needs how-to, new product, incident reports, training. Send complete ms.
Photos Reviews electronic format only: JPEG/TIFF/EPS files (300 dpi).
Columns/Departments Volunteers Corner; Training Notebook; Rescue Company; The Engine Company; The Truck Company; Fire Prevention Bureau; Apparatus; The Shops; Fire Service EMS; Fire Service Court; Speaking of Safety; Fire Commentary; Technology Today; and Innovations: Homegrown. Send complete ms.

FIRE FIGHTING IN CANADA

Canada's National Fire Magazine, P.O. Box 530, 105 Donly Dr. S., Simcoe Ontario N3Y 4N5 Canada. (888)599-2228. E-mail: lking@annexweb.com. Website: www.firefightingincanada.com. Magazine published 8 times/year covering fire fighting in Canada.

Nonfiction Needs general interest, interview, technical. Query.

$ $ FIREHOUSE MAGAZINE

Cygnus Business Media, 3 Huntington Quadrangle, Suite 301N, Melville NY 11747. (631)845-2700. Fax: (631)845-7218. E-mail: editors@firehouse.com. Website: www.firehouse.com. **85% freelance written. Works with a small number of new/unpublished writers each year.** Monthly magazine. *Firehouse* covers major fires nationwide, controversial issues and trends in the fire service, the latest firefighting equipment and methods of firefighting, historical fires, firefighting history and memorabilia. Fire-related books, fire safety education, hazardous-materials incidents, and the emergency medical services are also covered. Estab. 1976. Circ. 127,000. Byline given. Pays on publication. No kill fee. Accepts queries by mail, e-mail, fax. Sample copy for sae with 9x12 envelope and 8 First-Class stamps. Guidelines available online.

Nonfiction Needs book excerpts, of recent books on fire, EMS, and hazardous materials, historical, great fires in history, fire collectibles, the fire service of yesteryear, how-to, fight certain kinds of fires, buy and maintain equipment, run a fire department, technical, on almost any phase of firefighting, techniques, equipment, training, administration, trends in the fire service. No profiles of people or departments that are not unusual or innovative, reports of nonmajor fires, articles not slanted toward firefighters' interests. No poetry. **Buys 100 mss/year.** Query. Length: 500-3,000 words. **Pays $50-400 for assigned articles.**

Photos Send photos Captions, identification of subjects required. Pays $25-200 for transparencies and color prints. Cannot accept negatives.

Columns/Departments Training (effective methods); Book Reviews; Fire Safety (how departments teach fire safety to the public); Communicating (PR, dispatching); Arson (efforts to combat it). Length: 750-1,000 words. 50 Query or send complete ms. **Pays $100-300.**

Tips Have excellent fire service credentials and be able to offer our readers new information. Read the magazine to get a full understanding of the subject matter, the writing style, and the readers before sending a query or manuscript. Send photos with manuscript or indicate sources for photos. Be sure to focus articles on firefighters.

FIRE NEWS

146 S. Country Rd., Bellport NY 11713. (631)776-0500. Fax: (631)776-1854. E-mail: chuck@firenews.com. Website: www.firenews.com. Monthly magazine for Long Island fire fighters. Estab. 1973.

Nonfiction Needs general interest, how-to, interview, new product, technical. Query.

FIRE PROTECTION CONTRACTOR

550 High St., Suite 220, Auburn CA 95603. (530)823-0706. Fax: (530)823-6937. E-mail: info@fpcmag.com. Website: www.fpcmag.com. Monthly magazine for the benefit of fire protection contractors, engineers, designers, sprinkler fitters, apprentices, fabricators, manufacturers and distributors of fire protection products used in automatic fire sprinkler systems. Estab. 1978.

Nonfiction Needs general interest, how-to, interview, new product, technical. Query.

$ $ FIRE-RESCUE MAGAZINE

Jems Communications, 525 B St., Suite 1900, San Diego CA 92101. Fax: (619)699-6396. E-mail: jems.editor@elsevier.com. Website: www.jems.com. **75% freelance written**. Monthly magazine covering technical aspects of being a firefighter/rescuer. Estab. 1988. Circ. 50,000. Pays on publication. No kill fee. Buys first North American serial rights, buys one-time rights. Submit seasonal material 6 months in advance. Accepts queries by mail. Responds in 3 weeks to queries. Responds in 2 months to mss. Sample copy and writer's guidelines for 9x12 SAE with 5 first-class stamps or online. Guidelines available online.

Nonfiction Needs how-to, new product, photo feature, technical, incident review/report. fire suppression, incident command, vehicle extrication, rescue training, mass-casualty incidents, water rescue/major issues facing the fire service. **Buys 15-20 mss/year.** Send complete ms. Length: 1,000-3,000 words. **Pays $125-250.** Sometimes pays expenses of writers on assignment.

Photos Send photos Reviews contact sheets, negatives, 2—Š2 and 35mm transparencies, 5—Š7 prints. Offers $20-200 Buys one time rights.

Tips Read our magazine, spend some time with a fire department. We focus on all aspects of fire and rescue. Emphasis on techniques and new technology, with color photos as support.

FIRE SERVICES JOURNAL

6 Hillman Dr., Ajax ON L1S 6X9 Canada. (905)428-8465. Fax: (905)683-9572. E-mail: fire@interlog.com. Website: www.fsj.on.ca. Bimonthly magazine for the fire services industry.

Nonfiction Needs general interest, new product. Query.

FOREIGN SERVICE JOURNAL

2101 E St. NW, Washington DC 20037. (202)338-4045. Fax: (202)338-6820. E-mail: journal@afsa.org. Website: www.afsa.org. **75% freelance written**. Monthly magazine for foreign service personnel and others interested in foreign affairs and related subjects. Estab. 1924. Byline given. Pays on publication. No kill fee. Publishes ms an average of 3 months after acceptance. Buys first North American serial rights. Accepts queries by mail, e-mail, fax. Responds in 1 month to queries. Sample copy for $3.50 and 10x12 SAE with 6 first-class stamps. Guidelines for #10 sase.

Nonfiction Uses articles on diplomacy, professional concerns of the State Department and foreign service, diplomatic history and articles on foreign service experiences. Much of our material is contributed by those working in the profession. Informed outside contributions are welcomed, however. Needs essays, expose, humor, opinion, personal experience. **Buys 15-20 unsolicited mss/year.** Send complete ms. Length: 1,000-3,000 words.

Tips We're more likely to want your article if it has something to do with diplomacy or US foreign policy.

GOVERNMENT NEWS

The International Group, Ltd., P.O. Box 55, Glebe NSW 2037 Australia. (61)(2)9660-2113. Fax: (61)9660-4419. E-mail: info@intermedia.com.au. Website: www.intermedia.com.au. Monthly magazine covering important issues in every state and territory. *Government News* is dedicated to bringing together relevant news and product information for public sector workers and those in public office.

Nonfiction Needs general interest, new product. Query.

HOMELAND DEFENSE JOURNAL

4301 Wilson Blvd., Suite 1003, Arlington VA 22203-1867. (301)455-5633. E-mail: dp@homelanddefensejournal.com. Website: www.homelanddefensejournal.com. **50% freelance written**. Monthly magazine covering homeland defense, emergency management and security. *Homeland Defense Journal* is an Arlington, Virginia-based monthly magazine focusing on homeland security and emergency management throughout the U.S. Our readers are primarily decision makers in government, military and civilian areas at federal, state and regional levels. They include government and federal department officials, politicians, EM/HS operational directors, sheriffs, heads of law enforcement agencies, chief officers of local authorities, fire chiefs, airport and seaport general managers and so on. Estab. 2001. Circ. 35,000. Byline given. Pays on publication. Offers 50% kill fee. Publishes ms an average of 2 months after acceptance. Buys all rights. Editorial lead time 1-2 months. Accepts queries by e-mail. Responds in 1 week to queries. Responds in 1 month to mss. Sample copy free. Guidelines free.

Nonfiction Needs how-to, interview, new product, opinion, technical. Does not want articles promoting companies or their products and services. **Buys 200 mss/year.** Query. Length: 800-3,000 words. **Pays negotiable amount.** Sometimes pays expenses of writers on assignment.

Photos Send photos Captions, identification of subjects required. Reviews GIF/JPEG files. Offers no additional payment for photos accepted with ms. Buys one time rights.

Columns/Departments Periscope (IT developments as they relate to homeland security); Executive Showcase (industry appointments, major contract wins); Technical Showcase (new products/services that relate to homeland security), all 300-500 words. Query.

Tips Call or e-mail. Always willing to listen.

$ $ LAW ENFORCEMENT TECHNOLOGY MAGAZINE

Cygnus Business Media, P.O. Box 803, 1233 Janesville Ave., Fort Atkinson WI 53538-0803. (920)568-8334. Fax: (920)563-1702. E-mail: tabatha.wethal@cygnuspub.com. Website: www.officer.com. **40% freelance written**. Monthly magazine covering police management and technology. Estab. 1974. Circ. 30,000. Byline given. Pays on publication. No kill fee. Publishes ms an average of 4 months after acceptance. Buys first North American serial rights, buys electronic rights. Editorial lead time 6 months. Responds in 1 month to queries. Responds in 2 months to mss Guidelines available online

Nonfiction Needs how-to, interview, photo feature, police management and training. **Buys 30 mss/year.** Query. Length: 1,200-2,000 words. **Pays $75-400 for assigned articles.**

Reprints Send typed manuscript with rights for sale noted and information about when and where the material previously appeared. Payment negotiable.

Photos Send photos Captions required. Reviews contact sheets, negatives, 5x7 or 8x10 prints. Offers no additional payment for photos accepted with ms. Buys one time rights.

Tips "Writer should have background in police work or currently work for a police agency. Most of our articles are technical or supervisory in nature. Please query first after looking at a sample copy. Prefers mss, queries and images be submitted electronically."

$ $ 9-1-1 MAGAZINE

Official Publications, Inc., 18201 Weston Place, Tustin CA 92780-2251. (714)544-7776. Fax: (714)838-9233. E-mail: publisher@9-1-1magazine.com. Website: www.9-1-1magazine.com. **85% freelance written**. Trade magazine published 9 times/year for knowledgeable emergency communications professionals and those associated with this respectful profession. Serving law enforcement, fire, and emergency medical services, with an emphasis on communications, *9-1-1 Magazine* provides valuable information to readers in all aspects of the public safety communications and response community. Each issue contains a blending of product-related, technical, operational, and people-oriented stories, covering the skills, training, and equipment which these professionals have in common. Estab. 1989. Circ. 19,000. Byline given. Pays on publication. Offers 20% kill fee. Publishes ms an average of 4-6 months after acceptance. Buys first rights. Accepts queries by mail, e-mail, fax. Responds in 1 month to queries. Responds in 1 month to mss. Sample copy for sae with 9x12 envelope and 5 First-Class stamps. Guidelines available online.

Nonfiction Needs new product, photo feature, technical, incident report. **Buys 15-25 mss/year.** Query by e-mail. We prefer queries, but will look at manuscripts on speculation. Most positive responses to queries are considered on spec, but occasionally we will make assignments. Length: 1,000-2,500 words. **Pays 10-20¢/word.**

Photos Send photos Captions, identification of subjects required. Reviews color transparencies, prints, high-resolution digital (300 dpi). Offers $50-100/interior, $300/cover. Buys one time rights.

Tips We are looking for writers knowledgable in this field. As a trade magazine, stories should be geared for professionals in the emergency services and dispatch field, not the lay public. We do not use poetry or fiction. Our primary considerations in selecting material are: quality, appropriateness of material, brevity, knowledge of our readership, accuracy, accompanying photography, originality, wit and humor, a clear direction and vision, and proper use of language.

$ $ $ PLANNING

American Planning Association, 122 S. Michigan Ave., Suite 1600, Chicago IL 60603. (312)431-9100. Fax: (312)431-9985. E-mail: slewis@planning.org. Website: www.planning.org. **Contact:** Sylvia Lewis, editor. **30% freelance written.** Monthly magazine emphasizing urban planning for adult, college-educated readers who are regional and urban planners in city, state, or federal agencies or in private business, or university faculty or students. Estab. 1972. Circ. 44,000. Byline given. Pays on publication. No kill fee. Publishes ms an average of 2 months after acceptance. Buys all rights. Accepts queries by mail, e-mail, fax. Responds in 5 weeks to queries. Sample copy for 9x12 SAE with 6 first-class stamps Guidelines available online.

Nonfiction "It's best to query with a fairly detailed, 1-page letter or e-mail. We'll consider any article that's well written and relevant to our audience. Articles have a better chance if they are timely and related to planning, and if they appeal to a national audience. All articles should be written in magazine-feature style." Needs expose, on government or business, but topics related to planning, housing, land use, zoning, general interest, trend stories on cities, land use, government, how-to, successful government or citizen efforts in planning, innovations, concepts that have been applied, technical, detailed articles on the nitty-gritty of planning, transportation, computer mapping, but no footnotes or mathematical models. Transportation Issue; Technology Issue. Also needs news stories up to 500 words. **Buys 44 features and 33 news story mss/year.** Length: 500-3,000 words. **Pays $150-1,500.**

Photos "We prefer authors supply their own photos, but we sometimes take our own or arrange for them in other ways." State availability Captions required. Pays $100 minimum for photos used on inside pages and $300 for cover photos. Buys one time rights.

$ $ POLICE AND SECURITY NEWS

DAYS Communications, Inc., 1208 Juniper St., Quakertown PA 18951-1520. (215)538-1240. Fax: (215)538-1208. E-mail: jdevery@policeandsecuritynews.com. **40% freelance written.** Bimonthly tabloid on public law enforcement and Homeland Security. Our publication is designed to provide educational and entertaining information directed toward management level. Technical information written for the expert in a manner the nonexpert can understand. Estab. 1984. Circ. 22,000. Byline given. Pays on publication. No kill fee. Publishes ms an average of 2 months after acceptance. Buys first North American serial rights. Accepts queries by mail, e-mail, fax, phone. Accepts simultaneous submissions. Sample copy and writer's guidelines for 10x13 SAE with $2.53 postage.

Nonfiction Contact: Al Menear, articles editor. Needs expose, historical, how-to, humor, interview, opinion, personal experience, photo feature, technical. **Buys 12 mss/year.** Query. Length: 200-2,500 words. **Pays 10¢/word. Sometimes pays in trade-out of services.**

Reprints Send tearsheet, photocopy or typed ms with rights for sale noted and information about when and where the material previously appeared.

Photos State availability Reviews 3x5 prints. Offers $10-50/photo. Buys one time rights.

Fillers Needs facts, newsbreaks, short humor. 6 Length: 200-2,000 words. **10¢/word.**

SPRINKLER AGE

12750 Merit Dr., Suite 350, Dallas TX 75251. (214)349-5965, ext. 117. Fax: (214)343-8898. E-mail: jknowles@firesprinkler.org. Website: www.firesprinkler.org. **Contact:** Janet R. Knowles. Monthly magazine providing readers with up-to-date information on the latest developments in the fire sprinkler industry. "*Sprinkler Age* has been called 'the magazine' for technical information." Circ. 4,000. Guidelines by email.

Nonfiction Needs technical. Query.

$ $ $ $ YOUTH TODAY

The Newspaper on Youth Work, American Youth Work Center, 1200 17th St. NW, 4th Floor, Washington DC 20036. (202)785-0764. E-mail: pboyle@youthtoday.org. Website: www.youthtoday.org. **50% freelance**

written. 10 times/yr. newspaper covering businesses that provide services to youth. Audience is people who run youth programs—mostly nonprofits & government agencies. They want help in providing services, getting funding. Estab. 1994. Circ. 9,000. Byline given. Pays on acceptance. Offers $200 kill fee. Buys first North American serial rights, buys electronic rights. Editorial lead time 2 months. Accepts queries by mail, e-mail. Accepts simultaneous submissions. Responds in 2 weeks to queries. Responds in 1 month to mss. Sample copy for $5. Guidelines available online.
Nonfiction Needs expose, general interest, technical. No feel-good stories about do-gooders. We examine the business of youth work. **Buys 30 mss/yr. mss/year.** Query. Length: 500-2,000 words. **Pays $0.75-$1/word max. for assigned articles.** Pays expenses of writers on assignment.
Photos Identification of subjects required. Offers no additional payment for photos accepted with ms. Buys one time rights.
Tips Business writers have the best shot. Focus on evaluations of programs, or why a program succeeds or fails. Please visit online.

GROCERIES & FOOD PRODUCTS

$ $ $ DISTRIBUTION CHANNELS

AWMA's Magazine for Candy, Tobacco, Grocery, Foodservice and General Merchandise Marketers, American Wholesale Marketers Association, 2750 Prosperity Ave., Suite 530, Fairfax VA 22031. Fax: (703)573-5738. E-mail: tracic@awmanet.org. Website: www.awmanet.org. **70% freelance written**. Magazine published 10 times/year. "We cover trends in candy, tobacco, groceries, beverages, snacks, and other product categories found in convenience stores, grocery stores, and drugstores, plus distribution topics. Contributors should have prior experience writing about the food, retail, and/or distribution industries. Editorial includes a mix of columns, departments, and features (2-6 pages). We also cover AWMA programs." Estab. 1948. Circ. 11,000. Byline given. Pays on acceptance. No kill fee. Publishes ms an average of 2 months after acceptance. Editorial lead time 4 months. Accepts queries by mail, e-mail, fax. Guidelines available online.
Nonfiction Needs how-to, technical, industry trends; also profiles of distribution firms. No comics, jokes, poems, or other fillers. **Buys 40 mss/year.** Query with published clips. Length: 1,200-3,600 words. **Pays 50¢/word.** Pays expenses of writers on assignment.
Photos Authors must provide artwork (with captions) with articles.
Tips "We're looking for reliable, accurate freelancers with whom we can establish a long-term working relationship. We need writers who understand this industry. We accept very few articles on speculation. Most are assigned. To consider a new writer for an assignment, we must first receive his or her resume, at least 2 writing samples, and references."

FOOD MANAGEMENT NEWS (FMN)

Yaffa Publishing, 17-21 Bellevue St., Surry Hills NSW 2010 Australia. (61)(2)9281-2333. Fax: (61)(2)9281-2750. E-mail: yaffa@yaffa.com.au. Website: www.yaffa.com.au. Magazine published 11 times/year covering Australia's food, beverage and ingredients sectors. *FMN* provides an objective and colorful diet of news, features, new products and industry trends. Estab. 1975.
Nonfiction Needs expose, general interest, interview, new product, technical. Query.

$ $ $ NATURAL FOOD NETWORK MAGAZINE

Supporting the Business of Natural & Organic Food Supply, 760 Market St., Suite 432, San Francisco CA 94102. (415)839-5067. Fax: (415)398-3511. E-mail: news@naturalfoodnet.com. Website: www.naturalfoodnet.com. **70% freelance written**. Bimonthly magazine covering natural and certified organic food industry (domestic and international). Estab. 2003. Circ. 15,000. Byline given. Pays on publication. Offers 10% up to $50 maximum kill fee. Publishes ms an average of 2 months after acceptance. Buys first North American serial rights. Editorial lead time 2 months. Submit seasonal material 2 months in advance. Accepts queries by e-mail. Accepts simultaneous submissions. Responds in 1 week to queries. Responds in 1 month to mss. Sample copy free. Guidelines free.
Nonfiction Our publication circulates entirely to retail and supply professionals. Does not want work with a consumer angle. **Buys 50 mss/year.** Query. Length: 250-1,500 words. **Pays $250-750.** Sometimes pays expenses of writers on assignment.
Photos State availability Captions, identification of subjects required. Reviews JPEG files. Offers no additional payment for photos accepted with ms. Buys all rights.
Columns/Departments Q&A with industry leaders (natural and organic specialists in academia, trade associations and business); Worldview (interviews with internationally recognized leaders in organic food supply), both 750 words. 6 Query. **Pays $500.**
Tips Our magazine encourages writers to work closely with editors using online story pitch and assignment software. This collaborative software permits writers to see what is being pitched (anonymously) and to track their own assignments, download materials like story guidelines and monitor deadlines.

$ $ PRODUCE MERCHANDISING

Vance Publishing Corp., 10901 W. 84th Terrace, Lenexa KS 66214. (913)438-8700. Fax: (913)438-0691. E-mail: ccrawford@producemerchandising.com. Website: www.producemerchandising.com. **10% freelance written**. Monthly magazine. The magazine's editorial purpose is to provide information about promotions, merchandising, and operations in the form of ideas and examples. *Produce Merchandising* is the only monthly journal on the market that is dedicated solely to produce merchandising information for retailers. Circ. 12,000. Byline given. Pays on acceptance. No kill fee. Publishes ms an average of 3 months after acceptance. Buys all rights. Editorial lead time 3 months. Accepts queries by mail. Responds in 2 weeks to queries. Sample copy free.

Nonfiction Needs how-to, interview, new product, photo feature, technical, contact the editor for a specific assignment. **Buys 48 mss/year.** Query with published clips. Length: 1,000-1,500 words. **Pays $200-600.** Pays expenses of writers on assignment.

Photos State availability of or send photos Captions, identification of subjects, model releases required. Reviews color slides and 3x5 or larger prints. Offers no additional payment for photos accepted with ms. Buys all rights.

Columns/Departments Contact: Contact editor for a specific assignment. 30 Query with published clips. **Pays $200-450.**

Tips Send in clips and contact the editor with specific story ideas. Story topics are typically outlined up to a year in advance.

$ $ THE PRODUCE NEWS

800 Kinderkamack Rd., Suite 100, Oradell NJ 07649. (201)986-7990. Fax: (201)986-7996. E-mail: groh@theproducenews.com. Website: www.theproducenews.com. **10% freelance written. Works with a small number of new/unpublished writers each year.** Weekly magazine for commercial growers and shippers, receivers and distributors of fresh fruits and vegetables, including chain store produce buyers and merchandisers. Estab. 1897. Pays on publication. No kill fee. Publishes ms an average of 2 weeks after acceptance. Accepts queries by mail, e-mail, fax. Responds in 1 month to queries. Sample copy and writer's guidelines for 10X13 SAE and 4 first-class stamps.

Nonfiction News stories (about the produce industry). Buys profiles, spot news, coverage of successful business operations and articles on merchandising techniques. Query. **Pays $1/column inch minimum.** Sometimes pays expenses of writers on assignment.

Photos Black and white glossies or color prints. Pays $8-10/photo.

Tips Stories should be trade oriented, not consumer oriented. As our circulation grows in the next year, we are interested in stories and news articles from all fresh-fruit-growing areas of the country.

$ $ WESTERN GROCER MAGAZINE

Mercury Publications Ltd., 1740 Wellington Ave., Winnipeg MB R3H 0E8 Canada. (204)954-2085. Fax: (204)954-2057. Website: www.mercury.mb.ca/. **75% freelance written**. Bimonthly magazine covering the grocery industry. Reports profiles on independent food stores, supermarkets, manufacturers and food processors, brokers, distributors, and wholesalers. Estab. 1916. Circ. 15,500. Byline given. Pays 30-45 days from receipt of invoice. Offers 33% kill fee. Buys all rights. Submit seasonal material 3 months in advance. Sample copy and writer's guidelines free

- Assigns stories to Canadian writers based on editorial needs of publication.

Nonfiction Needs how-to, interview. Industry reports and profiles on companies. Query with published clips. Length: 500-9,000 words. **Pays 25-35¢/word.** Sometimes pays expenses of writers on assignment.

Photos State availability Captions required. Reviews negatives, transparencies, 3x5 prints, JPEG, EPS, or TIF files. Negotiates payment individually Buys all rights.

Tips E-mail, fax, or mail a query outlining your experience, interest, and pay expectations. Include clippings.

HARDWARE

AUSTRALIAN HARDWARE JOURNAL

Glenvale Publications, P.O. Box 50, Mt. Waverley VIC 3149 Australia. (61)(03)9544-2233. Fax: (61)(03)9543-1150. E-mail: thomas@glenv.com.au. Website: www.hardwarejournal.com.au. Magazine for hardware retailers, suppliers, agents and distributors all over Australia. *The Australian Hardware Journal* consistently delivers a strong mix of the latest news, industry trends, product and marketing innovation that leads to more informed decision making. Estab. 1886. Circ. 6,200.

Nonfiction Needs general interest, how-to, interview, new product, technical. Query.

HOME FURNISHINGS & HOUSEHOLD GOODS

FINE FURNISHINGS INTERNATIONAL

FFI, Grace McNamara, Inc., 4215 White Bear Parkway, Suite 100, St. Paul MN 55110. (651)293-1544. Fax: (651)653-4308. E-mail: ffiedit@gracemcnamarainc.com. Website: www.ffimagazine.com. Quarterly magazine covering the high-end furniture industry. Estab. 1997. Circ. 25,000. Pays on publication. Buys all rights. Editorial lead time 3-5 months. Accepts queries by mail, e-mail. Sample copy for $5.

Nonfiction Interior designer profiles, high-end residential furnishings, international trade events, and interior-design associations are all featured in our trade publication.

Tips Writers must have a knowledge of interior design and furnishings that allows them to speak with authority to our to-the-trade audience of interior designers and architects.

$ $ HOME FURNISHINGS RETAILER

National Home Furnishings Association (NHFA), 3910 Tinsley Dr., High Point NC 27265. (336)801-6156. Fax: (336)801-6102. E-mail: tkemerly@nhfa.org. **75% freelance written.** Monthly magazine published by NHFA covering the home furnishings industry. We hope home furnishings retailers view our magazine as a profitability tool. We want each issue to help them make or save money. Estab. 1927. Circ. 15,000. Byline given. Pays on acceptance. No kill fee. Publishes ms an average of 6 weeks after acceptance. Buys first North American serial rights. Editorial lead time 3 months. Accepts queries by mail, e-mail. Responds in 1 month to queries. Sample copy available with proper postage Guidelines for #10 sase.

Nonfiction Query with published clips. 3,000-5,000 words (features) **Pays $350-500.**

Photos State availability Identification of subjects required. Reviews transparencies. Negotiates payment individually. Buys one time rights.

Columns/Departments Columns cover business and product trends that shape the home furnishings industry. Advertising and Marketing; Finance; Technology; Training; Creative Leadership; Law; Style and Operations. Length: 1,200-1,500 words. Query with published clips.

Tips Our readership includes owners of small `Ma and Pa' furniture stores, executives of medium-sized chains (2-10 stores), and executives of big chains. Articles should be relevant to retailers and provide them with tangible information, ideas, and products to better their business.

HOME LIGHTING & ACCESSORIES

Doctorow Communications, Inc., 1011 Clifton Ave., Clifton NJ 07013. (973)779-1600. Fax: (973)779-3242. Website: www.homelighting.com. **25% freelance written. Prefers to work with published/established writers.** Monthly magazine for lighting showrooms/department stores. Estab. 1923. Circ. 10,000. Pays on publication. No kill fee. Publishes ms an average of 6 months after acceptance. Buys first rights. Submit seasonal material 6 months in advance. Accepts queries by mail. Responds in 2 months to queries. Sample copy for sae with 9x12 envelope and 4 First-Class stamps.

Nonfiction Needs interview, with lighting retailers, personal experience, as a businessperson involved with lighting, technical, concerning lighting or lighting design, profile (of a successful lighting retailer/lamp buyer). Outdoor (March); Tribute To Tiffanies (August) **Buys less than 10 mss/year.** Query.

Reprints Send tearsheet and information about when and where the material previously appeared.

Photos State availability Captions required. Offers no additional payment for 5x7 or 8x10 b&w glossy prints.

Tips "Have a unique perspective on retailing lamps and lighting fixtures. We often use freelancers located in a part of the country where we'd like to profile a specific business or person. Anyone who has published an article dealing with any aspect of home furnishings will have high priority."

PWC MAGAZINE

Painting & Wallcovering Contractor, 403 Briarwood Rd., Wallingford PA 19086-6502. (888)590-8942. Fax: (888)590-8942. E-mail: mchollet@paintsquare.com. Website: www.paintstore.com. **75% freelance written.** 8 issues/year magazine covering all aspects of the painting and wallcovering contracting industry. Circ. 25,000+. Pays within 30 days of acceptance. No kill fee.

Nonfiction Needs only topics specifically related to the painting and wallcovering industries; no generic submissions, please. See Editorial Calendar for topics. Submit query or cover letter and bio. **Pays variable amount.**

Photos Writer solicits as part of assignment. No Photographers needed.

WINDOW FASHIONS

Grace McNamara, Inc., 4215 White Bear Pkwy., Suite 100, St. Paul MN 55110. Fax: (651)653-4308. E-mail: linda@gracemcnamarainc.com. Website: www.window-fashions.com. **30% freelance written.** Monthly magazine dedicated to the advancement of the window fashions industry, *Window Fashions* provides comprehensive information on design and business principles, window fashion aesthetics, and product applications. The magazine serves the window-treatment and wall-coverings industry, including designers, retailers, dealers, specialty stores, workrooms, manufacturers, fabricators, and others associated with the field of interior design. Writers should be thoroughly knowledgable on the subject, and submissions need to be comprehensive. Estab. 1981. Circ. 30,000. Byline given. Pays on publication. No kill fee. Publishes ms an average of 3 months after acceptance. Buys all rights. Editorial lead time 3 months. Submit seasonal material 4 months in advance. Accepts queries by mail, e-mail. Accepts simultaneous submissions. Sample copy for $5.

Nonfiction Needs how-to, window fashion installation, interview, of designers, personal experience, specific topics within the field. No broad topics not specific to the window fashions industry. **Buys 24 mss/year.** Query or send complete ms Length: 800-1,000 words.

Tips The most helpful experience is if a writer has knowledge of interior design or, specifically, window treatments. We already have a pool of generalists, although we welcome clips from writers who would like to be considered for assignments. Our style is professional business writing—no flowery prose. Articles tend to be to the point, as our readers are busy professionals who read for information, not for leisure. Most of all we need creative ideas and approaches to topics in the field of window treatments and interior design. A writer needs to be knowledgeable in the field because our readers would know if information was inaccurate.

HOSPITALS, NURSING & NURSING HOMES

ALZHEIMER'S CARE GUIDE

Freiberg Press Inc., P.O. Box 612, Cedar Falls IA 50613. (319)553-0642. Fax: (319)553-0644. E-mail: bfreiberg@cfu.net. Website: www.care4elders.com. **25% freelance written**. Bimonthly magazine covering Alzheimer's care. Aimed at caregivers of Alzheimer's patients. Interested in either inspirational first-person type stories or features/articles involving authoritative advice or caregiving tips. Estab. 1992. Circ. 10,000. Byline sometimes given. Pays on acceptance. No kill fee. Buys all rights. Accepts queries by e-mail.

- Query first. Only pays for assigned articles.

Nonfiction Needs book excerpts, interview, personal experience, technical. **Buys 50 mss/year.** Query. Length: 500-2,000 words.

AUSTRALIAN NURSING JOURNAL

Level 2, 21 Victoria St., Melbourne VIC 3000 Australia. (61)(3)9639-5211. Fax: (61)(3)9652-0567. E-mail: anj@anf.org.au. Website: www.anf.org.au. Monthly magazine covering nursing issues in Australia. *ANJ* welcomes articles written by nurses for nurses. Please contact the editor first to make sure your article is appropriate for the journal. Publishes ms an average of 3-12 months after acceptance. Responds in 3 months to queries. Guidelines available online.

Nonfiction Needs general interest, how-to, interview, opinion, technical. Query. Length: 400-2,000 words.

$ $ CURRENT NURSING IN GERIATRIC CARE

Freiberg Press Inc., P.O. Box 612, Cedar Falls IA 50613. (319)553-0642. E-mail: bfreiberg@cfu.net. Website: www.care4elders.com. **25% freelance written**. Bimonthly trade journal covering medical information and new developments in research for geriatric nurses and other practitioners. Estab. 2006. Byline sometimes given. Pays on acceptance. No kill fee. Buys all rights. Accepts queries by e-mail. Sample copy free.

Nonfiction Query. Length: 500-1,500 words. **Pays 15¢/word for assigned articles.**

Photos State availability

$ $ $ HOSPITALS & HEALTH NETWORKS

Health Forum, 1 N. Franklin, 29th Floor, Chicago IL 60606. (312)422-2100. E-mail: bsantamour@healthforum.com. Website: www.hhnmag.com. **25% freelance written**. Monthly magazine covering hospitals. We are a business publication for hospital and health system executives. We use only writers who are thoroughly familiar with the hospital field. Submit rÃˆsumÃˆ and up to 5 samples of health care-related articles. We assign all articles and do not consider manuscripts. Estab. 1926. Circ. 85,000. Byline given. Pays on acceptance. Offers variable kill fee. Publishes ms an average of 3 months after acceptance. Buys all rights. Editorial lead time 2-3 months. Accepts queries by e-mail. Responds in 2-4 months to queries.

Nonfiction Contact: Bill Santamour, managing editor. Needs interview, technical. Query with published clips. Length: 350-2,000 words. **Pays $300-1,500 for assigned articles.**

Tips If you demonstrate via published clips that you are thoroughly familiar with the business issues facing health-care executives, and that you are a polished reporter and writer, we will consider assigning you an article for our InBox section to start out. These are generally 350 words on a specific development of interest to hospitals and health system executives. Persistence does not pay with us. Once you've sent your résumé and clips, we will review them. If we have no assignment at that time, we will keep promising freelance candidates on file for future assignments.

$ $ LONG TERM CARE

The Ontario Long Term Care Association, 345 Renfrew Dr., Suite 102-202, Markham ON L3R 9S9 Canada.

(905)470-8995. Fax: (905)470-9595. E-mail: hlrpublishing@bellnet.ca. Website: www.oltca.com. Quarterly magazine covering professional issues and practical articles of interest to staff working in a long-term care setting (nursing home, retirement home): Information must be applicable to a Canadian setting; focus should be on staff and for resident well being. Estab. 1990. Circ. 6,000. Byline given. Pays on publication. No kill fee. Publishes ms an average of 4 months after acceptance. Buys one-time rights. Editorial lead time 3 months. Submit seasonal material 5 months in advance. Responds in 3 months to queries. Sample copy free. Guidelines available online.

Nonfiction Needs general interest, how-to, practical, of use to long term care practitioners, inspirational, interview. No product-oriented articles. Query with published clips. Length: 800-1,500 words. **Pays up to $500 (Canadian).**

Photos Send photos Captions, model releases required. Reviews contact sheets, 5x5 prints. Offers no additional payment for photos accepted with ms. Buys one time rights.

Columns/Departments Query with published clips. **Pays up to $500 (Canadian).**

Tips Articles must be positive, upbeat, and contain helpful information that staff and managers working in the long term care field can use. Focus should be on staff and resident well being. Articles that highlight new ways of doing things are particularly useful. Please call the editor to discuss ideas. Must be applicable to Canadian settings.

$ $ $ NURSEWEEK

Heartland Edition, Gannett Healthcare Group, 2353 Hassell Rd., Suite 110, Hoffman Estates IL 60169-2170. (847)490-6666. Fax: (847)490-0419. E-mail: hcygon@gannetthg.com. Website: www.nurse.com. **98% freelance written**. Biweekly magazine covering nursing news. Registered nurses read our magazine, which they receive for free by mail. We cover nursing news about people, practice, and the profession. Estab. 1999. Circ. 155,000. Byline given. Pays on publication. Offers $200 kill fee. Publishes ms an average of 2 months after acceptance. Buys all rights. Editorial lead time 2-3 months. Submit seasonal material 4 months in advance. Accepts queries by mail, e-mail, fax, phone. Accepts simultaneous submissions. Sample copy free. Guidelines free.

Nonfiction Needs interview, personal experience. Wwe don't want poetry, fiction, technical pieces. **Buys 20 mss/year. mss/year.** Query. Length: 600-1,500 words. **Pays $200-800 for assigned articles. Pays $200-800 for unsolicited articles.**

Photos Send photos Captions, model releases required. Reviews contact sheets, GIF/JPEG files. Offers no additional payment for photos accepted with ms. Buys all rights.

Tips Pitch us nursing news, AP style, minimum 3 sources, incorporate references.

$ $ $ NURSING SPECTRUM

Greater Chicago Edition, Gannett Healthcare Group, 2353 Hassell Rd., Suite 110, Hoffman Estates IL 60169-2170. (847)490-6666. Fax: (847)490-0419. E-mail: hcygan@gannetthg.com. Website: www.nurse.com. **98% freelance written**. Biweekly magazine covering nursing news. All of our readers are registered nurses who receive our publication free in the mail. We cover people, practice, and the profession of nursing. Estab. 1987. Circ. 64,500. Byline given. Pays on publication. Offers $200 kill fee. Publishes ms an average of 2 months after acceptance. Buys all rights. Editorial lead time 2 months. Submit seasonal material 4 months in advance. Accepts queries by mail, e-mail, fax, phone. Accepts simultaneous submissions. Responds in 2 months to mss. Sample copy free.

Nonfiction Needs interview, personal experience. We do not want fiction or technical essays. **Buys 100 mss/year. mss/year.** Query with published clips. Length: 600-1,500 words. **Pays $200-800 for assigned articles. Pays $200-800 for unsolicited articles.**

Photos Send photos Captions, model releases required. Reviews contact sheets, GIF/JPEG files. Offers no additional payment for photos accepted with ms. Buys all rights.

Tips Pitch us stories only about nursing, 3 sources minimum, use AP style, no references!

$ $ $ NURSING SPECTRUM, FLORIDA

Florida Edition, Nursing Spectrum, 1001 W. Cypress Creek Rd., Suite 330, Ft. Lauderdale FL 33309. (954)776-1455. Fax: (954)776-1456. Website: www.nursingspectrum.com. **80% freelance written**. Biweekly magazine covering registered nursing. We support and recognize registered nurses. All articles must have at least one RN in byline. We prefer articles that feature nurses in our region, but articles of interest to all nurses are welcome, too. We look for substantive, yet readable articles. Our bottom line—timely, relevant, and compelling articles that support nurses and help them excel in their clinical and professional careers. Estab. 1991. Circ. 60,000. Byline given. Pays on publication. No kill fee. Buys all rights. Editorial lead time 3 months. Submit seasonal material 4 months in advance. Accepts queries by mail, fax, phone. Responds in 1 month to queries. Responds in 4 months to mss. Sample copy free. Guidelines available online.

Nonfiction Needs general interest, how-to, career management, humor, interview, personal experience, photo feature. Critical Care; Nursing Management. **Buys 125 plus mss/year.** Length: 700-1,200 words. **Pays $50-800 for assigned articles.** Sometimes pays expenses of writers on assignment.

Photos Captions, identification of subjects, model releases required. Negotiates payment individually. Buys one time rights.

Columns/Departments Humor Infusion (cartoon, amusing anecdotes). 75 Query with published clips. **Pays $50-120.**

Tips Write in `magazine' style—as if talking to another RN. Use to-the-point, active language. Narrow your focus. Topics such as `The Future of Nursing' or `Dealing With Change' are too broad and nonspecific. Use informative but catchy titles and subheads (we can help with this). If quoting others, be sure quotes are meaningful and add substance to the piece. To add vitality, you may use statistics and up-to-date references. Try to paint a complete picture, using pros and cons. Be both positive and realistic.

$ SCHOOL NURSE NEWS

Franklin Communications, Inc., 53 Stickle Ave., Rockaway NJ 07866. (973)625-8811. Fax: (973)625-7914. Website: www.schoolnursenews.org. **10% freelance written.** Magazine published 5 times/year covering school nursing. Estab. 1982. Circ. 7,500. Byline given. Pays on publication. Publishes ms an average of 3-6 months after acceptance. Buys first North American serial rights. Editorial lead time 3-6 months. Submit seasonal material 6 months in advance. Accepts queries by e-mail, phone. Sample copy free. Guidelines free.

Nonfiction Needs how-to, interview, new product, personal experience. **Buys 1-2 mss/year.** Query. **Pays $100.**

HOTELS, MOTELS, CLUBS, RESORTS & RESTAURANTS

AUSTRALIAN HOTELIER

NPG, Suite 67, The Lower Deck, James Bay Wharf, 26 Pirrama Rd., Pyrmont Point NSW 2009 Australia. (61)(2)9566-1777. Fax: (61)(2)9566-1333. E-mail: jwilkinson@npg.com.au. Website: www.npg.com.au. Monthly magazine servicing the hotel industry across Australia. *Australian Hotelier* investigates relevant aspects of this diverse and growing industry in a non-aligned editorial style, reflecting both sides of issues, from the latest news and views to the trends affecting the market place.

Nonfiction Needs general interest, how-to, interview, new product. Query.

BARS & CLUBS

NPG, Suite 67, The Lower Deck, James Bay Wharf, 26 Pirrama Rd., Pyrmont Point NSW 2009 Australia. (61)(2)9566-1777. Fax: (61)(2)9566-1333. E-mail: jwilkinson@npg.com.au. Website: www.npg.com.au. Magazine covering the ever-increasing bars, clubs and nightclub market.

Nonfiction Needs general interest, how-to, interview, new product. Query.

$ $ BARTENDER MAGAZINE

Foley Publishing, P.O. Box 158, Liberty Corner NJ 07938. (908)766-6006. Fax: (908)766-6607. Website: www.bartender.com. **100% freelance written. Prefers to work with published/established writers; eager to work with new/unpublished writers.** Quarterly magazine emphasizing liquor and bartending for bartenders, tavern owners, and owners of restaurants with full-service liquor licenses. Circ. 148,225. Byline given. Pays on publication. No kill fee. Publishes ms an average of 3 months after acceptance. Buys first North American serial rights, buys first rights, buys one-time rights, buys second serial (reprint) rights, buys simultaneous rights, buys all rights. Submit seasonal material 3 months in advance. Accepts simultaneous submissions. Responds in 2 months to mss. Sample copy for sae with 9x12 envelope and 4 First-Class stamps.

Nonfiction Needs general interest, historical, ho-to, humor, interview with famous bartenders or ex-bartenders, new product, opinion, personal experience, photo feature, travel, nostalgia, unique bars, new techniques, new drinking trends, bar sports, bar magic tricks. Annual Calendar and Daily Cocktail Recipe Guide. Send complete ms and SASE. Length: 100-1,000 words.

Reprints Send tearsheet and information about when and where the material previously appeared. Pays 25% of amount paid for an original article.

Photos Send photos Captions, model releases required. Pays $7.50-50 for 8x10 b&w glossy prints; $10-75 for 8x10 color glossy prints.

Columns/Departments Bar of the Month; Bartender of the Month; Creative Cocktails; Bar Sports; Quiz; Bar Art; Wine Cellar; Tips from the Top (from prominent figures in the liquor industry); One For the Road (travel); Collectors (bar or liquor-related items); Photo Essays. **Length:** 200-1,000 words. Query by mail only with SASE. **Pays $50-200.**

Fillers Needs anecdotes, newsbreaks, short humor, clippings, jokes, gags. Length: 25-100 words. **Pays $5-25.**

Tips "To break in, absolutely make sure that your work will be of interest to all bartenders across the country. Your style of writing should reflect the audience you are addressing. The most frequent mistake made by writers in completing an article for us is using the wrong subject."

CHEF

The Food Magazine for Professionals, Talcott Communications Corp., 20 W. Kinzie, 12th Floor, Chicago IL 60610. (312)849-2220. Fax: (312)849-2174. Website: www.chefmagazine.com. **40% freelance written.** Monthly magazine covering chefs in all food-service segments. *Chef* is the one magazine that communicates food production to a commercial, professional audience in a meaningful way. Circ. 42,000. Byline given. No kill fee. Buys first North American serial rights, buys second serial (reprint) rights. Editorial lead time 2 months. Submit seasonal material 4 months in advance. Accepts queries by mail, e-mail, fax. Guidelines free.

Nonfiction Needs book excerpts, essays, expose, general interest, historical, how-to, create a dish or perform a technique, inspirational, interview, new product, opinion, personal experience, photo feature, technical. **Buys 30-50 mss/year.** Query. Length: 750-1,500 words.

Photos State availability Captions, identification of subjects required. Reviews transparencies. Buys one time rights.

Columns/Departments Flavor (traditional and innovative applications of a particular flavor) 1,000-1,200 words; Dish (professional chef profiles), 1,000-1,200 words; Savor (themed recipes), 1,000-1,500 words. 12-18 Query.

Tips Know food and apply it to the business of chefs. Always query first, after you've read our magazine. Tell us how your idea can be used by our readers to enhance their businesses in some way.

CLUB MANAGEMENT

The Resource for Successful Club Operations, Finan Publishing Co., 107 W. Pacific Ave., St. Louis MO 63119. (314)961-6644. Fax: (314)961-4809. Website: www.club-mgmt.com. Bimonthly magazine covering club management, private club market, hospitality industry. Estab. 1925. Circ. 16,702. Pays on publication. No kill fee. Publishes ms an average of 2 months after acceptance. Buys first North American serial rights, buys electronic rights. Accepts queries by mail, e-mail, fax.

Nonfiction Needs general interest, historical, how-to, interview, personal experience, photo feature, technical, travel. **Buys 100 mss/year.** Query with published clips. Length: 2,000-2,500 words.

Photos State availability

Columns/Departments Sports (private club sports: golf, tennis, yachting, fitness, etc.).

Tips We don't accept blind submissions. Please submit a resume and clips of your work. Send copies, not originals.

$ $ EL RESTAURANTE MEXICANO

P.O. Box 2249, Oak Park IL 60303-2249. (708)488-0100. Fax: (708)488-0101. E-mail: kfurore@restmex.com. Bimonthly magazine covering Mexican and other Latin cuisines. "*El Restaurante Mexicano* offers features and business-related articles that are geared specifically to owners and operators of Mexican, Tex-Mex, Southwestern, and Latin cuisine restaurants and other foodservice establishments that want to add that type of cuisine." Estab. 1997. Circ. 27,000. Byline given. Pays on publication. No kill fee. Publishes ms an average of 3 months after acceptance. Buys first North American serial rights. Responds in 2 months to queries. Sample copy free.

Nonfiction Looking for stories about unique Mexican restaurants and about business issues that affect Mexican restaurant owners. No specific knowledge of food or restaurants is needed; the key qualification is to be a good reporter who knows how to slant a story toward the Mexican restaurant operator. **Buys 4-6 mss/year.** Query with published clips. Length: 800-1,200 words. **Pays $250-300.** Pays expenses of writers on assignment.

Tips "Query with a story idea, and tell how it pertains to Mexican restaurants."

$ $ FLORIDA HOTEL & MOTEL JOURNAL

The Official Publication of the Florida Hotel & Motel Association, Accommodations, Inc., P.O. Box 1529, Tallahassee FL 32302-1529. (850)224-2888. Fax: (850)668-2884. E-mail: journal@fhma.net. Website: www.flahotel.com. **10% freelance written. Prefers to work with published/established writers.** Bimonthly magazine acting as a reference tool for managers and owners of Florida's hotels, motels, and resorts. Estab. 1978. Circ. 8,500. Byline given. Pays on publication. No kill fee. Publishes ms an average of 1-2 months after acceptance. Buys first rights. Editorial lead time 1-9 months. Submit seasonal material 4-5 months in advance. Accepts queries by mail. Accepts previously published material. Responds in 2-4 months to queries. Sample copy free. Guidelines available online.

Nonfiction Needs how-to, pertaining to hotel management, interview, new product, personal experience, technical. No travel tips or articles aimed at the traveling public, and no promotion of individual property, destination, product, or service. Query with published clips. Length: 500-1,500 words. **Pays 10¢/published word.** Sometimes pays expenses of writers on assignment.

Photos State availability Captions, identification of subjects, model releases required. Offers no additional payment for photos accepted with ms. Buys all rights.

Columns/Departments Management Monograph, 500-1,000 words (expert information for hotel and motel management); Florida Scene, 500 words (Florida-specific, time-sensitive information for hotel managers or owners); National Scene, 500-1,000 words (USA-specific, time-sensitive information for hotel managers or owners); Fillers and Features, 500-700 words (information specific to editorial focus for the issue). Query. **Pays in contributor copies.**

Fillers Needs anecdotes, facts, short humor. Length: 50-1,000 words. **Pays in contributor copies**

Tips We use press releases provided to this office that fit the profile of our magazine's departments, targeting items of interest to the general managers of Florida's lodging operations. Feature articles are written based on an editorial calendar. We also publish an annual buyer's guide that provides a directory of all FH&MA member companies and allied member companies.

$ $ $ $ HOSPITALITY TECHNOLOGY

Edgell Communications, 4 Middlebury Blvd., Randolph NJ 07869. (973)252-0100. Fax: (973)252-9020. E-mail: alorden@edgellmail.com. Website: www.htmagazine.com. **70% freelance written**. Magazine published 9 times/year. We cover the technology used in foodservice and lodging. Our readers are the operators, who have significant IT responsibilities. Estab. 1996. Circ. 16,000. Byline given. Pays on acceptance. No kill fee. Publishes ms an average of 1 month after acceptance. Buys all rights. Makes work-for-hire assignments. Editorial lead time 2 months. Accepts queries by mail, e-mail, fax, phone. Responds in 2 weeks to queries.

- This publication will not respond to all inquiries—only those that are of particular interest to the editor.

Nonfiction Needs how-to, interview, new product, technical. We publish 2 studies each year, the Restaurant Industry Technology Study and the Lodging Industry Technology Study. No unsolicited mss. **Buys 40 mss/year.** Query with published clips. Length: 800-1,200 words. **Pays $1/word.** Sometimes pays expenses of writers on assignment.

Tips Given the vast amount of inquiries we receive, it's impossible for us to respond to all. We can only respond to those that are of particular interest.

$ $ HOTELIER

Kostuch Publications, Ltd., 23 Lesmill Rd., Suite 101, Don Mills ON M3B 3P6 Canada. (416)447-0888. Fax: (416)447-5333. E-mail: rcaira@foodservice.ca. Website: www.foodserviceworld.com. **40% freelance written**. Magazine published 8 times/year covering the Canadian hotel industry. Estab. 1989. Circ. 9,000. Byline given. Pays on publication. No kill fee. Buys first North American serial rights. Editorial lead time 3 months. Submit seasonal material 2 months in advance. Accepts queries by mail, fax. Sample copy and writer's guidelines free.

Nonfiction Needs how-to, new product. No case studies. **Buys 30-50 mss/year.** Query. Length: 700-1,500 words. **Pays 35¢/word (Canadian) for assigned articles.** Sometimes pays expenses of writers on assignment.

Photos Send photos Offers $30-75/photo.

$ $ INSITE

Christian Camp and Conference Association, P.O. Box 62189, Colorado Springs CO 80962-2189. (719)260-9400. Fax: (719)260-6398. E-mail: editor@ccca.org. Website: www.ccca.org. **75% freelance written. Prefers to work with published/established writers.** Bimonthly magazine emphasizing the broad scope of organized camping with emphasis on Christian camps and conference centers. "All who work in youth camps and adult conferences read our magazine for inspiration and to get practical help in ways to serve in their operations." Estab. 1963. Circ. 8,500. Byline given. Pays on publication. No kill fee. Publishes ms an average of 4 months after acceptance. Buys first rights. Accepts queries by mail, e-mail. Responds in 1 month to queries. Sample copy for $4.95 plus 9x12 SASE. Guidelines available by request.

Nonfiction Needs general interest, trends in organized camping in general, Christian camping in particular, how-to, anything involved with organized camping, including motivating staff, programming, healthcare, maintenance, and camper follow-up, inspirational, interested in profiles and practical applications of Scriptural principles to everyday situations in camping, interview, with movers and shakers in Christian camping. **Buys 15-20 mss/year.** Query required. Length: 500-1,700 words. **Pays 20¢/word.**

Reprints Send photocopy and information about when and where the material previously appeared. Pays 50% of amount paid for an original article.

Photos Price negotiable for 35mm color transparencies and high-quality digital photos.

Tips "The most frequent mistake made by writers is that they send articles unrelated to our readers. Review our publication guidelines first. Interviews are the best bet for freelancers."

$ $ MOUNTAIN RESORT MAGAZINE

Skinner Media, Vail CO 81657. Phone/Fax: (252)261-3437. E-mail: editor@mountainresortmag.com. Website: www.mountainresortmag.com. **50% freelance written**. Bimonthly magazine covering the ski and snowboard resort industry. We are exclusively an area operations, marketing, and management resource for local, regional, and national mountain destinations. We combine humor with information and images with explanations, and understand the spark it takes to work in black snow pants 175 days a year. We will gladly trade publishing credits for real experience on the front lines. And, we readily understand that although travel writers and old-school journalists are invariably handsome, brilliant, and uber-masters of the sport, they have little cred with those who actually do the job. We do not preach, but utilize the voices in the industry to help share authentic experience. Estab. 2004. Circ. 4,200. Byline given. Pays on acceptance. Offers 20% kill fee. Buys first North American serial rights. Editorial lead time 2 months. Submit seasonal material 3 months in advance. Accepts queries by e-mail. Accepts simultaneous submissions. Responds in 1 week to queries. Responds in 1 month to mss. Guidelines by email.

Nonfiction Needs historical, how-to, humor, interview, new product, technical. Please do not confuse the retail or travel end of skiing and riding with the operations community (management, marketing, lift operators). **Buys 15 mss/year.** Query. Length: 1,200-2,000 words. **Pays $500**

Photos Please contact the editor if you have taken operations photography. (This does not include pictures of your buddy doing some trick in the park.)

Columns/Departments Bullwheel (informative spew about interesting and funny operations developments), 200 words. 1 Query. **Pays $100 maximum.**

Tips Our angle is experience from the front lines. We've of course had dozens of travel writers pawning their wares, but are more interested in actual resort employees' voices than consumer writing credits. Shoot ideas by e-mail, and please include any relevant on-hill experience. Be young; be funny. Tell us a story you heard in a locker room rather than drone on about what's happening in a board room.

$ $ $ PIZZA TODAY

The Monthly Professional Guide to Pizza Profits, Macfadden Protech, LLC, 908 S. 8th St., Suite 200, Louisville KY 40203. (502)736-9500. Fax: (502)736-9502. E-mail: jwhite@pizzatoday.com. Website: www.pizzatoday.com. **40% freelance written. Works with published/established writers; occasionally works with new writers.** Monthly magazine for the pizza industry, covering trends, features of successful pizza operators, business and management advice, etc. Estab. 1983. Circ. 47,000. Byline given. Pays on acceptance. No kill fee. Publishes ms an average of 2 months after acceptance. Buys all rights. Submit seasonal material 3 months in advance. Accepts queries by mail, e-mail, fax. Responds in 2 months to queries. Responds in 3 weeks to mss. Sample copy for sae with 10x13 envelope and 6 First-Class stamps. Guidelines for #10 sase.

Nonfiction Needs interview, entrepreneurial slants, pizza production and delivery, employee training, hiring, marketing, and business management. No fillers, humor, or poetry. **Buys 85 mss/year.** Length: 1,000 words. **Pays 50¢/word, occasionally more.** Sometimes pays expenses of writers on assignment.

Photos Captions required. Reviews contact sheets, negatives, transparencies, color slides, 5 x 7 prints.

Tips Our most pressing need is for articles that would fall within our Front of the House section. Review the magazine before sending in your query.

$ $ $ N SANTÉ MAGAZINE

On-Premise Communications, 100 South St., Bennington VT 05201. 802-442-6771. Fax: 802-442-6859. E-mail: mvaughan@santemagazine.com. Website: www.isantemagazine.com. **75% freelance written**. 9 issues per year magazine covering food, wine, spirits, and management topics for restaurant professionals. *"Santé's* readers are restaurant professionals who look to the magazine for information and specific advice on operating a profitable food and beverage program. Writers should 'speak' to readers on a professional-to-professional basis, under the assumption that readers have a greater knowledge of the material being covered than the average restaurant patron." Estab. 1996. Circ. 55,000. Byline given. Pays on publication. Offers 50% kill fee. Publishes ms an average of 2 months after acceptance. Buys first North American serial rights. Editorial lead time 6 months. Submit seasonal material 6 months in advance. Accepts queries by e-mail. Responds in 2 weeks to queries. We do not accept mss. Sample copy for with 7 envelope. Guidelines by email.

- "Articles should be concise and to the point and should closely adhere to the assigned word count. Our readers have many demands on their time and will only read articles that provide useful information in a readily accessible format. Where possible, articles should be broken into stand-alone sections that can be boxed or otherwise highlighted."

Nonfiction Needs interview, Restaurant business news. "We do not want consumer-focused pieces." **Buys 95 mss/year. mss/year.** Query with published clips. Length: 650-1,800 words. Sometimes pays expenses of writers on assignment.

Photos State availability Captions required. Reviews 8 x 10 at 300 dpi transparencies, GIF/JPEG files. Offers no additional payment for photos accepted. Buys one time rights.

Columns/Departments "Due to a Redesign, 650 words; Bar Tab (focuses on one bar's unique strategy for success), 1,000 words; Restaurant Profile (a business-related look at what qualities make one restaurant successful), 1,000 words; Maximizing Profits (covers one great profit-maximizing strategy per issue from several sources), Chef's Seminar (highlights one chef's unique style), Appellations (an in-depth look at a high-profile wine-producing region), Distillations (a detailed study of a particular type of spirit), 1,500 words; Provisions (like The Goods only longer; an in-depth look at a special ingredient), 1,500 words. 95 mss/year. Query with published clips. **Pays $300-$800.**

Tips "Present 2 or 3 of your best ideas via e-mail. Include a brief statement of your qualifications. Attach your resume and 3 electronic clips. The same format may be used to query via postal mail if necessary."

SPA AUSTRALASIA

The Intermedia Group, Ltd., P.O. Box 55, Glebe NSW 2037 Australia. (61)(2)9660-2113. Fax: (61)(2)9660-4419. E-mail: kirien@spaguru.com.au. Website: www.intermedia.com.au. Quarterly magazine covering existing spas and spas in planning and development.

- Query before submitting.

$ $ WESTERN HOTELIER MAGAZINE

Mercury Publications, Ltd., 1740 Wellington Ave., Winnipeg MB R3H 0E8 Canada. (204)954-2085. Fax: (204)954-2057. Website: www.mercury.mb.ca/. **33% freelance written**. Quarterly magazine covering the hotel industry. *Western Hotelier* is dedicated to the accommodation industry in Western Canada and U.S. western border states. *WH* offers the West's best mix of news and feature reports geared to hotel management. Feature reports are written on a sector basis and are created to help generate enhanced profitability and better understanding. Circ. 4,342. Byline given. Pays 30-45 days from receipt of invoice. Offers 33% kill fee. Buys all rights. Submit seasonal material 3 months in advance. Accepts queries by mail, fax. Accepts simultaneous submissions. Responds in 2 weeks to queries. Sample copy and writer's guidelines free

Nonfiction Needs how-to, train staff, interview. Industry reports and profiles on companies. Query with published clips. Length: 500-9,000 words. **Pays 25-35¢/word.** Sometimes pays expenses of writers on assignment.

Photos State availability Captions required. Reviews negatives, transparencies, 3x5 prints, JPEG, EPS or TIF files. Negotiates payment individually Buys all rights.

Tips E-mail, fax, or mail a query outlining your experience, interests and pay expectations. Include clippings.

$ $ WESTERN RESTAURANT NEWS

Mercury Publications, Ltd., 1740 Wellington Ave., Winnipeg MB R3H 0E8 Canada. (204)954-2085. Fax: (204)954-2057. Website: www.mercury.mb.ca/. **20% freelance written**. Bimonthly magazine covering the restaurant trade. Reports profiles and industry reports on associations, regional business developments, etc. *Western Restaurant News Magazine* is the authoritative voice of the foodservice industry in Western Canada. Offering a total package to readers, *WRN* delivers concise news articles, new product news, and coverage of the leading trade events in the West, across the country, and around the world. Estab. 1994. Circ. 14,532. Byline given. Pays 30-45 days from receipt of invoice. Offers 33% kill fee. Buys all rights. Submit seasonal material 3 months in advance. Accepts queries by mail, fax. Accepts simultaneous submissions. Sample copy and writer's guidelines free

Nonfiction Needs how-to, interview. Industry reports and profiles on companies. Query with published clips. Length: 500-9,000 words. **Pays 25-35¢/word.** Sometimes pays expenses of writers on assignment.

Photos State availability Captions required. Reviews negatives, transparencies, 3x5 prints, JPEG, EPS, or TIFF files. Negotiates payment individually Buys all rights.

Fillers Length: words.

Tips E-mail, fax, or mail a query outlining your experience, interests and pay expectations. Include clippings.

INDUSTRIAL OPERATIONS

CANADIAN PLASTICS

The Business Information Group, 12 Concorde Place, Suite 800, Toronto ON M3C 4J2 Canada. (800)387-0273. Fax: (416)510-5134. E-mail: mstephen@canplastics.com. Website: www.canplastics.com. **Contact:** Mark Stephen, Managing Editor. **20% freelance written**. Magazine published 7 times/year covering plastics. "*Canadian Plastics Magazine* reports on and interprets development in plastics markets and technologies for plastics processors and end-users based in Canada." Estab. 1943. Circ. 10,000. Byline always given. Pays on publication. Publishes ms an average of 3 months after acceptance. Editorial lead time 2 months. Submit seasonal material 4 months in advance. Responds in 2 weeks to queries. Responds in 1 month to mss. Sample copy available online.

Does not accept unsolicited editorial material.

Nonfiction Needs technical, industry news (Canada only). **Buys 6 mss/year.** Query with published clips. Length: 400-1,600 words.

Photos State availability

$ $ CAST POLYMER CONNECTION

International Cast Polymer Alliance of the American Composites Manufacturers Association, 1010 N. Glebe Rd., Suite 450, Arlington VA 22201-5761. (703)525-0511. Fax: (703)525-0743. E-mail: jgorman@acmanet.org. Website: www.icpa-hq.org. Bimonthly magazine covering cultured marble and solid surface industries. Articles should focus on small business owners and manufacturers. Circ. 2,000. Byline given. Pays on

publication. No kill fee. Publishes ms an average of 3 months after acceptance. Buys all rights. Accepts queries by mail, e-mail.
Nonfiction We are interested in how-to articles on technical processes, industry-related manufacturing techniques, and small-business operations. Needs historical, how-to, interview, photo feature, technical. **Buys 3-5 mss/year.** Query. Length: 2,000-5,000 words. **Pays $200-350.** Sometimes pays expenses of writers on assignment.

$ $ COMMERCE & INDUSTRY

Mercury Publications, Ltd., 1740 Wellington Ave., Winnipeg MB R3H 0E8 Canada. (204)954-2085. Fax: (204)954-2057. Website: www.mercury.mb.ca/. **75% freelance written**. Bimonthly magazine covering the business and industrial sectors. Industry reports and company profiles provide readers with an in-depth insight into key areas of interest in their profession. Estab. 1947. Circ. 18,876. Byline given. Pays 30-45 days from receipt of invoice. Offers 33% kill fee. Buys all rights. Submit seasonal material 3 months in advance. Accepts queries by mail, e-mail, fax. Accepts simultaneous submissions. Responds in 2 weeks to queries. Sample copy and writer's guidelines free or by e-mail
Nonfiction Needs how-to, interview. Industry reports and profiles on companies. Query with published clips. Length: 500-9,000 words. **Pays 25-35¢/word.** Sometimes pays expenses of writers on assignment.
Photos State availability Captions required. Reviews negatives, transparencies, 3x5 prints, JPEG, EPS or TIF files. Negotiates payment individually Buys all rights.
Tips E-mail, fax, or mail a query outlining your experience, interests and pay expectations. Include clippings.

$ $ MODERN MATERIALS HANDLING

Reed Business Information, 275 Washington St., Newton MA 02458. (617)964-0154. Fax: (617)558-4327. E-mail: noel.bodenburg@reedbusiness.com. Website: www.mmh.com. **40% freelance written**. Magazine published 11 times/year covering warehousing, distribution centers, inventory. *Warehousing Management* is an 11 times-a-year glossy national magazine read by managers of warehouses and distribution centers. We focus on lively, well-written articles telling our readers how they can achieve maximum facility productivity and efficiency. Heavy management components. We cover technology, too. Estab. 1945. Circ. 42,000. Byline given. Pays on acceptance (allow 4-6 weeks for invoice processing). No kill fee. Publishes ms an average of 1 month after acceptance. Editorial lead time 3 months. Accepts queries by mail, e-mail, fax. Sample copy free. Guidelines free.
Nonfiction Articles must be on-point, how-to pieces for managers. Needs how-to, new product, technical. State-of-the-Industry Report, Peak Performer, Salary and Wage survey, Warehouse of the Year Doesn't want to see anything that doesn't deal with our topic—warehousing. No general-interest profiles or interviews. **Buys 25 mss/year.** Query with published clips. **Pays $300-650.**
Photos State availability Captions, identification of subjects required. Reviews negatives, transparencies, prints. Offers no additional payment for photos accepted with ms. Buys all rights.
Tips Learn a little about warehousing, distributors and write well. We typically don't accept specific article queries, but welcome introductory letters from journalists to whom we can assign articles. But authors are welcome to request an editorial calendar and develop article queries from it.

$ $ $ PEM PLANT ENGINEERING & MAINTENANCE

CLB Media, Inc., 240 Edward St., Aurora ON L4G 3S9 Canada. (905)727-0077. Fax: (905)727-0017. E-mail: rrobertson@clbmedia.ca. Website: www.pem-mag.com. **30% freelance written**. Bimonthly magazine looking for informative articles on issues that affect plant floor operations and maintenance. Circ. 18,500. Byline given. Pays on publication. No kill fee. Publishes ms an average of 3 months after acceptance. Buys one-time rights. Editorial lead time 4 months. Submit seasonal material 4 months in advance. Accepts simultaneous submissions. Responds in 3 weeks to queries. Responds in 1 month to mss. Sample copy free. Guidelines available online.
Nonfiction Needs how-to, keep production downtime to a minimum, better operate an industrial operation, new product, technical. **Buys 6 mss/year.** Query with published clips. Length: 750-4,000 words. **Pays $500-1,400 (Canadian).** Sometimes pays expenses of writers on assignment.
Photos State availability Captions required. Reviews transparencies, prints. Negotiates payment individually. Buys one time rights.
Columns/Departments .
Tips Information can be found at our website. Call us for sample issues, ideas, etc.

QUALITY DIGEST

P.O. Box 1769, Chico CA 95927-1769. (530)893-4095. Fax: (530)893-0395. E-mail: mrichman@qualitydigest.com. Website: www.qualitydigest.com. **75% freelance written**. Monthly magazine covering quality improvement. Estab. 1981. Circ. 75,000. Byline given. Pays on acceptance. No kill fee. Buys all rights. Submit seasonal material 4 months in advance. Accepts queries by mail, e-mail, fax. Accepts simultaneous submissions. Responds in 3 months to mss. Sample copy and writer's guidelines free.

Nonfiction Needs book excerpts, how-to, implement quality programs and solve problems for benefits, etc., interview, opinion, personal experience, technical. Send complete ms. Length: 800-3,000 words.
Reprints Send tearsheet and information about when and where the material previously appeared.
Photos Send photos Captions, identification of subjects, model releases required. Reviews any size prints. Offers no additional payment for photos accepted with ms. Buys one time rights.
Tips Please be specific in your articles. Explain what the problem was, how it was solved and what the benefits are. Tell the reader how the technique described will benefit him or her. We feature shorter, tighter, more focused articles than in the past. This means we have more articles in each issue. We're striving to present our readers with concise, how-to, easy-to-read information that makes their job easier.

SPECIALTY FABRICS REVIEW

Industrial Fabrics Association International, 1801 County Rd. B W., Roseville MN 55113-4061. (651)222-2508. Fax: (651)225-6966. E-mail: gdnordstrom@ifai.com. Website: www.ifai.com. **Contact:** Galynn Norstrom, senior editor. **50% freelance written**. Monthly magazine covering industrial textiles and products made from them for company owners, salespeople, and researchers in a variety of industrial textile areas. Estab. 1915. Circ. 11,000. Byline given. Pays on publication. No kill fee. Publishes ms an average of 2 months after acceptance. Buys all rights. Accepts queries by mail, e-mail, phone. Responds in 1 month to queries.

- Break in by"researching the industry/magazine audience and editorial calendar. We rarely buy materials not specifically directed at our markets."

Nonfiction Needs technical, marketing, and other topics related to any aspect of industrial fabric industry from fiber to finished fabric product. New Products; New Fabrics; Equipment. No historical or apparel-oriented articles. **Buys 50-60 mss/year.** Query with phone number. Length: 1,200-3,000 words.
Tips "We encourage freelancers to learn our industry and make regular, solicited contributions to the magazine. We do not buy photography."

$ $ WEIGHING & MEASUREMENT

WAM Publishing Co., P.O. Box 2247, Hendersonville TN 37077. (615)824-6920. Fax: (615)824-7092. E-mail: wampub@wammag.com. Website: www.wammag.com. Bimonthly magazine for users of industrial scales. Estab. 1914. Circ. 13,900. Byline given. Pays on acceptance. Offers 20% kill fee. Buys all rights. Accepts queries by mail, e-mail, fax, phone. Responds in 2 weeks to queries. Sample copy for $2.
Nonfiction Needs interview, with presidents of companies, personal experience, guest editorials on government involvement in business, etc., technical, Profile (about users of weighing and measurement equipment). **Buys 15 mss/year.** Query on technical articles; submit complete ms for general interest material. Length: 1,000-2,500 words. **Pays $175-300.**

INFORMATION SYSTEMS

$ $ $ CARD TECHNOLOGY

The Magazine of Smart Cards, Networks, and ID Solutions, 550 W. Van Buren, Suite 1110, Chicago IL 60607. (312)913-1334. Fax: (312)913-1369. E-mail: Daniel.Bolaban@wanadoo.fr. Website: www.cardtechnology.com. **20% freelance written**. Monthly magazine covering smart cards, biometrics, and related technologies. *Card Technology* covers all uses of smart cards worldwide, as well as other advanced plastic card technologies. Aimed at senior management, not technical staff. Our readership is global, as is our focus. Estab. 1996. Circ. 22,000. Byline given. Pays on acceptance. Offers negotiable kill fee. Buys all rights. Editorial lead time 1 month. Submit seasonal material 2 months in advance. Accepts queries by e-mail. Responds in 1 week to queries. Responds in 1 month to mss. Sample copy free.
Nonfiction Needs interview, opinion. **Buys 15 mss/year.** Query with published clips. Length: 2,000-4,000 words. **Pays $500-1,500.** Sometimes pays expenses of writers on assignment.
Photos State availability Identification of subjects required. Reviews contact sheets, negatives, transparencies, prints. Negotiates payment individually. Rights negotiable.
Tips We are especially interested in finding freelancers outside of North America who have experience writing about technology issues for business publications.

CIO

Fairfax Business Media, P.O. Box 6813,, Wellesley Street, Auckland 1031 New Zealand. (64)(9)375-6012. E-mail: webmaster@fairfaxbm.co.nz. Website: www.cio.co.nz/. Monthly magazine covering management information for IT professionals. Articles deal with business issues, aligning information technology with business strategy, change management, and technology on a strategic level. Case studies should ask If you had to do this project again, what would you do differently? No kill fee.

- Query before submitting.

$ $ $ DESKTOP ENGINEERING

Design Solutions from Concept Through Manufacture, Level 5 Communications, Inc., P.O. Box 1039, Dublin NH 03444. (603)563-1631. Fax: (603)563-8192. E-mail: de-editors@deskeng.com. Website: www.deskeng.com. **90% freelance written**. "Monthly magazine covering computer hardware/software for hands-on design and mechanical engineers, analysis engineers, and engineering management. Ten special supplements/year.". Estab. 1995. Circ. 63,000. Byline given. Pays in month of publication. Kill fee for assigned story. Publishes ms an average of 2 months after acceptance. Buys all rights. Editorial lead time 3 months. Accepts queries by mail, e-mail. Responds in 2 weeks to queries. Responds in 1 month to mss. Sample copy for free with 8x10 SASE. Writer's guidelines by e-mail to jgourlay@deskeng.com

Nonfiction Needs how-to, new product, reviews, technical, design. No fluff. **Buys 50-70 mss/year.** Query. Length: 750-1,500 words. **Pays per project. Pay negotiable for unsolicited articles.** Sometimes pays expenses of writers on assignment.

Photos Send photos Captions required. Negotiates payment individually.

Columns/Departments Product Briefs (new products), 50-100 words; Reviews (software, hardware), 500-1,500 words

Tips Call the editors or e-mail them for submission tips.

$ $ $ GAME DEVELOPER

CMP Media LLC, 600 Harrison St., 6th Floor, San Francisco CA 94107. (415)947-6000. Fax: (415)947-6090. E-mail: jduffy@cmp.com. Website: www.gdmag.com. **90% freelance written**. Monthly magazine covering computer game development. Estab. 1994. Circ. 35,000. Byline given. Pays on publication. No kill fee. Publishes ms an average of 3-6 months after acceptance. Buys first North American serial rights, buys first rights, buys electronic rights, buys all rights. Editorial lead time 3 months. Submit seasonal material 4 months in advance. Accepts queries by e-mail. Sample copy free. Guidelines available online.

Nonfiction Needs how-to, personal experience, technical. **Buys 50 mss/year.** Query. Length: 3,000-5,000 words. **Pays $150/page.**

Photos State availability

Tips We're looking for writers who are professional game developers with published game titles. We do not target the hobbyist or amateur market.

INFONOMICS MAGAZINE

1100 Wayne Ave., Silver Spring MD 20910. (301)916-7182. Fax: (240)494-2690. E-mail: bherring@aiim.org. Website: www.infonomicsmag.com. **Contact:** Benjamin L. Herring, editor-in-chief. **30% freelance written. Prefers to work with writers with business/high tech experience.** Bimonthly magazine. "Infonomics is definied as 'the intelligent management of information to drive core processes,' and is published by AIIM, the Enterprise Content Management association that provides education, research, and best practices to help organizations find, control, and optimize their information. For over 60 years, AIIM has been leading nonprofit organization focused on helping users to understand the challenges associated with managing documents, content, records, and business processes. Specifically, we feature coverage of the business issues surrounding the implementation and use of document and information management technologies." Estab. 1943. Circ. 35,000. Byline given. Pays on submission. Offers $50 kill fee. Publishes ms an average of 6 months after acceptance. Buys first North American serial rights, buys second serial (reprint) rights. Accepts queries by mail, e-mail, fax, phone. Accepts simultaneous submissions. Sample copy available online. Guidelines available online.

Nonfiction Needs interview, photo feature, technical. **Buys 10-20 mss/year.** Query first. Length: 1,500 words. Sometimes pays expenses of writers on assignment.

Photos State availability Captions, identification of subjects required. Reviews negatives, 4x5 transparencies. Offers no additional payment for photos accepted with ms. Buys all rights.

Columns/Departments Trends (developments across industry segments); Technology (innovations of specific technology); Management (costs, strategies of managing informaiton); Point/Counterpoint. Length: 500-1,500 words. Query.

Tips "We would encourage freelancers who have access to our editorial calendar to contact us regarding article ideas, inquiries, etc. Our feature section is the area where the need for quality freelance coverage of our industry is most desirable. The most likely candidate for acceptance is someone who has a proven background in business writing, and/or someone with demonstrated knowledge of high-tech industries as they relate to information management."

$ JOURNAL OF INFORMATION ETHICS

McFarland & Co., Inc., Publishers, P.O. Box 611, Jefferson NC 28640. (336)246-4460. E-mail: hauptman@stcloudstate.edu. **90% freelance written**. Semiannual scholarly journal. Addresses ethical issues in all of the information sciences with a deliberately interdisciplinary approach. Topics range from electronic mail monitoring to library acquisition of controversial material. The *Journal*'s aim is to present thoughtful considerations of ethical dilemmas that arise in a rapidly evolving system of information exchange and dissemination. Estab. 1992. Byline given. Pays on publication. No kill fee. Publishes ms an average of 2 years after acceptance. Buys all rights. Submit seasonal material 8 months in advance. Accepts queries by mail, e-mail, phone. Sample copy for $30. Guidelines free.

Nonfiction Needs essays, opinion, book reviews. **Buys 10-12 mss/year.** Send complete ms. Length: 500-3,500 words. **Pays $25-50 depending on length.**

Tips Familiarize yourself with the many areas subsumed under the rubric of information ethics, e.g., privacy, scholarly communication, errors, peer review, confidentiality, e-mail, etc. Present a well-rounded discussion of any fresh, current, or evolving ethical topic within the information sciences or involving real-world information collection/exchange.

R & D MAGAZINE

Where Innovation Begins, Advantage Business Media, 100 Enterprise Dr., Suite 600, Box 912, Rockaway NJ 07866. Website: www.rdmag.com. Monthly magazine. *R & D Magazine* serves research scientists, engineers, and technical staff members at laboratories around the world. Estab. 1959. Circ. 85,000. Byline given. No kill fee. Editorial lead time 2 months. Guidelines available online.

Nonfiction "The best way to promote your idea is to write us a single-page letter containing: 1) Suggested title or topic heading for your article; 2) One-paragraph synopsis or outline of the story idea, indicating its significance and why it should be published in *R & D Magazine*; 3) Sentence or two about yourself (and any co-authors) indicating why you are qualified to write it." Query. **Pays 4 contributor copies.**

Photos Contact: Contact: Editor-in-Chief. Captions, identification of subjects required. Reviews 2 ¼x2 ¼ transparencies, 6x9 prints, TIFF/EPS files (300 dpi) or 35mm slides.

Tips "All articles in *R & D Magazine* must be original, accurate, timely, noncommercial, useful to our readers, and exclusive to our magazine."

$ $ $ SYSTEM INEWS

Penton Technology Media, 221 E. 29th St., Loveland CO 80538. (970)203-2824. Fax: (970)663-3285. E-mail: editors@systeminetwork.com; vhamend@penton.com. Website: www.iseriesnetwork.com. **40% freelance written**. Magazine published 12 times/year. Programming, networking, IS management, technology for users of IBM AS/400, iSERIES, SYSTEM i, AND IBM i platform. Estab. 1982. Circ. 30,000 (international). Byline given. Pays on publication. Offers 50% kill fee. Publishes ms an average of 3 months after acceptance. Buys first rights, buys second serial (reprint) rights, buys all rights. Editorial lead time 4 months. Submit seasonal material 4 months in advance. Accepts queries by mail, e-mail, fax, phone. Responds in 3 weeks to queries. Responds in 5 weeks to mss Guidelines available online

Nonfiction Needs opinion, technical. Query. Length: 1,500-2,500 words. **Pays 25-30¢/word for assigned articles.** Sometimes pays expenses of writers on assignment.

Reprints Send photocopy. Payment negotiable.

Photos State availability Offers no additional payment for photos accepted with ms.

Columns/Departments Guest Viewpoint (computer industry opinion), 1,500 words; Load'n'go (complete utility). 24 Query. **Pays $250-1,000.**

Tips "Be familiar with IBM AS/400/iSERIES/SYSTEM i/IBM i computer platform."

$ $ $ $ TECHNOLOGY REVIEW

MIT, 1 Main St., 7th Floor, Cambridge MA 02142. (617)475-8000. Fax: (617)475-8042. Website: www.technologyreview.com. Magazine published 10 times/year covering information technology, biotech, material science, and nanotechnology. *Technology Review* promotes the understanding of emerging technologies and their impact. Estab. 1899. Circ. 310,000. Byline given. Pays on acceptance. Accepts queries by mail, e-mail.

- Contact specific editor via e-mail using firstname.lastname@technologyreview.com

Nonfiction We place a high premium on in-depth, original reporting that produces stories rich in description, containing lively quotes from key researchers and industry analysts. Summaries of other companies or labratories doing similar work typically supplement articles. Looking for feature articles. Length: 2,000-4,000 words. **Pays $1-3/word.**

Fillers Short tidbits that relate laboratory prototypes on their way to market in 1-5 years. Length: 150-250 words. **Pays $1-3/word.**

INSURANCE

$ $ $ $ ADVISOR TODAY

NAIFA, 2901 Telestar Court, Falls Church VA 22042. (703)770-8204. E-mail: amseka@naifa.org. Website: www.advisortoday.com. **25% freelance written**. Monthly magazine covering life insurance and financial planning. Writers must demonstrate an understanding at what insurance agents and financial advisors do to earn business and serve their clients. Estab. 1906. Circ. 110,000. Pays on acceptance or publication (by mutual agreement with editor). No kill fee. Publishes ms an average of 3 months after acceptance. Makes work-for-hire assignments. Editorial lead time 3 months. Submit seasonal material 6 months in advance. Accepts queries by mail, e-mail, fax, phone. Sample copy free. Guidelines available online.

Nonfiction Insurance **Buys 8 mss/year.** Query. Length: 1,500-6,000 words. **Pays $800-2,000.**

$ $ AGENT'S SALES JOURNAL

Summit Business Media, 1255 Cleveland St., Suite 200, Clearwater FL 33755. Fax: (727)446-1166. E-mail: cpellett@agentmediacorp.com. Website: www.agentssalesjournal.com. **40% freelance written**. Monthly magazine covering life and health insurance industry. We are a how-to publication for life and health-licensed insurance agents. All editorial is nonpromotional and dedicated to helping our readerse do a better job. Circ. 50,000. Byline given. Pays on acceptance. Offers 50% kill fee. Publishes ms an average of 2 months after acceptance. Buys first North American serial rights, buys electronic rights. Editorial lead time 2 months. Accepts queries by e-mail. Accepts simultaneous submissions. Sample copy available online. Guidelines free.

Nonfiction Contact: Christina Pellett, managing editor. Needs how-to, selling insurance, technical, Industry trend pieces. No articles promoting specific companies, products or services. No consumer-oriented material-please keep in mind audience is insurance agents. **Buys 24 mss/year mss/year.** Query with published clips. Length: 1,200-1,700 words. **Pays $350-450 for assigned articles.**

Columns/Departments Pays **$$350-$450.**

$ $ GEICO DIRECT

K.L. Publications, 2001 Killebrew Dr., Suite 105, Bloomington MN 55425-1879. (952)854-0155. Fax: (952)854-9440. E-mail: janklpub@aol.com. **60% freelance written**. Semiannual magazine published for the Government Employees Insurance Company (GEICO) policyholders. Estab. 1988. Circ. 7,000,000 total. Byline given. Pays on acceptance. No kill fee. Accepts queries by mail, e-mail. Responds to all queries as soon as possible. Quicker response by e-mail. Sample copy for 9x12 envelope w/3 first-class stamps. For Writer's Guidelines, submit email or #10 SASE.

Nonfiction "Driving, auto, and home safety; car care; lifestyle relating to safety and how-to for: single 20-somethings/young families/empty nesters/retirees; Americana/uniquely American; auto and home technology; travel (similar destinations—i.e. museums, aquariums, state parks, etc.—chosen from around the U.S. to get good regional and version-based (single 20-somethings/young families/empty nesters/retirees) mix." Query with published clips. Length: 1,000-2,200 words. **Pays $400-800.**

Photos Reviews 35mm transparencies, websites. Payment varies

Columns/Departments Safety FYI; Your Car. Length: 450-550 words Query with published clips. **Pays $275-350.**

Tips "We prefer work from published/established writers, especially those with specialized knowledge of the insurance industry, safety issues, and automotive topics."

JEWELRY

AUSTRALIAN JEWELLER

Phoenix Media & Publishing, Locked Bag 26, South Melbourne VIC 3205 Australia. (61)(3)9696-7200. Fax: (61)(3)9696-8313. E-mail: ajed@phoenixmags.com.au. Website: www.australianjewellermagazine.com.au. Monthly magazine containing regular features on local and international news, new products, tips on selling and opinion pieces. Accepts queries by mail, e-mail. Guidelines available online.

Nonfiction Needs general interest, new product, opinion. Query.

Tips Story ideas can be submitted via post or e-mail, but all story submissions should be delivered via e-mail in a Microsoft Word file and titled as follows: StoryName.doc.

$ $ COLORED STONE

Lapidary Journal/Primedia, Inc., 300 Chesterfield Parkway, Suite 100, Malvern PA 19355. (610)232-5700. Fax: (610)232-5756. E-mail: morgan.beard@primedia.com. Website: www.colored-stone.com. **50% freelance written**. Bimonthly magazine covering the colored gemstone industry. *Colored Stone* covers all aspects of the colored gemstone (i.e., no diamonds) trade. Our readers are manufacturing jewelers and jewelry designers, gemstone dealers, miners, retail jewelers, and gemologists. Estab. 1987. Circ. 11,000. Byline given. Pays on acceptance. No kill fee. Publishes ms an average of 2 months after acceptance. Buys one-time rights, buys all rights. Editorial lead time 2 months. Submit seasonal material 4 months in advance. Accepts queries by mail, e-mail, fax. Accepts simultaneous submissions. Responds in 1 month to queries. Responds in 2 months to mss. Sample copy free. Guidelines available online.

Nonfiction Needs expose, interview, new product, technical. No articles intended for the general public. **Buys 35-45 mss/year.** Query with published clips. Length: 400-2,200 words. **Pays $200-600.**

Photos State availability Captions, identification of subjects, model releases required. Reviews any size transparencies, 4x6 prints and up. Offers $15-50/photo. Buys one time rights.

Tips A background in the industry is helpful but not necessary. Please, no recycled marketing/new technology/etc. pieces.

$ THE DIAMOND REGISTRY BULLETIN

580 Fifth Ave., #806, New York NY 10036. (212)575-0444. Fax: (212)575-0722. Website: www.diamondregistry.com. **50% freelance written**. Monthly newsletter. Estab. 1969. Pays on publication. No kill fee. Buys all rights. Submit seasonal material 1 month in advance. Accepts queries by mail, e-mail. Accepts simultaneous submissions. Responds in about 3 weeks to mss. Sample copy for $5.

Nonfiction Needs how-to, ways to increase sales in diamonds, improve security, etc., interview, of interest to diamond dealers or jewelers, prevention advice (on crimes against jewelers). Send complete ms. Length: 50-500 words. **Pays $75-150.**

Tips We seek ideas to increase sales of diamonds.

$ $ THE ENGRAVERS JOURNAL

P.O. Box 318, Brighton MI 48116. (810)229-5725. Fax: (810)229-8320. E-mail: editor@engraversjournal.com. Website: www.engraversjournal.com. **70% freelance written**. Monthly magazine covering the recognition and identification industry (engraving, marking devices, awards, jewelry, and signage). We provide practical information for the education and advancement of our readers, mainly retail business owners. Estab. 1975. Byline given Pays on acceptance. No kill fee. Publishes ms an average of 3-9 months after acceptance. Buys one-time rights. Makes work-for-hire assignments. Accepts queries by mail, e-mail, fax. Responds in 2 weeks to mss. Sample copy free. Guidelines free.

Nonfiction Needs general interest, industry related, how-to, small business subjects, increase sales, develop new markets, use new sales techniques, etc., technical. No general overviews of the industry. Length: 1,000-5,000 words. **Pays $200 and up.**

Reprints Send tearsheet, photocopy or typed ms with rights for sale noted and information about when and where the material previously appeared. Pays 50-100% of amout paid for original article.

Photos Send photos Captions, identification of subjects, model releases required. Pays variable rate

Tips Articles should always be down to earth, practical, and thoroughly cover the subject with authority. We do not want the `textbook' writing approach, vagueness, or theory—our readers look to us for sound practical information. We use an educational slant, publishing both trade-oriented articles and general business topics of interest to a small retail-oriented readership.

$ $ LUSTRE

The Luxury Jeweler's Design & Lifestyle Magazine, Cygnus Publishing Co., 19 W. 44th St., Suite 1401, New York NY 10036. (212)921-1091. Fax: (212)921-5539. Website: www.lustremag.com. Bimonthly magazine covering fine jewelry and related accessories. *Lustre*'s focus is on the latest lifestyle and fashion trends of the most affluent consumers in the United States. Editorial includes model fashion and still life photography with emphasis on forecasting trends 6-8 months prior to retail deliveries. Estab. 1997. Circ. 5,000. Byline given. Pays on publication. Offers 50% kill fee. Publishes ms an average of 4 months after acceptance. Buys all rights. Editorial lead time 4 months. Submit seasonal material 4 months in advance. Accepts queries by mail. Responds in 4 weeks to queries. Sample copy free.

Nonfiction Needs how-to, new product. **Buys 18 mss/year.** Query with published clips. Length: 1,000-2,500 words. **Pays $500.** Sometimes pays expenses of writers on assignment.

Photos State availability Captions, identification of subjects required. Offers no additional payment for photos accepted with ms. Buys one-time rights, plus usage for 1 year after publication date (but not exclusive usage).

Columns/Departments Trend Talk (color, society, runway, item), 500-1,000 words; Marketing/Merchandising (to the affluent market), 1,000-2,000 words.

MODERN JEWELER

Cygnus Business Media, 3 Huntington Quadrangle, Suite 301N, Melville NY 11747. (631)845-2700. Fax: (631)845-7109. Website: www.modernjeweler.com. **20% freelance written**. Monthly magazine covering fine jewelry and watches. Estab. 1901. Circ. 33,000. Byline given. Pays on acceptance. No kill fee. Publishes ms an average of 2 months after acceptance. Buys all rights. Editorial lead time 2 months. Submit seasonal material 2 months in advance. Accepts queries by mail, fax. Responds in 3 weeks to queries. Responds in 3 months to mss. Sample copy for SAE.

Nonfiction Needs technical.

Photos State availability Reviews transparencies, prints.

Tips Requires knowledge of retail business, experience in dealing with retail and manufacturing executives and analytical writing style. We don't frequently use writers who have no ties to or experience with the jewelry manufacturing industry.

JOURNALISM & WRITING

$ $ $ $ AMERICAN JOURNALISM REVIEW

1117 Journalism Bldg., University of Maryland, College Park MD 20742. (301)405-8803. Fax: (301)405-8323. E-mail: editor@ajr.umd.edu. Website: www.ajr.org. **80% freelance written**. Bimonthly magazine covering print, broadcast, and online journalism. Mostly journalists subscribe. We cover ethical issues, trends in the industry, coverage that falls short. Circ. 25,000. Byline given. Pays within 1 month after publication. Offers 25% kill fee. Publishes ms an average of 2 months after acceptance. Buys first North American serial rights, buys electronic rights. Editorial lead time 1 month. Accepts queries by mail, e-mail, fax. Responds in 1 month to queries. Sample copy for $4.95 pre-paid or online. Guidelines available online.

Nonfiction Needs expose, personal experience, ethical issues. **Buys many mss/year.** Send complete ms. Length: 2,000-4,000 words. **Pays $1,500-2,000.** Pays expenses of writers on assignment.

Fillers Needs anecdotes, facts, short humor, short pieces. Length: 150-1,000 words. **Pays $100-250.**

Tips Write a short story for the front-of-the-book section. We prefer queries to completed articles. Include in a page what you'd like to write about, who you'll interview, why it's important, and why you should write it.

AUSTRALIAN AUTHOR

Australian Society of Authors, P.O. Box 1566, Strawberry Hills NSW 2012 Australia. (61)(2)9318-0877. Fax: (61)(2)9318-0530. E-mail: asa@asauthors.org. Website: www.asauthors.org. Magazine published 3 times/year covering issues of importance to Australian authors.

Nonfiction Needs general interest. Query.

$ AUTHORSHIP

National Writers Association, 10940 S. Parker Rd., #508, Parker CO 80134. (303)841-0246. E-mail: natlwritersassn@hotmail.com. Website: www.webmaster@nationalwriters.com. Quarterly magazine covering writing articles only. "Association magazine targeted to beginning and professional writers. Covers how-to, humor, marketing issues. Disk and e-mail submissions preferred." Estab. 1950s. Circ. 4,000. Byline given. Pays on acceptance. No kill fee. Buys first North American serial rights, buys second serial (reprint) rights. Editorial lead time 3 months. Submit seasonal material 6 months in advance. Accepts simultaneous submissions. Responds in 2 months to queries. Sample copy for 8½x11 envelope.

Nonfiction Writing only. Poetry (January/February). **Buys 25 mss/year.** Query or send complete ms. Length: 900 words. **Pays $10, or discount on memberships and copies.**

Photos State availability Identification of subjects, model releases required. Reviews 5x7 prints. Offers no additional payment for photos accepted with ms. Buys one time rights.

Tips "Members of National Writers Association are given preference. Writing conference in Denver every June."

$ BOOK DEALERS WORLD

North American Bookdealers Exchange, P.O. Box 606, Cottage Grove OR 97424. (541)942-7455. Website: www.bookmarketingprofits.com. **50% freelance written**. Quarterly magazine covering writing, self-publishing, and marketing books by mail. Circ. 20,000. Byline given. Pays on publication. No kill fee. Publishes ms an average of 3 months after acceptance. Buys first North American serial rights, buys second serial (reprint) rights. Accepts simultaneous submissions. Responds in 1 month to queries. Sample copy for $3.

Nonfiction Needs book excerpts, writing, mail order, direct mail, publishing, how-to, home business by mail, advertising, interview, of successful self-publishers, positive articles on self-publishing, new writing angles, marketing. **Buys 10 mss/year.** Send complete ms. Length: 1,000-1,500 words. **Pays $25-50.**

Reprints Send typed manuscript with rights for sale noted and information about when and where the material previously appeared. Pays 80% of amount paid for an original article.

Columns/Departments Publisher Profile (on successful self-publishers and their marketing strategy). Length: 250-1,000 words. 20 Send complete ms. **Pays $5-20.**

Fillers Fillers concerning writing, publishing, or books. 6 Length: 100-250 words. **Pays $3-10.**

Tips "Query first. Get a sample copy of the magazine."

$ BYLINE

P.O. Box 111, Albion NY 14411. (585)355-8172. E-mail: mpreston@bylinemag.com. Website: www.bylinemag.com. **80% freelance written. Eager to work with new/unpublished writers or experienced ones.** Magazine published 11 times/year for writers and poets. Estab. 1981. Byline given. Pays on acceptance. No kill fee. Publishes ms an average of 3 months after acceptance. Buys first North American serial rights. Editorial lead time 3-4 months. Submit seasonal material 6 months in advance. Accepts queries by mail, e-mail. Accepts simultaneous submissions. Responds in 2 months or less. Sample copy for $5 postpaid. Guidelines available online.

- *Do not send* complete mss by e-mail.

Nonfiction We're always searching for appropriate, well-written features on topics we haven't covered for a couple of years. Needs articles of 1,500-1,800 words connected with writing and selling. No profiles of writers. **Buys approximately 75 mss/year.** Prefers queries; will read complete mss. Send SASE. Length: 1,500-1,800 words. **Pays $75.**
Columns/Departments End Piece (humorous, philosophical, or motivational personal essay related to writing), 700 words, **pays $35**; First Sale (account of a writer's first sale), 250-300 words, **pays $20**; Only When I Laugh (writing-related humor), 50-400 words; **pays $15-25**; Great American Bookstores (unique, independent bookstores), 500-600 words. Send complete ms. **Pays $30-40.**
Fiction Needs mainstream, genre, literary. No science fiction, erotica, or extreme violence. **Buys 11 mss/year.** Send complete ms. Length: 2,000-4,000 words. **Pays $100.**
Poetry Contact: Contact: Sandra Soli, poetry editor. Needs free verse, haiku, light verse, traditional. All poetry should connect in some way with the theme of writing or the creative process. **Buys 100 poems/year.** Submit maximum 3 poems. Under 30 lines. **Pays $10, plus free issue.**
Tips We're open to freelance submissions in all categories. We're always looking for clear, concise feature articles on topics that will help writers write better, market smarter, and be more successful. Strangely, we get many more short stories than we do features, but we buy more features. If you can write a friendly, clear, and helpful feature on some aspect of writing better or selling more work, we'd love to hear from you.

$ $ CANADIAN SCREENWRITER

Writers Guild of Canada, 366 Adelaide St. W., Suite 401, Toronto ON M5V 1R9 Canada. (416)979-7907. Fax: (416)979-9273. E-mail: info@wgc.ca. Website: www.wgc.ca/magazine. **80% freelance written**. Magazine published 3 times/year covering screenwriting for television, film, radio and digital media. *Canadian Screenwriter* profiles Canadian screenwriters, provides industry news and offers practical writing tips for screenwriters. Estab. 1998. Circ. 4,000. Byline given. Pays on acceptance. Offers 50% kill fee. Publishes ms an average of 1 month after acceptance. Buys first rights, buys electronic rights. Editorial lead time 2 months. Submit seasonal material 2 months in advance. Accepts queries by e-mail. Accepts previously published material. Responds in 1 week to queries. Responds in 1 month to mss. Sample copy free. Guidelines by email.
Nonfiction Needs how-to, humor, interview. Does not want writing on foreign screenwriters. The focus is on Canadian-resident screenwriters. **Buys 12 mss/year.** Query with published clips. Length: 750-2,200 words. **Pays 50¢/word.** Sometimes pays expenses of writers on assignment.
Photos State availability Identification of subjects required. Reviews GIF/JPEG files. Negotiates payment individually. Buys one time rights.
Tips Read other Canadian film and television publications.

$ CANADIAN WRITER'S JOURNAL

P.O. Box 1178, New Liskeard ON P0J 1P0 Canada. (705)647-5424. Fax: (705)647-8366. E-mail: cwj@cwj.ca. Website: www.cwj.ca. **75% freelance written**. Bimonthly magazine for writers. Accepts well-written articles by all writers. Estab. 1984. Circ. 350. Byline given. Pays on publication. No kill fee. Publishes ms an average of 9 months after acceptance. Buys one-time rights. Accepts queries by mail, e-mail, fax, phone. Responds in 2 months to queries. Sample copy for $8, including postage. Guidelines available online.
Nonfiction Looking for articles on how to break into niche markets. Needs how-to, articles for writers. **Buys 200 mss/year.** Query optional. **Pays $7.50/published magazine page (approx. 450 words).**
Reprints Send typed manuscript with rights for sale noted and information about when and where the material previously appeared.
Fiction Requirements being met by annual contest. Send SASE for rules, or see guidelines on website. Does not want gratuitous violence, sex subject matter.
Poetry Short poems or extracts used as part of articles on the writing of poetry.
Tips We prefer short, tightly written, informative how-to articles. U.S. writers note that U.S. postage cannot be used to mail from Canada. Obtain Canadian stamps, use IRCs, or send small amounts in cash.

$ CROSS & QUILL

The Christian Writers Newsletter, Christian Writers Fellowship International, 1624 Jefferson Davis Rd., Clinton SC 29325-6401. (864)697-6035. E-mail: cwfi@aol.com. Website: www.cwfi-online.org. **75% freelance written**. Bimonthly journal featuring information and encouragement for writers. We serve Christian writers and others in Christian publishing. We like informational and how-to articles. Estab. 1976. Circ. 1,000. Byline given. Pays on publication. No kill fee. Publishes ms an average of 6-12 months after acceptance. Buys first rights, buys second serial (reprint) rights. Editorial lead time 6 months. Submit seasonal material 6 months in advance. Accepts queries by mail, e-mail: CQArticles@aol.com and CQArticles@cwfi-online.org. Responds in 1 month to queries. Responds in 2 months to mss. Sample copy for $2 with 9—Š11 SAE and 2 first-class stamps. Writer's guidelines at cwfi-online.org/crossquil.htm or for SAE.
Nonfiction Needs Have an immediate need for 200-800 word features on fiction writing, writing for young readers, how-to plan and write almost any writing form, any phase of marketing, testimonies of how God worked in your life and career while attending a writers conference. We also need articles on almost any

topic on participating in or leading writers groups (200-800) and fillers to 100 words on almost any writing topic or poetry (12 lines max)., devotional. **Buys 25 mss/year.** Send complete ms. Length: 200-800 words. **Pays $10-50.**

Photos State availability

Poetry Needs free verse, haiku, light verse, traditional. **Buys 10 poems/year.** Submit maximum 3 poems. Length: 12 lines. **Pays $5.**

Fillers to 100 words on almost any writing topic. **$5.**

Tips Study guidelines and follow them. Acceptances of philosophical, personal reflection, or personal experiences is rare. Paste article submissions into an e-mail form. We prefer not to download submissions as attached files. Double-space between paragraphs. Please use plain— not html text. Do not use boldface or bullets.

$ $ $ E CONTENT MAGAZINE

Digital Content Strategies & Resources, Online, Inc., 88 Danbury Rd., Suite 1D, Wilton CT 06897. (203)761-1466. Fax: (203)761-1444. E-mail: michelle.manafy@infotoday.com. Website: www.econtentmag.com. **90% freelance written**. Monthly magazine covering digital content trends, strategies, etc. *E Content* is a business publication. Readers need to stay on top of industry trends and developments. Estab. 1979. Circ. 12,000. Byline given. Pays within 1 month of publication. Offers 20-50% kill fee. Buys all rights. Editorial lead time 4 months. Accepts queries by e-mail. Responds in 3 weeks to queries. Responds in 1 month to mss. Sample copy and writer's guidelines online.

Nonfiction Needs expose, how-to, interview, new product, opinion, technical, news features, strategic and solution-oriented features. No academic or straight Q&A. **Buys 48 mss/year.** Query with published clips. Length: 500-700 words. **Pays 40-50¢/word.** Sometimes pays expenses of writers on assignment.

Photos State availability Captions required. Negotiates payment individually Buys one time rights.

Columns/Departments Profiles (short profile of unique company, person or product), 1,200 words; New Features (breaking news of content-related topics), 500 words maximum. 40 Query with published clips. **Pays 30-40¢/word**

Tips Take a look at the website. Most of the time, an e-mail query with specific article ideas works well. A general outline of talking points is good, too. State prior experience.

$ FELLOWSCRIPT

InScribe Christian Writers' Fellowship, PO Box 26016, 650 Portland St., Dartmouth NS B2W 6P3 Canada. E-mail: submissions@inscribe.org. Website: www.inscribe.org. **Contact:** Joanna Mallory, acq. ed. **100% freelance written**. Quarterly writers' newsletter featuring Christian writing. "Our readers are Christians with a commitment to writing. Among our readership are best-selling authors and unpublished beginning writers. Submissions to us should include practical information, something the reader can immediately put into practice." Estab. 1983. Circ. 200. Byline given. Pays on publication. No kill fee. Publishes ms an average of 2-12 months after acceptance. Buys one-time rights, buys second serial (reprint) rights, first or reprint rights. Editorial lead time 3 months. Submit seasonal material 4 months in advance. Accepts queries by e-mail, prefers full ms by email; postal submissions only accepted from InScribe members. Accepts simultaneous submissions. Responds in 1 month to queries. Responds in 2-6 months to mss. Sample copy for $3.50, 9 x 12 SAE, and 2 first-class stamps (Canadian) or IRCs. Guidelines available online.

Nonfiction All must pertain to writing and the writing life. Needs essays, expose, how-to, for writers, interview, new product. Does not want poetry, fiction, personal experience, testimony or think piece, commentary articles. **Buys 30-45 mss/year.** Send complete ms. Length: 400-1,200 words. **Pays 2 ½¢/word (first rights); 1 ½¢/word reprints (Canadian funds).**

Columns/Departments Book reviews, 150-300 words; Market Updates, 50-300 words. 1-3. Send complete ms. **Pays 1 copy.**

Fillers Needs facts, newsbreaks. 5-10 Length: 25-300 words. **Pays 1 copy.**

Tips Send your complete manuscript by e-mail (pasted into the message, no attachments). E-mail is preferred. Tell us a bit about yourself. Write in a casual, first-person, anecdotal style. Be sure your article is full of practical material, something that can be applied. Most of our accepted freelance submissions fall into the 'how-to' category, and involve tasks, crafts, or procedures common to writers. Please do not send inspirational articles (i.e., 'How I sold My First Story')."

$ FREELANCE MARKET NEWS

An Essential Guide for Freelance Writers, The Writers Bureau Ltd., Sevendale House, 7 Dale St., Manchester M1 1JB England. (44)(161)228-2362. Fax: (44)(161)228-3533. E-mail: fmn@writersbureau.com. Website: www.freelancemarketnews.com. **15% freelance written**. Monthly newsletter covering freelance writing. Estab. 1968. Byline given. Pays on acceptance. No kill fee. Publishes ms an average of 3 months after acceptance. Buys all rights. Editorial lead time 3 months. Submit seasonal material 3 months in advance. Accepts queries by mail, e-mail, fax. Accepts previously published material. Accepts simultaneous submissions. Sample copy available online. Guidelines available online.

- "Send complete manuscripts rather than a query."

Nonfiction Needs how-to sell your writing/improve your writing. **Buys 12 mss/year.** 700 words **Pays £50/1,000 words.**
Columns/Departments New Markets (magazines which have recently been published); Fillers & Letters; Overseas Markets (obviously only English-language publications); Market Notes (established publications accepting articles, fiction, reviews, or poetry). All should be between 40 and 200 words. **Pays £40/1,000 words.**

$ $ FREELANCE WRITER'S REPORT

CNW Publishing, Inc., 45 Main St., P.O. Box A, North Stratford NH 03590-0167. (603)922-8338. E-mail: fwrwm@writers-editors.com. Website: www.writers-editors.com. **25% freelance written.** Monthly newsletter. *"FWR* covers the marketing and business/office management aspects of running a freelance writing business. Articles must be of value to the established freelancer; nothing basic." Estab. 1982. Byline given. Pays on publication. No kill fee. Publishes ms an average of 6 months after acceptance. Buys one-time rights. Editorial lead time 2 months. Submit seasonal material 2 months in advance. Accepts simultaneous submissions. Responds in 1 week to queries. Responds in 2 weeks to mss. Sample copy for 6x9 SAE with 2 first-class stamps (for back copy); $4 for current copy. Guidelines and sample copy available online.
Nonfiction Needs book excerpts, how-to (market, increase income or profits). "No articles about the basics of freelancing." **Buys 50 mss/year.** Send complete ms by e-mail. Length: Up to 900 words. **Pays 10¢/word.**
Tips "Write in a terse, newsletter style."

KIRKUS REVIEWS

Nielsen Business Media, 770 Broadway, 7th Floor, New York NY 10003. (646)654-4715. E-mail: info@kirkusreviews.com. Website: www.kirkusreviews.com. Children's/YA Editor: Vicky Smith. **Contact:** Editorial Coordinator: Mary-Kate Figur. **100% freelance written.** Biweekly trade journal that reviews 5,000 prepublication books each year—mainstream fiction, nonfiction, children's books, and young adult books—for libraries, booksellers, publishers, producers, and agents. Estab. 1933. Circ. 2,100. No byline given. Pays on acceptance. No kill fee. Editorial lead time 3-4 months.
Tips Please visit our Web site for details.

$ MAINE IN PRINT

Maine Writers & Publishers Alliance, 318 Glickman Family Library, P.O. Box 9301, 314 Forest Ave., Portland ME 04104. (207)228-8263. Fax: (207)228-8150. E-mail: info@mainewriters.org. Website: www.mainewriters.org. Quarterly newsletter for writers, editors, teachers, librarians, etc., focusing on Maine literature and the craft of writing. Estab. 1975. Circ. 3,000. Byline given. Pays on publication. No kill fee. Publishes ms an average of 2 months after acceptance. Buys one-time rights. Editorial lead time 2 months. Accepts queries by mail. Accepts simultaneous submissions. Sample copy and writer's guidelines free.
Nonfiction Needs essays, how-to, writing, interview, technical. No creative writing, fiction, or poetry. **Buys 20 mss/year.** Query with published clips. Length: 400-1,500 words. **Pays $25-50 for assigned articles.**
Reprints Send tearsheet and information about when and where the material previously appeared. Pays $25.
Photos State availability Offers no additional payment for photos accepted with ms.
Columns/Departments Front-page articles (writing related), 500-1,500 words. 20 Query. **Pays $25 minimum.**
Tips Become a member of Maine Writers & Publishers Alliance. Become familiar with Maine literary scene.

$ $ 🌐 MSLEXIA

For Women Who Write, Mslexia Publications Ltd., P.O. Box 656, Newcastle upon Tyne NE99 1PZ United Kingdom. (44)(191)261-6656. E-mail: postbag@mslexia.demon.co.uk. Website: www.mslexia.co.uk. **60% freelance written.** Quarterly magazine offering advice and publishing opportunities for women writers, plus poetry and prose submissions on a different theme each issue. *Mslexia* tells you all you need to know about exploring your creativity and getting into print. No other magazine provides *Mslexia*'s unique mix of advice and inspiration; news, reviews, interviews; competitions, events, grants; all served up with a challenging selection of new poetry and prose. *Mslexia* is read by authors and absolute beginners. A quarterly master class in the business and psychology of writing, it's the essential magazine for women who write. Estab. 1998. Circ. 12,000. Byline given. Pays on publication. Offers 50% kill fee. Publishes ms an average of 1 month after acceptance. Buys one-time rights. Editorial lead time 3 months. Submit seasonal material 3 months in advance. Accepts queries by mail, e-mail, phone. Accepts simultaneous submissions. Responds in 3 months to mss. Sample copy available online. Writer's guidelines online or by e-mail.

- This publication does not accept e-mail submissions except from overseas writers.

Nonfiction Needs how-to, interview, opinion, personal experience. No general items about women or academic features. We are only interested in features (for tertiary-educated readership) about women's writing and literature. **Buys 40 mss/year.** Query with published clips. Length: 500-2,000 words. **Pays $70-400 for assigned articles. Pays $70-300 for unsolicited articles.** Sometimes pays expenses of writers on assignment.

Columns/Departments We are open to suggestions, but would only commission 1 new column/year, probably from a UK-based writer. 12 Query with published clips.

Fiction Contact: Helen Christie, editorial assistant. See guidelines on our website. Submissions not on one of our current themes will be returned (if submitted with a SASE) or destroyed. **Buys 30 mss/year.** Send complete ms. Length: 50-3,000 words.

Poetry Contact: Helen Christie, editorial assistant. Needs avant-garde, free verse, haiku, traditional. **Buys 40 poems/year.** Submit maximum 4 poems.

Tips Read the magazine; subscribe if you can afford it. *Mslexia* has a particular style and relationship with its readers which is hard to assess at a quick glance. The majority of our readers live in the UK, so feature pitches should be aware of this. We never commission work without seeing a written sample first. We rarely accept unsolicited manuscripts, but prefer a short letter suggesting a feature, plus a brief bio and writing sample.

$ NEW WRITER'S MAGAZINE

Sarasota Bay Publishing, P.O. Box 5976, Sarasota FL 34277-5976. (941)953-7903. E-mail: newriters@aol.com. **95% freelance written**. Bimonthly magazine. "*New Writer's Magazine* believes that *all* writers are *new* writers in that each of us can learn from one another. So, we reach pro and nonpro alike." Estab. 1986. Circ. 5,000. Byline given. Pays on publication. No kill fee. Buys first rights. Accepts queries by mail. Responds in 1 month to queries and to mss. Guidelines for #10 SASE.

Nonfiction Needs general interest, historical, how-to, for new writers, humor, interview, opinion. **Buys 50 mss/year.** Send complete ms. Length: 700-1,000 words. **Pays $10-50.**

Photos Send photos Captions required. Reviews 5x7 prints. Offers no additional payment for photos accepted with ms.

Fiction Needs experimental, historical, humorous, mainstream, slice-of-life vignettes-of-life vignettes. "Again, we do *not* want anything that does not have a tie-in with the writing life or writers in general." **Buys 2-6 mss/year.** Send complete ms. Length: 700-800 words. **Pays $20-40.**

Poetry Needs free verse, light verse, traditional. Does not want anything *not* for writers. **Buys 10-20 poems/year.** Submit maximum 3 poems. Length: 8-20 lines. **Pays $5 minimum.**

Fillers For cartoons, writing lifestyle slant. Buys 20-30/year. Pays $10 maximum. Needs anecdotes, facts, newsbreaks, short humor. 5-15 Length: 20-100 words. **$5 maximum.**

Tips "Any article with photos has a good chance, especially an up close and personal interview with an established professional writer offering advice, etc. Short profile pieces on new authors also receive attention."

NEW ZEALAND AUTHOR

New Zealand Society of Authors, P.O. Box 7701, Wellesley St., Auckland 1141 New Zealand. Phone/Fax: (64) (9)379-4801. E-mail: nzsa@clear.net.nz. Website: www.authors.org.nz. Bimonthly newsletter. Articles are on professional development for writers, plus local and overseas news and information on competitions, awards, and fellowships. Circ. 1,200. No kill fee.

- Query before submitting.

$ $ NOVEL & SHORT STORY WRITER'S MARKET

F+W Media, Inc., 4700 E. Galbraith Rd., Cincinnati OH 45236. E-mail: alice.pope@fwmedia.com. **Contact:** Alice Pope, editor. **80% freelance written**. Annual resource book covering the fiction market. "In addition to thousands of listings for places to get fiction published, we feature articles on the craft and business of fiction writing, as well as interviews with successful fiction writers, editors, and agents. Our articles are unique in that they always offer an actionable take-away. In other words, readers must learn something immediately useful about the creation or marketing of fiction." Estab. 1981. Byline given. Pays on acceptance plus 30 days. Offers 25% kill fee. Buys exclusive first serial rights and nonexclusive electronic rights for reproduction on website. Accepts queries by e-mail only. Include "NSSWM query" in the subject line. Responds in 1 week to queries.

- Accepts proposals during the summer.

Nonfiction Needs how-to, write, sell and promote fiction; find an agent; etc., interview, personal experience. **Buys 20+ mss/year.** Length: 1,000-3,0000 words. **Pays $350-700.**

Photos Send photos Identification of subjects required. Reviews prints, GIF/JPEG files (hi-res). Offers no additional payment for photos accepted with ms.

Tips "The best way to break into this book is to review the last few years' editions and look for aspects of the fiction industry that we haven't covered recently. Send me a specific, detailed pitch stating the topic, angle, and 'takeaway' of the piece, what sources you intend to use, and what qualifies you to write this article. Freelancers who have published fiction and/or have contacts in the industry have an advantage."

$ $ POETS & WRITERS MAGAZINE

90 Broad Street, 2100, New York NY 10004. E-mail: editor@pw.org. Website: www.pw.org. **95% freelance written**. Bimonthly professional trade journal for poets and fiction writers and creative nonfiction writers. Estab. 1987. Circ. 60,000. Byline given. Pays on acceptance of finished draft. Offers 25% kill fee. Publishes

ms an average of 4 months after acceptance. Buys first North American serial rights, buys nonexclusive reprint rights shared 50/50 thereafter rights. Submit seasonal material 4 months in advance. Accepts queries by mail, e-mail. Responds in 2 months to mss. Sample copy for $5.95 to Sample Copy Dept. Guidelines available online.

- No poetry or fiction submissions.

Nonfiction Needs how-to, craft of poetry, fiction or creative nonfiction writing, interviews, with poets or writers of fiction and creative nonfiction,, personal essays about literature, regional reports of literary activity, reports on small presses, service pieces about publishing trends. "We do not accept submissions by fax." **Buys 35 mss/year.** Send complete ms. Length: 500-2,500 (depending on topic) words.
Photos State availability Reviews b&w prints. Offers no additional payment for photos accepted with ms.
Columns/Departments Literary and Publishing News, 500-1,000 words; Profiles of Emerging and Established Poets, Fiction Writers and Creative Nonfiction Writers, 2,000-3,000 words; Regional Reports (literary activity in US and abroad), 1,000-2,000 words. Query with published clips or send complete ms. **Pays $150-500.**

$ $ QUILL & SCROLL MAGAZINE

Quill and Scroll International Honorary Society for High School Journalists, E346 Adler Journalism Bldg., Iowa City IA 52242-2004. (319)335-3321. Fax: (319)335-3989. E-mail: quill-scroll@uiowa.edu. Website: www.uiowa.edu/~quill-sc. **20% freelance written.** bimonthly during school year magazine covering scholastic journalism-related topics. Our primary audience is high school journalism students working on and studying topics related to newspapers, yearbooks, radio, television, and online media; secondary audience is their teachers and others interested in this topic. Estab. 1926. Circ. 10,000. Byline given. acceptance & publication. No kill fee. Publishes ms an average of 4 months after acceptance. Buys all rights. Makes work-for-hire assignments. Editorial lead time 2 months. Accepts queries by mail, e-mail. Accepts simultaneous submissions. Responds in 2 weeks to queries. Guidelines available.
Nonfiction Needs essays, how-to, humor, interview, new product, opinion, personal experience, photo feature, technical, travel, types on topic. Articles not pertinent to high school student journalists. Query. Length: 600-1,000 words. **Pays $100-500 for assigned articles. Pays complementary copy - $200 max. for unsolicited articles.** Sometimes pays expenses of writers on assignment.
Photos State availability Reviews GIF/JPEG files. Offers no additional payment for photos accepted with ms.

$ $ $ QUILL MAGAZINE

Society of Professional Journalists, 3909 N. Meridian St., Indianapolis IN 46208. Fax: (317)920-4789. E-mail: jskeel@spj.org. Website: www.spj.org/quill.asp. **75% freelance written.** Monthly magazine covering journalism and the media industry. *Quill* is a how-to magazine written by journalists. We focus on the industry's biggest issues while providing tips on how to become better journalists. Estab. 1912. Circ. 10,000. Byline given. Pays on acceptance. Offers 25% kill fee. Publishes ms an average of 2 months after acceptance. Buys first rights, buys electronic rights. Editorial lead time 2-3 months. Submit seasonal material 2-3 months in advance. Accepts queries by e-mail. Accepts previously published material. Accepts simultaneous submissions. Sample copy available online.
Nonfiction Needs general interest, how-to, technical. Does not want personality profiles and straight research pieces. **Buys 12 mss/year.** Query. Length: 800-2,500 words. **Pays $150-800.**

$ THE WRITER'S CHRONICLE

The Association of Writers & Writing Programs (AWP), MS 1E3, George Mason Univ., Fairfax VA 22030. (703)993-4301. Fax: (703)993-4302. E-mail: awp@awpwriter.org. Website: www.awpwriter.org. **75% freelance written.** 6 times during the academic year. magazine covering essays on the craft and art of writing poetry, fiction, and nonfiction. *The Writer's Chronicle* strives to: present the best essays on the craft and art of writing poetry, fiction, and nonfiction; help overcome the over-specialization and balkanization of the literary arts by presenting a public forum for the appreciation, debate, and analysis of contemporary literature; present the diversity of accomplishments and points of view within contemporary literature; provide serious and committed writers and students of writing the best advice on how to manage their professional lives; provide the members and subscribers with a literary community; provide information on publishing opportunities, grants, and awards; promote the good works of AWP, its programs, and its individual members. Estab. 1967. Circ. 30,000. Byline given. Pays on publication. No kill fee. Publishes ms an average of 6 months after acceptance. Buys first North American serial rights, buys electronic rights. Editorial lead time 1 month. Accepts queries by mail, e-mail. Accepts simultaneous submissions. Responds in 2 weeks to queries. Responds in 3 months to mss. Sample copy free. Guidelines free.
Nonfiction Needs essays, interview, opinion. We do not want personal essays. **Buys 5 mss/year. mss/year.** Send complete ms. Length: 3,000-7,000 words. **$11 for every 100 words. for assigned articles.**

$ $ THE WRITER

Kalmbach Publishing Co., 21027 Crossroads Circle, P.O. Box 1612, Waukesha WI 53187-1612. E-mail: queries@writermag.com. Website: www.writermag.com. **90% freelance written. Prefers to buy work of published/**

established writers. Estab. 1887. Pays on acceptance. No kill fee. Buys first North American serial rights. Accepts queries by mail, e-mail. Sample copy for $5.95. Guidelines available online.

- No phone queries.

Nonfiction Practical articles for writers on how to write fiction and nonfiction for publication, and how and where to market manuscripts in various fields. Considers all submissions generally in 1-2 months. Assignments go to writers who have published in the magazine. Length: 700-3,400 words. **Pays $50-500.**
Reprints Send tearsheet or photocopy and information about when and where the material previously appeared.
Tips We are looking for articles with plenty of practical, specific advice that writers can apply to their own work. We are particularly interested in articles done in our 'step by step' format; a memo is available on this format. Query first on step by step articles, and only if you have a strong record of publication.

$ $ $ WRITER'S DIGEST

F+W Media, Inc., 4700 E. Galbraith Rd., Cincinnati OH 45236. (513)531-2690. E-mail: wdsubmissions@fwmedia.com. Website: www.writersdigest.com. **75% freelance written**. Bimonthly magazine for those who want to write better, get published and participate in the vibrant culture of writers. "Our readers look to us for specific ideas and tips that will help them succeed, whether success means getting into print, finding personal fulfillment through writing or building and maintaining a thriving writing career and network." Estab. 1920. Byline given. Pays on acceptance. Offers 25% kill fee. Publishes ms an average of 6-9 months after acceptance. Buys first North American print and perpetual world digital rights. Pays 25% print reprint fee. Accepts queries by e-mail only. Responds in 2 months to queries. Responds in 2 months to mss. Guidelines available online and on editorial calendar.

- The magazine does not accept or read e-queries with attachments.

Nonfiction "Although we welcome the work of new writers, we believe the established writer can better instruct our readers. Please include your publishing credentials related to your topic with your submission." Needs essays, how-to, humor, inspirational, interviews, profiles. Does not accept phone, snail mail, or fax queries. "We don't buy newspaper clippings or reprints of articles previously published in other writing magazines. Book and software reviews are handled in-house, as are most *WD* interviews." **Buys 40 mss/year.** Send complete ms. Length: 800-1,500 words. **Pays 30-50¢/word.**
Tips "InkWell is the best place for new writers to break in. We recommend you consult our editorial calendar before pitching feature-length articles. Check our writer's guidelines for more details."

$ WRITERS' JOURNAL

The Complete Writer's Magazine, Val-Tech Media, P.O. Box 394, Perham MN 56573-0394. (218)346-7921. Fax: (218)346-7924. E-mail: writersjournal@writersjournal.com. Website: www.writersjournal.com. **Contact:** Leon Ogroske. **60% freelance written**. Bimonthly magazine covering writing. "*Writers' Journal* is read by thousands of aspiring writers whose love of writing has taken them to the next step: writing for money. We are an instructional manual giving writers the tools and information necessary to get their work published. We also print works by authors who have won our writing contests." Estab. 1980. Circ. 22,000. Byline given. Pays on publication. No kill fee. Publishes ms an average of 4 months after acceptance. Buys first rights, buys second serial (reprint) rights. Accepts queries by mail, e-mail, fax. Responds in 6 weeks to queries. Responds in 6 months to mss. Sample copy for $6. Guidelines available online.
Nonfiction Needs how-to, write, publish, market. **Buys 25 mss/year.** Send complete ms. Length: 800-2,500 words. **Pays $30.**
Photos Send photos Model releases required. Reviews transparencies, 8x10 prints, GIF/JPEG files. Offers no addition payment for photos accepted with ms; offers $50/cover photo. Buys one time rights.
Fiction "We only publish winners of our fiction contests—16 contests/year." Length: 2,000 words.
Poetry Contact: Contact Esther Leiper, poetry editor. Needs light verse. Does not want anything boring. **Buys 30 poems/year.** Submit maximum 2 poems. Length: 15 lines. **Pays $5.**
Fillers Needs facts, gags, short humor. 20 Length: 10-200 words. **Pays up to $10.**
Tips "Appearance must be professional with no grammatical or spelling errors, submitted on white paper, double spaced with easy-to-read font. We want articles that will help writers improve technique in writing, style, editing, publishing, and story construction. We are interested in how writers use new and fresh angles to break into the writing markets."

$ WRITING THAT WORKS

The Business Communications Report, Communications Concepts, Inc., 7481 Huntsman Blvd., #720, Springfield VA 22153-1648. (703)643-2200. E-mail: concepts@writingthatworks.com. Website: www.apexawards.com. Monthly newsletter on business writing and communications. Our readers are company writers, editors, communicators, and executives. They need specific, practical advice on how to write well as part of their job. Estab. 1983. Byline sometimes given. Pays within 45 days of acceptance. No kill fee. Publishes ms an average of 3 months after acceptance. Buys all rights. Editorial lead time 3 months. Accepts queries by mail, e-mail. Responds in 1 month to queries. Sample copy and writer's guidelines online.
Nonfiction Practical, short, how-to articles and quick tips on business writing techniques geared to company

writers, editors, publication staff and communicators. We're always looking for shorts—how-to tips on business writing. Needs how-to. **Buys 90 mss/year.** Accepts electronic final mss. Length: 100-600 words. **Pays $35-150.**

Columns/Departments Writing Techniques (how-to business writing advice); Style Matters (grammar, usage, and editing); Online Publishing (writing, editing, and publishing for the Web); Managing Publications; PR & Marketing (writing).

Fillers Short tips on writing or editing. Mini-reviews of communications websites for business writers, editors, and communicators. Length: 100-250 words. **Pays $35.**

Tips We do not use material on how to get published or how to conduct a freelancing business. Format your copy to follow *Writing That Works* style. Include postal and e-mail addresses, phone numbers, website URLs, and prices for products/services mentioned in articles.

$ $ $ $ WRITTEN BY

The Magazine of the Writers Guild of America, West, 7000 W. Third St., Los Angeles CA 90048. (323)782-4522. Fax: (323)782-4800. Website: www.wga.org. **40% freelance written**. Magazine published 9 times/year. "*Written By* is the premier magazine written by and for America's screen and TV writers. We focus on the craft of screenwriting and cover all aspects of the entertainment industry from the perspective of the writer. We are read by all screenwriters and most entertainment executives." Estab. 1987. Circ. 12,000. Byline given. Pays on acceptance. Offers 10% kill fee. Publishes ms an average of 2 months after acceptance. Buys first North American serial rights, buys electronic rights. Editorial lead time 4 months. Submit seasonal material 4 months in advance. Accepts queries by mail, e-mail, fax, phone. Guidelines for #10 SASE.

Nonfiction Needs book excerpts, essays, historical, humor, interview, opinion, personal experience, photo feature, technical, software. No beginner pieces on how to break into Hollywood, or how to write scripts. **Buys 20 mss/year.** Query with published clips. Length: 500-3,500 words. **Pays $500-3,500 for assigned articles.** Sometimes pays expenses of writers on assignment.

Photos State availability Captions, identification of subjects, model releases required. Reviews transparencies. Offers no additional payment for photos accepted with ms. Buys one time rights.

Columns/Departments Pays $1,000 maximum.

Tips "We are looking for more theoretical essays on screenwriting past and/or present. Also, the writer must always keep in mind that our audience is made up primarily of working writers who are inside the business; therefore all articles need to have an `insider' feel and not be written for those who are still trying to break in to Hollywood. We prefer a hard copy of submission or e-mail."

LAW

$ $ $ $ ABA JOURNAL

The Lawyer's Magazine, American Bar Association, 321 N. Clark St., Chicago IL 60610. (312)988-6018. Fax: (312)988-6014. E-mail: releases@abanet.org. Website: www.abajournal.com. **10% freelance written**. Monthly magazine covering law. The *ABA Journal* is an independent, thoughtful, and inquiring observer of the law and the legal profession. The magazine is edited for members of the American Bar Association. Circ. 380,000. Byline given. Pays on acceptance. No kill fee. Makes work-for-hire assignments. Accepts queries by mail, e-mail. Sample copy free. Guidelines available online.

Nonfiction We don't want anything that does not have a legal theme. No poetry or fiction. **Buys 5 mss/year.** Query with published clips. Length: 500-3,500 words. **Pays $300-2,000 for assigned articles.**

Columns/Departments The National Pulse/Ideas from the Front (reports on legal news and trends), 650 words; eReport (reports on legal news and trends), 500-1,500 words. The *ABA Journal eReport* is our weekly online newsletter sent out to members. 25 Query with published clips. **Pays $300, regardless of story length**

ALTERNATIVE LAW JOURNAL

The Legal Service Bulletin Co-operative, Ltd., Law Faculty, Monash University VIC 3800 Australia. E-mail: deb.candy@Law.monash.edu.au. Website: www.altlj.org. Quarterly magazine covering the promotion of social justice issues, legal system, development of alternative practice, community legal education and support of law reform activity. Guidelines available online.

Nonfiction Needs general interest, interview. Send complete ms. Length: 800-4,000 words.

Fillers Length: 100-150 words.

Tips Heavy, scholarly or overly legalistic articles are not encouraged. We particularly discourage excessive footnotes.

$ $ $ BENCH & BAR OF MINNESOTA

Minnesota State Bar Association, 600 Nicollet Mall #380, Minneapolis MN 55402. (612)333-1183. Fax: (612)333-4927. Website: www.mnbar.org. **5% freelance written**. Magazine published 11 times/year. Audience

is mostly Minnesota lawyers. *Bench & Bar* seeks reportage, analysis, and commentary on trends and issues in the law and the legal profession, especially in Minnesota. Preference to items of practical/professional human interest to lawyers and judges. Estab. 1931. Circ. 17,000. Byline given. Pays on acceptance. No kill fee. Publishes ms an average of 3 months after acceptance. Buys first North American serial rights. Makes work-for-hire assignments. Responds in 1 month to queries. Guidelines for free online or by mail.
Nonfiction Needs Needs analysis and exposition of current trends, developments and issues in law, legal profession, esp, in Minnesota. Balanced commentary and "how-to" considered. We do not want one-sided opinion pieces or advertorial. **Buys 2-3 mss/year.** Send query or complete ms. Length: 1,000-3,500 words. **Pays $500-1,500.** Some expenses of writers on assignment.
Photos State availability Identification of subjects, model releases required. Reviews 5x7 prints. Pays $25-100 upon publication Buys one time rights.

DE REBUS

P.O. Box 36626, Menlo Park 0102 South Africa. (27)(12)362-0969. Fax: (27)(12)362-1729. E-mail: derebus@mweb.co.za. Website: www.derebus.org.za. Trade journal published 11 times/year for South African attorneys. Preference is given to articles written by attorneys. No kill fee. Accepts queries by mail, e-mail. Guidelines available online.
Nonfiction Needs interview, opinion, law book reviews, case notes. Length: 3,000 words (articles); 1,000 words (case notes/opinions).

$ $ $ $ INSIDECOUNSEL

(formerly *Corporate Legal Times*), 222 S. Riverside Plaza, Suite 620, Chicago IL 60606. (312)654-3500. E-mail: rvasper@insidecounsel.com. Website: www.insidecounsel.com. **50% freelance written**. Monthly tabloid. *InsideCounsel* is a monthly national magazine that gives general counsel and inhouse attorneys information on legal and business issues to help them better manage corporate law departments. It routinely addresses changes and trends in law departments, litigation management, legal technology, corporate governance and inhouse careers. Law areas covered monthly include: intellectual property, international, technology, project finance, e-commerce and litigation. All articles need to be geared toward the inhouse attorney's perspective. Estab. 1991. Circ. 45,000. Byline given. Pays on publication. No kill fee. Publishes ms an average of 3 months after acceptance. Buys all rights. Editorial lead time 3 months. Submit seasonal material 3 months in advance. Accepts queries by mail, e-mail. Responds in 3 weeks to queries. Sample copy for $17. Guidelines available online.
Nonfiction Needs interview, news about legal aspects of business issues and events. **Buys 12-25 mss/year.** Query with published clips. Length: 500-3,000 words. **Pays $500-2,000.**
Photos Freelancers should state availability of photos with submission. Identification of subjects required. Reviews color transparencies, b&w prints. Offers $25-150/photo. Buys all rights.
Tips Our publication targets general counsel and inhouse lawyers. All articles need to speak to them—not to the general attorney population. Query with clips and a list of potential in-house sources.

$ $ $ JCR

National Court Reporters Association, 8224 Old Courthouse Rd., Vienna VA 22180. E-mail: jschmidt@ncrahq.org. Website: www.ncraonline.org. **10% freelance written**. Monthly, except bimonthl July/Aug and Nov/Dec. magazine covering court reporting, captioning, and CART provision. The JCR has two complementary purposes: to communicate the activities, goals and mission of its publisher, the National Court Reporters Association; and, simultaneously, to seek out and publish diverse information and views on matters significantly related to the court reporting and captioning professions. Estab. 1899. Circ. 20,000. Byline sometimes given. Pays on acceptance. No kill fee. Publishes ms an average of 4-5 months after acceptance. Buys first North American serial rights, buys simultaneous rights, buys electronic rights. Makes work-for-hire assignments. Editorial lead time 4 months. Submit seasonal material 4 months in advance. Accepts queries by mail, e-mail. Sample copy free. Guidelines free.
Nonfiction Needs book excerpts, how-to, interview, technical, legal issues. **Buys 6-10 mss/year mss/year.** Query. Length: 1,000-2,500 words. **Pays $1,000 maximum for assigned articles. Pays $100 maximum for unsolicited articles.** Sometimes pays expenses of writers on assignment.
Columns/Departments Language (proper punctuation, grammar, dealing with verbatim materials); Technical (new technologies, using mobile technology, using technology for work); Book excerpts (language, crime, legal issues), all 1,000 words. **Pays $-$100.**

$ $ $ N JOURNAL OF COURT REPORTING

National Court Reporters Association, 8224 Old Courthouse Rd., Vienna VA 22180. E-mail: jschmidt@ncrahq.org. Website: www.ncraonline.org. **10% freelance written**. Monthly (bimonthly July/August and November/December) magazine. "The *Journal of Court Reporting* has two complementary purposes: to communicate the activities, goals and mission of its publisher, the National Court Reporters Association; and, simultaneously, to seek out and publish diverse information and views on matters significantly related to the court reporting and captioning professions." Estab. 1899. Circ. 20,000. Byline sometimes given. Pays on acceptance. No kill fee. Publishes ms an average of 4-5 months after acceptance. Buys first North American serial rights, buys simultaneous rights, buys electronic rights. Makes work-for-hire assignments; rights as needed. Editorial lead time 4 months. Submit seasonal material 4 months in advance. Accepts queries by mail, e-mail. Accepts simultaneous submissions. Sample copy free Guidelines free

Nonfiction Needs book excerpts, how-to, interview, technical, legal issues. **Buys 10 mss/year.** Query. Length: 1,000-2,500 words. **Pays 1,000 max. for assigned articles. Pays $100 max. for unsolicited articles.** Sometimes pays expenses of writers on assignment.

Columns/Departments Language (proper punctuation, grammar, dealing with verbatim materials); Technical (new technologies, using mobile technology, using technology for work); Book excerpts (language, crime, legal issues), all 1,000 words; Puzzles (any, but especially word-related games). **Pays $- $100.**

LAW OFFICE COMPUTING

James Publishing, P.O. Box 25202, Santa Ana CA 92799. (714)755-5450. Fax: (714)751-5508. E-mail: aflatten@jamespublishing.com. Website: www.lawofficecomputing.com. **90% freelance written**. Bimonthly magazine covering legal technology industry. *Law Office Computing* is a magazine written for attorneys and other legal professionals. It covers the legal technology field and features software reviews, profiles of prominent figures in the industry, and `how-to' type articles. Estab. 1991. Circ. 7,000. Byline given. Pays on publication. No kill fee. Publishes ms an average of 2 months after acceptance. Buys first North American serial rights. Editorial lead time 4 months. Submit seasonal material 4 months in advance. Accepts queries by mail, e-mail, fax. Sample copy free. Guidelines available online.

Nonfiction Needs how-to, interview, new product, technical. **Buys 30 mss/year.** Query. Length: 2,000-3,500 words. **Pays on a case-by-case basis.** Sometimes pays expenses of writers on assignment.

Photos State availability

Columns/Departments Tech profile (profile firm using technology), 1,200 words; My Solution, 1,200 words; Software reviews: Short reviews (a single product), 600 words; Software Shootouts (2 or 3 products going head-to-head), 1,000-1,500 words; Round-Ups/Buyer's Guides (8-15 products), 300-500 words/product. 6 Query. **Pays on a case-by-case basis**

Tips If you are a practicing attorney, legal MIS, or computer consultant, try the first-person My Solution column or a short review. If you are a professional freelance writer, technology profiles or a news story regarding legal technology are best, since most of our other copy is written by legal technology professionals.

$ LEGAL ASSISTANT TODAY

James Publishing, Inc., P.O. Box 25202, Santa Ana CA 92799. (714)755-5468. Fax: (714)751-5508. E-mail: rhughes@jamespublishing.com. Website: www.legalassistanttoday.com. Bimonthly magazine geared toward all legal assistants/paralegals throughout the United States and Canada, regardless of specialty (litigation, corporate, bankruptcy, environmental law, etc.). How-to articles to help paralegals perform their jobs more effectively are most in demand, as are career and salary information, and timely news and trends pieces. Estab. 1983. Circ. 8,000. Byline given. Pays on publication. No kill fee. Buys first North American Serial rights, electronic rights, non-exclusive rights to use the article, author's name, image, and biographical data in advertising and promotion. Editorial lead time 10 weeks. Submit seasonal material 3 months in advance. Accepts queries by mail, e-mail, fax. Accepts simultaneous submissions. Responds in 2 months to mss. Sample copy and writer's guidelines free. Guidelines available online.

Nonfiction Needs interview, unique and interesting paralegals in unique and particular work-related situations, news (brief, hard news topics regarding paralegals), features (present information to help paralegals advance their careers). **Pays $25-100.**

Photos Send photos

Tips Fax a detailed outline of a 2,500 to 3,000-word feature about something useful to working legal assistants. Writers must understand our audience. There is some opportunity for investigative journalism as well as the usual features, profiles, and news. How-to articles are especially desired. If you are a great writer who can interview effectively, and really dig into the topic to grab readers' attention, we need you.

$ $ $ $ NATIONAL

Practice Trends and Legal Insights, The Canadian Bar Association, 500-865 Carling Ave., Ottawa ON K1S 5S8 Canada. (613)237-2925. Fax: (613)237-0185. E-mail: jordanf@cba.org. Website: www.cba.org/national. **90% freelance written**. Magazine published 8 times/year covering practice trends and business developments in the law, with a focus on technology, innovation, practice management and client relations. Estab. 1993. Circ. 37,000. Byline given. Pays on acceptance. Offers 50% kill fee. Publishes ms an average of 2 months after acceptance. Buys first North American serial rights, buys electronic rights. Editorial lead time 2 months. Accepts queries by e-mail. Sample copy free.

Nonfiction Buys 25 mss/year. Query with published clips. Length: 1,000-2,500 words. **Pays $1/word.** Sometimes pays expenses of writers on assignment.

$ $ THE NATIONAL JURIST AND PRE LAW

Cypress Magazines, P.O. Box 939039, San Diego CA 92193. (858)300-3201. Fax: (858)503-7588. E-mail: njpl@

cypressmagazines.com. Website: www.nationaljurist.com. **25% freelance written**. Bimonthly magazine covering law students and issues of interest to law students. Estab. 1991. Circ. 100,000. Pays on publication. No kill fee. Buys all rights. Accepts queries by mail, e-mail, fax, phone.
Nonfiction Needs general interest, how-to, humor, interview. **Buys 4 mss/year.** Query. Length: 750-3,000 words. **Pays $100-500.**
Photos State availability Reviews contact sheets. Negotiates payment individually.
Columns/Departments Pays $100-500.

$ $ THE PENNSYLVANIA LAWYER

Pennsylvania Bar Association, P.O. Box 186, 100 South St., Harrisburg PA 17108-0186. E-mail: editor@pabar.org. **25% freelance written. Prefers to work with published/established writers**. Bimonthly magazine published as a service to the legal profession and the members of the Pennsylvania Bar Association. Estab. 1979. Circ. 30,000. Byline given. Pays on acceptance. No kill fee. Publishes ms an average of 6 months after acceptance. Buys first rights, buys one-time rights. Submit seasonal material 6 months in advance. Accepts queries by mail, e-mail. Responds in 2 months to queries and to mss. Sample copy for $2. Writer's guidelines for #10 SASE or by e-mail.
Nonfiction "All features must relate in some way to Pennsylvania lawyers or the practice of law in Pennsylvania." Needs how-to, interview, law-practice management, technology. **Buys 8-10 mss/year.** Query. Length: 1,200-2,000 words. **Pays $50 for book reviews; $75-400 for assigned articles. Pays $150 for unsolicited articles.** Sometimes pays expenses of writers on assignment.
Photos State availability Identification of subjects required. Reviews contact sheets. Negotiates payment individually. Buys one time rights.

THE PUBLIC LAWYER

American Bar Association Government and Public Sector Lawyers Division, 750 15th St. NW, Washington DC 20005. (202)662-1023. Fax: (202)662-1751. E-mail: gpsld@abanet.org. Website: www.governmentlawyer.org. **60% freelance written**. Semiannual magazine covering government attorneys and the legal issues that pertain to them. The mission of *The Public Lawyer* is to provide timely, practical information useful to all public lawyers regardless of practice setting. We publish articles covering topics that are of universal interest to a diverse audience of public lawyers, such as public law office management, dealing with the media, politically motivated personnel decisions, etc. Articles must be national in scope. Estab. 1993. Circ. 6,500. Byline given. Publishes ms an average of 4 months after acceptance. Buys first rights, buys electronic rights. Editorial lead time 6 months. Accepts queries by e-mail. Accepts simultaneous submissions. Responds in 1 month to queries. Responds in 2 months to mss. Sample copy free. Guidelines available online.
Nonfiction Needs interview, opinion, technical, book reviews. Does not want pieces that do not relate to the status of government lawyers or legal issues of particular interest to government lawyers. We accept very few articles written by private practice attorneys. **Buys 6-8 mss/year.** Query. Length: 2,000-5,000 words. **Pays contributor copies.**
Photos State availability Identification of subjects, model releases required. Reviews GIF/JPEG files. Offers no additional payment for photos accepted with ms. Buys one time rights.
Tips Articles stand a better chance of acceptance if they include one or more sidebars. Examples of sidebars include pieces explaining how government and public sector lawyers could use suggestions from the main article in their own practice, checklists, or other reference sources.

STUDENT LAWYER

The Membership Magazine of the American Bar Association's Law Student Division, c/o ABA Publishing, 321 N. Clark St., Chicago IL 60654. (312)988-6048. Fax: (312)988-6081. E-mail: studentlawyer@abanet.org. Website: www.abanet.org/lsd/studentlawyer. **Works with a small number of new writers each year**. Monthly magazine (September-May). "*Student Lawyer* is a legal-affairs features magazine that competes for a share of law students' limited spare time, so the articles we publish must be informative, well-researched, good reads. We are especially interested in articles that provide students with practical advice for navigating the challenges of law school and developing their careers." Estab. 1972. Circ. 35,000. Byline given. No kill fee. Buys first rights. Editorial lead time 6 months. Accepts queries by e-mail. Guidelines available online.
Nonfiction No fiction, please Query with published clips. Length: 2,000-2,500 words.
Tips "We are not a law review; we are a features magazine with law school (in the broadest sense) as the common denominator. Write clearly and well. Expect to work with editor to polish manuscripts to perfection. We do not make assignments to writers with whose work we are not familiar. If you're interested in writing for us, send a detailed, thought-out query with 3 previously published clips. We are always willing to look at material on spec. Sorry, we don't return manuscripts."

$ $ $ $ SUPER LAWYERS

Key Professional Media, 220 S. Sixth St., Suite 500, Minneapolis MN 55402. (612)313-1760. Fax: (612)335-

8809. E-mail: awahlberg@lawandpolitics.com. Website: www.superlawyers.com. **100% freelance written.** Monthly magazine covering law and politics. We publish glossy magazines in every region of the country. All serve a legal audience and have a storytelling sensibility. We write exclusively profiles of interesting attorneys. Estab. 1990. Byline given. Pays on acceptance. Offers 25% kill fee. Publishes ms an average of 1 month after acceptance. Buys first rights, buys electronic rights. Editorial lead time 6 months. Submit seasonal material 6 months in advance. Accepts queries by mail, e-mail. Accepts simultaneous submissions. Sample copy free. Guidelines free.
Nonfiction Needs general interest, historical. Query. Length: 500-2,000 words. **Pays 50¢-$1.50/word.**

LUMBER

ALABAMA FORESTS

Alabama Foresty Association, 555 Alabama St., Montgomery AL 36104-4395. Website: www.alaforestry.org. **0-5% freelance written.** Quarterly we also publish a bi-monthly electronic newsletter. We write of, by, and for the forestry industry in Alabama. Estab. 1958. Circ. 2,000. Pays on acceptance. No kill fee. Publishes ms an average of 3-6 months after acceptance. Buys first rights. Editorial lead time 6-12 months. Submit seasonal material 3-6 months in advance. Accepts queries by e-mail. Accepts previously published material. Accepts simultaneous submissions. Responds in 2-4 weeks to queries. Responds in 3-6 months to mss. Sample copy by email. Guidelines available.
Nonfiction Needs book excerpts, historical, how-to, new product, photo feature, "If you have something you've already had published that you would like to share with our readers, we might want to do that and give you 5-10 copies for your portfolio and the exposure to our membership, which includes most of the key players in forestry in Alabama (the pulp and paper companies, large and small sawmills, veneer mills, plywood mills, consulting foresters, furniture and other types of secondary wood manufacturers, landowners, etc.". **Buys Sometimes a couple, sometimes none. mss/year.** Send complete ms. Length: 700-1,500 words.
Photos Contact: Sam Duvall. Send photos Captions, identification of subjects required. Reviews GIF/JPEG files (300 dpi at 1-2 MB). Offers no additional payment for photos accepted with ms. Negotiates payment individually. Buys one time rights.
Tips "We have a 'New Products & Services' section where we preview new forestry products for our members. I am also interested in insightful & informative stories about hunting & fishing in Alabama. Also, stories that give a new slant to forestry-specific issues & practices. Reading the magazine will help some. I do a lot of the writing of feature/personal interest-type articles myself."

$ $ PALLET ENTERPRISE

Industrial Reporting Inc., 10244 Timber Ridge Dr., Ashland VA 23005. (804)550-0323. Fax: (804)550-2181. E-mail: editor@ireporting.com. Website: www.palletenterprise.com. **40% freelance written.** Monthly magazine covering lumber and pallet operations. Articles should offer technical, solution-oriented information. Anti-forest articles are not accepted. Articles should focus on machinery and unique ways to improve profitability/make money. Estab. 1981. Circ. 14,500. Pays on publication. Buys first rights, buys one-time rights, buys electronic rights. Makes work-for-hire assignments. May buy all rights. Rights purchased depends on the writer and the article. Editorial lead time 2 months. Submit seasonal material 2 months in advance. Accepts queries by mail, e-mail, fax, phone. Accepts previously published material. Accepts simultaneous submissions. Sample copy available online. Guidelines free.
Nonfiction Contact: Tim Cox, editor. We only want articles of interest to pallet manufacturers, pallet recyclers, and lumber companies/sawmills. Needs interview, new product, opinion, technical, industry news, environmental, forests operation/plant features. No lifestyle, humor, general news, etc. **Buys 20 mss/year.** Query with published clips. Length: 1,000-3,000 words. **Pays $200-400 for assigned articles. Pays $100-400 for unsolicited articles.** Sometimes pays expenses of writers on assignment.
Photos State availability Captions, identification of subjects required. Reviews 3x5 prints. Negotiates payment individually. Buys one time rights and Web rights
Columns/Departments Contact: Tim Cox, editor. Green Watch (environmental news/opinion affecting US forests), 1,500 words. 12 Query with published clips. **Pays $200-400.**
Tips Provide unique environmental or industry-oriented articles. Many of our freelance articles are company features of sawmills, pallet manufacturers, pallet recyclers, and wood waste processors.

$ $ SOUTHERN LUMBERMAN

Hatton-Brown Publishers, P.O. Box 2268, Montgomery AL 36102. (334)834-1170. Fax: (334)834-4525. E-mail: rich@hattonbrown.com. Website: www.southernlumberman.com. **20% freelance written. Works with a small number of new/unpublished writers each year**. Monthly journal for the sawmill industry. Estab. 1881. Circ. 15,000. Byline given. Pays on publication. No kill fee. Publishes ms an average of 3 months after acceptance. Buys first North American serial rights. Submit seasonal material 6 months in advance. Responds in 1 month to queries. Responds in 2 months to mss. Sample copy for $3 and 9x12 SAE with 5 first-class stamps Guidelines for #10 sase.

Nonfiction Needs how-to, sawmill better, technical, equipment analysis, sawmill features. **Buys 10-15 mss/year.** Send complete ms. Length: 500-2,000 words. **Pays $150-350 for assigned articles. Pays $100-250 for unsolicited articles.** Sometimes pays expenses of writers on assignment.

Reprints Send tearsheet or photocopy of article and information about when and where the article previously appeared. Pays 25-50% of amount paid for an original article.

Photos Always looking for news feature types of photos featuring forest products, industry materials, or people. Send photos Captions, identification of subjects required. Reviews transparencies, 4x5 color prints. Pays $10-25/photo

Tips Like most, we appreciate a clearly-worded query listing the merits of a suggested story—what it will tell our readers they need/want to know. We want quotes, we want opinions to make others discuss the article. Best hint? Find an interesting sawmill operation owner and start asking questions—what's he doing bigger, better, different. I bet a story idea develops. We need color photos, too. We're interested in new facilities, better marketing, and improved production.

$ $ TIMBERLINE

Timber Industry Newsline/Trading Post, Industrial Reporting, Inc., 10244 Timber Ridge Dr., Ashland VA 23005. (804)550-0323. Fax: (804)550-2181. E-mail: editor@ireporting.com. Website: www.timberlinemag.com. **50% freelance written.** Monthly tabloid covering the forest products industry. Articles should offer technical, solution-oriented information. Anti-forest products, industry articles are not accepted. Articles should focus on machinery and unique ways to improve profitability and make money. Estab. 1994. Circ. 30,000. Byline given. Pays on publication. Buys first rights, buys one-time rights, buys electronic rights. Makes work-for-hire assignments. May purchase all rights. Rights purchased depends on the writer and the article. Editorial lead time 2 months. Submit seasonal material 2 months in advance. Accepts queries by mail, e-mail, fax, phone. Accepts previously published material. Accepts simultaneous submissions. Sample copy available online. Guidelines free.

Nonfiction Contact: Tim Cox, editor. We only want articles of interest to loggers, sawmills, wood treatment facilities, etc. Readers tend to be pro-industry/conservative, and opinion pieces must be written to appeal to them. Needs historical, interview, new product, opinion, technical, industry news, environmental operation/plant features. No lifestyles, humor, general news, etc. **Buys 25 mss/year.** Query with published clips. Length: 1,000-3,000 words. **Pays $200-400 for assigned articles. Pays $100-400 for unsolicited articles.** Sometimes pays expenses of writers on assignment.

Photos State availability Captions, identification of subjects required. Reviews 3x5 prints. Negotiates payment individually. Buys one time rights and Web rights

Columns/Departments Contact: Tim Cox, editor. From the Hill (legislative news impacting the forest products industry), 1,800 words; Green Watch (environmental news/opinion affecting US forests), 1,500 words. 12 Query with published clips. **Pays $200-400.**

Tips Provide unique environmental or industry-oriented articles. Many of our freelance articles are company features of logging operations or sawmills.

$ $ TIMBERWEST

Timber/West Publications, LLC, P.O. Box 610, Edmonds WA 98020-0160. Fax: (425)771-3623. E-mail: timberwest@forestnet.com. Website: www.forestnet.com. **75% freelance written.** Monthly magazine covering logging and lumber segment of the forestry industry in the Northwest. We publish primarily profiles on loggers and their operations—with an emphasis on the machinery—in Washington, Oregon, Idaho, Montana, Northern California, and Alaska. Some timber issues are highly controversial and although we will report on the issues, this is a pro-logging publication. We don't publish articles with a negative slant on the timber industry. Estab. 1975. Circ. 10,000. Byline given. Pays on acceptance. No kill fee. Buys first North American serial rights, buys second serial (reprint) rights. Editorial lead time 3 months. Accepts queries by mail, fax. Responds in 3 weeks to queries. Sample copy for $2. Guidelines for #10 sase.

Nonfiction Needs historical, interview, new product. No articles that put the timber industry in a bad light—such as environmental articles against logging. **Buys 50 mss/year.** Query with published clips. Length: 1,100-1,500 words. **Pays $350.** Pays expenses of writers on assignment.

Photos Send photos Captions, identification of subjects required. Reviews contact sheets, transparencies, prints, GIF/JPEG files. Offers no additional payment for photos accepted with ms Buys all rights.

Fillers Needs facts, newsbreaks. 10 Length: 400-800 words. **Pays $100-250.**

Tips We are always interested in profiles of loggers and their operations in Alaska, Oregon, Washington, Montana, and Northern California. We also want articles pertaining to current industry topics, such as fire abatement, sustainable forests, or new technology. Read an issue to get a clear idea of the type of material *TimberWest* publishes. The audience is primarily loggers and topics that focus on an `evolving' timber industry versus a `dying' industry will find a place in the magazine. When querying, a clear overview of the article will enhance acceptance.

MACHINERY & METAL

$ $ $ AMERICAN MACHINIST

Penton Media, 1300 E. 9th St., Cleveland OH 44114. (216)931-9240. Fax: (216)931-9524. E-mail: ameditor@penton.com. Website: www.americanmachinist.com. **10% freelance written**. Monthly magazine covering all forms of metalworking. *American Machinist* is the oldest magazine dedicated to metalworking in the United States. Our readers are the owners and managers of metalworking shops. We publish articles that provide the managers and owners of job shops, contract shops, and captive shops the information they need to make their operations more efficient, more productive, and more profitable. Our articles are technical in nature and must be focused on technology that will help these shops to become more competitive on a global basis. Our readers are skilled machinists. This is not the place for lightweight items about manufacturing, and we are not interested in articles on management theories. Estab. 1877. Circ. 80,000. Byline sometimes given. Offers 20% kill fee. Publishes ms an average of 1-2 months after acceptance. Buys all rights. Makes work-for-hire assignments. Editorial lead time 3-6 months. Submit seasonal material 4-6 months in advance. Accepts queries by mail, e-mail, phone. Responds in 1-2 weeks to queries. Responds in 1 month to mss. Sample copy available online.

Nonfiction Needs general interest, how-to, new product, opinion, personal experience, photo feature, technical. Query with published clips. Length: 600-2,400 words. **Pays $300-1,200.** Sometimes pays expenses of writers on assignment.

Photos State availability Captions, identification of subjects, model releases required. Reviews GIF/JPEG files. Negotiates payment individually. Buys all rights.

Fillers Needs anecdotes, facts, gags, newsbreaks, short humor. 12-18 Length: 50-200 words. **Pays $25-100.**

Tips With our exacting audience, a writer would do well to have some background working with machine tools.

$ $ $ CUTTING TOOL ENGINEERING

CTE Publications, Inc., 40 Skokie Blvd., Northbrook IL 60062. (847)714-0175. Fax: (847)559-4444. E-mail: alanr@jwr.com. Website: www.ctemag.com. **40% freelance written**. Monthly magazine covering industrial metal cutting tools and metal cutting operations. "*Cutting Tool Engineering* serves owners, managers and engineers who work in manufacturing, specifically manufacturing that involves cutting or grinding metal or other materials. Writing should be geared toward improving manufacturing processes." Circ. 48,000. Byline given. Pays on publication. Offers 50% kill fee. Publishes ms an average of 2 months after acceptance. Buys all rights. Editorial lead time 2 months. Accepts queries by mail, fax. Responds in 2 months to mss. Sample copy and writer's guidelines free

Nonfiction Needs how-to, opinion, personal experience, technical. "No fiction or articles that don't relate to manufacturing." **Buys 10 mss/year.** Length: 1,500-3,000 words. **Pays $750-1,500.** Pays expenses of writers on assignment.

Photos State availability Captions required. Reviews transparencies, prints. Negotiates payment individually. Buys all rights.

Tips "For queries, write 2 clear paragraphs about how the proposed article will play out. Include sources that would be in the article."

$ $ ✪ EQUIPMENT JOURNAL

Pace Publishing, 5160 Explorer Dr., Unit 6, Mississauga ON L4W 4T7 Canada. (800)667-8541. Fax: (905)629-7988. E-mail: editor@equipmentjournal.com. Website: www.equipmentjournal.com. **10% freelance written**. 17 times/year. "Canada's National Equipment Newspaper. We publish product information, jobsite stories, and 15 features a year that are relevant to the material handling, construction, mining, forestry, and transportation industries." Estab. 1966. Circ. 25,000. Byline given. Pays on publication. No kill fee. Publishes ms an average of 1-2 months after acceptance. Buys first rights, buys second serial (reprint) rights. Editorial lead time 2-3 months. Submit seasonal material 2 months in advance. Accepts queries by mail, e-mail, fax, phone. Accepts previously published material. Accepts simultaneous submissions. Sample copy and guidelines free.

Nonfiction Needs how-to, interview, new product, photo feature, technical. No material that falls outside of *EJ*'s mandate—the Canadian equipment industry. **Buys 15/year mss/year.** Send complete ms. Length: 500-1,000 words. **$250-$400 for assigned and unsolicited articles.** Sometimes pays expenses of writers on assignment.

Photos State availability. Identification of subjects required. 4 x 6 prints. Negotiates payment individually. Buys all rights.

Tips "We are looking for new product release stories of products made by Canadian manufacturers and field application stories that take place in Canada."

$ $ $ THE FABRICATOR

833 Featherstone Rd., Rockford IL 61107. (815)399-8700. Fax: (815)381-1370. E-mail: kateb@thefabricator.

com. Website: www.thefabricator.com. **15% freelance written.** Monthly magazine covering metal forming and fabricating. Our purpose is to disseminate information about modern metal forming and fabricating techniques, machinery, tooling, and management concepts for the metal fabricator. Estab. 1971. Circ. 58,000. Byline given. Pays on publication. No kill fee. Buys all rights. Editorial lead time 6 months. Accepts queries by mail, e-mail. Responds in 2 weeks to queries. Responds in 1 month to mss. Sample copy free. Guidelines available online.

Nonfiction Needs how-to, technical, company profile. Query with published clips. Length: 1,200-2,000 words. **Pays 40-80¢/word.**

Photos Request guidelines for digital images. State availability Captions, identification of subjects required. Reviews transparencies, prints. Negotiates payment individually Rights purchased depends on photographer requirements

$ $ $ GASES & WELDING DISTRIBUTOR

Penton Media, 1300 E. 9th St., Cleveland OH 44114. (216)931-9240. Fax: (216)931-9524. E-mail: weldingeditor@penton.com. Website: www.weldingdesign.com. **10% freelance written.** Bimonthly magazine covering the distribution business for welding supplies and industrial gases. *Gases & Welding Distributor* provides information to the owners and managers of distributorships that sell welding equipment and industrial gases. We include information on federal regulations, business technology for distributorships, technological developments in welding, and feature stories on how our distributors are doing business with the goal of helping our readers to be more productive, efficient and competitive. These shops are very local in nature, and need to be addressed as small businessmen in a field that is consolidating and becoming more challenging. We do not write about business management theory as much as we write about putting into practice good management techniques that have proved to work at similar businesses. Estab. 1966. Circ. 20,000. Byline sometimes given. Pays on publication. Offers 20% kill fee. Publishes ms an average of 1-2 months after acceptance. Buys all rights. Makes work-for-hire assignments. Editorial lead time 3-6 months. Submit seasonal material 4-6 months in advance. Accepts queries by mail, e-mail, phone. Responds in 1-2 weeks to queries. Responds in 1 month to mss. Sample copy available online.

Nonfiction Needs general interest, how-to, new product, opinion, personal experience, photo feature, technical. Query with published clips. Length: 600-2,400 words. **Pays $300-1,200.** Sometimes pays expenses of writers on assignment.

Photos State availability Captions, identification of subjects, model releases required. Reviews GIF/JPEG files. Negotiates payment individually. Buys all rights.

Fillers Needs anecdotes, facts, gags, newsbreaks, short humor. 12-18 Length: 50-200 words. **Pays $25-100.**

Tips Writers should be familiar with welding and/or the industrial distribution business. With that, calling or e-mailing me directly is the next best approach. We are interested in information that will help to make machine shops more competitive, and a writer should have a very specific idea before approaching me.

MACHINE DESIGN

Penton Media, Penton Media Bldg., 1300 E. 9th St., Cleveland OH 44114. (216)931-9412. Fax: (216)621-8469. E-mail: mdeditor@penton.com. Website: www.machinedesign.com. Semimonthly magazine covering machine design. Covers the design engineering of manufactured products across the entire spectrum of the idustry for people who perform design engineering functions. Circ. 185,163. No kill fee. Editorial lead time 10 weeks. Accepts queries by mail, e-mail.

Nonfiction Needs how-to, new product, technical. Send complete ms.

Columns/Departments Query with or without published clips or send complete ms.

MACHINERY LUBRICATION MAGAZINE

Noria Corporation, 1328 East 43rd Court, Tulsa OK 74105. (918)749-1400, ext. 120. Fax: (918)746-0925. E-mail: jkucera@noria.com. Website: noria.com. Bimonthly hardcopy magazine and website covering machinery lubrication, oil analysis, tribology. Estab. 2001. Circ. >39,000. Byline given. No kill fee. Publishes ms an average of 3-6 months after acceptance. Editorial lead time 3 months. Accepts queries by e-mail. Accepts previously published material. Responds in 2 weeks to queries. Responds in 3 months to mss. Sample copy available online. Guidelines available online.

Nonfiction Contact: Jenny Kucera, managing editor. Needs how-to, new product, technical. No heavy commercial, opinion articles. Query. Length: 1,000-2,000 words.

Photos Contact: Jenny Kucera. Send photos Captions, identification of subjects required. Reviews GIF/JPEG files. Offers no additional payment for photos accepted with ms.

Tips Please request editorial guidelines by sending email.

MANUFACTURING BUSINESS TECHNOLOGY

Reed Business Information, 2000 Clearwater Dr., Oak Brook IL 60523-8809. (630)288-8757. Fax: (630)288-8105. E-mail: nancy.bartels@reedbusiness.com. Website: www.mbtmag.com. Monthly magazine about the use of information technology to improve productivity in discrete manufacturing and process industries. Estab. 1984. Circ. 97,000. Byline sometimes given. Pays on publication. No kill fee. Publishes ms an average

of 3 months after acceptance. Buys all rights. Editorial lead time 3 months. Submit seasonal material 4 months in advance. Accepts queries by e-mail. Sample copy free. Guidelines available online.
Nonfiction Needs technical. **Buys 30 mss/year.** Query.
Photos Captions required. No additional payment for photos.

$ MATERIAL HANDLING WHOLESALER

Specialty Publications International, Inc., P.O. Box 725, Dubuque IA 52004-0725. (877)638-6190 or (563)557-4495. Fax: (563)557-4499. E-mail: editorial@mhwmag.com. Website: www.mhwmag.com. **100% freelance written.** *MHW* is published monthly for new and used equipment dealers, equipment manufacturers, manufacturer reps, parts suppliers, and service facilities serving the material handling industry. Estab. 1979. Circ. 9,200. Byline given. Pays on publication. No kill fee. Publishes ms an average of 2 months after acceptance. Buys first rights. Editorial lead time 1 month. Submit seasonal material 2 months in advance. Accepts queries by mail, e-mail, fax. Accepts simultaneous submissions. Sample copy for $31 annually (3rd clas). Guidelines free.
Nonfiction Needs general interest, how-to, inspirational, new product, opinion, personal experience, photo feature, technical, material handling news.
Photos Send photos Reviews 3x5 prints. Offers no additional payment for photos accepted with ms. Buys all rights.
Columns/Departments Aftermarket (aftermarket parts and service); Battery Tech (batteries for lifts-MH equipment); Marketing Matters (sales trends in MH industry); Human Element (HR issues); all 1,200 words. 3 Query. **Pays $0-50.**

MODERN APPLICATIONS NEWS

The Authoritative source for Job Shop Solutions, Nelson Publishing Inc., 6001 Cochran Rd., Suite 104, Solon OH 44139. (440)248-1125, ext. 210. E-mail: pnofel@nelsonpub.com. Website: www.modernapplicationsnews.com. **10% freelance written.** Monthly magazine covering the machining and metalworking industry. *Modern Applications News* is geared toward the owners and employees of metalworking job shops and contract manufacturers who are in search of case histories that show how a product or process provides solutions that increase efficiency or save time, money, or effort in specifically-stated amounts in dollars or percentages. Estab. 1967. Circ. 75,000. Byline sometimes given. Rarely pays for contributions. Offers 10% kill fee. Publishes ms an average of 2 months after acceptance. Buys first North American serial rights. Editorial lead time 4 months. Accepts queries by e-mail. Accepts previously published material. Responds in 1 week to queries. Responds in 1 week to mss. Sample copy free. Guidelines available online.
Nonfiction Needs new product, opinion, technical, Industrial case histories. We do not want articles that do not deal with machining or metalworking. Query. Length: 950-2,400 words.
Photos Send photos Identification of subjects required. Reviews GIF/JPEG files. Offers no additional payment for photos accepted with ms. Buys one time rights.
Columns/Departments The Last Word (an opinion piece by a leader in the machining industry), 750 words. 12 mss/year Send complete ms.
Tips Almost all of *Modern Applications News's* content is provided by public relations and advertising agencies or manufacturer representatives in the metalworking industry. Freelancers should contact the agencies or manufacturers to offer their services. Case histories should describe the problem faced by a job shop and how a manufacturer's product solved the problem with explicitly-stated benefits; but the articles should not 'hype' the manufacturer's product.

$ $ ORNAMENTAL AND MISCELLANEOUS METAL FABRICATOR

National Ornamental And Miscellaneous Metals Association, 1535 Pennsylvania Ave., McDonough GA 30253. (888)516-8585. Fax: (770)288-2006. E-mail: editor@nomma.org. **20% freelance written.** "Bimonthly magazine to inform, educate, and inspire members of the ornamental and miscellaneous metalworking industry.". Estab. 1959. Circ. 9,000. Byline given. Pays on publication. No kill fee. Buys one-time rights. Editorial lead time 1-2 months. Accepts queries by mail, e-mail, fax. Responds by e-mail in 1 month (include e-mail address in query). Guidelines by email.
Nonfiction Needs book excerpts, essays, general interest, historical, how-to, humor, interview, opinion, personal experience, photo feature feature, technical. **Buys 8-12 mss/year.** Query. Length: 1,200-2,000 words. **Pays $250-400.**
Reprints Send tearsheet, photocopy or typed ms with rights for sale noted and information about when and where the material previously appeared. Pays 100% of amount paid for an original article.
Photos Artwork and sidebars preferred. State availability Model releases required. Reviews contact sheets, negatives, transparencies, prints.
Columns/Departments 700-900 words. **Pays $ 50-100.**
Tips "Please request and review recent issues. Contacting the editor for guidance on article topics is welcome."

$ $ $ PRACTICAL WELDING TODAY

FMA Communications, Inc., 833 Featherstone Rd., Rockford IL 61107-6302. (815)227-8282. Fax: (815)381-1370. E-mail: amandac@thefabricator.com. Website: www.thefabricator.com. **15% freelance written**. Bimonthly magazine covering welding. We generally publish how-to and educational articles that teach people about a process or how to do something better. Estab. 1997. Circ. 40,000. Byline given. Pays on publication. No kill fee. Buys all rights. Editorial lead time 6 months. Accepts queries by mail, e-mail. Responds in 2 weeks to queries. Responds in 2 months to mss. Sample copy free. Guidelines available online.

Nonfiction Needs how-to, technical, company profiles. Forecast issue on trends in welding (January/February) No promotional, one-sided, persuasive articles or unsolicited case studies. **Buys 5 mss/year.** Query with published clips. Length: 800-1,200 words. **Pays 40-80¢/word.** Sometimes pays expenses of writers on assignment.

Photos State availability Captions, identification of subjects required. Reviews contact sheets. Negotiates payment individually Rights purchased depends on photographer requirements

Tips Follow our author guidelines and editorial policies to write a how-to piece from which our readers can benefit.

$ $ SPRINGS

The International Magazine of Spring Manufacturers, Spring Manufacturers Institute, 2001 Midwest Rd., Suite 106, Oak Brook IL 60523-1335. (630)495-8588. Fax: (630)495-8595. Website: www.smihq.org. **10% freelance written**. Quarterly magazine covering precision mechanical spring manufacture. Articles should be aimed at spring manufacturers. Estab. 1962. Circ. 10,800. Byline given. Pays on publication. No kill fee. Publishes ms an average of 3-6 months after acceptance. Buys first rights. Editorial lead time 4 months. Accepts simultaneous submissions. Sample copy free. Guidelines available online.

Nonfiction Needs general interest, how-to, interview, opinion, personal experience, technical. **Buys 4-6 mss/year.** Length: 2,000-10,000 words. **Pays $100-600 for assigned articles.**

Photos State availability Captions required. Reviews prints, digital photos. Offers no additional payment for photos accepted with ms. Buys one time rights.

Tips Call the editor. Contact springmakers and spring industry suppliers and ask about what interests them. Include interviews/quotes from people in the spring industry in the article. The editor can supply contacts.

$ $ $ STAMPING JOURNAL

Fabricators & Manufacturers Association (FMA), 833 Featherstone Rd., Rockford IL 61107. (815)399-8700. Fax: (815)381-1370. E-mail: kateb@thefabricator.com. Website: www.thefabricator.com. **15% freelance written**. Bimonthly magazine covering metal stamping. We look for how-to and educational articles—nonpromotional. Estab. 1989. Circ. 35,000. Byline given. Pays on publication. No kill fee. Buys all rights. Editorial lead time 6 months. Accepts queries by mail, e-mail, fax, phone. Responds in 2 weeks to queries. Responds in 2 months to mss. Sample copy and writer's guidelines free

Nonfiction Needs how-to, technical, company profile. Forecast issue (January) No unsolicited case studies. **Buys 5 mss/year.** Query with published clips. 1,000 words **Pays 40-80¢/word.** Sometimes pays expenses of writers on assignment.

Photos State availability Captions, identification of subjects required. Reviews contact sheets. Negotiates payment individually Rights purchased depends on photographer requirements

Tips Articles should be impartial and should not describe the benefits of certain products available from certain companies. They should not be biased toward the author's or against a competitor's products or technologies. The publisher may refuse any article that does not conform to this guideline.

$ $ $ $ TODAY'S MACHINING WORLD

Screw Machine World, Inc., 4235 W. 166th St., Oak Forest IL 60452. (708)535-2200. Fax: (708)535-0103. E-mail: jill@todaysmachiningworld.com. Website: www.todaysmachiningworld.com. **40% freelance written**. Monthly magazine covering metal turned parts manufacturing U.S./global. We hire writers to tell a success story or challenge regarding our industry. There are **no** advertorials coming from advertisers. Estab. 2001. Circ. 18,500. Byline given. Pays on publication. Offers $500 kill fee. Publishes ms an average of 2 months after acceptance. Makes work-for-hire assignments. Editorial lead time 2-4 months. Submit seasonal material 2 months in advance. Responds in 1 month to mss. Guidelines free.

Nonfiction Needs general interest, how-to. We do not want unsolicited articles. **Buys 12-15 mss/year. mss/year.** Query. Length: 1,500-2,500 words. **Pays $1,500-2,000 for assigned articles.**

Photos State availability Captions required. Reviews GIF/JPEG files. Negotiates payment individually. Buys one time rights.

Columns/Departments Shop Doc (manufacturing problem/solution), 500 words. Query. **Pays $-$250.**

Tips You may submit an idea related to manufacturing that would be of interest to our readers. If you pitch it, we'll respond!

$ $ $ TPJ—THE TUBE & PIPE JOURNAL

Fabricators & Manufacturers Association (FMA), 833 Featherstone Rd., Rockford IL 61107. (815)399-8700. Fax: (815)381-1370. Website: www.thefabricator.com. **15% freelance written**. Magazine published 8 times/year covering metal tube and pipe. Educational perspective—emphasis is on how-to articles to accomplish a particular task or improve on a process. New trends and technologies are also important topics. Estab. 1990. Circ. 30,000. Byline given. Pays on publication. No kill fee. Buys all rights. Editorial lead time 6 months. Accepts queries by mail, e-mail. Responds in 2 weeks to queries. Responds in 2 months to mss. Sample copy free. Guidelines available online.

Nonfiction Any new or improved tube production or fabrication process—includes manufacturing, bending, and forming tube (metal tube only). Needs how-to, technical. Forecast issue (January) No unsolicited case studies. **Buys 5 mss/year.** Query with published clips. Length: 800-1,200 words. **Pays 40-80¢/word.** Sometimes pays expenses of writers on assignment.

Photos State availability Captions, identification of subjects required. Reviews contact sheets. Negotiates payment individually Rights purchased depends on photographer requirements

Tips Submit a detailed proposal, including an article outline, to the editor.

$ $ $ WELDING DESIGN & FABRICATION

Penton Media, 1300 E. 9th St., Cleveland OH 44114. (216)931-9240. Fax: (216)931-9524. E-mail: weldingeditor@penton.com. Website: www.weldingdesign.com. **10% freelance written**. Bimonthly magazine covering all facets of welding and running a welding business. *Welding Design & Fabrication* provides information to the owners and managers of welding shops, including business, technology and trends. We include information on engineering and technological developments that could change the business as it is currently known, and feature stories on how welders are doing business with the goal of helping our readers to be more productive, effecient, and competitive. Welding shops are very local in nature and need to be addressed as small businessmen in a field that is consolidating and becoming more challenging and more global. We do not write about business management theory as much as we write about putting into practice good management techniques that have proved to work at similar businesses. Estab. 1930. Circ. 40,000. Byline given. Pays on publication. Offers 20% kill fee. Publishes ms an average of 1-2 months after acceptance. Buys all rights. Makes work-for-hire assignments. Editorial lead time 3-6 months. Submit seasonal material 4-6 months in advance. Accepts queries by mail, e-mail, phone. Responds in 1-2 weeks to queries. Responds in 1 month to mss. Sample copy available online.

Nonfiction Needs general interest, how-to, new product, opinion, personal experience, photo feature, technical. Query. Length: 600-2,400 words. **Pays $300-1,200.** Sometimes pays expenses of writers on assignment.

Photos State availability Captions, identification of subjects, model releases required. Reviews GIF/JPEG files (300 dpi). Negotiates payment individually. Buys all rights.

Fillers Needs anecdotes, facts, gags, newsbreaks, short humor. 12-18 Length: 50-200 words. **Pays $25-100.**

Tips Writers should be familiar with welding and/or metalworking and metal joining techniques. With that, calling or e-mailing me directly is the next best approach. We are interested in information that will help to make welding shops more competitive, and a writer should have a very specific idea before approaching me.

$ $ WIRE ROPE NEWS & SLING TECHNOLOGY

Wire Rope News LLC, P.O. Box 871, Clark NJ 07066. (908)486-3221. Fax: (732)396-4215. Website: www.wireropenews.com. **100% freelance written**. Bimonthly magazine published for manufacturers and distributors of wire rope, chain, cordage, related hardware, and sling fabricators. Content includes technical articles, news and reports describing the manufacturing and use of wire rope and related products in marine, construction, mining, aircraft and offshore drilling operations. Estab. 1979. Circ. 4,300. Byline sometimes given. Pays on acceptance. No kill fee. Publishes ms an average of 6 months after acceptance. Buys all rights. Editorial lead time 2 months. Submit seasonal material 2 months in advance. Accepts queries by mail, fax. Accepts simultaneous submissions.

Nonfiction Needs general interest, historical, interview, photo feature, technical. **Buys 30 mss/year.** Send complete ms. Length: 2,500-5,000 words. **Pays $300-500.**

Photos Send photos Identification of subjects required. Reviews contact sheets, 5x7 prints, digital. Offers no additional payment for photos accepted with ms. Buys all rights.

Tips We are accepting more submissions and queries by e-mail.

THE WORLD OF WELDING

Hobart Institute of Welding Technology, 400 Trade Square East, Troy OH 45373. (937)332-5603. Fax: (937)332-5220. E-mail: hiwt@welding.org. Website: www.welding.org. **10% freelance written**. Quarterly magazine covering welding training and education. "The content must be educational and must contain welding topic information." Estab. 1990. Circ. 6,500. Byline given. Publishes ms an average of 3 months after acceptance. Buys all rights. Editorial lead time 3 months. Submit seasonal material 3 months in advance. Accepts queries by mail, e-mail, fax. Accepts simultaneous submissions. Responds in 1 week to queries. Responds in 3

months to mss. Sample copy free. Guidelines free.
Nonfiction Needs general interest, historical, how-to, interview, personal experience, photo feature, technical, welding topics. Query with published clips.
Photos Send photos Captions, identification of subjects, model releases required. Reviews GIF/JPEG files. Offers no additional payment for photos accepted with ms.
Fiction Needs adventure, historical, mainstream, welding. Query with published clips.
Fillers Needs facts, newsbreaks.
Tips "Writers must be willing to donate material on welding and metallurgy related topics, welded art/ sculpture, personal welding experiences. An editorial committee reviews submissions and determines acceptance."

MAINTENANCE & SAFETY

$ $ AMERICAN WINDOW CLEANER MAGAZINE

Voice of the Professional Window Cleaner, P.O. Box 98, Bedford NY 10506. (910)693-2644. Fax: (910)246-1681. Website: www.awcmag.com. **20% freelance written**. Bimonthly magazine window cleaning. Articles to help window cleaners become more profitable, safe, professional, and feel good about what they do. Estab. 1986. Circ. 8,000. Byline given. Pays on acceptance. Offers 33% kill fee. Publishes ms an average of 4-8 months after acceptance. Buys first rights. Editorial lead time 2 months. Submit seasonal material 3 months in advance. Responds in 2 weeks to queries. Responds in 1 month to mss. Sample copy free. Guidelines available online.
Nonfiction Needs how-to, humor, inspirational, interview, personal experience, photo feature, technical, add on business. We do not want PR-driven pieces. We want to educate—not push a particular product. **Buys 20 mss/year.** Query. Length: 500-5,000 words. **Pays $50-250.**
Photos State availability Captions required. Reviews contact sheets, transparencies, 4x6 prints. Offers $10 per photo. Buys one time rights.
Columns/Departments Window Cleaning Tips (tricks of the trade); 1,000-2,000 words; Humor-anecdotes-feel good-abouts (window cleaning industry); Computer High-Tech (tips on new technology), all 1,000 words 12 Query. **Pays $50-100.**
Tips *American Window Cleaner Magazine* covers an unusual niche that gets people's curiosity. Articles that are technical in nature and emphasize practical tips or safety, and how to work more efficiently, have the best chances of being published. Articles include: window cleaning unusual buildings, landmarks; working for well-known people/celebrities; window cleaning in resorts/casinos/unusual cities; humor or satire about our industry or the public's perception of it. At some point, we make phone contact and chat to see if our interests are compatible.

CANADIAN OCCUPATIONAL SAFETY

CLB Media, Inc., 240 Edward St., Aurora ON L4G 3S9 Canada. (905)727-0077. Fax: (905)727-0017. E-mail: tphillips@clbmedia.ca. Website: www.cos-mag.com. **40% freelance written**. Bimonthly magazine. We want informative articles dealing with issues that relate to occupational health and safety in Canada. Estab. 1989. Circ. 14,000. Byline given. Pays on publication. No kill fee. Publishes ms an average of 3 months after acceptance. Buys one-time rights. Editorial lead time 4 months. Submit seasonal material 4 months in advance. Accepts queries by mail, e-mail, fax, phone. Responds in 3 weeks to queries. Responds in 1 month to mss. Sample copy and writer's guidelines free.
Nonfiction Needs how-to, interview. **Buys 30 mss/year.** Query with published clips. Length: 500-2,000 words. **Payment varies** Sometimes pays expenses of writers on assignment.
Photos State availability Captions required. Reviews transparencies. Negotiates payment individually. Buys one time rights.
Tips Present us with an idea for an article that will interest workplace health and safety professionals, with cross-Canada appeal.

$ CLEANING BUSINESS

3693 E. Marginal Way S., Seattle WA 98134. Fax: (206)622-6876. Website: www.cleaningbusiness.com. **80% freelance written**. Quarterly magazine. We cater to those who are self-employed in any facet of the cleaning and maintenance industry and seek to be top professionals in their field. *Cleaning Business* is published for self-employed cleaning professionals, specifically carpet, upholstery and drapery cleaners; janitorial and maid services; window washers; odor, water and fire damage restoration contractors. Our readership is small but select. We seek concise, factual articles, realistic but definitely upbeat. Circ. 6,000. Byline given. Pays 1 month after publication. No kill fee. Publishes ms an average of 3 months after acceptance. Buys all rights. Makes work-for-hire assignments. Submit seasonal material 6 months in advance. 3 months or less. Sample copy for $3 and 8x10 SAE with 3 first-class stamps. Guidelines for #10 sase.
Nonfiction Needs expose, safety/health business practices, how-to, on cleaning, maintenance, small business

management, humor, clean jokes, cartoons, interview, new product, must be unusual to rate full article—mostly obtained from manufacturers, opinion, personal experience, technical. What's New? (February) No wordy articles written off the top of the head, obviously without research, and needing more editing time than was spent on writing. **Buys 40 mss/year.** Query. Length: 500-3,000 words. Pa;ys expenses of writers on assignment with prior approval only.

Photos Magazine size is 8 ½x11—photos need to be proportionate. Also seeks full-color photos of relevant subjects for cover. State availability Captions, identification of subjects, model releases required. Pays $5-25 for Buys one time rights.

Columns/Departments Ten regular columnists now sell four columns per year to us. We are interested in adding Safety & Health and Fire Restoration columns (related to cleaning and maintenance industry). We are also open to other suggestions—send query. 36 Query with or without published clips. **Pays $15-85.**

Fillers Needs anecdotes, gags, newsbreaks, short humor, jokes, gags, poetry. 40 Length: 3-200 words. **Pays $1-20.**

Tips We are constantly seeking quality freelancers from all parts of the country. A freelancer can best break in to our publication with fairly technical articles on how to do specific cleaning/maintenance jobs; interviews with top professionals covering this and how they manage their business; and personal experience. Our readers demand concise, accurate information. Don't ramble. Write only about what you know and/or have researched. Editors don't have time to rewrite your rough draft. Organize and polish before submitting.

$ $ EXECUTIVE HOUSEKEEPING TODAY

The International Executive Housekeepers Association, 1001 Eastwind Dr., Suite 301, Westerville OH 43081. (614)895-7166. Fax: (614)895-1248. E-mail: ldigiulio@ieha.org. Website: www.ieha.org. **50% freelance written**. Monthly magazine for nearly 5,000 decision makers responsible for housekeeping management (cleaning, grounds maintenance, laundry, linen, pest control, waste management, regulatory compliance, training) for a variety of institutions: hospitality, healthcare, education, retail, government. Estab. 1930. Circ. 5,500. Byline given. Pays on acceptance. No kill fee. Publishes ms an average of 6 months after acceptance. Buys first North American serial rights. Editorial lead time 2 months. Submit seasonal material 3 months in advance. Accepts queries by mail, e-mail, fax, phone.

Nonfiction Needs general interest, interview, new product, related to magazine's scope, personal experience, in housekeeping profession, technical. **Buys 30 mss/year.** Query with published clips. Length: 500-1,500 words. **Pays $150-250.**

Photos State availability Identification of subjects required. Offers no additional payment for photos accepted with ms. Buys one time rights.

Columns/Departments Federal Report (OSHA/EPA requirements), 1,000 words; Industry News; Management Perspectives (industry specific), 500-1,500 words. Query with published clips. **Pays $150-250.**

Tips Have a background in the industry or personal experience with any aspect of it.

$ $ PEST CONTROL MAGAZINE

7500 Old Oak Blvd., Cleveland OH 44130. (216)706-3735. Fax: (216)706-3711. E-mail: pestcon@questex.com. Website: www.pestcontrolmag.com. Monthly magazine for professional pest management professionals and sanitarians. Estab. 1933. Circ. 20,000. Pays on publication. No kill fee. Licenses rights. Submit seasonal material 3 months in advance. Accepts queries by mail, e-mail, phone. Responds in 1 month to mss. Guidelines available online.

Nonfiction Prefers contributors with pest control industry background. All articles must have trade or business orientation. Needs how-to, humor, inspirational, interview, new product, personal experience, stories about pest management operations and their problems, case histories, new technological breakthroughs. No general information type of articles desired. **Buys 3 mss/year.** Query. Length: 1,000-1,400 words. **Pays $150-400 minimum.**

Photos Digital photos accepted; please query on specs. State availability No additional payment for photos used with ms.

Columns/Departments Regular columns use material oriented to this profession, 550 words.

MANAGEMENT & SUPERVISION

APICS MAGAZINE

APICS The Association for Operations Management, 8430 W. Bryn Mawr Ave., Suite 1000, Chicago IL 60631. (773)867-1777. E-mail: editorial@apics.org. Website: www.apics.org. **15% freelance written**. Bimonthly magazine covering operations management, enterprise, supply chain, production and inventory management, warehousing and logistics. Be clear, conversational, and to the point. Estab. 1987. Circ. 45,000. Byline given. Pays on acceptance. Offers 50% kill fee. Publishes ms an average of 2 months after acceptance. Buys all rights. Editorial lead time 3-4 months. Submit seasonal material 3-4 months in advance. Accepts queries by e-mail. Accepts simultaneous submissions.

Nonfiction Needs technical, General research/reporting. We don't want vendor-driven articles. **Buys 3-5 mss/year mss/year.** Query. Length: 1,250-2,500 words.

HR MAGAZINE

On Human Resource Management, Society for Human Resource Management, 1800 Duke St., Alexandria VA 22314-3499. (703)548-3440. E-mail: hrmag@shrm.org. Website: www.shrm.org. **Contact:** Nancy M. Davis, editor. **90% freelance written.** Monthly magazine covering human resource management profession with special focus on business news that affects the workplace, including compensation, benefits, recruiting, training and development, outsourcing, management trends, court decisions, legislative actions, and government regulations. Accepts queries and mss via website; responds in 45 days. Estab. 1948. Circ. 250,000. Byline given. Pays on acceptance. No kill fee. Publishes ms an average of 2 months after acceptance. Buys all rights. Editorial lead time 4 months. Sample copy free. Guidelines available online.

- Must submit queries via website.

Nonfiction Needs technical, expert advice and analysis, news features. **Buys 75 mss/year.** Query. Length: 1,800-2,500 words. Pays expenses of writers on assignment.

Photos State availability Identification of subjects, model releases required. Buys one time rights.

Tips "Readers are members of the Society for Human Resource Management (SHRM), mostly HR managers with private employers ranging from small to very large in size. Our stories must balance business acumen with a concern for the well-being and productivity of employees."

$ $ $ HUMAN RESOURCE EXECUTIVE

LRP Publications Magazine Group, P.O. Box 980, Harsham PA 19044. (215)784-0910. Fax: (215)784-0275. E-mail: dshadovitz@lrp.com. Website: www.hrexecutive.com. **30% freelance written.** Monthly magazine serving the information needs of chief human resource professionals/executives in companies, government agencies, and nonprofit institutions with 500 or more employees. Estab. 1987. Circ. 75,000. Byline given. Pays on acceptance. Offers kill fee. Pays 50% kill fee on assigned stories. Publishes ms an average of 2 months after acceptance. Buys all rights. Accepts queries by mail, e-mail, fax. Responds in 1 month to mss. Guidelines available online.

Nonfiction Needs book excerpts, interview. **Buys 16 mss/year.** Query with published clips. Length: 1,800 words. **Pays $200-1,000.** Sometimes pays expenses of writers on assignment.

Photos State availability Identification of subjects required. Reviews contact sheets. Offers no additional payment for photos accepted with ms. Buys first and repeat rights

$ $ INCENTIVE

VNU Business Publications, 770 Broadway, New York NY 10003. (646)654-4485. Fax: (646)654-7650. Website: www.incentivemag.com. Monthly magazine covering sales promotion and employee motivation: managing and marketing through motivation. Estab. 1905. Circ. 41,000. Byline given. Pays on acceptance. No kill fee. Publishes ms an average of 3 months after acceptance. Buys all rights. Accepts queries by mail, e-mail, fax. Responds in 1 month to queries. Responds in 2 months to mss. Sample copy for sae with 9x12 envelope.

Nonfiction Needs general interest, motivation, demographics, how-to, types of sales promotion, buying product categories, using destinations, interview, sales promotion executives, travel, incentive-oriented, corporate case studies. **Buys 48 mss/year.** Query with published clips. Length: 1,000-2,000 words. **Pays $250-700 for assigned articles. does not pay for unsolicited articles. for unsolicited articles.** Pays expenses of writers on assignment.

Reprints Send tearsheet and information about when and where the material previously appeared. Pays 50% of the amount paid for an original article.

Photos Send photos Identification of subjects required. Reviews contact sheets, transparencies. Offers some additional payment for photos accepted with ms.

Columns/Departments

Tips Read the publication, then query.

PEOPLE MANAGEMENT

Chartered Institute of Personnel and Development, 17-18 Britton St., London England EC1M 5TP United Kingdom. (44)(207)324-2729. E-mail: editorial@peoplemanagement.co.uk. Website: www.peoplemanagement.co.uk. Biweekly magazine publishing articles on all aspects of managing and developing people at work. Circ. 135,000. No kill fee. Editorial lead time 2 months. Only responds to proposals if interested. Guidelines available online.

Nonfiction Needs general interest, features with a theoretical/strategic/policy theme or investigations of current developments/case studies, how-to, step-by-step hints/tips for best practices to use in everyday work. Submit 2-page proposal, bio. Length: 1,000-2,500 words.

Columns/Departments Learning Centre (training/development matters aimed to provoke discussion), 350 words; Viewpoint (addresses a key topical issue), 600 words; Research (academics summarize their latest findings or review other research in a particular area), 500 words); Troubleshooter (overview of a HR dilemma and/or a solution to that dilemma), 350 words/dilemma and 400 words/solution.

$ $ PLAYGROUND MAGAZINE

The National Magazine for Today's Playground Design & Standards, Harris Publishing, 360 B St., Idaho Falls ID 83402. (208)542-2271. Fax: (208)522-5241. E-mail: shannon@playgroundmag.com. Website: www.playgroundmag.com. **25% freelance written**. Magazine published 7 times/year covering playgrounds, play-related issues, equipment and industry trends. *Playground Magazine* targets a park and recreation management, elementary school teachers and administrators, child care facilities and parent-group leader readership. Articles should focus on play and the playground market as a whole, including aquatic play and surfacing. Estab. 2000. Circ. 35,000. Byline given. Pays on publication. No kill fee. Publishes ms an average of 6 months after acceptance. Buys first North American serial rights, buys electronic rights. Editorial lead time 2 months. Submit seasonal material 1 year in advance. Accepts queries by mail, e-mail. Accepts simultaneous submissions. Responds in 1 month to queries. Responds in 2 months to mss. Sample copy for $5. Guidelines for #10 sase.

Nonfiction Needs how-to, interview, new product, opinion, personal experience, photo feature, technical, travel. *Playground Magazine* does not publish any articles that do not directly relate to play and the playground industry. **Buys 4-6 mss/year.** Query. Length: 800-1,500 words. **Pays $50-300 for assigned articles.** Sometimes pays expenses of writers on assignment.

Photos State availability of or send photos Captions, identification of subjects, model releases required. Reviews 35mm transparencies, GIF/JPEG files (350 dpi or better). Offers no additional payment for photos accepted with ms. Buys one time rights.

Columns/Departments Dream Spaces (an article that profiles a unique play area and focuses on community involvement, unique design, or human interest), 800-1,200 words. 2 Query. **Pays $100-300.**

Tips We are looking for articles that managers can use as a resource when considering playground construction, management, safety, etc. Writers should find unique angles to playground-related features. We are a trade journal that offers up-to-date industry news and features that promote play and the playground industry.

MARINE & MARITIME INDUSTRIES

ASIA PACIFIC SHIPPING

Baird Publications, 135 Sturt St., Southbank VIC 3006 Australia. (61)(3)9645-0411. Fax: (61)(3)9645-0475. E-mail: marinfo@baird.com.au. Website: www.baird.com.au. Monthly magazine aimed at those involved in operating and supplying equipment and services to the shipping and port industries of Asia, Australia, New Zealand and the South Pacific. *Asia Pacific Shipping* provides its readers with information and ideas as to how to improve the efficiency and profitability of their business operations through the adoption of new vessels, technology and equipment, improved management and operational techniques and systems, and by simply providing them with the information required to make the right business decisions.

Nonfiction Needs general interest, how-to, new product, technical. Query.

$ $ CURRENTS

Marine Technology Society, 5565 Sterrett Pl., Suite 108, Columbia MD 21044-2665. (410)884-5330. Fax: (410)884-9060. E-mail: publications@mtsociety.org. Website: www.mtsociety.org. **0% freelance written**. Bimonthly newsletter covering commercial, academic, scientific marine technology. Estab. 1963. Circ. 2,600. Byline given. Pays on acceptance. No kill fee. Buys all rights. Makes work-for-hire assignments. Editorial lead time 1-2 months. Accepts queries by e-mail. Accepts previously published material. Accepts simultaneous submissions. Responds in 4 weeks to queries Sample copy free

- "Our readers are engineers and technologists who design, develop and maintain the equipment and instruments used to understand and explore the oceans. The newsletter covers society news, industry news, science and technology news, and similar news."

Nonfiction Needs interview, technical. **Buys 1-6 mss/year mss/year.** Query. Length: 250-500 words. **Pays $100-500 for assigned articles.** Sometimes pays expenses of writers on assignment.

MARINE BUSINESS

Yaffa Publishing, 17-21 Bellevue St., Surry Hills NSW 2010 Australia. (61)(2)9281-2333. Fax: (61)(2)9281-2750. E-mail: yaffa@yaffa.com.au. Website: www.yaffa.com.au. Monthly magazine covering Australia's boating industry.

Nonfiction Needs general interest, interview, new product. Query.

$ $ MARINE BUSINESS JOURNAL

The Voice of the Marine Industries Nationwide, 330 N. Andrews Ave., Ft. Lauderdale FL 33301. (954)522-5515. Fax: (954)522-2260. E-mail: sboating@southernboating.com. Website: www.marinebusinessjournal.com. **25% freelance written**. Bimonthly magazine that covers the recreational boating industry. *The Marine Business Journal* is aimed at boating dealers, distributors and manufacturers, naval architects, yacht brokers, marina owners and builders, marine electronics dealers, distributors and manufacturers, and anyone involved in the U.S. marine industry. Articles cover news, new product technology, and public affairs affecting the industry. Estab. 1986. Circ. 26,000. Byline given. Pays on publication. No kill fee. Publishes ms an average of 1 month after acceptance. Buys first North American serial rights, buys one-time rights, buys second serial (reprint) rights. Accepts queries by mail, e-mail. Responds in 2 weeks to queries. Sample copy for $2.50, 9x12 SAE with 7 first-class stamps.

Nonfiction Buys 20 mss/year. Query with published clips. Length: 500-1,000 words. **Pays $200-500.**

Photos State availability Captions, identification of subjects, model releases required. Reviews 35mm or larger transparencies, 5x7 prints. Offers $50/photo. Buys one time rights.

Tips Query with clips. It's a highly specialized field, written for professionals by professionals, almost all on assignment or by staff.

$ $ PROFESSIONAL MARINER

Journal of the Maritime Industry, Navigator Publishing, P.O. Box 569, Portland ME 04112. (207)822-4350. Fax: (207)772-2879. E-mail: editors@professionalmariner.com. Website: www.professionalmariner.com. **75% freelance written.** Bimonthly magazine covering professional seamanship and maritime industry news. Estab. 1993. Circ. 29,000. Byline given. Pays on publication. No kill fee. Buys all rights. Editorial lead time 3 months. Accepts queries by mail, e-mail, fax, phone. Accepts simultaneous submissions.

Nonfiction For professional mariners on vessels and ashore. Seeks submissions on industry news, regulations, towing, piloting, technology, engineering, business, maritime casualties, and feature stories about the maritime industry. Does accept sea stories and personal professional experiences as correspondence pieces. **Buys 15 mss/year.** Query. varies; short clips to long profiles/features. **Pays 25¢/word.** Sometimes pays expenses of writers on assignment.

Photos Send photos Captions, identification of subjects required. Reviews prints, slides. Negotiates payment individually. Buys one time rights.

Tips Remember that our audience comprises maritime industry professionals. Stories must be written at a level that will benefit this group.

SEA BREEZES

Sea Breezes Publications Ltd, Media House, Cronkbourne, Douglas, Isle of Man IM4 4SB. E-mail: sb.enquiries@seabreezes.co.im. Website: www.seabreezes.co.im. "*Sea Breezes* publishes factual tales of ships, seamen, and the sea that are of interest to professional seamen or those with a deep knowledge of ships and shipping." Estab. 1919. Pays at the end of each publication month. No kill fee. Accepts queries by mail, e-mail. Guidelines by email.

Nonfiction Does not accept fiction, poetry, cartoons, crosswords, quizzes, puzzles, or anything that smacks of the romance of the sea. Length: 1,000-6,000 words. **Pays 14£/page.**

Photos State availability of or send photos Captions required. 5£/photo; 10£/cover photo; 30£/centrespread photo

WORK BOAT WORLD

Baird Publications, 135 Sturt St., Southbank VIC 3006 Australia. (61)(3)9645-0411. Fax: (61)(3)9645-0475. E-mail: marinfo@baird.com.au. Website: www.baird.com.au. Monthly magazine covering all types of commercial, military and government vessels to around 130 meters in length. Maintaining close contact with ship builders, designers, owners and operators, suppliers of vessel equipment and suppliers of services on a worldwide basis, the editors and journalists of *Work Boat World* seek always to be informative. They constantly put themselves in the shoes of readers so as to produce editorial matter that interests, educates, informs and entertains. Estab. 1982.

Nonfiction Needs general interest, how-to, interview, new product. Query.

MEDICAL

CALIFORNIA

$ $ SOUTHERN CALIFORNIA PHYSICIAN

LACMA Services, Inc., 707 Wilshire Blvd., Suite 3800, Los Angeles CA 90017. (213)683-9900. Fax: (213)226-0350. E-mail: cheryle@socalphys.com. Website: www.socalphys.com. **25% freelance written.** Monthly magazine covering non-technical articles of relevance to physicians. We want professional, well-researched articles covering policy, issues, and other concerns of physicians. No personal anecdotes or patient viewpoints. Estab. 1908. Circ. 18,000. Byline given. Pays on acceptance. Offers 10% kill fee. Publishes ms an average of 2-3 months after acceptance. Buys first North American serial rights, buys second serial (reprint) rights, buys electronic rights. Editorial lead time 2-3 months. Accepts queries by e-mail. Accepts simultaneous submissions. Responds in 4 weeks to queries. Responds in 2 months to mss. Sample copy available online.

Nonfiction Needs general interest. **Buys 12-24 mss/year. mss/year.** Query with published clips. Length: 600-3,000 words. **Pays $200-600 for assigned articles.**
Photos State availability
Columns/Departments Medical World (tips/how-to's), 800-900 words. Query with published clips. **Pays $$200-$600.**

$ $ ADVANCE FOR HEALTHY AGING

Merion Publications, 2900 Horizon Dr., King of Prussia PA 19406. (800)355-5627. Fax: (610)278-1425. E-mail: mwolf@advanceweb.com. Website: www.advanceweb.com/healthyaging. **5% freelance written**. Bimonthly magazine covering health careÃ³the science of aging well. *"Healthy Aging* is a magazine for physicians who are interested in providing wellness and skin services to their baby boomer patients. Writers should be able to write to a physician's level. This means researching studies and doing thorough interviewing to understand medical topics, ranging from nutraceuticals, and preventative health topics. Articles must be well-researched and objective—speaking to the mission of the magazine." Estab. 2005. Circ. 30,000. Byline given. Pays on publication. Publishes ms an average of 3 months after acceptance. Buys first North American serial rights. Editorial lead time 5 months. Submit seasonal material 3 months in advance. Accepts queries by mail. Responds in 3 months to queries. Guidelines available online.
Nonfiction Needs interview, technical. "Nothing touting miracle cures for aging or favoring a product or specific approach. Articles must be research-driven and provide realistic portrayals." **Buys 6 mss/year.** Query with published clips. Length: 1,800-2,500 words. **Pays $150-300.**
Tips "Authors should be able to take medical information and make it easy to read for a physician-level audience, and prove their information will be objective with research, interviews, etc. We are looking for consumer-oriented articles that are taken a part for physician's practical use."

$ ADVANCE FOR RESPIRATORY CARE PRACTITIONERS

Merion Publications, Inc., 2900 Horizon Dr., King of Prussia PA 19406-0956. (610)278-1400. Fax: (516)275-1425. E-mail: venge@merion.com. Website: www.advanceweb.com?rcp. **50% freelance written**. Biweekly magazine covering respiratory diseases and therapies. *ADVANCE for Respiratory Care Practitioners* is available only to respiratory therapists and related health care personnel. We are a forum for educating our readers about new therapies and equipment and some of the changes and innovations taking place in the field of respiratory care. Estab. 1988. Circ. 45,500. Byline given. Pays on publication. Offers 75% kill fee. Publishes ms an average of 6 months after acceptance. Buys all rights. Editorial lead time 1 month. Submit seasonal material 3 months in advance. Accepts queries by mail, e-mail, fax, phone. Accepts simultaneous submissions. Responds in 2 weeks to queries. Responds in up to 6 months to mss. Sample copy available online. Guidelines available online.
Nonfiction Needs technical. Because we are an exclusive respiratory care publication, we do not want to see articles beyond that reach. We also do not want to get general information articles about specific respiratory care related diseases. For example, our audience is all too familiar with cystic fibrosis, asthma, COPD, bronchitis, Alpha 1 Antitrypsin Defiency, pulmonary hypertension and the like. **Buys 2-3 mss/year.** Query. **Pays $150.** Sometimes pays expenses of writers on assignment.
Photos State availability Captions, identification of subjects, model releases required. Reviews GIF/JPEG files. Negotiates payment individually. Buys all rights.
Tips The only way to truly break into the market for this publication on a freelance basis is to have a background in health care (preferably in respiratory care). All of our columnists are caregivers; most of our freelancers are caregivers. Any materials that come in of a general nature like 'contact me for freelance writing assignments or photography' are discarded.

$ ADVANCE NEWSMAGAZINES

Merion Publications Inc., 2900 Horizon Dr., King of Prussia PA 19406. (610)278-1400. Fax: (610)278-1425. Website: www.advanceweb.com. More than 30 magazines covering allied health fields, nursing, age management, long-term care and more. Byline given. Pays on publication. Buys first North American serial rights. Editorial lead time 3 months. Accepts queries by e-mail, phone.
Nonfiction Needs interview, new product, personal experience, technical. Query with published clips. Length: 2,000 words.

$ $ $ AHIP COVERAGE

America's Health Insurance Plans, 601 Pennsylvania Ave., Suite 500, Washington DC 20004. (202)778-8493. Fax: (202)331-7487. E-mail: ahip@ahip.org. Website: www.ahip.org. **75% freelance written**. Bimonthly magazine. *AHIP Coverage* is geared toward administrators in America's health insurance companies. Articles should inform and generate interest and discussion about topics on anything from patient care to regulatory issues. Estab. 1990. Circ. 12,000. Byline given. Pays within 30 days of acceptance of article in final form. Offers 30% kill fee. Publishes ms an average of 2 months after acceptance. Buys all rights. Editorial lead time 2 months. Submit seasonal material 4 months in advance. Accepts queries by mail, e-mail, fax. Accepts simultaneous submissions. Sample copy free.

Nonfiction Needs book excerpts, how-to, how industry professionals can better operate their health plans, opinion. We do not accept stories that promote products. Send complete ms. Length: 1,800-2,500 words. **Pays 65¢/word minimum.** Pays phone expenses of writers on assignment.
Photos Buys all rights.
Tips Look for health plan success stories in your community; we like to include case studies on a variety of topics—including patient care, provider relations, regulatory issues—so that our readers can learn from their colleagues. Our readers are members of our trade association and look for advice and news. Topics relating to the quality of health plans are the ones more frequently assigned to writers, whether a feature or department. We also welcome story ideas. Just send us a letter with the details.

AMERICA'S PHARMACIST

National Community Pharmacists Association, 100 Daingerfield Rd., Suite 205, Alexandria VA 22314. (703)683-8200. Fax: (703)683-3619. E-mail: mike.conlan@ncpanet.org. Website: www.ncpanet.org. **10% freelance written**. Monthly magazine. *America's Pharmacist* publishes business and management information and personal profiles of independent community pharmacists, the magazine's principal readers. Estab. 1904. Circ. 25,000. Byline given. Pays on publication. No kill fee. Publishes ms an average of 3 months after acceptance. Buys all rights. Editorial lead time 3 months. Submit seasonal material 3 months in advance. Accepts queries by mail, e-mail, fax. Accepts simultaneous submissions. Responds in 1 week to queries. Responds in 2 weeks to mss. Sample copy free.
Nonfiction Needs interview, business information. **Buys 3 mss/year.** Query. Length: 1,500-2,500 words.
Photos State availability Captions, identification of subjects, model releases required. Reviews contact sheets. Negotiates payment individually Buys one time rights.

$ AT THE CENTER

At the Center Webzine, P.O. Box 309, Fleetwood PA 19522. (800)588-7744 ext. 2. Fax: (800)588-7744. E-mail: publications@rightideas.us. Website: www.atcmag.com. **20% freelance written**. Webzine published 4 times/year that provides encouragement and education to the staff, volunteers, and board members working in crisis pregnancy centers. Estab. 2000. Circ. 30,000. Byline given. Pays on publication. No kill fee. Publishes ms an average of 1 year after acceptance. Buys first North American serial rights, buys first rights, buys one-time rights, buys electronic rights. Editorial lead time 6 months. Submit seasonal material 1 year in advance. Accepts queries by mail, e-mail, fax. Accepts simultaneous submissions. Responds in 1 month to queries. Responds in 3-4 months to mss. Online at www.atcmag.com. Writer's guidelines for #10 SASE or by e-mail.
Nonfiction Relevant topics include abstinence programs and counseling, adoption, counseling pregnant moms in a crisis, post-abortion stress. **Buys about 12 mss/year.** Query. Length: 800-1,200 words. **Pays $150 for assigned articles. Pays $50-150 for unsolicited articles.**
Tips Generally, we don't have enough space to print personal stories. If your story is relevant to the things you want to share with staff and volunteers of the centers, your best chance to get it published is to keep it brief (a couple paragraphs). Any scripture references should be quoted from KJV or ESV.

AUSTRALIAN COSMETIC SURGERY MAGAZINE

Bella Media, Level 2, 294 New South Head Rd., Double Bay NSW 2028 Australia. (61)(2)9362-1555. Fax: (61)(2)9362-1556. E-mail: acsmag@bellamedia.com.au. Website: www.cosmeticsurgerymagazine.com.au. Quarterly magazine containing information about individual procedures written by experts in the field, plus doctor interviews, technology updates, and the latest health and beauty news.
Nonfiction Needs general interest, interview, new product, technical. Query.

AUSTRALIAN FAMILY PHYSICIAN

Royal Australian College of General Practitioners, 1 Palmerston Crescent, South Melbourne VIC 3205 Australia. E-mail: afp@racgp.org.au. Website: www.racgp.org.au. Monthly magazine dedicated to meeting the ongoing educational requirements of general practitioners. Guidelines available online.
Nonfiction Needs technical. Send complete ms. Length: 1,500 words.

$ $ $ BIOTECHNOLOGY HEALTHCARE

A Guide for Decision Makers on the Biotechnology Revolution, BioCommunications LLC, 780 Township Line Rd., Yardley PA 19067. (267)685-2783. Fax: (267)685-2966. E-mail: editors@biotechnologyhealthcare.com. Website: www.biotechnologyhealthcare.com. **75% freelance written**. Bimonthly magazine. "We are a business magazine (not an academic journal) that covers the economic, regulatory, and health policy aspects of biotech therapies and diagnostics. Our audience includes third-party payers, employer purchasers of healthcare, public healthcare agencies, and healthcare professionals who prescribe biotech therapies. Articles should be written in business magazine-style prose and should be focused on the concerns of these audiences." Estab. 2004. Circ. 36,000 (digital); 12,431 (print). Byline given. Pays on acceptance. Offers $300 kill fee. Publishes ms an average of 3 months after acceptance. Buys all rights. Editorial lead time 4 months. Accepts queries by mail, e-mail, fax. Responds in 2 weeks to queries. Responds in 1 month to mss. Sample copy available online. Guidelines by email.

Nonfiction Needs book excerpts, essays, how-to, manage the cost of biologics, case studies, interview, opinion, technical, about biotech therapies, diagnostics, or devices, regulatory developments, cost analyses studies, coverage of hot-button issues in the field. **Buys 24 mss/year.** Query with published clips. Length: 1,650-3,300 words. **Pays 75-85¢/word. Pays $300-1,870 for unsolicited articles.** Pays expenses of writers on assignment.
Photos Contact: Philip Denlinger, design director. State availability Captions, identification of subjects required. Reviews contact sheets, 4X6 or larger, color only prints, PowerPoint slides, TIF files that are 200 dpi or higher. Negotiates pay individually Buys one time rights.
Columns/Departments Our columns are 'spoken for,' but I am always interested in pitches for new columns from qualified writers. 18 Query with published clips. **Pays $300 minimum for a full piece; 75¢/word maximum for ms 600-1,200 words**
Fillers Needs gags. 3 cartoons **Pays $300 for cartoons upon publication**
Tips "Biotechnology represents a new age of medicine, and our readers—who struggle with how to provide healthcare benefits to employees and health insurance enrollees in an affordable way—have a strong interest in learning about how these cutting-edge, but very expensive, treatments will affect how they do their jobs. Keep in mind the interests of the managed care medical or pharmacy director, the employer HR/benefits department, the state Medicaid director, or the clinician who provides biotech therapies to patients. Our audience is highly educated, but not versed in the deep science of biotechnology, so write up to their level but be conversational and stay away from jargon. Please avoid sending consumer-health pitches, as we are not a consumer publication."

$ $ BIOWORLD PERSPECTIVES

3525 Piedmont Rd., Bldg. 6, Suite 400, Atlanta GA 30305. (404)262-5545. Fax: (404)262-5555. E-mail: amanda.lyle@ahcmedia.com. Website: www.bioworld.com. **Contact:** Amanda Lyle. **75% freelance written.** Weekly e-zine Biotechnology. "We're open to a variety of articles, so long as there's a tie-in to biotech. So far, topics have included Michael Moore's film, *Sicko*, Michael Crichton's book, *Next* and its presentation of biotech patents, a comparison of real biotech innovations to those mentioned in sci-fi, personal accounts of people's experiences with diseases, critiques of science education in the West, and how immigration can help the biotech industry. Usually there is some connection to current events, an ethical debate, or a top-of-mind issue." Estab. 2007. Circ. 3,500. Byline given. Pays on publication. No kill fee. Publishes ms an average of 1 month after acceptance. Buys all rights. Editorial lead time 2 months. Submit seasonal material 2 months in advance. Accepts queries by e-mail. Responds in 2 weeks to queries. Sample copy free. Guidelines free.
Nonfiction Needs essays, humor, inspirational, interview, opinion, personal experience. **Buys 25 mss/year mss/year.** Query with published clips. Length: 1,000-1,200 words.

$ $ JEMS

The Journal of Emergency Medical Services, Elsevier Public Safety, 525 B St., Suite 1900, San Diego CA 92101. Fax: (619)699-6396. E-mail: jems.editor@elsevier.com. Website: www.jems.com. **95% freelance written**. Monthly magazine directed to personnel who serve the pre-hospital emergency medicine industry: paramedics, EMTs, emergency physicians and nurses, administrators, EMS consultants, etc. Estab. 1980. Circ. 45,000. Byline given. Pays on publication. No kill fee. Publishes ms an average of 6 months after acceptance. Buys all North American serial rights. Submit seasonal material 6 months in advance. Accepts queries by mail, e-mail, fax. Responds in 2-3 months to queries. Sample copy and writer's guidelines free Guidelines available online.
Nonfiction Needs essays, expose, general interest, how-to, humor, interview, new product, opinion, personal experience, photo feature, technical, continuing education. **Buys 50 mss/year.** Query. **Pays $200-400.**
Photos State availability Identification of subjects, model releases required. Reviews 4x6 prints, digital images. Offers $25 minimum per photo Buys one time rights.
Columns/Departments Length: 850 words maximum. Query with or without published clips. **Pays $50-250.**
Tips "Please submit a 1-page cover letter with your manuscript. Your letter should answer these questions: 1) What specifically are you going to tell *JEMS* readers about prehospital medical care? 2) Why do *JEMS* readers need to know this? 3) How will you make your case (i.e., literature review, original research, interviews, personal experience, observation)? Your query should explain your qualifications, as well as include previous writing samples. Please submit online to www.eeselsevier.com/jems."

EMERGENCY MEDICINE NEWS

Emergency Medicine's Only Independent News Magazine, Lippincott Williams & Wilkins, Wolters Kluwer Health, 333 7th Ave., 19th Floor, New York NY 10001. E-mail: emn@lww.com. Website: www.em-news.com. **100% freelance written.** Monthly publication covering emergency medicine only, not emergency nursing, EMTs, PAs. "*Emergency Medicine News* provides breaking coverage of advances, trends and issues within the field, as well as clinical commentary with a CME activity by Editorial Board Chairman James R. Roberts, MD, a leader in the field." Estab. 1978. Circ. 30,000. Byline given. Pays on acceptance. Offers 25% kill fee. Buys first North American serial rights, buys electronic rights. Editorial lead time 2 months. Submit seasonal material 4 months in advance. Accepts queries by e-mail. Responds in 2 weeks to queries. Responds in 1 month to mss. Sample copy available online.

Nonfiction Query.

Tips "Best way to break in is to read publication online and pitch unique idea. No queries just touting experience or looking for assignment."

$ $ $ MANAGED CARE

780 Township Line Rd., Yardley PA 19067-4200. (267)685-2784. Fax: (267)685-2966. E-mail: editors@managedcaremag.com. Website: www.managedcaremag.com. **75% freelance written**. Monthly magazine. We emphasize practical, usable information that helps HMO medical directors and pharmacy directors cope with the options, challenges, and hazards in the rapidly changing health care industry. Estab. 1992. Circ. 44,000. Byline given. Pays on acceptance. Offers 20% kill fee. Publishes ms an average of 6 weeks after acceptance. Buys all rights. Editorial lead time 3 months. Submit seasonal material 4 months in advance. Accepts queries by mail, e-mail, fax. Responds in 3 weeks to queries. Responds in 2 months to mss. Sample copy free. Writer's guidelines on request.

Nonfiction I strongly recommend submissions via e-mail. You'll get a faster response. Needs book excerpts, general interest, trends in health-care delivery and financing, quality of care, and employee concerns, how-to, deal with requisites of managed care, such as contracts with health plans, affiliation arrangements, accredidation, computer needs, etc., original research and review articles that examine the relationship between health care delivery and financing. Also considered occasionally are personal experience, opinion, interview/profile, and humor pieces, but these must have a strong managed care angle and draw upon the insights of (if they are not written by) a knowledgeable managed care professional. **Buys 40 mss/year.** Query with published clips. Length: 1,000-3,000 words. **Pays 75¢/word.** Pays expenses of writers on assignment.

Photos State availability Reviews contact sheets, negatives, transparencies, prints. Negotiates payment individually Buys first-time rights

Tips Know our audience (health plan executives) and their needs. Study our website to see what we cover.

MEDESTHETICS

Business Education for Medical Practitioners, Creative Age Publications, 7628 Densmore Ave., Van Nuys CA 91406. E-mail: ihansen@creativeage.com. Website: www.medestheticsmagazine.com. **50% freelance written**. Bimonthly magazine covering noninvasive medical aesthetic services such as laser hair removal, skin rejuvenation, injectable fillers, and neurotoxins. "*Medesthetics* is a business to business magazine written for and distributed to dermatologists, plastic surgeons and other physicians offering noninvasive medical aesthetic services. We cover the latest equipment and products as well as legal and management issues specific to medspas, laser centers and other medical aesthetic practices." Estab. 2005. Circ. 20,000. Byline given. Pays on acceptance. Publishes ms an average of 3 months after acceptance. Buys first rights, buys electronic rights. Editorial lead time 3 months. Submit seasonal material 3 months in advance. Accepts queries by e-mail. Responds in 1 month to queries.

Nonfiction Needs new product, technical. "Does not want articles directed at consumers." **Buys 25 mss/year.** Query.

Photos State availability Identification of subjects, model releases required. Reviews transparencies, prints. Negotiates payment individually. Buys one time rights.

Tips "We work strictly on assignment. Query with article ideas; do not send manuscripts. We respond to queries with article assignments that specify article requirements."

$ $ $ $ MEDICAL ECONOMICS

123 Tice Blvd., Suite 300, Woodcliff Lake NJ 07677. (201)690-5411. Fax: (201)690-5420. E-mail: jsabatie@advanstar.com. Website: www.memag.com. Semimonthly magazine (24 times/year). *Medical Economics* is a national business magazine read by M.D.s and D.O.s in office-based practice. Our purpose is to be informative and useful to practicing physicians in the professional and financial management of their practices. We look for contributions from writers who know—or will make the effort to learn—the nonclinical concerns of today's physician. These writers must be able to address those concerns in feature articles that are clearly written and that convey authoritative information and advice. Our articles focus very narrowly on a subject and explore it in depth. Circ. 210,000. Pays on acceptance. Offers 25% kill fee. Buys all rights. Accepts queries by mail, e-mail, fax. Sample copy available online. Guidelines available online.

Nonfiction Articles about private physicians in innovative, pioneering, and/or controversial situations affecting medical care delivery, patient relations, or malpractice prevention/litigation; personal finance topics. We do not want overviews or pieces that only skim the surface of a general topic. We address physician readers in a conversational, yet no-nonsense tone, quoting recognized experts on office management, personal finance, patient relations, and medical-legal issues. Query with published clips. Length: 1,000-1,800 words. **Pays $1,200-2,000 for assigned articles.** Pays expenses of writers on assignment. Expenses over $100 must be approved in advance—receipts required. Will negotiate an additional fee for photos, if accepted for publication.

Photos Will negotiate an additional fee for photos accepted for publication.

Tips We look for articles about physicians who run high-quality, innovative practices suited to the age of managed care. We also look for how-to service articles—on practice-management and personal-finance topics—which must contain anecdotal examples to support the advice. Read the magazine carefully, noting its style and content. Then send detailed proposals or outlines on subjects that would interest our mainly primary-care physician readers.

MEDICAL IMAGING

6100 Center Dr., Suite 1000, Los Angeles CA 90045. (310)642-4400 ext. 257. Fax: (310)641-0831. E-mail: danderson@ascendmedia.com. Website: www.medicalimagingmag.com. **80% freelance written**. Monthly magazine covering diagnostic imaging equipment and technology. Estab. 1986. Circ. 26,000. Byline given. Pays on publication. No kill fee. Publishes ms an average of 2 months after acceptance. Buys all rights. Editorial lead time 2 months. Sample copy on request.

Nonfiction Needs interview, technical. No general interest/human interest stories about healthcare. Articles *must* deal with our industry, diagnostic imaging. **Buys 6 mss/year.** Query with published clips. Length: 1,500-2,500 words.

Photos State availability Identification of subjects, model releases required. Reviews negatives. Offers no additional payment for photos accepted with ms Buys all rights.

Tips Send an e-mail or a letter with an interesting story idea that is applicable to our industry, diagnostic imaging. Then follow up with a phone call. Areas most open to freelancers are features and technology profiles. You don't have to be an engineer or radiologist, but you have to know how to talk and listen to them.

MIDWIFERY TODAY

P.O Box 2672, Eugene OR 97402. Fax: (541)344-1422. E-mail: editorial@midwiferytoday.com. Website: www.midwiferytoday.com. **Contact:** Cheryl K. Smith. **95% freelance written**. Quarterly magazine. "Through networking and education, *Midwifery Today*'s missions is to return midwifery to its rightful position in the family; to make midwifery care the norm throughout the world; and to redefine midwifery as a vital partnership with women." Estab. 1986. Circ. 3,000. Byline given. No kill fee. Publishes ms an average of 5 months after acceptance. Editorial lead time 3-9 months. Submit seasonal material 6 months in advance. Accepts queries by e-mail. Accepts simultaneous submissions. Responds in 2 weeks to queries. Responds in 1 month to mss. Sample copy available online. Guidelines available online.

Nonfiction Contact: Cheryl K. Smith. "All articles must relate to pregnancy or birth and provide something of value to birth practitioners." Needs book excerpts, essays, how-to, humor, inspirational, interview, opinion, personal experience, photo feature, clinical research, herbal articles, birth stories, business advice. **Buys 60 mss/year.** Send complete ms. Length: 300-3,000 words.

Photos Contact: Cathy Guy, Layout Designer. State availability Model releases required. Reviews prints, GIF/JPEG files. $15-$50 per photo Buys one time rights.

Columns/Departments Contact: Cheryl K. Smith. News: "In My Opinion" (150-750 words). 8 Send complete ms.

Poetry Contact: Cheryl K. Smith. Needs avant-garde, haiku, light verse, traditional. Does not want poetry unrelated to pregnancy or birth. **Buys 4/year poems/year.** Maximum line length of 25

Fillers Contact: Jan Tritten. Needs anecdotes, facts, newsbreaks. Length: 100-600 words.

Tips "Use Chicago Manual of Style formatting."

$ $ $ $ MODERN PHYSICIAN

Essential Business News for the Executive Physician, Crain Communications, 360 N. Michigan Ave., 5th Floor, Chicago IL 60601. (312)649-5439. Fax: (312)280-3183. E-mail: dburda@crain.com. Website: www.modernphysician.com. **10% freelance written**. Monthly magazine covering business and management news for doctors. *Modern Physician* offers timely topical news features with lots of business information—revenues, earnings, financial data. Estab. 1997. Circ. 32, 552. Byline given. Pays on acceptance. No kill fee. Publishes ms an average of 2 months after acceptance. Buys all rights. Editorial lead time 2 months. Accepts queries by mail, e-mail. Responds in 6 weeks to queries. Sample copy free. Writer's guidelines sent after query.

Nonfiction Length: 750-1,000 words. **Pays 75¢-$1/word.**

Tips Read the publication, know our audience, and come up with a good story idea that we haven't thought of yet.

THE NEW ZEALAND JOURNAL OF PHYSIOTHERAPY

New Zealand Society of Physiotherapists, P.O. Box 27386, Wellington New Zealand. (64)(4)801-6500. Fax: (64)(4)801-5571. E-mail: nzsp@physiotherapy.org.nz. Website: www.physiotherapy.org.nz. "Acadmic journal publishing papers relevant to the theory and practice of physiotheraphy." No kill fee.

Nonfiction Research reports, scholarly papers (clinical or professional perspective), clinical commentary, literature review, case study, case report, book/software/video review. Send complete ms.

NEW ZEALAND JOURNAL OF SPORTS MEDICINE

Sports Medicine of New Zealand, Inc., 40 Logan Park Dr., Dunedin New Zealand. (64)(3)477-7887. Fax:

(64)(3)477-7882. E-mail: smnznat@xtra.co.nz. Website: www.sportsmedicine.co.nz. Semiannual magazine covering articles of interest to medical/surgical specialists, general practitioners, physiotherapists, podiatrists, nutritionalists, and sports scientists. No kill fee.

- Query before submitting.

THE NEW ZEALAND MEDICAL JOURNAL

Dept. of Surgery, Christchurch Hospital, P.O. Box 4345, Christchurch New Zealand. (64)(3)364-1277. Fax: (64)(3)364-1683. E-mail: nzmj@cdhb.govt.nz. Website: www.nzma.org.nz/journal. **Contact:** Brennan Edwardes, prod. ed. No kill fee. Accepts queries by e-mail. Guidelines available online.

Nonfiction Editorials (1,200 words), Obituaries (600 words and a photo), Case Reports (600 words and a photo), Viewpoints (3,000 words), Medical Image (50-200 words and 1-4 images), Letters and Original Articles. Send complete ms.

$$ OPTICAL PRISM

Canada's leading magazine for optical professionals, Nusand Publishing, 250 The East Mall, Suite 1113, Toronto ON M9B 6L3 Canada. (416)233-2487. Fax: (416)233-1746. E-mail: kedwards@opticalprism.ca. Website: www.opticalprism.ca. **30% freelance written**. Magazine published 9 times/year covering Canada's optical industry. We cover the health, fashion and business aspects of the optical industry in Canada. Estab. 1982. Circ. 10,000. Byline given. Pays on publication. Publishes ms an average of 2 months after acceptance. Buys first rights, buys electronic rights. Editorial lead time 3 months. Submit seasonal material 3 months in advance. Accepts queries by mail, e-mail. Accepts previously published material. Accepts simultaneous submissions.

Nonfiction Needs interview, related to optical industry. Query. Length: 1,000-1,600 words. **Pays 40¢/word (Canadian).** Sometimes pays expenses of writers on assignment.

Columns/Departments Insight (profiles on people in the eyewear industry—also sometimes schools and businesses), 700-1,000 words. 5 Query. **Pays 40¢/word.**

Tips Please look at our editorial themes, which are on our Web site, and pitch articles that are related to the themes for each issue.

$$ PLASTIC SURGERY NEWS

American Society of Plastic Surgeons, 444 E. Algonquin Rd., Arlington Heights IL 60005. Fax: (847)981-5458. E-mail: mss@plasticsurgery.org. Website: www.plasticsurgery.org. **15% freelance written**. Monthly tabloid covering plastic surgery. *Plastic Surgery News* readership is comprised primarily of plastic surgeons and those involved with the specialty (nurses, techs, industry). The magazine is distributed via subscription and to all members of the American Society of Plastic Surgeons. The magazine covers a variety of specialty-specific news and features, including trends, legislation and clinical information. Estab. 1960. Circ. 7,000. Byline given. Pays on acceptance. Offers 25% kill fee. Publishes ms an average of 1-2 months after acceptance. Buys first North American serial rights, buys simultaneous rights, buys electronic rights. Editorial lead time 1-3 months. Accepts queries by e-mail. Accepts simultaneous submissions. Responds in 2 weeks to queries. Responds in 3 months to mss. Sample copy for 10 First-Class stamps. Guidelines by email.

Nonfiction Needs expose, how-to, new product, technical. Does not want celebrity or entertainment based pieces. **Buys 20 mss/year.** Query with published clips. Length: 1,000-3,500 words. **Pays 20-40¢/word.** Sometimes pays expenses of writers on assignment.

Columns/Departments Digital Plastic Surgeon (technology), 1,500-1,700 words.

$$ PODIATRY MANAGEMENT

Kane Communications, Inc., P.O. Box 750129, Forest Hills NY 11375. (718)897-9700. Fax: (718)896-5747. E-mail: bblock@podiatrym.com. Website: www.podiatrym.com. Magazine published 9 times/year for practicing podiatrists. "Aims to help the doctor of podiatric medicine to build a bigger, more successful practice, to conserve and invest his money, to keep him posted on the economic, legal, and sociological changes that affect him." Estab. 1982. Circ. 16,500. Byline given. Pays on publication. $75 kill fee. Buys first North American serial rights, buys second serial (reprint) rights. Submit seasonal material 4 months in advance. Accepts queries by e-mail. Accepts simultaneous submissions. Responds in 2 weeks to queries. Sample copy for $5 and 9x12 SAE Guidelines for #10 SASE.

Nonfiction "Book excerpts, general interest (taxes, investments, estate, estate planning, recreation, hobbies), how-to (establish and collect fees, practice management, organize office routines, supervise office assistants, handle patient relations), interview/profile (about interesting or well-known podiatrists), personal experience. These subjects are the mainstay of the magazine, but offbeat articles and humor are always welcome." **Buys 35 mss/year.** Length: 1,500-3,000 words. **Pays $350-600.**

Reprints Send photocopy. Pays 33% of amount paid for an original article.

Photos State availability Pays $15 for b&w contact sheet. Buys one time rights.

Tips "Articles should be tailored to podiatrists, and preferably should contain quotes from podiatrists."

$$ PRIMARY CARE OPTOMETRY NEWS

The Leading Clinical Newspaper for Optometrists, SLACK Incorporated, 6900 Grove Rd., Thorofare NJ 08086. (856)848-1000. Fax: (856)848-6091. E-mail: editor@PCONSuperSite.com. Website: www.pconsupersite.com. **5% freelance written**. Monthly tabloid covering optometry. *Primary Care Optometry News* strives to be the optometric professional's definitive information source by delivering timely, accurate, authoritative and balanced reports on clinical issues, socioeconomic and legislative affairs, ophthalmic industry and research developments, as well as updates on diagnostic and thereapeutic regimens and techniques to enhance the quality of patient care. Estab. 1996. Circ. 39,000. Byline given. Pays on publication. Offers 50% kill fee. Publishes ms an average of 2 months after acceptance. Buys all rights. Editorial lead time 2 months. Accepts queries by mail, e-mail, fax, phone. Responds in 2 weeks to queries. Sample copy available online. Guidelines by email.

Nonfiction Needs how-to, interview, new product, opinion, technical. **Buys 20 mss/year.** Query. Length: 800-1,000 words. **Pays $350-500.** Sometimes pays expenses of writers on assignment.

Photos State availability Captions, model releases required. Reviews GIF/JPEG files. Offers no additional payment for photos accepted with ms. Buys all rights.

Columns/Departments What's Your Diagnosis (case presentation), 800 words. 40 Query. **Pays $100-500.**

Tips Either e-mail or call the editor-in-chief with questions or story ideas.

$$ STITCHES

The Journal of Medical Humour, Stitches Publishing, Inc., 240 Edward St., Aurora ON L4G 3S9 Canada. (905)713-4336. Fax: (905)727-0017. E-mail: simon@stitchesmagazine.com. **90% freelance written**. Bimonthly magazine covering humor for physicians. *Stitches* is read primarily by physicians in Canada. Stories with a medical slant are particularly welcome, but we also run a lot of nonmedical material. It must be funny and, of course, brevity is the soul of wit. Estab. 1990. Circ. 44,000. Byline given. Pays on publication. No kill fee. Publishes ms an average of 3-4 months after acceptance. Buys first North American serial rights, buys electronic rights. Editorial lead time 1 month. Submit seasonal material 4 months in advance. Responds in 6 weeks to queries. Responds in 2 months to mss. Sample copy and writer's guidelines free.

Nonfiction Needs humor, personal experience. **Buys 20 mss/year.** Send complete ms. Length: 200-1,500 words. **Pays 25¢/word to US contributors.**

Fiction Needs humorous. **Buys 20 mss/year.** Send complete ms. Length: 200-1,500 words. **Pays 25¢/word (US) to US contributors.**

Poetry Humorous. **Buys 5 poems/year.** Submit maximum 5 poems. Length: 2-30 lines. **Pays 35¢/word (US) to US contributors.**

Tips Due to the nature of humorous writing, we have to see a completed manuscript, rather than a query, to determine if it is suitable for us. Along with a short cover letter, that's all we require.

$$$$ UNIQUE OPPORTUNITIES

The Physician's Resource, U O, Inc., 214 S. 8th St., Suite 502, Louisville KY 40202. Fax: (502)587-0848. E-mail: bett@uoworks.com. Website: www.uoworks.com. **55% freelance written**. Bimonthly magazine covering physician relocation and career development. Published for physicians interested in a new career opportunity. It offers physicians useful information and first-hand experiences to guide them in making informed decisions concerning their first or next career opportunity. It provides features and regular columns about specific aspects of the search process, practice management and career development. Estab. 1991. Circ. 80,000 physicians. Byline given. Pays 1 month after acceptance. Offers 10% kill fee. Publishes ms an average of 2 months after acceptance. Buys first North American serial rights, buys electronic rights. Editorial lead time 3 months. Submit seasonal material 6 months in advance. Responds in 2 months to queries. Sample copy for sae with 9x12 envelope and 6 First-Class stamps. Guidelines available online.

Nonfiction Features: Practice options and information of interest to physicians in career transition. **Buys 14 mss/year.** Query with published clips. Length: 1,500-3,500 words. **Pays $750-2,000.** Sometimes pays expenses of writers on assignment.

Photos State availability Identification of subjects, model releases required. Negotiates payment individually. Buys electronic rights

Columns/Departments Remarks (opinion from physicians and industry experts on physician career issues), 900-1,500 words. **No payment.**

Tips Submit queries via letter or e-mail with ideas for articles that directly pertain to physician career issues, such as specific or unusual practice opportunities, relocation, or practice establishment subjects, etc. Feature articles are most open to freelancers. Physician sources are most important with tips and advice from both the physicians and business experts. Physicians like to know what other physicians think and do, and appreciate suggestions from other business people.

MUSIC TRADE

$ CLASSICAL SINGER MAGAZINE

Classical Publications, Inc., P.O. Box 1710, Draper UT 84020. (801)254-1025, ext. 14. Fax: (801)254-3139. E-mail: editorial@classicalsinger.com. Website: www.classicalsinger.com. Monthly magazine covering classical singers. Estab. 1988. Circ. 7,000. Byline given, plus bio and contact info Pays on publication. No kill fee. Publishes ms an average of 3 months after acceptance. Buys second serial (reprint) rights, buys all rights. Editorial lead time 3 months. Submit seasonal material 3 months in advance. Accepts queries by e-mail. Accepts previously published material. Responds in 1 month to queries. Potential writers will be given password to website version of magazine and writer's guidelines online.

Nonfiction Editorial calendar available on request. The best way to find materials for articles is to look on the General Interest forum on our website and see what singers are interested in. Needs book excerpts, expose, carefully done, how-to, humor, interview, new product, personal experience, photo feature, religious, technical, travel, crossword puzzles on opera theme. Does not want reviews unless they are assigned. Query with published clips. Length: 500-3,000 words. **Pays 5¢/word ($50 minimum). Writers also receive 10 copies of the magazine.** Pays telephone expenses of writers with assignments when Xerox copy of bill submitted.

Photos Send photos Captions required. Buys all rights.

Tips *Classical Singer Magazine* has a full-color glossy cover and glossy b&w and color pages inside. It ranges in size from 56 pages during the summer to 120 pages in September. Articles need to meet this mission statement: 'Information for a classical singer's career, support for a classical singer's life, and enlightenment for a classical singer's art.'

CLAVIER COMPANION

Frances Clark Center, P.O. Box 651, Kingston NJ 08528. (714)226-9785. Fax: (714)226-9733. Website: www.claviercompanion.com. **Contact:** Peter Jutras, editor-in-chief. **1% freelance written**. Magazine published 6 times/year featuring practical information on teaching subjects that are of value to studio piano teachers and interviews with major artists. Estab. 1937. Circ. 14,000. Byline given. Pays on publication. No kill fee. Publishes ms an average of 18 months after acceptance. Buys all rights. Submit seasonal material 6 months in advance. Accepts queries by mail, fax, phone. Responds in 6 weeks to queries. Sample copy and writer's guidelines free

Nonfiction "Articles should be of interest and direct practical value to concert pianists, harpsichordists, and organists who are teachers of piano, organ, harpsichord, and electronic keyboards. Topics may include pedagogy, technique, performance, ensemble playing, and accompanying." Needs historical, how-to, interview, photo feature. 10-12 double-spaced pages. **Pays small honorarium.**

Reprints Occasionally we will reprint a chapter in a book.

Photos Digital artwork should be sent in TIFF, EPS, JPEG files for Photoshop at 300 dpi. Send photos Identification of subjects required. Reviews negatives, 2¼x2¼ transparencies, 3x5 prints. Offers no additional payment for photos accepted with ms. Buys all rights.

$ ⊘ INTERNATIONAL BLUEGRASS

International Bluegrass Music Association, 2 Music Circle S., Suite 100, Nashville TN 37203. (615)256-3222. Fax: (615)256-0450. E-mail: info@ibma.org. Website: www.ibma.org. www.discoverbluegrass.com. **10% freelance written**. Bimonthly newsletter. We are the business publication for the bluegrass music industry. IBMA believes that our music has growth potential. We are interested in hard news and features concerning how to reach that potential and how to conduct business more effectively. Estab. 1985. Circ. 4,500. Byline given. Pays on publication. No kill fee. Publishes ms an average of 2 months after acceptance. Buys one-time rights. Submit seasonal material 4 months in advance. Accepts queries by mail, e-mail, phone. Accepts simultaneous submissions. Responds in 1 month to queries. Sample copy for sae with 6x9 envelope and 2 First-Class stamps.

Nonfiction Unsolicited mss are not accepted, but unsolicited news about the industry is accepted. Needs book excerpts, essays, how-to, conduct business effectively within bluegrass music, new product, opinion. No interview/profiles/feature stories of performers (rare exceptions) or fans. **Buys 6 mss/year.** Query. Length: 1,000-1,200 words. **Pays up to $150/article for assigned articles.**

Reprints Send photocopy of article and information about when and where the article previously appeared. Does not pay for reprints.

Photos Send photos Captions, identification of subjects, True required. Offers no additional payment for photos accepted with ms. Buys one time rights.

Columns/Departments Staff written.

Tips We're interested in a slant strongly toward the business end of bluegrass music. We're especially looking for material dealing with audience development and how to book bluegrass bands outside of the existing market.

$ $ $ MIX MAGAZINE

Primedia Business Magazines, 6400 Hollis St., Suite 12, Emeryville CA 94608. Fax: (510)653-5142. E-mail:

tkenny@mixonline.com. Website: www.mixonline.com. **50% freelance written**. Monthly magazine covering pro audio. *Mix* is a trade publication geared toward professionals in the music/sound production recording and post-production industries. We include stories about music production, sound for picture, live sound, etc. We prefer in-depth technical pieces that are applications-oriented. Estab. 1977. Circ. 50,000. Byline given. Pays on publication. Offers 50% kill fee. Publishes ms an average of 3 months after acceptance. Buys all rights. Editorial lead time 10 weeks. Submit seasonal material 3 months in advance. Responds in 2 weeks to queries. Responds in 1 month to mss. Sample copy for $6. Guidelines free.

Nonfiction Needs how-to, interview, new product, technical, project/studio spotlights. Sound for picture supplement (April, September), Design issue **Buys 60 mss/year.** Query. Length: 500-2,000 words. **Pays $300-800 for assigned articles. Pays $300-400 for unsolicited articles.**

Photos State availability Captions, identification of subjects required. Reviews 4x5 transparencies, prints. Negotiates payment individually. Buys one time rights.

$ $ THE MUSIC & SOUND RETAILER

Testa Communications, 25 Willowdale Ave., Port Washington NY 11050. (516)767-2500. E-mail: bberk@testa.com. Website: www.msretailer.com. **20% freelance written**. Monthly magazine covering business to business publication for music instrument products. *The Music & Sound Retailer* covers the music instrument industry and is sent to all dealers of these products, including Guitar Center, Sam Ash, and all small independent stores. Estab. 1983. Circ. 11,700. Byline given. Pays on acceptance. Offers $100 kill fee. Buys first North American serial rights. Editorial lead time 1 month. Submit seasonal material 2 months in advance. Accepts queries by e-mail. Accepts simultaneous submissions. Responds in 2 weeks to queries. Responds in 1 month to mss. Sample copy for #10 sase. Guidelines free.

Nonfiction Needs how-to, new product, opinion, (does not mean letters to the editor), personal experience. Our 25th anniversary issue will be published in November with material due on October 1. Historical news or features will be considered. Concert and CD reviews are never published; interviews with musicians. **Buys 25 mss/year. mss/year.** Query with published clips. Length: 1,000-2,000 words. **Pays $300-450 for assigned articles. Pays $300-450 for unsolicited articles.** Sometimes pays expenses of writers on assignment.

Photos Send photos Captions required. Reviews GIF/JPEG files. Offers no additional payment for photos accepted with ms. Buys one time rights.

MUSIC CONNECTION

The National Music Industry Trade Magazine, Music Connection, Inc., 14654 Victory Blvd., Encino CA 91436. (818)995-0101. Fax: (818)995-9235. E-mail: markn@musicconnection.com. Website: www.musicconnection.com. **40% freelance written**. Monthly magazine geared toward working musicians and/or other industry professionals, including producers/engineers/studio staff, managers, agents, publicists, music publishers, record company staff, concert promoters/bookers, etc. Estab. 1977. Circ. 75,000. Byline given. Pays after publication. Offers kill fee. Kill fee varies. Publishes ms an average of 2 months after acceptance. Buys all rights. Editorial lead time 2 months. Submit seasonal material 2 months in advance. Sample copy for $5.

Nonfiction Needs how-to, music industry related, interview, new product, technical. Query with published clips. Length: 1,000-5,000 words. **Payment varies** Sometimes pays expenses of writers on assignment.

Tips "Articles must be informative 'how-to' music/music industry-related pieces, geared toward a trade-reading audience comprised mainly of musicians. No fluff."

$ $ $ OPERA NEWS

Metropolitan Opera Guild, Inc., 70 Lincoln Center Plaza, New York NY 10023-6593. (212)769-7080. Fax: (212)769-8500. Website: www.operanews.com. **75% freelance written**. Monthly magazine for people interested in opera; the opera professional as well as the opera audience. Estab. 1936. Circ. 105,000. Byline given. Pays on publication. No kill fee. Publishes ms an average of 4 months after acceptance. Buys first serial rights only. Editorial lead time 4 months. Sample copy for $5.

Nonfiction Most articles are commissioned in advance. Monthly issues feature articles on various aspects of opera worldwide. Emphasis is on high quality writing and an intellectual interest to the opera-oriented public. Needs historical, interview, informational, think pieces, opera, CD, and DVD reviews. Query. Length: 1,500-2,800 words. **Pays $450-1,200.** Sometimes pays expenses of writers on assignment.

Photos State availability Buys one time rights.

Columns/Departments 24

$ OVERTONES

Official Bimonthly Journal of the American Guild of English Handbell Ringers, American Guild of English Handbell Ringers, P.O. Box 1765, Findlay OH 45839. E-mail: editor@agehr.org. Website: www.agehr.org. **80% freelance written**. Bimonthly magazine covering English handbell ringing and conducting. AGEHR is dedicated to advancing the musical art of handbell/handchime ringing through education, community and communication. The purpose of 'Overtones' is to provide a printed resource to support that mission. We offer how-to articles, inspirational stories and interviews with well-known people and unique ensembles. Estab. 1954. Circ. 8,000. Byline given. Pays on publication. No kill fee. Publishes ms an average of 4 months after acceptance. Buys all rights. Editorial lead time 4 months. Submit seasonal material 4 months in advance. Accepts queries by mail, e-mail. Accepts previously published material. Responds in 1 month to queries. Responds in 1 month to mss. Sample copy by email. Guidelines by email.

Nonfiction Needs essays, general interest, historical, how-to, inspirational, interview, religious, technical. Does not want product news, promotional material. **Buys 8-12 mss/year.** Send complete ms. Length: 1,200-2,400 words. **Pays $120.** Sometimes pays expenses of writers on assignment.

Photos State availability of or send photos Captions required. Reviews 8x10 prints, JPEG/TIFF files. Offers no additional payment for photos accepted with ms. Buys one time rights.

Columns/Departments Handbells in Education (topics covering the use of handbells in school setting, teaching techniques, etc.); Handbells in Worship (topics and ideas for using handbells in a church setting); Nuts & Bolts (variety of topics from ringing and conducting techniques to score study to maintenance); Community Connections (topics covering issues relating to the operation/administration/techniques for community groups); Music Reviews (recommendations and descriptions of music following particular themes, i.e., youth music, difficult music, seasonal, etc.), all 800-1,200 words. Query. **Pays $80.**

Tips When writing profiles/interviews, try to determine what is especially unique or inspiring about the individual or ensemble and write from that viewpoint. Please have some expertise in handbells, education, or church music to write department articles.

$ $ VENUES TODAY

The News Behind the Headlines, 18350 Mount Langley, #200, Fountain Valley CA 92708. Fax: (714)378-0040. E-mail: linda@venuestoday.com. Website: www.venuestoday.com. **70% freelance written.** Weekly magazine covering the live entertainment industry and the buildings that host shows and sports. We need writers who can cover an exciting industry from the business side, not the consumer side. The readers are venue managers, concert promoters, those in the concert and sports business, not the audience for concerts and sports. So we need business journalists who can cover the latest news and trends in the market. Estab. 2002. Byline given. Pays on publication. Publishes ms an average of 1 month after acceptance. Buys all rights. Editorial lead time 1-2 months. Submit seasonal material 1-2 months in advance. Accepts queries by mail, e-mail, fax. Accepts simultaneous submissions. Responds in 1 week to queries. Sample copy available online. Guidelines free.

Nonfiction Needs interview, photo feature, technical, travel. Does not want customer slant, marketing pieces. Query with published clips. Length: 500-1,500 words. **Pays $100-250.** Pays expenses of writers on assignment.

Photos State availability Captions, identification of subjects required. Reviews GIF/JPEG files. Negotiates payment individually. Buys one time rights.

Columns/Departments Venue News (new buildings, trend features, etc.); Bookings (show tours, business side); Marketing (of shows, sports, convention centers); Concessions (food, drink, merchandise). Length: 500-1,200 words. 250 Query with published clips. **Pays $100-250.**

Fillers Needs gags. 6 **Pays $100-300.**

OFFICE ENVIRONMENT & EQUIPMENT

$ $ OFFICE DEALER

Updating the Office Products Industry, OfficeVision, Inc., 252 N. Main St., Suite 200, Mt. Airy NC 27030. (336)783-0000. Fax: (336)783-0045. E-mail: scullen@os-od.com. Website: www.os-od.com. **80% freelance written.** Bimonthly magazine covering the office product industry. *Office Dealer* serves independent resellers of office supplies, furniture, and equipment. Estab. 1987. Circ. 15,300. Byline given. Pays on publication. No kill fee. Buys all rights. Editorial lead time 3 months. Submit seasonal material 5 months in advance. Accepts queries by mail, e-mail, fax. Accepts simultaneous submissions. Responds in 1 month to queries. Sample copy and writer's guidelines free

Nonfiction Needs interview, new product, technical. **Buys 10 mss/year.** Length: 700-1,500 words. **Pays $300-500.**

Tips See editorial calendar posted online. Feature articles are written by our staff or by freelance writers. We may accept corporate `byline' articles. Queries should be a single page or less and include an SASE for response. Samples of a writer's past work and clips concerning the proposed story are helpful.

$ $ OFFICE SOLUTIONS

The Magazine for Office Professionals, OfficeVision Inc., 252 N. Main St., Suite 200, Mt. Airy NC 27030. (336)783-0000. Fax: (336)783-0045. E-mail: scullen@os-od.com. Website: www.os-od.com. **80% freelance written.** Bimonthly magazine covering the office personnel and environment. *Office Solutions* subscribers are responsible for the management of their personnel and office environments. Estab. 1984. Circ. 81,250. Byline given. Pays on publication. No kill fee. Buys all rights. Editorial lead time 3 months. Submit seasonal material 4 months in advance. Accepts queries by mail, e-mail, fax. Accepts simultaneous submissions.

Responds in 1 month to queries. Sample copy and writer's guidelines free
Nonfiction Our audience is responsible for general management of an office environment and personnel, so articles should be broad in scope and not too technical in nature. Needs interview, new product, technical, human resources. **Buys 18 mss/year.** Query. Length: 1,500-2,200 words. **Pays $200-450.**
Tips See editorial calendar posted online. Feature articles are written by our staff or by freelance writers. Queries should be a single page or less and include an SASE for response. Samples of a writer's past work and clips concerning the proposed story are helpful.

PACKAGING NEWS
Yaffa Publishing, 17-21 Bellevue St., Surry Hills NSW 2010 Australia. (61)(2)9281-2333. Fax: (61)(2)9281-2750. E-mail: yaffa@yaffa.com.au. Website: www.yaffa.com.au. Magazine published 11 times/year for packaging buyers.
Nonfiction Needs general interest, how-to, interview, new product, technical. Query.

STATIONERY NEWS
Yaffa Publishing, 17-21 Bellevue St., Surry Hills NSW 2010 Australia. (61)(2)9281-2333. Fax: (61)(2)9281-2750. E-mail: yaffa@yaffa.com.au. Website: www.yaffa.com.au. Monthly magazine covering office product reselling chain. Circ. 6,000.
Nonfiction Needs general interest, interview, new product, technical. Query.

PAPER

$ $ THE PAPER STOCK REPORT
News and Trends of the Paper Recycling Markets, McEntee Media Corp., 9815 Hazelwood Ave., Cleveland OH 44149. (440)238-6603. Fax: (440)238-6712. E-mail: ken@recycle.cc. Website: www.recycle.cc. Biweekly newsletter covering market trends, news in the paper recycling industry. Audience is interested in new innovative markets, applications for recovered scrap paper, as well as new laws and regulations impacting recycling. Estab. 1990. Circ. 2,000. Byline given. Pays on publication. No kill fee. Publishes ms an average of 1 month after acceptance. Buys first rights, buys all rights. Editorial lead time 2 months. Submit seasonal material 2 months in advance. Accepts queries by mail, e-mail, fax, phone. Accepts simultaneous submissions. Responds in 1 month to queries. Sample copy for #10 SAE with 55¢ postage.
Nonfiction Needs book excerpts, essays, expose, general interest, historical, interview, new product, opinion, photo feature, technical, all related to paper recycling. **Buys 0-13 mss/year.** Send complete ms. Length: 250-1,000 words. **Pays $50-250 for assigned articles. Pays $25-250 for unsolicited articles.** Pays expenses of writers on assignment.
Photos State availability Identification of subjects required. Reviews contact sheets. Negotiates payment individually.
Tips Article must be valuable to readers in terms of presenting new market opportunities or cost-saving measures.

PULP & PAPER CANADA
1 Holiday St., #705, East Tower, Pointe-Claire QC H9R 5N3 Canada. (514)630-5955. Fax: (514)630-5980. E-mail: anyao@pulpandpapercanada.com. **5% freelance written**. Monthly magazine. Prefers to work with published/established writers. Estab. 1903. Circ. 10,361. Byline given. Pays on publication. Offers kill fee. Negotiates kill fee. Buys first North American serial rights. Accepts queries by mail, e-mail. Responds in 1 month to queries. Sample copy free.
Nonfiction Articles with photographs or other good quality illustrations will get priority review. Needs how-to, related to processes and procedures in the industry, interview, of Canadian leaders in pulp and paper industry, technical, relevant to modern pulp and/or paper industry. No fillers, short industry news items, or product news items. **Buys 5 mss/year.** Send complete ms. 2,200 words maximum (with photos).
Tips Any return postage must be in either Canadian stamps or International Reply Coupons only.

$ $ RECYCLED PAPER NEWS
Independent Coverage of Environmental Issues in the Paper Industry, McEntee Media Corp., 9815 Hazelwood Ave., Cleveland OH 44149. (440)238-6603. Fax: (440)238-6712. E-mail: rpn@recycle.cc. Website: www.recycle.cc. **10% freelance written**. Monthly newsletter. We are interested in any news impacting the paper recycling industry, as well as other environmental issues in the paper industry, i.e., water/air pollution, chlorine-free paper, forest conservation, etc., with special emphasis on new laws and regulations. Estab. 1990. Pays on publication. No kill fee. Publishes ms an average of 2 months after acceptance. Buys first

rights, buys all rights. Editorial lead time 1 month. Submit seasonal material 1 month in advance. Accepts queries by mail, e-mail, fax, phone. Accepts simultaneous submissions. Responds in 2 months to queries. Sample copy for 9x12 SAE and 55¢ postage. Guidelines for #10 sase.
Nonfiction Needs book excerpts, essays, how-to, interview, new product, opinion, personal experience, photo feature, technical, new business, legislation, regulation, business expansion. **Buys 0-5 mss/year.** Query with published clips. **Pays $10-500.**
Columns/Departments Query with published clips. **Pays $10-500.**
Tips We appreciate leads on local news regarding recycling or composting, i.e., new facilities or businesses, new laws and regulations, unique programs, situations that impact supply and demand for recyclables, etc. International developments are also of interest.

PETS

$ $ PET AGE

H.H. Backer Associates, Inc., 18 S. Michigan Ave., Suite 1100, Chicago IL 60603. (312)578-1818. Fax: (312)578-1819. E-mail: hhbacker@hhbacker.com. **90% freelance written**. Monthly magazine for pet/pet supplies retailers, covering the complete pet industry. Prefers to work with published/established writers. Will consider new writers. Estab. 1971. Circ. 23,022. Byline given. Pays on acceptance. No kill fee. Publishes ms an average of 3 months after acceptance. Buys first North American serial rights, buys one-time rights. Sample copy and writer's guidelines available.
Nonfiction How-to articles on marketing/merchandising companion animals and supplies; how-to articles on retail store management; industry trends and issues; animal health care and husbandry. No profiles of industry members and/or retail establishments or consumer-oriented pet articles. **Buys 80 mss/year.** Query with published clips. Length: 1,500-2,200 words. **Pays 15¢/word for assigned articles.** Pays documented telephone expenses.
Photos Captions, identification of subjects required. Reviews transparencies, slides, and 5x7 glossy prints. Buys one time rights.
Tips This is a business publication for busy people, and must be very informative in easy-to-read, concise style. Articles about animal care or business practices should have the pet-retail angle or cover issues specific to this industry.

$ $ PET PRODUCT NEWS INTERNATIONAL

BowTie News, P.O. Box 6050, Mission Viejo CA 92690. (949)855-8822. Fax: (949)855-3045. Website: www.bowtieinc.com. **70% freelance written**. Monthly magazine. *Pet Product News* covers business/legal and economic issues of importance to pet product retailers, suppliers, and distributors, as well as product information and animal care issues. We're looking for straightforward articles on the proper care of dogs, cats, birds, fish, and exotics (reptiles, hamsters, etc.) as information the retailers can pass on to new pet owners. Estab. 1947. Circ. 26,000. Byline given. Pays on publication. Offers $50 kill fee. Buys first North American serial rights. Editorial lead time 3 months. Submit seasonal material 4 months in advance. Accepts queries by mail, fax. Responds in 2 weeks to queries. Sample copy for $5.50. Guidelines for #10 sase.
Nonfiction Needs general interest, interview, new product, photo feature, technical. No cute animal stories or those directed at the pet owner. **Buys 150 mss/year.** Query. Length: 500-1,500 words. **Pays $175-350.**
Columns/Departments The Pet Dealer News™ (timely news stories about business issues affecting pet retailers), 800-1,000 words; Industry News (news articles representing coverage of pet product suppliers, manufacturers, distributors, and associations), 800-1,000 words; Pet Health News™ (pet health and articles relevant to pet retailers); Dog & Cat (products and care of), 1,000-1,500 words; Fish & Bird (products and care of), 1,000-1,500 words; Small Mammals (products and care of), 1,000-1,500 words; Pond/Water Garden (products and care of), 1,000-1,500 words. 120 Query. **Pays $150-300.**
Tips Be more than just an animal lover. You have to know about health, nutrition, and care. Product and business articles are told in both an informative and entertaining style. Talk to pet store owners and see what they need to know to be better business people in general, who have to deal with everything from balancing the books and free trade agreements to animal rights activists. All sections are open, but you have to be knowledgeable on the topic, be it taxes, management, profit building, products, nutrition, animal care, or marketing.

PLUMBING, HEATING, AIR CONDITIONING & REFRIGERATION

CLIMATE CONTROL NEWS

Yaffa Publishing, 17-21 Bellevue St., Surry Hills NSW 2010 Australia. (61)(2)9281-2333. Fax: (61)(2)9281-

2750. E-mail: yaffa@yaffa.com.au. Website: www.yaffa.com.au. Monthly magazine for consulting/design engineers and architects, contractors and wholesalers in the HVAC/R industry. Circ. 7,000.
Nonfiction Needs general interest, interview, new product, technical. Query.

$ $ HVACR NEWS

Trade News International, 4444 Riverside Dr., #202, Burbank CA 91505-4048. Fax: (818)848-1306. E-mail: news@hvacrnews.com. Website: www.hvacrnews.com. Monthly tabloid covering heating, ventilation, air conditioning, and refrigeration. We are a national trade publication writing about news and trends for those in the trade. Estab. 1981. Circ. 50,000. Byline sometimes given. Pays on publication. No kill fee. Buys first North American serial rights. Editorial lead time 2 months. Submit seasonal material 2 months in advance. Accepts queries by mail, e-mail. Responds in 1 month to queries. Sample copy available online. Guidelines by email.
Nonfiction Needs general interest, how-to, interview, photo feature, technical. **Buys 25 mss/year.** Query with published clips. Length: 250-1,000 words. **Pays 25¢/word.** Sometimes pays expenses of writers on assignment.
Photos Send photos Identification of subjects required. Offers $10 minimum. Negotiates payment individually. Buys one time rights.
Columns/Departments Technical only. 24 **Pays 20¢/word.**
Tips Writers must be knowledgeable about the HVACR industry.

$ $ SNIPS MAGAZINE

BNP Media, 2401 W. Big Beaver Rd., Suite 700, Troy MI 48084. (248)244-6416. Fax: (248)362-0317. E-mail: mcconnellm@bnpmedia.com. Website: www.snipsmag.com. **2% freelance written**. Monthly magazine for sheet metal, heating, ventilation, air conditioning, and metal roofing contractors. Estab. 1932. No kill fee. Publishes ms an average of 3 months after acceptance. Buys all rights. Accepts queries by mail, e-mail, fax, phone. Call for writer's guidelines
Nonfiction Material should deal with information about contractors who do sheet metal, heating, air conditioning, ventilation, and metal roofing work; also about successful advertising and/or marketing campaigns conducted by these contractors and the results. Under 1,000 words unless on special assignment. **Pays $200-300.**
Photos Negotiable.

PRINTING

$ $ IN-PLANT GRAPHICS

North American Publishing Co., 1500 Spring Garden St., Suite 1200, Philadelphia PA 19130. (215)238-5321. Fax: (215)238-5457. E-mail: bobneubauer@napco.com. Website: www.ipgonline.com. **40% freelance written**. *"In-Plant Graphics* features articles designed to help in-house printing departments increase productivity, save money, and stay competitive. *IPG* features advances in graphic arts technology and shows in-plants how to put this technology to use. Our audience consists of print shop managers working for (nonprint related) corporations (i.e., hospitals, insurance companies, publishers, nonprofits), universities, and government departments. They often oversee graphic design, prepress, printing, bindery, and mailing departments." Estab. 1951. Circ. 23,100. Byline given. Pays on publication. No kill fee. Publishes ms an average of 3 months after acceptance. Buys all rights. Editorial lead time 2 months. Submit seasonal material 3 months in advance. Accepts queries by mail, e-mail, fax. Guidelines available online.
Nonfiction "Stories include profiles of successful in-house printing operations (not commercial or quick printers); updates on graphic arts technology (new features, uses); reviews of major graphic arts and printing conferences (seminar and new equipment reviews)." Needs new product, graphic arts, technical, graphic arts/printing/prepress. No articles on desktop publishing software or design software. No Internet publishing articles. **Buys 5 mss/year.** Query with published clips. Length: 800-1,500 words. **Pays $350-500.**
Photos State availability Captions, identification of subjects required. Reviews transparencies, prints. Negotiates payment individually. Buys one time rights.
Tips "To get published in *IPG*, writers must contact the editor with an idea in the form of a query letter that includes published writing samples. Writers who have covered the graphic arts in the past may be assigned stories for an agreed-upon fee. We don't want stories that tout only one vendor's products and serve as glorified commercials. All profiles must be well balanced, covering a variety of issues. If you can tell us about an in-house printing operation is doing innovative things, we will be interested."

$ $ SCREEN PRINTING

407 Gilbert Ave., Cincinnati OH 45202-2285. (513)421-2050. Fax: (513)421-5144. E-mail: tom.frecska@stmediagroup.com. Website: www.screenweb.com. **30% freelance written**. Monthly magazine for the screen printing industry, including screen printers (commercial, industrial, and captive shops), suppliers and

manufacturers, ad agencies, and allied professions. Works with a small number of new/unpublished writers each year. Estab. 1953. Circ. 17,500. Byline given. Pays on publication. No kill fee. Publishes ms an average of 3 months after acceptance. Buys all rights. Accepts queries by mail, e-mail, fax. Sample copy available. Guidelines for #10 sase.

Nonfiction Because the screen printing industry is a specialized but diverse trade, we do not publish general interest articles with no pertinence to our readers. Subject matter is open, but should fall into 1 of 4 categories—technology, management, profile, or news. Features in all categories must identify the relevance of the subject matter to our readership. Technology articles must be informative, thorough, and objective—no promotional or 'advertorial' pieces accepted. Management articles may cover broader business or industry specific issues, but they must address the screen printer's unique needs. Profiles may cover serigraphers, outstanding shops, unique jobs and projects, or industry personalities; they should be in-depth features, not PR puff pieces, that clearly show the human interest or business relevance of the subject. News pieces should be timely (reprints from nonindustry publications will be considered) and must cover an event or topic of industry concern. Unsolicited mss not returned. **Buys 10-15 mss/year.** Query. **Pays $400 minimum for major features.**

Photos Cover photos negotiable; b&w or color. Published material becomes the property of the magazine.

Tips Be an expert in the screen-printing industry with supreme or special knowledge of a particular screen-printing process, or have special knowledge of a field or issue of particular interest to screen-printers. If the author has a working knowledge of screen printing, assignments are more readily available. General management articles are rarely used.

$ $ THE BIG PICTURE

The Business of Wide Format, ST Media Group International, 11262 Cornell Park Dr., Cincinnati OH 45242. (513)263-9377. E-mail: lauren.mosko@stmediagroup.com. Website: www.bigpicture.net. **20% freelance written**. Monthly magazine covering wide-format digital printing. *The Big Picture* covers wide-format printing as well as digital workflow, finishing, display, capture, and other related topics. Our 21,500 readers include digital print providers, sign shops, commercial printers, in-house print operations, and other print providers across the country. We are primarily interested in the technology and work processes behind wide-format printing, but also run trend features on segments of the industry (innovations in point-of-purchase displays, floor graphics, fine-art printing, vehicle wrapping, textile printing, etc.). Estab. 1996. Circ. 21,500 controlled. Byline given. Pays on publication. Offers 20% kill fee. Publishes ms an average of 2 months after acceptance. Buys first print and Web rights. Editorial lead time 2 months. Accepts queries by e-mail. Accepts previously published material. Accepts simultaneous submissions. Responds in 2 weeks to queries. Responds in 1 month to mss. Sample copy available online. Guidelines available.

Nonfiction Needs how-to, interview, new product, technical. Does not want broad consumer-oriented pieces that don't speak to the business and technical aspects of producing print for pay. **Buys 15-30 mss/year. mss/ year.** Query with published clips. Length: 1500-2500 words. **Pays $500-700 for assigned articles.** Sometimes (limit agreed upon in advance)

Photos Send photos Reviews GIF/JPEG files hi-res. Offers no additonal payment for photos accepted with ms.

Tips Interest in and knowledge of the printing industry will position you well to break into this market.

PROFESSIONAL PHOTOGRAPHY

CAPTURE

Commercial Photography Magazine, Yaffa Publishing, 17-21 Bellevue St., Surry Hills NSW 2010 Australia. (61) (2)9281-2333. Fax: (61)(2)9281-2750. E-mail: yaffa@yaffa.com.au. Website: www.yaffa.com.au. Bimonthly magazine covering all aspects of running a successful photography business, from equipment, studios and techniques, to staffing, marketing, copyright and legal issues.

Nonfiction Needs how-to, interview, new product, technical. Query.

$ $ IMAGING BUSINESS

(formerly *Photographic Processing*), Cygnus Business Media, 3 Huntington Quad., Suite 301N, Melville NY 11747. (631)845-2700. Fax: (631)845-7109. E-mail: bill.schiffner@cygnusb2b.com. Website: www.labsonline.com. **30% freelance written**. Monthly magazine covering photographic (commercial/minilab) and electronic processing markets. Estab. 1965. Circ. 19,000. Byline given. Pays on publication. Offers $75 kill fee. Publishes ms an average of 4 months after acceptance. Editorial lead time 3 months. Submit seasonal material 3 months in advance. Accepts simultaneous submissions. Sample copy and writer's guidelines free

Nonfiction Needs how-to, interview, new product, photo processing/digital imaging features. **Buys 20-30 mss/year.** Query with published clips. Length: 1,500-2,200 words. **Pays $275-350 for assigned articles. Pays $250-275 for unsolicited articles.**

Photos Looking for digitally manipulated covers. Send photos Captions required. Reviews 4x5 transparencies,

4x6 prints. Offers no additional payment for photos accepted with ms. Buys one time rights.
Columns/Departments Surviving in 2000 (business articles offering tips to labs on how to make their businesses run better), 1,500-1,800 words; Business Side (getting more productivity out of your lab). 10 Query with published clips. **Pays $150-250.**

$ $ NEWS PHOTOGRAPHER

National Press Photographers Association, Inc., 6677 Whitemarsh Valley Walk, Austin TX 78746. E-mail: magazine@nppa.org. Website: www.nppa.org. Published 12 times/year. *News Photographer* magazine is dedicated to the advancement of still and television news photography. The magazine presents articles, interviews, profiles, history, new products, electronic imaging, and news related to the practice of photojournalism. Estab. 1946. Circ. 11,000. Byline given. Pays on acceptance. Offers 100% kill fee. Publishes ms an average of 4 months after acceptance. Buys one-time and archival electronic rights. Editorial lead time 2 months. Submit seasonal material 2 months in advance. Accepts queries by mail, e-mail, fax, phone. Accepts previously published material. Accepts simultaneous submissions. Responds in 1 month to queries. Sample copy for sae with 9x12 envelope and 3 First-Class stamps. Guidelines free.
Nonfiction Needs historical, how-to, interview, new product, opinion, personal experience, photo feature, technical. **Buys 10 mss/year.** Query. 1,500 words **Pays $300.** Pays expenses of writers on assignment.
Photos State availability Captions, identification of subjects required. Reviews high resolution, digital images only. Negotiates payment individually. Buys one time rights.
Columns/Departments Query.

PHOTO & IMAGING TRADE NEWS

Yaffa Publishing, 17-21 Bellevue St., Surry Hills NSW 2010 Australia. (61)(2)9281-2333. Fax: (61)(2)9281-2750. E-mail: yaffa@yaffa.com.au. Website: www.yaffa.com.au. Monthly magazine covering product information, news and business ideas for the photo retail industry. *Photo & Imaging Trade News* combines expert industry analysis on all aspects of running a photo business, including new products, marketing, promotions, pricing and the latest trends from overseas. It also publishes exclusive market statistics.
Nonfiction Needs general interest, how-to, interview, new product, technical. Query.

$ $ THE PHOTO REVIEW

140 E. Richardson Ave., Suite 301, Langhorne PA 19047. (215)891-0214. Fax: (215)891-9358. E-mail: info@photoreview.org. Website: www.photoreview.org. **50% freelance written**. Quarterly magazine covering art photography and criticism. "*The Photo Review* publishes critical reviews of photography exhibitions and books, critical essays, and interviews. We do not publish how-to or technical articles." Estab. 1976. Circ. 2,000. Byline given. Pays on publication. No kill fee. Publishes ms an average of 9-12 months after acceptance. Buys first rights. Editorial lead time 3 months. Submit seasonal material 6 months in advance. Accepts queries by mail. Accepts simultaneous submissions. Responds in 2 months to queries. Responds in 3 months to mss. Sample copy for $7. Guidelines for #10 SASE.
Nonfiction Needs interview, photography essay, critical review. No how-to articles. **Buys 20 mss/year.** Send complete ms. 2-20 typed pages **Pays $10-250.**
Reprints "Send tearsheet, photocopy or typed ms with rights for sale noted and information about when and where the material previously appeared." Payment varies.
Photos Send photos Captions required. Reviews contact sheets, transparencies, prints. Offers no additional payment for photos accepted with ms. Buys all rights.

SHUTTERBUG

Primedia, 1419 Chaffee Dr., Suite 1, Titusville FL 32780. Fax: (321)225-3149. E-mail: editorial@shutterbug.com. Website: www.shutterbug.com. **90% freelance written**. Monthly covering photography and digial imaging. Written for the avid amateur, part-time, and full-time professional photographers. Covers equipment techniques, profiles, technology and news in both silver-halide and digital imaging. Estab. 1972. Circ. 90,000. Byline given. Pays on publication. Buys first North American serial rights, buys second serial (reprint) rights, buys electronic rights. Editorial lead time 3 months. Submit seasonal material 6 months in advance. Accepts queries by mail, e-mail. Responds in 1 month to queries. Responds in 1 month to mss.
Nonfiction Query. Length: 1,000-1,500 words. **Payment rate depends on published length, including photographs**
Photos Send photos Captions, model releases required. Reviews contact sheets, transparencies, CD-ROMs. Offers no additional payment for photos

REAL ESTATE

$ $ AREA DEVELOPMENT MAGAZINE

Sites and Facility Planning, Halcyon Business Publications, Inc., 400 Post Ave., Westbury NY 11590. (516)338-

0900, ext. 211. Fax: (516)338-0100. E-mail: gerri@areadevelopment.com. Website: www.areadevelopment.com. **80% freelance written. Prefers to work with published/established writers.** Bimonthly magazine covering corporate facility planning and site selection for industrial chief executives worldwide. Estab. 1965. Circ. 45,000. Byline given. Pays on publication. No kill fee. Publishes ms an average of 2 months after acceptance. Buys all rights. Accepts queries by mail, e-mail, fax. Responds in 3 months to queries. Sample copy free. Guidelines for #10 sase.

Nonfiction Related areas of site selection and facility planning such as taxes, labor, government, energy, architecture, and finance. Needs historical, if it deals with corporate facility planning, how-to, experiences in site selection and all other aspects of corporate facility planning, interview, corporate executives and industrial developers. **Buys 75 mss/year.** Query. Length: 1,500-2,000 words. **Pays 40¢/word.** Sometimes pays expenses of writers on assignment.

Photos State availability Captions, identification of subjects required. Reviews JPEGS of at least 300 dpi . Negotiates payment individually.

AUSTRALIAN PROPERTY INVESTOR

Australian Commercial Publishing, Ltd., P.O. Box 1434, Toowong Business Centre QLD 4066 Australia. (61)(7)3720-9422. Fax: (61)(7)3720-9322. E-mail: editor@apimagazine.com.au. Website: www.apimagazine.com.au. Monthly magazine covering issues of importance to Australian property investors.

Nonfiction Needs general interest, how-to, inspirational, interview, technical. Query.

$ $ CANADIAN PROPERTY MANAGEMENT

Mediaedge Communications Inc., 5255 Yonge St., Suite 1000, Toronto ON M2N 6P4 Canada. (416)512-8186. Fax: (416)512-8344. E-mail: claret@mediaedge.ca. Website: www.mediaedge.ca. **10% freelance written.** Magazine published 8 times/year covering Canadian commercial, industrial, institutional (medical and educational), residential properties. *Canadian Property Management* magazine is a trade journal supplying building owners and property managers with Canadian industry news, case law reviews, technical updates for building operations and events listings. Building and professional profile articles are regular features. Estab. 1985. Circ. 14,500. Byline given. Pays on publication. No kill fee. Publishes ms an average of 3 months after acceptance. Buys all rights. Editorial lead time 2 months. Submit seasonal material 2 months in advance. Accepts queries by mail, e-mail, fax, phone. Accepts simultaneous submissions. Responds in 3 weeks to queries. Responds in 2 months to mss. Sample copy for $5, subject to availability. Guidelines free.

Nonfiction Needs interview, technical. No promotional articles (i.e., marketing a product or service geared to this industry)! Query with published clips. Length: 700-1,200 words. **Pays 35¢/word.**

Photos State availability Captions, identification of subjects, model releases required. Reviews transparencies, 3x5 prints, digital (at least 300 dpi). Offers no additional payment for photos accepted with ms

Tips We do not accept promotional articles serving companies or their products. Freelance articles that are strong, information-based pieces that serve the interests and needs of property managers and building owners stand a better chance of being published. Proposals and inquiries with article ideas are appreciated the most. A good understanding of the real estate industry (management structure) is also helpful for the writer.

COMMERCIAL INVESTMENT REAL ESTATE

CCIM, 430 N. Michigan Ave., Suite 800, Chicago IL 60611-4092. (312)321-4460. Fax: (312)321-4530. E-mail: magazine@ccim.com. Website: www.ciremagazine.com. **10% freelance written.** Bimonthly magazine. *CIRE* offers practical articles on current trends and business development ideas for commercial investment real estate practitioners. Estab. 1982. Circ. 17,000. Byline given. Pays on acceptance. No kill fee. Publishes ms an average of 4 months after acceptance. Buys all rights. Editorial lead time 4 months. Submit seasonal material 4 months in advance. Accepts queries by mail, e-mail, fax. Responds in 2 weeks to queries. Responds in 1 month to mss. Sample copy available online. Guidelines available online.

Nonfiction Needs how-to, technical, business strategies. **Buys 3-4 mss/year.** Query with published clips. Length: 1,800-3,000 words. **Pays .**

Photos May ask writers to have sources. Send images to editors.

Tips Always query first with a detailed outline and published clips. Authors should have a background in writing on business or real estate subjects.

$ $ THE COOPERATOR

The Co-op and Condo Monthly, Yale Robbins, Inc., 102 Madison Ave., 5th Floor, New York NY 10016. (212)683-5700. Fax: (646)405-9768. E-mail: editorial@cooperator.com. Website: www.cooperator.com. **70% freelance written.** Monthly tabloid covering real estate in the New York City metro area. *The Cooperator* covers condominium and cooperative issues in New York and beyond. It is read by condo unit owners and co-op shareholders, real estate professionals, board members and managing agents, and other service professionals. Estab. 1980. Circ. 40,000. Byline given. Pays on publication. No kill fee. Publishes ms an average of 3 months after acceptance. Buys all rights. Makes work-for-hire assignments. Submit seasonal material 3 months in advance. Accepts queries by mail, e-mail, fax. Responds in 1 month to queries. Sample copy and writer's guidelines free.

Nonfiction All articles related to co-op and condo ownership. Needs interview, new product, personal experience. No submissions without queries. Query with published clips. Length: 1,500-2,000 words. **Pays $325-425.** Sometimes pays expenses of writers on assignment.

Photos State availability

Columns/Departments Profiles of co-op/condo-related businesses with something unique; Building Finance (investment and financing issues); Buying and Selling (market issues, etc.); Design (architectural and interior/exterior design, lobby renovation, etc.); Building Maintenance (issues related to maintaining interior/exterior, facades, lobbies, elevators, etc.); Legal Issues Related to Co-Ops/Condos; Real Estate Trends, all 1,500 words. 100 Query with published clips.

Tips You must have experience in business, legal, or financial. Must have published clips to send in with resume and query.

$ $ FLORIDA REALTOR MAGAZINE

Florida Association of Realtors, 7025 Augusta National Dr., Orlando FL 32822-5017. (407)438-1400. Fax: (407)438-1411. E-mail: flrealtor@far.org. Website: floridarealtormagazine.com. **Contact:** Doug Damerst, editor-in-chief. **70% freelance written.** Journal published 11 times/year covering the Florida real estate profession. "As the official publication of the Florida Association of Realtors, we provide helpful articles for our 125,000 members. We report new practices that lead to successful real estate careers and stay up on the trends and issues that affect business in Florida's real estate market." Estab. 1925. Circ. 112,205. Byline given. Pays on publication. No kill fee. Publishes ms an average of 2 months after acceptance. Buys one-time rights, buys electronic rights. Editorial lead time 3 months. Accepts queries by mail, e-mail, fax. Sample copy available online.

Nonfiction Book excerpts, how-to, inspirational, interview/profile, "new product—all with a real estate angle. Florida-specific is good." No fiction or poetry. **Buys varying number of mss/year.** Query with published clips. Length: 800-1,500 words. **Pays $500-700.** Sometimes pays expenses of writers on assignment.

Photos State availability Captions, identification of subjects, model releases required. Negotiates payment individually. Buys one-time print rights and internet use rights.

Columns/Departments Some written in-house: Know the Law, 900 words; Market It, 900 words; Technology & You, 1,000 words; ManageIt, 900 words. varying number of **Payment varies.**

Tips "Build a solid reputation for specializing in real estate business writing in state/national publications. Query with specific article ideas."

NATIONAL RELOCATION & REAL ESTATE

RIS Media, 50 Water St., Norwalk CT 06854. (203)855-1234. Fax: (203)852-7208. E-mail: maria@rismedia.com. Website: rismedia.com. **10-30% freelance written.** Monthly magazine covering residential real estate and corporate relocation. Our readers are professionals within the relocation and real estate industries; therefore, we require our writers to have sufficient knowledge of the workings of these industries in order to ensure depth and accuracy in reporting. Estab. 1980. Circ. 45,000. Byline usually given. Pays on acceptance. Offers kill fee. Buys all rights. Editorial lead time 2 months. Accepts queries by mail, e-mail. Responds in 2 weeks to queries. Sample copy free.

Nonfiction Needs expose, how-to, use the Internet to sell real estate, etc., interview, new product, opinion, technical. Query with published clips. Length: 250-1,200 words. Sometimes pays expenses of writers on assignment.

Photos Prefers digital media via e-mail. Send photos Captions required. Reviews transparencies. Offers no additional payment for photos accepted with ms.

Columns/Departments Query with published clips.

Tips All queries must be done in writing. Phone queries are unacceptable. Any clips or materials sent should indicate knowledge of the real estate and relocation industries. In general, we are open to all knowledgeable contributors.

$ $ OFFICE BUILDINGS MAGAZINE

Yale Robbins, Inc., 102 Madison Ave., New York NY 10016. (212)683-5700. Fax: (212)545-0764. Website: www.officebuildingsmagazine.com. **15% freelance written.** Annual magazine covering market statistics, trends, and thinking of area professionals on the current and future state of the real estate market. Estab. 1987. Circ. 10,500. Byline sometimes given. Pays 1 month after publication. Offers kill fee. Buys all rights. Editorial lead time 2 months. Accepts queries by mail, e-mail, fax. Sample copy and writer's guidelines free.

Nonfiction Survey of specific markets. **Buys 15-20 mss/year.** Query with published clips. Length: 1,500-2,000 words. **Pays $600-700.** Sometimes pays expenses of writers on assignment.

$ $ PROPERTIES MAGAZINE

Properties Magazine, Inc., P.O. Box 112127, Cleveland OH 44111. (216)251-0035. Fax: (216)251-0064. E-mail: kkrych@propertiesmag.com. **25% freelance written.** Monthly magazine covering real estate, residential, commerical construction. *Properties Magazine* is published for executives in the real estate, building, banking, design, architectural, property management, tax, and law community—busy people who need the facts presented in an interesting and informative format. Estab. 1946. Circ. over 10,000. Byline given. Pays on publication. No kill fee. Publishes ms an average of 2 months after acceptance. Buys first rights. Editorial lead time 2 months. Submit seasonal material 2 months in advance. Accepts queries by mail, fax. Responds in 3 weeks to queries. Sample copy for $3.95.

Nonfiction Needs general interest, how-to, humor, new product. Environmental issues (September); Security/Fire Protection (October); Tax Issues (November); Computers In Real Estate (December). **Buys 30 mss/year.** Send complete ms. Length: 500-2,000 words. **Pays 50¢/column line.** Sometimes pays expenses of writers on assignment.

Photos Send photos Captions required. Reviews prints. Offers no additional payment for photos accepted with ms. Negotiates payment individually. Buys one time rights.

Columns/Departments 25 Query or send complete ms. **Pays 50¢/column line.**

$ $ REM

The Real Estate Magazine, 2255 B #1178 Queen St. East, Toronto ON M4E 1G3 Canada. (416)425-3504. E-mail: jim@remonline.com. Website: www.remonline.com. **35% freelance written**. Monthly trade journal covering real estate. *REM* provides Canadian real estate agents and brokers with news and opinions they can't get anywhere else. It is an independent publication and not affiliated with any real estate board, association, or company. Estab. 1989. Circ. 45,000. Pays on acceptance. Offers 25% kill fee. Publishes ms an average of 2 months after acceptance. Buys first Canadian serial rights and and rights to use on the REM web site. Editorial lead time 3 months. Submit seasonal material 3 months in advance. Accepts queries by mail, e-mail, fax. Accepts previously published material. Accepts simultaneous submissions. Sample copy free.

Nonfiction Needs book excerpts, expose, inspirational, interview, new product, personal experience. "No articles geared to consumers about market conditions or how to choose a realtor. Must have Canadian content." **Buys 60 mss/year.** Query. Length: 500-1,500 words. **Pays $200-400.**

Photos Send photos Captions, identification of subjects required. Reviews transparencies, prints, GIF/JPEG files. Offers $25/photo. Buys one time rights.

Tips "Stories must be of interest or practical use for Canadian realtors. Check out our website to see the types of stories we require."

$ $ ZONING PRACTICE

American Planning Association, 122 S. Michigan Ave., Suite 1600, Chicago IL 60603-6107. (312)431-9100. Fax: (312)431-9985. E-mail: zoningpractice@planning.org. Website: www.planning.org/zoningpractice/index.htm. **90% freelance written**. Monthly newsletter covering land-use regulations including zoning. "Our publication is aimed at practicing urban planners and those involved in land-use decisions, such as zoning administrators and officials, planning commissioners, zoning boards of adjustment, land-use attorneys, developers, and others interested in this field. The material we publish must come from writers knowledgeable about zoning and subdivision regulations, preferably with practical experience in the field. We do not need to hear from people who simply have opinions about zoning. Anything we publish needs to be of practical value to our audience in their everyday work." Estab. 1984. Circ. 2,900. Byline given. Pays on publication. Offers 50% kill fee. Publishes ms an average of 3 months after acceptance. Buys all rights. Editorial lead time 6 months. Accepts queries by mail, e-mail, fax, phone. Responds in 2 weeks to queries. Responds in 1 month to mss. Sample copy free. www.planning.org/zoningpractice/contribguidelines.htm

Nonfiction Needs technical. "See our description. We do not need general or consumer-interest articles about zoning because this publication is aimed at practitioners." **Buys 12 mss/year. mss/year.** Query. Length: 3,000-5,000 words. **Pays $300 min. for assigned articles.** Sometimes pays expenses of writers on assignment.

Photos State availability Captions required. Reviews GIF/JPEG files. Negotiates payment individually. Buys all rights.

Tips "Breaking in is easy if you know the subject matter and can write in plain English for practicing planners. We are always interested in finding new authors. We generally expect authors will earn another $200 premium for participating in an online forum called, Ask the Author, in which they respond to questions from readers about their article. This requires a deep practical sense of how to make things work with regard to your topic."

RESOURCES & WASTE REDUCTION

$ $ COMPOSTING NEWS

The Latest News in Composting and Scrap Wood Management, McEntee Media Corp., 9815 Hazelwood Ave., Cleveland OH 44149. (440)238-6603. Fax: (440)238-6712. E-mail: ken@recycle.cc. **5% freelance written**. Monthly newsletter. We are interested in any news impacting the composting industry including new laws, regulations, new facilities/programs, end-uses, research, etc. Estab. 1992. Circ. 1,000. Pays on publication.

No kill fee. Publishes ms an average of 1 month after acceptance. Buys first rights, buys all rights. Editorial lead time 1 month. Submit seasonal material 1 month in advance. Accepts queries by mail, e-mail, fax, phone. Accepts previously published material. Accepts simultaneous submissions. Responds in 2 months to queries. Sample copy for 9x12 SAE and 55¢ postage. Guidelines for #10 sase.
Nonfiction Needs book excerpts, essays, general interest, how-to, interview, new product, opinion, personal experience, photo feature, technical, new business, legislation, regulation, business expansion. **Buys 0-5 mss/year.** Query with published clips. Length: 100-5,000 words. **Pays $10-500.**
Columns/Departments Query with published clips. **Pays $10-500.**
Tips We appreciate leads on local news regarding composting, i.e., new facilities or business, new laws and regulations, unique programs, situations that impact supply and demand for composting. International developments are also of interest.

$ $ $ EROSION CONTROL

The Journal for Erosion and Sediment Control Professionals, Forester Communications, Inc., 2946 De La Vina St., Santa Barbara CA 93105. (805)682-1300. Fax: (805)682-0200. E-mail: eceditor@forester.net. Website: www.erosioncontrol.com. **60% freelance written**. Magazine published 7 times/year covering all aspects of erosion prevention and sediment control. "*Erosion Control* is a practical, hands-on, `how-to' professional journal. Our readers are civil engineers, landscape architects, builders, developers, public works officials, road and highway construction officials and engineers, soils specialists, farmers, landscape contractors, and others involved with any activity that disturbs significant areas of surface vegetation." Estab. 1994. Circ. 20,000. Byline given. Pays 1 month after acceptance. No kill fee. Publishes ms an average of 3 months after acceptance. Buys all rights. Editorial lead time 4 months. Submit seasonal material 4 months in advance. Accepts queries by mail, e-mail, fax, phone. Responds in 3 weeks to queries. Sample copy and writer's guidelines free.
Nonfiction Needs photo feature, technical. **Buys 15 mss/year.** Query with published clips. Length: 3,000-4,000 words. **Pays $700-850.** Sometimes pays expenses of writers on assignment.
Photos Send photos Captions, identification of subjects, model releases required. Reviews transparencies, prints. Offers no additional payment for photos accepted with ms. Buys all rights.
Tips "Writers should have a good grasp of technology involved and good writing and communication skills. Most of our freelance articles include extensive interviews with engineers, contractors, developers, or project owners, and we often provide contact names for articles we assign."

$ $ MSW MANAGEMENT

The Journal for Municipal Solid Waste Professionals, Forester Communications, Inc., P.O. Box 3100, Santa Barbara CA 93130. (805)682-1300. Fax: (805)682-0200. E-mail: editor@forester.net. Website: www.mswmanagement.com. **Contact:** John Trotti, group editor. **70% freelance written**. Bimonthly magazine. "*MSW Management* is written for public sector solid waste professionals—the people working for the local counties, cities, towns, boroughs, and provinces. They run the landfills, recycling programs, composting, incineration. They are responsible for all aspects of garbage collection and disposal; buying and maintaining the associated equipment; and designing, engineering, and building the waste processing facilities, transfer stations, and landfills." Estab. 1991. Circ. 25,000. Byline given. Pays 30 days after acceptance No kill fee. Buys all rights. Editorial lead time 4 months. Submit seasonal material 4 months in advance. Accepts queries by mail, e-mail, fax, phone. Accepts simultaneous submissions. Responds in 6 weeks to queries. Responds in 2 months to mss. Sample copy and writer's guidelines free. Guidelines available online.
Nonfiction Needs photo feature, technical. "No rudimentary, basic articles written for the average person on the street. Our readers are experienced professionals with years of practical, in-the-field experience. Any material submitted that we judge as too fundamental will be rejected." **Buys 15 mss/year.** Query. Length: 3,000-4,000 words. **Pays $350-750.** Sometimes pays expenses of writers on assignment.
Photos Send photos Captions, identification of subjects, model releases required. Reviews transparencies, prints. Offers no additional payment for photos accepted with ms. Buys all rights.
Tips "We're a small company, easy to reach. We're open to any and all ideas as to possible editorial topics. We endeavor to provide the reader with usable material, and present it in full color with graphic embellishment whenever possible. Dry, highly technical material is edited to make it more palatable and concise. Most of our feature articles come from freelancers. Interviews and quotes should be from public sector solid waste managers and engineers—not PR people, not manufacturers. Strive to write material that is `over the heads' of our readers. If anything, attempt to make them `reach.' Anything submitted that is too basic, elementary, fundamental, rudimentary, etc., cannot be accepted for publication."

$ $ $ STORMWATER

The Journal for Surface Water Quality Professionals, Forester Communications, Inc., 2946 De La Vina St., Santa Barbara CA 93105. (805)682-1300. Fax: (805)682-0200. E-mail: sweditor@forester.net. Website: www.stormh2o.com. **10% freelance written**. Magazine published 8 times/year. "*Stormwater* is a practical business journal for professionals involved with surface water quality issues, protection, projects, and programs. Our readers are municipal employees, regulators, engineers, and consultants concerned with stormwater management."

Estab. 2000. Circ. 20,000. Byline given. Pays 1 month after acceptance. No kill fee. Publishes ms an average of 3 months after acceptance. Editorial lead time 4 months. Submit seasonal material 4 months in advance. Accepts queries by mail, e-mail. Responds in 3 weeks to queries. Guidelines free.

Nonfiction Needs technical. **Buys 8-10 mss/year.** Query with published clips. Length: 3,000-4,000 words. **Pays $700-850.** Sometimes pays expenses of writers on assignment.

Photos Send photos Captions, identification of subjects, model releases required. Offers no additional payment for photos accepted with ms. Buys all rights.

Tips "Writers should have a good grasp of the technology and regulations involved in stormwater management and good interviewing skills. Our freelance articles include extensive interviews with engineers, stormwater managers, and project owners, and we often provide contact names for articles we assign. See past editorial content online."

WASTE AGE MAGAZINE

The Business Magazine For Waste Industry Professionals, Intertec Publishing, 6151 Powers Ferry Rd. NW, Atlanta GA 30339-2941. (770)618-0310. Fax: (770)618-0349. E-mail: ptom@primediabusiness.com. **50% freelance written**. Monthly magazine. *Waste Age* reaches individuals and firms engaged in the removal, collection, processing, transportation, and disposal of solid/hazardous liquid wastes. This includes: private refuse contractors; landfill operators; municipal, county, and other government officials; recyclers and handlers of secondary materials; major generators of waste, such as plants and chain stores; engineers, architects, and consultants; manufactures and distributors of equipment; universities, libraries, and associations; and legal, insurance, and financial firms allied to the field. Readers include: owners, presidents, vice-presidents, directors, superintendents, engineers, managers, supervisors, consultants, purchasing agents, and commissioners. Estab. 1958. Circ. 40,000. Byline given. Pays on publication. No kill fee. Publishes ms an average of 4 months after acceptance. Editorial lead time 2 months. Responds in 1 week to queries. Responds in 1 month to mss. Sample copy free. Guidelines free.

Nonfiction Needs how-to, practical information on improving solid waste management, i.e., how-to rehabilitate a transfer station, how-to improve recyclable collection, how-to manage a landfill, etc., interview, of prominent persons in the solid waste industry. No feel-good 'green' articles about recycling. Remember our readers are not the citizens but the governments and private contractors. No 'why you should recycle' articles. **Buys over 50 mss/year.** Query. Length: 500-2,000 words. Pays expenses of writers on assignment.

Photos Send photos Identification of subjects required. Reviews contact sheets, negatives, transparencies, prints, digital. Negotiates payment individually.

Tips Read the magazine and understand our audience. Write useful articles with sidebars that the readers can apply to their jobs. Use the Associated Press style book. Freelancers can send in queries or manuscripts, or can fax or e-mail a letter of interest (including qualifications/resume) in possible assignments. Writers must be deadline-oriented.

$ $ WATER WELL JOURNAL

National Ground Water Association, 601 Dempsey Rd., Westerville OH 43081. Fax: (614)898-7786. Website: www.ngwa.org. **25% freelance written**. Monthly magazine covering the ground water industry; well drilling. Each month the *Water Well Journal* covers the topics of drilling, rigs and heavy equipment, pumping systems, water quality, business management, water supply, on-site waste water treatment, and diversification opportunities, including geothermal installations, environmental remediation, irrigation, dewatering, and foundation installation. It also offers updates on regulatory issues that impact the ground water industry. Estab. 1948. Circ. 25,000. Byline given. Pays on publication. No kill fee. Publishes ms an average of 3 months after acceptance. Buys all rights. Editorial lead time 6 weeks. Submit seasonal material 3 months in advance. Accepts queries by mail. Responds in 2 weeks to queries. Responds in 1 month to mss. Guidelines free.

Nonfiction Needs essays, sometimes, historical, sometimes, how-to, recent examples include how-to chlorinate a well; how-to buy a used rig; how-to do bill collections, interview, new product, personal experience, photo feature, technical, business management. No company profiles or extended product releases. **Buys up to 30 mss/year.** Query with published clips. Length: 1,000-3,000 words. **Pays $150-400.**

Photos State availability Captions, identification of subjects required. Offers $50-250/photo

Tips "Some previous experience or knowledge in groundwater/drilling/construction industry helpful. Published clips are a must."

SELLING & MERCHANDISING

$ THE AMERICAN SALESMAN

National Research Bureau, 320 Valley St., Burlington IA 52601. (319)752-5415. E-mail: national@willinet.net (articles@salestrainingandtechniques.com). Website: www.national-research-bureau.com. www.salestrainingandtechniques.com. **80% freelance written**. Monthly magazine covering sales and marketing. *The American Salesman Magazine* is designed for sales professionals. Its primary objective is to provide informative articles which develop the attitudes, skills, personal and professional qualities of sales representatives, allowing them to use more of their potential to increase productivity and achieve goals. Byline given. Publishes ms an average of 1 month after acceptance. Buys all rights. Editorial lead time 1 month. Submit seasonal material 2 months in advance. Accepts queries by e-mail. Sample copy free. Guidelines by email.

Nonfiction Needs personal experience. **Buys 24 mss/year.** Send complete ms. Length: 500-1,000 words. **Pays 4¢/word.**

APPLIANCE RETAILER

The Intermedia Group, Ltd., P.O. Box 55, Glebe NSW 2037 Australia. (61)(2)9660-2113. Fax: (61)(2)9660-4419. E-mail: info@intermedia.com.au. Website: www.intermedia.com.au. Monthly magazine covering industry events and issues as well as in depth product features and category reviews. *Appliance Retailer* is the leading trade magazine for the Australian electrical appliance industry servicing manufacturers and retailers of portable appliances, audio visual equipment, whitegoods as well as heating and cooling products.

- Query before submitting.

AUSTRALIAN GIFTGUIDE

The Intermedia Group, Ltd., Unit 39, 100 Harris St., Pyrmont NSW 2009 Australia. (61)(2)9660-2113. Fax: (61)(2)9660-4419. E-mail: marion@intermedia.com.au. Website: www.intermedia.com.au. Quarterly magazine covering the very latest products, trends, industry news and trade fairs around the world. *Australian Giftguide* magazine has been serving the gift and homewares industry for 30 years and is widely regarded as 'the bible of the trade.' It is recognized as an essential business tool by tens of thousands of gift and homewares retailers throughout Australia and New Zealand.

Nonfiction Needs general interest. Query.

$ $ BALLOONS AND PARTIES MAGAZINE

Partilife Publications, 65 Sussex St., Hackensack NJ 07601. (201)441-4224. Fax: (201)342-8118. E-mail: mark@balloonsandparties.com. Website: www.balloonsandparties.com. **10% freelance written**. International trade journal published 4 times/year for professional party decorators and gift delivery businesses. Estab. 1986. Circ. 7,000. Byline given. Pays on publication. No kill fee. Publishes ms an average of 3 months after acceptance. Buys all rights. Submit seasonal material 6 months in advance. Accepts queries by mail, e-mail, fax, phone. Responds in 6 weeks to queries. Sample copy for sae with 9x12 envelope.

Nonfiction Needs essays, how-to, interview, new product, personal experience, photo feature, technical, craft. **Buys 12 mss/year.** Send complete ms. Length: 500-1,500 words. **Pays $100-300 for assigned articles. Pays $50-200 for unsolicited articles.** Sometimes pays expenses of writers on assignment.

Reprints Send typed manuscript with rights for sale noted and information about when and where the material previously appeared. Length: up to 2,500 words. Pays 10¢/word.

Photos Send photos Captions, identification of subjects, model releases required. Reviews 2—Š2 transparencies, 3—Š5 prints. Buys all rights.

Columns/Departments Problem Solver (small business issues); Recipes That Cook (centerpiece ideas with detailed how-to), 400-1,000 words. Send complete ms with photos.

Tips Show unusual, lavish, and outstanding examples of balloon sculpture, design and decorating, and other craft projects. Offer specific how-to information. Be positive and motivational in style.

C&I RETAILING

Berg Bennett, Ltd., Suite 6, The Atrium, 340 Darling St., Balmain NSW 2041 Australia. (61)(2)9555-1355. Fax: (61)(2)9555-1434. E-mail: magazine@c-store.com.au. Website: www.c-store.com.au. "Bimonthly magazine covering retail store layout, consumer packaged goods, forecourt, impulse retailing as well as convenience food.". Circ. 20,431.

Nonfiction Needs general interest, how-to, new product, industry news. Query.

$ $ CASUAL LIVING MAGAZINE

Voice of the Leisure Market, Reed Business Information, 7025 Albert Pick Rd., Suite 200, Greensboro NC 27409-9519. (336)605-1122. Fax: (336)605-1158. E-mail: cwingram@reedbusiness.com. Website: www.casualliving.com. **10% freelance written**. Monthly magazine covering outdoor furniture and accessories, barbecue grills, spas and more. We write about new products, trends and casual furniture retailers plus industry news. Estab. 1958. Circ. 10,000. Pays on publication. Publishes ms an average of 1-2 months after acceptance. Buys all rights. Editorial lead time 1-2 months. Submit seasonal material 2 months in advance. Accepts queries by mail, e-mail. Responds in 2 weeks to queries. Sample copy available online.

Nonfiction Needs how-to, interview. **Buys 20 mss/year.** Query with published clips. Length: 300-1,000 words. **Pays $300-700.** Sometimes pays expenses of writers on assignment.

Photos Contact: Courtney Paschal, associate editor. Identification of subjects required. Reviews GIF/JPEG files. Negotiates payment individually. Buys all rights.

$ $ $ $ CONSUMER GOODS TECHNOLOGY

Edgell Communications, 4 Middlebury Blvd., Randolph NJ 07869. (973)252-0100. Fax: (973)252-9020. E-mail: tclark@edgellmail.com. Website: www.consumergoods.com. **40% freelance written**. Monthly tabloid benchmarking business technology performance. Estab. 1987. Circ. 25,000. Byline given. Pays on publication. No kill fee. Publishes ms an average of 2 months after acceptance. Buys first North American serial rights, buys second serial (reprint) rights, buys electronic rights, buys all rights. Editorial lead time 3 months. Accepts queries by e-mail. Sample copy available online. Guidelines by email.

Nonfiction We create several supplements annually, often using freelance. Needs essays, expose, interview. **Buys 60 mss/year.** Query with published clips. Length: 700-1,900 words. **Pays $600-1,200.** Sometimes pays expenses of writers on assignment.

Photos Identification of subjects, model releases required. Negotiates payment individually. Buys all rights.

Columns/Departments Columns 400-750 words—featured columnists. 4 Query with published clips. **Pays 75¢-$1/word**

Tips All stories in *Consumer Goods Technology* are told through the voice of the consumer goods executive. We only quote VP-level or C-level CG executives. No vendor quotes. We're always on the lookout for freelance talent. We look in particular for writers with an in-depth understanding of the business issues faced by consumer goods firms and the technologies that are used by the industry to address those issues successfully. 'Bits and bytes' tech writing is not sought; our focus is on benchmarketing the business technology performance of CG firms, CG executives, CG vendors, and CG vendor products. Our target reader is tech-savvy, CG C-level decision maker. We write to, and about, our target reader.

$ $ CONVENIENCE STORE DECISIONS

Penton Media, Inc., Two Greenwood Square, #410, Bensalem PA 19020. (215)245-4555. Fax: (215)245-4060. E-mail: jgordon@penton.com. Website: www.c-storedecisions.com. **15-20% freelance written**. Monthly magazine covering convenience retail/petroleum marketing. *CSD* is received by top-level executives in the convenience retail and petroleum marketing industry. Writers should have knowledge of the industry and the subjects it encompasses. Estab. 1990. Circ. 42,000. Byline given. Pays on publication. No kill fee. Buys all rights. Makes work-for-hire assignments. Editorial lead time 2-4 months. Submit seasonal material 3 months in advance. Accepts queries by mail, e-mail, fax. Accepts simultaneous submissions. Responds in 3 weeks to queries. Sample copy and writer's guidelines free.

Nonfiction Needs interview, retailers, photo feature, technical. No self-serving, vendor-based stories. **Buys 12-15 mss/year.** Query with published clips. Length: 400-2,000 words. **Pays $200-600 for assigned articles.** Sometimes pays expenses of writers on assignment.

Photos State availability Identification of subjects required. Negotiates payment individually. Buys all rights.

Tips Offer experience. We get queries from freelancers daily. We are looking for writers with industry experience. We need real-life, retailer-based work. Bring us a story.

$ $ COUNTRY SAMPLER'S COUNTRY BUSINESS

The Magazine for Retailers of Country Gifts and Accessories, Emmis Publishing LP, 707 Kautz Rd., St. Charles IL 60174. (630)377-8000. Fax: (630)377-8194. E-mail: cbiz@sampler.emmis.com. Website: www.countrybusiness.com. **50% freelance written**. Magazine published 7 times/year covering independent retail, gift and home decor. *Country Business* is a trade publication for independent retailers of gifts and home accents. Estab. 1993. Circ. 32,000. Byline given. Pays 1 month after acceptance of final ms. Offers $50 kill fee. Publishes ms an average of 4-6 months after acceptance. Buys all rights. Editorial lead time 4-6 months. Submit seasonal material 8-10 months in advance. Accepts queries by mail, e-mail, fax. Accepts previously published material. Accepts simultaneous submissions. Usually responds in 4-6 weeks (only if accepted). Sample articles are available on website Guidelines by email.

Nonfiction Needs how-to, pertaining to retail, interview, new product, finance, legal, marketing, small business. No fiction, poetry, fillers, photos, artwork, or profiles of businesses, unless queried and first assigned. **Buys 20 mss/year.** Send complete ms. Length: 1,000-2,500 words. **Pays $275-500 for assigned articles. Pays $200-350 for unsolicited articles.** Sometimes pays expenses of writers on assignment. Limit agreed upon in advance

Columns/Departments Display & Design (store design and product display), 1,500 words; Retailer Profile (profile of retailer—assigned only), 1,800 words; Vendor Profile (profile of manufacturer—assigned only), 1,200 words; Technology (Internet, computer-related articles as applies to small retailers), 1,500 words; Marketing (marketing ideas and advice as applies to small retailers), 1,500 words; Finance (financial tips and advice as applies to small retailers), 1,500 words; Legal (legal tips and advice as applies to small retailers), 1,500 words; Employees (tips and advice on hiring, firing, and working with employees as applies to small retailers), 1,500 words. 15 Query with published clips or send complete ms. **Pays $250-350.**

$ $ $ $ DIRECT SELLING NEWS

Video Plus, 200 Swisher Rd., Lake Dallas TX 75067. E-mail: nlaichas@directsellingnews.com. Website: www.directsellingnews.com. **20% freelance written**. Monthly magazine covering direct selling/network marketing industry. Though we are a business publication, we prefer feature-style writing rather than a newsy approach.

Circ. 6,000. Byline given. Pays 30 days after publication. Publishes ms an average of 1-2 months after acceptance. Makes work-for-hire assignments. Editorial lead time 3 months. Submit seasonal material 3 months in advance. Accepts queries by e-mail. Responds in 3 weeks to queries. Sample copy available online.
Nonfiction Needs general interest, how-to. Query. Length: 1,500-3,000 words. **Pays 50¢-$1/word.**

$ EVENTS MEDIA NETWORK, INC.

P.O. Box 1132, Medford NJ 08055. (609)953-9544. Fax: (609)953-2010. **20% freelance written**. Bimonthly magazine covering special events across North America, including festivals, fairs, auto shows, home shows, trade shows, etc., and attractions including museums, amusement parks, and zoos. Covers 15 categories of shows/events. Byline given. No kill fee. Buys first rights. Submit seasonal material 3 months in advance. Accepts queries by mail. Sample copy and writer's guidelines free.
Nonfiction Needs how-to, interview, new product, event review. Annual special event directory, covering over 38,000 events No submissions unrelated to selling at events. Query. Length: 400-750 words. **Pays $2.50/column inch.**
Reprints Send photocopy of article and information about when and where the article previously appeared.
Photos Send photos Captions required. Reviews contact sheets. Offers $20/photo. Buys one time rights.
Columns/Departments Five columns monthly (dealing with background of event, special events, and attractions, or unique facets of industry in North America). Length: 250-500 words. Query with published clips. **Pays $3/column inch.**

$ $ GIFTWARE NEWS

Talcott Corp., 20 W. Kinzie, 12th Floor, Chicago IL 60610. (312)849-2220. Fax: (312)849-2174. **20% freelance written**. Monthly magazine covering gifts, collectibles, and tabletops for giftware retailers. Estab. 1976. Circ. 35,000. Byline given. Pays on publication. No kill fee. Publishes ms an average of 2 months after acceptance. Buys all rights. Submit seasonal material 6 months in advance. Responds in 2 months to mss. Sample copy for $8.
Nonfiction Needs how-to, sell, display, new product. **Buys 20 mss/year.** Send complete ms. Length: 1,500-2,000 words. **Pays $400-500 for assigned articles. Pays $200-300 for unsolicited articles.**
Photos Send photos Identification of subjects required. Reviews 4x5 transparencies, 5x7 prints, electronic images. Offers no additional payment for photos accepted with ms.
Columns/Departments Stationery, giftbaskets, collectibles, holiday, merchandise, tabletop, wedding market and display—all for the gift retailer. Length: 1,500-2,500 words. 10 Send complete ms. **Pays $100 250.**
Tips We are not looking so much for general journalists but rather experts in particular fields who can also write.

🌐 GREETINGS & GIFTS

Yaffa Publishing, 17-21 Bellevue St., Surry Hills NSW 2010 Australia. (61)(2)9281-2333. Fax: (61)(2)9281-2750. E-mail: alisonleader@yaffa.com.au. Website: www.yaffa.com.au. Bimonthly magazine for owners and managers of gift and specialist greeting card shops.
Nonfiction Needs general interest, how-to, interview, new product, technical. Query.

🌐 MHD

Supply Chain Solutions, The Intermedia Group, Ltd., P.O. Box 55, Glebe NSW 2037 Australia. (61)(2)9660-2113. Fax: (61)(2)9660-4419. E-mail: charles@intermedia.com.au. Website: www.intermedia.com.au. Bimonthly magazine covering logistic and supply chain management issues. *MHD* contains case studies of innovative applications and technology covering materials planning and scheduling, just-in-time manufacturing, materials handling, order picking and packing, distribution and occupational health and safety.
Nonfiction Needs general interest, how-to, new product, technical. Query.

$ $ NEW AGE RETAILER

2183 Alpine Way, Bellingham WA 98225. (800)463-9243. Fax: (360)676-0932. E-mail: Kathy@newageretailer.com. Website: www.newageretailer.com. **60% freelance written**. Bimonthly magazine for retailers of spiritual and New Age books, music, and giftware. The goal of the articles in *New Age Retailer* is usefulness—we strive to give store owners and managers practical, in-depth information they can begin using immediately. We have 3 categories of articles: retail business methods that give solid information about the various aspects of running an independent store; inventory articles that discuss a particular New Age subject or trend; and education articles that help storeowners and managers gain knowledge and stay current in New Age subjects. Estab. 1987. Circ. 10,000. Byline given. Pays on publication. Offers 10% kill fee. Publishes ms an average of 4 months after acceptance. Buys first North American serial rights, buys second serial (reprint) rights, buys simultaneous rights, buys electronic rights. Editorial lead time 4 months. Submit seasonal material 4 months in advance. Accepts queries by mail, e-mail, fax, phone. Accepts simultaneous submissions. Responds in 1 month to queries. Responds in 2 months to mss. Sample copy for $5. Guidelines available online.
Nonfiction Needs book excerpts, how-to, interview, new product, opinion, personal experience, technical, business principles, spiritual. No self-promotion for writer's company or product. Writer must understand

independent retailing or New Age subjects. **Buys approximately 25 mss/year.** Query with published clips. Length: 2,500-3,500 words. **Pays $150-350 for assigned articles. Pays $100-300 for unsolicited articles.**
Photos State availability of or send photos Captions required. Reviews 2X3 minimum size prints, digital images at 300 dpi. Negotiates payment individually. Buys one time rights.
Tips Describe your expertise in independent retailing or the New Age market and independent retailing. Have an idea for an article ready to pitch. Promise only what you can deliver.

$ $ NICHE

The Magazine For Craft Gallery Retailers, The Rosen Group, 3000 Chestnut Ave., Suite 304, Baltimore MD 21211. (410)889-3093. Fax: (410)243-7089. E-mail: kstewart@rosengrp.com. **80% freelance written**. Quarterly trade magazine for the progressive craft gallery retailer. Each issue includes retail gallery profiles, store design trends, management techniques, financial information, and merchandising strategies for small business owners, as well as articles about craft artists and craft mediums. Estab. 1988. Circ. 25,000. Byline given. Pays on publication. No kill fee. Publishes ms an average of 9 months after acceptance. Buys first North American serial rights. Editorial lead time 9 months. Submit seasonal material 1 year in advance. Accepts queries by mail, e-mail, fax. Responds in 6-8 weeks to queries. Responds in 3 months to mss. Sample copy for $3.
Nonfiction *Niche* is looking for in-depth articles on store security, innovative merchandising/display, design trends, or marketing and promotion. Stories of interest to independent retailers, such as gallery owners, may be submitted. Needs interview, photo feature, articles targeted to independent retailers and small business owners. **Buys 20-28 mss/year.** Query with published clips. **Pays $300-700.** Sometimes pays expenses of writers on assignment.
Photos Send photos Captions required. Reviews transparencies, slides, e-images. Negotiates payment individually.
Columns/Departments Retail Details (short items at the front of the book, general retail information); Artist Profiles (biographies of American Craft Artists); Retail Resources (including book/video/seminar reviews and educational opportunities pertaining to retailers). Query with published clips. **Pays $25-100.**

$ O&A MARKETING NEWS

KAL Publications, Inc., 559 S. Harbor Blvd., Suite A, Anaheim CA 92805. (714)563-9300. Fax: (714)563-9310. E-mail: kathy@kalpub.com. Website: www.kalpub.com. **3% freelance written**. Bimonthly tabloid. *O&A Marketing News* is editorially directed to people engaged in the distribution, merchandising, installation, and servicing of gasoline, oil, TBA, quick lube, carwash, convenience store, alternative fuel, and automotive aftermarket products in the 13 Western states. Estab. 1966. Circ. 7,500. Byline sometimes given. Pays on publication. No kill fee. Publishes ms an average of 2 months after acceptance. Buys first rights, buys electronic rights. Editorial lead time 1 month. Submit seasonal material 1 month in advance. Accepts queries by mail, e-mail, fax. Accepts simultaneous submissions. Responds in 2 months to queries. Responds in 2 months to mss. Sample copy for sae with 9—Š13 envelope and 10 First-Class stamps.
Nonfiction Needs interview, photo feature, industry news. Nothing that doesn't pertain to the petroleum marketing industry in the 13 Western states. **Buys 35 mss/year.** Send complete ms. Length: 100-500 words. **Pays $1.25/column inch.**
Photos State availability of or send photos Captions, identification of subjects required. Reviews contact sheets, 4x6 prints. Offers $5/photo. Buys electronic rights
Columns/Departments Oregon News (petroleum marketing news in state of Oregon) 7 Send complete ms. **Pays $1.25/column inch.**
Fillers Needs gags, short humor. 7 Length: 1-200 words. **Pays per column inch.**
Tips "Seeking Western industry news pertaining to the petroleum marketing industry. It can be something simple—like a new gas station or quick lube opening. News from 'outlying' states such as Montana, Idaho, Wyoming, New Mexico, and Hawaii is always needed—but any timely, topical news-oriented stories will also be considered."

$ $ $ $ OPERATIONS & FULFILLMENT

Primedia, Inc., 11 Riverbend Dr. S., P.O. Box 4949, Stamford CT 06907-2524. (203)358-4106. E-mail: barnn@primediabusiness.com. Website: www.opsandfulfillment.com. **25% freelance written**. Monthly magazine covering catalog/direct mail operations. *Operations & Fulfillment (O&F)* is a monthly publication that offers practical solutions for catalog online, and direct response operations management. The magazine covers such critical areas as material handling, bar coding, facility planning, transportation, call centers, warehouse management, information systems, online fulfillment and human resources. Estab. 1993. Circ. 17,600. Pays on publication. No kill fee. Publishes ms an average of 2 months after acceptance. Buys first North American serial rights. Editorial lead time 2 months. Accepts queries by mail, e-mail, phone. Responds in 1 week to queries. Sample copy and writer's guidelines free.
Nonfiction Needs book excerpts, how-to, interview, new product, technical. **Buys 4-6 mss/year.** Query with published clips. Length: 2,500-3,000 words. **Pays $1,000-1,800.**
Photos In addition to the main article, you must include at least one sidebar of about 400 words that contains a detailed example or case study of how a direct-to-customer catalog company implements or benefits from the

process you're writing about; a check list or set of practical guidelines (i.e., Twelve Ways to Ship Smarter) that describe how to implement what you suggest in the article; supporting materials such as flow charts, graphs, diagrams, illustrations and photographs (these must be clearly labeled and footnoted); and an author biography of no more than 75 words. Send photos Captions, identification of subjects required.

Tips Writers need some knowledge of the direct-to-customer industry. They should be able to deal clearly with highly technical material and provide attention to detail and painstaking research.

PARTY & PAPER RETAILER

P.O. Box 128, Sparta MI 49345. (616)887-9008. Fax: (616)887-2666. Website: www.partypaper.com. **80% freelance written**. Monthly magazine covering every aspect of how to do business better for owners of party and stationery shops. Tips and how-tos on display, marketing, success stories, merchandising, operating costs, e-commerce, retail technology, etc. Estab. 1986. Circ. 20,000. Pays on publication. Offers 15% kill fee. Buys first North American serial rights. Editorial lead time 6 months. Submit seasonal material 6 months in advance. Accepts queries by mail, e-mail, fax. Responds in 2 months to queries. Sample copy for $6.

Nonfiction Needs book excerpts, how-to, (retailing related), new product. No articles written in first person. **Buys 100 mss/year.** Query with published clips. Length: 800-1,500 words. Phone expenses only

Reprints Send tearsheet or photocopy of article and information about when and where the article previously appeared.

Photos State availability Captions, identification of subjects required. Reviews transparencies. Negotiates payment individually. Buys one time rights.

Columns/Departments Shop Talk (successful party/stationery store profile), 1,500 words; Storekeeping (selling, employees, market, running store), 800 words; Cash Flow (anything finance related), 800 words. 30 Query with published clips. **Payment varies.**

🌐 RETAIL TECHNOLOGY

The Intermedia Group, Ltd., P.O. Box 55, Glebe NSW 2037 Australia. (61)(2)9660-2113. Fax: (61)(2)9660-4419. E-mail: Branko@intermedia.com.au. Website: www.intermedia.com.au. Quarterly magazine covering retail technology solutions. *Retail Technology* informs retailers of technology products, services and developments; explains issues and trends in an easy-to-read sytle; and showcases examples of innovative technology at work through retail case studies.

Nonfiction Needs general interest, new product, technical. Query.

$ $ TRAVEL GOODS SHOWCASE

The source for luggage, business cases, and accessories, Travel Goods Association, 5 Vaughn Dr., Suite 105, Princeton NJ 08540. (609)720-1200. Fax: (609)720-0620. E-mail: cathy@travel-goods.org. Website: www.travel-goods.org. **Contact:** Cathy Hays, senior editor. **5-10% freelance written**. Magazine published quarterly covering travel goods, accessories, trends, and new products. "*Travel Goods Showcase* contains articles for retailers, dealers, manufacturers, and suppliers about luggage, business cases, personal leather goods, handbags, and accessories. Special articles report on trends in fashion, promotions, selling and marketing techniques, industry statistics, and other educational and promotional improvements and advancements." Estab. 1975. Circ. 11,000. Byline given. Pays on acceptance. Offers $50 kill fee. Publishes ms an average of 2 months after acceptance. Editorial lead time 3 months. Submit seasonal material 2 months in advance. Accepts queries by mail, e-mail. Responds in 2 weeks to queries. Responds in 1 month to mss. Sample copy and writer's guidelines free.

Nonfiction Needs interview, new product, technical, travel, retailer profiles with photos. No manufacturer profiles. **Buys 3 mss/year.** Query with published clips. Length: 1,200-1,600 words. **Pays $200-400.**

$ $ $ VERTICAL SYSTEMS RESELLER

The news source for channel management, Edgell Communications, Inc., 4 Middlebury Blvd., Suite 1, Randolph NJ 07869. (973)252-0100. Fax: (973)252-9020. E-mail: alorden@edgellmail.com. Website: www.verticalsystemsreseller.com. **60% freelance written**. Monthly journal covering channel strategies that build business. Estab. 1992. Circ. 30,000. Byline given. Pays on acceptance. No kill fee. Publishes ms an average of 2 months after acceptance. Editorial lead time 3 months. Accepts queries by mail, e-mail, fax. Accepts simultaneous submissions. Responds in 2 weeks to queries. Responds in 2 months to mss. Sample copy available online.

Nonfiction Needs interview, opinion, technical, technology/channel issues. **Buys 36 mss/year.** Query with published clips. Length: 1,000-1,700 words. **Pays $200-800 for assigned articles.** Sometimes pays expenses of writers on assignment.

Photos Send photos Identification of subjects, model releases required. Offers no additional payment for photos accepted with ms.

$ $ $ VM+SD

S.T. Media Group International, 407 Gilbert Ave., Cincinnati OH 45202. (513)421-2050. Fax: (513)421-5144. E-mail: steve.kaufman@stmediagroup.com. Website: www.vmsd.com. **10% freelance written**. Monthly magazine covering retailingÃ³store design, store planning, visual merchandising, brand marketing. Our articles need to get behind the story, tell not only what retailers did when building a new store, renovating an existing store, mounting a new in-store merchandise campaign, but also why they did what they did: specific goals, objectives, strategic initiatives, problems to solve, target markets to reach, etc. Estab. 1872. Circ. 20,000. Byline given. Pays on acceptance. Offers $100 kill fee. Publishes ms an average of 1-2 months after acceptance. Buys all rights. Editorial lead time 2-3 months. Submit seasonal material 3-4 months in advance. Accepts queries by e-mail. Sample copy free. Guidelines free.

Nonfiction Buys 2-3 mss/year. Query. Length: 500-1,000 words. **Pays $400-1,000.**

Photos Contact: Contact Matthew Hall, managing editor. Send photos Reviews GIF/JPEG files. Negotiates payment individually. Buys one time rights.

Columns/Departments Contact: Contact Anne Dinardo, senior associate editor. Please ask for an editorial calendar. 5-6 Query. **Pays $500-750.**

Tips We need to see a demonstrated understanding of our industry, its issues and major players; strong reporting and interviewing skills are also important. Merely facile writing is not enough for us.

SPORT TRADE

HORSE RACING

NEW ZEALAND BLOODHORSE

The Magazine for the Thoroughbred Industry, P.O. Box 272-1316, Papakura New Zealand. (64)(9)269-2264. Fax: (64)(9)269-2265. E-mail: editor@nzbloodhorse.co.nz. Website: www.nzbloodhorse.co.nz. Monthly magazine providing information for trainers, breeders, owners, and administrators. Articles cover management and personnel involved in producing each year's foals, yearling sales, extensive coverage of racetrack performances, and the importing of stallions and mares from the world's racing showcases. No kill fee.

- Query before submitting.

$ $ AQUATICS INTERNATIONAL

Hanley-Wood, LLC, 4160 Wilshire Blvd., Los Angeles CA 90010. Fax: (323)801-4986. E-mail: gthill@hanleywood.com. Website: www.aquaticsintl.com. Magazine published 10 times/year covering public swimming pools and waterparks. Estab. 1989. Circ. 30,000. Byline given. Pays on publication. No kill fee. Publishes ms an average of 3 months after acceptance. international rights in perpetuity and makes work-for-hire assignments. Editorial lead time 3 months. Responds in 1 month to queries. Sample copy for $10.50.

Nonfiction Needs how-to, interview, technical. **Buys 6 mss/year.** Query with published clips. Length: 1,500-2,500 words. **Pays $525 for assigned articles.**

Columns/Departments Pays $ 250.

Tips Send query letter with samples.

$ $ ARROWTRADE MAGAZINE

A Magazine for Retailers, Distributors & Manufacturers of Bowhunting Equipment, Arrow Trade Publishing Corp., 3479 409th Ave. NW, Braham MN 55006. (320)396-3473. Fax: (320)396-3206. E-mail: arrowtrade@northlc.com. **60% freelance written.** Bimonthly magazine covering the archery industry. "Our readers are interested in articles that help them operate their business better. They are primarily owners or managers of sporting goods stores and archery pro shops." Estab. 1996. Circ. 11,000. Byline given. **Pays on publication.** No kill fee. Publishes ms an average of 2 months after acceptance. Buys first North American serial rights. Editorial lead time 2 months. Accepts queries by mail, e-mail, fax. Responds in 2 weeks to queries. Responds in 2 weeks to mss. Sample copy for sae with 9x12 envelope and 10 First-Class stamps.

Nonfiction Needs interview, new product. Generic business articles won't work for our highly specialized audience. **Buys Buys 24 mss/year. mss/year.** Query with published clips. Length: 1,800-3,800 words. **Pays $350-550.**

Photos Send photos Captions required. Must provide digital photos on CD or DVD. Offers no additional payment for photos accepted with ms.

Columns/Departments Product Focus (digging into the design and function of an innovative single product); Behind the Brand (profiling a firm that's important to the bowhunting industry). **Buys 24 mss/year.** Query with published clips. **Pays $250-375.**

Tips "Our readers are hungry for articles that help them decide what to stock and how to do a better job selling or servicing it. Articles needed typically fall into one of these categories: business profiles on outstanding retailers, manufacturers or distributors; equipment articles that cover categories of gear, citing trends in the market and detailing why products have been designed a certain way and what type of use they're best suited for; basic business articles that help dealers do a better job of promoting their business, managing their inventory, training their staff, etc. Good interviewing skills are a must, as especially in the equipment articles we like to see a minimum of 6 sources."

$ $ BOATING INDUSTRY INTERNATIONAL

The Management Magazine for the Recreational Marine Industry, Ehlert Publishing Group, 6420 Sycamore Lane, Suite 100, Maple Grove MN 55369. (763)383-4448. Fax: (763)383-4499. Website: www.boating-industry.com. **10-20% freelance written**. Bimonthly magazine covering recreational marine industry management. We write for those in the industry—not the consumer. Our subject is the business of boating. All of our articles must be analytical and predictive, telling our readers where the industry is going, rather than where it's been. Estab. 1929. Circ. 23,000. Byline given. Pays on acceptance. Offers 50% kill fee. Publishes ms an average of 2 months after acceptance. Buys first rights, buys electronic rights. Editorial lead time 2 months. Submit seasonal material 2 months in advance. Accepts queries by mail, e-mail, fax. Responds in 1 month to queries. Sample copy available online. Guidelines free.

Nonfiction Needs technical, business. **Buys 30 mss/year.** Query with published clips. Length: 250-2,500 words. **Pays $25-250.** Sometimes pays expenses of writers on assignment.

Photos State availability Captions, identification of subjects required. Reviews 2X2 transparencies, 4x6 prints. Negotiates payment individually. Buys one time rights.

$ $ BOWLING CENTER MANAGEMENT

Trade Magazine for Bowling Center Operators, Luby Publishing, 122 S. Michigan Ave., Suite 1506, Chicago IL 60603. (312)341-1110. Fax: (312)341-1469. E-mail: mikem@lubypublishing.com. Website: www.bcmmag.com. **50% freelance written**. Monthly magazine covering bowling centers, family entertainment. "Our readers are looking for novel ways to draw more customers. Accordingly, we look for articles that effectively present such ideas." Estab. 1995. Circ. 12,000. Byline given. Pays on acceptance. Publishes ms an average of 3 months after acceptance. Buys first North American serial rights. Editorial lead time 3 months. Submit seasonal material 6 months in advance. Accepts queries by e-mail. Accepts previously published material. Accepts simultaneous submissions. Responds in 2-3 weeks to queries. Sample copy for $10.

Nonfiction Needs how-to, interview. **Buys 10-20 mss/year.** Query. Length: 750-1,500 words. **Pays $150-350.**

Tips "Send a solid, clever query by e-mail with knowledge and interest in an industry trend."

BREEDING & RACING MAGAZINE

Gadfly Media, Level 1, 645 Harris St., Ultimo, Sydney NSW 2007 Australia. (61)(2)9281-7523. Fax: (61)(2)9281-7529. E-mail: rchapman@gadfly.net.au. Website: www.breedingracing.com. Monthly magazine covering the thoroughbred breeding and racing industry across Australia, New Zealand and Southeast Asia.

Nonfiction Needs general interest. Query.

$ $ CROSSFIRE

Paintball Digest, 570 Mantus Rd., P.O. Box 690, Sewell NJ 08080. (888)834-6026. E-mail: editor@paintball2xtremes.com. Website: www.crossfiremag.com. **100% freelance written**. Monthly magazine covering paintball sport. *Crossfire* will cover all aspects of the paintball industry from tactics to safety. Byline given. Pays on publication. No kill fee. Makes work-for-hire assignments. Editorial lead time 1 year. Submit seasonal material 2 months in advance. Accepts queries by mail, e-mail, fax. Accepts simultaneous submissions. Responds in 2 weeks to queries. Sample copy free.

Nonfiction Needs how-to, humor, interview, new product, personal experience, photo feature, technical, travel, Tournament coverage, industry news. **Buys 1-3 mss/year.** Send complete ms. Length: 700-1,900 words. **Pays 7-22¢/word.**

Photos Send photos Captions, identification of subjects, model releases required. Reviews negatives. Negotiates payment individually. Buys all rights.

Fillers Needs facts, gags, newsbreaks. 24 Length: 25-100 words. **7-22¢/word**

Tips Paintball or extreme sport participation is a plus.

GOLF BUSINESS

National Golf Course Owners Association, 291 Seven Farms Dr., 2nd Floor, Charleston SC 29492. (843)881-9956. Fax: (843)856-3288. E-mail: rmusselwhite@ngcoa.org. Website: www.golfbusiness.com. **Contact:** Ronnie Musselwhite, Editor. **80% freelance written**. Monthly magazine covering the business of golf course ownership. "*Golf Business* is the official publication of the National Golf Course Owners Association. The editorial content is designed to promote the exchange of information and ideas among course owners and senior industry executives to improve the profitability of their operations. Articles cover all areas of management and operations, including course design and maintenance, pro shop merchandising, marketing and inventory control, food and beverage operations, insurance and liability issues, legislative updates, finance and human resources. Regular features include in-depth reviews of agronomic issues, environmental policies, technology, highlights of new golf course equipment, plus merchandising strategies for golf apparel, equipment and accessories." Estab. 1996. Circ. 18,000. Byline given. Pays on publication. No kill fee. Buys first rights. Editorial lead time 3 months. Accepts queries by e-mail. Guidelines available online.

$ $ GOLF COURSE MANAGEMENT

Golf Course Superintendents Association of America, 1421 Research Park Dr., Lawrence KS 66049. (800)472-7878. Fax: (785)832-3665. E-mail: shollister@gcsaa.org. Website: www.gcsaa.org. **50% freelance written.** Monthly magazine covering the golf course superintendent. *GCM* helps the golf course superintendent become more efficient in all aspects of their job. Estab. 1924. Circ. 40,000. Byline given. Pays on acceptance. No kill fee. Publishes ms an average of 6 months after acceptance. Buys first North American serial rights, Web rights, and makes work-for-hire assignments. Editorial lead time 6 months. Submit seasonal material 6 months in advance. Accepts simultaneous submissions. Responds in 3 weeks to queries. Responds in 1 month to mss. Sample copy and writer's guidelines free.

Nonfiction Needs how-to, interview. No articles about playing golf. **Buys 40 mss/year.** Query. Length: 1,500-2,500 words. **Pays $400-600.** Sometimes pays expenses of writers on assignment.

Photos Send photos Identification of subjects required. Offers no additional payment for photos accepted with ms. Buys all rights.

Tips Writers should have prior knowledge of golf course maintenance, agronomy and turfgrass science and the overall profession of the golf course superintendent.

IDEA FITNESS JOURNAL

IDEA Health & Fitness Association, Inc., 10455 Pacific Center Court, San Diego CA 92121. (858)535-8979. Fax: (858)535-8234. E-mail: websters@ideafit.com. Website: www.ideafit.com. **70% freelance written.** Magazine published 10 times/year for fitness professionals—personal trainers, group fitness instructors, and studio and health club owners—covering topics such as exercise science, nutrition, injury prevention, entrepreneurship in fitness, fitness-oriented research, and program design. Estab. 1984. Circ. 20,000. Byline given. Pays on acceptance. No kill fee. Publishes ms an average of 4 months after acceptance. Buys all rights. Accepts queries by mail, e-mail, fax. Accepts simultaneous submissions. Responds in 2 months to queries. Sample copy for $5. Guidelines available online.

Nonfiction Needs how-to, technical. No general information on fitness; our readers are pros who need detailed information. **Buys 15 mss/year.** Query. Length: 1,000-3,000 words. **Payment varies**

Photos State availability Model releases required. Offers no additional payment for photos with ms. Buys all rights.

Columns/Departments Research (detailed, specific info—must be written by expert), 750-1,500 words; Industry News (short reports on research, programs, and conferences), 150-300 words; Fitness Handout (exercise and nutrition info for participants), 750 words. 80 Query. **Payment varies.**

Tips We don't accept fitness information for the consumer audience on topics such as why exercise is good for you. Writers who have specific knowledge of, or experience working in, the fitness industry have an edge.

$ $ INTERNATIONAL BOWLING INDUSTRY

B2B Media, Inc., 13245 Riverside Dr., Suite 501, Sherman Oaks CA 91423. Fax: (818)789-2812. E-mail: info@bowlingindustry.com. Website: www.bowlingindustry.com. **40% freelance written.** Monthly magazine covering ownership and management of bowling centers (alleys) and pro shops. "*IBI* publishes articles in all phases of bowling center and bowling pro shop ownership and management, among them finance, promotion, customer service, relevant technology, architecture and capital improvement. The magazine also covers the operational areas of bowling centers and pro shops such as human resources, food and beverage, corporate and birthday parties, ancillary attractions (go-karts, gaming and the like), and retailing. Articles must have strong how-to emphasis. They must be written specifically in terms of the bowling industry, although content may be applicable more widely." Estab. 1993. Circ. 10,200. Byline given. Pays on acceptance. Offers $50 kill fee. Publishes ms an average of 3 months after acceptance. Buys all rights. Submit seasonal material 3 months in advance. Accepts queries by mail, e-mail, fax. Accepts simultaneous submissions. Responds in 2 weeks to queries. Responds in 1 month to mss. Sample copy for #10 SASE. Guidelines free.

Nonfiction Needs how-to, interview, new product, technical. **Buys 40 mss/year.** Send complete ms. Length: 1,100-1,400 words. **Pays $250.** Sometimes pays expenses of writers on assignment.

Photos State availability Identification of subjects required. Reviews JPEG photos. Offers no additional payment for photos accepted with ms. Buys all rights.

Tips "Please supply writing samples, applicable list of credits and bio."

$ $ NSGA RETAIL FOCUS

National Sporting Goods Association, 1601 Feehanville Dr., Suite 300, Mt. Prospect IL 60056-6035. (847)296-6742. Fax: (847)391-9827. E-mail: info@nsga.org. Website: www.nsga.org. **20% freelance written. Works with a small number of new/unpublished writers each year.** Bimonthly magazine. *NSGA Retail Focus* serves as a bimonthly trade journal for sporting goods retailers who are members of the association. Estab. 1948. Circ. 2,000. Byline given. Pays on publication. Offers kill fee. Offers kill fee Publishes ms an average of 1 month after acceptance. Buys first rights, buys second serial (reprint) rights, buys electronic rights. Submit seasonal material 6 months in advance. Accepts queries by e-mail. Sample copy for sae with 9x12 envelope and 5 First-Class stamps.

Nonfiction Needs interview, photo feature. No articles written without sporting goods retail businesspeople in mind as the audience. In other words, no generic articles sent to several industries. **Buys 12 mss/year.** Query with published clips. **Pays $150-300.** Sometimes pays expenses of writers on assignment.

Photos State availability Reviews high-resolution, digital images. Payment negotiable Buys one time rights.

Columns/Departments Personnel Management (succinct tips on hiring, motivating, firing, etc.); Sales Management (in-depth tips to improve sales force performance); Retail Management (detailed explanation of merchandising/inventory control); Store Design; Visual Merchandising, all 1,500 words. 12 Query. **Pays $150-300.**

$ $ PADDLER MAGAZINE

A Publication of Paddlesports Publishing, Inc., Paddlesport Publishing, Inc., 12040 98th Ave. NE, Suite 205, Kirkland WA 98034. (425)814-4140. E-mail: mike@paddlermagazine.com. Website: www.paddlermagazine.com. **70% freelance written**. Quarterly magazine covering the canoeing, kayaking and rafting industry. Estab. 1993. Circ. 7,500. Byline given. 1 month after publication. No kill fee. Publishes ms an average of 6 months after acceptance. Buys first North American serial and one-time electronic rights. Editorial lead time 2 months. Submit seasonal material 6 months in advance. Accepts queries by mail, e-mail. Accepts simultaneous submissions. Responds in 3 months to queries. Sample copy for 8 ½x11 SAE and $1.78. Guidelines for #10 sase.

Nonfiction Needs new product, technical, business advice. **Buys 8 mss/year.** Query or send complete ms. Length: 2,300 words. **Pays 15-20¢/word.** Sometimes pays expenses of writers on assignment.

Photos State availability Reviews transparencies, hi-res digital images (300 dpi at 5x7). Buys one time rights.

Columns/Departments Profiles, how-to, great ideas, computer corner. 12 Query or send complete ms. **Pays 10-20¢/word.**

$ $ POOL & SPA NEWS

Hanley-Wood, LLC, 6222 Wilshire Blvd., Los Angeles CA 90048. (323)801-4972. Fax: (323)801-4986. E-mail: etaylor@hanleywood.com. Website: poolspanews.com. **15% freelance written**. Semimonthly magazine covering the swimming pool and spa industry for builders, retail stores, and service firms. Estab. 1960. Circ. 16,300. Pays on publication. No kill fee. Publishes ms an average of 2 months after acceptance. Buys all rights. Accepts queries by mail, e-mail. Responds in 1 month to queries. Sample copy for $5 and 9x12 SAE and 11 first-class stamps.

Nonfiction Needs interview, technical. Send resume with published clips. Length: 500-2,000 words. **Pays $150-550.** Pays expenses of writers on assignment.

Reprints Send typed manuscript with rights for sale noted and information about when and where the material previously appeared. Payment varies

Photos Payment varies

Columns/Departments Payment varies.

$ $ REFEREE

Referee Enterprises, Inc., P.O. Box 161, Franksville WI 53126. Fax: (262)632-5460. E-mail: submissions@referee.com. Website: www.referee.com. **75% freelance written**. Monthly magazine covering sports officiating. *Referee* is a magazine for and read by sports officials of all kinds with a focus on baseball, basketball, football, softball, and soccer officiating. Estab. 1976. Circ. 40,000. Byline given. Pays on acceptance. Offers kill fee. Kill fee negotiable. Publishes ms an average of 6 months after acceptance. Buys all rights. Editorial lead time 6 months. Accepts queries by mail, e-mail, fax. Responds in 2 weeks to queries. Responds in 1 month to mss. Sample copy for #10 sase. Guidelines available online.

Nonfiction Needs book excerpts, essays, historical, how-to, sports officiating related, humor, interview, opinion, photo feature, technical, as it relates to sports officiating. We don't want to see articles with themes not relating to sport officiating. General sports articles, although of interest to us, will not be published. **Buys 40 mss/year.** Query with published clips. Length: 500-2,500 words. **Pays $100-400.** Sometimes pays expenses of writers on assignment.

Photos State availability Identification of subjects required. Reviews contact sheets, negatives, transparencies, prints. Offers $35-40 per photo. Purchase of rights negotiable.

Tips Query first and be persistent. We may not like your idea but that doesn't mean we won't like your next one. Professionalism pays off.

$ $ THE RINKSIDER

Independent Voice of the Industry, Target Publishing Co., Inc., 2470 E. Main St., Columbus OH 43209. (614)235-1022. Fax: (614)235-3584. E-mail: rinksider@rinksider.com. Website: www.rinksider.com. **90% freelance written**. Bimonthly magazine of interest to owners/operators of roller skating facilitiesÃ³promotions, games, snack bars, roller hockey competitive programs, music, decor, features on new or successful skating centers, competitive amusements, etc. Estab. 1953. Circ. 1,600. Byline given. Pays on publication. Offers

100% (unless poorly done) kill fee. Publishes ms an average of 2 months after acceptance. Buys first rights, buys exclusive of competitive journals rights. Editorial lead time 1 month. Accepts queries by e-mail. Accepts previously published material. Accepts simultaneous submissions. Responds in 2 weeks to queries. Responds in 1 month to mss. Sample copy for $5. Guidelines free.

Nonfiction Needs essays, historical, how-to, humor, inspirational, interview, new product, personal experience, photo feature, travel. Does not want opinion pieces. Query with published clips. Length: 250-1,000 words. **Pays $75-200.**

Photos Send photos Reviews prints. Offers no additional payment for photos accepted with ms. Buys all rights.

Columns/Departments Finance; Roller Skating News; Marketing; Technology. 20 Query with published clips. **Pays $75-200.**

$ $ SKI AREA MANAGEMENT

Beardsley Publications, P.O. Box 644, Woodbury CT 06798. (203)263-0888. Fax: (203)266-0452. Website: www.saminfo.com. **85% freelance written**. Bimonthly magazine covering everything involving the management and development of ski resorts. We are the publication of record for the North American ski industry. We report on new ideas, developments, marketing, and regulations with regard to ski and snowboard resorts. Everyone from the CEO to the lift operator of winter resorts reads our magazine to stay informed about the people and procedures that make ski areas successful. Estab. 1962. Circ. 4,500. Byline given. Pays on publication. Offers kill fee. Offers kill fee. Buys all rights. Editorial lead time 2 months. Submit seasonal material 3 months in advance. Accepts queries by mail, e-mail. Responds in 2 weeks to queries. Sample copy for 9x12 SAE with $3 postage or online. Guidelines for #10 sase.

Nonfiction Needs historical, how-to, interview, new product, opinion, personal experience, technical. We don't want anything that does not specifically pertain to resort operations, management, or financing. **Buys 25-40 mss/year.** Query. Length: 500-2,500 words. **Pays $50-400.**

Photos Send photos Identification of subjects required. Reviews transparencies, prints. Offers no additional payment for photos accepted with ms. Buys one-time rights or all rights.

Tips Know what you are writing about. We are read by people dedicated to skiing and snowboarding and to making the resort experience the best possible for their customers. It is a trade publication read by professionals.

STONE, QUARRY & MINING

THE AUSIMM BULLETIN

P.O. Box 660, Carlton South VIC 3053 Australia. (61)(3)9662-3166. Fax: (61)(3)9662-3662. E-mail: editor@ausimm.com.au. Website: www.ausimm.com.au. Bimonthly magazine. *The Bulletin* informs its readership of the latest AusIMM news from branch activities to education and lobbying initiatives. Each issue has a regional focus on an area in Australasia comprising an overview of the projects and developments and articles on issues and companies/sites particular to the profiled region. Circ. 7,900. Accepts queries by e-mail.

Nonfiction Needs general interest, interview, technical. Query.

$ $ CANADIAN MINING JOURNAL

Business Information Group, 12 Concorde Place, Suite 800, Toronto ON M3C 4J2 Canada. (416)510-6742. Fax: (416)510-5138. E-mail: jwerniuk@canadianminingjournal.com. **5% freelance written**. Magazine covering mining and mineral exploration by Canadian companies. *Canadian Mining Journal* provides articles and information of practical use to those who work in the technical, administrative, and supervisory aspects of exploration, mining, and processing in the Canadian mineral exploration and mining industry. Estab. 1882. Circ. 11,000. Byline given. Pays on publication. No kill fee. Publishes ms an average of 3 months after acceptance. Buys one-time rights, buys electronic rights. Makes work-for-hire assignments. Submit seasonal material 3 months in advance. Accepts queries by mail, e-mail, fax, phone. Responds in 1 week to queries. Responds in 1 month to mss.

Nonfiction Needs opinion, technical, operation descriptions. **Buys 6 mss/year.** Query with published clips. Length: 500-1,400 words. **Pays $100-600.** Pays expenses of writers on assignment.

Photos State availability Captions, identification of subjects, True required. Reviews 4x6 prints or high-resolution files. Negotiates payment individually. Buys one time rights.

Columns/Departments Guest editorial (opinion on controversial subject related to mining industry), 600 words. 3 Query with published clips. **Pays $150.**

Tips I need articles about mine sites it would be expensive/difficult for me to reach. I also need to know the writer is competent to understand and describe the technology in an interesting way.

$ $ COAL PEOPLE MAGAZINE

Al Skinner, Inc., 629 Virginia St. W, P.O. Box 6247, Charleston WV 25362. (304)342-4129. Fax: (304)343-3124.

E-mail: alskinner@ntelos.net. Website: www.coalpeople.com. **50% freelance written**. Monthly magazine. Most stories are about people or historical—either narrative or biographical on all levels of coal people, past and present—from coal execs down to grass roots miners. Most stories are upbeat—showing warmth of family or success from underground up! Estab. 1976. Circ. 11,000. Byline given. Pays on publication. No kill fee. Publishes ms an average of 3 months after acceptance. Buys first rights, buys second serial (reprint) rights. Makes work-for-hire assignments. Submit seasonal material 2 months in advance. Accepts queries by e-mail. Responds in 3 months to mss. Sample copy for sae with 9x12 envelope and 10 First-Class stamps.

Nonfiction Needs book excerpts, and film if related to coal, historical, coal towns, people, lifestyles, humor, including anecdotes and cartoons, interview, for coal personalities, personal experience, as relates to coal mining, photo feature, on old coal towns, people, past and present. Calendar issue for more than 300 annual coal shows, association meetings, etc. (January); Surface Mining/Reclamation Award (July); Christmas in Coal Country (December). No poetry, fiction, or environmental attacks on the coal industry. **Buys 32 mss/year.** Query with published clips. Length: 750-2,500 words. **Pays $150-250.**

Reprints Send tearsheet and information about when and where the material previously appeared. Pays 50% of amount paid for an original article.

Photos Send photos Captions, identification of subjects required. Reviews contact sheets, transparencies, 5x7 prints. Buys one-time reprint rights.

Columns/Departments Length: 300-500 words. Editorials—anything to do with current coal issues (nonpaid); Mine'ing Our Business (bull pen column—gossip—humorous anecdotes); Coal Show Coverage (freelance photojournalist coverage of any coal function across the US). 10 Query. **Pays $50.**

Fillers Needs anecdotes. Length: 300 words. **Pays $35.**

Tips We are looking for good feature articles on coal professionals, companies—past and present, color slides (for possible cover use), and b&w photos to complement stories. Writers wanted to take photos and do journalistic coverage on coal events across the country. Slant stories more toward people and less on historical. More faces and names than old town, company store photos. Include more quotes from people who lived these moments! The following geographical areas are covered: North America and overseas.

$ CONTEMPORARY STONE & TILE DESIGN

Business News Publishing Co., 210 Route 4 E., Suite 311, Paramus NJ 07652. (201)291-9001. Fax: (201)291-9002. E-mail: jennifer@stoneworld.com. Website: www.stoneworld.com. Quarterly magazine covering the full range of stone and tile design and architecture—from classic and historic spaces to current projects. Estab. 1995. Circ. 14,000. Byline given. Pays on publication. No kill fee. Publishes ms an average of 3 months after acceptance. Buys first rights. Submit seasonal material 6 months in advance. Responds in 3 weeks to queries. Sample copy for $10.

Nonfiction Overall features on a certain aspect of stone design/tile work, or specific articles on individual architectural projects. Needs interview, prominent architect/designer or firm, photo feature, technical, architectural design. **Buys 8 mss/year.** Query with published clips. Length: 1,500-3,000 words. **Pays $6/column inch.** Pays expenses of writers on assignment.

Photos State availability Captions, identification of subjects required. Reviews transparencies, prints. Pays $10/photo accepted with ms. Buys one time rights.

Columns/Departments Upcoming Events (for the architecture and design community); Stone Classics (featuring historic architecture); question and answer session with a prominent architect or designer. Length: 1,500-2,000 words. **Pays $6/inch**

Tips The visual aspect of the magazine is key, so architectural photography is a must for any story. Cover the entire project, but focus on the stonework or tile work and how it relates to the rest of the space. Architects are very helpful in describing their work and often provide excellent quotes. As a relatively new magazine, we are looking for freelance submissions and are open to new feature topics. This is a narrow subject, however, so it's a good idea to speak with an editor before submitting anything.

$ $ PIT & QUARRY

Questex Media Group, 600 Superior Ave. E., Suite 1100, Cleveland OH 44114. (216)706-3725. Fax: (216)706-3710. E-mail: info@pitandquarry.com. Website: www.pitandquarry.com. **10-20% freelance written.** Monthly magazine covering nonmetallic minerals, mining, and crushed stone. Audience has knowledge of construction-related markets, mining, minerals processing, etc. Estab. 1916. Circ. 25,000. Byline given. Pays on acceptance. No kill fee. Publishes ms an average of 2 months after acceptance. Buys first North American serial rights. Editorial lead time 2 months. Accepts queries by e-mail. Accepts simultaneous submissions. Responds in 1 month to queries. Responds in 4 months to mss.

Nonfiction Needs how-to, interview, new product, technical. No humor or inspirational articles. **Buys 3-4 mss/year.** Query. Length: 2,000-2,500 words. **Pays $250-500 for assigned articles. Pays nothing for unsolicited articles.** Sometimes pays expenses of writers on assignment.

Photos State availability Identification of subjects, model releases required. Offers no additional payment for photos accepted with ms. Buys one time rights.

Columns/Departments Brand New; Techwatch; E-business; Software Corner; Equipment Showcase. Length: 250-750 words. 5-6 Query. **Pays $250-300.**

Tips Be familiar with quarry operations (crushed stone or sand and gravel), as opposed to coal or metallic minerals mining. Know construction markets. We always need equipment-focused features on specific quarry operations.

QUARRY

Phoenix Media & Publishing, Locked Bag 26, South Melbourne VIC 3205 Australia. (61)(3)9696-7200. Fax: (61)(3)9696-8313. E-mail: quarry@phoenixmags.com.au. Website: www.quarrymagazine.com.au. Monthly magazine providing the latests industry, technical and management information as well as profiling industry people and companiesÃ³from small 1-man operations to multi-national giants. *Quarry* is the official journal of the Institute of Quarrying Australia, which was established to promote education and professional recognition of the quarry industry. Accepts queries by mail, e-mail. Guidelines available online.
Nonfiction Needs general interest, interview, new product, technical. Query. Length: 400-2,500 words.
Photos Reviews JPEG files (300 dpi).
Tips Story ideas can be submitted via post or e-mail, but all story submissions should be delivered via e-mail in a Microsoft Word file and titled as follows: StoryName.doc.

$ STONE WORLD

BNP Media, 210 Route 4 E., Suite 203, Paramus NJ 07652. (201)291-9001. Fax: (201)291-9002. E-mail: michael@stoneworld.com. Website: www.stoneworld.com. Monthly magazine on "natural building stone for producers and users of granite, marble, limestone, slate, sandstone, onyx and other natural stone products.". Estab. 1984. Circ. 21,000. Byline given. Pays on publication. No kill fee. Publishes ms an average of 4 months after acceptance. Buys first North American serial rights, buys second serial (reprint) rights. Submit seasonal material 6 months in advance. Responds in 2 months to queries. Sample copy for $10.
Nonfiction Needs how-to, fabricate and/or install natural building stone, interview, photo feature, technical, architectural design, artistic stone uses, statistics, factory profile, equipment profile, trade show review. **Buys 10 mss/year.** Send complete ms. Length: 600-3,000 words. **Pays $6/column inch.** Pays expenses of writers on assignment.
Reprints Send photocopy with rights for sale noted and information about when and where the material previously appeared. Pays 50% of amount paid for an original article.
Photos State availability Captions, identification of subjects required. Reviews transparencies, prints, slides, digital images. Pays $10/photo accepted with ms. Buys one time rights.
Columns/Departments News (pertaining to stone or design community); New Literature (brochures, catalogs, books, videos, etc., about stone); New Products (stone products); New Equipment (equipment and machinery for working with stone); Calendar (dates and locations of events in stone and design communities). Query or send complete ms. Length 300-600 words. **Pays $6/inch.**
Tips "Articles about architectural stone design accompanied by professional color photographs and quotes from designing firms are often published, especially when one unique aspect of the stone selection or installation is highlighted. We are also interested in articles about new techniques of quarrying and/or fabricating natural building stone."

TOY, NOVELTY & HOBBY

$ $ MODEL RETAILER

21027 Crossroads Circle, P.O. Box 1612, Waukesha WI 53187. (262)796-8776. Fax: (262)796-1383. E-mail: hmiller@modelretailer.com. Website: www.modelretailer.com. **5% freelance written**. Monthly magazine. *Model Retailer* covers the business of hobbies, from financial and shop management issues to industry trends and the latest product releases. Our goal is to provide hobby shop entrepreneurs with the tools and information they need to be successful retailers. Estab. 1987. Circ. 6,000. Byline given. Pays on acceptance. No kill fee. Publishes ms an average of 3 months after acceptance. Buys one-time rights, buys electronic rights. Editorial lead time 3 months. Submit seasonal material 6 months in advance. Accepts queries by mail, e-mail, fax. Sample copy and writer's guidelines free Guidelines available online.
Nonfiction Needs how-to, business, new product. No articles that do not have a strong hobby or small retail component. **Buys 2-3 mss/year.** Query with published clips. Length: 750-1,500 words. **Pays $250-500 for assigned articles. Pays $100-250 for unsolicited articles.** Sometimes pays expenses of writers on assignment.
Photos State availability Captions, identification of subjects required. Reviews 4—Š6 prints. Negotiates payment individually. Buys one time rights.
Columns/Departments Shop Management; Sales Marketing; Technology Advice; Industry Trends, all 500-750 words. 2-3 Query with published clips. **Pays $100-200.**

PEN WORLD

World Publications, Inc., 3946 Glade Valley Dr., Kingwood TX 77339-2059. (281)359-4363. Fax: (281)359-

5748. E-mail: editor@penworld.com. Website: www.penworld.com. Magazine published 6 times/year. Published for writing instrument enthusiasts. Circ. 30,000. No kill fee.

TRANSPORTATION

BUS CONVERSIONS

The First and Foremost Bus Converters Magazine, MAK Publishing, 7246 Garden Grove Blvd., Westminster CA 92683. (714)799-0062. Fax: (714)799-0042. E-mail: editor@busconversions.com. Website: www.busconversions.com. **95% freelance written**. Monthly magazine covering the bus conversion industry. Estab. 1992. Circ. 10,000. Pays on publication. No kill fee. Buys first North American serial rights. Accepts queries by mail, e-mail.

Nonfiction Each month, *Bus Conversions* publishes a minimum of 2 coach reviews, usually anecdotal stories told by those who have completed their own bus conversion. Publishes some travel/destination stories (all of which are related to bus/RV travel). Looking for articles on engine swaps, exterior painting, and furniture. Needs how-to, articles on the electrical, plumbing, mechanical, decorative, and structural aspects of bus conversions; buses that are converted into RVs.

Photos Include color photos (glossy) with submission. Photos not returned unless SASE is included.

Columns/Departments Industry Update; Products of Interest; Ask the Experts; One For the Road; Road Fix.

Tips Most of our writers are our readers. Knowledge of bus conversions and the associated lifestyle is a prerequisite.

DIESEL

The Intermedia Group, Ltd., P.O. Box 55, Glebe NSW 2037 Australia. (61)(2)9660-2113. Fax: (61)(2)9660-4419. E-mail: steve@intermedia.com.au. Website: www.intermedia.com.au. Bimonthly magazine covering Australian road transport industry. With sharp news stories and bold feature articles that tap deep into the heart of trucking in the new millenium, *Diesel* presents the people and products of the Australian road transport industry in a style and format that is modern, informative and entertaining.

Nonfiction Needs general interest. Query.

LIMOUSINE DIGEST

(*Limousine Digest*), Digest Publications, 29 Fostertown Rd., Medford NJ 08055. (609)953-4900. Fax: (609)953-4905. E-mail: info@limodigest.com. Website: www.limodigest.com. **Contact:** Susan Rose, editor/assistant publisher. **10% freelance written**. Monthly magazine covering ground transportation. *"Limousine Digest* is `the voice of the luxury ground transportation industry.' We cover all aspects of ground transportation from vehicles to operators, safety issues, and political involvement." Estab. 1990. Circ. 14,000. Byline given. Pays on publication. No kill fee. Publishes ms an average of 3 months after acceptance. Makes work-for-hire assignments. Editorial lead time 1 year. Submit seasonal material 3 months in advance. Accepts queries by mail, e-mail, fax. Accepts simultaneous submissions. Sample copy free.

Nonfiction Needs historical, how-to, start a company, market your product, humor, inspirational, interview, new product, personal experience, photo feature, technical, travel, industry news, business. **Buys 7-9 mss/year.** Send complete ms. Length: 700-1,900 words. **Negotiates flat-fee and per-word rates individually. Will pay authors in advertising trade-outs.**

Photos Must include photos to be considered. Send photos Captions, identification of subjects, model releases required. Reviews negatives. Negotiates payment individually. Buys all rights.

Columns/Departments New Model Showcase (new limousines, sedans, buses), 1,000 words; Player Profile (industry members profiled), 700 words; Hall of Fame (unique vehicles featured), 500-700 words. 5 Query. **Negotiates flat-fee and per-word rates individually. Will pay authors in advertising trade-outs.**

$ $ METRO MAGAZINE

Bobit Publishing Co., 3520 Challenger St., Torrance CA 90503. (310)533-2400. Fax: (310)533-2502. E-mail: info@metro-magazine.com. Website: www.metro-magazine.com. **10% freelance written**. Magazine published 10 times/year covering transit bus, passenger rail, and motorcoach operations. *Metro Magazine* delivers business, government policy, and technology developments that are *industry specific* to public transportation. Estab. 1904. Circ. 20,500. Byline given. Pays on acceptance. Offers 10% kill fee. Publishes ms an average of 2 months after acceptance. Buys all rights. Editorial lead time 3 months. Submit seasonal material 3 months in advance. Accepts queries by e-mail. Responds in 2 weeks to queries. Responds in 1 month to mss. Sample copy for $8. Guidelines by email.

Nonfiction Needs how-to, interview, of industry figures, new product, related to transit—bus and rail—private bus, technical. **Buys 6-10 mss/year.** Query. Length: 400-1,500 words. **Pays $80-400.**

Photos State availability Captions, identification of subjects, model releases required. Negotiates payment individually Buys all rights.

Columns/Departments Query. **Pays 20¢/word**

$ $ SCHOOL BUS FLEET

Bobit Business Media, 3520 Challenger St., Torrance CA 90503. (310)533-2400. Fax: (310)533-2502. E-mail: sbf@bobit.com. Website: www.schoolbusfleet.com. **10% freelance written**. Magazine covering school transportation of K-12 population. Most of our readers are school bus operators, public and private. Estab. 1956. Circ. 24,000. Byline given. Pays on acceptance. Offers kill fee. Offers 25% kill fee or $50. Publishes ms an average of 3 months after acceptance. Buys first North American serial rights. Editorial lead time 3 months. Submit seasonal material 3 months in advance. Accepts queries by mail, e-mail, fax. Responds in 1 month to queries. Sample copy free. Guidelines free.

Nonfiction Needs interview, new product, technical. **Buys 6 mss/year.** Query with published clips. Length: 600-1,800 words. **Pays 20-25¢/word.** Sometimes pays expenses of writers on assignment.

Photos State availability Captions, identification of subjects required. Reviews transparencies, 4x6 prints, digital photos. Negotiates payment individually. Buys one time rights.

Columns/Departments Shop Talk (maintenance information for school bus mechanics), 650 words. 2 Query with published clips. **Pays $100-150.**

Tips Freelancers should submit ideas about innovations in school bus safety and operations.

TRAVEL TRADE

$ $ $ CRUISE INDUSTRY NEWS

Cruise Industry News, 441 Lexington Ave., Suite 809, New York NY 10017. (212)986-1025. Fax: (212)986-1033. E-mail: oivind@cruiseindustrynews.com. Website: www.cruiseindustrynews.com. **20% freelance written**. Quarterly magazine covering cruise shipping. We write about the business of cruise shipping for the industry. That is, cruise lines, shipyards, financial analysts, etc. Estab. 1991. Circ. 10,000. Byline given. Pays on acceptance or on publication. Offers 25% kill fee. Publishes ms an average of 4 months after acceptance. Buys first rights. Editorial lead time 3 months. Accepts queries by mail. Reponse time varies. Sample copy for $15. Guidelines for #10 sase.

Nonfiction Needs interview, new product, photo feature, business. No travel stories. **Buys more than 20 mss/year.** Query with published clips. Length: 500-1,500 words. **Pays $500-1,000 for assigned articles.** Sometimes pays expenses of writers on assignment.

Photos State availability Pays $25-50/photo. Buys one time rights.

$ $ LEISURE GROUP TRAVEL

Premier Tourism Marketing, 4901 Forest Ave., Downers Grove IL 60515. (630)964-1431. Fax: (630)852-0414. E-mail: johnk@premiertourismmarketing.com. Website: www.premiertourismmarketing.com. **35% freelance written**. Bimonthly magazine covering group travel. We cover destinations and editorial relevant to the group travel market. Estab. 1994. Circ. 15,012. Byline given. Pays on publication. No kill fee. Buys first rights, including online publication rights. Editorial lead time 6 months. Submit seasonal material 6 months in advance. Accepts queries by mail, e-mail. Sample copy available online.

Nonfiction Needs travel. **Buys 75 mss/year.** Query with published clips. Length: 1,200-3,000 words. **Pays $0-1,000.**

Tips Experience in writing for 50+ travel marketplace a bonus.

LL&A MAGAZINE

Media Diversified, Inc., 96 Karma Rd., Markham ON L3R 4Y3 Canada. (905)944-0265. Fax: (416)296-0994. E-mail: info@mediadiversified.com. Website: www.mediadiversified.com. **5% freelance written**. Quarterly magazine for the luggage, leathergoods and accessories market. Estab. 1966. Circ. 4,500. Byline given. Pays on publication. No kill fee. Buys first rights. Editorial lead time 6 weeks. Accepts queries by e-mail. Sample copy free Guidelines free

Nonfiction Needs general interest, how-to, new product, technical.

$ $ MIDWEST MEETINGS®

Hennen Publishing, 302 6th St. W., Brookings SD 57006. Fax: (605)692-9031. E-mail: serenity@midwestmeetings.com. Website: www.midwestmeetings.com. **20% freelance written**. Quarterly magazine covering meetings/conventions industry. We provide information and resources to meeting/convention planners with a Midwest focus. Estab. 1996. Circ. 28,500. Byline given. Pays on acceptance. Publishes ms an average of 5 months after acceptance. Buys one-time rights, buys electronic rights. Editorial lead time 3 months. Submit seasonal material 3 months in advance. Accepts queries by mail, e-mail, fax. Sample copy free. Guidelines by email.

Nonfiction Needs essays, general interest, historical, how-to, humor, interview, personal experience, travel. Does not want marketing pieces related to specific hotels/meeting facilities. **Buys 15-20 mss/year.** Send complete ms. Length: 500-1,000 words. **Pays 5-50¢/word.**

Photos Send photos Captions, identification of subjects required. Reviews GIF/JPEG files (300 dpi). Offers no additional payment for photos accepted with ms. Buys one time rights.

Tips If you were a meeting/event planner, what information would help you to perform your job better? We like lots of quotes from industry experts, insider tips, etc. If you're not sure, e-mail the editor. We're friendly.

$ $ $ RV BUSINESS

TL Enterprises, Inc., 2575 Vista del Mar Dr., Ventura CA 93001. (805)667-4100. Fax: (805)667-4484. E-mail: bhampson@affinitygroup.com. Website: www.rvbusiness.com. **50% freelance written**. Monthly magazine. *RV Business* caters to a specific audience of people who manufacture, sell, market, insure, finance, service and supply, components for recreational vehicles. Estab. 1972. Circ. 21,000. Byline given. Pays on acceptance. Offers kill fee. Offers kill fee. Publishes ms an average of 2 months after acceptance. Buys first North American serial rights. Editorial lead time 3 months. Accepts queries by mail, e-mail. Sample copy free.

Nonfiction Needs new product, photo feature, industry news and features. No general articles without specific application to our market. **Buys 300 mss/year.** Query with published clips. Length: 125-2,200 words. **Pays $50-1,500.** Sometimes pays expenses of writers on assignment.

Columns/Departments Top of the News (RV industry news), 75-400 words; Business Profiles, 400-500 words; Features (indepth industry features), 800-2,000 words. 300 Query. **Pays $50-1,500.**

Tips Query. Send 1 or several ideas and a few lines letting us know how you plan to treat it/them. We are always looking for good authors knowledgeable in the RV industry or related industries. We need more articles that are brief, factual, hard hitting, and business oriented. Review other publications in the field, including enthusiast magazines.

$ $ SCHOOL TRANSPORTATION NEWS

STN Media Co., 5334 Torrance Blvd., 3rd Floor, Torrance CA 90503. (310)792-2226. Fax: (310)792-2231. E-mail: info@stnonline.com. Website: www.stnonline.com. **Contact:** Ryan Gray, editor-in-chief. **20% freelance written**. Monthly magazine covering school bus and pupil transportation industries in North America. "Contributors to *School Transportation News* must have a basic understanding of K-12 education and automotive fleets and specifically of school buses. Articles cover such topics as manufacturing, operations, maintenance and routing software, GPS, security and legislative affairs. A familiarity with these principles is preferred. Additional industry information is available on our Web site. New writers must perform some research of the industry or exhibit core competencies in the subject matter." Estab. 1991. Circ. 23,633. Byline given. Pays on publication. No kill fee. Buys one-time rights. Editorial lead time 1-2 months. Submit seasonal material 3 months in advance. Accepts queries by e-mail. Accepts simultaneous submissions. Sample copy free. Guidelines free.

Nonfiction Needs book excerpts, general interest, historical, humor, inspirational, interview, new product, personal experience, photo feature, technical. "Does not want strictly localized editorial. We want articles that put into perspective the issues of the day." Query with published clips. Length: 600-1,200 words. **Pays $150-300.** Sometimes pays expenses of writers on assignment.

Photos Contact: Contact Vince Rios, director. Captions, model releases required. Reviews GIF/JPEG files. Offers $150-200/photo. Buys all rights.

Columns/Departments Creative Special Report, Cover Story, Top Story; Book/Video Reviews (new programs/publications/training for pupil transporters), both 600 words. 40 Query with published clips. **Pays $150.**

Tips "Potential freelancers should exhibit a basic proficiency in understanding school bus issues and demonstrate the ability to report on education, legislative and business affairs, as well as a talent with feature writing. It would be helpful if the writer has previous contacts within the industry. Article pitches should be e-mailed only."

$ $ SPECIALTY TRAVEL INDEX

Alpine Hansen, P.O. Box 458, San Anselmo CA 94979. (415)455-1643. Fax: (415)455-1648. E-mail: info@specialtytravel.com. Website: www.specialtytravel.com. **90% freelance written**. Semiannual magazine covering adventure and special interest travel. Estab. 1980. Circ. 35,000. Byline given. Pays on receipt and acceptance of all materials. No kill fee. Buys one-time rights. Editorial lead time 3 month. Submit seasonal material 3 months in advance. Accepts queries by mail, e-mail. Writer's guidelines on request.

Nonfiction Needs how-to, personal experience, photo feature, travel. **Buys 15 mss/year.** Query. Length: 1,250 words. **Pays $300 minimum.**

Reprints Send tearsheet. Pays 100% of amount paid for an original article.

Photos State availability Captions, identification of subjects required. Reviews EPS/TIFF files. Negotiates payment individually.

Tips Write about group travel and be both creative and factual. The articles should relate to both the travel agent booking the tour and the client who is traveling.

$ STAR SERVICE

NORTHSTAR Travel Media, 200 Brookstown Ave., Suite 301, Winston-Salem NC 27101. (336)714-3328. Fax: (336)714-3168. E-mail: csheaffer@ntmllc.com. Website: www.starserviceonline.com. "Eager to work with experienced writers as well as those working from a home base abroad, planning trips that would allow time for hotel reporting, or living in major ports for cruise ships. Worldwide guide to accommodations and cruise ships, sold to travel professionals on subscription basis. Estab. 1960. No byline given. Pays 1 month after acceptance. No kill fee. Buys all rights. Accepts queries by e-mail preferred. Writer's guidelines provided.

- E-mail queries preferred.

Nonfiction "Objective, critical evaluations of hotels and cruise ships suitable for international travelers, based on personal inspections. Freelance correspondents ordinarily are assigned to update an entire state or country or individual hotels in their local market. Assignment involves on-site inspections of all hotels and cruise ships we review; revising and updating published reports; and reviewing new properties. Qualities needed are thoroughness, precision, perseverance, and keen judgment. Solid research skills and powers of observation are crucial. Travel writing and hotel experience is highly desirable. Reviews must be colorful and clear. We accept no advertising or payment for listings, so reviews should dispense praise and criticism where deserved. Query should include details on writer's experience in travel and writing, clips, specific forthcoming travel plans, and how much time would be available for hotel or ship inspections. Sponsored trips are acceptable." **Buys 4,500 mss/year. Pays $30-40/report used.**

Tips "We may require sample hotel or cruise reports on facilities near freelancer's hometown before giving the first assignment. No byline because of sensitive nature of reviews."

TRAVEL AGENT MAGAZINE

Questex Media, 1 Park Ave., 2nd Floor, New York NY 10016. (917)326-6196. E-mail: omcdonald@advanstar.com. Website: www.travelagentcentral.com/travelagentcentral. Weekly magazine serving travel agents.

Nonfiction Needs general interest, interview, travel. Query.

$ $ TRAVEL TIPS

Premier Tourism Marketing, 4901 Forest Ave., Downers Grove IL 60515. (630)964-1431. Fax: (630)852-0414. E-mail: johnk@premiertourismmarketing.com. Website: www.premiertourismmarketing.com. **75% freelance written**. Bimonthly magazine covering group travel. We cover destinations and editorial relevant to the group travel market. Estab. 1994. Circ. 12,500. Byline given. Pays on publication. Buys first rights, buys electronic rights. Editorial lead time 6 months. Submit seasonal material 6 months in advance. Accepts queries by mail, e-mail. Sample copy available online.

Nonfiction Needs travel. **Buys 36-50 mss/year.** Query with published clips. Length: 1,200-3,000 words. **Pays $0-500.**

Tips Experience in writing for 50+ travel marketplace a bonus.

VETERINARY

$ $ VETERINARY ECONOMICS

Business Solutions for Practicing Veterinarians, Advanstar Veterinary Healthcare Communications, 8033 Flint, Lenexa KS 66214. (913)492-4300. Fax: (913)492-4157. E-mail: ve@advanstar.com. Website: www.vetecon.com. **20% freelance written**. Monthly magazine covering veterinary practice management. We address the business concerns and management needs of practicing veterinarians. Estab. 1960. Circ. 54,000. Byline given. Pays on publication. No kill fee. Publishes ms an average of 6 months after acceptance. Buys all rights. Editorial lead time 3 months. Submit seasonal material 3 months in advance. Accepts queries by mail, e-mail, fax. Accepts simultaneous submissions. Responds in 3 months to queries. Sample copy free. Guidelines available online.

Nonfiction Needs how-to, interview, personal experience. **Buys 24 mss/year.** Send complete ms. Length: 1,000-2,000 words. **Pays $50-400.**

Photos Send photos Captions, identification of subjects required. Reviews transparencies, prints. Offers no additional payment for photos accepted with ms. Buys one time rights.

Columns/Departments Practice Tips (easy, unique business tips), 200-300 words. Send complete ms. **Pays $40.**

Tips Among the topics we cover: veterinary hospital design, client relations, contractual and legal matters, investments, day-to-day management, marketing, personal finances, practice finances, personnel, collections, and taxes. We also cover news and issues within the veterinary profession; for example, articles might cover the effectiveness of Yellow Pages advertising, the growing number of women veterinarians, restrictive-covenant cases, and so on. Freelance writers are encouraged to submit proposals or outlines for articles on these topics. Most articles involve interviews with a nationwide sampling of veterinarians; we will provide the names and phone numbers if necessary. We accept only a small number of unsolicited manuscripts each year; however, we do assign many articles to freelance writers. All material submitted by first-time contributors is read on speculation, and the review process usually takes 12-16 weeks. Our style is concise yet conversational, and all manuscripts go through a fairly rigorous editing process. We encourage writers to provide specific examples to illustrate points made throughout their articles.

VETZ MAGAZINE

Main Street Publishing Group, 608 Hampton Dr., Venice CA 90291. (310)452-3900. Fax: (310)452-3909. E-mail: contact@vetzmagazine.com. Website: www.vetzmagazine.com. **50% freelance written**. Magazine published 8 times/year covering the lifestyles, health, and practice management of veterinarians. Estab. 2005. Circ. 19,000. Byline given. No kill fee. Publishes ms an average of 2 months after acceptance. Buys all rights. Editorial lead time 2 months. Submit seasonal material 4 months in advance. Accepts queries by mail, e-mail, fax. Accepts previously published material. Responds in 3 weeks to queries. Responds in 2 months to mss. Sample copy online or via e-mail.

Nonfiction Needs book excerpts, how-to, humor, new product, lifestyle. **Buys 6 mss/year.** Query with published clips. **Does not pay for articles at this time. Offers byline, photo, and link to author's e-mail.**

Photos Identification of subjects required. Reviews GIF/JPEG files. Negotiates payment individually. Buys one time rights.

Columns/Departments Lifestyle; Health; Finance; Technology, all 750 words. 3 Query with published clips. **Does not pay for articles at this time. Offers byline, photo, and link to author's e-mail.**

Fiction Length: 750-900 words. **Does not pay for articles at this time. Offers byline, photo, and link to author's e-mail.**

MARKETS

Newspapers

Over the past several years, newspapers have been struggling, but it would be foolish to think they're dead or dying. There are still thousands of dailies and weeklies covering city and regional beats across the country. And while most newspapers have been forced to consolidate efforts and cut staff to remain competitive, they still need to provide newsworthy content to fill pages, which opens the door of opportunity for freelancers.

Staff writers will continue to handle the obvious stories of national, regional and local importance, but a freelancer can make sales by searching out those stories of real interest that are not as obvious, as well as the stories that demand special connections or a certain sensitivity to write. Your uniqueness as a freelancer is something you should communicate in your query letter. (For more information on query letters, read "Query Letter Clinic," on page 14.)

Listings

In addition to smaller circulation newspapers, *Writer's Market* lists many of the highest circulation newspapers in the country. As a result of these being the highest circulation newspapers, the information they freely share with freelancers is scarce. While it is always advised that you query before submitting to a newspaper, that rule holds especially true for the higher circulation papers.

Most newspapers have several departments with a specific editor handling all the material within each. It is important that you take the extra step to find out who the current contact is for the department you wish to submit your query. While it can seem like a lot of legwork, that is exactly the kind of professionalism that will be required if you expect to successfully freelance for newspapers.For more informationTo find out more on the relationship between freelancers and newspapers, including the best ways to break in and work with editors, read "Freelance Newspaper Writing 101'' on page 23.

ABLE NEWSPAPER

The Newspaper For, By, and About the Disabled, Melmont Printing, P.O. Box 395, Old Bethpage NY 11804. Fax: (516)939-0540. E-mail: ablenews@aol.com. Website: www.ablenews.com. Estab. 1991. Circ. 35,000. Accepts 20% of material on one-time basis. **30 features purchased/year.** all news including, but not limited to, legislation, advocacy, health, transportation, and housing issues. "*Able* focuses on news for people with disabilities." Accepts queries by e-mail, fax. Buys first rights. Pays on publication. Byline given. Sample copy and guidelines free.

Needs Query with published clips. Length: 400-600 words. **Pays $50 minimum.**

THE AGE

Fairfax Media Limited, P.O. Box 257C, Melbourne VIC 8001 Australia. (61)(3)9601-2250. E-mail: newsdesk@theage.com.au. Website: www.theage.com.au. Estab. 1854. Circ. 200,000. Daily. Pays on Pays on publication. "Nominal kill fee on commissioned pieces which do not run."

- Query before submitting.

AKRON BEACON JOURNAL

Sound Publishing, Inc., P.O. Box 640, Akron OH 44309. (330)996-3000. Fax: (330)376-9235. Website: www.ohio.com/mld/beaconjournal. Estab. 1839. Circ. 165,527. Daily. No kill fee.

- Mostly staff written.

ANTIQUE SHOPPE NEWSPAPER

Specialty General Service Publications, Inc., P.O. Box 2175, Keystone Heights FL 32656. (352)475-1679. Fax: (352)475-5326. E-mail: antshoppe@aol.com. Website: www.antiqueshoppefl.com. Estab. 1986. Circ. 20,000. Accepts 25% of material under contract. Accepts 25% of material on one-time basis. **100 features purchased/year.** Works with 10-12 writers/year. Accepts queries by mail, e-mail, phone. Responds in 1 week to queries. Buys one-time rights. Pays on publication. Editorial lead time 3-4 weeks. No kill fee. Byline given. Accepts previously published submissions. Accepts simultaneous submissions. Returns submission with SASE. Sample copy free. Guidelines free.

Needs Query with published clips. Length: 1,000-1,750 words. **Pays $50.**

Photos Send photos Reviews prints, GIF/JPEG files. Buys one time rights. Offers no additional payment for photos accepted with ms. Captions required.

Tips "Writers should have knowledge on expertise in the antique/collectibles industry."

THE ARIZONA REPUBLIC

Gannett Newspapers, 200 E. Van Buren St., Phoenix AZ 85004. (602)444-6397. E-mail: newstips@arizonarepublic.com. Website: www.arizonarepublic.com. Letters to the Editor: P.O. Box 2244, Phoenix AZ 85002. Fax: (602)444-8933. Estab. 1890. Circ. 486,000. Daily. No kill fee.

- Generally, stories written and submitted by the public are not accepted for publication.

ASIAN PAGES

Kita Associates, Inc., P.O. Box 11932, St. Paul MN 55111-1932. (952)884-3265. Fax: (952)888-9373. E-mail: asianpages@att.net. Website: www.asianpages.com. Estab. 1990. Circ. 75,000. Accepts 40% of material on one-time basis. **50-60 features purchased/year.** Biweekly. "*Asian Pages* celebrates the achievements of the Asian community in the Midwest and promotes a cultural bridge among the many different Asian groups that the newspaper serves." Accepts queries by mail. Responds in 1 month to queries. Responds in 2 months to mss. Buys first North American serial rights. Pays on publication. Editorial lead time 4 months. Offers 50% kill fee. Byline given. Accepts simultaneous submissions. Sample copy for SASE with 9x12 envelope and 3 First-class stamps. Guidelines for #10 SASE.

Needs All articles must have an Asian slant. We're interested in articles on the Asian New Years, banking, business, finance, sports/leisure, home and garden, education, and career planning. No culturally insensitive material. Send complete ms. Length: 500-700 words. **Pays $40.**

Columns/Departments Query with exceptional ideas for our market and provide 1-2 sample columns. 100

ATLANTA JOURNAL-CONSTITUTION

Cox Newspapers, Inc., 72 Marietta St., NW, Atlanta GA 30303. (404)526-5151. Fax: (404)526-5610. Website: www.ajc.com. Circ. 405,000. Daily. No kill fee.

- Mostly staff written.

THE BALTIMORE SUN

Tribune Co., 501 N. Calvert St., P.O. Box 1377, Baltimore MD 21278. (410)332-6000. Fax: (410)323-2898. E-mail: feedback@baltimoresun.com. Website: www.baltimoresun.com. Circ. 304,000. Daily. No kill fee.

- Mostly staff written.

BIGNEWS

Mainchance Publishing, 120 E. 32nd St., New York NY 10016. (212)679-4535. Fax: (212)679-4573. E-mail: bignewsmag@aol.com. Website: www.mainchance.org. Estab. 2000. Circ. 25,000. Accepts 75% of material on one-time basis. **30 features purchased/year.** "Our paper is a monthly art and literature publication sold on the streets of New York by homeless and formerly homeless vendors. We present stories and essays from an 'alternative' or 'outsider' viewpoint." Accepts queries by mail, e-mail, fax, phone. Responds in 1 week to queries. Responds in 1 month to mss. Buys one-time, electronic rights. Pays on publication. Editorial lead time 2 months. Offers 50% kill fee. Byline given. Accepts simultaneous submissions. Sample copy free. Guidelines available online.

Needs Send complete ms. Length: 1,000-5,000 words. **Pays $35-65.**

Photos State availability Reviews GIF/JPEG files. Buys one time rights. Negotiates payment individually. Captions required, identification of subjects required.

Tips "We usually look for the 'outcast' point of view, so keep that in mind."

BIRMINGHAM WEEKLY

Magnolia Media, 2257 Highland Ave. S., Birmingham AL 35205. (205)939-4030. E-mail: editor@bhamweekly.com. Estab. 1997. Circ. 30,000. Accepts 40% of material on one-time basis. We are edgy, hip, well written, but based in solid journalism. Our audience is 18-54, educated with disposable income and an irreverant but intelligent point of view. Accepts queries by mail, e-mail. Responds in 2 weeks to queries. Pays on publication. Editorial lead time 3 weeks. Byline given. Accepts simultaneous submissions. Sample copy free.

Needs We are strictly interested in stories that have a Birmingham connection, except in reviews, where the requirement is for readers to be able to buy the CD or book or see the film in Birmingham. No opinion columns, i.e., op-ed stuff. Query. Length: 750-2,000 words. **Payment varies. for no answer.** Sometimes pays expenses of writers on assignment.

Columns/Departments Sound Advice (CD Reviews), 200 words; Book Reviews, 300-750 words.

BOOKPAGE

Promotion, Inc., 2143 Belcourt Ave., Nashville TN 37212. (615)292-8926. Fax: (615)292-8249. Website: www.bookpage.com. Circ. 500,000. Monthly. "*BookPage* reviews almost every category of new books including popular and literary fiction, biography, memoir, history, science, and travel." Accepts queries by e-mail only. Editorial lead time 3 months. Byline given. Guidelines free.

- "*BookPage* editors assign all books to be reviewed, choosing from the hundreds of advance review copies we receive each month. We do not publish unsolicited reviews. We also publish additional reviews and interviews on our Website, BookPage.com."

Tips "If you are interested in being added to our large roster of freelance reviewers, send an e-mail to the editor with a brief bio, a description of your reading interests, and samples of your writing—particularly any book reviews you have written. We prefer experienced writers who can effectively communicate, with imagination and originality, what they liked about a particular book."

⊘ THE CHARLOTTE OBSERVER

Knight Ridder, P.O. Box 30308, Charlotte NC 28230. (704)358-5000. Fax: (704)358-5022. E-mail: localnews@charlotteobserver.com. Website: www.charlotteobserver.com. Estab. 1886. Circ. 242,000. Daily. No kill fee.

- Mostly staff written.

⊘ CHICAGO SUN-TIMES

Sun-Times Media Group, Inc., 350 N. Orleans, Chicago IL 60654. (312)321-3000. Fax: (312)321-3084. Website: www.suntimes.com. Circ. 450,000. Daily. No kill fee.

- Mostly staff written, but accepts freelance queries by mail.

⊘ CHICAGO TRIBUNE

Tribune Co., 435 N. Michigan Ave., Chicago IL 60611. (312)222-3232. Fax: (312)222-2550. Website: www.chicagotribune.com. Estab. 1847. Circ. 689,000. Daily. No kill fee.

- Mostly staff written.

⊘ THE CINCINNATI ENQUIRER

Gannett Newspapers, 312 Elm St., Cincinnati OH 45202. (513)768-8000. Fax: (513)768-8340. Website: www.enquirer.com. Circ. 191,000. Daily. No kill fee.

- Mostly staff written.

⊘ THE COLUMBUS DISPATCH

The Dispatch Printing Co., 34 S. 3rd St., Columbus OH 43215. (614)461-5000. Fax: (614)461-7580. Website: www.dispatch.com. Circ. 261,000. Daily. No kill fee.

- Mostly staff written.

⊘ DAILY NEWS (NY)

Daily News LP, 450 W. 33rd St., New York NY 10001. (212)210-2100. Fax: (212)643-7832. E-mail: news@edit.nydailynews.com. Website: www.nydailynews.com. Circ. 737,000. Daily. No kill fee.

- Mostly staff written.

⊘ THE DALLAS MORNING NEWS

A.H. Belo Corp., P.O. Box 655237, Dallas TX 75265. (214)977-8429. Fax: (214)977-8319. E-mail: metro@dallasnews.com. Website: www.dallasnews.com. Estab. 1885. Circ. 515,000. Daily. No kill fee.

- Mostly staff written.

⊘ DENVER POST

MediaNews Group, 101 W. Colfax Ave., Denver CO 80202. (303)820-1010. Fax: (303)820-1201. E-mail: newsroom@denverpost.com. Website: www.denverpost.com. Circ. 300,000. Daily. No kill fee.

- Mostly staff written. Contact specific editor.

⊘ DES MOINES REGISTER

Gannett Newspapers, P.O. Box 957, Des Moines IA 50304. (515)284-8000. Fax: (515)286-2504. E-mail: metroiowa@dmreg.com. Website: www.desmoinesregister.com. Estab. 1849. Circ. 155,000. Daily. No kill fee.

- Mostly staff written.

⊘ THE DETROIT NEWS

Gannett Newspapers, 615 W. Lafayette Blvd., Detroit MI 48226. (313)222-6400. Fax: (313)222-2335. E-mail: metro@detnews.com. Website: www.detnews.com. Circ. 233,000. Daily. No kill fee.

- Mostly staff written.

EVANGEL

Free Methodist Publishing House, P.O. Box 535002, Indianapolis IN 46253-5002. (317)244-3660. Estab. 1897. Circ. 13,000. Accepts 100% of material on one-time basis. **125 features purchased/year.** Weekly take home paper for adults. Accepts queries by mail. Responds in 4-6 weeks to queries. Buys second serial (reprint), simultaneous rights. Pays on publication. No kill fee. Sample copy for #10 SASE. Guidelines for #10 SASE.

Needs fiction, personal experience, poetry Religious themes dealing with contemporary issues from a Christian frame of reference, finding a solution to a problem common to young adults, coping with handicapped child, for instance, or with a neighborhood problem, story of how God-given strength or insight saved a situation, free verse, light verse, traditional, religious. Send complete ms. Length: 300-1,000 words. **Pays 4¢/word.**

Photos Purchased with accompanying ms.

Tips "Seasonal material will get a second look. Write an attention-grabbing lead followed by an article that says something worthwhile. All material should fit the mission of the publication as described in the guidelines. Lack of SASE brands author as a nonprofessional."

⊘ FORT WORTH STAR-TELEGRAM

Knight Ridder, 400 W. 7th, Fort Worth TX 76102. (817)390-7400. Fax: (817)390-7789. E-mail: newsroom@star-telegram.com. Website: www.star-telegram.com. Estab. 1906. Circ. 228,000. Daily. No kill fee.

- Mostly staff written.

⊘ THE GREENVILLE NEWS

Gannett Newspapers, P.O. Box 1688, Greeville SC 29602-1688. (864)298-4100. Fax: (864)298-4395. E-mail: localnews@greenvillenews.com. Website: www.greenvilleonline.com. Other Address: 305 S. Main St., Greenville SC 29601-2640. Estab. 1874. Circ. 87,622. Daily. No kill fee.

- Mostly staff written. Direct story ideas to the appropriate section editor (e-mail addresses provided on website).

⊘ THE HARTFORD COURANT

Tribune Co., 285 Broad St., Hartford CT 06115. (860)241-6200. Fax: (860)241-3865. Website: www.ctnow.com. Circ. 190,000. Daily. No kill fee.

- Mostly staff written. Submit story ideas to the appropriate section editor (e-mail addresses provided on website).

HOME TIMES FAMILY NEWSPAPER

(formerly *Palm Beach Conservative*), Neighbor News, Inc., P.O. Box 22547, West Palm Beach FL 33416. (561)439-3509. E-mail: hometimes2@aol.com. Website: hometimesnewspaper.org. **Contact:** Dennis Lombard, ed. & publ. Estab. 1990. Circ. 8,000. Accepts 50% of material under contract. Accepts 100% of material on one-time basis. **12 features purchased/year.** Works with Works with several local stringers. writers/year. Monthly tabloid mailed to subscribers throughout Palm Beach and Martin Counties in Southeast Florida. *"Home Times* is a conservative newspaper written for the general public but with a Biblical worldview and family-values slant. It is not religious or preachy." Accepts queries by Does not accept queries. 2-4 weeks to full articles only. Buys one-time and reprint rights. Makes work-for-hire assignments. Pays on publication. Editorial lead time 12 weeks. No kill fee. Byline given. Accepts simultaneous submissions. Returns submission with SASE. Sample copy for $3. Guidelines for #10 SASE.

Needs Buys one-shot features. Does not want devotionals. Send complete ms. Length: 500-1,000 words. **Pays $10-50 for assigned articles.** Other Sometimes pays expenses of writers on assignment.

Columns/Departments Home & Family; Arts & Entertainment, Science, Sports, Advice, Lifestyles; Personal

Finances, all shorts and features. 12

Fillers anecdotes, facts, short humor good quotes 100 word maximum.

Photos Can scan any size prints but prefer emailed digital photos. Send photos Reviews 4x5 prints or gif/tif/jpeg files. Buys one time rights. Offers $5-25/photo. Captions required, identification of subjects, model releases required, if appropriate.

Tips "We strongly suggest writers get guidelines plus READ the paper. Your $3 gets you three consecutive issues. Writer's subscription on $19."

HOUSTON CHRONICLE

Hearst Newspapers, P.O. Box 4260, Houston TX 77210. (713)362-7171. Fax: (713)362-6677. E-mail: online@chron.com. Website: www.houstonchronicle.com. Circ. 548,000. Daily. No kill fee.

- Mostly staff written.

THE INDIANAPOLIS STAR

Gannett Newspapers, P.O. Box 145, Indianapolis IN 46206. (317)444-4000. Fax: (317)444-6600. E-mail: info@indystar.com. Website: www.indystar.com. Estab. 1903. Circ. 255,000. Daily. No kill fee.

- Mostly staff written.

THE KANSAS CITY STAR

Knight Ridder, 1729 Grand Blvd., Kansas City MO 64108. (816)234-4636. Fax: (816)234-4926. E-mail: thestar@kcstar.com. Website: www.kcstar.com. Estab. 1880. Circ. 273,000. Daily. No kill fee.

- Mostly staff written.

KIDS VT

Vermont's Family Newspaper, Kids VT Publications, Inc., P.O. Box 1089, Shelburne VT 05482. (802)985-5482. Fax: (802)985-5479. E-mail: editorial@kidsvt.com. Website: www.kidsvt.com. Estab. 1994. Circ. 21,000. Accepts 80% of material on one-time basis. **25-40 features purchased/year.** Monthly. Accepts queries by mail, e-mail, fax. local, Vermont rights. Pays on publication. Editorial lead time 2 months. Accepts previously published submissions. Accepts simultaneous submissions. Guidelines available online.

Needs Query. Length: 400-1,600 words. **Pays $10-40.**

Photos State availability Buys one time rights. Negotiates payment individually. Captions required.

Tips Send unsolicited mss.

LAS VEGAS REVIEW-JOURNAL

Stephens Media Group, P.O. Box 70, Las Vegas NV 89125. (702)383-0211. Fax: (702)383-4676. Website: www.lvrj.com. Estab. 1905. Circ. 170,000. Daily. No kill fee.

- Mostly staff written.

LIVING

Media For Living, 1251 Virginia Ave., Harrisonburg VA 22802-2434. E-mail: mediaforliving@gmail.com. Website: www.livingforthewholefamily.com. **Contact:** Dorothy Hartman. Estab. 1992. Circ. 250,000. Accepts 90% of material on one-time basis. **40-50 features purchased/year.** Quarterly. "*Living* is a quarterly 'good news' paper published to encourage and strengthen family life at all stages, directed to the general newspaper-reading public." Responds in 2 months to queries. Responds in 6 months to mss. Pays on publication. Editorial lead time 6 months. Byline given. Accepts previously published submissions. Accepts simultaneous submissions. Sample copy for SASE with 9x12 envelope and 4 First-class stamps. Guidelines available by e-mail.

Needs Send complete ms. Length: 500-1,000 words. **Pays $35-60.**

Photos State availability of or send photos Reviews 3x5 or larger prints. Buys one time rights. Offers $25/photo. Identification of subjects required.

Tips "This paper is for a general audience in the community, but written from a Christian-value perspective. It seems to be difficult for some writers to understand our niche—*Living* is not a religious periodical, but handles an array of general interest family topics and mentions Christian values or truths as appropriate. Writing is extremely competitive and we attempt to publish only high-quality writing."

LIVING LIGHT NEWS

Living Light Ministries, 5306 89th St., #200, Edmonton AB T6E 5P9 Canada. (780)468-6397. Fax: (780)468-6872. E-mail: shine@livinglightnews.com. Website: www.livinglightnews.org. Estab. 1995. Circ. 75,000. Accepts 100% of material on one-time basis. **50 features purchased/year.** Bimonthly. "Our publication is a seeker-sensitive, evangelical, outreach-oriented newspaper focusing on glorifying God and promoting a personal relationship with Him." Accepts queries by e-mail, phone. Responds in 2 weeks to queries and to mss. Buys first North American serial, first, one-time, second serial (reprint), simultaneous, all rights. Makes work-for-hire assignments. Editorial lead time 2 months. Offers 100% kill fee. Byline sometimes given. Accepts previously published submissions. Accepts simultaneous submissions. Sample copy for 10x13 SAE with $3.50 in IRCs. Guidelines available online.

Needs Profiles on 'celebrity Christians' in sports, business and entertainment, plus amazing stories of hope, redemption and transformation through Jesus Christ. We have a special Christian college supplement called

'New Horizons' each spring. No issue-oriented, controversial stories. Query with published clips. Length: 300-1,000 words. **Pays $30-100 for assigned articles.** Sometimes pays expenses of writers on assignment. pays expenses of writers on assignment.

Columns/Departments 40

Photos State availability Reviews 3x5 prints, GIF/JPEG files. Buys all rights. Offers $20/photo. Identification of subjects required.

Tips "Please visit our website for a sample of our publication. All of our stories must be of interest to both Christians and non-Christians. We look for lively writing styles that are friendly, down-to-earth, and engaging. We especially like celebrity profiles."

LOS ANGELES DAILY JOURNAL

Daily Journal Corp., 915 E. First St., Los Angeles CA 90012. (213)229-5300. Fax: (213)625-0945. Website: www.dailyjournal.com. **Contact:** David Houston, editor. Estab. 1877. Circ. 17,500. Accepts 5% of material on one-time basis. **variable number of features purchased/year.** Daily. Content "must be of interest to lawyers and others interested in legal and governmental affairs." Accepts queries by mail, e-mail, fax, phone. Buys first, electroic rights. Makes work-for-hire assignments. Pays on publication. Offers kill fee. Offers variable kill fee. Byline given. Accepts simultaneous submissions.

Needs Query with published clips. Length: 500-5,000 words. **Payment varies (negotitates individually). for no answer.** Sometimes pays expenses of writers on assignment.

Photos State availability Buys all rights. Negotiates payment individually. Captions required, identification of subjects required.

⊘ LOS ANGELES TIMES

Tribune Co., 202 W. 1st St., Los Angeles CA 90012. (213)237-5000. Fax: (213)237-4712. E-mail: op-ed@latimes.com. Website: www.latimes.com. Circ. 945,000. Daily. No kill fee.

- Mostly staff written. Break in on the Op-Ed page.

Photos Photos should be b&w and no smaller than 5x7. Unable to return unsolicited photos. Captions required.

⊘ MIAMI HERALD

Knight Ridder, 1 Herald Plaza, Miami FL 33132. (305)350-2111. Fax: (305)376-5287. E-mail: nationalnews@herald.com. Website: www.herald.com. Estab. 1903. Circ. 328,000. Daily. No kill fee.

- Mostly staff written.

⊘ MILWAUKEE JOURNAL SENTINEL

Journal Communications, P.O. Box 661, Milwaukee WI 53201. (414)224-2413. Fax: (414)224-2047. Website: www.jsonline.com. Estab. 1837. Circ. 257,000. Daily. No kill fee.

- Mostly staff written.

N THE MOUNTAIN MESSENGER

P.O. Drawer A, Downieville CA 95936. (530)289-3262. Fax: (530)289-3262. E-mail: mtnmess@cwo.com. Estab. 1853. Circ. 2,500. Accepts 10% of material under contract. Accepts 5% of material on one-time basis. **20 features purchased/year.** Weekly. Accepts queries by mail, e-mail. Buys one-time rights. Pays on publication. Editorial lead time 1 week. No kill fee. Byline given. Accepts previously published submissions. Accepts simultaneous submissions. Returns submission with SASE. Sample copy free. Guidelines available by e-mail.

Needs Buys one-shot features. Buys article series. April Fools' edition (first Thursday of April). Query. Length: 350-1,200 words. **Pays $5-100.** Pays expenses of writers on assignment.

Columns/Departments Local History (slants opinionated, revisionist, or well researched).

Photos Contact: Don Russell, editor. State availability Buys one time rights. Negotiates payment individually. Identification of subjects required.

Tips "We prefer outrageously opinionated, funny stories. This is our editorial policy from page one on."

⊘ NEWSDAY

Tribune Co., 235 Pinelawn Rd., Melville NY 11747. (631)843-2020. Fax: (631)843-2953. E-mail: news@newsday.com. Website: www.newsday.com. Estab. 1940. Circ. 579,000. Daily. No kill fee.

- Mostly staff written.

⊘ THE NEW YORK TIMES

The New York Times Co., 229 W. 43rd St., New York NY 10036. (212)556-1234. Fax: (212)556-3815. E-mail: news-tips@nytimes.com. Website: www.nytimes.com. Estab. 1851. Circ. 1,130,000. Daily. No kill fee.

- Mostly staff written.

N ⊕ THE NORTHERN ADVOCATE

P.O. Box 210, 88 Roberts St., Whangerei New Zealand. E-mail: editor@northernadvocate.co.nz. Website: www.northernadvocate.co.nz. Estab. 1875. Circ. 15,321. Daily. No kill fee.

- Query before submitting.

Newspapers

NZ AVIATION NEWS
P.O. Box 9711, Newmarket Auckland 1149 New Zealand. (64)(9)307-7849. Fax: (64)(9)307-7854. E-mail: editor@aviationnews.co.nz. Website: www.aviationnews.co.uz. Estab. 1978. Circ. 15,000. Monthly newspaper covering the aviation industry and recreational activity in New Zealand and the Pacific region No kill fee.
Photos Reviews negatives, prints, JPEG files.

THE OKLAHOMAN
Oklahoma Publishing Co., P.O. Box 25125, Oklahoma City OK 73125. (405)478-7171. Fax: (405)475-3970. Website: www.newsok.com. Circ. 222,000. Daily. No kill fee.
- Mostly staff written; submit story ideas through the website.

THE OREGONIAN
Newhouse Newspapers, 1320 SW Broadway, Portland OR 97201. (503)221-8327. Fax: (503)227-5306. E-mail: newsroom@news.oregonian.com. Website: www.oregonian.com. Circ. 344,000. Daily. No kill fee.
- Mostly staff written.

ORLANDO SENTINEL
Tribune Co., 633 N. Orange Ave., Orlando FL 32801. (407)420-5000. Fax: (407)420-5350. Website: www.orlandosentinel.com. Circ. 266,000. Daily. No kill fee.
- Mostly staff written.

THE PALM BEACH POST
Cox Newspapers, Inc., P.O. Box 24700, West Palm Beach FL 33416. (561)820-4100. Fax: (561)820-4407. E-mail: pbonline@pbpost.com. Website: www.pbpost.com. Estab. 1894. Circ. 181,000. Daily. No kill fee.
- Mostly staff written.

PHILADELPHIA INQUIRER
Knight Ridder, P.O. Box 8263, Philadelphia PA 19101. (215)854-2000. Fax: (215)854-5099. E-mail: inquirer.letters@phillynews.com. Website: www.philly.com. Estab. 1829. Circ. 386,000. Daily. No kill fee.
- Mostly staff written.

THE PLAIN DEALER
Newhouse Newspapers, 1801 Superior Ave. E., Cleveland OH 44114. (216)999-5000. Fax: (216)999-6366. E-mail: editor@cleveland.com. Website: www.cleveland.com. Circ. 373,000. Daily. No kill fee.
- Mostly staff written.

THE PROVIDENCE JOURNAL
75 Fountain St., Providence RI 02902. (401)277-7000. Fax: (401)277-7346. E-mail: pjnews@projo.com. Website: www.projo.com. Estab. 1829. Circ. 165,000. Daily. No kill fee.
- Mostly staff written.

RICHMOND TIMES-DISPATCH
Media General, Inc., P.O. Box 85333, Richmond VA 23293. (804)649-6000. Fax: (804)775-8059. E-mail: news@timesdispatch.com. Website: www.timesdispatch.com. Circ. 217,000. Daily. No kill fee.
- Mostly staff written.

ROCKY MOUNTAIN NEWS
E.W. Scripps Co., P.O. Box 719, Denver CO 80201. (303)892-5000. Fax: (303)892-2841. E-mail: metro@rockymountainnews.com. Website: www.rockymountainnews.com. Circ. 300,000. Daily. No kill fee.
- Mostly staff written. Contact specific editor.

SACRAMENTO BEE
McClatchy Newspapers, P.O. Box 15779, Sacramento CA 95816. (916)321-1000. Fax: (916)321-1109. Website: www.sacbee.com. Estab. 1857. Circ. 300,000. Daily. No kill fee.
- Mostly staff written.

SACRAMENTO VALLEY MIRROR
138 W. Sycamore, City Willows CA 95988. (530)934-9511. Fax: (530)934-9208. E-mail: vmtim@pulsarco.com. Estab. 1991. Circ. 2,954. Accepts 10%% of material under contract. Accepts 5%% of material on one-time basis. **50/yr. features purchased/year.** Works with 15 writers/year. "Semiannual magazine covering general news. Accepts queries by mail, e-mail, fax. Responds in 1 week to queries. Buys first North American serial, electronic rights. Pays on publication. Editorial lead time 2 weeks. No kill fee. Byline given. SASE returns. Sample copy for #10 SASE.
- Much muckraking.

Needs Buys one-shot features. Does not want homilies, cooking items, 'I remember when.'; No general gooey, syrupy style items. Query with resume only. **Pays $25-200 for assigned articles.** Sometimes pays expenses of writers on assignment. pays expenses.

Photos State availability of photos. Reviews JPEG files. Buys all rights. Payment can be negotiated on major stories.
Tips "We need bright, tight, sharp writing. Tight leads. Compact and complete nut grafs. Stories must be well-sourced and on the record. Caution: We want news, not 'placed' items."

⊘ ST. LOUIS POST-DISPATCH

Pulitzer Newspapers, Inc., 900 N. Tucker Blvd., Saint Louis MO 63101. (314)340-8000. Fax: (314)340-3050. E-mail: pdeditor@post-dispatch.com. Website: www.post-dispatch.com. Estab. 1878. Circ. 286,000. Daily. No kill fee.

- Mostly staff written.

⊘ ST. PETERSBURG TIMES

490 First Ave. S., Saint Petersburg FL 33701. (727)893-8111. Fax: (727)893-8675. E-mail: local@sptimes.com. Website: www.sptimes.com. Estab. 1884. Circ. 354,000. Daily. No kill fee.

- Mostly staff written.

⊘ THE SAN DIEGO UNION-TRIBUNE

Copley Press, P.O. Box 120191, San Diego CA 92112. (619)299-3131. Fax: (619)293-1896. E-mail: letters@uniontrib.com. Website: www.uniontrib.com. Estab. 1868. Circ. 346,000. Daily. No kill fee.

- Mostly staff written.

SAN FRANCISCO CHRONICLE

Hearst Newspapers, 901 Mission St., San Francisco CA 94103. (415)777-1111. Fax: (415)543-7708. E-mail: metro@sfchronicle.com. Website: www.sfgate.com. Circ. 500,000. Daily. No kill fee. Guidelines available online.

- Very competitive market.

Needs Query. Length: 250-2,000 words. **Pays up to $500.**
Photos Contact: images@sfchronicle.com. We are looking for arresting images—of all points of view—that speak without accompanying text. Send photos Reviews JPEG files.

⊘ SAN JOSE MERCURY NEWS

Knight Ridder, 750 Ridder Park Dr., San Jose CA 95190. (408)920-5000. Fax: (408)288-8060. E-mail: letters@sjmercury.com. Website: www.mercurynews.com. Estab. 1851. Circ. 275,000. Daily. No kill fee. Guidelines available online.

- Mostly staff written. Contact specific editor.

⊘ SEATTLE POST-INTELLIGENCER

Hearst Newspapers, P.O. Box 1909, Seattle WA 98111. (206)448-8000. Fax: (206)448-8166. E-mail: citydesk@seattlepi.com. Website: www.seattlepi.com. Estab. 1863. Circ. 155,000. Daily. No kill fee.

- Mostly staff written.

⊘ THE STAR-LEDGER

Newhouse Newspapers, 1 Star Ledger Plaza, Newark NJ 07102. (973)392-4141. Fax: (973)392-5845. E-mail: eletters@starledger.com. Website: www.nj.com/starledger. Circ. 407,000. Daily. No kill fee.

- Mostly staff written.

⊘ STAR TRIBUNE

McClatchy Newspapers, 425 Portland Ave., Minneapolis MN 55488. (612)673-4000. Fax: (612)673-4359. E-mail: metrostate@gw.startribune.com. Website: www.startribune.com. Circ. 375,000. Daily. No kill fee.

- Mostly staff written.

⊘ THE TAMPA TRIBUNE

Life. Printed Daily., Media General, Inc., P.O. Box 191, Tampa FL 33601. (813)259-7600. Fax: (813)225-7676. E-mail: news@tampatrib.com. Website: www.tampatrib.com. Circ. 238,000. Daily. No kill fee.

- Mostly staff written.

⊘ THE TENNESSEAN

Gannett Newspapers, 1100 Broadway, Nashville TN 37203. (615)259-8000. Fax: (615)259-8093. E-mail: newstips@tennessean.com. Website: www.tennessean.com. Estab. 1812. Circ. 181,000. Daily. No kill fee.

- Mostly staff written.

TREASURE CHEST

The Information Source & Marketplace for Collectors and Dealers of Antiques and Collectibles, Sun Chronicle, 34 S. Main St., P.O. Box 1120, Attleboro MA 02703. (508)236-0378. Fax: (508)236-0463. Estab. 1988. Circ. 45,000. Accepts 90% of material on one-time basis. **60-80 features purchased/year.** Monthly. Responds in 2 months to mss. Buys first, second serial (reprint) rights. Pays on publication. Byline given. Accepts previously published submissions. Sample copy for $2 and 9x12 SASE. Guidelines for #10 SASE.
Needs Primarily interested in feature articles on a specific field of antiques or collectibles with reproducable photographs. Send complete ms. Articles on disk or via e-mail preferred. Length: 750-1,000 words. **Pays $30-**

40.

Tips Learn about your subject by interviewing experts—appraisers, curators, dealers.

⊘ USA TODAY

Gannett Newspapers, 7950 Jones Branch Dr., McLean, VA 22108 (703)854-3400. Fax: (703)854-2078. E-mail: editor@usatoday.com. Website: www.usatoday.com. Circ. 2,250,000. Daily. No kill fee.

- Mostly staff written.

⊘ THE VINDICATOR

Vindicator Printing Company, P.O. Box 780, Youngstown OH 44501-0780. (330)747-1471. Fax: (330)747-6712. Website: www.vindy.com. Other Address: 107 Vindicator Square, Youngstown OH 44503-1136. Circ. 67,523. Daily. No kill fee.

- Mostly staff written.

THE WALL STREET JOURNAL

Dow Jones & Co., Inc., 200 Liberty St., New York NY 10281. (212)416-2000. Fax: (212)416-2255. E-mail: edit.features@wsj.com. Website: www.wsj.com. Circ. 1,890,000. Daily. Accepts queries by e-mail. No kill fee. Guidelines available online.

- Op-Ed pieces must be exclusive to the *Journal*.

Needs Submit by e-mail complete ms, cover letter, and contact info. Length: 600-1,200 words.

THE WASHINGTON POST

Washington Post Co., 1150 15th St. NW, Washington DC 20071. (202)334-6000. Fax: (202)334-5672. E-mail: oped@washpost.com. Website: www.washingtonpost.com. Estab. 1877. Circ. 796,000. Daily. No kill fee.

- Mostly staff written. Break in with Op-Ed piece.

Needs Op-Ed pieces must be written exclusively for *The Post*. around 700 words.

THE WASHINGTON POST (TRAVEL SECTION)

1150 15th St. NW, Washington DC 20071. (202)334-7750. Fax: (202)912-3609. E-mail: travel@washpost.com. **Contact:** Nancy McKeon, travel editor. Accepts 40 (prefers to work with published/established writers) % of material on one-time basis. Weekly. Responds in 1 month to queries. Buys first North American serial rights. Pays on publication. Offers kill fee. There is no fixed kill fee. Byline given.

- No unsolicited mss. "We are now emphasizing staff-written articles as well as quality writing from other sources. Stories are rarely assigned; all material comes in on speculation. Travel must not be subsidized in any way."

Needs "Emphasis is on travel writing with a strong sense of place, color, anecdote, and history." Query with published clips. 1,500-2,500 words, plus sidebar for practical information.

Photos State availability

MARKETS

Screenwriting

Writers do not often get into screenwriting for the fame. Most of the glory shines on the directors, actors and actresses. But every great movie and TV show relies upon a great script that was crafted by a screenwriter. And though there may not be much in the way of fame, successful screenwriters do tend to bring in a healthy income. In fact, "How Much Should I Charge?'' on page 61 states that screenwriters make anywhere from $56,500 to $106,070 for an original screenplay.

Writing for TV

To break into TV you must have spec scripts—work written for free that serves as a calling card and gets you in the door. A spec script showcases your writing abilities and gets your name in front of influential people. Whether a network has invited you in to pitch some ideas, or a movie producer has contacted you to write a first draft for a feature film, the quality of writing in your spec script got their attention and that may get you the job.

It's a good idea to have several spec scripts, perhaps one each for three of the top five shows in the format you prefer to work, whether it's sitcom (half-hour comedies), episodic (one-hour series), or movie of the week (two-hour dramatic movies). For TV and cable movies, you should have completed original scripts (not sequels to existing movies) and you might also have a few for episodic TV shows.

In choosing the shows you write spec scripts for, you must remember one thing: Don't write a script for a show you want to work on. If you want to write for *CSI*, for example, you'll send a *Cold Case* script and vice versa. It may seem contradictory, but it's standard practice. It reduces the chances of lawsuits, and writers and producers can feel very proprietary about their shows and their stories. They may not be objective enough to fairly evaluate your writing. In submitting another similar type of show you'll avoid these problems while demonstrating comparable skills.

Writing for the movies

An original movie script contains characters you have created, with story lines you design, allowing you more freedom than you have in TV. However, your writing must still convey believable dialogue and realistic characters, with a plausible plot and high-quality writing carried through roughly 120 pages.

Many novice screenwriters tend to write too many visual cues and camera directions into their scripts. Your goal should be to write something readable, like a "compressed novella.'' Write succinct resonant scenes and leave the camera technique to the director and producer.

N 100 PERCENT TERRY CLOTH
421 Waterview Street, Playa Del Ray CA 90293 United States. (325)515-3787. Fax: (419)791-3378. E-mail: TM@terencemichael.com. Website: www.terencemichael.com.

ALLIED ARTISTS, INC.
9360 W. Flamingo Rd., Unit 110-189, Las Vegas NV 89147. (702)991-9011. E-mail: query@alliedartistsonline.com. Website: www.alliedartistsonline.com. Estab. 1990. Produces material for broadcast and cable television, home video, and film. **Buys 3-5 scripts/year. Works with 10-20 writers/year.** Buys first or all rights. Accepts previously produced material. Submit synopsis, outline. Responds in 2 months to queries. Responds in 3 months to mss. Pays in accordance with writer's guild standards.
Needs films, videotapes, social issue TV specials (30-60 minutes), special-interest home video topics, positive values feature screenplays.
Tips "We are looking for positive, uplifting dramatic stories involving 'real people' situations. Future trend is for more reality-based programming, as well as interactive television programs for viewer participation. Send brief e-mail query only. Do not send scripts or additional material until requested. No phone pitches accepted."

AMERICAN BLACKGUARD, INC.
P.O. Box 680686, Franklin TN 37068 United States. (615)599-4032. E-mail: contact@americanblackguard.com. Website: www.americanblackguard.com. "See website for current needs.".

AMERICAN WORLD PICTURES, INC.
16027 Ventura Blvd., Suite 320, Encino CA 91436. (818)380-9100. Fax: (818)380-0050. E-mail: jason@americanworldpictures.com. Website: www.americanworldpictures.com. **Contact:** Jason Corey, acquisitions. **Buys 4 scripts/year. Works with 5 writers/year.** Buys all rights. Accepts previously produced material. Query. Responds in 2 months to queries. Responds in 3 months to mss. Pays only $15,000 for scripts. Do not contact if price is more than that.

O-- Needs feature-length films. Send DVD/VHS to the Acquisitions Department.

Tips "Use strong characters and strong dialogue."

BIG EVENT PICTURES
3940 Laurel Canyon Blvd., #1137, Studio City CA 91604. E-mail: bigevent1@bigeventpictures.com. **Contact:** Michael Cargile, president. "Produces G, PG, and R-rated feature films for theaters, cable TV, and home video.". Query by e-mail. Producers will respond if interested.
Tips "Interesting query letters intrigue us—and tell us something about the writer. Query letter should include a short log line or pitch encapsulating what this story is about and should be no more than 1 page in length. We look for unique stories with strong characters and would like to see more action and science fiction submissions. We make movies that we would want to see. Producers are known for encouraging new/unproduced screenwriters and giving real consideration to their scripts."

SAM BLATE ASSOCIATES, LLC
10331 Watkins Mill Dr., Montgomery Village MD 20886-3950. (301)840-2248. Fax: (301)990-0707. E-mail: info@writephotopro.com. Website: www.writephotopro.com. **Contact:** Sam Blate, CEO. Produces educational and multimedia for marine, fishing, boating, business, education, institutions and state and federal governments. **Works with 2 local writers/year on a per-project basis—it varies as to business conditions and demand.** Buys first rights when possible Query with writing samples and SASE for return. Responds in 1 month to queries. Payment depends on contact with client. Pays some expenses.
Tips Writers must have a strong track record of technical and aesthetic excellence.

BURRUD PRODUCTIONS, INC.
468 N. Camden Drive, 2nd Floor, Beverly Hills CA 90210. (310)860-5158. Fax: (562)595-5986. E-mail: info@burrud.com. Website: www.burrud.com.

COOKIE JAR ENTERTAINMENT INC.
4100 Alameda Ave., Burbank CA 91505 United States. (818)955-5400. Fax: (818)955-5696. E-mail: info@thecookiejarcompany.com. Website: www.cookiejarentertainment.com. John Vandervelde.

CORNER OF THE SKY ENTERTAINMENT
1635 N Cahuenga Blvd., Los Angeles CA 90028. (323)860-1572. Fax: (323)860-1574. E-mail: George@cornerofthesky.com. Website: www.cornerofthesky.com.

LEE DANIELS ENTERTAINMENT
315 W. 36th St., Suite 1002, New York NY 10018. (212)334-8110. Fax: (212)334-8290. E-mail: info@leedanielsentertainment.com. Website: www.leedanielsentertainment.com. VP of Development. We work in all aspects of entertainment, including film, television, and theater. All nonagency scripts must be accompanied by a signed copy of the submission release form, which can be downloaded from the Web site. All scripts should be registered or copyrighted for your protection. All scripts should be in standard screenplay format. Include a synopsis, logline, and character breakdown (including lead and supporting roles). Do not send any extraneous

materials.

Tips Lee Daniels produced *Monster's Ball* and *The Woodsman*, and produced/directed *Shadowboxer*. He is the first African-American sole producer of an Academy-Award-winning film.

EDCON PUBLISHING GROUP

30 Montauk Blvd., Oakdale NY 11769-1399. (631)567-7227. Fax: (631)567-8745. E-mail: editor@edconpublishing.com. Website: www.edconpublishing.com. **Contact:** Janice Cobas, editor. Estab. 1971. Produces supplementary materials for elementary-high school students, either on grade level or in remedial situations. **100% freelance written.** All scripts/titles are by assignment only. Do not send manuscripts. Employs video, CD, book, and personal computer media. Buys all rights. Responds in 1 month to outline, 6 weeks on final scripts Pays $300 and up.

Needs Currently seeking Basic Math assessments in print/software format.

Tips "High interest/low readability."

ENERGY ENTERTAINMENT

999 N. Doheny Dr., #711, Los Angeles CA 90069. (310)274-3440. Website: www.energyentertainment.net. **Contact:** Brooklyn Weaver, owner/manager-producer. Estab. 2001. Submit query via website.

FAST CARRIER PICTURES, INC.

820 Majorca Place, Los Angeles CA 90049. (213)300-1896. E-mail: fastcarriervp@aol.com. Website: www.fastcarrier.com. **Contact:** Rory Aylward. Estab. 2000. Mass market motion picture/TV audience. **Buys 1-2 scripts/year. Works with 1-2 writers/year.** No options or cash up front. Query with synopsis.

- Our bread basket is cable, broadcast, and smaller theatrical films in the following genres: women in jeopardy, low-budget family movies tied to a holiday, low-budget westerns, horror, and romantic comedy.

Needs No teen sex comedies, large science fiction movies, historical epics, serial killer movies, or gross violence and humor at the expense of women, children, or minorities.

GINTY FILMS

16255 Ventura Blvd., Suite 625, Encino CA 91436. (310)277-1408. E-mail: ginty@robertginty.com. Website: www.robertginty.com. **Contact:** Robert Ginty. Estab. 1989. Commercial audience. **Buys 12-15 scripts/year. Works with 10-20 writers/year.** Buys first rights, all rights. Accepts previously produced material. Query with synopsis. Responds in 1 month to queries. Responds in 1 month to mss. Pays in accordance with writer's guild standards.

GREY LINE ENTERTAINMENT

115 W. California Blvd., #310, Pasadena CA 91105-3005. (626)943-0950. E-mail: submissions@greyline.net. Website: www.greyline.net. **Contact:** Sara Miller, submissions coordinator. Grey Line Entertainment is a full-service motion picture production and literary management company. We offer direct management of all services associated with the exploitation of stories. When our clients' motion picture screenplays are ready for the marketplace, we place them directly with studios or with major co-producers who can assist in packaging cast and/or director before approaching financiers (Warner Bros., New Line, Fox, Disney, etc.), or broadcasters (HBO, Showtime, etc.). Query via e-mail only. No attachments. Review online submission guidelines before sending. Responds in 2 weeks to queries.

- Queries for screenplays and treatments should consist of a compelling and business-like letter giving us a brief overview of your story and a 1-sentence pitch. Be sure to include your return address and a phone number. No multiple submissions. Treatments and screenplays submitted without a completed and signed Grey Line submission form will be discarded. Include SASE for reply. We recommend you register your screenplays/treatments with the copyright office or WGA before submitting.

Tips Your work must be finished and properly edited before seeking our representation (meaning proofread, spell-checked, and rewritten until it's perfect).

HUGHES CAPITAL ENTERTAINMENT

22817 Ventura Blvd., #471, Woodland Hills CA 91364. (818)484-3205. Fax: (818)484-3205. E-mail: info@trihughes.com. Website: www.hughescapitalentertainment.com. **Contact:** Faye, creative executive; Patrick Huges, producer; Karen Rabesa, VP production/development. Estab. 2006. Produces 2 movies/year. Send query and synopsis, or submit complete ms. Mostly accepts agented submissions. Responds in 3 weeks to queries.

- "We are looking to produce and develop feature-length screenplays, produced stage plays, well-developed pitches, and detailed treatments. Focus is on broad comedies, urban comedies, socially smart comedies, family films (family adventure), ground-breaking abstract projects, and new writers/directors with an extremely unique and unparalleled point of view. Don't focus on budget, cast, or locations. The story is key to getting things done here."

Tips "Don't back your screenplay or book into a budget. Let the creative lead the way. Never talk about a low budget and a star that's attached or that pre-sold in Egypt for $100 million. We don't care. We care about a unique voice—a filmmaker willing to take risks. Scripts that push the limits without trying for shock value. We care about filmmakers and good writers here."

ARNOLD LEIBOVIT ENTERTAINMENT

P.O. Box 33544, Santa Fe NM 87594-3544. E-mail: director@scifistation.com. Website: www.scifistation.com. **Contact:** Barbara Schimpf, vice president, production; Arnold Leibovit, director/producer. Estab. 1988. "Produces material for motion pictures and television.". **Works with 1 writer/year.** Query with log line and synopsis via e-mail. Do not send full script unless requested. A submission release must be included with all scripts. Responds in 2 months to queries. Pays in accordance with writer's guild standards.
Needs films, 35mm, videotapes. Does not want novels, plays, poems, treatments, or submissions on disk.

LEO FILMS

6548 Country Squire Ln., Omaha NE 68152. (323)459-5574. E-mail: lustgar@pacbell.net. Website: www.leofilms.com. **Contact:** Steve Lustgarten, president. Estab. 1989. Has released over 75 feature films. **Buys 5 scripts/year. Works with 8 writers/year.** Buys all rights. Query by e-mail with synopsis. Responds in 1 week to queries. Responds in 2 months to mss. Payment varies—options and sales.
Tips "Will also consider novels, short stories, and treatments that have true movie potential."

MAINLINE RELEASING

A Film & TV Production and Distribution Co., 301 Arizona Ave., 4th Floor, Santa Monica CA 90401. (301)255-7999. Fax: (310)255-7998. E-mail: hilda@lightning-ent.com. Website: www.mainlinereleasing.com. **Contact:** Hilda Somarriba, coordinator, sales, acquisitions and marketing. Estab. 1997. Produces family films, drama, thrillers, and erotic features.

THE MARSHAK/ZACHARY CO.

8840 Wilshire Blvd., 1st Floor, Beverly Hills CA 90211. Fax: (310)358-3192. E-mail: marshakzachary@aol.com; alan@themzco.com. **Contact:** Alan W. Mills, associate. Estab. 1981. "Audience is film goers of all ages and television viewers.". **Buys 3-5 scripts/year. Works with 10 writers/year.** Rights purchased vary. Query with synopsis. Responds in 2 weeks to queries. Responds in 3 months to mss. Payment varies
Tips "Submit logline (1-line description), a short synopsis of storyline, and a short biographical profile (focus on professional background). SASE required for all mailed inquiries. If submissions are sent via e-mail, subject must include specific information or else run the risk of being deleted as junk mail. All genres accepted, but ideas must be commercially viable, high concept, original, and marketable."

MONAREX HOLLYWOOD CORP.

11605 W. Pico Blvd., Suite 200, Los Angeles CA 90064. (310)478-6666. Fax: (310)478-6866. E-mail: monarexcorp@aol.com. **Contact:** Chris D. Nebe, president. Estab. 1978. All audiences. **Buys 3-4 scripts/year. Works with 5-10 writers/year.** Buys all rights. Query with synopsis. Responds in 1 month to queries. Pays in accordance with writer's guild standards.

NHO ENTERTAINMENT

8931 Beverly Blvd., #249, Los Angeles CA 90048. E-mail: info@nho.la. Website: www.nhoentertainment.com. **Contact:** Mark Costa, partner. Estab. 1999. All audiences. **Buys 5 scripts/year. Works with 10 writers/year.** Buys all rights. Accepts previously produced material. Query with synopsis, resume, writing samples, production history via e-mail. Responds in 1 month to queries. Catalog for #10 SASE. Pays in accordance with writer's guild standards.
Needs films, videotapes, multi kits, tapes, cassettes.

NITE OWL PRODUCTIONS

126 Hall Rd., Aliquippa PA 15001. (724)775-1993. Fax: (801)881-3017. E-mail: niteowlprods@aol.com; mark@niteowlproductionsltd.com. Website: www.niteowlproductionsltd.com. **Contact:** Bridget Petrella. Estab. 2001. Production credits include *Shopping Cart Commandos* and *American Playhouse: Three Sovereigns for Sarah*. Send a 1-page, single-spaced query letter via e-mail or mail.

- We will be producing at least 5-10 feature films in the next 2-5 years. We are searching for polished, well-structured, well-written, and professional-looking screenplays that are ready for production. If your screenplay does not meet these standards, do not send us a query. All screenplays must be in English and be in standard industry format. Provide a working title for your screenplay.

Tips All submissions must include a dated and signed Submission Release Form or they will be discarded immediately. All full-length feature film screenplays must be 80-130 pages in length. One-hour TV spec scripts must be 55-65 pages in length. Do not send us computer disks. One hardcopy of your screenplay will suffice. Do not cheat on your margins—we will notice. Proofread your screenplay thoroughly before submitting to avoid typos and punctuation and grammar mistakes. Copyright your script with the US Copyright Office and register it with the WGA. All screenplays must be firmly bound and include a cover page with the title of the work and your name, address, and contact information. Your materials will not be returned.

POP/ART FILM FACTORY

23679 Calabasas Rd., Suite 686, Calabasas CA 91302. E-mail: popartfilms@earthlink.net. Website: popartfilmfactory.com. **Contact:** Daniel Zirilli, CEO/director. Estab. 1990. Produces material for all audiences/feature films. Query with synopsis. Pays on per project basis

O― "We also have domestic and international distribution, and are always looking for finished films. We're producing 3 feature films/year and 15-20 music-oriented projects."

Needs films, any format, multi kits, documentaries.

Tips "Send a query/pitch letter and let me know if you are willing to write on spec (for the first job only; you will be paid if the project is produced). Be original. Do not play it safe. If you don't receive a response from anyone you have ever sent your ideas to, or you continually get rejected, don't give up if you believe in yourself. Good luck and keep writing!"

THE PUPPETOON STUDIOS

P.O. Box 33544, Santa Fe NM 87594-3544. E-mail: director@scifistation.com. Website: www.scifistation.com. **Contact:** Arnold Leibovit, director/producer. Estab. 1987. Wants plays geared toward a broad audience. **Works with 1 writers/year.** Query with logline and synopsis via e-mail. Do not send script unless requested. Submission release required with all scripts. Responds in 2 month to queries. Pays in accordance with writer's guild standards.

Needs films, 35mm. No novels, plays, poems, treatments, or submissions on disk.

RANDWELL PRODUCTIONS, INC.

185 Pier Ave., Suite 103, Santa Monica CA 90405. E-mail: randwellprods@yahoo.com. Website: www.randwell.com. **Contact:** Christina Wanke, development. Estab. 1997. TV and features audience. **Buys 3-4 scripts/year. Works with 2-3 writers/year.** Buys all rights. Query with synopsis. Responds in 2 weeks to queries. Responds in 3 months to mss. Pays in accordance with writer's guild standards.

Needs films, 35mm. No sci-fi, no westerns.

Tips Please keep synopsis to no more than one page. We hardly if ever request a copy of unsolicited material so don't be surprised if we pass.

SHORELINE ENTERTAINMENT, INC.

1875 Century Park E., Suite 600, Los Angeles CA 90067. (310)551-2060. Fax: (310)201-0729. E-mail: info@shorelineentertainment.com. Website: www.shorelineentertainment.com. Production credits include *Glengarry Glen Ross, The Visit, The Man From Elysian Fields*. Estab. 1993. Mass audience. **Buys 8 scripts/year. Works with 8 writers/year.** Buys all rights. Query. Responds in 1 week to queries.

Needs films, 35, 70mm.

Tips Looking for character driven films that are commercial as well as independent. Completed screenplays only. Especially looking for big-budget action, thrillers. We accept submissions by mail, e-mail or fax. No unsolicited screenplays, please.

SILENT SOUND FILMS, LTD.

United Kingdom. E-mail: thj@silentsoundfilms.co.uk. Website: www.silentsoundfilms.co.uk. **Contact:** Timothy Foster, MD. Estab. 1997. "Stage and fiction movies only. TV: arts/travel documentary.". Query with synopsis. Writers paid in accordance with WGA standards or the UK 'pact' agreement, if British production.

O― "We are interested in excellent writing (specifically musicals, art house, stage plays) with well-developed plot themes and original characters. So if you have a story that is nonparochial, we would be interested to see an e-mailed package that comprises: a 1-page synopsis, no more than 8 pages of scenario, and brief biography. Do not send images, complete screenplays, or large attachments. If it's something that grabs our attention, you will certainly hear from us."

Needs films, 35mm. "Does not want U.S.-based movies, nor storylines with principally American characters set anywhere else. This is because we are involved in what is unreliably called art house films and the best American art house films are made by Americans. So why compete?"

Tips "We seek the filmic equivalent of literature as opposed to bestseller."

SPENCER PRODUCTIONS, INC.

P.O. Box 2247, Westport CT 06880. E-mail: spencerprods@yahoo.com. **Contact:** Bruce Spencer, general manager; Alan Abel, creative director. Produces material for high school students, college students and adults. Occasionally uses freelance writers with considerable talent. Query. Responds in 1 month to queries. Payment negotiable

Needs tapes cass.

Tips "For a comprehensive view of our humor requirements, we suggest viewing our feature film production, *Is There Sex After Death* (Rated R), starring Buck Henry. It is available at video stores. Or read *Don't Get Mad . Get Even* and *How to Thrive on Rejection* by Alan Abel (published by W.W. Norton), both available from Barnes & Noble or Amazon. Also Books-on-Tape. Send brief synopsis (one page) and outline (2-4 pages)."

TOO NUTS PRODUCTIONS, L.P.

925 Lakeville St., Petaluma CA 94952. (310)967-4532. E-mail: info@toonutsproductions.com. **Contact:** Ralph Scott and Daniel Leo Simpson, co-executive producers. Estab. 1994. "Produces illustrated kids books, CDs, DVDs, animation shorts for internet, and half-hour tv/video with a twist. Among our storylines in development: Our Teacher is a Creature, Toad Pizza, The Salivating Salamander, The Suburban Cowboys, The Contest-Ants,

The De-Stinktive Skunk, and Sneeks Peaks. Audience is children, typically ages 3-6 and 7-9. Always looking for talented, new kidlit illustrators as well.". **Buys 4-10 scripts/year. Works with 4-6 writers/year.** Buys both first rights and all rights Query with synopsis. Submit resume. Submit writing samples. Submit production history. creative but brief cover letter/e-mail; Works with 1% first time writers. Illustrators query with creative but brief cover letter, samples of work by e-mail or hyperlink to your online portfolio. Responds in less than 3 months to queries. Responds in 6 months to mss. pays royalty and makes outright purchase

Really good original — clean — content.

Needs videotapes, multi kits, tapes cass, synopses, audio CDs, CD-ROMs. "Please do not submit anything with violence, chainsaws, axes, ice picks, and general blood and guts. We're producing for children, not monsters, or those who aspire to become them."

Tips "Suggestion: Use the words 'Too Nuts' at least twice in your query. (Do the math.) If you don't know how to giggle all the way to the bank, you may want to try someone else. If you've already exorcised your inner child, lizard, monkey, etc., that's a 'no no.' Please visit our website before querying. We receive too many submissions about axe murderers and adult themes. Even if you're still searching for your inner child through your writing, those subjects are clearly not for our audience. If you send us anything like this, expect a very 'spirited' response. Find your inner child on your own time!"

TREASURE ENTERTAINMENT

468 N. Camden Dr., Suite 200, Beverly Hills CA 90210. (310)860-7490. Fax: (310)943-1488. E-mail: info@treasureentertainment.net. Website: www.treasureentertainment.net. **Contact:** Mark Heidelberger, Treasure Entertainment co-chairman/chief executive officer. Estab. 2000. Management consideration given to writers with produced credits only. Intended audience is theatrical, festival, television, home video/DVD, Internet. **Buys 1-2 scripts/year. Works with 8-10 writers/year.** Accepts previously produced material. Query. Responds in up to 6 months to queries. Responds in up to 6 months to mss. Pays 1-10% royalty. Makes outright purchase of $1-100,000.

Needs films, 35 mm and 16mm, videotapes, multi kits.

Tips "We reserve the right to reject or return any unsolicited material. We also reserve the right not to purchase any material if we don't feel that any submissions are of sufficient merit. Our needs tend to change with the market and will vary from year to year. We are agreeing to look at writer's queries only. Queries should be sent by mail or e-mail only."

VALEO FILMS

P.O. Box 1500, Lindale TX 75771. (903)592-2495. E-mail: screenplays@valeofilms.com. Website: www.valeofilms.com. Query by e-mail or mail.

Currently considering projects that contain 1 or more of the following: character or story driven, identifies moral values, romance/love story, educational/documentary, presents the human condition, strong visual imagery, coming of age/learning, or intellectual drama/mystery.

Tips We require that you provide your name, phone number, address, title of your work, and WGA registration or copyright number. We will send an Unsolicited Project Release letter for you to sign and return with a sing copy of your screenplay/treatment. We don't want projects that contain the following characteristics: 1 character saves the world, SFX based, highly action based, extreme/grotesque violence, high sexual content, or strong explicit language. Although we do have a vast array of production resources available to us, we are a relatively small production copmany who prefers to limit the number of projects we have in production. Consequently, we tend to be very selective when it comes to choosing new material.

MARKETS

Playwriting

Where TV and movies have a diminished role for writers in the collaboration that produces the final product, whether a show or a film, theater places a very high value on the playwright. This may have something to do with the role of the scripts in the different settings.

Screenplays are often in a constant state of "in progress," where directors make changes; producers make changes; and even actors and actresses make changes throughout the filming of the TV show or movie. Plays, on the other hand, must be as solid as a rock, because the script must be performed live night after night.

As a result, playwrights tend to have more involvement in the productions of their scripts, a power screenwriters can only envy. Counterbalancing the greater freedom of expression are the physical limitations inherent in live performance: a single stage, smaller cast, limited sets and lighting, and, most importantly, a strict, smaller budget. These conditions not only affect what but also how you write.

Listings

The following listings include contact information, submission details, current needs, and other helpful tips to help you find a home for your finished and polished play. As with any market, it is advised that after you pinpoint a listing that you then follow up with them to find out their most current submission policy and to ask who you should address your submission. This might seem like a lot of work, but writing plays is a competitive business. Your professionalism will go a long way in separating you from other "wanna-be" playwrights.

For more information

To find out more about writing and submitting plays, contact the Dramatists Guild (www.dramaguild.com) and the Writers Guild of America (www.wga.org). Both organizations are great for networking and for learning the basics needed to build a successful career crafting plays.

ABINGDON THEATRE CO.

312 W. 36th St., 6th Floor, New York NY 10018. (212)868-2055. Fax: (212)868-2056. E-mail: literary@abingdontheatre.org. Artistic Director: Jan Buttram. **Contact:** Literary Manager: Kim T. Sharp. Estab. 1993. **Produces 2-3 Mainstage and 2-3 Studio productions/year.** Professional productions for a general audience. Submit full-length script in hard copy, cast breakdown, synopsis and development history, if any. No one-act. Include SASE for return of manuscript. Responds in 4 months. Buys variable rights. **Payment is negotiated.**

Needs All scripts should be suitable for small stages. No musicals where the story line is not very well-developed and the driving force of the piece.

Tips Check website for updated submission guidelines.

ACT II PLAYHOUSE

P.O. Box 555, Ambler PA 19002. (215)654-0200. Fax: (215)654-9050. **Contact:** Stephen Blumenthal, literary manager. Estab. 1998. **Produces 5 plays/year.** Submit query and synopsis. Include SASE for return of submission. Responds in 1 month. **Payment negotiable.**

Needs Contemporary comedy, drama, musicals. Full length. 6 character limitation; 1 set or unit set. Does not want period pieces. Limited number of scenes per act.

ACTORS THEATRE OF LOUISVILLE

316 W. Main St., Louisville KY 40202-4218. (502)584-1265. Fax: (502)561-3300. E-mail: awegener@actorstheatre.org. **Contact:** Amy Wegener, literary manager. Estab. 1964. **Produces approximately 25 new plays of varying lengths/year.** "Professional productions are performed for subscription audience from diverse backgrounds. Agented submissions only for full-length plays, will read 10-page samples of unagented full-length works. Open submissions to National Ten-Minute Play Contest (plays 10 pages or less) are due November 1." Responds in 9 months to submissions, mostly in the fall. Buys variable rights. **Offers variable royalty.**

Needs We are interested in full-length and 10-minute plays and in plays of ideas, language, humor, experiment and passion.

ALLEYWAY THEATRE

One Curtain Up Alley, Buffalo NY 14202. (716)852-2600. Fax: (716)852-2266. E-mail: newplays@alleyway.com. **Contact:** Literary Manager. Estab. 1980. **Produces 4-5 full-length, 6-12 one-act plays/year.** Submit complete script; include CD for musicals. Alleyway Theatre also sponsors the Maxim Mazumdar New Play Competition. See the Contest & Awards section for more information. Responds in 6 months. Seeks first production rights. **Pays 7% royalty.**

Needs "Works written uniquely for the theatre. Theatricality, breaking the fourth wall, and unusual settings are of particular interest. We are less interested in plays which are likely to become TV or film scripts."

ALLIANCE THEATRE

1280 Peachtree St. NE, Atlanta GA 30309. (404)733-4650. Fax: (404)733-4625. Website: www.alliancetheatre.org. **Contact:** Literary Intern. Estab. 1969. **Produces 11 plays/year.** Professional production for local audience. Only accepts agent submissions and unsolicited samples from Georgia residents only. Electronic correspondence preferred. Query with synopsis and sample or submit through agent. Enclose SASE. Responds in 9 months.

Needs Full-length scripts and scripts for young audiences no longer than 60 minutes.

Tips "As the premier theater of the southeast, the Alliance Theatre sets the highest artistic standards, creating the powerful experience of shared theater for diverse people."

⊘ AMERICAN CONSERVATORY THEATER

30 Grant Ave., 6th Floor, San Francisco CA 94108-5800. (415)834-3200. Artistic Director: Carey Perloff. **Contact:** Pink Pasdar, associate artistic director. Estab. 1965. **Produces 8 plays/year.** Plays are performed in Geary Theater, a 1,000-seat classic proscenium. No unsolicited scripts.

APPLE TREE THEATRE

1850 Green Bay Rd., Suite 100, Highland Park IL 60035. (847)432-8223. Fax: (847)432-5214. E-mail: info@appletreetheatre.com. **Contact:** Eileen Boevers. Estab. 1983. **Produces 4 plays/year.** "Professional productions intended for an adult audience mix of subscriber base and single-ticket holders. Our subscriber base is extremely theater-savvy and intellectual." Return SASE submissions only if requested. Rights obtained vary. **Pays variable royalty.**

Needs "We produce a mixture of musicals, dramas, classical, contemporary, and comedies." Length: 90 minutes-2 ½ hours. Small space, unit set required. No fly space, theatre in the round. Maximum actors 5.

Tips "No farces or large-scale musicals. Theater needs small shows with 1-unit sets due to space and financial concerns. Also note the desire for nonlinear pieces that break new ground. *Please do not submit unsolicited manuscripts—send letter and description along with tapes for musicals*; if we want more, we will request it."

ARENA STAGE

1101 6th St. SW, Washington DC 20024. (202)554-9066. Fax: (202)488-4056. Artistic Director: Molly Smith. **Contact:** Mark Bly, senior dramaturg. Estab. 1950. **Produces 8 plays/year.** Only accepts scripts from writers with agent or theatrical representation.

Needs "Plays that illuminate the broad canvas of American work, with a commitment to aesthetic, cultural, and geographic diversity. Arena is committed to showcasing the past, present, and future of American theatre." Seeks only full-length plays and musicals in all genres.

ARIZONA THEATRE CO.

P.O. Box 1631, Tucson AZ 85702. (520)884-8210. Fax: (520)628-9129. **Contact:** Literary Department. Estab. 1966. **Produces 6-8 plays/year.** "Arizona Theatre Company is the State Theatre of Arizona and plans the season with the population of the state in mind." Only Arizona writers may submit unsolicited scripts, along with production history (if any), brief bio, and SASE. Out-of-state writers can send a synopsis, 10-page sample dialogue, production history (if any), brief bio, and SASE. Responds in 4-6 months. **Payment negotiated.**

Needs Full length plays of a variety of genres and topics and full length musicals. No one-acts.

Tips "Please include in the cover letter a bit about your current situation and goals. It helps in responding to plays."

ARTISTS REPERTORY THEATRE

1515 SW Morrison, Portland OR 97205. (503)241-1278. Fax: (503)241-8268. Estab. 1982. **Produces** Plays performed in professional theater with a subscriber-based audience. Send synopsis, résumé, and sample (maximum 10 pages). No unsolicited mss accepted. Responds in 6 months. **Pays royalty.**

Needs Full-length, hard-hitting, emotional, intimate, actor-oriented shows with small casts (rarely exceeds 10-13, usually 2-7). Language and subject matter are not a problem. No one-acts or children's scripts.

ART STATION THEATRE

5384 Manor Dr., Stone Mountain GA 30083. (770)469-1105. E-mail: info@artstation.org. **Contact:** Jon Goldstein, program manager. Estab. 1986. **Produces 3 plays/year.** ART Station Theatre is a professional theater located in a contemporary arts center in Stone Mountain, GA, which is part of Metro Atlanta. Audience consists of middle-aged to senior, suburban patrons. Query with synopsis and writing samples. Responds in 1 year. **Pays 5-7% royalty.**

Needs Full length comedy, drama and musicals, preferably relating to the human condition in the contemporary South. Cast size no greater than 6.

ASIAN AMERICAN THEATER CO.

55 Teresita Blvd., San Francisco CA 94127. E-mail: aatcspace@gmail.com. **Contact:** Artistic Director. Estab. 1973. **Produces 4 plays/year.** Produces professional productions for San Francisco Bay Area audiences. Submit complete script. **Payment varies.**

Needs The new voice of Asian American theater. No limitations in cast, props or staging.

Tips Looking for plays from the new Asian American theater aesthetic—bold, substantive, punchy. Scripts from Asian Pacific Islander American women and under-represented Asian Pacific Islander ethnic groups are especially welcome.

ASOLO THEATRE CO.

5555 N. Tamiami Trail, Sarasota FL 34234. (941)351-9010. Fax: (941)351-5796. Estab. 1960. **Produces 7-8 plays/year.** A LORT theater with 2 intimate performing spaces. **Negotiates rights and payment.**

Needs Play must be full length. We operate with a resident company in rotating repertory.

ATTIC THEATRE & FILM CENTRE

5429 W. Washington Blvd., Los Angeles CA 90016-1112. (323)525-0600. Website: www.attictheatre.org. Artistic Director: James Carey. **Contact:** Literary Manager. Estab. 1987. **Produces 4 plays/year.** "We are based in Los Angeles and play to industry and regular Joes. We use professional actors; however, our house is very small, and the salaries we pay, including the royalties are very small because of that." Send query and synopsis or check out website. Returns submissions with SASE. Responds in 4 months. Buys first producer rights. **Payment is negotiated on a case by case basis.**

Needs "We will consider any type of play except musicals and large cast historical pieces with multiple hard sets. One Act plays are only accepted through the Denise Ragan Wiesenmeyer One Act Marathon Competition. Please see website for contest rules and regulations. One Acts can not be any longer than 30 minutes."

Tips "Please send an SASE and read our guidelines on the website. Follow all the directions."

BAILIWICK REPERTORY

Bailiwick Arts Center, 1229 W. Belmont Ave., Chicago IL 60657-3205. (773)883-1090. Fax: (773)883-2017. E-mail: bailiwick@bailiwick.org. **Contact:** David Zak, artistic director. Estab. 1982. **Produces 5 mainstage plays (classic and newly commissioned) each year; 12 one-acts in annual Directors Festival.** Pride

Performance Series (gay and lesbian), includes one-acts, poetry, workshops, and staged adaptations of prose. Submit year-round. One-act play fest runs July-August. Responds in 9 months for full-length only. **Pays 6% royalty.**

Needs We need daring scripts that break the mold. Large casts or musicals are OK. Creative staging solutions are a must.

Tips Know the rules, then break them creatively and boldly! Please send SASE for manuscript submission guidelines *before you submit* or get manuscript guidelines at our website.

BAKER'S PLAYS PUBLISHING CO.

45 W. 25th St., New York NY 10010. E-mail: publications@bakersplays.com. **Contact:** Managing Editor. Estab. 1845. **Publishes 20-30 straight plays and musicals. Works with 2-3 unpublished/unproduced writers annually. 80% freelance written. 75% of scripts unagented submissions.** Plays performed by amateur groups, high schools, children's theater, churches and community theater groups. Submit complete script with news clippings, resume, production history. Submit complete cd of music with musical submissions. See our website for more information about e-submissions. Responds in 3-6 months. **Pay varies; negotiated royalty split of production fees; 10% book royalty.**

Needs We are finding strong support in our new division—plays from young authors featuring contemporary pieces for high school production.

Tips We are particularly interested in adaptation of lesser-known folk tales from around the world. Also of interest are plays which feature a multicultural cast and theme. Collections of one-act plays for children and young adults tend to do very well. Also, high school students: Write for guidelines (see our website)for information about our High School Playwriting Contest.

MARY BALDWIN COLLEGE THEATRE

Mary Baldwin College, Staunton VA 24401. Fax: (540)887-7139. **Contact:** Terry K. Southerington, professor of theater. Estab. 1842. **Produces 5 plays/year.** 10% of scripts are unagented submissions. "An undergraduate women's college theater with an audience of students, faculty, staff and local community (adult, somewhat conservative)." Query with synopsis. Responds in 1 year. Buys performance rights only. **Pays $10-50/ performance.**

Needs "Full-length and short comedies, tragedies, and music plays geared particularly toward young women actresses, dealing with women's issues both contemporary and historical. Experimental/studio theater not suitable for heavy sets. Cast should emphasize women. No heavy sex; minimal explicit language."

Tips "A perfect play for us has several roles for young women, few male roles, minimal production demands, a concentration on issues relevant to contemporary society, and elegant writing and structure."

BARTER THEATRE

P.O. Box 867, Abingdon VA 24212-0867. (276)628-2281. Fax: (276)619-3335. E-mail: dramaturge@ bartertheatre.com. **Contact:** Catherine Bush, dramaturge. Estab. 1933. **Produces 17 plays/year.** "Plays performed in residency at 2 facilities, a 500-seat proscenium theater and a smaller 167-seat flexible theater. Our plays are intended for diversified audiences of all ages." Submit synopsis and dialogue sample only with SASE. Barter Theatre often premieres new works. Responds in 9 months. **Pays negotiable royalty.**

Needs "We are looking for good plays, comedies and dramas that entertain and are relevant; plays that examine in new and theatrical ways the human condition and contemporary issues. We prefer casts of 4-12, single or unit set. Strong language may lessen a play's appeal for Barter audiences."

Tips "We are looking for material that appeals to diverse, family audiences. We accept no one act play queries."

BLOOMSBURG THEATRE ENSEMBLE

226 Center St., Bloomsburg PA 17815. E-mail: jsatherton@bte.org. Ensemble Director:Gerard Stropnicky. **Contact:** J. Scott Atherton, manager of admin. and development. Estab. 1979. **Produces 9 plays/year.** Professional productions for a non-urban audience. Submit query and synopsis. Responds in 9 months. Buys negotiable rights **Pays 6-9% royalty. Pays $50-70/performance.**

Needs Because of our non-urban location, we strive to expose our audience to a broad range of theatre—both classical and contemporary. We are drawn to language and ideas and to plays that resonate in our community. We are most in need of articulate comedies and cast sizes under 6.

Tips Because of our non-urban setting we are less interested in plays that focus on dilemmas of city life in particular. Most of the comedies we read are cynical. Many plays we read would make better film scripts; static/relationship-heavy scripts that do not use the 'theatricality' of the theatre to an advantage.

BOARSHEAD THEATER

425 S. Grand Ave., Lansing MI 48933. (517)484-7800. Fax: (517)484-2564. **Contact:** Kristine Thatcher, artistic director. Estab. 1966. **Produces 8 plays/year (6 mainstage, 2 Young People's Theater productions inhouse), 4 or 5 staged readings.** Mainstage Actors' Equity Association company; also Youth Theater—touring to schools by our intern company. Submit synopsis, character breakdown, 20 pages of sample dialogue, bio, production history (if any) via mail or e-mail. **Pays royalty for mainstage productions, transport/per diem for staged readings.**

Needs Thrust stage. Cast usually 8 or less; occasionally up to 20; no one-acts and no musicals considered. Prefers staging which depends on theatricality rather than multiple sets. Send materials for full-length plays (only) to Kristine Thatcher, artistic director. For Young People's Theater, send one-act plays (only); 4-5 characters.
Tips Plays should not have multiple realistic sets—too many scripts read like film scripts. Focus on intelligence, theatricality, crisp, engaging humorous dialogue. Write a good play and prove it with 10 pages of great, precise dialogue.

BROADWAY PLAY PUBLISHING

56 E. 81st St., New York NY 10028-0202. (212)772-8334. Fax: (212)772-8358. E-mail: sara@broadwayplaypubl.com; broadwaypl@aol.com. This publisher does not read play mss. It will only publish a play if the playwright is an American-born resident; the play is not in print elsewhere; the play is full-length (at least 1 hour); the play has contemporary subject matter; the play is for at least 2 actors; the play has been professionally produced for at least 12 pefromances; there is acceptable color artwork for the cover; there are a few sentences from print media complimenting the play.

CELEBRATION THEATRE

7985 Santa Monica Blvd., #109-1, Los Angeles CA 90046. Fax: (323)957-1826. E-mail: celebrationthtr@earthlink.net. Artistic Director: Michael Matthews. **Contact:** Literary Management Team. Estab. 1983. **Produces 4 plays/year.** Performed in a small theatre in Los angeles. For all audiences, but with gay and lesbian characters at the center of the plays. Submit query and synopsis. Responds in 5 months. **Pays 6-7% royalty.**
Needs Produce works with gay and lesbian characters at the center of the narrative. There aren't any limitations, but simple productions work best. Don't send coming-out plays/stories.

CHAMBER THEATRE

158 N. Broadway, Milwaukee WI 53202. (414)276-8842. Fax: (414)277-4477. E-mail: mail@chamber-theatre.com. **Contact:** C. Michael Wright, artistic director. Estab. 1975. **Produces 5 plays/year.** Plays produced for adult and student audience. Submit query and synopsis. Submissions accompanied by a SASE will be returned. Responds in 3 months. **Pays royalty.**
Needs Produces literary, thought-provoking, biographical plays. Plays require small-unit settings. No plays for a large cast.

CHILDSPLAY, INC.

P.O. Box 517, Tempe AZ 85280. (480)350-8101. Fax: (480)350-8584. E-mail: info@childsplayaz.org. **Contact:** Artistic Director. Estab. 1978. **Produces 5-6 plays/year.** Professional touring and in-house productions for youth and family audiences. Submit synopsis, character descriptions and 7- to 10-page dialogue sample. Responds in 6 months. **Pays royalty of $20-35/performance (touring) or pays $3,000-8,000 commission. Holds a small percentage of royalties on commissioned work for 3-5 years.**
Needs Seeking theatrical plays on a wide range of contemporary topics. Our biggest market is K-6. We need intelligent theatrical pieces for this age group that meet touring requirements and have the flexibility for in-house staging. The company has a reputation, built up over 30 years, of maintaining a strong aesthetic. We need scripts that respect the audience's intelligence and support their rights to dream and to have their concerns explored. Innovative, theatrical and small is a constant need. Touring shows limited to 5 actors; in-house shows limited to 6-10 actors.
Tips No traditionally-handled fairy tales. Theater for young people is growing up and is able to speak to youth and adults. The material must respect the artistry of the theater and the intelligence of our audience. Our most important goal is to benefit children. If you wish your materials returned send SASE.

🅰 CLEVELAND PLAY HOUSE

8500 Euclid Ave., Cleveland OH 44106. E-mail: sgordon@clevelandplayhouse.com. Artistic Director: Michael Bloom. **Contact:** Seth Gordon, associate artistic director. Estab. 1915. **Produces 10 plays/year.** We have five theatres, 100-550 seats. Submit 10-page sample with synopsis. Will return submissions if accompanied by SASE. Responds in 6 months. **Payment is negotiable.**
Needs All styles and topics of new plays.

COLONY THEATRE CO.

555 N. Third St., Burbank CA 91502. (818)558-7000. Fax: (818)558-7110. E-mail: colonytheatre@colonytheatre.org. **Contact:** Michael David Wadler, literary manager. **Produces 6 plays/year.** Professional 276-seat theater with thrust stage. Casts from resident company of professional actors. Submit query and synopsis. Negotiated rights. **Pays royalty for each performance.**
Needs Full length (90-120 minutes) with a cast of 4-12. Especially interested in small casts of 4 or fewer. No musicals or experimental works.
Tips We seek works of theatrical imagination and emotional resonance on universal themes.

A CONTEMPORARY THEATRE

700 Union St., Seattle WA 98101. (206)292-7660. Fax: (206)292-7670. Estab. 1965. **Produces 5-6 mainstage plays/year.** ACT performs a subscription-based season on 3 stages: 2 main stages (a thrust and an arena) and a smaller, flexible 99-seat space. Although our focus is towards our local Seattle audience, some of our notable productions have gone on to other venues in other cities. *Agented submissions only* or through theatre professional's recommendation. Query and synopsis only for Northwest playwrights. Responds in 6 months. **Pays 5-10% royalty.**

Needs ACT produces full-length contemporary scripts ranging from solo pieces to large ensemble works, with an emphasis on plays that embrace the contradictions and mysteries of our contemporary world and that resonate with audiences of all backgrounds through strong storytelling and compelling characters.

Tips ACT is looking for plays that offer strong narrative, exciting ideas, and well-drawn, dimensional characters that will engage an audience emotionally and intellectually. These may sound like obvious prerequisites for a play, but often it seems that playwrights are less concerned with the story they have to tell than with the way they're telling it, emphasizing flashy, self-conscious style over real substance and solid structure.

CREEDE REPERTORY THEATRE

P.O. Box 269, Creede CO 81130-0269. (719)658-2541. E-mail: litmgr@creederep.com. **Contact:** Frank Kuhn, Literary Manager. Estab. 1966. **Produces 6 plays/year.** Plays performed for a smaller audience. Submit synopsis, 10-page dialogue sample, letter of inquiry, resume; electronic submissions only. Responds in 6 months. **Royalties negotiated with each author—paid on a per performance basis.**

Needs "Special consideration given to plays focusing on the cultures and history of the American West and Southwest."

Tips "We seek new adaptations of classical or older works as well as original scripts."

DALLAS CHILDREN'S THEATER

Rosewood Center for Family Arts, 5938 Skillman, Dallas TX 75231. E-mail: artie.olaisen@dct.org. **Contact:** Artie Olaisen, assoc. artistic dir. Estab. 1984. **Produces 10 plays/year.** "Professional theater for family and student audiences." Query with synopsis, number of actors required, any material regarding previous productions of the work, and a demo tape or lead sheets (for musicals). No materials will be returned without a SASE included. Responds in up to 8 months. Rights negotiable. **Pays negotiable royalty.**

Needs "Seeking substantive material appropriate for youth and family audiences. Most consideration given to full-length, non-musical works, especially classic and contemporary adaptations of literature. Also interested in social, topical, issue-oriented material. Very interested in scripts which enlighten diverse cultural experiences, particularly Hispanic and African-American experiences. Prefers scripts with no more than 15 cast members; 6-12 is ideal."

Tips "No adult experience material. We are a family theater. Not interested in material intended for performance by children or in a classroom. Productions are performed by professional adults. Children are cast in child-appropriate roles. We receive far too much light musical material that plays down to children and totally lacks any substance. Be patient. We receive an enormous amount of submissions. Most of the material we have historically produced has had previous production. We are not against perusing non-produced material, but it has rarely gone into our season unless we have been involved in its development. No phone calls."

DARLINGHURST THEATRE COMPANY

19 Greenknowe Ave., Potts Pointe NSW 2011 Australia. (61)(2)9331-3107. E-mail: theatre@darlinghursttheatre.com. Submission period ends September 15. Seeks to expose the audience to a diverse range of work, included narratives, non-narratives, Australian content, and international work. Classics are not excluded, though work new to Sydney is encouraged. Financial issues are a part of the selection process, so discuss your proposal with Glenn Terry before submitting. If asked, send complete ms or outline. See website for more submission details.

DETROIT REPERTORY THEATRE

13103 Woodrow Wilson, Detroit MI 48238-3686. (313)868-1347. Fax: (313)868-1705. **Contact:** Barbara Busby, literary manager. Estab. 1957. **Produces 4 plays/year.** Professional theater, 194 seats operating on A.E.A. SPT contract Detroit metropolitan area. Submit complete ms in bound folder, cast list, and description with SASE. Responds in 6 months. **Pays royalty.**

Needs Wants issue-oriented works. Cast limited to no more than 7 characters. No musicals or one-act plays.

DIVERSIONARY THEATRE

4545 Park Blvd., Suite 101, San Diego CA 92116. (619)220-6830. E-mail: dkirsch@diversionary.org. **Contact:** Dan Kirsch, executive director. Estab. 1986. **Produces 5-6 plays/year.** "Professional non-union full-length productions of gay, lesbian, bisexual and transgender content. Ideal cast size is 2-6." Submit application and 10-15 pages of script. Responds in 6 months.

DIXON PLACE

258 Bowery, 2nd Floor, New York NY 10012. (212)219-0736. Fax: (212)219-0761. **Contact:** Leslie Strongwater, artistic director. Estab. 1986. **Produces 12 plays/year.** Submit full script. Does not accept submissions from writers outside the NYC area. Looking for new work, not already read or workshopped in full in New York. **Pays flat fee.**

Needs Particularly interested in non-traditional, either in character, content, structure and/or themes. We almost never produce kitchen sink, soap opera-style plays about AIDS, coming out, unhappy love affairs, getting sober or lesbian parenting. We regularly present new works, plays with innovative structure, multi-ethnic content, non-naturalistic dialogue, irreverent musicals and the elegantly bizarre. We are an established performance venue with a very diverse audience. We have a reputation for bringing our audience the unexpected. Submissions accepted year-round.

🄰 DORSET THEATRE FESTIVAL

Box 510, Dorset VT 05251-0510. (802)867-2223. Estab. 1976. **Produces 5 plays/year (1 a new work).** Our plays will be performed in our Equity theater and are intended for a sophisticated community. Agented submissions only. **Rights and compensation negotiated.**

Needs Looking for full-length contemporary American comedy or drama. Limited to a cast of 6.

Tips Language and subject matter must be appropriate to general audience.

DRAMATIC PUBLISHING

311 Washington St., Woodstock IL 60098. (800)448-7469. Fax: (800)334-5302. **Contact:** Linda Habjan, submissions editor. **Publishes 40-50 titles/year.** Publishes paperback acting editions of original plays, musicals, adaptations, and translations. **Receives 250-500 queries and 600 mss/year.** Catalog and script guidelines free. **Pays 10% royalty on scripts; performance royalty varies.**

Needs Interested in playscripts appropriate for children, middle and high schools, colleges, community, stock and professional theaters. Send full ms.

Tips We publish all kinds of plays for the professional, stock, amateur, high school, elementary and children's theater markets: full lengths, one acts, children's plays, musicals, adaptations.

DRAMATICS MAGAZINE

2343 Auburn Ave., Cincinnati OH 45219. (513)421-3900. Fax: (513)421-7077. E-mail: dcorathers@edta.org. **Contact:** Don Corathers, editor. Estab. 1929. **Publishes** For high school theater students and teachers. Submit complete script. Responds in 3 months. Buys first North American serial rights only.

Needs We are seeking one-acts to full-lengths that can be produced in an educational theater setting.

Tips No melodrama, musicals, farce, children's theater, or cheap knock-offs of TV sitcoms or movies. Fewer writers are taking the time to learn the conventions of theater—what makes a piece work on stage, as opposed to film and television—and their scripts show it. We're always looking for good interviews with working theatre professionals.

EAST WEST PLAYERS

120 N. Judge John Aiso St., Los Angeles CA 90012. (213)625-7000. Fax: (213)625-7111. E-mail: jliu@eastwestplayers.org. Artistic Director: Tim Dang. **Contact:** Jeff Liu, literary manager. Estab. 1965. **Produces 4 plays/year.** Professional 240-seat theater performing under LOA-BAT contract, presenting plays which explore the Asian Pacific American experience." Submit ms with title page, résumé, cover letter, and SASE. Responds in 3-9 months. **Pays royalty against percentage of box office.**

Needs Whether dramas, comedies, or musicals, all plays must either address the Asian American experience or have a special resonance when cast with Asian American actors.

ELDRIDGE PUBLISHING CO.

P.O. Box 14367, Tallahassee FL 32317. E-mail: editorial@histage.com. Managing Editor: Nancy Vorhis. **Contact:** Editor: Susan Shore. Estab. 1906. **Publishes 65 new plays/year for junior high, senior high, church, and community audience.** Query with synopsis (acceptable). Please send CD with any musicals. Responds in 1-2 months. Buys all dramatic rights. **Pays 50% royalties for amateur productions, 80% for professional productions and 10% copy sales in general market. Makes outright purchase of $100-600 in religious market.**

Needs "We are most interested in full-length plays and musicals for our school and community theater market. Nothing lower than junior high level, please. We always love comedies but also look for serious, high caliber plays reflective of today's sophisticated students. We also need one-acts and plays for children's theater. In addition, in our religious market we're always searching for holiday plays. No plays which belong in a classroom setting as part of a lesson plan. Unless it is for Christmas, no other religious musicals considered."

Tips "Please have your work performed, if at all possible, before submitting. The quality will improve substantially."

THE ENSEMBLE STUDIO THEATRE

549 W. 52nd St., New York NY 10019. (212)247-4982. Fax: (212)664-0041. E-mail: firman@

ensemblestudiotheatre.org. Website: www.ensemblestudiotheatre.org. Artistic Director: William Carden. **Contact:** Linsay Firman, artistic director. Estab. 1972. **Produces 250 projects/year for off-off Broadway developmental theater in a 100-seat house, 60-seat workshop space.** Do not fax mss or resumes. Submit complete ms. Responds in 10 months.

Needs "Full-length plays with strong dramatic actions and situations and solid one-acts, humorous and dramatic, which can stand on their own. Special programs include Going to the River Series, which workshops new plays by African-American women, and the Sloan Project, which commissions new works on the topics of science and technology. Seeks original plays with strong dramatic action, believable characters and dynamic ideas. We are interested in writers who respect the power of language. No verse-dramas or elaborate costume dramas. Accepts new/unproduced work only."

ENSEMBLE THEATRE OF CINCINNATI

1127 Vine St., Cincinnati OH 45248. (513)421-3555. Fax: (513)562-4104. E-mail: lynn.meyers@cincyetc.com. **Contact:** D. Lynn Meyers, producing artistic director. Estab. 1987. **Produces 12 plays/year, including a staged reading series.** Professional year-round theater. Query with synopsis, submit complete ms or submit through agent. Responds in 6 months. **Pays 5-10% royalty.**

Needs Dedicated to good writing of any style for a small, contemporary cast. Small technical needs, big ideas.

THE ESSENTIAL THEATRE

P.O. Box 8172, Atlanta GA 30306. (404)212-0815. E-mail: pmhardy@aol.com. **Contact:** Peter Hardy, artistic director. Estab. 1987. **Produces 3 plays/year.** Professional theatre on a small budget, for adventurous theatregoers interested in new plays. Submit complete script by regular mail, or e-mail in Word format to: pmhardy@aol.com Include SASE for return of submission. Responds in 10 months.

Needs Accepts unproduced plays of any length by Georgia writers only, to be considered for Essential Theatre Playwriting Award.

Tips Submission deadline: April 23

THE FOOTHILL THEATRE CO.

P.O. Box 1812, Nevada City CA 95959. (530)265-9320. Fax: (530)265-9325. E-mail: info@foothilltheatre.org. Artistic Director: Carolyn Howarth. **Contact:** Literary Manager. Estab. 1977. **Produces 6-9 plays/year.** We are a professional theater company operating under an Actors' Equity Association contract for part of the year, and performing in the historic 246-seat Nevada Theatre (built in 1865) and at an outdoor amphitheatre on the north shore of Lake Tahoe. We also produce a new play development program called New Voices of the Wild West that endeavors to tell the stories of the non-urban Western United States. The audience is a mix of locals and tourists. Query by e-mail. Responds in 6 months-1 year. Buys negotiable rights. **Payment varies.**

Needs We are most interested in plays which speak to the region and its history, as well as to its current concerns. No melodramas. Theatrical, above all.

Tips At present, we're especially interested in unproduced plays that speak to the rural and semi-rural American West for possible inclusion in our new play reading and development program, New Voices of the Wild West. History plays are okay, as long as they don't sound like you wrote them with an encyclopedia open in your lap. The best way to get our attention is to write something we haven't seen before, and write it well.

FOUNTAIN THEATRE

5060 Fountain Ave., Los Angeles CA 90029. (323)663-2235. Fax: (323)663-1629. E-mail: ftheatre@aol.com. Artistic Directors: Deborah Lawlor, Stephen Sachs. **Contact:** Simon Levy, dramaturg. Estab. 1990. Produces both a theater and dance season. Produced at Fountain Theatre (99-seat equity plan). *Professional recommendation only*. Query with synopsis to Simon Levy, producing director/dramaturg. Responds in 6 months. Rights acquired vary. **Pays royalty.**

Needs Original plays, adaptations of American literature, material that incorporates dance or language into text with unique use and vision.

THE FREELANCE PRESS

P.O. Box 548, Dover MA 02030-2207. (508)785-8250. Fax: (508)785-8291. **Contact:** Narcissa Campion, managing director. Estab. 1984. Submit complete ms with SASE. Responds in 4 months. **Pays 70% of performance royalties to authors. Pays 10% script and score royalty.**

Needs We publish original musical theater to be performed by young people, dealing with issues of importance to them. Also adapt 'classics' into musicals for 8- to 16-year-old age groups to perform. Large cast, flexible.

SAMUEL FRENCH, INC.

45 W. 25th St., New York NY 10010. (212)206-8990. Fax: (212)206-1429. E-mail: publications@samuelfrench.com. **Contact:** Editorial Department. Estab. 1830. **Publishes 50-60 titles/year.** Publishes paperback acting editions of plays. Receives 1,500 submissions/year, mostly from unagented playwrights. 10% of publications are from first-time authors; 20% from unagented writers. **Pays 10% royalty on retail price, plus amateur and stock royalties on productions.**

Needs Comedies, mysteries, children's plays, high school plays.

Tips Broadway and Off-Broadway hit plays, light comedies and mysteries have the best chance of selling to our firm. Our market is comprised of theater producers—both professional and amateur—actors and students. Read as many plays as possible of recent vintage to keep apprised of today's market; write plays with good female roles; and be 100% professional in approaching publishers and producers. We recommend (not require) that submissions be in the format used by professional playwrights in the US, as illustrated in *Guidelines*, available for $4 (postpaid).

WILL GEER THEATRICUM BOTANICUM

P.O. Box 1222, Topanga CA 90290. (310)455-2322. Fax: (310)455-3724. **Contact:** Ellen Geer, artistic director. Estab. 1973. **Produces 4 classical and 1 new play if selected/year.** Professional productions for summer theater. Botanicum Seedlings new plays selected for readings and one play each year developed. Contact: Jennie Webb. Send synopsis, sample dialogue and tape if musical. Responds in 6 months. **Pays 6% royalty or $150 per show.**
Needs Socially relevant plays, musicals; all full-length. Cast size of 4-10 people. "We are a large outdoor theatre—small intimate works could be difficult."
Tips "September submissions have best turn around for main season; year-round for 'Botanicum Seedlings.'"

GEORGE STREET PLAYHOUSE

9 Livingston Ave., New Brunswick NJ 08901. (732)246-7717. Artistic Director: David Saint. **Contact:** Literary Associate. **Produces 6 plays/year.** Professional regional theater (LORT C). Proscenium/thurst stage with 367 seats. *No unsolicited scripts. Agent or professional recommendation only.*
Tips It is our firm belief that theater reaches the mind via the heart and the funny bone. Our work tells a compelling, personal, human story that entertains, challenges and stretches the imagination.

GEVA THEATRE CENTER

75 Woodbury Blvd., Rochester NY 14607. (585)232-1366. **Contact:** Marge Betley, literary manager. **Produces 7-11 plays/year.** Professional and regional theater, modified thrust, 552 seats; second stage has 180 seats. Subscription and single-ticket sales. Query with sample pages, synopsis, and resume. Responds in 3 months.
Needs Full-length plays, translations, and adaptations.

THE GOODMAN THEATRE

170 N. Dearborn St., Chicago IL 60601-3205. (312)443-3811. Fax: (312)443-3821. E-mail: artistic@goodman-theatre.org. **Contact:** Tanya Palmer, literary manager. Estab. 1925. **Produces 9 plays/year.** The Goodman is a professional, not-for-profit theater producing a series in both the Albert Theatre and the Owen Theatre, which includes an annual New Play Series. The Goodman does not accept unsolicited scripts, nor will it respond to synopsis of plays submitted by playwrights unless accompanied by a stamped, self-addressed postcard. The Goodman may request plays to be submitted for production consideration after receiving a letter of inquiry or telephone call from recognized literary agents or producing organizations. Responds in 6 months. Buys variable rights. **Pays variable royalty.**
Needs Full-length plays, translations, musicals; special interest in social or political themes.

GRETNA THEATRE

P.O. Box 578, Mt. Gretna PA 17064. Fax: (717)964-2189. E-mail: larryfrenock@gretnatheatre.com. **Contact:** Larry Frenock, producing director. Estab. 1927. Plays are performed at a professional equity theater during summer. Agent submissions only. **Pays negotiable royalty (6-12%).**
Needs We produce full-length plays for a summer audience—subject, language and content are important. Prefer package or vehicles which have star role.
Tips No one-acts. Given that we re a summer stock theatre, the chances of producing a new play are extremely remote, though we have produced play readings in the past.

GRIFFIN THEATRE COMPANY

13 Craigend St., Kings Cross NSW 2011 Australia. (61)(2)9332-1052. Fax: (61)(2)9331-1524. Gives consideration and feedback if the author has had a play professionally produced, has an agent, has been shortlisted for the Griffin Award, or has had a play workshopped at Griffin. If you don't meet these requirements, you may still send a 1-page outline and a 10-page sample. If interested, we will request the full manuscript.

HARTFORD STAGE CO.

50 Church St., Hartford CT 06103. (860)525-5601. Fax: (860)525-4420. Estab. 1963. **Produces 6 plays/year.** Regional theater productions with a wide range in audience.
Needs Classics, new plays, musicals. *Agented submissions only.* No queries or synopses.

HORIZON THEATRE CO.

P.O. Box 5376, Atlanta GA 31107. (404)523-1477. Fax: (404)584-8815. **Contact:** Literary Manager. Estab. 1983. **5+ plays/year, and workshops 6 plays as part of New South Playworks Festival** Professional productions. Accepts unsolicited résumés, samples, treatments, and summaries with SASE. Responds in 1 year. Buys

rights to produce in Atlanta area.
Needs "We produce contemporary plays that seek to bridge cultures and communities, utilizing a realistic base but with heightened visual or language elements. Particularly interested in comedy, satire, plays that are entertaining and topical, but thought provoking. Also particular interest in plays by women, African-Americans, or that concern the contemporary South. No more than 8 in cast."

ILLINOIS THEATRE CENTRE

371 Artists' Walk, P.O. Box 397, Park Forest IL 60466. (708)481-3510. Fax: (708)481-3693. E-mail: ilthctr@sbcglobal.net. Estab. 1976. **Produces 8 plays/year.** Professional Resident Theatre Company in our own space for a subscription-based audience. Query with synopsis or agented submission. Responds in 2 months. Buys casting and directing and designer selection rights. **Pays 7-10% royalty.**
Needs All types of 2-act plays, musicals, dramas. Prefers cast size of 6-10.
Tips Always looking for mysteries and comedies. Make sure your play arrives between November and January when play selections are made.

INDIANA REPERTORY THEATRE

140 W. Washington St., Indianapolis IN 46204-3465. (317)635-5277. E-mail: rroberts@irtlive.com. Website: www.irtlive.com. Artistic Director: Janet Allen. Dramaturg: Richard Roberts. "Modified proscenium stage with 600 seats; thrust stage with 300 seats." Send synopsis with résumé via e-mail to the dramaturg. No unsolicited scripts. Submit year-round (season chosen by January). Responds in 6 month.
Needs Full-length plays, translations, adaptations, solo pieces. Also interested in adaptations of classic literature and plays that explore cultural/ethnic issues with a midwestern voice. Special program: Discovery Series (plays for family audiences with a focus on youth). Cast size should be 6-8.
Tips "The IRT employs a playwright-in-residence from whom the majority of our new work is commissioned. We occasionally place other subject-specific commissions."

INTERACT THEATRE CO.

The Adrienne, 2030 Sansom St., Philadelphia PA 19103. (215)568-8077. Fax: (215)568-8095. E-mail: pbonilla@interacttheatre.org. **Contact:** Peter Bonilla, literary associate. Estab. 1988. **Produces 4 plays/year.** Produces professional productions for adult audience. Query with synopsis and bio. No unsolicited scripts. Responds in 6 months. **Pays 2-8% royalty or $25-100/performance.**
Needs Contemporary dramas and comedies that explore issues of political, social, cultural or historical significance. Virtually all of our productions have political content in the foregound of the drama. Prefer plays that raise interesting questions without giving easy, predictable answers. We are interested in new plays. Limit cast to 8. No romantic comedies, family dramas, agit-prop.

A INTIMAN THEATRE

201 Mercer St., Seattle WA 98109. (206)269-1901. Fax: (206)269-1928. E-mail: literary@intiman.org. Artistic Director: Bartlett Sher. **Contact:** Sheila Daniels. Estab. 1972. **Produces 6 plays/year.** LORT C Regional Theater in Seattle. Best submission time is October through March. *Agented submissions only* or by professional recommendation. Responds in 8 months.
Needs Well-crafted dramas and comedies by playwrights who fully utilize the power of language and character relationships to explore enduring themes. Prefers nonnaturalistic plays and plays of dynamic theatricality.

JEWEL BOX THEATRE

3700 N. Walker, Oklahoma City OK 73118-7099. (405)521-7031. Fax: (405)525-6562. **Contact:** Charles Tweed, production director. Estab. 1956. **Produces 6 plays/year.** Amateur productions. 3,000 season subscribers and general public. **Pays $500 contest prize.**
Needs Annual Playwriting Competition: Send SASE in September-October. Deadline: mid-January.

JEWISH ENSEMBLE THEATRE

6600 W. Maple Rd., West Bloomfield MI 48322. (248)788-2900. E-mail: e.orbach@jettheatre.org. **Contact:** Evelyn Orbach, artistic director. Estab. 1989. **Produces 4-6 plays/year.** Professional productions at the Aaron DeRoy Theatre (season), The Detroit Institue of Arts Theatre, and Scottish Rite Cathedral Theatre (schools), as well as tours to schools. Submit complete script. Responds in 1 year. Obtains rights for our season productions and staged readings for festival. **Pays 6-8% royalty for full production or honorarium for staged reading—$100/full-length play.**
Needs We do few children's plays except original commissions; we rarely do musicals. Cast limited to a maximum of 8 actors
Tips We are a theater of social conscience with the following mission: to produce work on the highest possible professional level; to deal with issues of community & humanity from a Jewish perspective; to provide a platform for new voices and a bridge for understanding to the larger community.

KITCHEN DOG THEATER

3120 McKinney Ave., Dallas TX 75204. (214)953-2258. Fax: (214)953-1873. **Contact:** Chris Carlos, co-artistic director. Estab. 1990. **Produces 5 plays/year.** Kitchen Dog has two performance spaces: a 100-seat black box

and a 150-seat thrust. Submit complete manuscript with SASE. Each year the deadline for submissions is March 1 (received by). Writers are notified by May 15. Buys rights to full production. **Pays $1,000 for winner of New Works Festival.**
Needs We are interested in experimental plays, literary adaptations, historical plays, political theater, gay and lesbian work, culturally diverse work, and small musicals. Ideally, cast size would be 1-5, or more if doubling roles is a possibility. No romantic/light comedies or material that is more suited for television than the theater.
Tips We are interested in plays that are theatrical and that challenge the imagination—plays that are for the theater, rather than TV or film.

KUMU KAHUA

46 Merchant St., Honolulu HI 96813. (808)536-4222. Fax: (808)536-4226. E-mail: kumukahuatheatre@hawaiiantel.net. **Contact:** Artistic Director. Estab. 1971. **Produces 5 productions, 3-4 public readings/year.** Plays performed at new Kumu Kahua Theatre, flexible 120-seat theater, for community audiences. Submit complete script. Responds in 4 months. **Pays royalty of $50/performance; usually 20 performances of each production.**
Needs Plays must have some interest for local Hawai'i audiences.

LILLENAS PUBLISHING CO.

P.O. Box 419527, Kansas City MO 64141-6527. (816)931-1900. Fax: (816)412-8390. **Contact:** Kim Messer, product manager. Estab. 1926. "We publish on 2 levels: 1) Program Builders—seasonal and topical collections of recitations, sketches, dialogues, and short plays; 2) Drama Resources which assume more than 1 format: a) full-length scripts; b) one-acts, shorter plays, and sketches all by 1 author; c) collection of short plays and sketches by various authors. All program and play resources are produced with local church and Christian school in mind. Therefore there are taboos." Queries are encouraged, but synopses and complete scripts are read. This publisher is interested in collections of and individual sketches. There is also a need for short pieces that are seasonal and on current events. Responds in 3 months. First rights are purchased for Program Builders scripts. For Drama Resources, we purchase all print rights. **Drama Resources are paid on a 12% royalty, whether full-length scripts, one-acts, or sketches. No advance.**
Needs 98% of Program Builders materials are freelance written. Scripts selected for these publications are outright purchases; verse is minimum of 25¢/line, prose (play scripts) are minimum of $5/double-spaced page. "Lillenas Drama Resources is a line of play scripts that are, for the most part, written by professionals with experience in productions as well as writing. While we do read unsolicited scripts, more than half of what we publish is written by experienced authors whom we have already published."
Tips "All plays need to be presented in standard play script format. We welcome a summary statement of each play. Purpose statements are always desirable. Approximate playing time, cast and prop lists, etc., are important to include. Contemporary settings generally have it over Biblical settings. Christmas and Easter scripts must have a bit of a twist. Secular approaches to these seasons (Santas, Easter bunnies, and so on), are not considered. We sell our product in 10,000 Christian bookstores and by catalog. We are in the forefront as a publisher of religious drama resources. Request a copy of our newsletter and/or catalog."

Ⓐ ⊘ LONG WHARF THEATRE

222 Sargent Dr., New Haven CT 06511. (203)787-4284. Fax: (203)776-2287. **Contact:** Literary Dept. Estab. 1965. **Produces 6-8 plays/year.** Professional regional theater. *Agented submissions only.*
Needs Full-length plays, translations, adaptations. Special interest: Dramatic plays and comedies about human relationships, social concerns, ethical and moral dilemmas.
Tips "We no longer accept queries."

LOS ANGELES DESIGNERS' THEATRE

P.O. Box 1883, Studio City CA 91614-0883. E-mail: ladesigners@juno.com. **Contact:** Richard Niederberg, artistic dir. Estab. Established 1970. **Produces 8-20 plays/year.** "Professional shows/industry audience." Submit proposal only (i.e., 1 page in #10 SASE) We want highly commercial work without liens, 'understandings,' or promises to anyone. Does not return submissions accompanied by a SASE. Reports in 3 months (minimum) to submission. Purchases rights by negotiation, first refusal for performance/synchronization rights only. **Payment varies.**
Needs All types. "No limitations—We seek design challenges. No boring material. Shorter plays with musical underscores are desirable; nudity, street language, and political themes are OK."

MAGIC THEATRE

Fort Mason Center, Bldg. D, 3rd Floor, San Francisco CA 94123. (415)441-8001. Fax: (415)771-5505. E-mail: info@magictheatre.org. Artistic Director: Chris Smith. **Contact:** Mark Routhier, director of artistic development. Estab. 1967. **Produces 6 mainstage plays/year, plus monthly reading series and several festivals each year which contain both staged readings and workshop productions.** Regional theater. Bay area residents can send complete ms or query with cover letter, résumé, 1-page synopsis, SASE, dialogue sample (10-20 pages). Those outside the Bay area can query or submit through an agent. Responds in 6-8 months. **Pays royalty or per performance fee.**

Needs Plays that are innovative in theme and/or craft, cutting-edge sociopolitical concerns, intelligent comedy. Full-length only, strong commitment to multicultural work.
Tips Not interested in classics, conventional approaches and cannot produce large-cast (over 10) plays. Send query to Mark Routhier, literary manager.

MALTHOUSE THEATRE

113 Sturt St., Southbank VIC 3006 Australia. (61)(3)9685-5100. Fax: (61)(3)9685-5111. E-mail: admin@malthousetheatre.com.au. **Contact:** Michael Kantor, artistic director. We are dedicated to contemporary Australian theatre. Writers should have had at least 1 professional production of their work. Proposals are called for on March 1, July 1, and October 1. Mail 1-page synopsis, brief author bio, and 10-page sample. Responds in 3 months if interested.

MANHATTAN THEATRE CLUB

311 W. 43rd St., 8th Floor, New York NY 10036. (212)399-3000. Fax: (212)399-4329. E-mail: questions@mtc-nyc.org. Director of Artistic Development: Paige Evans. **Contact:** Raphael Martin, literary manager. **Produces 7 plays/year.** 1 Broadway and 2 Off-Broadway theatres, using professional actors. *Solicited and agented submissions only.* No queries. Responds within 6 months.
Needs We present a wide range of new work, from this country and abroad, to a subscription audience. We want plays about contemporary concerns and people. All genres are welcome. MTC also maintains an extensive play development program.

MCCARTER THEATRE

91 University Place, Princeton NJ 08540. E-mail: literary@mccarter.org. Artistic Director: Emily Mann. **Contact:** Literary Manager. **Produces 5 plays/year; 1 second stage play/year.** Produces professional productions for a 1,077-seat and 360-seat theaters. Agented submissions only. Responds in 4-6 months. **Pays negotiable royalty.**
Needs Full length plays, musicals, translations.

MELBOURNE THEATRE COMPANY

129 Ferrars St., Southbank VIC 3006 Australia. (61)(3)9684-4500. Fax: (61)(3)9696-2627. E-mail: info@mtc.com.au. **Contact:** Aiden Fennessey, associate director. "MTC produces classic plays, modern revivals and the best new plays from Australia and overseas. Victorian work is given emphasis. MTC does not accept unsolicited manuscripts and it is our strict policy to return them unread. MTC does not produce work from previously unproduced Australian playwrights. New Australian plays generally come from three sources: by the commissioning of established writers; by the invitation to submit work to emerging writers with a track record and the potential to write for a mainstream subscription audience; and through a recommendation from an industry body, such as the Australian Script Centre or any of the major playwriting competitions." Responds in 3 months.

MERIWETHER PUBLISHING, LTD.

885 Elkton Dr., Colorado Springs CO 80907-3557. Fax: (719)594-9916. E-mail: merpcds@aol.com. President: Mark Zapel. Associate Editor: Arthur L. Zapel. **Contact:** Ted Zapel, associate editor. Estab. 1969. We publish how-to theatre materials in book and video formats. We are interested in materials for middle school, high school, and college-level students only. Query with synopsis/outline, résumé of credits, sample of style, and SASE. Catalog available for $2 postage. Responds in 1 month to queries; 2 months to full-length mss. **Offers 10% royalty.**
Needs Musicals for a large cast of performers, one-act or two-act comedy plays with large casts, and book mss on theatrical arts subjects. We are now looking for scenebooks with special themes: scenes for young women, comedy scenes for 2 actors, etc. These need not be original, provided the compiler can get letters of permission from the original copyright owner. We are interested in all textbook candidates for theater arts subjects. Christian children's activity book manuscripts also accepted. We will consider elementary-level religious plays, but no elementary-level children's secular plays.
Tips We publish a wide variety of speech contest materials for high-school students. We are publishing more full-length play scripts and musicals parodies based on classic literature or popular TV shows. Our educational books are sold to teachers and students at college and high-school levels. Our religious books are sold to youth activity directors, pastors, and choir directors. Another group of buyers is the professional theater, radio, and TV category. We will be especially interested in full-length (two- or three-act) plays with name recognition (either the playwright or the adaptation source).

METROSTAGE

1201 N. Royal St., Alexandria VA 22314. (703)548-9044. Fax: (703)548-9089. **Contact:** Carolyn Griffin, producing artistic director. Estab. 1984. **Produces 5-6 plays/year.** Professional productions for 130-seat theatre, general audience. Agented submissions only. Responds in 3 months. **Pays royalty.**
Needs Contemporary themes, small cast (up to 6 actors), unit set.
Tips Plays should have *already* had readings and workshops before being sent for our review. Do not send plays that have never had a staged reading.

NEBRASKA THEATRE CARAVAN

6915 Cass St., Omaha NE 68132. Fax: (402)553-6288. E-mail: info@omahaplayhouse.com. Artistic Director: Carl Beck. **Contact:** Alena Furlong, development director. Estab. 1976. **Produces 4-5 plays/year.** Nebraska Theatre Caravan is a touring company which produces professional productions in schools, arts centers, and small and large theaters for elementary, middle, high school and family audiences. Submit query and synopsis. Responds in 3 weeks. Negotiates production rights unless the work is commissioned by us. **Pays $20-50/performance.**

Needs All genres are acceptable bearing in mind the student audiences. We are truly an ensemble and like to see that in our choice of shows; curriculum ties are very important for elementary and hich school shows; 75 minutes for middle/high school shows. No sexually explicit material.

Tips We tour eight months of the year to a variety of locations. Flexibility is important as we work in both beautiful performing arts facilities and school multipurpose rooms.

THE NEW GROUP

410 W. 42nd St., New York NY 10036. (212)244-3380. Fax: (212)244-3438. E-mail: info@thenewgroup.org. Artistic Director: Scott Elliott. **Contact:** Ian Morgan, associate artistic director. Estab. 1991. **Produces 4 plays/year.** Off-Broadway theater. Submit 10-page sample, cover letter, résumé, synopsis, and SASE. No submissions that have already been produced in NYC. Include SASE for return of script. Responds in 9 months to submissions. **Pays royalty. Makes outright purchase.**

Needs We produce challenging, character-based scripts with a contemporary sensibility. Does not want to receive musicals, historical scripts or science fiction.

NEW JERSEY REPERTORY COMPANY.

179 Broadway, Long Branch NJ 07740. (732)229-3166. Fax: (732)229-3167. E-mail: njrep@njrep.org. Website: www.njrep.org. Artistic Director: SuzAnne Barabas. **Contact:** Literary Manager. Estab. 1997. **Produces 6-7 plays/year and 20-25 script-in-hand readings.** Professional productions year round. Previously unproduced plays and musicals only. Submit via e-mail with synopsis, cast breakdown, playwright bio. For musicals, e-mail mp3 of songs or send CD. Responds in 1 year if interested. Rights negotiable.

Needs Full-length plays with a cast size no more than 4. Simple set.

Tips "Annual Theatre Brut Festival of Short Plays. Previously unproduced. 1-4 actors; simple set, no more than 10 minutes in length. Theme for 2009-2010 festival: Creation."

NEW REPERTORY THEATRE

200 Dexter Ave., Waterton MA 02472. (617)923-7060. Fax: (617)923-7625. E-mail: artistic@newrep.org. **Contact:** Rick Lombardo, producing artistic director. Estab. 1984. **Produces 5 plays/year.** Professional theater, general audience. Query with synopsis and dialogue sample. Buys production and subsidiary rights. **Pays 5-10% royalty.**

Needs Idea laden, all styles, full-length only. New musicals.

Tips No sitcom-like comedies. Incorporating and exploring styles other than naturalism.

NEW STAGE THEATRE

1100 Carlisle, Jackson MS 39202. (601)948-3533. Fax: (601)948-3538. E-mail: mail@newstagetheatre.com. **Contact:** Artistic Director. Estab. 1965. **Produces 8 plays/year.** Professional productions, 8 mainstage, 1 in our 'second space.' We play to an audience comprised of Jackson, the state of Mississippi and the Southeast. Submit query and synopsis. Exclusive premiere contract upon acceptance of play for mainstage production. **Pays 5-8% royalty. Pays $25-60/performance.**

Needs Southern themes, contemporary issues, small casts (5-8), single set plays.

NEW THEATRE

4120 Laguna St., Coral Gables FL 33146. (305)443-5373. Fax: (305)443-1642. E-mail: tvodihn@new-theatre.org. **Contact:** Tara Vodihn, literary manager. Estab. 1986. **Produces 7 plays/year.** Professional productions. Submit query and synopsis. Responds in 3-6 months. Rights subject to negotiation. **Payment negotiable.**

Needs Interested in full-length, non-realistic, moving, intelligent, language-driven plays with a healthy dose of humor. No musicals or large casts.

Tips No kitchen sink realism. Send a simple query with synopsis. Be mindful of social issues.

NEW THEATRE

542 King St., Newtown NSW 2042 Australia. (61)(2)9519-3403. Fax: (61)(2)9519-8960. E-mail: newtheatre@bigpond.com. **Contact:** Administrator. Estab. 1932. We welcome the submission of new scripts. Submissions are assessed by playreaders and the artistic director. Submit complete ms and SASE.

NEW YORK STATE THEATRE INSTITUTE

37 First St., Troy NY 12180. (518)274-3200. Fax: (518)274-3815. E-mail: nysti@capital.net. **Contact:** Patricia DiBenedetto Snyder, producing artistic director. **Produces 6 plays/year.** Professional regional productions for adult and family audiences. Submit query and synopsis. Responds in 6 weeks. **Payment varies.**

Needs We are not interested in material for 'mature' audiences. Submissions must be scripts of substance

and intelligence geared to family audiences.
Tips Do not submit complete script unless invited after review of synopsis.

NEW YORK THEATRE WORKSHOP

83 E. 4th St., New York NY 10003. Fax: (212)460-8996. Artistic Director: James C. Nicoloa. **Contact:** Literary Department. Estab. 1979. **Produces 6-7 full productions and approximately 50 readings/year.** Plays are performed off-Broadway. Audience is New York theater-going audience and theater professionals. Query with cover letter, synopsis, 10-page dialogue sample, 2 letters of recommendation. Include tape/CD/video where appropriate. Responds in 6-10 months.
Needs Full-length plays, translations/adaptations, music theater pieces; proposals for performance projects. Socially relevant issues, innovative form, and language.
Tips No overtly commercial and conventional musicals or plays.

NORTHLIGHT THEATRE

9501 Skokie Blvd., Skokie IL 60077. (847)679-9501. Fax: (847)679-1879. **Contact:** Meghan Beals McCarthy, dramaturg. Estab. 1975. **Produces 5 plays/year.** We are a professional, equity theater, LORT C. We have a subscription base of over 8,000 and have a significant number of single ticket buyers. Query with 10-page dialogue sample, synopsis, resume/bio, and SASE/SASPC for response. Send SASE. Responds in 3-4 months. Buys production rights, plus royalty on future mountings. **Pays royalty.**
Needs Full-length plays, translations, adaptations, musicals. Interested in plays of 'ideas'; plays that are passionate and/or hilarious; accessible plays that challenge, incite, and reflect the beliefs of our society/community. Generally looking for cast size of 6 or fewer, but there are exceptions made for the right play.
Tips As a mainstream regional theater, we are unlikely to consider anything overtly experimental or absurdist. We seek good stories, vivid language, rich characters, and strong understandings of theatricality.

NORTH SHORE MUSIC THEATRE AT DUNHAM WOODS

P.O. Box 62, Beverly MA 01915. (978)232-7200. Fax: (978)921-7874. Estab. 1955. **Produces 8 plays/year.** Plays are performed at Arena theater for 27,500 subscribers. Submit letter of interest, synopsis, production details, music tape/CD, SASE. Responds in 4 months. Rights negotiable. **Payment negotiable.**
Needs Musicals only (adult and children's), with cast size under 20.
Tips No straight plays, opera.

ODYSSEY THEATRE ENSEMBLE

2055 S. Sepulveda Blvd., Los Angeles CA 90025. (310)477-2055. Fax: (310)444-0455. **Contact:** Sally Essex-Lopresti, director of literary programs. Estab. 1969. **Produces 9 plays/year.** Plays performed in a 3-theater facility. All 3 theaters are Equity 99-seat theater plan. We have a subscription audience of 4,000 for a nine-play main season, and they are offered a discount on our rentals and co-productions. Remaining seats are sold to the general public. No unsolicited material. Query with resume, synopsis, 10 pages of sample dialogue, and cassette if musical Does not return scripts without SASE. Responds in 2 weeks. Buys negotiable rights. **Pays 5-7% royalty.**
Needs Full-length plays only with either an innovative form and/or provocative subject matter. We desire highly theatrical pieces that explore possibilities of the live theater experience. We are not reading one-act plays or light situation comedies.

OMAHA THEATER CO./ROSE THEATER

2001 Farnam St., Omaha NE 68102. (402)345-9718. E-mail: jlarsonotc@msn.com. **Contact:** James Larson, artistic dir. **Produces 6-10 plays/year.** "Our target audience is children, preschool through high school, and their parents." Submit query and synopsis. Send SASE. Responds in 9 months. **Pays royalty.**
Needs Plays must be geared to children and parents (PG rating). Titles recognized by the general public have a stronger chance of being produced. Cast limit: 25 (8-10 adults). No adult scripts.
Tips Unproduced plays may be accepted only after a letter of inquiry (familiar titles only!).

ONE ACT PLAY DEPOT

Box 335, Spiritwood Saskatchewan S0J 2M0 Canada. E-mail: submissions@oneactplays.net. "Accepts unsolicited submissions only in February of each year." Submit complete script by mail or via e-mail as a plain .txt file or pasted into the body of the message.
Needs Interested only in one-act plays. Does not want musicals or farces. Do not mail originals. Our main focus will be black comedy, along with well-written dramatic and comedic pieces.

THE O'NEILL PLAYWRIGHTS CONFERENCE

305 Great Neck Rd., Waterford CT 06385. (860)443-5378. Fax: (860)443-9653. E-mail: info@theoneill.org; playwrights@theoneill.org. **Contact:** Jill Mauritz, general manager. Estab. 1964. **Produces 7-8 plays/year.** The O'Neill Center theater is located in Waterford, Connecticut, and operates under an Equity LORT contract. There are 4 theaters: Barn—250 seats, Edith Oliver Theater—150 seats, Dina Merrill—188 seats. Please send #10 SASE for guidelines in the fall, or check online. Decision by late April. We accept submissions September 1-October 1 of each year. Conference takes place during June/July each summer. Playwrights selected are in

residence for one month and receive a four-day workshop and two script-in-hand readings with professional actors and directors. **Pays stipend plus room, board and transportation.**

EUGENE O'NEILL THEATER CENTER, O'NEILL MUSIC THEATER CONFERENCE

305 Great Neck Rd., Waterford CT 06385. (860)443-5378. Fax: (860)443-9653. **Contact:** Jill A. Mauritz, general manager. Developmental process for new music theater works. Creative artists are in residence with artistic staff and equity company of actors/singers. Public and private readings, script in hand, piano only. For guidelines and application deadlines, send SASE to address above. **Pays stipend, room and board.**

OREGON SHAKESPEARE FESTIVAL

15 S. Pioneer St., Ashland OR 97520. Fax: (541)482-0446. Artistic Director: Bill Rauch. **Contact:** Director of Literary Development and Dramaturgy. Estab. 1935. **Produces 11 plays/year.** OSF directly solicits playwright or agent, and does not accept unsolicited submissions.

PERTH THEATRE COMPANY

P.O. Box 3514, Adelaide Terrace, Perth WA 6832 Australia. (61)(8)9323-3433. Fax: (61)(8)9323-3455. E-mail: frontdesk@perththeatre.com.au. **Contact:** Alan Becher, artistic director. Estab. 1983. Seeks to develop new West Australian theatre and provide opportunities to talented local artists. Develops most of its scripts through the Writer's Lab program. Do not send an unsolicited ms unless it is submitted by or accompanied by a letter of recommendation from a writer's agency, script development organization, or professional theatre company. Make sure to include a SASE.

PHILADELPHIA THEATRE CO.

230 S. Broad St., Suite 1105, Philadelphia PA 19102. (215)985-1400. Fax: (215)985-5800. **Contact:** Literary Office. Estab. 1974. **Produces 4 plays/year.** Agented submissions only. No e-mail submissions, letter of inquiry, summaries or excerpts please.

Needs Philadelphia Theatre Company produces contemporary American plays and musicals.

Tips Our work is challenging and risky—look to our history for guidance.

PIONEER DRAMA SERVICE, INC.

P.O. Box 4267, Englewood CO 80155-4267. (303)779-4035. Fax: (303)779-4315. E-mail: submissions@pioneerdrama.com. Publisher: Steven Fendrich. **Contact:** Lori Conary, submissions editor. Estab. 1963. **Publishes** Plays are performed by schools, colleges, community theaters, recreation programs, churches, and professional children's theaters for audiences of all ages. Query or submit complete ms All submissions automatically entered in Shubert Fendrich Memorial Playwriting Contest. Guidelines for SASE. Responds in about 2 weeks to queries; 4-6 months to submissions. Retains all rights. **Pays royalty.**

Needs Comedies, mysteries, dramas, melodramas, musicals and children's theater. Two-acts up to 90 minutes; children's theater (1 hour); one-acts no less than 20 minutes. Prefers large ensemble casts with many female roles, simple sets, and costumes. Plays need to be appropriate for amateur groups and family audiences. Interested in adaptations of classics of public domain works appropriate for children and teens. Also plays that deal with social issues for teens and preteens.

Tips Check out our website to see what we carry and if your material would be appropriate for our market. Make sure to include proof of productions and a SASE if you want your material returned.

PITTSBURGH PUBLIC THEATER

621 Penn Ave., Pittsburgh PA 15222. (412)316-8200. Fax: (412)316-8216. Artistic Director: Ted Pappas. **Contact:** Dramaturg. Estab. 1975. **Produces 7 plays/year.** O'Reilly Theater, 650 seats, thrust seating. Submit full script through agent, or query with synopsis, cover letter, 10-page dialogue sample, and SASE. Responds in 4 months.

Needs Full-length plays, adaptations and musicals.

PLAYSCRIPTS, INC.

325 W. 38th St., Suite 305, New York NY 10018. E-mail: submissions@playscripts.com. Estab. 1998. Audience is professional, community, college, high school and children's theaters worldwide. See website for complete submission guidelines. Materials accompanied by SASE will be returned; however, e-mail submissions are preferred. Response time varies. Buys exclusive publication and performance licensing rights. **Pays negotiated book and production royalties.**

Needs We are open to a wide diversity of writing styles and content. Musicals are not accepted.

Tips Playscripts, Inc. is a play publishing company dedicated to new work by established and emerging playwrights. We provide all of the same licensing and book production services as a traditional play publisher, along with unique promotional features that maximize the exposure of each dramatic work. Be sure to view our guidelines before submitting.

THE PLAYWRIGHTS' CENTER'S PLAYLABS

2301 Franklin Ave. E., Minneapolis MN 55406. (612)332-7481. Fax: (612)332-6037. E-mail: info@pwcenter.org. Producing Artistic Director: Polly K. Carl. Estab. 1971. PlayLabs is a 2-week developmental workshop for new plays. The program is held in Minneapolis and is open by script competition. Up to 5 new plays are given reading performances and after the festival, a script sample and contact link are posted on the Center's website. Announcements of playwrights by May 1. Playwrights receive honoraria, travel expenses, room and board.

Needs We are interested in playwrights with ambitions for a sustained career in theater, and scripts that could benefit from development involving professional dramaturgs, directors, and actors. US citizens or permanent residents only. Participants must attend entire festival. Submission deadline in October; see Web site for application and exact deadline. No previously produced materials.

PLAYWRIGHTS HORIZONS

416 W. 42nd St., New York NY 10036. (212)564-1235. Fax: (212)594-0296. Artistic Director: Tim Sanford. **Contact:** Adam Greenfield, literary manager (plays); send musicals Attn: Kent Nicholson, Director of Musical Theater. Estab. 1971. **Produces 6 plays/year.** Plays performed off-Broadway for a literate, urban, subscription audience. Submit complete ms with author bio; include CD for musicals. Responds in 6-8 months. Negotiates for future rights. **Pays royalty. Makes outright purchase.**

Needs We are looking for new, full-length plays and musicals by American authors.

Tips "We do not accept one-acts, one-person shows, non-musical adaptations, translations, children's shows, screenplays, or works by non-US writers. We dislike synopses because we accept unsolicited manuscripts. We look for plays with a strong sense of language and a clear dramatic action that truly use the resources of the theater."

PLAYWRIGHTS' PLATFORM

398 Columbus Ave., #604, Boston MA 02116. **Contact:** Jerry Bisantz, producing director. Estab. 1972. **Produces approximately 50 readings/year** Plays are read in staged readings at Hovey Players on Spring St. (Walthan MA). Accepts scripts on a face-to-face basis. Submit script and SASE (or e-mail or hand deliver). Responds in 2 months.

Needs Any types of plays. We will not accept scripts we think are sexist or racist. Massachusetts residents only. There are no restrictions on length or number of characters, but it's more difficult to schedule full-length pieces.

Ⓐ PLAYWRIGHTS THEATRE OF NEW JERSEY

P.O. Box 1295, Madison NJ 07940-1295. (973)514-1787. Fax: (973)514-2060. Artistic Director: John Pietrowski. **Contact:** Alysia Souder, director of program development. Estab. 1986. **Produces 3 plays/year.** We operate under a Small Professional Theatre Contract (SPT), a development theatre contract with Actors Equity Association. Readings are held under a staged reading code. Responds in 1 year. For productions we ask the playwright to sign an agreement that gives us exclusive rights to the play for the production period and for 30 days following. After the 30 days we give the rights back with no strings attached, except for commercial productions. We ask that our developmental work be acknowledged in any other professional productions. **Makes outright purchase of 750.**

Needs Any style or length; full length, one acts, musicals.

Tips We are looking for American plays in the early stages of development—plays of substance, passion, and light (comedies and dramas) that raise challenging questions about ourselves and our communities. We prefer plays *that can work only on the stage* in the most theatrical way possible—plays that are not necessarily `straight-on' realistic, but rather ones that use imagery, metaphor, poetry and musicality in new and interesting ways. Plays can go through a 3-step development process: A roundtable, a concert reading, and then a workshop production.

Ⓐ PLOWSHARES THEATRE CO.

2870 E. Grand Blvd., Suite 600, Detroit MI 48202-3146. (313)872-0279. Fax: (313)872-0067. **Contact:** Gary Anderson, producing artistic director. Estab. 1989. **Produces 5 plays/year.** Professional productions of plays by African-American writers for African-American audience and those who appreciate African-American culture. *Agented submissions only*. Responds in 8 months.

Tips "Submissions are more likely to be accepted if written by an African-American with the willingness to be developed. It must also be very good, and the writer should be ready to make a commitment."

PORTLAND STAGE CO.

P.O. Box 1458, Portland ME 04104. (207)774-1043. Fax: (207)774-0576. E-mail: info@portlandstage.com. Artistic Director: Anita Stewart. **Contact:** Daniel Burson, literary manager. Estab. 1974. **Produces 7 plays/year.** Professional productions at Portland Stage Company. Send first 10 pages with synopsis. Responds in 3 months. Buys 3- or 4-week run in Maine. **Pays royalty.**

Needs Developmental Staged Readings: Little Festival of the Unexpected.

Tips Work developed in Little Festival generally will be more strongly considered for future production.

Ⓐ PRIMARY STAGES CO., INC.

131 W. 45th St., 2nd Floor, New York NY 10036. (212)840-9705. Fax: (212)840-9725. **Contact:** Tessa LaNeve, literary manager. Estab. 1985. **Produces 4 plays/year.** All plays are produced professionally off-Broadway at 59E59 Theatres' 199 seat theatre. Agented submissions only Guidelines online. **Pays flat fee.**

Needs Full-length plays, small cast (6 or fewer) musicals. New York City premieres only. Small cast (1-6), unit set or simple changes, no fly or wing space.
Tips Best submission time: September-June. Chances: Over 1,000 scripts read, 4-5 produced. Women and minorities encouraged to submit.

PRINCE MUSIC THEATER

100 S. Broad St., Suite 650, Philadelphia PA 19110. (215)972-1000. Fax: (215)972-1020. **Contact:** Marjorie Samoff, producing artistic director. Estab. 1984. **Produces 4 musicals/year.** Professional musical productions. Send synopsis and sample audio tape with no more than 4 songs. Responds in 6 months. **Pays royalty.**
Needs Song-driven music theater, varied musical styles. Nine in orchestra, 10-14 cast, 36x60 stage.
Tips "Innovative topics and use of media, music, technology a plus. Sees trends of arts in technology (interactive theater, virtual reality, sound design); works are shorter in length (1-1 & ½ hours with no intermissions or 2 hours with intermission)."

PRINCETON REP COMPANY

44 Nassau St., Suite 350, Princeton NJ 08542. E-mail: prcreprap@aol.com. **Contact:** New Play Submissions. Estab. 1984. Plays are performed in site-specific venues, outdoor amphitheatres, and indoor theatres with approximately 199 seats. Princeton Rep Company works under Actors' Equity contracts, and its directors are members of the SSDC. Query with synopsis, SASE, résumé, and 10 pages of sample dialogue. Submissions accompanied by a SASE will be returned. Responds in up to 2 years. Rights are negotiated on a play-by-play basis. **Payment negotiated on a play-by-play basis.**
Needs Stories that investigate the lives of middle and working class people. Love stories of the rich, famous, and fatuous. If the play demands a cast of thousands, please don't waste your time and postage. No drama or comedy set in a prep school or ivy league college.

THE PUBLIC THEATER

425 Lafayette St., New York NY 10003. (212)539-8500. Artistic Director: Oskar Eustis. **Contact:** Literary Department. Estab. 1964. **Produces 6 plays/year.** Professional productions. Query with synopsis,10-page sample, letter of inquiry, cassette with 3-5 songs for musicals/operas. Responds in 3 months.
Needs Full-length plays, translations, adapatations, musicals, operas, and solo pieces. All genres, no one-acts.

⊘ PULSE ENSEMBLE THEATRE

266 W. 36th St., 22nd Floor, New York NY 10018. (212)695-1596. Fax: (212)594-4208. E-mail: theatre@pulseensembletheatre.org. **Contact:** Brian Richardson. Estab. 1989. **Produces 3 plays/year.** No unsolicited submissions. Only accepts new material through the Playwright's Lab. Include SASE for return of submission. Buys variable rights. **Usually pays 2% of gross.**
Needs Meaningful theater. No production limitations. Does not want to see fluff or vanity theater.

THE PURPLE ROSE THEATRE CO.

137 Park St., Chelsea MI 48118. (734)433-7782. Fax: (734)475-0802. **Contact:** Guy Sanville, artistic director. Estab. 1990. **Produces 4 plays/year.** PRTC is a regional theater with an S.P.T. equity contract which produces plays intended for Midwest/Middle American audience. Query with synopsis, character breakdown, and 10-page dialogue sample. Responds in 9 months. **Pays 5-10% royalty.**
Needs Modern, topical full length, 75-120 minutes. Prefers scripts that use comedy to deal with serious subjects. 8 cast maximum. No fly space, unit set preferable. Intimate 168 seat ¾ thrust house.

QUEENSLAND THEATRE COMPANY

P.O. Box 3310, South Brisbane QLD 4101 Australia. (61)(7)3010-7600. Fax: (61)(7)3010-7699. E-mail: mail@qldtheatreco.com.au. **Contact:** Michael Gow, artistic director. "Seeks timeless classics, modern classics, and new plays from Australia and overseas. Only considers unsolicited scripts if the playwright has had at least 1 play professionally produced if the script has been submitted by an agent, or recommended by a professional theatre company or script development agency." Responds in 3 months.
Needs "Works specifically aimed at child/youth audiences are less likely to be considered."

RED LADDER THEATRE CO.

3 St. Peter's Buildings, York St., Leeds LS9 1AJ United Kingdom. (44)(113)245-5311. E-mail: rod@redladder.co.uk. **Contact:** Rod Dixon, artistic director. Estab. 1969. **Produces 2 plays/year.** Our work tours nationally to young people, aged 13-25, in youth clubs, community venues and small scale theatres. Submit query and synopsis. Responds in 6 months. **Offers ITC/Equity writers contract.**
Needs One hour in length for cast size no bigger than 5. Work that connects with a youth audience that both challenges them and offers them new insights. We consider a range of styles and are seeking originality. Small scale touring. Does not want to commission single issue drama. The uses of new technologies in production (DVD, video projection). Young audiences are sophisticated.
Tips Please do not submit full length plays. Get in touch with us first. Tell us about yourself and why you would like to write for Red Ladder. We like to hear about ideas you may have in the first instance.

RESOURCE PUBLICATIONS

160 E. Virginia St., Suite 290, San Jose CA 95112-5876. (408)286-8505. Fax: (408)287-8748. E-mail: editor@rpinet.com. Estab. 1973. Audience includes laity and ordained seeking resources (books/periodicals/software) in Christian ministry, worship, faith formation, education, and counseling (primarily Roman Catholic, but not all). Submit query and synopsis via e-mail. Responds in 3 months.

Needs Needs materials for those in pastoral ministry, faith formation, youth ministry, and parish administration. No fiction, children's books, or music.

ROUND HOUSE THEATRE

P.O. Box 30688, Bethesda MD 20824. (240)644-1099. Fax: (240)644-1090. Producing Artistic Director: Blake Robison. **Contact:** Danisha Crosby, associate producer. **Produces 5-7 plays/year.** Professional AEA Theatre. Query with synopsis; no unsolicited scripts accepted. Responds in 2-12 months. **Pays negotiated percentage for productions.**

SALTWORKS THEATRE CO.

569 N. Neville St., Pittsburgh PA 15213. (412)621-6150. Fax: (412)621-6010. E-mail: nalrutz@saltworks.org. **Contact:** Norma Alrutz, executive director. Estab. 1981. **Produces 8-10 plays/year.** Submit query and synopsis. Responds in 2 months. Obtains regional performance rights for educational grants. **Pays $25/performance.**

Needs Wants plays for children, youth, and families that address social issues like violence prevention, sexual responsibility, peer pressures, tobacco use, bullying, racial issues/diversity, drug and alcohol abuse (grades 1-12). Limited to 5 member cast, 2 men/2 women/1 either.

Tips Check website for current play contest rules and deadlines.

SEATTLE REPERTORY THEATRE

P.O. Box 900923, Seattle WA 98109. E-mail: bradena@seattlerep.org. Artistic Director: David Esbjornson. **Contact:** Braden Abraham, literary manager. Estab. 1963. **Produces 8 plays/year.** Send query, resume, synopsis and 10 sample pages. Responds in 6 months. Buys percentage of future royalties. **Pays royalty.**

Needs The Seattle Repertory Theatre produces eclectic programming. We welcome a wide variety of writing.

SECOND STAGE THEATRE

307 W. 43rd St., New York NY 10036. (212)787-8302. Fax: (212)397-7066. **Contact:** Sarah Bagley, literary manager. Estab. 1979. **Produces 6 plays/year.** Professional off-Broadway productions. Adult and teen audiences. Query with synopsis and 10-page writing sample or agented submission. Responds in 6 months. **Payment varies.**

Needs We need socio-political plays, comedies, musicals, dramas—full lengths for full production.

Tips No biographical or historical dramas, or plays in verse. Writers are realizing that audiences can be entertained while being moved. Patience is a virtue but persistence is appreciated.

SHAW FESTIVAL THEATRE

P.O. Box 774, Niagara-on-the-Lake ON L0S 1J0 Canada. (905)468-2153. Fax: (905)468-7140. **Contact:** Jackie Maxwell, artistic director. Estab. 1962. **Produces 12 plays/year.** Professional theater company operating 3 theaters (Festival: 869 seats; Court House: 327 seats; Royal George: 328 seats). Shaw Festival presents the work of George Bernard Shaw and his contemporaries written during his lifetime (1856-1950) and in 2000 expanded the mandate to include contemporary works written about the period of his lifetime. Query with SASE or SAE and IRC's, depending on country of origin. We prefer to hold rights for Canada and northeastern US, also potential to tour. **Pays 5-10% royalty.**

Needs We operate an acting ensemble of up to 75 actors; and we have sophisticated production facilities. During the summer season (April-November) the Academy of the Shaw Festival organizes workshops of new plays commissioned for the company.

SOUTH COAST REPERTORY

P.O. Box 2197, Costa Mesa CA 92628-2197. (714)708-5500. Fax: (714)545-0391. Website: www.scr.org. Artistic Directors: Martin Benson and David Emmes. **Contact:** Kelly Miller, literary manager. Estab. 1964. **Produces 14 plays/year.** Professional nonprofit theater; a member of LORT and TCG. "We operate in our own facility which houses the 507-seat Segerstrom stage and 336-seat Julianne Argyros stage. We have a combined subscription audience of 18,000." Query with synopsis and 10 sample pages of dialogue, and full list of characters. Responds in 1-2 months on queries; 4-6 months on full scripts. Acquires negotiable rights. **Pays royalty.**

Needs "We produce full-length contemporary plays, as well as theatre for young audiences, scripts geared toward a 4th grade target audience with a running time of approximately 65 minutes. We prefer plays that address contemporary concerns and are dramaturgically innovative. A play whose cast is larger than 15-20 will need to be extremely compelling, and its cast size must be justifiable."

Tips "We don't look for a writer to write for us—he or she should write for him or herself. We look for honesty and a fresh voice. We're not likely to be interested in writers who are mindful of any trends. Originality and craftsmanship are the most important qualities we look for."

SOUTHERN APPALACHIAN REPERTORY THEATRE (SART)

Mars Hill College, P.O. Box 1720, Mars Hill NC 28754. (828)689-1384. E-mail: sart@mhc.edu. Managing Director: Rob Miller. Estab. 1975. **Produces 5-6 plays/year.** Since 1975 the Southern Appalachian Repertory Theatre has produced over 50 world premieres in the 166-seat Owen Theatre on the Mars Hill College campus. SART is a professional summer theater company whose audiences range from students to senior citizens. SART also conducts an annual playwrights conference in which 4-5 playwrights are invited for a weekend of public readings of their new scripts. The conference is held in March or May each year. Submissions must be postmarked by September 30. If a script read at the conference is selected for production, it will be given a fully-staged production in the following summer season. Playwrights receive honorarium and housing. Enclose SASE for return of script.

Needs Comedies, dramas and musicals. No screenplays, translations, or adaptations. Please send complete scripts of full-length plays and musicals, synopsis, and a recording of at least 4 songs (for musicals). Include name and contact information only on a cover sheet. New plays are defined as those that are unpublished and have not received a fully-staged professional production. Workshops and other readings do not constitute a fully-staged production.

STAGE LEFT THEATRE

3408 N. Sheffield, Chicago IL 60657. (773)883-8830. E-mail: scripts@stagelefttheatre.com. **Contact:** Kevin Heckman, producing artistic director. Estab. 1982. **Produces 3-4 plays/year.** Professional productions (usually in Chicago), for all audiences (usually adult). Submit script through an agent or query with cover letter, 10-page excerpt, 1-page synopsis, SASE, supporting material, and résumé. Submissions accompanied by a SASE will be returned. Responds in 3 months. **Pays 6% royalty.**

Needs Any length, any genre, any style that fits the Stage Left mission—to produce plays that raise debate on political and social issues. We do have an emphasis on new work.

🄰 STAMFORD THEATRE WORKS

307 Atlantic St., Stamford CT 06901. (203)359-4414. Fax: (203)356-1846. E-mail: stwct@aol.com. **Contact:** Steve Karp, producing director. Estab. 1988. **Produces 4-6 plays/year.** Professional productions for an adult audience. *Agented submissions* or queries with a professional recommendation. Include SASE for return of submission. Responds in 3 months. **Pays 5-8% royalty.**

Needs Plays of social relevance; contemporary work. Limited to unit sets; maximum cast of about 8.

🄰 STEPPENWOLF THEATRE CO.

758 W. North Ave., 4th Floor, Chicago IL 60610. (312)335-1888. Fax: (312)335-0808. Artistic Director: Martha Lavey. **Contact:** Edward Sobel, director of new play development. Estab. 1976. **Produces 9 plays/year.** 500-, 250- and 100-seat performance venues. Many plays produced at Steppenwolf have gone to Broadway. We currently have 20,000 savvy subscribers. Agented submissions only with full scripts. Others please check our website for submission guidelines. Unrepresented writers may send a 10-page sample along with cover letter, bio, and synopsis. Responds in 6-8 months. Buys commercial, film, television, and production rights. **Pays 5% royalty.**

Needs Actor-driven works are crucial to us, plays that explore the human condition in our time. We max at around 10 characters.

Tips No musicals, one-person shows, or romantic/light comedies. Plays get produced at STC based on ensemble member interest.

STONEHAM THEATRE

395 Main St., Stoneham MA 02180. E-mail: weylin@stonehamtheatre.org. **Contact:** Weylin Symes, artistic director. Estab. 1999. **Produces 7 plays/year.** Plays will be produced on-stage in our 350-seat SPT-7 theater—either as part of the Mainstage Season or our Emerging stages series of new works. Submit complete script via mail or e-mail. Submissions accompanied by a SASE will not be returned. Responds in 3 months. Rights acquired varies according to script. **Pays royalty.**

Needs Anything of quality will be considered. We look for exciting new work with a fresh voice, but that can still appeal to a relatively mainstream audience. Does not want anything with a cast size over 18 for a musical or 9 for a play.

🄰 STUDIO ARENA THEATRE

710 Main St., Buffalo NY 14202. (716)856-8025. E-mail: jblaha@studioarena.com. **Contact:** Jana Blaha, executive assistant. Estab. 1965. **Produces 6-8 plays/year.** Professional productions. Agented submissions only.

Needs Full-length plays. No fly space.

Tips Do not fax or send submissions via the Internet. Submissions should appeal to a diverse audience. We do not generally produce musicals. Please send a character breakdown and 1-page synopsis for a faster reply.

TADA!

15 W. 28th St., 3rd Floor, New York NY 10001. (212)252-1619. Fax: (212)252-8763. E-mail: jgreer@tadatheater.com. **Contact:** Literary Manager. Estab. 1984. **Produces 3 musical plays/year.** TADA! produces original musicals performed by children and teens, ages 8-18. Productions are for family audiences. Submit a brief summary of the musical, 10 pages from the scripts, and a CD or cassette with songs from the score. TADA! also sponsors an annual one-act playwriting contest for their Spring Staged Reading Series. Works must be original, unproduced and unpublished one-acts. Plays must be geared toward teen audiences. Call or e-mail for guidelines. Responds in 2-3 months. **Pays 5% royalty. Commission fee.**

Needs Generally pieces run 1 hour long. Must be enjoyed by children and adults and performed by a cast of children ages 8-18.

Tips "No redone fairy tales or pieces where children are expected to play adults. Plays with animals and non-human characters are highly discouraged. Be careful not to condescend when writing for children's theater."

TEATRO VISIÓN

1700 Alum Rock Ave., Suite 265, San José CA 95116. (408)272-9926. Fax: (408)928-5589. E-mail: elisamarina@teatrovision.org. **Contact:** Elisa Marina Alvarado, artistic director. Estab. 1984. **Produces 3 plays/year.** Professional productions for a Latino population. Query with synopsis or submit complete ms. Responds in 6 months.

Needs We produce plays by Latino playwrights—plays that highlight the Chicano/Latino experience.

N THE TEN-MINUTE MUSICALS PROJECT

P.O. Box 461194, West Hollywood CA 90046. E-mail: info@tenminutemusicals.org. **Contact:** Michael Koppy, producer. Estab. 1987. **Produces 1-10 plays/year.** "Plays performed in Equity regional theaters in the US and Canada. Deadline August 31; notification by November 30." Submit complete script, lead sheets and, cassette/CD Submission guidelines for #10 SASE. Buys first performance rights. **Pays $250 royalty advance upon selection, against equal share of performance royalties when produced.**

Needs Looking for complete short stage musicals lasting 7-14 minutes. Limit cast to 10 (5 women, 5 men).

THEATER AT LIME KILN

P.O. Box 1244, Lexington VA 24450. Estab. 1984. **Produces 3 (1 new) plays/year.** Outdoor summer theater (May through October) and indoor space (October through May, 144 seats). Submit query and synopsis. Include SASE for return of submitted materials. Responds in 3 months. Buys performance rights. **Pays $25-75/performance.**

Needs Plays that explore the history and heritage of the Appalachian region. Minimum set required.

Tips Searching for plays that can be performed in outdoor space. Prefer plays that explore the cultural and/or history of the Appalichian region.

THEATER BY THE BLIND

306 W. 18th St., New York NY 10011. (212)243-4337. Fax: (212)243-4337. E-mail: gar@nyc.rr.com. **Contact:** Ike Schambelan, artistic director. Estab. 1979. **Produces 2 plays/year.** Off Broadway, Theater Row, general audiences, seniors, students, disabled. If play transfers, we'd like a piece. Submit complete script. Responds in 3 months. **Pays $1,000-1,500/production.**

Needs Genres about blindness.

THEATRE BUILDING CHICAGO

1225 W. Belmont Ave., Chicago IL 60657. (773)929-7367 ext. 222. Fax: (773)327-1404. E-mail: jsparksco@aol.com. **Contact:** John Sparks, artistic director. "Produces readings of new musicals and Stages Festival, some works developed in our workshop. Some scripts produced are unagented submissions. Developmental readings and workshops performed in 3 small off-Loop theaters are seating 148 for a general theater audience, urban/suburban mix." Submit synopsis, sample scene, CD or cassette tape and piano/vocal score of three songs, and author bios along with Stages Festival application, available on our website. Responds in 3 months.

Needs "Musicals *only*. We're interested in all forms of musical theater including more innovative styles. Our production capabilities are limited by the lack of space, but we're very creative and authors should submit anyway. The smaller the cast, the better. We are especially interested in scripts using a younger (35 and under) ensemble of actors. We mostly look for authors who are interested in developing their scripts through workshops, readings and production. No one-man shows or 'single author' pieces."

Tips "We would like to see the musical theater articulating something about the world around us, as well as diverting an audience's attention from that world. Offers Script Consultancy—A new program designed to assist authors and composers in developing new musicals through private feedback sessions with professional dramaturgs and musical directors. For further info contact John Sparks, (773)929-7367, ext. 222."

THEATRE IV

114 W. Broad St., Richmond VA 23220. (804)783-1688. Fax: (804)775-2325. E-mail: j.serresseque@theatreivrichmond.org. **Contact:** Janine Serresseque. Estab. 1975. **Produces approximately 20 plays/year.** National tour of plays for young audiences—maximum cast of 5, maximum length of an hour. Mainstage plays for young audiences in 600 or 350 seat venues. Submit query and synopsis. Include SASE for return of submission. Responds in 1 month. Buys standard production rights. **Payment varies.**

Needs Touring and mainstage plays for young audiences. Touring—maximum cast of 5, length of 60 minutes.

THEATRE THREE

P.O. Box 512, 412 Main St., Port Jefferson NY 11777-0512. (631)928-9202. Fax: (631)928-9120. **Contact:** Jeffrey Sanzel, artistic director. Estab. 1969. We produce an Annual Festival of One-Act Plays on our Second Stage. Deadline for submission is September 30. Send SASE for festival guidelines or visit website. SASE for festival guidelines. Responds in 6 months. We ask for exclusive rights up to and through the festival. **Pays $75 for the run of the festival.**

Needs One-act plays. Maximum length: 40 minutes. Any style, topic, etc. We require simple, suggested sets and a maximum cast of 6. No adaptations, musicals or children's works.

Tips Too many plays are monologue-dominant. Please—reveal your characters through action and dialogue.

THEATRE THREE

2800 Routh St., #168, Dallas TX 75201. (214)871-3300. Fax: (214)871-3139. E-mail: admin@theatre3dallas.com. **Contact:** Jac Alder, executive producer-director. Estab. 1961. **Produces 7 plays/year.** Professional regional theatre, in-the-round. Audience is college age to senior citizens. Query with synopsis; agented submissions only. Responds in 6 months. **Contractual agreements vary.**

Needs Musicals, dramas, comedies, bills of related one-acts. Modest production requirement; prefer casts no larger than 10. Theatre Three also produces in a studio theatre (its former rehearsal hall) called Theatre Too. The space is variously configured according to demands of the show. Shows in that space include cabaret type revues, experimental work, dramas with small casts and staged readings or concert versions of musicals.

Tips No parodies or political commentary/comedy. Most produced playwrights at Theatre Three (to show taste of producer) are Moliere, Sondheim, Ayckbourne, Miller, Stoppard, Durang (moralists and irony-masters).

THEATRE WEST

3333 Cahuenga Blvd. W., Hollywood CA 90068-1365. (323)851-4839. Fax: (323)851-5286. E-mail: theatrewest@theatrewest.org. **Contact:** Chris DiGiovanni and Doug Haverty, moderators of the Writers Workshop. Estab. 1962. 99-seat waiver productions in our theater. Audiences are primarily young urban professionals. Residence in Southern California is vital as it's a weekly workshop. Submit script, résumé and letter requesting membership. Responds in 4 months. Contracts a percentage of writer's share to other media if produced on MainStage by Theatre West. **Pays royalty based on gross box office.**

Needs Full-length plays only, no one-acts. Uses minimalistic scenery, no fly space.

Tips Theatre West is a dues-paying membership company. Only members can submit plays for production. So you must first seek membership to the Writers Workshop. We accept all styles of theater writing, but theater only—no screenplays, novels, short stories or poetry will be considered for membership.

THEATREWORKS

P.O. Box 50458, Palo Alto CA 94303. (650)463-1950. Fax: (650)463-1963. E-mail: kent@theatreworks.org. **Contact:** Kent Nicholson, new works director. Estab. 1970. **Produces 8 plays/year.** Specializes in development of new musicals. Plays are professional productions intended for an adult audience. Submit synopsis, 10 pages of sample dialogue, and SASE. Include SASE for return of submission. Responds in 6-8 months. Buys performance rights. **Payment varies per contract.**

Needs TheatreWorks has a high standard for excellence. We prefer well-written, well-constructed plays that celebrate the human spirit through innovative productions and programs inspired by our exceptionally diverse community. There is no limit on the number of characters, and we favor plays with multi-ethnic casting possibilities. We are a LORT C company. Plays are negotiated per playwright. Does not want one-acts, plays with togas. We are particularly interested in plays with musical elements.

Tips Guidelines are online—check out our website for Submission Checklist Request and the New Works Program under New Works.

THEATREWORKS/USA

151 W. 26th St., 7th Floor, New York NY 10001. (212)647-1100. Fax: (212)924-5377. Estab. 1961. **Produces 3-4 plays/year.** Professional equity productions for young audiences. Weekend series at Equitable Towers, NYC. Also, national and regional tours of each show. Submit query and synopsis only. *No unsolicited submissions.* Responds in 1 month. Obtains performing rights. **Pays 6% royalty.**

UNICORN THEATRE

3828 Main St., Kansas City MO 64111. (816)531-7529 ext. 23. Fax: (816)531-0421. Producing Artistic Director: Cynthia Levin. **Contact:** Herman Wilson, literary assistant. **Produces 6-8 plays/year.** "We are a professional Equity Theatre. Typically, we produce plays dealing with contemporary issues." Send complete script (to Herman Wilson) with brief synopsis, cover letter, bio, character breakdown. Send #10 SASE for results. Does not return scripts. Responds in 4-8 months.

Needs Prefers contemporary (post-1950) scripts. Does not accept musicals, one-acts, or historical plays.

URBAN STAGES

555 8th Avenue #1800, New York NY 10018. (212)421-1380. Fax: (212)421-1387. E-mail: urbanstage@aol.com. **Contact:** Frances Hill. Estab. 1986. **Produces 2-4 plays/year.** Professional productions off Broadway—throughout the year. General audience. Submit complete script. Enter Emerging Playwright Award competition. There is a reading fee of $10 per script. Prize is $1,000, plus NYC production. Responds in 4 months. If produced, option for 1 year. **Pays royalty.**

Needs Full-length; generally 1 set or styled playing dual. Good imaginative, creative writing. Cast limited to 3-6.

Tips We tend to reject `living-room' plays. We look for imaginative settings. Be creative and interesting. No one acts. No e-mail submissions, scripts are not returned.

UTAH SHAKESPEAREAN FESTIVAL

New American Playwright's Project, 351 W. Center St., Cedar City UT 84720-2498. (435)586-7884. Fax: (435)865-8003. Founder/Executive Producer Emeritus: Fred C. Adams. **Contact:** Charles Metten, director. Estab. 1993. **Produces 9 plays/year.** Travelling audiences ranging in ages from 6-80. Programming includes classic plays, musicals, new works. Submit complete script; no synopsis. No musicals. Returns submissions accompanied by a SASE. Responds in 3-4 months. **Pays travel, housing, and tickets for USF productions only.**

Needs "The USF is only interested in material that explores characters and ideas that focus on the West and our western experience, spirit, and heritage. Preference is given to writers whose primary residence is in the western United States. New plays are for staged readings only. These are not fully mountable productions. Cast size is a consideration due to the limited time of rehearsal and the actors available during the USF production period. Does not want plays that do not match criteria or plays longer than 90 pages."

Tips "We want previously unproduced plays with western themes by western playwrights."

WALNUT STREET THEATRE

Ninth and Walnut Streets, Philadelphia PA 19107. (215)574-3550. Fax: (215)574-3598. Producing Artistic Director: Bernard Havard. **Contact:** Literary Office. Estab. 1809. **Produces 10 plays/year.** Our plays are performed in our own space. WST has 3 theaters—a proscenium (mainstage), 1,052 seats; and 2 studios, 79-99 seats. We have a subscription audience—the largest in the nation. Query with synopsis, 10-20 pages of dialogue, character breakdown, and bio. Include SASE for return of materials. Responds in 5 months. Rights negotiated per project. **Pays negotiable royalty or makes outright purchase.**

Needs Full-length dramas and comedies, musicals, translations, adaptations, and revues. The studio plays must have a cast of no more than 4 and use simple sets.

Tips Bear in mind that on the mainstage we look for plays with mass appeal, Broadway-style. The studio spaces are our off-Broadway. No children's plays. Our mainstage audience goes for work that is entertaining and light. Our studio season is where we look for plays that have bite and are more provocative.

WILLOWS THEATRE CO.

636 Ward St., Martinez CA 94553-1651. Artistic Director: Richard Elliott. **Produces 6 plays/year.** Professional productions for a suburban audience. Accepting only commercially viable, small-medium size comedies right now. Guidelines are online at website. Send synopsis, character breakdown, resume, SASE. Do not send full script unless invited to do so. Do not email submission or email the office for information on your submission. Responds in 6 months to scripts. **Pays standard royalty.**

Needs Commercially viable, small-medium size musicals or comedies that are popular, rarely produced, or new. Certain stylized plays or musicals with a contemporary edge to them (e.g., *Les Liasons Dangereuses, La Bete, Candide*). No more than 15 actors. Unit or simple sets with no fly space, no more than 7 pieces. We are not interested in 1-character pieces.

Tips "Our audiences want light entertainment, comedies, and musicals. Also, have an interest in plays and musicals with a historical angle."

THE WILMA THEATER

265 S. Broad St., Philadelphia PA 19107. (215)893-9456. Fax: (215)893-0895. E-mail: wcb@wilmatheater.org. **Contact:** Walter Bilderback, dramaturg and literary manager. Estab. 1980. **Produces 4 plays/year.** LORT-C 300-seat theater, 7,500 subscribers. *Agented submissions only* for full mss. Accepts queries with cover letter, résumé, synopsis, and sample if recommended by a literary manager, dramaturg, or other theater professional. Responds in 6 months.

Needs Full-length plays, translations, adaptations, and musicals from an international repertoire with emphasis on innovative, bold staging; world premieres; ensemble works; works with poetic dimension; plays with music; multimedia works; social issues, particularly the role of science in our lives. Prefers maximum cast size of 12. Stage 44'x46'.

Tips Before submitting any material to The Wilma Theater, please research our production history. Considering the types of plays we have produced in the past, honestly assess whether or not your play would suit us. In general, I believe researching the various theaters to which you send your play is important in the long and short run. Different theaters have different missions and therefore seek out material corresponding with those goals. In other words, think through what is the true potential of your play and this theater, and if it is a compatible relationship.

WOMEN'S PROJECT AND PRODUCTIONS

55 West End Ave., New York NY 10023. (212)765-1706. Fax: (212)765-2024. **Contact:** Megan E. Carter, Associate Artistic Director. Estab. 1978. **Produces 3 plays/year.** Professional Off-Broadway productions. Agented submissions only. Please see website for submission guidelines and details.

Needs "We are looking for full-length plays written by women."

WOOLLY MAMMOTH THEATRE CO.

641 D St. NW, Washington DC 20004. (202)289-2443. E-mail: elissa@woollymammoth.net. Artistic Director: Howard Shalwitz. **Contact:** Elissa Goetschius, literary manager. Estab. 1980. **Produces 5 plays/year.** Produces professional productions for the general public. Solicited submissions only. Responds in 6 months to scripts; very interesting scripts often take much longer. Buys first- and second-class production rights. **Pays variable royalty.**

Needs We look for plays with a distinctive authorial voice. Our work is word and actor driven. One-acts and issue-driven plays are not used. Cast limit of 5

MARKETS

Greeting Cards

Greeting cards are an intricate part of American culture. There are, of course, cards tied to holidays, birthdays, graduations, and weddings. There are "thinking of you'' cards, condolences cards, thank you cards, get well cards, and humor cards. And many of these cards are specialized to mom, dad, mother-in-law, father-in-law, son, daughter, cousin, and even ex-girlfriend's roommate from college (OK, that may be stretching it—but only slightly). Point is, they are here; they've all got a special message to deliver; and someone has to write them.

Freelance realities

Writers who make a decent income writing greeting cards are almost always staff writers or those who are on contract. Freelance writers do not typically earn enough to use greeting card sales as any more than a supplemental source of income.In the most recent "How Much Should I Charge?'' survey (on page 61), freelancers made $50 on the low end to $300 on the high end per card. And that is from a more experienced set of freelancers. It is known that some freelancers settle for payment as low as $5 to $10 per card idea, which makes it harder for newer writers to negotiate higher payments.

Listings

Each listing includes contact information, submission specs, needs, and payment details. While we work to give you the most up-to-date listing information, it is still recommended that you either contact the companies or check out their Web sites to confirm specific submission policies and needs. This little bit of extra work is what often sets apart professional writers from the rest of the pack. In a competitive market such as greeting cards, professionalism goes a long way toward ensuring success.

For more information

To learn even more about the greeting card industry, check out the Greeting Card Association (GCA) Web site at www.greetingcard.org. It provides industry statistics, tips, and information on specific greeting card companies.

⊘ AMERICAN GREETINGS

One American Rd., Cleveland OH 44144-2398. (216)252-7300. Fax: (216)252-6778. No unsolicited material. Experienced, talented writers should submit a cover letter and résumé describing their education and content experience for contract-to-permanent staff writing positions.

Needs humorous.

Tips In this competitive arena, we're only looking for gifted humor writers and cartoonists who are interested in adapting their skillsets to the uniqueness of greeting card composition.

BLUE MOUNTAIN ARTS, INC.

P.O. Box 1007, Boulder CO 80306. (303)449-0536. Fax: (303)447-0939. E-mail: editorial@sps.com. **Bought over 200 freelance ideas last year.** Submit seasonal/holiday material 4 months in advance. Responds in 2-4 months. Buys worldwide, exclusive rights, or anthology rights. Pays on publication. Request writer's guidelines through website.

- No rhymed poetry, religious verse, or one-liners. No poems that sound like the ones we've already published.

Needs "Submissions should reflect a message, feeling, or sentiment that one person would want to share with another. Full book manuscripts or proposals are also accepted for possible publication by our book division, Blue Mountain Press." **Pays $300 for the first work chosen for publication on a card (payment scale escalates after that); $50 for anthology rights; payment schedule for books will be discussed at time of acceptance.**

Other Product Lines Calendars, gift books, prints, mugs.

Tips "Familiarize yourself with our products before submitting material, although we caution you not to study them too hard. We want poetry that expresses real emotions and feelings, so we suggest that you have someone specific in mind (a friend, relative, etc.) as you write. We prefer that submissions be typewritten, one poem per page, with name and address on every page. Only a small portion of the freelance material we receive is selected each year, either for publication on a notecard or in a gift anthology, and the review process can also be lengthy, but every ms. is given serious consideration."

DESIGNER GREETINGS

11 Executive Ave., Edison NJ 08817. (732)662-6700. Fax: (732)662-6701. E-mail: info@designergreetings.com. Website: www.designergreetings.com. **50% freelance written. Receives 200-300 submissions/year.** Submit seasonal/holiday material 6 months in advance. Responds in 2 months. Buys greeting card rights. Pays on acceptance. Guidelines online.

Needs conventional, humorous, informal, inspirational, juvenile, sensitivity, soft line, studio. Accepts rhymed and unrhymed verse ideas.

EPHEMERA, INC.

P.O. Box 490, Phoenix OR 97535. (541)535-4195. Fax: (541)535-5016. **Contact:** Editor. Estab. 1980. "We have been producing Novelty Buttons, Magnets, and Stickers. You'll find our stuff all over the place.cutting edge card & gift shops, bookstores, music stores, gay & left wing shops, porno stores, coffee shops, etc. Some of our best designs end up on products made by companies we license to for T-shirts, cards, books, towels, mugs, calendars, etc." **95% freelance written. Receives 2,000 submissions/year.** Buys nearly 200 slogans for novelty buttons, stickers, and magnets each year. Responds in 1-5 months. Buys all rights. Pays on acceptance. Writer's guidelines for SASE or online Complete full-color catalog online or for $4

- "Be fresh, original, and concise. Ephemera has a reputation for having the most irreverent, provocative and outrageously funny material on the market. We encourage you to be as weird, twisted and rude as you like."

Needs "We produce irreverent, provocative, and outrageously funny buttons, magnets, and stickers. You'll find them in cutting-edge shops that sell cards, gifts, books, music, coffee, pipes, porn, etc. We're looking for snappy slogans about politics, women and bitchiness, work, parenting, coffee, booze, pot, drugs, religion, food, aging, teens, gays and lesbians, sexual come-ons and put-downs, etc. Pretty please, don't limit yourself to these topics. Surprise us!" **Pays $50/slogan.**

Tips "We're looking for fresh, interesting, original material. Our buttons and magnets are small, so we crave concise and high-impact gems of wit. We urge you to be as off-the-wall and obscene as you like. We want humor that makes us laugh out loud. See the retail store online to get an idea of what we like."

GALLANT GREETINGS CORP.

4300 United Parkway, Schiller Park IL 60176. Gallant is a publisher of traditional, religious, and humorous greeting cards for all occasions and seasons. All card ideas are purchased from freelance writers. Payment is $45/card idea purchased.

⊘ HALLMARK CARDS

P.O. Box 419034, Kansas City MO 64141. At this time, Hallmark does not accept unsolicited freelance submissions, and our employment opportunities would involve relocating to the Kansas City area.

INNOVATIVE ART

100 Smith Ranch Rd., San Rafael CA 94903. **25% freelance written. Receives 400 submissions/year. Bought 100 freelance ideas last year.** Responds in 2 months. Pays on acceptance.

Needs humorous, informal, inspirational, Other. **Pays flat fees. Buys exclusive rights.**

Other Product Lines Calendars, posters, matted/framed prints.

Tips Upscale, cute, alternative, humorous cards for bookstores, card stores, chain stores, and college bookstores.

KALAN LP

97 S. Union Ave., Lansdowne PA 19050. (610)623-1900. E-mail: editorial@kalanlp.com. **Contact:** David Umlauf. "Please enter submissions at our online website." **80% freelance written. Receives 500-800 submissions/year. Bought 80-100 freelance ideas last year.** Submit seasonal/holiday material 8-10 months in advance. Responds in 6-8 months. Buys all rights. Pays on acceptance. Guidelines available for free.

Needs humorous. Accepts rhymed and unrhymed verse ideas. **Pays $100-150. Pays $100/card concept; $60/one-liners.**

Other Product Lines Bumper stickers; post cards; posters; key rings; shot glasses; lighters; buttons; mugs; magnets.

Tips "Target to contemporary women of all ages. We want humor anywhere from subtle, to risqué, to downright rude. No flowery prose."

KOEHLER COMPANIES, INC.

8758 Woodcliff Rd., Bloomington MN 55438. (952)942-5666. Fax: (952)942-5208. E-mail: bob@koehlercompanies.com. "We manufacture a decorative plaque line that utilizes verse and art. We are not a greeting card company. We combine art and message to create a product that a consumer will like enough to want to look at for a year or longer." **65% freelance written. Receives 100 submissions/year. Bought 25 freelance ideas last year.** Responds in 1 month. Pays on acceptance.

Needs humorous, inspirational. **We pay $125/selected verse and limit the use to our products so that writers may resell their work for other uses.**

Other Product Lines Framed Prints.

Tips "We sell wholesale to the retail market and the mail order catalog industry as well. Lengthy verse is sometimes challenging. Usually under 6 lines is best. We prefer to have work submitted by e-mail or mail."

MARIAN HEATH GREETING CARDS

9 Kendrick Rd., Wareham MA 02571. **90% freelance written. Receives 75-100 submissions/year. Bought 200-250 freelance ideas last year.** Submit seasonal/holiday material 4 months in advance. Responds in 2 weeks. Buys greeting card rights. Pays on publication. Guidelines for #10 SASE.

Needs Accepts wide range of writing styles—casual or coversational, meaningful, inspirational, humorous. Prefers unrhymed verse ideas.

Tips Verses that are sincere and complimentary in a conversational tone tend to do best. For humor, we avoid 'put down' type of jokes and try to stay positive. Target audience is women over 18 and Baby Boomers.

MOONLIGHTING CARDS

P.O. Box 4670, Vallejo CA 94590. Fax: (707)554-9366. E-mail: robin@moonlightingcards.com. Submit seasonal/holiday material 12 months in advance. Pays on publication. Guidelines online.

Needs announcements, conventional, humorous, informal, inspirational, invitations, juvenile, sensitivity, soft line, studio. Prefers unrhymed verse ideas. Send as many ideas at one time as you like. But if we see you have not paid attention to our guidelines, we will not sort through 100 queries to find 1 gem. **Pays $25-25.**

Tips Currently, we are reviewing quotes for 'year-round LOVE cards' (aka Valentine's that don't say 'Happy Valentine's Day'). Birthday, thank you, and everyday wisdom all do well for us. Review the cards on our Web site and our guidelines to get a sense of what works for us.

NOVO CARD PUBLISHERS, INC.

3630 W. Pratt Ave., Lincolnwood IL 60712. (847)763-0077. Fax: (847)763-0020. E-mail: art@novocard.net. **80% freelance written. Receives 500 submissions/year. Bought 200 freelance ideas last year.** Submit seasonal/holiday material 8 months in advance. Responds in 2 months. Buys worldwide greeting card rights. Pays on acceptance. Guidelines for #10 SASE. Market list available on mailing list basis.

Needs announcements, conventional, humorous, informal, inspirational, invitations, juvenile, soft line, Other.

OATMEAL STUDIOS

P.O. Box 138WP, Rochester VT 05767. (802)767-3171. E-mail: dawn@oatmealstudios.com. **85% freelance written. Bought 200-300 freelance ideas last year.** Responds in 6 weeks. Pays on acceptance. Current market list for #10 SASE.

- Humor—conversational in tone and format—sells best for us.

Needs humorous, Other. Will review concepts. Humorous material (clever and very funny) year-round. Prefers unrhymed verse ideas. **Current pay schedule available with guidelines.**

Other Product Lines Notepads, stick-on notes.

Tips The greeting card market has become more competitive with a greater need for creative and original ideas. We are looking for writers who can communicate situations, thoughts, and relationships in a funny way and apply them to a birthday, get well, etc., greeting. We are willing to work with them in targeting our style. We will be looking for material that says something funny about life in a new way.

THE PAPER MAGIC GROUP, INC.

401 Adams Ave., Scranton PA 18501. (800)278-4085. **50% freelance written. Receives 500 submissions/ year.** Submit seasonal/holiday material 6 months in advance. Pays on acceptance. No market list

Needs Christmas boxed cards only. Submit Christmas sentiments only. relative titles, juvenile.

PAPYRUS DESIGN

500 Chadbourne Rd., Fairfield CA 94533. Fax: (707) 428-0641. Website: www.papyrusonline.com. **Contact:** Nikki Burton. Estab. 1950. **10% freelance written. Bought 35 freelance ideas last year.** Responds in 2 months.

Needs Submit 10 ideas per batch with SASE. Inspirational, humor, sentimental, contemporary, romance, friendship, seasonal, and everyday categories. "Prefers unrhymed verse, but on juvenile cards rhyme is OK."

Tips "Seeking text that goes beyond the standard generic verse. Conversational (modern voice), sophisticated, clever, flirty, whimsical, hot topics, and heartfelt text concepts are needed. We are always looking for unique ways to approach the following captions: birthday, friendship, wedding, anniversary, new baby, and sympathy. Poetry and off-color humor are not appropriate for our line. Heartfelt or sentimental text works best if it is short and elegant. The target market is female, stylish, professional, and savvy."

P.S. GREETINGS

5730 N. Tripp Ave., Chicago IL 60646. (773)267-6150. Fax: (773)267-6055. **Bought 200-300 freelance ideas last year.** Submit seasonal/holiday material 6 months in advance. Responds in 1 month. Pays on acceptance. Writer's guidelines/market list for #10 SASE or online.

Needs conventional, humorous, inspirational, invitations, juvenile, sensitivity, soft line, studio, Other. Accepts rhymed and unrhymed verse ideas. **Pays one-time flat fee.**

Other Product Lines Stationary, notepads.

RECYCLED PAPER GREETINGS

111 N. Canal St., Chicago IL 60606. (800)777-9494. Website: www.recycledpapergreetings.com. **100% freelance written. Bought 3,000 freelance ideas last year.** Responds in 2 months.

Needs "Please send ideas for specific occasions, such as birthday, friendship, thank you, miss you, and thinking of you."

Tips "Find our guidelines online. We do not accept submissions that include a message without any accompanying artwork. Be sure to label each card idea with your name, address, and phone number, and include a SASE. We accept simultaneous submissions."

ROCKSHOTS, INC.

20 Vandam St., New York NY 10013. (212)243-9661. Fax: (212)604-9060. **Bought 75 greeting card verse (or gag) freelance ideas last year.** Responds in 1 month. Buys greeting card rights. Guidelines for #10 SASE.

Needs humorous. "Looking for a combination of sexy and humorous come-on type greeting (sentimental is not our style); and insult cards (looking for cute insults). Card gag can adopt a sentimental style, then take an ironic twist and end on an off-beat note." sentimental or conventional material. **Pays $50/gag line.**

Tips "Rockshots is an outrageous, witty, adult, and sometimes shocking card company. Our range of style starts at cute and whimsical and runs the gamut all the way to totally outrageous and unbelievable. Rockshots' cards definitely stand out from all the 'mainstream' products on the market today. Some of the images we are famous for include 'sexy' photos of 500- to 600-pound female models, smart-talking grannies, copulating animals, and, of course, incredibly sexy shots of nude and seminude men and women. Some of our best-selling cards are photos with captions that start out leading the reader in one direction, and then zings them with a punch line totally out of left field, but also hysterically apropos. As you can guess, we do not shy away from much. Be creative, be imaginative, be funny, but most of all, be different. Do not hold back because of society's imposed standards, but let it all pour out. It's always good to mix sex and humor, as sex always sells. Remember that 70% to 80% of our audience is women, so get in touch with your 'feminine' side, your bitchy feminine side. Your gag line will be illustrated by a Rockshots photograph or drawing, so try and think visually. It's always a good idea to preview our cards at your local store or on our Web site, if this is possible, to give you a feeling of our style."

SNAFU DESIGNS, INC.

2500 University Ave. W., Suite C-10, St. Paul MN 55114. E-mail: info@snafudesigns.com. Responds in 6 weeks. Buys all rights. Pays on Acceptance. Guidelines for #10 SASE.

Needs Humorous, Informal. "Specifically seeking birthday, friendship, thank you, anniversary, congratulations, get well, new baby, Christmas, wedding, pregnancy, retirement, Valentines Day and Mother's Day ideas." **Pays $100/idea.**

Tips "Our cards use clever ideas that are simple and concisely delivered and are aimed at a smart, adult audience. We like 'off the wall' irreverent humor that often has a little bite to it. Well done 'bathroom humor' is great! Please do not submit anything cute."

MARKETS

Contests & Awards

The contests and awards listed in this section are arranged by subject. Nonfiction writers can turn immediately to nonfiction awards listed alphabetically by the name of the contest or award. The same is true for fiction writers, poets, playwrights and screenwriters, journalists, children's writers, and translators. You'll also find general book awards, fellowships offered by arts councils and foundations, and multiple category contests.

New contests and awards are announced in various writer's publications nearly every day. However, many lose their funding or fold—and sponsoring magazines go out of business just as often. We have contacted the organizations whose contests and awards are listed here with the understanding that they are valid through 2008-2009. **Contact names**, **entry fees**, and **deadlines** have been highlighted and set in bold type for your convenience.

To make sure you have all the information you need about a particular contest, always send a SASE to the contact person in the listing before entering a contest. The listings in this section are brief, and many contests have lengthy, specific rules and requirements that we could not include in our limited space. Often a specific entry form must accompany your submission.

When you receive a set of guidelines, you will see that some contests are not applicable to all writers. The writer's age, previous publication, geographic location, and length of the work are common matters of eligibility. Read the requirements carefully to ensure you don't enter a contest for which you are not qualified. You should also be aware that every year, more and more contests, especially those sponsored by "little'' literary magazines, are charging entry fees.

Winning a contest or award can launch a successful writing career. Take a professional approach by doing a little extra research. Find out who the previous winner of the award was by investing in a sample copy of the magazine in which the prize-winning article, poem, or short story appeared. Attend the staged reading of an award-winning play. Your extra effort will be to your advantage in competing with writers who simply submit blindly.

Information on contests and awards listed in the previous edition of *Writer's Market*, but not included in this edition, can be found in the General Index.

ANDERBO POETRY PRIZE

Anderbo Poetry Prize, 270 Lafayette St., Suite 1412, New York NY 10012. Website: www.anderbo.com. **Contact:** Rick Rofihe. Estab. 2005. "Poet must have have been previously published on anderbo.com. Limit 6 poems per poet. Poems should be typed on 8½ x 11 paper with the poet's name and contact info on the upper right corner of each poem. Mail submissions. Enclose SASE to receive names of winner and honorable mentions. See guidelines online at website. All entries are non-returnable." **Postmarked by Nov. 1, 2009. Charges $10 reading fee. Check or money order payable to Rick Rofihe.** Prize $500, publication on anderbo.com. William Logan for 2009, assisted by Charity Burns

N ART AFFAIR WRITING CONTEST

Art Affair, P.O. Box 54302, Oklahoma City OK 73154. E-mail: artaffair@aol.com. Website: www.shadetreecreations.com. **Contact:** Barbara Shepherd. "Fiction and poems must be unpublished. Multiple entries accepted and may be mailed in the same packet. For (general) Short Story, double-space in 12-point font (put page and word count in upper right-hand corner of first page—5,000 word limit. Include cover page with writer's name, address, phone number, and title of story. For Western Short Story, follow same directions but type 'Western' on cover page. For Poetry, submit original poems on any subject, in any style, no more than 60 lines (put line count in the upper right-hand corner of first page). Include cover page with poet's name, address, phone number, and title. Do not include SASE; mss will not be returned." To encourage new and established writers and to publicly recognize them for their efforts. Open to any writer or poet. **Oct. 1 (every year). Charges $5/each short story, each western short story; $3/each poem. Make check payable to Art Affair.** Prize Short Story: 1st Prize: $50; 2nd Prize: $25; 3rd Prize: $15. Western Short Story: 1st Prize: $50; 2nd Prize: $25; 3rd Prize: $15. Poetry: 1st Prize: $40; 2nd Prize: $25; 3rd Prize: $15. (all winners also receive certificates. Additional certificates for Honorable Mentions will be awarded at discretion of the judges). Winners' list will be published on our website in Dec. Short Story, Western Short Story, Poetry. highly-qualified and professional judges—different each year (blind judging).

Tips "Guidelines and entry forms available for SASE and on website."

N MARILYN BAILLIE PICTURE BOOK AWARD

The Canadian Children's Book Centre, 40 Orchard View Blvd., Suite 101, Toronto ON M4R 1B9 Canada. (416)975-0010. Fax: (416)975-8970. Website: www.bookcentre.ca. Estab. 2006. "To be eligible, the book must be an original work in English, aimed at children ages 3-8, written and illustrated by Canadians and first published in Canada. Eligible genres include fiction, nonfiction and poetry. Books must be published between Jan. 1 and Dec. 31 of the previous calendar year." "Honours excellence in the illustrated picture book format." **Jan. 15.** Prize $20,000 a jury selected by the Canadian Children's Book Centre.

Tips "Please visit website for submission guidelines and eligibility criteria."

N CENTRAL COAST WRITERS SPRING WRITING CONTEST

Central Coast Writers Spring Writing Contest, Central Coast Writers Branch of the California Writers Club, P.O. Box 997, Pacific Grove CA 93950. E-mail: info@centralcoastwriters.org or cow-contests@comcast.net. Website: www.centralcoastwriters.org. **Contact:** Michael Thomas, contest chair. "All entries are considered for publication. Buys first rights. All rights revert to author upon publication." Submissions required to be unpublished. "To recognize and reward writers of the best short story and poem submitted and to feature their work on the Central Coast Writers website and in *The Homestead Review*, the literary journal of Hartnell College." **Entry period from Sept. 15, 2009 through January 15, 2010. Same each year. Charges $15 per story, $5 per poem.** Prize $500 for the winning story and $500 for the winning poem. poetry and fiction Prof. Maria Garcia Teutsch and Dr. Jessica Breheny, published authors in their respective fields of poetry and fiction.

Tips "See website for guidelines."

N ERIC HOFFER AWARD

Hopewell Publications, LLC, Annual contest for previously published books., P.O. Box 11, Titusville NJ 08560-0011. Fax: (609)964-1718. E-mail: info@hopepubs.com. **Contact:** Christopher Kim, chair. "Annual contest for previously published books. Recognizes excellence in independent publishing in many unique categories: Art (titles capture the experience, execution, or demonstration of the arts); General Fiction (nongenre-specific fiction); Commercial Fiction (genre-specific fiction); Children (titles for young children); Young Adult (titles aimed at the juvenile and teen markets); Culture (titles demonstrating the human or world experience); Memoir (titles relating to personal experience); Business (titles with application to today's business environment and emerging trends); Reference (titles from traditional and emerging reference areas); Home (titles with practical applications to home or home-related issues, including family); Health (titles promoting physical, mental, and emotional well-being); Self-help/spiritual (titles involving the mind and spirit, including religion); Legacy (titles over 2 years of age that hold particular relevance to any subject matter or form). Open to any writer of published work within the last 2 years." "This contest recognizes excellence in independent publishing in many unique categories: Art, General Fiction, Commercial Fiction, Children, Young Adult, Culture, Memoir, Business,

Reference, Home, Health, Self-help/spiritual, and Legacy (fiction & nonfiction)." **January 25. Charges $45.** Prize $1,500, press/media, and international coverage in *The US Review of Books & Best New Writing.* authors, editors, agents, publishers, book producers, artists, experienced category readers, and health and business professionals.

N FOOD VERSE CONTEST

Literal Latte, 200 East 10th St., Suite 240, New York NY 10003. (212)260-5532. E-mail: litlatte@aol.com. Website: www.literal-latte.com. **Contact:** Jenine Gordon Bockman, editor. "Open to any writer. Submissions required to be unpublished. Guidelines and entry forms are available for SASE and online at website. Literal Latte acquires first rights." "Annual contest to give support and exposure to great writing." **Jan. 31 every year. Charges $10.** Prize $500 the Editors.

N GLIMMER TRAIN'S BEST START CONTEST

Glimmer Train Press, Inc., 1211 NW Glisan St., #207, Portland OR 97209. Fax: (503)221-0837. E-mail: eds@glimmertrain.org. Website: www.glimmertrain.org. **Contact:** Linda Swanson-Davies. Estab. 2009. "Offered quarterly to encourage new writers, open to any writer whose fiction has not appeared in a nationally distributed print publication with a circulation over 3,000. Word count: up to 1,000. Open all during the months of March, June, September, and December. See complete writing guidelines and submit online at website." **Charges $10 fee/story.** Prize Best 50 entries each get $50 and make Glimmer Train's Best Start List, which will be announced in their respective bulletin month, on their website, and in a number of other online publications.

N LITERAL LATTE ESSAY AWARD

Literal Latte, 200 E. 10th St., Suite 240, New York NY 10003. (212)260-5532. E-mail: litlatte@aol.com. Website: www.literal-latte.com. **Contact:** Jenine Gordon Bockman. "Open to any writer. Send previously unpublished personal essays, 6,000 words max. All topics accepted. Include SASE or email address for reply." Acquires first rights. To give support and exposure to great writing. **Sept. 15. Charges $10.** Prize 1st Prize: $1,000; 2nd: $300; 3rd: $200. The Editors

Tips "Go to website for guidelines."

N LITERAL LATTE SHORT SHORTS CONTEST

Literal Latte, 200 E. 10th St., Suite 240, New York NY 10003. (212)260-5532. E-mail: litlatte@aol.com. Website: www.literal-latte.com. **Contact:** Jenine Gordon Bockman. Estab. Annual contest. Send unpublished shorts. 2,000 words max. All styles welcome. Postmark by June 30th. Name, address, phone number, email address (optional) on cover page only. Include SASE or email address for reply. All entries considered for publication.". **Postmark June 30th. Charges $10 for up to 3, or $15 per set of 6 shorts.** Prize $500 the Editors

N THE LOFTS INROADS PROGRAM

Native American writings, The Loft Literary Center, 1011 Washington Ave. S., Suite 200, Open Book, Minneapolis MN 55415. (612)215-2575. Fax: (612)215-2576. E-mail: loft@loft.org. Website: www.loft.org. **Contact:** Bao Phi, coordinator. "Program offers up to eight writers the opportunity to engage in nine weeks of craft seminars, individual conferences, and public readings with an established local mentor who shares their ethnic heritage. Open to Native American writers who write in any genre. Mentor: Gwen Westerman Griffin." Prize $200 stipend.

N THE LOFT MENTOR SERIES IN POETRY AND CREATIVE PROSE

prose and poetry, The Loft Literary Center, 1011 Washington Ave. S., Suite 200, Open Book, Minneapolis MN 55415. (612)215-2575. Fax: (61)215-2576. **Contact:** Jerod Santek. "Offers twelve emerging Minnesota writers the opportunity to work intensively with six nationally acclaimed writers of prose and poetry." See guidelines and follow carefully and exactly. **June 3, 5:00 p.m.** Prize stipend

N MCKNIGHT ARTIST FELLOWSHIPS FOR WRITERS, LOFT AWARD(S) IN CHILDREN'S LITERATURE/CREATIVE PROSE/POETRY

fellowships/awards, The Loft Literary Center, 1011 Washington Ave. S., Suite 200, Open Book, Minneapolis MN 55415. (612)215-2575. Fax: (612)215-2576. E-mail: loft@loft.org. Website: www.loft.org. **Contact:** Jerod Santek. "The Loft administers the McKnight Artists Fellowships for Writers. Five $25,000 awards are presented annually to accomplished Minnesota writers and spoken word artists. Four awards alternate annually between creative prose (fiction and creative nonfiction) and poetry/spoken word. The fifth award is presented in children's literature and alternates annually for writing for ages 8 and under and writing for children older than 8." The awards provide the writers the opportunity to focus on their craft for the course of the fellowship year. Prize $25,000

Tips "See guidelines and follow carefully and exactly."

N MINNESOTA WRITERS' CAREER INITIATIVE GRANT

The Loft Literary Center, fellowships and awards, 1011 Washington Ave. S., Suite 200, Open Book, Minneapolis

MN 55415. (612)215-2575. Fax: (612)215-2576. E-mail: loft@loft.org. Website: www.loft.org. **Contact:** Jerod Santek. "The Minnesota Writers' Career Initiative Program provides financial support and professional assistance to advanced Minnesota writers. Up to four winners each year will receive grants of up to $10,000 to underwrite career development plans. Applicants must have published a book or have one slated for publication during the award year." **June 2010. Watch for application guidelines in Dec. 2009.**

MUSE ANNUAL LITERARY COMPETITION

MUSE, The Lit, Best of MUSE Writing Contest, 2570 Superior Ave., Suite 203, Cleveland OH 44114. (216)694-0000. E-mail: judith@the-lit.org. Website: www.the-lit.org. **Contact:** Judith Mansour-Thomas. "Fiction and creative nonfiction not to exceed 2,000 words. Poetry limited to 3 poems per entry - max. 2 typewritten pages per poem. Writers on writing entry not to exceed 2,000 words (prose) or max. 3 poems per entry. Prizes awarded in each category. First-place winners published in a special edition of MUSE. Announcement of winners and honorable mentions in April/May Issue MUSE. Sponsored by MUSE and The Lit." "Entries will be judged anonymously. Do not put name on mss pages. Attach entry form (or facsimile) to submission." **Dec. 31, 2009. Charges $25 per category; each additional entry within a category, add $10. Make check payable to The Lit and mail.** Prize Up to $500. fiction, poetry, creative nonfiction.

Tips "Ms. will not be returned." Include SASE for list of winners."

THE PRIZE FOR BEST MUSIC THEATRE SCRIPT

Victorian Premier's Literary Awards, State Government of Victoria, State Library of Victoria, 328 Swanston St. C, Melbourne VIC 3000 Australia. (613)8664 7277. E-mail: pla@slv.vic.gov.au. Website: www.slv.vic.gov.au/pla. **Contact:** Project Officer. "Prize offered for music theatre scripts produced in Australia and first performed during the eligible period. Recognizes up to 4 co-authors." **Usually May each year. Charges $44.** Prize Up to AUD $30,000

Tips "Guidelines and entry forms available on our website."

THE PRIZE FOR INDIGENOUS WRITING

Victorian Premier's Literary Awards, State Government of Victoria, State Library of Victoria, 328 Swanston Street C, Melbourne VIC 3000 Australia. (613)8664 7277. E-mail: pla@slv.vic.gov.au. Website: www.slv.vic.gov.au/pla. **Contact:** Project Officer. "This biennial prize is designed to reward and promote books in all literary categories. The prize is open to those who are of Aboriginal and Torres Strait Islander descent, who identify as Aboriginal and Torres Strait Islanders, and who are accepted as such by the communities in which they live. The Prize is not offered in 2009." **Deadline: Usually in May. Charges $44.** Prize Up to AUD $30,000

Tips "Guidelines and entry forms are on our website."

SHABO AWARD FOR CHILDREN'S PICTURE BOOK WRITERS

The Loft Literary Center, 1011 Washington Ave. S., Suite 200, Open Book Minneapolis MN 55415. (612)215-2575. Fax: (612)215-2576. E-mail: loft@loft.org. Website: www.loft@loft.org. **Contact:** Jerod Santek. Estab. 2005. "The Shabo Award is offered to children's picture book writers to develop 'nearly there' manuscripts into publishable pieces. Up to eight advanced writers will be chosen annually. Participants should have few, or no, publications to date. Guidelines available online in early May with an early June deadline."

TD CANADIAN CHILDREN'S LITERATURE AWARD

The Canadian Children's Book Centre, 40 Orchard View Blvd., Suite 101, Toronto ON M4R 1B9 Canada. (416)975-0010. Fax: (416)975-8970. Website: www.bookcentre.ca. Estab. 2004. "All books, in any genre, written by Canadian and for children ages 1-12 are eligible. Only books first published in Canada are eligible for submission. Books must be published between January 1 and December 31 of the previous calendar year. Open to Canadian citizens and/or permanent residents of Canada. "To honour the most distinguished book of the year for young people in both English and French." **Jan. 15.** Prize Two prizes of $25,000, one for English, one for French. $10,000 will be divided among the Honour Book English titles and Honour Book French titles, to a max. of four; $2,500 shall go to each of the publishers of the English and French grand-prize winning books for promotion and publicity. a jury selected by the Canadian Children's Book Centre.

Tips "Please visit website for submission guidelines and eligibility criteria."

THE CHARITON REVIEW SHORT FICTON PRIZECHARITON REVIEW SHORT FICTION PRIZE, THE

Truman State University Press, 100 East Normal Ave., Kirksville MO 63501-4221. **Contact:** Nancy Rediger. An annual award for the best unpublished short fiction on any theme up to 5,000 words in English. Enclose a SASE if you want to be notified when your ms is received. Mss will not be returned. **August 31, 2009 (postmarked). Charges Include a nonrefundable reading fee of $20 for each ms submitted. Check payable to: Truman State University Press. If you prefer to pay by Visa, MasterCard, or Discover, include your credit card number, expiration date, cardholder name, and signature.** Prize $1,000 prize and publication in *The Chariton Review*. Three finalists will also be published in the Spring issue. All U.S. entrants receive a one-year subscription (two

issues) to *The Chariton Review*. Entrants outside the U.S. receive the prizewinning issue only. The final judge will be announced after the finalists have been selected in January.
Tips "Current Truman State University faculty, staff, or students are not eligible to compete."

THE SCENT OF AN ENDING™
White Eagle Coffee Store Press, P.O. Box 383, Fox River Grove IL 60021-0383. (847)639-9200. E-mail: wecspress@aol.com. Website: www.whiteeaglecoffeestorepress.com or www.thescentofanending.com. **Contact:** Frank Edmund Smith, pub. "Contest is offered annually for unpublished submissions. We're searching for the best bad ending to an imaginary novel—an ending that's a real stinker. We're looking for a memorably bad ending to a novel that has not been written. Submit the invented Title of the Novel and the final 25-125 words. The entry must be completely your own invention and cannot be taken from or closely based on anything actually published. " "All winners will be required to sign a contract verifying originality." **Final deadline is Sept. 30 each year. Charges $6.37.** Prize 1st Place $89.25, 2nd Place $67.32, 3rd Place $31.18 plus dubious fame and publication for all winners and finalists. Initial publication on website, then in chapbook format. Editors of White Eagle Coffee Store Press
Tips "Rolling entry. Rights to any winning and published materials revert to author on publication."

DENISE RAGAN WIESENMEYER ONE ACT MARATHON
Attic Theatre & Film Center, One Act plays, 5429 W. Washington Blvd., Los Angeles CA 90016. (323)525-0600. Fax: (323)482-1081. Website: www.attictheatre.org. **Contact:** Jaime Gray. "Open to all writers. Submissions required to be previously unpublished. No entry fee. Guidelines and entry forms available for SASE or go to our website and download." "The Marathon will take a 6-month option on all material that is produced at the ATTIC in the contest without pay. If a production is forthcoming from any of the contest finalists, discussions with the author will take place at that time." "Offered annually to find and support new work by established and up and coming writers with production and contest and publishing opportunities." **Dec. 31 each year.** Prize $300 for first place; $150 for second place. All finalists are invited to be published by the ATTIC and sold at our online store. "Judged by industry professionals in the L.A. area. Last year the Literary Director for the Geffen Playhouse and assistant Literary Director for the Mark Taper acted as judges."

PLAYWRITING & SCRIPTWRITING

"SET IN PHILADELPHIA" SCREENWRITING COMPETITION
Greater Philadelphia Film Office, 100 S. Broad Street, Suite 600, Philadelphia PA 19110. (215)686-2668. Fax: (215)686-3659. E-mail: sip@film.org. Website: www.film.org. Screenplays must be set primarily in the Greater Philadelphia area (includes the surrounding counties). All genres and storytelling approaches are acceptable. Screenplays must be between 85-130 pages in length. There are different awards, such as an award for the best script for writers under 25, as well as the best script for a regional writer. See the Web site for full details. **Charges $45-65.** Prize $10,000 grand prize, with other prizes offered.

20/20 SCREENWRITING CONTEST
3639 Malibu Vista Drive, Malibu CA 90265. (310)454-0971. Fax: (310)573-3868. E-mail: 2020contest@screenbrokers.com. Website: www.2020contest.com. "Send in the first 20 pages of your scripts for the first round and then go from there." Electronic submissions accepted. **Deadline: June 20. Charges $20 basic, $40 expanded feedback.** Prize "You will win a WGA-signatory, veteran agency representation. In addition, winners will also receive either a pass to the next Screenwriters' Expo, or a four DVDs from past Expo speakers." All genres; 20-page excerpt from script.

ACTORS' CHOICE AWARDS
The Screenwriting Conference in Santa Fe, PO Box 29762, Santa Fe NM 87592. (866)424-1501. Fax: (505)424-8207. E-mail: writeon@scsfe.com. **Deadline: May 15. Charges $25.** Prize All 5 winners receive free admission to the PAGEawards screenwriting competition. In addition, scripts are forwarded to producers attending Producers seminar. All genres.

ALBERTA PLAYWRITING COMPETITION
Alberta Playwrights' Network, 2633 Hochwald Ave. SW, Calgary AB T3E 7K2 Canada. (403)269-8564. Fax: (403)265-6773. Offered annually for unproduced plays with full-length and Discovery categories. Discovery is open only to previously unproduced playwrights. Open only to residents of Alberta. **Deadline: March 31. Charges $40 fee (Canadian).** Prize Full length: $3,500 (Canadian); Discovery: $1,500 (Canadian); plus a written critique, workshop of winning play, and possible reading of winning plays at a Showcase Conference

AMERICAN GEM SHORT CONTEST
FilmMakers Magazine, American Gem Short Screenplay Contest, P.O. Box 4678, Mission Viejo CA 92690.

Contest is held annually. Short scripts only. **Deadline: April 30; late deadline: June 15. Charges $29-$59.**

ANNUAL INTERNATIONAL ONE-PAGE PLAY COMPETITION
Lamia Ink!, P.O. Box 202, Prince Street Station, New York NY 10012. **Contact:** Cortland Jessup, founder/artistic director. Offered annually for previously published or unpublished 1-page plays. Acquires the rights to publish in our magazine and to be read or performed at the prize awarding festival. "We will publish and award prizes annually, but may not in every year hold a public performance of the finalist plays. In years without a live performance festival we will award prizes via mail and list all finalists on website." Playwright retains copyright. There are 3 rounds of judging with invited judges that change from year to year. There are up to 12 judges for finalists round. Guidelines available online. The competition is a short-form theatrical exercise created to nurture aspiring writers, challenge established writers and encourage a wide range of experimentation. **Deadline: March 15. Charges $2/play; $5/3 plays (maximum).** Prize $200 for the winner; all finalists will be published.
Tips "Send SASE for guidelines or download them from the website."

ANNUAL NATIONAL PLAYWRITING COMPETITION
Wichita State University, School of Performing Arts, 1845 Fairmount, Wichita KS 67260-0153. (316)978-3360. Fax: (316)978-3202. E-mail: bret.jones@wichita.edu. **Contact:** Bret Jones, Director of Theatre. Offered annually for full-length plays (minimum of 90 minutes playing time), or 2-3 short plays on related themes (minimum of 90 minutes playing time). Open to all undergraduate and graduate students enrolled at any college or university in the US (indicate school affiliation). **Deadline: March 15.** Prize Production by the Wichita State University Theatre. Winner announced April 15. No plays returned after February 15.

ANNUAL ONE-ACT PLAYWRITING CONTEST
TADA!, 15 W. 28th St., 3rd Floor, New York NY 10001. (212)252-1619, ext. 17. Fax: (212)252-8763. E-mail: jgreer@tadatheater.com. Website: www.tadatheater.com. **Contact:** Joanna Greer, associate artistic director. Offered annually to encourage playwrights to develop new plays for teen and family audiences. Call or e-mail for guidelines. **Deadline: January 31, 2010.** Prize Cash award and staged readings.

ARIZONA SCREENPLAY SEARCH
Phoenix Film Foundation, 1700 N. Seventh Ave., Suite 250, Phoenix AZ 85007. (602)955-6444. This contest is actually multiple contests in one. One contest only accepts scripts where the plot happens in the state. The other contest is open to all plots. **Charges fee varies by year.** Prize Cash prizes offered.

AUSTIN FILM FESTIVAL SCREENPLAY COMPETITION
1604 Nueces, Austin TX 78701. (512)478-4795. Fax: (512)478-6205. E-mail: info@austinfilmfestival.com. **Deadline: May 15June 1. Charges $30-$40.** Prize Cash prizes. Some of the contest winning scripts, such as *Excess Baggage*, have gone on to be not only bought, but produced. Multiple genres.

BIG BEAR LAKE SCREENWRITING COMPETITION
P.O. Box 1981, Big Bear Lake CA 92315-1981. (909)866-3433. E-mail: BigBearFilmFest@aol.com. **Deadline: April 1. Charges $40.** Prize No confirmed money prizes, but winners receive software and their script submitted to studios.

THE BRITISH SHORT SCREENPLAY COMPETITION
c/o Pinewood Film Studios, Pinewood Road, Iver Heath, Buckinghamshire SL0 0NH United Kingdom. E-mail: info@kaosfilms.co.uk. Website: www.kaosfilms.co.uk/rules/. The British Short Screenplay Competition is open to writers of any nationality from any country. The entered screenplay must not have been previously optioned, sold or produced. Screenplays must be written in English language. The screenplay must be no less than five-minutes and no more than fifteen minutes screen time. **Charges 25-35 British pounds.** All genres.

BUNTVILLE CREW'S AWARD BLUE
Buntville Crew, 118 N. Railroad Ave., Buckley IL 60918-0445. E-mail: buntville@yahoo.fr. **Contact:** Steven Packard, artistic dir. "Presented annually for the best unpublished/unproduced play script under 15 pages, written by a student enrolled in any Illinois high school. Submit 1 copy of the script in standard play format, a brief biography, and a SASE (scripts will not be returned). Include name, address, telephone number, age, and name of school." **Deadline: May 31.** Prize Cash prize and possible productions in Buckley and/or New York City. panel selected by the theater.

BUNTVILLE CREW'S PRIX HORS PAIR
Buntville Crew, 118 N. Railroad Ave., Buckley IL 60918-0445. E-mail: buntville@yahoo.fr. Website: www.buntville@yahoo.com. **Contact:** Steven Packard, artistic dir. "Annual award for unpublished/unproduced play script under 15 pages. Plays may be in English, French, German, or Spanish (no translations, no adaptations). Submit 1 copy of the script in standard play format, a résumé, and a SASE (scripts will not be returned). Include

name, address, and telephone number." **Deadline: May 31**. **Charges $8.** Prize $200 and possible production in Buckley and/or New York City. panel selected by the theater.

CALIFORNIA YOUNG PLAYWRIGHTS CONTEST

Playwrights Project, 2356 Moore St., #204, San Diego CA 92110-3019. (619)239-8222. Fax: (619)239-8225. E-mail: write@playwrightsproject.org. Website: www.playwrightsproject.org. **Contact:** Cecelia Kouma, managing director. "Offered annually for previously unpublished plays by young writers to stimulate young people to create dramatic works, and to nurture promising writers. Scripts must be a minimum of 10 standard typewritten pages; send 2 copies. Scripts will *not* be returned. If requested, entrants receive detailed evaluation letter. Writers must be California residents under age 19 as of the deadline date. Guidelines available online." **Deadline: June 1**. Prize Professional production of 3-5 winning plays at a professional theatre in San Diego, plus royalty

CHRISTIAN SCREENWRITE

P.O. Box 447, Bloomfield NJ 07003. (201)306-5093. E-mail: info@christianscreenwrite.com. Website: www.christianscreenwrite.com. Contemporary Christian screenplays only. The contest is "looking for films that spread the messages and principles and Christianity." **Deadline: July 2009-September 2009. Charges $40.** Prize Cash prizes offered for top three winners.

CINEQUEST FILM FESTIVAL SCREENPLAY COMPETITION

Cinequest Film Festival, 22 N. Almaden Ave., San Jose CA 95110. (408)295-3378(FEST). Fax: (408)995-5713. E-mail: info@cinequest.org. All genres and lengths of screenplays (up to 125 pages) are accepted, from low-budget Indie dramas to mega-money flicks. **Charges $35-40.** Prize Multiple prizes, with a $5,000 grand prize. Winning scripts will be passed on to moviemakers.

CITA SKETCH WRITING AND PLAY CONTEST

Christians in Theatre Arts, P.O. Box 26471, Greenville SC 29616. (864)679-1898. E-mail: admin@cita.org. Website: www.cita.org. "Annual sketch contest for CITA members: to encourage excellence in theatrical sketch writing, focusing on material created to minister in worship services, evangelistic outreach, street theatre, or educational, amateur, or professional theatre performance. Sketches must in some way reflect Christian truth, values, or questions. Sketches may be presentational, slice-of-life, monologue, mime, or any combination of forms. Prize winners of Drama and comedy categories will receive a plaque at a general session of the CITA National Conference in June. See website for guidelines. Annual play contest: The goal of this competition is to encourage CITA playwrights by providing the competition winner with exposure and connection with organizations related to CITA which may then consider it for further development and/or production." **Deadline: February 1. Charges $10/entry for sketch contest; $20/entry for play contest.** Prize Staged readings/productions of these works may also be a part of the conference at the discretion of the judges. Works may be published in the CITA magazine, *Christianity and Theatre*, with the author's permission. All further production rights will be reserved by the author.

COE COLLEGE PLAYWRITING FESTIVAL

Coe College, 1220 First Ave. NE, Cedar Rapids IA 52402-5092. (319)399-8624. Fax: (319)399-8557. E-mail: swolvert@coe.edu. **Contact:** Susan Wolverton. Estab. 1993. "Offered biennially for unpublished work to provide a venue for new works for the stage. We are interested in full-length productions, not one-acts or musicals. There are no specific criteria although a current resume and synopsis is requested. Open to any writer." **Deadline: November 1, even years. Notification: January 15, odd years**. Prize $500, plus 1-week residency as guest artist with airfare, room and board provided.

CREATIVE WORLD AWARDS (CWA) SCREENWRITING COMPETITION

PO Box 10699, Marina del Rey CA 90295. E-mail: info@creativeworldawards.com; submissions@creativeworldawards.com. **Contact:** Marlene Neubauer/Heather Waters. "The CWA is an international screenwriting contest devoted to discovering and advancing the hottest new screenwriters in the industry. With direct access to top level producers and industry executives, this contest has become a prominent source for promoting talented writers. It is open to all writers 18 years or older whose total earnings from all film screenwriting may not exceed $30,000." All screenplays must be in English, between 90-120 pages and in standard spec screenplay format. See website's Basic FAQ page for more detailed information. Feature length screenplays only. Short screenplays are not accepted. **Deadline: June 30, 2009. Charges $45-65.** Prize One Grand Winner, 4 Category Winners - Over $16,000 in cash and prizes awarded.

DAYTON PLAYHOUSE FUTUREFEST

The Dayton Playhouse, 1301 E. Siebenthaler Ave., Dayton OH 45414-5357. (937)424-8477. **Contact:** Amy Brown, executive director. Three plays selected for full productions, three for staged readings at July FutureFest weekend. The six authors will be given travel and lodging to attend the festival. Professionally adjudicated. Guidelines online. **Deadline: October 31**. Prize $1,000

Contests & Awards

DC SHORTS SCREENWRITING COMPETITION

DC Shorts Film Festival, 1317 F Street, NW, Ste 920, Washington DC 20004. (202)393-4266. **Contact:** Jon Gann. DC Shorts is proud to present a different kind of screenwriting competition. A panel of judges consisting of filmmakers, screenwriters and critics will review and provide condensed coverage (feedback) for scripts of 15 pages or less. A set of finalists (no more than 7) will be selected to be featured during the festival weekend, which the screenwriters are invited to attend, and cast a live reading of the script from a bank of actors and directors. The live readings will be performed in front of an audience, who will vote on their favorite. These votes, along with the scores of the judges, will determine a competition winner. Prize One script will receive $1,000 up front, plus a $1,000 upon completion of the final film. The final film is guaranteed entry into DC Shorts 2010.

DUBUQUE FINE ARTS PLAYERS ANNUAL ONE-ACT PLAY CONTEST

Dubuque Fine Arts Players, 1686 Lawndale, Dubuque IA 52001. E-mail: gary.arms@clarke.edu. **Contact:** Gary Arms. "We select 3 one-act plays each year. We award cash prizes of up to $600 for a winning entry. We produce the winning plays in August. Offered annually for unpublished and unproduced work. Guidelines and application form for SASE." **Deadline: January 31**. **Charges $10.** Prize 1st Place: $600; 2nd Place: $300; 3rd Place: $200. Five groups who read all the plays; each play is read at least twice. Plays that score high enough enter the second round. The top 10 plays are read by a panel consisting of 3 directors and 2 other final judges.

ESSENTIAL THEATRE PLAYWRITING AWARD

The Essential Theatre, 1414 Foxhall Lane, #10, Atlanta GA 30316. (404)212-0815. E-mail: pmhardy@aol.com. **Contact:** Peter Hardy. "Offered annually for unproduced, full-length plays by Georgia resident writers. No limitations as to style or subject matter." **Deadline: April 23**. Prize $600 and full production.

THE LOUIS ESSON PRIZE FOR DRAMA

Victorian Premier's Literary Awards, State Government of Victoria, State Library of Victoria, 328 Swanston St. C, Melbourne VIC 3000 Australia. (61)(3)8664-7277. E-mail: pla@slv.vic.gov.au. Website: www.slv.vic.gov.au/pla. **Contact:** Project Officer. "Annual prize for theatre or radio scripts produced between May 1 and April 30. The State Library of Victoria reserves the right to place a copy of all nominated works in its collection. Further copyright remains with the author. Authors must be Australian citizens or permanent residents." **Deadline: Usually May each year**. Prize AUD $15,000

Tips "For guidelines and nomination forms please visit our website."

FADE IN AWARDS

287 S. Robertson Blvd., #467, Beverly Hills CA 90211. (310)275-0287. "The Fade In Awards were established in 1996 to assist talented new writers and writer/directors in getting recognized within the Hollywood community in order to begin a career as a working filmmaker." Prize Cash prizes offered, and industry exposure to agents, producers, & executives. Open to any writer worldwide. Seven categories and two formats to choose from.

Tips "You can enter the contest online or mail in a submission."

FEATURE LENGTH SCREENPLAY COMPETITION

Austin Film Festival, 1801 Salina St., Austin TX 78702. (512)478-4795. Fax: (512)478-6205. E-mail: alex@austinfilmfestival.com. Offered annually for unproduced screenplays. The Austin Film Festival is looking for quality screenplays which will be read by industry professionals. This year AFF will be providing 'Readers Notes' to all Second Rounders (top 10%) and higher for no additional charge. Two main categories: Drama Category and Comedy Category. Two optional Award Categories (additional entry of $20 per category); Latitude Productions Award and Sci-Fi Award. For guidelines for SASE or call (800)310-3378. The writer must hold the rights when submitted; work must be original and not under option. The screenplay must be feature length and in industry standard format. **Deadline: May 15 (early); June 1 (late)**. **Charges $40/early entry; $50/late entry.** Prize $5,000 in Comedy and Drama; $2,500 for Latitude Productions Award and Sci-Fi Award.

FESTIVAL OF NEW AMERICAN PLAYS

Firehouse Theatre Project, 1609 W. Broad St., Richmond VA 23220. (804)355-2001. E-mail: info@firehousetheatre.org. Website: www.firehousetheatre.org. **Contact:** Carol Piersol, artistic director. "Annual contest designed to support new and emerging American playwrights. Scripts must be full-length and previously unpublished/unproduced. (Readings are acceptable if no admission was charged.) Submissions should be mailed in standard manuscript form. This means no disks, no emails. All author information must be on a title page separate from the body of the manuscript and no reference to the author is permitted in the body of the script. Scripts must be accompanied by a letter of recommendation from a theater company or individual familiar with your work. Letters of recommendation do not need to be specific to the play submitted; they may be general recommendations of the playwright's work. All letters must be received with the script, not under separate cover. Scripts received without a letter will not be considered. Due to the volume of mail, manuscripts cannot be returned. All American playwrights welcome to submit their work." **Deadline: June 30 postmark**. Prize 1st Place: $1,000 and a staged reading; 2nd Place: $500 and a staged reading. All plays are initially read by a panel of individuals with experience in playwriting and literature. Previous judges have included Lloyd Rose (former *Washington Post* theatre critic), Bill Patton (frequent Firehouse director), Richard Toscan (dean of the Virginia Commonwealth University School for the Arts), and Israel Horovitz (playwright). All finalists are asked to sign a contract with the Firehouse Theatre Project that guarantees performance rights for the staged reading in January and printed credit for Firehouse Theatre Project if the play is produced/published in the future.

FILMMAKERS INTERNATIONAL SCREENWRITING AWARDS
P.O. 4678, Mission Viejo CA 92690 USA. E-mail: info@filmmakers.com. Website: www.filmmakers.com. **Deadline: May 31; late deadline: June 30. Charges $49-$69.**

FIREHOUSE THEATRE PROJECT NEW PLAY COMPETITION
The Firehouse Theatre Project, 1609 W. Broad St., Richmond VA 23220. (804)355-2001. **Contact:** Literary Manager FTP. Calls for previously unpublished full-length works with non-musical and non-children's themes. Submissions must be in standard play format. Scripts should be accompanied by a letter of recommendation from a company or individual familiar with your work. Submissions must be unpublished. Visit website for complete submission guidelines. "We're receptive to unusual, but well-wrought works." Acquires the right to produce the winning scripts in a staged reading for the FTP Festival of New American Plays. Following the Festival production dates, all rights are relinquished to the author. Open to US residents only. **Deadline: June 30**. Prize 1st Prize: $1,000; 2nd Prize: $500 a committee selected by the executive board of the Firehouse Theatre Project.

JOHN GASSNER MEMORIAL PLAYWRITING COMPETITION
New England Theatre Conference, 215 Knob Hill Dr., Hamden CT 06158. Fax: (203)288-5938. E-mail: mail@netconline.org. "We annually seek unpublished full-length plays and scripts. Open to all. Playwrights living outside New England may participate." **Deadline: April 15. Charges $10 fee.** Prize 1st Place: $1,000; 2nd Place: $500

GOTHAM SCREEN FILM FESTIVAL AND SCREENPLAY CONTEST
603 W. 115th St., Suite 384, New York NY 10025. E-mail: info@gothamscreen.com. "Submit via Withoutabox account or download form at Website." "The contest is open to anyone. Feature length screenplays should be properly formatted and have an approximate length of 80-120 pages. On the cover page, please put the title, the writer's name(s) and the contact details." **Deadline: September. Charges $35-50.** Prize $2,500. In addition, excerpts from selected contest entries will be performed live by professional actors at a staged reading during the festival. Drama, comedy, adventure, horror, thriller/suspense, family, romantic comedy, documentary. **Tips** "Include an e-mail address to be notified."

GOVERNOR GENERAL'S LITERARY AWARD FOR DRAMA
Canada Council for the Arts, 350 Albert St., P.O. Box 1047, Ottawa ON K1P 5V8 Canada. (613)566-4414, ext. 5573. Fax: (613)566-4410. "Offered for the best English-language and the best French-language work of drama by a Canadian. Publishers submit titles for consideration." **Deadline: March 15, June 1, or August 7, depending on the book's publication date**. Prize Each laureate receives $25,000; nonwinning finalists receive $1,000.

AURAND HARRIS MEMORIAL PLAYWRITING AWARD
The New England Theatre Conference, Inc., 215 Knob Hill Dr., Hamden CT 06518. Fax: (203)288-5938. E-mail: mail@netconline.org. "Offered annually for an unpublished full-length play for young audiences. Guidelines available online or for SASE. 'No phone calls, please.' Open to all." **Deadline: May 1. Charges $10 fee.** Prize 1st Place: $1,000; 2nd Place: $500

HENRICO THEATRE COMPANY ONE-ACT PLAYWRITING COMPETITION
Henrico Recreation & Parks, P.O. Box 27032, Richmond VA 23273. (804)501-5138. Fax: (804)501-5284. E-mail: per22@co.henrico.va.us. **Contact:** Amy A. Perdue. "Offered annually for previously unpublished or unproduced plays or musicals to produce new dramatic works in one-act form. Scripts with small casts and simpler sets given preference. Controversial themes and excessive language should be avoided." **Deadline: July 1**. Prize $300; Runner-Up: $200. Winning entries may be produced; videotape sent to author

HOLIDAY SCREENPLAY CONTEST
P.O. Box 450, Boulder CO 80306. (303)629-3072. E-mail: Cherubfilm@aol.com. Website: www.HolidayScreenplayContest.com. "Scripts must be centered on a holiday. The screenplay must be centered around one Holiday (New Year's Day, President's Day, Valentine's Day, St. Patrick's Day, April Fool's Day, Easter, 4th of July, Halloween, Thanksgiving, Hanukkah, Christmas, Kwanzaa, or any other world holiday you would like to feature). This contest is limited to the first 400 entries." Screenplays must be in English.

Screenplays must not have been previously optioned, produced, or purchased prior to submission. Multiple submissions are accepted but each submission requires a separate online entry and separate fee. Screenplays must be between 90 - 125 pages. **Deadline: November**. **Charges $30.** Prize Up to $500.

HORROR SCREENPLAY CONTEST

Cherub Productions, P.O. Box 540, Boulder Co 80306. (303)629-3072. E-mail: Cherubfilm@aol.com. "This contest is looking for horror scripts." This contest is limited to the first 600 entries. Screenplays must be between 90 - 125 pages. **Charges $35.** Prize More than $5000 in cash and prizes.

INTERNATIONAL FAMILY FILM FESTIVAL (IFFF)

4531 Empire Ave., #200, Burbank CA 91505. (661)257-3131. Fax: (818)847-1184. E-mail: info@iffilmfest.org. "IFFF advocates, promotes and encourages excellence in films produced for a general audience by emerging screenwriters, filmmakers and studios worldwide. "Friz Award" for Lifetime Achievement in Animation, Lifetime Achievement in Film, IFFF "Spirit" Award, IFFF Directors Gold Award, Top Applause Award. " Short screenplays and feature screenplays reviewed. Features should be fewer than 120 pages, and shorts should be fewer than 45 pages. With entry form, you will need to include a 50-word synopsis as well as character descriptions. **Deadline: January**. **Charges $30 (short); $60 (full).** Drama, comedy, animation, sci-fi/fantasy, musical.

KUMU KAHUA/UHM THEATRE DEPARTMENT PLAYWRITING CONTEST

Kumu Kahua Theatre, Inc./University of Hawaii at Manoa, Dept. of Theatre and Dance, 46 Merchant St., Honolulu HI 96813. (808)536-4222. Fax: (808)536-4226. E-mail: kumakahuatheatre@hawaiiantel.net. Website: www.kumukahua.com. **Contact:** Harry Wong III, artistic director. Offered annually for unpublished work to honor full-length and short plays. Guidelines available every September. First 2 categories open to residents and nonresidents. For Hawaii Prize, plays must be set in Hawaii or deal with some aspect of the Hawaiian experience. For Pacific Rim prize, plays must deal with the Pacific Islands, Pacific Rim, or Pacific/Asian-American experience—short plays only considered in 3rd category. **Deadline: January 2**. Prize Hawaii: $600; Pacific Rim: $450; Resident: $250.

L.A. DESIGNERS' THEATRE-COMMISSIONS

L.A. Designers' Theatre, P.O. Box 1883, Studio City CA 91614-0883. (323)650-9600 or (323)654-2700 T.D.D. Fax: (323)654-3210. E-mail: ladesigners@juno.com. **Contact:** Richard Niederberg, artistic director. Estab. 1970. "Quarterly contest to promote new work and push it onto the conveyor belt to filmed or videotaped entertainment. All submissions must be registered with copyright office and be unpublished. Material will not be returned. Do not submit anything that will not fit in a #10 envelope. No rules, guidelines, fees, or entry forms. Just present an idea that can be commissioned into a full work. Proposals for uncompleted works are encouraged. Unpopular political, religious, social, or other themes are encouraged; 'street' language and nudity are acceptable. Open to any writer." **Deadline: March 15, June 15, September 15, December 15**. Prize Production or publication of the work in the Los Angeles market. We only want 'first refusal.'

LAS VEGAS INTERNATIONAL FILM FESTIVAL SCREENPLAY COMPETITION

Las Vegas International Film Festival, 10300 W. Charleston Blvd., Las Vegas NV 89135. (502)371-8037. E-mail: info@lvfilmfest.com. Website: www.lvfilmfest.com/Filmmakers/Screenplay_Competition.aspx. "This annual screenplay competition was created to help aspiring screenwriters break into the entertainment industry as well as to support emerging new talent." Scripts may be submitted via hardcopy or electronic file. Scripts should be no longer than 180 pages. **Charges $30.** Prize Cash prizes are awarded to the First, Second, and Third place winners.

MAXIM MAZUMDAR NEW PLAY COMPETITION

Alleyway Theatre, 1 Curtain Up Alley, Buffalo NY 14202. (716)852-2600. Fax: (716)852-2266. E-mail: newplays@alleyway.com. **Contact:** Literary Manager. Estab. 1989. Annual competition. Full Length: Not less than 90 minutes, no more than 10 performers. One-Act: Less than 20 minutes, no more than 6 performers. Musicals must be accompanied by audio CD. Finalists announced October 1; winners announced November 1. Playwrights may submit work directly. There is no entry form. Writers may submit once in each category, but pay only 1 fee. Please specify if submission is to be included in competition. Alleyway Theatre must receive first production credit in subsequent printings and productions. **Deadline: July 1**. **Charges $25.** Prize Full length: $400, production; One-act: $100, production.

MCKNIGHT ADVANCEMENT GRANT

The Playwrights' Center, 2301 Franklin Ave. E., Minneapolis MN 55406-1099. (612)332-7481, ext. 10. Fax: (612)332-6037. Estab. 1981. Offered annually for either published or unpublished playwrights to recognize those whose work demonstrates exceptional artistic merit and potential and whose primary residence is in the state of Minnesota. The grants are intended to significantly advance recipients' art and careers, and can be used to support a wide variety of expenses. Applications available mid-October. Guidelines for SASE. Additional funds of up to $2,000 are available for workshops and readings. The Playwrights' Center evaluates each application and forwards finalists to a panel of 3 judges from the national theater community. Applicant must have been a citizen or permanent resident of the US and a legal resident of the state of Minnesota since July 1, 2009. (Residency must be maintained during fellowship year.) Applicant must have had a minimum of 1 work fully produced by a professional theater at the time of application. **Deadline: February 3**. Prize $25,000 which can be used to support a wide variety of expenses, including writing time, artistic costs of residency at a theater or arts organization, travel and study, production, or presentation

MCLAREN MEMORIAL COMEDY PLAY WRITING COMPETITION
Midland Community Theatre, 2000 W. Wadley, Midland TX 79705. (432)682-2544. Fax: (432)682-6136. Estab. 1990. "Offered annually in 2 divisions: one-act and full-length. All entries must be comedies for adults, teens, or children; musical comedies are *not* accepted. Work must have never been professionally produced or published. See website for competition guidelines and required entry form." **Deadline: Jan1-Feb28**. **Charges $20/script.** Prize $400 for winning full-length play; $200 for winning one-act play; staged readings for full length finalist.

MEXICO INTERNATIONAL FILM FESTIVAL SCREENPLAY COMPETITION
Mexico International Film Festival, 20058 Ventura Blvd., Suite 123, Woodland Hills CA 91364. E-mail: info@mexicofilmfestival.com. **Charges $30.** Awards are based solely on overall merits of the screenplays.

MONTEREY SCREENPLAY COMPETITION
Monterey County Film Commission, 801 Lighthouse Ave, Suite 104, Monterey CA 93940. (831)646-0910. Fax: (831) 655-9250. E-mail: info@filmmonterey.org. Feature scripts must be between 90 and 120 pages. A completed and signed Entry Form and Entry Fee must accompany each submission. The act of signing and submitting the form constitutes acceptance without reservation of all rules and requirements of the Monterey Screenplay Competition and all decisions rendered by its judges. **Deadline: May 19July 31**. **Charges $40-$50.**

MOVIE SCRIPT CONTEST (FEATURE & SHORT)
P.O. Box 6336, Burbank CA 91510-6336. Fax: (818)688-3990. E-mail: info@moviescriptcontest.com. **Contact:** Jason Zimmatore, Contest Coordinator. To discover & promote new writing talent. **Deadline: July 31**. Prize $1,000 for 1st Place Short Script Winner. Golden Brad Trophey and promotion for 1st through 3rd place Winners in our feature contest, and the top 10 loglines are read by our producer partners.

MUSICAL STAIRS
West Coast Ensemble, P.O. Box 38728, Los Angeles CA 90038. (818)786-1900. Fax: (818)786-1905. **Contact:** Les Hanson. Offered annually for unpublished writers to nurture, support, and encourage musical creators. Permission to present the musical is granted if work is selected as finalist. **Deadline: June 30**. Prize $500 and presentation of musical

NANTUCKET FILM FESTIVAL SCREENPLAY COMPETITION
Nantucket Film Festival, 1633 Broadway, suite 15-333, New York NY 10019. (212)708-1278. Fax: (212)708-7490. E-mail: info@nantucketfilmfestival.org. Screenplays must be standard feature film length (90-130 pages) and standard U.S. format only. **Charges $50.**

NATIONAL CHILDREN'S THEATRE FESTIVAL
Actors' Playhouse at the Miracle Theatre, 280 Miracle Mile, Coral Gables FL 33134. (305)444-9293, ext. 615. Fax: (305)444-4181. E-mail: maulding@actorsplayhouse.org. **Contact:** Earl Maulding. Offered annually for unpublished musicals for young audiences. Target age is 4-12. Script length should be 45-60 minutes. Maximum of 8 actors to play any number of roles. Prefer settings which lend themselves to simplified scenery. Bilingual (English/Spanish) scripts are welcomed. Call or visit website for guidelines. Open to any writer. **Deadline: April 1**. **Charges $10 fee.** Prize $500 and full production.
Tips "Travel and lodging during the festival based on availability."

NATIONAL TEN-MINUTE PLAY CONTEST
Actors Theatre of Louisville, 316 W. Main St., Louisville KY 40202-4218. (502)584-1265. Offered annually for previously (professionally) unproduced 10-minute plays (10 pages or less). "Entries must *not* have had an Equity production." One submission/playwright. Scripts are not returned. Please write or call for submission guidelines. Open to US residents. **Deadline: November 1 (postmarked)**. Prize $1,000

NEVADA FILM OFFICE SCREENWRITER'S COMPETITION
555 E. Washington Ave., Ste. 5400, Las Vegas NV 89101. 1-877-NEV-FILM. "At least 75% of the locations in the script must be filmable in Nevada." **Deadline: August 30**. **Charges $25 for pdf submission or $50 for hardcopy.**

NEW AMERICAN COMEDY WORKSHOP

Ukiah Players Theatre, 1041 Low Gap Rd., Ukiah CA 95482. (707)462-9226. Fax: (707)462-1790. E-mail: info@ukiahplayerstheatre.org. **Contact:** Nathan O. Bell, exec. dir. "Offered every 2 years to playwrights seeking to develop their unproduced, full-length comedies into funnier, stronger scripts. Two scripts will be chosen for staged readings; 1 of these may be chosen for full production. Guidelines for SASE are online." **Deadline: November 30 of odd-numbered years.** Prize Playwrights chosen for readings will receive a $25 royalty/performance. The playwright chosen for full production will receive a $50 royalty/performance, travel (up to $500) to Ukiah for development workshop/rehearsal, lodging, and per diem.

NEW JERSEY SHORT FILM SCREENPLAY COMPETITION

New Jersey State Short Film Festival / Cape May Film Society, PO 595, Cape May NJ 08204. (609)823-9159. Fax: (609) 884-6700. E-mail: info@njstatefilmfestival.com. **Contact:** chair. "The initial emphasis on short films speaks to an avenue ignored by most screenplay competitions, which tend to favor features. Who is eligible: all New Jersey residents; students at New Jersey colleges; anyone else who uses New Jersey as the principal setting for the script." Short scripts should be 12 pages or fewer. (1) Entry form—Can be downloaded from the festival's website closer to submission schedule . Copy must be included with preview DVD. (2) DVD. Both case and tape must be labeled with the title, running time and contact information. (3) Optional: Still from film (photograph or jpeg file). (4) Optional: Promotional material. Notification: Filmmakers will be notified via e-mail. Films must be received, fee paid, no later than October 2, 2009 to be accepted for screening. "To encourage and reward New Jersey film writers." **Deadline: Aug. 15-$10 (early); Sept. 15-$15 (reg.); Oct. 2-$25 (late)**. Prize Grand prize: Manuscript made into a movie.

Tips "Can submit electronically."

NEW VOICE SERIES

Remembrance Through the Performing Arts, P.O. Box 162446, Austin TX 78716. E-mail: RemPerArts@aol.com. **Contact:** Rosalyn Rosen, artistic director. Offered annually to find talented American playwrights who are in the early stages of script development. We develop plays on the page, provide staged readings, work in progress productions, then produce our most developed 'production ready' during our mainstage season. Playwrights must query through e-mail only. Send bio and brief synopsis. Open to Texas playwrights only. **Deadline: Ongoing**.

DON AND GEE NICHOLL FELLOWSHIPS IN SCREENWRITING

Academy of Motion Picture Arts & Sciences, 1313 N. Vine St., Hollywood CA 90028-8107. (310)247-3010. E-mail: nicholl@oscars.org. Website: www.oscars.org/nicholl. Estab. 1985. Offered annually for unproduced screenplays to identify talented new screenwriters. Open to writers who have not earned more than $5,000 writing for films or TV. **Deadline: May 1. Charges $30 fee.** Prize Up to five $30,000 fellowships awarded each year.

ONE ACT MARATHON

Attic Theatre Ensemble, 5429 W. Washington Blvd., Los Angeles CA 90016-1112. (323)525-0600. E-mail: info@attictheatre.org. **Contact:** Literary Manager. "Offered annually for unpublished and unproduced work. Scripts should be intended for mature audiences. Length should not exceed 40 minutes. Guidelines for SASE or online." **Deadline: December 31**. Prize 1st Place: $300; 2nd Place: $100.

ONE-ACT PLAY CONTEST

Tennessee Williams/New Orleans Literary Festival, 938 Lafayette St., Suite 328, New Orleans LA 70113. (504)581-1144. E-mail: info@tennesseewilliams.net. Website: www.tennesseewilliams.net. **Contact:** Paul J. Willis. "Annual contest for an unpublished play." "The One-Act Play Competition is an opportunity for playwrights to see their work fully produced before a large audience during one of the largest literary festivals in the nation, and for the festival to showcase undiscovered talent." **Deadline: December 1. Charges $15.** Prize $1,000 and a staged reading at the festival. The play will also be fully produced at the following year's festival. The Tennessee Williams/New Orleans Literary Festival reserves the right to publish. an anonymous expert panel.

Tips "Guidelines and entry forms can be found on the website, or send a SASE."

ONE IN TEN SCREENPLAY CONTEST

Cherub Productions, P.O. Box 540, Boulder CO 80306. E-mail: Cherubfilm@aol.com. Website: www.OneInTenScreenplayContest.com. Scripts that provide a positive potrayal of gays and lesbians. A requirement of the competition is that at least one of the primary characters in the screenplay be gay or lesbian (bisexual, transgender, questioning, and the like) and that gay and lesbian characters must be portrayed positively. All writers are encouraged to enter! **Deadline: September 1. Charges $45.** Prize $1,000

PAGE INTERNATIONAL SCREENWRITING AWARDS, THE

7510 Sunset Blvd., #610, Hollywood CA 90046-3408. E-mail: info@pageawards.com. **Contact:** Zoe Simmons, contest coor. "Annual competition to discover the most talented new screenwriters from across the country and around the world. Each year, awards are presented to 31 screenwriters in 10 different genre categories. Guidelines and entry forms are available online. Open to all writers over 18 years of age who have not previously earned more than $25,000 writing for film and/or television." Adaptations of books, plays, or other source material written by another author are not eligible under any circumstances; nor are scripts adapted from books, plays, or other source material written by you if your source material has been sold, produced, or is currently under option to any third party. Scripts adapted from your own self-published books, plays, or other source material are eligible if you have retained all rights to your work. **Jan. 15 (early); March 1 (regular); April 1 (late). Charges Entry fees: $39 (early); $49 (regular); -$59 (late).** Prize Over $50,000 in cash and prizes, including a $25,000 Grand Prize, plus Gold, Silver, and Bronze Prizes in all 10 categories. Most importantly, the award-winning writers receive extensive publicity and industry exposure. action/adventure, comedy, drama, family, historical, sci-fi/fantasy, thriller/horror, short film script, TV drama pilot, and TV sitcom pilot. The contest is judged by Hollywood professionals, including industry script readers, consultants, agents, managers, producers, and development executives.

THE PAGE INTERNATIONAL SCREENWRITING AWARDS

The PAGE Awards Committee, 7510 Sunset Blvd., #610, Hollywood CA 90046-3408. E-mail: info@PAGEawards.com. **Contact:** Zoe Simmons, contest coordinator. Annual competition to discover the most talented new screenwriters from across the country and around the world. "Each year, awards are presented to 31 screenwriters in 10 different categories: action/adventure, comedy, drama, family film, historical film, science fiction/fantasy, thriller/horror, short film script, TV drama pilot, and TV sitcom pilot. Guidelines and entry forms are online. The contest is open to all writers 18 years of age and older who have not previously earned more than $25,000 writing for film and/or television. Please visit contest Web site for a complete list of rules and regulations." **Deadline: January 15 (early); March 1 (regular); April 1 (late). Charges $39 (early); $49 (regular); $59 (late).** Prize Over $50,000 in cash and prizes, including a $10,000 grand prize, plus gold, silver, and bronze prizes in all 10 categories. Most importantly, the award-winning writers receive extensive publicity and industry exposure. Judging is done entirely by Hollywood professionals, including industry script readers, consultants, agents, managers, producers, and development executives. Entrants retain all rights to their work.

THE PEN IS A MIGHTY SWORD

The Virtual Theatre Project, 1901 Rosalia Rd., Los Angeles CA 90027. (877)787-8036. Fax: (323)660-5097. E-mail: pen_sword2008@yahoo.com. **Contact:** Whit Andrews. "Annual contest open to unproduced plays written specifically for the stage. Contest opens January 1, 2010. Plays should be bold, compelling, and passionate. Guidelines for SASE or online." **Deadline: June 30. Charges $10.** Prize 1st Place: $2,000 and staged reading; 2nd Place: $1,000 and a staged reading; 3rd Place: $500 and a reading. In addition, up to 7 honorable mentions receive $100 each. Judged by a panel of professional writers, directors, and producers.

ROBERT J. PICKERING AWARD FOR PLAYWRIGHTING EXCELLENCE

Coldwater Community Theater, c/o 89 Division, Coldwater MI 49036. (517)279-7963. Fax: (517)279-8095. **Contact:** J. Richard Colbeck, committee chairperson. Estab. 1982. Contest to encourage playwrights to submit their work and to present a previously unproduced play in full production. Must be previously unproduced monetarily. Submit script with SASE. "We reserve the right to produce winning script." **Deadline: December 31.** Prize 1st Place: $300; 2nd Place: $100; 3rd Place: $50

PILGRIM PROJECT GRANTS

156 Fifth, #400, New York NY 10010. (212)627-2288. Fax: (212)627-2184. E-mail: davida@firstthings.com. **Contact:** Davida Goldman. Grants for a reading, workshop production, or full production of plays that deal with questions of moral significance. **Deadline: Ongoing.** Prize Grants of $1,000-7,000

PRAXIS FALL SCREENWRITING COMPETITION

Praxis Centre for Screenwriters, 515 W. Hastings St., Suite 3120, Vancouver BC V6B 5K3 Canada. (778)782-7880. Fax: (778)782-7882. E-mail: praxis@sfu.ca. "We are looking for feature film scripts of any genre. Each writer remains anonymous to the jury until a short list has been identified. Must be Canadian citizens or landed immigrants." **Deadline: 06/27/2009. Charges $75.**

RHODE ISLAND INTERNATIONAL FILM FESTIVAL FEATURE SCREENPLAY COMPETITION

P.O. Box 162, Newport RI 02840. (401)861-4445. Fax: (401)861-7590. E-mail: adams@film-festival.org. Website: www.film-festival.org/enterascreenplay.php. "This contest for the festival looks for feature length scripts." Scripts not to exceed 130 pages. "The purpose of the contest is to promote, embolden and cultivate screenwriters in their quest for opportunities in the industry." **Deadline: July 5.** All genres.

Tips "Screenplays will be judged on creativity, innovation, vision, originality and the use of language. The key element is that of communication and how it complements and is transformed by the language of film."

RHODE ISLAND INTERNATIONAL FILM FESTIVAL SHORT SCREENPLAY COMPETITION

PO Box 162, Newport RI (401)861-4445. Fax: (401)490-6735. E-mail: adams@film-festival.org. Website: www.film-festival.org/enterascreenplay.php. "This second contest for the festival looks for short and feature length scripts." "The purpose of the contest is to promote, embolden and cultivate screenwriters in their quest for opportunities within the industry."

RICHARD RODGERS AWARDS IN MUSICAL THEATER

American Academy of Arts and Letters, 633 W. 155th St., New York NY 10032-7599. (212)368-5900. Fax: (212)491-4615. Website: www.artsandletters.org. **Contact:** Jane E. Bolster. Estab. 1978. "The Richard Rodgers Awards subsidize full productions, studio productions, and staged readings by nonprofit theaters in New York City of works by composers and writers who are not already established in the field of musical theater. Authors must be citizens or permanent residents of the US. Guidelines and application for SASE or online." **Deadline: November 1**.

SCREENWRITING EXPO SCREENPLAY COMPETITION

6404 Hollywood Blvd., Ste 415, Los Angeles CA 90028. (323)957-1405. Fax: (323)957-1406. E-mail: contests@screenwritingexpo.com. **Contact:** Pasha McKenley, contest coordinator. "Writers must be at least 18 years old and have not earned more than $8,000 for writing services in film or television. Submitted screenplays must be the unproduced, unoptioned, and wholly original work of the writer(s). There must be no dispute about the ownership of submitted screenplays or the writers' right to submit screenplay. Submitted teleplays will adhere to the industry "spec script" practice of being a derivative work based on a pre-existing television series, however submitted teleplays must contain original story and dialogue. For teleplays, any characters created by the writer(s) must be wholly original work. Pilots for unproduced television shows or episodes of an unproduced series will not be accepted." **Deadline: multiple deadlines**. **Charges $45-65.** Prize $20,000 grand prize, a trip to LA for the Expo, and four genre prizes totaling $10,000. Action-Adventure, Thriller, Sci-Fi, Comedy, Family, Animation, Low Budget Indie, Horror, Fantasy.

SCRIPTAPALOOZA SCREENPLAY COMPETITION

Writers Guild of America west Registry and sponsored by Write Brothers, Inc., 7775 Sunset Blvd., PMB #200, Hollywood CA 90046. (323)654-5809. E-mail: info@scriptapalooza.com. Estab. 1998. "Annual competition for unpublished scripts from any genre. Open to any writer, 18 or older. Submit one copy of a 90- to 130-page screenplay. Body pages must be numbered, and scripts must be in industry-standard format. All entered scripts will be read and judged by more than 90 production companies." **Early Deadline: January 7; Deadline: March 5; Late Deadline: April 15. Charges $40 (early); $45 (regular deadline); $50 (late).** Prize 1st Place: $10,000 and software package from Write Brothers, Inc.; 2nd Place, 3rd Place, and 10 Runners-Up: Software package from Write Brothers, Inc. The top 100 scripts will be considered by over 90 production companies.

SCRIPTAPALOOZA TELEVISION WRITING COMPETITION

7775 Sunset Blvd., PMB #200, Hollywood CA 90046. (323)654-5809. E-mail: info@scriptapalooza.com. "Biannual competition accepting entries in 4 categories: reality shows, sitcoms, original pilots, and 1-hour dramas. There are more than 25 producers, agents, and managers reading the winning scripts. Two past winners won Emmys because of Scriptapalooza and 1 past entrant now writes for Comedy Central." **Deadline: October 15 and April 15**. **Charges $40.** Prize 1st Place: $500; 2nd Place: $200; 3rd Place: $100 (in each category).

SHRIEKFEST HORROR/SCI-FI FILM FESTIVAL & SCREENPLAY COMPETITION

PO Box 920444, Sylmar CA 91392. E-mail: shriekfest@aol.com. Website: www.shriekfest.com. **Contact:** Denise Gossett/Todd Beeson. "No, we don't use loglines anywhere, we keep your script private." We accept award winning screenplays, no restrictions as long as it's in the horror/thriller or scifi/fantasy genres. We accept shorts and features. No specific lengths. "Our awards are to help screenwriters move their script up the ladder and hopefully have it made into a film. Our winners take that win and parlay it into agents, film deals, and options." **Deadline: May 22 and June 30**. **Charges $25-55.** Prize Trophies, product awards, usually cash. Our awards are updated all year long as sponsors step onboard. The winners go home with lots of stuff. The contest is open to any writer, all ages, we have an under 18 category too. And we are an international contest. We have at least 15-20 judges and they are all in different aspects of the entertainment industry, such as producers, directors, writers, actors, agents."

DOROTHY SILVER PLAYWRITING COMPETITION OF THE MANDEL

The Mandel Jewish Community Center of Cleveland, 26001 S. Woodland, Beachwood OH 44122. (216)831-0700. Fax: (216)831-7796. E-mail: dbobrow@clevejcc.org. Website: www.clevejcc.org. **Contact:** Deborah Bobrow, competition coordinator. "All entries must be original works, not previously produced, suitable for a full-length presentation, and directly concerned with the Jewish experience." **Deadline: December 31, notification by end of March.** Prize Cash award and a staged reading

SOUTHEASTERN THEATRE CONFERENCE NEW PLAY PROJECT

Dept. of Theatre & Dance, Austin Peay State Univ., 681 Summer St., Clarksville TN 37044. E-mail: hardinb@apsu.edu. **Contact:** Chris Hardin, chair. "Annual award for full-length plays or related one acts. No musicals or children's plays. Submissions must be unproduced/unpublished. Readings and workshops are acceptable. Submit application, synopsis, and 1 copy of script on CD or as an e-mail attachment (preferred). Send SASE or visit website for application. Entries will be accepted between March 1st and June 1st. One submission per playwright only." Eligibility: Playwrights who reside in the SETC region (or who are enrolled in a regionally accredited educational institution in the SETC region) or who reside outside the region but are SETC members are eligible for consideration. SETC Region states include Alabama, Florida, Georgia, Kentucky, Mississippi, North Carolina, South Carolina, Tennessee, Virginia, West Virginia. Mission: The SETC New Play Project is dedicated to the discovery, development and publicizing of worthy new plays and playwrights. **Deadline: June 1**. Prize $1,000 and a staged reading.

Tips "Text should be in 12 pt type and in a plain font such as Times New Roman. Plays must be submitted by email attachment in Microsoft Word or PDF format with the following guidelines: Script must include page numbers at the bottom of each page. The author's name should not appear anywhere in the script. Do not include resumes, playwright biographies or a history of the play. 1 copy, Word or PDF format, attached to an email. Completed Application Form included as separate email attachment. Electronic signatures will be accepted.The decision of the panel of readers will be announced in November of each year."

SOUTHERN PLAYWRIGHTS COMPETITION

Jacksonville State University, 700 Pelham Rd. N., Jacksonville AL 36265-1602. (256)782-5469. Fax: (256)782-5441. E-mail: jmaloney@jsu.edu; swhitton@jsu.edu. Website: www.jsu.edu/depart/english/southpla.htm. **Contact:** Joy Maloney, Steven J. Whitton. Estab. 1988. "Offered annually to identify and encourage the best of Southern playwriting. Playwrights must be a native or resident of Alabama, Arkansas, District of Columbia, Florida, Georgia, Kentucky, Louisiana, Missouri, North Carolina, South Carolina, Tennessee, Texas, Virginia, or West Virginia." **Deadline: January 15**. Prize $1,000 and production of the play

TELEPLAY COMPETITION

Austin Film Festival, 1801 Salina St.,, Austin TX 78702. (512)478-4795. Fax: (512)478-6205. E-mail: alex@austinfilmfestival.con. Offered annually for unproduced work to discover talented television writers and introduce their work to industry professionals. Categories: drama and sitcom (must be specific scripts for currently airing cable or network shows). Contest open to writers who do not earn a living writing for television or film. **Deadline: June 1. Charges $30.** Prize $1,000 in each category

THEATRE BC'S ANNUAL CANADIAN NATIONAL PLAYWRITING COMPETITION

Theatre BC, P.O. Box 2031, Nanaimo BC V9R 6X6 Canada. (250)714-0203. Fax: (250)714-0213. E-mail: pwc@theatrebc.org. **Contact:** Robb Mowbray, executive director. Offered annually "to unpublished plays to promote the development and production of previously unproduced new plays (no musicals) at all levels of theater." Categories: Full Length (75 minutes or longer); One-Act (less than 75 minutes); and an open Special Merit (juror's discretion). Guidelines for SASE or online. Winners are also invited to New Play Festival: Up to 16 hours with a professional dramaturg, registrant actors, and a public reading in Kamloops (every Spring). Production and publishing rights remain with the playwright. Open to Canadian residents. All submissions are made under pseudonyms. E-mail inquiries welcome. **Deadline: Fourth Monday in July. Charges $40/entry; optional $25 for written critique.** Prize Full Length: $1,000; One-Act: $750; Special Merit: $500

TRUSTUS PLAYWRIGHTS' FESTIVAL

Trustus Theatre, Box 11721, Columbia SC 29211-1721. (803)254-9732. Fax: (803)771-9153. E-mail: sarahkhammond@gmail.com. Website: www.trustus.org. **Contact:** Sarah Hammond, literary manager. Offered annually for professionally unproduced full-length plays; cast limit of 8. Prefers challenging, innovative dramas and comedies. No musicals, plays for young audiences, or "hillbilly" southern shows. Send SASE or consult Trustus Web site for guidelines and application. Festival for 2009 has been suspended for production of in-house play. **Deadline: for 2011 festival: December 1, 2009-February 28, 2010.** Prize $500 and a 1-year development period with full production and travel/accommodations to attend the public opening.

UNICORN THEATRE NEW PLAY DEVELOPMENT

Unicorn Theatre, 3828 Main St., Kansas City MO 64111. (816)531-7529, ext. 22. Fax: (816)531-0421. **Contact:** Herman Wilson, literary assistant. Offered annually to encourage and assist the development of an unpublished and unproduced play. We look for nonmusical, issue-oriented, thought-provoking plays set in contemporary times (post 1950s) with a cast limit of 10. Submit cover letter, brief bio/résumé, short synopsis, complete character breakdown, complete ms, SASE. Does not return scripts. **Deadline: Ongoing.**

VAIL FILM FESTIVAL SCREENPLAY COMPETITION

Vail Film Institute, PO Box 747, Vail CO 81657. (970)476-1092. Fax: (646)349-1767. E-mail: info@vailfilmfestival.

org. Feature Scripts must be between 70-125 pages in length. Short Scripts must be between 3-45 pages in length. **Charges $35-65.** Prize 2 Filmmaker Passes to the 2010 Vail Film Festival, 1 domestic air ticket to Denver, 3 night hotel accomodations in Vail, screenplay read by established film production companies. Staged reading of excerpt of winning screenplay during the Vail Film Festival.

WICHITA STATE UNIVERSITY PLAYWRITING COMPETITION

School of Performing Arts, Wichita State University, 1845 N. Fairmount, Campus Box 153, Wichita KS 67260-0153. (316)978-3360. Fax: (316)978-3202. E-mail: brett.jones@wichita.edu. **Contact:** Bret Jones, Director of Theatre. Estab. 1974. Offered for unpublished, unproduced (a) Full-length plays in one or more acts should be a minimum of 90 minutes playing time; (b) Two or three short plays on related themes by the same author will be judged as one entry. The total playing time should be a minimum of 90 minutes; (c) Musicals should be a minimum of 90 minutes playing time and must include a CD of the accompanying music. Contestants must be graduate or undergraduate students in a US college or university. **Deadline: March 15**. Prize Production of winning play (ACTF) Judged by a panel of faculty.

WRITERS ON THE STORM SCREENPLAY COMPETITION

Coverage, Ink., P.O. Box 899, Venice CA 90294. (310)582-5880. E-mail: writerstorm@gmail.com. Website: www.writerstorm.com. "We're all about empowering the writer, because we ARE writers. Yes, a contest that's actually by writers, for writers. Our prizes are deliberately development-heavy because we believe knowledge is power. Must be 18 years of age or older. Open to anyone who has earned less than $10,000 career earnings as a screenwriter." **Deadline: July 27, 2009. Charges $40.** Prize $22,000 in prizes.

THE WRITERS PLACE SCREENPLAY CONTEST

525 E. 72nd St., #18A, New York NY 10021. (310)429-5181. E-mail: contact2@thewritersplace.org. **Deadline: January 1-May 15, 2009. Charges $55.**

WRITESAFE PRESENT-A-THON

3767 MC 5026, Saint Joe AR 72675. (870)449-2488. E-mail: admin@writesafe.com. "A quarterly contest with these deadlines:The first Present-A-Thon of each year starts January 1 and ends March 31. The second Present-A-Thon of each year starts April 1 and ends June 30. The third Present-A-Thon of each year starts July 1 and ends September 30. The fourth Present-A-Thon of each year starts October 1 and ends December 31." **Deadline: March 31, June 30, September 30 and December 31**. Prize First Prize is consideration for publication, production, or representation by a panel of experts. Second Prize is consideration for publication, production, or representation. More prizes awarded.

YEAR END SERIES (YES) FESTIVAL OF NEW PLAYS

Dept. of Theatre, Nunn Dr., Northern Kentucky University, Highland Heights KY 41099-1007. (859)572-6362. Fax: (859)572-6057. E-mail: forman@nku.edu. **Contact:** Sandra Forman, project director. "Receives submissions from May 1 until September 30 in even-numbered years for the festivals which occur in April of odd-numbered years. Open to all writers." **Deadline: October 1**. Prize $500 and an expense-paid visit to Northern Kentucky University to see the play produced

YOUNG PLAYWRIGHTS INC. WRITE A PLAY! NYC COMPETITION

Young Playwrights, Inc., P.O. Box 5134, New York NY 10185. (212)594-5440. Fax: (212)684-4902. E-mail: literary@youngplaywrights.org. **Contact:** Literary Department. "Offered annually for stage plays of any length (no musicals, screenplays, or adaptations) by NYC elementary, middle, and high school students only." **Deadline: April 1**. Prize Prize varies.

ANNA ZORNIO MEMORIAL CHILDREN'S THEATRE PLAYWRITING COMPETITION

University of New Hampshire, Dept. of Theatre and Dance, PCAC, 30 Academic Way,, Durham NH 03824-3538. (603)862-3044. E-mail: mike.wood@unh.edu. **Contact:** Michael Wood. "Offered every 4 years for unpublished well-written plays or musicals appropriate for young audiences with a maximum length of 60 minutes. May submit more than 1 play, but not more than 3. All plays will be performed by adult actors and must be appropriate for a children's audience within the K-12 grades. Guidelines and entry forms available as downloads on the website. Open to all playwrights in US and Canada. All ages are invited to participate." **Deadline: March 2, 2012**. Prize Up to $500. The play is also produced and underwritten as part of the 2013-2014 season by the UNH Department of Theatre and Dance. Winner will be notified on or after Dec. 15, 2012.

ARTS COUNCILS & FELLOWSHIPS

ALABAMA STATE COUNCIL ON THE ARTS FELLOWSHIP-LITERATURE

Alabama State Council on the Arts, 201 Monroe St., Montgomery AL 36130-1800. (334)242-4076, ext. 224. Fax:

(334)240-3269. E-mail: randy.shoults@arts.alabama.gov. Website: www.arts.alabama.gov. **Contact:** Randy Shoults. "Literature fellowship offered every year (for previously published or unpublished work) to set aside time to create and improve skills. Two-year Alabama residency required. Guidelines available." **Deadline: March 1**. Prize $10,000 or $5,000

ALASKA STATE COUNCIL ON THE ARTS CAREER OPPORTUNITY GRANT AWARD

Alaska State Council on the Arts, 411 W. 4th Ave., Suite 1E, Anchorage AK 99501-2343. (907)269-6610. Fax: (907)269-6601. E-mail: andrea.noble@alaska.gov. **Contact:** Charlotte Fox, executive director. Grants help artists take advantage of impending, concrete opportunities that will significantly advance their work or careers. Open to residents of Alaska only. Professional artists working in the literary arts who are requesting support for unique, short-term opportunities are eligible. **Deadline: Applications accepted quarterly.** Prize Up to $1,000 **Tips** "Guidelines available on website. Accepts inquiries by fax, phone and e-mail."

ARROWHEAD REGIONAL ARTS COUNCIL INDIVIDUAL ARTIST CAREER DEVELOPMENT GRANT

Arrowhead Regional Arts Council, 1301 Rice Lake Rd., Suite 111, Duluth MN 55811. (218)722-0952 or (800)569-8134. E-mail: info@aracouncil.org. **Contact:** Jean Sramek, program assistant. Applicants must live in the 7-county region of Northeastern Minnesota. Award to provide financial support to regional artists wishing to take advantage of impending, concrete opportunities that will advance their work or careers. **Deadline: November 30, April 24 and August 28**. Prize Up to $1,000. ARAC Board.

BUSH ARTIST FELLOWS PROGRAM

The Bush Foundation, 332 Minnesota St., Suite E-900, St. Paul MN 55101. (651)227-0891. Fax: (651)297-6485. Website: www.bushfoundation.org. **Contact:** www.artists@bushfoundation.org. Estab. 1976. "Fellowships for US citizens or permanent residents and residents of Minnesota, North Dakota, South Dakota. Applicants must be 25 years or older (students are not eligible) and want to further his/her own work. All application categories rotate on a 2-year cycle. Applications available in September." **Deadline: October/November 2010**. Prize Up to 15 fellowships/year of $50,000 each. Smaller project grants- $3,000-$6,000- Also available for writers who are residents of North Dakota or South Dakota through a program called Dakota creative connections. Deadline: April 2011.

CHLA RESEARCH GRANTS

Children's Literature Association, P.O. Box 138, Battle Creek MI 49016-0138. (269)965-8180. Fax: (269)965-3568. E-mail: info@childlitassn.org. **Contact:** ChLA Grants Chair. Offered annually. "The grants are awarded for proposals dealing with criticism or original scholarship with the expectation that the undertaking will lead to publication and make a significant contribution to the field of children's literature in the area of scholarship or criticism." Funds are not intended for work leading to the completion of a professional degree. Guidelines available online or send SASE to ChLA office for a print copy. **Deadline: February 1**. Prize $500-1,500

DELAWARE DIVISION OF THE ARTS

820 N. French St., Wilmington DE 19801. (302)577-8278. Fax: (302)577-6561. E-mail: kristin.pleasanton@state.de.us. **Contact:** Kristin Pleasanton, coordinator. Award offered annually to help further the careers of Delaware's emerging and established professional artists. Open to Delaware residents only **Deadline: August 1**. Prize $10,000 for masters; $6,000 for established professionals; $3,000 for emerging professionals. out-of-state professionals in each division.

GRANTS FOR WRITERS

NC Arts Council, Department of Cultural Resources, MSC #4632, Raleigh NC 27699-4632. (919)807-6500. Fax: (919)807-6532. E-mail: jeff.pettus@ncdcr.org. **Contact:** Jeff Pettus, Senior Program Director. Offered every 2 years to serve writers of fiction, poetry, literary nonfiction, and literary translation in North Carolina, and to recognize the contribution they make to this state's creative environment. Guidelines available on Web site. Writer must have been a resident of NC for at least a year as of the application deadline and may not be enrolled in any degree-granting program at the time of application. Prize $10,000 grants every 2 years

THE HODDER FELLOWSHIP

Joseph Henry House, Princeton University, Princeton NJ 08544. Website: www.princeton.edu/arts/lewis_center/society_of_fellows. "The Hodder Fellowship will be given to writers of exceptional promise to pursue independent projects at Princeton University during the 2010-11 academic year. Typically the fellows are poets, playwrights, novelists, creative nonfiction writers, and translators who have published one highly acclaimed work and are undertaking a significant new project that might not be possible without the "studious leisure" afforded by the fellowship. Preference is given to applicants outside academia. Candidates for the PhD are not eligible. Submit a resume, sample of previous work (10 pages maximum, not returnable), and a project proposal of 2-3 pages. Guidelines available on website. Princeton University is an equal opportunity employer and complies with applicable EEO and affirmative action regulations." **Deadline: November 1 (postmarked)**. Prize $62,000 stipend

CHRISTOPHER ISHERWOOD FELLOWSHIPS

Christopher Isherwood Foundation, PMB 139, 1223 Wilshire Blvd., Santa Monica CA 90403-5040. E-mail: james@isherwoodfoundation.org. **Contact:** James P. White, executive director. "Several awards are given annually to selected writers who have published a novel." **Deadline: September 1-October 1 (send to the address posted on the website)**. Prize Fellowship consists of $4,000. advisory board.

JENNY MCKEAN/MOORE VISITING WRITER

English Department, George Washington University, Washington DC 20052. (202)994-6180. Fax: (202)994-7915. E-mail: faymos@gwu.edu. **Contact:** Faye Moskowitz. "Offered annually to provide 1-year visiting writers to teach 1 George Washington course and 1 free community workshop each semester. Guidelines for SASE or online. This contest seeks someone specializing in a different genre each year." **Deadline: November 15**. Prize Annual stipend varies, depending on endowment performance; most recently, stipend was $58,000, plus reduced-rent townhouse (not guaranteed).

LITERARY GIFT OF FREEDOM

A Room of Her Own Foundation, P.O. Box 778, Placitas NM 87043. E-mail: info@aroomofherownfoundation.org. Website: www.aroomofherownfoundation.org. **Contact:** Tracey Cravens-Gras, associate director. Award offered every other year to provide very practical help—both materially and in professional guidance and moral support with mentors and advisory council—to women who need assistance in making their creative contribution to the world. Guidelines and deadlines available at www.aroomofherownfoundation.org. Open to any female resident citizen of the US. **Deadline: February 1 (for fiction writers)**. **Charges Application: $35.** Prize Award is $50,000 over 2 years in support of the production of a particular creative project.

MINNESOTA STATE ARTS BOARD ARTIST INITIATIVE GRANT

Minnesota State Arts Board, Park Square Court, Suite 200, 400 Sibley St., St. Paul MN 55101-1928. (651)215-1600 or (800)866-2787. Fax: (651)215-1602. E-mail: erin.mclennon@arts.state.mn.us. **Contact:** Erin McLennon. "The grant is meant to support and assist artists at various stages in their careers. It encourages artistic growth adn career development, nurtures artistic creativity, and recognizes the contributions individual artists make to the creative environment of the state of Minnesota. Literary categories include prose, poetry, playwriting, and screenwriting. Open to Minnesota residents." **July 30.** Prize Bi-annual grants of $2,000-6,000

NEBRASKA ARTS COUNCIL INDIVIDUAL ARTISTS FELLOWSHIPS

Nebraska Arts Council, 1004 Farnam St., Plaza Level, Omaha NE 68102. (402)595-2122. Fax: (402)595-2334. E-mail: jayne.hutton@nebraska.gov. **Contact:** J.D. Hutton. Estab. 1991. Offered every 3 years (literature alternates with other disciplines) to recognize exemplary achievements by originating artists in their fields of endeavor and support the contributions made by Nebraska artists to the quality of life in this state. Generally, distinguished achievement awards are $5,000 and merit awards are $1,000-2,000. Funds available are announced in September prior to the deadline. Must be a resident of Nebraska for at least 2 years prior to submission date; 18 years of age; and not enrolled in an undergraduate, graduate, or certificate-granting program in English, creative writing, literature, or related field. **Deadline: November 15.**

NORTH CAROLINA ARTS COUNCIL REGIONAL ARTIST PROJECT GRANTS

North Carolina Arts Council, Dept. of Cultural Resources, MSC #4632, Raleigh NC 27699-4634. (919)807-6500. Fax: (919)807-6532. E-mail: jeff.pettus@ncdcr.gov. **Contact:** Jeff Pettus, Senior Program Director. **Deadline: Generally late summer/early fall**. Prize $500-3,000 awarded to writers to pursue projects that further their artistic development. Open to any writer living in North Carolina. See website for contact information for the local arts councils that distribute these grants.

NORTH CAROLINA WRITERS' FELLOWSHIPS

North Carolina Arts Council, Dept. of Cultural Resources, Raleigh NC 27699-4632. (919)807-6500. Fax: (919)807-6532. E-mail: jeff.pettus@ncdcr.gov. **Contact:** Jeff Pettus, Senior Program Director. Offered every even year to support writers of fiction, poetry, literary nonfiction, literary translation, and spoken word. See website for guidelines and other eligibility requirements. Writers must be current residents of North Carolina for at least 1 year, must remain in residence in North Carolina during the grant year, and may not pursue academic or professional degrees while receiving grant. Contest offered to support writers in the development and creation of their work. **Deadline: November 1, 2008**. Prize $10,000 grant. A panel of literary professionals (writers and editors).

OREGON LITERARY FELLOWSHIPS

Literary Arts, Inc., 224 NW 13th Ave., Suite 306, Portland OR 97209. (503)227-2583. E-mail: susan@literary-arts.org. **Contact:** Susan Denning, dir. of programs & events. "The annual Oregon Literary Fellowships support Oregon writers with a monetary award. Guidelines for SASE or online. Open to Oregon residents only." **Deadline: last Friday in June**. Prize $2,500-3,000. out-of-state judges who are selected for their expertise in a genre.

JAMES D. PHELAN LITERARY AWARD

The San Francisco Foundation, Intersection for the Arts, 446 Valencia St., San Francisco CA 94103. (415)626-2787. E-mail: kevin@theintersection.org. **Contact:** Kevin B. Chen, program director. Estab. 1935. "Offered annually for unpublished, work-in-progress fiction, nonfiction, short story, poetry, or drama by a California-born author age 20-35." **Deadline: March 31**. Prize Three awards of $2,000

RHODE ISLAND ARTIST FELLOWSHIPS AND INDIVIDUAL PROJECT GRANTS

Rhode Island State Council on the Arts, One Capitol Hill, 3rd Floor, Providence RI 02908. (401)222-3880. Fax: (401)222-3018. E-mail: cristina@arts.ri.gov. **Contact:** Cristina DiChiera, director of individual artist programs. Annual fellowship competition is based upon panel review of mss for poetry, fiction, and playwriting/screenwriting. Project grants provide funds for community-based arts projects. Rhode Island artists may apply without a nonprofit sponsor. Applicants for all RSCA grant and award programs must be at least 18 years and not currently enrolled in an arts-related degree program. **Deadline: April 1 and October 1**. Prize Fellowship awards: $5,000 and $1,000. Grants range from $500-10,000 with an average of around $3,000.

WALLACE STEGNER FELLOWSHIPS

Creative Writing Program, Stanford University, Dept. of English, Stanford CA 94305-2087. (650)723-0011 or (650)725-1208. Fax: (650)723-3679. E-mail: mpopek@stanford.edu. Website: www.creativewriting.stanford.edu. **Contact:** Mary Popek, program administrator. "A 2-year, non-degree granting program at Stanford offered annually for emerging writers to attend the Stegner workshop to practice and perfect their craft under the guidance of the creative writing faculty. Guidelines available online." **Deadline: December 1 (postmarked)**. **Charges $60 fee.** Prize Living stipend (currently $26,000/year) and required workshop tuition of $7,479/year

VERMONT ARTS COUNCIL

136 State St., Drawer 33, Montpelier VT 05633-6001. (802)828-5425. Fax: (802)828-3363. E-mail: srae@vermontartscouncil.org. **Contact:** Sonia Rae. Grants awarded once per year for specific projects. Creation Grants for writers of poetry, plays, screenplays, fiction, non-fiction. Community Arts Grants and Arts Learning Grants for not-for-profit organizations (including writing programs and not-for-profit presses). Available are rolling grants in the following categories: Artist Development Grants providing professional development funds for individual artists and Technical Assistance Grants providing grants for organizational development to non-profit arts organizations. Open to Vermont residents only. Prize $250-5,000

WRITERS' & NEW WRITERS' BURSARIES

Scottish Arts Council, 12 Manor Place, Edinburgh EH3 7DD Scotland. (44)(131)240-2444. E-mail: help.desk@scottisharts.org.uk. Writers' Bursaries are awarded to assist published writers of literary work and playwrights, based in Scotland, who need finance for a period of concentrated work on their next book or play. For more information on deadlines and grant levels, please contact the help desk.

FICTION

AMERICAN SHORT FICTION SHORT STORY CONTEST

American Short Fiction, P.O. Box 301209, Austin TX 78703. (512)538-1305. Fax: (512)538-1306. E-mail: editors@americanshortfiction.org. Website: www.americanshortfiction.org. **Contact:** Stacey Swann, editor. Contest offered annually to reward the unpublished best short fiction being written. Submissions accepted only via the online submission manager on website. See website for full guidelines. **Deadline: September 15-December 1**. **Charges $20 to *American Short Fiction*.** Prize 1st Place: $1,000 and publication; 2nd Place: $500.

ANNUAL GIVAL PRESS NOVEL AWARD

Gival Press, LLC, P.O. Box 3812, Arlington VA 22203. (703)351-0079. E-mail: givalpress@yahoo.com. **Contact:** Robert L. Giron. "Offered annually for a previously unpublished original novel (not a translation). It must be in English with at least 30,000-100,000 words of literary quality. Guidelines online, via e-mail, or by mail with SASE." **Deadline: May 30**. **Charges $50 (USD) reading fee.** Prize $3,000, plus publication of book with a standard contract.

ANNUAL GIVAL PRESS SHORT STORY AWARD

Gival Press, LLC, P.O. Box 3812, Arlington VA 22203. (703)351-0079. E-mail: givalpress@yahoo.com. **Contact:** Robert L. Giron. "Offered annually for a previously unpublished original short story (not a translation). It must be in English with at least 5,000-15,000 words of literary quality. Guidelines by mail with SASE, by e-mail, or online." To award the best literary short story submitted. **Deadline: August 8**. **Charges $25 (USD) reading fee.** Prize $1,000, plus publication on website. The editor narrows entries to the top ten; previous winner chooses the top 5 and the winner—all done anonymously.

Tips "Open to any writer as long as the work is original, not a translation, and written in English. The copyright remains in the author's name; certain rights fall under the contract."

THE BALTIMORE REVIEW FICTION CONTEST

The Baltimore Review, P.O. Box 36418, Towson MD 21286. Website: www.baltimorereview.org. **Contact:** Susan Muaddi Darraj. "The Annual Fiction Award aims to recognize the best new fiction today, from Baltimore and beyond. Submit one short story per entry fee. All styles and forms are accepted. Maximum word count is 6,000. Simultaneous submissions are fine, but alert us if your story has been accepted elsewhere. Judges vary each year." **Deadline: December 1. Charges $20; $25 for fee and 1-year subscription.** Prize 1st Place: $500 and publication; 2nd Place: $250; 3rd Place: $100.

BARD FICTION PRIZE

Bard College, P.O. Box 5000, Annandale-on-Hudson NY 12504-5000. (845)758-7087. E-mail: bfp@bard.edu. Estab. 2001. Open to younger American writers. "The Bard Fiction Prize is intended to encourage and support young writers of fiction to pursue their creative goals and to provide an opportunity to work in a fertile and intellectual environment. **Deadline: July 15.** Prize $30,000 and appointment as writer-in-residence at Bard College for 1 semester.

BINGHAMTON UNIVERSITY JOHN GARDNER FICTION BOOK AWARD

Binghamton University, Dept. of English, General Literature & Rhetoric, P.O. Box 6000, Binghamton NY 13902-6000. (607)777-2713. **Contact:** Maria Mazziotti Gillan, creative writing prog. dir. Estab. 2001. "Contest offered annually for a novel or collection of fiction published in previous year. Offered annually for a novel or collection of short stories published that year in a press run of 500 copies or more. Each book submitted must be accompanied by an application form. Publisher may submit more than 1 book for prize consideration. Send 3 copies of each book. Guidelines available online or for SASE." **Deadline: March 1.** Prize $1,000. Judged by professional writer not on Binghamton University faculty.

N BOSTON REVIEW SHORT STORY CONTEST

Boston Review, 35 Medford St., Suite 302, Somerville MA 02143. Stories should not exceed 4,000 words and must be previously unpublished. **Deadline: Summer 2010. Charges $20 fee (check or money order payable to *Boston Review*).** Prize $1,500 and publication in a later issue of *Boston Review*

BOULEVARD SHORT FICTION CONTEST FOR EMERGING WRITERS

Boulevard Magazine, 6614 Clayton Rd., PMB #325, Richmond Heights MO 63117. (314)862-2643. Website: www.richardburgin.net/boulevard. **Contact:** Richard Burgin, senior editor. Offered annually for unpublished short fiction to a writer who has not yet published a book of fiction, poetry, or creative nonfiction with a nationally distributed press. "We hold first North American rights on anything not previously published." Open to any writer with no previous publication by a nationally known press. Guidelines for SASE or on website. **Deadline: December 15. Charges $15 fee/story; includes 1-year subscription to *Boulevard*.** Prize $1,500, and publication in 1 of the next year's issues.

CANADIAN AUTHORS ASSOCIATION MOSAID TECHNOLOGIES INC. AWARD FOR FICTION

P.O. Box 581, Stn. Main, Orillia ON L3V 6K5 Canada. (705)653-0323 or (866)216-6222. E-mail: admin@canauthors.org. **Contact:** Anita Purcell. Offered annually for a full-length novel by a Canadian citizen or permanent immigrant. Entry form required. Obtain entry form from contact name or download from website. **Deadline: December 15. Charges $35 fee (Canadian).** Prize $2,500 and a silver medal

THE ALEXANDER PATTERSON CAPPON FICTION AWARD

New Letters, University of Missouri-Kansas City, 5101 Rockhill Rd., Kansas City MO 64110. (816)235-1168. Fax: (816)235-2611. E-mail: newletters@umkc.edu. **Contact:** Amy Lucas. Offered annually for unpublished work to discover and reward new and upcoming writers. Buys first North American serial rights. Open to any writer. **Deadline: Third week in May. Charges $15 (includes cost of a 1-year subscription).** Prize 1st Place: $1,500 and publication in a volume of *New Letters*; runner-up will receive a complimentary copy of a recent book of poetry or fiction courtesy of BkMk Press. All entries will be given consideration for publication in future issues of *New Letters*.

G. S. SHARAT CHANDRA PRIZE FOR SHORT FICTION

BkMk Press, University of Missouri-Kansas City, 5100 Rockhill Rd., Kansas City MO 64110-2499. (816)235-2558. Fax: (816)235-2611. E-mail: bkmk@umkc.edu. Website: www.umkc.edu/bkmk. "Offered annually for the best book-length ms collection (unpublished) of short fiction in English by a living author. Translations are not eligible. Initial judging is done by a network of published writers. Final judging is done by a writer of national reputation. Guidelines for SASE, by e-mail, or on website." **Deadline: January 15 (postmarked). Charges $25 fee.** Prize $1,000, plus book publication by BkMk Press.

THE ARTHUR C. CLARKE AWARD

246E Bethnal Green Rd., London E2 0AA U.K. E-mail: clarkeaward@gmail.com. **Contact:** Tom Hunter, award administrator. "Annual award presented to the best science fiction novel, published between January 1 and December 31 of the year in question, receiving its first British publication during the calendar year." **Deadline: 2nd week in December**. Prize £2,009 (rising by £1 each year), and an engraved bookend. Judged by representatives of the British Science Fiction Association, the Science Fiction Foundation, and the SF Crowsnest Web site.

CAROLYN A. CLARK FLASH FICTION PRIZE

National League of American Pen Women, Nob Hill, San Francisco Branch, The Webhallow House, 1544 Sweetwood Dr., Broadmoor Village CA 94015-2029. E-mail: pennobhill@aol.com. Website: www.soulmakingcontest.us. **Contact:** Eileen Malone. "Three flash fiction (short-short) stories per entry, under 500 words. Previously published material is accepted. Indicate category on each story. Identify only with 3X5 card. Open annually to any writer." **Deadline: November 30. Charges $5/entry (make checks payable to NLAPW, Nob Hill Branch).** Prize 1st Place: $100; 2nd Place: $50; 3rd Place: $25.

COFFEE HOUSE FICTION

Coffeehousefiction.com, P.O. Box 399, Forest Hill MD 21050. E-mail: info@coffeehousefiction.com. **Contact:** Sherri Cook Woosley, contest director. Estab. 2004. "Annual contest to encourage unpublished fiction writers who have chosen a vocation with such a high frustration rate. Each of our judges either loves literature or is a writer, and understands firsthand the emotional highs and lows of the road to publication. Guidelines for SASE, via e-mail, or online. Writers keep all rights to their work." The story must be original, unpublished and not exceed 3,500 words. You may submit multiple entries. **Deadline: Jan. 31. Charges $17.** Prize 1st Place: $350 plus 5 copies of chapbook anthology; 2nd Place: $125 plus 2 copies of chapbook; 3rd Place: $75 plus 1 copy; 4th Place: $50 plus 1 copy. All winners are published on Coffeehousefiction.com with bios and pictures. Patricia Valdata of Cloudstreet Communications; Sherri Cook Woosley, M.A. in English Literature from Univ. of Maryland; May Kuroiwa, Critique Director for MWA; Nancy Adler, graduate work from Johns Hopkins University.

Tips "Your short fiction work must be submitted in accordance with the submission guidelines. No entry fees will be returned. This contest is void where prohibited or restricted by law."

JACK DYER FICTION PRIZE

Crab Orchard Review, Dept. of English, Southern Illinois Univ. Carbondale, Carbondale IL 62901-4503. E-mail: jtribble@siu.edu. **Contact:** Jon C. Tribble, man. ed. "Offered annually for unpublished short fiction. *Crab Orchard Review* acquires first North American serial rights to all submitted work. Open to any writer. Open to US citizens only." **March 1 - April 30. Charges $10/entry (can enter up to 3 stories, each story submitted requires a separate fee and can be up to 6,000 words), which includes one copy of *Crab Orchard Review* featuring the winners.** Prize $1,500 and publication.

THE EUREKA! FELLOWSHIP FOR SHORT STORY WRITING

The Writers' Colony at Dairy Hollow, 515 Spring St., Eureka Springs AR 72632. (479)253-7444. Fax: (479)253-9859. E-mail: director@writerscolony.org. **Contact:** Vicki Kell-Schneider, coor. "Fellowship offerings include full and partial stipends for two- and four-week fellowships in arts writing, travel writing, culinary writing and more. Fellowships offer gifted writers room, board and time to focus fully on their work at the Writers' Colony at Dairy Hollow, Eureka Springs, Arkansas." **Deadlines vary. Charges $35.** Prize 1-month residency, all-expense paid fellowship at the Writers' Colony at Dairy Hollow, Eureka Springs, Arkansas. Transportation to and from the colony is not included. Judge by literary professionals.

FIRSTWRITER.COM INTERNATIONAL SHORT STORY CONTEST

firstwriter.com, United Kingdom. **Contact:** J. Paul Dyson, man. ed. "Accepts short stories up to 3,000 words on any subject and in any style." **Deadline: April 1. Charges $7.50 for 1 short story; $12 for 2; $15 for 3; and $20 for 5.** Prize total about $300. Ten special commendations will also be awarded and all the winners will be published in *firstwriter* magazine and receive a$30 subscription voucher, allowing an annual subscription to be taken out for free All submissions are automatically considered for publication in *firstwriter* magazine and may be published there online. *firstwriter* magazine editors.

FISH INTERNATIONAL SHORT STORY COMPETITION

Fish Publishing, Durrus, Bantry, Co. Cork Ireland (353)(21)275-5645. E-mail: info@fishpublishing.com. Website: www.fishpublishing.com. **Contact:** Prize Coordinator. Estab. 1994. Offered annually for unpublished fiction mss (maximum 5,000 words). **Deadline: November 30. Charges $30 USD per story.** Prize 1st Prize: 10,000 Euro (approximately $13,400 USD); 2nd Prize: 1 week at Anam Cara Writers' Retreat in West Cork and 250 Euro (approximately $150 USD); 3rd Prize: 250 Euro. Twelve runners-up will receive 100 Euro. All 15 winning authors will be published in the annual Fish Short Story Anthology and invited to the launch at the

West Cork Literary Festival in June. Winners announced March 17. Judged by a panel of international judges which changes every year.
Tips "Enter online. See www.fishpublishing.com for One Page Story Prize, Historical Short Fiction Prize, and Unpublished Novel Award."

FISH UNPUBLISHED NOVEL AWARD

Fish Publishing, Durrus, Bantry, Co. Cork Ireland. E-mail: info@fishpublishing.com. Website: www.fishpublishing.com. **Contact:** Clem Cairns and Jula Walton. A competition for the best unpublished novel entered. **Deadline: September 30. Charges $50 USD.** Prize 1st Prize: Publication of winning novel and cash. "This is not an annual award, but is run every so often."

FLASH FICTIONS COMPETITION

NSW Writers' Centre, P.O. Box 1056, Rozelle NSW 2039 Australia. (61)(2)9555-9757. E-mail: nswwc@nswwriterscentre.org.au. **Contact:** Sue Boaden, exec. dir. "Competition for a 500-word short story in any genre of speculative fiction (science fiction, horror, fantasy)." **Deadline: February 24. Charges $5.** Prize Book vouchers from Infinitas Bookshop. Tim Martin, Chris Barnes, Cat Sparks

DANUTA GLEED LITERARY AWARD FOR FIRST BOOK OF SHORT FICTION

The Writers' Union of Canada, 90 Richmond St. E., Suite 200, Toronto ON M5C 1P1 Canada. (416)703-8982. Fax: (416)504-9090. E-mail: dwindsor@writersunion.ca. **Contact:** Deborah Windsor. Offered annually to Canadian writers for the best first collection of published short stories in the English language. Must have been published in the previous calendar year. Submit 5 copies. **Deadline: January 31.** Prize 1st Place: $10,000; $500 to each of 2 runners-up

GLIMMER TRAIN'S FAMILY MATTERS CONTEST

Glimmer Train Press, Inc., 1211 NW Glisan St., Suite 207, Portland OR 97209. Fax: (503)221-0837. E-mail: eds@glimmertrain.org. **Contact:** Linda Swanson-Davies. "Offered for unpublished stories about family. Word count: 500-12,000. See complete writing guidelines and submit onilne at website. Open Jan. 1-31, April 1-30, July 1-31, October 13-31. Winners will be called and results will be announced in their respective bulletins, on their website, and in a number of additional print and online publications." **Charges $15 fee/story.** Prize 1st Place: $1,200, publication in *Glimmer Train Stories*, and 20 copies of that issue; 2nd Place: $500; 3rd Place: $300.

GLIMMER TRAIN'S FICTION OPEN

Glimmer Train, Inc., Glimmer Train Press, Inc., 1211 NW Glisan St., Suite 207, Portland OR 97209. (503)221-0836. Fax: (503)221-0837. E-mail: eds@glimmertrain.org. **Contact:** Linda Swanson-Davies. "Offered as a platform for all themes, all lengths (2,000-20,000 words), and all writers. See complete writing guidelines and submit online at website. Open all during the months of March, June, September and December. Winners will be called and results will be announced in their respective bulletin month, on their website, and in a number of additional print and online publications." **Charges $20/story.** Prize 1st Place: $2,000, publication in *Glimmer Train Stories*, and 20 copies of that issue; 2nd Place: $1,000 and consideration for publication; 3rd Place: $600.

GLIMMER TRAIN'S MAY SHORT-STORY AWARD FOR NEW WRITERS

Glimmer Train Press, Inc., 1211 NW Glisan St., Suite 207, Portland OR 97209. (503)221-0836. Fax: (503)221-0837. E-mail: eds@glimmertrain.org. **Contact:** Linda Swanson-Davies. "Offered for any writer whose fiction hasn't appeared in a nationally distributed publication with a circulation over 5,000." Word count: 1,200-12,000 words. **Open May 1-31.** Follow submission procedure on Web site. Winners will be called and results will be announced in their August bulletin, on their website, and in a number of additional print and online publications. **Charges $15 fee/story.** Prize Winner receives $1,200, publication in *Glimmer Train Stories* and 20 copies of that issue; second place, $500; third place, $300.

GLIMMER TRAIN'S SHORT-STORY AWARD FOR NEW WRITERS (NOVEMBER)

Glimmer Train Press, Inc., 1211 NW Glisan St., Suite 207, Portland OR 97209. (503)221-0836. Fax: (503)221-0837. E-mail: eds@glimmertrain.org. **Contact:** Linda Swanson-Davies. "Offered for any writer whose fiction hasn't appeared in a nationally-distributed publication with a circulation over 5,000. Word count: 500-12,000 words. **Open November 1-30.** See complete writing guidelines and submit online at website. Winners will be called and results will be announced in their February bulletin, on their website, and in a number of additional print and online publications." **Charges $15 fee/story.** Prize Winner receives $1,200, publication in *Glimmer Train Stories*, and 20 copies of that issue; 2nd Place: $500; 3rd Place: $300.

GLIMMER TRAIN'S VERY SHORT FICTION CONTEST (AUGUST)

Glimmer Train Press, Inc., 1211 NW Glisan St., 207, Portland OR 97209. (503)221-0836. Fax: (503)221-0837. E-mail: eds@glimmertrain.org. **Contact:** Linda Swanson-Davies. "Offered to encourage the art of the very short story. Word count: 3,000 maximum. Open August 1-31. See complete writing guidelines and submit online at website. Winners will be called and results will be announced in their November bulletin, on their website, and in a number of additional print and online publications." **Charges $15 fee/story.** Prize First Place: $1,200, publication in Glimmer Train Stories, and 20 copies of that issue; 2nd Place: $500; 3rd Place: $300.

GLIMMER TRAIN'S VERY SHORT FICTION AWARD (FEBRUARY)
Glimmer Train Press, Inc., 1211 NW Glisan St., #207, Portland OR 97209. (503)221-0836. Fax: (503)221-0837. E-mail: eds@glimmertrain.org. **Contact:** Linda Swanson-Davies. "Offered to encourage the art of the very short story. Word count: 3,000 maximum. Open February 1-28. See complete writing guidelines and submit online at website. Winners will be called and results will be announced in their May bulletin and in a number of additional print and online publications." **Charges $15 fee/story.** Prize Winner receives $1,200, publication in *Glimmer Train Stories,* and 20 copies of that issue; 2nd Place: $500; 3rd Place: $300.

GOVERNOR GENERAL'S LITERARY AWARD FOR FICTION
Canada Council for the Arts, 350 Albert St., P.O. Box 1047, Ottawa ON K1P 5V8 Canada. (613)566-4414, ext. 5573. Fax: (613)566-4410. Offered annually for the best English-language and the best French-language work of fiction by a Canadian. Publishers submit titles for consideration. **Deadline: March 15, June 1, or August 7, depending on the book's publication date.** Prize Each laureate receives $25,000; nonwinning finalists receive $1,000.

LYNDALL HADOW/DONALD STUART SHORT STORY COMPETITION
Fellowship of Australian Writers (WA), P.O. Box 6180, Swanbourne WA 6911. (61)(8)9384-4771. Fax: (61)(8)9384-4854. E-mail: admin@fawwa.org.au. Website: www.fawwa.org.au. Annual contest for unpublished short stories (maximum 3,000 words). "We reserve the right to publish entries in an FAWWA publication or on its website." Guidelines online or for SASE. **Deadline: June 1. Charges $10/story.** Prize 1st Place: $400; 2nd Place; $100; Highly Commended: $50.

LORIAN HEMINGWAY SHORT STORY COMPETITION
Hemingway Days Festival, P.O. Box 993, Key West FL 33041-0993. (305)294-0320. E-mail: shortstorykw@aol.com. Website: www.shortstorycompetition.com. Estab. 1981. Offered annually for unpublished short stories up to 3,000 words. Guidelines available via mail, e-mail, or online. **Deadline: May 15. Charges $12/story postmarked by May 1, $17/story postmarked by May 15; no stories accepted after May 15.** Prize 1st Place: $1,000; 2nd-3rd Place: $500; honorable mentions will also be awarded

TOM HOWARD/JOHN H. REID SHORT STORY CONTEST
c/o Winning Writers, 351 Pleasant St., PMB 222, Northampton MA 01060-3961. (866)946-9748. E-mail: johnreid@mail.qango.com. Website: www.winningwriters.com. **Contact:** John Reid. Estab. 1993. "Both unpublished and published work accepted (maximum 5,000 words). Guidelines for SASE or online." **Deadline: March 31. Charges $15 USD/story/essay/prose work.** Prize 1st Place: $3,000; 2nd Place: $1,000; 3rd Place: $400; 4th Place: $250; plus 5 high distinction awards of $200 each and 6 most highly commended awards of $150 each. The top 10 entries will be published on the Winning Writers Web site. Judged by John H. Reid; assisted by Dee C. Konrad.

L. RON HUBBARD'S WRITERS OF THE FUTURE CONTEST
P.O. Box 1630, Los Angeles CA 90078. (323)466-3310. E-mail: contests@authorservicesinc.com. **Contact:** Contest Administrator. "Offered for unpublished work to find, reward, and publicize new speculative fiction writers so they may more easily attain professional writing careers." Open to new and amateur writers who have not professionally published a novel or short novel, more than 1 novelette, or more than 3 short stories. Eligible entries are short stories or novelettes (under 17,000 words) of science fiction or fantasy. Guidelines for SASE, online, or via e-mail. No entry fee. Entrants retain all rights to their stories. **Deadline: December 31, March 31, June 30, September 30.** Prize Awards quarterly 1st Place: $1,000; 2nd Place: $750; and 3rd Place: $500. Annual Grand Prize: $5,000. Judged by professional writers only.

INDIANA REVIEW FICTION CONTEST
Indiana Review, Ballantine Hall 465, Indiana University, Bloomington IN 47405-7103. (812)855-9535. Fax: (812)855-4253. E-mail: inreview@indiana.edu. Website: www.indiana.edu/~inreview. Only 1 story per entry fee, 35 double-spaced pages maximum. 12 pt. font. Offered annually for unpublished work. Guidelines on website and with SASE request. **Deadline: October. Charges $15 fee (includes a 1-year subscription).** Prize $1,000 Judged by guests; 2009 prize judged by Ron Carlson

THE INNERMOONLIT AWARD FOR BEST FIRST CHAPTER OF A NOVEL
E-mail: timescythe11@yahoo.com. **Contact:** Brian Agincourt Massey. Annual contest for an unpublished novel chapters. Maximum length: 2,000 words. Guidelines available online. No entry fee. Open to all writers 18 years and older. **Deadline: March 1.** Prize 1st Place: $100; 2nd Place: $50; 3rd Place: $25 Brian and Maria Massey.

THE INNERMOONLIT AWARD FOR BEST SHORT-SHORT STORY

E-mail: timescythe11@yahoo.com; masseym@winthrop.edu. **Contact:** Brian Agincourt Massey. "Annual contest for unpublished short-short stories that do not exceed 500 words. Guidelines available online at website. No entry fee. Open to all writers 18 years and older." **Deadline: September 1. Charges No entry fee.** Prize 1st Place: $100; 2nd Place: $50; 3rd Place: $25. Brian and Maria Massey

INTERNATIONAL 3-DAY NOVEL CONTEST

200-341 Water St., Vancouver BC V6B 1B8 Canada. E-mail: info@3daynovel.com. Website: www.3daynovel.com. **Contact:** Melissa Edwards. Estab. 1977. "Offered annually for the best novel written in 3 days (Labor Day weekend). To register, send SASE (IRC if from outside Canada) for details, or entry form available online. Open to all writers. Writing may take place in any location." **Deadline: Friday before Labor Day weekend. Charges $50 fee (lower group rates available).** Prize 1st place receives publication; 2nd place receives $500; 3rd place receives $100.

JESSE H. JONES AWARD FOR BEST WORK OF FICTION

6335 W. Northwest Hwy., #618, Dallas TX 75225. (214)363-7253. E-mail: franvick@aol.com. **Contact:** Fran Vick. Offered annually by Texas Institute of Letters for work published January 1-December 31 of year before award is given to recognize the writer of the best book of fiction entered in the competition. Writers must have been born in Texas, have lived in the state for at least 2 consecutive years at some time, or the subject matter of the work should be associated with the state. See website for guidelines. **Deadline: January 1.** Prize $6,000

JAMES JONES FIRST NOVEL FELLOWSHIP

Wilkes University, Department of English, 245 S. River St., Wilkes-Barre PA 18766. (570)408-4534. Fax: (570)408-3333. E-mail: Jamesjonesfirstnovel@wilkes.edu. Offered annually for unpublished novels, novellas, and closely-linked short stories (all works in progress). "The award is intended to honor the spirit of unblinking honesty, determination, and insight into modern culture exemplified by the late James Jones." The competition is open to all American writers who have not previously published novels. **Deadline: March 1. Charges $25 fee.** Prize $10,000; 2 runners-up get $750 honorarium

E.M. KOEPPEL $1,100 SHORT FICTION ANNUAL AWARD

Writecorner Press, Koeppel Contest, P.O. Box 140310, Gainesville FL 32614-0310. Website: writecorner.com. **Contact:** Mary Sue Koeppel, Robert B. Gentry. Estab. 2004. "Any number of unpublished stories under 3,000 words may be entered by any writer. Send 2 title pages. Put only the title on one title page. List the title and the author's name, address, phone, e-mail, and short bio on the second title page. Guidelines online or SASE." **Deadline: October 1-April 30. Charges $15/story; $10/additional story.** Prize 1st Place: $1,100; Editor's Choices: $100 each; P.L. Titus Scholarship: $500.

THE LAWRENCE FOUNDATION AWARD

Prairie Schooner, 201 Andrews Hall, P.O. Box 880334, Lincoln NE 68588-0334. (402)472-0911. Fax: (402)472-9771. E-mail: kgrey2@unl.edu. **Contact:** Hilda Raz. Offered annually for the best short story published in *Prairie Schooner* in the previous year. Prize $1,000

LITERAL LATTÉ FICTION AWARD

Literal Latté, 200 E. 10th St., Suite 240, New York NY 10003. (212)260-5532. E-mail: litlatte@aol.com. Website: www.literal-latte.com. **Contact:** Edward Estlin, contributing ed. "Award to provide talented writers with 3 essential tools for continued success: money, publication, and recognition. Offered annually for unpublished fiction (maximum 6,000 words). Guidelines for SASE, by e-mail, or online. Open to any writer." **Deadline: January 15.** Prize 1st Place: $1,000 and publication in *Literal Latté*; 2nd Place: $300; 3rd Place: $200; also up to 7 honorable mentions.

Tips "Winners notified by phone. List of winners available in late April for SASE or by e-mail."

LONG STORY CONTEST, INTERNATIONAL

White Eagle Coffee Store Press, P.O. Box 383, Fox River Grove IL 60021. (847)639-9200. E-mail: wecspress@aol.com. **Contact:** Frank E. Smith, publisher. "Offered annually since 1993 for unpublished work to recognize and promote long short stories of 8,000-14,000 words (about 30-50 pages). Sample of previous winner: $6.95, including postage. Open to any writer; no restrictions on materials." **Deadline: December 15. Charges $15 fee; $10 for second story in same envelope.** Prize A. E. Coppard Prize: $1,000, publication, and 25 copies of chapbook

LUMINA WRITING CONTEST

Lumina, Sarah Lawrence College's Literary Magazine, Slonim House, 1 Mead Way, Bronxville NY 10708-5999. "Lumina, the literary journal of Sarah Lawrence College's graduate writing program, accepts previously unpublished fiction, nonfiction, poetry, and art; holds annual writing contest. **Deadline: January 8. Charges $10 for up to 2 pieces; $5 per additional piece.** Prize 1st Prize: $500, publication of your work, and 2 copies of the publication; 2nd Prize: $100, publication of your work, and 2 copies of the publication; 3rd Prize: publication of your work, and 2 copies of the publication.

THE MARY MACKEY SHORT STORY PRIZE

Soul-Making Literary Competition, National League of American Pen Women, Nob Hill, San Francisco Bay Area, The Webhallow House, 1544 Sweetwood Dr., Broadmoor Village CA 94015-2029. E-mail: pennobhill@aol.com. **Contact:** Eileen Malone. "One story/entry, up to 5,000 words. All prose works must be typed, page numbered, and double-spaced. Identify only with 3X5 card. Open annually to any writer." **Deadline: November 30. Charges $5/entry (make checks payable to NLAPW, Nob Hill Branch).** Prize 1st Place: $100; 2nd Place: $50; 3rd Place: $25.

THE MALAHAT REVIEW NOVELLA PRIZE

The Malahat Review, University of Victoria, P.O. Box 1700 STN CSC, Victoria BC V8W 2Y2 Canada. (250)721-8524. E-mail: malahat@uvic.ca. **Contact:** John Barton, Editor. "Held in alternate years with the Long Poem Prize. Offered to promote unpublished novellas. Obtains first world rights. After publication rights revert to the author. Open to any writer." **Deadline: February 1 (even years). Charges $35 CAD fee for Canadian entrants; $40 US for American entrants; $45 US for entrants from elsewhere (includes a 1-year subscription to *Malahat*).** Prize $500, plus payment for publication ($40/page) and an additional year's subscription.

MARY MCCARTHY PRIZE IN SHORT FICTION

Sarabande Books, P.O. Box 4456, Louisville KY 40204. (502)458-4028. Fax: (502)458-4065. E-mail: info@sarabandebooks.org. **Contact:** Kirby Gann, managing editor. Offered annually to publish an outstanding collection of stories, novellas, or short novel (less than 250 pages). All finalists considered for publication. **Deadline: January 1-February 15. Charges $25 fee.** Prize $2,000 and publication (standard royalty contract).

MARJORIE GRABER MCINNIS SHORT STORY AWARD

ACT Writers Centre, Gorman House Arts Centre, Ainslie Ave., Braddon ACT 2612 Australia. Phone/Fax: (61)(2)6262-9191. E-mail: admin@actwriters.org.au. "Open theme for a short story with 1,500-3,000 words. Guidelines available on Web site. Open only to unpublished emerging writers residing within the ACT or region." **Deadline: September 25. Charges $7.50/nonmembers; $5/members.** Prize $600 and publication. Five runners-up receive book prizes. All winners may be published in the ACT writers centre newsletter and on the ACT writers centre Web site.

MILKWEED NATIONAL FICTION PRIZE

Milkweed Editions, 1011 Washington Ave. S., Suite 300, Minneapolis MN 55415. (612)332-3192. Fax: (612)215-2550. Website: www.milkweed.org. **Contact:** The Editors. Estab. 1986. "Annual award for unpublished works. Milkweed is looking for a novel, novella, or a collection of short stories written in English. Mss should be of high literary quality and must be double-spaced and between 150-400 pages in length. Enclose a SASE for response, or a mailer-sized SASE with postage or a $5 check for return of ms. All mss submitted to Milkweed will automatically be considered for the prize. Submission directly to the contest is no longer necessary. Writers are recommended to have previously published a book of fiction or 3 short stories (or novellas) in magazines/journals with national distribution. Catalog available on request for $1.50. Guidelines for SASE or online." **Deadline: Open**. Prize Publication by Milkweed Editions and a cash advance of $5,000 against royalties agreed upon in the contractual arrangement negotiated at the time of acceptance

C. WRIGHT MILLS AWARD

The Society for the Study of Social Problems, 901 McClung Tower, University of Tennessee, Knoxville TN 37996-0490. (865)689-1531. Fax: (865)689-1534. E-mail: mkoontz3@utk.edu. **Contact:** Michele Smith Koontz, admin. officer & meeting man. "Offered annually for a book published the previous year that most effectively critically addresses an issue of contemporary public importance; brings to the topic a fresh, imaginative perspective; advances social scientific understanding of the topic; displays a theoretically informed view and empirical orientation; evinces quality in style of writing; and explicitly or implicitly contains implications for courses of action." **Deadline: January 15**. Prize $500 stipend

KATHLEEN MITCHELL AWARD

Cauz Group Pty., Ltd., Cauz Group Pty., Ltd., P.O. Box 229, Pymble BC 2073 Australia. (61)(2)9144-2415. Fax: (61)(2)9326-5514. E-mail: psalter@cauzgroup.com.au. **Contact:** Petrea Salter. Estab. 1996. "Offered in even years for novels published in the previous 2 years. Author must have been under age 30 when the novel was published. Entrants must be Australian or British born or naturalized Australian citizens, and have resided in Australia for the last year. The award is for a novel of the highest literary merit." **Deadline: February 19, 2010**. Prize $7,500 (Australian).

NATIONAL WRITERS ASSOCIATION NOVEL WRITING CONTEST

The National Writers Association, 10940 S. Parker Rd. #508, Parker CO 80134. (303)841-0246. Fax: (303)841-2607. **Contact:** Sandy Whelchel, director. Annual contest to help develop creative skills, to recognize and reward outstanding ability, and to increase the opportunity for the marketing and subsequent publication of novel mss. **Deadline: April 1. Charges $35 fee.** Prize 1st Place: $500; 2nd Place: $250; 3rd Place: $150.

NATIONAL WRITERS ASSOCIATION SHORT STORY CONTEST

The National Writers Association, 10940 S. Parker Rd. #508, Parker CO 80134. (303)841-0246. Fax: (303)841-2607. **Contact:** Sandy Whelchel, director. Annual contest to encourage writers in this creative form, and to recognize those who excel in fiction writing. **Deadline: July 1. Charges $15 fee.** Prize 1st Place: $200; 2nd Place: $100; 3rd Place: $50.

THE NELLIGAN PRIZE FOR SHORT FICTION

Colorado Review/Center for Literary Publishing, 9105 Campus Delivery, Dept. of English, Colorado State University, Ft. Collins CO 80523-9105. (970)491-5449. E-mail: creview@colostate.edu. **Contact:** Stephanie G'Schwind, editor. Offered annually to an unpublished short story. Guidelines for SASE or online. **Deadline: March 12. Charges $15.** Prize $1,500 and publication of story in *Colorado Review*.

THE FLANNERY O'CONNOR AWARD FOR SHORT FICTION

The University of Georgia Press, 330 Research Dr., Athens GA 30602-4901. (706)369-6130. Fax: (706)369-6131. Estab. 1981. Mss must be 200-275 pages long. Authors do not have to be previously published. Does not return mss. **Deadline: April 1-May 31. Charges $20 fee.** Prize $1,000 and publication under standard book contract

ORANGE PRIZE FOR FICTION

Orange PCS, c/o Booktrust, Book House, 45 E. Hill, Wandsworth, London SW18 2QZ United Kingdom. Fax: (44)(208)516-2978. E-mail: tarryn@booktrust.org.uk. Website: www.orangeprize.co.uk. **Contact:** Tarryn McKay. "This annual award is for a full-length novel written by a woman that fulfills the criteria of excellence in writing, relevance to people's everyday and imaginative lives, accessibility, and originality. The award is open to any full-length novel written in English between April 1 and the following March 31 by a woman of any nationality and published in the UK by a UK publisher. Translations are not eligible, neither are novellas or collections of short stories. Books from all genres are encouraged, but all books must be unified and substantial works written by a single author. All entries must be published in the UK between the publication dates, but may have been previously published outside the UK." **Deadline: End of November**. Prize £30,000 and a statuette known as The Bessie. Judged by a panel of high-profile, professional women.

THE VANCE PALMER PRIZE FOR FICTION

Victorian Premier's Literary Awards, State Government of Victoria, State Library of Victoria, 328 Swanston St. C, Melbourne VIC 3000 Australia. (61)(3)8664-7277. E-mail: pla@slv.vic.gov.au. Website: www.slv.vic.gov.au/pla. **Contact:** Project Officer. "Prize for a novel or collection of short stories published May 1-April 30. Authors must be Australian citizens or permanent residents. Previously published entries must have appeared in print between 1 May and 30 April each year (subject to change)." **Deadline: Usually May each year (subject to change). Charges $44.** Prize Up to AUD $30,000
Tips "For guidelines and nomination forms please visit our website."

PATERSON FICTION PRIZE

PCCC, Poetry Center, One College Blvd., Paterson NJ 07505-1179. (973)684-6555. Fax: (973)523-6085. E-mail: mgillan@pccc.edu. **Contact:** Maria Mazziotti Gillan, executive director. Offered annually for a novel or collection of short fiction published the previous calendar year. Guidelines for SASE or online. **Deadline: April 1**. Prize $1,000

PEN/FAULKNER AWARDS FOR FICTION

PEN/Faulkner Foundation, 201 E. Capitol St., Washington DC 20003. (202)675-0345. Fax: (202)675-0360. E-mail: jneely@penfaulkner.org. **Contact:** Jessica Neely, Executive Director. Offered annually for best book-length work of fiction by an American citizen published in a calendar year. **Deadline: October 31**. Prize $15,000 (one Winner); $5,000 (4 Finalists)

THE PINCH FICTION LITERARY AWARDS

The University of Memphis/Hohenberg Foundation, Dept. of English, 471 Patterson Hall, Memphis TN 38152. (901)678-4591. E-mail: editor@thepinchjournal.com. Offered annually for unpublished short stories of 5,000 words maximum. Guidelines for SASE or on website. **Deadline: March 15. Charges $20/story, which is put toward a 1-year subscription for *River City*.** Prize 1st Place: $1,500 and publication; 2nd Place: possible publication and 1-year subscription.

THE KATHERINE ANNE PORTER PRIZE FOR FICTION

Nimrod International Journal, The University of Tulsa, 800 S. Tucker Dr., Tulsa OK 74104. (918)631-3080. Fax: (918)631-3033. E-mail: nimrod@utulsa.edu. **Contact:** Francine Ringold. "This annual award was established to discover new, unpublished writers of vigor and talent. Open to US residents only." **Deadline: April 30. Charges $20 (includes a 1-year subscription to *Nimrod*).** Prize 1st Place: $2,000 and publication; 2nd Place: $1,000 and publication. *Nimrod* retains the right to publish any submission. the *Nimrod* editors select the finalists and a recognized author selects the winners.

PRISM INTERNATIONAL ANNUAL SHORT FICTION, POETRY, AND LITERARY NONFICTION CONTESTS

Prism International, Creative Writing Program, UBC, Buch E462, 1866 Main Mall, Vancouver BC V6T 1Z1 Canada. (604)822-2514. Fax: (604)822-3616. E-mail: prism@interchange.ubc.ca. Website: prism.arts.ubc.ca. **Contact:** (See website for appropriate editor). "Offered annually for unpublished work to award the best in contemporary fiction, poetry, drama, translation, and non-fiction. Works of translation are eligible. Guidelines are available on website. Acquires first North American serial rights upon publication, and limited Web rights for pieces selected for website. Open to any writer except students and faculty in the Creative Writing Department at UBC, or people who have taken a creative writing course at UBC within 2 years of the contest deadline." **Deadline: January 29. Charges $28/entry; $7 each additional entry (outside Canada pay US currency); includes subscription.** Prize 1st Place: $1,500-2,000; Runners-up (3): $200-300 each (depends on contest); winners published.

THE PRIZE FOR AN UNPUBLISHED MANUSCRIPT BY AN EMERGING VICTORIAN WRITER

Victorian Premier's Literary Awards, State Government of Victoria, State Library of Victoria, 328 Swanston St. C, Melbourne VIC 3000 Australia. (61)(3)8664-7277. E-mail: pla@slv.vic.gov.au. Website: www.slv.vic.gov.au/pla. **Contact:** Project Officer. "Annual prize for an unpublished ms which may be a novel or a collection of short stories. Open to unpublished authors who are residents of Victoria. **Deadline: Usually May each year.** Prize AUD $15,000 and 20 hours of professional assistance from the Victorian Writers' Centre.

Tips "Guidelines and entry forms available online."

THOMAS H. RADDALL ATLANTIC FICTION PRIZE

Writers' Federation of Nova Scotia, 1113 Marginal Rd., Halifax NS B3H 4P7 Canada. (902)423-8116. Fax: (902)422-0881. E-mail: talk@writers.ns.ca. **Contact:** Jane Buss, executive director. Estab. 1990. "Full-length books of fiction written by Atlantic Canadians, and published as a whole for the first time in the previous calendar year, are eligible. Entrants must be native or resident Atlantic Canadians who have either been born in Newfoundland, Prince Edward Island, Nova Scotia, or New Brunswick, and spent a substantial portion of their lives living there, or who have lived in 1 or a combination of these provinces for at least 24 consecutive months prior to entry deadline date." "Publishers: Send 4 copies and a letter attesting to the author's status as an Atlantic Canadian, and the author's current mailing address and telephone number." "To recognize the best Atlantic Canadian adult fiction." **Deadline: First Friday in December. Charges No fee or form.** Prize $15,000.

Tips "WFNS does not open attachments. Please copy and paste such material in the body of our reply."

REAL WRITERS

Real Writers Support & Appraisal Service, P.O. Box 170, Chesterfield S40 1FE United Kingdom. E-mail: info@real-writers.com. **Contact:** Lynne Patrick, coordinator.

THE ROGERS WRITERS' TRUST FICTION PRIZE

The Writers' Trust of Canada, 90 Richmond St. E., Suite 200, Toronto ON M5C 1P1 Canada. (416)504-8222. Fax: (416)504-9090. E-mail: info@writerstrust.com. **Contact:** Amanda Hopkins. "Awarded annually for a distinguished work of fiction—either a novel or short story collection—published within the previous year. Presented at the Writers' Trust Awards event held in Toronto each Fall. Open to Canadian citizens and permanent residents only." Prize $25,000 and $3,500 to four finalists.

RROFIHE TROPHY

Open City, 270 Lafayette St., #1412, New York NY 10012. Website: http://opencity.org/rrofihe.html. **Contact:** Rick Rofihe c/o Open City. "Sixth annual contest for an unpublished short story (up to 5,000 words). Stories should be typed, double-spaced, on 8 ½ X 11 paper with the author's name and contact information on the first page, and name and story title on the upper right corner of remaining pages. Limit 1 submission/author. Author must not have been previously published in *Open City*. Enclose SASE to receive names of winner and honorable mentions. All mss are nonreturnable and will be recycled. First North American serial rights (from winner only)." **Deadline: October 15 (postmarked). Charges $10 (make check payable to RRofihe).** Prize $500, a trophy, and publication in *Open City*. Judge: Rick Rofihe

JOANNA CATHERINE SCOTT NOVEL EXCERPT PRIZE

National League of American Pen Women, Nob Hill, San Francisco Bay Area Branch, The Webhallow House, 1544 Sweetwood Dr., Broadmoor Village CA 94015. E-mail: pennobhill@aol.com. **Contact:** Eileen Malone. "Send first chapter or the first 20 pages, whichever comes first. Include a 1-page synopsis indicating category at top of page. Identify with 3X5 card only. Open annually to any writer." **Deadline: November 30. Charges $5/ entry (make checks payable to NLAPW, Nob Hill Branch).** Prize 1st Place: $100; 2nd Place: $50; 3rd Place: $25.

MICHAEL SHAARA AWARD FOR EXCELLENCE IN CIVIL WAR FICTION

Civil War Institute at Gettysburg College, 300 N. Washington St., Campus Box 435, Gettysburg PA 17325. (717)337-6590. Fax: (717)337-6596. E-mail: civilwar@gettysburg.edu. Estab. 1997. Offered annually for fiction published for the first time in January 1-December 31 of the year of the award to encourage examination of the Civil War from unique perspectives or by taking an unusual approach. All Civil War novels are eligible. To nominate a novel, send 10 copies of the novel to the address above with a cover letter. Nominations should be made by publishers, but authors and critics can nominate as well. **Deadline: December 31.** Prize $2,500

MARY WOLLSTONECRAFT SHELLEY PRIZE FOR IMAGINATIVE FICTION

Rosebud, N3310 Asje Rd., Cambridge WI 53523. (608)423-4750. Fax: (608)423-9976. E-mail: jrodclark@smallbytes.net. Website: www.rsbd.net. **Contact:** J. Roderick Clark, editor. Biennial (odd years) contest for unpublished stories. Entries are welcome any time. Acquires first rights. Open to any writer. **Deadline: October 15. Charges $10/story.** Prize $1,000, plus publication in *Rosebud*. 4 runner-ups receive $100 and publication in *Rosebud*.

SKYLINE MAGAZINE ANNUAL SHORT STORY CONTEST

Skyline Arts & Entertainment Magazine, Skyline Review, P.O. Box 295, Stormville NY 12582-0295. E-mail: skylineeditor@hotmail.com. **Contact:** Victoria Valentine, pub. "Annual anthology of short stories, poetry & art. Complete submission information listed online. Submissions are evaluated on originality, subject interest, writing style, grammar, and punctuation. We look for storylines that grab our attention, flow smoothly, with strong, unique characterizations and imagery. Powerful conclusions and/or surprise endings are a must. Read all guidelines before submitting online website form. Electronic submissions only!" Victoria Valentine, Phaedra Valentine.

ELIZABETH SIMPSON SMITH FICTION AWARD

9136 Joyce Kilmer Dr., Charlotte NC 28213. E-mail: kcburrow.uncc.edu. **Contact:** Ken Burrows. "Offered annually for unpublished short stories (maxiumum 4,000 words) by US residents. Send SASE or see guidelines online." **Deadline: May 31. Charges $20 fee.** Prize $500 and publication in anthology.

SPOKANE PRIZE FOR SHORT FICTION

Eastern Washington University Press, 534 E. Spokane Falls Blvd., Suite 203, Spokane WA 99202. (800)508-9095. Fax: (509)368-6596. E-mail: ewupress@mail.ewu.edu. **Contact:** Christopher Howell. Annual award to publish the finest work the literary world has to offer. Please visit our website for full details. **Deadline: May 15. Charges $25.** Prize $3,000 and publication.

🌐 SUNFLOWER BOOKSHOP SHORT STORY AWARD

City of Eira, P.O. Box 42, Caulfield South VIC 3162 Australia. E-mail: arts@gleneira.vic.gov.au. Website: www.gleneira.vic.gov.au. "Award for a 3,000-word short story. Open to people who reside, work, or study in the city of Glen Eira. Entries preferred by email or CD; winner to be published in etchings." **Deadline: June 19. Charges $10.** Prize 1st Place: $500; 2nd Place: $300; 3rd Place: $200. Judge: Cate Kennedy

THE DAME LISBET THROCKMORTON FICTION CONTEST

Coffeehousefiction.com, P.O. Box 399, Forest Hill MD 21050. E-mail: contest@coffeehousefiction.com. **Contact:** Sherri Cook Woosley. "Annual contest for unpublished fiction (3,500 words or less). It's meant to encourage writers who have chosen a vocation with such a high frustration rate. Each judge either loves literature or is a writer and understands firsthand the emotional highs and lows of the road to publication." **Deadline: Jan. 31. (Critiques are also available for an additional $25.). Charges $17.** Prize 1st Prize: $350 plus 5 copies of resulting anthology; 2nd Prize: $125 plus 2 copies of anthology; 3rd Prize: $75 plus one copy; 4th Prize: $50 plus one copy. All winners are published on Coffeehousefiction.com with bios and pictures. Sherri Cook Woosley, Patricia Valdata, May Kuroiwa and Nancy Adler.

STEVEN TURNER AWARD FOR BEST FIRST WORK OF FICTION

6335 W. Northwest Hwy., #618, Dallas TX 75225. (214)363-7253. E-mail: franvick@aol.com. **Contact:** Fran Vick. Offered annually for work published January 1-December 31 for the best first book of fiction. Writers must have been born in Texas, have lived in the state for at least 2 consecutive years at some time, or the subject matter of the work should be associated with the state. Guidelines online. **Deadline: January 3.** Prize

$1,000

24-HOUR SHORT STORY CONTEST

WritersWeekly.com, P.O. Box 2399, Bangor ME 04402. E-mail: writersweekly@writersweekly.com. **Contact:** Angela Hoy. "Quarterly contest in which registered entrants receive a topic at start time (usually noon CST) and have 24 hours to write a story on that topic. All submissions should be returned via e-mail. Each contest is limited to 500 people. Guidelines via e-mail or online." **Deadline: Quarterly—see Web site for dates. Charges $5.** Prize 1st Place: $300; 2nd Place: $250; 3rd Place: $200. There are also 20 honorable mentions and 60 door prizes. The top 3 winners' entries are posted on WritersWeekly.com (non-exclusive electronic rights only). Writers retain all rights to their work. Angela Hoy (publisher of WritersWeekly.com and Booklocker.com).

GARY WILSON SHORT FICTION AWARD

descant, Texas Christian University's literary journal, TCU, Box 297270, Fort Worth TX 76129. (817)257-6537. Fax: (817)257-6239. E-mail: descant@tcu.edu. **Contact:** David Kuhne, editor. Offered annually for an outstanding story in an issue. Prize $250

N THOMAS WOLFE FICTION PRIZE

North Carolina Writers' Network, P.O. Box 21591, Winston-Salem NC 27120-1591. (919)336-293-8844. Fax: (919)929-0535. E-mail: mail@ncwriters.org. **Contact:** Ed Southern, exec. dir. Offered annually for unpublished work "to recognize a notable work of fiction—either short story or novel excerpt—while honoring one of North Carolina's best writers—Thomas Wolfe." Past judges have included Anne Tyler, Barbara Kingsolver, C. Michael Curtis and Randall Kenan. **See website, www.ncwriters.org. Charges $15 fee for members of the NC Writers' Network, $25 for non-members.** Prize $1,000 and potential publication.

WOW! WOMEN ON WRITING QUARTERLY FLASH FICTION CONTEST

Wow! Women on Writing, 740 S. Van Buren St., Suite D, Placentia CA 92870. E-mail: contestinfo@wow-womenonwriting.com. Website: www.wow-womenonwriting.com/contest.php. **Contact:** Angela Mackintosh, CEO. Contest offered quarterly. We are open to all themes and genres, although we do encourage writers to take a close look at our guest judge for the season and the flavor of our Web site, if you are serious about winning. We love creativity, originality and light-hearted reads. Entries must be 250-500 words. **Deadline: August 31, November 30, February 29, May 31. Charges $10.** Prize 1st Place: $200 cash prize,1 Year Premium-Green Writers' Markets subscription ($48 value), goodie bag worth $100, story published on WOW! Women On Writing, interview on blog; 2nd Place: $150 cash prize, 1 year Premium-Green Writers' Markets Subscription ($48 value), goodie bag world $100, story published on WOW! Women On Writing, interview on blog; 3rd Place: $100 cash prize, 1 Year Premium-Green Writers' Markets Subscription ($48 value), goodie bag worth $100, story published on WOW! Women On Writing, interview on blog; 7 Runners-Up: goodie bag worth $100, story published on WOW! Women On Writing. a literary agent.

WRITERS' JOURNAL ANNUAL FICTION CONTEST

Val-Tech Media, P.O. Box 394, Perham MN 56573. (218)346-7921. Fax: (218)346-7924. E-mail: writersjournal@writersjournal.com. **Contact:** Leon Ogroske (editor@writersjournal.com). Offered annually for previously unpublished fiction. Open to any writer. Guidelines for SASE or online. **Deadline: January 30. Charges $15 reading fee.** Prize 1st Place: $500; 2nd Place: $200; 3rd Place: $100; plus honorable mentions. Prize-winning stories and selected honorable mentions are published in *Writers' Journal*.

WRITERS' JOURNAL ANNUAL HORROR/GHOST CONTEST

Val-Tech Media, P.O. Box 394, Perham MN 56573. (218)346-7921. Fax: (218)346-7924. E-mail: writersjournal@writersjournal.com. **Contact:** Leon Ogroske. "Offered annually for previously unpublished works. Open to any writer. Guidelines for SASE or online." **Deadline: March 30. Charges $7 fee.** Prize 1st Place: $250; 2nd Place: $100; 3rd Place: $50; plus honorable mentions. Prize-winning stories and selected honorable mentions are published in *Writers' Journal*.

WRITERS' JOURNAL ANNUAL ROMANCE CONTEST

Val-Tech Media, P.O. Box 394, Perham MN 56573. (218)346-7921. Fax: (218)346-7924. E-mail: writersjournal@writersjournal.com. **Contact:** Leon Ogroske. Offered annually for previously unpublished works. Open to any writer. Guidelines for SASE or online. **Deadline: July 30. Charges $7 fee.** Prize 1st Place: $250; 2nd Place: $100; 3rd Place: $50; plus honorable mentions. Prize-winning stories and selected honorable mentions are published in *Writers' Journal*.

WRITERS' JOURNAL ANNUAL SHORT STORY CONTEST

Val-Tech Media, P.O. Box 394, Perham MN 56573. (218)346-7921. Fax: (218)346-7924. E-mail: writersjournal@writersjournal.com. **Contact:** Leon Ogroske. Offered annually for previously unpublished short stories. Open to any writer. Guidelines for SASE or online. **Deadline: May 30. Charges $10 reading fee.** Prize 1st Place: $350; 2nd Place: $125; 3rd Place: $75; plus honorable mentions. Prize-winning stories and selected honorable mentions are published in *Writers' Journal*.

ZOETROPE SHORT FICTION CONTEST

Zoetrope: All-Story, 916 Kearny St., San Francisco CA 94133. **Contact:** Francis Ford Coppola, publisher. Annual contest for unpublished short stories. Guidelines by SASE or on website. Open to any writer. Please clearly mark envelope short fiction contest. **Deadline: October 1. Charges $15 fee.** Prize 1st Place: $1,000, 2nd Place: $500, 3rd Place: $250, plus 7 honorable mentions

Tips "The winners and honorable mentions will be considered for representation by leading literary agencies."

NONFICTION

AMWA MEDICAL BOOK AWARDS COMPETITION

American Medical Writers Association, 40 W. Gude Dr., Suite 101, Rockville MD 20850-1192. (301)294-5303. Fax: (301)294-9006. E-mail: slynn@amwa.org. **Contact:** Book Awards Committee. Offered annually to honor the best medical book published in the previous year in each of 3 categories: Books for Physicians, Books for Allied Health Professionals, and Trade Books. **Deadline: March 1. Charges $50 fee.**

ANTHEM ESSAY CONTEST

The Ayn Rand Institute, P.O. Box 57044, Irvine CA 92619-7044. (949)222-6550. Fax: (949)222-6558. E-mail: essay@aynrand.org. Estab. 1992. "Offered annually to encourage analytical thinking and excellence in writing (600-1,200 word essay), and to expose students to the philosophic ideas of Ayn Rand. For information contact your English teacher or guidance counselor or visit our website. Open to 8th, 9th and 10th graders." **Deadline: March 20**. Prize 1st Place: $2,000; 2nd Place (5): $500; 3rd Place (10): $200; Finalist (45): $50; Semifinalist (175): $30

ATLAS SHRUGGED ESSAY CONTEST

The Ayn Rand Institute, P.O. Box 57044, Irvine CA 92619-7044. (949)222-6550. Fax: (949)222-6558. E-mail: essay@aynrand.org. "Offered annually to encourage analytical thinking and excellence in writing, and to expose students to the philosophic ideas of Ayn Rand. Essays are judged both on style and content. Essay length: 800-1,600 word essay. Guidelines on website. Open to 12th graders and college undergraduate and graduate students." **Deadline: September 17**. Prize 1st Place: $10,000; 2nd Place (3 awards): $2,000; 3rd Place (5 awards): $1,000; Finalists (20 awards): $100; Semifinalists (20 awards): $50.

BANCROFT PRIZE

Columbia University, c/o Office of the University Librarian, 517 Butter Library, Mail Code 1101, 535 W. 114th St., New York NY 10027. **Contact:** Bancroft Prize Committee. "Offered annually for work published in previous year. Winning submissions will be chosen in either or both of the following categories: American history (including biography) and diplomacy. Open to all writers except previous recipients of the Bancroft Prize." **Deadline: November 1**. Prize $10,000 for the winning entry in each category

RAY ALLEN BILLINGTON PRIZE

Organization of American Historians, 112 N. Bryan Ave., P.O. Box 5457, Bloomington IN 47408-5457. (812)855-7311. Fax: (812)855-0696. **Contact:** Award and Prize Committee Coordinator. Offered in even years for "the best book in American frontier history, defined broadly so as to include the pioneer periods of all geographical areas and comparison between American frontiers and others." Guidelines available online. **Deadline: October 1 of even-numbered years**. Prize $1,000

BRITISH CZECH AND SLOVAK ASSOCIATION WRITING COMPETITION

24 Ferndale, Tunbridge Wells Kent TN2 3NS England. E-mail: prize@bcsa.co.uk. **Contact:** Prize Administrator. "Annual contest for original writing (1,500-2,000 words) in English on the links between Britain and the Czech/Slovak Republics, or describing society in transition in the Republics since 1989. Entries can be fact or fiction. Topics can include history, politics, the sciences, economics, the arts, or literature." **Deadline: June 30**. Prize 1st Place: £300; 2nd Place: £100.

JOHN BULLEN PRIZE

Canadian Historical Association, 395 Wellington St., Ottawa ON K1A 0N4 Canada. (613)233-7885. Fax: (613)567-3110. E-mail: cha-shc@lac-bac.gc.ca. Offered annually for an outstanding historical dissertation for a doctoral degree at a Canadian university. Open only to Canadian citizens or landed immigrants. **Deadline: November 30**. Prize $500

CANADIAN LIBRARY ASSOCIATION STUDENT ARTICLE CONTEST

Canadian Library Association, 328 Frank St., Ottawa ON K2P 0X8 Canada. (613)232-9625, ext. 301. Fax:

(613)563-9895. **Contact:** Valerie Delrue. Offered annually to unpublished articles discussing, analyzing, or evaluating timely issues in librarianship or information science. Open to all students registered in or recently graduated from a Canadian library school, a library techniques program, or faculty of education library program. Submissions may be in English or French. **Deadline: March 31**. Prize 1st Place: $150 and trip to CLA's annual conference; 1st runner-up: $150 and $75 in CLA publications; 2nd runner-up: $100 and $75 in CLA publications.

THE DOROTHY CHURCHILL CAPPON CREATIVE NONFICTION AWARD

New Letters, University of Missouri-Kansas City, 5101 Rockhill Rd., Kansas City MO 64110. (816)235-1168. Fax: (816)235-2611. E-mail: newletters@umkc.edu. **Contact:** Amy Lucas. Contest is offered annually for unpublished work to discover and reward emerging writers and to give experienced writers a place to try new genres. Acquires first North American serial rights. Open to any writer. Guidelines for SASE or online. **Deadline: Third week of May. Charges $15 fee (includes cost of a 1-year subscription).** Prize 1st Place: $1,500 and publication in a volume of *New Letters*; runner-up will receive a copy of a recent book of poetry or fiction courtesy of BkMk Press. All entries will receive consideration for publication in future editions of *New Letters*.

THE SHAUGHNESSY COHEN PRIZE FOR POLITICAL WRITING

The Writers' Trust of Canada, 90 Richmond St. E., Suite 200, Toronto ON M5C 1P1 Canada. (416)504-8222. Fax: (416)504-9090. E-mail: info@writerstrust.com. **Contact:** Amanda Hopkins, program coor. "Awarded annually for a nonfiction book of outstanding literary merit that enlarges our understanding of contemporary Canadian political and social issues. Presented at the Politics & the Pen event each spring in Ottawa. Open to Canadian citizens and permanent residents only." **Deadline: November 6**. Prize $25,000 and $3,500 to four finalists.

CARR P. COLLINS AWARD

The Texas Institute of Letters, 6335 W. Northwest Hwy., #618, Dallas TX 75225. (214)363-7253. E-mail: franvick@aol.com. Website: texasinstituteofletters.org. **Contact:** Fran Vick. Offered annually for work published January 1-December 31 of the previous year to recognize the best nonfiction book by a writer who was born in Texas, who has lived in the state for at least 2 consecutive years at one point, or a writer whose work has some notable connection with Texas. See website for guidelines. **Deadline: January 3**. Prize $5,000

COMPETITION FOR WRITERS OF BC HISTORY

British Columbia Historical Federation, P.O. Box 5254, Station B, Victoria BC V8R 6Nr Canada. (604)274-6449. E-mail: info@bchistory.ca. Website: www.bchistory.ca. "Offered annually to nonfiction books containing a facet of BC history and published during contest year. Books become the property of BC Historical Federation." **Deadline: December 31**. Prize Cash, a certificate of merit, and an invitation to the BCHF annual conference. The contest winner receives the Lieutenant-Governor's Medal for Historical Writing.

AVERY O. CRAVEN AWARD

Organization of American Historians, P.O. Box 5457, Bloomington IN 47408-5457. (812)855-7311. Fax: (812)855-0696. **Contact:** Award and Prize Committee Coordinator. Estab. 1985. "Offered annually for the most original book on the coming of the Civil War, the Civil War years, or the Era of Reconstruction, with the exception of works of purely military history. Guidelines available online." **Deadline: October 1**. Prize $500

A CUP OF COMFORT

Adams Media Corp./F+W Publications Co., 57 Littlefield St., Avon MA 02322. Fax: (508)427-6790. E-mail: cupofcomfort@adamsmedia.com. A Cup of Comfort is the best-selling book series featuring inspiring true stories about the relationships and experiences that deeply affect our lives. Stories must be true, written in English, uplifting, and appropriate for a mainstream audience. This prize includes publication in an anthology. Contest is offered 6-8 times/year. Deadline is 6-12 months prior to publication. Call for submissions and guidelines on website, for SASE, or by e-mail. Open to aspiring and published writers. Allow 6-9 months for response. Limited rights for a specified period of time; applies only to those stories selected for publication. Prize $500 grand prize; $100 for all other stories published in each book (50 stories/anthology).

MERLE CURTI AWARD

Organization of American Historians, P.O. Box 5457, 112 N. Bryan Ave., Bloomington IN 47408-5457. (812)855-7311. Fax: (812)855-0696. **Contact:** Award and Prize Committee Coordinator. Offered annually for books in the fields of American social and/or intellectual history. Guidelines available online. **Deadline: October 1**. Prize $2,000 (or $1,000 should 2 books be selected).

THE ALFRED DEAKIN PRIZE FOR AN ESSAY ADVANCING PUBLIC DEBATE

Victorian Premier's Literary Awards, State Government of Victoria, State Library of Victoria, 328 Swanston St. C, Melbourne VIC 3000 Australia. (61)(3)8664-7277. E-mail: pla@slv.vic.gov.au. Website: www.slv.vic.gov.au/pla. **Contact:** Project Officer. "Annual prize for an individual essay that contributes to the national debate through the quality of its writing. Must have been published between May 1 and April 30 (each year) in the form of a book or a print, electronic, or newspaper article. Authors must be Australian citizens or permanent residents." **Deadline: Usually May each year**. Prize AUD $15,000

Tips "For guidelines and entry forms please see our website."

GORDON W. DILLON/RICHARD C. PETERSON MEMORIAL ESSAY PRIZE

American Orchid Society, Inc., 16700 AOS Ln., Delray Beach FL 33446-4351. (561)404-2043. Fax: (561)404-2045. E-mail: jmengel@aos.org. Website: www.aos.org. **Contact:** Jane Mengel. Estab. 1985. "Annual contest open to all writers. The theme is announced each May in *Orchids* magazine. All themes deal with an aspect of orchids, such as repotting, growing, hybridizing, etc. Unpublished submissions only. Themes in past years have included Orchid Culture, Orchids in Nature, and Orchids in Use. Acquires one-time rights." **Deadline: November 30**. Prize Cash award and a certificate. Winning entry usually published in the May issue of *Orchids* magazine.

THE DONNER PRIZE

The Award for Best Book on Canadian Public Policy, The Donner Canadian Foundation, 394A King St. E., Toronto ON M5A 1K9 Canada. (416)368-8253 or (416)368-3763. E-mail: sherry@mdgassociates.com. Website: www.donnerbookprize.com. **Contact:** Sherry Naylor. "Offered annually for nonfiction published January 1-December 31 that highlights the importance of public policy and to reward excellent work in this field. Entries must be published in either English or French. Open to Canadian citizens." **Deadline: November 30**. Prize $30,000; 5 shortlist authors get $5,000 each.

EDUCATOR'S AWARD

The Delta Kappa Gamma Society International, P.O. Box 1589, Austin TX 78767-1589. (888)762-4685. Fax: (512)478-3961. E-mail: societyexec@deltakappagamma.org. Website: www.deltakappagamma.net. **Contact:** Educator's Award Committee. "Offered annually for quality research and nonfiction published January-December of previous year. This award recognizes educational research and writings of female authors whose work may influence the direction of thought and action necessary to meet the needs of today's complex society. The book must be written by 1 or 2 women who are citizens of any country in which The Delta Kappa Gamma Society International is organized: Canada, Costa Rica, Denmark, Estonia, Finland, Germany, Great Britain, Guatemala, Iceland, Mexico, The Netherlands, Norway, Puerto Rico, Sweden, US. Guidelines (required) for SASE. **Deadline: February 1**. Prize $2,500

EVANS BIOGRAPHY & HANDCART AWARDS

Mountain West Center for Regional Studies, Utah State University, 0700 Old Main Hill, Logan UT 84322-0700. (435)797-3630. Fax: (435)797-3899. E-mail: mwc@cc.usu.edu. Estab. 1983. Offered to encourage the writing of biography about people who have played a role in Mormon Country (not the religion, the region—Intermountain West with parts of Southwestern Canada and Northwestern Mexico). Publishers or authors may nominate books. Criteria for consideration: Work must be a biography or autobiography on someone who lived in our significantly contributed to the history of the Interior West; must be submitted for consideration for publication year's award; new editions or reprints are not eligible; mss are not accepted. Submit 5 copies. **Deadline: January 1**. Prize $10,000 and $1,000

DINA FEITELSON RESEARCH AWARD

International Reading Association, Division of Research & Policy, 800 Barksdale Rd., Newark DE 19714-8139. (302)731-1600, ext. 423. Fax: (302)731-1057. E-mail: research@reading.org. **Contact:** Marcella Moore. "Dina Feitelson Research Award is an award for an exemplary work published in English in a refereed journal that reports on an empirical study investigating aspects of literacy acquisition, such as phonemic awareness, the alphabetic principle, bilingualism, or cross-cultural studies of beginning reading. Articles may be submitted for consideration by researchers, authors, et al. Copies of the applications and guidelines can be downloaded in pdf format from the website." **Deadline: September 1**. Prize Monetary award and recognition at the International Reading Association's annual convention.

WALLACE K. FERGUSON PRIZE

Canadian Historical Association, 395 Wellington St., Ottawa ON K1A 0N4 Canada. (613)233-7885. Fax: (613)567-3110. E-mail: cha-shc@lac-bac.gc.ca. **Contact:** Michel Duquet, executive coordinator. Offered to a Canadian who has published the outstanding scholarly book in a field of history other than Canadian history. Open to Canadian citizens and landed immigrants only **Deadline: December 2**. Prize $1,000

GOVERNOR GENERAL'S LITERARY AWARD FOR LITERARY NONFICTION

Canada Council for the Arts, 350 Albert St., P.O. Box 1047, Ottawa ON K1P 5V8 Canada. (613)566-4414, ext. 5573. Fax: (613)566-4410. Offered annually for the best English-language and the best French-language work of literary nonfiction by a Canadian. **Deadline: March 15, June 1 or August 7, depending on the book's publication date**. Prize Each laureate receives $25,000; non-winning finalists receive $1,000.

JAMES T. GRADY—JAMES H. STACK AWARD FOR INTERPRETING CHEMISTRY FOR THE PUBLIC

American Chemical Society, 1155 16th St. NW, Washington DC 20036-4800. E-mail: awards@acs.org. "Offered annually for previously published work to recognize, encourage, and stimulate outstanding reporting directly to the public, which materially increases the public's knowledge and understanding of chemistry, chemical engineering, and related fields. Guidelines online at website. Rules of eligibility: A nominee must have made noteworthy presentations through a medium of public communication to increase the American public's understanding of chemistry and chemical progress. This information shall have been disseminated through the press, radio, television, films, the lecture platform, books, or pamphlets for the lay public." **Deadline: November 1**. Prize $3,000, medallion with a presentation box, and certificate, plus travel expenses to the meeting at which the award will be presented.

JOHN GUYON LITERARY NONFICTION PRIZE

Crab Orchard Review, English Department, Southern Illinois Univ. Carbondale, Carbondale IL 62901-4503. E-mail: jtribble@siu.edu. **Contact:** Jon C. Tribble, managing ed. "Offered annually for unpublished work. This competition seeks to reward excellence in the writing of creative nonfiction. This is not a prize for academic essays. *Crab Orchard Review* acquires first North American serial rights to submitted works. Open to US citizens only." **March 1 - April 30. Charges $10/essay (limit of 3 essays of up to 6,500 words each), which includes one copy of** *Crab Orchard Review* **featuring the winners.** Prize $1,500 and publication.

ALBERT J. HARRIS AWARD

International Reading Association, Division of Research and Policy, 800 Barksdale Rd., Newark DE 19714-8139. (302)731-1600, ext. 423; (800)336-7323. Fax: (302)731-1057. E-mail: research@reading.org. **Contact:** Marcella Moore. "Offered annually to recognize outstanding published works focused on the identification, prevention, assessment, or instruction of learners experiencing difficulty learning to read. Articles may be nominated by researchers, authors, and others. Copies of the applications and guidelines can be downloaded in PDF format from the website." **Deadline: September 1**. Prize Monetary award and recognition at the International Reading Association's annual convention.

ELLIS W. HAWLEY PRIZE

Organization of American Historians, P.O. Box 5457, 112 N. Bryan Ave., Bloomington IN 47408-5457. (812)855-9852. Fax: (812)855-0696. **Contact:** Award and Prize Committee Coordinator. "Offered annually for the best book-length historical study of the political economy, politics, or institutions of the US, in its domestic or international affairs, from the Civil War to the present. Guidelines available online." **Deadline: October 1**. Prize $500

CREATIVE NONFICTION PRIZE

National League of American Pen Women, Nob Hill, San Francisco Branch, The Webhallow House, 1544 Sweetwood Dr., Broadmoor Village CA 94015-2029. E-mail: pennobhill@aol.com. **Contact:** Eileen Malone. All prose works must be typed, page numbered, and double-spaced. Each entry up to 3,000 words. Identify only with 3X5 card. Open annually to any writer. **Deadline: November 30. Charges $5/entry (make checks payable to NLAPW, Nob Hill Branch)**. Prize 1st Place: $100; 2nd Place: $50; 3rd Place: $25.

KATHERINE SINGER KOVACS PRIZE

Modern Language Association of America, 26 Broadway, 3rd Floor, New York NY 10004-1789. (646)576-5141. Fax: (646)458-0030. E-mail: awards@mla.org. **Contact:** Coordinator of Book Prizes. Estab. 1990. Offered annually for a book published during the previous year in English or Spanish in the field of Latin American and Spanish literatures and cultures. Books should be broadly interpretive works that enhance understanding of the interrelations among literature, the other arts, and society. Author must be a current member of the MLA. **Deadline: May 1**. Prize $1,000 and a certificate

LERNER-SCOTT PRIZE

Organization of American Historians, P.O. Box 5457, 112 N. Bryan Ave., Bloomington IN 47408-5457. (812)855-9852. Fax: (812)855-0696. **Contact:** Award and Prize Committee Coordinator. "Offered annually for the best doctoral dissertation in US women's history. Guidelines available online." **Deadline: October 1 for a dissertation completed during the previous academic year (July 1-June 30)**. Prize $1,000

LINCOLN PRIZE AT GETTYSBURG COLLEGE

Gettysburg College and Lincoln & Soldiers Institute, 300 N. Washington St., Campus Box 435, Gettysburg PA 17325. (717)337-6590. Fax: (717)337-6596. E-mail: lincolnprize@gettysburg.edu. Offered annually for the "finest scholarly work in English on the era of the American Civil War. The award will usually go to a book published in the previous year; however articles, essays, and works of fiction may be submitted." Guidelines for SASE or online. **Deadline: November 1**. Prize $50,000.

LITERARY NONFICTION CONTEST

(formerly Rogers Communication Literary Nonfiction Contest), PRISM International, Creative Writing Program, UBC, Buch E462—1866 Main Mall, Vancouver BC V6T 1Z1 Canada. (604)822-2514. Fax: (604)822-3616. E-mail: prism@interchange.ubc.ca. Website: www.prismmagazine.ca. **Contact:** contest manager. Offered annually for published and unpublished writers to promote and reward excellence in literary nonfiction writing. "*PRISM* buys first North American serial rights upon publication. We also buy limited Web rights for pieces selected for the website. Open to anyone except students and faculty of the Creative Writing Program at UBC or people who have taken a creative writing course at UBC in the 2 years prior to contest deadline." All entrants receive a 1-year subscription to *PRISM*. Guidelines for SASE (Canadian postage only), via e-mail, or visit our website. **Deadline: November 30. Charges $28/piece; $7/additional entry.** Prize $1,500 for the winning entry, plus $20/page for the publication of the winner in *PRISM*'s winter issue

TONY LOTHIAN PRIZE

under the auspices of the Biographers' Club, 119a Fordwych Rd., London NW2 3NJ United Kingdom. (44) (20)8452 4993. E-mail: anna@annaswan.co.uk. **Contact:** Anna Swan. "Entries should consist of a 10-page synopsis and 10 pages of a sample chapter for a proposed biography. Open to any biographer who has not previously been published or commissioned or written a book." **Deadline: August 1. Charges £10.** Prize £2,000. Judges have included Michael Holroyd, Victoria Glendinning, Selina Hastings, Frances Spalding, Lyndall Gordon, Anne de Courcy, Nigel Hamilton, Anthony Sampson, and Mary Lovell.
Tips "Further details at www.biographersclub.co.uk."

WALTER D. LOVE PRIZE

North American Conference on British Studies, History Department, 0119 Sutherland Bldg., Penn State University, Abington PA 19001. E-mail: axa24@psu.edu. **Contact:** Andrew August. "Offered annually for best article in any field of British Studies. Open to American or Canadian writers." **Deadline: April 1.** Prize $150

SIR JOHN A. MACDONALD PRIZE

Canadian Historical Association, 395 Wellington St., Ottawa ON K1A 0N4 Canada. (613)233-7885. Fax: (613)567-3110. E-mail: cha-shc@lac-bac-gc.ca. **Contact:** Michel Duquet, executive coordinator. Offered annually to award a previously published nonfiction work of Canadian history judged to have made the most significant contribution to an understanding of the Canadian past. Open to Canadian citizens only. **Deadline: December 2.** Prize $1,000

LINDA JOY MYERS MEMOIR PRIZE

National League of American Pen Women, Nob Hill, San Francisco Branch, Webhallow House, 1544 Sweetwood Dr., Broadmoor Village CA 94015-20029. E-mail: pennobhill@aol.com. **Contact:** Eileen Malone. "One memoir/entry, up to 3,000 words, double spaced. Previously published material is acceptable. Indicate category on first page. Identify only with 3X5 card. Open annually to any writer." **Deadline: November 30. Charges $5/entry (make checks payable to NLAPW, Nob Hill Branch).** Prize 1st Place: $100; 2nd Place $50; 3rd Place $25.

NATIONAL WRITERS ASSOCIATION NONFICTION CONTEST

The National Writers Association, 10940 S. Parker Rd., #508, Parker CO 80134. (303)841-0246. Fax: (303)841-2607. E-mail: natlwritersassn@hotmail.com. **Contact:** Sandy Whelchel, director. "Annual contest to encourage writers in this creative form and to recognize those who excel in nonfiction writing." **Deadline: December 31. Charges $18 fee.** Prize 1st Place: $200; 2nd Place: $100; 3rd Place: $50.

THE FREDERIC W. NESS BOOK AWARD

Association of American Colleges and Universities, 1818 R St. NW, Washington DC 20009. (202)387-3760. Fax: (202)265-9532. E-mail: info@aacu.org. **Contact:** Bethany Sutton. Offered annually for work published in the previous year. Each year the Frederic W. Ness Book Award Committee of the Association of American Colleges and Universities recognizes books which contribute to the understanding and improvement of liberal education. Guidelines for SASE or online. "Writers may nominate their own work; however, we send letters of invitation to publishers to nominate qualified books." **Deadline: May 1.** Prize $2,000 and a presentation at the association's annual meeting—transportation and 1 night hotel for meeting are also provided.

FRANK LAWRENCE AND HARRIET CHAPPELL OWSLEY AWARD

Southern Historical Association, Dept. of History, University of Georgia, Athens GA 30602-1602. (706)542-8848. Fax: (706)542-2455. **Contact:** Southern Historical Association. Estab. 1934. Offered in odd-numbered years for recognition of a distinguished book in Southern history published in even-numbered years. Publishers usually submit the books. **Deadline: March 1.**

THE NETTIE PALMER PRIZE FOR NONFICTION

Victorian Premier's Literary Awards, State Government of Victoria, State Library of Victoria, 328 Swanston St. C, Melbourne VIC 3000 Australia. (61)(3)8664-7277. E-mail: pla@slv.vic.gov.au. Website: www.slv.vic.gov.au/

pla. **Contact:** Project Officer. "Prize offered annually for a work of nonfiction previously published May 1-April 30 each year. Authors must be Australian citizens or permanent residents." **Deadline: Usually May each year. Charges $44.** Prize Up to AUD $30,000
Tips "For guidelines and nomination forms please visit our website."

LOUIS PELZER MEMORIAL AWARD

Organization of American Historians, *Journal of American History*, 1215 E. Atwater Ave., Bloomington IN 47401. (812)855-2816. Fax: (812)855-9939. "Offered annually for the best essay in American history by a graduate student. The essay may be about any period or topic in the history of the US, and the author must be enrolled in a graduate program at any level, in any field. Length: 7,000 words maximum (including endnotes). Guidelines available online." **Deadline: December 1**. Prize $500 and publication of the essay in the *Journal of American History*.

PRESERVATION FOUNDATION CONTESTS

The Preservation Foundation, Inc., 2213 Pennington Bend, Nashville TN 37214. E-mail: preserve@storyhouse.org. Website: www.storyhouse.org. **Contact:** Richard Loller, pub. "Contest offered annually for unpublished nonfiction. General nonfiction category (1,500-5,000 words)—any appropriate nonfiction topic. Travel nonfiction category (1,500-5,000 words)—must be true story of trip by author or someone known personally by author. E-mail entries only (no mss). **First entry in each category is free; $10 fee for each additional entry (limit 3 entries/category)**. Open to any previously unpublished writer. Defined as having made no more than $750 by creative writing in any previous year." **Deadline: August 31**. Prize 1st Place: $100 in each category; certificates for finalists.

THE PRIZE FOR A FIRST BOOK OF HISTORY

Victorian Premier's Literary Awards, State Government of Victoria, State Library of Victoria, 328 Swanston St. C, Melbourne VIC 3000 Australia. (61)(3)8664-7277. E-mail: pla@slv.vic.gov.au. Website: www.slv.vic.gov.au/pla. **Contact:** Project Officer. "Biennial prize for an author's first solely written history book published during the eligible period. Not offered in 2009. Authors must be Australian citizens or permanent residents." **Deadline: Usually in May (but not offered in 2009)**. Prize AUD $15,000
Tips "Guidelines and entry forms available on our website."

THE PRIZE FOR SCIENCE WRITING

Victorian Premier's Literary Awards, State Government of Australia, State Library of Victoria, 328 Swanston St. C, Melbourne VIC 3000 Australia. (61)(3)8664-7277. E-mail: pla@slv.vic.gov.au. Website: www.slv.vic.gov.au/pla. **Contact:** Project Officer. "Biennial prize (held in odd-numbered years) for popular science books for nonspecialist readers published May 1-April 30. The prize aims to encourage discussion and understanding of scientific ideas in their broadest sense in the wider community and nurture a culture of innovation in Victoria. Authors must be Australian citizens or permanent residents." **Deadline: Usually May.** Prize AUD $15,000
Tips "See guidelines and entry forms on our website."

JAMES A. RAWLEY PRIZE

Organization of American Historians, P.O. Box 5457, 112 N. Bryan Ave., Bloomington IN 47408-5457. (812)855-7311. Fax: (812)855-0696. **Contact:** Award and Prize Committee Coordinator. "Offered annually for a book dealing with the history of race relations in the US. Books must have been published in the current calendar year. Guidelines available online." **Deadline: October 1; books to be published after October 1 of the calendar year may be submitted as page proofs.** Prize $1,000

PHILLIP D. REED MEMORIAL AWARD FOR OUTSTANDING WRITING ON THE SOUTHERN ENVIRONMENT

Southern Environmental Law Center, 201 W. Main St., Suite 14, Charlottesville VA 22902-5065. (434)977-4090. Fax: (434)977-1483. E-mail: cmccue@selcva.org. **Contact:** Cathryn McCue, writing award coor. Offered annually for nonfiction pieces that most effectively tell stories about the South's environment. Categories include Journalism and Book. Entries must have been published during the previous calendar year and have a minimum of 3,000 words. Guidelines online or for SASE. **Deadline: early January**. Prize $1,000 for winner in each category. See www.southernenvironment.org/about/reed_award/.

EVELYN RICHARDSON NONFICTION AWARD

Writers' Federation of Nova Scotia, 1113 Marginal Rd., Halifax NS B3H 4P7 Canada. (902)423-8116. Fax: (902)422-0881. E-mail: talk@writers.ns.ca. **Contact:** Jane Buss, executive director. "This annual award is named for Nova Scotia writer Evelyn Richardson, whose book *We Keep a Light* won the Governor General's Literary Award for nonfiction in 1945. There is **no entry fee** or form. Full-length books of nonfiction written by Nova Scotians, and published as a whole for the first time in the previous calendar year, are eligible. Publishers: Send 4 copies and a letter attesting to the author's status as a Nova Scotian, and the author's current mailing address and telephone number.: **Deadline: First Friday in December**. Prize $2,000.

THE CORNELIUS RYAN AWARD

The Overseas Press Club of America, 40 W. 45th St., New York NY 10036. (212)626-9220. Fax: (212)626-9210. **Contact:** Sonya Fry, executive director. Offered annually for best nonfiction book on international affairs. Generally publishers nominate the work, but writers may also submit in their own name. The work must be published and on the subject of foreign affairs. **Deadline: End of January**. **Charges $175 fee.** Prize $1,000 and a certificate

FRANCIS B. SIMKINS AWARD

Southern Historical Association, Dept. of History, University of Georgia, Athens GA 30602-1602. (706)542-8848. Fax: (706)542-2455. Estab. 1934. Editor: John B. Boles. The award is sponsored jointly with Longwood College. Offered in odd-numbered years for recognition of the best first book by an author in the field of Southern history over a 2-year period. **Deadline: March 1**.

CHARLES S. SYDNOR AWARD

Southern Historical Association, Dept. of History, University of Georgia, Athens GA 30602. (706)542-8848. Fax: (706)542-2455. **Contact:** Southern Historical Association. Offered in even-numbered years for recognition of a distinguished book in Southern history published in odd-numbered years. Publishers usually submit books. **Deadline: March 1**.

FREDERICK JACKSON TURNER AWARD

Organization of American Historians, P.O. Box 5457, 112 N. Bryan Ave., Bloomington IN 47408-7311. (812)855-9852. Fax: (812)855-0696. **Contact:** Award and Prize Committee Coordinator. "Offered annually for an author's first book on some significant phase of American history and also to the press that submits and publishes it. The entry must comply with the following rules: the work must be the first book-length study of history published by the author; if the author has a PhD, he/she must have received it no earlier than 7 years prior to submission of the ms for publication; the work must be published in the calendar year before the award is given; the work must deal with some significant phase of American history. Guidelines available online." **Deadline: October 1**. Prize $1,000

WESTERN WRITERS OF AMERICA

MSC06 3770, 1 University of New Mexico, Albuquerque NM 87131-0001. (505)277-5234. Fax: (505)277-5275. E-mail: wwa@unm.edu. **Contact:** Paul Hutton, exec. dir. "17 Spur Award categories in various aspects of the American West."

THE ELIE WIESEL PRIZE IN ETHICS ESSAY CONTEST

The Elie Wiesel Foundation for Humanity, 555 Madison Ave., 20th Floor, New York NY 10022. Fax: (212)490-6006. Estab. 1989. This annual competition is intended to challenge undergraduate juniors and seniors in colleges and universities throughout the US to analyze ethical questions and concerns facing them in today's complex society. All students are encouraged to write thought-provoking, personal essays. **Deadline: December 9**. Prize 1st Prize: $5,000; 2nd Prize: $2,500; 3rd Prize: $1,500; Honorable Mentions (2): $500. a distinguished panel of readers who evaluate all contest entries. A jury, including Elie Wiesel, chooses the winners.

WRITERS' JOURNAL ANNUAL SCIENCE FICTION/FANTASY CONTEST

Val-Tech Media, P.O. Box 394, Perham MN 56573. (218)346-7921. Fax: (218)346-7924. E-mail: writersjournal@writersjournal.com. **Contact:** Leon Ogroske. Offered annually for unpublished work (maximum 2,000 words). No e-mail submissions accepted. Guidelines for SASE or online. **Deadline: November 30**. **Charges $7 fee.** Prize 1st Place: $250; 2nd Place: $100; 3rd Place: $50, plus honorable mentions. Prize-winning stories and selected honorable mentions will be published in *Writer's Journal* magazine

THE WRITERS' TRUST NONFICTION PRIZE

The Writers' Trust of Canada, 90 Richmond St. E., Suite 200, Toronto ON M5C 1P1 Canada. (416)504-8222. Fax: (416)504-9090. E-mail: info@writerstrust.com. **Contact:** Amanda Hopkins. "Offered annually for a work of nonfiction published in the previous year. Award presented at The Writers' Trust Awards event held in Toronto each Fall. Open to Canadian citizens and permanent residents only." Prize $25,000 (Canadian), and $3,500 to four finalists.

WRITING FOR CHILDREN & YOUNG ADULTS

ASTED/GRAND PRIX DE LITTERATURE JEUNESSE DU QUEBEC-ALVINE-BELISLE

Association pour l'avancement des sciences et des techniques de la documentation, 2065 Parthenais, #387, Montreal QC H2K 3TI Canada. (514)281-5012. Fax: (514)281-8219. E-mail: info@asted.org. Website: www.asted.org. Prize granted for the best work in youth literature edited in French in the Quebec Province. Authors and editors can participate in the contest. Offered annually for books published during the preceding year. **Deadline: June 1**. Prize $1,000.

Tips "French translations of other languages are not accepted."

THE GEOFFREY BILSON AWARD FOR HISTORICAL FICTION FOR YOUNG PEOPLE

The Canadian Children's Book Centre, 40 Orchard View Blvd., Suite 101, Toronto ON M4R 1B9 Canada. (416)975-0010. Fax: (416)975-8970. Website: www.bookcentre.ca. "Created in Geoffrey Bilson's memory in 1988. Offered annually for a previously published 'outstanding work of historical fiction for young people by a Canadian author.' Open to Canadian citizens and residents of Canada for at least 2 years." **Deadline:December 15**. Prize $5,000. a jury selected by the Canadian Children's Book Centre.

Tips "Please visit website for submission guidelines and eligibility criteria."

BOOKTRUST EARLY YEARS AWARDS

c/o Booktrust, Book House, 45 E. Hill, Wandsworth, London SW18 2QZ United Kingdom. Fax: (44)(208)516-2978. E-mail: tarryn@booktrust.org.uk. Website: www.booktrust.org.uk. **Contact:** Tarryn McKay. Estab. 1999. "Annual awards are given to the best books, first published in the UK between September 1 and the following August 31, in the opinion of the judges in each category. The categories are: Baby Book Award, Pre-School Award, and Best Emerging Illustrator Award. Authors and illustrators must be of British nationality, or other nationals who have been residents in the British Isles for at least 5 years. Books can be any format." **Deadline: May**. Prize £2,000 and a crystal award to each winner. Money to be shared between author and illustrator. In addition, the publisher receives a crystal award naming them as one of The Booktrust Early Years Awards Publisher of the Year, and the best emerging illustrator receives a piece of original artwork.

DELACORTE PRESS CONTEST FOR A FIRST YOUNG ADULT NOVEL

Random House Children's Books/Random House, Inc., 1745 Broadway, 9th Floor, New York NY 10019. Offered annually to encourage the writing of contemporary young adult fiction. Open to US and Canadian writers who have not previously published a young adult novel. Guidelines on website. **Deadline: October 1-December 31 (postmarked)**. Prize $1,500 cash, publication, and $7,500 advance against royalties the editors of Delacorte Press Books for Young Readers.

DELACORTE YEARLING CONTEST FOR A FIRST MIDDLE-GRADE NOVEL

Delacorte Press Books for Young Readers, Random House, Inc., 1745 Broadway, New York NY 10019. (212)782-9000. Fax: (212)782-8234. Estab. 1992. Offered annually for an unpublished fiction ms (96-160 pages) suitable for readers 9-12 years of age, set in North America, either contemporary or historical. Guidelines available online. **Deadline: April 1-June 30**. Prize $1,500, publication, and $7,500 advance against royalties. World rights acquired

THE NORMA FLECK AWARD FOR CANADIAN CHILDREN'S NONFICTION

The Canadian Children's Book Centre, 40 Orchard View Blvd., Suite 101, Toronto ON M4R 1B9 Canada. (416)975-0010. Fax: (416)975-8970. E-mail: info@bookcentre.ca. **Contact:** Shannon Howe, program coordinator. "The Norma Fleck Award was established by the Fleck Family Foundation and the Canadian Children's Book Centre in 1999 to recognize and raise the profile of exceptional Canadian nonfiction books for young people." Presented annually for books published between January 1 and December 31 of the previous calendar year. Open to Canadian citizens or landed immigrants. **Deadline: January 15**. Prize $10,000 Judged by a jury selected by the Canadian Children's Book Centre.

FRIENDS OF THE AUSTIN PUBLIC LIBRARY AWARD FOR BEST CHILDREN'S AND BEST YOUNG ADULT'S BOOK

6335 W. Northwest Hwy, #618, Dallas TX 75225. (214)363-7253. E-mail: franvick@aol.com. **Contact:** Fran Vick. Offered annually for work published January 1-December 31 of previous year to recognize the best book for children and young people. Writer must have been born in Texas, have lived in the state for at least 2 consecutive years at one time, or the subject matter must be associated with the state. See website for judges and further information. **Deadline: First week of January**. Prize $500 for each award winner.

GOVERNOR GENERAL'S LITERARY AWARD FOR CHILDREN'S LITERATURE

Canada Council for the Arts, 350 Albert St., P.O. Box 1047, Ottawa ON K1P 5V8 Canada. (613)566-4414, ext. 5573. Fax: (613)566-4410. Offered for the best English-language and the best French-language works of children's literature by a Canadian in 2 categories: text and illustration. Publishers submit titles for consideration. **Deadline: March 15, June 1, or August 1, depending on the book's publication date**. Prize Each laureate receives $25,000; non-winning finalists receive $1,000.

INTERNATIONAL READING ASSOCIATION CHILDREN'S AND YOUNG ADULTS' BOOK AWARDS

International Reading Association, P.O. Box 8139, Newark DE 19714-8139. (302)731-1600, ext. 221. Fax: (302)731-1057. Website: www.reading.org. "Offered annually for an author's first or second published book in fiction and nonfiction in 3 categories: primary (preschool-age 8), intermediate (ages 9-13), and young adult (ages 14-17). Recognizes newly published authors who show unusual promise in the children's book field. Guidelines and deadlines for SASE." Prize $1,000, and a medal for each category

THE VICKY METCALF AWARD FOR CHILDREN'S LITERATURE

The Writers' Trust of Canada, 90 Richmond St. E., Suite 200, Toronto ON M5C 1P1 Canada. (416)504-8222. Fax: (416)504-9090. E-mail: info@writerstrust.com. **Contact:** Amanda Hopkins. The Metcalf Award is presented to a Canadian writer for a body of work in children's literature at The Writers' Trust Awards event in Toronto each Fall. Open to Canadian residents only. Prize $20,000

MILKWEED PRIZE FOR CHILDREN'S LITERATURE

Milkweed Editions, 1011 Washington Ave. S., Suite 300, Minneapolis MN 55415. (612)332-3192. Fax: (612)215-2550. E-mail: editor@milkweed.org. **Contact:** The Editors. Estab. 1993. Annual prize for unpublished works. The Milkweed Prize for Children's Literature will be awarded to the best ms for children ages 8-13 that Milkweed accepts for publication during each calendar year by a writer not previously published by Milkweed Editions. Mss should be of high literary quality and must be double-spaced, 90-200 pages in length. All mss submitted to Milkweed will automatically be considered for the prize. Submission directly to the contest is not necessary. Must review guidelines, available online or for SASE. Catalog for $1.50 postage. Prize $10,000 advance on royalties agreed upon at the time of acceptance.

MUNICIPAL CHAPTER OF TORONTO IODE JEAN THROOP BOOK AWARD

Toronto Municipal Chapter IODE, 40 St. Clair Ave. E., Suite 200, Toronto ON M4T 1M9 Canada. (416)925-5078. Fax: (416)925-5127. **Contact:** Theo Heras (Lillian Smith Library, 239 College St., Toronto). Offered annually for childrens' books published by a Canadian publisher. Author and illustrator must be Canadian citizens residing in or around Toronto. **Deadline: November 1**. Prize $1,000

PATERSON PRIZE FOR BOOKS FOR YOUNG PEOPLE

The Poetry Center at Passaic County Community College, One College Blvd., Paterson NJ 07505-1179. (973)684-6555. Fax: (973)523-6085. E-mail: mgillan@pccc.edu. Website: www.pccc.edu/poetry. **Contact:** Maria Mazziotti Gillan, exec. dir. "Offered annually for books published the previous calendar year. Three categories: pre-kindergarten-grade 3; grades 4-6; grades 7-12. Open to any writer." **Deadline: March 15**. Prize $500 in each category.

PEN/PHYLLIS NAYLOR WORKING WRITER FELLOWSHIP

PEN American Center, 588 Broadway, Suite 303, New York NY 10012. (212)334-1660, ext. 108. Fax: (212)334-2181. E-mail: awards@pen.org. **Contact:** Nick Burd. Offered annually to a writer of children's or young-adult fiction in financial need, who has published 2 books for children and young adults which may have been well reviewed and warmly received by literary critics, but which have not generated sufficient income to support the author. Previous works must be released through a US publisher. Writers must be nominated by an editor or fellow writer. **Deadline: January 15**. Prize $5,000

PRIX ALVINE-BELISLE

Association pour L'avancement des sciences et des techniques de la documentation, ASTED, Inc., 2065 Parthenau, #387, Montreal QC H2K 3T1 Canada. (514)281-5012. Fax: (514)281-8219. E-mail: info@asted.org. **Contact:** Francois Farley-Chevier, executive director. Offered annually for work published the year before the award to promote authors of French youth literature in Canada. **Deadline: April 1**. Prize $1,000

SYDNEY TAYLOR MANUSCRIPT COMPETITION

Association of Jewish Libraries, Sydney Taylor Manuscript Award Competition, 204 Park St., Montclair NJ 07042. E-mail: stmacajl@aol.com. **Contact:** Aileen Grossberg. Material should be a work of fiction in English, with universal appeal of Jewish content for readers aged 8-11 years. "It should deepen the understanding of Judaism for all children, Jewish and nonJewish, and reveal positive aspects of Jewish life." No poems or plays. Length: 64-200 pages. Rules, entry forms available at website: www.jewishlibraries.org. Judged by 5 AJL member librarians. Open to any writer. Must be unpublished. **Deadline: December 15**. Prize $1,000

RITA WILLIAMS YOUNG ADULT PROSE PRIZE

National League of American Pen Women, Nob Hill, San Francisco Branch, Category of the Soul-Making Literary Competition, The Webhallow House, 1544 Sweetwood Dr., Broadmoor Vig. CA 94015-2029. E-mail: pennobhill@aol.com. **Contact:** Eileen Malone. "Up to 3,000 words in story, essay, journal entry, creative nonfiction, or memoir by writer in grades 9-12. Indicate age and category on each first page. Identify with 3X5 card only. Open annually to young adult writers." **Deadline: November 30**. **Charges $5/entry (make checks payable to NLAPW, Nob Hill Branch).** Prize 1st Place: $100; 2nd Place: $50; 3rd Place: $25.

PAUL A. WITTY SHORT STORY AWARD
Executive Office, International Reading Association, P.O. Box 8139, Newark DE 19714-8139. (302)731-1600, ext. 221. Fax: (302)731-1057. E-mail: exec@reading.org. "Offered to reward author of an original short story published in a children's periodical during 2009 which serves as a literary standard that encourages young readers to read periodicals. Write for guidelines or download from website." **Deadline: December 1**. Prize $1,000

WORK-IN-PROGRESS GRANT
Society of Children's Book Writers and Illustrators (SCBWI), 8271 Beverly Blvd., Los Angeles CA 90048. (323)782-1010. E-mail: scbwi@scbwi.org. Website: www.scbwi.org. Four grants—1 designated specifically for a contemporary novel for young people, one for nonfiction, one for an unpublished writer, one general fiction—to assist SCBWI members in the completion of a specific project. Open to SCBWI members only. **Applications received only between February 15 and March 15**.

WRITE A STORY FOR CHILDREN COMPETITION
Academy of Children's Writers, P.O. Box 95, Huntingdon Cambridgeshire PE28 5RL England. Phone/Fax: (44) (148)783-2752. E-mail: enquiries@childrens-writers.co.uk. **Contact:** Contest Director. Annual contest for the best unpublished short story writer for children. Guidelines and entry forms online or send SAE/IRC. Open to any unpublished writer over the age of 18. **Deadline: March 31. Charges $10 (US) Bill. No checks; £2.70 (UK).** Prize 1st Place: £2,000; 2nd Place: £300; 3rd Place: £200. a panel appointed by the Academy of Children's Writers.

WRITERS' LEAGUE OF TEXAS CHILDREN'S BOOK AWARDS
Writers' League of Texas, 1501 W. Fifth St., Suite E-2, Austin TX 78703. (512)499-8914. Fax: (512)499-0441. E-mail: wlt@writersleague.org. Website: www.writersleague.org. **Contact:** Kristy Bordine, program and membership coordinator. Offered annually for work published January 1-December 31. Honors 2 outstanding books for children. Writer's League of Texas dues may accompany entry fee. **Deadline: April 31. Charges $25 fee.** Prize Two prizes of $1,000 and trophies.

WRITING FOR CHILDREN COMPETITION
The Writers' Union of Canada, 90 Richmond St. E., Suite 200, Toronto ON M5C 1P1. (416)703-8982, ext. 226. Fax: (416)504-9090. E-mail: competitions@writersunion.ca. **Contact:** Competitions Coordinator. Offered annually to discover developing Canadian writers of unpublished children's/young adult fiction or nonfiction. Open to Canadian citizens or landed immigrants who have not been published in book format by a commercial or university press in any genre and who do not currently have a contract with a publisher. **Deadline: April 24. Charges $15 entry fee.** Prize $1,500; the winner and 11 finalists' pieces will be submitted to 3 Canadian publishers of children's books

GENERAL

ARTSLINK PROJECTS AWARD
CEC Artslink, 435 Hudson St., 8th Floor, New York NY 10014. (212)643-1985, ext. 21. Fax: (212)643-1996. E-mail: tmiller@cecartslink.org. **Contact:** Tamalyn Miller, program man. "Offered annually to enable artists of all media to work in Central and Eastern Europe, Russia, Central Asia and the Caucasus with colleagues there on collaborative projects. Check website for deadline and other information." Prize up to $10,000.

AUSTRALIAN CHRISTIAN BOOK OF THE YEAR AWARD
Australian Christian Literature Society, c/o SPCK-Australia, P.O. Box 198, Forest Hill Victoria 3131 Australia. E-mail: acls@spcka.org.au. **Contact:** Book of the Year Coordinator. "Annual contest for an Australian Christian book published between April 1 and March 31. Book must be submitted by a publisher." Book must be submitted by a publisher. **Deadline: March 31. Charges $50 per title.**

AUSTRALIAN SOCIETY OF INDEXERS MEDAL
P.O. Box 680, Belgrave VIC 3160 Australia. E-mail: simmo27au@yahoo.com.au. Website: www.aussi.org. **Contact:** John Simken. "Award presented to the most outstanding index to a book or periodical compiled in Australia or New Zealand even though the text to which it refers may have originated elsewhere. The index must be in print and published after 2004. The judges may also make 'highly commended' awards. **Deadline: December 14**. Prize Certificate

THE BOARDMAN TASKER AWARD FOR MOUNTAIN LITERATURE
The Boardman Tasker Charitable Trust, Pound House, Llangennith, Swansea West Glamorgan SA3 1JQ United Kingdom. Phone/Fax: (44)(179)238-6215. E-mail: margaretbody@lineone.net. **Contact:** Margaret Body.

"Offered annually to reward a work of nonfiction or fiction, in English or in translation, which has made an outstanding contribution to mountain literature. Books must be published in the UK between November 1 of previous year and October 31 of year of the prize. Writers may obtain information, but entry is by publishers only. No restriction of nationality, but work must be published or distributed in the UK. Guidelines for SASE or online." **Deadline: August 15.** Prize £3,000.

DAFOE BOOK PRIZE

J.W. Dafoe Foundation, 351 University College, University of Manitoba, Winnipeg MB R3T 2M8 Canada. **Contact:** Dr. James Fergusson. The Dafoe Book Prize was established to honor John Dafoe, editor of the *Winnipeg Free Press* from 1900 to 1944, and is awarded each year to the book that best contributes to our understanding of Canada and/or its relations abroad by a Canadian or author in residence. Books must be published January-December of previous publishing year — ie 2009 Award is for books published in 2008. Co-authored books are eligible, but not edited books consisting of chapters from many different authors. Submit 4 copies of book. Authors must be Canadian citizens or landed immigrants. **Deadline: December 6.** Prize $10,000. board members and academics.

THE DEBUT DAGGER

Crime Writers' Association, New Writing Competition, P.O. Box 273, Borehamwood Herts WD6 2XA England. Website: www.thecwa.co.uk. **Contact:** L. Evans. "An annual competition for unpublished crime writers. Submit the opening 3,000 words of a crime novel, plus a 500-1,000 word synopsis of its continuance. Open to any writer who has not had a novel commercially published in any genre." Entries will not be returned. **Charges fees vary each year.** Prize See website for details and for prize information

ROSALIE FLEMING MEMORIAL HUMOR PRIZE

National League of American Pen Women, The Webhallow House, 1544 Sweetwood Dr., Broadmoor Village CA 94015-2029. E-mail: pennobhill@aol.com. **Contact:** Eileen Malone. "Make judge Mary Eastham laugh in 2,500 words or less. Must be original and unpublished. Any form (poem, story, essay, etc.) is acceptable. Only 1 piece allowed/entry. Indicate category on first page. Identify only with 3X5 card." **Deadline: November 30. Charges $5/entry (make checks payable to NLAPW, Nob Hill Branch).** Prize 1st Place: $100; 2nd Place: $50; 3rd Place: $45.

THE FOUNTAINHEAD ESSAY CONTEST

The Ayn Rand Institute, P.O. Box 57044, Irvine CA 92619-7044. E-mail: essay@aynrand.org. Estab. 1985. "Offered annually to encourage analytical thinking and excellence in writing, and to expose students to the philosophic ideas of Ayn Rand. For information contact your English teacher or guidance counselor, or visit our website. Length: 800-1,600 words. Open to 11th and 12th graders." **Deadline: April 25.** Prize 1st Place: $10,000; 2nd Place (5): $2,000; 3rd Place (10): $1,000; Finalist (45): $100; Semifinalist (175): $50.

THE JANE GESKE AWARD

Prairie Schooner, 201 Andrews Hall, P.O. Box 880334, Lincoln NE 68588-0334. (402)472-0911. Fax: (402)472-9771. E-mail: jenglehardt2@unl.edu. **Contact:** Hilda Raz. Offered annually for work published in *Prairie Schooner* in the previous year. Prize $250.

THE GLENNA LUSCHEI PRAIRIE SCHOONER AWARD

Prairie Schooner, 201 Andrews Hall, P.O. Box 880334, Lincoln NE 68588-0334. (402)472-0911. Fax: (402)472-9771. E-mail: jengelhardt2@unl.edu. **Contact:** Hilda Raz. "Offered annually for work published in *Prairie Schooner* in the previous year." Prize $1,000.

OHIOANA WALTER RUMSEY MARVIN GRANT

Ohioana Library Association, 274 E. First Ave., Suite 300, Columbus OH 43201. (614)466-3831. Fax: (614)728-6974. E-mail: ohioana@ohioana.org. **Contact:** Linda Hengst. Offered annually to encourage young writers; open to writers under age 30 who have not published a book. Entrants must have been born in Ohio or have lived in Ohio for at least 5 years. Enter 1-6 pieces of prose totaling 10-60 pages (double space, 12 pt. font). **Deadline: January 31.** Prize $1,000.

THE PRAIRIE SCHOONER READERS' CHOICE AWARDS

Prairie Schooner, 201 Andrews Hall, P.O. Box 880334, Lincoln NE 68588-0334. (402)472-0911. Fax: (402)472-9771. E-mail: jengelhardt2@unl.edu. "Annual awards (usually 4-6) for work published in *Prairie Schooner* in the previous year." Prize $250.

PUSHCART PRIZE

Pushcart Press, P.O. Box 380, Wainscott NY 11975. (631)324-9300. Website: www.pushcartprize.com. **Contact:** Bill Henderson. Estab. 1976. All short stories, poetry, and essays must be nominated by an editor from a publishing house or little magazine. **Deadline: December 1.**

DAVID RAFFELOCK AWARD FOR PUBLISHING EXCELLENCE

National Writers Association, 10940 S. Parker Rd., #508, Parker CO 80134. (303)841-0246. Fax: (303)841-2607. E-mail: natlwritersassn@hotmail.com. Website: www.nationalwriters.com. **Contact:** Sandy Whelchel. "Contest is offered annually for books published the previous year." Its purpose is to assist published authors in marketing their works and to reward outstanding published works. **Deadline: May 15. Charges $100 fee.** Prize Publicity tour, including airfare, valued at $5,000.

JOHN LLEWELLYN RHYS PRIZE

Booktrust Book House, 45 E. Hill, Wandsworth, London SW18 2QZ United Kingdom. Fax: (44)(208)516-2978. E-mail: tarryn@booktrust.org.uk. **Contact:** Tarryn McKay. The prize was founded in 1942 by Jane Oliver, the widow of John Llewellyn Rhys, a young writer killed in action in World War II. This is one of Britain's oldest and most prestigious literary awards, with an unequalled reputation of singling out the fine young writers—poets, novelists, biographers, and travel writers—early in their careers. Entries can be any work of literature written by a British or Commonwealth writer aged 35 or under at the time of publication. Books must be written in English and published in the UK between January 1 and December 31 the year of the prize. Translations are not eligible. **Deadline: August**. Prize £5,000 to the winner and £500 to shortlisted authors.

ROCKY MOUNTAIN ARTISTS' BOOK COMPETITION

Hemingway Western Studies Center, Boise State University, 1910 University Dr., Boise ID 83725. (208)426-1999. Fax: (208)426-4373. E-mail: ttrusky@boisestate.edu. Website: www.boisestate.edu/hemingway/. **Contact:** Tom Trusky. "Offered annually to publish multiple edition artists' books of special interest to Rocky Mountain readers. Topics must be public issues (race, gender, environment, etc.). Authors may hail from Topeka or Ulan Bator, but their books must initially have regional appeal. Acquires first rights. Open to any writer." **Deadline: September 1-December 1**. Prize $500, publication, and standard royalties.

THE GROLLO RUZZENE FOUNDATION PRIZE FOR WRITING ABOUT ITALIANS IN AUSTRALIA

Victorian Premier's Literary Awards, State Government of Australia, State Library of Victoria, 328 Swanston St. C, Melbourne VIC 3000 Australia. (61)(3)8664-7277. E-mail: pla@slv.vic.gov.au. **Contact:** Project Officer. "Biennial prize (held in odd-numbered years) for a ms published May 1-April 30 that encourages people from all backgrounds to write about the experiences of Italians in Australia. Migration studies, histories, travel narratives, published plays and screenplays, biographies, and collections of poems/novels for adults/children are accepted. Authors must be Australian citizens or permanent residents." **Deadline: Usually May each year**. Prize $15,000

Tips "Guidelines and entry forms available on our website."

TEXAS INSTITUTE OF LETTERS AWARD FOR MOST SIGNIFICANT SCHOLARLY BOOK

The Texas Institute of Letters, (214)363-7253. E-mail: dpayne@mail.smu.edu. "Offered annually for submissions published January 1-December 31 of previous year to recognize the writer of the book making the most important contribution to knowledge. Writer must have been born in Texas, have lived in the state at least 2 consecutive years at some time, or the subject matter of the book should be associated with the state. See website for guidelines." **Generally one week after Jan. 1.** Prize $2.500

THE WRITERS' TRUST NOTABLE AUTHOR AWARD

The Writers' Trust of Canada, 90 Richmond St. E., Suite 200, Toronto ON M5C 1P1 Canada. (416)504-8222. Fax: (416)504-9090. E-mail: info@writerstrust.com. **Contact:** James Davies. The Writers' Trust Notable Author Award is presented annually at The Writers' Trust Awards Event, held in Toronto each Spring, to a Canadian writer for a body of work in hope of continued contribution to the richness of Canadian literature. Open to Canadian citizens and permanent residents only. Prize $25,000

FRED WHITEHEAD AWARD FOR BEST DESIGN OF A TRADE BOOK

Texas Institute of Letters, 6335 W. Northwest Hwy., #618, Dallas TX 75225. (214)363-7253. E-mail: franvick@aol.com. **Contact:** Fran Vick, secretary. Offered annually for the best design for a trade book. Open to Texas residents or those who have lived in Texas for 2 consecutive years. See website for guidelines. **Deadline: January 3**. Prize $750

WHITING WRITERS' AWARDS

Mrs. Giles Whiting Foundation, 1133 Avenue of the Americas, 22nd Floor, New York NY 10036-6710. Estab. 1985. "The Foundation gives annually $50,000 each to up to 10 writers of poetry, fiction, nonfiction, and plays. The awards place special emphasis on exceptionally promising emerging talent. Direct applications and informal nominations are not accepted by the Foundation. Literary professionals are contacted by the foundation to make nominations." 6-7 writers of distinction and accomplishment.

WRITERS' LEAGUE OF TEXAS MANUSCRIPT CONTEST

Writers' League of Texas, 611 S. Congress Ave., Suite 130, Austin TX 78704. (512)499-8914. Fax: (512)499-0441.

E-mail: wlt@writersleague.org. **Contact:** Kristy Bordine. Annual contest for unpublished work in 9 categories: narrative nonfiction, mainstream fiction, mystery, thriller/action-adventure, romance, science fiction/fantasy, children's middle grade, young adult, and historical fiction. Guidelines for SASE or online. **Deadline: March 7, 2008. Charges $50 fee for score sheet.** Prize Recognition at Agents & Editors Conference, and meeting with an agent who selected winner.

JOURNALISM

AAAS KAVLI SCIENCE JOURNALISM AWARDS

American Association for the Advancement of Science, Office of News and Information, 1200 New York Ave. NW, Washington DC 20005. Website: www.aaas.org/SJAwards. **Contact:** Awards Coordinator. Estab. 1945. Offered annually for previously published work to reward excellence in reporting on the sciences, engineering, and mathematics. Sponsored by The Kavli Foundation. **Deadline: August 1.** Prize $3,000 and a trip to AAAS Annual Meeting committees of reporters and editors.

AMY WRITING AWARDS

The Amy Foundation, P.O. Box 16091, Lansing MI 48901. (517)323-6233. Fax: (517)321-2572. E-mail: amyfoundtn@aol.com. Estab. 1985. Offered annually to recognize creative, skillful writing that applies biblical principles. Submitted articles must be published in a secular, non-religious publication (either printed or online) and must be reinforced with at least one passage of scripture. The article must have been published between January 1 and December 31 of the current calendar year. **Deadline: January 31.** Prize 1st Prize: $10,000; 2nd Prize: $5,000; 3rd Prize: $4,000; 4th Prize: $3,000; 5th Prize: $2,000; and 10 prizes of $1,000

ERIK BARNOUW AWARD

Organization of American Historians, P.O. Box 5457, 112 N. Bryan Ave., Bloomington IN 47407-5457. (812)855-7311. Fax: (812)855-0696. **Contact:** Award & Prize Committee Coordinator. Estab. 1983. "One or 2 awards are given annually in recognition of outstanding reporting or programming on network or cable television, or in documentary film, concerned with American history, the study of American history, and/or the promotion of history. Entries must have been released the year of the contest. Guidelines available online." **Deadline: December 1.** Prize $1,000 (or $500 should 2 films be selected)

THE WHITMAN BASSOW AWARD

Overseas Press Club of America, 40 W. 45th St., New York NY 10036. (212)626-9220. Fax: (212)626-9210. **Contact:** Sonya Fry, executive director. Offered annually for best reporting in any medium on international environmental issues. Work must be published by US-based publications or broadcast. **Deadline: End of January. Charges $175 fee.** Prize $1,000 and a certificate

HEYWOOD BROUN AWARD

The Newspaper Guild-CWA, 501 Third St. NW, Washington DC 20001-2797. (202)434-7177. Fax: (202)434-1472. E-mail: azipser@cwa-union.org. **Contact:** Andy Zipser. Offered annually for works published the previous year. This annual competition is intended to encourage and recognize individual journalistic achievement by members of the working media, particularly if it helps right a wrong or correct an injustice. First consideration will be given to entries on behalf of individuals or teams of no more than 2. Guidelines for SASE or online. **Deadline: Last Friday in January.** Prize $5,000 and plaque.

CONGRESSIONAL FELLOWSHIP PROGRAM

American Political Science Association, 1527 New Hampshire Ave. NW, Washington DC 20036-1206. (202)483-2512. Fax: (202)483-2657. **Contact:** Program Coordinator. Estab. 1953. Offered annually for professional journalists who have 2-10 years of full-time professional experience in newspaper, magazine, radio, or television reporting at time of application to learn more about the legislative process through direct participation. Visit our website for deadlines. Open to journalists and scholars. **Deadline: December 1.** Prize $38,000, and travel allowance for 3 weeks' orientation and legislation aide assignments December-August

CONSUMER JOURNALISM AWARD

National Press Club, General Manager's Office, National Press Bldg., 529 14th St. NW, Washington DC 20045. (202)662-8744. Fax: (202)662-7512. E-mail: jbooze@npcpress.org. **Contact:** Joann Booze. "Offered annually to recognize excellence in reporting on consumer topics in the following categories: newspapers, periodicals, television, and radio. Guidelines available online." **Deadline: May 1.** Prize $750 for each category

ANN COTTRELL FREE ANIMAL REPORTING AWARD

National Press Club, General Manager's Office, National Press Bldg., 529 14th St. NW, Washington DC 20045. (202)662-8744. Fax: (202)662-7512. E-mail: jbooze@npcpress.org. **Contact:** Joann Booze. "Award honors excellence in reporting about animals. Established by the family of journalist and longtime Press Club member Ann Cottrell Free, who wrote extensively about animals and their welfare, this prize recognizes serious work by journalists that informs and educates the public about threats facing animals." Guidelines available online. Prize $750

THE JOHN CURTIN PRIZE FOR JOURNALISM

Victorian Premier's Literary Awards, State Goverment of Victoria, State Library of Victoria, 328 Swanston St. C, Melbourne VIC 3000 Australia. (61)(3)8664-7277. E-mail: pla@lsv.vic.gov.au. Website: www.slv.vic.gov.au/pla. **Contact:** Project Officer. "Annual prize in any medium (print or electronic newspaper, journal, or broadcast as a television or radio item) for a piece of journalism about the Australian experience. Must be published May 1-April 30 each year. Authors must be Australian citizens or permanent residents." **Deadline: Usually May each year**. Prize AUD $15,000

Tips "See guidelines and entry forms on our website."

JOAN M. FRIEDENBERG ONLINE JOURNALISM AWARD

National Press Club, General Manager's Office, National Press Bldg., 529 14th St. NW, Washington DC 20045. (202)662-7532. Fax: (202)662-7512. E-mail: jbooze@npcpress.org. **Contact:** Joann Booze. Offered annually in memory of Joan M. Friedenberg "for original reporting and the use of online technology in order to provide a thorough and graphically attractive report. Judges especially interested in the use of multimedia." **Deadline: May 1**. Prize $750

EDWIN M. HOOD AWARD FOR DIPLOMATIC CORRESPONDENCE

General Manager's Office, National Press Club, National Press Bldg., 529 14th St. NW, Washington DC 20045. (202)662-8744. E-mail: jbooze@npcpress.org. **Contact:** Joann Booze. "Offered annually to recognize excellence in reporting on diplomatic and foreign policy issues. Categories: print, online, and broadcast. Guidelines available online." **Deadline: May 1**. Prize $750 in each category.

SANDY HUME MEMORIAL AWARD FOR EXCELLENCE IN POLITICAL JOURNALISM

National Press Club, General Manager's Office, National Press Bldg., 529 14th St. NW, Washington DC 20045. (202)662-8744. Fax: (202)662-7512. E-mail: jbooze@npcpress.org. **Contact:** Joann Booze. Offered annually for work published in the previous calendar year. This award honors excellence and objectivity in political coverage by reporters 34 years old or younger. **Deadline: May 1**. Prize $750

ANSON JONES, M.D. AWARD

Texas Medical Association, 401 W. 15th St., Austin TX 78701-1680. (512)370-1381. Fax: (512)370-1629. E-mail: brent.annear@texmed.org. **Contact:** Brent Annear, media relations manager. "Offered annually to the media of Texas for excellence in communicating health information to the public. Open only to Texas general interest media for work published or aired in Texas during the previous calendar year. Guidelines posted online." **Deadline: January 15**. Prize $1,000 for winners in each of the categories.

FRANK LUTHER MOTT-KAPPA TAU ALPHA RESEARCH AWARD IN JOURNALISM

University of Missouri School of Journalism, 76 Gannett Hall, Columbia MO 65211-1200. (573)882-7685. E-mail: umcjourkta@missouri.edu. **Contact:** Dr. Keith Sanders, exec. dir., Kappa Tau Alpha. "Offered annually for best researched book in mass communication. Submit 6 copies; no forms required." **Deadline: December 7**. Prize $1,000

NEWSLETTER JOURNALISM AWARD

General Manager's Office, National Press Club, National Press Bldg., 529 14th St. NW, Washington DC 20045. (202)662-8744. Website: npc.press.org. "This competition acknowledges excellence in newsletter journalism for best analytical or interpretive reporting piece. Entries must be published by an independent newsletter." Guidelines online. **Deadline: April 1**. Prize $750

PEARL AWARDS FOR OUTSTANDING INTERNATIONAL INVESTIGATIVE REPORTING, DANIEL

International Consortium of Investigative Journalists, A Project of the Center for Public Integrity, 910 17th St. NW, 7th Floor, Washington DC 20006. (202)466-1300. Fax: (202)466-1101. E-mail: mwalker@icij.org. **Contact:** Marina Walker Guevara, Deputy Director. Offered biennially for work produced in print, broadcast, and online media. The story or series must involve reporting in at least two countries and must have been first published or broadcast in general information media between January 1, 2008 and December 31, 2009. **Deadline: January 15, 2010.** Prize Offers Two $5,000 first prizes; one to a U.S.-based reporter or news organization and the other to a non-U.B.-based journalist or news organization.

THE MADELINE DANE ROSS AWARD

Overseas Press Club of America, 40 West 45th Street, New York NY 10036. (212)626-9220. Fax: (212)626-9210. E-mail: sonya@opcofamerica.org. **Contact:** Sonya Fry, Executive Director. "Offered annually for best international reporting in the print medium showing a concern for the human condition. Work must be published by US-based publications or broadcast. Printable application available online." **Deadline: Late January; date changes each year. Charges $175 fee.** Prize $1,000 and certificate

N ARTHUR ROWSE AWARD FOR PRESS CRITICISM

General Manager's Office, National Press Club, National Press Bldg., 529 14th St. NW, Washington DC 20045. (202)662-7532. Website: www.npc.press.org. Offered annually for work published or broadcast the previous calendar year. This award, sponsored by former *US News & World Report* reporter Arthur Rowse, "honors excellence in examining the role and work of the news media. All entries must focus on criticism of journalistic practices or reporting on the industry, and must encourage responsible media behavior." Categories: 1. newspapers, magazines, newsletters, and online. 2. Broadcast. Submit up to 5 articles or broadcasts; must be accompanied by a letter explaining the significance of the work and any subsequent actions resulting from its publication or airing. **Deadline: April 1**. Prize $1,000 in each category

JOSEPH D. RYLE AWARD FOR EXCELLENCE IN WRITING ON THE PROBLEMS OF GERIATRICS

National Press Club, General Manager's Office, National Press Bldg., 529 14th St. NW, Washington DC 20045. (202)662-7532. Fax: (202)662-7512. E-mail: jbooze@npcpress.org. **Contact:** Joann Booze. Offered annually for work published in the previous year. This award honors excellence and objectivity in coverage of the problems faced by the elderly. **Deadline: May 1**. Prize $2,000.

SANOFI PASTEUR MEDAL FOR EXCELLENCE IN HEALTH RESEARCH JOURNALISM

Canadians for Health Research, P.O. Box 126, Westmount QC H3Z 2T1 Canada. (514)398-7478. Fax: (514)398-8361. E-mail: info@chrcrm.org. "Offered annually for work published the previous calendar year in Canadian newspapers or magazines. Applicants must have demonstrated an interest and effort in reporting health research issues within Canada. Guidelines available from CHR or on website." **Deadline: March 12 (postmarked)**. Prize $2,500 bursary and a medal.

SCIENCE IN SOCIETY AWARDS

National Association of Science Writers, Inc., P.O. Box 7905, Berkeley CA 94707. (510)647-9500. E-mail: director@nasw.org. Website: www.nasw.org. **Contact:** Tinsley Davis. Estab. 1972. Offered annually for investigative or interpretive reporting about the sciences and their impact for good and bad. Categories: books, commentary and opinions, Science reporting, and Science reporting with a local or regional focus. Material may be a single article or broadcast, or a series. Works must have been first published or broadcast in North America between June 1 and May 31 of the previous year. **Deadline: February 1**. Prize $1,000, and a certificate of recognition in each category.

SOVEREIGN AWARD

The Jockey Club of Canada, P.O. Box 66, Station B, Etobiwke ON M9W 5K9 Canada. (416)675-7756. Fax: (416)675-6378. E-mail: jockeyclub@bellnet.ca. Website: www.jockeyclubcanada.ca. **Contact:** Bridget Bimm, exec. dir. Estab. 1973. "Offered annually to recognize outstanding achievement in the area of Canadian thoroughbred racing journalism published November 1-October 31 of the previous year." "Submissions for these media awards must be of Canadian Thoroughbred racing or breeding content. They must have appeared in a media outlet recognized by The Jockey Club of Canada. The writer may submit no more than 1 entry/category. A copy of the newspaper article or magazine story must be provided along with a 3.25 disk containing the story in an ASCII style format. Submissions to the photograph category should include a newspaper cut of the photo and 10 8½x11 photos. Submission to the Outstanding Film/Video/Broadcast category should be made by sending a letter detailing what the video is about, the names of the editor, producer, etc., and a VHS or Beta tape of the program, including the date the show aired and where." **Deadline: October 31, 5:00 p.m. (EDT)**. Outstanding Newspaper Article, Outstanding Feature Story, Outstanding Photograph, Outstanding Film/Video/Broadcast.

STANLEY WALKER JOURNALISM AWARD FOR BEST WORK OF JOURNALISM APPEARING IN A NEWSPAPER OR SUNDAY SUPPLEMENT

The Texas Institute of Letters, 6335 W. Northwest Hwy., #618, Dallas TX 75225. (214)363-7253. E-mail: franvick@aol.com. **Contact:** Fran Vick, secretary. Offered annually for work published January 1-December 31 of previous year to recognize the best writing appearing in a daily newspaper. Writer must have been born in Texas, have lived in the state for 2 consecutive years at some time, or the subject matter of the article must be associated with the state. See website for guidelines. **Deadline: First week of January**. Prize $1,000

WASHINGTON REGIONAL REPORTING AWARD

National Press Club, General Manager's Office, National Press Bldg., 529 14th St. NW, Washington DC 20045. (202)662-7532. Fax: (202)662-7512. E-mail: jbooze@npcpress.org. **Contact:** Joann Booze. "This prize recognizes the work of Washington-based regional reporters who provide a clear understanding of events, issues and politics of importance to a city, state or region. This contest honors reporters who demonstrate excellence and versatility in covering Washington from a local angle." **Deadline: May 1**. Prize $750

TRANSLATION

AMERICAN TRANSLATORS ASSOCIATION STUDENT TRANSLATION AWARD

American Translators Association, 225 Reinekers Lane, Suite 590, Alexandria VA 22314. (703)683-6100. Fax: (703)683-6122. E-mail: ata@atanet.org. Grant-in-aid is granted for a promising literary or sci-tech translation, or translation-related project to an unpublished student enrolled in a translation program at a US college or university. Must be sponsored by a faculty member. **Deadline: April 16**. Prize Certificate of recognition and up to $500 toward expenses for attending the ATA Annual Conference

ASF TRANSLATION PRIZE

The American-Scandinavian Foundation, 58 Park Ave., New York NY 10016-3007. (212)879-9779. Fax: (212)686-2115. Offered annually to a translation of Scandinavian literature into English of a Nordic author born within the last 200 years. "The prize is for an outstanding English translation of poetry, fiction, drama, or literary prose originally written in Danish, Finnish, Icelandic, Norwegian, or Swedish that has not been previously published in the English language." **Deadline: June 1**. Prize $2,000, publication of an excerpt in an issue of *Scandinavian Review*, and a commemorative bronze medallion. Runner-up receives the Leif and Inger Sjoberg Prize of $1,000, publication of an excerpt in an issue of *Scandinavian Review*, and a commemorative bronze medallion.

DIANA DER-HOVANESSIAN TRANSLATION PRIZE

New England Poetry Club, 2 Farrar St., Cambridge MA 02138. (617)744-6034. E-mail: contests@nepoetryclub.org. **Contact:** NEPC Contest Coordinator. Annual contest for a poem translated into English. Please enclose a copy of the original poem. **Deadline: June 30. Charges $10/up to 3 poems.** Prize $250
Tips "Send two copies of your entry: one original and one with the translator's name and address on it."

SOEURETTE DIEHL FRASER TRANSLATION AWARD

6335 W. Northwest Hwy., #618, Dallas TX 75225. (214)528-2655. E-mail: franvick@aol.com. Website: http://texasinstituteofletters.org. **Contact:** Fran Vick. Offered every 2 years to recognize the best translation of a literary book into English. Translator must have been born in Texas or have lived in the state for at least 2 consecutive years at some time. **Deadline: January 3**. Prize $1,000

GERMAN PRIZE FOR LITERARY TRANSLATION

American Translators Association, 225 Reinekers Ln., Suite 590, Alexandria VA 22314. (703)683-6100, ext. 3006. Fax: (703)683-6122. E-mail: ata@atanet.org. **Contact:** Jonathan Mendoza. Offered in odd-numbered years for a previously published book translated from German to English. In even-numbered years, the Lewis Galentiere Prize is awarded for translations other than German to English. **Deadline: May 15**. Prize $1,000, a certificate of recognition, and up to $500 toward expenses for attending the ATA Annual Conference

GOVERNOR GENERAL'S LITERARY AWARD FOR TRANSLATION

Canada Council for the Arts, 350 Albert St., P.O. Box 1047, Ottawa ON K1P 5V8 Canada. (613)566-4414, ext. 5573. Fax: (613)566-4410. Offered for the best English-language and the best French-language work of translation by a Canadian. Publishers submit titles for consideration **Deadline: March 15, June 1, or August 7, depending on the book's publication date**. Prize Each laureate receives $25,000; non-winning finalists receive $1,000.

JAPAN-U.S. FRIENDSHIP COMMISSION PRIZE FOR THE TRANSLATION OF JAPANESE LITERATURE

Donald Keene Center of Japanese Culture at Columbia University, 507 Kent Hall, MC 3920, Columbia University, New York NY 10027. (212)854-5036. Fax: (212)854-4019. E-mail: donald-keene-center@columbia.edu. Website: www.donaldkeenecenter.org. Annual award of $6,000 in Japan-U.S. Friendship Commission Prizes for the translation of Japanese literature. "A prize is given for the best translation of a modern work or a classical work, or the prize is divided between equally distinguished translations. To qualify, works must be book-length translations of Japanese literary works: novels, collections of short stories, literary essays, memoirs, drama, or poetry. Submissions are judged on the literary merit of the translation and the accuracy with which it reflects the spirit of the Japanese original. Eligible works include unpublished mss, works in press, or books published during the 2 years prior to the prize year. Applications are accepted from translators or their publishers. Previous winners are ineligible. Must be a U.S. Citizen or permanent resident." **Deadline: December 31**.

THE HAROLD MORTON LANDON TRANSLATION AWARD

The Academy of American Poets, 584 Broadway, Suite 604, New York NY 10012-3210. (212)274-0343. Fax: (212)274-9427. E-mail: awards@poets.org. **Contact:** Awards Coordinator. Offered annually to recognize a published translation of poetry from any language into English. Open to living US citizens. **Deadline: December 31**. Prize $1,000

PEN TRANSLATION PRIZE

PEN American Center, 588 Broadway, Suite 303, New York NY 10012. (212)334-1660, ext. 108. Fax: (212)334-2181. E-mail: awards@pen.org. **Contact:** Literary Awards Manager. Offered for a literary book-length translation into English published in the calendar year. No technical, scientific, or reference books. Publishers, agents, or translators may submit 3 copies of each eligible title. All eligible titles must have been published in the US. **Deadline: December 15**. Prize $3,000

RAIZISS/DE PALCHI FELLOWSHIP

The Academy of American Poets, 584 Broadway, Suite 604, New York NY 10012. (212)274-0343, ext. 18. Fax: (212)274-9427. E-mail: cevans@poets.org. **Contact:** Awards Coordinator. Offered in alternate years to recognize outstanding unpublished translations of modern Italian poetry into English. Applicants must verify permission to translate the poems or that the poems are in the public domain. Open to any US citizen. Guidelines online or for SASE. **Deadline: December 31.** Prize $5,000

POETRY

AKRON POETRY PRIZE

The University of Akron Press, 374B Bierce Library, Akron OH 44325-1703. (330)972-5342. Fax: (330)972-8364. E-mail: uapress@uakron.edu. **Contact:** Mary Biddinger, editor and award dir. Annual book contest for unpublished poetry. "The Akron Poetry Prize brings to the public writers with original and compelling voices. Books must exhibit 3 essential qualities: mastery of language, maturity of feeling, and complexity of thought." Competition receives 500+ entries. The final selection will be made by a nationally prominent poet. The University of Akron Press has the right to publish the winning ms, inherent with winning the poetry prize. Open to all poets writing in English Winner will be posted on website by Sept. 30." "Intimate friends, relatives, current and former students of the final judge (students in an academic, degree-conferring program or its equivalent) are not eligible to enter)." **Entries accepted May 1-June 15 only. Charges $25 fee.** Prize Offers annual award of $1,000 plus publication of book-length ms. 2009: Martin Espada.

Tips "Submissions must be unpublished. Considers simultaneous submissions (with notification of acceptance elsewhere). Submit 48 or more pages, typed, single-spaced; optional SA postcard for confirmation. Mss will not be returned. So not send mss bound or enclosed in covers. See website for complete guidelines."

ANHINGA PRIZE FOR POETRY

Anhinga Press, Drawer W, P.O. Box 10595, Tallahassee FL 32302. (850)442-1408. Fax: (850)442-6323. Estab. 1983. Offered annually for a book-length collection of poetry by an author who has not published more than 1 book of poetry. Guidelines for SASE or on website. Open to any writer writing in English. **Deadline: February 15-May 1. Charges $25 fee.** Prize $2,000, and publication

ANNUAL GIVAL PRESS OSCAR WILDE AWARD

Gival Press, LLC, P.O. Box 3812, Arlington VA 22203. (703)351-0079. E-mail: givalpress@yahoo.com. **Contact:** Robert L. Giron. "Award given to the best previously unpublished original poem—written in English of any length, in any style, typed, double-spaced on 1 side only—which best relates gay/lesbian/bisexual/transgendered life, by a poet who is 18 or older. Entrants are asked to submit their poems without any kind of identification (with the exception of titles) and with a separate cover page with the following information: name, address (street, city, and state with zip code), telephone number, e-mail address (if available) and a list of poems by title. Checks drawn on American banks should be made out to Gival Press, LLC." **Deadline: June 27 (postmarked). Charges $5 (USD) reading fee per poem.** Prize $100 (USD), and the poem, along with information about the poet, will be published on the Gival Press website.

THE ANNUAL PRAIRIE SCHOONER STROUSSE AWARD

Prairie Schooner, 201 Andrews Hall, P.O. Box 880334, Lincoln NE 68588-0334. (402)472-0911. Fax: (402)472-9771. E-mail: http://prairieschooner.unl.edu. **Contact:** Hilda Raz. Offered annually for the best poem or group of poems published in *Prairie Schooner* in the previous year. Prize $500.

ARTS QUEENSLAND THOMAS SHAPCOTT PRIZE

The Queensland Writers Centre, Level 2, 109 Edward St., Brisbane QLD 4000 Australia. (61)(7)3839-1243. "Prize for an unpublished poetry ms (48-100 pages) by an emerging Queensland poet." **Deadline: July 13.** Prize $3,000 and a publishing contract with Univ. of Queensland Press. Thomas Shapcott, Nigel Krauth, and Bronwyn Lea

ATLANTIC POETRY PRIZE
Writers' Federation of Nova Scotia, 1113 Marginal Rd., Halifax NS B3H 4P7 Canada. (902)423-8116. Fax: (902)422-0881. E-mail: talk@writers.ns.ca. **Contact:** Jane Buss, executive director. Full-length books of adult poetry written by Atlantic Canadians, and published as a whole for the first time in the previous calendar year, are eligible. Entrants must be native or resident Atlantic Canadians who have either been born in Newfoundland, Prince Edward Island, Nova Scotia, or New Brunswick, and spent a susbstantial portion of their lives living there, or who have lived in one or a combination of these provinces for at least 24 consecutive months prior to entry deadline date. Publishers: Send 4 copies and a letter attesting to the author's status as an Atlantic Canadian and the author's current mailing address and telephone number. **Deadline: First Friday in December**. Prize $2,000.

THE BALTIMORE REVIEW POETRY CONTEST
The Baltimore Review, P.O. Box 36418, Towson MD 21286. Website: www.baltimorereview.org. **Contact:** Susan Muaddi Darraj. "The Annual Poetry Award aims to recognize the best new poetry today, from Baltimore and beyond. Submit up to four poems per entry fee. All styles and forms are accepted. Simultaneous submissions are fine, but alert us if your poem has been accepted elsewhere. Judges vary each year." **Deadline: July 1. Charges $15; $20 for fee and 1-year subscription.** Prize 1st Place: $300 and publication; 2nd Place: $150; 3rd Place: $50.

THE BASKERVILLE PUBLISHERS POETRY AWARD & THE BETSY COLQUITT POETRY AWARD
descant, Texas Christian University's literary journal, TCU, Box 297270, Fort Worth TX 76129. (817)257-6537. Fax: (817)257-6239. E-mail: descant@tcu.edu. **Contact:** Dave Kuhne, editor. "Annual award for an outstanding poem published in an issue of *descant*." **Deadline: September-April**. Prize $250 for Baskerville Award; $500 for Betsy Colquitt Award. Publication retains copyright, but will transfer it to the author upon request.

BLUE LYNX PRIZE FOR POETRY
Eastern Washington University Press, 705 W. First Ave., Spokane WA 99201. (800)508-9095. Fax: (509)623-4283. E-mail: ewupress@mail.ewu.edu. **Contact:** Christopher Howell. Annual award to publish the finest work the literary world has to offer. Send book-length mss of at least 48 pages. Guidelines available online or for SASE. Entries are judged anonymously. Please visit website for full details. **Deadline: May 15. Charges $25.** Prize $2,000 and publication.

BLUE MOUNTAIN ARTS/SPS STUDIOS POETRY CARD CONTEST
P.O. Box 1007, Boulder CO 80306. (303)449-0536. Fax: (303)447-0939. E-mail: poetrycontest@sps.com. Website: www.sps.com. "We're looking for original poetry that is rhyming or non-rhyming, although we find no-rhyming poetry reads better. Poems may also be considered for possible publication on greeting cards or in book anthologies. Contest is offered biannually. Guidelines available online." **Deadline: December 31 and June 30**. Prize 1st Place: $300; 2nd Place: $150; 3rd Place: $50. Blue Mountain Arts editorial staff.

BOSTON REVIEW POETRY CONTEST
Boston Review, 35 Medford St., Suite 302, Somerville MA 02143. Submit up to 5 unpublished poems, no more than 10 pages total. **Deadline: June 1. Charges $20 fee (check or money order payable to *Boston Review*).** Prize $1,500 and publication in the October/November issue of *Boston Review*

BARBARA BRADLEY PRIZE
New England Poetry Club, 2 Farrar St., Cambridge MA 02138. E-mail: contests@nepoetryclub.org. **Contact:** NEPC Contest Coordinator. Offered annually for a poem under 21 lines, written by a woman. **Deadline: June 30. Charges $10 for 3 poems.** Prize $200

Tips Send 2 copies of each entry with your name, address and phone number on one copy.

BRITTINGHAM PRIZE IN POETRY; FELIX POLLAK PRIZE IN POETRY
University of Wisconsin Press, Dept. of English, 600 N. Park St., University of Wisconsin, Madison WI 53706. E-mail: rwallace@wisc.edu. **Contact:** Ronald Wallace, contest director. Estab. 1985. "Offered for unpublished book-length mss of original poetry. Submissions must be received by the press during the month of September, accompanied by a required SASE for contest results. Does not return mss. One entry fee covers both prizes. Guidelines for SASE or online." **Charges $25 fee (payable to Univ. of Wisconsin Press).** Prize $2,500 ($1,000 cash prize and $1,500 honorarium for campus reading) and publication of the 2 winning mss.

GERALD CABLE BOOK AWARD
Silverfish Review Press, P.O. Box 3541, Eugene OR 97403. (541)344-5060. E-mail: sfrpress@earthlink.net. **Contact:** Rodger Moody, series editor. "Purpose is to publish a poetry book by a deserving author who has yet to publish a full-length book collection. For guidelines send SASE, or request by e-mail." **Deadline: October 15. Charges $20 reading fee.** Prize $1,000, 25 copies, and publication by the press for a book-length ms of original poetry.

Tips "Now accepting email submissions (save money on postage and photocopying); use Paypal for reading fee payment, see website for instructions."

THE CENTER FOR BOOK ARTS POETRY CHAPBOOK COMPETITION

The Center for Book Arts, 28 W. 27th St., 3rd Floor, New York NY 10001. (212)481-0295. Fax: (866)708-8994. E-mail: info@centerforbookarts.org. Website: www.centerforbookarts.org. **Contact:** Sarah Nicholls. Offered annually for unpublished collections of poetry. Individual poems may have been previously published. Collection must not exceed 500 lines or 24 pages. **Deadline: December 1 (postmarked). Charges $25 fee.** Prize $500 award, $500 honorarium for a reading, publication, and 10 copies of chapbook. Judged by Sharon Dolin and Terrance Hayes (2010).

JOHN CIARDI POETRY AWARD FOR LIFETIME ACHIEVEMENT

Italian Americana, URI/CCE, 80 Washington St., Providence RI 02903-1803. Fax: (401)277-5100. E-mail: bonomoal@etal.uri.edu. **Contact:** Carol Bonomo Albright, editor. Offered annually for lifetime achievement to a mature Italian American poet who has published in all aspects of poetry: creative, critical, etc. Applicants should have at least 2 books published and engage in activities promoting poetry. Open to Italian-Americans only. Prize $1,000

THE COLORADO PRIZE FOR POETRY

Colorado Review/Center for Literary Publishing, Dept. of English, Colorado State University, 9105 Campus Delivery, Ft. Collins CO 80523-9105. (970)491-5449. E-mail: creview@colostate.edu. **Contact:** Stephanie G'Schwind, editor. "Offered annually to an unpublished collection of poetry. Guidelines available for SASE or online at website." **Deadline: January 14. Charges $25 fee (includes subscription).** Prize $1,500 and publication of book

N CRAB ORCHARD SERIES IN POETRY OPEN COMPETITION

1000 Faner Dr., Southern Illinois University, Carbondale IL 62901-4503. **Contact:** Jon C. Tribble, series ed. "Offered annually for collections of unpublished poetry. Visit website for current deadlines. Open to US citizens and permanent residents." **Charges $25 fee.** Prize Two winners selected: both receive $3,500 and publication.

BRUCE DAWE NATIONAL POETRY PRIZE

Faculty of the Arts, University of Southern Queensland, Toowoomba QLD 4350 Australia. (61)(7)4631-1065. Fax: (61)(7)4631-1063. E-mail: daweprize@usq.edu.au. **Contact:** Prize Coordinator. "Annual award for an original unpublished poem not exceeding 50 lines. Open to citizens and permanent residents of Australia." **Deadline: August 14. Charges $6/poem.** Prize $1,500 Judged by the university's English literature staff.

THE CJ DENNIS PRIZE FOR POETRY

Victorian Premier's Literary Awards, State Government of Victoria, State Library of Victoria, 328 Swanston St. C, Melbourne VIC 3000 Australia. (61)(3)8664-7277. E-mail: pla@slv.vic.gov.au. Website: www.slv.vic.gov.au/pla. **Contact:** Project Officer. "Annual prize for a significant selection of new work by a poet published in a book between May 1 and April 30 each year. Authors must be Australian citizens or permanent residents. **Deadline: Usually May each year.** Prize AUD $15,000

Tips "For guidelines and nomination forms please visit our website."

ALICE FAY DI CASTAGNOLA AWARD

Poetry Society of America, 15 Gramercy Park S., New York NY 10003. (212)254-9628. Fax: (212)673-2352. **Contact:** Programs Associate. Offered annually for a manuscript-in-progress of poetry or verse-drama. Guidelines for SASE or online. Award open only to PSA members. "It is strongly encouraged that applicants read the complete contest guidelines on the PSA website before submitting. Open to members only." **Deadline: October 1-December 22.** Prize $1,000

JANICE FARRELL POETRY PRIZE

The Soul-Making Literary Competition, National League of American Pen Women, Nob Hill, San Francisco Branch, The Webhallow House, 1544 Sweetwood Dr., Broadmoor Village CA 94015-2029. E-mail: pennobhill@aol.com. **Contact:** Eileen Malone. "Poetry may be double- or single-spaced. One-page poems only, and only 1 poem/page. All poems must be titled. 3 poems/entry. Indicate category on each poem. Identify with 3X5 card only. Open annually to all writers." **Deadline: November 30. Charges $5/entry (make checks payable to NLAPW, Nob Hill Branch).** Prize 1st Place: $100; 2nd Place: $50; 3rd Place: $25. Judged by a local San Francisco successfully published poet.

FIELD POETRY PRIZE

Oberlin College Press/FIELD, 50 N. Professor St., Oberlin OH 44074-1091. (440)775-8408. Fax: (440)775-8124. E-mail: oc.press@oberlin.edu. Website: www.oberlin.edu/ocpress/prize.htm. **Contact:** Linda Slocum, managing editor. "Offered annually for unpublished work. Contest seeks to encourage the finest in contemporary poetry writing. Open to any writer." **Deadline: Submit in May only. Charges $25 fee, which includes a 1-year subscription.** Prize $1,000 and the book is published in Oberlin College Press's FIELD Poetry Series.

FIVE POINTS JAMES DICKEY PRIZE FOR POETRY

Five Points, Georgia State University, P.O. Box 3999, Atlanta GA 30302-3999. (404)413-5812. Fax: (404)413-5877. "Offered annually for unpublished poetry. Send 3 unpublished poems, no longer than 50 lines each, name and address on each poem, SASE for receipt and notification of winner. Winner announced in Spring issue." **Deadline: December 1. Charges $20 fee (includes 1-year subscription).** Prize $1,000, plus publication.

ALLEN GINSBERG POETRY AWARDS

The Poetry Center at Passaic County Community College, One College Blvd., Paterson NJ 07505-1179. (973)684-6555. Fax: (973)684-5843. E-mail: mgillan@pccc.edu. **Contact:** Maria Mazziotti Gillan, exec. dir. "Offered annually for unpublished poetry to honor Allen Ginsberg's contribution to American literature. The college retains first publication rights. Open to any writer." **Deadline: April 1. Charges $18, which includes the cost of a subscription to *The Paterson Literary Review*.** Prize $1,000

GIVAL PRESS POETRY AWARD

Gival Press, LLC, P.O. Box 3812, Arlington VA 22203. (703)351-0079. E-mail: givalpress@yahoo.com. **Contact:** Robert L. Giron. "Offered annually for a previously unpublished poetry collection as a complete ms, which may include previously published poems; and previously published poems must be acknowledged & poet must hold rights. The competition seeks to award well-written, original poetry in English on any topic, in any style. Guidelines for SASE, by e-mail, or online. Entrants are asked to submit their poems without any kind of identification (with the exception of the titles) and with a separate cover page with the following information: name, address (street, city, state, and zip code), telephone number, e-mail address (if available), short bio, and a list of the poems by title. Checks drawn on American banks should be made out to Gival Press, LLC." **Deadline: December 15 (postmarked). Charges $20 reading fee (USD).** Prize $1,000, publication, and author's copies. The editor narrows entries to the top 10; previous winner selects top 5 and the winner—all done anonymously.

Tips "Open to any writer, as long as the work is original, not a translation, and is written in English. The copyright remains in the author's name; certain rights fall to the publisher per the contract."

GIVAL PRESS POETRY COMPETITION

Gival Press, LLC, P.O. Box 3812, Arlington VA 22203. (703)351-0079. Fax: (703)351-0079. E-mail: givalpress@yahoo.com. **Contact:** Robert L. Giron. Offered annually for previously unpublished poetry manuscript. The competition seeks to award well-written original poetry in English. Guidelines for SASE or by e-mail. Open to all poets, national as well as international, who write in English. **Deadline: December 15. Charges $20.** Prize $1,000, plus publication

GOVERNOR GENERAL'S LITERARY AWARD FOR POETRY

Canada Council for the Arts, 350 Albert St., P.O. Box 1047, Ottawa ON K1P 5V8 Canada. (613)566-4414, ext. 5573. Fax: (613)566-4410. Offered for the best English-language and the best French-language work of poetry by a Canadian. Publishers submit titles for consideration. **Deadline: March 15, June 1, or August 7, depending on the book's publication date.** Prize Each laureate receives $25,000; nonwinning finalists receive $1,000.

KATHRYN HANDLEY PROSE POEM PRIZE

National League of American Pen Women, Nob Hill, San Francisco Branch, The Webhallow House, 1544 Sweetwood Dr., Colma CA 94015-2029. E-mail: pennobhill@aol.com. **Contact:** Eileen Malone. Poetry may be double- or single-spaced. 1-page poems only, and only 1 prose poem/page. 3 poems/entry. Indicate category on each poem. Identify only with 3X5 card. Open annually to all writers. **Deadline: November 30. Charges $5/entry (make checks payable to NLAPW, Nob Hill Branch).** Prize 1st Place: $100; 2nd Place: $50; 3rd Place: $25.

THE BEATRICE HAWLEY AWARD

Alice James Books, 238 Main St., Farmington ME 04938. Phone/Fax: (207)778-7071. E-mail: ajb@umf.maine.edu. Website: www.alicejamesbooks.org. **Contact:** Lacy Simons, managing editor. "Offered annually for unpublished full-length poetry collection. Open to US residents only. Guidelines online or for SASE." **Deadline: December 1. Charges $25.** Prize $2,000, and publication

CECIL HEMLEY MEMORIAL AWARD

Poetry Society of America, 15 Gramercy Park, New York NY 10003. (212)254-9628. Fax: (212)673-2352. E-mail: tom@poetrysociety.org. **Contact:** Thomas Hummel, awards coordinator. Offered for unpublished lyric poems on a philosophical theme. Line limit: 100. Guidelines subject to change. *Open to PSA members only.* Guidelines for SASE or online. **Deadline: October 1-December 22.** Prize $500

IRA LEE BENNETT HOPKINS PROMISING POET AWARD

International Reading Association, P.O. Box 8139, Newark DE 19714-8139. (302)731-1600 ext 221. Fax: (302)731-1057. E-mail: exec@reading.org. Website: www.reading.org. "Offered every 3 years to a promising new poet of children's poetry (for children and young adults up to grade 12) who has published no more than 2 books of children's poetry. Download application from Web site after May 2009." **Deadline: December 1, 2009 for published poem books during 2007-2009**. Prize $500.

FIRMAN HOUGHTON PRIZE

New England Poetry Club, 2 Farrar Street, Cambridge MA 02138. E-mail: contests@nepoetryclug.org. Website: www.nepoetryclub.org/contests.htm. **Contact:** NEPC Contest Coordinator. Offered annually for a lyric poem in English. **Deadline: June 30**. **Charges $10 for 3 poems payable to New England Poetry Club. Members free.** Prize $250

Tips "Send two copies of your entry: one original and one with the writer's name and address on it."

INDIANA REVIEW POETRY PRIZE

Indiana Review, Ballantine Hall 465, Indiana University, Bloomington IN 47405-7103. (812)855-3439. Fax: (812)855-9535. **Contact:** Grady Jaynes, editor. Offered annually for unpublished work. Judged by guest judges; 2009 prize judged by Natasha Trethewey. Open to any writer. Send no more than 3 poems per entry. Guidelines on web site and with SASE request. **Deadline: Late March**. **Charges $15 fee (includes a 1-year subscription).** Prize $1,000.

IOWA POETRY PRIZES

University of Iowa Press, 100 Kuhl House, Iowa City IA 52242. (319)335-2000. Fax: (319)335-2055. Offered annually to encourage poets and their work. Submit mss by April 30; put name on title page only. Open to writers of English (US citizens or not). Manuscripts will not be returned. Previous winners are not eligible. **Deadline: April**. **Charges $20 fee.**

ROBINSON JEFFERS TOR HOUSE PRIZE FOR POETRY

Robinson Jeffers Tor House Foundation, P.O. Box 223240, Carmel CA 93922. (831)624-1813. Fax: (831)624-3696. E-mail: thf@torhouse.org. **Contact:** Poetry Prize Coordinator. "The contest honors well-crafted, unpublished poetry in all styles, ranging from experimental work to traditional forms, including short narrative poems." **Deadline: November 1-March 15**. **Charges $10 for first 3 poems; $15 for up to 6 poems; $2.50 for each additional poem.** Prize $1,000; $200 for Honorable Mention. Preliminary judging by a distinguished panel of published poets and editors. Final judging by a nationally known poet.

BARBARA MANDIGO KELLY PEACE POETRY AWARDS

Nuclear Age Peace Foundation, PMB 121, 1187 Coast Village Rd., Suite 1, Santa Barbara CA 93108-2794. (805)965-3443. Fax: (805)568-0466. E-mail: wagingpeace@napf.org. "he Barbara Mandigo Kelly Peace Poetry Contest was created to encourage poets to explore and illuminate positive visions of peace and the human spirit. The annual contest honors the late Barbara Kelly, a Santa Barbara poet and longtime supporter of peace issues. Awards are given in 3 categories: adult (over 18 years), youth between 12 and 18 years, and youth under 12. All submitted poems should be unpublished." **Deadline: July 1 (postmarked)**. **Charges $15/up to 3 poems; no fee for youth entries.** Prize Adult: $1,000; Youth (13-18): $200; Youth (12 and under): $200. Honorable Mentions may also be awarded. A committee of poets selected by the Nuclear Age Peace Foundation. The foundation reserves the right to publish and distribute the award-winning poems, including honorable mentions.

Tips "Poets should keep copies of all entries as we will be unable to return them. Copies of the winning poems from the 2003 Awards will be posted on the Nuclear Age Peace Foundation website after October 1, 2009."

THE LEDGE POETRY AWARDS COMPETITION

The Ledge Magazine & Press, 40 Maple Ave., Bellport NY 11713. E-mail: info@theledgemagazine.com. **Contact:** Timothy Monaghan. "Offered annually for unpublished poems of exceptional quality and significance. No restrictions on form or content. All poems are considered for publication in the magazine. Guidelines online or for SASE. Open to any writer." **Deadline: April 30**. **Charges $10/first 3 poems; $3/additional poem. $20 subscription to *The Ledge Magazine* gains free entry for the first three poems.** Prize 1st Place: $1,000 and publication in *The Ledge Magazine*; 2nd Place: $250 and publication; 3rd Place: $100 and publication.

LITERAL LATTÉ POETRY AWARD

Literal Latté, 200 E. 10th St., Suite 240, New York NY 10003. (212)260-5532. E-mail: LitLatte@aol.com. **Contact:** Jenine Gordon Bockman, ed. "Offered annually to any writer for unpublished poetry (maximum 2,000 words per poem). All styles welcome. Winners published in *Literal Lattè*." Acquires first rights. **Deadline: July 15**. **Charges $10/up to 6 poems; $15/set of 10 poems.** Prize 1st Place: $1,000; 2nd Place: $300; 3rd Place: $200 The Editors

FRANCES LOCKE MEMORIAL POETRY AWARD

The Bitter Oleander Press, 4983 Tall Oaks Dr., Fayetteville NY 13066-9776. (315)637-3047. Fax: (315)637-5056. E-mail: info@bitteroleander.com. **Contact:** Paul B. Roth. Offered annually for unpublished, imaginative poetry. Open to any writer. **Deadline: June 15. Charges $10 for 5 poems; $2/additional poem.** Prize $1,000, publication in the autumn issue, and 5 copies of that issue

LOUISE LOUIS/EMILY F. BOURNE STUDENT POETRY AWARD

Poetry Society of America, 15 Gramercy Park S., New York NY 10003. (212)254-9628. Fax: (212)673-2352. Website: www.poetrysociety.org. **Contact:** Programs Associate. Offered annually for unpublished work to promote excellence in student poetry. Open to American high school or preparatory school students (grades 9-12). Guidelines for SASE and online. Judged by prominent American poets. It is strongly encouraged that applicants read the complete contest guidelines before submitting. **Deadline: October 1-December 22. Charges $5 for a student submitting a single entry; $20 for a high school submitting unlimited number of its students' poems.** Prize $250

LYRIC POETRY AWARD

Poetry Society of America, 15 Gramercy Park, New York NY 10003. (212)254-9628. Fax: (212)673-2352. E-mail: tom@poetrysociety.org. **Contact:** Thomas Hummel, awards coordinator. Offered annually for unpublished work to promote excellence in lyric poetry. Line limit 50. Guidelines subject to change. *Open to PSA members only*. Guidelines for SASE or online. **Deadline: October 1-December 23.** Prize $500

NAOMI LONG MADGETT POETRY AWARD

Lotus Press, Inc., P.O. Box 21607, Detroit MI 48221. E-mail: lotuspress@comcast.net. **Contact:** Constance Withers. "Offered annually to recognize an unpublished poetry ms by an African American. Guidelines for SASE, by e-mail, or online." **Deadline: January 2-March 31.** Prize $500 and publication by Lotus Press.

THE MALAHAT REVIEW LONG POEM PRIZE

The Malahat Review, Box 1700 STN CSC, Victoria BC V8W 2Y2 Canada. E-mail: malahat@uvic.ca (queries only). **Contact:** John Barton, Editor. "Long Poem Prize offered in alternate years with the Novella Contest. Open to unpublished long poems. Preliminary reading by editorial board; final judging by 3 recognized poets. Obtains first world rights. After publication rights revert to the author. Open to any writer." **Deadline: February 1 (odd years). Charges $35 CAD fee for Canadian entrants; $40 US for American entrants; $45 US for entrants from elsewhere (includes a 1-year subscription to the *Malahat*, published quarterly).** Prize of $500 (for two), plus payment for publication ($40/page), and additional 1-year subscription.

MORTON MARR POETRY PRIZE

Southwest Review, P.O. Box 750374, Dallas TX 75275-0374. (214)768-1037. Fax: (214)768-1408. E-mail: swr@mail.smu.edu. **Contact:** Willard Spiegelman. "Annual award given to a poem by a writer who has not yet published a first book of poetry. Contestants may submit no more than 6 poems in a traditional form (i.e., sonnet, sestina, villanelle, rhymed stanzas, blank verse, etc.). A cover letter with name, address, and other relevant information may accompany the poems which must be printed without any identifying information. Guidelines for SASE or online. Open to any writer who has not yet published a first book of poetry." **Deadline: September 30. Charges $5/poem.** Prize 1st Place: $1,000; 2nd Place: $500; publication in *The Southwest Review*.

LUCILLE MEDWICK MEMORIAL AWARD

Poetry Society of America, 15 Gramercy Park, New York NY 10003. (212)254-9628. Fax: (212)673-2352. **Contact:** Brett Fletcher Lauer, awards coordinator. Original poem in any form on a humanitarian theme. Line limit: 100. Guidelines subject to change. *Open to PSA members only*. Guidelines for SASE or online. **Deadline: October 1-December 23.** Prize $500

KATHRYN A. MORTON PRIZE IN POETRY

Sarabande Books, P.O. Box 4456, Louisville KY 40204. (502)458-4028. Fax: (502)458-4065. E-mail: info@sarabandebooks.org. **Contact:** Jennifer Woods, associate editor. Offered annually to publish an outstanding collection of poetry. All finalists considered for publication. **Deadline: January 1-February 15. Charges $25 fee.** Prize $2,000 and publication with standard royalty contract

SHEILA MOTTON AWARD

New England Poetry Club, 2 Farrar St., Cambridge MA 02138. E-mail: contests@nepoetryclub.org. For a poetry book published in the last 2 years. Send 2 copies of the book and **$10 entry fee.** Prize $500

ERIKA MUMFORD PRIZE

New England Poetry Club, 2 Farrar Street, Cambridge MA 02138. E-mail: contests@nepoetryclub.org. Offered annually for a poem in any form about foreign culture or travel. **Deadline: June 30. Charges $10/up to 3**

entries in NEPC contests. Prize $250

NATIONAL FEDERATION OF STATE POETRY SOCIETIES ANNUAL POETRY CONTEST

National Federation of State Poetry Societies, P.O. Box 270554, West Hartford CT 06127. E-mail: connpoetry@comcast.netahoo.com. Website: www.nfsps.org/poetry_contests. **Contact:** Christine Beck. Estab. 1959. "Contest for previously unpublished poetry. Has 50 categories. Flier lists them all. Guidelines for SASE. Must have guidelines to enter. All awards are announced in June. Only the top awards (not honorable mentions) are published the following June." **Deadline: March 15.** Prize TBA.

NATIONAL WRITERS ASSOCIATION POETRY CONTEST

The National Writers Association, 10940 S. Parker Rd. #508, Parker CO 80134. (303)841-0246. Fax: (303)841-2607. **Contact:** Sandy Whelchel, director. Annual contest to encourage the writing of poetry, an important form of individual expression but with a limited commercial market. **Charges $10 fee.** Prize 1st Place: $100; 2nd Place: $50; 3rd Place: $25.

HOWARD NEMEROV SONNET AWARD

The Formalist, 320 Hunter Dr., Evansville IN 47711. Website: www2.evansville.edu/theformalist/. Offered annually for an unpublished sonnet to encourage poetic craftsmanship and to honor the memory of the late Howard Nemerov, third US Poet Laureate. Acquires first North American serial rights for those sonnets chosen for publication. Upon publication all rights revert to the author. Open to the international community of writers. Guidelines available online or for SASE. **Deadline: November 15. Charges $3/sonnet.** Prize $1,000 and publication in *Measure: A Review of Formal Poetry*.

THE PABLO NERUDA PRIZE FOR POETRY

Nimrod International Journal, 800 S. Tucker Dr., Tulsa OK 74104. (918)631-3080. Fax: (918)631-3033. E-mail: nimrod@utulsa.edu. **Contact:** Francine Ringold. Annual award to discover new writers of vigor and talent. Open to US residents only. **Deadline: April 30. Charges $20 (includes a 1-year subscription).** Prize 1st Place: $2,000 and publication; 2nd Place: $1,000 and publication. *Nimrod* retains the right to publish any submission. the *Nimrod* editors (finalists). A recognized author selects the winners.

THE OHIO STATE UNIVERSITY PRESS/THE JOURNAL AWARD IN POETRY

The Ohio State University Press and *The Journal*, 1070 Carmack, Columbus OH 43210. (614)292-6930. Fax: (614)292-2065. E-mail: ohiostatepress@osu.edu. **Contact:** Poetry Editor. Offered annually for unpublished work, minimum of 48 pages of original poetry. **Deadline: Entries accepted September 1-30. Charges $25 fee.** Prize $3,000 and publication

GUY OWEN AWARD

Southern Poetry Review, Dept. of Languages, Literature, and Philosophy, Armstrong Atlantic State University, 11935 Abercorn St., Savannah GA 31419-1997. (912)344-3196. Fax: (912)344-3494. E-mail: james.smith@armstrong.edu. Website: www.spr.armsrong.edu. **Contact:** James Smith. Send 3-5 unpublished poems (maximum 10 pages) and SASE for response only. Include contact information on cover sheet only. All entries considered for publication. Please indicate simultaneous submissions. **Deadline: March 1-June 15 (postmarked). Charges $15 entry fee (includes 1-year subscription).** Prize $1,000 and publication of winning poem in *Southern Poetry Review*. Final judge will be a distinguished poet.

THE PATERSON POETRY PRIZE

The Poetry Center at Passaic County Community College, One College Blvd., Paterson NJ 07505-1179. Fax: (973)523-6085. E-mail: mgillan@pccc.edu. **Contact:** Maria Mazziotti Gillan, Exec. Director. "Offered annually for a book of Poetry published in the previous year. Guidelines available online or send SASE to above address." **Deadline: February 1.** Prize $1,000

PAUMANOK POETRY AWARD

English Department, Knapp Hall, Farmingdale State University of New York, 2350 Broadhollow Rd., Route 110, Farmingdale NY 11735. Fax: (631)420-2051. E-mail: brownml@farmingdale.edu. **Contact:** Margery L. Brown, director, Visiting Writers Program. "Offered annually for published or unpublished poems. Send cover letter, 1-paragraph bio, 3-5 poems (name and address on each poem). Include SASE for notification of winners. (Send photocopies only; mss will *not* be returned.)" **Deadline: September 15. Charges $25 fee, payable to Farmingdale State University VWP.** Prize 1st Place: $1,000, plus expenses for a reading in series; Runners-up (2): $1,000, plus expenses for a reading in series

PEARL POETRY PRIZE

Pearl Editions, 3030 E. Second St., Long Beach CA 90803. (562)434-4523. Fax: (562)434-4523. E-mail: pearlmag@aol.com. **Contact:** Marilyn Johnson, editor/publisher. "Offered annually to provide poets with further opportunity to publish their poetry in book-form and find a larger audience for their work. Mss must be original works written in English. Guidelines for SASE or online. Open to all writers." **Deadline: July 15. Charges $20.** Prize $1,000 and publication by Pearl Editions

PERUGIA PRESS PRIZE

Perugia Press, Celebrating Poetry by Women since 1997, P.O. Box 60364, Florence MA 01062. E-mail: info@perugiapress.com. **Contact:** Susan Kan. "The contest is for first or second poetry books by women. Some poems in the submission may be previously published, but the ms as a whole must be unpublished. Send SASE or visit our Web site for guidelines. The contest is open to women poets who are US residents and who have not published more than 1 book." **Deadline: November 15. Charges $22.** Prize $1,000 and publication

THE PINCH POETRY LITERARY AWARDS

The University of Memphis/Hohenberg Foundation, Dept. of English, 471 Patterson Hall, Memphis TN 38152. (901)678-4591. E-mail: editor@thepinchjournal.com. Offered annually for unpublished poems of 2 pages maximum. Guidelines for SASE or on website. **Deadline: March 15. Charges $20 fee for up to 3 poems.** Prize 1st Place: $1,000 and publication; 2nd and 3rd Place: Publication and a 1-year subscription

RAINMAKER AWARDS IN POETRY

ZONE 3, Austin Peay State University, P.O. Box 4565, Clarksville TN 37044. (931)221-7031. Fax: (931)221-7149. E-mail: wallacess@apsu.edu. **Contact:** Susan Wallace, managing editor. "Offered annually for unpublished poetry. Previous judges include Carolyn Forché, Margie Piercy, Maxine Kumin, Stephen Dunn, Mark Jarman, and Michael Collier. Open to any poet." **Charges $10 fee (includes 1-year subscription).** Prize 1st Place: $500; 2nd Place: $300; 3rd Place: $100.

MARGARET REID POETRY CONTEST FOR TRADITIONAL VERSE

c/o Winning Writers, 351 Pleasant St., PMB 222, Northampton MA 01060-3961. E-mail: johnreid@mail.qango.com. Website: www.winningwriters.com. **Contact:** John Reid. Estab. 2004. "Seeks poems in traditional verse forms, such as sonnets." Both unpublished and published work accepted. Guidelines for SASE or on Web site. **Deadline: June 30. Charges $7 for every 25 lines of poetry.** Prize 1st Place: $3,000; 2nd Place: $1,000; 3rd Place: $400; 4th Place: $250; plus 6 Most Highly Commended awards of $150 each. The top 10 entries will be published on the Winning Writers Web site. Judged by John H. Reid and Dee C. Konrad

RIVER STYX INTERNATIONAL POETRY CONTEST

River Styx Magazine, 3547 Olive St., Suite #107, St. Louis MO 63103-1014. (314)533-4541. Fax: (314)289-4019. **Contact:** Michael Nye, Managing Editor. Offered annually for unpublished poetry. Poets may send up to 3 poems, not more than 14 pages. **Deadline: May 31. Charges $20 reading fee (which includes a 1-year subscription).** Prize $1,500 and publication in August issue Judged by Stephen Dunn in 2009. Past judges include Dorianne Laux, Rodney Jones, Maura Stanton, Billy Collins, Molly Peacock, and Philip Levine.

BENJAMIN SALTMAN POETRY AWARD

Red Hen Press, P.O. Box 3537 Attn: Benjamin Saltman Award, Granada Hills CA 91394. (818)831-0649. Fax: (818)831-6659. E-mail: editors@redhen.org. **Contact:** Kate Gale. Estab. 1998. Offered annually for unpublished work to publish a winning book of poetry. Open to any writer. Name on cover sheet only, 48 page, minimum. Send SASE for notification. **Deadline: October 31. Charges $25 fee.** Prize $3,000 and publication

SAWTOOTH POETRY PRIZE

Ahsahta Press, Boise State University, 1910 University Dr., MS 1525, Boise ID 83725-1525. (208)426-3134. Poets writing in English are eligible. Previous book publication is not a consideration. No students or former students of Boise State Univ. or of the judge; no close friends of the judge. No email or faxed entries. **Eligibility between Jan. 1, 2010 and Mar. 1, 2010. Charges $25 reading fee; a copy of the winning book will be sent if a 7"X10" mailer with priority postage is included with submission.** Prize $1,500 for a book of poems upon publication plus 25 copies of the book; announcements in national publications, featured on our website. Rae Armantrout

SILVER WINGS ANNUAL POETRY CONTEST

Silver Wings, P.O. Box 2340, Clovis CA 93613. (559)347-0194. E-mail: cloviswings@aol.com. **Contact:** Jackson Wilcox. Estab. 1983. "The annual contest is sponsored by Silver Wings, a small bi-monthly poetry magazine." We would like to encourage new writers of poetry with a Christian message or thought. **Deadline: December 31. Charges $3.** Prize 1st Place: $100; 2nd Place: $50; 3rd Place: $35; 4th Place: $30; 5th Place: $25; 6th Place: $20; 7th Place: $15. A few Honorable Mentions are also published with no cash prize. Purchases first rights with permission to publish in *Silver Wings*. Poetry on Wings board in February.

Tips "Contest poems must be original and never before published."

SLIPSTREAM ANNUAL POETRY CHAPBOOK COMPETITION

Slipstream, Box 2071, Niagara Falls NY 14301. E-mail: editors@slipstreampress.org. Website: www.

slipstreampress.org. **Contact:** Dan Sicoli, co-editor. "Offered annually to help promote a poet whose work is often overlooked or ignored. Open to any writer." Winner is featured prominently on the Slipstream website for one year, as well as in all Slipstream catalogs, press releases, and promotional material. Winning chapbooks are submitted by Slipstream for review by various national and international poetry/writing pubications and may also be featured in the Grants & Awards section of Poets & Writers magazine. **Deadline: December 1. Charges $20.** Prize $1,000 and 50 copies of published chapbook. (Everyone who enters receives a copy of the winning chapbook plus one complimentary issue of *Slipstream* magazine.
Tips "Winner announced in late spring/early summer."

HELEN C. SMITH MEMORIAL AWARD FOR BEST BOOK OF POETRY

(formerly the Natalie Ornish Poetry Award), The Texas Institute of Letters, 6335 W. Northwest Hwy., #618, Dallas TX 75225. (214)363-7253. E-mail: franvick@aol.com. **Contact:** Fran Vick, secretary. Offered annually for the best book of poems published January 1-December 31 of previous year. Poet must have been born in Texas, have lived in the state at some time for at least 2 consecutive years, or the subject matter must be associated with the state. See website for guidelines. **Deadline: January 1.** Prize $1,200

THE SOW'S EAR CHAPBOOK PRIZE

The Sow's Ear Poetry Review, P.O. Box 127, Millwood VA 22646. (540)955-3955. E-mail: rglesman@gmail.com. **Contact:** Robert Lesman, managing editor. Estab. 1988. Offered for poetry mss of 22-26 pages. Guidelines for SASE, by e-mail, or on Web site. **Deadline: Submit March-April. Charges $20 fee; $24 for Canadian addresses, 436 elsewhere; includes subscription.** Prize $1,000, 25 copies, and distribution to subscribers

SPOON RIVER POETRY REVIEW EDITORS' PRIZE

Spoon River Poetry Review, Campus Box 4241, Publications Unit, Illinois State University, Normal IL 61790-4241. (309)438-3025. Offered annually for unpublished poetry to identify and reward excellence. Guidelines available online. Open to all writers. **Deadline: April 15. Charges $16 (entitles entrant to a 1-year subscription valued at $15).** Prize 1st Place: $1,000 and publication; Runners-Up (2): $100 each and publication.

THE EDWARD STANLEY AWARD

Prairie Schooner, 201 Andrews Hall, P.O. Box 880334, Lincoln NE 68588-0334. (402)472-0911. Fax: (402)472-9771. E-mail: kgrey2@unl.edu. **Contact:** Hilda Raz. Offered annually for poetry published in *Prairie Schooner* in the previous year. Prize $1,000.

THE ELIZABETH MATCHETT STOVER MEMORIAL AWARD

Southwest Review, Southern Methodist University, P.O. Box 750374, Dallas TX 75275-0374. (214)768-1037. Fax: (214)768-1408. E-mail: swr@mail.smu.edu. **Contact:** Jennifer Cranfill,Senior Editor and Willard Spiegelman, Editor-In-Chief. "Offered annually to the best works of poetry that have appeared in the magazine in the previous year. Please note that mss are submitted for publication, not for the prizes themselves. Guidelines for SASE and online." Prize $300 Jennifer Cranfill and Willard Spiegelman.

HOLLIS SUMMERS POETRY PRIZE

Ohio University Press, 19 Circle Dr., The Ridges, Athens OH 45701. (740)593-1155. Fax: (740)593-4536. **Contact:** David Sanders. Offered annually for unpublished poetry mss. Mss will be eligible even if individual poems or sections have been published previously. Open to any writer. Guidelines for SASE or online. **Deadline: October 31. Charges $20.** Prize $1,000 and publication of the ms in book form

TRANSCONTINENTAL POETRY AWARD

Pavement Saw Press, 321 Empire Street, Montpelier OH 43543. (419)485-0524. E-mail: info@pavementsaw.org. Website: pavementsaw.org. **Contact:** David Baratier, editor. "Offered annually for a first book of poetry. Judged by the editor and a guest judge. Guidelines available online." **Deadline: August 15. Charges $20 fee.** Prize $1,000, 50 copies for judge's choice, and standard royalty contract for editor's choice. All writers receive 2 free book for entering.

UTMOST CHRISTIAN POETRY CONTEST

Utmost Christian Writers Foundation, 121 Morin Maze, Edmonton AB T6K 1V1 Canada. The purpose of this annual contest is "to promote excellence in poetry by poets of Christian faith. All entries are eligible for most of the cash awards, but there is a special category for rhyming poetry with prizes of $150 and $100. All entries must be unpublished." **Deadline: February 28. Charges $20/poem (maximum 5 poems).** Prize 1st Place: $1,500; 2nd Place: $500; 3rd Place: $350. Four prizes of $100 are offered for honorable mention, as well as twenty prizes of $50 for merit. Rights are acquired to post winning entries on the organization's website. Judged by a committee of the Directors of Utmost Christian Writers Foundation (who work under the direction of Barbara Mitchell, chief judge).

Contests & Awards

DANIEL VAROUJAN AWARD

New England Poetry Club, 2 Farrar Street, Cambridge MA 02138. E-mail: contests@nepoetryclub.org. Website: www.nepoetryclub.org/contests.htm. **Contact:** NEPC Contest Coordinator. "Offered annually for an unpublished poem worthy of Daniel Varoujan, a poet killed by the Turks at the onset of the first genocide of the 20th century which decimated three-fourths of the Armenian population." Send poems in duplicate, with name and address of poet on one copy only. **Deadline: June 30. Charges $10/up to 3 entries made payable to New England Poetry Club. Members free.** Prize $1,000

CHAD WALSH POETRY PRIZE

Beloit Poetry Journal, P.O. Box 151, Farmington ME 04938. (207)778-0020. E-mail: bpj@bpj.org. **Contact:** Lee Sharkey and John Rosenwald, editors. "Offered annually to honor the memory of poet Chad Walsh, a founder of the *Beloit Poetry Journal*". The editors select an outstanding poem or group of poems from the poems published in the journal that year. Open to the author of the poem or group of poems that are judged to be outstanding during the previous year. Prize $2,500

WAR POETRY CONTEST

Winning Writers, 351 Pleasant St., PMB 222, Northampton MA 01060-3961. (866)946-9748. Fax: (413)280-0539. E-mail: adam@winningwriters.com. **Contact:** Adam Cohen. Estab. 2002. "This annual contest seeks outstanding, unpublished poetry on the theme of war. Up to 3 poems can be submitted, with a maximum total of 500 lines. English language only; translations accepted if you wrote the original poem." Submit online or by mail. Guidelines for SASE or see Web site. nonexclusive right to publish submissions on WinningWriters.com, in e-mail newsletter, and in press releases. **Deadline: November 15-May 31. Charges $15.** Prize 1st Place: $2,000 and publication on WinningWriters.com; 2nd Place: $1,200 and publication; 3rd Place: $600 and publication; Honorable Mentions (12): $100 and publication. 2008 winner was Aliene Pylant for "Unerring Mercy and Pure Grace." Judge: award-winning poet Jendi Reiter.

THE WORD WORKS WASHINGTON PRIZE

Dearlove Hall, Adirondack Community College, 640 Bay Rd., Queensbury NY 12804. E-mail: editor@wordworksdc.com. **Contact:** Nancy White, Washington Prize Admin. Estab. 1981. Offered annually "for the best full-length poetry manuscript (48-64 pp.) submitted to The Word Works each year. The Washington Prize contest is the only forum in which we consider unsolicited manuscripts." Acquires first publication rights. Open to any American writer. **Deadline: January 15-March 1. Charges $25 fee.** Prize $1,500 and book publication; all entrants receive a copy of the winning book

WERGLE FLOMP HUMOR POETRY CONTEST

Winning Writers, 351 Pleasant St., PMB 222, Northampton MA 01060-3961. (866)946-9748. Fax: (413)280-0539. E-mail: adam@winningwriters.com. **Contact:** Adam Cohen. Estab. 2002. "This annual contest seeks the best parody poem that has been sent to a vanity poetry contest as a joke. Vanity contests are characterized by low standards. Their main purpose is to entice poets to buy expensive products like anthologies, chapbooks, CDs, plaques, and silver bowls. Vanity contests will often praise remarkably bad poems in their effort to sell as much stuff to as many people as possible. The Wergle Flomp Prize will be awarded for the best bad poem. One poem of any length should be submitted, along with the name of the vanity contest that was spoofed. The poem should be in English. Inspired gibberish is also accepted. See website for guidelines, examples, and to submit your poem. nonexclusive right to publish submissions on WinningWriters.com, in e-mail newsletter, and in press releases." **Deadline: August 15-April 1.** Prize 1st Place: $1,359; 2nd Place: $764; 3rd Place: $338. Twelve Honorable Mentions get $72.95 each. All prize winners receive publication at WinningWriters.com. Non-US winners will be paid in US currency (or PayPal) if a check is inconvenient. Judged by Jendi Reiter.

Tips "Submissions may be previously published and may be entered in other contests. Competition receives about 800 entries/year. Winners are announced on August 15 at WinningWriters.com. Entrants who provide a valid e-mail address will also receive notification. The 2008 winner was Benjamin Taylor Lally for "First Edition, 2008."

WICK OPEN POETRY CHAPBOOK COMPETITION

Wick Poetry Center, 301 Satterfield Hall, Kent State University, P.O. Box 5190, Kent OH 44242-0001. (330)672-2067. Fax: (330)672-3333. E-mail: wickpoet@kent.edu. **Contact:** Maggie Anderson, director. Offered annually for a chapbook of poems (15-25 pages) by a poet currently living in Ohio. Guidelines available online or for SASE. **Deadline: October 31. Charges $15 fee for open competition; no fee for student competition.** Prize Publication of the chapbook by the Kent State University Press

STAN AND TOM WICK POETRY PRIZE

Wick Poetry Center, 301 Satterfield Hall, Kent State University, P.O. Box 5190, Kent OH 44242-0001. (330)672-2067. Fax: (330)672-3333. E-mail: wickpoet@kent.edu. **Contact:** Maggie Anderson, director. Open to anyone writing in English who has not previously published a full-length book of poems (a volume of 50 pages or more published in an edition of 500 or more copies). Send SASE or visit the website for guidelines. **Deadline: May 1. Charges $20 reading fee.** Prize $2,000 and publication by the Kent State University Press

WILLIAM CARLOS WILLIAMS AWARD

Poetry Society of America, 15 Gramercy Park S., New York NY 10003. (212)254-9628. Fax: (212)673-2352. **Contact:** Programs Associate. Offered annually for a book of poetry published by a small press, nonprofit, or university press. Winning books are distributed to PSA Lyric Circle members while supplies last. Books must be submitted directly by publishers. Entry forms are required. It is strongly encouraged that applicants read the complete contest guidelines on the PSA website before submitting. **Deadline: October 1-December 22. Charges $20 fee.** Prize $500-1,000

ROBERT H. WINNER MEMORIAL AWARD

Poetry Society of America, 15 Gramercy Park, New York NY 10003. (212)254-9628. Fax: (212)673-2352. **Contact:** Brett Fletcher Lauer, awards coordinator. This award acknowledges original work being done in mid-career by a poet who has not had substantial recognition. Send manuscript of 10 poems (up to 20 pages). Guidelines for SASE or online. Open to poets over 40 who are unpublished or have 1 book. **Deadline: October 1-December 23. Charges $15/nonmembers; free to PSA members.** Prize $2,500

N WRITECORNER PRESS $500 POETRY AWARD

Writecorner Press, P.O. Box 140310, Gainesville FL 32614. (352)338-7778. Website: www.writecorner.com. **Contact:** Mary Sue Koeppel, Robert B. Gentry, coeditors. "Offered annually for unpublished poetry. Poetry may be in any style and on any subject. Maximum poem length is 40 lines. Only unpublished poems are eligible. No limit on number of poems entered by any 1 poet. The winning poem is published, as are the editors' choices poems. Copyright then returns to the authors. Guidelines for SASE or online." **Deadline: March 31, 2010. Submit between Oct. 1 - March 31 annually. Charges $5/poem; $3 each additional poem.** Prize $500 and publication on www.writecorner.com Mary Sue Koeppel and Robert B. Gentry, editors
Tips "Writecorner Press also sponsors the annual $1,100 E.M. Koeppel Short Fiction Award."

THE WRITER MAGAZINE/EMILY DICKINSON AWARD

Poetry Society of America, 15 Gramercy Park, New York NY 10003. (212)254-9628. Fax: (212)673-2352. **Contact:** Brett Fletcher Lauer, awards coordinator. Offered annually for a poem inspired by Emily Dickinson, though not necessarily in her style. Line limit: 30. Guidelines for SASE or online. Guidelines subject to change. *Open to PSA members only.* **Deadline: October 1-December 23.** Prize $250

WRITERS' JOURNAL POETRY CONTEST

Val-Tech Media, P.O. Box 394, Perham MN 56573. (218)346-7921. Fax: (218)346-7924. E-mail: writersjournal@writersjournal.com. **Contact:** Esther M. Leiper. Offered for previously unpublished poetry. Guidelines for SASE or online. **Deadline: April 30, August 30, December 30. Charges $3/poem.** Prize 1st Place: $50; 2nd Place: $25; 3rd Place: $15. First, second, third, and selected honorable mention winners will be published in *Writers' Journal* magazine.

MULTIPLE WRITING AREAS

ABILENE WRITERS GUILD ANNUAL CONTEST

Abilene Writers Guild, P.O. Box 2562, Abilene TX 79604. E-mail: AWG@abilenewritersguild.org. "Offered annually for unpublished work in ten categories. All rights remain with the writer." **Deadline: October 1-November 30. Charges $10 for each novel entry and $5 each for all other category entries.** Prize Prizes up to $100. professional writers and editors; different judges each year.
Tips "Details available on our website after August 1st."

ALLIGATOR JUNIPER AWARD

Alligator Juniper/Prescott College, 220 Grove Ave., Prescott AZ 86301. (928)350-2012. Fax: (928)776-5102. E-mail: aj@prescott.edu. **Contact:** Jeff Fearnside, managing editor. Offered annually for unpublished fiction, nonfiction and poetry. Guidelines online. Acquires first North American rights **Deadline: October 1 postmark. Charges $10 (includes the winning issue).** Prize $500 and publication. Judged by the staff and occasional guest judges.

AMERICAN MARKETS NEWSLETTER COMPETITION

American Markets Newsletter, 1974 46th Ave., San Francisco CA 94116. E-mail: sheila.oconnor@juno.com. **Contact:** Sheila O'Connor. "Accepts fiction and nonfiction up to 2,000 words. Entries are eligible for cash prizes and all entries are eligible for worldwide syndication whether they win or not. Here's how it works: Send us your double-spaced manuscripts with your story/article title, byline, word count, and address on the first page above your article/story's first paragraph (no need for separate cover page). There is no limit to the number of entries you may send." **Deadline: December 31 and July 31. Charges $12 for 1 entry; $15 for 2 entries; $20 for 3 entries; $25 for 4 entries; $30 for 5 entries.** Prize 1st Place: $300; 2nd Place: $100; 3rd Place: $50. a panel of independent judges.

ANNUAL U.S. MARITIME LITERATURE AWARDS

P.O. Box 264, Fulton TX 78358. E-mail: maritimeliterature@yahoo.com. **Contact:** Captain Richard Lamb. Accepts nonfiction maritime books published in the previous calendar year in these divisions: young readers (audiences 12 and under); adult (audiences 13 and above); foreign country (published outside the U.S.). Publishers are welcome to submit nominations. **Deadline: January 1-May 31**. Prize Glass-etched trophy and award ceremony. The winner's names are forwarded to The White House and First Family.

ANNUAL WRITING CONTEST

Lumina, the literary journal of Sarah Lawrence College, Sarah Lawrence College Slonim House, One Mead Way, Bronxville NY 10708. E-mail: lumina@slc.edu. **Contact:** Lani Scozzari. "Annual writing contest in poetry, fiction, or creative nonfiction (varies by year). Please visit http://slc.edu/lumina in late August for complete and updated contest rules." Typical reading period: Sept. 1 - Nov. 15. Electronic submissions only. **Charges $10.** Prize 1st Place: $500; 2nd Place: $100; 3rd Place: $50.

ARIZONA AUTHORS' ASSOCIATION ANNUAL NATIONAL LITERARY CONTEST AND BOOK AWARDS

Arizona Authors' Association, 6145 W. Echo Ln., Glendale AZ 85302. (623)847-9343. E-mail: info@azauthors.com. Website: www.azauthors.com. Offered annually for previously unpublished poetry, short stories, essays, novels, and articles. New awards for published books in fiction, anthology, nonfiction, and children's. Winners announced at an award banquet in Glendale in November, and short pieces and excerpts published in *Arizona Literary Magazine*. **Deadline: July 1. Charges $10 fee for poetry; $15 for short stories and essays; $30 for unpublished novels and published books.** Prize $100 and publication, and/or feature in the *Arizona Literary Magazine*.

ATLANTIC WRITING COMPETITION FOR UNPUBLISHED MANUSCRIPTS

Writers' Federation of Nova Scotia, 1113 Marginal Rd., Halifax NS B3H 4P7. (902)423-8116. Fax: (902)422-0881. E-mail: talk@writers.ns.ca. **Contact:** Bonita Hatcher,program coordinator. Estab. 1975. "Annual contest for beginners to try their hand in a number of categories: novel, short story, poetry, writing for younger children, writing for juvenile/young adult, magazine article/essay. Only 1 entry/category is allowed. Established writers are also eligible, but must work in an area that's new to them. Because our aim is to help Atlantic Canadian writers grow, judges return written comments when the competition is concluded. Anyone residing in the Atlantic Provinces for at least 6 months prior to the contest deadline is eligible to enter." **Deadline: First Friday in December. Charges $25 fee for novel ($20 for WFNS members); $15 fee for all other categories ($10 for WFNS members).** Prize **Novel**—1st Place: $200; 2nd Place: $150; 3rd Place: $100. **Writing for Younger Children and Juvenile/Young Adult**—1st Place: $150; 2nd Place: $75; 3rd Place: $50. **Poetry, Essay/Magazine Article, and Short Story**—1st Place: $100; 2nd Place: $75; 3rd Place: $50. a team of 2-3 professional writers, editors, booksellers, librarians, or teachers.

AWP AWARD SERIES

Association of Writers & Writing Programs, Carty House, Mail Stop 1E3, George Mason University, Fairfax VA 22030. (703)993-4301. Fax: (703)993-4302. E-mail: awp@awpwriter.org. **Contact:** Supriya Bhatnagar. Offered annually to foster new literary talent. Categories: poetry (Donald Hall Poetry Prize), short fiction (Grace Paley Prize in Short Fiction), novel, and creative nonfiction. Guidelines for SASE or online. Open to any writer. **Deadline: January 1-February 28 (postmarked). Charges $25/nonmembers; $10/members.** Prize Cash honorarium—4,000 for Donald Hall Prize for Poetry and Grace Paley Prize in Short Fiction, and $2,000 each for novel and creative nonfiction—and publication by a participating press.

BOROONDARA LITERARY AWARDS

City of Boroondara, 8 Inglesby Rd., Camberwell VIC 3124 Australia. E-mail: bla@boroondara.vic.gov.au. **Contact:** Awards Coordinator. "Contest for unpublished work in 2 categories: Young Writers, 7th-9th grade and 10th-12th grade (prose and poetry on any theme) and Open Short Story (2,000-3,000 words). Entries are only eligible if submitted on floppy disk or CD-ROM." **Deadline: August 31. Charges $8.40/short story; free entry for Young Writers.** Prize **Young Writers**—1st Place: $300; 2nd Place: $150; 3rd Place: $100. **Open Short Story**—1st Place: $1,500; 2nd Place: $500; 3rd Place $250.

THE BOSTON AUTHORS CLUB BOOK AWARDS

The Boston Authors Club, 79 Moore Road, Wayland MA 01778. E-mail: lawson@bc.edu. Website: www.bostonauthorsclub.org. **Contact:** Alan Lawson. "Julia Ward Howe Prize offered annually for books published the previous year. Two awards are given, 1 for trade books of fiction, nonfiction, or poetry, and the second for children's books. Authors must live or have lived within 100 miles of Boston. No picture books or subsidized publishers." **Deadline: January 15**. Prize $1,000 in each category. Books may also be cited as Finalist or Recommended with no cash award.

BURNABY WRITERS' SOCIETY CONTEST

E-mail: info@bws.bc.ca. **Contact:** Eileen Kernaghan. "Offered annually for unpublished work. Open to all residents of British Columbia. Categories vary from year to year. Send SASE for current rules. For complete guidelines: www.bws.bc.ca." Purpose is to encourage talented writers in all genres. **Deadline: May 31. Charges $5 fee.** Prize 1st Place: $200; 2nd Place: $100; 3rd Place: $50; and public reading.

CANADIAN HISTORICAL ASSOCIATION AWARDS

Canadian Historical Association, 395 Wellington, Ottawa ON K1A 0N3 Canada. (613)233-7885. Fax: (613)567-3110. E-mail: cha-shc@lac-bac.gc.ca. **Contact:** Michel Duquet, executive coordinator. Offered annually. Categories: Regional history, Canadian history, history (not Canadian), women's history (published articles, English or French), doctoral dissertations. Open to Canadian writers. **Deadline: Varies**. Prize Varies.

THE CITY OF VANCOUVER BOOK AWARD

Cultural Services Department, 453 W. 12th Ave., Vancouver BC V5Y 1V4 Canada. (604)871-6434. Fax: (604)871-6005. E-mail: marnie.rice@vancouver.ca. "Offered annually for books published in the previous year which exhibit excellence in the categories of content, illustration, design, and format. The book must contribute significantly to the appreciation and understanding of the city of Vancouver and heighten awareness of 1 or more of the following: Vancouver's history, the city's unique character, or achievements of the city's residents. The book may be fiction, nonfiction, poetry, or drama written for adults or children, and may deal with any aspects of the city—history, geography, current affairs, or the arts. Guidelines online." Prize $2,000

COLORADO BOOK AWARDS

Colorado Center for the Book, 1490 Lafayette St., Suite 101, Denver CO 80218. (303)894-7951, ext. 21. Fax: (303)864-9361. E-mail: long@coloradohumanities.org. **Contact:** Margaret Coval, exec. dir., or Jennifer Long, Prog. Adjudicator. Offered annually for work published by December of previous year. "The purpose is to champion all Colorado authors, editors, illustrators, and photographers, and in particular, to honor the award winners raising the profiles of both their work and Colorado as a state whose people promote and support reading, writing, and literacy through books. The categories are generally: children's literature, young adult and juvenile literature, fiction, genre fiction (romance, mystery/thriller, science fiction/fantasy, historical), biography, history, anthology, poetry, pictorial, graphic novel/comic, creative nonfiction, and general nonfiction, as well as other categories as determined each year. Open to authors who reside or have resided in Colorado." **Deadline: January 31. Charges $50 fee.**

COMMONWEALTH CLUB OF CALIFORNIA BOOK AWARDS

595 Market St., San Francisco CA 94105. (415)597-6700. Fax: (415)597-6729. E-mail: bookawards@commonwealthclub.org. Website: www.commonwealthclub.org/bookawards. **Contact:** Gina Baleria, Director, Literary Events. Estab. 1931. "Offered annually for published submissions appearing in print January 1-December 31 of the previous year. Purpose of award is the encouragement and production of literature in California. Can be nominated by publisher as well. Open to California residents (or residents at time of publication)." **Deadline: December 18, 2009 for books published in 2009**. Prize Medals and cash prizes to be awarded at publicized event fiction, nonfiction, poetry, first work of fiction, juvenile up to 10 years old, young adult 11-16, works in translation, notable contribution to publishing and Californiana.
Tips "Guidelines available on website."

CORDON D 'OR - GOLD RIBBON ANNUAL INTERNATIONAL CULINARY ACADEMY AWARDS

Cordon d 'Or - Gold Ribbon Inc., P.O. Box 40868, St. Petersburg FL 33743. (727)347-2437. E-mail: cordondor@aol.com. **Contact:** Noreen Kinney. "Contest promotes recognition of food authors, writers, and culinary magazines and websites, food stylists and food photographers and other professionals in the culinary field. See website: www.cordondorcuisine.com for full details. Open to any writer. on all categories can be found on the Web site. Open to any writer. The only criteria is that all entries must be in the English language." The entry fee varies with each category (see Web site). **Deadline: Nov. 30**. Prize Cordon d 'Or - Gold Ribbon Crystal Globe Trophies (with stands and engraved marble bases) will be presented to winners in each category. An outstanding winner chosen by the judges from among all entries will also win a cash award of $1,000. professionals in the fields covered in the awards program.

DAFFODIL DAY ARTS AWARDS

Cancer Council Victoria, 1 Rathdowne St., Carlton VIC 3053 Australia. (61)(3)0065-6585. Fax: (61)(3)9635-5240. E-mail: arts.awards@cancervic.org.au. Website: www.cancervic.org.au/artsawards. **Deadline: April 3. Charges $10.** Judged by high-profile and well-respected artists/specialists.

DANA AWARDS IN THE NOVEL, SHORT FICTION AND POETRY

www.danaawards.com, 200 Fosseway Dr., Greensboro NC 27445. (336)644-8028. E-mail: danaawards@pipeline.com. **Contact:** Mary Elizabeth Parker, chair. "Three awards offered annually for unpublished work written in English. Purpose is monetary award for work that has not been previously published or received monetary award, but will accept work published simply for friends and family. Works previously published online are not eligible. No work accepted by or for persons under 16 for any of the 3 awards. Awards: **Novel**—For the first 50 pages of a novel completed or in progress. **Fiction**—Short fiction (no memoirs) up to 10,000 words. **Poetry**—For best group of 5 poems based on excellence of all 5 (no light verse, no single poem over 100 lines). See website for full guidelines on varied reading fees." **Deadline: October 31 (postmarked). Charges $25 per novel entry; $15 per short fiction entry; $15 per poetry entry.** Prize $1,000 for each of the 3 awards.

EATON LITERARY AGENCY'S ANNUAL AWARDS PROGRAM

Eaton Literary Agency, P.O. Box 49795, Sarasota FL 34230. (941)366-6589. Fax: (941)365-4679. E-mail: eatonlit@aol.com. Website: www.eatonliterary.com. **Contact:** Richard Lawrence, V.P. "Offered annually for unpublished mss." **Deadline: March 31 (mss under 10,000 words); August 31 (mss over 10,000 words).** Prize $2,500 (over 10,000 words); $500 (under 10,000 words). Judged by an independent agency in conjunction with some members of Eaton's staff.

THE VIRGINIA FAULKNER AWARD FOR EXCELLENCE IN WRITING

Prairie Schooner, 201 Andrews Hall, P.O. Box 880334, Lincoln NE 68588-0334. (402)472-0911. Fax: (402)472-9771. E-mail: jengelhardt2@unl.edu. **Contact:** Hilda Raz. "Offered annually for work published in *Prairie Schooner* in the previous year." Prize $1,000.

THE FLORIDA REVIEW EDITOR'S PRIZE

Dept. of English, P.O. Box 161346, University of Central Florida, P.O. Box 161346, Orlando FL 32816. (407)823-2038. E-mail: flreview@mail.ucf.edu. Annual awards for the best unpublished fiction, poetry, and creative nonfiction. first rights **Deadline: Spring Yearly. Check Web site for specifics. Charges $15.** Prize $1,000 (in each genre) and publication in *The Florida Review*. Judged by the editors in each genre. Judging is blind, so names should not appear on mss.

FUGUE'S POETRY AND PROSE CONTEST

Fugue, P.O. Box 441102, 200 Brink Hall, English Department, University of Idaho, Moscow ID 83844-1102. Website: www.uidaho.edu/fugue/contest. **Contact:** Genre Editor (Poetry or Nonfiction). Annual award for poetry, every 2 years for nonfiction and poetry, to recognize the most compelling work being produced. 2009: Poetry and Nonfiction. 2010: Reading for Poetry and Fiction. Acquires first North American serial rights and electronic rights." **Deadline: May 1. Charges $20/submission, 1 year subscription included with cost.** Prize $1,000 and publication for 1st-place winner; publication for 2nd- and 3rd-place winners.

INDIANA REVIEW ½ K (SHORT-SHORT/PROSE-POEM) PRIZE

Indiana Review, Ballantine Hall 465, Indiana University, Bloomington IN 47405-7103. (812)855-3439. Fax: (812)855-4253. E-mail: inreview@indiana.edu. **Contact:** Grady Jaynes. Maximum story/poem length is 500 words. Offered annually for unpublished work. **Deadline: Early June. Charges $15 fee for no more than 3 pieces (includes a 1-year subscription). Check Web site for guidelines.** Prize $1,000 Guest judges; Lydia Davis 2009 judge

IOWA AWARD IN POETRY, FICTION, & ESSAY

The Iowa Review, 308 EPB, Iowa City IA 52242. (319)335-0462. Fax: (319)335-2535. Website: www.iowareview.org. **Deadline: January 2-31 (postmarked). Charges $20 entry fee.** Prize $1,000 and publication

LAMBDA LITERARY AWARDS

The Lambda Literary Foundation, 5482 Wilshire Blvd., Los Angeles CA 90036-4218. (323)936-5876. E-mail: awards@lambdaliterary.org. **Contact:** Charles Flowers. Annual contest for published books in approximately 20 categories: Anthology; Arts & Culture; Bisexual; Chilren's/Young Adult; Debut Fiction (1 gay, 1 lesbian); Drama/Theater; Erotica; Fiction (1 men's, 1 women's; LGBT Nonfiction; LGBT Studies; Memoir/Biography (1 men's, 1 women's); Mystery (1 men's, 1 women's); Poetry (1 men's, 1 women's); Romance (1 men's, 1 women's); Science Fiction/Fantasy/Horror; Transgender. **Deadline: December 1. Charges $20.** Prize The debut gay and lesbian fiction awards have cash honorarium

LET'S WRITE LITERARY CONTEST

The Gulf Coast Writers Association, P.O. Box 10294, Gulfport MS 39505. E-mail: gcwriters@aol.com. **Contact:** Victoria Olsen. **Deadline: April 15. Charges $10 for each fiction or nonfiction entry and $5 for poetry.** Prize 1st Prize: $75; 2nd Prize: $50; 3rd Prize: $25. 5 professional writers.

THE HUGH J. LUKE AWARD

Prairie Schooner, 201 Andrews Hall, P.O. Box 880334, Lincoln NE 68588-0334. (402)472-0911. Fax: (402)472-9771. E-mail: jengelhardt2@unl.edu. **Contact:** Hilda Raz. Offered annually for work published in *Prairie Schooner* in the previous year. Prize $250.

THE MCGINNIS-RITCHIE MEMORIAL AWARD

Southwest Review, P.O. Box 750374, Dallas TX 75275-0374. (214)768-1037. Fax: (214)768-1408. E-mail: swr@mail.smu.edu. **Contact:** Jennifer Cranfill, senior editor and Willard Spiegelman, editor-in-chief. "The McGinnis-Ritchie Memorial Award is given annually to the best works of fiction and nonfiction that appeared in the magazine in the previous year. Manuscripts are submitted for publication, not for the prizes themselves. Guidelines for SASE or online." Prize Two cash prizes of $500 each. Jennifer Cranfill and Willard Spiegelman.

MIDLAND AUTHORS AWARD

Society of Midland Authors, P.O. Box 10419, Chicago IL 60610-0419. E-mail: writercc@aol.com. **Contact:** Carol Jean Carlson. Offered annually for published fiction, nonfiction, poetry, biography, children's fiction, and children's nonfiction published in the previous calendar year. Authors must reside in, have been born in, or have strong connections to the states of Illinois, Indiana, Iowa, Kansas, Michigan, Minnesota, Missouri, Nebraska, North Dakota, South Dakota, Wisconsin, or Ohio. Guidelines online. **Deadline: February 1.** Prize Monetary award given to winner in each category.

NATIONAL OUTDOOR BOOK AWARDS

921 S. 8th Ave., Stop 8128, Pocatello ID 83209. (208)282-3912. E-mail: wattron@isu.edu. Website: www.noba-web.org. **Contact:** Ron Watters. "Nine categories: History/biography, outdoor literature, instructional texts, outdoor adventure guides, nature guides, childrens' books, design/artistic merit, natural history literature, and nature and the environment. Additionally, a special award, the Outdoor Classic Award, is given annually to books which, over a period of time, have proven to be exceptionally valuable works in the outdoor field. Application forms and eligibilty requirements are available online." **Deadline: September 1. Charges $65 fee.** Prize Winning books are promoted nationally and are entitled to display the National Outdoor Book Award (NOBA) medallion.

NEW LETTERS LITERARY AWARDS

New Letters, UMKC, University House, Room 105, 5101 Rockhill Rd., Kansas City MO 64110-2499. (816)235-1168. Fax: (816)235-2611. Award has 3 categories (fiction, poetry, and creative nonfiction) with 1 winner in each. Offered annually for previously unpublished work. Guidelines for SASE or online. first North American serial rights. **Deadline: May 18. Charges $15 fee (includes a 1-year subscription to *New Letters* magazine).** Prize 1st Place: $1,500, plus publication; First Runners-Up: A copy of a recent book of poetry or fiction courtesy of our affiliate BkMk Press. Preliminary judges are regional writers of prominence and experience. All judging is done anonymously. Winners picked by a final judge of national repute. Previous judges include Maxine Kumin, Albert Goldbarth, Charles Simic, Janet Burroway.

NEW MILLENNIUM WRITING AWARDS

New Millennium Writings, Room M2, P.O. Box 2463, Knoxville TN 37901. Website: www.newmillenniumwritings.com/awards.html. **Contact:** Contest Coordinator. Offered biannually for unpublished fiction, poetry, essays or nonfiction prose to encourage new writers and bring them to the attention of the publishing industry. **Deadline: June 17 & Jan31. Charges $17/submission.** Prize $1,000 each for best poem, fiction, and nonfiction; winners published in *NMW* and on website.

THE NOMA AWARD FOR PUBLISHING IN AFRICA

Kodansha Ltd., Japan, P.O. Box 128, Witney, Oxon OX8 5XU United Kingdom. (44)(1993)775-235. Fax: (44)(1993)709-265. E-mail: maryljay@aol.com. Website: www.nomaaward.org. **Contact:** Mary Jay, secretary to the Noma Award Managing Committee. Estab. 1979. "The Noma Award, sponsored by Kodansha LTD., Japan, is open to African writers and scholars whose work is published in Africa. The spirit within which the annual award is given is to encourage and reward genuinely autonomous African publishers, and African writers. The award is given for an outstanding new book in any of these 3 categories: scholarly or academic; books for children; and literature and creative writing (including fiction, drama, poetry, and essays on African literature). Entries must be submitted by publishers in Africa, who are limited to 3 entries (in any combination of the eligible categories). The award is open to any author who is indigenous to Africa (a national, irrespective of place of domicile). Guidelines at website or from Secretariat." **Deadline: April 30.** Prize $10,000 (US). "The managing committee is an impartial committee chaired by Mr. Walter Bgoya, comprising African scholars, book experts, and representatives of the international book community. This Managing Committee is the jury. The jury is assisted by independent opinion and assessment from a large and distinguished pool of subject specialists from throughout the world, including many in Africa."

PNWA LITERARY CONTEST

Pacific Northwest Writers Association, PMB 2717-1420 NW Gilman Blvd, Ste, Issaquah WA 98027. (425)673-2665. Fax: (206)824-4559. E-mail: pnwa@pnwa.org. Website: www.pnwa.org. **Contact:** Kelli Liddane. "Annual contest for unpublished writers. Over $12,000 in prize monies. Categories include: Mainstream; Historical; Romance; Mystery/Thriller; Science Fiction/Fantasy; Young Adult Novel; Nonfiction Book/Memoir; Screenwriting; Poetry; Adult Short Story; Children's Picture Book/Chapter Book; Adult Short Topics. Each entry receives 2 critiques. Guidelines online." **Deadline: February 19. Charges $35/entry (members); $50/entry (nonmembers).** Prize 1st Place: $600; 2nd Place: $300; 3rd Place: $150. Each prize is awarded in all 12 categories.

POSTCARD STORY COMPETITION

The Writers' Union of Canada, 90 Richmond St. E., Suite 200, Toronto ON M5C 1P1 Canada. (416)703-8982. Fax: (416)504-9090. **Contact:** Competitions Coordinator. "Offered annually for original and unpublished fiction, nonfiction, prose, verse, dialogue, etc., with a maximum length of 250 words. Open to Canadian citizens or landed immigrants only." **Deadline: February 14. Charges $5 entry fee.** Prize $500

PRAIRIE SCHOONER BOOK PRIZE

Prairie Schooner and the University of Nebraska Press, 201 Andrews Hall, University of Nebraska, Lincoln NE 68588-0334. (402)472-0911. E-mail: jengelhardt2@unlnotes.unl.edu. **Contact:** Hilda Raz, editor. "Annual book series competition publishing 1 book-length collection of short fiction and 1 book-length collection of poetry. **Submission Period: January 15-March 15.**" **Charges $25.** Prize $3,000 and publication through the University of Nebraska Press (1 award in fiction and 1 award in poetry). Also awards $1,000 runner-up prize in each category. Hilda Raz, editor of *Prairie Schooner*, and members of the Book Series Literary Board.

THE PRESIDIO LA BAHIA AWARD

Sons of the Republic of Texas, 1717 Eighth St., Bay City TX 77414-5033. (979)245-6644. Fax: (979)244-3819. E-mail: srttexas@srttexas.org. **Contact:** Scott Dunbar, chairman. Offered annually to promote suitable preservation of relics, appropriate dissemination of data, and research into Texas heritage, with particular attention to the Spanish Colonial period. **Deadline: September 30**. Prize $2,000 total; 1st Place: Minimum of $1,200, 2nd and 3rd prizes at the discretion of the judges Judged by members of the Sons of the Republic of Texas on the Presidio La Bahia Award Committee.

PUDDING HOUSE CHAPBOOK COMPETITION

Pudding House Publications, 81 Shadymere Ln., Columbus OH 43213. (614) 986-1881. E-mail: jen@puddinghouse.com. Website: www.puddinghouse.com. **Contact:** Jennifer Bosveld. "Ms must be 10-36 pages (prefers around 24-28 pages). Some poems may be previously published but not the collection as a whole. Guidelines on website." **Deadline: September 30. Charges $12.** Prize $1,000, publication, and 20 copies of the chapbook.

QWF LITERARY AWARDS

Quebec Writers' Federation, 1200 Atwater Ave., Montreal QC H3Z 1X4 Canada. (514)933-0878. E-mail: info@qwf.org. "Offered annually for a book published October 1-September 30 to honor excellence in English-language writing in Quebec. Categories: fiction, nonfiction, poetry, first book, children's and young adult, and translation. Author must have resided in Quebec for 3 of the past 5 years. Guidelines online." **Deadline: May 31 for books published before May 16; August 15 for books/bound proofs published after May 16. Charges $20/entry.**

SUMMERFIELD G. ROBERTS AWARD

Sons of the Republic of Texas, 1717 Eighth St., Bay City TX 77414-5033. (979)245-6644. Fax: (979)244-3819. E-mail: srttexas@srttexas.org. **Contact:** Sam F. Clark, Jr., chairman. Offered annually for submissions published during the previous calendar year to encourage literary effort and research about historical events and personalities during the days of the Republic of Texas, 1836-1846, and to stimulate interest in the period. **Deadline: January 15**. Prize $2,500 the last 3 winners of the contest.

THE ROSS FORTUNE WRITE COLOR AWARDS

Ross Fortune's Interactive, Design Head Cottage, New No. 66, Old No. 30 B. South Boag Rd., T. Nagar, Chennai-Madras, Tamil Nadu 600017 India. (91)(44)4207-1020. E-mail: editors@rossfortune.com. Website: www.rossfortune.com. **Contact:** Tariq Hyder, editorial director. Annual contest to discover and promote talented, unpublished writers in all genres, including fiction, nonfiction, graphic novels and photography. All entries must be original and not submitted elsewhere. Usually no rights are acquired, but rules vary from year to year. Participating sponsors might acquire all rights. Open to writers worldwide under the age of 50. **Deadline: September 30**. Prize Award varies each year from $100 (USD) to a maximum of $1,000 (USD). Winning works are published in a sponsoring magazine, newspaper or website. Internships are awarded to young finalists. All participants receive certificates suitable for framing. Judged by a panel of respected journalists, established writers, critics, and popular bloggers.

SASKATCHEWAN BOOK OF THE YEAR AWARD

Saskatchewan Book Awards, Inc., 205B, 2314 11th Ave., Regina SK S4P OK1 Canada. (306)569-1585. Fax: (306)569-4187. E-mail: director@bookawards.sk.ca. **Contact:** Jackie Lay, executive director. Offered annually for work published September 15-September 14 annually. This award is presented to a Saskatchewan author for the best book, judged on the quality of writing. Books from the following categories will be considered: children's; drama; fiction (short fiction by a single author, novellas, novels); nonfiction (all categories of nonfiction writing except cookbooks, directories, how-to books, or bibliographies of minimal critical content); poetry. Visit website for more details. **Deadline: First deadline: July 31; Final deadline: September 14. Charges $20 (Canadian).** Prize $3,000

SASKATOON BOOK AWARD

Saskatchewan Book Awards, Inc., Box 1921, Regina SK S4P 3E1 Canada. (306)569-1585. Fax: (306)569-4187. E-mail: director@bookawards.sk.ca. **Contact:** Jackie Lay, executive director. Offered annually for work published September 15-September 14. In recognition of the vitality of the literary community in Saskatoon, this award is presented to a Saskatoon author for the best book, judged on the quality of writing. Books from the following categories will be considered: children's; drama; fiction (short fiction by a single author, novellas, novels); nonfiction (all categories of nonfiction writing except cookbooks, directories, how-to books, or bibliographies of minimal critical content); poetry. **Deadline: First deadline: July 31; Final deadline: September 14. Charges $20 (Canadian).** Prize $2,000

MARGARET & JOHN SAVAGE FIRST BOOK AWARD

Halifax Public Libraries, 60 Alderney Dr., Dartmouth NS B2Y 4P8 Canada. (902)490-5991. Fax: (902)490-5889. E-mail: mackenh@halifaxpubliclibraries.ca. **Contact:** Heather MacKenzie. "Recognizes the best first book of fiction or nonfiction written by a first-time published author residing in Atlantic Canada. Books may be of any genre, but must contain a minimum of 40% text, be at least 49 pages long, and be available for sale. No anthologies. Publishers: Send 4 copies of each title and submission form for each entry." Children's Books not accepted. **Deadline: December 4. Charges $10 (submission fee must accompany entry- cheques to be made payable to the Halifax Regional Municipality).**

THE MONA SCHREIBER PRIZE FOR HUMOROUS FICTION & NONFICTION

15442 Vista Haven Place, Sherman Oaks CA 91403. E-mail: brad.schreiber@att.net. Website: www.brashcyber.com. **Contact:** Brad Schreiber. "The purpose of the contest is to award the most creative humor writing, in any form less than 750 words, in either fiction or nonfiction, including but not limited to stories, articles, essays, speeches, shopping lists, diary entries, and anything else writers dream up." **Deadline: December 1. Charges $5 fee/entry (payable to Mona Schreiber Prize).** Prize 1st Place: $500; 2nd Place: $250; 3rd Place: $100. Brad Schreiber, author, journalist, consultant, and instructor at MediaBistro.com. Complete rules and previous winning entries on Web site.

Tips "No SASE's, Please."

SHORT GRAIN WRITING CONTEST

Grain Magazine, Box 67, Saskatoon SK S7K 3K1 Canada. (306)244-2828. Fax: (306)244-0255. E-mail: grainmag@sasktel.net. **Contact:** Mike Thompson, Business Administrator. "Two categories with four prizes in each: poetry in any form including prose poem; short fiction of any style including postcard story. All entrants receive a 1-year subscription to *Grain Magazine*." Guidelines available by fax, e-mail, or on Web site. **Deadline: April 1 annually. Charges $30 fee for maximum of 2 entries in one category; US and international entries $36 in US funds.** Prize Two first prizes of $1,250; two second prizes of $750; four runner-up prizes of $500, plus publication.

SHORT PROSE COMPETITION FOR DEVELOPING WRITERS

The Writers' Union of Canada, 90 Richmond St. E., Suite 200, Toronto ON M5C 1P1 Canada. (416)703-8982. Fax: (416)504-9090. **Contact:** Nancy MacLeod, Competitions Coordinator. Offered annually "to discover developing Canadian writers of unpublished prose: fiction and nonfiction." Length: 2,500 words maximum. Open to Canadian citizens or landed immigrants who have not been published in book format by a commercial or university press, and who do not currently have a contract with a publisher. **Deadline: November 3. Charges $25 entry fee.** Prize $2,500 and possible publication in a literary journal.

THE BERNICE SLOTE AWARD

Prairie Schooner, 201 Andrews Hall, PO Box 880334, Lincoln NE 68588-0334. (402)472-0911. Fax: (402)472-9771. E-mail: jengelhardt2@unl.edu. **Contact:** Hilda Raz. "Offered annually for the best work by a beginning writer published in *Prairie Schooner* in the previous year." Prize $500

KAY SNOW WRITING AWARDS

Willamette Writers, 9045 SW Barbur Blvd., Suite 5A, Portland OR 97219. (503)452-1592. Fax: (503)452-0372. E-mail: wilwrite@willamettewriters.com. "Contest offered annually to offer encouragement and recognition to writers with unpublished submissions. Acquires right to publish excerpts from winning pieces one time in their newsletter." **Deadline: April 23. Charges $15 fee; no fee for student writers.** Prize 1st Place: $300; 2nd Place: $150; 3rd Place: $50; excerpts published in Willamette Writers newsletter, and winners acknowledged at banquet during writing conference. Student writers win $50 in categories for grades 1-5, 6-8, and 9-12. The Liam Callen Award of $500 goes to the best overall entry in all divisions.

Tips "This contest has many different categories, including film scripts."

THE ERIC HOFFER AWARD (PROSE)

Best New Writing, P.O. Box 11, Titusville NJ 08560. Fax: (609)964-1718. E-mail: info@hopepubs.com. **Contact:** Christopher Klim, Exec. editor. "Annual contest for new and unpublished prose. Purchases first publication and one-time anthology rights for winning entries." "The Eric Hoffer Award (formerly the Writers' Notes Award) for short prose (i.e., fiction and creative nonfiction - 10,000 words or less) was established at the start of the 21st century as a means of opening a door to writing of significant merit. It honors the memory of the great American philosopher Eric Hoffer by highlighting salient writing. The winning stories and essays are published in *Best New Writing*." **March 31. Charges Free.** Prize $500; publication contract. Judges include authors, editors, journalists, agents, and experienced category readers.

THE ERIC HOFFER AWARD (BOOKS)

Best New Writing, P.O. Box 11, Titusville NJ 08560-0011. Fax: (609)818-1913. E-mail: info@hopepubs.com. **Contact:** Christopher Klim, senior editor. Annual contest recognizing excellence in publishing. "This contest recognizes excellence in independent publishing in 14 distinct categories. Honors by press type (academic, independent, small press, and self-published). Also awards the Montaigne Medal for most thought provoking book and the Da Vinci Eye for best cover. Results published in the US Review of Books." **Deadline: January 25. Charges $45.** Prize $1,500 Judge by authors, editors, agents, publishers, book producers, artists, experienced category readers, and health and business professionals.

TORONTO BOOK AWARDS

City of Toronto c/o Toronto Protocol, 100 Queen St. W., 2nd Floor, West Tower, City Hall, Toronto ON M5H 2N2 Canada. (416)392-8191. Fax: (416)392-1247. E-mail: bkurmey@toronto.ca. **Contact:** Bev Kurmey, protocol officer. "Offered annually for previously published fiction or nonfiction books for adults or children that are evocative of Toronto." **Deadline: March 31.** Prize Awards total $15,000; $1,000 goes to shortlist finalists (usually 4-6) and the remainder goes to the winner. Judged by independent judging committee of 5 people chosen through an application and selection process.

THE BRONWEN WALLACE MEMORIAL AWARD

The Writers' Trust of Canada, 90 Richmond St. East, Suite 200, Toronto, Ontario M5C 1P1 Canada. (416)504-8222. Fax: (416)504-9090. E-mail: info@writerstrust.com. Website: www.writerstrust.com. **Contact:** Amanda Hopkins. Presented annually to "a Canadian writer under the age of 35 who is not yet published in book form. The award, which alternates each year between poetry and short fiction, was established in memory of poet Bronwen Wallace." Prize $5,000 and $1,000 to two finalists

ROBERT WATSON LITERARY PRIZES

The Greensboro Review MFA Writing Program, 3302 Moore Humanities and Research Admin. Bldg, P.O. Box 26170, Greensboro NC 27402-6170. (336)334-5459. E-mail: anseay@uncg.edu. Website: www.greensbororeview.org. **Contact:** Allison Seay, assoc. editor. Estab. 1966. "Offered annually for fiction (7,500 word limit) and poetry recognizing the best work published in the spring issue of *The Greensboro Review*. Sample issue for $5." **Deadline: September 15.** Prize $500 each for best short story and poem. Rights revert to author upon publication.

WESTERN HERITAGE AWARDS

National Cowboy & Western Heritage Museum, 1700 NE 63rd St., Oklahoma City OK 73111-7997. (405)478-6404. Fax: (405)478-4714. E-mail: ssimpson@nationalcowboymuseum.org. **Contact:** Shayla Simpson, PR director. Offered annually for excellence in representation of great stories of the American West published November 30-December 1. Competition includes 7 literary categories: nonfiction, western novel, juvenile book, art book, photography, poetry book, and magazine article. Guidelines available online. **Charges $50 entry fee.** Prize bronze Wrangler statue.

WESTERN MAGAZINE AWARDS

Western Magazine Awards Foundation, 875 Prairie Ave., Port Coquitlam, Vancouver BC V3B 1R9 Canada. (604)945-3711. E-mail: corey@westernmagazineawards.ca. "Offered annually for magazine work published January 1 - December 31 of previous calendar year. Entry categories include business, culture, science, technology and medicine, entertainment, fiction, political issues, and much more. The work must have been published in a magazine whose main editorial office is in Western Canada, the Northwest Territories, and Yukon. Guidelines for SASE or online. Applicant must be a Canadian citizen or full-time resident." **Deadline: February 25. Charges Entry fees change annually.** Prize $750 - $1,000

WESTMORELAND POETRY & SHORT STORY CONTEST

Westmoreland Arts & Heritage Festival, 252 Twin Lakes Rd., Latrobe PA 15650-9415. (724)834-7474. Fax: (724)850-7474. E-mail: info@artsandheritage.com. **Contact:** Diana Morreo. Offered annually for unpublished work. Two categories: Poem & Short Story. Short story entries no longer than 4,000 words. Family-oriented festival and contest. **Deadline: April 3. Charges $10/story or for 2 poems.** Prize Up to $200 in prizes.

JOHN WOOD COMMUNITY COLLEGE WRITING CONTEST

1301 S. 48th St., Quincy IL 62305. (217)641-4940. Fax: (217)641-4900. **Contact:** Kelli Langston, community education specialist. Categories include nonfiction and fiction. No identification should appear on manuscripts, but send a separate 3x5 card for each entry with name, address, phone number, e-mail address, title of work, and category in which each work should be entered. Only for previously unpublished work: poetry (2 page/poem maximum), fiction (2,000 words maximum), nonfiction (2,000 words maximum). Accepts traditional rhyming poetry, nonrhyming poetry, and other poetry forms such as haiku, limericks, etc. Entries are accepted March 1-April 3. Guidelines for SASE or online. **Charges $5/poem; $7/fiction or nonfiction. Critiquing service is available for $5/poem; $15/story.** Prize Cash prizes dictated by the number of entries received.

THE WORD GUILD CANADIAN WRITING AWARDS

The Word Guild, Box 28087, Waterloo, ON N2L 6J8 Canada. (519)886-4196. E-mail: questions@thewordguild.com. Website: www.thewordguild.com. The Word Guild is an association of Canadian writers and editors who are Christian, and who are committed to encouraging one another and to fostering standards of excellence in the art, craft, practice and ministry of writing. Memberships available for various experience levels. Yearly conference Write! Canada is held in June in Guelph, Ontario, and features plenary speakers, continuing classes and workshops. Editors and agents on site. Critiques available. The Word Guild offers three contests: Best New New Canadian Christian Author contest, The Word Guild Canadian Christian Writing Awards, and the God Uses Ink Novice contests. Best New Canadian Christian Author contest is for completed book manuscripts for unpublished authors. Deadline is November. Prize: publishing of ms. The TWG Canadian Christian Writing Awards is for work published in the past year, in many categories including books, articles, songs, poetry. Deadlines are October and January. Cash prizes offered. The God Uses Ink Novice contest is for writers who have never been paid, in three age categories. Entrants write on an assigned theme. **Deadline: March.** Prize Registration for Write! Canada conference Judged by writers, editors, etc.

WORLD'S BEST SHORT SHORT STORY FICTION CONTEST, NARRATIVE NONFICTION CONTEST & SOUTHEAST REVIEW POETRY CONTEST

English Department, Florida State University, Tallahassee FL 32306. **Contact:** Jessica Pitchford, ed. Estab. 1979. "Annual award for unpublished short short stories (500 words or less), poetry, and narrative nonfiction (5,000 words or less) for unpublished short short story (no more than 300 words)." **Deadline: March 15. Charges $15 reading fee for up to 3 stories or poems, $10 reading fee per nonfiction entry.** Prize $500 for short short and poetry winner, $250 for nonfiction winner. Winners will be published in *The Southeast Review*. Nine finalists in short fiction and poetry and two finalists in nonfiction will also be published.

WRITER'S DIGEST WRITING COMPETITION

Writer's Digest, a publication of F+W Media, Inc., 700 E. State Street, Iola WI 54990. (513)531-2690, ext. 1328. E-mail: writing-competition@fwpubs.com. **Contact:** Nicki Florence. Writing contest with 10 categories: Inspirational Writing (spiritual/religious, maximum 2,500 words); Memoir/Personal Essay (maximum 2,000 words); Magazine Feature Article (maximum 2,000 words); Short Story (genre, maximum 4,000 words); Short Story (mainstream/literary, maximum 4,000 words); Rhyming Poetry (maximum 32 lines); Nonrhyming Poetry (maximum 32 lines); Stage Play (first 15 pages and 1-page synopsis); TV/Movie Script (first 15 pages and 1-page synopsis). Entries must be original, in English, unpublished/unproduced (except for Magazine Feature Articles), and not accepted by another publisher/producer at the time of submission. *Writer's Digest* retains one-time publication rights to the winning entries in each category. **Deadline:May 15/late entry June 1, additional fee for late entries. Charges $10/first poetry entry; $5/additional poem. All other entries are $15/first ms; $10/additional ms.** Prize Grand Prize: $2,500 and a trip to New York City to meet with editors and agents; 1st Place: $1,000, ms critique and marketing advice from a *Writer's Digest* editor, commentary from an agent, and $100 of Writer's Digest Books; 2nd Place: $500 and $100 of Writer's Digest Books; 3rd Place: $250 and $100 of Writer's Digest Books; 4th Place: $100 and a subscription to *Writer's Digest*; 5th Place: $50 and a subscription to *Writer's Digest*' 6th-10th place $25 and a subscription to *Writer's Digest*.

WRITERS-EDITORS NETWORK ANNUAL INTERNATIONAL WRITING COMPETITION

Florida Freelance Writers Association, P.O. Box A, North Stratford NH 03590-0167. E-mail: contest@writers-editors.com. **Contact:** Dana K. Cassell, executive director. "Annual award to recognize publishable talent. Categories: Nonfiction (previously published article/essay/column/nonfiction book chapter; unpublished or self-published article/essay/column/nonfiction book chapter); Fiction (unpublished or self-published short story or novel chapter); Children's Literature (unpublished or self-published short story/nonfiction article/book chapter/poem); Poetry (unpublished or self-published free verse/traditional)." **Deadline: March 15. Charges $5 (active or new CNW/FFWA members) or $10 (nonmembers) for each fiction/nonfiction entry under 3,000 words; $10 (members) or $20 (nonmembers) for each entry of 3,000 words or longer; $3 (members) or $5 (nonmembers) for each poem.** Prize 1st Place: $100; 2nd Place: $75; 3rd Place: $50. All winners and Honorable Mentions will receive certificates as warranted. Judged by editors, librarians, and writers.

WRITERS' LEAGUE OF TEXAS BOOK AWARDS

Writers' League of Texas, 1501 W. Fifth St., Suite E-2, Austin TX 78703. (512)499-8914. Fax: (512)499-0441. E-mail: wlt@writersleague.org. **Contact:** Kristy Bordine, program and membership coordinator. Offered annually for work published June 1-May 31. Honors 3 outstanding books published in fiction, nonfiction, and literary categories. Membership dues may accompany entry fee. **Deadline: April 31. Charges $25 fee.** Prize Three $1,000 prizes and trophies

RESOURCES

Professional Organizations

AGENTS' ORGANIZATIONS

Association of Authors' Agents (AAA), 14 Vernon St., London W14 0RJ, United Kingdom. (44)(20)7471-7900. E-mail: philippa@lawagency.co.uk. Web site: www.agentsassoc.co.uk.

Association of Authors' Representatives (AAR). E-mail: info@aar-online.org. Web site: www.aar-online.org.Association of Talent Agents (ATA), 9255 Sunset Blvd., Suite 930, Los Angeles CA 90069. (310)274-0628. Fax: (310)274-5063. E-mail: shellie@agentassociation.com. Web site: www.agentassociation.com.

WRITERS' ORGANIZATIONS

Academy of American Poets 584 Broadway, Suite 604, New York NY 10012-5243. (212)274-0343. Fax: (212)274-9427. E-mail: academy@poets.org. Web site: www.poets.org.

American Crime Writers League (ACWL), 17367 Hilltop Ridge Dr., Eureka MO 63205. Web site: www.acwl.org. American Medical Writers Association (AMWA), 40 W. Gude Dr., Suite 101, Rockville MD 20850-1192. (301)294-5303. Fax: (301)294-9006. E-mail: amwa@amwa.org. Web site: www.amwa.org.

American Screenwriters Association (ASA), 269 S. Beverly Dr., Suite 2600, Beverly Hills CA 90212-3807. (866)265-9091. E-mail: asa@goasa.com. Website: www.asascreenwriters.com.

American Translators Association (ATA), 225 Reinekers Lane, Suite 590, Alexandria VA 22314. (703)683-6100. Fax: (703)683-6122. E-mail: ata@atanet.org. Web site: www.atanet.org.

Education Writers Association (EWA), 2122 P St., NW Suite 201, Washington DC 20037. (202)452-9830. Fax: (202)452-9837. E-mail: ewa@ewa.org. Web site: www.ewa.org.

Garden Writers Association (GWA), 10210 Leatherleaf Ct., Manassas VA 20111. (703)257-1032. Fax: (703)257-0213. E-mail: info@gardenwriters.org. Web site: www.gardenwriters.org.

Horror Writers Association (HWA), 244 5th Ave., Suite 2767, New York NY 10001. E-mail: hwa@horror.org. Web site: www.horror.org.

The International Women's Writing Guild (IWWG),P.O. Box 810, Gracie Station, New York NY 10028-0082. (212)737-7536. Fax: (212)737-9469. E-mail: dirhahn@iwwg.org. Web site: www.iwwg.com.

Mystery Writers of America (MWA), 17 E. 47th St., 6th Floor, New York NY 10017. (212)888-8171. Fax: (212)888-8107. E-mail: mwa@mysterywriters.org. Web site: www.mysterywriters.org.

National Association of Science Writers (NASW), P.O. Box 890, Hedgesville WV 25427. (304)754-5077. E-mail: diane@nasw.org. Web site: www.nasw.org.

National Association of Women Writers (NAWW), 24165 IH-10 W., Suite 217-637, San Antonio TX 78257. Phone/Fax: (866)821-5829. Web site: www.naww.org.

Organization of Black Screenwriters (OBS). Web site: www.obswriter.com. Outdoor Writers Association of America (OWAA), 121 Hickory St., Suite 1, Missoula MT 59801. (406)728-7434. Fax: (406)728-7445. E-mail: krhoades@owaa.org. Web site: www.owaa.org.

Poetry Society of America (PSA), 15 Gramercy Park, New York NY 10003. (212)254-9628. Web site: www.poetrysociety.org. Poets & Writers, 90 Broad St., Suite 2100, New York NY 10004. (212)226-3586. Fax: (212)226-3963. Web site: www.pw.org.

Romance Writers of America (RWA), 16000 Stuebner Airline Rd., Suite 140, Spring TX 77379. (832)717-5200. Fax: (832)717-5201. E-mail: info@rwanational.org. Web site: www.rwanational.org.

Science Fiction and Fantasy Writers of America (SFWA), P.O. Box 877, Chestertown MD 21620. E-mail: execdir@sfwa.org. Web site: www.sfwa.org.

Society of American Business Editors & Writers (SABEW), University of Missouri, School of Journalism, 385 McReynolds, Columbia MO 65211. (573)882-7862. Fax: (573)884-1372. E-mail: sabew@missouri.edu. Web site: www.sabew.org.

Society of American Travel Writers (SATW), 7044 S. 13 St., Oak Creek WI 53154. (414)908-4949. Fax: (414)768-8001. E-mail: satw@satw.org. Web site: www.satw.org.

Society of Children's Book Writers & Illustrators (SCBWI), 8271 Beverly Blvd., Los Angeles CA 90048. (323)782-1010. Fax: (323)782-1892. E-mail: scbwi@scbwi.org. Web site: www.scbwi.org.

Washington Independent Writers (WIW), 1001 Connecticut Ave. NW, Suite 701, Washington DC 20036. (202)775-5150. Fax: (202)775-5810. E-mail: info@washwriter.org. Web site: www.washwriter.org.

Western Writers of America (WWA). E-mail: spiritfire@kc.rr.com. Web site: www.westernwriters.org.

INDUSTRY ORGANIZATIONS

American Booksellers Association (ABA), 200 White Plains Rd., Suite 600, Tarrytown NY 10591. (914)591-2665. Fax: (914)591-2720. E-mail: info@bookweb.org. Web site: www.bookweb.org.

American Society of Journalists & Authors (ASJA), 1501 Broadway, Suite 302, New York NY 10036. (212)997-0947. Fax: (212)937-2315. E-mail: director@asja.org. Web site: www.asja.org.

Association for Women in Communications (AWC), 3337 Duke St., Alexandria VA 22314. (703)370-7436. Fax: (703)370-7437. E-mail: info@womcom.org. Web site: www.womcom.org.

Association of American Publishers (AAP), 71 5th Ave., 2nd Floor, New York NY 10003. (212)255-0200. Fax: (212)255-7007. Or, 50 F St. NW, Suite 400, Washington DC 20001. (202)347-3375. Fax: (202)347-3690. Web site: www.publishers.org.

The Association of Writers & Writing Programs (AWP), Mail Stop 1E3, George Mason University, Fairfax VA 22030. (703)993-4301. Fax: (703)993-4302. E-mail: services@awpwriter.org.

Web site: www.awpwriter.org.

The Authors Guild, Inc., 31 E. 32nd St., 7th Floor, New York NY 10016. (212)563-5904. Fax: (212)564-5363. E-mail: staff@authorsguild.org. Web site: www.authorsguild.org.

Canadian Authors Association (CAA), Box 419, Campbellford ON K0L 1L0 Canada. (705)653-0323. Fax: (705)653-0593. E-mail: admin@canauthors.org. Web site: www.canauthors.org.

Christian Booksellers Association (CBA), P.O. Box 62000, Colorado Springs CO 80962-2000. (800)252-1950. Fax: (719)272-3510. E-mail: info@cbaonline.org. Web site: www.cbaonline.org.

The Dramatists Guild of America, 1501 Broadway, Suite 701, New York NY 10036. (212)398-9366. Fax: (212)944-0420. Web site: www.dramatistsguild.com.

National League of American Pen Women (NLAPW), 1300 17th St. NW, Washington DC 20036-1973. (202)785-1997. Fax: (202)452-8868. E-mail: nlapw1@verizon.net. Website: www.americanpenwomen.org.

National Writers Association (NWA), 10940 S. Parker Rd., #508, Parker CO 80134. (303)841-0246. Fax: (303)841-2607. E-mail: natlwritersassn@hotmail.com. Web site: www.nationalwriters.com.

National Writers Union (NWU), 113 University Place, 6th Floor, New York NY 10003. (212)254-0279. Fax: (212)254-0673. E-mail: nwu@nwu.org. Web site: www.nwu.org.

PEN American Center, 588 Broadway, Suite 303, New York NY 10012-3225. (212)334-1660. Fax: (212)334-2181. E-mail: pen@pen.org. Web site: www.pen.org.

The Playwrights Guild of Canada (PGC), 54 Wolseley St., 2nd Floor, Toronto ON M5T 1A5 Canada. (416)703-0201. Fax: (416)703-0059. E-mail: info@playwrightsguild.ca. Web site: www.playwrightsguild.com.

Volunteer Lawyers for the Arts (VLA), One E. 53rd St., 6th Floor, New York NY 10022. (212)319-2787. Fax: (212)752-6575. Web site: www.vlany.org.

Women in Film (WIF), 8857 W. Olympic Blvd., Suite 201, Beverly Hills CA 90211. (310)657-5144. Fax: (310)657-5154. E-mail: info@wif.org. Web site: www.wif.org.

Women's National Book Association (WNBA), P.O. Box 237, FDR Station, New York NY 10150. (212)208-4629. Fax: (212)208-4629. E-mail: publicity@bookbuzz.com. Web site: www.wnba-books.org.

Writers Guild of Alberta (WGA), 11759 Groat Rd., Edmonton AB T5M 3K6 Canada. (780)422-8174. Fax: (780)422-2663. E-mail: mail@writersguild.ab.ca. Web site: writersguild.ab.ca.

Writers Guild of America-East (WGA), 555 W. 57th St., Suite 1230, New York NY 10019. (212)767-7800. Fax: (212)582-1909. Web site: www.wgaeast.org.

Writers Guild of America-West (WGA), 7000 W. Third St., Los Angeles CA 90048. (323)951-4000. Fax: (323)782-4800. Web site: www.wga.org.

Writers Union of Canada (TWUC), 90 Richmond St. E., Suite 200, Toronto ON M5C 1P1 Canada. (416)703-8982. Fax: (416)504-9090. E-mail: info@writersunion.ca. Web site: www.writersunion.ca.

Resources

RESOURCES

Glossary

#10 Envelope. A standard, business-size envelope.

Advance. A sum of money a publisher pays a writer prior to the publication of a book. It is usually paid in installments, such as one-half on signing the contract; one-half on delivery of a complete and satisfactory manuscript.

Agent. A liaison between a writer and editor or publisher. An agent shops a manuscript around, receiving a commission when the manuscript is accepted. Agents usually take a 10-15% fee from the advance and royalties.

ARC. Advance reader copy.

Assignment. Editor asks a writer to produce a specific article for an agreed-upon fee.

Auction. Publishers sometimes bid for the acquisition of a book manuscript that has excellent sales prospects. The bids are for the amount of the author's advance, advertising and promotional expenses, royalty percentage, etc. Auctions are conducted by agents.

Avant-garde. Writing that is innovative in form, style, or subject.

Backlist. A publisher's list of its books that were not published during the current season, but that are still in print.

Bimonthly. Every two months.

Bio. A sentence or brief paragraph about the writer; can include education and work experience.

Biweekly. Every two weeks.

Blurb. The copy on paperback book covers or hard cover book dust jackets, either promoting the book and the author or featuring testimonials from book reviewers or well-known people in the book's field. Also called flap copy or jacket copy.

Boilerplate. A standardized contract.

Bound galleys. A prepublication edition of a book, usually prepared from photocopies of the final galley proofs; also known as ``bound proofs.'' Designed for promotional purposes, bound galleys serve as the first set of review copies to be mailed out.

Byline. Name of the author appearing with the published piece.

Category fiction. A term used to include all types of fiction.

Chapbook. A small booklet—usually paperback—of poetry, ballads or tales.

Circulation. The number of subscribers to a magazine.

Clips. Samples, usually from newspapers or magazines, of a writer's published work.

Coffee-table book. An heavily illustrated oversize book.

Commercial novels. Novels designed to appeal to a broad audience. These are often broken down into categories such as western, mystery and romance. See also *genre*.

Contributor's copies. Copies of the issues of magazines sent to the author in which the author's work appears.

Co-publishing. Arrangement where author and publisher share publications costs and profits of a book. Also known as cooperative publishing.

Copyediting. Editing a manuscript for grammar, punctuation, printing style and factual accuracy.

Copyright. A means to protect an author's work. See "Minding the Details" on page 51 for more information.

Cover letter. A brief letter that accompanies the manuscript being sent to and agent or editor.

Creative nonfiction. Nonfictional writing that uses an innovative approach to the subject and creative language.

Critiquing service. Am editing service in which writers pay a fee for comments on the salability or other qualities of their manuscript. Fees vary, as do the quality of the critiques.

CV. Curriculum vita. A brief listing of qualifications and career accomplishments.

Electronic rights. Secondary or subsidiary rights dealing with electronic/multimedia formats (i.e., the Internet, CD-ROMs, electronic magazines).

Electronic submission. A submission made by modem or on computer disk.

Erotica. Fiction or art that is sexually oriented.

Evaluation fees. Fees an agent may charge to evaluate material. The extent and quality of this evaluation varies, but comments usually concern the salability of the manuscript.

Fair use. A provision of the copyright law that says short passages from copyrighted material may be used without infringing on the owner's rights.

Feature. An article giving the reader information of human interest rather than news.

Filler. A short item used by an editor to ``fill'' out a newspaper column or magazine page. It could be a joke, an anecdote, etc.

Film rights. Rights sold or optioned by the agent/author to a person in the film industry, enabling the book to be made into a movie.

Foreign rights. Translation or reprint rights to be sold abroad.

Frontlist. A publisher's list of books that are new to the current season.

Galleys. The first typeset version of a manuscript that has not yet been divided into pages.

Genre. Refers either to a general classification of writing, such as the novel or the poem, or to the categories within those classifications, such as the problem novel or the sonnet.

Ghostwriter. A writer who puts into literary form an article, speech, story or book based on another person's ideas or knowledge.

Graphic novel. A story in graphic form, long comic strip, or heavily illustrated story; of 40 pages or more.

Hi-lo. A type of fiction that offers a high level of interest for readers at a low reading level.

High concept. A story idea easily expressed in a quick, one-line description.

Honorarium. Token payment—small amount of money, or a byline and copies of the publication.

Hook. Aspect of the work that sets it apart from others and draws in the reader/viewer.

How-to. Books and magazine articles offering a combination of information and advice in describing how something can be accomplished.

Imprint. Name applied to a publisher's specific line of books.

Joint contract. A legal agreement between a publisher and two or more authors, establishing provisions for the division of royalties the book generates.

Kill fee. Fee for a complete article that was assigned and then cancelled.

Lead time. The time between the acquisition of a manuscript by an editor and its actual publication.

Literary fiction. The general category of serious, non-formulaic, intelligent fiction.

Mainstream fiction. Fiction that transcends popular novel categories such as mystery, romance and science fiction.

Marketing fee. Fee charged by some agents to cover marketing expenses. It may be used to cover postage, telephone calls, faxes, photocopying or any other expense incurred in marketing a manuscript.

Mass market. Non-specialized books of wide appeal directed toward a large audience.

Memoir. A narrative recounting a writer's (or fictional narrator's) personal or family history; specifics may be altered, though essentially considered nonfiction.

Middle grade or mid-grade. The general classification of books written for readers approximately ages 9-11. Also called middle readers.

Midlist. Those titles on a publisher's list that are not expected to be big sellers, but are expected to have limited/modest sales.

Model release. A paper signed by the subject of a photograph giving the photographer permission to use the photograph.

Multiple contract. Book contract with an agreement for a future book(s).

Multiple submissions. Sending more than one book or article idea to a publisher at the same time.

Narrative nonfiction. A narrative presentation of actual events.

Net royalty. A royalty payment based on the amount of money a book publisher receives on the sale of a book after booksellers' discounts, special sales discounts and returns.

Novella. A short novel, or a long short story; approximately 7,000 to 15,000 words.

On spec. An editor expresses an interest in a proposed article idea and agrees to consider the finished piece for publication "on speculation." The editor is under no obligation to buy the finished manuscript.

One-time rights. Rights allowing a manuscript to be published one time. The work can be sold again by the writer without violating the contract.

Option clause. A contract clause giving a publisher the right to publish an author's next book.

Payment on acceptance. The editor sends you a check for your article, story or poem as soon as he decides to publish it.

Payment on publication. The editor doesn't send you a check for your material until it is published.

Pen name. The use of a name other than your legal name on articles, stories or books. Also called a pseudonym.

Photo feature. Feature in which the emphasis is on the photographs rather than on accompanying written material.

Picture book. A type of book aimed at preschoolers to 8-year-olds that tells a story using a combination of text and artwork, or artwork only.

Platform. A writer's speaking experience, interview skills, Web site and other abilities which help form a following of potential buyers for that author's book.

Proofreading. Close reading and correction of a manuscript's typographical errors.

Proposal. A summary of a proposed book submitted to a publisher, particularly used for nonfiction manuscripts. A proposal often contains an individualized cover letter, one-page overview of the book, marketing information, competitive books, author information, chapter-by-chapter outline, and two to three sample chapters.

Query. A letter that sells an idea to an editor or agent. Usually a query is brief (no more than one page) and uses attention-getting prose.

Remainders. Copies of a book that are slow to sell and can be purchased from the publisher at a reduced price.

Reporting time. The time it takes for an editor to report to the author on his/her query or manuscript.

Reprint rights. The rights to republish a book after its initial printing.

Royalties, standard hardcover book. 10 percent of the retail price on the first 5,000 copies sold; 121/2 percent on the next 5,000; 15 percent thereafter.

Royalties, standard mass paperback book. 4-8 percent of the retail price on the first 150,000 copies sold.

Royalties, standard trade paperback book. No less than 6 percent of list price on the first 20,000 copies; 71/2 percent thereafter.

SASE. Self-addressed, stamped envelope; should be included with all correspondence.

Self-publishing. In this arrangement the author pays for manufacturing, production and marketing of his book and keeps all income derived from the book sales.

Semimonthly. Twice per month.

Semiweekly. Twice per week.

Serial. Published periodically, such as a newspaper or magazine.

Serial fiction. Fiction published in a magazine in installments, often broken off at a suspenseful spot.

Serial rights. The right for a newspaper or magazine to publish sections of a manuscript.

Short-short. A complete short story of 1,500 words.

Sidebar. A feature presented as a companion to a straight news report (or main magazine article) giving sidelights on human-interest aspects or sometimes elucidating just one aspect of the story.

Simultaneous submissions. Sending the same article, story or poem to several publishers at the same time. Some publishers refuse to consider such submissions.

Slant. The approach or style of a story or article that will appeal to readers of a specific magazine.

Slice-of-life vignette. A short fiction piece intended to realistically depict an interesting moment of everyday living.

Slush pile. The stack of unsolicited or misdirected manuscripts received by an editor or book publisher.

Subagent. An agent handling certain subsidiary rights, usually working in conjuction with the agent who handled the book rights. The percentage paid the book agent is increased to pay the subagent.

Subsidiary rights. All right other than book publishing rights included in a book publishing contract, such as paperback rights, book club rights and movie rights. Part of an agent's job is to negotiate those rights and advise you on which to sell and which to keep. For more information, read "Minding the Details" on page **51**.

Subsidy publisher. A book publisher who charges the author for the cost to typeset and print his book, the jacket, etc., as opposed to a royalty publisher who pays the author.

Synopsis. A brief summary of a story, novel or play. As part of a book proposal, it is a comprehensive summary condensed in a page or page and a half, single-spaced.

Tabloid. Newspaper format publication on about half the size of the regular newspaper page.

Tearsheet. Page from a magazine or newspaper containing your printed story, article, poem or ad.

TOC. Table of Contents.

Trade book. Either a hardcover or softcover book; subject matter frequently concerns a special interest for a general audience; sold mainly in bookstores.

Trade paperback. A soft-bound volume, usually around 5X8, published and designed for the general public; available mainly in bookstores.

Translation rights. Sold to a foreign agent or foreign publisher.

Unsolicited manuscript. A story, article, poem or book that an editor did not specifically ask to see.

YA. Young adult books.

Book Publishers Subject Index

FICTION

Adventure

Amateur sleuth

Comic books

Confession

Contemporary

Erotica

Erotic romance

Ethnic

Experimental

Fantasy

Feminist

Gay

General

Gothic

Hard science fiction/technological

Historical

Subject Index

Horror

Humor

Inspirational

Juvenile

Lesbian

Literary

Mainstream

Military

Multicultural

Mystery

Mystery/suspense

Occult

Picture books

Plays

Poetry

Poetry in translation

Police procedural

Problem novels

Regional

Religious

Romance

Science fiction

Short story collections

Translation

War

Western

Young adult

NONFICTION

Agriculture

Alternative

Alternative lifestyles

Americana

Animals

Anthropology

Archaeology

Archeology

Architecture

Art

Audio

Business

Subject Index

Career guidance

Child guidance

Cinema

Community

Computers

Contemporary culture

Cooking

Counseling

Crafts

Creative nonfiction

Dance

Economics

Education

Electronics

Entertainment

Environment

Ethnic

Fashion

Film

Finance

Foods

Games

Gardening

Gay

Government

Government/politics

Health

History

Subject Index

Hobbies

Horses

Horticulture

Humanities

Subject Index

Language

Lesbian

Literary criticism

Literature

Medicine

Memoirs

Military

Money

Multicultural

Music

Muticultural

Nature

New Age

Subject Index

Photography

Psychology

Reading comprehension

Real estate

Recreation

Regional

Religion

Science

Sex

Social sciences

Sociology

Software

Spirituality

Sports

Stage

Translation

Transportation

Travel

True crime

War

Womens issues

Womens studies

World affairs

Young adult

General Index

General Index

C

D

E

F

G

General Index

H

I

J

M

O

P

S

General Index

T

X

Y

Z